AA Publishing, a trading name of AA Media Limited, whose registered office is
, Basing View, Basingstoke, Hampshire RG21 4EA.
mber 06112600.

ublished 2013
imited 2013

Please contact
Advertisement Sales: advertisingsales@theaa.com
Editorial Department: lifestyleguides@theaa.com

Typeset and repro by Servis Filmsetting Ltd, Stockport. Printed by Trento SRL, Italy.

This directory is compiled by AA Lifestyle Guides; managed in the Librios Information
Management System and generated by the AA establishment database system.

AA Restaurant Guide edited by Fiona Griffiths.

Restaurant descriptions have been contributed by the following team of writers: Fiona Griffiths, Hugh Morgan,
Mike Pedley, Carina Simon, Allen Stidwill, Stuart Taylor, Andrew Turvil.

A CIP catalogue for this book is available from the British Library.

ISBN: 978-0-7495-7475-8

A04981

Maps prepared by the
Mapping Services Department
of AA Publishing.

Maps © AA Media Limited 2013.

Contains Ordnance Survey data
© Crown copyright and database right 2013.

 Land &   This is based upon Crown
Property   Copyright and is reproduced
Services.   with the permission of Land &
Property Services under delegated authority from the
Controller of Her Majesty's Stationery Office.

© Crown copyright and database rights 2013
Licence number 100,363.
Permit number 130063

 Ordnance
Survey
Ireland's National Mapping Agency

Republic of Ireland mapping based
on © Ordnance Survey Ireland/
Government of Ireland Copyright
Permit number MP000913

Information on National Parks in England provided by
the Countryside Agency (Natural England).

Information on National Parks in Scotland provided
by Scottish Natural Heritage.

Information on National Parks in Wales provided by
The Countryside Council for Wales.

Contents

Welcome to the Guide 4

How to Use the Guide 6

How the AA Assesses for Rosette Awards 9

AA Chefs' Chef 2013–2014 10

AA Lifetime Achievement Award 2013–2014 12

AA Food Service Award 2013–2014 13

AA Restaurants of the Year 14

AA Wine Awards 16

Well Equipped: modern cooking techniques 18

Call of the Wild: the rise of foraged ingredients 26

It's a Grape Life: a day in the life of a sommelier 30

The Top Ten Per Cent 40

England 46

London 240

Channel Islands 536

Scotland 548

Wales 618

Northern Ireland 644

Republic of Ireland 652

Maps 676

Index 701

Welcome to the Guide

As ever, it's been a busy year for the AA hotel and restaurant inspectors, who have been travelling the length and breadth of the country making anonymous visits and giving new awards to some 200 restaurants which have now entered the guide for the first time this year. It's a heartening prospect to see so many new restaurants opening, and longer-established restaurants thriving, when the country remains in tough economic times: despite tighter household incomes, it seems eating out is one luxury people aren't prepared to let go of if they can possibly help it.

Good Times

The UK public has every reason to be enthusiastic about eating out these days – this, the 21st edition of *The AA Restaurant Guide*, is packed full of over 2,000 restaurants that are extremely deserving of the nation's hard-earned cash.

When the guide first started most of the best restaurants were in London, but now, wherever you may be in the UK or Ireland, there's likely to be a restaurant with an AA Rosette just a short distance away.

That's the beauty of this guide – it recognises restaurants of all types, from pubs to hotels to small bistros and high-end fine-dining restaurants. If they serve good food, they all have a chance of gaining an AA Rosette and a place in the guide.

Trend Setters

As a constantly evolving guide, we're well positioned to gain a good insight into emerging trends in the UK dining scene, and there are a couple of significant movements that have been gaining momentum in the last few years.

Firstly, the move towards chefs using a variety of different cooking techniques and equipment – including some with the kind of kit you'd be more likely to find in a science lab – is something that we explore in our feature 'Well Equipped' on page 18. If you've looked at a menu lately and seen the words 'Josper grill' or 'espuma' mentioned, and not had a clue what they are, then our feature will reveal all.

We've also seen an increasing use by chefs in all sectors of wild and foraged foods: chickweed, wood sorrel, dandelions,

they're all cropping up on menus and it seems like a trend that's only set to grow as our guest chef for this edition, Mat Follas of The Wild Garlic in Dorset, explains on page 26.

Unsung Heroes

There are certain areas of the restaurant profession that we felt we hadn't really given enough recognition to in the past – that of wine service and front-of-house service in general.

We've spent a day with a sommelier, namely Alan Holmes at The Vineyard near Newbury in Berkshire, learning all about what his job entails (page 30), and we've also launched a new award for 2014 – the AA Food Service Award – to recognise true excellence in restaurant service (turn to page 13 to see our inaugural winner).

Changing Places

The typically transient nature of the hospitality industry means that chefs move around all the time, restaurants change hands or, sadly, go out of business. This year we've seen a particularly high number of chef departures at three and four Rosette level; as these higher awarded restaurants require a series of inspections to verify their award, and due to a lack of time before publication, some of these restaurants appear in the guide with their Rosette level unconfirmed.

However, our inspections are ongoing throughout the year so you can be assured that we'll get to these specific restaurants very soon, and once their award is confirmed it will be published in the restaurants section on theAA.com.

Tell us what you think

We welcome your feedback about the restaurants included in this guide, and about the guide itself. A Readers' Report form appears at the back of the book, so please write in, or e-mail us at: lifestyleguides@theaa.com.

The restaurants, along with guest accommodation, pubs, golf courses, days out and hotels feature on The AA website: theAA.com, and on a number of AA mobile apps.

How to Use the Guide

1 MAP REFERENCE

Each town or village is given a map reference – the map page number and a two-figure reference based on the National Grid. For example: **Map 15 SJ39**
15 refers to the page number of the map section at the back of the guide
SJ is the National Grid lettered square (representing 100,000sq metres) in which the location will be found
3 is the figure reading across the top and bottom of the map page
9 is the figure reading down at each side of the map page. For Central London and Greater London, there is a 13-page map section starting on page 246.

2 LOCATION

Restaurants are listed in country and county order, then by town and then alphabetically within the town. There is an index by restaurant at the back of the guide and a similar one for the Central & Greater London sections on page 242.

3 RESTAURANT NAME

Details of opening times and prices may be omitted from an entry when the establishment has not supplied us with up-to-date information. This is indicated where an establishment name is shown in *italics*.

4 THE AA ROSETTE AWARD

Restaurants are awarded one or more Rosettes, up to a maximum of five.
See page 9.

5 FOOD STYLE

Food style summary

6 PHOTOGRAPHS

Restaurants are invited to enhance their entry with up to two photographs.

7 CHEF(S) AND OWNER(S)

The names of the chef(s) and owner(s) are as up-to-date as possible at the time of going to press, but changes in personnel

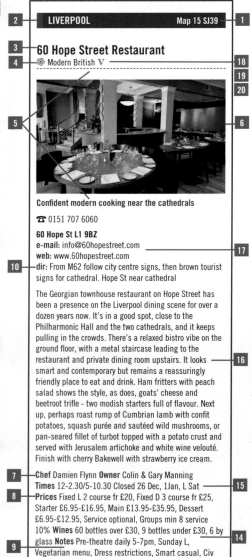

2 LIVERPOOL Map 15 SJ39 **1**

3
60 Hope Street Restaurant
4 ❀ Modern British V **18**
19
20

5 **6**

Confident modern cooking near the cathedrals

☎ 0151 707 6060

60 Hope St L1 9BZ
e-mail: info@60hopestreet.com
web: www.60hopestreet.com **17**
10 **dir:** From M62 follow city centre signs, then brown tourist signs for cathedral. Hope St near cathedral

The Georgian townhouse restaurant on Hope Street has been a presence on the Liverpool dining scene for over a dozen years now. It's in a good spot, close to the Philharmonic Hall and the two cathedrals, and it keeps pulling in the crowds. There's a relaxed bistro vibe on the ground floor, with a metal staircase leading to the restaurant and private dining room upstairs. It looks **16** smart and contemporary but remains a reassuringly friendly place to eat and drink. Ham fritters with peach salad shows the style, as does, goats' cheese and beetroot trifle - two modish starters full of flavour. Next up, perhaps roast rump of Cumbrian lamb with confit potatoes, squash purée and sautéed wild mushrooms, or pan-seared fillet of turbot topped with a potato crust and served with Jerusalem artichoke and white wine velouté. Finish with cherry Bakewell with strawberry ice cream.

7 **Chef** Damien Flynn **Owner** Colin & Gary Manning
Times 12-2.30/5-10.30 Closed 26 Dec, 1Jan, L Sat **15**
8 **Prices** Fixed L 2 course fr £20, Fixed D 3 course fr £25, Starter £6.95-£16.95, Main £13.95-£35.95, Dessert £6.95-£12.95, Service optional, Groups min 8 service 10% **Wines** 60 bottles over £30, 9 bottles under £30, 6 by **14**
9 glass **Notes** Pre-theatre daily 5-7pm, Sunday L, Vegetarian menu, Dress restrictions, Smart casual, Civ
13 Wed 50 **Seats** 90, Pr/dining room 40 **Children** Portions, Menu **Parking** On street

11 **12**

often occur, and may affect both the style and quality of the restaurant.

8 PRICES

Prices are for fixed lunch (2 courses) and dinner (3 courses) and à la carte dishes. Note: Prices quoted are an indication only, and are subject to change. We ask restaurants the following questions about service charge (their responses appear under Prices):
• Is service optional?
• Is service charge included?
• Is service charge added but optional, and what percentage?

9 NOTES

Additional information e.g. availability of vegetarian dishes, civil weddings, Sunday lunch prices etc.

10 DIRECTIONS

Short directions are given.

11 PARKING DETAILS

On-site parking or nearby parking.

12 CHILDREN

Menu, portions, age restrictions etc.

13 NUMBER OF SEATS

Number of seats in the restaurant, followed by private dining room (Pr/dining room).

14 NUMBER OF WINES

Number of wines under and over £30, and available by the glass.

15 DAILY OPENING AND CLOSING TIMES

Daily opening and closing times, the days of the week when closed and seasonal closures. Some restaurants offer all-day dining. Note that opening times are liable to change without notice. It is wise to telephone in advance.

16 DESCRIPTION

Description of the restaurant and the food.

17 E-MAIL ADDRESS AND WEBSITE

18 VEGETARIAN MENU

V Indicates a vegetarian menu. Restaurants with some vegetarian dishes available are indicated under Notes (see 9, above).

19 NOTABLE WINE LIST

🍷 **NOTABLE WINE LIST** This symbol, where present, indicates a notable wine list (see pages 16–17).

20 LOCAL AND REGIONAL PRODUCE

🍃 This symbol, where present, indicates the use of local and regional produce. More than 50% of the restaurant food ingredients are produced within a 50-mile radius.

Smoking Regulations
From July 2007 smoking was banned in all enclosed public places in the United Kingdom and Ireland. Internal communal areas must be smoke-free.

Facilities for Disabled Guests
The Equality Act 2010 provides legal rights for disabled people including access to goods, services and facilities, and means that service providers may have to consider making adjustments to their premises. For more information about the Act see www.gov.uk/government/policies/creating-a-fairer-and-more-equal-society or www.gov.uk/definition-of-disability-under-equality-act-2010.

The establishments in this guide should be aware of their obligations under the Act.

We recommend that you phone in advance to ensure that the establishment you have chosen has appropriate facilities.

Website Addresses
Where website addresses are included they have been supplied and specified by the respective establishment. Such websites are not under the control of AA Media Limited and as such AA Media Limited has no control over them and will not accept any responsibility or liability in respect of any and all matters whatsoever relating to such websites including access, content, material and functionality. By including the addresses of third-party websites the AA does not intend to solicit business or offer any security to any person in any country, directly or indirectly.

How the AA Assesses for Rosette Awards

The AA's Rosette award scheme was the first nationwide scheme for assessing the quality of food served by restaurants and hotels.

A consistent approach

The Rosette scheme is an award, not a classification, and although there is necessarily an element of subjectivity when it comes to assessing taste, we aim for a consistent approach throughout the UK. Our awards are made solely on the basis of a meal visit or visits by one or more of our hotel and restaurant inspectors, who have an unrivalled breadth and depth of experience in assessing quality. They award Rosettes annually on a rising scale of one to five.

So what makes a restaurant worthy of a Rosette award?

For our inspectors, the top and bottom line is the food. The taste of a dish is what counts, and whether it successfully delivers to the diner the promise of the menu. A restaurant is only as good as its worst meal. Although presentation and competent service should be appropriate to the style of the restaurant and the quality of the food, they cannot affect the Rosette assessment as such, either up or down. The summaries below indicate what our inspectors look for, but are intended only as guidelines. The AA is constantly reviewing its award criteria, and competition usually results in an all-round improvement in standards, so it becomes increasingly difficult for restaurants to reach an award level. For more detailed Rosette criteria, please visit theAA.com.

⊛ One Rosette

These are excellent restaurants that stand out in their local area featuring:
- Food prepared with care, understanding and skill
- Good quality ingredients

Around 50% of restaurants in this guide have one Rosette.

⊛⊛ Two Rosettes

The best local restaurants with:
- Higher standards
- Better consistency
- Greater precision apparent in the cooking
- Obvious attention to the quality and selection of ingredients

About 40% of restaurants in this guide have two Rosettes.

⊛⊛⊛ Three Rosettes

Outstanding restaurants demanding recognition well beyond their local area featuring:
- Selection and sympathetic treatment of highest quality ingredients
- Consistent timing, seasoning and judgement of flavour combinations
- Excellent, intelligent service and a well-chosen wine list

Around 10% of restaurants in this guide have three Rosettes.

⊛⊛⊛⊛ Four Rosettes

Dishes demonstrate:
- Intense ambition
- A passion for excellence
- Superb technical skills
- Remarkable consistency
- Appreciation of culinary traditions combined with desire for exploration and improvement
- Cooking demands national recognition

Twenty-nine restaurants in this guide have four Rosettes.

⊛⊛⊛⊛⊛ Five Rosettes

Cooking stands comparison with the best in the world:
- Highly individual cooking
- Breathtaking culinary skills
- Setting the standards to which others aspire
- Knowledgeable and distinctive wine list

Eleven restaurants in this guide have five Rosettes.

Tom Kerridge

This year's AA Chefs' Chef Award goes to Tom Kerridge of The Hand and Flowers in Marlow, Buckinghamshire

Tom Kerridge almost went into a life of acting – he played several small television roles as a child – but thankfully for his many food-loving fans, he chose a career in the culinary arts instead.

At the age of 18, this West Country lad went to catering school in Cheltenham, having developed a love of cooking at home that was partly inspired by Marco Pierre White's cookbook *White Heat*.

His first role in a professional kitchen came in 1991 as a commis chef at Calcot Manor in Tetbury, Gloucestershire, and after working at several country house hotels and restaurants in his home county, he eventually moved to London as sous chef under Gary Rhodes at Rhodes in the Square, in 1999.

After a two-year spell as sous chef at Odette's in Primrose Hill, he took up his first head chef position at Bellamys Dining Room in Vauxhall, and from there became head chef at Great Fosters in Egham, Surrey.

Then it was back to London as senior sous chef at the much lauded Monsieur Max in Hampton, before Kerridge moved to the renowned Adlards in Norwich as head chef for two years.

It was in 2005 that he and his wife Beth took over The Hand and Flowers in the upmarket Buckinghamshire town of Marlow (see entry on page 76), quickly transforming it from an ordinary pub into the destination restaurant (with four guest suites) that it is today.

> **Within its first year the restaurant picked up three AA Rosettes**

Within its first year the restaurant picked up three AA Rosettes along with a string of other accolades for Kerridge's highly individual, robustly flavoured, unpretentious modern British cooking.

This year The Hand and Flowers has joined the elite group of just 32 restaurants in the UK to hold four AA Rosettes, and counting amongst its biggest fans are several of Kerridge's fellow chefs – as the award of AA Chefs' Chef 2013-2014 testifies.

Ironically, despite abandoning a potential acting career some years ago, Kerridge is increasingly gracing our television screens through his talent for cooking, with regular appearances on the *Great British Menu*, *Saturday Kitchen* and, in 2013, his very own BBC Two cookery programme *Tom Kerridge's Proper Pub Food*.

On The Menu

Crispy pig's head with rhubarb,
pancetta and Greek cress

Spiced tranche of Cornish monkfish with roasted
cauliflower, peanut crumble and verjus

Hand & Flowers chocolate and ale cake with
salted caramel and muscovado ice cream

PREVIOUS WINNERS

Chris and Jeff Galvin
Galvin La Chapelle,
London E1
page 259

Michael Caines
Gidleigh Park, Chagford,
Devon
page 135

Andrew Fairlie
Andrew Fairlie @ Gleneagles,
Auchterarder, Perth &
Kinross
page 604

Germain Schwab
Winteringham Fields
(former chef), Lincolnshire
page 238

Raymond Blanc
Le Manoir aux Quat' Saisons,
Great Milton, Oxfordshire
page 410

Shaun Hill
Walnut Tree Inn,
Abergavenny,
Monmouthshire
page 633

Heston Blumenthal
The Fat Duck, Bray,
Berkshire
page 54

Jean-Christophe Novelli

Gordon Ramsay
Restaurant Gordon Ramsay,
London SW3
page 303

Rick Stein
The Seafood Restaurant,
Padstow, Cornwall
page 100

Marco Pierre White
Wheeler's
London SW1
page 300

Kevin Viner

Philip Howard
The Square,
London W1
page 351

Marcus Wareing
Marcus Wareing at
The Berkeley,
London SW1
page 290

Martin Wishart
Restaurant Martin Wishart,
Leith, Edinburgh
page 579

Pierre Koffmann
Koffmann's,
London SW1 page 289

AA Lifetime Achievement Award 2013-2014

Harry Murray

Lucknam Park Hotel & Spa in Wiltshire is the epitome of luxury – a world-class hotel recognised for its superlative standards of hospitality with five AA red stars and three AA Rosettes. And it has Harry Murray, managing director from 1997 to 2010, and now chairman, to thank for its meteoric rise to super-star hotel status.

But it's not just Lucknam Park where Murray has stamped his mark: in a career spanning more than 50 years, the 73-year-old has been instrumental in raising standards across the hospitality industry.

He's still just as passionate today about hotels as he was at the tender age of 13, when he stood outside The Midland Hotel in Manchester, watching all the comings and goings of international footballers

visiting to play against Manchester United, and decided he wanted to manage a luxury five-star hotel.

By the age of 27 he'd already achieved his first general manager position – at the North Stafford Hotel in Stoke-on-Trent – and by 32 he was managing his first five-star hotel, The President, in Johannesburg.

It was as general manager of The Imperial Hotel in Torquay from 1976 to 1994 when he really showed his worth: at a time when holidays abroad were getting cheaper, it was a struggle for British seaside hotels to keep going, so Murray introduced a whole array of gastronomic, art and antique, gardening, musical, and murder mystery weekends to attract customers, and succeeded in really putting The Imperial on the map.

As career highlights go, hosting a banquet for the Queen and President Mandela (while managing the InterContinental Cape Sun in Cape Town) is hard to beat, but there are many others, not least being appointed MBE

for services to the hospitality industry in 2005 and, of course, overseeing the £20 million refurbishment of Lucknam Park that transformed it into the leading country-house hotel it is today.

Although Murray retired as general manager of Lucknam Park in 2010, he is still heavily involved in operations there, as well as being a tireless ambassador for the industry, with his many roles including director of the UK's first hotel school (The Edge at Essex University), a governor of the Academy of Culinary Arts, patron of the hospitality industry charity Hospitality Action, and life patron of Springboard, the organisation that assists young people to enter a career in hospitality.

Harry Murray is no stranger to receiving awards for his outstanding contribution to the hospitality sector, and as he continues to work towards raising standards with such boundless enthusiasm and energy, we can be sure he has much more to achieve yet.

The Waterside Inn, Bray, Berkshire

For the first time in *The Restaurant Guide's* 21-year history, the AA is launching an award to recognise those who work on the customer-facing side of the restaurant profession.

From the 2000-plus AA Rosetted restaurants across the UK, candidates were shortlisted by our inspection team that fitted the following criteria:

- Consistently deliver excellent standards of restaurant service and hospitality.
- Technical service skills and food and beverage knowledge of the highest standard.
- Clear commitment to staff training and development.

There was little argument over the inaugural winner: The Waterside Inn in Bray, Berkshire (see entry on page 55), is revered in the UK hospitality industry and beyond as a beacon of excellence.

Our inspectors commented that The Waterside Inn sets service standards for others to aspire to, with its winning combination of faultlessly professional service and natural hospitality.

Michel Roux's Thames-side restaurant, run since 2002 by his son Alain, is justly renowned for the seamless professionalism of its front-of-house team, led by director and general manager Diego Masciaga.

Masciaga, who has been with The Waterside Inn for some 30 years, is a true master of his craft, directing his charges with boundless energy and enthusiasm to provide unfalteringly impeccable service, and delivering the same warm welcome to every guest, whether regular or first-timer.

Indeed, the atmosphere in the classically elegant restaurant is far from stuffy and starchy – as can often be the case at this level – and instead it's relaxed, informal and constantly buzzing. In this setting, the front-of-house team consistently pull off an extremely clever trick that not many others manage – that of spotting a guest's every need and being at their side in an instant to assist, quietly and unobtrusively.

Of course, all this stems from superb training, and the Waterside is an industry leader on that front. A great amount of time and care is taken to train all staff to the highest possible standards – it's no wonder people in the hospitality sector come from around the world to spend time at The Waterside Inn learning just how it's done.

The award's two runners-up were The Three Chimneys on the Isle of Skye and Sketch in London.

A word about our sponsor, People 1st

The People 1st Training Company's highly acclaimed WorldHost™ customer service programme has been used to train over one-million people worldwide, including volunteers and staff at the London 2012 Olympic and Paralympic Games. Hundreds of UK service businesses have already trained their staff to WorldHost™ standards and achieved WorldHost™ Recognised Business status.

Diego Masciaga (left)

AA Restaurants of the Year

Potential Restaurants of the Year are nominated by our team of full-time inspectors based on their routine visits. In selecting a Restaurant of the Year, we look for somewhere that is exceptional in its chosen area of the market. Whilst the Rosette awards are based on the quality of the food alone, Restaurant of the Year takes into account all aspects of the dining experience.

ENGLAND

THE ARTICHOKE ⊛⊛⊛
AMERSHAM, BUCKINGHAMSHIRE page 70

Chef-patron Laurie Gear made excellent use of the enforced closure of his restaurant (by a fire in the neighbouring premises in 2008) to spend a period in the legendary Noma in Copenhagen, returning reinvigorated and inspired. The Artichoke, which he runs with wife Jacqueline, sits in pole position on the market square of lovely Old Amersham, the building combining the best of its original 16th-century features with a chic 21st-century sheen. From the open kitchen comes food that's inventive, ambitious, often quite complex, and supported by top-class technical ability. Ingredients (locally sourced, foraged too) are as good as you'll get, and flavours unapologetic, as in a full-throttle starter of pan-fried quail's breast with crispy stuffed leg, pickled artichokes, watercress, toasted hazelnut, and hazelnut mayonnaise. A punchy fish and meat combo comprising braised Dingley Dell pork cheeks, langoustines, star anise carrot purée, fennel salad, roast carrot, and bacon and star anise crumb might precede a well-judged dessert of Michel Cluizel white chocolate ganache with amaretti biscuits, Amalfi lemon and olive oil jelly, and lemon and thyme sherbet.

LONDON

MEDLAR ⊛⊛⊛
LONDON SW10 page 310

It can be a fine line between success and failure in the restaurant game, but some people manage to make success look very easy indeed. Joe Mercer Nairne and David O'Connor are such people. Medlar is one of those restaurants that goes about its business with a quiet confidence: the menu reads (and eats) like a foodie's dream, the service is slick but not overbearing, and the prices are reasonable. It looks good from the street, with its cool, muted colour tones, awning, and doors that open up to give that European vibe in the warmer months. Inside it is simply elegant, not casual, but not overly smart either – tables are dressed in white linen, the designer touches are present but held in check. The food has a rustic charm about it, but it is far from unsophisticated: wild garlic soup with a poached pheasant's egg and morels, perhaps, followed by roast poussin with sautéed spätzle, caramelised shallot, girolles and cauliflower purée. For dessert, lemon curd ice cream with blackcurrant compôte and meringues maintains the high standards to the very end.

SCOTLAND

ONDINE

EDINBURGH page 577

There's always a lively buzz at Ondine – in fact it's got such a loyal following, it's hard to believe the place hasn't been here for years. The central horseshoe-shaped crustacea bar is both a feature in the room and a declaration of intent – this place is about seafood, and top-notch sustainable Scottish seafood at that. Just off the Royal Mile, on George IV Bridge, it's a modish space with great views out over the old town. Start with rock oysters (Loch Fyne, Cumbrae, Carlingford), either as they come or cooked (tempura or thermidor, perhaps), or something like a textbook fish and shellfish soup with the trad accompaniments of rouille, gruyère and croutons. Chef Roy Brett shows a sensibly steady hand when it comes to treating the first-class piscine produce at his disposal, so nothing is overworked and everything tastes just so. Thus main course might be a simple roast shellfish platter, risotto nero with grilled chilli squid, Shetland mussel marinière, fish curry, or good, old-fashioned deep-fried haddock and chips with minted pea purée.

WALES

YE OLDE BULLS HEAD INN

BEAUMARIS, ISLE OF ANGLESEY page 621

This particular Bull has impeccable pedigree. Dating from the 15th century, the inn stands just a stone's throw from the walls of Beaumaris Castle and comes with a serious weight of history. Having undergone numerous transformations over the years, it now offers swish boutique accommodation for the style-conscious 21st-century traveller. In the Loft Restaurant, formerly the hayloft serving the stables, the ancient beams extend over a classy and intimate contemporary space clothed in shades of oatmeal and cream. Head chef Hefin Roberts deals in imaginative and stylishly-presented modern British dishes built from premium Welsh ingredients, starting, perhaps, with the punchy flavours of poached gurnard fillet with spiced crab meat, garlic gnocchi, toasted seed quinoa, and sweet and sour vegetables. Next up, roast loin and marinated rump of Anglesey lamb comes with the Mediterranean notes of courgettes, spiced aubergine purée, red onions, spinach, cumin-spiced potatoes, and an intense jus. Full-on flavours keep coming all the way to a dessert of pistachio and chocolate cake with spiced chocolate and orange mousse, and chocolate oil.

AA Wine Awards

The AA Wine Awards

The annual AA Wine Awards attracted a huge response from our AA recognised restaurants, with over 1,300 wine lists submitted for judging. Three national winners were chosen – Northcote, Blackburn for England; The Witchery by the Castle, Edinburgh, for Scotland; and Park House in Cardiff for Wales. The Witchery was also selected as the Overall Winner of the award for the UK – the first ever Scottish entrant to achieve this – with a member of their wine team set to enjoy the prize of an all-expenses-paid trip to Willi Opitz's vineyards at Illmitz in Austria's Burgenland.

All 2,000 Rosetted restaurants in this year's guide were invited to submit their wine lists and, from these, the panel selected a shortlist of over 260 establishments, identified in the guide with the Notable Wine List symbol ![NOTABLE WINE LIST].

The shortlisted establishments were asked to choose wines from their list (within a budget of £80 per bottle) to accompany a menu designed by last year's winner L'Etranger in London. The final judging panel included Simon Numphud, AA Hotel Services Business Manager, and Ibi Issolah, Director of L'Etranger. The judges' comments are shown under the award winners on the opposite page.

Other wine lists that stood out in the final judging included those from Terroirs, London; The Chester Grosvenor, Chester; Castle Terrace, Edinburgh and Ellenborough Park, Cheltenham.

What makes a wine list notable?

We are looking for high-quality wines, with diversity across grapes and/ or countries of origin and style, the best individual growers and vintages. The list should be well presented, ideally with some helpful notes and, to reflect the demand from diners, a good choice of wines by the glass.

To reach the final shortlist, we look for a real passion for wine, which should come across to the customer, a fair pricing policy (depending on the style of the restaurant), and an interesting coverage (not necessarily a large list), which might include areas of specialism, perhaps a particular wine area, sherries or larger formats such as magnums.

What disappoints the judges are spelling errors, wines under incorrect regions or styles, split vintages (which are still far too common), lazy purchasing (all wines from a country from just one grower or negociant) and confusing layouts. Sadly, many restaurants still do not pay much attention to wine, resulting in ill considered lists.

The Witchery by the Castle – Winning Wine Selection

Menu	Wine selection
Canapés	Billecart-Salmon, Brut, NV
Starter – Pan-fried foie gras, cinnamon and date pudding, yuzu infused caramelised endive	Gewurztraminer, Cuvee des Seigneurs De Ribeaupierre, Trimbach 2005
Fish course – Black and white roasted wild Chilean sea bass fillets served on an Aohoba leaf	Puligny-Montrachet, Etienne Sauzet 2009
Main course – Kudu antelope with chocolate and kidney sauce	Côte-Rôtie, Robert and Patrick Jasmin 2006
Cheese – Mature Stilton pannacotta with walnut bread	Torcolato Breganze, Vino Dolce, Maculan 2006
Dessert – Kalamansi ravioli with lemongrass	Château Doisy-Daëne 2003
Coffee and chocolates	Macallan 18-year-old whisky

WINNER FOR SCOTLAND AND OVERALL WINNER

THE WITCHERY BY THE CASTLE ◉

EDINBURGH page 582

Where so many strive for individuality by adding 'boutique' character, The Witchery is as strikingly memorable, intriguing and lavish as they come. The two dining rooms (Witchery and Secret Garden) leave a lasting impression: the former with its fabulous oak panelling and tapestries, the latter with its ornately painted ceiling and French windows opening onto a secluded terrace with great views. On the menu is some smart Scottish cooking, rooted in tradition but with a contemporary sheen, complemented by a comprehensive list of over 500 wines put together by owner and wine enthusiast James Thomson. The highly diverse list includes a wide selection of burgundies, over 30 champagnes, and 17 wines available by the glass.

Judges' comments: A superb list which holds your interest throughout. There's clear strength and depth to the expertly chosen selection, along with a great pricing policy ensuring good value at all levels. Intelligent tasting notes are the icing on the cake.

WINNER FOR ENGLAND

NORTHCOTE ◉◉◉◉

LANGHO, LANCASHIRE page 226

Craig Bancroft and Nigel Haworth have owned and run Northcote, overlooking the lush Ribble Valley, since the early 1980s and have evolved it to become one of the best hotel and restaurants in the UK. Achieving four AA Rosettes in 2011, Haworth's reputation is well deserved and he is a passionate champion of Lancashire's culinary history and producers. Meanwhile, Bancroft oversees the running of both hotel and restaurant, including the excellent wine list which he has developed over the years. The comprehensive offering – some 400 bins – has been created with the enjoyment of food and wine at its heart, and includes a wide range of half bottles designed to be matched with Haworth's gourmet menus.

Judges' comments: A beautifully presented list which has quality selections throughout. There's a well chosen range by the glass and it's great to see under-appreciated areas such as Portugal being championed.

WINNER FOR WALES

PARK HOUSE ◉◉

CARDIFF page 622

Once a private club, Park House, which overlooks the gardens of the National Museum of Wales, was designed by William Burges, one of the premier practitioners of the Gothic Revival. The architect is celebrated in the name of the restaurant, which is done out in tones of pinks and peaches against solid oak panel background. Here, chef Jonathan Edwards offers an ambitiously lengthy menu featuring a great deal of prime produce and showcasing a mastery of contemporary technique. The lovingly assembled wine list focuses on highlighting varietal and regional differences, and many of the wines come direct from the cellars of vineyards to ensure the provenance of each bottle is of the highest quality.

Judges' comments: A clear passion and commitment to wine is very evident in this list, with some great depth in vintages. The larger formats listing, wide range of Australian wines and the selection of champagnes are impressive.

Above: Aiden Byrne's sea, soil and oxtail starter involves a multitude of different cooking techniques and equipment

Well Equipped

By Fiona Griffith.

Have you ever wondered how some chefs manage to cook a piece of meat to stunning perfection, how they make a light-as-air foam, or produce an optical illusion on the plate? Today's chefs are using a whole array of techniques and equipment to make their food stand out from the crowd, as Fiona Griffiths has been finding out...

It's the middle of March, 2013, and in a little kitchen above an Italian restaurant in Didsbury, Greater Manchester, some strange looking apparatus has appeared amongst the pots and pans. All tubes, pumps, gauges, funnels and beakers, gleaming white and clinically clean, it looks like the kind of stuff you'd expect to find in a chemistry lab.

In fact, it's enough to make you think Heston Blumenthal has taken over the kitchen, but no, the bespectacled one hasn't made a move north: this scientific paraphernalia belongs to Aiden Byrne, chef-patron of The Church Green British Grill in nearby Lymm, and a finalist in the BBC's *Great British Menu* 2013.

So what's it – and the man himself – doing here? Well, Byrne is temporarily camping out in this rather cramped space while he works on dishes for his new restaurant – Manchester House – which is due to open in Manchester in five months' time.

Located in the city's Spinningfields district, the restaurant will be a whole world away from the kind of simple grills and comfort food dishes he serves at two AA Rosette The Church Green: instead, it will see Byrne return to the fine-dining style of cooking he loves (he used to be head chef at Tom Aikens' eponymous Chelsea restaurant and The Grill at The Dorchester), although every single dish on the menu will be completely new, and will use a multitude of techniques to create the kind of culinary fireworks he hopes will put Manchester House on the global foodie map.

"I've ripped up my old recipes and put them in the bin because I don't want to cook food I've cooked in the past," explains Byrne.

"It's quite easy for a chef, especially when opening a new restaurant, to revert to their default dishes, but having been out of the high-end fine-dining scene for five years, I'm desperate to come up

Aiden Byrne's bacon and onion brioche with pea butter and pea juice

with something brand new and to do something I've never done before."

Hence Byrne has equipped himself with all the latest cheffy gadgets, including a centrifuge, distillation machine, freeze-dryer, rotary evaporator, gastro-vac and homogeniser, and has been developing recipes for his new venture since September [2012].

"The first three months was about getting to understand the equipment," says Byrne.

"Usually this technology would be sold to chemical companies, but the lab equipment suppliers have seen a new market.

"However, it's up to us chefs to work out what we can do with it – for instance, the distillation machine only comes with instructions for distilling water and ethanol, but it's brilliant for clarifying sauces and purées, and you can use it to make a tomato consommé within minutes."

Peas Please

Byrne uses his centrifuge to make a pea butter for his bacon and onion brioche at the new restaurant: frozen peas are boiled and then put in the centrifuge which separates them out into a pure pea water at the top, a pea paste in the middle and a dry pulp at the bottom.

"We mix up the pea paste with whipped butter and the result is fantastic – we couldn't do it any other way," says Byrne, adding that he thinks the centrifuge (which costs around £2,000–£3,000) will be the next staple bit of kit in professional kitchens.

It's certainly a staple in his super-duper new all-induction kitchen at Manchester House, along with a whole load of other, less way-out but equally must-have equipment, such as water baths, an

"Usually this technology would be sold to chemical companies..."

spuma (a cream-whipper for making foams) and a Primo indoor barbecue.

For one of his new dishes – simply called potato and artichoke salad – he uses the espuma to make some 'false white truffles': milk flavoured with parmesan and truffle oil and set with gelatine is put into an espuma canister, before being squirted out onto a palette knife, dropped into liquid nitrogen to freeze it solid, and then rolled in cep powder so it looks like a white truffle.

Multi-tasking

Many of his new creations involve using a combination of different cooking methods, such as cooking meat or fish sous-vide (in a vacuum-sealed bag in a water bath) before finishing off in the barbecue.

"That way you still achieve that really delicate texture that you can get from sous-vide because it slowly cooks the piece of meat or fish, but with a just-roasted flavour from the bars of the grill," explains Byrne.

His 'sea, soil and oxtail' dish, which harks back to the Manchester of the Industrial Revolution, is an incredibly complex starter which utilises practically every bit of equipment at his disposal.

"It's the whole kitchen coming together in one dish with modern techniques and traditional cooking methods," says Byrne.

First he makes an oxtail consommé in a pressure-cooker, and then a beetroot water to add to the consommé to "make it less meaty".

"We put the beetroot through a juicer and then into the distillation machine. Without this machine if I wanted something to evaporate I would need to boil it, but because the beetroot juice is under pressure in the distillation machine, I can take it to just 35–40°C and it will give me a vapour that's

unspoilt, pure beetroot water – it's absolutely amazing" explains Byrne.

The beef component of the dish – a piece of oxtail – is put in the barbecue to give it a smoky flavour before being cooked sous-vide for 100 hours at 50°C.

"That way all the flavour of the smoke in the bag is infused into the oxtail," says Byrne.

As for the oysters, they're kept alive and fed with triple-filtered beetroot juice for 48 hours, which turns them bright red. They're then served in their natural state, as well as being used, along with some samphire, to make an oyster and seaweed vapour in the distillation machine, and an oyster mayonnaise in the homogeniser.

Lastly, Byrne makes an oxtail doughnut to dip in the oyster mayonnaise: oxtail meat is used to make a beef sauce which is reduced down until sticky and then coated with a savoury doughnut batter and deep-fried.

Precision job

Clearly, without all this high-tech, science-y equipment, the menu at Manchester House would be very different, but would it be worse for it?

Byrne believes it wouldn't be as interesting – either for himself or his customers – and his dishes would certainly be less precise.

"I'm 40 now and really thrilled to be in a position where I can do something new and exciting for myself as well as my customers," says Byrne. "I was trained by French traditional chefs and I love that classic way of cooking and don't want to come away from that, but what I do want this equipment to do is enhance that."

He adds: "People may criticise the whole molecular gastronomy movement, but at the end of the day it's given us an understanding of the science that's

happening every time we cook, so we can gain greater control over what we're doing and get much more precise results."

Wishful Thinking

Mark Poynton, chef-patron of Restaurant Alimentum in Cambridge, holder of three AA Rosettes, has a less high-tech kitchen than his counterpart in Manchester, but he's "trying to twist the investor's arm" for some new kit.

Top of his wish-list is a freeze-dryer, but he'd also like the latest Pacojet (a device that micro-purées frozen foods into an ultra-light mousse, cream or sauce without thawing) and, if money was no object, an induction kitchen.

Aiden Byrne's distillation machine

"With a freeze-dryer you can literally freeze-dry anything. So you can make a mousse, freeze-dry it, and it intensifies the flavour because you lose all the water.

"You can also freeze-dry something like asparagus when it's coming towards the end of its season, so you can carry on using the asparagus flavour," says Poynton.

"I think induction is going to be the next big thing every chef wants – having the ability to cook something, take your pan off the heat and then within five-to-ten seconds that area's cool again is just brilliant. It cuts down the heat in the kitchen, saves on gas and saves on man hours because it doesn't take as much cleaning."

As for the Pacojet, he has the original version of the device, which he uses all the time for making instant ice creams and starters like an ultra-light pork liver and foie gras parfait.

"I think the Pacojet and the water bath are the two greatest revolutions in cooking in the last 15 years – the Pacojet because it's made ice creams and sorbets so much more accessible, and the water bath because it's brought more consistency to cooking, providing you know what you're doing," says Poynton.

Combination Cooking

And like Byrne, Poynton has become a big fan in the last year – since he bought a Primo indoor barbecue – of using a combination of sous-vide cooking and grilling.

"I like to combine sous-vide with other techniques like the indoor barbecue – for instance I can achieve a perfect lamb rump by cooking it at 60° C for 30 minutes in the water bath, and then barbecuing it to add a smoky flavour," he says.

He also uses pressure-cookers to cook things quickly that would normally take hours, such as pig cheeks and beef cheeks.

"I can cook a whole ox tongue in 20 minutes in a pressure-cooker, which would otherwise take four hours. They're also brilliant for making sauces and stocks because the cooking time is halved and you're not losing any of the flavour through evaporation," explains Poynton.

He believes his style of food has changed greatly in the last couple of years thanks to the additional kit in his kitchen, but he does have to discipline himself not to rely too heavily on just one piece of equipment.

"The pressure-cookers have enabled me to get fresher and more intense flavours, and the barbecue has just brought a totally different style of cooking I would never have thought of before.

"However, the last thing you want as a customer is to go to a restaurant where there are five main courses and two of them are barbecued, so it's important not to get fixated on one method of cooking."

Spoilt for Choice

There shouldn't be any danger of Ashley Palmer-Watts getting fixated on one particular cooking technique: the executive chef at Dinner by Heston Blumenthal in London's Knightsbridge has just about every gadget and gizmo (and more traditional equipment such as a spit-roast) a chef could possibly desire in his multi-million-pound kitchen.

> "I think the Pacojet and the water bath are the two greatest revolutions in cooking in the last 15 years..."

Mark Poynton uses an espuma to make an apricot mousse and a Pacojet to make a sorbet for his battenburg, apricot and Amaretto dessert

If he had to choose one item as his most essential piece of kit though, it would have to be the water bath.

"I've heard some people say that sous-vide [cooking in a water bath] isn't proper cooking, that it's not teaching chefs how to cook with skill. Our stance on that is that it probably teaches them more skills because you have to understand how to use it and how to get the best out of the particular food you're cooking," says Palmer-Watts.

"We love it because of the consistency we can generate by cooking that way. I've got 57 chefs working in shifts, doing two services a day, 300 covers in total, so to have that consistency running through the kitchen is really, really important."

Two-way Treatment

Several of his dishes start off in the water bath and are finished in the Josper grill (an enclosed, indoor barbecue – see The Thrill of the Grill), such as his black foot pork chop with spelt, ham hock, turnip and Robert sauce.

Palmer-Watts explains: "Because it's a nice thick pork chop with lots of marbling, if we were to just put it into the Josper we'd have to char it too much to get the heat through to the centre, so we temper it for 5 minutes first in the water bath at 35°C to warm it up.

"However, with our spiced pigeon dish we cook it sous-vide all the way and then just roast the skin on the plancha [a metal plate grill]. We also braise a lot of vegetables by cooking them sous-vide."

Consistency is Key

Palmer-Watts is constantly on the quest for new pieces of equipment that will reduce the margin for error and, in turn, make the food at Dinner more consistent. One of the most used items in his kitchen ("it's as much part of the kitchen as a spatula") is a refractometer, which measures the amount of sugar in a fruit purée.

"When you're making something from raspberries for instance, their sweetness is going to vary according to the season and where they've come from, so once you've got your raspberry purée you can look at it through your refractometer and then add stock syrup as necessary to make it sweeter – otherwise you're just guessing, and what's the sense in that?" says Palmer-Watts.

And another piece of kit he wouldn't be without is a dehydrator, which is used for drying purées or crystalising ingredients.

"When I first started cooking, if you wanted to dry something out it was very much a case of leave it under the house lights or in the hot cupboard, and it was a bit finger-in-the-air guesswork, whereas with a dehydrator you've got more control," explains Palmer-Watts. "Of course, it's not essential to have a dehydrator, there are ways around it, but it's the same with all of these things – they just help every chef who uses them achieve better results, and the less you waste as well the more efficient you become."

Ashley Palmer-Watts' blackfoot pork chop with spelt, ham hock, turnip, and Robert sauce

The Thrill of the Grill

If there's one piece of kit on most chefs' wish-lists at the moment, it's a Josper Grill or an Inka Charcoal Oven.

Both are enclosed indoor barbecues, and right now it seems every new restaurant has one or the other (those with a bigger budget opt for the Josper which, at about £12,000, is around twice the price of the Inka).

Aiden Byrne has a Josper at his British Grill at The Macdonald Craxton Wood Hotel in Chester, sister restaurant to The Church Green, where he has an Inka. He says the biggest advantage of cooking meats in an enclosed barbecue (other popular brands are the Primo, Bertha and Green Egg), is the intensity of flavour.

"If you put a burger on an open grill it's going to colour and flavour one side, then you would turn it over and colour and flavour the other side. With these enclosed grills, because the heat is coming from all around rather than just underneath, you're cooking and flavouring the whole thing at once so the flavour is much more intense," explains Byrne.

At The Three Horseshoes in Leek, Staffordshire, brothers Mark and Steve Kirk decided they wanted to showcase the excellent meats they buy from local farmers, so in May 2012 they bought an Inka oven and transformed their two AA Rosette fine-dining restaurant into a grill.

"Our menu was starting to go in a few different directions, so we decided to specialise in grills and we haven't looked back," says Steve. "We decided to rename the restaurant The Inka Grill – using the brand name has been a good move because it makes people curious to find out what it's all about. We've gone from selling 20 burgers a week to selling 80–100, and we do a lot of mid-week trade now."

It's not just burgers and steaks they use the Inka for – trout, flat-breads, leeks (for a lamb dish) and even Thai-style mussels are cooked over charcoal in the oven.

Steve has also been on a course to learn how to cook sous-vide, so several dishes, including a beef fillet, belly pork and marinated ribs, are now cooked in the water bath and then finished in the Inka.

Mark adds: "You've got to move forward as a business and try and keep up with what's going on in the industry."

Call of the Wild

By Mat Follas

Pennywort, bog myrtle, hen of the wood — strange sounding foraged ingredients are cropping up on menus everywhere. But do they taste any good or is this just another passing food fad? Here, foraging fan Mat Follas, winner of the BBC's *MasterChef* in 2009 and chef-patron of The Wild Garlic in Iwerne Minster, Dorset, shares his view.

All European countries have a deep-rooted culture and understanding of wild foods, yet in Britain, foraging is generally seen as something for the sandal-wearing hippy crowd, and is often referred to in the same breath as collecting road-kill and other unsavoury practices. Historically, though, we foraged for key ingredients as much as any European country, yet this seems to have been lost as a result of land clearances during and after the Second World War, and the rise in the 1970s of ready meals as a status symbol, which really meant that eating meals prepared from wild foods was looked down upon as lower status dining.

Thankfully, this is something that is slowly beginning to change.

Led by restaurants like L'Enclume and Le Champignon Sauvage, who consistently produce some of the best cuisine in the world, highly skilled chefs with a passion for amazing food are showing us how it can be enhanced by the remarkable flavours that wild ingredients can give.

My personal inspiration for wild foods came as a foreigner to this country: I saw one of my neighbours come back from a walk with a basket of leaves and flowers he'd collected, which he then proceeded to turn into an amazing meal, with the only additions being a few potatoes and some chicken wings, bought for 10p each from the butcher. His thrift was more than a little admirable, but what shocked me was the explosion of remarkable flavours he achieved, and the underlying fun of what, to him, was an everyday occurrence. It's no surprise though that he hasn't introduced foraging to his family, despite it being a lifelong habit (he's a man in his 80s) as, he says, "they wouldn't eat this type of food".

My first wild food dish was scallops I'd dived for myself, barbecued and tossed in some melted butter with a few wild garlic leaves chopped through. Simple but absolutely delicious, and flavours that no shop-bought scallops or regular garlic could have provided. It's a dish I replicated when I was on *MasterChef* and gained huge praise for from the judges. It made me appreciate how lucky I am to live in this part of Britain, and was the start of my journey to understand the produce that's freely available.

The revival of wild food in popular culture has to be laid at the feet of Hugh Fearnley-Whittingstall, who brought an awareness that the green things often can be eaten, can be fun and, more than anything, can taste good.

A bunch of red-nosed farmers in a shed sampling scrumpy cider in the depths of winter is about as far away from the overly corporatised, manufactured life that so many of us were leading; it seemed a kind of nirvana, but in a terribly British way.

It led us to Dorset on holiday, and we were lucky enough to get the opportunity to make the break from our old lives to something more real – we moved to Dorset and found ourselves in an area where farming and living off the land are part of the everyday. That way of living is a delight to us and part of the experience we want our guests to enjoy too.

Not everything about wild food foraging is great. It needs to be remembered that just because you can eat something, it doesn't necessarily mean it's good – a lot of things that you can eat to survive frankly don't taste very nice, or of anything, so why bother?

I've seen cooks making the mistake of using a foraged ingredient to be trendy rather than trusting their taste buds when it's obvious the ingredient is really adding very little to their dish.

I'm also not a fan of using wild ingredients sourced a long distance from a restaurant – I believe it should be something special about the area the restaurant is in and that the picking of the wild ingredients is tightly controlled to minimise damage to the environment. Many plants I pick in small amounts for personal use I would never use in my restaurant as the impact on the environment would be too great.

Keeping it local can often seem like a buzzword, but restaurants that do it well, like those in this guide, do bring something truly special to the whole dining experience.

We need to be sensible when foraging: wild chervil and hogweed are great unusual ingredients, but they also often grow alongside a variety of hemlock that can be misidentified and is very poisonous – as Socrates found out to his cost. Similarly, lords and ladies, which is known to cause anaphylactic shock, often grows alongside wild garlic, and without care can be picked by mistake. A death cap mushroom looks, to the untrained eye, like a common field mushroom.

My advice is never, ever start to forage using just a book to identify. Begin with two or three simple plants, such as wild garlic, nettles and blackberries, and then get someone with proper experience to show you.

I recommend you don't forage for mushrooms at all unless you are really committed to learning and take care –

Mat Follas discovers a bumper crop of wild garlic growing in the woods

here are plenty of very good cultivated mushrooms for very little cost.

However, there are some mushrooms that are more identifiable: hedgehog, chanterelle, puffballs and porcini are the only mushrooms I forage for – the rest leave to the real experts.

A good friend of mine and a forager who used to supply our restaurant, the late Jo Francis, spent her life learning about mushrooms, and she had the best philosophy on the subject I've come across – there are 50 or so varieties of mushrooms that you can eat, and frankly only about ten of them taste any good.

I believe her philosophy holds just as strongly for most wild foods. It is worth the effort to have, say, a top ten plants which are simple to identify, create flavour combinations that cultivated plants can't easily achieve, and have a minimal impact on the environment. As you might have guessed, wild garlic would be at the top of my list!

Restaurants are windows to different worlds. There's the classic formal restaurant we all know, with white starched tablecloths, silver service and fawning waiting staff, which still has its place in modern restaurant culture, but at the other end of the scale, where The Wild Garlic sits, is more experiential, albeit a fairly gentle introduction to some of the more unusual flavours that can be found in this part of the UK.

Others certainly do it better than us: L'Enclume, Le Champignon Sauvage, The Elephant – all three AA Rosette awarded and above. We're still on our journey and frankly delighted to be one of just 19 restaurants in Dorset to hold two AA Rosettes. We choose a casualness of style that reflects the type of restaurant we like to dine in, but have seen foraged ingredients used

Mat's 'cheese and pickles' dish features leaves and flowers from wild chervil (cow parsley)

abundantly in far more formal dining environments too.

So what next for foraging as a food trend ?

Trends come and go by their nature. We now see that Copenhagen's Noma, where foraged ingredients are at the heart of the operation, is no longer ranked as the number one restaurant in the world, and The Fat Duck and other restaurants that focus on molecular gastronomy are now struggling to stay in the top 50.

The next movement, in my humble opinion, will focus on elegance of presentation and using a mixture of recent trends – molecular gastronomy and foraged and unusual ingredients – but with a deep-rooted style based on classic techniques and classic dishes.

By classic, I mean classic to that region, country and culture, and in that, I think British restaurants really can, and do, hold their own. We have a rich heritage of traditional dishes, many of which are being re-introduced into restaurant culture as we start to take a real pride in great British dishes, cooked well.

As part of that whole movement, I believe foraging is now moving into the mainstream, as many restaurants now use ingredients that would have been considered foraged and really quite daring only a few years ago. Samphire is now readily available; specialist companies supplying the restaurant trade now grow ingredients like sea kale, a Victorian delicacy that was cultivated until the 1970s and is now making a slow comeback.

I'm delighted to have played a small part in bringing wild food foraging into the mainstream of the restaurant trade and into the public awareness – it's a special and fun part of our cultural heritage that should not be lost.

You can learn more about foraging by joining Mat Follas on one of his one-day wild food courses. The course starts with a drink and a chat about edible wild plants, followed by a few hours exploring the countryside and seashore looking for plants of culinary value, before heading back to The Wild Garlic for a late three-course lunch hosted by Mat. For more details visit thewildgarlic.co.uk

It's all about wine at The Vineyard at Stockcross near Newbury

It's a Grape Life

By Fiona Griffiths

If you have a passion for wine, working as a sommelier must surely be your dream job. But what does the role entail? Fiona Griffiths spent a day with Alan Holmes, director of wine at five AA red star hotel The Vineyard, near Newbury in Berkshire, to find out.

For a hotel that specialises in wine, with 3,000 bottles on the list, 100 wines available by the glass, and two tasting menus with a different wine matched to each dish, having a glass-washer out of action over a busy Easter weekend is nothing short of a disaster.

It's little wonder Alan Holmes is looking rather tired when we meet: he was polishing glasses until 2am at the weekend to keep up with the demand.

"We sell 80 per cent of our wines by the glass which is a huge undertaking, especially on a Saturday night when you've got 100 guests in the restaurant all having between five and seven courses, and each course having a matching wine. It certainly means a lot of glass washing," says Holmes.

"We're doing a refurbishment of our glass storage room where the main glass-washer is and it was only meant to take a week, but it's turned into three weeks.

"We've got a smaller glass-washer but it's slower and only takes 12 glasses at a time, so over Easter we had to bring in extra staff who were literally polishing glasses from 7.30am until 2am, and I had to help out too."

So it's not all overseas trips to vineyards and tastings of Chateau Margaux when you reach the top of your game as a sommelier (although there is a fair amount of that) – from time to time you still have to do the sommelier equivalent of shelling peas.

In fact, as I quickly discover, Holmes's job is full of variety – on any one day he might be giving a wine masterclass (perhaps on how temperature affects flavour or how to set up a cellar), taking some guests on a cellar tour and private tasting, running a wine school event (anything from 'ten wines to try before you die' to 'the classics explained'), doing a stock-take in the cellar, or selecting wines for a corporate function, wedding or wine dinner.

This afternoon he's heading over to The Vineyard's nearby sister property, The Donnington Valley hotel, to lead a staff training session on spirits, followed by a meeting and tasting session with a supplier.

With a name like The Vineyard, you might think there are vines to be tended as well, but the vineyard in question – rather, there are three of them – is actually out in California, and owned, like the hotel, by local entrepreneur Sir Peter Michael. Around 20 per cent of the wines on the list are from the Peter Michael Winery and other top Californian producers, although the rest of the world gets a very good showing too.

Holmes admits he knew comparatively little about Californian wine when he was interviewed for the job at The Vineyard in November 2012, but he soon got a crash course when he was sent out to California a few days later.

A Sommelier's life: Alan Holmes (left) tastes the stock

"I was due to have a couple of weeks off after leaving my old job and I got a call asking if I could spare the time to go out to California. I went out with James Hocking, who runs The Vineyard's sister business Vineyard Cellars [a specialist Californian wine merchant], and we visited 25 wineries in one week.

"It was funny because everywhere we went people would ask how long I'd been at The Vineyard, and I had to say I hadn't actually started working there yet!"

Since then, Holmes has been out to California again – this time with his girlfriend as a part holiday/part work trip – and he's clearly now able to share in the passion Sir Peter Michael has for the wines of the American west coast.

That's just as well, as many of the wine-related activities at The Vineyard are centered, naturally, around Californian wines.

The hotel's wine bar – where most tasting sessions are held – is named the California Bar and is decorated with a huge, specially-commissioned painting depicting the Judgement of Paris competition in 1976 when a selection of the finest French Bordeauxs and Californian cabernet sauvignons were pitted against each other in blind tastings, and the Californian wines came out on top.

"We try to pair the wines up as much as possible, but we do want people to see there's a difference between France and California"

The competition provides the inspiration for the seven-course Judgement tasting menu in the restaurant; go for the optional wine pairings (if you can afford to splash out another £86 a head on top of the £89 for the food) and Holmes or a member of his team will present you with six Californian wines and six French (in 125ml measures), and it's up to you to vote for your favourite.

Holmes explains: "We try to pair the wines up as much as possible, but we do want people to see there's a difference between France and California – to show there are characteristics that are quite similar, but also slight variances."

That evening in the restaurant, my Cornish brill with chanterelles, salsify and Swiss chard comes with a glass of Saintsbury chardonnay 2010 from California's Napa Valley, matched against a glass of Domaine Testut chablis 2011 (one point to California). And my Balmoral Estate venison with butternut squash, pearl barley and hazelnut is accompanied by Peter Michael's Bordeaux Blend (a blend of cabernet franc, cabernet sauvignon, petit verdot and merlot) 2008, and a glass of Chateau Cos d'Estournel St Estephe 2nd cru classe 2003 (another point to California).

Just to make things a little more fun, some of the wines are served in black glasses (mimicking the blind tasting of the Judgement of Paris), with your challenge to guess whether the contents are French or Californian and the grape variety.

Thus my ballotine of guinea fowl with lemon and walnuts comes with a black glass which turns out to contain a biodynamic pinot gris from California's Sonoma Valley 2010 – suffice to say I didn't manage to guess the country or the grape variety correctly, but it was an interesting test.

The alternative tasting menu – aptly named The Discovery – is possibly even more eye-opening.

This time there are five courses (at £49 a head) matched (for an extra £45) with five wines from lesser-known areas around the world.

That might translate to a malagousia from Greece, a riesling from Slovakia, a koshu from Japan or a cabernet sauvignon from China.

"It's grapes you wouldn't normally choose and countries or regions you would maybe pass by," explains Holmes.

"We tend to use the Discovery menu as an opportunity to try different things and get feedback from the guests, because you can go to trade tastings and try a wine in a line up and think it's great, but then you get it back here and try it in a

The California Bar with its giant mural of the Judgement of Paris wine competition

food scenario and it maybe doesn't show up as well.

"Often we'll buy one or two cases of something and if it's not favourably received we won't buy anymore."

The Discovery menu may be a good way of trying out wines from unusual places, but it's not all about novelty.

"It's no good having something interesting as a wine if it doesn't go with the dish. The idea is to create a wow factor with the wine, the food, and then the two perfectly matched together," says Holmes.

Creating that 'wow factor' can't be easy, so how does he do it? How does he select a wine that's both interesting and that complements a particular dish to a tee?

Well, having a chef – in the shape of Frenchman Daniel Galmiche – who understands the task at hand is paramount to begin.

With 30,000 bottles in the cellar, 3,000 wines and a whopping 100 available by the glass, keeping track of vintages, making sure nothing gets past its best and ensuring stocks don't get too low is a mammoth task

Galmiche knows to steer clear of powerful, dominating flavours in his cooking ("artichokes are a stand out no-no, as are very strong vinaigrettes or very strong spices") and to make his dishes adaptable so they can be matched with the variety of different wines available.

Holmes explains: "On a regular basis chef will put a dish up on the pass and say this is an idea I'm thinking of doing, and I'll go away, look at the key elements and maybe come up with three or four different wines I think will work.

"We'll then taste them with the dish, see how the wine affects the food and the food affects the wine, and if there's an element of the dish that's a standout problem with the wines he'll tell me what he can do to temper the acidity, saltiness, richness or whatever it may be.

"The other thing we have to make sure with the tasting menus is that the set up is right so you get a flow of the wines, as it's no good jumping back and forth between different flavours."

With 30,000 bottles in the cellar, 3,000 wines and a whopping 100 available by the glass, keeping track of vintages, making sure nothing gets past its best and ensuring stocks don't get too low is a mammoth task.

It's for that reason that Holmes changes the by-the-glass list – or 'The Short List' as it's known – every two weeks.

Climbing the ladder

Alan Holmes originally set out to be a chef and went to catering college full of dreams of one day opening his own restaurant. But during his course he spent some time front-of-house and found he enjoyed being customer-facing instead of tucked away in a kitchen.

"I really enjoyed the guest interaction and I found I was also really interested in the drinks side. I was intrigued as to how two wines made from the same grape in the same year from two villages side by side could taste so different from each other," he says.

At college he won a food and wine service competition for which the prize was two weeks' work experience, shadowing the head sommelier, at Hambleton Hall in Rutland.

His first job quickly followed – working as a commis wine waiter at the renowned Sharrow Bay in the Lake District – before moving on two years later to Paul Heathcote in Lancashire as an assistant sommelier. From there he moved to London to work at Gordon Ramsay's Petrus for three years.

"There I had the opportunity to taste some of the most amazing wines in the world, including a 1961 Petrus in both bottle and magnum side by side," says Holmes.

After three years at Petrus he went to Chewton Glen in Hampshire where he stayed for eight years, working his way up from head sommelier to wine and beverage manager, before taking up his position as director of wine at The Vineyard at the end of 2012.

Alan Holmes (right) shares a drink with chef Daniel Galmiche

"With 100 wines by the glass we have to change them regularly because we've got to keep it moving through the Discovery and Judgement menus and wine matching with the a la carte," says Holmes. "If we've got a busy weekend coming up I'll plan for the weekend by going through the dishes on the three menus and working out which wines we'll pair up with what.

"Every week I'll also choose something light and crisp from the cellar for our Friday night liquid amuse-bouche – we'll send a couple of glasses to guests' rooms with their luggage when they arrive to refresh the palate after a long journey and get them in the mood for the weekend."

The main list (or 'The Long List') also gets updated on an ongoing basis as wines sell out, vintages change or new wines come in.

"The main list is changing all the time – every week we do vintage checks and we'll reprint certain pages of the list, then every six weeks we'll do a complete reprint.

"With 3000 wines you do get to a point where certain lines are irreplaceable and we're always bringing in new wines. We regularly get samples in from our suppliers as we're always looking for new things," explains Holmes.

A three-monthly stocktake by a specialist wine auditor helps him keep track, but he and his team also need to carefully monitor sales.

"The auditor does the nitty gritty of counting all the bottles but the rest of the time it's a case of backtracking deliveries and invoices against our sales and doing spot-checks on a regular basis," says Holmes. "Although the wines are kept at the optimum condition in our cellars they can get past their vintage or use by date so we're very careful to make sure they don't get too far down the line. Having started here in December [2012] I know there are a few things that are getting too mature, so we'll give them away as staff incentives, and anything starting to show signs of oxidation we'll give to the kitchen or use for staff training."

And having a good knowledge of what's in the cellars and what's drinking well enables Holmes to pick an 'icon wine' to offer to guests every Saturday night. The chosen wine – "either a great vintage, a unique wine or a rarity" – is offered by the glass at just slightly above cost price.

"For example, we might offer a top burgundy for £40 or £50 a glass that would be £600–£800 a bottle on our list. It's great for people who are big enough wine aficionados that they'd like to try something like that and to know whether an £800 bottle of wine is worth it, but who won't ever be able to afford to buy a bottle," says Holmes.

Of course, Holmes has tried his fair share of great wines himself: amongst his top five are Henschke Hill of Grace Shiraz 1975 ("a remarkable wine – the nose when I opened it was of white chocolate, very creamy almost"), Angelo Gaja Sori San Lorenzo Barbaresco 1985 ("a magnificent wine that showed a variety of aromas from dried rose petals through to white truffle"), and Dom Ruinart Rose 1982 ("very mature but astounding with a lamb dish drunk in the cellars at Ruinart when I attended the European Sommelier of the Year dinner").

Surely, for a sommelier, these kinds of tasting experiences must be the best part of the job? Surprisingly, Holmes says not.

"The thing that gives me the most enjoyment is the guest satisfaction – it's the moment when you give a guest a glass of a wine that they're not expecting and you see them taste it and go 'wow, that's actually really good'. That's the best bit for me."

Let's all raise a glass to that.

> "I was intrigued as to how two wines made from the same grape in the same year from two villages side by side could taste so different from each other"

Alan Holmes's most memorable wine moment

"I was in a small fish restaurant in Canada about 12 years ago and the wine list was literally just the name of the wine and the price. There was a Corton Charlemagne white Burgundy for $85 (the exchange rate was $3 to the pound) which the restaurant owner said he thought was a '95 vintage. When it turned out to be an '85 vintage he said he didn't think it was going to be any good, but it was from one of the best producers [Domaine Bonneau] and we were selling it for around £300 a bottle from quite recent vintages in London, so we said we'll have it. We drank it and it was amazing. I gave the man a glass and it was brilliant seeing his face as he realised what a fantastic wine it was.

I then confessed to my sommelier profession and asked him what he had in the way of red, and he got quite excited. He went off to unlock a wardrobe that was full of bottles of red wine. He wanted me to tell him what I knew ... I picked a bottle of Ornellaia from Bolgheri in Tuscany ... at the end of the meal he wouldn't let me pay a thing because he was just so thrilled I'd enlightened him about his wine collection.

To find these hidden gems in a small seafood restaurant above a shop in Vancouver was just amazing."

FARMHOUSE TOUCH –
AT HOME WITH THE PRESENT,
INSPIRED BY THE PAST.

The captivating charm of Farmhouse Touch makes any occasion a special occasion. Relaxed, informal and designed for the way we live today. Mix and match the white and Blueflowers versions to express your individuality, or combine with Farmhouse Touch cutlery and glassware to create a perfect sense of home.

Villeroy & Boch
1748

SPONSORING THE AA AWARDS

Villeroy & Boch are proud to have presented the AA Awards for the past 22 years. Quality and inspiration are the defining qualities of a great restaurant. They are also the values that have made Villeroy & Boch, with its tradition of innovation dating back to 1748, the leading tableware brand in Europe. Dining with friends and family, and enjoying good food and drink together are special to all of us, and these occasions are made all the more special when served on beautiful tableware from Villeroy & Boch. Our distinctive and original designs have consistently set the pace for others to follow and provide the perfect setting chosen by many of the world's leading chefs to frame their award-winning creations. Villeroy & Boch offer a wide range of stunning designs to suit any lifestyle and décor, and create the perfect ambience for successful entertaining and stylish family living.

UK and Ireland customer services line: 0208-871-0011
line open Monday-Friday 9am-5pm

JOIN OUR 1748 CLUB

Subscribe to our FREE 1748 Club email newsletter, and you'll find it packed with:
• Recipes
• New products
• Exclusive Members' offers
• Top tips from our stylist
• Competitions
• Chef's corner
• Table style advice
• Product care
• How to guides
And much more besides. Just register online at **www.1748club.co.uk/newsletter**
Incidentally, our 1748Club web site was recently voted 'web site of the week' by a leading women's weekly magazine.

AA MEMBERS SAVE 10%

As an AA member you enjoy **10% off** when shopping online using this link:
www.theaa.com/rewards
In addition, members of the AA also receive **10% off** full price products in any of our Concession Stores on presentation of an AA membership card. For a list of stockists go to www.1748club.co.uk and click on Where Can I See.

Visit our community web site at:
www.1748club.co.uk

The Top Ten Per Cent

Each year all the restaurants in the AA Restaurant Guide are awarded a specially commissioned plate that marks their achievement in gaining one or more AA Rosettes. The plates represent a partnership between the AA and Villeroy & Boch – two quality brands working together to recognise high standards in restaurant cooking.

Restaurants awarded three, four or five AA Rosettes represent the Top Ten Per Cent of the restaurants in this Guide. The pages that follow list those establishments that have attained this special status.

5 ROSETTES

LONDON

Marcus Wareing at The Berkeley
The Berkeley, Wilton Place, Knightsbridge, SW1
020 7235 1200

Tom Aikens
43 Elystan Street, SW3
020 7584 2003

Hibiscus
29 Maddox Street, Mayfair, W1
020 7629 2999

Sketch (Lecture Room & Library)
9 Conduit Street, W1
020 7659 4500

ENGLAND

BERKSHIRE
The Fat Duck
High Street, BRAY, SL6 2AQ
01628 580333

CAMBRIDGESHIRE
Midsummer House
Midsummer Common, CAMBRIDGE, CB4 1HA
01223 369299

CUMBRIA
L'Enclume
Cavendish Street, CARTMEL, LA11 6PZ
015395 36362

DEVON
Gidleigh Park
CHAGFORD, TQ13 8HH
01647 432367

NOTTINGHAMSHIRE
Restaurant Sat Bains with Rooms
Lenton Lane, Trentside NOTTINGHAM, NG7 2SA
0115 986 6566

OXFORDSHIRE
Le Manoir aux Quat' Saisons
Church Road GREAT MILTON, OX44 7PD
01844 278881

SURREY
Michael Wignall at The Latymer
Pennyhill Park Hotel & Spa, London Road, BAGSHOT, GU19 5EU
01276 471774

4 ROSETTES

LONDON

Seven Park Place by William Drabble
St James's Hotel and Club, 7-8 Park Place, SW1
020 7316 1600

Restaurant Gordon Ramsay
68 Royal Hospital Road, SW3
020 7352 4441

Alain Ducasse at The Dorchester
The Dorchester, 53 Park Lane, W1
020 7629 8866

Hélène Darroze at The Connaught
Carlos Place, W1
020 3147 7200

Murano
20-22 Queen Street, W1
020 7495 1127

Pied à Terre
34 Charlotte Street, W1
020 7636 1178

Pollen Street Social
8-10 Pollen Street, W1
020 7290 7600

The Square
6-10 Bruton Street Mayfair, W1
020 7495 7100

Launceston Place Restaurant
1a Launceston Place, W8
020 7937 6912

LONDON, GREATER

Chapter One
Farnborough Common, Locksbottom, BROMLEY, BR6 8NF
01689 854848

ENGLAND

BERKSHIRE
Waterside Inn
Ferry Road, BRAY, SL6 2AT
01628 620691

L'ortolan
Church Lane, SHINFIELD, RG2 9BY
0118 988 8500

BRISTOL
Casamia Restaurant
38 High Street, Westbury-on-Trym, BRISTOL, BS9 3DZ
0117 959 2884

BUCKINGHAMSHIRE
Adam Simmonds at Danesfield House
Henley Road, MARLOW, SL7 2EY
01628 891010

The Hand & Flowers
126 West Street MARLOW, SL7 2BP
01628 482277

CHESHIRE
Simon Radley at The Chester Grosvenor
Chester Grosvenor & Spa, Eastgate, CHESTER, CH1 1LT
01244 324024

GLOUCESTERSHIRE
Le Champignon Sauvage
24-28 Suffolk Road,
CHELTENHAM,
GL50 2AQ
01242 573449

LANCASHIRE
Northcote
Northcote Road,
LANGHO, BB6 8BE
01254 240555

RUTLAND
Hambleton Hall
Hambleton,
OAKHAM,
LE15 8TH
01572 756991

SUSSEX, WEST
**The Pass Restaurant at
South Lodge Hotel**
Brighton Road,
LOWER BEEDING,
RH13 6PS
01403 891711

WILTSHIRE
Whatley Manor Hotel and Spa
Easten Grey,
MALMESBURY,
SN16 0RB
01666 822888

JERSEY
**Ocean Restaurant
at the Atlantic Hotel**
Le Mont de la Pulente,
ST BRELADE, JE3 8HE
01534 744101

SCOTLAND
CITY OF EDINBURGH
The Kitchin
78 Commercial Quay,
Leith, EDINBURGH,
EH6 6LX
0131 555 1755

Restaurant Martin Wishart
54 The Shore,
Leith,
EDINBURGH,
EH6 6RA
0131 553 3557

21212
3 Royal Terrace,
EDINBURGH,
EH7 5AB
0131 523 1030

HIGHLAND
Boath House
Auldearn,
NAIRN,
IV12 5TE
01667 454896

PERTH & KINROSS
**Andrew Fairlie @
Gleneagles**
The Gleneagles Hotel,
AUCHTERARDER,
PH3 1NF
01764 694267

REPUBLIC OF IRELAND
DUBLIN
**Restaurant Patrick
Guilbaud**
Merrion Hotel,
21 Upper Merrion Street,
DUBLIN
01 676 4192

CO WATERFORD
The Cliff House Hotel
ARDMORE
024 87800

3 ROSETTES

LONDON
E1
Galvin La Chapelle
St. Botolph's Hall,
35 Spital Square
020 7299 0400

E2
Viajante
Patriot Square,
Bethnal Green
020 7871 0461

EC1
Club Gascon
57 West Smithfield
020 7600 6144

EC2
1901 Restaurant
ANdAZ London,
40 Liverpool Street
020 7618 7000

NW1
Odette's Restaurant & Bar
130 Regent's Park Road
020 7586 8569

SW1
**Ametsa with Arzak
Instruction**
The Halkin Hotel,
5 Halkin Street
020 7333 1234

**Apsleys at
The Lanesborough**
Hyde Park Corner
020 7333 7254

**Dinner by
Heston Blumenthal**
Mandarin Oriental,
Hyde Park,
66 Knightsbridge
020 7201 3833

Koffmann's
The Berkeley, Wilton Place
020 7235 1010

One–O–One
The Park Tower,
Knightsbridge,
101 Knightsbridge
020 7290 7101

Pétrus
1 Kinnerton Street,
Knightsbridge
020 7592 1609

The Rib Room
Jumeirah Carlton,
Tower Hotel, Cadogan Place
020 7858 7250

**Thirty Six by Nigel
Mendham at Dukes London**
35–36 St James's Place
020 7491 4840

SW3
Outlaw's at The Capital
22-24 Basil Street,
Knightsbridge
020 7589 5171

Rasoi Restaurant
10 Lincoln Street
020 7225 1881

SW4
Trinity Restaurant
4 The Polygon,
Clapham
020 7622 1199

SW10
Medlar Restaurant
438 King's Road
020 7349 1900

SW17
Chez Bruce
2 Bellevue Road,
Wandsworth Common
020 8672 0114

continued overleaf

3 ROSETTES

CONTINUED

W1
**Alyn Williams at
The Westbury**
Bond Street
020 7078 9579

Arbutus Restaurant
63–64 Frith Street
020 7734 4545

L'Autre Pied
5–7 Blandford Street,
Marylebone Village
020 7486 9696

Brasserie Chavot
41 Conduit Street,
Mayfair
020 7183 6425

Corrigan's Mayfair
28 Upper Grosvenor Street
020 7499 9943

CUT at 45 Park Lane
45 Park Lane
020 7493 4545

Dabbous
39 Whitfield St
020 7323 1544

**Galvin at Windows
Restaurant & Bar**
London Hilton on
Park Lane,
22 Park Lane
020 7208 4021

Gauthier Soho
21 Romilly Street
020 7494 3111

Le Gavroche Restaurant
43 Upper Brook Street
020 7408 0881

The Greenhouse
27a Hay's Mews
020 7499 3331

Hakkasan Mayfair
17 Bruton Street
020 7907 1888

Locanda Locatelli
8 Seymour Street
020 7935 9088

Maze
London Marriott Hotel,
10–13 Grosvenor Square
020 7107 0000

The Ritz Restaurant
150 Piccadilly
020 7300 2370

Roka
37 Charlotte Street
020 7580 6464

Sketch (The Gallery)
9 Conduit Street
020 7659 4500

Social Eating House
58–59 Poland Street
020 7993 3251

Texture Restaurant
DoubleTree by Hilton
Hotel, 34 Portman Street
020 7224 0028

Theo Randall
1 Hamilton Place,
Hyde Park Corner
020 7318 8747

Umu
14–16 Bruton Place
020 7499 8881

Wild Honey
12 Saint George Street
020 7758 9160

W6
The River Café
Thames Wharf Studios,
Rainville Road
020 7386 4200

W8
Kitchen W8
11-13 Abingdon Road,
Kensington
020 7937 0120

Min Jiang
Royal Garden Hotel,
2–24 Kensington,
High Street
020 7361 1988

W11
The Ledbury
127 Ledbury Road,
020 7792 9090

WC2
L'Atelier de Joël Robuchon
13–15 West Street
020 7010 8600

Clos Maggiore
33 King Street
020 7379 9696

LONDON, GREATER

The Glasshouse
14 Station Parade,
KEW, TW9 3PZ
020 8940 6777

Bingham
61–63 Petersham Road,
RICHMOND-UPON-
THAMES, TW10 6UT
020 8940 0902

ENGLAND

BEDFORDSHIRE
Paris House Restaurant
London Road, Woburn
Park, WOBURN
MK17 9QP
01525 290692

BERKSHIRE
Restaurant Coworth Park
Blacknest Road,
ASCOT SL5 7SE
01344 876600

Royal Oak at Paley Street
Littlefield Green,
MAIDENHEAD, SL6 3JN
01628 620541

The Vineyard
Stockcross, NEWBURY
RG20 8JU
01635 528770

BUCKINGHAMSHIRE
The Artichoke
9 Market Square,
Old Amersham,
AMERSHAM HP7 0DF
01494 726611

**Aubergine at
The Compleat Angler**
Marlow Bridge,
MARLOW, SL7 1RG
01628 405405

Humphry's at Stoke Park
Park Road, STOKE POGES
SL2 4PG
01753 717171

Stoke Place
Stoke Green, STOKE
POGES SL2 4HT
01753 534790

CAMBRIDGESHIRE
Restaurant Alimentum
152–154 Hills Road,
CAMBRIDGE, CB2 8PB
01223 413000

CHESHIRE
The Alderley Restaurant
Alderley Edge Hotel,
Macclesfield Road,
ALDERLEY EDGE
SK9 7BJ
01625 583033

**1851 Restaurant at
Peckforton Castle**
Stonehouse Lane,
PECKFORTON,
CW6 9TN
01829 260930

CORNWALL &
ISLES OF SCILLY
Hell Bay
BRYHER, TR23 0PR
01720 422947

Paul Ainsworth at No. 6
6 Middle Street
PADSTOW,
PL28 8AP
01841 532093

The Seafood Restaurant
Riverside, PADSTOW,
PL28 8BY
01841 532700

Driftwood
Rosevine, PORTSCATHO
TR2 5EW
01872 580644

Restaurant Nathan Outlaw
The St Enodoc Hotel,
ROCK, PL27 6LA
01208 863394

Hotel Tresanton
27 Lower Castle Road,
ST MAWES, TR2 5DR
01326 270055

CUMBRIA
Rogan & Company Restaurant
The Square, CARTMEL
LA11 6QD
015395 35917

Hipping Hall
Cowan Bridge,
KIRKBY LONSDALE,
LA6 2JJ
015242 71187

Gilpin Hotel & Lake House
Crook Road,
WINDERMERE,
LA23 3NE
015394 88818

Holbeck Ghyll Country House Hotel
Holbeck Lane,
WINDERMERE, LA23 1LU
015394 32375

Linthwaite House Hotel & Restaurant
Crook Road,
WINDERMERE,
LA23 3JA
015394 88600

The Samling
Ambleside Road,
WINDERMERE,
LA23 1LR
015394 31922

DERBYSHIRE
Fischer's Baslow Hall
Calver Road,
BASLOW,
DE45 1RR
01246 583259

The Peacock at Rowsley
Bakewell Road,
ROWSLEY, DE4 2EB
01629 733518

DEVON
The Old Inn
DREWSTEIGNTON,
EX6 6QR
01647 281276

The Elephant Restaurant & Brasserie
3/4 Beacon Terrace,
TORQUAY,
TQ1 2BH
01803 200044

DORSET
Sienna
36 High West Street,
DORCHESTER
DT1 1UP
01305 250022

Summer Lodge Country House Hotel, Restaurant & Spa
Fore Street,
EVERSHOT DT2 0JR
01935 482000

CO DURHAM
Wynyard Hall Hotel
Wynyard,
BILLINGHAM
TS22 5NF
01740 644811

Rockliffe Hall
Rockliffe Park,
Hurworth on Tees,
DARLINGTON,
DL2 2DU
01325 729999

GLOUCESTERSHIRE
Ellenborough Park
Southam Road,
CHELTENHAM,
GL52 3NH
01242 545454

The Feathered Nest Country Inn
NETHER WESTCOTE,
OX7 6SD
01993 833030

Lords of the Manor
UPPER SLAUGHTER,
GL54 2JD
01451 820243

Cotswolds88 Hotel
Kemps Lane,
PAINSWICK, GL6 6YB
01452 813688

GREATER MANCHESTER
The French by Simon Rogan
Peter Street,
MANCHESTER,
M60 2DS
0161 236 3333

HAMPSHIRE
The Montagu Arms Hotel
Palace Lane,
BEAULIEU
SO42 7ZL
01590 612324

36 on the Quay
47 South Street,
EMSWORTH
PO10 7EG
01243 375592

Hartnett Holder & Co
Lime Wood,
Beaulieu Road,
LYNDHURST
SO43 7FZ
023 8028 7167

Chewton Glen Hotel & Spa
Christchurch Road,
NEW MILTON
BH25 6QS
01425 282212

JSW
20 Dragon Street,
PETERSFIELD
GU31 4JJ
01730 262030

Avenue Restaurant at Lainston House Hotel
Woodman Lane, Sparsholt
WINCHESTER
SO21 2LT
01962 776088

HERTFORDSHIRE
Colette's at The Grove
Chandler's Cross,
RICKMANSWORTH
WD3 4TG
01923 807807

Auberge du Lac
Brocket Hall Estate,
Brocket Road,
WELWYN, AL8 7XG
01707 368888

KENT
The West House
28 High Street,
BIDDENDEN
TN27 8AH
01580 291341

Apicius
23 Stone Street,
CRANBROOK TN17 3HF
01580 714666

The Marquis at Alkham
Alkham Valley Road,
Alkham, DOVER
CT15 7DF
01304 873410

Thackeray's
85 London Road,
TUNBRIDGE WELLS
TN1 1EA
01892 511921

LANCASHIRE
The Freemasons at Wiswell
8 Vicarage Fold,
Wiswell, WHALLEY
BB7 9DF
01254 822218

LINCOLNSHIRE
Harry's Place
17 High Street,
Great Gonerby,
GRANTHAM
NG31 8JS
01476 561780

Winteringham Fields
WINTERINGHAM
DN15 9ND
01724 733096

MERSEYSIDE
Fraiche
11 Rose Mount,
Oxton Village,
BIRKENHEAD
CH43 5SG
0151 652 2914

continued overleaf

3 ROSETTES

CONTINUED

MERSEYSIDE continued

Stewart Warner at Hillbark
Hillbark Hotel and Spa,
Royden Park, FRANKBY
CH48 1NP
0151 625 2400

The Lawns Restaurant
Thornton Hall Hotel,
Neston Road, THORNTON
HOUGH, CH63 1JF
0151 336 3938

NORFOLK
Morston Hall
Morston, Holt,
BLAKENEY, NR25 7AA
01263 741041

**The Neptune Restaurant
with Rooms**
85 Old Hunstanton Road,
HUNSTANTON
PE36 6HZ
01485 532122

**Roger Hickman's
Restaurant**
79 Upper St Giles Street
NORWICH, NR2 1AB
01603 633522

Titchwell Manor Hotel
TITCHWELL, PE31 8BB
01485 210221

NORTHAMPTONSHIRE
**Rushton Hall Hotel
& Spa**
Rushton,
KETTERING
NN14 1RR
01536 713001

OXFORDSHIRE
The Sir Charles Napier
Sprigg's Alley,
CHINNOR
OX39 4BX
01494 483011

Orwells
Shiplake Row, Binfield
Heath, HENLEY-ON-
THAMES RG9 4DP
0118 940 3673

SHROPSHIRE
Fishmore Hall
Fishmore Road,
LUDLOW SY8 3DP
01584 875148

SOMERSET
Abbey Hotel Bath
1 North Parade,
BATH, BA1 1LF
01225 461603

**Bath Priory Hotel,
Restaurant & Spa**
Weston Road,
BATH BA1 2XT
01225 331922

**The Dower House
Restaurant**
The Royal Crescent Hotel,
16 Royal Crescent,
BATH, BA1 2LS
01225 823333

**The Olive Tree at
The Queensberry Hotel**
4–7 Russel Street,
BATH, BA1 2QF
01225 447928

Little Barwick House
Barwick Village,
YEOVIL, BA22 9TD
01935 423902

SUFFOLK
The Bildeston Crown
104 High Street,
BILDESTON, IP7 7EB
01449 740510

Tuddenham Mill
High St, Tuddenham St Mary,
NEWMARKET IP28 6SQ
01638 713552

SURREY
Drake's Restaurant
The Clock House, High St,
RIPLEY, GU23 6AQ
01483 224777

SUSSEX, WEST
**Ockenden Manor Hotel
& Spa**
Ockenden Lane,
CUCKFIELD, RH17 5LD
01444 416111

Gravetye Manor Hotel
Vowells Lane, West
Hoathly, EAST
GRINSTEAD, RH19 4LJ
01342 810567

Langshott Manor
Langshott Lane, Horley
GATWICK AIRPORT
(LONDON), RH6 9LN
01293 786680

**AG's Restaurant at
Alexander House Hotel**
East Street, TURNERS
HILL RH10 4QD
01342 714914

TYNE & WEAR
Jesmond Dene House
Jesmond Dene Road,
NEWCASTLE UPON
TYNE, NE2 2EY
0191 212 3000

WARWICKSHIRE
Mallory Court Hotel
Harbury Lane,
Bishop's Tachbrook,
ROYAL LEAMINGTON
SPA, CV33 9QB
01926 330214

**Restaurant 23 &
Morgan's Bar**
34 Hamilton Terrace,
ROYAL LEAMINGTON
SPA, CV32 4LY
01926 422422

WEST MIDLANDS
Loves Restaurant
The Glasshouse, Canal
Square, Browning Street
BIRMINGHAM, B16 8FL
0121 454 5151

Purnell's
55 Cornwall Street,
BIRMINGHAM, B3 2DH
0121 212 9799

Simpsons
20 Highfield Road,
Edgbaston,
BIRMINGHAM, B15 3DU
0121 454 3434

WILTSHIRE
**The Bybrook at the Manor
House Hotel**
CASTLE COMBE
SN14 7HR
01249 782206

The Park Restaurant
Lucknam Park Hotel &
Spa, COLERNE, SN14 8AZ
01225 742777

**The Harrow at
Little Bedwyn**
LITTLE BEDWYN
SN8 3JP
01672 870871

WORCESTERSHIRE
**Brockencote Hall Country
House Hotel**
CHADDESLEY CORBETT
DY10 4PY
01562 777876

YORKSHIRE, NORTH
The Angel Inn
HETTON BD23 6LT
01756 730263

Samuel's at Swinton Park
Swinton, MASHAM
HG4 4JH
01765 680900

**The Black Swan
at Oldstead**
OLDSTEAD, YO61 4BL
01347 868387

**Judges Country
House Hotel**
Kirklevington, YARM
TS15 9LW
01642 789000

YORKSHIRE, WEST
Box Tree
35-37 Church Street
ILKLEY
LS29 9DR
01943 608484

JERSEY

Bohemia Restaurant
The Club Hotel & Spa,
Green Street,
ST HELIER
JE2 4UH
01534 880588

Grand Jersey
The Esplanade,
ST HELIER
JE2 3QA
01534 722301

Longueville Manor Hotel
ST SAVIOUR
JE2 7WF
01534 725501

SCOTLAND

ANGUS
Gordon's
Main Street,
INVERKEILOR DD11 5RN
01241 830364

ARGYLL & BUTE
Airds Hotel & Restaurant
PORT APPIN, PA38 4DF
01631 730236

AYRSHIRE, SOUTH
Glenapp Castle
BALLANTRAE
KA26 0NZ
01465 831212

Lochgreen House Hotel
Monkton Hill Road,
Southwood, TROON
KA10 7EN
01292 313343

The James Miller Room
Turnberry Resort Scotland,
Maidens Road,
TURNBERRY
KA26 9LT
01655 331000

DUMFRIES & GALLOWAY
Knockinaam Lodge
PORTPATRICK,
DG9 9AD
01776 810471

DUNBARTONSHIRE, WEST
Martin Wishart at Loch Lomond
Cameron House on Loch
Lomond, BALLOCH
G83 8QZ
01389 722504

EDINBURGH, CITY OF
Castle Terrace Restaurant
33–35 Castle Terrace,
EDINBURGH,
EH1 2EL
0131 229 1222

Norton House Hotel & Spa
Ingliston, EDINBURGH
EH28 8LX
0131 333 1275

Number One, The Balmoral
1 Princes Street,
EDINBURGH,
EH2 2EQ
0131 557 6727

Plumed Horse
50–54 Henderson Street,
Leith, EDINBURGH
EH6 6DE
0131 554 5556

Pompadour by Galvin
The Caledonian,
A Waldorf Astoria Hotel,
Princes Street,
EDINBURGH, EH1 2AB
0131 222 8975

FIFE
The Peat Inn
PEAT INN, KY15 5LH
01334 840 206

Road Hole Restaurant
Old Course Hotel, Golf
Resort & Spa
ST ANDREWS,
KY16 9SP
01334 474371

Rocca Grill
Macdonald Rusacks Hotel
The Links
ST ANDREWS,
KY16 9JQ
01334 472549

GLASGOW, CITY OF
Hotel du Vin at One Devonshire Gardens
1 Devonshire Gardens,
GLASGOW, G12 0UX
0844 736 4256

HIGHLAND
Inverlochy Castle Hotel
Torlundy, FORT WILLIAM
PH33 6SN
01397 702177

The Torridon Restaurant
TORRIDON, IV22 2EY
01445 791242

SCOTTISH BORDERS
Cringletie House
Edinburgh Road,
PEEBLES,
EH45 8PL
01721 725750

STIRLING
Roman Camp Country House Hotel
CALLANDER,
FK17 8BG
01877 330003

The Ardeonaig Hotel & Restaurant
South Loch Tay Side,
KILLIN, FK21 8SU
01567 820400

SCOTTISH ISLANDS

SKYE, ISLE OF
The Three Chimneys
COLBOST, Isle of Skye
IV55 8ZT
01470 511258

Kinloch Lodge
Sleat, ISLE ORNSAY,
IV43 8QY
01471 833214

WALES

ANGLESEY, ISLE OF
Ye Olde Bulls Head Inn
Castle Street,
BEAUMARIS, LL58 8AP
01248 810329

CEREDIGION
Plas Ynyshir Hall Hotel
EGLWYS FACH
SY20 8TA
01654 781209

CONWY
Tan-y-Foel Country House
Capel Garmon,
BETWS-Y-COED
LL26 0RE
01690 710507

Bodysgallen Hall and Spa
LLANDUDNO
LL30 1RS
01492 584466

MONMOUTHSHIRE
The Walnut Tree
Llandewi Skirrid,
ABERGAVENNY
NP7 8AW
01873 852797

NEWPORT
Terry M at the Celtic Manor Resort
Coldra Woods,
NEWPORT
NP18 1HQ
01633 413000

NORTHERN IRELAND

BELFAST
Deanes Restaurant
36–40 Howard Street,
BELFAST
BT1 6PF
028 9033 1134

REPUBLIC OF IRELAND

CO CLARE
Gregans Castle
BALLYVAUGHAN
065 7077005

CO KILKENNY
The Lady Helen Restaurant
Mount Juliet Hotel
THOMASTOWN
056 7773000

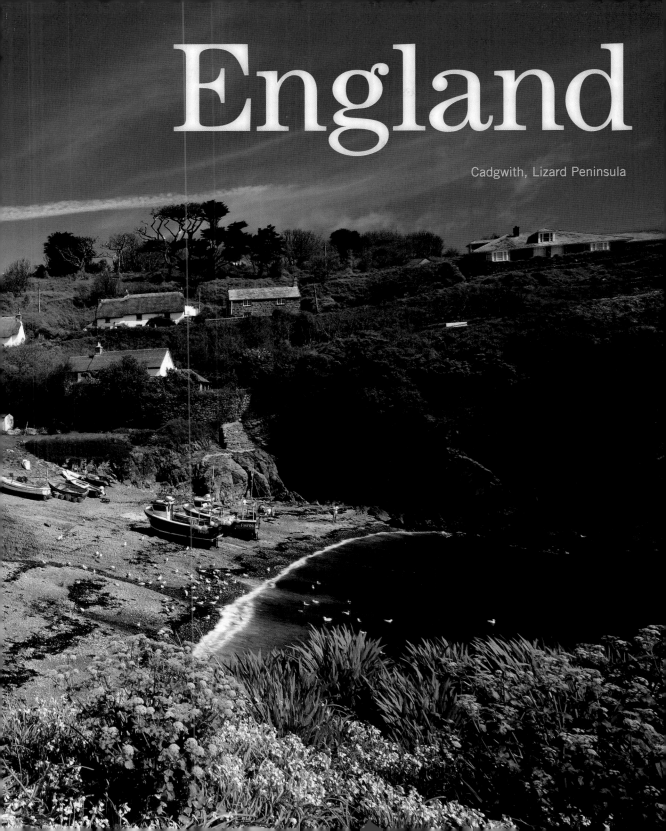

England

Cadgwith, Lizard Peninsula

BEDFORDSHIRE

BEDFORD
Map 12 TL04

The Bedford Swan Hotel

◉ Traditional & Modern British V

18th-century hotel with modish menu

☎ 01234 346565
The Embankment MK40 1RW
e-mail: info@bedfordswanhotel.co.uk
web: www.bedfordswanhotel.co.uk
dir: M1 junct 13, take A421 following signs to city centre
(one way system). Turn left to The Embankment, car park
on left after Swan statue

The handsome Georgian Swan, like its namesake bird,
presents a serene façade to the world, but there's an
awful lot going on beneath the surface. In the case of this
hotel by the River Great Ouse, that amounts to a swish
spa, some impressive period details (oak panels, ornate
plasterwork and the like), boutique-style bedrooms, bar,
terrace and a charming riverside restaurant. A recent
makeover has left no stone unturned to create a
contemporary venue with plenty of swagger. The River
Room restaurant takes a modish brasserie approach, so
there are steaks and burgers - with local beef - to the
likes of Gloucestershire Old Spot gammon with a fried
egg, pineapple and chips, or seared sea bass with warm
fennel slaw and lobster sauce. Start with a pork and
chicken pie with piccalilli and go home content after a
Cambridge burnt custard with home-made shortbread.

Chef Jason Buck **Owner** BDL **Times** 12-3/6-10
Prices Fixed L 2 course £12.95-£17.95, Fixed D 3 course
£20-£40, Tasting menu £35, Starter £5-£8, Main
£12-£20, Dessert £5-£6 **Wines** 6 by glass **Notes** Sunday
L, Vegetarian menu, Dress restrictions, Smart casual, Civ
Wed 100 **Seats** 90, Pr/dining room 20 **Children** Portions,
Menu **Parking** 90

BOLNHURST
Map 12 TL05

The Plough at Bolnhurst

◉ Modern British ♨ NOTABLE WINE LIST ♨

Classy modern menu in Tudor pub

☎ 01234 376274
Kimbolton Rd MK44 2EX
e-mail: theplough@bolnhurst.com
dir: A14/A421 onto B660 for approx 5m to Bolnhurst
village

This whitewashed 15th-century country inn has period
charm in spades - doughty Tudor beams and timbers,
tiny windows, and welcoming open fires in its cosy bars.
So the contemporary restaurant in an expansive, light-
bathed room comes as a striking contrast. Fizzing with
life at lunchtime - when chalkboards suggest ideas such

as deep-fried whitebait with tartare sauce and lemon, or
local Dexter steak pie with Savoy cabbage and duck fat
roast potatoes - the mood segues into a more intimate,
candlelit vibe in the evening. Top-class local produce is
translated into big-flavoured modern dishes on a daily-
changing menu that could open with pan-fried pigeon
breast with beetroot purée, pancetta, trompette
mushrooms and juniper, and follow with corn-fed
Goosnargh duck breast with turnip gratin, roast shallots
and Armagnac sauce. Awaiting at the end, perhaps cider
and apple mousse with caramelised apple tart and
caramel ice cream.

Chef Martin Lee **Owner** Martin Lee, Jayne Lee, Michael
Moscrop **Times** 12-2/6.30-9.30 Closed 27 Dec-14 Jan,
Mon, D Sun **Prices** Fixed L 2 course £13-£20, Starter
£6.75-£10, Main £15.50-£26.95, Dessert £1.75-£8,
Service optional **Wines** 91 bottles over £30, 12 by glass
Notes Sunday L £21-£25, Vegetarian available **Seats** 96,
Pr/dining room 34 **Children** Portions **Parking** 30

FLITWICK
Map 11 TL03

Menzies Hotels Woburn Flitwick Manor

◉ Modern, Traditional

Modern country-house cooking in a Georgian manor

☎ 01525 712242
Church Rd MK45 1AE
e-mail: steven.essex@menzieshotels.co.uk
web: www.menzieshotels.co.uk
dir: M1 junct 12, follow Flitwick after 1m turn left into
Church Rd. Manor 200 yds on left

Surrounded by acres of grounds, the manor is a splendid
Georgian property with all the trappings of a country-
house hotel, from deep sofas and antiques, to period
features and four-poster beds, while the restaurant is a
handsome room, with upholstered seats at white-linen-
draped tables. The kitchen gives a modern twist to
country-house style, pairing pan-fried scallops with
cauliflower bhaji and purée, and serving poached chicken
ballotine with cep broth, cocotte potatoes and purple-
sprouting broccoli. More familiar-sounding offerings are
handled equally well, seen in a well-made terrine of
pressed ham hock with apple purée, and meat-packed
game pie with port jus, honey-roast vegetables and kale.
Ingredients are well selected, timings are properly judged,
and dishes deliver all the promised flavours: blackberry
frangipane tart, for instance, with vibrant mixed berry
compôte and cinnamon ice cream, or chocolate fondant
with a salt caramel centre accompanied by rum and
raisin ice cream.

Times 12-3/7-10

LUTON
Map 6 TL02

Adam's Brasserie at Luton Hoo

◉ Modern British

**Brasserie cooking in the smartened up stables at Luton
Hoo**

☎ 01582 734437 & 698888
**Luton Hoo Hotel, Golf and Spa, The Mansion House
LU1 3TQ**
e-mail: reservations@lutonhoo.co.uk
dir: M1 junct 10A, 3rd exit to A1081 towards Harpenden/
St Albans. Hotel less than a mile on left

Part of the fabulous Luton Hoo estate, complete with golf
course, wonderful gardens, a luxurious hotel, spa, and
elegant fine-dining restaurant (see entry for the Wernher
Restaurant), Adam's Brasserie is yet another string to
their bow. Situated in the former stables, now the country
club, the high-ceilinged and many-windowed room is
adorned with pictures of movie stars who have filmed on
the estate over the years, and serves up a pleasing array
of brasserie-style dishes. That amounts to meats from
the grill (Casterbridge beef sirloin, for example), herb-
crusted fillet of cod, and butternut squash ravioli. Start
with pan-seared scallops with a black pudding bonbon or
home-smoked fillet of trout (smoked in Jasmine tea and
thyme), and finish with a traditional rice pudding, or
caramelised pear Pavlova.

Chef Kevin Clark **Owner** Elite Hotels **Times** 12-3/6-10
Closed D Sun **Prices** Starter £6-£8.95, Main £14.50-£21,
Dessert £6.75-£8, Service optional **Wines** 18 bottles over
£30, 19 bottles under £30, 8 by glass **Notes** Sun Jazz L,
Sunday L £35, Vegetarian available, Civ Wed 120
Seats 90, Pr/dining room 120 **Children** Portions, Menu
Parking 100

Menzies Hotels London Luton - Strathmore

◉ International ✎

International brasserie dishes in a town-centre hotel

☎ 01582 734199
Arndale Centre LU1 2TR
e-mail: strathmore@menzieshotels.co.uk
web: www.menzieshotels.co.uk
dir: Exit M1 junct 10a towards town centre, adjacent to The Mall Centre car park

A mere couple of miles from Luton Airport, the Strathmore is a modern corporate hotel, accessed through the Arndale shopping mall in the centre of town. The spacious brasserie, with banquette seating in fetching flame-orange and a wiggly-patterned carpet, fulfills its brief by offering standard international dishes, the whole place enthusiastically kitting itself out to suit gastronomic idioms such as Mediterranean, Chinese and so forth on the twice-weekly theme nights. Otherwise, expect enterprising combinations such as surf clams and smoked haddock in mustardy Florentine sauce, or classic seared scallops with black pudding and minted pea purée, to start, before the main-course choice brings on salmon en croûte in creamy Cointreau sauce, a vegetarian dish of chargilled vegetable penne, or a canonical chicken tikka masala with coriander rice and all the works. Favourite desserts include caramelised lemon tart, and vanilla pannacotta with vodka and basil jelly.

Chef Kerry Gent **Owner** Menzies Hotels **Times** 12-3/7-9.45 **Prices** Fixed L 2 course fr £15, Fixed D 3 course fr £19.50, Starter £4.75-£8.50, Main £13.25-£19.95, Dessert £5.25-£5.75, Service optional **Wines** 3 bottles over £30, 30 bottles under £30, 12 by glass **Notes** Sunday L, Vegetarian available, Civ Wed 120 **Seats** 90, Pr/dining room 250 **Children** Portions, Menu **Parking** 22

Wernher Restaurant at Luton Hoo

◎◎ Modern European

Magnificent country estate with modern cooking

☎ 01582 734437
Luton Hoo Hotel, Golf and Spa, The Mansion House LU1 3TQ
e-mail: reservations@lutonhoo.co.uk
dir: M1 junct 10A, 3rd exit to A1081 towards Harpenden/St Albans. Hotel less than a mile on left

The 'Hoo' in question is actually an old Saxon word for the spur of a hill. Straddling the counties of Hertfordshire and Bedfordshire, Luton Hoo is a striking and rather stately house with impeccable credentials: Robert Adam and Sir Robert 'British Museum' Smirke are responsible for the magnificent façade, 'Capability' Brown sorted out the gardens, and Elite Hotels have provided every comfort for the 21st-century visitor. There's a golf course, spa facilities, splendidly handsome rooms and a restaurant which is done-out in a lavish, elegant manner, with marble panelling, ornate chandeliers, opulent fabrics and immaculately dressed tables. The menu is based around well-sourced produce and follows a modish path. Start, perhaps, with crispy goats' cheese with braised rocket, tomato, pine nut and red onion sauce, before the likes of roast rack of lamb with beetroot pommes purée, sautéed kale, roast baby turnips and thyme jus, and, to finish,

warm roasted fig tart with orange ice cream and crème anglaise. Adam's Brasserie (see entry) offers an alternative.

Wernher Restaurant at Luton Hoo

Chef Kevin Clark **Owner** Elite Hotels **Times** 12.30-2/7-10 Closed Mon-Tue **Prices** Fixed L 2 course fr £47.50, Fixed D 3 course fr £52.50, Tasting menu fr £62.50, Service optional **Wines** 50 bottles over £30, 3 bottles under £30, 13 by glass **Notes** Speciality menu, Sunday L, Vegetarian available, Dress restrictions, Jacket or tie, Civ Wed 390 **Seats** 80, Pr/dining room 280 **Children** Portions, Menu **Parking** 316

See advert below

Paris House Restaurant

British, French **V**

Creative contemporary cooking in a magnificent mock-Tudor house

☎ 01525 290692
London Rd, Woburn Park MK17 9QP
e-mail: info@parishouse.co.uk
dir: M1 junct 13. From Woburn take A4012 Hockliffe, 1m out of Woburn village on left

Part of The 10 in 8 Fine Dining Group (see also entries for La Bécasse and L'ortolan), Paris House is a jewel in the county of Bedfordshire. The house really is quite something. It's a magnificent faux-Tudor black-and-white building with a curious history that saw the Duke of Bedford ship it over from Paris, lock, stock and chimneys, where it had been part of a display representing a piece of old England at The Paris International Exhibition in 1878. But enough history, for there is very good reason to visit regardless of the splendour of the house, or in fact the beauty of the 22 acres of grounds, and that is for the superb food on offer. Chef-patron Phil Fanning's cooking is refined, creative, but rooted in good sense, with superb produce at the heart of everything. Choose either the six-, eight- or ten-course tasting menus - or if you really want to push the boat out, book the chef's table beside the pass for a close-up view of all the cheffy action and a 14-course tasting menu specifically tailored to your party. Whichever route you choose, be assured that the flavours will all be spot on and everything will look beautiful on the plate. Braised English snails (from Aylesbury) might come with smoked potato, mushroom soil and garden herbs on the eight-course 'Gourmand' menu, followed a little later on by Woburn Estate venison with smoked heart, turnips and ceps chutney. From the show-stopping ten-course 'Surprise' comes crab and marinated butternut squash with soft-shelled crab tempura and lemon purée, and Redborne pig with ash-rolled swede, sprouting broccoli, wild mushroom and sage stuffing. These are dishes of real craft and creativity, with modern cooking techniques used to good effect when necessary. There's a pre-dessert before the likes of raspberry soufflé with raspberry sorbet and oats, or rhubarb trifle with poached rhubarb, duck egg custard and coconut sorbet.

Chef Phil Fanning **Owner** Alan Murchison
Times 12-2/6.30-9 Closed Mon, L Tue, D Sun & 26 Dec-8 Jan **Prices** Tasting menu £71-£115, Service added but optional 12.5% **Wines** 150 bottles over £30, 4 bottles under £30, 10 by glass **Notes** Gourmand menu 6/8/10 course. Chefs table L £110/D £200, Sunday L £37-£95, Vegetarian menu, Dress restrictions, Smart casual **Seats** 37, Pr/dining room 14 **Children** Portions, Menu **Parking** 24

WOBURN   Map 11 SP93

The Inn at Woburn

◎◎ Modern British, French

High-impact Anglo-French cooking on the Woburn estate

☎ 01525 290441
George St MK17 9PX
e-mail: inn@woburn.co.uk
web: www.woburn.co.uk/inn
dir: 5 mins from M1 junct 13. Follow signs to Woburn. Inn in town centre at x-rds, parking to rear via Park St

If watching the big cats feeding at the Woburn Abbey estate's safari park has brought on an appetite, head for the Georgian coaching inn where chef Olivier Bertho delivers refined Anglo-French cooking in a smart country-house setting. The venue is rather posher than its 'inn' title suggests; Olivier's Restaurant is furnished with clubby buttoned leather seating at bare wooden tables, displays of lilies in blue-and-white Chinese vases, and gilt mirrors on neutral cream and mushroom-hued walls. The food is a labour-intensive take on the modern French idiom - grilled scallops with pea purée, beetroot coulis and chervil oil is one way to start, before turning to something like an assiette of pork with cider jus, comprising belly pork with red cabbage, pork fillet on colcannon with apple jam, and mini meatballs with sage and tomato coulis. Leave room for a multi-faceted dessert such as an 'assiette du verger' (orchard assiette) involving tarte Tatin, blackberry pannacotta and vanilla crème brûlée.

Chef Olivier Bertho **Owner** Bedford Estates
Times 12-2/6.30-9.30 **Prices** Starter £5.20-£9.95, Main

£13.50-£18.95, Dessert £6.95-£8.60, Service optional
Wines 22 bottles over £30, 22 bottles under £30, 18 by glass **Notes** Sunday L £20-£25, Vegetarian available, Civ Wed 60 **Seats** 40, Pr/dining room 90 **Children** Portions, Menu **Parking** 80

See advert opposite

Paris House Restaurant

◎◎◎ *– see opposite*

WYBOSTON   Map 12 TL15

Wyboston Lakes Hotel

◎ British, International

Cosmopolitan eating by a lake

☎ 0333 700 7667
Great North Rd MK44 3BA
e-mail: restaurant@wybostonlakes.co.uk
dir: Off A1/A428, follow brown Cambridge signs. Wyboston Lakes Hotel on right, marked by flags

With 350 acres of Bedfordshire to call its own, Wyboston Lakes has an awful lot going on: conference, golf and spa facilities are a big part of its appeal, and they can sort out your wedding or private function if you're in the market for one. There is a lake, of course, (more than one in fact) and the Waterfront Restaurant has a good view with picture windows and a terrace to make the best of it. The kitchen keeps things relatively modern in a gentle and globe-trotting manner, so there are steaks and maize-fed chicken cooked on the grill, or something a little more adventurous such as roasted harissa-marinated rump of lamb with Gorgonzola garganelli, or ginger-glazed sea bream with pak choi and Thai vegetable salad. Start with pan-fried squid with chorizo and lime crème fraîche, and finish with passionfruit cheesecake or pistachio parfait.

Chef Fergus Martin **Times** 12-2.30/6.30-9.30
Closed Xmas & New Year **Prices** Prices not confirmed
Wines 7 bottles over £30, 33 bottles under £30, 20 by glass **Notes** Sunday L, Vegetarian available, Civ Wed 130 **Seats** 90, Pr/dining room 24 **Children** Portions **Parking** 100

BERKSHIRE

ASCOT   Map 6 SU96

The Barn at Coworth

◎ British

Converted barn with a local flavour

☎ 01344 876600
Blacknest Rd SL5 7SE
e-mail: restaurants.CPA@dorchestercollection.com
dir: M25 junct 13 S onto A30 to Sunningdale. Hotel on left 2 min past Wentworth Golf Club

Polo is the game at Coworth Park, a lavish country hotel and spa which is part of the Dorchester group. There's a fine-dining restaurant, of course - see separate entry - but also this converted barn near the stable area where you can tuck into some classy brasserie-style food. It looks great with its open-to-view kitchen, unbuttoned vibe and cheerful service team sporting orange polo tops, and there's a fabulous terrace, too, with gorgeous views over the grounds. There are some good local ingredients on the menu such as trout from the River Test, potted and served with horseradish crème fraîche and lamb's lettuce, or main-course Bramble Farm chicken with creamed potatoes, New Forest mushrooms, cabbage and bacon. There're also the likes of a posh burger and fish and chips. Among desserts, free-range egg custard tart might come with Yorkshire rhubarb in season.

Chef Brian Hughson **Owner** Dorchester Collection
Times 12.30-2.45/6-9.30 **Prices** Fixed L 2 course fr £25, Fixed D 3 course fr £35, Starter £8-£12.50, Main £15-£27.50, Dessert £8-£12.50, Service added but optional 12.5% **Wines** 48 bottles over £30, 4 bottles under £30, 4 by glass **Notes** Fixed L & D Mon-Fri, Sunday L, Vegetarian available, Civ Wed 300 **Seats** 75 **Children** Portions, Menu **Parking** 100

Bluebells Restaurant & Garden Bar

◎◎ Modern, International ✦

Smart setting for contemporary cooking

☎ 01344 622722
Shrubbs Hill, London Rd, Sunningdale SL5 0LE
e-mail: info@bluebells-restaurant.co.uk
dir: From M25 junct 13, A30 towards Bagshot. Restaurant between Wentworth & Sunningdale

You wouldn't know it from the slick interior, but a 300-year-old building is at the heart of this stylish contemporary restaurant. Bluebells was conceived with a high-end clientele from nearby Ascot and Windsor in mind, so a designer makeover has transformed the interior with a glossy magazine look - gauzy voile curtains divide the open-plan space into bar, main restaurant and conservatory areas without reducing the sense of wide-open space, while exposed brick, darkwood floors, white-leather seats and a muted olive colour scheme give the place a highly-polished feel. Smartly engineered dishes offer a light touch, like a dainty trio of crab cakes dressed in a fresh sweet chilli sauce. Next, flavours, colours and

continued

ASCOT *continued*

textures all combine perfectly in a dish of slow-braised belly pork with apple and cider foam, red onion marmalade and bubble-and-squeak. Creative and confident to the end, the curtain comes down on a ginger-infused winter fruit pudding with home-made honeycomb ice cream coated in crushed pistachios.

Chef Adam Turley **Owner** John Rampello **Times** 12-2.30/6.30-9.45 Closed 25-26 Dec, 1-11 Jan, BH, Mon, D Sun **Prices** Fixed L 2 course fr £15, Starter £8.25-£16.50, Main £18-£28, Dessert £8-£9.50, Service added but optional 10% **Wines** 74 bottles over £30, 30 bottles under £30, 12 by glass **Notes** Sunday L £22.50-£27, Vegetarian available, Dress restrictions, Smart casual **Seats** 90, Pr/dining room 14 **Children** Portions, Menu **Parking** 100

Macdonald Berystede Hotel & Spa

🌐 British, European

Up-to-date brasserie cooking near Legoland and the racing

☎ 01344 623311 & 0844 879 9104
Bagshot Rd, Sunninghill SL5 9JH
e-mail: general.berystede@macdonald-hotels.co.uk
web: www.berystede.com
dir: M3 junct 3/A30, A322 then left onto B3020 to Ascot or M25 junct 13, follow signs for Bagshot. At Sunningdale turn right onto A330

The Berystede is handy for both Legoland and the racing at Ascot, depending on how you get your kicks, and is a handsome red-brick mansion with a rather impressive glassed walkway to the entrance. With spa and business facilities, it's the image of a modern corporate hotel, yet one with some character, and an impressive restaurant, Hyperion, furnished with curving banquettes and quality table appointments. The kitchen brigade brings its creative exertions to bear on seasonal produce in up-to-date brasserie dishes that can look a little busy but deliver on flavour. Start with a poppy-seeded goats' cheese pannacotta with red pepper sorbet and tapenade, which constitutes an artful study in contrasts, before going on to Highland lamb two ways (the tender-as-anything shank getting the vote) with rösti, slow-cooked tomatoes and puréed aubergine in red wine jus. Evenly glazed, pleasantly zesty lemon tart for afters comes with intense raspberry ice cream and coulis.

Chef Jon Machin **Owner** Macdonald Hotels **Times** 12.30-2/7-9.45 Closed L Sat **Prices** Prices not confirmed Service added but optional 12.5% **Wines** 12 by glass **Notes** Sunday L, Vegetarian available, Civ Wed 150 **Seats** 100, Pr/dining room 24 **Children** Portions, Menu **Parking** 120

Restaurant Coworth Park

◉◉◉ *— see opposite*

BRACKNELL   Map 5 SU86

Coppid Beech

🌐 European, Pacific Rim

Alpine atmosphere and modern food by the Thames

☎ 01344 303333
John Nike Way RG12 8TF
e-mail: sales@coppidbeech.com
web: www.coppidbeech.com
dir: M4 junct 10 take Wokingham/Bracknell onto A329. In 2m take B3408 to Binfield at rdbt. Hotel 200yds on right

You may think that the Thames Valley is not known for its skiing and Alpine chalets, but that is because you haven't yet discovered the Coppid Beech Hotel. The smart modern hotel not only has the look of a Swiss chalet, but there's the chance to strap on the planks too as there's a dry-ski slope, an ice rink and toboggan run in the complex. With an appetite suitably sharpened by the year-round winter sports, move on to Rowans, the hotel's upscale dining option. It is an eye-catching space, with plush drapes and linen-clothed tables beneath a soaring timbered ceiling hung with crystal chandelier as a backdrop to a menu that covers a fair amount of modern European territory. Start with wood pigeon en croûte served with beetroot carpaccio, and orange and beetroot jus, followed by sirloin steak with mushrooms, parsnip purée, garlic spinach and marchand de vin sauce. Finish with a Thai-influenced coconut pannacotta with sweet-and-sour pineapple, and basil jelly.

Chef Paul Zolik **Owner** Nike Group Hotels Ltd **Times** 12-2/7-9.45 Closed L Sat, D Thu, Sun **Prices** Fixed D 3 course £25.50-£33, Starter £5.95-£9.25, Main £15.25-£23, Dessert £6.25-£10.50, Service optional **Wines** 20 bottles over £30, 20 bottles under £30, 15 by glass **Notes** Sunday L, Vegetarian available, Dress restrictions, Smart casual, Civ Wed 300 **Seats** 120 **Children** Portions, Menu **Parking** 350

BRAY   Map 6 SU97

Caldesi in Campagna

◉◉ Traditional Italian 🍃

Refined Italian eatery in Bray

☎ 01628 788500
Old Mill Ln SL6 2BG
e-mail: campagna@caldesi.com
dir: M4 junct 8/9, at rdbt exit A308 Bray/Windsor. Continue for 0.5m, left B3028 Bray village, right Old Mill Lane, restaurant in 400yds on right

As if to prove that nobody in Bray need be stuck for somewhere to eat out, yet another fine-dining venue springs up, this one a two-handed operation from Italian chef Giancarlo Caldesi and his wife Katie, a food writer specialising in Italy. The restaurant is in a small white house on the outskirts of the village, the refined but simple décor extending to beige tones, parquet flooring, a brick fireplace and quality tableware. There's bar seating too, as well as an outdoor area, and when the Berkshire sun comes out, you might just fancy you were in Tuscany. The more so as Caldesi's cooking pulls off that very 21st-century trick of using British (mainly local) sustainable ingredients to give a convincing impression of the food of somewhere else entirely. The carpaccio is made from Scotch beef, and comes properly dressed with shaved parmesan, rocket, rosemary and balsamic, gaining true succulence from its being served warm. Squid is slow-cooked to tenderness and married with tomatoes and chilli for a fine crostini topping, and the home-made pasta that encases sea bass in ravioli, or tangles up clams, garlic and chilli in spaghetti, is the real thing. Fish cookery is spot-on, the timing of a piece of fried stone bass flawless, while meat might be classic saltimbocca Romana, or Barbary duck breast crusted in pink peppercorns with mashed potato in red grape sauce.

Chef Gregorio Piazza **Owner** Giancarlo Caldesi **Times** 12-2.30/6-10.30 Closed Xmas for approx 5 days, Mon, D Sun **Prices** Fixed L 2 course fr £14.50, Starter £10.50-£15, Main £10-£25, Dessert £6-£9, Service added but optional 12.5% **Wines** 116 bottles over £30, 19 bottles under £30, 13 by glass **Notes** Sunday L, Vegetarian available, Dress restrictions, **Seats** 50 **Children** Portions, Menu **Parking** 8

Save on Hotels. Book at theAA.com/hotel

BERKSHIRE 53 ENGLAND

The Crown

◉◉ Modern British ◔

Heston's proper pub

☎ 01628 621936
High St SL6 2AH
e-mail: reservations@thecrownatbray.co.uk
dir: M4 junct 8/9, follow signs for Maidenhead Central, left towards Windsor, right to Bray

With low-beamed ceilings, real fires, leaded windows, secretive little nooks and crannies, and a no-frills bar for drinkers, The Crown is a classic 16th-century inn. However, the location in the gastro-Mecca of Bray might set you wondering who owns it, and although there is no obvious clue to that effect, it is indeed owned (along with The Hinds Head - see entry) by one Heston Blumenthal. But fear not: a visit to the bank manager is not needed, and the place has not been whizzed upmarket into high-falutin' gastro territory. That said, the food is clearly a cut or two above the average pub grub. Founded on first-class ingredients, you can expect modern British pub classics with added refinement. Chicken liver parfait is served with toasted brioche and sweet and sour onions, while fillet of hake is accompanied by charred leeks, celeriac purée, ceps and cep sauce in a simple but perfectly executed main course. Finish with Earl Grey pannacotta with lemon crumble, or flag-waving British cheeses such as Barkham Blue and Lyburn Old

Winchester with fig and date chutney and raisin and hazelnut bread.

Chef Nick Galer **Owner** Heston Blumenthal
Times 12-2.30/6-9.30 **Prices** Service added but optional 12.5% **Wines** 18 bottles over £30, 16 bottles under £30, 14 by glass **Notes** Sunday L £13-£23.50, Vegetarian available **Seats** 40 **Children** Portions, Menu

The Fat Duck

◉◉◉◉◉ — *see page 54*

Hinds Head

◉◉ British ◭ NOTABLE WINE LIST

Heston's modern take on old-English hearty fare

☎ 01628 626151
High St SL6 2AB
e-mail: info@hindsheadbray.com
dir: M4 junct 8/9, at rdbt take exit to Maidenhead Central, next rdbt take exit Bray & Windsor, after 0.5m take B3028 to Bray

One of Heston Blumenthal's three Bray outposts (see entries for The Fat Duck and The Crown) is a traditional inn dating from the 15th century, complete with oak panelling and beams, open fires, comfortable leather-look seats and a child-friendly, casual atmosphere. There's

none of Heston's molecular gastronomy here; rather, the intention is to revive the traditions of hostelry dining, keeping things simple and straightforward, with dishes defined by bold, upfront flavours. Chicken liver parfait is a textbook example, and other starters could be snail hash (from an 1884 recipe, says the menu), and a salad of beetroot, goats' curd, orange and pumpkin seeds. Quality and timings are never in doubt, seen in roast fillet of cod with celeriac purée, sultanas and salt cod, a winning combination, and veal chop with cabbage and onions and classic sauce Reform. Desserts recreate some long-forgotten dishes: try rhubarb and custard quaking pudding, or wassailing caramelised butter loaf with apple and Pomona.

Chef Kevin Love **Owner** Hinds Head Ltd
Times 12-2.30/6.30-9.30 Closed 25-26 Dec, D 1 Jan, BHs, Sun **Prices** Starter £7.50-£11.75, Main £17.95-£29.50, Dessert £7.95-£9.50, Service added but optional 12.5% **Wines** 56 bottles over £30, 25 bottles under £30, 14 by glass **Notes** Tasting menu available 7 course, with 24 hr notice, Sunday L, Vegetarian available **Seats** 100, Pr/dining room 22 **Children** Portions, Menu **Parking** 40

Restaurant Coworth Park

ASCOT | MAP 6 SU96

Modern British ◭ NOTABLE WINE LIST

Contemporary cooking in a luxury hotel

☎ 01344 876600
Blacknest Rd SL5 7SE
e-mail: restaurants.CPA@dorchestercollection.com
dir: M25 junct 13 S onto A30 to Sunningdale. Hotel on left 2 min past Wentworth Golf Club

Just outside Ascot, and with Her Maj as a neighbour in Windsor Great Park, Coworth Park does five-star English country house glamour with knobs on. And that's hardly surprising when you consider that this is the aristocratic country cousin to the West End's glitzy Dorchester Hotel. There are 240 acres of lush Berkshire countryside wrapped around the elegant 17th-century manor house, with the Coworth Park Equestrian Centre handy for a

quick game of polo, or you might recharge the batteries in the eco-friendly spa. Food-wise, you're spoilt for choice: the modish Spatisserie located in the spa (geddit?) serves healthy options and scrummy cakes, the converted oak and stone barn is the spot for bistro-dining (The Barn - see entry), the swish Drawing Room in the main house does all-day dining and afternoon tea, a swanky bar with a terrace overlooks the croquet lawn and sunken gardens, and then there's the fine-dining option, The Restaurant, a series of elegant Georgian rooms done out in muted browns and greens, with a centrepiece artwork of shimmering leaves and twigs dominating the ceiling, curvy toffee-hued leather seats and impeccably dressed tables. Head chef Brian Hughson, a veteran of stellar kitchens in London, has recently moved out from The Grill at The Dorchester to drive this high-end operation. Although rooted in classical thinking, the cooking is glossy, contemporary and full of invention. Soused Cornish mackerel with smoked mussels, fennel crisps and crumb, samphire and curry cream balances out into

a satisfying whole, while an equally accomplished main course comprising loin of rose veal topped with melted Comté cheese is matched with crispy sweetbread, English truffle granola and shallot purée. Finally, rhubarb stars in a dessert of crumble, sorbet, parfait and crisps with almond cassonade and rosemary custard.

Chef Brian Hughson **Owner** Dorchester Collection
Times 12.30-3/6.30-9.30 Closed Mon, D Sun **Prices** Fixed L 3 course fr £29.95, Fixed D 3 course fr £40, Tasting menu £85, Service added but optional 12.5% **Wines** 600+ bottles over £30, 4 bottles under £30, 18 by glass **Notes** Fixed L Tue-Fri, D Tue-Thu, Tasting menu 7 course, Sunday L, Vegetarian available, Dress restrictions, Smart casual, Civ Wed 300 **Seats** 66, Pr/dining room 16 **Children** Portions, Menu **Parking** 100

The Fat Duck

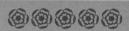

Modern British V ⬥ NOTABLE WINE LIST

Mind-boggling culinary creations old and new at Heston HQ

☎ 01628 580333
High St SL6 2AQ
dir: M4 junct 8/9 (Maidenhead) take A308 towards Windsor, turn left into Bray. Restaurant in centre of village on right

The pale-grey-painted former pub looks so insignificant and unassuming as you pass by on the main road through Bray, but how looks can deceive. Behind that neutral, understated frontage there are some mind-blowing culinary fireworks going off, and the momentum has been kept up now for some 18 years. Heston (we all think of him by his first name these days) may not be at the stoves in the tiny kitchen out back anymore, but despite his TV work and other commitments, he's often to be found in the 'laboratory' kitchen across the road, working on his next creation (some dishes take years in the planning and days to make for each service, so it's little wonder the cost of a meal now almost breaks the £200 mark). The small dining room is just as low-key as the outside of the building, with smartly-laid tables (only 14 of them) and a relaxed ambience helped along by the extremely efficient, friendly and knowledgeable staff. For those lucky enough to bag a table (bookings are only available up to two months in advance), a 14-course menu full of multi-sensory stimulation (smell, taste, sight, sound) and lots of fun awaits - and it's an experience you're unlikely ever to forget. Some dishes are fixtures, while others are swapped in and out or reworked to keep things exciting and interesting, not that many guests are likely to dine here more than once. The curtain is raised in typical Heston style with some 'nitro poached aperitifs': a flavoured espuma (your choice of vodka and lime sour, gin and tonic or Campari soda) is poached in liquid nitrogen at -196 degrees C, and as it dissolves on your tongue it releases an intense hit of clean, crisp flavour that really is the ultimate palate cleanser. There could be a deeply flavourful red cabbage gazpacho next, before a playful trio of savoury ice lollies - a Rocket Waldorf (walnut, celery, apple and grape), a Twister (smoked salmon and wasabi), and a foie gras Feast (an ultra smooth foie gras mousse with fig jelly and toasted hazelnuts). Snail porridge is a menu stalwart, the fine oats bound in a vivid green parsley and garlic sauce, with some earthy-tasting snails, some finely shredded Ibérico Bellota ham, micro-herbs and shaved fennel. Roast foie gras with some nicely tart pink rhubarb and a salty and crisp crab biscuit is an inspired combination, while the short rib of Wagyu beef, slow-cooked and packed full of flavour, needs no other embellishment than its accompanying piccalilli garnish. Back at the zanier end of the spectrum, the 'Mad Hatter's tea party' - mock turtle soup, pocket watch and toast sandwich - is a piece of pure theatre, while 'sound of the sea' stimulates all the senses, with an iPod in a shell playing crashing wave sounds to heighten the enjoyment of a superb fish composition (a 'shoreline' of tapioca 'sand', deep-fried sardine, a foam of vegetable stock and milk, three varieties of seaweed, and ultra-fresh kingfish, abalone and mackerel). And that's just a handful of the culinary marvels on offer. Amongst the sweeter courses, 'the BFG' never ceases to wow with its clearly defined Black Forest gâteau flavours, while new creation 'the candle' (white chocolate, dark chocolate, passion fruit and popping candy) provides another dose of theatre as the waiting staff light it, blow it out, and then cut chunks off with cigar cutters to reveal the delicious contents.

Chef Heston Blumenthal, Jonny Lake **Owner** Fat Duck Ltd **Times** 12-2/7-9 Closed 2 wks at Xmas, Sun-Mon **Prices** Tasting menu £195, Service added but optional 12.5% **Wines** 500 bottles over £30, 13 by glass **Notes** Tasting menu only, Vegetarian menu **Seats** 40 **Children** Portions **Parking** Two village car parks

Save on Hotels. Book at **theAA.com/hotel**

BERKSHIRE 55 **ENGLAND**

Waterside Inn

French **NOTABLE WINE LIST**

The Roux family's riverside restaurant four decades on

☎ 01628 620691
Ferry Rd SL6 2AT
e-mail: reservations@waterside-inn.co.uk
dir: M4 junct 8/9, A308 (Windsor) then B3028 to Bray. Restaurant clearly signed

The Waterside Inn celebrated its 40th birthday in 2012, and it's hard to imagine it won't still be going strong in another 40 years. The restaurant which was a rundown old pub before Michel and Albert Roux took it over in the early '70s remains at the forefront of French gastronomy in the UK - in the hearts of a good many regulars who return again and again for the consistently superb cooking, impeccable service and enchanting riverside setting. You might think a restaurant of this standing would be stuffy and formal, but far from it. Indeed, it is lavishly furnished, the staff are immaculately turned out, there's a doorman to greet you and your car will be valet-parked, but at the same time the place has an easy, relaxed and ever-buzzing vibe, with every guest - regular or first-timer - treated like a valued friend. If the weather is kind you can watch the birds and boats on the water from the lovely terrace while sipping a glass of champagne and nibbling on some top-notch canapés - amongst them perhaps mini Welsh rarebits and anchovy straws. A

comfortable lounge and small bar provide alternatives if need be, before moving through to the classically elegant restaurant, where floor-to-ceiling windows provide everyone with a view of the river, and the service, led by Diego Masciaga, a true master of his craft, really is second to none. These days the kitchen is headed up by Michel Roux's son Alain, and clearly the art of gastronomy is in the blood. He still cooks some of the traditional dishes of his father's day, but there are injections of modernity and innovation on the menu, thus keeping the old-timers who've been coming for decades just as happy as the younger guests looking for something a little more of-the-moment - it's a delicate balance that's achieved admirably well. The menu - in fact, there are three to choose from, including the entry level menu gastronomique at £79.50 for three courses (lunch only) - changes faithfully with the seasons, and showcases the finest ingredients money can buy, many from the UK. You could start with something very traditionally French but interpreted in a contemporary style, such as ravioli and diablotins (soft, mousse-like dumplings) of Burgundy snails flavoured with parsley and garlic, served in a delicate chicken bouillon scented with lemongrass - a delightful dish with great contrasts in texture and rich, fresh flavours. Pan-fried lobster medallions is another way to go, the lobster ultra-fresh and perfectly cooked, served with a light white port sauce, with an Asian twist from some ginger flavoured julienned vegetables. Staying with seafood,

main-course pan-fried fillet of sea bass is faultless in every way, served with a crispy kromesky fritter filled with potted brown shrimps and given a lightly citrusy lift with a Menton lemon emulsion. If you prefer to go down a meatier route, try and persuade a dining partner to share the saddle of milk-fed lamb stuffed with morels and spinach, which is sliced at the table and served with a lovely selection of al dente baby vegetables and a minted hollandaise - you won't be disappointed. When it comes to dessert, you can bet there will always be a seasonal soufflé (warm rhubarb with raspberries perhaps, or orange with cranberries), although the layered sweet almond and apple dessert is a very good contender, served with a Granny Smith apple granité that just tastes of pure fresh apple. It has to be said that a meal at The Waterside doesn't come cheap, but dining here is an experience every one should enjoy at least once.

Chef Alain Roux **Owner** Alain Roux
Times 12-2/7-10 Closed 26 Dec-23 Jan, Mon-Tue **Prices** Fixed L 2 course fr £45.50, Tasting menu fr £152.50, Starter £30.50-£48.50, Main £50.50-£57, Dessert £30-£40.50, Service included
Wines 1000+ bottles over £30, 1 bottle under £30, 14 by glass **Notes** Tasting menu 6 course, Sun L 3 course, Sunday L £79.50, Vegetarian available, Dress restrictions, Smart casual, Civ Wed 70
Seats 75, Pr/dining room 8 **Children** Menu
Parking 20

BRAY *continued*

The Riverside Brasserie

◉◉ Modern European

Accomplished cooking by the Thames

☎ 01628 780553
Bray Marina, Monkey Island Ln SL6 2EB
e-mail: info@riversidebrasserie.co.uk
dir: Off A308, signed Bray Marina

If you like to make a grand entrance, why not arrive by boat, as this hidden gem is tucked away beside the Thames in Bray Marina. The waterside decked terrace is perfect for alfresco dining, but if summer sets in with its customary severity and drives you indoors, the simple interior oozes understated class and an easygoing ambience. Full-length glass doors mean the river views are still there, while the chefs working in an open-to-view kitchen turn out straightforward yet skillfully cooked brasserie food. Chicken liver and foie gras parfait with onion marmalade and toasted brioche is a classic starter, done right, while splendid ingredients bring lustre to an uncomplicated main course comprising spanking fresh cod with crunchy choucroute, pea purée and crispy Parma ham. Elsewhere, there may be Romney Marsh lamb rump, cooked sous-vide for maximum tenderness, and served with green beans and Sicilian pesto. To finish, a great combo of sweet and salty flavours comes courtesy of a chocolate ganache and salted caramel tart served with milk ice cream.

Times 12-2.30/7-9.30 Closed Mon-Thu (Oct-Mar), L Fri (Oct-Mar)

Waterside Inn

◉◉◉◉ — *see page 55*

CHIEVELEY   Map 5 SU47

The Crab at Chieveley

◉◉ Modern British

Idiosyncratic seafood restaurant in the wilds of Berkshire

☎ 01635 247550
Wantage Rd RG20 8UE
e-mail: info@crabatchieveley.com
dir: M4 junct 13, towards Chieveley. Left into School Rd, right at T-junct, 0.5m on right. Follow brown tourist signs

The Crab has unique selling points coming out of its ears. It's a restaurant-with-rooms fashioned out of a large country cottage, the guestrooms furnished in emulation of famous international hotel rooms from Waikiki Beach to Bora Bora, while the dining is a single-minded celebration of the bounty of the sea, as indicated by the seashell-filled nets dangling from the ceilings. The kitchen casts its own net with a vigorous lunge from landlocked Berkshire to the southwest boats of Brixham, Newlyn and Looe, for dishes that mix intelligent design with simplicity. Starters might be seared king scallops with black pudding bonbons and raisin purée, or brill tartare with blood-orange jelly and ginger crème fraîche, before a straightforward main such as tranche of crisp-skinned halibut on the bone with fat chips, crushed peas and béarnaise. If you're here for the namesake dish, Salcombe crab comes thermidored, garlic-buttered, or Thai-style with coconut, lime and coriander. Dessert might be a praline chocolate bar, its accompanying scoop of caramel ice cream wearing a bangle of spun sugar.

Times 12-2.30/6-9.30 Closed D 25 Dec

COOKHAM   Map 6 SU88

The White Oak

◉◉ European **NEW**

The epitome of a gastropub in a charming Thames-side village

☎ 01628 523 043
The Pound SL6 9QE
e-mail: info@thewhiteoak.co.uk
dir: M4 junct 8/9 onto A308(M) towards Maidenhead Central, continue towards Marlow. Right at lights Switchback Road South to Gardener Road. At rdbt 1st exit B4447 Switchback Road North to Cookham, right at mini-rdbt to The Pound

As if there weren't enough reasons to pay a visit to Cookham (the River Thames, the art gallery, lovely walks, quaint old buildings), there's now another in the form of The White Oak - an old village inn that's been transformed in recent years into a truly decent modern gastropub. Against a contemporary backdrop of wooden floors, neutral colours on the walls, splashes of modern artwork, unclothed chunky wooden tables and lots of natural light flooding in through a skylight and patio doors to the garden, chef Clive Dixon serves a pleasingly simple European repertoire that changes daily. Ingredients are of the highest quality and it shows in dishes like soupe de poisson with rouille and gruyère and the seasonal twist of pumpkin sippets (in place of traditional croutons). Main course might be an unctuous, melt-in-the-mouth Scottish beef cheek with red cabbage - both pickled and braised (a pleasing combination of textures) - and parsnip purée, while dessert ends on a fun and moreish note with hot brioche doughnuts served with raspberry purée and vanilla sauce for dipping. With proprietor Henry Cripps heading up the front-of-house team you can expect service that's truly on the ball, along with a relaxed and friendly atmosphere.

Chef Clive Dixon **Owner** Henry & Katherine Cripps
Times 12-2.30/6.30-9.30 **Prices** Fixed L 2 course £15, Fixed D 3 course £19, Service optional, Groups min 7 service 12.5% **Notes** Tasting menu 5,6,7 course, Sunday L, Vegetarian available

FRILSHAM
Map 5 SU57

The Pot Kiln

◎◎ Traditional British, European ◎

Confident country cooking in rural inn

☎ 01635 201366
RG18 0XX
e-mail: info@potkiln.org
dir: From Yattendon follow Pot Kiln signs, cross over motorway. Continue for 0.25m pub on right

A pub first and foremost, The Pot Kiln is the kind of pub every village deserves: one which serves a proper pint, grows its own vegetables, and sources the rest of the produce used with a good deal of care. And the fact it has a penchant for game, well, that's just a bonus. Of course, it is not the red-brick pub that is doing all this, but the owners, Mike and Katie Robinson. Mike is on the telly a fair bit, usually spreading the good word in support of British game, and he practices what he preaches. So seated at unadorned wooden tables in a thoroughly pubby atmosphere, you might tuck into a salad of Berkshire wood pigeon with black pudding, bacon and Jerusalem artichoke purée, or go your own way with cider-steamed River Fowey mussels. Pavé of Lockinge fallow deer is hard to ignore in this company, but everything is cooked with care and attention and presented with a contemporary touch or two. There's a bar menu too, serving up a cracking ploughman's, sandwiches and the like.

Chef Mike Robinson, Ben Fisher **Owner** Mike & Katie Robinson **Times** 12-2.30/7-9.30 Closed 25 Dec, Tue, D Sun **Prices** Prices not confirmed Service added but optional 10% **Wines** 6 by glass **Notes** Sunday L, Vegetarian available **Seats** 48 **Children** Portions **Parking** 70

HUNGERFORD
Map 5 SU36

The Bear Hotel

◎ Modern European

Contemporary cooking in an updated coaching inn

☎ 01488 682512
41 Charnham St RG17 0EL
e-mail: info@thebearhotelhungerford.co.uk
web: www.thebearhotelhungerford.co.uk
dir: M4 junct 14, follow A338/Hungerford signs. 3m to T-junct turn right onto A4 over 2 rdbts. Hotel 500yds on left

A long roll call of monarchs have enjoyed the hospitality of this seriously historic 15th-century coaching inn. The place is looking rather clean-cut and contemporary in the bar and snug these days, but the vast open fireplace in the lounge and massive black beams in the restaurant hint at its past. The latter is a soothing space: plain white walls hung with bright artwork, and tables set with crisp cloths and highly polished cutlery make a suitable setting for the kitchen's unfussy modern cooking. Chilli-spiced duck and vegetable spring rolls served with sweet and sour plum sauce set the ball rolling, ahead of pan-fried sea bass partnered by prawn and sesame noodles with a soya reduction. Those in the market for something meaty might find roast wood pigeon with turnip and swede purée, hot-pot potatoes and crispy black pudding, and for afters, perhaps bread and butter pudding with rum syrup.

Times 12-3/7-9.30 Closed D Sun, BHs

Littlecote House Hotel

◎◎ Modern British ◎

Appealing modern menu in an historic house

☎ 01488 682509
Chilton Foliat RG17 0SU
dir: From A4 Hungerford, follow brown signs

The house in question dates back to the 16th century, but the site is even older than that: a Roman mosaic and the remains of a Roman settlement can be seen in the grounds. Oliver Cromwell's soldiers were said to have been billeted here in the Civil War, an historic fact that's referenced in the name of the more exclusive of the hotel's dining options - Oliver's Bistro. The modern, minimalist dining room looks smart, with views over the immaculate gardens and slick service. An exciting menu showcases local suppliers and dishes are attractively presented. A good range of global wines complements the likes of duo of Cornish mackerel - well-made pâté and pan-seared fillet with a crisp skin - pointed up by gooseberry jam and onion marmalade. Then you might take rump of Gloucester lamb, moist and full of flavour, with garden peas, garlic and salsa verde. Honey crème brûlée with poached rhubarb brings proceedings to a simple but highly effective close.

Chef Matthew Davies **Owner** Warner Leisure Hotels **Times** 6.30-9 Closed Mon, L all week **Prices** Prices not confirmed Service optional **Wines** 3 by glass **Notes** Vegetarian available, Civ Wed 60 **Seats** 40, Pr/dining room 8 **Parking** 200

HURLEY
Map 5 SU88

Black Boys Inn

◎◎ Modern French

Modern French cooking in a Chilterns village

☎ 01628 824212
Henley Rd SL6 5NQ
e-mail: info@blackboysinn.co.uk
web: www.blackboysinn.co.uk
dir: M40 junct 4, A404 towards Henley, then A4130. Restaurant 3m from Henley-on-Thames & Maidenhead

This 16th-century coaching inn got its name from Charles II's clandestine visit in 1651 after the Battle of Worcester: it was the fond moniker given him by his soldiers because of his swarthy complexion. Today, a modern gloss adds a degree of sophistication to the oak beams, polished floors and unclothed tables, while the kitchen's style suits the environment to a T, its roots based firmly in French provincial cooking. Thus, mussels marinière may be followed by goose confit accompanied by Alsace-style apple and red cabbage flavoured with Calvados. There can be a welcome contemporary pitch to dishes too, seen in a salad of smoked eel, beetroot and apple with wasabi crème fraîche, and roast duck breast flavoured with lime in Armagnac sauce. Desserts are prepared with care, whether homely apple and plum crumble with custard or Sicilian-style lemon posset.

Chef Adrian Bannister **Owner** Adrian & Helen Bannister **Times** 12-2/7-9 Closed D Sun **Prices** Fixed L 2 course fr £12.50, Starter £5.95-£10.50, Main £17.50-£22.50, Dessert £6.25-£9.50, Service optional **Wines** 57 bottles over £30, 25 bottles under £30, 20 by glass **Notes** Carte du jour 2/3 courses, Sunday L £17.95-£22.50, Vegetarian available **Seats** 45, Pr/dining room 12 **Children** Portions **Parking** 45

The Olde Bell Inn

◎◎ Modern British

Classy, creative cooking in a smartly revamped coaching inn

☎ 01628 825881
High St SL6 5LX
e-mail: oldebellreception@coachinginn.co.uk
web: www.theoldebell.co.uk
dir: M4 junct 8/9 follow signs for Henley. At rdbt take A4130 to Hurley, turn right to Hurley Village, 800yds on right

A 12th-century coaching inn with bags of original features it certainly is, but the 'olde' sits well alongside the more fashionable at the Bell, with a sympathetic modern facelift that delivers a good deal of designer chic. The restaurant looks rather smart with its muted colours and wooden floors, while a mix of table and seating styles (from broad-oak tables to booth-style seating around the walls) delivers a relaxed, upbeat vibe. The cooking matches the surroundings, built on classical foundations but showcasing a modern approach with plenty of flair and imagination. Fresh local, seasonal produce and flavour drive the appealing roster: perhaps stuffed saddle of rabbit teamed with crosnes (Chinese artichoke), chanterelle and parsnip dauphinoise, or perhaps roast flounder with shallot purée, English asparagus, sea vegetables and confit garlic. To finish, expect the likes of treacle tart, clotted cream and raisin caramel. A separate bar menu, large garden and smart bedrooms put the icing on the cake.

Times 12.30-2.30/6-10 Closed Xmas, New Year, D Sun

HURLEY *continued*

Red Lyon

◎ Modern British ○

Good honest cooking in a whitewashed country inn

☎ 01628 823558
Henley Rd SL6 5LH
e-mail: info@redlyon.co.uk
web: www.redlyon.co.uk
dir: M4 junct 8/9 onto A4130, restaurant on left after Burchetts Green rdbt. Adjacent to Temple Golf Club

It's a toss-up as to when the Red Lyon is at its best: in winter when you can sit by a roaring log fire, or in summer when the garden is a flowering oasis. Whenever you choose to visit, the Red Lyon remains a pub - real ales on tap - that happens to serve up some pretty fine food. Nothing too fancy mind, but lots of local ingredients and bags of good ideas. Share one of the deli boards crammed with the likes of pork pie, mature cheddar, brie, piccalilli, coleslaw and pickled onions, or settle in for a three-course meal which might take you from pan-roasted Scottish scallops with fennel, parmesan and herbs, via braised shoulder of lamb with rosemary crushed potatoes and red cabbage, to apple and cinnamon crumble with custard. There are daily specials, plus a bespoke children's menu to add to its appeal.

Chef Simon Pitney-Baxter **Owner** Simon Pitney-Baxter, David Thompson **Times** 12-2.30/6-9.30 Closed 31 Dec, D 25-26 Dec, BH **Prices** Fixed L 2 course £15.70-£24.45, Fixed D 3 course £20.65-£30.95, Starter £4.75-£6.95, Main £10.95-£17.50, Dessert £4.95-£6.50, Service optional, Groups min 10 service 10% **Wines** 11 by glass **Notes** Sunday L, Vegetarian available **Seats** 70, Pr/dining room 35 **Children** Portions, Menu **Parking** 60

MAIDENHEAD   Map 6 SU88

Boulters Riverside Brasserie

◎◎ Modern British ○

Modern brasserie dining by the river

☎ 01628 621291
Boulters Lock Island SL6 8PE
e-mail: info@boultersrestaurant.co.uk
dir: M4 junct 7 onto A4 towards Maidenhead, cross Maidenhead bridge, right at rdbt. Restaurant 0.5m on right

The to-die-for Thames-side location overlooking Boulters Lock, where the river ambles past Maidenhead Bridge, is

a very good reason to head to this buzzy, contemporary brasserie. There may be nothing but glass walls between diners and the river, but Boulters is not a place to let the food take a back seat while the views pull in the punters: the ground-floor fine-dining brasserie is flooded with light and looks stylishly neutral with its bare darkwood tables and wooden floors. The food fits the setting to a T - well-executed contemporary brasserie dishes wrought from quality local produce, all impeccably presented. Roast pumpkin and Parmesan risotto gets a herby kick from marjoram and deeper earthy notes from truffle butter, while main course delivers splendidly fresh baked cod with a cheese crust, fondant potato, wilted spinach and wholegrain mustard sauce. For dessert, only Valrhona's finest will do for a hot chocolate fondant with pistachio parfait.

Chef Daniel Woodhouse **Owner** The Dennis family **Times** 12-2.45/6.30-9.30 Closed Mon, D Sun **Prices** Fixed L 2 course fr £15.95, Service added but optional 12.5% **Wines** 78 bottles over £30, 42 bottles under £30, 22 by glass **Notes** Sunday L £21.95-£26.95, Vegetarian available **Seats** 70, Pr/dining room 12 **Children** Portions, Menu **Parking** 20

Fredrick's Hotel Restaurant Spa

◎◎ Modern European

Modern European dishes in an unusual spa hotel

☎ 01628 581000
Shoppenhangers Rd SL6 2PZ
e-mail: reservations@fredricks-hotel.co.uk
web: www.fredricks-hotel.co.uk
dir: From M4 junct 8/9 take A404(M), then turning (junct 9A) for Cox Green/White Waltham. Left on to Shoppenhangers Rd, restaurant 400 mtrs on right

A classy spa hotel has been coaxed out of what looks a bit of an architectural hodge-podge, a grand suburban dwelling with towering pinnacles like industrial chimneys attached. The gardens and pool have been cleverly designed to make the most of the space, and an aura of the country house has been evoked in the principal dining room, where royal blue and gold upholstery is the regal setting for cooking that wears its modern European credentials on its sleeve. A duo of crab and home-smoked sea trout is accompanied by the bite of celeriac and apple remoulade for an appetising opener, and may be succeeded by monkfish bundled up in prosciutto with black olive gnocchi and tomato relish. Prosciutto wrapping might also be favoured for pork fillet, where it seems more of a tautology, although the accompaniments of caramelised balled apple and sage-scented mash are good, and a brave attempt at pannacotta flavoured with watermelon just about comes off, helped along by its garnishes of pistachio ice cream and lightly glazed blackberries.

Chef Craig Smith **Owner** R Takhar **Times** 12-2.30/7-9.30 Closed 23-27 Dec **Prices** Fixed L 2 course fr £31, Fixed D 3 course fr £39, Starter £12.50-£15.50, Main £25.50-£29.50, Dessert £6.50-£8, Service optional **Wines** 7 by glass **Notes** Sunday L, Vegetarian available,

Dress restrictions, Smart casual, Civ Wed 100 **Seats** 60, Pr/dining room 140 **Children** Portions **Parking** 90

The Royal Oak Paley Street

◎◎◎ *– see opposite*

NEWBURY   Map 5 SU46

Donnington Valley Hotel & Spa

◎◎ Modern British 📖 NOTABLE WINE LIST ○

Engaging modern cooking in a golfing and spa hotel

☎ 01635 551199
Old Oxford Rd, Donnington RG14 3AG
e-mail: general@donningtonvalley.co.uk
web: www.donningtonvalley.co.uk
dir: M4 junct 13, A34 towards Newbury. Take immediate left signed Donnington Hotel. At rdbt take right, at 3rd rdbt take left, follow road for 2m, hotel on right

There's plenty on offer at Donnington Valley, from tip-top business facilities, golf, a luxurious spa and, in the Wine Press restaurant, some good food to be had, too. It's a smart, modern hotel on a large scale, with no less than 111 bedrooms to choose from. The restaurant is a clear-headed space (no chintz here), set over two levels and decorated in mellow neutral tones, with artworks and fresh flowers adding splashes of colour. The kitchen delivers a slate of broadly modern British dishes based on high quality produce. Ham hock and foie gras terrine, for example, with beetroot chutney and toasted brioche, or from the Market Menu, chicken and duck liver parfait with tomato chutney. There are steaks from the grill, plus modish ideas such as seared monkfish tail with saag aloo, cauliflower beignet, courgette flower and lemon foam, which shows off the sound technical abilities in the kitchen. For dessert, try the rocky road baked cheesecake with hazelnut ice cream. Given the restaurant's name, it's no surprise that the wine list is well worth exploring.

Chef Kelvin Johnson **Owner** Sir Peter Michael **Times** 12-2/7-10 **Prices** Fixed L 2 course fr £18, Fixed D 3 course fr £28, Starter £8-£12, Main £17-£23, Dessert £8, Service optional **Wines** 250 bottles over £30, 50 bottles under £30, 21 by glass **Notes** Sunday L, Vegetarian available, Dress restrictions, Smart casual, Civ Wed 160 **Seats** 120, Pr/dining room 130 **Children** Portions, Menu **Parking** 150

The Royal Oak Paley Street

MAIDENHEAD   MAP 6 SU88

British, European NOTABLE WINE LIST

First-class modern British cooking in a spruced up country pub

☎ 01628 620541
Paley St, Littlefield Green SL6 3JN
e-mail: info@theroyaloakpaleystreet.com
web: www.theroyaloakpaleystreet.com
dir: M4 junct 8/9. Take A308 towards Maidenhead Central, then A330 to Ascot. After 2m, turn right onto B3024 to Twyford. Second pub on left

Nick Parkinson's place in the Berkshire countryside is in many ways a sustainable archetype for the future of the great British pub. The white-painted inn dating back to the 17th century may well have fallen by the wayside like so many had it not been for the vision of Nick, son of Sir Michael, to create a place to enjoy a proper pint of beer, great wines and some first-class, clearly-focused British food. It's a foodie destination these days, thanks to the canny appointment of Dominic Chapman, who has headed up the stoves for half-a-dozen years now. Black-and-white photos of the great and the good adorn the walls and a pubby informality (beamed ceilings, wooden floors, exposed brickwork) and bonhomie runs right through, but make no mistake, there's some seriously good food to be had and the service is slick

and professional. The restaurant has been extended and now includes The Oak Room private dining and function area. Dominic seeks out the very best produce, most of which is British, a significant proportion local, and creates menus filled with things you'll want to eat. Lasagna of wild rabbit, for example, with wood blewits and chervil, is a first course that oozes class, or there's all the comfort of a Jerusalem artichoke soup with anchovy toast. Black Angus oxtail and kidney pie is a cut above your average, or go for the line-caught sea bass with samphire, cockles and mussels. The menu follows the seasons with due vigilance. Yorkshire rhubarb trifle or Cox's apple tart with vanilla ice cream are traditional ideas executed with flair and craft, whilst the cheeseboard brims with good stuff from Britain and France. You can simply pop in for a pint if you wish, there's a cracking list of wines with a good choice by the glass, and the terrace is a lovely spot in the warmer months.

Chef Dominic Chapman **Owner** Nick Parkinson **Times** 12-2.30/6-9.30 Closed D Sun **Prices** Fixed L 2 course fr £25, Fixed D 3 course fr £30, Starter £7-£12.50, Main £16-£35, Dessert £6.50-£9.50, Service added but optional 12.5% **Wines** 400 bottles over £30, 80 bottles under £30, 20 by glass **Notes** Fixed D menu available Mon-Thu, L Mon-Sat, Sunday L, Vegetarian

available **Seats** 80, Pr/dining room 20 **Parking** 70

NEWBURY *continued*

Newbury Manor Hotel

Modern European

Romantic waterside setting for classically-inspired cooking

☎ 01635 528838
London Rd RG14 2BY
e-mail: enquiries@newbury-manor-hotel.co.uk
dir: M4 junct 13, A34 Newbury, A4 Thatcham, 0.5m on right

Newbury Manor is a handsome Grade II-listed Georgian house set in nine delicious acres of woodlands and water meadows. The River Bar & Restaurant lies just a short stroll from the main house through fragrant herb gardens and across wooden bridges. It's in an old watermill at the confluence of the Kennet and Lambourn Rivers, with a decking terrace above the tranquil pool where the electric blue flash of a kingfisher is a frequent sight. The cooking suits the comfortable and relaxed tone of the place with its straightforward menus of seasonally-driven dishes. Local produce is the bedrock of flavour-led ideas such as seared king scallops and balsamic-glazed pork belly with apple and celeriac remoulade, while among main courses you might find a duo of salt marsh lamb cutlet and braised shoulder teamed with fine beans and shallots, or pan-fried monkfish with pea and smoked bacon risotto, and maple-dressed salad.

Chef Jan Papcun **Owner** Heritage Properties & Hotels **Times** 12-2.30/6-10 **Prices** Fixed L 2 course £14.95, Fixed D 3 course £19, Starter £6-£10, Main £11.50-£22.50, Dessert £5-£6.50, Service optional **Wines** 10 bottles over £30, 25 bottles under £30, 12 by glass **Notes** Sunday L, Vegetarian available, Civ Wed 160 **Seats** 48, Pr/dining room 160 **Children** Portions **Parking** 80

Regency Park Hotel

Modern European **NEW**

Good brasserie cooking in modern spa hotel

☎ 01635 871555
Bowling Green Rd, Thatcham RG18 3RP
e-mail: info@regencyparkhotel.com
web: www.regencyparkhotel.co.uk
dir: M4 junct 13, follow A339 to Newbury for 2m, then take the A4 (Reading), the hotel is signed

Tucked into the Berkshire hinterland between Newbury and Thatcham, the Regency Park is a modern corporate spa hotel. If you've just hot-footed it from a visit to nearby Highclere Castle (TV's *Downton Abbey* in its other life), it will look a bit prosaic by comparison, but creature comforts are conspicuous by their abundance, and the Watermark restaurant is kitted out in restful spring-like shades, along with a water-feature. The cooking keeps to a simple brasserie formula, but achieves a convincing success rate with the likes of seared scallops and gingered carrots in coriander oil, or duck liver parfait with spiced plum chutney to start, and then perhaps pink-cooked rump of lamb with flageolets and spinach in an outstanding garlic and rosemary jus. A more ambitious fish dish might see hazelnut-crusted turbot turn up with turnips in a red wine and shallot sauce, while dessert could be firm-textured orange cheesecake with sharply contrasting rhubarb compôte.

The Vineyard

NEWBURY   **MAP 5 SU46**

Modern French **V** NOTABLE WINE LIST

World-class wines and finely tuned modern French cuisine amid five-star splendour

☎ 01635 528770
Stockcross RG20 8JU
e-mail: general@the-vineyard.co.uk
web: www.the-vineyard.co.uk
dir: From M4 take A34 towards Newbury, exit at 3rd junct for Speen. Right at rdbt then right again at 2nd rdbt

They don't make wine at The Vineyard - nor do they have any grapevines - but they do serve some pretty amazing wines from a cellar that runs to a whopping 30,000 bottles. A good deal of those amazing wines come from California and, more specifically, from owner Sir Peter Michael's vineyards (so the name does make some sense after all).

No matter what kind of wine floats your boat, there'll be something for you on the 3,000-strong list and, even better, around 100 of them are available by the glass. Of course, it's not all about wine here: the hotel offers luxurious accommodation, a swish spa and the classy, contemporary French cooking of Daniel Galmiche, served in the elegant restaurant, where a sweeping staircase with a balustrade fashioned as if it were a coiling grapevine connects the two levels, and an unstuffy front-of-house team are fully versed in both the menu and - rather impressively - the wine list. When it comes to choosing what to eat, the idea is to choose four or five dishes and then put your trust in the eminently capable sommelier to match each up to a suitable wine. Alternatively, you can go for one of the two tasting menus - the seven-course Judgement whereby dishes are paired up with both Californian and French wines so you can vote for your favourite, or the Discovery with matching wines chosen from lesser-known parts of the world. Whichever route you choose, expect some surprises, some excellent marriages of flavour, and a lot of fun. Ballottine of guinea fowl with lemon and walnuts is an intelligently composed, elegant dish of superb textural contrasts and ingredients of the highest quality. Next up, wonderfully fresh, precisely cooked Cornish brill comes in a delightful partnership with chanterelles, salsify and Swiss chard. Jimmy Butlers' free-range pork rib-eye - with spinach and onion seeds - is tender, moist, packed with flavour and beautifully presented, and it all ends on a high with technically impressive and creative desserts like English rhubarb with Victoria sponge and lime meringue, or dark chocolate with zingy ginger ice cream, pineapple and tonka bean emulsion.

Chef Daniel Galmiche **Owner** Sir Peter Michael **Times** 12-2/7-9.30 **Prices** Fixed L 2 course £17-£33, Fixed D 3 course £35-£59, Tasting menu £49-£89, Starter £7-£14, Main £18-£22, Dessert £7-£10, Service optional **Wines** 2800 bottles over £30, 60 bottles under £30, 120 by glass **Notes** ALC 2/3 course £62/£72, Tasting menu 5/7 course, Sunday L, Vegetarian menu, Civ Wed 120 **Seats** 86, Pr/dining room 120 **Children** Portions, Menu **Parking** 100

Save on Hotels. Book at **theAA.com/hotel**

BERKSHIRE 61 **ENGLAND**

Chef Laurent Guyon **Owner** Planned Holdings Ltd **Times** 12.30-2/7-10 Closed L Sat **Prices** Fixed L 2 course £14.95, Fixed D 3 course £29, Starter £7-£10, Main £15-£25, Dessert £7-£14.95, Service optional **Wines** 16 bottles over £30, 24 bottles under £30, 16 by glass **Notes** Sunday L, Vegetarian available **Seats** 90, Pr/dining room 40 **Children** Portions, Menu **Parking** 150

The Vineyard

◉◉◉ – *see opposite*

PANGBOURNE Map 5 SU67

The Elephant at Pangbourne

◉ Modern British, European ◉

Contemporary cooking in a colonial setting

☎ 0118 984 2244
Church Rd RG8 7AR
e-mail: reception@elephanthotel.co.uk
web: www.elephanthotel.co.uk
dir: A4 Theale/Newbury, right at 2nd rdbt signed Pangbourne. Hotel on left

Prepare to enjoy the opulence of the former British Empire at this smart boutique hotel in Pangbourne, beside the River Thames. Throughout, handcrafted Indian furniture and fabrics set the scene - be it in the more casual BaBar bistro or Christoph's stylish fine-dining restaurant. There's an enclosed garden, if the weather lives up to the theme. The menu sometimes harks back to the UK's colonial past with the use of the accordant spicing, but it's broadly modish European in focus; start, perhaps, with pecan, chicken and pork pâté served with rustic bread, apple juice and jelly before poppadom-encrusted coley with Bombay potatoes and sweet curry sauce, and finish with an Elephant knickerbocker glory or bitter chocolate parfait with rosewater and cardamom ice cream.

Owner Hillbrooke Hotels **Times** 12-2.30/7-9 **Prices** Prices not confirmed Service optional **Wines** 10 bottles over £30, 21 bottles under £30, 11 by glass **Notes** Sunday L, Vegetarian available, Civ Wed 100 **Seats** 40, Pr/dining room 77 **Children** Portions, Menu **Parking** 15

READING Map 5 SU77

Cerise Restaurant at The Forbury Hotel

◉◉ Modern British

Sharply delineated brasserie cooking in a cherry-red basement

☎ 0118 952 7770
26 The Forbury RG1 3EJ
e-mail: reception@theforburyhotel.co.uk

The hotel frontage is a stolid porticoed affair that does nothing to prepare you for the dramatic ambience of the basement Cerise Restaurant. High side-windows let in plenty of natural light, avoiding the gloomy air that can afflict subterranean dining rooms. Indeed, the restaurant lives up to its name with cherry-red the prevailing tone, while mock-crocodile banquette seating and tub chairs at smartly set tables look the part. Expect a lively menu of pop brasserie food, cooked to order, with sharply delineated flavours and attention to often surprisingly classical detail. A pair of fat croquettes of haddock and mussel arrive on a bed of dill-sauced leeks for a bravura opener, which may be followed by something gamey such as sautéed breast of partridge with a little pie of the confit leg, honey-glazed spicy parsnips, sweet potato and a deeply rich and satisfying game jus. Pastry-work for desserts is top-notch, crisp and brittle for a glazed prune and Armagnac filling, served alongside candied kumquats and a mild-mannered but impressive milk sorbet.

Chef Michael Parke **Times** 12-3/5-10.30 **Prices** Starter £7.50-£10, Main £14-£21, Dessert £8.50-£10.50, Service optional **Wines** 70 bottles over £30, 24 bottles under £30, 11 by glass **Notes** Sunday L, Vegetarian available, Civ Wed 50 **Seats** 72, Pr/dining room 35 **Children** Portions, Menu **Parking** 18

Forbury's Restaurant

◉ French, European ◉ NOTABLE WINE LIST ◉

Refined, confident cooking in smartly contemporary venue

☎ 0118 957 4044
1 Forbury Square RG1 3BB
e-mail: forburys@btconnect.com
dir: In town centre, opposite Forbury Gardens

If this stylish modern restaurant feels more big-city cool than Reading central - with its floor-to-ceiling windows overlooking swanky Forbury Square - it will come as no surprise to hear that the striking glass office block in which it is located was designed by the same architect who created Canary Wharf. Smartly decked out in an appropriately modish manner, Forbury's comes with large canvases of modern art, leather chairs, rich colours and

linen-clad tables. There's a buzzy wine bar area and large fair-weather terrace to cover all bases. The kitchen delivers a progressive take on the classic French theme, with reliance on fresh quality produce, clean flavours and creative presentation. Expect pan-roasted Barbury duck breast teamed with a cassoulet of Puy lentils and sprout tops, or wild sea bass fillet with fricassée of truffled potatoes, broad beans and chanterelle mushrooms. To finish, there might be a warm Amedei chocolate fondant with pistachio ice cream.

Chef Gavin Young **Owner** Xavier Le-Bellego **Times** 12-2.15/6-10 Closed 26-28 Dec, 1-2 Jan, Sun **Prices** Fixed L 2 course £13.50, Fixed D 3 course £23, Tasting menu £65-£75, Starter £7.50-£12.50, Main £12.50-£28, Dessert £7.50-£9.50, Service optional, Groups min 4 service 12.5% **Wines** 11 by glass **Notes** Tasting menu 6 course, Early bird D 3 course £20, Vegetarian available **Seats** 80, Pr/dining room 16 **Children** Portions **Parking** 40

The French Horn

◉◉ Traditional French V ◉

Classical French dining on the Thames

☎ 0118 969 2204
Sonning RG4 6TN
e-mail: info@thefrenchhorn.co.uk
dir: From Reading take A4 E to Sonning. Follow B478 through village over bridge, hotel on right, car park on left

The cooking at The French Horn may not be at the cutting edge of culinary trends, but you know you'll be treated to the delights of timeless Gallic gastronomy in an idyllic, quintessentially English Thames-side setting. The elegant glass-fronted dining room revels in old-school refinement, and opens onto a waterfront terrace where manicured lawns give way to ancient willows dipping their fronds into the river. As you sip a glass of fizz, you might catch a waft of the signature dish - caneton rôti à l'anglaise - that's spit-roast duck, which turns fragrantly above the fire, and comes to table with apple purée, sage stuffing and rich duck jus. Otherwise, you might start with pan-fried foie gras with caramelised pear and blackcurrant sauce, followed by pheasant casserole, and bow out French-style with crêpes Suzette, or do things the British way with bread-and-butter pudding and custard.

Chef J Diaga **Owner** Emmanuel family **Times** 12-2.30/7-10 Closed 1-4 Jan **Prices** Fixed L 2 course fr £19.50, Fixed D 3 course fr £26.50, Starter £8.50-£24.60, Main £17.95-£37.45, Dessert £8.10-£11.80, Service included **Wines** 14 by glass **Notes** Sunday L, Vegetarian menu, Dress restrictions, No shorts or sleeveless shirts **Seats** 70, Pr/dining room 24 **Children** Portions **Parking** 40

READING *continued*

Holiday Inn Reading M4 Jct 10

@@ Modern European, Indian NEW ✪

Imaginative fusion cooking in a smart new Holiday Inn

☎ 0118 944 0444
Wharfedale Rd, Winnersh Triangle RG41 5TS
e-mail: reservations@hireadinghotel.com
web: www.meridianleisurehotels.com/reading
dir: M4 junct 10/A329(M) towards Reading (E), 1st exit
signed Winnersh/Woodley/A329, left at lights into
Wharfedale Rd. Hotel on left

You sense that they're not exactly going for the romantic
tryst market with that road-atlas hotel name, but this is
in fact a brand-new flagship for the group, not far from
either Heathrow or Legoland, depending on your business,
and designed with an impressive degree of contemporary
flair. Airy spaciousness is the tone of the public areas,
and a helical chandelier on the staircase provides a
talking point, while the Caprice dining room boasts smart
linen, fresh flowers, a pianist, and the skills of Graham
Weston, an accomplished country-house chef. Melding
Mediterranean and Asian modes in the approved idiom,
he offers a thoughtful menu that rises above corporate
homogeneity. Tuna tataki with avocado and wasabi is a
palate-sharpener, or there may be foie gras mousse with
smoked duck and poached pear to kick things off. Home-
made linguine garnishes a well-balanced main course of
baked stone bass in smoked salmon and vegetable broth,
or there could be a roulade of chicken, guinea fowl and
pigeon served with rösti and creamed spinach. A biscuit-
based baked cheesecake of rum and raisin pairs well
with citrus sorbet.

Chef Graham Weston **Owner** Meridian Reading
Times 12-3/6-11 **Prices** Fixed L 2 course fr £18.95, Fixed
D 3 course fr £22.95, Starter £6.25-£8.25, Main
£15.50-£24.95, Dessert £5.25-£6.95, Service optional
Wines 60 bottles over £30, 25 bottles under £30
Notes Sunday L, Vegetarian available, Civ Wed 260
Seats 120, Pr/dining room 20 **Children** Portions, Menu
Parking 130

Malmaison Reading

@ Modern European

Enlivening brasserie cooking in a restyled railway hotel

☎ 0118 956 2300 & 956 2302
Great Western House, 18-20 Station Rd RG1 1JX
e-mail: reading@malmaison.com
web: www.malmaison.com
dir: Next to Reading station

The Reading branch of the much-loved Mal chain is a
sparkling-white balustraded edifice, formerly the Great
Western Railway Hotel, hence its interior proliferation of
rail-related memorabilia. Homage duly paid to an era

when the trains ran on time, the rest is as breathlessly
in-the-moment as can be imagined. A sleek, dark bar is
consecrated to premium cocktails and stylistically listed
wines, while the street-facing restaurant comes equipped
with blinded windows, bare brick walls, exposed
ductwork, back-to-back bench seating recalling the old
railway couchettes, and lights that look ready to
illuminate a Hollywood film-set. A menu of enlivening
brasserie food might open with a fun platter of 'lollipops'
(chicken satay, prawn tempura, crab spring roll, Thai
pork and fishcake bonbon), or a retooled prawn cocktail of
admirable simplicity, before moving to coriander-coated
rack of lamb with minty yoghurt, or lobster thermidor. A
Valrhona chocolate tart brings up the rear.

Chef Harcin Worzalla **Owner** MWB Malmaison Holdings
Ltd **Times** 12-2.30/6-10.30 Closed L Sat, D 25 Dec
Prices Fixed L 2 course £14.95, Fixed D 3 course £19.95,
Service added but optional 10% **Wines** 18 by glass
Notes Sunday L, Vegetarian available, Civ Wed 35
Seats 64, Pr/dining room 40 **Children** Portions, Menu
Parking NCP across road

Millennium Madejski Hotel Reading

@@ British, International Ⅴ ✪

Modern British dishes in a glam football hotel

☎ 0118 925 3500
Madejski Stadium RG2 0FL
e-mail: reservations.reading@millenniumhotels.co.uk
web: www.millenniumhotels.co.uk
dir: 1m N from M4 junct 11. 2m S from Reading town
centre

The fortunes of Reading FC may not exactly be in the
ascendant, but their home, the Madejski Stadium
complex, incorporates a winningly contemporary hotel in
voguish monochrome and glass. If you're not a supporter,
you'll need to know it's junction 11 off the M4. Cilantro is
the main restaurant, reached via a stylish champagne
bar. With smartly attired tables and staff, it all feels
suitably executive-boxish, and there is some vibrant
modern British food in prospect. Nanny Williams blue
goats' cheese is the ingredient in a starter soufflé, which
comes with the fitting companion of a Granny Smith
sorbet, looking for all the world like a dessert. Mains
might include wonderful seasonal grouse with creamed
cabbage, game chips, watercress and gutsy Cumberland
sauce, or steamed John Dory with a scallop and wild
mushrooms. Finish with orange millefeuille and white
chocolate parfait, daringly seasoned with rosemary. There
is also a Menu Gourmand taster, in both regular and
vegetarian versions.

Chef Denzil Newton **Owner** Madejski Hotel Co **Times** 7-10
Closed 25 Dec, 1 Jan, BH, Sun-Mon, L all week
Prices Prices not confirmed **Wines** 12 by glass
Notes Gourmand menu 7 course £47, Vegetarian menu,
Dress restrictions, Smart casual **Seats** 55, Pr/dining room
12 **Children** Portions **Parking** 100

Mya Lacarte

@ Modern British ✪

Carefully-sourced British produce on the high street

☎ 0118 946 3400
5 Prospect St, Caversham RG4 8JB
e-mail: eat@myalacarte.co.uk
dir: M4 junct 10, continue onto A3290/A4 signed
Caversham. At Crown Plaza Hotel continue over
Caversham Bridge, restaurant 3rd left

With a love of food that extends to promoting
sustainability and environmental conservation, the team
behind Mya Lacarte show a good and healthy approach to
life. The menu indicates veggie dishes and points out
what to go for if you have various allergies and
intolerances, and first-and-foremost the idea is to keep
things as local and seasonal as possible. So you might
start with local beetroot (puréed, pickled and confit)
partnered with Shropshire goats' cheese, or go for
Watlington pork belly carpaccio. Follow on with pan-fried
Gressingham duck with the accompanying leg, honey-
roasted parsnips, red cabbage, cranberry chutney and
duck jus, or the fishy catch of the day, finishing with
chocolate and beetroot pudding. Situated right in the
heart of Caversham, this unpretentious, modish
establishment is a fine example of a contemporary
neighbourhood restaurant. More power to its elbow.

Chef Justin Le Stephany **Owner** Matthew Siadatan
Times 12-3/5-10.30 Closed 25-26 Dec, 1 Jan, D Sun
Prices Fixed L 2 course £14.95, Fixed D 3 course £18.95,
Tasting menu £65-£75, Starter £5.95-£9.95, Main
£13.95-£22, Dessert £3-£8, Service optional, Groups min
5 service 10% **Wines** 10 bottles over £30, 20 bottles
under £30, 10 by glass **Notes** Sunday L, Vegetarian
available, Dress restrictions, Smart casual **Seats** 35, Pr/
dining room 12 **Children** Portions **Parking** NCP

SHINFIELD	**Map 5 SU76**

L'ortolan

@@@ – *see opposite*

Save on Hotels. Book at **theAA**.com/hotel

BERKSHIRE 63 ENGLAND

L'ortolan

SHINFIELD   MAP 5 SU76

Modern French V ⬧ NOTABLE WINE LIST

Consummate modern French style in a former vicarage

☎ 0118 988 8500
Church Ln RG2 9BY
e-mail: info@lortolan.com
web: www.lortolan.com
dir: From M4 junct 11 take A33 towards Basingstoke. At 1st lights turn left, after garage turn left, 1m turn right at Six Bells pub. Restaurant 1st left (follow tourist signs)

Alan Murchison's 10 in 8 enterprise emphatically doesn't work as a chain with the same signature stamped on each outpost, but is made up of a heterogeneous collection of venues stretching from Shropshire, through Bedfordshire and Berkshire, down to Hampshire. L'ortolan was the first, and still feels in many ways like a flagship. It's a red-brick former vicarage tucked away down a lane, in a sizeable but pleasantly tranquil village not far from Reading and the M4. With conservatory extensions looking over the pretty gardens, and interiors decorated to a high order, it looks every inch the destination restaurant. Three private dining rooms are part of the appeal, and the place is run with knowledgeable aplomb by a cosmopolitan European brigade of staff. Head chef Nick Chappell is a consummate practitioner of the modern French style, bringing a nice delicacy of judgment to dishes that manage that elusive balance of looking neat and light while being constructed of powerful, concentrated elements in bold counterpoint. Multi-course tasting menus are the principal drivers of the operation: five stages at lunch, six for the Signature, seven for the Gourmand, ten for the Prestige, with vegetarian versions too. Classical French technique is the foundation, with increasingly evident Indian and other Asian seasoning and spicing conferring distinctiveness. Lunch might begin with a serving of firm-textured Goosnargh duck terrine with pickled rhubarb, granola and a sharp rhubarb sorbet, or a warm pavé of salmon with salt-baked beetroot in all colours, and a purée of kalamansi. Those Indian notes resound in the lightly curried mussels that accompany a main course of stone bass, together with shaved white radish, lentil dhal and pickles, or there may be braised and roasted pork belly, its buttery tenderness matched by a serving of full-throttle macaroni cheese, with garnishes of apple Parisienne and a deeply resonant Calvados sauce. Main courses on the lengthier menus may include succulent venison haunch with charred cauliflower, sauced with port and chocolate, and roast fillet and braised shin of veal in liquorice with burnt onion (charred veg are a speciality) and Madeira sauce, while the corresponding vegetarian option may be spinach and mushroom agnolotti with truffled cep purée. The professional finish to dishes is maintained through to dazzling desserts such as the vibrantly colourful blood orange cream with pistachio meringue and pistachio ice cream, or parsnip and almond cake with parsnip sorbet and bitter chocolate ganache.

Chef Alan Murchison, Nick Chappell **Owner** Newfee Ltd **Times** 12-2/7-9 Closed 2 wks Xmas-New Year, Sun-Mon **Prices** Fixed L 2 course £28, Tasting menu £39-£105, Service added but optional 12.5% **Wines** 200 bottles over £30, 8 bottles under £30, 11 by glass **Notes** Tasting menu 7/10 course, Chef's table available, Vegetarian menu, Dress restrictions, Smart casual, Civ Wed 58 **Seats** 58, Pr/dining room 22 **Children** Portions **Parking** 30

The Greene Oak

@ Modern British NEW

Modern pub dining in a welcoming country inn

☎ 01753 864 294
Oakley Green SL4 5UW
e-mail: info@thegreeneoak.co.uk

The Greene Oak probably couldn't be greener if it tried: the exterior of the pub is painted green, and inside the theme continues, with pale green banquettes and chairs, green legs on chunky wooden tables, green panels on some of the walls and splashes of green in the patterned cushions and blinds. It all makes for a very fresh and vibrant look, which is reflected in the waiting staff who are as cheery and welcoming as they come. The modern pub food takes its influences from Europe and beyond, and relies on top-notch, seasonal British ingredients. The carte is supplemented by a daily-changing set menu at lunchtime and some blackboard specials, the latter possibly bringing forth breaded beef rib fingers with braised red cabbage to start: an unusual dish with good textural contrast (moist, tender beef, crispy coating) and great flavour. Main course could be as simple as a sea-fresh roast skate wing with fat-cut chips, seasonal greens and caper and butter sauce, while dessert could end on a fruity note with warm spiced poached plums sitting atop a nicely made pear and almond tart.

Chef Richard Stearn **Owner** Henry & Katherine Cripps **Times** 12-3/6-10 **Prices** Fixed L 2 course £12-£15, Starter £4.50-£12, Main £12.50-£29, Dessert £5-£7.50, Service optional, Groups min 7 service 12.5% **Wines** 24 bottles over £30, 27 bottles under £30, 21 by glass **Notes** Vegetarian available **Seats** 85 **Children** Portions, Menu **Parking** 50

Macdonald Windsor Hotel

@ Scottish, Modern British NEW

Scottish dining opposite Windsor Castle

☎ 0844 8799101
23 High St SL4 1LH
e-mail: gm.windsor@macdonaldwindsor.co.uk
dir: M4 junct 6 A355, take A332, rdbt 1st exit signed town centre. In 0.7m turn left into Bachelors Acre

Right opposite the castle, the Macdonald group's boutique hotel was once a John Lewis store. You may well wonder whether it's Balmoral across the street rather than Windsor, as the culinary compass is firmly set to north of the border, with a strong Scottish note informing the menus in the cool and contemporary Caley's restaurant. A Josper charcoal grill rules the roost in the kitchen, turning out fabulous rib-eye steaks cooked à point, with thick chips and béarnaise, as well as lemon sole, Highland lamb cutlets, and chicken glazed in heather honey and thyme. Starters might be Scotch broth or haggis in whisky sauce, and there are sharing platters of John Ross Jr smoked fish, while desserts are unabashedly populist in their appeal, with hot chocolate

fudge cake and rich vanilla ice cream, peach Melba and knickerbocker glory on offer.

Chef Gareth Long **Owner** Macdonald Hotels **Times** 7-10 All-day dining **Prices** Fixed L 2 course £15-£19, Starter £2.50-£8.50, Main £9.50-£27.50, Dessert £5.50-£8.90, Service optional **Notes** Buffet £15, Sunday L £19-£22, Vegetarian available, Civ Wed 120 **Seats** 70, Pr/dining room 24 **Children** Portions, Menu **Parking** 30, Pre-booked and chargeable

Mercure Windsor Castle Hotel

@@ Modern British

Bright modern cooking by the castle

☎ 0870 400 8300 & 01753 851577
18 High St SL4 1LJ
e-mail: h6618@accor.com
web: www.mercure.com
dir: M25 junct 13 take A308 towards town centre then onto B470 to High St. M4 junct 6 towards A332, at rdbt first exit into Clarence Rd, left at lights to High St

You get a ringside seat for the Changing of the Guard at Windsor Castle at this 16th-century coaching inn in the heart of Windsor. The place is rather more than a simple inn these days, of course - kitted out with bare darkwood tables and contemporary hues of aubergine and grey, Restaurant Eighteen sports a clean-cut 21st-century look that matches its imaginative, French-influenced modern menu. The kitchen sends out well-balanced and clear-flavoured dishes and has the confidence to try out interesting combinations - perhaps flavouring a pannacotta with Stilton and rosemary and serving it with roast figs, caramelised walnuts and sherry-like vin de curé vinegar. Main course might run to a modish duo of spring lamb - roast rack and confit shoulder teamed with sautéed samphire, butternut purée, celeriac fondant and roast shallots - and to finish, perhaps rhubarb parfait with poached rhubarb crumble, and strawberry consommé.

Times 12-2.30/6.30-9.45

Oakley Court Hotel

@@ Modern European NEW V 🖐

Creative modern European cooking amid Victorian Gothic extravagance

☎ 01753 609988
Windsor Rd, Water Oakley SL4 5UR
e-mail: reservations@theoakleycourthotel.com
web: www.theoakleycourthotel.com
dir: M4 junct 6 to Windsor. At rdbt right onto A308. Hotel 2.5m on right

The British Isles don't lack for magnificent Gothic castles that turn out to have been built during the reign of Queen Victoria. Oakley Court is a prime example, with its turrets and stepped gables and 37 acres of well-tended grounds. The place is a hive of sporting activity, with golf, tennis and swimming on tap, or you can get beautified in the treatment rooms. The half-panelled dining room, with its crisply clothed tables and formal service, is the place to

head to for some creative modern European cooking featuring plenty of local ingredients. The contemporary classic pairing of shellfish and pig is celebrated in an opener that combines caramelised scallops with Ibérico ham, a ham croquette, pea purée and pickled cauliflower. Pink-cooked herb-crusted lamb loin is the real deal, teamed with a little shepherd's pie, with traditional veg accoutrements and a rich jus, while fish might be salmon served with a stew of broad beans and clams and saffron potatoes. Finish with coffee semi-fredo and white chocolate biscotti in coffee syrup.

Chef Michael Mealey **Owner** The Oakley Court Hotel Ltd **Times** 12-2.30/6.30-9.30 Closed L Sat **Prices** Starter £8-£9, Main £22-£25, Dessert £9-£10, Service added but optional 8% **Notes** Sunday L £23.50-£29.95, Vegetarian menu, Civ Wed 170 **Seats** 100, Pr/dining room 33 **Children** Portions, Menu **Parking** 200

Sir Christopher Wren Hotel and Spa

@ Modern British NEW 🖐

Modish cooking by the River Thames

☎ 01753 442400
Thames St SL4 1PX
e-mail: wrens@sarova.co.uk
dir: M4 junct 6, 1st exit from relief road, follow signs to Windsor, 1st major exit on left, turn left at lights

Right next to Eton Bridge, with the river flowing past, there's no quibbling about the name of the Thames View Restaurant - it's a peach of a position, and the windows are expansive enough to give everyone a view. The man himself - Sir Christopher - had connections to Windsor but didn't design the hotel, but that's not to say it isn't a handsome and characterful building, and there's even room for spa and leisure facilities. The restaurant is smart and comfortable, with linen-clad tables and a menu that follows a modern British path. Start with ham hock and foie gras terrine with spiced plums and sakura cress, or oak-smoked salmon with capers, shallots and lemon, before a main course such as sea bass with crab and saffron risotto, confit fennel and saffron cream sauce. To finish, dark chocolate truffle torte with raspberry sorbet hits the spot.

Chef Nenad Bibic **Owner** Sarova Hotels **Times** 12.30-2.30/6.30-10 **Prices** Starter £6-£10.50, Main £12-£21.50, Dessert £6.50-£8, Service optional, Service added but optional **Wines** 20 bottles over £30, 35 bottles under £30, 10 by glass **Notes** Pre-theatre D available, Sunday L £29.95, Vegetarian available, Dress restrictions, Smart casual preferred, Civ Wed 100 **Seats** 65, Pr/dining room 100 **Children** Portions, Menu **Parking** 14, Pre-bookable only, Riverside train station

Save on Hotels. Book at **theAA.com/hotel**

BRISTOL 65 **ENGLAND**

BRISTOL

BRISTOL
Map 4 ST57

The Avon Gorge Hotel

Modern British

Splendid Clifton location and modern British cooking

☎ 0117 973 8955
Sion Hill, Clifton BS8 4LD
e-mail: rooms@theavongorge.com
dir: From S: M5 junct 19, A369 to Clifton Toll, over suspension bridge, 1st right into Sion Hill. From N: M5 junct 18A, A4 to Bristol, under suspension bridge, follow signs to bridge, exit Sion Hill

The Victorian builders of the hotel chose their site well: at one end of Brunel's landmark suspension bridge, overlooking the gorge and the bridge itself. In the restaurant, floor-to-ceiling windows open on to a terrace with some of the city's best views. There's more to the cooking than the self-styled modern British tag would suggest, with the enterprising kitchen turning out grilled sardines with warm tomato vinaigrette, spring vegetable tarte Tatin with rocket pesto and mozzarella, and confit pork belly with cider and brandy sauce and bubble-and-squeak made with black pudding. There's also ham hock terrine with piccalilli and cider jelly, followed by a choice of steaks with béarnaise, or perhaps seared chicken breast with potato and garlic salad and mushrooms. Fish options are worth exploring - pan-fried halibut fillet with broad beans, peas and lemon butter perhaps - and to cap a meal might be steamed nectarine pudding with custard.

Chef Luke Trott **Owner** Swire Hotels **Times** 12-4/6-10 **Prices** Fixed L 2 course fr £9.95, Starter £5.50-£8.95, Main £10.95-£17.50, Dessert £5.75-£7.95, Service added but optional **Wines** 21 bottles under £30, 24 by glass **Notes** Sunday L £15.95-£18.95, Vegetarian available, Civ Wed 100 **Seats** 50, Pr/dining room 20 **Children** Portions, Menu **Parking** 25

Best Western Henbury Lodge Hotel

Modern British

Charming Georgian country-house hotel near Bristol

☎ 0117 950 2615
Station Rd, Henbury BS10 7QQ
e-mail: info@henburyhotel.com
web: www.henburyhotel.com
dir: M5 junct 17/A4018 towards city centre, 3rd rdbt right into Crow Ln. At end turn right, hotel 200mtrs on right

This elegant small hotel fashioned from a Georgian mansion is a country house in the city, stylishly made over with a pared-back contemporary look. The Blaise Restaurant sports a light and airy décor involving creamy yellow walls hung with gilt-framed mirrors, wooden floors, toffee-brown leather chairs at bare blond-wood tables, and French doors leading out to a terrace in the pretty walled garden. The kitchen makes the most of local ingredients and seasonal produce in its straightforward modern ideas, as in a tasty starter of potted ham served

with hot toast and home-made crab apple jelly. Main course is a well-matched trio of guinea fowl breast with caramelised apples and cider cream sauce, or there could be roasted cod with creamed Savoy cabbage, and mustard and parsley sauce. Finish with a dark chocolate and orange mousse with cinnamon shortbread.

Chef Paul Bullard **Owner** Tim & Rosalind Forester **Times** 7-10 Closed Xmas-New Year, Sun, L all week **Prices** Fixed D 3 course £24.95-£26.95, Service optional, Groups min 6 service 10% **Wines** 1 bottle over £30, 16 bottles under £30, 14 by glass **Notes** Vegetarian available **Seats** 22, Pr/dining room 12 **Children** Portions **Parking** 20

Bordeaux Quay

Modern European

Modern warehouse conversion covering all bases on the Bristol waterfront

☎ 0117 943 1200
V-Shed, Canons Way BS1 5UH
e-mail: info@bordeaux-quay.co.uk
dir: Canons Rd off the A4, beyond Millennium Square car park

The converted warehouse is named after the stretch of city waterfront on which it stands, so called because it once stored imported Sauternes. Lighter bar options and an all-day brasserie are on the ground floor, while the main restaurant, with its industrial ducting and smart, breezy décor, is upstairs. There's a cookery school in there too. Modern European stylings are the name of the game. Cornish crab gratin topped with gruyère is garnished with pink grapefruit for an appealing starter. At main course, salmon en croûte comes with a white wine sauce, or go for ballottine of chicken breast with preserved lemon, creamed cabbage and pommes Anna. An inventive way with rhubarb sees a portion of poached surmounting a layer of set rice pudding flavoured with the same, on a base of firm pistachio parfait.

Chef Alex Murray, Andy Pole **Owner** Alex & Luke Murray **Prices** Starter £4.50-£6.50, Main £8.50-£18.50, Dessert £5.50, Service added but optional 12.5% **Wines** 40 bottles over £30, 40 bottles under £30, 30 by glass **Notes** Breakfast from 8 Mon-Fri, 9 Sat-Sun, Sunday L £12.50-£18.50, Vegetarian available **Seats** Pr/dining room 28 **Children** Portions, Menu **Parking** Millennium Square

---

Bristol Marriott Royal Hotel

Modern

Modern brasserie food in a magnificent Victorian hotel

☎ 0117 925 5100
College Green BS1 5TA
e-mail: bristol.royal@marriotthotels.co.uk
web: www.marriott.co.uk
dir: Next to cathedral by College Green

The Victorians seldom missed the opportunity to build big and grand, and the Bristol Marriott is such a place, right next to the cathedral and close to the historic waterfront.

It has all those magnificent Victorian proportions on the inside, too, plus a four-star décor that makes it a prime mover in the city's hotel scene. Walter's is the newly made-over restaurant with a swish design that blends old and new to create a modish space. There's a decidedly West of England feel to the menu, which keeps a regional flavour in starters such as Cornish breaded goats' cheese and pea salad with a cider reduction. Another starter of potted hazelnut with black pudding mousse served with eggy bread shows there's a creative team in the kitchen. Main courses might deliver free-range chicken breast with leek compôte and ham hock pie, or steaks from the grill, and, to finish, raspberry and lemon tart with elderflower custard.

Chef Martyn Watkins **Owner** Marriott International **Times** 5-10 Closed Sun, L every day **Prices** Starter £5-£8.50, Main £12-£20, Dessert £5-£8, Service optional **Notes** Pre-theatre meals available, Vegetarian available, Dress restrictions, Smart casual, Civ Wed 250 **Seats** 140 **Parking** 190

Casamia Restaurant

– *see page 66*

Glass Boat Restaurant

Modern French

Modern bistro fare on a glamorous barge

☎ 0117 929 0704
Welsh Back BS1 4SB
e-mail: bookings@glassboat.co.uk
dir: Moored below Bristol Bridge in the old centre of Bristol

Not a mere glass-bottomed boat, please note, but an extensively glazed former barge that floats in the Severn Estuary at the old Bristol docklands, this is one of the city's more individually styled eateries. You may need your sea-legs if the current is high, but the ambience of walnut floors, a beautiful marble bar at the bow end, and pictures that crowd the walls is too glamorous to miss for the sake of a bit of bobbing about. The menu offers modern bistro fare with plenty of imagination, plying a course from smoked trout with pickled fennel, or scallops with salted caramel and Jerusalem artichoke galette, to venison loin with poached pear and caramelised walnuts. Lighter lunchtime dishes are full of appeal too - perhaps something like dill-laced salmon and prawn fishcakes with wilted spinach and hollandaise. Finish with zesty lemon posset and biscotti. Theatre-goers can enjoy a good-value supper until 7pm.

Chef Freddy Bird, Charlie Hurrell **Owner** Arne Ringer **Times** 12-2.30/5.30-10.30 Closed 24-26 Dec, 1-10 Jan, L Mon, D Sun **Prices** Fixed L 2 course £10, Fixed D 3 course £20, Starter £6.50-£12.50, Main £13-£22.50, Dessert £6-£7.50, Service optional, Groups min 8 service 12.5% **Wines** 7 by glass **Notes** Sunday L, Vegetarian available, Civ Wed 100 **Seats** 120, Pr/dining room 40 **Children** Portions, Menu **Parking** NCP Queen Charlotte St

Casamia Restaurant

Modern

Exciting progressive cooking following the seasons

☎ 0117 959 2884
38 High St, Westbury Village, Westbury-on-Trym BS9 3DZ
e-mail: info@casamiarestaurant.co.uk
dir: Close to Westbury College Gatehouse

It's a family business as you might expect from a restaurant called 'my house'. It first opened its doors in 1999, and with all respect to Paco and Susan Sanchez-Iglesias, things really started to happen when their sons Peter and Jonray took over the kitchen and began to develop their style of bold modern cooking. These days the restaurant is right at the sharp pointy end of the cutting edge. The entrance is reminiscent of holidays in Spain - the wrought iron gate, the exposed-brick corridor - and it adds to the anticipation, and, these days, the expectation. There's a homeliness to the interior, with its beamed ceiling and confident neutrality, and decorative touches to reflect the seasons: as the menu changes, so the décor changes. The seasons rule the roost around here. The team in the kitchen brings a touch of theatre to the experience, delivering the food to the table and giving detailed and passionate explanations of each dish; the service is charming all round. This is multi-course territory with 12 being the magic number (there's a shorter lunch option available, too), and it is very much a case of choosing a bottle of wine and putting your trust in Peter and Jonray. You're in safe hands though: their food makes full use of the contemporary cooking canon and every dish is developed and crafted for maximum flavour impact. It all looks beautiful, too - vivid colours, cocktail glasses, a mix of plates, perfect swipes - but first and foremost it's about taste. Take a dish of parsley spelt risotto, for example, a simple enough idea which is executed perfectly, with a deeply intense flavour and some puffed spelt on top, or the John Dory with spring greens and cider, the fish topped with a sliver of citrus jelly - a stunning dish. There's rainbow trout with variations of cabbage (a real stunner), and lamb with an allium stew and mint sauce. For dessert you might be treated to the apple pie that featured on the BBC's *Great British Menu* in 2013, or perhaps the dark chocolate lollipop, another good-looker, standing proud in its wooden block. Upstairs there's a state-of-the-art kitchen and demonstration room.

Chef Peter & Jonray Sanchez-Iglesias **Owner** Paco & Susan Sanchez-Iglesias **Times** 12.30-2/7-9 Closed 25-26 Dec, Sun-Mon **Prices** Tasting menu £38-£88, Service optional, Groups min 6 service 12.5% **Wines** 20 by glass **Notes** Tasting menu 4/6/13 course, Vegetarian available, Dress restrictions, Smart casual **Seats** 40 **Parking** On street

Save on Hotels. Book at theAA.com/hotel

BRISTOL 67 ENGLAND

BRISTOL *continued*

Goldbrick House

◎◎ Modern British ◎

Mod Brit cooking in a multi-purpose city-centre venue

☎ 0117 945 1950
69 Park St BS1 5PB
e-mail: info@goldbrickhouse.co.uk
dir: M32, follow signs for city centre. Left side of Park St, going up the hill towards museum

Goldbrick House is a multi-tasking sort of operation in the heart of Bristol. Housed in a pair of stylishly converted Georgian townhouses, it's a buzzy place where you could breeze into the all-day café/bar for anything from eggs Benedict for breakfast, to pan-fried lamb burger with chips and tzatziki for lunch or dinner. Otherwise, head upstairs for a glass of fizz in the champagne and cocktail bar, and push on into the stylish contemporary restaurant, where there are keenly-priced early-evening menus to set you up for a concert at nearby St George's Hall, a set menu with five choices at each stage, or the full-on carte which majors in unpretentious modern ideas. Venison ragù with pappardelle and shaved pecorino, perhaps, or mussel and pancetta chowder with chives to set the ball rolling, then steamed duck leg pudding with Creedy Carver duck breast, braised chard and orange jus, or if you're in the mood for fish, monkfish scampi with chunky chips, mustard cress and radish salad, pepper ketchup and lemon mayo. Round things off with honey and thyme crème brûlée with lavender, rosewater and lemon shortbreads.

Chef Matthew Peryer **Owner** Dougal Templeton, Alex Reilley, Mike Bennett **Times** noon-10.30 Closed 25-26 Dec, 1 Jan, Sun **Prices** Fixed L 2 course £10, Fixed D 3 course £26, Starter £5.50-£7.50, Main £12.95-£21.50, Dessert £5-£7.50, Service added but optional 10% **Wines** 12 by glass **Notes** Early D menu 6-7pm, Vegetarian available, Civ Wed 90 **Seats** 180, Pr/dining room 40 **Children** Portions, Menu **Parking** On street, NCP

Hotel du Vin Bristol

◎ French ◆NOTABLE WINE LIST ◎

Contemporary brasserie fare and exceptional wine list

☎ 0844 736 4252
The Sugar House, Narrow Lewins Mead BS1 2NU
e-mail: info.bristol@hotelduvin.com
web: www.hotelduvin.com
dir: From M4 junct 19, M32 into Bristol. At rdbt take 1st exit & follow main road to next rdbt. Turn onto other side of carriageway, hotel 200yds on right

The HdV formula is familiar enough: the Bristol outpost is found in an 18th-century building near the waterfront and features bare floorboards, banquettes, unclothed wooden tables with candles, and references to wine all over the place (the list is massive). It's normally lively and cheery, helped along by well-drilled, friendly staff. Much of the appeal is down to the contemporary take on well-worn brasserie fare, with a good balance between seafood and meat, so expect dressed crab, or devilled kidneys, followed by moules frites, or roast belly pork with Agen prune sauce and mustard dauphinoise. Raw materials are of the top order and the kitchen's care and attention evident in, for instance, tender, lean steak tartare, then a classic example of properly timed lemon sole meunière. Finish with something like rich chocolate pavé offset by crunchy candied pistachios and vanilla ice cream.

Chef Marcus Lang **Owner** HotelduVin
Times 12-2.30/6-10.30 Closed L 31 Dec **Prices** Tasting menu £65-£85, Starter £5.95-£11.50, Main £12.50-£25.95, Dessert £5.95-£8.50, Service added but optional 10% **Wines** 45 bottles over £30, 18 bottles under £30, 20 by glass **Notes** Pre-theatre D 2 main course for price of 1 until 7.30pm, Sunday L £19.95, Vegetarian available, Civ Wed 65 **Seats** 85, Pr/dining room 72 **Children** Portions, Menu **Parking** 8, NCP Rupert St

Juniper

◎ Modern ◎

Buzzy neighbourhood place with creative cooking

☎ 0117 942 1744 & 07717 277490
21 Cotham Road South BS6 5TZ
e-mail: enq@juniperrestaurant.co.uk

A neighbourhood restaurant with a good deal of ambition, Juniper serves up some bright and creative food to the people of Cotham and Kingsdown. The vivid blue frontage stands out on Cotham Road South, and once inside all is relaxed and unpretentious - just what you want in a neighbourhood restaurant. The menu pays due respect to the seasons, and the produce of the region, to deliver inventive and full-flavoured dishes. Seared king scallops, for example, nicely caramelised on top, come with a piece of crispy pork belly, sticky coconut rice and oriental stock in a creative twist on a modern classic. Main-course pavé of aged Somerset beef doesn't want for flavour either, partnered with creamed cheddar leeks, baby onions, chorizo- and tomato-flavoured potatoes, and a cabernet jus. Finish with a warm apple pudding with butterscotch sauce and vanilla bean ice cream.

Chef Nick Kleiner, Simon Line **Owner** Anita & Nick Kleiner **Times** 6.30-12 Closed 26-30 Dec, L all week **Prices** Fixed D 3 course £18-£20, Starter £6.50-£8.95, Main £12.95-£18.95, Dessert £6.50, Service added but optional 10% **Notes** Tasting menu 8 course, Vegetarian available **Seats** 70, Pr/dining room 30 **Children** Portions

The Muset Restaurant

◎◎ Modern British NEW ◎

Inventive, entertaining cooking

☎ 0117 973 7248
12-16 Clifton Rd BS8 1AF
e-mail: eat@themuset.com

This stalwart of the foodie scene in the affluent Clifton postcode has been around for over 30 years in one form or another, and now wears a new set of clothes after a recent refurbishment. First impressions are of a thriving and relaxed neighbourhood restaurant: the stylish décor of wooden floors, darkwood tables and exposed brickwork contrasting with panels of funky statement wallpaper is suited perfectly to its well-conceived contemporary cooking. The service team is welcoming and unstuffy, while the kitchen clearly knows its onions, sourcing high-quality produce for its technically-accomplished repertoire. An intensely-flavoured amuse-bouche of game broth served with a crisp pork beignet sets the tone for what is to come. Eclectic flavour and textural combinations are a hallmark, as in a starter of chargrilled quail which is teamed inventively with quinoa, mackerel, fromage blanc and quenelles of pistachio and pesto. A more conventional marriage of beef fillet with crisp tongue and cheek matched with celeriac, horseradish and smoked leek follows, while dessert celebrates Valrhona's splendid chocolate in the form of a rich sponge and dark mousse served with an off-the-wall sangria sorbet.

Chef Jethro Lawrence **Owner** Mike Fitzpatrick **Times** 12-2.30/6-9.30 Closed 25-26 Dec, 1-2 Jan, Mon, D Sun **Prices** Fixed L 2 course £10, Fixed D 3 course £22, Tasting menu £45-£65, Starter £8-£11, Main £17-£32, Dessert £6.50-£7.50, Service added but optional 10% **Wines** 72 bottles over £30, 36 bottles under £30, 16 by glass **Notes** Sunday L, Vegetarian available **Seats** 70 **Children** Portions, Menu **Parking** On street

No.4 Clifton Village

◎ Modern European ◎

Bistro cooking in Clifton

☎ 0117 970 6869
Rodney Hotel, 4 Rodney Place, Clifton BS8 4HY
e-mail: bookings@no4cliftonvillage.co.uk
dir: M5 junct 19, follow signs across Clifton Bridge. At mini rdbt turn onto Clifton Down Rd. Hotel 150yds on right

With its ever-changing backdrop of local artworks, No. 4 is situated in the smart Rodney Hotel, a spiffing Georgian townhouse in Clifton. The restaurant is a relaxed and unpretentious space, with huge sash windows, ornate ceilings and oak floorboards, and the promise of a table in the secluded garden when the weather allows. There's a decidedly bistro feel to the place, and on the menu, too, where the choice changes daily and the seasons are respected. Start with goats' cheese on thyme crostini with beetroot purée, for example, or crispy duck leg with steamed bok choy and orange. Next up, go for whole grilled plaice, or seasonal vegetable risotto with parmesan and pesto, and for dessert, gooseberry and toffee crunch tart, or summer berry Eton mess. Side dishes such as hand-cut chips and glazed Chantenay carrots bump up the prices a little.

Chef David Jones **Owner** Hilary Lawson **Times** 6-10 Closed Xmas, Sun, L all week **Prices** Fixed D 3 course £19.95-£25.95, Starter £5.95-£7.50, Main £11.50-£17.50, Dessert £5.95-£7.50, Service added but optional 10% **Wines** 5 by glass **Notes** Vegetarian available **Seats** 35, Pr/dining room 42 **Children** Portions

BRISTOL *continued*

The Pump House

◎◎ Modern British ⬍ NOTABLE WINE LIST ✆

Thriving dockside pub-restaurant with serious approach to food

☎ 0117 927 2229
Merchants Rd, Hotwells BS8 4PZ
e-mail: info@the-pumphouse.com
web: www.the-pumphouse.com
dir: A4 Clevedon to city centre, left before swing bridge

The Victorians gave many of their industrial buildings rather more architectural appeal than was strictly necessary for their original purposes - in this case, a hydraulic pumping station. Down on the dock, chef-proprietor Toby Gritten has made great use of the scale of the building and the position by the water to create a pub and restaurant of vim and vigour. You can eat downstairs in the pub part of the operation (or outside by the water's edge) or head upstairs for a little more refinement and a little less hubbub. There's a good deal of regional produce on the menu and a steady hand in the kitchen turning out dishes of genuine appeal. Cornish crab is wrapped up cannelloni-style in thin slices of grapefruit, and served with apple textures (sorbet and crisp) and curried granola to start. Main-course Cornish hake is paired with Creedy Carver chicken wings, salsify and crown prince (a squash) purée. Desserts are no less creative - 'citrus', for example, consists of a lime posset, lemon sherbet, orange curd and grapefruit sorbet.

Chef Toby Gritten, Jack Williams, Hayden Botha **Owner** Toby Gritten & Dan Obern **Times** 12-3.30/6.30-9.30 Closed 25 Dec, Mon-Wed, L Thu, D Sun **Prices** Fixed L 2 course fr £12.50, Fixed D 3 course fr £15, Tasting menu fr £45, Starter £5.50-£9.50, Main £13-£21, Dessert £5.50-£8, Service added but optional 10% **Wines** 118 bottles over £30, 47 bottles under £30, 22 by glass **Notes** Sunday L, Vegetarian available **Seats** 50 **Children** Portions **Parking** 20

riverstation

◎ Modern European ✆

Buzzy riverside setting and modish brasserie food

☎ 0117 914 4434 & 914 5560
The Grove BS1 4RB
e-mail: relax@riverstation.co.uk
dir: On harbour side in central Bristol between St Mary Redcliffe church & Arnolfini

With its acres of glass and two terraces, it should be possible to see the water wherever you sit. But truth be told, this place is all about the atmosphere and the food. It looks thoroughly modern in the industrial-chic manner - the building was once a river police station - and there's a buzzy café-bar downstairs and cool restaurant on the first floor. The food is serious stuff, based on first-rate seasonal ingredients, and inspiration is drawn from far and wide without ever losing focus. Spice crab börek, for example, come with pickled green tomatoes and sweet chilli dressing, while haricot bean and almond soup is served with mandarin oil and chervil root. These are bright, modish dishes rooted in good culinary sense. Fillet of Cornish gurnard is paired with wild red rice, pak choi and black bean sauce among main courses, and to finish, warm pear and quince crumble with vanilla ice cream is a winning combo.

Chef Toru Yanada, Peter Taylor **Owner** J Payne & P Taylor **Times** 12-2.30/6-10.30 Closed 24-26 Dec, D Sun (except BH) **Prices** Fixed L 2 course £12.75, Fixed D 3 course £18.50, Starter £5.50-£11, Main £15.50-£19.75, Dessert £5.50-£7, Service optional, Groups min 6 service 10% **Wines** 37 bottles over £30, 33 bottles under £30, 14 by glass **Notes** Pre-theatre £10 Mon-Fri 6-7.15pm, Fixed D 2/3 course Mon-Fri, Sunday L, Vegetarian available, Civ Wed 130 **Seats** 120, Pr/dining room 26 **Children** Portions, Menu **Parking** Pay & display, meter parking opposite

The Rockfish Grill & Seafood Market

◎ Mediterranean, Seafood

Fantastically fresh seafood cooked as simply as possible

☎ 0117 973 7384
128 Whiteladies Rd, Clifton BS8 2RS
e-mail: enquiries@rockfishgrill.co.uk
dir: From city centre follow signs for Clifton, restaurant halfway along Whiteladies Rd

The Rockfish is another plank in Mitch Tonks's single-minded campaign to bring rigorously straightforward seafood cookery to a wide arc of southwest England, from the Dartmouth riverfront to the seething metropolis of Bristol (or as seething as Clifton gets, anyway). The operation here is simple: either buy your fish from the market to take home, or sit down next-door and let the busy team in the open kitchen cook it for you. 'The enjoyment is in the freshness,' Tonks declares, a manifesto statement with which few would disagree, and which produces Brixham mussels done in garlic and chilli, roasted bream with fennel and onions, halibut steamed in a paper packet with a few tomatoes and olive oil, and charcoal-grilled red gurnard with salsa verde. It's a winning formula that others would do well to emulate. Desserts are pretty simple too, perhaps a vivid jelly of Campari and prosecco with creamy vanilla ice.

Chef James Davidson **Owner** Mitch Tonks **Times** 12-2.30/6-10.30 Closed 25 Dec, 1 Jan, Sun-Mon **Prices** Prices not confirmed Service optional **Wines** 12 by glass **Notes** Fixed L 2 course menu available before 7pm, Vegetarian available **Seats** 52 **Children** Portions **Parking** On street

Second Floor Restaurant

◎◎ Modern European ⬍ NOTABLE WINE LIST

Lots of style and plenty of substance

☎ 0117 961 8898
Harvey Nichols, 27 Philadelphia St, Quakers Friars BS1 3BZ
e-mail: Reception.Bristol@harveynichols.com

The Bristol outpost of the lux shopping outlet is housed in a nifty modern building in the city's Cabot Circus development, and you can expect the usual heady mix of designer clothes, fabulous food market and contemporary restaurant and bar. Up on the second floor (which is the top one), the restaurant is a good-looking space with bags of contemporary bravura and an upmarket brasserie-style menu. This is creative, well-crafted cooking, based on excellent produce, a good deal of which comes from the region. Steamed grey mullet and Brixham crab, for example, might come in a broth flavoured with ginger, chilli, lime and coconut, and vegetarians (or anyone else for that matter) will find happiness in the form of a Jerusalem artichoke tart, soft poached egg, hollandaise and herb salad. Main-course slow-cooked shoulder and seared rump of lamb is served with crisp sweetbreads and barley risotto, and, to finish, there might be individual treacle tart with roast banana and clotted cream. The excellent wine list is worth more than a moment of your time.

Chef Louise McCrimmon **Owner** Harvey Nichols Restaurants Ltd **Times** 12-3/6-10 Closed 25 Dec, 1 Jan, Etr Sun, D Sun-Mon **Prices** Fixed L 2 course £17, Fixed D 3 course £20, Starter £7.50-£9.50, Main £18-£24, Dessert £5-£8, Service added but optional 10% **Wines** 250 bottles over £30, 50 bottles under £30, 14 by glass **Notes** Sun brunch 11-4, Afternoon tea daily 3-5, Vegetarian available **Seats** 60, Pr/dining room 10 **Children** Portions, Menu **Parking** NCP/Cabot Circus car park

Save on Hotels. Book at theAA.com/hotel

BUCKINGHAMSHIRE   69   ENGLAND

BUCKINGHAMSHIRE

AMERSHAM   Map 6 SU99

AA RESTAURANT OF THE YEAR FOR ENGLAND

The Artichoke

◎◎◎ — see page 70

The Crown

◎ Modern British NEW ✿

Good eating in a modernised coaching inn

☎ 01494 721541
16 High St HP7 0DH
e-mail: crownreception@coachinginn.co.uk
web: www.thecrownamersham.co.uk

This historic, timber-framed coaching inn has benefitted from an impressive refurbishment and now boasts an eclectic mixture of traditional character features and modern design. There are inglenook fireplaces and crooked floors aplenty, along with a cobbled courtyard and, in the restaurant - The Crown Chop House - a rustic but comfortable décor of bare wooden tables and chairs, banquette-style seating with colourful throws, stripped-back dark floors and white walls with Tudor beams. Small Kilner jars of salt, pewter side plates and tea lights in fine glass holders decorate the tables. Leisurely service and seasonal cooking - featuring vegetables from the inn's garden and grilled meats from the Josper oven - complete the package. From a list of inventive starters, duck pâté, foie gras, air-dried ham and pear hits the spot, before Cornish hake, creamed Savoy cabbage and red wine sauce, or 28-day aged feather blade from the Josper. Gypsy tart and marmalade ice cream is memorable for its simplicity and depth of flavour.

Chef Will Hughes **Times** Closed D Sun **Prices** Starter £5.50-£8.50, Main £12.50-£22, Dessert fr £5.50, Service added but optional **Notes** Afternoon tea available, Sunday L £22.50-£27.50, Vegetarian available, Dress restrictions, Smart casual, Civ Wed 50 **Seats** 24, Pr/dining room 30 **Children** Portions, Menu **Parking** 40

Gilbey's Restaurant

◎ Modern British

Imaginative modern cooking in a former school building

☎ 01494 727242
1 Market Square HP7 0DF
e-mail: oldamersham@gilbeygroup.com
dir: M40 junct 2, A355 exit Beaconsfield/Amersham

Gilbey's Old Amersham restaurant occupies a former grammar school building dating from the 17th century, and serves its local clientele as a textbook reliable neighbourhood bistro. There are low ceilings, wood flooring and cheerful art on sky-blue walls to create an ambience of stylish, intimate rusticity, while the friendly staff help foster a congenial, upbeat vibe. The kitchen makes a virtue of simplicity, working an intelligent vein of appealing modern British ideas that bring together spiced pickled red mullet with red pepper bavarois and black olive tapenade toast, or pork and pink peppercorn terrine with cider jelly, and leek vinaigrette. The same inventive streak partners herb-crusted Scottish cod with caramelised onion fregola, spiced aubergine and tomato compôte, or roast loin of lamb with a mini shepherd's pie, mint-crushed peas and redcurrant sauce. To finish, a zippy lemon tart is served to good effect with pistachio ice cream.

Chef Adam Whitlock **Owner** Michael, Bill, Caroline & Linda Gilbey **Times** 12-2.30/6.45-9.45 Closed 24-29 Dec, 1 Jan **Prices** Fixed L 2 course £19.50, Fixed D 3 course £25.50, Starter £6.50-£10.75, Main £16.50-£25.50, Dessert £7.55-£9.50, Service added but optional 12.5% **Wines** 6 bottles over £30, 16 bottles under £30, 10 by glass **Notes** Sunday L, Vegetarian available **Seats** 50, Pr/dining room 12 **Children** Portions **Parking** On street & car park

AYLESBURY   Map 11 SP81

Hartwell House Hotel, Restaurant & Spa

◎◎ Modern British NOTABLE WINE LIST ✿

Ambitious country-house cooking in a rococo stately home

☎ 01296 747444
Oxford Rd HP17 8NR
e-mail: info@hartwell-house.com
web: www.hartwell-house.com
dir: 2m SW of Aylesbury on A418 (Oxford road)

A claimant to the French throne, Louis XVIII, waited out part of his exile during the Napoleonic era at this stately house, kicking his heels in the full company of his court amid the Aylesbury ducks. The landscaped grounds and rococo ceilings must have felt at least a little like home, and certainly make a suitably opulent setting these days for a refined spa hotel. Furnished in shimmering primrose, with ornate mirrors and swags, the dining room is a grand setting for Daniel Richardson's ambitious country-house cooking, which draws in many modern ideas. Finely sliced smoked eel might be sent out with a horseradish pannacotta and shrimp and caper salad to set things going, while mains produce excellent veal fillet with its braised shin and sweetbread, alongside sweetcorn purée, ceps and chard in tomato jus, a well-orchestrated plate of flavours. That much-maligned dessert, the Pavlova, is given fresh impetus in a lemon and white chocolate version, with poached strawberries, strawberry sorbet and crystallised rose petals.

Chef Daniel Richardson **Owner** Historic House Hotels/National Trust **Times** 12.30-1.45/7.30-9.45 Closed L 31 Dec **Prices** Fixed L 3 course £24.75, Fixed D 3 course £29.95, Tasting menu £67, Service included **Wines** 325 bottles over £30, 11 bottles under £30, 15 by glass **Notes** Tasting menus available, Sunday L, Vegetarian available, Dress restrictions, Smart casual, No jeans, tracksuits/trainers, Civ Wed 120 **Seats** 56, Pr/dining room 36 **Children** Portions **Parking** 50

BEACONSFIELD   Map 6 SU99

Crazy Bear Beaconsfield

◎ British, International ✿

Bright modern menus in flamboyant setting

☎ 01494 673086
75 Wycombe End, Old Town HP9 1LX
e-mail: enquiries@crazybear-beaconsfield.co.uk
dir: M40 junct 2, 3rd exit from rdbt, next rdbt 1st exit. Over 2 mini-rdbts, on right

The shell of the coaching inn may date from the 15th century, but internally it's been given a flamboyant, even eccentric look, the English-themed restaurant (there are other eating options) featuring chequerboard-patterned cloth walls, chandeliers, cream bench seating, and low light levels. It's a fun, lively place, with a menu that covers a lot of ground, with starters of tuna sashimi with salade Niçoise, steak tartare, and grilled lobster. A global tilt can be detected among main courses too, so tiger prawns 'pil pil', served with Caesar salad, may appear alongside properly timed pan-fried fillet of halibut with crab bisque and a herby potato cake. Finish with classic crêpe Suzette or remain native with English trifle with sloe gin sabayon.

Chef Martin Gallon **Owner** Jason Hunt **Times** 12-12 **Prices** Fixed L 2 course £14.50, Starter £8.95-£14.95, Main £11.95-£26.50, Dessert £8.95-£12.50, Service added but optional 12.5% **Wines** 20 by glass **Notes** Sunday L, Vegetarian available, Dress restrictions, Smart casual, no ripped jeans or trainers, Civ Wed 40 **Seats** 75, Pr/dining room 22 **Children** Portions **Parking** 20, On street

The Artichoke

AA RESTAURANT OF THE YEAR FOR ENGLAND

AMERSHAM   MAP 6 SU99

Modern European NOTABLE WINE LIST

Highly creative and technically impressive cooking with a local flavour

☎ 01494 726611
9 Market Square, Old Amersham HP7 0DF
e-mail: info@artichokerestaurant.co.uk
web: www.artichokerestaurant.co.uk
dir: M40 junct 2. 1m from Amersham New Town

Proving the dictum that 'it's an ill wind that blows no good', chef-patron Laurie Gear made excellent use of the enforced closure of his restaurant (by a fire in the neighbouring premises in 2008) to spend a period in the legendary Noma in Copenhagen. He returned reinvigorated and inspired, and together with his wife Jacqueline, who takes care of front-of-house, actually expanded The Artichoke into that fire-damaged neighbouring property - in fact the Scandinavian sojourn even inspired the interior décor of the revamped operation. The Artichoke sits in pole position on the market square of the lovely old town, the Grade II listed building combining the best of its original 16th-century features - a huge open fireplace, oak beams, and painted brick walls - with a chic 21st-century sheen involving designer chairs, walnut tables and modern art in three stylish dining areas, one sharing space with a new open kitchen. And you can rest assured that what emerges from that kitchen is inventive, ambitious, often quite complex, and supported by top-class technical ability. Ingredients (locally sourced, foraged too) are as good as you'll get, and flavours unapologetic, as witnessed in a full-throttle starter of pan-fried quail's breast with crispy stuffed leg, pickled artichokes, watercress, toasted hazelnut, and hazelnut mayonnaise. A more delicate accompaniment of cauliflower purée, pickled romanesco, baby spinach, and chervil foam supports a main course of roast hake; elsewhere, the flavours are turned back up to 11 in a punchy fish and meat combo comprising braised Dingley Dell pork cheeks, langoustines, star anise carrot purée, fennel salad, roast carrot, and bacon and star anise crumb. There's plenty going on, too, in a well-judged dessert of Michel Cluizel white chocolate ganache with amaretti biscuits, Amalfi lemon and olive oil jelly, and lemon and thyme sherbet.

Chef Laurie Gear, Ben Jenkins
Owner Laurie & Jacqueline Gear
Times 12-3/6.30-11 Closed 1 wk Xmas & Apr, 2 wks Aug/Sep, Sun-Mon
Prices Fixed L 2 course £21.50, Fixed D 3 course £45, Tasting menu £65-£113, Starter £12-£14, Main £18.50-£22.50, Dessert £6.50-£8.50, Service added but optional 12.5% **Wines** 5 bottles over £30, 5 bottles under £30, 11 by glass **Notes** Tasting menu 7 course, Vegetarian available **Seats** 48, Pr/dining room 16 **Children** Portions **Parking** On street, nearby car park

BEACONSFIELD *continued*

The Jolly Cricketers

◉ Modern British

Assured cooking in village pub with a cricketing theme

☎ 01494 676308

24 Chalfont Rd, Seer Green HP9 2YG

e-mail: jacl.baker@virgin.net

dir: M40 junct 2, take A355 N, at rdbt 1st exit onto A40, next rdbt 2nd exit onto A355, turn right into Longbottom Ln, turn left into School Ln & continue into Chalfont Rd

Jolly cricketers are indeed depicted on the pub sign outside, a promising indicator of the warm-hearted and congenial atmosphere within this traditional old village pub. A range of real ales and a crowd-pleasing but sensibly concise menu, which underscores the cricketing theme, are all part of the draw. You might start with soft-boiled quail's eggs given a kick from caviar and anchovy mayonnaise, or go for the earthier flavours of pressed ox tongue with pickled shallots and mustard. Traditionalists need look no further than ale-braised ham with colcannon and parsley sauce, or steak and kidney pie, while other main-course offerings may run to fillet of black bream with brown shrimps, caper butter, spinach and crushed ratte potatoes. End with a 'Sticky Wicket': perhaps bread-and-butter pudding with custard, or Valrhona chocolate brownie with cherries and pistachio ice cream.

Chef Matt Lyons **Owner** A Baker & C Lillitou **Times** 12-2.30/6.30-9 Closed 25-26 Dec, D Sun **Prices** Starter £6-£9.50, Main £9.50-£19.50, Dessert £6-£8, Service optional, Groups min 6 service 10% **Wines** 21 bottles over £30, 16 bottles under £30, 16 by glass **Notes** Sunday L £14.50-£15.50, Vegetarian available **Seats** 36 **Children** Portions, Menu **Parking** 10, On street

BLETCHLEY   Map 11 SP83

The Crooked Billet

◉ Modern British 🌿

Thatched country pub with city-smart menu

☎ 01908 373936

2 Westbrook End, Newton Longville MK17 0DF

e-mail: john@thebillet.co.uk

dir: M1 junct 14 follow A421 towards Buckingham. Turn left at Bottledump rdbt to Newton Longville. Restaurant on right on entering village

It's a pub with a bar serving up real ales, but this thatched gem of a place is a destination for food- and wine-lovers first and foremost. The 17th-century building has plenty of period charm to be sure - inglenook fireplaces, oak beams and the like - along with a menu that wouldn't look amiss in a chic city brasserie. Mackerel might turn up in a terrine, with caviar crème fraîche, toasted soda bread and sweet and sour cucumber, and among main courses there could be grilled Barnsley chop with crispy sweetbreads, fondant potato, minted peas and a creamy thyme reduction. There's some good cooking at dessert stage, too: baked lime tart, for

example, with lime posset, a biscuit and a caipirinha sorbet. When it comes to wine, you'll find a staggering 200 choices by the glass, which is pretty much everything except the most expensive bins.

Chef Emma Gilchrist **Owner** John & Emma Gilchrist **Times** 12-2/7-10 Closed 27-28 Dec, L Mon, D Sun **Prices** Fixed L 2 course fr £16.75, Fixed D 2 course fr £16.75, Starter £5-£10, Main £9-£19, Dessert £5-£6.50, Service optional, Groups min 6 service 12% **Wines** 170 by glass **Notes** Tasting menu 8 course, with wine £90, Sunday L, Vegetarian available **Seats** 70, Pr/dining room 16 **Children** Portions **Parking** 30

BUCKINGHAM   Map 11 SP63

Villiers Hotel

◉◉ Modern British 🌿

Straightforward brasserie cooking in the medieval quarter

☎ 01280 822444

3 Castle St MK18 1BS

e-mail: reservations@villiershotels.com

web: www.villiers-hotel.co.uk

dir: Town centre - Castle Street is to the right of Town Hall near main square

The white-fronted Villiers Hotel looks a picture in summer, with its overflowing window-boxes. Situated in the medieval district of Buckingham, it makes a good destination for eating out in a generally under-served area. A smart contemporary-styled dining room in rich reds and white overlooks a courtyard, and is clearly popular with in-the-know locals. The straightforward menu of brasserie favourites is not above the odd innovative touch here and there, starting perhaps with roast pigeon and pancetta, garnished with quail's eggs, radicchio and walnuts, and moving on to fillets of lemon sole with crayfish, pea and lemon risotto and spiced cauliflower beignets. More classic offerings lack for nothing in quality, especially the flavourful herb-roasted chicken breast that comes with peas and girolles, smoked bacon, puréed wild mushrooms and thyme-scented jus. More thyme might crop up in an ice cream to accompany tarte Tatin, or there may be bracingly tangy lemon meringue torte with lemon curd ice cream. Good-value market menus at a fixed price are a tempting option.

Chef Paul Stopps **Owner** Oxfordshire Hotels Ltd **Times** 12-2.30/6-9.30 **Prices** Fixed L 2 course £12.95-£16.95, Fixed D 3 course £20.95-£25.95, Starter £4.75-£7.95, Main £11.95-£19.50, Dessert £6.95-£7.90, Service optional, Groups min 6 service 10% **Wines** 17 bottles over £30, 32 bottles under £30, 13 by glass **Notes** Sunday L, Vegetarian available, Civ Wed 150 **Seats** 70, Pr/dining room 150 **Children** Portions **Parking** 52

BURNHAM   Map 6 SU98

Burnham Beeches Hotel

◉ Modern British, European 🌿

Confident cooking in an early Georgian hotel

☎ 0844 736 8603 & 01628 600150

Burnham Beeches, Grove Rd SL1 8DP

e-mail: burnhambeeches@corushotels.com

web: www.corushotels.com

dir: off A355, via Farnham Royal rdbt

An early Georgian house in 10 acres of grounds, the corporately owned Burnham Beeches stands in a rural spot sufficiently tranquil to have inspired Thomas Gray to have composed his celebrated Elegy here. He is honoured in the name of Gray's Restaurant, a pair of interlinked rooms, one panelled, with views over the attractive gardens. The kitchen turns out a confident version of modern British food, adding a portion of grilled gilt head bream to Niçoise salad in citrus dressing to start, and then garnishing rump of lamb with cumin-spiked couscous and chargrilled veg. Finish with rhubarb and apple crumble with ginger ice cream and vanilla sauce.

Chef Rafal Wysocki **Owner** Corus Hotels **Times** 12-2/7-9.30 **Prices** Starter £6.50-£9.50, Main £15.50-£24, Dessert £6.50-£9.50 **Wines** 28 bottles over £30, 17 bottles under £30, 9 by glass **Notes** Sunday L £19.95-£24.95, Vegetarian available, Dress restrictions, Smart casual, Civ Wed 160 **Seats** 70, Pr/dining room 120 **Children** Portions, Menu **Parking** 150

The Grovefield House Hotel

◉◉ Modern

Uncomplicated cooking and garden views

☎ 01628 603131

Taplow Common Rd SL1 8LP

e-mail: info.grovefield@classiclodges.co.uk

web: www.grovefieldhotel.co.uk

dir: From M4 junct 7, left on A4 towards Maidenhead. Next rdbt turn right under railway bridge. Straight over mini rdbt, garage on right. Continue for 1.5m, hotel on right

In seven and a half acres of its own private grounds, Grovefield was originally a country retreat built for the Fuller family of Fuller's beer fame. These days it does business as a grand, country-house hotel with luxurious, modern accommodation and a smart restaurant, Hamilton's, serving simple, modern British cuisine. Large windows offer views out over the well-manicured lawns as you tuck into the likes of ham hock terrine with apple and cider dressing - a generous portion served with good toasted brioche - or crab ravioli with red pepper dressing and asparagus tips. Superb, full-flavoured roast canon of English lamb might follow, complemented well by a first-class ratatouille and gratin potato, while fish fans can't go far wrong with pan-fried fillet of brill with sautéed potatoes and champagne sauce. Pear, almond and cranberry tart with spiced pear sorbet shows no lack of

continued

BURNHAM *continued*

skill at dessert, or you might go for dark chocolate torte with strawberries and a tuile biscuit.

Chef Immad Nazzak **Owner** Classic Lodges Ltd **Times** 12-2.30/7-10.30 Closed L Sat **Prices** Fixed L 2 course £15.95, Fixed D 3 course £29.95, Service optional **Wines** 4 by glass **Notes** Sunday L, Vegetarian available, Dress restrictions, No T-shirts, trainers, Civ Wed 150 **Seats** 60, Pr/dining room 50 **Children** Portions, Menu **Parking** 140

CHENIES   Map 6 TQ09

The Bedford Arms Hotel

◉ Modern International

Hotel restaurant with confident cooking

☎ 01923 283301
WD3 6EQ
e-mail: contact@bedfordarms.co.uk
web: www.bedfordarms.co.uk
dir: M25 junct 18/A404 towards Amersham, after 2m follow signs on right for hotel

The red-brick Bedford Arms has a lot up its sleeve, from a traditional beamed bar and an oak-panelled restaurant, to a pretty garden, and even a license for civil weddings. Tables in the restaurant are dressed up in white linen cloths and the service team runs the show with charm and confidence. The cooking does not try to rock the boat, but neither is it stuck in the past, so crisp whitebait with cayenne mayonnaise sits alongside black tiger prawn tempura amongst first courses. Pan-fried sea bass might feature in a main course with braised celery, toasted chestnuts and truffle vinaigrette, or go for the rack of Devonshire lamb with pea purée and buttered broad beans. Vanilla pannacotta with blackcurrant sauce and shortbread competes for your attention at dessert stage with chocolate fondant with rum and raisin ice cream.

Chef Christopher Cloonan **Owner** Peter & Alisa Ratcliffe **Times** 12-2.30/7-9.30 Closed 26 Dec-5 Jan, D Sun **Prices** Prices not confirmed Service optional, Groups min 6 service 10% **Wines** 10 by glass **Notes** Tasting menu available, Sunday L, Vegetarian available, Dress restrictions, Smart casual, Civ Wed 55 **Seats** 55, Pr/ dining room 24 **Children** Portions **Parking** 55

CUBLINGTON   Map 11 SP82

The Unicorn

◉◉ Traditional & Modern British ☙

The kind of pub every village should have

☎ 01296 681261
12 High St LU7 0LQ
e-mail: theunicornpub@btconnect.com
web: www.theunicornpub.co.uk
dir: 2m N of A418 (between Aylesbury & Leighton Buzzard). In village centre

The welcome is warm and sincere, the menu chock-full of the sort of unfussy modern pub food that makes you want a bit of everything, and the 17th-century interior is replete with low beams, open fires, homely mismatched wooden furniture, and old pictures of village life on the walls. The place is the hub of local life too, selling home-made bread, milk, wine, butter, stamps and Cublington greetings cards. And the food lives up to its promise, whether it is a cooked breakfast on Saturday mornings, coffee and afternoon tea with home-made cakes throughout the week - which is rather nice out in the lovely garden - or a doorstop sandwich and a pint of real ale. If you want to put the kitchen through its paces properly, go for the full three-courses: smoked wood pigeon and chicory salad with apple chutney and toasted pumpkin seeds to start, then slow-roast pork belly with mash, braised red cabbage, and sage and cider jus. Wrap it all up with toffee and date pudding with clotted cream and toffee sauce.

Chef Christopher George **Owner** Mr S D George **Times** 12-2.30/6.30-9 **Prices** Fixed L 2 course £13.50-£16.50, Fixed D 3 course £16.50-£19.50, Starter £5-£7, Main £11-£23, Dessert £5-£7, Service optional, Groups min 10 service 10% **Wines** 3 bottles over £30, 26 bottles under £30, 8 by glass **Notes** Sunday L, Vegetarian available **Seats** 60, Pr/dining room 20 **Children** Portions, Menu **Parking** 20

GERRARDS CROSS   Map 6 TQ08

The Bull Hotel

◉ Modern British **NEW**

Smart hotel restaurant on the high street

☎ 01753 885995
Oxford Rd SL9 7PA
e-mail: bull@sarova.co.uk
dir: M40 junct 2 follow Beaconsfield on A355. After 0.5m 2nd exit at rdbt signed A40 Gerrards Cross for 2m. The Bull on right

The old Bull has borne witness to over 300 years of passing life on the road between London and Oxford, and to prove it isn't all forgotten, the smartly traditional bar is named after a famous highwayman, Jack Shrimpton. The one-time coaching inn is these days a swish four-star hotel with tip-top facilities and a restaurant, Beeches, that has a decidedly contemporary feel: think bold tones of burgundy and cream, and plenty of space between the darkwood tables. The menu is an up-to-date offering, too: parsnip and Cox's apple soup with root vegetable crisp and parmesan might be amongst starters. Follow on with pan-fried sea trout with surf clams, saffron potatoes, samphire and a lemon and chive butter, or pan-seared duck breast with glazed silver skin onion and cherry port jus (among other things). Go home happy after burnt English cream with marinated seasonal berries.

Chef Simon Dunn **Owner** Sarova Hotels **Times** 12-2.30/7-9 Closed L Sat **Prices** Fixed L 2 course £17.95, Starter £5.50-£6.95, Main £14.50-£22.50, Dessert £4.95-£7.50, Service added but optional **Wines** 4 bottles over £30, 15 bottles under £30, 10 by glass **Notes** Live Jazz Sun L 12-2.30, Sunday L £13.95-£21.50, Vegetarian available, Civ Wed 130 **Seats** 110, Pr/dining room 150 **Children** Portions, Menu **Parking** 100

GREAT MISSENDEN   Map 6 SP80

Nags Head Inn & Restaurant

◉ British, French ♨

Charming pub offering well-cooked Anglo-French food

☎ 01494 862200 & 862945
London Rd HP16 0DG
e-mail: goodfood@nagsheadbucks.com
web: www.nagsheadbucks.com
dir: N from Amersham on A413 signed Great Missenden, left at Chiltern Hospital onto London Rd (1m S of Great Missenden)

There's nothing knackered or tired about this Nag; the 15th-century red-brick hostelry - set in the rolling Chilterns - comes sporting a modern makeover that has fashioned it into a stylish foodie pub with rooms serving creative Anglo-French cooking. At heart though, it's still a quaint, intimate old inn, inviting enough to have tempted various Prime Ministers to call in for a pint on their way to Chequers. And, thanks to erstwhile regular Roald Dahl, it appeared in the film of his children's book *Fantastic Mr Fox*, while colourful artworks on the walls are based on Dahl characters. You can certainly see its appeal: a fire blazes away in the inglenook beneath ancient oak beams in the small bar, while the equally cosy restaurant areas on either side are all carpeted comfort. Fresh organic produce - local where possible - drives the kitchen's accomplished output; take sea bream fillet with sour apple-pickled cockles served with cider vinegar white butter, and perhaps a warm apple and rhubarb tart finale.

Chef Alan Bell, Howard Gale, Claude Paillet **Owner** Alvin, Adam & Sally Michaels **Times** 12-11 Closed 25 Dec **Prices** Prices not confirmed Service optional, Groups min 6 service 10% **Wines** 95 bottles over £30, 31 bottles under £30, 16 by glass **Notes** Sunday L, Vegetarian available, Dress restrictions, Smart casual **Seats** 60 **Children** Portions **Parking** 35

LONG CRENDON   Map 5 SP60

The Angel Restaurant

◉ Modern European V ♦ NOTABLE WINE LIST ♨

Confident cooking in 16th-century coaching inn

☎ 01844 208268
47 Bicester Rd HP18 9EE
e-mail: info@angelrestaurant.co.uk
dir: M40 junct 7, beside B4011, 2m NW of Thame

The Angel may sound like a pub, and does indeed have a bar serving real ales with comfy leather sofas around an open fire, but food is the main thing these days. Inside it has the chic good looks of a switched-on 21st-century restaurant, blending age-old wattle-and-daub walls, gnarled timbers, and slate floors with funky fabrics and scrubbed pine tables. Whether you eat in the cosy bar, luminous conservatory, or outdoors on the heated terrace, expect up-to-date ideas shot through with Mediterranean or Asian inspiration. The coast may be some way off, but daily deliveries of fish keep the kitchen well-supplied with the materials for specials - crispy fillet of sea bass on chargrilled Mediterranean vegetables with sweet chilli and basil dressing, perhaps. Elsewhere there may be a trio of Sandy Lane pork - a fillet wrapped in Parma ham, cider-glazed belly and braised cheek with potato purée, roast baby fennel, and morel sauce. Remember to leave space for afters as it would be a shame to miss out on warm treacle tart with butterscotch sauce and honeycomb ice cream.

Chef Trevor Bosch **Owner** Trevor & Annie Bosch **Times** 12-2.30/7-9.30 Closed D Sun **Prices** Starter £3.25-£8.50, Main £10.25-£12.75, Service optional, Groups min 8 service 10% **Wines** 12 by glass **Notes** Sunday L, Vegetarian menu **Seats** 75, Pr/dining room 14 **Children** Portions **Parking** 30

MARLOW   Map 5 SU88

Adam Simmonds at Danesfield House

◉◉◉◉ — *see page 74*

Aubergine at the Compleat Angler

◉◉◉ — *see page 75*

Bowaters

◉◉ Modern British

Modern British food served in a charming Thames-side setting

☎ 0844 879 9128 & 01628 405406
Macdonald Compleat Angler, Marlow Bridge SL7 1RG
e-mail: compleatangler@macdonald-hotels.co.uk
dir: M4 junct 8/9 or M40 junct 4. A404 to rdbt, take Bisham exit, 1m to Marlow Bridge, hotel on right

Fabulously located on the banks of the River Thames overlooking the rushing water at Marlow Weir, the handsome Georgian Compleat Angler Hotel was named after the famous angler Izaak Walton. It's hard to imagine a more charming spot on a summer's evening, with tables laid on the riverside lawn, flickering candles reflected on the water, a view of Marlow church, and the distant thunder of that aforementioned weir. If the weather isn't up to it, the suave setting of Bowaters restaurant won't disappoint, where classic pastel shades meet contemporary style - and you get those watery views come rain or shine. The kitchen delivers an intelligent menu of accessible contemporary dishes with clearly defined flavours presented with a distinct wow factor. Seared scallops might appear in a trio with pancetta and a warm chicory and asparagus salad, followed by tender medallions of veal with deep earthy flavoured sweetbreads and a well-reduced Madeira sauce, and a deliciously moist almond tart with sweet rhubarb and a zesty yoghurt sorbet. Aubergine (see entry) is the hotel's other restaurant option.

Chef Neal Dove **Owner** Macdonald Hotels **Times** 12.30-2/7-10 Closed D Sun **Prices** Fixed L 2 course fr £20.50, Fixed D 3 course fr £23.50, Service added but optional 12.5% **Wines** 13 by glass **Notes** ALC 1/2/3 course £25/£32/£39, Sunday L, Vegetarian available, Civ Wed 100 **Seats** 90, Pr/dining room 120 **Children** Portions, Menu **Parking** 100

Crowne Plaza Marlow

◉◉ Modern British

Modern lakeside dining in contemporary hotel

☎ 01628 496800
Field House Ln SL7 1GJ
e-mail: reservations@crowneplazamarlow.co.uk
web: www.cpmarlow.co.uk
dir: A404 exit to Marlow, left at mini rdbt, left into Field House Lane

Located in five acres of Buckinghamshire countryside, this modern, low-rise hotel benefits from a lakeside view. Its proximity to the motorway network, as well as to London, Windsor and Henley, makes it popular with a mixture of conference guests, tourists, and wedding parties, but in this instance it's not all about location, location, location. The contemporary Glaze Restaurant, with its darkwood tables, raspberry-hued banquettes and lovely lakeside views, is well worth a visit. Expect good, honest food with a nod to the seasons, served by friendly staff. Kick off with crisp, nicely presented goats' cheese croquettes with mustard foam and honey and lemon dressing, before a generous portion of pressed pork belly pointed up by apple sauce, caramelised apple, sage rösti and sour apple foam. Failing that, go for a steak, burger, or sausages from the grill section of the menu. A cooked-to-order bitter chocolate fondant is properly oozy and comes with honeycomb ice cream to round things off.

Chef Stuart Hine **Owner** BDL Hotels **Times** 6.30-10 **Prices** Fixed D 3 course fr £30, Service added but optional 12.5% **Wines** 11 by glass **Notes** Vegetarian available, Civ Wed 400 **Seats** 150 **Children** Portions, Menu **Parking** 300

Adam Simmonds at Danesfield House

Modern European NOTABLE WINE LIST

Technical wizardry and high formality in a shimmering pastiche castle

☎ 01628 891010
Henley Rd SL7 2EY
e-mail: reservations@danesfieldhouse.co.uk
web: www.danesfieldhouse.co.uk
dir: M4 junct 4/A404 to Marlow. Follow signs to Medmenham and Henley. Hotel is 3m outside Marlow

After various prototypes in earlier centuries, the Danesfield that rises before us today was built at the very end of the Victorian era as a last gasp of 19th century architectural pastiche. Designed ostensibly in the manner of the Italian Renaissance, it resembles nothing so much as a fairy-tale castle done in crenellated sugar-frosting (locally quarried chalk, in fact), best seen at a distance when it shimmers white in the sunlight behind mists of lavender in the formal gardens. Commanding superlative views over the upper reaches of the Thames, it is kitted out in fine plutocratic style, most notably in the Grand Hall, where the roaring fires of winter make a comforting backdrop to afternoon tea. Outdoor tables make the most of the surroundings. In a dining room named after its executive chef, the tone is one of tautly maintained formality, imbued with a due sense of gastronomic occasion. Dishes are borne from the kitchen on light wood trays, to be conveyed to your table with full descriptive ceremony by the maître d', like a butler announcing the arrival of esteemed guests at a soirée. As of May 2013, the main restaurant is devoted to tasting menus and a fixed-price lunch and dinner menus, the carte having been relocated to the less formal Orangery. Adam Simmonds' style remains intact, of course - a highly burnished rendition of the contemporary European idiom, complete with ingenious juxtapositions, and demonstrating a healthy curiosity about the role of texture, along with a fair bit of scientific wizardry. The components of an opening dish indicate the range: roasted Scottish scallops with firmly textured, profoundly pungent truffle purée and another of artichoke, as well as garnishes of shaved winter truffle and lardo. Somehow, amid the competing flavours, a balance is struck. A flawlessly timed confit fillet of sea bass turns up with a dazzling entourage of fennel coleslaw, delicately cooked lettuce, and gentle dumplings of cuttlefish. The meat centrepiece of a tasting menu might be venison, a slow-roasted fillet, alongside confit celeriac, puréed chestnuts and crunchy bacon, while dessert might offer a pair of lemon textures - parfait and curd, together with fennel pollen ice cream and olive oil fruit paste - or else a serving of tenderly poached rhubarb with a tube of vanilla pannacotta wrapped in rhubarb jelly, plus a spray of crumble and a sub-Arctically cold ginger granita.

Chef Adam Simmonds
Times 12-2/7-9.30 Closed 18 Aug-2 Sep, 23 Dec-7 Jan, BHs, Sun-Mon, L Tue-Wed **Prices** Fixed L 3 course fr £65, Fixed D 3 course fr £65, Tasting menu fr £82, Service added but optional 12.5% **Wines** 350 bottles over £30, 50 bottles under £30, 14 by glass **Notes** Tasting menu 7 course, Vegetarian available, Dress restrictions, Smart casual, Civ Wed 30 **Seats** 24, Pr/dining room 14 **Children** Portions **Parking** 100

MARLOW *continued*

The Hand & Flowers

◉◉◉◉ *— see page 76*

The Vanilla Pod

◉◉ British, French **V** ◐

Intelligently constructed dishes in central townhouse

☎ 01628 898101
31 West St SL7 2LS
e-mail: contact@thevanillapod.co.uk
dir: From M4 junct 8/9 or M40 junct 4 take A404, A4155 to Marlow. From Henley take A4155

The Vanilla Pod is a charming little restaurant where dimmed lighting and the buzz of conversation add to the intimate feel of the place. Walls are a warm cream, tables are well dressed, and service is clued-up. The kitchen superimposes modern British tastes on classic French lines, so a terrine of ham hock and chicken with prunes may precede fillet of lamb with lentils and Madeira jus, and it pulls off some robust flavour combinations: earthy girolles and the aniseed kick of fennel confit for lemon sole in a herb crust, coffee-infused celeriac for slowly cooked duck breast, while the eponymous vanilla pod goes into a jus for lightly seared scallops with shallots in red wine. Vanilla and olive

breads have been applauded, and puddings could run to rich, light chocolate and orange fondant with none other than vanilla ice cream.

Chef Michael Macdonald **Owner** Michael & Stephanie Macdonald **Times** 12-2/7-10 Closed 24 Dec-3 Jan, Sun-Mon **Prices** Fixed L 2 course fr £15.50, Fixed D 3 course fr £45, Tasting menu £55-£64, Service optional, Groups min 10 service 12.5% **Wines** 80 bottles over £30, 12 bottles under £30, 10 by glass **Notes** ALC 3 course £45, Tasting menu 8 course, Vegetarian menu, Dress restrictions, Smart casual **Seats** 28, Pr/dining room 8 **Parking** West Street car park

---

MILTON KEYNES	Map 11 SP83

Mercure Milton Keynes Parkside Hotel

◉ Modern British

Modernised traditional dishes in a boutique hotel

☎ 01908 661919
Newport Rd, Woughton on the Green MK6 3LR
e-mail: h6627-gm@accor.com
web: www.mercure.com
dir: M1 junct 14, A509 towards Milton Keynes. 2nd exit on H6 follow signs to Woughton on the Green

Set in the Ouzel Valley Park, and yet only a short hop from the hurly-burly of Milton Keynes, the Grade II listed,

white-painted building has been stylishly made over inside to give it a boutique hotel feel. Simply laid bare-wood tables and framed pictures set the tone in the dining room, where a menu of confidently rendered brasserie favourites is offered. Sea trout smoked over Earl Grey and rosemary, served with horseradish mayonnaise, is an aromatically compelling starter, and might precede Gressingham duck breast with honey-roasted chicory and plums, or chargrilled tuna with roasted vine tomatoes and chips in the skins. If deconstructed puddings are your thing, try the apple pie, which arrives as a hollowed-out baked apple filled with the cooked fruit, alongside a slice of crisp sweet pastry, with an accompanying jug of very fine vanilla custard.

Times 12-2/6.30-9.30 Closed D Sun

STOKE POGES	Map 6 SU98

Humphry's at Stoke Park

◉◉◉ *— see page 77*

Aubergine at the Compleat Angler

MARLOW	MAP 5 SU88

Modern European

Contemporary flair and top-quality ingredients beside the Thames

☎ 01628 405405 & 0844 879 9128
Marlow Bridge SL7 1RG
e-mail: aubergineca@londonfinedininggroup.com
web: www.auberginemarlow.com
dir: M4 junct 8/9 or M40 junct 4. A404 to rdbt, take Bisham exit, 1m to Marlow Bridge, hotel on right

This Thames-side hotel next to Marlow weir takes its name from the work penned by the 17th-century writer Izaak Walton, while Aubergine's namesake is the restaurant formerly at London's Park Walk where Gordon Ramsay once ran the stoves. The Aubergine here has the stylish good looks and décor in keeping with a hotel of

this calibre, along with views of the weir as well as into the kitchen; smartly uniformed staff are well trained, professional and always on hand to guide you through the menus and excellent wine list. Tim O'Shea's cooking draws on the best modern European ideas updated root and branch for the 21st century. Fillets of sea bass, for instance, are served boldly with baby octopus and octopus carpaccio, chorizo jam, olive oil jelly and black olives. Dishes may, indeed, have a number of layers, but they are remarkable for their cohesive mixing and matching. The menus offer plenty of choice, including the expected extravagances: sautéed foie gras, for example, with orange purée, and another starter of succulent Scottish langoustines successfully partnered by braised pork cheek with apple. Ingredients are outstanding, timing and seasoning are spot on, and the structure of each dish is intelligently considered so nothing ever appears out of place. The main event might be aged fillet of beef with ox cheek and Madeira jus, served with spinach purée and truffle and foie gras cromesquis, or

perhaps roast partridge in cooking juices with a boudin of leg meat, pear tarte Tatin and pearl barley. Extras like breads and amuse-bouche hold form, and desserts are well up to snuff too: try blueberry soufflé with banana ice cream, or compressed pineapple with white chocolate jelly, cashew nut crunch, and lemongrass and pineapple sorbet - a stunning finale.

Chef Tim O'Shea **Owner** London Fine Dining Group **Times** 12-2.30/7-10.30 **Prices** Fixed L 2 course fr £23, Fixed D 3 course fr £50, Tasting menu fr £55, Service added but optional 12.5% **Wines** 125 bottles over £30, 7 bottles under £30, 6 by glass **Notes** Gourmand menu 5 course from £55 (with wine £95), Sunday L, Vegetarian available, Dress restrictions, Smart casual **Seats** 49 **Children** Portions **Parking** 100

The Hand & Flowers

MARLOW   MAP 5 SU88

British, French

Big flavours and traditional techniques in an outstanding gastro inn

☎ 01628 482277
126 West St SL7 2BP
e-mail: reservations@
thehandandflowers.co.uk
web: www.thehandandflowers.co.uk
dir: M40 junct 4/M4 junct 8/9 follow
A404 to Marlow

The rejuvenated country pub movement has gone from strength to strength in the past generation, so much so that the term 'gastro-pub', which was once an exclamation of surprise that there was something worth eating in a mere tavern, might profitably be retired now. At the forefront of developments have been establishments like The Hand & Flowers, although it's perhaps as well to note that there's nowhere quite like it, not for miles around. The old inn, which has four stunning guest bedrooms, is a tribute to Tom and Beth Kerridge, who only took it on in 2005 and have since created one of the country's most outstanding venues. It's been spruced up, certainly, and yet the place really does retain the feel of a simple village hostelry, with its bare-boarded floor, rustic furniture and brick fireplace. The tables don't have cloths, but do have rather good dining ware, and the service approach is as warmly hospitable as

you like. Tom Kerridge is a West Country boy who worked under some of the premier names of the London dining scene for some years, before striking out on his own. What he offers here is the culmination of that experience, brought to bear on the pick of seasonal British ingredients, many of them locally sourced, in dishes that look to traditional domestic preparations for their influence, and always boast lots of robust, unabashed flavour. Smoking, pickling, salt-curing and blowtorching are favoured techniques, and ingredients such as tart apple, wild garlic, blue cheese and oxtail lend the requisite depth. A bowl of lovage soup is thus garnished with smoked eel, Bramley apple and blue cheese tortellini for maximum impact, while another starter presents a 'Scotch egg' of smoked mackerel and garlic on onion soubise with charred whole onion. The menu choice is surprisingly wide, with dishes built up of many tempting layers, which may make choosing nigh-on impossible. Mains run to red mullet cooked in beef dripping with oxtail and bayleaf dressing, tenderloin and malt-glazed cheek of pork with pickled mustard leaves, garlic sausage and dauphinoise, or a very superior fillet steak with chips and béarnaise, and on Sundays there's roast beef and Yorkshire pudding. Desserts sustain that commitment to big, loud, often old-school flavours with pistachio sponge cake and marzipan, served with

melon sorbet, or banana soufflé with gingerbread custard. The superb wine list opens with a good selection by the glass.

Chef Tom Kerridge **Owner** Tom & Beth Kerridge **Times** 12-2.45/6.30-9.45 Closed 24-26 Dec, D Sun, 1 Jan **Prices** Prices not confirmed Service added but optional 12.5%, Groups min 6 service 12.5% **Wines** 107 bottles over £30, 16 bottles under £30, 17 by glass **Notes** Sunday L, Vegetarian available **Seats** 50 **Children** Portions **Parking** 20

Humphry's at Stoke Park

STOKE POGES   **MAP 6 SU98**

Modern British

Highly refined, modern cooking in a grand country club

☎ 01753 717171 & 717172
Park Rd SL2 4PG
e-mail: info@stokepark.com
dir: M4 junct 6 or M40 junct 2, take A355 towards Slough, then B416. Stoke Park in 1.25m on right

As you approach Stoke Park down the long, sweeping drive that meanders through the estate's 27-hole championship golf course, your eyes are met with an undeniably impressive sight: a handsome, palatial mansion, painted snow-white, with all the period elegance that you'd hope for in a building designed by George III's architect James Wyatt in the late 1700s. If the place looks familiar at all, that's probably because you've seen it in a movie or two - it was used as a filmset for the Bond film *Dr No* and *Bridget Jones's Diary*, amongst others. The golf course was added in Edwardian times, when Stoke Park became Britain's first ever country club, and today the place still operates in the same vein, as well as being a hotel open to non-members and non-residents. Aside from the golf (and the tennis, the spa and the gym), the hotel's biggest draw has to be its Humphry's restaurant (named after Humphry Repton who was commissioned

in 1791 to upgrade Lancelot 'Capability' Brown's landscaping of the grounds). Here, high ceilings, soft-fabric wall coverings, antique mirrors, a feature fireplace and full-height windows looking out across the estate's 300 acres of parkland - including the bridge over the lake designed by Humphry himself - create a gently calming atmosphere in which to enjoy the innovative, contemporary cooking of head chef Chris Wheeler. Menus change with the seasons and feature a good deal of local produce. A playful amuse-bouche of beetroot macaroon with salmon mousse gets things off to a flying start, before a first course of pan-fried scallops (perfectly cooked) with an ultra-smooth and light celeriac purée, crispy pancetta and caviar. Technical skill abounds in a flavour-rich main course of roast tournedos of beef with bone marrow, a light and fluffy horseradish mash, wild mushrooms and 'Shardeloes Farm English red wine sauce', while rhubarb and lavender jelly with a vanilla pannacotta and pan-fried almond cake turns out to be a match made in heaven at dessert.

Chef Chris Wheeler **Owner** Roger King **Times** 12-2.30/7-10 Closed 24-26 Dec, 1st wk Jan **Prices** Fixed L 2 course £25, Fixed D 3 course £48-£58, Tasting menu £75, Starter £9.50-£16.50, Main £17.50-£28.50, Dessert £9-£12.50, Service added but optional 12.5% **Wines** 78 bottles over £30, 11 bottles

under £30, 18 by glass **Notes** ALC L only, Vegetarian available, Dress restrictions, Smart casual, no trainers or T-shirts, Civ Wed 120 **Seats** 50, Pr/dining room 120 **Children** Portions **Parking** 400

STOKE POGES continued

Stoke Place

◉◉◉ – see below

Taplow House Hotel

◉◉ Modern British

Intelligent British cooking in an eye-catching Georgian mansion

☎ 01628 670056
Berry Hill SL6 0DA
e-mail: reception@taplowhouse.com
dir: M4 junct 7 towards Maidenhead, at lights follow signs to Berry Hill

You don't have to be an architecture anorak to be struck by the crenallated red-brick and white-stucco façade of this Georgian house on the Berks-Bucks border, and its gardens are equally out of the ordinary, with their centuries-old tulip trees and Cedar of Lebanon. In Berry's restaurant, tall French windows are framed with heavy, swagged drapes and a crystal chandelier hangs above plush traditional table settings. The food, however, has taken a contemporary country-house route, using great ingredients in intelligent combinations, with plenty of European accents, as in a starter that matches poussin and foie gras terrine with prune purée and grape dressing. Next out, a very fine slab of pan-fried turbot shares a plate with Parisienne potatoes, confit cherry tomatoes, and broccoli with artichoke cream. To wrap things up, there's a banana tarte Tatin with rum and raisin ice cream.

Times 12-2/7-9.30 Closed L Sat

The Terrace Dining Room, Cliveden

◉◉ Modern, Traditional **NEW V** 🍷NOTABLE WINE LIST

Iconic country house with confident team in the kitchen

☎ 01628 668561
Cliveden Estate SL6 0JF
e-mail: info@clivedenhouse.co.uk
web: www.clivedenhouse.co.uk
dir: M4 junct 7, A4 towards Maidenhead, 1.5m, onto B476 towards Taplow, 2.5m, hotel on left

There is a sense of exhilaration on arrival at Cliveden, one of the nation's great country houses. It's the history, the imposingly majestic façade, the scale of the place, the grandeur - it has to be seen. The hotel lives up to all that expectation with its luxurious finish, which is being added to as we go to print with an all-encompassing, multi-million-pound refurbishment in full swing. The Terrace Dining Room is a suitably traditional space, with lovely views over the parterre gardens and River Thames, lots of period details and portraits to admire, and first-class service. The cooking displays some exemplary technical skills and brings first-rate ingredients to the table: veal sweetbreads, for example, in a starter with salsify and champ purée, and a grelot onion Tatin. Main-course West Country partridge with smoked potato purée, poached beetroot and root vegetable pressing shows great balance of flavours and textures, and, to finish, white chocolate crème brûlée comes with a winning passionfruit and banana sorbet. The wine list has a few surprises up its sleeve.

Chef Carlos Martinez **Owner** SRE Hotels
Times 12-2.30/7-9.30 **Prices** Fixed L 3 course £28-£60, Fixed D 3 course £60, Tasting menu £95, Starter £15, Main £32.50, Dessert £15, Service optional **Wines** 481 bottles over £30, 9 bottles under £30, 11 by glass **Notes** Tasting menu 7 course, Vegetarian menu, Dress restrictions, Smart casual, Civ Wed 140 **Seats** 60 **Children** Portions, Menu

---

Stoke Place

Modern European 🍷NOTABLE WINE LIST

Stunning modern cooking in a rural idyll a world away - but five minutes by car - from Slough

☎ 01753 534790
Stoke Green SL2 4HT
e-mail: enquiries@stokeplace.co.uk
dir: M4 junct 6, A355, right at 1st lights to A4 Bath Rd. At 1st rdbt take 2nd exit onto Stoke Rd. B416 to Stoke Green. Hotel 200mtrs on right

Stoke Place may have a Slough postcode, but don't let that put you off: it's as far removed from the gritty, urban sprawl of Slough as it could possibly be, sitting in 26 acres in the decidedly upmarket village of Stoke Poges. They describe Stoke Place as a 'modern country house', and by that they're referring to its attitude, which is aimed at encouraging you to let your hair down. No stuffiness here, please; they love to throw a party. But if all that sounds a little 'free', worry not, for this is a very civilised kind of partying, where attention to detail and quality are watchwords. The scene is set by the splendid William and Mary-era house and those gorgeous grounds landscaped by none other than Lancelot 'Capability' Brown. So far, so good. And then there is the restaurant, in the hands of chef Craig 'equally capable' van der Meer, whose innovative contemporary cooking really puts Stoke Place on the foodie map. There are lovely views across the wide open expanse of grass, leading down to the lake, from the restaurant, which is done out with pleasingly rustic-chic simplicity (sans linen tablecloths), while on the menu, well-sourced materials are turned into smart modern food showing a good deal of skill and creativity. Plenty of the ingredients come from their own garden, but everything else is sourced with care and attention. A first course dish of seared pigeon includes a kohlrabi remoulade, blood orange and pistachios in an imaginative combo, followed, perhaps, by seared loin of venison, celeriac purée, Brussels sprouts, a modish chocolate jelly and bone marrow jus. Everything on the plate plays its part in creating the whole, every flavour and texture works in harmony, and it all looks beautiful, too. To finish, fried brioche, poached plums, milk chocolate and crème fraîche ice cream is a true winner.

Chef Craig van der Meer **Owner** Mr & Mrs Dhillon
Times 12-2.30/7-9.30 Closed 24 Dec-9 Jan, L Sun
Prices Fixed L 2 course £15.50, Tasting menu £55-£65, Starter £15, Main £20, Dessert £10, Service added but optional 12.5% **Wines** 347 bottles over £30, 61 bottles under £30, 24 by glass **Notes** Sunday L £19.50-£23.50, Vegetarian available, Dress restrictions, Smart casual, Civ Wed 120 **Seats** 36, Pr/dining room 14 **Children** Menu **Parking** 120

The Five Arrows

◎◎ Modern European **NEW** V

Contemporary dining on the Rothschild estate

☎ 01296 651727
High St HP18 0JE
e-mail: five.arrows@nationaltrust.org.uk

The Five Arrows in question are the family emblem of the Rothschilds, each arrow representing one of the five sons who was sent off to establish banking houses in Europe's financial capitals. The rest, as the saying goes, is history. The small Victorian hotel stands at the gates of Waddesdon Manor, and other than a mock-Tudor flourish here and there, has none of the airs and graces of the grand French château-style stately home. The restaurant sports a smartly contemporary look with unclothed darkwood tables and Rothschild wine-related prints on the walls, and a refreshingly relaxed ambience. The repertoire displays a commendable seasonal focus that delivers bright contemporary ideas, starting with a ballottine of chicken and black pudding matched with honey-poached cranberries, cauliflower purée, celery and lemon oil. Next up, the Waddesdon Estate supplies the venison (pan-fried loin and braised haunch) that comes with the hearty accompaniments of herb mash, braised red cabbage, girolles, and redcurrant jus, and for pudding there's hazelnut and vanilla iced parfait with caramelised hazelnuts and hazelnut tuile.

Chef Karl Penny **Times** 12-2.15/7-9.15 Closed D 25-26 Dec **Prices** Fixed L 2 course £13.75 **Notes** Sunday L, Vegetarian menu

Chequers Inn

◎◎ British, French

French-influenced bistro cooking in an old coaching inn

☎ 01628 529575
Kiln Ln HP10 0JQ
e-mail: info@chequers-inn.com
web: www.chequers-inn.com
dir: M40 junct 2, A40 through Beaconsfield Old Town towards High Wycombe. 2m from town left into Broad Ln. Inn 2.5m on left

The Chequers hides its 17th-century pedigree rather well from the outside, but the oak beams and flagstoned floors within tell their own story. Its dining room has been coaxed boldly into the modern era with white-painted walls, contemporary light fixtures and big mirrors, but the crisp white linen remains. A small covered patio is pressed into service on those elusive warmer days. A French-inflected, resourceful bistro cooking style informs the menus, and dishes are turned out well. Sautéed foie gras with roasted fig and cherry syrup makes a bold opening statement, while a reworking of classic cock-a-leekie sees a chicken croquette added to leek fondue, with a compôte of prunes included for good measure.

A two-way lamb main course offers roast rack and confit shoulder alongside a mélange of broad beans, peas and baby onions, a dish that needs some seasoning adjustment, and dessert might bring a fruity assemblage into play in the form of watermelon and strawberry salsa and rhubarb compôte as accompaniment to traditional vanilla-speckled pannacotta in port syrup.

Chef Pascal Lemoine **Owner** PJ Roehrig
Times 12-2.30/7-9.30 Closed D Sun, 25 Dec, 1 Jan
Prices Fixed L 2 course £13.95, Fixed D 3 course fr £25.95, Tasting menu fr £49.95, Starter £6.95-£9.95, Main £14.95-£26.95, Dessert £6.95-£8.50, Service optional **Wines** 11 bottles over £30, 27 bottles under £30, 11 by glass **Notes** Sunday L, Vegetarian available **Seats** 60, Pr/dining room 60 **Children** Portions **Parking** 50

CAMBRIDGESHIRE

The Black Bull Inn

◎ Modern British **NEW**

Thatched country pub with creative team in the kitchen

☎ 01223 893844
27 High St CB21 4DJ
e-mail: info@blackbull-balsham.co.uk
dir: A11 Balsham exit, in centre of village

The old inn is as pretty as a picture with its mop of thatch and neat white-painted façade, and it does not shirk from its pub duties, with real ale on tap and a fabulous garden and terrace designed by a chap with Chelsea flower medals to his name. Food is a highlight of any visit, with the main event taking place in a barn with a high-vaulted ceiling, a tastefully neutral colour scheme and high quality solid oak tables. The menu takes a broadly modish approach to proceedings, so among first courses there are things like ham hock and foie gras terrine with piccalilli and home-made brioche bun, or beetroot salmon gravad lax with beetroot textures, quail's egg, horseradish jelly and brie ice cream. Follow one of those with roast cod with ruby chard, crushed potatoes, mussel curry and courgettes, and finish with white chocolate and ginger biscuit cheesecake served with a berry sauce.

Chef Peter Friskey **Owner** Alex Clarke **Prices** Fixed L 2 course £13, Starter £5.50-£9.50, Main £9.50-£22, Dessert £2.50-£9, Service optional, Groups min 8 service 10% **Wines** 7 bottles over £30, 23 bottles under £30, 12 by glass **Notes** Sunday L £12-£17, Vegetarian available **Children** Portions

Best Western Plus Cambridge Quy Mill Hotel

◎◎ Modern European ☺

Confident cooking in a former watermill

☎ 01223 293383
Church Rd, Stow-Cum-Quy CB25 9AF
e-mail: info@cambridgequymill.co.uk
web: www.cambridgequymill.co.uk
dir: exit A14 at junct 35, E of Cambridge, onto B1102 for 50yds. Entrance opposite church

The original watermill was built in 1830 and still lies at the heart of Quy Mill, although the place is now a smart contemporary hotel and health club complex set in 11 acres of riverside meadows. Recently refurbished in a contemporary country inn style, the Mill House Restaurant capitalises on its setting in the miller's house, overlooking the waterwheel and mill race: at night it is an intimate place with open fires and candlelight, cool jazz floating in the background, and a friendly, upbeat ambience. The skilled kitchen team likes to keep things imaginative, using spot-on accuracy of timing, careful balance and thoughtful composition to make an impact. The menu keeps a keen eye on the seasons, cleverly contrasting leek and cauliflower pannacotta with the sharpness of pickled winter vegetables, while roast halibut fillet arrives with scallops, prawn and lobster sauce, and winter greens. Meatier fare might run to pan-roasted beef fillet with slow-cooked oxtail, onions, olive oil mash and spinach mousse. Dessert brings on a faultless baked custard tart with caramel ice cream.

Chef Andrew Walker **Owner** David Munro
Times 12-2.30/6.30-9.45 Closed 25-26 Dec **Prices** Fixed L 2 course £12.50-£25, Fixed D 3 course £25-£35, Starter £6-£9.05, Main £11-£26, Dessert £6-£9, Service optional, Groups min 8 service 10% **Wines** 27 by glass **Notes** Complimentary bread & amuse bouche with all A La Carte, Sunday L, Vegetarian available, Dress restrictions, Smart dress/smart casual - no shorts (men), Civ Wed 80 **Seats** 48, Pr/dining room 80 **Children** Portions **Parking** 90

CAMBRIDGE continued

Hotel du Vin Cambridge

◉ French ☺

Classic bistro dining in the city centre

☎ 01223 227330
15-19 Trumpington St CB2 1QA
e-mail: info.cambridge@hotelduvin.com
web: www.hotelduvin.com
dir: M11 junct 11 Cambridge S, pass Trumpington Park & Ride on left. Hotel 2m on right after double rdbt

The Cambridge branch of the Hotel du Vin chain, bang in the city centre, follows the well-trusted concept of wooden floors, banquettes, unclothed tables, restored fireplaces, plenty of prints and much evidence of viniculture. The kitchen is open to view and the team here put their focus on sourcing top-quality ingredients, with the knowhow to treat them comme il faut. Familiar bistro classics come in the shape of escargots bourguignon, or smoked haddock and leek gougère with gruyère sauce, then cassoulet, or sole Véronique. Dishes are accurately timed and combinations judiciously considered, from seared scallops with Serrano ham and smooth pea purée, through grilled steaks, perhaps with béarnaise, to crisp-skinned, tender roast cod with salsa verde and buttered leeks. To finish? What else but crème brûlée or tarte Tatin?

Chef Jonathan Dean **Owner** MWB **Times** 12-2/6-10 **Prices** Fixed L 2 course fr £15.50, Starter £5.95-£11.50, Main £12.50-£29.50, Service added but optional 10% **Wines** 25 by glass **Notes** Sunday L £19.95, Vegetarian available **Seats** 76, Pr/dining room 24 **Children** Portions **Parking** Valet parking service

Hotel Felix

◉◉ Modern British

Intricate modern cooking in a boutique hotel

☎ 01223 277977
Whitehouse Ln, Huntingdon Rd CB3 0LX
e-mail: help@hotelfelix.co.uk
web: www.hotelfelix.co.uk
dir: M11 junct 13. From A1 N take A14 turn onto A1307. At City of Cambridge sign turn left into Whitehouse Ln

A bow-fronted Victorian villa is the setting for a rather distinctive boutique hotel, in which the battleship-grey interiors are offset with splashes of abstract-art colour, and outdoor tables on a terrace overlooking the attractive gardens make the most of the punting weather. Contemporary brasserie cooking is the draw in Graffiti, where braised shoulder of mutton might be a starter portion, served with chargrilled aubergine and red pepper jam. Main courses resound to French and Italian notes, either for salt hake with petits pois and violet potatoes Parisienne, or poached ballottine of local rabbit wrapped in coppa, with walnut gnocchi, prune purée and Armagnac cream. The flavours of these busy dishes ring clearly and harmoniously through them, and the momentum is maintained in desserts such as lemon

polenta cake, served warm with plum compôte and Margarita crème fraîche.

Owner Jeremy Cassel **Times** 12-2/6.30-10 **Prices** Fixed L 2 course £14.50, Starter £4.50-£8.25, Main £11.50-£21.75, Dessert £5.50-£8.50, Service added but optional 10% **Wines** 20 bottles over £30, 22 bottles under £30, 19 by glass **Notes** Sunday L £14.50-£18.50, Vegetarian available, Civ Wed 60 **Seats** 45, Pr/dining room 60 **Children** Portions, Menu **Parking** 90

Menzies Cambridge Hotel & Golf Club

◉ Modern, International

Confident brasserie cooking in a golfing hotel

☎ 01954 249988
Bar Hill CB23 8EU
e-mail: cambridge@menzieshotels.co.uk
web: www.menzieshotels.co.uk
dir: M11 N & S to A14 follow signs for Huntingdon. A14 turn off B1050 Bar Hill, hotel 1st exit on rdbt

There's a lot going on at this modern hotel on the outskirts of Cambridge. There's a championship golf course, for a start, and with 200 acres to explore, plus a spa with swimming pool, there's plenty to keep just about anyone happy. The Brasserie restaurant is worth a visit, too, an open-plan space with mezzanine floors lit by an atrium-style roof; it's all very relaxed and un-starchy. Kick off with a chicken liver parfait with melba toast and onion marmalade, before moving on to Tuscan chicken with tomato broth, olive and oregano mash or Thai green curry. Wild mushroom and tarragon linguine with garlic ciabatta is a good veggie option, whilst carnivores might go for a steak cooked on the chargrill. For dessert, something like apple crumble with custard or tiramisù is sure to satisfy.

Chef Adrian Gaiu **Owner** Menzies Hotels **Times** 1-2.30/7-9.30 Closed L Sat (by appt only) **Prices** Service included **Wines** 20 bottles under £30, 11 by glass **Notes** Sunday L £8.95-£21.95, Vegetarian available, Dress restrictions, Smart, Civ Wed 180 **Seats** 170, Pr/dining room 50 **Children** Portions, Menu **Parking** 200

Midsummer House

◉◉◉◉◉ – *see page 82*

See advert opposite

Restaurant Alimentum

◉◉◉ – *see page 83*

Restaurant 22

◉ Modern European ☺

Modish cooking in charming little venue

☎ 01223 351880
22 Chesterton Rd CB4 3AX
e-mail: enquiries@restaurant22.co.uk
dir: M11 junct 13 towards Cambridge, turn left at rdbt onto Chesterton Rd

As the name implies, look out for that number 22 - with a cream frontage and green door and shutters - to track down this converted Victorian townhouse restaurant on Chesterton Road. Inside, the small dining room is set out with close-up, white-linen-decked tables, decorated with flickering candles. The cooking keeps things sensibly simple too, but with an appealing contemporary European sheen. Salted-cod croquettes, perhaps, with lamb's lettuce, garlic and caper berry aïoli, or white bean and thyme soup with garlic croûtons to start. Next up on the fixed price menu is a sorbet, followed by main-courses such as pan-fried pork cutlet teamed with potato rösti, creamed leeks, porcini mushrooms and sage. To finish, the flavours of the Med are laid bare in a dish of clementine and polenta cake with Limoncello cream.

Chef Mr Kipping **Owner** Mr A & Mrs S Tommaso **Times** 7-9.45 Closed 25 Dec & New Year, Sun-Mon, L all week **Prices** Fixed D 3 course fr £33.95, Service optional **Wines** 26 bottles over £30, 52 bottles under £30, 6 by glass **Notes** Vegetarian available **Seats** 26, Pr/dining room 14 **Children** Portions **Parking** On street

---

DUXFORD   Map 12 TL44

Duxford Lodge Hotel

◉ British, European

Confident cooking in historic country house

☎ 01223 836444
Ickleton Rd CB22 4RT
e-mail: admin@duxfordlodgehotel.co.uk
web: www.duxfordlodgehotel.co.uk
dir: M11 junct 10, onto A505 to Duxford. 1st right at rdbt, hotel 0.75m on left

Just a few minutes from the famous airfield and its museum, Edwardian Duxford Lodge is steeped in wartime history, having played host in the 1940s to stars and bigwigs such as Bing Crosby, Churchill and Douglas Bader. Le Paradis restaurant is a soothing, pastel-hued venue where crisp white linen, comfy chairs and smartly turned-out staff add an old-style charm to proceedings. The European-influenced food maintains a healthy attachment to familiar ideas - chicken liver and foie gras pâté for example, followed by loin of pork with black pudding mash, and apple and cider jus, or a seared fillet of sea bass with sun-blushed tomatoes, fennel gremolata and Provençal herbs to add a touch of southern sunshine. To finish, there are comforting old friends such as sticky toffee pudding with toffee sauce.

Times 12-2/7-9.30 Closed 24 Dec-2 Jan, L Mon, Fri-Sat

MIDSUMMER HOUSE

Midsummer House is located in the heart of historic Cambridge. This Victorian Villa encapsulates Daniel Clifford's vision for culinary perfection and is home to some seriously stylish food.

Daniel Clifford's quest for culinary perfection has taken the restaurant to another level over the past 13 years; his cooking has a modern-focus which is underpinned by classical French technique offering seriously sophisticated food with dishes arriving dressed to thrill.

Upstairs there is a private dining room, and a sophisticated bar and terrace for alfresco drinks with river views. Our private dining room is the perfect location for small weddings, lavish birthday celebrations, simple family gatherings or corporate entertaining.

Midsummer Common, Cambridge CB4 1HA
Tel: 01223 369299 • **Fax:** 01223 302672
Website: www.midsummerhouse.co.uk • **Email:** reservations@midsummerhouse.co.uk

Midsummer House

CAMBRIDGE   MAP 12 TL45

Modern British **NOTABLE WINE LIST**

Stellar cooking from a chef at the top of his game

☎ 01223 369299
Midsummer Common CB4 1HA
e-mail: reservations@midsummerhouse.co.uk
web: www.midsummerhouse.co.uk
dir: Park in Pretoria Rd, then walk across footbridge. Restaurant on left

The setting is idyllic: on the edge of Midsummer Common, with cattle grazing on the lush green grass, and the River Cam flowing by, the Victorian villa sits in a beautiful, countrified spot which makes it hard to believe you're still within the city boundary. It's been a restaurant for many years, run since 1998 by chef Daniel Clifford, who's worked tirelessly and with unwavering energy and enthusiasm in that time (even selling all of his cookery books so he wouldn't lose focus on his own dishes) to put Midsummer House well and truly on the gastronomic map. He's certainly succeeded in that aim, with his restaurant now recognised as one of the finest in the country, and a good deal of TV exposure under his belt (Clifford was a winner in the BBC's *Great British Menu* in 2012 and 2013). Everything about Midsummer House - not just the creative, contemporary cooking - makes it the kind of place where you want to spend a good deal of your time: the two-storey building is decorated in a sleek, modern style, with a small bar upstairs for drinks, which opens out onto a delightful terrace with river views. The conservatory dining room overlooks the attractive and immaculately maintained walled garden, and is decorated in natural shades of cream and brown, with crisp linen on the tables, comfortable, smartly upholstered seating, and a window into the kitchen providing glimpses of Clifford and his fairly sizeable brigade at work. Service is slick and on the ball, and the attention to detail here is impressive, from the care with which the building has been furnished (check out the expensive antique radiators), to the sourcing of ingredients and the intensity of work put into peripherals like canapés, home-made breads and petits fours. Clifford's cooking bears the hallmarks of a chef trained in the French classics, whilst being thoroughly modern, innovative and exciting. There are three menus to choose from - the Classic, Market and Taste of Midsummer - each changing with the seasons and each showcasing fantastic produce which is always allowed to shine. An amuse-bouche of cauliflower velouté with smoked salmon and cucumber shows the serious intent of the kitchen, before (from the Taste of Midsummer menu) ultra-fresh mackerel arrives tartare-style with a wonderfully crispy skin and accompanying flavours of chervil, fennel and passionfruit. Next up comes a clever dish of a hollowed out leek stuffed with pristine slices of scallop and Jersey royal potatoes, before roast wild sea bass, perfectly cooked and with a superb crispy skin, is partnered with surf clams, cucumber, wasabi and sorrel and finished with grated lime to add extra freshness. Roast quail leg and supreme of quail is perfectly timed and full of flavour, and served with sliced red grapes, celery, and a shallot purée and toasted sourdough on the side. Amongst desserts, apple crumble with baked yoghurt and vanilla is an inventive and fantastically fresh-tasting take on the comfort-food classic: a cone-shaped glass is layered with finely diced apple, a set vanilla yoghurt, an ultra fine purée of apple, a crunchy topping with a hint of cinnamon, a quenelle of smooth apple sorbet with a deep apple flavour, and finished with a wafer-thin slice of apple that simply melts in the mouth - stunning. Do make use of the sommelier's expertise when it comes to choosing something from the extensive wine list.

Chef Daniel Clifford **Owner** Midsummer House Ltd **Times** 12-1.45/7-9.30 Closed 2 wks Xmas, Sun-Mon, L Tue **Prices** Prices not confirmed Service added but optional 12.5% **Wines** 12 by glass **Notes** Fixed D 3 course Tue-Thu, 6 course Tue-Sat £75-£95, Vegetarian available **Seats** 45, Pr/dining room 16 **Children** Portions **Parking** On street

Restaurant Alimentum

Modern European 🍷 NOTABLE WINE LIST

Impeccable ingredients and classy, contemporary cooking

☎ 01223 413000
152-154 Hills Rd CB2 8PB
e-mail: reservations@
restaurantalimentum.co.uk
web: www.restaurantalimentum.co.uk
dir: Opposite Cambridge Leisure Park

Travelling along Hills Road out of the city, it's easy to miss Restaurant Alimentum: it's discretely located on the ground floor of a modern apartment block, but those who are in the know (and that includes a growing number of Londoners who catch the train up to the nearby station) beat a path to chef-patron Mark Poynton's door for his immaculate, precise, inventive, contemporary European cooking. The bar has recently had a makeover, so it's worth stopping off here for an aperitif - accompanied by some live music on Friday and Saturday nights - before moving through to the restaurant with its sharp, modern looks (smoked glass, shimmering black-lacquered tables, red padded walls above leather banquettes) and a window into the nerve centre that is the kitchen. The service team are slick and professional whilst managing to keep things relaxed, and if you go for a flight of wine to match your food, you can expect some excellent marriages

courtesy of the expert sommelier. Choose between the à la carte, the seven-course tasting menu or the ten-course 'surprise' menu, and whichever route you take, expect some beautifully presented plates of food cooked with skill using a variety of modern and traditional techniques. Breast and legs of quail with broccoli, lime and peanut is a starter where all the flavours sing together in harmony and the cooking is as accurate as can be, while smoked eel, apple, horseradish and truffle is a perfectly balanced, wonderfully fresh-tasting dish. For the main event, a sea-fresh piece of halibut is roasted to perfection and served with the sweetness of butternut squash along with cabbage and crunchy toasted pumpkin seeds, while faultlessly cooked duck breast is partnered with smoky-tasting celeriac, wild garlic and potato in another winning combination. An apricot and almond Battenberg cake with an apricot cannelloni filled with a light amaretto mousse might bring up the rear, or perhaps a passionfruit curd successfully partnered with coffee ice cream and a saffron granita. Wonderful homemade breads and excellent petits fours show this is a kitchen that's firing on all cylinders.

Chef Mark Poynton **Owner** Mark Poynton **Times** 12-2.30/6-10 Closed 24-30 Dec, BHs, L 31 Dec, D Sun **Prices** Fixed L 2 course fr £18.50, Fixed D 3 course fr £24.50, Tasting menu fr £72, Starter

£13, Main £23, Dessert £13, Service added but optional 12.5% **Wines** 121 bottles over £30, 16 bottles under £30, 22 by glass **Notes** Tasting menu 'surprise' 10 course £85, Sunday L, Vegetarian available **Seats** 62, Pr/dining room 34 **Children** Portions **Parking** NCP Cambridge Leisure Centre (3 min walk)

ELY
Map 12 TL58

The Anchor Inn

🌐 Modern British **NEW** 🎋

Local flavours in Fen country

☎ 01353 778537
Bury Ln, Sutton Gault, Sutton CB6 2BD
e-mail: anchorinn@popmail.bta.com
dir: Signed off B1381 in Sutton village, 7m W of Ely via A142

Sitting beside the New Bedford River or 'The Hundred Foot Drain' as locals know it, The Anchor was built around 1650 to house workers digging the canals to drain the Fens. Just seven miles from Ely, and with the big skies of Fenland all around, the setting feels remote, but inside there's the cosy ambience of period oak panelling, low-beamed ceilings and rustic pine tables on quarry tiled floors - all in all a pleasing backdrop for imaginative modern cooking. Using seasonal East Anglian produce - crabs from Cromer, Brancaster oysters and mussels, fresh local asparagus, and venison from the Denham Estate - hearty menus take in the likes of seared scallops with chorizo jam, sweet potato purée and crisps, ahead of pork tenderloin wrapped in Parma ham and filled with sage and onion cream cheese, served with black pudding potato croquette, sautéed leeks and Calvados jus. Chocolate fondant with beetroot sorbet and marshmallow sauce makes an alluring finale.

Chef Maciej Bilewski **Owner** Black Rock Inns
Times 12-3.30/7-11 **Prices** Fixed L 2 course £13.95, Starter £5.50-£9.75, Main £11.50-£23.95, Dessert £5.75-£8.25, Service optional, Groups min 10 service 10% **Wines** 12 bottles over £30, 38 bottles under £30, 10

by glass **Notes** Sunday L £12.95, Vegetarian available **Seats** 70 **Children** Portions, Menu **Parking** 16

See advert opposite

HINXTON
Map 12 TL44

The Red Lion Inn

🌐 Modern British 🎋

Appealing modern cooking in a pretty country inn

☎ 01799 530601
32 High St CB10 1QY
e-mail: info@redlionhinxton.co.uk
dir: M11 junct 10, at rdbt take A505 continue to A1301 signed Saffron Walden/Hinxton for 0.75m & follow signs for Hinxton

Bags of period character and a lovely location in the pretty conservation village of Hinxton make this charming Grade II 16th-century pub and restaurant with rooms a popular haunt. Expect exposed oak beams, low ceilings, roaring fires and Chesterfield sofas in the buzzy restaurant. Plus there's a tranquil garden in the shadow of the village church for warmer days. The best local and seasonal ingredients are the bedrock of the cooking here, with a daily specials board supplementing the carte. Start, perhaps, with seared scallops in an interesting partnership of sweetcorn mousse, black pudding purée, boiled quail's eggs and truffle. The creative ideas continue into main courses such as honey-glazed duck breast, fondant potato, parsnip textures, steamed broccoli, veal jus and vanilla, while pudding might be pear and almond pannacotta, poached blackcurrants, nut crunch millefeuille, apple purée and plum fool. Four local ales on draught add to the local feel.

Chef Peter Friskey **Owner** Alex Clarke **Times** 12-2/6.30-9 **Prices** Fixed L 2 course £14, Starter £5.50-£9.50, Main £10-£22, Dessert £2.50-£9, Service optional, Groups min 8 service 10% **Wines** 7 bottles over £30, 13 bottles under £30, 12 by glass **Notes** Tasting menus available, Pudding Club, Sunday L £12-£17, Vegetarian available **Seats** 60 **Children** Portions **Parking** 43

HUNTINGDON
Map 12 TL27

The Old Bridge Hotel

🌐🌐 Modern British 🍷 NOTABLE WINE LIST

Distinctive cooking and exceptional wines

☎ 01480 424300
1 High St PE29 3TQ
e-mail: oldbridge@huntsbridge.co.uk
web: www.huntsbridge.com
dir: From A14 or A1 follow Huntingdon signs. Hotel visible from inner ring road

The handsome, ivy-covered, 18th-century Old Bridge is all things to all men: a combination of townhouse hotel, bustling inn and destination restaurant, with people here for a coffee, a pint of real ale, a glass of champagne or a full gourmet evening. There's plenty to entice and enjoy on a menu that shows a kitchen taking a pretty global

approach, from a crab starter, accompanied by fennel, radicchio and pomegranate salad, to a main course of slow-cooked lamb shoulder, tender and full of flavour, with roast pepper couscous, spinach, olives and salsa verde. Dishes are carefully planned with flavours in mind, from bresaola with rocket, radish, parmesan and balsamic to pan-fried wild sea bass with spinach and cockle, mussel and potato chowder. Flexibility means you could pop in for just traditional cod and chips, and then be tempted to stay on for one of the irresistible puddings like chocolate délice with salted caramel and barley ice cream.

Chef James Claydon **Owner** J Hoskins **Times** 12-2/6.30-10 **Prices** Fixed L 2 course £14.95, Starter £7-£12, Main £13-£26, Dessert £6-£8, Service optional **Wines** 300 bottles over £30, 75 bottles under £30, 35 by glass **Notes** Sunday L £29.50, Vegetarian available, Civ Wed 80 **Seats** 100, Pr/dining room 60 **Children** Portions, Menu **Parking** 60

KEYSTON
Map 11 TL07

Pheasant Inn

🌐🌐 Modern British

Imaginative country cooking in a family-owned thatched inn

☎ 01832 710241
Loop Rd PE28 0RE
e-mail: info@thepheasant-keyston.co.uk
dir: 0.5m off A14, clearly signed, 10m W of Huntingdon, 14m E of Kettering

This pheasant has roosted in a tranquil farming village to the west of Huntingdon, and looks every square inch the image of an utterly charming country inn. It's a low-slung building with a thatched roof, all beams and open fires within, and dotted with tables throughout for the diners, as well as having a more formal dedicated dining room. After an interregnum, the Hoskins family (who had owned it since the 1960s) reacquired the Pheasant, and the place exudes well-managed efficiency and cheer. Simon Cadge works some interesting ideas into the well-trodden country pub route, seen in a starter of home-cured bresaola with chunks of hot beetroot, a dollop of white bean purée and truffle-oiled saladings. That might be succeeded by crisp-skinned sea bream with saffroned potato gratin in a buttery tiger prawn broth, corn-fed chicken with pancetta and pied de mouton mushrooms, or a pub stalwart like cottage pie. Finish with good artisan cheeses and walnut bread, or raisin ice cream doused in PX sherry.

Chef Simon Cadge **Owner** John Hoskins
Times 12-2/6.30-9.30 Closed 2-15 Jan, Mon, D Sun **Prices** Fixed L 2 course £15, Starter £5.95-£9.95, Main £11-£25, Dessert £5-£8, Service optional **Wines** 50 bottles over £30, 25 bottles under £30, 12 by glass **Notes** Sunday L £25, Vegetarian available **Seats** 80, Pr/dining room 30 **Children** Portions **Parking** 40

LITTLE WILBRAHAM
Map 12 TL55

Hole in the Wall

Modern British

Classic country inn with sound seasonal cooking

☎ 01223 812282
2 High St CB21 5JY
dir: A14 junct 35. A11 exit at The Wilbrahams

The name comes from a long-gone beer collection system whereby farm labourers collected their refilled jugs and barrels on the way home from work, but nowadays Alex Rushmer and Ben Maude attract custom to the heavily-beamed 15th-century inn with rather more substantial fare. Inside, it is the archetypal country pub: logs crackling in inglenook fireplaces, low beams garlanded with hopbines, and scrubbed pine tables squeezed in elbow-to-elbow to feed into the convivial ambience. The kitchen aims for full-flavoured cooking wrought with an eye to local supplies and seasonality, which is reflected on the specials board and monthly menus. Heart-warming winter offerings could see roasted bone marrow served with pickled shallots and parsley, or duck liver brûlée with pineapple and passionfruit preceding venison loin with parsnip, haggis fritters, port sauce and coffee. Desserts mine a similar fortifying vein - perhaps warm treacle tart with locally-milled oats and raspberry ripple ice cream.

Chef Alex Rushmer **Owner** Alex Rushmer & Ben Maude
Times 12-2/7-9 Closed 2 wks Jan, Mon, L Tue, D Sun
Prices Fixed L 2 course £14, Starter £6-£9, Main £12-£18, Dessert £6, Service optional **Wines** 10 by glass **Notes** Sunday L £23-£30, Vegetarian available **Seats** 75, Pr/dining room 40 **Children** Portions **Parking** 30

PETERBOROUGH
Map 12 TL19

Best Western Plus Orton Hall Hotel & Spa

Modern British

Grand old building with well-crafted menu

☎ 01733 391111
The Village, Orton Longueville PE2 7DN
e-mail: reception@ortonhall.co.uk
web: www.bw-ortonhallhotel.co.uk
dir: off A605 E, opposite Orton Mere

The history of the house built in this spot goes back to the 11th century, but the main part of today's structure is a stripling by comparison, built as it was in 1835. It's an impressive complex of buildings set in a 20-acre estate, which includes some specimen trees, and there's a decidedly traditional feel on the inside too. The Huntly Restaurant has plenty of period detailing, rich fabrics and smartly dressed tables. The menu sets a nice balance, offering pigeon and vegetable broth alongside spiced dry-cooked mackerel crostini among first courses, and pan-roasted fillet of Lincolnshire beef with onion and thyme purée and grain mustard butter, or baked tilapia with garlic mash and sweet peppers among mains. The stables has been converted into an inn, and the old library is the hotel's lounge bar.

Chef Kevin Wood **Owner** Abacus Hotels
Times 12.30-2/7-9.30 Closed 25 Dec, L Mon-Sat
Prices Fixed D 3 course £30, Service optional **Wines** 6 by glass **Notes** Sunday L, Vegetarian available, Civ Wed 90 **Seats** 34, Pr/dining room 40 **Parking** 200

Bull Hotel

Modern European

Modernised classic dishes in a 17th-century coaching inn

☎ 01733 561364
Westgate PE1 1RB
e-mail: rooms@bull-hotel-peterborough.com
web: www.peelhotels.co.uk
dir: Off A1, follow city centre signs. Hotel opposite Queensgate Shopping Centre. Car park on Broadway adjacent to library

The 17th-century Bull Hotel is in the Westgate area of town, where most of Peterborough's business and entertaining goes on. It's a characterful building that was once a coaching inn, and has at its heart a contemporary brasserie done in muted pale colours with unclothed tables and a pleasingly informal air. Modern spins on classic dishes are the favoured theme, though the classic dishes themselves may hail from far and wide. Smoked duck breast with a salad of spring onions, chilli and ginger in toasted sesame dressing kicks things off in Oriental style, and might be followed by lamb Wellington with pea mousse in shallot gravy, or sea bream on crab and chilli linguine in vegetable broth. Banish any thought of winter colds with a honey-and-lemon hot toddy, served as an accompaniment to lemon posset and gingerbread cake.

Chef Jason Ingram **Owner** Peel Hotels plc
Times 12-2/6.30-9.45 **Prices** Fixed D 3 course fr £23.50, Starter £6.50-£8.50, Main £14-£22.50, Dessert £6-£7.50, Service optional **Notes** Sunday L, Vegetarian available, Dress restrictions, Smart casual, Civ Wed 100 **Seats** 80, Pr/dining room 200 **Children** Portions **Parking** 100

PIDLEY
Map 12 TL37

Marcello@ the barn

◉ Modern British NEW ⊛

Modish cooking in a handsome barn

☎ 01487 842204
Fen Rd PE28 3DE
e-mail: marcello.cambridge@gmail.com
dir: A141 from Huntingdon to Warboys. At rdbt right into Fenton Rd (B1040). Left into Fen Rd, follow brown signs for Lakeside Lodge Complex. Approx 0.75m, right to restaurant

The premises is indeed a barn - a newly constructed one, built of green oak, extending over two floors and looking pretty fine inside and out. The chef-patron is indeed called Marcello - Marcello da Silveira, who hails from Brazil. It all takes place on an upmarket caravan and camping site near St Ives (we're in Cambridgeshire, note), and there's a decidedly modern European spin to the menus, plus plenty of regional produce on show. Start with a breast of partridge with a chorizo and bean stew, for example, or the chef's take on an old favourite: battered halibut cheek, potato salad and pea purée. Main course serves up the likes of slow-roasted rump of lamb with mash, greens and a bourguignon sauce, and patience brings its due reward in the form of banana and pistachio soufflé.

Chef Marcello da Silveira **Owner** Marcello da Silveira **Times** 12.15-2.30/6.30-9.30 Closed 1st 2 wks Jan, Mon-Tue, D Sun **Prices** Prices not confirmed Service optional, Groups min 6 service 10% **Wines** 11 by glass **Notes** 6 course tasting menu, Sunday L, Vegetarian available **Seats** 56 **Parking** 32

ST NEOTS
Map 12 TL16

The George Hotel & Brasserie

◉◉ Modern British ⊛

Popular brasserie with well-judged dishes

☎ 01480 812300
High St, Buckden PE19 5XA
e-mail: mail@thegeorgebuckden.com
web: www.thegeorgebuckden.com
dir: Off A1, S of junct with A14

The George, with its distinctive frontage of timbering and columns, was originally a coaching inn and today combines a boutique hotel with a wine bar and brasserie-style restaurant (as well as a ladies' fashion shop). The

Italian chef brings more than a hint of his homeland to the menus, from crayfish lasagne with white wine and basil velouté to properly roasted partridge with boar lardo, pearl barley orzotto, glazed beetroot and horseradish crème fraîche, a dish of great flavour combinations. Otherwise the menu combines a modern British approach with a classical perspective and an eye on the seasons: tempura squid with harissa and spring onion sauce, sirloin steak with Café de Paris butter, then vanilla crème brûlée, or grenadine-poached rhubarb with meringue and rhubarb sorbet.

Chef José Graziosi **Owner** Richard & Anne Furbank **Times** 12-2.30/7-9.30 **Prices** Fixed L 2 course £16, Starter £5.95-£12.95, Main £12.95-£24.95, Dessert £5.95-£7.50, Service optional **Wines** 42 bottles over £30, 70 bottles under £30, 18 by glass **Notes** Sunday L £18-£22, Vegetarian available, Dress restrictions, Smart casual, Civ Wed 60 **Seats** 60, Pr/dining room 30 **Children** Portions **Parking** 25

STILTON
Map 12 TL18

Bell Inn Hotel

◉ Modern British V ⊛

Modish cooking in rambling old coaching inn

☎ 01733 241066
Great North Rd PE7 3RA
e-mail: reception@thebellstilton.co.uk
web: www.thebellstilton.co.uk
dir: A1(M) junct 16, follow Stilton signs. Hotel in village centre

Dick Turpin used to pop into this rambling mellow-stone old coaching inn, and no doubt he'd recognise the fireplaces and rustic beams if he walked in today. The first-floor restaurant might look familiar to him too, with its vaulted ceiling and impressive wooden staircase leading to a gallery. The menus are more cutting edge and cosmopolitan than the surroundings would suggest, though, with seared scallops appearing with black pudding, cauliflower purée and garlic sauce, and a main course of saffron-poached salmon fillet accompanied by herby lemon risotto and a trio of beetroot. The kitchen is led by the seasons, so expect game in winter - perhaps roast breast of guinea fowl with rocket and potato croquettes, tempura broccoli and redcurrant jus - and it comes as no surprise to see no fewer than six stiltons alongside desserts of chocolate tart with pistachio ice cream, or the creative-sounding coconut and lime risotto with chocolate sorbet.

Chef Robin Devonshire **Owner** Mr Liam McGivern **Times** 12-2/7-9.30 Closed 25 Dec, 31 Dec, L Mon-Sat, D Sun **Prices** Fixed L 2 course £14.95, Fixed D 3 course £29.50-£37.65, Starter £4.95-£8.95, Main £9.95-£18.75, Dessert fr £5.25, Service optional **Wines** 6 bottles over £30, 36 bottles under £30, 8 by glass **Notes** Sunday L, Vegetarian menu, Dress restrictions, Smart casual, Civ Wed 100 **Seats** 60, Pr/dining room 20 **Children** Portions, Menu **Parking** 30

WANSFORD
Map 12 TL02

The Haycock Hotel

◉ Modern British ⊛

Bright, modish cooking in historic inn

☎ 01780 782223 & 781124
London Rd PE8 6JA
e-mail: phil.brette@thehaycock.co.uk
dir: In village centre accessible from A1/A47 intersection

Part of the Macdonald group, The Haycock has served customers heading north or south for over 300 years and shows no sign of slacking off. These days the handsome old stone building can even sort out your wedding needs, but it is still very much the place to slake a thirst or tuck into some good food. The public rooms have bags of character - real fires et al - while the restaurant offers a little bit of cosseting refinement. On the menu is a broadly inspired range of modish dishes, where seared scallops come with black pudding purée, cauliflower couscous and apple salad, and ham hock and foie gras terrine with wild mushrooms, celeriac purée and herbs croûtes. Among main courses, the menu delivers sous-vide lamb rump alongside beer-battered cod, or, for the vegetarian traveller, something like open wild mushroom lasagna with butternut squash purée and sage butter.

Chef Luke Holland **Owner** Judith Carter **Times** 12-2.30/6.30-9.30 Closed D Sun, 24 & 31 Dec **Prices** Fixed L 2 course £14.95-£24.95, Fixed D 3 course £29.95-£49.95, Tasting menu £39.95-£49.95, Starter £5.50-£8.50, Main £14.50-£21, Dessert £6-£9.50, Service optional **Wines** 17 bottles over £30, 21 bottles under £30, 16 by glass **Notes** Sunday L, Vegetarian available, Dress restrictions, Smart casual, Civ Wed 100 **Seats** 32, Pr/dining room 25 **Children** Portions, Menu **Parking** 300

WISBECH
Map 12 TF40

Crown Lodge Hotel

◉ Modern, Traditional ⊛

All-comers' hotel menu in a converted car showroom

☎ 01945 773391
Downham Rd, Outwell PE14 8SE
e-mail: office@thecrownlodgehotel.co.uk
web: www.thecrownlodgehotel.co.uk
dir: 5m SE of Wisbech on A1122, 1m from junct with A1101, towards Downham Market

On the banks of Welle Creek at Outwell, just outside Wisbech, the Crown Lodge is a modern hotel that utilises what were the expansive spaces of a car showroom to resplendent effect. An open-plan bar, lounge and restaurant allows plenty of breathing space, and looks smart and modern. It's a popular local venue, and a glance at the all-encompassing menu, which ranges from light snacks to brasserie dishes of big appeal, reveals why. A salad of goats' cheese and beetroot dressed in red wine vinegar and walnut oil is one modish way to start, three scallops with minted pea purée and hollandaise another. Main course could be mozzarella-glazed gammon steak with a sun-dried tomato and olive salad, or lemon- and thyme-crusted salmon on creamy spinach with asparagus, while comfort is assured at the finishing line in the form of a warm chocolate brownie, offset by raspberry sorbet.

Chef Jamie Symons **Owner** Mr W J Moore
Times 12-2.30/6-10 Closed 25-26 Dec, 1 Jan
Prices Service optional **Wines** 4 bottles over £30, 52 bottles under £30, 10 by glass **Notes** Sunday L £10.50-£19, Vegetarian available, Dress restrictions, Smart casual **Seats** 40, Pr/dining room 100 **Children** Portions, Menu **Parking** 50

CHESHIRE

ALDERLEY EDGE   Map 16 SJ87

The Alderley Restaurant

@@@ – *see page 88*

BROXTON   Map 15 SJ45

De Vere Carden Park

@ Modern British

Contemporary British cooking in a modern golfing hotel

☎ 01829 731000
CH3 9DQ
e-mail: reservations.carden@devere-hotels.com
web: www.cardenpark.co.uk
dir: A41 signed Whitchurch to Chester, at Broxton rdbt turn on to A534 towards Wrexham. After 2m turn into Carden Park Estate

Carden Park's Redmonds Restaurant is a smart, split-level modern setting kitted out with leather armchairs and smart wicker chairs at unclothed dark mahogany tables, and a relaxed ethos that aims for an unbuttoned approach to fine dining. Using top-quality produce to good effect, the kitchen works in a straightforward contemporary idiom, setting the ball rolling with butter-poached salmon terrine with smoked salmon, watercress mayonnaise and sun-blushed tomato and olive salad, ahead of a well-thought-out main course involving slow-braised belly pork with bubble and squeak, parsnip purée and crisps, black pudding fritter and root vegetable jus. To finish, vanilla pannacotta gets the exotic treatment with coconut ice cream and mango and pineapple salsa. You'll have no trouble working off the calories here: the sprawling mock-Tudor hotel is lost among 1,000 acres of verdant Cheshire countryside with woodland walks, two championship golf courses, and a spa with 20 treatment rooms.

Times 12.30-2.30/7-10 Closed L Mon-Sat, D Sun

CHESTER   Map 15 SJ46

La Brasserie at The Chester Grosvenor & Spa

@@ Modern, European

Top-end brasserie dining at landmark hotel

☎ 01244 324024
Eastgate CH1 1LT
e-mail: restaurants@chestergrosvenor.co.uk
dir: A56 follow signs for city centre hotels. On Eastgate St next to the Eastgate clock

La Brasserie is reached through the ground-floor colonnades of this impressive half-timbered hotel and has an upmarket air with its bare wooden floors, black-leather sofas, granite tabletops and a giant hand-painted glass skylight. Given the name, it might be a surprise to find that the kitchen is not stuck in the classical French repertoire, so under 'hors d'oeuvres' there may be, for instance, mi-cuit salmon with tandoori spices, mussels and almonds, and Umbrian-style lentil soup with corned ox and a brioche dumpling. Beautifully presented, well-timed scallops come with creamed cauliflower, juicy raisins and boudin fritters adding sweet and sharp counterpoints. Materials are from the top drawer, combinations are well considered and techniques never in doubt, so Josper-grilled Barnsley chop with saffron mousseline and Greek salad is overall an impressive main course. Fish options might extend to sea bass with salsa verde, brown shrimps and cress, and expectations are well met by puddings like a light Grand Marnier savarin with a vibrant orange salad, orange cream and caramel.

Chef Simon Radley, John Retallick **Owner** Grosvenor - Duke of Westminster **Times** 12-10.30 Closed 25-26 Dec, All-day dining **Prices** Fixed L 2 course £19.50, Starter £6.95-£13.95, Main £15.95-£48, Dessert £4-£8.50, Service optional, Groups min 8 service 12.5% **Wines** 7 bottles over £30, 19 bottles under £30, 26 by glass **Notes** £29.50, Vegetarian available, Civ Wed 250 **Seats** 80, Pr/dining room 228 **Children** Portions, Menu **Parking** 250, NCP attached to hotel

Fifteen Thirty Nine Bar & Restaurant

@ Modern British **NEW** 🍃

Ambitious modish cooking overlooking the racecourse

☎ 01244 304600 & 304610
Chester Race Company Limited, The Racecourse CH1 2LY
e-mail: restaurant1539@chester-races.com
dir: Located in Chester racecourse, access via main car park entrance or by foot from Nun's Road

A day at the races can be a very urbane event these days, especially if you head for Chester and grab a table in Restaurant 1539. With its 180 degree views over the racecourse through floor-to-ceiling windows, and contemporary good looks inside, it's a smart setting for some sharp modern food. There's a bar and roof terrace, too. The kitchen rightfully makes a big deal of regional

ingredients and there's a good amount of creativity on show. Treacle-cured trout gravad lax with red pepper caramel and 10-hour squid is a starter which demonstrates the ambition here. Move on to a steak from the Vale of Clwyd (rib-eye, perhaps), or butter-poached turbot with a parmesan and basil cream and ratatouille tortellini. And finish with a funky iced buttermilk parfait with rosewater jelly and macerated strawberries. The lunch menu is a steal and the wine list designed to impress.

Chef Darren Gallagher **Owner** Chester Race Company **Times** 12-3/6-9.30 Closed D Sun **Prices** Fixed L 2 course fr £10, Starter £4.75-£12.95, Main £12.95-£22.95, Dessert £4.75-£6.50, Service optional **Wines** 13 by glass **Notes** Sunday L fr £14.95, Vegetarian available **Seats** 160, Pr/dining room 60 **Children** Portions, Menu

Grosvenor Pulford Hotel & Spa

@ Mediterranean, European

The flavours of Italy in a smart hotel

☎ 01244 570560
Wrexham Rd, Pulford CH4 9DG
e-mail: enquiries@grosvenorpulfordhotel.co.uk
web: www.grosvenorpulfordhotel.co.uk
dir: M53/A55 at junct signed A483 Chester/Wrexham & North Wales. Left onto B5445, hotel 2m on right

The Grosvenor Pulford, in its own grounds a five-minute drive from the city centre, is a luxury hotel, with Ciro's brasserie at its heart. It's a remarkable room, light and airy, with stucco paintwork, Romanesque arches and murals. What's on offer is Italy's cuisine, with some other influences along the way, all using fresh seasonal produce. Terrine de prosciutto turns out to be pressed game terrine with celeriac purée and mulled pear, or go for twice-baked cheese soufflé with pickled beetroot and rocket. Main courses show a kitchen on its game - well-timed seared sea bass fillet and scallops with crisp basil and spinach, tournedos Rossini, and pollo arrosto with crisp pancetta and red wine sauce - as do desserts of apple and cinnamon soufflé with a mini toffee apple.

Chef Paul Prescott **Owner** Harold & Susan Nelson **Times** 12-2/6-9.30 Closed L Sat **Prices** Starter £5.10-£9.95, Main £9.10-£28, Dessert £6.50, Service optional **Wines** 15 bottles over £30, 29 bottles under £30, 10 by glass **Notes** Sunday L £10.95, Vegetarian available, Civ Wed 250 **Seats** 120, Pr/dining room 200 **Children** Portions, Menu **Parking** 200

The Alderley Restaurant

Modern British V

Dynamic modern British cooking amid the Cheshire smart set

☎ 01625 583033
Alderley Edge Hotel, Macclesfield Rd SK9 7BJ
e-mail: reception@alderleyedgehotel.com
dir: A538 to Alderley Edge, then B5087 Macclesfield Rd

The Edge (as locals call the hotel) has a new string to its bow in the form of a brasserie with a good deal of art-deco swagger and a menu described as 'retro classics', but the main Alderley Restaurant is the real deal dining destination here, continuing to impress year on year with its contemporary and dynamic cooking. It all takes place in a lovely spot, with lush woodland and views over the countryside, and gardens that were built to amuse the Victorian captain of industry who built the place back in the 1850s. There are good views from the conservatory restaurant, a swish and comfortable space with plenty of room between the smartly-dressed tables. Chef Chris Holland appeared on the BBC's *Great British Menu* in 2013, but has long been a star in the North West. His cooking is bold and creative but with a decidedly regional flavour thanks to the superb produce brought into the kitchen. This is the kind of kitchen that delivers from the off, with the canapés a treat in themselves - oxtail tart with horseradish mash, for example, or a salmon doughnut - and an amuse-bouche such as English cauliflower espuma with parmesan crumble. And that's just to get you revved up. The main event might kick off with pork pie with sweetcorn and apple, which may sound a little humble and rustic, but delivers a delicious porky extravaganza of fritter, slow-cooked belly and cider-braised cheek with a sweetcorn purée - a stellar dish. Next up, main-course wild halibut includes charred leeks and a smoked haddock and potato broth, or local pheasant might come two ways with pickled cranberry, sprout leaves and parsnip. Desserts are no less creative and well crafted: lemon meringue cheesecake, perhaps, which is a compelling combination of flavours and textures, or a Bramley apple crumble 'hot and cold' that combines an iced apple parfait with a hot apple and cinnamon compôte.

Chef Chris Holland **Owner** J W Lees (Brewers) Ltd **Times** 12-2/7-10 Closed 1 Jan, L 31 Dec, D 25-26 Dec **Prices** Fixed L 2 course fr £20.95, Fixed D 3 course £34.50, Tasting menu £58.50-£91.50, Starter £11.95-£12.75, Main £23.50-£24.25, Dessert £10.50, Service optional **Wines** 300 bottles over £30, 19 bottles under £30, 16 by glass **Notes** Sunday L, Vegetarian menu, Dress restrictions, Smart casual, Civ Wed 150 **Seats** 80, Pr/dining room 130 **Children** Portions, Menu **Parking** 82

CHESTER *continued*

Oddfellows

◉ Modern British

Skillful cooking in idiosyncratic hotel

☎ 01244 400001
20 Lower Bridge St CH1 1RS
e-mail: reception@oddfellows.biz
web: www.oddfellows.biz

The elegant Georgian façade of this townhouse hotel conceals a rather contemporary operation within. One whole wall in The Garden restaurant is a vast window, bare wooden tables are set with candles and quality fittings, and staff dressed in black are friendly and knowledgeable. Overseen by the formidable culinary talents of Simon Radley (see entry at The Chester Grosvenor), the kitchen takes an unmistakably contemporary path to deliver a menu bursting with inspiration from the Mediterranean. You might start with scallops with oxtail pudding, roast garlic, and potato purée, or smoked salmon with beetroot, apple jelly and horseradish, then follow with roast fillet of cod in a crab and parmesan crust, teamed with asparagus, gnocchetti, and vierge butter. Meat main courses come in for similarly full-flavoured treatment - perhaps lamb rump with aubergine purée, butternut squash and pomodorino chutney. It all culminates in desserts such as chocolate tart with peanut butter ice cream.

Times 12-3/5-10

Rowton Hall Country House Hotel & Spa

◉ Traditional British 🍃

Classic menus in a Georgian manor

☎ 01244 335262
Whitchurch Rd, Rowton CH3 6AD
e-mail: reception@rowtonhallhotelandspa.co.uk
web: www.rowtonhall.co.uk
dir: M56 junct 12, A56 to Chester. At rdbt left onto A41 towards Whitchurch. Approx 1m, follow hotel signs

Just a couple of miles outside Chester's city walls, Georgian Rowton Hall sits in eight acres of splendid gardens. It still has all of the grand Adam fireplaces, oak panelling and carved central staircase you would expect in a house of this vintage, as well as a swanky health and beauty spa to take care of the pampering angle. The fetching blend of period elegance and restrained contemporary style continues in the Langdale restaurant with Lloyd Loom seating at linen-clothed tables on wooden floors. The kitchen continues to deal in straightforward dishes, offering among starters crab ravioli with spinach and horseradish foam, and mains that can be as classic as rib-eye steak with Pont-Neuf potatoes, field mushrooms, watercress and horseradish butter, or monkfish wrapped in Parma ham with Puy lentils and buttered spinach. Puddings have the soothing familiarity of apple crumble and sauce anglaise, or vanilla crème brûlée with a sablé biscuit.

Chef Jamie Leon **Owner** Mr & Mrs Wigginton
Times 12-2/7-9.30 **Prices** Fixed L 2 course £9.95, Fixed D 3 course £19.95-£26.50, Starter £4.95-£9.50, Main £9.95-£26.50, Dessert £4.50-£6.95, Service optional **Notes** Sunday L, Vegetarian available, Dress restrictions, Casually elegant, Civ Wed 170 **Seats** 70, Pr/dining room 120 **Children** Portions, Menu **Parking** 200

Simon Radley at The Chester Grosvenor

◉◉◉◉ *— see page 90*

— see page 90

CREWE   Map 15 SJ75

Crewe Hall

◉ Modern European

Contemporary brasserie in a 17th-century stately home

☎ 01270 253333 & 259319
Weston Rd CW1 6UZ
e-mail: crewehall@qhotels.co.uk
web: www.qhotels.co.uk
dir: M6 junct 16 follow A500 to Crewe. Last exit at rdbt onto A5020. 1st exit next rdbt to Crewe. Crewe Hall 150yds on right

Crewe Hall is a seriously stately home that truly deserves its Grade I listed status. It is an undeniably magnificent slice of Jacobean architecture, but also manages to pull off a balancing act between displaying its abundant period character and blending seamlessly with 21st-century style, as typified in the Brasserie located in the contemporary west wing, where its light, fresh, neutral décor makes a complete contrast to the lavish interior of the main building. In tune with the surroundings, the kitchen turns out a straightforward modern repertoire, from openers like confit duck leg rillettes with pistachio purée, red radish cress, and pickled breakfast radish, to main course ideas along the lines of salt-crusted lamb shank with château potatoes, glazed carrots, fine beans and rosemary jus. Presentation is a forte, and flavours stay clean and well balanced through to desserts such as a modishly vegetable-based beetroot pannacotta and sorbet with walnut crisp.

Times All day

KNUTSFORD   Map 15 SJ77

Cottons Hotel & Spa

◉ Mediterranean, International

Broadly appealing menus in modern surroundings

☎ 01565 650333
Manchester Rd WA16 0SU
e-mail: cottons.dm@shirehotels.com
web: www.cottonshotel.com
dir: On A50, 1m from M6 junct 19

Cottons is a large, modern hotel with extensive facilities, including a restaurant that occupies two split-level rooms, smartly decorated along clean-cut, contemporary lines. Formal but friendly staff make recommendations as they hand out menus and also inform guests about the daily specials. The seasonally-changing carte offers much to appeal, from well-timed, tender seared scallops with pea purée and crisp pancetta, to roast rump of lamb (served pink, as requested) with salsa verde and crushed new potatoes. Gluten-free dishes are highlighted - among them perhaps scallops and salmon with samphire and saffron risotto - while puddings might run to crème brûlée, or summer berry meringue sundae.

Times 12-2/7-9.30 Closed L Sat-Sun

Mere Court Hotel & Conference Centre

◉ Mediterranean, Modern British 🍃

Arts and Crafts style and accomplished modern cooking

☎ 01565 831000
Warrington Rd, Mere WA16 0RW
e-mail: sales@merecourt.co.uk
web: www.merecourt.co.uk
dir: A50, 1m W of junct with A556, on right

Mere Court, built in 1903, is a perfect example of the Arts and Crafts style, seen internally in wood carving, metalwork and stained glass. The Arboreum Restaurant is a fine room with beams, panelling, a stone fireplace and views over the lake. The kitchen focuses on the repertory of modern British dishes, turning out ham hock terrine with piccalilli purée and pork crackling, and pan-fried chicken breast with parsley risotto, fennel purée, truffled vinaigrette and beetroot crisps. But it shows flexibility too, so before beef Rossini may come tempura prawns with authentic Thai green sauce, or duck spring roll, with white chocolate pannacotta with basil ice cream to round things off.

Owner Mr Chawla **Times** 12-2/6.30-9.30 **Prices** Prices not confirmed Service optional **Wines** 4 by glass **Notes** Sunday L, Vegetarian available, Dress restrictions, Smart casual, Civ Wed 150 **Seats** 40, Pr/dining room 150 **Children** Portions, Menu **Parking** 150

Simon Radley at The Chester Grosvenor

CHESTER MAP 15 SJ46

Modern French V NOTABLE WINE LIST

Cooking of grand excitement in Chester's crown jewel hotel

☎ 01244 324024 & 895618
Chester Grosvenor & Spa, Eastgate CH1 1LT
e-mail: hotel@chestergrosvenor.co.uk
dir: A56 follow signs for city centre hotels. On Eastgate St next to the Eastgate clock

It looks like it's always been here and it has, pretty much, since the Elizabethan era at least, in one form or other. It's part of the fabric of the city. Standing within the Roman walls next to the landmark Eastgate Clock, the grand black-and-white fronted premises has bags of period character, and was reinvented when Victoria was on the throne. It is part of the Duke of Westminster's rather extensive property portfolio (Grosvenor being the family name), and has a luxurious finish within that can't fail to impress; it is swish, classy and kitted out to satisfy the most dedicated sybarite. Among its treasures is a spa and numerous eating and drinking options. La Brasserie (see separate entry) serves up a thoroughly authentic French feel, The Arkle Bar and Lounge is a fine place to while away a few hours (afternoon tea is a bit of a treat, especially with champagne), but the main event, the shining light, is

Simon Radley. The restaurant that bears his name is a splendidly pillared space done out with a sophisticated neutrality that is soothing and calming and sets the scene for what is to come. The immaculate service team ensures everything goes swimmingly. Simon Radley's food is dynamic and contemporary, with the ingredients given room to breathe and deliver impact on their own merits, and everything that appears on the plate is of staggering high quality. Each dish is given a single name, a moniker to catch your eye, so you might start with 'Arabica', which is a fabulous French squab with the flavours of pistachio, Medjool dates, dandelions and coffee, or 'Crown Prince', which delivers a saddle of French rabbit with hand-rolled smoked bacon macaroni, pumpkin and poached langoustine. The flavours work in harmony and everything looks fabulous on the plate. Among main courses, 'Herdwick' is that fine breed, mutton this time around (in various guises), served up with cabbage and cumin, spearmint jelly and ewes' curd. Or go for the 'Flavours of Bouillabaisse' which is a sophisticated impression with red mullet, fennel rouille, poached langoustine and sourdough crunch. The craft, skill and sheer delight continues into dessert stage: 'Sticky Rice' perhaps, with the flavours of coconut, poached lychee, iced guava and passionfruit, or 'Floating Island', another delightful interpretation, with

chilled blood orange nectar, poached and crisp vacherin and iced mandarin. There's a tasting menu, too, but you probably worked that out already, and a stellar wine list that fair beggars belief.

Chef Simon Radley, Ray Booker **Owner** Grosvenor - Duke of Westminster **Times** 6.30-9.30 Closed 25 Dec, 1 wk Jan, Sun-Mon, L all week (except Dec) **Prices** Fixed D 3 course £69, Tasting menu £90, Service added but optional 12.5% **Wines** 457 bottles over £30, 66 bottles under £30, 19 by glass **Notes** Tasting menu 8 course, Vegetarian menu, Dress restrictions, Smart dress, no shorts or sportswear, Civ Wed 250 **Seats** 45, Pr/dining room 228 **Parking** Car park attached to hotel (£10 24hrs)

KNUTSFORD *continued*

The Mere Golf Resort & Spa

◉ International NEW

A please-all menu in a modern lakeside hotel

☎ 01565 830155
Chester Rd, Mere WA16 6LJ
e-mail: reservations@themereresort.co.uk
dir: M6 junct 19 or M56 junct 7

Sitting beside a lake in extensive tree-filled grounds, this modern hotel has a lot going on. There's an 18-hole golf course, a luxury spa with swimming pool, and three restaurants, including the flagship Browns. Kick things off with a cocktail in Browns Bar before moving through to the contemporary, smartly kitted-out restaurant where the focus is on fresh, seasonal, local ingredients. Start with something like roasted quail breast with chicken liver parfait and date chutney, or go down the fishy route with Anglesey mussels with sweet wine, shallots and chervil. Main course might look to sunnier climes for something like pan-fried red mullet with crisp squid, black olive, tomato and capers, or you could stay closer to home with roasted loin of Scottish venison with carrot purée, baby turnips and roasted chestnuts, or perhaps a simple steak from the grill served with all the traditional accompaniments.

Prices Fixed D 3 course £34 **Notes** Sunday L **Parking** 400

LYMM Map 15 SJ68

The Church Green British Grill

◉◉ Modern British V 🍷

A class act in a refurbished village pub

☎ 01925 752068
Higher Ln WA13 0AP
e-mail: reservations@thechurchgreen.co.uk
dir: M6 junct 20 follow signs for Lymm along B5158 after 1.5m turn right at T-junct onto A56 towards Altrincham, on right after 0.5m

Aiden Byrne is a modern media-savvy British chef par excellence. Having made his bones in A-list kitchens - Tom Aikens, Pied à Terre, and The Grill at The Dorchester, among others - he has become a well-known face on the telly, written a cookbook and set up on his own account in The Church Green, a stylishly reinvented old pub in a Cheshire village. Inside is the bare brickwork, natural wood, leather seating and neutral hues you'd expect in a contemporary gastro set-up, and his wife Sarah presides over a switched-on front-of-house team. Byrne stays in touch with the zeitgeist, so in order to chime with the prevailing mood of belt-tightening austerity, he reined in the culinary concept from fine dining to a 'British Grill' with a simplified, more everyman appeal in 2012. Be assured, though, that the same uncompromising approach to sourcing the finest local and seasonal ingredients still drives the operation. There are homely classics - steak and kidney pudding, beef hotpot, sausages and mash - or potted Lancashire shrimps, a traditional dish brought bang up to date by adding nutmeg mayonnaise, toasted sourdough bread and apple and watercress salad to the deal. Seared over coconut husk charcoal on the Inka grill, 28-day dry-aged steaks sourced from small Cheshire farms are exemplary, as witnessed in a perfectly-timed and well-rested rib-eye with bonbons of bone marrow and stilton, beef dripping chips and béarnaise sauce. For those wanting to dig deeper into Byrne's culinary capacities, take a bunch of pals for the four-course 'Great British' menu, which must be shared by the whole table.

Chef Aiden Byrne, Ian Matsin **Owner** Aiden Byrne **Times** 12-9.30 Closed 25 Dec **Prices** Tasting menu £60, Service optional **Wines** 29 bottles over £30, 28 bottles under £30, 18 by glass **Notes** Tasting menu 5 course, Sunday L £14-£24, Vegetarian menu, Dress restrictions, Smart casual preferred **Seats** 50 **Children** Portions, Menu **Parking** 25

MACCLESFIELD Map 16 SJ97

Shrigley Hall Hotel, Golf & Country Club

◉ Modern British NEW

Modern British cooking in a stately Georgian hotel

☎ 01625 575757
Shrigley Park, Pott Shrigley SK10 5SB
web: www.pumahotels.co.uk/hotels/shrigley-hall-hotel/
dir: Exit A523 at Legh Arms towards Pott Shrigley. Hotel 2m on left before village

Built in 1825 for William Turner MP, in the days when second homes were less controversial, Shrigley is a late-Georgian pile that hasn't lost an iota of its grandeur over the past two centuries. The gorgeous painted domed ceiling above the grand staircase is not to be missed. A spacious, elegant room overlooking the grounds, with the distant Peaks as backdrop, the Oakridge dining room goes for a fittingly stately ethos, with swagged curtains, chandeliers and thick napery to luxuriate in. The culinary tone is classical with just a hint of the British demotic, so grilled cod with peas and bacon in a thin creamy sauce might turn up as a main course, as might sugar-baked gammon with silverskins in mustard sauce. Bookending those are the likes of chicken liver parfait with fig purée, or Stornoway black pudding with apple and bacon, and favourite puddings such as red fruit Pavlova, and a svelte chocolate tart on biscuit base with salted caramel and vanilla cream.

Times 7-9 **Prices** Prices not confirmed

NANTWICH Map 15 SJ65

Rookery Hall Hotel & Spa

◉◉ Modern British

Old-school comforts in an imposing Cheshire mansion

☎ 0845 0727 533
Main Rd, Worleston CW5 6DQ
e-mail: rookeryhall@handpicked.co.uk
web: www.handpickedhotels.co.uk/rookeryhall
dir: B5074 off 4th rdbt, on Nantwich by-pass. Hotel 1.5m on right

The hall is a stolidly imposing bolthole from the rigours of the kind of modern living that goes on in nearby Manchester and along the teeming M6. It stands serene amid 38 acres of rolling Cheshire, its late-Georgian magnificence making an impressive backdrop for the spa treatments and contemporary cooking we expect to find - in that order. Layers of table napery (fast disappearing elsewhere), gentling candlelight and formally drilled service aim to lull. So might an evening starter that looks like breakfast with its runny-yolked warm Scotch egg, black pudding, tomato, brown sauce, and buttered brioche in lieu of a muffin. Otherwise, poached pear has inched its way up the menu from third course to first - though still stained with red wine, it comes with Waldorf salad. Main could be a crisp-skinned rendition of Goosnargh duck confit, along with white bean purée and creamed cabbage in a light reduction sauce of redcurrant and rosemary. Lemon cheesecake comes with an intense cherry sorbet to round it all off.

Chef Mark Walker **Owner** Hand Picked Hotels **Times** 12-2/7-9.30 Closed L Sat **Prices** Service optional **Wines** 81 bottles over £30, 9 bottles under £30, 12 by glass **Notes** Sunday L fr £22.95, Vegetarian available, Dress restrictions, Smart casual, no jeans or trainers, Civ Wed 200 **Seats** 90, Pr/dining room 150 **Children** Portions, Menu **Parking** 100

PECKFORTON Map 15 SJ55

1851 Restaurant at Peckforton Castle

@@@ — *see below*

PUDDINGTON Map 15 SJ37

Macdonald Craxton Wood Hotel

@@ British V 🍷

Smart British cooking and top-notch ingredients

☎ 0151 347 4000 & 347 4016
Parkgate Rd, Ledsham CH66 9PB
e-mail: events.craxton@macdonald-hotels.co.uk
web: www.macdonaldhotels.co.uk/craxtonwood
dir: from M6 take M56 towards N Wales, then A5117/A540 to Hoylake. Hotel on left 200yds past lights

The eponymous woodland is 27 acres of leafy grounds that surround this traditional hotel, which houses an outpost of Aiden Byrne's British Grill (See also entry for The Church Green British Grill in Lymm). The style is smart and understated as suggested by the 'grill' tag, so slate and grey tones, photos on the walls pointing up the direction of the menu (lots of local agricultural scenes and farm animals aplenty), and bare tables. The efficient service team is smartly turned out in long aprons. There are plenty of classics on the menu (fish and chips the trad way), a Josper Grill to max out the flavours in the steaks (and lamb and duck), plus sharing platters and well-judged main courses such as slow-cooked pork belly with exemplary crackling, thyme mash, roasted apple and broccoli. Top quality ingredients shine through in dishes presented in a fashionable manner - think slate bread boards and a richly flavoured chicken liver parfait served in a jar, alongside toasted brioche, truffle Madeira jelly and sweet onion marmalade. The ideas are straightforward enough, but the level of technical skill on display is high. Rice pudding mousse with raspberries and cream makes a highly satisfying finish.

Chef David Ashton **Owner** Macdonald Hotels & Resorts **Times** 12-11 Closed L Mon-Sat **Prices** Starter £6.50-£10, Main £11-£27, Dessert £6-£7.50, Service optional **Wines** 32 bottles over £30, 28 bottles under £30, 12 by glass **Notes** Sunday L £12-£18, Vegetarian menu, Dress restrictions, Civ Wed 250 **Seats** 100, Pr/dining room 12 **Children** Portions, Menu **Parking** 300

SANDIWAY Map 15 SJ67

Nunsmere Hall Hotel

@@ British, European 🍷

Accomplished modern cooking in plush restaurant

☎ 01606 889100
Tarporley Rd, Oakmere CW8 2ES
e-mail: reservations@nunsmere.co.uk
web: www.nunsmere.co.uk
dir: M6 junct 18, A54 to Chester, at x-rds with A49 turn left towards Tarporley, hotel 2m on left

Dating from the turn of the last century, this mansion is surrounded on three sides by a 60-acre lake. It's now a luxury country-house hotel, its Crystal Restaurant, which overlooks the south-facing terrace and sunken Italian garden, a room of distinction, with yards of fabrics everywhere, an intricate ceiling, gilt-framed mirrors and

1851 Restaurant at Peckforton Castle

PECKFORTON MAP 15 SJ55

Modern British, French

Food fit for a king in a mock-medieval castle

☎ 01829 260930
Stonehouse Ln CW6 9TN
e-mail: info@peckfortoncastle.co.uk
web: www.peckfortoncastle.co.uk
dir: 15m from Chester, situated near Tarporley

If you like gothic mansions, you'll love this: Peckforton Castle is a Victorian-built, mock-medieval fortress on a grand scale, surrounded by impeccable grounds in the heart of the Cheshire countryside. It was built in 1851 - hence the restaurant's name - for a wealthy Cheshire landowner and MP, and at the time it so impressed the architect Gilbert Scott (famous for his gothic-style design of St Pancras Station) that he called it, "the largest and most carefully and learnedly executed gothic mansion of the present". Praise indeed. Today, in the hands of the Naylor family who fell in love with the castle and bought it after their eldest son got married here, it continues to wow the many visitors who pass through its doors. And many pass through its doors specifically to dine in the elegant and stylish 1851 Restaurant, with its deep-pile tartan carpets, thick napery, highly polished glassware and sparkling silverware - a truly magnificent setting for the assured modern British cooking of head chef Mark Ellis. Only the finest Cheshire produce, including salmon, cheese, Goosnargh duck and beef, finds its way onto the menu, and dishes display classic French techniques but with a modern interpretation. A meal may begin with some excellent homemade bread, perhaps flavoured with cheese and onion, before an amuse-bouche of mushroom velouté with a gentle accent of sage. Seared fillet of mackerel, faultlessly cooked, may follow, served with 'beetroot textures' (firm pieces and a sweet purée), along with apple and an appropriately cooling 'horseradish yoghurt'. For the main event corn-fed Goosnargh poulet with 'langoustine pot au feu, pressed then pan-fried knuckle, poché- grillé breast, truffled soft egg' might appeal: an immaculately presented, imaginative dish of contrasting textures and flavours that all come together as one delicious whole. A skilled hand at pastry is in evidence at dessert stage in a morello cherry frangipane with fine, crisp pastry and a perfectly textured filling with sharp and richly flavoured cherries, complemented by liquorice and blackcurrant ice cream.

Chef Mark Ellis **Owner** Naylor family **Times** 6-8.45 Closed L Mon-Sat **Prices** Fixed D 3 course £46, Service optional, Service added but optional 10% **Wines** 24 bottles over £30, 30 bottles under £30, 9 by glass **Notes** Sun L served all day 12.30-8.45pm, Sunday L, Vegetarian available, Dress restrictions, Smart casual, no trainers **Seats** 60, Pr/dining room 165 **Children** Portions, Menu **Parking** 100

Save on Hotels. Book at **theAA.com/hotel**

CHESHIRE 93 **ENGLAND**

a wooden floor topped by a rug. The kitchen sources materials conscientiously and corrals them into well-conceived dishes that are never unnecessarily fussy. Start off with potted shrimps with potato salad and pickled cucumber, or a subtly flavoured warm salad of baby leeks, chorizo, parmesan and a soft-boiled egg drizzled with truffle oil, before a gutsy main course like slowly braised shin of beef served with horseradish mash and bourguignon-style sauce. Lemon sole is cooked with pinpoint accuracy and comes with a light truffle and parsley butter served with spring onion mash and French-style beans, and to crown proceedings may be a prettily presented dessert like dark chocolate mousse with chocolate sponge, cherry sorbet and jelly, and sour cream parfait.

Chef Craig Malone **Owner** Prima Hotels
Times 12-2/7-9.30 **Prices** Fixed L 2 course £16.95-£18.95, Fixed D 3 course £34.50-£36.50, Tasting menu fr £49.50, Service added but optional 12.5% **Wines** 66 bottles over £30, 32 bottles under £30, 15 by glass **Notes** Tasting menu available, Sunday L, Vegetarian available, Dress restrictions, No jeans, trainers or shorts, Civ Wed 80 **Seats** 60, Pr/dining room 80 **Children** Portions, Menu **Parking** 80

TARPORLEY
Map 15 SJ56

Macdonald Portal Hotel Golf & Spa

◉ Modern British

Sophisticated country-club setting for classic cuisine

☎ 0844 879 9082
Cobbiers Cross Ln CW6 0DJ
e-mail: general.portal@macdonald-hotels.co.uk
dir: Off A49 in village of Tarporley

With three courses spread around its expansive acreages of rolling Cheshire countryside, it is odds-on that most guests are up for a spot of golf at this upscale contemporary hotel, and those not bearing a weighty bag of clubs will no doubt be heading for some serious pampering in the glossy spa. Named after the 12th-century Earl of Chester who built nearby Beeston Castle, the classy Ranulf Restaurant has a clubby feel thanks to a butch décor of sleek contemporary wall panelling, tobacco-hued leather banquettes and bare darkwood tables, softened by romantic candlelight in the evening. The kitchen sources its materials well, and has the sense not to faff around with them, offering among starters Stornoway black pudding with caramelised apple and bacon salad, or fishcakes with caper mayonnaise. Main courses continue the theme of tried-and-true classics - Scottish sirloin or rib-eye steaks sizzling from the grill, or pan-fried fillet of wild sea bass with new potatoes and seasonal greens. Puds are equally comforting - perhaps Eton Mess or a straight-up crème brûlée.

Times 6-9.30 Closed L all week

WARMINGHAM
Map 15 SJ76

The Bear's Paw

◉ Modern European

Refined gastro-pub cooking near Crewe

☎ 01270 526317
School Ln CW11 3QN
e-mail: info@thebearspaw.co.uk
web: www.thebearspaw.co.uk
dir: M6 junct 17, A534, A533 signed Middlewich & Northwich. Continue on A533, left into Mill Ln, left into Warmingham Ln. Right into Plant Ln, left into Green Ln

In a village just outside Crewe, The Bear's Paw is a large inn with a stylish open-plan layout and lots of wood: floor, panelling, bare tables. Candles, flowers and prints on the walls add character, and there's a lounge area with tub leather-look chairs and a log fire. The menus are conventional enough, with few surprises, but the kitchen sources the best materials it can find, free-range whenever possible, and treats them with integrity. Pan-fried calves' liver, with bacon, creamy mash and onion gravy, is given a lift from deep-fried haggis, and there may be baked hake fillet with samphire, tomato ragout and paprika-spiced potato. Some dishes can be ordered as a starter or a main - salmon and smoked haddock fishcake with tartare sauce for instance - and to finish there may be a copybook example of vanilla crème brûlée.

Chef Matt Castelli **Owner** Harold & Susan Nelson
Times 12-9.30 All-day dining **Prices** Starter £4.75-£7.50, Main £9.95-£23.95, Dessert £4.50-£9.95, Service optional **Wines** 13 bottles over £30, 30 bottles under £30, 10 by glass **Notes** Sunday L £12.95, Vegetarian available **Seats** 150 **Children** Portions, Menu **Parking** 75

WILMSLOW
Map 16 SJ88

Stanneylands Hotel

◉◉ Modern British

Well-executed British food in smart country hotel

☎ 01625 525225
Stanneylands Rd SK9 4EY
e-mail: sales@stanneylandshotel.co.uk
web: www.stanneylandshotel.co.uk
dir: from M56 at airport turn off, follow signs to Wilmslow. Left into Station Rd, onto Stanneylands Rd. Hotel on right

From its humble origins in the 18th century as a farmhouse, Stanneylands has ascended the social ladder to trade as a relaxing country hotel handy for Manchester airport and for forays into the city centre. With its oak panelling and well-drilled, professional staff, the restaurant makes an intimate setting for a well-conceived repertoire of modern ideas appealing to classic culinary sensibilities. Ham hock and parsley terrine with home-made piccalilli is a guaranteed crowd pleaser - as long as it is done well - and this example hits all the right notes. Next up, seared venison tenderloin with caramelised shallots, curly kale, Vichy carrots and Madeira jus delivers a fine depth of flavours; to finish, warm cherry Bakewell tart with clotted cream could hardly do more to oblige.

Chef Richard Maun **Owner** Prima Hotel Group
Times 12-2.30/7-9.45 **Prices** Fixed L 2 course fr £14.50, Fixed D 3 course fr £31.50, Starter £5.95-£7.95, Main £14.50-£23.50, Dessert £6.95-£8.50, Service optional **Wines** 66 bottles over £30, 32 bottles under £30, 15 by glass **Notes** Tasting menu available, Sunday L, Vegetarian available, Dress restrictions, Smart casual, Civ Wed 120 **Seats** 60, Pr/dining room 120 **Children** Portions, Menu **Parking** 110

CORNWALL & ISLES OF SCILLY

BODMIN
Map 2 SX06

Trehellas House Hotel & Restaurant

◉ Traditional & Modern British ☙

Cornish produce put to good effect in converted courthouse

☎ 01208 72700
Washaway PL30 3AD
e-mail: enquiries@trehellashouse.co.uk
web: www.trehellashouse.co.uk
dir: Take A389 from Bodmin towards Wadebridge. Hotel on right 0.5m beyond road to Camelford

Trehellas House has worn a few hats over the years since it was built in the early 18th century: initially an inn that also served as the local court house (trials must have been entertaining after a few flagons of ale...), then a farm, and a pub once more in the '70s. Nowadays it has traded up to a country-house hotel with an appealing restaurant, where low beams and slate-flagged floors set the scene for punchy modern cooking. Effective dishes are delivered without undue fuss, and Cornish produce is at the heart of it all. Start with partridge and juniper casserole with peppercorn rice and parsnip crisps, followed by St Ives Bay sea bass with ginger, lemon and pepper linguine and mussel cream. Artisan Cornish cheeses are hard to resist, but the incurably sweet of tooth might finish with sticky toffee pudding with toffee sauce and clotted cream.

Chef Tim Parsons **Owner** Alistair & Debra Hunter **Times** 12-2/6.30-9 **Prices** Starter £6-£10, Main £14-£25, Dessert £6, Service included **Wines** 25 bottles under £30, 6 by glass **Notes** Sunday L £10-£16, Vegetarian available **Seats** 40 **Children** Portions, Menu **Parking** 25

BOSCASTLE
Map 2 SX09

The Wellington Hotel

◉◉ Modern British ☙

Creative contemporary cooking in popular fishing village

☎ 01840 250202
The Harbour PL35 0AQ
e-mail: info@wellingtonhotelboscastle.com
web: www.wellingtonhotelboscastle.com
dir: A30, A395 at Davidstowe follow Boscastle signs. B3266 to village. Right into Old Rd

With a top spot overlooking the harbour, The Wellington is a local landmark, its castellated tower keeping watch over the village. It dates from the 16th century, the name changing in the 19th in honour of the Iron Duke, and the restaurant is called The Waterloo to maintain the theme. And there's exciting things happening here in the 21st century. The restaurant has a soothing traditional Georgian charm about it, maintaining period dignity without a single iota of chintz, and the cooking shows ambition. Chef Steve Marsh seeks out top-notch regional produce and demonstrates some acute technical skills in

the execution of dishes. Start, perhaps, with a pressing of rabbit confit, plus seared loin, served with poppyseed bread, capers and red-veined sorrel, or blow-torched scallops with home-cured coppa, vanilla, spinach and caviar. The modish thinking continues at main-course stage, too, with halibut with oxtail, bok choy, cockles, grelot onions and udon noodles, and desserts like blackberry and orange 'Arctic roll' with a salad of hedgerow blackberries, candy orange, sorbet and pistachio pannacotta.

Chef Stephen Marsh **Owner** Cornish Coastal Hotels Ltd **Times** 12-3/6-9 Closed L all week, D Mon-Tue **Prices** Prices not confirmed Service optional **Wines** 10 by glass **Notes** Vegetarian available **Seats** 35, Pr/dining room 28 **Children** Portions, Menu **Parking** 15

BUDE
Map 2 SS20

The Castle Restaurant

◉ Modern European ☙

Wharfside castle with good, honest fare

☎ 01288 350543
The Wharf EX23 8LG
e-mail: enquiries@thecastlerestaurantbude.co.uk
web: www.thecastlerestaurantbude.co.uk
dir: From A39 into Bude at mini-rdbt go straight ahead along The Crescent. Then 1st turn on right & to The Castle Heritage Centre. Restaurant within centre

Bude Castle is now an arts and heritage centre and also houses this small, busy restaurant, which has more the feel of a bistro, with lots of bare wood, compactly spaced tables and efficient, chatty staff. The menu hints of a bistro too, taking in as it does tasty ham hock terrine with onion jam, crispy duck confit with truffled jus, mash and broad beans, and crème brûlée, although there's also a tasting menu if you want to spread your wings, ranging from fried scallops with cauliflower purée and curry oil, and rump of beef with salt beef cottage pie and greens. Produce is judiciously sourced, from a beautifully fresh portion of hake in beer batter with sauce gribiche and chips, to a platter of local cheeses.

Chef Kit Davis **Owner** Kit Davis **Times** 12-2.30/6-9.30 Closed D Sun **Prices** Fixed L 2 course fr £12.50, Fixed D 3

course fr £26.50, Starter £5.50-£8, Main £12-£21, Dessert £5-£7, Service optional **Wines** 7 by glass **Notes** Tasting menu available, Sunday L, Vegetarian available, Civ Wed 100 **Seats** 40 Pr/dining room 60 **Children** Portions, Menu **Parking** Parking nearby

CALLINGTON
Map 3 SX36

Langmans Restaurant

◉◉ Modern British ☙

Pedigree local produce on a six-course tasting menu

☎ 01579 384933
3 Church St PL17 7RE
e-mail: dine@langmansrestaurant.co.uk
dir: From the direction of Plymouth into town centre, left at lights and second right into Church St

The Butterys have carved out a glittering reputation for themselves at their highly singular restaurant in this pleasant market town, drawing custom in from Plymouth and beyond. Hung about with work by local artists, and driven by produce from local growers and farmers, it's a distinctively regional operation, and distinctive too in that the format is a six-course tasting menu for all. Most of this is table d'hôte, perhaps opening with a portion of 36-hour pork belly with a strip of crunchy crackling and Cox's apple purée. A soup could be rich and silky butternut squash topped with a halved scallop, before the fish course, a serving of beautifully timed brill with salsify and oyster mushrooms in a creamy sauce. Meat may well offer a choice, maybe chump of lamb sauced with red wine and star anise, or truffled beef sirloin, with a showboat of wonderful vegetables. Pause for some West Country cheeses, and then set about the dessert trio, served on a compartmented glass plate - chocolate tart, passionfruit and chocolate tower, and rhubarb and ginger cheesecake, served with variously complementary ice creams.

Chef Anton Buttery **Owner** Anton & Gail Buttery **Times** 7.30-close Closed Sun-Wed, L all week **Prices** Tasting menu fr £40, Service optional **Wines** 45 bottles over £30, 50 bottles under £30, 11 by glass **Notes** Tasting menu 6 course, Vegetarian available, Dress restrictions, Smart casual preferred **Seats** 24 **Parking** Town centre car park

FALMOUTH
Map 2 SW83

Falmouth Hotel

◉ British V

Victorian coastal hotel with confident cooking

☎ 01326 312671
Castle Beach TR11 4NZ
e-mail: reservations@falmouthhotel.com
web: www.falmouthhotel.com
dir: A30 to Truro then A390 to Falmouth. Follow signs for beaches, hotel on seafront near Pendennis Castle

The Victorian Grande Dame of Falmouth's coastline stands in a commanding position overlooking Pendennis Castle, the sandy beaches and the sea. In case the splendid view out of the window isn't enough, model ships and maritime pictures remind you of the port's seagoing heritage in the Trelawney dining room, where the kitchen draws on fine Cornish and West Country produce for its repertoire of modern dishes. Expect Cornish seafood terrine with lemon and dill crème fraîche, followed by pan-fried cutlets and braised shoulder of lamb with rosemary mash, sweet red cabbage and broad bean jus. Given the location, you may be in the mood for fish - perhaps red wine-poached brill fillet with wild mushroom risotto, sautéed salsify, and Merlot. Local cheeses or bitter lemon tart with orange marmalade and Cornish clotted cream provide a satisfying finish.

Chef Mark Aldred **Owner** Richardson Hotels of Distinction **Times** 12-2/6.45-8.45 **Prices** Fixed D 3 course £29.95, Service optional **Wines** 15 bottles over £30, 15 bottles under £30, 7 by glass **Notes** Wed L 1/2/3 course £6/£8/£10, Sunday L, Vegetarian menu, Civ Wed 150 **Seats** 150, Pr/dining room 40 **Children** Portions, Menu **Parking** 65

The Greenbank Hotel

@@ Modern International 🍴

Dual-purpose menu with panoramic estuary views

☎ 01326 312440
Harbourside TR11 2SR
e-mail: reception@greenbank-hotel.co.uk
web: www.greenbank-hotel.co.uk
dir: Approaching Falmouth from Penryn, take left along North Parade. Follow sign to Falmouth Marina and Greenbank Hotel

Superbly positioned on the estuary, The Greenbank overlooks the backwaters of the Fal towards the marina, as well as the hotel's own private quay, from where a water taxi plies the route into town. Panoramic windows survey the scene from the first-floor restaurant, where a bare wood floor and clothed tables with chairs upholstered in contrasting primary colours set a stripped-down modern tone. The menu divides its wares into Classics and Fusions, depending on whether you're in the mood for smoked chicken pâté and piccalilli, followed by fish in Betty Stogs beer batter with chunky chips, or a more speculative journey that leads from crispy beef tongue with celeriac remoulade in port and orange glaze, to seared breast and confit leg of duck with butternut squash purée and kale. An eclectic mix of culinary styles reinforces the point: smoked bratwurst hot dog with sauerkraut, and lamb loin with ras el hanout, couscous and tzatziki. A technically unimpeachable crème brûlée comes with honeycomb, shortbread and rhubarb sorbet.

Chef Fiona Were **Owner** Greenbank Hotel (Falmouth) Ltd **Times** 12-2/6.30-9.15 **Prices** Starter £5.50-£9.95, Main £13.50-£23, Dessert £6.50-£8.95, Service optional **Wines** 51 bottles over £30, 35 bottles under £30, 9 by glass **Notes** Sunday L £7-£14, Vegetarian available, Civ Wed 90 **Seats** 60, Pr/dining room 16 **Children** Portions **Parking** 60

The Royal Duchy Hotel

@@ Modern British 🍴

Well-judged modish dishes overlooking Falmouth Bay

☎ 01326 313042
Cliff Rd TR11 4NX
e-mail: reservations@royalduchy.co.uk
web: www.brend-hotels.co.uk
dir: on Cliff Rd, along Falmouth seafront

If it is a piece of classic seaside grandeur you're after, The Royal Duchy can deliver. The view across the bay over towards Pendennis Castle and out to sea is magnificent and if you're seated on the terrace, well, you've got the best seat in town. The dining room, with its rich red tones, crisp white linen-clad tables and chandeliers, is a reassuringly traditional setting for some gently contemporary cooking. A first-course ravioli, for example, is filled with fresh crab and ginger and topped with a light ginger foam, or there might be salt-beef terrine with celeriac remoulade and pickled sultanas. A first-rate piece of haddock stars in a main course with watercress purée and lemon sabayon, the balance of flavours just right, whilst vegetarians will find satisfaction in the form of a roasted beetroot risotto with rocket and watercress salad. End on a high with Key lime pie with dark chocolate sorbet.

Chef John Mijatovic **Owner** Brend Hotel Group **Times** 12.30-2/6-9 Closed L Mon-Sat **Prices** Fixed L 2 course £13.50, Fixed D 3 course £35, Service optional **Wines** 18 bottles over £30, 25 bottles under £30, 16 by glass **Notes** Sunday L, Vegetarian available, Dress restrictions, Smart casual, Civ Wed 150 **Seats** 100, Pr/dining room 24 **Children** Portions, Menu **Parking** 40

St Michael's Hotel and Spa

@ Modern Mediterranean **NEW**

Seductive sea views and contemporary cooking

☎ 01326 312707
Gyllyngvase Beach, Seafront TR11 4NB
e-mail: info@stmichaelshotel.co.uk
dir: Follow signs for seafront & beaches

If it's a sea view you're after, St Michael's can deliver, and it's all the better when seen from the beautiful sub-tropical gardens, or the terrace. The hotel's Flying Fish Restaurant bags the fabulous vista, but even if the weather prevents you gazing out to sea, there's plenty on the menu to keep you happy. It's a bright, contemporary restaurant, with floor-to-ceiling windows and well-spaced

tables dressed in white linen. There's a genuine local flavour to the contemporary menus, with lots of Cornish seafood on offer: whole dressed crab, oysters, Thai-style crabcakes, or the Newlyn seafood grill. There's meat, too, in the form of steaks from Lower Carnebone Farm, or a trio of Cornish pork (slow-cooked belly, seared loin and braised cheek). And for dessert, iced cappuccino parfait with mini doughnuts, chocolate sugar cubes and latte anglaise shows the ambition and skill of the kitchen team.

Times 12-2/6.30-9

FOWEY   Map 2 SX15

The Fowey Hotel

@ Modern European **V** 🍴

Modish cooking and soothing harbour views

☎ 01726 832551
The Esplanade PL23 1HX
e-mail: reservations@thefoweyhotel.co.uk
web: www.richardsonhotels.co.uk
dir: A30 to Okehampton, continue to Bodmin. Then B3269 to Fowey for 1m, on right bend left junct then right into Dagands Rd. Hotel 200mtrs on left

The Fowey Hotel has a good deal of seaside appeal with its grand Victorian façade and position overlooking the Fowey River - the sea is just around the corner. Its restaurant - Spinnakers - has splendid Victorian proportions and features, but does not feel stuck in the past with its smart décor and tables dressed in white linen. There's a good deal of local produce on the menu, not least seafood landed on the nearby quay: pan-seared mackerel, for example, with Niçoise salad and sauce vierge, or pan-seared scallops with belly pork, creamed leeks and cauliflower coulis. Among main courses, West Country lamb might turn up in the company of scallion potato purée, wilted greens, Chantenay carrots, broad beans and a mint and balsamic jus, and to finish, all the exoticism of passionfruit soup with mango parfait and honeycomb ice cream.

Chef Mark Griffiths **Owner** Keith Richardson **Times** 12-3/6.30-9 **Prices** Fixed D 3 course £35-£44.90, Service optional **Wines** 12 bottles over £30, 49 bottles under £30, 15 by glass **Notes** Sunday L, Vegetarian menu, Dress restrictions, Smart casual, no torn denim, trainers, shorts, Civ Wed 70 **Seats** 60, Pr/dining room 22 **Children** Portions, Menu **Parking** 20

GOLANT   Map 2 SX15

Cormorant Hotel & Restaurant

⊚⊚ Modern British V 🍷

Creative contemporary cooking and glorious estuary views

☎ 01726 833426
PL23 1LL
e-mail: relax@cormoranthotel.co.uk
web: www.cormoranthotel.co.uk
dir: A390 onto B3269 signed Fowey. In 3m left to Golant, through village to end of road, hotel on right

Built above the Fowey Estuary, this charming small hotel has panoramic views over the water from a terrace as well as from the stylish restaurant, with its wooden floor, pastel colours and mirrors. A glance at the short menu shows that this is a kitchen with its fingers on the culinary pulse, turning out starters like seared scallops with a roe beignet, pear purée and parsnip crisps, and chicken liver and foie gras parfait with grape and balsamic chutney, Madeira jelly and a toasted beetroot brioche. Dishes are thoughtfully constructed to make the most of flavours without too much fiddle, and high culinary standards are applied to quality produce. Poached fillet of local lemon sole, for instance, is accompanied by cockle and mussel chowder, cockle 'scampi', lemon mash, green beans and parsley purée, and roast guinea fowl breast is stuffed with pesto mousse and served with a poached egg and mustard mash. Puddings seem like labours of love if lemon tart is anything to go by: it comes with lemon posset, blood orange sorbet and meringue drops.

Chef Dane Watkins **Owner** Mrs Mary Tozer
Times 12-2/6.30-9.30 **Prices** Fixed D 3 course fr £32.50, Tasting menu £42.50, Starter £7-£12, Main £14-£23, Dessert £7-£8, Service optional, Groups min 7 service 12% **Wines** 21 bottles over £30, 46 bottles under £30, 6 by glass **Notes** Tasting menu, incl vegetarian 6 course, Vegetarian menu, Dress restrictions, Smart casual, no shorts **Seats** 30 **Children** Portions **Parking** 20

HAYLE   Map 2 SW53

Rosewarne Manor

⊚⊚ Modern British NEW

Ambitious cooking in renovated 1920s manor

☎ 01209 610414
20 Gwinar Rd TR27 5JQ
e-mail: enquiries@rosewarnemanor.co.uk
dir: A30 Camborne West towards Connor Downs, left into Gwinear Rd. 0.75m to Rosewarne Manor

After a period when this grand 1920s building had fallen into neglect, the current owners have resurrected Rosewarne as a venue with a keen eye to the weddings and functions market, and with good food to boot. The modern British repertoire is driven by seasonality and local sourcing, and the confident cooking delivers well-defined flavours. The menu gives little away in terms of description or cooking methods, so you will need to quiz

the helpful staff about what, exactly, is involved at each stage. You might set the ball rolling with Cornish blue cheese pannacotta, matched inventively with apple textures and gingerbread, then progress to an unusual assemblage of pork belly with dark chocolate, cauliflower and apple, or there could be a modish fish and meat combo involving line-caught sea bass with beef shin, Savoy cabbage and beurre noisette. To finish, egg custard tart with lemon curd and pistachio crumb might catch the eye, or you could round things off on a savoury note with the excellent artisan Cornish cheeses.

Times 12-2.30/6-9 Closed Mon-Tue **Prices** Fixed D 3 course £30

HELSTON   Map 2 SW62

New Yard Restaurant

⊚⊚ Modern British

Quality local produce and confident modern cooking

☎ 01326 221595
Trelowarren Estate, Mawgan TR12 6AF
e-mail: kirsty.newyardrestaurant@trelowarren.com
web: www.trelowarren.com
dir: 5m from Helston

Trelowarren, on the Lizard Peninsula, is a working estate of 1,000 acres, plus tourist accommodation, and The New Yard is at its heart. It's been converted from the coach house, the old arched doorways now windows looking over the courtyard with its olive trees in giant pots. Almost 90 per cent of the kitchen's produce comes from within a 10-mile radius, with vegetables, herbs, fruit and game from the estate itself, the last appearing as a main course of roast pheasant wrapped in pancetta. The kitchen tends to keep things simple, and there's a strong comfort factor to its output: pork belly with braised red cabbage and celeriac, for instance, or spicy monkfish tail with cauliflower, lentils and curry oil. More voguish ideas are equally well handled, seen in starters of crab tortellini with fennel and apple salad, and curd cheese and beetroot salad. At dessert stage, a theme on lemon (posset, cake, tart and sorbet) might fight for attention with warm chocolate mousse.

Times 12-2/7-9 Closed Mon (mid Sep-Whitsun), D Sun

LIZARD   Map 2 SW71

Housel Bay Hotel

⊚ Modern British

Dramatic clifftop location and compelling cooking

☎ 01326 290417 & 290917
Housel Cove TR12 7PG
e-mail: info@houselbay.com
dir: A30 from Exeter, exit Truro and take A34/A394 to Helston & A3083 to Lizard

The solid-looking stone property was planned and built as a hotel as long ago as the 1890s, and its founders had a good eye for location: it stands dramatically on top of a cliff looking down over the sea, with the coast path running through the gardens. The kitchen's requirements are met by small Cornish producers, and just about everything is made on the premises. The menu is a slate of interesting ideas, so guinea fowl rillette is given a black Cajun yoghurt dip as well as gherkins, and chargrilled tuna steak comes with a dollop of pineapple salsa and horseradish and a portion of creamy potato and spring onion salad. Elements generally combine or contrast to produce a harmonious end result, as in main-course grilled sea bass fillet with clam and coconut velouté, celeriac rösti, Parma ham snaps, green and broad beans and roast tomatoes, or flavourful, tender rump of lamb with sweetbreads, forestière jus, celeriac fondant, grilled aubergine and samphire. Coconut pannacotta with lemon tart is a refreshing way to end.

Times 12-2.30/7-9.30 Closed Jan

LOOE   Map 2 SX25

Barclay House

⊚⊚ Modern British V 🍷

Coastal cuisine with exquisite sea views

☎ 01503 262929
St Martin's Rd PL13 1LP
e-mail: info@barclayhouse.co.uk
web: www.barclayhouse.co.uk
dir: 1st house on left on entering Looe from A38

Colourful artworks and blond-wood seats at crisp linen-clad tables bright tone in the dining room of Barclay House, a snow-white country villa perched on the sylvan hillsides above Looe harbour. Those keen on keeping food miles to an absolute minimum will be heartened to learn that the fish and seafood comes fresh off the day boats down on the quayside, and the kitchen has Cornish produce as an abiding theme in its light and punchy cooking. On the seafood front, dishes range from Looe Bay scallops with pea purée, chorizo and organic watercress, to Fowey River mussels steamed in Cornish Orchards cider with shallots, garlic, thyme and cream, while West Country meat could be represented by local duck breast with truffled mash, braised red cabbage, and red wine and blackberry jus. The deep comfort of a saffron bread-and-butter pudding becomes more indulgent still with the addition of a dollop of Cornish clotted cream, and there's a Cornish cheeseboard too, served with onion marmalade.

Chef Joe Sardari **Owner** Malcolm, Graham & Gill Brooks **Times** 7-9 Closed Sun, L all week (except by arrangement) **Prices** Fixed D 2 course £32, Tasting menu £39, Service added but optional 10% **Wines** 17 bottles over £30, 29 bottles under £30, 11 by glass **Notes** Tasting menu 6 course, Vegetarian menu, Dress restrictions, Smart casual, Civ Wed 70 **Seats** 60 **Children** Portions, Menu **Parking** 25

Trelaske Hotel & Restaurant

◎◎ Modern British ⊙

Local produce in verdant Cornwall

☎ 01503 262159
Polperro Rd PL13 2JS
e-mail: info@trelaske.co.uk
dir: B252 signed Looe. Over Looe bridge signed Polperro. 1.9m, hotel signed on right

Run with great charm by hands-on owners, this lovely small-scale hideaway sits in four acres of woodland and pretty, well-tended gardens between Looe and Polperro. Chef-proprietor Ross Lewin is clearly a man who likes to go his own way - self-taught and, to a certain degree, self-sufficient thanks to harvests of fruit, vegetables and herbs grown in the hotel's own poly tunnels, he delivers an accomplished modern British repertoire, built on Cornish materials. Fish fresh from the Looe day boats stars in dishes such as cod fillet with cauliflower couscous and lemon sauce, while Cornish Black pork loin is matched with vanilla mash, hog's pudding and glazed pear. Staying with the local terroir, you could wind proceedings up with Cornish cheeses, crackers and home-made chutney, or go for the comforts of spotted dick with pouring cream.

Chef Ross Lewin **Owner** Ross Lewin & Hazel Billington **Times** 12-2/7-9 Closed 22-26 Dec, L Mon-Sat **Prices** Fixed L 2 course £19.95, Fixed D 3 course £33.50, Service optional **Wines** 8 by glass **Notes** Sunday L, Vegetarian available, Dress restrictions, Smart casual, no shorts **Seats** 40 **Children** Portions **Parking** 60

LOSTWITHIEL   Map 2 SX15

Asquiths Restaurant

◎◎ Modern British ⊙

Minimal fuss, maximum flavours

☎ 01208 871714
19 North St PL22 0EF
e-mail: info@asquithsrestaurant.co.uk
dir: Opposite St Bartholomews church

Opposite the medieval church in Lostwithiel, there's a serenity about Asquiths that is wholly inviting. The smart interior is monochrome, except for works by Penzance artist Steve Slimm on the exposed stone walls, and staff are easygoing but nevertheless on the ball. A serious restaurant, then, but not one that takes itself so seriously as to be intimidating. Food-wise, there are no smoke and mirrors here, just well-sourced, cleverly-conceived and skilfully-cooked modern dishes. Cornish credentials are evident throughout, from the beers and wines to the duck livers that appear with a creamy sage and mushroom sauce and potato gnocchi to open proceedings. Next up, crispy-skinned black bream is matched with buttered spinach, crab and chilli potato cake and a well-made citrus beurre blanc, or there might be slow-cooked belly and faggot of local pork with potato purée, white beans and grain mustard. This is confident, mature cooking that shows its final flourish of class with a pannacotta with Monbazillac jelly, raspberry sorbet, and biscotti crumbs.

Chef Graham Cuthbertson **Owner** Graham & Sally Cuthbertson **Times** 7-9 Closed Xmas, Jan, Sun-Mon, L all week **Prices** Starter £5-£7, Main £12-£16, Dessert £5.50-£7, Service optional **Wines** 2 bottles over £30, 35 bottles under £30, 4 by glass **Notes** Vegetarian available **Seats** 28, Pr/dining room 10 **Children** Portions **Parking** Car park at rear

---

MARAZION   Map 2 SW53

Mount Haven Hotel & Restaurant

◎◎ Modern British ⊙

Accomplished modern cooking in family-run hotel

☎ 01736 710249
Turnpike Rd TR17 0DQ
e-mail: reception@mounthaven.co.uk
web: www.mounthaven.co.uk
dir: From centre of Marazion, up hill E, hotel 400yds on right

The local landmark of St Michael's Mount standing guard in the bay doesn't look any better than when surveyed from the terrace at the Mount Haven, glass of wine in hand of course. The 19th-century coach house is these days a chic hotel with a restaurant that is a cut above the competition. There's good use of natural tones in the décor and a friendly and unpretentious approach to service. The menu shows plenty of local influence, giving a sense of place, and the composition of dishes follows a

---

broadly contemporary path. Pea and ham hock soup, for example, comes with a parsley beignet, and local John Dory is served with celeriac carpaccio among first courses. Main course might bring forth some local venison in a well-balanced partnership with roasted root vegetables, celeriac purée, potato fondant and port jus. If the sea views have whet your appetite, go for pan-roasted pollock with smoked haddock chowder, mussels and crispy leeks, and to finish, apple fritters with cinnamon ice cream and vanilla syrup.

Owner Orange & Mike Trevillion **Times** 12-2.30/6.30-9.30 Closed 27-30 Dec **Prices** Starter £5.50-£7.95, Main £15.50-£22.50, Dessert £6-£7.50, Service optional **Wines** 21 bottles over £30, 20 bottles under £30, 11 by glass **Notes** Vegetarian available, Dress restrictions, Smart casual **Seats** 50 **Children** Portions, Menu **Parking** 30

MAWGAN PORTH   Map 2 SW86

The Scarlet Hotel

◎◎ Modern European V ⊙

Confident contemporary cooking and wonderful sea views

☎ 01637 861800
Tredragon Rd TR8 4DQ
e-mail: stay@scarlethotel.co.uk
dir: A39, A30 towards Truro. At Trekenning rdbt take A3059, follow Newquay Airport signs. Right after garage signed St Mawgan & Airport. Right after airport, right at T-junct signed Padstow (B3276). At Mawgan Porth left. Hotel 250yds on left

Huge windows opening on to the terrace, with wonderful views of the beach, sea and headland, dominate the restaurant at this modern hotel, which was built along eco-friendly lines. The kitchen's larder has been 'grown, reared, caught or foraged to taste as it should', according to the hotel, and indeed dishes are praiseworthy for the freshness of the ingredients and the clear flavour combinations. Langoustine consommé with tortellini and pickled celery is straight out of today's cookery school, and could be followed by the more orthodox lamb rump with rosemary jus, fondant potato and broccoli, or you might start with venison terrine with toast and pears poached in red wine and move on to grilled plaice in a crab and herb crust, accompanied by garlic-flavoured spinach, beetroot and mash. Vegetarians are properly catered for, and desserts have the wow factor, among them ginger pannacotta with sea buckthorn sorbet and micro shoots.

Chef Tom Hunter **Owner** Red Hotels Ltd **Times** 12.30-2.15/7-9.30 Closed 3-31 Jan **Prices** Fixed L 3 course £22.50, Fixed D 3 course £42.50, Service optional **Wines** 69 bottles over £30, 19 bottles under £30, 39 by glass **Notes** Sunday L, Vegetarian menu, Civ Wed 74 **Seats** 70, Pr/dining room 20 **Parking** 37, In village

| MAWNAN SMITH | Map 2 SW72 |

Budock Vean - The Hotel on the River

Traditional British V

Well-crafted dishes in a traditional country house

☎ 01326 252100
TR11 5LG
e-mail: relax@budockvean.co.uk
web: www.budockvean.co.uk
dir: from A39 follow tourist signs to Trebah Gardens. 0.5m to hotel

Wrapped in 65 unforgettable acres of organically-managed subtropical gardens on the Helford River, and bathed in Cornwall's balmy climate, it's no wonder that Budock Vean has a loyal following of guests who return again and again. Tradition is the watchword at this country house, whose reassuringly formal mood is defined by the jacket-and-tie dress code at dinner. The kitchen hauls in the finest local, seasonal produce as the bedrock of menus that blend traditional and more modern ideas. Things start simply enough with home-smoked breast of Barbary duck with orange fig and toasted pine nuts, then move on to pan-roasted suprême of Cornish turbot served with leeks, crab and parmesan mash, and chive butter sauce; dyed-in-the-wool traditionalists might rejoice at roast sirloin of local beef with duck fat-roasted potatoes, parsnips, onions, Yorkshire pudding and gravy. Dessert delivers the homely comfort of apple and peach crumble with vanilla crème anglaise.

Chef Darren Kelly **Owner** Barlow family
Times 12-2.30/7.30-9 Closed 3 wks Jan **Prices** Starter £7.75-£20, Main £18.25-£36, Dessert £6.95, Service optional **Wines** 33 bottles over £30, 59 bottles under £30, 10 by glass **Notes** 5 course L £39.95, Sunday L £19.95, Vegetarian menu, Dress restrictions, Jacket & tie (ex school hols), Civ Wed 80 **Seats** 100, Pr/dining room 40 **Children** Portions, Menu **Parking** 100

| MOUSEHOLE | Map 2 SW42 |

The Cornish Range Restaurant with Rooms

Traditional British

Locally-caught seafood in a charming village restaurant

☎ 01736 731488
6 Chapel St TR19 6SB
e-mail: info@cornishrange.co.uk
dir: From Penzance 3m S to Mousehole, via Newlyn. Follow road to far side of harbour

Squirrelled away down one of Mousehole's skinny back lanes (leave your car at the outskirts of the village) this delightful stone-built restaurant with rooms is rooted deep in local fishing heritage, since it was once a factory for salting and packing the local pilchard catch. And as Newlyn is just up the road, prime fish and seafood still drives the activity here, albeit in a more sophisticated manner. Inside, the feel is homely but smart, with

scrubbed pine tables and colourful local art on the walls. Hard at it in the open-to-view kitchen, Keith Terry cooks confident, forthright dishes with robust flavours, opening with the likes of grilled mackerel fillets with seared scallops, Serrano ham and horseradish cream, followed by baked hake fillet with monkfish in prosciutto, braised Puy lentils and herb pesto or, for die-hard carnivores, a chargrilled rib-eye steak with tomato and garlic confit, wild mushroom gratin and balsamic glaze.

Chef Keith Terry **Owner** Chad James & Keith Terry **Times** 10-2.15/5.30-9.30 Closed L winter **Prices** Fixed D 2 course £16.50, Starter £5.95-£8.95, Main £11.95-£20.95, Dessert £5.95, Service optional **Wines** 6 bottles over £30, 18 bottles under £30, 6 by glass **Notes** Vegetarian available **Seats** 42 **Children** Portions, Menu **Parking** Harbour car park

| MULLION | Map 2 SW61 |

Mullion Cove Hotel

Modern British

Sea views and accomplished modern cooking

☎ 01326 240328
TR12 7EP
e-mail: enquiries@mullion-cove.co.uk
web: www.mullion-cove.co.uk
dir: A3083 towards The Lizard. Through Mullion towards Mullion Cove. Hotel in approx 1m

The hotel's location could hardly be bettered: it's perched on the top of cliffs overlooking Mullion's harbour, with spectacular coastal views. There's a timeless elegance to the aptly named Atlantic Restaurant, where window tables are inevitably at a premium, but wherever you sit pleasant and efficient staff ensure guests are well looked after. The menus change daily, with local fishing boats providing the kitchen's seafood stock-in-trade: perhaps a full-flavoured main course of prawn and mussel broth infused with saffron, accompanied by roast fillet of pollock and new potatoes, or bouillabaisse with crab and dill linguine. Combinations are well considered and dishes deliver plenty of punchy flavours, among them a starter of roast guinea fowl with spring onion and chorizo roulade, sweetcorn purée and pickled mushrooms. Meals can end memorably with the likes of raspberry and chocolate pannacotta with fruit salad and lemon ice cream.

Chef Lee Brooking **Owner** Matthew Grose **Times** 12-2/7-8.45 Closed L Mon-Sat **Prices** Fixed D 3 course fr £36, Service optional **Wines** 25 bottles over £30, 30 bottles under £30, 12 by glass **Notes** Sunday L, Vegetarian available, Dress restrictions, Jackets req for men **Seats** 60 **Children** Portions, Menu **Parking** 45

| PADSTOW | Map 2 SW97 |

Margot's

British

High-impact bistro cookery amid the Padstow bustle

☎ 01841 533441
11 Duke St PL28 8AB
e-mail: bazbeachdog@aol.com

Amid the brash commercialism that has overtaken Padstow in recent years, Margot's is a haven of appealing modesty, a little bistro with a marine-blue frontage tucked away in the narrow streets of the town centre. Simple wood tables, colourful artworks and a Brains beer flag adorning the ceiling set the tone for some straightforward, direct and high-impact bistro cookery from chef-patron Adrian Oliver. Padstow runs on fresh fish, and just as well when you contemplate a starter of grilled mackerel dressed in cucumber, capers and lemon, or a main such as whole lemon sole in citrus oil. Meats are good too though, perhaps a confit leg of duck with crisped ham and spring onion mash in red wine sauce. A fine finisher is the chocolate pannacotta, its dense richness thrown into relief by the tang of raspberries, with a brandy-snap for added crunch.

Chef Adrian Oliver, Lewis Cole, Claire Drake **Owner** Adrian & Julie Oliver **Times** 12-2/7-9 Closed Nov, Jan, Sun-Mon **Prices** Prices not confirmed Service optional **Wines** 5 bottles over £30, 16 bottles under £30, 5 by glass **Notes** Tasting menu 6 course, Vegetarian available **Seats** 22 **Children** Portions **Parking** Harbour car park

The Metropole

Modern British

Harbourside restaurant with an assured team in the kitchen

☎ 01841 532486 & 0800 005 2244
Station Rd PL28 8DB
e-mail: reservations@the-metropole.co.uk
web: www.the-metropole.co.uk
dir: M5/A30 past Launceston, follow signs for Wadebridge and N Cornwall. Then take A39 and follow signs for Padstow

'The Met' to its friends is just about Padstow's most imposing building, a Victorian grande dame that is a local landmark. From its lofty perch on a hill above town it looks across the estuary to the comings and goings of the local fishing boats, so window seats are much in demand in the dignified traditional surroundings of the Harbour Restaurant. Thanks to a certain Mr Stein, Padstow has become foodie central in this part of Cornwall, and The Met is not about to let the side down, particularly when the rich local bounty of land and sea turns up practically on the doorstep. Such prime produce might appear in a surf and turf-style combo of seared scallops with hog's pudding, butternut squash purée and a maple syrup jus to start, followed, perhaps, by confit duck leg with braised Puy lentils, onion purée and wilted spinach. To finish, how about lemon posset with blackcurrant ice cream and homemade shortbread?

Chef Michael Corbin **Owner** Richardson Hotels Ltd
Times 6.30-9 Closed L Mon-Sat **Prices** Starter £7.50,
Main £18.50, Dessert £7, Service optional **Wines** 7 bottles
over £30, 24 bottles under £30, 9 by glass **Notes** Sunday
L £12-£15, Vegetarian available, Dress restrictions,
Smart casual, Civ Wed 100 **Seats** 70, Pr/dining room 30
Children Portions, Menu **Parking** 50

Paul Ainsworth at No. 6

⊛⊛⊛ – see page 100

St Petroc's Hotel and Bistro

⊛ Traditional, Mediterranean ☺

Rick Stein's lively seafood bistro

☎ 01841 532700
4 New St PL28 8EA
e-mail: reservations@rickstein.com
dir: Follow one-way around harbour, 1st left,
establishment 100yds on right

In the fifth-oldest building in Padstow, Rick Stein's bistro
has bare wooden tables, white walls hung with bold
artwork, and a courtyard and garden for alfresco dining.
The focus, as expected, is on seafood in various guises,
although there are a few token meat dishes in the shape
of pan-fried chicken breast with black pudding, and
steaks. Plainly grilled lemon sole with béarnaise, or
bourride of brill, salt cod and red mullet take centre
stage, preceded perhaps by crab tart with garlic, tomato
and tarragon, or smoked trout with horseradish cream.
For dessert, expect something like pannacotta with
vanilla-poached rhubarb.

Chef Paul Harwood **Owner** R & J Stein **Times** 12-2/7-10
Closed 25-26 Dec, 1 May, D 24 Dec **Prices** Fixed L 2
course fr £16.50, Fixed D 3 course fr £27, Starter
£6.90-£8.95, Main £14.95-£29.50, Dessert £4.80-£6.90,
Service optional **Wines** 7 bottles over £30, 18 bottles
under £30, 12 by glass **Notes** Fixed L menu available
winter, Vegetarian available **Seats** 54 **Children** Portions,
Menu **Parking** Car park up hill

The Seafood Restaurant

⊛⊛⊛ – see page 100

PENZANCE   Map 2 SW43

The Bay @ Hotel Penzance

⊛⊛ Seafood V ☺

Splendid cooking and sea views

☎ 01736 366890 & 363117
Britons Hill TR18 3AE
e-mail: eat@thebaypenzance.co.uk
web: www.thebaypenzance.co.uk
dir: from A30, left at last rdbt for town centre. 3rd right
onto Britons Hill. Restaurant on right

The Bay Restaurant in the Hotel Penzance is a light and
relaxed room, with a bar at one end, unclothed tables,
artwork on the walls, and views over rooftops to Mount's
Bay. Staff are friendly, polite and on the ball - which it
has to be, with four menus to cope with: one for vegans, a
tasting menu, one devoted to shellfish (24 hours' notice
required), taking in lobster thermidor with new potatoes,
and fruits de mer, and the main event. The last
showcases local produce, and the cooking is assured and
uncluttered. Among starters, smoked eel is served with
buckwheat blinis and an apple and fennel compôte, and
pan-fried rabbit loin with salsify, wild mushrooms, a fried
quail's egg and Calvados jus. Fish is a strong suit,
judging by a thick fillet of crisp-skinned grilled red mullet
accompanied by cauliflower purée and diced beetroot and
beetroot foam. Meat-eaters could opt for belly pork fillet
and hogs pudding with an apple and cider reduction, and
dessert is often the star of the show: maybe fig
frangipane tart with fig purée and star anise and honey
ice cream.

Chef Ben Reeve **Owner** Yvonne & Stephen Hill **Times** 11-9
Closed 1st 2 wks Jan, L Sat **Prices** Fixed L 2 course fr
£11.50, Fixed D 3 course fr £32, Tasting menu fr £49,
Service optional, Groups min 8 service 10% **Wines** 23
bottles over £30, 21 bottles under £30, 12 by glass
Notes Vegan menu available, Sunday L, Vegetarian menu,
Dress restrictions, Smart casual, no shorts, Civ Wed 60
Seats 60, Pr/dining room 12 **Children** Portions, Menu
Parking 12, On street

Ben's Cornish Kitchen

⊛ British NEW ☺

Appealing modern food in relaxed surroundings

☎ 01736 719200
West End, Marazion TR17 0EL
e-mail: ben@benscornishkitchen.com
dir: On coast road opposite St Michael's Mount

Relaxed and easygoing, Ben Prior's friendly
neighbourhood restaurant ticks all of the right boxes with
its unfussily voguish setting - wooden floors, plain wood
tables and raffia chairs, whitewashed and stone walls

---

decorated with local art - and the sort of straightforward
contemporary food made from lovingly-sourced seasonal
ingredients that we all want to eat these days. The
recently-opened first-floor dining room not only lets more
lucky punters in, but also gives sweeping sea views to St
Michael's Mount. The kitchen uses excellent regional
ingredients to good effect, delivering the likes of home-
cured beef with Parmesan custard, watercress and
capers, which might be followed by a more ambitious
idea involving tenderloin and crispy belly of local pork
matched with roast and puréed cauliflower, hazelnuts,
verjus onions, and smoked apple and tonka bean purée.
Just the ticket, too, is a well-made dessert of vanilla
pannacotta, berry compôte and honeycomb.

Chef Ben Prior **Owner** Ben Prior **Times** 12-2/6.30-9
Closed Sun, L Mon **Prices** Fixed L 2 course fr £15, Tasting
menu fr £49, Starter £5-£10, Main £13-£24, Dessert
£5-£8, Service optional **Wines** 65 bottles over £30, 65
bottles under £30, 25 by glass **Notes** Vegetarian
available **Seats** 45, Pr/dining room 25 **Children** Portions,
Menu

The Coldstreamer Inn

⊛ Modern British ☺

Modern Cornish cooking at a village hostelry

☎ 01736 362072
Gulval TR18 3BB
e-mail: info@coldstreamer-penzance.co.uk
dir: 1m NE of Penzance on B3311, right turn into School
Ln in Gulval, opposite church

Once the New Inn, the pub was renamed after WWII in
honour of a son of its then owners, a Coldstream
Guardsman who had died on active service. Standing
across from the church, it's very much the local hostelry
of the little village of Gulval, only a mile or so from
Penzance. A reassuringly rustic ambience has been
allowed to prevail, with a bare wood floor and pine tables
in the separate dining area. In the evenings, candles are
lit and a contented babble rises from the room. What's
contenting them is the modern Cornish cooking of Tom
Penhaul, which is based on Newlyn fish, locally grown
fresh produce and meat from a Penzance butcher. A
breast of pigeon has been a modish starter for a while
now, and appears here in tenderly pink guise under a
welter of hazelnuts, orange and sorrel. That may be
followed by a well-crisped and forthrightly seasoned fillet
of black bream, dressed in lemon oil and partnered by
asparagus and rainbow chard risotto, while meats take in
roast sirloin with a flat mushroom, kale and béarnaise.

Chef Tom Penhaul **Owner** Richard Tubb **Times** 12-3/6-9
Closed 25 Dec **Prices** Service optional **Wines** 13 bottles
over £30, 28 bottles under £30, 7 by glass **Notes** Sunday
L fr £9.95, Vegetarian available **Seats** 40
Children Portions, Menu **Parking** Village square

Paul Ainsworth at No. 6

PADSTOW   **MAP 2 SW97**

Modern British **V**

Bold, flavour-driven cooking from a true culinary maestro

☎ 01841 532093
6 Middle St PL28 8AP
e-mail: enquiries@number6inpadstow.co.uk
dir: A30 follow signs for Wadebridge then sign to Padstow

Padstow has long been a foodie magnet, thanks to a certain Mr Stein and his Seafood Restaurant (see entry). But in a sense it's now the turn of Mr Ainsworth to pull in the food-loving crowds, especially after his appearances representing the South West on BBC Two's *Great British Menu*. A small Georgian townhouse - No. 6 - just off Padstow's main high street is where you'll find him (unless he's filming for the telly, of course). He put his

name above the door of this 18th century building in 2008, having honed his skills in London working with some of the top names in the business (including Gordon Ramsay and Marcus Wareing). It's a smart, contemporary-looking restaurant spread across several small rooms, with tightly set tables and a warm, buzzy vibe with gentle music playing and friendly, eager to please staff. The food surely can't fail to please: based on peerless Cornish produce, rooted in the classics but brought bang up-to-date with lashings of imaginative ideas and slick presentation, it's the kind of food that makes you want to come back for more - and more. Smoked cod's roe with crackling and superb mini loaves of hot, home-made bread give a hint of the delights to come, before a meal gets properly underway with something like blow-torched mackerel, accurately cooked and with a chargrilled flavour, served with a textbook celeriac remoulade, Parma ham and pickled cucumber - a simple, flavour-packed starter. Main-course 'salmon and lobster' comes as a lightly cooked piece of sea-fresh

fish, a succulent lobster tail and claw and a perfectly made ravioli, with English mustard, sea purslane and cheddar cleverly bringing the whole dish together. 'Chocolate cake - pistachio, Caramac, dark chocolate sorbet' is an inspired dessert, the 'cake' actually being pistachio, embedded with crunchy glazed nuts, and the chocolate coming as a ganache covered with thin chocolate, which turns into a wickedly indulgent molten chocolate and caramel sauce when the liquid Caramac is poured over.

Chef Paul Ainsworth **Owner** Paul Ainsworth
Times 12-3/6-10 Closed 24-26 Dec, 7-31 Jan, Sun-Mon
Prices Fixed L 2 course £18, Fixed D 3 course fr £17, Tasting menu £65, Starter £11-£12, Main £25-£31, Dessert £9-£21, Service optional **Wines** 53 bottles over £30, 18 bottles under £30, 16 by glass **Notes** Vegetarian menu **Seats** 40, Pr/dining room 22 **Children** Portions, Menu **Parking** Harbour car park and on street

The Seafood Restaurant

PADSTOW   **MAP 2 SW97**

Traditional, International Seafood **V** 🍷 NOTABLE WINE LIST

Inspired seafood cooking at the Stein flagship

☎ 01841 532700
Riverside PL28 8BY
e-mail: reservations@rickstein.com
dir: Follow signs for town centre. Restaurant on left of riverside

The large, ever-packed restaurant on the quayside is where the Stein brand started out, humbly enough, and although the empire has mushroomed, the mothership still embraces the basic concept of taking the catch straight from where it is landed in through the kitchen door to be treated simply - no foams, fussing or fads here, thank you. Spread around a central seafood bar, where you can watch the brigade assembling those

magnificent platters of super-fresh crustaceans, the restaurant is an airy, bustling space of blond wood, white walls, colourful splashes of contemporary art, and tables dressed in their best linen. Things haven't stood still, though: as armchair cooks may have noted, Stein's many TV travel cookery programmes have had a major influence on the repertoire, so while the roots, and indeed heart, are still clearly in France, the classic platters of fresh seafood are now outnumbered by ideas that take their inspiration from Spain, southeast Asia, Japan, and the swampy southern states of the USA. Essentially, though, the Stein culinary ethos has always been about keeping things simple, avoiding ephemeral fashions, and sticking to the business of dishing up seafood of exemplary quality and freshness in a relaxed and buzzy ambience. And things don't come much more straightforward and home-grown than a pile of deep-fried Hereford river prawns with aïoli to get things of the blocks, or you might go for palourde clams grilled a la plancha and served with olive oil, parsley and lemon juice. Main courses bring out the big

guns of the fish world, which are often at their best when given simple, classic treatment, as in a roast slab of turbot with hollandaise sauce. Elsewhere, a luxuriant Newlyn fish pie, packed with lobster, prawns, monkfish and scallops in a seafood velouté with truffle oil competes for your attention with Indonesian seafood curry with monkfish, squid and prawns.

Chef Stephane Delourme **Owner** R & J Stein
Times 12-2/7-10 Closed 25-26 Dec, 1 May, D 24 Dec
Prices Fixed L 3 course £29.95-£37, Starter £9.50-£25.50, Main £18-£49.50, Dessert £8.90-£9.20, Service optional **Wines** 31 bottles over £30, 25 bottles under £30, 22 by glass **Notes** Vegetarian menu **Seats** 120 **Children** Portions, Menu **Parking** Pay & display opposite

Save on Hotels. Book at **theAA.com/hotel**

CORNWALL & ISLES OF SCILLY 101 ENGLAND

PENZANCE *continued*

Harris's Restaurant

◉ Modern European 🍷

Clearly focused, unfussy food just off the high street

☎ 01736 364408
46 New St TR18 2LZ
e-mail: contact@harrissrestaurant.co.uk
dir: Located down narrow cobbled street opposite Lloyds TSB & the Humphry Davy statue

Harris's is an unshowy, reassuringly traditional restaurant with wooden floors, clothed tables, and an engaging atmosphere generated in part by unflappable and friendly service. The emphasis is on seafood, carefully and unfussily prepared, from a simple starter of smoked salmon with white crabmeat, or grilled scallops with herb dressing, to accurately timed roast John Dory with pesto, or a whole lobster in buttery lemon sauce. For meat-eaters there's gutsy duck terrine with green tomato chutney, followed by noisettes of local lamb with rosemary sauce and fennel purée, and a meal could be capped off by iced lemon soufflé in a dark chocolate case.

Chef Roger Harris **Owner** Roger & Anne Harris **Times** 12-2/7-9.30 Closed 3 wks winter, 25-26 Dec, 1 Jan, Sun (also Mon in winter), L Mon **Prices** Starter £8.50-£8.95, Main £14.95-£29.50, Dessert £7.85, Service added but optional 10% **Wines** 6 by glass **Notes** Vegetarian available, Dress restrictions, Smart casual **Seats** 40, Pr/dining room 20 **Parking** On street, local car park

The Navy Inn

◉ Modern British 🍷

Enterprising seafood dishes - and more - just off the seafront

☎ 01736 333232
Lower Queen St TR18 4DE
e-mail: keir@navyinn.co.uk
dir: In town centre, follow Chapel St for 50yds, right into Queen St to end

The Navy is a small whitewashed pub just off the seafront, with a boarded floor and a nautical theme. It's an atmospheric place, with customers chatting over a pint at the bar, pleasant and willing service, and an enthusiastic and dedicated brigade in the kitchen. Seafood comes from nearby Newlyn fish market and meat from Cornish farms or the local butcher, and it all gets turned into some bright contemporary dishes. Start with well-timed chargrilled John Dory fillet with lime and smoked haddock salad, and move on to seared scallops with black pudding purée and quince paste. Dedicated meat-eaters could opt for duck terrine with rhubarb purée and pickled vegetables, then seared venison loin served with tomato gnocchi, braised shallots and roast tomatoes. All comers could end with an enterprising dessert like a trio of apple (rich curd, fritters and sorbet with cinnamon).

Chef Keir Meikle, Jay Orrey **Owner** Keir Meikle **Times** 12-10 Closed 26 Dec **Prices** Starter £4.50-£8.95, Main £10.50-£17.95, Dessert £5.95-£8.95, Service optional **Wines** 7 bottles over £30, 30 bottles under £30, 9 by glass **Notes** Sunday L £11.50-£13.50, Vegetarian available **Seats** 46 **Children** Portions, Menu **Parking** 30 mtrs free parking on promenade

| **PERRANUTHNOE** | Map 2 SW52 |

The Victoria Inn

◉ Modern British 🍷

Top-notch ingredients in lovely village inn

☎ 01736 710309
TR20 9NP
e-mail: enquiries@victoriainn-penzance.co.uk
dir: A30 to Penzance, A394 to Helston. After 2m turn right into Perranuthnoe, pub is on right on entering the village

Good beaches and lovely pubs are not quite 10-a-penny in Cornwall, but the county has more than its fair share. And Perranuthnoe has a couple of crackers. The beach is a draw for holiday-makers, whilst The Victoria Inn attracts anyone who knows a good thing when they see it. It is still an unspoilt pub with all the natural west-country charm you'd hope for, with real ales on tap and a lack of pretension all round, whilst Stewart Eddy's straight-up, clearly focused cooking elevates the place still further. Whether you eat in the bar or the marginally more formal dining area, you'll get fine, fresh regional produce and clear-headed food. There's Cornish crab, of course, but this time with warm garlic toast, pickled fennel and herb salad and aïoli; next up, perhaps slow-roasted Primrose Herd belly of pork, or wild mushroom and local vegetable risotto with Lyburn cheese. Valrhona dark chocolate and espresso mousse with Cornish sea salt and caramel sauce and coffee ice cream reveals the chef's experience under the tutelage of the great and the good.

Chef Stewart Eddy **Owner** Stewart & Anna Eddy **Times** 12-2/6.30-9 Closed 25-26 Dec, 1 Jan, Mon (off season), D Sun **Prices** Starter £5-£7.95, Main £10.95-£18.95, Dessert £5.95-£8.25, Service optional **Wines** 4 bottles over £30, 34 bottles under £30, 7 by glass **Notes** Sunday L £9.95-£18.95, Vegetarian available **Seats** 60 **Children** Portions, Menu **Parking** 10, On street

| **PORTHLEVEN** | Map 2 SW62 |

Kota Restaurant with Rooms

◉ British, Pacific Rim 🍷

Asian-influenced modern British cooking by the sea

☎ 01326 562407
Harbour Head TR13 9JA
e-mail: kota@btconnect.com
dir: B3304 from Helston into Porthleven, Kota on harbour head opposite slipway

Chef-proprietor Jude Kereama has Maori, Chinese and Malaysian blood in his veins, so you can expect vibrant pacific rim fusion cooking in his relaxed bistro in an 18th-century corn mill on Porthleven harbour. In such a setting, local fish naturally plays a starring role (Kota is Maori for shellfish, by the way): exciting and inventive dishes see Far-Eastern flavours colliding creatively with tastes from elsewhere - so you could start with Falmouth Bay oysters au naturel with shallot vinegar, or take them tempura-battered with wasabi tartare, while Cornish mussels could arrive with tamarind, chilli and coconut broth. The good ideas keep coming: pan-fried hake with prawn and green pea risotto, samphire and a rich bisque sauce hits all the right notes, and if you're in a meaty mood, the likes of Cornish sirloin steak teamed with a beef and mushroom pie, spinach, horseradish mash and watercress purée will satisfy. Finish with a millefeuille of rhubarb parfait with green apple sorbet.

Chef Jude Kereama **Owner** Jude & Jane Kereama **Times** 5.30-9 Closed 25 Dec, Jan, Sun (also Mon off season), L all week **Prices** Prices not confirmed Service optional, Groups min 6 service 10% **Wines** 13 by glass **Notes** Vegetarian available **Seats** 40 **Children** Portions, Menu **Parking** On street

| **PORTLOE** | Map 2 SW93 |

The Lugger Hotel

◉◉ European

Enterprising cooking by the harbour

☎ 01872 501322
TR2 5RD
e-mail: reservations.lugger@ohiml.com
web: www.luggerhotel.com
dir: A390 to Truro, B3287 to Tregony, A3078 (St Mawes Rd), left for Veryan, left for Portloe

Dating from the 16th century, now a luxury hotel, The Lugger overlooks the sea and tiny harbour of this picturesque Roseland Peninsula village, with a terrace outside the smart restaurant for summer dining. Local ingredients are the kitchen's linchpin, particularly seafood, which might appear as moules marinière, or crab salad, followed by cod fillet with caper and lemon butter. Elsewhere, look for contemporary treatments of maple-glazed pork belly with a scallop and cauliflower cream, and pigeon with beetroot and pomegranate salad, then pheasant breast with basil polenta, dried tomatoes and game chips, and saddle of venison with bitter chocolate jus, spinach and dauphinoise potatoes. Cornish cheeses are alternatives to puddings like orange pannacotta with poached rhubarb.

Times 12.30-2.30/7-9

PORTSCATHO — Map 2 SW83

Driftwood

◎◎◎ – *see opposite*

ROCK — Map 2 SW97

Restaurant Nathan Outlaw

◎◎◎ – *see opposite*

ST AGNES — Map 2 SW75

Rose-in-Vale Country House Hotel

◎ Traditional and Modern British

Modern country cooking in a Cornish valley

☎ 01872 562202
Mithian TR5 0QD
e-mail: reception@rose-in-vale-hotel.co.uk
web: www.rose-in-vale-hotel.co.uk
dir: Take A30 S towards Redruth. At Chiverton Cross rdbt take B3277 signed St Agnes. In 500mtrs turn at tourist info sign for Rose-in-Vale. Into Mithian, right at Miners Arms, down hill

The creeper-clad, stone-built Georgian country house hides in its own little valley in Cornwall, amid highly attractive gardens. It's run with exemplary solicitude by the Evans family, and has at its heart an elegantly attired, chandeliered white dining room called The Valley, where floral curtains frame the pastoral view. Contemporary country-house cooking is the order of the day, starting perhaps with Exe Estuary mussels given the marinière treatment, or smoked haddock and leek risotto. Main courses draw on local fish landed at St Agnes - maybe sea bass stuffed with a mousse of scallops and tarragon, and accompanied by asparagus and a raviolo of lobster - but there may also be pan-roasted rump of local lamb with ratatouille and crushed potatoes. Hazelnut and muscovado tart with salted caramel ice cream is the trendy way to finish. Attention to detail extends to canapés and amuse-bouche, and Sundays see a carvery operation spring into action.

Times 12-2/7-9 Closed 2 wks Jan, L Mon-Wed (winter)

ST AUSTELL — Map 2 SX05

Austell's

◎◎ Modern British ♨

Sophisticated dining near the beach

☎ 01726 813888
10 Beach Rd PL25 3PH
e-mail: brett@austells.net
dir: From A390 towards Par, 0.5m after Charlestown rdbt at 2nd lights turn right. Left at rdbt. Restaurant 600yds on right

In a small parade of shops on the road to Carlyon Bay, Austell's is a restaurant of cool, uncluttered elegance, with a wooden floor, artwork on plain walls and slatted-back chairs at wooden tabletops; it's split-level, with diners on the raised area so they can see the chefs at work in the open-plan kitchen. Seasonality means the menus change regularly, and everything is made in-house, from breads (among them maybe rosemary and pesto) to petits fours. The cooking, based on contemporary British ideas, is honest, accurate and of clearly defined upfront flavours. Typical of starters is a plate of seared scallops (local, of course) with chorizo, pea mousse and herb salad - a good balance of tastes and textures. Among main courses, peach purée and jus infused with foie gras add an extra oomph to pink, crisp-skinned duck breast, served with wilted spinach and sautéed potatoes. End with a theatrical flourish with basil crème brûlée, served flaming, the sugar still caramelising, accompanied by velvety poached strawberries and punchy strawberry ice cream.

Chef Brett Camborne-Paynter **Owner** Brett Camborne-Paynter **Times** 6-10 Closed 1-15 Jan, Mon, L Mon-Sat **Prices** Service optional **Wines** 8 bottles over £30, 32 bottles under £30, 11 by glass **Notes** £14.95-£19.95, Vegetarian available **Seats** 48 **Children** Portions **Parking** 30

Carlyon Bay Hotel

◎ Modern & Traditional British **NEW**

Simple traditions on the St Austell clifftop

☎ 01726 812304
Sea Rd, Carlyon Bay PL25 3RD
e-mail: reservations@carlyonbay.com
web: www.carlyonbay.com
dir: From St Austell, follow signs for Charlestown. Carlyon Bay signed on left, hotel at end of Sea Rd

Surveying the rugged Cornish coast from its clifftop perch above St Austell, the creeper-curtained Carlyon Bay Hotel is an imposing presence above the bay. Within its 250 acres of grounds you'll find a full complement of spa and leisure facilities, including its own championship golf course. Taking care of the gastronomic side of things is the aptly-named Bay View Restaurant, where huge windows allow maximum exposure to the sea views, and everything is smartly turned out, from the linen-swathed tables to the amicable, black-and-white-uniformed staff. The kitchen tacks a pretty traditional course, keeping things simple and relying on the quality and provenance of its ingredients to win plaudits. Cornish mussels with cider, cream and garlic is a good way to start, then follow with roast rump of new season's lamb with pea purée, creamed potato, and rosemary and redcurrant sauce. To finish, vanilla pannacotta gets a lift from tangy poached rhubarb and crunchy pistachio.

Times 12-2/7-9.30 **Prices** Starter £4-£11.50, Main £8.50-£29.50 **Notes** Fixed Table D'hote & L menu available, Sunday L, Dress restrictions, Smart casual, no ripped denim or sportswear

The Cornwall Hotel, Spa & Estate

◎ British, International ♨

Smart manor house with modish cooking

☎ 01726 874050 & 874051
Pentewan Rd, Tregorrick PL26 7AB
e-mail: enquiries@thecornwall.com
dir: A391 to St Austell then B3273 towards Mevagissey. Hotel approx 0.5m on right

If you have a lovely stay here and can't drag yourself away, you could always buy one of the holiday homes in the surrounding 43 acres of parkland. But fear not if your budget won't run to that, for you can simply return to eat here again in either the smart Arboretum restaurant, the more informal Acorns Brasserie, or sit out in the sunshine on the Parkland Terrace. There's a lot going on here. You'll find the Arboretum restaurant in the old White House part of the hotel - once a private mansion - and it's a classy space (two spaces really) done out in fashionably muted colour tones. The menu here takes a broadly contemporary path, drawing inspiration from far and wide whilst making good use of regional ingredients. So you might start with hoisin duck spring rolls with a sweet chilli dip, followed by pan-seared line-caught sea bass with Thai purée and vegetable stir-fry.

Chef Carl Milton **Owner** Rudrum Holdings **Times** 12.30-2.30/6.30-9.30 **Prices** Fixed D 3 course £25-£35, Service optional **Wines** 16 bottles over £30, 19 bottles under £30, 12 by glass **Notes** Sunday L, Vegetarian available, Dress restrictions, Smart casual, Civ Wed 60 **Seats** 38, Pr/dining room 16 **Children** Portions, Menu **Parking** 100

Driftwood

PORTSCATHO	MAP 2 SW83

Modern European

Accomplished cooking in a stunning coastal setting

☎ 01872 580644
Rosevine TR2 5EW
e-mail: info@driftwoodhotel.co.uk
dir: 5m from St Mawes off the A3078, signed Rosevine

If Cornwall has been redefined in recent years as a more thrusting and dynamic county, then Driftwood has been at the forefront. It has an awful lot going for it. Take the location, for a start, more Cornish than a pasty on a surfboard, the clifftop setting above the azure (ish) sea and crashing waves is spectacular, best enjoyed from the decked terrace of course, glass of wine in hand. And the hotel itself has a beachcomber vibe going on, which is both chic and relaxed, and entirely on the money. The restaurant, for example, has a contemporary neutrality that seems entirely fitting in the circumstances, with muted natural shades, pale wood floor, and expanses of

whiteness. Chris Eden heads up the team in the kitchen with local pride, considerable skill, and bags of good ideas. This is modern contemporary cooking out of the top drawer. There's a definite local flavour to the menu - provenance is a watchword - and there is no lack of creativity and modish thinking. Flavour is to the fore, for example, in a first course dish of roast quail, with confit leg, pancetta, chanterelles, celery purée and sunflower seeds, and in main-course poached brill, the fish cooked perfectly and served with quinoa, chunks and purée of Ironbark pumpkin, monk's beard and oyster leaves, and an accompanying crab emulsion. For dessert, a dark chocolate cylinder with sea salt caramel and caramelised white chocolate ends the meal on a real high. The service style suits the mood of the place, being both relaxed and entirely on the ball, and everything - including the excellent canapés, amuse, breads, and pre-desserts - adds up to an impressive whole.

Chef Christopher Eden **Owner** Paul & Fiona Robinson **Times** 12-2/7-9.30 Closed early Dec-early Feb, L all week (ex Thu-Sat, Jun-Sep) **Prices** Fixed D 3 course fr £50,

Tasting menu fr £80, Service optional **Wines** 40 bottles over £30, 17 bottles under £30, 6 by glass **Notes** Tasting menu available, Vegetarian available **Seats** 34 **Parking** 20

Restaurant Nathan Outlaw

ROCK	MAP 2 SW97

Modern British, Seafood V 🍷 NOTABLE WINE LIST

Refined multi-course seafood dining from a modern master

☎ 01208 863394 & 862737
The St Enodoc Hotel PL27 6LA
e-mail: mail@nathan-outlaw.co.uk
dir: M5/A30/A39 to Wadebridge. B3314 to Rock

Such is Nathan Outlaw's enduring affection for Cornwall, its landscapes, produce and people, that he has put down deep roots here. It's a long slog to London to do a TV slot on *Saturday Kitchen*, but he has weathered the challenge of running a fine-dining destination restaurant at Rock (plus Outlaw's Seafood & Grill here and now at The Capital Hotel in Knightsbridge) with the media demands our modern culinary masters face, and managed it better than most. The St Enodoc Hotel is a sparely elegant

contemporary refuge, with natural hues from slate floors and solid wood, the neutrality of which avoids detracting from the sumptuous views over the Camel Estuary. The dining room has a monochrome look, but a gentle rather than stark one, and offers porthole peeps of the kitchen activity at one end. The fixed-menu drill continues to be refined and elaborated: now six fish dishes, followed by cheese and a brace of desserts, it's an even-paced gastronomic experience to write home about. Some of the dishes may seem familiar if you're lucky enough to be a regular, but there is actually a creative degree of remixing going on, whereby accompaniments are tried out with different principals, and the same species may appear cooked one night and raw the next. A slice of uncooked turbot is scented with basil and orange, before the famous soused mackerel appears, perhaps simply garnished with cucumber and dill this time. Proper tartare dressing, all punchy acidity, adorns full-flavoured roast cod for your third course, followed by scallops along with a fried oyster, hazelnuts and watercress. Next, red

mullet benefits from a Mediterranean treatment, with squid, tomato and paprika, and as if all that weren't enough, your sixth course might be a light spin on bouillabaisse, comprising sea bass, gurnard and brill in Porthilly sauce, a smooth amalgam of mussels and clams from the nearby bay. Excellent south-western cheeses provide the bridgehead to desserts, perhaps burnt gooseberry and ginger custard, and then caramelised bread-and-butter pudding with raspberries. The wine choices served optionally with the menu are inspirational, worth the extra outlay for Koshu from Japan, Pecorino from eastern Italy and Canadian ice wine, via the local Camel Valley Pinot Noir sparkler, of course.

Chef Nathan Outlaw, Chris Simpson **Owner** Nathan Outlaw **Times** 7-9 Closed Xmas, Jan, Sun-Mon, L all week **Prices** Tasting menu £99, Service added but optional 12.5% **Wines** 180 bottles over £30, 2 bottles under £30, 40 by glass **Notes** Tasting menu 10 course, Vegetarian menu, Dress restrictions, Smart casual **Seats** 20 **Parking** 30

Carbis Bay Hotel

◉ Traditional, Mediterranean

Contemporary cooking and panoramic views

☎ 01736 795311
Carbis Bay TR26 2NP
e-mail: info@carbisbayhotel.co.uk
web: www.carbisbayhotel.co.uk
dir: A3074, through Lelant. 1m, at Carbis Bay 30yds
before lights turn right into Porthrepta Rd to sea & hotel

Dating from the late 19th century, the family-run Carbis
Bay Hotel has stunning views over the eponymous waters
from its lofty position. The panoramic view can also be
appreciated from the Sands restaurant, a spacious,
traditionally decorated room, where the menus are
evidence of a kitchen working in the modern vein, with
starters encompassing battered haloumi on minted pea
purée with beetroot and balsamic dressing, and duck and
bean sprout spring roll with hoisin dipping sauce. The
same broad sweep of styles is seen in main courses of
honey-glazed duck breast with an orange and Cointreau
sauce accompanied by patatas bravas and asparagus,
and well-timed fried cod served on parmesan mash with
creamed leeks and a Noilly Prat reduction. Crème brûlée
is a classical rendition, flavoured with Baileys and
garnished with raspberries.

Times 12-3/6-9 Closed 3 wks Jan

Garrack Hotel & Restaurant

◉ Modern British

Inventive cooking and stunning views

☎ 01736 796199 & 792910
Burthallan Ln, Higher Ayr TR26 3AA
e-mail: reception@garrack.com
dir: Exit A30 for St Ives, then from B3311 follow brown
signs for Tate Gallery, then brown Garrack signs

From its lofty position high above the tourist crowds of
the town centre, this ivy-clad granite hotel's show-
stopping views over Porthmeor beach and the Atlantic are
a diner's dream-ticket. The unstuffy, light-and-airy
restaurant's simple design blends traditional and
contemporary elements to allow those stunning vistas
pride of place, while menus likewise demonstrate a
kitchen making the most of Cornwall's natural resources
in accomplished modern dishes of creativity and
ambition. Seafood rightly scores high in the billing;
perhaps seared fillets of red mullet teamed with pea
risotto, tapenade of black olives and wilted spinach,
while from the land, perhaps another dish with a sunny-
climes influence like pan-roasted breast of free-range
chicken with chorizo, root vegetable and white bean stew
with saffron aïoli. To finish, vanilla pannacotta with
forced rhubarb, red berry reduction and fresh strawberries
fits the bill.

Times 12.30-2/6-9 Closed 5 days Xmas, L Mon-Sat

Porthminster Beach Restaurant

◉ Modern Mediterranean V ☺

Seafood-led fusion cookery on the beach at St Ives

☎ 01736 795352
TR26 2EB
e-mail: pminster@btconnect.com
dir: On Porthminster Beach, beneath the St Ives Railway
Station

They got there early and bagged themselves a prime spot
on the beach at St Ives, beneath the towering eminence
of Porthminster Point, the better to look out over the
crashing waves breaking on spotless sands. It's a classic
contemporary seafood venue, with chilled-out staff, the
tiled interior opening onto outdoor decking, where you
might sit and set about a dish of crisp-fried salt-and-
spice squid with citrus miso under the Cornish sun. An
Australian chef ensures there's a lot of knowledgeable
fusion thinking going on, as in a main course of baked
pollock with smoked pancetta, celeriac, almonds, salsa
verde, a razor clam and truffled parcel of egg yolk. Or go
with the much simpler crab linguine with Fowey mussels,
dressed in chilli, garlic, parsley and lemon. There are
good vegetarian dishes too, and sweet treats such as
coconut rice pudding with mandarin sorbet, mango and
peanut brittle.

Chef M Smith **Owner** Jim Woolcock, David Fox, Roger &
Tim Symons, M Smith **Times** 12-3.30/6-9.30 Closed 25
Dec, Mon (Winter) **Prices** Prices not confirmed Service
optional **Wines** 16 bottles over £30, 26 bottles under £30,
9 by glass **Notes** Vegetarian menu **Seats** 60
Children Portions **Parking** 300yds (railway station)

The Queens

◉ Modern British ☺

Purposeful pub cooking near the harbour

☎ 01736 796468
2 High St TR26 1RR
e-mail: info@queenshotelstives.com
dir: A3074 to town centre. With station on right, down hill
to High St

The catering side of the operation may have been taken
up a gear with refurbishment in 2011, but this is still
pre-eminently a local pub, and a friendly and welcoming
one at that. A short stroll from the harbour, it's a granite-
fronted Georgian building, with a pleasing ambience of
unclothed tables, sofas and bare floorboards inside. The
short menu is chalked up on boards, and the approach is
nice and relaxed. That said, the cooking has a real sense
of purpose and drive these days, with straightforward
dishes cooked and presented with simple flair. Good
husbanding of leftovers results in a starter of massively
enjoyable pork bubble-and-squeak with seared hog's
pudding and a poached egg, while the right attention to
detail produces a piece of crisp-skinned, moist-fleshed
stone bass for main, served with a fondue dressing of
mussels, tomato and saffron. A generous pairing of

meats might furnish a leg of confit duck with guinea
fowl, alongside roots and Puy lentils, and heritage
puddings such as apple crumble with vanilla ice cream
are bound to please.

Chef Matt Perry **Owner** Neythan Hayes
Times 12.30-2.30/6.30-9 Closed 25 Dec, Mon (Nov-Mar),
D Sun **Prices** Starter £3.50-£8, Main £8-£16, Dessert
£4-£6, Service optional **Wines** 3 bottles over £30, 20
bottles under £30, 12 by glass **Notes** Sunday L £9.50,
Vegetarian available **Seats** 50 **Children** Portions, Menu
Parking Station car park

Seagrass Restaurant

◉ Modern British NEW ☺

Splendid seafood straight from the bay

☎ 01736 793763
Fish St TR26 1LT
e-mail: info@seagrass-stives.com
dir: On Fish Street opposite the Sloop Pub

Its location on Fish Street is a serendipitous address for
this exciting newcomer to the St Ives foodie scene;
Seagrass has already made quite a splash with its
modern seafood-oriented cooking. Tucked away just off
the seafront, a secretive doorway leads up to the rather
cool, stylish first-floor restaurant, where the focus is
firmly on top-class seasonal Cornish produce. The kitchen
cuts no corners here, making everything - breads, stocks,
ice cream - from scratch, and maintaining strong supply
lines to local fishermen to ensure the shellfish that make
up the platters of fruits de mer are plucked fresh from the
bay. Make a start with pan-fried Cornish scallops with
cucumber, lime and avocado, then move on to salted cod
loin, matched enterprisingly with seafood cannelloni,
roast tomato velouté, peas, samphire and crispy sea
lettuce, and round off with pink grapefruit tart with
candied walnuts and crème fraîche.

Chef Tom Pryce **Owner** Scott & Julia Blair
Times 12.30-2.30/5.30-9.30 Closed Sun-Mon (Nov-Apr ex
BH), L all week (Oct-Apr ex BH), D 25 Dec,1 Jan
Prices Fixed D 3 course £19.95, Starter £7.95-£9.50,
Main £13.95-£22.95, Dessert £6.25-£9.50, Service
optional **Wines** 10 bottles over £30, 22 bottles under £30,
10 by glass **Notes** Vegetarian available **Seats** 32
Children Portions, Menu **Parking** The Sloop Car park

Save on Hotels. Book at **theAA.com/hotel**

CORNWALL & ISLES OF SCILLY 105 ENGLAND

ST MAWES
Map 2 SW83

Hotel Tresanton

◉◉◉ – see below

ST MELLION
Map 3 SX36

St Mellion International Resort

◉◉ Modern International

Accomplished cosmopolitan cooking in large golfing resort

☎ 01579 351351
PL12 6SD
e-mail: stmellion@crown-golf.co.uk
dir: On A388 about 4m N of Saltash

Surrounded by 450 acres of prime Cornish countryside, St Mellion is a modern development complete with golf course, spa and a restaurant - An Boesti - which is well worth a look. The room is spacious and elegant, and the team in the kitchen clearly sets itself high standards. The menu follows a modern cosmopolitan path, offering the likes of carpaccio with wasabi, pickled radish and mustard dressing, and sea bass fillet with a crab bhaji, asparagus, fennel herb, and sea foam. Dishes are intelligently judged - a starter of seared scallops with softly textured pork belly, black pudding and apple is a subtle assembly of flavours - and fine local produce is

treated with care: witness a simple and effective main course of roast pigeon, successfully partnered by shallot purée, beetroot and mushrooms. Breads are so good that most people ask for more, but don't overdo it if you want a pudding, such as a trio of chocolate, or deconstructed apple and blackberry crumble with saffron custard and blackberry parfait.

Chef Kevin Hartley **Owner** Crown Golf **Times** 6.30-9.30 Closed Xmas, New Year, Mon-Tue (off season), L all week **Prices** Prices not confirmed Service optional **Wines** 7 by glass **Notes** Sunday L, Vegetarian available, Dress restrictions, Smart casual, Civ Wed 300 **Seats** 60 **Children** Portions **Parking** 750

TALLAND BAY
Map 2 SX25

Talland Bay Hotel

◉◉ Modern

Coastal views and imaginative cooking

☎ 01503 272667
PL13 2JB
e-mail: info@tallandbayhotel.co.uk
web: www.tallandbayhotel.co.uk
dir: Signed from x-rds on A387 between Looe and Polperro

Dating back around 400 years, this charming whitewashed hotel is set about 150 feet above sea level in a quiet rural location between Looe and Polperro, just a few hundred yards from the beach. Inside there's lots of swagger - the style is decidedly contemporary with copious natty artworks - whilst the oak-panelled restaurant benefits from huge picture-windows opening out onto a terrace area with fab views across the bay. Local ingredients, particularly seafood, abound in imaginative dishes cooked with much flair and a lightness of touch. Expect the likes of Gevrik goats' cheese mousse with apricot and walnut bread and walnut dressing, followed by main-course seared Cornish seafood with new potatoes, smoked tomatoes, fennel céviche, olive tapenade and spiced fish velouté. Great local cheeses vie for attention alongside puds such as burnt cinnamon custard, apple doughnut and hazelnut tuile.

Times 12.30-2.30/6.30-9.30 Closed L Mon-Sat (Oct-mid Apr)

Hotel Tresanton

ST MAWES
MAP 2 SW83

British, Mediterranean

Bright modern cooking in super-stylish seafront hotel

☎ 01326 270055
27 Lower Castle Rd TR2 5DR
e-mail: info@tresanton.com
dir: On the waterfront in town centre

A quiet lane skirting the water's edge leads to this über-chic bolthole in fashionable St Mawes. Arriving at road level, you may wonder where the place actually is, but the discreet entrance leads a few steps up the hillside, and all is revealed: straggling different levels above the waterfront, the classy boutique hotel is fashioned from a cluster of old cottages that was once home to the yachting club. The nautical brigade are long gone, and a sprinkle of design magic by Olga Polizzi in the 1990s completed the hotel's transformation into one of Cornwall's A-list weekend retreats. The gorgeous terrace comes into its own on balmy summer days - just soak up those sea views sweeping all the way towards Pendennis Castle in Falmouth. If the weather forces you indoors, there's certainly no need to despair, as the restaurant has vast windows to give you the same views. The space is suffused with immaculately tasteful nautical stylishness and Mediterranean-inspired luminosity - jaunty seaside colours, vanilla-painted tongue-and-groove walls, and blue seats at pristine, white linen-clad tables on mosaic-tiled floors all add up to a delightful setting for the zesty modern Mediterranean-accented cooking. The culinary inspiration might come from the sun-drenched south, but raw materials are resolutely local throughout. A delicious pairing of John Dory with River Fal scallops, green beans and beetroot salsa, or Newlyn sardines with pizza bread, mozzarella, tomato and basil might set things up for a main course of herb crusted brill supported by potato gratin, leeks and pancetta. Local meat is always a good bet too - perhaps an imaginative coupling of Cornish duck with roast pork belly, lettuce hearts, green beans and pearl onions. West Country cheeses served with oatcakes and apple chutney are the alternative to sweet offerings such as pannacotta with champagne rhubarb.

Chef Paul Wadham **Owner** Olga Polizzi **Times** 12-2.30/7-9.30 Closed 2 wks Jan **Prices** Fixed L 2 course £22, Starter £8-£12, Main £18-£24, Dessert £6-£10, Service optional **Wines** 47 bottles over £30, 13 bottles under £30, 8 by glass **Notes** Sunday L £28, Vegetarian available, Civ Wed 45 **Seats** 60, Pr/dining room 45 **Children** Menu **Parking** 30

TRURO
Map 2 SW84

Bustophers Bar Bistro

◉ British, French ◎

Friendly neighbourhood bistro using good local produce

☎ 01872 279029
62 Lemon St TR1 2PN
e-mail: info@bustophersbarbistro.com
dir: Located on right, past Plaza Cinema up the hill

This longstanding neighbourhood bistro has a loyal following in Truro and it's easy to see why. An infectiously buzzy atmosphere is heightened by an open kitchen and a separate bar area, where some 20 wines are available by the glass. Staff are welcoming and the place holds equal appeal for romantic couples, business suits at lunchtime, and friends grabbing a few drinks for a post work catch-up. The décor is elegant and minimalist, broken up by some bold artwork on the walls, and tables outside are popular in the summertime. Modern bistro food using quality local ingredients is the name of the game here and daily specials are chalked up on the blackboard. You might start with a simple ham hock terrine with piccalilli, following on with turbot with crab risotto and spinach, or perhaps go for a classic moules marinières or the house burger. Custard tart with apple crumble ice cream hits the spot for dessert.

Chef Matt Long **Owner** Simon & Sue Hancock **Times** 12-2.30/5.30-9.30 Closed 25-26 Dec, 1 Jan **Prices** Fixed D 3 course £18, Starter £5-£8, Main £11-£21, Dessert £5-£8, Service optional, Groups min 8 service 10% **Wines** 20 bottles over £30, 40 bottles under £30, 19 by glass **Notes** Sunday L, Vegetarian available **Seats** 110, Pr/dining room 30 **Children** Portions, Menu **Parking** Moorfield NCP at rear of property

Indaba Fish

◉ Modern British, Seafood ◎

Modish seafood dishes in the city centre

☎ 01872 274700
Tabernacle St TR1 2EJ
e-mail: eating@indabafish.co.uk
dir: 100yds off Lemon Quay

On a quiet street, Indaba Fish is a buzzy restaurant with wooden floors and tables, high ceilings, banquettes and brown and cream leather-look seats, and some 'fish shoal' lampshades reflecting the seafood credentials of the place. Flavourful dishes with a pleasing lack of pretension are what to expect, the kitchen clearly in its element working in a variety of styles. Start with razor clams cooked with ginger, spring onions, chilli and soy, or prawn and squid escabèche with noodles. Crabs are chosen from a tank, and the whole of the kitchen's arsenal has been determined with quality in mind: tip-top monkfish tail, for instance, fried in vanilla flour served with spicy clams, butternut squash, peppers and coconut, or roast loin of cod with a gratin of mussels, pancetta, leeks and spinach. There are a couple of meat dishes,

and to finish might be rich chocolate and honeycomb tart with raspberry coulis.

Chef Robert Duncan **Owner** Stephen Shepherd **Times** 12-2.30/5.30-9.30 Closed Sun **Prices** Starter £5-£9, Main £12-£22, Dessert £6-£8, Service optional, Groups min 10 service 10% **Wines** 6 bottles over £30, 24 bottles under £30, 12 by glass **Notes** Pre-theatre menu 5.30-6.45 Mon-Sat 2/3 course £13.95/£16.95, Vegetarian available **Seats** 40, Pr/dining room 24 **Children** Portions **Parking** Car park opposite

Probus Lamplighter Restaurant

◉◉ Modern British ◎

Charming village restaurant with a local flavour

☎ 01726 882453
Fore St, Probus TR2 4JL
e-mail: maireadvogel@aol.com
dir: 5m from Truro on A390 towards St Austell

Chef-patron Robert Vogel used to be head chef on the QE2, where he got his sea legs and learned a thing or two about fancy presentation. His family-run restaurant, tucked away in Probus village, between St Austell and Truro, is in a 300-year-old former farmhouse with bags of period features (oak beams, roaring log fires), plus a charming country vibe. The food is unpretentious, seasonal stuff, with top West Country produce put to good use in satisfying modern British dishes. Start with a light and fluffy Cornish blue cheese soufflé with poached pears and walnut dressing, moving on to herb-crusted best end of Trudgian Farm lamb with a rolled, braised shoulder, dauphine potatoes and Merlot jus, or fillet of brill with herbed potatoes and saffron sauce. Finish with a chocolate tart paired with bourbon ice cream.

Chef Robert Vogel **Owner** Robert & Mairead Vogel **Times** 7-10 Closed Sun-Mon, L all week **Prices** Fixed D 3 course £32 **Wines** 7 by glass **Notes** Vegetarian available, Dress restrictions, Smart casual **Seats** 32, Pr/dining room 8 **Children** Portions **Parking** On street & car park

Tabb's

◉◉ Modern European ◎

Skilful contemporary cooking a short stroll from the city centre

☎ 01872 262110
85 Kenwyn St TR1 3BZ
e-mail: n.tabb@virgin.net
dir: Down hill past train station, right at mini rdbt, 200yds on left

London-trained Nigel Tabb forsook the smoke for the pleasant reaches of Cornwall, first in Portreath and latterly at this welcoming venue a short stroll from the centre of Truro. It's a neighbourhood restaurant of considerable charm, from the lavender walls to the cornucopia of local produce on offer, and the formidable range of skill that the chef-patron brings to his essentially simple modern dishes. Thinly sliced ballottine of pork and duck combines superlative meats, with good complements from warm tomato sauce and piccalilli.

Mains exhibit similarly fine judgment in the timing of a grilled fillet of hake, bedded on creamed mushroom and leek, in a vanilla-scented tomato dressing, or in offering a pair of venison cuts - fried fillet and pot-roasted shoulder - alongside caramelised orange, shallot cream and shredded parsnips in a port reduction. A burst of vibrant flavour provides a dazzling finale in the form of lime and Earl Grey cheesecake with strawberry and black pepper sorbet and orange sauce. Pedigree southwestern cheeses are the alternative.

Chef Nigel Tabb **Owner** Nigel Tabb **Times** 12-2/5.30-9.30 Closed 25 Dec, 1 Jan, 1 wk Jan, Sun-Mon, L Sat **Prices** Fixed L 2 course £19.50, Starter £7.25-£10.50, Main £15.75-£20.50, Dessert £7.50, Service optional **Wines** 18 bottles over £30, 28 bottles under £30, 15 by glass **Notes** L & Pre-theatre menu 5.30-6.45pm bookings only, Vegetarian available **Seats** 30 **Children** Portions **Parking** 200yds

VERYAN
Map 2 SW93

The Nare

◉ Traditional British ◎

Traditional cooking with panoramic views of the south Cornish coast

☎ 01872 501111
Carne Beach TR2 5PF
e-mail: stay@narehotel.co.uk
web: www.narehotel.co.uk
dir: From Tregony follow A3078 for approx 1.5m. Left at Veryan sign, through village towards sea & hotel

Traditional five-course table d'hôte dining is the deal in The Nare's main dining room, so expect well-drilled staff gliding unobtrusively between linen-clothed tables to deliver classic silver service each evening, with hors d'oeuvre and sweet trolleys trundled out to start and finish proceedings. The setting is one to savour, as the hotel perches above a secluded sandy beach, and with full-length windows on three sides there's nothing to intrude on spectacular views across Gerrans Bay. The kitchen isn't planning to push the culinary envelope here, preferring to put its faith in high calibre produce - particularly excellent local fish and seafood - cooked simply and accurately. Twice-baked Stilton soufflé with creamed leeks sets the ball rolling, while main course delivers roasted celeriac, spinach, wild mushrooms and pommes Anna as the accompaniment to a pavé of Cornish lamb. The Quarterdeck - see entry - is the more casual dining option.

Chef Richard James **Owner** T G H Ashworth **Times** 12.30-2.30/7.30-10 Closed L Mon-Sat **Prices** Service optional **Wines** 150 bottles over £30, 50 bottles under £30, 18 by glass **Notes** Fixed D 5 course £50, Sunday L £33, Vegetarian available, Dress restrictions, Jacket and tie **Seats** 75 **Children** Portions, Menu **Parking** 70

The Quarterdeck at the Nare

⍟⍟ Traditional British ⏲

Superb local produce, creative cooking and fab sea views

☎ 01872 500000
Carne Beach TR2 5PF
e-mail: stay@narehotel.co.uk
dir: From Tregony follow A3078 for approx 1.5m. Left at Veryan sign, through village towards sea & hotel

Overlooking a heavenly sandy beach, The Nare hotel has much to recommend it, including a brace of excellent restaurants. The Quarterdeck has its own entrance and a different, more unbuttoned vibe to its sister venue, the Dining Room (see entry for The Nare). The view is worth going out of your way for, and you get it whether you're out on the idyllic terrace breathing in the salty air, or indoors on a typically severe English summer's day, taking it all in through vast full-length windows in a yachtie-themed setting of polished teak, gingham seats and square rails. The kitchen ensures that peerless piscine produce from the local waters gets star billing in its confident modern dishes - perhaps seared scallops partnered with parsnip purée and truffled mushrooms, then John Dory with cider and thyme mussels, roast garlic and chive mash. Local meat fans will be pleased to learn that the prime protein hasn't clocked up many food miles either - loin of venison is served with butternut squash purée, girolles and potato gnocchi, while two could sign up to a rib of Heligan beef, and wrap things up with Valrhona chocolate fondant, rum ice cream and white chocolate sauce.

Chef Richard James **Owner** Toby Ashworth
Times 12.30-2.30/7-9.30 Closed 25 Dec, D 31 Dec
Prices Starter £7.50-£9, Main £14.50-£40, Dessert £7.50-£8.50, Service optional **Wines** 150 bottles over £30, 50 bottles under £30, 18 by glass **Notes** Vegetarian available, Dress restrictions, Smart casual after 7pm **Seats** 60 **Children** Portions, Menu **Parking** 60

WATERGATE BAY	Map 2 SW86

Fifteen Cornwall

⍟ Italian ⏲

Italian cooking, Jamie-style, on the beach

☎ 01637 861000
On The Beach TR8 4AA
e-mail: restaurant@fifteencornwall.co.uk
dir: M5 to Exeter & join A30 westbound. Exit Highgate Hill junct, following signs to airport and at T-junct after airport, turn left & follow road to Watergate Bay

Fifteen Cornwall reopened early in 2013 after a refit that saw the addition of a new antipasti bar and an improved kitchen, still open-to-view, now centred around a charcoal-fired Josper oven. It's a large restaurant, with a wooden floor, round-backed chairs at square and circular tables, teardrop-style lampshades and fabulous beach views. Jamie Oliver's principle hasn't changed: to give young people a solid grounding in kitchen skills and experience (he now has 20 apprentices here), and it seems to be working well judging by the quality of the food. Straightforward, unfussy Italian cooking is the order of the day, with dishes of upfront rustic flavours. Start with pasta - gnocchi with oxtail and sage, or taglierini with squid and mussels - and proceed to a steak with marrowbone and horseradish, monkfish with cime di rapa and rosemary, or duck with polenta and salsa verde. Had enough of tiramisù? Then go for lemon tart with rhubarb and clotted cream.

Chef Andy Appleton **Owner** Cornwall Foundation of Promise **Times** 12-2.30/6.15-9.45 **Prices** Fixed L 2 course £28, Tasting menu £60-£80, Starter £8-£11, Main £19-£20, Dessert £6-£8, Service optional **Wines** 13 by glass **Notes** Tasting menu D 5 course, ALC L only, Vegetarian available **Seats** 120, Pr/dining room 12 **Children** Portions, Menu **Parking** In front of restaurant & on site P&D

SCILLY, ISLES OF	

BRYHER	Map 2 SV81

Hell Bay

⍟⍟⍟ — *see below*

Hell Bay

BRYHER	MAP 2 SV81

Modern British **V**

Magisterial cooking on a barely inhabited island

☎ 01720 422947
TR23 0PR
e-mail: contactus@hellbay.co.uk
web: www.hellbay.co.uk
dir: Access by boat from Penzance, plane from Exeter, Newquay or Land's End

Bryher is the smallest of the five inhabited Scillies, less than a mile across at its widest point and about a mile-and-a-half top to bottom. A little to the west of Tresco, which looks like a bustling metropolis by comparison, it consists of a gentle undulation of granite hills, leading down to sweeping sandy beaches crunchy with seashells. Hell Bay may sound like something out of the Wild West, but the west of Bryher is entirely peaceable, and makes a supremely relaxing location for this Atlantic-facing boutique hotel in its little cove. A stunning art collection includes works by Barbara Hepworth and Patrick Heron, as well as contemporary Scillonian and Cornish painters, and the abstract work in particular looks superb in the daylight-filled, blond-wood ambience of the public rooms. As you would expect, fine fresh seafood is a strong suit of the kitchen, with local crabs and saltwater fish in evidence on the daily-changing menus, supplemented by thoroughbred Tresco beef, the latter perhaps appearing in a main course of seared fillet and braised blade, with glazed shallots and onion purée in red wine jus. A magisterial confidence in the cooking is evidenced by the willingness to leave well alone rather than strive for constant novelty, so brill might simply turn up in a saffron-scented mussel broth with braised baby gem, but nor are interesting ideas lacking. A starter of salt cod cured in Indian spices, with parsnip salsa and korma sauce, efficiently primes the taste buds, while main might involve partnering lobster ravioli with roast monkfish tail in bouillabaisse-style sauce. Desserts span the technical range, from apple tarte fine with Calvados sauce and vanilla ice cream, to dark chocolate samosa with caramelised banana, banoffee ice cream and a sesame seed tuile, or there are excellent cheeses, most likely including creamy Yarg and the Gorgonzola-ish Cornish Blue.

Chef Richard Kearsley **Owner** Tresco Estate
Times 12-2/7-9.30 Closed 2 Nov-17 Mar **Prices** Fixed D 3 course fr £39, Service optional **Wines** 20 bottles over £30, 30 bottles under £30, 11 by glass **Notes** Vegetarian menu, Dress restrictions, Smart casual **Seats** 70, Pr/dining room 12 **Children** Portions

TRESCO — Map 2 SV81

New Inn

◉ Modern, Traditional

Simple and direct cooking at a welcoming Scillies inn

☎ 01720 423006 & 422867
TR24 0QQ
e-mail: newinn@tresco.co.uk
web: www.tresco.co.uk
dir: Ferry or light plane from Land's End, Newquay or Exeter; 250yds from harbour (private island, contact hotel for details)

A popular venue for Tresco walkers, the New Inn is reliably full of banter and bonhomie, with eating spread across the main bar, the residents' dining room and a pavilion. It all feels reassuringly lived-in, and outdoor eating in the garden with sea views (it's only a short hop back from the waterfront) is a real treat, as is getting bedded in here on a rough winter's night. Scilly crab and baby leek tart blends its fine components into a soufflé-like filling, garnished with dressed leaves, and could be followed by seared venison steak with braised red cabbage, fine beans and truffle-oiled mash, a simple, direct and uncluttered way of presenting a great piece of meat. Finish with enjoyably bitter chocolate and pecan brownie, served hot with vanilla ice cream.

Chef Alex Smith **Owner** Mr Robert Dorrien-Smith
Times 12-2/6.30-9 **Prices** Starter £3-£7, Main £8-£25, Dessert £5-£6, Service optional **Wines** 11 by glass
Notes Sunday L £12.50-£14, Vegetarian available
Seats 30 **Children** Portions, Menu **Parking** Car free Island

CUMBRIA

ALSTON — Map 18 NY74

Lovelady Shield Country House Hotel

◉◉ Modern British ◉

Refined modern dining in intimate country house

☎ 01434 381203
CA9 3LF
e-mail: enquiries@lovelady.co.uk
dir: 2m E of Alston, signed off A689 at junct with B6294

The seductively situated Lovelady Shield sits among three acres of lush gardens with the River Nent running past, and its charming Georgian features succeed in enhancing further any romantic notions. It looks pretty peachy on the inside, with those generous Georgian proportions and a comfortingly smart and traditional décor. The dining room is suitably elegant with its pastel hues, and service from the friendly and approachable team is just the ticket. The menus follow the seasons and there's a gentle modernism to the output. Seared scallops might come with a poached mousse and trio of cauliflower preparations, for example, or there might be seared pigeon breast with a potato pancake, braised red cabbage, Jerusalem artichoke purée and pancetta crisp. Next up, roast loin of venison with ox tongue, rösti potato gâteau and Scotch quail's egg competes for your attention with poached whiting with smoked haddock brandade and mussel minestrone. There's plenty of modish thinking among desserts, too: Amalfi lemon tart with raspberry 'accompaniments' and gin and tonic gel, for example.

Chef Anthony Muir **Owner** Peter & Marie Haynes
Times 12-2/7-8.30 Closed L Mon-Sat **Prices** Tasting menu fr £58.50, Service optional **Wines** 100 bottles over £30, 50 bottles under £30, 11 by glass **Notes** 4 course D £46.50, Sunday L, Vegetarian available, Dress restrictions, No shorts, Civ Wed 100 **Seats** 30 **Children** Portions, Menu **Parking** 20

AMBLESIDE — Map 18 NY30

Drunken Duck Inn

◉◉ Modern British ◉

Superb local produce and contemporary seasonal cooking

☎ 015394 36347
Barngates LA22 0NG
e-mail: info@drunkenduckinn.co.uk
web: www.drunkenduckinn.co.uk
dir: Take A591 from Kendal, follow signs for Hawkshead (from Ambleside), in 2.5m sign for inn on right, 1m up hill

High above Lake Windermere, with breathtaking views of the fells, the inn is a combination of bar, restaurant and hotel. There may be the usual ceiling beams and wooden floors, but this is a slick, classy operation without any hint of chintz. The lunch menu, with orders placed at the bar, is a pretty impressive listing (think cheese soufflé, sirloin steak with béarnaise and fries, Cullen skink with pancetta and a poached egg), while the evening carte ups the ante. An amuse-bouche of perhaps pea and mint soup raises expectations before the arrival of a well-conceived, tasty starter of, say, lamb fillet on a dollop of mash surrounded by cockles and samphire in a tomato and tarragon jus, or crab ravioli in shellfish bisque. Main courses are along the lines of contemporary brasserie-style dishes, from ox cheek braised in red wine served with mash and bourguignon sauce, to crisp-skinned, succulent sea bass with a selection of accurately cooked vegetables. To finish, try Manchester tart with vanilla ice cream.

Chef Jonny Watson **Owner** Stephanie Barton
Times 12-4/6.30-9 Closed 25 Dec **Prices** Prices not confirmed Service optional **Wines** 26 by glass
Notes Sunday L, Vegetarian available **Seats** 52
Children Portions **Parking** 40

Rothay Manor

◉ Traditional British **V** ◉

Accurate cooking in a well-established hotel

☎ 015394 33605
Rothay Bridge LA22 0EH
e-mail: hotel@rothaymanor.co.uk
web: www.rothaymanor.co.uk
dir: In Ambleside follow signs for Coniston (A593). Manor 0.25m SW of Ambleside opposite rugby pitch

Rothay Manor has the sense of deep-seated tradition that comes from being run by the same family for 45 years. The Regency manor was built in 1822 by a Liverpool shipping merchant and is close by Ambleside, yet cushioned from its bustle by an acre of lovingly-maintained grounds. The restaurant goes for time-honoured Lakeland charm: candlelit mahogany tables are laid with crystal, china, silver and linen napkins, and tended by correctly formal but unstuffy staff. Flexibility has crept into the five-course dinner format, allowing diners to choose as many dishes as they are happy to take on; going for three courses from the gently-modernised country-house cooking, you might kick off with stilton, apricot and walnut pâté with home-made oat biscuits, then progress to Holker Hall wild mallard braised with damson gin, and served with juniper berry jus, braised red cabbage, and rosemary potatoes. At the end, choose between local cheeses or vanilla pannacotta with a compôte of rum-soaked raisins, and hazelnut ice cream.

Rothay Manor

Chef Jane Binns **Owner** Nigel Nixon **Times** 12.30-1.45/7-9 Closed 2-17 Jan, L 1 Jan, D 25 Dec **Prices** Fixed L 2 course fr £15.50, Fixed D 3 course £39.50-£50, Service optional **Wines** 10 by glass **Notes** ALC L only, Sunday L, Vegetarian menu, Dress restrictions, Smart casual **Seats** 65, Pr/dining room 34 **Children** Portions, Menu **Parking** 35

Waterhead Hotel

🏵 Modern British

Vibrant brasserie cooking on the edge of Windermere

☎ 015394 32566
Lake Rd LA22 0ER
e-mail: waterhead@englishlakes.co.uk
web: www.englishlakes.co.uk
dir: A591 into Ambleside, hotel opposite Waterhead Pier

The Waterhead is a townhouse hotel near Ambleside, so named for its strategic siting on the northern edge of Lake Windermere. It hardly needs saying that the surrounding countryside is breathtaking in its quiet majesty, and the hotel is a good place to stay for those on the Lakeland cultural trail. Wordsworth lived nearby, and don't forget Beatrix Potter, readings of whose works are thoughtfully piped into the lavatories for you. Don't get too engrossed in there, though, or you might miss the vibrant brasserie dining going on in the modernist Bar and Grill, with its blue glassware and purple-lit ceiling. Start with a meaty sharing platter of barbecue ribs, chipolata and fell-bred beef carpaccio, or something like sticky-toffee duck leg with wilted greens. Mains might offer a whole poussin with Cumbrian pancetta in red wine jus, or herbed lemon sole in smoked salmon butter, and then there's Grasmere gingerbread cheesecake to finish.

Times 11.30-7/7-9.30 Closed Xmas, New Year (only open to residents), L Mon-Sat

---

APPLEBY-IN-WESTMORLAND   **Map 18 NY62**

Appleby Manor Country House Hotel

🏵 Modern British

Peaceful rural views and modern country-house cooking

☎ 017683 51571
Roman Rd CA16 6JB
e-mail: reception@applebymanor.co.uk
web: www.applebymanor.co.uk
dir: M6 junct 40/A66 towards Brough. Take Appleby turn, then immediately right. Continue for 0.5m

This Victorian sandstone country-house hotel was sited in such a way that all the public rooms, including the oak-panelled restaurant and the conservatory extension, have unparalleled views over Appleby Castle and the Eden Valley towards the fells of the Lake District. The kitchen makes good use of local ingredients and generally follows a well-tried route: pan-fried calves' liver, for instance, with truffled celeriac purée, caramelised onions and crispy bacon, followed by Lancashire hotpot, or pan-fried Goosnargh duck breast with orange sauce, bubble-and-squeak and onion tarte Tatin. Fashionable and exotic touches are sometimes introduced, adding shrimp foam to seared scallops with pea purée, say, stir-fried Asian vegetables and hot-and-sour prawn soup to grilled mackerel, and chocolate and chilli ice cream to an assiette of chocolate to finish, or go for the familiarity of sticky toffee pudding.

Times 12-2/7-9 Closed 24-26 Dec

BARROW-IN-FURNESS   **Map 18 SD26**

Clarence House Country Hotel & Restaurant

🏵🏵 British, International V

Modern British versatility in an orangery setting

☎ 01229 462508
Skelgate, Dalton-in-Furness LA15 8BQ
e-mail: clarencehsehotel@aol.com
web: www.clarencehouse-hotel.co.uk
dir: A590 through Ulverston & Lindal, 2nd exit at rdbt & 1st exit at next. Follow signs to Dalton, hotel at top of hill on right

The white-fronted hotel in Dalton-in-Furness, not far from Barrow, is perfectly poised between sandy beaches and the lush green acres of Lakeland. A dining room designed like an orangery, with windows on three sides, affords covetable views over the St Thomas Valley, and terrace tables make the best of the sun. The menus are defined by that resourcefully versatile reach that has come to be the hallmark of the modern British idiom, offering

Chinese-style slow-roasted duck in plum sauce with cashews and pomegranate to start, or a tian of Cornish crab set in avocado, tomato and basil. For main, there may be grilled salmon garnished with crisp pancetta and a pea and mint risotto, or roast chump of Cumbrian lamb with provençale accompaniments of aubergine, confit peppers and tapenade. A grill section offers various steaks and chops with a choice of sauces. Friday night is carvery night.

Chef Mr Alan Forsyth **Owner** Mrs Pauline Barber **Times** 12-2/7-9 Closed D Sun **Prices** Starter fr £5.95, Main fr £18.95, Dessert fr £6.95, Service included **Wines** 8 by glass **Notes** Fri D carvery £29.95, Sun L 12-3, Sunday L £25.95, Vegetarian menu, Dress restrictions, Smart dress, Civ Wed 100 **Seats** 100, Pr/dining room 14 **Children** Portions **Parking** 40

BASSENTHWAITE   **Map 18 NY23**

Armathwaite Hall Country House & Spa

🏵 British, French V ☙

Fine dining with lake views

☎ 017687 76551
CA12 4RE
e-mail: reservations@armathwaite-hall.com
web: www.armathwaite-hall.com
dir: From M6 junct 40/A66 to Keswick then A591 towards Carlisle. Continue for 7m and turn left at Castle Inn

Hard by Bassenthwaite Lake, the hall is a magnificent-looking property hung with creepers. Updating has brought all the mod cons expected in a 21st-century hotel, including a spa, while the Lake View Restaurant is a lovely high-ceilinged room with oak panelling, rich golds and reds and comfortable chairs at formally set tables. Attentive staff are smartly attired - as you'd expect of a restaurant with a dress code. The kitchen steers a course between the traditional and the contemporary, turning out starters like smoked chicken liver parfait with Cumberland sauce, and creamy smoked haddock risotto flavoured with fines herbes and parmesan. Sauces are a strength, judging by a broad bean butter one to accompany halibut fillet wrapped in cabbage with salmon and dill mousse, and one of leek and bacon butter for pan-fried chicken breast. Desserts hit the spot too, among them perhaps white chocolate pannacotta, or cherry Pavlova with rhubarb coulis and vanilla cream.

Chef Kevin Dowling **Owner** Graves family **Times** 12.30-1.45/7.30-9 **Prices** Prices not confirmed Service optional **Wines** 6 by glass **Notes** Fixed D 5 course £45.95, Sunday L, Vegetarian menu, Dress restrictions, Smart casual, no jeans, T-shirts or trainers **Seats** 80 **Children** Portions **Parking** 100

BASSENTHWAITE *continued*

The Pheasant

@ Modern British

Charming period coaching inn with clearly focused, seasonal menu

☎ 017687 76234
CA13 9YE
e-mail: info@the-pheasant.co.uk
web: www.the-pheasant.co.uk
dir: M6 junct 40, take A66 (Keswick and North Lakes). Continue past Keswick and head for Cockermouth. Signed from A66

With period charm to spare, The Pheasant is in a peaceful spot near Bassenthwaite Lake. A coaching inn since the 16th century, a gently contemporary restaurant is now part of the package, but rest assured the wonderfully atmospheric bar still dispenses local ales, and there's also a bistro if you're after something a little less formal. The Fell Restaurant is imbued with a pleasing understated refinement, with wood-panelled walls, upholstered chairs, linen-clad tables and smartly dressed staff (donning pheasant emblazoned ties) who maintain the air of civility. Good local produce shines through in nicely presented seasonal British dishes such as ham hock terrine with piccalilli purée and celeriac remoulade, followed by slow-cooked loin of Holker Hall venison with parsnip confit, buttered cabbage, thyme gnocchi and chocolate-scented jus.

Chef Malcolm Ennis **Owner** Trustees of Lord Inglewood **Times** 12-1.30/7-9 Closed 25 Dec, D Sun-Mon **Prices** Prices not confirmed Service optional, Groups min 8 service 10% **Wines** 12 by glass **Notes** Daily changing menu, Sunday L, Vegetarian available, Dress restrictions, Smart casual, No jeans, T-shirts, trainers **Seats** 45, Pr/dining room 12 **Parking** 40

BORROWDALE Map 18 NY21

Leathes Head Hotel

@ British ☺

Traditional country-house cooking and lovely views

☎ 017687 77247
CA12 5UY
e-mail: reservations@leatheshead.co.uk
dir: 3.75m S of Keswick on B5289, set back on the left

A warm welcome awaits visitors to this small hotel in the heart of the beautiful Borrowdale Valley. The Leathes Head was originally built in Edwardian times as a gentleman's residence, and is full of original features in its 11 bedrooms and its traditionally decorated public rooms, including the intimate restaurant. Here, with views of the two-and-a-half acres of gardens and the unspoilt fells beyond, you can enjoy some traditional, country-house-hotel cooking based on plenty of locally-sourced ingredients. Cream of butternut squash soup with cumin and herb croûtons might kick things off, with poached haddock with seasonal vegetables and Lancashire brown shrimps and prawns in a bisque sauce to follow. Black Forest chocolate pot with Bakewell tart ice cream and Amaretto is an ambitious but altogether winning dessert.

Chef David Jackson **Times** 6.30-8.30 Closed mid Nov-mid Feb **Prices** Fixed D 2 course fr £24.95, Service optional **Wines** 23 bottles over £30, 31 bottles under £30, 10 by glass **Notes** Coffee incl, Fixed D 4 course £32.50, Vegetarian available **Seats** 24 **Parking** 15

BRAITHWAITE Map 18 NY22

The Cottage in the Wood

@@ Modern European

Inventive cooking and stunning mountain views

☎ 017687 78409
Whinlatter Forest CA12 5TW
e-mail: relax@thecottageinthewood.co.uk
dir: M6 junct 40, A66 signed Keswick. 1m after Keswick take B5292 signed Braithwaite, hotel in 2m

Located at the heart of the Whinlatter Forest, this 17th-century former coaching inn sits in one of the most stunningly beautiful and tranquil parts of the Lake District National Park, yet is only a short drive away from bustling Keswick. The Mountain View restaurant is at the forefront of the small operation and has just undergone a refurbishment, not that many diners will be looking at the décor with such breathtaking views of the Skiddaw range

and forest to be admired through the full-length windows. Head chef Ryan Blackburn is a Cumbrian lad and his passion for what's on the doorstep shines through in his imaginative menus that take the best the region has to offer as their bedrock. A flavoursome first course of Scottish chanterelles with organic spelt risotto and parmesan might be followed by a perfectly cooked Whitehaven-landed turbot, with trotter cromesquis, coastal herbs and cockle vinaigrette. It's worth pre-ordering the Cumberland apple pudding and rum butter sauce - a soft, rich, deeply satisfying pudding that's really rather special.

Times 12.30-2.30/6-9 Closed Jan, Mon, D Sun

BRAMPTON Map 21 NY56

Farlam Hall Hotel

@@ Modern British V

Updated classics and relaxing pastoral views

☎ 016977 46234
Hallbankgate CA8 2NG
e-mail: farlam@relaischateaux.com
web: www.farlamhall.co.uk
dir: On A689, 2.5m SE of Brampton (not in Farlam village)

Farlam Hall has been around since the 16th century, but owes most of its current splendour to a wealthy Victorian industrialist who created the glorious gardens and the old-school grandeur of its interiors. The same family have run Farlam for over 30 years, so you can expect well-polished service and an air of continuity. The dining room is well-lit by floor-to-ceiling windows overlooking the ornamental lake, and tables are formally turned-out with gleaming crystal and silver on starched linen, but there is no other presence of starch, least of all in the delightfully relaxed service. A daily-changing menu offers classic English country-house cooking with subtle modern tweaks - perhaps smoked and fresh salmon fishcake with buttered leeks and cream, dill and white wine sauce, followed by tenderloin of local Cumbrian pork wrapped in air-dried ham matched with apple mashed potato, apple sauce tartlet and Calvados sauce. Well-kept English cheeses intervene before time-honoured puddings such as glazed lemon tart with fruit coulis.

Chef Barry Quinion **Owner** Quinion family **Times** 8-8.30 Closed 24-30 Dec, 4-15 Jan, L all week **Prices** Prices not confirmed Service optional **Wines** 37 bottles over £30, 24 bottles under £30, 12 by glass **Notes** Vegetarian menu, Dress restrictions, Smart casual, no shorts, Civ Wed 40 **Seats** 40, Pr/dining room 20 **Children** Portions **Parking** 25

Save on Hotels. Book at **theAA.com/hotel**

CUMBRIA 111 ENGLAND

L'Enclume

CARTMEL MAP 18 SD37

Modern British V 🍷NOTABLE WINE LIST 🖐

A world-class dining experience in a little Cumbrian village

☎ 015395 36362
Cavendish St LA11 6PZ
e-mail: info@lenclume.co.uk
dir: Follow signs for A590 W, turn left for Cartmel before Newby Bridge

Anyone who follows Simon Rogan will know that he's a chef who never stands still. He's always working on the next project, whether that be a new dish, a new restaurant, growing a new kind of vegetable, experimenting with a new ingredient picked from the wild, expanding his farm (it now spans 23 acres across five different sites) - the man is constantly on the quest for new discoveries, new opportunities, excitement and, ultimately, perfection. So it's no surprise then that in a year when he opened two new restaurants (The French by Simon Rogan at The Midland in Manchester - see entry, to be joined at the hotel by Mr Cooper's House & Garden in September 2013), he's made a huge investment of money and energy in revamping the mothership, L'Enclume. As we go to print, work is underway to vastly extend, strip out and replace the kitchen, while the dining room is getting a top-to-toe facelift which will ultimately preserve all of the period character of the 700-year-old former forge but with a much more polished feel. Part

of the project involves knocking down the wall dividing the kitchen and the restaurant to create a semi-open kitchen, allowing diners to get a good insight into the culinary action on the other side of the pass. You can bet that once all the work has been done, the place will still have the same pleasingly unpretentious feel as before, with lots of natural materials in the design (stone floors and walls, bare wood tables), and friendly, charming and totally on-the-ball serving staff. They're all very well versed in the menu, which is a good thing when you consider that a meal here is a succession of dishes all made up of multiple, often unusual, components. At the heart of everything is Rogan's true passion - super-fresh ingredients, many picked just hours ago at his organic farm nearby, or foraged from the local countryside. Livestock are also reared on the farm, and what Rogan doesn't produce himself he sources from trusted local suppliers; you can be assured that only the very best will do in his kitchen. The freshly baked breads get things off to a highly promising start, and every dish that follows simply bursts with fresh, powerful flavours and vibrant, natural colours, with edible flowers often used to stunning effect. Modern cooking techniques are used aplenty, but natural flavours are never, ever compromised, and dishes are judged to a tee. Cod 'yolk', sage cream, pea shoots, salt and vinegar demonstrates the level of creative genius at work here, while valley venison - a sublime piece of meat - comes inventively

with charcoal oil, mustard and fennel. Sea-fresh hake is partnered with the most carroty-tasting grilled carrots you'll probably ever experience, along with Manx queenies (precision-cooked) and celandine. Mussels come in their own juice (a fantastically rich flavoured juice) with cabbage and leek, and Reg's guinea hen is partnered with turnip shoots, potato, offal and scurvy grass (a member of the cabbage family) - this is healthy high-end dining. Sea buckthorn, buttermilk, liquorice and butternut is an inspired dessert, full of interesting, complementary flavours and contrasting textures, while rhubarb with brown butter, wild sorrel and apple offers the perfect balance of sweet and tart. There are 15 lovely bedrooms if you wish to enjoy the experience to the full - and why wouldn't you?

Chef Simon Rogan **Owner** Simon Rogan, Penny Tapsell **Times** 12-1.30/6.30-9.30 Closed L Mon-Tue **Prices** Tasting menu £95, Service optional, Groups min 8 service 10% **Wines** 190 bottles over £30, 4 bottles under £30, 10 by glass **Notes** Tasting menu L 8 course D 12 course £32.50, Vegetarian menu **Seats** 50, Pr/dining room 10 **Parking** 7, On street

CARLISLE
Map 18 NY35

Crown Hotel

◉ Modern British

Modern British cooking in a country conservatory

☎ 01228 561888
Station Rd, Wetheral CA4 8ES
e-mail: info@crownhotelwetheral.co.uk
web: www.crownhotelwetheral.co.uk
dir: M6 junct 42, B6263 to Wetheral, right at village shop, car park at rear of hotel

Just off the A69, outside Carlisle, the peaceful village of Wetheral is home to this attractive country hotel in its own gardens, views of which are on offer all round in the raftered conservatory restaurant. Unclothed darkwood tables and friendly service indicate the laidback approach, and the food is at the gentler end of the modern British spectrum. Producing black pudding in-house is a commendable venture, and a thick slice of it might turn up with spicy chorizo and salad, garnished with mustard mayonnaise, as a hearty starter. Roast lamb rump comes with grain mustard mash and confit root vegetables, a main course that delivers tender, flavourful meat and a robust jus. Fish may be fried trout with wilted greens, pesto mash and lemon butter. For pudding, you may be tempted by the northern classic Cumberland rum nicky, a concoction of dried fruits in ginger and rum, fashioned here into a tart and served with clotted cream.

Chef Paul Taylor **Owner** David Byers
Times 12-2.30/7-9.30 Closed L Sat **Prices** Fixed L 2 course fr £15.25, Fixed D 3 course £26-£29.95, Starter £5.95-£9.99, Main £17.95-£24.95, Dessert £5.95-£9.95, Service optional **Wines** 5 bottles over £30, 29 bottles under £30, 12 by glass **Notes** Sunday L, Vegetarian available, Civ Wed 120 **Seats** 80, Pr/dining room 120 **Children** Portions, Menu **Parking** 70

CARTMEL
Map 18 SD37

Aynsome Manor Hotel

◉ Traditional & Modern British 🍃

Traditional country-house dining with a daily-changing menu

☎ 015395 36653
LA11 6HH
e-mail: aynsomemanor@btconnect.com
dir: M6 junct 36, A590 signed Barrow-in-Furness towards Cartmel. Left at end of road, hotel before village

Once a country residence of the Pembrokes, the manor is an elegant little country house at the head of the Cartmel Valley, looking southwards towards the fabled Norman priory, the stretching meadows and the woods. Inside it has an old-school feel, but in a good way, with clothed tables, silverware and gleaming glasses, deep windows and portraits in oils gazing down from the walls. Pick any number of courses from the daily-changing menu, or go for the full five, perhaps opening with pigeon breast and local black pudding with raspberry-dressed saladings, and then steamed sea trout with samphire, and a sharply contoured sauce of tomato, olives and tarragon. In between comes a soup such as parsnip and apple, and it's all rounded off with a dessert such as impressively fragile vanilla pannacotta with gooseberry compôte, or dark chocolate, pecan and maple syrup tart with minted raspberry coulis, and then perhaps good British cheeses with biscuits.

Chef Gordon Topp **Owner** Christopher & Andrea Varley **Times** 7-8.30 Closed 25-26 Dec, 2-28 Jan, L Mon-Sat, D Sun (ex residents) **Prices** Fixed D 3 course £29-£30, Service optional **Wines** 20 bottles over £30, 45 bottles under £30, 6 by glass **Notes** Sunday L, Vegetarian available, Dress restrictions, Smart dress **Seats** 28 **Children** Portions, Menu **Parking** 20

L'Enclume

◉◉◉◉◉ – *see page 111*

Rogan & Company Restaurant

◉◉◉ – *see opposite*

CROSTHWAITE
Map 18 SD49

The Punchbowl Inn at Crosthwaite

◉◉ Modern British 🍃

Smartly updated inn with carefully crafted, appealing dishes

☎ 015395 68237
Lyth Valley LA8 8HR
e-mail: info@the-punchbowl.co.uk
dir: A590 then A5074 signed Bowness/Crosthwaite. Inn within 3m on right

The whitewashed old inn, in a stunning rural spot at the heart of the Lyth Valley, is a stylish place indeed, always busy, with a slate-topped bar and a restaurant with a polished oak floor, leather chairs and a stone fireplace. The same menu is served throughout, the carefully composed dishes based on fine Lakeland produce. Seared scallops are served with a ball of black pudding and apple purée, a drizzle of caramel adding a welcome touch of sweetness, and garlicky potato soup is jazzed up by slices of chorizo. Main courses are no less appreciated: slow-cooked rolled pork belly with a tasty faggot, creamy mash and Savoy cabbage with bacon, say, and well-timed roast loin of cod with leek and bacon chowder and sweetcorn purée. Ambition extends into puddings too: witness chocolate mousse not just with raspberry sorbet but with popping candy and elderflower foam.

Chef Scott Fairweather **Owner** Richard Rose **Times** 12-9 **Prices** Starter £4.50-£9.95, Main £12.95-£19.95, Dessert £5.95-£6.95, Service optional, Groups min 10 service 10% **Wines** 74 bottles over £30, 33 bottles under £30, 14 by glass **Notes** Sunday L, Vegetarian available, Civ Wed 60 **Seats** 50, Pr/dining room 16 **Children** Portions, Menu **Parking** 40

ELTERWATER   Map 18 NY30

Langdale Hotel & Spa

◉◉ Modern British ✋

Well-crafted, modish cooking in a rustic setting

☎ 015394 37302 & 38080
The Langdale Estate LA22 9JD
e-mail: purdeys@langdale.co.uk
web: www.langdale.co.uk
dir: M6 junct 36, A591 or M6 junct 40, A66, B5322, A591

Set in a Victorian former gunpowder factory in a 35-acre estate dotted with streams, ponds, and an original waterwheel and millstones, there's no lack of charm at the Langdale Hotel. Its Purdey's Restaurant is a smartly rustic venue, with exposed Lakeland stone walls climbing to the raftered roof above wooden tables and chairs; an original cannon used for testing is a talking point, although the only sparks flying around nowadays come from the skilled kitchen team, who make a real effort to keep things seasonal and local. The menus follow a broadly modern British script, starting out with a full-flavoured pairing of seared scallops with crispy veal sweetbreads and salsa verde. Ingredients are well sourced and compositions convincing: a tasting of free-range pork is evidence of sound technical skills, and comes pointed up with pickled apple purée and sage jus. Elsewhere, inspiration may come from far-off shores - perhaps coconut and lemongrass curry to add oomph to spiced monkfish and mussels. For puddings, Yorkshire rhubarb cheesecake is delivered with vanilla-poached rhubarb and gingerbread ice cream.

Chef Graham Harrower **Owner** Langdale Leisure Ltd **Times** 6.30-9.30 Closed L ex groups - booking essential **Prices** Tasting menu £49.50, Starter £5.95-£12.50, Main £13.95-£22.50, Dessert £6.50-£7.95, Service optional **Wines** 9 by glass **Notes** Tasting menu 7 course, Vegetarian available, Dress restrictions, Smart casual, Civ Wed 60 **Seats** 80, Pr/dining room 40 **Children** Portions, Menu **Parking** 50

GLENRIDDING   Map 18 NY31

The Inn on the Lake

◉◉ Modern European V ✋

Modern cooking on the shore of Ullswater

☎ 017684 82444
CA11 0PE
e-mail: innonthelake@lakedistricthotels.net
web: www.lakedistricthotels.net
dir: M6 junct 40, A66 Keswick, A592 Windermere

The lake in question is Ullswater and it is indeed set before you, a beautiful vista that is Lakeland through-and-through. The hotel has 15 acres of fabulous grounds to explore as well, so there is plenty of opportunity to really connect with this impressive landscape. The interior matches the charming period spaces with some well-chosen furniture, creating smart and comfortable rooms, not least the Lake View Restaurant, which certainly serves up quite a panorama. The team in the kitchen makes good use of the excellent produce available in this region and they don't lack for technical skills and good ideas either. You might start, for example, with confit of Goosnargh duck leg with orange and Cointreau jelly and celeriac purée, or Appleby goats' cheese with textures of beetroot. Bright, modish stuff then. Local lamb might come three ways (fillet, mini-cutlet and shoulder), or try the seared wild sea trout with mussel beignet, shaved fennel and saffron rice broth. Things end on a high with dark chocolate terrine with buttermilk ice cream and marinated blackberries.

Chef Fraser Soutar **Owner** Charles & Kit Graves **Times** 12-2/7-9 **Prices** Fixed L 2 course £16.95, Fixed D 3 course fr £32, Service optional **Wines** 8 by glass **Notes** Sunday L, Vegetarian menu, Dress restrictions, Smart casual, Civ Wed 110 **Seats** 100, Pr/dining room 40 **Children** Portions, Menu **Parking** 100

Rogan & Company Restaurant

CARTMEL   MAP 18 SD37

Modern British ✋

Top-class cooking at L'Enclume's younger sibling

☎ 015395 35917
The Square LA11 6QD
e-mail: reservations@roganandcompany.co.uk
dir: From M6 junct 36 follow signs for A590. Turn off at sign for Cartmel village

If you can't get a table at L'Enclume, Simon Rogan's hugely celebrated restaurant and holder of the ultimate five Rosettes (see entry), dining at Rogan & Company is by no means a poor substitute. L'Enclume's little sister sits beside the river in a lovely old building right in the centre of the small village of Cartmel. It's just a short stroll away from L'Enclume, so although you won't find the man himself behind the stoves here on a daily basis, you can be assured that he's here regularly, keeping a good eye on things and making sure head chef Danielle Barry and her team faithfully execute his unique style of contemporary, natural cooking. Cool, mellow beats, staff casually dressed in long black aprons, and bare-wood tables simply set with Lakeland slate table-mats and high quality glassware help create a laidback, relaxed feel in the ground-floor dining room - the perfect backdrop to showcase Rogan's technically brilliant food. Every dish is visually stunning, the ingredients vibrantly colourful and tasting as fresh as fresh can be - little wonder when many of them have been foraged from the local countryside or gathered that morning from Rogan's own farm down the road. Dinner might begin on a meaty note with smoked loin and rillettes of pork with pickled mushrooms, served with the added bonus of a crispy pig's ear to give good textural contrast and nasturtium to bring freshness of flavour and colour to the plate. For the main event wild bass with salsify, shrimp and curly kale could be one way to go, or perhaps the braised shoulder of Herdwick hogget - a fine piece of meat, perfectly cooked, bursting with flavour and ably supported by some barbecued and crushed broccoli, potatoes and onions. Dessert could be something as simple - yet highly effective - as a deeply fruity black cherry sponge with a textbook white chocolate mousse, or as out-of-the-ordinary as chocolate pizza with sweet cheese ice cream, or cider cream, thyme custard and crispy yoghurt.

Chef Simon Rogan, Danny Barry **Owner** Simon Rogan, Penny Tapsell **Times** 12-2.30/6.30-9 Closed Mon-Tue **Prices** Fixed L 3 course £29.50-£38.50, Tasting menu £29.50-£38.50 **Wines** 14 bottles over £30, 23 bottles under £30, 14 by glass **Notes** Vegetarian available **Seats** 40, Pr/dining room 10 **Children** Portions **Parking** On street

---

GRANGE-OVER-SANDS   Map 18 SD47

Clare House

◉ Modern British 🍴

Wonderful views and modern country-house cooking

☎ 015395 33026
Park Rd LA11 7HQ
e-mail: info@clarehousehotel.co.uk
web: www.clarehousehotel.co.uk
dir: Off A590 onto B5277, through Lindale into Grange,
keep left, hotel 0.5m on left past Crown Hill & St Paul's
Church

This elegant Victorian country house stands in well-
maintained gardens leading down to the expansive
waters of Grange-over-Sands. The restaurant is split into
two nicely done out rooms with artwork hung on the
modern wallpaper and clothed and unclothed tables set
with fresh flowers. The kitchen team turns out a happy
blend of modern and traditional dishes, on a well-judged
carte (not too long, not too short) and based on a good
amount of local ingredients. On the five-course evening
menu you might find a twice-baked cheese soufflé, the
final baking with cream and gruyère, and main courses
such as hearty roast tenderloin and belly of pork with
grain mustard and parsley mash, purple sprouting
broccoli, apple sauce, crackling and herb jus. To finish,
lemon posset with spiced summer berries and East
Yorkshire sugar cakes fits the bill.

Chef Andrew Read, Mark Johnston **Owner** Mr & Mrs D S
Read **Times** 12-2.30/6.30-7.30 Closed Dec-Apr
Prices Prices not confirmed **Wines** 3 by glass **Notes** Fixed
D 5 course £36, Light L menu Mon-Sat, Sunday L,
Vegetarian available **Seats** 36 **Children** Portions
Parking 16

GRASMERE   Map 18 NY30

Macdonald Swan Hotel

◉ Traditional British

Good honest cooking in smart Lakeland inn

☎ 0844 879 9120
LA22 9RF
e-mail: sales/oldengland@macdonald-hotels.co.uk
web: www.macdonaldhotels.co.uk
dir: M6 junct 36, A591 towards Kendal, A590 to Keswick
through Ambleside. Hotel on right on entering village

Name-checked in Wordsworth's *The Waggoner*, the Swan
is part of Lakeland history. Sitting at the foot of rolling
hills, it dates from the 1650s when it opened its doors as
a coaching inn, and today, the white-painted building,
although much updated, doesn't lack for character. It
looks handsome on the inside, with plenty of period
details, warming log fires, a bar called Walkers' and a
restaurant named The Waggoners. The latter is a smart-

looking space with a broad menu that runs from classics
such as prawn cocktail and potted shrimps, to the likes
of pumpkin ravioli with sage butter. There are steaks
cooked on the grill - thickly cut sirloin, for example -
served with traditional sauces, and hearty things like
beef cheeks with stout and herb dumplings. To finish,
there might be Grasmere gingerbread cheesecake with
Cumbrian honey ice cream.

Chef Robert Ryan **Owner** Macdonald Hotels & Resorts
Times 12.30-3.30/6-9 Closed L Mon-Sat **Prices** Prices
not confirmed Service optional **Wines** 12 by glass
Notes Sunday L, Vegetarian available, Dress restrictions,
Smart casual, no trainers or T-shirts, Civ Wed 70
Seats 60, Pr/dining room 20 **Children** Portions, Menu
Parking 60

Oak Bank Hotel

◉◉ Modern British 🍴

Stylish modern cooking in Lakeland country house

☎ 015394 35217
Broadgate LA22 9TA
e-mail: info@lakedistricthotel.co.uk
web: www.lakedistricthotel.co.uk
dir: N'bound: M6 junct 36 onto A591 to Windermere,
Ambleside, then Grasmere. S'bound: M6 junct 40 onto
A66 to Keswick, A591 to Grasmere

Go for a stroll through the well-tended gardens running
down to the River Rother at this Victorian hotel before
relaxing over a drink in front of the log fire in the lounge.
Then make your way into the conservatory restaurant, its
elegance uplifted by redecoration. Dinner might kick off
with salt-cod cream with crackling and pea textures
(purée, parfait and shoots), bringing the taste buds to
life before something like accurately roasted scallops on
piquillo pepper salsa, the plate dotted with triangles of
air-dried ham and romesco crumbs. The kitchen is
painstaking about sourcing locally and has a good eye for
presentation, evident in a main course of Holker Estate
partridge, roast breast, braised leg and pithivier
strategically plated with dauphinoise, swede purée and
fondant, and sauced with game jus. Turbot poached in
red wine, with potato purée and a fricassée of baby gem,
mushrooms and salsify, might be an alternative, and the
meal might end with a memorable theme on chocolate
and orange.

Chef Darren Comish **Owner** Glynis & Simon Wood
Times 6.30-8.30 Closed 21-26 Dec, 2-16 Jan, 3-15 Aug, L
all week **Prices** Fixed D 3 course £30.50-£39, Service
optional, Groups min 6 service 10% **Wines** 6 bottles over
£30, 43 bottles under £30, 6 by glass **Notes** Vegetarian
available, Dress restrictions, Smart casual **Seats** 32
Children Portions **Parking** 14

Rothay Garden Hotel

◉◉ Modern European

**Well-balanced modern dishes in a chintz-free
conservatory**

☎ 015394 35334
Broadgate LA22 9RJ
e-mail: stay@rothaygarden.com
web: www.rothaygarden.com
dir: From N M6 junct 40, A66 to Keswick, then S on A591
to Grasmere. From S M6 junct 36 take A591 through
Windermere/Ambleside to Grasmere. At N end of village
adjacent to park

On the edge of Grasmere, the refurbished hotel sits in a
couple of acres of riverside gardens, with the panoramic
sweep of the Lakeland fells as background.
Chintzophobes need have no fear; dining goes on in a
thoroughly modern conservatory-style room with bare floor
and smartly clothed tables, with restful views of the
gardens all around. Andrew Burton has the balance right
between country-hotel and modern edge in his cooking,
offering a savoury Charlotte of spring onion and tomato,
along with a seared scallop and crab, with rouille
dressing and wilted spinach to start. Next up could be
sautéed guinea fowl breast in sherry cream sauce, with
ravioli of sun-blushed tomato and feta, as well as wild
mushrooms and asparagus, before the finishing flourish
sees Cassis coulis trickled into a black treacle soufflé, or
a medley of orange and lemon flavours applied to posset,
mousse and sablé.

Times 12-1.45/7-9.30

Wordsworth Hotel & Spa

◉◉ British 🍴

**Creative country-house cooking in the heart of the
Lakes**

☎ 015394 35592
LA22 9SW
e-mail: enquiry@thewordsworthhotel.co.uk
web: www.thewordsworthhotel.co.uk
dir: Off A591 centre of village adjacent to St Oswald's
Church

What a setting: two acres of riverside gardens with
stunning views of Grasmere Vale and the mountains all
around mean that before you even sit down to eat, this
classic country house - built originally in 1870 as a
hunting lodge for the Earl of Cadogan - feels like
Lakeland on a plate. The Signature Restaurant - with the
bonus of an airy conservatory extension - goes for a
plush, rather romantic look, with moody lighting and
piano music to set the ambience. The kitchen pulls out all
the stops to impress: imaginative ideas appear with
colourful presentation, foams and espumas adding gloss
to a solid bedrock of fine Cumbrian ingredients. Crisp cod

cheeks are winningly matched with salt-cod pannacotta, carrot mousse, red chard and pancetta crumb, ahead of Cumbrian lamb - slow-cooked loin and shoulder and sweetbreads - with broad bean fricassée, rosemary confit potatoes and grelot onions. Macerated strawberries with basil, mascarpone mousse, black pepper sablé biscuit and cinder toffee makes a bright and well-balanced ending.

Chef Jaid Smallman **Owner** Iain & Jackie Garside **Times** 12.30-2/6.30-9.30 **Wines** 40 bottles over £30, 12 bottles under £30, 10 by glass **Notes** Sunday L £19-£29, Vegetarian available, Dress restrictions, Smart casual, Civ Wed 100 **Seats** 65, Pr/dining room 18 **Children** Portions, Menu **Parking** 50

HOWTOWN   Map 18 NY41

Sharrow Bay Country House Hotel

◉◉ British, International

Classically-based cuisine by the majestic tranquillity of Ullswater

☎ 017684 86301
Sharrow Bay CA10 2LZ
e-mail: info@sharrowbay.co.uk
web: www.sharrowbay.co.uk
dir: M6 junct 40. From Pooley Bridge right fork by church towards Howtown. Right at x-rds, follow lakeside road for 2m

If any view is guaranteed to bring out the landscape artist or poet manqué in you, it ought to be the majestic, tranquil prospect over Ullswater enjoyed by Sharrow Bay. The hotel is a venerable old trooper of the country-house movement. At its heart is the defiantly unreconstructed dining room, a place of heavily draped comfort, all pink flounce and cultivated, flawlessly courteous service. The deal here is classically based cuisine that flies the flag proudly for Cumbrian produce, with a wide range of choice. A trio of seafood makes a compendious opener, offering dressed crab, a seared scallop and lobster tortellino, before the intermediate courses, the first a soup or fish dish (salmon with prawn risotto, perhaps), the second a citrus sorbet. Main course might be best end of Herdwick lamb, or fillet of Matterdale venison, the latter appearing with braised red cabbage, apple and raisins, puréed roast butternut squash, and a strong sauce founded on brandy and port. Some new-fangled thinking - orange polenta cake with blood orange jelly and Cointreau mascarpone cream - inveigles itself among the traditional likes of nougat glacé and toffee pudding for dessert, and then there are fine British cheeses to bring down the curtain.

Times 1-8

IREBY   Map 18 NY23

Overwater Hall

◉◉ Modern British ✿

Creative modish cooking in splendid Georgian country-house hotel

☎ 017687 76566
CA7 1HH
e-mail: welcome@overwaterhall.co.uk
dir: A591 at Castle Inn take road towards Ireby. After 2m turn right at sign

A fine Georgian house with a stately facade, Overwater Hall was ripe for conversion to a hotel (which happened in the late 1960s), and it has been under the same private ownership since 1992. Nowadays, it is a splendidly handsome country house replete with winding driveway and 18 acres of pretty gardens and woodland, and a décor rich with elegant, traditional charms. The dining room is appropriately formal with the tables sharply dressed with white linen and fresh flowers. The kitchen follows four-course tradition, with a fish course such as fillet of hake in a creamy sauce with prawns and fresh herbs following a starter of a whole quail pan-fried with orange and thyme on a smoked bacon rösti with honey-glazed shallots and hedgerow jus. There's a good deal of regional produce on the menu, and lots of flavours on the plate: main-course pan-fried saddle of venison comes with beetroot purée, pithivier of pheasant and wild mushrooms, potato and pancetta terrine, and damson jus.

Chef Adrian Hyde **Owner** Adrian & Angela Hyde, Stephen Bore **Times** 12.30-2/7-8.30 Closed 1st 2 wks Jan, L Sun-Mon **Prices** Starter £6-£8.50, Main £12.50-£18.50, Dessert £6.50, Service optional **Wines** 30 bottles over £30, 40 bottles under £30, 9 by glass **Notes** ALC L only, Light L Tue-Sat 12.30-2, 4 course D £45, Vegetarian available, Dress restrictions, Smart casual, Civ Wed 30 **Seats** 30 **Children** Portions **Parking** 15

KENDAL   Map 18 SD59

Best Western Castle Green Hotel in Kendal

◉◉ Modern British

Well-crafted dishes in a smart modern hotel

☎ 01539 734000
Castle Green Ln LA9 6RG
e-mail: reception@castlegreen.co.uk
web: www.castlegreen.co.uk
dir: M6 junct 37, A684 towards Kendal. Hotel on right in 5m

This substantial hotel sits in 14 acres of gardens and woodland overlooking Kendal Castle and the fells, making it an ideal bolt-hole for exploring Lakeland. The smartly

contemporary Greenhouse Restaurant is a light and airy venue where visual entertainment comes two ways: a glass 'theatre window' lets you watch the chefs in action without the inconvenience of noise and smells; look the other way, and sweeping picture windows open onto views of Kendal and its castle. The kitchen bangs the drum for locally-produced ingredients (a Cumbrian tasting menu revolves around supplies from a 55-mile radius), brings an imaginative approach to its work and has a deft touch in its handling of the modern British idiom. A perfectly-timed pan-fried brill fillet with cauliflower fritters, pea purée, watercress, and shellfish sauce makes a fine opening gambit, followed by roast breast and confit leg of mallard matched with swede, chestnuts, red cabbage and an interesting twist from smoked mash. It all concludes with treacle tart with chocolate ice cream and the palate-cleansing sharpness of apricot sauce.

Times 12-2/6-10

KESWICK   Map 18 NY22

Morrels

◉ Modern British

Relaxed contemporary dining

☎ 017687 72666
34 Lake Rd CA12 5DQ
e-mail: info@morrels.co.uk
dir: Between the market square & the Keswick Theatre by the Lake

Bang in the centre of Keswick between the market and the Theatre by the Lake, the exterior of Morrels may have the look of a classic Lakeland stone-built townhouse, but the stripped-out contemporary interior is a slice of metropolitan style that wouldn't look out of place in a big city. It is a slick act, all pine floors, bare wooden tables, chocolate and cream high-backed chairs, etched glass screens and an eclectic modern menu to match. The kitchen takes its inspiration from around the world, and pulls it all together in simple, contemporary ideas such as pan-fried scallops with chorizo and sweet potato purée, which you might follow with slow-roast pork belly with black mash, apple sauce, crackling and gravy, or steamed sea bass fillet with fennel, tomato and dill ragoût. Friendly staff and a laid-back modern soundtrack make for an easygoing ambience.

Times 5.30 Closed Mon, L all week

KESWICK *continued*

Swinside Lodge Country House Hotel

◉◉ Modern British V ▮NOTABLE WINE LIST ☙

Enticing table d'hôte menu near Derwentwater's edge

☎ 017687 72948
Grange Rd, Newlands CA12 5UE
e-mail: info@swinsidelodge-hotel.co.uk
web: www.swinsidelodge-hotel.co.uk
dir: M6 junct 40, A66, left at Portinscale. Follow to Grange for 2m ignoring signs to Swinside & Newlands Valley

There is simply no excuse for not coming to dinner with a well-honed appetite at Swinside Lodge. The trim, whitewashed Georgian house lies at the foot of Catbells, just a five-minute stroll from the shore of Derwentwater, and evocatively-named fells - Skiddaw, Blencathra, and Causey Pike - crowd all around, beckoning you to pull on the boots to get the view from the top. Lakeland tradition holds sway at the dinner table: a four-course table d'hôte format, with a choice at pudding stage, and the option to squeeze in a cheese course. Menus change daily and with the seasons, thus a winter spread opens with galantine of pheasant and venison with pickled red cabbage, prune and brandy jelly, then on via soup (carrot and ginger with cumin yoghurt) to baked salmon with smoked salmon and cucumber, celeriac, fennel and spinach in a white wine and tarragon sauce. Dessert is an orange polenta sponge pudding with Grand Marnier sauce and mascarpone.

Chef Clive Imber **Owner** Mike & Kath Bilton
Times 7.30-10.30 Closed Dec-Jan, L all week
Prices Prices not confirmed Service optional **Wines** 88 bottles over £30, 42 bottles under £30, 12 by glass
Notes 4 course D £38, Vegetarian menu, Dress restrictions, Smart casual **Seats** 18 **Children** Portions **Parking** 12

KIRKBY LONSDALE   Map 18 SD67

Hipping Hall

◉◉◉ – see below

The Sun Inn

◉ Modern British V ☙

Friendly old inn with a local flavour

☎ 015242 71965
6 Market St LA6 2AU
e-mail: email@sun-inn.info
web: www.sun-inn.info
dir: From A65 follow signs to town centre. Inn on main street

The Sun, dating from the 17th century, is a warm and characterful inn with the expected flagstone and oak floors, beams and log fires, while its restaurant has a modern feel, with bright fabrics and chairs made by Gillows of Lancaster. You can eat here or in the bar, and there are a number of options, from the 'Posh Nosher's' menu and lunchtime favourites like sausages and mash. Throughout, dishes are carefully composed making maximum use of local produce. Expect potted crab with roast garlic and dill mayonnaise, or beetroot Tatin with celeriac remoulade, then slow-roast shoulder of Lune lamb with rosemary and redcurrant jus, or fried sea bream fillets with crayfish sauce, finishing with something trad like rhubarb crumble.

Chef Charlotte Norfolk **Owner** Lucy & Mark Fuller
Times 12-6/6.30-9 Closed L Mon **Prices** Prices not confirmed Service optional **Wines** 14 bottles over £30, 32 bottles under £30, 7 by glass **Notes** Sunday L, Vegetarian menu **Seats** 36 **Children** Portions, Menu **Parking** On street & nearby car park

---

LUPTON   Map 18 SD58

The Plough Inn Lupton

◉ Modern British ☙

Smart contemporary looks and modish pub food

☎ 015395 67700
Cow Brow LA6 1PJ
e-mail: info@theploughatlupton.co.uk
dir: M6 junct 36 onto A65 signed Kirkby Lonsdale

The Plough had fallen on hard times before being given a shot in the arm by the good people behind the Punchbowl

---

Hipping Hall

KIRKBY LONSDALE   MAP 18 SD67

Modern British V

Classically based modern cooking in a fine medieval dining room

☎ 015242 71187
Cowan Bridge LA6 2JJ
e-mail: info@hippinghall.com
web: www.hippinghall.com
dir: 8.5m E of M6 junct 36 on A65

Hipping-stones once allowed travellers on foot to cross the stream that runs past the old wash-house at the hall that is named after them. Built of local grey stone, it once housed a humble smithy, but rather came up in the world when an early 17th century owner married the daughter of a local bigwig, and went on to acquire a title. It stands amid the rugged lunar landscape on the Cumbria - Lancashire border, a refuge from the wilds of the northern weather. The old conservatory has been upgraded to a smart new orangery for lounging, and the hall boasts a fine medieval dining room, complete with minstrels' gallery, stately fireplace and raftered ceiling. A choice of two menus is offered here each evening - a straightforward three-course structure with a choice of four dishes at each stage, or a seven-course tasting extravaganza, including pre-dessert, with cheese as an optional extra. Menu specifications go for the laconic listings approach, even to the extent of listing 'smoke' as one of the components of a starter of turbot terrine and cucumber, but the combinations of ingredients are mostly classically informed. Thus, ballottine and parfait of duck come with fig, for the all-important fruity note, and brioche, while the main-course exploration of hogget from a local farmer offers herb-crumbed meat with belly and kidney, as well as puréed swede. Robust accompaniments for fish are favoured, so halibut may be bolstered by artichoke, wild mushrooms and leek, while chestnuts are the surprise addition to sea bass and cockles on the tasting menu. Comfort is piled upon comfort in a dessert that comprises honeycomb mousse, treacle tart and a brandy snap with golden raisins, crumbled honeycomb and whisky ice cream. The vegetarian seven-course menus are quite as imaginative, built around courses such as chestnut cannelloni with wild mushrooms and broccoli, and shallot tart with puréed celeriac and walnuts.

Chef Brent Hulena **Owner** Andrew Wildsmith
Times 12-2/7-9.30 Closed L Mon-Fri **Prices** Fixed L 3 course £32.50, Fixed D 3 course £55, Tasting menu £65, Service optional **Wines** 58 bottles over £30, 17 bottles under £30, 10 by glass **Notes** Tasting menu 7 course, Sunday L, Vegetarian menu, Civ Wed 45 **Seats** 26 **Children** Portions **Parking** 20

Save on Hotels. Book at **theAA.com/hotel**

CUMBRIA 117 **ENGLAND**

Inn in Crosthwaite (see entry). It's surely never looked better. The refurbishment has maintained the best of the pubby elements - wooden floors, beams, real fires and the like - and given the place a classy finish with well-chosen colours, leather sofas, and a Brathay slate-topped bar. There are real ales and a decent slate of wines by the glass alongside a broad menu of Brit-focused food. Start with something like salt and pepper tempura squid, or pan-fried Stornoway black pudding with caramelised apple and a poached hen's egg, and follow on with braised lamb shank with garlic potatoes, spring greens and a rosemary and redcurrant jus. There are old favourites like whole tail breaded scampi and a good burger (8oz Aberdeen Angus), and, for dessert, bread and butter pudding with vanilla-poached apricots.

Chef Mark Swanton **Owner** Richard Rose **Times** 12-9 All-day dining **Prices** Starter £3.95-£6.50, Main £9.95-£19.95, Dessert £4.95-£5.95, Service optional, Groups min 15 service 10% **Wines** 28 bottles over £30, 38 bottles under £30, 14 by glass **Notes** Sunday L £10.95-£13.95, Vegetarian available **Seats** 120, Pr/dining room 8 **Children** Portions, Menu **Parking** 40

NEAR SAWREY Map 18 SD39

Ees Wyke Country House

◉ Modern, Traditional

Confident country-house cooking in elegant Georgian hotel

☎ 015394 36393
LA22 0JZ
e-mail: mail@eeswyke.co.uk
web: www.eeswyke.co.uk
dir: On B5285 on W side of village

A Georgian house above Esthwaite Water, with glorious fell views, Ees Wyke was at one time Beatrix Potter's holiday home before she bought Hill Top and moved to the village. It's now a comfortable, and comforting, country-house hotel, with dinner served in the dining room overlooking the lake. In typical Lakeland style, everyone takes their seats simultaneously for a daily-changing, five-course menu with a couple of choices per course. Good local sourcing is clear, and the kitchen combines classical ideas with gently modern notions, devising well-balanced meals. Start with seared scallops with balsamic dressing before broccoli and onion quiche, then go on to the main course: pink pan-fried noisettes of lamb with a wine jus hinting of mint and garlic, or gilt head bream fillets grilled with pancetta, thyme and oregano. Puddings might be a toss-up between sticky toffee sponge and pears poached in Muscat with honey and cinnamon, before a choice of local cheeses.

Times 7.30-close

NEWBY BRIDGE Map 18 SD38

Lakeside Hotel Lake Windermere

◉◉ Modern British V ☺

Lakeside dining with a choice of restaurants

☎ 015395 30001
Lakeside LA12 8AT
e-mail: sales@lakesidehotel.co.uk
web: www.lakesidehotel.co.uk
dir: M6 junct 36 follow A590 to Newby Bridge, straight over rdbt, right over bridge. Hotel within 1m

Originally a simple 17th-century coaching inn, the Lakeside Hotel has spread its wings to cater for the influx of visitors who want a piece of its splendid setting and a spot of me-time in the spa. Embraced by thickly-wooded hills and overlooking nothing but the boats nodding at anchor on Lake Windermere, the Lakeside Hotel certainly delivers on the promise. Luckily, the building's expansion has not been at the expense of its period charm - there are cosy lounges and snug traditional bars for an aperitif, before you head for the more formal oak-panelled Lakeview restaurant. Local produce forms the backbone of the modern British menu, which might kick off by putting up bacon jelly, creamed cabbage and pancetta crisp as the supporting cast for pigeon breast, then follow with pan-fried sea bass, crab ravioli, langoustine foam and lentils. Desserts show a similar propensity for delivering varied textures - perhaps an assemblage of chocolate mocha parfait, pannacotta, passionfruit mousse and white chocolate gel.

Chef Richard Booth **Owner** Mr N Talbot
Times 12.30-2.30/6.45-9.30 Closed 23 Dec-15 Jan **Prices** Fixed D 3 course £42, Service included **Wines** 12 by glass **Notes** Vegetarian menu, Dress restrictions, Smart casual, no jeans, Civ Wed 80 **Seats** 70, Pr/dining room 30 **Children** Portions, Menu **Parking** 200

Whitewater Hotel

◉ Modern, Traditional British

Punchy modern British cooking by the River Leven

☎ 015395 31133
The Lakeland Village LA12 8PX
e-mail: enquiries@whitewater-hotel.co.uk
web: www.whitewater-hotel.co.uk
dir: M6 junct 36 follow signs for A590 Barrow, 1m through Newby Bridge. Right at sign for Lakeland Village, hotel on left

The Whitewater is a resort hotel in Lakeland Village, constructed around a converted stone-built mill, offering the latest in spa treatments in an area that's all about tranquil relaxation in its own right. A thoroughly hospitable dining room uses the paradoxically soothing effect of rough stone walls, hung with Lakeland scenes, against a setting of smart table linen, high-backed chairs and views through expansive windows of the cascading River Leven. Whether you feel you need the Michael Bublé as well is a matter of taste. The modern British food on offer is full of punchy, vivid flavours and subtle technique, teaming goats' cheese and basil pannacotta with beetroot carpaccio, powdered dried olives, pine nuts and honey, for a winning start. Inspiration comes from far and wide, including North Africa for rump of lamb in Moroccan herbs with chickpea purée, preserved lemon, cumined carrots and harissa. Fruit-focused desserts might include raspberry clafoutis with lemon mascarpone.

Times 12-2/7-9 Closed L Mon-Sat

PENRITH Map 18 NY53

North Lakes Hotel & Spa

◉ Modern British ☺

Comfort eating for all the family at a Cumbrian spa hotel

☎ 01768 868111
Ullswater Rd CA11 8QT
e-mail: nlakes@shirehotels.com
web: www.shirehotels.com
dir: M6 junct 40 at junct with A66

The North Lakes is well-placed for those who want to explore the great outdoors, but if hill-walking isn't your bag, there's also a plethora of more sedate spa treatments plus a pool and Jacuzzi to help you let off steam. In the restaurant and bar, oak beams and six real fires help create the feel of a hunting lodge, while the tables are unclothed, adding to the laidback vibe. The crowd-pleasing menus - including children's and early bird - major on comfort food, so you could kick off with heritage beetroot and goats' cheese salad with toasted pine nuts and pomegranate, or baked French onion soup with gruyère cheese. Then go for fish and chips or confit of duck shepherd's pie with slow-braised red cabbage - a rich and warming dish for a cold winter's day. Valrhona chocolate mousse with cherry ice cream pairs classic

continued

PENRITH *continued*

flavours to good effect. Don't forget to try one of the locally brewed Daniel Thwaites ales before you leave.

Chef Mr Doug Hargeaves **Owner** Shire Hotels Ltd **Times** 12.15-1.45/7-9.15 **Prices** Prices not confirmed Service optional **Wines** 14 by glass **Notes** Vegetarian available, Dress restrictions, Smart casual, Civ Wed 150 **Seats** 112 **Children** Portions, Menu **Parking** 120

RAVENGLASS	Map 18 SD09

The Pennington Hotel

◎ British NEW

Imaginative cooking and estuary views

☎ 0845 450 6445
CA18 1SD
e-mail: info@penningtonhotels.com
dir: M6, junct 36 to A590 Barrow, right Greenodd A5092, joining A595 Muncaster/Ravenglass. Located in village centre

In the heart of Ravenglass overlooking the estuary, The Pennington Hotel welcomes with its appealing blend of period character (it started life as a 16th-century coaching inn) and smart contemporary style gained from its recent refurbishment. The place is just a stone's throw from the sea and Muncaster Castle, which is a spot of luck since the castle's historic kitchen gardens provide freshly picked seasonal fruit and herbs. The Pennington's kitchen focuses on care and skill rather than convoluted complexity, as demonstrated by a twice-baked soufflé of Blue Whinnow cheese with pear and rocket salad and hazelnut dressing. The same goes for a main course of cod suprême teamed with potato rösti, spinach, Romanesco cauliflower, Chantenay carrots and chervil. For dessert, 'rhubarb and custard' is a well-balanced dish of vanilla pannacotta with poached rhubarb and jelly, and vanilla soup.

Times 12-2.30/7-9 **Prices** Prices not confirmed **Notes** Breakfast brunch last Sun each month 11-2 £10.95

SEASCALE	Map 18 NY00

Sella Park House Hotel

◎ Traditional British NEW

Local supplies and a modern approach

☎ 0845 450 6445 & 01946 841601
Calderbridge CA20 1DW
e-mail: info@penningtonhotels.com
dir: From A595 at Calderbridge, follow sign for North Gate. Hotel 0.5m on left

Six acres of lovely gardens running down to the River Calder make this historic 16th-century manor house a popular venue for tying the knot, but you don't have to be heading for a wedding to see what the kitchen can do. There's no faulting the splendid seasonal Cumbrian produce it hauls in as the basis of its up-to-date cooking:

vegetables, fruit and herbs are plucked fresh from the kitchen garden at nearby Muncaster Castle, and great care is taken in tracking down the best local meat and fish. The Priory Restaurant makes a traditional setting for ideas that run the gamut from a tried-and-tested pairing of local hand-dived scallops and home-made black pudding lifted by crisp sage and quince jelly, to a main course of Goosnargh duck breast with butternut squash and orange purée, braised red cabbage and spicy duck jus. For dessert, apple tarte Tatin rounds things off nicely.

Chef Jon Fell **Times** 12-3/6-9 **Prices** Prices not confirmed Service optional

---

TEMPLE SOWERBY	Map 18 NY62

Temple Sowerby House Hotel & Restaurant

◎◎ Modern British ⏴

Imaginative modern cooking in an intimate country-house hotel

☎ 017683 61578
CA10 1RZ
e-mail: stay@templesowerby.com
web: www.templesowerby.com
dir: 7m from M6 junct 40, midway between Penrith & Appleby, in village centre

Set amid the verdant fells of the Eden Valley close to Ullswater, this small-scale 18th-century country-house hotel overlooks the village green and makes a great base for exploring the northern Lake District. When you come in from hiking the hills, you can warm up by a real fire in the winter, or on balmy days, sip an aperitif in the pretty walled garden before moving indoors to the smart dining room. The skilled kitchen brigade turn out an inventive bang-up-to-date British menu crammed with fine Cumbrian produce and local game - rabbit, for example, which is delivered as lasagne and smoked loin with wild mushrooms and local pancetta. Next up, pan-roasted pollock is perfectly timed and matched with crisp crab cakes, lobster bisque and squid ink gnocchi. Elsewhere, local meat fans might be treated to roast rump and slow-cooked shoulder of Cumbrian lamb with pease pudding, lettuce, smoked onions, and lamb jus. Round things off with the deep comforts of hot chocolate tart, Horlicks ice cream, orange marshmallow, and cookie crumble.

Chef Ashley Whittaker **Owner** Paul & Julie Evans **Times** 7-9 Closed 8 days Xmas, L all week **Prices** Fixed D 3 course £39.50, Service optional **Wines** 10 bottles over £30, 30 bottles under £30, 7 by glass **Notes** Vegetarian available, Dress restrictions, Smart casual preferred, Civ Wed 40 **Seats** 24, Pr/dining room 24 **Parking** 20

WATERMILLOCK	Map 18 NY42

Macdonald Leeming House

◎ Modern British

Ambitious country-house cooking on the shores of Ullswater

☎ 0844 879 9142
CA11 0JJ
e-mail: leeminghouse@macdonald-hotels.co.uk
web: www.macdonald-hotels.co.uk
dir: M6 junct 40, continue on A66 signed Keswick. At rdbt follow A592 towards Ullswater, at T-junct turn right, hotel 3m on left

This 200-year-old Lakeland manor certainly knows how to capitalise on its splendid location on the edge of Ullswater, offering fishing rights to the rod and line brigade, and making sure that the tables by the French windows of the Regency Restaurant bask in glorious views of the lake. Leeming House takes a traditional approach to the grande-luxe country-house dining experience: a polished front-of-house team deliver correctly formal service, while the kitchen delivers gently modern ideas along the lines of goats' cheese fondue teamed with beetroot in the form of jelly, mousse and caviar. Main courses major in grilled rib-eye and sirloin of Scottish beef, or there might be grilled wild sea bass with creamed potato, broccoli and salsa verde.

Chef Gary Fothersgill **Owner** Macdonald Hotels **Times** 12-2/6.45-9 **Prices** Starter £7-£7.50, Main £15-£23.50, Dessert £6.50, Service optional **Notes** Reservations recommended, Sunday L, Vegetarian available, Dress restrictions, Smart casual, No jeans or T-shirts, Civ Wed 80 **Seats** 60, Pr/dining room 24 **Children** Portions, Menu **Parking** 50

Rampsbeck Country House Hotel

◎◎ Modern British

Smart modern cooking in a refined lakeside setting

☎ 017684 86442
CA11 0LP
e-mail: enquiries@rampsbeck.co.uk
web: www.rampsbeck.co.uk
dir: M6 junct 40, A592 to Ullswater, T-junct turn right at lake's edge. Hotel 1.25m

Rampsbeck is the tranquil country hideaway par excellence: you can wander through 18 acres of splendid

Save on Hotels. Book at **theAA.com/hotel**

CUMBRIA 119 **ENGLAND**

grounds down to the hotel's own lake shore, and drink in the luscious views over Ullswater and the distant fells. The traditional 18th-century house is replete with antiques, grand marble fireplaces and ornate ceilings, its elegant dining room is presided over by staff who deliver polished service in an ambience of calm, well-practiced professionalism, while local materials provide the backbone of a modern repertoire that looks to the French classics for its inspiration. Roast loin of Cartmel Valley hare with pancetta, potato cake, wild mushrooms, beetroot purée and natural jus is an opener composed intelligently of happy bedfellows, while main course brings more luxury in a full-flavoured combination of veal medallions in a foie gras and marjoram crust with thyme-roasted new potatoes, asparagus, and port jus. At dessert, a mint chocolate cylinder is pointed up with coconut foam, but the array of artisan Cumbrian cheeses will prove impossible to ignore for some.

Rampsbeck Country House Hotel

Chef Ian Jackson **Owner** Blackshaw Hotels Ltd **Times** 12-1.45/7-9 **Prices** Prices not confirmed Service optional **Wines** 11 by glass **Notes** Sunday L, Vegetarian available, Dress restrictions, Smart casual, no shorts, Civ Wed 60 **Seats** 40, Pr/dining room 15 **Children** Portions **Parking** 30

WINDERMERE   Map 18 SD49

Beech Hill Hotel

⊛ Modern British **V**

Modern cooking on Windermere

☎ 015394 42137
Newby Bridge Rd LA23 3LR
e-mail: reservations@beechhillhotel.co.uk
web: www.beechhillhotel.co.uk
dir: M6 junct 36, A591 to Windermere. Left onto A592 towards Newby Bridge. Hotel 4m from Bowness-on-Windermere

On the shore of Windermere, Beech Hill naturally has wonderful views over the waters to the fells beyond, and diners can enjoy the vista from the restaurant, a large and smartly kitted-out room, where the menus offer an appealing range of dishes, the kitchen clearly in touch with contemporary tastes. Salmon and watercress fishcake with a poached egg and chive hollandaise might appear next to another starter of more unorthodox grilled smoked wood pigeon with a stir-fry of sprouts, lentils and bacon, and among main courses roast local chicken

breast with dauphinoise, mushrooms and tarragon might compete for your attention alongside tender, moist loin of venison in prosciutto with a broth of pearl barley, apples and celeriac. Fish is not overlooked - perhaps fillet of sea bass with pea hash, fennel tempura and tartare sauce - and puddings could extend to raspberry Alaska.

Chef Christopher Davies **Owner** Mr F Richardson **Times** 7-9 Closed L all week except party booking, D 25 Dec **Prices** Fixed D 3 course £32.95-£36.95, Starter £5-£8, Main £10-£20, Dessert £5-£9, Service optional **Wines** 25 bottles over £30, 25 bottles under £30, 8 by glass **Notes** Fixed D 5 course £37.95, Vegetarian menu, Dress restrictions, Smart casual, no denim or trainers, Civ Wed 120 **Seats** 130, Pr/dining room 90 **Children** Portions, Menu **Parking** 60

Cedar Manor Hotel & Restaurant

⊛⊛ Modern British 🍃

Soothing Lakeland hotel restaurant with impressive cooking

☎ 015394 43192
Ambleside Rd LA23 1AX
e-mail: info@cedarmanor.co.uk
dir: From A591 follow signs to Windermere. Hotel on left just beyond St Mary's Church at bottom of hill

This one-time gentleman's residence lies on the outskirts of Windermere in mature walled gardens, where the 200-year-old cedar that gives the place its name takes centre stage. Dinners here are a soothing affair: the candlelit restaurant looks smart with its high-backed leather chairs and crisp linen, while chef Roger Pergl-Wilson has established a strong local following for food that impresses with its classic culinary sensibilities and well-defined flavours. Ingredients are sourced carefully, and an eye is always kept on the calendar, thus an early spring menu might begin with venison terrine with juniper and pistachio, and progress to slow-cooked belly pork, which is cider-braised and honey-glazed and served with mustard mash. The chef's travels are reflected in forays into exotica, such as Cambodian marinated beef served with lime and black pepper dipping sauce and spicy potato wedges. At the end, local cheeses from a fine supplier in Kendal make a savoury alternative to the likes of nutmeg custard with cardamom doughnuts and raspberry jam sorbet.

Chef Roger Pergl-Wilson **Owner** Caroline & Jonathan Kaye **Times** 6.30-8.30 Closed Xmas & 6-25 Jan, L all week **Prices** Fixed D 3 course £39.95, Service optional **Wines** 11 bottles over £30, 26 bottles under £30, 7 by glass **Notes** Vegetarian available, Dress restrictions, Smart casual, no mountain wear **Seats** 22, Pr/dining room 10 **Children** Portions **Parking** 12

Gilpin Hotel & Lake House

⊛⊛⊛ – *see page 120*

Holbeck Ghyll Country House Hotel

⊛⊛⊛ – *see page 121*

Jerichos

⊛⊛ Modern British 🍃

Inventive cooking in a busy evening-only restaurant

☎ 015394 42522 & 45026
College Rd LA23 1BX
e-mail: info@jerichos.co.uk
dir: M6 junct 36. A591 to Windermere. 2nd left towards Windermere then 1st right onto College Rd. Restaurant 300mtrs on right

Jerichos is a thoroughly modern town-centre restaurant with rooms in a Victorian building, sporting a clean-cut look of white walls, pine floors, and black leather seats at bare wooden tables. The vibe is contemporary and relaxed, while menu descriptions might sound a tad involved, the sourcing of materials, spot-on presentation and evident technical skills shows a confident hand in the kitchen, working always with the seasons. A summer dinner starts with a vibrant fresh pea and garden herb risotto with crispy pancetta and goats' cheese. At main course stage, a pan-fried fillet of lemon sole arrives on butter-glazed samphire, along with Jersey potatoes with spinach and lemon dressing, Avruga caviar and crispy potato, with each element adding to the overall composition. Creativity doesn't flag in a finale of salted dark chocolate and almond butter mousse with home-made nutmeg ice cream.

Chef Chris Blaydes **Owner** Chris & Jo Blaydes **Times** 7-9.30 Closed 1st wk Nov, 24-26 Dec, last wk Dec, 1 Jan, last 3 wks Jan, Mon & Thu, L all week **Prices** Starter £4.95-£9.50, Main £16.50-£27.50, Dessert £6.50-£11, Service optional, Groups min 6 service 10% **Wines** 24 bottles over £30, 23 bottles under £30, 2 by glass **Notes** Vegetarian available **Seats** 28 **Children** Portions **Parking** 13

Gilpin Hotel & Lake House

Modern British

Dynamic contemporary cooking in fabulous family-run hotel

☎ 015394 88818
Crook Rd LA23 3NE
e-mail: hotel@gilpin.co.uk
web: www.gilpin.co.uk
dir: M6 junct 36 take A590/A591 to rdbt N of Kendal, then B5284 for 5m

The Cunliffe family have associations with this lovely house going back to the beginning of the 20th century. They've now reached the landmark 25th year running the place as a country-house hotel, and over that time have not for one second rested on their laurels, or slowed down in their quest to provide the very best levels of hospitality. Gilpin is surrounded by 22 acres of magnificent Lakeland countryside, with soaring trees and beautiful gardens, and the hotel itself is done out with a good deal of style and not an iota of chintz. The original features of the house (built in 1901) remain, but the impression within is of contemporary luxury and comfort (not modern and minimalist, but timeless and luxurious). There's also Lake House a short drive away which gives six more beautiful bedrooms, a lakeside vista, spa and a complimentary chauffeur service up to the hotel for dinner. As of 2012 there's a new man in the kitchen - Dan Grigg - and eating

here remains, as ever, a highlight of a stay. The cooking is thrillingly contemporary, but clearly focused at the same time. There are plenty of creative ideas and preparations on show, everything looks wonderful on the plate, and the ingredients are second to none. Take a first-course salt cod dish - salt cod korma - which sees delightfully flavoursome fish topped with a fine curried crust and partnered with an iced raita and crisp rice - a winning combination. Follow on with a dish of Gloucestershire Old Spot pork that shows sharp technical ability: perfectly slow-cooked belly, succulent cheek and a crisp 'quaver' served up with liquid Granny Smith and celeriac. Dessert might bring forth a baba with charred pineapple and rum and raisin ice cream, or a malted mousse with caraway, quince and ginger crumb. There are wine suggestions for every dish, even on the light lunch menu, and the staff run the show with charm and professionalism.

Chef Daniel Grigg **Owner** Cunliffe family **Times** 12-2/6.30-9.15 **Prices** Fixed L 3 course £30-£35, Starter £6-£8.50, Main £14-£18, Dessert £7.50-£8.50, Service optional **Wines** 200 bottles over £30, 12 bottles under £30, 14 by glass **Notes** Fixed D 5 course £58.50, ALC L only, Sunday L £30-£35, Vegetarian available, Dress restrictions, Smart Casual **Seats** 60, Pr/dining room 20 **Parking** 40

Save on Hotels. Book at **theAA.com/hotel**

CUMBRIA 121 **ENGLAND**

Holbeck Ghyll Country House Hotel

WINDERMERE MAP 18 SD49

Modern British V NOTABLE WINE LIST

Breathtaking views and classy cooking

☎ 015394 32375
Holbeck Ln LA23 1LU
e-mail: stay@holbeckghyll.com
dir: 3m N of Windermere on A591, right into Holbeck Lane (signed Troutbeck), hotel 0.5m on left

It's hardly surprising that everyone swoons over Holbeck Ghyll's unrivalled location and outstanding views. Anticipation builds as you draw near along the driveway, then the panorama unfurls over Lake Windermere to some of Lakeland's best-known peaks - Scafell Pike, Coniston Old Man and the Langdale Pikes. It is something to tuck away in your memory forever. And the house itself is no wallflower: it is far enough from the madding crowds to offer restorative tranquillity, while its baronial oak panelled walls, stained glass, artworks, and rugs on burnished wood floors all add up to a taste of the good things in life.

Country house chic is delivered in spades throughout, and diners are treated to those fabulous Lakeland views from a setting of oak-panelled opulence; manning it all is a fine-tuned service team who live up to the surroundings. The food aims to impress with its serious intent, contemporary vitality and technical accomplishment. Chef David McLaughlin has been at the sharp end for over a decade so has a well-established supply line of superlative local growers and producers, and always keeps a sharp eye on the seasons. Tian of crab is tempered with avocado and pink grapefruit, while rillettes of rabbit could be served with crostini and truffle cream vinaigrette. Attention to detail in timing and presentation is immaculate all the way through a main course of Goosnargh duck breast served pink and tender and matched with creamed cabbage and thyme jus, while fish could be roasted brill with soused vegetables, asparagus and white bean foam. To finish, a dazzling dessert explores a cherry theme involving clafoutis with almond ice cream, and cherry sorbet, sauce and confit. If you can fit it in, the heavily-laden trolley delivers a splendid array of perfectly ripened cheeses from the UK and Europe.

Chef David McLaughlin **Owner** Stephen Leahy
Times 12.30-2/7-9.30 **Prices** Fixed L 2 course fr £26, Fixed D 3 course fr £70, Tasting menu £90, Service optional **Wines** 270 bottles over £30, 29 bottles under £30, 13 by glass
Notes Sunday L, Vegetarian menu, Dress restrictions, Smart casual, Civ Wed 60 **Seats** 50, Pr/dining room 20
Children Portions, Menu **Parking** 50

Linthwaite House Hotel & Restaurant

WINDERMERE MAP 18 SD49

Modern British V NOTABLE WINE LIST

Adventurous contemporary cooking with captivating Lakeland views

☎ 015394 88600
Crook Rd LA23 3JA
e-mail: stay@linthwaite.com
web: www.linthwaite.com
dir: A591 towards The Lakes for 8m to large rdbt, take 1st exit (B5284), 6m, hotel on left. 1m past Windermere golf club

Linthwaite makes an excellent base for tourists on the William Wordsworth and Beatrix Potter trails, but is also in a prime position to enjoy some of Lakeland's most captivating views, either on the terrace in fine weather, or from the snugness of the conservatory if it's turned a bit blowy. Lake Windermere is right on the doorstep, and the prospect extends over rolling woodland to the fells beyond. For a relatively modestly sized house, it packs a lot in, with spa treatments and wedding parties going on, and the decorative style is fresh and airy, with softer shades predominating and a restraining hand on the frills and furbelows. A suite of three dining rooms makes an expansive setting for Chris O'Callaghan's contemporary cooking, which draws on first-division local suppliers and novel techniques to craft a more adventurous style than many Lake District hotel restaurants attempt. Start with a chargrilled pigeon breast, resting on a bed of crunchy sweetcorn granola, and given a discreet sweet note with a scattering of poached blueberries, or opt for a witty spin on a favourite aperitif, combining gin-cured salmon and a tonic sorbet with a sharply tangy purée of lemon. Satisfying textures crop up again in a main course of curry-crusted halibut with tempura-battered soft-shell crab, Indian-spiced sweet potato and Madras-flavoured foam, or there may be

a more conventional serving of roast Herdwick lamb with roasted turnip and swede purée. To finish, there could be white chocolate cheesecake with piña colada ice cream and passionfruit, or a technically proficient caramel soufflé with apple and quince compôte and positively flavoured vanilla ice cream. A six-course tasting menu covers all bases. The wine list is a model of its kind, with helpful, unpretentious tasting notes and an impressive range of choice, from the European heartlands to the southern hemisphere.

Chef Chris O'Callaghan **Owner** Mike Bevans
Times 12.30-2/6.45-9.30 Closed Xmas & New Year (ex residents) **Prices** Fixed L 2 course fr £14.95, Fixed D 3 course fr £52, Tasting menu fr £69.50, Service optional **Wines** 25 bottles over £30, 25 bottles under £30, 14 by glass **Notes** Sunday L, Vegetarian menu, Dress restrictions, Smart casual, Civ Wed 60 **Seats** 64, Pr/dining room 16 **Children** Portions, Menu **Parking** 40

WINDERMERE *continued*

Lindeth Howe Country House Hotel & Restaurant

◉◉ Modern British ◐

Confident modern cooking chez Beatrix Potter

☎ 015394 45759
Lindeth Dr, Longtail Hill LA23 3JF
e-mail: hotel@lindeth-howe.co.uk
web: www.lindeth-howe.co.uk
dir: 1m S of Bowness onto B5284, signed Kendal and Lancaster. Hotel 2nd driveway on right

With its sylvan setting and views over Lake Windermere and mountains, this is a slice of heaven and no mistake. It's a classic country house with a pedigree - Lakeland doyenne Beatrix Potter lived and wrote a couple of her tales here. So after consuming the delicious views and exploring the verdant grounds, it is back for dinner in the handsome, newly decorated dining room. Chef Marc Guibert hails from France and is passionate about regional produce, seeking out first-class ingredients and serving up a menu of contemporary and creative dishes. Everything looks beautiful on the plate and everything is on the plate for a reason. Confit of Cartmel salmon takes centre stage in a starter with rhubarb, ginger, star anise,

duck croquette and rhubarb gel, followed perhaps by slow-cooked blade of beef with a lemon and parsley risotto, glazed vegetables and veal jus, and, to finish, orange mousse with a dark chocolate tuile, orange sponge, chocolate soil, orange gel and coriander cress.

Chef Marc Guibert **Owner** Lakeinvest Ltd
Times 12-2.30/6.30-9 **Prices** Fixed L 2 course £10-£12.50, Tasting menu £49.50, Starter £5.95-£9.50, Main £19.95-£28.50, Dessert £5.95-£7.95, Service optional **Wines** 8 by glass **Notes** Fixed D 5 course £49.50, Trilogy menu £48, Sunday L £14.95-£19.95, Vegetarian available, Dress restrictions, Smart casual, no jeans or sleeveless T-shirts **Seats** 70, Pr/dining room 20
Children Portions, Menu **Parking** 50

Linthwaite House Hotel & Restaurant

◉◉◉ — *see page 121*

Macdonald Old England Hotel & Spa

◉◉ Traditional British, European

Stylish modern dining and stunning lake views

☎ 0844 879 9144
23 Church St, Bowness LA23 3DF
e-mail: sales.oldengland@macdonald-hotels.co.uk
web: www.macdonaldhotels.co.uk
dir: Through Windermere to Bowness, straight across at mini-rdbt. Hotel behind church on right

There is something rather wonderful about dining with a view over water, and with its lakeside setting, the Number 23 Church Street Restaurant at the Macdonald Old England serves up a very nice one indeed. It's Lake Windermere, of course, that you'll see through the floor-to-ceiling windows (or better still the terrace), but there're plenty of other good reasons to come here. The Victorian mansion is much extended these days and includes a spa amongst its many attractions. The restaurant has a good deal to offer, from steaks cooked on the grill, through to some gently contemporary dishes based on top quality regional ingredients. You might start with a ballottine of confit duck leg with honey-pickled vegetables, or a twice-baked cheese soufflé with a fricassée of roasted butternut squash. Those steaks - rib-eye, perhaps - come with plum tomatoes, field

The Samling

WINDERMERE	MAP 18 SD49

Modern British V ◈NOTABLE WINE LIST ◐

Experimental British cooking in a winsome Windermere retreat

☎ 015394 31922
Ambleside Rd LA23 1LR
e-mail: info@thesamlinghotel.co.uk
web: www.thesamlinghotel.co.uk
dir: M6 junct 36, A591 through Windermere towards Ambleside. 2m. 300yds past Low Wood Water Sports Centre just after sharp bend turn right into hotel entrance

A winsomely attractive, white-fronted country house overlooking Lake Windermere, The Samling is another Lakeland bolthole set amid 67 acres of grounds. How do they cram them all in? Thankfully, they do, and this is one of the more lusciously sited. You can sail on the lake,

wallow in the outdoor hot tub, knock croquet balls about on the lawn, get married, anything really... The dining is spread over two rooms, one on either side of the house, and the décor is as quietly understated as the location requires, with bare wood floors, plain painted walls and clothed tables offering nothing to distract from the fine prospect over the lake, other than outstanding British food using local ingredients in dishes that essay the odd foray into today's scientific experimentalism. There are eureka moments aplenty in a repertoire that encompasses a mélange of poached lobster and ribbons of Périgord foie gras, dressed in chicory jam and fresh coconut, sashimi tuna with Ibérico ham and mandarin in vanilla oil, or quail and prawn ravioli with brown shrimps and mango, scattered with soy-roasted seeds. Locally farmed meats steal the show at main, for twice-cooked beef rib, served with a snail cigar, parsley bonbon and shallot marmalade, or anatomised suckling pig, the belly, loin and shoulder of which appear with spring greens, morels and cider jelly, in a sauce pungent with wild garlic and

truffle. For dessert, you'd have to have a heart of stone not to want the chocolate rock, a kind of sprayed parfait alongside soft mousse, seasoned with flavours of pomegranate and beetroot, but the sloe gin crème brûlée with blackberry ice cream has garnered the accolades of ITV cookery judges (on *Britain's Best Dish*), or you might feel it's worth leaving space for the arrival of the chariot that comes laden with British and European cheeses.

Chef Ian Swainson **Owner** Mr Danson
Times 12-1.30/6.30-9.30 **Prices** Fixed L 3 course £25-£50, Fixed D 3 course £50, Tasting menu £65, Service optional **Wines** 22 by glass **Notes** Tasting menu 7 course, Sunday L, Vegetarian menu, Dress restrictions, Smart casual **Seats** 22, Pr/dining room 8
Children Portions, Menu **Parking** 20

mushrooms and hand-cut chips, or go for grilled fillet of grey mullet with fennel purée and poached potatoes. For dessert, chocolate and stem ginger tart with ginger ice cream shows a lightness of touch.

Times 6.30-9.30 Closed L all week

Miller Howe Hotel

◉◉ Modern British V ▲NOTABLE WINE LIST ✋

Romantic lakeside setting and polished country-house cooking

☎ 015394 42536
Rayrigg Rd LA23 1EY
e-mail: info@millerhowe.com
dir: M6 junct 36. Follow the A591 bypass for Kendal. Enter Windermere, continue to mini rdbt, take left onto A592. Miller Howe is 0.25m on right

Miller Howe is something of a Lakeland icon, with its landscaped grounds and stunning views over Windermere and the fells. Staying here is an indulgent experience, a new bar area a recent addition, and no less cosseting is dining in the restaurant, with its plush décor and romantic views of the lake. Put yourselves in the hands of chef Andrew Beaton and go for his tasting menu, or make the more difficult choice of something from the carte, with its handful of dishes per course. One way to start is with the extravagance of poached lobster with lobster cream, Jerusalem artichokes and tarragon gnocchi, or the more earthy delight of ham hock ballottine with piccalilli, vegetables and purée. Dishes impress with the technical care applied to quality produce and intelligent balance, whether time-honoured pink-roast saddle of lamb with crispy neck, glazed root vegetables and rosemary jus, or more adventurous baked cod fillet with tandoori-style roast scallops, cauliflower, apples and tandoori oil. Assiettes and tastings are a favoured approach to desserts, perhaps of chocolate or passionfruit.

Chef Andrew Beaton **Owner** Martin & Helen Ainscough
Times 12.30-1.45/6.45-8.45 Closed 2 wks Jan
Prices Fixed L 2 course £19-£25, Fixed D 3 course £45, Tasting menu £55, Starter £14-£16, Main £24-£28, Dessert £8-£12, Service optional **Wines** 100 bottles over £30, 50 bottles under £30, 12 by glass **Notes** Sunday L, Vegetarian menu, Dress restrictions, Smart casual
Seats 80, Pr/dining room 30 **Children** Portions
Parking 40

The Samling

◉◉◉ – *see opposite*

Storrs Hall Hotel

◉◉ Modern British

Creative vision and old-school standards in a creamy-white Windermere mansion

☎ 015394 47111
Storrs Park LA23 3LG
e-mail: storrshall@englishlakes.co.uk
web: www.englishlakes.co.uk
dir: on A592 2m S of Bowness, on Newby Bridge road

There's an appetising look to the creamy-white façade of the Grade II listed Georgian mansion sitting in 17 acres of grounds by Lake Windermere. Inside, the old-school approach is what fine Lakeland dining is all about, and its appeal is heightened when you contemplate the sensational view over gardens and lake. Game dishes show up well, as witness chestnut-crumbed breast of Cartmel grouse with red wine salsify and bacon choucroute, and the technical wizardry that underpins many dishes is nowhere more dazzlingly on show than in a serving of rabbit, the confit leg appearing in tempura batter with prunes, the loin poached, with sweet and sour garnishes of dessert wine jelly and pickled shimejis. 'Cheeky' is the provocative name given to an ingenious main that pairs cheeks of beef and monkfish, the former braised to a tee, both gaining from their accompaniments of truffled artichoke purée, sautéed wild mushrooms and lentils. A dessert plate offers white chocolate pavé with blackberry ripple ice cream and jelly and what the menu calls 'rustic' praline.

Times 12.30-2/7-9

ASHBOURNE   Map 10 SK14

Callow Hall Hotel

◉◉ Traditional British

Classic British cuisine in family-run country-house hotel

☎ 01335 300900
Mappleton Rd, Mappleton DE6 2AA
e-mail: info@callowhall.co.uk
dir: A515 through Ashbourne towards Buxton, left at Bowling Green pub, then 1st right

What's not to like about this quintessentially English Victorian country-house retreat in 44 acres of woodlands and gardens on the edge of the Peak District National Park, overlooking the Dove Valley and Bentley Brook? Its ivy-festooned walls enfold an old-school set up of antiques, opulent fabrics, fancy plasterwork and oak panels galore, and the vibe in the elegant dining room isn't about to rock that particular boat. A sure-footed kitchen team still does things the old way, smoking and curing meats and fish in-house and doing all of its own baking. The result is country-house cooking in the classic mould; dinner starts with a textbook lobster bisque served with crème fraîche and chives, and a little skewer of tiger prawns and scallops, then moves via an intermediate course - gilt head bream with tomato and black olive tapenade - to mains, perhaps boned roast quail with home-made sausage stuffing, kale, cranberry and apple and rich game jus. To close the show, warm raspberry and blueberry frangipane tart comes with an exemplary vanilla ice cream.

Times 12-1.45/7.15-9

BAKEWELL   Map 16 SK26

Piedaniel's

◉ Traditional French

French bistro dishes with an air of contemporary chic

☎ 01629 812687
Bath St DE45 1BX
dir: From Bakewell rdbt in town centre take A6 Buxton exit. 1st right into Bath St (one-way)

The stone-built timbered look suggests a traditional country inn, but this appealing venue has an air of contemporary chic about it indoors, with smartly dressed tables, whitewashed stone walls and splashes of spring green in the décor. The order of the day is bistro dishes that reliably deliver to their specifications, starting perhaps with saffron-scented mussel soup, or scallops and tiger prawns provençale, and bringing out the big guns at main-course stage, when best end of lamb is served in its cooking juices with basil couscous and tomato confit, or chicken is swathed in smoked Black Forest ham and served with ratatouille sauce. Finish up with a wodge of chocolate truffle torte with raspberry sorbet.

Times 12-2/7-10 Closed Xmas & New Year, 2 wks Jan, 2 wks Aug, Mon, D Sun

BASLOW
Map 16 SK27

Cavendish Hotel

◉◉ Modern British V 🍃

Modish cooking in historic coaching inn

☎ 01246 582311
Church Ln DE45 1SP
e-mail: info@cavendish-hotel.net
web: www.cavendish-hotel.net
dir: M1 junct 29 follow signs for Chesterfield. From
Chesterfield take A619 to Bakewell, Chatsworth & Baslow

On the Chatsworth Estate, the Duke and Duchess of
Devonshire's country seat, the Cavendish Hotel is a
supremely civilised place to stay and eat. There's been an
inn on this spot for a good while (even local historians
aren't sure when it first opened its doors, but it was a
long time ago), and today's incarnation has plenty of
period charm. It's been done out with a good deal of good
taste by the Duke and Duchess with lots of antiques and
original paintings. The Gallery restaurant is a traditional
and elegant room, with smartly laid tables and a service
team who are entirely on the ball. On the menu is some
ambitious and creative food based on good local
ingredients. Start, perhaps, with Gressingham duck in a
terrine with foie gras, prunes and Armagnac, its richness
cut with the accompanying pineapple, plus pain d'épice.
Next up, slow-cooked belly of pork with Thai flavours,
seared scallop and satay sauce, and, to finish, glazed
lemon tart with raspberry doughnuts, consommé, powder
and basil sorbet.

Chef Mike Thompson **Owner** Chatsworth Estates
Times 12-2.30/6.30-10 Closed D 25 Dec **Prices** Fixed L 2
course £35, Fixed D 3 course £45, Service added 5%
Wines 34 bottles over £30, 24 bottles under £30, 11 by
glass **Notes** Sunday L, Vegetarian menu, Dress
restrictions, No trainers, T-shirts or jeans **Seats** 50, Pr/
dining room 18 **Children** Portions **Parking** 40

Fischer's Baslow Hall

◉◉◉ – *see opposite*

BEELEY
Map 16 SK26

The Devonshire Arms at Beeley

◉◉ Modern British 🍃

Accomplished cooking in an up-to-date country inn

☎ 01629 733259
Devonshire Square DE4 2NR
e-mail: enquiries@devonshirebeeley.co.uk
web: www.devonshirebeeley.co.uk
dir: 6m N of Matlock & 5m E of Bakewell, located off
B6012

Set in a charming little village on the Chatsworth Estate,
The Devonshire Arms looks for all it's worth the
quintessential mellow-stone English country inn. Inside,
though, that is not the whole story. The expected classic
look of the cosy bar with oak beams, exposed-stone walls
and wood-burning fires leads on to a light, modishly-
styled brasserie extension rich with bold colours, tub
dining chairs and vibrant modern artwork. The estate's
produce rightly figures prominently on a repertoire that
keeps things intelligently straightforward and seasonal.
Start with warm scallop and cockle salad dressed in basil
oil, or rabbit and mushroom tortellini with carrot and
orange purée. There are classic pub dishes such as
bangers (courtesy of one Mr Hancock) served with mash
and red wine and onion gravy, or more the more modish
tempura skate wing with Russian salad, lobster sauce
and duck ham. To finish, Mrs Hill's (the chef's mum)
lemon tart with sweet Chantilly cream is a fixture. There's
a flexible approach here, with the same menu taken in
the bar.

Chef Alan Hill **Owner** Duke of Devonshire
Times 12-3/6-9.30 **Prices** Starter £5.25-£8, Main
£11.95-£25, Dessert fr £5.95, Service optional **Wines** 20
by glass **Notes** Sunday L, Vegetarian available **Seats** 60
Children Portions **Parking** 30

BRADWELL
Map 16 SK18

The Samuel Fox Country Inn

◉◉ Modern British 🍃

Local produce and accomplished modern cooking

☎ 01433 621562
Stretfield Rd S33 9JT
e-mail: enquiries@samuelfox.co.uk
dir: M1 junct 29, A617 towards Chesterfield, onto A619
towards A623 Chapel-en-le-Frith. B6049 for Bradwell,
restaurant located on left

If you've had cause to put up a folding umbrella during
your time here in the wild hills of the Peak District, say a
word of thanks to Samuel Fox, the local man who invented

the device. The old village boozer that bears his name
has been revamped to good effect in recent years in a
fresh, modern style, with an airy open-plan layout and
lovely views of the Hope Valley through the windows. The
kitchen sources the best materials it can lay its hands on
and takes a creative modern approach that has firmly
established the place on the local foodie scene. Dishes
score highly on their unfussy attitude and full-on
flavours, starting typically with devilled sprats with lime
and garlic mayonnaise, before effective, big-hearted
pairings such as slow-cooked belly pork with chorizo,
white beans and roasted garlic, or braised haunch of
venison with celeriac, cabbage and red wine. Puddings
put a clever spin on old favourites by matching
something like burnt vanilla cream with blueberries and
brioche doughnuts.

Chef James Duckett **Owner** Johnson Inns
Times 12-2.30/6-9.30 Closed 2-31 Jan, D 25 Dec
Prices Fixed L 2 course £10, Starter £4.50-£7, Main
£11.50-£18.50, Dessert £3.50-£8.50, Service optional
Wines 8 bottles over £30, 35 bottles under £30, 14 by
glass **Notes** Sunday L £19-£24, Vegetarian available
Seats 50 **Children** Portions, Menu **Parking** 15

BREADSALL
Map 11 SK33

Breadsall Priory, A Marriott Hotel & Country Club

◉ Traditional

Honest British cooking in historical property

☎ 01332 832235
Moor Rd, Morley DE7 6DL
web: www.marriottbreadsallpriory.co.uk
dir: M1 junct 25, A52 to Derby, then follow Chesterfield
signs. Right at 1st rdbt, left at next. A608 to Heanor Rd.
In 3m left then left again

In 300 acres that include two golf courses, Breadsall
Priory is a handsome building with its roots in the 13th
century. An archway in the Priory Restaurant, a beamed
room with leaded windows looking out on to the grounds,
was part of the original property. The menu doesn't stray
too far beyond these shores, and the kitchen delivers
admirably straightforward and uncluttered starters,
among them perhaps ham hock terrine with piccalilli,
and seared scallops with celeriac purée and pickled
apple. Main courses show the same sort of restraint,
teaming well-timed fillet of bream with chive tagliolini
and creamed leeks, and roast guinea fowl with port jus.
Grilled steaks, with a choice of sauces, are popular
choices, and comforting puddings may include steamed
chocolate sponge.

Times 7-10 Closed Mon, L Tue-Sat

Save on Hotels. Book at **theAA.com/hotel**

DERBYSHIRE 125 ENGLAND

Fischer's Baslow Hall

Modern European V

Bold, creative cooking in an elegant country house

☎ 01246 583259
Calver Rd DE45 1RR
e-mail: reservations@fischers-baslowhall.co.uk
dir: From Baslow on A623 towards Calver. Hotel on right

Reaching the 25-year landmark here in 2013 - raise a glass, why not? - Max and Susan Fischer have turned this Edwardian country house into a restaurant with rooms of the highest order. It is special. Even one's arrival down the winding tree-lined driveway lowers the blood-pressure, and lower still when the house, built in the style of a 17th-century manor, comes into view. The garden is a joy to behold and even pays its dues by contributing vegetables, fruits and herbs for the table. Inside, it's a class act, too, with a soothingly traditional demeanour, plenty of period character, and everything from paintings to furniture chosen with a keen eye. The team in the kitchen - headed up by Rupert Rowley - has really put Fischer's on the map: this is a kitchen that embraces the new, respects the old, and puts the ingredients centre stage. Things get off to a flying start with the canapés and fabulous breads (stout and treacle anyone?), before a first course red mullet fillet, cooked over burning coals, with red pepper, aubergine and Ibérico chorizo, or mosaic of rabbit wrapped in carrot, with textures of carrot and liquorice gel. There's craft, balance and intelligence to the food here. The 'Classic Menu' is supported by a 'Taste of Britain' tasting menu that puts first-class seasonal, regional ingredients to the fore, and the vegetarian menu delivers punchy, enticing flavours, too. A steamed bone marrow and oxtail pudding might turn up at main course stage, with roast sweetbreads, ox tongue, braised golden turnip and red wine sauce, but there are compelling fishy alternatives: pan-fried John Dory, perhaps, with white truffle gnocchi, Wye Valley asparagus and Sauternes sauce. Presentation is never less than eye-catching, as with a dessert of chocolate 'tree trunk', with hazelnut granité, chocolate mousse and coconut sorbet.

Chef Rupert Rowley **Owner** Mr & Mrs M Fischer **Times** 12-1.30/7-8.30 Closed 25-26 & 31 Dec **Prices** Fixed L 2 course fr £20.13, Fixed D 3 course £48-£72, Tasting menu £50-£72, Starter £12.50-£13.75, Main £24.50-£25.95, Dessert £8.50-£9, Service optional **Wines** 110 bottles over £30, 20 bottles under £30, 6 by glass **Notes** Sunday L, Vegetarian menu, Dress restrictions, Smart casual, no jeans, sweatshirts, trainers, Civ Wed 38

Seats 55, Pr/dining room 38
Children Portions **Parking** 20

BUXTON — Map 16 SK07

Best Western Lee Wood Hotel

Traditional & Modern British

Modish cooking (with nostalgic classics) in a Georgian manor house

☎ 01298 23002
The Park SK17 6TQ
e-mail: reservations@leewoodhotel.co.uk
web: www.leewoodhotel.co.uk
dir: M1 junct 24, A50 towards Ashbourne, A515 to Buxton. From Buxton town centre follow A5004 Long Hill to Whaley Bridge. Hotel approx 200mtrs beyond University of Derby campus

Lee Wood can put on an impressive wedding if you're in the market for one, but no matter if not, for the hotel's Elements Restaurant is worth a visit in its own right. The rather handsome Georgian manor house is in a good spot to explore all that the Buxton area has to offer (which is a great deal), while its ambitious restaurant awaits to provide satisfying sustenance at lunch and dinner. The conservatory dining room is the setting for some creative modern cooking. Start, perhaps, with a confit of duck leg with a chilli jelly, spiced bread crisp and pineapple purée. There's more traditional stuff, too, such as first-course cod fishcakes with lemon and parsley sauce, and main-courses range from fish and chips to fillet of sea bass with puréed basil potatoes, peperonata and pesto sauce. Finish with chocolate and hazelnut marquise with caramelised hazelnut and liquorice caviar.

Times 12-2/5.30-9.15 Closed 24-25 Dec

CHESTERFIELD — Map 16 SK37

Casa Hotel

Modern European

Celebrate all things Spanish in a lopsided 'pomo' hotel

☎ 01246 245990
Lockoford Ln S41 7JB
e-mail: cocina@casahotels.co.uk
web: www.casahotels.co.uk
dir: M1 junct 29 to A617 Chesterfield/A61 Sheffield, 1st exit at rdbt, hotel on left

A hunk of Catalonian postmodernism landed in Chesterfield with the opening of the Spanish-themed Casa, the long blocks of its uneven storeys looking as if assembled by a gigantic five-year-old. Cool, in other words. The interior design counterpoints sober wood tones with splashes of mural colour, including in the second-floor Cocina restaurant, where a dazzlingly illuminated night-time cityscape draws the eye. A tapas repertoire and sharing platters of charcuterie set the compass needle quivering on the menus, with albondigas, pan con tomate and salt-cod croquetas all up to the mark. Mains might tempt by swaddling monkfish in Parma ham and serving it with crab risotto in a sudden eastwards lurch towards Italy, but the star of the show is the charcoal-fired Josper grill, which lends smoky savour to organically reared Belted Galloway rib-eye, sirloin and fillet, hung for four weeks and served with a sauce choice and chips. Finish appropriately with crema catalana and spiced shortbread, or by pondering your selection from the dual-nationality cheese trolley. Spanish wines lead the charge on the list.

Chef Andrew Wilson **Owner** Steve Perez **Times** 12-2/6-10 Closed L Mon-Sat, D Sun **Prices** Fixed D 3 course fr £19.50, Starter £5-£9.50, Main £12-£27, Dessert £5-£8, Service optional **Wines** 31 bottles over £30, 34 bottles under £30, 12 by glass **Notes** Early bird menu available D 6-7pm Mon-Sat, Sunday L, Vegetarian available, Dress restrictions, Smart casual, Civ Wed 280 **Seats** 100, Pr/dining room 200 **Children** Portions **Parking** 200

CLOWNE — Map 16 SK47

Hotel Van Dyk

Modern British

Boutique Georgian hotel with fine modern cooking

☎ 01246 810219
Worksop Rd S43 4TD
e-mail: info@hotelvandyk.co.uk
dir: M1 junct 30, towards Worksop, at rdbt 1st exit, next rdbt straight over. Through lights, hotel 100yds on right

This boutique hotel, a grand Grade II listed building, has two eating options, The Bowden being the fine-dining venue, a splendid room with panelled walls, luxurious fabrics, chandeliers and a self-playing baby grand. The kitchen hits a few international notes, steaming mussels and clams in a starter with coconut, lemongrass and chilli and serving them with wild rice salad, and marinating rump of lamb and plating it with vegetable tagine, spicy apricot chutney and tzatziki dressing. Smoked duck breast might come with pancetta and cherry compôte, followed by beef bourguignon, or roast halibut fillet accompanied by saffron fondant potatoes, broccoli, sorrel purée and lemon beurre blanc.

Times 12-9.30 Closed Mon-Tue

DALBURY — Map 10 SK23

The Black Cow

Modern British NEW

Good cooking on the village green

☎ 01332 824297
The Green, Dalbury Lees DE6 5BE
e-mail: enquiries@theblackcow.co.uk
dir: From Derby A52 signed Ashbourne, Kirk Langley; turn into Church Lane, then Long Lane, follow signs to Dalbury Lees

On the corner of the village green, The Black Cow looks every inch the rural village pub, complete with pretty hanging baskets. It's a freehouse, so you'll find some interesting ales on tap, including from local breweries with names like Dancing Duck and Peakstone Rock. There are bedrooms, too, if you want to stay over. It's been gently updated inside, so it still feels like a pub, but is done out in muted contemporary tones and, in the dining area, smart high-backed leather chairs stand at chunky darkwood tables. On the menu, the chef takes on British, European and some Asian ideas, starting perhaps with black tiger prawns with peanut, chilli and coconut sauce, and sticky rice, or pressed ham hock and apricot terrine with red onion marmalade. For main course, you might choose a steak or something like pan-fried fillet of sea bass with saffron risotto, roasted butternut squash and sweet pepper dressing.

Chef Jazwant Singh **Owner** Mark & Sean Goodwin **Times** 12-2/6-9 **Prices** Starter £3.95-£7.50, Main £9.50-£16.95, Dessert £4.50-£6.95, Service optional **Wines** 1 bottle over £30, 17 bottles under £30, 8 by glass **Notes** Sunday L fr £40, Vegetarian available **Seats** 30, Pr/dining room 25 **Children** Portions, Menu **Parking** 12, On street

DARLEY ABBEY — Map 11 SK33

Darleys Restaurant

Modern British V

Modern British cooking by the water's edge

☎ 01332 364987
Haslams Ln DE22 1DZ
e-mail: info@darleys.com
web: www.darleys.com
dir: A6 N from Derby (Duffield road). Right in 1m into Mileash Ln, to Old Lane, right, over bridge. Restaurant on right

This converted silk mill on the banks of the River Derwent - rather appropriately once a mill workers' canteen - is a fab location on fair-weather days with its smart decked terrace overlooking the weir. The interior is bang up-to-date, so shades of darkwood, chocolate and toffee are joined by vibrant fabrics giving splashes of colour. Likewise, the kitchen takes a modern approach to the cooking, driven by quality local and seasonal produce. A soundly-priced lunch menu might feature braised lamb shoulder with colcannon potato cake, while dinner cranks up the ante serving up smoked haddock chowder with cauliflower bhaji, followed by a trio of pork accompanied by root vegetable terrine and cider sauce. Baby meringues with broken shortbread and Daiquiri curd and sorbet

Save on Hotels. Book at **theAA.com/hotel**

DERBYSHIRE 127 **ENGLAND**

makes for a stylish finale. Plenty of the inside tables benefit from the watery views.

Chef Jonathan Hobson, Mark Hadfield **Owner** Jonathan & Kathryn Hobson **Times** 12-2/7-9.30 Closed BHs, 1st 2 wks Jan, D Sun **Prices** Prices not confirmed Service optional **Wines** 15 by glass **Notes** Sunday L, Vegetarian menu **Seats** 70 **Children** Portions **Parking** 12

DERBY
Map 11 SK33

Masa Restaurant

◉◉ Modern European **V** 🥂

Modern classic brasserie dishes in a converted Wesleyan chapel

☎ 01332 203345

The Old Chapel, Brook St DE1 3PF

e-mail: enquiries@masarestaurantwinebar.com

dir: 8m from M1 junct 25. Brook St off inner ring road near BBC Radio Derby

A stone chapel of the Wesleyan persuasion is the converted home to Masa, a city-centre venue that comprises a bustling ground-floor bar with a galleried restaurant divided into a number of different levels. Modern classic brasserie dishes contribute to the urban cool of the place, and staff make impressively short work of all the steps to bring them to you. Expect seared scallops with cauliflower purée, or ham hock and chicken terrine with piccalilli, to start, followed by beef fillet and dauphinoise, or sea bass with crushed new potatoes, roasted Mediterranean veg and basil oil. The ideas may not be exactly cutting edge, but they are rendered with convincing panache and with palpably good prime materials. Finish with lemon tart, served with vanilla ice cream and raspberry coulis.

Chef Adam Harvey **Owner** Didar & Paula Dalkic **Times** 12-2/6-9.30 Closed Mon-Tue **Prices** Fixed L 2 course £17, Fixed D 3 course £25, Tasting menu £25, Starter £5-£8.50, Main £12.50-£22.50, Dessert £5.95-£7.95, Service optional, Groups min 8 service 10% **Wines** 12 bottles over £30, 34 bottles under £30, 11 by glass **Notes** Tasting menu 5 course, Sunday L, Vegetarian menu, Dress restrictions, Smart casual, black tie when specified, Civ Wed 100 **Seats** 120 **Children** Portions **Parking** On street (pay & display), Car park Brook St

---

FROGGATT
Map 16 SK27

The Chequers Inn

◉ Traditional, European 🥂

Homely country inn in the Peak District

☎ 01433 630231

S32 3ZJ

e-mail: info@chequers-froggatt.com

dir: On A625 between Sheffield & Bakewell, 0.75m from Calver

Originally four 18th-century cottages, The Chequers stands above Calver Bridge on the steep banks of Froggatt Edge. Follow a visit to nearby Chatsworth House, or end an invigorating moorland ramble, with a meal at this traditional inn, which offers good pub food and comfortable accommodation. Look to the printed menu for a good choice of pub favourites (local sausages, mash and gravy, hot roast beef sandwiches) or, for something more modern and adventurous, order from the specials board, perhaps confit duck leg with roasted plums followed by seafood risotto with saffron, or pork shoulder with parsley mash and apple and vanilla compôte. Décor has the homely feel of a country cottage, with simple wooden furniture, bare boards, pine dressers and rag-washed yellow walls.

Chef Graham Mitchell **Owner** Jonathan & Joanne Tindall **Times** 12-2.30/6-9.30 Closed 25 Dec **Prices** Starter £6.50-£7, Main £12.50-£16, Dessert £5.75, Service optional **Wines** 3 bottles over £30, 34 bottles under £30, 10 by glass **Notes** Sunday L £14, Vegetarian available **Seats** 90 **Children** Portions, Menu **Parking** 50

GRINDLEFORD
Map 16 SK27

The Maynard

◉◉ Modern British 🥂

Glorious views, a dash of boutique style and contemporary cooking

☎ 01433 630321

Main Rd S32 2HE

e-mail: info@themaynard.co.uk

dir: M1/A619 into Chesterfield, onto Baslow, A623 to Calver right into Grindleford

The glorious rolling Peak District opens up in front of this rather grand old house, now a decidedly swish boutique hotel. Needless to say, a drink on the terrace is a particularly good idea when the sun is up, laying bare a spectacularly green and pleasant vista, but indoors is no less eye-catching. With clever use of bold colours and artworks, and a mix of textures and materials, the lounge has a good deal of contemporary swagger, whilst the restaurant is done out with hand-painted murals, classy blue tones and smartly dressed tables. The cooking is equally of the moment, with plenty of regional flavours and bags of good ideas. Start, perhaps, with a confit

duck and smoked chicken terrine, the luscious richness perfectly cut with rhubarb and pear chutney, or a vibrant Thai hot-and-sour broth with garlicky tiger prawns. Next up, breast of guinea fowl is roasted and comes with creamed Savoy cabbage, butternut squash and potato fondant, while oven-baked sea trout is accompanied by dauphinoise and a chive and caviar cream sauce. To finish, warm chocolate tart comes in a happy union with a red berry sorbet.

Chef Mark Vernon **Owner** Jane Hitchman **Times** 12-2/7-9 Closed L Sat **Prices** Prices not confirmed Service optional **Wines** 7 by glass **Notes** Sunday L, Vegetarian available, Civ Wed 140 **Seats** 50, Pr/dining room 140 **Children** Portions, Menu **Parking** 60

HARDSTOFT
Map 16 SK46

The Shoulder at Hardstoft

◉◉ Modern British 🥂

Food-driven pub with passion for local produce

☎ 01246 850276

Deep Ln S45 8AF

e-mail: info@thefamousshoulder.co.uk

dir: Follow signs to Hardwick Hall, take 1st right after turning off B6039

This one-time down-at-heel village boozer has been given a 'more-gastro-than-pub' contemporary makeover. Stone-built and 300-years old, the re-branded Shoulder is essentially a pub and restaurant with rooms, though still with a friendly, relaxed attitude. The restaurant itself is a light, clean-lined space of pale-wood floors and tables, fashionable high-back seating and red, cream or boldly papered walls. There's a snug bar, real fires and leather sofas to chill-out on, while the aroma of home-baked loaves (for sale on the bar) heightens anticipation and displays the kitchen's passion for local, home-made, home-smoked and home-grown produce. The cooking takes a modern, precise approach without being too showy: shoulder and loin venison Wellington, perhaps, with foie gras, braised red cabbage, baby leeks and smoked garlic jus. To finish, vanilla crème brûlée, shortbread and freeze-dried raspberries hits the spot. A bar menu is also available, but you can eat whatever you want wherever you want.

Chef Simon Johnson **Owner** Simon Johnson **Times** 12-9 Closed D Sun **Prices** Service included **Wines** 5 bottles over £30, 23 bottles under £30, 10 by glass **Notes** Sunday L £8-£12, Vegetarian available **Seats** 60, Pr/dining room 12 **Children** Portions, Menu **Parking** 50

HARTSHORNE	Map 10 SK32

The Mill Wheel

◉ Modern British ◔

Locally-based cooking in a 17th-century mill

☎ 01283 550335
Ticknall Rd DE11 7AS
e-mail: info@themillwheel.co.uk
web: www.themillwheel.co.uk
dir: M42 junct 2, A511 to Woodville, left onto A514 towards Derby to Hartshorne

An inn only since the 1980s, The Mill Wheel is a converted 17th-century mill, still full of period detail in its stone walls, beamed ceilings and - most majestically of all - the original water-powered wheel, turning sedately in the midst of the bar which has been designed around it. Real ales and comfortable leather sofas are the plus points, and upstairs is a beamed restaurant, done in uncluttered modern style with contemporary artworks and light wooden furniture. Assiduously sourced local produce informs the modern British menus, which take in the likes of a trio of smoked fish with salmon keta and orange salad to start, followed by a pork duo - tenderloin and smoked belly - accompanied by crushed sage potatoes, wild mushrooms and Calvados cream, or sea bass with smoked bacon and peas. An excellent, chunky bread-and-butter pudding with plenty of crème anglaise is the star finale. Pudding Table nights once a month offer a fixed-price three-course dinner with as many puddings as you feel you deserve.

Chef Russel Burridge **Owner** Colin & Jackie Brown
Times 12-2.15/6-9.15 **Prices** Starter £3.95-£5.95, Main £7.95-£19.95, Dessert £4.50-£5.95, Service optional **Wines** 1 bottle over £30, 15 bottles under £30, 9 by glass **Notes** Champagne breakfast 4 course £19.95, Sunday L £9.95-£16.95, Vegetarian available **Seats** 52 **Children** Portions, Menu

HATHERSAGE	Map 16 SK28

George Hotel

◉◉ Modern British ◔

Well-considered flavours in a 500-year-old former coaching inn

☎ 01433 650436
Main Rd S32 1BB
e-mail: info@george-hotel.net
web: www.george-hotel.net
dir: In village centre on junction of A625/B6001

This 500-year-old Peak District coaching inn comes with all the low beams, open fires, stone walls and bare wooden floors that one might expect in an inn mentioned by Charlotte Brontë in *Jane Eyre*. But times change and the inn has morphed into a rather stylish hotel and restaurant, overlaid with a cool, contemporary décor involving funky fabrics and modish patterned wallpapers. The cooking takes a similarly on-trend route, taking as its bedrock top-class materials from local suppliers, and doing it all the hard way, making breads, pastries and ice creams in-house. When summer peas are in season, they appear in an inventive combo of pea pannacotta, tempura crayfish tails, pea shoot salad and thermidor mayonnaise, while a winter main course could see steamed chestnut and venison pudding partnered with roasted root vegetables, juniper sauce and parsnip crisps. Whatever the time of year, treacle tart with vanilla sauce, banana and clotted cream ice cream and caramelised walnuts makes a stonking finish.

Chef Helen Heywood **Owner** Eric Marsh
Times 12-2.30/7-10 Closed D 25 Dec **Prices** Prices not confirmed Service added 5% **Wines** 16 bottles over £30, 36 bottles under £30, 11 by glass **Notes** Early bird menu Mon-Fri 6.30-7.30pm, Sunday L, Vegetarian available, Dress restrictions, Smart casual, no T-shirts or trainers, Civ Wed 70 **Seats** 45, Pr/dining room 70 **Children** Portions **Parking** 45

The Plough Inn

◉ Modern British ◔

Peak District riverside inn with Mediterranean-accented cooking

☎ 01433 650319
Leadmill Bridge S32 1BA
e-mail: sales@theploughinn-hathersage.co.uk
web: www.theploughinn-hathersage.co.uk
dir: 1m SE of Hathersage on B6001. Over bridge, 150yds beyond at Leadmill

The Tudor inn on the River Derwent exudes a sense of country-pub tradition, from the tartan carpeting in the bar, the open fires and the informal dining area with its pub furniture. The same menu is served throughout the place, and is comprised of modern British specials with a Mediterranean accent. Flash-fried whitebait with lime and coriander mayo, butternut squash, goats' cheese and sage risotto, and spatchcocked poussin marinated in lemon and oregano with Greek salad are what to expect. Go east for a fish dish such as seaweed-battered red mullet with bok choy in black bean sauce, and back home again for original Bakewell pudding with poached blueberries and custard.

Chef Robert Navarro **Owner** Robert & Cynthia Emery
Times 11.30-2.30/6.30-9.30 Closed 25 Dec **Prices** Fixed L 2 course £15-£20, Fixed D 3 course £21.50-£27.50, Starter £6-£10, Main £14-£25, Dessert £6-£7.50, Service optional **Wines** 14 by glass **Notes** Sunday L, Vegetarian available, Dress restrictions, Smart casual **Seats** 40, Pr/dining room 24 **Children** Portions **Parking** 40

HIGHAM   Map 16 SK35

Santo's Higham Farm Hotel

◉ Modern International ✪

Pleasingly unfussy cooking in the lush Amber Valley

☎ 01773 833812
Main Rd DE55 6EH
e-mail: reception@santoshighamfarm.co.uk
web: www.santoshighamfarm.co.uk
dir: M1 junct 28, A38 towards Derby, then A61 to Higham, left onto B6013

This 15th-century farmstead has evolved over the years into a rambling small-scale hotel run with sincere charm by hands-on owner Santo Cusimano. It is a hideaway made for hiking through Derbyshire's wild landscapes, and even if you're not up to taking on the great outdoors, armchair ramblers can bask in uplifting views over the Amber Valley. The comfy candlelit dining room is done out in a reassuringly traditional way with linen-clad tables, and the food is equally unpretentious, comforting stuff wrought from well-chosen local ingredients. Expect Italian-inspired ideas along the lines of pheasant meatballs with tomato sauce and parmesan crisp, followed by classic combinations such as goose fillet with cranberry relish, fondant potato, braised chicory and port jus, or daube of beef with root vegetables and red wine sauce. Finish with white chocolate pannacotta served with a spiced apple samosa.

Chef Lee Sanderson **Owner** Santo Cusimano
Times 12-3/7-9.30 Closed BHs, L Mon-Sat, D Sun
Prices Starter £4.50-£7.50, Main £12.50-£21, Dessert £4.50-£6.50, Service added but optional 5% **Wines** 6 by glass **Notes** Sunday L £10.50-£19, Vegetarian available, Dress restrictions, Smart casual, Civ Wed 100 **Seats** 50, Pr/dining room 34 **Children** Portions **Parking** 100

HOPE   Map 16 SK18

Losehill House Hotel & Spa

◉◉ Modern British V ✪

Glorious Peak District views and contemporary country-house cooking

☎ 01433 621219
Lose Hill Ln, Edale Rd S33 6AF
e-mail: info@losehillhouse.co.uk
web: www.losehillhouse.co.uk
dir: A6187 into Hope. Take turn opposite church into Edale Rd. 1m, left & follow signs to hotel

Losehill House, in the Arts and Crafts style, was originally built as a walking hostel, which accounts for its fantastic Peak District location. Meals are served in the Orangery Restaurant, a light, contemporary room with comfortable upholstered chairs and views of sheep-grazed fields. Dishes are put together creatively and are generally straightforward and uncluttered, taking in perfectly cooked lamb fillet with a mini shepherd's pie and crispy shoulder together with carrots and cauliflower cheese, or fillet of sea bass set off by tarragon foam with seasonal asparagus and broad beans. Starters are brought off successfully too, judging by tender monkfish cheek with prosciutto, aubergine purée and sultana dressing, and a meal might end with honey (from local bees) crème brûlée with summery gooseberry and elderflower sorbet, or a theme on rhubarb.

Chef Darren Goodwin **Owner** Paul & Kathryn Roden
Times 12-2.30/6.30-9 **Prices** Fixed L 2 course £14.50-£19.50, Fixed D 3 course £35, Tasting menu £45, Service optional **Wines** 6 by glass **Notes** Taste of Losehill 7 course £45, Sunday L, Vegetarian menu, Civ Wed 80 **Seats** 50, Pr/dining room 12 **Children** Portions **Parking** 20

MATLOCK   Map 16 SK35

Stones Restaurant

◉◉ Modern British V ✪

Modern dining with a riverside terrace

☎ 01629 56061
1c Dale Rd DE4 3LT
e-mail: info@stones-restaurant.co.uk

Tucked away behind a wooden fence in the heart of this perennially charming spa town, Stones is every inch the contemporary eatery. A blank white room with exposed wood flooring and florally patterned upholstery (plus a newly extended tiled riverside terrace overlooked by trees, if you're ready to bask in the Derbyshire sun) makes a refreshing setting for Kevin Stone's modern British stylings. Home-made black pudding with a poached egg and garlic hollandaise is worth a punt, while the scallops come with lemon and dill arancini, dressed in tomato and capers, for a more Mediterranean mood. Mains embrace an Asian take on halibut, which comes with a crab spring roll and pak choi in buttery sauce Jacqueline, a variety of lamb cuts with pea pannacotta in mint and caper jus, or a positively old-school breast of free-range chicken with wild mushrooms and blue cheese in watercress sauce. Desserts are tastes, textures and studies, but there might be a simple crème brûlée in there too, redolent of vanilla, and served with pistachio ice cream and shortbread.

Chef Kevin Stone **Owner** Kevin Stone, Jade Himsworth, Katie Temple **Times** 12-2/6.30-9 Closed 26 Dec, 1 Jan, Sun-Mon, L Tue **Prices** Fixed L 2 course £16.50, Fixed D 3 course £30-£34, Service optional **Wines** 10 bottles over £30, 25 bottles under £30, 8 by glass **Notes** Vegetarian menu **Seats** 50 **Children** Portions, Menu **Parking** Matlock train station

MELBOURNE   Map 11 SK32

The Bay Tree

◉◉ Modern British

Modish cooking in a tranquil market town

☎ 01332 863358
4 Potter St DE73 8HW
e-mail: enquiries@baytreerestaurant.co.uk
dir: From M1(N) junct 23A or junct 24 (S) take A453 to Isley Walton, turn right & follow signs to Melbourne town centre

The charming market town of Melbourne has a gem of a local restaurant in The Bay Tree. And it's a restaurant that takes inspiration from far beyond the Derbyshire countryside - chef Rex Howell has drawn on his experience around the world, especially the Far East, to deliver his style of modern British cooking. There is nothing to scare the horses, though, and flavour combinations are well judged. Cornish crab salad comes with avocado and pickled kohlrabi, for example, or go for Keralan-style green mango and king prawn curry with a spicy home-made tomato chutney. The butternut squash purée that accompanies a rack of English lamb is flavoured with cumin, and star anise infuses the sauce accompanying line-caught sea bass. The village has an old-world feel, but inside The Bay Tree there's a soothing contemporary shimmer and pleasing absence of country chintz.

Times 10.30-3/6.30-10.30 Closed 25 & 31 Dec, BHs, Mon-Tue, D Sun

The Peacock at Rowsley

Modern British V

Contemporary and populist cooking in a lustrous Peak District hotel

☎ 01629 733518
Bakewell Rd DE4 2EB
e-mail: reception@thepeacockatrowsley.com
web: www.thepeacockatrowsley.com
dir: A6, 3m before Bakewell, 6m from Matlock towards Bakewell

Owned by Lord Edward Manners, and restyled by Parisian design guru India Mahdavi, The Peacock spreads its lustrous tail-feathers amid the rugged austerity of the Peak District. The interfacing of 17th century stolidity and modern style lends the interiors a classy dash, not least in the bar, where the rough-stone walls and log fire are offset by a sleek, marble-topped counter, and the prevailing juxtaposition of aubergine and leafy-green in the furnishings offers more visual stimulation than today's ubiquitous beige and coffee hues tend to. In the restaurant, tables set with gleaming glasses but not cloths look out over the gardens, and the mood is one of relaxing civility. Dan Smith is a confirmed localist, inveigling black pudding, beef, fresh produce and Cropwell Bishop Stilton from the environs onto menus that have a distinct undercurrent of populism (beer-battered haddock and chips, venison

faggots, neeps and tatties in onion gravy, apple and rhubarb crumble with ginger custard on Sundays) beneath the more obviously contemporary flourishes. That latter tendency sees a partnering of pork cheek and black pudding with parmesan polenta, accompanied by pineapple and chicory, for starters, and a possible follow-up of spiced monkfish in coconut and mussel sauce with lentils, carrots and squash, or duck breast and liver with quinoa, turnip, rhubarb and gingerbread crumbs. Desserts tend to the lighter end of the spectrum - perhaps fromage frais mousse with pink peppercorn meringue and mint oil - but aren't above indulging the constituency that will always fall for a wodge of warm chocolate cake with peanut shortbread and caramel, accompanied by a sorbet flavoured with breakfast cereal and milk. The savoury option could be a properly melting serving of Vacherin Mont d'Or with an Eccles cake, Medjool dates, apple and Brazils.

Chef Daniel Smith **Owner** Rutland Hotels **Times** 12-2/7-9 Closed D 24-26 Dec **Prices** Fixed L 3 course £16.50-£17.50, Fixed D 3 course £55.50-£60, Starter £7-£13, Main £28.50-£40, Dessert £8.50-£9.50, Service optional **Wines** 40 bottles over £30, 11 bottles under £30, 18 by glass **Notes** Sunday L, Vegetarian menu, Civ Wed 20 **Seats** 40, Pr/dining room 20 **Children** Portions **Parking** 25

The Peacock at Rowsley

The Peacock at Rowsley is a small luxury hotel located in the famous Peak District in the heart of England, and conveniently close to the major towns of Chesterfield, Sheffield, Manchester, Nottingham and Derby.

Owned by Lord Edward Manners, owner of nearby *Haddon Hall*, the hotel has been refurbished throughout and styled by award winning designer India Mahdavi.

Dan Smith, Head Chef, worked with Tom Aikens in London and has since returned to Derbyshire. He has prepared and designed tantalising menus for our restaurant and bar, using, wherever possible, locally sourced ingredients.

We aim to provide a relaxed and comfortable experience whether you are coming for a weekend in the country, a special occasion, or just to eat and drink.

The Peacock at Rowsley, Derbyshire DE4 2EB • **Tel:** 01629 733518 • Fax: 01629 732671
Website: www.thepeacockatrowsley.com • **Email:** reception@thepeacockatrowsley.com

MORLEY — Map 11 SK34

The Morley Hayes Hotel

🏵🏵 Modern British

Modern-classic cooking on a converted farm estate

☎ 01332 780480
Main Rd DE7 6DG
e-mail: enquiries@morleyhayes.com
web: www.morleyhayes.com
dir: 4m N of Derby on A608

Morley Hayes near Derby has been a farm estate and an orphanage in its time, but has been run as a family hotel since the 1980s. The Dovecote, its principal dining room, is to be found on the raftered first floor of a separate former farm building, overlooking the golf course and surrounding countryside. The cooking is as trend-conscious as can be, with many modern-classic dishes and some novel ideas in evidence. King prawn ravioli with a seared scallop in lemongrass sauce may whet the appetite for Gressingham duck breast with bok choy, radishes, honey-roast carrots and a pastilla of the leg meat. Finish with rhubarb jelly and sorbet, served with buttermilk pannacotta, or else they'll happily deconstruct a Black Forest gâteau for you.

Chef Nigel Stuart **Owner** Robert & Andrew Allsop/Morley Hayes Leisure Ltd **Times** 12-2/7-9.30 Closed 27 Dec, 1 Jan, L Sat, Mon **Prices** Prices not confirmed Service

optional **Wines** 22 bottles over £30, 30 bottles under £30, 12 by glass **Notes** Sunday L, Vegetarian available, Dress restrictions, Smart casual, Civ Wed 80 **Seats** 100, Pr/dining room 24 **Children** Portions, Menu **Parking** 250

RISLEY — Map 11 SK43

Risley Hall Hotel & Spa

🏵 European

Modern cooking in a venerable Saxon manor

☎ 0115 939 9000
Derby Rd DE72 3SS
e-mail: reservations.risleyhall@bespokehotels.com
web: www.bespokehotels.com/risleyhall
dir: M1 junct 25, Sandiacre exit into Bostock Ln. Left at lights, hotel on left in 0.25m

Risley's baronial hall is a big hit with the wedding crowd, hardly surprisingly given that it's an impressively handsome room, but then again, there's much to admire here. The creeper-covered 11th-century house has grown up over the years to include some pretty swanky mod cons (a spa and the like), and in its Abbey's Restaurant there's some good food to be had. It's an elegant and well-proportioned room done out in a traditional style with tables draped in white linen. The cooking follows a broadly modern path, but gently so. You might start with an interesting salad of oxtail, Stilton, spring onion and watercress, followed by pan-fried chicken breast with dauphinoise potatoes, the dish finished with a thyme and red wine jus. For dessert, fig and almond tart with lime crème fraîche has a good balance of flavours.

Times 12-6.30/7-10.30

ROWSLEY — Map 16 SK26

East Lodge Country House Hotel

Rosettes not confirmed at time of going to print – see below

The Peacock at Rowsley

🏵🏵🏵 – see page 130

See advert on page 131

East Lodge Country House Hotel

Rosettes not confirmed at time of going to print

ROWSLEY — Map 16 SK26

Modern British 🍃

Contemporary country-house cooking in the Peak District

☎ 01629 734474
DE4 2EF
e-mail: info@eastlodge.com
web: www.eastlodge.com
dir: On A6, 5m from Matlock & 3m from Bakewell, at junct with B6012

Please note: the Rosette award for this establishment has been suspended due to a change of chef. Reassessment will take place in due course under the new chef.

This was once the hunting lodge of Haddon Hall and is now a small country-house hotel oozing style and charm surrounded by pretty gardens (ideal for strolling) and ten acres of landscaped grounds. The furnishings and décor are sumptuous without being in the slightest bit intimidating, while the staff are knowledgeable and genuinely hospitable. Have a drink with nibbles in the conservatory bar before moving on to the restaurant, an elegant room with a green and cream colour scheme, large mahogany tables, soft carpeting and gentle lighting. Don't expect any cutting-edge culinary firework's; rather, the kitchen's approach is a gently updated version of classical country-house cooking, thus you might start with a smooth duck liver and port parfait with beetroot and orange relish and sourdough bread, before chicken breast roasted with tarragon and served with carrot purée, glazed shallots and pommes Anna. Fine local, and therefore seasonal, produce is at the heart of the operation, some from the hotel's own garden, and flavours are clearly defined. A tasting of pork - thin slices of cheek, ham hock terrine, barbecued kebab and chunks of scratching - interspersed with crisp slices and poached cubes of artichoke is an ambitious dish that pays off, while moist and meaty fillet of sea bass comes winningly supported by brown shrimp sauce, celeriac purée, tender celery hearts and butter-poached new potatoes. Desserts can be a delight - witness velvety iced white chocolate and vanilla parfait with a soft centre of strawberry sorbet, and bursts of fresh flavours from an accompanying salad of champagne marinated strawberries with candied orange and mint. Interesting breads (perhaps cheese and bacon) and delicate petits fours add to the all-round pleasure.

Owner Elyzian Hospitality Ltd **Times** 12-2/6.30-9 **Prices** Fixed D 3 course £39.50, Tasting menu £55, Service optional **Notes** Tasting menu 6 course, Chef's table 8 course £65, Vegetarian available, Dress restrictions, Smart casual, no jeans or trainers, Civ Wed 150 **Seats** 80, Pr/dining room 72 **Children** Portions, Menu **Parking** 40

DEVON

ASHBURTON　　　　　　　　　　Map 3 SX77

Agaric

◉ Modern British ✪

Well-judged menu in engaging restaurant with rooms

☎ 01364 654478
30 North St TQ13 7QD
e-mail: eat@agaricrestaurant.co.uk
dir: Opposite town hall. Ashburton off A38 between Exeter & Plymouth

Nick and Sophie Coiley's restaurant with rooms with its mushroomy name and dedication to the harvest of the local land and sea is a foodies' paradise. Everything is made in-house, much of the produce comes from their own garden, and they've even planted olive trees with the cunning plan to produce their own olive oil in the future. There's a charming rusticity to the interior and a definite lack of stuffiness all round - that goes for the cheerful service team, too - and you can buy some of their preserves, oils and the like to bolster your own store cupboard. The food focuses on flavour and avoids needless over-embellishment. Start with venison, rabbit, pork, prunes and Armagnac terrine, served with their Agaric onion marmalade, followed by breaded fillets of sole with herb and cream sauce and cucumber salad. And to finish, blood orange, vanilla and star anise parfait with blood orange sorbet, mixed berry coulis and an almond biscuit.

Chef Nick Coiley **Owner** Mr N & Mrs S Coiley
Times 12-2/7-9.30 Closed 2 wks Aug, Xmas, 1 wk Jan, Sun-Tue, L Sat **Prices** Fixed L 2 course £14.95-£16.95, Starter £5.95-£9.50, Main £15.95-£24.50, Dessert £6.95-£9.50, Service optional, Groups min 8 service 10% **Wines** 6 by glass **Notes** Brunch Sat 9.30-1.30, Vegetarian available **Seats** 30 **Children** Portions **Parking** Car park opposite

AXMINSTER　　　　　　　　　　Map 4 SY29

Fairwater Head Hotel

◉ Modern British ✪

Straightforward brasserie cooking on the Jurassic Coast

☎ 01297 678349
Hawkchurch EX13 5TX
e-mail: info@fairwaterheadhotel.co.uk
web: www.fairwaterheadhotel.co.uk
dir: A358 into Broom Lane at Tytherleigh, follow signs to Hawkchurch & hotel

Four miles outside Axminster, the hotel stands on the Jurassic Coast, England's first ever designated World Heritage Site. In a stripped-wood ambience, the creatively spelt Greenfields Brazzerie does what it says on the tin, offering un-mucked about classic dishes presented efficiently and with flair. Vulscombe goats' cheese terrine with apple and nut salad utilises one of modern Devon's premier dairy products, while mains go in for braised daube of beef with horseradish mash in red wine jus, or

simple grilled plaice in chive butter. The generous dessert choice runs from Eton Mess with winter berries to apple and sultana crumble with ice cream and custard.

Chef Jeremy Woollven **Owner** Adam & Carrie Southwell
Times 12-2/7-9 Closed Jan, L Mon-Tue, Thu-Fri
Prices Fixed L 2 course £12.50, Starter £4.95-£8, Main £12.50-£19, Dessert £5-£7.50, Service optional **Wines** 6 bottles over £30, 62 bottles under £30, 12 by glass **Notes** Sunday L fr £10, Vegetarian available, Dress restrictions, Smart casual, Civ Wed 65 **Seats** 60, Pr/dining room 18 **Children** Portions, Menu **Parking** 40

BEESANDS　　　　　　　　　　Map 3 SX84

The Cricket Inn

◉ Modern British ✪

Quaint seaside inn serving tip-top seafood and more besides

☎ 01548 580215
TQ7 2EN
e-mail: enquiries@thecricketinn.com
web: www.thecricketinn.com
dir: From Kingsbridge follow A379 towards Dartmouth, at Stokenham mini-rdbt turn right for Beesands

When the crabs, lobster and scallops are hauled in from the sea in front of where you're sitting, you know you're in for a treat. But that's not to say that this gem of an inn on the shingly beach of Start Bay neglects the bounty of the land, which turns up in the shape of locally-reared lamb chop served with cabbage, smoked bacon and black pudding mash. Smartly refurbished, The Cricket Inn still hangs on to its quaint traditional fishing inn character with old photos of Beesands village and fishing paraphernalia in the bar, while the airy restaurant extension is done out in a pared-back New England style. Those diver-caught scallops from the bay might be delivered with shiitaki mushrooms, cauliflower purée, and crispy Parma ham, while lemon sole of the same provenance could turn up simply with lemon and chive butter, or there may be brill with a crab and ginger reduction and deep-fried angel hair noodles.

Chef Scott Simon **Owner** Nigel & Rachel Heath
Times 12-2.30/6-8.30 Closed 25 Dec **Prices** Starter £5.50-£9, Main £11-£20, Dessert £4.50-£6, Service optional **Wines** 2 bottles over £30, 26 bottles under £30, 12 by glass **Notes** Sunday L £11-£20, Vegetarian available **Seats** 65, Pr/dining room 40 **Children** Portions, Menu **Parking** 30

BIDEFORD　　　　　　　　　　Map 3 SS42

Yeoldon House Hotel

◉ British ✪

Nostalgic cooking by the Torridge estuary

☎ 01237 474400
Durrant Ln, Northam EX39 2RL
e-mail: yeoldonhouse@aol.com
web: www.yeoldonhousehotel.co.uk
dir: A39 from Barnstaple over River Torridge Bridge. At rdbt right onto A386 towards Northam, then 3rd right into Durrant Lane

Newspaper cuttings and pictures from times gone by adorn the walls of the dining room at the Steeles' Victorian hotel, which also enjoys sweeping views of the Torridge estuary. Brian runs an industrious kitchen, often single-handedly, producing well-crafted food that has a nostalgic feel to it, and is none the worse for that. Chicken liver and cranberry terrine comes with an intensely flavoured onion marmalade, and could be followed by a generous portion of bracingly fresh baked cod with an old-school white wine and saffron cream sauce incorporating finely chopped fennel. Meats include fine West Country lamb chump on parsnip and horseradish mash, with traditional redcurrant and rosemary, while the pudding vote goes once more to the treacle and ginger tart, served with excellent ginger ice cream.

Chef Brian Steele **Owner** Brian & Jennifer Steele
Times 7-8 Closed Xmas, Sun, L all week **Prices** Fixed D 3 course £35, Service optional **Wines** 4 bottles over £30, 25 bottles under £30, 6 by glass **Notes** Vegetarian available, Dress restrictions, Smart casual, Civ Wed 50 **Seats** 30 **Children** Portions **Parking** 30

BLACKAWTON　　　　　　　　　　Map 3 SX85

The Normandy Arms

◉ British **NEW**

Impressive cooking in stylish village inn

☎ 01803 712884
Chapel St TQ9 7BN
e-mail: info@normandyarms.co.uk
dir: On A3122 Kingsbridge to Dartmouth road, turn right at Forces Tavern

Nestled between the fabulous South Hams coast and the rugged expanses of Dartmoor, this long-established village inn is rooted into the fabric of Blackawton. The interior has been reworked with the sort of clean-cut contemporary look you would expect of a switched-on dining pub, blending leather sofas, chunky wooden tables, and colourful art on whitewashed walls with the timeless feel of exposed stone walls and flagstoned floors. Chef-proprietor Andrew West-Letford knows his way around the modern British repertoire and clearly relishes the bounty of local produce on his doorstep - his Salcombe crab tart with marinated cucumber and chive salad is worth the trip alone. Main course brings roast

continued

BLACKAWTON *continued*

haunch of venison with spiced red cabbage, parsnips and potato galette, another clean, uncluttered dish with subtle contrasts of flavour and texture that shows a confident hand at the stoves. Hazelnut slice with sour cherry sorbet and griottine cherries closes the show on a high note.

Chef Andrew West-Letford **Times** 12.30-2.30/6.30-9.30 Closed D Sun **Prices** Fixed D 3 course £18, Starter £5-£7, Main £13-£18, Dessert £4-£9 **Notes** Menu du jour Tue-Thu D, Coffee mornings Wed & Fri 9-11.30, Sunday L

BRIXHAM — Map 3 SX95

Quayside Hotel

Modern British

The freshest seafood by the harbour

☎ 01803 855751
41-49 King St TQ5 9TJ
e-mail: reservations@quayside.co.uk
dir: From Exeter take A380 towards Torquay, then A3022 to Brixham

The fish landed in Brixham ends up on menus around the country, but at the Quayside Hotel you can tuck into the fruits of these waters within sight of the fishing boats. The family-run hotel carved out of old fishermen's cottages has views over the harbour and bay beyond and its kitchen makes good use of the bounty on its doorstep. Salt-and-pepper Start Bay squid is one way to begin, or you might fancy their house prawn cocktail, served on chicory leaves. The availability of fish is dependent on the catch of course, so you might find black bream, red mullet and skate, or you might not. Baked monkfish with a citrus beurre blanc stars a fine piece of fish, but there are some meat options if you insist (confit duck, perhaps). River Dart oysters are a treat when available, and the plateau de fruits de mer is a tantalising choice if you can persuade someone to share it with you.

Chef Andy Sewell **Owner** Mr & Mrs C F Bowring **Times** 6.30-9.30 Closed L all week **Prices** Prices not confirmed Service optional **Wines** 10 by glass **Notes** Vegetarian available, Dress restrictions, Smart casual preferred **Seats** 40, Pr/dining room 18 **Children** Portions, Menu **Parking** 30

BURRINGTON — Map 3 SS61

Northcote Manor

Modern British V

Tranquil country-house setting and well-sourced modern British food

☎ 01769 560501
EX37 9LZ
e-mail: rest@northcotemanor.co.uk
web: www.northcotemanor.co.uk
dir: M5 junct 27 towards Barnstaple. Left at rdbt to South Molton. Follow A377, right at T-junct to Barnstaple. Entrance after 3m, opposite Portsmouth Arms railway station and pub. (NB do not enter Burrington village)

The 18th-century manor house used to be a Benedictine monastery and it maintains a sense of peacefulness today that the monks may well have appreciated. The 20 acres of sweeping lawns and patio overlooking the Japanese Garden offer plenty of opportunities for reflection, but a cream tea in the sunshine offers a more immediate form of gratification. In keeping with the unfettered elegance of it all, the stylishly understated restaurant serves up a daily-changing menu which pledges to use local ingredients wherever possible. So you might find medallions of Cornish cod in a light soda water and beer batter with crisp potatoes, lemon crème fraîche and pea purée, then move on to breast of Crediton Aylesbury duckling with gratin potatoes, wilted baby spinach, oven-baked fig and red wine gravy. Finish with an unctuous dark chocolate fondant with caramelised banana, white chocolate ice cream and hot chocolate drink.

Chef Richie Herkes **Owner** J Pierre Mifsud **Times** 12-2/7-9 **Prices** Prices not confirmed Service optional **Wines** 10 by glass **Notes** Sunday L, Vegetarian menu, Dress restrictions, Smart casual preferred, no jeans, Civ Wed 80 **Seats** 34, Pr/dining room 50 **Children** Portions, Menu **Parking** 30

CHAGFORD — Map 3 SX78

Gidleigh Park

– see opposite

---

22 Mill Street Restaurant & Rooms

Modern British

Lively modern cooking in Dartmoor village

☎ 01647 432244
22 Mill St TQ13 8AW
e-mail: info@22millst.com
dir: A382/B3206 enter village into main square, Mill St is on the right

Chagford can't have changed all that much in the last several hundred years, except for all the cars. But down a little lane a short stroll from the centre of the village is a restaurant with rooms that definitely feels of these times.

It's perfectly traditional on the outside, but within it has a light and gently contemporary finish - lots of pale wood, fashionably neutral colour tones and well-chosen furniture - and makes an appealing setting for the classy cooking. And there is some good cooking going on here. The menu deals in high quality regional ingredients, everything is made in-house, and there are lots of tempting combinations. Start, perhaps, with haddock poached in brown butter with goats' milk, almonds and sorrel, or a whole carrot cooked in dripping and served with warm Sharpham brie, steamed nettles and ale. Next up, braised and roasted pork belly with smoked cockles, sea vegetables and stout and cockle juice, and to finish, warm rice pudding with aired milk and a jam and sloe sorbet. There's a tasting menu, too.

Times 12-4/6.30-10 Closed 2 wks Jan, Mon

DARTMOUTH — Map 3 SX85

The Dart Marina Hotel

Traditional & Modern British V

Confident modern cooking in contemporary riverside hotel

☎ 01803 832580
Sandquay Rd TQ6 9PH
e-mail: reception@dartmarinahotel.com
web: www.dartmarina.com
dir: A3122 from Totnes to Dartmouth. Follow road which becomes College Way, before Higher Ferry. Hotel sharp left in Sandquay Rd

You won't lack for sensory stimulation at the classy waterfront Dart Marina Hotel: if the views over the marina and the watery action on the River Dart aren't enough, there's a spa, plus foodie pleasures courtesy of the recently refurbished and extended River Restaurant. It's a cool, clean-cut space done out with a neutral white, cream and tan palette; full-length windows make the most of its riverfront spot. The seasons are duly noted and South Devon's excellent produce is pressed into service as the foundation of an appealing menu of up-to-date classics. Slow-cooked salmon ballotine with fine herbs, gribiche sauce, and fennel and lemon salad is a well-composed opener, which might be followed by slow-cooked shoulder of Blackawton lamb with cocotte potatoes and roasted root vegetables. Finish with warm cherry Bakewell pudding with passionfruit cream and butternut squash and vanilla ice cream.

Chef Tom Woods **Owner** Richard Seton **Times** 12-2/6-9 Closed 23-26 & 30-31 Dec, L Mon-Sat **Prices** Fixed D 3 course £37.50, Service optional **Wines** 38 bottles over £30, 21 bottles under £30, 19 by glass **Notes** Sunday L, Vegetarian menu, Dress restrictions, Smart casual **Seats** 86 **Children** Portions, Menu **Parking** 100

continued

Save on Hotels. Book at **theAA.com/hotel**

DEVON 135 ENGLAND

Gidleigh Park

CHAGFORD MAP 3 SX78

Modern European V NOTABLE WINE LIST

Stunning contemporary cooking in wonderful Dartmoor isolation

☎ 01647 432367
TQ13 8HH
e-mail: gidleighpark@gidleigh.co.uk
web: www.gidleigh.com
dir: From Chagford Sq turn right at Lloyds TSB into Mill St, after 150yds right fork, across x-rds into Holy St. Restaurant 1.5m

Depending on the season, Gidleigh Park may well appear a refuge from the seething multitudes, not just of the big city, but of nearby Chagford, where the tourist footfall can thicken to a stampede. Standing in majestic isolation on a Dartmoor hillside, the place was built on the site of an old ruined estate in the late 1920s for an Australian shipping magnate, who only lived for three years after its completion. It looks as grand today as was the intention then, a piece of bravura mock Tudor stuffed with artworks and antiques, with views over the River Teign below the lawns. Gidleigh remains the jewel in executive chef Michael Caines' crown, the place where his culinary philosophy finds its most eloquent expression. In a suite of three interlinked dining rooms panelled in oak and decorated with good-humoured lithographs, the scene is one of understated formality. Staff are impeccably attired, and know what they are about, including full familiarity with the menus. There are residual touches of classical French cuisine in evidence, for instance in a brilliantly textured terrine of foie gras with Madeira jelly and truffled green bean salad to start, but the kitchen's magnetic north is modern Britain, which pours forth regional supplies, not least from Gidleigh's own kitchen garden. Brixham scallops with caramelised cauliflower purée in sweet raisin vinaigrette is a confident interpretation of a contemporary classic dish, and the sound judgment with fish extends to a main course of Cornish salt cod and Beesands crab, the former rolled in paprika and slow-cooked, the latter adding freshness to a composition deepened with the spicy bite of chorizo and the acid tang of little jewels of lemon purée. Pairings of principal items are popular throughout, as is also seen in a duo of venison and pork belly with jasmine-scented raisins and puréed chestnut, the kind of production that's easier to pull off when you have a large brigade at your disposal. Desserts retain the fun factor, rather than making us eat up our veg: a plate of orange variations marshals a tartlet, mousse and sorbet, as well as preserved mandarin, while banana parfait is accompanied by lime-spiked butterscotch sauce, a lime sorbet and salted peanuts. Breads and petits fours show that attention is fiercely focused down to the finest details, and the selection of southwestern cheeses includes the brilliantly titled Devon's Little Stinky, a washed-rind cow's milk specimen worth the aromatic onslaught. With a cellar running to an incredible 1,300 bins, you'd be wise to seek the expert guidance of the sommelier when it comes to choosing something fabulous to complete your dining experience.

Chef Michael Caines MBE
Owner Andrew and Christina Brownsword **Times** 12-2/7-9.45
Prices Fixed L 2 course £35-£42, Tasting menu £120-£135, Service optional **Wines** 11 by glass
Notes Tasting menu 5, 8 course, ALC 3 course £110, Vegetarian menu, Dress restrictions, Shirt with collar, no jeans or sportswear **Seats** 52, Pr/dining room 22 **Children** Portions, Menu **Parking** 45

DARTMOUTH *continued*

The Seahorse

◉◉ Mediterranean, Seafood

Enterprising seafood cooking by the Dart

☎ 01803 835147

5 South Embankment TQ6 9BH

e-mail: enquiries@seahorserestaurant.co.uk

There's something comfortably relaxing about Mitch Tonks's seafood restaurant a few paces from the River Dart. Large button-back banquettes on each side form the foundation of the design, a wall of wines makes a strong visual impact, the open-plan kitchen adds movement, and there's generally a contented buzz in the air. The menus change daily, and the philosophy is to keep things simple and not muck about with whatever's been delivered fresh that morning, with an open charcoal fire the favoured cooking medium. Scallops roasted in the shell with garlic and white port show the style, perhaps followed by vibrantly fresh turbot roasted with basil and tomato and served with garlicky spinach. More modish treatments get a look in - clams served with braised pork, sherry and peas, for instance - and with a Mediterranean slant to the menu, particularly towards Italy, you can also expect octopus carpaccio, and fritto misto di mare. Meat-eaters aren't entirely overlooked, and puddings like caramel pannacotta topped with espresso sauce complete a polished act.

Chef Mat Prowse, Mitch Tonks **Owner** Mat Prowse, Mitch Tonks **Times** 12-3/6-10 Closed 25 Dec, 1 Jan, Mon, L Tue, D Sun **Prices** Fixed L 2 course £20, Fixed D 2 course £20, Starter £7.50-£13.50, Main £18-£32.50, Dessert £3.90-£13.50, Service optional **Wines** 6 by glass **Notes** Sunday L, Vegetarian available **Seats** 40 **Children** Portions **Parking** On street

DOWN THOMAS   Map 3 SX55

Langdon Court Hotel & Restaurant

◉◉ Traditional British **NEW V** ⊙

Country-house cooking in the lush South Hams countryside

☎ 01752 862358

Adams Ln PL9 0DY

e-mail: enquiries@langdoncourt.com

dir: signed from A379 at Elburton rdbt

Langdon Court is a real architectural gem, a 16th-century manor house in the lush South Hams countryside, sitting amid formally laid-out gardens full of ornamental ponds and topiary. Its regal credentials are such that it once played host to Edward VII and Lillie Langtry and, in earlier times, Elizabeth I. Antique furnishings make a refined statement in the main dining room, where the cooking aims for the high-toned country-house idiom. Crab lasagna is bursting with freshness and flavour, with thin pasta layers and a garnish of cucumber balls edged with caviar, or there could be a modish pairing of scallops and chorizo dressed with red pepper salsa. A rich vein of classicism brings on a main course of corn-fed chicken breast in morel sauce with a bouquet of vivid green veg, as well as local beef fillet with wild mushrooms and glazed winter roots. Light tiramisù with positively flavoured coffee granita is a satisfying way to finish.

Chef Robbie Hill **Owner** Emma & Geoffrey Hill **Times** 12-3/6.30-9.30 **Prices** Tasting menu £12.95-£21.95, Starter £5.50-£7.50, Main £17.50-£22.50, Dessert £6.50-£8.50, Service optional **Wines** 26 bottles over £30, 26 bottles under £30, 8 by glass **Notes** Sunday L, Vegetarian menu, Dress restrictions, Smart, Civ Wed 75 **Seats** 36, Pr/dining room 20 **Children** Portions

DREWSTEIGNTON   Map 3 SX79

The Old Inn

◉◉◉ — *see below*

The Old Inn

DREWSTEIGNTON   MAP 3 SX79

Modern European **V**

Intelligent, flavour-packed cooking of verve and vigour

☎ 01647 281276

EX6 6QR

e-mail: enquiries@old-inn.co.uk

dir: A30 W, exit Cheriton Bishop, Drewsteignton, Castle Drogo, turn left at Crockenwell, follow signs to Drewsteignton. A38 to A382 Bovey Tracy, Mortonhampstead, turn right at Sandy Park, continue past Castle Drogo, follow signs to Drewsteignton

The in-vogue olive-green heritage colour of the woodwork is the only clue that something out of the ordinary might be going on behind the doors of this whitewashed, 17th-century cottagey restaurant in a chocolate-box-pretty village on the fringes of Dartmoor. Once inside you're greeted with a deliciously unpretentious atmosphere courtesy of a cosy parquet-floored lounge with squashy sofas by a woodburner, modern art on the walls and a pair of retrievers to welcome guests; in the brace of cosy dining rooms are stylish oak tables on white-painted floorboards, claret and sage-green walls hung with eclectic art, and not a chichi designer touch in sight. Chef-patron Duncan Walker brings a solid pedigree to the job: he came down from the north-east 25 years ago to work with Shaun Hill at Gidleigh Park, and seems to have been bitten by the Devon bug. After a brief rest from the stoves, he's now back in his whites doing what he does so well - there are no gimmicks or smoke and mirrors to his cooking, just top-class regional produce well-chosen for its ability to get along together and not fight it out on the plate. And with just 17 diners to cater for, the results are truly extraordinary. The waffle-free menu tends to undersell itself, since it is hard to do justice in so few words to the turbo-charged flavours that Walker extracts from the humblest of ingredients. Risotto of rabbit with parmesan and thyme, or open ravioli of lobster, red peppers and basil are typical starters, while main course compositions and timings are pin-sharp, as when grilled fillet of brill appears with saffron, mussels, parsley and white wine, or grilled loin of venison with glazed figs and port. Nothing misses a beat all the way through to desserts - and remember, Walker is the soufflé king, so wind things up with a prune and Armagnac version with burnt honey ice cream. There's a trio of lovely bedrooms if you can afford the time to stay over.

Chef Duncan Walker **Owner** Duncan Walker **Times** 12-2/7-9 Closed Sun-Tue, L Sun-Thu **Prices** Fixed L 3 course £29.50, Fixed D 3 course £42.50, Service included **Wines** 17 bottles over £30, 21 bottles under £30, 2 by glass **Notes** Service flexible, pre book, tables 6 or more by arrangement, Vegetarian menu **Seats** 17, Pr/dining room 10 **Parking** Village square

Save on Hotels. Book at **theAA.com/hotel**

DEVON 137 **ENGLAND**

EGGESFORD
Map 3 SS61

Fox & Hounds Country Hotel

◉ British 🍷

Tip-top local ingredients cooked without fuss

☎ 01769 580345
EX18 7JZ
e-mail: relax@foxandhoundshotel.co.uk
web: www.foxandhoundshotel.co.uk
dir: M5 junct 27, A361 towards Tiverton. B3137 signed
Witheridge. After Nomansland follow signs to Eggesford
Station, hotel in 50mtrs

The traditional country name is an apt one for this hotel
on the River Taw. Rural pursuits are all around - fishing
is on the doorstep, rough shooting on the surrounding
hills, or you could simply hike the Tarka Trail through
Eggesford Forest and spot deer, woodpeckers and otters
on the river. The Fox & Hounds has been spruced up for
contemporary tastes, although the bar takes pride in its
original beer engines dispensing local ales, and the dog-
friendly ethos means Rover can warm himself by the fire.
Eat here if you like - it's the same menu as in the
restaurant, which means uncomplicated British classics
in a hearty West Country vein, brimming with local
ingredients. Ham hock terrine with pear chutney might
set the ball rolling, then mignons and braised belly of
locally-reared pork turn up in the company of caramelised
apples and crushed potatoes. And for pud, baked Alaska
flavoured with coconut rum, or go for the West Country
cheeseboard.

Chef Alex Pallatt **Owner** Nick & Tara Culverhouse
Times 12-2.30/6.30-9 **Prices** Fixed D 3 course
£25-£27.50, Starter £5.75-£9.50, Main £12.95-£18.25,
Dessert £5.95-£7.95, Service optional **Wines** 3 bottles
over £30, 30 bottles under £20, 6 by glass **Notes** Sunday
L, Vegetarian available, Civ Wed 120 **Seats** 60, Pr/dining
room 120 **Children** Portions, Menu **Parking** 100

ERMINGTON
Map 3 SX65

Plantation House

◉ Modern British **NEW** 🍷

Confident cooking in boutique bolthole

☎ 01548 831100
Totnes Rd PL21 9NS
e-mail: info@plantationhousehotel.co.uk

This Georgian parish rectory looks out over the River Elme
with a stately elegance that fits perfectly with its
contemporary boutique styling. The interiors are
immaculate throughout, and the operation runs with
faultless attention to detail that makes the place a
heavenly gastro getaway. Dining goes on in a brace of
intimate and tasteful rooms with a sun-kissed terrace for
summer aperitifs, and the kitchen rightly places
carefully-sourced produce at the heart of things, whether
it's West Country meats and cheeses, locally-landed
sustainable fish, or seasonal foraged materials. This all
translates into flavour-driven dishes of real integrity,
starting with a modishly retro tian of home-smoked

salmon and prawns with avocado and home-made Marie
Rose sauce. Next up, roast rump of lamb is matched with
Puy lentils, roast shallots, pea purée, and green
peppercorn and Merlot jus. The cooking retains
undeniable depth through to a dessert of vanilla
pannacotta with Campari and orange jelly and orange
galette.

Chef Richard Hendey, John Raines **Owner** Richard Hendey
Times 7-9 Closed L all week **Prices** Fixed D 3 course £25,
Service included **Notes** 4 course D £36-£39.50, Breakfast
7.30-9.30, Vegetarian available **Seats** 28, Pr/dining room
12 **Children** Portions

EXETER
Map 3 SX99

Barton Cross Hotel & Restaurant

◉ Traditional British, French

Reliably good food in thatched hotel

☎ 01392 841245 & 841584
Huxham, Stoke Canon EX5 4EJ
e-mail: bartonxhuxham@aol.com
web: www.thebartoncrosshotel.co.uk
dir: 0.5m off A396 at Stoke Canon, 3m N of Exeter

In the Exe Valley four miles from the city centre, Barton
Cross has been converted from a thatched longhouse, its
restaurant showing signs of its age in an inglenook, cob
walls, beams and an impressive gallery under a raftered
ceiling. The kitchen deals in Anglo-European cooking with
some polish, turning out chicken liver parfait with orange
chutney alongside smoked salmon risotto spiked with dill
and lemon, followed by beef fillet with oxtail cottage pie
and port-based gravy, and well-timed fillet of sea bass
with tangerine butter and chargrilled fennel. The
occasional idea surfaces from further afield - pan-fried
monkfish with coconut and curry sauce, say - and
enterprising desserts may run to chocolate tart with
marmalade and whisky ice cream.

Times 12.30-2.30/6.30-11.30 Closed L Mon-Thu

The Olive Tree Restaurant at the Queens Court Hotel

◉◉ Modern British

Confident, creative cooking in a townhouse hotel

☎ 01392 272709
Queens Court Hotel, 6-8 Bystock Ter EX4 4HY
e-mail: enquiries@queenscourt-hotel.co.uk
web: www.queenscourt-hotel.co.uk
dir: Exit dual carriageway at junct 30 onto B5132
(Topsham Rd) towards city centre. Hotel 200yds from
Central Station

There is much to enjoy at this restaurant in a townhouse
hotel on a quiet, leafy square just a short stroll from the
city centre. The pared-back monochrome décor - black
leather high-backed chairs at linen-clad tables and
snow-white walls - has a certain gloss thanks to
contemporary chandeliers and Venetian masks on the
walls - a nod, perhaps, to the Mediterranean warmth that
informs the modern cooking on offer. Sound sourcing
lends substance to the whole operation, backed by the
kitchen brigade's thoughtful approach and sound
technical ability to pull off ideas such as boudin of rabbit
mousseline and poached garlic served with lightly-spiced
pickled red cabbage and a port reduction. Local roots are
celebrated via a herb-crusted rack of West Country lamb,
partnered with a slow-braised lamb shank faggot with
Lyonnaise potatoes and carrot purée, while creative
desserts run to a tiramisù-inspired coffee and
mascarpone mousse-filled chocolate macaroon served
with miniature jellies and espresso syrup.

Times 12-2/6.30-9.30 Closed Xmas, New Year, L Sun

EXMOUTH
Map 3 SY08

Les Saveurs

◉ Modern French 🍷

French fish cookery near the Exe estuary

☎ 01395 269459
9 Tower St EX8 1NT
e-mail: lessaveurs@yahoo.co.uk
dir: A376 to Exmouth, left at rdbt. Right at next rdbt onto
one way system Rolle St. Tower St on right

With a skilled and sensitive French craftsman at work in
the kitchen, it's no surprise to see the menu opening with
a classic rich fish soup with rouille, grated emmental,
and garlic croûtons at this family-run fish restaurant

continued

EXMOUTH continued

tucked down a little lane just a stone's throw from the sandy beach. Let your nose lead the way to the delicious wafts from the stock pot, which emanate from a delightfully romantic space done out with exposed brick walls, distressed-effect chairs and snow-white linen, and pile into a pot of Exmouth mussels marinières, followed perhaps by Lyme Bay turbot fillet with champagne sauce and mash, or gilt head bream with foraged nettle sauce and samphire. Meat eaters are sorted out by the likes of roast lamb rump with wild mushroom and Madeira sauce and gratin dauphinoise. End with a classic tarte Tatin, crème brûlée, or crêpes Suzette done with authentic French flair.

Chef Olivier Guyard-Mulkerrin **Owner** Olivier & Sheila Guyard-Mulkerrin **Times** 7-10.30 Closed Nov-Apr advance bookings only, Sun-Mon, ex by special arrangement, L all week **Prices** Starter £7-£8.50, Main £16.50-£25, Dessert £6.50, Service optional, Groups min 6 service 10% **Wines** 10 bottles over £30, 19 bottles under £30, 5 by glass **Notes** Vegetarian available, Dress restrictions, Smart casual **Seats** 30, Pr/dining room 36 **Parking** On street/council offices

HAYTOR VALE   Map 3 SX77

Rock Inn

@ British 🍷

Simple, honest food at a traditional Dartmoor inn

☎ 01364 661305 & 661556
TQ13 9XP
e-mail: reservations@rockinn.co.uk
dir: From A38 at Drum Bridges, onto A382 to Bovey Tracey. In 2m take B3387 towards Haytor for 3.5m, follow brown signs

The 18th-century Rock Inn is a haven of civility and good cheer amid the wild, wind-blasted tors of Dartmoor - the sort of place you should factor in to a day's hiking or car touring in the area. Run by the same family for nigh-on 30 years, it's still a proper pub with oak furniture, gleaming brasses and locally-brewed real ales in the bar, and the all-round feelgood factor that comes from roaring log fires, cosy nooks and romantically candlelit tables. The food is simple, effective and flavour-packed, with a good showing of local produce on a menu that gives due credit to suppliers of the principal component of each main course - perhaps pan-fried wild sea bass from Brixham partnered by chorizo risotto and tomato pesto, or for fans of local meat, pan-roasted rump of lamb with fine beans, rosemary fondant potato, beetroot purée and red wine jus. At the end, West Country cheeses are mighty tempting, or you could go for a vanilla pannacotta with rhubarb compôte and shortbread.

Chef Sophie Collier, Mark Tribble **Owner** Mr C Graves **Times** 12-2.15/6.30-9 Closed 25-26 Dec **Prices** Fixed L 2 course fr £13.50, Fixed D 3 course fr £24, Starter £6.95-£8.95, Main £10.95-£18.95, Dessert £5.45-£7.25, Service optional, Groups min 6 service 10% **Wines** 20 bottles over £30, 50 bottles under £30, 16 by glass **Notes** Sunday L, Vegetarian available, Dress restrictions,

No shorts (pm only) **Seats** 75, Pr/dining room 20 **Children** Portions, Menu **Parking** 25

HONITON   Map 4 ST10

The Holt Bar & Restaurant

@@ Modern British 🍷

Imaginative cooking in a vibrant local pub

☎ 01404 47707
178 High St EX14 1LA
e-mail: enquiries@theholt-honiton.com
dir: At west end of High St

Situated on the main street in Honiton, The Holt is the place to go for a convivial atmosphere, local beer and creative gastro-pub cooking. Downstairs is rustic with comfy sofas, while upstairs there's an airy open-plan dining room. You're guaranteed a good pint here as it's owned by the Otter Brewery and serves a range of regular and seasonal ales on tap. Indeed drinkers are as welcome as those coming to sample the elegant cooking. Local suppliers are utilised to full effect and, as there's now an offshoot smoking business, expect to find plenty of home-smoked goodies on the menu (printed on recycled paper made from discarded hops, malt, yeast and beer labels, no less). Crisp cod croquette with smoked prawn tails and tartare sauce is a clever dish of contrasting flavours and textures, while breast of guinea fowl with bubble and squeak, sweet peas and green beans is simple yet moreish. Finish with vanilla pannacotta, raspberry sauce and biscotti. If you fancy something different, there's also a selection of tapas available.

Chef Angus McCaig, Billy Emmett **Owner** Joe & Angus McCaig **Times** 12-2/6.30-10 Closed 25-26 Dec, Sun-Mon **Prices** Starter £5-£6.50, Main £13.50-£16.50, Dessert £5.50-£7.50, Service optional **Wines** 6 bottles over £30, 25 bottles under £30, 6 by glass **Notes** Vegetarian available **Seats** 50 **Children** Portions **Parking** On street, car park 1 min walk

Monkton Court

@@ Modern British 🍷

Artistically presented modern cooking in a former vicarage

☎ 01404 42309
Monkton EX14 9QH
e-mail: enquiries@monktoncourthotel.co.uk
dir: 2m E A30

The greystone roadside inn on the A30 is an obvious stopping-off point on the way into the deep southwest. It sits in four acres on the fringes of the Blackdown Hills, and was once a rather grand vicarage. Mullioned windows and a multitude of period features lend the place an effortless charm, although the dining room goes for a more modern look, with simple table settings and a light and airy feel. Service forgoes the airs and graces in order to encourage conviviality, and the kitchen runs a well-honed instinct for artistry, constructing impressive compositions on the plate, but without forgetting culinary principle. A starter of twice-baked Devon Blue soufflé on

walnut-dressed tomato salad with spiced pear chutney is a fine essay in textural and flavour contrasts. The Blackdown lamb trio - sautéed loin, shoulder spring roll and breaded sweetbreads - remains abidingly popular, or there may be sea bass with razor clams and pak choi in bouillabaisse sauce. A wait at the end is rewarded with sticky pear Tatin and Calvados ice cream.

Chef Joe Nagy **Owner** Colin & Jennifer Wheatley-Brown, Joe Nagy **Times** 12-2.30/6.30-9.30 **Prices** Fixed D 3 course fr £36, Service optional **Wines** 6 by glass **Notes** ALC 2/3 course £28.50/£36, Sunday L, Vegetarian available, Dress restrictions, Smart casual **Seats** 60, Pr/dining room 12 **Children** Portions, Menu **Parking** 40

ILFRACOMBE   Map 3 SS54

11 The Quay

@ Modern, Traditional 🍷

Brasserie cooking in a restaurant decorated by Damien Hirst

☎ 01271 868090 & 868091
11 The Quay EX34 9EQ
e-mail: info@11thequay.co.uk
dir: Follow signs for harbour and pier car park. Restaurant on left before car park

The Hirst name is enough to draw attention to 11 The Quay, although its handsome red-brick and stone façade would be an inviting prospect even without the promise of the artist's work on the walls within. Forget formaldehyde-marinated sharks and shock tactics though - the pieces up in the Atlantic Room restaurant and the Harbourside space are more along the nostalgic lines of children's seashell friezes, and will do nothing to dent your appetite for the straightforward modern brasserie food on offer. Seated beneath the Atlantic Room's ceiling, which arches like the hull of an upturned boat, and with ocean views as a backdrop, a plate of Lundy Island crab claws with chilli mayonnaise is an apt choice among starters, or foie gras with Seville marmalade and toasted brioche might tempt. Next up, a rib-eye of Exmoor Angus steak with goose fat chips and béarnaise is a classic trio done just right, before a textbook crème brûlée ends things on another faultless note.

Chef Tom Frost, Henry Sowden **Owner** Damien Hirst **Times** 12-2.30/6-9 Closed 25-26 Dec **Prices** Starter £4-£12, Main £8.50-£24.50, Dessert £5.50-£9, Service optional **Wines** 10 bottles over £30, 19 bottles under £30, 10 by glass **Notes** Sunday L £13.95-£22, Vegetarian available **Seats** 45, Pr/dining room 26 **Children** Portions, Menu **Parking** Pier car park 100yds

Sandy Cove Hotel

◉ Modern British ✸

Simple cooking, local produce, views to die for

☎ 01271 882243
Old Coast Rd, Combe Martin Bay, Berrynarbor EX34 9SR
e-mail: info@sandycove-hotel.co.uk
dir: A339 to Combe Martin, through village towards
Ilfracombe for approx 1m. Turn right just over brow of hill
marked Sandy Cove

With its huge picture windows, the restaurant in this
lovely family-run hotel makes the most of the magnificent
views of the rugged North Devon coast and the rolling
hills of Exmoor. On a fine day, things get better still when
you can eat out on the sea decks overlooking the cove,
and what's on your plate comes from the waves and
fields of the landscape all around. There are no
extravagant combinations or elaborate presentations
here, just unpretentious, unchallenging ideas from a
kitchen that has the confidence to bring splendid
ingredients together in harmonious combinations and let
them speak for themselves. Seared wood pigeon breast is
matched with bubble-and-squeak, beetroot purée and a
poached quail's egg, ahead of duck breast with braised
fennel, orange and thyme carrots, dauphinoise potato
and red wine sauce, and for pudding there's vanilla
pannacotta with fruit compôte and clotted cream.

Chef Debbie Meaden **Owner** Dawn Ten-Bokkel
Times 12-2/6.30-9 **Prices** Fixed D 3 course £30, Starter
£4.95, Main £17, Dessert £5.95, Service optional **Wines** 3
bottles over £30, 28 bottles under £30, 3 by glass
Notes Sunday L, Vegetarian available, Dress restrictions,
Smart casual, Civ Wed 200 **Seats** 150, Pr/dining room 30
Children Portions, Menu **Parking** 50

ILSINGTON — Map 3 SX77

Ilsington Country House Hotel

◉◉ Modern European ✸

Great Dartmoor views and confident cooking

☎ 01364 661452
TQ13 9RR
e-mail: hotel@ilsington.co.uk
web: www.ilsington.co.uk
dir: A38 to Plymouth, exit at Bovey Tracey. 3rd exit from
rdbt to Ilsington, then 1st right, hotel on right in 3m

Ilsington presses all the right classy country-house
buttons: a Dartmoor bolt-hole set in ten acres of grounds
that includes a health club and spa pool. The large airy
restaurant maintains the theme, its floor-to-ceiling
picture windows offering cracking views across to Haytor
Rocks and beyond from well-dressed tables. The kitchen
goes the extra mile in its quest for quality ingredients,
including using their own eggs, foraging for wild herbs in
the grounds and curing fish and meats in their own
smokehouse. Otherwise, quality locally-sourced produce
forms the basis of the modern approach here,
underpinned by a classical French theme. Take seared
rump of lamb served with confit shoulder, sweetbreads
and a rosemary sauce, for instance, or fillet of sea bream

with spring onion and tomato crushed potatoes, root
vegetable nage and Avruga caviar chive oil. Finish with
lime leaf pannacotta teamed with port braised plum and
lemongrass gel.

Chef Mike O'Donnell **Owner** Hassell family
Times 12-2/6.30-9 Closed L Mon-Sat **Prices** Fixed D 3
course fr £36, Service included **Wines** 12 bottles over
£30, 32 bottles under £30, 7 by glass **Notes** Sunday L,
Vegetarian available, Civ Wed 100 **Seats** 75, Pr/dining
room 70 **Children** Portions **Parking** 60

KINGSBRIDGE — Map 3 SX74

Buckland-Tout-Saints

◉ Modern British **NEW**

Classic country-house dining in refined ambience

☎ 01548 853055
Goveton TQ7 2DS
e-mail: buckland@tout-saints.co.uk
dir: Turn off A381 to Goveton. Follow brown tourist signs
to St Peter's Church. Hotel 2nd right after church

Deep in lush South Hams countryside, there's lots to
admire at this impressive William and Mary manor house
set in four acres of immaculately tended gardens and
woodland. Huge windows make for a luminous interior,
which works a classic country-house look replete with
antiques, wood panelling, opulent fireplaces and sheaves
of fresh flowers. Not to be outfaced by such luxury, the
Queen Anne Restaurant is quite a looker too with its
burnished Russian pine panelling, ornate plasterwork
ceiling, windows framed by opulent swagged drapes, and
well-spaced tables swathed in crisp white linen. In such
a setting, the kitchen isn't looking to push the culinary
envelope, preferring to focus on top-notch ingredients
brought together in tried and true combinations - chicken
and parsley terrine with Waldorf salad and mustard
mayonnaise, for example, and well-conceived mains such
as baked cod with noisette potatoes, wilted spinach, and
caper and parsley beurre noisette.

Chef Ted Ruewell **Owner** Eden Hotel Collection
Prices Prices not confirmed

KNOWSTONE — Map 3 SS82

The Masons Arms

◉◉ Modern British ✸

**Strong contemporary cooking in the lush western
countryside**

☎ 01398 341231
EX36 4RY
e-mail: enqs@masonsarmsdevon.co.uk
dir: Signed from A361, turn right once in Knowstone

A genuinely delightful thatched medieval country inn that
maintains strong links to excellent local growers and
suppliers, The Masons also manages to retain the
atmosphere of a village pub. Deep in the lush countryside
on the border between Devon and Somerset, it is
surrounded by rolling hills, and is full of cheer on winter

evenings when the fire crackles, and in summer too for an
outdoor meal. The celestial ceiling mural in the dining
room has to be seen to be believed. Mark Dodson once
cooked under Michel Roux at Bray (see entry, Waterside
Inn, Berkshire), which might explain the flair and
precision evident in the dishes here. Good strong
contemporary thinking informs a starter of wood pigeon
breasts, flash-fried and tender, accompanied by puréed
beetroot and pine nuts in blueberry jus, while the main-
course pairing of local beef fillet and oxtail in its truffled,
Madeira-rich juices continues to be a triumph of timing
and seasoning. Fish could be something almost as
robust, perhaps sea bass alongside Jerusalem artichoke
purée, butter beans and flageolets with smoked garlic in
red wine jus, and dessert closes things with a fitting
flourish in the form of lemon mascarpone mousse with
passionfruit syrup, or an apple trio with Granny Smith
sorbet.

Chef Mark Dodson **Owner** Mark & Sarah Dodson
Times 12-2/7-9 Closed 1st wk Jan, 1 wk Aug BH, Mon, D
Sun **Prices** Fixed L 2 course fr £20, Starter £8.75-£12.80,
Main £17.50-£24.50, Dessert £8.50-£9.50, Service
optional **Wines** 41 bottles over £30, 17 bottles under £30,
9 by glass **Notes** Sunday L £36, Vegetarian available
Seats 28 **Children** Portions **Parking** 10

LEWDOWN — Map 3 SX48

Lewtrenchard Manor

***Rosettes not confirmed at time of going to print – see
page 140***

LIFTON — Map 3 SX38

Arundell Arms

◉◉ Modern British **V** ✸

Assured cooking in an 18th-century coaching inn

☎ 01566 784666
Fore St PL16 0AA
e-mail: reservations@arundellarms.com
dir: Just off A30 in Lifton, 3m E of Launceston

After a hard day's hunting, shooting or fishing (the inn
has 20 miles of fly-fishing rights on the Tamar), the
Arundell Arms will welcome you with open arms and the
comfy, classically chintzy embrace of squashy sofas,
antiques and log fires. It's an elegant and sophisticated
place, where you don't need to turn up in a waxed Barbour
jacket and Hunter wellies to feel welcome. In the stylishly
decorated restaurant, as you'd hope, there's game in
season and fish from the river, while well-chosen local
suppliers feature prominently on a menu that champions
fabulous West Country produce. The cooking takes an
unmistakably modern line that might see braised pork
cheeks paired with spinach, apple and vanilla purée,
smoked bacon, and cider sauce as a starter, with perhaps
a ragoût of John Dory and monkfish with lentils, Pernod,
leeks and pea shoots to follow. Desserts could run to
blood orange parfait with coffee ice cream and marinated
oranges.

continued

LIFTON *continued*

Chef Steven Pidgeon **Owner** Adam Fox-Edwards
Times 12.30-2.30/7.30-10 **Prices** Fixed L 2 course £19,
Fixed D 3 course £42.50, Tasting menu £47.50, Service
optional **Wines** 7 by glass **Notes** Sunday L, Vegetarian
menu, Dress restrictions, Smart casual, Civ Wed 80
Seats 70, Pr/dining room 24 **Children** Portions, Menu
Parking 70

Tinhay Mill Guest House and Restaurant

⊛ British, French V ⊙

Traditional atmosphere and well-crafted food in revamped 15th-century mill

☎ 01566 784201
Tinhay PL16 0AJ
e-mail: tinhay.mill@talk21.com
web: www.tinhaymillrestaurant.co.uk
dir: From M5 take A30 towards Okehampton/Launceston.
Lifton off A30 on left. Follow brown tourist signs.
Restaurant at bottom of village near river

Emblazoned on the masthead of the menu of this
restaurant with rooms is the phrase 'Where time stands
still', and there is indeed an element of unchanging
tradition in 15th-century Tinhay Mill's whitewashed walls,
oak beams and crackling log fires. Its popularity with

locals and peripatetic gourmets is due in no small way to
the hands-on charm of owners Margaret and Paul Wilson.
Margaret has been cooking all her life and insists on the
best of the local larder as the basis for her honest, well-
crafted Anglo-French cooking. It is all made in-house,
starting with cracked green pepper bread straight from
the oven to go with a faultless cream of celeriac soup.
Main course delivers a choux bun filled with super-fresh
monkfish, scallops and king prawns and white wine,
chive and saffron sauce. To finish, there's ginger
pannacotta with fresh pineapple, citrus syrup and
coconut biscuits.

Chef Margaret Wilson **Owner** Mr P & Mrs M Wilson
Times 7-9.30 Closed 4 wks Xmas & New Year, 3 wks Feb
& Mar, Sun & Mon (ex residents), L all week
Prices Starter £5.25-£9.75, Main £16.50-£25.50, Dessert
£5.50-£9.25, Service optional, Groups min 8 service 10%
Wines 9 bottles over £30, 7 bottles under £30, 4 by glass
Notes Vegetarian menu, Dress restrictions, Smart casual,
no T-shirts, trainers or shorts **Seats** 24, Pr/dining room
24 **Parking** 10

LYDFORD   Map 3 SX58

Dartmoor Inn

⊛⊛ Modern British

Passionate cooking in a charmingly restored coaching inn

☎ 01822 820221
EX20 4AY
e-mail: info@dartmoorinn.co.uk
web: www.dartmoorinn.com
dir: On A386 (Tavistock to Okehampton road)

On the edge of Dartmoor's elemental moorland and just a
short drive from Lydford, you'll find Karen and Philip
Burgess's 16th-century roadside inn. If you're expecting a
darkly-beamed Devon hostelry, think again, as the
delightful contemporary interior owes more to the clean-

Lewtrenchard Manor

Rosettes not confirmed at time of going to print

LEWDOWN   Map 3 SX48

Modern British ⊙

Majestic old manor with exemplary modern food

☎ 01566 783222
EX20 4PN
e-mail: info@lewtrenchard.co.uk
dir: Take A30 signed Okehampton from M5 junct 31. 25m,
exit at Sourton Cross. Follow signs to Lewdown, then
Lewtrenchard

**The Rosette award for this establishment has been
suspended due to a change of chef. Reassessment will
take place in due course under the new chef.**

It's not much of a drive off the A30 to get to this fine
country-house hotel, and yet once you arrive you feel like
you're miles from anywhere, such is the peace and quiet
in this secluded spot. The house, a Jacobean manor
dating back to the early 1600s (an earlier property on the

site is mentioned in the Domesday Book), sits in a valley
beneath the wild tors of Dartmoor. It's been run as a hotel
since 1949 and is now back in the hands of Sue and
James Murray who originally bought it in the 1980s (for a
brief spell it was owned by the now-collapsed von Essen
hotel group). With the Murrays once again at the helm,
Lewtrenchard has a warm and welcoming feel and a
relaxed atmosphere despite its grand proportions. The
building's many period charms are all present and correct
- oak panels, stained-glass windows, ornate
plasterworks, feature fireplaces - and the gardens are
certainly worth a pre (or post) -prandial stroll with their
streams, ponds and many exotic plants. The grounds are
also home to a walled kitchen garden that supplies head
chef John Hooker with much of what he needs of the
vegetable and fruit variety - with the rest taken care of by
local and regional suppliers. Hooker changes the menu
daily, depending on what seasonal produce is available,
and his skills lie in delivering bright, imaginative dishes
using contemporary techniques and with immaculate

presentation. 'Newlyn plaice, coconut, lemongrass, spiced
onion' gets things off to a promising start, the fish sea-
fresh and accurately cooked, served in a broth of sweet
coconut with pickled cauliflower, and with mini onion
bhajees for extra textural and flavour contrast. Ultra-
tender loin of venison comes with flavour-packed pork
cheek, a textbook potato terrine, a super-smooth parsnip
purée and capers in a deeply satisfying main course,
while moist, warm banana bread with a thin cylinder of
peanut parfait and banoffee sorbet brings things to a
close in style. The Purple Carrot private dining room
adjoining the kitchen offers the chance of an eight-course
tasting menu and a close-up view of the action.

Owner The Murray family **Times** 12-1.30/7-9 **Prices** Fixed
L 2 course fr £19.50, Fixed D 3 course fr £49.50, Tasting
menu fr £69, Service optional **Wines** 50 bottles over £30,
10 bottles under £30, 13 by glass **Notes** Fixed L 4 course
£24, D 5 course £49.50, Sunday L, Vegetarian available,
Dress restrictions, Smart casual, Civ Wed 100 **Seats** 45,
Pr/dining room 22 **Children** Portions, Menu **Parking** 40

Save on Hotels. Book at **theAA.com/hotel**

DEVON 141 **ENGLAND**

cut, light and airy style of Scandinavia and New England. That said, this is no starchy gastro establishment: traditional creature comforts are present and correct, so you can sup a pint by a crackling fire in winter, and keep things simple with a great bar menu - twice-fried chip butty, or scallop fritters, anyone? But chef Philip is capable of rather more than this. Bag a seat in one of the interconnecting dining rooms where the menu delves into the realms of black bream fritters with green mayonnaise, followed by charcoal-grilled lamb cutlets with a herb crust and piquant mint sauce. There's no attempt to reinvent the wheel here, just well-executed food with big flavours and generosity of spirit, finishing with vanilla pannacotta with lime jelly and walnut crumble.

Chef Philip Burgess, Andrew Honey **Owner** Karen & Philip Burgess **Times** 12-2.15/6.30-9.30 Closed Mon, D Sun **Prices** Starter £4.95-£8.95, Main £12.95-£21.95, Dessert £2.75-£8.50, Service optional, Groups min 10 service 10% **Wines** 6 by glass **Notes** Seasonal set menus, Sunday L £19.95-£23.95 **Seats** 65, Pr/dining room 20 **Children** Portions, Menu **Parking** 35

LYNMOUTH — Map 3 SS74

Rising Sun Hotel

◉ British, French

Modern British cooking in a convivial harbourside inn

☎ 01598 753223
Harbourside EX35 6EG
e-mail: reception@risingsunlynmouth.co.uk
web: www.risingsunlynmouth.co.uk
dir: M5 junct 23 (Minehead). Take A39 to Lynmouth. Opposite the harbour

The Sun rises on a sloping road overlooking a little harbour in a pretty corner of Devon. It's a profoundly charming thatched inn dating from the 14th century, its weathered panelling, wonky ceilings and creaking floorboards having seen their fair share of smugglers' business in the past. Today, the business is altogether more wholesome, with a menu of locally sourced ingredients being served in both the bar and the more formal dining room, where tables are smartly clothed. The style is mainstream modern British, with many of the familiar combinations of the most recent generation in evidence. Warm crab tart with lime and coriander mayonnaise, or pigeon breast with beetroot purée and shallot dressing, are the winning ways of starting, while mains follow on with roast cod, deep-fried mussels and creamy mash in red wine jus, or confit duck leg on tomato and olive ragoût, served with salt-roasted new potatoes.

Chef Ben Meill **Owner** Personally Run Hotels Ltd **Times** 7-9 Closed L all week **Prices** Prices not confirmed Service optional **Wines** 5 by glass **Notes** Dress restrictions, Smart casual requested **Seats** 32

Tors Hotel

◉ Modern **NEW** 🍽

Antiques, harbour views and well-judged modern cooking

☎ 01598 753236
EX35 6NA
e-mail: torshotel@torslynmouth.co.uk
dir: Adjacent to A39 on Countisbury Hill just before entering Lynmouth from Minehead

This long-established hotel in five acres of woodland on the elemental Exmoor coastline has been in the hands of Martin Miller (of Miller's Antiques guides renown) for the last couple of years, during which time he has put his unmistakable signature on the place, stuffing it with antiques and objets d'art. Looking down to Lynmouth straggling along the harbour, the restaurant has glorious bay views as a backdrop to the unfussy repertoire of modern classics. The cooking is accurate, and dishes such as pan-roasted Cornish scallops with pea purée, black pudding crumbs and candied pancetta, have a clear sense of purpose. A well-judged main course sees chicken ballotine with sage, prosciutto and parmesan matched with fondant potatoes, seasonal vegetables, and chicken and grape jus. It all ends with a nicely balanced trio of custard pannacotta pointed up with the tartness of rhubarb and the crunch of vanilla shortbread.

Chef Andy Collier **Owner** Martin Miller **Times** 12-2.30/7-9 Closed Nov-Feb, L all week **Prices** Service added but optional 10%, Groups min 8 service 10% **Wines** 12 bottles over £30, 18 bottles under £30, 6 by glass **Notes** Sunday L £11.50-£17.50, Vegetarian available, Dress restrictions, No trainers **Seats** 60 **Children** Portions, Menu **Parking** 30

PLYMOUTH — Map 3 SX45

Artillery Tower Restaurant

◉ Modern British 🍽

Confident cooking in historic maritime building

☎ 01752 257610
Firestone Bay, Durnford St PL1 3QR
dir: 1m from city centre & rail station

Built in the early 1500s to protect the deep water passage into Plymouth Sound, the old Firestone Bay gunnery tower on Plymouth's seafront can certainly claim to be a part of the town's history. And it still looks the part. Inside, the circular room is very atmospheric, what with its three-foot-thick exposed stone walls, walnut ceilings, wood-burning stove and neatly laid wooden tables to remind you what you're here for. Peter and Debbie Constable's restaurant is refreshingly focused on the ingredients - superb stuff, sourced locally which are cooked with skill and simplicity, everything made in-house. Start with Devon crab and avocado salad, for example, with Bloody Mary sauce, or roast quail with bacon and lentils. Next up, roast duck breast with confit leg, pear and ginger, or a superb piece of John Dory served with scallops and a tomato and basil sauce. To finish there might be vanilla cheesecake with rhubarb and jelly.

Chef Peter Constable **Owner** Peter & Debbie Constable **Times** 12-2.15/7-9.30 Closed Xmas, New Year, Sun-Mon, L Sat **Prices** Starter £5-£12, Main £12-£30, Dessert £5.50-£10, Service optional, Groups min 8 service 6% **Wines** 5 bottles over £30, 20 bottles under £30, 6 by glass **Notes** Vegetarian available **Seats** 26, Pr/dining room 16 **Children** Portions **Parking** 20, Evening only

Barbican Kitchen

◉ Modern **V** 🍽

Convincing brasserie food from the Tanner bros

☎ 01752 604448
Plymouth Gin Distillery, 60 Southside St PL1 2LQ
e-mail: info@barbicankitchen.com
web: www.barbicankitchen.com
dir: On Barbican, 5 mins walk from Bretonside bus station

The Tanner brothers of Tanners Restaurant (see entry) and telly fame opened their lively, vibrant brasserie in the famous Plymouth Gin distillery in 2006, and it's going from strength to strength. It looks great: bold, bright colours, contemporary prints on the wall (Banksy is just the ticket) - it's informal and fun. There's an open-kitchen on the upper floor and cheery staff throughout. The menu is reasonably priced, with bags of choice, and everything is cooked with care and attention. West Country crab on toast with curried mayo and apple is a light snack or a starter depending on your mood. There's a house burger, steaks, pasta (chorizo penne with sherry vinegar cream maybe), and stirring main courses such as the teriyaki bowl (chicken or Loch Duart salmon) with sesame noodles, or maple-roast pork belly with pears, potatoes and grain mustard sauce. For pud, perhaps dark chocolate tart with mascarpone or summer pudding with clotted cream.

Chef Christopher & James Tanner, Ben Palmer **Owner** Christopher & James Tanner **Times** 12-2.30/5-9.30 Closed 25-26 & 31 Dec **Prices** Fixed L 2 course fr £10.95, Fixed D 3 course fr £14.95, Starter £4.50-£9.99, Main £5.95-£17.95, Dessert £5.95-£6.25, Service included **Wines** 5 bottles over £30, 25 bottles under £30, 13 by glass **Notes** Fixed 2/3 course L menu also available pre-theatre, Sunday L, Vegetarian menu **Seats** 80 **Children** Portions, Menu **Parking** Drakes Circus, Guildhall

PLYMOUTH *continued*

Duke of Cornwall Hotel

◉ Modern British, European **V** ☺

Modern cooking in a Victorian hotel

☎ 01752 275850 & 275855
Millbay Rd PL1 3LG
e-mail: enquiries@thedukeofcornwall.co.uk
web: www.thedukeofcornwall.co.uk
dir: City centre, follow signs 'Pavilions', hotel road is opposite

The Duke of Cornwall has been a landmark building in Plymouth since 1863. It certainly stands out from the crowd with its Victorian gothic architecture, while inside it's all oak panels, elaborate ceiling roses and sparkling chandeliers in generously proportioned public rooms. The elegant, traditionally-furnished dining room is the setting for some modern cooking with a European flavour, with menus founded in the best of West Country produce from land and sea. Mini Scotch eggs with smoked salmon and spicy roast red pepper purée might get the ball rolling, followed by pork fillet with pommes purée, crisp pancetta and a red wine and pork jus. Desserts range from a richly indulgent dark chocolate truffle terrine with Crème de Menthe crème anglaise, to a lemon and mascarpone slice with red berry compôte.

Chef Darren Kester **Owner** W Combstock, J Morcom **Times** 7-10 Closed 26-31 Dec, L all week **Prices** Fixed D 3 course £15, Starter £5-£8, Main £10-£14, Dessert £5-£8 **Wines** 8 by glass **Notes** Vegetarian menu, Dress restrictions, Smart casual, Civ Wed 200 **Seats** 80, Pr/dining room 30 **Children** Portions, Menu **Parking** 40, Also on street

Rhodes@ The Dome

◉ British **NEW** ☺

Modern bistro dining beneath the dome

☎ 01752 266600
Barbican PL1 2NZ
e-mail: info@rhodesatthedome.co.uk
dir: On Plymouth Hoe

The impressive setting for TV chef Gary Rhodes's latest restaurant is a rather glam contemporary affair in a former museum up on Plymouth Hoe. The huge circular bar set beneath the titular glass dome is the obvious place to begin proceedings with nibbles and a cocktail, while taking in the magnificent views of Smeaton's Tower looming above, and Plymouth Sound spread before you. Thankfully, the décor doesn't try to compete with the vista: neutral shades, well-spaced darkwood tables and clean-lined modern style are the order of the day, while the food satisfies current tastes for unbuttoned, ingredients-led bistro dishes. It's a style that allows a croque monsieur to be turbocharged with warm smoked

salmon, or straight-up grilled Devon Ruby sirloin steak with béarnaise, semi-dried tomatoes and mushrooms to share the billing with roast fillet of locally-caught cod served with lemon, capers, shrimps and crushed champ potatoes. Puddings play to the crowd with the likes of glazed lemon tart with local cream.

Chef Gary Rhodes, Kevin Robertson-Wells **Owner** Edward Steven **Times** 12-4/5.30-10 **Prices** Fixed L 2 course £14, Fixed D 3 course £17, Starter £5-£9, Main £11-£24, Dessert £5-£6, Service optional **Wines** 6 bottles over £30, 18 bottles under £30, 7 by glass **Notes** Sunday L, Vegetarian available **Seats** 150, Pr/dining room 25 **Children** Portions **Parking** On street

Tanners Restaurant

◉◉ Modern European ⚓ NOTABLE WINE LIST ☺

Stimulating modern cookery in a venerable Barbican house

☎ 01752 252001
Prysten House, Finewell St PL1 2AE
e-mail: enquiries@tannersrestaurant.com
web: www.tannersrestaurant.co.uk
dir: Town centre. Behind St Andrew's Church on Royal Parade

Tucked away in the oldest part of Plymouth, the historic Barbican district, the Tanner brothers' striking venue is a venerable-looking stone-built house that has been sympathetically kitted out to serve an enthusiastic local constituency. Good table appointments and sleek modern furniture look well against the ancient stone walls, and the service is as polished as the glassware. Stimulating contemporary ideas flow through the menu, producing a starter of seared scallops with smoked prawns and chorizo in a white bean cassoulet (the beans just needing a shade longer perhaps), or straightforward dressed Devon crab, and mains like whole lemon sole from Looe, served with Fowey mussels and sea-greens. Meats are top-drawer, perhaps Bodmin Moor venison loin, interestingly presented amid an east-west culture clash of tarka dhal and cavolo nero, a surprisingly successful piece of inspiration, or slow-cooked ox cheek with horseradish mash and purple sprouting broccoli. Desserts include firm-based fig frangipane tart with cream cheese

ice cream, and there are fine artisan cheeses served with walnut and sultana bread and fruit jellies.

Chef Martyn Compton, Christopher & James Tanner **Owner** Christopher & James Tanner **Times** 12-2.30/7-9.30 Closed 25 & 31 Dec, 1st wk Jan, Sun-Mon **Prices** Fixed L 2 course fr £14, Fixed D 3 course fr £20, Tasting menu £55-£100, Starter £7.50-£9.95, Main £19.95-£23.95, Dessert £7.95, Service optional, Groups min 8 service 10% **Wines** 30 bottles over £30, 25 bottles under £30, 20 by glass **Notes** Tasting menu 6 course, Vegetarian available, Dress restrictions, Smart casual preferred, no trainers **Seats** 45, Pr/dining room 26 **Children** Portions **Parking** On street, church car park next to restaurant

---

PLYMPTON Map 3 SX55

Treby Arms

◉◉ Modern European **NEW** ☺

Skilled cooking from a *MasterChef* victor in a revamped village inn

☎ 01752 837363
Sparkwell PL7 5DD
e-mail: trebyarms@hotmail.co.uk
dir: A38 Plympton turn off towards Langage and Dartmoor Zoological Park, signed

This pleasant old inn in the backwoods of Dartmoor has pulled off that tricky balancing act of going gastro without losing its original identity as a village pub. A cosy, rustic bar with a crackling fire caters for those who just fancy a pint and a bit of banter, while the bulk of the space has been refurbished with the clean-cut, rustic-chic look of a switched-on dining pub: black-beamed ceiling, slate floors and bare scrubbed pine tables. Chef-proprietor Anton Piotrowski certainly delivers the goods via snappy, inventive ideas realised with the sort of razor-sharp technique that goes way beyond the realms of pub fodder (he did win the BBC's *MasterChef* in 2012, after all) as demonstrated by a knockout starter of frog's legs with beer-battered snails, black pudding, confit garlic, and parsley purée. Main course unites spot-on pan-fried bream fillet with creamy mash, crispy squid, chorizo, and clam beurre blanc, then dessert scores another hit: a meltingly delicious chocolate caramel log is matched with digestive biscuit, banana purée and parfait, and lifted with yuzu foam.

Chef Anton Piotrowski **Owner** Anton & Clare Piotrowski **Times** 12-3/6-9.30 Closed 25-26 Dec **Prices** Prices not confirmed **Groups** min 10 service 12.5% **Wines** 11 bottles over £30, 28 bottles under £30, 9 by glass **Notes** Sunday L, Vegetarian available **Children** Portions

Save on Hotels. Book at **theAA.com/hotel**

DEVON 143 **ENGLAND**

| **ROCKBEARE** | **Map 3 SY09** |

The Jack In The Green Inn

◉◉ Modern British V 🕒

A creative powerhouse in a Devon country pub

☎ 01404 822240
EX5 2EE
e-mail: info@jackinthegreen.uk.com
web: www.jackinthegreen.uk.com
dir: 3m E of M5 junct 29 on old A30

The Jack, as it's known to its dedicated local fan-base, is a sensitively refurbished country pub-cum-restaurant not far from Exeter, where the original frame of roughcast stone walls and beams houses, among its various nooks and crannies, a bright, contemporary-styled eatery done in pale lemon. The powerhouse combination of proprietor Paul Parnell and his skilled head of culinary operations, Matthew Mason, stamp the place with bundles of personality, bolstered by a cornucopia of thoroughbred Devon produce, including fine ales, ciders and fruit juices. For the 'Totally Devon' route through the menu, aim for the items highlighted in bold. The food can be as straightforward as chicken breast with mushrooms and tarragon, or salmon with watercress hollandaise, but a creative streak also brings on five-course tasting menus which may feature the likes of sea bass in Thai broth, herb-crusted beef fillet with shallot purée in balsamic, and white chocolate mousse with lemon curd and fennel pollen ice cream, with a pause for regional cheeses before dessert. Vegetarian and vegan menus ensure nobody feels neglected.

Chef Matthew Mason **Owner** Paul Parnell
Times 12-2/6-9.30 Closed 25 Dec-5 Jan **Prices** Fixed L 3 course £25, Fixed D 3 course £25, Starter £4.95-£8.50, Main £18.50-£26.50, Dessert £5.95-£8.50, Service optional **Wines** 60 bottles over £30, 40 bottles under £30, 12 by glass **Notes** Tasting menu available, Sunday L, Vegetarian menu, Dress restrictions, Smart casual

Seats 80, Pr/dining room 60 **Children** Portions, Menu **Parking** 120

| **SALCOMBE** | **Map 3 SX73** |

Soar Mill Cove Hotel

◉◉ Modern British 🕒

Top-notch West Country produce and fab sea views

☎ 01548 561566
Soar Mill Cove, Marlborough TQ7 3DS
e-mail: info@soarmillcove.co.uk
web: www.soarmillcove.co.uk
dir: A381 to Salcombe, through village follow signs to sea

Few things set you up for a good feed better than salty air and a sea view, and this low-slung hotel is tucked away in 2000 acres of National Trust-managed coastal heaven with the waves practically lapping at the door. The Serendipity restaurant is looking great after a makeover bringing in a beachcomber-chic, New England-style décor of powder-blue tongue-and-groove wall panelling to match baby-blue seating and polished wood floors; and fear not, the floor-to-ceiling windows are still there, with those uplifting sea views. West Country produce, often organic, anchors the daily-changing menu, and with the fishing fleets of Salcombe and Brixham close to hand, fish and seafood are naturally high on the agenda. Salcombe scallops with spicy chorizo and tomato dressing should stimulate the appetite, while main courses take in the likes of turbot fillet steamed over an infusion of ginger and lemon and teamed with saffron potatoes and citrus sauce. End with a choc-fest of rich chocolate tart with chocolate sauce and sorbet.

Chef I Macdonald **Owner** Mr & Mrs K Makepeace & family
Times 10.30-5/7.15-9 Closed Jan, L all week **Prices** Fixed D 3 course fr £42.50, Starter £7.50-£9, Main £10-£16.50, Service optional **Wines** 21 bottles over £30, 25 bottles under £30, 6 by glass **Notes** Vegetarian available, Civ Wed 150 **Seats** 60 **Children** Portions, Menu **Parking** 25

Tides Reach Hotel

◉ Modern British 🕒

Stunning seaside setting for good British food

☎ 01548 843466
South Sands TQ8 8LJ
e-mail: enquire@tidesreach.com
web: www.tidesreach.com
dir: Take cliff road towards sea and Bolt Head

This relaxed family-run hotel in Devon's splendid South Hams certainly lives up to its name: when the tide is in, the waves are practically lapping at the doorstep. The salty air and seaside vibes are enough to conjure up a healthy appetite for the kitchen's uncomplicated cooking, served to uplifting views of the idyllic South Sands cove in Salcombe Estuary through sweeping picture windows in the Garden Room restaurant. The provenance of superb West Country ingredients is painstakingly annotated on a menu that kicks off with smoked eel with an entertaining trio of onion preparations - marmalade, purée and pickles. Next out, gurnard fillet arrives with chive beurre

---

blanc, stir-fried purple sprouting broccoli, leeks and smoked bacon, and sauté potatoes. At the end, perhaps a Sachertorte-inspired sponge with Grand Marnier chocolate cream, and cranberry compôte and sorbet.

Chef Finn Ibsen **Owner** Edwards family **Times** 7-9 Closed Dec-Jan, L all week **Prices** Fixed D 3 course £36, Service included **Wines** 11 by glass **Notes** Vegetarian available, Dress restrictions, Smart casual, no jeans or T-shirts **Seats** 80 **Parking** 80

| **SAUNTON** | **Map 3 SS43** |

Saunton Sands Hotel

◉ Modern, Traditional V 🕒

Assured local cooking beside a North Devon beach

☎ 01271 890212
EX33 1LQ
e-mail: reservations@sauntonsands.com
web: www.sauntonsands.com
dir: Exit A361 at Braunton, signed Croyde B3231, hotel 2m on left

If the North Devon beach location evokes a flicker of déjà vu, it may be because you recognise it from the video for Robbie Williams' '*Angels*' - or the cover of Pink Floyd's '*A Momentary Lapse of Reason*' for older readers. The white art deco-ish hotel sits on an eminence, gazing loftily over the sand dunes out to the Atlantic and the UNESCO biosphere that is Braunton Burrows. A smart clientele rolls up here for poolside lounging and spa pampering, and not least for Ian Worley's assured southwestern cooking. Original ideas abound, from a starter of smoked haddock carpaccio with quail's egg arancini, trompettes and curried mayonnaise, to the Exmoor venison with three styles of parsnip, chestnuts and bitter chocolate. More mainstream dishes - chicken liver and foie gras parfait, Lancashire hotpot with pickled red cabbage - are rendered with imaginative aplomb too. Chocolate Bakewell tart has fine buttery pastry, and is nicely cut with praline ice cream and a clutch of rum-soaked raisins.

Chef I Worley, D Turland **Owner** Brend Hotels **Times** 12.30-2/6.45-9.30 **Prices** Fixed L 2 course £16.50-£19.95, Fixed D 3 course £36-£55.95, Starter £8.50, Main £18-£25, Dessert £8.50, Service optional **Wines** 53 bottles over £30, 54 bottles under £30, 15 by glass **Notes** Sunday L, Vegetarian menu, Dress restrictions, Smart, jacket & tie preferred, no sportswear, Civ Wed 200 **Seats** 200, Pr/dining room 20 **Children** Portions **Parking** 140

SHALDON   Map 3 SX97

ODE dining

◉◉ British ⊙

Top-quality local and organic produce in coastal village

☎ 01626 873977
21 Fore St TQ14 0DE
e-mail: contact@odetruefood.com
dir: Cross bridge from Teignmouth then 1st left into Fore St

After a career globetrotting around the kitchens of the world, Tim and Clare Bouget are now intent that travel should be as minimal as possible - at least where local produce is concerned. ODE is a discreet little venue with a loud-and-proud commitment to green credentials. The three-storey Georgian townhouse was made over using environmentally-friendly materials, and nothing gets through the door unless it is line-caught, traditionally-reared or organically grown - except of course, the customers. The result is a vibrant modern British repertoire, cooked with subtlety and intelligence. A parfait of Duckaller Farm pork with crisp bread, and port and red onion compôte opens with a fine chorus of flavours and textures, then slow-cooked haunch of Haldon fallow deer arrives in the good honest company of English cabbage, bacon and glazed shallots. For pudding, treacle tart with lemon verbena cream hits just the right note.

Chef Tim Bouget **Owner** Tim & Clare Bouget **Times** 7-9.30 Closed 25 Dec, BHs, Sun-Tue, L all week **Prices** Fixed D 3 course £40, Service optional, Groups min 6 service 10% **Wines** 5 by glass **Notes** Vegetarian available **Seats** 24 **Parking** Car park 3 mins walk

SIDMOUTH   Map 3 SY18

Riviera Hotel

◉ Modern British ⊙

Seafront restaurant with a local flavour

☎ 01395 515201
The Esplanade EX10 8AY
e-mail: enquiries@hotelriviera.co.uk
web: www.hotelriviera.co.uk
dir: From M5 junct 30 take A3052 to Sidmouth. Situated in centre of The Esplanade

In a prime seafront location, the bay-fronted Hotel Riviera is a classic slice of Regency elegance from the days when ladies and gentlemen paraded along Sidmouth's prom, attracted, perhaps, by the cachet of holidaying in a place favoured by royalty and literati. When the sun plays ball, the restaurant terrace is a glorious spot, with its views over Lyme Bay; indoors, a traditionally elegant dining room is the setting for the kitchen's locally-based modern British cooking. Try ham hock and flageolet bean terrine with pineapple crisps, and pineapple and chilli compôte to begin, followed perhaps by seared spiced salmon with pepper couscous, rösti potatoes, spring onion crème fraîche and caviar.

Chef Matthew Weaver **Owner** Peter Wharton
Times 12.30-2/7-9 **Prices** Starter £10.50-£14, Main £16-£32, Dessert £6.50-£10.50, Service optional **Wines** 43 bottles over £30, 33 bottles under £30, 6 by glass **Notes** Fixed L 5 course £29.50 D 6 course £42, Sunday L, Vegetarian available **Seats** 85, Pr/dining room 65 **Children** Portions, Menu **Parking** 26

The Salty Monk

◉◉ Modern British V ⊙

Gentle modern British food in a former salthouse

☎ 01395 513174
Church St, Sidford EX10 9QP
e-mail: saltymonk@btconnect.com
web: www.saltymonk.co.uk
dir: From M5 junct 30 take A3052 to Sidmouth, or from Honiton take A375 to Sidmouth, 200yds on right opposite church in village

The Salty Monk has a new string to its bow - or should that be belt to its habit? - in the form of a brasserie where the old lounge bar used to be (the lounge has moved to the old Gallery Room). It's business as usual, though, in the main restaurant with its warming colour scheme and soothing candle-lit ambience. Andy and Annette Witheridge's charming restaurant with rooms, located in a 16th-century building built to store the salt traded by local monks, has plenty of character and a genuine focus on top-notch regional ingredients: check-out the suppliers on the menu. To begin, a smoked fish quiche comes straight out of the oven, or there might be duck liver parfait with melba toast and raisins marinated in Madeira. The splendid West Country produce includes fish such as sea bass, served pan-fried with rösti potatoes and a red wine glaze, and the pork which comes as a trio (roast loin, slow-braised belly and rillettes) with apple fondant and creamed potatoes. Finish with a classic lemon tart.

Chef Annette & Andy Witheridge, Scott Horn **Owner** Annette & Andy Witheridge
Times 12-1.30/6.30-9.30 Closed 1 wk Nov, Jan, L Mon-Wed **Prices** Fixed L 3 course fr £29.50, Fixed D 3 course £42.50-£48, Tasting menu fr £62.50, Service optional, Groups min 8 service 10% **Wines** 14 by glass **Notes** Tasting menu 8 course Fri-Sat, Sunday L, Vegetarian menu, Dress restrictions, Smart casual **Seats** 45 **Children** Portions **Parking** 20

The Victoria Hotel

◉ Traditional

Turn-of-the-century splendour beside the sea

☎ 01395 512651
The Esplanade EX10 8RY
e-mail: reservations@victoriahotel.co.uk
web: www.victoriahotel.co.uk
dir: At western end of The Esplanade

Standing proud in five acres of landscaped grounds at the end of Sidmouth's gorgeous Georgian esplanade, the handsome Victoria basks in sweeping views of the cliff-bracketed bay. Old-school tradition reigns within, from the high ceilings and ornate plasterwork, down to the dress code requiring gentlemen to turn up in jacket and tie at dinner, when a pianist or chamber orchestra provides the soundtrack. Expect straightforward cooking that aims to soothe rather than to challenge diners, and local materials as the bedrock of the output, starting with a silky smooth chicken liver parfait teamed with spiced fruit chutney and toasted brioche, ahead of loin of lamb with dauphinoise potatoes, petits pois with Parma ham, and minted jus. Apple tarte Tatin ends on an aptly classic note.

Chef Delroy Budraham **Owner** Brend Hotels
Times 1-2/7-9 **Prices** Prices not confirmed **Notes** Dress restrictions, Jacket & tie **Seats** 120, Pr/dining room 30

SOUTH BRENT   Map 3 SX66

Glazebrook House

◉ Traditional British ⊙

Unfussy, consistent cooking in a Dartmoor country house

☎ 01364 73322
TQ10 9JE
e-mail: enquiries@glazebrookhouse.com
web: www.glazebrookhouse.com
dir: From A38, between Ivybridge & Buckfastleigh exit at South Brent, follow hotel signs

A small-scale country house that was once home to a Georgian gentleman of some substance makes a relaxed and intimate setting for a family-run hotel. On the southern fringe of Dartmoor, it sits in four acres, and its owners, the Cashmores, run the place with charm. Their chef has been with them a good many years, and achieves an impressive level of consistency for unfussy food that uses the pick of southwestern produce. A voguish salad features warm baby beetroot with excellent goats' cheese and walnuts, and may be followed by carefully timed fillet of well-hung local venison in a shiny, deeply flavoured red wine reduction. Properly made tarte Tatin is a dependably satisfying dessert.

Chef David Merriman **Owner** Dave & Caroline Cashmore
Times 7-9 Closed 2 wks Jan, 1 wk Aug, Sun, L all week **Prices** Fixed D 3 course fr £19.50, Starter £4.50-£6.50, Main £16.50-£24.50, Dessert £4.50-£5.95, Service optional **Wines** 23 bottles under £30, 7 by glass **Notes** Vegetarian available, Civ Wed 80 **Seats** 60, Pr/dining room 12 **Children** Portions **Parking** 40

The Laughing Monk

◉ Modern British 🍴

Top-notch local produce cooked with care and attention

☎ 01803 770639
Totnes Rd TQ6 0RN
e-mail: thelaughingmonk@btconnect.com
dir: A38 & follow signs towards Dartmouth, 700yds past Dartmouth Golf Club take right turn to Strete. Restaurant on left just past church

Book-ended by the heavenly South Hams beaches of Blackpool Sands and Slapton, this Victorian school house was given a pared-back modern look - local art, bare wooden floors and tables, and sections of exposed stone wall - when Ben and Jackie Handley took over in 2008. It all makes a fitting backdrop for Ben's no-nonsense cooking, which delivers feisty dishes of ingredient-driven modern food. It helps, of course that this part of the world is blessed with outstanding locally-landed and reared produce, and the seafood doesn't come any fresher than the hand-dived Start Bay scallops that might come with butternut squash purée and crispy pancetta, or the John Dory that is pan-fried and served with smoked salmon potato cake, warm vegetable salad and vine tomato dressing. Meat eaters can sink their teeth into Dartmoor-bred, 28-day aged Devon Ruby Red sirloin from the chargrill, and for pudding there could be Bakewell tart with Devon clotted cream and raspberry sauce.

Chef Ben Handley **Owner** Ben & Jackie Handley **Times** 6.30-9 Closed Xmas, Jan, Sun, L all week **Prices** Fixed D 3 course fr £24, Starter £6.50-£11.50, Main £12-£22, Dessert £6.50-£7.50 **Wines** 1 bottle over £30, 25 bottles under £30, 5 by glass **Notes** Early supper menu available Mon-Sat, Vegetarian available **Seats** 60 **Parking** 4, On street

Bedford Hotel

◉ British

Contemporary menus in a comfortable old hotel

☎ 01822 613221
1 Plymouth Rd PL19 8BB
e-mail: enquiries@bedford-hotel.co.uk
web: www.bedford-hotel.co.uk
dir: M5 junct 31, A30 (Launceston/Okehampton). Then A386 to Tavistock, follow town centre signs. Hotel opposite church

The Bedford, built by the ducal family who give it its name, is unmistakable, with its Gothic-style castellated façade. Its restaurant is special too, with moulded ceilings, panelled walls and candlelight. The menu is very much of the 21st century, though, with pan-fried duck breast with caramelised onion and fig tart and raisin jus followed by roast salmon fillet with a brown shrimp, lime and chilli beurre blanc, accompanied by buttered greens and rösti. Local produce is put to good use: River Exe

mussels, served with leek and shallot ragout and parsley tagliatelle, then fillet of Devon beef, with thyme jus, oxtail ravioli, roast beetroot and dauphinoise potatoes, and, to finish, West Country cheeses are an alternative to something like treacle tart with raspberry coulis.

Chef Matt Carder **Owner** Warm Welcome Hotels **Times** 12-2.30/7-9.30 Closed L Mon-Sat **Prices** Fixed D 3 course £29.95, Service optional **Wines** 18 bottles over £30, 15 bottles under £30, 6 by glass **Notes** Sunday L, Vegetarian available, Dress restrictions, Smart casual, no jeans **Seats** 55, Pr/dining room 24 **Children** Portions, Menu **Parking** 48

The Horn of Plenty

◉◉ Modern British 🍴

Confident contemporary cooking and glorious valley views

☎ 01822 832528
Gulworthy PL19 8JD
e-mail: enquiries@thehornofplenty.co.uk
web: www.thehornofplenty.co.uk
dir: From Tavistock take A390 W for 3m. Right at Gulworthy Cross. In 400yds turn left, hotel in 400yds on right

Built in the 19th century for the Duke of Bedford's mine captain, The Horn of Plenty has a soul-soothing setting of beguiling tranquillity amid five acres of wild orchards and gardens, including a handy kitchen garden that earns its keep in stocking the larder with seasonal materials. Ravishing views across the wooded Tamar Valley are framed by picture windows in the restaurant, where chef Scott Paton leads an ambitious and enthusiastic brigade who aim high and score palpable hits from the off, delivering invention, excitement and razor-sharp technique in equal measure. Well-conceived, contemporary dishes built from carefully-sourced ingredients are the deal here: an impressive pan-fried turbot fillet teamed with celeriac fondant and soy and truffle vinaigrette starts the show, ahead of a simple-sounding breast of corn-fed chicken with purple sprouting broccoli and brown butter hollandaise, which gains lustre from the quality of its ingredients and impeccable execution. The new season's rhubarb is showcased in a clever dessert comprising the vegetable served poached, in a sorbet, with creamy curd and toasted white chocolate.

Chef Scott Paton **Owner** Julie Leivers & Damien Pease **Times** 12-2.15/7-10.15 **Prices** Fixed L 2 course £19.50, Fixed D 3 course £49.50, Tasting menu £59.50, Service optional, Groups min 10 service 10% **Wines** 29 bottles over £30, 32 bottles under £30, 17 by glass **Notes** Tasting menu available, Sunday L, Vegetarian available, Dress restrictions, Smart casual, smart Sat D, Civ Wed 80 **Seats** 60, Pr/dining room 14 **Children** Portions, Menu **Parking** 20

The Library @ Browns

◉◉ Modern British

Accomplished contemporary cooking in smart boutique hotel

☎ 01822 618686
80 West St PL19 8AQ
e-mail: info@brownsdevon.com
dir: B3250 onto A386 to Tavistock

Dating from the 17th century, the old girl still boasts open fires, oak beams, exposed stone and slate flags, although a makeover gives a contemporary sheen. Dining takes place in The Library, a small and intimate room with soft music, polished oak tables, vivid artwork and an eponymous wall of books. The kitchen hits the spot with modern British and classic dishes, with flavour as king and an eye for presentation. Start with tender, moist quail on a bed of Jerusalem artichoke risotto, with a scattering of girolles and hazelnuts adding depth, while home-made haggis adds a further dimension to a main course of Dartmoor venison paired with bubble-and-squeak and honey-roast roots. West Country produce plays a starring role throughout. Cornish gurnard might appear with mussel and clam chowder, before the likes of local pork with black pudding, bacon, apple, mustard sauce and Savoy cabbage, and, to finish, crème brûlée is a classic. Chocoholics can get their fix with the 'everything chocolatey'.

Times 12-3/7-10.30

Thurlestone Hotel

◉ British 🍴

Stunning sea views and well-judged cooking

☎ 01548 560382
TQ7 3NN
e-mail: enquiries@thurlestone.co.uk
web: www.thurlestone.co.uk
dir: A38 take A384 into Totnes, A381 towards Kingsbridge, onto A379 towards Churchstow, onto B3197 turn into lane signed to Thurlestone

The location - a delicious coastal hotspot near Salcombe - would be reason enough to visit this part of the world, but the Thurlestone Hotel's 19 acres of subtropical gardens overlooking the sea and cliffs makes this a location to savour. That splendid panorama of the coastline across Bigbury Bay can be appreciated at leisure in the elegant Margaret Amelia restaurant, since floor-to-ceiling picture windows mean it stays as a backdrop throughout proceedings. The kitchen deals in well-conceived modern British dishes wrought from excellent local produce - South Devon crab, perhaps, which might share a plate with avocado pannacotta, tomato jelly and basil shoots, while mains run from chargrilled fillet steak with oxtail ravioli and horseradish hollandaise to herb-crusted hake with spinach, saffron

continued

THURLESTONE *continued*

mash and lobster butter sauce. Dessert could be a chocolate and orange torte with hazelnut ice cream.

Chef Hugh Miller **Owner** Grose family
Times 12.30-2.30/7.30-9 Closed 4-20 Jan, L Mon-Sat
Prices Service optional **Wines** 119 bottles over £30, 26 bottles under £30, 9 by glass **Notes** 4 course £38.50, Fish tasting menu, Sunday L £22.50, Vegetarian available, Dress restrictions, Jacket, Civ Wed 150 **Seats** 150, Pr/dining room 150 **Children** Portions, Menu **Parking** 120

TORQUAY   Map 3 SX96

The Elephant Restaurant and Brasserie

🌹🌹🌹 – *see below*

Grand Hotel

🌹 Modern European 🍷

Expansive grand-hotel cooking on the English Riviera

☎ 01803 296677
Torbay Rd TQ2 6NT
e-mail: reservations@grandtorquay.co.uk
web: www.grandtorquay.co.uk
dir: M5 junct 31, follow signs for Torquay. At the Penn Inn rdbt follow signs for seafront

Local girl Dame Agatha Christie was so fond of her hometown that she continued to holiday here long after she had moved on, and indeed spent a honeymoon at The Grand. With the railway station just behind it, and Torquay's section of the English Riviera coastline right in front, it could hardly be more handily positioned, and the 1881 dining room (commemorating the year the place opened) capitalises on those balmy views. Richard Hunt cooks with a free rein, offering an expansive menu of modern grand-hotel food. A seafood-themed starter might see skate and crayfish bound into fishcakes with tomato concasse in vivid green pea and rocket velouté, before breast of guinea fowl comes along in the company of sautéed wild mushrooms and pancetta and confit swede in red wine jus. A medley of bright, tangy flavours enlivens a dessert of coconut parfait with pineapple salsa and lime and cassis ripple ice cream.

Chef Richard Hunt **Owner** Keith Richardson
Times 12.30-3/6.30-9.30 Closed L Mon-Sat **Prices** Fixed D 3 course fr £29.95, Service optional **Wines** 19 bottles over £30, 25 bottles under £30, 11 by glass **Notes** Sunday L, Vegetarian available, Dress restrictions, Smart casual, Civ Wed 100 **Seats** 160, Pr/dining room 40 **Children** Portions, Menu **Parking** 30, Station car park opposite

---

The Imperial Hotel

🌹 Modern British **NEW**

Updated Classical cooking and stunning views

☎ 01803 294301
Park Hill Rd TQ1 2DG
e-mail: imperialtorquay@pumahotels.co.uk
web: www.pumahotels.co.uk
dir: M5 to Exeter, A380 then A3022 to Torquay. Park Hill Rd off Torwood St/Babbacombe Rd, just N of New Harbour

This Torquay landmark was built in 1866 on a clifftop, giving wonderful views over the bay and English Channel. Those views are perhaps best appreciated from the Regatta Restaurant, a stylish, light and airy room, where staff are correct but unstuffy. The kitchen follows a more or less traditional path, with some modern twists, and changes the menu weekly, with daily fish specials available depending on the catch. A highly professional team is at work, sourcing top-end produce and turning

---

The Elephant Restaurant and Brasserie

TORQUAY   MAP 3 SX96

Modern British

Fine dining and brasserie dishes near the harbour

☎ 01803 200044
3-4 Beacon Ter TQ1 2BH
e-mail: info@elephantrestaurant.co.uk
dir: Follow signs for Living Coast, restaurant opposite

Simon Hulstone's convivial, stylish venue sits at an oblique angle to the bobbing boats in Torquay harbour, but still makes the most of fine marine views, particularly from the first-floor bar and its adjacent dining space, the Room. Here, for six of the best months of the year, he offers a full-dress version of contemporary British cooking, while the ground-floor Brasserie trades in the more everyday likes of goats' cheese and beetroot, venison burgers, and steak and skinny chips, but also

fish dishes with a difference, such as poached and glazed smoked haddock with truffled macaroni cheese. It's upstairs, though, where the stops are pulled out, for all that there has been a slight edging towards a more conservative approach of late, which perhaps suits the straitened times. Sea bass makes an appearance with a risotto of spider-crab and peas, given summery lift with lemon verbena cream and courgette flowers. A technically curious roulade constructed of well-trimmed lamb on one side and chicken breast on the other doesn't quite add up to more than the sum of its halves, though its accompaniments of smoked garlic, asparagus, pea mousse and shallot and thyme purée lack nothing in resonance. Starters may be where the fireworks dazzle most, as in a serving of halibut poached in beurre noisette, with a beignet of smoked eel and foie gras, accompanied by lovage jelly and pickled apple. To finish, the famous sphere of strawberry and lemon mascarpone, garnished with elderflower cream and strawberry juice, is another architectonic marvel, or choose a trio of

impeccable West Country cheeses from the trolley. The service approach of understated, but precisely efficient, civility ensures people get treated as the old friends many of them have indeed become. A well-chosen wine list has some attractive selections by the glass, not least Gosset's Brut Excellence, the house champagne.

Chef Simon Hulstone **Owner** Peter Morgan, Simon Hulstone **Times** 12-2/7-9 Closed 1st 2wks Jan, Sun-Mon **Prices** Fixed L 2 course fr £16.95, Fixed D 3 course £49.50, Tasting menu £55-£85, Starter £7-£9.25, Main £16.50-£23.50, Dessert £6-£7.50, Service added but optional 10% **Wines** 24 bottles over £30, 30 bottles under £30, 8 by glass **Notes** Tasting menu available, Vegetarian available **Seats** 75, Pr/dining room 12 **Parking** Opposite restaurant

out well-executed, visually attractive dishes. Duck and prune confit is a good example of the beast, served with red onion chutney and a crisp, well-dressed salad, and could be followed by grilled pork steak, tender and moist, with the expected accompaniments of grain mustard sauce, apple purée, Savoy cabbage and fondant potato. A dab hand with pastry is evident when it comes to puddings: perhaps smooth and tangy lemon tart complemented by crème Chantilly and sharp mango coulis.

Chef Jacek Gorney **Owner** Puma Hotels **Times** 7-9.30 Closed L all week **Prices** Fixed D 3 course £22-£29, Starter £6-£9, Main £17-£24, Dessert £5.50-£9, Service optional **Wines** 15 bottles over £30, 47 bottles under £30, 18 by glass **Notes** Vegetarian available, Dress restrictions, Smart casual, Civ Wed 300 **Seats** 170, Pr/dining room 350 **Children** Portions, Menu **Parking** 110, NCP - Torquay Town Centre

Orestone Manor

◉◉ Modern, European NEW V ⏂

Capable cooking in boutique manor house

☎ 01803 328098
Rockhouse Ln TQ1 4SX
e-mail: info@orestonemanor.com
dir: A379 to Shaldon. Follow road through, hotel signed on left (beware sharp turn)

This handsome Georgian manor house sits in landscaped grounds overlooking Lyme Bay. Family-run, and with just 11 stylish bedrooms, it combines stylish intimacy with a serious attitude to gastronomy. The views from the smart conservatory-style bistro are of the landscaped gardens and out to sea, while the menu proposes uncomplicated, please-all dishes along the lines of seafood or antipasti platters, local steaks and burgers, bolstered by daily blackboard specials. At dinner, there's a more ambitious à la carte menu served on linen-clothed tables in the more formal restaurant. The kitchen allies sound technique with thorough use of quality local produce, setting out with well-made chicken liver parfait with red onion marmalade and toasted brioche, followed by the comfort of crispy pork belly with Savoy cabbage, lardons and pork jus. If the nearness of the briny puts you in the mood for fish, something like roast Cornish cod fillet with buttered spinach, clams and mussel cream should fit the bill. Finish with a classic vanilla crème brûlée with shortbread.

Chef Daniel Morris **Owner** Neil & Catherine D'Allen **Times** 12-2.30/6.30-9.30 Closed 3-30 Jan **Prices** Fixed L 2 course £18-£21, Fixed D 3 course £25-£30, Tasting menu £44.50-£47.50, Starter £5.50-£11.50, Main £14.50-£22.50, Dessert £6.50, Service optional **Wines** 22 bottles over £30, 45 bottles under £30, 18 by glass **Notes** Tasting menu at wknds or by arrangement, Sunday L, Vegetarian menu, Civ Wed 120 **Seats** 55, Pr/dining room 22 **Children** Portions, Menu **Parking** 38

TOTNES   Map 3 SX86

The Riverford Field Kitchen

◉ Modern British ⏂

Vegetables take a starring role at organic Devon farm

☎ 01803 762074
Riverford TQ11 0JU
e-mail: fieldkitchen@riverford.co.uk
dir: From A38 Buckfastleigh, take A384 to Totnes. Turn off to Landscove & Woolston Green & follow signs to Riverford Organics

As the name suggests, this is no place for high heels and designer suits, with Riverford (the renowned supplier of organically grown fruit and veg) offering a homely, communal, refectory-style dining experience at its farm restaurant just outside Totnes. There's just one sitting for lunch and dinner and you share tables (and food) with your fellow diners, while chef Rob Andrew deals in whatever's seasonal and picked from the fields that day at his open-to-view kitchen. As such there's no menu, rather each table is given one main meat dish and around five creative veg dishes to share - vegetables are king here. It's a three-course affair, so leave plenty of room for mains such as slow-roast lamb shoulder with salsa verde, plus a whole array of veggie side-plates, perhaps taking in Swiss chard and anchovy gratin and red cabbage with blue cheese and walnuts. Steamed marmalade sponge or sticky toffee pudding end things comfort style.

Chef Rob Andrew **Owner** Guy Watson
Times 12.30-3/7.30-11.30 Closed D Sun-Wed (winter) **Prices** Fixed L 3 course £22.50, Fixed D 3 course £26.50, Service optional **Wines** 1 bottle over £30, 15 bottles under £30, 6 by glass **Notes** Sunday L, Vegetarian available **Seats** 72 **Children** Portions **Parking** 30

TWO BRIDGES   Map 3 SX67

Two Bridges Hotel

◉ Modern British

Scenic moorland spot and bold cooking

☎ 01822 892300
PL20 6SW
e-mail: enquiries@twobridges.co.uk
web: www.twobridges.co.uk
dir: 8m from Tavistock on B3357, hotel at junct with B3312

One bridge (check), two bridges (check), the setting is true Dartmoor, the bridges built of old stone with history in their sturdy frames. The hotel has 60 acres to call its own, but nature is all around. The traditional Tors Restaurant is the setting for some rather daringly contemporary food, the good use of regional produce giving it all a sense of place. Home-made bread, an amuse-bouche and petits fours show the serious intentions of the kitchen crew. Devon rabbit - tender loin, soft confit - with quail's egg, carrot purée, salsify and candied orange is a creative first course, followed perhaps by Crediton chicken with onion bhaji, sag aloo,

almonds, dates and apricots, or fillet of sea bass with chorizo, butternut squash, gem lettuce and crab. And to finish, in season you might find rhubarb and custard with meringue, lemon and pistachios.

Times 12-2/6.30-9.30

WOODBURY   Map 3 SY08

Woodbury Park Hotel and Golf Club

◉ Modern British ⏂

Attractive brasserie food at a golfing and fitness hotel

☎ 01395 233382 & 234735
Woodbury Castle EX5 1JJ
e-mail: enquiries@woodburypark.co.uk
web: www.woodburypark.co.uk
dir: M5 junct 30, take A376/A3052 towards Sidmouth, turn right opposite Halfway Inn onto B3180 towards Budleigh Salterton to Woodbury Common, hotel signed on right

Exeter is one of those cities that doesn't require too much of a trek outwards in order to come across the rolling acres of the English countryside. There are 550 of them around Woodbury Park, some consecrated to a pair of golf courses, while inside the hotel is a hive of activity, with keep-fit machines, swimming and massages. All of which provide various ways of honing an appetite for the straightforward, aesthetically presented brasserie food on offer in the Atrium Restaurant. Expect grilled mackerel from Brixham, subtly chillied-up and served with tomato jelly and red onion, and then herb-crusted cod with ratatouille and dauphinoise, or a right royal beef platter comprised of a quarter-pound fillet steak, chargrilled ribeye and oxtail pudding. Vanilla pannacotta has that just-set consistency, its creamy blandness offset with a clutch of sharply balsamic-dressed strawberries. A West Country cheeseboard offers the region's finest, served with membrillo and olives.

Chef Matthew Pickett **Owner** Sue & Robin Hawkins **Times** 12.30-2.30/6.30-9.30 Closed L Mon-Sat, D 31 Dec **Prices** Fixed D 3 course £25, Starter £6.50-£8, Main £16-£18, Dessert £6, Service optional **Wines** 7 bottles over £30, 39 bottles under £30, 10 by glass **Notes** Sunday L, Vegetarian available, Dress restrictions, Smart casual, Civ Wed 150 **Seats** 120, Pr/dining room 180 **Children** Portions **Parking** 350

WOOLACOMBE — Map 3 SS44

Watersmeet Hotel

Traditional British, European

Superb coastal views and confident cooking

☎ 01271 870333
Mortehoe EX34 7EB
e-mail: info@watersmeethotel.co.uk
web: www.watersmeethotel.co.uk
dir: M5 junct 27. Follow A361 to Woolacombe, right at beach car park, 300yds on right

Dramatically perched on the cliffside, this elegant hotel is traditionally decorated throughout and has an old style charm and relaxing ambience. Floor-length windows in the west-facing dining room promise views of incredible sunsets at dinner; every seat in the house enjoys views of the spectacular coastline, sandy beach and across to Lundy Island. The kitchen takes high quality produce and delivers consistently well-executed food with some European influences, with dishes on the daily changing menu demonstrating an impressive lightness of touch. Home-cured pigeon ham (moist and tender) comes with an appealing combination of celeriac, beetroot, apple and hazelnuts - a dish of nicely contrasting colours and textures - while main-course loin and breast of lamb with flageolet bean purée, sweetbread and balsamic reduction is an equally well-considered plate of food. Caramel pannacotta, honeycomb and poached pear balances all the flavours perfectly or, for the savoury-toothed, the board of English cheeses, seasonal chutney and pickled celery is an alternative way to finish. The newly opened bistro offers more informal dining.

Chef John Prince **Owner** Mrs James **Times** 12-2/7-9 **Prices** Prices not confirmed Service optional **Notes** Sunday L, Vegetarian available, Dress restrictions, Smart casual, jacket, no jeans or T-shirts, Civ Wed 65 **Seats** 56, Pr/dining room 18 **Children** Portions, Menu **Parking** 40

DORSET

BEAMINSTER — Map 4 ST40

BridgeHouse

Modern International

Up-to-date cooking in a 13th-century building

☎ 01308 862200
3 Prout Bridge DT8 3AY
e-mail: enquiries@bridge-house.co.uk
web: www.beaminsterbrasserie.co.uk
dir: From A303 take A356 towards Dorchester. Turn right onto A3066, 200mtrs down hill from town centre

The 700-year-old stone-built BridgeHouse was originally a home to priests, and while there's no lack of old-world charm, sympathetic renovation has brought modern-day style to the hotel. The restaurant (the Beaminster Brasserie) comes in three distinct areas: a more formal panelled and candlelit main room with an Adam fireplace and intimate ambience, a lighter, modern conservatory and canvassed-over terrace overlooking the walled garden. The kitchen's creative modern cooking is inspired by the abundant local larder and comes with a nod to France and sunnier climes, as well as the occasional influence from even further afield. Crispy Lyme Bay hake fillet is served with tiger prawn and squid paella, and lobster, broad bean and pea bisque, or Creedy Carver chicken tikka saag with tandoori leg, crispy liver, peshwari rice, crispy skin and cucumber raita. Desserts extend to pineapple tarte Tatin or dark chocolate fondant.

Times 12-2.30/6.30-9.30

The Wild Garlic

Modern British

Careful sourcing and considered cooking from
MasterChef **winner**

☎ 01308 861446
4 The Square DT8 3AS
e-mail: mail@thewildgarlic.co.uk
web: www.thewildgarlic.co.uk
dir: From A303, exit A3066 Crewkerne and follow signs for Bridport. Restaurant in Town Sq

Please note: as we go to press this restaurant is about to relocate to Iwerne Minster, near Blandford, Dorset.

There's no doubt winning *MasterChef* in 2009 played its part early on in getting punters through the door of Mat Follas's Wild Garlic, but it goes from strength to strength because it's a damn fine restaurant. The 16th-century one-time tollhouse on the square has been spruced up with a nicely chilled-out vibe (Follas was brought up in New Zealand after all), with rough-hewn solid-oak tables on wooden floors, white and sage-green half-panelled walls and chalkboards announcing the day's specials. Produce is sourced with due diligence from around these parts, with many foraged ingredients cropping up here and there but only where they have a place. Confit duck leg and chorizo cassoulet is a hearty way to start, or there might be something like a red onion Tatin with goats' cheese sauce. Main courses have equal appeal, perhaps a venison loin with spelt and a chocolate and espresso sauce, or one of the fish of the day from the board. Desserts such as blood orange posset, lemonade and rose ice cream prove this is a creative kitchen on song.

Chef Mat Follas **Owner** Mat & Amanda Follas **Times** 12-2/7-11 Closed BHs, Sun-Tue **Prices** Fixed L 2 course £14, Tasting menu £45-£50, Starter £6-£8, Main £17-£25, Dessert £7-£12, Service optional, Groups min 10 service 10% **Wines** 12 bottles over £30, 14 bottles under £30, 9 by glass **Notes** Vegetarian available

Seats 40 **Children** Portions **Parking** Car park at front of building

BOURNEMOUTH — Map 5 SZ09

Best Western The Connaught Hotel

Modern British

Gentle modern British cooking in fashionable Bournemouth

☎ 01202 298020
30 West Hill Rd, West Cliff BH2 5PH
e-mail: reception@theconnaught.co.uk
web: www.theconnaught.co.uk
dir: Follow Town Centre West & BIC signs

Bournemouth is in vogue. Its glorious sandy beaches were declared among the best in Europe by the EU in 2012, and it has gradually shaken off its image as a sedate resort of the venerable, and put on a new suit of fashionable clothes. That said, it still does old-school elegance well, as may be witnessed at The Connaught, which gazes imperiously out over those aforesaid beaches from the eminence of the West Cliff. The smart Blakes dining room is done in café crème, and offers a congenial version of the modern British idiom, with no alarming combos to cause palpitations. Start with cured seared salmon in an aïoli salad of fennel, radish and caviar, and then follow on with Creedy Carver duck breast with three-cheese potato gratin and Savoy cabbage, in a sauce of morels and red wine. After which, it's surely worth a 15-minute pause to await a hot banana soufflé, served with matching ice cream and chocolate sauce.

Best Western Connaught Hotel

Chef David Hutcheson **Owner** Franklyn Hotels Ltd **Times** 6.30-9 Closed L all week (private lunches by arrangement) **Prices** Starter £6-£8.50, Main £15-£24.95, Dessert £6-£9.45, Service added but optional 10% **Wines** 20 bottles over £30, 29 bottles under £30, 15 by glass **Notes** Pre-theatre menu available must pre-book, Vegetarian available, Dress restrictions, Smart casual, no jeans, T-shirts or mobiles, Civ Wed 120 **Seats** 80, Pr/dining room 16 **Children** Menu **Parking** 66

Bournemouth Highcliff Marriott Hotel

◉◉ Modern British

Smart cooking in a Victorian clifftop hotel gone cool

☎ 01202 557702
St Michael's Rd, West Cliff BH2 5DU
e-mail: reservations.bournemouth@marriotthotels.co.uk
web: www.highcliffgrill.co.uk
dir: Take A338 dual carriageway through Bournemouth, then follow signs for International Centre to West Cliff Rd, then 2nd right

The aptly-titled Highcliff Marriott Hotel lords it from its perch on Bournemouth's West Cliff, basking in views across the resort and its Blue Flag beaches. Externally, the place is still a snow-white grande dame of Victorian vintage, but once inside, it is clear that the chintz has been well and truly chucked. Right in tune with the new image, the Highcliff Grill is looking pretty slick with its modern brasserie-style decor involving bare darkwood tables and funky cherry and lime green seating. The cooking plays a straight bat: contemporary, but sticking to the unfussy grill concept with a mix of modern and classic dishes built on well-sourced materials. Chicken liver and Madeira parfait with pear chutney and pickled walnuts is a tried-and-true starter done right, then grilled fillet of sea trout appears in the company of a fluffy potato crêpe, intense beetroot confit, curly kale and chervil hollandaise. Awaiting at the end is a textbook melting centre within a chocolate fondant teamed with chocolate ice cream and a crunchy praline.

Times 1-3/6-9.30 Closed L Mon-Sat

The Crab at Bournemouth

◉◉ Seafood ☺

Imaginative ways with seafood near the pier

☎ 01202 203601
Exeter Rd BH2 5AJ
e-mail: info@crabatbournemouth.com
dir: Follow signs to B.I.C, restaurant opposite

Opposite Bournemouth International Centre, moments from the pier, The Crab, like its sister in Chieveley (see entry, Berkshire), is a seafood restaurant, and, if the name isn't enough, fishy plates on the chunky darkwood tables and piscine shapes in the wrought-iron room dividers are reminders. Daily deliveries from the West Country mean everything is spankingly fresh, timings are accurate, and glazes, sauces and broths add further interest to dishes. Classics like moules marinière and lobster thermidor jostle for attention among more contemporary choices: seared scallops with black pudding, or prawn and pork dumpling, presented in a steamer with a teriyaki dipping sauce, followed by a meaty chunk of cod with a brown shrimp and mussel broth, served with saffron potatoes and spinach, or John Dory fillets with macaroni cheese and lobster bisque. Meat-eaters are not entirely overlooked, and desserts can

be as inventive as apple cheesecake with caramel ice cream.

Chef Dave Horridge **Owner** Julie Savage
Times 12-2.30/5.30-10 **Prices** Fixed D 3 course fr £20.95, Starter £6.50-£12, Main £15-£39.95, Dessert £4.95-£7.95, Groups min 6 service 10% **Wines** 18 bottles over £30, 24 bottles under £30, 19 by glass **Notes** Sunday L, Vegetarian available, Dress restrictions, Smart casual **Seats** 80 **Children** Portions, Menu **Parking** B.I.C

Cumberland Hotel

◉◉ British

Hip contemporary dining in an art-deco hotel

☎ 01202 290722 & 556529
27 East Overcliff Dr BH1 3AF
e-mail: kwood@cumberlandbournemouth.co.uk
dir: A35 towards East Cliff & beaches, right onto Holdenhurst Rd, straight over 2 rdbts, left at junct to East Overcliff Drive, hotel on seafront

Overlooking the sea on Bournemouth's East Cliff, the Cumberland is a bright-white temple to art-deco architecture that brings a touch of Miami Beach style to the English seaside with its palm-lined poolside terrace. Recently made over with a loud-and-proud funky contemporary style to appeal to a vibrant crowd, the Ventana Brasserie is the focus of culinary endeavours, serving a roll-call of unfussy crowd-pleasing modern dishes wrought from local materials. Start with duck liver pâté with crispy smoked bacon, piccalilli and granary toast rubbed with English mustard, before moving into the well-trodden territory of steaks and burgers from the grill, or monkfish with red pepper coulis and stir-fried vegetables. To finish, almond and raspberry tiramisù offers a creative take on an old favourite.

Chef Mateusz Nowatkowski **Owner** Kevin Wood
Times 12-10 **Prices** Service optional, Groups min 6 service 10% **Wines** 4 bottles over £30, 24 bottles under £30, 9 by glass **Notes** Sunday L £11.95-£21.95, Vegetarian available, Dress restrictions, Smart casual, Civ Wed 90 **Seats** 90, Pr/dining room 40 **Children** Menu **Parking** 55, On street

The Green House

◉ Modern British NEW

Inventive, eco-friendly and exciting cooking

☎ 01202 498900
4 Grove Rd BH1 3AX
e-mail: info@thegreenhousehotel.com

The USP of this trendy revamped Victorian hotel is its impeccable eco-friendly credentials - hence the 'green' element of its title. Sustainability drives everything from the chic boutique furnishings through to the Green Room Restaurant's exciting contemporary British output, so you can expect the provenance of the kitchen's raw materials to be of the highest order, often organic and sourced from within a 50-mile radius; the wine list, too, is based on organic or bio-dynamic wines. The menu is tweaked daily to capitalise on the best of what's seasonal and fresh in

the local area, and there's clearly an inventive spirit at work to come up with off-the-wall combos such as a starter of duck egg omelette with smoked eel, goats' cheese foam and pumpkin purée. Next up, Laverstoke Park buffalo liver arrives with foraged St George's mushrooms, pea risotto and fennel, and to finish, baked vanilla yoghurt comes with brownie ice cream and dried cherries.

Prices Fixed L 2 course £14.99, Starter £5.50-£7, Main £15.50-£16.50, Dessert £7-£9.50 **Notes** Sun Jazz L 4 course £22.50, Sunday L

Hermitage Hotel

◉ Modern British

Seafront hotel with good, honest food

☎ 01202 557363
Exeter Rd BH2 5AH
e-mail: info@hermitage-hotel.co.uk
web: www.hermitage-hotel.co.uk
dir: Follow A338 (Ringwood-Bournemouth) & signs to pier, beach & BIC. Hotel directly opposite

The Hermitage sits centre-stage in Bournemouth, opposite the splendid pier and the promenade running alongside the town's celebrated golden beaches, and lies a handily short stroll from the Pavilion Theatre and whatever is going down in the Bournemouth International Centre. The old girl has been smartly refurbished and still has a sense of majesty in the high-ceilinged dining room with its grand decorative fireplaces. The cooking here ploughs a crowd-pleasing furrow, delivering uncomplicated ideas along the lines of a retro prawn and crayfish cocktail with Marie Rose sauce to start, then classic steaks or braised lamb shank with creamed potato, crispy pancetta, green beans and rosemary and redcurrant sauce. End with dark chocolate fondant with vanilla ice cream and chocolate sauce.

Times 6-9 Closed L Mon-Sat

Menzies Hotels Bournemouth - Carlton

◉ Traditional & Modern British

Sea views and classical cooking

☎ 01202 552011
East Overcliff BH1 3DN
e-mail: carlton@menzieshotels.co.uk
web: www.menzieshotels.co.uk
dir: M3/M27, follow A338 (Bournemouth). Follow signs to town centre & East Overcliff. Hotel is on seafront

This traditional hotel makes the most of its spectacular location on Bournemouth's East Cliff. The dining room has fab views over the outdoor pool and decking area to the sea beyond, and when the sun shines you might even forget you're in the UK. In Frederick's restaurant, with its high ceilings adorned with chandeliers and swag drapes, a formal dress code applies, which certainly helps maintain that sense of grandeur. Unfussy, classical food is what to expect; smoked haddock and chive ravioli, for

continued

BOURNEMOUTH *continued*

example, with a mussel and vegetable broth, or chicken, basil and mint terrine with home-made chutney. Next up, best end of English lamb is served pink with goats' cheese glazed dauphinoise potatoes and seasonal greens, with chocolate and coffee layer mousse with roasted hazelnut ganache a star turn for dessert.

Chef Richard Allsopp **Owner** Menzies Hotels
Times 12.30-2/7-9.45 **Prices** Fixed L 3 course fr £16.95, Fixed D 3 course fr £24.95, Starter £7-£10.50, Main £16.50-£25.50, Dessert £4.50-£6.50, Service optional **Wines** 8 by glass **Notes** Sunday L, Vegetarian available, Dress restrictions, Smart casual, Civ Wed 80 **Seats** 120, Pr/dining room 180 **Children** Portions, Menu **Parking** 76

The Print Room & Ink Bar & Brasserie

◎◎ Classic Brasserie ◎

Cosmopolitan menu in a magnificent art-deco venue

☎ 01202 789669
Richmond Hill BH2 6HH
e-mail: info@theprintroom-bournemouth.co.uk
web: www.theprintroom-bournemouth.co.uk
dir: Just off town centre in *Daily Echo* newspaper building

The impressive art deco premises of the *Daily Echo* building make a setting of considerable grandeur for this vast brasserie, cafe and bar. Black-and-white chequerboard floors, maple booths, mirrors, Swarovski chandeliers and black lacquer tables all feed into the Depression-era feel - not that there's anything remotely downbeat about this operation: there's something going on all day here, kicking off with breakfast in the Ink Bar for early birds, until The Print Room takes over with its buzzy brasserie cooking. Modern European ideas appear alongside British classics on a wide-ranging menu built on plenty of local materials. Start inventively with pan-fried scallops with diced chorizo and Bloody Mary butter, ahead of pan-seared free-range chicken breast teamed with sautéed potatoes and pancetta, and white wine and tarragon cream sauce. Elsewhere, a fillet of sea bass might get more exotic treatment with the addition of shiitake mushrooms, baby sweetcorn, pak choi, bean shoots and an Asian broth. To finish, a well-made, correctly wobbly pannacotta is served with poached figs.

The Print Room & Ink Bar & Brasserie

Chef Nick Hewitt, Edgarus Cekauskas **Owner** Print Room Dorset Ltd **Times** 12-3/6-11 Closed D Sun **Prices** Fixed L 2 course fr £12.50, Fixed D 3 course £22-£35, Starter £4.50-£9.50, Main £10.95-£25, Dessert £5.75-£7, Service optional, Groups min 10 service 10% **Wines** 18 bottles over £30, 29 bottles under £30, 12 by glass **Notes** Pre-theatre menu available, Sunday L, Vegetarian available **Seats** 120, Pr/dining room 22 **Children** Portions, Menu **Parking** NCP - 100yds

Rock Restaurant

◎ Modern British NEW

Modern British dining in an old Methodist church

☎ 01202 765696
Landseer Rd, Westbourne BH4 9EH
e-mail: westbourne@rockrestaurants.co.uk

A former Methodist church with a Tesco Express on the ground floor and a restaurant above is a rather unusual combination, but so it is here in classy Westbourne. Head up the winding staircase to the first floor and enter Rock to be greeted by the sight of a beautiful stained-glass window plus several other original features of the 18th-century church, such as antique oak panelling and a vaulted ceiling. Providing further visual stimulation is a theatre-kitchen, where you can watch head chef Nick Atkins at work crafting top-notch local and seasonal ingredients into some classics of the modern British idiom, such as plump and juicy seared scallops with pork belly, celeriac purée and apple caramel to start. Main course could be something as simple as a home-made burger in a brioche bun with roasted pepper dressing and all the trimmings, or perhaps a comfort food dish of unctuous slow-cooked featherblade of Dorset beef with a smooth horseradish mash, Savoy cabbage and butter-poached carrots.

Chef Nick Atkins **Times** 12-11 Closed D Sun **Prices** Fixed L 2 course £15, Groups min 10 service 10%

West Beach

◎ Modern, Seafood ◎

Sophisticated seafood dishes on the beach

☎ 01202 587785
Pier Approach BH2 5AA
e-mail: enquiry@west-beach.co.uk
web: www.west-beach.co.uk
dir: 100yds W of the pier

For a seafood restaurant, West Beach couldn't have a better location: it's almost on the beach, with a fabulous decked terrace and great views. It's a friendly place with clued-up staff, done out in pastels and light woods and with an open-plan kitchen. Some meat and vegetarian dishes are on the menu, but it would be churlish to arrive here and pass up on the spankingly fresh seafood. A few preparations are pulled out of the classical repertoire - moules marinière, lobster thermidor - but in general the kitchen leaves no modern culinary stone unturned, giving hake the bourguignon treatment and serving it with spinach and mash, and partnering pan-fried John Dory with ham hock ballottine and emulsion and accompanying it with braised baby gem, celeriac and fondant potato. You could start with accurately pan-fried scallops, served with carrot purée and couscous, pickled raisins and coriander, go on to fish pie, and finish with a dessert from the short list: perhaps plum trifle.

Chef Nick Hewitt **Owner** Andrew Price
Times 12-3.30/6-10 Closed 25 Dec, D 26 Dec, 1 Jan **Prices** Starter £5.50-£10, Main £12.75-£19.50, Dessert £5-£9.50, Service optional, Groups min 10 service 10% **Wines** 27 bottles over £30, 42 bottles under £30, 26 by glass **Notes** Tasting menu available, Pre-theatre 2 course

Save on Hotels. Book at **theAA.com/hotel**

DORSET 151 **ENGLAND**

£14.95, Sunday L fr £12.50, Vegetarian available, Dress restrictions, No bare feet or bikinis **Seats** 90 **Children** Portions, Menu **Parking** NCP 2 mins

---

BRIDPORT
Map 4 SY49

Riverside Restaurant

◎ Seafood, International ◐

The pick of local seafood in a waterside setting

☎ 01308 422011
West Bay DT6 4EZ
e-mail: neilriverside@hotmail.com
web: www.thefishrestaurant-westbay.co.uk
dir: A35 Bridport ring road, turn to West Bay at Crown rdbt

Lonnie Donegan was top of the pops with '*My Old Man's a Dustman*' when the Watson family set up shop in their unaffected restaurant. Over half a century later, it is still going great guns and has never deviated from its prime directive: serving generous, fuss-free dishes of fish and seafood fresh off the local Lyme Bay boats. With water all around, the setting is retro beachcomber-chic, with hues of lavender blue and pale wood tables, and the kitchen's approach admirably uncheffy and to the point - what appears at the table depends on what the boats have brought in: deep-fried squid with saffron aïoli needs no further adornment, as is the case with Portland crab and sweetcorn chowder. Next up, there are whole fish grilled on the bone, platters of shellfish, or the daily specials may offer grilled brill with a celeriac, coriander and horseradish remoulade.

Chef A Shaw, E Webb, G Leech **Owner** Mr & Mrs A Watson **Times** 12-2.30/6.30-9 Closed 30 Nov-12 Feb, Mon (ex BHs), D Sun **Prices** Fixed L 2 course £19.55, Starter £4.95-£10.50, Main £12.95-£27.50, Dessert £4.95-£7.50, Service optional, Groups min 7 service 10% **Wines** 15 bottles over £30, 45 bottles under £30, 10 by glass **Notes** Sunday L, Vegetarian available **Seats** 80, Pr/dining room 30 **Children** Portions, Menu **Parking** Public car park 40 mtrs

---

CHRISTCHURCH
Map 5 SZ19

Captain's Club Hotel and Spa

◎◎ Modern European ◐

Contemporary spa hotel with appealing riverside restaurant

☎ 01202 475111
Wick Ferry, Wick Ln BH23 1HU
e-mail: enquiries@captainsclubhotel.com
web: www.captainsclubhotel.com
dir: Hotel just off Christchurch High St, towards Christchurch Quay

Any skipper should be happy to hang his hat at the Captain's Club, with its position at Christchurch Quay on the River Stour and the seafood offered up on the menu. Whatever your maritime credentials, though, this modern hotel has bags of appeal, including a delicious spa, classy accommodation, and an impressive restaurant. With floor-to-ceiling windows, live music in the piano bar and a large terrace for when the weather is kind, there is a lot of 21st-century style hereabouts. There's an all-day menu which can sort you out with everything from sandwiches (crab, maybe) to omelette Arnold Bennett, or rib-eye steak with all the expected trimmings. But for lunch and dinner there's also crustacea such as whole crab with lemon and herb mayo, fish main courses such as halibut with crab and asparagus salad and fennel purée, and meaty mains like duck breast served with the confit leg meat mixed into bubble-and-squeak, plus a fried duck egg. Finish with warm spotted dick with custard and berry jam.

Chef Andrew Gault **Owner** Platinum One Hotels Ltd **Times** 11.30-10 **Prices** Prices not confirmed Service optional **Wines** 12 by glass **Notes** Sunday L, Vegetarian available, Civ Wed 120 **Seats** 100, Pr/dining room 120 **Children** Portions, Menu **Parking** 41

Christchurch Harbour Hotel

◎◎ Modern British ◐

Chic waterside restaurant for fresh seafood and stunning views

☎ 01202 483434
95 Mudeford BH23 3NT
e-mail: aj@thejetty.co.uk
web: www.christchurch-harbour-hotels.co.uk
dir: A35/A337 to Highcliffe. Right at rdbt, hotel & restaurant 1.5m on left

Newly relaunched as the Upper Deck, the restaurant at the 18th-century Christchurch Harbour is looking ultra-cool with its swanky bar (for cocktails and light bites), and its laidback, contemporary coastal design. The

glorious view over Mudeford Quay to Hengistbury Head on the other side of the water is still there, of course, and you can enjoy it through large windows in the restaurant or, if you're lucky, from the lovely terrace. Not surprisingly, deliveries of fish arrive daily, and may be simply grilled, fried or baked without too much fuss or elaboration: lemon sole fillet, say, or fillet of cod with seasonal crushed peas, potatoes and herb velouté. Fish soup is something of a stalwart among starters, with alternatives varying from retro prawn cocktail with Marie Rose sauce to bolder seared scallops with braised pork cheek and apple dressing. Those who must have meat could opt for classic duck confit terrine, served with spicy rhubarb chutney, followed by roast chicken breast with the no-nonsense accompaniments of wilted greens and creamy mashed potato.

Chef Clyde Hollett **Owner** Harbour Hotels Group **Times** 12-2.30/6-9.45 **Prices** Fixed L 2 course £15.50, Fixed D 3 course fr £25, Tasting menu fr £39.50, Starter £4.25-£11.50, Main £15.50-£27.50, Dessert £6.50-£7.95, Service added but optional 10% **Wines** 30 bottles over £30, 30 bottles under £30, 12 by glass **Notes** Sunday L, Vegetarian available, Dress restrictions, Smart casual, Civ Wed 100 **Seats** 95, Pr/dining room 20 **Children** Portions **Parking** 100

Crooked Beam Restaurant

◎ Modern British

Friendly, family-run restaurant with well-judged menu

☎ 01202 499362
Jumpers Corner, 2 The Grove BH23 2HA
e-mail: info@crookedbeam.co.uk
dir: Situated on corner of Barrack Rd A35 and The Grove

'Mind your head' says a sign on the beams, but the slight risk of a bump is a small price to pay for the experience of eating at this delightful little restaurant. The 300-year old building wears its antiquity well and is suitably cosy and traditional within. Husband-and-wife-team Simon and Vicki Hallam run the show - he in the kitchen, she out front - and they know what their customers want. Good quality produce is at the heart of things, with the menu following a broad and crowd-pleasing path. Potted crab, for example, comes with dressed leaves and walnut and raisin toast, and chicken liver and pistachio parfait with a nicely-judged plum chutney and toasted brioche. Main course might deliver sea bass marinated in chilli and coriander served with a warm green bean and tomato salad, and to finish, perhaps a treacle tart with raspberry coulis and Calvados cream.

Times 12-2/7-11 Closed Mon, L Sat, D Sun

CHRISTCHURCH *continued*

The Jetty

◉◉ Modern British

Sleek modish venue with sharp, unfussy cooking

☎ 01202 400950
95 Mudeford BH23 3NT
e-mail: dine@thejetty.co.uk
dir: A35/A337 to Highcliffe. Right at rdbt, hotel & restaurant 1.5m on left

If it's a winning waterside location you're after, head on over to The Jetty in the grounds of the Christchurch Harbour hotel. It sits in a glorious position overlooking the water to Mudeford Quay, and the building is a bit of a looker itself: a contemporary carbon-neutral construction built of wood and glass. Every customer is guaranteed the view through the floor-to-ceiling windows, but the terrace has got to be first choice when the weather is warm. The kitchen is under the auspices of Alex Aitken, a man who knows how to let the ingredients do the talking; the provenance of what appears on the plate is taken very seriously indeed. Start, perhaps, with a Scotch egg, but with a difference: the egg is wrapped in salt-cod brandade and fried in tempura batter. Seafood is king here, so follow on with a fine piece of halibut served with hand-dived Weymouth scallops and tempura Poole Bay rock oyster. There are good meat offerings, too, such as rib-eye steak with hand-cut chips, watercress and béarnaise sauce.

Times 12-2.30/6-10

The Lord Bute & Restaurant

◉ British, Mediterranean ♨

Well-heeled surroundings for local ingredients

☎ 01425 278884
179-185 Lymington Rd, Highcliffe BH23 4JS
e-mail: mail@lordbute.co.uk
web: www.lordbute.co.uk
dir: Follow A337 to Lymington, opposite St Mark's churchyard in Highcliffe

Set above the beach, the hotel dates from the 18th century; parts of the property used to be the entrance lodges to Highcliffe Castle. Nowadays the restaurant is a delightful, elegant room with an orangery extension, its walls hung with paintings, with plenty of space between tables, and attentive and swift service. Using organic, GM-free local produce, the kitchen has assembled a crowd-pleasing menu, from New Forest asparagus topped with a poached egg and mustard and chive hollandaise, or light foie gras parfait with apple and apricot chutney, to well-timed, tender rump of Romsey lamb with shepherd's pie and redcurrant and mint sauce, or grilled local sea bass fillet with caper and brown shrimp butter. Among a half-dozen or so desserts may be iced praline parfait with butterscotch sauce and clotted cream.

Chef Kevin Brown **Owner** S Box & G Payne
Times 12-2/7-9.30 Closed Mon, L Sat, D Sun
Prices Service optional **Wines** 13 bottles over £30, 35 bottles under £30, 10 by glass **Notes** Sunday L £23.95, Vegetarian available, Dress restrictions, Smart casual, no jeans or T-shirts **Seats** 95 **Children** Portions **Parking** 50

Splinters Restaurant

◉ Modern International ♨

Superior cooking in lively neighbourhood restaurant

☎ 01202 483454
12 Church St BH23 1BW
e-mail: eating@splinters.uk.com
web: www.splinters.uk.com
dir: Directly in front of Priory gates

With over half a century of service now under its belt, Splinters boasts an enviable local following among Christchurch's foodies. The jaunty green frontage stands out on the cobbled street leading to the Priory, and takes its name from the work-related injuries suffered by the carpenters who built the cosy booth seating within. It is a welcoming family-run set-up with a bar-lounge for aperitifs and canapés, and a warren of appealing dining rooms with nooks and corners for a romantic soirée. The kitchen cuts no corners, making everything in house from top-class local materials. The result is a crowd-pleasing repertoire of broadly modern European ideas, starting, perhaps, with a chicken liver parfait served with orange marmalade and toasted brioche. Main course could be honey-roasted duck breast with dauphinoise potato and cranberry compôte, with walnut and caramel tart with vanilla ice cream for pud.

Chef Paul Putt **Owner** Paul & Agnes Putt
Times 11-2/6.30-10 Closed 26 Dec, 1-10 Jan, Sun-Mon
Prices Fixed L 2 course fr £13.50, Fixed D 3 course fr £26.50, Service optional, Groups min 8 service 10%
Wines 30 bottles over £30, 50 bottles under £30, 5 by glass **Notes** ALC 2/3 course £31.95/£38.95, Vegetarian available, Dress restrictions, Smart casual **Seats** 42, Pr/dining room 30 **Children** Portions **Parking** Priory car park

Mortons House Hotel

◉◉ British ♨

Confident cooking in an Elizabethan manor

☎ 01929 480988
East St BH20 5EE
e-mail: stay@mortonshouse.co.uk
web: www.mortonshouse.co.uk
dir: In village centre on A351

There's a lot of history around these parts - Corfe Castle itself had the job of guarding the main route through the Purbeck Hills - and Mortons House has been around to bear witness to over 400 years of it. Built in 1590 or so, these days it's a hotel and restaurant with a good deal of period charm and character. The interior has been done up to meet contemporary needs without affecting the historic integrity of the building. The restaurant is a suitably traditional space with well-dressed tables and a menu that is most definitely not stuck in the past. Start, perhaps, with butternut and sage ravioli with baby spinach and crispy pancetta, or Cornish red mullet with a watercress risotto and romesco dressing. There's a confidence and focus to the kitchen's output, which extends to main courses such as fillet of cod with braised Puy lentils and sautéed wild mushrooms, and fillet of local beef with smoked veal tongue, beetroot dauphinoise potatoes, pickled beetroot, parsnip purée and cavolo nero. For dessert, warm strawberry Bakewell tart with Dorset clotted ice cream ends things in fine style.

Chef Ed Firth **Owner** Mrs Woods, Mr & Mrs Clayton
Times 12-1.45/7-9 **Prices** Fixed D 3 course £39.50-£100, Service optional, Groups min 20 service 10% **Wines** 22 bottles over £30, 32 bottles under £30, 4 by glass **Notes** Sunday L, Vegetarian available, Dress restrictions, Smart casual preferred, Civ Wed 60 **Seats** 60, Pr/dining room 22 **Children** Portions, Menu **Parking** 40

Sienna

◉◉◉ *— see opposite*

Save on Hotels. Book at **theAA.com/hotel**

DORSET 153 ENGLAND

Sienna

DORCHESTER   MAP 4 SY69

Modern British

Small is beautiful on Dorchester's high street

☎ 01305 250022
36 High West St DT1 1UP
e-mail: browns@siennarestaurant.co.uk
dir: Near top of town rdbt in Dorchester

Reaching the ten-year milestone in April 2013, Russell and Elena Brown have achieved great things at their diminutive restaurant in historic Dorchester. With just 15 customers at any given time, chef-patron Russell is able to ensure a remarkable level of consistency, and can even offer a tasting menu which extends to seven enticing courses. There's nothing fussy about the interior - its calming neutrality extends to ash tables against hues of ochre and cream, with mirrors and colourful splashes of artwork by way of relief. Elena runs the front-of-house with charm and professionalism. The menu follows the seasons with due diligence and focuses on regional produce (looking due west). Russell is technically gifted, adept at balancing flavours and textures, and manages to produce dishes that are creative without being overblown. Landed in the West Country, and caught by line, cod might turn up amongst starters with parsley root purée and red wine-braised baby onions, whilst local Blackacre Farm hen's eggs go into the pappardelle, served with roasted onions, thyme and fontina cheese. Every ingredient on the plate makes a contribution to the sum of the whole dish. Saddle of wild venison with caramelised quince, chestnuts, potato purée and game jus is a main course of balance and bite, or go for something fishy such as monkfish saltimbocca with potato and radicchio casserole and sage beurre noisette. Desserts are no less appealing: Yorkshire forced rhubarb frangipane tart, for example, with orange custard and rhubarb sorbet. West Country cheeses are a temptation, too. The lunch menu (three choices per course) is terrific value for money.

Chef Russell Brown **Owner** Russell & Elena Brown **Times** 12.30-2/7-9 Closed 2 wks Feb/Mar, 2 wks Sep/Oct, Sun-Mon, L Tue **Prices** Fixed L 2 course £25.50, Fixed D 3 course £45, Tasting menu fr £60, Service optional **Wines** 20 bottles over £30, 19 bottles under £30, 7 by glass **Notes** Tasting menu 7 course, Vegetarian available **Seats** 15 **Parking** On street, top of town car park

Summer Lodge Country House Hotel, Restaurant & Spa

EVERSHOT   MAP 4 ST50

Modern British 🍷 NOTABLE WINE LIST

Assured modish cooking in peaceful surroundings

☎ 01935 482000
Fore St DT2 0JR
e-mail: summerlodge@rchmail.com
dir: 1m W of A37 halfway between Dorchester & Yeovil

This grand Georgian house was extended in the Victorian era, the plans drawn up by no less than Thomas Hardy (author, architect, and local hero), and it makes a fabulous country house, brimming with traditional charm and all the luxuriating extras that make a stay memorable. The four acres of gardens are a treat and there's an indoor pool and all-weather tennis court, too. The handsomely-proportioned house is done-out with a good deal of opulence, with fine fabrics and furniture, not least in the conservatory dining room with its swagged curtains and elegantly dressed tables. Service from the slick and professional team is a highlight of any visit, including the excellent sommelier on hand to guide you through the top-notch wine list. On the menu is some well-judged, gently updated classical cooking. A shot-glass of spinach velouté might get the ball rolling, before an amuse bouche (lobster salad with citrus jelly, perhaps), and a starter of marbled foie gras and port terrine with ginger bread, grapes and golden raisins. Next up, a beautifully cooked fillet of Cornish turbot comes in the good company of chestnut gnocchi, beetroot purée and thyme butter, or try the Exmoor venison with sweet potato gratin, creamed white onions and a port and sage jus. The astute technical abilities and nous of the kitchen team continues in desserts such as hot Granny Smith soufflé with praline espuma and caramelised apple tart.

Chef Steven Titman **Owner** Mrs Bea Tollman **Times** 12-2.30/7-9.30 **Prices** Fixed L 2 course £23, Fixed D 3 course £40, Tasting menu £78-£210, Starter £18-£19, Main £20-£29, Dessert £11-£13, Service optional, Groups min 12 service 12.5% **Wines** 1400 bottles over £30, 8 bottles under £30, 25 by glass **Notes** Tasting menu 8 course available with/out wines, Sunday L, Vegetarian available, Dress restrictions, Jackets preferred, no T-shirts or shorts, Civ Wed 40 **Seats** 60, Pr/dining room 20 **Children** Portions, Menu **Parking** 60

EVERSHOT — Map 4 ST50

The Acorn Inn

◉ British

Modern gastro-pub fare in Hardy country

☎ 01935 83228
28 Fore St DT2 0JW
e-mail: stay@acorn-inn.co.uk
web: www.acorn-inn.co.uk
dir: From A37 between Yeovil & Dorchester, follow
Evershot & Holywell signs, 0.5m to inn

In a pretty village at the heart of Hardy's Wessex, this
16th-century coaching inn is a gem, with a warm and
welcoming bar (low ceiling, open fire, brick walls and its
own snacky menu) and a stylishly cottagey restaurant with
local artwork, antiques and Persian rugs. Scrupulously
sourced ingredients bring on locally-smoked venison with
classic celeriac remoulade, and Dorset cheddar and
walnut soufflé with thyme butter and celery cream. Main
courses cover a range of flavours, from chicken, mushroom
and tarragon pie with spring onion mash, to a winter
hotpot of venison served with caramelised onions and
braised red cabbage. Fish might appear as pan-fried hake
fillet with salsa verde, and among puddings may be
almond tart with a poached pear and vanilla ice cream.

Times 12-2/7-9

George Albert Hotel

◉ Modern British **NEW** 🍷

Uncomplicated cooking in smart modern hotel

☎ 01935 483430
Wardon Hill DT2 9PW
e-mail: enquiries@gahotel.co.uk
dir: On A37 (between Yeovil & Dorchester). Adjacent to
Southern Counties Shooting Ground

There's plenty of scope for working up an appetite at the
George Albert since this smart modern hotel is handily
placed for exploring the many attractions of Dorset. At its
culinary heart is the Kings Restaurant, an expansive
open-plan room kitted out in a neutral style, its well-
spaced tables swathed in white linen, and tended by
friendly, smartly-uniformed staff. The kitchen takes a
modern approach to dishes built on good quality, often
local, materials, and its strengths lie in the fact that it
sticks to tried-and-tested themes - ham hock terrine with
home-made piccalilli being a case in point, although you
might equally opt to open with beetroot tarte Tatin with
horseradish cream. Confit shoulder of Dorset lamb with
mini shepherd's pie, pea purée, carrots and lamb jus
could turn up for substantial satisfaction at main course
stage, before it all concludes on an exotic note with
passionfruit pannacotta, pineapple salsa and mango
sauce.

Chef Andy Pike **Owner** G Crook & Sons
Times 12-2.30/6.30-9 **Prices** Service optional **Wines** 10
bottles over £30, 21 bottles under £30, 14 by glass
Notes Sunday L £11-£18, Vegetarian available, Civ Wed
200 **Seats** 40 **Children** Portions, Menu **Parking** 200

Summer Lodge Country House Hotel, Restaurant & Spa

◉◉◉ — **see page 153**

LYME REGIS — Map 4 SY39

The Mariners

◉ British, International 🍷

**Updated old coaching inn with consistently interesting
food**

☎ 01297 442753
Silver St DT7 3HS
e-mail: enquiries@hotellymeregis.co.uk
dir: S onto B3261 from A35, on left opposite right turn to
the Cobb

This low-slung pink building was a coaching inn back in
the 17th century, but after a smart makeover to take on
the more refined needs of 21st-century diners, its
restaurant now sports a shipshape, uncluttered modern
look with wooden floors, wall lights and wooden tables. If
you grab one of the best tables you get views over the
rooftops towards Lyme Bay as a backdrop to unfussy
modern cooking that puts well-sourced Dorset produce at
the heart of things. Local seafood is a good bet, so you
might set the ball rolling with Lyme Bay scallops with
chorizo crumb and tarragon mayonnaise. Main course
could see Dorset lamb supported by celeriac dauphinoise,
asparagus in Parma ham, and lamb jus, or perhaps more
of that splendid local fish in the shape of grilled lemon
sole with samphire, prawns and herbs and buttered new
potatoes. Comfort-oriented desserts run to sticky toffee
pudding with butterscotch sauce and toffee ice cream.

Chef Richard Reddaway, Chris Higgs **Owner** Jerry
Ramsdale **Times** 12-2/6.30-9 Closed D 25 Dec
Prices Fixed L 2 course £12-£18.95, Fixed D 3 course
£24.95-£29.95, Starter £4.95-£7.50, Main £8.95-£22.95,
Dessert £5-£6.75, Service optional **Wines** 3 bottles over
£30, 27 bottles under £30, 9 by glass **Notes** Sunday L,
Vegetarian available **Seats** 36 **Children** Portions, Menu
Parking 20, Car park 200mtrs

MAIDEN NEWTON — Map 4 SY59

Le Petit Canard

◉ Modern British, French 🍷

**Honest, accomplished cooking in pretty village
restaurant**

☎ 01300 320536
Dorchester Rd DT2 0BE
e-mail: craigs@le-petit-canard.co.uk
web: www.le-petit-canard.co.uk
dir: In centre of Maiden Newton, 8m W of Dorchester

The location in a cottagey terrace building - once a
coaching inn by all accounts - and the traditional, homely
décor is not exactly the cutting-edge of restaurant design,
but no matter, for this is a delightful place run with
passion by Gerry and Cathy Craig. The tables are neatly
laid with linen cloths and topped with flowers and
candles, and the original features of the property -
wooden beams and some exposed stonework - add to its
charm. Gerry's cooking does not try to reinvent the wheel,
but neither is it stuck in the past. Seared scallops with
celeriac purée, for example, is a gently modish
construction, or go for the bresaola with rocket, olive oil
and parmesan shavings. Main-course roast breast of
duck comes with a plum and ginger sauce, and loin fillet
of local wild venison with pear chutney, while dessert
might be a textbook crème brûlée.

Chef Gerry Craig **Owner** Mr & Mrs G Craig **Times** 12-2/7-9
Closed Mon, L all week (ex 1st & 3rd Sun in month), D
Sun **Prices** Fixed D 3 course £33-£35.95, Service optional
Wines 4 bottles over £30, 26 bottles under £30, 6 by
glass **Notes** Sun L 1st & 3rd Sun only, Vegetarian
available, Dress restrictions, Smart casual preferred
Seats 28 **Parking** On street/village car park

Save on Hotels. Book at **theAA.com/hotel**

DORSET 155 ENGLAND

POOLE
Map 4 SZ09

Harbour Heights

◎◎ Modern European ☺

Spectacular views and modern bistro food

☎ 01202 707272
73 Haven Rd, Sandbanks BH13 7LW
e-mail: enquiries@harbourheights.net
web: www.fjbhotels.co.uk
dir: From A338 follow signs to Sandbanks, restaurant on
left past Canford Cliffs

Breathtaking views over Poole Harbour come as standard
at this elegant, revamped, 1920s art deco hotel. You can
take in the scene either sitting on the south-facing
decked terrace whilst sipping a pre-dinner cocktail or a
glass of wine, or from the open-plan bistro with its floor-
to-ceiling windows. With a new French chef at the helm,
you can expect a menu of modern European food with an
emphasis on what's local and in season, including fish
landed at Poole Quay which is displayed on the fresh fish
counter in the restaurant. So you might start with a
meaty first course of beef oxtail ravioli with braised onion
and consommé, moving on to perfectly cooked lemon sole
with a supporting cast of smoked prawn butter, braised
Puy lentils, cabbage and sweet and sour onions. A rich
chocolate marquise, baby poached pear and fromage
blanc sorbet is not for the faint-hearted at dessert, or
why not try bay leaf pannacotta, passion fruit and crackle
crystals?

Chef Loic Gratadoux **Owner** FJB Hotels
Times 12-2.30/7-9.30 **Prices** Prices not confirmed
Service included **Wines** 11 by glass **Notes** Chef's table,
Sunday L, Vegetarian available, Dress restrictions, Smart
casual **Seats** 90, Pr/dining room 100 **Children** Portions,
Menu **Parking** 50

The Haven

◎◎ Modern British **V** ☺

**Delightful Poole Bay views and confident modern
cooking**

☎ 01202 707333
161 Banks Rd, Sandbanks BH13 7QL
e-mail: reservations@havenhotel.co.uk
web: www.havenhotel.co.uk
dir: Follow signs to Sandbanks Peninsula; hotel next to
Swanage ferry departure point

On sunny days, with views across the waves and
waterborne action from tables on the terrace of the
water's-edge La Roche restaurant, there's a real touch of
the Riviera. The stylish art-deco era hotel itself - once the
home of radio pioneer Guglielmo Marconi - sits at the
southernmost tip of the Sandbanks strip and overlooks
the sweep of Poole Bay. Inside, the brasserie-style
restaurant's tiered tables make the best of the views too,
while two large fish tanks continue the watery theme.
Likewise, the sharp, French-influenced menu makes the
most of the local larder, especially (given the location)
sea-fresh locally-landed fish and shellfish. Pan-fried cod
fillet might be served with cod cakes, brandade and a
mussel sauce, South Coast native lobster is grilled or
served thermidor-style, or for meat-lovers, perhaps rump
of lamb with fondant potato, ratatouille and shallot
purée. Finish with baked vanilla cheesecake with textures
of apple and blackberries.

Chef Jason Hornbuckle **Owner** Mr J Butterworth
Times 12-2.30/7-9.30 **Prices** Prices not confirmed
Service optional **Wines** 11 by glass **Notes** Sunday L,
Vegetarian menu, Dress restrictions, No shorts or beach
wear, Civ Wed 99 **Seats** 80, Pr/dining room 156
Children Portions, Menu **Parking** 90

Hotel du Vin Poole

◎ Modern British, French ☺

Bistro cooking in an elegant Georgian house

☎ 0844 7489265
Mansion House, Thames St BH15 1JN
web: www.hotelduvin.co.uk
dir: A350 into town centre follow signs to Channel Ferry/
Poole Quay, left at bridge, 1st left is Thames St

The elegant Virginia-creeper-clad Georgian mansion sits
just off the old quayside. In a former life it was the
Mansion House hotel until 2008, when it got the HdV
trademark makeover, a winning formula that takes
interesting old buildings, and reworks them with a
smartly-casual wine and bistro food-oriented focus. The
Poole outpost offers a smart bar, wine cellar and wine-
tasting room, plus the open-plan bistro at its beating
heart, which follows the familiar style of banquette
seating, unclothed wooden tables, and sunny ochre-
washed walls hung with wine-related images. It's an

amenable setting for good bistro food backed by an
impressive, French-orientated wine list, while the walled
outdoor terrace is a major pull on balmy days. Expect
good honest cooking that respects the quality of the raw
materials - a moules marinière starter is as good as
anything you'll find across the nearby Channel.
Elsewhere, there's steak tartare or dressed crab with
walnut toast, while main course brings seared salmon
with warm salad Niçoise and Lyonnaise potatoes.

Chef Darren Rockett **Owner** Hotel Du Vin/SLK
Times 12.30-2/5.30-10 **Prices** Starter £5.95-£11.50,
Main £12.50-£25.95, Dessert £6.95, Service added but
optional 10% **Wines** 10 by glass **Notes** Pre-theatre 1
course, wine & coffee £12.95, Sunday L £22.95-£24.95,
Vegetarian available, Dress restrictions, Smart casual,
Civ Wed 35 **Seats** 85, Pr/dining room 36
Children Portions, Menu **Parking** 300

The Sandbanks

◎ Mediterranean, European **V**

Unfussy bistro dishes with bracing marine views

☎ 01202 707377 & 709884
15 Banks Rd, Sandbanks BH13 7PS
e-mail: reservations@sandbankshotel.co.uk
web: www.fjbhotels.co.uk
dir: From Poole or Bournemouth, follow signs to
Sandbanks Peninsula. Hotel on left along peninsula

Seven miles of Blue Flag beach on the doorstep and
splendid views across Poole Bay mean that this upscale
seaside hotel will always be a magnet for summer's day
dining, particularly when alfresco eating on the
beachfront terrace is on the cards. Whether you're indoors
in the relaxed octagonal brasserie, or out on the terrace,
there's a real jet-set Riviera buzz to the place and a
simple menu of appropriately contemporary
Mediterranean-accented dishes. You might get going
with in-house-smoked and marinated salmon with crab,
brown shrimp, prawns and lemongrass dressing, then
proceed to rump of local lamb with seasonal vegetables
and gratin dauphinoise, and wind proceedings up with
chocolate crème brûlée with almond biscuits.

Chef Wayne Jones **Owner** Mr J Butterworth
Times 12-3/6-10 Closed Mon-Tue, D Sun **Prices** Service
optional **Wines** 17 by glass **Notes** Sunday L £18.95,
Vegetarian menu, Dress restrictions, Smart casual, Civ
Wed 80 **Seats** 65, Pr/dining room 25 **Children** Portions,
Menu **Parking** 112

PORTLAND   Map 4 SY67

The Bluefish Restaurant

⚜ Modern

Well-judged cooking next to Chesil Beach

☎ 01305 822991
15-17a Chiswell DT5 1AN
e-mail: thebluefish@tesco.net
dir: Take A354 by Chesil Bank, off Victoria Square in Portland, over rdbt towards Chesil Beach, next to 72hr free car park

On the Isle of Portland, next to Chesil Beach, The Bluefish is an easygoing, relaxed and child-friendly restaurant with stone walls and a mishmash of chairs at plain wooden tables, with popular outdoor seating under parasols. It's the sort of place that people return to again and again, drawn by the atmosphere and the quality of the cooking. The Anglo-European, modern menu might kick off with split-pea and ham soup with a duck egg and go on to beef broth with pasta and vegetables. Fish and shellfish are expertly cooked, turning up in palate-pleasing combinations: perhaps pan-fried local scallops with sweetcorn purée, black pudding and orange butter, followed by sea bass fillet poached in olive oil with Serrano ham, faggots, beetroot and port sauce. Desserts are no less appealing, from lemon posset with berries to chocolate fondant with poached cherries and lemon curd.

Times 12-3/7-9 Closed Xmas, Mon-Tue, L Wed-Fri, D Sun (in winter)

POWERSTOCK   Map 4 SY59

Three Horseshoes Inn

⚜ British 🍃

Proper pub, proper pub food

☎ 01308 485328
DT6 3TF
e-mail: threehorseshoespowerstock@live.co.uk
dir: 3m from Bridport. Powerstock signed off A3066 Bridport to Beaminster

You wouldn't normally go out of your way for Scotch eggs and burgers, but this classic Dorset village inn has elevated pubby classics to a higher plane - that burger being made of Dorset veal and bone marrow, and teamed with barbecue pulled short rib, celeriac slaw and triple-cooked chips. But first, serpentine, skinny lanes have to be negotiated before you arrive to a warm greeting and a fine pint of Palmers ale in the convivial bar - take a table here if you prefer the cheerful country pub vibe, or move through to the cosy restaurant decorated with works (for sale) by local artists, or on fine days, head outside for valley views from the terrace and lovely garden. The kitchen is driven by an enthusiasm for local produce and working with the seasons, and lines up a cast of ideas we'd all like to see in our local: wild boar Scotch egg (a quail's egg, that is) with a venison sausage roll, crispy pig's ears and pickles is a starter that should be on every pub's menu, while mains bring on a proper pub pie - a deep, pastry-topped dish of beef chunks in a rich sauce

of Guinness and oysters, served with clotted cream mash, and honey-roasted parsnips and carrots.

Chef Karl Bashford **Owner** Mr K Bashford, Ms Prekopova **Times** 12-2.30/6.30-9.30 Closed L Mon, D Mon (winter only) **Prices** Starter £5-£9, Main £10-£22, Dessert £5-£7, Service optional **Wines** 8 by glass **Notes** Sunday L £10, Vegetarian available **Seats** 60 **Children** Portions, Menu **Parking** 20

SHAFTESBURY   Map 4 ST82

Best Western Royal Chase Hotel

⚜ Modern British

Nicely unfussy cooking in Thomas Hardy country

☎ 01747 853355
Salisbury Rd SP7 8DB
e-mail: reception@theroyalchasehotel.co.uk
web: www.theroyalchasehotel.co.uk
dir: Close to rdbt junct with A350 & A30 (avoid town centre)

Formerly a 17th-century monastery, the Best Western Royal Chase is housed in beautiful tree-lined grounds close to the centre of Shaftesbury. Its tucked-away location adds a soothing sense of calm, and the friendly local service team don't burst the bubble. In the Byzant restaurant, the kitchen turns out unfussy dishes such as forestière terrine with home-made chutney, Dorset leaves and home-baked bread, followed perhaps by the likes of pan-fried fillet of sea bass with dauphinoise potatoes, shellfish bisque and samphire, and for dessert, chocolate cheesecake with pistachio ice cream. If you've got the kids in tow, check out their special menu in the family-orientated country bar.

Times 12-2/7-9.30

La Fleur de Lys Restaurant with Rooms

⚜⚜ Modern French 🍃

Former girls' school turned smart restaurant with rooms

☎ 01747 853717
Bleke St SP7 8AW
e-mail: info@lafleurdelys.co.uk
web: www.lafleurdelys.co.uk
dir: Junct A350/A30

With over twenty years under their belt, the owners of this welcoming restaurant with rooms in the heart of Shaftesbury have evolved a polished act that keeps the loyal regulars knocking at their door. The feel inside is homely and traditional - there's a comfy lounge with squidgy sofas to sink into for a pre-dinner drink, and the dining room is a plushly kitted-out space with linen-clothed tables and smart glassware and cutlery. As the name may hint, modern French cooking is the deal here, based on top-class local supplies brought together in confident, ambitious combinations starting, typically, along the lines of pan-fried breast of quail and duck liver with celeriac purée, and asparagus tips in truffle sauce. Main courses run to grilled Dover sole with langoustines, baby leeks, and light caviar sauce, or roast breast of

Creedy Carver duck with broad beans, spring onions and passionfruit sauce. Finally, hot lime soufflé might arrive with dark chocolate ice cream and lime sauce.

Chef D Shepherd, M Preston **Owner** D Shepherd, M Preston & M Griffin **Times** 12-2.30/7-10.30 Closed 3 wks Jan, L Mon-Tue, D Sun **Prices** Fixed L 2 course £27, Fixed D 3 course £33, Service optional **Wines** 50 bottles over £30, 50 bottles under £30, 8 by glass **Notes** Sunday L, Vegetarian available, Dress restrictions, Smart casual, No T-shirts **Seats** 45, Pr/dining room 12 **Children** Portions **Parking** 10

SHERBORNE   Map 4 ST61

Best Western The Grange at Oborne

⚜⚜ Modern British 🍃

Pleasing contemporary ideas in a rural setting

☎ 01935 813463
Oborne DT9 4LA
e-mail: reception@thegrange.co.uk
web: www.thegrangeatoborne.co.uk
dir: From A30 turn left at sign & follow road through village to hotel

This 200-year-old manor built of Purbeck stone in a tiny hamlet near Sherborne does brisk business as a country-house hotel with a nice line in weddings these days. The romantic candlelit restaurant seems tailor-made for such occasions, as it looks through graceful Georgian windows over a fountain and gardens which are floodlit at night. The kitchen goes in for a modernised style of country cooking perfectly in keeping with the surroundings, with the boxes ticked for seasonality and regional sourcing. Start with venison terrine, its gamey richness tamed by kumquat jam, then follow with fillet of beef served with a cottage pie, roasted banana shallot purée, glazed carrots and truffle jus. Desserts end on a high with a fresh apricot and almond tarte Tatin balanced by a zesty peach and mango sorbet.

Chef Nick Holt **Owner** Mr & Mrs K E Mathews **Times** 12-1.30/7-9 **Prices** Fixed L 2 course £21, Fixed D 3 course £35, Service optional **Wines** 10 bottles over £30, 34 bottles under £30, 7 by glass **Notes** Sunday L, Vegetarian available, Dress restrictions, Smart casual, Civ Wed 120 **Seats** 30, Pr/dining room 120 **Children** Portions, Menu **Parking** 50

Eastbury Hotel

⚜⚜ Modern British NEW 🍃

Contemporary cooking in an attractive Dorset townhouse

☎ 01935 813131
Long St DT9 3BY
e-mail: enquiries@theeastburyhotel.com
web: www.theeastburyhotel.com
dir: 5m E of Yeovil, follow brown signs for Eastbury Hotel

Life changes down a gear or two to a soothingly sedate pace at this boutique Georgian townhouse bolt-hole set in an acre of delightful walled gardens. Hands-on owners

Save on Hotels. Book at theAA.com/hotel

DORSET 157 ENGLAND

lend the operation a family-run feel, while cheery, attentive staff play their part in ensuring friendly and personal service in the dining room, which splits between the main building and a conservatory-style extension. The view looks out over a kitchen garden that does its bit in providing fresh seasonal ingredients, a commendable attitude to provenance that extends to rearing their own pigs and keeping bees. Modern menus are thoroughly in tune with the local market and the seasons, serving up skillfully cooked, well-thought-out dishes, beginning with a full-flavoured opener involving Lyme Bay scallops, veal tongue, cuttlefish, parsnips and toasted seeds. Fantastic ingredients also distinguish a main course of stone bass matched with crab cannelloni, fennel, charred sea leeks, pollen, and shellfish bisque. At the end, superb, fresh and vibrant raspberry jam makes a perfect foil to the nursery delights of caramelised clotted cream rice pudding.

Chef Brett Sutton **Owner** Mr & Mrs P King
Times 12-2/7-9.30 **Prices** Fixed L 2 course £17, Tasting menu £45, Starter £7.50-£9.50, Main £15-£19.50, Dessert £7.50-£8.50, Service optional, Groups min 6 service 10% **Wines** 23 bottles over £30, 48 bottles under £30, 6 by glass **Notes** Tasting menu 7 course, Sunday L, Vegetarian available, Civ Wed 80 **Seats** 40, Pr/dining room 12 **Children** Portions, Menu **Parking** 20

The Green

◉◉ Modern British ◐

Creative modern dishes in picture-postcard property

☎ 01935 813821
3 The Green DT9 3HY
e-mail: info@greenrestaurant.co.uk
dir: A30 towards Milborne Port, at top of Greenhill turn right at mini rdbt. Restaurant on left

A new chef-proprietor has taken over this picture-postcard property, a Grade II listed building, with its heavily beamed interior. He brings with him a wealth of know-how and experience gained at some top restaurants and has introduced short, daily-changing menus that reflect his commitment to local ethically sourced ingredients. A trio of Dorset crab (landed just the night before) makes a compelling - and popular - starter: with tomato in a Mediterranean-style soup, a savoury crème brûlée and in a parmesan tuile. Duck liver pâté sounds pretty standard but here it's given an extra dimension by beetroot and gherkin 'vinaigrette'. Dishes have a good balance without being too complex, seen in main courses of slowly cooked hogget with Jerusalem artichokes and mint nage, and Lyme Bay gurnard with red pepper and champagne sauce, and the kitchen puts a great deal of effort - and innovation - into its desserts, from meadowsweet mousse with citrus zest and caramelised walnuts, to ginger sticky toffee pudding with lime leaf ice cream and Cointreau caramel sauce.

Chef Alexander Matkevich **Owner** Alexander Matkevich
Times 12-2.30/7-9.30 Closed Sun-Mon **Prices** Fixed L 2 course £17.95, Fixed D 3 course £20, Starter £5.50-£11, Main £13.95-£18, Dessert £6-£7.95, Service optional, Groups min 8 service 10% **Wines** 8 by glass **Notes** Vegetarian available **Seats** 40, Pr/dining room 30 **Parking** On street, car park

---

SYDLING ST NICHOLAS   Map 4 SY69

The Greyhound Inn

◉ British ◐

Popular village inn with good, unfussy cooking

☎ 01300 341303
26 High St DT2 9PD
e-mail: info@dorsetgreyhound.co.uk

This relaxed 17th-century inn is still a proper boozer with hand-pulled real ales, but good wines and contemporary cooking are equally part of the equation these days. The Greyhound lies in a postcard-pretty Dorset village in verdant Thomas Hardy country, and its easy-on-the-eye good looks take in a flagstoned bar buzzing with convivial banter, exposed stone and brick walls, and a glassed over well where coachmen once hauled water for their horses. The kitchen keeps things simple, leaving the quality of top-notch local materials to do the talking. Seafood fresh from the Dorset coast has the opening shout - Weymouth squid sliced and sautéed with spicy chorizo, shallots and lemon. Main course could be as forthright as a local rib-eye steak with hand-cut chips, field mushrooms and béarnaise sauce, or fish fans could go for wild sea bass tempura with pea purée, chips and sauce gribiche. Honey and ginger cheesecake with vanilla ice cream keeps things squarely in the comfort zone.

Chef Lou Jones **Owner** Martin Frizell **Times** 12-2/6.30-9 Closed D Sun **Prices** Service optional **Wines** 6 bottles over £30, 10 bottles under £30, 6 by glass **Notes** Sunday L £9.50-£12.50, Vegetarian available **Seats** 60, Pr/dining room 30 **Children** Portions, Menu **Parking** 20

WAREHAM   Map 4 SY98

Kemps Country House

◉ Traditional, International

Simple but effective cooking in a Dorset country house

☎ 0845 8620315 & 01929 462563
East Stoke BH20 6AL
e-mail: info@kempscountryhouse.co.uk
web: www.kempshotel.com
dir: A352 between Wareham & Wool

Kemps is a commodious country house in a south-facing position looking over the Frome Valley towards the Purbeck Hills, a particularly picturesque slice of Dorset (and handy for the local Monkey World, primate-fans). The prettily decorated white dining room with its net curtained ceiling makes a relaxing venue for the brasserie-style cooking the place trades in. Start with a painstakingly constructed parcel of duck confit in filo pastry with dressed leaves, before considering a shank of local lamb, served with roast honeyed root veg, creamy mash and redcurrant jus, or battered cod with chips and mushy peas. It's simple, but effective, hearty food, concluding perhaps with chocolate and raspberry tart, served with densely rich clotted cream ice cream.

Times 12-3/6.30-9.30

WIMBORNE MINSTER   Map 5 SZ09

Les Bouviers Restaurant with Rooms

◉◉ French ◐

Francophile cooking in an elegant restaurant with rooms

☎ 01202 889555
Arrowsmith Rd, Canford Magna BH21 3BD
e-mail: info@lesbouviers.co.uk
web: www.lesbouviers.co.uk
dir: 1.5m S of Wimborne on A349, turn left onto A341. In 1m turn right into Arrowsmith Rd. 300yds, 2nd property on right

James Coward has now confidently embarked on a third decade running Les Bouviers, which moved to its current site a few years ago, offering half-a-dozen guest rooms as well as a smartly appointed restaurant in shades of red and gold. The feel of being invited to dine in a private home results in a particularly congenial atmosphere, but the culinary standards are some way above the domestic, not least in the breadth of choice. France is the premier amour, as is evident in classic bouillabaisse with garlic rouille to start, with breast of guinea fowl and foie gras-stuffed ballottine on braised red cabbage following on. Other influences are woven carefully into the mix too, though, perhaps for a starter of smoked haddock and butternut squash risotto with truffle oil, or peppered monkfish with pickled veg, chillied peppers and pimento oil. A host of signature desserts awaits for the grand finale, including mango, apricot and thyme crème brûlée with Earl Grey granité, or the classic lemon tart with saffron ice cream.

Chef James Coward **Owner** James & Kate Coward
Times 12-2.15/7-9.30 Closed D Sun **Prices** Fixed L 2 course fr £17.95, Fixed D 3 course fr £35.95, Service optional, Groups min 7 service 10% **Wines** 24 by glass **Notes** ALC 2/3 course £41/£46, Tasting menu 7 course, Sunday L, Vegetarian available, Dress restrictions, No ripped jeans or shorts, Civ Wed 120 **Seats** 50, Pr/dining room 120 **Children** Portions, Menu **Parking** 50

Number 9

◉◉ Modern British ◐

Bags of charm and well-sourced produce close to the theatre

☎ 01202 887557
West Borough BH21 1LT
e-mail: no9wimborne@aol.com
dir: 150 yds from The Square before Tivoli Theatre, on West Borough

Just off the market square and a couple of doors down from the town's Tivoli Theatre, Number 9 occupies a Grade II listed building full of charm and character. It looks inviting with its natural, neutral colour scheme both inside and out, and its side terrace for alfresco drinks and dining when the weather allows (there's also a small walled

continued

WIMBORNE MINSTER *continued*

garden at the back), and you can stop off for tea and home-made cake, coffee and morning pastries, a light snack or a full-blown meal. Lunchtime brings forth the likes of steamed Cornish rope-grown mussels in a white wine, garlic and cream sauce with fries, spot-on fish and chips, and hot- and cold-smoked salmon, artichoke and chicory tagliatelle. In the evenings, chef Greg Etheridge cranks things up a notch or two, turning out the likes of braised shin of beef sausage roll to start, followed by baked fillet of trout and clams with Parmentier potatoes, English asparagus, dandelion leaf, pea tops, pea crème fraîche and crisp wild garlic. The menu changes with the seasons, March, for example, bringing forth a dessert of poached rhubarb and custard millefeuille.

Chef Greg Etheridge **Owner** Roy & Linda Tazzyman **Times** 12-2.30/6-9.30 Closed Xmas, BH Mon, D Mon **Prices** Fixed D 3 course £25-£40, Starter £3.95-£7.95, Main £11.95-£24.95, Dessert £4.95-£8.50, Service optional, Groups min 8 service 10% **Wines** 3 bottles over £30, 18 bottles under £30, 9 by glass **Notes** Pre-theatre menu available, Sunday L, Vegetarian available **Seats** 50, Pr/dining room 30 **Children** Portions, Menu **Parking** On street or car park

| WYKE REGIS | Map 4 SY67 |

Crab House Café

◉ British, Seafood ◐

The freshest seafood in a laid-back beach hut

☎ 01305 788867
Ferrymans Way, Portland Rd DT4 9YU
e-mail: info@crabhousecafe.co.uk
web: www.crabhousecafe.co.uk
dir: A354 along Westwey once onto Portland Rd continue for just under a mile, at rdbt take 2nd exit for restaurant

The Crab House Café is a little slice of seafood heaven on the Dorset coast, overlooking Chesil Beach and the owner's oyster farm. The beachcomber-vibe with its wooden shack setting only adds to its charm, and if you're lucky you'll have the weather on your side so you can sit outside and breathe in the sea air. The Portland oysters farmed in the beds below will delight fans of the bivalves, and can be eaten au naturel, or with pesto and parmesan, or bacon and cream. There are crabs too, of course, to crack into, but much more besides: mussels in garlic, lemon and thyme, say, or home-cured sea trout, and for main course, perhaps fillet of ling with Thai spring cabbage and broccoli curry with preserved lemon

and coriander rice. The fish is landed in nearby Weymouth, Poole or Brixham, and the menu changes daily depending on the catch. Why aren't there more places like this in the UK?

Crab House Café

Chef Nigel Bloxham, Adam Foster **Owner** Nigel Bloxham **Times** 12-2/6-9 Closed mid Dec-Jan, Mon-Tue (except 8 wks in summer), D Sun (Oct-Mar) **Prices** Starter £4.95-£10.50, Main £11.95-£36, Dessert £4.95-£6.50, Service optional, Groups min 8 service 8% **Wines** 16 by glass **Notes** Sunday L, Vegetarian available **Seats** 40 **Children** Portions **Parking** 40

CO DURHAM

| BARNARD CASTLE | Map 19 NZ01 |

The Morritt

◉◉ British, International ◐

Historic country house with flavoursome cooking

☎ 01833 627232
Greta Bridge DL12 9SE
e-mail: relax@themorritt.co.uk
web: www.themorritt.co.uk
dir: 3m S of Barnard Castle off A66. 9m W of Scotch Corner from A1 (Darlington)

Named after a local artist, Major Morritt, whose paintings hang in the hotel, this 18th-century coaching inn turned country-house hotel has a long history of feeding travellers well before sending them on their way. Nowadays, the restaurant's dark oak panelling and herringbone parquet floors have been jollied up with a gently contemporary look involving lively artwork, silk window blinds and moody lighting; it all adds up to an amenable setting for good French-inspired cooking that straddles the border between the classics and more modern ideas. Pan-fried mackerel is pointed up with rhubarb, toasted seeds and pea purée, and there's plenty of generosity and flavour in a main course of braised lamb neck fillet with sweet potato, wild mushrooms, and butternut squash purée. Dessert ends on a high note with a rich dark chocolate tart with white chocolate ice cream and an espresso shot poured affogato-style on top.

Chef Lee Stainthorpe **Owner** B A Johnson & P J Phillips **Times** 12-3/6-9 **Prices** Service optional **Wines** 19 bottles over £30, 44 bottles under £30, 18 by glass **Notes** Fixed L Sun only, Sunday L £18, Vegetarian available, Dress restrictions, Smart, No shorts, T-shirts or flip flops, Civ Wed 200 **Seats** 60, Pr/dining room 24 **Children** Portions, Menu **Parking** 30

| BILLINGHAM | Map 19 NZ42 |

Wynyard Hall Hotel

◉◉◉ – *see opposite*

| DARLINGTON | Map 19 NZ21 |

Headlam Hall

◉◉ British, French ◐

Country mansion with well-crafted, contemporary food

☎ 01325 730238
Headlam, Gainford DL2 3HA
e-mail: admin@headlamhall.co.uk
web: www.headlamhall.co.uk
dir: 8m W of Darlington off A67

With its partly creeper-covered façade and elegant period detailing within, Headlam Hall is a rather grand old girl. The main building dates from the 17th century but has moved with the times: there's a swish spa to deliver 21st century levels of pampering, and a smart restaurant serving up some sparky modern food. The eating takes place in a series of rooms: the Panelled Room is as described, the Orangery a warm and luminous space with well-chosen neutral colours and well-spaced, linen-clad tables. The suppliers of what is to come are listed on the menu - good quality local stuff - and much is produced on their own farm, or comes from the hotel's garden. These fine ingredients are treated with respect by the team in the kitchen and served up in a broadly modish European, good-looking manner. Goats' cheese parfait, for example, with toasted nuts and seeds, red-wine-poached gingerbread and red wine syrup might precede pan-fried haunch of venison with venison ragu, onion purée, fondant potato, roasted shallot and a blueberry and venison jus.

Chef David Hunter **Owner** J H Robinson **Times** 12-2.30/7-9.30 Closed 25-26 Dec **Prices** Fixed L 2 course £14.50, Starter £6-£9, Main £14-£25, Dessert £5-£7, Service optional **Wines** 20 bottles over £30, 38 bottles under £30, 10 by glass **Notes** Sunday L £22.50, Vegetarian available, Dress restrictions, Smart casual, no shorts or T-shirts, Civ Wed 120 **Seats** 70, Pr/dining room 30 **Children** Portions, Menu **Parking** 80

Rockliffe Hall

◉◉◉ – *see page 160*

See advert opposite

Save on Hotels. Book at theAA.com/hotel

CO DURHAM 159 ENGLAND

Wynyard Hall Hotel

BILLINGHAM MAP 19 NZ42

Modern British V

Boldly original cooking in a lavish country mansion setting

☎ 01740 644811
Wynyard TS22 5NF
e-mail: enq@wynyardhall.co.uk
web: www.wynyardhall.co.uk
dir: A19 onto A1027 towards Stockton. At rdbt 3rd exit B1274 (Junction Rd). At next rdbt 3rd exit onto A177 (Durham Rd). Right onto Wynyard Rd signed Wolviston. Left into estate at gatehouse

Charles Dickens, Disraeli, Sir Robert Peel, Churchill, King Edward VII, Elizabeth II and the Duke of Wellington are all past guests at Wynyard Hall, a hugely imposing mansion beside its own lake that is these days one of the North East's finest hotels. Golden gates flank the entrance, and as you approach the hall via a long, winding drive and cross over the lion-topped bridge, you start to get a sense of what's to come: gold-painted interiors, glass-fronted display cases, wonderful oil portraits and a fabulously lavish dining room - The Wellington Restaurant - decorated with magnificent floral displays and with sofa seating for some tables. In surroundings like this the food can struggle to compete for your attention, but Alan O'Kane's imaginative, contemporary cooking is more than up to the task. Menu descriptions are not overly wordy, as in a starter of 'chicken wings, chicken consommé, crispy skin, salt-baked Jerusalem artichoke' - a nicely balanced dish with some clever textural contrasts and pleasing to the eye, too. Whitby crab shows up in another starter, teamed with 'carrot and walnut variations', while hand-dived scallops (plump and juicy) come in a classic pairing with a pressing of Middlewhite pork, caramelised apple and boudin noir bon-bons. 'Variations of corn-fed duck, apple, blackberry, salsify, pickled walnuts' makes for a fine main course, or you could go for another surf and turf type combination (of the luxury variety) of slow-cooked John Dory with belly pork, preparations of langoustine, scampi anglaise and seashore vegetables. Tip-top pastry skills are on show in a dessert of coffee soufflé, coffee soil and biscotti ice cream, while chocolate lovers will be in heaven with the 'layered chocolate, cherry seven-ways'.

Chef Alan O'Kane **Owner** Allison Antonopoulos **Times** 12-3/7-9.30 **Prices** Fixed L 2 course £24.50, Fixed D 3 course £31.50, Tasting menu £55, Service optional **Wines** 51 bottles over £30, 30 bottles under £30, 10 by glass **Notes** Sunday L, Vegetarian menu, Dress restrictions, Smart casual, Civ Wed 250 **Seats** 80, Pr/dining room 30 **Children** Portions, Menu **Parking** 200

Rockliffe Hall

Modern British NOTABLE WINE LIST

Inventive cooking in an ornately refurbished orangery

☎ 01325 729999
Rockliffe Park, Hurworth-on-Tees DL2 2DU
e-mail: enquiries@rockliffehall.com
web: www.rockliffehall.com
dir: A1(M) junct 57, A66 (M), A66 towards Darlington, A167, through Hurworth-on-Tees. In Croft-on-Tees left into Hurworth Rd, follow signs

Built towards the close of the 18th century, Rockliffe - known initially as Pilmore House - has progressed through various periods of colourful private ownership to be handed down to us as a handsomely maintained, top-drawer estate hotel. Standing in 375 acres by the River Tees, outside the village of Hurworth, near Darlington, it offers the full luxury package expected nowadays, from nuptials to massages to golf, with an elegantly refurbished, ornate dining room in the old orangery, all gilt pillars against an ivory-white background, the walls crowded with little prints and mirrors. In 2013, Dan Shotton stepped up to head chef when the previous incumbent left, and keeps his foot on the gas with stylish, artfully inventive modern dishes that are full of surprises. Rolled confit rabbit sprinkled with dandelion leaves, pickled carrots and

hazelnuts is a confident overture to a dinner that might continue with aromatic chervil-braised turbot, chaperoned by a big fat langoustine, in shellfish emulsion sauce, garnished with baby plum tomatoes on the vine. An alternative route might be to start with a pressed terrine of pink fir potato and goats' cheese, vividly accompanied by candied golden beetroot in a lemony, mustardy dressing, before moving to Yorkshire wood-pigeon with poached rhubarb in celeriac and bitter chocolate jus. Veggie choices might include ravioli of chalky-textured Monk's Folly cheese from Yorkshire, with braised gem lettuce and kalamata olives, or a fried duck egg with parsley gnocchi and white asparagus in truffled hollandaise. Finish with a luxuriously rich egg custard tart, served with gariguette strawberries and a swipe of creamed pistachio, or milk chocolate timbale with honeycomb, raisins and praline ice cream. Alternatively, await the next circuit of the trolley, which is encouragingly laden with local, as well as other premium British, cheeses. A pedigree wine list is under the knowledgeable care of an accomplished young sommelière.

Chef Dan Shotton **Owner** Rockliffe Hall **Times** 12.30-2/6.30-9.30 Closed L Fri-Sat, D Sun **Prices** Fixed L 2 course £19.50, Tasting menu £65-£100, Starter £8-£25, Main £20-£35, Dessert £9-£10, Service optional **Wines** 500 bottles over £30, 3 bottles under £30, 23 by glass **Notes** Tasting menu L £50, Vegetarian available, Dress restrictions, Smart attire, collared shirts/jackets for men **Seats** 60

Save on Hotels. Book at **theAA.com/hotel**

CO DURHAM 161 ENGLAND

Bistro 21

◉ Modern British V ☙

Upbeat bistro cooking in a former farmhouse

☎ 0191 384 4354
Aykley Heads House, Aykley Heads DH1 5TS
e-mail: admin@bistrotwentyone.co.uk
dir: Off B6532 from Durham centre, pass County Hall on right & Dryburn Hospital on left. Turn right at double rdbt into Aykley Heads

From the outside, the bistro has a cottagey look, a feeling of rusticity extending inside via stone floors, bare brick walls and low ceilings, although a central atrium adds a more modern touch. There's something reassuringly familiar about the menu, featuring as it does calves' liver with bacon, and a chunk of perfectly timed grilled cod with tartare sauce, chips and crushed peas, although the appeal is broadened by the likes of starters of Asian-style duck breast dressed with honey and mustard served with bean sprouts, and jasmine-cured salmon with watermelon and cucumber, and a main course like chicken breast with Moroccan-style couscous and lemon crème fraîche. Puddings are an enticing slate, from knickerbocker glory to steamed ginger sponge with rhubarb compôte and custard.

Chef Rauri McKay **Owner** Terence Laybourne
Times 12-2/6-10.30 Closed 25 Dec, 1 Jan, D Sun
Prices Fixed L 2 course £15.55, Fixed D 3 course £18, Starter £6.50, Main £12-£16.50, Dessert £5.50, Service added but optional 10% **Wines** 6 bottles over £30, 18 bottles under £30, 9 by glass **Notes** Early D menu available, Sunday L, Vegetarian menu **Seats** 65, Pr/dining room 30 **Children** Portions, Menu **Parking** 11

Honest Lawyer Hotel

◉ Modern British ☙

Something for everybody in a modern city hotel

☎ 0191 378 3780
Croxdale Bridge, Croxdale DH1 3SP
e-mail: enquiries@honestlawyerhotel.com
dir: A1 junct 61

This wryly-named hotel is a smart, cleanly-designed modern operation with impeccably well-kept guest rooms spread around a courtyard. Food is taken care of by Bailey's Restaurant, a venue with friendly, unpretentious charm, done out in cheering hues of purple and pink. A crowd-pleasing output from the cosmopolitan kitchen ranges from modern European brasserie cooking, to classic Brit comfort food. Local supplies turn up in a starter of ham hock and smoked Ribblesdale cheese terrine with tomato chutney and toasted brioche, while main courses cover a lot of ground from a hearty plateful comprising slow-braised confit duck leg, fondant potatoes, Puy lentils, green beans, a fried duck egg and port wine jus, to slabs of Northumbrian steak, real home-made burgers, or Black Sheep beer-battered haddock with fat chips and minted mushy peas. Finish with a

proper home-made pear and frangipane tart with cinnamon ice cream and pear purée.

Chef Harry Bailie **Owner** John Sanderson **Times** 11-9.30 All-day dining **Prices** Starter £2.95-£6.25, Main £10.95-£18.95, Dessert £5.95-£6.95, Service included **Wines** 2 bottles over £30, 27 bottles under £30, 7 by glass **Notes** Sunday L, Vegetarian available **Seats** 50, Pr/dining room 60 **Children** Portions, Menu **Parking** 150

Ramside Hall Hotel

◉ International NEW

Carnivore heaven in golf-oriented hotel

☎ 0191 386 5282
Carrville DH1 1TD
e-mail: mail@ramsidehallhotel.co.uk
web: www.ramsidehallhotel.co.uk
dir: A1(M) junct 62, A690 to Sunderland. Straight on at lights. 200mtrs after rail bridge turn right

A grand house has stood on the site of Ramside Hall since Elizabethan times, but the sprawling complex you see today has at its heart a largely Victorian house, beefed up in the late 20th century with lots more rooms and three loops of nine holes to set the emphasis firmly on the pursuit of golf. The crowd-pleasing culinary options run from straightforward carvery and rôtisserie dishes, to the menu in the brasserie-style Rib Room, which 'does what it says on the tin', majoring in slabs of locally-reared 28-day-aged beef. Just choose your cut (there's a 20oz rib-eye if you're feeling particularly peckish) and it arrives with roasted mushrooms, braised onions and a choice of classic sauces; non-carnivores could go for grilled lobster or halibut. Preceding this there might be Provençal fish soup with rouille and croûtons, and to finish, comfort-oriented puddings such as a retro knickerbocker glory or classic crème brûlée.

Times 7-10 **Prices** Prices not confirmed **Notes** Sunday L

The Oak Tree Inn

◉◉ Modern British ☙

Confident, creative cooking in a converted village inn

☎ 01833 627371
DL11 7HH
e-mail: claireross67@hotmail.com
dir: 7m W on A66 from Scotch Corner

Locals still prop up the bar at this traditional inn in a quiet little village, but the majority of people come from further afield to dine. It's easy to see what the attractions are: beams and panelled walls, an open fire, and, in the dining room, wooden tables and high-backed leather-look seats on a red carpet, and an informal atmosphere. The menus change according to availability and quality, so roast pheasant may appear in season, accompanied by sticky red cabbage, bacon, apple, and parsnip purée. Ideas are sophisticated and modern, so cheddar and mushroom rarebit comes with roast fillet of beef and

crushed new potatoes, and chorizo and steamed mussels with crisp-skinned fillet of sea bass and new potatoes. Starters are no less compelling, among them perhaps beetroot and goats' cheese tart with olives and tomato, while invention doesn't flag in desserts like passionfruit crème brûlée.

Chef Alastair Ross **Owner** Alastair & Claire Ross
Times 6.30-9.30 Closed 24-27 & 31 Dec, 1-2 Jan, Mon, L all week **Prices** Starter £5.50-£8.50, Main £19.50-£23.50, Dessert £4.50-£8, Service optional **Wines** 12 bottles over £30, 40 bottles under £30, 8 by glass **Notes** Vegetarian dishes & children's portions by prior arrangement **Seats** 20, Pr/dining room 20 **Children** Portions **Parking** 3, On street

Redworth Hall Hotel

◉ Modern British

Gentle modern British cooking in a 17th-century manor

☎ 01388 770600
DL5 6NL
e-mail: redworthhall@pumahotels.co.uk
web: www.pumahotels.co.uk
dir: From A1(M) junct 58 take A68 towards Corbridge. At 1st rdbt take A6072 towards Bishop Auckland. At next rdbt take 2nd exit (A6072). Hotel on left

Redworth was built at the end of the 17th century, in architectural homage to the Jacobean style of the early 1600s. It's an expansive turreted manor house that retains some aspects of its original look, most notably in the splendid galleried Great Hall and the sort of spiral stone staircase on which you could imagine a swashbuckling swordfight unfolding. Any thoughts of clashing steel are banished by soothing spa treatments these days, along with the further care and attention lavished on you in the elegant, smartly decorated dining room with its linen-clad tables. Modern British dishes of a gentle disposition are the bill of fare, ranging from pork and sage rillettes with pickled vegetables, through sea bass with spring greens in crab and vermouth sauce, or confit duck leg in redcurrant jus, to fruity finishers such as chocolate and orange torte with raspberry coulis, or a mango and passionfruit mousse with a salsa of chopped fruits.

Times 12-2/6.30-9.30 Closed 25 Dec

ROMALDKIRK — Map 18 NY92

Rose & Crown Hotel

◎◎ British, French ◐

Classically-based cuisine in a lovely old inn

☎ 01833 650213
DL12 9EB
e-mail: hotel@rose-and-crown.co.uk
web: www.rose-and-crown.co.uk
dir: 6m NW of Barnard Castle on B6277

Rubbing shoulders with a doughty Saxon church known as the Cathedral of the Dale, and bracketed by three village greens, the stone-built 18th-century Rose & Crown is a haven of sybaritic pleasures among the fells and meadows of remote Teesdale. There's fine hand-pulled ale to quaff by the crackling log fire in the bar, and a rather classy oak-panelled and candlelit dining room, where the four-course dinner menus are built on local, seasonal produce and inspired by neatly-dovetailed classic and contemporary trends. A wild mushroom and spinach risotto with crisp leeks to give textural contrast shows the style, then comes a soup - perhaps butternut squash and sweet potato with a rich, natural taste. Main course might be pan-fried best end of lamb - tender and packed full of flavour - with a mini shepherd's pie, seared kidneys, mange tout, parsnip purée and a wild mushroom jus. A textbook chocolate tart with a crisp pastry base and high cocoa content, accompanied by Baileys ice cream, closes the show on a high.

Chef Andrew Lee, Henritetta Croslad **Owner** The Robinson family **Times** 12-2.30/7.30-9.30 Closed 23-27 Dec **Prices** Fixed L 2 course fr £14.50, Starter £5-£8.50, Main £12-£23, Dessert £4-£8, Service optional **Wines** 20 bottles over £30, 25 bottles under £30, 10 by glass **Notes** Sunday L fr £19.50, Vegetarian available, Dress restrictions, Smart dress **Seats** 30 **Children** Portions, Menu **Parking** 25

SEAHAM — Map 19 NZ44

The Ozone Restaurant

◎ Asian Fusion NEW

Asian flavours in a glamorous five-star hotel

☎ 0191 516 1400
Seaham Hall Hotel, Lord Byron's Walk SR7 7AG
e-mail: info@seaham-hall.co.uk
dir: Leave A1018 onto A19 at rdbt take 2nd exit onto B1285/Stockton Rd. Turn left at Lord Byron Walk in 0.3m turn right

Built in the 1790s, Seaham Hall is quite a pad. It was saved from rack and ruin back at the turn of the century to be reborn as a rather magnificent five-star hotel. Its White Room restaurant is under refurbishment as we go to print, but fear not, for the flame-coloured Ozone Restaurant serves up some impressive Pan-Asian food in a cool and chilled-out setting. There's an open kitchen, views over the grounds (especially good from the terrace) and a menu packed with great flavours. Start with king prawn and mango salad with lime dressing, or Filipino-style lollipop (chicken wings stuffed with minced pork and prawns with a teriyaki and sweet chilli sauce). Sharing and grazing is the best way to approach things. Main-course deep-fried sea bass comes with tamarind sauce, Thai herbs and jasmine rice, or go for crispy pork belly with pak choi, green beans, shiitake mushrooms and a garlic and soy sauce.

Times 11-5/6-9 Closed 25 Dec, D Sun

SEDGEFIELD — Map 19 NZ32

Best Western Hardwick Hall Hotel

◎ Modern British V ◐

Steaks and more in parkland hotel

☎ 01740 620253
TS21 2EH
e-mail: info@hardwickhallhotel.co.uk
dir: Off A1(M) junct 60 towards Sedgefield, left at 1st rdbt, hotel 400mtrs on left

Within acres of parkland, this is a luxury hotel with lavishly appointed bedrooms, banqueting and conference facilities and the basement Rib Room restaurant. The kitchen's focus is on 28-day-aged steaks, all from local farms, on display in a glass-fronted meat locker. Take your pick from anything between a six-ounce fillet to Chateaubriand (for two people) - the chefs will cook it the way you want and serve it with your choice of sauce. A spread of starters, many also served as a main course, runs from crab and apple salad with chard and tomato vinaigrette, to Provençal fish soup with rouille and croûtons, and if meat's not your thing you could proceed to baked halibut fillet with a Sicilian sauce, or lobster Thermidor with salad and fries. End with an irresistible knickerbocker glory.

Chef Mark Flood **Owner** Ramside Estates **Times** 6-10 Closed L all week **Prices** Service optional **Wines** 26 bottles over £30, 49 bottles under £30, 12 by glass **Notes** Sunday L £15.95-£19.95, Vegetarian menu, Dress restrictions, Smart casual, Civ Wed 200 **Seats** 90, Pr/dining room 15 **Children** Portions, Menu **Parking** 350

ESSEX

BRENTWOOD — Map 6 TQ59

Marygreen Manor Hotel

◎◎ Modern European V

Enterprising modern food in a Tudor mansion

☎ 01277 225252
London Rd CM14 4NR
e-mail: info@marygreenmanor.co.uk
web: www.marygreenmanor.co.uk
dir: M25 junct 28, onto A1023 over 2 sets of lights, hotel on right

The endearingly asymmetrical timbered Tudor mansion was once the home of one Henry Roper, a manservant of Catherine of Aragon. Nice work if you could get it. It retains much of the panelling, oak beams and ornate ceilings of the 16th century, and has been gently eased into the modern hotel trade with sensitivity and class. An attractive courtyard garden makes a fine venue for sunny days, and you can bet the log fire will have been lit to cheer the scene in winter's chill. The Tudors dining room is a sight for sore eyes, with its heavy beams, helical stanchions of weathered oak and chairs with Gothic-arched backs, but the cooking doesn't restrict itself to any English yesteryear. Start with a dish of English garden snails and French bulots (the kind that look like whelks), girolles, baby squid and confit garlic, a something-for-everyone assemblage of good things, which may be succeeded by locally-reared roebuck with variations on beetroot (pickled, puréed and sorbet). Dessert could be jasmine tea chiboust with passionfruit ice cream.

Chef Mr Majid Bourote **Owner** Mr S Bhattessa **Times** 12.30-2.30/7.15-10.15 Closed L Mon, D Sun, BHs **Prices** Prices not confirmed Service added but optional 12% **Wines** 72 bottles over £30, 51 bottles under £30, 7 by glass **Notes** Tasting menu 6 course, Sunday L, Vegetarian menu, Dress restrictions, Smart casual, no jeans or trainers, Civ Wed 60 **Seats** 80, Pr/dining room 85 **Children** Portions **Parking** 100

Save on Hotels. Book at **theAA.com/hotel**

ESSEX 163 **ENGLAND**

CHELMSFORD Map 6 TL70

County Hotel

◉ Modern European ✿

British and Mediterranean flavours in town-centre hotel

☎ 01245 455700
29 Rainsford Rd CM1 2PZ
e-mail: kloftus@countyhotelgroup.co.uk
web: www.countyhotelgroup.co.uk
dir: Off Chelmsford ring road close to town centre and
A12 junct 18

A conveniently short stroll from the railway station and
town centre, the County Hotel is done out in a cheery
modern style, as typified in the County Kitchen restaurant,
where oak floors and leather seats in summery pastel
hues of mustard, mint and tangerine add colour to
neutral contemporary décor. Uncomplicated modern
European cooking using local materials is the kitchen's
stock in trade, starting along the lines of venison and
confit pheasant terrine with celeriac remoulade and
toasted walnut bread; mains might bring fillet steak with
potato rösti, butternut squash purée, curly kale and red
wine jus, or a burst of Mediterranean warmth in the form
of Ligurian fish stew. For dessert, there could be dark
chocolate fondant with clotted cream ice cream.

Chef Wayne Browning **Owner** Michael & Ginny Austin
Times 12-2.30/6-10 Closed L Sat **Prices** Fixed L 2 course
£14.95-£22.95, Fixed D 3 course £19.95-£28.50, Starter
£4.95-£8.50, Main £11.95-£22.95, Dessert £4.95-£5.50
Wines 18 bottles over £30, 22 bottles under £30, 6 by
glass **Notes** Pre-theatre menu available, Sunday L,
Vegetarian available, Civ Wed 80 **Seats** 64, Pr/dining
room 135 **Children** Portions, Menu **Parking** 70

COGGESHALL Map 7 TL82

Baumann's Brasserie

◉◉ French, European

Gutsy cooking in buzzy brasserie

☎ 01376 561453
4-6 Stoneham St CO6 1TT
e-mail: food@baumannsbrasserie.co.uk
web: www.baumannsbrasserie.co.uk
dir: A12 from Chelmsford, exit at Kelvedon into
Coggeshall. Restaurant in centre opposite clock tower

Originally launched by legendary restaurateur Peter
Langan, chef-patron Mark Baumann's buzzy brasserie
has been a fixture on the local dining scene for almost 30
years. The setting may be a 16th-century timbered house,
and continental-style pavement tables hint at a classic
French bistro, but there's nothing stuck in the past about
Baumann's inventively-tweaked French and British
dishes. Inside, the mood is laid-back and cosmopolitan
and the one-off décor is akin to an eclectic art gallery
done out with antique linen-clothed tables. Smart, on-
the-money food is the deal here, delivered via no-
nonsense menus that follow the seasons rather than the
vagaries of culinary trends. Beetroot tarte Tatin with
chive-whipped goats' cheese and sugar-roasted
chestnuts makes a cracking starter, then you might
continue with something from the daily fish menu - fillet
of monkfish, for example, gets the robust flavours of Thai
red curry crust and king prawns in garlic and ginger. It
all ends on a high note with an excellent traditional
marmalade steamed sponge with vanilla custard.

Times 12-2/7-9.30 Closed 2 wks Jan, Mon-Tue

COLCHESTER Map 13 TL92

The North Hill Hotel

◉◉ Modern British ✿

Well-prepared food in popular, modern-day hotel bistro

☎ 01206 574001
51 North Hill CO1 1PY
e-mail: info@northhillhotel.com
dir: Follow directions for town centre, down North Hill,
hotel on left

North Hill's sunny yellow façade paints a cheery face onto
the exterior of a handsome Georgian building in the
historic heart of Colchester, giving a gentle hint at the
breezy, rather funky contemporary décor within. Bright
and swirly artwork feeds into the cool, pared-back look of
the Green Room bistro, where plain wooden tables and
chairs are set against sage-green walls, and an
unbuttoned vibe completes the setting for the upbeat
modern cooking. The kitchen's output is driven by well-
sourced local ingredients treated without undue fuss:
perhaps warm smoked duck breast with a fig, green bean
and grape salad to open the show, ahead of well-timed
sea bass fillets with toasted almond and caper butter,
wilted spinach, and herb-crushed new potatoes. Meatier
fare runs to slow-cooked venison with mushrooms and
smoked bacon puff pastry pie. For dessert, there could be
elderflower pannacotta served with a warm vanilla
doughnut.

Chef John Riddleston **Owner** Rob Brown
Times 12-2.30/6-9.30 **Prices** Starter £4.50-£7.50, Main
£10.50-£22.50, Dessert £5.25-£6.95, Service optional

Wines 14 by glass **Notes** Sunday L fr £10.50, Vegetarian
available **Seats** 45, Pr/dining room 30 **Children** Portions,
Menu **Parking** NCP opposite

Stoke by Nayland Hotel, Golf & Spa

◉◉ Modern British ✿

Complex contemporary cooking overlooking the golf

☎ 01206 262836 & 265835
Keepers Ln, Leavenheath CO6 4PZ
e-mail: winston.wright@stokebynayland.com
web: www.stokebynayland.com
dir: From A134, pass through the village of Nayland,
ignoring signs to Stoke-By-Nayland. Continue on A134,
shortly after Hare & Hounds turn right on to B1068 signed
Stoke by Nayland Golf Club. In approx 1.5m right

There's an awful lot going on here on the Suffolk-Essex
border. There are two championship golf courses on the
300-acre site for a start, plus the hotel of course, spa
facilities, and, in the shape of the Lakes Restaurant, a
rather good dining option. A wall of sliding glass doors
ensures everyone gets a glimpse of the water and the
greens - better still, bag a table on the terrace - and
inside it is a smart and airy space with plenty of room
between tables. The menus show a kitchen with a clear
fondness for carefully-sourced British ingredients,
deployed in a broad-minded European-influenced
repertoire. Start with lambs' sweetbreads with purple-
sprouting broccoli, potato crisp and wild garlic pesto, or
pan-fried cod cheeks with saffron-pickled quail's egg,
spiced pear and lotus root. Next up, butter roasted fillet of
halibut is topped with a cauliflower and pistachio crust
and is served alongside ras el hanout-flavoured carrots,
beluga lentils, saffron sauce, rosewater oil and a
barbecue date jam.

Chef Alan Paton **Owner** The Boxford Group
Times 12.30-2.30/6.30-10 **Prices** Fixed D 3 course fr
£25, Starter £4.50-£7.50, Main £11-£19, Dessert
£5.50-£6.95, Service optional **Wines** 12 by glass
Notes Sunday L, Vegetarian available, Civ Wed 200
Seats 90, Pr/dining room 60 **Children** Portions
Parking 350

Wivenhoe House Hotel

◉◉ Modern British **NEW** ⚑ NOTABLE WINE LIST ✿

Innovative ideas in splendid 18th-century hotel

☎ 01206 863666
Wivenhoe Park CO4 3SQ
e-mail: info@wivenhoehouse.co.uk
web: www.wivenhoehouse.co.uk
dir: A12 take A133 towards Clacton, then B1027 to
Wivenhoe, turn right into Boundary Road, right into Park
Road

Wivenhoe House is a magnificent 18th-century property in
well-landscaped grounds, with a modern garden wing
housing a separate brasserie. The house's 18th-century
occupants would be flummoxed by much of what's on the

continued

COLCHESTER *continued*

menu in Signatures, the smart, traditionally styled restaurant, and indeed today's guests may have to ask staff to elucidate dishes like '40-degree umami salmon, cucumber, liquorice, fennel pollen, plate essence', and 'not quite duck à l'orange'. That caveat aside, the menu is a slate of thoroughly modern, inventive ideas, and the kitchen clearly has a good eye when it comes to buying its raw materials. Starters might take in a well-composed duck liver parfait with blackberries, walnuts and gingerbread, or an artfully presented mosaic of game and Monbazillac with baby vegetables. Main courses are in similar vein, with smoked bone marrow mayonnaise and pickled walnuts to accompany roast beef cheeks, and beetroot, baby turnips, sprout leaves and radish for nicely timed scallops. Breads get the nod, and among puddings chocolate brownie is a good rendition, served with novel smoky bacon ice cream.

Chef Paul Boorman **Owner** Essex University **Times** 12-10 All-day dining **Prices** Tasting menu £45, Starter £5-£7, Main £11-£19, Dessert £5.50, Service optional **Wines** 192 bottles over £30, 86 bottles under £30 **Notes** Sunday L £12.95-£21.95, Vegetarian available **Seats** 80, Pr/dining room 12 **Children** Portions **Parking** 40

DEDHAM — Map 13 TM03

milsoms

◉ Modern International ✋

Global food in a contemporary setting

☎ 01206 322795
Stratford Rd CO7 6HN
e-mail: milsoms@milsomhotels.com
web: www.milsomhotels.com
dir: 7m N of Colchester, just off A12

There's no booking at Milsoms contemporary brasserie and bar, serving food all day in the village of Dedham. It's a set-up that's served them so well, they've also replicated it at Kesgrave Hall near Ipswich (see entry, Suffolk). The rustic and airy split-level restaurant has scrubbed pine tables, wooden floors and colourful artwork and gets its buzz from the 'engine room', or open-plan kitchen, plus the happy hum of contented diners, of course. The terrace is cushioned from the extremes of the weather by a huge sail and is a lovely spot in the warmer months. Expect crowd-pleasing brasserie-style dishes (sometimes influenced by more exotic climes) along the lines of rabbit schnitzel with sauerkraut, poached egg, caper and anchovy butter, or blackened 'Essex bird' chicken breast with tabouleh, aubergine and Greek

yoghurt and harissa. Finish with triple chocolate brownie with butterscotch sauce, crushed pecan nuts and vanilla ice cream.

Chef Sarah Norman, Ben Rush **Owner** Milsom family **Times** 12-9.30 All-day dining **Prices** Starter £6-£10.95, Main £10.50-£26, Dessert £5.95-£6.95, Service optional **Wines** 20 bottles over £30, 45 bottles under £30, 20 by glass **Notes** Sunday L £21-£28, Vegetarian available **Seats** 80, Pr/dining room 30 **Children** Portions, Menu **Parking** 80

The Sun Inn

◉ Italian, Modern British ⓘ NOTABLE WINE LIST ✋

A taste of Italy in a village inn

☎ 01206 323351
High St CO7 6DF
e-mail: office@thesuninndedham.com
dir: In village centre opposite church

The Sun is a proper village inn, and an old one at that, in the heart of Constable country. The 15th-century property has lots of character inside and out, and, as well as open fires, friendly service and a good range of real ales, there's a serious approach to food. The kitchen has decidedly Italian leanings, with a suggested aperitivo on the menu to get you in the mood. Sharing the antipasti platter is one way to begin, with local Mersea oysters joining the Italian meats, chicken liver crostino and the like if you're lucky. Mussels braised with celery, tomato and thyme and served with a roast garlic focaccia is another starter, followed perhaps by roast Telmara Farm duck breast with its braised leg, root vegetable purée, celery, grapes and walnuts. The theme carries on into desserts such as pannacotta with Grappa and caramelised blood oranges.

Chef Ugo Simonelli **Owner** Piers Baker **Times** 12-2.30/6.30-9.30 Closed 25-26 Dec, 3-4 Jan **Prices** Fixed L 2 course £15-£25, Fixed D 3 course £15.50, Starter £5-£7.50, Main £8.75-£20, Dessert £5.95-£7.50, Service optional **Wines** 44 bottles over £30, 46 bottles under £30, 20 by glass **Notes** Breakfast available Fri-Sun, Sunday L, Vegetarian available **Seats** 70 **Children** Portions, Menu **Parking** 15

Le Talbooth

◉◉ Modern British ⓘ NOTABLE WINE LIST ✋

Consistent high standards by the River Stour

☎ 01206 323150
Gun Hill CO7 6HN
e-mail: talbooth@milsomhotels.com
web: www.milsomhotels.com
dir: 6m from Colchester follow signs from A12 to Stratford St Mary, restaurant on the left before village

Refurbishment has brought Le Talbooth contrasting tactile materials like wood and leather, the introduction of theatrical chandeliers and new curtains at the windows that give the same pastoral views of the River Stour from the ancient former toll house. Thankfully, the kitchen's standards remain consistently high, with a nicely varied menu that takes in ham hock and duck liver terrine with piccalilli mousse, Iberico ham and onion bread, and poached fillet of red gurnard with fennel, gnocchi, tomato and cucumber. Dishes are well composed, seen in a starter of crab ravioli set atop a velouté of pancetta, spring onions, and sweetcorn, and main-course saddle of new season's lamb accompanied by a deeply flavoured jus, deep-fried crumbed sweetbreads, sea beet and borlotti and broad beans. The kitchen is equally confident handling some less familiar ideas: witness main-course fillet of turbot, braised pork belly, clams and carrot consommé. Freshly-made breads get the thumbs up, as do puddings like toothsome chocolate mousse layered with cappuccino sabayon served with nougat ice cream.

Chef Zack Deakins **Owner** Milsom family **Times** 12-2/6.30-9 Closed D Sun (Oct-Apr) **Prices** Fixed L

2 course £24.50, Starter £9.50-£16.75, Main £19.50-£32, Dessert £8.75-£10.50, Service optional **Wines** 250 bottles over £30, 46 bottles under £30, 19 by glass **Notes** Sunday L £34.50, Vegetarian available, Dress restrictions, Smart casual, No jeans, Civ Wed 50 **Seats** 80, Pr/dining room 34 **Children** Portions, Menu **Parking** 50

GESTINGTHORPE   Map 13 TL83

The Pheasant

British **NEW**

Foodie satisfaction in charming country inn

☎ 01787 465010 & 461196
Audley End CO9 3AU

Since chef-proprietor James Donoghue took over at The Pheasant in 2006, the mustard-yellow-painted country pub on the Suffolk-Essex border has flourished. The interior has the light and uncluttered looks of a switched-on contemporary dining pub, and food is placed passionately at the heart of the operation. There's now a smokehouse, plus a large plot across the road providing organic fruit and vegetables, and Donoghue also keeps bees. The uncomplicated, flavour-driven approach offers plenty to tempt: sweet and tender smoked shell-on prawns are pointed up with saffron aïoli and excellent home-baked brown bread, while a vibrant home-made spicy chicken and tomato pie makes a virtue of simplicity and fresh, flavour-packed raw materials. A pannacotta lifted by delicious strawberry sauce concludes the theme of tried-and-true ideas done really well. Five classy boutique-style B&B rooms mean you can stay over and really loosen the belt at dinner.

Chef James Donoghue **Owner** James & Diana Donoghue
Times 12-3/6.30-9 **Prices** Starter £5.50-£6.25, Main £10.50-£18.95, Dessert £5.50-£6.95

GREAT TOTHAM   Map 7 TL81

The Bull & Willow Room at Great Totham

Traditional & Modern British

Accomplished cooking in made-over pub

☎ 01621 893385 & 894020
2 Maldon Rd CM9 8NH
e-mail: reservations@thewillowroom.co.uk

The Bull is an Essex pub with lots of period charm and a good deal of contemporary appeal. It really does look the business with its splendid 16th-century façade neatly spruced up, its characterful bar packed with original features, and decorative colours chosen from the favoured neutral and natural palette. There's just the one menu throughout these days, whether you stick in the bar or head into The Willow Room, which offers a touch of

refinement in the shape of elegant upholstered chairs and tables dressed in white linen. On the menu is some smart, modish cooking alongside some old favourites. So you could choose to go for prawn cocktail with brown bread and butter followed by steak and kidney pudding, or kick off with smoked ham hock terrine with piccalilli and knacker bread, before moving on to honey-glazed Gressingham duck breast with roasted red plums and endive. To finish, the British artisan cheese platter offers stiff competition to desserts such as chocolate tart with black olive caramel (or you could always have both).

Chef Luke Stevens **Owner** David Milne
Times 12-2.30/5-9.45 **Prices** Fixed L 2 course £12.95, Fixed D 2 course £15.45, Starter £4.95-£9.25, Main £10.95-£21.95, Dessert £3-£8.95, Service optional, Groups min 8 service 10% **Wines** 19 bottles over £30, 46 bottles under £30, 9 by glass **Notes** Fixed D Mon-Fri, Menus/prices change 8-10 wks, Sun L ALC, Sunday L, Vegetarian available, Dress restrictions, Smart casual **Seats** 75, Pr/dining room 20 **Children** Portions, Menu **Parking** 80

GREAT YELDHAM   Map 13 TL73

The White Hart

British, European

Characterful old inn with skillful contemporary cooking

☎ 01787 237250
Poole St CO9 4HJ
e-mail: mjwmason@yahoo.co.uk
dir: On A1017, between Halstead & Haverhill

As its black and white timbered Tudor frontage attests, The White Hart has been in business since the dawn of the 16th century, and as long as folk hanker for this romantic image of Olde England it looks set to prosper. Oak panelling, inglenooks piled with logs, leaded windows, burnished oak tables and head-grazing beams set a suitably historic scene, while the culinary thrust aims at flavour-driven modern British dishes produced from impeccably-sourced materials - home-grown herbs and veg from a nearby field, for instance. This is an intelligent kitchen team firing on all cylinders to deliver well-balanced, technically adept dishes: hand-dived scallops are matched with black pudding fritters, cauliflower purée and bacon foam, ahead of Blythburgh free-range pork (braised belly and slow-roast tenderloin) in a hazelnut and herb crust, with pommes dauphine and Calvados caramel apples. A finale of pear frangipane tart with honeycomb, honey ice cream (from the hotel's own beehives) and pear cider foam is also right on the money.

Chef Mr Wu Zhenjang, Mr K White **Owner** Matthew Mason
Times noon-mdnt Closed 25 Dec D, Mon, L Tue
Prices Starter £6.95-£12.95, Main £16.95-£24.95, Dessert £5.95-£10.95, Service optional, Groups min 7 service 10% **Wines** 8 by glass **Notes** Sun L 1,2 or 3

course 12-3, under 12 eat free (T&C apply), Sunday L, Vegetarian available, Dress restrictions, Smart casual, Civ Wed 200 **Seats** 44, Pr/dining room 200 **Children** Portions, Menu **Parking** 50

HARWICH   Map 13 TM23

The Pier at Harwich

Modern British, Seafood

Spankingly fresh seafood and harbour views

☎ 01255 241212
The Quay CO12 3HH
e-mail: pier@milsomhotels.com
web: www.milsomhotels.com
dir: A12 to Colchester then A120 to Harwich Quay

What better setting could there be for a restaurant that celebrates the fruits of the sea than Harwich's quay? Watch the boats glide silently by from the first-floor windows of the light and airy Harbourside Restaurant and peruse a menu that takes in the traditional as well as more exotic ideas, so among starters may be deeply-flavoured fish soup with rouille, garlic toasts and parmesan, and crab (from Harwich, naturally) tacos with guacamole and chipotle dressing. Lobster (small, medium or large) gets varied treatments, from thermidor to cold poached, served with celeriac remoulade, truffled potatoes and tomato and watercress salad; Dover sole meunière, perfectly timed, is a classic example, served with lightly cooked green vegetables, and hardliners could always opt for beer-battered fish with triple-cooked chips and pea purée. Meat-eaters are not entirely overlooked, and an imaginative touch with puddings brings on coconut pannacotta with mango, chilli and pineapple salsa, and ginger-braised pineapple with Eccles cake ice cream. The ground-floor Ha'penny Bistro is a more informal but equally popular alternative.

continued

HARWICH *continued*

The Pier at Harwich

Chef Tom Bushell **Owner** Milsom family
Times 12-2/6-9.30 Closed Mon-Tue **Prices** Fixed L 2
course £20, Starter £7.95-£13.75, Main £16.50-£39,
Dessert £6.50-£8, Service optional **Wines** 70 bottles over
£30, 35 bottles under £30, 16 by glass **Notes** Sunday L
£29, Vegetarian available, Civ Wed 50 **Seats** 80, Pr/
dining room 16 **Children** Portions, Menu **Parking** 12

MANNINGTREE	Map 13 TM13

The Mistley Thorn

◉◉ British, Italian 🍽️

Italian influenced modern cooking on the Stour Estuary

☎ 01206 392821
High St, Mistley CO11 1HE
e-mail: info@mistleythorn.co.uk
dir: From A12 take A137 for Manningtree & Mistley

A combined bar and restaurant with rooms, The Mistley
Thorn is directly opposite the swan basin designed by
Robert Adam. It was built as a coaching inn in 1723, but
the bistro-style restaurant has a modern look. Seafood
gets a good airing on the imaginative, daily-changing
menus, from lobster with garlic mayonnaise, to grilled
lemon sole with ginger butter. Good local ingredients are
handled with skill, and a love of Italian cooking is evident
throughout, seen in a plate of superior charcuterie
(salamis, prosciutto and bresaola), venison carpaccio
with fricò (fried cheese), and fritto misto di mare. Sauces
and accompaniments are well considered adjuncts to the
main event: salsa verde for roast skate wing, say, plum
and red wine sauce for seared duck breast, and tomato,
orange and coriander sauce for seared fillet of brill. Some
puddings have a French accent - crème brûlée, St-
Emilion au chocolat - but then there's also affogato, with
Sherri's Mom's cheesecake highlighting chef-patron
Sherri Singleton's Californian origins.

Chef Sherri Singleton, Karl Burnside **Owner** Sherri
Singleton, David McKay **Times** 12-2.30/6.30-9.30
Prices Fixed L 2 course £10.95-£12.95, Fixed D 3 course
£15-£15.95, Starter £4.95-£7.95, Main £10.95-£18.95,
Dessert £5.25-£5.95, Service optional, Groups min 8
service 10% **Wines** 17 by glass **Notes** Sunday L,
Vegetarian available **Seats** 75, Pr/dining room 28
Children Portions, Menu **Parking** 7

ORSETT	Map 6 TQ68

Orsett Hall Banqueting & Conference Centre

◉◉ Modern British **NEW** 🍽️

Inspiring modern cookery in a glassed garden terrace

☎ 01375 891402
Prince Charles Av RM16 3HS
dir: M25 junct 29/A127 Southend, then A128 Tilbury,
hotel 3m on right

The hall as it stands today is a painstakingly
reconstructed facsimile of the original 17th-century
manor house that stood on the same spot, but sadly
burned to a shell in 2007. A brisk trade in corporate
business and weddings is a mainstay of many such
places, but not everywhere boasts such a head-turning
dining room as Orsett has. Designed as a glassed terrace
overlooking the gardens, it's a riot of bold colours and
floral patterns. Coloured glass chandeliers catch the
sunlight, while cream wood panelling provides a calming
backdrop: an appropriately contemporary and interesting
setting in which to enjoy the inspired, intelligent cooking
of chef Robert Pearce. A range of flavours and textures
distinguishes a starter of pigeon, in which the breast is
smoked and the legs served sweet-and-sour, alongside
contrasting purée and crisps of parsnip. Seafood is
showcased in a dazzlingly presented main course of red
snapper and spiced scallops in crab bisque, with lemon
jelly and lime foam. Aromatically beguiling desserts
include rosewater-glazed pineapple with coconut
arancini, yoghurt sorbet and lime.

Chef Robert Pearce **Owner** Apex Property Holdings ltd
Times 12-11 **Prices** Fixed L 2 course £20.95, Fixed D 3
course £26.50, Tasting menu £24.95, Starter
£6.50-£7.95, Main £16.25-£18.95, Dessert £6.50-£8.95,
Service optional **Wines** 15 bottles over £30, 18 bottles
under £30, 6 by glass **Notes** Sunday L, Vegetarian
available, Dress restrictions, Smart dress, Civ Wed 120
Seats 50 **Children** Portions, Menu **Parking** 250

SOUTHEND-ON-SEA	Map 7 TQ88

The Roslin Beach Hotel

◉ British **NEW** 🍽️

Well-conceived dishes by the sea

☎ 01702 586375
Thorpe Esplanade, Thorpe Bay SS1 3BG
e-mail: info@roslinhotel.com
web: www.roslinhotel.com
dir: On Thorpe Esplanade 2.5m past Southend Pier
towards Shoeburyness

The Roslin Beach's restaurant, a relaxing, stylish room
where the tables focus on the glass frontage looking over
the terrace then the sea, goes from strength to strength.
Scallops with asparagus, artichoke purée and black

pudding is the sort of bright, modern composition to
expect among starters, alongside more traditional duck
and chicken liver parfait with peach and red onion
chutney. Among main courses, a steak from the grill with
a choice of sauces is one option - sirloin with garlic and
parsley butter, say - or look elsewhere for more invention:
impressive three ways with pork (belly, loin and shoulder,
all properly timed, moist and full of flavour), with buttery
mash, or skate tail pan-fried with spring onions
partnered by crispy squid and lime salsa. End with
steamed toffee, pecan and banana pudding with custard,
or something lighter like chocolate pyramid.

Chef Wayne Hawkins **Owner** Regis Entertainment Ltd
Times 12-2.45/6-9.30 **Prices** Fixed L 2 course £15,
Starter £4.50-£7.95, Main £12.95-£26.95, Dessert
£4.95-£9.95, Service added but optional 10% **Wines** 18
bottles over £30, 53 bottles under £30, 10 by glass
Notes Sunday L £19.95-£25.50, Vegetarian available,
Dress restrictions, smart casual, Civ Wed 100 **Seats** 70,
Pr/dining room 30 **Children** Portions, Menu **Parking** 57

STOCK	Map 6 TQ69

The Hoop

◉ Modern British

Assured modern cooking in an old pub

☎ 01277 841137
High St CM4 9BD
e-mail: thehoopstock@yahoo.co.uk
dir: A12 Billericay Galleywold junct, on B1007

Over 450 years old, The Hoop is on two levels, a ground-
floor bar dispensing real ales with a small fireplace and
the real ambience of a country pub, and the upstairs Oak
Room restaurant, with a beamed ceiling, bare wooden
tables and prints on the walls. The lively menu focuses on
modern British flavours, which translates into starters of
ham knuckle and guinea fowl terrine with pickled
vegetables, and seared scallops with a salt-cod beignet
and cauliflower purée. Dishes are well composed so
individual components add up to a satisfying whole: a
well-timed fillet of John Dory on creamed potatoes
surrounded by a ragout of tomato and plump mussels,
and pork belly and fillet with a sauce of caramel, vanilla
and apple served with pancetta, roast shallots and a
potato croquette.

Chef Phil Utz **Owner** Michelle Corrigan **Times** 12-2.30/6-9
Closed Beer festival week, Mon, L Sat, D Sun
Prices Starter £5.95-£9.50, Main £12.95-£25.95, Dessert
£5.95-£8.95, Groups min 6 service 10% **Wines** 11 bottles
over £30, 33 bottles under £30, 14 by glass
Notes Seasonal tasting menu available, Sunday L £25,
Vegetarian available **Seats** 40 **Children** Portions
Parking Village hall

The Fat Goose

@ Modern British 🕯

Rustic cooking in a charming old pub

☎ 01255 870060
Heath Rd CO16 0BX
e-mail: eat@fat-goose.co.uk
dir: A120 to Horsley Cross, follow B1035 to Tendring/
Thorpe-le-Soken. 1.5m on right

The Goose hits all the right notes for switched-on,
comfort-oriented dining. Slate floors, high barn-like
wooden beams, and chunky wooden chairs and tables set
a suitably rustic tone for punchy food with a big heart. The
chef-proprietor believes in doing things the slow way with
no corners cut, so everything from stocks to bread is made
from scratch, in-house, using local produce, and it is all
priced to put an extra smile on your face. The menu is
packed with the sort of dishes you want to eat: twice-
baked ham and gruyère soufflé with a cheese and chive
glaze ahead of roast rump of new season lamb with gratin
dauphinoise, confit shallots, roast garlic and rosemary
jus, or a posh burger made from Sandringham Estate
venison on caramelised onion focaccia, served with blue
cheese, redcurrant and shallot chutney, Adnams-cured
bacon and Pont-Neuf potatoes. Slacken the belt, and end
with apple and sultana steamed pudding with cinnamon
crème anglaise and Calvados ice cream.

Chef Philip Hambrook-Moore **Owner** Philip Hambrook-
Moore **Times** 12-2.30/6.30-9.30 Closed Mon **Prices** Prices
not confirmed Service optional, Groups min 8 service 10%
Wines 17 by glass **Notes** Tasting menu available for
groups 6-8, Sunday L, Vegetarian available **Seats** 100,
Pr/dining room 50 **Children** Portions, Menu **Parking** 50

Catch 22 Restaurant

@ Seafood NEW 🕯

Super-fresh seafood near the Essex coast

☎ 01621 868888
**Crowne Plaza Resort, Colchester - Five Lakes,
Colchester Rd CM9 8HX**
e-mail: enquiries@cpcolchester.co.uk
dir: From Colchester on A120, then A12, turn onto B1024,
then B1023

The UK's first Crowne Plaza resort spreads its wings
across 320 acres of rolling Essex countryside, an
upmarket package that comes fully loaded with country
club-style sporting and leisure facilities. The brasserie
deals in easy-eating comfort food (see entry below), but
when you want something more refined than straight-up
steaks, the Catch 22 Restaurant moves into fish mode,
since its USP is spanking fresh fish and seafood (the
day's 'catch', geddit?) landed in nearby Mersea. The
kitchen is right at home when it comes to on-trend
contemporary flavours - an opener such as beetroot-cured
salmon with wasabi, seaweed, ginger and sake jelly,
mizuna and yuzu dressing, for example. Main courses

could see a terrine of red mullet and seaweed, smoked
artichoke and squid delivered as a foil to grilled gurnard,
while more local flavour turns up in the Maldon salt
caramel that accompanies warm chocolate fondant with
vanilla ice cream.

Chef Anthony Molnar **Owner** A3 Hotels
Times 12.30-2.30/6.30-9.30 All-day dining **Prices** Fixed L
2 course £16, Fixed D 3 course £24.95, Starter
£5.50-£12.50, Main £15-£29.95, Dessert £5.50-£9,
Service optional **Wines** 4 bottles over £30, 5 bottles under
£30, 9 by glass **Notes** Vegetarian available, Dress
restrictions, Smart casual **Seats** 60 **Children** Portions

Crowne Plaza Resort Colchester - Five Lakes

@ Modern British

**Modern British brasserie cooking in a multi-resourced
hotel**

☎ 01621 868888
Colchester Rd CM9 8HX
e-mail: enquiries@cpcolchester.co.uk
web: www.cpcolchester.co.uk
dir: M25 junct 28, then on A12. At Kelvedon take B1024
then B1023 to Tolleshunt Knights, clearly marked by
brown tourist signs

Following a multi-million-pound refurbishment at this
resort hotel - with its two 18-hole golf courses, country
club and swish spa - the spacious main restaurant has
been re-branded 'Brasserie 1'. In tune with its relaxed,
contemporary outlook, the kitchen's classic British
comfort food - with emphasis on quality ingredients and
freshness - fits the bill to a tee. Expect the likes of a fillet
of sea bass teamed with pesto and lemon barley risotto,
watercress and a parmesan tuile, or loin of local pork
served with mustard mash and a cider sauce, while a
range of steaks (21-day dry-aged rib-eye, maybe, with
vine tomatoes, flat mushrooms, thick chips and Café de
Paris butter) are a perennial favourite. Finish with a
warm Bakewell tart and raspberry ripple ice cream.

Times 7-10 Closed 26 & 31 Dec, 1 Jan, Sun-Mon

GLOUCESTERSHIRE

Aztec Hotel & Spa

@ Modern British

Eclectic modern menu in a vibrant room

☎ 01454 201090
Aztec West BS32 4TS
e-mail: quarterjacks@shirehotels.com
dir: M5 junct 16/A38 towards city centre, hotel 200mtrs
on right

Taking its name from an iconic Bristol clock, the large,
fashionable Quarter Jacks Restaurant at the modern
Aztec Hotel & Spa scores high on the cool stakes. A
thoroughly contemporary affair it may be, but it has
managed to incorporate recycled Jacobean timbers into

its Nordic-styling. The high-vaulted ceiling, big rustic
stone fireplace, polished wooden floors, leather seating
and eye-catching modern abstract art certainly make a
strong impression. The vibe is relaxed and unstuffy, a bit
like the food, which takes good regional produce and
deals with it in an uncomplicated, crowd-pleasing
manner. Grilled venison sausages might be partnered
with mash and pickled red cabbage, or go for the more
modish pan-seared sea bass fillets with brown shrimp
and saffron risotto. Desserts can be as comforting as
sticky toffee pudding or apple and blackberry crumble.

Times 12.30-2/7-9.30 Closed L Sat, D 25-26 Dec

Alveston House Hotel

@ Modern European 🕯

Georgian country house with good seasonal cooking

☎ 01454 415050
Davids Ln BS35 2LA
e-mail: info@alvestonhousehotel.co.uk
web: www.alvestonhousehotel.co.uk
dir: On A38, 3.5m N of M4/M5 interchange. M5 junct 16
N'bound or junct 14 S'bound

Whitewashed and Georgian on the outside, yet revamped
in a clean-cut contemporary style inside, Alveston House
Hotel sits in lovely walled gardens near to Bristol. A
secluded walled garden is just the spot for alfresco
aperitifs before settling into the soothing caramel and
cream hued setting of Carriages restaurant for
seasonally-changing menus which make the most of fine
regionally-sourced produce. Simple, trustworthy
combinations set the tone - perhaps smoked haddock
and salmon fishcakes with lemon and dill mayonnaise,
followed by honey-glazed rump of lamb with aubergine
and anchovy confit, or pan-fried sea bass fillet on a bed
of spinach with mushroom and tarragon sauce. End
indulgently with chocolate, rum and raisin fondant with
honeycomb ice cream.

Chef Ben Halliday **Owner** Julie Camm
Times 12-1.45/7-9.30 **Prices** Fixed L 2 course £20, Fixed
D 3 course £25, Starter £5.75-£6.25, Main
£15.50-£17.75, Dessert £5.75-£7.25, Service optional
Wines 6 bottles over £30, 29 bottles under £30, 5 by
glass **Notes** Sunday L, Vegetarian available, Civ Wed 75
Seats 75, Pr/dining room 40 **Children** Portions, Menu
Parking 60

ARLINGHAM	Map 4 SO71

The Old Passage Inn

◉◉ Seafood

Seafood specialities overlooking a bend in the Severn

☎ 01452 740547
Passage Rd GL2 7JR
e-mail: oldpassage@btconnect.com
dir: M5 junct 13/A38 towards Bristol, 2nd right to Frampton-on-Severn, over canal, bear left, follow to river

Set on an ox-bow bend of the Severn where a ford once crossed the river, the Old Passage is a restaurant-with-rooms done in shimmering green and consecrated to the best of West Country and Welsh seafood. Cornish lobsters and oysters are mainstays of the menu, the latter offered fried, with garlic mayonnaise for dipping, or au naturel. Things get a little exotic when soft-shell crab comes with kumquat chutney, but old-school classicism is celebrated in main courses such as richly sauced lobster thermidor gratinated under parmesan, while lighter tastes might be served by whole roasted lemon sole in beurre noisette. Good beer-battered fish and hand-sliced chips are a stalwart, and if you're determined on meat, there's usually one option, but one that's much more than an afterthought, perhaps saddle of venison with oxtail and spinach arancini, puréed celeriac and braised red cabbage. Treacle tart is respectably gooey and comes with zesty marmalade ice cream. Special breakfasts are held on the days when the Severn is in full bore.

Chef Mark Redwood **Owner** Sally Pearce
Times 12-2/7-9.30 Closed 25-26 Dec, Mon, D Sun, Tue-Wed Jan-Feb **Prices** Fixed L 2 course fr £15, Tasting menu fr £68, Starter £8.50-£14, Main £18-£49, Dessert

£7.65-£9.65, Service optional **Wines** 29 bottles over £30, 16 bottles under £30, 15 by glass **Notes** ALC menu only, Sunday L, Vegetarian available **Seats** 60, Pr/dining room 12 **Children** Portions **Parking** 40

BARNSLEY	Map 5 SP00

Barnsley House

◉◉ Modern European 🍃

Uncomplicated country cooking overlooking the kitchen garden

☎ 01285 740000
GL7 5EE
e-mail: info@barnsleyhouse.com
dir: 4m N of Cirencester on B4425 between Cirencester & Burford

The initials BB engraved above the garden door are the seal of ownership imprinted on the property by the Barnsley village squire for whom it was originally built, one Brereton Bouchier. It dates from the end of the 17th century, and is a slice of soft-focus grandeur in Cotswold stone, its gardens laid out by Rosemary Verey in the 1950s. Contemporary styling within produces a plain-looking long dining room, The Potager, framed in blond wood tones, with views over the kitchen garden from which it takes its name. Dishes are kept simple, the better to celebrate the provenance and quality of their materials. First up could be an assemblage of watermelon, spiced cashews and feta, or grilled cuttlefish with courgette and pepper salad, before mains such as superbly flavoured local chicken, with green beans, dauphinoise and bacon, or salmon from the Wear lightly dressed in fennel, basil and lemon. A side-dish of heirloom tomato salad is a must-have in the circumstances. Desserts maintain the straightforward style, matching bitter chocolate tart with praline parfait, or adding plums to glazed rice pudding.

Chef Graham Grafton **Owner** Calcot Health and Leisure
Times 12-2.30/7-9.30 **Prices** Fixed L 2 course £21, Starter £6.50-£10, Main £13.50-£26.50, Dessert £7.50-£8, Service included **Wines** 40 bottles over £30, 20 bottles under £30, 10 by glass **Notes** Sunday L, Vegetarian available, Dress restrictions, Smart casual preferred, Civ Wed 120 **Seats** 40, Pr/dining room 14 **Children** Portions, Menu **Parking** 25

The Village Pub

◉ Traditional & Modern British V 🍃

Local produce in a delightful Cotswold pub

☎ 01285 740421
GL7 5EF
e-mail: info@thevillagepub.co.uk
web: www.thevillagepub.co.uk
dir: B4425 from Cirencester to Bibury

Located just outside Cirencester, The Village Pub is true to its name at the heart of the community, combining a delightful traditional pub atmosphere with some first-class dining. Owned by the people behind Barnsley House and Calcot Manor (see entries), cosy, yet simple décor with unclothed wooden tables sets the scene inside, while out back there's a small terrace for dining alfresco on warmer days. It's a popular place so it's worth booking, especially at weekends. Local and seasonal produce, including trout from up the road in Bibury, is competently handled on a broadly modern British menu, with some well-executed pub classics for the purists. A punchy shredded Asian confit duck leg with chilli and coriander salad might precede local Ozleworth Estate half grouse wrapped in bacon and sage with dauphinoise potatoes and Savoy cabbage. Finish with chocolate and chestnut torte. A decent range of real ales on tap and some well chosen wines completes the experience.

Chef Graham Grafton **Owner** Richard Ball
Times 12-2.30/6-9.30 **Prices** Starter £7-£9, Main £11-£20, Dessert £6.50, Service optional **Wines** 16 bottles under £30, 3 by glass **Notes** Sunday L £13.95-£15.95, Vegetarian menu **Seats** 60 **Children** Portions

BIBURY	Map 5 SP10

Bibury Court Hotel

◉◉ Modern British 🍃

Intricate modern British food in a Jacobean manor house

☎ 01285 740337
GL7 5NT
e-mail: hello@biburycourt.com
web: www.biburycourt.com
dir: On B4425 between Cirencester & Burford; hotel behind church

Bibury has weathered its entertainingly louche history as the seat of illegitimate sons and bigamous husbands over the centuries, losing not one iota of its Jacobean dignity. With abundant charm and character exuding from every pore, the interiors are done in striking Adam Calkin wallpaper of botanical design, to offset the heavy stone walls and leaded windows. A conservatory lets a little daylight in on the magic, while the Oak Room comes, as the owners themselves playfully put it, with 'a little more starch to the cloth'. Conceptually intricate modern British dishes are the stock-in-trade, so expect to start with crab martini in bisque jelly, with devilled crab toast, avocado ice cream and caviar, before roasted white chicken breast rolls up, accompanied by a mousse of Gloucestershire chorizo, or hot-smoked salmon with a potato pancake and samphire in hollandaise. Bringing up the rear might be a spin on frangipane tart, an apricot version on puff pastry, with well-gauged rosemary ice cream on a heap of chocolate powder, and jellies of apricot and almond.

Chef Adam Montgomery **Owner** John Lister
Times 12-2/7-9 **Prices** Prices not confirmed Service added but optional 10% **Wines** 20 bottles over £30, 8 bottles under £30, 8 by glass **Notes** Sunday L, Vegetarian available, Civ Wed 32 **Seats** Pr/dining room 14 **Children** Portions **Parking** 100

Swan Hotel

◉ Traditional British, European

Appealing cooking in a Cotswold idyll

☎ 01285 740695
GL7 5NW
e-mail: info@swanhotel.co.uk
web: www.cotswold-inns-hotels.co.uk/swan
dir: 9m S of Burford A40 onto B4425. 6m N of Cirencester A4179 onto B4425. In town centre by bridge

A thoroughly relaxing country experience is on offer at the Bibury Swan, a Cotswold retreat in an idyllic setting. The Gallery dining room is so named in acknowledgement of the display of pony pictures by a Dartmoor artist. Logs are stacked against the wall, tables are properly clothed, and there's a pleasant buzz of bonhomie about the place. The menu invites you to 'commence' with something like sea trout escabèche, pickled cucumber and saffron aïoli, and then 'continue' with chargrilled sirloin and dauphinoise with béarnaise, or a whole baked lemon sole with olive beurre blanc. You'll then want to 'complete' the experience with honey and hazelnut tart, served with vanilla ice cream and caramel sauce.

Times 7-9.30 Closed L Mon-Sat

CHARINGWORTH   Map 10 SP13

Charingworth Manor Hotel

◉ French, Mediterranean

Charming country-house hotel with unfussy contemporary cooking

☎ 01386 593555
GL55 6NS
e-mail: gm.charingworthmanor@classiclodges.co.uk
web: www.classiclodges.co.uk
dir: M40 exit at signs for A429/Stow. Follow signs for Moreton-in-Marsh. From Chipping Camden follow signs for Charingworth Manor

This honey-coloured stone manor has stood on this plot for some 700 years and is a vision deserving of a place on any biscuit tin. It will come as no surprise to hear the place is a big hit on the wedding scene - it's romantic, and then some. The interior matches old and new with a keen eye and there are spa and leisure facilities to ensure maximum pampering. The business of eating takes place in the John Greville Restaurant, with its splendid oak beams, shimmering candles, and fabulous views out over the pretty countryside. The kitchen keeps things relatively uncomplicated, so you might start with chicken liver pâté with toasted brioche and apple chutney, or roast parsnip and thyme soup finished with honey and cream. Next up, main course delivers the likes of roast breast of free-range chicken with ceps duxelle stuffing and Madeira jus, or honey-roasted belly of pork with crispy crackling and five spice-scented jus.

Times 12-2.30/7-10

CHELTENHAM   Map 10 SO92

Le Champignon Sauvage

◉◉◉◉ *— see page 170*

Cheltenham Park Hotel

◉ International **NEW**

Classic and contemporary dining beside a lake

☎ 01242 222021
Cirencester Rd, Charlton Kings GL53 8EA
e-mail: cheltenhampark@pumahotels.co.uk
web: www.pumahotels.co.uk

Whether you have had a winner or lost your shirt on the gee gees at nearby Cheltenham racecourse, the Lakeside Restaurant of this smart country hotel is the place to end the day with a meal of celebration or consolation. The bright and airy space is flooded with light from walls of floor-to-ceiling windows overlooking the gardens and lake, and cheerfully kitted out with tangerine, burgundy, and grey high-backed seats at bare darkwood tables - a setting that sits well with the uncomplicated, please-all repertoire of classic and gently modern cooking. The kitchen sources its materials diligently and delivers well-executed dishes along the lines of chicken liver parfait with fruit chutney and melba toast, followed by braised shoulder of lamb with gratin potatoes, spinach,

asparagus and roasted parsnips. End in comfort mode with sticky toffee pudding with butterscotch sauce and clotted cream.

Chef Mr Summit **Times** 12.30-2.30/7-9.30 Closed L Mon-Sat **Prices** Prices not confirmed **Notes** Vegetarian available, Dress restrictions, Smart casual **Seats** Pr/dining room 22 **Children** Menu **Parking** 170

The Curry Corner

◉ Bangladeshi, Indian ☺

Upmarket Bangladeshi cuisine with a Cotswold leaning

☎ 01242 528449
133 Fairview Rd GL52 2EX
e-mail: info@thecurrycorner.com
dir: From A40 turn right into Hewlett Rd, at mini-rdbt turn left

Father and daughter Shamsul and Monrusha Krori's restaurant on a corner - funnily enough - not far from the centre of town brings a flavour of Bangladesh to Cheltenham. There is nary a cliché in sight, for this is the real deal. There's the smart décor, for a start, with its distinctive Indian carvings and sari bolsters against a backdrop of ruby-red wall coverings and tapestries, and then there's the menu, which contains a few things you won't have seen before, and a few you will; Bangladeshi home-cooking is the watchword. Ingredients come from the sub-continent and from the Cotswolds. Start, perhaps, with kakra kofta, which is two Bengal-style crab samosas filled with crab from Brixham, potato and spices, with an accompanying fresh tomato and tamarind sauce, and follow on with raan gusht - lamb shank marinated in 16 spices and cooked in a masala sauce. The excellent breads are made in-house, and vegetable sides are notably good.

Chef Shamsul Krori, Monrusha Krori **Owner** Shamsul & Saleha Krori **Times** 12-2/5.30-11.30 Closed 25 Dec, Mon (open some BHs), L Fri **Prices** Fixed L 2 course fr £10, Fixed D 3 course £25-£36, Starter £4.95-£8.95, Main £10.95-£23, Dessert £6.50-£7.95, Service added but optional 10% **Wines** 19 bottles over £30, 32 bottles under £30, 7 by glass **Notes** Pre-theatre set menu 2 course £20 5.30-6.30 except Fri-Sat, Sunday L, Vegetarian available, Dress restrictions, Smart casual, no caps **Seats** 52, Pr/dining room 40 **Children** Menu **Parking** On street, St James car park

Le Champignon Sauvage

CHELTENHAM MAP 10 SO92

Modern French

Daring, thoughtful cooking in a supremely civilised setting

☎ 01242 573449
24-28 Suffolk Rd GL50 2AQ
e-mail: mail@lechampignonsauvage.co.uk
dir: S of town centre, on A40, near Cheltenham College

The silver anniversary clocked up in 2012, the good old Champignon endures. It has become almost commonplace to celebrate its longevity, but the thing about longevity is that it gets, by definition, more awe-inspiring with every passing year. David and Helen Everitt-Matthias have put their hearts and souls into this supremely civilised place, and the cookbooks that have issued forth from it over the years add up to fascinating snapshots of the British restaurant dining of the past quarter-century. The name itself appears to acknowledge a time when wild mushrooms were an on-trend ingredient in a newly confident post-nouvelle era, but the truth is that David Everitt-Matthias has always been a chef to move with the times, reflecting what is interesting and best about new directions without feeling the need to sign up for every last bit of flim-flam. He is a keen and canny buyer, an enthusiastic forager and, best of all, a great thinker of modern cooking, truly one of the country's prime movers. The context is a refined, comfortable room, its mixture of sunny yellow, cornflower blue and striking modern paintings setting the relaxing scene over which Helen continues to preside with unflappable aplomb. The art of thoughtful combining remains important, as seen in a first course like Cornish mackerel fillet, its intrinsic sea-fresh tang deepened with salt-baked kohlrabi and hazelnuts, and an umami-laden oyster dressing. Pointedly sharp seasonings lift a pairing of Dexter beef tartare and corned beef that is accompanied by pickled shimeji mushrooms and dressed in wasabi mayonnaise. Main courses are all about shining the spotlight on outstanding principal components, whether for a tranche of roasted halibut served with both Jerusalems and globe artichokes, so rarely found together despite the accidental coincidence of their common names, sauced in spiced red wine, or for seasonal partridge, its gamey richness underscored by puréed ceps, braised walnuts and chicory. There is daring in partnering local lamb with cockles and woodruff-scented parsnips, and a reassuring feeling for elevated comfort food in the serving of Winchcombe venison that appears with a bolognaise of the shank, sweetened with beetroot and fig. Aromatic herb and spice flavours confer individualism on now familiar but still bewitching desserts such as caramel-poached pineapple with pineapple-verbena sorbet, bitter chocolate and green aniseed tart with fennel ice cream, and bergamot parfait with orange jelly and liquorice cream. Lunch produces a shorter, but not one whit the less beguiling, range.

Chef David Everitt-Matthias **Owner** Mr & Mrs D Everitt-Matthias
Times 12.30-1.30/7.30-8.45 Closed 10 days Xmas, 3 wks Jun, Sun-Mon
Prices Fixed L 2 course £48, Fixed D 3 course £59, Service optional **Notes** ALC Fixed L/D incl dessert & cheese £69
Seats 40 **Parking** Public car park (Bath Rd)

CHELTENHAM *continued*

The Daffodil

◉ British, European

Charcoal-grilled steaks and live jazz in old Art Deco cinema

☎ 01242 700055
18-20 Suffolk Pde, Montpellier GL50 2AE
e-mail: eat@thedaffodil.com
dir: S of town centre, just off Suffolk Rd, near Cheltenham Boys' College

Where converted banks were once the dominant restaurant trend, old Art Deco cinemas now follow. The Daffodil is housed in a peach of a venue, Cheltenham's very first picture palace, opening in the silent film era of the early twenties with a screening of the now totally forgotten horse-racing thriller, Thunderclap. Nothing of the drama is lost in refashioning it as a modern eatery, with its open kitchen where the screen once was, live jazz and sizzling Josper charcoal oven. That last turns out sirloins, ribeyes and chateaubriands of fabulous Cotswold beef, dry-aged for a month and served with crunchy chips and spot-on béarnaise. They might follow twice-baked Double Gloucester soufflé dressed in truffle oil, Carlingford oysters in shallot vinegar and Tabasco, or potted crab, with a finale of chilli-dressed pineapple

carpaccio, mango salsa and coconut sorbet to leave the taste buds tingling. Superb English and Welsh cheeses are well-chosen and carefully described.

Chef Tom Rains **Owner** Mark Stephens & James McAlpine **Times** 12-3/6-10 Closed 1-7 Jan, Sun **Prices** Fixed L 2 course £13.50, Fixed D 3 course £15.50, Tasting menu £49.50, Starter £4.95-£10.95, Main £13.50-£24.50, Dessert £4.95-£6.50, Service added but optional 10% **Wines** 35 bottles over £30, 20 bottles under £30, 18 by glass **Notes** Fixed price menu Mon-Sat until 7.30pm, Bar menu all day, Vegetarian available, Civ Wed 100 **Seats** 140 **Children** Portions, Menu **Parking** On street, NCP

Ellenborough Park

◉◉◉ — *see below*

The Greenway Hotel & Spa

◉◉ Modern British, French Ⅴ 📖 NOTABLE WINE LIST 🍷

Vibrant modern cooking in the Cotswolds

☎ 01242 862352
Shurdington Rd GL51 4UG
e-mail: info@thegreenway.co.uk
web: www.thegreenwayhotelandspa.com
dir: 3m S of Cheltenham on A46 (Stroud) & through Shurdington

With eight acres of glorious Cotswold countryside to call its own, The Greenway is a beautiful 16th-century manor house covered in ivy and steeped in history. It's a splendid setting for the country-house experience. The interior matches period features - grand stone fireplaces and arches, wooden floors and the like - with a blend of well-chosen bespoke furniture and antiques. On the dining front, the Orchard Brasserie is the less formal option, whilst the business of fine dining goes on in the lavish, oak-panelled Garden Restaurant, which does indeed look over the sunken garden. The complex and creative menu might see you kicking off with an assiette of beetroot, which is a riot of glorious colours, the beets joined by goats' cheese and honey bonbons, pickled shimeji mushrooms and orange peel. Next up, Challans duck - breast and confit rillettes - alongside butternut squash, cauliflower, plums and a sticky reduction sauce. Finish with a vanilla crème brûlée, which has its crispy top created at the table, and comes with pineapple carpaccio and caramelised banana.

Chef Robin Dudley **Owner** Sir Peter Rigby **Times** 12-2.30/7-9.30 **Prices** Fixed L 2 course fr £18.95, Fixed D 3 course £49.50-£65, Tasting menu £25.50-£35, Service added but optional 10% **Wines** 200 bottles over £30, 40 bottles under £30, 11 by glass **Notes** ALC 3 course £49.50, Sunday L, Vegetarian menu, Dress restrictions, Smart casual, Civ Wed 60 **Seats** 60, Pr/dining room 22 **Children** Portions, Menu

Ellenborough Park

CHELTENHAM   **MAP 10 SO92**

Modern British 📖 NOTABLE WINE LIST

Stunning manor-house hotel with dynamic cooking and a luxurious finish

☎ 01242 545454
Southam Rd GL52 3NH
e-mail: info@ellenboroughpark.com
dir: A46 right after 3m onto B4079, merges with A435, 4m, over 3 rdbts, left onto Southam Lane, right onto Old Road, right onto B4632, hotel on right

With its elevated position in rolling parkland overlooking Cheltenham racecourse, and its mightily impressive façade, historic Ellenborough Park makes a fine first impression. The palatial grandeur of the Cotswold-stone building cannot be overstated. And with its swanky spa, 21st-century business facilities, smart bedrooms and two

restaurants, there's a lot to like. The Brasserie is a useful second string to its bow, but the main event is the fine-dining Beaufort Dining Room with its Tudor fireplaces, stained-glass Oriel windows and acres of burnished oak panels. It's an impeccable setting for the finely-crafted, inspired cooking of David Kelman. There are lots of bright modish ideas on show, but this is a kitchen with a classical grounding. A smoked salmon starter, for example, is of the highest order: Uig Lodge smoked salmon, expertly carved at the table, is served with dressed salad leaves and soft-boiled quail's egg. Main-course ballottine of corn-fed poussin comes with the roast leg meat in an accompanying bonbon, plus a riot of fabulous vegetables, gem lettuce with smoked bacon and a shallot sauce. There's the likes of Chateaubriand of Hereford Cross beef, too, served with roast château potatoes, béarnaise sauce and red wine jus. The execution of dishes is spot on and the balance of flavours judged perfectly. For dessert, buttermilk and vanilla pannacotta has just the right amount of wobble and

comes with cider-poached pear, green apple and toffee caramel cannelloni, or go for a taste of the summer with iced strawberry parfait with Pimm's jelly and lemonade foam. There are first-rate cheeses, too, with a fabulous selection from the British Isles to choose from. The excellent 500-strong wine list shows this to be a high-end establishment from top to bottom, and there's plenty of help on hand from the sommelier and his team.

Chef David Kelman **Times** 7-10 Closed Mon, L Mon-Sat, D Sun **Prices** Fixed D 3 course fr £55, Service optional **Wines** 510 bottles over £30, 25 bottles under £30, 12 by glass **Notes** Sunday L, Vegetarian available, Dress restrictions, Smart casual, Civ Wed 150 **Seats** Pr/dining room 20 **Children** Portions, Menu **Parking** 123

CHELTENHAM *continued*

Hotel du Vin Cheltenham

◉ British, European

Bistro dining in Cheltenham's restaurant quarter

☎ 01242 588450
Parabola Rd GL50 3AQ
e-mail: info.cheltenham@hotelduvin.com
web: www.hotelduvin.com
dir: M5 junct 11, follow signs for city centre. At rdbt opposite Morgan Estate Agents take 2nd left, 200mtrs to Parabola Rd

The Cheltenham outpost of this popular boutique hotel brand is located in the trendy Montpelier area, and its decorative showpiece is a large spiral staircase down which diners descend from the bar to the busy bistro. Here, the look is as you'd expect: empty wine bottles as decoration, every part of available walls covered with wine related prints and memorabilia, wooden floorboards, simply-laid unclothed tables, black leather chairs and banquettes. Good quality ingredients are treated with care and respect in bistro-style dishes and, of course, the wine list impresses with its mainly French selection, including plenty by the glass. Dressed crab and walnut toast or moules frites start things off on a sound footing, before something like half a Normandy chicken with a jus rôti, or steak haché with fried duck egg and bois bourdain. A classic crêpe Suzette makes a fitting finale.

Times 12-2/6.30-10.30

Lumière

◉◉ Modern British V ✋

High-octane modern cooking from masterful chef

☎ 01242 222200
Clarence Pde GL50 3PA
e-mail: info@lumiere.cc
web: www.lumiere.cc
dir: Town centre, near bus station

Refurbishment has given a clean, elegant and serene ambience to Lumière, with its crisply starched linen, pin-striped carpet, banquettes and gilt mirrors, a bar at one end and a window giving on to the kitchen. Chef Jon Howe brings his own highly distinctive stamp to the style of the cooking, giving dishes a degree of refined complexity witnessed in a pairing of scallops with belly pork served with cumin caramel, carrot, orange and a purée of star anise. His skills and thoughtfulness pay off, producing an

attractive, palate-pleasing starter of deep-fried, thinly breaded beef cheek balls, moist and of superb flavour, with corned beef and bresaola, accompanied by wasabi, anchovies and beetroot, each element working well without overpowering the others. Invention extends to desserts along the lines of pineapple carpaccio with stunning Kalamansi sorbet, passionfruit, and coconut marshmallows with peanuts, ginger and chilli. Extras like breads and canapés are well up to snuff, and meals end memorably with a selection of petits fours with coffee.

Lumière

Chef Jon Howe **Owner** Jon Howe & Helen Aubrey
Times 12-1.30/7-9 Closed 2 wks winter, 2 wks summer, Sun-Mon, L Tue **Prices** Fixed L 3 course £28, Fixed D 3 course £49, Tasting menu £55-£70, Groups min 7 service 10% **Wines** 58 bottles over £30, 15 bottles under £30, 18 by glass **Notes** Tasting menu 6/9 course, Vegetarian menu **Seats** 25 **Parking** On street

Monty's Brasserie

◉◉ Modern British ✋

Smart brasserie cooking in stylish Grade II listed hotel

☎ 01242 227678
George Hotel, 41 St Georges Rd GL50 3DZ
e-mail: info@montysbraz.co.uk
web: www.montysbraz.co.uk
dir: M5 junct 11, follow signs to town centre. At lights (TGI Fridays) turn left onto Gloucester Rd. Straight on, at lights turn right, Monty's 0.75m on left

The George delivers all the Regency style one hopes for in Cheltenham - Grade II listed no less, so plenty of period details inside and out, and grand Georgian proportions. There's a cocktail bar in the basement with a decidedly contemporary sheen, and in fact the whole place is done out with a good degree of finesse. Monty's matches the modish tone with its brasserie good looks - lots of darkwood, smart lighting - and a lively carte, backed with daily specials, and based on good quality ingredients. Start with a classic moules marinière done well, or chicken liver and black truffle parfait, before a main course such as Cotswold beef Wellington, or loin of monkfish wrapped in Serrano ham with confit grelot onions, creamed potatoes, carrot purée, creamed potatoes

and a thyme and red wine sauce. The acute technical abilities of the team in the kitchen are on display again at dessert stage in the form of an excellent tiramisù cheesecake.

Chef Renark Cousins **Owner** Jeremy Shaw
Times 12-2/6-11 Closed 25-26 Dec **Prices** Fixed L 2 course £12.50, Fixed D 3 course £15, Starter £7-£10, Main £16-£26, Dessert £6-£7, Service added but optional 10% **Wines** 17 bottles over £30, 25 bottles under £30, 7 by glass **Notes** Sunday L, Vegetarian available **Seats** 40, Pr/dining room 32 **Children** Portions, Menu **Parking** 30

The Kings

◉◉ Modern British

Georgian Cotswold townhouse with energetic brasserie cooking

☎ 01386 840256
The Square, High St GL55 6AW
e-mail: info@kingscampden.co.uk
dir: In centre of town square

The Kings may be a classic Georgian townhouse built in honey-hued Cotswold stone right on Chipping Campden's square, but the traditional chintz and twee country hotel look has been chucked out. Instead, the place wears the style of a smartly casual modern operation - that's to say comfy banquettes, mismatched furniture and polished wooden floors in the brasserie, and in the beamed restaurant, unclothed antique tables, a flagged floor, a log fire and moody lighting. The up-to-date approach carries through to what appears on the plate: modern food built on splendid seasonal ingredients. The menus have something for everyone, whether it's a well-thought-out array of duck-based flavours and textures comprising slices of duck breast, creamy duck mousse and a duck confit parcel, all mixing well with sliced cherries, rich cherry sauce and almond biscotti, or a main course of Cotswold chicken breast with gnocchi, sautéed Mediterranean vegetables, broccoli and chorizo cream. End with something that adds a clever twist to classic ideas like elderflower pannacotta with lemon tart ice cream and olive oil biscuits.

Times 12-2.30/6.30-9.30

Seagrave Arms

◉ Modern British ✋

Local ingredients at a beautifully sited Georgian inn

☎ 01386 840192
Friday St, Weston-Sub-Edge GL55 6QH
e-mail: info@seagravearms.co.uk
web: www.seagravearms.co.uk
dir: A44 Oxford/Evesham, exit Broadway & follow B4632 towards Stratford-upon-Avon

A Georgian Cotswold country inn between Chipping Campden and Broadway, the Seagrave is a Grade II listed building that looks out over some of the lushest scenery in England. The kitchen sources assiduously from local farms and suppliers, bakes its own bread, and makes its own chutneys and ice creams. Daily specials and fish dishes are chalked up on the blackboard, to supplement the likes of grilled herring with stewed white beans in shellfish sauce, roast chicken breast with chicken and leek 'cannelloni' in a sauce of Rioja, and banana cake with salt caramel, rum and raisin ice cream and peanut crumble. Local cheeses come with apple chutney.

Chef Julien Atrous **Owner** Kevin & Sue Davies
Times 12-3/6-10 Closed 2nd wk Jan, Mon **Prices** Starter £5.50-£7.50, Main £13.50-£16.95, Dessert £5.95-£6.50, Service optional **Wines** 2 bottles over £30, 18 bottles under £30, 14 by glass **Notes** Sunday L, Vegetarian available **Seats** 36, Pr/dining room 14 **Children** Portions, Menu **Parking** 14

Three Ways House

⊕ Modern British 🍷

Well-conceived dishes at the home of the Pudding Club

☎ 01386 438429
Chapel Ln, Mickleton GL55 6SB
e-mail: reception@puddingclub.com
web: www.threewayshousehotel.com
dir: On B4632, in village centre

Let us begin at the end, with a warning that Three Ways House is the Cotswolds seat of the Pudding Club, so skipping dessert just won't do. However, there's plenty to take in here before afters hove into view. The Victorian building has heaps of period charm, although the restaurant sports a more contemporary, eclectic look with good use of mirrors to boost the feeling of space. As you might expect, the cooking is punchy, big-hearted British stuff, with a flag-waving dedication to local raw materials balanced by a multi-cultural approach to flavour combinations. Thus a starter tian of crab and red pepper with a mango and lime salsa does not have an especially Gloucestershire ring about it, while main course brings things closer to home with a juniper-crusted loin of venison with curly kale and port wine jus. And so to pudding which could be a selection of steamed puds with lashings of custard, or a heretical plate of British cheeses.

Chef Mark Rowlandson **Owner** Simon Coombe, Peter Henderson **Times** 12-2.30/7-9.30 Closed L Mon-Sat **Prices** Fixed D 3 course fr £37, Service optional **Wines** 13 by glass **Notes** Sunday L, Vegetarian available, Civ Wed 80 **Seats** 80, Pr/dining room 70 **Children** Portions, Menu **Parking** 37, On street

Jesse's Bistro

⊕ Modern British 🍷

Appealing bistro food down a cobbled alley

☎ 01285 641497 & 07932 150720
14 Blackjack St GL7 2AA
e-mail: info@jessesbistro.co.uk
web: www.jessesbistro.co.uk
dir: In town centre between the parish church & Roman Museum, behind Jesse Smith the Butchers

The bistro is to be found in a converted stable down a little cobbled alley in the centre of town, behind a butcher's shop of the same name. The exposed stone walls, wrought-iron fitments and beams of the interior, which is divided into three spaces, provide a characterful backdrop, and there's a small mezzanine area for group bookings. A compact courtyard opens on fine days. An Anglo-French approach to the bistro ethic brings on simple dishes that are carefully presented and deliver plenty of flavour. Ham, duck and foie gras terrine with red onion marmalade and toasted date bread is a typical starter, or the idiom may be stretched to encompass panko-crumbed soft-shelled crab with glass noodle salad in teriyaki-style soy dressing. The quality and proportions of a main-course serving of well-timed sea bass with buttered spinach and puréed fennel in basil and lime oil are impressive, while the slow-braised pork belly comes with a glazed apple tart.

Chef Paul Driver-Dickenson, David Witnall, Andrew Parffrey **Owner** Watermoor Meat Supply **Times** 12-3/7-10 Closed Xmas, Sun, D Mon **Prices** Starter £6-£13.50, Main £12.50-£30, Dessert £6-£8, Service optional, Groups min 8 service 10% **Wines** 35 bottles over £30, 25 bottles under £30, 15 by glass **Notes** Vegetarian available, Dress restrictions, Smart casual preferred **Seats** 55, Pr/dining room 12 **Children** Portions **Parking** Old station car park

Tudor Farmhouse Hotel & Restaurant

⊕⊕ Modern British V 🍷

Clear modern flavours in an ancient ex-farmhouse

☎ 01594 833046
High St GL16 8JS
e-mail: info@tudorfarmhousehotel.co.uk
web: www.tudorfarmhousehotel.co.uk
dir: Off A4136 onto B4228, through Coleford, turn right into Clearwell, hotel on right just before War Memorial Cross

In a sleepy village deep in the Forest of Dean this converted farmhouse restaurant, as the name suggests, has inglenooks, wood panelling, venerable beams and exposed stone walls to attest to its origins, but what comes out of the kitchen these days is far from stuck in the past. Driven by seasonal and local ingredients, the menus are full of fresh, modern ideas, among which you might find a terrine of confit chicken, shiitaki mushrooms and pancetta, served with raisin purée, while main courses run to braised shoulder of locally-farmed lamb with poached apple, carrot purée and red wine jus. To finish, head for chestnut and maple tart with vanilla mascarpone cream and orange caramel syrup. This is genuine, unaffected cooking and it's all backed by personable staff who provide efficient, friendly service.

Chef Martin Adams **Owner** Colin & Hari Fell **Times** 12-2/6.30-9 Closed 2-5 Jan **Prices** Tasting menu £45, Starter £6-£9, Main £10-£23, Dessert £6-£10, Service optional **Wines** 25 bottles over £30, 40 bottles under £30, 10 by glass **Notes** Sunday L £16.95-£20, Vegetarian menu **Seats** 36, Pr/dining room 22 **Children** Portions, Menu **Parking** 30

The Wyndham Arms Hotel

⊕ Modern British

Polished gastro-pub fare in old village inn

☎ 01594 833666
GL16 8JT
e-mail: stay@thewyndhamhotel.co.uk
dir: Exit B4228. Hotel in village centre on B4231

Clearwell is a picturesque village near Offa's Dyke Path between the Wye Valley and the Forest of Dean, and this characterful old inn is at its centre. Local ales and cider are dispensed in the rustic-style bar, and meals are served in the stone-walled, vaulted restaurant. The pub keeps Gloucestershire Old Spot pigs (and sells its own takeaway sausages and burgers), which turn up in pork and ham hock terrine, and as roast loin with apple and potato mash and cider cream. Elsewhere, starters can take in home-smoked duck breast with raspberry vinaigrette, or sardine escabèche in a salad with crayfish and citrus dressing, with pubby main courses like grilled gammon steak with fried eggs and chips, or more classically orientated pan-fried fillet of sea bass with barigoule sauce and saffron-flavoured potatoes.

Times 12-2/6.30-9 Closed 1st wk Jan, L some days in winter, D some Sun

COLN ST ALDWYNS
Map 5 SP10

The New Inn at Coln

◎ Traditional & Modern British

Tranquil country inn with appealingly modish menu

☎ 01285 750651

GL7 5AN

dir: 8m E of Cirencester, between Bibury & Fairford

The New Inn has carved itself a niche as a destination on the local foodie scene, and it is quite a looker too: a creeper-clad, honey-hued stone inn, made over in the country-chic vein with rugs on flagstone floors, inglenooks and beams, all overlaid with slick contemporary design touches. The kitchen aims at all-round satisfaction with a keenly-priced set lunch option and a wide-ranging main menu full of local accents and unpretentious modern ideas. You might start with a sharing slate of charcuterie or seafood, or a simple well-thought-out opener along the lines of home-smoked pigeon breast with watercress and balsamic dressing, followed by something from the grill - perhaps Gloucestershire Old Spot T-bone pork chop with wholegrain mustard mash, spiced red cabbage and thyme jus. Otherwise, saffron-battered haddock with minted mushy peas, skinny chips and home-made tartare sauce might hit the spot. At the end, how about tempura-battered apple fritters with caramel sauce and black pepper ice cream?

Times 12.30-2.30/7-9

CORSE LAWN
Map 10 SO83

Corse Lawn House Hotel

◎◎ British, French Ⅴ 🍷 NOTABLE WINE LIST 🍷

Extensive menus in an appealing rural setting

☎ 01452 780771

GL19 4LZ

e-mail: enquiries@corselawn.com

web: www.corselawn.com

dir: 5m SW of Tewkesbury on B4211, in village centre

Bedded in among the Cotswolds, the Malverns and the Forest of Dean, Corse Lawn is an appealing country retreat fronted by a large ornamental pond that originally served as a coach-wash. Family-owned by the Hines for the past generation, it's run with an eye to old-school formality, but not to the detriment of a palpable sense of enjoyment in both the principal dining room and the less formal bistro. The menus cater for all eventualities, and include a separate vegetarian menu offering the likes of Jerusalem artichoke bavarois with chestnuts and tarragon, followed perhaps by pumpkin ravioli with walnut sauce. Elsewhere you might find Thai fishcakes with coriander and chilli, or oxtail terrine with horseradish cream to start, followed by chargrilled salmon with crushed peas in beurre blanc, or Chinese-spiced belly pork with ginger and honey. A riot of seasonal fruits from the grounds forms the backbone of the extensive dessert listing, embracing raspberry soufflé and sorbet, as well as the richness of chocolate torte with marmalade ice cream.

Chef Andrew Poole, Martin Kinahan **Owner** Hine family **Times** 12-2/7-9.30 Closed 24-26 Dec **Prices** Fixed L 2 course £15-£22.50, Fixed D 3 course £20-£33.50, Tasting menu £30-£35, Starter £5.95-£10.95, Main £14.95-£22.50, Dessert £5.75-£7.75, Service optional **Wines** 220 bottles over £30, 80 bottles under £30, 10 by glass **Notes** Sunday L, Vegetarian menu, Civ Wed 70 **Seats** 50, Pr/dining room 28 **Children** Portions, Menu **Parking** 60

DAYLESFORD
Map 10 SP22

Daylesford Farm Café

◎ Modern British 🍃

Organic produce cooked with flair in converted barn

☎ 01608 731700

GL56 0YG

e-mail: thefarm@daylesfordorganic.com

dir: From Cheltenham take A40 & A436 through Stow-on-the-Wold, follow signs to Daylesford farmshop

As one-stop, top-quality food shopping experiences go, the original Daylesford Deli in a lovely converted Cotswold stone barn is hard to beat. Here you can load up with a cornucopia of organic goodies from a butcher, baker, creamery, fishmonger and grocer, but there's a lot more going on than just the deli these days: you can also get blissed out with a spot of meditation and pampering in the Hay Barn spa, before lunching organically on the best produce the season has to offer. The café is a clean-lined space with a chic New England style and a relaxed, buzzy vibe. When the raw materials are as good as this, no kitchen worth its salt would mess about with them, so dishes are prepared with minimal fuss to let the flavours speak for themselves - a starter of warm Dorset crab on fresh sourdough toast being a case in point. When something more substantial is called for, there's grilled Aberdeen Angus steak sandwich with balsamic roasted onions, horseradish cream, and rosemary potato wedges, and a chocolate nemesis with vanilla cream.

Chef Gaven Fuller **Owner** Carole Bamford **Times** 12-3/7-9.30 Closed 25-26 Dec, 1 Jan **Prices** Starter £6-£10, Main £10-£15, Dessert £4.50-£8, Service added but optional 10% **Wines** 9 bottles over £30, 10 bottles under £30, 9 by glass **Notes** Sunday L £14-£18, Vegetarian available **Seats** 75, Pr/dining room 60 **Children** Portions **Parking** 100

EBRINGTON
Map 10 SP14

The Ebrington Arms

◎◎ Modern British

Village inn with great food

☎ 01386 593223

GL55 6NH

e-mail: reservations@ebringtonarms.co.uk

web: www.theebringtonarms.co.uk

dir: From Chipping Campden take B4035 towards Shipston-on-Stour, left to Ebrington

This gem of a 17th-century village inn - tucked away in green-and-pleasant Cotswold countryside - brims with the genuine charm and character of a proper old-style pub, and is justly revered by its locals who huddle around its small bar. Cotswold-stone walls, oak beams and big open fireplaces are all present and correct, as are real ales on tap. The restaurant continues the rustic-chic theme, decked out with old darkwood tables, while the kitchen turns up the gas with a decidedly modern approach based around quality local seasonal produce and something of a nod to sunnier climes. From a spring menu might come rack of top quality new season Cotswold lamb served with provençale vegetables and confit tomato tapenade, or perhaps a classic bouillabaisse (monkfish, red mullet, king prawns and sea bass with rouille and croûtes), while a cleverly presented rhubarb and custard tart with ginger ice cream might provide the finale.

Times 12-2.30/6.30-9.30 Closed 25 Dec, D Sun

GLOUCESTER
Map 10 SO81

The Wharf House Restaurant with Rooms

◎ Modern European 🍃

Broadly appealing cooking in a former lockhouse by the Severn

☎ 01452 332900

Over Waterside, Over GL2 8DB

e-mail: enquiries@thewharfhouse.co.uk

web: www.thewharfhouse.co.uk

dir: From Over rdbt take A40 westbound to Ross-on-Wye, 1st right in 50 yds

Owned by the Herefordshire & Gloucestershire Canal Trust, profits from this restaurant with rooms by the River Severn go towards the upkeep of 34 miles of canals in the two counties. It really comes into its own when the weather allows for eating on the terrace overlooking the water, but it's a pleasant space if you're dining indoors, with its wooden tables, parquet floor and fashionably neutral colour palette. The menu suits the relaxed and informal setting, offering a large choice of well-prepared and unfussy dishes. Start with a tart filled with leeks and stilton, or a salad enriched with crab and mango salsa, before main-course rainbow trout with tangy tomato chutney, or rack of Herefordshire lamb with leek and potato dauphinoise and rich honey and rosemary sauce.

Save on Hotels. Book at **theAA.com/hotel**

GLOUCESTERSHIRE 175 ENGLAND

Chef David Penny **Owner** H & G Canal Trust **Times** 12–6
Closed 26–27 & 31 Dec, 1 Jan, D 24–25 Dec
Prices Tasting menu £45.99–£52.99, Starter
£5.99–£11.99, Main £13.99–£22.99, Dessert
£4.99–£12.99, Service optional, Groups min 6 service
10% **Wines** 20 bottles over £30, 31 bottles under £30, 7
by glass **Notes** Sunday L £15.99, Vegetarian available,
Dress restrictions, Smart casual **Seats** 40
Children Portions **Parking** 32

LOWER SLAUGHTER   Map 10 SP12

Lower Slaughter Manor

◎◎ Modern British V ✹

**Classically based innovation in the honeyed heart of
the Cotswolds**

☎ 01451 820456
GL54 2HP
e-mail: info@lowerslaughter.co.uk
web: www.lowerslaughter.co.uk
dir: Off A429, signed 'The Slaughters'. 0.5m into village
on right

Lower Slaughter is the distilled essence of the Cotswolds,
right down to that slightly Miss Marpleish name. A manor
house dating from the time of the Commonwealth, it's a
superbly relaxing environment, with plenty of public
rooms for lounging, the interiors done with colourful
panache but without excess clutter. Jamie Raftery arrived
in the spring of 2013 to take up the cudgels, and makes
an instant splash, maintaining the calmly innovative
style of his predecessor, for food that combines
discerning local buying with a modernist approach to
classical principles. Start with a silky-smooth goats'
cheese mousse, perfectly married with beetroot, candied
walnuts and apple, for a dish that combines sweet, salty
and bitter elements in glorious harmony. Main course
might be breast and confit leg of Creedy Carver duck, the
latter encased in a fragile pancake, served with bok choi
and a sauce that balances the classic note of orange
with the punctuating Asianisms of five-spice and ginger -
a bravura production. Rhubarb is some sort of benchmark
test of a chef's dessert ingenuity nowadays, and Raftery
steps up with an array of mousse, jelly, sorbet, purée and
crumble, the poached batons topped with a dollop of
superlative clotted cream.

Chef Jamie Raftery **Owner** Brownsword Hotels
Times 12.15–2/7–9.30 **Prices** Fixed L 2 course fr £20,
Fixed D 3 course £65, Tasting menu £85, Service optional
Wines 350 bottles over £30, 20 bottles under £30, 12 by
glass **Notes** Sunday L, Vegetarian menu, Dress
restrictions, Smart, no jeans or trainers, Civ Wed 70
Seats 55, Pr/dining room 20 **Children** Portions, Menu
Parking 30

MORETON-IN-MARSH   Map 10 SP23

Manor House Hotel

◎◎ Modern British V

Classy, modern cooking in a 16th-century gem

☎ 01608 650501
High St GL56 0LJ
e-mail: info@manorhousehotel.info
web: www.cotswold-inns-hotels.co.uk/manor
dir: Off A429 at south end of town

In a happy blend of old and new, period character rubs
along nicely with aesthetics in tune with contemporary
tastes in this mellow yellow Cotswold-stone classic. The
Manor House comes from blue-blooded stock: Henry VIII
bequeathed the house to the Dean and Chapter of
Westminster in 1539, and the trencherman royal would no
doubt give the kitchen's output the seal of approval.
Highly-refined country-house cooking in the modern
British mould is the name of the game in the Mulberry
Restaurant. Escabèche of Brixham monkfish appears with
smoked salmon mousse and wafer thin shards of
pancetta to create a well-conceived opener, while mains
go down the inventive route of partnering tenderloin and
braised shoulder of pork with Madeira-poached apple,
black pudding crumble, leeks and a soft quail's egg.
Popping candy injects a note of frivolity to an entertaining
rosemary pannacotta with pineapple salsa and Piña
Colada sorbet.

Chef Nick Orr **Owner** Michael & Pamela Horton
Times 12–2.30/7–9.30 Closed L Mon-Sat **Prices** Fixed D 3
course £39, Tasting menu £55, Service added but
optional 10% **Wines** 20 bottles over £30, 20 bottles under
£30, 8 by glass **Notes** Tasting menu 8 course, Sunday L,
Vegetarian menu, Dress restrictions, Smart casual, no
shorts or trainers, Civ Wed 120 **Seats** 55, Pr/dining room
120 **Children** Portions **Parking** 32

Redesdale Arms

◎ British

Relaxed dining in historic Cotswold inn

☎ 01608 650308
High St GL56 0AW
e-mail: info@redesdalearms.com
dir: On A429, 0.5m from rail station

This fine old Cotswold-stone inn has been a part of the
bustling, picture-postcard-pretty Moreton scene for
centuries, today offering a classy fusion of old and
modern. It successfully blends venerable wood panelling,
oak floorboards and exposed stone walls with a relaxed
contemporary style, using tobacco-hued sofas, modern
art and muted colour schemes. Dinner is served in the
modern brasserie-styled rear conservatory, with its
please-all menus conjured from quality, local and
seasonal produce with simplicity and flavour to the fore.
Take an opener of warm Cotswold goats' cheese and
caramelised red onion tartlet with dressed leaves and
balsamic and port wine syrup, and to follow, perhaps
pan-seared Cornish sea bass fillet with sautéed potatoes,
wilted spinach and a caviar and lemon butter sauce. To

close, Greek yoghurt pannacotta with winter berry
compôte.

Chef Daniel Ciobotiaru **Times** 12–2.30/6.30–9
Prices Starter £4.95–£6.95, Main £11.95–£23.95, Dessert
£4.95–£6.50, Groups min 8 service 10% **Notes** Bistro
menu available daily (exc Tue, market day menu), Sunday
L, Dress restrictions, Smart casual

White Hart Royal Hotel

◎ Traditional British ✹

Enterprising cooking in a Cotswold coaching inn

☎ 01608 650731
High St GL56 0BA
e-mail: whr@bpcmail.co.uk
web: www.whitehartroyal.co.uk
dir: In town centre

The 17th-century former coaching inn of Cotswold stone
looks a picture in summer when festooned with hanging
baskets. It stands in the centre of this delightful market
town at the top of the Evenlode Valley, the quintessence
of pastoral England. Since everywhere built in this era
has to have sheltered either Cromwell or Charles I at
some point, be it noted that the King holed up here for a
night after the battle of Marston Moor in 1644. A pair of
lounges, a flagstoned snug with original inglenook and
the courtyard restaurant, which includes tables en plein
air for the sunny days, come as standard. After a starter
of 'Soup of the Moment', or a tri-coloured stack of Marie
Rose prawns, crab salad and avocado mousse, the main
courses try out some enterprising ideas, such as
Balinese-style fish (red snapper, king prawn and catfish)
wrapped in a banana leaf, served with lemongrass and
coconut broth and saffron rice. Impressively tender lamb
is two lumps of rump seared on all sides, accompanied
by silky-smooth minted pea purée in red wine and
rosemary reduction. Recline into the comfort-zone at the
end with the likes of steamed lemon and honey pudding.

Chef Carl Chappell **Owner** Bulldog Hotel Group Ltd
Times 11–3/6–10 Closed L Mon-Sat **Prices** Prices not
confirmed Service optional **Wines** 7 bottles over £30, 30
bottles under £30, 11 by glass **Notes** Sunday L,
Vegetarian available **Seats** 44, Pr/dining room 12
Children Portions **Parking** 6, On street

NAILSWORTH — Map 4 ST89

Wild Garlic Restaurant and Rooms

◉◉ Modern British V 🕙

Imaginative modern cooking in former blacksmith's

☎ 01453 832615

3 Cossack Square GL6 0DB

e-mail: info@wild-garlic.co.uk

dir: M4 junct 18. A46 towards Stroud. Enter Nailsworth, turn left at rdbt and then an immediate left. Restaurant opposite Britannia Pub

This sweet, small-yet-perfectly-formed modern restaurant is a stylish, relaxed place with enthusiastic staff to match. Chef-prop Matthew Beardshall's kitchen takes an admirable hands-on approach making everything in-house, from organic bread and pasta to sorbets and ice cream, while the concise brasserie-style menu changes monthly to reflect seasonality and make the very best use of the regional larder. On a late spring menu, expect simplicity and flavour from the likes of a fillet of South Coast turbot teamed with a slow-roast tomato salad and samphire, or perhaps Cotswold white chicken Kiev served with wild garlic butter (wild garlic rightly making an appearance on the plate; it's abundant in the area), plus potato, smoked bacon and watercress salad. To finish, maybe rhubarb and custard with champagne and poached rhubarb jelly and almond tuile.

Chef Matthew Beardshall **Owner** Matthew Beardshall **Times** 12-2.30/7-9.30 Closed 1st 2 wks Jan, Mon-Tue, L Wed, D Sun **Prices** Tasting menu £35-£45, Starter £6.95-£8.95, Main £14.95-£19.95, Dessert £6.95, Service optional, Groups min 7 service 10% **Wines** 12 bottles over £30, 32 bottles under £30, 10 by glass **Notes** Tasting menu 4/6 course, Sunday L, Vegetarian menu **Seats** 42 **Children** Portions, Menu **Parking** NCP, parking on street

NETHER WESTCOTE — Map 10 SP22

The Feathered Nest Country Inn

◉◉◉ — *see below*

Three Choirs Vineyards

◉ Modern British, European 🕙

Award-winning wines, good food and more

☎ 01531 890223

GL18 1LS

e-mail: ts@threechoirs.com

web: www.threechoirs.com

dir: 2m N of Newent on B4215, follow brown tourist signs

With grape varieties such as seyval blanc and huxelrebe grown on the gently sloping Herefordshire hills, the Three Choirs Vineyard is a reminder if you need it that the UK viniculture business is in fine fettle. It makes a good trip out, what with a shop, wine tasting and cookery classes

available, and you can even leave with bottles of their own cider and beer if that doesn't seem too heretical. The Vineyard Restaurant and terrace has prime views over the estate and those precious vines, and is the setting for an unfussy menu that deals in well-judged flavour combinations, plus plenty of regional produce. Start with ham hock fritter with celeriac, apples and English mustard, or a crispy free-range egg served up with broad beans and truffle mayonnaise, before 21-day aged Hereford rib-eye or beetroot tarte Tatin, beet purée and Cerney Ash goats' cheese cream. They even have their own dessert wine to accompany the likes of vanilla brulée, Herefordshire raspberries and shortbread.

Chef Siobhan Hartley **Owner** Three Choirs Vineyards Ltd **Times** 12-2/7-9 Closed Xmas, New Year **Prices** Fixed L 2 course £24.50, Fixed D 3 course £37.50, Starter £5.75-£12.50, Main £13-£21.50, Dessert £5.50-£6.50, Service optional, Groups min 10 service 10% **Wines** 8 bottles over £30, 28 bottles under £30, 14 by glass **Notes** Sunday L, Vegetarian available, Dress restrictions, Smart casual **Seats** 50, Pr/dining room 20 **Children** Portions, Menu **Parking** 50

PAINSWICK — Map 4 SO80

Cotswolds88Hotel

◉◉◉ — *see opposite*

The Feathered Nest Country Inn

NETHER WESTCOTE — MAP 10 SP22

Modern British 🍷 NOTABLE WINE LIST

A gem of a country pub in a beautiful Cotswold village

☎ 01993 833030

OX7 6SD

e-mail: info@thefeatherednestinn.co.uk

web: www.thefeatherednestinn.co.uk

dir: On A424 between Burford & Stow-on-the-Wold, signed

Pub food has come a long way in the last few years, especially at this particular pub anyway. Since Tony and Amanda Timmer took over the former 17th-century malthouse in the pretty Cotswold village of Nether Westcote in 2009, they've transformed it from a rundown pub into a stylish country inn with four luxurious bedrooms and a big foodie following. The place has a friendly, welcoming vibe and a pleasing mix of contemporary style (check out the riding saddle stools in the bar) and original features such as open

fireplaces and wooden beams. There's a large terrace for fine-weather dining, with fabulous views across the surrounding countryside. But it's the kitchen's consistently impressive output that most people come here for: the seasonally changing menu showcases the very best local produce in a range of interesting, modern twists on classic dishes. Red mullet with artichoke and vegetable broth, fennel pollen, caper berries and olives is a starter that simply sings with flavour, the fish moist and fresh, the artichoke crisp, the broth light, and the caper berries adding a contrasting firm texture and a welcome saltiness. Main-course suckling pig comes four ways: in a pie with a crisp, buttery pastry, as loin and shoulder, and in a paper-thin terrine, all faultlessly cooked, rich-tasting and complemented well by carrot quinoa, rainbow chard and Calvados sauce. A chocolate bavoir - clearly made from top-quality chocolate - with a superb chestnut ice cream and chocolate crumb, ends things on a high. Breads are made freshly on-site every day, and if you want a decent coffee you'll find it here, complete with a duo of excellent petits fours - perhaps a Baileys and milk chocolate truffle and a pistachio macaroon. The award-winning wine list of over 220 bins - several available by the

glass - is well worth exploring, and there's a good selection of local cask-conditioned ales.

Chef Kuba Winkowski **Owner** Tony Timmer **Times** 12-2.30/6.30-9.30 Closed 25 Dec, Mon, D Sun **Prices** Prices not confirmed Service optional, Groups min 8 service 12.5% **Wines** 215 bottles over £30, 29 bottles under £30, 19 by glass **Notes** Sunday L, Vegetarian available, Civ Wed 200 **Seats** 60, Pr/dining room 16 **Children** Portions, Menu **Parking** 45

Save on Hotels. Book at **theAA.com/hotel**

GLOUCESTERSHIRE 177 ENGLAND

Cotswolds88Hotel

Modern British

Imaginative modern British cooking in a hip boutique hotel

☎ 01452 813688
Kemps Ln GL6 6YB
e-mail: reservations@cotswolds88hotel.com
web: www.cotswolds88hotel.com
dir: M4 junct 15, follow A419 past Swindon & Cirencester to Stroud. Turn off to Painswick

If you still associate the Cotswolds with twee little tea rooms and starchy country-house hotels, think again. Cotswolds88 may well have the achingly handsome stone exterior you might expect in this neck of the woods, but what lies within is a flourish of designer whimsy and bold boutique ambition. But rest assured there is substance to all this playfulness, not least in the output of the Juniper restaurant, which is a big hitter in the regional culinary stakes. Canapés in the bar - carefully made stuff such as ham hock beignet - gets things off on the right foot before moving into the restaurant for the main event: there's a touch of theatre here, perhaps it's the almost stage-set nature of the décor. Chicken and chive boudin with celeriac fondant and purée, pickled apple and split chicken jus is a first course of serious craft - and graft - as is dressed shellfish with lemon, curd

ham, horseradish snow and tuba radishes. These ambitious dishes are executed with a good deal of skill and understanding of modern techniques, while the balance of flavours remains intact. Slow-cooked venison, beautifully cooked, comes in a main course with a bitter tonka bean jus, a tarte fine made of the haunch meat, watercress purée and red cabbage ketchup. A fish main course might be pan-fried halibut with beetroot, baby fennel, orange and cardamom emulsion and crab crushed potatoes. With dishes this complex it is easy to lose one's way, but that does not happen here. A dessert of sticky toffee pudding with caramelised bananas and banana ice cream sounds relatively simple, but isn't, and British cheeses await if you've any room. When the weather is up to snuff, don't miss a stroll around the pretty gardens to take in the view and admire the impressive house.

Chef Lee Scott **Owner** Mr & Mrs Harris **Times** 12-2.30/6.30-10 Closed 1 wk Jan, Mon-Tue **Prices** Fixed D 3 course £45, Tasting menu £55-£65, Starter £7.50-£12.50, Main £13.75-£28.50, Dessert £6.95-£9.95, Service added but optional 12.5% **Wines** 60 bottles over £30, 40 bottles under £30, 10 by glass **Notes** Tasting menu 5/7 course, Sunday L, Vegetarian available, Civ Wed 120 **Seats** 42, Pr/dining room 14 **Parking** 17, Public car park

PAXFORD
Map 10 SP13

Churchill Arms

◎◎ Traditional ⊕

Superior cooking in a Cotswolds pub

☎ 01386 594000
GL55 6XH
e-mail: info@thechurchillarms.com
dir: A429 from The Fosse, then A44 to Bourton-on-the-Hill. Turn right at end of village to Paxford via Blockley

Its location in a charming Cotswolds village makes this 18th-century honey-coloured stone inn well worth seeking out, and another reason for doing so is the quality of the cooking. It's an informal place, with beams in the ceiling, boarded and flagstoned floors, an inglenook and old furnishings. Straightforward dishes, short on fuss but long on flavours, are the order of the day, with the kitchen reliant on good quality local ingredients. Kick off with something like ham hock terrine with grape chutney, rocket and sourdough, gravad lax with beetroot, new potatoes and crème fraîche, or push the boundaries with salt cod Scotch egg with green bean salad. Fish is accurately timed - seen in pan-fried sea bream with pesto, spinach, and new potatoes - otherwise perhaps go for rump of lamb with dauphinoise and an olive and tomato jus. Old stalwarts have their place, among them grilled venison sausages with mustard mash and caramelised onion jus, and there's a choice of steaks. For the finale comes sticky toffee pudding with cream, or chocolate mousse with raspberries.

Chef Neal Heyworth **Owner** Richard Shore
Times 12-2/6.30-9 Closed 25 Dec **Prices** Service optional, Groups min 10 service 10% **Wines** 9 by glass **Notes** Sunday L £11-£14, Vegetarian available **Seats** 56 **Children** Portions, Menu **Parking** On street

STOW-ON-THE-WOLD
Map 11 SP12

Fosse Manor

◎◎ Modern British

Smart country-house hotel with a local flavour

☎ 01451 830354
GL54 1JX
e-mail: enquiries@hydefosse.co.uk
web: www.fossemanor.co.uk
dir: 1m S on A429, 300yds past junct with A424

The classic Cotswolds honey-stone, creeper-clad exterior of this former rectory looks like it conceals a scene of country-house chintz, but inside the picture is one of pared-back, neutral-hued contemporary style. You'll find Fosse Manor on the fringes of Stow-on-the-Wold in five acres of idyllic grounds and gardens that provide the backdrop to dining in the smart restaurant. The kitchen too, has stayed in touch with current trends, serving up appealing menus of uncomplicated modern British ideas built on top-grade local produce. A terrine of local game, duck and foie gras with pear chutney might be one way to start, while main course could showcase Lighthorn lamb in a trio of rump, sweetbread and hotpot, served with

tomato and basil, and red wine sauce. At the end, local cheeses are always a good bet, or you could bow out sweetly with dark chocolate torte with vanilla ice cream and cherries in Kirsch.

Chef Mark Coleman **Owner** Fosse Manor Hotel Ltd
Times 12-2/7-9 **Prices** Prices not confirmed Service optional **Notes** Sunday L, Vegetarian available **Seats** 80 **Children** Portions, Menu **Parking** 40

The Kings Head Inn

◎ British

Refined pub fare in an atmospheric village inn

☎ 01608 658365
The Green, Bledington OX7 6XQ
e-mail: info@kingsheadinn.net
web: www.kingsheadinn.net
dir: On B4450, 4m from Stow-on-the-Wold

The King's Head is a textbook example of a switched-on village pub. The scene is idyllic: honey-hued Cotswold houses huddle around the village green where ducks and bantams play in a trickling brook; inside are wobbly flagstone floors, log fires and head-skimming beams. A commendable balance is struck between food and drink - the place is still the village boozer serving a fine pint of Hook Norton, while the cooking is a definite notch or two above your average pub. A menu in the modern British mould showcases local free-range and organic materials, starting with super-fresh grilled sardines with fennel, mint and chilli, then perhaps an Aberdeen Angus steak reared on the family farm, or roast haunch of Cotswold venison with mash, green beans and beetroot jus.

Times 12-2/7-9.30 Closed 25-26 Dec

Number Four at Stow Hotel & Restaurant

◎◎ British, European ⊕

Stylish modern restaurant serving imaginative food

☎ 01451 830297
Fosseway GL54 1JX
e-mail: reservations@hotelnumberfour.co.uk
dir: Situated on A424 Burford Road, at junct with A429

A building dating from the 17th century is home to this stylish boutique hotel in the heart of the Cotswolds. Number Four is one of those places that gets everything pitch perfect, from the opulent contemporary look, to the sort of prescient service that anticipates guests' needs, and, in the oldest part of the house, light and modern cooking in the characterful beamed and painted wood-panelled Cutler's Restaurant. Head chef Brian Cutler uses local, seasonal produce from a well-chosen network of suppliers to good effect in well-executed dishes. Salad of Cornish crab and smoked salmon, or chicory tarte Tatin with blue cheese and artichoke might open proceedings, while mains extend to well-conceived pairings of flavour and texture - medallions of Cotswold venison with walnut spätzle, or suprême of sea bass with scallop cannelloni, say. Finish with something like strawberry parfait with marshmallow.

Chef Brian Cutler **Owner** Caroline & Patricia Losel
Times 12-2/7-9 Closed Xmas, D Sun **Prices** Fixed L 2 course fr £14.50, Starter £6-£10.50, Main £14.50-£23, Dessert £6.50-£10.50, Service optional **Wines** 15 bottles over £30, 15 bottles under £30, 10 by glass Sunday L £24.50-£28.50, Vegetarian available **Seats** 50, Pr/dining room 40 **Children** Portions, Menu **Parking** 50

Wyck Hill House Hotel & Spa

◎◎ Modern British ⊕

Stylish contemporary cooking in smart Cotswolds hotel

☎ 01451 831936
Burford Rd GL54 1HY
e-mail: info.wyckhillhouse@bespokehotels.com
dir: A429 for Cirencester, pass through 2 sets of lights in Stow-on-the-Wold, at 3rd set of lights bear left signed Burford, then A424 signed Stow-on-the-Wold, hotel 7m on left

Expectations are heightened at first sight of the old Cotswolds property with lovely views of the Windrush Valley, expectations fully met by the interior of antique-furnished lounges, an oak-panelled bar, and a smartly kitted-out dining room of neutral-shaded walls, comfortable upholstered chairs and French windows looking over the estate. The menu is in the contemporary idiom, with ideas pulled in from here and there for each dish, so pan-fried king scallops are served with carrot and raisin salsa and wasabi mayonnaise, and warm smoked breast of wood pigeon comes with black pudding, a quail's egg, crisp pancetta and spicy lentils. Interest is well maintained into main courses: crab risotto with sautéed butternut squash might take your fancy, while traditionalists' needs will be well met by roast fillet of beef with béarnaise and the usual accompaniments. A lot of work goes into puddings, with enjoyable results: lemongrass custard and coconut sorbet accompany pineapple sponge pudding, and frosted pecans and plums infused in red wine liven up a vanilla crème brûlée.

Chef Mark Jane **Owner** Bespoke Hotels
Times 12.30-2/7-9.30 **Prices** Fixed L 2 course fr £15.95, Fixed D 3 course fr £39, Service optional **Wines** 40 bottles over £30, 30 bottles under £30, 10 by glass **Notes** Sunday L, Vegetarian available, Civ Wed 120 **Seats** 50, Pr/dining room 120 **Children** Portions, Menu **Parking** 120

STROUD
Map 4 SO80

Burleigh Court Hotel

◎◎ British, European

Grand old house, confident cooking

☎ 01453 883804
Burleigh, Minchinhampton GL5 2PF
e-mail: burleighcourt@aol.com
web: www.burleighcourthotel.co.uk
dir: 2.5m SE of Stroud, off A419

Guests at this Cotswold stone manor house have none other than Clough Williams-Ellis of Portmeirion fame to thank for the superb view of the Golden Valley, since he designed its terraced gardens in the 1930s to provide a perfect viewing platform to take it all in. Built at the outset of the 19th century, Burleigh Court is every inch the classic English country-house retreat: an oak-panelled lounge bar is the venue for a snifter before dinner in the formal, old-school elegance of the dining room. The kitchen revisits classical ideas with a modern eye, using top-drawer ingredients together with home-grown seasonal herbs and veg. It's a straightforward way of doing things that produces accomplished partnerships all the way: a twice-baked goats' cheese soufflé with roasted pears, pine nuts and rocket, ahead of sautéed Cornish mullet and scallops with spring onion and herb potato, creamed leeks, and lemon and dill dressing. To close the show, a summer assiette of lime brings on rose and lime jelly, lime curd tart, and iced lime parfait.

Chef Adrian Jarrad **Owner** Louise Noble **Times** 12-2/7-9 Closed 24-26 Dec **Prices** Fixed L 2 course fr £20, Starter £6.50-£14, Main £15.95-£25.95, Dessert £7.25-£9.95, Service optional **Wines** 8 bottles over £30, 8 bottles under £30, 8 by glass **Notes** Sunday L fr £25.50, Vegetarian available, Civ Wed 50 **Seats** 34, Pr/dining room 18 **Children** Portions, Menu **Parking** 28

TETBURY   Map 4 ST89

Calcot Manor

◎◎ Modern British ✿

Charming 14th-century Cotswold retreat with vibrant modern cuisine

☎ 01666 890391
Calcot GL8 8YJ
e-mail: reception@calcotmanor.co.uk
web: www.calcotmanor.co.uk
dir: M4 junct 18, A46 towards Stroud. At x-roads junct with A4135 turn right, then 1st left

Set in 220 acres of prime Cotswolds countryside, Calcot Manor left behind its seven-centuries-old origins as a lowly farmhouse long ago. Nowadays, it is the full-dress boutique-style country hotel package, offering luxurious rooms and a state-of-the-art spa pitched squarely at style-conscious sybarites. Foodie palates also get a stimulating workout in the chic, stylishly revamped Conservatory Restaurant. The kitchen has let go of its erstwhile focus on fine dining, and now looks to the sunny cuisines of the Mediterranean for spiritual inspiration, while local suppliers furnish the building blocks for its skillfully-wrought modern output. The wide-ranging menu has all bases covered, whether you just want to graze on nibble-sized portions of skate nuggets with tartare sauce, or Scotch quail's eggs with black pudding, or go for the full two or three courses. Should you prefer the latter, you might set out with herb-crusted Cornish mackerel with piccalilli, then look to the wood oven for hay-roasted rack of lamb with potato gratin and fine beans, or go for a whole Dover sole griddled on the plancha.

Chef Michael Benjamin **Owner** Richard Ball (MD) **Times** 12-2/7-9.30 **Prices** Starter £7.50-£12, Main £12-£31, Dessert £8.95, Service optional **Wines** 36 bottles over £30, 14 bottles under £30, 24 by glass **Notes** Sunday L, Vegetarian available, Civ Wed 100 **Seats** 100, Pr/dining room 16 **Children** Portions, Menu **Parking** 150

Hare & Hounds Hotel

◎◎ Modern British

Charming Cotswold hotel with confident team in the kitchen

☎ 01666 881000
Westonbirt GL8 8QL
e-mail: reception@hareandhoundshotel.com
web: www.cotswold-inns-hotels.co.uk
dir: 2.5m SW of Tetbury on A433

The Hare & Hounds has some pretty fancy neighbours in the form of the National Arboretum and the Beaufort Polo Club, but it is quite capable of making an impression on its own merits. The handsome Cotswold-stone house was built in 1928 and cuts quite a dash these days as a country-house hotel, with the Beaufort Restaurant really putting it on the map. The vaulted hammer-beamed ceiling and stone mullioned windows strike an elegant pose, whilst the well-designed chairs and smartly laid tables suggest this place is not stuck in the past. And so it proves on the menu. The well-crafted modern British dishes show adroit technical skills and impressive management of flavours. Start with a carrot velouté in a creative partnership with coconut pannacotta and a sweet and sour ginger relish, moving on to braised shoulder and loin of lamb with choucroute, confit garlic, baby carrots and potato crisp. Everything looks beautiful on the plate, not least desserts such as raspberry and basil vacherin with a lemon and basil parfait and raspberry gel.

Times 7-9.30 Closed L Mon-Sat

THORNBURY   Map 4 ST69

Ronnie's of Thornbury

◎◎ Modern European ✿

Modern European cooking in a 17th-century schoolhouse

☎ 01454 411137
11 St Mary St BS35 2AB
e-mail: info@ronnies-restaurant.co.uk

Hidden away in an unlikely location in the town's shopping precinct, Ronnie's became an instant hit with locals when it opened in 2007, and it's easy to see why: whether you pop in for brunch or dinner, the vibe is easygoing, and the modern European cooking keeps things local, seasonal and to the point. The 17th-century building wears its contemporary look well: stone walls, beamed ceilings, wooden floors and neutral hues are pointed up by paintings and photos by West Country artists. Ronnie Faulkner's team will send you away happy, whether you turn up to kick start the day with coffee and eggs Benedict, or round it off with intelligent, precisely-cooked dinner ideas such as cassoulet with confit duck and a fashionable quail's Scotch egg, followed by roasted pork loin matched with a pork and apricot pie, butternut squash, caramelised apple and pork crackling. For pudding, there may be almond sponge with ginger and rhubarb pannacotta, or you could go for a savoury finish with the splendid array of English artisan cheeses.

Chef Ron Faulkner, George Kostka **Owner** Ron Faulkner **Times** 12-3/6.30-10.30 Closed 25-26 Dec, 1 Jan, Mon, D Sun **Prices** Fixed L 2 course fr £15, Fixed D 3 course £25-£30, Tasting menu fr £45, Service added but optional 10%, Groups min 7 service 10% **Wines** 44 bottles over £30, 52 bottles under £30, 25 by glass **Notes** Menu of the day 2/3 course £10/£13, Sunday L, Vegetarian available **Seats** 68 **Children** Portions **Parking** Car park

---

Thornbury Castle

◎◎ Modern British 🍷 NOTABLE WINE LIST 🏅

Modern cuisine served up in a genuine Tudor castle

☎ 01454 281182
Castle St BS35 1HH
e-mail: info@thornburycastle.co.uk
web: www.thornburycastle.co.uk
dir: M5 junct 16, N on A38. 4m to lights, turn left. Follow brown historic castle signs. Restaurant behind St Mary's church

In days of yore you needed to be a serious bigwig to stay at Thornbury - Henry VIII, say, who courted Anne Boleyn here, or Queen Mary I, who lived within its walls for many years. A historic place, then, but nowadays anyone with the price of a meal to hand is welcome at Thornbury, the only Tudor castle in England to be run as a hotel. Once inside, everything is predictably castley - arrow-slit windows, roaring log fires, oak panelled walls, suits of armour, tapestries - but medieval hog roast banquets are no longer on the menu. The kitchen takes a rather more contemporary, country-house view of things, deploying well-sourced local ingredients - herbs and vegetables from the garden, wines from the castle's own vineyard - in creative combinations. Foie gras parfait with apple crumble, cider reduction and wild sorrel opens things on a luxurious footing; next comes a three-way serving of Middlewhite pork comprising shoulder, belly and loin served with baby vegetables, creamed potato and rich braising juices. Finally, apple tarte Tatin is matched with blackberry bubbles and decadent clotted cream ice cream.

Chef Mark Veale **Owner** LFH **Times** 11.45-2/7-9 **Prices** Fixed L 2 course £15.50-£25, Fixed D 3 course fr £50, Tasting menu fr £65, Service optional **Wines** 7 by glass **Notes** Sunday L, Vegetarian available, Dress restrictions, Smart casual, No jeans, trainers or T-shirts, Civ Wed 50 **Seats** 72, Pr/dining room 22 **Children** Portions, Menu **Parking** 50

UPPER SLAUGHTER — Map 10 SP12

Lords of the Manor

◎◎◎ — *see below*

WICK — Map 4 ST77

Masons at Tracy Park

◎◎ Modern British

Focused, unfussy cooking in a posh country club

☎ 0117 937 1800 & 07973 797555
Bath Rd BS30 5RN
e-mail: info@tracypark.co.uk
dir: Just off A420

Tracy Park is a handsome pile indeed, dating from the early 19th century, with two championship golf courses, lush parkland, and stables that inspired the author of *Black Beauty*. It's handsomely done out on the inside as well, and it's easy to see why the place is a hit on the wedding scene. Masons restaurant is a bit of a hit, too, situated in an old Masonic lodge, it has a soaring arched ceiling, exposed stonework walls, lots of atmospheric darkwood and plushly upholstered chairs: a smart setting for some smart, gently modish cooking. Kick off with mackerel pâté with horseradish butter and rye toast, before moving on to slow-cooked pork belly with dauphinoise potatoes, confit shallot and sage jus, or grilled Scottish salmon with fennel salad, lemon and cream dressing. Pear and almond tart with raspberry sorbet or a selection of local cheeses will send you home happy.

Chef Daniel Kasieczka **Owner** Tracy Park Golf & Country Club **Times** 12-2.30/7-9 Closed Xmas, L Mon-Sat **Prices** Starter £5.25-£6.25, Main £14.45-£19.25, Dessert £5.25-£6.80, Service optional **Wines** 22 bottles under £30, 6 by glass **Notes** Sun L 3 course , reservations preferred, Sunday L £19.95, Vegetarian available, Civ Wed 130 **Seats** 36, Pr/dining room 130 **Children** Portions, Menu **Parking** 250

WINCHCOMBE — Map 10 SP02

Wesley House

◎◎ Modern European

Impressive modern cooking in a period house

☎ 01242 602366
High St GL54 5LJ
e-mail: enquiries@wesleyhouse.co.uk
web: www.wesleyhouse.co.uk
dir: In centre of Winchcombe

The 15th century merchant's house gets its name from the Methodist preacher who stayed here in the 18th century. Period features like beamed ceilings, an inglenook fireplace and bare stone walls in the traditional main dining room have been brought up to date with contemporary flair - expect colour-changing lighting and big flower displays. There's also a stylish conservatory with stunning views of the surrounding countryside. The

---

Lords of the Manor

UPPER SLAUGHTER — MAP 10 SJ12

Modern British 🍴 NOTABLE WINE LIST 🍷

Accomplished modern cooking in a picture-postcard Cotswold house

☎ 01451 820243
GL54 2JD
e-mail: reservations@lordsofthemanor.com
web: www.lordsofthemanor.com
dir: Follow signs towards The Slaughters 2m W of A429. Hotel on right in centre of Upper Slaughter

The Cotswolds isn't short of handsome, honey-stoned old properties surrounded by beautiful grounds, but surely this has to be one of the loveliest? The 17th-century former rectory in eight acres of landscaped gardens and parkland bordered by the River Eye looks simply idyllic, and once inside it's a welcoming and homely place despite its glossy interiors magazine décor (think funky modern fabrics and sexy splashes of colour mingling rather successfully with the antiques, grand fireplaces and mullioned windows). In the restaurant the approach is a pleasingly gentle interpretation of country-chic, with tables dressed in their finest linen, extremely comfortable upholstered seats and fine art on the walls. The staff are formally dressed and highly skilled (do make use of the sommelier's expertise when choosing from the superb list), but do their utmost to make guests feel relaxed. New head chef Richard Edwards' cooking is right on the money, taking the finest ingredients and using a good measure of modern technique to produce dishes of considerable flair. Softly-poached breast of quail with a cannelloni of the leg meat is an immaculately prepared and presented starter, the quail wonderfully tender and flavoursome, the pasta thin and perfectly cooked, with the flavours of sage and onion bringing the whole dish together. Combinations are classically based but given a modern interpretation, and flavour is always king, as in main-course braised halibut - a wonderfully fresh piece of fish, precision cooked - served with shredded iceberg lettuce combined with fresh Cornish crabmeat, farfalle pasta and a smooth and creamy truffle butter sauce. A textbook raspberry soufflé might round things off, indulgently served with a thick white chocolate sauce and a refreshing quenelle of raspberry sorbet. A meal here is certainly an occasion to savour, with canapés, excellent breads, amuse-bouches and pre-desserts all part of the highly polished package.

Chef Richard Edwards **Owner** Empire Ventures **Times** 12-2.30/7-9.30 Closed L Mon-Sat **Prices** Fixed D 3 course £69, Tasting menu £92, Service optional **Wines** 490 bottles over £30, 10 bottles under £30, 15 by glass **Notes** Tasting menu 7/10 course available, Sunday L, Vegetarian available, Dress restrictions, Smart casual, no trainers or jeans, Civ Wed 80 **Seats** 50, Pr/dining room 30 **Children** Portions, Menu **Parking** 40

food is certainly rooted in the 21st century, with the kitchen team's modern European output bringing together interesting combinations of ingredients with aplomb. Crab tortellini with coriander and chilli, steamed vegetables and lemongrass cream certainly doesn't stint on the crabmeat, while the ingredients work together a treat. Roasted Loomswood duck breast, balsamic-glazed vegetables, shallot rösti and thyme sauce is equally well-balanced, but save room for the highlight of the meal - properly chewy dark chocolate and nougatine torte with Greek yoghurt sorbet and passionfruit jelly. The wine list features plenty of choice by the glass and bottle and the lunchtime wine flights are a popular way to go.

Chef Cedrik Rullier **Owner** Matthew Brown
Times 12-2/7-9 Closed Mon, D Sun **Prices** Fixed L 2 course fr £14.50, Fixed D 3 course fr £25, Starter £6-£9, Main £16-£25, Dessert £5.50-£6.50, Service optional **Wines** 43 bottles over £30, 48 bottles under £30, 11 by glass **Notes** Sunday L, Vegetarian available, Civ Wed 70 **Seats** 70, Pr/dining room 24 **Children** Portions **Parking** In the square

See advert below

Wesley House Wine Bar & Grill

◉ European

Trend-setting brasserie next-door to Wesley House

☎ 01242 602366
High St GL54 5LJ
e-mail: enquiries@wesleyhouse.co.uk
dir: In the centre of Winchcombe

Historic Wesley House - built for a merchant back in the 15th century - has a few tricks up its sleeve these days, not least its Wine Bar & Grill, which is a delightful 21st-century interloper amid all the antiquity. Next-door's fine-dining restaurant (see separate entry) has a rival in the shape of this funky, modern venue, where you can sip on a cocktail and tuck into some sparky brasserie-style food. With mirror-balls, purple lighting, and zebra-skin barstools, there's no lack of contemporary swagger about it. Start with something like steamed Fowey mussels with roasted fennel, coconut and cardamom, before a steak cooked on the grill, or sticky black bean pork belly with coriander mash and stir-fried oriental vegetables. There's a daily tapas selection board, too, plus desserts such as hot chocolate fondant with home-made raspberry sorbet.

Chef Cedrik Rullier **Owner** Matthew Brown
Times 12-2/6-10 Closed 25-26 Dec, 1 Jan, Sun-Mon **Prices** Fixed L 2 course fr £10.50, Starter £5-£6, Main £11-£22, Dessert £5, Service optional **Wines** 3 bottles over £30, 24 bottles under £30, 21 by glass **Notes** Vegetarian available, Civ Wed 70 **Seats** 50 **Children** Portions

WOTTON-UNDER-EDGE   Map 4 ST79

Tortworth Court Four Pillars Hotel

◉ Modern British **NEW**

Handsome Victorian hotel with brasserie-style menu

☎ 01454 263000
Tortworth GL12 8HH
e-mail: tortworth@four-pillars.co.uk
web: www.four-pillars.co.uk
dir: M5 junct 14. Follow B4509 towards Wotton. Turn right at top of hill onto Tortworth Rd, hotel 0.5m on right

The impressive Victorian house was built in the middle of the 19th century for the 2nd Earl of Ducie and its listed status will come as no surprise. It's a cracking example of Victorian architecture, with vast gables and soaring chimneys: ideal material, then, for the country-house hotel treatment. With 30 acres of lovely gardens, including its own arboretum, spa facilities and a range of restaurants and bars, there's plenty to admire. The house is magnificent inside, too, splendidly proportioned, not least Moreton's, the main dining room, with its ornately carved panels and huge mullioned windows in what was originally the library. The brasserie-style menu might see you start with a tartlet of red onion and Jerusalem artichoke with a pesto dressing, or fresh mussels and bacon cooked in Stowford Press cider. Main courses are in a similar vein, so Thai vegetable curry sits alongside braised duck leg with blackberry and red wine sauce.

Times 12-2.30/6.30-10 Closed Sun-Mon, L Sat

GREATER MANCHESTER

ALTRINCHAM Map 15 SJ78

Earle by Simon Rimmer

◉ Modern European NEW ☺

Vibrant modern cooking in village brasserie

☎ 0161 929 8869
4 Cecil Rd, Hale WA15 9PA
e-mail: info@earlerestaurant.co.uk
dir: M56 junct 7 onto A556 towards Altrincham, follow
signs to Hale

Telly chef Simon Rimmer's operation in the busy little
village of Hale is a contemporary brasserie that ticks all
the right boxes for locally sourced and seasonal
ingredients. The vibe is buzzy yet relaxed and the look is
stylish without trying too hard - herringbone wood
panelling and floors, exposed red-brick walls and
unclothed wooden tables - and you may see the man
himself at work in the open-to-view kitchen. A simple
approach sees classic comfort dishes alongside bright
modern ideas, while the 'Ten-Mile Meal' champions local
suppliers. Get going with hot-smoked salmon and
spinach frittata with crab mayonnaise, mint and radish,
then consider pan-roast rump of lamb with lamb and
mint ravioli, braised peas and baby gem lettuce.
Rimmer's Manchester establishment, Greens, is
vegetarian, so you can expect some creative veggie
dishes, such as truffled mushroom and pearl barley stew
with pickled red cabbage and celeriac hash. Finish with
lemon polenta cake with lemon meringue Eton mess.

Chef Simon Rimmer **Owner** Simon Rimmer
Times 12-2/5.30-9.30 Closed 25-26 Dec, 1 Jan, L Mon
Prices Fixed L 2 course £16.95, Fixed D 3 course £20.95,
Starter £4.50-£10.95, Main £12.95-£25.95, Dessert
£6.25, Service optional, Groups min 6 service 10%
Wines 17 bottles over £30, 20 bottles under £30, 10 by
glass **Notes** Sunday L, Vegetarian available **Seats** 65, Pr/
dining room 14 **Children** Portions, Menu **Parking** Station
car park

BOLTON Map 15 SD70

Egerton House Hotel

◉ Modern British ☺

Well-tuned English cuisine

☎ 01204 307171
Blackburn Rd BL7 9PL
e-mail: sales@egertonhouse-hotel.co.uk
web: www.egertonhouse-hotel.co.uk
dir: M61, A666 (Bolton road), pass ASDA on right. Hotel
2m on just past war memorial on right

A handsome country mansion built by a Victorian textile
baron, Egerton House sits in gorgeous landscaped
gardens on the fringes of the Lancashire hills - a
peaceful retreat that is equally handy for business in
Bolton. It offers a nice balance of country-house comfort
and contemporary style; with its polished pine floors,
claret-hued walls hung with gilt-framed pictures, and
bare darkwood tables, the dining room makes a sharp
modern setting for cooking that adds intelligent touches
to traditional pairings. That might translate as smoked
Applewood cheese soufflé with celery and apple salad to
open, then roast pork tenderloin with spring bean
cassoulet and mashed potato. Round things off with the
nursery comfort of steamed syrup sponge pudding and
custard.

Owner Jan Hampton **Times** 12-3/7-11 Closed BHs, L Mon-
Sat, D Sun **Prices** Fixed D 3 course £24.95, Service
optional **Wines** 5 by glass **Notes** Sunday L, Vegetarian
available, Civ Wed 130 **Seats** 50, Pr/dining room 120
Children Portions, Menu **Parking** 90

See advert opposite

MANCHESTER Map 16 SJ89

The Dining Rooms @ Worsley Park

◉ Modern British ☺

Accomplished cooking on country club estate

☎ 0161 975 2000
Walkden Rd, Worsley M28 2QT
e-mail: bernard.walker@marriotthotels.com
web: www.marriottworsleypark.co.uk
dir: M60 junct 13, over 1st rdbt take A575. Hotel 400yds
on left

This country club and hotel is on a 200-acre estate (once
the Duke of Bridgewater's) that includes an 18-hole golf
course, yet it is only seven miles from the centre of
Manchester. The Dining Rooms - three of them - are
decorated in contemporary style, an appropriate backdrop
for some ambitious modern cooking that might include
starters of pan-fried sea trout with black pudding,
spinach and mustard dressing, and smoked bacon and
artichoke tart with pea purée and shoots. The Bolton
Abbey Estate is the source of beef and lamb - perhaps
well-timed rump with chunky chips and watercress - with
plenty of variety in other main courses: game pie with
sweet potato mash and buttered greens, say. Cheeses are
all from the north-west, and puddings may extend to
rhubarb and custard parfait.

Chef Chris Marshall **Owner** Marriott Hotels **Times** 6.30-10
Prices Starter £6-£11.50, Main £14.50-£24, Dessert
£6-£9, Service optional **Wines** 14 bottles over £30, 19
bottles under £30, 20 by glass **Notes** Sunday L £21-£31,
Vegetarian available, Civ Wed 180 **Seats** 140, Pr/dining
room 14 **Children** Portions, Menu **Parking** 250

The French by Simon Rogan

◉◉◉ *– see opposite*

Save on Hotels. Book at theAA.com/hotel

GREATER MANCHESTER 183 ENGLAND

The French by Simon Rogan

MANCHESTER MAP 16 SJ89

British, French NEW

A cutting-edge revolution for The French

☎ 0161 236 3333
Peter St M60 2DS
e-mail: midlandsales@qhotels.co.uk
web: www.qhotels.co.uk
dir: M602 junct 3, follow Manchester Central Convention Complex signs, hotel opposite

No, Mr Rogan has not taken time off from his envelope-pushing culinary innovation at L'Enclume (see entry) to write a sociological history of the Gallic race: this is the title of his new venture within The Midland Hotel's time-warp bubble of belle époque elegance. The French has always been one of Manchester's hot tickets, the place to go when only a hit of old-school Gallic glamour will do, but the time-honoured guéridon service has gone into retirement with the arrival of the young Turk on the scene. The décor, too, has been reworked within the confines of the venue's sacrosanct period features: there are huge twinkly disco ball chandeliers and bare pale wooden tables, custom-made from sustainable timber, all overlaid with muted contemporary tones. Multi-course tasting menus are the means by which Rogan delivers his unique take on gastronomy, each intriguing combination of taste and texture presented on bespoke plates made from natural materials such as glazed stone, slates or slabs of wood, and each dish provokes thought: you read the sparse description, then wonder how the often alien-sounding elements will work out on the plate. And at the heart of things, Rogan's food is all about ingredients - fresh, seasonal, foraged even - and cutting-edge techniques are deployed to wring from them every last molecule of flavour. Goats' cheese brings together a dish of beetroot, salted hazelnuts and apple marigold in the same way that a just-poached egg yolk links the flavours and textures of razor clams, celeriac and sea herbs. Progressing, highlights include rib-eye ox tartare dressed with 'coal oil' and partnered by pumpkin seeds, kohlrabi and sunflower shoots, while fish fans will be thrilled by hake fillet with buckwheat, watercress and smoked roe butter. The combinations continue to excite, entertain and puzzle in equal measure, through to desserts such as pear with meadowsweet and rye, buttermilk and linseeds.

Times 7-11 Closed BHs, Sun-Mon, L all week

MANCHESTER *continued*

Greens

◉ Modern Vegetarian V

Veggie Mancunian star

☎ 0161 434 4259
43 Lapwing Ln, West Didsbury M20 2NT
e-mail: simoncgreens@aol.com
dir: Between Burton Rd & Palatine Rd

Greens has grown in reputation and size since it opened back in 1990 in its trendy Didsbury base, in part down to TV chef and co-owner Simon Rimmer's media profile. It's a relaxed modern brasserie-style outfit; a fashionable confection of darkwood tables and chairs, wooden floor, leather banquettes and a feature wall of bold-patterned wallpaper. The modern vegetarian food comes with verve and vigour to match the on-cue surroundings, taking inspiration from the global larder in simply presented dishes with flavour to the fore. Thus homely Cheshire cheese and sage sausages might come with bubble-and-squeak, beer gravy and tomato chutney, or perhaps an Asian-influenced Indian-spiced chick pea parcel with spinach and sweet potato served with yellow mustard seed and tomato sauce. To finish, there's lemon tart with raspberry sauce.

Chef Simon Rimmer **Owner** Simon Connolly & Simon Rimmer **Times** 12-2/5.30-10.30 Closed 25-26 Dec, 1 Jan, L Mon **Prices** Fixed L 2 course £15, Starter £4.50-£6.25, Main £10.50-£13.50, Dessert £4.95-£5.95, Service optional, Groups min 6 service 10% **Wines** 4 bottles over £30, 23 bottles under £30, 15 by glass **Notes** Sunday L £12.95, Vegetarian menu **Seats** 84 **Children** Portions, Menu **Parking** On street

Harvey Nichols Second Floor Restaurant

◉◉ Modern European V

Chic department store with trendy modish cooking

☎ 0161 828 8898
21 New Cathedral St M1 1AD
e-mail: secondfloor.reservations@harveynichols.com
dir: Just off Deansgate, town centre. 5 min walk from Victoria Station, on Exchange Sq

Manchester city centre's outpost of the much-loved brand houses a striking restaurant in-keeping with the city's industrial image. Round metal spiked chairs, girders, tiled flooring, black walls and grey table cloths with white covers meet expectations. The large windows bring the bustling landscape in, and there's also a chance to watch the landmark big wheel turn. Business types make up a large part of the lunchtime clientele, but all-comers get to tuck into unfussy, imaginative modern European food. Flavours sing out in the likes of crisp oxtail salad with roast garlic, onion jam and pickled mushroom, followed by stone bass with fennel risotto, artichoke, chard and lemon dressing. Puddings are equally voguish; beetroot parfait with yoghurt mousse, chocolate soil and pickled blackberries, perhaps, or popcorn pannacotta with maple syrup jelly and caramel mousse.

Chef Sam Everett, Matthew Horsfield **Owner** Harvey Nichols **Times** 12-3/6-9.30 Closed 25-27 Dec, Etr Sun, D Sun-Mon **Prices** Prices not confirmed Service added but optional 10% **Wines** 20 by glass **Notes** Menu Gourmand 6 course £55, Sunday L, Vegetarian menu **Seats** 50 **Children** Portions, Menu **Parking** NCP under store opposite

The Lowry Hotel

◉◉ Modern International ◐

Super-stylish hotel with talent in the kitchen

☎ 0161 827 4000 & 827 4041
50 Dearmans Place, Chapel Wharf, Salford M3 5LH
e-mail: hostess@roccofortehotels.com
web: www.roccofortecollection.com
dir: M6 junct 19, A556/M56/A5103 for 4.5m. At rdbt take A57(M) to lights, right onto Water St. Left to New Quay St/ Trinity Way. At 1st lights right onto Chapel St for hotel

The River Irwell which flows past the five-star Lowry marks the boundary between Manchester and Salford, and the heart of the city is just a stroll away on the other side of the landmark Trinity Bridge. With its acres of glimmering glass, the hotel makes a bold statement - this place is big, glamorous and classy, and with its River Restaurant, it has a dining venue to match. The position by the river means the terrace is a hotspot when the north-western weather is kind, but the immaculate dining room is a hit year-round. It is all calming contemporary neutrality inside, with white linen tableclothes and smart duck-egg blue leather chairs, and the service style is slick and polished. The menu draws inspiration from a broadly modish European template, so you might get a bit of autumnal Mediterranean sunshine in the form of a salad of roasted pumpkin with ricotta, sage and beurre noisette, followed by a bit of northern charm in the form of lamb noisette with Lancashire hotpot, wild mushrooms and Shrewsbury sauce (a port and redcurrant jelly combo).

Owner Sir Rocco Forte & family **Times** 12-2.30/6-10.30 **Prices** Fixed L 2 course £15-£21, Fixed D 3 course £19.95, Starter £5-£22.50, Main £11-£29, Dessert £5.50-£9.50, Service added but optional 10% **Wines** 12 by glass **Notes** Sunday L, Vegetarian available, Civ Wed 400 **Seats** 85, Pr/dining room 20 **Children** Portions, Menu **Parking** 100, RCP

Macdonald Manchester Hotel

◉ Modern British, Scottish ◐

Traditional Scottish food in the middle of Manchester

☎ 0161 272 3200
London Rd M1 2PG
e-mail: general.manchester@macdonald-hotels.co.uk
dir: Opposite Piccadilly Station

Hard by Piccadilly Station, the Macdonald Manchester is a tower-block hotel in the modern style. A re-conceptualisation of the eating options has imbued the informal dining room with a Scottish vibe, so Highland business visitors needn't feel all at sea. John Ross Jr of

Aberdeen supplies the smoked fish platters - salmon, trout and mackerel with horseradish cream - which are a good place to start, while haggis, neeps and tatties in whisky sauce comes in two sizes. For mains, grilled meats with various sauces, including one made with Dunsyre Blue, are done on the Josper charcoal grill, or you might opt for fried halibut with new potatoes and seasonal greens. Scottish desserts are conspicuous by their absence, but sticky toffee pudding and New York cheesecake won't lack for takers.

Chef Stuart Duff **Owner** Macdonald Hotels **Times** 5-10 Closed L all week **Prices** Prices not confirmed Service included, Groups min 10 service 10% **Wines** 13 by glass **Notes** Vegetarian available **Seats** 140 **Children** Portions, Menu **Parking** 85, Fee for parking

Malmaison Manchester

◉ Modern International ◐

Broadly appealing menus in chic city-centre hotel

☎ 0161 278 1000
1-3 Piccadilly M1 1LZ
e-mail: manchester@malmaison.com
web: www.malmaison.com
dir: From M56 follow signs to Manchester, then to Piccadilly

An old linen warehouse formed the infrastructure for Manchester's Malmaison, a cool, hip hotel, its laid-back restaurant furnished with red leather-look banquettes and funky tables. The menu is a good match for the place, with ideas picked up from around the globe, the Josper grill turning out steaks, lamb cutlets, barbecue ribs, and so on. Elsewhere, look for mutton masala with saffron rice and raita, Thai-style vegetable, miso and noodle soup, or salmon fishcake with spinach and parsley sauce, preceded by the likes of chicken liver and foie gras parfait with grape chutney, or corn chowder, and followed by Valrhona chocolate tart.

Chef Kevin Whiteford **Owner** Malmaison Limited **Times** 12-2.30/6-11 **Prices** Prices not confirmed Service added but optional 10% **Wines** 21 by glass **Notes** Sunday L, Vegetarian available **Seats** 85, Pr/dining room 10 **Children** Portions **Parking** NCP 100 mtrs

Room Manchester

◉◉ Modern British

Reinvented retro food stylings in a jaw-dropping mega-brasserie

☎ 0161 839 2005
81 King St M2 4AH
e-mail: jamie@roomrestaurants.com

A jaw-dropping venue in the city centre, in one of the buildings where Churchill held wartime meetings, is brimming over with in-your-face contemporary styling. Climb the stairs to the Room itself, an electrifying mega-brasserie with light fittings big enough to live in, hanging from a sky-high ceiling, a glamorous cocktail bar run by bottle-tossing bartenders, and tall arched windows with views of celebs arriving in the street below. In such a wowzer atmosphere, it would be a trifle anticlimactic if the cooking simply dealt in deadpan brasserie staples, but it doesn't. There is an almost tongue-in-cheek retro note running through the menus, but the dishes are ingeniously retooled and often performed at the table, as when a bowl of neatly arranged seafood chowder ingredients has its leek soup poured over it by the waiter. Rollmop herrings come with beetroot pickled in vodka, main-course rabbit loin with a carrot cannelloni tube of shredded shoulder and Pink Fir apples, and dessert might be toasted marshmallows in cherry soup, or beetroot and goats' cheese Eton mess.

Times 12-2.45/5.30-10 Closed 24-26 Dec, BHs, Sun

Sweet Mandarin

◉ Chinese V

A vibrant modern setting for fab Chinese food

☎ 0161 832 8848
19 Copperas St M4 1HS
e-mail: lisa@sweetmandarin.com
dir: Top end of High Street opposite Old Smithfield Fish Market façade in Northern Quarter

On a standout glass-fronted corner site opposite the old Smithfield market, Sweet Mandarin is run by three sisters whose USP is that they produce home-style 'fresh, healthy and authentic' Chinese food that stands out from the norm. Inside, the décor goes for a modern de-cluttered look with a nod to traditions in the customary red napkins and lanterns. Quoting their grandmother as a major influence, the ladies send out a mix of classics, as well as more contemporary fusion ideas, all built on a sound basis of quality ingredients. Family heritage recipes take in Mabel's claypot chicken, cooked with ginger, spring onions, mushrooms, and the special ingredient - a Chinese sausage called lap cheung. Seafood makes a good showing too, in the likes of sizzling scallops or 'firecracker' prawns, heated up with a kung pao sauce of chilli, garlic and peanuts.

Chef Lisa Tse **Owner** Helen Tse **Times** 5-11 Closed 25-26 Dec, Mon, L all week **Prices** Fixed D 2 course £20-£35, Starter £3.50-£10.95, Main £9.95-£16.95, Service added but optional 10% **Wines** 1 bottle over £30, 13 bottles under £30, 7 by glass **Notes** Vegetarian menu **Seats** 85 **Children** Portions **Parking** Shudehill car park

MANCHESTER AIRPORT Map 15 SJ88

Etrop Grange Hotel

◉◉ Modern British

Georgian elegance and modern cooking a stone's throw from the airport

☎ 0161 499 0500
Thorley Ln M90 4EG
e-mail: fandb@etrophotel.co.uk
dir: Off M56 junct 5. Follow signs to Terminal 2, take 1st left (Thorley Ln), 200yds on right

The Georgian Grade II listed house dating from 1780 finds itself right next to Manchester Airport these days, which

is rather handy. It is surrounded by pretty grounds and feels nicely secluded and, with its WineGlass restaurant, it's a lot more than a useful stopover address. Decorated in a smart and traditional manner, the restaurant has lots of period charm and overlooks a courtyard garden. The menu takes a broadly modish path but also offers its own posh burger, steaks cooked on the grill and fish and chips. From the more contemporary 'Chef's Dinner Menu', you might start with wood pigeon with pumpkin, shallots and almonds, or sweetcorn 'cheesecake' with Guinness, popcorn and walnut. This is creative and ambitious stuff. Main-course rabbit (loin and leg) stars moist and tender meat with beetroot, aubergine and spelt. There's imagination in the desserts, too, with a bitter chocolate cremeux with salted peanut butter parfait and carrots (purée and thinly sliced).

Chef Ernst Van Zyl **Owner** Sonoma Hotels **Times** 12-2/6.30-9.30 **Prices** Fixed L 2 course £17.50, Tasting menu £50-£90, Starter £5.50-£9.50, Main £13.95-£24, Dessert £7-£10, Service optional **Wines** 12 bottles over £30, 26 bottles under £30, 34 by glass **Notes** Tasting menu, Wine tasting evening, Sunday L, Vegetarian available, Dress restrictions, Smart casual, Civ Wed 94 **Seats** 40, Pr/dining room 20 **Children** Portions, Menu **Parking** 90

OLDHAM Map 16 SD90

The White Hart Inn

◉ Modern British V

Modern British cooking in a traditional Lancashire inn

☎ 01457 872566
51 Stockport Rd, Lydgate OL4 4JJ
e-mail: bookings@thewhitehart.co.uk
dir: M62 junct 20, A627, continue to end of bypass, then A669 to Saddleworth. Enter Lydgate turn right onto Stockport Rd. White Hart Inn 50yds on left

The centre of Oldham is not far off, but when you're ensconced in this cosy old coaching inn on the fringes of the wild moors, the city feels a long way away. Real fires and fine local ales add a glow of conviviality to the Tap Room, although eating is the core business these days, whether you go for the brasserie menu, which is also served in the rustic Barn Room, or trade up to the more contemporary-styled restaurant. The food is good, hearty unpretentious stuff - Morteau sausage and Puy lentil casserole followed by braised beef in red wine with smoked mash and glazed carrots, perhaps, from the brasserie menu, while the restaurant menu might propose foie gras two ways with pear sorbet and hazelnuts, then loin of local venison with turnip gratin, quince and chanterelles. Make sure to leave room for pudding, which could be rhubarb crumble soufflé with thyme and ginger ice cream, or pannacotta with Armagnac-poached Agen prunes.

Chef Mike Shaw **Owner** Charles Brierley **Times** 12-2.30/6-9.30 Closed 26 Dec, 1 Jan, Tue, L Mon-Sat, D Sun **Prices** Fixed L 2 course £13.50, Fixed D 3 course £16.50, Tasting menu £47.50, Starter £6-£9, Main £14-£26, Dessert £5.80-£6, Service optional **Wines** 70 bottles over £30, 70 bottles under £30, 10 by glass

Notes Tasting menu 7 course, Sunday L, Vegetarian menu, Civ Wed 180 **Seats** 50, Pr/dining room 32 **Children** Portions, Menu **Parking** 75

PRESTWICH Map 15 SD80

Aumbry

◉◉ British V ☺

Innovative cooking in friendly and relaxed restaurant

☎ 0161 798 5841
2 Church Ln M25 1AJ
e-mail: enquiries@aumbryrestaurant.co.uk
dir: M60 junct 17, A56 signed Manchester/Prestwich. Turn right into Church Ln

Aumbry (the name for a small cupboard in the wall of a church) is a compact restaurant in two knocked-together red-brick Victorian cottages with a cobbled frontage. Dishes may sound simple, but the thought and workmanship behind them are impressive. Slow-cooked Ringley pork, black peas, vinegar and apple turns up melt-in-the-mouth meat, served with contrastingly crisp crackling, smooth apple purée and perfectly cooked peas topped with vinegar-filled battered teardrops. Quality is high and timings just so, seen in roast wild turbot with robustly flavoured smoked eel pudding, tender deep-fried frog's leg, parsley root purée and verjuice. Starters show the same sort of mixings and matchings: black pudding Scotch eggs (rich and runny quail's eggs) served on tomato ketchup and mushroom relish, or home-smoked mackerel with poached rhubarb and a smear of mustard cream. Beetroot and chocolate cakes prove to be a successful combination, served with beetroot-flavoured marshmallow, honey, hazelnuts, caraway and pollen.

Chef Laurence Tottingham, Mary-Ellen McTague **Owner** Laurence Tottingham, Mary-Ellen McTague **Times** 12-2.30/6-9.30 Closed Xmas, 1st week Jan, Sun-Mon, L Tue-Thu **Prices** Fixed L 2 course £20, Tasting menu £70-£90, Service optional, Groups min 6 service 10% **Wines** 100 bottles over £30, 25 bottles under £30, 15 by glass **Notes** Fixed D 4/6 course £40/£55, Tasting menu 9/12 course, Sunday L, Vegetarian menu **Seats** 34 **Children** Portions, Menu **Parking** On street

ROCHDALE Map 16 SD81

Nutters

◉◉ Modern British V NOTABLE WINE LIST ☺

Gifted chef creatively cooking with Lancashire ingredients

☎ 01706 650167
Edenfield Rd, Norden OL12 7TT
e-mail: enquiries@nuttersrestaurant.com
dir: From Rochdale take A680 signed Blackburn. Edenfield Rd on right on leaving Norden

Andrew Nutter is no shy and retiring wallflower and his restaurant (family owned and run) in a rather grand 18th-century manor house in six acres of well-cared for parkland, does not want for personality either. The

continued

ROCHDALE *continued*

restaurant with its stone arches and high ceilings has bags of vitality and is the setting for some fine cooking with some excellent regional produce. There's no lack of fun and personality in the food, either, but first and foremost this is technically impressive and enjoyable stuff. Each dish is stamped with Nutter's personality and his take on classical and contemporary cooking, thus crispy Dingley Dell pork and apple beignets with bacon bits and golden delicious salsa might kick things off, before corn-fed chicken supreme with wild herb stuffing, potato 'hush puppy' and a yellow pepper and shallot dressing. For pudding, there is much fun to be had too; warm treacle tart, perhaps, served with baby Baileys profiteroles and rum and raisin ice cream. A vegetarian menu ensures everyone can come out to play, and there's a 'surprise' six-course gourmet menu if you're up for the adventure.

Chef Andrew Nutter **Owner** The Nutter family
Times 12-2/6.30-9.30 Closed 1-2 days after both Xmas & New Year, Mon **Prices** Fixed L 2 course fr £13.95, Starter £4.80-£9.50, Main £14.80-£23, Dessert £4.40-£7.80, Service optional, Groups min 8 service 10% **Wines** 107 bottles over £30, 90 bottles under £30, 9 by glass **Notes** Gourmet menu 6 course £42, Sunday L £23.50, Vegetarian menu, Dress restrictions, Smart casual, Civ Wed 120 **Seats** 143, Pr/dining room 30 **Children** Portions, Menu **Parking** 100

The Peacock Room

◉◉ Modern British

Luxe art-deco look and smart modish food

☎ 01706 368591
Crimble Hotel, Crimble Ln, Bamford OL11 4AD
e-mail: crimble@thedeckersgroup.com
web: www.thedeckersgroup.com
dir: M62 junct 20 follow signs for Blackburn, left onto B6222 (Bury road) contine for 1m Crimble Lane on left

Within the Crimble Hotel, dating from the 17th century, the ornate Peacock Room restaurant makes a powerful visual statement with its art-deco styling recalling the days of the great ocean liners. Indeed the opulent chandeliers hail from a cruise ship and sit nicely with the lush furnishings, swag curtains, gold effect cornicing, mirrored ceiling and tables dressed in their best whites. Outside the eponymous peacocks strut their stuff in the grounds. The passion in the kitchen shines through in contemporary British dishes such as hand-dived scallops with a caper and angelica purée, cauliflower and raisin

dressing, or an aesthetically pleasing main-course Texal lamb four ways, served with roasted pumpkin, roasted seeds, chervil root fondants and rosemary jus. Among fish main courses might be fillet of halibut with roast garlic risotto, pak choi, soused cherry tomatoes and golden tomato vierge, and among desserts perhaps a Manchester tart with raspberry sorbet.

The Peacock Room

Times 12-2.30/6.30-10 Closed Mon-Tue, L Sat, D Sun

WIGAN · Map 15 SD50

Macdonald Kilhey Court Hotel

◉ Modern British

Peaceful garden views and sound cooking

☎ 01257 472100
Chorley Rd, Standish WN1 2XN
e-mail: general.kilheycourt@macdonald-hotels.co.uk
web: www.macdonaldhotels.co.uk
dir: M6 junct 27, through village of Standish. Take B5239, left onto A5106, hotel on right

The hotel dates from 1884, when it was built by a local brewer, and its Laureate Restaurant occupies a large conservatory on three levels, its atmosphere relaxed and informal, overlooking the hotel's grounds. The kitchen puts fresh seasonal produce to good effect in such tried-and-trusted classics as Stornoway black pudding with caramelised apple and bacon salad, or shrimp cocktail with Marie Rose sauce, then coq au vin, steaks from the grill or pan-fried fillet of sea bass with seasonal vegetables. Vegetarians can go for pumpkin ravioli with sage butter, and to finish, we're all in it together with Eton Mess and crème brûlée.

Times 12.30-2.30/6.30-9.30 Closed L Sat

Wrightington Hotel & Country Club

◉ Modern International ◐

Unfussy cooking and top-notch leisure facilities

☎ 01257 425803
Moss Ln, Wrightington WN6 9PB
e-mail: info@bennettsrestaurant.com
dir: M6 junct 27, 0.25m W, hotel on right after church

The leisure and conference facilities place the modern Wrightington Hotel firmly on the local map, with its location close to the M6 (albeit in a quiet countryside setting) delivering a steady flow of business customers and pleasure seekers. Bennett's Restaurant is a large open-plan space with darkwood tables, warm colours and a menu that includes a section called 'Lancashire Classics'. Duck liver parfait with brandied sultanas, tomato chutney and brioche gets the ball rolling, with an individual hotpot with carrot and swede purée flying the regional flag. Finish with a warm melting Belgium chocolate pudding.

Chef Ian Snape **Times** 6-9.30 Closed Sun, L all week **Prices** Starter £4.75-£5.75, Main £12.95-£22.95, Dessert £4.75-£5.75, Service added but optional 4% **Wines** 17 by glass **Notes** Vegetarian available, Dress restrictions, Smart casual **Seats** 75 **Children** Portions **Parking** 220

HAMPSHIRE

ALTON · Map 5 SU73

The Anchor Inn

◉◉ British ◐

Unspoilt country inn with a British (and sometimes Italian) flavour

☎ 01420 23261
Lower Froyle GU34 4NA
e-mail: info@anchorinnatlowerfroyle.co.uk
dir: From A31, turn off to Bentley

Dating back to the 16th century, The Anchor is a picturesque country inn in Lower Froyle, close to Alton. Open fireplaces and low beams are what to expect, plus a slate of smart bedrooms all named after war poets. Classical furnishings spruce up the restaurant, where pictures recalling the history of this country take pride of place. This is country pursuit territory, so you might work up an appetite with a bit of fly fishing and shooting before cosying up for some impressive British (ish) food. Local, seasonal ingredients crop up on the menu which incorporates some Italian influences and balances the flavours very well indeed. You might start with haricot beans on toast with chorizo, rocket and parmesan, then move on to Ryland lamb loin with roast beetroot and mash, flageolet bean and lamb shoulder crumble, and finish with sticky date pudding with fudge sauce and clotted cream.

Chef Kevin Chandler **Owner** The Millers Collection **Times** 12-2.30/6.30-9.30 Closed 25 Dec, D 26 Dec, 1 Jan **Prices** Prices not confirmed Service optional **Wines** 9 by glass **Notes** Vegetarian available, Civ Wed 60 **Seats** 70, Pr/dining room 20 **Children** Portions, Menu **Parking** 36

Save on Hotels. Book at theAA.com/hotel

HAMPSHIRE 187 ENGLAND

ANDOVER   Map 5 SU34

Esseborne Manor

@@ Modern British 🍴

Timeless country-house setting for updated classics

☎ 01264 736444
Hurstbourne Tarrant SP11 0ER
e-mail: info@esseborne-manor.co.uk
web: www.esseborne-manor.co.uk
dir: Halfway between Andover & Newbury on A343, just
1m N of Hurstbourne Tarrant

In curvaceous countryside high above the beautiful
Bourne Valley, Esseborne Manor is a pleasantly intimate
and comfortingly traditional take on the country house
idiom. The Victorian house has the feel of a private home,
albeit a rather plush and handsomely decorated one, with
an opulent dining room where walls are hung with red
and gold fabric, and immaculately-laid tables look
through large sash windows to the gardens. A herb
garden plays its part in furnishing the kitchen's needs,
together with quality materials sourced largely from
Hampshire and Berkshire. The cooking tacks an
ambitious modern course through a European-accented
repertoire of classic flavour combinations. Expect starters
along the lines of cauliflower soup with parmesan foam,
while main course delivers crisp belly, stuffed fillet and
breaded cheek of local pork, sage polenta chips and pear.

Chef Dennis Janssen **Owner** Ian Hamilton
Times 12-2/7-9.30 **Prices** Fixed L 2 course £15, Fixed D 3
course £30, Tasting menu £55, Starter £4.75-£6.50, Main
£12.50-£20, Dessert £5-£7, Service optional **Wines** 34
bottles over £30, 59 bottles under £30, 12 by glass
Notes Sunday L, Vegetarian available, Dress restrictions,
Smart dress, Civ Wed 100 **Seats** 35, Pr/dining room 80
Children Portions **Parking** 40

The Plough Inn

@@ Modern British NEW V 🍴

Gordon Ramsay protégé lands in Longparish

☎ 01264 720358
Longparish SP11 6PB
e-mail: eat@theploughinn.info

Villages don't come much more quintessentially English
than Longparish in the unspoilt Test Valley near Andover,
and pub food doesn't come an awful lot better than that
served at The Plough Inn. The creeper-clad old inn at the
heart of the village has been spruced up nicely by its new
owner, Gordon Ramsay protégé James Durrant - formerly
executive chef at Maze in London (see entry) - and these
days it goes for a minimalist look of whitewashed walls,
exposed beams, wooden floors, an open fire and unclothed
wooden tables. The original bar remains, along with a
small seating area for drinkers, but the majority of the
pub is given over to the business of eating from Durrant's
modern British, seasonally changing menu. Dishes are
built from top-notch ingredients and show no lack of skill
and a keen eye for presentation. A richly flavoured Cornish
fish soup with the traditional accompaniments of aioli,
croutons and grated cheese - this time local Lyburn Gold

- is a deeply satisfying way to start, before following on
with a sublimely tender braised shoulder of lamb along
with onion purée, red onions and a flavour-packed salt
marsh mutton shepherd's pie served in a mini lidded
casserole. If the weather is playing ball there's a lovely
garden for alfresco drinking and dining.

Chef James Durrant **Owner** James & Louise Durrant
Times 12-2.30/6-9.30 Closed D Sun **Prices** Starter
£6.50-£9, Main £12.50-£22, Dessert £5.50-£6.50, Service
optional **Wines** 19 bottles over £30, 14 bottles under £30,
11 by glass **Notes** Sunday L £13.50-£14.50, Vegetarian
menu **Seats** 48 **Children** Portions, Menu **Parking** 25

BARTON-ON-SEA   Map 5 SZ29

Pebble Beach

@ British 🍴

Upbeat brasserie cooking with a clifftop sun terrace

☎ 01425 627777
Marine Dr BH25 7DZ
e-mail: mail@pebblebeach-uk.com
dir: Follow A35 from Southampton onto A337 to New
Milton, turn left onto Barton Court Av to clifftop

The place to be seen in Barton is this modern clifftop
venue overlooking The Needles and the sea, where a local
in-crowd packs the spacious terrace with its broadly
parasoled tables on warmer days. Upbeat modern
brasserie cooking is the drill, incorporating plenty of
super-fresh fish, such as scallops with shredded parsnips
and curried apple purée, followed by John Dory with
broccoli gratin and almond tapenade, or brill roasted with
garlic and thyme. Meats might encompass slow-cooked
leg of lamb in Provençal herbs, tomato and garlic, or
chargrilled calf's liver and bacon with mash and onion
gravy, and proceedings end with the likes of chocolate
shortbread tart spiked with lime zest, served with mango
sorbet and a riot of superfluous sauces. The menu
helpfully suggests a different sweet wine as
accompaniment to each dessert. If you want to enjoy that
panorama a little longer you can book a room with a view
and stay overnight.

Chef Pierre Chevillard **Owner** Michael Caddy
Times 11-2.30/6-11 Closed D 25 Dec, 1 Jan **Prices** Fixed
L 2 course £24.50, Fixed D 3 course £28.50, Starter
£5.95-£11.50, Main £13.60-£25.70, Dessert £6.99,
Service optional, Groups min 10 service 10% **Wines** 2
bottles over £30, 52 bottles under £30, 16 by glass
Notes Sunday L, Vegetarian available, Dress restrictions,
Smart casual, no beach wear **Seats** 90, Pr/dining room 8
Children Portions **Parking** 20

BASINGSTOKE   Map 5 SU65

Apollo Hotel

@ International

Smart and stylish modern hotel dining

☎ 01256 796700
Aldermaston Roundabout RG24 9NU
e-mail: admin@apollo-hotels.com
web: www.apollohotels.com
dir: From M3 junct 6 follow ring road N & signs for
Aldermaston/Newbury. Then follow A340 (Aldermaston)
signs, at rdbt take 5th exit onto Popley Way. Hotel
entrance 1st left

Handy for the M3, doing business, or whatever brings you
to the Basingstoke area, the luxurious modern Apollo
Hotel also offers gastronomic satisfaction in its fine-
dining Vespers restaurant. It is a clean-lined
contemporary space furnished with curvaceous wood and
leather chairs at linen-clothed tables, neutral tones, and
vibrant modern abstract art to inject a note of contrasting
colour. In case the name isn't enough of a clue, it is a
dinner-only venue, where the kitchen delivers a please-all
repertoire of inventive modern dishes. Smoked lamb loin
with feta cheese, green bean salad and raspberry
dressing could give way to fillet steak with smoked garlic
béarnaise, thyme-roasted potatoes and oxtail jus. After
that, apple pannacotta with cinnamon doughnut and
butterscotch sauce might provide a satisfying finish.

Times 12-3/7-11 Closed BHs, 1 Jan, L Mon-Sat

Audleys Wood

@@ Modern British 🍴

Local ingredients cooked with flair

☎ 01256 817555 & 0845 072 7405
Alton Rd RG25 2JT
e-mail: audleyswood@handpicked.co.uk
web: www.handpickedhotels.co.uk/thesimondsroom
dir: M3 junct 6. From Basingstoke take A339 towards
Alton, hotel on right

As its name might hint, Audleys Wood Hotel is surrounded
by woodland, but the Victorian country house also comes
with its own seven acres of well-kept grounds, and the
all-round appeal of an upmarket operation run with style
and thoroughly contemporary levels of service. The fine-
dining Simonds Room provides an impressive setting
with a contemporary sheen to go with its period oak
panelling - recycled, so it is said, from Tewkesbury Abbey.
A Gallic undercurrent drifts through the modern English
cooking, but that said, local Hampshire ingredients are
the kitchen's building blocks and they are handled with
seasonal sensitivity and technical aplomb. Go for the
'Taste of Hampshire' menu, and the exact provenance of
the principal components is spelled out in detail. There's
no lack of creativity either: confit rainbow trout might
start things off in the company of quinoa, celeriac, and
sea urchin and cumin velouté, while mains could see
noisette of new season lamb partnered by pea cannelloni,
fricassée of sweetbreads and cockles, and beans. Fishy

continued

BASINGSTOKE *continued*

ideas might run to roast turbot with ratte potatoes, crab and spring onion beignets, samphire, and oyster and sorrel velouté, while desserts such as New Forest rhubarb and custard stick with the local theme.

Chef Adam Fargin **Owner** Hand Picked Hotels **Times** 7-9 Closed Sun-Mon, L all week **Prices** Prices not confirmed Service optional **Wines** 70 bottles over £30, 9 bottles under £30, 18 by glass **Notes** Vegetarian available, Civ Wed 100 **Seats** 20, Pr/dining room 40 **Parking** 70

Basingstoke Country Hotel

◎ Modern European

Good simple cooking in country hotel

☎ 01256 764161
Scures Hill, Nately Scures, Hook RG27 9JS
e-mail: basingstokecountry.reception@puma hotels.co.uk
web: www.pumahotels.co.uk
dir: On A30 between Nateley Scures & Hook

A contemporary hotel and country club in four acres of Hampshire countryside just off the M3, the Basingstoke Country Hotel has broad appeal. If you're here for the spa, a business meeting or such like, take time to eat in the hotel's Scures Brasserie. The room won't win any style awards but it is a bright space with a lack of pretension - no starchy tablecloths here. The team in the kitchen takes a classical approach but the food is not stuck in the past. Take a starter of cured salmon and crab, for example, which comes with avocado cream and pickled fennel to bolster its impact. Next up, slow-roasted pork belly, the fat perfectly rendered, comes with soft and tender braised belly and a black pudding bonbon. Dessert might serve up a lemon posset complete with a chocolate cookie.

Chef Corrie Barnard **Owner** Puma Hotels **Times** 7-10 Closed 23-27 Dec, L all week **Prices** Fixed D 3 course £21.50-£30.50, Starter £5.25-£8.95, Main £15.25-£21.25, Dessert £5.95-£8.95, Service optional **Wines** 15 bottles over £30, 47 bottles under £30, 12 by glass **Notes** Vegetarian available, Dress restrictions, Smart casual, no shorts, Civ Wed 120 **Seats** 85 **Children** Portions, Menu **Parking** 200

Oakley Hall Hotel

◎◎ Modern British ◒

Modern brasserie cooking and Jane Austen connections

☎ 01256 783350
Rectory Rd, Oakley RG23 7EL
e-mail: enquiries@oakleyhall-park.com
web: www.oakleyhall-park.com
dir: M3 junct 7, follow Basingstoke signs. In 500yds before lights turn left onto A30 towards Oakley, immediately right onto unclass road towards Oakley. In 3m left at T-junct into Rectory Rd. Left onto B3400. Hotel signed 1st on left

The grand old house - built in 1795 and extended in the 19th century as was the wont of the Victorians - presents a handsome face to the world. It has literary associations, for it was once owned by friends of Jane Austen, who lived in a nearby village. These days in its life as a luxury hotel it has plenty to offer the modern guest, not least in the form of the Winchester Restaurant, a modish space with banquette seating, wall mirrors and unclothed tables. The kitchen turns out some nicely contemporary food, so Thai-spiced brown crabcake with coriander mayo and mooli salad might compete for your attention with pan-fried pork belly with garlic flageolet beans and apple purée among first courses. Follow on, perhaps, with roasted sea bass with turnip gratin, Orange Beauty scallops and vanilla emulsion, and finish in the comfort zone with treacle tart with stem ginger ice cream.

Chef Justin Mundy **Owner** Jon Huxford **Times** 12-2/7-9.30 **Prices** Prices not confirmed Service included **Wines** 8 by glass **Notes** Sunday L, Vegetarian available, Dress restrictions, Smart, no jeans or T-shirts, Civ Wed 100 **Seats** 40, Pr/dining room 200 **Children** Portions, Menu **Parking** 100

BAUGHURST   Map 5 SU56

The Wellington Arms

◎◎ Modern British ◒

Good pub food crafted from the most local of local produce

☎ 0118 982 0110
Baughurst Rd RG26 5LP
e-mail: hello@thewellingtonarms.com
dir: M4 junct 12 follow Newbury signs on A4. At rdbt left signed Aldermaston. Through Aldermaston. Up hill, at 2nd rdbt 2nd exit signed Baughurst, left at T-junct, pub 1m on left

With its neatly trimmed bushes and unassuming elegance, this place certainly looks like a much loved English pub. That's not the half of it, though, for the dedication and passion of its hands-on owners, Simon Page and Jason King, runs deep. Their desire to be sustainable extends to recycling every conceivable item and you need only look in the garden and paddock to see their passion for provenance - Tamworth pigs, rare-breed Longwool sheep, chickens, bees, vegetables and herbs for

the pot are all present and correct. And what they can't produce themselves is sourced with genuine care. Inside it's traditional and charming, more food destination than boozer, and blackboards display what delights lie ahead. Terrine of rabbit and wood pigeon with tomato chutney and grilled toast is a robust and well-made beginning, whilst main-course gurnard comes with lentils and sautéed spinach. It is not complicated stuff, but just what you want to eat. For dessert, baked vanilla sponge with home-made custard is gloriously light and satisfying.

Chef Jason King **Owner** Simon Page & Jason King **Times** 12-2.30/6.30-9.30 Closed D Sun **Prices** Prices not confirmed Service added but optional 10% **Wines** 45 bottles over £30, 21 bottles under £30, 9 by glass **Notes** Sunday L, Vegetarian available **Seats** 34, Pr/dining room 20 **Children** Portions **Parking** 25

BEAULIEU   Map 5 SU30

Beaulieu Hotel

◎ British ◒

Contemporary British cooking at a New Forest country house

☎ 023 8029 3344
Beaulieu Rd SO42 7YQ
e-mail: beaulieu@newforesthotels.co.uk
web: www.newforesthotels.co.uk
dir: On B3056 between Lyndhurst & Beaulieu. Near Beaulieu Road railway station

A former coaching inn standing on open heathland in the New Forest, the Beaulieu Hotel is just the place for an escape to landscapes where wild ponies outnumber the hikers. There's no lack of grandeur in the smart country-house interiors, while the cream and lemon-panelled Exbury dining room is a handsome space with French windows opening onto the patio where you can dine alfresco overlooking the landscaped gardens when the weather plays ball. A well thought-out menu delivers up-to-date compositions built on the eminently sound foundations of well-sourced local ingredients, thus Hampshire pigeon breast might share a plate with blue cheese dauphinoise and pear, ahead of a three-way presentation of local free-range pork, comprising belly, tenderloin and hock with apple purée. Desserts take the classic route of crème brûlée, or apple tarte Tatin with Bramley apple sorbet.

Chef Michael Mckell **Owner** New Forest Hotels plc **Times** 7-9 Closed L all week **Prices** Starter £4.50-£7.95, Main £16-£21.45, Dessert £4.50-£6.50, Service optional **Wines** 8 bottles over £30, 30 bottles under £30, 8 by glass **Notes** Vegetarian available, Civ Wed 300 **Seats** 60, Pr/dining room 80 **Children** Portions, Menu **Parking** 60

The Montagu Arms Hotel

◎◎◎ *– see opposite*

Save on Hotels. Book at **theAA.com/hotel**

HAMPSHIRE 189 **ENGLAND**

BOTLEY   Map 5 SU51

Macdonald Botley Park, Golf & Spa

Modern British, European

Simple, honest cooking in relaxed hotel

☎ 01489 780888
Winchester Rd, Boorley Green SO32 2UA
e-mail: botleypark@macdonald-hotels.co.uk
web: www.macdonald-hotels.co.uk/botleypark
dir: M27 junct 7, A334 towards Botley. At 1st rdbt left, past M&S store, over the next 5 mini rdbts. At 6th mini rdbt turn right. In 0.5m hotel on left

Botley Park is a sprawling modern country hotel in 176 acres of landscaped grounds just a short hop from Southampton Airport and the M3. When you have worked up an appetite on its 18-hole championship golf course and steamed away the stress in the spa, the Winchester Restaurant offers a smart contemporary setting for an uncomplicated repertoire of unpretentious cooking. Expect well-sourced, high-quality ingredients in starters such as Stornoway black pudding with caramelised apple and bacon salad, followed by a prime slab of Scottish steak from the grill, or slow-roasted shoulder of lamb with boulangère potatoes and ratatouille. End with the comfort of fig sponge pudding with walnut praline and crème anglaise.

Times 12.30-2.30/7-9.45 Closed L Sat

BRANSGORE   Map 5 SZ19

The Three Tuns

British, European

Appealing varied menu in a traditional thatched inn

☎ 01425 672232
Ringwood Rd BH23 8JH
e-mail: threetunsinn@btconnect.com
web: www.threetunsinn.com
dir: On A35 at junct for Walkford/Highcliffe follow Bransgore signs, 1.5m, restaurant on left

The weather might help you decide: is it a drink in the oak-beamed snug bar or out on the terrace surrounded by mature trees? This traditional 17th-century thatched inn has bags of character and country charm, and a long menu that can doubtless meet your needs whatever the time of day; there's a good showing of regional ingredients, too. Whether you're on the look-out for a thick-cut sandwich, light salad, something traditional like fish and chips, or the more modish winter squash risotto, the kitchen can sort you out. There's also the likes of calves' liver with apple, bacon and mash, alongside pan-fried Mudeford sea bass with roast chervil root, porcini mushrooms, shaved fennel, truffle, red wine zabaglione, New Forest mushroom dust and dauphinoise potatoes, and puddings run from quince turnover with maple pear and crème fraîche to New Forest ice creams and sorbets.

Chef Colin Nash **Owner** Nigel Glenister
Times 12-2.15/6-9.15 Closed 25-26 & 31 Dec
Prices Starter £4.95-£9, Main £9.95-£22.95, Dessert £6-£8.95, Service optional **Wines** 11 by glass
Notes Sunday L, Vegetarian available, Dress restrictions, Smart casual **Seats** 60, Pr/dining room 50
Children Portions **Parking** 50

The Montagu Arms Hotel

BEAULIEU   MAP 5 SU30

Modern French V

Log fires, oak panels and local ingredients in a traditional country house

☎ 01590 612324
Palace Ln SO42 7ZL
e-mail: reservations@montaguarmshotel.co.uk
web: www.montaguarmshotel.co.uk
dir: From M27 junct 2 take A326 & B3054 for Beaulieu

Deep in the New Forest, and perfectly placed for the fabled motor museum, The Montagu Arms is a 17th-century country house with poignantly pretty gardens, and a sense of unabashed traditionalism throughout. It's been a hotel for two centuries, although the present façade dates back only to the 1880s. In the colder months, they bank up the log-fires so you can feel truly bedded in against the elements. The range of dining options takes in Monty's Inn, where pub stalwarts are served in a rustic atmosphere, while the true business of gastronomy goes on in the elegant Terrace restaurant, where an old-school look of oak panelling and crisp table linen complements the alluring views over the gardens. Matthew Tomkinson is an apostle of localism, where 'local' means starting with the hotel's own kitchen garden and chicken coop, whence vegetables, herbs and fresh eggs issue forth. For much of the rest, 'the New Forest is my larder,' Tomkinson declares, with game and pork sourced within its boundaries, as well as foraged ingredients, while fish is hauled up from the South Coast. Dishes are in the modern French mould, unafraid of a certain level of complexity, but always cleverly managing to maintain balance. Starting things off might be a fascinating pairing of pork belly with sautéed squid, accompanied by roast pumpkin and toasted peanuts, while mains offer well-timed sea bass with artichokes and home-cured ham in red wine sauce, or roast saddle, confit belly and crisp-fried sweetbread of lamb, with goats' curd and capers. A separate vegetarian menu isn't all goats' cheese and butternut squash, but might take in roasted garlic gnocchi with romaine and preserved lemon, followed by lusciously caramelised onion tarte Tatin with sautéed artichokes, cured tomatoes and more onions pickled in beer. Finish with passionfruit and white chocolate cheesecake, served with orange sorbet.

Chef Matthew Tomkinson **Owner** Greenclose Ltd, Mr Leach **Times** 12-2.30/7-9.30 Closed Mon, L Tue
Prices Fixed L 2 course £22.50, Fixed D 3 course £65, Tasting menu £85-£160, Service optional **Wines** 12 by glass **Notes** D 3 course ALC £70, Sunday L, Vegetarian menu, Dress restrictions, Smart casual **Seats** 60, Pr/dining room 32 **Children** Portions **Parking** 45

BROCKENHURST — Map 5 SU30

The Balmer Lawn Hotel

Modern British

Fine dining at grand New Forest hotel

☎ 01590 623116 & 625725
Lyndhurst Rd SO42 7ZB
e-mail: info@balmerlawnhotel.com
dir: Take A337 towards Brockenhurst, hotel on left after
'Welcome to Brockenhurst' sign

This imposing pavillion-style Victorian hunting lodge
turned country hotel has hosted prime ministers and
presidents over the years, no doubt drawn by its charming
New Forest setting. Reinvented with panache for the
modern world, the friendly, family-run operation aims
more at pampering or business these days, with its
excellent spa, sports and conference facilities.
Beresford's restaurant is the fine-dining option, an
impressive, grandly-proportioned space done out with
understated contemporary style - high-backed black
leather seats at unclothed darkwood tables, and a warm
palette of toffee and chocolate. The kitchen deals in
modern cooking with a healthy showing of prime-quality,
often local, materials. Seared scallops matched with
breaded Romsey pork belly and black pudding, and apple
and vanilla sauce opens the show, ahead of partridge
stuffed with Madeira-marinated prunes and chestnuts,
and braised Puy lentils, soured white cabbage, and
celeriac purée. To round it all off, there's classic apple
tarte Tatin with vanilla sauce.

Chef Jim Wright **Owner** Mr C Wilson
Times 12.30-2.30/7-9.30 **Prices** Starter £7.50-£10, Main
£17-£20, Dessert £7.50-£10, Service added but optional
10%, Groups min 10 service 12.5% **Wines** 30 bottles over
£30, 21 bottles under £30, 9 by glass **Notes** Tasting
menu 8 course, 2 for 1 L Mon-Fri, Sunday L, Vegetarian
available, Dress restrictions, Smart casual, no jeans or
trainers, Civ Wed 120 **Seats** 80, Pr/dining room 100
Children Portions, Menu **Parking** 100

Careys Manor Hotel & Senspa

Thai V

Imaginative cooking in the New Forest

☎ 01590 623551
Lyndhurst Rd SO42 7RH
e-mail: zengarden@senspa.co.uk
web: www.thezengarden.co.uk
dir: M27 junct 2, follow Fawley/A326 signs. Continue over
3 rdbts, at 4th rdbt right lane signed Lyndhurst/A35.
Follow A337 (Lymington/Brockenhurst)

Careys Manor, the original building dating from 1888, is
in a delightful spot in the New Forest. It has three
eateries: a French bistro, the Thai Zen Garden (see entry),
and the cream of the crop, the Manor Restaurant, where
the skilled kitchen team applies some culinary wizardry to
fresh seasonal produce. Seared pigeon breast with red
wine reduction, sweet potato and cumin purée and rocket
sounds mainstream enough, but an alternative may be
butter-poached sea trout with seaweed-marinated mooli

and cucumber dressing. Technical precision is evident
throughout, and combinations thoughtful. Thus, confit
pork belly comes with black pudding purée, potato gratin
and a sage jus, and slices of roast Dorset rump of veal
are plated on spinach and accompanied by pommes
Anna, caramelised onion purée and rich thyme-infused
gravy. Fish gets a decent showing: perhaps glazed
salmon fillet creatively partnered by saffron gratin with
kale, caper and raisin purée, prawn shavings and lemon
butter. Bread and extras get nods of approval, and
desserts are as well made as everything else, among
them perhaps honey parfait with raspberry sorbet.

Chef Chris Wheeldon, Thosaporn Wongsasube
Owner Greenclose Ltd **Times** 12-2.30/7-10 Closed D Mon
Prices Prices not confirmed Service optional **Wines** 9
bottles over £30, 12 bottles under £30, 8 by glass
Notes Vegetarian available, Vegetarian menu **Seats** 50,
Pr/dining room 12 **Parking** 20

The Pig

British V

Home-grown and foraged food in a New Forest hotel

☎ 01590 622354
Beaulieu Rd SO42 7QL
e-mail: info@thepighotel.com
dir: M27 junct 2, follow A326 Lyndhurst, then A337
Brockenhurst onto B3055 Beaulieu Road. 1m on left up
private road

Snuggling deep in the New Forest is a flagship venue for
the brave new world of British gastronomy, in which chefs
get out into the wilds to forage for some of their
ingredients, grow a great deal more in a walled kitchen
garden, and source most of the rest from within a 25-
mile radius. That it proves such a winning formula is
heartening indeed, especially as it's presented here with
no over-earnest preachiness. The fruit cages, herb and
veg patches and the little garden shed that does duty as
a smoke-house are worth a look, and the interior styling
with green walls, a Kew Garden's worth of potted plants,
and mounted boars' heads, is agreeably quirky.
Memorable dishes include a starter plate of mixed garden
veg fritters with lemon and shallot mayo and crispy tripe,
Gloucestershire Old Spot pork chop with apple and fennel
mash, wilted greens and grain mustard sauce, and
seared mackerel with beetroot carpaccio in lemon
verbena vinaigrette, scattered with nasturtiums. To
finish, a pot of lemon posset is garnished with candied
orange zest and wonderful home-made biscuits.

Chef James Golding **Owner** Robin Hutson
Times 12-2.30/6.30-9.30 **Prices** Starter £5-£16, Main
£14-£26, Dessert £7, Service added but optional 12.5%
Wines 59 bottles over £30, 38 bottles under £30, 14 by
glass **Notes** Sunday L £17.50, Vegetarian menu **Seats** 85,
Pr/dining room 14 **Children** Portions, Menu **Parking** 40

Rhinefield House

Modern British

**Well-handled resonant flavours in eye-popping
Victorian mansion**

☎ 01590 622922
Rhinefield Rd SO42 7QB
e-mail: rhinefieldhouse@handpicked.co.uk
web: www.handpickedhotels.co.uk/rhinefieldhouse
dir: M27 junct, A337 to Lyndhurst, then A35 W towards
Christchurch. 3.5m, left at sign for Rhinefield House.
Hotel 1.5m on right

Built in 1887 in a mix of Tudor and Gothic styles,
Rhinefield House has been superbly updated into a luxury
hotel with leisure and spa facilities. The degree of
craftsmanship that went into the interior is mind-
blowing: the Alhambra Room, for instance, modelled on
Granada's palace, took two years to build, while the
restaurant, under its ornate ceiling, is dominated by a
magnificent carving of the Spanish Armada. The menu is
a slate of thoroughly modern ideas, with foams a
favoured component of many dishes - a subtle one of
apple for a starter of crab risotto, for instance - and the
cooking is marked out by some vibrant combinations,
with seared scallops in another starter paired with pork
belly carpaccio and Granny Smith dressing. Timings are
well judged, so roast rack of lamb is tender and pink and
wrapped in black pudding, which seems subdued
compared with the forthright tastes of cod fillet with
clams, Caesar sauce, red pepper mousse and almonds.
End with the comparatively mundane strawberry sorbet
with lemon meringue.

Chef Craig Dunn **Owner** Hand Picked Hotels Ltd
Times 12-5/7-10 **Prices** Prices not confirmed Service
optional **Wines** 18 by glass **Notes** Sunday L, Vegetarian
available, Dress restrictions, Smart casual preferred, Civ
Wed 130 **Seats** 58, Pr/dining room 12 **Children** Portions,
Menu **Parking** 150

The Zen Garden Restaurant

Thai NEW V

Vibrant Thai cooking in a spa

☎ 01590 623219 & 623551
**The SenSpa, Careys Manor Hotel, Lyndhurst Rd
SO42 7RH**
e-mail: zengarden@senspa.co.uk
dir: A337 from Lyndhurst signed Lymington,
Brockenhurst, within Careys Manor Hotel

If you go down to the woods today you're in for a big
surprise, for within the SenSpa at Careys Manor Hotel in
the New Forest is a smart Thai restaurant. Perhaps not a
huge surprise these days, but a pleasing one nonetheless.

Save on Hotels. Book at theAA.com/hotel

HAMPSHIRE 191 ENGLAND

The Zen Garden Restaurant looks the part with its gold columns, bamboo ceiling and darkwood tables and chairs, and there's an ethical approach when it comes to sourcing materials for the traditional menus. Start with something like soft-shelled crab - perfectly cooked - with a Thai salad and a rich, sticky sauce, or taro fritters with a red curry paste and lime leaves. There are soups such as the classic tom yam, and stir-fried dishes such as goong phad prik (tiger prawns with chilli, peppers, red cabbage and spring onion). Beef sirloin comes in a main course with a spicy marinade, crushed roasted rice and a papaya salad with chilli, mint and tamarind.

Chef Thosporn Wongsasube **Owner** Greenclose Ltd **Times** 12-2.30/7-10 Closed D Mon **Prices** Fixed L 2 course £19.20-£26.45, Fixed D 3 course £26.15-£34.40, Tasting menu £34.50, Starter £6.25-£9.50, Main £12.95-£16.95, Dessert £6.95-£7.95 **Wines** 10 bottles over £30, 12 bottles under £30, 9 by glass **Notes** Sunday L, Vegetarian menu, Dress restrictions, Smart casual **Seats** 50, Pr/dining room 16 **Parking** 130

BROOK
Map 5 SU21

The Bell Inn

◉ Modern English

New Forest setting for brasserie-style cooking

☎ 023 8081 2214
SO43 7HE
e-mail: bell@bramshaw.co.uk
web: www.bellinnbramshaw.co.uk
dir: M27 junct 1 onto B3079, hotel 1.5m on right

Squirrelled away in the heart of the New Forest and part-owned by the Bramshaw Golf Club, The Bell is a handsome Georgian hotel and something of a '19th hole' for golf enthusiasts. A traditional vibe and original features grace the cosy bar, while the Oak Room restaurant aims for a more modern style, blending period character with a smart contemporary look. The kitchen takes a serious approach to keeping things local - much of the produce comes from the New Forest and game from their own estate, while fish is caught by day-boats on the coast nearby. Wherever you choose to sit, the accomplished brasserie-style output pleases all; think slow-cooked lamb rump served with gratin potatoes and ratatouille to a selection of steaks from the grill, or from the sea, a fillet of Lymington sea bass with mussel and clam chowder.

Chef Gavin Sinden **Owner** Crosthwaite Eyre family **Times** 12-2.30/6.30-9.30 **Prices** Starter £5.95-£8.25, Main £13.25-£23.95, Dessert £5.50-£6.50, Service optional **Wines** 13 bottles over £30, 20 bottles under £30, 12 by glass **Notes** Sunday L, Vegetarian available **Seats** 50, Pr/dining room 40 **Children** Portions, Menu **Parking** 40

BURLEY
Map 5 SU20

Moorhill House Hotel

◉ Traditional & Modern British ☺

Modern cooking with a local flavour in the New Forest

☎ 01425 403285
BH24 4AG
e-mail: moorhill@newforesthotels.co.uk
web: www.newforesthotels.co.uk
dir: Exit A31 signed Burley Drive, through village, turn right opposite cricket pitch

A drive through the ancient woodland of the New Forest is an unparalleled scene-setter, and as the sight of ponies roaming the grounds gives way to croquet and badminton on the hotel lawns, it's clear you've left city life far behind. You can take a retrospective look over the grounds and the woods from the raised patio that the Burley Restaurant gives on to. Ben Cartwright enthusiastically utilises local produce here, including the famed Burley cider, which might be the foundation of a sauce to go with slow-roast pork belly. Modern classic dishes are cooked with confidence and brio, as witness scallops with butternut squash purée and broccoli tempura, served on a slate, and seared haunch of venison with caramelised red cabbage in cranberry jus. Finish with pecan pie, which comes with orange ice cream and vanilla sauce, but note also the tempting selection of fine New Forest cheeses, served with fruity chutney.

Chef Ben Cartwright **Owner** New Forest Hotels **Times** 12-2/6.30-9 Closed L Mon-Sat **Prices** Starter £4.50-£6, Main £15.50-£19.50, Dessert £5-£7.95, Service optional **Wines** 3 bottles over £30, 28 bottles under £30, 8 by glass **Notes** Sunday L, Vegetarian available, Dress restrictions, Smart casual, Civ Wed 90 **Seats** 60, Pr/dining room 40 **Children** Portions, Menu **Parking** 50

CADNAM
Map 5 SZ21

Bartley Lodge Hotel

◉ Traditional British ☺

Elegant surroundings for country-house cooking

☎ 023 8081 2248
Lyndhurst Rd SO40 2NR
e-mail: bartley@newforesthotels.co.uk
web: www.newforesthotels.co.uk
dir: M27 junct 1, A337, follow signs for Lyndhurst. Hotel on left

Part of the small family of New Forest Hotels, Bartley Lodge conforms to the group's format of country retreats tucked away in the forested tracts of Hampshire. A long drive meanders through landscaped grounds to the door of the 18th-century hunting lodge, which has been extensively made-over and spruced-up in recent years whilst leaving its ample period character intact. Housed in the original library, the Crystal Restaurant (named presumably after the elegant centrepiece chandelier) is a spacious, high-ceilinged room done out in Wedgwood blue and gold - a setting that sits well with the repertoire of straightforward country-house cooking. Duck liver

parfait with red onion marmalade is a trusty starter, while main course delivers lamb two ways - rare roasted and slow-braised - served with dauphinoise potatoes and red cabbage. At dessert, a classic vanilla crème brûlée comes with lavender and crab apple jelly and lime shortbread.

Chef Stuart White **Owner** New Forest Hotels **Times** 12-2/7-9 Closed L Mon-Sat **Prices** Starter £5-£9, Main £15-£19.50, Dessert £5-£6.50, Service optional **Wines** 8 bottles over £30, 32 bottles under £30, 8 by glass **Notes** Sunday L £19.95, Vegetarian available, Dress restrictions, Smart casual, Civ Wed 80 **Seats** 60 **Children** Portions, Menu **Parking** 90

DOGMERSFIELD
Map 5 SU75

Four Seasons Hotel Hampshire

◉◉ Modern French, European V ☺

Modish regionally-inspired cooking in a grand Georgian manor

☎ 01252 853000 & 853100
Dogmersfield Park, Chalky Ln RG27 8TD
e-mail: reservations.ham@fourseasons.com
dir: M3 junct 5 onto A287 Farnham. After 1.5m take left to Dogmersfield, hotel 0.6m on left

The Hampshire address in the Four Seasons portfolio is all you might hope it to be: grand, glamorous and luxurious. The house certainly makes a fine first impression with its red-brick Georgian handsomeness, and the Dogmersfield Estate provides a lush English backdrop for it all. Inside it's all epic period detail and slick contemporary design, including in the Seasons restaurant, with its tables dressed in white linen and polished service. Here the kitchen delivers modish cooking based on a good deal of splendid Hampshire produce. Fridays are now dedicated to fresh fish and seafood, with a separate menu offering the likes of steamed cockles with chilli, or Lymington fisherman's pie with leeks and smoked haddock. Seafood still gets a look-in the rest of the week, but instead you might start with ham hock, foie gras and smoked partridge terrine with Jerusalem artichoke and raisin purée, followed by local lamb three ways (smoked shoulder, noisette and rack). There's a Taste of Hampshire tasting menu, too.

Chef Cyrille Pannier **Owner** Four Seasons Hotels & Resorts **Times** 6-10.30 Closed Mon, L Tue-Sat, D Sun **Prices** Fixed D 3 course £49, Tasting menu £55, Starter £11-£14, Main £22-£36, Dessert £9-£11, Service added but optional 12.5% **Wines** 75 bottles over £30, 15 by glass **Notes** Fixed D 5 course £55, Sunday L, Vegetarian menu, Dress restrictions, Smart casual **Seats** 100, Pr/dining room 24 **Children** Portions, Menu **Parking** 100

DROXFORD
Map 5 SU61

Bakers Arms

Traditional British

Favourites and fancier in a homely Hampshire pub

☎ 01489 877533
High St SO32 3PA
e-mail: adam@thebakersarmsdroxford.com
dir: Off A32

Droxford sits in the Meon Valley, within the boundaries of the South Downs National Park, an appealing little village with this equally appealing whitewashed local hostelry at its heart. A stag's head peers down from a wall hung with framed pictures of the place in bygone days, and the rustic furniture, blazing fires and merciful absence of muzak stamp the interior scene with the seal of authenticity. Good local beers and a menu of well-thought pub favourites such as chicken liver parfait, sausages and mash with onion gravy, and rice pudding with clotted cream seem to guarantee satisfaction. Things can get productively fancier too though, as in pigeon and smoked bacon salad with apple sauce, followed by seared sea bass with curly kale in lentil and herb dressing, with brilliant chips. Chunked-up poached pear on a caramel layer spooned over with creamy yoghurt is a harmonious finale. Don't miss the superb home-made fennel-seed bread.

Chef Richard Harrison, Adam Cordery **Owner** Adam & Anna Cordery **Times** 11.45-3/6-11 Closed Mon, D Sun **Prices** Fixed L 2 course £13, Fixed D 2 course £13, Starter £6.50-£7.50, Main £10.95-£18.95, Dessert £5.50-£6.50, Service optional, Groups min 8 service 10% **Wines** 12 bottles over £30, 23 bottles under £30, 10 by glass **Notes** Sunday L £14.95, Vegetarian available **Seats** 45 **Children** Portions **Parking** 30

EMSWORTH
Map 5 SU70

Fat Olives

British, Mediterranean

Locally-inspired modern cooking near the quay

☎ 01243 377914
30 South St PO10 7EH
e-mail: info@fatolives.co.uk
dir: In town centre, 1st right after Emsworth Square, 100yds towards the Quay. Restaurant on left with public car park opposite

Refurbishment has given a touch of contemporary comfort to this 17th-century fisherman's cottage about 25 yards from the quay. The kitchen remains as enthusiastic as ever, cooking everything on the premises from delicious bread to peanut butter ice cream (to accompany caramel mousse and a chocolate brownie) and buying its supplies from the local area. The menu is a slate of modern, successful ideas, from smoked trout, leek and potato terrine in a cress emulsion, or pig's head balanced by apple purée and slaw, to roast gurnard with a buttery sauce of sage and verjuice, served with cippolini onions and butternut squash, or the full-on flavours of roast pork loin with a black pudding faggot and quince and trotter sauce.

Chef Lawrence Murphy **Owner** Lawrence & Julia Murphy **Times** 12-2/7-9 Closed 1 wk Xmas, 1 wk Mar, 2 wks Jun, Sun-Mon **Prices** Fixed L 2 course fr £17.95, Starter £6.25-£10.75, Main £15.50-£27, Dessert £6.50-£7.95, Service optional, Groups min 8 service 10% **Wines** 23 bottles over £30, 24 bottles under £30, 8 by glass **Notes** Sat L no min age for children, Vegetarian available **Seats** 25 **Parking** Opposite restaurant

36 on the Quay

— see below

---

36 on the Quay

EMSWORTH
MAP 5 SU70

Modern British NOTABLE WINE LIST

Superlative cooking on Chichester Harbour

☎ 01243 375592 & 372257
47 South St PO10 7EG
e-mail: info@36onthequay.co.uk
dir: Last building on right in South St, which runs from square in centre of Emsworth

Ramon and Karen Farthing's exemplary restaurant with rooms occupies a 17th-century cottage right on the quayside looking out over Chichester Harbour. Under the Farthings' stewardship, 36 has rooted itself into the local gastronomic landscape for many years, and it's easy to see why: the waterside setting is a dream, the dining room is smartly neutral with local art on the walls, and should you want to stay over to indulge fully in the remarkably high-achieving cooking, the bedrooms are stylish boltholes. Ramon Farthing is the man in charge of the engine room, where confident, intricately-inventive modern ideas are the order of the day. It is no surprise that fish is high on the agenda on a choice of either set-price or full-works tasting menus: a starter of pan-seared scallops is matched with deeply-flavoured creamed fresh crab, the crunch of sugar snap peas, and chestnut mushrooms in a silky-smooth shellfish sabayon, while a magnificent piece of turbot plays the starring role in a main course, served alongside a punchy caponata, steamed leeks, nicely-caramelised roasted salsify, a basil and orange beignet, and light chicken infusion. It may sound a touch complex and labour-intensive, but the talented kitchen team develops and road tests its ideas to ensure that flavours are clearly delineated and sing together in harmony. By contrast, meat can receive more robust treatments: perhaps a two-way serving of veal, loin pan-roasted in hay and compressed breast with wild nettles, mousseline potatoes, charred Savoy cabbage heart and caramelised onion sauce. It all ends on a high note with a deconstructed take on apple pie with vanilla ice cream with pressed apple and apple parfait layered with disks of apple crisp, or there might be a five-part dessert that works a riff on lemon, for example. The final fanfare sounds for a wine list of great depth and interest with exciting bottles from around the world.

Chef Ramon Farthing, Gary Pearce **Owner** Ramon & Karen Farthing **Times** 12-2/7-9.30 Closed 1st 2/3 wks Jan, 1 wk end May & Oct, 25-26 Dec, Sun-Mon **Prices** Fixed L 2 course £23.95, Tasting menu £70, Service optional **Wines** 7 by glass **Notes** Tasting menu complete tables only Sun-Thu. ALC menu £57.95, Vegetarian available, Dress restrictions, Smart casual, no shorts **Seats** 45, Pr/dining room 12 **Children** Portions **Parking** Car park nearby

Solent Hotel & Spa

◎ British, European

Skillful cooking and wide-ranging menus

☎ 01489 880000
Rookery Av, Whiteley PO15 7AJ
e-mail: solent@shirehotels.com
web: www.shirehotels.com
dir: M27 junct 9, hotel on Solent Business Park

A modern hotel with spa facilities among meadows and woodland, The Solent's Terrace Restaurant is a dimly lit room, enhanced by candles, separated from the bar by an open fireplace; tables are clothed and correctly set, and the atmosphere is at the same time relaxed and formal. The longish and wide-ranging menu is likely to appeal to all-comers, with starters ranging from crispy Asian duck with watercress, cucumber and coriander salad, to prawn and lobster salad with Marie Rose sauce. Main courses can be reassuringly familiar - exemplary duck leg confit, its meat falling off the bone, with red wine jus, crisp potatoes and honey-infused carrots for instance - although the kitchen also presents more contemporary ideas, among them perhaps roast scallops with black pudding accompanied by pommes purée and red wine sauce. Finish with creamy, light and tangy lemon posset with seasonal berries and a spiced sugar cake, or sticky toffee pudding.

Chef Peter Williams **Owner** Shire Hotels
Times 12.15-2/7-9.30 Closed L Sat **Prices** Prices not confirmed Service optional **Wines** 15 by glass
Notes Sunday L, Vegetarian available, Dress restrictions, No T-shirts, Civ Wed 160 **Seats** 130, Pr/dining room 40 **Children** Portions, Menu **Parking** 200

Aviator

◎ Modern European ♨

Innovative food in a monument to wristwatches and flying

☎ 01252 555890
Farnborough Rd GU14 6EL
e-mail: brasserie@aviatorfarnborough.co.uk
web: www.aviatorfarnborough.co.uk
dir: A325 to Aldershot, continue for 3m. Hotel on right

The TAG company's contemporary hotel overlooking the airfield at Farnborough is oriented to the twin compass points of luxury timepieces (as in the eponymous wristwatch) and the great days of aviation, when nobody had heard of check-in queues and bag searches. In the glitzed-up surroundings, the décor in the Brasserie is

agreeably un-brasserie-like, all aubergine and pigeon-egg in its understatement, though the neatly framed portraits of screen stars add glamour. Steaks of locally farmed, dry-aged beef done on the Josper grill, served with triple-cooked chips, are a centrepiece, but there are some more innovative touches too. Crisp-skinned sea bass in a chowder of clams, fennel and star-anise is singing with aromatic intensity. That might follow a well-built terrine of rabbit and smoked bacon with liver parfait, apple and grape compôte, and crumbled salty pistachios, while the finale could be a bewitchingly scented lavender parfait with matching marshmallow, served with warm poached pear and green apple sorbet.

Chef Luk Wheaton **Owner** TAG **Times** 12-2.30/6-10.30
Prices Service optional **Wines** 44 bottles over £30, 18 bottles under £30, 16 by glass **Notes** Tasting menu available, Sunday L £18-£21, Vegetarian available, Civ Wed 90 **Seats** 150, Pr/dining room 8 **Children** Portions, Menu **Parking** 169

The Bugle

◎ Modern British

Contemporary food in lovingly-restored riverside inn

☎ 023 8045 3000
High St SO31 4HA
e-mail: manager@buglehamble.co.uk
dir: M27 junct 8 to Hamble-Le-Rice. In village follow signs to foreshore

With its textbook rustic interior of bare-brick walls, doughty timbers, flagstone and wooden floors, oak slab bar, and warming wood-burning stove, it's hard to believe that this historic waterside pub was once in line for demolition. Luckily, a campaign by villagers rescued the place, and English Heritage pitched in to oversee its restoration and put this well-loved inn firmly back at the heart of local life. Casual 'small plates' such as pork and chorizo sausage rolls or warm home-made scotch egg with celery salt give a taste of what's on offer. The menu is peppered with classic pub grub done right - local ale battered fish with triple-cooked chips, crushed peas and tartare sauce, as well as beef shin and Bowman Ale puff pastry pie with mash; elsewhere there could be slow-roasted pork belly teamed with celeriac gratin, spiced pear, and perry gravy. It's hard to pass by the local artisan cheeses, but the incurably sweet of tooth could head for bread-and-butter pudding with real custard. On a fine day, tuck in out on the terrace to a picturesque backdrop of boats nodding at anchor on the River Hamble.

Times 12-2.30/6-9.30 Closed 25 Dec

Langstone Hotel

◎◎ Modern British

Accomplished cooking in harbourside hotel

☎ 023 9246 5011
Northney Rd PO11 0NQ
e-mail: info@langstonehotel.co.uk
web: www.langstonehotel.co.uk
dir: From A27 signed Havant/Hayling Island follow A3023 across roadbridge onto Hayling Island & take sharp left on leaving bridge

Positioned on the north side of the island, views of the boats in the harbour and the estuary are big attractions at this up-to-date hotel with a buzzy, welcoming atmosphere. That said, it's the Langstone's Brasserie restaurant that elevates it above the opposition. With its circular design, high ceilings, large windows and a terrace, good views are guaranteed, and the modish food matches the unbuttoned, smart-casual setting. This is a kitchen that serves up an amuse-bouche - salmon and chorizo fishcake with a mango salsa, maybe - and delivers well-focused contemporary dishes. Pan-seared mackerel salad, for example, with braised chicory and crème fraîche, or chicken liver parfait with Earl Grey, parsley tea and toast soldiers. Ingredients are well sourced, including the pork belly served with black pudding beignets, pea purée, sage jus and apple foam, and for dessert, a chocolate orange fondant with white chocolate ice cream and orange tuile has excellent balance of flavours.

Chef James Parsons **Owner** BDL Hotels
Times 12.30-2/6.30-9.30 **Prices** Starter £7-£10, Main £12.50-£17, Dessert £6.95, Service optional **Wines** 17 bottles over £30, 24 bottles under £30, 7 by glass
Notes Sunday L £15.95-£18.95, Vegetarian available **Seats** 120, Pr/dining room 120 **Children** Portions, Menu **Parking** 132

Hartnett Holder & Co

Hartnett Holder & Co is a relaxed, stylish and comfortable upscale restaurant - full of character, yet unpretentious. Angela Hartnett and Lime Wood's Luke Holder, with their team, create locally sourced English dishes with a respectful nod to the seasons and to Italian culinary ideologies. This collaboration is reflected in their fresh, confident approach ensuring that this is "fun dining, not fine dining".

Hartnett and Holder's food is out-and-out British yet comes with the much loved Italian approach to eating – where sharing and provenance is everything. The style is chefs' home-cooked food not chefs' food cooked for restaurants. Both Angela and Luke are famed for their informal, grounded style of cooking and their respect for local produce.

Expect a menu of Italian influenced forest dishes with English classics, pulling together both chefs' much admired signature styles, which will remain constant and other dishes on the menu will change daily with forest and seasonality being the driver. Sample dishes include salad of duck egg, duck heart, toast and turnips or polenta ravioli with Dorset truffles and artichokes.

Lime Wood, Beaulieu Road, Lyndhurst, Hampshire SO43 7FZ • **Tel:** 02380 287177
Website: www.hhandco.co.uk • **Email:** info@hhandco.co.uk

Save on Hotels. Book at theAA.com/hotel

HAMPSHIRE 195 ENGLAND

LYMINGTON
Map 5 SZ39

Stanwell House Hotel

◉◉◉ Modern European ✱

Bright, modish cooking in boutique hotel

☎ 0844 704 6820
14-15 High St SO41 9AA
e-mail: enquiries@stanwellhouse.com
dir: M27 junct 1, follow signs to Lyndhurst into Lymington
centre & High Street

A classy boutique operation close by Lymington's quay on
the edge of the New Forest, Stanwell House occupies a
Georgian coaching inn that was once a finishing school
for young ladies, and now delivers refinement in a more
edible form. Two dining venues - Seafood at Stanwell
House and The Bistro - take advantage of excellent
Hampshire produce: as its name suggests, the former
deals in fishy tapas and piscine pleasures such as seared
fillet of brill with shellfish velouté, poached scallops and
tomato and basil, or monkfish in Parma ham with squid
ink risotto, pickled lemon, and saffron aïoli, while The
Bistro's four menus work a more wide-ranging remit of
contemporary European dishes in a glossy, modern space
overlooking the inviting terrace. Here, you might start
with haggis ravioli with braised cabbage, whisky foam
and veal jus, and follow with steaks from the grill, or
cheek, loin and belly of pork with pickled carrots, haricot
beans and orange oil.

Chef Mr Stuart White **Owner** Mrs V Crowe, Mr R Milton
Times 12-3/6-10 **Prices** Prices not confirmed Service
included **Notes** Sunday L, Vegetarian available, Civ Wed
70 **Seats** 70, Pr/dining room 18 **Children** Portions
Parking Public car park or on street

LYNDHURST
Map 5 SU30

The Glasshouse

◉◉ Modern British ✱

**Contemporary-style restaurant with well-judged
cooking**

☎ 023 8028 6129 & 8028 3677
**Best Western Forest Lodge, Pikes Hill, Romsey Rd
SO43 7AS**
e-mail: enquiries@theglasshousedining.co.uk
web: www.theglasshousedining.co.uk
dir: M27 junct 1, A337 towards Lyndhurst. In village, with
police station & courts on right, take 1st right into Pikes
Hill

A former dower house built in the Georgian period, this
hotel has been given a thoroughly modern look inside, the
restaurant with a dramatic décor of black and gold, with
striking artwork on the walls. The kitchen prides itself on
sourcing ingredients locally and pays due respect to

seasonality, so haunch of venison might appear,
accompanied by game jus, confit garlic, creamed
potatoes and a selection of vegetables. The menus offer
plenty of variety, from chicken tikka with pickled
cucumber, mango and an onion bhaji, to confit duck with
plum sauce and jelly, spring onions, cucumber and a
poppadom. Fish is not overlooked - pavé of haddock is
poached in red wine and accompanied by crushed new
potatoes, roast mooli and beans - and in colder months
the kitchen might put winter fruits into a crumble and
serve it with juniper pannacotta and clotted cream ice
cream.

Chef Richard Turner **Owner** New Forest Hotels
Times 12-2/7-9.30 Closed Mon, D Sun **Prices** Starter
£6-£8.50, Main £17.50-£18.50, Dessert £6.50-£8.50,
Service optional **Wines** 16 bottles over £30, 26 bottles
under £30, 2 by glass **Notes** Sun L 2/3 course, Sunday L
£15.50-£18.50, Vegetarian available, Dress restrictions,
Smart dress, Civ Wed 90 **Seats** 40, Pr/dining room 10
Parking 60

Hartnett Holder & Co

◉◉◉ — see page 196

See advert opposite

NEW MILTON
Map 5 SZ29

Chewton Glen Hotel & Spa

◉◉◉ — see page 198

See advert on page 197

OLD BURGHCLERE
Map 5 SU45

The Dew Pond Restaurant

◉ British, European

Country restaurant with fine views and modern cooking

☎ 01635 278408
RG20 9LH
dir: Newbury A34 South, exit Tothill. Follow signs for
Highclere Castle, pass castle entrance on right, down hill
& turn left signed Old Burghclere & Kingsclere, restaurant
on right in approx 0.25m

The Dew Pond is a place that embeds itself forever in the
memory if you come to dine alfresco on the decking
terrace on a summer's day. The unforgettable view at this
idyllic country restaurant in a pair of converted 16th-
century drovers' cottages sweeps across the eponymous
dew pond to Watership Down and Highclere Castle. But
all is not lost should the weather keep you indoors, as the
two cosy dining rooms exude the comfort of ancient oak
beams, calming pastel shades and colourful local
artwork. Chef-patron Keith Marshall looks to the local
area for his peerless supplies (including wines from

Hampshire) and rejects fads, fashions and fireworks in
favour of solid technical ability, turning out appealingly
uncomplicated yet thoughtful compositions, along the
lines of roasted scallops with chorizo, saffron aïoli,
tomato and basil, while saddle of local roe deer is
matched with celeriac purée, field mushrooms, shallots,
gratin dauphinoise and red wine jus. Flavours stay full-
throttle for a caramelised lemon tart with meringue and
raspberry sorbet.

Times 7-9.30 Closed 2 wks Xmas & New Year, 2 wks Aug,
Sun-Mon, L served by appointment only

OTTERBOURNE
Map 5 SU42

The White Horse

◉ Traditional & Modern British

Modern pub grub done right

☎ 01962 712830
Main Rd SO21 2EQ
e-mail: manager@whitehorseotterbourne.co.uk
dir: M3 junct 12/A335 1st exit at 1st rdbt & 2nd exit at
next 2 rdbts, via Otterbourne Hill into Main Rd.
Restaurant on left

When you come down from a hike along the lofty spine of
the South Downs - the western end of the South Downs
Way is at nearby Winchester - you couldn't ask for a more
fortifying pitstop. After a top-to-toe refurb by the team
behind The White Star in Southampton and The Bugle in
Hamble (see entries) this run-down village boozer now
looks every inch the modern dining pub with its wooden
and quarry-tiled floors, bare beams, cheerful heritage
hues, and mismatched vintage tables. The mood is
unbuttoned and family-friendly, while the kitchen is
driven by an enthusiasm for local ingredients, served up
in a straightforward contemporary vein. This might
translate as fried squid with smoked paprika aïoli,
followed by beef shin suet pudding paired with seared
fillet, braised red cabbage and mash. Puddings take a
similarly comfort-oriented route - perhaps Bramley apple
syrup sponge with custard.

Times 12-2.30/6-9.30

Hartnett Holder & Co

British, Italian **NEW** NOTABLE WINE LIST

Italian family cooking in a sophisticated New Forest hotel

☎ 023 8028 7167 & 8028 7177
Lime Wood, Beaulieu Rd SO43 7FZ
e-mail: info@limewood.co.uk
dir: A35 through Ashurst for 4m, then left in Lyndhurst signed Beaulieu, 1m to hotel

Formerly a prep school for the children of the landed gentry, Lime Wood, a Regency manor-house hotel in the heart of the New Forest, was acquired by its present ownership in 1999. A sense that the place is a continual work-in-progress is reinforced by the further enhancement of the boutique interiors, with Martin Brudnizki and David Collins having both taken a recent hand, and the kitchen is also now a collaborative venture, with Lime Wood's Luke Holder joined by in-demand Angela Hartnett (she of London's Murano - see entry) to confer a touch of Italianate simplicity on the upscale productions. With the compass point oscillating between Tuscany and Hampshire, you might expect cheerful chaos, but the results are a streamlined blend of honest, clearly focused and genuinely enjoyable dishes that are probably best experienced in the form of 'Il Tavolo della Cucina', a menu sorpresa of sharing dishes in homage to traditional familial dining. The results are eloquent: braised treviso with raisins and toasted breadcrumbs, gammon broth with smoked toasted cheese, pasta dishes such as tagliatelle with brown shrimps, or gnocchi with rabbit bolognese, all sound convincingly true Italian chords. At main, superior protein fixes arrive in the form of a chunk of fennel-crusted hake with clams, or gurnard with white beans and crab, or there may be local rose veal chop crusted in parmesan, served with artichokes. The sharing principle continues into party-piece main courses like roast native rib-eye with smoked bone marrow and charred red onion, or even a whole brill in lemon butter. A side of peperonata or deep-fried zucchini completes the mood, and if you're hankering for a slice of Blighty after all the Italiana, finish with rhubarb fool, or apple pie and toffee ice cream. A handful of modern Italian charmers has been inveigled among the imaginative selection of wines by the glass.

Chef Luke Holder, Angela Hartnett
Owner Lime Wood Group **Times** 12-11
Closed L Mon All-day dining
Prices Fixed L 2 course £25, Starter £6.50-£11, Main £12-£26, Dessert £7-£11, Service added but optional 12.5% **Wines** 565 bottles over £30, 34 bottles under £30, 13 by glass
Notes Tavolo Familiare 5 courses, Sunday L, Vegetarian available, Civ Wed

60 **Seats** 70, Pr/dining room 16
Children Portions, Menu **Parking** 60

Chewton Glen Hotel & Spa

NEW MILTON   MAP 5 SZ29

Modern British V **NOTABLE WINE LIST**

Classy cooking in luxury country-house hotel

☎ 01425 282212
Christchurch Rd BH25 6QS
e-mail: reservations@chewtonglen.com
web: www.chewtonglen.com
dir: Off A35 (Lyndhurst) turn right through Walkford, 4th left into Chewton Farm Rd

There's no shortage of country house hotels in the UK, but few are quite as special as Chewton Glen. Just a short distance from the sea and on the edge of the New Forest National Park, the gracious red-brick mansion looks splendid as you pull up in the flower-filled courtyard and hand over your car keys to the valet. As first impressions go, it's right up there, and when you step inside, your expectations are perfectly met by the elegant modern country-house décor, and the unfailingly courteous, efficient, warm and welcoming staff. The look in the restaurant, Vetiver, is similarly chic and contemporary, with lime-green banquettes, black-velvet covered chairs, black and cream walls and large windows looking out onto the lovely gardens (there are 130 acres in total, including an orchard, beehives, and a walled kitchen garden providing vegetables, herbs and salad leaves).

The restaurant is spread across five rooms, including two light-filled conservatories which open out onto the terrace for alfresco dining on warmer days. The flexible, crowd-pleasing menu offers something for everyone, whether you simply want a steak from the grill, or a bowl of pasta like Poole Bay mussel and clam linguini with preserved lemon and parsley, or a full-blown three courses. Classic French technique and first-class ingredients, many of them sourced locally, underpin every dish. The twice-baked emmental soufflé is a fixture, and very good it is too, while Scottish scallops - faultlessly cooked - with apple, raisins and mini onion bhajees provides a more of-the-moment alternative. Roast grouse with confit legs, braised lentils and smoked chocolate is an inspired main course that shows a good deal of technical skill, while Thai-style lobster curry with jasmine rice is rich and fragrant with a generous proportion of fresh, meaty lobster. There are some traditional elements to the service style, such as grilled Dover sole filleted at the table, and a daily-changing roast from the trolley. Indecisive types might struggle at dessert stage, when the likes of passionfruit soufflé with mango ice cream, and warm chocolate fondant with lavender and salt caramel emulsion, compete for your attention with tipsy plum pudding with brandy cream. The set lunch menu is a steal at £25 for three courses, and do make use of the sommelier's expertise when it comes to choosing from the extensive wine list.

Chef Andrew Du Bourg, Luke Matthews **Owner** Chewton Glen Hotels Ltd **Times** 12-2.30/6-10 **Prices** Fixed L 3 course fr £25, Tasting menu £70-£75, Starter £9.50-£19.50, Main £19.50-£39.50, Dessert £7.50-£12.50, Service added but optional 12.5% **Wines** 500 bottles over £30, 27 bottles under £30, 16 by glass **Notes** Tasting menu 7 course, Seasonal menu £60, Sunday L fr £39.50, Vegetarian menu, Civ Wed 140 **Seats** 164, Pr/dining room 50 **Children** Portions, Menu **Parking** 150

Save on Hotels. Book at **theAA.com/hotel**

HAMPSHIRE 199 **ENGLAND**

Annie Jones Restaurant

◉ Modern European

Ingenious European cooking and classic tapas near the station

☎ 01730 262728
10a Lavant St GU32 3EW
e-mail: info@anniejones.co.uk
dir: From A3 into town centre, following Winchester direction. Restaurant is in Lavant St (the road leading to rail station)

A couple of minutes' walk from the railway station, Annie Jones is a broad-fronted converted shop with a big picture window. Inside is a stylish ambience of bare wood floor, lavishly dressed tables and a pile of logs by the fireplace. Towards the back is a tapas bar area with unclothed tables and tall stools for Spanish-style snacking. Steven Ranson goes for a modern European style with simple, clean presentations that avoid overly precious lily-gilding, and flavours that speak out loud and clear. Salmon fishcake to start is a large spherical agglomerate of juicy flaked fish, fluffy potato and chives, and comes inventively with a portion of smoked haddock ravioli. For the main event a pair of Barbary duck breasts come properly rested, pink but flavourful, and offset fruitfully with Williams pear purée, caramelised fig, poached blackberries and breadcrumbed mash. Nutmeggy custard tart is a little overwhelmed by the tart berry compôte it comes with, or there may be chocolate and hazelnut torte with white chocolate sorbet.

Chef Steven Ranson **Owner** Steven Ranson, Jon Blake **Times** 12-2/6-late Closed 25-26 Dec, 1 Jan, Mon, L Tue, D Sun (winter) **Prices** Fixed L 2 course fr £14.95, Fixed D 3 course fr £35, Service added 12% **Wines** 10 bottles over £30, 15 bottles under £30, 6 by glass **Notes** Tasting menu 7 course, early bird Tue-Thu 6-7.30pm, Sunday L, Vegetarian available **Seats** 32 **Children** Portions **Parking** On street or Swan Street car park

JSW

◉◉◉ — see below

Langrish House

◉◉ Modern British 🍷

Vigorous modern British cooking at a South Downs house with a past

☎ 01730 266941
Langrish GU32 1RN
e-mail: frontdesk@langrishhouse.co.uk
web: www.langrishhouse.co.uk
dir: A3 onto A272 towards Winchester. Hotel signed, 2.5m on left

Langrish House's singular place in English history is assured. In the 17th century, when it was built, it became a repository for Royalist prisoners during the Civil War (they were put to work digging the vaults), while one of the forebears of the present generation of Talbot-Ponsonbys was a thoroughgoing eccentric, revered as the Emperor Frederick by the family, in whose ironic honour an imperial crest was designed, on display in the dining room named after him to this day. The culinary style would once have been thought as eccentric as Frederick, but is these days recognisable as a vigorous expression of the modern British idiom. Expect to start, perhaps, with black tiger prawns on a risotto of preserved lemon and chorizo in beurre noisette, before moving on to pork tenderloin with twice-baked cauliflower strudel, glazed beetroot, plum and vanilla jam and curry oil, before coming to rest with passionfruit pannacotta, cheesecake ice cream and pine nut brittle.

Chef Adrian Wilson **Owner** Mr & Mrs Talbot-Ponsonby **Times** 12-2/7-9.30 Closed 1-17 Jan **Prices** Fixed L 2 course £18.95, Starter £6.50-£8.95, Main £16.50-£19.50, Dessert £7.95-£9.95, Service added but optional 12.5% **Wines** 17 bottles over £30, 19 bottles under £30, 11 by glass **Notes** Sunday L £18.95-£21.95, Vegetarian available, Dress restrictions, Smart casual, Civ Wed 80 **Seats** 24, Pr/dining room 80 **Children** Portions **Parking** 100

JSW

◉◉◉

Modern British V 🔖 NOTABLE WINE LIST

Dynamic contemporary cooking in a made-over old inn

☎ 01730 262030
20 Dragon St GU31 4JJ
e-mail: jsw.restaurant@btconnect.com
dir: A3 to town centre, follow one-way system to College St which becomes Dragon St, restaurant on left

The chef-proprietor's initials provide the name for this relaxed restaurant in an immaculately whitewashed 17th-century former coaching inn. Jake Saul Watkins is a Hampshire lad who has been plying his trade in Petersfield for a dozen years or so, and in this current venue since 2006. He's not the sort of chef who puts his initials above the door then turns up once in a while to oversee the action - you can expect him to be there at the sharp end, giving his all at every service. The dining room has plenty of character: the antiquity of its exposed oak beams is overlaid with a subtly understated contemporary décor - neutral hues, generously-sized tables dressed decorously in cream floor-length linen, and a front-of-house team who know how to interact with customers to provide a memorable, relaxed time without slacking off on professional efficiency. If you're staying over in one of the three stylish rooms, the treats start at breakfast, with splendid freshly-made breads and pâtisserie from Rungis market in Paris demonstrating that sourcing of top-quality produce is the bedrock of the whole operation. This is confident, refined cooking but at its heart there's an intelligent simplicity that reminds you it is all meant to be eaten rather than cooed over. Whether you go for the entry-level two-course set menu, the carte, or splurge on the five- or seven-course tasting menus, everything is made in-house with top-level creativity and skills. Partridge with shallot tarte Tatin is pointed up with squares of coffee jelly and creamy coffee sauce - a first-class opener with clear flavours and great presentation. Timing, too, is impeccable, producing an exemplary translucent fillet of local wild turbot with creamy fennel risotto, cut through with a powerful red wine sauce. At the end, honeycomb parfait with salted caramel doughnuts and peanut brittle is a master-class in flavours and textures. The 700-bin wine list is notable for its remarkable global spread and fair mark-ups.

Chef Jake Watkins **Owner** Jake Watkins **Times** 12-1.30/7-9.30 Closed 2 wks Jan, May & summer, Sun-Mon **Prices** Fixed L 2 course £19.50, Fixed D 3 course £32.50, Service added but optional 10%, Groups min 10 service 10% **Wines** 9 by glass **Notes** Tasting menu L/D 5/7 course, Vegetarian menu **Seats** 58, Pr/dining room 18 **Children** Portions **Parking** 19

PETERSFIELD *continued*

The Old Drum

Modern British NEW

Robust and creative British cooking in renovated town-centre pub

☎ 01730 300544
16 Chapel St GU32 3DR
e-mail: info@theolddrum.co.uk
web: www.theolddrum.co.uk

The Old Drum has the appealing feel of a country pub that's upped sticks and moved to town. Exploratory renovation has uncovered its original beamed and tongue-and-groove ceilings, and it's been decorated with an agreeable mix of fresh, light colours, reconditioned timber flooring and some quirky touches (like a chair upholstered in the Stars and Stripes). Efficient staff and Digby the dog help to radiate as much hospitality as there was when HG Wells used to drink here. Simon Hartnett cooks the kinds of dishes that underpin today's hang-loose British catering. Robust ham hock and brawn terrine with warm pease pudding, parsley jelly and a sage biscuit will put hairs on your chest, and could be followed by 28-day-aged ribeye steak accompanied by a boozy and spicy Bloody Mary tomato, thick mushroom ketchup and chips cooked in dripping. The world larder is raided for inspiration in dishes such as hake with potato and onion bhaji and spiced lentils in cauliflower velouté. Creative tweaks continue through to desserts such as bread-and-butter pudding made with banana brioche, with a banana fritter and tonka ice cream.

Chef Simon Hartnett **Owner** Simon & Suzi Hawkins
Times 12-2/6.30-9.30 Closed 1st wk Jan, D Sun
Prices Starter £5.20-£7.50, Main £9-£19.95, Dessert £6-£9, Service optional **Wines** 7 bottles over £30, 21 bottles under £30, 8 by glass **Notes** £12.95-£14.50, Vegetarian available **Seats** 45 **Children** Portions **Parking** Adjacent car park

The Thomas Lord

Modern British

Inventive country pub cooking

☎ 01730 829244
High St, West Meon GU32 1LN
e-mail: info@thethomaslord.co.uk
dir: M3 junct 9, A272 towards Petersfield, right at x-rds onto A32, 1st left

A real village pub just off the main road through West Meon, The Thomas Lord is named after the founder of the famous cricket ground in north London. A restoration by new owners has stayed true to the ethos of the place, which is why the good people of West Meon reliably fill it with a convivium of chatter and cheer. Vegetables, salads and herbs are grown in the garden, the eggs come from the pub's own free-range chickens, and the place is under the same ownership as Upham Brewery near Winchester, which supplies its fine ales. The kitchen deals in inventive, dependable country-pub cooking of a high order, starting with a fortifying bowl of creamed

cauliflower soup with lardons and cheddar, or chunky chicken and mushroom terrine with artichokes and shallot relish. Mains show off prime materials in the form of sirloin of local beef seared in treacle, its braised shin-meat fashioned into a croquette, in red wine and horseradish jus. Meringue-topped lemon tart comes with resonant star-anise ice cream for afters.

Chef Fran Joyce **Owner** Upham Ales **Times** 12-2.30/6-9.30 Closed 25 Dec **Prices** Starter £5.50-£8, Main £11-£20, Dessert £6-£8, Service optional, Groups min 8 service 10% **Wines** 16 bottles over £30, 21 bottles under £30, 10 by glass **Notes** Sunday L £12-£15, Vegetarian available **Seats** 70, Pr/dining room 20 **Children** Portions **Parking** 20

PORTSMOUTH & SOUTHSEA   Map 5 SU60

Portsmouth Marriott Hotel

Modern, Seafood

Lively hotel restaurant near the marina

☎ 0870 400 7285 & 023 9238 3151
Southampton Rd PO6 4SH
web: www.portsmouthmarriott.co.uk
dir: M27 junct 12, keep left to lights, turn left. Hotel on left

Not far from all the main action in Portsmouth, with Gunwharf Quays and the Spinnaker Tower on hand, the Marriott won't endear many with its rather stolid apartment-block look, but inside is a deal more cheering. The Sealevel restaurant is a big open space, furnished with semi-circular booths as well as regular tables, and with an infectiously lively atmosphere. White canvas covers attached to the booths suggest the sails on view in the nearby marina. The cooking nails its colours to a fairly conservative version of modern British, with nothing too startling, but treating quality raw materials with respect. Crab cakes are appetisingly textured and offset with a crisp fennel salad, while well-timed venison comes with a big spinach-topped potato rösti and puréed celeriac in redcurrant jus. For fish-lovers, monkfish is poached in smoked pancetta broth and served with saffron potatoes, and proceedings close with hot chocolate fondant, or pear Bakewell and clotted cream.

Chef Jaap Schep **Times** 12-3/6.30-10 **Prices** Service optional **Wines** 21 by glass **Notes** Sunday L £12.95-£15.95, Vegetarian available **Seats** 70 **Children** Portions, Menu **Parking** 196

Restaurant 27

Modern European

European and Asian modes in a relaxing venue near the seafront

☎ 023 9287 6272
27a South Pde PO5 2JF
e-mail: info@restaurant27.com
dir: M27 junct 12, take M275 to A3, follow A288 South Parade, left Burgoyne Rd

The single-storey whitewashed building a little way off the seafront at Southsea may look a touch prosaic from

the outside, but inside has been decorated with some verve. An artist's impression of kitchen scenes hangs over the bar to orientate us, and the darkwood unclothed tables are furnished with simple but stylish implements. Kevin Bingham cooks to a taut, four dishes to choose from per course formula, employing European and Asian technique in persuasive synthesis. A spin on crab cocktail offers fine local crabmeat with the sharpening flavours of pickled vegetables, puréed tomato and dill, and may be followed by 30-hour pork belly, which offers beautifully moist but not gelatinous meat of excellent flavour, along with hazelnut gnocchi, roasted sweetcorn and girolles, or a pairing of scallops and king prawns in lemongrass and palm-sugar broth. Crème brûlée is caramelised to order, resulting in a variety of temperature layers beneath, which doesn't please everybody, but its accompaniments of basil meringue, lemon and lime jelly and late-summer berries take it to another dimension altogether.

Chef Kevin Bingham, Annie Smith, Danny Wilson, Matt Barnes **Owner** Kevin & Sophie Bingham
Times 12-2.30/7-9.30 Closed Xmas, New Year, Mon-Tue, L Wed-Sat, D Sun **Prices** Fixed D 3 course £40, Tasting menu £35, Service optional **Wines** 29 bottles over £30, 19 bottles under £30, 14 by glass **Notes** Tasting menu 7 course Wed-Thu, Sunday L, Vegetarian available **Seats** 34 **Children** Portions **Parking** On street

---

PRESTON CANDOVER   Map 5 SU64

Purefoy Arms

British, Spanish NEW

A food-focused pub with a Spanish and local flavour

☎ 01256 389777
Alresford Rd RG25 2EJ
e-mail: info@thepurefoyarms.co.uk

The red-brick Purefoy Arms is a pub run by a husband-and-wife-team with a passion for food and wine. He's a chef, and Spanish, and she's a Brit with experience in the wine trade. It's a match made in heaven in this traditional English pub with its spruced-up rustic charm, which means wooden tables, leather sofas, and blackboards revealing what's good to eat that day. Portland crab on toast wins with its simplicity (and generosity), or go for smoked chicken terrine with basil pesto. The produce is sourced with a good deal of care and the menu changes daily. Spiced Ibérico pork cheeks with judion beans and pata negra sauce is a taste of the old country for chef (there are tapas-style bar snacks, too), but there's also Dexter beef burger with dripping-cooked chips or ray wing with sea kale, brown shrimps and black butter. With well-chosen wines, real ales, and desserts such as strawberry millefeuille with thyme ice cream, there's plenty of reason to linger a while. And the large garden is a fair-weather treat.

Chef Andres Alemany **Owner** Andres & Marie-Lou Alemany
Times 12-3/6-10 Closed 26 Dec, 1 Jan, Mon, D Sun
Prices Fixed L 2 course £14.50, Starter £6-£12, Main £11.95-£28.50, Dessert £5-£9.50, Service added but optional 10% **Wines** 50 bottles over £30, 40 bottles under £30, 10 by glass **Notes** Sunday L £14.50-£15.50 **Seats** 60 **Children** Portions **Parking** 30, On street

Map 5 SU32

The Three Tuns

@ Modern British

Skillful and appealing gastro-pub cooking

☎ 01794 512639
58 Middlebridge St SO51 8HL
e-mail: manager@the3tunsromsey.co.uk
dir: A27 bypass on A3030

Just five minutes from the Market Square, The Three Tuns has all the hallmarks of an old country pub: panelling, bare brick walls, lots of polished wood, slate floors, beams, open fires and real ales. What lifts it out of the country-pub mould is the quality of the cooking; there's no cheffy skulduggery here, just well-considered combinations in carefully cooked dishes using fine local ingredients. Try smoked salmon with celeriac remoulade and a caper and shallot dressing with toasted rye bread, or rustic-sounding black pudding Scotch egg with home-made brown sauce. For main course, the Tuns' pie is a model of its kind - ox cheek slowly cooked with mushrooms and horseradish, rich and full of flavour, in impeccable pastry, served with seasonal vegetables. To top things off may be nicely wobbly vanilla pannacotta with stewed rhubarb, or zingy berry crumble and custard.

Chef Andrew Yates, Damian Brown **Owner** M Dodd, D Brown, I Longhorn **Times** 12-2.30/6-9 Closed 25-26 Dec **Prices** Starter £5.50-£7.50, Main £9.95-£14.95, Dessert £5.50-£6.50, Service optional **Wines** 16 bottles under £30, 10 by glass **Notes** Sunday L fr £12.50, Vegetarian available **Seats** 35 **Children** Portions, Menu **Parking** 14, On street

The White Horse Hotel & Brasserie

@@ Modern British 🍃

Modern British classics in an ancient coaching inn

☎ 01794 512431
19 Market Place SO51 8ZJ
e-mail: reservations@silkshotels.com
web: www.silkshotels.com
dir: M27 junct 3, follow signs for Romsey, right at Broadlands. In town centre

Established as a coaching inn 600 years ago, The White Horse is plumb in the middle of the charming market town of Romsey. Retaining much of its period detail, it offers a boldly decorated bar where orders are taken, as well as a plush dining room with smartly clothed tables. The cooking style is all about modern British classics, delivered with considerable panache. Seared scallops sit on their now canonical cauliflower purée, given texture with crisp-fried shallots and a deeper note of seasoning with curry oil. Duck three ways (breast, confit leg and foie gras) seems the best of all worlds, with its accurately cooked meat and liver, unified with a well-judged white wine jus of orange and grape, while satisfaction is assured in the sticky department with Jamaica gingerbread chocolate fondant, served with caramelised banana ice cream.

The White Horse Hotel & Brasserie

Chef Chris Rock **Owner** Mr Nuttall **Times** 12-3/6-10 **Prices** Fixed L 2 course fr £14.50, Fixed D 3 course fr £16.50, Starter £5-£9.50, Main £9.50-£22, Dessert £5-£8.50, Service optional **Wines** 11 by glass **Notes** Sunday L, Vegetarian available, Dress restrictions, Smart casual, Civ Wed 65 **Seats** 85, Pr/dining room 40 **Children** Portions, Menu **Parking** Car park nearby

ROTHERWICK — Map 5 SU75

Tylney Hall Hotel

◉◉◉ Traditional British ✋

A decorative treasure-house with fine country-hotel cooking

☎ 01256 764881
Ridge Ln RG27 9AZ
e-mail: sales@tylneyhall.com
web: www.tylneyhall.com
dir: M3 junct 5, A287 to Basingstoke, over junct with A30, over rail bridge, towards Newnham. Right at Newnham Green. Hotel 1m on left

Tylney Hall is a magnificent house with more than its fair share of period elegance in its Florentine rococo ceilings, scrolled cornicings and original walnut panelling (the latter you can admire to your heart's content while taking pre-dinner drinks in the comfortable library). In the Oak Room restaurant, swagged French windows look out over the expansive manicured gardens (laid out by Gertrude Jekyll, no less), while starched table linen and posies set the scene for some professionally rendered, traditional country-house cooking, with some flourishes of modernity here and there. Start, perhaps, with sautéed tiger prawns with caramelised orange in green peppercorn and coriander dressing, or duck and foie gras terrine with a sweetened tomato chutney. The centrepiece of the short dinner menu is the roast of the evening - rack of local lamb or Angus sirloin maybe - which is carved from the trolley at your table. Alternatively there could be glazed Gressingham duck breast served with fine celeriac gratin, apple and blackberries. Finish with orange and lemon cheesecake.

Tylney Hall Hotel

Chef Stephen Hine **Owner** Elite Hotels
Times 12.30-2/7-10 **Prices** Fixed L 2 course fr £19.50, Fixed D 3 course fr £39.50, Starter fr £13.50, Main fr £25, Dessert fr £11, Service optional **Wines** 350 bottles over £30, 5 bottles under £30, 10 by glass **Notes** Bill of Fayre menu 3 course £46, Sunday L, Vegetarian available, Dress restrictions, Jacket & tie at D, no jeans Fri-Sat, Civ Wed 120 **Seats** 80, Pr/dining room 120 **Children** Portions, Menu **Parking** 150

See advert on page 201

SHEDFIELD — Map 5 SU51

Meon Valley, A Marriott Hotel & Country Club

◉ Traditional & Modern British ✋

Modern leisure hotel with appealing contemporary menu

☎ 01329 836826
Sandy Ln SO32 2HQ
web: www.marriottmeonvalley.co.uk
dir: M27 junct 7 take A334 towards Wickham & Botley, continue past Botley and vineyard, hotel on left in 1m

Within the modern Meon Valley Marriott Hotel & Country Club, which as you might expect from the name excels in health, leisure and golf facilities, the smart Broadstreet restaurant is a beacon of civility. It all stands in 225 acres of beautiful grounds, just a short hop from the motorway. In the restaurant, smartly dressed staff are on the ball and the unfussy, gently modish food hits the spot. Start with ham hock and parsley terrine with apple and cider chutney and toasted brioche, before moving on to grilled leg of lamb steak with dauphinoise potatoes, chilli-roasted butternut squash, wilted spinach and rosemary jus. Two cheeses from the county (served with quince jelly and fig and raisin bread) is an alternative to a sweet such as iced lemon meringue parfait with mango coulis.

Chef Paul Watts, Sattish Yerimali **Owner** Marriott Hotels
Times 6.30-9.30 Closed Mon, L Mon-Sat, D Sun-Mon
Prices Starter £6-£11, Main £12-£25, Dessert £6, Service optional **Wines** 13 by glass **Notes** Sunday L £15.92-£20.95, Vegetarian available, Dress restrictions, Smart casual, Civ Wed 90 **Seats** 75, Pr/dining room 90 **Children** Portions, Menu **Parking** 350

SOUTHAMPTON — Map 5 SU41

Botleigh Grange Hotel

◉ Traditional British, Modern European

Straightforward cooking in 17th-century country house

☎ 0844 411 9050
Grange Rd, Botley SO30 2GA
e-mail: res-botleighgrange@legacy-hotels.co.uk
web: www.legacy-hotels.co.uk
dir: On A334, 1m from M27 junct 7

A classic country house in 14 acres of well-tended gardens and grounds, Botleigh Grange combines the grandeur of a 17th-century mansion with the de rigueur spa, conference and wedding facilities. An aperitif in the oak-panelled cocktail lounge beneath a magnificent Victorian ceiling is always a good idea before moving through to the dining room in a modern glass-domed extension overlooking the gardens. In tune with this quintessentially English setting, the kitchen sticks to an uncomplicated repertoire of traditional country house fare, enlivened with a hint of European flair here and there. King scallops with samphire and garlic and parsley butter is a feel-good way to start, followed by pan-fried medallions of pork, richly sauced with Calvados, and partnered by sautéed spinach and potato cake. For dessert, crème brûlée is flavoured with Cointreau and orange and served with almond biscotti.

Times 12.30-2.30/7-9.30

Mercure Southampton Centre Dolphin Hotel

◉ Modern International ✋

Historic hotel with crowd-pleasing menu

☎ 023 8038 6460
34-35 High St SO14 2HN
e-mail: H7876@accor.com
web: www.mercure.com
dir: A33 follow signs for Docks & Old Town/IOW ferry, at ferry terminal turn right into High Street, hotel 400yds on left

Formerly a 17th-century coaching inn boasting the likes of Jane Austen, Queen Victoria and Admiral Nelson among its former guests, several million pounds and a takeover from the Mercure chain later, this is a striking and characterful place to stay and to eat. In the Signature Restaurant, contemporary tones abound and it all looks suitably modish and unstuffy - darkwood tables, plenty of period character, and a menu that doesn't stray far from traditional, brasserie-style comforts. Baked ramekin of

Save on Hotels. Book at **theAA.com/hotel**

HAMPSHIRE 203 **ENGLAND**

Hampshire pear with stilton cream and watercress salad might precede steak and kidney pie, half a roast poussin with bubble-and-squeak and bread sauce, or a Casterbridge steak from the grill.

Chef Tibor Suli **Owner** Longrose Buccleuch **Times** 12-2.30/7-9.45 **Prices** Prices not confirmed Service included **Wines** 8 bottles over £30, 24 bottles under £30, 12 by glass **Notes** Vegetarian available, Civ Wed 120 **Seats** 80 **Children** Portions, Menu **Parking** 80

White Star Tavern, Dining and Rooms

@@ British

Seasonal local food amid ocean-liner décor

☎ 023 8082 1990
28 Oxford St SO14 3DJ
e-mail: reservations@whitestartavern.co.uk
web: www.whitestartavern.co.uk
dir: M3 junct 14 onto A33, towards Ocean Village

Housed in an old shipping line hotel once owned by the White Star Line (forever associated with a certain RMS Titanic) this buzzy gastro-pub and restaurant celebrates Southampton's maritime heritage with rooms that pay homage to the bygone era of great ocean-liners. After an aperitif in the lively bar, head for the smart banquette seating in the wood-floored and panelled dining rooms, where contemporary brasserie-style dishes featuring plenty of Hampshire produce take in the likes of braised

duck meat Scotch egg with bacon bits and sherry vinaigrette as a prelude to loin of New Forest venison with thyme polenta, spinach, mushrooms, and pomegranate dressing. Day boat fish might be battered (with local ale in the mix) and served with triple-cooked chips, mushy peas and tartare sauce, while splendid local cheeses offer a savoury alternative to baked rhubarb crumble cheesecake with stem ginger ice cream.

Times 12-2.30/6-9.30 Closed 25-26 Dec

STOCKBRIDGE   Map 5 SU33

The Greyhound on the Test

@@ Modern British ◔

Good eating in a revamped 15th-century riverside pub

☎ 01264 810833
31 High St SO20 6EY
e-mail: info@thegreyhoundonthetest.co.uk
dir: 9m NW of Winchester, 8m S of Andover. Off A303

The 15th-century Greyhound in the lovely village of Stockbridge is under new ownership and has a new look to show for it. The place has been spruced up in its entirety (the seven bedrooms included), with a new bar area added and splashes of colourful modern artwork on the walls, but happily none of the charm of the ancient building has been lost. In fact, period character abounds, with low oak beams, wonky floors and open fires. Venture

out back, and you'll find the building sits right beside the River Test, a truly idyllic setting for drinks and dining if the weather allows, and a lovely spot for fishing if you're so inclined. Chef Alan Haughie draws on the best regional ingredients for his varied menu of modern and more traditional ideas. Start, perhaps, with braised cod cheeks with a creamy curried saffron sauce and linguine, following on with pan-fried hake (perfectly cooked) with purple sprouting broccoli and lemon butter, or braised pork belly and cheek with celeriac purée and white beans. End firmly in the comfort zone with a textbook apple crumble.

Chef Alan Haughie **Owner** Lucy Townsend **Times** 12-4/7-9 Closed 25-26 & 31 Dec, 1 Jan, D Sun (winter) **Prices** Fixed L 2 course fr £11.95, Starter £4-£7.50, Main £9.85-£24, Dessert £4.95-£6.95 **Wines** 8 by glass **Notes** Sunday L, Vegetarian available **Seats** 52, Pr/dining room 20 **Children** Portions **Parking** 20

Avenue Restaurant at Lainston House Hotel

WINCHESTER   MAP 5 SU42

Modern British V ❖ NOTABLE WINE LIST

Creative modern cooking in 17th-century country-house hotel

☎ 01962 776088
Woodman Ln, Sparsholt SO21 2LT
e-mail: enquiries@lainstonhouse.com
web: www.exclusivehotels.co.uk
dir: B3049 Stockbridge road, junct with Woodman Ln

Red-brick Lainston House, a charming and cosseting country-house hotel, dates from the 17th century when it was a hunting lodge, and stands in 63 acres of parkland; the ruins of a 12th-century chapel are a short stroll away. It's a stunningly beautiful building in a lovely rural setting, though only a few miles from historic Winchester. A dining area has been added to the kitchen garden, with

a wood-fired oven for summer barbecues, and alfresco eating on the terrace is on the cards in warm weather. When the weather isn't being kind, the Avenue Restaurant offers an equally pleasant environment in which to dine. It takes its name from the mile-long stretch of limes glimpsed through its windows, and diners are in safe hands from a kitchen with a solid foundation of culinary skills based on years of experience, with local produce - including many fruits and vegetables from the garden and meat from the resident pigs - forming the bedrock of its output. Venison carpaccio with lemon curd, a crisp quail's egg and truffled mayonnaise, and seared scallops with salted curry sauce, cauliflower purée, bacon crisps and apple are the sort of well-executed bright ideas among starters. Main course might bring on pink slices of lamb saddle on a bed of artichoke along with braised shoulder, minted apple jelly, black garlic and spiced wine gravy, with a fish option among the handful of choices of perhaps accurately timed halibut fillet fashionably partnered by oxtail, served with parsnips, pickled walnut

and pearl barley. British cheeses are an alternative to such innovative puddings as rich salted chocolate and peanut millefeuille with creamy burned butter ice cream, or pears poached in orange blossom. The excellent breads are all baked in-house, and the extensive wine list is well worth a moment of your time.

Chef Andy MacKenzie, Phil Yeomans **Owner** Exclusive Hotels **Times** 12-2/7-10 **Prices** Fixed L 2 course £22, Fixed D 3 course £55, Tasting menu £65, Starter £11, Main £34, Dessert £10-£20, Service added but optional 10% **Wines** 302 bottles over £30, 21 bottles under £30, 291 by glass **Notes** Sunday L, Vegetarian menu, Dress restrictions, Smart casual, Civ Wed 120 **Seats** 60, Pr/dining room 120 **Children** Portions, Menu **Parking** 200

STOCKBRIDGE *continued*

The Peat Spade Inn

◉ Modern British

Classic British dishes in charming dining inn

☎ 01264 810612
SO20 6DR
e-mail: info@peatspadeinn.co.uk
dir: M3 junct 8, A303 W approx 15m, then take A3057 Stockbridge/Andover

Sitting on the banks of the River Test in Hampshire's historic fly fishing country, this dining pub is well-placed for sourcing the area's finest ingredients. With simple scrubbed pine tables, bare floorboards, and deep green and burgundy walls hung with old photos and prints, the dining rooms are full of character. The kitchen believes in keeping it simple, relying for its effect on the quality of local produce, including game from the Leckford Estate and wild ingredients from the New Forest. It is the attention to detail that counts here - toasted home-made Guinness bread, for instance, served with chicken liver parfait and onion marmalade. Main courses could see pub classics - beer-battered haddock and triple-cooked chips, or slow-cooked steak and ale pie - alongside ballottine of wood pigeon with crispy black cabbage, creamed potato, beetroot, capers and jus.

Times 12-2.30/6.30-9.30 **Prices** Prices not confirmed **Notes** Pre-booking strongly recommended, menu changes daily, Sunday L, Vegetarian available

---

WINCHESTER	Map 5 SU42

Avenue Restaurant at Lainston House Hotel

◉◉◉ — *see page 203*

The Black Rat

◉◉ Modern British

Former pub serving up seriously good food

☎ 01962 844465 & 841531
88 Chesil St SO23 0HX
e-mail: reservations@theblackrat.co.uk
dir: M3 junct 9/A31 towards Winchester & Bar End until T-junct. Turn right at lights, restaurant 600yds left

A one-time pub, dating from the 18th century, is these days home to a restaurant of distinction. There's a lot of the old pub character remaining on the inside, with beams, brickwork and fireplaces, but that is where the similarity to the old boozer ends, for this place serves up contemporary British food which is as sharp as a pin. There's a lack of pretension to the place - chunky wooden tables to sit at, for example, and a relaxed service style - but it feels smart and comfortable. And what turns up on the plate is high quality ingredients, sourced from (mostly) named regional suppliers or grown on their own allotment, and cooked with precision and imagination. Partridge, foie gras and ham hock are happy bedfellows

indeed in a first-course terrine served with crushed egg, fabulous home-made mustard and new potato crisps. Main-course Loch Duart salmon and hand-dived scallop is flavoured with Douglas Fir and comes with crumbled gingerbread, crushed pumpkin and crow garlic, while blood orange and olive oil cake with Pedro Ximenez jelly and toasted almonds is a revelatory finale.

Chef Jamie Stapleton-Burns **Owner** David Nicholson **Times** 12-2.15/7-9.30 Closed 2 wks Etr, 2 wks Oct/Nov, 2 wks Xmas & New Year, L Mon-Fri **Prices** Fixed L 2 course £22.95, Starter £8.25-£9.50, Main £19.95-£22.95, Dessert £7.25-£9.25, Service optional, Groups min 10 service 10% **Wines** 6 by glass **Notes** Fixed L Sat-Sun only, Sunday L, Vegetarian available **Seats** 40, Pr/dining room 16 **Parking** Car park opposite

The Chesil Rectory

◉ Modern British

Modernised British dishes in a medieval house

☎ 01962 851555
1 Chesil St SO23 0HU
e-mail: enquiries@chesilrectory.co.uk
dir: S from King Alfred's statue at bottom of The Broadway, cross small bridge, turn right, restaurant on left, just off mini rdbt

Winchester's oldest house makes a suitably atmospheric setting for eating out, with its ancient doorways, timbering and exposed floorboards. Taller diners should beware of the low lintels as they pick their way about. The little windows can make the place quite dark, but with the fire crackling on a chilly day, that only adds to the appeal. The menu announces 'great British dining', a heartwarming prospect, the more so since it's a gently modernised version. Guinea fowl and prune terrine with spiced pear chutney, followed by smoked haddock gratin with hispi cabbage, gives some indication of the style. Risotto frankly isn't a strong suit, and has nothing to do with British dining anyway, ancient or modern, but a main course of venison from Blackmoor delivers exceptional meat, well-timed and tender, with shredded veg, silky mash and a chocolate-boosted jus. Finish with rhubarb fool, or sticky toffee pudding with butterscotch and mascarpone.

Chef Damian Brown **Owner** Mark Dodd, Damian Brown, Iain Longhorn **Times** 12-2.20/6-9.30 Closed 1 wk Xmas, BH Mons **Prices** Fixed L 2 course £15.95, Fixed D 3 course £19.95, Starter £6.95-£8.50, Main £13.95-£20, Dessert £6.95, Service optional, Groups min 10 service 10% **Wines** 33 bottles under £30, 9 by glass **Notes** Set menu Mon-Sat 12-2.20/6-7, Sun 6-9, Sunday L, Vegetarian available **Seats** 75, Pr/dining room 14 **Children** Portions **Parking** NCP Chesil St adjacent

Holiday Inn Winchester

◉ European, International **NEW** ❧

Modern hotel with brasserie menu

☎ 01962 670700
Telegraph Way, Morn Hill SO21 1HZ
e-mail: info@hiwinchester.co.uk

This modern hotel has all the bells and whistles for putting on a conference or wedding, plus, in the shape of its Morn Hill Brasserie, a suitably contemporary and appealing dining venue. The large open-plan room looks smart and inviting, with a lack of stuffiness and a menu that has something for everyone. There's a pretty good showing of Hampshire produce, from the rib-eye steak cooked on the chargrill, through to the cheeses served with home-made chutney. Under the heading 'Old Favourites' you'll find the Morn Hill burger and pie of the day, there's a 'Pasta & Risotto' section too, or dip into the 'Something Special' to sample the likes of home-made duck spring roll with oriental leaves, chilli, ginger and soya dipping sauce, followed by braised pork cheek with fondant potato, sautéed curly kale and cider sauce. Apple and blackberry crumble with sauce anglaise is a typically comforting dessert.

Chef Paul Bentley **Owner** Zinnia Hotels **Times** 12-2/6.30-9.30 **Prices** Starter £4.20-£6.95, Main £12.25-£18.25, Dessert £5-£8, Service optional **Wines** 17 bottles over £30, 34 bottles under £30, 10 by glass **Notes** Tasting menu available 3 course, Sunday L £11.95-£14.95, Vegetarian available, Civ Wed 150 **Seats** 128, Pr/dining room 200 **Children** Portions, Menu **Parking** 170

Hotel du Vin Winchester

◉◉ Traditional British, French 🏅 NOTABLE WINE LIST

Bustling bistro and great wines in Georgian townhouse hotel

☎ 01962 841414
14 Southgate St SO23 9EF
e-mail: info@winchester.hotelduvin.co.uk
web: www.hotelduvin.com
dir: M3 junct 11, follow signs to Winchester town centre, located on left

The Winchester branch is where the HdV brand got started with a formula that goes like this: take a characterful old building (in this case an elegant early-Georgian townhouse near the cathedral), add upmarket, style-driven bedrooms, and a wine-themed, retro-French-style bistro serving simple but well-prepared contemporary brasserie-style classics built from top-class local materials. Et voilà, as the French say. It's a lively space, done out with lots of wood - bare floorboards, burnished wooden tables - and wine-related memorabilia to go with an eager-to-please menu that might offer dressed crab with walnut toast as an opening gambit, then move on to duck confit with Puy lentils, or roast cod with buttered leeks and salsa verde. Tarte au citron or crêpes Suzette are desserts as beret-wearingly Gallic as the bulk of the excellent wine list.

Times 12-1.45/7-10

Save on Hotels. Book at **theAA.com/hotel**

HAMPSHIRE 205 **ENGLAND**

Marwell Hotel

◎◎ Modern European **NEW** 🌱

Creative cooking in a smart leisure hotel

☎ 01962 777681
Thompsons Ln, Colden Common, Marwell SO21 1JY
e-mail: info@marwellhotel.co.uk
web: www.marwellhotel.co.uk
dir: B3354 through Twyford. 1st exit at rdbt (B3354), left
onto B2177 signed Bishop Waltham. Left into Thompsons
Ln after 1m, hotel on left

A short drive from Winchester and all its historic charms,
and with Marwell Zoo right on the doorstep, the Marwell
Hotel is a good base for exploring this part of Hampshire.
There are leisure facilities aplenty on site, including an
indoor pool, and the place is a big hit on the wedding
scene. Do note, though, that the main restaurant is worth
a visit on its own merits. Regional ingredients are given
pride of place on the menu and the cooking is
contemporary, accurate and really rather good. You might
start with squab pigeon, for example, perfectly tender,
and served in the company of onion jam, port jus and
blackberries. Next up, Hampshire lamb features in a
complex dish with the shoulder meat in a pastilla, along
with a herb cutlet, an almond-crusted sweetbread, and
goats' cheese, black olive mash and port and fig purée.
For dessert there might be a creative take on the theme of
rhubarb and custard, or a hot Valrhona chocolate fondant
with green tea ice cream and cumin caramel.

Chef Richard Cameron **Owner** Bastian family
Times 5.30-10 Closed 25 Dec **Prices** Starter £7-£11.50,
Main £14-£20.75, Dessert £5.75-£6.75, Service optional
Wines 10 bottles over £30, 10 bottles under £30
Notes Vegetarian available, Civ Wed 200 **Seats** 80, Pr/
dining room 120 **Children** Portions, Menu **Parking** 100

Running Horse Inn

◎◎ Modern International

Innovative cooking in upgraded inn

☎ 01962 880218
88 Main Rd, Littleton SO22 6QS
e-mail: runninghorseinn@btconnect.com
web: www.runninghorseinn.co.uk
dir: B3049 out of Winchester 1.5m, turn right into
Littleton after 1m, Running Horse on right

Three miles from the centre of Winchester, The Running
Horse combines the functions of bar, restaurant and
small hotel. It's a relaxed and informal sort of place, with
the restaurant featuring modern art on battleship-grey
walls, and wicker-back chairs at plain wooden tables.
Fresh, seasonal food that's big on flavours is what to
expect here. Roast pigeon breast, with a black pudding
fritter, beetroot purée, confit garlic and thyme jus, is an
impressive starter, or there might be a trio of ravioli
(trout, crab and crayfish) with pea purée and bisque
foam. Timings are accurate - witness pink, moist,
flavourful roast rack of lamb, served with braised neck
along with pea and mint pannacotta and rosemary and
garlic gratin - and even complicated dishes seem to

work: poached fillets of plaice are rolled in spinach and
served with shellfish sauce, shrimp and cucumber jelly,
vanilla potato purée and roast tomatoes. Stick to a simple
dessert like espresso crème brûlée with Amaretto cream.

Chef Paul Down **Owner** Light Post Ltd **Times** 12-2/6-9.30
Prices Prices not confirmed Service optional, Groups min
6 service 10% **Wines** 14 by glass **Notes** Sunday L,
Vegetarian available **Seats** 50 **Children** Portions, Menu
Parking 40

The Winchester Hotel and Spa

◎ Modern European

Contemporary brasserie fare in a modern hotel

☎ 01962 709988
Worthy Ln SO23 7AB
e-mail: info@thewinchesterhotel.co.uk
web: www.thewinchesterhotel.co.uk
dir: A33 then A3047, hotel 1m on right

Smack in the centre of Winchester, Hutton's Brasserie at
The Winchester Hotel comes with a glossy interior of
polished floorboards, darkwood tables, creamy leather
chairs and banquettes, and chillout music in the
background. Switched-on staff look the part, and the
kitchen delivers a crowd-pleasing repertoire of classic
and modern European ideas. A terrine of rabbit, ham hock
and morels with apricot chutney might kick off
proceedings, followed by venison medallions with garlic
mash, buttered purple broccoli, and port wine jus, or
baked fillet of red snapper with broad beans, peppers and
lemon dressing. Bringing up the rear, there might be dark
chocolate crème brûlée with walnut biscotti.

Chef Neil Dore **Owner** Quantum Hotels Ltd
Times 12.30-2/7-9.30 **Prices** Fixed L 2 course £19, Fixed
D 3 course £23.50, Service optional **Wines** 15 bottles over
£30, 25 bottles under £30, 9 by glass **Notes** Sunday L,
Vegetarian available, Dress restrictions, Smart casual,
Civ Wed 150 **Seats** 80, Pr/dining room 40
Children Portions, Menu **Parking** 70

The Wykeham Arms

◎◎ Modern British **NEW**

**Rustic, historic pub delivering exciting, crowd-pleasing
food**

☎ 01962 853834
75 Kingsgate St SO23 9PE
e-mail: wykehamarms@fullers.co.uk
dir: S out of city along Southgate St. Take 3rd turning L
into Canon St, inn on R at end

This historic pub is rustically styled: pewter tankards,
school caps and several pictures adorn the walls, while
tables are an eclectic mix of shapes and sizes. Open log
fires warm up the traditional, old-style bar, and the
garden is a must in the summer months. There's
something for everyone on the varied menu. The 28-day
aged beef and oyster stew from the 'House Comforts'
section is just the job to warm you up on a cold winter's
day, while elsewhere there are some technically
impressive and exciting dishes, such as an intricate

poached and roasted English quail, textures of shallots
and parmesan to start. Main course could be roast South
Coast hake with coriander-infused shiitake mushroom,
pak choi, spring onion and soy broth, or you might choose
juniper and orange-infused venison saddle with
dauphinoise potato, beetroot and blackberries. There's a
lot going on in coffee and praline pannacotta, cocoa nibs,
lime, and salt caramel ice cream to finish. The great
selection of high quality wines is accessibly priced.

Chef Adam Thomason **Owner** Fuller, Smith & Turner
Times 12-3/6-9.30 Closed D 25 Dec **Prices** Fixed L 2
course fr £13, Fixed D 3 course fr £21, Tasting menu
£50-£75, Starter £6-£10, Main £11-£22, Service optional,
Groups min 6 service 10% **Wines** 24 bottles over £30, 41
bottles under £30, 20 by glass **Notes** Vegetarian
available, Dress restrictions, Smart casual **Seats** 90
Parking Town centre car park

WOODLANDS Map 5 SU31

Woodlands Lodge Hotel

◎ Modern British **NEW** 🌱

Forest hotel with an accent on fresh local produce

☎ 023 8029 2257
Bartley Rd SO40 7GN
e-mail: reception@woodlands-lodge.co.uk
web: www.woodlands-lodge.co.uk
dir: M27 junct 2, rdbt towards Fawley, 2nd rdbt right
towards Cadnam. 1st left at White Horse Pub onto
Woodlands Road, over cattle grid, hotel on left

Perfect for working up an appetite for lunch, the lovely
gardens of this hotel open straight into the dappled
glades of the New Forest. The spruce-looking
whitewashed building is reputed to have been a royal
hunting lodge, a past that is reflected in the name of its
Hunters Restaurant, an airy Victorian addition done out in
soothing pastel shades and furnished decorously with
tables swathed in floor-length linen; a luminous
conservatory extension opens out views over the gardens
and forest. The kitchen's trump card is a restored walled
kitchen garden that provides organically-grown seasonal
fruit and veg, while liberated ex-battery hens now live the
good life in exchange for their free-range eggs. The
straightforward repertoire starts typically with chicken
liver parfait with brioche and red onion jam, moves on to
rump of lamb with herb mash, ratatouille and mint jus,
and finishes with apple and forest berry crumble.

Chef John Oyard **Owner** Robert Anglaret
Times 12-2.30/7-9 **Prices** Fixed D 3 course fr £30,
Service optional **Wines** 5 by glass **Notes** Fixed L 3 course,
Fixed D 4 course, Sunday L, Vegetarian available, Civ Wed
120 **Seats** 30, Pr/dining room 35 **Children** Portions
Parking 80

HEREFORDSHIRE

HEREFORD · Map 10 SO53

Castle House

◎◎ Modern British

Classy townhouse hotel with innovative style of cooking

☎ 01432 356321
Castle St HR1 2NW
e-mail: info@castlehse.co.uk
web: www.castlehse.co.uk
dir: City centre, follow signs to Castle House Hotel

It might be in the city centre, hard by the cathedral, but Castle House has a peaceful setting, its restaurant looking over gardens to the Wye. This is a comfortable room, with vivid artworks on pastel-green walls and candles on the tables. The kitchen makes good use of local suppliers, and comes up with some bright, modern ideas, pairing crisp pork belly with scallops, sweetcorn purée and chilli jam, and grilled Cornish mackerel with a trio of gooseberries (fruit, jam and jelly). Sound techniques and an eye for presentation are clear in main courses: perhaps accurately cooked loin of lamb set atop little gems and peas and mint-infused braised shoulder, with fondant potato, or roast grey mullet with clams, shrimps, fennel and broad bean tartare. To finish, expect something equally labour-intensive: perhaps lavender crème brûlée, with raspberry Pavlova to one side and three tiny quenelles of lime and honey pickle adding contrasting sharpness.

Times 12-2/6.30-9.30

See advert opposite

Holme Lacy House Hotel

◎◎ Modern British

Quality dining in the Wye Valley

☎ 01432 870870
Holme Lacy HR2 6LP
e-mail: holmelacy@bourne-leisure.co.uk
web: www.warnerleisurehotels.co.uk
dir: B4399 at Holme Lacy, take lane opposite college. Hotel 500mtrs on right

Set in the Wye Valley, Holme Lacy House is a listed Georgian mansion in 20 acres of parkland (note the topiary), with an interior boasting ornate ceilings in the lounges, a grand central staircase, and the Orchard Restaurant panelled in oak with a fireplace. The menu offers much to interest the palate and the eye, and ingredients are well chosen, with starters like langoustine risotto with tomato fondant and parmesan crisps, and pork faggot with shallot purée, crispy leeks and cider-roast apple. Main courses make an impact too, with nothing too fancy or gimmicky: moist, flavourful roast chicken breast, for instance, served on cabbage, accompanied by confit leg, baby carrots, boulangère potatoes and a well-made jus, or a well-conceived fish alternative of roast halibut fillet with citrus-braised mussels, fennel and dauphinoise potatoes. End with a fruity pudding like pineapple tart with pineapple and Malibu sorbet and coconut mousse, or perhaps the 'quartet of chocolate', or alternatively a plate of top-notch local cheeses.

Chef Douglas Elliman **Owner** Bourne Leisure **Times** 6-9 Closed L all week **Prices** Fixed L 2 course £17.95, Fixed D 3 course £19.95, Starter £6.50-£7.50, Main £17.50-£21.50, Dessert £6.50-£10.50, Service optional **Wines** 11 bottles over £30, 26 bottles under £30, 11 by glass **Notes** Vegetarian available, Dress restrictions, Smart casual **Seats** 50 **Parking** 200

KINGTON · Map 9 SO25

The Stagg Inn and Restaurant

◎◎ Modern British **V** ☙

First-class gastro-pub in rural Herefordshire

☎ 01544 230221
Titley HR5 3RL
e-mail: reservations@thestagg.co.uk
dir: Between Kington & Presteigne on B4335

Whitewashed and handsome from the outside and comfortably rustic within, The Stagg stands in tiny Titley amid unspoilt Welsh border country. Here the Marches are a treasure-trove of fine raw ingredients, put to best use by the Roux-trained chef-patron Steve Reynolds. His passion for food may have put this rural local on the culinary map but it's still very much the local pub, with jolly, pint-drinking farmers and walkers filling the homely, pine-furnished bar. His short daily menus bristle with local produce, from estate game to sausages, faggots and chorizo from their own pigs, and fresh fruits and vegetables from the kitchen garden. Expect to find gutsy

modern British dishes, cooked with an assured, yet restrained touch, allowing key flavours to shine through. Perhaps kick off with a full-flavoured crabcake served with watercress and a vibrant tartare sauce. Follow with a succulent, accurately cooked chicken breast, accompanied by girolles, spinach, creamy dauphinoise and tomato purée, then round off with a light and silky honey pannacotta with Marsala baked figs, or a plate of impressive local cheeses.

Chef S Reynolds, M Handley **Owner** Steve & Nicola Reynolds **Times** 12-2/6.30-9 Closed 2 wks Jan-Feb, 1st 2 wks Nov, Mon, D Sun **Prices** Prices not confirmed Service optional **Wines** 8 by glass **Notes** Sunday L, Vegetarian menu **Seats** 70, Pr/dining room 30 **Children** Portions, Menu **Parking** 22

LEDBURY · Map 10 SO73

Feathers Hotel

◎ Modern British ☙

Atmospheric brasserie in a historic inn

☎ 01531 635266
High St HR8 1DS
e-mail: mary@feathers-ledbury.co.uk
web: www.feathers-ledbury.co.uk
dir: M50 junct 2. Ledbury on A449/A438/A417. Hotel on main street

Holding court in this historic town since 1564, it is probably fair to call the Feathers an institution. The timbered old coaching inn is these days a smart hotel with two eating options to satisfy the needs of the 21st-century traveller. Quills Restaurant is the smarter of the two spaces, whilst Fuggles Brasserie provides lots of atmosphere and a broadly appealing menu. With its exposed brick walls, chunky wooden tables, and dried hops adorning the ceiling (fuggles is a type of hops), the cooking follows a broadly modern British path where European techniques are fair game and local produce gets a good showing. There are steaks (Herefordshire, of course) from the grill with a selection of sauces, or you might start with baby monkfish tails with chorizo and orange salad and saffron dressing, before moving on to Redmarley pork fillet with a pressing of belly and black pudding, apple and parsnip purée, and spiced red cabbage.

Chef Susan Isaacs **Owner** David Elliston **Times** 12-2/6.30-9.30 **Prices** Fixed D 3 course fr £22, Starter £5.95-£7.75, Main £9.50-£21.95, Dessert £5.95, Service added but optional 10% **Wines** 42 bottles over £30, 95 bottles under £30, 12 by glass **Notes** Sunday L, Vegetarian available, Civ Wed 120 **Seats** 55, Pr/dining room 60 **Children** Portions **Parking** 30

LEINTWARDINE   Map 9 SO47

The Lion

◉ Modern British ♔

Modern British dishes in an idyllic English inn

☎ 01547 540203 & 540747
High St SY7 0JZ
e-mail: enquiries@thelionleintwardine.co.uk
web: www.thelionleintwardine.co.uk
dir: On A4113. At bottom of High Street by bridge

Set beside the River Teme in a peaceful Herefordshire hamlet, The Lion is a sensitively restored village local with a patio area looking over extensive gardens, and riverside tables under the trees. An English idyll, it was once the local of Sir Banastre Tarleton, who distinguished himself controversially in the American War of Independence, albeit on the losing side. The bare floorboards, leather sofas and beams make all the right noises within, while the kitchen offers a polished repertoire of modern British dishes. A pressed terrine of Devon crab and smoked langoustine has good flavour, and is accompanied by a light watercress pannacotta and baby pear, while prime materials are in evidence in a

pairing of best end and herbed breast of spring lamb, which comes with beech mushrooms and mash, or there could be a bracing early summer risotto of green beans, peas and red mint, served with gremolata, lemon yoghurt and pecorino. Modern menus would be lost without their 'textures', here manifesting as doughnut, mousse, ice cream and sherbet sprinkle, composed of different apple varieties.

The Lion

Chef Paul Halmshaw **Owner** Mr & Mrs W Watkins **Times** 12-2.30/6-9.30 Closed 25 Dec **Prices** Fixed D 3 course fr £25, Starter £5.95-£8.50, Main £10.95-£18.95, Dessert £5.50-£7.95 **Wines** 12 bottles over £30, 38 bottles under £30, 13 by glass **Notes** Sunday L, Vegetarian available, Dress restrictions, Smart casual **Seats** 50, Pr/dining room 20 **Children** Portions, Menu **Parking** 20

ROSS-ON-WYE   Map 10 SO52

The Chase Hotel

◉ British, European ♔

Georgian country-house hotel with modish restaurant

☎ 01989 763161
Gloucester Rd HR9 5LH
e-mail: res@chasehotel.co.uk
web: www.chasehotel.co.uk
dir: M50 junct 4 onto A449. Take A40 towards Gloucester, turn right at rdbt into Ross-on-Wye. Hotel on left 0.25m

Every bit the contemporary dining room, Harry's - set in a large Georgian mansion which is The Chase Hotel (with 11 acres of grounds) - is named after the owner's grandson. Shades of cream, tan and black, modern furnishings and silk drapes blend quite happily with the room's original features - high ceilings, ornate plaster covings and tall windows included. Fresh, quality local ingredients drive the kitchen's equally modern roster of dishes, with things like slow-roasted lamb shank (with a mixed bean cassoulet) lining up alongside those with a nod to sunnier climes, perhaps cod fillet saltimbocca (served on creamed potatoes with a chorizo and paprika Mediterranean sauce). Desserts follow suit, with the ubiquitous Brit sticky toffee pudding favourite strutting its stuff alongside a classic tiramisù or tarte Tatin.

Chef Richard Birchall **Owner** Camanoe Estates Ltd **Times** 12-2/7-10 Closed 24-27 Dec **Prices** Fixed L 2 course £15.50, Fixed D 3 course £27.50, Starter £5.50-£9.95, Main £12.50-£24, Dessert £5.50-£7.95, Service included **Wines** 12 bottles over £30, 33 bottles under £30, 13 by glass **Notes** Sunday L, Vegetarian available, Civ Wed 150 **Seats** 70, Pr/dining room 300 **Children** Portions, Menu **Parking** 75

ROSS-ON-WYE *continued*

Glewstone Court Country House Hotel & Restaurant

🏵 Modern British, French 🍷

West Country produce in an attractive Wye Valley Georgian hotel

☎ 01989 770367
Glewstone HR9 6AW
e-mail: info@glewstonecourt.com
web: www.glewstonecourt.com
dir: From Ross Market Place take A40/A49 (Monmouth/Hereford) over Wilton Bridge. At rdbt left onto A40 (Monmouth/S Wales), after 1m turn right for Glewstone. Hotel 0.5m on left

Set in lovely gardens in the Wye Valley, just three miles from Ross-on-Wye and with views of the Forest of Dean, Glewstone Court is a friendly, family-run Georgian country house. The elegant house has preserved many period features, not least a fine curving Regency staircase, while the candlelit dining room goes for a gently-updated style offset by fancy plasterwork cornicing and crystal chandeliers. This is the right spot for sourcing the fine bounty of the Marches - Welsh lamb, Gloucester pork, and Hereford beef - which might be put to good use as pan-fried strips of steak with lemongrass, chilli and garlic in a Thai-spiced salad. Next, Abergavenny venison turns up with honeyed figs and sloe gin jus, before a dreamy honey pannacotta with raspberry confit wraps things up in fine style.

Chef Christine Reeve-Tucker, Vicky Lyons **Owner** C & W Reeve-Tucker **Times** 12-2/7-10 Closed 25-27 Dec **Prices** Fixed L 2 course fr £14, Fixed D 3 course £26-£27, Starter £5.75-£8.95, Main £14-£21, Dessert £6.95-£7.95, Service optional **Wines** 11 by glass **Notes** Sunday L, Vegetarian available, Dress restrictions, No baseball caps, Civ Wed 72 **Seats** 36, Pr/dining room 40 **Children** Portions, Menu **Parking** 28

Wilton Court Restaurant with Rooms

🏵🏵 Modern British 🍷

Skillful modern cooking in a riverside setting

☎ 01989 562569
Wilton Ln HR9 6AQ
e-mail: info@wiltoncourthotel.com
dir: M50 junct 4 onto A40 towards Monmouth at 3rd rdbt turn left signed Ross-on-Wye then take 1st right, hotel on right

In a bucolic setting on the banks of the River Wye, this small-but-perfectly-formed restaurant with rooms displays its Elizabethan pedigree in the shape of stone-mullioned windows and ancient oak beams. Inside, however, the décor works a light and airy look in step with contemporary tastes, particularly in the light-flooded Mulberry Restaurant, where a conservatory extension overlooks the 300-year-old tree that gives the place its name. The kitchen's emphasis remains on local produce - Hereford beef and lamb, Gloucestershire pork, and splendid regional cheeses - all name-checked on a modern British menu featuring openers such as local Dorstone goats' cheese matched with pine nut and sun-blushed tomato rissole and plum compôte, or Wye Valley asparagus with quail's egg and Parmesan salad and hollandaise sauce. Main course sees slow-roasted Gloucestershire belly pork served with perfect crunchy crackling, black pudding, apple and potato croquette, and cider reduction, and to wind proceedings up, hot chocolate fondant is jazzed up with raspberry sorbet, although the superb artisan cheeses from Herefordshire and Gloucestershire are hard to pass by.

Chef Martyn Williams **Owner** Roger & Helen Wynn **Times** 12-2.15/7-9 **Prices** Fixed L 2 course £16.95, Fixed D 3 course £32.50, Tasting menu £52.50, Starter £5.95-£8.95, Main £16.50-£22.95, Dessert £6.95-£7.50, Service optional **Wines** 7 bottles over £30, 31 bottles under £30, 8 by glass **Notes** Tasting menu 7 course (complete tables only), Sunday L, Vegetarian available, Dress restrictions, Smart casual preferred **Seats** 40, Pr/dining room 12 **Children** Portions, Menu **Parking** 25

WOOLHOPE **Map 10 SO63**

Butchers Arms

🏵 British, European 🍷

Up-to-date country cooking in an old-fashioned rural pub

☎ 01432 860281
HR1 4RF
e-mail: food@butchersarmswoolhope.com
dir: 0.5m out of village, on Ledbury road

The black-and-white half-timbered Butchers is about eight miles' drive out of Hereford, in a splendidly unspoiled rural locale. Happily, it hasn't been inappropriately prettied up inside, but retains its centuries-old heavy wooden beams and foursquare pub furniture. The kitchen draws on local beef, ducks and venison, fruit and veg from farms and gardens in the vicinity, and fish from the Cornish boats, to craft an appealing style of country cooking that's as up-to-date as the surroundings aren't. Start with haggis fritters and beetroot relish, or a soft-boiled duck egg with prosciutto-wrapped asparagus, before going on with grey mullet in brown shrimp and herb butter. Versions of pub staples all look highly alluring, whether it be beef and chorizo burger in smoked paprika butter, or meaty pork sausages with rosemary and garlic from a local butcher, served with smooth mash and an excellent shallot gravy. The warm ginger cake with treacle toffee ice cream is still a popular way to finish, or there might be rum and coconut pannacotta with caramelised banana.

Chef Fran Snell **Owner** Stephen & Annie Bull **Times** 12-2.15/6.30-9 Closed Mon (except BHs), D Sun **Prices** Starter £3.95-£8.50, Main £10.50-£17.50, Dessert £5.75, Service optional **Wines** 8 by glass **Notes** Sunday L £19.50-£24.50, Vegetarian available **Seats** 60, Pr/dining room 24 **Children** Portions **Parking** 40

HERTFORDSHIRE

BERKHAMSTED   Map 6 SP90

The Gatsby

◉ Modern European 🍷

Movies and brasserie cooking in a retooled Art Deco cinema

☎ 01442 870403
97 High St HP4 2DG
e-mail: thegatsby@live.co.uk
dir: M25 junct 20/A41 to Aylesbury in 3m take left turn to Berkhamsted following town signs. Restaurant on left on entering High St

As the name at the top of the frontage announces, The Gatsby shares these premises with the original Rex cinema, a beautiful piece of 1930s British Art Deco from the era of Basil Rathbone and Nova Pilbeam, its heritage traced in the screen-stars of the golden age who dot the walls, and the show-tunes the restaurant pianist rolls out. The modern brasserie menu feels just right in the glitzy surroundings, and makes a fine prelude or supplement to a film upstairs. Seared pigeon breast with a vegetable pastilla in hazelnut and cumin dressing raises the curtain on a performance that might go on to feature Thai fish broth with red mullet and bok choi, alight with lemongrass and ginger, or roast guinea fowl with truffled parsnip purée in a sauce of ceps. Desserts run to dark chocolate fondant with cherry and lime frozen yoghurt, or there are English and French cheeses.

Chef Matthew Salt **Owner** Nick Pembroke
Times 12-2.30/5.30-10.30 Closed 25-26 Dec **Prices** Fixed L 2 course £14.95, Fixed D 3 course fr £20.90, Starter £6.95-£9.25, Main £16.25-£27.95, Dessert £7.95-£8.95, Service optional, Groups min 6 service 12.5% **Wines** 25 bottles over £30, 27 bottles under £30, 16 by glass **Notes** Pre cinema menu Mon-Sat 12-2.30 & 5.30-6.30, Sunday L, Vegetarian available, Dress restrictions, Smart casual **Seats** 65 **Children** Portions **Parking** 10

DATCHWORTH   Map 6 TL21

The Tilbury

◉ Modern British V 🍷

Proper village pub serving up well-sourced, carefully-cooked food

☎ 01438 815550
1 Watton Rd SG3 6TB
e-mail: info@thetilbury.co.uk
dir: A1(M) junct 7, A602 signed Ware & Hertford. At Bragbury End right into Bragbury Lane to Datchworth

Paul Bloxham is a flag-waving supporter of regional and seasonal British food, and if he can serve it up in a smartly renovated pub, so much the better. Known for his TV appearances, Bloxham has plenty of energy left over for pulling tired old boozers up by their bootstraps (the buildings, that is, rather than the clientele) and that is exactly what he has done here in the village of Datchworth. The Tilbury goes for a shabby-chic look with darkwood flooring and tables and bold slabs of colour on the walls, and the vibe is laid-back: a switched-on, food-oriented modern pub, in other words. Food miles are kept to a minimum, but that doesn't preclude shellfish from Scotland and Welsh salt marsh lamb from appearing on the menu, since quality first and foremost is what drives the kitchen's output. Wild boar and quail make an inviting duo for posh Scotch eggs, served with Guinness and mango ketchup, while mains span everything from roast rump of Herdwick mutton with braised white onion, spinach and capers, to steamed Norfolk mussels in saffron, leek and perry cream with chips. Pudding could be a trendy prune and Armagnac sandwich with rice pudding ice cream.

Chef Paul Bloxham, Mark Thurlow **Owner** Paul Bloxham & Paul Andrews **Times** 12-3/6-late Closed 1 Jan, some BHs, D Sun **Prices** Fixed L 2 course £13.95-£18.95, Fixed D 3 course £17.95-£22.95, Starter £4.95-£10.95, Main £9.95-£24.95, Dessert £5.50-£6.95, Service optional, Groups min 6 service 10% **Wines** 32 by glass **Notes** Sunday L, Vegetarian menu **Seats** 70, Pr/dining room 14 **Children** Portions, Menu **Parking** 40

FLAUNDEN   Map 6 TL00

Bricklayers Arms

◉ British, French 🍷

Traditional country inn with well-crafted Anglo-French cooking

☎ 01442 833322 & 831722
Black Robin Ln, Hogpits Bottom HP3 0PH
e-mail: goodfood@bricklayersarms.com
web: www.bricklayersarms.com
dir: M25 junct 20, A451 towards Chipperfield. Into Dunny Ln, 1st right into Flaunden Ln. 1m on single track

An assemblage of three 18th-century cottages that once housed a blacksmith's forge and a butcher's is now a country inn, surrounded by rolling English acres and the walking country of the Chess Valley. Inside is as rustic as you like, with low ceilings, oak beams and a log fire in winter, and there are tables on the terrace and dotted around the garden for when the sun shines on Hertfordshire. Anglo-French food based on plenty of local produce is the name of the game, and dishes are carefully crafted and attractively presented. Start with lightly battered king scallops with stir-fried seafood and spicy tomato coulis, or a signature selection of smoked fish with lemon coriander butter. A potato-topped pie is a familiar enough sight in a country inn, but not perhaps one incorporating partridge, pheasant and venison in red wine and game stock. Sticky toffee pudding or apple and rhubarb tart turn the comfort factor up to max. A splendid wine list and fine selection of local ales completes a thoroughly cheering picture.

Chef Claude Paillet **Owner** Alvin & Sally Michaels
Times 12-2.30/6.30-9.30 Closed 25 Dec **Prices** Fixed L 2 course £15, Fixed D 3 course £20, Starter £5.95-£12.95, Main £11.95-£24.95, Dessert £4.75-£6.95, Service optional, Groups min 6 service 10% **Wines** 96 bottles over £30, 34 bottles under £30, 16 by glass **Notes** Sunday L, Vegetarian available **Seats** 95, Pr/dining room 50 **Children** Portions **Parking** 40

HATFIELD — Map 6 TL20

Beales Hotel

Modern British

Contemporary architecture and vibrant contemporary cooking

☎ 01707 288500 & 288518
Comet Way AL10 9NG
e-mail: outsidein@bealeshotels.co.uk
web: www.bealeshotels.co.uk
dir: On A1001 opposite Galleria Shopping Mall - follow signs for Galleria

The striking modernist design has the look of a Scandinavian design, all smoked glass panels suspended within a cage of cedarwood and steel girders, but this is actually the Hatfield outpost of the Beales Hotels group. Well done for picking up on the art reference, though, since the place really does house a substantial collection of contemporary art from the University of Hertfordshire. The Outsidein Restaurant follows the theme of funky Nordic-style minimalism, using designer ceiling lights above darkwood tables, groovy fabrics on seats and sofas, and pale wood all around on the walls and floors. Thankfully the operation is not a case of style over substance, since creative ideas and bags of flavour emanate from the kitchen. Tried-and-true combos such as pan-fried scallops with cauliflower purée, chorizo and pancetta crisp aren't going to set the world on fire, but are executed with the skill required to tease out all the flavours and textures. A main course of venison Wellington with swede rösti, chestnut purée and honey jus hits all the right autumnal notes, and a finale of pear frangipane tart is matched effectively with honey soup and caramel.

Times 12-2.30/6-10

HITCHIN — Map 12 TL12

Redcoats Farmhouse Hotel

Traditional European

Vibrant flavours in an ancient former farmhouse

☎ 01438 729500
Redcoats Green SG4 7JR
e-mail: sales@redcoats.co.uk
web: www.redcoats.co.uk
dir: A602 to Wymondley. Turn left to Redcoats Green. At top of hill straight over at junct

The same family have lived in this charming 15th-century farmhouse in four acres of pleasant countryside for over a century, and they are proud to share its delights with guests. Redcoats is a warm, welcoming and homely place with a light-flooded conservatory dining room looking over the grounds providing an airy summery vibe to the kitchen's full-flavoured seasonal cooking. A classic winter main course of partridge served with watercress, game chips and game gravy is bookended by a starter of pan-seared wasabi crabcakes with lime and sweet chilli dressing, and an inventive finale of bay leaf-infused crème brûlée pointed up with greengage coulis and gingersnap biscuit.

Chef Scott Liversedge **Owner** Mr P Butterfield & Mrs J Gainsford **Times** 12-2.30/6.30-9 Closed 1 wk after Xmas, BH Mons, D Sun **Prices** Fixed L 2 course fr £18, Fixed D 3 course fr £30, Starter £6-£12, Main £18-£40, Dessert £7-£8.50, Service optional, Groups min 8 service 10% **Wines** 117 bottles over £30, 42 bottles under £30, 11 by glass **Notes** Sunday L, Vegetarian available, Dress restrictions, Smart casual, No jeans or T-shirts, Civ Wed 80 **Seats** 70, Pr/dining room 24 **Children** Portions **Parking** 30

RICKMANSWORTH — Map 6 TQ09

Colette's at The Grove

— see below

Colette's at The Grove

RICKMANSWORTH — MAP 6 TQ09

Modern European — NOTABLE WINE LIST

Technical innovation and natural flavours in a spa hotel near the M25

☎ 01923 807807
Chandler's Cross WD3 4TG
e-mail: info@thegrove.co.uk
web: www.thegrove.co.uk
dir: M25 junct 19, follow signs to Watford. At 1st large rdbt take 3rd exit. 0.5m entrance on right

A comprehensively equipped modern spa hotel only minutes from the M25, The Grove is on hand to provide all the smoothing of feathers that life in the nearby metropolis has ruffled up. It's a Georgian mansion house with golf and mudpacks according to taste in relaxation, and a pair of options for dining: the informal Stables (see separate entry) and Colette's, the fine-dining alternative. Done in today's preferred pastel shades, it makes a neutral but soothing backdrop for Russell Bateman's culinary pyrotechnics, which come in the form of variously proportioned menus given names from the aesthetic repertoire: Haiku, Sonnet and Symphony, depending on whether you're in the market for a bit of Basho, a shot of Shakespeare or the full Mahler. An organic walled garden supplies much of the fresh produce, and the style is about using technical innovation to emphasise natural flavours. Roast Landes foie gras with carrot ketchup and nasturtiums is one eye-catching way to start, as is venison tartare with pickled pear, 100% cocoa and parsnip. Thus primed, the relative classicism of Cotswold chicken roasted with Périgord truffle stuffed under the skin and an enriching note from Vacherin cheese comes as a more than pleasant surprise; cauliflower variations (pickled, roasted and raw) add the requisite note of modernity. Red meats are subjected to complexes of flavours as when Cornish lamb is tricked out with artichokes, pomegranate, ceps and marjoram, while the currently fashionable pairing of chicken wings and fish (in this case turbot) is buttressed by leeks, salsify, chestnuts and tarragon. Apple varieties from the orchard - Cox, Russet, Braeburn and Granny Smith - get a thorough workout in a dessert plate that combines poached, diced, creamed and sorbet elements, together with caramel jelly, or there could be an assemblage of Manjari chocolate, Valencia orange, brioche, olive oil and sea salt.

Chef Russell Bateman **Owner** Ralph Trustees Ltd **Times** 6.30-10 Closed Sun-Mon (ex BHs), L all week **Prices** Fixed D 3 course £65, Tasting menu £75-£85, Service optional **Wines** 24 by glass **Notes** ALC 3 course £65, Occasional market menu £35 Tue-Thu, Vegetarian available, Civ Wed 500 **Seats** 40, Pr/dining room 24 **Parking** 300

Save on Hotels. Book at **theAA.com/hotel**

HERTFORDSHIRE 211 **ENGLAND**

The Stables Restaurant at The Grove

◉ Modern British

Creative modern cooking in George Stubbs' favourite stables

☎ 01923 807807 & 296015
Chandler's Cross WD3 4TG
e-mail: restaurants@thegrove.co.uk
dir: M25 junct 19, A411 towards Watford. Hotel on right

The former stable block was illustrious enough in its day to have brought Britain's foremost equine painter George Stubbs here in search of his models. It now forms the restaurant of a country house reinvented as The Grove hotel, and is an informal, raftered dining space with open-to-view kitchen, complete with wood-burning oven for pizzas and a chargrill for the steaks. Starters draw inspiration from dessert ideas, such as poached pear with blue cheese and walnuts in ginger dressing, or goats' cheese cheesecake with hazelnut base, garnished with roasted figs. Mains might take in a duo of lamb - best end and shoulder - with hotpot potatoes and roots, or fillets of lemon sole with cavolo nero in Jerusalem artichoke butter. Substantial puddings include treacle tart and clotted cream, simply but classically rendered. Colette's (see entry) is the fine-dining option at The Grove.

Chef Christopher Mouyiassi **Owner** Ralph Trustees Ltd
Times 12-3/6-9.30 Closed 25 & 31 Dec **Prices** Starter £8-£11.20, Main £10-£32, Dessert £6-£8, Service optional **Wines** 11 bottles over £30, 10 bottles under £30, 10 by glass **Notes** Sunday L, Vegetarian available **Seats** 120, Pr/dining room 16 **Children** Portions, Menu **Parking** 300

ST ALBANS   Map 6 TL10

Chez Mumtaj

◉◉ French, Asian

French-Asian fusion in opulent surroundings

☎ 01727 800033
Centurian House, 136-142 London Rd AL1 1PQ
e-mail: info@chezmumtaj.com
web: www.chezmumtaj.com

What's in a name? Well this one says it all in two words: modern Franco-Asian cuisine is the deal at Chez Mumtaj, and the décor takes its cue from a gentlemen's club with mahogany panelled walls, glass screens etched with a regimental-style coat of arms, and cream leather banquettes. The kitchen team serves up a wide-ranging, eclectic repertoire that travels as extensively as a gap-year backpacker through the cuisines of southeast Asia and Europe, bringing it all together with classic French cooking techniques. Expect to see pan-seared spice-crusted Scottish scallops teamed with sautéed wild mushrooms and shallots, almond, cardamom, and saffron cappuccino foam, ahead of main-course hybrids involving 28-day-aged rib-eye beef crusted with sumac and pepper, and partnered with herb butter, potato fondant, Madeira cardamom glaze, ceps, spinach, celeriac purée and veal jus.

Chez Mumtaj

Chef Chad Rahman **Owner** Chad Rahman
Times 12-2.30/6-11 Closed 25 Dec, Mon **Prices** Prices not confirmed Service added but optional 10% **Wines** 14 by glass **Notes** Tasting & early bird D menus available, Sunday L, Vegetarian available, Dress restrictions, Smart casual **Seats** 100, Pr/dining room 16 **Parking** On street & car park nearby

See advert below

ST ALBANS *continued*

St Michael's Manor

◉◉ British, European ✪

Classically-based cooking in a Tudor manor

☎ 01727 864444
Fishpool St AL3 4RY
e-mail: reservations@stmichaelsmanor.com
web: www.stmichaelsmanor.com
dir: At Tudor Tavern in High St into George St. After abbey & school on left, road continues onto Fishpool St. Hotel 1m on left

Just a short stroll from the cathedral and city centre, St Michael's is an Elizabethan manor house in five acres of well-kept grounds with a lake at the centre - a view which you can appreciate at leisure from the elegant orangery-style Lake Restaurant. Attentively professional service boosts still further the sense of well-being in this luminous space, while the kitchen steers a broadly modern British course, delivering frequently-changing menus of technically-adept, classically-based cooking with modish touches here and there, as in the roasted shoulder lollipops that are matched with venison carpaccio and shallot and hazelnut dressing. Elsewhere, line-caught sea bass is paired to great effect with crab and dill beignets, purple sprouting broccoli, crushed Jersey Royals and pinot grigio cream, while meat-eaters could get a more robust pairing of shin of beef and oxtail suet pudding with roasted shallots, broccoli Mornay, and duck fat-roasted potatoes. Creative desserts run to galette of Cox's apple with Calvados cream, mint opaline and black butter ice cream.

Chef Mr Perry Butler **Owner** Sheila Newling Ward
Times 12-2/7-9.30 Closed L 31 Dec, D 25 Dec
Prices Fixed L 2 course £17, Fixed D 3 course £21, Starter £8.50-£12.50, Main £18.50-£23.50, Dessert £8-£12, Service added but optional 12.5% **Wines** 39 bottles over £30, 38 bottles under £30, 15 by glass **Notes** Sunday L, Vegetarian available, Dress restrictions, Smart casual,

Civ Wed 100 **Seats** 130, Pr/dining room 24
Children Portions, Menu **Parking** 60

Sopwell House

◉ Modern British **NEW** ✪

Smart country club near historic St Albans

☎ 01727 864477
Cottonmill Ln, Sopwell AL1 2HQ
e-mail: enquiries@sopwellhouse.co.uk
web: www.sopwellhouse.co.uk
dir: M25 junct 22, A1081 St Albans. At lights left into Mile House Ln, over mini-rdbt into Cottonmill Ln

The one-time country residence of Lord Mountbatten is a handsome Georgian house indeed, white-painted, and standing in 12 acres of pretty gardens. It makes an impressive country-house hotel and has all the spa facilities you might imagine. The restaurant is suitably modish in its aspirations, with decoration chosen from the soothing contemporary colour palette and tables dressed up in white linen cloths. A smart setting, then, for some sharp contemporary cooking. Start, perhaps, with quail served with parsley purée, black truffle and pistachio arancini, or king scallop with confit belly of pork, broad beans and sweetcorn purée. Follow on with crab-crusted salmon fillet with a saffron risotto, king prawns and a poppy seed salad, or a duo of Barbary duck with autumn vegetables and orange jus. Dessert might bring forth iced banana parfait with dark chocolate sauce and honeycomb.

Chef James Chapman **Times** 12-3/7-10 **Prices** Prices not confirmed Service optional **Notes** Sunday L £25

Pendley Manor Hotel

◉◉ Modern British

Handsome manor house with modern cooking

☎ 01442 891891
Cow Ln HP23 5QY
e-mail: sales@pendley-manor.co.uk
web: www.pendley-manor.co.uk
dir: M25 junct 20, A41 (Tring exit). At rdbt follow Berkhamsted/London signs. 1st left signed Tring Station & Pendley Manor

Although Pendley's history stretches back a thousand years and gets a mention in the Domesday Book, the current incarnation is part Victorian neo-Tudor, built in 1872 after a fire destroyed the original, and part modern annexe, built to extend significantly its events and conference capacity. The Victorian section offers period grandeur in spades, particularly in the Oak Restaurant where oak flooring, lofty ceilings, colourful patterned wallpaper, and swagged-back drapes at vast bay windows make for an imposing setting. The refined cooking avoids risk taking in favour of well-tried mainstream ideas: a starter of seared yellowfin tuna with spiced crab, scallop fritter and guacamole saffron mayonnaise is convincing and well executed, while excellent Cornish lamb - a cutlet and 12-hour-braised

shoulder, to be precise - is teamed to equally good effect with wild mushroom mousse, confit garlic, and pea purée with thyme jus. Finally, chocolate fondant releases a rich melting centre just as it should, to mingle with pistachio ice cream and crunchy meringue.

Chef Martin White **Owner** Craydawn Pendley Manor
Times 12.30-2.30/7-9.30 Closed L Sat **Prices** Fixed L 2 course £20.50, Fixed D 3 course £27.50, Starter £8.50-£11.25, Main £18.75-£32, Dessert £7.50-£9, Service optional **Wines** 13 bottles over £30, 33 bottles under £30, 7 by glass **Notes** Sunday L, Vegetarian available, Dress restrictions, Smart casual, Civ Wed 180 **Seats** 75, Pr/dining room 200 **Children** Portions, Menu **Parking** 150

Hanbury Manor, A Marriott Hotel & Country Club

◉◉ French, Mediterranean

Imaginative modern cooking in a Jacobean manor

☎ 01920 487722
SG12 0SD
e-mail: wendy.traynor@marriotthotels.com
web: www.marriotthanburymanor.co.uk
dir: From M25 junct 25, take A10 towards Cambridge, for 12m. Leave A10 Wadesmill/Thundridge/Ware. Right at rdbt, hotel on left

Hanbury Manor is a fine example of Jacobean architecture, with all the hallmarks expected in a property of the period - oak panelling, oil paintings and tapestries - as well as the 21st-century requisites of spa and golf course. Dining in the Zodiac Restaurant takes place under a vaulted ceiling, with the signs of the zodiac in gold leaf, along with panelled walls, a grand fireplace and formally dressed tables. The menus are as contemporary as the surroundings are historic, with ideas culled from around Europe, and the kitchen has a discerning eye for quality produce. Well-timed scallops are served with cauliflower purée and powerful agrodolce sauce, and may be followed by breast of Gressingham duck, of excellent quality and great flavour, with rösti enhanced by shredded leg confit, baby beets, pear and an unusual café au lait sauce. Canapés are prepared with the same amount of care as the rest of the package, and puddings might include an imaginative take on Black Forest gâteau with a cherry lolly and cherry foam.

Times 12-2.30/7-10.30 Closed Mon-Tue, L Wed-Sat, D Sun

Save on Hotels. Book at **theAA.com/hotel**

HERTFORDSHIRE 213 **ENGLAND**

WELWYN	Map 6 TL21

Auberge du Lac

◉◉◉ — see page 214

See advert below

Tewin Bury Farm Hotel

◉◉ Modern British

- -

Up-to-the-minute modern cookery in 500 acres of Hertfordshire farmland

☎ 01438 717793
AL6 0JB
e-mail: restaurant@tewinbury.co.uk
dir: A1M junct 6 (signed Welwyn Garden City), 1st exit A1000. 0.25m to B1000 Hertford Rd. Hotel on left

Although this is still a working farm in the best part of 500 acres of lush Hertfordshire countryside with the dinky River Mimram threading through, the Williams family diversified to set up lovely guest rooms and a restaurant in the complex of converted barns. The results are light, contemporary - almost Scandinavian - in the use of pale natural oak for tables and chairs, flooring, and rough-hewn rafters. Logs are stacked ready for use in the wood-fired oven, which lies at the heart of the kitchen's output

of sunny, French-accented contemporary dishes. Vegetables, herbs and trout are produced on the farm, while other materials are kept as local as possible. Well-judged ideas such as lime-marinated mackerel with black olive caramel, hazelnut and green beans lead on to mains of Hertfordshire beef fillet with bone marrow dumplings, sweet garlic purée, wilted sorrel, ale foam and beef jus. The switched-on creativity continues through to desserts, which could bring warm carrot cake with cream cheese mousse, cinnamon ice cream and caramelised walnuts.

Times 12-2.30/6.30-9.30

The Waggoners

◉ French ◐

- -

Authentic French cooking in lovely village inn

☎ 01707 324241
Brickwall Close, Ayot Green AL6 9AA
e-mail: laurent@thewaggoners.co.uk
dir: A1(M) junct 6 to B197, right into Ayot and 1st left Brickwall Close

The bi-lingual menu is a clue to what's going on in the kitchen of this smartly revamped 17th-century coaching inn: hands-on French owners Laurent and Aude Brydniak

have injected a hit of Gallic flair into the quintessentially English setting. Ancient blackened beams, an inglenook fireplace, and walls festooned with copper pans and pewter mugs make for a cosy space, and cheery staff add a pleasant tone to proceedings. The menu is packed with well-executed classics to bring a smile to Francophile foodies - there could be foie gras ballottine with apricot and peach purée or frogs' legs sautéed with garlic and parsley butter, then a pause for a palate-cleansing trou normand - apple, rosemary and honey granita with Calvados - before mushroom and rosemary-stuffed roast leg of lamb with parsnip mash, asparagus and Marsala jus. Dessert could be a French fancy such as a praline chiboust cream-filled Paris-Brest cake served with Grand Marnier ice cream.

Chef Pierre Kolabukoff **Owner** Laurent & Aude Brydniak **Times** 12-2.30/6.30-9 Closed Mon, D Sun **Prices** Fixed L 2 course fr £14.50, Starter £5.50-£14, Main £13-£23, Dessert £5.95-£7, Service optional, Groups min 6 service 10% **Wines** 40 bottles over £30, 60 bottles under £30, 22 by glass **Notes** Sunday L fr £13, Vegetarian available, Dress restrictions, Smart casual **Seats** 65, Pr/dining room 35 **Children** Portions **Parking** 70

Auberge du Lac

French, European V NOTABLE WINE LIST

Refined and modish cooking in a lakeside hunting lodge

☎ 01707 368888
**Brocket Hall Estate, Brocket Rd
AL8 7XG**
e-mail: auberge@brocket-hall.co.uk
web: www.brocket-hall.co.uk
dir: A1(M) junct 4, B653 to Wheathampstead. In Brocket Ln take 2nd gate entry to Brocket Hall

The Brocket Hall Estate encloses 543 acres of quintessentially English countryside, and now makes a living as an upmarket complex for corporate get-togethers, glossy weddings and a spot of golf. But that all melts into the distance when you're seated in the dreamy setting of the Auberge du Lac, especially if you're lucky enough to be dining alfresco on the lakeside terrace. The stately pile's former hunting lodge - a red-brick mini country mansion - has dipped its toes into the idyllic waterside location by Broadwater Lake since the 18th century. Inside it retains plenty of period character, and the mood is enhanced by perfectly-paced service that never misses a beat. Chef Phil Thompson leads a talented kitchen team, growing in confidence from year to year since he took the reins in 2005, and constantly fine-tuning the output to deliver seriously well-crafted, creative

and dynamic modern food anchored firmly in French classicism. Superb produce is at the heart of it all and seasonality is a cornerstone, so a winter meal might start with a pairing of veal sweetbreads and roast bone marrow, served with turnip and sour cream, then continue with cod served alongside roast salsify, almond butter, razor clams and chicken skin. There are unusual strokes among meat dishes too - perhaps hare partnered by Jerusalem artichoke, confit yolk, mushroom duxelle, and home-made black pudding. The technique is sufficiently assured to bring off these daring productions with convincing flair, and such refined pleasures are also open to vegetarians via a carte and six-course tasting menus - perhaps a 62-degree poached egg with brown bread foam, seeds and nuts, followed by hand-rolled tagliatelle with wild mushrooms and aged parmesan. Equally impressive deserts could celebrate chocolate together with salt caramel, candied hazelnuts, buttermilk and shortbread. A skilled sommelier will guide you through the 750-bin wine list, which reads as a *Who's Who* of stellar French producers alongside splendid stuff from elsewhere.

Chef Phil Thompson **Owner** CCA International **Times** 12-2.30/7-9.30 Closed 27 Dec-17 Jan, Sun-Mon **Prices** Fixed L 3 course £39.50, Fixed D 3 course £60, Tasting menu £69-£79.50, Service added but optional 10% **Wines** 14 by glass **Notes** ALC fixed 3 course £60, Tasting menu 6/9 course, Vegetarian menu, Dress restrictions, No jeans or trainers, Civ Wed 62 **Seats** 70, Pr/dining room 32 **Children** Portions, Menu **Parking** 50

Save on Hotels. Book at **theAA.com/hotel**

HERTFORDSHIRE – KENT 215 **ENGLAND**

WELWYN *continued*

The Wellington

◉ Modern British **NEW** ✪

Village inn with an appealing menu

☎ 01438 714036
High St AL6 9LZ
e-mail: info@wellingtonatwelwyn.co.uk
dir: A1M junct 6, on High Street in Welwyn village across from St Mary's Church

Going strong since AD 1352, The Wellington, on Welwyn's pretty high street, is an old coaching inn which takes a contemporary approach to the business of hospitality. A makeover a few years ago has opened up the place, seen the addition of some rather cool bedrooms, and put the focus firmly on the gastro side of the pub spectrum. It looks good with its rustic-chic exposed brick walls, real fires and bar stocked with proper beers. The menu keeps things simple and unpretentious, so you might choose to tuck into a hearty beef and Wellington ale pie. If you're up for the full works, however, you might start with crispy duck and hoisin dumpling, or go for one of the daily specials such as crab and tarragon bonbons with samphire, radish, cucumber and tarragon oil. Next up, a fillet burger, fish pie, or something a little more adventurous such as braised ox cheek with an oxtail lollipop.

Chef John Beardsworth **Owner** Christopher Gerard
Times 12-10 All-day dining **Prices** Fixed L 2 course £12.95, Fixed D 2 course £12.95, Starter £5.95-£7.95, Main £11.95-£23.50, Dessert £5.95-£6.95, Groups min 8 service 10% **Wines** 10 bottles over £30, 40 bottles under £30, 30 by glass **Notes** Sunday L fr £13.95, Vegetarian available **Seats** 90 **Children** Portions **Parking** 40

The White Hart Hotel

◉ Modern British ✪

Pub cooking with panache in an old coaching inn

☎ 01438 715353
2 Prospect Place AL6 9EN
e-mail: bookings@whitehearthotel.net
web: www.thewhitehearthotel.net
dir: A1(M) junct 6, follow signs to Welwyn shops

A 17th-century coaching-inn in a thriving Hertfordshire village ticks all the boxes for bucolic charm. The flagstone floors, brick fireplace and uneven beams inside tell a venerable story, but the modernisation job in the décor has resulted in an elegant look to the dining room, with deep violet walls and quality table settings. An upbeat, friendly air pervades, and the place is understandably popular with locals who lunch, as well as travelling custom motoring over for a relaxing dinner. Pub stalwarts are rendered with some panache, from hearty carrot and coriander soup with croûtons, venison with pearl barley and dumplings, and a rather sophisticated rhubarb syllabub, and there are enterprising fish specialities too, such as baked cod in clam and bacon chowder.

Chef Paul Ribbands **Owner** Piers Lyon
Times 12-2.30/6.30-9.30 **Prices** Fixed L 2 course £18.95, Tasting menu £40-£80, Starter £5.65-£10.50, Main £10.50-£18.95, Dessert £5.95-£9.50, Service optional **Wines** 17 bottles over £30, 26 bottles under £30, 13 by glass **Notes** Sunday L £14.95-£21.95, Vegetarian available **Seats** 44, Pr/dining room 40 **Children** Portions, Menu **Parking** 22

WILLIAN Map 12 TL23

The Fox

◉ Modern British ✪

Creative cooking in a smart local pub

☎ 01462 480233
SG6 2AE
e-mail: info@foxatwillian.co.uk
dir: A1(M) junct 9 towards Letchworth, 1st left to Willian, The Fox 0.5m on left

The picturesque village of Willian may have just the one pub, but the stylish Fox has all the attributes that anyone could reasonably ask for: a proper pubby locals' bar bristling with well-kept real ales, a smart contemporary open-plan dining room hung with original artwork beneath a glazed atrium ceiling, and a skilled kitchen whose ambition goes way beyond pub grub staples. Under the same ownership as The White Horse in Brancaster Staithe (see entry), supply lines to fish and seafood from the Norfolk coast are strong, so a Mediterranean stew of mussels fresh from the beds next to its seaside sibling might open the show, followed by pan-roasted fillet of hake with chorizo fricassée, Parmentier potatoes and citrus aïoli. Meaty mains also come with contemporary European accents - perhaps a duo of local lamb (roast rump and mini shepherd's pie) with basil mashed potato, confit tomatoes, and red wine and mint jus.

Chef Harry Kodagoda **Owner** Clifford Nye
Times 12-2/6.45-9.15 Closed D Sun **Prices** Starter £4.95-£8.95, Main £12.95-£19.95, Dessert £4.95-£6.95, Service added but optional 10% **Wines** 16 bottles over £30, 29 bottles under £30, 15 by glass **Notes** Sunday L £12.50-£14.95, Vegetarian available **Seats** 70 **Children** Portions **Parking** 40

KENT

ASHFORD Map 7 TR04

Eastwell Manor

◉◉ British, French ✪

Creative, classical cooking in a grand manor house

☎ 01233 213000
Eastwell Park, Boughton Lees TN25 4HR
e-mail: enquiries@eastwellmanor.co.uk
dir: From M20 junct 9 take 1st left (Trinity Rd). Through 4 rdbts to lights. Left onto A251 signed Faversham. 0.5m to sign for Boughton Aluph, 200yds to hotel

It's a stately pile and no mistake, a breath-taking house with a history that goes back to Norman times. Sure, it has been extended over the years, but it has lost none of its sense of magnificence. The extension means there's room for swish leisure facilities for a start, and it will come as no surprise to hear the place is a popular wedding venue. It stands in over 60 acres of glorious grounds and inside is no less impressive with its ornate plasterwork, carved oak panelling, baronial fireplaces and antiques at every turn. The Manor Restaurant fits in very nicely indeed with its traditional fine-dining finish, and ambitious, well-crafted, gently updated classic cooking. Start with gravad lax with horseradish cream and beetroot purée, or ham hock croquette with carrot and ginger purée and home-made piccalilli, and move on to roast rack of Smarden lamb with braised shoulder confit, red cabbage purée and dauphinoise potatoes. Desserts are equally on the money: warm chocolate fondant, for example, with dark chocolate sauce and tonka bean ice cream.

Chef Neil Wiggins **Owner** Turrloo Parrett
Times 12-2.30/7-10 **Prices** Fixed L 2 course £15.50-£19.50, Fixed D 3 course £32, Service added but optional 10% **Wines** 20 by glass **Notes** Gourmet champagne evenings, Sunday L, Vegetarian available, Dress restrictions, Smart collared shirt D, no denim/sportswear, Civ Wed 250 **Seats** 80, Pr/dining room 80 **Children** Portions **Parking** 120

ASHFORD *continued*

The Wife of Bath

@@ Modern British @

Intimate, stylish village restaurant with accomplished cooking

☎ 01233 812232
4 Upper Bridge St, Wye TN25 5AF
e-mail: relax@thewifeofbath.com
dir: 4m NE of Ashford. M20 junct 9, A28 for Canterbury, 3m right to Wye

This stylish small restaurant with rooms brings a touch of contemporary class to the pretty medieval Kentish village of Wye. On the accommodation side, the rooms deliver a high comfort factor if you fancy slackening off the belt and staying over in order to put the kitchen team through its paces. The ambience is laid-back and intimate, while fashionable patterned wallpaper, modern art and linen-clothed tables add up to a fresh, uncluttered, setting. The kitchen doesn't labour the point, but the lion's share of its ingredients come from local Kentish producers, and are brought together in well-conceived dishes showing plenty of flair and imagination, resulting in some off-the-wall combinations - smoked duck delivered with a whisky and tobacco-infused vinaigrette, for example. Grilled hake arrives wearing a gruyère crust, and matched with a punchy crayfish velouté, spiced broccoli, and smooth mash, while dessert brings down the curtain with an enterprising combination of roasted sesame seed and orange parfait, orange liquid gel, and a shredded marmalade garnish.

Chef Robert Hymers **Owner** Rupert & Victoria Reeves
Times 12-2/6.30-9.30 Closed 25 Dec, Mon, L Tue, D Sun
Prices Prices not confirmed Service optional **Wines** 11 by glass **Notes** Sunday L, Vegetarian available **Seats** 42, Pr/dining room 12 **Children** Portions, Menu **Parking** 12

AYLESFORD   Map 6 TQ75

Hengist Restaurant

@@ Modern European

Polished cooking in sophisticated setting

☎ 01622 719273
7-9 High St ME20 7AX
e-mail: restaurant@hengistrestaurant.co.uk
dir: M20 junct 5 & 6, follow signs to Aylesford

History buffs might be interested to note that Hengist is named after the man who invaded across the Medway with his brother Horsa in AD 449 and rewarded themselves with the titles of Kings of Kent. But enough of history. Within the 16th-century building, oak beams, brick and stonework are juxtaposed with a rather decadent Paul Smith-designed contemporary look involving chocolate suede walls, smoked glass and twinkling chandeliers. Under the guidance of Richard Phillips (see entry for Thackeray's, Tunbridge Wells) the kitchen deals in modern European ideas underpinned by well-sourced local produce, inventive combinations and punctilious attention to detail. Pistachio-wrapped foie

gras with Sauternes jelly, celeriac purée and Kentish cherries shows the refined style, while main courses could deliver Barolo-poached wild sea bass partnered inventively with creamed cauliflower salad, buttered girolles, caper raisin dressing and cauliflower velouté. The same high-gloss values continue to the end in an exquisite modern take on cheesecake, flavoured with citrus and vanilla and served with raspberries, lemon meringue and mint ice cream.

Times 12-2.30/6.30-10 Closed 26 Dec & 1 Jan, Mon, D Sun

BEARSTED   Map 7 TQ85

Soufflé Restaurant

@ Modern European @

Charming village setting for modish cooking

☎ 01622 737065
31 The Green ME14 4DN
e-mail: soufflerestaurant@hotmail.com
web: www.soufflerestaurant.net
dir: M20 junct 7 follow Maidstone signs, bear left towards Bearsted straight over at rdbt, towards Bearsted Green at next mini-rdbt, continue for approx 1.5m to the green. Restaurant on left, turn left just before Soufflé sign & park at rear of restaurant

With its lovely location on Bearsted's pretty village green, you're already off to a flying start at this charming 16th-century timbered cottage restaurant - especially when fine weather lets you dine out on the front terrace. Inside, the old-world charm is bolstered further still by gnarled, head-skimming timbers, bare brickwork, and a crackling winter log fire. Add in the lure of creative cooking that puts a modern spin on classic ideas, and has impeccably-sourced ingredients at the centre of things, and it's no wonder Nick Evenden's place is a long-running stalwart of the local dining scene. Expect pan-fried scallops served on a ham and parsley terrine with pea purée and mustard foam, followed by roast saddle of rabbit wrapped in pancetta and stuffed with black pudding, and to finish, perhaps a rhubarb-fest involving crème brûlée, compôte and sorbet.

Soufflé Restaurant

Chef Nick Evenden **Owner** Nick & Karen Evenden
Times 12-2/7-9.30 Closed Mon, L Sat, D Sun **Prices** Fixed L 2 course £14-£17, Fixed D 3 course fr £25, Starter £7.50-£11, Main £19-£26, Dessert £7.50-£8.50, Service optional **Wines** 20 bottles over £30, 50 bottles under £30, 7 by glass **Notes** Sunday L, Vegetarian available **Seats** 40, Pr/dining room 25 **Children** Portions **Parking** 12, On street

---

BIDDENDEN   Map 7 TQ83

The West House

@@@ *— see opposite*

BOUGHTON MONCHELSEA   Map 7 TQ75

The Mulberry Tree

@@ Modern British @

Serious cooking in Kent countryside setting

☎ 01622 749082 & 741058
Hermitage Ln ME17 4DA
e-mail: info@themulberrytreekent.co.uk
dir: B2163 turn into Wierton Rd straight over x-rds, 1st left East Hall Hill

If you're expecting a typical weatherboarded and tile-hung Kentish hostelry, the clean-lined modern building may come as a surprise in the time-warp bucolic setting of Boughton Monchelsea. The former pub has been reinvented as a stylish and relaxed contemporary bar and restaurant done out with leather sofas on wooden floors, set against a warm colour scheme and boldly-patterned designer wallpapers. It is all clearly abreast of current trends, as is the team in the kitchen who send out daily-changing menus of well-tuned modern British food with a European accent. Having supply lines to the 'Garden of England's' finest ingredients would keep many a kitchen happy, but here they go the whole nine yards, raising their own turkeys and Kentish Middlewhite pigs in the field at the back and cultivating a productive kitchen garden. Roasted brill with chargrilled potato, braised leek, and smoked bacon and cockle vinaigrette, and rump of lamb with broad beans, wild garlic and dauphinoise potatoes are typical mains, and you might follow that with spiced ginger pannacotta with caramelised pear and pear macaroon.

Chef Mark Pearson **Owner** Karen Williams & Mark Jones
Times 12-2/6.30-9.30 Closed 26 Dec, Mon, D Sun
Prices Fixed L 2 course fr £14.50, Fixed D 3 course fr £17.50, Starter £6.95-£8.50, Main £16.75-£21.50,

Save on Hotels. Book at **theAA.com/hotel**

KENT 217 **ENGLAND**

Dessert £6.50, Service optional, Groups min 10 service 10% **Wines** 30 bottles over £30, 31 bottles under £30, 54 by glass **Notes** Sunday L, Vegetarian available, Civ Wed 70 **Seats** 70, Pr/dining room 12 **Children** Portions, Menu **Parking** 60

BRANDS HATCH — Map 6 TQ56

Brandshatch Place Hotel & Spa

◎◎ Modern British

Grand location for modern British food

☎ 01474 875000
Brands Hatch Rd, Fawkham DA3 8NQ
e-mail: brandshatchplace@handpicked.co.uk
web: www.handpickedhotels.co.uk/brandshatchplace
dir: M25 junct 3/A20 West Kingsdown. Left at paddock entrance/Fawkham Green sign. 3rd left signed Fawkham Rd. Hotel 500mtrs on right

Nothing can disturb the peace at this luxurious and handsome Georgian hotel, not even the iconic racetrack nearby. For here everything is calm, serene and built (by the Duke of Norfolk, no less) with a good deal of panache. It makes a splendid country-house hotel with plenty of room to spread out and forget about the real world. The restaurant is certainly a reason to visit in its own right: with its fine Georgian features, views over the garden, and tables dressed up for the business of fine dining, it's the perfect setting for some smart contemporary cooking.

Each dish on the menu comes with an accompanying wine recommendation, and the kitchen sources from Kent where possible. Start, perhaps, with pressed ham hock terrine with home-made piccalilli, or wild garlic and white onion soup. Follow on with a spankingly fresh fillet of hake with kohlrabi fondant, spinach and pancetta, and finish with vanilla pannacotta with a shortbread tuile and blood orange sorbet.

Chef Carl Smith **Owner** Hand Picked Hotels
Times 12-2/7-9.30 **Prices** Fixed L 2 course £28, Fixed D 3 course £36, Starter £9.95-£12.50, Main £12.95-£26.95, Dessert £7.95-£8.50, Service optional **Wines** 88 bottles over £30, 11 bottles under £30, 18 by glass **Notes** Sunday L, Vegetarian available, Civ Wed 70 **Seats** 60, Pr/dining room 110 **Children** Portions, Menu **Parking** 100

CANTERBURY — Map 7 TR15

The Dove Inn

◉ British, French

Attractive food-focused country pub

☎ 01227 751360
Plum Pudding Ln, Dargate ME13 9HB
e-mail: doveatdargate@hotmail.com
dir: 6m NW of Canterbury. A299 Thanet Way, turn off at Lychgate service station

Head down the evocative-sounding Plumpudding Lane in the village of Dargate and you'll find this splendid Georgian country pub. It's got a lovely rural aspect and a charmingly respectable rusticity to its interior, and the focus is very much on food. Sit at a chunky wooden table, or outside if the weather is playing ball, and tuck into some intelligently put together food, much of it sourced locally (some of it from the pub's own garden), and cooked with flair. You might start with smoked haddock macaroni with a poached duck egg, or pumpkin and sage risotto flavoured with truffle oil, and move on to roasted marsh lamb with black cabbage and pearl barley, or breast of local duck with potato gratin and purple sprouting broccoli. The menu shows British and French leanings, not least at dessert stage where you might find a classic crème brûlée with home-made shortbread, or lemon posset with vanilla cream cheese mousse.

Chef Phillip MacGregor **Owner** Phillip & Sarah MacGregor
Times 12-2.30/7-9 Closed Mon, D Sun, Tue **Prices** Prices not confirmed Service added but optional 10%, Groups min 6 service 10% **Wines** 12 by glass **Notes** Sunday L, Vegetarian available **Seats** 26 **Children** Portions **Parking** 15, On street

---

The West House

BIDDENDEN — MAP 7 TQ83

Modern European ◈ NOTABLE WINE LIST

Self-assured cooking in a delightful setting

☎ 01580 291341
28 High St TN27 8AH
e-mail: thewesthouse@btconnect.com
dir: Junct of A262 & A274. 14m S of Maidstone

There are some lovely villages in Kent and Biddenden is amongst that number, with a church, a green, and a nice line in Flemish weavers' cottages. It is in one such 16th-century cottage that Graham Garrett (and his family - this is very much a family affair) has set up shop and made a name for himself, even gaining a place on our TV screens in shows such as the *Great British Menu*. It looks great inside with its cleverly sensitive mix of old and new, where chunky oak beams and an inglenook are set

against a classily-understated contemporary décor with darkwood tables on bare floorboards, buttery-coloured leather seats and food-oriented art on plain white walls. Like most chefs at this level, Garrett is pathologically scrupulous about the provenance of the ingredients he works with, and he allows the natural flavours to take centre stage. There are a good many modern cooking techniques on show, but they are used sensitively, and in context, so dishes are well balanced and not in the least bit namby pamby. There's a tasting menu, with optional wine flight, a mightily tempting lunch menu (25 quid for three cracking courses) and a reasonably-priced carte. A Rye Bay scallop comes in the fine company of a treatise on the great British carrot - roast heritage, mousse, pickled and salad - or start instead with a sausage roll (a posh one, mind) with Huntsham Farm pork and truffle and a Madeira sauce. Next up, the likes of slow-cooked shoulder of lamb with pastilla, aubergine purée and couscous, and grilled fillet of sole with curried mussel chowder keep up the momentum. The creativity continues

with desserts - how about a 'mojito'? Well, the rum cake with lime curd, mint sorbet and granita certainly hits the spot, or try the poached banana with hazelnut crumble and chocolate 'rocks'.

Chef Graham Garrett **Owner** Jackie Hewitt & Graham Garrett **Times** 12-2/7-9.30 Closed 25 Dec-1 Jan, Mon, L Sat, D Sun **Prices** Fixed L 2 course £35-£40, Fixed D 3 course £40, Service added but optional 12.5% **Wines** 15 by glass **Notes** Sunday L **Seats** 32 **Children** Portions **Parking** 7

CANTERBURY *continued*

The Goods Shed Restaurant

◉ British ♥

Hearty modern dishes overlooking the farmers' market

☎ 01227 459153
Station Road West CT2 8AN
e-mail: restaurant@thegoodsshed.co.uk
dir: Adjacent to Canterbury West train station

Right next to Canterbury West railway station, the former rail depot now plays host to a thriving covered food market, with an on-site eatery on a raised level overlooking proceedings. Blackboard menus announce the day's bill of fare, there are blankets to swaddle yourself in on chilly evenings, and the kitchen team can be seen beavering away at the freshest produce. A bowl of Crown Prince squash soup is a restorative treat in winter, or there may be modern brasserie favourites such as scallops with Jerusalem artichoke purée and bacon. Following up might come pheasant with chestnuts and chorizo, pollock and mussels in garlicky cider cream, or a well-timed piece of hake with lentils and pungent aïoli. Finish with thin-shelled lemon and basil tart and balsamic ice cream, although shipwreck tart, a boozy, rough-textured treacle tart served with clotted cream, is the most luxurious way to harden the arteries.

Chef Rafael Lopez **Owner** Rafael Lopez **Times** 12-2.30/6-mdnt Closed 25-26 Dec, 1-2 Jan, Mon, D Sun **Prices** Starter £6-£10, Main £13-£22, Dessert £6.50-£8.50, Service optional **Wines** 8 by glass **Notes** Banquet menu £35, Sunday L £14.50-£22, Vegetarian available **Seats** 80 **Children** Portions **Parking** 40

CRANBROOK   Map 7 TQ73

Apicius

◉◉◉ – *see opposite*

DARTFORD   Map 6 TQ57

Rowhill Grange Hotel & Utopia Spa

◉◉ Modern European V ♥

Soothing modernised dishes in Kentish rural tranquillity

☎ 01322 615136
Wilmington DA2 7QH
e-mail: admin@rowhillgrange.com
web: www.alexanderhotels.co.uk
dir: M25 junct 3, take B2173 towards Swanley, then B258 towards Hextable. Straight on at 3 rdbts. Hotel 1.5m on left

A Georgian house set in acres of trimly manicured grounds, complete with a duck-dotted lake, Rowhill has the virtue of rural tranquillity going for it. Its newly styled principal dining room, RG's, is a gently lit space done in mother-of-pearl shades, with quality table linen and modern artworks. The kitchen works to today's best-practice watchwords of seasonality and regionality and

modernising takes on bastions of culinary tradition. Thus, green pea soup comes garnished with a poached egg and truffle oil, or smoked salmon with a pickled cucumber salad, for starters. Mains go in for soothing textures and classic combinations, as when butter-poached South Coast lobster is served on linguine with spinach and beetroot purée, or poached and grilled chicken is supported by truffled potatoes and peas and broad beans with pancetta. A slate of grill options for mixing and matching with sauces is a popular feature.

Chef Luke Davis **Owner** Peter & Deborah Hinchcliffe **Times** 12-2.30/7-9.30 **Prices** Prices not confirmed Service added but optional 12.5% **Wines** 34 bottles over £30, 26 bottles under £30, 10 by glass **Notes** Sunday L, Vegetarian menu, Dress restrictions, No sportswear, Civ Wed 150 **Seats** 100 **Children** Portions, Menu **Parking** 300

DEAL   Map 7 TR35

Dunkerleys Hotel & Restaurant

◉◉ Modern British ♥

Seafood-based menu in a long-running seafront hotel

☎ 01304 375016
19 Beach St CT14 7AH
e-mail: ddunkerley@btconnect.com
web: www.dunkerleys.co.uk
dir: Turn off A2 onto A258 to Deal - situated 100yds before Deal Pier

Ian and Linda Dunkerley have already celebrated the 25th anniversary of their seafront hotel in Deal, and look set to clock up another good few years yet. Why change a winning formula? The place exudes a gaily inviting air, with its flagpoles and flower-baskets, and the newly refurbed dining room looks the part, with smart white linen and high-backed chairs, unless the Kentish sunshine tempts you out on to the terrace. Seafood has got to be the main deal in Deal, and crops up reliably in the shape of Carlingford rock oysters on ice, seared king scallops in sweet-and-sour livery with puréed Bramleys, together with main dishes like grilled Dover sole with parsley butter, or Kingsdown sea bass given the Asian treatment with hot-and-sour veg, pak choi and rice. If you're a meatier customer, there are roast lamb rump with ratatouille in redcurranted wine reduction, or fillet steak with chunky chips and a mushroom-topped croûte instead. Meals end with the likes of banana tarte Tatin, served with rum-laced praline ice cream.

Chef Ian Dunkerley, Josh Hackett **Owner** Ian & Linda Dunkerley **Times** 12-2.30/7-9.30 Closed Mon, D Sun **Prices** Fixed L 2 course fr £11.95, Fixed D 3 course £28.95-£43.95, Service optional **Wines** 24 bottles over £30, 61 bottles under £30, 9 by glass **Notes** Sunday L, Vegetarian available, Dress restrictions, Smart casual preferred **Seats** 50 **Children** Portions **Parking** Public car park adjacent

---

DOVER   Map 7 TR34

The Marquis at Alkham

◉◉◉ – *see opposite*

Wallett's Court Country House Hotel & Spa

◉◉ Modern British

Creative cooking in historic manor

☎ 01304 852424
Westcliffe, St Margaret's-at-Cliffe CT15 6EW
e-mail: dine@wallettscourt.com
web: www.wallettscourthotelspa.com
dir: M2/A2 or M20/A20, follow signs for Deal (A258), 1st right for St-Margaret's-at-Cliffe. Restaurant 1m on right

The unassuming whitewashed exterior of this family-run country-house hotel hides a 17th-century Jacobean manor, but if staying in a room built of ancient bricks and mortar is too prosaic for your tastes, you could go 'glamping' in a Navajo tipi in the lovely grounds instead. At dinner, though, it's back to the past among the oak beams, inglenook fireplaces and candlelit tables of the romantic restaurant, where the modern British idiom gets a workout to produce dishes based on carefully-sourced materials from Kent and Sussex. The kitchen keeps things straightforward, setting off along the lines of Kentish rabbit terrine with tarragon emulsion and toasted sourdough bread, followed, perhaps, by a 40-day-matured sirloin of Sussex Red beef with roasted salsify, girolles, pommes purées and Madeira jus. In winter, there may be Christmas pudding soufflé with mulled wine sorbet and brandy sauce to wrap things up.

Times 12-2.30/7-9 Closed 25-26 Dec, L Mon-Sat (ex group bookings 10+)

EDENBRIDGE   Map 6 TQ44

Haxted Mill Restaurant

◉ Modern French, Mediterranean

Popular dishes in a country inn with waterwheel

☎ 01732 862914
Haxted Rd TN8 6PU
e-mail: david@haxtedmill.co.uk
dir: M25 junct 6, A22 towards East Grinstead. Through Blindley Heath, after Texaco garage left at lights, in 1m 1st left after Red Barn PH. 2m to Haxted Mill

They were grinding grain for flour here until just after the Great War, but the watermill is still fully functional, and quite an education to behold. The restaurant is housed in the stables with their steeply sloping beamed ceilings, and also on a pair of terraces under sunshades. Should you wish to defy the elements on cooler evenings, the staff will provide shawls for draping yourself in. A populist menu of international brasserie classics might guide you from sautéed squid with chorizo, tomato and peppers, through roast rack of lamb with minted veg, or salmon marinated in soy sauce and maple syrup, to the final satisfaction of chocolate profiteroles with vanilla ice cream.

Chef David Peek **Owner** David & Linda Peek **Times** 12-2/7-9 Closed 23 Dec-1 Apr, Mon, D Sun **Prices** Prices not confirmed Service added but optional 10% **Wines** 16 by glass **Notes** Sunday L, Vegetarian available, Dress restrictions, Smart casual **Seats** 52 **Parking** 100

Apicius

CRANBROOK   MAP 7 TQ73

Modern European

Imaginative star quality in a small high-street venue

☎ 01580 714666
23 Stone St TN17 3HF
dir: In town centre, opposite Barclays Bank, 50yds from church

If every small town in the country had a restaurant like Apicius in its midst we might truly be able to claim national culinary greatness. As it is though, this is far from the case, and lucky Cranbrook can rejoice. The name references a Roman cookery writer - well, why not? - and the framed menus on the walls suggest that chef-patron Tim Johnson's love of the culinary arts runs deep: he's worked with some top chefs in his time. It's a small place - some 30 covers - and the décor is smart and neat and charming, the atmosphere unintimidating and unpretentious, with tables neatly laid. The food does the talking. High quality ingredients are at the heart of every dish, and the cooking is bright, bold, even a little daring at times, and with a focus and clarity that never fails to impress: a starter of sautéed wild mushrooms, for example, with brioche, parmesan crisps and ceps sauce is a dish with real heart and soul. Deep-fried frogs' legs is another first course packed with flavour, coming with celeriac purée, garlic crisps and parsley salad. Fish is cooked with flair, too: sea bass, perhaps, in a main course with fennel and orange, baby artichokes and roast garlic. Slow-roasted shoulder of Kentish pork with braised endive, prune purée and turnip galette is another dish with Francophile leanings and robust, thrilling flavours. Desserts show no less astute thinking and precise execution: poached winter rhubarb with wild strawberry jelly, hibiscus ice cream and vanilla syrup, for example, or medjool date sponge with apricot salad, pistachio coulis and honey ice cream.

Chef Timothy Johnson **Owner** Timothy Johnson, Faith Hawkins **Times** 12-2/7-9 Closed 2 wks Xmas-New Year, 2 wks summer, Mon-Tue, L Sat, D Sun **Prices** Fixed L 2 course £26.50, Fixed D 3 course £40, Service added but optional 12.5% **Wines** 10 by glass **Notes** Sunday L, Vegetarian available **Seats** 30 **Parking** Public car park at rear

The Marquis at Alkham

DOVER   MAP 7 TR34

Modern British V ◆ NOTABLE WINE LIST

Creative cooking and boutique chic deep in the Kent countryside

☎ 01304 873410
Alkham Valley Rd, Alkham CT15 7DF
e-mail: reception@themarquisatalkham.co.uk
web: www.themarquisatalkham.co.uk
dir: M20 continue to A2. Take A260 exit & turn on to the Alkham Valley Rd

It's hard to believe that this was at one time a rundown old pub: a major renovation project a few years back has seen The Marquis of Granby (as it used to be) utterly transformed into a strikingly contemporary restaurant with rooms. Sitting in the heart of the delightful Kent Downs village of Alkham, within striking distance of the tiny cricket pitch (one of the smallest in England, apparently), the smart, white-painted building is in an idyllic spot. And once inside it's all just as lovely: whitewashed walls broken up with splashes of modern art, real-wood floors, fine furnishings, beautiful fabrics and subtle lighting set the tone in the restaurant, lounge and bar, and there are ten chic designer bedrooms (plus accommodation in two cottages at the restaurant's nearby sister business, the Chalksole Estate Vineyard). If the weather's playing ball you can sit outside on the lovely garden terrace and take in the views over the luscious Alkham Valley - perhaps with a glass of Chalksole Estate bubbly to get you in the mood for the creative cooking that's to come. Chef Charlie Lakin has made a well-deserved name for himself of late with his robust, imaginative food which unfailingly champions the best of Kentish produce along with a good measure of foraged ingredients. Menus are varied and there's a daily changing table d'hôte as well as a seasonally changing carte and Kent tasting menu. Fantastic freshly-made bread - white and brown sliced and caramelised onion rolls - with good quality butter gets things off to a promising start before a first course of tender fillets of pheasant served with razor-thin slices of crisp ham, roasted apples and ramson berries. Next up, a first-rate fillet of cod is teamed with finely shredded Savoy cabbage, smoked salmon dauphines (nicely crisp on the outside and fluffy in the middle) and a rich Dijon mustard sauce and confit vegetables. A chestnut millefeuille is a pudding lover's dream - an excellent chestnut cream sandwiched between wonderfully crisp rectangles of puff pastry, accompanied by a crunchy 'nut soil', pumpkin praline and vanilla ice cream.

Chef Charles Lakin **Owner** Tony Marsden & Hugh Oxborrow **Times** 12-2.30/6.30-9 Closed L Mon **Prices** Fixed L 2 course fr £9.50, Fixed D 2 course fr £22.50, Tasting menu £30-£55, Starter £6-£16, Main £14.50-£29.50, Dessert £6-£11, Service added but optional 10% **Wines** 300 bottles over £30, 12 bottles under £30, 14 by glass **Notes** Tasting menu available, Sunday L £14.50-£24.50, Vegetarian menu, Civ Wed 55 **Seats** 60, Pr/dining room 20 **Children** Portions **Parking** 26

Read's Restaurant

◉◉ Modern British ▮NOTABLE WINE LIST ◔

Sophisticated modern British cooking in red-brick Georgian manor

☎ 01795 535344
Macknade Manor, Canterbury Rd ME13 8XE
e-mail: enquiries@reads.com
dir: From M2 junct 6 follow A251 towards Faversham. At T-junct with A2 (Canterbury road) turn right. Hotel 0.5m on right

Read's occupies a classically proportioned Georgian house in its own grounds, its restaurant a room of charm and elegance, with pictures on the walls, drapes over the windows and candles on clothed tables. Chef-proprietor David Pitchford places a high priority on his sources, buying local meat and game, fish from Whitstable and Hythe, and growing vegetables and herbs in his own garden. He has an unerring grasp of what works together, serving sautéed tiger prawns on a bed of pak choi with slow-braised teriyaki pork and coriander, and a winter starter of roast quail and cobnuts on celeriac tart with leaves dressed in orange and tarragon. The same imaginative and intelligent approach pervades main courses too: witness pink-roast lamb loin with glazed apricots, croustillante of slow-braised shoulder, Savoy cabbage and carrot purée. Fish-eaters might have the chance of precisely timed pan-fried halibut fillet with caramelised cauliflower purée and a pomegranate, caper and raisin dressing, while a dessert of rhubarb soufflé with ginger ice cream will appeal to all comers.

Chef David Pitchford **Owner** David & Rona Pitchford **Times** 12-2.30/7-10 Closed BHs, Sun-Mon **Prices** Fixed L 3 course fr £25, Fixed D 3 course fr £60, Tasting menu fr £60, Service optional **Wines** 100 bottles over £30, 45 bottles under £30, 18 by glass **Notes** Tasting menu 7 course, Vegetarian available, Dress restrictions, Smart casual, Civ Wed 60 **Seats** 50, Pr/dining room 30 **Children** Portions **Parking** 30

Rocksalt Rooms

◉◉ Modern British

Fabulous harbourside setting and a local flavour

☎ 01303 212070
2 Back St CT19 6NN
e-mail: info@rocksaltfolkestone.co.uk
dir: M20 junct 13, follow A259 Folkestone Harbour, then left to Fish Market

The niftily designed building right on the harbour is actually cantilevered out over the water, so if you're lucky enough to bag a table on the terrace, you're right over the briny. It's a great building, with a huge glass wall to make the most of the view over the boats in the harbour and open sea beyond, and a smart, well-designed interior. Chef Mark Sergeant is a Ramsay protégé with a passion for provenance, and here he's able to grab the

freshest possible seafood from local boats and harvest herbs and some vegetables from a farm under the same ownership as the restaurant. Seafood gets a good showing on the menu, but there's also salt marsh lamb shank hotpot or a Boston rib steak to keep all-comers happy. Start with potted Dungeness shrimps or Rocksalt fish soup, and move on to herb-crusted Folkestone cod with razor clams and ransoms, or pan-fried red gurnard with cockles and sea purslane. For dessert, find happiness with a Kentish gypsy tart or lemon meringue pie.

Times 12-3/6.30-10

Who'd A Thought It

◉ Modern British NEW ◔

Wacky setting for simple contemporary food

☎ 01622 858951
Headcorn Rd ME17 2AR
e-mail: joe@whodathoughtit.com
dir: M20 junct 8, A20 towards Lenham. 1m take Grafty Green turn, follow brown tourist signs for 4.5m

The funky approach to interior design at this restaurant with rooms has resulted in a one-off jungle boudoir look involving sexy shades of caramel, chocolate and cream matched with tigerskin seats and leopard print carpets, plushly padded suede booths and walls studded with rhinestones, and low and moody lighting reflected in gilt-framed mirrors. The place is billed as a champagne and oyster bar, so the requisite bivalves and bubbly are a good way to start - native Colchesters and a good choice of fizz by the glass should hit the spot - otherwise the wide-ranging modern menu kicks off with salt and pepper squid with an Asian-inspired salad of lightly-pickled vegetables, lime emulsion and coriander shoots, followed by pork belly braised in Stowford Press cider with red cabbage, baby onions, diced potatoes, parsnip purée, and crackling. It's all full of flavour and well executed, and standards don't slip at dessert either with a properly comforting sticky toffee pudding with butterscotch sauce and toffee ice cream.

Chef Tim Ward **Owner** Joe Mallett **Times** 11.30-3/6-9 Closed 1 Jan **Prices** Starter £4-£10, Main £14-£32, Dessert £6, Service optional **Wines** 80 bottles over £30, 23 bottles under £30, 14 by glass **Notes** Tasting small plate menu, Sunday L £9-£11, Vegetarian available **Seats** 50 **Children** Portions **Parking** 45

Chilston Park Hotel

◉◉ Modern British ◔

Splendid Georgian mansion with elegant restaurant

☎ 01622 859803
Sandway ME17 2BE
e-mail: chilstonpark@handpicked.co.uk
web: www.handpickedhotels.co.uk/chilstonpark
dir: M20 junct 8

There's a decidedly stately air to this Georgian country-house hotel in the Kent countryside. The handsomeness of the façade gives a fine first impression, while the interior is jam-packed with splendid antiques, crystal chandeliers and period details such as ornate fireplaces; it will come as no surprise to hear the place was once owned by the authors of Miller's Antiques guide. Culpeper's Restaurant is a suitably fine-dining affair, located in the house's original dining hall, with smartly laid tables and a menu of gently modern British dishes. Among first courses, the modern classic that is scallops with black pudding, smoked bacon and pea purée stars nicely seared South Coast bivalves, or there might be beetroot-cured salmon gravad lax with beetroot purée, pickled fennel and micro cress. Presentation is a strength, as in main-course braised blade of beef with its accompanying pommes purée, creamed Savoy cabbage and pancetta. To finish, warm rice pudding comes with Ruby pears, honey and cardamom ice cream and a port wine reduction, or there might be roast pecan soufflé.

Chef Andrew Williams **Owner** Hand Picked Hotels **Times** 7-9.30 Closed L Mon-Sat **Prices** Fixed D 3 course £36, Starter £8.50-£10.50, Main £28-£32.50, Dessert £8.50-£12.50, Service optional **Wines** 60 bottles over £30, 15 bottles under £30, 18 by glass **Notes** Seasonal Gourmet menu available, Sunday L, Vegetarian available, Dress restrictions, Smart casual, Civ Wed 100 **Seats** 45, Pr/dining room 20 **Children** Portions, Menu **Parking** 100

Fish on the Green

◉ British, French ◔

Refreshingly simple fish and seafood in a Kentish village

☎ 01622 738300
Church Ln, Bearsted Green ME14 4EJ
dir: N of A20 on village green

The venue, in a tranquil location in Bearsted, a village east of Maidstone, was once the stable-block for the inn next door. Fishing-related artworks set the tone for the maritime menu, which offers the bounty of the seas in refreshingly straightforward culinary formats. Baked spiced crab with wholemeal toast, or steamed mussels in leeks, bacon and cider, are among the possible curtain-raisers for whole grilled lemon sole with brown shrimp and mace butter, or halibut with wilted spinach and chive hollandaise. If you're not into fish, a main course such as slow-roast pork belly with winter greens and

Save on Hotels. Book at theAA.com/hotel

KENT 221 ENGLAND

pancetta, apple purée and thyme jus should fit the bill. Finish with rhubarb and ginger crumble, served with clotted cream.

Chef Peter Baldwin **Owner** Alexander Bensley
Times 12-2.30/6.30-10 Closed Xmas, Mon (some), D Sun (some) **Prices** Fixed L 2 course £15.95, Fixed D 3 course £28.95-£44.95, Service optional **Wines** 7 by glass **Notes** Vegetarian available **Seats** 50 **Children** Portions **Parking** 50

MARGATE
Map 7 TR37

The Ambrette

⊛ Modern Indian V ☺

Modern Anglo-Indian food based on prime Kentish produce

☎ 01843 231504
44 King St CT9 1QE
e-mail: info@theambrette.co.uk
dir: A299/A28, left into Hawley St B2055. Restaurant on right corner King St

Dev Biswal has cannily spotted a gap in the culinary market, and moved to fill it with this restaurant in Margate and another by the same name in Rye. This isn't modern Indian food as such: it's 'modern British with Indian influences'. The Margate Ambrette is a light, breezy venue with chunky wood tables, minimally adorned walls and engagingly informative service. A strong aesthetic sense informs the presentations of dishes that both look good and deliver a panoply of upstanding flavours. Start with a grilled fillet of claresse (a freshwater member of the European catfish family) crusted in black pepper, coriander and sesame, or aromatically spiced calves' liver in Madeira jus. Kentish pork loin in a fennel and cinnamon coat comes with Goan-style garlic and vinegar sauce, with aubergine and chick pea timbale and basmati, or opt for stir-fried crab done in mustard oil, cinnamon and cardamom. Vegetarian specials and side-orders bring bright, spicy flavours to humble ingredients.

Chef Dev Biswal **Owner** Dev Biswal
Times 11.30-2.30/5.30-9.30 Closed 26 Dec, Mon **Prices** Prices not confirmed Service added but optional 12.5% **Wines** 14 bottles over £30, 18 bottles under £30, 11 by glass **Notes** Pre-theatre menu until 6.30 & after 9pm, Sunday L, Vegetarian menu, Dress restrictions, Smart casual **Seats** 52 **Children** Portions **Parking** 10

ROCHESTER
Map 6 TQ76

Topes Restaurant

⊛⊛ Modern British ☺

An atmospheric gem in historic Rochester

☎ 01634 845270
60 High St ME1 1JY
e-mail: julie.small@btconnect.com
web: www.topesrestaurant.com
dir: M2 junct 1, through Strood High St over Medway Bridge, turn right at Northgate onto High St

Born again Dickens fans might like to know that the 15th-century building which houses Topes gets a name check in his last novel, *The Mystery of Edwin Drood*. The gnarled beams and narrow stairs climbing to the kitchen and dining room certainly have a Dickensian feel, but the interior has had a nip here and a tuck there to give it a more contemporary look. The mood is relaxed and chef-proprietor Chris Small's cooking taps into the current appetite for ingredients-led, unpretentious dishes with forthright flavours. Excellent Kentish produce underpins a gutsy starter of wild rabbit and pork terrine teamed with rabbit rillettes, pickled walnuts and grape chutney, before main course sees wood pigeon breasts sharing a plate with black pudding and bacon forestière and butternut squash purée. To finish, a British cheeseboard fights it out with the likes of bread-and-butter pudding with crème anglaise, caramelised pineapple and butterscotch ice cream.

Chef Chris Small **Owner** Chris & Julie Small
Times 12-2.30/6.30-9 Closed Mon-Tue, D Sun **Prices** Fixed L 2 course £16, Fixed D 3 course £22, Starter £6.50-£8.50, Main £15-£18, Dessert £6.50, Service optional **Wines** 10 by glass **Notes** Sunday L, Vegetarian available **Seats** 55, Pr/dining room 16 **Children** Portions, Menu **Parking** Public car park

---

SANDWICH
Map 7 TR35

The Lodge at Prince's

⊛⊛ Modern British NEW ☺

Golf-centric hotel with modern brasserie

☎ 01304 611118
Princes Dr, Sandwich Bay CT13 9QB
e-mail: j.george@princesgolfclub.co.uk
web: www.princesgolfclub.co.uk

This newly-built golf and function-oriented hotel hunkers down among the rolling greensward of its championship golf links, which are, of course, reason enough for many guests to come here. But even if mashies and niblicks aren't your bag, there is much to admire in the views across the wide-open dunes to the Bay of Sandwich and the white cliffs of Ramsgate. On the food front, the smart, contemporary brasserie-styled restaurant deals in creative modern British dishes founded on well-sourced local materials, served in a clean-cut, rather masculine ambience of neutral shades, pale wooden floors and bare darkwood tables. Crown Prince tortellini are filled with pumpkin and served with velvety sage beurre noisette sauce, while a splendid fillet of beef gets unusual treatment - rolled in ash, and matched with wild mushrooms, meadow grass and milk skin; elsewhere, local fish might get a showing - roast brill, for example, partnered with red wine-poached salsify and chanterelles with a truffle dressing. Desserts run to apple crumble soufflé or banana tarte Tatin with banana ice cream.

Chef Michael Fowler **Owner** Mr M McGuire
Times 12-2.30/6.30-9 **Prices** Fixed L 2 course £12.50-£20, Fixed D 3 course £28.50, Tasting menu £45-£55, Starter £7-£14, Main £18-£24, Service optional **Wines** 10 bottles over £30, 30 bottles under £30, 8 by glass **Notes** Sunday L, Vegetarian available **Seats** 55, Pr/dining room 20 **Children** Portions **Parking** 100

SEVENOAKS
Map 6 TQ55

Gavin Gregg Restaurant

⊛⊛ Modern British, European ☺

Popular high street operation with hands-on owners

☎ 01732 456373
28-30 High St TN13 1HX
dir: 1m from Sevenoaks train station. 500yds from top of town centre towards Tonbridge on left

Now into its 13th year, the 17th-century timbered house on the high street has become a stalwart of the foodie scene in the Sevenoaks area. Inside, the décor is simplicity itself: head-skimming black beams juxtaposed with cream and bright-orange-painted walls, and the restaurant's twirly 'g' logo displayed prominently in the windows. Gavin Gregg heads a team of four serving up supremely confident modern dishes with great clarity, depth and balance of flavour. Starters could get straight down to a display of technique, drawing the contrasts from Loch Duart salmon ballottine done three ways - slow-poached, vodka-cured and smoked - with potato and chive salad and caviar. Main course brings pan-seared honeyed duck breast with confit duck leg pithivier, celeriac purée, buttered leeks and Savoy cabbage, and boulangère potatoes; to finish, fine ingredients are again in evidence in an intense chocolate and honey cheesecake served with caramelised hazelnuts, and honey and yoghurt ice cream. If you're after top value, the fixed price menus are hard to beat.

Chef Gavin Gregg **Owner** Gavin & Lucinda Gregg
Times 12-2/6.30-9.30 Closed BH, Mon-Tue, D Sun **Prices** Fixed L 2 course £13.50-£18.50, Fixed D 3 course £23-£30, Tasting menu £45-£60, Service added but optional 10% **Wines** 9 by glass **Notes** Sunday L, Vegetarian available **Seats** 80, Pr/dining room 32 **Children** Portions **Parking** Town centre

SITTINGBOURNE — Map 7 TQ96

Hempstead House Country Hotel

◉ Traditional European ◐

Classical cooking in a charming Victorian hotel

☎ 01795 428020
London Rd, Bapchild ME9 9PP
e-mail: info@hempsteadhouse.co.uk
web: www.hempsteadhouse.co.uk
dir: 1.5m from town centre on A2 towards Canterbury

The Lake family who built the original Hempstead House in 1850 and had its four acres of mature landscaped gardens to themselves until it became a country-house hotel and spa in 1990 are honoured in the name of its restaurant. The conservatory-style space has a plush look that reflects the old house's Victorian character, involving swagged drapes, plasterwork ceilings, crystal chandeliers and swanky tables laid with fine china, silver and glassware. The kitchen steers an accessible course that is clearly rooted in French classics, starting out with the likes of pan-seared pigeon breast with roasted leeks, wild mushrooms and tarragon butter, followed by brill fillet teamed with braised fennel, saffron pommes dauphinoise and anchovy sauce. Desserts run to caramel and apple bavarois with apple sorbet and bitter apple compôte.

Chef Paul Field, Peter Gilbey Owner Mr & Mrs A J Holdstock Times 12-2.30/7-10 Closed D Sun (non residents) Prices Fixed L 2 course fr £14.50, Fixed D 3 course fr £27.50, Starter £5.95-£9.50, Main £16.95-£22.50, Dessert £7.95, Service optional Wines 16 bottles over £30, 53 bottles under £30, 4 by glass Notes Sunday L, Vegetarian available, Dress restrictions, Smart casual, Civ Wed 150 Seats 70, Pr/dining room 30 Children Portions, Menu Parking 200

TENTERDEN — Map 7 TQ83

Swan English Restaurant

◉ British NEW ◐

Winning winery with an English flavour on the menu

☎ 01580 761616
Chapel Down Winery, Small Hythe Rd TN30 7NG
e-mail: bookings@loveswan.co.uk
dir: B2082 between Tenterden and Rye

Make sure there's plenty of room in your boot when you visit the Chapel Down winery so you can head home fully stocked. The Swan is an English restaurant on the first floor of a handsome structure of oak and galvanised steel that houses the wine and food shop, and it's a cool and contemporary space with neutral colour tones and lots of natural wood. It's a sibling to The Swan at West Malling (see entry) and treads a thoroughly English furrow. Start with a lobster and crab chowder, perhaps, packed with shellfish, and follow on with honey-roast pork served with a pudding made with smoked bacon, mashed potatoes and grain mustard. For dessert, rhubarb and custard consists of poached fruit and a set vanilla custard. When it comes to drink, how about some refreshing English rosé to start, followed by a nice cool glass of bacchus?

Times 12-3/6-10.30 Prices Fixed L 2 course £14.95, Starter £6.50-£12, Main £11-£27, Dessert £5.25-£8.80, Service added but optional 12.5% Notes Garden menu 2/3 course Mon-Fri 12-3, advance booking req, Sunday L Seats Pr/dining room 20

TUNBRIDGE WELLS (ROYAL) — Map 6 TQ53

Hotel du Vin Tunbridge Wells

◉ French, British ⬛ NOTABLE WINE LIST ◐

Anglo-French bistro favourites and a vineyard out back

☎ 01892 526455
Crescent Rd TN1 2LY
e-mail: reception.tunbridgewells@hotelduvin.com
web: www.hotelduvin.com
dir: Follow town centre to main junct of Mount Pleasant Rd & Crescent Rd/Church Rd. Hotel 150yds on right just past Phillips House

The HdV group's outpost in Royal Tunbridge Wells is a good-looking sandstone mansion built in 1762. It overlooks the broad acres of Calverley Park from the rear, as well as the hotel's own vineyard. The ambience in the Bistro is classically simple, with dark floorboards, creamy walls, gentle lighting and framed prints, and the food follows suit, with a range of Anglo-French bistro favourites. Fish cookery is impressive, as witness a main course of accurately timed monkfish in a Burgundian-influenced sauce comprised of pearl onions, pancetta and wild mushrooms, or you might opt for the house cassoulet, replete with confit duck and Toulouse sausage. Those might be preceded by devilled lamb's kidneys on toast, or beef carpaccio, watercress and parmesan in horseradish dressing, while tarte Tatin with crème Normande makes a punchy finale. It goes without saying that the wine list offers a wide range of styles and prices to suit all budgets and tastes.

Chef Daniel McGarey Owner Hotel du Vin Ltd Times 12-2.30/5.30-10 Prices Prices not confirmed Service added but optional 10% Wines 16 by glass Notes Pre-theatre meal offer on selected nights, Vegetarian available, Civ Wed 84 Seats 80, Pr/dining room 84 Children Portions, Menu Parking 30, NCP

Montrose Restaurant

◉ Modern European

Smart seasonal cooking in stylish setting

☎ 01892 513161
15a Church Rd, Southborough TN4 0RX
e-mail: bookings@montroserestaurant.co.uk
dir: M25 junct 5 to A21. Exit A21 Tunbridge Wells/Tonbridge, to Southborough. Restaurant on right after cricket green

Behind a stirring late-Victorian façade, the Montrose makes no less of an impact on the inside: swish black chandeliers, black clothed tables and lavishly upholstered chairs combine to give the space a sense of occasion. The kitchen keeps it simple with good quality, locally-sourced ingredients the star of the show in its modish output. You might encounter braised rabbit ravioli with caramelised shallots, carrot crisps and jus, followed by supreme of guinea fowl stuffed with brie and apple, prosciutto ham, balsamic sauce and pomme mousseline, and bring down the curtain with a liquorice and Pernod parfait served with lime syrup. Wine is a big deal here - the co-owner is a dedicated oenophile and it shows in an interesting list.

Times 12-2.30/6.30-late Closed D Sun

The Spa Hotel

◉ Modern, Traditional British ◐

Country-house dining beneath crystal chandeliers

☎ 01892 520331
Mount Ephraim TN4 8XJ
e-mail: reservations@spahotel.co.uk
web: www.spahotel.co.uk
dir: On A264 leaving Tunbridge Wells towards East Grinstead

Built in the middle of the 18th century, this handsome mansion first opened its doors as a hotel in the Victorian era to capitalise on the perceived value of the waters around here - an original spa hotel. And today's tip-top spa facilities more than meet contemporary expectations. The house stands in 14 acres of grounds - walking is an alternative fitness therapy after all - and inside the place has a good deal of boutique style to go with the impressive Georgian features. The Chandelier Restaurant is appropriately named and comes dressed up in grand style with well-spaced, well-dressed tables. The menu mixes some traditional and contemporary ideas and is based on good quality ingredients. Start with a risotto of mushrooms with pecorino and truffles, or crispy coconut king prawn with chilli and lime dipping sauce, before a grilled sirloin steak or pan-fried lamb fillets with tarragon cream, parsley sponge, potato cake and soft green cabbage.

Chef Steve Cole Owner Scragg Hotels Ltd Times 12.30-2/7-9.30 Closed L Sat Prices Service included Wines 8 by glass Notes Sunday L £19.50-£25, Vegetarian available, Dress restrictions, Smart casual, No jeans or T-shirts Seats 80, Pr/dining room 200 Children Portions, Menu Parking 150

Save on Hotels. Book at **theAA.com/hotel**

KENT 223 ENGLAND

Thackeray's

◉◉◉ – see below

The Swan

◉◉ Modern British ✿

Smart modish cooking in a contemporary Kentish inn

☎ 01732 521910
35 Swan St ME19 6JU
e-mail: info@loveswan.co.uk
dir: M20 junct 4 follow signs for West Malling, left into
Swan St. Approx 200yds on left

The one-time coaching inn got a millennium makeover
back in 2000 and was reborn as a bar and brasserie, and
all remains well with the world. The classic-looking 15th-
century pub on the pretty high street looks great with its
stainless steel, granite and wood, funky modern artworks
and mirrors beneath the original oak beams. And in the
summer the 'secret garden' - well, it's out back - with its
decidedly urban-cool vibe is a great spot to chill and be
chilled. The menu matches the good-looking,
contemporary attitude with a good deal of swagger of its
own, which includes some bright ideas, appealing flavour
combinations, and plenty of regional ingredients.
Beautifully cooked Rye Bay scallops, for example, might
turn up in a first course with pork belly, fennel and a

nicely-judged harissa, and main-course duck (from just
down the road) with crumbed confit leg, beets and a rich
Madeira jus. For pud gypsy tart shows fine pastry work
and spot-on balance of sweetness with its accompanying
bee pollen ice cream and honeycomb.

Chef Scott Goss **Owner** Swan Brasserie Ltd
Times 12-3.30/5.30-10 **Prices** Fixed L 2 course fr £15,
Fixed D 3 course fr £18, Starter £6-£11.80, Main
£12.90-£29, Dessert £5-£7, Service added but optional
12.5% **Wines** 12 by glass **Notes** Fixed menu 2 course
5.30-7pm, Sunday L, Vegetarian available, Dress
restrictions, Smart casual, Civ Wed 100 **Seats** 90, Pr/
dining room 20 **Children** Portions, Menu **Parking** Long-
stay car park

The Sportsman

◉◉ Modern British ✿

**Bracing freshness and absence of pretension in a
Kentish pub**

☎ 01227 273370
Faversham Rd, Seasalter CT5 4BP
e-mail: contact@thesportsmanseasalter.co.uk
dir: On coast road between Whitstable & Faversham,
3.5m W of Whitstable

The environs of Seasalter have been in the catering trade,
one way or another, since the 12th century, when the land
provisioned the kitchens of Canterbury Cathedral,
struggling to cope with an influx of pilgrim trade
following that unpleasant business in 1170. These days,
a shoot of the productive Harris family looks after the
white-fronted inn with its glassed-in terrace and blond
wood dining room. Simplicity and honest industry reign
throughout, from the churning of butter in-house to the
willing, warm-hearted staff. Blackboard menus and a
seven-course taster offer local farm-grown and sea-
sourced produce via straightforward preparations such
as grilled slip-sole in seaweed butter, roast chicken with
bread sauce, chestnuts and bacon, and seared thornback
ray in brown butter, served with cockles and sherry
vinegar. The bracing freshness of it all, coupled with the
lack of pretentiousness, exercise a potent allure, and
there's chocolate to finish, in the form of a warm mousse,
accompanied by salted caramel and milk sorbet.

Chef Stephen Harris, Dan Flavell **Owner** Stephen & Philip
Harris **Times** 12-2/7-9 Closed 25-26 Dec, 1 Jan, Mon, D
Sun **Prices** Tasting menu £65, Starter £6.95-£9.95, Main
£18.95-£22.95, Dessert £6.95, Service optional, Groups
min 6 service 10% **Wines** 10 bottles over £30, 39 bottles
under £30, 10 by glass **Notes** Pre-order tasting menu
available Mon-Fri, 48 hrs notice req, Sunday L, Vegetarian
available **Seats** 50 **Children** Portions **Parking** 20

Thackeray's

Modern French, European V

**Superior contemporary French cooking in elegant
surroundings**

☎ 01892 511921
85 London Rd TN1 1EA
e-mail: reservations@thackerays-restaurant.co.uk
dir: A21/A26, towards Tunbridge Wells. On left 500yds
after the Kent & Sussex Hospital

Thackeray's, one-time home of the novelist, occupies the
oldest house in Tunbridge Wells, something that's
difficult to believe given its modern interior: the highly
polished floorboards may be original, but the rest is a
cool, elegant décor of honey and cream, with comfortable
upholstered dining chairs and brown banquettes. And
lovers of alfresco dining will be thrilled by the Japanese

Terrace, with its water feature and heated canopy. Chef-
proprietor Richard Phillips is uncompromising about
where he buys his raw materials, never straying beyond
Kent and Sussex unless he has to, and works around a
modern French repertory based on classical techniques.
Starters are often vibrant combinations of flavours with a
degree of complexity: pan-fried foie gras (from Les
Landes), for instance, comes not only with its own
cooking juices and poached rhubarb but with
Gewürztraminer jelly, vanilla purée and toasted oats, and
crab salad with buttered lobster, lime-cured mooli,
avocado, chargrilled pomelo and a crab tuile. If main
courses seem a little calmer, they are assembled with the
same level of intelligence, bringing on perfectly timed
roast turbot with a creamy fish velouté, smoked cod
flakes, violet potatoes and purple-sprouting broccoli, and
roast beef with sauce Marco Polo, sautéed ceps, roast
beetroot and potatoes creamed with black truffle. The
same attention to detail and presentation goes into
puddings, among them perhaps dark chocolate and

mandarin cylinder with white chocolate and orange
cannelloni, kumquats and mandarin sorbet, and apricot
and tonka bean soufflé with apricot sorbet and hazelnut
'soup'.

Chef Richard Phillips, Daniel Hatton **Owner** Richard
Phillips, Paul Smith **Times** 12-2.30/6.30-10.30
Closed Mon, D Sun **Prices** Fixed L 2 course £16.95, Fixed
D 3 course fr £25.50, Tasting menu fr £75, Starter
£9.95-£12.95, Main £23.95-£26.95, Dessert
£10.95-£14.70, Service added but optional 12.5%
Wines 75 bottles over £30, 20 bottles under £30, 23 by
glass **Notes** Sunday L, Vegetarian menu, Dress
restrictions, Smart casual **Seats** 70, Pr/dining room 16
Children Portions **Parking** On street in evening, NCP

The Bull

◉ Modern British ✋

Contemporary cooking in old village inn

☎ 01732 789800
Bull Ln TN15 7RF
e-mail: info@thebullhotel.com
web: www.thebullhotel.com
dir: In centre of village

The Bull, a pub in a peaceful village on the North Downs Way (and just off the M20), has a bit of a past. It dates back to the 14th century, and pilgrims to Canterbury would have stopped here; more recently it was a source of solace for Second World War pilots from nearby airfields. It's still a haven, with a popular bar and a beamed restaurant with two wood-burners. The cooking has more cutting edge than might be expected in a village inn; starters of beetroot-cured gravad lax, or smoked pigeon breast with apple and celeriac remoulade might be followed by sea bass fillet with pancetta and a tarragon and langoustine sauce. Meats are from local farms - pork chop, say, served with a fried duck egg, black pudding and baby vegetables - and puddings such as champagne syllabub are a highlight.

Chef James Hawkes, David Evans **Owner** Martin Deadman **Times** 12-2.30/6-9 **Prices** Starter £6-£7.50, Main £13-£18.95, Dessert fr £5.95, Service added but optional 10% **Wines** 28 bottles over £30, 29 bottles under £30, 9 by glass **Notes** Sunday L fr £13, Vegetarian available **Seats** Pr/dining room 12 **Children** Portions **Parking** 18

LANCASHIRE

The Clog & Billycock

◉ Traditional British ✋

Unpretentious pub with great local flavour

☎ 01254 201163
Billinge End Rd, Pleasington BB2 6QB
e-mail: enquiries@theclogandbillycock.com
dir: M6 junct 29/M65 junct 3. Follow signs to Pleasington

The name has a suitably northern ring for a gastro-pub whose ethos is all about championing local suppliers. Part of chef Nigel Haworth's (see entry for Northcote) trio of Ribble Valley Inns, The Clog & Billycock is a genuine crowd pleaser, with a warm and welcoming vibe thanks to its open fires, rough-stone floors and well-kept, locally-brewed real ales on the pulls. Regional 'food heroes' are honoured in black and white photos on the wall and on place-mats on bare wooden tables, while Lancashire's rich larder turns up in simple, seasonal ideas on the plate. A rough-cut Goosnargh chicken liver pâté is served in a jar capped by shallot butter, with golden sultanas, chicken scratchings and warm toast, ahead of a brace of skewers - pheasant with bacon and duck with prunes - teamed effectively with juniper and orange butter, celeriac mash and braised red cabbage.

Chef Steve Peel **Owner** Nigel Haworth, Craig Bancroft, Richard Matthewman **Times** 12-2/5.30-8.30 Closed Xmas **Prices** Fixed L 2 course £11.50, Fixed D 3 course £15, Starter £3.75-£6.85, Main £8.50-£19.50, Dessert £5, Service optional **Wines** 7 bottles over £30, 30 bottles under £30, 10 by glass **Notes** Fixed L & D 2/3 course available Mon-Thu, Sunday L **Seats** 130 **Children** Portions, Menu **Parking** 75

The Millstone at Mellor

◉◉ British ✋

Fine Lancashire produce in a smart village inn

☎ 01254 813333
Church Ln, Mellor BB2 7JR
e-mail: info@millstonehotel.co.uk
dir: 4m from M6 junct 31 follow signs for Blackburn. Mellor is on right 1m after 1st set of lights

It's always a treat to find an inn that puts equal importance on food and drink - such is The Millstone. This Ribble Valley local serves a fine pint of Thwaites, the renowned Lancashire brewing company, the founding-father of which is buried in the cemetery next door. And if you really want to sample the beers, go for the 'Thoroughly Thirds', which is a taster board of three different ales. And the wine list ain't no slouch either. There is a rustic handsomeness to the bar and eating areas, but rough and ready it most certainly is not. Chef-patron Anson Bolton is passionate about produce and the provenance of what turns up on the plate is never in doubt. There are pub classics (Bowland steak, kidney and Thwaites' Wainwright's ale suet pudding), deli boards (local cheeses among them), steaks cooked on the grill,

and seasonally-changing dishes such as grilled Middlewhite pork cutlet with black pudding rösti, pork scratching and apple purée. Start with baked goats' cheese on buttered crumpet and finish with baked ginger parkin with cinnamon ice cream and treacle sauce.

Chef Anson Bolton **Owner** Thwaites Inns of Character **Times** 12-9.30 Closed D 25-26 Dec, 1 Jan All-day dining **Prices** Starter £4.95-£7.95, Main £10.95-£24.45, Dessert £5.95-£6.95, Service optional **Wines** 9 bottles over £30, 32 bottles under £30, 9 by glass **Notes** Sunday L, Vegetarian available **Seats** 90, Pr/dining room 20 **Children** Portions, Menu **Parking** 45, On street

---

The Highwayman

◉ Traditional British ✋

Regional cooking in a restored country inn

☎ 015242 73338
LA6 2RJ
e-mail: enquiries@highwaymaninn.co.uk
dir: M6 junct 36 to A65 Kirkby Lonsdale, off A683

Although you might well just drop in for a jar of one of the well-kept local ales, The Highwayman is certainly no run-of-the-mill local. The gently reworked pub is a popular, unpretentious place offering simple wooden tables, roaring fires, and food you would cross the county for - which is no surprise when you learn that this is one of Nigel Haworth and Craig Bancroft's pubs (see entries for The Clog & Billycock and The Three Fishes). No jabbering games machines or muzak here, thank you - just the happy thrum of people hanging out with friends and tucking into straightforward, ingredients-led dishes: Scotch egg with coronation Goosnargh chicken and curry tartare for starters, then a fish pie stuffed to the gills with chunks of fish and prawns. Elsewhere, there might be Morecambe Bay shrimps with blade mace butter and toasted muffin, or a pukka Lancashire hotpot made with Cumbrian fell-bred lamb, then a retro pudding such as old English lemonade jelly with vanilla ice cream.

Chef Matt Thompson **Owner** Nigel Haworth, Craig Bancroft, Richard Matthewman **Times** 12-2/5.30-8.30 Closed Xmas, Mon (ex BHs) **Prices** Fixed L 2 course £11.50, Fixed D 3 course £15, Starter £3.75-£5.50, Main £8-£19.50, Dessert £5 **Wines** 7 bottles over £30, 30 bottles under £30, 10 by glass **Notes** Fixed L & D Tue-Thu, Sunday L, Vegetarian available **Seats** 120 **Children** Portions, Menu **Parking** 45

Save on Hotels. Book at **theAA.com/hotel**

LANCASHIRE 225 **ENGLAND**

CHORLEY — Map 15 SD51

The Red Cat

@@ Modern British **V** ☺

Intelligent modern British cooking in relaxed setting

☎ 01257 263966
114 Blackburn Rd, Whittle-le-Woods PR6 8LL
e-mail: enquiries@theredcat.co.uk
dir: M61 junct 8 signed Wheelton, left off A674

Look out for the red cat motif etched into a large glass panel by the door in this former farmhouse, turned local pub, turned restaurant, just outside Chorley. Neutral tones complement the modern look with the lounge and interconnecting dining rooms divided by glass panels, and wooden tables are elegantly set with candles. It's a popular place, with its smart look and relaxed feel, but they come for the food, which is unfussy yet refined, imaginatively presented, and based on tip-top local Lancashire produce. Fleetwood smoked haddock, for example, comes with crushed peas, and mussel and herb velouté, and fillet of Bowland beef with bourguignon garnish, crushed thyme potatoes and seared foie gras. For dessert, lemon curd pannacotta is paired with rhubarb milkshake.

Chef Chris Rawlinson **Owner** Chris & Mike Rawlinson
Times 12-2/6-mdnt Closed Mon-Tue, D Sun **Prices** Fixed L 2 course £17.50, Fixed D 3 course £22.50, Tasting menu £55, Starter £6.95-£11.95, Main £16.95-£26.95, Dessert £6.95-£8.95, Service added but optional 10% **Wines** 18 bottles over £30, 34 bottles under £30, 9 by glass
Notes Tasting menu 5 course, Sunday L, Vegetarian menu
Seats 50 **Children** Portions **Parking** 100

GISBURN — Map 18 SD84

Stirk House Hotel

@ Traditional, Modern ☺

Modern Lancashire cooking in a Tudor manor

☎ 01200 445581
BB7 4LJ
e-mail: reservations@stirkhouse.co.uk
web: www.stirkhouse.co.uk
dir: M6 junct 32, W of village, on A59. Hotel 0.5m on left

Deep in the Ribble Valley, and with the Forest of Bowland and Ribble Hill close by, the wild Lancashire setting of 16th-century Stirk House is a treat in itself. The stone manor house comes with a priest-hole within its ancient walls, but otherwise, the place has been revamped in a tasteful contemporary style. Original plasterwork ceilings, wooden floors and an ornate fireplace add character to the restaurant, where friendly young staff are keen to please and well-briefed on the menu. Relying on splendid Lancashire produce, the cooking keeps things classic and straightforward. Smooth chicken liver parfait comes with red onion jam and toasted sourdough bread, followed by roast duck breast matched with fresh cherry compôte, green beans and colcannon mash. Rounding things off, there's white chocolate pannacotta with fresh raspberries

and a glass of sweet botrytis semillon wine, or a slate of Lancashire cheeses with home-made chutney.

Chef Chris Dobson **Owner** Paul Caddy
Times 12.30-2.30/7-9 Closed Xmas **Prices** Starter £4.95-£7.25, Main £10.95-£19.50, Dessert £5.95-£7.50, Service optional **Wines** 9 bottles over £30, 23 bottles under £30, 9 by glass **Notes** Sunday L £16.50-£19.50, Vegetarian available, Civ Wed 95 **Seats** 40, Pr/dining room 50 **Children** Portions, Menu **Parking** 300

LANGHO — Map 18 SD73

WINNER OF THE AA WINE AWARD FOR ENGLAND

Northcote

@@@@ – see page 226

See advert on page 227

LYTHAM ST ANNES — Map 18 SD32

Bedford Hotel

@ Modern British **NEW** ☺

Clearly-focused cooking in seaside resort hotel

☎ 01253 724606
307-313 Clifton Drive South FY8 1HN
e-mail: reservations@bedfordhotel.com
web: www.bedfordhotel.com
dir: From M55 follow signs for airport to last lights. Left through 2 sets of lights. Hotel 300yds on left

Within walking distance of the town's famous golf course (host of the 2012 British Open) and its genteel seafront with lovely sandy beach, the Bedford is a large Victorian hotel with lots going on, from spa and gym to coffee shop. The Cartland Restaurant has plenty of traditional charm, with decorative plasterwork, warm pastel tones, black-and-white prints of film stars and neatly laid tables. The cooking is classically inspired and makes good use of Lancashire produce, ensuring the place keeps a sense of identity. Thus you might start with Lytham shrimp risotto, or local partridge and pheasant in a terrine served with Bramley apple and pear chutney and warm olive bread. Next up, pot-roasted blade of beef, perhaps, with spring onion mash and red wine sauce, or a traditional salmon en croûte with a chive velouté. The good ideas and careful execution continues at dessert stage with the likes of lemon posset with basil sugar.

Chef Paul Curran **Owner** Baker family
Times 10-5/6.30-8.30 **Prices** Fixed L 2 course £10-£15, Fixed D 3 course £23.50, Starter £3.75-£7.95, Main £15.50-£19.50, Dessert £4.25-£8.95, Service optional **Wines** 1 bottle over £30, 22 bottles under £30, 4 by glass **Notes** Sunday L, Vegetarian available, Dress restrictions, Smart casual, Civ Wed 120 **Seats** Pr/dining room 120 **Children** Portions **Parking** 20, On street (no charge)

Clifton Arms Hotel

@ British ☺

Modern British cooking on the seafront

☎ 01253 739898
West Beach FY8 5QJ
e-mail: welcome@cliftonarms-lytham.com
web: www.cliftonarms-lytham.com
dir: On A584 along seafront

The Clifton Arms, a Grade II listed red-brick hotel, is in a prime spot on the seafront, and its restaurant has fab sea views. White-clothed tables are correctly set, candles are lit in the evening, and smartly dressed staff are formal but friendly. The kitchen makes the most of its location, buying Bowland beef - the fillet, perhaps, accompanied by braised blade with root vegetables served with creamed potatoes - Goosnargh chicken, and fish from Fleetwood, and creating a menu along modern lines. Seared scallops with crisp pork belly, cauliflower purée, and five-spice jus, might start you off, followed by roast cannon of lamb served with tomato and basil butter and chargrilled vegetables. Cheeses are all from Lancashire, and treacle tart with berry compôte and vanilla ice cream may be among desserts.

Chef Justin Jerome **Owner** David Webb
Times 12-2.30/6.30-9 **Prices** Fixed D 3 course fr £25, Starter fr £6, Main fr £14, Dessert fr £6, Service optional **Wines** 14 bottles over £30, 36 bottles under £30, 12 by glass **Notes** Sunday L, Vegetarian available, Civ Wed 100 **Seats** 60, Pr/dining room 140 **Children** Portions **Parking** 50

Northcote

LANGHO   MAP 18 SD73

Modern British V 🍷 NOTABLE WINE LIST

Dynamically creative Lancashire cooking in a grand Victorian house

☎ 01254 240555
Northcote Rd BB6 8BE
e-mail: reception@northcote.com
web: www.northcote.com
dir: M6 junct 31, 9m to Northcote. Follow Clitheroe (A59) signs. Hotel on left before rdbt

Northcote was built as a grand private house in the 1880s for a spinster of the parish, one Mary Yates, who had her family's coat of arms nailed up over the door, and then promptly lost interest in the place. Successive changes of ownership during the last century saw it pass through the hands of various local magnates, Lancashire grandees of the cornflour and (inevitably) cotton trades, until it arrived safely in the hands of a local entrepreneur in the 1980s, who nursed ambitions to turn the place into a country hotel with just a handful of bedrooms and the reputation of a culinary lighthouse for the region. Not far from Blackburn, it overlooks the lush Ribble Valley, views that are a verdant rebuke to those who think of the northwest as being all windswept desolation and satanic mills. The partnership of chef Nigel Haworth and wine expert Craig Bancroft

- today's custodians of the Victorian red-brick pile - is one of Lancashire gastronomy's glittering ornaments, and while Lisa Allen is chef de cuisine, Haworth is not above pitching in still on occasion. Thirty years of water under the bridge doesn't flow by without steady evolution, but the vicissitudes of culinary fashion here are subtly and thoughtfully incorporated. A strong underpinning of regional produce has always been a given, and the notional appellations contrôlées of Lancashire are proudly evident: a porridge of Southport shrimps comes with Banks tomatoes and tarragon pesto, while a local farmer's beetroot is salt-baked and paired with a cheese fondue made with Shorrock's Lancashire Bomb. Technical skills are outstanding, both for fish, as in an opener of lightly charred turbot with seared cucumber, butter beans, a stunning smoked oyster and sea flora, and for main-course meats such as Cumbrian roe deer with a potato-wrapped portion of black pudding, the flavours boldly deepened with blackcurrant and liquorice, alongside a portion of reimagined coleslaw. Pop-culture references bring on crispy quavers (no, not that sort) with fillet and cheek of rare-breed milk-fed pork, alongside pearl barley risotto and chorizo, while dessert could be a ginger take on melting fondant, served with full-cream ice cream and caramel custard. Gourmet menus, tasters, veggie alternatives: the repertoire accommodates just about any way you care to go, with the assurance that

dynamic creativity and bright ideas are in full spate throughout, along with some truly superb wines from a masterpiece of a wine list.

Chef Nigel Haworth, Lisa Allen **Owner** Nigel Haworth, Craig Bancroft, Richard Matthewman **Times** 12-2/7-9.30 Closed 25 Dec, Food & Wine Festival **Prices** Fixed L 3 course fr £27.75, Tasting menu £85, Starter £10.50-£15, Main £28.50-£36, Dessert £11-£12.50, Service added but optional 10% **Wines** 297 bottles over £30, 40 bottles under £30, 11 by glass **Notes** Fixed Gourmet D 5 course £60, Tasting menu 7 course, Sunday L £36, Vegetarian menu, Dress restrictions, No jeans or trainers **Seats** 70, Pr/dining room 36 **Children** Portions, Menu **Parking** 60

Save on Hotels. Book at **theAA.com/hotel**

LANCASHIRE 227 **ENGLAND**

Enjoy the real taste of Lancashire

Take an AA four Rosette restaurant. Add the winning chefs from the BBC2's Great British Menu.

Combine with the freshest, most delicious ingredients from the pick of the region's artisan producers. Blend with fine wines chosen by a master of art. And finish with rooms sumptuously refurbished to be the ultimate in luxury and comfort. Could this be the recipe for the perfect treat?

- **Relaxing lunch or decadent dinner**
- **Overnight stay in one of our 14 stunning bedrooms**
- **Unforgettable Gourmet Breaks**
- **Enjoy exclusive private dining in The Louis Roederer Room**

Nigel Haworth, Craig Bancroft, Lisa Allen and all the team welcome you to the jewel in the crown of the food capital of Great Britain. Northcote.

Northcote Road, Langho, Blackburn, Lancashire BB6 8BE
Tel 01254 240 555 www.northcote.com

northcote

JUST 10 MILES FROM M6 JUNCTION 31 AND LESS THAN 6 MILES FROM M65 JUNCTION 6

LYTHAM ST ANNES *continued*

Greens Bistro

Modern British 🌢

Charming basement bistro with Lancashire cooking

☎ 01253 789990

3-9 St Andrews Road South, St Annes-on-Sea FY8 1SX
e-mail: info@greensbistro.co.uk
dir: Just off St Annes Sq

Paul and Anna Webster's intimate, basement bistro is a popular neighbourhood venue with plenty of smart rustic character thanks to its low ceilings and plenty of little hideaway nooks and alcoves. It's quite the spot for a cosy tête-à-tête, with the reassuring background hum of contented diners and a good buzz and bustle provided by friendly staff who are happy to engage in a bit of chat with customers. The cooking is straightforward, rustic modern bistro food and unapologetically pro-Lancashire in its sourcing of local ingredients. Get things going on a sound footing with a well-made twice-baked Lancashire cheese soufflé with red onion jam and a green salad, ahead of wild sea trout fillet served with sautéed new potatoes, green summer vegetables and hollandaise sauce. Meatier fare might run to medallions of pork tenderloin with bubble and squeak, apple and sauce, sage gravy, and Bury black pudding - the best, locals say, but they would, wouldn't they? Home-spun puddings include baked egg custard with seasonal berries and shortbread.

Chef Paul Webster **Owner** Paul & Anna Webster
Times 6-10 Closed 25 Dec, BHs, 2 wks Jan, 1 wk summer, Sun-Mon, L all week **Prices** Fixed D 3 course £17.95, Starter £4-£5.75, Main £13.95-£16.95, Dessert £4.95-£5.25, Service optional, Groups min 8 service 10% **Wines** 7 by glass **Notes** Vegetarian available **Seats** 38 **Children** Portions **Parking** On street

---

PRESTON   Map 18 SD52

The Pines Hotel

Traditional British 🌢

Classy cooking in charming hotel

☎ 01772 338551

570 Preston Rd, Clayton-Le-Woods PR6 7ED
e-mail: mail@thepineshotel.co.uk
dir: M6 junct 28/29 off A6 & S of B5256

Owned and run by Betty Duffin since the year The Beatles released *Please Please Me* (that's 1963 by the way),

there's, perhaps unsurprisingly, a charm and confidence to The Pines. The one-time Victorian cotton mill owner's residence stands in four pretty acres of landscaped gardens and mature woodland, and these days does a brisk trade in weddings and conferences. The traditional-looking Haworth Restaurant is another string to The Pines' bow, with its smartly laid tables and its broadly appealing menu. Start, perhaps, with pan-fried Scottish king scallops with pea and truffle purée, pancetta and crispy black pudding, or French onion soup with gruyère croûte. Follow on with classic moules marinière, or rack of lamb with Anna potatoes, aubergine salsa and red wine jus, or a steak from the grill. Finish with a white chocolate parfait and peanut butter with a berry compôte.

The Pines Hotel

Chef Imi Luhacs **Owner** Betty Duffin
Times 12-2.30/6-9.30 **Prices** Fixed L 2 course fr £12.50, Fixed D 3 course fr £17, Service optional **Wines** 7 by glass **Notes** Sunday L, Vegetarian available, Civ Wed 250 **Seats** 95, Pr/dining room 46 **Children** Portions, Menu **Parking** 150

See advert opposite

THORNTON   Map 18 SD34

Twelve Restaurant and Lounge Bar

Modern British 🌢

Lancastrian cooking in contemporary setting next to a windmill

☎ 01253 821212

Marsh Mill Village, Marsh Mill-in-Wyre, Fleetwood Road North FY5 4JZ
e-mail: info@twelve-restaurant.co.uk
web: www.twelve-restaurant.co.uk
dir: A585 follow signs for Marsh Mill Complex. Turn right into Victoria Rd East, entrance 0.5m on left

Right next to a working windmill in Thornton Cleveleys (yes, they've got one), Twelve is a stripped-down contemporary eatery that wouldn't look out of place in a

city-centre redevelopment. Stark clean lines frame the interior styling, where Pop Art montages, vermilion walls and cubist bar stools make a statement. Lancastrian cooking with flourishes of Français is the business, ranging from starters such as pig's head croquette with Puy lentils and apple purée to mains along the lines of roast breast and confit leg of guinea fowl with parsnip purée, or fried cod with fennel vierge and mini-fondant potatoes. Threesomes are popular, whether for cuts of beef, bits of lamb, or the local cheese selection, but desserts may go one better, with four in one under the distinctly vernacular rubric of 'Banana Butty'.

Twelve Restaurant and Lounge Bar

Chef Paul Moss **Owner** Paul Moss & Caroline Upton
Times 12-3/6.30-12 Closed 1st 2 wks Jan, Mon, L Tue-Sat **Prices** Fixed L 3 course £16.95, Fixed D 3 course £20.90-£24.95, Starter £5.95-£13.50, Main £17.95-£26.50, Dessert £5.95-£8.25, Service optional **Wines** 18 bottles over £30, 39 bottles under £30, 12 by glass **Notes** Sunday L, Vegetarian available **Seats** 90 **Children** Portions **Parking** 150

See advert on page 230

Save on Hotels. Book at **theAA.com/hotel**

LANCASHIRE 229 **ENGLAND**

The Pines Hotel is independently owned and has been in the same family since 1963. Over the years the Victorian cotton mill owner's house has been extensively extended. His once billiard room is now, some might say, the best 300 seat function room in the North West.

The hotel restaurant, "Haworth's" (the owner's maiden name), has enjoyed the accolade of being awarded the acclaimed AA Rosette since 2003.

The menu is of classic English style which is in keeping with the style & décor of the restaurant. All produce is sourced locally except the meat, which is from Donald Russell in Aberdeenshire, Scotland, who supplies premium meats to some of the finest restaurants and hotels.

The menu includes Scallops, Sea Bass, Rack of Lamb, Venison and Chateaubriand. To complete your meal the Assiette of Desserts is mouth watering.

In such beautiful & comfortable surroundings, a meal at The Pines is always a memorable occasion.

The Pines Hotel & Haworth Restaurant
570 Preston Road, Clayton-le-Woods, Chorley, Lancashire PR6 7ED
T: 01772 338551 | E: mail@thepineshotel.co.uk | W: www.thepineshotel.co.uk

TWELVE
RESTAURANT & LOUNGE BAR

- Situated beneath a beautifully restored 18th century windmill
- Contemporary- styled restaurant and lounge bar
- 5 minute drive from Blackpool
- Traditional British cuisine with a modern twist using fresh seasonal produce

OPEN
Tuesday – Sunday evenings for dinner
and Sundays 12pm – 2pm

AWARDS
2 AA Rosettes   2007 – 2013

TEL 01253 82 12 12 | www.twelve-restaurant.co.uk

WE ARE LOCATED
Marsh Mill Village
Thornton Cleveleys
Lancashire
FY5 4JZ

The Freemasons at Wiswell

WHALLEY   **MAP 18 SD73**

Modern British ⚑ NOTABLE WINE LIST

Skillful cooking from a talented chef in an old village inn

☎ 01254 822218
8 Vicarage Fold, Wiswell BB7 9DF
e-mail: steve@freemasonswiswell.co.uk
dir: A59, located on the edge of Whalley village near Clitheroe

There's much to recommend in this part of the country: the Ribble Valley has interesting little towns, beautiful countryside and some truly excellent food producers, so it's hardly surprising chef Steven Smith has returned to his Lancashire roots and set himself up in an old pub in the chocolate-box village of Wiswell. The Freemasons was once three small cottages, one of which was a freemasons' lodge, but these days it's progressed from being a traditional inn to an out and out stylish but rustic gastropub complete with open fires, flagstoned floors, antique rugs, huntin' shootin' fishin'-themed paintings on the walls and mismatched antique furniture. The place has a warm and homely atmosphere, helped along by the friendly and impressively knowledgeable staff. Blackburn-born Smith honed his skills in many of the North's top kitchens, and it shows in his assured and innovative adaptations of classic dishes. Produce is top-notch, seasonal at all times and sourced from an army of suppliers in the Ribble Valley, including daily fish deliveries from Wellgate Fisheries in nearby Clitheroe. A September lunch might begin with venison tartare, butternut squash, pickled damsons, smoked almonds and chocolate: the venison singing with flavour and with a perfect texture, the discs and purée of squash giving earthy sweetness, enhanced by the chocolate, and the almonds adding textural contrast. The market fish of the day could be the route to take at main course, perhaps beautifully cooked, sea-fresh halibut topped with buttery Southport shrimp and Southport tenderstem broccoli. Meals here tend to finish on a high with something like a vanilla slice - layers of fine pastry and a gently flavoured vanilla cream topped with caramelised pears in a rich and sticky ginger syrup. Of course, it's not all about the food: the bar has an impressive selection of traditional cask ales from award-winning independent breweries, while the cellar stocks over 250 wines from around the world.

Chef Steven Smith, Matthew Horsefall **Owner** Steven Smith **Times** 12-2.30/5.30-9.30 Closed 2 Jan for 2 wks, Mon **Prices** Fixed L 2 course £16.95, Fixed D 3 course £19.95, Tasting menu £60, Starter £7.95-£16.95, Main £15.95-£29.95, Dessert £7.95-£11.95, Service optional **Wines** 75 bottles over £30, 75 bottles under £30, 30 by glass **Notes** Fixed L 3 course seasonal menu also offered early supper, Sunday L, Vegetarian available **Seats** 70, Pr/dining room 12 **Children** Portions **Parking** In village

Save on Hotels. Book at **theAA.com/hotel**

LANCASHIRE 231 **ENGLAND**

WHALLEY Map 18 SD73

The Freemasons at Wiswell

◉◉◉ – *see opposite*

The Three Fishes

◉ British ☕

Refined traditional food in a rural pub

☎ 01254 826888
Mitton Rd, Mitton BB7 9PQ
e-mail: enquiries@thethreefishes.com
dir: M6 junct 31, A59 to Clitheroe. Follow Whalley signs,
B6246, 2m

The Three Fishes has the sort of look you'd hope for in a
400-year-old inn in a tiny village: stone walls, rugs on a
slate floor, log fires, upholstered benches and wooden
tables, and better still, it is part of the group run by Nigel
Haworth and Craig Bancroft of Northcote fame (see
entry). The kitchen is dedicated to supporting 'local food
heroes' and building on Lancashire's culinary traditions.
A high level of integrity is evident here; dishes tend to be
uncomplicated, flavours clear, presentation attractive.
Bury black pudding with onion relish and mustard or
treacle-cured salmon with pikelets may precede fish pie,
Lancashire hotpot, or a chargrilled steak. A trio of
'European classics' includes daube de boeuf, and
desserts are unabashedly English, from parkin to moreish
sticky toffee pudding.

Chef Andy McCarthy **Owner** Craig Bancroft, Nigel
Haworth, Richard Matthewman **Times** 12-2/5.30-8.30
Closed 25 Dec **Prices** Fixed L 2 course £11.50, Fixed D 3
course £15, Starter £3.75-£6.50, Main £8.50-£19.50,
Dessert £5, Service optional **Wines** 7 bottles over £30, 30
bottles under £30, 10 by glass **Notes** Fixed L & D 2/3
course Mon-Thu, Sunday L, Vegetarian available
Seats 140 **Children** Portions, Menu **Parking** 70

WHITEWELL Map 18 SD64

The Inn at Whitewell

◉ Modern British ☕

Traditional rural inn with a local flavour

☎ 01200 448222
Forest of Bowland, Clitheroe BB7 3AT
e-mail: reception@innatwhitewell.com
dir: From S M6 junct 31 Longridge follow Whitewell signs.
From N M6 junct 33 follow Trough of Bowland & Whitewell
signs

This rural 16th-century inn overlooking the River Hodder
has bags of appeal. The Forest of Bowland along the
valley makes for quite a view for a start, while stone
floors, old beams, roaring fires and antique furniture are
all you might hope for within. Take a seat wherever the
mood takes you, be it in the informal bar area with
wooden tables or the plusher main restaurant complete
with linen tablecloths and smart table settings. Local
ingredients make a good showing on the menu; start
perhaps with seared scallops with grilled black pudding,
minted pea purée, smoked bacon lardons and a
watercress dressing, before moving on to roast rack of
Burholme Lonk lamb cooked with cumin, tomatoes and
garlic. Puddings take the comfort route - banoffee pie
with dark chocolate, for example.

Chef Jamie Cadman **Owner** Charles Bowman
Times 12-2/7.30-9.30 **Prices** Starter £5-£8.75, Main
£15.50-£27.50, Dessert £6, Service optional **Wines** 50
bottles over £30, 40 bottles under £30, 20 by glass
Notes Sunday L £14, Vegetarian available, Civ Wed 80
Seats 60, Pr/dining room 20 **Children** Portions
Parking 70

WREA GREEN Map 18 SD33

The Spa Hotel at Ribby Hall Village

◉◉ Modern British NEW V

Confident cooking in smart spa hotel

☎ 01772 674484
Ribby Hall Village, Ribby Rd PR4 2PR
e-mail: brasserie@ribbyhall.co.uk
web: www.ribbyhall.co.uk/spa-hotel
dir: M55 junct 33 follow A585 towards Kirkham & brown
tourist signs for Ribby Hall Village. Straight across 3
rdbts. Ribby Hall Village 200yds on left

There are some pretty swanky spa facilities at the
eponymously named hotel and it's an adult-only venue,
so the idea is you leave the kids at home and pamper
yourself. So far so good. The Brasserie is another string to
its bow, and it is well worth the trip out on its own merits.
It occupies a modishly done out space with plenty of room

between the darkwood tables, and serves up some smart
modern food. There's a good showing of regional
ingredients on the menu and a decidedly modern British
approach all round. Start, for example, with a soft boiled
duck's egg served with two ham hock croquettes and
home-made salad cream, or go for the pressed belly pork
with apple, black pudding and Grasmere gingerbread.
Follow on with Goosnargh duck breast - the skin nicely
rendered - with crystalised turnip, confit fennel and
orange, or roast loin of cod with samphire, potted shrimps
and shellfish foam. And for dessert there may be treacle
tart with orange anglaise, chocolate crumb and clotted
cream.

Chef Michael Noonan **Times** 12-2/6-9 **Prices** Prices not
confirmed Service optional **Notes** Booking advisable L&D,
Vegetarian menu, Dress restrictions, Smart casual

WRIGHTINGTON Map 15 SD51

Corner House

◉ Modern British ☕

Victorian hostelry with pub classics and modern dishes

☎ 01257 451400
Wrightington Bar WN6 9SE
e-mail: info@themulberrytree.info
dir: 4m from Wigan. From M6 junct 27 towards Parbold,
right after motorway exit, by BP garage into Mossy Lea
Rd. On right after 2m

Formerly the Mulberry Tree, the whitewashed inn a short
tootle from the M6 dates back to the early Victorian era,
and has seen service as a wheelwright's and
blacksmith's premises over the years. The restaurant is
kitted out in dark woods and white walls, and run by
friendly, efficient staff, who serve forth an extensive
menu of pub classics and more speculative modern
dishes. Expect to begin with something like seared
scallops on pea, asparagus and lemon risotto, before
progressing to a steak from the grill, market-fresh fish
such as sea bass or salmon with crushed new potatoes
and a choice of sauces, or one of the daily specials that
add lustre to the occasion - perhaps rump of lamb with a
minty lamb sausage, sautéed potatoes and red wine jus.
Vegetarians are properly looked after, as are the sweet of
tooth, who might go for amaretto pannacotta with warm
chocolate sauce.

Chef Mr Lawson **Owner** Ross Lawson & Helen Hunter
Times 12-2.30/5-8.30 Closed 26 Dec **Prices** Starter
£4.95-£7.95, Main £9.95-£20.95, Dessert £5.95-£7.50,
Service added but optional 10% **Wines** 9 bottles over
£30, 26 bottles under £30, 8 by glass **Notes** Early Bird 2
course £14.50, Sunday L £14.95-£17.95, Vegetarian
available **Seats** 60 **Children** Portions, Menu **Parking** 80

LEICESTERSHIRE

CASTLE DONINGTON

For restaurant details see East Midlands Airport

EAST MIDLANDS AIRPORT   Map 11 SK42

Best Western Premier Yew Lodge Hotel & Spa

◎◎ British 🍴

Peaceful country hotel with creative cooking

☎ 01509 672518
Packington Hill DE74 2DF
e-mail: info@yewlodgehotel.co.uk
web: www.yewlodgehotel.co.uk
dir: M1 junct 24. Follow signs to Loughborough & Kegworth on A6. On entering village, 1st right, after 400yds hotel on right

Although it sits just minutes from the motorway network and East Midlands airport, the Yew Lodge Hotel is a surprisingly peaceful hideaway. The split-level bistro-style Orchard Restaurant is tended by smartly-uniformed and welcoming staff who play their part in ensuring the place is as well-supported by locals as it is by hotel residents. The skilled kitchen takes classic ideas and adds a contemporary spin here and there, perhaps surprise ingredients such as white chocolate and champagne added to a classic pairing of seared scallops and black pudding, or the sharpness of radish, carrot and citrus to cut the richness of a hay-smoked salmon cheesecake. Mains could bring on pork Wellington with pig's cheek, apple and wild mushrooms, or fish, in the shape of turbot fillet with mussels, curry, coriander, onion and garlic. Dessert could be a playful 'Night at the Movies' assemblage of popcorn, Oreo biscuit, Cola, candyfloss, caramel and retro sweets.

Chef Trevor Bearder **Owner** Pick family
Times 12–2/6.30–9.30 Closed L Sat **Prices** Fixed L 2 course £12.95, Fixed D 3 course £22.35–£33.85, Starter £5.50–£6.95, Main £10.95–£20.95, Dessert £5.95, Service optional **Wines** 2 bottles over £30, 26 bottles under £30, 10 by glass **Notes** Sunday L, Vegetarian available, Dress restrictions, Smart casual, Civ Wed 250 **Seats** 90, Pr/dining room 20 **Children** Portions, Menu **Parking** 188

The Priest House Hotel

◎◎ Modern British 𝐕

Ambitious modern cooking in historic country-house hotel

☎ 0845 072 7502
Kings Mills DE72 2RR
e-mail: thepriesthouse@handpicked.co.uk
web: www.handpickedhotels.co.uk/thepriesthouse
dir: M1 junct 24, onto A50, take 1st slip road signed Castle Donington. Right at lights, hotel in 2m

With its peaceful rural setting on the River Trent and period charm in spades, this country-house hotel is understandably a popular wedding venue. It's also a dining destination, with a bright, modern menu and a characterful restaurant with beams, stone walls and leaded windows. The kitchen's a busy place, judging by starters like confit leg and smoked loin of rabbit served with carrot purée, redcurrants and tarragon and mustard dressing, and roast scallops paired with confit belly pork accompanied by pear purée and pink peppercorn vinaigrette. Dishes are marked out by the quality of the ingredients and often bold combinations bringing out forthright flavours: roast turbot, for instance, comes with oxtail tortellini, salsify poached in red wine and a sauce of clams and red wine, and breast of guinea fowl roasted with pancetta is served with garlic purée, dauphinoise and thyme and marjoram crumble. Just as labour-intensive are appealing puddings like apple and caramel custard trifle with pain perdu and apple sorbet and crystalline.

Chef David Humphreys **Owner** Hand Picked Hotels
Times 12–2.30/7–9.30 Closed L Mon-Sat, D Sun
Prices Fixed D 3 course £36–£43, Service optional
Wines 74 bottles over £30, 11 bottles under £30, 18 by glass **Notes** Sunday L, Vegetarian menu, Civ Wed 120 **Seats** 34, Pr/dining room 100 **Children** Portions, Menu **Parking** 100

HINCKLEY   Map 11 SP49

Sketchley Grange Hotel

◎◎ British, European

Sound modern British cooking in a spa retreat

☎ 01455 251133
Sketchley Ln, Burbage LE10 3HU
e-mail: reservations@sketchleygrange.co.uk
web: www.sketchleygrange.co.uk
dir: From M69 junct 1 take B4109 (Hinckley). Straight on 1st rdbt, left at 2nd rdbt & immediately right into Sketchley Lane. Hotel at end of lane

Just inside Leicestershire, right on the border with Worcestershire, Sketchley Grange is a mock-Tudor country house which has been extended and upgraded over the years to create a luxurious hotel with a range of top-notch facilities. There are lovely grounds to explore, a spa to relax in, and a choice of restaurants including The Dining Room – an elegant and intimate setting in which to enjoy some contemporary fine-dining. You might start with chilli and coriander beef carpaccio with horseradish and cornichon, then follow with steamed fillet of wild sea bass partnered with seared scallops, parsley potatoes, leeks, sun-dried tomatoes and a langoustine and basil cream. Chocoholics will rejoice in the 'tasting of chocolate' – a combination of a milk chocolate pannacotta, dark chocolate brownie and a scoop of white chocolate and basil ice cream.

Times 7–9.30 Closed Mon, L Tue-Sat, D Sun

KEGWORTH

For restaurant details see East Midlands Airport

LEICESTER   Map 11 SK50

Hotel Maiyango

◎ Modern European 🍴

Fab décor and smart modern European cooking

☎ 0116 251 8898
13-21 St Nicholas Place LE1 4LD
e-mail: reservations@maiyango.com
dir: M1 junct 21, A5460 for 3.5m. Turn right onto A47 round St Nicholas Circle onto St Nicholas Place

The buzzy rooftop cocktail bar of this city centre boutique hotel is just the spot to soak up an aperitif with the cityscape vista of spires and rooftops. The combo of slick bolthole, cool bar and modish restaurant is a winner here, with the restaurant going for an ethnic chic Moroccan and Middle Eastern-inspired look. The food surprisingly veers off from Arabia, taking a more modern European tack, spiked here and there with global influences, while the kitchen's commitment to local sourcing means that supplies come from as close to home as possible. Lobster and crayfish ravioli is matched with carrot and lemongrass broth, then for the main event, chicken breast is wrapped around a punchy pairing of basil mousse and pigeon breast and served with roast sweet potato fondant, smoked beetroot purée and wild mushroom jus. At the end, a blueberry and almond pannacotta comes with caramelised peaches and Bellini sorbet.

Chef Phillip Sharpe **Owner** Aatin Anadkat
Times 12.30–2.30/6.30–9.45 Closed 25 Dec, 1 Jan, L Sun-Tue **Prices** Fixed L 2 course fr £16.50, Fixed D 3 course fr £30, Service optional, Groups min 6 service 10% **Wines** 19 bottles over £30, 35 bottles under £30, 12 by glass **Notes** Tasting & pre-theatre menus available, Vegetarian available **Seats** 55, Pr/dining room 80 **Children** Portions **Parking** NCP

LONG WHATTON   Map 11 SK42

The Royal Oak

Modern British V

Skillful modern cooking in a smartly modernised village inn

☎ 01509 843694
26 The Green LE12 5DB
e-mail: enquiries@theroyaloaklongwhatton.co.uk

No longer a pub starved of love and attention, the 21st-century incarnation of The Royal Oak is a thriving gastro-pub in the contemporary manner. The facelift undertaken over the last few years has resulted in a smart interior, the addition of some natty bedrooms, and a focus on food. That said, real ale is all part of the plan, and a few 'pub classics' remain on the menu to ensure the place remains part of the community (a proper pub in other words). The kitchen buys local where possible and turns out bright modish stuff such as chicken liver parfait with red onion jam, or Cullen skink arancini to start. There are sharing platters filled with goodies, and impressive main courses such as grilled fillet of hake with caper and tarragon butter, served with a ham hock bubble-and-squeak and confit egg yolk. To finish, tiramisù with Kahlua eggnog and cinnamon-infused compôte.

Chef James & Charles Upton, Shaun McDonnell **Owner** Alex & Chris Astwood **Times** 12-2.30/5.30-9.30 Closed D Sun **Prices** Fixed D 3 course fr £15, Starter £4.50-£7.95, Main £11.50-£23.95, Dessert £3.75-£6.50, Service optional **Wines** 5 bottles over £30, 23 bottles under £30, 9 by glass **Notes** Early doors menu Mon-Fri 5.30-6.30, Sunday L, Vegetarian menu **Seats** 45 **Children** Portions, Menu **Parking** 30

MELTON MOWBRAY   Map 11 SK71

Stapleford Park

Modern French, British

Ambitious cooking in opulent surroundings

☎ 01572 787000 & 787019
Stapleford LE14 2EF
e-mail: reservations@stapleford.co.uk
web: www.staplefordpark.com
dir: A1 to Colsterworth onto B676, signed Melton Mowbray. In approx 9m turn left to Stapleford

Set in landscaped grounds modelled by 'Capability' Brown, this magnificent mansion has the sort of grand interior of a stately home, with stunning plasterwork, paintings and huge fireplaces, with rich upholstery and drapes adding to the feeling of opulence. The Grinling Gibbons Restaurant, with its beautifully appointed tables, candlelight and crystal chandeliers, takes its name from the master craftsman who carved the superb mantelpiece; if the setting seems dauntingly formal, friendly, switched-on staff make every effort to engage

with guests. Menus are thoughtfully compiled and nicely balanced, and what stands out is the quality of the produce along with the kitchen's imagination and flair. Canapés are promising auguries, well matched by starters of rillette of sea trout with rocket and crème fraîche mousse, or game terrine wrapped in Parma ham with fig chutney. Timings are spot on, from roast beef for Sunday lunch to an imaginative dish of wild halibut and smoked haddock with a Scotch egg, mushroom 'ketchup' and pickled vegetables. Desserts are equally successful, among them an assiette of chocolate and one of passionfruit and coconut.

Times 11.30-2.30/7-9.30 Closed exclusive use days, D Sun-Tue

NORTH KILWORTH   Map 11 SP68

Kilworth House Hotel & Theatre

Modern British V

Modern country-house cooking in a luxury hotel

☎ 01858 880058
Lutterworth Rd LE17 6JE
e-mail: info@kilworthhouse.co.uk
web: www.kilworthhouse.co.uk
dir: A4304 towards Market Harborough, after Walcote, hotel 1.5m on right

Period authenticity runs through this Italianate 19th-century mansion thanks to a top-to-toe restoration overseen by the eagle eyes of English Heritage. Only two families lived in it for 120 years before it became an upmarket country-house hotel in the noughties with all the plush style, fittings and furniture befitting a hotel of this standing (including, these days, an open-air theatre in the grounds). If you want to see what the chefs can do, the Wordsworth Restaurant is the fine-dining venue, a truly remarkable confection of stained-glass windows, rich red patterned wallpaper and burnished antique tables beneath a lanterned dome of elaborate plasterwork and twinkling chandeliers; in short, the sort of place you feel that best bib and tucker is required. The scene thus set, what's on the menu is classic country-house cooking brought gently up to date - seared scallops with spiced tomato relish and parsnip purée, for example, while at main course duck is served three ways as breast, confit and rillettes, with pommes Anna, pickled cabbage and orange. If you're in the market for fish, consider brill with sweet potato and coconut curry and red lentil salsa.

Chef Carl Dovey **Owner** Mr & Mrs Mackay **Times** 12-2.30/7-9.30 **Prices** Fixed L 2 course £22, Fixed D 3 course £29.50, Tasting menu fr £49.50, Starter £6.50-£10.95, Main £14.95-£24.45, Dessert £6.50-£8, Service optional **Wines** 44 bottles over £30, 35 bottles under £30, 10 by glass **Notes** Theatre menu in season 3 course £28, Tasting menu Wed-Sat, Sunday L, Vegetarian menu, Dress restrictions, No jeans or trainers, Civ Wed 150 **Seats** 70, Pr/dining room 130 **Children** Portions, Menu **Parking** 140

QUORN   Map 11 SK51

Quorn Country Hotel

Modern British NEW

Simple British dishes in a stylish country hotel

☎ 01509 415050
Charnwood House, 66 Leicester Rd LE12 8BB
e-mail: sales@quorncountryhotel.co.uk
web: www.quorncountryhotel.co.uk
dir: M1 junct 23/A6 towards Leicester, follow signs for Quorn

Built around the originally 17th-century Charnwood House, the Quorn is a distinctly stylish country hotel just outside Loughborough. Oak panelling and chandeliers are much in evidence, although gentler pastoral murals confer a sense of serenity on the Shires dining room, where smartly dressed tables and professional service are up to snuff. The kitchen goes in for a carefully judged version of modern British cooking that doesn't try to overreach itself, opening meals with the familiar likes of ham hock terrine and piccalilli, or a single scallop with puréed cauliflower and a rasher of crisp streaky bacon. Simple mains run to grilled mackerel with potato and watercress in sorrel butter, or rump of new season's lamb with samphire and rosemary and a good, deeply flavoured jus. To finish, there could be chocolate marquise accompanied by a poached pear and lime cream, or a nutmeggy custard tart made with duck eggs, served with clotted cream.

Chef James Lonergan **Owner** Mr Walshe **Times** 12-2/7-9 Closed L Sat **Prices** Fixed L 2 course fr £24.95, Service optional **Wines** 48 bottles over £30, 12 bottles under £30, 5 by glass **Notes** Sunday L, Vegetarian available, Civ Wed 120 **Seats** 112, Pr/dining room 240 **Children** Portions, Menu **Parking** 120

WOODHOUSE EAVES — Map 11 SK51

The Woodhouse

◉◉ Modern British 🍷

Vibrant cooking in stylish village restaurant

☎ 01509 890318
43 Maplewell Rd, Woodhouse Eaves LE12 8RG
e-mail: info@thewoodhouse.co.uk
web: www.thewoodhouse.co.uk
dir: M1 junct 23 towards Loughborough, right into
Nanpantan Rd, left into Beacon Rd, right in Main St &
again into Maplewell Rd

The unassuming whitewashed cottagey exterior of this
restaurant, tucked away in a little village near Leicester,
conceals a vibrant, contemporary-looking interior. A
recent revamp has toned down the once racy décor,
leaving a thoroughly modern and stylish venue where you
might kick off with cocktails in the jazzy bar before
proceeding to the chic dining area. There are upholstered
dining chairs at properly set tables, art on the walls, and
a relaxed, informal vibe, while the cooking intrigues with
its imaginative juxtapositions of flavour and texture,
presented simply, and solidly grounded in sound locally-
sourced materials. It's clear from the off that there is
ambition and no lack of technical ability here: monkfish
cheeks are flaked and set against crisp chicken wings,
summer minestrone and freshly-made tagliatelle, while
main course brings lamb rump and sweetbreads with
vanilla mash, lettuce, peas, cucumber, and mint foam.
The same sense of enthusiastic experimentation creeps
into desserts as well: a deconstructed Black Forest
gâteau delivers a chocolate torte with almond, vanilla
meringue and Amaretto ice cream.

Chef Paul Leary **Owner** Paul Leary **Times** 12-3/6.30-12
Closed BHs, Mon, L Sat, D Sun **Prices** Fixed L 2 course
£12.95, Fixed D 3 course £21.95, Tasting menu £45-£65,
Starter £8.95, Main £22.50, Dessert £8.95, Service
optional **Wines** 39 bottles over £30, 37 bottles under £30,
10 by glass **Notes** Fixed ALC 3 course £37.50, Sunday L
Seats 50, Pr/dining room 40 **Children** Portions
Parking 15

WYMESWOLD — Map 11 SK62

Hammer & Pincers

◉◉ Modern European NEW V 🍷

Inventive cooking in smart rural restaurant

☎ 01509 880735
5 East Rd LE12 6ST
e-mail: info@hammerandpincers.co.uk

Gastropub? Country restaurant? It doesn't matter what
label you tag onto the Hammer & Pincers - what's beyond
argument is that lucky locals in the Leicestershire village
of Wymeswold have great food on their doorstep. Run by
husband and wife team Danny and Sandra Jimminson
who trained in big-name kitchens, this smart rural
restaurant is a stylish, contemporary space with bright
artworks on exposed brickwork walls. Its serious intent is
made clear with keenly-priced multi-course grazing and
gourmet menus to bolster a repertoire of creative modern
European cuisine. A small card on each table, written
with a touch of humour and snippets of personal
information, shows the strength of their relationship with
local suppliers, and staff are on the ball and happy to
chat about the menus, which read like a dream. Chunky
ham hock and parsley terrine with piccalilli and toasted
walnut and raisin bread is big on flavour, while pan-
roasted salmon fillet served with parmesan gnocchi and
crayfish velouté makes for a colourful, well-constructed
main course. Refined puds include chocolate and orange
oil délice with Grand Marnier clementines and milk ice
cream.

Chef Daniel Jimminson **Owner** Daniel & Sandra
Jimminson **Times** 12-2/6-9 **Prices** Fixed L 2 course fr
£15, Fixed D 3 course fr £18, Tasting menu fr £35, Starter
£6-£11, Main £15-£24, Dessert £5-£6.50, Service
optional **Wines** 18 bottles over £30, 26 bottles under £30,
16 by glass **Notes** Sunday L, Vegetarian menu **Seats** 46
Children Portions, Menu **Parking** 40

LINCOLNSHIRE

GRANTHAM — Map 11 SK93

Harry's Place

◉◉◉ – *see opposite*

HORNCASTLE — Map 17 TF26

Magpies Restaurant with Rooms

◉◉ British, European 🍷

Bright, modish cooking in the Lincolnshire Wolds

☎ 01507 527004
73 East St LN9 6AA
dir: 0.5m from town centre on A158 towards Skegness

The market town of Horncastle is home to Andrew and
Caroline Gilbert's restaurant with rooms, lovingly formed
out of three 200-year-old black and cream cottages. It's
all very charming and traditional on the inside, too, with
a log-burning stove in the comfortable sitting room to
melt away any winter chill, before you head into the
dining room with its neatly laid tables and warm pastel
tones. On the menu you'll find lots of local ingredients
and plenty of imaginative and appealing combinations.
Start with confit of veal with a spinach pithivier and
sautéed wild mushrooms, or go for the chef's fish pie with
seared king scallop and parsley sauce. Among main
courses, baked cod might be partnered with a lemongrass
and ginger beurre blanc, and local partridge boned and
stuffed with chestnuts and foie gras. The cheese trolley
makes an entrance near the end, but you might well be
tempted by sticky toffee pudding with salted caramel
shortbread, white chocolate and fudge semi-fredo and
caramel sauce.

Chef Andrew Gilbert **Owner** Caroline Gilbert
Times 12-2/7-9.30 Closed 27 Dec, 1st wk Jan, Mon-Tue, L
Sat **Prices** Fixed L 2 course £20, Fixed D 3 course £45,
Service optional **Wines** 72 bottles over £30, 72 bottles
under £30, 7 by glass **Notes** Magpie menu 3 course D
Wed-Thu & Sun £19.95, Sunday L, Vegetarian available,
Dress restrictions, Smart casual **Seats** 34
Children Portions **Parking** On street

Save on Hotels. Book at theAA.com/hotel

LINCOLNSHIRE 235 ENGLAND

HOUGH-ON-THE-HILL Map 11 SK94

The Brownlow Arms

◉ British ◠

Country-pub cooking in an elegant village inn

☎ 01400 250234
High Rd NG32 2AZ
e-mail: armsinn@yahoo.co.uk
web: www.thebrownlowarms.com
dir: Take A607 (Grantham to Sleaford road). Hough-on-the-Hill signed from Barkston

A Lincolnshire village inn that has come up in the world, The Brownlow is as elegantly appointed as an interiors magazine country house, with tapestry-backed chairs and gilt-framed mirrors in a panelled dining room. Attentive, friendly service puts everyone at their ease though, and the menu stays within the familiar territory of classic country-pub cooking. Devilled lamb's kidneys in a puff pastry basket make a robust opener, or there might be battered tiger prawns dressed Thai-style in lime, coriander and green chilli. The Asian note might be struck again in a main of sesame-crusted duck with pak choi and a little rhubarb tart, or there may be a fish assemblage of plaice, salmon and scallops, served with crushed peas in lemon and chive beurre blanc. A successful dessert is the griottine cherry frangipane tart, with creamy praline parfait and Frangelico ice cream. Cheeses are served with grapes and membrillo.

Chef Oliver Snell **Owner** Paul & Lorraine Willoughby **Times** 12-3/6.30-9.30 Closed 25-26 Dec, Mon, L Tue-Sat, D Sun **Prices** Fixed D 3 course £21.95, Service optional **Wines** 5 by glass **Notes** Sunday L, Vegetarian available **Seats** 80, Pr/dining room 26 **Parking** 26, On street

LINCOLN Map 17 SK97

Branston Hall Hotel

◉◉ Modern British V

Complex modern British food with lake and parkland views

☎ 01522 793305
Lincoln Rd, Branston Park, Branston LN4 1PD
e-mail: info@branstonhall.com
web: www.branstonhall.com
dir: On B1188, 3m S of Lincoln. In village, hotel drive opposite village hall

Branston Hall is an exuberant Victorian country house, with decorative gables and pinnacle chimneys reaching for the stars. Eighty-eight acres of mature parkland do wonders for the feeling of gracious living the place exudes, and it serves its purpose as a retreat hotel in the Lincolnshire countryside with great aplomb. The Lakeside dining room is a restful place, with views over the park to the said stretch of water, and it majors in today's unmistakable culinary style of mingled classical and modern. An appetising array of flavours is assembled in a terrine of rabbit, pistachios and sultanas, accompanied by pickled carrots and Agen prunes. The same may be said of complex but well-balanced main courses such as a double-act of cep-crusted monkfish and sticky salt beef, served with pease pudding and clams, while desserts sing something simpler in the key of liquorice parfait or almond tart.

Chef Miles Collins **Owner** Southsprings Ltd **Times** 12-2/7-9.30 **Prices** Prices not confirmed Service optional **Wines** 14 by glass **Notes** Sunday L, Vegetarian menu, Dress restrictions, Smart casual, no jeans, T-shirts or trainers, Civ Wed 120 **Seats** 75, Pr/dining room 28 **Children** Portions **Parking** 75

Harry's Place

GRANTHAM MAP 11 SK93

Modern French

Outstanding quality in a restaurant built for ten

☎ 01476 561780
17 High St, Great Gonerby NG31 8JS
dir: 1.5m NW of Grantham on B1174

From the outside, Harry's Place looks like a private residence, a very elegant Georgian house on the outskirts of Grantham, to be precise, sitting quietly behind tall trees in a pleasant garden. In fact, the place is so unassuming that you could pass right by without realising that Harry and Caroline Hallam's bijou operation is one of Britain's finest (and smallest) foodie addresses. In some ways, it is a perfect business model: the place is booked up way in advance since there are only ten lucky diners to cater for at each sitting, which means that attention to detail and quality control are of the highest order. And as the Hallams are running it from home, they avoid the worrying overheads of separate business premises. No staff are needed: chef-patron Harry cooks single-handedly out back in the kitchen, while Caroline runs front-of-house single-handedly and with easygoing conviviality - there are just three well-spaced tables to tend, after all. This set-up has worked admirably for around a quarter of a century, and it all takes place in a homely-yet-elegant dining room. Top-class materials are provided by a well-established network of trusted suppliers, and they are brought together with razor-sharp classical French technique and an unerring eye for balance in flavour and texture. Wonderful breads are freshly baked in-house twice a day, and the hand-written menu proposes just two choices at each of three courses. Escalopes of wild sea trout with a sauce of shallots, Sauternes and chives, accompanied by some perfectly-cooked samphire might start you off, or perhaps a soup, say really intense and earthy mushroom with truffle oil. Sticking with fish for main course, fillet of wild sea bass could arrive lightly-seared, with a red wine, basil and coriander sauce, on mango relish and braised lentils, while the meaty alternative could bring Aberdeen Angus beef fillet with blueberries, a sauce of red wine and Armagnac, and a horseradish hollandaise. Vibrant desserts are simplicity itself - apricot ice cream with Cointreau syrup, perhaps - and there are plenty of perfectly ripe cheeses to indulge in.

Chef Harry Hallam **Owner** Harry & Caroline Hallam **Times** 12.30-3/7-8.30 Closed 2 wks from 25 Dec, 1 wk Aug, Sun-Mon **Prices** Starter £9.50-£18.50, Main £37.50-£39.50, Dessert £8, Service optional **Wines** 20 bottles over £30, 7 bottles under £30, 4 by glass **Notes** Vegetarian meal on request at time of booking, Vegetarian available **Seats** 10 **Children** Portions **Parking** 4

LINCOLN *continued*

The Lincoln Hotel

® Modern British V ℭ

Sharp modern dishes in designer-led hotel

☎ 01522 520348
Eastgate LN2 1PN
e-mail: vandrews@thelincolnhotel.com
web: www.thelincolnhotel.com

The Lincoln is a modern hotel, hard by the 12th-century cathedral, with a designer-chic interior that's bang up to the minute. The Green Room restaurant is a serenely decorated, chandelier-hung space with drapes over the windows, and a menu that's as sharp and modern an assembly as the surroundings would suggest. Chicken liver and foie gras parfait balanced by mulled cranberry chutney might start you off, followed by monkfish tail wrapped in Parma ham with tomato and merguez sausage cassoulet and butter bean and basil purée. Prime ingredients are cooked with care, and combinations are carefully considered, as in a starter of scallops with apple purée, black pudding crumb and smoked bacon foam, and main-course pan-fried chicken breast, full of flavour, in its own cooking juices accompanied by candied carrots, celeriac purée and hasselback potatoes. Professional but relaxed service, some notable breads, and puddings along the lines of chocolate and pear tart, all add to the pleasure.

Chef James Maulgue **Owner** Christopher Nevile, Lady Arnold **Times** 6-9.30 Closed Sun-Mon, L all week **Prices** Prices not confirmed Service optional **Notes** Vegetarian menu **Seats** 30, Pr/dining room 12 **Children** Portions, Menu

The Old Bakery

®® Modern British ℭ

Smart former bakery with local ingredients to the fore

☎ 01522 576057
26-28 Burton Rd LN1 3LB
e-mail: enquiries@theold-bakery.co.uk
dir: From A46 follow directions for Lincoln North then follow brown signs for The Historic Centre

Close to Lincoln Cathedral, this former bakery turned restaurant with rooms is a charmingly rustic place, partly thanks to plenty of surviving period features, and note there's now a fabulous deli from which you can take home all sorts of goodies. The restaurant still has the old ovens in situ (now defunct), plus the original hand-operated wooden mixing vat has been split and made into bench seating, with the rustic-chic dining rooms extending into a conservatory-style garden room. The passionate Italian chef-patron and his small kitchen team deliver clearly flavoured, carefully crafted dishes based on local, seasonal Lincolnshire produce. The weekly-changing menu brings together contemporary British and Italian ideas, so after tucking into home-made foccacia presented in white bags as per a bakery, you can tuck into Eden Farm organic roasted butternut squash and garlic soup with sherry-braised onion crostino and crème fraîche jelly. And for main course Peter Lundgren slow-roasted Gloucestershire Old Spot baby pig might come with stir-fried garlic potato, cinnamon-braised apple and red cabbage, and smoked pancetta cream.

Chef Ivano de Serio **Owner** Alan & Lynn Ritson, Tracey & Ivano de Serio **Times** 12-1.30/7-9 Closed 26 Dec, 1 Jan, Mon, D Sun **Prices** Fixed L 2 course fr £12.50, Fixed D 3 course £20, Tasting menu £38-£45, Starter £5.95-£10.95, Main £15.50-£24.50, Dessert £4.95-£7.95, Service optional **Wines** 65 bottles over £30, 53 bottles under £30, 9 by glass **Notes** Tasting menu 7/10 course, 5/8 course with wine £53-£65, Sunday L, Vegetarian available, Dress restrictions, Smart casual **Seats** 65, Pr/dining room 15 **Children** Portions **Parking** On street, public car park 20mtrs

Tower Hotel

® Modern **NEW** ℭ

Bright modern cooking in the cathedral quarter

☎ 01522 529999
30 Westgate LN1 3BD
e-mail: tower.hotel@btclick.com
web: www.lincolntowerhotel.com
dir: Next to Lincoln Castle

The Tower is in the cathedral quarter with the old town on its doorstep and the centre 10 minutes down the hill. The restaurant's décor is quite simple, with high-backed wicker chairs at clothed tables, a wooden floor and a mirrored wall on one side. The kitchen exhibits a high level of skill and imagination, turning out starters like Thai-style haddock and tuna fishcake, artistically presented with sweet-and-sour pineapple and lime mayonnaise (a well-considered combination), and a playful rabbit trifle and lollipop with pea custard, celeriac mash and gingerbread. Among main courses, properly timed pan-fried duck breast with maple dressing is complemented by a salty, crumbly goats' cheese bonbon, celeriac fondant, wild mushrooms and baby spinach, while roast bream comes with vanilla mash, leeks braised with fennel seeds, and orange vierge. Lactose- and gluten-free dishes are available, and puddings may extend to Calvados and raisin pannacotta with apple dip and buttermilk ice cream.

Chef Darren Rogan **Owner** P Creasey **Times** 12-5/6-9.30 Closed 25-26 Dec, 1 Jan **Prices** Starter £5.75-£7.25, Main £10.75-£24.95, Dessert £5.75-£26, Service optional **Wines** 5 bottles over £30, 20 bottles under £30, 8 by glass **Notes** Sunday L £9.95-£17.50, Vegetarian available **Seats** 48 **Children** Portions, Menu **Parking** NCP opposite

Washingborough Hall Hotel

® Modern British

Modern cooking in Georgian country house

☎ 01522 790340
Church Hill, Washingborough LN4 1BE
e-mail: enquiries@washingboroughhall.com
dir: B1190 into Washingborough. Right at rdbt, hotel 500yds on left

Washingborough Hall is a haven of civility: a delightful Georgian manor house earning its living as a switched-on small-scale country-house hotel at the heart of a sleepy Lincolnshire village. Its three acres of glorious grounds aren't just for show - a garden provides herbs for the kitchen, which turns out an enticing line in unaffected modern cooking. The Dining Room restaurant exudes quietly understated class with its restrained heritage colours, unclothed tables, pale wooden floors, ornate marble fireplace and floor-to-ceiling Georgian windows overlooking the garden. The hoped-for Lincolnshire

Save on Hotels. Book at **theAA.com/hotel**

LINCOLNSHIRE 237 **ENGLAND**

ingredients turn up in inventive contemporary ideas that respect the seasons and aim to soothe rather than challenge; expect starters along the lines of pig's cheek croquette with pineapple salsa salad and wild garlic mayonnaise, followed by rack of local lamb in a Moroccan-inspired casserole with apricot couscous and curly kale.

Times 12-2/6.30-9

LOUTH
Map 17 TF38

Brackenborough Hotel

@ Modern British 🍷

Modish bistro in a rural setting

☎ 01507 609169

Cordeaux Corner, Brackenborough LN11 0SZ

e-mail: reception@brackenborough.co.uk

web: www.oakridgehotels.co.uk

dir: Hotel located on main A16 Louth to Grimsby Rd

With its winning location in the open countryside outside Louth, the Brackenborough Hotel takes pole position when it comes to eating, too, with a bistro that has a lot to offer. It's a spacious and contemporary space, with high vaulted ceilings and a chic, modish finish, and views out over the pretty gardens in daylight hours. The menu does not attempt to subvert its bistro moniker, rather it embraces all that is great about the much-loved, unpretentious formula. Start with leek and potato soup served hot or cold as you prefer it, or a traditional Lincolnshire haslet (meatloaf) with apple chutney, and you might follow on with an Aberdeen Angus steak cooked on the grill with a choice of sauces. There's a classic coq au vin, too, and fish and chips, or go for the pan-fried sea bass with parsnip purée and crisps, and caramelised garlic. To finish, perhaps a chocolate and milk tart.

Chef Steven Legg **Owner** Ashley Lidgard **Times** 11.30-2.30/5-9.30 **Prices** Starter £3.95-£5.95, Main £7.95-£17.95, Dessert £4.95-£6.50, Service optional **Wines** 36 bottles over £30, 47 bottles under £30, 11 by glass **Notes** Fixed D 2 main courses £17.90, Sunday L £14.95-£17.95, Vegetarian available, Civ Wed 100 **Seats** 78, Pr/dining room 120 **Children** Portions, Menu **Parking** 80

MARKET RASEN
Map 17 TF18

The Advocate Arms

@ Modern European 🍷

Confident cooking in a town-centre restaurant with rooms

☎ 01673 842364

2 Queen St LN8 3EH

e-mail: info@advocatearms.co.uk

dir: Located just off Market Place, High Street

Right in the centre of town, the 18th-century Advocate Arms is a restaurant with rooms with a contemporary sheen and a lot to offer. The bar and bedrooms fit the bill if that's what you're looking for - maybe you've been at the nearby races - while the restaurant serves up some gently inventive things alongside some old favourites. There're steaks, for example, served in the traditional manner, but equally you might go for belly pork strudel with potato rösti, caramelised apple purée and a honey and cider sauce. To start, the smoked fish platter catches the eye, as do pheasant rillettes with home-made cranberry compôte and melba toast. Desserts also display a degree of creativity, with their version of sticky toffee coming as a tart with toffee sauce and condensed milk ice cream, or there's the modish dark chocolate cheesecake with salted caramel, chocolate soil and mascarpone.

Chef Mike Watts **Owner** Darren Lince **Times** 7am-9.30pm Closed D Sun (last orders 6.30) All-day dining **Prices** Fixed L 2 course £7.95-£18.95, Fixed D 3 course £15.95-£16.95, Starter £3.95-£7.95, Main £9.95-£22.95, Dessert £5.25, Service optional **Wines** 8 bottles over £30, 32 bottles under £30, 12 by glass **Notes** Sunday L, Vegetarian available **Seats** 65, Pr/dining room 16 **Children** Portions, Menu **Parking** 6, Short walk

SCUNTHORPE
Map 17 SE81

Forest Pines Hotel & Golf Resort

@ Modern British 🍷

Sustainable seafood in a country-house hotel

☎ 01652 650770

Ermine St, Broughton DN20 0AQ

e-mail: forestpines@qhotels.co.uk

web: www.qhotels.co.uk

dir: From M180 junct 4, travel towards Scunthorpe on A18. Continue straight over rdbt, hotel is situated on left

Say the name 'Grimsby' and the port's fishing heritage immediately springs to mind. The fine-dining restaurant at the swish Forest Pines Hotel & Golf Resort a few miles inland in the North Lincolnshire countryside is called Eighteen57 in honour of the year Grimsby's main fish dock opened. Its interior follows a snazzy piscine theme involving blue mosaic-tiled walls, and pictures, reliefs and murals to celebrate the maritime world. Naturally, local fish and seafood feature prominently, but by no means exclusively, on an enticing modern repertoire produced by a kitchen that has an eye to sustainability in its sourcing policy. Scarborough crabcakes with lemon and chive crème fraîche are a good way to start, followed by line-caught Brixham sea bass with mussel, crab and scampi risotto. As fish is tricky to incorporate into pudding, how about a straightforward vanilla crème brûlée with chocolate chip cookie?

Owner Q Hotels **Times** 6.30-10 Closed Sun (ex lunch)-Mon, L Mon-Sat **Prices** Starter £5.45-£8.95, Main £13.75-£23.95, Dessert £5.25-£7.95, Service included **Wines** 7 by glass **Notes** 4 course carvery £26 available 7-9pm Fri-Sun, Sunday L £12-£16, Vegetarian available, Dress restrictions, Smart casual, no ripped jeans **Seats** 70 **Children** Menu **Parking** 400

SLEAFORD   Map 12 TF04

The Bustard Inn & Restaurant

Modern British

Sensitively refurbished old inn in peaceful village

☎ 01529 488250
44 Main St, South Rauceby NG34 8QG
e-mail: info@thebustardinn.co.uk
dir: A17 from Newark, turn right after B6403 to Ancaster. A153 from Grantham, after Wilsford, turn left for South Rauceby

The local community lost its original boozer when it was demolished in the 19th century to make way for a new entrance to the Rauceby Hall estate, and it got this Victorian inn as its replacement in 1860. Now smartly revitalised with a contemporary country-chic look involving a pared-back décor of dove-grey painted chairs on a flagstone floor, and a solid oak bar, The Bustard now puts food at the heart of the operation. Exposed stone walls, ancient timbers and an ornate oriel window are its original features, which combine with solid ash tables and tapestry chairs in a smart, relaxed setting for modern cooking with its feet on the ground and its roots in local, seasonal ingredients. Start out along the lines of pan-fried scallops with butternut squash purée and chorizo, then move on to loin of Belton Park venison teamed with potato gratin, carrot purée, blackberries and chestnuts, and wrap things up with a Lincolnshire plum bread-and-butter pudding with vanilla ice cream.

Chef Phil Lowe **Owner** Alan & Liz Hewitt
Times 12-2.30/6-9.30 Closed 1 Jan, Mon, D Sun
Prices Fixed L 2 course £12.50, Starter £5.50-£8.50, Main £11.50-£25.50, Dessert £5.75-£8.90, Service optional **Wines** 15 bottles over £30, 29 bottles under £30, 10 by glass **Notes** Sunday L £14.50-£23.50, Vegetarian available, Civ Wed 60 **Seats** 66, Pr/dining room 12 **Children** Portions, Menu **Parking** 18, On street

STAMFORD   Map 11 TF00

The Bull & Swan at Burghley

Traditional British

Fuss-free classics in historic inn

☎ 01780 766412
St Martins PE9 2LJ
e-mail: enquiries@thebullandswan.co.uk

A bunch of gentlemen reprobates who called themselves the Honourable Order of Little Bedlam must have made The Bull & Swan a colourful local back in the 17th century. Nowadays they would all get ASBOs, but would no doubt be relieved to find the eating and drinking business still in full swing, with local ales to quaff, and the local area's finest produce, including game from the Burghley Estate, to feast upon. The stylishly reworked interior is what you'd hope to find in a switched-on dining pub - darkwood floors and bare tables, and caramel-hued leather chairs. The kitchen's output is seasonal, no-nonsense stuff along the lines of pan-seared king scallops with butternut squash purée, pancetta and toasted hazelnuts, followed by a classic rib-sticking dish of venison Wellington with sautéed potatoes, baby leeks and carrots, and game jus. The hearty approach ends with something like sticky toffee pudding with caramel sauce and clotted cream.

Times 12-2.30/6-9

Winteringham Fields

WINTERINGHAM   MAP 17 SE92

Modern British, European

Surrealist sculptural cookery in a hospitable former farmhouse

☎ 01724 733096
1 Silver St DN15 9ND
e-mail: reception@winteringhamfields.co.uk
dir: Village centre, off A1077, 4m S of Humber Bridge

Colin McGurran's career has taken him from catering college in Bournemouth to Michelin-starred luxe on the Loire, grand hoteling in the United Arab Emirates and a Yorkshire country inn, to arrive at the fabled Winteringham in the Humber estuary. With his wife and three daughters in close support, he has succeeded in bringing a warmly hospitable air to bear on this converted farmhouse, with its labyrinth of swagged and fabricked rooms, not least a dining room that's all soft-focus swathes of linen and gilt-framed mirrors. McGurran's food is the last word in intricately worked sculptural innovation, distantly recalling the architectural extravaganzas of Victorian banqueting. The famous quail main course, as seen on TV (on the BBC's *Great British Menu*), features a miniature recreation of a forest complete with tree bark, moss and foliage, an autumnal mist swirling down in the form of dry ice poured over at table. There is some food in there too, the quail perched on a branch, its skin crisply roasted, the leg confit, and there's a pretty arrangement of blackberries, pear, and a cigar of foie gras parfait, as well as a delicious pan jus. This jaw-dropping main course is best approached via a simple starter such as smoked haddock chowder, or a single big tomato, although that turns out to be a gelatine-sealed container for gazpacho mousse, served with garden salad in a soil made of black olives. Finish with another spherical job, of coconut pannacotta with mango sorbet. The menus are tantalisingly reticent about how each dish will look: never has steak tartare with corned-beef hash and mustard cream, followed by salt cod risotto with cockles and garlic, and then egg custard tart with Sauternes-soaked raisins and amaretto ice cream, been more likely to be a racketing voyage into the unknown. If it all sounds like Bizarro World surrealism, be warned that there is a full *Alice in Wonderland* themed menu.

Chef Colin McGurran **Owner** Colin McGurran
Times 12-1.30/7-9 Closed 2 wks Xmas, last 2 wks Aug, Sun-Mon **Prices** Fixed L 3 course fr £39.95, Fixed D 3 course fr £59, Service optional **Wines** 20 by glass
Notes Menu surprise 10 course £79, Vegetarian available, Dress restrictions, Smart dress preferred, Civ Wed 55 **Seats** 60, Pr/dining room 12 **Children** Portions
Parking 20

Save on Hotels. Book at **theAA.com/hotel**

LINCOLNSHIRE 239 **ENGLAND**

The George of Stamford

◉ Traditional British ▲ NOTABLE WINE LIST

Historical institution treasured for its traditional values and cooking

☎ 01780 750750
71 St Martins PE9 2LB
e-mail: reservations@georgehotelofstamford.com
web: www.georgehotelofstamford.com
dir: From A1(N of Peterborough) turn onto B1081 signed Stamford and Burghley House. Follow road to 1st set of lights, hotel on left

It is not often that you can sup a pint in a place where pilgrims and knights of the Holy Sepulchre stopped off on the journey to Jerusalem, but not many inns come with The George's thousand years of history. The Great North Road no longer has the same importance as the days when 40 coaches stopped here each day, but you can still tap into something of the feel of bygone times in the splendid oak-panelled restaurant. There is still a nostalgic adherence to old ways here: roast sirloin of English beef is carved on a trolley at your table, and a straight-up grilled Dover sole is expertly de-boned. Modernists are kept happy too with the likes of confit leg of wood pigeon with cep risotto and espresso jus, followed by a fashionable trio of lamb - seared cutlet, confit shoulder and a little shepherd's pie with spinach purée and roast garlic. Things rewind to a traditional ending when trolleys of cheeses and desserts are wheeled out.

Chef Chris Pitman, Paul Reseigh **Owner** Lawrence Hoskins **Times** 12.30-2.30/7.30-10.30 **Prices** Prices not confirmed Service optional **Wines** 91 bottles over £30, 47 bottles under £30, 21 by glass **Notes** Walk in L menu, Sunday L, Vegetarian available, Dress restrictions, Jacket required, no jeans or sportswear, Civ Wed 50 **Seats** 90, Pr/dining room 40 **Children** Portions **Parking** 110

Jim's Yard

◉ British, European V

Bistro cooking in a conservatory restaurant

☎ 01780 756080
3 Ironmonger St PE9 1PL
e-mail: jim@jimsyard.biz

As its name might hint, Jim's Yard is secreted away in two dinky knocked-together cottages in a hidden courtyard in Stamford's historic centre. The luminous dining room opens into a conservatory area with café-style tables and an alfresco terrace in a pretty walled garden; upstairs is a contemporary loft-style space of bare stone walls hung with black-and-white photos of old Stamford. Throughout, the vibe is relaxed and family-run, and the cooking is in the classic bistro mould, starting with a terrine of confit chicken and chorizo wrapped in Parma ham, followed, perhaps, by fillet of sea bream with saffron potatoes, spinach, and mussel butter sauce. End on a resolutely Gallic note with a pukka tarte Tatin with vanilla ice cream.

Chef James Ramsay **Owner** James & Sharon Trevor **Times** 12-2.30/6.30-9.30 Closed 24 Dec 2 wks, last wk Jul-1st wk Aug, Sun-Mon **Prices** Fixed L 2 course £14.50, Fixed D 3 course £19.50, Starter £4.50-£7, Main £13-£19.50, Dessert £5-£7, Service optional **Wines** 43 bottles over £30, 54 bottles under £30, 13 by glass **Notes** Pre-theatre menu Tue-Thu 6-7pm, Vegetarian menu **Seats** 55, Pr/dining room 14 **Children** Portions **Parking** Broad St

The William Cecil

◉ Modern British ◔

Assured cooking within the Burghley Estate

☎ 01780 750070
High St PE9 2LG
e-mail: enquiries@thewilliamcecil.co.uk
dir: Exit A1 signed Stamford & Burghley Park. Continue & hotel 1st building on right on entering town

The William Cecil gets its name from Elizabeth I's great statesman, who built Stamford's Burghley House (the hotel is actually on the estate). The stylish restaurant has been given a contemporary look while retaining original features like wood panelling. Smartly dressed, informal staff keep the wheels turning, delivering starters like seared scallops with confit belly pork, apple purée and caper dressing, and carpaccio with gherkins, baby onions, truffle and parmesan. Sound techniques and quality produce are hallmarks, seen also in main courses of accurately seared turbot fillet with champagne butter, crushed new potatoes and sautéed samphire, and classic beef Wellington with white bean purée, confit garlic, roast tomatoes and port jus. Crème brûlée seems to be a signature dessert, and there may be the indulgence of melting dark chocolate fondant with honeycomb and clotted cream ice cream. There's a large terrace for outdoor eating.

Chef Phil Kent **Owner** Hillbrooke Hotels Ltd **Times** 12-3/6-9 **Prices** Starter £5.95-£13, Main £14.95-£25, Dessert £7-£12, Service added but optional 10% **Wines** 25 bottles over £30, 23 bottles under £30, 11 by glass **Notes** Sunday L £14.95-£28.95, Vegetarian available, Civ Wed 100 **Seats** 72, Pr/dining room 100 **Children** Portions **Parking** 70

WINTERINGHAM Map 17 SE92

Winteringham Fields

◉◉◉ – see page opposite

London

HMS Belfast and Tower Bridge

Index of London Restaurants

This index shows rosetted restaurants in London in alphabetical order, followed by their postcodes and map references. Page numbers precede each entry.

0-9

353	10 Greek St, W1	Plan 3 A2
340	140 Park Lane Restaurant & Bar, W1	Plan 2 F1
267	1901 Restaurant, EC2	Plan 3 H3
271	28-50 Wine Workshop & Kitchen, EC4	Plan 3 D2

A

306	The Abbeville Kitchen, SW5	Plan 4 A3
380	A Cena, TWICKENHAM	Plan 1 C2
283	Al Duca, SW1	Plan 4 J6
314	Alain Ducasse at The Dorchester, W1	Plan 4 G6
314	Alloro, W1	Plan 2 J1
272	Almeida Restaurant, N1	Plan 1 F4
314	Alyn Williams at The Westbury, W1	Plan 2 H2
284	Amaya, SW1	Plan 4 G4
284	Ametsa with Arzak Instruction, SW1	Plan 4 G5
276	The Anchor & Hope, SE1	Plan 5 E5
314	Andrew Edmunds, W1	Plan 2 J1
357	Angelus Restaurant, W2	Plan 2 D1
360	Anglesea Arms, W6	Plan 1 D3
266	L' Anima, EC2	Plan 3 H4
268	Apex City of London Hotel, EC3	Plan 3 H1
284	Apsleys at The Lanesborough, SW1	Plan 4 G5
316	Aqua Kyoto, W1	Plan 2 J2
316	Aqua Nueva, W1	Plan 2 J2
317	Arbutus Restaurant, W1	Plan 2 K2
357	Assaggi, W2	Plan 2 A1
368	L'Atelier de Joël Robuchon, WC2	Plan 3 A2
317	Athenaeum Hotel & Apartments, W1	Plan 4 H6
317	Aurelia, W1	Plan 2 J1
317	L'Autre Pied, W1	Plan 2 G3
284	Avenue, SW1	Plan 4 J6
318	Avista, W1	Plan 2 G1

B

282	Babur, SE23	Plan 1 G2
361	Babylon, W8	Plan 4 B5
377	Bacco Restaurant Italiano, RICHMOND UPON THAMES	Plan 1 C2
308	Baglioni Hotel, SW7	Plan 4 C5
368	Balthazar, WC2	Plan 3 B1
284	Bar Boulud, SW1	Plan 4 F5
318	Bar Trattoria Semplice, W1	Plan 2 H2
270	Barbecoa, EC4	Plan 3 F2
379	The Barn Hotel, RUISLIP	Plan 1 A5
318	Barrafina, W1	Plan 2 K2
281	Bella Vista Cucina Italiana, SE3	Plan 1 H3
319	Bellamy's, W1	Plan 2 H1
362	Belvedere, W8	Plan 1 E3
319	Benares Restaurant, W1	Plan 2 H1
319	Bentley's Oyster Bar & Grill, W1	Plan 2 J1
300	Bibendum Restaurant, SW3	Plan 4 E3
377	Bingham, RICHMOND UPON THAMES	Plan 1 C2
305	Bistro Union, SW4	Plan 1 E2
263	Bistrot Bruno Loubet, EC1	Plan 3 E4

263	The Bleeding Heart, EC1	Plan 3 D3
307	Blue Elephant, SW6	Plan 1 E3
319	Bocca di Lupo, W1	Plan 2 K1
284	Boisdale of Belgravia, SW1	Plan 4 H3
266	Boisdale of Bishopsgate, EC2	Plan 3 H3
308	Bombay Brasserie, SW7	Plan 4 C3
266	Bonds, EC2	Plan 3 G2
320	Brasserie at the Cumberland, W1	Plan 2 F2
320	Brasserie Zedel, W1	Plan 2 J2
261	Brawn, E2	Plan 3 K5
270	Bread Street Kitchen, EC4	Plan 3 F2
276	Brigade, SE1	Plan 5 H6
308	Bulgari Hotel & Residences, SW7	Plan 4 F5
311	The Butcher & Grill, SW11	Plan 1 E3
377	La Buvette, RICHMOND UPON THAMES	Plan 1 C2

C

323	C London, W1	Plan 2 H1
357	Le Café Anglais, W2	Plan 2 B1
264	Le Café du Marché, EC1	Plan 3 E3
258	Café Spice Namasté, E1	Plan 3 J1
306	Cambio de Tercio, SW5	Plan 4 C2
312	Cannizaro House, SW19	Plan 1 D1
276	Cantina del Ponte, SE1	Plan 5 J6
277	Cantina Vinopolis, SE1	Plan 5 F6
307	Capote y Toros, SW5	Plan 4 C2
286	Le Caprice, SW1	Plan 4 J6
269	Caravaggio, EC3	Plan 3 H2
300	Cassis Bistro, SW3	Plan 4 E4
286	Cavendish London, SW1	Plan 4 J6
321	Cecconi's, W1	Plan 2 J1
286	Le Cercle, SW1	Plan 4 G3
286	Chabrot, SW1	Plan 4 F5
366	Chakra, W11	Plan 1 E3
269	Chamberlains Restaurant, EC3	Plan 3 H2
270	The Chancery, EC4	Plan 3 D2
374	Chapter One, BROMLEY	Plan 1 H1
282	Chapters All Day Dining, SE3	Plan 1 H3
359	Charlotte's Place, W5	Plan 1 C3
262	Chef Collin Brown, E14	Plan 6 D3
309	Chelsea Riverside Brasserie, SW10	Plan 1 E3
321	The Chesterfield Mayfair, W1	Plan 4 H6
312	Chez Bruce, SW17	Plan 1 E2
323	China Tang at The Dorchester, W1	Plan 4 G6
270	Chinese Cricket Club, EC4	Plan 3 E1
277	Chino Latino London, SE1	Plan 5 G5
369	Christopher's, WC2	Plan 3 C1
310	Chutney Mary Restaurant, SW10	Plan 1 E3
368	Cibo, W14	Plan 1 D3
264	Cicada, EC1	Plan 3 E4
323	Cielo, W1	Plan 2 J2
369	Cigalon, WC2	Plan 3 D2
286	The Cinnamon Club, SW1	Plan 5 A4
266	Cinnamon Kitchen, EC2	Plan 3 H3
362	Clarke's, W8	Plan 4 A6

369 Clos Maggiore, WC2 — Plan 3 B1
263 Club Gascon, EC1 — Plan 3 E3
323 Cocochan, W1 — Plan 2 G2
287 Colbert, SW1 — Plan 4 G3
357 Colchis, W2 — Plan 2 A1
273 La Collina, NW1 — Plan 1 E4
300 Le Colombier, SW3 — Plan 4 D2
264 Le Comptoir Gascon, EC1 — Plan 3 E3
376 The Continental Hotel, HEATHROW AIRPORT (LONDON) — Plan 1 B2
267 Coq d'Argent, EC2 — Plan 3 G2
287 Corinthia Hotel London, SW1 — Plan 5 B6
323 Corrigan's Mayfair, W1 — Plan 2 G1
323 Criterion, W1 — Plan 2 K1
360 Crowne Plaza London - Ealing, W5 — Plan 1 C4
324 CUT at 45 Park Lane, W1 — Plan 4 G6

D

324 Dabbous, W1 — Plan 4 G6
305 The Dairy, SW4 — Plan 1 E2
324 Degò, W1 — Plan 2 J2
324 Dehesa, W1 — Plan 2 J1
371 The Delaunay, WC2 — Plan 3 C2
312 The Depot, SW14 — Plan 1 D3
371 Les Deux Salons, WC2 — Plan 3 B1
270 Dicianove, EC4 — Plan 3 E1
325 Dinings, W1H — Plan 2 E3
287 Dinner by Heston Blumenthal, SW1 — Plan 4 F5
366 The Dock Kitchen, W10 — Plan 1 D4
325 Downton Mayfair, W1 — Plan 2 J1
271 The Drapers Arms, N1 — Plan 1 F4
326 DSTRKT, W1 — Plan 2 K1
267 Duck & Waffle, EC2 — Plan 3 H2
377 The Dysart Arms, RICHMOND UPON THAMES — Plan 1 C2

E

367 E&O, W11 — Plan 1 D4
367 Edera, W11 — Plan 1 D3
301 Eight Over Eight, SW3 — Plan 4 D1
357 El Pirata Detapas, W2 — Plan 2 A2
261 The Empress, E9 — Plan 1 G4
312 Enoteca Turi, SW15 — Plan 1 D2
311 Entrée Restaurant and Bar, SW11 — Plan 1 E2
326 L'Escargot - The Ground Floor Restaurant, W1 — Plan 3 A2
308 L'Etranger, SW7 — Plan 4 C4
268 Eyre Brothers, EC2 — Plan 3 H4

F

272 Fifteen London - The Restaurant, N1 — Plan 3 G5
327 Fino, W1 — Plan 2 J3
327 Flemings Mayfair, W1 — Plan 4 H6
327 Four Seasons Hotel London at Park Lane, W1 — Plan 4 G6
262 Four Seasons Hotel London at Canary Wharf, E14 — Plan 6 A3
313 The Fox & Grapes, SW19 — Plan 1 D2
282 Franklins, SE22 — Plan 1 F2
272 Frederick's Restaurant, N1 — Plan 1 F4
380 The French Table, SURBITON — Plan 1 C1
377 Friends Restaurant, PINNER — Plan 1 B5

G

327 Galvin at Windows Restaurant & Bar, W1 — Plan 4 G6
327 Galvin Bistrot de Luxe, W1 — Plan 2 G3
258 Galvin Café a Vin, E1 — Plan 3 H3
259 Galvin La Chapelle, E1 — Plan 3 H3
360 The Gate, W6 — Plan 1 D3
328 Gauthier Soho, W1 — Plan 3 A1
328 Le Gavroche Restaurant, W1 — Plan 2 G1
273 The Gilbert Scott, NW1 — Plan 3 B5
273 Gilgamesh Restaurant Lounge, NW1 — Plan 1 E4
278 Gillray's Steakhouse & Bar, SE1 — Plan 5 C5
377 The Glasshouse, KEW — Plan 1 C3
328 Goodman, W1 — Plan 2 J1
288 The Goring, SW1 — Plan 4 H4
328 Great British Restaurant, W1 — Plan 2 G1
371 Great Queen Street, WC2 — Plan 3 B2
371 Green Man and French Horn, WC2 — Plan 3 B1
328 The Greenhouse, W1 — Plan 4 H6
278 Gregg's Bar and Grill, SE1 — Plan 5 H4
328 The Grill At The Dorchester, W1 — Plan 4 G6
376 Grim's Dyke Hotel, HARROW WEALD — Plan 1 B5
262 The Gun, E14 — Plan 6 D2

H

278 H10 London Waterloo Hotel, SE1 — Plan 5 E5
328 Hakkasan, W1 — Plan 2 K2
328 Hakkasan Mayfair, W1 — Plan 2 H1
331 Haozhan, W1 — Plan 3 A1
311 Harrison's, SW12 — Plan 1 E2
307 The Harwood Arms, SW6 — Plan 1 E3
358 Hedone, W4 — Plan 1 D3
331 Hélène Darroze at The Connaught, W1 — Plan 2 H1
276 Hendon Hall Hotel, NW4 — Plan 1 D5
331 Hibiscus, W1 — Plan 2 J1
358 High Road Brasserie, W4 — Plan 1 D3
331 Hix, W1 — Plan 2 J1
334 Hix Mayfair, W1 — Plan 2 J1
264 Hix Oyster & Chop House, EC1 — Plan 3 E3

I

334 Iberica Marylebone, W1 — Plan 2 H4
288 Il Convivio, SW1 — Plan 4 G3
374 Incanto Restaurant, HARROW ON THE HILL — Plan 1 B5
288 Inn the Park, SW1 — Plan 5 A5
358 Island Restaurant & Bar, W2 — Plan 2 D1
371 The Ivy, WC2 — Plan 3 A1

J

372 J. Sheekey & J. Sheekey Oyster Bar, WC2 — Plan 3 B1
371 Jamie's Italian, WC2 — Plan 3 B1
334 JW Steakhouse, W1 — Plan 2 G1

K

334 Kai Mayfair, W1 — Plan 4 G6
273 Karpo, NW1 — Plan 3 B5
372 Kaspar's Seafood Bar & Grill, WC2 — Plan 3 C1
288 Ken Lo's Memories of China, SW1 — Plan 4 H3
363 Kensington Place, W8 — Plan 4 A6

335 Kitchen Joël Antunès at Embassy Mayfair, W1   Plan 2 J1
363 Kitchen W8, W8   Plan 4 A4
289 Koffmann's, SW1   Plan 4 G5
372 Kopapa, WC2   Plan 3 B2
372 Kyashii, WC2   Plan 3 B1

L

311 Lamberts, SW12   Plan 1 E2
313 The Lambourne, SW19   Plan 1 E1
335 Latium, W1   Plan 2 J3
363 Launceston Place Restaurant, W8   Plan 4 C4
314 The Lawn Bistro, SW19   Plan 1 D2
367 The Ledbury, W11   Plan 1 E4
335 Levant, W1   Plan 2 G2
314 The Light House Restaurant, SW19   Plan 1 D1
335 Lima, W1   Plan 2 K3
335 Little Social, W1   Plan 2 H2
335 Locanda Locatelli, W1H   Plan 2 G2
376 London Heathrow Marriott Hotel, HEATHROW AIRPORT   Plan 1 A3
368 Lonsdale, W11   Plan 1 E4
376 Lujon, KESTON   Map 6 TQ46
271 Lutyens Restaurant, EC4   Plan 3 E2
258 The Luxe, First-Floor Brasserie, E1   Plan 3 J3

M

278 Magdalen, SE1   Plan 5 H6
363 The Mall Tavern, W8   Plan 4 A6
264 Malmaison Charterhouse Square, EC1   Plan 3 E3
337 The Mandeville Hotel, W1   Plan 2 G2
301 Manicomio, SW3   Plan 4 F3
268 Manicomio - City, EC2   Plan 3 F2
275 Manna, NW3   Plan 1 E4
308 Marco, SW6   Plan 1 E3
258 Marco Pierre White Steak & Alehouse, E1   Plan 3 H3
289 Marcus Wareing at the Berkeley, SW1   Plan 4 G5
372 Massimo Restaurant & Oyster Bar, WC2   Plan 5 B6
337 Maze, W1   Plan 2 G1
337 Maze Grill, W1   Plan 2 G1
310 Medlar Restaurant, SW10   Plan 4 D1
337 Mele e Pere, W1   Plan 2 J1
273 Meliá White House, NW1   Plan 2 H4
337 Mennula, W1   Plan 2 K3
337 Le Meridien Piccadilly, W1   Plan 2 J1
338 Mews of Mayfair, W1   Plan 2 H1
274 Michael Nadra Primrose Hill, NW1   Plan 1 E4
365 The Milestone Hotel, W8   Plan 4 B5
309 Millennium Bailey's Hotel London Kensington, SW7   Plan 4 C4
365 Min Jiang, W8   Plan 4 B5
289 Mint Leaf, SW1   Plan 5 A6
289 Mitsukoshi, SW1   Plan 2 K1
268 Miyako, EC2   Plan 3 H3
264 The Modern Pantry, EC1   Plan 3 E4
373 Mon Plaisir, WC2   Plan 3 B2
338 The Montagu, W1   Plan 2 F2
368 The Montague on the Gardens, WC1   Plan 3 B3
265 The Montcalm London City at The Brewery, EC1 Plan 3 G4
265 Morgan M, EC1   Plan 3 E3
265 Moro, EC1   Plan 3 D4
291 MU at Millennium Knightsbridge, SW1   Plan 4 F4
338 Murano, W1   Plan 4 H6

N

307 New Lotus Garden, SW5   Plan 4 B3
338 Newman Street Tavern, W1   Plan 2 J3
358 Nipa, W2   Plan 2 D1
338 Nobu, W1   Plan 5 H6
338 Nobu Berkeley ST, W1   Plan 4 H6
340 NOPI, W1   Plan 2 J3
340 Novikov Asian Restaurant, W1   Plan 4 H6
340 Novikov Italian Restaurant, W1   Plan 4 H6
361 Novotel London West, W6   Plan 1 D3
301 Nozomi, SW3   Plan 4 E4

O

274 Odette's Restaurant & Bar, NW1   Plan 1 E4
291 One-O-One, SW1   Plan 4 F5
340 The Only Running Footman, W1   Plan 4 H6
373 The Opera Tavern, WC2   Plan 3 C1
340 Orrery, W1   Plan 2 G3
373 Orso, WC2   Plan 3 C1
291 Osteria Dell'Angolo, SW1   Plan 5 A4
301 Outlaw's at The Capital, SW3   Plan 4 F5
279 The Oxo Tower Restaurant, SE1   Plan 3 D1
341 Ozer Restaurant, W1   Plan 2 H2

P

310 The Painted Heron, SW10   Plan 1 E3
282 The Palmerston, SE22   Plan 1 F2
368 Paramount, WC1   Plan 3 A2
279 Park Plaza County Hall, SE1   Plan 5 C5
341 Park Plaza Sherlock Holmes, W1   Plan 2 F3
292 Park Plaza Victoria London, SW1   Plan 4 J3
279 Park Plaza Westminster Bridge, SE1   Plan 5 C5
366 Park Terrace Restaurant, W8   Plan 4 B5
269 The Perkin Reveller, EC3   Plan 5 J6
379 The Petersham Hotel, RICHMOND UPON THAMES   Plan 1 C2
379 Petersham Nurseries Café, RICHMOND UPON THAMES   Plan 1 C2
341 La Petite Maison, W1   Plan 2 H1
292 Pétrus, SW1   Plan 4 G5
341 Pied à Terre, W1   Plan 2 J3
279 Pizarro, SE1   Plan 5 H4
262 Plateau, E14   Plan 6 B3
341 Plum Valley, W1   Plan 2 K1
341 Pollen Street Social, W1   Plan 2 J2
341 Polpo, W1   Plan 2 J1
280 Le Pont de la Tour, SE1   Plan 5 J6
269 Prism Brasserie and Bar, EC3   Plan 3 H3
344 The Providores and Tapa Room, W1   Plan 2 G3
274 Pullman London St Pancras   Plan 3 A5

Q

292 Quaglino's, SW1   Plan 4 J6
292 Quilon, SW1   Plan 4 J4
344 Quo Vadis, W1   Plan 2 K2

R

301 Racine, SW3   Plan 4 E4
311 Ransome's Dock, SW11   Plan 1 E3
301 Rasoi Restaurant, SW3   Plan 4 F3
344 The Red Fort, W1   Plan 2 K2
301 Restaurant Gordon Ramsay, SW3   Plan 4 F1

358	Restaurant Michael Nadra, W4	Plan 1 D3
270	Restaurant Sauterelle, EC3	Plan 3 G2
280	Restaurant Story, SE1	Plan 5 J5
380	Retro, TEDDINGTON	Plan 1 C1
294	The Rib Room, SW1	Plan 4 F4
379	Richmond Hill Hotel, RICHMOND UPON THAMES	Plan 1 C2
344	The Riding House Café, W1	Plan 2 J3
345	Ristorante Semplice, W1	Plan 2 H2
345	The Ritz Restaurant, W1	Plan 1 J6
361	The River Café, W6	Plan 1 D3
280	Roast, SE1	Plan 5 G6
345	Roka, W1	Plan 2 J3
262	Roka, E14	Plan 6 C3
345	Roti Chai, W1	Plan 2 G2
294	Roux at Parliament Square, SW1	Plan 5 B5
346	Roux at The Landau, W1	Plan 2 H4
374	Royal Chace Hotel, ENFIELD	Map 6 TQ39
294	The Royal Horseguards, SW1	Plan 5 B6
281	RSJ, The Restaurant on the South Bank, SE1	Plan 5 D6
294	The Rubens at the Palace, SW1	Plan 4 H4

S

361	Sagar, W6	Plan 1 D3
294	St Ermin's Hotel, SW1	Plan 4 K4
265	St John, EC1	Plan 3 E3
260	St John Bread & Wine, E1	Plan 3 J3
275	St Pancras Grand Brasserie, NW1	Plan 3 B6
294	Sake No Hana, SW1	Plan 4 J6
297	Salloos Restaurant, SW1	Plan 4 G5
346	Salt Yard, W1	Plan 2 J3
359	Sam's Brasserie & Bar, W4	Plan 1 D3
297	Santini Restaurant, SW1	Plan 4 H4
347	Sartoria, W1	Plan 2 J1
374	Savoro Restaurant with Rooms, BARNET	Map 6 TQ29
373	Savoy Grill, WC2	Plan 3 C1
347	Scott's Restaurant, W1	Plan 2 G1
297	Season at The Fifth Floor Restaurant, SW1	Plan 4 F5
297	Seven Park Place by William Drabble, SW1	Plan 4 J6
347	Shogun, Millennium Hotel Mayfair, W1	Plan 2 G1
347	Sketch (Lecture Room & Library), W1	Plan 2 J1
347	Sketch (The Gallery), W1	Plan 2 J1
347	Sketch (The Parlour), W1	Plan 2 J1
281	Skylon, SE1	Plan 5 C6
266	Smiths of Smithfield, Top Floor, EC1	Plan 3 E3
350	So Restaurant, W1	Plan 2 J1
350	Social Eating House, W1	Plan 2 J2
376	Sofitel London Heathrow, HEATHROW AIRPORT (LONDON)	Plan 1 A2
297	Sofitel London St James, SW1	Plan 4 K6
312	Sonny's Kitchen, SW13	Plan 1 D3
350	The Square, W1	Plan 2 H1
299	The Stafford London by Kempinski, SW1	Plan 4 J6
350	Sumosan Restaurant, W1	Plan 2 H1
260	Super Tuscan, E1	Plan 3 H3
305	Sushinho, SW3	Plan 4 D1
268	Sushisamba London, EC2	Plan 3 H2

T

353	Tamarind, W1	Plan 4 H6
373	Terroirs, WC2	Plan 3 B1
353	Texture Restaurant, W1	Plan 2 F2

353	Theo Randall, W1	Plan 4 G5
299	Thirty Six by Nigel Mendham at Dukes London, SW1	Plan 4 J6
353	Time & Space, W1	Plan 2 H1
299	Tinello, SW1	Plan 4 G2
305	Tom Aikens, SW3	Plan 4 E3
309	Tom Ilic, SW8	Plan 1 E3
305	Tom's Kitchen, SW3	Plan 4 E2
305	Trinity Restaurant, SW4	Plan 1 E2
353	Trishna, W1	Plan 2 G3
260	Les Trois Garçons, E1	Plan 3 J4
359	La Trompette, W4	Plan 1 D3
272	Trullo, N1	Plan 1 F4
306	Tsunami, SW4	Plan 1 F2

U

353	Umu, W1	Plan 2 H1

V

359	Le Vacherin, W4	Plan 1 D3
271	Vanilla Black, EC4	Plan 3 D2
355	Vasco & Piero's Pavilion Restaurant, W1	Plan 2 J2
355	Veeraswamy Restaurant, W1	Plan 2 J1
355	Verru Restaurant, W1	Plan 2 G3
261	Viajante, E2	Plan 1 G4
355	Villandry, W1	Plan 2 H3

W

260	Wapping Food, E1	Plan 1 F3
374	West Lodge Park Hotel, HADLEY WOOD	Map 6 TQ29
300	Wheeler's, SW1	Plan 4 J6
271	The White Swan Pub & Dining Room, EC4	Plan 3 D3
260	Whitechapel Gallery Dining Room, E1	Plan 3 J3
355	Wild Honey, W1	Plan 2 H1
275	The Winter Garden, NW1	Plan 2 F3
355	The Wolseley, W1	Plan 4 J6

X

276	XO, NW3	Plan 1 E4

Y

356	Yauatcha, W1	Plan 2 J2
356	YMing Restaurant, W1	Plan 3 A1

Z

300	Zafferano, SW1	Plan 4 F4
366	Zaika of Kensington, W8	Plan 4 B5
281	Zucca, SE1	Plan 5 H4
309	Zuma, SW7	Plan 4 F5

London Plan 1

Central London Congestion Charging Zone

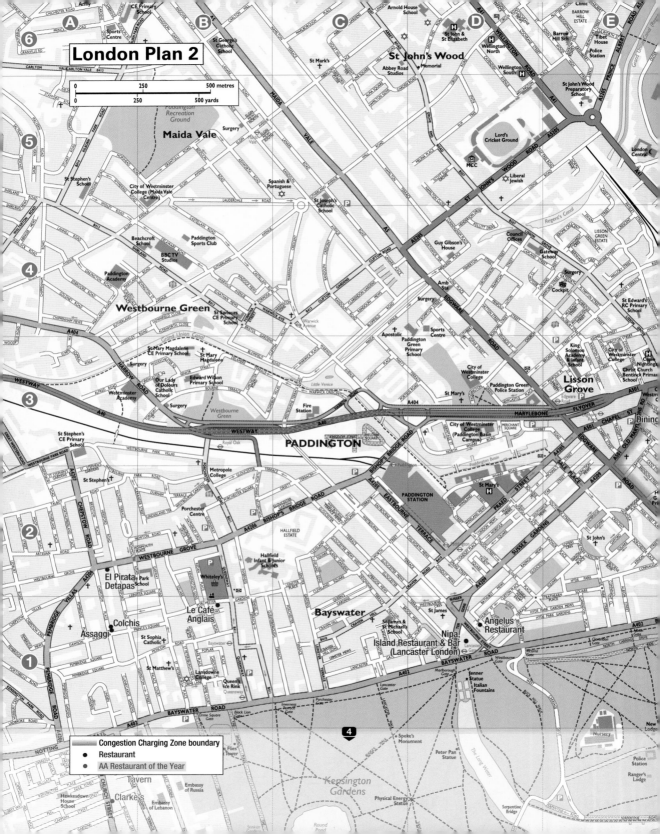

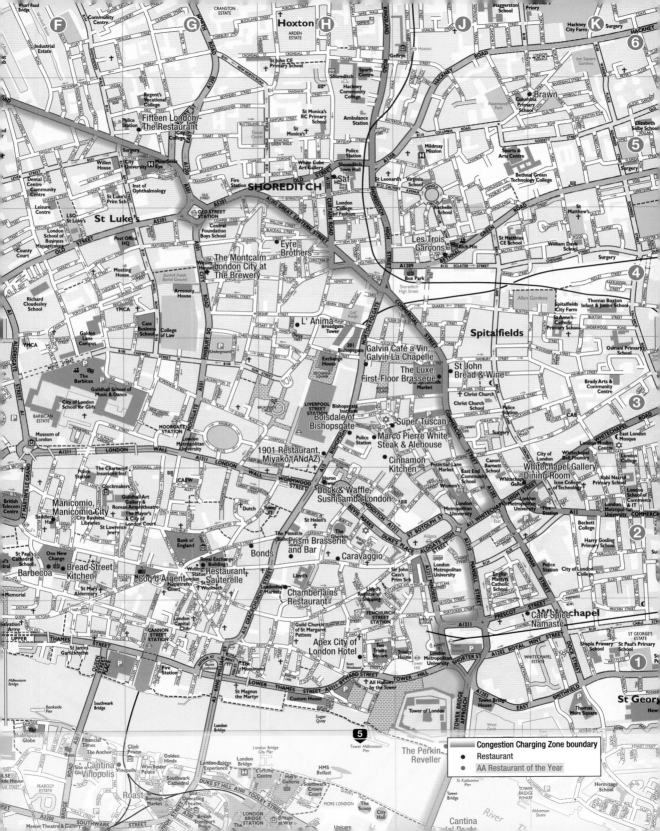

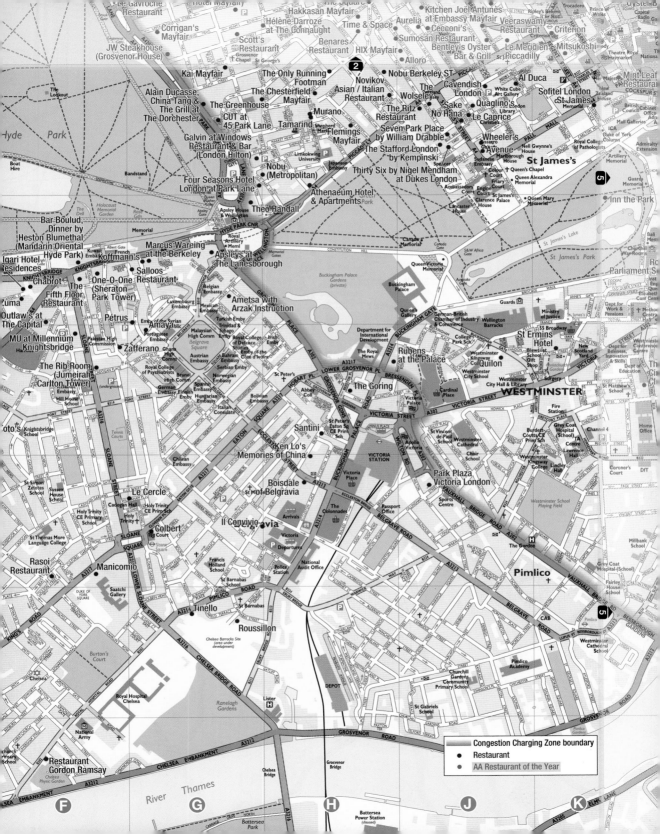

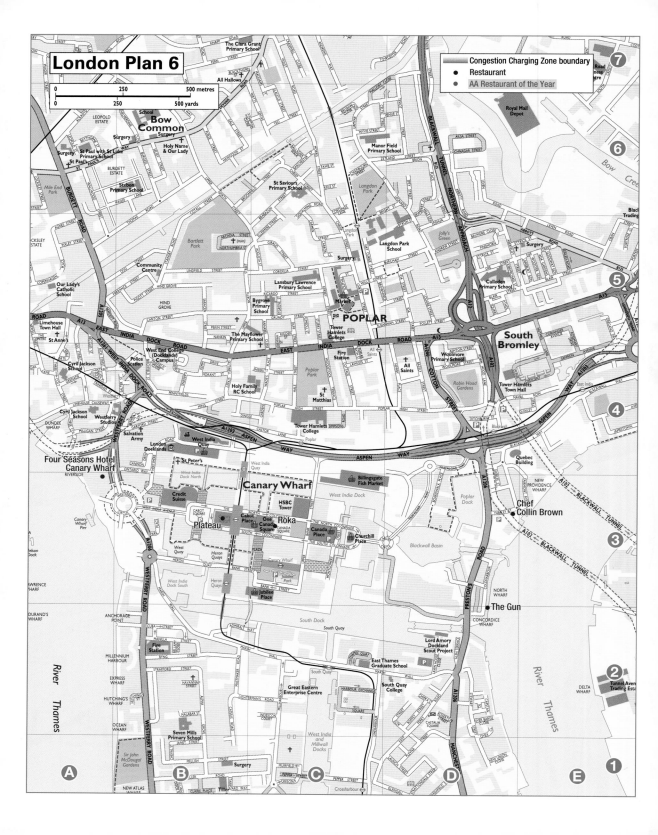

LONDON

Greater London Plans 1-6, pages 246-256. (Small scale maps 6 & 7 at back of Guide.) Restaurants are listed below in postal district order, commencing East, then North, South and West, with a brief indication of the area covered. Detailed plans 2-6 show the locations of restaurants with AA Rosette Awards within the Central London postal districts. If you do not know the postal district of the restaurant you want, please refer to the index preceding the street plans for the entry and map pages. The plan reference for each restaurant also appears within its directory entry.

LONDON E1

Café Spice Namasté
PLAN 3 J1

◉ Indian

Vibrant modern Indian cooking in Whitechapel

☎ 020 7488 9242
16 Prescot St E1 8AZ
e-mail: binay@cafespice.co.uk
dir: Nearest station: Tower Gateway (DLR), Aldgate, Tower Hill. Walking distance from Tower Hill

This longstanding Indian may be set in an imposing red-brick Victorian block, but its colourful interior is far more Mumbai than Whitechapel. Here, vibrantly-painted walls and colourful fabrics are matched by friendly service headed by the effervescent Pervin Todiwala, while husband Cyrus's refined, confidently spiced, inventive modern cooking draws on his Parsee roots and the best of seasonal British ingredients. From menus with detailed notes, perhaps start with street-food style Dahi Saev Batata Poori (explosive mouthfuls of crisp, wafer-thin puffed poories filled with crushed potato, spiced yoghurt, and tamarind and date chutney, sprinkled with chick pea vermicelli and fresh coriander). Specials up the ante - perhaps sea-fresh line-caught cod fillet for the main event, marinated with tamarind, crushed pepper, yoghurt and garlic, then chargrilled and served with coconut curry sauce. Otherwise, try a traditional Parsee-style chicken curry (Murgh Ni Curry Nay Papaeto): rich and exotic with spiced attitude and cooling coconut in equal parts.

Chef Cyrus Todiwala **Owner** Cyrus & Pervin Todiwala **Times** 12-3/6.15-10.30 Closed Xmas, BHs, Sun, L Sat **Prices** Fixed L 3 course £35-£70, Fixed D 3 course £35-£70, Tasting menu fr £70, Starter £5.55-£12.50, Main £15.50-£19.50, Dessert £5.50-£7.25, Service added but optional 12.5% **Wines** 7 by glass **Notes** Vegetarian available, Dress restrictions, Smart casual **Seats** 120 **Children** Portions **Parking** On street, NCP

Galvin Café a Vin
PLAN 3 H3

◉◉ French, Italian

Bustling City wine café with good bistro cooking

☎ 020 7299 0404
35 Spital Square E1 6DY
e-mail: info@galvinrestaurants.com
dir: Nearest station: Liverpool St. Close to Spitalfields Market, 5 min walk from Liverpool St Station

Next door to La Chapelle (see entry, opposite), part of the burgeoning empire of the frères Galvin, the clue to this café's true heart is in its name. The interesting, often biodynamic, organic or natural wines on offer come in a variety of measures, and you can sample them sitting at the burnished zinc bar, at a table in the pint-sized interior, or on the heated and covered garden terrace at the back (you can also dine where you wish, too). A jazz pianist plays on Monday and Saturday evenings to boost the already-lively vibe. Jack Boast cooks to an Anglo-French template, doing onion soup with Gruyère croûtons and escargots à la bourguignonne, with perhaps bream fillet in anchovy dressing and purple sprouting broccoli to follow. It's well-wrought modern bistro cooking with the emphasis on hang-loose informality, justifiably popular at lunchtimes and early evening, when a value prix-fixe with a pair of choices at each course might offer soused herrings, then cured pork ribeye with green beans and mash. Finish with rum baba and Chantilly, or rhubarb cheesecake. Cheeses are from Spitalfields specialists Androuet.

Chef Jack Boast, Jeff Galvin **Owner** Chris & Jeff Galvin, Ken Sanker **Times** 12-3/6-10.30 Closed 24-26 Dec, 1 Jan, D 23 Dec **Prices** Fixed L 2 course £14.95, Fixed D 3 course £18.50, Starter £6-£9, Main £11-£17.50, Dessert £5.50-£6.50, Service added but optional 12.5% **Wines** 50 bottles over £30, 28 bottles under £30, 29 by glass **Notes** Fixed D 6-7pm, Sunday L, Vegetarian available **Seats** 47 **Children** Portions, Menu **Parking** On street

Galvin La Chapelle
PLAN 3 H3

◉◉◉ – see opposite

The Luxe, First-Floor Brasserie
PLAN 3 J3

◉ Modern British

Brasserie dining in fashionably remodelled Victorian market building

☎ 020 7101 1751
109 Commercial St E1 6BG
e-mail: reservations@theluxe.co.uk
dir: Nearest station: Liverpool Street

Sibling to *MasterChef* host John Torode's Smiths of Smithfield (see entry), The Luxe is a similarly trendy, multi-level, multi-faceted venue that sits comfortably in its Old Spitalfields Flower Market setting. The beautifully restored Victorian building delivers a fashionable warehouse-look in the all-day café/bar on the ground floor, while in the basement there's another bar with DJs and live music from 6pm 'til late. But you'll need to head up to the first-floor Brasserie for the main culinary action: here the smart dining space comes with on-trend Cherner chairs, silk wallpaper, red brick and polished wood flooring, while the modern, seasonal British ingredient-led cooking is delivered from an open kitchen. Start perhaps with sumac-spiced scallops (excellent quality, perfectly timed) with cauliflower purée and pancetta, following on with tender new season lamb with olive-crushed Jersey Royals, spinach and mint jelly, or treat yourself to a top-drawer steak (rare-breed, 28-day-dry-aged) - either fillet, rib, sirloin or chateaubriand.

Chef Paul Daniel **Times** 12-3/6-11 **Prices** Starter £5.75-£9.75, Main £13-£65

Marco Pierre White Steak & Alehouse
PLAN 3 H3

◉ Modern European V

Quality City steakhouse in bright basement setting

☎ 020 7247 5050
East India House, 109-117 Middlesex St E1 7JF
e-mail: info@mpwsteakandalehouse.org
dir: Nearest station: Liverpool Street

This roll-out brand offers a brasserie-style roster of dishes with timeless English appeal and plenty of ideas from France and Italy. Thus Brit classics like York ham with home-made piccalilli meet tuna steak provençale or wild halibut à la Sicilienne. Meat is the mainstay, with Scottish steaks (from fillet to top-drawer Chateaubriand for two - with the usual choice of sauces) to the likes of calves' liver and dry-cured bacon. Expect well-sourced ingredients and cooking that's not too showy, but factor-in necessary side order veg, while desserts tend to stay on the nursery slopes (Eton Mess to sticky toffee pudding). Throw in well-selected wines and good cocktails and all bases are covered. The basement setting - hidden away from the Bishopsgate mayhem - is a light, clean-cut space, decked out with wooden flooring, red leather chairs, white linen-clad tables and walls lined with JAK cartoons (Mail on Sunday fame).

Chef Juan Lopez **Owner** James & Rachael Robertson **Times** 12-3/5.30-10 Closed 25 Dec, 1 Jan **Prices** Fixed L 3 course £21.50-£39.50, Fixed D 3 course £21.50-£39.50, Starter £6.75-£21.50, Main £16.75-£65, Dessert £7.50-£9.50, Service added but optional 12.5% **Wines** 100 bottles over £30, 23 bottles under £30, 19 by glass **Notes** Sunday L, Vegetarian menu **Seats** 80, Pr/dining room 34 **Children** Portions **Parking** On street after 6.30pm

Galvin La Chapelle

LONDON E1

LONDON E1   **PLAN 3 H3**

French ⬛ NOTABLE WINE LIST

Consummate French class in a majestic City venue

☎ 020 7299 0400
St. Botolph's Hall, 35 Spital Square E1 6DY
e-mail: info@galvinrestaurants.com
web: www.galvinrestaurants.com
dir: Nearest station: Liverpool Street. Close to Old Spitalfields Market

One of the more eye-catching jewels in the constantly enlarging Galvin brothers' crown, La Chapelle has been fashioned from what was originally the gymnasium of a Victorian girls' school. The restored brickwork and beams confer real character on the space, and the mezzanine level provides for tantalising bird's-eye views of the action below. Immaculately dressed tables and a professional service team add distinction and class to the occasion, and a fine wine list is built on the sturdy foundations of a run of vintages of the great north Rhône red, Hermitage La Chapelle, one of France's finest utterances of the Syrah grape. In keeping with that, the prevailing culinary winds are distinctly cross-Channel, with much Français menu lingo (pavés, étuvées and such), and classic Gallic ingredients and techniques in evidence. The truffled onion velouté is garnished with roast

frogs' legs, while a pressed terrine comprised of Landes chicken, Bayonne ham and foie gras could hardly be more fondly Francophile unless it were delivered by a waiter singing *La Marseillaise*. That said, the odd more obviously modern-Brit note intervenes productively, as when pickled mackerel with shaved fennel and apple and cucumber 'condiment' delivers plenty of pugnacious punch on the prix-fixe. But then look at the cuisine grand-mère simplicity of roast corn-fed chicken and petits pois à la française: it's an object-lesson in how to make a relatively simple dish to a stunning standard, its wonderfully moist meat offset with crisp skin and a classic, creamy, garden-fresh garnish. Fish is gently, rather than robustly, treated, so a fricassée of Jersey Royals, broad beans and samphire does wonders for a slab of sea trout, and the closer might be a garnished cheese course, perhaps Fourme d'Ambert with pear chutney and walnuts, or an unexpectedly Italian excursion into the territory of orange pannacotta with candied kumquats and biscotti.

Chef Zac Whittle, Jeff Galvin
Owner Chris Galvin, Jeff Galvin, Ken Sanker **Times** 12-2.30/6-10.30
Closed 24-26 Dec, 1 Jan, L 23 Dec
Prices Fixed L 2 course fr £29.50, Fixed D 3 course fr £29.50, Tasting menu £70-£120, Starter £8-£18.50, Main £24.50-£32.50, Dessert £9-£12.50, Service added but optional 12.5%

Wines 285 bottles over £30, 18 bottles under £30, 42 by glass **Notes** Fixed price D 6-7pm, Sunday L, Vegetarian available **Seats** 110, Pr/dining room 16 **Children** Portions **Parking** On street, NCP

LONDON E1 *continued*

St John Bread & Wine
PLAN 3 J3

British

Gutsy British cooking in Spitalfields

☎ 020 3301 8069
94-96 Commercial St E1 6LZ
e-mail: reservations@stjohnbreadandwine.com
dir: Nearest station: Liverpool Street/Aldgate East

Across the street from Spitalfields Market, this younger, smaller sister of St John (see entry) concentrates, like the original, on seasonal, indigenous produce and promotes the concept of 'the whole beast', so crispy pig's skin (with chicory and mustard) and ox heart (with celeriac) are as likely to feature as prime cuts. There's little distinction between starters and main courses, so sharing is encouraged. The kitchen takes a no-nonsense approach, turning out straightforward dishes strong on flavour. Start with, or share, pigeon with pickled red cabbage or smoked sprats with horseradish, and proceed to faggots with turnip and black cabbage, or black bream with green sauce. Breads are exceptional, and British desserts make an impact: perhaps rhubarb Eton Mess or bread pudding.

Chef Lee Tiernan **Owner** Trevor Gulliver & Fergus Henderson **Times** 9-11 Closed 24 Dec-1 Jan **Prices** Starter £4.90-£8.90, Main £10.90-£17.10, Dessert £6.50-£7.10, Service optional, Groups min 6 service 12.5% **Wines** 70 bottles over £30, 15 bottles under £30, 12 by glass **Notes** Vegetarian available **Seats** 60 **Parking** On street

Super Tuscan
PLAN 3 H3

Italian

An authentic enoteca in Spitalfields

☎ 020 7247 8717
8A Artillery Passage E1 7LJ
e-mail: info@supertuscan.co.uk
dir: Nearest station: Liverpool Street. 5 min walk from Liverpool Street Station, Bishopsgate exit

An unassuming entrance leads into a parquet-floored restaurant with brown banquettes along one wall, plain wooden chairs, some booths, and tall stools at a long bar, the sort of functional interior, like many enotecas, that doesn't distract attention from the gutsy Italian food on offer here - or from the intelligently chosen Italian wines. Start with 'sample-sized portions', to use menu-speak: arancini di prosciutto (fried rice balls stuffed with ham, parmesan and béchamel) or polpette di vitello (veal meatballs poached in stock with peas and potatoes), or go for an antipasti platter of assorted meats or regional cheeses for sharing, and proceed to a classic Tuscan dish of chargrilled sausages with fennel seeds. Ingredients, sourced from Italy, are used in authentic Italian recipes, and dishes are big on flavour. Finish with ricotta-stuffed doughnuts with a scoop of outstanding ice cream.

Chef Nick Grossi **Owner** Nick Grossi
Times 12-2.30/5.30-10 Closed Xmas, New Year, Sat-Sun **Prices** Starter £4-£7.50, Main £10-£20, Dessert £4-£7,

Service optional **Wines** 28 bottles over £30, 28 bottles under £30, 17 by glass **Notes** Vegetarian available **Seats** 30 **Children** Portions

Les Trois Garçons
PLAN 3 J4

French

Theatrical surroundings for some smart fine dining

☎ 020 7613 1924
1 Club Row, Shoreditch E1 6JX
e-mail: info@lestroisgarcons.com
web: www.lestroisgarcons.com
dir: Nearest station: Liverpool Street. From station, head along Bishopsgate towards Shoreditch High St. Turn right after bridge onto Bethnal Green Rd. Restaurant on left

An inspired choice for a date or a flamboyant venue for a City business lunch, this one-time Shoreditch pub turned unique French restaurant - just five minutes' walk from Bishopsgate - is a jaw-dropping exercise in chic, high-camp interior design. Sit beneath dangling retro handbags, bejewelled chandeliers or perhaps a stuffed giraffe's head craning from the wall, and yes, that tiger is wearing a necklace and that chimpanzee a tiara. Okay, it might be something of a Marmite venue - you'll either love it or hate it - but it is wonderfully surreal and glamorous, especially by candlelight, and there's no denying the quality and flair of its modern, clear-flavoured and well-dressed French-inspired food. Take rabbit saddle and mushroom roulade with lasagne of its leg, baby carrots and pea shoots to open, and to follow, perhaps Chateaubriand served with roasted potatoes, green beans, Szechuan pepper jus and béarnaise. Finish with frozen coconut 'nougat' and passionfruit coulis. Charming and knowledgeable service and a French-led wine list complete the picture.

Chef Michael Chan **Owner** Stefan Karlson, Hassan Abdullah, Michel Lassere **Times** 12-2.30/6-9.30 Closed Xmas, New Year, Sun, L Mon-Wed, Sat **Prices** Fixed L 2 course £17.50, Tasting menu fr £66, Starter £7-£14.50, Main £14.50-£32.50, Dessert £7-£9.50, Service added but optional 12.5% **Wines** 90 bottles over £30, 10 bottles under £30, 13 by glass **Notes** Vegetarian available **Seats** 65, Pr/dining room 10 **Parking** On street

Wapping Food
PLAN 1 F3

Modern International

Fashionable cooking in an out-of-the-ordinary setting

☎ 020 7680 2080
Wapping Hydraulic, Power Station, Wapping Wall E1W 3SG
dir: Nearest station: Shadwell DLR, Wapping. Between Wapping Wall & King Edward VII Memorial Park, parallel to the river opposite the Prospect of Whitby

Set in the now-cool, rejuvenated London Docks, this former hydraulic pumping station turned restaurant and gallery is a rather hip, unique setting for dinner. The cavernous, hard-edged, warehouse-like space feels like a gigantic Tracy Emin-style art installation, with its trendy, simple, modern furniture sitting amid massive old machinery, girders, chains and pulleys, green tiled and painted brick walls and towering windows, the whole softened by a myriad of flickering candles, a dangling mirror ball, and a bar and open kitchen. The daily-changing, modern menu takes a light, healthy approach that lets the prime-quality ingredients shine. Witness brill teamed with chicory, pea purée, lardo and sorrel, or duck breast with beetroot, cherries, chicory and dandelion leaf. End on a high with a moist and light pistachio and lemon cake with cherries and crème fraîche. The equally inspired all-Aussie wine list has as much personality as the surroundings and food.

Times 12-3/6.30-11 Closed 24 Dec-3 Jan, BHs, L Mon-Fri, D Sun

Whitechapel Gallery Dining Room
PLAN 3 J3

Modern British

Forthright flavours at the go-ahead gallery

☎ 020 7522 7896
77-82 Whitechapel High St E1 7QX
e-mail: dining@whitechapelgallery.org
dir: Nearest station: Aldgate East

The Whitechapel Gallery has perhaps not received the attention it deserves over the years compared to some of the big-hitters up town, but this is the gallery that displayed Picasso's *Guernica* in 1938, and it has a bold and brave reputation in the art world. And when it comes to dining, it thinks big these days too, with Angela Hartnett - her off the telly - acting as a consultant. It's a suitably modish dining space with lots of blond wood and an appropriately relaxed vibe. Emma Duggan heads up the team in the kitchen, delivering a focused daily-changing menu that keeps things seasonal, relatively simple, quietly contemporary and highly appealing. Roast squash, Treviso, feta and toasted walnuts shows the Hartnett influence, as does Jerusalem artichoke risotto, but there're also main courses (they call them small plates and bigger plates) such as Creedy Carver chicken and chestnut mushroom pie, and beer-battered Cornish pollock. The cheeses are British, note, just in case you're not tempted by chocolate torte with salted caramel ice cream.

Times 12-2.30/6-11 Closed 24 Dec-2 Jan, Mon, D Sun & Tue

LONDON E2

Brawn
PLAN 3 K5

◉◉ Traditional European

Smart, honest cooking in trendy East London

☎ 020 7729 5692
49 Columbia Rd E2 7RG
e-mail: enquiries@brawn.co
dir: Nearest station: Liverpool St, Bethnal Green. From Liverpool Street, follow Shoreditch High St, right Hackney Rd, right Columbia Rd

On the Columbia Road - of flower market fame - this sister of Terroirs (see entry) is a vibrant place with quirky artwork, a definite buzz and fabulously hearty food. The broadly European-focused daily-changing menu (particularly France and Italy) is straightforward enough - and that's the genius of it. Top-notch produce is served without a jot of flim-flam (as Boris might say), and our piggie friends get their own section on the menu. Thus pork rillettes or a selection of charcuterie may get the ball rolling, plus there's the likes of potted brown shrimps and toast; foie gras and confit shallots; snails and polenta; or oxtail and kidney ravioli and hispi cabbage. It's advisable to linger long enough to sample chocolate ganache with crème anglaise and praline. Cheeses and sourdough bread hail from East London and the wine list focuses on sustainable, biodynamic and organic varieties.

Chef Owen Kenworthy **Owner** Ed Wilson, Oli Barker **Times** 12-3/6-11 Closed Xmas, New Year, BHs, L Mon-Wed, D Sun **Prices** Starter £8-£12, Main £12-£19, Dessert £5-£6, Service added but optional 12.5% **Wines** 98 bottles over £30, 33 bottles under £30, 12 by glass **Notes** Sunday L £25-£35, Vegetarian available **Seats** 70 **Parking** On street

Viajante
PLAN 1 G4

◉◉◉ – *see below*

LONDON E9

The Empress
PLAN 1 G4

◉ Modern British

Laid-back crowd-pleaser with simple, feisty dishes

☎ 020 8533 5123
130 Lauriston Rd, Victoria Park E9 7LH
dir: Nearest station: Cambridge Heath, Mile End. A10 S towards Dalston, left Hackney Rd, then right onto A107, left into Old Ford Rd and left again into Grove Rd

With the generous proportions of a Victorian pub and the white walls, bare brickwork, claret Chesterfield banquettes, modern art and canteen-like simplicity of an on-trend contemporary urban eatery, The Empress slots right into the easygoing vibe of its Victoria Park

neighbourhood. The kitchen brigade is led by Hackney resident Elliott Lidstone who comes hot-foot from the high-achieving L'ortolan (see entry), and while there's none of that high-falutin' stuff going on here, the emphasis is still firmly on quality produce cooked with care and skill. The simple approach delivers retro ham croquettes, which doesn't sound like it will get your motor running, but they are well-made, creamy and crunchy, or there are similar offerings along the lines of pig's ears, or crab on toast, which you could treat as either bar snacks or nibbly starters. A brace of roasted quails on top of chargrilled spring salad shares the stage with snails with bone marrow and wild garlic, or there might be rainbow trout with Jersey Royals and braised lettuce. End with ginger pannacotta with rhubarb or chocolate mousse with peanut brittle and lime.

Chef Elliott Lidstone **Owner** Michael Buurman **Times** 12-3.30/6-10.15 Closed 25-26 Dec, L Mon (ex BHs) **Prices** Starter £4.60-£7, Main £12.50-£23, Dessert fr £5.60, Service optional, Groups min 5 service 12.5% **Wines** 19 bottles over £30, 37 bottles under £30, 17 by glass **Notes** Brunch available Sat-Sun 10-12, Sunday L £12.50-£15.70, Vegetarian available **Seats** 49 **Children** Portions **Parking** On street

Viajante

LONDON E2
PLAN 1 G4

Modern, International **V**

Cutting-edge cooking in Bethnal Green

☎ 020 7871 0461
Patriot Square, Bethnal Green E2 9NF
e-mail: info@viajante.co.uk
dir: Nearest station: Bethnal Green. Entrance Cambridge Heath Road

There's nothing wrong with seeking comfort from tried and tested dishes, but at times you may wish to be challenged by your food, and if that's the mood you're in then you've come to the right place. The restaurant's name means 'traveller' in Portuguese, and chef-patron Nuno Mendes has done a fair bit of globetrotting since leaving his native Portugal, including a formative stint at the game-changing El Bulli - a period that has clearly

contributed much to the development of his own boldly creative cooking. Suffice it to say that you need to be up for Mendes's foodie journey, as what turns up is avant-garde, thrillingly creative stuff. The setting is the grand old Edwardian town hall in Bethnal Green, now a swish boutique hotel, and as one might expect, Viajante is quite a looker with its up-to-date light wood and pale blue hues, unclothed tables, local contemporary artworks, and an open-to-view kitchen that is designed to be an integral part of the experience - so 'open', in fact, as to practically be in the room. The format is three, six, nine or 12 courses (the three being at lunch only, the 12 at dinner only) with recommended wines to heighten each dish. Presentation is never less than memorable, sometimes quite remarkable, and there is much to entertain along the way. Scallops with parsnips and watercress might get the 12-course menu off the starting line, followed by langoustine with Brussels sprouts and rye, then pike with roe and egg yolk. Cutting-edge techniques and head-spinning flavour and textural

combinations keep the show on the road, always moving on to something new, something exhilarating. Brill with vanilla and daikon, maybe, or pig tail with pecan molé, bay leaf yoghurt and sweet cornbread, ahead of salsify with spruce bark and black truffle. At journey's end, perhaps black carrot with toasted caraway ice cream.

Chef Nuno Mendes **Owner** Nuno Mendes, Peng Loh **Times** 12-2/6-9.30 Closed BHs, Mon-Tue, L Wed-Thu **Prices** Fixed D 3 course £35, Tasting menu £35-£95, Service added but optional 12.5% **Wines** 180 bottles over £30, 14 by glass **Notes** Tasting menu L 3/6/9 course, D 6/9/12 course, Sunday L, Vegetarian menu **Seats** 40, Pr/dining room 16 **Parking** On street

LONDON E14

Chef Collin Brown
PLAN 6 D3

◉ Caribbean

Authentic Caribbean flavours in the Docklands

☎ 020 7515 8177
2 Yabsley St E14 9RG
e-mail: info@chefcollinbrown.com
dir: Nearest station: Blackwall

Almost in the shadow of Canary Wharf's skyscrapers and with the Thames a few paces away, Chef Collin Brown's Caribbean restaurant is a smart, modern affair yet with a genuine laid-back neighbourhood vibe. A glass-fronted semi-circular space occupying a corner site below an apartment complex, the décor comes with a touch of Caribbean flamboyance. Luxuriant wall-coverings in gold and black meet glitzy chandeliers and gilded mirrors, high-back, plum-coloured dining chairs, parquet flooring and a funky Caribbean soundtrack. The man himself was born in Jamaica and brings his passion for the Caribbean to the table in uncomplicated dishes that are bold and expressive. Witness classic mains like a highly seasoned boneless goat curry, or succulent, high-octane jerk chicken breast, while a light, boozy signature rum, cognac and almond sponge-cake dessert or mango cheesecake finish things off in tropical style. Cocktails take you straight back to holidays in the sun.

Times 5-11.30 Closed Xmas, New Year, L all week

Four Seasons Hotel London at Canary Wharf
PLAN 6 A3

◉ Italian **V** ◐

Traditional northern Italian cooking at Canary Wharf

☎ 020 7510 1858 & 7510 1999
46 Westferry Circus, Canary Wharf E14 8RS
e-mail: restaurant.quadrato.caw@fourseasons.com
web: www.fourseasons.com/canarywharf
dir: Nearest station: Canary Wharf. Just off Westferry Circus rdbt

You may be enveloped within the corporate embrace of Canary Wharf, but the Four Seasons does its best to disavow the setting with its terrace tables looking on to the little courtyard garden and pool. Inside the Quadrato restaurant proper, a slick modern ambience of chocolate-brown banquettes, white cubic pillars and an open kitchen is the setting for a light approach to fairly traditional northern Italian cooking. A soft-boiled duck egg on a potato cake dressed in truffle oil is an appetising starter, and might be followed by one of the customary intermediate risottos or pastas, perhaps creamy-sauced smoked salmon penne with broccoli. A carefully timed slab of grilled tuna with puréed basil is a refreshing main dish, as an alternative to duck breast with figs in balsamic sauce, or grilled lamb cutlets with caponata. Classic tiramisù, or honey pannacotta with an emulsion of orange and pistachio, round things off in style.

Chef Moreno Casaccia **Owner** Four Seasons Hotels and Resorts **Times** 12-3/6-10.30 **Prices** Starter £8-£15, Main £14-£28, Dessert £7, Service optional, Groups min 6 service 12.5% **Wines** 8 bottles under £30, 22 by glass **Notes** Sunday L £45, Vegetarian available, Vegetarian menu, Dress restrictions, Smart casual, Civ Wed 200 **Seats** 90 **Children** Portions, Menu **Parking** 26

The Gun
PLAN 6 D2

◉ Modern British

Gutsy British food in an historic waterside pub

☎ 020 7515 5222
27 Coldharbour E14 9NS
e-mail: info@thegundocklands.com
dir: Nearest station: South Quay DLR, Canary Wharf. A12/A13 exit A1206. From South Quay DLR, E down Marsh Wall to mini rdbt, turn left, over bridge, 1st right

This handsomely remodelled former dockers' boozer comes with a hot-ticket Thames-side setting and is entirely worth the short cab ride from Canary Wharf. Views across the water of the O2 Arena and 2012 Olympic park are part of the package, along with a vibrant, lively atmosphere and big-hearted gastro-pub cooking. There's a smart dining room in the main bar at the front, a smaller bar with two cosy snugs at the back, and it's all decked out with polished wood floorboards, framed naval art on white walls, and burgundy leather seating. Dishes are generous and fashioned from quality ingredients, and the menu runs from classics like beer-battered cod and wiener schnitzel, to more modish offerings such as curried haddock croquettes or monkfish tail served with smoked bacon and peas, baby gem and a butter sauce. In the summer months The Gun's Portuguese barbecue joint - A Grelha - 'pops up' beside the river to offer an alternative dining option.

Chef Quinton Bennett **Owner** Tom & Ed Martin **Times** 12-3/6-10.30 Closed 25-26 Dec **Prices** Starter £6-£13.50, Main £14-£28, Dessert £5-£9.50, Service added but optional 12.5% **Wines** 86 bottles over £30, 33 bottles under £30, 23 by glass **Notes** Sunday L, Vegetarian available **Seats** 40, Pr/dining room 22 **Children** Portions, Menu **Parking** On street, NCP

Plateau
PLAN 6 B3

◉◉ Modern French 🍷 NOTABLE WINE LIST

Sophisticated, contemporary fine dining in futuristic landscape

☎ 020 7715 7100
4th Floor, Canada Place, Canada Square, Canary Wharf E14 5ER
e-mail: plateau@danddlondon.com
dir: Nearest station: Canary Wharf DLR/Tube. Facing Canary Wharf Tower and Canada Square Park

There are show-stopping views over Canary Wharf's high-rise cityscape from the aptly named Plateau - a sleek, glass-and-steel roof-top restaurant set four floors up above the shopping mall. The long, lightdrenched space is divided into two zones by a central theatre-style

kitchen, each with its own bar and outdoor terrace. The hip Bar & Grill (cocktails and brasserie menu) is up first, while the restaurant on the other side is calmer and more sophisticated. The design mixes retro styling with warm, restrained neutral tones in the restaurant; think funky white plastic 'tulip' swivel dining chairs and curvy upholstered banquettes, white marble-topped tables, huge arching stainless-steel floor lamps, stunning flower arrangements and changing art displays. But it's not all style over substance here, the ambitious, light, well-dressed modern European cooking - underpinned by a classic French theme - shows real pedigree, driven by quality seasonal materials. Take a duo of fine-tuned signature dishes from the carte: English parsley risotto with sauté of snails, garlic butter and red wine jus, and main-course honey-spiced Goosnargh duck with braised endive and port-marinated radish. Desserts keep up the style count, perhaps organic lemon posset with kalamansi crush and jelly, while the wine list is one of distinction.

Chef Allan Pickett **Owner** D & D London **Times** 12-2.30/6-10.15 Closed 25-26 Dec, Sun, L Sat **Prices** Fixed L 2 course £22, Fixed D 3 course £25, Tasting menu £49, Starter £6.50-£14.50, Main £17.50-£32, Dessert £5-£7.50, Service added but optional 12.5% **Wines** 400 bottles over £30, 30 bottles under £30, 24 by glass **Notes** Vegetarian available, Dress restrictions, Smart casual, Civ Wed 150 **Seats** 120, Pr/dining room 30 **Children** Menu **Parking** 500

Roka
PLAN 6 C3

◉◉ Japanese

Top-flight Japanese cooking in Canary Wharf

☎ 020 7636 5228
1st Floor, 40 Canada Square E14 5FW
e-mail: info@rokarestaurant.com
dir: Nearest station: Canary Wharf. 5 min walk from Canary Wharf tube

Overlooking Canada Square, Roka is a flavour of the East in Canary Wharf and though times may be hard, it still seems to be pulling in the punters. The interior, like its sister restaurant in Charlotte Street (see entry), has acres of wood offering a pleasing contrast to all that glass and concrete outside, and the robata grill doesn't quite hold centre stage as it does up west. Nevertheless, this is an appealing contemporary space and a fine place to enjoy the divertingly confident Japanese food. Sushi and sashimi remain a highlight and a good way to kick off a meal, but whichever way you go, quality runs right through. The negi toro maki roll is made with first-class tuna, or you might go for a fresh water eel version with avocado and cucumber. From the robata grill, spiced chicken wings are perked up with Sancho salt and lime, and black cod is marinated in yuzu miso. Desserts are no afterthought, and if the weather is up to scratch, there's a terrace from which you might actually be able to smell the money.

Chef Cristian Bravaccini **Owner** Rainer Becker, Arjun Waney **Times** 12-3.30/5.30-11.30 Closed 25 Dec **Prices** Prices not confirmed Service added but optional

Save on Hotels. Book at **theAA.com/hotel**

LONDON, CENTRAL (E14 – EC1) 263 **ENGLAND**

12.5% **Wines** 152 bottles over £30, 13 by glass **Notes** Sun brunch £42, with champagne £54, Vegetarian available, Dress restrictions, Smart casual **Seats** 88 **Children** Portions, Menu **Parking** On street

LONDON EC1

Bistrot Bruno Loubet
PLAN 3 E4

@@ Modern French

Proper bistro cooking in a trendy Clerkenwell hotel

☎ 020 7324 4444 & 7324 4567
The Zetter Hotel, St John's Square, 86-89 Clerkenwell Rd EC1M 5RJ
e-mail: info@thezetter.com
dir: Nearest station: Farringdon. From west A401, Clerkenwell Rd A5201. Hotel 200mtrs on left

French chef Bruno Loubet has been a mover and shaker on London's dining scene on and off for a couple of decades. As we go to print he's about to open another restaurant in King's Cross, called Grain Store, where the humble vegetable is to be given elevated status on the menu (although it won't be a vegetarian restaurant by any means). Here, at the trendy Zetter Hotel in Clerkenwell, the offering in the laid-back, modern Bistrot is of a much more meaty variety. While dishes may be aesthetically presented, they are at heart proper bistro food, with a pleasantly peasanty undertow. A fat little boudin blanc in a bowl of garbure (ham stew) is the kind

of starter Londoners were starved of during the ascendancy of molecular cooking, and is all the more welcome a prospect for its rustic richness. That might be followed by fried grey mullet with salt cod and celeriac, the skin of the mullet singed but the flavour loud and proud, or perhaps the signature hare royale, or a hearty rabbit ragoût with tagliatelle. Flawlessly neat apple tart with crème fraîche and cinnamon sugar makes a fine finish.

Chef Bruno Loubet **Owner** Bruno Loubet, Michael Benyan, Mark Sainsbury **Times** 12-2.30/6-10.30 Closed 23-27 Dec **Prices** Starter £2.50-£10, Main £6.50-£19, Dessert £3.25-£6.50, Service added but optional 12.5% **Wines** 23 bottles under £30, 19 by glass **Notes** Plat du Jour £12.75, Sunday L £17.50, Vegetarian available **Seats** 90, Pr/dining room 40 **Children** Portions, Menu **Parking** NCP

The Bleeding Heart
PLAN 3 D3

@ Modern French 🍷 NOTABLE WINE LIST

Discreet and romantic Hatton Garden favourite

☎ 020 7242 2056
Bleeding Heart Yard, Off Greville St EC1N 8SJ
e-mail: bookings@bleedingheart.co.uk
dir: Nearest station: Farringdon. Turn right out of Farringdon Station onto Cowcross St, continue along Greville St for 50mtrs. Turn left into Bleeding Heart Yard

Secreted away in a rather Dickensian cobbled courtyard, this bastion of French cooking has bags of character and

atmosphere; its name recalls the macabre murder of society beauty Lady Elizabeth Hatton, killed by her jealous lover back in the 17th century. The cellar restaurant itself has charm by the bucket-load; a trio of intimate, romantic, warmly toned subterranean rooms, with low-beamed ceilings, panelling, fireplaces and wine-themed prints. White linen, burgundy leather seating and slick Gallic service up the ante for some modish, unapologetically French fare: think roast rump of Suffolk Blackface lamb teamed with caramelised root vegetables, pommes mousseline and rosemary jus to a classic finish of warm chocolate fondant with orange ice cream. A serious wine list impresses, including bottles from their own Hawkes Bay estate, while all carte dishes come with recommendations by the glass.

Chef Julian Marshall **Owner** Robert & Robyn Wilson **Times** 12-3/6-10.30 Closed Xmas & New Year (10 days), Sat-Sun (Bistro open Sat) **Prices** Fixed L 3 course £25, Fixed D 3 course £30, Starter £6-£13, Main £14-£29, Dessert £6.95, Service added but optional 12.5% **Wines** 360 bottles over £30, 40 bottles under £30, 23 by glass **Notes** Vegetarian available, Dress restrictions, Smart casual **Seats** 110, Pr/dining room 40 **Parking** 20 evening only, NCP nearby

Club Gascon

LONDON EC1
PLAN 3 E3

Modern French V 🍷 NOTABLE WINE LIST

Vanguard southwest French food in a palatial room

☎ 020 7600 6144
57 West Smithfields EC1A 9DS
e-mail: info@clubgascon.com
dir: Nearest station: Barbican, Farringdon, St Paul's

The grand frontage of Pascal Aussignac's destination eatery in Smithfield recalls the days when teahouses (it was once a Lyon's) came in stately guise, and the tone is sustained in the palatial interior. A high-ceilinged marble hall with impressively dressed tables and big mirrors is dominated by a gargantuan floral display on the bar counter, the imposing mood softened by jazzy piano music and the encyclopedically knowledgeable staff, who not only look great in their long black aprons, but are

sufficiently fluent in Aussignac-ien to be able to explain the menus to you. The bill of fare is vanguard French modernism with a tenacious commitment to the patron's native southwest, evinced in the importation every week of speciality ingredients from Gascony. A lunchtime prix-fixe of impeccable value, a seasonal tasting menu of market-led dishes, and the full carte are alike overflowing with culinary marvel, the menu linguistics indicating the distinctiveness of it all - pine-smoked prawns, pink tapioca pearls and frosted oyster; black pudding tart with artichoke crush; strawberry gazpacho, espelette crust, tarragon sorbet and Pimm's - while the evidence on the plate is of pitch-perfect judgment, dish after dish. Crackled capon wings make a rich and flavourful opener, alongside scallop mousse rolled in nuts, topped with lovage foam, to be followed by anchovy-stuffed squid with piperade, romanesco florets and red pepper coulis, or goose à l'orange with pickled beetroot and samphire. Dessert might be almost straightforward, perhaps a high-intensity milk chocolate mousse on a nutty biscuit

base, alongside a scoop of dreamy violet ice cream. The drinks list is a spellbinder too, with a cornucopia of superb southwestern wines to go at, as well as bracing pastis. And in case you were wondering, that floral display is also the handiwork of the multi-talented Aussignac. Is there anything he can't do?

Chef Pascal Aussignac **Owner** P Aussignac & V Labeyrie **Times** 12-2/6.30-10 Closed Xmas, New Year, BHs, Sun, L Sat **Prices** Fixed L 2 course £25, Fixed D 3 course £28, Tasting menu £60-£90, Starter £11-£14.50, Main £19-£22.50, Dessert £10, Service added but optional 12.5% **Wines** 400 bottles over £30, 30 bottles under £30, 15 by glass **Notes** Tasting menu 5 course, Vegetarian menu, Dress restrictions, Smart casual **Seats** 40 **Children** Portions **Parking** NCP opposite restaurant

LONDON EC1 *continued*

Le Café du Marché
PLAN 3 E3

🍽 French

Rustic, Gallic cooking in a classically converted warehouse

☎ 020 7608 1609
Charterhouse Mews, Charterhouse Square EC1M 6AH
dir: Nearest station: Barbican

When the urge for Gallic gastronomy strikes, head down a cobbled alley off Charterhouse Square for this authentic slice of France. The place drips classic cross-Channel style with its bare-brick walls, French posters, jazz pianist and candlelit starched linen-dressed tables set in a rustic-chic converted Victorian warehouse. The scene thus set, you can expect unreconstructed French provincial dishes on an uncomplicated two- or three-course fixed price menu - honest, peasant cooking that has stood the test of time, starting with fish soup or grilled lamb's tongues with sauce gribiche, and progressing to a côte de boeuf with béarnaise sauce for two, or duck confit en croûte with Savoy cabbage and Agen prunes. Finish with the bavarois du jour, or the splendid selection of French cheeses.

Chef Simon Cottard **Owner** Anna Graham-Wood
Times 12-2.30/6-10 Closed Xmas, New Year, Etr, BHs, Sun, L Sat **Prices** Prices not confirmed Service added but optional 12.5% **Notes** Vegetarian available **Seats** 120, Pr/dining room 65 **Children** Portions **Parking** Next door (small charge)

Cicada
PLAN 3 E4

🍽 Pan-Asian

Authentic Pan-Asian cooking in trendy Clerkenwell

☎ 020 7608 1550
132-136 St John St EC1V 4JT
e-mail: cicada@rickerrestaurants.com
dir: Nearest station: Farringdon

Will Ricker's first outlet (see also entries for E&O, Eight Over Eight and XO) has had a bit of a refurb, but it remains a popular, fun place, people drawn by its reasonably priced Pan-Asian cooking. The kitchen assiduously sources authentic Eastern ingredients and turns out convincing renditions, from dim sum - pumpkin and spinach gyoza, say, or chicken siu mai - to whole sea bream chargrilled with garlic and chilli. Dishes like tempura soft-shelled crab, a plate of sashimi, Wagyu beef with sesame and shallots, and chicken phad thai all share the billing, in grazing-size portions, attractively presented, to encourage experimentation. Sticky coconut rice with banana and vanilla may be the real thing, but Western chocolate pudding may be harder to resist.

Chef Neil Witney **Owner** Will Ricker **Times** 12-3/6-11 Closed Xmas, BHs, Sun, L Sat **Prices** Fixed L 2 course £18-£30, Fixed D 3 course £22-£40, Tasting menu £24-£40, Starter £3.50-£15, Main £10.50-£28, Dessert £4.50-£6, Service added but optional 12.5% **Wines** 44 bottles over £30, 16 bottles under £30, 12 by glass

Notes Vegetarian available **Seats** 90, Pr/dining room 40 **Parking** On street

Club Gascon
PLAN 3 E3

🍽🍽🍽 *– see page 263*

Le Comptoir Gascon
PLAN 3 E3

🍽 Traditional French

Gutsy French dishes by Smithfield Market

☎ 020 7608 0851
61-63 Charterhouse St EC1M 6HJ
e-mail: info@comptoirgascon.com
dir: Nearest station: Farringdon, Barbican, St Paul's. In front of Smithfield Market

The casual, bustling, petite bistro-deli sibling of heavyweight Club Gascon (see entry), Comptoir deals in the gutsy food of southwest France. The feel is one of true cuisine terroir, with simple market-driven cooking and full-on flavours: duck confit and garbure béarnaise, for example, or a traditional Toulousain cassoulet. Lighter things might include crispy squid Basquaise with garlic and mixed herbs, while desserts - like lemon tart or a classic chocolate fondant - keep things simple yet show acute technical ability in their making. The décor fits the bill with its modern-rustic vibe; exposed brickwork and ducting, dinky elbow-to-elbow wooden tables, small velour-covered chairs and copious wines tantalising from their cabinets. The fixed-price blackboard lunch menu offers good value, while the miniscule deli counter - with displays of breads, conserves, pastries and the like - offers supplies to takeaway. Well-selected wines are from southwest France... where else?

Chef John Kent **Owner** Vincent Labeyrie, Pascal Aussignac **Times** 12-2.30/7-10 Closed 25 Dec-1 Jan, BHs, Sun-Mon **Prices** Fixed L 2 course £14.50, Starter £6-£13, Main £9-£14.50, Dessert £3.50-£6, Service added but optional 12.5% **Wines** 19 bottles over £30, 13 bottles under £30, 11 by glass **Notes** Vegetarian available **Seats** 32 **Children** Portions **Parking** NCP 50 mtrs

Hix Oyster & Chop House
PLAN 3 E3

🍽 Modern British

No-nonsense British cooking in chilled-out Clerkenwell

☎ 020 7017 1930
36-37 Greenhill Rents, Cowcross St EC1M 6BN
e-mail: chophouse@restaurantetcltd.co.uk
dir: Nearest station: Farringdon. Turn left out of underground station (approx 1min walk)

A wooden floor, white-tiled walls, visible pipes, revolving overhead fans, and tightly packed tables ready and waiting with ketchup and vinegar bottles, all create an unfussy, roughcast sort of atmosphere at Mark Hix's buzzy Clerkenwell restaurant. The kitchen takes an equally straightforward, no-nonsense approach to its output, turning out steaks, fish fingers with mushy peas and chips, and beef flank and oyster pie. As well as the expected oysters, starters may take in tender and full-

flavoured veal dumpling wrapped in cawl and served with bashed neeps, a fine example of winter comfort food, and squid with ink-cooked spelt. Go out on a high with an excellent chocolate and orange sponge with orange sorbet, while for the impecunious there's credit crunch ice cream with hot chocolate sauce.

Times 12-11 Closed BHs, L Sat

Malmaison Charterhouse Square
PLAN 3 E3

🍽🍽 French, European

Boutique hotel with a chic brasserie

☎ 020 7012 3700
18-21 Charterhouse Square, Clerkenwell EC1M 6AH
e-mail: athwaites@malmaison.com
web: www.malmaison.com
dir: Nearest station: Barbican

With Smithfield meat market practically on the doorstep, there's no difficulty for the London Mal's kitchen to lay its hands on slabs of prime protein. Tucked discreetly away in a cobbled courtyard off Charterhouse Square, the slick basement brasserie caters to all-comers, whether it's city slickers doing deals over a grilled rib-eye with bone marrow, or lunch to refuel after a hit of retail therapy and pampering. The chic setting conforms to the Malmaison house style: intimate tables for two are tucked into secretive alcoves, amid sexy contemporary boudoir textures of velvet, bare wood and exposed brickwork, and hues of purple and burgundy. In tune with the Moulin Rouge vibe, classic French-accented brasserie dishes built on top-quality ingredients are the thing here. Expect the likes of braised oxtail with smoked and crispy polenta, followed by something gamey - pan-fried partridge with cauliflower purée, Savoy cabbage and tarragon jus, say. Elsewhere there are comfort classics such as Toulouse sausages with caramelised onion and red wine jus, and for fish fans, perhaps roast monkfish with fines herbes, cream of haricot blanc and trompette de mort mushrooms. Stay with the French theme and finish with a crème brûlée.

Times 12-2.30/6-10.30 Closed 23-28 Dec, L Sat

The Modern Pantry
PLAN 3 E4

🍽 Modern 🍽

Creative fusion food in a fashionable part of town

☎ 020 7553 9210
47-48 St John's Square, Clerkenwell EC1V 4JJ
e-mail: enquiries@themodernpantry.co.uk
dir: Nearest station: Farringdon, Barbican

The word 'fusion' is hardly a new term in the foodie firmament these days, but chef-proprietor Anna Hansen has been at the forefront of this particular style of cooking since it first hit these shores in the mid-1990s. The venue is a gem of a conversion of two listed Georgian townhouses in a trendy part of town, and it serves up plenty of options: modish café (and traiteur) on the ground floor and a coolly smart first-floor restaurant where the tables are poshed up with white linen cloths. Food is served all day and flavours come from far and wide. A pear, for example, is roasted with pomegranate molasses and tonka beans and served up in a salad with golden beetroots, Stichelton, bull's blood, sorrel and spiced pecans. Among main courses, roast Gloucestershire Old Spot pork belly might come with mushroom and date purée, choucroute and green pepper relish, and pan-fried cod with smoky red-wine-braised octopus. Matching wines are suggested on the menu.

Chef Anna Hansen **Owner** Anna Hansen **Times** 12-10.30 Closed Xmas, New Year, Aug BH, All-day dining **Prices** Fixed L 2 course £21.50, Starter £4.80-£9.50, Main £15.50-£22, Dessert £2.80-£8, Service added but optional 12.5% **Wines** 90 bottles over £30, 27 bottles under £30, 19 by glass **Notes** Sunday L £21.50-£76.50, Vegetarian available **Seats** 110, Pr/dining room 60 **Children** Portions **Parking** On street (meter)

The Montcalm London City at The Brewery   PLAN 3 G4

◉ Traditional British **NEW**

Smart hotel with a taste of Britain on the menu

☎ 020 7614 0100
52 Chiswell St EC1Y 4SB
e-mail: reservations@themontcalmlondoncity.co.uk
dir: Nearest station: Liverpool St, Barbican, Moorgate. From Gatwick M23 N to M25 signed Heathrow Airport/ Central London to M4. From Heathrow M4 E 9m, Great West Road towards Shaftesbury Avenue, right New Oxford Street, right Drake Street and left Edward Street. At the rdbt 1st exit Aldersgate St, right Beech St, Hotel on left

The last beer was brewed here in what was originally the Whitbread brewery in 1976. Now the old girl has taken on a new lease of life as a five-star luxury hotel, but you can still get a decent pint in the Jugged Hare gastro-pub or the main restaurant, the Chiswell Street Dining Rooms. The latter has sharp pastel-coloured tones in wood and leather, a cocktail bar if you're up for it, and on the menu some breezy, gently modish food with a definite British streak: baked Dorset crab and Shetland mussels, to start perhaps, with creamed leek gratin, or an Atlantic king prawn cocktail. Follow on with slow-cooked rump of Herdwick lamb with celeriac and parsnip gratin and a shallot and smoked bacon casserole, or 35-day aged Cumbrian rib-eye steak. Finish with an orange and almond sponge with Amaretto ice cream.

Chef Richard O'Connell **Owner** Montcalm London Hotels Ltd **Times** 11.45-3.30/5.45-11 **Prices** Prices not confirmed **Notes** Pre/post-theatre 5.30-6.30/10-10.45pm

Morgan M   PLAN 3 E3

◉◉ Modern French **V**

French master in the City

☎ 020 7609 3560
50 Long Ln, Barbican EC1A 9EJ
dir: Nearest station: Barbican, Farringdon. Opposite Smithfield Market, left out of Barbican Tube, 2 mins walk

Islington house prices are doubtless robust enough to survive the loss, but Morgan Meunier's departure from the borough will have saddened the hearts of a good many locals. The City is the beneficiary, for Monsieur M has moved just around the corner from the Barbican, opposite Smithfield Market. And very smart it looks too, with its olive-green frontage and etched glass windows. Inside, there's a decidedly natural quality to the chosen colour palette, with patterned wallpaper and natural wood floors to match. Wherever he pitches up, Morgan's food will garner a following, built as it is on robust French foundations and a good deal of craft and endeavour. His cooking is a harmonious meeting of modern refinement and seasonally-led classicism. Ravioli of snails in Chablis, for example, is rich with earthy flavours, topped with garlic froth and finished with red wine jus, while main-course pavé of halibut comes with wild mushroom tempura that gets the light batter just right and packs a wonderful punch. To finish, tarte paysanne is a skillfully constructed dessert, with an accompanying olive oil and lime ice cream, and all the high-class incidentals such as amuse-bouche, pre-dessert and excellent bread (served with wonderful butter) only add to the whole experience.

Chef M Meunier, S Soulard **Owner** Morgan Meunier **Times** 12-2.30/6-10.30 Closed 24-30 Dec, Sun, L Sat **Prices** Fixed L 2 course fr £21.50, Fixed D 3 course fr £25.50, Tasting menu £48-£52, Starter £9.50-£15.50, Main £19.50-£26.50, Dessert £9.50-£12.50, Service added but optional 12.5% **Wines** 81 bottles over £30, 17 bottles under £30, 9 by glass **Notes** Tasting menu 6 course, Grazing tasting dishes, Vegetarian menu, Dress restrictions, Smart casual **Seats** 59 **Children** Portions **Parking** Long Lane

Moro   PLAN 3 D4

◉ Islamic, Mediterranean **NOTABLE WINE LIST** 🍽

Moreish Moorish and Spanish cuisine in a long-stayer

☎ 020 7833 8336
34-36 Exmouth Market EC1R 4QE
e-mail: info@moro.co.uk
dir: Nearest station: Farringdon, Angel. 5 mins walk from Sadler's Wells theatre, between Farringdon Road and Rosebery Avenue

Moro has been a stalwart of the Exmouth Market scene for 16 years. Its popularity is easy to understand: regulars return time and again for the full-on flavours of its vibrant take on Spanish and Moorish cuisine. Diners spill out onto pavement tables in fine weather, while indoors it's a sparsely-furnished, high-decibel venue where you can perch at the bar washing down tapas with the splendid range of sherries and Iberian wines, or sink into a harem-style bolster cushion at one of the closely-packed tables. Get the show on the road with a crispy seafood brik with harissa; next, from the open kitchen might come a straight-talking main course like wood-roasted pork with wilted frisée, pomegranate and migas (pan-fried bacon and breadcrumbs to the uninitiated), or charcoal-grilled sea bass with sprouting broccoli, Seville orange sauce and Canarian-style wrinkled potatoes. For dessert, perhaps sublime chocolate and apricot tart, or exemplary rosewater and cardamom ice cream. Friendly, well-briefed staff keep it all nicely together.

Chef Samuel & Samantha Clark **Owner** Mr & Mrs S Clark **Times** 12-2.30/6-10.30 Closed Xmas, New Year, BHs, D Sun **Prices** Starter £7-£9, Main £16.50-£21, Dessert £6-£9, Service added but optional 12.5% **Wines** 72 bottles over £30, 21 bottles under £30, 12 by glass **Notes** Sunday L, Vegetarian available, Civ Wed 70 **Seats** 90 **Children** Portions **Parking** NCP Farringdon Rd

St John   PLAN 3 E3

◉◉ British

Nose-to-tail eating at its best

☎ 020 3301 8069
26 St John St EC1M 4AY
e-mail: reservations@stjohnrestaurant.com
dir: Nearest station: Farringdon. 100yds from Smithfield Market, northside

Firmly entrenched on the London dining scene (and with a younger brother in the form of St John Bread & Wine - see entry), this trailblazer of the 'nose-to-tail' eating approach still packs them in. Set up in 1994 by Fergus Henderson and Trevor Gulliver in a former smokehouse just up from Smithfield Market, its utilitarian look and championing of unglamorous, lesser-used cuts has certainly caught on. A wrought-iron staircase leads up from the bare-bones ground-floor bar and bakery counter to the equally pared-down dining room: here it's all exposed floorboards, coat-hook-lined white walls, ranks of white-paper-clothed tables with café-style chairs, staff dressed in long white aprons and an open kitchen adding to the buzz. On the food front, others may have copied the robust, gutsy style, but few come close to achieving St John's unvarnished, honest simplicity. Roast bone marrow with parsley salad is a menu stalwart, but you might also encounter rabbit offal and radishes, devilled kidneys, or mallard and Jerusalem artichokes. It's not all aimed at meat-eaters though - how about brill with leeks and butter beans, or fennel and Berkswell? Desserts are equally comfort-spun, from the signature Eccles cake and Lancashire cheese, to treacle steamed pudding.

Times 12-3/6-11 Closed Xmas, New Year, BHs, L Sat, D Sun

LONDON EC1 *continued*

Smiths of Smithfield, Top Floor

PLAN 3 E3

Modern British

Terrific London views, a buzzy vibe and spot-on ingredients

☎ 020 7251 7950

(Top Floor), 67-77 Charterhouse St EC1M 6HJ
e-mail: reservations@smithsofsmithfield.co.uk
dir: Nearest station: Farringdon, Barbican, Chancery Lane. Opposite Smithfield Market

From the top floor of this Grade II listed former meat warehouse by Smithfield Market the views across to St Paul's are mightily impressive. Up here is the most refined restaurant of the bunch - Top Floor - but it's still a relaxed place with floor-to-ceiling windows to catch that view. Wherever you eat - breakfast or brunch or alcoholic milkshakes at ground-floor level, or the dining room on the second floor - clued-up staff pitch the balance of banter and knowledgeable efficiency just right. With the market just opposite, you'd expect top quality produce on the menu and SOS absolutely delivers, particularly on rare breed meats. Up on the Top Floor a flavoursome shellfish risotto and tempura soft-shelled crab is a nicely judged first course, followed perhaps by duck breast with bok choy, mango, chilli and star anise sauce. Almond sponge with poached Cox's Orange Pippin apple and toffee sauce is a fine finale.

Chef Tony Moyse, Michael Lecouteur **Owner** John Torode **Times** 12-3.30/6.30-11 Closed 25-26 Dec, 1 Jan, L Sat, D Sun **Prices** Fixed L 2 course £22.50, Starter £8.50-£14, Main £18-£39, Dessert £6.95-£7.25, Service added but optional 12.5% **Wines** 148 bottles over £30, 14 bottles under £30, 15 by glass **Notes** Sunday L £19.95-£30, Vegetarian available **Seats** 80, Pr/dining room 30 **Children** Portions **Parking** NCP: Snowhill

LONDON EC2

L' Anima

PLAN 3 H4

Italian

A contemporary take on regional Italian cooking

☎ 020 7422 7000

1 Snowden St, Broadgate West EC2A 2DQ
e-mail: info@lanima.co.uk
dir: Nearest station: Liverpool Street

Occupying part of the ground floor of a large office block, L'Anima is anything but soulless. The name means soul, for a start, and there is nothing bland about the look of the place. There's a stark brilliance to the space, in fact, from its white leather seats and white linen on the tables, to the bar which fizzes with energy and is separated from the restaurant by a glass wall. It's a super-cool, minimalist look which is more Milan than City of London. And so to Francesco Mazzei's menu, which is equally sharp and exciting, founded on the principles of regional Italian cooking, and full of things you really want to eat. A starter of octopus, for example, cooked a la plancha and

served with cannellini beans, ricotta mustia and paprika oil is simply perfection. Home-made squid ink cavatelli with clams and peas might follow, or perhaps roast veal with roast potatoes and mammole artichokes. For dessert, raspberry soufflé is a spot-on version, served with vanilla ice cream and raspberry purée.

Times 11.45-3/5.30-11 Closed BHs, Sun, L Sat

Boisdale of Bishopsgate

PLAN 3 H3

Traditional British

Cooking showcasing Scotland's best produce

☎ 020 7283 1763

Swedeland Court, 202 Bishopsgate EC2M 4NR
e-mail: manager@boisdale-city.co.uk
dir: Nearest station: Liverpool Street. Opposite Liverpool St station

In a narrow alley near Petticoat Lane market, Boisdale's City branch (see also Boisdale of Belgravia) occupies a subtly lit vaulted basement, its vivid red-painted walls hung with a plethora of photographs and prints, with booth seating, upright timbers, and, to underline its Scottish credentials, a tartan carpet; there's also a champagne and oyster bar. The cooking is founded on thoroughbred Scottish meats and seafood, starters including various ways with smoked salmon - perhaps as céviche with pea and avocado purée - the range broadened by the likes of a haggis Scotch egg with piccalilli, and crab with lobster jelly, horseradish and fennel cream. Main courses tend to be safe bets: prime steaks with béarnaise or foie gras and truffle shavings, along with Dover sole meunière with Jersey Royals and spinach, or Hebridean mutton with confit potato, smoked onion purée, and spring greens with pickled raisins.

Times 11-3/6-9 Closed Xmas, 31 Dec, BHs, Sat-Sun

Bonds

PLAN 3 G2

British, European

Ambitious modern cooking in the splendour of a former banking hall

☎ 020 7657 8088 & 7657 8090

Threadneedles, 5 Threadneedle St EC2R 8AY
e-mail: bonds@theetoncollection.co.uk
dir: Nearest station: Bank. Bank Tube station exit 3, follow Threadneedle St for 200m, then cross Finch Lane, entrance on right

Set in the swish Threadneedles (a former Victorian banking hall turned boutique hotel), the aptly named Bonds is a handsome City bar and restaurant on a grand scale. The look successfully blends the past with the current day: dramatic soaring columns, high decorative ceiling, vast windows and contemporary features like American walnut flooring, oak furnishings, fashionable burgundy leather seating and white linen. The light, well-tuned modern European cooking is rooted in top-notch ingredients and employs a good dose of technical artistry. A smooth and light foie gras parfait with toasted brioche and a fig and watercress salad might start you off, followed by wonderfully tender new-season rump of lamb

with crushed Jersey Royals, Puy lentils and a rosemary jus. If fish is more your thing, the steamed halibut teamed with buttered spinach, potato gnocchi tartare, crispy squid, chorizo and a red wine jus should hit the spot, while desserts, like cherry dark chocolate (cherry parfait, dark chocolate mousse and cherry jelly) come dressed to thrill. The daily-changing fixed-price menu is a steal.

Chef Stephen Smith **Owner** Westmont Hospitality Group **Times** 12-2.30/6-10 Closed BHs, Sat-Sun **Prices** Fixed L 2 course £20, Fixed D 3 course £24, Starter £9.50-£14.50, Main £13.50-£26.50, Dessert £6.50, Service added but optional 12.5% **Wines** 65 bottles over £30, 15 bottles under £30, 19 by glass **Notes** Vegetarian available, Dress restrictions, Smart casual **Seats** 80, Pr/dining room 16 **Children** Portions **Parking** NCP Finsbury Sq

Cinnamon Kitchen

PLAN 3 H3

Modern Indian

Modern Indian cuisine in former spice warehouse

☎ 020 7626 5000 & 7397 9611

9 Devonshire Square EC2M 4YL
e-mail: info@cinnamon-kitchen.com
dir: Nearest station: Liverpool St. Follow New St (off Bishopsgate) into Devonshire Sq

Tucked away in Devonshire Square close to Liverpool Street Station, the 'Kitchen' is the younger, livelier City sibling of Westminster's Cinnamon Club (see entry). Aptly occupying the former East India Company's spice warehouse, the large dining space has a cool, industrial-chic look, kitted out with classy leather seating, polished wooden tables, eye-catching lantern-esque lighting, modern artworks and, at the back, a pewter and black granite tandoor bar. The modern Indian cuisine, fashioned from prime seasonal produce, is as bold as the surroundings, with clean-cut dishes of punchy flavour and well-judged spicing. Witness Kolhapuri-style spiced saddle of Kentish lamb served with pilau rice, or perhaps chargrilled halibut with Rajasthani-style 'kadhi' sauce, while Westernised desserts might take in stem ginger and anise pannacotta with peach compôte. A serious wine list comes with plenty of spice-friendly options, but if cocktails are more your thing, head next-door to the buzzy and coolly sophisticated Anise Bar.

Chef Vivek Singh, Abdul Yaseen **Owner** Indian Restaurants Ltd **Times** 12-2.30/6-10.30 Closed 25-26 Dec, 1 Jan, some BHs, Sun, L Sat **Prices** Fixed L 2 course £15, Fixed D 3 course £21, Tasting menu £60-£135, Starter £5.50-£15, Main £12.50-£40, Dessert £6-£15, Service added but optional 12.5% **Wines** 222 bottles over £30, 17 bottles under £30, 21 by glass **Notes** Pre & post theatre menu, Tasting menu 6 course, Vegetarian available **Seats** 130, Pr/dining room 16 **Children** Portions **Parking** NCP Rodwell Hse on Bishopsgate

Coq d'Argent   PLAN 3 G2

◉◉ French NOTABLE WINE LIST ✆

Traditional French food and rooftop views

☎ 020 7395 5000
1 Poultry EC2R 8EJ
e-mail: coqdargent.co.uk
dir: Nearest station: Bank. Use exit 9 Bank Station

With what must be some of the best rooftop views in central London, Coq d'Argent is a smart contemporary setting for some confident French cooking. Divided into a brasserie (food at lunchtimes, lively bar in the evening) and a restaurant with a reception area in between, both have terraces which are a big pull when the sun shines on the City. The restaurant has tables dressed up for serious dining and service which matches the formality without ever taking itself too seriously. Both menus are printed in French with English translations; from the restaurant menu you might kick off with a foie gras parfait with pear and ginger relish, before moving on to baked stone bass with fennel, courgette, tomato and saffron casserole. Desserts to send you home (or back to work) happy include apple tart with roasted cardamom ice cream, and frozen passionfruit and vanilla vacherin.

Chef Mickael Weiss **Owner** D and D London **Times** 11.30-3/6-10 Closed BH, L Sat, D Sun **Prices** Fixed L 2 course £26, Fixed D 3 course £29, Starter £9.50-£14.50, Main £16.50-£37.50, Dessert £7.50-£12, Service added but optional 12.5% **Wines** 600 bottles over £30, 60 bottles under £30, 30 by glass **Notes** Top table 3 course £25, Sunday L, Vegetarian available, Dress restrictions, Smart casual **Seats** 150 **Children** Portions, Menu

Duck & Waffle   PLAN 3 H2

◉ British, European **NEW**

Mesmerising views 24/7

☎ 020 3640 7310
Heron Tower, 100 Bishopsgate EC2N 4AY
e-mail: dwreservations@sushisamba.com
dir: Nearest station: Liverpool Street

Got a head for heights? You might like to look elsewhere if you don't as the Duck & Waffle is on the 40th floor of the City's Heron Tower. The view is a-m-a-z-i-n-g. It's actually open all day and all night, so it can sort you out for breakfast, lunch, dinner, cocktails, a late supper, the lot. There are no sharply pressed linen tablecloths here - it's not that sort of place - and the food takes a broad sweep through the UK and mainland Europe. The eponymous dish of duck and waffle is present and correct - confit duck with a fried duck's egg and mustard-maple syrup - but you might prefer to start with pearl barley and wild garlic risotto and move on to whole baked sea bass with warm roasted fennel and chilli. The late night menu is much the same, only shorter, so you can tuck into spicy ox cheek doughnut with apricot jam in the wee small hours.

Chef Daniel Doherty **Times** mdnt-mdnt All-day dining **Prices** Prices not confirmed Service added but optional 12.5% **Notes** Open 24hrs, Sunday L, Vegetarian available, Dress restrictions, No trainers or sportswear **Seats** 260, Pr/dining room 18 **Children** Portions

1901 Restaurant

LONDON EC2   **PLAN 3 H3**

British **V**

Modern British brasserie cooking in a great white ballroom

☎ 020 7618 7000
ANdAZ London, 40 Liverpool St EC2M 7QN
e-mail: london.restres@andaz.com
dir: Nearest station: Liverpool Street. On corner of Liverpool St & Bishopsgate, attached to Liverpool St station

The name may recall the beginning of the Edwardian era, but the dining venue that has been fashioned from the ballroom of the old Great Eastern, once the railway hotel serving Liverpool Street station, is firmly in the now. The great glass domed ceiling somehow survived the Blitz and the stonking great pillars endure, but the space has a clean, fresh, oxygenated feel, with coloured light panels glowing gently behind the wine-store, and a programme of live music on certain evenings. On the last Wednesday of the month, the whole room is lit with hundreds of candles, a sight to behold in a city used to clinical minimalism and restaurants that look like offices. If you're all for mucking in, a communal table in the cheese-and-wine tasting cellar makes an interesting divertissement. The cooking comes straight out of the modern British brasserie drawer, with the provenances of main ingredients indicated; it may not be country-house localism, but you're in the City of London after all. Crab makes its way from Dorset to be presented as dumplings and a tartare, alongside sweetcorn pannacotta, dressed in mango and coriander, while the lentils have a longer journey (from Oldham, Lancashire) to comprise the principal attraction of a veggie starter array of couscous, sweet potato, pomegranate and spinach purée. Mains offer the likes of Gressingham duck (breast and confit leg) with fruit and veg alternations of spiced pineapple, turnips, orange and peas, or perhaps Devon sole with brown shrimps and grapes under caper and lemon foam. Desserts look surprisingly trad after all that, featuring as they do crème brûlée, Eton Mess, or blueberry cheesecake and lemon sorbet. Breakfasts and afternoon tea are served, and it's worth allowing time for a cocktail, when the barman steps out from behind the traditional divide of the counter to mix your drink.

Chef Hameed Fareds **Owner** Hyatt **Times** 12-2.30/6.30-10 Closed Xmas, New Year, BHs, Sun, L Sat **Prices** Fixed L 2 course £24, Fixed D 3 course £30, Tasting menu £60, Starter £10-£14, Main £17-£28, Dessert £9-£10, Service added but optional 12.5% **Wines** 235 bottles over £30, 16 bottles under £30, 50 by glass **Notes** Tasting menu 6 course, Vegetarian menu **Seats** 100 **Parking** NCP London Wall

LONDON EC2 *continued*

Eyre Brothers　　　　　　　　PLAN 3 H4

◉◉ Spanish, Portuguese

Big, enticing Iberian flavours in the City

☎ 020 7613 5346
70 Leonard St EC2A 4QX
e-mail: eyrebros@btconnect.com
dir: Nearest station: Old Street Exit 4

Doing its authentic Iberian thing in the City's northern hinterland since 2001, this modern, urban-cool outfit rather slips under the radar of its West-End counterparts. David Eyre's cooking draws inspiration from across the Iberian Peninsula, with full-on flavours created from top-notch produce treated with integrity and skill. Take an opener of Viscaya salted anchovies on grilled bread teamed with pimentos de piquillo, black olives, capers and a soft-boiled egg to evoke those sun-drench flavours, or a big-hearted signature main course of grilled fillet of acorn-fed Ibérica pig (marinated with smoked paprika, thyme and garlic) delivered with patatas pobres (oven potatoes with green peppers, onions, garlic and white wine). Tapas are served at the all-day bar, while well-matched Spanish and Portuguese wines patriotically take their cue from the cuisine. It's a stylish place without trying too hard, with full-drop windows, classy wood veneer and brown leather banquettes and matching chairs, while a hip backing track of jazz music and friendly service keeping it humming along nicely.

Chef Dave Eyre, Joao Cleto **Owner** Eyre Bros Restaurants Ltd **Times** 12-3/6.30-11 Closed Xmas-New Year, BHs, Sun, L Sat **Prices** Prices not confirmed Service optional **Wines** 14 by glass **Notes** Vegetarian available **Seats** 100 **Parking** On street

Manicomio - City　　　　　　　PLAN 3 F2

◉ Modern Italian

Contemporary Italian with a cool City vibe

☎ 020 7726 5010
Gutter Ln EC2V 8AS
e-mail: gutterlane@manicomio.co.uk
dir: Nearest station: St Paul's. Just off Cheapside

Secreted away on a narrow lane between Cheapside and Gresham Street, the sleek, effortlessly cool modernism of Manicomio's Sir Norman Foster-designed glass building shimmers in the sunlight. Sibling to the Chelsea original (see entry), this three-tiered City version is a resolutely business-suit affair, covering all the bases. A parasol-covered little terrace comes screened from the street, joined at ground-floor level by a lively café-bar/takeaway (open from breakfast). However, for the real culinary action, head upstairs to the more formal yet unstuffy first-floor restaurant: a clean-lined, equally fashionable set up, with high-back leather banquettes or chairs and white-linen-clad tables. The light and fresh modern Italian cooking pays due respect to the provenance, seasonality and quality of its ingredients. Take grilled Cornish turbot teamed with fried artichokes, tomato pulp and green and yellow beans, or perhaps chargrilled Devon

rib-eye with roast heritage tomatoes, aubergine and rocket pesto. The Roundhouse on the top floor incorporates a vibrant cocktail bar.

Chef Tom Salt **Owner** Andrew & Ninai Zarach **Times** 12-3/6-10 Closed 1 wk Xmas, Sat-Sun **Prices** Starter £8.75-£11.50, Main £13.50-£25, Dessert £5-£10.50, Service added but optional 12.5% **Wines** 101 bottles over £30, 33 bottles under £30, 14 by glass **Notes** Vegetarian available **Seats** 95, Pr/dining room 60 **Children** Portions

Miyako　　　　　　　　　　　PLAN 3 H3

◉ Japanese **V**

Authentic cooking in buzzing Japanese restaurant

☎ 020 7618 7100
ANdAZ London, 40 Liverpool St EC2M 7QN
e-mail: london.restres@andaz.com
dir: Nearest station: Liverpool Street. On corner of Liverpool St & Bishopsgate

It may be the Japanese dining option at the sprawling ANdAZ hotel, but Miyako, with its own street entrance, certainly has the buzz of a stand-alone restaurant. The bustling sushi counter up front services the health-conscious City suits and heels who pile in at lunchtimes for take-out boxes of sashimi and sushi, while off to one side, the dining room has something of a calmer vibe. Small but perfectly formed, the look is modern and clean-lined, with pale-wood or bamboo-panelled walls, and low-slung black lacquered tables and chairs. The menu deals in an appealing range of authentic Japanese cooking given a modern spin, and covers all the bases from sashimi (such as sea bass or turbot) to hand-rolled sushi, inside-out rolls, various tempura (perhaps soft shelled crab), and specials like sea bass goma ankake (deep-fried with a sesame seed crust and vegetable sauce). Desserts shouldn't be overlooked - witness chocolate cake with ginger cream and plum sake jelly.

Chef Sueharu Hamaue **Owner** Hyatt **Times** 12-5/5-10 Closed Xmas, New Year, Sun, L Sat **Prices** Starter £3-£7, Main £8-£29, Dessert £5.50, Service added but optional 12.5% **Wines** 4 bottles over £30, 3 bottles under £30, 9 by glass **Notes** Vegetarian available, Vegetarian menu **Seats** 30 **Parking** NCP London Wall

1901 Restaurant　　　　　　　PLAN 3 H3

◉◉◉ – *see page 267*

Sushisamba London　　　　　　PLAN 3 H2

◉◉ Japanese, Brazilian, Peruvian **NEW**

Trendy Japanese-meets-South American cuisine with capital views

☎ 020 3640 7330
Heron Tower, 110 Bishopsgate EC2N 4AY
e-mail: reservationslondon@sushisamba.com
dir: Nearest station: Liverpool Street. Exit Liverpool Street station, South on Bishopsgate. The Heron Tower is on the left side of the street

While the name announces Sushisamba's Japanese-meets-South-American theme, nothing quite prepares you for the Formula 1 speed of the glass elevator ride to its 38th-floor setting in the Heron building. The view from up here is spectacular, and you can enjoy it (and some seriously good people watching too) from a series of cocktail bars (one on the 39th floor), alfresco terraces and a sushi counter. It's a shame the dining room itself looks east, excluding the capital's most historic landmarks, but the décor is pleasingly sleek and contemporary, with tiled floors, a bamboo-covered high ceiling, unclothed tables and funky leather seating, and the kitchen's Japanese/Brazilian/Peruvian fusion food is dressed to thrill and delicious to eat. The menu is in the all-day grazing style, so you might share some superb green bean tempura with rich and powerful black truffle aïoli to begin, moving on to exquisitely fresh black cod miso from the robata (charcoal grill) served with large, sweet Peruvian corn, or maybe succulent duck breast with tangy sansho pepper vinaigrette.

Times 11.30am-mdnt All-day dining **Prices** Starter £5-£17, Main £8-£49, Dessert £9.50-£12, Service added but optional 12.5% **Notes** Dress restrictions, Smart casual

LONDON EC3

Apex City of London Hotel　　　PLAN 3 H1

◉ Modern European

Smart European flavours in a swanky City hotel

☎ 020 7977 9580 & 0845 365 0002
1 Seething Ln EC3N 4AX
e-mail: addendum@apexhotels.co.uk
web: www.apexhotels.co.uk
dir: Nearest station: Tower Hill. Follow Lower Thames St, left onto Trinity Square, left into Muscovy St, right into Seething Ln, opposite Seething Ln gardens

The Apex Hotel's Addendum Restaurant is a softly-lit contemporary-looking space with floor-to-ceiling windows, sleek oak panelling and tables, charcoal granite flooring, and cream leather seats, all enlivened by splashes of colourful artwork - a smart setting that is clearly a big hit with the suited and booted denizens of the Square Mile. The scene thus set, the kitchen delivers seasonally-attuned, straightforward modern European cooking that aims for all-round satisfaction, based on good quality materials brought together in sensibly reined-in combinations. Bath chap terrine is served with the contrasting flavours of apple and grain mustard sauce, ahead of chicken ballottine with pearl barley and roasted leeks, or there might be hearty satisfaction in the shape of pork faggots with parsnip mash and onion rings. To finish, pistachio puts a creative spin on a well-made crème brûlée, pointed up with a tangy cherry sorbet.

Times 12-2.30/6-10

Caravaggio PLAN 3 H2

◉ Modern Italian

Smart City Italian in former banking hall

☎ 020 7626 6206
107-112 Leadenhall St EC3A 4DP
e-mail: caravaggio@etruscarestaurants.com
web: www.caravaggiorestaurant.co.uk
dir: Nearest station: Aldgate, Fenchurch St. Close to Leadenhall Market & the Lloyd's building

The ornate high ceilings, splendid art-deco light fittings, and a grand staircase sweeping up to a mezzanine gallery certainly add a touch of class to this smart Square Mile Italian in a revamped banking hall. The décor has a retro feel recalling the days of luxurious ocean liners, a theme that finds its reflection in the eclectic mix of classic and contemporary regional Italian cooking. Alongside standard fare such as saffron risotto with fresh seafood, and grilled rib-eye of Argentinian beef with hand-cut chips and béarnaise, there are some interesting options: home-made chestnut maccheroncini with turnip tops and fresh tomato, followed by roasted loin of venison with cavolo nero, potato gratin and cranberry jus. Desserts follow the theme with a panettone tiramisù, or you could go for a savoury finish: mature pecorino sheeps' cheese and a shot of venerable grappa. The vibe is buzzy and service is as slick as the lunchtime City suits.

Chef Faliero Lenta **Owner** Enzo & Piero Quaradeghini **Times** 12-3/6.30-10 Closed Xmas, BHs, Sat-Sun **Prices** Fixed L 2 course £17.50, Starter £7-£12, Main £12.80-£26.50, Dessert £6.20-£12.50, Service added but optional 12.5% **Wines** 113 bottles over £30, 33 bottles under £30, 14 by glass **Notes** Vegetarian available, Dress restrictions, Smart casual **Seats** 150 **Parking** On street

Chamberlains Restaurant PLAN 3 H2

◉◉ Modern British, Seafood

Super-fresh fish in the heart of the City

☎ 020 7648 8690
23-25 Leadenhall Market EC3V 1LR
e-mail: info@chamberlains.org
dir: Nearest station: Bank, Monument

Long-established Billingsgate fishmongers Chamberlain and Thelwell are behind this classy City venture, so no surprises that fish and seafood are its main stock in trade. Spread over three floors and sitting pretty amid the Victorian splendour of Leadenhall Market, Chamberlains buzzes with the power-lunch crowd. There's an all-weather front terrace (beneath the market's glazed roof), while inside huge windows give views over the action from the lively brasserie-like ground floor and mezzanine balcony. Blond-wood floors, red seating, white linen and subtle nautical references keep things light and breezily fashionable. Upstairs there's a more formal room, and a 'chill-out' bar (with a separate menu) hides in the vaulted basement. Sea-fresh seafood is what to expect, with provenance and sourcing rightly to the fore. The menu mixes classics (lobster thermidor or skate wing with brown nut butter) with more modern thinking (wild sea bass with braised oxtail, endive and hazelnut dressing). Some dishes are simply cooked without frills, others a little more intricate, and there's a few meat options too (assiette of lamb, for instance).

Chef Andrew Jones **Owner** Chamberlain & Thelwell **Times** 12-9.30 Closed Xmas, New Year & BHs, Sat-Sun **Prices** Starter £9.50-£16, Main £18.50-£38.50, Dessert £6.50-£11, Service added but optional 12.5% **Wines** 41 bottles over £30, 13 bottles under £30, 11 by glass **Notes** Vegetarian available **Seats** 150, Pr/dining room 65 **Children** Portions

The Perkin Reveller PLAN 5 J6

◉◉ British, Fish NEW

Seasonal British cooking and stunning Thames views

☎ 020 3166 6949
The Wharf, at The Tower of London EC3N 4AB
e-mail: info@perkinreveller.co.uk
dir: Nearest station: Fenchurch Street, Tower Hill. Adjacent to the Tower of London East Gate

Don't be put off by the wacky name (a merry character from Chaucer's *The Cook's Tale*) as this restaurant with show-stopping views of Tower Bridge and the brooding walls of the Tower of London is no touristy pit-stop. Light, contemporary and hard-edged, the glass-walled dining space comes kitted out with solid pale-wood furniture (including long refectory-style tables) set on dark slate-tiled flooring. Of its two bars, one is located in the adjoining tower gatehouse, with its haunting, romantic atmosphere. The kitchen's not stuck in the past though, instead celebrating modern British cooking of flair and panache with a light touch, fashioned from premium seasonal produce. Well-dressed plates might take in signature salt marsh lamb three ways (succulent rump, melt-in-the-mouth slow-cooked shoulder, and crisp fried tongue) served with swede fondant, while desserts could deliver a light, moist carrot cake teamed with marmalade ice cream. The outdoor terrace is a must on a sunny day, and the place is also open for breakfast and afternoon tea.

Chef Andrew Donovan **Owner** Historic Royal Palaces **Times** 11.30-3.30/5.30-10.30 **Prices** Fixed L 2 course £15, Starter £2-£8.50, Main £12.50-£28, Dessert £6, Service added but optional 12.5% **Notes** Sunday L **Parking** City Quay, Arch

Prism Brasserie and Bar PLAN 3 H2

◉◉ Modern European

Accomplished brasserie cooking in the City

☎ 020 7256 3888
147 Leadenhall St EC3V 4QT
e-mail: prism.events@harveynichols.com
dir: Nearest station: Bank, Monument. Take exit 4 from Bank tube station, 5 mins walk

The grand surroundings of the former Bank of New York bring a touch of style and class to this fashionable Harvey Nichols' heart-of-the-City outpost. Soaring Doric columns and lofty decorative ceilings sit alongside fashionable red leather chairs, white-clothed tables, striking flower displays and mood artwork to deliver a touch of colour to the dining quarter's lunching bankers and brokers. The large bar area comes with low-slung matching seating and a baby grand piano that hints at more relaxed evening service. The versatile brasserie menu covers all the bases, with the kitchen's fresh, clean-flavoured, modern approach driven by top-notch produce, including ingredients from their own rooftop kitchen garden. Pot-roasted duck breast, for example, served with forestière potatoes, steamed curly kale and pan juices, or from the grill, 50-day dry-aged Longhorn rib-eye. For dessert, perhaps prune and almond tart served with prune and Armagnac ice cream.

Times 11.30-3/6-10 Closed Xmas, BHs, Sat-Sun

LONDON EC3 *continued*

Restaurant Sauterelle PLAN 3 G2

@@ Modern European

Confident contemporary cooking in landmark building

☎ 020 7618 2483
The Royal Exchange EC3V 3LR
e-mail: pierrem@danddlondon.com
dir: Nearest station: Bank. In heart of business centre.
Bank tube station exit 3

Sitting beneath glazed arches on the mezzanine floor of the magnificent Royal Exchange, classy Sauterelle certainly has 'wow factor', its best tables looking down on the inner courtyard glistening with high-end jewellers, boutiques and the bustle of the Grand Café below. All carpeted comfort, white linen and modern tub-style chairs or banquettes, the intimate space is lined with wine racks at one end and has an open kitchen 'window' at the other. The vibe is chic, the service slickly professional, and the wines speak with a strong French accent. Avignon-born chef Arnaud Delannay's cooking is inspired by his southern French roots and delivers a light, contemporary touch, clean, fresh flavours and well-dressed presentation. Witness a signature starter of sea-fresh Orkney Isle scallops teamed with a perfectly balanced accompaniment of curried cauliflower purée, sauce vièrge and micro basil, or a main-event top-notch venison haunch of full-on flavour, served with braised red cabbage, celeriac purée and saffron poached quince.

Times 12-2.30/6-10 Closed BHs, Sat-Sun

LONDON EC4

Barbecoa PLAN 3 F2

@ Modern

Jamie's bbq joint

☎ 020 3005 8555
20 New Change Passage EC4M 9AG
dir: Nearest station: St Paul's. Opposite St Paul's Cathedral

Expect a buzzy, vibrant atmosphere, a stylishly cool interior, stunning views of St Paul's Cathedral, and some top-notch meat at Jamie Oliver and Adam Perry Lang's barbecue steakhouse in the City. Cooking by fire, smoke and charcoal is the central theme here, which means robata grills, tandoor ovens and Texan smokers among other bits of snazzy kit. The flames and smoke from the semi-open kitchen add a touch of theatre in the first-floor restaurant, where floor-to-ceiling windows offer great views of the cathedral. The meat comes directly from the farm and is prepared in the downstairs butchery, with beef being hung on-site for five to eleven weeks. Tuck into a plate of Lyme Bay crab with avocado, chervil and tomato before the main event, perhaps lamb chops from the wood oven, served with butter beans and Swiss chard, or dry-aged sirloin steak from the grill with a cep and rosemary cream.

Times 11.30-11

Bread Street Kitchen PLAN 3 F2

@@ Modern British, European ✋

Vibrant, city-cool brasserie from the Gordon Ramsay stable

☎ 020 3030 4050
10 Bread St EC4M 9AJ
e-mail: info@breadstreetkitchen.com
dir: Nearest station: Mansion House

From Gordon Ramsay Holdings comes Bread Street Kitchen, an ambitious, 230-cover, two-floored space at the One New Change shopping mall in the City. It's an open-all-day joint, rather cool, with a high-octane, industrial warehouse look - very New York with a pinch of art deco. And, at a reputed cost of £5m, it's a good job it looks good. With gantries, creative lighting (dangling retro-glass lampshades and an army of angle-poises), black-and-white floor tiles and leather banquettes, BSK makes an impression. The first-floor level is a long, large-windowed room with an open theatre kitchen stretching its length, while above there's an eye-catching balconied wine gallery. The kitchen turns out quick-fire dishes from a lengthy all-day roster (including breakfast weekdays); take salmon céviche with ruby grapefruit, jalapeño, lime and coriander from the 'raw bar', perhaps slow-roasted Dingley Dell pork belly with spiced apple sauce from the 'wood stone' oven, or Herdwick mutton and potato pie (with Worcestershire sauce) from the 'hot kitchen'. Do factor in the necessity for side orders and some very light portioning, though good cocktails, global wines and an army of staff keep things on track.

Chef Erion Karaj **Owner** Gordon Ramsay Holdings
Times 11-3/5.30-11 **Prices** Starter £7.50-£15, Main £12.50-£43, Dessert £7-£10, Service added but optional 12.5% **Notes** Late L menu available Mon-Sat 3-5.30pm, Vegetarian available, Dress restrictions, Casual **Seats** 275 **Children** Portions, Menu

The Chancery PLAN 3 D2

@@ Modern British, French

Intimate, fine-tuned dining in legal land

☎ 020 7831 4000
9 Cursitor St EC4A 1LL
e-mail: reservations@thechancery.co.uk
dir: Nearest station: Chancery Lane. Situated between High Holborn and Fleet St, just off Chancery Ln

A bijou, understated outfit secreted away in the heart of lawyerland, the aptly named Chancery is a sharp-suited yet unstuffy affair. Effortlessly urbane and dressed as smartly as its clientele with mellow pastel shades, polished-wood floors, white linen, fashionable leather seating, mirrors and modern abstract art, there are two intimate dining rooms on the ground floor and an even cosier eating area in the basement. Alice Churchill's kitchen deals in immaculately presented, inventive modern European dishes such as a starter of seared tuna (accurately timed) with crispy tempura squid, chilli, ginger and spring onions. Mains might turn to the Mediterranean for inspiration, as in roast cod teamed

with a stuffed courgette flower, chorizo and heritage tomatoes, or perhaps there might be a more classic roasted rump of new season lamb served with crisp sweetbreads and navarin of baby vegetables. A richly indulgent Amedei mousse with ginger, kumquats and marmalade ice cream hits the spot at dessert. A considered wine list with several by the glass options rounds off a class act.

Times 12-2.30/6-10.30 Closed Xmas, Sun, L Sat

Chinese Cricket Club PLAN 3 E1

@ Chinese V

Classy Chinese in a modern City hotel

☎ 020 7438 8051
Crowne Plaza London - The City, 19 New Bridge St EC4V 6DB
e-mail: loncy.ccc@ihg.com
dir: Nearest station: Temple, St Paul's, Blackfriars. Opposite Blackfriars underground (exit 8)

Named after the four-year-old Chinese national cricket team, this restaurant is one of two in the Crowne Plaza London City hotel (see also entry for Diciannove). Cooking-themed images of rural China adorn the neutral modern space, along with plenty of cricket memorabilia and Chinese calligraphy prints. Well-paced service is delivered by smartly dressed staff who are happy to explain the predominantly Szechuan menu, where traditional dishes sit comfortably alongside more contemporary imaginings. You might start with a beautifully balanced hot and sour soup, or prawn and pork sui mai from the dim sum section, before diced chicken with ginger, scallions and sesame, or a signature dish like crispy orange beef or fried perch with garlic chives. Desserts, chawan mushi (steamed egg custard) aside, are more European - try banana toffee cake, or hot chocolate pudding. Various set menus, including a vegetarian version and a chef's tasting menu supplement the carte.

Chef Guanghao Wu **Owner** Blackfriars hotel group
Times 12-2.30/6-10 Closed Xmas & Etr, L 10 Jan
Prices Tasting menu fr £25, Service added but optional 12.5% **Wines** 10 by glass **Notes** Vegetarian menu, Civ Wed 160 **Seats** 65 **Parking** On street

Diciannove PLAN 3 E1

@ Italian

Elegant Italian dining in the City

☎ 020 7438 8052 & 7438 8055
Crowne Plaza London - The City, 19 New Bridge St EC4V 6DB
e-mail: ciao@diciannove19.com
web: www.diciannove19.com
dir: Nearest station: Blackfriars. On New Bridge St, opposite Blackfriars underground (exit 8)

Formerly Giorgio Locatelli's Refettorio, the renamed and relaunched Diciannove in the Crowne Plaza hotel is a masculine, minimalist environment where the deal is slick yet simple Italian cooking prepared from carefully sourced ingredients. Dark wood, sparkling glassware, low-level lighting and booth seating set the tone, and there's a cool bar backlit in yellow where you can perch on a leather stool and take in the atmosphere before dinner. Start with a fresh and flavoursome dish of grilled prawns, rocket leaves, pine kernels and tomatoes - a suitably light option that should leave you room for the home-made pasta: perhaps tagliatelle with beef and pork ragout, or pumpkin filled tortelli with sage, amaretto and butter sauce. Next you might go for calves' liver, braised white onions, pine nuts and raisins, finishing with amaretto parfait with an intense chocolate sauce.

Chef Alessandro Bay **Owner** Crowne Plaza
Times 12-2.30/6-10.30 Closed Xmas, 24-30 Jan, Etr & BHs, Sun, L Sat **Prices** Prices not confirmed Service added but optional 12.5% **Wines** 12 by glass **Notes** Pretheatre D menu £25, Bi-monthly seasonal menu from £35, Vegetarian available, Dress restrictions, Smart casual, Civ Wed 160 **Seats** 100, Pr/dining room 33 **Children** Portions **Parking** NCP - Queen Victoria St

Lutyens Restaurant   PLAN 3 E2

◎◎ Modern European 🍷 NOTABLE WINE LIST 🍷

Accomplished modern brasserie cooking in stylish setting

☎ 020 7583 8385
85 Fleet St EC4Y 1AE
e-mail: info@lutyens-restaurant.com
dir: Nearest station: Chancery Lane, St Pauls, Blackfriars. Adjacent to St Bride's Church

In the shadow of St Bride's Church, this stylish outfit occupies an elegant Lutyens-designed building that was once home to Reuters and the Press Association. These days its coolly sophisticated interior - pastel tones, pale wood, white linen and towering floral displays - bears the Conran stamp, and the multi-faceted space encompasses a restaurant, all-day bar up front (serving breakfasts from 7.30am), raw bar (for oysters, tartares, carpaccios and céviche) and, in the basement, private dining rooms and a members' club. Chef Henrik Ritzen's cooking is rooted in classic French technique but with a suitably light and sophisticated modern touch. A simple and elegant starter of slow-cooked hen's egg with girolles and lardons shows the style, as does main-course monkfish, clams, samphire and broad beans - a winning dish full of fresh flavours, accurately cooked and stylishly presented. Dessert could be a classic lemon soufflé with the added bonus of some raspberry ripple ice cream and a raspberry Madeleine. Superb breads are freshly baked, and the wine list is an absolute corker.

Chef Henrik Ritzen **Owner** Peter Prescott & Terence & Vicki Conran **Times** 12-3/6-10 Closed Xmas & BHs, Sat-Sun **Prices** Fixed L 2 course fr £22, Fixed D 3 course fr £26, Starter £8-£19, Main £14-£36, Dessert £6-£9, Service added but optional 12.5% **Wines** 514 bottles over £30, 37 bottles under £30, 40 by glass **Notes** Vegetarian available **Seats** 120, Pr/dining room 26 **Children** Portions

28-50 Wine Workshop   PLAN 3 D2
& Kitchen

◎◎ French, European 🍷

Serious about wine, serious about food

☎ 020 7242 8877
140 Fetter Ln EC4A 1BT
e-mail: info@2850.co.uk
dir: Nearest station: Chancery Lane. At the bottom of Fetter Ln, close to the corner of Fleet St

Wine steals the show at 28-50, the digits referencing the latitude range within which the world's vineyards are planted. It's a relaxed, uptempo basement affair (from the team behind Texture - see entry) and comes kitted out in a dark-green colour scheme, with wine the theme at every turn (displays of bottles, pictures, corks and boxes). Floorboards, exposed brick, porthole mirrors and knowledgeable service add to the on-cue vibe. Simple French bistro-inspired fare is the name of the game, wrought from premium produce and accessibly priced. Witness succulent rump of lamb served with panisse (chick pea fritter), exemplary ratatouille and basil, or perhaps top-dollar sirloin (28-day aged US grain-fed beef) teamed with braised shallots, watercress and classic béarnaise. And then there are the fairly priced wines, with 30 served by the glass, carafe or bottle on the every-day selection. Alternatively, take your pick from the Collector's List with some starry vintages and more wallet-busting prices. (There's a second branch in Marylebone and another about to open as we go to print in Mayfair.)

Chef Paul Walsh **Owner** Xavier Rousset, Agnar Sverrisson **Times** 12-2.30/6-9.30 Closed Xmas, New Year, BHs, Sat-Sun **Prices** Starter £6.50-£8.50, Main £10.95-£16.95, Dessert £4.50-£8.50, Service added but optional 12.5% **Wines** 65 bottles over £30, 15 bottles under £30, 30 by glass **Notes** Lunch menu 2 course £15.95 **Seats** 60, Pr/dining room 12 **Parking** NCP

Vanilla Black   PLAN 3 D2

◎◎ Modern Vegetarian V 🍷

Classy vegetarian cookery in a hidden London location

☎ 020 7242 2622
17-18 Tooks Court EC4A 1LB
e-mail: vanillablack@btconnect.com
dir: Nearest station: Chancery Lane. Exit 4 from Chancery Lane tube station. 2nd left into Chancery Ln, left into Cursitor St, left into Tooks Court

Andrew Dargue and Donna Conroy's upscale vegetarian restaurant is to be found in an almost hidden location down a side street near Chancery Lane, but the venue itself is expansive and spacious, its clean modern design overlaid with echoes of art deco. There's a good deal of excitement around British vegetarian gastronomy these days, and here's why: interesting, innovative dishes that combine high-quality ingredients, up-to-the-minute technique and a sound approach to texture and flavour contrasts. A brace of Yukon Gold potato cakes start a meal off boldly, gaining plenty of savoury depth from

their garnishes of smoked mayonnaise, pickled cucumber ketchup, vinegar dust and crisps. On offer for main may be something strongly redolent of bracing seaside air - seared seaweed, cabbage and pickled potatoes, with soda bread sauce and seaside veg. If something cheesy appeals, try a winning combination of celery pannacotta and blue Wensleydale profiteroles, with charred celery and carrots in a precisely and distinctively flavoured apple sauce. The inventiveness doesn't stop there - how about white chocolate and cep tart with a cornflake cake, picpoul wine sorbet and fried tarragon?

Chef Andrew Dargue **Owner** Andrew Dargue & Donna Conroy **Times** 12-2.30/6-10 Closed 2wks Xmas & New Year, BH Mons, Sun, L Sat **Prices** Fixed L 2 course £18.50, Fixed D 3 course £35, Service added but optional 12.5% **Wines** 10 by glass **Notes** Vegetarian menu **Seats** 45 **Children** Portions **Parking** On street (metered) or NCP

The White Swan Pub   PLAN 3 D3
& Dining Room

◎ Modern British

City gastro-pub with classy first-floor restaurant

☎ 020 7242 9696
108 Fetter Ln EC4A 1ES
e-mail: info@thewhiteswanlondon.com
dir: Nearest station: Chancery Lane. Fetter Lane runs parallel with Chancery Lane

In fair weather, this smart Holborn pub - sibling of The Gun (see entry) - is picked out by the throng of after-work drinkers pitched up on the pavement outside. The remodelled character panelled bar comes complete with boars' heads and deer antlers mounted on the walls, plus a mezzanine balcony from which to take in the action below. The bar offers more traditional sustenance, while the dapper top-floor dining room is the place to head to for the main culinary action. It's a bright, fashionable room with windows on two sides, a mirrored ceiling, modern leather seating, white linen-clad tables and a patterned-wood floor. The kitchen delivers appropriately modern, well-flavoured dishes with an eye on presentation: witness pan-fried tranche of lemon sole with razor clam, samphire, fennel gratin and clam velouté, or perhaps herb-crusted loin of Herdwick mutton teamed with grilled tongue, violet artichoke, glazed carrots and garlic purée. Check out the sophisticated wine list.

Times 12-3/6-10 Closed Xmas, New Year, BHs, Sat-Sun (except private parties)

LONDON N1

Almeida Restaurant
PLAN 1 F4

French

Honest French cooking opposite the theatre

☎ 020 7354 4777

30 Almeida St, Islington N1 1AD
e-mail: almeida-reservations@danddlondon.com
dir: Nearest station: Angel, Highbury & Islington. Turn right from station, along Upper St, past church

A little walk from the hustle and bustle of Islington's busy centre rewards with good honest French food in a contemporary setting. The eponymous theatre is opposite. In the airy room, dressed in fashionable contemporary neutrality, large windows look out onto the street where parasols are set along the pavement for eating outside in the warmer months. White linen tablecloths adorn the tables at the back of the space, whilst up front is a tad less formal; both areas, though, hum with a heartfelt Gallic bonhomie. The food carries its French allegiances lightly, with some standout seasonal British ingredients taking centre stage. Cornish crab ravioli comes with buttered lettuce and beurre blanc in a well-crafted first course, followed by Denham Estate venison à la bourguignon with gratin dauphinoise which is brim full of flavour. Finish with a textbook crème brûlée à la vanille and a warm madeleine.

Times 12-2.30/5.30-11 Closed 26 Dec, 1 Jan, L Mon, D Sun

The Drapers Arms
PLAN 1 F4

British

Real gastro-pub serving no-nonsense modern British food

☎ 020 7619 0348

44 Barnsbury St N1 1ER
e-mail: info@thedrapersarms.com
dir: Nearest station: Highbury & Islington, Angel. Just off Upper St, situated between Angel/Highbury & Islington tube stations, opposite town hall

The handsome, Georgian-era Drapers Arms is an inviting neighbourhood pub, tucked away in a leafy, upscale residential quarter of Islington. With real ales on hand-pump, a well-chosen wine list (with an admirable by-glass and carafe selection) and a kitchen that cuts its cloth on truly seasonal ingredients delivered via a daily-changing menu, the Drapers certainly earns the 'gastro-pub' billing so inappropriately used by many other pubs. A light-filled, u-shaped bar with high ceilings and tall windows, scuffed floorboards and retro furniture creates a relaxed environment in which to enjoy the no-nonsense, gutsy British food, such as pigeon and prune pie, bream with cockles, samphire and tarragon butter, or, following the Glorious Twelfth, roast grouse with pâté, toast and blackberries. Puddings, likewise, take the comfort route - maybe a buttermilk pudding with raspberries. Lighter bar snacks are available too, and there's a great little courtyard garden for those sunnier days.

Times 12-3.30/6-10

Fifteen London - The Restaurant
PLAN 3 G5

Modern British

Turning lives around by means of vibrant seasonal cooking

☎ 020 3375 1515

15 Westland Place N1 7LP
dir: Nearest station: Old Street. Exit 1 from Old Street tube station, walk up City Rd, opposite Moorfields Eye Hospital

Sailing into its second decade of operations, the original incarnation of Jamie Oliver's philanthropic restaurant enterprise continues to draw in the punters, though with a completely new look and style. The former warehouse has been completely refurbished to give it more of a neighbourhood vibe, there's a new head chef in place, and gone is the Italian menu and instead the deal is a range of smaller and larger plates for sharing, all based on prime seasonal ingredients and delivering big, fresh flavours. So you might start with devilled egg and smoked anchovy, duck ham and quince, or beef and barley buns and horseradish, moving on to cockles, pig's cheek, butterbeans and laver bread, and braised lamb shoulder with purple sprouting broccoli and new season garlic. The place still continues in its original purpose though - to take in young unemployed people and prepare them for a career in the kitchen - so you can feel good about yourself as you feast on rotisserie Norfolk chicken with violet artichokes and lovage mayo.

Times 12-2.45/6.30-9.30 Closed 25 Dec, 1 Jan, L 26 Dec

Frederick's Restaurant
PLAN 1 F4

Modern British

Popular dining spot among Islington's antique shops

☎ 020 7359 2888

106-110 Islington High St, Camden Passage, Islington N1 8EG
e-mail: dine@fredericks.co.uk
dir: Nearest station: Angel. From underground 2 mins walk to Camden Passage. Restaurant among the antique shops

Built in 1789 as a pub, and rebuilt in 1834, Frederick's has been a stalwart of the Islington dining scene since the late 1960s and is still going strong. It's an attractive space, its brick walls hung with abstracts; a recent addition has been the Club Room, a contemporary private dining room. Its appeal lies in its broadly based menu and consistently high-quality cooking. Straightforwardly pleasing starters might take in crab and avocado salad with cucumber jelly, and prawns fried with garlic butter. Among main courses, monkfish gets the bourguignon treatment, served with Charlotte potatoes, while in season may come roast breast of guinea fowl with an onion tart, pepper and cumin purée and purple-sprouting broccoli. Chocoholics could end with rich chocolate fondant cut by cinnamon ice cream, while others could go for something like three ways with rhubarb.

Chef Adam Hilliard **Owner** Nick Segal
Times 12-2.30/5.45-11.30 Closed Xmas, New Year, BHs, Sun (ex functions) **Prices** Fixed L 2 course fr £15.50, Fixed D 3 course fr £19.50, Starter £6.50-£14.50, Main £15-£30, Dessert £5.50-£8.50, Service added but optional 12.5% **Wines** 25 by glass **Notes** Vegetarian available **Seats** 150, Pr/dining room 50 **Children** Portions, Menu **Parking** NCP Business Design Centre

Trullo
PLAN 1 F4

Italian

The epitome of a true neighbourhood Italian in North London

☎ 020 7226 2733

300-302 St Paul's Rd N1 2LH
e-mail: enquiries@trullorestaurant.com
dir: Nearest station: Highbury & Islington

Look for the black awning of this neat little glass-fronted Italian, inauspiciously tucked away amongst the jumble of shops just off Highbury Corner roundabout. An effortlessly likeable and popular outfit, Trullo serves up honest, affordable Italian food and wine. Simply decked out with darkwood floors, white walls, low-hanging lights, closely set wooden tables with paper cloths and an open kitchen, the place feels every inch a classic Italian trattoria. The seasonally focused, daily-changing and commendably short menu puts the emphasis on flavour, with well-sourced ingredients (including some lesser-used cuts) treated with respect and minimal fuss, while fresh hand-made pasta and the charcoal grill provide the kitchen's main thrust. Witness big-hearted pappardelle with beef shin ragu or ravioli of calves' brains and cime di rapa with sage butter, or from the grill, perhaps line-caught sea bass served with castelluccio lentils and salsa rossa. End on a similarly authentic note with Amalfi lemon tart or vanilla and caramel pannacotta.

Chef Tim Siadatan **Owner** Jordan Frieda, Tim Siadatan
Times 12.30-2.30/6-10.30 Closed 25 Dec-3 Jan, D Sun **Prices** Fixed L 2 course £12, Starter £6.50-£9, Main £14-£17, Dessert £4.50-£9, Service optional, Groups min 7 service 12.5% **Wines** 40 bottles over £30, 11 bottles under £30, 11 by glass **Notes** Large table menus available £25-£45, Sunday L £30, Vegetarian available **Seats** 40, Pr/dining room 35 **Children** Portions **Parking** On street

LONDON NW1

La Collina   PLAN 1 E4

Italian

A taste of Italy in pretty Primrose Hill

☎ 020 7483 0192
17 Princess Rd, Chalk Farm NW1 8JR
e-mail: info@lacollinarestaurant.co.uk
dir: Nearest station: Chalk Farm, Camden Town

At La Collina the cooking is as authentic as anyone could reasonably ask for, while amiable Italian staff add an extra layer of Latin feel to this smart neighbourhood venue. A recent refurb has kept the pared-back interior at the top of its game with the addition of a new bar; there's a pleasing simplicity to the place - whitewashed walls, stripped wood floors - which spreads itself through a ground-floor room and a pint-sized basement where you can watch the culinary action in the open kitchen. The homespun regional Italian cooking produces quality, ingredient-led dishes with the odd modern interjection. Typical starters run to salt cod with pepper and anchovy sauce, then look to the specials for home-made ravioli stuffed with pheasant and partridge, served with game jus. On the carte might be salt-baked sea bass with spinach, or chicken paillard with salad and roast potatoes. The all-Italian wines add to the appeal.

Chef Diana Rinaldo **Owner** Patrick Oberto, Diana Rinaldo **Times** 12-3/6-11 Closed Xmas wk, L Mon **Prices** Prices not confirmed Service added but optional 12.5% **Wines** 25 bottles over £30, 20 bottles under £30, 7 by glass **Notes** Vegetarian available, Dress restrictions, Smart casual **Seats** 40 **Children** Portions **Parking** Free on street after 6pm & weekends

The Gilbert Scott   PLAN 3 B5

British

Nostalgic cooking that trumpets the best of British

☎ 020 7278 3888
Renaissance St Pancras Hotel, Euston Rd NW1 2AR
e-mail: reservations@thegilbertscott.co.uk
dir: Nearest station: St Pancras. On Euston Rd at front of St Pancras Station

The rebirth of what was once the Midland Grand Hotel in St Pancras station has not lacked for media attention, and if you want to see what the whole shebang looks like after £200 million, give or take, pull up a chair in The Gilbert Scott restaurant. GS himself was the Victorian architect who oversaw the building of the whole Gothic-revival fantasy pile, and he would surely have felt at home with both the clubby grandeur of the cavernous dining room's soaring plasterwork ceilings, gilt mirrors and claret-hued, buttoned banquettes, and Marcus Wareing's nostalgic take on the heritage cooking of old time England. The menu covers a lot of ground and makes for a good read with intriguing listings such as Dorset snail and chicken pie, soles in coffins, and 'tweed kettle'. What turns up on the plate is all very appealing, starting with nettle and watercress soup with confit egg yolk and crème fraîche, followed by rump and breast of

Cumbrian spring lamb teamed with broad beans and minted yoghurt. For pudding, it's playtime with a quirkily entertaining orange marmalade Jaffa cake with Earl Grey ice cream.

Chef Nick Ward **Owner** Marcus Wareing **Times** 12-3/5.30-11 **Prices** Fixed L 2 course fr £19, Fixed D 3 course fr £23, Starter £7-£13.50, Main £14-£32, Dessert £6.50-£8.50, Service added but optional 12.5% **Wines** 200 bottles over £30, 2 bottles under £30, 17 by glass **Notes** Sunday L, Vegetarian available **Seats** 110, Pr/dining room 20 **Children** Portions **Parking** 12, NCP St Pancras

Gilgamesh Restaurant Lounge   PLAN 1 E4

Pan-Asian

Pan-Asian dishes in a psychedelic re-creation of ancient Babylon (in Camden)

☎ 020 7482 5757 & 7428 4922
The Stables Market, Chalk Farm Rd NW1 8AH
e-mail: reservations@gilgameshbar.com
dir: Nearest station: Chalk Farm, Camden Town. Stables Market on Chalk Farm Rd, next to Camden Lock. Entrance by Camden Lock Place (off Chalk Farm Road) close to railway Bridge

First the red carpet treatment, then an escalator to transport you up above Camden's riotous Stables Market to the gargantuan Gilgamesh might seem over-the-top, but then the mind-boggling themed interiors are inspired by the legendary excesses of Babylon. Think hand-carved wooden furniture, extravagant fabrics, a lapis lazuli inlaid 50-metre bar, ornate walls of beaten bronze panels, marble pillars, palm trees, vast windows and nightclub-esque psychedelic lighting. When it comes to the cooking, it's by no means exotic imagery over substance, with Ian Pengelley's menus inspired by the food halls of Asia and confidently covering all the bases from sushi and sashimi (prepared by Japanese chefs) or tempura to Chinese dim sum, Thai green chicken curry, Malaysian beef Penang or hoba miso Chilean sea bass. East meets west at dessert in something like a chocolate and lemongrass brûlée with exotic sorbet, while Asian-inspired cocktails, sake and well-selected wines keep everyone in high spirits.

Times 12-2.30/6-mdnt

Karpo   PLAN 3 B5

Modern European, British

Funky all-day restaurant serving up seasonal flavours

☎ 020 7843 2221
23-27 Euston Rd, St Pancras NW1 2SD
e-mail: info@karpo.co.uk
dir: Nearest station: King's Cross, St Pancras

Named in honour of the Greek goddess of the fruits of the earth, there's a good deal of modernity on show here, not least at the front of the building (the Megaro Hotel) which is covered in vivid graffiti-style artwork. It's easy to spot at any rate, just opposite St Pancras International station. And it is suitably modern and funky on the inside,

too: a mix of contemporary furnishings, colourful artworks, a 'living wall' of plants, and a mixture of canteen-style benches and tables, plus counter dining and an open kitchen. It's a relaxed, easygoing place, with friendly staff and food available all day. The menu shows no particular international allegiances, but is more British than anything else, with the available seasonal produce rightly leading the way. Start with flame-grilled mackerel with oyster and cucumber, before a main course such as Herdwick lamb with pickled carrots and sheep's cheese, with Cox's apple crumble and clotted cream for dessert.

Chef Joe Sharratt **Owner** Antonio Megaro **Times** 12-11 All-day dining **Prices** Fixed L 2 course £15, Fixed D 3 course £25-£30, Starter £6-£10, Main £12-£18, Dessert £4-£6, Service added but optional 12.5% **Wines** 10 by glass **Notes** Sunday L, Vegetarian available **Seats** 140, Pr/dining room 36 **Children** Portions **Parking** On street

Meliá White House   PLAN 2 H4

Spanish, Mediterranean

Ambitious Spanish cooking in an art-deco hotel

☎ 020 7391 3000
Albany St, Regent's Park NW1 3UP
e-mail: melia.white.house@melia.com
dir: Nearest station: Great Portland St, Regent's Park, Warren St. Opposite Gt Portland St underground station

Close to Regent's Park, and an easy stroll from Oxford Street, the Iberian-owned art-deco hotel pays homage to its national cuisine in the elegant fine-dining Spanish restaurant, L'Albufera. It is a glossy space, all polished wooden floors, black-clothed tables and cream upholstered chairs as a backdrop to vibrant cooking that straddles both traditional and modern Spanish schools. Materials are sourced from the homeland for maximum authenticity, so Serrano ham is carved from a trolley, and there are tapas dishes - crab croquettes, or cod tongues in pilpil sauce with shiitaki mushrooms, say - if that's the route you want to take, otherwise you might start with in-house-smoked sea trout with marinated baby beetroot and citrus dressing, then move on to slow-cooked turbot in a crab crust with fondant potatoes and fennel consommé. For dessert, a mojito could be deconstructed as brown rum parfait with mint sorbet and lime foam, or finish instead with exemplary Spanish cheeses served with figs and tarragon oil.

Chef Gines Lorente Barcelona **Owner** Melia White House (Biosphere Hotel Co) **Times** 7-10.30 Closed Sun, BHs, L all week **Prices** Fixed D 3 course fr £30, Tasting menu £30, Starter £7.50-£17, Main £16.50-£19.50, Dessert £6, Service added but optional 12.5% **Wines** 12 bottles under £30, 21 by glass **Notes** Buffet L only available daily in The Place, Vegetarian available, Dress restrictions, Smart casual, Civ Wed 180 **Seats** 62, Pr/dining room 12 **Children** Portions, Menu **Parking** On street

LONDON NW1 *continued*

Michael Nadra Primrose Hill   PLAN 1 E4

@@ Modern European NEW 🌱

Classy modern food, with surroundings to match, by the canal

☎ 020 7722 2800 & 7722 2809
42 Gloucester Av NW1 8JD
e-mail: primrose@restaurant-michaelnadra.co.uk
dir: Nearest station: Chalk Farm, Camden Town. 5 mins walk along the Regent's Canal from Camden Market

Chef-patron Michael Nadra made his name in Chiswick before branching out with this second, more ambitious canal-side venue in leafy Primrose Hill. Scoring high in the cool stakes, the interior ranges over different levels, with a martini bar at its centre, along with a subterranean vaulted-and-cobbled area (formerly a tunnel for barge horses), and there's a terrace for alfresco dining. Dark slate floors, fashionable leather seating, exposed brick and large windows all add up to some seriously good looks, while service is slickly professional but friendly. The cooking fits the contemporary style of the place: light, clean, bold-flavoured, skilful dishes that aren't overworked and allow prime ingredients to sing. Combinations are creative and everything is founded in well-honed classical technique. Thinly sliced roast rib-eye with cauliflower purée, rocket, parmesan and truffle jus is a starter that's big on flavour, and might be followed by

succulent lamb rump teamed with sautéed sweetbreads, swede fondant, Savoy cabbage and cracking rosemary jus. A first-class fishy alternative could be grilled halibut accompanied by sautéed scallops, celeriac purée, truffled leeks and bisque sauce. If you can't wait 20 minutes for a classic apple tarte Tatin finale, go for wobbly vanilla pannacotta perfection.

Chef Michael Nadra **Owner** Michael Nadra
Times 12-2.30/6-10.30 Closed 24 Dec, 1 Jan **Prices** Fixed L 2 course £14-£27, Fixed D 3 course £32-£47, Tasting menu £49-£81, Starter £8-£12, Main £18-£25, Dessert £6-£10, Service added but optional 12.5% **Wines** 150 bottles over £30, 25 bottles under £30, 16 by glass **Notes** Fixed D 2/3 course £18-23 Mon-Sat, Tasting menu whole table, Sunday L, Vegetarian available **Seats** 100, Pr/dining room 40 **Children** Portions **Parking** On street

Odette's Restaurant & Bar   PLAN 1 E4

@@@ *– see below*

Pullman London St Pancras   PLAN 3 A5

@ Modern European, International NEW

International menu in a contemporary railway hotel

☎ 020 7666 9000 & 7666 9038
100-110 Euston Rd NW1 2AJ
e-mail: h5309@accor.com
web: www.accorhotels.com/5309
dir: Nearest station: King's Cross, Euston, St Pancras Int. 3 min walk from St Pancras International. Hotel adjacent to the British Library

The hotel is ideally placed to receive weary travellers debouching from the Eurostar at St Pancras International, five minutes off. A major refurbishment has generally glitzed things up, though the main restaurant has gone for the anonymous feel of an astronautical control centre, with grey seating at regulation-spaced tables and dark nets screening the street view. The global menu is flagged with international wine suggestions for each dish, and the neatly presented items encompass enjoyable risotto nero with ink and flesh of chargrilled calamari, sautéed skate with roast beets in beurre noisette, and Josper-grilled rib-eye with hefty pont-neuf chips and vigorously seasoned portobello mushroom. 'Timeless Specialities' include a beef and oyster pie made with ox cheek, smoked oysters and caramelised onions in puff pastry. A slim slice of Valrhôna chocolate tart served warm is nicely contrasted with a scoop of milky ice

---

Odette's Restaurant & Bar

LONDON NW1   **PLAN 1 E4**

Modern British V

Confident modern British cooking in a long-standing neighbourhood restaurant

☎ 020 7586 8569
130 Regent's Park Rd NW1 8XL
e-mail: info@odettesprimrosehill.com
dir: Nearest station: Chalk Farm

If ever there were an obvious restaurant du quartier in the leafy reaches of north London, it would have to be Odette's. With quiet persistence and continuity, it has been a local beacon since the late 1970s, discreetly going its own way amid the raging riptides of London food fashion, sailing on to the delight not just of Primrose Hill's cognoscenti, but to many from further afield. The place has never shied away from opening itself up to the

elements, and as well as the tables out front, there is a wonderful garden at the back with properly clothed tables and cushioned seating, the next best thing to picnicking in the big city. Bryn Williams has been a foodie since his Welsh childhood and has racked up a starry CV working with the likes of Marco Pierre White, Michel Roux Jr and Chris Galvin. What he offers here is the best kind of modern British cooking, making much of the Welsh materials of his own heritage (mutton, beef, farmhouse cheeses and bara brith), in menu formats that encourage experimentation, including six-course tasters in both omni and veggie versions. Seafood is treated with confident verve, enfolding crayfish into a little starter 'lasagne' with Chinese-style salt-and-pepper squid and shellfish sauce, while Cornish mackerel acquires its traditional sharpness of focus through the less traditional elements of poached rhubarb, apple and hazelnuts. That Welsh mutton may appear in dual guise, as roast loin and hotpot, with shallots, capers and mint, while a Gascon note resounds in a main of roast duck breast with confit

gizzards and sweet-and-sour beetroot. A soft landing is provided at meal's end by a pistachio cake that comes with caramelised apple and Calvados cream, or lemon meringue parfait with blueberries in lemongrass syrup.

Chef Bryn Williams **Owner** Bryn Williams
Times 12-2.30/6-10.30 Closed 25-26 Dec, 1 Jan **Prices** Fixed L 2 course £17-£22, Fixed D 3 course £25, Tasting menu fr £50, Starter £6-£9, Main £16-£22, Dessert £8-£10, Service added but optional 12.5% **Wines** 36 bottles over £30, 16 bottles under £30, 16 by glass **Notes** Fixed D 2/3 course 6-7pm, Tasting/Vegetarian menu 6 course, Sunday L, Vegetarian menu **Seats** 70, Pr/dining room 25 **Children** Portions **Parking** On street

cream, or there may be crema catalana garnished with caramelised ginger.

Chef Rees Smith **Owner** Accor UK **Times** 12-2.30/6-11 Closed L Sat-Sun **Prices** Starter £6.95-£9, Main £14-£27, Dessert £7, Service added but optional 10% **Wines** 46 bottles over £30, 12 bottles under £30, 310 by glass **Notes** Vegetarian available **Seats** 92 **Children** Portions, Menu

St Pancras Grand Brasserie   PLAN 3 B6

◉ British ☕

British classics in the international terminus

☎ 020 7870 9900
St Pancras International NW1 9QP
e-mail: stpg@searcys.co.uk
dir: Nearest station: King's Cross, St Pancras

Below the magnificent arched roof of the stunningly made-over St Pancras station, The Grand - on the upper Eurostar concourse - revives something of the spirit and romance of rail-travel's heyday. The art-deco styled room fittingly has a hint of classic French brasserie, with globe lighting, leather banquettes and booths, warm woods, bevelled and etched glass, brass fittings and a gold-leaf ceiling, while the atmosphere bustles with the clink of champagne glasses and the comings-and-goings of international travellers. There's an oyster bar at one end of the room and a whisky bar at the other, and the place is constantly on the move, serving everything from breakfast to elevenses, lunch, afternoon tea and dinner. The please-all menu covers all bases with a roll-call of British favourites and more modish options, driven by well-sourced produce: think dressed Weymouth crab, whole South Coast plaice served with brown shrimps and new potatoes, or perhaps Cumberland sausage with mash and onion gravy.

Chef Chris Dines **Owner** Searcys **Times** 11am-mdnt Closed 25-26 Dec, All-day dining **Prices** Service added but optional 12.5% **Wines** 28 bottles over £30, 19 bottles under £30, 24 by glass **Notes** Sunday L £6-£25, Vegetarian available **Seats** 160, Pr/dining room 2 **Children** Portions, Menu

The Winter Garden   PLAN 2 F3

◉◉ British, Mediterranean

Classical cooking under a soaring glass roof

☎ 020 7631 8000 & 7631 8230
The Landmark London, 222 Marylebone Rd NW1 6JQ
e-mail: restaurants.reservation@thelandmark.co.uk
web: www.wintergarden-london.com
dir: Nearest station: Marylebone. M25/A40 follow signs for West End. Continue along Marylebone Rd for 300 mtrs. Restaurant on left

The Landmark Hotel started off life in the late 1800s as a grand railway hotel and has been stylishly and expensively restored. The Winter Garden has the prime spot: right in the middle of the grand atrium which goes up and up (through eight storeys to be precise) to the glass roof. It's like being outdoors, really. Adding to the sense of occasion, a pianist can be heard tinkling away amid the palm trees. Classical-minded dishes hit the spot, and it's worth checking out the luxurious Sunday champagne brunch if you're in the mood to spoil yourself. From the carte you might begin with Cornish crab lasagne and chive butter sauce. Next up, rack of Cotswold lamb comes with a herb crust, aubergine and roasted red peppers, and rosemary sauce, while Dover sole is served off the bone with lemon, parsley and brown shrimps. Finish with a chocolate délice, orange, kumquats, salted caramel and Cointreau ice cream.

Times 11.30-3/6-10.45

Manna   PLAN 1 E4

◉ International Vegan

Long-running neighbourhood vegetarian in leafy Primrose Hill

☎ 020 7722 8028
4 Erskine Rd, Primrose Hill NW3 3AJ
e-mail: geninfo@manna.com
dir: Nearest station: Chalk Farm. 500 mtrs from underground station

Perhaps it's not altogether surprising that Manna - a '60s veggie/vegan trailblazer - should be tucked away down a side street off fashionable Primrose Hill's main drag, not a million miles from Camden. Manna has moved with the times and these days serves up smart-looking, creative dishes based on high quality ingredients to a well-heeled crowd. The menu takes inspiration from around the globe, backpacking its way from starters like spiced jerk tofu, plantain and sweet potato kebabs to mains like enchilada casserole, root vegetable tagine or organic bangers (fennel and pumpkin seed) and mash. The understated, modish, natural-toned décor suits dressing up or down, with wooden floors and furniture given a touch of pizzazz with elegant wallpaper featuring silhouetted trees and birds and branch-themed ceiling lights. Add to this a relaxed mood, friendly service and organic, biodynamic and vegan wines, and it's easy to see why Manna is sill going strong.

Owner R Swallow, S Hague **Times** 12-3/6.30-11 Closed Xmas & New Year, Mon, L variable **Prices** Prices not confirmed Service added but optional 12.5% **Wines** 8 by glass **Seats** 50 **Children** Portions **Parking** On street

LONDON NW3 *continued*

XO
PLAN 1 E4

◉ Pan-Asian

Asian variety act in well-heeled Belsize Park

☎ 020 7433 0888
29 Belsize Ln NW3 5AS
e-mail: xo@rickerrestaurants.com
dir: Nearest station: Swiss Cottage, Belsize Park. From Havistock Hill, right into Ornan Rd (before BP garage). Restaurant on right

This northern outpost of Will Ricker's stable of trendy bar-restaurants brings a touch of big-city cool to a leafy enclave of Belsize Park. The fashionably minimalist space is divided between bar and dining room and dotted with modern oriental touches: think black lacquered surfaces, funky chandeliers, decorative ironwork, low-slung booth-style leather seating and under-lit wall mirrors so you can check out who's in the house as you graze through the menu of voguish Pan-Asian dishes. The kitchen's repertoire is designed for sharing and takes in everything from dim sum (roast pumpkin and spinach gyoza, perhaps) to sashimi and sushi (salmon and avocado maki maybe), tempura (such as tiger prawn, lime and salt), curries, barbecued dishes and roasts (including the ever-popular black cod with sweet miso). Eye-catching cocktails, well-chosen wines and up-tempo music complete a polished package.

Chef Tom Cajone **Owner** Will Ricker **Times** 12-3/6-11 Closed 25-26 Dec & 1 Jan **Prices** Fixed L 2 course fr £15, Fixed D 3 course fr £18, Starter £5.50-£17, Main £9.50-£30, Dessert £5-£6, Service added but optional 12.5% **Wines** 33 bottles over £30, 19 bottles under £30, 16 by glass **Notes** Sunday L, Vegetarian available **Seats** 92, Pr/dining room 22 **Children** Portions, Menu **Parking** On street

LONDON NW4

Hendon Hall Hotel
PLAN 1 D5

◉◉ Modern British

Historic North London mansion with contemporary cooking

☎ 020 8457 2200
Ashley Ln, Hendon NW4 1HF
e-mail: hendonhall@handpicked.co.uk
web: www.handpickedhotels.co.uk/hendonhall
dir: Nearest station: Hendon Central. M1 junct 2. A406. Right at lights into Parson St. Next right into Ashley Lane, Hendon Hall on right

The impressive North London mansion dates from the 16th century and has earned a crust as a hotel since 1911. Nowadays, the place has a light contemporary look that blends well with a host of period features, including crystal chandeliers, a grand staircase and handsomely-proportioned rooms. Named after the 18th-century actor and manager of the eponymous Drury Lane theatre, who once owned the hall, the fine-dining Garrick Restaurant works an upmarket modern look with contemporary art on

the walls and smart russet and gold high-backed chairs at formally-laid tables. The kitchen continues to score palpable hits with its up-to-date cooking, setting out with a well-made terrine of confit duck, guinea fowl and foie gras matched creatively with red wine pear purée and parsnip. Next up, roast fillet of hake comes with capers and leek fondue, and jus noisette. The modern, creative thinking continues at dessert stage too with a well-thought-out composition of flavours and textures involving whipped lemon curd, meringue, citrus jelly and lemonade granita.

Times 12-2.30/6.30-9.30

LONDON SE1

The Anchor & Hope
PLAN 5 E5

◉◉ British

Thrilling gastro-pub with big-hearted cooking

☎ 020 7928 9898
36 The Cut SE1 8LP
e-mail: anchorandhope@btconnect.com
dir: Nearest station: Southwark, Waterloo. On left approaching from Waterloo Rd towards Blackfriars Rd, just past Young Vic Theatre

This tumultuous Waterloo gastro-pub is a roaring success - roaring being the operative word when it is rammed and you're in the high-decibel bar with a pint of real ale waiting your turn for a table in the eating area (you can't book to eat, except for Sunday lunch). The Anchor & Hope still looks and feels like a pub with its pared-back, no-frills interior - oxblood walls hung with modern art, and well-worn wooden tables and mismatched chairs. The food suits the mood of the place: flannel-free, unpretentious dishes built on quality seasonal ingredients. The menu changes each session, and descriptions rarely go beyond a handful of words, so forget three-course formality and just order whatever grabs your attention - warm snail and bacon salad or grilled razor clams might get the juices flowing, followed by roast Swaledale beef rump with dripping potatoes and horseradish. Otherwise three of you (or a greedy pair) could sign up for roast kid's leg 'saltimbocca' with chips and aïoli. Puds stay on message, perhaps raspberry Bakewell tart with clotted cream.

Chef Jonathon Jones **Owner** Robert Shaw, Mike Belben, Jonathon Jones, Harry Lester **Times** 12-2.30/6-10.30 Closed BHs, 25 Dec-1 Jan, L Mon, D Sun **Prices** Starter £5.80-£10, Main £11-£18, Dessert £2.40-£6.40, Service optional **Wines** 36 bottles over £30, 21 bottles under £30, 13 by glass **Notes** Sunday L, Vegetarian available **Seats** 58 **Parking** On street

Brigade
PLAN 5 H6

◉ British ◉

Turning up the heat in an old fire station

☎ 0844 346 1225
The Fire Station, 139 Tooley St SE1 2HZ
e-mail: info@thebrigade.co.uk
dir: Nearest station: London Bridge. Between station & Tower Bridge

Brigade isn't only so-called because of its location in an old fire station. The name also references the brigade in the kitchen as they're mostly apprentices who have been at risk of homelessness or have lived on the streets, and are on a six-month chef training scheme aimed at giving them the skills, qualifications and confidence to turn their lives around. The scheme is being run in conjunction with Southwark College and the Beyond Food Foundation charity, founded by Brigade chef-patron Simon Boyle. The restaurant has a contemporary look with leather high-backed chairs and banquettes, and black lacquered tables, and the lively atmosphere is helped along by the sounds, sights and smells of the centrally positioned open kitchen (grab a seat at the counter if you want to be really close to the action). The menu is broadly modern British, using plenty of top-notch seasonal, British ingredients. Hand-dived Scottish scallops with beetroot and chilli risotto is one way to start, perhaps followed by one of the best burgers in town, made from rump steak and with shredded oxtail sitting on top.

Chef Simon Boyle **Owner** DeVere & PWC **Times** 12-3/5.30-10 Closed Sun, L Sat **Prices** Starter £5.95-£12.95, Main £9.95-£28, Dessert £4.95-£8.95, Service added but optional 12.5% **Wines** 30 bottles over £30, 18 bottles under £30, 18 by glass **Notes** Deposit £10 per person for groups over 10, Vegetarian available **Seats** 89, Pr/dining room 45 **Children** Portions

Cantina del Ponte
PLAN 5 J6

◉ Italian ◉

Relaxed Italian dining by the Thames

☎ 020 7403 5403
The Butlers Wharf Building, 36c Shad Thames SE1 2YE
e-mail: cantinareservations@danddlondon.com
dir: Nearest station: Tower Hill, London Bridge. SE side of Tower Bridge, on river front

The name says it all really: a modern-day take on the Italian trattoria sitting plum on the Thames-side promenade overlooking Tower Bridge. On warm days there's a definite hint of the Med, with its big awning-covered terrace a magnet for watching the world. Inside, rollback glass doors offer year-round vistas too, while fashionable furnishings combine with terracotta floor tiles, black-and-white wall tiles and a huge Italian market mural to deliver a stylish but relaxed Latin vibe. The authentic regional Italian cooking sits perfectly with the 'cantina' billing, keeping things simple and rustic and driven by prime produce. Think veal chop Milanese, or perhaps red gurnard fillet served with mussels, fresh tomato and courgettes. Linguine with lobster, chilli and fresh tomato is a popular pasta choice, while desserts might feature a classic pannacotta (served with plums cooked in syrup). The all-Italian wine list and friendly service hit just the right note too.

Chef Angelo Albera **Owner** D and D London
Times 12-3/6-11 Closed 24-26 Dec, L 31 Dec
Prices Fixed L 2 course £10-£15, Fixed D 3 course £18.95-£22.95, Starter £5-£12, Main £15-£34, Dessert £5.50-£7, Service optional, Groups min 8 service 12.5%
Wines 12 bottles over £30, 17 bottles under £30, 11 by glass **Notes** Sunday L, Vegetarian available **Seats** 110 **Children** Portions **Parking** NCP Gainsford St

Cantina Vinopolis   PLAN 5 F6

◉ Mediterranean ♦ NOTABLE WINE LIST

Dining underneath the arches at the South Bank's wine emporium

☎ 020 7940 8333
1 Bank End SE1 9BU
e-mail: cantina@vinopolis.co.uk
dir: Nearest station: London Bridge. 5 min walk from London Bridge on Bankside, between Southwark Cathedral & Shakespeare's Globe Theatre

The soaring arches of a Victorian railway viaduct near London Bridge Station make an impressive cathedral-like space for worshipping the grape in its multifarious forms. Part of the Vinopolis complex, Cantina is the place to head for Mediterranean-accented dining in a modish setting of oak tables and leather banquettes beneath cavernous vaulted brick ceilings, with the rumble of overhead trains as an evocative soundtrack. It's run by staff who are passionate about food and wine, and in case you had forgotten that this is a temple to good wines, there are displays of bottles and a splendid list to jog the memory. Expect straight-talking ideas along the lines of duck foie gras terrine with home-made bread, followed by pheasant served with potato fondant, braised black cabbage, green lentils and vegetable stew, or if you

fancy fish, perhaps lemon sole with spinach, new potatoes, capers and passionfruit marinière. Stay with the wine theme and treat yourself to a glass of something sticky to go with prune and almond tart served with vanilla ice cream.

Times 12-3/6-10.30 Closed Xmas, BHs, Sun, L Mon-Wed

Chino Latino London   PLAN 5 G5

◉◉ Modern Pan-Asian V ♨

East Asian food and western cocktails in a South Bank hotel

☎ 020 7769 2500
Park Plaza Riverbank London, 18 Albert Embankment SE1 7TJ
e-mail: london@chinolatino.co.uk
web: www.chinolatino.co.uk
dir: Nearest station: Vauxhall. Between Vauxhall & Lambeth bridge

Latino cocktails and a Pan-Asian menu is the thing at this hot-spot on the South Bank. Part of an international franchise - with branches in the UK and Germany - it scores high in the cool stakes: all cream leather and darkwood set to a backdrop of striking ruby-coloured glass panels, back-lit cocktail bar and a sushi station with a busy chorus of chefs. The fashionable Pan-Asian menu - where fish and seafood make a strong showing - comes highlighted with signature dishes, plus there's a

trio of tasting options. Expect dim sum of chicken sui mai with foie gras and shiitake mushrooms to tempura of stuffed red chilli and soft-shelled crab. Among main courses monkfish tail with yuzu kusho dressing and yuzu jelly, black cod with miso, and pork belly with shiso apple cider and popcorn crackling show the style. Sharp cocktails and a good range of sake stay true to the theme.

Chino Latino London

Chef Sebastian Francis **Owner** Park Plaza Hotels
Times 12-2.30/6-10.30 Closed 1 Jan, L Sat-Sun
Prices Tasting menu £38-£50, Starter £4.50-£13, Main £13-£36, Dessert £7.95-£15.50, Service added but optional 12.5% **Wines** 29 bottles over £30, 18 bottles under £30, 12 by glass **Notes** Three tasting menus available, Vegetarian menu, Dress restrictions, Smart casual, no sportswear or fancy dress **Seats** 85 **Children** Portions, Menu **Parking** Q-park at Waterloo station

See advert below

LONDON SE1 *continued*

Gillray's Steakhouse & Bar PLAN 5 C5

◎◎ English NEW ✪

English cooking with pride and Thames views

☎ 020 7928 5200
**Marriott Hotel County Hall, Westminster Bridge Rd,
County Hall SE1 7PB**
e-mail: gareth.bowen@marriotthotels.com
web: www.gillrays.com
dir: Nearest station: Westminster, Waterloo

Enjoying a prime position on the South Bank, close to the
London Eye, Gillray's shows off its pride in all things
English through diligently sourced top-notch produce.
Peruse the list of 39 English gins or choose from one of
the many inventive cocktails in the bar before heading
into the somewhat masculine wood-panelled dining room.
Crystal chandeliers, a long chesterfield sofa and views
across to Big Ben and the Houses of Parliament make a
fine setting for an unpretentious patriotic menu. Instead
of bread comes a generous Yorkshire pudding filled with
English cheddar and horseradish crème fraîche. You
might then choose plump, rich Devonshire crab cakes
with mustard and dill mayonnaise. For the main event,
steaks - 35-day-aged Aberdeen Angus no less - are
obviously the big draw: perhaps you might go for a
perfectly cooked 260g rib-eye with red wine and bone
marrow sauce, baked bone marrow and truffled chips.
Standards don't slip at dessert - a zingy lemon meringue
pie on a buttery pastry base provides a delightful finish.

Chef Gareth Bowen **Owner** Marriott Hotels **Times** 11-11
All-day dining **Prices** Fixed L 2 course fr £22, Fixed D 3
course fr £29, Tasting menu fr £65, Starter £7-£14.50,
Main £14-£55, Dessert £5-£9, Service included, Service
added but optional 12.5% **Wines** 22 bottles over £30, 2
bottles under £30, 18 by glass **Notes** Sunday L,
Vegetarian available **Seats** 108, Pr/dining room 16
Children Portions, Menu **Parking** 25

Gregg's Bar and Grill PLAN 5 H4

◎ Modern British ✪

**Simple cooking and a relaxed vibe courtesy of Gregg
Wallace**

☎ 020 7378 2450
**Bermondsey Square Hotel, Bermondsey Square, Tower
Bridge Rd SE1 3UN**
e-mail: restaurantmanager@bermondseysquarehotel.co.
uk
dir: Nearest station: London Bridge, Borough,
Bermondsey. From station exit towards Guys Hospital, left
into Saint Thomas St, 200mtrs right into Bermondsey St,
400mtrs cross Abbey St into Bermondsey Sq

Just past a lovely pewter-topped bar in the Bermondsey
Hotel, Gregg's Bar & Grill (that's Wallace of *MasterChef*
fame) is an un-starchy, relaxed kind of place, open for
breakfast through to brunch, lunch and dinner. The
expansive room has somewhat of a New England feel,
with boarded walls and pillars painted in appealing
pastel shades, plus an open-to-view kitchen. Share a few

'small plates' with friends - perhaps salt and pepper
squid with black ink garlic mayo or country terrine with
toasted sourdough and plum and apricot chutney - before
moving on to something comforting like scallop, shellfish
and Brixham smoked haddock pie with a puff-pastry
topper, or a steak from the grill (perhaps Black Angus 40-
day aged rib-eye). Pudding could be a clever twist on a
classic, such as pumpkin crème brulée with pumpkin
ganache, or - for chocolate lovers - a 'chocolate bomb'.

Chef Jordi Vila **Owner** Robin Sheppard **Times** 12-3/6-11
Prices Fixed L 2 course £12-£20, Fixed D 3 course
£20-£35, Starter £4.50-£7, Main £9.50-£24, Dessert
£2-£8, Service added but optional 12.5% **Wines** 4 bottles
over £30, 16 bottles under £30, 9 by glass **Notes** Brunch
Sat & Sun, Paella night, Sunday L, Vegetarian available,
Civ Wed 90 **Seats** 70, Pr/dining room 25
Children Portions, Menu **Parking** NCP 10 mins walk

H10 London Waterloo Hotel PLAN 5 E5

◎ Mediterranean NEW

Cool Mediterranean food in a new Waterloo hotel

☎ 020 7928 4062
384-302 Waterloo Rd SE1 8RQ
e-mail: h10.london.waterloo@h10hotels.com
dir: Nearest station: Waterloo, Lambeth North. 450mtrs
from Waterloo Station & approx 5min walk from Lambeth
North station, located near the London Eye

The freshly minted H10 in Waterloo is a prime piece of
London new-build from a dynamic international hotel
group, a sharp-edged wedge of a building close to the
station. Interior styling is as up-to-the-minute as can be,
with postmodern graphic panels in the clinically white
lobby, and a design tone in the first-floor Three O Two
restaurant that recalls an upmarket cafeteria, with its
geometrically perfect lines of unclothed tables for two.
Grab a window table for the best views of what's
happening down on Waterloo Road. Light Mediterranean
brasserie food is what to expect, perhaps starting with an
attentively timed dried tomato and asparagus risotto,
dressed in olive oil and balsamic, moving on to lamb
confit, cooked at a laid-back temperature for ideal
tenderness, and bedded on sweet potato dauphinoise
with glazed shallots, and concluding with assertively
nutmegged crema catalana of authentic texture (ie a
shade looser than crème brûlée).

Prices Prices not confirmed **Parking** NCP Library St or
Elephant & Castle

Magdalen PLAN 5 H6

◎◎ British, European

Reassuringly focused cooking by London Bridge

☎ 020 7403 1342
152 Tooley St SE1 2TU
e-mail: info@magdalenrestaurant.co.uk
web: www.magdalenrestaurant.co.uk
dir: Nearest station: London Bridge. 5 min walk from
London Bridge exit. Restaurant 300yds on right opposite
Unicorn Theatre

Magdalen is run by a husband-and-wife-team with fine
CVs (The Fat Duck and the Mandarin Oriental to name but
two previous employers) and a passion for clear-headed,
flavourful food. In the thriving London Bridge setting,
their restaurant is an unfussy space, on the smart side of
casual (or the casual side of smart) with its richly
coloured walls, wooden floor, contemporary artworks and
tables laid with white linen cloths. With the provenance
of the produce to the fore, whether best of British or
quality European imports, the menu is packed full of food
you want to eat, cooked without fuss. Kick off with crisp
fried pig's head and gribiche, or nettle soup with goats'
curd toast, then follow on with roast diver-caught
scallops with lentils, broad beans and wild garlic, or
grilled veal's heart served with potato cake, watercress
and béarnaise. East India sherry and raisin ice cream or
excellent cheeses bring things to a close.

Chef James & Emma Faulks, David Abbott **Owner** Roger &
James Faulks **Times** 12-2.30/6.30-10 Closed Xmas, BHs,
Sun, L Sat **Prices** Fixed L 2 course £15.50, Starter
£7.50-£12.50, Main £13.50-£22, Dessert £6-£6.50,
Service added but optional 12.5% **Wines** 58 bottles over
£30, 15 bottles under £30, 12 by glass **Notes** Vegetarian
available **Seats** 90, Pr/dining room 30 **Parking** On street

Save on Hotels. Book at **theAA.com/hotel**

LONDON, CENTRAL (SE1) 279 ENGLAND

The Oxo Tower Restaurant PLAN 3 D1

Modern, Traditional British V NOTABLE WINE LIST

Captivating views and modish food

☎ 020 7803 3888
8th Floor, Oxo Tower Wharf, Barge House St SE1 9PH
e-mail: oxo.reservations@harveynichols.com
web: www.harveynichols.com
dir: Nearest station: Blackfriars, Waterloo, Southwark.
Between Blackfriars & Waterloo Bridge on the South Bank

The view is 24-carat gold. Up on the eighth floor of the
old Oxo building, this bar, brasserie and restaurant
combo overlooks the river and St Paul's Cathedral, a
position which never ceases to impress, day or night. A
table on the outdoor terrace is a prized possession indeed
(when the weather's right, of course), but it's impressive
enough from behind the vast wall of glass. The
contemporary cooking matches the modish neutrality of
the décor, whilst the well turned-out staff are a reminder
that the restaurant is no afterthought. Lobster tempura
served alongside a well-flavoured consommé and daikon
and wasabi salad demonstrates the kitchen is not beyond
a bit of globe-trotting, but the cooking is more broadly
focused on European preparations. Monkfish, for example,
with smoked ham hock croquettes and quince and vanilla
purée, or South Devon fillet of beef with pickled girolles,
truffle mash and Madeira sauce. To finish, you'll need a
friend to join you for the Bramley apple soufflé with
Calvados ice cream, and do allow some time to peruse
the wine list.

Chef Jeremy Bloor **Owner** Harvey Nichols & Co Ltd
Times 12-3/6-11.30 Closed 25 Dec, D 24 Dec
Prices Fixed L 3 course fr £36.50, Fixed D 2 course fr £35,
Starter £14.50-£19.50, Main £21.50-£35, Dessert
£7.50-£14.50, Service added but optional 12.5%
Wines 14 by glass **Notes** Pre-theatre menu 2 course £35,
Vegetarian menu, Civ Wed 300 **Seats** 250
Children Portions, Menu **Parking** On street, NCP

Park Plaza County Hall PLAN 5 C5

Italian

Italian favourites in Thames-side landmark building

☎ 020 7021 1919 & 7021 1800
1 Addington St SE1 7RY
e-mail: ppchres@pphe.com
web: www.parkplazacountyhall.com
dir: Nearest station: Waterloo

This glossy contemporary hotel on the South Bank sits
right by the County Hall building next to Westminster
Bridge and the London Eye. Amongst its 14 storeys, the
stylish restaurant is on the mezzanine floor overlooking
the ground-floor bar, with a wide-screen vista of the
cityscape through a wall of glass. The modern, minimal
look - cream leather chairs at unclothed white tables,
moody colour-shifting lighting, and bright modern art -
stays unchanged, but the culinary goings-on have
evolved in step with its new name, L'Italiano. A
traditional clay wood-burning oven takes care of
authenticity in the pizza department; elsewhere there are
old favourites among the antipasti, such as aubergine
parmigiana, plus simple pasta dishes like seafood
linguine. If the charcoal grill catches your eye, go for sea
bass served with sautéed spinach in garlic oil and
braised lentils, then wrap it up with a classic tiramisù.

Chef Mark Dancer **Owner** Park Plaza **Times** 5.30-10.30
Closed L all week **Prices** Starter £4.50-£7.95, Main
£5.50-£14.50, Dessert £4.50-£8, Service added but
optional 12.5% **Wines** 12 bottles over £30, 18 bottles
under £30, 13 by glass **Notes** Vegetarian available, Civ
Wed 50 **Seats** 104, Pr/dining room 50 **Children** Portions,
Menu **Parking** U Park Ltd

Park Plaza Westminster Bridge PLAN 5 C5

French NEW

Vibrant modern brasserie dishes on the South Bank

☎ 020 7620 7200
SE1 7UT
e-mail: ppwlres@pphe.com
dir: Nearest station: Westminster, Waterloo

In a perfect riverside location near to the South Bank's
attractions (London Eye, London Aquarium, National
Theatre, etc) and just across the bridge from Big Ben and
the Houses of Parliament, the Park Plaza Westminster
Bridge is a contemporary colossus with over 500 stylish
rooms, and is also home to French-style Brasserie Joël. It
is a clean-cut, darkly minimalist space with bare black-
lacquered tables, black and cream banquettes, moody
red lighting, and a huge showpiece olive tree as a nod to
the culinary style. Uncomplicated modern brasserie
dishes aim to please, so dig in and start with blue cheese
tart with caramelised shallots and lamb's lettuce, then
move on to roast rack of lamb with garlic confit and
watercress, or if you're in the market for fish, go for a
whole sea bass chargrilled in the Josper oven and served
with fennel confit and bouillabaisse sauce. End with
roast pear millefeuille with chestnut cream.

Chef Walter Ishizuka **Times** 12-2/5.30-10.30 Closed L Sat
Prices Prices not confirmed Service added but optional
12.5% **Notes** Pre-theatre menu available, Sunday L
Seats 180 **Children** Menu

Pizarro PLAN 5 H4

Spanish NEW

Spanish cooking at its best in foodie Bermondsey

☎ 020 7378 9455
194 Bermondsey St SE1 3TQ
dir: Nearest station: Bermondsey, Borough, London
Bridge. From Earl's Court Road take A3220 to Kennington
Lane. Take A3 Newington Butts, left A201 Elephant &
Castle & left New Kent Road. At rdbt 2nd exit Tower
Bridge & follow signs for Bermondsey A2205, restaurant
on left

If you've fallen in love with the tapas served at José at
104 Bermondsey Street, then you might want to hotfoot it
down to number 194 where the eponymous José Pizarro
has opened a stylish and casual restaurant serving a full
menu of authentic and modern Spanish cuisine. Floor-to-
ceiling windows fill the room with natural light, while the
open kitchen adds to the buzz and you can take your pick
of places to sit (on a stool at the bar, beside the window
for some people watching, or a more intimate booth at
the back). The regularly-changing menu is bolstered by
daily specials, and the kitchen deals in top-notch
ingredients put together in simple, unfussy combinations.
Lamb's sweetbreads with PX sherry is one way to begin,
the sweetbreads moist and rich and served with an
intense but well balanced sauce, while Iberico pork presa
with Jerusalem artichokes and pear purée makes a fine
main course (precisely cooked meat complemented
perfectly by sweet pear and earthy artichokes). Round
things off with a textbook vanilla cheesecake with fresh
raspberries.

Chef José Pizarro **Owner** José Pizarro **Times** 12-3/6-11
Closed 4 days over Xmas **Prices** Fixed L 2 course fr £17,
Starter £6-£8.50, Main £11-£17.50, Dessert £5, Service
optional **Wines** 20 bottles over £30, 15 bottles under £30,
27 by glass **Notes** All day menu Sat, Sun brunch
10am-2pm, Sunday L £8-£17.50, Vegetarian available
Seats 75, Pr/dining room 10 **Parking** On street, NCP car
park

LONDON SE1 *continued*

Le Pont de la Tour

PLAN 5 J6

⊚⊚ Modern French ▮ NOTABLE WINE LIST

Great views and assured French cooking

☎ 020 7403 8403
The Butlers Wharf Building, 36d Shad Thames SE1 2YE
e-mail: lepontres@danddlondon.com
web: www.lepontdelatour.co.uk
dir: Nearest station: Tower Hill, London Bridge. SE of Tower Bridge

In the league table of London's restaurants with a view, Le Pont de la Tour is definitely in the Premiership. The name translates as Tower Bridge, and that's what lies before you, whether you're dining out on its planter-lined terrace, or indoors taking in the scene through vast floor-to-ceiling windows. The setting owes a debt to the gracious lines of art deco style and everything is just right - correctly-paced service, a chic ambience that evokes 1930s Paris, and food that is rooted in the French classics. The spotlight is always on seafood here and luxury ingredients are liberally pressed into service, as in a generously filled lobster raviolo served with spinach and sauce Nantua. A wintery dish of venison comes in a spicy peppery crust with salsify, braised red cabbage and sauce poivrade, or you might go for roasted wild sea bass with tomato fondue, courgette ribbons and olive crumb. Sticking with the Gallic theme, apple tarte Tatin is served with vanilla ice cream and honeycomb tuile. If your wallet can stand the strain, the place is well known for its cracking wine list.

Chef Tom Cook **Owner** Des Gunewardena
Times 12-3/6-11 **Prices** Starter £10.50-£11, Main £19.50-£80, Dessert £7-£14, Service optional, Groups min 8 service 12.5% **Wines** 150 bottles over £30, 20 bottles under £30, 35 by glass **Notes** Sunday L fr £26, Vegetarian available, Dress restrictions, No trainers in main restaurant **Seats** 140, Pr/dining room 24
Children Portions, Menu **Parking** On street & car park

Restaurant Story

PLAN 5 J5

Rosettes not confirmed at time of going to print – see below

Roast

PLAN 5 G6

⊚ British V ♨

Great British produce overlooking Borough Market

☎ 0845 034 7300
The Floral Hall, Borough Market, Stoney St SE1 1TL
e-mail: info@roast-restaurant.com
web: www.roast-restaurant.com
dir: Nearest station: London Bridge

Any restaurant would be hard pushed to find a better location for getting its hands on top-drawer raw materials than this one-off operation perched above the colourful cornucopia of Borough Market, and accordingly, sourcing and provenance are the keystones of this kitchen's output. The wow factor of the cool conservatory-like setting in the old Floral Hall is undeniable: turn up for breakfast to experience the hubbub of the market below, while knockout views of floodlit St Paul's alongside

---

Restaurant Story

Rosettes not confirmed at time of going to print

LONDON SE1   **Plan 5 J5**

Modern British

Red-hot opening from rising-star chef

☎ 020 7183 2117
201 Tooley St SE1 2UE
e-mail: dine@restaurantstory.co.uk
dir: Nearest station: London Bridge, Tower Hill. Located at end of Tooley St near Tower Bridge

Tom Sellers has honed his skills with big-hitters Tom Aikens in London, Thomas Keller at Per Se in New York and René Redzepi at Noma in Copenhagen, so you can be sure he's a chef who really knows his onions. And now he's opened his first solo venture, Story, which looks set to be a real page-turner. Set in a Nordic-styled wood-clad new building at the Tower Bridge end of Tooley Street, it perhaps looks a little out of place (the spot was previously home to a Victorian toilet block). Floor-to-ceiling windows offer views of The Shard and the maddening rush of traffic outside, while inside it's all clean-lined modernity, with polished concrete floors, chocolate-brown leather chairs and blonde-wood tables, and a chorus of chefs on show in the open kitchen. The menu follows the tasting format - either six or ten courses - delivering a succession of small dishes that reflect Sellers' journey through life, with some clever plays on childhood memories. Take signatures like 'bread and dripping' to start: a Wee Willie Winkie-style candle made of beef dripping that melts so you can dip the fantastic sourdough bread in. There's the Three Bears' porridge dilemma finale (one too rich, one too salty and one just right), while a Tunnock's-like teacake - here infused with rosewater - appears with coffee. Everything - from the small rabbit 'sandwich' to a nasturtium flower filled with oyster emulsion - is technically brilliant, wonderfully creative and simply bursting with flavour. Milky-white sashimi-esque scallop spheres teamed brilliantly with cucumber balls dusted in dill ash is a joyously simple dish when compared with some of Sellers' more complex creations, such as perfectly timed pigeon with wafer-thin spheres of high-octane summer truffle and pine. Presentation all the way through is nothing short of stunning, and combinations are full of interest and intrigue - just like any good Story.

Chef Tom Sellers **Owner** Tom Sellers
Times 12-2.30/6.30-9.30 Closed 2 wks Xmas, Sun-Mon
Prices Service added but optional 12.5% **Notes** Fixed menu L/D 6 course £45, 10 course £65, Vegetarian available **Seats** 40 **Parking** On street

the bright lights of the Shard are a draw in the evening. Forget fads and fashions: menus are designed to showcase simple, robust, traditional Brit dishes. You may find pan-fried Manx queenies with wild garlic butter to start, then chargrilled Newlyn squid with spicy tomato and herb relish alongside ham hock and Herefordshire snail pie with pease pudding, while daily roasts might bring slow-roasted shoulder of lamb with rosemary-roasted root vegetables and mint relish.

Chef Marcus Verberne **Owner** Iqbal Wahhab **Times** 12-3/5.30-11 Closed D Sun **Prices** Fixed L 3 course £30, Starter £7.75-£12.75, Main £15.75-£35, Dessert £7.50-£8.25, Service added but optional 12.5% **Wines** 21 by glass **Notes** Tasting menu with matching wines, Sunday L, Vegetarian menu, Dress restrictions, Smart casual **Seats** 120 **Children** Portions, Menu **Parking** NCP Kipling St

RSJ, The Restaurant on the South Bank

PLAN 5 D6

@ Modern European

Pleasingly unfussy food and notable Loire wines

☎ 020 7928 4554
33 Coin St SE1 9NR
e-mail: tom.king@rsj.uk.com
dir: Nearest station: Waterloo. Towards Waterloo Bridge & the IMAX cinema. At rdbt, right into Stamford St. RSJ on the corner of Coin St, 2nd right

RSJ's proximity to the National Theatre and other delights of the ever-improving South Bank makes it a big hit with culture vultures stopping by for the pre- and post-theatre menus. The wine list is a big draw too, or so it should be, with its focus on the Loire; many of the wines are organic and have been selected by the owner who's been visiting France for 'research purposes' for over 30 years. In the kitchen, simple food is elevated by intelligent flavour combinations and sound cooking in the likes of Essex ham hock with oxtail and foie gras terrine, served with piccalilli, or a main-course braised pork belly with honey-glazed celeriac, parsnips, butternut squash, poached apple and sage jus. Finish with a pear and hazelnut tart with home-made honey ice cream.

Chef Chris Whittle **Owner** Nigel Wilkinson **Times** 12-2.30/5.30-11.30 Closed Xmas, 1 Jan, Sun, L Sat **Prices** Prices not confirmed Service added but optional 12.5% **Wines** 6 by glass **Seats** 100, Pr/dining room 25

Skylon

PLAN 5 C6

@ Modern British **NEW V**

Smart riverside dining at the Royal Festival Hall

☎ 020 7654 7800
Royal Festival Hall, Southbank Centre SE1 8XX
e-mail: skylonreservations@danddlondon.com
dir: Nearest station: Waterloo Station

With a name that may suggest an empire in a galaxy, far, far away, Skylon is in fact in the Royal Festival Hall on the Southbank of the River Thames. There's a cool bar, a swish grill, and a restaurant headed up by executive chef Adam Gray. The restaurant occupies a large, high-ceilinged space facing the water, and there's a vast wall of glass so you won't miss a thing. It looks very sharp with its well-spaced (there is plenty of room after all), linen-clad tables, muted colour tones and impressive designer light fittings. On the menu are some smart classical ideas gently updated in places, based on good quality produce, and with a modern British flavour. Start, perhaps, with pressed duck foie gras and Lincolnshire smoked eel terrine with apple jelly and warm brioche, and follow on with pan-fried halibut with creamed celeriac, wild mushrooms, smoked bacon and red wine gravy.

Chef Adam Gray **Owner** D and D London **Times** 12-2.30/5.30-10 Closed 15 Dec **Prices** Fixed L 2 course fr £25, Fixed D 3 course fr £27.50, Tasting menu fr £60, Service added but optional 12.5% **Wines** 260 bottles over £30, 16 bottles under £30, 18 by glass **Notes** Pre-theatre menu available, Sunday L, Vegetarian menu, Dress restrictions, Smart casual **Seats** 100, Pr/dining room 33 **Children** Menu

Zucca

PLAN 5 H4

@@ Modern Italian ©

Vibrant, compelling modern Italian cooking and a lively atmosphere

☎ 020 7378 6809
184 Bermondsey St SE1 3TQ
e-mail: reservations@zuccalondon.com
dir: Nearest station: London Bridge. Ten minutes' walk from London Bridge tube. At the Long Lane end of Bermondsey St

Zucca woos both the critics and crowds with its vibrant modern Italian cooking and prime people-watching through its large, floor-to-ceiling windows. The emphasis here is on tip-top seasonal ingredients, simply but accurately cooked with passion to deliver light, fresh, clean dishes that sing with flavour. The compact menu changes daily, and the pricing is commendably reasonable for food of this quality. Antipasti (set for sharing) includes namesake zucca fritti (zucca meaning pumpkin in Italian) or perhaps sea bass carpaccio, while a smattering of unmissable home-made pasta might feature taglierini with new-season mushrooms and parmesan. For mains, try grilled swordfish with Sicilian

aubergines and chick peas, or a veal chop with spinach and lemon, while desserts - like pistachio and raspberry tart with vanilla ice cream - shouldn't be overlooked. Super home-baked breads, informed service and some corking Italian wines all add up to a class act, while the minimalist surroundings - an open kitchen, white walls broken up by a few abstracts, wooden flooring and white Formica-style tables and chairs - fit the relaxed café-style vibe.

Chef Sam Harris **Owner** Sam Harris **Times** 12-3/6-10 Closed 25 Dec, 1 Jan, Etr, Mon, D Sun **Prices** Starter £4.25-£6, Main £15-£16.95, Dessert £2-£8.95, Service optional **Wines** 100 bottles over £30, 10 bottles under £30, 12 by glass **Notes** Sunday L £15-£16.95, Vegetarian available **Seats** 64, Pr/dining room 10 **Children** Portions **Parking** On street

LONDON SE3

Bella Vista Cucina Italiana

PLAN 1 H3

@ Italian

Italian classics in vibrant setting

☎ 020 8318 1143
3/5 Montpelier Vale, Blackheath SE3 0TA
dir: Nearest station: Blackheath

Blackheath Village's Bella Vista is a lot of fun, a taste of Italy as a jaded copywriter might say. That 'vista' is over Blackheath Village, all the street action clearly visible through the floor-to-ceiling windows to the front. It looks pretty tasty inside with a contemporary-rustic-chic vibe going on, some exposed brick, darkwood tables, and some authentic Italian foodie products on shelves to bring a touch of 'cucina' to proceedings. The menu is devised by Piero Marenghi and the place is from the same stable as Chapters All Day Dining (see entry) and the high-flying Chapter One (see entry). So what's on the menu? You might start with some fabulous burrata cheese with basil pesto and cherry tomatoes, or the more substantial fritto misto, and pasta and risottos are a good bet too (pappardelle with new season lamb ragu, maybe, or wild mushroom risotto). Main-courses bring forth the likes of tagliata (sliced rib-eye with soft polenta, pine nuts, raisin and truffle sauce), and to finish, vanilla pannacotta with blood oranges and biscotti.

Times 12-3/6-11

LONDON SE3 *continued*

Chapters All Day Dining PLAN 1 H3

@@ Modern British ○

Blackheath Village eatery buzzing all day long

☎ 020 8333 2666
43-45 Montpelier Vale, Blackheath Village SE3 0TJ
e-mail: chapters@chaptersrestaurants.co.uk
web: www.chaptersrestaurants.com
dir: Nearest station: Blackheath. 5 mins from Blackheath
Village train station

With a super location overlooking the heath from its
alfresco pavement tables or through floor-to-ceiling
windows, Chapters (relaxed sibling of big-hitting big-
brother restaurant Chapter One - see entry) is an all-
round hot ticket. Fashionable good looks (floorboards,
banquettes, exposed brick, mirrors, dangling globe lights
and a zinc-topped bar) pull in an appreciative young and
young-at-heart crowd to the two-floored dine-all-day
outfit at the heart of trendy Blackheath Village. It covers
all the bases, from breakfast to weekend brunch, morning
coffee to modern brasserie classics at lunch and dinner.
Throw in daily specials, a fixed-price lunch option, kids'
dishes, well-chosen wines (with plenty by glass and pichet)
and accessible prices and everyone's happy. Conjured
from quality ingredients, well-presented, clean-flavoured
dishes might take in slow-roasted belly of Gloucestershire
Old Spot pork with colcannon, caramelised apple and a
cider velouté, or perhaps smoked haddock fishcake with
creamed spinach, beurre blanc sauce and frisée salad,
while from the Josper grill there might be rib-eye steak or
Kentish double Barnsley lamb chop. Comfort desserts
(Eton Mess, baked vanilla cheesecake) round off an
accomplished, neighbourhood-restaurant act.

Chef Alex Tyndall **Owner** Selective Restaurants Group
Times 8am-11pm Closed 2-3 Jan, All-day dining
Prices Service added but optional 12.5% **Wines** 22
bottles over £30, 40 bottles under £30, 17 by glass
Notes Lunch set menu Mon-Thu 2/3 course

£12.95/£14.95, Sunday L £8.95-£25.25, Vegetarian
available **Seats** 100 **Children** Portions, Menu **Parking** Car
park by station

LONDON SE22

Franklins PLAN 1 F2

@ British ○

Hearty British cooking on East Dulwich high street

☎ 020 8299 9598
157 Lordship Ln, East Dulwich SE22 8HX
e-mail: info@franklinsrestaurant.com
dir: Nearest station: East Dulwich. 0.5m S from East
Dulwich Station travel via Dog Kennel Hill & Lordship Ln

Among the shops, pubs and coffee bars on busy Lordship
Lane, Franklins stands out from the crowd with its in-
vogue rendition of gutsy British cooking. It divides into a
pubby front bar and a pared-back small bistro at the
rear, all exposed brick, bare floorboards, big Victorian
mirrors, paper-clothed tables and an open window into
the kitchen. The daily-changing concise menu deals in
seasonal British produce, with provenance and simplicity
the key. There's small-plate snacking (black pudding on
toast, for example) to top-end blow-outs like roast grouse
with bread sauce and liver pâté, while, in between,
starters like chicken hearts with sweet dumpling squash,
or mains such as calves' faggots and rainbow chard,
further illustrate the hearty, no-frills style. Puds stay in
the treacle tart and chocolate truffle cake comfort zone.

Chef Ralf Wittig **Owner** Tim Sheehan & Rodney Franklin
Times 12-12 Closed 25-26 & 31 Dec, 1 Jan **Prices** Fixed L
2 course fr £13.95, Starter £9-£9, Main £12-£21, Dessert
£5.50-£6.50, Service optional, Groups min 6 service 10%
Wines 16 bottles over £30, 30 bottles under £30, 15 by
glass **Notes** Sunday L £5-£18, Vegetarian available
Seats 42, Pr/dining room 24 **Children** Portions
Parking Bawdale Road

The Palmerston PLAN 1 F2

@ Modern British, European ○

Quality eating and drinking in a proper Dulwich pub

☎ 020 8693 1629
91 Lordship Ln, East Dulwich SE22 8EP
e-mail: info@thepalmerston.net
dir: Nearest station: East Dulwich. 2m from Clapham,
0.5m from Dulwich Village, 10min walk from East
Dulwich station

The real deal when it comes to the much-overused term
'gastro-pub', the trademark green façade of The
Palmerston helps place it a cut above the rest on bustling
Lordship Lane. The old made-over corner boozer may offer
a handful of tables for drinkers, but there's no mistaking
its food-led credentials. Darkwood abounds in well-
trodden floorboards, wall panelling and furniture, paired
with green-leather wall banquettes, dangling globe
lighting and black chandeliers. Jamie Younger (once head
chef at swanky Bibendum in Chelsea) heads up the
kitchen, taking a modern European approach that pays
respect to quality ingredients while delivering generous,

punchy flavoured, well-dressed dishes. Pan-fried wild
brill fillet with potato purée, ceps, garlic, parsley and
beurre rouge, and roast Iberico bellota pork shoulder
teamed with San Isidro red cabbage, chorizo, apple crisps
and oregano gravy (for two) show the style. A serious wine
list (many by the glass and carafe), hand-pump ales and
friendly, relaxed service round off a classy act.

Chef Jamie Younger, James Donnelly **Owner** Jamie
Younger, Paul Rigby, Remi Olajoyegbe **Times** 12-2.30/7-
mdnt Closed 25-26 Dec, 1 Jan **Prices** Fixed L 2 course
£13, Starter £6.50-£9, Main £14-£19, Dessert £5-£7,
Service added but optional 10% **Wines** 40 bottles over
£30, 20 bottles under £30, 30 by glass **Notes** Light menu
available daily 3-6pm, Sunday L £14, Vegetarian
available **Seats** 70 **Children** Portions **Parking** On street

LONDON SE23

Babur PLAN 1 G2

@@ Modern Indian

Modern Indian cuisine in a cool brasserie-style setting

☎ 020 8291 2400
119 Brockley Rise, Forest Hill SE23 1JP
e-mail: mail@babur.info
web: www.babur.info
dir: Nearest station: Honor Oak Park. Turn left from Honor
Oak Park station, continue for 150mtrs to first lights,
right again for 100mtrs along Brockley Rise

With a prowling, life-size tiger on the roof, newcomers
could be forgiven for thinking this is just another flock-
wallpapered curry house, but Babur takes a thoroughly
creative approach to cuisine as well as décor. Inside the
look is classy and modern: walnut veneer, exposed
brickwork and blue limestone flooring meets brown-
leather banquettes and industrial ducting - throw in a
gallery of striking ethnic artworks and funky pendant
lighting and the place really comes to life. The cooking
certainly doesn't hold back either, delivering a colourful
blend of traditional and contemporary thinking. Quality
ingredients - many not widely encountered in Indian
cooking - and judicious spicing are joined by well-dressed
presentation. Witness ostrich (clove-smoked and
marinated in Rajasthani spices) or goat patties (with
tamarind and raisin chutney) to start, followed by mains
like well-spiced Kerala-inspired coconut lamb with
tomato rice. Desserts follow the East-meets-West theme
- perhaps a spiced chocolate fondant or mango brûlée -
while wines are spice-friendly and the menu includes
recommendations to match each main course.

Babur

Chef Jiwan Lal **Owner** Babur 1998 Ltd
Times 12-2.30/6-11.30 Closed 26 Dec, L 27 Dec, D 25
Dec **Prices** Starter £6.75-£8.50, Main £11.95-£16.95,
Dessert £4.75-£5.95, Service optional **Wines** 3 bottles
over £30, 39 bottles under £30, 11 by glass **Notes** Tasting
menu available Jul-Aug, Sunday L, Vegetarian available
Seats 72 **Parking** 15, On street

See advert below

LONDON SW1

Al Duca　　　　　　　PLAN 4 J6

🏵 Modern Italian

Buzzy, fairly priced Italian in St James

☎ 020 7839 3090
4-5 Duke of York St SW1Y 6LA
e-mail: alduca@btconnect.com
dir: Nearest station: Green Park. 5 mins walk from station
towards Piccadilly. Right into St James's, left into Jermyn
St. Duke of York St halfway along on right

Contemporary good looks, a buzzy ambience and sensible
pricing all add up to a package that keeps happy
customers returning to this eternally popular St James's
Italian. A modern interior provides a quick trip to the Med
with its stone floors, light oak furniture, and Italian tones
of olive and terracotta, the mood of well-being boosted by
a roll-back glass frontage for alfresco eating on fine
days; smartly turned-out, chatty and knowledgeable staff
and a spot-on all-Italian wine list play their part too. The
kitchen's repertoire of uncomplicated classic and gently-
modernised Italian dishes built on top-class ingredients
has stood the test of time: home-made pasta is as good
as you'd hope, particularly if pappardelle with venison
ragoût and seasonal mushrooms is up for grabs. Next up,
pan-fried duck breast benefits from the bittersweet tones
of grilled radicchio, pumpkin sauce and a Marsala
reduction, before a textbook tiramisù winds things up on
top form.

Chef Giovanni Andolfi **Owner** Cuisine Collection, Claudio
Pulze **Times** 12-11 Closed Xmas, BHs, Sun **Prices** Fixed L
2 course fr £23.50, Fixed D 3 course fr £28, Service added
but optional 12.5% **Wines** 160 bottles over £30, 20
bottles under £30, 13 by glass **Notes** Pre & post theatre
menu 2/3 course £16.50/£19, Vegetarian available, Dress
restrictions, Smart casual **Seats** 56 **Children** Portions
Parking Jermyn St, Duke St

LONDON SW1 *continued*

Amaya
PLAN 4 G4

☺☺ Indian ⚑NOTABLE WINE LIST

Fine Indian cuisine with plenty of kitchen theatre

☎ 020 7823 1166

Halkin Arcade, Motcomb St SW1X 8JT

e-mail: amaya@realindianfood.com

dir: Nearest station: Knightsbridge

Amaya certainly has seductive style in spades. Located in Knightsbridge's glossy Halkin Arcade, it is as well-dressed as its customers: by day, light floods in through a glazed atrium roof; at night, textures of black granite, rosewood and leather are set against white walls splashed with bold modern artwork, plus there's the added culinary drama of chefs doing their thing in an impressive open kitchen. The cooking takes a three-pronged approach using traditional methods - the clay tandoor oven, sigri (a grill with a coal flame) and tawa (a thick iron hot-plate). Food arrives as and when it is ready, rather than in the conventional starter/main course format, so be prepared to share and graze through a succession of ideas, taking in flash-grilled rock oysters with coconut and ginger moilee sauce, or griddled sea bass with a coconut and herb crust, and on via tandoori monkfish tikka and Punjabi chicken wing lollipops to boned tandoori quail.

Chef Karunesh Khanna **Owner** R Mathrani, N&C Panjabi **Times** 12.30-2.15/6.30-11.30 Closed D 25 Dec **Prices** Fixed L 3 course £19.50-£35, Fixed D 3 course £60, Tasting menu £55-£110, Starter £11-£24, Main £10-£36, Dessert £8-£9, Service added but optional 12.5% **Wines** 19 by glass **Notes** Fixed D 2 course, Vegetarian tasting menu, Vegetarian available **Seats** 99, Pr/dining room 14 **Parking** NCP

Ametsa with Arzak Instruction PLAN 4 G5

☺☺☺ – *see opposite*

Apsleys at The Lanesborough PLAN 4 G5

☺☺☺ – *see opposite*

Avenue
PLAN 4 J6

☺ Modern British ⚑

Buzzy, contemporary restaurant and bar

☎ 020 7321 2111

7-9 St James's St SW1A 1EE

e-mail: avenuereservations@danddlondon.com

dir: Nearest station: Green Park. Turn right past The Ritz, 2nd turning into St James's St

There's an air of chic modern refinement at Avenue, with its long bar, a predominantly plum and rust décor, some banquettes at closely set clothed tables, and smartly clad professional staff. It's a popular place, people drawn by the appealing, largely modern British menu as much by the atmosphere. Crab tart, given bite by an accompanying fennel salad, can get a meal off to a flying start, or there may be more robust-sounding braised pork cheeks with Jerusalem artichokes and chanterelles. Fish is handled well, judging by a fresh and moist fillet of sea bass, with a golden crisp skin, sauced with orange beurre blanc, served atop spring greens with pan-fried cauliflower stalks. Meat-eaters could opt for chicken breast intriguingly offset by bacon vinaigrette served with pears and parsnips, and to finish there could be a classic rendition of tarte Tatin with vanilla ice cream.

Chef Kimmo Makkonen **Owner** D and D London **Times** 12-3/5.45-11 Closed 25-26 Dec, 1 Jan, BH, Sun, L Sat **Prices** Fixed L 2 course £19.50-£27.50, Starter £6.50-£13.50, Main £14-£29.50, Dessert £5-£7, Service added but optional 12.5%, Groups min 8 service 12.5% **Wines** 43 bottles over £30, 19 bottles under £30, 19 by glass **Notes** Pre-theatre menu, ALC not available at L, Vegetarian available, Civ Wed 130 **Seats** 150, Pr/dining room 20 **Children** Portions **Parking** Parking meters on streets

Bar Boulud
PLAN 4 F5

☺☺ French, American ⚑NOTABLE WINE LIST

Classy bistro cooking from superstar chef

☎ 020 7201 3899

Mandarin Oriental Hyde Park, 66 Knightsbridge SW1X 7LA

e-mail: barboulud@mohg.com

dir: Nearest station: Knightsbridge. Opposite Harvey Nichols

Sister restaurant to internationally acclaimed chef Daniel Boulud's New York outpost, if you want somewhere fashionably glossy with a genuine buzz and a lesson in stunning bistro food, this is the place to come. Housed in the Mandarin Oriental in the heart of Knightsbridge, it's not the place to linger over a long, slow meal - there's usually a two-hour limit on tables - but what you get instead is bags of Gallic atmosphere. Settle in with a drink at the long zinc-topped bar before moving onto the charcuterie counter overlooking the kitchen, or perhaps a red leather banquette in one of the inter-connected dining rooms. Wine plays a central role here, as evinced from framed wine-stained muslins, duly labelled with the vintage and used as decoration. Boulud's Lyonnaise birthplace shines through in a big menu of elegantly presented pâtés, terrines, charcuterie and platters of seafood jazzed up by a New York state of mind. Start with boudin blanc or truffled white sausage and mashed potato, or terrine of duck, foie gras and figs with myrtle liquor and chestnut compôte, before the DBGB 'piggie burger' pairing of beef patty with barbecue pulled pork and green chilli mayonnaise, or a rather more classic roasted chicken breast with carrot purée, Swiss chard and spiced cranberries. To finish, coupe peppermint - a flourless sponge, hot chocolate sauce, mint ice cream and chocolate sorbet - stands out alongside ile flottante with caramel sauce, crème anglaise and apple sorbet.

Chef Dean Yasharian, Daniel Boulud **Owner** Daniel Boulud **Times** 12-11 All-day dining **Prices** Fixed L 3 course £23, Fixed D 3 course £23, Starter £8.50-£15.50, Main £11.75-£29, Dessert £2.75-£10, Service added but optional 12.5% **Wines** 500 bottles over £30, 6 bottles under £30, 28 by glass **Notes** Sunday L, Vegetarian available **Seats** 168, Pr/dining room 20 **Children** Portions **Parking** NCP Sloane St

Boisdale of Belgravia
PLAN 4 H3

☺ Traditional British

A bit of Scotland imported to London

☎ 020 7259 1257

15 Eccleston St SW1W 9LX

e-mail: info@boisdale.co.uk

dir: Nearest station: Victoria. Left along Buckingham Palace Rd, Eccleston St is 1st on right

A combination of jazz venue, bar and restaurant, Boisdale of Belgravia is spread over a number of rooms in a handsome townhouse, with a clubby décor and red walls hung with a profusion of pictures. As at its sibling in Bishopsgate (see entry), the cooking is built on fine Scottish produce, skilfully and accurately worked. Seared scallops with haggis and saffron-mashed potatoes are a happy blend of flavours, an alternative to another starter of seasonal asparagus with a poached duck egg and truffle vinaigrette. Top-quality Aberdeenshire steaks with a choice of sauces may vie for attention with the luxury of grilled lobster with garlic and parsley butter, although a gutsy dish of sautéed lamb's sweetbreads and braised kidneys, served with mustard and tarragon sauce, mash, and Savoy cabbage mixed with bacon, may be an option too.

Chef Colin Wint **Owner** Mr R Macdonald **Times** 12-3/7-11.15 Closed Xmas, New Year, Etr, BHs, Sun, L Sat **Prices** Fixed L 2 course £19.75, Fixed D 2 course £19.75, Starter £6-£22, Main £13.75-£36, Dessert £6.50-£7, Service added but optional 12.5% **Wines** 22 by glass **Notes** Vegetarian available, Dress restrictions, Smart casual **Seats** 140, Pr/dining room 40 **Parking** On street, Belgrave Sq

Ametsa with Arzak Instruction

LONDON SW1   PLAN 4 G5

New Basque **NEW**

Flavourburst Basque cuisine for a new age

☎ 020 7333 1234
The Halkin Hotel, 5 Halkin St, Belgravia SW1X 7DJ
e-mail: ametsa.thehalkin@comohotels.com
dir: Nearest station: Hyde Park Corner. Halkin Street just off Hyde Park Corner

So it's farewell, then, to David Thompson's Nahm, and hello to Ametsa with Arzak Instruction. The new moniker doesn't have quite the snappy ring of its previous incarnation, but foodies' ears are guaranteed to prick up at the mention of Arzak, the legendary nouveau Basque restaurant in San Sebastian where Juan Mari Arzak and his daughter Elena turn out modernist molecular cuisine (the Ametsa part means 'dream' in Basque). In case you can't make the pilgrimage to northern Spain, Arzak chef Mikel Sorazu has come to London to spread the family philosophy of pairing the Basque region's earthy flavours with surprising contemporary twists. The setting in the minimalist Halkin has all the prestige and gloss you would expect of its swanky Belgravia postcode: the interior is a true one-off with its ceiling fashioned from 7,000 golden glass test tubes filled with spices, oak flooring laid at an angle across the room, and whiter-than-white walls - the sort of dazzling whiteness that has a touch of the science laboratory about it. And the science element is appropriate, since the kitchen engages in a sort of alchemy, taking top-class, usually organic, British ingredients and treating them in a way designed to play with your head, taste buds and preconceptions about how food should behave. The meal begins in a pretty orthodox manner with an elegant dish of plump langoustine tails matched with crisp, straw-like potatoes, and an exemplary creamy and comforting sweetcorn velouté. Main course introduces more off-the-wall elements - 'pigeon with shot' serves the bird with tiny colourful spheres designed to resemble the shot, some fashioned from purple potato and vegetables, while the silver ones melt in the mouth with a burst of acidity as a foil to the remarkably tender, deeply-flavoured pigeon and its super-rich accompanying jus. Dessert delivers a simple, yet intriguing idea: two delicate parcels of French toast wrapped in thin slithers of mango and served on coconut soup.

Chef Sergio Sanz, Mikel Sorazu **Owner** Halkin by COMO **Times** 12-2.30/6.30-10.30 Closed 25 Dec, L Sun **Prices** Tasting menu £105, Service added but optional 12.5% **Wines** 126 bottles over £30, 13 by glass **Notes** Fixed L 4 course £52, Tasting menu 7 course, Vegetarian available, Dress restrictions, Smart casual **Seats** 68, Pr/dining room 28 **Children** Portions **Parking** On street (after 6pm)

Apsleys at The Lanesborough

LONDON SW1   PLAN 4 G5

Modern Italian, Mediterranean

Outstanding Italian cooking in luxury hotel

☎ 020 7333 7254 & 7333 7645
The Lanesborough, Hyde Park Corner SW1X 7TA
e-mail: apsleys@lanesborough.com
dir: Nearest station: Hyde Park Corner

Heinz Beck is a chef at the top of his game, with his La Pergola restaurant in Rome winning gongs galore. This German master may have his heart in Italy, but he's also set up at one of the poshest hotels in London to bring his style of phenomenal modern Italian cooking to the capital of the UK. The restaurant, Apsleys, is named in honour of the Duke of Wellington, whose former home is the other side of Hyde Park Corner, and it is as opulent and luxurious as any Venetian palazzo. That's very much the look they go for, by the way, with a glass atrium, deep, rich carpets, a striking mural and tables dressed up to the nines. Delivering the Beck style is head chef Heros De Agostinis, and he does so with flair and bravura. The bilingual menu kicks off with antipasti as you might imagine: veal terrine, perhaps, with baby artichokes, pea purée and balsamic vinaigrette, or tempura Sicilian prawns with red pepper couscous and marinated courgettes. The ingredients are first-class and the excellent technical abilities of the team in the kitchen bring the very best out of them. Pasta is as good as you might hope - spaghetti with aubergine, tomato coulis and salted ricotta, for example - and among secondi, leg of Pyrenean lamb awaits if you've a willing collaborator, or go for pigeon with crispy polenta, marinated figs and cauliflower. There is a tasting menu, with optional wine flight, if you want to really see what this kitchen is capable of. Desserts follow the modern Italian path and certainly don't lack impact or technical proficiency: orange jelly with bergamot ice cream, perhaps, or chocolate soufflé.

Chef Heinz Beck, Heros De Agostinis **Owner** St Regis Hotels and Resorts **Times** 12.30-2.30/7-10.30 **Prices** Fixed L 2 course fr £25, Fixed D 3 course fr £45, Tasting menu £65-£85, Starter £18.50-£35, Main £29-£68, Dessert £12.50-£15.50, Service added but optional 12.5% **Wines** 27 by glass **Notes** Tasting menu 5/7 course, Vegetarian available, Dress restrictions, Smart casual **Seats** 100, Pr/dining room 14 **Children** Portions, Menu **Parking** 25

LONDON SW1 *continued*

Le Caprice
PLAN 4 J6

@ Modern European **V** 🕐

Renowned Mayfair favourite

☎ 020 7629 2239 & 7016 5220
Arlington House, Arlington St SW1A 1RJ
e-mail: reservations@le-caprice.co.uk
dir: Nearest station: Green Park. Arlington St runs beside
The Ritz. Restaurant is at end

A 30th-anniversary refurb (September 2011) has kept the
iconic revolving front doors at this glam Mayfair classic -
tucked away behind The Ritz - with a terrace, cool bar,
and sleek new floor and windows ringing the changes.
The monochrome retro-cool '80s look remains, including
its celebrated gallery of black-and-white David Bailey
photographs. The much-loved simple classic dishes - like
salmon fishcakes or Caprice burger - haven't gone
anywhere either. Service is slick and professional, with
the charm offensive commencing as soon as you enter
through those doors. The please-all roster of reliable
European-brasserie comfort dishes includes the likes of
deep-fried fish with minted pea purée, chips and tartare,
plus seasonal specials like whole grilled Cornish
monkfish tail with béarnaise, or the more modish Thai-
baked sea bass with fragrant rice. Nursery desserts (aka,
lemon curd steamed sponge pudding) and a short
afternoon menu keep the fun rolling all day.

Chef Andy McLay **Owner** Caprice Holdings Ltd
Times 12-12 Closed 25-26 Dec, L 1 Jan, D 24 Dec All-
day dining **Prices** Fixed D 3 course £24.25, Starter
£6.50-£16.25, Main £15.75-£34.50, Dessert
£6.50-£10.75, Service added but optional 12.5%
Wines 60 bottles over £30, 5 bottles under £30, 28 by
glass **Notes** Weekend brunch menu, Sunday L, Vegetarian
menu **Seats** 86 **Parking** On street, NCP

Cavendish London
PLAN 4 J6

@ British 🕐

Well-sourced produce in a smart St James's hotel

☎ 020 7930 2111
81 Jermyn St SW1Y 6JF
e-mail: info@thecavendishlondon.com
web: www.thecavendishlondon.com
dir: Nearest station: Green Park, Piccadilly. From
Piccadilly (pass The Ritz), 1st right into Dukes St before
Fortnum & Mason

Given its Jermyn Street address, just behind Fortnum &
Mason, it will come as no surprise to hear that The
Cavendish is a swish four-star hotel. The vivid and bold
art that abounds, though, may well top expectations. The
Petrichor restaurant - named in honour of the scent that
arises from the earth after a dry spell has been broken by
the first rains - is up on the first floor and is a chic space
with vibrant artworks, smartly upholstered seating and
darkwood tables. The seasonally-minded menu is focused
on well-sourced ingredients and sustainability, and the
combinations are contemporary and enticing. Start with
Wicks Manor pork as slowly braised and fried pig's cheek

croquette, served with Scotch quail's egg, garlic purée,
pickled vegetables and piccalilli sauce. Follow on with
'sustainable fish pie' packed with salmon, mussels,
smoked haddock and scampi, or confit venison shoulder
with pumpkin purée, fondant potato and juniper berry
sauce.

Chef Nitin Padwal **Owner** Ascott Ltd
Times 12-2.30/5.30-10.30 Closed 25-26 Dec, 1 Jan, L
Sat-Sun & BH Mon **Prices** Fixed L 2 course £15.50,
Starter £6-£9.50, Main £16.50-£23, Dessert £6-£9.50,
Service added but optional 12.5% **Wines** 31 bottles over
£30, 12 bottles under £30, 10 by glass **Notes** Pre-theatre
menu Sun-Thu 5.30-6.30/Fri-Sat 5-6.30pm, Vegetarian
available **Seats** 80, Pr/dining room 70 **Children** Portions,
Menu **Parking** 60, Secure on-site valet parking

Le Cercle
PLAN 4 G3

@@ Modern French

**Modish basement restaurant serving up inspired
modern French dishes**

☎ 020 7901 9999
1 Wilbraham Place SW1X 9AE
e-mail: info@lecercle.co.uk
dir: Nearest station: Sloane Square. Just off Sloane St

From the same stable as Club Gascon (see entry), this
stylish modern basement dining room close to Sloane
Square is a lively place much of the day. The glamorous
interior boasts a mezzanine lounge area with secluded
booths where you can chillax with an inventive cocktail or
two, and an equally cool restaurant with polished wood
tables, smart leather seating and a glass-fronted wine
cellar. Creative modern French grazing-style dishes are
the order of the day, plus the occasional conventional
French favourite alongside good-value set lunch, pre-
theatre and 'Traditions' tasting menus. Clear flavours
and stylish presentation characterise the likes of onglet
tartare with smoked ketchup and mustard ice cream,
baby squid ragoût with crab bisque, and among the
larger plats, braised and seared venison with parsnip
and white chocolate pulp and artichoke macaroons.
Desserts are no less inventive: crème brûlée with
raspberry and hibiscus sorbet, for example. A racy French
wine list doesn't let standards slip.

Times 12-2.30/5.30-10.45 Closed Xmas, Sun-Mon

Chabrot
PLAN 4 F5

@@ French

Authentic French bistro in Knightsbridge

☎ 020 7225 2238
9 Knightsbridge Green SW1X 7QL
e-mail: info@chabrot.co.uk
dir: Nearest station: Knightsbridge

'Bistrot d'amis' heads up the menu, and indeed Chabrot
has the sort of friendly atmosphere typical of a bistro du
coin, helped along by characteristic bentwood chairs,
closely set tables covered by red and white cloths, and
friendly, informal service. The cooking is based on the
cuisine of southern France, the menu ranging from

grazing-sized plates of, for example, smoked herrings
with warm potato salad, or foie gras terrine with green
beans, to duck confit with a salad of potatoes, beans and
shallots. The kitchen puts tip-top French produce to good
effect: Brittany oysters with baby chorizo, andouille and
jambon de Bayonne in a platter of charcuterie, Périgord
truffle with poached Landais chicken breast, served with
vegetables, and, for two to share, Pyrenean lamb shoulder
roasted with spices, dried fruit and couscous. Wave the
tricolore at the end with prunes and Armagnac syrup.

Times 12-3.30/6.30-11 Closed Sun

The Cinnamon Club
PLAN 5 A4

@@ Modern Indian 🕐

Inventive Indian food in a grand listed building

☎ 020 7222 2555
**The Old Westminster Library, 30-32 Great Smith St
SW1P 3BU**
e-mail: info@cinnamonclub.com
dir: Nearest station: Westminster, St James's Park. Take
exit 6, across Parliament Sq, pass Westminster Abbey on
left. 1st left into Great Smith St

Close to Westminster's finest (Abbey, School and
Parliament), the historic Grade II listed Old Westminster
Library makes for an appealing dining venue. It's
certainly a characterful setting, with a decidedly
gentlemen's clubby vibe, with some inspired modern
Indian dishes on the menu. High ceilings, skylights,
parquet floor, darkwood and contemporary seating all
play their part, but it is the gallery of books above the
main dining room that sticks in the mind. The star turn
here (attracting political types and Westminster suits) is
the innovative, high calibre contemporary Indian food,
which comes well-dressed and driven by top-notch
ingredients and balanced spicing. Spiced crusted sea
bass, for example, with chick pea salad, green mango
and coconut chutney to start, followed by clove-smoked
grouse breast teamed with pumpkin pickle and green
moong 'tadka'. The same attention to detail is lavished
on desserts, perhaps coriander and corn cake delivered
with coconut parfait and spiced ice cream. Tasting
menus, a good value fixed-price lunch, professional but
smiley service and a spice-friendly corker of a wine list
complete the picture. (See also entry for the Cinnamon
Kitchen.)

Chef Vivek Singh **Owner** Indian Restaurants Limited
Times 12-2.45/6-10.45 Closed BHs, Sun, L 25 Dec
Prices Fixed L 2 course £22, Fixed D 3 course £24,
Tasting menu £75-£150, Starter £8-£17, Main £16-£34,
Dessert £7.50-£12.50, Service added but optional 12.5%
Wines 307 bottles over £30, 18 bottles under £30, 20 by
glass **Notes** Tasting menu D 7 course, with paired wines
£115-£150, Vegetarian available, Dress restrictions,
Smart casual, Civ Wed 40 **Seats** 130, Pr/dining room 60
Parking Abingdon St

Save on Hotels. Book at **theAA.com/hotel**

LONDON, CENTRAL (SW1) 287 ENGLAND

Colbert

PLAN 4 G3

◉ French **NEW**

France comes to Sloane Square

☎ 020 7730 2804
50-52 Sloane Square, Chelsea SW1W 8AX
e-mail: info@colbertchelsea.com
dir: Nearest station: Sloane Square. M25 junct 15
Heathrow Airport/London, follow A4 Great West Road. Turn
right Beauchamp Place, right Chesham Place & 2nd left
Lyall Street. Follow A317 Eaton Square, left Sloane
Square. Restaurant on left

Occupying a prominent corner site on Sloane Square,
Colbert is owned by the same team behind The Delaunay
and The Wolseley (see entries) and runs along a similar
all-day dining concept to the latter. Inspired by a classic
Parisian café, it's a trip back to the France of the Belle
Epoque or 1930s inside, with burgundy leather
banquettes, mirrors, wood panelling, artworks and
chessboard tiles. Except for the absence of Gauloises
smoke and stripy jumpers, the scene could hardly be
more Gallic - even the blackboard specials are written in
French. Expect fish soup with rouille and gruyère to taste
just as hearty and punchy as it would across the Channel,
before moving on to old friends such as chicken paillard,
steak tartare, navarin of lamb, or Toulouse cassoulet with
confit duck. Beret-wearing desserts feature the likes of
tarte fine aux pommes, crème caramel and chocolate
mousse.

Times 8am-11.30pm All-day dining **Prices** Prices not
confirmed Service added but optional 12.5% **Notes** Cover
charge £1.75 L & D

Corinthia Hotel London

PLAN 5 B6

◉◉ Modern British **V** ▲NOTABLE WINE LIST

Quality ingredients impeccably cooked in stylish hotel

☎ 020 7930 8181
Whitehall Place SW1A 2BD
e-mail: northallenquiry@corinthia.com
dir: Nearest station: Charing Cross, Embankment. M4
onto A4, follow Central London signs. Pass Green Park,
right into Coventry St, 1st right into Haymarket, left into
Pall Mall East, right into Trafalgar Sq, 3rd exit into
Whitehall Place

The Northall restaurant at the Corinthia, a luxury hotel
just off Whitehall, is a vast designer-led space of high
ceilings, tall windows, orange banquettes at correctly set
unclothed tables, and plenty of flowers in evidence. The
kitchen showcases the best of British produce (suppliers
are named under each dish) and has assembled a crowd-
pleasing menu of modern ideas as well as established
classics like crab bisque and steaks from the Josper grill.
Kick off with an indulgent starter of pan-fried foie gras
well complemented by roast mango and sauce Jacqueline,
or something more unusual like céviche of scallops
dressed with fermented lemons and edible flowers.
Timings are spot on and combinations well thought out,
so roast haunch of venison comes nicely caramelised
outside, pink inside, served with spicy red cabbage and
rich, sticky gravy. The kitchen's not too proud to turn its
hand to burgers and beer-battered haddock, but its full
creative talents are seen in puddings like a visually
pleasing plate of vanilla parfait offset by a flawless
cherry compôte and mint jelly.

Chef Garry Hollihead **Times** 12-3/5.30-11 **Prices** Fixed L
2 course £26.50, Fixed D 3 course £30, Starter £6-£15,
Main £14-£39, Dessert £8, Service added but optional
12.5%, Groups min 10 service 12.5% **Notes** 3 course incl
glass of champagne, Sunday L, Vegetarian menu, Dress
restrictions, **Seats** 82 **Children** Portions, Menu
Parking Valet parking

Dinner by Heston Blumenthal

PLAN 4 F5

◉◉◉ – **see below**

Dinner by Heston Blumenthal

LONDON SW1   PLAN 4 F5

British ▲NOTABLE WINE LIST

Heston looking back to move forward

☎ 020 7201 3833
**Mandarin Oriental Hyde Park, 66 Knightsbridge
SW1X 7LA**
e-mail: malon-dinnerhb@mohg.com
web: www.dinnerbyheston.com
dir: Nearest station: Knightsbridge. Opposite Harvey
Nichols

Let's talk about ice cream: an ice cream trolley is wheeled
over to your table and with a little bit of help from some
liquid nitrogen, bingo, fresh ice cream made just for you,
and served in a cone with popping candy or such like.
How cool is that? By the time you get to that stage,
though, you'll have admired the spacious and elegant
room, with its views over Hyde Park and stunning open
kitchen seen through a wall of glass, settled into your
table and been served with a good deal of charm and
efficiency, and eaten a memorable meal. Heston
Blumenthal needs no introduction, and his London
outpost, headed-up by the talented Ashley Palmer-Watts,
fulfills his vision to bring old recipes back to life,
reinvigorate them with amazingly high quality produce
and some modern cooking techniques and kit (note the
Josper Grill at the back of the kitchen). The recipes date
from 1390 to 1940 and every dish meets (and exceeds)
21st-century expectations when it comes to flavour,
texture and wow-factor; in other words, they deliver.
Savoury porridge (circa 1660) stars frog's legs (succulent
and tender) in a vivid green parsley porridge with smoked
beetroot, garlic and fennel - a beautifully balanced dish.
Battalia pie (back to 1660 for this one, too) is filled with
sweetbreads, lamb's tongue, devilled kidneys and pigeon,
in a rich and earthy dish of real class. Cod in cider with
chard and fired mussels brings us up to 1940. The
amazing mechanical rotisserie gives a golden glow to the
pineapples served with the tipsy cake (circa 1810), or try
the brown bread ice cream with salted butter caramel,
pear and malted yeast syrup. Dinner, or lunch at Dinner,
is a memorable experience but no novelty act - the craft,
the fabulous produce, and the attention to detail are sure
to impress.

Chef Ashley Palmer-Watts **Owner** Mandarin Oriental Hyde
Park **Times** 12-2.30/6.30-10.30 **Prices** Fixed L 3 course fr
£36, Starter £14.50-£17, Main £26-£38, Dessert £9-£12,
Service added but optional 12.5% **Wines** 20 by glass
Notes Vegetarian available, Dress restrictions, Smart
casual **Seats** 138, Pr/dining room 10 **Children** Portions
Parking Valet parking, NCP

LONDON SW1 *continued*

The Goring
PLAN 4 H4

@@ Traditional British 🍷 NOTABLE WINE LIST

Refined, classical English cooking in a grand hotel

☎ 020 7396 9000
Beeston Place SW1W 0JW
e-mail: reception@thegoring.com
web: www.thegoring.com
dir: Nearest station: Victoria. From Victoria St turn left into Grosvenor Gdns, cross Buckingham Palace Rd, 75yds turn right into Beeston Place

A starring role in the royal wedding in 2011 (the Middletons stayed here, you might recall) was surely among the highlights of the Goring family's hundred-plus year tenure of this fine piece of Belgravia real estate. It remains one of London's most luxurious and alluringly English hotels. The lavishly done out restaurant suits the mood, with its grand Edwardian proportions, moulded plasterwork, bespoke Swarovski chandeliers and precisely laid tables, watched over by a skilled service team who work in a formal manner. From the trolley comes a roast at lunch, with perhaps a beef Wellington in the evening, and, from the carte, dishes that follow the British seasons and are based on top quality produce. Goosnargh duck leg might come in a terrine with pickled red cabbage, followed by Lincolnshire ham knuckle with egg pithivier, pea purée and English mustard sauce, or wild mushroom and leek tart with a leek sauce. It's back to the trolley for desserts and cheeses.

Chef Derek Quelch **Owner** Goring family
Times 12.30-2.30/6-10 Closed L Sat **Prices** Fixed L 3 course fr £38, Fixed D 3 course fr £49.50, Service added but optional 12.5% **Wines** 364 bottles over £30, 4 bottles under £30, 22 by glass **Notes** Pre-theatre 2 course £35, Sunday L, Vegetarian available, Dress restrictions, Smart dress, Civ Wed 50 **Seats** 70, Pr/dining room 50
Children Portions, Menu **Parking** 7

Il Convivio
PLAN 4 G3

@@ Modern Italian

Modish Italian in smart Belgravia

☎ 020 7730 4099
143 Ebury St SW1W 9QN
e-mail: ilconvivio@etruscarestaurants.com
web: www.ilconvivio.co.uk
dir: Nearest station: Victoria, Sloane Square. 7 min walk from Victoria Station - corner of Ebury St and Elizabeth St

Named after Dante's poem which translates as 'a meeting over food and drink', Il Convivio offers creative modern Italian food based on high quality ingredients. Entering the Georgian townhouse restaurant on moneyed Ebury Street, the feeling is one of light and space, thanks to a glass frontage, a skylight in the main restaurant and the conservatory out back with a fully retractable roof to cope with the UK's unpredictable seasons. A deep red wall amongst the white continues the theme with inscriptions of Dante's poems, while limestone-tiled floors, cedar wooden panels and white linen add to the romantic atmosphere. The large Italian wine list has plenty to choose from by the glass. Start with all the simplicity of beef carpaccio with celery and basil infused olive oil, before moving on to tagliatelle with Cornish crab, rocket and black olive, and a main course such as monkfish fillet wrapped in courgette and Parma ham, served with fennel and mint salad.

Chef Jonathan Lees **Owner** Piero & Enzo Quaradeghini
Times 12-3.15/6-11.15 Closed Xmas, New Year, BHs, Sun **Prices** Fixed L 2 course fr £17.50, Fixed D 3 course fr £23.50, Starter £7.50-£17.50, Main £14-£24, Dessert £6-£7.50, Service added but optional 12.5% **Wines** 129 bottles over £30, 37 bottles under £30, 18 by glass **Notes** Vegetarian available, Dress restrictions, Smart casual **Seats** 65, Pr/dining room 14 **Parking** On street

Inn the Park
PLAN 5 A5

@ British

Good British cooking in St James's Park

☎ 020 7451 9999
St James's Park SW1A 2BJ
e-mail: reservations@innthepark.com
dir: Nearest station: St James's Park, Charing Cross, Piccadilly. 200mtrs down The Mall towards Buckingham Palace

With The Mall and Horseguards Parade close by, this smart wooden building with floor-to-ceiling glass has upped the ante as far as eating in a London park goes. There's a distinctly Scandinavian feel to the structure, but this is central London alright. A covered decked terrace is the place to be when the weather allows, but those windows ensure the lake and magnificent trees are visible all year round. It's a café, too, with the restaurant bit looking good with its comfy tubular chairs and orange-topped tables. As if to confirm its contemporary credentials, the kitchen is open to view. Expect good British produce prepared with a pleasing straightforwardness; grilled razor clams or crab salad with pea shoots and mint might kick things off, followed by green lentil, pea and toasted cashew burger, or honey-glazed spring chicken with wild garlic stuffing.

Times 12-3.30/5.30-9.30

Ken Lo's Memories of China
PLAN 4 H3

@ Chinese

Smart Chinese cooking in Belgravia

☎ 020 7730 7734
65-69 Ebury St SW1W 0NZ
e-mail: moc@londonfinedininggroup.com
dir: Nearest station: Victoria. At junction of Ebury Street & Eccleston St

Serving the well-heeled of Belgravia for some 30 years, Ken Lo's is a smart, upmarket restaurant with a loyal following. Chinese fabrics and red lanterns combine in a room divided by sandalwood screens, looked over by a slick service team. Authentic regional Chinese cooking is the order of the day, with lots of classic dishes featured in a range of set menus and on the mighty à la carte. You might start with three-spiced squid, siu mai dumplings or red oil-poached chicken dumplings, following on with a soup (Shanghai fish and crabmeat, perhaps). Next up, Peking quick-fried lamb with spring onion, Cantonese beef in black bean sauce, or a clay pot dish such as aubergine with minced prawns.

Chef Peter Shum Tsui **Owner** A-Z Restaurants
Times 12-2.30/6-11 Closed 25-26 Dec **Prices** Starter £4-£14.95, Main £12.50-£50, Dessert £5.95-£8.95, Service added but optional 13%, Groups min 15 service 15% **Wines** 6 by glass **Notes** Sunday L, Vegetarian available, Dress restrictions, Smart casual **Seats** 120, Pr/dining room 20 **Children** Portions **Parking** On street

Save on Hotels. Book at **theAA.com/hotel**

LONDON, CENTRAL (SW1) 289 **ENGLAND**

Koffmann's
PLAN 4 G5

⍟⍟⍟ – *see below*

Marcus Wareing at the Berkeley
PLAN 4 G5

⍟⍟⍟⍟⍟ – *see page 290*

Mint Leaf
PLAN 5 A6

⍟ Modern Indian 🥢

Upmarket Indian cooking in super-cool setting

☎ 020 7930 9020
Suffolk Place, Haymarket SW1Y 4HX
e-mail: reservations@mintleafrestaurant.com
web: www.mintleafrestaurant.com
dir: Nearest station: Piccadilly, Charing Cross. At the end of Haymarket, on corner of Pall Mall & Suffolk Pl

Enter the canopied door from the street, descend the stairs and make your way along the catwalk-style walkway that splits the two sides of this voguishly designed and furnished restaurant. Top-end Indian cooking is the deal, with dishes sourced from all over the sub-continent. Grilled chicken breast infused with lemon served with spicy mint sauce, plump and succulent prawns in a sweet-and-sour-style tomato sauce, and accurately seared scallops with star anise and green peppercorns show the style. Bite-sized pieces of lightly smoked chicken come in a well-balanced, velvety sauce of tomato and fenugreek leaves and incidentals like breads get the thumbs up. Gulab jamon might be given the brûlée treatment for pudding.

Mint Leaf

Chef Rajinder Pandey **Owner** Out of Africa Investments **Times** 12-3/5.30-11 Closed 25-26 Dec, 1 Jan, L Sat-Sun **Prices** Fixed L 2 course fr £13.95, Tasting menu fr £75, Starter £6.50-£12, Main £13-£19, Dessert fr £7.50, Service added but optional 12.5% **Wines** 100 bottles over £30, 17 bottles under £30, 13 by glass **Notes** Pre-theatre menu 5-7pm 2/3 course £13.95/£17.95, Vegetarian available, Dress restrictions, Smart casual, no scruffy jeans or trainers, Civ Wed 100 **Seats** 144, Pr/dining room 66 **Children** Portions **Parking** NCP, on street

Mitsukoshi
PLAN 2 K1

⍟ Japanese

Friendly, traditional, Japanese department store restaurant

☎ 020 7930 0317
Dorland House, 14-20 Lower Regent St SW1Y 4PH
e-mail: restaurant@mitsukoshi.co.uk
dir: Nearest station: Piccadilly Circus. Piccadilly Circus, exit Lower Regent St, entry via Mitsukoshi department store lower ground floor

In the basement below the Mitsukoshi department store, just a short stroll from all the Piccadilly Circus mêlée, this authentic, traditional-style Japanese restaurant is much loved by Japanese tourists and expats. It comes with separate sushi and cocktail bars, while the main dining area - a few steps below - is a modish space, decked out with red carpet and black lacquered furniture with red-leather upholstery; pale-wood booth-like dividers break up the large space. Authentic, polite and smiley service backs up an extensive carte of honest, traditional Japanese dishes, which include several set and fixed-priced options as well as sushi and sashimi. Expect king prawn tempura, grilled salmon with a spicy teriyaki sauce, or prime Scottish rib-eye steak with an onion soy dressing. For a touch of theatre, try the sukiyaki or shabu-shabu (hotpots) cooked in the pan at the table.

Times 12-2/6-10 Closed 25-26 Dec, 1 Jan, Etr

Koffmann's

LONDON SW1
PLAN 4 G5

French 🍷 NOTABLE WINE LIST

Top-grade regional French cooking from a virtuoso

☎ 020 7235 1010 & 7201 1665
The Berkeley, Wilton Place SW1X 7RL
e-mail: koffmanns@the-berkeley.co.uk
dir: Nearest station: Knightsbridge. 300mtrs from Hyde Park Corner along Knightsbridge

A taste of South West France in South West London has long been Pierre Koffmann's proposition, and from the early days of haute cuisine at La Tante Claire (over 35 years ago!) to today's slightly less haute approach, he remains one of the finest exponents in the country. The Berkeley makes a smart home for some smart - sometimes homely, sometimes luxurious - seasonal French cooking. Koffmann's has its own entrance and feels very much like a stand-alone restaurant, where the lack of natural daylight matters not a jot in the comfortable setting: warm neutral colours, foodie prints on textured walls and crisply set tables, supported by a formal French service team. Expect classical favourites alongside some of the great man's signature dishes, all based on fabulous ingredients. The bi-lingual menus offer up lobster bisque and hot foie gras pot-au-feu to get the ball rolling, or there might be a seasonal asparagus soup with great depth of flavour and little croûtons bringing a delightful textural contrast. Next up, cod might be steamed and served with fennel consommé or roasted and partnered with couscous delicately spiced up with North African aromatics. Scottish sirloin steak with black pepper sauce, or duck breast with orange sauce are traditional ideas executed with great attention to detail, or there might be Iberico pork with girolles. Desserts offer up some old favourites such as crêpe Suzette and rum baba, but if you can wait for 15 minutes, the delights of pistachio soufflé with pistachio ice cream await. The wine list is packed full of interesting selections to match the French regional cooking.

Chef Pierre Koffmann **Owner** Pierre Koffmann **Times** 12-2.30/6-10.30 **Prices** Fixed L 2 course £21.50, Tasting menu £100, Starter £9-£16, Main £18-£40, Dessert £8-£15, Service added but optional 12.5% **Wines** 250 bottles over £30, 10 bottles under £30, 12 by glass **Notes** Pre/post theatre menu 2/3 course £24/£28, Sunday L £22.50-£26, Vegetarian available, Dress restrictions, Smart casual **Seats** 120, Pr/dining room 18 **Children** Portions **Parking** Knightsbridge car park

Marcus Wareing at the Berkeley

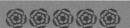

Modern European V ◆ NOTABLE WINE LIST

Cooking of the highest order from a hands-on super-chef

☎ 020 7235 1200
The Berkeley, Wilton Place, Knightsbridge SW1X 7RL
e-mail: marcuswareing@the-berkeley.co.uk
dir: Nearest station: Knightsbridge, Hyde Park Corner. 300mtrs from Hyde Park Corner along Knightsbridge

Marcus Wareing has become something of a household name since he became chef-patron of his eponymous restaurant at the swish Berkeley hotel in 2008. He's made a fair few TV appearances since then, particularly lending his immense expertise as a judge on the Beeb's *MasterChef* and *Great British Menu*, though most of the time you'll still find him here at the pass in Knightsbridge, making sure everything that leaves the kitchen meets his perfectionist standards. High standards are set by the team on the customer-facing side of the operation too: on arrival at the hotel you'll be greeted by the doormen and then escorted through to the restaurant - it's an approach that certainly makes for a sense of occasion. The dining room is a handsome looking space with walls covered in burgundy velvet, matching leather chairs and well spaced, finely dressed tables. The colour-scheme can make the room feel quite dark, but that just adds to an overall impression of cosseting warmth - of being in a safe haven away from the frenetic activity on the Knightsbridge streets outside. It's a good job there's lots of space, as trolleys laden with various gastronomic cargoes - perfectly ripe cheeses and brandies amongst them - regularly work the room. The front-of-house team are masters at making you feel relaxed and at home, whilst being unfalteringly attentive and highly skilled in the art of service. The menus run from a reasonably-priced set lunch (£38 for three courses, coffee and half a bottle of water) to the à la carte (with a vegetarian version), and two tasting menus, including the show-stopping chef's menu at £120. Things get off to a flying start with canapés and then an amuse-bouche (a carrot and coriander espuma, perhaps, topped with onion crisps) that demonstrate the kitchen's ability to get maximum flavour from its ingredients. It would be easy to fill yourself up on the wonderful breads served with home-made brown butter, but that would be a shame when there are so many treats to come. Dishes are largely simple in their construction without any of the pizzazz you might expect from such a Premier League dining destination, but that's the beauty of Wareing's cooking - it's less about technical wizardry and more about texture, freshness, seasonality, and flavour, flavour, flavour. The richness of exemplary quality foie gras is tempered with the sharpness of fresh rhubarb, and comes with a light and fluffy brioche in a simple but brilliantly executed starter, which might be followed by super-fresh Scottish halibut, precision cooked, partnered with the fresh flavours of fregola, blood orange and sea kale. Herdwick lamb, with an intense, natural flavour and as tender as can be, comes with broccoli and wild garlic in another stunning main course. For dessert there might be lemon, meringue and iced tea - a little like a deconstructed lemon meringue pie, with the perfect balance of tang and sweetness, and superb textural contrasts - or perhaps a textbook pear tarte Tatin. Don't skip the excellent coffee that comes with fabulous chocolates from master chocolatier Damian Allsop. As you might expect in a restaurant of this standing, the wine list is a work of art in itself.

Chef Marcus Wareing, Mark Froydenlund **Owner** Marcus Wareing Restaurants Ltd **Times** 12-2.30/6-11 Closed 1 Jan, Sun **Prices** Fixed L 2 course £30-£60, Fixed D 3 course fr £80, Tasting menu £98-£120, Service added but optional 12.5% **Wines** 700 bottles over £30, 15 by glass **Notes** Fixed D 8/10 course £98/£120, Vegetarian menu, Dress restrictions, Smart - jacket preferred, No jeans/trainers **Seats** 70, Pr/dining room 16 **Children** Portions **Parking** NCP, on street

LONDON SW1 *continued*

MU at Millennium Knightsbridge
PLAN 4 F4

◉ Chinese ❁

Refined Chinese cooking in modern hotel

☎ 020 7201 6330
17 Sloane St, Knightsbridge SW1X 9NU
e-mail: reservations.knightsbridge@millenniumhotels.
co.uk
web: www.millenniumhotels.co.uk
dir: Nearest station: Knightsbridge, Victoria. 200yds from
Knightsbridge Stn, near Harrods

The restaurant at this modern Sloane Street hotel has
morphed into Le Chinois, which has taken as its
inspiration Singapore's Orchard Hotel. The deal is now a
long carte of Chinese dishes, gently tempered to appeal
to refined Western palates. Vegetable spring rolls and
pan-fried chicken dumplings are conventional enough
starters, and there could also be sesame prawns on
toast. Among main courses, prime cuts and luxuries
jostle for attention with lesser ingredients, all handled
with the same high levels of skill: lobster comes with
ginger and spring onions on a bed of noodles, rib-eye is
sautéed in black bean sauce, and minced pork and tofu
are cooked in a clay pot. Vegetables are properly timed à
la minute - mushrooms stir-fried with seasonal greens,

say - and among desserts red bean pancake with ice
cream competes for your attention with more westernised
options like a classic tarte Tatin.

Chef Anthony Robinson **Owner** Millennium & Copthorne
Hotels **Times** 12-10.30 All-day dining **Prices** Prices not
confirmed Service added but optional 12.5% **Wines** 16
bottles over £30, 10 bottles under £30, 9 by glass
Notes Vegetarian available **Seats** 65 **Children** Portions,
Menu **Parking** 8, NCP Pavilion Rd

One-O-One
PLAN 4 F5

◉◉◉ – *see below*

Osteria Dell'Angolo
PLAN 5 A4

◉ Italian

Italian classics in the heart of Westminster

☎ 020 3268 1077
47 Marsham St SW1P 3DR
e-mail: osteriadell_angolo@btconnect.com
dir: Nearest station: St James's Park, Westminster.
Located off Horseferry Rd

The kitchen of this contemporary Italian in the heart of
Westminster near to the Houses of Parliament has its
finger firmly on the regional pulse of Tuscan cuisine. After
a glass of prosecco in the smart darkwood bar, take a

seat in the dining room where butch burgundy leather
contrasts with white linen and the Mediterranean warmth
of a yellow and amber colour scheme. Well-sourced
artisan produce from Italy and splendid true-Brit
materials work together in dishes such as grilled Cornish
squid filled with Swiss chard, capers, pine kernels,
stracciatella Pugliese cheese and black olives, while
home-made gnocchi are stuffed with goats' cheese and
served with wild mushrooms, pumpkin and sage sauce.
Full-flavoured mains run to roast monkfish with osso
buco sauce, sautéed radicchio, and toasted almond and
red wine sauce, or grilled Galloway beef fillet with turnip
tops and a timbale of borlotti beans and leeks.

Chef Massimiliano Vezzi **Owner** Claudio Pulze
Times 12-3/6-10.30 Closed Xmas, New Year, last 2 wks
Aug, BHs, Sun, L Sat **Prices** Fixed L 2 course £16.50,
Fixed D 3 course £27.95, Starter £8.50-£11.50, Main
£18-£24.50, Dessert £5.50, Service added but optional
12.5% **Wines** 200 bottles over £30, 8 bottles under £30,
12 by glass **Notes** Early supper menu Mon-Sat 6-7.30pm,
Vegetarian available **Seats** 80, Pr/dining room 22
Parking 6

One-O-One

LONDON SW1
PLAN 4 F5

French V ♦ **NOTABLE WINE LIST**

A temple of seafood in a Knightsbridge hotel

☎ 020 7290 7101
**The Park Tower Knightsbridge, 101 Knightsbridge
SW1X 7RN**
e-mail: oneoone@luxurycollection.com
web: www.oneoonerestaurant.com
dir: Nearest station: Knightsbridge. E from station, just
after Harvey Nichols, corner William St & Knightsbridge

Born in a fishing village in Brittany and with cooking in
his blood, Pascal Proyart is the undisputed big fish when
it comes to the cooking of seafood in the capital. He's
been here for 15 years now, and this restaurant in The
Park Tower Knightsbridge is a must-visit address for
anyone with a passion for the fruits of the sea. Rest

assured that ethical issues around sustainability, etc, are
high up the agenda and you can eat with a clear
conscience. The room is designed to evoke the shape of a
shucked oyster, right down to the seafood counter
representing the pearl at its centre, and it's a smart and
civilised space watched over by a thoroughly proficient,
well-drilled and charming service team. There's a
sustainable 'Petits Plats' menu available at lunchtime,
allowing you to choose from anywhere between two and
six courses, and priced accordingly. Alternatively, there's
a full-on tasting menu (which includes a meat course),
and an à la carte packed with good ideas. Monsieur
Proyart has adroit technical abilities and his
interpretation of modern French cooking shows plenty of
imagination and creativity, but ultimately respect for the
fabulous ingredients at his disposal. A first-course dish
of wild langoustines - fabulous, really - with pan-fried
duck foie gras, petit ravioli, hoisin froth and Peking duck
consommé balances flavours triumphantly, while the
oak-smoked Scottish salmon might come with crispy

braised pork belly, crushed potato with parsley and caper
butter, and balsamic and horseradish. There is an
inherent sense here of what works with what. Slow-
cooked wild Norwegian cod (from the Barents Sea) comes
in a main course with Ibérian chorizo risotto and squid
and prawns cooked à la plancha, and, to finish, there's
no less skill among desserts: perhaps white chocolate
mousse with juniper berries, lemon sorbet and soft gin
and tonic jelly.

Chef Pascal Proyart **Owner** Starwood Hotels & Resorts
Times 12-3/6.30-10 Closed 25 Dec, 1 Jan **Prices** Fixed L
2 course £17, Fixed D 2 course £49-£60, Starter £18-£28,
Main £28-£32, Dessert £9.50, Service optional, Groups
min 15 service 12.5% **Wines** 8 by glass **Notes** Tasting
menu 5 course, Sunday L, Vegetarian menu, Dress
restrictions, Smart casual **Seats** 51, Pr/dining room 10
Children Portions, Menu

LONDON SW1 *continued*

Park Plaza Victoria London PLAN 4 J3

◉ Modern French, Mediterranean

Modern hotel brasserie dining

☎ 020 7769 9772 & 7769 9999
239 Vauxhall Bridge Rd SW1V 1EQ
e-mail: gfernando@pphe.com
web: www.parkplaza.com
dir: Nearest station: Victoria. 2 min walk from Apollo
Victoria Theatre

Well placed for exploring London's history and heritage
and conveniently close to Victoria Station, the Park Plaza
is a smart modern hotel with stylish public areas. The
coffee bar is a popular daytime venue, and at cocktail
o'clock, the glossy bar is an inviting spot to linger a while
before moving on into JB's Restaurant. Staying with the
up-to-date theme, it has full-length windows for
watching the street bustle while you choose from a wide-
ranging menu of modern crowd pleasers. Ingredients are
well-sourced and treated without undue fuss, starting
perhaps, with grilled baby squid with lemon, parsley, red
pepper and chorizo, while mains may include roast pigeon
with grilled polenta, smoked pork belly and date sauce.
Finish with blackberry, limoncello and mascarpone trifle.

Times 6-10 Closed BHs, Sun, L all week

Pétrus PLAN 4 G5

◉◉◉ – *see opposite*

Quaglino's PLAN 4 J6

◉ French Brasserie

**Properly made brasserie-style dishes and a buzzing
atmosphere**

☎ 020 7930 6767
16 Bury St, St James's SW1Y 6AJ
e-mail: quaglinos@danddlondon.com
dir: Nearest station: Green Park, Piccadilly Circus. Bury St
is off Jermyn St

The sheer scale of Quaglino's cannot fail to impress even
regulars as they descend the staircase to the vast space
below, with its art-deco good looks and lively atmosphere,
especially when live music adds to the zing. The
seasonally-changing menu is a roll-call of modern

brasserie fare, albeit often using luxuries: foie gras
terrine with quince jelly, followed by Dover sole meunière,
for instance. Other ingredients are equally well chosen
(the kitchen utilises small and medium suppliers to
guarantee quality and freshness) and well handled, and,
surprisingly given the size of the operation, cooking
standards are consistently high. Start with dressed crab
on toast, or beef carpaccio, and go on to a succulent slab
of pork belly with apple sauce and ratte potatoes, or
smoked haddock fishcake with spinach and dill beurre
blanc. Finish with an old favourite like strawberry
meringue, or chocolate tart with orange sauce.

Chef Craig James **Owner** D & D London **Times** 12-3/5.30-
mdnt Closed 24-25 Dec, 1 Jan, L 31 Dec **Prices** Fixed L 2
course £15, Starter £8-£16.50, Main £15.50-£32.50,
Dessert £7.50, Service added but optional 12.5%
Wines 160+ bottles over £30, 2 bottles under £30, 25 by
glass **Notes** Fixed D pre/post-theatre 5.30-7/10-11pm
£18.50-£24.50, Vegetarian available, Dress restrictions,
Smart casual **Seats** 267, Pr/dining room 44
Children Portions, Menu **Parking** Arlington Street NCP

Quilon PLAN 4 J4

◉◉ Indian ⚘ NOTABLE WINE LIST

Classy Southern Indian coastal cooking

☎ 020 7821 1899
41 Buckingham Gate SW1E 6AF
e-mail: info@quilonrestaurant.co.uk
web: www.quilon.co.uk
dir: Nearest station: St James's Park, Victoria. Next to
Crowne Plaza Hotel St James

A complete makeover in 2012 has certainly raised the
stakes at Quilon, a haute-cuisine modern Indian that's
part of the swanky Crowne Plaza hotel, though you
wouldn't necessarily know that from the street as it has

its own entrance. The new Q Bar up front offers a smart,
intimate space for drinks and canapés, while the
L-shaped dining room is an equally sophisticated,
contemporary confection decorated with striking coastal-
inspired works by acclaimed artist Paresh Maity. Sriram
Aylur's cooking is focused on the seafood and vegetarian
dishes of the South-West Indian coastal region, though
meat dishes find their place too. Subtlety, balance and
refinement are trademarks, with the skilful blend of heat
and fragrance allowing top-notch seasonal produce to
shine. Take herb-crusted tilapia with mustard sauce or
Goan-spiced and seared whole sea bass with Goan green
and red masala. Vegetable dishes might include mango
curry (fresh ripe mango cooked with yoghurt and green
chillies and tempered with mustard seeds and curry
leaves), while meat lovers can't go wrong with the
braised lamb shank (slow-cooked with freshly ground
herbs, spices and chillies). Service is slick and discreet,
while a cracking wine list offers plentiful spice-friendly
bottles, plus there's an impressive selection of
international beers.

Quilon

Chef Sriram Aylur **Owner** Taj International Hotels Limited
Times 12-2.30/6-11 Closed 25 Dec **Prices** Fixed L 3
course £27-£45, Fixed D 3 course £48-£63, Tasting menu
£48-£85, Starter £8-£14, Main £15-£31, Dessert £7-£8,
Service added but optional 12.5% **Wines** 130 bottles over
£30, 4 bottles under £30, 16 by glass **Notes** Taster menu
from £48, Sunday L, Vegetarian available, Dress
restrictions, Smart casual **Seats** 90, Pr/dining room 16
Children Portions **Parking** On street, NCP

See advert opposite

Pétrus

LONDON SW1   PLAN 4 G5

Modern French V NOTABLE WINE LIST

High-achieving Ramsay kitchen in Knightsbridge

☎ 020 7592 1609
1 Kinnerton St, Knightsbridge SW1X 8EA
e-mail: petrus@gordonramsay.com
dir: Nearest station: Knightsbridge, Sloane Square

The name says it all: the legendary wine has always been a status symbol, the sort of name that people drop to show they know a thing or two about gastronomy. A good brand then, and the savvy Mr Ramsay, who knows a thing or two about the power of a brand, made sure he held on to the name of the restaurant where Marcus Wareing (see entry Marcus Wareing at the Berkeley) stamped his mark after the pair parted company. The rather odd-shaped space has an elegant, neutral look: cosseting shades of

beige, oyster and silver, swashes of claret in the fabrics and on the walls (a nod to its vinous namesake, no doubt) and circular linen-swagged tables arranged like satellites around a centre-piece glass wine tower looking rather like an accessory from the Tardis. It all exudes a decidedly luxe sheen that the denizens of Belgravia probably take for granted, although it's hard to remain unruffled by the confident modern French cooking of Sean Burbidge, which continues to impress with its immaculate attention to detail and striking presentations underpinned by the peerless quality of the materials. Hitting the luxury button from the off, Landes foie gras might come in a first course with apple jelly, smoked duck, hazelnut and blackberry crumble, or those in a truly Gallic mindset could go for crispy frogs' legs with broccoli purée, braised grelot onions, black garlic and parmesan. Main courses have no less appeal: braised Gigha halibut, perhaps, with chargrilled baby leeks and textures of chestnut, or a voluptuous loin and braised shin of Highland venison with Stilton macaroni, roast pear and juniper sauce. The

successes continue to dessert - maybe crème brûlée enlivened by star anise, caramelised pear and liquorice. If you want a piece of the action on a more modest budget, the set lunch menu offers fine value. And as you might expect of a restaurant named after the legendary Pomerol château, the wine list is a top-rank contender.

Chef Sean Burbidge **Owner** Gordon Ramsay Holdings **Times** 12-2.30/6.30-10.30 Closed 22-26 Dec, Sun **Prices** Fixed L 2 course fr £55, Fixed D 3 course fr £65, Tasting menu fr £75, Service added but optional 12.5% **Wines** 498 bottles over £30, 7 bottles under £30, 13 by glass **Notes** Chef's menu 5 course, Vegetarian menu, Dress restrictions, No sportswear **Seats** 55, Pr/dining room 7 **Children** Portions **Parking** On street (free after 6.30)/NCP Park Towers

LONDON SW1 *continued*

The Rib Room

PLAN 4 F4

@@@ *– see opposite*

Roux at Parliament Square

PLAN 5 B5

Rosettes not confirmed at time of going to print – see opposite and page 296

The Royal Horseguards

PLAN 5 B6

@@ Modern, Traditional British

Enterprising cooking near Whitehall

☎ 0871 376 9033 & 020 7451 9333
2 Whitehall Court SW1A 2EJ
e-mail: royalhorseguards@guoman.co.uk
web: www.theroyalhorseguards.co.uk
dir: Nearest station: Embankment, Charing Cross. From Trafalgar Sq take exit to Whitehall. Turn into Whitehall Place then into Whitehall Court

This regal Victorian pile was once home to the Secret Service in the First World War and now makes a suitably grand Thames-side hotel. The upmarket postcode is about as central as things get, handy for the London Eye, and a stone's throw from the Houses of Parliament and Trafalgar Square. The detectives of Scotland Yard were once based next-door, and their number - Whitehall 1212 - which was dialled in many a black-and-white noir thriller, now lives on in One Twenty One Two, the hotel's fine dining restaurant. The kitchen sources its materials from far and wide to ensure quality is always of the highest order, delivering well-crafted food in a gently modern vein, while never losing sight of its French roots. Dinner starts out with diver-caught scallops with truffle and cauliflower soup and garlic crisps, before moving on to buttered guinea fowl with pears, shallot purée, chestnut cream and grilled salsify. To finish, Valrhona's Dulcey blond chocolate stars in a mocha parfait, partnered by espresso cream, milk sorbet and home-made doughnut.

Times 12-3/5.30-10

The Rubens at the Palace

PLAN 4 H4

@@ Modern British

British food in a hotel with history

☎ 020 7834 6600
39 Buckingham Palace Rd SW1W 0PS
e-mail: bookrb@rchmail.com
web: www.redcarnationhotels.com
dir: Nearest station: Victoria. Opposite Royal Mews, 100mtrs from Buckingham Palace

The Rubens Hotel was originally built in the mews opposite Buck House to put up debutantes in the days when blue-blooded gels were presented to the world at

palace parties, and when all of that upstairs, downstairs world was swept aside by World War II, it was taken over by the Polish Resistance as their wartime HQ. These days the clubby Library restaurant still has a whiff of bygone times about it - it was plush armchairs upholstered with heraldic designs, and tables swathed in crisp white linen crisscrossed by red runners, as if flying the Cross of St George. What leaves the kitchen, however, is stamped firmly with the mark of the modern British idiom. The menu might start out with a modish composition of seared scallops with cauliflower purée, curry oil, piccalilli and micro herbs, or keep things staunchly traditional by serving smoked salmon carved at the table. A thoroughly modern main course could see peppered tenderloin of Gloucestershire Old Spot pork paired with white onion tarte Tatin, pearl barley and pancetta risotto, sage jus and spring greens, and to finish, perhaps an assiette of lemon comprising lemon and polenta cake, lemon posset and iced lemon parfait.

Chef Adrian Bailey **Owner** Red Carnation Hotels
Times 7.30-10.30 Closed 24-27 Dec, L all week
Prices Fixed D 3 course £32.50, Tasting menu £32.50, Starter £7-£12, Main £17-£35, Dessert £7-£10, Service added but optional 12.5% **Wines** 93 bottles over £30, 17 bottles under £30, 16 by glass **Notes** Vegetarian available, Dress restrictions, No shorts, tracksuits or trainers, Civ Wed 80 **Seats** 26, Pr/dining room 60 **Parking** NCP at Victoria Coach Station

St Ermin's Hotel

PLAN 4 K4

@@ Modern European ☺

Impressive cooking at luxury hotel

☎ 020 7222 7888
2 Caxton St, St James's Park SW1H 0QW
e-mail: reservations@sterminshotel.co.uk
dir: Nearest station: Victoria, St James's Park. Just off Victoria St, directly opposite New Scotland Yard

Carved out of what was a mansion block, St Ermin's is a grand luxury hotel, with a vast staircase sweeping up from the lobby and the Caxton Grill, a comfortable, light-filled room of soft colours with a calming, cosseting ambience. The menu is built on the modern European repertoire, and the cooking is based squarely on top-end raw materials. The kitchen is just as happy churning out pea velouté with ham hock (more commonly known as pea and ham soup) as it is with foie gras with pressed duck and pears. The Josper grill comes into its own for steaks and for the fish of the day, and another main course may be baked neck of organic lamb, tender and moist, with flavourful sweetbreads (the highlight), onion purée and fondant potato. Puddings can be as pretty as a glass of soft peanuts bound in honey (the hotel produces its own) topped first with caramel mousse, then by chocolate mousse, with a scoop of chocolate and cola ice cream.

Chef Adam Handling, Sylvan Chevereau **Owner** Amerimar
Times 12-2/6-10.30 Closed L Sat-Sun, 26 & 31 Dec

Prices Starter £8-£15, Main £20-£32, Dessert £8-£12, Service added but optional 12.5% **Wines** 45 bottles over £30, 16 bottles under £30, 25 by glass **Notes** Vegetarian available **Seats** 72, Pr/dining room 10 **Children** Portions, Menu **Parking** Valet parking

Sake No Hana

PLAN 4 J6

@@ Traditional Japanese

Sophisticated Japanese cooking in a smart part of town

☎ 020 7925 8988
23 St James's St SW1A 1HA
e-mail: reservations@sakenohana.com
dir: Nearest station: Green Park, Piccadilly Circus. From Green Park Station, head towards Piccadilly Circus, first right St James's St. Restaurant situated halfway down on right

Pause for a drink, perhaps a Japanese whisky or Velvet Haiku cocktail in the smart, contemporary bar before riding the escalator to the sophisticated first floor modern Japanese restaurant in well-to-do St James's. Here, large windows, a wooden lattice-decorated ceiling and full-length blinds to emulate sushi rolling mats make for an authentic Japanese feel. Light wooden tables oiled with tinted maple and light green leather banquettes are tended by charmingly attentive staff, happy to talk you through a menu which combines imported Japanese produce and UK ingredients to good effect in traditional and some fusion dishes. Wend your way through the enticing menu starting perhaps with white miso soup with wild mushrooms, or prawn and yam croquette with dashi. Deep-fried tofu with white miso, served with red miso and white miso with spinach, is a dish full of flavour, whilst slow-poached beef is beautifully tender and complemented by its accompanying light, creamy mashed potato with chestnuts, all set on a hoba leaf over charcoal. Mandarin semi-fredo with spiced caramel and roasted macadamia nuts makes for a fine fusion finale. Or pull up a chair at the sushi bar for a less formal experience.

Chef Daisuke Hayashi **Owner** Hakkasan Ltd
Times 12-2.30/6-11 Closed 24-25 Dec, Sun **Prices** Prices not confirmed Service added but optional 13% **Wines** 7 by glass **Notes** Vegetarian available, Dress restrictions, Smart casual **Seats** 100 **Parking** NCP

The Rib Room

LONDON SW1   PLAN 4 F4

British V

Classical dishes and more at Knightsbridge hotel

☎ 020 7858 7250 & 7858 7181
**Jumeirah Carlton Tower Hotel, Cadogan Place
SW1X 9PY**
e-mail: JCTinfo@jumeirah.com
web: www.jumeirah.com
dir: Nearest station: Knightsbridge. Follow road signs for
City Centre, towards Knightsbridge/Hyde Park/Sloane Sq,
then into Sloane St/Cadogan Place

The Rib Room, on the ground floor of the Jumeirah Carlton
Tower, is something of a time-honoured institution on the
Knightsbridge dining scene, and it's understandable:
comfortable upholstery, dark wooden furniture, a
profusion of courteous and efficient staff, prime British
produce, and consistently high culinary standards. The
eponymous roast rib of Aberdeen Angus is reassuring to
many, and the rest of the carte is an engaging package
of familiar classics, from beef tartare to lobster
thermidor, prawn cocktail with Marie Rose sauce to
chargrilled calves' liver and bacon with caramelised
onion sauce, all prepared and cooked to a T. Those
seeking wilder shores should focus on the seasonal
menu, which has an altogether more modern sweep.
Orkney scallops are teamed up with tamarind and date
purée, roasted cauliflower and lime caramel, for instance,
and may be an alternative to a gutsier starter of braised
lamb neck with marrowbone, onions and mushrooms.
Main courses are exemplary for their balance and
presentation: roast saddle of hare is served with a hotpot
of the leg, pickled red cabbage and apple purée, and
seared loin of monkfish with tomato and saffron purée
and a deep-tasting smoked eel velouté. End on an exotic
note with coconut and white rum mousse with pineapple
jelly and kalamansi curd, or stick closer to home and go
for baked custard tart with plum compôte. Good quality
breads with unsalted butter, and interesting petits fours
with coffee, complete the package.

Chef Ian Rudge **Owner** Jumeirah
Times 12.30-2.45/6.30-10.45 **Prices** Fixed L 2 course
£24-£49, Fixed D 3 course £58, Starter £8-£16, Main
£25-£44, Dessert £8, Service added but optional 15%
Wines 400 bottles over £30, 30 bottles under £30, 17 by
glass **Notes** Fixed ALC D fr £28, British experience menu
available, Sunday L, Vegetarian menu, Dress restrictions,
Smart casual **Seats** 88, Pr/dining room 16
Children Portions, Menu **Parking** 70

Roux at Parliament Square

Rosettes not confirmed at time of going to print

LONDON SW1 **PLAN 5 B5**

Modern European

High-flying candidate on Parliament Square

☎ 020 7334 3737
Parliament Square SW1P 3AD
e-mail: roux@rics.org
web: www.rouxatparliamentsquare.co.uk
dir: Nearest station: Westminster

Please note: the Rosette award for this establishment has been suspended due to a change of chef. Reassessment will take place in due course under the new chef.

The address may suggest a bastion of the British establishment, whilst the Roux name might imply a touch of classical refinement. But Roux at Parliament Square also has a decidedly contemporary sheen. Michel Roux jnr of Le Gavroche and *MasterChef* fame has a real winner up his sleeve here, a restaurant that might not hit the headlines on a regular basis, but is delivering some compellingly modern food, with head chef Steve Groves cooking up a storm. There's a bar with big ideas in the cocktail department, and two dining rooms done out in soothing neutral tones with a restrained contemporary finish to the space (the original building was designed by the chap who built the British Museum). The

service team does Monsieur Roux proud. A meal starts with a bang - fabulous breads and amuse-bouche set the bar high - before a first-course such as ballottine of Lincolnshire pork with mustard emulsion, pickled onions and smoked hock beignet. Technique is as sharp as a pin, flavours and textures perfectly judged, and it all looks beautiful on the plate. Main-course saddle of rabbit is stuffed with apple black pudding and comes with confit cabbage, macaroni and cider sauce, grilled fillet of Arctic char with an emulsion of sea vegetables and shellfish, plus Jersey Royals and white asparagus. To finish, poached Williams pear and almond sponge is lifted by the well-judged flavours of camomile and fennel. The wine list has all the verve and swagger of a Roux-inspired selection.

Chef Steve Groves **Owner** Restaurant Associates **Times** 12-2/6.30-10 Closed Xmas, New Year, BHs, Sat-Sun **Prices** Fixed L 3 course £35, Tasting menu £79, Starter £11-£16, Main £17-£27, Dessert £8-£14 **Wines** 21 by glass **Notes** Vegetarian available, Dress restrictions, Smart casual **Seats** 56, Pr/dining room 10 **Children** Portions **Parking** NCP Semley Place

LONDON SW1 *continued*

Salloos Restaurant   PLAN 4 G5

@ Pakistani

Authentic Pakistani cooking in Knightsbridge mews house

☎ 020 7235 4444
62-64 Kinnerton St SW1X 8ER
dir: Nearest station: Knightsbridge. Kinnerton St is opposite Berkeley Hotel on Wilton Place

Discreetly tucked away in a flower-decked corner mews house just across from The Berkeley hotel, Salloos is a genuine, family-run Pakistani outfit plying its trade here since 1976. Climb the stairs from the tiny bar to the intimate first-floor dining room to enjoy some of the Capital's most consistently sound Pakistani cooking. White linen, warm authentic colours and latticework-screened windows blend with modern seating, crystal chandeliers and contemporary artwork, while the atmosphere is traditional and the service formal (some might judge poker-faced). The kitchen's authentic, well-tuned Mughlai cuisine (the chef has been here almost 40 years so confident spicing is assured) is fashioned from quality produce on a repertoire that sees little change. Salloos is renowned for its tandooris like lamb chops or chicken or lamb shish kebab, and its house specialities such as a Khyber region chicken karahi (de-boned chicken cooked in fresh tomatoes, ginger, green chillies and fragrant coriander), while salan (curries) could include jheenga masala (small prawns cooked with onions, tomatoes and spices).

Chef Abdul Aziz **Owner** Mr & Mrs M Salahuddin **Times** 12-3/7-11.45 Closed Xmas, Sun **Prices** Starter £8-£12, Main £16-£18, Dessert £6.50, Service added but optional 12.5% **Wines** 2 by glass **Notes** Vegetarian available **Seats** 65 **Parking** Meters, car park Kinnerton St

Santini Restaurant   PLAN 4 H4

@ Italian

Faithful Italian cooking in ritzy surroundings

☎ 020 7730 4094
29 Ebury St SW1W 0NZ
e-mail: santini@santinirestaurant.com
web: www.santinirestaurant.com
dir: Nearest station: Victoria. Take Lower Belgrave St off Buckingham Palace Rd. Restaurant on 1st corner on left

This long-running Belgravia restaurant continues to produce carefully crafted Italian food in a sophisticated, upmarket décor of subtle pastel and soft grey shades, marble floor, and comfortable seating. The straightforward, honest cooking is based on quality ingredients and flavours ring true. Carpaccio and spaghetti carbonara may come as no surprise, but there's also crab salad with pomegranate, mint and parsley. Main courses take in classics like breadcrumbed veal chop, calves' liver with crisp pancetta, and plainly grilled Dover sole, with things ending memorably with the indulgence of chocolate and vanilla cheesecake.

Chef Christian Gardin **Owner** Mr G Santin **Times** 12-3/6-11 Closed Xmas, 1 Jan, Etr Sun-Mon, L Sat-Sun **Prices** Prices not confirmed Service added but optional 12.5% **Wines** 7 by glass **Notes** Pre-theatre menu, Vegetarian available, Dress restrictions, Smart casual **Seats** 65, Pr/dining room 30 **Children** Portions **Parking** Meters (no charge after 6.30pm)

Season at The Fifth Floor   PLAN 4 F5
Restaurant

@@ Modern International 🍷 NOTABLE WINE LIST

Market menus on the top floor at Harvey Nics

☎ 020 7235 5250
Harvey Nichols, 109-125 Knightsbridge SW1X 7RJ
e-mail: reception@harveynichols.com
dir: Nearest station: Knightsbridge, Hyde Park Corner. Entrance on Sloane St

It's all about great food and wine up on the top floor at Harvey Nics, with a classy food store, a café and the

flagship restaurant, the forerunner of all the various First, Second, Fourth, and indeed Forth Floors boasted by branches of the swish department store that have sprung up around the country. The restaurant has rebranded itself as Season, and as one might hope, its menus of bright contemporary brasserie-style dishes follow the seasons avidly, setting out with a gorgeous-looking terrine of smoked salmon served with herb butter, fresh crab and home-made tomato and mayonnaise sauces. At main course stage, the cooking stays accurate, delivering clean-cut flavours in easy-on-the-eye dishes: earthy girolles, carrot and nutmeg purée and spinach provide a perfect supporting cast for tender and pink roast duck breast, or you might prefer baked sea trout with Provençal vegetables, grilled fennel and sauce vierge. Ladies who lunch can kiss the diet goodbye with a warm chocolate mousse with mixed fresh berries and raspberry and red wine sorbet.

Times 12-3/6-11 Closed Xmas, Etr Sun, D Sun

Seven Park Place by   PLAN 4 J6
William Drabble

@@@@ – *see page 298*

Sofitel London St James   PLAN 4 K6

@ French, British

A touch of French style on Pall Mall

☎ 020 7968 2900
6 Waterloo Place SW1Y 4AN
e-mail: thebalcon.london@sofitel.com
dir: Nearest station: Piccadilly Circus. 3 mins' walk from Piccadilly Circus & Trafalgar Square

The hotel is an imposing piece of London real estate in an upmarket part of town, and The Balcon restaurant is suitably capacious and stylish (and rather glamorous with it). It's done out in the grand Parisian manner with double-height ceiling, soaring columns, a show-stopping duo of matching spiral staircases, plus a charcuterie and champagne bar. The menu ploughs a brasserie furrow with British and French influences along the way, and some excellent British ingredients on show. There are tarts and tartines (Welsh rarebit, for example) and superb charcuterie from Trealy Farm in Monmouthshire and Mas le Rouget in Cantal (south-central France). Start with a salad - perhaps roasted and pickled beetroots with Roquefort, candy walnuts and frisée - follow on with Label Anglais chicken cooked on the rotisserie, or beer-braised ox cheeks, and finish with a lemon pudding with lemon sauce.

Chef Vincent Menager **Owner** Accor UK **Times** 11-11 All-day dining **Prices** Fixed L 2 course £15, Fixed D 3 course £20, Starter £8-£14.25, Main £12-£25.50, Dessert £6-£8, Service added but optional 12.5% **Wines** 80 bottles over £30, 2 bottles under £30, 12 by glass **Notes** Sunday L, Vegetarian available **Seats** 100, Pr/dining room 16 **Children** Portions, Menu **Parking** NCP at Piccadilly

Seven Park Place by William Drabble

Modern French 🍷 NOTABLE WINE LIST

Assured classical French cooking in a riotously decorated St James's club

☎ 020 7316 1600
St James's Hotel and Club, 7-8 Park Place SW1A 1LS
e-mail: info@stjameshotelandclub.com
web: www.stjameshotelandclub.com
dir: Nearest station: Green Park. Off St James's St

Following some unpleasantness at a rival establishment in 1857, Earl Granville and a minister of the Sardinian government, the Marchese d'Azeglio, decided to found their own London club where they would be made welcome. Well, you would, wouldn't you? The St James's was the result, and instantly became a magnet not just for the idle rich, but for the more discerning artists of the day. By the turn of the century, Arthur Sullivan and Henry James were among those dropping in regularly. The place was relaunched in 2008 as a club-hotel with a refit that brought Murano chandeliers and cashmere-lined walls to a London about to be plunged into the financial crisis, followed the year after by William Drabble to head up a self-named restaurant. Drabble was for over a decade the incumbent at Aubergine in Chelsea, which he brought back to first-division status following Gordon

Ramsay's departure, and as such he represented a stellar acquisition for the St James's. The dining room décor, let it be said, isn't what you'd call understated. In fact, it's an argumentative hugger-mugger of geometric patterning in carpets and upholstery, with broad swathes of art-deco-ish foliage advancing up the brown walls. Not for the hung-over. It's perhaps all the more reassuring in the circumstances that Drabble's food is not about jarring sensory assault, but achieves wondrous results from dishes that make a show of themselves where it counts - on the palate. There is exquisite concentration and intensity in the cooking, which is impeccably seasonal in its use of ingredients, and in terms of the kind of weighting that works best, so lighter food in summer, more heartily rustic when the chill sets in. A seam of assured French classicism runs through the menus, which might open with seared foie gras in a dressing of roasted quince and hazelnuts, or a partnership of marinated scallops and Dorset crab with blood-orange mayonnaise. Following up comes an assiette of tenderly eloquent Lune Valley lamb with onions and thyme, or the gentle satisfaction of griddled sea bass on creamed leeks with mushrooms in red wine. If you're in the mood for something a little more peasanty, pig's head slow-cooked in Madeira with root veg should fill the bill. Paxton and Whitfield cheeses make a savoury

preamble on the gourmand menu to a dessert such as banana parfait with caramelised milk, or there may be technically perfect raspberry soufflé with chocolate sauce. All menus come with inspired wine-matching options.

Chef William Drabble **Times** 12-2/7-10 Closed Sun-Mon **Prices** Fixed L 2 course fr £25.50, Fixed D 3 course fr £58, Tasting menu fr £72, Service added but optional 12.5% **Wines** 257 bottles over £30, 16 bottles under £30, 8 by glass **Notes** Fixed 6 course Menu Gourmand, Vegetarian available, Civ Wed 40 **Seats** 34, Pr/dining room 40 **Parking** On street and NCP

Save on Hotels. Book at theAA.com/hotel

LONDON, CENTRAL (SW1) 299 ENGLAND

LONDON SW1 *continued*

The Stafford London by Kempinski

PLAN 4 J6

Traditional British **NOTABLE WINE LIST**

Luxurious hotel dining in exclusive location

☎ 020 7493 0111
16-18 St James's Place SW1A 1NJ
e-mail: info@thelyttelton.com
web: www.thelyttelton.com
dir: Nearest station: Green Park

It's easy to forget you're in central London when you're safely ensconced in The Stafford. Hidden away down a discreet street by Green Park, it is a luxurious St James's address that is worth knowing about. The American Bar, for a start, should put it on any map; head on down for a damn fine martini. If it is something more sustaining you're after, The Lyttelton restaurant does a nice line in classy British food, where fine UK produce gets treated with due diligence and turned into smart, gently refined dishes. It all takes place in a rather swanky room with tones of ivory and grey, smart contrasting floral fabrics, commissioned artwork and chandeliers. Start with tartare of beef with melba toast and quail's egg, move on to best-end of Daphne's lamb with celeriac dauphinoise and mint sauce, or risotto of wild mushrooms. End in style with Seville orange marmalade sponge with Grand Marnier custard.

Chef Brendan Fyldes **Owner** Dr A El Sharkawy
Times 12.30-2.30/5-10.30 All-day dining **Prices** Fixed L 2 course fr £19.12, Starter £9.50-£17.50, Main £19.50-£49.95, Dessert £9, Service added but optional 12.5% **Wines** 340 bottles over £30, 5 bottles under £30, 11 by glass **Notes** Pre-theatre menu 5.30-7pm 2/3 course £19.12/£24.12, Sunday L fr £19.12, Vegetarian available, Civ Wed 44 **Seats** 52, Pr/dining room 44 **Parking** NCP on Arlington Street

---

Thirty Six by Nigel Mendham at Dukes London

PLAN 4 J6

🌸🌸🌸 – *see below*

Tinello

PLAN 4 G2

🌸🌸 Italian 🍴

Classy Italian cooking in elegant restaurant

☎ 020 7730 6327 & 7730 3663
87 Pimlico Rd SW1W 8PH
e-mail: max@tinello.co.uk
dir: Nearest station: Sloane Square. From Sloane Square tube station, down Holbein Place. Left at T-junct

Tinello is a stylish place with its trendy dining chairs and brown banquettes at smartly set tables under dangling copper lampshades. It makes a classy backdrop to

straightforward modern Italian cooking built around prime ingredients. Antipasti (perhaps goats' cheese, beetroot and pumpkin salad) or 'small eats' like deep-fried squid are possibilities before skilfully made pasta: spaghetti vongole, or pappardelle with hare ragù, say. Don't expect gimmicks or fuss in main courses: steamed lemon sole, beautifully timed, is accompanied by nothing more than aubergine and basil sauce, a dish singing with flavours, and pan-fried veal cutlet by vibrantly flavoured fennel and lemon salad. Tiramisù seems to be a fixture among desserts, or there may be light frangipane pear tart with yoghurt ice cream.

Chef Federico Sali **Owner** Giorgio Locatelli
Times 12-2.30/6.15-10.30 Closed BH Mon, Sun
Prices Starter £1.35-£12.50, Main £9.50-£26.25, Dessert £4.75-£13.50, Service optional, Groups min 8 service 12.5% **Wines** 20 by glass **Notes** Vegetarian available, Dress restrictions, Smart casual **Seats** 75, Pr/dining room 25 **Children** Portions **Parking** On street, single yellow from 6.30pm

---

Thirty Six by Nigel Mendham at Dukes London

🌸🌸🌸

LONDON SW1   PLAN 4 J6

Modern British

Refined contemporary cooking in luxe Mayfair hotel

☎ 020 7491 4840
35-36 St James's Place SW1A 1NY
e-mail: thirtysix@dukeshotel.com
web: www.dukeshotel.com
dir: Nearest station: Green Park. From Pall Mall into St James's St. 2nd left into St James's Place. Hotel in courtyard on left

Nigel Mendham is a chef who does not salivate at the thought of every new gadget or buy the latest piece of technological wizardry. Mendham prefers tried-and-true cooking methods, but do you know what? His food is dynamic, contemporary and looks spectacular on the plate. It all takes place in the luxe Dukes Hotel, with its

impeccable address and luxurious, moneyed finish. The restaurant is named after the chef and the address, but it is no coincidence that 36 has associations with the solar square of ancient Western tradition, and is a favoured number in Chinese astrology. All that good luck has resulted in a smart, modish dining room with fine artworks and high comfort levels. There's a showpiece tasting menu in support of the à la carte, plus an early evening menu if you're in a hurry, or on a budget, and a good-value set lunch. The cooking is refined, intelligent and captivating. Start with a dish of 'pork textures', which sees the cheek, croquette and belly partnered with pickled and puréed onions, or hand-dived scallops with a savoury pannacotta, smoked bacon and parsley root purée. Among main courses, Highland venison stars with a lush suet pudding, winter vegetables and game jus, or there might be John Dory with spiced mussels, aubergine and herb quinoa. A contemporary interpretation of carrot cake appears at dessert stage with liquid carrot, iced cream cheese and spiced walnuts, or there's rhubarb and

custard (ginger crumble, sorbet and bourbon vanilla). There's a rather fabulous bar, too, where martinis are a bit of a speciality.

Chef Nigel Mendham **Times** 12-2.30/6-9.30 Closed L Mon, D Sun **Prices** Fixed L 2 course £25, Fixed D 3 course £60, Tasting menu £75, Service added but optional 12.5% **Wines** 13 by glass **Notes** Tasting menu 6 course, Sunday L, Vegetarian available, Dress restrictions, Smart casual, Civ Wed 80 **Seats** 36 **Children** Portions, Menu **Parking** Holiday Inn, Britannia car park

LONDON SW1 *continued*

Wheeler's

PLAN 4 J6

◎◎ Seafood

Seafood stalwart in St James's

☎ 020 7408 1440
72-73 St James's St SW1A 1PH
e-mail: info@wheelersrestaurant.org
dir: Nearest station: Green Park

If you're after a bit of spruced-up, old-school style and some classic seafood dishes, this long-running restaurant (opened in 1856) will sort you out. The fact it is co-owned by Sir Rocco Forte and Marco Pierre White should give a clue that there's a good deal of swagger and charm about the place, too. This is traditional, old-school dining for the modern age. Rich red walls are crammed with prints and photographs, some of which are of a risqué nature (we're talking scantily dressed ladies), tables are dressed up in white linen, and there's an art-deco sheen to the décor. On the menu is classic seafood done right, simply turned out, starting perhaps with a bisque of fresh crab Newburg, or calamari fritti alla Romana and tartare sauce, followed by wing of skate with winkles, jus à la Parisienne, or tranche of cod à la Viennoise and sabayon of champagne. British stouts, ales and ciders are the business, too.

Chef Marco Corsica **Times** 12-3/5.30-11 Closed Sun, L Sat **Prices** Fixed L 2 course £16.95, Fixed D 3 course £22.50 **Notes** Fixed L & D available Mon-Fri 12-3 & 5.30-7, Breakfast £7.50 **Seats** 120

Zafferano

PLAN 4 F4

◎◎ Modern Italian

Refined but authentic Italian cooking in Knightsbridge

☎ 020 7235 5800
15 Lowndes St SW1X 9EY
e-mail: zafferano@londonfinediningroup.com
dir: Nearest station: Knightsbridge. Located off Sloane St, behind Carlton Tower Hotel

Italian cooking has gone through a productive evolution in the capital over the past 20 years, with greater regional awareness, integrity of ingredients and the learning of a whole new lexicon undergirding it. Knightsbridge's Zafferano has been one of the prime movers in that development, offering refined, authentic food that doesn't lose sight of the foundational principle of simplicity, in a room that adopts the moneyed rustic look of candy-striped upholstery against stolid brickwork. The output has occasionally wavered with each new change of kitchen regime, but the menus still inspire confidence: seared scallops in saffron vinaigrette are a signature opener, or there may be richly deliquescent burrata with aubergine and sun-dried Piennolo tomatoes. After an interlude for pasta, gnocchi, or perhaps langoustine risotto, it's on to corn-fed chicken with cavolo nero in textbook peverada (a sauce combining the richnesses of chicken livers, sausage and anchovy), or maybe turbot in walnuts and capers. The lightest finish is

mulberry pannacotta decorated with dried figs, and there are fine Italian cheeses, too.

Chef Michele Nargi **Owner** A-Z Restaurants-London Fine Dining Group **Times** 12-3/7-11 Closed 3 days Xmas **Prices** Fixed L 2 course fr £21, Fixed D 3 course fr £46.50, Starter £11-£15, Main £9-£24, Dessert £7-£10, Service added 13.5%, Groups min 10 service 15% **Wines** 6 by glass **Notes** Vegetarian available, Dress restrictions, Smart casual **Seats** 85, Pr/dining room 20 **Children** Portions **Parking** NCP behind restaurant

LONDON SW3

Bibendum Restaurant

PLAN 4 E3

◎◎ British, French V ♦ NOTABLE WINE LIST

Modern classics at a Chelsea institution

☎ 020 7581 5817
Michelin House, 81 Fulham Rd SW3 6RD
e-mail: reservations@bibendum.co.uk
web: www.bibendum.co.uk
dir: Nearest station: South Kensington. Left out of South Kensington underground station on to Pelham St & walk as far as lights

Climb the stairs to the first-floor restaurant and take one of the comfortable seats at a well-spaced table amid the crisp, sharp décor, with its Michelin Man theme, not least his stained-glass depiction. Good-quality, honest modern British and European cooking is what Bibendum excels at, served with style by efficient staff. Seasonality plays its part, fresh and tasty gazpacho appearing in summer, a main course of roast quails in a foie gras croûte with mushrooms and Madeira sauce in winter. The odd interloper adds interest - say, tuna tataki with an Asian herb salad and soy, lime and ginger dressing - among popular fixtures such as deep-fried haddock and chips with tartare sauce, and calves' liver and bacon. Breads are excellent and puddings can be highlights: perhaps vibrantly flavoured blueberry and elderflower jelly with cherry compôte and crème Chantilly.

Chef Matthew Harris **Owner** Sir Terence Conran, Simon Hopkinson, Michael Hamlyn **Times** 12-2.30/7-11 Closed 25-26 Dec, 1 Jan, D 24 Dec **Prices** Fixed L 2 course £26.50, Starter £10.75-£25, Main £18-£33, Dessert

£8-£11, Service added but optional 12.5% **Wines** 521 bottles over £30, 22 bottles under £30, 14 by glass **Notes** Sun D 3 courses £30, Sunday L fr £32.50, Vegetarian menu **Seats** 80 **Children** Portions **Parking** On street

Cassis Bistro

PLAN 4 E4

◎◎ French

Classy Knightsbridge hangout with the flavours of the Med and more

☎ 020 7581 1101
232-236 Brompton Rd SW3 2BB
e-mail: reception@cassisbistro.co.uk
dir: Nearest station: Knightsbridge, South Kensington. Opposite V&A

A new chef has taken over the stoves at Cassis, giving an Italian tilt to the otherwise French menu (albeit a thoroughly contemporary one), marrying the two cultures with the addition of pistou to ribollita soup, for instance. The décor remains as classy as ever, with a wooden floor and tables, comfortable chairs and banquettes, and walls displaying some vivid artwork. There's not much of a bistro feel to the intelligently assembled menu, with luxury products no doubt de rigueur for this moneyed part of town: caramelised Landes foie gras, for instance, with rhubarb marmalade, followed by lobster with fennel and tarocco orange. Less exalted materials are handled equally well, among them cod brandade with olives and confit tomatoes, or tongue salad with French beans and pickled onions, then saddle of rabbit crepinette with potato gratin, or plainly poached turbot fillet with sweet mash. Classics from France and Italy show up among puddings: crème brûlée flavoured with lime and rosemary with citrus sorbet, and tiramisù with a scoop of coffee ice cream.

Chef Massimiliano Blasone **Owner** Marlon Abela **Times** 12-11 Closed 25 Dec **Prices** Fixed L 2 course £18, Tasting menu £55-£75, Starter £9-£20, Main £16-£29, Dessert £6-£15, Service added but optional 12.5% **Wines** 700 bottles over £30, 8 bottles under £30, 14 by glass **Notes** Vegetarian available **Seats** 90 **Children** Portions **Parking** On street

Le Colombier

PLAN 4 D2

◎ French

Unfussy brasserie cooking just off the Fulham Road

☎ 020 7351 1155
145 Dovehouse St SW3 6LB
e-mail: lecolombier1998@aol.com
dir: Nearest station: South Kensington. Dovehouse St is just off the Fulham Rd S of South Kensington underground station

If you're looking for a hit of pure France without the need to cross la Manche, head down to Chelsea, just off the Fulham Road, where Le Colombier will satisfy your cravings. The front conservatory is a lovely spot when the weather is fine, but the décor inside is perfectly sunny all year round; relaxing blue and cream tones, wooden floorboards, and white linen-clad tables. The formal service zips along nicely, making the place good for a working lunch. Expect classic French brasserie-style dishes; duck liver terrine, perhaps, served with fig jam and brioche, followed by grilled monkfish with wild rice and tomato and vermouth cream sauce. Desserts can be as classic as tarte Tatin and the all-French wine list has something for all pockets and preferences.

Chef Philippe Tamet **Owner** Didier Garnier
Times 12-3/6.30-10.30 **Prices** Fixed L 2 course £19.50, Starter £6.90-£15, Main £18.90-£35, Dessert £6.90-£8.50, Service added but optional 12.5%
Wines 178 bottles over £30, 40 bottles under £30, 10 by glass **Notes** Sunday L £23, Vegetarian available, Dress restrictions, Smart casual **Seats** 70, Pr/dining room 28 **Parking** Metered parking

Eight Over Eight PLAN 4 D1
Pan-Asian

Pan-Asian cooking in a cool, buzzy Chelsea favourite

☎ 020 7349 9934
392 King's Rd SW3 5UZ
e-mail: eightovereight@rickerrestaurants.com
dir: Nearest station: Sloane Sq, South Kensington

The ethnicity of the cuisine here is easy enough to work out, as the trend-central King's Road branch of Will Ricker's oriental fusion empire is named after the Chinese lucky number eight. The space is split between bar and restaurant and kitted out with an effortlessly cool and minimally chic décor. Well-conceived Pan-Asian grazing is what the kitchen does here, and happily, the food is no mere afterthought to the socialising. Dim sum are a reliably good way to get going (perhaps nori-wrapped chicken dumplings, or prawn and black cod gyoza), before exploring the other categories of the menu. Sushi and sashimi take in luxury Wagyu beef sashimi or spicy tuna ura maki; elsewhere are a barbecued rack of ribs with black pepper sauce or a spicy prawn and pumpkin curry. Desserts draw their inspiration from closer to home - perhaps chocolate fondant with green tea ice cream. Switched-on, upbeat service, and an eye-catching cocktail list complete the picture.

Times 12-3/6-11 Closed 24-29 Dec, Etr

Manicomio PLAN 4 F3
Modern Italian

Bustling modern Italian just off Sloane Square

☎ 020 7730 3366
85 Duke of York Square, Chelsea SW3 4LY
e-mail: info@manicomio.co.uk
dir: Nearest station: Sloane Square. Duke of York Sq 100mtrs along King's Rd from Sloane Sq

Built as the military asylum of the Duke of York barracks, Manicomio presents a cool, calming image, with its planked floor, wall banquettes and vivid artwork.

Contemporary Italian cooking is the draw, with many ingredients imported from the Motherland: perhaps speck d'Aosta in a starter with mozzarella and baby artichokes, and lentils from Umbria to accompany roast hake fillet, parsley pesto and spinach. The menu is evenly divided between fish and meat, the latter extending to chargrilled quail skewered with chicken livers on polenta with vin cotto sauce, followed by a winter main course of grilled sirloin with bone marrow, braised ox cheek and roast squash. Finish with the tiramisù or maybe treacle and lemon tart.

Chef Tom Salt **Owner** Ninai & Andrew Zarach
Times 12-3/6.30-10.30 Closed Xmas & New Year
Prices Prices not confirmed Service added but optional 12.5% **Wines** 18 by glass **Notes** Sunday L, Vegetarian available **Seats** 70, Pr/dining room 30 **Children** Portions **Parking** On street

Nozomi PLAN 4 E4
Japanese

Contemporary Japanese cooking in slick setting

☎ 020 7838 1500 & 7838 0181
14-15 Beauchamp Place, Knightsbridge SW3 1NQ
e-mail: info@nozomi.co.uk
dir: Nearest station: Knightsbridge. From Knightsbridge continue onto Brompton Road (A4). Left onto Beauchamp Place, Nozomi is halfway down Beauchamp Place

Make your way through the fashionable cocktail bar at the front and into the restaurant behind, a dimly lit space with a décor of silver and black and where the music, more foreground than background, is intended to 'relax inhibitions'. Authentic contemporary Japanese cuisine is the deal, with the long menu covering a lot of ground. Start with a selection of sushi - anything from tuna, crab and sea bass - or choose from an extensive list of maki rolls and temaki, plus small dishes such as tofu steak with aubergine and miso. Not surprisingly in this postcode, luxuries are littered about, among them whole tempura lobster with ponzu and daikon, pan-fried foie gras marinated in whisky, and chargrilled Wagyu beef steaks, although the same attention to detail is evident throughout from black cod with pickled daikon, to grilled lamb cutlets with mushrooms and yuzu-infused yoghurt, and pan-fried pork tenderloin and crispy ribs with grilled pear and soy.

Times 12-3/6.30-11.30 Closed L Mon **Prices** Prices not confirmed Service added but optional 15% **Wines** 10 by glass **Notes** Pre-theatre menu, Sunday L, Vegetarian available, Dress restrictions, Smart casual **Seats** 110, Pr/dining room 36 **Parking** 10, Valet parking & on street

Outlaw's at The Capital PLAN 4 F5
◎◎◎ *– see page 302*

Racine PLAN 4 E4
Traditional French

An authentic French brasserie opposite Brompton Oratory

☎ 020 7584 4477
239 Brompton Rd SW3 2EP
e-mail: bonjour@racine.com
dir: Nearest station: Knightsbridge, South Kensington

When you long for the French bourgeois cooking of the neighbourhood bistros and brasseries of Paris and the elbow-to-elbow bouchons of Lyon, Racine comes up with the goods: this is timeless dining built on the solid foundations of diligently-sourced, seasonal produce. The look is spot-on too, with wooden floors, chocolate leather banquettes, wall mirrors, soft-focus lighting and an easygoing vibe, all kept ticking over by correctly courteous staff. Slacken your belt and be prepared for big-hearted, robust, gutsy cooking. Seared foie gras with caramelised apple and Calvados makes a classic opener, or you might go for a visceral plate of calf's brains with black butter and capers. Mains plough a similarly Gallic furrow - grilled rabbit with mustard sauce and smoked bacon, or veal kidneys with creamed Fourme d'Ambert cheese, Espelette pepper jus and pommes purée.

Chef Henry Harris **Owner** Henry Harris
Times 12-3/6-10.30 Closed 25 Dec **Prices** Fixed D 3 course £17.75-£20, Starter £7-£13, Main £16.50-£28.50, Dessert £6.50-£9.50, Service added but optional 14.5% **Wines** 100 bottles over £30, 14 bottles under £30, 20 by glass **Notes** Sunday L, Vegetarian available **Seats** 60, Pr/dining room 22 **Children** Portions

Rasoi Restaurant PLAN 4 F3
◎◎◎ *– see page 302*

Restaurant Gordon Ramsey PLAN 4 F1
◎◎◎◎ *– see page 303*

Outlaw's at The Capital

LONDON SW3   **PLAN 4 F5**

British, Seafood **V** NOTABLE WINE LIST **NEW**

The best of Cornish seafood in London

☎ 020 7589 5171
22-24 Basil St, Knightsbridge SW3 1AT
e-mail: outlaws@capitalhotel.co.uk
web: www.capitalhotel.co.uk
dir: Nearest station: Knightsbridge. Off Sloane St, beside Harrods

Nathan Outlaw has made a name for himself metaphorically flying the flag of St Piran's - the white cross on the black background that is the Cornish standard - at his restaurant in Rock (see entry). He's actually from Kent, but his heart is out West. And now he's opened in London in the smartest setting imaginable: The Capital. This magnificent townhouse hotel just around the corner from Harrods is a little piece of five-star heaven: discreet, chic, refined...simply gorgeous. You know you're somewhere special when the liveried doorman ushers you inside. Outlaw's restaurant occupies the smart dining room with its touch of understated art-deco-esque civility and glamour. It's not a room to stir emotion, but it is in keeping with the confident, free-thinking independent nature of the hotel. There are no linen tablecloths, for example, but tables are set just-so, the decorative touches are of the highest quality, and the service team out of the top drawer. Nathan has put Pete Biggs, his right-hand man, in charge of the kitchen and the menu looks west, making full use of their existing supply lines. The kitchen does not deal exclusively with seafood, but it is the mainstay of the output. The cooking is creative and shows high levels of technical skill. The ingredients, though, are given room to shine. Take a starter of hand-picked crab with asparagus salad and English mustard dressing - simply perfection - or a main featuring a superb piece of hake which comes with lettuce and a beautifully refined tartare sauce. There might be raw scallops among first courses, with bacon, apple and white radish, and a meaty main course such as lamb rack with sweetbreads, roast onion and olive. This is a kitchen that is strong in all areas: witness a dessert of rhubarb crumble and its accompanying rhubarb and ginger beer sorbet - top stuff.

Chef Nathan Outlaw, Pete Biggs **Owner** Mr D Levin **Times** 12-2.30/6-10.30 Closed Sun **Prices** Fixed L 2 course £20, Tasting menu £70-£160, Starter £12-£16, Main £24-£32, Dessert £6-£10, Service added but optional 12.5% **Wines** 37 by glass **Notes** Sunday L, Vegetarian available, Vegetarian menu, Dress restrictions, Smart casual **Seats** 35, Pr/dining room 24 **Parking** 8

Rasoi Restaurant

LONDON SW3   **PLAN 4 F3**

Modern Indian **V**

The frontline of modern Indian cooking

☎ 020 7225 1881
10 Lincoln St SW3 2TS
e-mail: info@rasoirestaurant.co.uk
dir: Nearest station: Sloane Square. Near Peter Jones and Duke of York Sq

If you know your Hindi, you'll know that rasoi means kitchen, which might suggest a rather homely approach all round, and indeed you do have to ring the doorbell to get into Vineet and Rashima Bhatia's restaurant. But that is where all thoughts of domesticity end, for here you can expect thrilling and refined modern Indian cooking of the highest order. The Chelsea townhouse looks rather splendid inside and out, with a chic interior that has a sense of Asia and meets fine-dining expectations - silk wall hangings, elegant chairs, and tables draped in crisp white linen. As if to confirm its top-end status, there's a menu prestige in support of the fixed-price carte and set lunch menus, including a vegetarian version which should catch the eye of every non-meat eater in the Capital. The cooking is distinguished by phenomenal technical skill and compelling, finely-judged flavour combinations. Kick off, perhaps, with scallop and prawn brochette, beautifully fresh and cooked just-so, partnered with spring onion and crab khichdi (a dish of rice and dhal), or chilli paneer wrapped in banana leaf with a mushroom and peanut croquette and achari aubergine salsa. Among main courses, there might be a thoroughly contemporary two-way approach and even a foam or two: sea bass, for example, pan-seared and cooked in the tandoor, served with beetroot and pea upma, lemongrass and coconut sauce and a white tomato foam. The quality of ingredients is a stand-out feature here and every dish looks impressive on the plate, not least desserts such as rose petal brûlée, paired with a winter berry and rasgulla wheel, and pineapple and fennel sorbet. The wine list does not shy from the challenge of matching some excellent wines to the modern Asian flavours.

Chef Vineet Bhatia **Owner** Vineet & Rashima Bhatia **Times** 12-2.30/6-10.30 Closed Xmas, New Year, BH, L Sat **Prices** Fixed L 2 course £22-£27, Fixed D 3 course £50-£65, Tasting menu £79-£89, Starter £18-£20, Main £26-£35, Dessert £7.50-£15, Service added but optional 12.5% **Wines** 300 bottles over £30, 10 bottles under £30, 10 by glass **Notes** Tasting menu 7 course incl wine, Sunday L, Vegetarian menu, Dress restrictions, Smart casual **Seats** 35, Pr/dining room 14 **Parking** On street

Restaurant Gordon Ramsay

LONDON SW3   PLAN 4 F1

French, European **V** NOTABLE WINE LIST

The mothership of the Gordon Ramsay empire

☎ 020 7352 4441
68 Royal Hospital Rd SW3 4HP
e-mail: reservations@gordonramsay.com
dir: Nearest station: Sloane Square. At junct of Royal Hospital Road & Swan Walk

From the beginning of 2013 Clare Smyth became chef-patron of Restaurant Gordon Ramsay, which is testament to her abilities and Gordon Ramsay's willingness to let his protégés shine. She's been head chef since 2007 and now she's a business partner. Royal Hospital Road remains the flagship of the Ramsay brand, and if ever a chef was a brand, it is he. Ramsay is global, with nearly a dozen addresses in the USA alone, and the same sort of number in London. A busy man, then, and dependent on his most trusted lieutenants. This is where the road to global domination began, back in 1998, and it remains a bastion of Ramsay's style of refined, modern French cooking. Ramsay never sought to sink the ship of haute cuisine, happy instead to do it up until it has never looked so good, and keep the wind in its sails. And as the restaurant enters a new era, there's been a refurbishment to mark the new beginning, a subtle art-deco styling that remains soothingly muted and classy. There are several stand-out elements to a visit to Royal Hospital Road. Firstly, the service is supremely good: it's the kind of place where things happen just before your brain picks up they need attending to - they're one step ahead. Secondly, the quality of the produce: everything is staggeringly good, super-fresh, the best of the best. And thirdly, the cooking is as near perfect as it is possible to get (hence the accolades) and it all looks absolutely beautiful. A starter of pan-fried Isle of Skye scallops, for example, with heritage apples, walnuts, celery and cider emulsion is perfectly judged, the shellfish as fresh as can be and the timing of the cooking spot on. Another starter sees sautéed foie gras in the triumphant company of roasted veal sweetbreads, cabernet sauvignon vinegar and an almond velouté. Next up, main-course suckling pig comes as crisp and succulent belly, roasted loin and spiced shoulder, or go for Isle of Gigha halibut in the company of king crab, cauliflower couscous, finger lime and ras el hanout-infused broth. Desserts are no less impressive, creative and adroitly executed: the smoked chocolate cigar, for example, with blood orange and cardamom ice cream, or the classic tarte Tatin with Tahitian vanilla ice cream. The wine list contains some amazing stuff from the world's top producers, with prices to make your eyes water, but does not sideline those who want to drink on a more financially accessible level.

Chef Gordon Ramsay, Clare Smyth **Owner** Gordon Ramsay Holdings Ltd **Times** 12-2.15/6.30-10.15 Closed 1 wk Xmas, Sat-Sun **Prices** Fixed L 3 course £45, Fixed D 3 course £95, Service added but optional 12.5% **Wines** 176 bottles over £30, 1 bottle under £30, 18 by glass **Notes** ALC 3 course £95, Tasting menu 7 course, Vegetarian menu, Dress restrictions, Smart dress, no jeans, trainers or sportswear **Seats** 45 **Children** Portions **Parking**

Tom Aikens

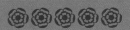

LONDON SW3   **PLAN 4 E3**

Modern European V NOTABLE WINE LIST

Art on a (hand-crafted) plate from a true culinary master

☎ 020 7584 2003
43 Elystan St SW3 3NT
e-mail: info@tomaikens.co.uk
dir: Nearest station: South Kensington, Sloane Square. Off Fulham Rd (Brompton Rd end)

There's certainly no danger of walking past Tom Aikens restaurant without noticing it - with its black, strikingly modern frontage it certainly stands out from the crowd in this largely residential corner of Chelsea. But once inside the look is contrastingly understated, with lots of natural wood (floors, tables, chairs) and neutral colours, and not a starched tablecloth or white linen napkin in sight. Staff are dressed casually too, and the general mood is relaxed and unpretentious - just the feel Aikens wanted to achieve when he gave the previously rather formal, fine-dining décor the heave-ho in 2012. It's true to say that some purists may feel the minimalist approach of bare wood tables and cushion-less wooden chairs isn't right in a restaurant at the pinnacle of gastronomy, where dinner can easily set you back £100 a head, but check out the workmanship in those bespoke, hand-crafted tables and (ultra-comfortable) chairs. In fact, skilled craftsmanship is a theme that runs right through everything here: the glassware, the decorative accoutrements on the tables, the vast array of different shaped and coloured dishes that frame Aikens' artfully created plates of food. With skilled service from a well trained, knowledgeable and utterly charming team, it all adds up to a highly enjoyable eating experience. Aikens' food is at once innovative, contemporary, clever, refined, bold, and full of fresh, fresh flavours and vibrant natural colours. If you're on a budget, go at lunchtime and dine from the excellent value set lunch menu, but if you can afford to push the boat out and order from the à la carte, you'll be justly rewarded for sure. Whichever route you choose, you'll get some wonderfully fresh bread - four superb rolls, served warm in a heated hessian bag and with three flavours of butter - to get things started. Then, (choosing from the carte) smoked eel with watercress emulsion, compressed cucumber and smoked apple is a starter made in heaven, full of fresh flavours and with the perfect balance of smokiness and acidity, while house-made ricotta with green olive juice, honey jelly and pine nuts elevates a collection of simple raw ingredients to a new level. Poached tails of monkfish with confit squid, piglet belly and white strawberries - a dish with real wow factor - might follow, or perhaps Udale lamb loin (the meat simply melting in the mouth) accompanied by creamed polenta, cipollini onion and dandelion. Technical dexterity is displayed again at dessert stage, when an exotic tasting coconut parfait with mango mousse and coconut sorbet competes for your affections with a richly indulgent frozen chocolate mousse, chocolate sorbet and grué de cocoa. It goes without saying that the petits fours are fabulous, as is the wine list, which runs to 350 bins from around the world and offers a decent amount of choice for those with shallower pockets.

Chef Tom Aikens **Owner** Tom Aikens Group Ltd **Times** 12-2.30/6.30-10.30 Closed 2 wks Xmas, Etr, BHs, Sun-Mon, L Sat **Prices** Fixed L 2 course £28, Tasting menu £90, Starter £15-£21, Main £29-£35, Dessert £12-£15, Service added but optional 12.5% **Wines** 350 bottles over £30, 30 bottles under £30, 15 by glass **Notes** Tasting menu D 7 course, ALC 2/3 course £28/£34, Vegetarian menu **Seats** 54, Pr/dining room 10 **Parking** Parking meters outside

LONDON SW3 *continued*

Sushinho
PLAN 4 D1

◉ Japanese, Brazilian

Japanese-Brazilian fusion cooking on the King's Road

☎ 020 7349 7496
312-314 King's Rd, Chelsea SW3 5UH
e-mail: info@sushinho.com
dir: Nearest station: Sloane Sq. On N side of King's Rd,
Between Old Church St & The Vale

Voguish interior styling and an exuberant backing track
of Latin-American sounds prove a hit with the Chelsea
set at Sushinho, a hybrid Japanese/Brazilian restaurant
inspired by the sushi joints of Rio and São Paolo (Brazil's
Japanese community is the largest outside Japan). Dishes
are designed for sharing and there's plenty of choice on
the cross-cultural menu, including straight-up Japanese
sushi, sashimi or tempura alongside more Latin American
dishes like feijoada (Brazil's big-flavoured black bean
stew) with succulent pork belly, kale and crackling, or
perhaps fusion dishes like melt-in-the-mouth blackened
butterfish partnered by the balanced heat of wasabi
guacamole. There are slabs of prime steak too (grain-fed
picanha maybe) with crisp cassava chips and fiery
chipotle mayo. Exposed brick, bamboo, low lighting and
the occasional palm tree inject a little extra exoticism
into the experience, as do the cocktail bar and dinky sushi
counter. There's now a second Sushinho in the City.

Times 12-3/6-10.30 Closed 25-26 Dec, 1 Jan, L Sun-Tue

Tom Aikens
PLAN 4 E3

◉◉◉◉◉ — *see opposite*

Tom's Kitchen
PLAN 4 E2

◉◉ British, French

First-class brasserie food from top-class chef

☎ 020 7349 0202
27 Cale St, South Kensington SW3 3QP
e-mail: info@tomskitchen.co.uk
dir: Nearest station: South Kensington, Sloane Square.
Cale St (Parallel to Kings Rd), midway between Chelsea
Green and St Luke's Church

With its utilitarian good looks, Tom's Kitchen fizzes with
life and bonhomie. The ethos is there for all to see: 'food
for everyone and anyone' it says engraved on a piece of
slate, and that's a fair statement, just as long as that
'someone' can pay seventeen quid for fish and chips. But
this is Chelsea (just around the corner from Tom Aikens'
flagship restaurant) and the prices are not unreasonable,
and perhaps most important of all, the quality is high.
Covering three floors of this handsome townhouse, there's
a space to suit your mood, and it is the all-day, ground-
floor brasserie where most of the action takes place at
tightly packed wooden tables. Spicy crabcake, perked up
with a tomato salsa and packed with a goodly amount of

crab, shows the way, or go for something along the lines
of baked scallops with garlic and lemon. Top-notch
produce is sourced with due diligence throughout.
Chicken, leek and bacon pie is a real cracker, and
desserts run to apple and blackberry crumble with
toasted almond ice cream. There's a second branch in
Somerset House in the West End and another in Canary
Wharf.

Chef Tim Brindley, Tom Aikens **Owner** Tom Aikens
Times 12-3/6-11 Closed 25-26 Dec, D 24 Dec
Prices Starter £9.50-£16.50, Main £14-£29.50, Dessert
£7, Service added but optional 12.5% **Wines** 24 bottles
over £30, 23 bottles under £30, 13 by glass **Notes** Sunday
L, Vegetarian available **Seats** 75, Pr/dining room 40
Children Portions **Parking** On street

LONDON SW4

Bistro Union
PLAN 1 E2

◉◉ British ◉

True-Brit food in neighbourhood bistro

☎ 020 7042 6400
40 Abbeville Rd, Clapham SW4 9NG
e-mail: eat@bistrounion.co.uk
dir: Nearest station: Clapham South. Left from Clapham
South tube onto Clapham Common south side. Continue
with park on left and take 4th right Narbonne Ave,
Abbeville Rd directly ahead

Chef-proprietor Adam Byatt certainly seems comfortable
in Clapham. His Trinity operation (see entry), which
opened in 2006, has gone from strength to strength to be
the top dog in the postcode, and it is now joined by this
new, more informal neighbourhood venture. A simple, de-
cluttered brasserie-style décor sits well with the local
clientele in the trendy Abbeville enclave: there are
stripped wood floors, chunky unclothed tables, and a
central bar where you can perch on wooden stools with
your cutlery and menu in individual drawers under the
counter, perusing a bar menu of on-trend nibbles (pork
scratchings, pickled quail's eggs, winkles and pickled
shallots, to name but three) hand-written onto a roll of
brown paper. The food is in the day-to-day hands of Karl
Goward who comes from Fergus Henderson's St John
Bread and Wine (see entry), so you can expect a no-
nonsense approach with a nod to the 'nose-to-tail' eating
style. What leaves the kitchen is creative, fun, and built
with British-led ingredients - perhaps beer and onion
soup with Welsh rarebit, or baked aubergine with cow's
curd and mint to start, then more of the same butch,
true-Brit ideas, along the lines of Cumberland toad in the
hole with Guinness onions.

Chef Karl Goward, Adam Byatt **Owner** Adam Byatt
Times 11-3/6-10 Closed D Sun **Prices** Fixed L 2 course fr
£14, Fixed D 3 course fr £18, Starter £5-£8, Main
£10-£22, Dessert £2-£5, Service added but optional
12.5% **Wines** 26 bottles over £30, 14 bottles under £30,
11 by glass **Notes** Sunday L, Vegetarian available
Seats 40 **Children** Portions, Menu

The Dairy
PLAN 1 E2

◉◉ Modern British NEW V

Relaxed bar-bistro serving innovative modern food

☎ 020 7622 4165
15 The Pavement, Clapham SW4 0HY
e-mail: bookings@the-dairy.co.uk
dir: Nearest station: Clapham Common. South circular
A205

Its central Clapham location - looking out over the
common just a few paces from the tube - isn't The Dairy's
only draw, as this relaxed, on-cue outfit is home to some
seriously fine cooking at accessible prices. From the
outside it looks unremarkable, but step inside and you'll
find it a friendly, welcoming and popular place, with a
dinky bar up front and a bistro behind with a pared-back
look of recycled and reclaimed furniture and fittings, flagstoned floors and an open kitchen. The cooking is clever
and innovative, producing well-crafted dishes that are
light and colourful with clean flavours and modern
presentation. Some of the seasonal ingredients used
come from The Dairy's own urban garden. Kick off with
some fresh sourdough bread with home-made smoked
bone marrow butter, then choose a selection of small
plates from the varied menu. You might begin with a
plate of potted salmon with Guinness soda bread, or
some slices of excellent salumi, moving on to garden-
fresh peas with celery, mint and fried bread, and perhaps
sea-fresh West Coast lemon sole teamed with maple
pancetta and ember oil buttermilk. For dessert, how
about Lincolnshire rhubarb (nicely tart) with contrasting
sweet hibiscus meringue, pumpkin seeds and rhubarb ice
cream?

Chef Robin Gill **Owner** Robin & Sarah Gill, Matt Wells
Times 12-11 Closed Xmas, Mon, L Tue, D Sun
Prices Tasting menu £40-£65, Service added but
optional 12.5% **Wines** 20 bottles over £30, 18 bottles
under £30, 7 by glass **Notes** Daily specials L, D, Bar &
snack menu, seasonal menu changes, Sunday L,
Vegetarian menu **Seats** 40 **Children** Portions

Trinity Restaurant
PLAN 1 E2

◉◉◉ — *see page 306*

LONDON SW4 *continued*

Tsunami
PLAN 1 F2

Japanese

Cool minimalism and Japanese fusion food

☎ 020 7978 1610
5-7 Voltaire Rd SW4 6DQ
e-mail: clapham@tsunamirestaurant.co.uk
dir: Nearest station: Clapham North. Off Clapham High Street

The Clapham branch of two Tsunami operations (the other is in Charlotte Street) is a big hit with those seeking a trendy locale and the mouth-filling flavours of Japanese fusion dining. The minimal club-like décor ticks all the right style boxes with its buzzy, brightly lit cocktail bar serving warm and cold sakes, and an open-plan eating area done out with darkwood tables, sleek banquettes, huge mirrors, and funky modern art; the modish open-to-view kitchen gives everyone a good look at the chefs doing their stuff. It's a high-decibel, sociable place, so the menu obliges with dishes that are meant for sharing and grazing - classic sushi, tempura, sashimi as you'd expect - but the kitchen isn't scared to cross borders and send out roast duck and foie gras nigiri, or grilled scallops flambéed with whisky to get things going. Mains offer everything from hira unagi (grilled marinated eel with rice and pickles) to a rib-eye with exotic mushrooms and truffle sauce.

Times 12.30-3.30/5.30-11 Closed 24-26 Dec, 1 Jan, L Mon-Fri

LONDON SW5

The Abbeville Kitchen
PLAN 4 A3

British, European **NEW**

Top-notch cooking with a nod to the Med in a buzzing neighbourhood restaurant

☎ 020 8772 1110 & 3163 0699
47 Abbeville Rd SW5 9QN
e-mail: food@abbevillekitchen.com
dir: Nearest station: Clapham Common, Clapham South. approx 2 min walk from Clapham Common South Side

The Abbeville Kitchen is the kind of neighbourhood restaurant every neighbourhood should have. Squeezed in amongst the shops and restaurants in a residential street near Clapham Common, it looks rather café-like from the outside, but behind that unassuming frontage there's an awful lot going on. The menu changes daily, so you can be assured the ingredients are always super-fresh, and pretty much everything, including some drinks, is made in-house. You can sit up at the small bar at the front or head for one of the wooden tables in the buzzy restaurant with its semi-open kitchen. The menu is mostly Spanish, with a bit of Italian and some British dishes thrown into the mix, so you might start with anticuchos - grilled skewers of herb-marinated ox heart, the meat wonderfully tender and full of flavour - or perhaps minestrone soup, or Hampshire pork and prune terrine. Main course could be as simple as a whole roast bream served with superb home-made chunky chips and aïoli, or roast lamb rump

---

with chick peas and wild garlic. Torta de Santiago with crème fraîche and blood orange is a textbook version of the Spanish classic.

Chef Kevin McFadden **Owner** Kevin Hastings
Times 12-3/6.30-11 Closed Xmas, 31 Dec, L Mon-Wed
Prices Fixed L 2 course fr £10, Starter £5-£7, Main £11-£16, Dessert £2-£6, Service optional **Wines** 19 bottles over £30, 23 bottles under £30, 10 by glass **Notes** Breakfast available Sat-Sun, Sunday L, Vegetarian available **Parking** On street

Cambio de Tercio
PLAN 4 C2

Spanish

Contemporary Spanish cooking in fun, vibrant atmosphere

☎ 020 7244 8970
163 Old Brompton Rd SW5 0LJ
dir: Nearest station: Gloucester Road. Close to junction with Drayton Gardens

With sibling tapas bars Capote y Toros (see entry) almost next door and Tendido Cero opposite, this stretch of Old Brompton Road is indelibly Spanish. Now with a swanky new entrance bar (including a few extra tables and impressive new kitchen below), Cambio feels more expansive and less frenetic than previously, though it still comes decked out in its wonderful trademark throbbing colours with large flamboyant artworks. Floors are covered in cool black slate, closely set tables are laid with white

---

Trinity Restaurant

LONDON SW4
PLAN 1 E2

British, European **V**

Dynamic modern cooking in Clapham

☎ 020 7622 1199
4 The Polygon, Clapham SW4 0JG
e-mail: dine@trinityrestaurant.co.uk
dir: Nearest station: Clapham Common. 200 yds from underground left towards Common & follow road keeping Common on left. Restaurant far side of The Polygon (an island block of buildings) opposite the Sun pub

There are many gems outside the bursting heart of central London, and Adam Byatt's restaurant in The Polygon on the north side of Clapham Common is such a place. It may well serve the neighbourhood very well indeed, but it is not a neighbourhood restaurant by definition - this is most definitely a destination

restaurant. It doesn't do neighbourhood prices, either, but it is not expensive when compared to other places of similar ambition and achievement. Good reason to head to Clapham, then. It's a smart-looking space with darkwood and white neutrality abounding, tables dressed in crisp white linen, and windows that open up to bring the outside in when the weather is up to snuff. Byatt's cooking is creative, confident, well-judged, and, best of all, very good to eat. The menu changes with the seasons, but new things come on board often enough to satisfy regulars; dishes such as these take time in the planning. Choose from the à la carte or two tasting menus (five or seven courses) and rest assured, whichever route you take, flavours will be bang on, presentation will impress, and satisfaction will be achieved. Dish descriptions keep it simple, so 'chicken consommé, baked celeriac, chicken oyster' is one way to start, followed by Dexter sirloin with Dorset snail persillade, scorched onions and truffle creamed potato. All of the ingredients are top-notch, from the scallops served as a céviche with pickle and charred

cucumber, to the gilt head bream with its accompanying pumpkin, chanterelles and oxtail dumplings. There's no less excitement at dessert stage: take lemon soufflé with crème fraîche sorbet, or passionfruit and bitter chocolate 'Mess'.

Chef Adam Byatt, Graham Squire **Owner** Angus Jones & Adam Byatt **Times** 12.30-2.30/6.30-10.30 Closed 24-26 Dec, 31 Jan, L Mon, D Sun **Prices** Fixed L 2 course £20, Tasting menu £45-£55, Starter £7-£12, Main £19-£33, Dessert £5-£9, Service added but optional 12.5% **Wines** 75 bottles over £30, 24 bottles under £30, 14 by glass **Notes** Sunday L £28-£35, Vegetarian menu **Seats** 63, Pr/dining room 12 **Children** Portions **Parking** On street

linen, while black banquettes and chairs afford the comforts. The food is similarly colourful and well dressed and comes with a sparkling touch of innovation and flair; nibbles might include fried manchego 'lollipops', for example, while the carte flouts three-course convention for tapas-sized portions for sharing. Traditionalists might go for crispy Serrano ham croquettes, while signature tapas like eight-hour cooked semi-dry tomatoes with sweet Oloroso sherry and cured Cecina beef crank it up a little. There are more substantial plates, too, such as flame-grilled Presa Iberica teamed with smoked chorizo mash, figs and vinegar carame, with an 'all lemon dessert' consisting of an airy sponge, ice cream, custard and jelly.

Times 12-2.30/7-11.30 Closed 2 wks at Xmas, New Year

Capote y Toros   PLAN 4 C2

🎖 Spanish **V**

Authentic tapas and fabulous range of sherries

☎ 020 7373 0567
157 Old Brompton Rd SW5 0LJ
e-mail: cambiodeterciogroup@btconnect.com
dir: Nearest station: South Kensington, Gloucester Road

Step into this pint-sized bodega on the Old Brompton Road and you're transported to a lively, sunny, neighbourhood bar in downtown Càdiz. It's another show-stopper from next-door-but-one big-brother outfit, Cambio de Tercio (see entry) and bills itself as a ham, tapas and sherry joint. Photos of matadors line one wall of the narrow, vibrant-coloured space, while Iberico hams hang from the ceiling above the tiny bar set amongst display racks of sherry and wine. There's a no booking policy, so catch a seat at the single row of modern pale-wood tables or perch on a high stool at the counter opposite and wait your turn over a glass of manzanilla. Sherry (a staggering 110 labels) is the thing, though all-Spanish wines roll out to 350 bins. Friendly, clued-up Spanish staff add to the fun, while the menu keeps things simple and accessible, offering first-class hams and charcuterie shipped in from southern Spain alongside traditional Andalucían tapas. Expect the likes of carpaccio of duck liver with Pedro Ximénez reduction; pork meatballs with Oloroso sherry sauce; Iberico pork with chorizo purée; and roasted codfish in a Sobrasada chorizo crust with courgette carpaccio. Olé!

Chef Luis Navacerrada Lanzadera **Owner** Abel Lusa **Times** 6-11.30 Closed Xmas, Sun-Mon, L all week **Prices** Fixed D 3 course £13.50-£44, Starter £4.50-£22, Main £4.50-£10.50, Dessert £4.75-£6.75, Service added but optional **Wines** 110 bottles over £30, 35 bottles under £30 **Notes** Vegetarian menu

New Lotus Garden   PLAN 4 B3

🎖 Chinese

Neighbourhood Chinese that really hits the spot

☎ 020 7244 8984
15 Kenway Rd SW5 0RP
e-mail: jiang.hubert@gmail.com
dir: Nearest station: Earl's Court

We could all do with a top-notch Chinese such as Hubert Jiang's welcoming little place in our neighbourhood. This is Chinese cooking as it should be done - precise, well-judged dishes of clean, clearly-defined flavours. You'll find it all on a quiet residential street close to Earl's Court, in a bijou room with maroon cloths on elbow-to-elbow tables, serving up a compendious repertoire of old favourites running from dim sum to Pekinese and Cantonese classics - soft-shelled crabs baked with garlic, salt and chilli, or crispy aromatic duck with wheaten pancakes to start, then sea bass steamed with ginger and spring onion, or twice-cooked belly pork with preserved vegetables. All the accompaniments like Fujian fried rice or Singapore noodles are top-class too.

Times 12-2.30/5-11.30 Closed 24-26 Dec, L Sat

LONDON SW6

Blue Elephant   PLAN 1 E3

🎖 Thai **V**

Lavish riverside setting for old Thai favourite

☎ 020 7751 3111
The Boulevard, Imperial Wharf, Townmead Rd SW6 2UB
e-mail: london@blueelephant.com
dir: Nearest station: Imperial Wharf

In its swanky new home since 2012, The Blue Elephant (originally on Fulham Broadway) pulls in an adoring crowd to the plush Thames-side development of Imperial Wharf. Some might find it a bit *Footballers' Wives* with its extravagant décor inspired by the Saran Rom palace in Bangkok: think wood carvings, warm colours, a forest of green foliage, chandeliers and drapes, and a gilded bar modelled on the Royal Barge of Thailand. The lengthy menu is a complicated beast, focusing on Thai cooking of 'the past', 'today' and 'tomorrow', while throwing in a couple of tasting options and a separate vegetarian section along the way. From the old days, perhaps lamb shank yellow curry, and, for something new, try wild-catch black pepper prawns (stir-fried with garlic and black pepper and topped with lemongrass). Service is charming and authentic and there's also a riverside alfresco terrace.

Chef Nooror Somany **Owner** Blue Elephant International Group **Times** 12-2.30/6-10.30 Closed 25-26 Dec, 1 Jan **Prices** Fixed L 2 course fr £14, Tasting menu £38-£55, Starter £7-£15, Main £13-£30, Dessert £6.50-£8.50, Service added but optional 12.5% **Wines** 14 by glass **Notes** Sunday L fr £30, Vegetarian menu, Dress restrictions, Smart casual **Seats** 150, Pr/dining room 8 **Parking** Car park next to Imperial Wharf tube station

The Harwood Arms   PLAN 1 E3

🎖🎖 British

Supplier-led British cooking in smart gastro-pub

☎ 020 7386 1847
27 Walham Grove, Fulham SW6 1QR
e-mail: admin@harwoodarms.com
dir: Nearest station: Fulham Broadway. Located on the corner of Farm Lane & Walham Grove

On an unassuming backstreet in trendy Fulham, the stylish Harwood Arms is one of Britain's top gastro-pubs, all the more so as it remains true to its roots as a cracking community local - Tuesday night is quiz night, there's a raft of real ales on tap, and the overall vibe is relaxed and informal. With Brett Graham of The Ledbury (see entry) and The Pot Kiln's (see entry) Mike Robinson as owners, you've a right to have high expectations. And they are duly met. Inside you could almost forget you're in London with photos of outdoor country pursuits hung on grey and cream walls, and rustic wooden tables. On the menu, first class, carefully-sourced English produce is cooked with confidence; Berkshire rabbit faggots, for example, with split peas, smoked bacon and pickled mushrooms is a robust way to start, before moving on to Gloucestershire Old Spot pork belly with root vegetable broth and ribs glazed in ginger beer, or wild sea bass with cauliflower, oat-crusted mussels and preserved lemon. And neither do desserts miss a beat: baked stem ginger custard with honeycomb ice cream is an unerringly satisfying finale.

Times 12-3/6.30-9.30 Closed 24-28 Dec, 1 Jan, L Mon

LONDON SW6 *continued*

Marco   PLAN 1 E3

◉◉ Anglo-French

MPW brasserie-style dishes at Stamford Bridge

☎ 020 7915 2929
**M&C Hotels At Chelsea FC, Stamford Bridge, Fulham Rd
SW6 1HS**
e-mail: info@marcorestaurant.org
dir: Nearest station: Fulham Broadway

Valet parking may seem a touch Hollywood for the UK, but
it can come in quite handy in the streets around
Chelsea's Stamford Bridge ground. Then again, if you
inhabit the world of Roman Abramovich and Marco Pierre
White, who have joined forces to set up this high-gloss
operation, such services are likely par for the course.
Although the Blues' supporters would no doubt appreciate
the excellent range of ales on offer inside, this is a world
a long, long way from the pies and hotdogs that fuel the
footie fans: a chic décor brings together charcoal-grey
walls, smoked mirrors, low-level lighting, and leather
banquettes and velour seats at linen-swathed tables. On
the culinary front, MPW's signature style of tried-and-
tested French brasserie dishes is stamped all over the
carte, and it is all driven by top-class ingredients,
sharply-defined flavours and classy execution. Artichokes
Barigoule à la Provençale sets out in fine Gallic style,
then line-caught sea bass is served à la marinière with
fresh clams; if you're in the market for meatier fare, there
are steaks, grilled calves' liver with bacon, or roast rump
of lamb à la Dijonnaise with gratin dauphinoise. The
menu comes back across the Channel to end with English
cheeses with quince jelly, or flag-waving puddings along
the lines of Eton Mess or Cambridge burnt cream.

Times 6-10.30 Closed 2 wks Jul-Aug, Sun-Mon, L all week

LONDON SW7

Baglioni Hotel   PLAN 4 C5

◉ Modern Italian

Modern Italian cooking in swish hotel

☎ 020 7368 5700
60 Hyde Park Gate, Kensington Rd SW7 5BB
e-mail: brunello.london@baglionihotels.com
dir: Nearest station: Kensington High Street. Hotel
entrance facing Hyde Park Gate & Kensington Palace

The Baglioni's Brunello restaurant is an open-plan bar-
lounge and stylish dining room with plush seating, rich
fabrics, chandeliers and charming and attentive staff,
mostly Italian. Ingredients are diligently sought out, many
from the motherland, to re-create the modern Italian
cooking style, as in a richly flavoured starter of caponata
and burrata cheese drizzled with olive oil, and smoked
swordfish with exotic fruit salad in a grape reduction.

Pasta dishes are given their due - perhaps pappardelle
with veal ragù and broad beans - and main courses have
included pink and succulent veal chop with creamy mash
and sautéed spinach, and chargrilled prawns and squid
with baby seasonal vegetables. There's a great range of
home-made breads, and among dolci might be vanilla
cheesecake with cherry sorbet.

Chef Antonio Bufi **Owner** Baglioni Hotels
Times 12-3/5.30-11 **Prices** Fixed L 2 course £18, Fixed D
3 course £29, Starter £9.50-£14.50, Main £16-£25,
Dessert £8-£15, Service added but optional 12.5%
Notes Pre-theatre menu 5.30-7pm all wk £25-£30,
Sunday L, Vegetarian available, Dress restrictions, Smart
casual, Civ Wed 60 **Seats** 70, Pr/dining room 60
Children Portions, Menu **Parking** 2, On street Kensington
Rd/De Vere Gardens

Bombay Brasserie   PLAN 4 C3

◉◉ Indian ✿

A taste of Mumbai near Gloucester Road

☎ 020 7370 4040
Courtfield Close, Courtfield Rd SW7 4QH
e-mail: info@bbrestaurant.co.uk
dir: Nearest station: Gloucester Road. Opposite tube
station

For three decades the Bombay Brasserie has been
offering a slice of Bombay (Mumbai) glamour to fans of
authentic Indian cuisine. It's a restaurant on a grand
scale, divided between two rooms, the first with a more
traditional Raj-era look and feel (gold chandeliers, gilt-
frame mirrors, plush patterned carpet, deep cushioned
banquettes), and the second a vast conservatory with a
much more contemporary and minimalist design (white
and black tiled floor, black modern chairs). Mumbai is a
melting pot of different cultures and hence its cuisine -
and the menu here - takes its influences from India's
many diverse regions and beyond. Much of the repertoire
will sound familiar - seekh kebab, chicken tikka, lamb
rogan josh, dal makhani - but this is no ordinary curry
house: ingredients are top quality, spicing is precise,
everything is cooked fresh to order using minimal fat, and
presentation is refined. Malabari soft-shelled crab - fried
in a light, crispy, subtly spiced batter - is a good way to
start. Keep with the fishy theme at main course with the
Goan halibut curry (chunks of fresh halibut simmered in
a tangy coconut and red chilli sauce), and make sure you
order one of the freshly-made, thin and light naan
breads. The desserts are all made in-house too.

Chef Prahlad Hegde **Owner** Taj International Hotels
Times 12-3/6.30-11.30 Closed 25-26 Dec **Prices** Prices
not confirmed Service added but optional 10% **Wines** 18
by glass **Notes** Fixed D 5 course £70, Tasting menu on
request, Sunday L, Vegetarian available, Dress
restrictions, Smart casual **Seats** 185, Pr/dining room 16
Parking Millennium Gloucester Hotel next door

Bulgari Hotel & Residences   PLAN 4 F5

◉◉ Modern Italian NEW ▲ NOTABLE WINE LIST

**Classy Italian cooking in incomparably stylish
surroundings**

☎ 020 7151 1010
171 Knightsbridge SW7 1DW
e-mail: london-info@bulgarihotels.com
dir: Nearest station: Knightsbridge. Almost opposite Hyde
Park

With a name like that, you'd expect something fairly
swish, and you won't be disappointed. The hotel is a
design-led temple of chic in the heart of Knightsbridge,
its lobby an expanse of gleaming battleship-grey, the
Ristorante accessed via a sweeping staircase more
obviously suited to a cruise-liner. The mahogany-floored
space is again monochrome, with semicircular booth-
style seating and clothed tables. The menus deal in
relatively simple but lively Italian classics from Genoa,
Milan, Naples and so forth. A seafood salad of prawns,
clams, squid and octopus on a bed of romaine leaves
scores highly for the quality of its rapidly sautéed prime
ingredients, while the traditional intermediaries
encompass bone marrow in saffron risotto, and a pasta
dish of ox cheek in a rich, casseroley sauce. Mains might
be perfectly rendered roast lamb with caponata, or nicely
judged fish specials such as sea bass with taggiasca
olives, minestrone vegetables and basil. A zinging citrus
selection to round things off incorporates an orange
tartlet with candied lemon and lemon-basil sorbet, and
the tiramisù is pretty nifty too. Home-made grissini and
breads underscore the class of the operation.

Chef Robbie Pepin **Times** 12-2.30/6.30-10.30
Prices Fixed L 3 course £30, Starter £9-£24, Main
£14-£38, Dessert £7-£14, Service added but optional
12.5% **Wines** 473 bottles over £30, 27 bottles under £30,
18 by glass **Notes** La Dolce Domenica Sun L £58,
Vegetarian available, Dress restrictions, Smart casual
Seats 80, Pr/dining room 18 **Children** Portions, Menu
Parking NCP Pavillion Road

L'Etranger   PLAN 4 C4

◉◉ French, Japanese ▲ NOTABLE WINE LIST

**A happy marriage between France and Japan in a
swanky setting**

☎ 020 7584 1118 & 7823 9291
36 Gloucester Rd SW7 4QT
e-mail: etranger@etranger.co.uk
dir: Nearest station: Gloucester Road. 5 mins walk from
tube station at junct of Queens Gate Terrace and
Gloucester Rd

Decked out in soothing shades of silver-grey with oak
flooring, fashionable dark-leather seating, mirrors,
striking floral displays and windows screened with

sparkling beads, intimate L'Etranger delivers a classy calmness that fits with its modern French credentials and flirtation with Japanese cooking. The private dining area has similar good looks and wine-bottle-lined walls. The kitchen's fine-tuned roster is driven by tip-top produce, a hint of luxury, flavour and well-dressed presentation. Take Scottish John Dory fillet say, perhaps teamed with a clam risotto, baby leeks and Riesling sauce, or an Asian-inspired caramelised Alaskan black cod with miso, sushi rice and pickled ginger. Desserts take up the theme too, running from a classic apple tarte Tatin to chocolate fondant with green tea ice cream. The location ensures some gold-card prices, though this is tempered by good-value lunch, early bird and weekend brunch offerings, and service is thoroughly professional and eager to please (including a sommelier for an absolute corking tome of a wine list). Downstairs, evenings-only venue Meursault offers a more casual take on the L'Etranger theme.

Chef Jerome Tauvron **Owner** Ibi Issolah
Times 12-3/5.30-11 Closed 26-27 Dec **Prices** Fixed L 2 course fr £16.50, Fixed D 3 course fr £48, Tasting menu fr £95, Starter £8.50-£18.50, Main £10.50-£69, Dessert £7.50-£24.50, Service added but optional 12.5%
Wines 1400 bottles over £30, 60 bottles under £30, 12 by glass **Notes** Degustation 5/6 course £65/£95, Early bird Mon-Fri 6-6.45pm, Sunday L, Vegetarian available, Dress restrictions, Smart casual **Seats** 64, Pr/dining room 20 **Children** Portions **Parking** NCP

Millennium Bailey's Hotel London Kensington
PLAN 4 C4

◉ Italian

Italian cooking in smart townhouse hotel

☎ 020 7331 6308
140 Gloucester Rd SW7 4QH
e-mail: olives.baileys@millenniumhotels.co.uk
web: www.millenniumhotels.co.uk
dir: Nearest station: Gloucester Road. Hotel opposite tube station

The setting may be a blue-blooded, beautifully restored Victorian townhouse in Kensington, but the language changes to Italian in the Olives Restaurant. Waiting staff bring an authentic Italian buzz to a modern setting of bare darkwood tables and contemporary artwork on rich blue walls, while an open kitchen adds a further dynamic element to proceedings. A glass of prosecco in the stylish bar should cement the feel-good mood before tucking into a mix of classic and updated dishes all made with well-sourced materials. Get going with excellent bread and olive oil, then follow with risotto of wood pigeon and artichokes, or venison ragoût with red wine and juniper berries. Main courses offer classic osso buco Milanese alongside oven-baked monkfish served with spelt and olives in clam guazzetto. Check out the keenly-priced lunch special and pre-theatre menus too.

Times 12-5/5-10.30

Zuma
PLAN 4 F5

◉◉ Modern Japanese

Buzzy modern Japanese in fashionable Knightsbridge

☎ 020 7584 1010
5 Raphael St, Knightsbridge SW7 1DL
e-mail: info@zumarestaurant.com
dir: Nearest station: Knightsbridge. Brompton Rd west, turn right into Lancelot Pl & follow road to right into Raphael St

With a network of branches spanning the planet from Miami to Hong Kong as well as Knightsbridge, Zuma is an expanding global brand. Its aim is to spread the word on the informal Japanese dining style, known as izakaya. The venue uses all the contemporary textures of blond wood, granite blocks, steel and glass you might expect in an über-chic, minimally Zen-like setting, but the vibe is the polar opposite of calm and relaxation when the crowds turn up (often in chauffeur-driven Bentleys - it's that sort of place) and fuel up on the 40 different types of sake in the buzzing bar. It is certainly not a case of style over substance: whether you are dining in the main restaurant or at the open robata grill and sushi counter, the cooking is defined by superb fresh ingredients, razor-sharp flavours and magnificent presentation. The sushi is exemplary and you could go about things tapas-style and graze through yellowtail sashimi with soy dashi, shallot and crispy garlic, then seared beef with soy, ginger, lime and coriander alongside pork skewers with yuzu mustard miso. Desserts can be a weaker element of the Japanese idiom, but a parfait-like caramelised chocolate saikoro with cocoa crumble holds its own.

Chef Bjoern Weissgerber **Owner** Rainer Becker & Arjun Waney **Times** 12-2.30/6-11 Closed 25 Dec **Prices** Prices not confirmed Service added but optional 15% **Wines** 17 by glass **Notes** Tasting menu min 2 people, Vegetarian available, Dress restrictions, Smart casual **Seats** 175, Pr/dining room 14 **Parking** On street

---

LONDON SW8

Tom Ilic
PLAN 1 E3

◉◉ Modern European

Robust flavours from seasoned chef in downtown Battersea

☎ 020 7622 0555
123 Queenstown Rd SW8 3RH
e-mail: info@tomilic.com
dir: Nearest station: Clapham Common. Close to Clapham Junct & Battersea Power Station

Though Tom Ilic's self-named shop-front restaurant may have the look of a workaday neighbourhood bistro, savvy locals and the capital's foodies know there's some smart cooking going on here. Expect imaginative and gutsy cooking with personality and full-on flavours served in generous portions, and at reasonable prices, too. Ilic's trademark skill with meat, and, in particular, things

porcine, is on show. Consider carte signatures like a starter of braised pig's cheek with chorizo (accompanied by garlic mash and crackling) to a main-event 'degustation of pork' (with pickled white cabbage and caramelised apple), while fish lovers are not ignored; witness baked fillet of line-caught sea bass with tomato fondue, crab and prawn tartlet. Fixed-price menus (lunch and dinner) offer more cracking value - twice-baked mature cheddar soufflé followed by baked fillet of salmon, for example - while the atmosphere has a relaxed, white-linen-free vibe, with modern art, leafy fronds and leather chairs providing a contemporary sheen.

Times 12-2.30/6-10.30 Closed last wk Aug, Xmas, Mon, L Tue, D Sun

---

LONDON SW10

Chelsea Riverside Brasserie
PLAN 1 E3

◉ Traditional British, French

Marina dining in the heart of London

☎ 020 7823 3000
Wyndham Grand London, Chelsea Harbour SW10 0XG
web: www.chelseariversidebrasserie.co.uk
dir: Nearest station: Fulham Broadway, Imperial Wharf. A4 to Earls Court Rd S towards river. Right into Kings Rd, left down Lots Rd. Chelsea Harbour in front

The high-gloss Wyndham Grand is pitched squarely at the jet-set crew who frequent Chelsea Harbour waterfront. The concept of the restaurant can change from one year to the next, but seems to be sticking with its incarnation as the Chelsea Riverside Brasserie for now. It is a glitzy space, naturally, filled with plush royal blue and cream seats at bare wooden tables, although a wall of windows inevitably focuses the attention on the alfresco terrace perched above the boats moored in the marina - a space that is in much demand when the sun decrees that outdoor dining season is open. The menu sticks to a simple modern style, opening with caramelised foie gras roulade with apple chutney and toasted brioche, and pursuing the brasserie theme with top-grade cuts of Scottish steak slapped on the grill and served with French fries and a classic béarnaise sauce. Lighter ideas could be Shetland mussels in a time-honoured garlic and white wine sauce, or organic salmon with crème fraîche potatoes, sautéed lentils and thyme jus. Conclude with a dainty pairing of elderflower and champagne mousse with pistachio ice cream and gooseberries.

Times 12-10.30 **Prices** Prices not confirmed Service added but optional 12.5% **Wines** 18 by glass **Notes** Vegetarian available **Seats** 105, Pr/dining room 12 **Children** Menu **Parking** NCP

LONDON SW10 *continued*

Chutney Mary Restaurant
PLAN 1 E3

◉◉ Indian

Stunning venue for Indian cooking that's a cut above

☎ 020 7351 3113
535 King's Rd, Chelsea SW10 0SZ
e-mail: chutneymary@realindianfood.com
dir: Nearest station: Fulham Broadway. On corner of King's Rd and Lots Rd

This glamorous Chelsea Indian has been going strong for more than two decades, and when you descend the staircase from the reception and first set eyes on the glittering spectacle that is the basement restaurant, you start to understand why. The place looks simply stunning, and the tricky decisions start before you've even looked at the menu: do you take a table in the opulently decorated split-level dining room, with its mirrored walls, rich orange hues, framed crystal-studded silk hangings and Raj-era sketches, or in the spacious conservatory, decked out greenhouse-style with trees and plants soaring towards the high ceiling? Wherever you sit, expect flickering candles on the linen-clad tables and friendly, professional service. The authentic Indian cooking is brought bang up-to-date with attractive, modern presentation, and the ingredients are top-notch. Start,

perhaps, with tokri chaat, a crispy straw potato basket filled with traditional Indian street foods and topped with strained yoghurt and chutneys - a dish full of contrasts in texture, flavour and colour. Roast shoulder of tender lamb in a brown onion based sauce with fine green beans is a suitably modern take on a lamb curry. Round things off in a slightly more Western vein with a first-class coconut pannacotta with black cherry sorbet.

Chef Mr Manar Tulli **Owner** R Mathrani, N & C Panjabi **Times** 12.30-3/6.30-11.30 Closed L Mon-Fri, D 25 Dec **Prices** Fixed L 3 course fr £24, Tasting menu fr £25, Starter £7-£14.50, Main £17.50-£31.50, Dessert fr £7, Service added but optional 12.5% **Wines** 18 by glass **Notes** Sunday L fr £26, Vegetarian available, Civ Wed 110 **Seats** 110, Pr/dining room 24 **Children** Menu **Parking** Parking meters outside

---

AA RESTAURANT OF THE YEAR FOR LONDON

Medlar Restaurant
PLAN 4 D1

◉◉◉ – *see below*

The Painted Heron
PLAN 1 E3

◉◉ Modern Indian

First-rate modern Indian near the river

☎ 020 7351 5232
112 Cheyne Walk SW10 0DJ
e-mail: thepaintedheron@btinternet.com
dir: Nearest station: South Kensington

Rather secreted away on the north bank of the Thames close to Battersea Bridge, this Chelsea Indian is a thoroughly modern affair. The clean-lined interiors - think black lacquered leather upholstered chairs, white linen-clothed tables and plain walls dotted with modern art - deliver a stylish, on-vogue edge to the deceptively roomy dining area. The cooking is equally smart and modern, underpinned by seasonality and judicious spicing, and making use of produce not readily encountered on many Indian repertoires: take tandoor grilled squab pigeon breasts in tamarind to open, followed by the likes of diced rabbit in a hot Kajasthani jungle curry, or perhaps guinea fowl supreme in Karahi masala with chick peas and fried green chillies. Otherwise try black cod (spice roasted) in a Malabari curry, or lamb neck fillet in a Pakistani 'nihari' curry with kholrabi. The dessert list looks to the west for something like a spot-on chocolate and pistachio fondant, while ancillaries (like naan or poppadoms and

---

Medlar Restaurant

AA RESTAURANT OF THE YEAR FOR LONDON

LONDON SW10 PLAN 4 D1

Modern European **NEW**

Highly skilled cooking and a refreshing lack of pretension

☎ 020 7349 1900
438 King's Rd, Chelsea SW10 0LJ
e-mail: info@medlarrestaurant.co.uk
dir: Nearest station: Sloane Square, Earl's Court. About 20 mins walk along King's Rd from Sloane Square underground station

It can be a fine line between success and failure in the restaurant game, but some people manage to make success look very easy indeed. Joe Mercer Nairne and

David O'Connor are such people. Medlar is one of those restaurants that goes about its business with a quiet confidence: the menu reads (and eats) like a foodie's dream, the service is slick but not overbearing, and the prices are reasonable. And all this on the King's Road. It looks good from the street - inviting, you might say - with its cool, muted colour tones, awning, and doors that open up to give that European vibe in the warmer months (there are actually a few tables outside as well). Inside it is simply elegant, not casual, but not overly smart either - tables are dressed in white linen, the designer touches are present but held in check. It is restrained, confident - a bit like the cooking. The food has a rustic charm about it, but it is far from unsophisticated: wild garlic soup with a poached pheasant's egg and morels - yes, please. One spring day you might fancy some new season's asparagus, and here it is, with jamon Ibérico, goats' cheese mousse and broad bean vinaigrette (spot on), or how about duck egg tart with red wine sauce, turnip purée, lardons and sautéed duck heart? And that's just

the starters. Next up, roast poussin with sautéed spätzle, caramelised shallot, girolles and cauliflower purée competes for your attention with wild turbot with ginger, mushroom and soy broth, white asparagus, pak choi and prawn dumpling. For dessert, lemon curd ice cream with blackcurrant compôte and meringues and crème chiboust with strawberries and honeycomb maintain the high standards to the very end.

Chef Joe Mercer Nairne **Owner** Joe Mercer Nairne, David O'Connor **Times** 12-3/6.30-10.30 **Prices** Fixed L 3 course £26-£30, Fixed D 3 course £42, Service added but optional 12.5% **Wines** 400+ bottles over £30, 15 by glass **Notes** Sunday L, Vegetarian available, Dress restrictions, Smart casual **Seats** 85, Pr/dining room 28 **Children** Portions, Menu **Parking** On street

pickles) maintain the good form. There's plenty of spice-friendly wines too, and cigar smokers have the luxury of their own lounge out back.

Times 12-3/6.30-11 Closed Xmas, Etr, L Sat

LONDON SW11

The Butcher & Grill
PLAN 1 E3

◉ Modern British

A carnivore's delight in relaxed, modern warehouse-style setting

☎ 020 7924 3999
39-41 Parkgate Rd, Battersea SW11 4NP
e-mail: info@thebutcherandgrill.com
dir: Nearest station: Clapham Junction, Battersea

This all-day combo of butcher's shop, deli, coffee bar, and no-frills grill restaurant ticks all the modern lifestyle boxes in its warehouse setting. Its butcher's-apron-style striped awning makes it easy to spot, while inside the look is all exposed floorboards and brick, modern wood furniture, leather banquettes and big monochrome photos of livestock to reinforce the meaty theme. Top-grade ethically-reared meat is the mainstay of the brasserie-style menu, which majors around the grill, offering fab dry-aged and big-flavoured steaks, or the likes of Gloucestershire Old Spot pork chops; it's all handled simply but with skill. And there's much more besides, including classics like pie and mash or blackboard specials such as day-boat fish - maybe whole plaice simply served with sautéed potatoes, spinach and a lemon butter sauce. Non-carnivores aren't forgotten either, with decent veggie options like roasted butternut squash with cep and parmesan Wellington and a balsamic glaze. A rear terrace overlooks a disused Thames wharf, and there's a sibling branch in Wimbledon.

Times 12-3/5.30-11 Closed 25-26 Dec, D Sun

Entrée Restaurant and Bar
PLAN 1 E2

◉◉ Modern European ♥

Buzzing neighbourhood restaurant and bar

☎ 020 7223 5147
2 Battersea Rise, Battersea SW11 1ED
e-mail: info@entreebattersea.co.uk
dir: Nearest station: Clapham Junction, Clapham Common. Just off the corner of Clapham Common, Battersea Rise at Lavender Walk

A casual, relaxed feel, a buzzy, lively atmosphere, live weekend jazz and a touch of theatre from an open kitchen all combine to make this unpretentious neighbourhood restaurant a real hit. Peruse the weekly-changing menu over pre-dinner drinks in the cocktail bar, then head upstairs to the intimate restaurant, where wooden floors, black leather banquettes and glowing candles on bare wooden tables set the laid-back tone. Thoughtfully presented modish dishes are built around top-notch British seasonal produce; start with the likes of pheasant and chestnut soup or chilled poached salmon with

Jerusalem artichoke and broccoli salad. For main course there may be venison with braised red cabbage, fondant potato and sultana purée, or stone bass with squid ink purée, Swiss chard and seafood parcels, and to finish, chocolate cake with white chocolate mousse and caramel ice cream.

Chef James McDonald **Owner** Jayke Mangion, Gerry O'Keefe **Times** 12-4/6-10.30 Closed 1 wk Xmas, L Mon-Fri **Prices** Prices not confirmed Service added but optional 12.5% **Wines** 8 by glass **Notes** Sunday L, Vegetarian available, Dress restrictions, Smart casual **Seats** 55 **Children** Portions **Parking** On street

Ransome's Dock
PLAN 1 E3

◉◉ Modern British ▮NOTABLE WINE LIST

Long-serving neighbourhood restaurant with canal views

☎ 020 7223 1611 & 7924 2462
35-37 Parkgate Rd, Battersea SW11 4NP
e-mail: chef@ransomesdock.co.uk
dir: Nearest station: Sloane Square, Clapham Junction. Between Albert Bridge & Battersea Bridge

Sitting alongside moored houseboats on a small canal leading to the Thames in Battersea, this relaxed neighbourhood restaurant and bar is an excellent all-day option. Owned by Martin and Vanessa Lam for over 20 years, the combination of charming location, warm, easygoing atmosphere, dynamic wine list and unpretentious, modish cooking remains a winner. Large windows serve up lovely views of the water and an outdoor terrace gets you even closer. Generous portions of hearty bistro-style dishes are what to expect, plus that superb award-winning wine list with plenty of interesting options, including a great selection of dessert wines. Start perhaps with warm Lincolnshire smoked eel fillets with buckwheat pancake and horseradish cream, then move on to Elizabeth David's spinach and ricotta gnocchi or English rose veal goulash with parsley dumplings. The kitchen shows its mettle with a fine warm chocolate and damson tart with crème fraîche.

Times 12-11 Closed Xmas, Aug BH, D Sun

LONDON SW12

Harrison's
PLAN 1 E2

◉ Modern British

Thriving neighbourhood brasserie with confident cooking

☎ 020 8675 6900
15-19 Bedford Hill, Balham SW12 9EX
e-mail: info@harrisonsbalham.co.uk
dir: Nearest station: Balham. Turn right from Balham High Rd opposite Waitrose, onto Bedford Hill. Restaurant on corner of Bedford Hill & Harberson Rd

This easygoing and suitably cool brasserie and bar is a winner with the Balham crowd (kids and all). Owner Sam Harrison (of big-brother Sam's Brasserie & Bar in Chiswick fame - see entry) is a one-time lieutenant of

Rick Stein, and he's pitched this place just right. An oval-shaped metal-formed bar is a great centrepiece to the room, encircling an open kitchen on one side and drinks counter on the other; low-slung lightshades, banquettes and simple wooden furniture complete the modern good looks, while staff are seemingly sunny natured. The cooking keeps things relatively straightforward with a pleasing roster of brasserie-style dishes but does not lack contemporary verve. The daily-changing carte is joined by fixed-price options, weekend breakfast and brunch, and bar and children's menus. Start with something as enticingly modish as prawn popcorn with Cajun aïoli and follow on with pan-seared sea bass with curried butternut squash purée, leeks and apple foam, or stick with a classic such as cheeseburger and fries. Inspiring cocktails and a fashionable wine list, with plenty by the glass and 500ml carafe, complete the picture.

Times 12-mdnt Closed 24-27 Dec, L 28 Dec

Lamberts
PLAN 1 E2

◉◉ Modern British

Conscientious seasonal cooking near Balham tube

☎ 020 8675 2233
2 Station Pde, Balham High Rd SW12 9AZ
e-mail: bookings@lambertsrestaurant.com
dir: Nearest station: Balham. Just S of Balham station on Balham High Rd

The sparely functional but smart south London eatery a minute or two from Balham tube station may look like many another compact urban brasserie with its exposed floorboards, serried ranks of tables and bland coffee colour scheme, but a beating heart of gastronomic passion drives the place. Ryan Lowery is as conscientious about conservation and quality as if he were cooking in a country pub in Wiltshire, sourcing organic and ethically produced materials from family smallholdings, and keeping a weather eye on the changing seasons. A lovage dressing fragrantly garnishes a starter of smoked mackerel with potato and anchovy salad, while a gastro-salad of pear, toasted walnuts, Devon's Harbourne Blue goats' cheese and watercress offers refreshment to an old bistro classic. Mains are built from apposite accumulations of ingredients, adding haricots, cavolo nero and artichoke crisps to hake and mussels, or parsnip and sprouting broccoli to a Herdwick lamb duo of rump and shoulder, the latter enthroned on a pastry shell. Celebrate the tang of the season's first rhubarb in an upside-down cake with vanilla custard.

Chef Ryan Lowery **Owner** Mr Joe Lambert **Times** 12.30-2.30/6-10 Closed 25 Dec, BH (except Good Fri), Mon, D Sun **Prices** Fixed L 2 course £15, Fixed D 3 course £20, Tasting menu £35-£50, Starter £7-£10, Main £15-£23, Dessert £6-£8, Service added but optional 12.5% **Wines** 22 bottles over £30, 31 bottles under £30, 14 by glass **Notes** Sunday L, Vegetarian available **Seats** 50 **Children** Portions, Menu **Parking** On street

LONDON SW13

Sonny's Kitchen
PLAN 1 D3

◉◉ Modern

Popular and highly regarded neighbourhood restaurant

☎ 020 8748 0393 & 8741 8451
94 Church Rd, Barnes SW13 0DQ
e-mail: manager@sonnyskitchen.co.uk
dir: Nearest station: Barnes. From Castelnau end of Church Rd on left by shops

Sonny's, part restaurant, part food store, has occupied its premises in a parade of shops for a generation. Chefs may come and go, but constant updating and reinvention keep the place ahead of the game, and changes in décor move with the times. It's comfortable, relaxing and welcoming, with a sensibly concise menu offering enough variety to keep its regulars returning again and again. Classic ideas might take in home-cured salmon with endive and dill, or linguine vongole, followed by duck à l'orange, or grilled sea bream fillet with anchovy butter. Standards are consistently high, as is quality, seen in starters of braised ox tongue with Charlotte potatoes, beetroot and horseradish, and a salad of avocado, smoked eel and bacon, and main courses like roast poussin with melted onions, thyme and garlic leaves. A few pizzas and steaks extend the range even further, and puddings end on a satisfying note: vanilla crème brûlée with griottine cherries and Kirsch, or rice pudding with rhubarb compôte.

Chef Tom Boland **Owner** Rebecca Mascarenhas, Phil Howard **Times** 12-2.30/6-10.30 Closed Xmas, New Year, D Sun **Prices** Fixed L 2 course £16.50, Starter £7.50-£9.50, Main £7.95-£21, Dessert £6.50-£10.50, Service added but optional 12.5% **Wines** 54 bottles over £30, 25 bottles under £30, 20 by glass **Notes** Sunday L, Vegetarian available **Seats** 100, Pr/dining room 18 **Children** Portions, Menu **Parking** On street

LONDON SW14

The Depot
PLAN 1 D3

◉ Modern British, European

Popular, relaxed, neighbourhood-style riverside brasserie

☎ 020 8878 9462
Tideway Yard, 125 Mortlake High St, Barnes SW14 8SN
e-mail: info@depotbrasserie.co.uk
dir: Nearest station: Barnes Bridge. Between Barnes Bridge & Mortlake stations

Thames-view tables in the dining room and bar are The Depot's principle draw-card, while a sunny terrace in the cobbled courtyard out front offers alfresco opportunities without the watery vista. The interior is relaxed and unstuffy rather than big-city cool: banquette seating and café-style chairs combine with pastel tones, simple wooden tables and herringbone-patterned floorboards. The service fits the unpretentious, upbeat vibe, while the kitchen's modern, simply constructed, please-all, brasserie-style roster comes with an occasional nod to sunnier climes. A classic bouillabaisse might start you off, followed by stone bass and scallops served with crayfish, tarragon and baby spinach risotto, or a grilled leg of lamb steak teamed with baby carrots, borlotti bean stew and spinach. Comfort-zone desserts might offer Eton Mess or the ubiquitous sticky toffee pudding. Fixed-price options and bar and children's menus help keep the Barnes locals returning.

Chef Gary Knowles **Owner** Tideway Restaurants Ltd **Times** 12-3.30/6-10 **Prices** Fixed L 2 course £12.95-£15.95, Fixed D 3 course £14.50-£17.50, Tasting menu £40-£45, Starter £5-£13.95, Main £10.50-£20.95, Dessert £5.95-£6, Service added but optional 12.5% **Wines** 13 bottles over £30, 33 bottles under £30, 20 by glass **Notes** Sunday L, Vegetarian available **Seats** 120, Pr/dining room 60 **Children** Portions, Menu **Parking** Parking after 6.30pm & at wknds

LONDON SW15

Enoteca Turi
PLAN 1 D2

◉ Italian 🍷 NOTABLE WINE LIST

Regional Italian food and wine in Putney

☎ 020 8785 4449
28 Putney High St SW15 1SQ
e-mail: enoteca@talktalk.net
dir: Nearest station: Putney Bridge. Opposite Odeon Cinema near bridge

Behind an unassuming frontage on Putney High Street, the family-run Enoteca has been serving regional Italian cooking to eager south Londoners for over 20 years. Wine is given a top billing here, too - there's over 300 to get through from across Italy, plus every dish is given a by-the-glass pairing. Seasonality and a light modern touch are evident in regional dishes along the lines of smoked duck breast with confit leg, white cabbage salad, quince preserve with cumin straws, and slow-cooked feather blade of organic beef with ricotta filled paccheri pasta, red wine and tomato sauce. Finish with a torta caprese - Capri chocolate and almond cake with limoncello cream.

Chef Mr G Turi **Owner** Mr G & Mrs P Turi **Times** 12-2.30/7-10.30 Closed 25-26 Dec, 1 Jan, Sun, L BHs **Prices** Fixed L 2 course £17.50, Fixed D 3 course £32.50, Starter £8.75-£12.50, Main £12.50-£28.50, Dessert £6.75-£9.75, Service added but optional 12.5% **Wines** 300 bottles over £30, 14 bottles under £30, 11 by glass **Notes** Vegetarian available, Dress restrictions, Smart casual **Seats** 85, Pr/dining room 18 **Children** Portions **Parking** Putney Exchange car park, on street

LONDON SW17

Chez Bruce
PLAN 1 E4

◉◉◉ – **see opposite**

LONDON SW19

Cannizaro House
PLAN 1 D1

◉◉ British, European ☺

Confident cooking in a parkland setting

☎ 020 8879 1464
West Side, Wimbledon Common SW19 4UE
e-mail: info@cannizarohouse.com
web: www.cannizarohouse.com
dir: Nearest station: Wimbledon. From A3 (London Rd) Tibbets Corner, take A219 (Parkside) right into Cannizaro Rd, then right into West Side

When you're just past your 300th birthday, even the most elegant old beauty needs a facelift. And the wraps came off this magnificent Georgian mansion surrounded by parkland within Wimbledon Common in March 2013, revealing opulent fabrics, designer wallpapers and silk lampshades galore in a restyled contemporary look. The kitchen, thankfully, sees no reason to change from its eminently sound policy of sourcing the finest organic, seasonal and local ingredients, uniting them using rock-solid classical techniques in a contemporary European menu of fresh, vibrant colours, tastes and textures. Dinner could open with a modern take on a French classic - tempura frogs' legs with garlic purée, parsley, lemon and wild garlic from the Surrey Downs - while well-conceived main courses handle multiple flavours with assurance, bringing together 36-hour-cooked, treacle-cured pork collar with brawn croquette, plums and amaretti, say, or roast fillet of John Dory with butter-poached langoustine, bisque risotto and prawn cracker. Desserts are no less creative, if heritage carrot cake with cream cheese, candied walnuts, and beetroot is anything to go by. For more informal eating head to the hotel's newly added Orangerie.

Chef Christian George **Owner** Bridgehouse Hotels **Times** 12-2.30/7-9.30 **Prices** Prices not confirmed Service optional **Wines** 12 by glass **Notes** Sunday L, Vegetarian available, Dress restrictions, No shorts, Civ Wed 100 **Seats** 60, Pr/dining room 120 **Children** Portions, Menu **Parking** 55

The Fox & Grapes   PLAN 1 D2

Traditional British

Pub food à la Claude Bosi

☎ 020 8619 1300

9 Camp Rd, Wimbledon SW19 4UN

e-mail: reservations@foxandgrapeswimbledon.co.uk

dir: Nearest station: Wimbledon

It may sound like a cosy old-fashioned boozer, but The Fox & Grapes has been transformed into a contemporary food-oriented pub with a cavernous open-plan interior of parquet floors, wood panelling, and chunky bare wooden tables and mismatched chairs wrapped around a central island bar. The man behind this radically reinvented gastro-pub on the edge of Wimbledon Common is none other than Claude Bosi of Mayfair restaurant Hibiscus fame (see entry), so if the prices at the West-End flagship are a bit rich for your blood, you can buy into his flavour-driven take on pub classics via crispy ox tongue with watercress and sauce gribiche, then mains taking in brown ale-battered hake and chips with mushy peas, or Cumberland sausage with chive mash and red onion gravy. For pudding, generous satisfaction might come in the shape of apple and rhubarb crumble with custard, or a platter of fine artisan British cheeses.

Chef Claude Bosi, Stephen Gadd **Owner** Claude Bosi **Times** 12-3/6-9.30 Closed 25 Dec **Prices** Prices not confirmed Service optional **Wines** 33 bottles over £30, 16 bottles under £30, 11 by glass **Notes** Vegetarian available **Seats** 90 **Children** Portions, Menu **Parking** On street

The Lambourne   PLAN 1 E1

Modern European

A buzz and bistro food in downtown Wimbledon

☎ 020 8545 8661

263 The Broadway, Wimbledon SW19 1SD

e-mail: info@lambournebarandgrill.com

dir: Nearest station: Wimbledon

At the less glam end of The Broadway, The Lambourne is a trendy address none the less, and it draws the crowds for its mix of vibrant bar and slick dining. You can sit in the high-ceilinged bar at blond-wood stools at high blond-wood tables (blond wood is a theme) and sip on a cocktail (cocktails are a theme), or head into the dining area which has a more intimate vibe with its slate floors and black banquettes and chairs. Wherever you sit, the decibels can be high and the please-all roster (including daily specials) remains the same - simple, well-executed, no-fuss bistro-style dishes at prices that won't alarm

your financial advisor. Battered calamari with grilled lime and tartare sauce to start perhaps, then roasted lamb rump with marinated Mediterranean vegetables and olive tapenade, or pan-fried skate wing with wilted spinach, capers and parsley noisette. Beef from Smithfield Market is cooked simply on the grill and served with triple-cooked chips.

Times 12-5-11 Closed 25-26 Dec, 1 Jan, L Mon-Fri **Prices** Prices not confirmed Service optional, Groups min 6 service 12.5% **Wines** 6 by glass **Notes** Pre-theatre menu available, Sunday L, Vegetarian available **Seats** 45 **Children** Portions, Menu **Parking** 22

Chez Bruce

LONDON SW17   PLAN 1 E2

Modern NOTABLE WINE LIST

Seriously good cooking by Wandsworth Common

☎ 020 8672 0114

2 Bellevue Rd, Wandsworth Common SW17 7EG

e-mail: enquiries@chezbruce.co.uk

dir: Nearest station: Wandsworth Common, Balham

Dining chez Bruce is an absolute pleasure. It's the kind of place chefs choose to eat, where the produce leads the way, the cooking enhances but never overpowers the ingredients, and fads and fashions are eschewed in favour of flavour. It's been here (opposite Wandsworth Common) for getting on for 20 years now, first opening its doors in 1995, and apart from nabbing the shop next-door for an extension, little has changed. The décor suits the style of the food, being both a little bit smart and a

little bit rustic, with wooden floors, well-chosen contemporary artworks and linen-clad tables, and a service team who fill you with confidence. The menu follows a broadly regional French path (sweeping across the Mediterranean) with no lack of good ideas and clear-headed thinking. Start, perhaps, with grilled baby squid served with cod brandade and saffron fritters, chick peas, chorizo, aïoli and piquillo peppers in a rich tomato sauce, or crostini of raw razor clam and scallop with tarragon, hazelnuts, pea shoots, avocado and fennel. The high quality of the ingredients is a stand-out feature, as is the skill level of the team in the kitchen. Main-course grilled Welsh lamb is a fabulous piece of meat with an accompanying glazed meatball, wild garlic, fresh goats' cheese and garlic bread. There's all the comfort of côte de boeuf with béarnaise and hand-cut chips, too, if you have a willing partner. For dessert, malt custard with coffee cream, toasted almond ice cream and chocolate almonds is a winner, but, then again, the cheeses are a

tantalising alternative. The wine list more than does justice to the food.

Chef Bruce Poole **Owner** Bruce Poole, Nigel Platts-Martin **Times** 12-2.30/6.30-10 Closed 24-26 Dec,1 Jan **Prices** Fixed L 3 course £27.50-£35, Fixed D 3 course £45, Service added but optional 12.5% **Wines** 18 by glass **Notes** Sunday L, Vegetarian available, Dress restrictions, Smart casual **Seats** 75, Pr/dining room 16 **Children** Portions **Parking** On street, station car park

LONDON SW19 *continued*

The Lawn Bistro
PLAN 1 D2

◎◎ British, European

Modern French pedigree in stylish neighbourhood bistro

☎ 020 8947 8278 & 8944 1031
67 High St, Wimbledon SW19 5EE
e-mail: info@thelawnbistro.co.uk
dir: Nearest station: Wimbledon

Well-heeled locals pack this modern French bistro in the heart of Wimbledon village, and it's not hard to see why: the setting has the charm you'd expect of a bourgeois neighbourhood venue, with its light oak flooring, unclothed wooden tables and olive-green leather-clad chairs and banquettes looking as sleek and chic as the trendy boutiques all around, while the food, courtesy of head chef Ollie Couillaud, is a blend of rusticity and refinement that doesn't miss a beat. Staff turned out smartly in long aprons, white shirts and dark ties run a tight ship, serving up a repertoire that is Franco-centric, with occasional brushstrokes of British, Spanish and Italian. Seared scallops and black pudding are matched with apple purée and lentil and hazelnut vinaigrette in a gutsy starter, then main course partners a top-class breast of free-range chicken with white asparagus, spring cabbage, Jersey Royals and a bowl of frothy truffle velouté. To finish, the flavours and textures of a Valrhona chocolate and caramel pot with salted pistachio praline are a match made in heaven, or two could sign up for a retro baked Alaska, flambéed at the table.

Chef Ollie Couillaud **Owner** Akbar Ashurov
Times 12-2.30/6.30-10.30 Closed Xmas, 1 Jan, D Sun
Prices Fixed L 2 course £14.95-£19.50, Fixed D 3 course £27.95-£37.50, Service added but optional 12.5%
Wines 78 bottles over £30, 32 bottles under £30, 11 by glass **Notes** Early D menu £24.95-£26.95, Sunday L, Vegetarian available, Dress restrictions, Smart casual
Seats 70, Pr/dining room 24 **Children** Portions

The Light House Restaurant
PLAN 1 D1

◎ British, International

Cheerful neighbourhood restaurant with appealing cooking

☎ 020 8944 6338
75-77 Ridgway, Wimbledon SW19 4ST
e-mail: info@lighthousewimbledon.com
dir: Nearest station: Wimbledon. From station right up Wimbledon Hill left at mini-rdbt onto Ridgway, restaurant on left

Light streams into this popular neighbourhood restaurant, adding to a bright and breezy atmosphere created in part by friendly service and a décor of pale wood and modern art hung on plain walls. There's more than just a hint of the Mediterranean to the broad-based menu, so there's plenty to interest regulars and newcomers alike. How about starting with seared rare tuna steak with daikon, chard and ponzu dressing, or steamed mussels with coconut red curry? If they don't appeal there may be chicken liver pâté with pumpkin chutney. The kitchen skilfully handles its choice produce and brings out distinctive flavours in dishes: pink-roast beef fillet, for instance, with potato and celeriac gratin, mushrooms and truffled port sauce, and spot-on baked cod fillet with crispy sage and sweet potato and parmesan mash. Who could fail to be won over by puddings like hot chocolate mousse with orange ice cream?

Chef Chris Casey **Owner** Mr Finch & Mr Taylor
Times 12-3/6-10.30 Closed 24-26 Dec, 1 Jan, D Sun
Prices Fixed L 2 course £14.95, Fixed D 3 course fr £19.95, Starter £5-£12.50, Main £12.50-£23.50, Dessert £5.50-£6.50, Service added but optional 12.5% **Wines** 48 bottles over £30, 28 bottles under £30, 16 by glass **Notes** Fixed D 3 course Mon-Thu, Sunday L, Vegetarian available **Seats** 80, Pr/dining room 14 **Children** Portions, Menu

LONDON W1

Alain Ducasse at The Dorchester
PLAN 4 G6

◎◎◎◎ – *see opposite*

Alloro
PLAN 2 J1

◎ Modern Italian

Upper-crust Italian off Piccadilly

☎ 020 7495 4768
19-20 Dover St W1S 4LU
e-mail: alloro@londonfinedininggroup.com
dir: Nearest station: Green Park. From station towards Piccadilly, Dover St is 2nd on left

Alloro has the sort of decoration and furnishings appropriate to this expensive part of town - papered walls, leather-look banquettes and dining chairs at formally laid tables, crisp napery and a marble floor - while the menu, in Italian with translations, brings the flavours of the warm South. Generally straightforward treatments are given to top-notch produce, often imported, bringing on effective starters like deep-fried tomatoes layered with creamy burrata cheese sprinkled with balsamic, or, in season, chargrilled asparagus with quails' eggs and summer truffle. Fish is well handled - chargrilled tuna steak, pink, as requested, with a simple tomato and rocket salad, say - and among meat main courses might be slowly cooked pork belly served with apple purée and pickled onion. Pasta is made in-house, and puddings might see mango doughnuts hinting of chilli served with pineapple consommé.

Times 12-2.30/7-10.30 Closed Xmas, 4 days Etr, BHs, Sun, L Sat

Alyn Williams at The Westbury
PLAN 2 H2

◎◎◎ – *see page 316*

Andrew Edmunds
PLAN 2 J1

◎ Modern European

Evergreen, rustic, Soho favourite

☎ 020 7437 5708
46 Lexington St, Soho W1F 0LW
dir: Nearest station: Oxford Circus

There's something almost Dickensian about this old townhouse on a Soho side street - with its dark, higgledy-piggledy tavern-esque atmosphere. There's been no 'contemporary makeover' here (and hurrah for that) and no-one can doubt its enduring popularity. Pint sized and bijou, the narrow ground floor and basement come decked out with old prints, tightly-packed paper-clothed tables and time-worn cottagey furniture. The kitchen takes an equally simple, honest approach, with seasonal, ingredient-led dishes on a daily-changing handwritten menu that has its feet firmly on the ground. Line-caught cod, for example, with new potatoes, spinach and tartare sauce or salt beef with roast potato wedges, dill pickle, mixed leaves and poached free-range egg, although the kitchen is equally comfortable with octopus carpaccio among possible first courses. There's plenty on the wine list to keep oenophiles interested.

Times 12.30-3/6-10.45 Closed Xmas, Etr

Alain Ducasse at The Dorchester

LONDON W1　　　　　　　　PLAN 4 G6

Modern French V

Dazzling classical cookery in an anonymous hotel dining room

☎ 020 7629 8866
The Dorchester, 53 Park Ln W1K 1QA
e-mail: alainducasse@thedorchester.com
dir: Nearest station: Hyde Park Corner, Marble Arch

At first blush, the Ducasse dining room at The Dorchester looks like one of those anonymised spaces, where all the effort and expense has gone into making the place look like nowhere in particular, a feeling that seems to suit an international superchef franchise. In London, you get a room done in an almost indefinable shade of watery green, with views through one-way glass of the Park Lane traffic. Staff, on the other hand, dazzle with their sartorial precision and professionalism, even if not always with their English. They are fully conversant with the menu, and the wine team inspires sound confidence. It's fair to say that Jocelyn Herland has eased himself into the rhythm here over the past several years. There were early reports of food that was rather humdrum for haute cuisine, the lunch menus in particular strangely unambitious, but of late there are signs that the kitchen is beginning to take wing, often with some of the same dishes that appeared less than scintillating before. Main courses to write home about include the brilliant sea bass (a dish created to mark the silver anniversary of Ducasse's arrival at the Louis XV in Monte Carlo, we're told). It's a handsomely silver-suited piece of impeccable fish, with a line of crumbled olive on top, accompanied by baby artichokes and garlic croquettes, an explosion of flavours. No less astonishing is the famous Limousin veal, butter-tender and pale as Keats, sauced with a moreish rich veal stock crowded with girolles and wafer-thin slices of culatello ham, the softness of texture offset by the crunch of fresh almonds. There's daring in the simplicity of these dishes, but genuine impact too. That seems just a touch less applicable to first courses such as the bundles of seasonal veg - cooked and crudités - garnished with Taggiasca olives and light tomato syrup, or the two-way serving of fine Dorset crab, a bowl of white meat seasoned with lemon and paprika, a bowl of brown with crab jelly and a row of julienned vegetables sitting in it. The quality isn't in question, but the point is being forcefully made that not all contemporary cuisine is about technical ingenuity. Desserts are as classical as rum baba doused in your choice of six rums, or a raspberry soufflé puffed up like a Lord High Chancellor, attended by vividly colourful raspberry sorbet.

Chef Jocelyn Herland, Angelo Ercolano
Owner The Dorchester Collection
Times 12-1.30/6.30-9.30 Closed 1-7 Jan, 29 Mar-1 Apr, 26-30 Dec, Sun-Mon, L Sat **Prices** Fixed L 2 course fr £60, Fixed D 3 course £85, Tasting menu £120, Service added but optional 12.5% **Wines** 14 by glass **Notes** Tasting menu 7 course, Fixed L inc wine & coffee, Vegetarian menu, Dress restrictions, Smart casual L, Smart D no jeans or trainers **Seats** 82, Pr/dining room 30 **Parking** 20

LONDON W1 *continued*

Aqua Kyoto

PLAN 2 J2

◉◉ Japanese

Classy Japanese food in super-cool roof-top setting

☎ 020 7478 0540
240 Regent St W1B 3BR
e-mail: reservation@aqua-london.com
dir: Nearest station: Oxford Street. Opposite the London Palladium, just behind Regent St

From the smart lobby entrance, you're whisked by lift to the 5th floor and the über-chic world of Aqua. The super-sexy Spirit cocktail bar is up first; it's shared by twin restaurants Aqua Nueva (Spanish tapas - see entry) and this modern Japanese outfit, and covers the top floor of the former Dickins & Jones building. There's great rooftop views from the terrace, while, like everything else here, Kyoto's ultra-designed dining room shimmers with contemporary style and teems with beautiful people, especially in the evenings when it becomes a high-energy 'destination' (lunch is quieter). Moody black, red and gold complement the theatre of a sunken centrepiece sushi bar, charcoal grill and jaw-dropping lantern-style light fitting. It's not design over substance: the cooking deserves serious attention, while friendly staff are happy to advise on the menus. Visually striking, well-constructed dishes and top-drawer ingredients are the thing; take king crab tempura with crab miso, or perhaps twice-cooked crispy pork belly with langoustine and yuzu pepper to high-rolling Wagyu beef with garlic ponzu and grape icicles. Otherwise there's cracking sushi and sashimi, fashionable wines and super cocktails.

Chef Jordan Sclare **Owner** David Yeo, Richard Ward **Times** 12-3/6-11.15 Closed 25-26 Dec, BH, D Sun **Prices** Tasting menu £35-£55, Service added but optional 12.5% **Wines** 12 by glass **Notes** Vegetarian available, Dress restrictions, Smart casual, no trainers or sportswear, Civ Wed 100 **Seats** 95, Pr/dining room 10 **Parking** Poland St

Aqua Nueva

PLAN 2 J2

◉◉ Spanish

Fashionable restaurant for Spanish wines and top-notch tapas

☎ 020 7478 0540
5th Floor, 240 Regent St W1B 3BR
e-mail: reservation@aqua-london.com
dir: Nearest station: Oxford Circus. Opposite London Palladium

Take the lift to the fifth floor, walk through the dark corridor dominated by an illuminated sculpture of a bull, and enter the ultra-chic, ultra-modern restaurant, a large, no-expense-spared designer-led space hung with thousands of wooden spindles. The roof terrace is an added attraction, while the new Cava bar offers some 15 different varieties of the Spanish sparkling wine by the glass and bottle. This is the sort of place where people come to see and be seen as much as for the faithful renditions of tapas based on top-end Spanish ingredients. Take your pick from the bilingual carte: perhaps fabada (traditional stew of white beans, blood sausage and Iberian ham), seared foie gras with caramelised hazelnuts and pear confit, scallops with sweetcorn velouté, or a selection of cheese. Those with heartier appetites could go for one of the main courses: among them may be roast loin of monkfish with garlic soup and paprika, and glazed ox cheek with pequillo peppers and potato purée. See also the entry for Aqua Kyoto.

Chef Alberto Hernandez **Owner** Aqua Restaurant Group **Times** 12-3/6-11.30 Closed Xmas, New Year, BHs, Sun **Prices** Fixed L 2 course £19.50, Service added but optional 12.5% **Wines** 13 by glass **Notes** Vegetarian available, Dress restrictions, Smart casual, no trainers or sportswear, Civ Wed 100 **Seats** 160, Pr/dining room 16

Alyn Williams at The Westbury

French, European V **NOTABLE WINE LIST**

Innovation, top-flight skills and heaps of glamour

☎ 020 7078 9579
Bond St W1S 2YF
e-mail: alynwilliams@westburymayfair.com
dir: Nearest station: Oxford Circus, Piccadilly Circus, Green Park

The man whose name has been over the door of the top-end dining venue of The Westbury for the last couple of years brings an unquestionable pedigree to the table. After many years in the kitchens of Gordon Ramsay and Marcus Wareing, Alyn Williams continues to cook at a rarefied level, impressing all comers with highly-refined, French-accented contemporary cooking and a commitment to technical excellence without resorting to flashy effects to sustain interest. The Westbury has an unassailable position among the A-list playground of Mayfair's hotels, so you can expect an interior of self-conscious glamour and opulence: art-deco-inspired Swarovski chandeliers and a Fendi-designed look in the über-glam Polo Bar, while the restaurant wears an understated yet unmistakably glossy décor of oatmeal-hued leather chairs at linen-swathed tables, set against softly burnished darkwood panels, huge mirrors, and romantic, subtly-backlit alcoves. Sparse menu descriptions do more to intrigue than to inform, but the juxtapositions of components shows that these are all intelligent, thought-provoking ideas realised with top-flight technical skills. You expect a hit of the high life in Mayfair, so the decadence of foie gras might come semi-fredo-style, supported creatively by the turbo-charged flavours of Amalfi lemon, liquorice and salted hazelnut caramel, while the very essence of the sea could be conjured by a main course involving Guernsey sea bass, sea urchin, seaweed, grilled shellfish and lemon gnocchi. It is all audacious and visually exciting stuff, yet it is anchored by finely-honed discipline. Meaty dishes gain lustre through the pedigree of their components - perhaps blanquette of Cumbrian lamb pointed up with late-season white truffle and young wild garlic - while desserts toss seldom-seen ingredients into the mix, as in an acorn crème Catalan with pear, pine, and winter truffle tuile. Vegetarians are not sidelined either, since they have an equally inventive meat-free tasting menu and carte to explore.

Chef Alyn Williams **Owner** Cola Holdings Ltd **Times** 12-2.30/6-10.30 Closed 1-2 Jan, Sun, L Sat **Prices** Fixed L 3 course £25, Fixed D 3 course £50, Tasting menu £60, Service added but optional 12.5% **Wines** 450 bottles over £30, 6 bottles under £30, 20 by glass **Notes** Fixed ALC 3 course £50, Tasting menu 7 course, Vegetarian menu, Dress restrictions, Smart casual, Civ Wed 20 **Seats** 65, Pr/dining room 20 **Children** Portions **Parking** 20

Arbutus Restaurant

PLAN 2 K2

@@@ – *see below*

Athenaeum Hotel & Apartments

PLAN 4 H6

@@ Modern British

Classy British cooking in a luxurious Mayfair hotel

☎ 020 7499 3464
116 Piccadilly W1J 7BJ
e-mail: info@athenaeumhotel.com
web: www.athenaeumhotel.com
dir: Nearest station: Hyde Park Corner, Green Park. On Piccadilly, opposite Green Park

The eye-catching vertical garden that spans the ten floors of the Athenaeum has helped make the place a bit of a landmark (watch as first-timers stare in amazement). But the hotel is no less impressive on the inside, with a luxurious five-star finish and bags of style. The place is also renowned for its afternoon teas, whilst the Whisky Bar is a favoured haunt of lovers of the grain. The restaurant with its cool black and white photos and discreet seating arrangements makes for a classy venue for some sharp, contemporary cooking. First-class ingredients feature in starters such as venison terrine with red onion marmalade, mixed seed toast and micro leaves, and mains such as saddle of rabbit wrapped in cured ham and served with wild garlic and woodland mushrooms, beetroot purée, truffle onions and crispy potatoes. For dessert, lemon posset with strawberry coulis and home-made shortbread biscuit, or chocolate marquise with milk sorbet hit the spot.

Chef David Marshall **Owner** Ralph Trustees Ltd
Times 12.30-2.30/5.30-10.30 **Prices** Starter £8-£16, Main £16-£37, Dessert £9.50, Service optional, Groups min 6 service 12.5% **Wines** 28 bottles over £30, 10 bottles under £30, 15 by glass **Notes** Sunday L £24.50-£29.50, Vegetarian available **Seats** 46, Pr/dining room 44 **Children** Portions, Menu **Parking** Close car park

Aurelia

PLAN 2 J1

@@ Italian, Mediterranean

Fashionable all-day dining inspired by the flavours of southern Europe

☎ 020 7409 1370
13-14 Cork St, Mayfair W1S 3NS
e-mail: info@aurelialondon.co.uk
dir: Nearest station: Piccadilly Circus, Green Park. On Cork street, between New & Old Bond Street

The latest see-and-be-seen offering from the people behind La Petite Maison, Zuma and Roka (see entries), Aurelia is tucked away in the heart of Mayfair with pricing to match the postcode. Like its siblings, it's a class act though, serious about its food and wine and open all day from breakfast. The modern Mediterranean menu takes its inspiration from the route of the ancient Roman coastal road, Via Aurelia, reflecting the best of Italian, French and Spanish cuisines from Rome to Valencia. The fashionable sharing-plate concept delivers those sun-drenched flavours via a lengthy please-all roster. Kick off with charcuterie (jamon Iberica de Bellota, perhaps) or sobrasada (warm, spicy Mallorcan sausage with honey and walnut crostini), while pasta might include pappardelle with wild boar ragù. Larger plates - say veal cutlet Milanese or from the rotisserie, salt marsh lamb leg with anchovies and salmorigilio sauce - deliver the same skilful simplicity and quality produce. Set over two floors, the ground floor comes dominated by its bar, while in the more formal basement, the open kitchen takes centre stage.

Chef Alex Simone **Owner** Arjun Waney
Times 12-3/6-11.30 Closed Xmas, Sun **Prices** Fixed L 2 course £24.50, Starter £5-£26.50, Main £13.50-£59, Dessert £6.50-£25, Service added but optional 12.5% **Wines** 12 by glass **Notes** Sunday L £40-£100, Vegetarian available **Seats** 120 **Children** Portions, Menu **Parking** On street

L'Autre Pied

PLAN 2 G3

@@@ – *see page 318*

Arbutus Restaurant

@@@

LONDON W1   PLAN 2 K2

Modern French

Adventurous cooking off Soho Square

☎ 020 7734 4545
63-64 Frith St W1D 3JW
e-mail: info@arbutusrestaurant.co.uk
dir: Nearest station: Tottenham Court Road. Exit tube station, turn left into Oxford St. Left onto Soho St, cross over or continue around Soho Sq, restaurant is on Frith St 25mtrs on right

There's always a friendly greeter to welcome you with a smile when you arrive at Arbutus, instantly making you feel relaxed and at home. First impressions are good then, and they're not let down by the look of the place as you pass the high bar and a few tables at the entrance and move into the restaurant proper: a long room looking on to Frith Street, lively and buzzing, with a wooden floor, darkwood tabletops, leather-look seats and minimalist walls - all very modern, and a perfect backdrop to Anthony Demetre's cooking, as his motto could very well be 'keep it simple'. His menus are short (around half a dozen items per course), succinctly worded and follow the seasons faithfully, so they could well change on a daily basis. The cooking may be unpretentious and straightforward but it belies the effort and precise timing that goes into each dish: moist and succulent roast breast and leg of chicken with watercress sauce, for instance. Dishes are composed so flavours are expressive and distinct, from crab with guacamole, peanuts and mango, to lamb breast served with sultanas, sweet potato and Madeira-braised celery. Fish may show up among main courses as Scottish salmon fillet with beetroot purée, colza oil, Swiss chard and hazelnuts, and lesser-used cuts of meat are vivid parts of the output, among them warm, crisp pig's head with potato purée and pickled turnip, and pieds et paquets (lamb's tripe, shoulder and trotters). Puddings are copybook stuff of the likes of pear clafoutis with vanilla ice cream, egg custard tart, and bitter chocolate mousse with mandarin sorbet. Note that virtually every wine on the entire list can be bought by the 250ml carafe - a great way to match wines with each course. London restaurants Wild Honey and Les Deux Salons are siblings (see entries).

Chef Anthony Demetre **Owner** Anthony Demetre, Will Smith **Times** 12-2.30/5-11.30 Closed 25-26 Dec, 1 Jan **Prices** Fixed L 2 course fr £17.95, Starter £5.95-£10.95, Main £17.95-£19.50, Dessert £4.95-£6, Service added but optional 12.5% **Wines** 40 bottles over £30, 10 bottles under £30, 50 by glass **Notes** Pre-theatre D 5-6.30pm 2/3 course £18.95/£20.95, Sunday L, Vegetarian available **Seats** 75 **Children** Portions

LONDON W1 *continued*

Avista

PLAN 2 G1

◉◉ Italian

Authentic Italian cooking in Grosvenor Square

☎ 020 7596 3399 & 7629 9400
**Millennium Hotel Mayfair, 39 Grosvenor Square
W1K 2HP**
e-mail: reservations@avistarestaurant.com
web: www.avistarestaurant.com
dir: Nearest station: Bond Street. Located on the south
side of Grosvenor Sq, 5 min walk from Oxford St

When Michele Granziera wanted to move on from
Zafferano to set up on his own, only the best would do: as
a home to Avista, the Millennium Hotel fits the bill. It is
the very image of moneyed Mayfair elegance, although
the restaurant also has its own equally posh entrance on
Grosvenor Square. The high-gloss setting fits the swanky
postcode: marble floors, vast interstices between linen-
swathed tables, and soft-focus tones of ivory, honey and
beige. A granite-topped workstation where chefs primp
dishes in readiness for presentation adds a touch of
drama to the hushed refinement. Granziera cherry-picks
his way around the Italian repertoire, bringing together
rustic and contemporary ideas that are taken to a higher
level by the sheer quality of the ingredients. In winter, a
robust fish stew of salmon, prawns and squid comes in
the hearty company of fregola and croûtons rubbed with
garlic and fresh parsley. Next up, a full-flavoured dish of

venison loin with roast polenta, quince, pears and red
wine jus, while fish could be represented by roast
monkfish with crispy Parma ham and celeriac purée.

Chef Michele Granziera **Owner** Millennium & Copthorne
Hotels **Times** 12-2.30/6-10.30 Closed 1 Jan, Sun, L Sat
Prices Fixed L 2 course £18, Fixed D 3 course £23.50,
Starter £9.50-£20, Main £9.50-£29, Dessert
£4.20-£10.80, Service added but optional 12.5%
Wines 103 bottles over £30, 13 bottles under £30, 14 by
glass **Notes** Vegetarian available **Seats** 75, Pr/dining
room 12 **Children** Portions, Menu **Parking** On street/NCP

Barrafina

PLAN 2 K2

◉ Spanish

Authentic casual tapas bar hitting the spot in Soho

☎ 020 7813 8016
54 Frith St W1D 4SL
e-mail: jose@barrafina.co.uk
dir: Nearest station: Tottenham Court Rd

Soho's homage to Catalonia takes the hugely appealing
form of this authentic and traditionally casual tapas bar.
An admirably democratic no-bookings policy means you
may be forced to sip a glass of Cava or a fine fino sherry
while you wait, but hey, life could be worse. Inside it is
not much more than a long L-shaped marble lined
counter with high bar stools in front of an open kitchen,
where the chefs whip up those little grazing plates in a
fun, buzzing vibe. Tapas stands or falls on the quality of

its raw materials, and here they are sourced impeccably
and treated with unfussy respect on a concise menu
bolstered by daily specials. There's top-grade charcuterie,
seafood - deep-fried soft-shelled crab or salt-cod fritters
- and old Iberian friends such as chorizo with potato, and
watercress and ham croquettes, or morcilla with quail's
eggs. For pudding there's classic crema Catalana or
Santiago tart, and to wash it all down, a cracking choice
of wines by the glass.

Chef Nieves Barragan **Owner** Sam & Eddie Hart
Times 12-3/5-11 Closed BHs **Prices** Prices not confirmed
Service added but optional 12.5% **Wines** 26 bottles over
£30, 19 bottles under £30, 34 by glass **Notes** Sunday L,
Vegetarian available **Seats** 23 **Children** Portions
Parking On street

Bar Trattoria Semplice

PLAN 2 H2

◉ Italian

Reliable Italian cooking just off Oxford Street

☎ 020 7491 8638
22 Woodstock St W1C 2AR
dir: Nearest station: Bond Street

The more relaxed and casual sibling of Ristorante
Semplice (see entry) is an uncluttered space of light wood
furniture, red walls, candles on the tables and friendly
staff. 'Semplice' describes the kitchen's output too: no-
frills but spot-on cooking using quality ingredients. Pasta
runs from tagliatelle with bolognese sauce to orecchiette

L'Autre Pied

Modern European V ◢ NOTABLE WINE LIST

**Upbeat contemporary cooking off Marylebone High
Street**

☎ 020 7486 9696
5-7 Blandford St, Marylebone Village W1U 3DB
e-mail: info@lautrepied.co.uk
dir: Nearest station: Bond St, Baker St

As expected in a restaurant a few yards off upmarket
Marylebone High Street, L'Autre Pied (younger sibling of
Charlotte Street's Pied à Terre - see entry) has a classy,
stylish look, with textured flower patterns on the walls
and rosewood tables at dark leather-look chairs and
burgundy-coloured banquettes. Chef Andrew McFadden
carefully chooses seasonal raw materials and takes as
his point of reference a broadly European base, calling on

ideas from here and there to suit each dish, with ras el
hanout perking up a spicy Moroccan stew, for instance, or
sambal with roast hogget, glazed aubergine and dried
olives. The menus bristle with exciting ideas, ideas that
the kitchen ably brings off, turning out artfully conceived
starters like scallop céviche with black quinoa, crème
fraîche, radish, fennel and dill, and roast foie gras with
tea-marinated prunes, glazed endive, pomegranate and
nutmeg. Main courses can be labour-intensive affairs,
the kitchen's efforts paying dividends on the plate:
witness accurately cooked cod fillet with carrot purée
flavoured with sea buckthorn, caramel velouté and
tarragon oil, or roast suckling pig with garlic and spinach
purée, charred pineapple, spring onions and walnuts.
Innovation doesn't flag in puddings either, seen in stem
ginger mousse with passionfruit and rhubarb, and
smoked almond pannacotta with caramelised banana,
orange and olive oil purée and mandarin sorbet.

Chef Andrew McFadden **Owner** David Moore
Times 12-2.45/6-10.45 Closed 4 days Xmas, 1 Jan, D Sun
Prices Fixed L 2 course £22-£25, Fixed D 3 course
£25.50-£30.50, Tasting menu £49-£70, Starter
£12.50-£15.50, Main £28-£32, Dessert £8.50-£13,
Service added but optional 12.5% **Wines** 200 bottles over
£30, 6 bottles under £30, 10 by glass **Notes** Sunday L,
Vegetarian menu **Seats** 53, Pr/dining room 15

with Italian sausage and broccoli, while the rest of the menu is a roll-call of the tried and tested. Carpaccio with rocket and parmesan, and deep-fried squid and courgettes with tartare sauce head up a carte that may go on to baby chicken diavola with sautéed new potatoes, or yellowfin tuna with caponata. Among familiar-sounding desserts may be pannacotta, perhaps flavoured with mango.

Times 12-3/6-11 Closed Xmas, New Year & BHs

Bellamy's   PLAN 2 H1
◉ French
- -
Classy brasserie just off Berkeley Square

☎ 020 7491 2727
18-18a Bruton Place W1J 6LY
e-mail: gavin@bellamysrestaurant.co.uk
dir: Nearest station: Green Park, Bond St. Off Berkeley Sq, parallel with Bruton St

Resolutely Mayfair, with its mews setting just off Berkeley Square, its effortlessly classy good looks and slickly professional service, Bellamy's epitomises the chic, timeless French brasserie genre. Dark-green leather banquettes, pale-yellow walls (lined with vibrant French posters and mirrors), white linen and staff in bowties and waistcoats add to the authentic look, while the classic brasserie cooking is conjured from premium seasonal produce. Simple, ungimmicky, clear-flavoured dishes are the kitchen's raison d'être, with menus written in franglais and sporting luxury at every turn - foie gras terrine, oysters, or caviar to start, Dover sole or Castle Mey beef entrecote to follow. Otherwise, try poached sea-fresh skate Grenobloise (set atop spinach and served with croûtons, capers and a buttery lemon sauce), and finish with a classic tarte Tatin. Fabulous all-French wines and an interconnecting oyster bar and food store complete the experience.

Chef Stephane Pacoud **Owner** Gavin Rankin and Syndicate **Times** 12-3/7-10.30 Closed Xmas, New Year, BHs, Sun, L Sat **Prices** Fixed L 2 course £25, Fixed D 3 course £29.50, Starter £8-£20, Main £18-£30, Dessert £6.50, Service added but optional 12.5% **Wines** 60 bottles over £30, 2 bottles under £30, 22 by glass **Notes** Vegetarian available, Dress restrictions, No shorts for men **Seats** 70 **Children** Portions **Parking** On street, NCP

Benares Restaurant   PLAN 2 H1
◉◉ Modern Indian V ◍
- -
New-wave Indian cooking on Berkeley Square

☎ 020 7629 8886 & 7514 2805
12a Berkeley Square W1J 6BS
e-mail: reservations@benaresrestaurant.com
dir: Nearest station: Green Park. E along Piccadilly towards Regent St. Turn left into Berkeley St and continue straight to Berkeley Square

Atul Kochhar is a busy man these days, what with a new venture in Kent and outposts in Dublin and on P&O cruise ships, but he remains adamant that this upscale Mayfair address on Berkeley Square is where his attention is most

closely focused. A broad staircase sweeps up to the stylish first-floor bar and dining room, complete with chef's table, and the place retains the feel of the sort of nightclub one probably couldn't afford to be a member of. Well-drilled staff take a serious approach, and the flash and fire of the new-wave Indian cooking is not one bit bedimmed. Start with a trio of crisp-shelled venison samosas with tamarind and pear chutney for a palate-priming overture, before going on to cumin-roasted monkfish with green pea upma (a kind of South Indian porridge) and saffron sauce, or tandoori blackleg chicken supreme stuffed with forest mushrooms, accompanied by fine biryani and raita. A subtle westernising inflection is discernible in certain dishes, notably a dessert such as apple crumble with Armagnac custard, though even here the crumble is fragrant with spices.

Chef Atul Kochhar **Owner** Atul Kochhar
Times 12-2.30/5.30-11 Closed 23-31 Dec, Sun, L Sat
Prices Fixed L 2 course £29, Fixed D 3 course £35, Tasting menu £78, Starter £12-£25, Main £24-£60, Dessert £8.50-£11, Service added but optional 12.5% **Wines** 300 bottles over £30, 10 bottles under £30, 17 by glass **Notes** Fixed D available until 6.30pm Tasting menu available, Sunday L, Vegetarian menu, Dress restrictions, Smart casual **Seats** 120, Pr/dining room 34 **Parking** On street

Bentley's Oyster Bar & Grill   PLAN 2 J1
◉ Modern British, Seafood ⚑ NOTABLE WINE LIST
- -

Lovingly restored seafood bar and restaurant in London's Piccadilly

☎ 020 7734 4756
11-15 Swallow St W1B 4DG
e-mail: reservations@bentleys.org
web: www.bentleys.org
dir: Nearest station: Piccadilly Circus. 2nd right after Piccadilly Circus, opposite St James Church

The ground floor oyster bar in the heart of London's Piccadilly originally opened in 1916. A mere eight years ago it was taken over by celebrated restaurateur Richard Corrigan (see entry for Corrigan's Mayfair), who has restored the old girl to all of her former glory. Enter through a nightclub-style curtain and pull up a stool at the original marble oyster bar or one of the red leather banquettes. Peruse a menu of oysters, céviches and simple seafood dishes, or head upstairs to the restaurant for a more full-blown meal from the wider menu. Striking William Morris wallpaper, blue leather chairs and bold artwork set the tone for traditional comfort food or more modish dishes. Start with a flavoursome fish soup or

homely macaroni of lobster and basil, before something like seared fillet of hake with roast shallot, bacon and razor clams. Save room for a perfectly oozing chocolate fondant with blood orange sorbet, honey and grapefruit.

Bentley's Oyster Bar & Grill

Chef Michael Lynch **Owner** Richard Corrigan
Times 12-3/6-11 Closed 25 Dec, 1 Jan, L Sat (Grill only)
Prices Fixed L 3 course fr £24.95, Starter £9.50-£21.50, Main £19-£48, Dessert £7.95-£10.95, Service added but optional 12.5% **Wines** 40 bottles over £30, 40 bottles under £30, 16 by glass **Notes** Pre-theatre menu 2/3 course £26/£29, Sunday L £45, Vegetarian available, Dress restrictions, Smart casual **Seats** 90, Pr/dining room 60 **Children** Menu **Parking** 10 yds away

See advert on page 320

Bocca di Lupo   PLAN 2 K1
◉ Italian ◍
- -
Regional Italian sharing plates in the heart of Soho

☎ 020 7734 2223
12 Archer St W1D 7BB
e-mail: info@boccadilupo.com
dir: Nearest station: Piccadilly Circus. Turn left off Shaftesbury Av into Gt Windmill St, then right into Archer St. Located behind the Lyric & Apollo theatres

Tucked away as it is behind a modest red-brick façade in a quiet Soho side street, you wouldn't imagine that the atmosphere inside Bocca di Lupo would be so electric. But it's a highly popular place, buzzing at lunch and from early evening (with the pre-theatre crowd) and until late. You can perch on a stool at the long marble bar, or head on into the restaurant proper, with its bare wood tables, contemporary brown leather chairs and bright art on the walls. On the long Italian menu everything is regionally name-checked and comes in small or large portions to encourage sharing. Standout dishes include hot and salty sage leaves filled with anchovy, a sweetly moreish rabbit, pearl barley and wild garlic orzotto, and comforting cime di rapa with garlic and chilli. Desserts are particularly strong, be it gelato from their own ice cream parlour - Gelupo - across the road, or torta Caprese 'bilivello' (chocolate and blood orange tart from Capri).

continued

LONDON W1 *continued*

Chef Jacob Kenedy **Owner** Jacob Kenedy, Victor Hugo **Times** 12.15-3.45/5.15-22.45 Closed Xmas **Prices** Starter £4-£12, Main £12-£27.50, Dessert £3-£8.50, Service added but optional 12.5% **Wines** 140 bottles over £30, 15 bottles under £30, 20 by glass **Notes** Pre-theatre 1 course menu, Sunday L, Vegetarian available **Seats** 75, Pr/dining room 32 **Children** Portions **Parking** NCP Brewer St

Brasserie at The Cumberland   PLAN 2 F2

@ Modern British &

Smart, contemporary brasserie cooking

☎ 020 7616 5930
The Cumberland Hotel, Great Cumberland Place W1H 7DL
e-mail: brasserie@guoman.co.uk
dir: Nearest station: Marble Arch

The popular Brasserie at The Cumberland no longer has Gary Rhodes overseeing culinary operations, but his former right-hand man Paul Welburn now leads the kitchen team in turning out smart, on-the-money reworkings of British and European brasserie dishes. The mood of the venue is laid-back and cosmopolitan, a feeling enhanced by the thoroughly up-to-date space done with big, bold colours and muted lighting. The repertoire sets out with flavour-driven starters such as home-made veal kidney sausage with sauce turbigo, button onions, diced kidneys, and tomatoes, then looks to the chargrill for West Country-bred beef or a T-bone of Blythburgh free-range pork served with a choice of classic sauces; if you're in the mood for fish, there could be something like pan-roasted haddock fillet with steamed potatoes and a cockle, leek and parsley casserole. Desserts tend to stick to the straightforward theme - perhaps passionfruit soufflé with orange ice cream and passionfruit sauce, or chocolate coffee pot with salted caramel, milk foam and chocolate sorbet.

Chef Paul Welburn **Owner** The Cumberland Hotel **Times** 12-2.15/6-8 **Prices** Fixed L 2 course fr £13.95, Starter £6.50-£9.50, Main £8.50-£54, Dessert £6-£8.50, Service added but optional 12.5%, Groups min 10 service 12.5% **Wines** 18 by glass **Notes** Pre-theatre main £9.95, 2/3 course £13.95/£17.95, Sunday L fr £26.95, Vegetarian available, Dress restrictions, Smart casual **Seats** 80, Pr/dining room 22 **Children** Portions **Parking** NCP at Marble Arch

Brasserie Chavot

@@@ *– see opposite*

Brasserie Zedel   PLAN 2 J2

@ French **NEW**

Authentic brasserie dining in the heart of Piccadilly

☎ 020 7734 4888
20 Sherwood St W1F 7ED
e-mail: reservations@brasseriezedel.com
dir: Nearest station: Piccadilly Circus

From seasoned restaurateurs Corbin and King (see entries for The Wolseley, The Delaunay and Colbert) comes Brasserie Zedel - an authentic Parisian brasserie in the heart of Piccadilly. The grand art deco interior boasts high ceilings, marble pillars and period lighting with deep red seating. The food is equally authentic. All in French (an English version is available on request), the extensive all-day menu is supplemented by a good value prix-fixe and plats du jour. Start with a simple and light foie gras parfait or fish soup with rouille, before a perfectly cooked and nicely presented spatchcock chicken supported by a tarragon vinaigrette, sautéed potatoes and green beans. Finish with a textbook tarte au citron. There's plenty of opportunity to explore the all-French wine list, as each wine is available by the glass and carafe. For some after dinner entertainment, The Crazy Coqs cabaret and jazz venue is also on site.

Times 11.30am-mdnt **Prices** Prices not confirmed **Notes** Pre-Fixe menu 2/3 course 11.30am-mdnt

Save on Hotels. Book at **theAA.com/hotel**

LONDON, CENTRAL (W1) 321   ENGLAND

Cecconi's

PLAN 2 J1

◎◎ Traditional Italian

Fine Italian cooking and bags of style

☎ 020 7434 1500

5a Burlington Gardens W1X 1LE

dir: Nearest station: Piccadilly Circus, Oxford Circus. Burlington Gdns between New Bond St and Savile Row

Tops for people watching and a magnet for the Mayfair beau monde, Cecconi's is a hot ticket indeed. The room has bags of style, with its black-and-white marble floor and central bar flanked by fashionable green leather high stools, with white linen-clad tables all around, and sassy blue velour Chesterfield banquettes to sink into. The service runs like clockwork and delivers the all-day menu with a good deal of charm. Whether you're up for breakfast or cichetti (Venetian tapas - chicken liver crostini, mushroom arancini and the like), to more substantial courses, it's all here without any three-course convention. Dishes of simply prepared Venetian-inspired food are the thing, driven by tip-top seasonal produce and clean flavours (albeit at Mayfair prices); expect calamari fritti and top-drawer pastas (pappardelle with lamb ragù), and veal milanese and pan-fried halibut with grilled asparagus and salsa verde.

Chef Mr Simone Serafini **Owner** Soho House Ltd
Times 7am-1am Closed Xmas, New Year **Prices** Fixed D 3 course £50, Starter £7-£15, Main £16-£30, Dessert £7, Service optional **Wines** 14 by glass **Seats** 80 **Children** Portions **Parking** On street

The Chesterfield Mayfair

PLAN 4 H6

◎◎ Traditional British 🍃

Cosseting luxury, Mayfair style

☎ 020 7491 2622

35 Charles St, Mayfair W1J 5EB

e-mail: bookch@rchmail.com
web: www.chesterfieldmayfair.com
dir: Nearest station: Green Park. From N side exit station left & first left into Berkeley St. Continue to Berkeley Sq left towards Charles St

The Chesterfield Mayfair goes all out to bathe guests in upmarket warmth with plenty of antiques and plush fabrics throughout, and if this puts you in the mood for a spot of old-school fine dining, Butler's restaurant delivers the goods. The setting is appropriately formal with crimson chairs at white linen-swathed tables, and traditional carving and flambéing trolleys working the room. Naturally, the cooking isn't trying to push the culinary envelope, but well-honed technical skills and the splendid quality of the produce work together to pull off a class act. A surf and turf starter of Orkney king scallops with pork cheek, sweetcorn and baby carrots might start

you off, while for mains you could stick with the familiarity of a fine Scottish steak or Dover sole from the grill, or go down the modernist route with herb-crusted loin of lamb with potato and goats' cheese terrine, artichokes, fennel purée and olives. Finish with the theatre of crêpes Suzette, or carrot cake with Earl Grey tea ice cream.

Chef Ben Kelliher **Owner** Red Carnation Hotels
Times 12-2.30/5.30-10 Closed L Sat-Sun **Prices** Fixed L 2 course £19.50, Fixed D 3 course £25.50, Starter £9-£18, Main £13-£40, Dessert £9-£13, Service added but optional 12.5% **Wines** 60 bottles over £30, 12 bottles under £30, 20 by glass **Notes** Pre-theatre menu available, Vegetarian available, Civ Wed 100 **Seats** 65, Pr/dining room 40 **Children** Portions, Menu **Parking** NCP 5 minutes

Brasserie Chavot

LONDON W1

Modern French **NEW**

Classy brasserie from a French master

☎ 020 7183 6425

41 Conduit St, Mayfair W1S 2YF

e-mail: reservation@brasseriechavot.com
dir: Nearest station: Bond Street, Kings Cross, Paddington. From Oxford Circus S down Regent St, right onto Conduit St, hotel at junct of Conduit St & Bond St

Magic can happen when a top chef goes back to his roots and chooses to cook the classics the right way. That is the case with Eric Chavot. He's earned the plaudits over the years for his beautifully-crafted, fine-dining dishes served up at the likes of The Capital, but now he's back in the capital (London, that is) at the super-swish Westbury Hotel with his glamorous new place, Brasserie Chavot. It's a brasserie alright, but ooh la la, it's good. The décor is dazzlingly swanky with its mosaic floor, mirrors, darkwood panels, chandeliers and flashes of rich red from the leather on the chairs and banquettes. There's a great buzz to the place, as at all the best brasseries. The bedrock of the menu is the top quality produce sourced by the kitchen from across the UK and France. Soft-shelled crab with whipped aïoli has the look of a long-running favourite, the crab perfectly cooked and full of flavour, or you might be tempted by the scallop céviche, or the steak tartare with capers and mustard dressing. Among main courses, the grill serves up côte du porc with honey and mustard, tiger prawns with chick peas and chorizo, and, of course, a rib-eye steak with béarnaise sauce. There're the likes of sea bream with tapenade dressing and fennel, and rump of Oisin venison with honey-glazed root vegetables, too. Among desserts the vanilla crème brûlée is a classic done perfectly, but then again there's baba au rhum and Mont Blanc as well. It will come as no surprise that the wine list looks across the Channel for the bulk of its wares, and note there is a good choice by the pichet and carafe if a glass or bottle doesn't fit the bill.

Chef Eric Chavot **Owner** Eric Chavot
Times 12-2.30/6-10.30 **Prices** Prices not confirmed
Wines 23 by glass **Notes** Sunday L

Corrigan's Mayfair

Modern British, Irish V NOTABLE WINE LIST

Finely crafted gutsy cuisine in Mayfair

☎ 020 7499 9943
28 Upper Grosvenor St W1K 7EH
e-mail: reservations@corrigansmayfair.com
web: www.corrigansmayfair.com
dir: Nearest station: Marble Arch. Off Park Ln, main entrance via Upper Grosvenor St

Richard Corrigan has a knack for putting together a menu that is jam packed with things you want to eat; a little bit Irish, a little bit British, always with fabulous ingredients, and with integrity, too. That's not easy. Wild boar, caramelised quince, scratchings...bring it on. And he's got an eye for a glamorous setting. Here in Mayfair, it's looking pretty swanky with the big man's name written in gold above the door. There's a 25-foot marble topped bar where you can sit and tuck into Carlingford oysters with Vietnamese dressing, plus a room packed with burnished darkwood tables, blue leather seats and banquettes, and a good deal of art-deco-esque-style and club-like luxury. It's a handsome spot and no mistake. There is a tasting menu if you want chef to take charge, plus an excellent value seasonal market menu available at lunchtimes in the week. Choosing from the à la carte, fish soup

with rouille and croûtons is a classic done right, or there might be Cornish crab cocktail, or spiced venison tartare with Douglas Fir and buttermilk. There's a happy blend of what can only be described as rustic-luxury about the food: lobster macaroni as a main course, for example, or game pie. The kitchen is equally happy with meat or seafood cookery, with game worth seeking out in season. Line-caught sea bass with celery, truffle and bacon is one way to go with fish, and note vegetarians get their own menu. Desserts are equally eye-catching: rosewater and rhubarb with ginger shortbread, perhaps, or Cox's apple tarte Tatin with Calvados crème fraîche. To cap it all off, the wine list is a fine piece of work, and there's a Cognac trolley working the room if it takes your fancy.

Chef Richard Corrigan, Chris McGowan
Owner Richard Corrigan
Times 12-2.30/6-11 Closed 23-27 Dec, L Sat **Prices** Fixed L 2 course £25, Fixed D 3 course fr £27, Service added but optional 12.5% **Wines** 40 bottles over £30, 40 bottles under £30, 12 by glass
Notes Tasting menu 6 course, Chef's table available, Sunday L, Vegetarian menu, Dress restrictions, Smart casual
Seats 85, Pr/dining room 25
Children Portions **Parking** On street

Save on Hotels. Book at **theAA.com/hotel**

LONDON, CENTRAL (W1) 323 ENGLAND

LONDON W1 *continued*

China Tang at The Dorchester PLAN 4 G6

◉◉ Classic Cantonese 🍷NOTABLE WINE LIST

Glamorous Cantonese cooking in five-star Park Lane surroundings

☎ 020 7629 9988
53 Park Ln W1K 1QA
e-mail: reservations@chinatanglondon.co.uk
dir: Nearest station: Hyde Park Corner

The glittering opulence of The Dorchester's Chinese restaurant was conceived with the glamour of colonial-era Shanghai in mind. Chinoiserie is naturally the name of the game, set against a backdrop of contemporary fish-themed Asian art and fabulous art-deco mirrored columns. The cooking toes the classic Cantonese party line, although the sheer quality of the produce ramps up the menu of familiar dishes and dim sum to a higher plane. Naturally in this setting, luxuries are liberally sprinkled around but you don't have to break the bank - pork satay makes a punchy starter, then you might follow with salt-and-pepper squid, Peking duck or join the high rollers with braised abalone with oyster sauce. Desserts are not usually a strong point in cuisine of this ethnicity, so it is rewarding to end strongly with an inspired pairing of poached plums with Chinese almond mousse.

Times 12-12 Closed 25 Dec

Cielo PLAN 2 J1

◉◉ Modern Italian

Upbeat setting and good Italian food

☎ 020 7297 2893
3 New Burlington St W1S 2JF
e-mail: info@luxx-london.com
dir: Nearest station: Oxford Circus

Located in the heart of Mayfair, Cielo is a trendy and glamorous venue, successfully combining a contemporary Italian restaurant with a cool cocktail lounge and buzzy nightclub. So, if you fancy sipping a few cocktails before sitting down to a fairly late dinner (the kitchen doesn't start serving until 8pm) and then dancing the night away, then Cielo is the perfect place for you. The food is top-notch Italian, with head chef Claudio Illuminati serving up such well-constructed and imaginative dishes as linguini with lobster and tomato, duck breast with black cabbage and spiced pear, venison with pink pepper, milk polenta and trevisano radish, and sea bass with spinach, artichoke and parsley sauce, with vanilla and coffee pannacotta among the puddings. The place has a nightclubby vibe and there's also a retractable roof in the bar for summer cocktails under the stars.

Times 7-11 Closed 25 Dec, Sun-Mon, L all week

C London PLAN 2 H1

◉◉ Italian

Venetian elegance and celeb spotting in Mayfair

☎ 020 7399 0500
23-25 Davies St W1K 3DE
e-mail: london@crestaurant.co.uk
dir: Nearest station: Bond Street. Located between Oxford Street & Brook Street

Formerly named (and still known to its faithful as) Cipriani, C London is sibling to Venice's famous Harry's Bar and is beloved by the international glitterati. Don't be surprised if the paparazzi are waiting outside as you arrive at the glass-fronted restaurant with its revolving door, such is its popularity on the celeb circuit. Once inside, meeter-greeters from a battalion of white-jacketed, slickly professional staff commence the charm offensive no matter what your status, and the large, snazzy dining room looks appealing with its impeccable art-deco styling complete with Murano glass chandeliers. It's certainly not all style over substance - the straightforward classic Italian cooking is founded on tip-top produce and doesn't disappoint. Take sea-fresh Dover sole simply partnered by zucchini, or from the grill, moist, full-flavoured corn-fed chicken with lovely crispy skin, served simply with mixed vegetables. Breads are fabulous, a Bellini aperitif is almost a requisite, and for dessert you might choose something like lemon meringue pie from the 'selection of home-made cakes'. Factor in a buzzing atmosphere, and prices that are certainly determined with the celebrity in mind.

Chef Guiseppe Marangi **Owner** Cipriani family
Times 12-3/6-11.45 Closed 25 Dec **Prices** Prices not confirmed Service added but optional 12.5% **Wines** 6 by glass **Notes** Dress restrictions, No shorts **Seats** 140, Pr/dining room 32 **Children** Portions

Cocochan PLAN 2 G2

◉ Chinese, Japanese

Pan-Asian fusion cooking in vibrant West End setting

☎ 020 7486 1000
38-40 James St, Marylebone W1U 1EU
e-mail: info@cococran.co.uk
web: www.cococran.co.uk
dir: Nearest station: Bond Street

Not far from the craziness of Oxford Street, Cocochan offers an escape to far away continents, for your taste buds at least, for this is Pan-Asian country, where the flavours of China, Japan, Vietnam, Thailand and Korea come together harmoniously. There's an eye-catching Eastern modernism to the three dining spaces (one of which is the outdoor terrace) in the form of metallic and mirrored latticework on the walls and bamboo tables, and it's all good fun. Crabcakes with jalapeño mayo and Thai salad sums it all up pretty nicely, but there's straight-up sushi and sashimi if you wish to keep it simple. Chargrilled lamb cutlets with kimchee and nashi pear shows textbook meat cookery, or go for calamari salad with shiitake mushrooms, shallots, Thai basil and yuzu soya. End European style with the likes of pannacotta with mixed berry compôte.

Chef Shu Qun Zen **Owner** Hrag Darakjian **Times** noon-mdnt Closed 25 Dec, 1 Jan **Prices** Fixed L 2 course £15-£45, Fixed D 3 course £35-£85, Starter £3.50-£14, Main £11-£30, Dessert £4.50-£7.50, Service added but optional 12.5% **Wines** 40 bottles over £30, 15 bottles under £30, 15 by glass **Notes** Sharing menu group 10 £30-£65, Bento box L min £13.50, Sunday L, Vegetarian available **Seats** 80, Pr/dining room 35 **Parking** On street

Corrigan's Mayfair PLAN 2 G1

◉◉◉ – *see advert on page 324*

See opposite

Criterion PLAN 2 K1

◉ Modern British, European 🍷

Spectacularly impressive room with passionate team in the kitchen

☎ 020 7930 0488
224 Piccadilly W1J 9HP
e-mail: reservations@criterionrestaurant.com
dir: Nearest station: Piccadilly Circus. Next to Eros statue

The Criterion's unique interior never fails to impress with its magnificent Byzantine opulence: all soaring arches to high ceilings, mosaics, mirrors, gold and marble. The kitchen's a busy place, making bread and pasta (pappardelle with sautéed wild mushrooms, say), smoking fish - salmon and eel in a starter with horseradish mousse - and even churning its own butter. Treatments vary from roasting (rack of lamb with aubergine purée, fondant potato and carrots) to poaching (cod with brown shrimps and caviar accompanied by Jerusalem artichokes and spinach), and the results are appreciated for their accurate seasoning and timing. A grounding in the classical repertoire is evident too, from moules marinière to crème brûlée.

Chef Matthew Foxon **Owner** Mr I Sopromadze
Times 12-2.30/5.30-11.30 Closed 25 Dec **Prices** Fixed L 2 course £19-£25, Fixed D 3 course £23-£30, Service added but optional 12.5%, Groups min 11 service 12.5% **Wines** 50 bottles over £30, 7 bottles under £30, 13 by glass **Notes** Fixed 2/3 course also available 5.30-7pm & 10-11.30pm, Sunday L, Vegetarian available, Civ Wed 70 **Seats** 104 **Children** Portions **Parking** Brewer Street

LONDON W1 *continued*

CUT at 45 Park Lane

PLAN 4 G6

⊛⊛⊛ – *see opposite*

Dabbous

PLAN 2 J3

⊛⊛⊛ – *see page 326*

Degò

PLAN 2 J2

⊛⊛ Modern Italian

New-wave Italian a few paces from Oxford Circus

☎ 020 7636 2207
4 Great Portland St W1W 8QJ
e-mail: info@degowinebar.co.uk
dir: Nearest station: Oxford Circus. From tube enter Great
Portland St, then first right

Tucked away just a stone's throw from the maddening
crowds at Oxford Circus, this contemporary Italian may
easily be overlooked, but it certainly stands out from the
crowd with its full-flavoured cooking and cracking Italian
wines. Kitted out in red and darkwood, it comes with a
trendy ground floor wine bar (including pavement tables)
and a sleek basement restaurant with suede- and
leather-textured wall tiles, snazzy lighting and booth-
style leather banquettes. The kitchen takes an equally
modern approach, while staying true to the Italian
philosophy of simplicity and letting prime ingredients
shine. Dine on fashionable small or large plate dishes,
choose a sharing platter, or go down the more
conventional three-course route. Take succulent
redcurrant glazed pork belly (cooked for 12 hours), its
sweetness balanced by balsamic and endive, while fresh
home-made pasta is a must, perhaps big-flavoured
smoked ricotta and spinach ravioli offset by sweet
braised red onions. A high-octane hot chocolate cake
finale is a chocoholic's dream.

Chef Massimo Mioli **Owner** Massimo Mioli
Times 12-3/5.30-11.30 Closed Xmas, Etr, Sun, L Mon
Prices Starter £6.70-£11.80, Main £9.80-£14.50, Dessert
£6.90-£8.50, Service added but optional 12.5%
Wines 175 bottles over £30, 45 bottles under £30, 14 by
glass **Notes** Pre-theatre & tasting menus available,
Vegetarian available, Dress restrictions, Smart casual
Seats 45 **Children** Portions

Dehesa

PLAN 2 J1

⊛ Spanish, Italian

First-rate tapas in Soho

☎ 020 7494 4170
25 Ganton St W1F 9BP
e-mail: info@dehesa.co.uk
dir: Nearest station: Oxford Circus. Close to station, half
way along Carnaby St on corner of Ganton & Kingly St

Dehesa comes from the same stable as Salt Yard and
Opera Tavern (see entries) and, like them, is a charcuterie
and tapas bar dedicated to the cuisines of Spain and
Italy. It's a small place and it's easy to see why it gets so
busy: quality ingredients are handled professionally,
following authentic recipes, to bring the flavours of those
two countries to life in London. Bar snacks of house-
cured duck breast, or jamón ibérico, with a glass of fino
make pleasing partners, or select from the full list of
unfussy hot and cold dishes. Venetian-style sardines with
sautéed onions, sultanas and pine nuts, and piquant
salt-cod croquettes with sauce romesco are among the
fish options, with tender confit pork belly with rosemary-
scented cannellini beans, and fried lamb cutlet with
broad beans, chilli and mint among the meat. You might
not need extra vegetables like patatas fritas, but leave
room for tempting puddings like chocolate cake with
cappuccino ice cream.

Save on Hotels. Book at **theAA.com/hotel**

LONDON, CENTRAL (W1) 325 **ENGLAND**

Chef Giancarlo Vatteroni **Owner** Simon Mullins, Sanja Morris **Times** 12-3/5-11 Closed 24-26 & 31 Dec, 1-2 Jan, D Sun, BHs **Prices** Fixed L 2 course £35-£40, Fixed D 2 course £35-£40, Starter £5-£11, Main £5-£11, Dessert £5-£7, Service added but optional 12.5% **Wines** 25 bottles over £30, 15 bottles under £30, 11 by glass **Notes** Sunday L £5-£11, Vegetarian available **Seats** 40, Pr/dining room 12 **Parking** NCP

Dinings
PLAN 2 E3

◉◉ Japanese, European

Pint-sized basement room doing dazzling Japanese tapas

☎ 020 7723 0666
22 Harcourt St W1H 4HH
dir: Nearest station: Edgware Rd

Exquisitely-crafted miniatures are a Japanese strong point, so the concept of Japanese tapas shows the savvy culinary synergy going on here at Dinings, where the creative kitchen fuses Japanese and modern European dishes into some extremely productive ideas. There's still a bonsai-sized traditional sushi bar on the ground floor where just six diners get to share elbow-to-elbow space, up close and personal with the chefs, but it is down in the utilitarian basement that a city-chic clientele turns up to be led through the hot, sour, sweet and savoury spectrum. Concrete floors, walls painted blue and cream, bare tables and leatherette seating amount to a pretty spartan setting, but you're not here for the interior design: check out the blackboard specials, then tackle the lengthy menu in the true tapas spirit by sharing a bunch of small dishes. Pan-fried padron peppers with garlic and shichimi pepper, tar-tar chips (home-made potato crisps filled with avocado, seafood, meat, vegetables and sauces) and - heading upmarket - seared Wagyu beef with chilli miso is a typical trio.

Chef Masaki Sugisaki, Keiji Fuku **Owner** Tomonari Chiba, Masaki Sugisaki **Times** 12-2.30/6-10.30 Closed Xmas, 31 Dec-1 Jan, Sun **Prices** Prices not confirmed Service added but optional 11.5% **Wines** 24 bottles over £30, 6 bottles under £30, 9 by glass **Notes** Fixed L menu available, Vegetarian available **Seats** 28 **Parking** On street & NCP

Downtown Mayfair
PLAN 2 J1

◉◉ Italian NEW

Italian glamour in Mayfair

☎ 020 3056 1001
15 New Burlington Place W1S 2HX
e-mail: info@downtownmayfair.com
dir: Nearest station: Charing Cross, Oxford Circus. Located between Savile Row & Regent Street

From the owners of C London (see entry) and Harry's Bar (see the wonderful city of Venice) comes Downtown Mayfair. Located in a modern building between Regent Street and Savile Row, the interior is a smart recreation of 1940s London, updated through the prism of 21st-century fashion. It looks good with its burnished panels, engraved glass, mosaic marble floors, chandeliers and linen-clad tables, and there's even a little 'library' area which forms an inviting booth. The menu, like its siblings, looks to Italy, and in particular the north of the country. Before you tuck in, though, there's the small matter of a Bellini, taken on the terrace if you're lucky. Start with king crab salad - no-one said it was cheap - and move onto something like calves' liver alla Veneziana or tagliolini with prosciutto. For dessert, the tiramisù is not obligatory, but it is always likely to be a favourite.

Chef Raffaele Trignani **Times** 12-11.45 Closed BH, Sun **Prices** Prices not confirmed **Notes** Vegetarian available, Dress restrictions, No sandals or shorts for men **Seats** 120, Pr/dining room 40 **Parking** Burlington, Broadwick Masterpark

CUT at 45 Park Lane

LONDON W1 PLAN 4 G6

Modern American

Stunning steaks from a king of Californian cuisine in Mayfair

☎ 020 7493 4545
45 Park Ln W1K 1BJ
e-mail: restaurants45L@dorchestercollection.com
dir: Nearest station: Hyde Park Corner. Park Lane, near The Dorchester

The Austrian chef and entrepreneur Wolfgang Puck's name may not spring as readily to mind as our home-grown celeb chefs, but he is a household name in the US, having helped to shape and define the concept of Californian cuisine (globetrotting gourmets might have heard of Spago). As the uppercase in the title might suggest, this is an operation that is big on branding, and the Puck empire has rolled out its presence Ramsay-style to a whole bunch of places around the world, including several under the CUT banner. This high-end Mayfair operation is his first foray into Europe, and the approach is a pretty simple proposition: CUT focuses on prime beef. Given pride of place in the 45 Park Lane hotel, needless to say it doesn't look like your typical steakhouse (this is über-rich Park Lane after all, and a meal here is never going to be on the cards for those on a budget); the long, narrow room is done out with mellow wood panelling, rich leather seating, striking chandeliers and shimmering curtains, all in a modishly neutral palette. It's not compulsory to head straight for the bovine protein, so start, perhaps, with Scottish scallop carpaccio with cucumber, onions and wasabi-kosho ponzu. Then it's steak time, and they are very, very good: go for a rib-eye of 35-day-aged USDA prime black Angus from Creekstone Farms in Kansas, a superbly tender, powerfully flavoured piece of beef (served with excellent French fries and tempura onion rings). Alternatively, go for a true-Brit cut of Devon-bred Angus, or maybe even push the boat out for Wagyu sourced from Australia and Chile. There's a range of cuts in the American style, plenty of sauces to choose from (Argentinean chimichurri, for example), and it all ends happily with splendid desserts such as dark Valrhona chocolate soufflé.

Chef David McIntyre **Owner** Dorchester Collection **Times** 12-2.30/6-10.45 **Prices** Fixed L 2 course £29, Starter £11-£26, Main £21-£88, Dessert £14-£21, Service added 12.5% **Wines** 25 by glass **Notes** Sunday L, Vegetarian available, Dress restrictions, Smart casual, Civ Wed 60 **Seats** 70 **Parking** Valet parking

LONDON W1 *continued*

DSTRKT
PLAN 2 K1

@@ Modern American NEW 🖐

Nightclub-style dining at the cutting edge

☎ 020 7317 9120
9 Rupert St W1D 6DG
e-mail: reservations@dstrkt.co.uk
dir: Nearest station: Piccadilly Circus

With a name that looks like it's written in Klingon, this new venture just off Piccadilly Circus is part of a central London restaurant scene in overdrive. The gastrodome wave has given place to a whole host of venues that feel like nightclubs - high on concept, but determined to prove that being seen and eating well don't have to be mutually incompatible endeavours. You descend a dark staircase into a voluminous witches' grotto in black and gold, interlaced with botanical forms and beautiful people, where the music is more foreground than back. Georgi Yaneff, an American chef of major repute, has blown in from Beverley Hills to take charge, and brings a forceful West Coast sense of sass with him, boldly melding continental cuisines with Pan-Asian modes into a gigantic global fusion. Starters are sized for pick'n'mixing: grilled octopus with caramelised chick peas and preserved lemon is zesty and textured, rabbit ravioli is garnished with shaved baby artichokes and a heavyish mascarpone sauce. At main-course stage

barbecued baby goat is pulled into shreds and tossed with mixed sprouts and beans, while Scottish rib-eye steak is sauced with Talisker single malt from Skye. Finish with a berry tart filled with crème patissière, seasoned with a few drops of Angostura bitters.

Chef Georgi Yaneff **Owner** Deyan Dobrev **Times** 5pm-3am Closed Sun-Mon, L all week **Prices** Tasting menu £40-£90, Starter £5.50-£12, Main £10-£25, Dessert £2-£7, Service added but optional 12.5% **Wines** 62 bottles over £30, 14 bottles under £30, 15 by glass **Notes** Tasting menu 12 course, pre-theatre menu £25, Vegetarian available, Dress restrictions, Smart casual **Seats** 90 **Parking** NCP 100mtrs

L'Escargot - The Ground Floor Restaurant
PLAN 3 A2

@@ French

Soho grandee delivering accomplished French bistro fare

☎ 020 7439 7474
48 Greek St W1D 4EF
e-mail: sales@lescargotrestaurant.co.uk
web: www.lescargotrestaurant.co.uk
dir: Nearest station: Tottenham Court Rd, Leicester Square

The legendary 'snail' of Soho has been on the scene since 1927, and if that venerable pedigree isn't enough to impress you, the remarkable collection of signed art by the likes of Miró, Chagall, Warhol, Hockney and Matisse should seal the deal. The eternally buzzing ground-floor

Dabbous

LONDON W1
PLAN 2 J3

British

Highly innovative, natural cooking with a wholly urban backdrop

☎ 020 7323 1544
39 Whitfield St, Fitzrovia W1T 2SF
e-mail: info@dabbous.co.uk
dir: Nearest station: Goodge Street

Few new openings in 2012 were talked about as much as Dabbous - and a table here is still one of the hottest tickets in town even now. Indeed, what's not to like in this contemporary urban restaurant brought to us by Ollie Dabbous, formerly head chef at Texture (see entry)? The cooking here is light and modern, demonstrating a clear understanding of flavours and an eye for presentation of the naturally colourful variety. Dishes are deceptively

simple, ingredients are first-rate and entirely seasonal, with much use of fresh herbs, fruits, vegetables, juices, infusions and wild foods, and little need for butter or cream, thus resulting in flavours that are clean and clearly distinguishable from every mouthful. The restaurant is set over two floors with a basement bar serving seasonal cocktails and a small street-level dining room. This is no fancy temple to gastronomy with plush carpets and heavy drapes, instead the look is quite the opposite: fashionably pared-back industrial is what we're talking, with plenty of bare brick and concrete, sheet metal, exposed piping, dangling light bulbs and closely-set wooden tables - in other words nothing to detract attention away from the food on the plate. Excellent warm, sliced seeded bread arrives in a brown paper bag before a vibrant, fresh-tasting first-course of mixed alliums - marinated red and white onions and chives - sitting in an incredible chilled pine infusion (the pine sourced from a wood in Kent, so says the waiter). Next up, melt-in-the-mouth barbecued Iberico pork takes centre

stage in an inspired dish with savoury acorn praline (with fantastic crunch and earthy acorn flavour), turnip tops and home-made apple vinegar, while main-course charred salmon (faultlessly cooked) comes in a winning partnership with elderflower, spring onions and crumbed almonds. Iced lovage appears as the perfect palate cleanser before a stunning finale in the form of a chocolate and virgin hazelnut oil ganache (looking, rather cleverly, like the bark of a tree) teamed with basil 'moss' and a light sheep's milk ice cream.

Chef Ollie Dabbous **Times** 12-3/5.30-11.30 Closed Sun-Mon **Prices** Tasting menu £59 **Notes** 4 course set L £28, Tasting menu whole tables only

Save on Hotels. Book at **theAA.com/hotel**

LONDON, CENTRAL (W1) 327 ENGLAND

bistro of this classy townhouse interior was reworked by designer du jour David Collins for a retro look blending cut-glass mirrors and elegant art nouveau lighting with contemporary neutral tones. The kitchen keeps the extrovert crowd of Soho types happy with modishly tweaked French bistro cooking, while on-the-ball French-accented service sets a suitably Gallic tone for reinvented classic ideas along the lines of sautéed frogs' legs with truffle croquette, parsley velouté and garlic purée. Mains could take in roast guinea fowl à la forestière with baby leeks and tarragon velouté, or black bass fillet with Swiss chard, salsify purée and beurre blanc sauce. Bow out with a French finale - tarte au citron with lemon sorbet, or Valrhona chocolate fondant with milk ice cream.

Owner Jimmy Lahoud **Times** 12-2.30/5.30-11.30 Closed 25-26 Dec, 1 Jan, Sun, L Sat **Prices** Fixed L 2 course £16.50, Fixed D 3 course £19.50, Starter £7.50-£13.50, Main £12.50-£27, Dessert £7.50-£9.50, Service added but optional 12.5% **Wines** 168 bottles over £30, 25 bottles under £30, 8 by glass **Notes** Fixed D 2/3 course available pre-theatre only, Vegetarian available **Seats** 80, Pr/dining room 60 **Children** Portions **Parking** NCP Chinatown, on street parking

Fino
PLAN 2 J3

◎◎ Spanish

Stylish basement restaurant serving classy tapas

☎ 020 7813 8010
33 Charlotte St W1T 1RR
e-mail: info@finorestaurant.com
dir: Nearest station: Goodge St, Tottenham Court Rd. Entrance on Rathbone St

Fino celebrated its tenth birthday in 2013, and to mark the event Sam and Eddie Hart installed a new marble floor. They also commissioned an exclusive Fino tenth birthday manzanilla bottled by Hidalgo. Otherwise, the set-up remains much the same: a large, stylish restaurant with a long bar with high stools, and pale-wood tables and banquette seating, serving a wide selection of first-rate tapas, plus lots of daily-changing dishes, specials and some main courses. Ingredients, many imported, are the real McCoy, and are honestly and confidently handled, recreating the true flavours of Spain (some familiar, some not so). Snack on platters of cold meats and Manchego cheese, or create a feast: perhaps seafood from the plancha - baby cuttlefish with fennel aïoli - or a meat dish such as morcilla with peppers and quail's eggs, or crisp pork belly. Add a couple of vegetable dishes like chips with brava sauce, and beetroot, picos and tarragon salad, and you'll soon be back on that Spanish holiday. There are textbook Spanish puddings too like Santiago tart, and leche frita.

Chef Nieves Barragan Mohacho **Owner** Sam & Eddie Hart **Times** 12-2.30/6-10.30 Closed Xmas, BHs, Sun, L Sat **Prices** Starter £3.20-£8, Main £10-£20.20, Dessert £3.50-£8.80, Service added but optional 12.5% **Wines** 9 by glass **Notes** Vegetarian available **Seats** 90 **Children** Portions

Flemings Mayfair
PLAN 4 H6

◎ Modern European NEW

Hotel grill with lots of charm

☎ 020 7499 0000
Half Moon St, Mayfair W1J 7BH
e-mail: guest@flemings.co.uk
dir: Nearest station: Green Park. On quiet residential street off Piccadilly, 3 mins walk from Green Park

The basement restaurant of this swish hotel, formed out of six smart Mayfair townhouses, has a sensibly concise menu and focuses on beef from British herds, dry-aged for a minimum of 28 days. The room looks richly opulent with its tones of red, brown and gold, plush Regency wallpaper, smartly upholstered chairs and leather banquettes. The staff are a professional bunch who ensure all goes well. The menu is based on first-rate produce and things are kept relatively simple and well judged. You might start, perhaps, with ham hock and parsley terrine with crispy quail's egg and dandelion, or grilled quail with quince jelly and rocket. Next up, the steaks are hard to ignore - rib-eye or bavette, perhaps - served with hand-cut chips and a choice of three sauces. Appealing alternatives might include a classic burger, or Cornish cod with potato purée, brown shrimp and sprouting broccoli.

Chef Braden Charlesworth **Times** 12-2/5.30-10.30 Closed L Sat-Sun **Prices** Starter £8.50-£10.50, Main £15.50-£22.50, Service added but optional 12.5%

Four Seasons Hotel London at Park Lane
PLAN 4 G6

◎◎ Italian V NOTABLE WINE LIST

Innovative Italian cooking in red-and-black splendour

☎ 020 7499 0888
Hamilton Place, Park Ln W1J 7DR
e-mail: reservations.lon@fourseasons.com
dir: Nearest station: Green Park, Hyde Park Corner. Hamilton Place, just off Hyde Park Corner end of Park Lane

A dramatic reworking of the interior of the grand old Four Seasons by Hyde Park Corner in 2011 has given the place an unapologetically opulent look. That extends to The Amaranto Restaurant, with its mirror-shined black marble flooring as a foil to deep-pile carpets, onyx and burnished dark-wood tabletops, abstract artworks, and theatrical hues of blood-red and jet-black, as well as a light-flooded conservatory and alfresco terrace. The cooking offers a nuova cucina take on Italian dishes using authentic Italian ingredients. Antipasti such as beef carpaccio with aged parmesan mousse, Jerusalem artichoke, almonds, celeriac, and green apple chutney show the style, before moving into the realms of black truffle ravioli with Tuscan pecorino sabayon or roast loin of venison with Swiss chard gratin and fontina cheese, celeriac foam, forest berries and dark chocolate-scented jus.

Chef Davide Degiovanni **Owner** Four Seasons Hotels & Resorts **Times** 12-2/6-10.30 **Prices** Fixed L 2 course £19.50, Tasting menu £95, Starter £9-£16, Main £22-£38, Dessert £8, Service added but optional 15% **Wines** 250 bottles over £30, 34 by glass **Notes** Tasting menu 6 course, Allegro £26, Pre-theatre D £19.50, Sunday L, Vegetarian menu, Civ Wed 500 **Seats** 58, Pr/dining room 10 **Children** Portions, Menu **Parking** 10

Galvin at Windows Restaurant & Bar
PLAN 4 G6

◎◎◎ – *see page 329*

Galvin Bistrot de Luxe
PLAN 2 G3

◎◎ French NOTABLE WINE LIST

Well-crafted French cooking in stylish bistro

☎ 020 7935 4007
66 Baker St W1U 7DJ
e-mail: info@galvinrestaurants.com
web: www.galvinrestaurants.com
dir: Nearest station: Baker Street. 5 min walk from tube station, on left near Dorset St

The appeal of a Parisian-style bistro has never waned, judging by the success of the Galvin brothers' faithful re-creation on Baker Street. It certainly looks the part, with bentwood chairs and banquettes at crisply-clothed tables, ball lights, and attentive white-aproned staff adding to the bustle. The menu is pitched just right too, offering exceptionally well-executed bistro classics of escargots bourguignon and steak tartare before crisp-skinned, rich duck confit, and daube de beuf provençale. A fish option might be spot-on pavé of cod with leek and potato fondue and Avruga caviar. Some dishes come from beyond France's frontier - perhaps lamb tagine with harissa and couscous - but desserts return to the fold, among them tarte Tatin and orange soufflé with chocolate and Grand Marnier sauce.

Chef Chris Galvin, Luigi Vespero **Owner** Chris & Jeff Galvin, Ken Sanker **Times** 12-2.30/6-10.30 Closed 25-26 Dec, 1 Jan, L 24 Dec **Prices** Fixed L 3 course £19.50, Fixed D 3 course £21.50, Starter £7-£15, Main £16.50-£27.50, Dessert £6.50-£8.50, Service added but optional 12.5% **Wines** 135 bottles over £30, 15 bottles under £30, 25 by glass **Notes** Prix fixe D available 6-7pm, Sunday L, Vegetarian available **Seats** 110, Pr/dining room 22 **Children** Portions, Menu **Parking** On street, NCP

LONDON W1 *continued*

Gauthier Soho
PLAN 3 A1

◉◉◉ — *see opposite*

Le Gavroche Restaurant
PLAN 2 G1

◉◉◉ — *see page 330*

Goodman
PLAN 2 J1

◉ British, American 🔌

American-style Mayfair steakhouse serving prime cuts

☎ 020 7499 3776
26 Maddox St W1S 1QH
e-mail: reservations@goodmanrestaurants.com
dir: Nearest station: Oxford Circus. From Oxford Circus to Piccadilly along Regent St, 3rd street on right

Goodman is every bit the upmarket New York-style steakhouse (though it's actually part of a Russian chain with outlets in the City and Canary Wharf too). The interior looks the part with its polished darkwood walls and floors, combined with liver-brown leather seating (including some booths). A meal here gets underway with a generous array of prime, aged-in-house cuts from traceable herds (perhaps 150-day-aged corn-fed USDA Angus, or Irish grass-fed) brought to your table by informed, friendly staff. There are extra daily cuts to choose from on the blackboard, and although it's by no means cheap, depth of flavour is priceless. Rib-eye, T-bone, sirloin and fillet (priced by weight) all find their place, each accurately cooked over charcoal, and served with a choice of sauces. For non-meat eaters there's the likes of lobster cocktail or Caesar salad, while desserts continue the theme, with baked New York cheesecake a fixture. The corking wine list is unsurprisingly big on beefy reds.

Chef John Cadieux **Owner** Michail Zelman
Times noon-10.30 Closed Xmas, New Year, BHs, Sun All-day dining **Prices** Starter £5-£15, Main £15-£60, Dessert £3.50-£6.50, Service added but optional 12.5% **Wines** 15 by glass **Seats** 95 **Parking** On street

Great British Restaurant
PLAN 2 G1

◉◉ British NEW

Top-notch British food at accessible prices in Mayfair

☎ 020 7741 2233
North Audley St W1K 6WE
e-mail: info@eatbrit.com
dir: Nearest station: Bond Street, Marble Arch. Follow A4202 turn right Upper Brook Street, left Park Street, then 2nd right Green Street, restaurant on left

The capital's hardly awash with eating places serving classy British food, but Mayfair's relaxed Great British

Restaurant sets about filling the void. Located just around the corner from all the Oxford Street mayhem, the narrow, darkwood-panelled room has something of a nostalgic clubby vibe, with its black-and-white tiled floor, tables topped with Victorian reclaimed tiles, and dark-green leather upholstered bench seating and café-style chairs, while walls are lined with monochrome photos of '70s and '80s Brit Pop icons. The kitchen champions the best of British too, with seasonality, sourcing and traceability key, while menus include refined classic fare alongside more modern light, clear-flavoured dishes. Go for something traditional like signature shepherd's pie or standout fish and chips, or a more modish day-boat Cornish turbot (super-fresh) served with shrimp butter and parsley. Top and tail that with Maize Farm salt beef, mustard pease pudding, radicchio and pickles, and a comfort pud like textbook Cox apple and fruit crumble with proper custard. British cheeses and English wines and ales stay true to the home-grown ethos. Brunch is available at the weekend.

Chef Pete Taylor **Owner** Tony Zoccola, George Hammer
Times 11-10.30pm Closed D Sun **Prices** Starter £5.95-£7.95, Main £12.95-£22.50, Dessert £5.95-£6.50 **Notes** Non fixed menu available L & Supper, Brunch menu Sat-Sun 9-3, Sunday L £19.50-£24.50

The Greenhouse
PLAN 4 H6

◉◉◉ — *see page 330*

The Grill at The Dorchester
PLAN 4 G6

◉◉ British V 🔌 NOTABLE WINE LIST 🔌

Top quality eating at a world-class hotel

☎ 020 7629 8888
The Dorchester, Park Ln W1K 1QA
e-mail: restaurants.TDL@thedorchester.com
dir: Nearest station: Hyde Park Corner. Halfway along Park Ln between Hyde Park Corner & Marble Arch

My goodness, there is some good eating to be had at The Dorchester this century. It's all you'd hope it to be and simply walking through the front door for the first time is a bit of a thrill. If Monsieur Ducasse will forgive us for a moment (see separate entry), we're here to talk about The Grill, a restaurant that is an essential part of The Dorchester package. It's an eye-catching room filled with rich fabrics and murals on a Scottish theme (so lots of tartan), looked over by exceptional staff, for whom gueridon service (carving from the trolley, etc.) is a specialty of the house. The quality of the produce is second to none, and the menu mixes tradition with more contemporary touches. Start with sardine cannelloni, grilled cucumber and dill juice (a fabulously punchy dish), or some home-smoked Loch Duart salmon and gravad lax carved at the table. Among main courses, grilled Dover sole and fabulous Black Angus beef sit alongside Romsey lamb with aubergine purée, watercress and potato risotto, and to finish, expect the likes of hazelnut and chocolate moelleux.

Chef Henry Brosi **Owner** Dorchester Collection
Times 12-2.30/6.30-10.30 **Prices** Fixed L 3 course £27, Fixed D 3 course £35, Tasting menu £55, Starter £11-£21, Main £21-£49, Dessert £9-£14, Service added but optional 12.5% **Wines** 400 bottles over £30, 15 bottles under £30, 15 by glass **Notes** Sunday L, Vegetarian menu, Dress restrictions, Smart casual **Seats** 75 **Children** Portions, Menu **Parking** 20

Hakkasan
PLAN 2 K2

◉◉ Chinese 🔌 NOTABLE WINE LIST

New-wave Chinese cooking in a see-and-be-seen basement setting

☎ 020 7927 7000
8 Hanway Place W1T 1HD
e-mail: reservation@hakkasan.com
dir: Nearest station: Tottenham Court Rd. From station take exit 2, then 1st left, 1st right, restaurant straight ahead

Hidden away in a secretive alley off Tottenham Court Road, Hakkasan has always been a magnet for the glitterati, thanks to its original founder Alan Yau, whose mission was to make Chinese food sexy and sophisticated. Hakkasan continues to raise the profile of Cantonese cuisine and make it worthy of serious attention within London's foodie fraternity. The ambience within is that of a louche basement nightclub, with sepulchral lighting and a high-decibel vibe courtesy of the cocktail bar. A creative menu of new-wave and classic dishes covers every imaginable base, and then some, from an exhaustive compendium of dim sum, to 'small eat' ideas such as lamb salad with spicy peanut dressing or fried soft-shelled crab with red chilli and curry leaves. Main dishes include spicy scallops with almonds, spring onion and ginger, and stewed organic pork belly with oysters. The cooking is good, the prices are high.

Times 12-3/6-mdnt Closed 25 Dec

Hakkasan Mayfair
PLAN 2 H1

◉◉◉ — *see page 331*

Galvin at Windows Restaurant & Bar

LONDON W1	**PLAN 4 G6**

French **NOTABLE WINE LIST**

Stunning bird's eye views and compelling French cooking

☎ 020 7208 4021
London Hilton on Park Ln, 22 Park Ln W1K 1BE
e-mail: reservations@galvinatwindows.com
dir: Nearest station: Green Park, Hyde Park Corner. On Park Lane, opposite Hyde Park

The glamorous 1930s-style restaurant on the 28th floor of the Park Lane Hilton has unparalleled wide-angle views over the capital, with a split-level design allowing everyone to share the unique panorama. As much of an attraction is the cooking from head chef André Garrett, who, together with chef-patron Chris Galvin, has developed a menu of bold and creative dishes based around the principles of modern French haute cuisine. That means the cooking eschews butter, cream and delicate sauces in favour of bright, vibrant flavours, with influences culled from all over, resulting in starters such as scallops céviche with kohlrabi, cucumber, blood orange and soy, and quail salad with pickled black mooli and a deep-fried quail's egg. Prime seasonal produce drives the output, with some luxuries showing up in the shape of lobster bisque with lemongrass and basil, agnolotti giving it a bit of body, and foie gras and chicken ballottine with celeriac and truffled mayonnaise. There's a more down-to-earth approach in some main courses, seen in loin of mutton with a mini shepherd's pie, onion textures, pearl barley and ruby chard, and fillet of beef with Bordelaise-style braised cheek. Fish is handled with impressive results: poached fillet of brill in a herby potato crust, for instance, is timed to the minute, sauced with a shellfish and dashi broth and accompanied by enoki mushrooms. Desserts are an irresistible bunch, among them perhaps an à la minute soufflé flavoured with banana, chocolate and caramelised peanuts, and white chocolate mousse with blueberries and green tea ice cream. The wine list is a cracker, and if you're wondering why the front-of-house staff seem so on the ball, all becomes clear when you spot Mr Service himself, Fred Sirieix, walking the floor.

Chef André Garrett **Owner** Hilton International **Times** 12-2.30/6-10.30 Closed BHs, 26 Dec, 9 Apr, 7 May, L Sat, D Sun, 25 Dec **Prices** Fixed L 2 course £25, Fixed D 3 course £65, Tasting menu £95-£195, Service added but optional 12.5% **Wines** 248 bottles over £30, 36 bottles under £30, 31 by glass **Notes** Tasting menu 6 course, Dégustation menu available, Sunday L, Vegetarian available, Dress restrictions, Smart casual **Seats** 105 **Children** Portions, Menu **Parking** NCP

Gauthier Soho

LONDON W1	**PLAN 3 A1**

French V **NOTABLE WINE LIST**

Outstanding modern French cooking in the heart of Soho

☎ 020 7494 3111
21 Romilly St W1D 5AF
e-mail: info@gauthiersoho.co.uk
dir: Nearest station: Leicester Square. Just off Shaftesbury Avenue, off Dean Street

Gauthier takes up a Georgian townhouse (ring the doorbell to get in), with two restaurant rooms and five private dining rooms spread over three floors. A clean, uncluttered look is produced by white walls and table covers, beige dining chairs, mirrors, and spotlights in the high ceilings, with splashes of colour from fresh flowers, while slick and tuned-in staff keep the wheels turning. 'You won't find any recipe books, measuring equipment or timing devices in this kitchen' declares the restaurant; rather, M Gauthier relies on his instincts, intuition and taste buds, and the results can be stunningly good. The menus follow a set-price formula, with two or three courses at lunch, up to five at dinner, priced according to number taken (trois plats £40, and so on). Excellent canapés and breads are an impressive foretaste of the main business to come, underlined by a first course of fine black truffle ravioli with mascarpone and brown butter. Impeccable sourcing is a hallmark, with ingredients imaginatively mixed and matched and treated with a high level of both artistry and respect, serving roast scallops, for instance, with turnips in a light ginger cream, with crunchy green apples and coral dressing. Spot-on cod fillet is given a boost by its accompanying toasted salsify with wild mushroom marmalade, and lettuce and fish velouté, while among meat options loin of venison gets lifted out of the ordinary by an unusual pumpkin and pepper jus and Williams pear and celeriac purée. Sure-footedness continues into not-to-be-missed desserts like passionfruit soufflé with yoghurt sorbet, and mandarin curd with a matching sorbet.

Chef Gerard Virolle, Alexis Gauthier **Owner** Alexis Gauthier **Times** 12-2.30/6.30-10.30 Closed Xmas, BHs, Sun-Mon **Prices** Fixed L 2 course fr £18, Fixed D 3 course fr £40, Tasting menu fr £68, Service added but optional 12.5%, Groups min 8 service 15% **Wines** 150 bottles over £30, 30 bottles under £30, 20 by glass **Notes** ALC Fixed L/D menu, Vegetarian menu, Dress restrictions, Smart casual, no trainers **Seats** 60, Pr/dining room 32 **Children** Portions **Parking** On street, NCP Chinatown

Le Gavroche Restaurant

French ⚑ NOTABLE WINE LIST

Pure class from top to bottom

☎ 020 7408 0881
43 Upper Brook St W1K 7QR
e-mail: bookings@le-gavroche.com
dir: Nearest station: Marble Arch. From Park Lane into Upper Brook St, restaurant on right

Michel Roux Jnr is a bit of a telly star these days: he's even the main presenter of the BBC's relaunched *Food & Drink* programme. And anyone who has seen him on the small screen will surely have noticed, first and foremost, his absolute love of food. He is passionate. His first love, of course, is the cooking of France, and if you want to see where a lifetime of passion and experience can take you, head over to Mayfair. Taking the mantle from his illustrious father and uncle back in 1991, Monsieur Roux has managed to keep true to his first love whilst ensuring Le Gavroche remains at the forefront of the mind of every London foodie: after all these years it's still a must-visit address. The basement setting seems only to add to its cossetting and luxurious appeal, and everything is in its place, every detail is attended to. That goes for the service team, too, who never seem to take a wrong step. Le Gavroche has never followed fad or fashion, but neither is it preserved in aspic, and the food embraces tradition whilst maintaining a light touch. It isn't cheap - you knew that, right? - but the bilingual menu is full of first-rate ingredients, cooked with precision, and presented beautifully on the plate. Soufflé Suissesse is a richly indulgent first course that could not possibly be removed from the menu, but equally you might choose to begin with marinated Var salmon with lemon and vodka jelly. Main-course Cumbrian rose veal with creamed morel mushroom sauce and mashed potatoes is another classic combination that lingers in the memory, or you might opt for sauté lobster in a sauce infused with lemongrass and coconut. Apricot and Cointreau soufflé is a dessert with va-va-voom. The wine list is a magnificent piece of work with some very high prices indeed (we can but dream).

Chef Michel Roux Jnr **Owner** Le Gavroche Ltd **Times** 12-2/6.30-11 Closed Xmas, New Year, BHs, Sun, L Sat **Prices** Fixed L 3 course £52.60, Tasting menu £112-£180, Starter £19-£58, Main £28-£42, Dessert £17-£36, Service added but optional 12.5% **Wines** 2500 bottles over £30, 25 bottles under £30, 25 by glass **Notes** Fixed L 3 course, Tasting menu 8 course, Vegetarian available, Dress restrictions, Smart casual, jacket required, no jeans **Seats** 60 **Children** Portions **Parking** NCP - Park Lane

The Greenhouse

French, European ⚑ NOTABLE WINE LIST

Top-level cuisine at an old favourite

☎ 020 7499 3331
27a Hay's Mews, Mayfair W1J 5NY
e-mail: reservations@greenhouserestaurant.co.uk
dir: Nearest station: Green Park, Bond St. Behind Dorchester Hotel just off Hill St

You don't just happen upon The Greenhouse, despite the fact that it is one of London's top destination restaurants: the entrance in a wide Mayfair mews is as discreet as you could ask for. A stroll along the quiet garden path, lined prettily with box hedges, bay trees and little fountains on the way to the front door, might cause a brief pang of regret that alfresco dining isn't an option, but the interior will soon dispel any such notions. The dining room is a serenely stylish space, where hyper-polished service plays its part in creating an oasis of calm and refinement. Natural, restful shades of beige and ivory are offset by modern darkwood floors, avocado-coloured leather banquettes and chairs, and a feature wall taken up by a filigree display of tree branches to emphasise the garden theme. Chef Arnaud Bignon is the latest in a succession of high-achieving practitioners of the culinary arts to ply his trade at The Greenhouse; he's a chef who cooks from the heart, scouring the globe for inspiration and returning to his roots in applying finely-honed classical French techniques to combinations of ingredients that aren't always immediately obvious. Remarkably inventive amuse-bouche announce that your taste buds are in for some particularly intense stimulation, as in a first-course Cornish crab with mint jelly, cauliflower, Granny Smith apple and curry spices - a bright array of explosive flavours. Next up, a stunningly-presented line-caught sea bass with green polenta and blobs of a vibrant green chlorophyll herb purée, the whole brought together by the citrus tang of creamy yuzu sauce poured at the table. At dessert, 'Pineapple' brings tiny cubes of freshly-poached fruit, together with warm pine nuts and a hint of lavender set in a light and moist sponge, all pointed up with lemon sorbet and foam.

Chef Arnaud Bignon **Owner** Marlon Abela Restaurant Corporation **Times** 12-2.30/6.45-11 Closed Xmas, BHs, Sun, L Sat **Prices** Fixed L 2 course £25, Fixed D 3 course £75, Tasting menu £90, Starter fr £20, Main fr £45, Dessert fr £15, Service added but optional 12.5% **Wines** 3300 bottles over £30, 25 bottles under £30, 30 by glass **Notes** Vegetarian available **Seats** 60, Pr/dining room 10 **Children** Portions **Parking** On street

LONDON W1 *continued*

Haozhan
PLAN 3 A1

◉ Modern Chinese

Chinatown restaurant serving exciting oriental fusion food

☎ 020 7434 3838
8 Gerrard St W1D 5PJ
e-mail: info@haozhan.co.uk
dir: Nearest station: Trafalgar Square, Piccadilly Circus. 10 min walk from nearest underground stations

At the heart of Chinatown, this modern Chinese restaurant has feature lampshades adorning the ceiling, simple black wooden tables, a wall of illuminated green and black and a bustling atmosphere - testament to the popularity of its cooking. The kitchen fuses elements of Far Eastern styles - Malaysia, Japan, Korea, among others - to create some truly original dishes. Chilli squid and Szechuan-style duck vie for attention with Thai chicken curry, wasabi prawns topped with vegetable seeds and tobiko, and Taiwan-style chicken baked in a clay pot with basil, peppers, chilli and spring onions. Those with a deep pocket could feast on Wagyu beef with miso, and lobster stir-fried with curry leaves and chilli served with a dash of rice wine. Enterprising puddings might run to deep-fried ice cream and lemongrass jelly with mixed fruit.

Chef Kim Loy Wong **Owner** Jimmy Kong **Times** 12-11.30 Closed 24-25 Dec, All-day dining **Prices** Fixed D 2 course £14.80, Tasting menu £30, Starter £5.20-£33.20, Main £9.70-£46, Dessert £5.80-£7.70, Service added but optional 12.5% **Wines** 18 bottles over £30, 44 bottles under £30, 13 by glass **Notes** Tasting menu for 2, Pre-theatre menu from £16.50, Vegetarian available **Seats** 80, Pr/dining room 40 **Parking** Chinatown

Hélène Darroze at The Connaught
PLAN 2 H1

◉◉◉◉ — *see page 332*

Hibiscus
PLAN 2 J1

◉◉◉◉ — *see page 333*

HIX
PLAN 2 J1

◉◉ British 🍷 NOTABLE WINE LIST

A celebration of British ingredients

☎ 020 7292 3518
66-70 Brewer St W1F 9UP
e-mail: reservations@hixsoho.co.uk
dir: Nearest station: Piccadilly Circus. Short walk from Piccadilly Circus station

You could easily pass by the giant wooden door on Soho's Brewer Street without ever knowing there's a bustling restaurant on the other side. The red neon 'HIX' sign leads the way, for this is one of Mark Hix's gaffs - the burgeoning empire now running to six venues (five in the capital). Here in Soho, the spacious dining room has an air of art-deco style about it, with reeded glass panels, white-tiled floor, mirrors, brown leather banquettes and a long silver-topped bar running the whole length of one wall. Colourful mobiles and neon signs by Hix's artist chums (including Damien Hirst and Tim Noble) hang from the high ceiling. No-nonsense, modern British cooking utilising excellent seasonal ingredients is what to expect, and first impressions are good, with a small loaf of hot sourdough bread brought to the table fresh from the oven. Spring herb soup with Ticklemore goats' cheese is a delightfully earthy starter, while herb roasted Loch Duart salmon and spring vegetable salad is as fresh as fresh can be. Yorkshire rhubarb pie, served hot with a great big dollop of cold, creamy custard on top, makes a smile-inducing finish. For drinks (and small plates of simple food) check out Mark's Bar in the basement.

Times 12-mdnt Closed 25-26 Dec, 1 Jan

Hakkasan Mayfair

LONDON W1 PLAN 2 H1

Chinese

Refined Chinese cooking in luxury surroundings

☎ 020 7907 1888 & 7355 7701
17 Bruton St W1J 6QB
e-mail: mayfairreservation@hakkasan.com
dir: Nearest station: Green Park. Just off Berkeley Square

Hakkasan Mayfair (see also entry for the Hanway Place original) has a decided air of luxury, the first hint of which is a doorman greeting guests. This feeling is heightened by a décor of marble flooring, highly polished wooden panels, comfortable banquettes complete with intricate, colourful dragon designs, low lights, and by an abundance of staff. As at its sister establishment, the menu here deals in some bold and unconventional, even radical, dishes, as well as familiar Chinese staples and European-inspired puddings. Kick off with a platter of dim sum - scallop shumai, har gau, prawn and chive dumpling and one of duck - each plump, elegantly presented and precisely cooked. Otherwise, there's the must-have signature dish of crispy duck - rich and of wonderfully deep flavours - with pomelo, pine nuts and shallots. Naturally, luxury ingredients have a place - black truffles with roast duck, lobster in rice wine, chilli and garlic sauce - with the kitchen handling all of its output with the same high levels of technical skill and imagination. Crab in black bean sauce with lily bulb and Thai spring onions is notable for its clear, fresh flavours, and rib-eye steak stir-fried with black pepper and merlot is praiseworthy for the quality and tenderness of the meat. Desserts never fail to make an impact on both eye and palate, like a multi-faceted one of warm pear and pistachio jalousie with caramelised pears, pistachio purée and lemon curd and vanilla ice cream.

Chef Tong Chee Hwee, Seng Han Tan **Owner** Tasameem **Times** 12-3.15/6-11.15 Closed 24-25 Dec, L 26 Dec, 1 Jan **Prices** Fixed L 3 course £35-£130, Fixed D 3 course £65-£130, Starter £8-£21.50, Main £16-£61, Dessert £7.50-£13.50, Service added but optional 13% **Wines** 9 by glass **Notes** Afternoon menu available 3.15-5pm, Vegetarian available, Dress restrictions, Smart casual, no trainers, hats or sportswear **Seats** 197, Pr/dining room 14 **Parking** NCP

Hélène Darroze at The Connaught

Modern French V NOTABLE WINE LIST

Stellar cooking from a French chef in a British institution

☎ 020 3147 7200
Carlos Place W1K 2AL
e-mail: creservations@the-connaught.co.uk
dir: Nearest station: Bond Street, Green Park. Between Grosvenor Sq and Berkeley Sq

As the Saxe-Coburg-Gotha family changed their name to Windsor during World War I, so the Coburg Hotel became The Connaught in 1917. First opening its doors in 1815, the hotel was transformed into the splendid building we see today towards the end of Queen Victoria's reign, and it remains a towering, handsome structure to this day, situated on the corner of a little Mayfair square. Within there is all the luxurious grandeur you might imagine at such an iconic address, and the place has kept with the times by meeting contemporary design expectations without chasing every passing fashion. There are places to sip champagne, consume a magnificent afternoon tea, tuck into an all-day brasserie menu, and then there's the main event, the raison d'être for many visiting foodies: Hélène Darroze at The Connaught. A protégée of the legendary Alain Ducasse, who encouraged her to

swap the business suit for chef's whites, she had already made a mark on the Parisian gastronomic scene with her eponymous Left Bank restaurant, and has now won plaudits here for her impeccably refined and inspired cooking, which has its roots in her native South-Western France. It all takes place in a deliciously luxurious room where designer India Mahdavi has brought a softer edge amid the original burnished oak panelling. The service team sing from the same song sheet, with nary a note out of tune, and the whole experience is beautifully orchestrated from start to finish. The good times start when the bread arrives - and what bread it is! - and continues through to the final offering from the sweetie trolley (yes, there's a sweetie trolley). A meal might start with wild bay scallop, roasted in its shell, with a marinière of razor clams, abalone and whelks, plus edamame and shiso leaves, bergamot marmalade, and a green curry foam infused with lemongrass - stunning flavours and beautiful presentation. Next up, black pork from the Basque region - larded chop with Périgord black truffle, crispy, slow-cooked belly - with more of those truffles in the accompanying mashed potatoes, plus braised lettuce, and a sauce flavoured with Cévennes onions. There is no less craft and creativity at dessert stage: Sicilian pistachio steamed sponge, for example, with ruby grapefruit, Greek yoghurt sorbet, dark

brown sugar shortbread and grapefruit 'paper'. The wine list, like everything else here, is a class act, with prices that reach some fairly dizzying heights.

Chef Hélène Darroze **Owner** Maybourne Hotel Group **Times** 12-2.30/6.30-10.30 Closed 1 wk Jan, 2 wks Aug, Sun-Mon **Prices** Fixed L 3 course £35-£42, Fixed D 3 course £80, Tasting menu £92-£115, Service added but optional 12.5% **Wines** 550 bottles over £30, 14 by glass **Notes** ALC Fixed menu £80, Signature menu 6, 9 course, Vegetarian menu, Dress restrictions, Smart, no jeans or sportswear **Seats** 64, Pr/dining room 20 **Children** Portions **Parking** Valet parking

Hibiscus

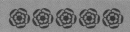

LONDON W1　　　PLAN 2 J1

Modern French V NOTABLE WINE LIST

Top-class modern French cooking from a master of his art

☎ 020 7629 2999
29 Maddox St, Mayfair W1S 2PA
e-mail: enquiries@hibiscusrestaurant.
co.uk
dir: Nearest station: Oxford Circus,
Marble Arch

Like many a great restaurant, Hibiscus doesn't look much from the outside. But once you step over the threshold and into the dining room, you just know you're somewhere special. A revamp in early 2013 has resulted in a classy, elegant look, with a pale-wood floor, white walls broken up with modern artworks, and plushly upholstered blue chairs and banquettes at tables draped in their best white linen. A magnificent central floral display provides a focal point in the room, while the lighting is subtle and the tables well spaced. The front-of-house team, led by Claire Bosi, manages the clever trick of always being on hand when you need something, but otherwise being almost invisible. The whole place exudes an air of confidence and refinement: it's little wonder it's firmly on the foodie map as a must-visit destination in the capital. Claude Bosi is a passionate chef who puts his all into sourcing the best ingredients, mostly from around the UK,

and turning them into stunning compositions on the plate. His early career saw him working in some of France's most stellar kitchens, and it's that classical French training, combined with a desire to celebrate the flavours of prime, seasonal produce in dishes which are bold, innovative and with just a hint of rusticity, that defines his own distinctive style. The idea of the tasting menu is given an unusual twist here: you merely choose how many courses you want - either three, six or eight - say whether there's anything in particular that you don't eat, and then leave it up to Bosi to do the rest. If you come for lunch - and at £34.95 per person for three courses why wouldn't you? - there's a more conventional menu to choose from, which is a great introduction to Bosi's modern take on the cusine of his homeland. Smoked guinea fowl and leek terrine with rapeseed emulsion and chicken liver parfait makes a fine opener, or you might go for the celeriac 'risotto' lifted with a good measure of three-year-old parmesan, egg yolk and pink grapefruit. Bosi's delicate touch with fish produces a perfectly moist roast Cornish cod, partnered with wild mushroom orzo and a deeply flavoured langoustine sauce, while rabbit leg confit in hay with glazed wild cabbage and Jerusalem artichokes is a wonderfully earthy-tasting main course which looks a picture on the plate. It's not unusual to see vegetables cropping up in desserts from time to

time, but a fine cream of white asparagus (with an incredibly intense flavour) is quite way-out, especially when it comes with black olive and coconut. It really works though, and there are more treats in store if you linger over coffee, with the petits fours including three different flavours of warm madeleines and some chocolates that are out of this world.

Chef Claude Bosi **Owner** Claude &
Claire Bosi **Times** 12-2.30/6.30-11
Closed 10 days Xmas, New Year, Sun-
Mon **Prices** Fixed L 3 course
£34.95-£49.50, Service added but
optional 12.5% **Notes** Tasting menu D
only 3/6/8 course, Vegetarian menu
Seats 48, Pr/dining room 18
Children Portions **Parking** On street

LONDON W1 *continued*

HIX Mayfair
PLAN 2 J1

◎◎ Traditional British **V**

Traditionally-inspired British cooking with bold British artworks

☎ 020 7518 4004
Brown's Hotel, Albemarle St W1S 4BP
e-mail: thealbemarle@roccofortehotels.com
web: www.roccofortehotels.com
dir: Nearest station: Green Park. Off Piccadilly between Green Park station & Bond St

Located in Brown's Hotel, the restaurant may bear Mark Hix's brand and have as its driving force his commitment to the best of British produce, but don't expect to see the man himself with his sleeves rolled up in the kitchen - that would be Lee Streeton. The Victorian dining room could never look staid with its remarkable collection of contemporary Brit art - Tracey Emin's pink neon 'I loved you more than I can love' and works by Cool Britannia names such as Bridget Riley and Rankin stand out in stark relief to the patrician oak panelling, plasterwork ceiling and white linen tables. But food, not art, is what we're here for, and a quick once-over of the extensive menu reveals the kitchen's belief in the virtues of traditional British food, whose provenance is naturally trumpeted loud and proud. A starter showcases Whitfield Estate partridge as both pan-seared breast and a rich pâté on toast with quince, while main course delivers a punchy combo of herb-baked Scottish razor clams with Bath Pig chorizo. A smattering of long-lost or foraged ingredients offers intrigue to the menu, turning up at dessert stage in the form of a sea buckthorn berry cheesecake.

Chef Mark Hix, Lee Streeton **Owner** Rocco Forte Hotels **Times** 12-3/5.30-11 **Prices** Prices not confirmed Service added but optional 12.5% **Wines** 18 by glass **Notes** Pre-theatre bookings 5.30-7.30pm Mon-Sat, Sunday L, Vegetarian menu, Dress restrictions, Smart casual **Seats** 80, Pr/dining room 70 **Children** Menu **Parking** Valet/Burlington St

Iberica Marylebone
PLAN 2 H4

◎◎ Modern Spanish

An authentic taste of Spain in the heart of Marylebone

☎ 020 7636 8650
195 Great Portland St W1W 5PS
e-mail: reservations@ibericalondon.co.uk
web: www.ibericalondon.co.uk
dir: Nearest station: Great Portland St, Regent's Park. Regent's Park end of Great Portland St

This hot-ticket venue is rightly a Great Portland Street destination, paying homage to Spain's culinary delights. Flooded by light from its huge windows, Iberica is every inch a stylish, contemporary space. Sit at the marble-topped L-shaped bar or tables around the edge of the double-height room, otherwise grab a pew in the delicatessen area amid artisan produce (including cheeses, hams, olive oils and wines) or upstairs on the more intimate mezzanine. Huge dangling lanterns, shutters, blue-and-white tiling and lightwood floors help create a warm Spanish vibe in which to enjoy an array of refined regional tapas and pinchos. Providence and ingredient quality are key, with flavours clear and uninhibited in well-presented dishes. Graze on cured meats - including the famous Jamón Iberico de Bellota - or cheeses, or perhaps go for the daily stew (Asturian white faba bean with chorizo, black pudding and saffron for instance), or classics like Serrano ham croquettes, octopus 'a la Gallega' with potatoes and pimenton, or seafood paella. Check out the impressive list of Spanish wines and sherries, and if you're over Docklands way, it's worth knowing there's a sister Iberica in Canary Wharf.

Chef Miguel Garcia & Nacho Mantano **Owner** Iberica Food & Culture Ltd **Times** 11.30-11 Closed 25-26 Dec, D Sun All-day dining **Prices** Prices not confirmed Service added but optional 12.5% **Wines** 53 bottles over £30, 20 bottles under £30, 79 by glass **Notes** Vegetarian available **Seats** 100, Pr/dining room 30 **Children** Portions

JW Steakhouse
PLAN 2 G1

◎ American

Carnivore heaven in top-end hotel grill

☎ 020 7499 6363 & 7399 8400
Grosvenor House, 86 Park Ln W1K 7TN
e-mail: info@jwsteakhouse.co.uk
web: www.jwsteakhouse.co.uk
dir: Nearest station: Marble Arch

The Grosvenor House Hotel, famous for putting on glitzy shindigs, is also the place to go if you're in the mood for some prime beef, American style. Creekstone Kansas Black Angus is the star of the show: New York Strip, perhaps, tender and delicious and served with gratin potatoes, onion rings and red wine sauce, or see what takes your fancy on the board. There are good burgers, too, or go for fish and chips or grilled jumbo shrimps with garlic butter. It all takes place in a big and classy room with dark, mellow tones, rich fabrics, banquette seating, darkwood tables and a switched on service team to ensure it all goes swimmingly. There's the rather swish Bourbon Bar, too. Start with calamari or a classic Caesar salad, and finish with peanut butter mousse with salted caramel ice cream, or warm apple pie with ice cream made in-house.

Times 12-2.30/6-10.30

Kai Mayfair
PLAN 4 G6

◎◎ Chinese

Vibrant Chinese cooking in opulent Mayfair setting

☎ 020 7493 8988
65 South Audley St W1K 2QU
e-mail: reservations@kaimayfair.co.uk
dir: Nearest station: Marble Arch. From tube station along Park Ln toward Hyde Park Cnr left after car showrooms into South St, continue to end & left into South Audley St. Restaurant on 20mtrs left

Spread over two floors, this swanky Chinese restaurant is decorated in red, gold and silver, with Chinese reliefs on the walls; tables are immaculately presented, seats are comfortable, and staff, friendly but relatively formal, are smartly attired. Kai aims to show the diversity of Chinese cuisine and the cooking is noted for its accurate timing, judicious use of spicing and seasoning, and its subtle combination of flavours and textures. Deep-fried soft-shelled crab, in a crisp batter with garlic, chilli and shallots, served with green mango julienne, and tender char siu with steamed pancakes and pickled cucumber can get a meal off to a flying start, followed perhaps by deep-fried prawns in a complex sauce of mandarin peel, yellow beans, soy, chilli, shallots, garlic and coriander, or tender marinated lamb cutlets with achar pickle. The menu opens with a page of desserts, showing how seriously they are taken here, and indeed 'mango, dragonfruit, coconut, sago', a combination of sorbet, mousse, jelly and foams, has been the crowning glory of a meal.

Times 12-2.15/6.30-10.45 Closed 25-26 Dec, 1 Jan

Kitchen Joël Antunès at Embassy Mayfair
PLAN 2 J1

◎◎ French

A slice of Provençal cool in chic Mayfair

☎ 020 7494 5660
29 Old Burlington St W1S 3AN
e-mail: reservations@embassymayfair.com
dir: Nearest station: Green Park, Piccadilly Circus. Just off Burlington Gardens (between Bond St & Regent St)

Respected French chef Joël Antunès' venture brings the South of France to the Embassy Mayfair. The light, airily remodelled interiors at Kitchen JA are inspired by a touch of retro-Riviera glamour, which amounts to patterned limestone tiled floors, white and spearmint-coloured leather chairs and banquettes, white linen and a marble-topped bar. There's a large terrace out front to enhance further the Mediterranean vibe (sunshine not guaranteed). Like the décor, the food is inspired by the South of France, with Provence the lynchpin and classic dishes given a light, well-dressed modern touch and based on good quality produce. Thus salad Niçoise stands alongside Provençal marinated red peppers with capers and anchovy to start, followed by traditional coq au vin or steak au poivre. At dinner, there's a couple of sharing dishes (perhaps roast suckling pork shoulder with baked apple), and for dessert tarte Tatin (of course) might rub shoulders with sablé noisette with milk chocolate Chantilly.

Times 12-2.30/6-11.30 Closed 25-26 Dec, 1 Jan, Good Fri L, Sun-Mon

Latium
PLAN 2 J3

◎◎ Italian

Regional Italian cooking with ravioli a speciality

☎ 020 7323 9123
21 Berners St W1T 3LP
e-mail: info@latiumrestaurant.com
dir: Nearest station: Goodge St, Oxford Circus

Latium, an L-shaped room with black chairs and banquettes at clothed tables, its plain walls covered with some vibrant artwork, gets its name from the Italian region Lazio (Latium). Much of the produce is imported direct, and the kitchen makes everything else, including pasta and bread each day. Such is chef Maurizio Morelli's dedication to his native shores that he has a separate ravioli menu: one of mushrooms in snail and tomato sauce, for instance, or mixed fish with bottarga, and sweet versions like chocolate pasta stuffed with ricotta, candied peel and pistachios in orange sauce. Elsewhere, the kitchen delivers the authentic goods in the shape of prosciutto with burrata cheese and mixed leaves, followed by seared scallops wrapped in pancetta with pearl barley cooked in squid ink and red pepper purée, and beef cheek braised with radicchio in red wine accompanied by seared polenta and baby onions. Flag-waving desserts may include wobbly pannacotta with apple and cinnamon sauce and figs poached in red wine.

Times 12-3/6.30-10.30 Closed BHs, Sun, L Sat

Levant
PLAN 2 G2

◉ Lebanese, Middle Eastern V ◐

The scents and flavours of the Middle East

☎ 020 7224 1111
Jason Court, 76 Wigmore St W1U 2SJ
e-mail: reservations@levant.co.uk
dir: Nearest station: Bond Street. From tube station, walk through St Christopher's Place, reach Wigmore St, restaurant across road

Secreted away in a basement just behind Oxford Street, the exotic fantasy world of Levant is reminiscent of a scene from *Arabian Nights*. Think brass lamps, flickering candles, incense, richly-coloured fabrics and carved wood, with nightly belly dancing and, at the weekends, a live Middle Eastern band and DJs to bring the place even more alive. Lunch is better for a quiet repas à deux, but whatever the time of day, the food is no afterthought: set up for sharing, the kitchen sends out an array of uncomplicated, warmly-spiced Middle Eastern food - with a strong Lebanese leaning - via fixed-price feast or meze menus and a carte. Kick off with some excellent falafel, or perhaps baba ghanoush or sambusak bil laham (spiced lamb and pine nuts in pastry), then move onto roasted sea bass fillet with citrus-scented rice, or cubed lamb marinated in lemon juice and spices grilled on skewers. Exotic cocktails and a range of Moroccan and Lebanese wines complete the experience.

Chef David Jones **Owner** Tony Kitous **Times** 12-mdnt Closed 25-26 Dec **Prices** Fixed L 2 course £10, Fixed D 2 course £28-£50, Starter £5.50-£18, Service added but optional 12.5%, Groups min 6 service 15% **Wines** 25 bottles over £30, 20 bottles under £30, 20 by glass **Notes** Sunday L, Vegetarian menu, Dress restrictions, Smart casual, Civ Wed 150 **Seats** 150, Pr/dining room 12 **Parking** Welbeck St

Lima
PLAN 2 K3

◉ Peruvian **NEW**

Buzzy, contemporary setting for a genuine taste of Peru

☎ 020 3002 2640
31 Rathbone Place, Fitzrovia W1T 1JH
e-mail: enquiry@limalondon.com
dir: Nearest station: Goodge Street, Tottenham Court Rd. From Goodge Street station head N.W Tottenham Court Road. Turn left Howland Street, left Charlotte Street, then right onto Percy Street. Rathbone Street 1st left, restaurant on right

Unless you've been to South America you're unlikely to have come across much Peruvian cuisine, but that's about to change: Lima is at the head of a new wave of London restaurants showcasing the unique melting pot of cultures (native Peruvian, European and Asian) that make up modern Peruvian cuisine. There's a fair chance you'll need a little help with the menu, which has been put together by one of Peru's most celebrated chefs, Virgilio Martinez, and covers all the bases from raw ('crudo') dishes such as céviches and tiraditos, to

starters and mains from the 'mar' and the 'tierra'. Sea bass causa with yellow pepper potato purée, crushed avocado and red shiso is a neatly presented and vibrantly colourful opener, full of fresh, clean flavours. Main course could be a precisely cooked confit of suckling pig in a well balanced dish with roasted Amazonian cashew, lentils and pear. Chocolate fans can't go wrong with the cacao porcelana 75 per cent, mango and hierbabuena granita and blue potato crystal - a rich chocolate parfait, partnered with a mango and mint granita and potato crisps, to you and me.

Chef Robert Ortiz, Virgilio Martinez **Owner** Gabriel Gonzalez, Virgilio Martinez, Jose Luis **Times** 12-2.30/5.30-11 Closed Sun **Prices** Fixed L 2 course £17.50, Starter £7-£12, Main £16-£26, Dessert £6-£8 **Notes** Pre-theatre 2/3 course 5.30-6pm, pre-bkg recommended

Little Social
PLAN 2 H2

◎◎ French, Modern European **NEW**

Jason Atherton's take on a Parisian bistro

☎ 020 7870 3730
5 Pollen St W1S 1NQ
e-mail: reservations@littlesocial.co.uk
dir: Nearest station: Charing Cross, Oxford Circus, Bond Street. Contact for directions

Across the road from its big brother - Pollen Street Social (see entry) - le petit social is a dose of Parisian bistro-style in London. And it isn't all that small by the way. It looks the part with vintage pictures cramming the walls, ox-blood-coloured banquette seating, darkwood tables, and a cocktail bar at the front. It fairly fizzes with bonhomie. The menu is a heady mix of French classics and more esoteric Atherton creations, and all based on tip-top (mostly) British ingredients. There's steak tartare, for example, steak frites, too, and a côte de boeuf for two to share (at a price). But equally you might start with crab, tomato and radish salad with miso tomato dressing and marinated beetroot, and follow on with pork chop with butternut squash purée, pine nut dressing and endive. Atherton has always been a dab hand at desserts, so save room for a classic tarte Tatin (for two again), or pink peppercorn meringue with lemon and lime curd and passionfruit.

Chef Carey Docherty **Owner** Jason Atherton **Times** 12-2.30/6-10.30 Closed D Sun **Prices** Starter £8.50-£11.50, Main £10-£20, Dessert £4.50-£12.50, Service added but optional 12.5% **Notes** Exclusive hire & Pre-fixe menu available **Parking** Burlington Car Park, Cavendish Square

Locanda Locatelli
PLAN 2 G2

◎◎◎ – *see page 336*

Locanda Locatelli

LONDON W1 PLAN 2 G2

Italian 🍷 NOTABLE WINE LIST

Fabulous Italian cooking of daring simplicity

☎ 020 7935 9088
8 Seymour St W1H 7JZ
e-mail: info@locandalocatelli.com
dir: Nearest station: Marble Arch. Opposite Marylebone police station

If your only experience of the celeb chef's work is watching his Italophile foodie travelogues on the telly, then it's worth splashing out to bag a table in his glossy West End venue. It is only with tongue firmly in cheek that anyone could call this ultra-chic Mayfair temple of the contemporary Italian culinary idiom a simple 'locanda': just north of Oxford Street, at the side of the Hyatt Regency Churchill Hotel, this is a seriously A-list hangout with a designer interior courtesy of David Collins. There are burnished parquet floors, textured wooden walls, beige leather bucket chairs, and booths divided by etched glass screens to give a veil of intimacy. The front-of-house team are a stand-out crew too, slickly and confidently working the floor, and always ready to chat intelligently about the food and wine. Coming from a well-established cooking dynasty, Locatelli himself has la cucina in his veins and a deeply-felt instinct for the low-intervention preparations that let the stunning quality of the ingredients take centre stage. The result is benchmark Italian food of verve and style that often amazes with its sheer simplicity. It all starts off on the right foot with really good cheese grissini to nibble, and a basket of first-class breads to dip into fantastic extra virgin olive oil. A simple salad of deep-fried calf's foot with mustard fruit arrives perfectly dressed, raising lowly peasant cooking to another level. Don't be tempted to skip the pasta course when there's oxtail ravioli, or risotto with Barolo wine and Castelmagno cheese, to be had. Main courses deliver the likes of roast brill with wild chicory, tomato and white beans, or roast rabbit leg with Parma ham, polenta and radicchio. Desserts embrace a tasting of gold-standard Amedei chocolate - which is as technically tricksy as Locatelli's food ever gets - or an Amalfi lemon take on Eton Mess. The head-spinning wine list is an in-depth exploration of Serie A Italian producers, with heaps of choice by the glass.

Chef Giorgio Locatelli **Owner** Plaxy & Giorgio Locatelli **Times** 12-3/6.45-11 Closed Xmas, BHs **Prices** Starter £10.50-£16.50, Main £18-£32.50, Dessert £6.50-£12.50, Service optional **Wines** 25 bottles under £30, 24 by glass **Notes** Vegetarian available **Seats** 70, Pr/dining room 50 **Children** Portions **Parking** NCP adjacent, parking meters

Maze

LONDON W1 PLAN 2 G1

French, Japenese V 🍷 NOTABLE WINE LIST

Exciting fusion cooking in Grosvenor Square

☎ 020 7107 0000
London Marriott Hotel, Grosvenor Square, 10-13 Grosvenor Square W1K 6JP
e-mail: maze@gordonramsay.com
web: www.gordonramsay.com/maze
dir: Nearest station: Bond Street

Gordon Ramsay's Maze has looked east from its French orientation since it opened, and now it's taken the step of adding a separate sushi bar, where a chef's menu takes away any dithering over what to choose. If you prefer to keep your destiny in your own hands though, the sushi carte takes in everything from salmon sashimi through California roll (crab, avocado, tobiko and sesame seeds), to hamachi (yellowtail) roll with cucumber and ume sauce. Moving away from the sushi bar into the main dining room, David Rockwell's slick interior design is as minimalist as it ever was, and the concept remains the same: tapas-size dishes to be ordered simultaneously to explore the full range of flavours and textures (although you can still order from the sushi menu here if you wish). Dishes sound intriguing and irresistible, and clearly a lot of trialling has been done to make sure sometimes unusual-sounding combinations actually work. There are no starters as such, so jump straight in to beetroot-soused mackerel with potato and horseradish salad and apple jelly; crisp chicken thigh with garlicky pesto, white onion and burned leek vinaigrette; and red mullet with crispy squid, garlic and lemon purée and red pepper vierge. Ingredients are out of the top drawer, with luxuries aplenty, so expect lobster and palourde clams with pork belly, braised apple and lobster and sake dressing, and foie gras, rabbit and smoked duck terrine with poached pear and Sauternes gel. Puddings are as inventive as the rest of the output and look as good too: go for quince Bakewell tart with apple and pear terrine and star anise ice cream, or clementine parfait with orange polenta cake, Cointreau gel and clove ice cream. Prices can mount up alarmingly, but this is Grosvenor Square, after all.

Chef Tristin Farmer **Owner** Gordon Ramsay Holdings Ltd **Times** 12-3/6-11 Closed 25 Dec **Prices** Starter fr £10, Main fr £10.50, Dessert £6.50-£13.50, Service added but optional 12.5% **Wines** 16 by glass **Notes** Fixed L/D 4 course £25, D 7 course £70, Vegetarian menu, Dress restrictions, No sportswear or shorts **Seats** 108 **Children** Portions **Parking** On street

LONDON W1 *continued*

The Mandeville Hotel
PLAN 2 G2

◉ Modern British

Masculine dining in a Marylebone hotel

☎ 020 7935 5599
Mandeville Place W1U 2BE
e-mail: info@mandeville.co.uk
web: www.mandeville.co.uk
dir: Nearest station: Bond St, Baker St. 3 mins walk from Bond St station

At the stylishly modern Mandeville Hotel in Marylebone, a big draw is its Reform Social and Grill restaurant inspired by classic Edwardian gentlemen's clubs. Sit on a brown leather stool at the pewter-topped bar and tuck into a bar snack such as miniature Welsh Wagyu beef burgers, or take your seat on a leather banquette at one of the wooden or marble-topped tables in the restaurant and choose something from the quintessentially British menu. Expect suitably manly portion sizes and lots of British ingredients in classical dishes, which pack a hearty flavour punch. Duck Scotch egg, black pudding, roast apple and oats is a robust start, which might lead to calves' liver and bacon, new potatoes and purple carrots. You might well need a doggy bag for the leftovers of an enormous sticky toffee pudding with clotted cream ice cream.

Times 12-3/7-11

Maze
PLAN 2 G1

◉◉◉ – *see opposite*

Maze Grill
PLAN 2 G1

◉◉ American

Gordon Ramsay's steakhouse overlooking Grosvenor Square

☎ 020 7495 2211
London Marriott Hotel, Grosvenor Square, 10-13 Grosvenor Square W1K 6JP
e-mail: mazegrill@gordonramsay.com
web: www.gordonramsay.com
dir: Nearest station: Bond St

Modern, chic and contemporary, Maze Grill is a relaxed and uncluttered sort of place, with eye-catching lights, much wood (floor, bar, tabletops) and a bustling atmosphere. The name is a bit of a giveaway - this is a New York-style grill specialising in prime steaks. The beef is of superb quality, properly aged and hung, and cooked on the charcoal-fired Josper grill. There's the prospect of Wagyu - at a price - or perhaps Dedham Vale grass- and grain-fed rump steak, aged for 31 days, served pink, succulent and of excellent texture, with Portobello mushrooms, fantastic chips and béarnaise. Starters might bring on barbecued pork belly, tender and full of flavour, served in a bun with coleslaw. There are

alternatives for non-meat-eaters, such as roasted cod with mash and a lemon and caper butter sauce, or grilled organic salmon with celeriac and chimmichurri. Sushi fans are also well served, and all comers can enjoy desserts like a simple but effective cherry Bakewell tart with a dollop of clotted cream.

Times 12-10.30

Mele e Pere
PLAN 2 J1

◉ Italian ☺

Rustic Italian food in modish surroundings

☎ 020 7096 2096
46 Brewer St, Soho W1F 9TF
e-mail: info@meleepere.co.uk
dir: Nearest station: Piccadilly Circus

The name means 'apples and pears', which explains why the plate glass window of this Soho Italian is full of Murano glass renditions of the fruits. You also have to descend the 'apples and pears' to reach the buzzy, modishly minimal basement restaurant - all chunky bleached wood tables lit by wall-mounted anglepoise lamps - a décor that perhaps prepares diners for the fact that this is not a comfort-food Italian serving the usual spag bol suspects. The chef-patron hails from northern Italy, and his repertoire takes the path of well-rendered rusticity, as typified in an unusual Italian take on a classic beef tartare accompanied by shaved parmesan and yellow Castelfranco radicchio. The concise menu continues with tagliatelle with rabbit and fresh peas, while mains run to sea bream with fregola and fennel, or pork belly with lentils and bean sprouts. Finish with a classic pannacotta or excellent Italian cheeses.

Chef A Mantovani **Owner** P Hughes, A Mantovani **Times** 12-11 Closed 25-26 Dec, 1 Jan **Prices** Prices not confirmed Service added but optional 12.5% **Wines** 16 by glass **Notes** Pre-theatre menu until 7pm £15.50-£17.50, Vegetarian available **Seats** 90 **Children** Portions **Parking** NCP

Mennula
PLAN 2 K3

◉◉ Modern Italian

Sicily brought to Fitzrovia

☎ 020 7636 2833 & 7637 3830
10 Charlotte St W1T 2LT
e-mail: santino@mennula.com
dir: Nearest station: Goodge Street, Tottenham Court Rd. 5 min walk from station

Charlotte Street has its fair share of restaurants, but head here for a taste of Sicily. It's a small, modern and warm place, with aubergine-coloured seating, a walnut floor and a stencil of an almond tree ('mennula' in Italian) on white walls. The kitchen has a firm foothold in Italian traditions, adding a Sicilian slant to its menus. Everything is made in-house, from commendable breads and pasta to tuma cheese, served warm as a starter on a

bed of winter leaves accompanied by quince marmalade, a refreshingly simple and tasty dish. Another starter may be a Sicilian salad of bottarga, orange, fennel and mint, then there's a run of pasta before the main event: the freshest of cod fillet in tempura with squash purée, tender spiced lentils and spicy chutney, or the full-on flavours of rabbit stuffed with sausage and pancetta in aubergine sauce with carrots, pine nuts and sultanas. What better way to finish than with a tasting platter of Sicilian desserts, among them semi-fredo and cassata siciliana?

Times 12-3/6-11 Closed Xmas, BHs, L Sat-Sun

Le Meridien Piccadilly
PLAN 2 J1

◉ British **NEW** V ☺

Airy dining in prime central London location

☎ 020 7734 8000
21 Piccadilly W1J 0BH
e-mail: piccadilly.terrace@lemeridien.com
dir: Nearest station: Piccadilly Circus

Occupying one of Piccadilly's grandest Regency edifices, Le Meridien has for many years stood up to be counted among the capital's swankiest addresses, and a recent megabucks refurbishment has given it a rather cool and contemporary look. Once you have made it past the temptations of the specialist gin bar, the prime West End location gets you unrivalled views over Piccadilly Circus if you choose to dine out on the terrace on a fine day, otherwise the glass-roofed restaurant is a totally glam split-level space with soaring columns, shimmering voile drapes and bare darkwood tables. The menu takes in a wide remit: starters cover all bases from a classic farmhouse terrine with Cumberland sauce to a more contemporary dish of pork belly with maple syrup dressing, watercress mayonnaise and apple compôte, while mains rely on prime quality meat and fish subjected to simple treatments - how about grilled Red Poll rump steak with béarnaise sauce, or steamed sea bass with mussels and Pernod?

Chef Michael Dutnall **Times** 12-2.30/5.30-10.30 Closed L Sun **Prices** Starter £2-£11, Main £20-£60, Dessert £8, Service added 12.5% **Wines** 52 bottles over £30, 8 by glass **Notes** Chef's table 5 course £99 (max 10 people), Sunday L, Vegetarian menu, Civ Wed 200 **Seats** 60 **Children** Portions, Menu

LONDON W1 *continued*

Mews of Mayfair   PLAN 2 H1

◉ Modern British **V** 🍃

High-flying cooking off Bond Street

☎ 020 7518 9388
10-11 Lancashire Court, New Bond St, Mayfair W1S 1EY
e-mail: info@mewsofmayfair.com
dir: Nearest station: Bond Street. Between Brook St & New Bond St. Opposite Dolce & Gabbana

This stylish bar and restaurant is indeed secreted away on a narrow, cobbled Mayfair mews just off Bond Street. There's a buzzy cocktail bar with a glamorous 18th-century chandelier and roll-back doors, and up on the first floor, the cool brasserie has a chic, light and airy décor - cream leather banquettes, wooden floors and chunky timber tables - and an equally attractive menu of crowd-pleasing contemporary dishes. Pulled Gloucestershire old spot pork pâté with cider-steeped apples and good old Colman's Mustard is a typically forthright starter, while main courses run the gamut from fish and chips with mushy peas and tartare sauce, to Orkney sea trout with seared scallops, asparagus, and pea purée, or grilled rump of Herdwick lamb with tinkerbell peppers and basil. Puddings head straight for the comfort zone: rhubarb and custard tart with ginger, and rhubarb ripple ice cream, say.

Chef Richard Sawyer **Owner** James Robson & Robert Nearn **Times** 12-4/6-12 Closed 25 Dec, D Sun **Prices** Starter £5.50-£12.50, Main £9.50-£38, Dessert £5-£10, Service added but optional 12.5% **Wines** 16 by glass **Notes** Sunday L £18, Vegetarian menu **Seats** 70, Pr/dining room 28 **Children** Portions, Menu **Parking** On street, NCP

The Montagu   PLAN 2 F2

◉◉ Modern British

Modern comfort food in smart West End venue

☎ 020 7299 2037
Hyatt Regency London, The Churchill, 30 Portman Square W1H 7BH
e-mail: montagu.hrlondon@hyatt.com
dir: Nearest station: Marble Arch. From Marble Arch rdbt, follow signs for Oxford Circus onto Oxford St. Left after 2nd lights into Portman St. Hotel on left

Faced with the presence of Locanda Locatelli in the same hotel (albeit with its own entrance; see entry) many a chef might throw in the towel, but the team at the stoves in the Hyatt Regency Churchill's Montagu restaurant are determined to give the stellar Italian operation a good run for its money. First impressions are suitably swanky: liveried doormen greet you at the door, and the restaurant - a clean-cut contemporary space, complete with open-plan kitchen - offers fine views over Portman Square. Uncomplicated, skilfully-cooked modern British dishes are the deal, starting with a posh version of prawn cocktail, the crustaceans poached in court-bouillon, or there might be chicken liver and port terrine with apple compôte and honey mustard bread. Main course delivers

venison loin with bacon, red cabbage and juniper jus, or pan-fried sea bass with wilted spinach, parsnip purée, and saffron sauce. The comfort classics continue at dessert stage with sticky toffee and date pudding with toffee sauce and vanilla ice cream.

Chef Carlos Teixeira **Owner** Hyatt Regency London-The Churchill **Times** 12-3/6-10.45 **Prices** Fixed L 2 course £25, Fixed D 3 course £25-£29, Tasting menu £75, Starter £7-£13, Main £19-£35, Dessert £6.50-£7, Service added but optional 12.5% **Wines** 54 bottles over £30, 12 bottles under £30, 13 by glass **Notes** Chef's table 3/5 course £55/£75 incl wine, Sunday L, Vegetarian available, Dress restrictions, Smart casual, Civ Wed 140 **Seats** 60 **Children** Portions **Parking** 48

Murano   PLAN 4 H6

◉◉◉◉ – *see opposite*

Newman Street Tavern   PLAN 2 J3

◉ Modern British **NEW**

Revamped pub with a passion for ingredients

☎ 020 3667 1445
48 Newman St W1T 1QQ
e-mail: info@newmanstreettavern.co.uk
dir: Nearest station: Goodge Street. Located corner of Newman & Goodge Streets, just off Charlotte Street

More restaurant than boozer these days, the Newman Street Tavern places food at the top of the agenda, and everything is sourced when at its very best - seasonality is the watchword. It's all very charming and relaxed on the inside with copious pictures of that produce from land and sea covering the walls, banquette seating in the windows, darkwood tables, and a marble-topped bar. There's a pleasing clarity and focus to the menus and a definite lack of fuss, so you might kick off a meal with country pâté with cornichons and silver skin onions and toast, or sweet-cured wild trout, before moving on to cottage pie, or Galloway beef with beetroot and horseradish. Helford fish and shellfish gratin is packed with the fruits of the sea, or there might be all the simplicity of ray wing with lemon and watercress. For dessert, Ayrshire cardamom kulfi competes for your attention with apple crumble and vanilla ice cream.

Times 12-11 Closed D Sun **Prices** Starter £5.50-£36, Main £12-£75, Dessert £5-£6.50, Service added but optional 12.5% **Notes** All day dining shellfish bar, L 12-3, D 5.30-11, Sunday L

Nobu   PLAN 5 H6

◉◉ Japanese

Top-end Japanese dining and views over Hyde Park

☎ 020 7447 4747
Metropolitan London, 19 Old Park Ln W1K 1LB
e-mail: london@noburestaurants.com
dir: Nearest station: Hyde Park Corner, Green Park

The Nobu brand now spans the globe from the Bahamas to Beijing, and this venue on the first-floor of the

Metropolitan Hotel overlooking Hyde Park was the first of its brace of London outposts. The pared-back décor of black banquettes, pale wood and stone hasn't dated since it opened in 1997, and has become something of a timeless classic. The same might be said of the Latino-Japanese fusion cooking, which revolutionised what diners expected from upscale Japanese dining by creatively applying a hit of South American fire to the subtle delicacy of Japanese food. Make no mistake, this is a slick, celeb-spotting Mayfair operation manned by clued-up staff who can talk the uninitiated through the alien terminology of sunomono, ponzu, or toban-yaki tataki, and politely remind you when it's time to leave your table to the next booking. Expect the traditional roll-call of sashimi and sushi, or the culinary fusion concept as typified by anti-cucho Peruvian-style tea-smoked lamb. Elsewhere, high-rollers can find Wagyu beef tartare with caviar, lobster tempura with creamy wasabi, or the unctuous overload of Wagyu and foie gras gyoza with spicy ponzu. Presentation is unfailingly exquisite, and meals might conclude with yoghurt mousse with Manuka honey ice cream, green apple compôte, and green tea and olive oil sponge.

Chef Mark Edwards **Owner** Nobuyuki Matsuhisa **Times** 12-2.15/6-10.15 **Prices** Fixed L 2 course £28.50-£32, Tasting menu £85-£95, Starter £7-£21.50, Main £13-£42, Service added but optional 15% **Wines** 8 by glass **Notes** Pre-theatre Bento box £33, Vegetarian available, Dress restrictions, Smart casual **Seats** 160, Pr/dining room 40 **Parking** Car park nearby

Nobu Berkeley ST   PLAN 4 H6

◉◉ Japanese

Super-cool Mayfair hot-spot for great Japanese food

☎ 020 7290 9222
15 Berkeley St W1J 8DY
e-mail: berkeleyst@noburestaurants.com
dir: Nearest station: Green Park

With a globe-spanning empire stretching from the Bahamas to Beijing, the Nobu brand still ranks among the A-list players on the Japanese cuisine scene. The über-chic Berkeley Street outpost is a high-energy, high-decibel magnet for Mayfair fashionistas who come for the see-and-be-seen buzz of the ground-floor bar, before winding up the spiral staircase to the cool David Collins-designed restaurant, where the décor plays a riff on an autumnal woodland theme. Black-clad staff aren't just there to look good either - they know their way around the menu, whose concept puts a lively spin onto classical high-end Japanese dining by applying the heat of Latin American fusion ideas. For traditionalists, there's a sushi bar, and a sunken hibachi table for fun DIY dining supervised by the chefs. Whichever path you take, expect first-rate ingredients, exquisite presentation, and the typical cleanness and precision of Japanese cooking. Open with a hybrid lobster taco, or perfect rock shrimp tempura, then move on to Wagyu rump tataki with ponzu and sansyo zuke salsa cooked in the wood oven.

Times 12-2.15/6-1am Closed 25 Dec, BH Mon

Murano

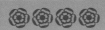

LONDON W1   **PLAN 4 H6**

Modern European, Italian
influence **V** **NOTABLE WINE LIST**

Top-drawer Italianish cooking in smart white surroundings

☎ 020 7495 1127
20-22 Queen St W1J 5PP
e-mail: muranorestaurant@angela-hartnett.com
dir: Nearest station: Green Park. Turn left from Piccadilly to Half Moon St, then left Curzon Street, right Queen Street

Angela Hartnett's career has followed one of the more fascinating London trajectories. She emerged from Gordon Ramsay's empire in the Aubergine days, and went on to become head chef at The Connaught (see entry), where she managed to prise the menus free of their attachment to the institutional Edwardian cooking of yesteryear. She has always maintained loyalty to her ancestral traditions of Italian eating, and now celebrates domestic foodways with Luke Holder at New Forest hotel Lime Wood (see entry, Lyndhurst, Hampshire). Here in Mayfair, the emphasis is less on peasant rustico, which is perhaps as well, and more on the opulence that comes with bespoke Venetian chandeliers, white leather upholstery and a clinically white, squeaky-clean feel that's hardly like sitting in a Tuscan albergo. And again, not all the food is necessarily, obviously Italian in inspiration. A dinner that progresses from scallop and sea bream céviche with herb tempura and orange vinaigrette, to loin and belly of rabbit with Dijon crème fraîche and croquet-monsieur, to finish with rice pudding soufflé and rum and raisin ice cream, will make an Italian native feel as though they'd bought the wrong flight tickets, however exquisite the results. Other dishes feel like crossovers. A lunch opener of fried lamb's sweetbreads is beautifully garnished with spring onions and shallot rings, a savoury purée of apple and shallot, and rich, buttery, warm mustard vinaigrette, for a highly satisfying prelude. Timing of fish is spot-on, as when a piece of monkfish turns up à point, offset cleverly with a topping of crushed almonds, alongside puréed broccoli, sautéed button mushrooms and a golden chicken jus, the touch of genius a shard of crisped chicken skin. For the echt Italian dishes, look to the signature pumpkin tortelli, its clean, resonant filling underscored by the lovely sheen of the sage butter, and a daring note of sweetness from crushed amaretti, while a main course of superb turbot with tender octopus, roasted cauliflower purée and Ibérico ham, shows a dab hand at the pairing of meat and fish. Full-on meat dishes might encompass Anjou pigeon with stem broccoli, pistachios and grilled foie gras. Desserts ring out clear as a bell with the expected richnesses, obviously so in the case of a complex layered chocolate cake with bitter orange, which has a hot black sauce poured on to melt through its brittle chocolate top and give an instant fondant centre.

Chef Diego Cardoso **Owner** Angela Hartnett **Times** 12-3/6.30-11 Closed 25-26 Dec, Sun **Prices** Fixed L 2 course fr £25, Fixed D 3 course fr £65, Service added but optional 12.5% **Wines** 17 by glass **Notes** 4/5 course £75/£85, Vegetarian menu **Seats** 46, Pr/dining room 12 **Children** Portions

LONDON W1 *continued*

NOPI   PLAN 2 J1

◉ Mediterranean, Middle Eastern

Vibrant Middle Eastern flavours Ottolenghi style

☎ 020 7494 9584
21-22 Warwick St W1B 5NE
e-mail: contact@nopi-restaurant.com
dir: Nearest station: Oxford Circus, Piccadilly Circus

NOPI (north of Piccadilly) is a brasserie on two levels, a more formal ground floor, with lots of marble and brass, and a basement with canteen-type tables and views into the kitchen. Owner Yotam Ottolenghi's cooking is based on the cuisine of the Middle East, with some input from other cultures, and dishes are meant to be shared. The menu is packed with interest, the food is full of zingy flavours, and if ingredients sound alien ask the staff to explain. Among vegetarian options have been shakshuka (North African braised eggs with pepper and tomato), burrata cheese with peach and fennel seeds, and chargrilled broccolini with skordalia and chilli oil, all demonstrating a masterly control of flavours. Meat and seafood hit the spot too: twice-cooked baby chicken with lemon myrtle oil and chilli sauce, and soft-shelled crab with nashi pear and pea shoots. Puddings are just as vigorous: try kaffir lime with meringue, tapioca, and honey mango.

Times 12-2.45/5.30-10.15 Closed D Sun

Novikov Asian Restaurant   PLAN 4 H6

◉ Chinese & Pan Asian **NEW**

Style-conscious Pan-Asian dining in Mayfair

☎ 020 7399 4330
50a Berkeley St W1J 8HA
dir: Nearest station: Charing Cross, Green Park. Approx 2min walk S.E from Green Park Tube station

Arkady Novikov's Mayfair food emporium is the dernier cri of hot-button, style-drenched dining. As well as an Italian section (see entry), there is an Asian Room, where Japanese, Chinese, Thai and Malaysian dishes coexist in perfect harmony. Granite walls and a lacquered ebony and jade bar counter create a busy but cool impression, while the glass-fronted kitchen is like watching a giant TV. Croissant-shaped dumplings of beef and foie gras, served on a banana leaf, are a fittingly stylish start, as are the unimpeachable sushi and maki rolls. They might be succeeded by Malay-style soft-shelled crab, classic Singapore noodles with pork and prawns, or spectacular meat dishes such as seared Wagyu rib-eye in ponzu, or roast duck with oriental mushrooms in truffle sauce. An unmoulded brûlée of green tea with guava sorbet keeps the taste buds humming at dessert stage, and there are more obviously western chocolate creations like semi-fredo with pear sorbet.

Chef Jeff Tyler **Times** 12-4 **Prices** Prices not confirmed Service added but optional 12.5% **Parking** NCP Carrington Street

Novikov Italian Restaurant   PLAN 4 H6

◉ Italian

Jaw-dropping temple of Italian (and Asian) gastronomy

☎ 020 7399 4330
50a Berkeley St W1J 8HA
e-mail: reservations@novikovrestaurant.co.uk
dir: Nearest station: Green Park

Arkady Novikov is an internationally known Russian restaurant entrepreneur with the resources to realise grandiose projects. The present complex is on the scale of a biblical temple, incorporating a sleek lounge-bar lit like a nightclub, a ground-floor Asian restaurant (see entry) and an Italian venue in the basement. Security-staff are on hand to ensure there are no sudden moves, and everywhere you look, there are shrines devoted to food and drink - mountains of oranges in wicker baskets, paniers of fresh produce in front of a long service counter, bottles of grappa crowded on to the top of a wine barrel. Once you get down to it, the Italian cooking is convincing, surprisingly rustic and honest, with some southern and Sardinian dishes for depth. Gossamer-thin slices of beef carpaccio with parmesan strips and rocket is the real deal, as is the asparagus salad with broad beans and Sardinian stone-dried red mullet bottarga. Calves' liver is top-drawer gear, lightly sautéed for melting texture, dressed in butter and sage.

Chef Arkady Novikov **Owner** Arkady Novikov
Times noon-11pm **Prices** Fixed L 2 course £19, Service added but optional 12.5% **Notes** Fixed L 4 course £26

140 Park Lane Restaurant PLAN 2 F1
& Bar

◉◉ Modern British

Prime produce simply cooked in central hotel

☎ 020 7493 7000 & 7647 5678
London Marriott Hotel, 140 Park Ln W1K 7AA
e-mail: mhrs.parklane@marriotthotels.com
web: www.140parklane.co.uk
dir: Nearest station: Marble Arch. From Hyde Park Corner, left A4202 Park Lane

At the Marble Arch end of Park Lane - handy for doing a spot of Oxford Street shopping - the London Marriott Hotel has views over Hyde Park and a luxurious interior with a relaxed and popular bar, and the smart bistro-style 140 Park Lane Restaurant. Prime seafood and steaks from grain-fed cattle are what it's all about here, and you can watch them being grilled to perfection in the open-to-view kitchen. Amongst the grills might be a 12oz USDA rib-eye or 8oz Scottish fillet, competing for your attention with lobster thermidor or a 7oz halibut steak. From elsewhere on the menu you might choose roast chicken, pleasantly moist and tasty, well matched by its accompanying onion purée, spinach and triple-cooked chips. Produce from the top drawer is used throughout: diver-caught scallops, for instance, here seared and served with smoked bacon and crisped cauliflower and purée. Breads are impressive, and the delights amongst

desserts include mandarin posset with segments of the fruit and crunchy pomegranate foam.

Times 11-3/5.30-10.30

The Only Running Footman   PLAN 4 H6

◉ Traditional British

Smart Mayfair pub with commitment to great food

☎ 020 7499 2988
5 Charles St, Mayfair W1J 5DF
e-mail: manager@therunningfootmanmayfair.com
dir: Nearest station: Green Park. Close to south end of Berkeley Sq

It looks like a pub, which indeed it is, but there's more than meets the eye to The Only Running Footman. The distinctive red-brick corner building in Mayfair has a ground-floor bar where you can have a drink and pick something off the all-day bar menu (from a sandwich to chargrilled Longhorn rib-eye steak), plus a smarter and quieter upstairs restaurant, where closely-packed tables are done-out in crisp white linen and all is a little more refined. (There's also a chef's table in a separate room which doubles up as a cookery school.) Upstairs you might start with sautéed Cornish squid and chorizo salad, followed by pan-fried sea bass with caramelised salsify and sauce vierge, finishing off with a berry Pavlova or cheeses from the Bath Cheese Company with pear chutney and pain aux fruits.

Chef Eddie Konadio **Owner** Barnaby Meredith
Times 12-2.30/6.30-10 Closed D 25 Dec **Prices** Fixed L 2 course £35-£42, Fixed D 3 course £35-£42, Starter £6-£9.85, Main £14.50-£49.95, Dessert £4.95-£6, Service added but optional 12.5% **Wines** 49 bottles over £30, 28 bottles under £30, 12 by glass **Notes** Chef's table available £70, Sunday L, Vegetarian available **Seats** 30, Pr/dining room 40 **Children** Portions **Parking** On street

Orrery   PLAN 2 G3

◉◉ Modern French V ⓔ

Stylish, elegant restaurant above designer store

☎ 020 7616 8000
55-57 Marylebone High St W1U 5RB
e-mail: orreryreservation@danddlondon.com
dir: Nearest station: Baker St, Regent's Park. At north end of Marylebone High St

Above the (Terence) Conran store at the top of fashionable Marylebone High Street, the landmark Orrery is a class act indeed. It's an elegantly streamlined, contemporary and understated space, the linear dining room flooded by light from large arched windows and roof skylights, with a glass wine cellar at one end and intimate bar tucked away at the other. Service is a strength here, professional certainly, but engaging, with a sommelier to advise on the excellent wine list. The modern cooking is underpinned by classical French thinking, with a refined touch and plenty of good ideas. Expect top-notch produce, a hint of luxury and meticulous presentation in dishes such as fillet of turbot with white asparagus, morels, peas and champagne velouté, or rump of Kentish lamb à la provençale served with pommes dauphinoise and rosemary jus, while a Melanosporum black truffle risotto is teamed with soft herbs and parmesan. A good value lunch du jour, plus a roof terrace and street-level Epicerie are all bonuses.

Chef Igor Tymchyshyn **Owner** D and D London **Times** 12-2.30/6.30-10.30 **Prices** Prices not confirmed Service added but optional 12.5%, Groups min 8 service 12.5% **Wines** 18 by glass **Notes** Sunday L, Vegetarian menu **Seats** 80, Pr/dining room 18 **Children** Portions **Parking** NCP, 170 Marylebone Rd

Ozer Restaurant   PLAN 2 H2

Turkish, Middle Eastern, Mediterranean

Busy upmarket Turkish restaurant near the BBC

☎ 020 7323 0505
5 Langham Place W1B 3DG
e-mail: ozer@ozer.co.uk
dir: Nearest station: Oxford Circus. 2 min walk towards Upper Regent St

If you're in a rush, this upmarket Turkish restaurant promises 'drinks in 2 minutes, starters in 5 minutes'. But why hurry? There's plenty to enjoy at leisure on a wide-ranging menu which is keen to show that there's more to the Turkish idiom than meze followed by kebabs, although the usual suspects such as spicy crisp lamb's liver, grilled sucuk sausage, lamb köfte meatballs, and ali nazik - sautéed lamb fillet with smoked aubergine caviar, yoghurt and garlic - are all present and correct. Near the BBC, the contemporary space is done out with cream leather seats at white linen tables set against vibrant red walls, and the place is always heaving, kept on the boil by energetic, personable waiters. The extensive repertoire strays from straightforward Turkish cuisine to include a wide range of Middle Eastern classics, as well as grilled steaks served with French fries, and Asian-accented seafood dishes including black cod with miso. Keeping it Turkish, finish with the house speciality 'Su Muhallebisi' - a confection of cubes of milk pudding, rose syrup, berries and nuts.

Times noon-11.30

Park Plaza Sherlock Holmes   PLAN 2 F3

British, European

Modern grill near the home of Holmes

☎ 020 7486 6161
108 Baker St W1U 6LJ
e-mail: info@sherlockholmeshotel.com
web: www.sherlockholmeshotel.com
dir: Nearest station: Baker Street. On Baker St, close to tube station

Located accurately in the fictional Edwardian sleuth's postcode, this slick Baker Street operation eschews the period theme in favour of a chic contemporary boutique hotel look. Polished wood floors and cream leather seats at black quartz inlaid tables set a smart, modern, city-slicker tone in the open-plan space of Sherlock's Bar & Grill. Holding centre stage is the kitchen team, hard at

work over charcoal grills and a wood-burning oven in the open-to-view kitchen. From a broadly European menu comes a generous serving of pan-fried king scallops with butternut squash purée and crispy bacon to set the ball rolling, then hot off the charcoal grill there might be veal escalope in breadcrumbs with roasted plum tomato and rocket, or from the wood-fired oven, Gressingham duck breast with caramelised plums and Swiss chard. For pudding, how about a good honest and homely version of apple and sultana crumble with cinnamon ice cream?

Chef Rachid Hammoum **Owner** Park Plaza Hotels **Times** 12-2.30/6-10.30 Closed D Sun, BHs **Prices** Fixed L 2 course £15, Fixed D 3 course £22, Starter £6-£12, Main £14-£20, Dessert £5.50-£7, Service added 12.5% **Wines** 6 bottles over £30, 11 bottles under £30, 10 by glass **Notes** Sunday L, Vegetarian available, Dress restrictions, Smart casual, Civ Wed 40 **Seats** 44, Pr/dining room 50 **Children** Portions, Menu **Parking** Chiltern St, NCP

La Petite Maison   PLAN 2 H1

French, Mediterranean

The flavours of the Midi in Mayfair

☎ 020 7495 4774
54 Brooks Mews W1K 4EG
e-mail: info@lpmlondon.co.uk
dir: Nearest station: Bond St

Modelled on and named after its sister restaurant in Nice, the light, open-plan, sunny room does have a breezily Mediterranean vibe. The Riviera-cool look takes in creamy walls with large frosted-glass windows, an open-to-view kitchen and an uptempo, see-and-be-seen atmosphere. A battalion of skilful staff respond without hovering at closely-set tables, while the cooking shows a light modern touch, keeping things simple and fresh, driven by top-notch produce in a procession of skilfully delivered dishes designed for sharing. Starters like a salad of French beans with foie gras or carpaccio of sea bream with salsa verde, precede mains along the lines of turbot served with artichokes and chorizo, or perhaps slow-cooked duck leg with orange glaze. Factor in two-hour table time slots or you could miss out on a vanilla crème brûlée or warm fig tart finale.

Times 12-3/6-11 Closed 25-26 Dec

Pied à Terre   PLAN 2 J3

– see page 342

Plum Valley   PLAN 2 K1

Chinese

Contemporary Cantonese cooking in Chinatown

☎ 020 7494 4366
20 Gerrard St W1D 6JQ
dir: Nearest station: Leicester Square

Behind its black frontage, multi-floored Plum Valley, with its dark décor and lots of dark wood, remains a bastion of Cantonese cooking. The kitchen eschews MSG, relying

instead on skilful techniques to bring out the natural, clean flavours of its ingredients, characteristically using a lot of chilli, garlic and ginger. Highlights among starters include crisp, golden prawn spring rolls, and crab 'crystal' dumpling: shredded crabmeat mixed with chopped prawns, coriander and ginger wrapped in rice-paper. More substantial dishes may run to minced pork dumpling and scallop wonton topped with a sliver of the shellfish - a good balance of flavours - and ample-sized pieces of chicken fried in a wok with spring onions and peppers, served in a light black bean sauce with crispy egg noodles.

Times noon-11.30 Closed 25 Dec **Prices** Prices not confirmed Service added but optional 12.5% **Notes** Vegetarian available **Seats** 90

Pollen Street Social   PLAN 2 J2

– see page 343

Polpo   PLAN 2 J1

Italian

Bustling Venetian-style bacaro in Soho

☎ 020 7734 4479
41 Beak St W1F 9SB
dir: Nearest station: Piccadilly Circus

Fizzing like a glass of prosecco, Polpo offers a trendy take on the bacaros of Venice, delivering on-vogue Italian-style tapas (cichetti) in a fabulously casual, high-energy atmosphere. Though Canaletto, the great Venetian master, may once have lived in this building, the décor is unapologetically stripped-back and designer distressed - think old tiles and exposed-brick walls, floorboards, dangling light bulbs and crammed-in tables. The street-level dining room comes with mandatory high-stool bar-dining (up front) and an open kitchen (out back), while there's a campari bar in the basement. It's high-octane when the place gets rammed (a given) and you can't book ahead in the evenings (so expect to queue), but that's all part of the relaxed fun of it all. Brown-paper menus double as placemats, staff are youthful but clued-up, while the kitchen sends out quick-fire, small plates for sharing (with very affordable price tags). It's authentic, simple, full-on flavoured stuff; perhaps potato and parmesan croquettes and wild mushroom piadina to fritto misto and lamb chump served with caponata and basil. The flourless orange and almond cake shouldn't be missed, while wines aptly reflect the northern Italian region too, served in tumblers by glass, carafe and bottle.

Times 12-11 Closed 25 Dec-1 Jan, D Sun

Pied à Terre

LONDON W1　　　　　**PLAN 2 J3**

Modern French **V** 🍾 NOTABLE WINE LIST

Art on a plate in one of London's finest and longest-standing restaurants

☎ 020 7636 1178
34 Charlotte St W1T 2NH
e-mail: info@pied-a-terre.co.uk
dir: Nearest station: Goodge Street. S of BT Tower and Goodge St

A firm fixture on many a gourmet's must-eat-at list, Pied à Terre has been going strong now for some 22 years. That's an incredibly long time in high-end restaurant circles, and it's testament to the passion with which the place is run by owner David Moore. Experienced restaurateur Moore certainly has the ability to pick out good chefs: Tom Aikens once headed up the kitchen here, then it was the supremely talented Shane Osborn, and now the equally skilful Marcus Eaves, who moved across from sister restaurant L'Autre Pied to take up the helm of the kitchen with impressive continuity. A quick look at the restaurant's website will tell you that the food here is no less than visually stunning, every dish a riot of colour and every component placed with extreme care to create a picture on the plate: never mind the works on the walls by the restaurant's yearly changing artist in residence, this is true art. Ingredients are of the highest order (herbs come from the restaurant's own roof garden) and are treated with the utmost respect to produce dishes with real wow factor. The two tasting menus (plus a vegetarian version) are the ultimate way to experience Eaves's cooking, but if your budget won't stretch to that, the à la carte presents itself with some tantalising dishes that inevitably make choosing tricky. The signature starter of roasted breasts and crispy leg of quail is a good way to begin, the breast-meat perfectly timed and succulent, the leg crisp on the outside and soft and velvety within, served with a fantastic quail Kiev, a vibrant green-coloured Douglas fir purée, and a hazelnut dressing. If you prefer fish, salad of Loch Duart salmon with razor clams, horseradish, cucumber and borage is a colourful dish full of fresh flavours and executed with precision. For the main event, try and persuade your dining partner to share the signature pan-fried fillet of halibut with bonito poached potatoes, sea kale, monk's beard and wakame emulsion - a fabulously inventive plate of food demonstrating some impressive technical skills and a real understanding of what works with what. The same level of creativity continues through to desserts such as a refreshing frozen rhubarb mousse with cardamom gel, rhubarb sorbet, yoghurt and vanilla foam, and rich and indulgent Valrhona chocolate crème with caramel sauce, salted peanut ice cream and chocolate jelly. As you'd expect, the vast wine list is outstanding, and it all takes place in a contemporary and elegant room watched over by a slickly professional but ever-friendly service team.

Chef Marcus Eaves **Owner** David Moore **Times** 12-2.45/6.15-11 Closed 2 wks Xmas & New Year, Sun, L Sat **Prices** Fixed L 2 course fr £27.50, Fixed D 3 course £75, Tasting menu £99-£145, Service added but optional 12.5% **Wines** 700 bottles over £30, 25 bottles under £30, 15 by glass **Notes** ALC 2/3 course £60/£75, Vegetarian menu **Seats** 40, Pr/dining room 12 **Parking** Cleveland St

Pollen Street Social

Modern British **V** NOTABLE WINE LIST

Refined bistro cooking and a buzzing atmosphere at Atherton's flagship

☎ 020 7290 7600
8-10 Pollen St W1S 1NQ
e-mail: reservations@
pollenstreetsocial.com
dir: Nearest station: Oxford Circus. 2 min walk from Oxford Circus, off Regent Street, between Hanover Street and Maddox Street

It seems there's no stopping Jason Atherton right now. With two new London openings in 2013 (see entries for Little Social and The Social Eating House), and two more in the pipeline as we go to print, let alone a growing portfolio of restaurants in Asia and the Middle East, there's an awful lot going on chez Atherton. But here, in the rather Dickensian-sounding Pollen Street, is where it's really at. Atherton may be spending more time abroad than ever before, but he's committed to working here in the kitchen of his flagship whenever he's in the UK. And when he is in the house you can watch him at work in the glass-fronted theatre kitchen, which only serves to add to the buzz of this ever-popular, lively and, ultimately, fun restaurant. The look is chic and contemporary, with a neutral colour palette (wooden floors and tables, white walls broken up with modern art, and

cool lighting) and a casual, cosmopolitan feel despite the high-class culinary output. You can start - and finish - with cocktails in the bar (the full menu is also served here, along with grazing options like a plate of hand-carved Ibérico ham), before taking a seat in the main dining room for Atherton's highly refined take on bistro cooking. There's an eight-course tasting menu, the à la carte, a dedicated vegetarian menu, and an amazing-value set lunch at £29.50 for three courses. Atherton ran Ramsay's Maze (see entry) before going it alone, so he's in the business of crafting high-calibre miniatures and taking a deconstructed approach to eating, thus expect plenty of pace-setting invention and cheeky combinations of taste and texture. Cornish crab vinaigrette with Nashi pear, cauliflower sweet-and-sour dressing and peanut powder is an exquisite, aromatic dish full of fresh, pure flavours and a perfect balance of sweet, salty and sour. Black Angus fillet, of superb quality and perfectly cooked to reveal its naturally rich flavour, comes partnered with charred eggplant, roasted salsify, charred onions, oxtail and marrowbone, while Cornish brill (a fantastic piece of fresh fish) is moist and succulent and imaginatively paired up with cauliflower and cheese purée, seaweed salt, and a cauliflower and cockle chowder. While everything - including the home-made breads and little extras such as a pre-dessert of

sangria mousse with blackberry granité and citrus curd - tastes wonderful, arguably Atherton saves the best till last, with the attention paid to pudding practically off the scale. Desserts are complex, highly creative and playful, and practically guaranteed to bring a smile to your face. Head up to the dessert bar for your final course if you can, so you can watch the pastry chefs skilfully assembling your sweet treat whilst also getting a bird's eye view of the kitchen. The 'PBJ' - peanut butter and jelly - is a delicious combination of peanut parfait, cherry yuzu sorbet, and nitro peanut, while chocolate lovers will likely find themselves in raptures over the 70 per cent cocoa chocolate ganache with banana ice cream, sesame crumble, Pedro Ximenez and chocolate coral.

Chef Jason Atherton **Owner** Jason Atherton **Times** 12-2.45/6-10.45 Closed BHs, Sun **Prices** Fixed L 2 course £26, Tasting menu £79, Service added but optional 12.5% **Wines** 19 by glass **Notes** Tasting menu 8 course, Vegetarian menu **Seats** 60, Pr/dining room 14 **Children** Portions **Parking** On street, car park Mayfair, Park Lane

LONDON W1 *continued*

The Providores and Tapa Room

PLAN 2 G3

◉◉ International 🏅 NOTABLE WINE LIST

High-excitement fusion food in fashionable Marylebone

☎ 020 7935 6175
109 Marylebone High St W1U 4RX
e-mail: anyone@theprovidores.co.uk
dir: Nearest station: Bond St, Baker St, Regent's Park. From Bond St station cross Oxford St, down James St, into Thayer St then Marylebone High St

When it comes to top-notch fusion food with a southern-hemisphere spin, Kiwi Peter Gordon is the man, and he has been serving up his highly inventive trademark cooking here on Marylebone High Street since 2001. Spread over two floors - an up-tempo, all-day, café-bar-style ground-floor Tapa Room (no bookings) and more grown-up (but still suitably chilled) restaurant upstairs - both are light and bright spaces, appealingly minimalist, with linen-clad tables and black leather banquettes the extent of the refinement in the restaurant. The creative cooking delivers all the colour and excitement required. Dish descriptions come with their enthralling array of esoteric ingredients (all excellent quality), and everything seems to work very well together. Tuna carpaccio to kick things off, perhaps, delivered on wakame, samphire and shiso cress salad with crunchy Cornish squid, wasabi tobikko and olive oil jelly. Next up, roast Elwy Valley lamb cannon is served on oregano corn bread with butter bean purée, raisin dressing and a kalamata olive tapioca crisp, showing the kitchen is quite comfortable with the flavours of the Mediterranean too. A star-turn New Zealand wine list only adds to its appeal. (See entry for sister restaurant Kopapa in Covent Garden.)

Chef Peter Gordon **Owner** P Gordon, M McGrath
Times 12-2.30/6-10 Closed 24 Dec-3 Jan, Etr Mon
Prices Fixed D 3 course £47, Starter £7.80-£15, Main £17-£21, Dessert £9.20-£9.80, Service added but optional 12.5% **Wines** 68 bottles over £30, 10 bottles under £30, 18 by glass **Notes** Fixed D 5 course £63, Tasting menu available 6 nights a week, Vegetarian available **Seats** 38 **Children** Portions

Quo Vadis

PLAN 2 K2

◉◉ Modern British

Brasserie-style cooking at a Soho institution

☎ 020 7437 9585
26-29 Dean St W1D 3LL
e-mail: reception@quovadissoho.co.uk
dir: Nearest station: Tottenham Court Road, Leicester Square

This glorious art deco gem was spruced up at the beginning of 2012 to bring in a lighter, more pared-back look in honour of the new broom in the kitchen, Jeremy Lee. Back-to-back tan leather banquettes divide up the space, and cream walls are hung with modern art in a setting that sits well with its original stained-glass windows, wall mirrors and wooden floors. Owned by restaurateur brothers Sam and Eddie Hart, who made their name with tapas joints Fino and Barrafina (see entries), the food here continues to plough a fairly classic brasserie-style furrow mixing simple modern comfort ideas with old school grills and braised dishes. After a cocktail or bubbles in the buzzy bar (which has its own nibbles menu) take a seat for seasonal delights - a taste of spring in a plate of tender squid with fennel, wild garlic and peas, followed by flawlessly-cooked brill with silky smooth olive oil mash pointed up with a punchy gremolata. At the end, almond tart with caramelised pear and vanilla ice cream is another hit.

Chef Jeremy Lee **Owner** Sam & Eddie Hart
Times 12-2.30/5.30-11 Closed 24-25 Dec, 1 Jan, BHs, Sun **Prices** Fixed L 2 course £17.50, Fixed D 3 course £20, Starter £4-£11, Main £16-£21.50, Dessert £6-£8.80, Service added but optional 12.5% **Wines** 131 bottles over £30, 14 bottles under £30, 10 by glass **Notes** Vegetarian available **Seats** 80, Pr/dining room 32 **Parking** On street or NCP

The Red Fort

PLAN 2 K2

◉ Traditional Indian **V**

Authentic contemporary Indian in the heart of Soho

☎ 020 7437 2525
77 Dean St, Soho W1D 3SH
e-mail: info@redfort.co.uk
dir: Nearest station: Leicester Square, Tottenham Court Road. Walk N on Charing Cross Rd. At Cambridge Circus left into Shaftesbury Av. Dean St 2nd right

Opened in 1983 and named after the eponymous Delhi landmark (although it no longer has a red façade), this smart and stylish Indian restaurant was one of the first in London to introduce regional cooking presented in a modern fashion. Nearly 30 years on and it continues to create innovative dishes, the unique Mogul Court cooking successfully combining great British produce with authentic sub-continental flavours. From the open kitchen may come a starter of spiced and roasted minced Devon lamb skewers with mint and onion salad, followed by such main courses as grilled stone bass with mustard, coconut milk and a curry leaf sauce, accompanied by a vegetable side dish, perhaps stir-fried okra with asparagus with tomato, onion and sun-dried spices. Dine in the subterranean Akhar bar or in the long ground floor dining room, with walls adorned with authentic artefacts amid ornate Mogul arches.

Chef M A Rahman **Owner** Amin Ali **Times** 12-4/5.30-11.30 Closed 25 Dec, L Sat-Sun **Prices** Fixed L 2 course £15-£25, Fixed D 3 course £18-£59, Tasting menu £49-£59, Starter £6-£14, Main £18-£38, Dessert £7-£16, Service added but optional 12.5% **Wines** 14 by glass **Notes** Tasting menu 4 course, Fixed pre-theatre D, Vegetarian menu, Dress restrictions, Smart casual **Seats** 84 **Parking** NCP

The Riding House Café

PLAN 2 J3

◉◉ Modern British

Buzzy all-day brasserie near Oxford Street

☎ 020 7927 0840
43-51 Great Titchfield St W1W 7PQ
e-mail: info@ridinghousecafe.co.uk
dir: Nearest station: Oxford Circus

If you're shopping on Oxford Street and looking for a pit-stop, then take a short diversion up Great Titchfield Street to The Riding House Café, where a fashionable all-day dining menu - everything from breakfasts to afternoon teas - is served in a lively, buzzing environment. Much more restaurant than café, The Riding House stands out from the crowd with its striking art-deco design (think large, 1930s-style windows all around, affording its diners great street views and plenty of light), whilst inside it is all parquet flooring and clubby wood panelling. You can perch on a swivel seat at the bar and watch the chefs at work or take an old wooden cinema seat at the long communal table to eat refectory-style; there are plenty of regular tables too if communal ain't your thing. Classic brasserie dishes are the order of the day at lunch and dinner: start with a couple of 'small plates', such as beautifully flavoured braised rabbit with soft polenta and parmesan, and crispy salt-cod fritters with red pepper aïoli, before tucking into a very fine fish and chips. The apple and sultana crumble for two with vanilla ice cream and custard is a very happy ending.

Times 12-3.30/6-10 Closed 25 Dec

Ristorante Semplice   PLAN 2 H2

@@ Italian

Elegant modern Italian a hop, skip and a jump from Oxford Street

☎ 020 7495 1509
10 Blenheim St W1S 1LJ
e-mail: info@ristorantesemplice.com
dir: Nearest station: Bond Street. Off New Bond Street, next to Bonhams

If you're shopping in Oxford Street and New Bond Street and fancy some sustenance of the sophisticated Italian kind, Ristorante Semplice, tucked away down a small side street near sister eatery Bar Trattoria Semplice (see entry), fits the bill. It may look expensive with its glamorous décor of piano-gloss rosewood panelling and gold textured walls, high-backed caramel and chocolate chairs and banquettes, and tables dressed in their finery, but you can still eat here for a snip at lunchtime if you go for the set menu (the à la carte is less of a bargain). The kitchen deals in modern Italian cooking based around superb ingredients, and shows a good deal of skill and creative flair. Start, perhaps, with a knock-out home-made tagliatelle with hare ragù and black cabbage, followed by super-fresh plaice fillets cooked Milanese style and served with roasted cauliflower and baby spinach leaves. It's well worth waiting the extra 12 minutes for the Domori chocolate fondant with a boozy

grappa pannacotta, deeply rich chocolate sorbet and crunchy croûtons of spiced bread.

Times 12-2.30/6.30-10.30 Closed Xmas, New Year, Sun, L Sat

The Ritz Restaurant   PLAN 4 J6

@@@ – *see below*

Roka   PLAN 2 J3

@@@ – *see page 346*

Roti Chai   PLAN 2 G2

@@ Modern Indian

Vibrant Indian street-food close to Oxford Street

☎ 020 7408 0101
3 Portman Mews South W1H 6HS
e-mail: infowala@rotichai.com
dir: Nearest station: Bond Street, Marble Arch. Short walk from Selfridges & Oxford St

Just off Oxford Street, close to M&S and Selfridges, Roti Chai takes its inspiration from the street stalls, roadside and railway cafés of the India sub-continent and brings a breath of fresh air to the West End shopping frenzy. There's an all-day Street Kitchen on the ground-floor with an up-tempo urban café vibe, while below there's a more

stylish evenings-only Dining Room, with its design inspired by India's famous rail transport (think luggage racks on walls and train-carriage like banquette seating). Expect intense, vibrant, robust flavours wherever you sit: Street Kitchen dishes might feature chicken lollipops (Keralan-spiced chicken wings) or railway lamb curry (lamb and potato served with chapatis), while the Dining Room still turns-out small 'street' plates alongside larger-options with a regional theme; perhaps awadhi lamb korma (flavoured with rosewater and saffron) or paneer pasanda (a speciality of the Mogul courts).

Times 12-11.45

The Ritz Restaurant

@@@

LONDON W1   **PLAN 4 J6**

British, French V 🍷 NOTABLE WINE LIST

Arresting dining in sumptuous restaurant

☎ 020 7300 2370
150 Piccadilly W1J 9BR
e-mail: ritzrestaurant@theritzlondon.com
web: www.theritzlondon.com
dir: Nearest station: Green Park. 10 min walk from Piccadilly Circus or Hyde Park Corner, less from Green Park station

'Ritz' has entered the vocabulary to mean luxury and glamour, and a visit to the world-famous hotel explains why, with its soft deep-pile carpets, glittering chandeliers and sconces, and yards of sumptuous fabrics. The restaurant is magnificent without being overwhelming, with an opulent Louis XVI-inspired décor, painted ceiling,

gold statuary, garlands of chandeliers sparkling in mirrored walls, and vast floor-to-ceiling windows hung with drapes overlooking Green Park. Impeccably liveried staff are skilled, knowledgeable and just the right side of formal without being stuffy. The menu pays due deference to the great Auguste Escoffier, the man who gave the world peach Melba, among other things, and, while the cooking is founded on the great French cuisine, executive chef John Williams has created his own distinctively contemporary repertory. Among starters, for instance, is pig's head, served with a slow-cooked duck egg and pickled vegetables, and steak tartare is unusually complemented by caviar and parsley. Given the surroundings, and the prices, luxuries abound as you'd expect, among them truffle in Jerusalem artichoke soup, and lobster as a main course with carrot fondant, ginger and lime. Elsewhere, ingredients are the best money can buy, often joined by humbler accompaniments, so beef tournedos, timed to the second, is served with deeply flavoured ox cheek and celeriac, and sea bass with pork

belly and kale. At dessert stage, put the kitchen to the test and order banana soufflé (it will be light and perfectly risen), served with malt ice cream, or go for crêpe Suzette for the theatricality of staff flambéing at the table.

Chef John T Williams MBE **Owner** The Ritz Hotel (London) Ltd **Times** 12.30-2/5.30-10 **Prices** Fixed L 3 course £47-£55, Fixed D 3 course £55-£95, Tasting menu £85-£175, Starter £16-£23, Main £36-£42, Dessert £14-£18, Service optional **Wines** 190 bottles over £30, 18 by glass **Notes** Menu Surprise 6 course £85, 'Live at the Ritz' menu £95, Sunday L, Vegetarian menu, Dress restrictions, Jacket & tie required, no jeans or trainers **Seats** 90, Pr/dining room 60 **Children** Portions, Menu **Parking** 10, NCP

LONDON W1 *continued*

Roux at The Landau

PLAN 2 H4

◉◉ Modern European V

Skilful Roux cookery in a luxurious dining room

☎ 020 7636 1000

The Langham London, Portland Place W1B 1JA
e-mail: reservations@thelandau.com
dir: Nearest station: Oxford Circus. N end of Regent St, at
Oxford Circus

The old-school elegance of The Langham has been gently
worked on in today's neutral shades by the David Collins
studio to make of the elliptically shaped Roux dining
room a place of great comfort and refinement, adorned
with horsey memorabilia. The place represents the return
of a collaboration between one of London gastronomy's
greats, Albert Roux, and his son, Michel, the vision
executed by the capable hands of the youthful Chris King.
What results is a style of contemporary French cuisine
that nonetheless also feels very 'London'. Cornish squid
with shaved cauliflower, seasoned with Meyer lemon and
dill, is impressive in its simplicity, but starters also
stretch to a pairing of spiced pork jowl and gambas a la
plancha, served on marjoram-scented arrocina beans.
North African modes inveigle a main course of aubergine
roasted in zatar, with bulgur pilaf and harissa
vinaigrette, while the chorizo is made in-house, to
accompany a roast Ibérico pork chop in thyme-spiked

Suffolk cider sauce. As you near the finishing-line, you'll
find the aromatic tendency still going strong in desserts
such as arabica coffee mousseline with Kahlúa jelly and
warm cinnamon doughnuts.

Chef Chris King **Owner** Langham Hotels International
Times 12.30-2.30/5.30-10.30 Closed BHs, Sun, L Sat
Prices Fixed D 3 course fr £35, Tasting menu £80-£140,
Starter £9.50-£18, Main £16-£45, Dessert £8.50-£15,
Service added but optional 12.5% **Wines** 200 bottles over
£30, 12 bottles under £30, 20 by glass **Notes** Vegetarian
menu, Dress restrictions, Smart casual, Civ Wed 40
Seats 100, Pr/dining room 18 **Children** Portions, Menu
Parking On street, NCP

Salt Yard

PLAN 2 J3

◉◉ Italian, Spanish

Top-notch tapas just off Tottenham Court Road

☎ 020 7637 0657

54 Goodge St W1T 4NA
e-mail: info@saltyard.co.uk
dir: Nearest station: Goodge St. Near Tottenham Court Rd

Part of a triumvirate of establishments where sharing is
king (see also The Opera Tavern and Dehesa), Salt Yard is
a lot of fun. It pulsates with positive energy. The cheerful
service team, laid-back, modish décor and Spanish-
Italian inspired food and wine combine to make a winning
formula. It takes a flexible approach, too, so you can

simply pop in for a glass of something in the first-floor
bar (reasonably-priced wines and an array of sherries
catch the eye) and partner it with some first-rate cured
meats or cheese, or stay a while in the thoroughly un-
oppressive basement and tuck into the likes of chargrilled
chicken with morcilla, pancetta and black bean stew. The
menu does not shy away from some of the great tapas
classics, so you can have your fill of tortilla and jamon
croquetas with Manchego, but this is a kitchen that is
prepared to cook a shoulder of lamb for seven hours and
partner it with roast rump, crushed pea and mint
vinaigrette, and serve up roast cod with warm mussel
escabèche.

Chef Benjamin Tish, Andrew Clarke **Owner** Sanja Morris &
Simon Mullins **Times** 12-3/5.30-11 Closed BHs, 10 days
Xmas, Sun **Prices** Prices not confirmed Service added but
optional 12.5% **Wines** 17 by glass **Notes** Vegetarian
available **Seats** 60 **Parking** NCP Cleveland St, meter
parking Goodge Place

Roka

LONDON W1

PLAN 2 J3

Japanese

Exquisite robata-grill cookery in London's Medialand

☎ 020 7580 6464

37 Charlotte St W1T 1RR
e-mail: info@rokarestaurant.com
dir: Nearest station: Goodge St, Tottenham Court Rd. 5
min walk from Goodge St

It seems a long time now since the London Japanese
dining scene was dominated by sober sushi restaurants
- these days, it rocks. There's another Roka in Canary
Wharf (see entry) and a third in Hong Kong, and it's a
sibling to the equally trend-setting Zuma (see entry).
These are über-cool places where the high-energy
atmosphere and sharp good-looks are not let down by the
food. Here in Charlotte Street - rather cool itself, it has to

be said - it all takes place in a light-filled corner-sited
venue, with full-drop glass doors that open out to create
a semi-alfresco vibe on sunny days, while outside,
pavement-side tables go the whole way. Inside, rich
hardwoods catch the eye under a warehouse-like ceiling,
while the thick grainy counter around the centrepiece
robata (charcoal) grill offers a ringside seat to all the
cheffy action. There's a tasting menu so you can submit
to a journey of the chef's choosing, or make your own way
with the help of the well-briefed service team. There's
sushi and sashimi (crispy prawn with avocado and dark
sweet soy, or soft-shelled crab with cucumber kimchi and
chilli mayonnaise) and everything is made with real skill
using wonderfully fresh and flavourful ingredients. The
robata grill serves up some pretty tantalising stuff such
as baby back ribs glazed with spiced master stock and
cashew nuts, or black cod marinated in yuzu miso.
There's also the likes of beef with ginger and sesame
dumplings, or rice hotpot with king crab and wasabi
tobiko. The craft and creativity carries on into desserts as

well, so you might find yoghurt and almond cake with
toffee banana and tonka bean ice cream. Downstairs in
the basement is the Shochu Lounge.

Chef Hamish Brown **Owner** Rainer Becker, Arjun Waney
Times 11.45-3/5.30-11 Closed 25 Dec **Prices** Prices not
confirmed Service added but optional 13.5% **Wines** 148
bottles over £30, 14 by glass **Notes** Average cost L/D
£50-£60, Vegetarian available, Dress restrictions, Smart
casual **Seats** 99 **Children** Portions, Menu **Parking** On
street, NCP in Brewers St

Sartoria
PLAN 2 J1

◎ Italian

Smart setting for modern Italian cooking

☎ 020 7534 7000 & 7534 7030
20 Savile Row W1S 3PR
e-mail: sartoriareservations@danddlondon.com
dir: Nearest station: Oxford Circus, Green Park, Piccadilly
Circus. Oxford Circus, exit 3, turn left down Regent St
towards Piccadilly Circus, 5th right into New Burlington
St, end of street on left

Named in honour of its location in the fine suiting and
booting world of Savile Row (the name is Italian for
tailor's shop), Sartoria is an immaculately turned-out
operation with a chic, Milanese-inspired interior and
switched-on, upbeat service from staff dressed to look
the part. On the menu is an earthy, uncomplicated roll-
out of creatively re-imagined modern Italian ideas.
Antipasti could take the shape of capon broth with
cappellacci 'Bishop's hat' ravioli, pumpkin and chestnut,
while pasta dishes run to Piemontese ravioli with sheep's
milk ricotta, spinach, walnuts and sage. Among main
courses might be braised lamb shank with celeriac purée,
or baked red mullet with spinach and gremolata, while
the dolci department offers layered Amedei chocolate
cake with passionfruit.
Chef Lukas Pfaff **Owner** D and D London
Times 12-3/5.30-11 Closed 24-26 Dec, 1-2 Jan, Etr Mon,
Sun (open for private parties only), L Sat **Prices** Fixed L 2
course £21, Fixed D 3 course £26, Starter £8.50-£21.50,
Main £16-£29, Dessert £6-£9.50, Service added but
optional 12.5% **Wines** 13 by glass **Notes** Pre-theatre
menu 5.30-7.30pm 2/3 course £15/£20, Vegetarian
available, Dress restrictions, Smart casual preferred, Civ
Wed 108 **Seats** 100, Pr/dining room 48 **Children** Portions
Parking On street

Scott's Restaurant
PLAN 2 G1

◎◎ British V

Bags of style and first-rate seafood

☎ 020 7495 7309
20 Mount St W1K 2HE
dir: Nearest station: Bond Street, Green Park. Just off
Grosvenor Sq, between Berkeley Sq & Park Ln

With its Mayfair address and art-deco good looks, Scott's
is quite the glamour puss. There are mosaics, huge
mirrors, oak-panelled walls, leather seats, and
impressive modern British artworks to catch the eye, plus
a menu brimming with top-notch seafood to enjoy. The
onyx-topped central crustacea bar sets the scene and
champagne is most definitely on the cards. There are
some meat and vegetarian choices on the menu, but
seafood is the thing. Those oysters might include
Lindisfarne rocks or West Mersea natives, whilst among
starters fried squid with chilli relish and lime shows the
style - fine fresh produce and careful execution. Seared

sea bass with lemon and herb butter hits the spot, or you
might push the boat out and go for lobster thermidor.
Among desserts, the Bakewell pudding with almond ice
cream is a bit of a show-stopper, as is the pear tarte
Tatin (if you've got a friend to share it with you). The
service is a bit of a highlight too.
Chef Dave McCarthy **Owner** Caprice Holdings
Times 12-10.30 Closed 25-26 Dec, 1 Jan, D 24 Dec
Prices Starter £7.75-£14.75, Main £18-£42, Dessert
£8.25-£9.75, Service added but optional 12.5%
Notes Sunday L, Vegetarian menu, Dress restrictions,
Smart casual **Seats** 120, Pr/dining room 40
Children Portions **Parking** NCP

Shogun, Millennium Hotel Mayfair
PLAN 2 G1

◎ Japanese

Traditional Japanese in a posh Mayfair hotel

☎ 020 7629 9400
Grosvenor Square W1A 3AN
e-mail: reservations.mayfair@millenniumhotels.co.uk
dir: Nearest station: Bond Street, Green Park. Located on
Grosvenor Square, within easy walking distance of Bond
Street and Green Park underground stations

Oddly secreted away in the rear courtyard of Grosvenor
Square's swanky Millennium Hotel, Shogun is an
unapologetically traditional Japanese outfit set in a
somewhat dated cellar. It does have a certain old-world
charm though, with its faux-stone wine cellar look
accessorised with heritage touches like a life-size
Samurai warrior statue, traditional prints and lantern
lighting, while unclothed tables are divided by display
racks of kyudo archery arrows. The simple, straight-up
traditional cooking fits the surroundings, the lengthy
roster fronted by a series of set house menus (perhaps
based around sashimi or tempura), otherwise, mains step
out with teriyaki of tuna, salmon, duck and Scotch sirloin,
or perhaps sliced pork fried with ginger or deep-fried
chicken. Among the Millennium's other dining options,
classy Italian Avista - see entry - is off the main foyer.
Chef Hiromi Mitsuka **Owner** Hiromi Mitsuka **Times** 6-11
Closed Mon, L all week **Prices** Prices not confirmed
Service added but optional 12.5% **Wines** 2 by glass
Notes Vegetarian available, Dress restrictions, Smart
Seats 60 **Children** Portions

Sketch (The Gallery)
PLAN 2 J1

◎◎◎ — see page 348

Sketch (Lecture Room & Library)
PLAN 2 J1

◎◎◎◎◎ — see page 349

Sketch (The Parlour)
PLAN 2 J1

◎◎ Modern European ✪

Art and eccentricity in Mayfair café and cocktail bar

☎ 020 7659 4500
9 Conduit St W1S 2XG
e-mail: info@sketch.uk.com
web: www.sketch.uk.com
dir: Nearest station: Oxford Circus, Green Park, Bond St.
From Oxford Circus, 5 min walk along Regent St, 4th
turning on right

A larger-than-life collaboration between French super-
chef Pierre Gagnaire and Mourad 'Momo' Mazouz, Sketch
spreads its whimsical wings around various eating and
drinking spaces in this arty, theatrical and totally
glamorous Mayfair playpen. In descending order of
fabulousness, the Lecture Room & Library, and The
Gallery (see separate entries) each have their singular
culinary and stylistic attractions for those whose pockets
have the necessary depth, while The Parlour is the entry-
level venue that serves as a funky place to see and be
seen all day long through breakfasts, informal lunches,
afternoon tea (with champers, why ever not?), before
morphing into an evening cocktail bar (members only
after 9). The one-off boudoir look involves an eccentric
mishmash of Louis XV antique chairs, sofas and divans,
crimson drapes and retro swirly designs. If you're doing
lunch, the all-day comfort food menu takes in everything
from French and Spanish charcuterie to beef cheek
bourguignon, or fishy ideas such as brandade with
parmesan and salmon roe. Cake fiends will revel in
chestnut gâteau or a hunk of something made with Agen
prunes poached in red wine and spices, and blackcurrant
marmalade.

Chef Pierre Gagnaire, Herve Deville **Owner** Mourad
Mazouz **Times** 12-10 Closed Xmas, 1 Jan **Prices** Starter
£8.50-£19, Main £12-£19, Dessert £5.50, Service added
but optional 12.5% **Wines** 23 bottles over £30, 4 bottles
under £30, 12 by glass **Notes** Vegetarian available
Seats 50 **Children** Portions, Menu **Parking** NCP Soho

Sketch (The Gallery)

LONDON W1   **PLAN 2 J1**

Modern European 🍷 NOTABLE WINE LIST

Virtuoso cooking in artist-designed restaurant

☎ 020 7659 4500
9 Conduit St W1S 2XG
e-mail: info@sketch.uk.com
web: www.sketch.uk.com
dir: Nearest station: Oxford Circus. 5 mins walk from station, take exit 3, along Regent St. Conduit St 4th on right

The Gallery's design by Turner Prize-winning artist Martin Creed was inspired by the 'boundaries of art and functionality', and he's created a truly unique environment. Walls are painted with strong lines, shapes and patterns of bright colours, the floor is a herringbone design in marble, and the furniture ranges from vintage to starkly modern designs. Staff, knowledgeable and chatty, are part of the artwork too, in their strongly patterned tops - as are the menus, with pop-up forks rising out as they're opened. 'Gastro-brasserie' is the restaurant's own description of its style, which seems to pay itself no favours, as Pierre Gagnaire's cooking is bold, imaginative and innovative. Twice-baked haddock soufflé with crunchy white cabbage salad sounds familiar enough, but another starter might bring on the complex flavours of an extravagant dish of foie gras terrine with girolles in vinegar, cranberry

chutney, quince paste and pistachios. Ingredients are impeccable, among them Dover sole meunière, Pyrenean lamb (braised, roasted and as a mini sausage), and wild venison (roast saddle, and shoulder in a stew), and world cuisines are plundered in the quest for originality, a quest that pays off handsomely with dishes like tomato concasse with coconut milk, lemongrass and ginger, marshmallow and burrata cheese ice cream, and fricassee of gambas with satay, avocado, turnip, pork scratchings, apple and mint. If the surroundings are a work of art, dishes can be too, particularly puddings which are triumphs of complementary flavours: try Manjari chocolate mousse with passionfruit and milk chocolate cream, coconut ganache and chocolate sorbet.

Chef Pierre Gagnaire, Herve Deville
Owner Mourad Mazouz
Times 12-2/6.30pm-2am Closed Xmas, New Year, BHs, L all week **Prices** Starter £12-£24, Main £16-£36, Dessert £8.50-£18, Service added but optional 12.5% **Wines** 85 bottles over £30, 9 bottles under £30, 15 by glass
Notes Vegetarian available, Dress restrictions, Smart casual, Civ Wed 650
Seats 150 **Children** Portions, Menu
Parking On street, NCP

Sketch (Lecture Room & Library)

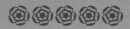

Modern European **V** NOTABLE WINE LIST

A dining experience like no other courtesy of a true French master

☎ 020 7659 4500
9 Conduit St W1S 2XG
e-mail: info@sketch.uk.com
web: www.sketch.uk.com
dir: Nearest station: Oxford Circus. 5 mins walk from station, take exit 3, along Regent St. Conduit St 4th on right

You could easily walk past Sketch on Mayfair's Conduit Street without even noticing it, such is its anonymous exterior (it's in a converted, cream-painted 18th century townhouse). But if you do get to the point of stepping inside, prepare to be blown away by the sheer wackiness of it all. There's a mixture of eating places within its four walls (see separate entries for The Gallery and The Parlour), but we're talking here about the cream of the crop, the Lecture Room & Library up on the first floor. There's a real sense of exclusivity to being escorted up the red and black staircase to the doors of the Lecture Room, which are then thrown open, almost Willy Wonka-style, to reveal the loud, colourful design of the elegantly proportioned Georgian space: think walls of studded cream leather, a hallucinogenic palette of orange, candy-pink, yellow and red, regularly-changing artwork, and other decorative objects such as giant, floor-standing vases and lantern-style lights. Some of the furniture has an air of the Middle East about it, which is more than likely thanks to the input of Algerian-born restaurateur Mourad 'Momo' Mazouz, creator of Sketch along with French super-chef Pierre Gagnaire. Tables are large but very well-spaced, and draped in white linen with the finest cutlery, glassware, and china you could

imagine. In the Lecture Room & Library all the menus - and there are several - are the work of the man himself (although he's not cooking here on a day-to-day basis), and if you need any help with deciphering them (as well you might), the friendly but highly professional staff are well-equipped to assist. Although first impressions might be of a rather whimsical place designed more to indulge its makers' fantasies than for the serious business of gastronomy, the cooking here is a thing of technical brilliance, with utterly complex but ultimately winning combinations of flavours and textures, and stunning presentations. Back to that choice of menus, there's a tasting menu and a vegetarian version, a truffle menu (with every dish featuring black truffle), the à la carte, and the gourmet rapide lunch - a steal at £40 for three courses including coffee and petits fours. From the à la carte, we're told that 'Perfume of the Earth' is inspired by one of Gagnaire's favourite perfumes, and consists of smoked cocotte of snails and vegetables, foie gras soup with white port, beef carpaccio, raw vegetables, beetroot syrup with Colman's mustard, sautéed Jerusalem artichokes, Sauternes jelly and baked ricotta - and that's just a starter. Follow on, perhaps, with skate wings meunière (superb quality fish, cooked with absolute precision) with steamed fennel with Dijon mustard, soft-boiled egg, Oscietra caviar and mackerel bouillon with seaweed, or perhaps go down a meatier path with a richly flavoured, harmonious dish of Challans duck with cinnamon and cumin sauce, red cabbage and blackcurrant marmalade, roasted foie gras, Morteau sausage, crunchy red onions, prune paste and Marguerite's potatoes. For the ultimate end to a meal it has to be 'Pierre Gagnaire's grand dessert', which consists of - deep breath... pink grapefruit marmalade, dragon fruit, candied red pepper, rose champagne granité, passionfruit, cream

cheese mousse, candied chestnut, shortbread, lemon and grappa sorbet, meringue, amarelli foam, candied lemon, coconut tapioca, roast pineapple, aloe vera, ginger, fresh coconut, kaffir lime, pear sorbet, Marc de gewürztraminer, milk chocolate, joconde cake, arabica coffee, gianduja, caramel with balsamic vinegar, chocolate sorbet, sharon fruit and tandoori. Food of this calibre doesn't come cheap, but for such labour-intensive culinary masterpieces, what would you expect?

Chef Pierre Gagnaire, Romain Chapel
Owner Mourad Mazouz **Times** 12-2.30/6.30-11 Closed 18-29 Aug, 23-30 Dec, 1 Jan, BHs, Sun-Mon, L Sat **Prices** Fixed L 2 course fr £35, Tasting menu £75-£95, Starter £33-£42, Main £43-£55, Dessert £13-£25, Service added but optional 12.5% **Wines** 730 bottles over £30, 70 bottles under £30, 20 by glass
Notes Tasting & Vegetarian tasting menu 6 course, Vegetarian menu, Civ Wed 50
Seats 50, Pr/dining room 24 **Children** Portions **Parking** NCP Soho, Cavendish Sq

LONDON W1 *continued*

Social Eating House   PLAN 2 J2

❀❀❀ – see below

So Restaurant   PLAN 2 J1

❀❀ Japanese

Modern Japanese with some top-notch European ingredients

☎ 020 7292 0767 & 7292 0760
3-4 Warwick St W1B 5LS
e-mail: info@sorestaurant.com
dir: Nearest station: Piccadilly Circus. Exit Piccadilly tube station via exit 1. Turn left along Glasshouse St. Restaurant next to The Warwick

Tucked away in Soho's hinterland just behind Piccadilly Circus, So is an unassuming but authentic, smart, modern Japanese. It spreads over two floors; a busy café-like ground floor with sushi bar and a more intimate, low-lit basement room. Laminate tables, an open-plan kitchen and a yobanyaki grill (where items are cooked over volcanic rocks imported from Mount Fuji) tick all the design boxes. The menu has a broad scope, from tempura (soft-shelled crab or squid), to sushi and sashimi, plus some European-inspired dishes; the kitchen makes good use of quality European produce, too, such as pan-fried foie gras served with Japanese mushrooms and teriyaki sauce, or half lobster meunière. There's fashionable stuff like black cod marinated in saikyo miso, too, plus good value West End lunch and bento box deals.

Chef Kaoru Yamamoto **Owner** Tetsuro Hama
Times 12-3/5.30-10.30 Closed Xmas-New Year, Sun
Prices Starter £3.50-£12, Main £14-£28, Dessert £5-£7.50, Service added but optional 12.5% **Wines** 25 bottles over £30, 16 bottles under £30, 8 by glass **Notes** Pre-theatre meal 3 course £19.95. Tasting menu 3 course, Vegetarian available **Seats** 70, Pr/dining room 6 **Parking** On street

The Square   PLAN 2 H1

❀❀❀❀ – see opposite

Sumosan Restaurant   PLAN 2 H1

❀❀ Japanese Fusion

Creative modern Japanese cooking

☎ 020 7495 5999
26B Albemarle St, Mayfair W1S 4HY
e-mail: info@sumosan.com
dir: Nearest station: Green Park. Between Dover St & Old Bond St

With a swanky Mayfair address - adjacent to Brown's Hotel and opposite The Royal Institute - Sumosan is a classy, fashionably modern Japanese restaurant with a clientele of international jet-setters and Mayfair beau monde, who come for some high-end Japanese grub. The décor is minimalist and neutrally toned, smart and contemporary, with pale-wood flooring, highly varnished wooden tables and designer lighting. The busy open kitchen puts out precisely cooked and well-dressed dishes from tip-top ingredients with some Western influences. There's highly accomplished sushi and sashimi, plus an extensive menu that runs to black cod with miso, toro stuffed with foie gras, or lamb chops furikaki, and, from the teppan-yaki, perhaps Wagyu beef with sweet potato purée. Head downstairs for pre-dinner cocktails in the bar, while a sommelier can guide you through the international wines and myriad of sake.

Chef Bubker Belkhit **Owner** Janina Wolkow
Times 12-3/6-11.30 Closed 26 Dec, New Year, L Sat-Sun
Prices Prices not confirmed Service added but optional 15% **Wines** 10 by glass **Notes** Fixed L 4, 7 course min £24.90, Tasting menu D 2 people, Vegetarian available, Dress restrictions, Smart casual **Seats** 100, Pr/dining room 32 **Parking** On street

Social Eating House

LONDON W1   **PLAN 2 J2**

Modern NEW

Informal, accessible dining in Soho courtesy of Jason Atherton

☎ 020 7993 3251
58-59 Poland St W1F 7NS
e-mail: reservations@socialeatinghouse.com
dir: Nearest station: Oxford Circus. Approx 4min walk N.W from Oxford Circus station

Anyone who's eaten at Pollen Street Social in Mayfair (see entry) will appreciate the fact that Jason Atherton is a chef who knows a thing or two about how to create a successful modern restaurant. And so it seems he's done it again over in Soho, where the Social Eating House is pulling in the punters left, right and centre for some perfectly pitched, vibrant, contemporary food, combined with a lively, buzzing atmosphere and comfortable, funky surroundings. The place is spread across three floors, with the restaurant (and a small bar) on street level, and the kitchen with 15-seat 'chef's bar' in the basement (along with the very attractively appointed toilets). The upper floor is given over to the trendy Blind Pig bar, where you can choose from an imaginative range of cocktails and some superior bar snacks, and where a floor-to-ceiling window at the front gives you a bird's-eye view of the comings-and-goings on the street below. Back to the restaurant proper, and the space is done out in a New York kind of style, with exposed brickwork, moss-green banquettes, mirrored ceiling, dark panelling and neon-signage. The man behind the accessibly-priced menu is Paul Hood, formerly Atherton's right-hand man at Pollen Street, who has developed a selection of dishes that at first glance appear quite simple, but in fact involve some serious skill in their execution. Kick things off with a 'jar to share' - perhaps a Middle-Eastern-inspired spiced aubergine with tomato and parsley, or meaty confit pork rillettes with grain mustard and cider vinegar - before a technically brilliant and powerfully flavoured ravioli of wild boar Bolognese, Berkswell, peppered hearts and kidneys. For the main event, lamb neck fillet is so tender it just melts in the mouth, and with its accompaniments of sheep's ricotta potato, monk's beard, garlic and parsley it's a dish to really savour. Baked curried hake - superb fresh fish - with roasted cauliflower and cheese makes a fine fishy alternative, while lemon curd pie with peppered pastry crumble, sour yoghurt sorbet and fennel provides a zingy, refreshing end to a memorable meal.

Chef Paul Hood **Owner** Paul Hood, Jason Atherton
Times 12-2.30/5.30-10.30 Closed 25-26 Dec, BH, Sun
Prices Fixed L 2 course £18, Starter £8.50-£10.50, Main £12-£23.50, Dessert £6.50, Service added but optional 12.5% **Notes** Dress restrictions, Smart casual **Parking** Soho or Broadwick masterpark

Save on Hotels. Book at **theAA.com/hotel**

LONDON, CENTRAL (W1) 351 ENGLAND

The Square

Modern French V NOTABLE WINE LIST

Shining star in the heart of Mayfair

☎ 020 7495 7100
6-10 Bruton St, Mayfair W1J 6PU
e-mail: reception@squarerestaurant.com
dir: Nearest station: Bond Street, Green Park

Philip Howard comes across as a cerebral chef, a thinker, and his vision of The Square has remained largely unchanged since it opened in 1991. He got it right first time around. That's 1991 - the year Michael Jackson was number one with *Black or White*, and the Booker Prize was won by Ben Okri's *Famished Road*. Sure the place has changed a little - a refurb here and there - but its essence remains the same, and the French-focused menu has kept with the times whilst steering clear of the many bandwagons that have passed by over the last 20 years or so. The room suits the Mayfair postcode but wears its luxe finish lightly, with its frosted glass and polished stone frontage, and striking abstract art on pearlescent walls within. The generously-spaced tables come clothed in crisp linen and the service team is a class act. Like all cooking at this level, the ingredients are of staggeringly high quality, everything selected at the peak of its seasonal perfect-ness. There is an undoubted classical soul here, with flavour combinations that inherently work, but be assured that the food feels contemporary, entirely of-the-moment and each dish is a joy to behold (and eat). Roast foie gras stars in a first course alongside a tarte fine of caramelised endive and burnt orange purée, whilst lasagne of Dorset crab with a cappuccino of shellfish and champagne foam is another starter which delivers technical perfection and an enticing balance of flavours. Glazed veal cheek with hand-rolled macaroni is another highlight (this kitchen can really make pasta) with crushed cauliflower, white asparagus and morels, or go for roast fillet of John Dory with crushed Jersey Royals, langoustine claws and a white asparagus velouté. Desserts are no less clearly focused and well crafted: banana soufflé, for example, with milk and granola ice cream, or new season's rhubarb with yoghurt parfait and vanilla. It is all creative and visually stunning enough to thrill from start to finish, and makes you resolve to save up and head back for the full-works tasting menu next time round. The thoroughly knowledgeable sommelier will help you find the right bottle from a head-spinning list of classic French heavyweights, with a remarkable showing from Burgundy.

Chef Philip Howard **Owner** N Platts-Martin & Philip Howard

Times 12-2.30/6.30-10.30 Closed 24-26 Dec, 1 Jan, L Sun, BHs **Prices** Fixed L 2 course £30, Fixed D 3 course £80, Tasting menu £105, Service added but optional 12.5% **Wines** 14 by glass **Notes** ALC 2/3 course £65/£80, Vegetarian menu, Dress restrictions, Smart casual, jacket & tie preferred **Seats** 75, Pr/dining room 18 **Children** Portions

Texture Restaurant

LONDON W1   **PLAN 2 F2**

Modern European V 🍷 NOTABLE WINE LIST

Creative and dynamic cooking with Icelandic soul

☎ 020 7224 0028
DoubleTree by Hilton Hotel, 34 Portman St W1H 7BY
e-mail: info@texture-restaurant.co.uk
web: www.texture-restaurant.co.uk
dir: Nearest station: Marble Arch, Bond St. On corner of Seymour St & Portman St

With a menu that brings a touch of Icelandic individuality to the modern European repertoire, plus its delicious champagne bar and a whizz-kid sommelier at the helm, Texture really is an address worth knowing about. Agnar Sverrisson (the Icelander, the chef-patron) and Xavier Rousset (the Frenchman, the wine guru) have developed a little empire over the last few years with their 28-50

wine bars bringing a welcoming pop to the London dining scene. It is here, though, where the pair have created a restaurant of class and confidence. Situated in the Mostyn Hotel, which is a grand Georgian building just off Oxford Street, the partnership is built on putting equal importance on food and wine. There are over 100 champagnes to choose from - the champagne bar at the front is a cool and sophisticated spot - and the wine list is a serious piece of work, too. The room itself is on a grand scale with high ceilings, ornate plasterwork, large windows and polished wooden floors, but, given the Scandinavian connections, there's nothing stuffy about it. The lightness of touch in first and main courses is in part down to the absence of cream and butter (that is saved for dessert!), and the technical skills on show are impressive. Start, perhaps, with Anjou pigeon, chargrilled and tender, with sweetcorn, shallots, bacon popcorn and red wine essence, or Scottish scallops céviche, Oscietra caviar, fennel and passionfruit. The cooking is distinguished by clear and harmonious flavours, textures

(of course) and creativity. Main-course organic duck breast with celeriac, bacon and Icelandic blueberries is a dish in perfect harmony, as is poached Cornish turbot with mussels, scallops, sea vegetables and bonito broth. The dairy products arrive at dessert stage: chocolate and Earl Grey ganache, perhaps, with Yorkshire rhubarb, milk ice cream and hazelnut crumbs. The set-lunch menu is terrific value and there are three tasting menus, including Scandinavian seafood and vegetarian versions. With its stellar wine list, and helpful sommelier to guide you, Texture is a compelling package.

Chef Agnar Sverrisson **Owner** Xavier Rousset & Agnar Sverrisson **Times** 12-2.30/6.30-11 Closed 2 wks Xmas, 2 wks Aug, 1 wk Etr, Sun-Mon **Prices** Prices not confirmed Service added but optional 12.5% **Wines** 500 bottles over £30, 6 bottles under £30, 14 by glass **Notes** Scandinavian fish tasting menu £68, Vegetarian menu, Dress restrictions, Smart casual **Seats** 52, Pr/dining room 16 **Children** Portions **Parking** NCP Bryanston St

Theo Randall

LONDON W1   **PLAN 4 G5**

Italian V 🍷 NOTABLE WINE LIST

Exciting Italian cooking in landmark hotel

☎ 020 7318 8747
Park Ln, 1 Hamilton Place, Hyde Park Corner W1J 7QY
e-mail: reservations@theorandall.com
dir: Nearest station: Hyde Park Corner, Green Park

Anyone who has followed the sparkling career path of Theo Randall - head chef and partner at Hammersmith's River Café (see entry) for a decade, and a stint at legendary Chez Panisse in California - will know that in spite of its über-glossy setting in Park Lane's InterContinental Hotel, his restaurant has its feet planted firmly in the rustic roots of Italian regional cooking. Refreshingly, despite its location on the ground floor of the soaring Hyde Park Corner landmark, it doesn't feel in

any way like a blandly corporate hotel restaurant either. It is a large and rather chic space, but not intimidatingly so: neutral walls hung with bright artwork and mirrors, and creamy green leather and darkwood chairs at crisply linen-clothed tables make it all very comfy and inviting, with a relaxed, easygoing feel. Randall's instinct for homing in on fresh, top-notch ingredients is kept sharp by regular trips to Italy. The daily-changing menu of rustic Italian cooking is driven by what's available from the markets or flown in each day, going straight to the earthy heart of things with flavours maxed out and the stamp of gutsy authenticity on each plate. Roll up your sleeves and dig in to the excellent freshly-made focaccia and bruschetta laden with olive oil, sweet cherry tomatoes and green herbs before opening with calamari in padella - pan-fried squid with fresh cannellini beans, chilli, anchovy, parsley and chopped rocket. As you'd rather hope, home-made pastas hit the spot - perhaps cappelletti stuffed with slow-cooked veal, pancetta, chanterelles and porcini mushrooms. The wood-fired oven

adds a deep caramelised dimension to a wood-roasted veal chop served with datterini tomatoes, spinach, fresh borlotti beans and vibrant salsa verde with a hint of mint. Pastry skills, as witnessed in an almond tart with roasted plums and crème fraîche, are outstanding, otherwise you might finish with pannacotta with brandy-marinated Agen prunes and hazelnut croquant.

Chef Theo Randall **Times** 12-3/6-11 Closed Xmas, New Year, BHs, Sun, L Sat **Prices** Fixed L 2 course £27-£30, Fixed D 3 course £33-£36, Tasting menu £65, Starter £12-£16, Main £27-£38, Dessert £7-£8, Service added 12.5% **Wines** 147 bottles over £30, 1 bottle under £30 **Notes** Sharing menu £55, Children's menu £8-£16, Vegetarian menu **Seats** 124, Pr/dining room 24 **Children** Portions, Menu

LONDON W1 *continued*

Tamarind
PLAN 4 H6

◎◎ Indian ☺

Classy, contemporary Indian cooking

☎ 020 7629 3561
20 Queen St, Mayfair W1J 5PR
e-mail: manager@tamarindrestaurant.com
web: www.tamarindrestaurant.com
dir: Nearest station: Green Park. Towards Hyde Park, take 4th right into Half Moon St to end (Curzon St). Turn left, 1st right into Queen St

Tamarind has been a hot ticket in the modern Indian fine-dining scene since the mid-90s. It may be in a basement, but this is Mayfair, so expect plenty of contemporary chic, with luxe hues of shimmering gold, bronze and silver and towering floral displays. Formally dressed staff and tables keep up sophisticated appearances, while a window onto the kitchen offers a glimpse of the action beyond. It impresses from the off with the opening gambit of poppadoms and chutneys a cut above the norm. Chef Alfred Prasad's food is inspired by the rich Mogul traditions of the Indian north-west, using top-drawer ingredients enhanced by sensitive spicing. Good use is made of the tandoor. A light, thoroughbred approach sees conventional thinking (rogan josh or Hyderabadi shank) lining up alongside the more innovative; pan-fried sea bass, for example, with fine beans and raw mango in a 'warmly spiced' sauce of tomato, mustard, curry leaves and coconut. Carte prices are on the high side, but lunch is a steal, and well-matched wines show that the attention to detail here runs deep.

Chef Alfred Prasad, Peter Joseph **Owner** Indian Cuisine Ltd **Times** 12-2.45/5.30-11 Closed 25-26 Dec, 1 Jan, L Sat **Prices** Tasting menu £56-£68, Service added but optional 12.5% **Wines** 134 bottles over £30, 2 bottles under £30, 14 by glass **Notes** Pre-theatre D £28.50 5.30-7pm, Sunday L fr £32, Vegetarian available, Dress restrictions, No jeans or shorts **Seats** 90 **Parking** NCP

10 Greek St
PLAN 3 A2

◎◎ Modern British NEW

Soho cool and good cooking too

☎ 020 7734 4677
10 Greek St W1D 4DH
e-mail: info@10greekstreet.com
dir: Nearest station: Charing Cross, Tottenham Court Rd. Approx 4min walk N from Tottenham Court Road station

There's no showboating here - not even a sign outside - but you should find it easy enough. The place has the fashionable insouciance that is endearingly all the rage in Soho these days - neutral colours, darkwood tables, old tiles, blackboards, some seating right on the pass, and simple food done really, really well. You gotta love it. The food is the star of the show, the ingredients take all the plaudits, but be assured the skill is to make this look easy. A starter of grilled asparagus with egg yolk ravioli and truffle oil says it all really, the yolk perfectly runny, the asparagus as fresh as a daisy. There's the likes of potted Dorset crab, too, with cucumber, mint and chilli, and main courses such as a whole lemon sole on the bone (wonderfully fresh) with samphire, fennel and sea radish, or Welsh Black beef with root vegetable mash, broccoli and horseradish. For pud, the chocolate pot with poached pear and vanilla cream is another winning dish.

Times 12-2.30/5.30-10.45 Closed Sun & some BH's, L bookings only **Prices** Prices not confirmed **Seats** Pr/dining room 12 **Parking** China Town, NCP Upper St Martins Lane

Texture Restaurant
PLAN 2 F2

◎◎◎ *– see opposite*

Theo Randall
PLAN 4 G5

◎◎◎ *– see opposite*

Time & Space
PLAN 2 H1

◎ British, European

Modish cooking amid Britain's scientific heritage

☎ 020 7670 2956
21 Albemarle St, Mayfair, Green Park W1S 4BS
e-mail: timeandspace@ri.ac.uk
dir: Nearest station: Green Park. In the Royal Institution of Great Britain building, close to underground

A contemporary London eatery that occupies the former library of the venerable Royal Institution in the heart of Mayfair, where you will also find the absorbing Michael Faraday Science Museum. Explore Britain's scientific heritage then relax over a meal at this sleek and modern restaurant, where old bookcases, glass cabinets displaying chemistry instruments, and a fine marble fireplace add an air of history and culture. Cooking is modern British and the menu offers a wide range of dishes, including some traditional favourites like London Pride battered fish and chips. Alternatively, try potted Severn and Wye smoked salmon, chicken liver parfait, cod in sweetcorn chowder with samphire, and Cambridge

burnt cream for pudding. The predominantly French wine list has a good range by the glass.

Chef Xavier Nicolau Oliver **Owner** Elior **Times** 12-3 Closed 24 Dec-3 Jan, Sat-Sun, D all week **Prices** Prices not confirmed Service added but optional 12.5% **Wines** 12 by glass **Notes** Vegetarian available, Dress restrictions, Smart casual **Seats** 50 **Children** Portions **Parking** Berkeley Square

Trishna
PLAN 2 G3

◎◎ Modern Indian V

The distinctive flavours of south-west India brought to Marylebone

☎ 020 7935 5624
15-17 Blandford St W1U 3DG
e-mail: info@trishnalondon.com
dir: Nearest station: Bond St, Baker St. S of Baker St station, along Baker St, 4th left after Marylebone Rd junct

Trishna's two small dining rooms are modern and minimalist in style, decorated in shades of blue and cream with wooden tables and chairs, pale oak flooring, and exposed bricks, with floor-to-ceiling windows opening on to the street in warm weather. This is where to head to for the coastal cuisine of south-west India, although the kitchen deploys British seasonal produce in its successful quest for authenticity. Dishes are designed to be shared, so diners can experience a mixture of flavours and styles. Lobster and shrimps with carom seeds, garlic and sweet chilli chutney, and broccoli and mushroom salad can precede the next wave: melt-in-the-mouth lamb, in a curry distinctively flavoured with cinnamon and coconut, crab with butter, pepper and garlic, and mixed seafood biryani. Vegetarians get a good deal, and desserts are taken seriously, among them light, well-made carrot halva topped with caramelised cashews with refreshing lychee sorbet.

Chef Karam Sethi **Owner** Karam Sethi **Times** 12-2.45/6-10.45 Closed 24-29 Dec, 1 Jan **Prices** Fixed L 2 course £17.50-£35, Tasting menu £20-£55, Starter £6.50-£13, Main £10-£22.50, Dessert £6.75-£8.50, Service added but optional 12.5% **Wines** 150 bottles over £30, 15 bottles under £30, 20 by glass **Notes** Early eve menu 4 course, Fixed D 5/7 course £38.50/£47.50, Sunday L £17.50-£40, Vegetarian menu **Seats** 65, Pr/dining room 12 **Parking** On street, NCP

Umu
PLAN 2 H1

◎◎◎ *– see page 354*

Umu

LONDON W1   PLAN 2 H1

Japanese **NOTABLE WINE LIST**

First-class Japanese dining off Berkeley Square

☎ 020 7499 8881
14-16 Bruton Place W1J 6LX
e-mail: reception@umurestaurant.com
web: www.umurestaurant.com
dir: Nearest station: Green Park, Bond St. Off Bruton St & Berkeley Sq

Past the modest entrance is a contemporary, uncluttered décor of dark and light wood furnishings, screens and mirrors, and subdued lighting, all as neat as a new pin. Executive chef Yoshinori Ishii certainly goes the extra mile for his guests, making all the tableware for the restaurant at his pottery wheel and painting watercolours for each new season to decorate the menu. And the menu in question has been reworked and refined by chef Ishii to focus more on the subtle nuances of Japanese cuisine and place greater emphasis on the provenance and integrity of the ingredients; he even goes fishing with new suppliers before agreeing to work with them in order to ensure the fish are caught via methods that preserve quality and minimise damage to marine wildlife, while all fish must be served within 24 hours of being caught. Such produce comes at a cost, of course. Perhaps gentler on the pocket might be one of the set-price lunches,

such as shokado bento, a bento box with a choice of grilled fish, poultry, seasonal simmered and cured dishes and a selection of sashimi, plus rice and home-made ice cream, sorbet or fruit. Timings are of pinpoint accuracy, and ingredients are from the top end of the quality spectrum, with some less common items amongst them. On the eight-wave kaiseki set-price menus (a good introduction to the culture), for instance, might be Cornish spider crab with quince purée and compôte and tosazu jelly; 'chain of winter flavours of burdock and kumquat, Jerusalem artichoke cake with blue tiger prawn'; and kabura-mushi (black Périgord truffle with abalone and scallops). Elsewhere, the accessible and comprehensive menu is split into 'today's market recommendations' (perhaps sake-steamed monkfish liver), a range of sushi and sashimi, soups and rice, vegetables, and a selection of dishes using Wagyu beef (perhaps tataki style - lightly charcoal-grilled, with vegetables and sesame-ponzu sauce) and wild Welsh eel - among them ibushi (smoked à la minute, with plum-shiso sauce). Desserts range from a cross-cultural version of tiramisù, to sticky toffee pudding with white miso ice cream.

Chef Yoshinori Ishii **Owner** Marlon Abela Restaurant Corporation
Times 12-2.30/6-11 Closed Xmas, New Year, BHs, Sun, L Sat **Prices** Starter £4-£28, Main £6-£65, Dessert £8-£14, Service added but optional 12.5%
Wines 650 bottles over £30, 1 bottle under £30, 28 by glass **Notes** Kaiseki menu £90, Vegetarian available
Seats 64, Pr/dining room 12
Children Portions **Parking** On street, NCP Hanover Hill

Save on Hotels. Book at theAA.com/hotel

LONDON, CENTRAL (W1) 355 **ENGLAND**

LONDON W1 *continued*

Vasco & Piero's Pavilion Restaurant

PLAN 2 J2

◉◉ Modern Italian

Seasonal Umbrian cooking in hospitable Soho favourite

☎ 020 7437 8774

15 Poland St W1F 8QE

e-mail: eat@vascosfood.com

dir: Nearest station: Oxford Circus. From station right towards Tottenham Court Rd, 5min right into Poland St. Restaurant on corner of Great Marlborough St & Noel St

If you're after some authentic Italian cooking and atmosphere, V & P's intimate, family-run restaurant won't disappoint. It's been a firm favourite in Soho for over 40 years now. Both the sunny Mediterranean décor and food are suitably unpretentious and to the point, with the unfussy Umbrian cooking concentrating on good quality ingredients (often imported from Italy) and allowing the flavours to shine through. Seasonality is celebrated with gusto here, so expect great things in the truffle season, and the likes of spring lamb will feature when at its best. Pasta is made in-house and the menus change twice daily, with good value early menus for post-work or pre-theatre brigades. Hand-made sea bass tortellini with fresh tomato, zucchini, carrots and celery is a fine version indeed, while strips of calves' liver and onions with sautéed cabbage also hits the spot. Finish with panettone bread-and-butter pudding with grappa-soaked raisins.

Chef Vasco Matteucci **Owner** Tony Lopez, Paul & Vasco Matteucci **Times** 12–3/5.30-10 Closed BHs, Sun, L Sat **Prices** Starter £6-£12, Main £14-£27, Dessert £6-£8.50, Service added but optional 12.5% **Wines** 35 bottles over £30, 19 bottles under £30, 12 by glass **Notes** Tasting menu on request, Vegetarian available, Dress restrictions, No shorts **Seats** 50, Pr/dining room 36 **Children** Portions **Parking** NCP car park opposite

Veeraswamy Restaurant

PLAN 2 J1

◉ Indian ⭐ NOTABLE WINE LIST

Reliable Indian cooking in long-established restaurant

☎ 020 7734 1401

Mezzanine Floor, Victory House, 99 Regent St W1B 4RS

e-mail: info@realindianfood.com

dir: Nearest station: Piccadilly Circus. Entrance near junct of Swallow St & Regent St, in Victory House

Veeraswamy opened its doors in 1926 and has been trading from the same premises ever since. The décor might have changed, but the turbans of the maharajas who frequented the restaurant are still on the walls and the silvered screens are still in place. Dishes are cooked to recipes that are true to their Indian roots, the kitchen uses good-quality raw materials, and the menu offers plenty of scope without being overly long. Monkfish tikka, and tandoor-baked venison with dates and tamarind are among the intriguing starters, and there's an option of sharing platters too. Among main courses, lamb biryani

sounds familiar enough, and others include raan akbari (baked lamb shank), lobster curry with coconut and mango, and grilled sea bass marinated in mint and cumin.

Chef Uday Salunkhe **Owner** R Mathrani, C & N Panjabi **Times** 12-2.30/5.30-11.30 Closed D 25 Dec **Prices** Fixed L 2 course £20-£27.50, Tasting menu £45-£75, Starter £6.75-£16.50, Main £19.50-£38.50, Dessert £7-£9, Service added but optional 12.5% **Wines** 18 by glass **Notes** Business L 2 course £27.50, ALC D only, Sunday L £24, Vegetarian available, Dress restrictions, Smart casual **Seats** 114, Pr/dining room 24 **Parking** On street after 8pm/wknds, NCP

Verru Restaurant

PLAN 2 G3

◉◉ Modern European

Inspired modern Baltic cooking in Marylebone village

☎ 020 7935 0858 & 07808 118191

69 Marylebone Ln W1U 2PH

e-mail: info@verru.co.uk

dir: Nearest station: Bond St, Baker St

Tucked just off Marylebone High Street, this pint-sized but perfectly formed restaurant delivers a delightful fusion of modern Baltic cooking, with Scandinavian and French overtones. Two small dining areas, one on street level and the other partially subterranean, deliver a smartly modish vibe with exposed brick and distressed glass blending with oak parquet flooring, pale-wood tables and leather seating in neutral-toned harmony. Oak wine racks and colourful photos of London life feature too, while well-pitched, friendly service negotiates the tight space and up-tempo atmosphere with aplomb. Chef-patron Andrei Lesment, who hails from Estonia, uses quality ingredients and cooks with a sure hand and a light modern touch. Kick off with an opener of Matjes herring and tartare with shaved fennel, pickled black radish and toasted Ryvita, and follow on with rump of lamb teamed with a samosa made from the shoulder meat, Jerusalem artichoke, spätzle, pine kernel, and bergamot preserve. Chocolate pavé with Kahlúa syrup is a finely tuned finale. Keenly-priced daily lunch and early-evening menus bolster the carte.

Chef Andrei Lesment **Owner** Andrei Lesment **Times** 12-3/6-10.30 Closed 25-26 Dec **Prices** Fixed L 2 course £15.95-£17.95, Fixed D 3 course £35-£45, Tasting menu £40, Starter £7.50-£9.95, Main £16.50-£22.50, Dessert £6.95, Service optional **Wines** 50 bottles over £30, 30 bottles under £30, 20 by glass **Notes** Pre-theatre menu daily 6-7pm £17.95, Sunday L, Vegetarian available **Seats** 26, Pr/dining room 8 **Children** Portions

Villandry

PLAN 2 H3

◉ French, European

Appealingly simple cooking in a foodie emporium

☎ 020 7631 3131

170 Great Portland St W1W 5QB

e-mail: contactus@villandry.com

dir: Nearest station: Great Portland Street, Oxford Circus. Entrance at 91 Bolsover St, between Great Portland St tube station & Oxford Circus

Thanks to new owners who have given the place a smart refurb, Villandry has voguish good looks. Billing itself as a grand café, it's an on-trend all-day food emporium, combining a café-bar with takeaway, a shop and patisserie counter, the 'red room' full of wines to drink in or take home, and a more formal restaurant at the rear. The flexible nature of the place means you can grab breakfast (eggs Benedict, say), have coffee and a pastry (salted caramel and walnut tart perhaps), moules frites with wine, or a full blown meal in the restaurant. Here, simple, sunny natured, French-Mediterranean dishes are prepared with a lightness of touch from seasonal produce. Tuck into something like cod with a high-impact chorizo crust, with wilted spinach, white beans and fresh tomatoes, or big-hearted Galloway fillet steak (28-day dry-aged) with chips and béarnaise. Dessert might deliver a pukka classic like apple tarte Tatin or warm chocolate fondant.

Times 12-3/6-10.30 Closed 25 Dec, Sun, BHs

Wild Honey

PLAN 2 H1

◉◉◉ – *see page 356*

The Wolseley

PLAN 4 J6

◉ Traditional European V ☺

Bustling landmark brasserie stylishly serving all day

☎ 020 7499 6996

160 Piccadilly W1J 9EB

e-mail: reservations@thewolseley.com

dir: Nearest station: Green Park. 500mtrs from Green Park station

Standing on the same glitzy strip of Piccadilly as The Ritz, The Wolseley is a landmark in its own right these days, and now has a gaggle of siblings: The Delaunay Colbert and Brasserie Zedel (see entries). A café-restaurant in the 'grand European tradition', everything is on a grand scale. It's big on glamour, atmosphere and art-deco style, with towering arches and pillars, dramatic chandeliers and marble floors. It bustles with life and is high on decibels, while battalions of well-drilled staff and all-encompassing menus keep up the tempo whatever the time of day. Breakfast serves up a full English or kedgeree among its many choices, and there are café and afternoon tea rosters to see you through the period between lunch and dinner. Crowd-pleasing timeless brasserie classics fill the lengthy lunch and dinner carte; from salad Niçoise to moules frites, wiener

continued

LONDON W1 *continued*

Holstein or duck confit with sautéed ceps and ratte potatoes. To finish, perhaps treacle tart or crème brûlée.

Chef Lawrence Keogh, Marc Benzimra **Owner** Chris Corbin & Jeremy King **Times** 7am-mdnt Closed D 24 Dec All-day dining **Prices** Starter £6.75-£24.75, Main £12.75-£32.75, Dessert £3.75-£8, Service added but optional 12.5% **Wines** 44 bottles over £30, 37 by glass **Notes** Sunday L, Vegetarian menu **Seats** 150, Pr/dining room 12 **Children** Portions **Parking** NCP Arlington St

Yauatcha
PLAN 2 J2

◉◉ Modern Chinese

Skilful dim sum in a trendy Soho address

☎ 020 7494 8888
15 Broadwick St W1F 0DL
e-mail: reservations@yauatcha.com
dir: Nearest station: Tottenham Court Rd, Piccadilly, Oxford Circus. On corner of Broadwick St & Berwick St

A contemporary dim sum tea house is how Yauatcha describes itself, and the tea house side of things greets you on the ground floor with an amazingly colourful array of pâtisserie. Down in the basement, however, things take a more glamorous turn, with bare brick walls studded with crucifix-shaped candle-lit mirrors, low-slung green leather banquettes at darkwood tables and a long, slim, illuminated fish tank (its occupants are not on the menu).

Staff are well versed in the extensive menu, which impresses with its excellent ingredients and intriguing blend of traditional Cantonese favourites and more esoteric contemporary compositions. Venison puffs are Wellington-style flaky pastry dim sum with notes of hoi sin, chilli and sesame, while more hardcore foodies might go for chicken feet in chilli black bean sauce. Larger plates also deliver full-throttle flavours - witness braised Somerset lamb with black pepper sauce, or for fish fans, there may be braised sea bass with shiitaki, bamboo shoots and wolfberry. Tea smoothies, unusual iced tea combinations and off-the-wall cocktails are the on-trend tipples of choice.

Times Noon-11.45 Closed 24-25 Dec

YMing Restaurant
PLAN 3 A1

◉ Traditional Chinese V 🏮

Chinese regional specialities in theatreland

☎ 020 7734 2721
35-36 Greek St W1D 5DL
e-mail: cyming2000@blueyonder.co.uk
dir: Nearest station: Piccadilly Circus. From Piccadilly Circus station, head towards Palace Theatre along Shaftesbury Av

The frantic bustle of Chinatown is close by this smart Soho Chinese, but Christine Yau's operation runs on helpful and friendly service that is a welcome change

from the infamously curt treatment meted out to diners across the other side of Shaftesbury Avenue. The setting is neat and clean, and the Cantonese and regional Chinese cooking reliably good, with a biblical carte from which to make your selection. Big mouth-filling flavours are driven by fresh, top-quality ingredients, while modern health-oriented sensibilities are assuaged by the use of leaner cuts and light oils. Authentic regional dishes start out with Beijing-style spare ribs spiced with cumin, black pepper, fennel seeds, garlic and fiery chillies, then move on to Shanghai with a 'treasure hunt' of pork, chicken, prawns and air-dried sausage. Elsewhere there's anise-flavoured gansu duck, or Tibetan garlic lamb.

Chef Tony Li Xiaosham **Owner** Christine Yau **Times** noon-11.45 Closed 25-26 Dec, 1 Jan, Sun (ex Chinese New Year) **Prices** Prices not confirmed Service added 10% **Wines** 20 bottles over £30, 18 bottles under £30, 8 by glass **Notes** Vegetarian menu, Dress restrictions, Smart casual **Seats** 60, Pr/dining room 25 **Parking** Chinatown car park

---

Wild Honey

LONDON W1   PLAN 2 H1

Modern European

Classy bistro cooking and great wines

☎ 020 7758 9160
12 Saint George St W1S 2FB
e-mail: info@wildhoneyrestaurant.co.uk
dir: Nearest station: Oxford Circus, Bond St

This younger sibling of Soho's Arbutus (see entry) may be in swanky Mayfair, but it puts on no airs and graces and sticks by its laudable ethos of serving up superb food at affordable prices. Run by the savvy team of chef Anthony Demetre and business partner Will Smith, tables are packed in fairly tightly, but that's just part of the equation that means prices aren't too Mayfair - in fact, if you want to get a taste of the action on a tighter budget, check out the lunch and theatre set menus, which are a

bit of a steal considering the postcode. But Wild Honey is not pitched at the bargain basement end of the market: the place was a gentlemen's club in its former life, and still exudes a certain blue-blooded clubbiness, as attested by its high ceilings, ornate plasterwork, and burnished wood panelling splashed with colourful contemporary art. At the heart of the action is a centrepiece onyx-topped bar with stools, otherwise red leather banquettes, yellow leather chairs and intimate booths sort out the seating. Anthony Demetre's food is confident, intelligent and skilfully crafted stuff that aims for full-throttle flavours from uniting high-end ingredients with more earthy items. Pressed chicken and eel terrine arrives with a deeply-flavoured chutney and toasted sourdough in a typically to-the-point starter, while main course delivers a simple, rather rustic risotto of Cornish silver mullet coloured vibrant green with parsley and well studded with mussels and shrimps. To finish, a classic bistro dessert of floating islands gets a novel spin from crunchy pink pralines inside light-as-air

meringue hovering in vanilla custard, but the perfectly ripened cheeses from La Fromagerie are also seriously tempting. Adding to the Gallic vibe, wines are available in 250ml carafes - a great way to match wines to individual dishes.

Chef Anthony Demetre **Owner** Anthony Demetre & Will Smith **Times** 12-2.30/6-11 Closed 25-26 Dec, 1 Jan **Prices** Fixed L 3 course £27, Fixed D 3 course £29.50, Starter £7.50-£15, Main £19.95-£34, Dessert fr £7, Service added but optional 12.5% **Wines** 45 bottles over £30, 6 bottles under £30, 50 by glass **Notes** Sunday L, Vegetarian available **Seats** 65 **Children** Portions **Parking** On street

LONDON W2

Angelus Restaurant   PLAN 2 D1

◉◉ Modern French 🏆 NOTABLE WINE LIST

Classy French brasserie with modish cooking

☎ 020 7402 0083
4 Bathurst St W2 2SD
e-mail: info@angelusrestaurant.co.uk
dir: Nearest station: Lancaster Gate, Paddington Station.
Opposite Royal Lancaster Hotel

A little piece of Parisian style near Hyde Park, Thierry Tomasin's brasserie de luxe has a good deal of charm. The art nouveau-inspired décor fits the bill with its original darkwood panelling, red leather banquettes and boudoir bar and lounge - in fact, it positively overflows with bonhomie. The cooking may well be founded in France, but there is plenty of modish thinking going on, and attention to detail is evident throughout. Start, perhaps, with spiced pork terrine with green peppercorns, apple glaze and a cider jelly, or tartlet filled with warm beetroot, Swiss chard and blue cheese. Next up, roast loin of venison with creamed kale, celeriac fondant and venison croustillante competes with sea bream with Szechuan sweet potato, sprout tops, clams and lemongrass. There's no less excitement in the desserts, where blood orange flavours a pannacotta and is served with a clementine consommé and orange tuile, or end on a savoury note with British and French cheeses with apple chutney and toasted hazelnut and prune bread.

Chef Joe Howley **Owner** Thierry Tomasin
Times 10am-11pm Closed 23 Dec-4 Jan **Prices** Fixed L 2 course £20, Tasting menu £75, Starter £10-£15, Main £20-£29, Dessert £9-£14, Service added but optional 12.5% **Wines** 600 bottles over £30, 16 bottles under £30, 4 by glass **Notes** Sunday L £20-£25, Vegetarian available **Seats** 40, Pr/dining room 22 **Children** Portions **Parking** On street

Assaggi   PLAN 2 A1

◉ Italian

Straightforward Italian dishes in relaxed surroundings

☎ 020 7792 5501
39 Chepstow Place W2 4TS
e-mail: nipi@assaggi.demon.co.uk
dir: Nearest station: Notting Hill Gate

Assaggi occupies a first-floor room above Georgian restaurant, Colchis (see entry). It may be possible to confuse the two entrances, though hardly the cuisine styles, since Assaggi has for years traded in the simple, straightforward Italian food that became popular with the first wave of Mediterranean cooking in Britain in the 1990s. The décor is minimal, rough-and-ready even, but by no means uncomfortable, and the relaxed air of contentment that pervades the place tells its own story. Simple classics are done with consummate brio, such as oozy burrata sandwiched by slices of grilled aubergine, or tip-top fritto misto comprised of mullet, sole, prawns and squid on straw potatoes and greens. The day's selection of desserts might furnish forth impressive, high-octane

chocolate torte, served warm with vanilla ice cream. Carta di musica crispbread and focaccia with good olive oil start things off well, and the wine list is teeming with fine Italian choices.

Chef Nino Sassu **Owner** Nino Sassu, Pietro Fraccari
Times 12.30-2.30/7.30-11 Closed 2 wks Xmas, BHs, Sun **Prices** Prices not confirmed Service optional **Wines** 6 by glass **Notes** Vegetarian available **Seats** 35 **Children** Portions

Le Café Anglais   PLAN 2 B1

◉ Modern British

Classic brasserie cooking in a beautiful art-deco room

☎ 020 7221 1415
8 Porchester Gardens W2 4DB
e-mail: info@lecafeanglais.co.uk
dir: Nearest station: Bayswater, Queensway

As far as surprises are concerned, finding Le Café Anglais up on the first floor of Whiteley's shopping centre in Queensway is as pleasant as they come. Entering via the street or through the mall itself, Rowley Leigh's take on a French bistro (of the de luxe variety for sure) is brimful of art-deco style and even a touch of glamour. The open-plan kitchen ensures the place buzzes with life and energy, and the appealing smells drifting across the room make choosing what to order even harder. There are oysters (fines de Claire, perhaps), birds cooked on the rotisserie (pheasant with apples and sprout tops), and Thai green curry and steak and kidney pie to emphasise the egalitarian nature of the place. Cheeses are of course both English and French, and desserts might include a classic tarte Tatin or quince and sherry trifle.

Chef Rowley Leigh **Owner** Rowley Leigh & Charlie McVeigh
Times 12-3.30/6.30-10.30 Closed 25-26 Dec, 1 Jan
Prices Fixed L 2 course £20, Fixed D 3 course £29.50-£45, Starter £5-£12.50, Main £9.50-£32.50, Dessert £6-£9.50, Service added but optional 12.5% **Wines** 60 bottles over £30, 10 bottles under £30, 14 by glass **Notes** Sunday L, Vegetarian available **Seats** 120, Pr/dining room 26 **Children** Portions, Menu **Parking** 120

Colchis   PLAN 2 A1

◉ Modern European

A taste of Georgia in trendy Notting Hill

☎ 020 7221 7620
39 Chepstow Place W2 4TS
e-mail: info@colchisrestaurant.co.uk
dir: Nearest station: Notting Hill Gate, Bayswater. From Notting Hill Gate take Pembridge Garden, then Pembridge Square, then Chepstow Place

A revamped pub below the well-known Italian restaurant Assaggi (see entry) is home to this newcomer exploring the food and wine of Georgia - that's the East European country, not the US state. It's a stylish, light, contemporary place with little to announce its Georgian influences until you view the menu. Up front is an all-day bar with feature wine wall display and brass-topped bar counter, plus a mix of low and high tables, chairs and

banquettes. Colours are neutral, seat coverings leather, suede and fabric, while quirky lighting catches the eye. The dining room (to the rear) follows the theme and colour palette, with the dinner carte delivering authentic staples like khinkali (Georgian dumplings with mince beef and pork, eaten by nibbling a small hole in one side then sucking out the warm broth before eating the filling) or lobio mchadit (black-eyed bean stew with corn cakes), to the more Western-inspired sea bass with grilled vegetables. The small plates and sharing platters are a hit, and the wine list includes some Georgian numbers.

Chef Paul Cosgrove **Owner** Paata Lemonzhdava
Times 12-2/6-11 Closed L Mon-Fri **Prices** Starter £7-£9.50, Main £14-£21, Dessert £7-£7.50, Service added but optional 12.5% **Wines** 20 bottles over £30, 5 bottles under £30, 6 by glass **Notes** Sunday L £25-£45, Vegetarian available **Seats** 60 **Children** Portions **Parking** Bayswater Car Park

El Pirata Detapas   PLAN 2 A2

◉ Modern Spanish 🟢

Classy, creative tapas and a good buzz

☎ 020 7727 5000
115 Westbourne Grove W2 4UP
e-mail: info@elpiratadetapas.co.uk
dir: Nearest station: Notting Hill Gate. Located junct Westbourne Grove & Hereford Rd

This offshoot of El Pirata in Mayfair gives off infectiously buzzy vibes in a long, sleek room done out with elbow-to-elbow darkwood tables, and a bar counter at the back that hits the spot for the trendy Westbourne Grove and Notting Hill crew. Things are buzzing away in the kitchen too, which serves up authentic Spanish flavours in its cracking repertoire of on-trend tapas dishes. Iberian hams are hanging in the basement just waiting to be carved, and if everyone at the table is up for it, there are keenly-priced tasting menus. You could stay with tried-and-tested sunny Spanish flavours - charcuterie and cheese platters, grilled prawns with garlic olive oil and parsley - or go for something more contemporary like pork cheeks with braised shallots and carrot purée, or wood pigeon with fig purée, red cabbage and red wine jus.

Chef Omar Allishoy, Esperanza Mateos **Owner** Detapas Restaurant Ltd **Times** 12-3/6-11 Closed 25-26 & 31 Dec, D 24 Dec **Prices** Fixed L 2 course £21-£25, Tasting menu £21-£25, Starter £3-£10, Main £11-£15, Dessert fr £4.50, Service added but optional 12.5% **Wines** 15 by glass **Notes** Chef menu £25, Degustation menu £21 fr £9.95, Vegetarian available **Seats** 90, Pr/dining room 30 **Children** Portions **Parking** Queensway

LONDON W2 *continued*

Island Restaurant & Bar

PLAN 2 D1

◉◉ Modern European 🌿

Polished brasserie-style cooking with Hyde Park views

☎ 020 7551 6070

Lancaster London Hotel, Lancaster Ter W2 2TY
e-mail: eat@islandrestaurant.co.uk
web: www.islandrestaurant.co.uk
dir: Nearest station: Lancaster Gate. Adjacent to
Lancaster Gate station, 5 min walk to Paddington Station

The Island Grill at this modern hotel cocoons diners from
the roar of the traffic on the one-way system outside. It's
a well-groomed sort of place, with a smart contemporary
décor, floor-to-ceiling windows looking over Hyde Park
(and the traffic) and a brasserie-style menu. Influences
are plucked from near and far: chargrilled smoked
chicken breast, for instance, is served in a salad with
avocado, pomegranate, baba ganoush and flatbread, and
crisp-fried squid with tomato and chilli jam and
preserved lemons. Traditionalists will be pleased with a
retro main course of veal Holstein, but more
representative of what the kitchen is capable of in terms
of imagination and skill is perhaps a braised faggot and
haggis mash to accompany grilled pork cutlet, and
crabcake with red pepper salsa and a salad of pequillo
peppers, radicchio and pickled shallots. To crown a meal
might be home-made Eccles cake with maple custard, or
the enticement of baked vanilla custard with coffee
bavarois, Valrhona chocolate sorbet and crushed
amaretti.

Chef Eibhear Coyle **Owner** Khun Jatuporn
Sihanatkathakul **Times** 7am-10.30pm **Prices** Fixed L 2
course fr £9.50, Fixed D 3 course £20-£25, Starter
£5.25-£7.95, Main £8.55-£17.95, Dessert £4-£5.50,
Service added but optional 12.5% **Wines** 10 bottles over
£30, 8 bottles under £30, 6 by glass **Notes** Sunday L,
Vegetarian available **Seats** 68 **Children** Portions, Menu
Parking Hotel or on street

Nipa

PLAN 2 D1

◉◉ Thai

**Precise Thai cooking in an authentic setting
overlooking Hyde Park**

☎ 020 7551 6039

Lancaster London Hotel, Lancaster Ter W2 2TY
e-mail: nipa@lancasterlondon.com
dir: Nearest station: Lancaster Gate. Adjacent to
Lancaster Gate station, 5 min walk to Paddington Station

Twinned with the homonymous Nipa at The Landmark
Hotel in Bangkok, The Lancaster's version is one of fewer
than 20 Thai restaurants in the UK to receive its home
country's Thai Select award. A panoramic window
overlooks Hyde Park, while the décor does its best to
persuade you, via carved wooden artefacts, orchids and
chopsticks, that you've been beamed to Southeast Asia.
The impression is helped along by the uniformly excellent
Thai staff, standing ready to offer unpatronising
guidance through the menus for non-initiates. Fire up the

taste buds with pancake-wrapped balls of minced
chicken and peanuts, served with mango salad, or crisp-
fried prawn cake with chilli plum sauce, before
progressing to a bowl of scorching-hot tom yum kai soup.
Main dishes are timed and spiced with flawless precision,
as in roast duck with pineapple and holy basil in coconut
broth, and stir-fried chicken with chilli and basil. A range
of set menus offers a good introduction, and meals can
end with the unexpected, such as a steamed banana
cake with sugared flaked almonds and ginger ice cream.

Chef Nongyao Thoopchoi **Owner** Lancaster London
Times 12-2/6.30-10.30 Closed 25 Dec, 1 Jan, L Sat-Mon
Prices Fixed L 2 course fr £12.95, Starter £6.50-£8.50,
Main £8.50-£16, Dessert £7, Service added but optional
Wines 23 bottles over £30, 8 bottles under £30, 21 by
glass **Notes** 4 course D £29-£34, Vegetarian available,
Dress restrictions, Smart casual **Seats** 55
Children Portions, Menu

LONDON W4

Hedone

PLAN 1 D3

◉◉ Modern European NEW

Chiswick temple to superb produce cooked with flair

☎ 020 8747 0377

301-303 Chiswick High Rd W4 4HH
e-mail: Aurelie@hedonerestaurant.com
dir: Nearest station: Chiswick Park, Gunnnersbury

It may be located at the less fashionable end of Chiswick
High Road, but don't be fooled, this is a restaurant with
serious credentials. The man behind it is food blogger
and ingredient-expert-turned-chef Mikael Jonsson, whose
background defines his kitchen's philosophy: to cook with
only the finest seasonal produce. Thus menus change
daily, and dishes show an intelligent simplicity and
balance, allowing those prime ingredients to shine. It's
hard to stop eating the home-baked sourdough bread,
but you wouldn't want to be too full to do justice to a
starter like poached Cornish rock oysters (wonderfully
fresh and juicy) with Granny Smith apple and shallots,
followed by pan-fried Dorset wild turbot (a fine specimen)
teamed with baby artichokes, white piattoni beans and
the sweetest, juiciest confit marinda tomatoes you'll likely
ever experience. Succulent English spring lamb (timed to
pink perfection) comes with Italian peas, salsa verde,
lardo di Colonnata and wonderful smoked Jersey Royals
with potato-skin foam (worth coming for alone). Desserts
are equally well-crafted: 'lemon variations' is a lovely
light, millefeuille-style confection of perfect meringue
and alternate lemon cream layers topped with lemon jelly
inset with lemon balm leaves and lemon shards, and
accompanied by lemon-infused milk yoghurt. It all takes
place in a modern, pared-back room with an open
kitchen, where the service is slick but relaxed, and the
atmosphere constantly buzzing.

Times 12-2.30/6.30-9.30 Closed Sun-Mon, L Tue-Wed
Prices Fixed L 3 course £35, Fixed D 3 course £55
Notes Tasting menus available with wine pairing
Seats Pr/dining room 16

High Road Brasserie

PLAN 1 D3

◉ European

Buzzy brasserie serving good, honest food all day

☎ 020 8742 7474

162 Chiswick High Rd W4 1PR
e-mail: cheila@highroadhouse.co.uk
dir: Nearest station: Turnham Green. Exit station, left
onto Turnham Green Terrace (B491). Left onto Chiswick
High Rd

A Soho House Group outfit (see also entry for Cecconi's),
the High Road Brasserie is a typically stylish, on-trend
hotspot on Chiswick's main drag. Awnings shield plenty
of pavement tables for alfresco dining, while inside the
fashionable brasserie look is brought together with
darkwood panelling, a patchwork of coloured floor tiles,
marble-topped bar and smart lighting. The place is open
all day, from breakfast to dinner and everything in-
between, and the please-all modern European menu
takes simplicity and good quality ingredients as its
watchwords. Get started with a small plate or two
(perhaps salt cod croquettes), moving on to a
straightforward chicken, bacon and avocado salad, or
mackerel Niçoise. Then, for the main event, cod, fine
beans and café de Paris butter, or perhaps another
classic done well in the form of fillet steak with béarnaise
and fries.

Chef Jesse Dunford Wood **Owner** Soho House Group
Times 7-mdnt All-day dining **Prices** Prices not confirmed
Service added but optional 12.5% **Notes** Breakfast, daily
specials, Sunday L, Vegetarian available **Seats** 120
Children Portions, Menu

Restaurant Michael Nadra

PLAN 1 D3

◉◉ Modern European

Classy modish cooking in Chiswick

☎ 020 8742 0766

6/8 Elliott Rd, Chiswick W4 1PE
dir: Nearest station: Turnham Green

An Edwardian villa with shop-front windows looking onto
the road is home to Michael Nadra's restaurant. You
might describe it as a neighbourhood restaurant, but
don't go thinking it is parochial in any way, for this is a
classy address with some well-crafted food on offer.
Burnished wooden tables come set with crisp white linen
napkins, and leatherette banquettes and chairs give a
touch of urban chic. The menu is packed with good ideas
that manage to be sophisticated and clearly focused at
the same time. Black tiger prawn, scallop and chive
dumplings, for example, come with a delicious spinach
and broccoli velouté and crisp red onions to start, whilst
for main course roasted cod is partnered with ratte
potatoes, samphire, fennel salad and chervil cream. The
quality of the ingredients and the composition of dishes
is spot on. And there's no less craft and creativity at
dessert stage: blueberry and almond sponge, perhaps,
with Greek yoghurt sorbet and blueberry granité. There's
a sister Restaurant Michael Nadra in Primrose Hill (see
entry).

Chef Michael Nadra **Owner** Michael Nadra
Times 12-2.30/6-10 Closed Xmas, 1 Jan, D Sat
Prices Fixed L 2 course fr £19.50, Fixed D 3 course fr £35,
Tasting menu £39-£49, Service added but optional
12.5% **Wines** 16 by glass **Notes** Tasting menu available
6 course, Sunday L, Vegetarian available, Dress
restrictions, Smart casual **Seats** 55 **Children** Portions
Parking On street

Sam's Brasserie & Bar   PLAN 1 D3

◉ Modern European

All-day brasserie in a factory conversion

☎ 020 8987 0555
11 Barley Mow Passage, Chiswick W4 4PH
e-mail: info@samsbrasserie.co.uk
web: www.samsbrasserie.co.uk
dir: Nearest station: Chiswick Park, Turnham Green.
Behind Chiswick High Rd, next to green, off Heathfield
Terrace

Exposed girders, pipes and bare brickwork are a nod to
this buzzy neighbourhood brasserie's former life as a
paper factory. Of course, the postcode is rather des-res
these days, tucked away just off Chiswick High Road, so
the look goes for a loft-style urban edge in its bare pale
wood tables and menus with something for all-comers
printed on brown paper table mats. It's easy to see the
appeal of the place: the big bar provides a tempting
diversion on entering the large, open-plan space before
moving on to the mezzanine dining area, where chatty
staff dressed sharply in long black aprons and white
shirts keep things ticking over nicely, and the kitchen is
open to view. Quality ingredients are deployed with
aplomb in a starter of lamb's belly fritters with pumpkin
purée and salsa verde, then a splendid crisp-skinned
slab of line-caught Atlantic cod arrives with buttered
leeks, clams, and chervil pesto. Two- and three-course
set menus deliver top value for the bargain hunter.

Times 9am-10.30pm Closed 25-26 Dec

La Trompette   PLAN 1 D3

◉◉ Modern European 🍷 NOTABLE WINE LIST

Assured modern French cooking in Chiswick

☎ 020 8747 1836
5-7 Devonshire Rd, Chiswick W4 2EU
e-mail: reception@latrompette.co.uk
dir: Nearest station: Turnham Green. From station follow
Turnham Green Terrace to junct with Chiswick High Rd.
Cross road & bear right. Devonshire Rd 2nd left

One of the trio of high-achieving operations that takes in
Wandsworth's Chez Bruce and Kew's Glasshouse (see
entries), La Trompette has been delighting the residents
of this well-heeled Chiswick enclave for over a decade.
The place is looking smart as a button after a recent
refurb, the cooking is still firmly rooted in France, and
while there may be a degree of rusticity to it, it's neither
clumsy nor prissy. Ravioli of suckling pig with grilled
turnip tops, pickled walnuts and creamy bacon sauce
sets out in fine style, delivering balance and full-bore
flavours, before main course brings on an equally
intensely flavoured and perfectly cooked slow-roasted
short rib of beef with smoked bone marrow, scorched
shallots, and field mushrooms. Fish main courses come
in for similarly robust treatments, perhaps pairing roast
John Dory with black rice, broccoli, Dorset crab and
tarragon. Attention to detail is impressive all the way
through to a dessert of chocolate millefeuille with salted
caramel mousse and roast pear.

Chef Rob Weston **Owner** Nigel Platts-Martin, Bruce Poole
Times 12-2.30/6.30-10.30 Closed 25-26 Dec, 1 Jan
Prices Fixed L 2 course £23.50-£27.50, Fixed D 3 course
fr £45, Service added but optional 12.5% **Wines** 450
bottles over £30, 100 bottles under £30, 15 by glass
Notes Sunday L, Vegetarian available **Seats** 88, Pr/dining
room 16 **Children** Portions **Parking** On street

Le Vacherin   PLAN 1 D3

◉◉ French 🍷

French classics in smart, relaxed neighbourhood bistro

☎ 020 8742 2121
76-77 South Pde W4 5LF
e-mail: info@levacherin.com
dir: Nearest station: Chiswick Park. From Chiswick Park
tube station turn left, restaurant 400mtrs on left

There's plenty of Gallic bonhomie over in Chiswick in the
form of Le Vacherin, a restaurant named in honour of a
fine French cheese or an iconic dessert, depending,
perhaps, on which is your favourite. It looks the part with
its polished-wood floors, burgundy leather banquettes
and mirror-friezes on cream walls hung with French-
themed posters, and the kitchen's output doesn't let the
side down either. If a judge of a good restaurant is doing
the simple things well, a plate of sautéed new season's
ceps with garlic and parsley is a very good sign indeed.
There's Bayonne ham with remoulade and classic onion
soup, too, and main courses such as confit duck leg with

Puy lentils and fillet of sea bass with salsify and
samphire. Wild rabbit with Morteau sausage and Dijon
mustard is a good dose of rustic authenticity, and, for
dessert, iced prune and Armagnac parfait or a good old
crème brûlée hit the spot. The prix-fixe menu is
particularly good value in any language.

Chef Malcolm John **Owner** Malcolm & Donna John
Times 12-3/6-11 Closed New Year & BHs, L Mon
Prices Fixed L 2 course £18.50-£22.50, Starter
£6.50-£13.50, Main £16-£23, Dessert £5.50-£13, Service
added but optional 12.5% **Wines** 200 bottles over £30,
15 bottles under £30, 12 by glass **Notes** Steak & wine
offer £9.95 Mon-Thu/Sun before 8pm, Sunday L £20-£25,
Vegetarian available, Civ Wed 70 **Seats** 72, Pr/dining
room 36 **Children** Portions **Parking** On street (metered)

LONDON W5

Charlotte's Place   PLAN 1 C3

◉◉ Modern European NEW V 🌱

Splendid seasonal food in a neighbourhood gem

☎ 020 8567 7541
16 St Matthews Rd, Ealing Common W5 3JT
e-mail: restaurant@charlottes.co.uk
dir: Nearest station: Ealing Common, Ealing Broadway

This sparkling neighbourhood bistro has impeccable
ethical credentials, sourcing its materials from like-
minded local suppliers and working in tune with the
seasons to ensure there's always something to catch the
interest on its breezy modern menus. The setting suits the
food: an unpretentious yet stylish blend of black leather
seats at unclothed darkwood tables on well-trodden
wooden floors, all framed by plain cream walls hung with
colourful prints. Top-notch pastry skills distinguish a
splendid tart of line-caught mackerel matched with a
lively accompaniment of olives, peppers, parmesan,
anchovy and balsamic. A Mediterranean warmth infuses
a main course of well-timed hake teamed with braised
octopus, sautéed potatoes, chorizo and croûtons cooked
in chorizo oil, all rounded off with a punchy salsa verde;
meat comes in for robust treatment - perhaps onglet skirt
steak with bone marrow fritter, celeriac, roast onions and
sauce Bordelaise. In summer, English raspberries are
showcased fresh and as a coulis to go with a wobbly
pannacotta pointed up with mint, Moscato d'Asti jelly and
a Breton biscuit.

Chef Greg Martin **Owner** Alex Wrethman
Times 12-3/6-9.30 Closed 26 Dec, 1 Jan, D 25 Dec
Prices Fixed L 2 course £16.95-£20.95, Fixed D 3 course
£29.95, Service added but optional 12.5% **Wines** 121
bottles over £30, 25 bottles under £30 **Notes** Early D daily
6-7pm 3 course & aperitif £26.95, Sunday L, Vegetarian
menu **Seats** 54, Pr/dining room 20 **Children** Portions
Parking On street

LONDON W5 *continued*

Crowne Plaza London - Ealing PLAN 1 C4

◉ Modern British, European
- -
Alluring British brasserie dishes in a stylish (on the inside) hotel

☎ 020 8233 3278
Western Av, Hanger Ln, Ealing W5 1HG
e-mail: west5@cp-londonealing.co.uk
web: www.cp-londonealing.co.uk
dir: Nearest station: Hanger Lane. A40 from central London towards M40. Exit at Ealing & North Circular A406 sign. At rdbt take 2nd exit signed A40. Hotel on left

If the Hanger Lane gyratory system can be said to have a distinguishing feature, the Crowne Plaza Ealing would be it. To be fair, it's a bit of an anonymous lump from the outside, but the public rooms are considerably more stylish than you may be led to expect. A dripping chandelier in the lobby and a bar upholstered in lavender lead on to the neutral but smart West 5 Brasserie, where modern dishes in the British idiom make up an alluring menu that doesn't just stick to the tried-and-tested. A crab terrine is served warm to emphasise its Gruyère content, and is offset by a pleasant cloudy citrus jelly, while mains run to whole baked mackerel with fennel and lemongrass citrus butter, or rosemary-crusted rack of lamb with a faggot of the shank meat, celeriac rösti, steamed cabbage and redcurrant jus. Fruity notes

continue into desserts such as passionfruit brûlée tart with coordinating sorbet.

Chef Ross Pilcher **Owner** Pedersen (Ealing) Ltd **Times** 12-9.45 Closed D 31 Dec **Prices** Prices not confirmed Service optional **Wines** 9 by glass **Notes** Vegetarian available **Seats** 106, Pr/dining room 60 **Children** Portions, Menu **Parking** 82

LONDON W6

Anglesea Arms PLAN 1 D3

◉ Modern British
- -
Superior cooking in pioneering gastro-pub

☎ 020 8749 1291
35 Wingate Rd, Ravenscourt Park W6 0UR
dir: Nearest station: Ravenscourt Park, Goldhawk Rd, Hammersmith. From Ravenscourt Park tube, walk along Ravenscourt Rd, turn left onto Paddenswick then right onto Wellesley Rd

The Anglesea was one of the pioneering London gastro-pubs, and its successful formula means it's as popular today as it ever has been: a buzzy, laid-back atmosphere, a flexible approach (eat as much or as little as you like) and good, honest, unfussy but appealing cooking that bats well above the weight of other establishments. The daily-changing menu is brimful of interesting ideas, sending people into dithering over starters like cured

trout with fennel and watercress salad, or a tartlet of sautéed lamb's kidneys with Swiss chard. Technical accuracy and well-judged combinations mark out the cooking, seen in main courses like cod fillet with sautéed bacon, Cornish mids and turnip tops, and lamb loin and shepherd's pie with carrots and cabbage. Finish with traditional apple crumble with custard or something like rhubarb trifle.

Chef Philip Harrison **Owner** Michael Mann, Jill O' Sullivan **Times** 12.30-2.45/7-10.30 Closed 25-27 Dec **Prices** Starter £5.95-£9, Main £9.50-£22, Dessert £5.50-£7.50, Service optional, Groups min 6 service 12.5% **Wines** 38 bottles over £30, 17 bottles under £30, 23 by glass **Notes** Sunday L £17.25-£32.50, Vegetarian available **Seats** 70 **Children** Portions **Parking** On street, pay & display (free at wknds)

The Gate PLAN 1 D3

◉ Modern Vegetarian V ◔
- -
Globally-inspired vegetarian cooking

☎ 020 8748 6932
51 Queen Caroline St, Hammersmith W6 9QL
e-mail: hammersmith@thegate.tv
dir: Nearest station: Hammersmith. From Hammersmith Apollo Theatre, continue down right side for approx 40 yds

If you have never tried the delights of the vegetarian cooking here before, get ready for a voyage of discovery at this bohemian eatery in the converted studio of artist Sir

The River Café

LONDON W6 PLAN 1 D3

Italian ⬥NOTABLE WINE LIST

Unimpeachable produce and cooking to soothe the soul

☎ 020 7386 4200
Thames Wharf Studios, Rainville Rd W6 9HA
e-mail: info@rivercafe.co.uk
dir: Nearest station: Hammersmith. Restaurant in converted warehouse. Entrance on S side of Rainville Rd at junct with Bowfell Rd

The pioneering partnership of Ruth Rogers and the late Rose Gray established The River Café a quarter of a century ago, with the intention of putting the very best, most authentic Italian cuisine on a plate without fussing and faffing about. Since then, the place has become a household name with a series of best-selling cookery books under its belt, and a remarkable roll-call of chefs

- Jamie Oliver and Hugh Fearnley-Whittingstall amongst them - who have trained in its kitchen. The hand of Ruth's hubby, architect Lord Rogers, is evident in the reclaimed industrial Thames-side premises, and once inside, the appeal of the sleek and luminous minimalist interior, the enthusiasm of the contagiously passionate staff and the alfresco garden area overlooking the Thames path and the water add up to an irresistible formula. Centre-stage is the huge white dome of the wood-burning oven, which is about as high-tech as cooking methods get around here; it is a much-overused foodie cliché, but the cooking here really is all about an unwavering commitment to top-quality ingredients - some shipped in from Italy, some from closer to home - treated with as little intervention as possible. A dedicated Italophile can rack up a frightening bill by working through four courses, but that's the price you pay for the very best materials. After exemplary home-made bread with house-brand Tuscan olive oil for dipping, you might start with ultra-fresh crab teamed with sea kale,

capers, grumolo rosso (baby red radicchio) and thick-skinned Sicilian Cedro lemon, then perhaps perfectly-made taglierini with violet artichokes, thyme, butter and pecorino cheese. Fish, such as chargrilled wild sea bass, slashed and stuffed with herbs, is delivered with spinach and slow-cooked Florence fennel, while a whole Anjou wood pigeon might be wood-roasted in Chianti wine and rounded off with sage, cavolo nero, polenta, butter and parmesan. Finish with pannacotta with grappa and champagne rhubarb, or superb Italian artisan cheeses.

Chef Joseph Trivelli, Ruth Rogers, Sian Owen **Owner** Ruth Rogers **Times** 12.30-3/7-11 Closed 24 Dec-1 Jan, BHs, D Sun **Prices** Starter £14-£24, Main £35-£45, Dessert £9, Service added but optional 12.5% **Wines** 230 bottles over £30, 14 by glass **Notes** Sunday L, Vegetarian available **Seats** 120, Pr/dining room 18 **Children** Portions **Parking** 29, Valet parking evening & wknds, Pay & display

Save on Hotels. Book at **theAA.com/hotel**

LONDON, CENTRAL (W6 – W8) 361

Frank Brangwyn. The minimally-furnished space sits beneath a high loft-style vaulted ceiling and is lit by a large window; when the weather plays ball, you can eat out in a lovely walled garden. This is the sort of vibrant cooking that easily dispels vegetarianism's lingering image problems - there are no nut cutlet clichés here, just fresh, first-class seasonal materials driving the kitchen's output, starting out with ideas such as wasabi potato cake stuffed with roasted shiitaki, ginger and chilli, served with pickled vegetables, while mains might run to a colourful risotto alla contadina, made with fava beans, peas, French beans, courgettes, lemon, mint and parsley, or aubergine teriyaki. Desserts return from the globetrotting theme with the likes of hazelnut Eton Mess, or rhubarb, pear and ginger crumble. The restaurant is currently closed for refurbishment and is expected to reopen in autumn 2013.

Chef Adrian Daniel, Mariusz Wegrodski **Owner** Adrian & Michael Daniel **Times** 12-2.30/6-10.30 Closed 23 Dec-3 Jan, Good Fri & Etr Mon **Prices** Fixed D 2 course £15, Starter £5.50-£6, Main £11-£14, Dessert £5-£5.50, Service added but optional 12.5% **Wines** 2 bottles over £30, 23 bottles under £30, 12 by glass **Seats** 60 **Parking** On street

Novotel London West
PLAN 1 D3

◉ Modern British

Notable cooking in a modern hotel

☎ 020 8741 1555
1 Shortlands W6 8DR
e-mail: H0737@accor.com
web: www.novotellondonwest.co.uk
dir: Nearest station: Hammersmith. M4 (A4) & A316 junct at Hogarth rdbt. Along Great West Rd, left for Hammersmith before flyover. On Hammersmith Bridge Rd to rdbt, take 5th exit. 1st left into Shortlands, 1st left to hotel main entrance

The Artisan Grill is the prime eating venue at this sizeable hotel. It's a large room, but not impersonal, with a contemporary décor, comfortable seating, friendly and attentive service and a glass façade separating it from the reception area. The cooking is based on the classic British repertory, with the menu broad enough to accommodate most tastes, and what it does the kitchen does well. Starters may run from charred asparagus with wild mushrooms to smoked haddock timbale with distinctively flavoured crayfish broth spiked with tarragon. For main course, choose something from the grill - steaks, or perhaps grilled cod fillet with tartare sauce - or go for mussels marinière with chips, or a duo of moist, well-timed Gloucestershire Old Spot pork (belly and fillet) topped with black pudding, served with braised red chard and jus flavoured with apple and cinnamon. End with a perfect rendition of chocolate fondant with white chocolate ice cream.

Chef Roy Thompson **Owner** Accor UK **Times** 12-2.30/5.30-10.30 Closed L Sat-Sun **Prices** Starter £6-£9, Main £14-£25, Dessert £5-£8, Service optional **Wines** 11 bottles over £30, 20 bottles under £30, 30 by glass **Notes** Vegetarian available **Seats** 42, Pr/dining room 10 **Children** Menu **Parking** 240

The River Café
PLAN 1 D2

◉◉◉ – *see opposite*

Sagar
PLAN 1 D3

◉ Indian Vegetarian **V**

Cracking-value South Indian vegetarian dining

☎ 020 8741 8563
157 King St, Hammersmith W6 9JT
e-mail: info@sagarveg.co.uk
dir: Nearest station: Hammersmith. 10 mins from Hammersmith Tube

Set on Hammersmith's main shopping drag, to the uninitiated Sagar might appear like just another modern-look high-street curry house rather than a well-regarded Southern Indian vegetarian outfit. Behind the full-drop glass frontage, pale-wood walls dotted with brass figurines (backlit at night), and tightly packed tables set the tone. Expect well-crafted dishes, smartly attired service and some recession-busting prices. The roster focuses on the crisp paper-thin dosas (rice and lentil pancakes with various fillings) and uthappams (lentil 'pizzas'), while starters include idli (fluffy rice and lentil steamed dumplings) and Bombay chowpati (street snacks) like crispy puri (perhaps a pani puri version, served with chick peas and sour-and-spicy consommé). Curries (maybe bhindi bhajee - fresh okra cooked in fresh tomato with South Indian spices) and all-inclusive thalis add to the lengthy menu, while the menu also helpfully indicates vegan options, plus nut, onion and garlic, and wheat-free dishes. (Sibling branches in Covent Garden and Bloomsbury.)

Chef S Sharmielan **Owner** S Sharmielan **Times** 12-3/5.30-10.45 Closed 25-26 Dec **Prices** Fixed L 3 course £5.95, Fixed D 3 course £15.95, Starter £2.30-£5.25, Main £4.45-£8.25, Dessert £2.50-£4, Service optional **Wines** 911 bottles under £30, 8 by glass **Notes** Vegetarian menu **Seats** 60 **Parking** On street

Babylon
PLAN 4 B5

◉◉ Modern British

South London skyline views and modern British cooking

☎ 020 7368 3993
The Roof Gardens, 99 Kensington High St W8 5SA
e-mail: babylon@roofgardens.virgin.com
web: www.babylon.roofgardens.virgin.com
dir: Nearest station: High Street Kensington. From High St Kensington tube station, turn right, then right into Derry St. Restaurant on right

Owned by Richard Branson, Babylon is a sleek and modern dining venue framed by the lush greenery of the famous Roof Gardens one floor below. The glass-sided dining room has booths, white linen and vivid green décor, and does nothing to detract from the stunning views over the London skyline - best enjoyed from the decked terrace. The food is also worth a look. The modern British menu is driven by quality seasonal produce and the kitchen is not scared of using luxury ingredients nor of indulging in butter and cream in the saucing. Dishes remain relatively light, though, and are creatively presented. Kick off, perhaps, with hot smoked halibut with beetroot spaghetti and potato mousse, moving on to duck leg braised in red wine with walnut gnocchi, sprouting broccoli and Jerusalem artichokes. To finish, try the pistachio sponge with citrus mousse, raspberry glaze and mandarin ice cream.

Chef Ian Howard **Owner** Virgin Limited Edition **Times** 12-2.30/7-10.30 Closed D Sun **Prices** Fixed L 2 course £21.50, Fixed D 3 course £46.50, Starter £9-£14.50, Main £19.50-£35, Dessert £8-£10, Service added but optional 12.5% **Wines** 22 by glass **Notes** Fixed L Mon-Fri, Sat 2/3 course £22-£25, Sunday L, Vegetarian available, Dress restrictions, Smart Casual **Seats** 180, Pr/dining room 12 **Children** Portions, Menu **Parking** NCP Young St

See advert on page 362

LONDON W8 *continued*

Belvedere
PLAN 1 E3

◉◉ British, French

Modern brasserie-type dishes in Holland Park

☎ 020 7602 1238
Abbotsbury Rd, Holland House, Holland Park W8 6LU
e-mail: sales@belvedererestaurant.co.uk
web: www.belvedererestaurant.co.uk
dir: Nearest station: Holland Park. Off Abbotsbury Rd
entrance to Holland Park

Dating from the 17th century, surrounded by lawns and a
flower garden with a fountain, The Belvedere must have
one of the most remarkable interiors in the capital: a
spacious, high-ceilinged room with a parquet floor, a
large mural of butterflies, images of Marilyn Monroe,
shell-like lampshades and a marble staircase sweeping
up to a mezzanine. The menu sticks mainly within the
Anglo-French traditions, so expect caramelised pork belly
with boudin noir and apple sauce, followed by halibut
fillet baked in a herb crust with spinach and mustard
sabayon. Ingredients are well chosen, and the kitchen
puts out consistently accomplished dishes: smoked
mackerel pâté with chicory and hazelnut dressing, for
instance, then roast Goosnargh duck breast with duck
hash, green beans and port jus, and an assiette of
chocolate with raspberry coulis, or rhubarb and ginger
mousse.

Chef Gary O'Sullivan **Owner** Jimmy Lahoud
Times 12-2.30/6-10.30 Closed 26 Dec, 1 Jan, D Sun
Prices Fixed L 2 course fr £16.50, Starter £8.95-£15.50,
Main £15.50-£24.95, Dessert £7.50-£10.50, Service
added but optional 12.5%, Groups min 13 service 15%
Wines 120 bottles over £30, 12 bottles under £30, 12 by
glass **Notes** Wknds L menu 3 course £27.50, Sunday L
£27.50, Vegetarian available, Dress restrictions, Smart
casual, no shorts D **Seats** 90 **Children** Portions
Parking Council car park

Clarke's
PLAN 4 A6

◉◉ Modern British, Mediterranean ⬤

Full-on flavours chez Sally

☎ 020 7221 9225
124 Kensington Church St W8 4BH
e-mail: restaurant@sallyclarke.com
dir: Nearest station: Notting Hill Gate. Turn right out of
Notting Hill Gate & then right into Kensington Church St.
Restaurant on left

Sally Clarke's eponymous restaurant is on two levels: a
light-filled ground-floor room and a larger basement with
an open-to-view kitchen. Her cooking is founded on the
best, freshest produce available in the markets each day,
which means the menu changes at each session, and
focuses on the integrity of that produce. Vegetables,
herbs and salad leaves are often brought from Sally's
own garden, the last going into a typical, clear-tasting
starter with mozzarella, pears and blood orange with
citrus dressing, or a heartier one of rare roast duck breast
and grilled heart with balsamic and beetroot dressing.
Main-course meats and fish are often chargrilled or
roasted to bring out the maximum flavour: a large veal
chop, precisely grilled, for instance, with well-chosen
vegetables, or roast monkfish tail with anchovy salsa
verde, baked artichoke and desiree potatoes. Imaginative
puddings could run to rhubarb trifle or chocolate tart, its
pastry light and crisp.

Chef Sally Clarke **Owner** Sally Clarke
Times 12.30-2/6.30-10 Closed 8 days Xmas & New Year,
D Sun **Prices** Prices not confirmed Service added but
optional 12.5% **Wines** 8 by glass **Notes** Vegetarian
available **Seats** 80, Pr/dining room 40 **Parking** On street

Kensington Place   PLAN 4 A6

◉ British

Buzzy brasserie starring seafood

☎ 020 7727 3184
201-209 Kensington Church St W8 7LX
e-mail: kensingtonplace@danddlondon.com
dir: Nearest station: Notting Hill Gate

It's over a quarter of a century since Kensington Place
first made a splash on the London dining scene. Now part
of the D&D London restaurant group, KP concentrates on
the fruits of the sea (there's even a wet fish shop next
door), serving up seafood from Billingsgate market or
direct from the Cornish coast. The setting on Kensington
Church Street remains a cracker, with its floor-to-ceiling
windows and bright and breezy vibe. The daily market
menu might deliver a tranche of turbot or skate wing
(add extras such as triple-cooked chips and green
beans), or stick to the carte and choose from the likes of
Cornish mackerel tartare with beetroot and anchovy
caviar, followed by marinated squid and prawn salad, or
confit organic salmon. There are meat and veggie options
too. Finish with plum and almond tart with iced orange
curd.

Chef Daniel Loftin **Owner** D & D London
Times 12-3/6.30-10.30 Closed L Mon, D Sun **Prices** Fixed
L 2 course £17, Starter £5.50-£8.50, Main £12.50-£24,
Dessert £5-£8.50, Service added but optional 12.5%
Wines 43 bottles over £30, 16 bottles under £30, 19 by
glass **Notes** Sunday L £12.50-£24, Vegetarian available
Seats 110, Pr/dining room 40 **Children** Portions, Menu
Parking On street

Kitchen W8   PLAN 4 A4

◉◉◉ – *see below*

Launceston Place   PLAN 4 C4
Restaurant

◉◉◉◉ – *see page 364*

The Mall Tavern   PLAN 4 A6

◉◉ Traditional British

**Appealingly innovative gastro-pub cooking near the
tube**

☎ 020 7229 3374
71-73 Palace Gardens Ter, Notting Hill W8 4RU
e-mail: info@themalltavern.com
dir: Nearest station: Notting Hill Gate. Exit Notting Hill
station towards KFC, right Palace Gardens Terrace

A Victorian pub a stone's throw from Notting Hill Gate
tube station, The Mall Tavern has a bar for drinkers but

the majority of people troop into the light and airy dining
room - a clean, uncluttered space of bare wooden floor,
wall banquettes and plain wooden tables. There's also a
tiny enclosed garden for sunny lunches. Friendly and
relaxed staff deliver menus - including a good value
fixed-price lunch - of sparklingly fresh ideas. How about
dandelion salad with ricotta, a pheasant egg and black
pudding, followed by the signature cow pie? The cooking
is marked out by its lack of fuss and gimmick but dishes
are intelligently composed to allow flavours to shine, with
the kitchen not averse to a bit of innovation. Chestnut
hummus with rosemary pitta bread is an unusual but
effective starter, offered alongside chicken liver pâté with
pickled red onions, while main courses might take in
'pork-o-bucco' with braised lentils, and smoked salmon
fishcakes with broccoli and sauce maltaise. Desserts are
an irresistible bunch, among them chocolate caramel tart
with orange salad.

Chef Asher Abramowitz **Owner** Perritt & Perritt Ltd
Times noon-10 Closed 24 Dec-2 Jan **Prices** Fixed L 2
course £10, Starter £1-£7, Service added but optional
12.5% **Wines** 8 bottles over £30, 8 bottles under £30, 17
by glass **Notes** Sunday L £12-£15, Vegetarian available
Seats 45, Pr/dining room 15 **Children** Portions

Kitchen W8

LONDON W8   **PLAN 4 A4**

Modern British

Exciting modern cooking off the High Street

☎ 020 7937 0120
11-13 Abingdon Rd, Kensington W8 6AH
e-mail: info@kitchenw8.com
dir: Nearest station: High Street Kensington. From station
left onto High St for 500mtrs & left into Abingdon Rd

The smart black façade and awning hint that this is
going to be a special sort of place, expectations borne out
by the equally slick interior: vivid art on the walls,
unusual wall lights, good-looking upholstered chairs at
neatly set tables and an attractive décor. This is a
combined enterprise from Philip Howard and Rebecca
Mascarenhas (see entries for The Square and Sonny's
Kitchen respectively), who, with their years of experience,

have built up a network of producers and suppliers all
over the country. 'Integrity and simplicity' are the buzz
words behind the kitchen's output, although dishes have
a higher level of ambition and complexity than the second
of those nouns would suggest: caramelised scallops with
beurre noisette are also plated with pear, Swiss chard,
hazelnuts and roast chicken skin, for instance, and that's
just a starter. But there's no point quibbling over
semantics when dishes are as well conceived and
precisely cooked as they are here. Ravioli of veal
sweetbreads and tongue, served with truffled cauliflower
and roasting juices, is a deeply satisfying starter, jostling
for attention with the upfront flavours of mackerel rillette
with smoked eel, pickled onions, mustard, dill and rye.
Dishes are a treasury of bright modern ideas, ingredients
are of the first order, and the amount of effort that goes
on in the kitchen can be mind-blowing. Roast wood
pigeon with wilted mustard leaves, bulgar wheat, quince
and beetroot, and roast cod fillet with hand-rolled crab
farfalle, broccoli and citrus crumbs are two standout

main courses that will surely send you home happy. And
the momentum extends into desserts that might range
from a simple rhubarb sorbet to white chocolate rice
pudding with date ice cream and a ginger financier.

Chef Mark Kempson **Owner** Philip Howard & Rebecca
Mascarenhas **Times** 12-2.30/6-10 Closed 25-26 Dec, BHs
Prices Fixed L 2 course fr £17.50, Starter £9.50-£15.95,
Main £19.50-£27.95, Dessert £5.95-£7.95, Service added
but optional 12.5% **Wines** 89 bottles over £30, 20 bottles
under £30, 14 by glass **Notes** Fixed D 6-7pm 2/3 course
£21.50/£24.50, Sunday L £25-£29.50, Vegetarian
available **Seats** 75 **Children** Portions **Parking** On street,
NCP High St

Launceston Place Restaurant

Modern British ⌇ NOTABLE WINE LIST

Sensational European cookery in a genteel Kensington mews

☎ 020 7937 6912
1a Launceston Place W8 5RL
e-mail: lpevents@danddlondon.com
dir: Nearest station: Gloucester Road, High Street Kensington. Just south of Kensington Palace, 10 min walk from Royal Albert Hall

Launceston Place has been a foodie destination through various incarnations in recent decades. Its location a few minutes away from the commercial whirl of High Street Ken has always been one of its attractions, but it's safe to say that it hasn't necessarily been intent on creating one of the bigger splashes on the capital's fine-dining scene. Tim Allen's arrival in 2012 from the country-house world of Wiltshire changed all that. Great things are now going on here, as is indicated by the extra Rosette gained this year. A composite of four early Victorian corner houses, the place slinks behind a sober, dark exterior, while inside the charcoal and plain fawn carpet and upholstery (a redecoration was in the offing as we were going to print) are tastefully offset with boldly assertive abstract artworks. Service is as highly polished as the cutlery, and fully in line with the profile of the place, where meals are taken at a gentler, subtler pace than is the hectic London norm. You're here to relax, even if you're hot-footing straight afterwards to an evening at the Albert Hall. As well as the early evening deal, there's a six-course taster, and a fair old welter of choice on the principal Market Menu. Allen's style is broadly modern European, utilising components such as Morteau sausage, Landes quail, Pata Negra lardo, brandade, Ibérico tenderloin and aged sherry vinegar in dishes that draw on the artillery of modern technique, but so as to emphasise the inherent characters of prime materials, rather than swamping them in counter-intuitive flavours. That Morteau appears in chunky cubes in a first course built around a perfectly judged, slow-cooked duck egg, along with just-tender braised white beans, and duck confit on toast topped with tiny delicate onion rings, the whole thing unified with a punchy duck stock reduction. Next up might be translucently well-timed roast cod, its skin appealingly brittle, accompanied by vivid flat-leaf parsley purée, cockles cooked in the Spanish manner on a plancha, and a salt-cod brandade of booming intensity, or possibly rump of veal roasted in aromatic herbs, with a single king oyster, glazed carrot, technically fascinating charred lettuce and puréed mushrooms in a jus gras. Virunga 70 percent cocoa chocolate from the eastern Congo lights up a brilliantly vibrant mousse, served with poached pear, salted caramel and praline soil, its stellar quality reinforced by a fantastically concentrated pear sorbet and a caramelised pistachio tuile.

Chef Timothy Allen **Owner** D & D London **Times** 12-2.30/6-10.30 Closed Xmas, New Year, Etr, L Mon **Prices** Fixed L 3 course £25, Fixed D 3 course £48, Tasting menu £65, Service added but optional 12.5% **Wines** 375 bottles over £30, 15 bottles under £30, 13 by glass **Notes** Early D 6-6.30pm 3 course £30, booking essential, Sunday L, Vegetarian available **Seats** 60, Pr/dining room 10 **Children** Portions **Parking** Car park off Kensington High St

LONDON W8 *continued*

The Milestone Hotel   PLAN 4 B5

  Modern British

Elegant hotel dining with a taste of luxury

☎ 020 7917 1000
1 Kensington Court W8 5DL
e-mail: bookms@rchmail.com
web: www.milestonehotel.com
dir: Nearest station: High St Kensington. From Warwick Rd right into Kensington High St. Hotel 400yds past Kensington tube

This Grade II listed boutique hotel with 24-hour butler service in Kensington prides itself on its professionalism and luxurious interior and aims to pamper guests unreservedly. The ornate Cheneston's restaurant (deriving its name from an early spelling of Kensington) doesn't

break the mould: it's an intimate space with traditional, cosseting service. An open fireplace, one of several original features, and candles on the tables at night lend a cosy air, while mahogany furniture and correctly laid tables add to the formal feel. The broadly modern British menu includes some of Bea Tollman's (founder and president of the Red Carnation Hotel Collection, of which The Milestone is part) favourite dishes. Wild sea trout with pickled cucumber, apple and radish salad makes a fine start to a meal, and might be followed by moist and flavoursome roast cannon of Welsh lamb with shallot purée, baby beetroot and potato fondant. Signature puddings include The Milestone quartet of desserts and Milestone rice pudding - vanilla rice pudding, Chantilly cream, salted caramel and candied nuts. The excellent wine list showcases many bottles from the owner's estate in South Africa.

Owner The Red Carnation Hotels **Times** 12-3/5.30-11 **Prices** Fixed L 2 course £25-£27, Fixed D 3 course £29-£34, Starter £10.50-£27.50, Main £19-£41, Dessert £9.50-£12, Service added but optional 12.5% **Wines** 12 by glass **Notes** Vegetarian available, Dress restrictions, Smart casual **Seats** 30, Pr/dining room 8 **Children** Portions, Menu **Parking** NCP Young Street off Kensington High Street

Min Jiang   PLAN 4 B5

 — see below

Min Jiang

LONDON W8   PLAN 4 B5

Chinese

Adventurous Chinese cooking and park views

☎ 020 7361 1988
Royal Garden Hotel, 2-24 Kensington High St W8 4PT
e-mail: reservations@minjiang.co.uk
web: www.minjiang.co.uk
dir: Nearest station: High Street Kensington. Adjacent to Kensington Palace & Gardens on 10th floor of Royal Garden Hotel

From its tenth-floor eyrie in the Royal Garden Hotel, Min Jiang has sweeping views over Kensington Gardens and Hyde Park to London's skyline. The restaurant is kitted out with lots of darkwood, with a décor predominantly of cream, the eyes drawn by a gallery of photographs and a collection of Chinese vases. Contemporary Chinese

cooking is the package, focusing on Szechuan and Cantonese dishes, from praiseworthy dim sum to steamed slices of abalone with dried ham and Chinese mushrooms. The kitchen's culinary credentials are evident in every dish, and there's no stinting on the quality of raw materials. Start off with, say, crispy fried squid with dried chilli and garlic, or Szechuan-style chicken, then go on to braised pork belly in a rich sauce with Chinese buns, or grilled rack of lamb in garlic-infused soy sauce, and throw in a vegetarian dish like asparagus with lotus root and black pepper, plus a bowl of rice or noodles. Fish and shellfish get a decent chunk of the long menu, from sea bass (whole or fillet) steamed with ginger and spring onions, through stir-fried Scottish scallops in spicy bean curd sauce, to sautéed lobster with XO sauce. Desserts are well worth exploring, among them Szechuan pancake with vanilla ice cream, and snowy flake (jasmine tea) tiramisù with a chocolate tuile. Ordering an assortment of dishes can send the final bill

soaring, but you wouldn't expect anything else in a hotel of this calibre and location.

Chef Lan Chee Vooi **Owner** Goodwood Group **Times** 12-3/6-10.30 **Prices** Starter £7-£12.90, Main £12-£60, Dessert £6.50-£8, Service optional, Groups min 8 service 10% **Wines** 133 bottles over £30, 4 bottles under £30, 15 by glass **Notes** Sunday L, Vegetarian available, Dress restrictions, Smart casual **Seats** 100, Pr/dining room 20 **Parking** 200

LONDON W8 *continued*

Park Terrace Restaurant PLAN 4 B5

◎◎ Modern British

Sophisticated modern British cuisine overlooking Kensington Gardens

☎ 020 7361 0602
Royal Garden Hotel, 2-24 Kensington High St W8 4PT
e-mail: reservations@parkterracerestaurant.co.uk
web: www.royalgardenhotel.co.uk
dir: Nearest station: High Street Kensington. Adjacent to Kensington Palace & Gardens, within Royal Garden Hotel

On the ground floor just off the marble-floored foyer of the swanky Royal Garden Hotel, the aptly-named Park Terrace comes with leafy views over Kensington Gardens through floor-to-ceiling windows running the full length of the room. Okay, it may not have the glamour of the hotel's other dining option, Min Jiang, up on the 10th floor (see entry), but it doesn't disappoint either. The contemporary décor cleverly reflects the park-life theme, with a natural colour palate, wood veneer and large black-and-white images of trees. Steve Munkley's modern British cooking is light, clear-flavoured and uncomplicated, and shows a strong commitment to local British suppliers and seasonality. Expect a duo of daily fish (perhaps salmon and scallop) served with cocotte potatoes and a tomato and olive salsa at lunch, while dinner ups the ante with lavender-and-herb crusted Essex lamb rump teamed with French beans, pea purée and confit potato, and desserts like a hot chocolate and cherry soufflé with cherry sorbet. Service is smartly attired and friendly, while the value lunch keeps the Kensington ladies on-side.

Chef Steve Munkley **Owner** Goodwood Group
Times 12-3/6-10.30 **Prices** Fixed L 2 course £16.50, Fixed D 3 course £36.50, Starter £10.50, Main £19, Dessert £8.50, Service optional, Groups min 8 service 10%
Wines 70 bottles over £30, 6 bottles under £30, 13 by glass **Notes** Pre-theatre menu available daily, Sunday L, Vegetarian available, Dress restrictions, Smart casual **Seats** 90, Pr/dining room 40 **Children** Portions, Menu **Parking** 200

Zaika of Kensington PLAN 4 B5

◎◎ Indian V ✋

New-wave Indian cooking in an opulent setting

☎ 020 7795 6533
1 Kensington High St W8 5NP
e-mail: Zaikareservations@Zaika-restaurant.co.uk
web: www.zaika-restaurant.co.uk
dir: Nearest station: High Street Kensington. Opposite Kensington Palace & Royal Garden Hotel

Zaika was at the forefront of the modern Indian culinary movement in the early 1990s that changed the parameters of Indian cooking in the UK forever (and for the better). It is fitting, perhaps, that it has now become part of the Tamarind group, whose Mayfair outpost (see entry) was similarly there at the beginning of the revolution. Here in Kensington, the one-time bank with its tall windows and sky-high carved ceiling avoids cliché and serves up smart, contemporary cooking in a stylish, comfortable environment. The intelligently put-together repertoire includes the likes of pan-seared spiced scallops with sautéed cavolo nero and pumpkin sauce, or a chicken tikka medley among starters. Next up, main-courses such as slow-cooked supreme of mallard with semolina pulao and a vindaloo sauce, or pan-fried sea bream with spiced cassava mash and mango and ginger sauce. The creativity and craft continues at dessert stage in the form of duo of kulfi flavoured with pistachio and lychee extract. There's tasting and pre-theatre menus, too.

Chef Alfred & Navin Prasad **Owner** Zaika Restaurant Ltd
Times 12-2.45/5.30-10.45 Closed Xmas, New Year, L Mon
Prices Tasting menu fr £55, Service added but optional 12.5% **Wines** 130 bottles over £30, 1 bottle under £30, 14 by glass **Notes** Tasting menu 6 course, Pre-theatre 2 course £22.50, Sunday L fr £17, Vegetarian menu, Dress restrictions, Smart casual preferred **Seats** 84 **Children** Portions **Parking** On street

LONDON W10

The Dock Kitchen PLAN 1 D4

◎ Fusion

Appealingly eclectic cooking beside the canal

☎ 020 8962 1610
Portobello Docks, 344/342 Ladbroke Grove W10 5BU
e-mail: reception@tomdixon.net
dir: Nearest station: Ladbroke Grove

Stevie Parle's former pop-up restaurant in Tom Dixon's furniture design gallery has gone from strength-to-strength since becoming a permanent fixture called The Dock Kitchen. Set in a new building smack beside the Grand Union Canal, the restaurant is a cool and contemporary dining space, with an open-to-view, glass-walled kitchen at its heart, and floor-to-ceiling glass on the water-facing side giving great canal views. Tom Dixon's furniture still gets a showing in the dining area, the wooden and metal tables un-clothed and accessorised with flowers and tea lights. Parle's cooking is influenced by his travels around the world, and so the menu offers an eclectic mix of dishes ranging from Middle Eastern to Italian to Indian. Norfolk cod roe on toast with raw peas, broad beans, dill and crème fraîche is typical of the simple approach, as is a main of hake roasted in white wine and herbs with samphire, lentils, Marinda tomatoes and mayonnaise.

Times 12-2.30/7-9.30

LONDON W11

Chakra PLAN 1 E3

◎ Indian NEW

Smart Indian restaurant in Notting Hill

☎ 020 7229 2115
157-159 Notting Hill Gate W11 3LF
e-mail: info@chakralondon.com
dir: Nearest station: Notting Hill Gate

Named after the energy points of the body according to Hindu and Buddhist tradition, the chakras are vital in aligning mind, body and soul. Chef Andy Varma has similar plans to invigorate and energise you with his food. It all takes place in a smart room a million miles from curry-house cliché, where the walls and banquettes are covered in cream-coloured leather, crisp white linen adorns the tables, and chandeliers hang from the ceiling. The cooking is most definitely a cut-above, too. The menu serves up lots of less familiar ideas and flavours are nicely judged throughout. Start with venison galouti, yam chaat, or masala asparagus, and move on to main courses such as chicken Jalandhar, which is a version of the Punjabi classic - tandoor grilled chicken with fine tomato and masala sauce, served with a roti. There's Chakra black cod, roasted quail, and Bengal fish curry, too, plus vegetarian dishes such as kadhai paneer and black dhal.

Chef Andy Varma **Times** 12-3/6-11 Closed D Sun **Prices** Prices not confirmed

E&O
PLAN 1 D4

◉ Pan Asian

East Asian grazing plates for the Notting Hill cognoscenti

☎ 020 7229 5454
14 Blenheim Crescent, Notting Hill W11 1NN
e-mail: eando@rickerrestaurants.com
dir: Nearest station: Notting Hill Gate, Ladbroke Grove. From station turn right, at mini rdbt turn into Kensington Park Rd, restaurant 10min down hill

The joint still jumps at E&O, one of the central supports of Will Ricker's era-defining restaurant group, providing Pan-Asian mini-plates to the grazers and hangers-out of Notting Hill. It's more than proved itself a winning formula since opening in 2001: people pack the place whatever the weather for finely honed, highly spiced, cleanly presented food sourced from the principal East Asian traditions. Chilli salt squid and crispy pork belly in black rice vinegar, the latter upholstered with an eye-popping layer of fat, are as authentic-seeming as anything in Chinatown, and a paper cone of tempura soft-shelled crab with creamy jalapeño dipping sauce is fun. The westernmost extremities of Pan-Asia are drawn with sufficient elastic to allow Ibérico pork a look-in, in the form of a firm pre-sliced chop with shimeji mushrooms and soba noodles, or you might choose whole crispy sea bass with chilli jam and spiced mango.

Desserts head west too for mango pannacotta and lime granita, or banoffee pie.

Chef Simon Treadway **Owner** Will Ricker **Times** 12-3/6-11 Closed 25-26 Dec, 1 Jan, Aug BH **Prices** Service added but optional 12.5%, Groups min 10 service 15% **Wines** 37 bottles over £30, 13 bottles under £30, 15 by glass **Notes** Fixed price D available reserved private dining only, Sunday L £10-£33, Vegetarian available **Seats** 86, Pr/dining room 18 **Children** Portions, Menu **Parking** On street

Edera
PLAN 1 D3

◉ Modern Italian

Well-liked neighbourhood Italian in leafy Holland Park

☎ 020 7221 6090
148 Holland Park Av W11 4UE
e-mail: roberto@edera.co.uk
dir: Nearest station: Holland Park. Exit Holland Park tube, left Holland Park Ave A40

Decked out on tiered levels, with blond-wood floors, light walls hung with big mirrors and linen-dressed tables, this minimally-styled Holland Park eatery pulls in a well-heeled crowd for its fashionable Sardinian-accented Italian cooking. Pavement tables fill early on warm sunny days despite traffic passing close by. The kitchen certainly knows its stuff, keeping things simple and straightforward, allowing the excellent ingredients to

speak for themselves. There is much that is familiar from the Italian mainland, bolstered by a daily specials list featuring the likes of chargrilled sea bream with courgettes and basil oil, and baked salted sea bass with potato salad, but the chef is Sardinian, so there might be spaghetti with grey mullet roe, and Sicilian cannoli for pudding.

Times 12-11 Closed 25-26 & 31 Dec

The Ledbury
PLAN 1 E4

◉◉◉ – see below

The Ledbury

LONDON W11
PLAN 1 E4

British, French V NOTABLE WINE LIST

Imaginative cooking from a supremely talented, tirelessly focused chef

☎ 020 7792 9090
127 Ledbury Rd W11 2AQ
e-mail: info@theledbury.com
dir: Nearest station: Westbourne Park, Notting Hill Gate. 5 min walk along Talbot Rd from Portobello Rd, on corner of Talbot Rd & Ledbury Rd

The Ledbury has rightly won awards and plaudits aplenty in recent years, such is the startlingly imaginative, creative, skilful cooking of Aussie chef Brett Graham. The place certainly looks the part of a high-end dining destination with its sophisticated, contemporary, neutral-toned décor, with leather seating, a parquet floor, high

ceilings, waiter stations and a mirrored wall giving the impression of space to the relatively small and intimate room. Smartly dressed serving staff are ever-attentive and friendly, adding to the sheer pleasure of a meal here. Graham's menus - including a tasting, set lunch (a very reasonable £35 for three courses), and à la carte - are all founded in the finest ingredients, some of which he actually goes out and gets himself (namely during the game season). Graham worked during his early career with Phil Howard at The Square (see entry), so you can be assured he knows just what to do to get the most flavour from the raw ingredients at his disposal, without anything ever feeling overworked. Céviche of scallops with radishes, seaweed and herb oil and frozen English wasabi is a thoroughly modern starter just singing with fresh flavours, which might compete for your affections with flame grilled mackerel (a beautiful piece of fish, cooked to perfection, with a delightful chargrilled taste) partnered with pickled vegetables, Celtic mustard and shiso. Everything looks beautiful on the plate, from

main-course roast sea bass (precisely timed) with broccoli stem, ultra-fresh crab and black quinoa, to fillet of roe deer with beetroots, pinot lees and crisp potato - a dish with all the rich, earthy flavours you could wish for on a cold December day. Desserts are equally impressive - perhaps a rich, but by no means cloying, pavé of chocolate with milk purée and lovage ice cream, or pear cooked in brown butter with the crunch of crispy porridge and the sweet nuttiness of a walnut oil parfait. Make sure you factor in the excellent wine list when it comes to planning your budget for dinner.

Chef Brett Graham **Owner** Nigel Platts-Martin, Brett Graham & Philip Howard **Times** 12-6.30 Closed 25 Dec, Aug BH, L Mon **Prices** Fixed L 2 course £30, Tasting menu £105-£175, Service added but optional 12.5% **Notes** Fri-Sat Tasting menu only, Sunday L fr £50, Vegetarian menu **Seats** 50 **Parking** Talbot Rd (metered)

LONDON W11 *continued*

Lonsdale
PLAN 1 E4

Modern British

Trendy Notting Hill lounge bar dining

☎ 020 7727 4080
48 Lonsdale Rd W11 2DE
e-mail: info@thelonsdale.co.uk
dir: Nearest station: Notting Hill, Ladbroke Grove. Parallel to Westbourne Grove, between Portobello Rd & Ledbury Rd

Tucked away on a residential street, this hip Notting Hill/Westbourne Grove hangout is an up-tempo evenings-only affair. The lively front bar gets rammed on busy nights, with cocktails and fizz de rigueur before moving on to the equally funky lounge-style dining area behind. Red mock-croc, low-backed banquettes, darkwood tables, gold walls and a centrepiece light feature deliver a low-lit nightclub vibe for a backing track of trendy music, youthful service and high decibels. The equally well-dressed but straightforward modish cooking is driven by quality ingredients and suits the mood; perhaps haunch of venison with juniper and chocolate sauce or pan-roasted sea bass with a fricassée of mussels, samphire and sorrel. Steaks from the Lake District (35-day hung) and starters such as black figs with Gervic goats' cheese fit the bill.

Chef Luke Keating **Owner** Tim Gardner **Times** 6-12 Closed 25-26 Dec, 1 Jan, Sun-Mon, L all week **Prices** Fixed D 3 course £29.50-£35, Starter £7-£10, Main £13-£36, Dessert £4-£7, Service added but optional 12.5% **Wines** 23 bottles over £30, 17 bottles under £30, 11 by glass **Notes** Vegetarian available **Seats** 80, Pr/dining room 30 **Parking** On street

LONDON W14

Cibo
PLAN 1 D3

Italian

W14's Italian flagship

☎ 020 7371 2085
3 Russell Gardens W14 8EZ
e-mail: ciborestaurant@aol.com
dir: Nearest station: Olympia, Shepherds Bush. S of Shepherds Bush station, right off Holland Rd into Russell Gdns

In a parade of shops on a small side street off busy Holland Road, Cibo is a small and unpretentious restaurant, a destination for lovers of Italian food. A bar dominates the room, decoration is provided by nude reliefs, ornaments and ceramic pots, and Italian staff are knowledgeable and helpful. Bread - focaccia, carta di musica - and nibbles like olives are promising openers before starters along the lines of smooth polenta topped with a tomato-based ragù of fennel-infused luganega sausage, or crudo di tonno with capers. Pasta is the real thing - perhaps ravioli, cooked al dente, stuffed with smooth minced pheasant in wild mushroom sauce, a well-balanced dish - and the kitchen's care with quality ingredients, some imported, shines throughout, from

whole sea bass plainly grilled with lemon and herbs, to pan-fried venison fillet served with agnolotti pasta filled with apple in venison sauce. Puddings are convincing renditions of the classics, from tiramisù to zabaglione.

Chef Piero Borrell **Owner** Gino Taddei **Times** 12.15-3/6.15-11 Closed Xmas, Etr BHs, L Sat, D Sun **Prices** Fixed L 2 course £19.50, Service added but optional 12.5% **Wines** 4 by glass **Notes** Sunday L, Vegetarian available **Seats** 50, Pr/dining room 14 **Children** Portions **Parking** On street

LONDON WC1

The Montague on the Gardens
PLAN 3 B3

British

Stylish hotel bistro with modern comfort classics

☎ 020 7612 8416 & 7612 8412
15 Montague St, Bloomsbury WC1B 5BJ
e-mail: pbradley@rchmail.com
web: www.montaguehotel.com
dir: Nearest station: Russell Square, Holborn. Just off Russell Sq, 10 min from Covent Garden, adjacent to British Museum

A discreet brass name plaque and bowler-hatted doorman at the entrance announce that the chic boutique Montague on the Gardens hotel is a cut above the norm. In a tranquil corner of Bloomsbury by the British Museum, its Blue Door Bistro is an appropriately cosseting and elegant operation with well-oiled service, and clean-lined contemporary looks - leather director's chairs at linen-clad tables, mahogany panelling, and a wall frieze of Dickensian London. Uncomplicated, comfort-oriented classics are the kitchen's stock in trade, starting with a properly made winter vegetable soup, ahead of a quirky take on cottage pie - made in this case with a rich filling of duck, and served with baby carrots and leeks. Otherwise you might splash out on a fillet of beef with wild mushroom and artichoke fricassée, fondant potato and Merlot jus, and wind things up with rice pudding with salted caramel sauce and candied mixed nuts.

Chef Martin Halls **Owner** Red Carnation Hotels **Times** 12.30-2.30/5.30-10.30 **Prices** Fixed L 2 course £19.50, Starter £5.50-£10.50, Main £13.50-£38, Dessert £5.50-£9.50, Service added but optional 12.5% **Wines** 61 bottles over £30, 25 bottles under £30, 24 by glass **Notes** Sunday L £5.50-£38, Vegetarian available, Civ Wed 120 **Seats** 40, Pr/dining room 100 **Children** Portions, Menu **Parking** On street, Bloomsbury Sq

Paramount
PLAN 3 A2

Modern European

Amazing views and appealing menu

☎ 020 7420 2900
Centre Point, 101-103 New Oxford St WC1A 1DD
e-mail: reservations@paramount.uk.net
dir: Nearest station: Tottenham Court Rd

Thirty-two-floors up in the Centre Point building, the panorama is paramount. Once you've stepped out of the

lift you're confronted with spectacular views across the capital which are worth the trip on their own, but there's some good eating and drinking to be had whilst you're up here. The Paramount restaurant and bar have fabulous views day and night through huge windows. The cool décor has darkwood floors, funky-ish lime green upholstered seating and copper tables (matching its copper cocktail bar) inlaid with black lacquered tops. And on the menu is some broadly appealing, gently contemporary food. You might start with carrot and coriander soup, but equally there's smoked eel risotto with sorrel and soft herbs, or seared scallop with black pudding and cauliflower purée. Next up, pan-fried whole plaice comes in traditional guise with caper and brown shrimp butter, and braised pork belly with Morteau sausages, lentils and carrots.

Chef Mark Kay **Owner** Pierre & Kathleen Condou **Times** 12-3/5.30-11 Closed Xmas, 1 Jan **Prices** Fixed L 2 course fr £23.50, Starter £8.50-£12.50, Main £16.50-£27.50, Dessert £6.50-£19.50, Service added but optional 12.5% **Wines** 10 by glass **Notes** Sunday L, Vegetarian available, Dress restrictions, Smart casual, Civ Wed 100 **Seats** Pr/dining room 30

LONDON WC2

L'Atelier de Joël Robuchon
PLAN 3 A2

– *see opposite*

Balthazar
PLAN 3 B1

French, European NEW

All-day French brasserie fare and an electric atmosphere

☎ 020 3301 1155
4-6 Russell St WC2B 5HZ
e-mail: info@balthazarlondon.com
dir: Nearest station: Covent Garden

The hottest ticket in Covent Garden right now, the much-hyped Balthazar - set in the old Theatre Museum just off the piazza - has played to packed houses ever since it opened in spring 2013. The London outpost of Keith McNally's legendary New York brasserie, it's a real looker, a large, elegant, high-ceilinged room decked out with mosaic floors, darkwood panelling, impressive art deco lighting, red-leather banquette seating and giant antique mirrors. And with an army of sunny natured staff, a swanky bar, and a constant turnover of animatedly enthusiastic diners, the place really rocks. The all-day offer takes in breakfast, lunch, afternoon tea and dinner (plus weekend brunch), with menus delivering a wide range of classic French brasserie fare, from fruits de mer to salad Niçoise, moules frites to steak au poivre. Some dishes get a more modish treatment, such as roasted cod fillet with crushed potatoes, superb olive tapenade and pistachios, while desserts are mostly comfort classics like apple tart Tatin and profiteroles.

Chef Robert Reed, Alexis Guillemot **Times** 7.30-mdnt All-day dining **Prices** Prices not confirmed **Notes** Vegetarian available **Seats** 175 **Children** Portions **Parking** NCP - Parker Street

Christopher's   PLAN 3 C1

◉ Contemporary American

A taste of the States in Covent Garden

☎ 020 7240 4222
18 Wellington St, Covent Garden WC2E 7DD
e-mail: reservations@christophersgrill.com
dir: Nearest station: Embankment, Covent Garden. Just by Strand, overlooking Waterloo Bridge

This bustling Covent Garden operation opened its doors in 1991 and has been trading in America's classic cuisine ever since, other than a brief hiatus in early 2013 when it closed for a top-to-tail refurbishment. The end results are a more art-deco-inspired look, more flexible all-day serving, and new American dishes to show that stateside cooking goes beyond steaks and burgers. That said, shellfish and steaks (some imported from the USA) form a sizeable chunk of the menu, but elsewhere there may be foie gras and chicken liver parfait with orange Muscat jelly and pineapple and chilli relish, or slow-cooked belly pork with Boston baked beans, feta and celeriac slaw. The Stars and Stripes is represented by Caesar salad among starters, the range broadened by the likes of carpaccio, and goats' cheese soufflé, while bringing up the rear are New York-style cheesecake, and pecan maple tart with vanilla ice cream.

Chef Francis Agyepong **Owner** Christopher Gilmour
Times 12-3/5-11 Closed 24 Dec-2 Jan, D Sun

Prices Fixed D 3 course £22, Starter £8-£14, Main £15-£68, Dessert £7-£12, Service added but optional 12.5% **Wines** 100+ bottles over £30, 5 bottles under £30, 12 by glass **Notes** Fixed D theatre Mon-Sat 5-6.15 & 10-11.30, Sun Supper menu **Seats** 110, Pr/dining room 40 **Children** Menu

Cigalon   PLAN 3 D2

◉◉ French

Friendly, relaxed and classy Provençal paradise in legal land

☎ 020 7242 8373
115 Chancery Ln WC2A 1PP
e-mail: bookings@cigalon.co.uk
dir: Nearest station: Chancery Lane, Temple

Blink and you could almost be on a sun-drenched Provençal veranda rather than the dusty legal world of Chancery Lane, courtesy of Cigalon's inspired design that brings the outside indoors via an atrium-like glass ceiling and open patio-style kitchen. Embellishing the illusion, pastel-striped banquettes, silver bamboo and curving lavender-coloured central booths come set to a soundtrack of chirpy birdsong and cicada. But it's not all good looks over substance: the operation - founded by some former Club Gascon folk - scores on all fronts. The kitchen itself focuses on the grill to deliver its sunny, seasonal Provençal menu of simple, robust, punchy flavoured classics. Witness an opener cassoulet of snails

and anchovies, or perhaps blowsier beef onglet teamed with baby onions, gnocchi and full-throttle red wine jus. Desserts might feature a warm black chocolate and nuciola tart with quenching pear sorbet to cut through its richness, while wines are exclusively French, focusing on Provence (with a nod to Corsica) like the food. (Baranis, their trendy bar, sits in the basement.)

Chef Julien Carlon **Owner** Vincent Labeyrie
Times 12-2.30/5.45-10 Closed Xmas, New Year, BHs, Sat-Sun **Prices** Fixed L 2 course fr £19.50, Fixed D 3 course fr £24.50, Starter £8-£13.50, Main £9.50-£18.50, Dessert £6-£8.50, Service added but optional 12.5% **Wines** 75 bottles over £30, 22 bottles under £30, 9 by glass **Notes** Vegetarian available, Dress restrictions, Smart casual **Seats** 60, Pr/dining room 8 **Children** Portions **Parking** On street

Clos Maggiore   PLAN 3 B1

◉◉◉ – *see page 370*

L'Atelier de Joël Robuchon

LONDON WC2   **PLAN 3 A2**

Modern French V

Concept dining with a clubby feel from a French master-chef

☎ 020 7010 8600
13-15 West St WC2H 9NE
e-mail: info@joelrobuchon.co.uk
dir: Nearest station: Leicester Sq, Covent Gdn, Tottenham Court Rd. Left off Cambridge Circus & Shaftesbury Av

Monsieur Robuchon has a dozen Ateliers dotted around the world, lucky London included, where his style of creative and exquisitely-crafted food is served up in decidedly cool and contemporary club-like settings - atelier means workshop after all. Although this is no temple to haute cuisine, it does have quality running through it from top to bottom. Here in London there are

three floors to choose from - L'Atelier on the ground floor, La Cuisine one floor up, and the Salon Bar and Terrace on top - and you can sit where you like depending on your mood, it's that kind of place. The ground-floor space is dominated by the granite bar-counter with high red stools, where diners get close to the kitchen action, and a dynamically interactive mood reigns. Staff are great at helping you through the menus, which consist in the main of Franco-Mediterranean dishes with some Japanese umami for good measure. Small-plated multi-course eating is the way to go downstairs if you really want to get a taste of the place. Upstairs there's more of a usual restaurant vibe with a striking monochrome décor and an open kitchen. Wherever you choose to sit, some rather thrilling food awaits. Foie gras terrine with toasted country bread seems like a good option given the provenance of the man himself, and indeed it is, but there's also crispy langoustine fritters with basil pistou, or pan-fried scallops with black truffle and pumpkin risotto. The quality of the ingredients is second to none

and the cooking doesn't betray that investment in the best produce. Roasted sea bass is cooked in a wasabi and black pepper sauce to deliver an Asian flavour, or there might be caramelised pork with endive, creamy polenta and black truffles. There's no less craft and creativity at dessert stage: royal gala apple compôte, hibiscus flower and Calingo cream, for example.

Chef Olivier Limousin **Owner** Joel Robuchon
Times 12-3/5.30-11 Closed 25-26 Dec, 1 Jan, Aug BH **Prices** Fixed L 2 course £28-£37, Tasting menu £129-£215, Starter £9-£40, Main £18-£43, Dessert £11, Service added but optional 13% **Wines** 4 bottles over £30, 2 bottles under £30, 26 by glass **Notes** Pre-theatre menu 2/4 course £28/£39, Sunday L, Vegetarian available, Vegetarian menu, Dress restrictions, Smart casual **Seats** 43 **Children** Portions **Parking** Valet parking service

Clos Maggiore

Modern French V 🍷 NOTABLE WINE LIST

An intimate oasis in the heart of Covent Garden

☎ 020 7379 9696
33 King St, Covent Garden WC2E 8JD
e-mail: enquiries@closmaggiore.com
web: www.closmaggiore.com
dir: Nearest station: Covent Garden, Leicester Sq. 1 min walk from Covent Garden piazza & Royal Opera House

An intimate ambience and a blossom-filled courtyard at its heart mean that this dreamy oasis in buzzing Covent Garden will always require seriously advance booking if you're lining it up for a Valentine's Day assignation. Once inside, the frenetic tourist hordes evaporate, and you're transported to a classy auberge in Provence or Tuscany, with elegantly dressed tables on stone floors, and a retractable roof allowing you to gaze up at blue sky or twinkling stars; in the winter months, a crackling log fire in the open stone hearth adds a cosseting element into the mix. If the courtyard is booked, don't despair: the other dining rooms offer an ambience of dark mahogany, an open fire, plush fabrics and soft-focus lighting to lend a sheen of Orient Express luxury. Marcellin Marc's contemporary French cooking is a perfect partnership with the location, his dishes underpinned by well-honed classical technique and driven by high-

quality ingredients. Prix-fixe, and pre- and post-theatre menus offer remarkable value for such an in-demand venue, but hey, you're here on a romantic big date, so splash out on the carte and start with scallops poached in seaweed butter served with leek fondue and oyster leaf, followed by roasted leg of Landes corn-fed chicken stuffed with Morteau sausage and partnered by roasted ratte potatoes, raspberry onion, and Alsace bacon sauce. Non-meat-eaters are not sidelined either: pan-roasted wild sea bass is accompanied by salted haddock and herb brandade, and fennel salad; there are enticing vegetarian dishes too. At the end, dark Valrhona chocolate fondant with blood orange sorbet is hard to resist. A wine list of serious scope and class is a good excuse to linger in one of the capital's most romantic destinations.

Chef Marcellin Marc **Owner** Tyfoon Restaurants Ltd **Times** 12-2.30/5-11 Closed 24-25 Dec **Prices** Fixed L 2 course fr £15.50, Fixed D 3 course fr £19.50, Tasting menu fr £59, Starter £6.90-£16.50, Main £17.50-£29.50, Dessert £6.90-£8.90, Service added but optional 12.5% **Wines** 1900 bottles over £30, 10 bottles under £30, 21 by glass **Notes** Pre & post theatre menus Mon-Sat 5-6, Sun 5-11pm, Sunday L, Vegetarian menu, Dress restrictions, Smart casual **Seats** 70, Pr/dining room 23 **Children** Portions **Parking** On street, NCP

Save on Hotels. Book at **theAA.com/hotel**

LONDON, CENTRAL (WC2) 371 **ENGLAND**

LONDON WC2 *continued*

The Delaunay
PLAN 3 C2

® European

All day brasserie dining in the grand European tradition

☎ 020 7499 8558
55 Aldwych WC2B 4BB
e-mail: reservations@thedelaunay.com
dir: Nearest station: Holborn, Covent Garden

If the Wolseley (see entry) is your bag, then you'll adore its Aldwych sibling. The Delaunay, like the ever-popular Piccadilly original, gets its inspiration from the grand café-restaurants of central Europe. The David Collins' design follows the same winning formula, as does the extensive all-day dining repertoire, though the Delaunay's swish interior has a rather warmer tone. Darkwood panelling, marble surfaces, green leather upholstered banquettes and chairs, linen-clothed tables, brass lighting and white-and-grey tiled floors set a classy tone, alongside a roomy bar-café area. It's an equally vibrant, glamorous spot, great for people watching and with slick, well-pitched service. And the show never stops; from breakfast and an all-day carte, plus afternoon tea, you can expect the likes of omelette Arnold Bennett, moules frites or croquet-monsieur to more substantial things such as roasted rump of lamb with spinach fregola or Wiener schnitzel. Not leaving room for desserts - like apple and marzipan strudel or baked vanilla cheesecake - would be a mistake. The Delaunay Counter - with separate entrance - offers a takeaway service, including fabulous patisserie.

Times 11.30-mdnt

Les Deux Salons
PLAN 3 B1

®® French

Covent Garden's re-created Parisian brasserie

☎ 020 7420 2050
40-42 William IV St WC2N 4DD
e-mail: info@lesdeuxsalons.co.uk
dir: Nearest station: Charing Cross, Leicester Square. Near National Portrait Gallery & Trafalgar Sq

The third venture from Anthony Demetre and Will Smith (see Arbutus and Wild Honey), Les Deux Salons is about as authentic a French brasserie as you'll find short of hopping on Eurostar, with its banquettes, globe lights, mosaic marbled floors and bustling ambience. The menu encapsulates everything you could hope for in a modern brasserie, from leek tart, or jambon persillé, to robust main courses of accurately timed roast cod with onions, cabbage and bacon, or beef slowly braised in red wine with carrots. Seasonality plays its part, autumn bringing on pork cheeks with honey and sherry vinegar and root vegetables, and Wednesday's plat du jour may be lapin à la moutarde, Thursday's cassoulet. Puddings are as French as can be, among them Paris-Brest and glazed lemon tart.

Chef Colin Layfield **Owner** Will Smith & Anthony Demetre **Times** 12-11 Closed 25-26 Dec, 1 Jan **Prices** Starter £2.50-£9.50, Main £8.50-£29.50, Dessert £2.95-£6.50, Service added but optional 12.5% **Wines** 37 bottles over £30, 11 bottles under £30, 40 by glass **Notes** Menu Prix-

Fixe £9.95. Menu Formule £19.75, Sunday L, Vegetarian available **Seats** 160, Pr/dining room 34 **Children** Portions **Parking** On street

Great Queen Street
PLAN 3 B2

® British, European

Best of British at bustling gastro-pub

☎ 020 7242 0622
32 Great Queen St WC2B 5AA
e-mail: greatqueenstreet@googlemail.com
dir: Nearest station: Covent Garden, Holborn

Younger stablemate of Waterloo's Anchor & Hope (see entry), Great Queen Street rocks week long. The long pub-like room - with a bar down one side (set for bar dining) and an open kitchen at the back - comes decked out in dark red walls, while elbow-to-elbow wooden tables (constantly being turned) and mismatched chairs fit with its back-to-basics ethos and high-decibel atmosphere. Wines are served in tumblers and specials get chalked -up, while the twice-daily-changing menu deals in quality produce where seasonality, sourcing and provenance are king. Intelligently simple, unfussy Brit fare with gutsy, big flavours is the kitchen's preference. There's no three-course formality, with dishes laid out in ascending price order, so mix-and-match with smaller plates (pork terrine to cured sprats, salsify and creamed horseradish) or large dishes like smoked Gloucestershire Old Spot and choucroute or braised hare with polenta.

Chef Tom Norrington-Davies, Sam Hutchins **Owner** R Shaw, T Norrington-Davies, J Jones, M Belben **Times** 12-2.30/6-10.30 Closed last working day in Dec-1st working day in Jan, BHs, D Sun **Prices** Prices not confirmed Service added but optional, Groups min 6 service 12.5% **Wines** 13 by glass **Notes** Sunday L, Vegetarian available **Seats** 70

Green Man and French Horn
PLAN 3 B1

®® French NEW ✦NOTABLE WINE LIST

Gutsy Gallic food matched with Loire wines

☎ 020 7836 2645
54 St Martins Ln WC2N 4EA
dir: Nearest station: Leicester square. Opposite the Salisbury theatre

This newcomer to the Covent Garden foodie scene (younger sibling to Terroirs, see entry) takes its inspiration from France, or to be more precise, dishes associated with the lands along the River Loire that are a match made in heaven when paired with the wines of the region. The operation occupies an old pub done out unfussily with bare brick walls, well-worn parquet floors, wooden tables and banquettes, and the formula works a treat: plates of rich, robust food matched with interesting, sensibly-priced wines, including an excellent choice by the glass. You might go for a plat du jour - grilled sardines with lemon, garlic and parsley, say - with a glass of wine for a mere tenner, or set out with a hearty slab of terrine made from pork belly, shoulder and liver served with cornichons and excellent sourdough bread, then move on to rabbit matched with salsify and cider.

For dessert, a splendid tarte vigneronne - winemaker's tart - is another treat from the Loire, a slim puff pastry tarte fine of apple set in red wine jelly.

Chef Ed Wilson **Owner** Ed Wilson, Oliver Barker **Times** 12-3/5.30-11 Closed Xmas, New Year, BH, Sun **Prices** Starter £7-£9.25, Main £10-£25, Dessert £6.50-£7.50, Service added but optional 12.5% **Notes** Plat du jour & glass of wine £10, Vegetarian available **Seats** 55 **Parking** On street

The Ivy
PLAN 3 A1

® British, International **V**

Ever-popular Theatreland legend

☎ 020 7836 4751
1-5 West St, Covent Garden WC2H 9NQ
dir: Nearest station: Leicester Square. Leicester Sq station exit 3 right, along Charing Cross Rd, 2nd right into Litchfield St. Restaurant entrance is around left hand corner on West St, opposite St Martin's Theatre

It still takes advance planning to get a table, but once inside all is comforting, woody, and rather dignified with its clubby oak panelling and green leather seating. The Ivy shows no sign of losing its lustre. Charming staff keep everything ticking along with a smile, despite the rapid turnover of tables throughout the day. The brasserie-style menu is dominated by ideas from the comforting end of the spectrum, hopping between staples such as shellfish bisque with Armagnac or salt-beef hash, to bang bang chicken, and main courses such as pan-fried sea bream with slow-braised peppers and wild garlic, or Bannockburn rib steak served on the bone. Desserts are such fun things as wild strawberry and prosecco jelly with ripple ice cream.

Chef Gary Lee **Owner** Caprice Holdings **Times** 12-11.30 Closed 25-26 Dec, 1 Jan, All-day dining **Prices** Starter £7-£16.75, Main £13.50-£34.50, Dessert £7.50-£9.75 **Notes** Sunday L, Vegetarian menu, Dress restrictions, Smart casual **Seats** 100, Pr/dining room 60 **Children** Portions **Parking** NCP, on street

Jamie's Italian
PLAN 3 B1

® Modern Italian

Jamie does the West End

☎ 020 3326 6390
11 Upper St Martin's Ln, Covent Garden WC2H 9FB
e-mail: covent@jamiesitalian.com
dir: Nearest station: Covent Garden, Leicester Square

In a prime position between Covent Garden and Leicester Square, Jamie Oliver's West End gaff (the group grows and grows) packs them in; avoid peak times to beat the queues. The place fairly buzzes from noon to midnight, the closely-set tables leading to quite a chorus. Jamie's hallmark Italian food is the name of the game, with good quality seasonal produce featuring in unfussy, fresh and vibrant dishes brimful with chilli, lemon and herby flavours. Pasta is made in-house and bread is baked twice daily in their artisan bakery next door. From the seasonal menu and chalkboard specials, perhaps kick off

continued

LONDON WC2 *continued*

with carpaccio of braised octopus with olives, rocket and herbs, then follow with a tender, full-flavoured feather steak, flash-grilled with sage and prosciutto, and served with a spicy tomato, basil and chilli salsa and a side dish of excellent polenta chips flavoured with rosemary and parmesan. Finish with a text-book smooth, creamy and precisely-flavoured vanilla pannacotta with fruit compôte.

Chef Andrea Cavenaghi, Zak Greggory **Owner** Jamie Oliver **Times** noon-11.30 Closed 25-26 Dec, All-day dining **Prices** Fixed L 3 course £25-£30, Fixed D 3 course £25-£30, Starter £3.75-£7.50, Main £6.25-£20.50, Dessert £4.90-£5.25, Service optional, Groups min 6 service 10% **Wines** 16 by glass **Notes** Vegetarian available **Seats** 190 **Children** Portions, Menu

J. Sheekey & J. Sheekey Oyster Bar
PLAN 3 B1

@ Seafood

Renowned theatreland fish restaurant

☎ 020 7240 2565
32-34 St Martin's Court WC2N 4AL
dir: Nearest station: Leicester Square. Leave station by exit 1 left into Charing Cross Rd. St Martin's Court is 2nd left

Very much London legend, this enduring and much-loved seafood restaurant in the heart of theatreland began life as a seafood stall in the 19th century. J Sheekey expanded the business into adjoining properties and it has been a haunt of the great and the good ever since, including theatrical types who ply their trade on the surrounding boards. Inside is a warren of snug wood-panelled dining rooms, plus a seafood and oyster bar, and a menu listing relatively straightforward fish and shellfish dishes prepared from superb quality raw ingredients. Start with a classic Catalan-inspired dish of razor clams with chorizo and broad beans, or a choice of oysters if you want to keep it simple, followed by a superb cod fillet on buttered leeks with meaty Isle of Mull mussels and wilted sea aster. A-listers might go for Beluga with blinis and sour cream (£195 for 30g), but everyone else can take comfort in a plum and almond tart.

Times 12-3/5.30-12 Closed 25-26 Dec, 1 Jan, D 24 Dec

Kaspar's Seafood Bar & Grill
PLAN 3 C1

@@ Seafood NEW ☺

Super-fresh seafood and more in a stunning art deco setting

☎ 020 7836 4343
The Savoy, Strand WC2R 0EU
e-mail: savoy@fairmont.com
dir: Nearest station: Embankment, Covent Garden, Charing Cross. Halfway along The Strand between Trafalgar Sq & Aldwych

When The Savoy reopened after its multi-million-pound overhaul a few years back, The River Restaurant was

preserved exactly as it was: a formal, traditional, old-school hotel dining room. But that's all changed now. It still overlooks the river, but every trace of the original has been erased and replaced with an informal, buzzy seafood bar and grill. Named Kaspar's after the legend of Kaspar the cat (ask one of the friendly staff for the full story), the room looks stunning with its central seafood bar and 1920s-inspired décor of gold and black patterned tiling, blue leather banquettes and tub-style chairs, mirrors, decorative glass panels and unusual light fittings. You can sit up at the seafood bar and watch as the chef prepares you a fruit de mer platter or a plate of smoked fish, or head to a table and order something from the extensive and varied carte - perhaps smoked sand shrimp and eel cocktail (a brilliant take on the classic prawn cocktail) to start, followed by a simple lobster club sandwich with fries, or monkfish kebabs from the grill.

Chef James Pare **Owner** Fairmont **Times** 12-11.30 **Prices** Starter £7-£39, Main £15-£39, Dessert £8-£15, Service added but optional 12.5% **Wines** 40 bottles over £30, 40 by glass **Notes** Vegetarian available, Dress restrictions, Smart casual, Civ Wed 400 **Seats** 114, Pr/dining room 12 **Children** Portions

Kopapa
PLAN 3 B2

@@ Fusion

Culinary Covent Garden alchemy from a master of fusion cuisine

☎ 020 7240 6076
32-34 Monmouth St, Seven Dials, Covent Garden WC2H 9HA
e-mail: information@kopapa.co.uk
dir: Nearest station: Covent Garden

The Seven Dials sister of Providores in Marylebone (see entry), Kopapa is another piece of fusion heaven from Kiwi trail-blazer Peter Gordon. It can pretty much sort you out any time of the day - breakfast, brunch, lunch, dinner, small plates, big plates, sharing (or not), it's up to you. And it has a chilled out vibe, too, with a marble-topped bar (bar snacks available, of course), and a relaxed attitude that keeps the customers coming back. On the menu is some creative fusion food, which means anything from Europe and Asia is fair game: deep-fried sesame and Urfa chilli-salted squid with sumac mayonnaise (small plate), or twice-cooked Middlewhite pork belly with sweet potato purée, cucumber lychee salad, peanuts and sweet chilli coconut sauce, for example. To finish, apple and quince Charlotte with preserved lemon custard competes for your attention with peanut butter parfait served with a délice made with Original Beans 75% Piura Criolla chocolate, plus sea salt caramel and chocolate crumble.

Chef Peter Gordon, Greig Hunter **Owner** Peter Gordon, Adam Willis, Brandon Allan, Michael McGrath **Times** 12-10.45 Closed 25-26 Dec All-day dining **Prices** Prices not confirmed Service added but optional 12.5% **Notes** Pre-theatre menu until 7pm Mon-Sat, Sun 9.30pm, Vegetarian available, Dress restrictions, Smart Casual **Seats** 66 **Parking** On street

Kyashii
PLAN 3 B1

@ Japanese

Creative Japanese food to share

☎ 020 7836 5211
4a Upper St Martin's Ln, Covent Garden WC2H 9NY
e-mail: info@kyashii.co.uk
dir: Nearest station: Covent Garden

Eye-catchingly trendy with its glass-fronted entrance and futuristically-styled interior, Kyashii is an über-cool contemporary Japanese restaurant close to Covent Garden and the West End theatres. Dazzling white seating, yellow neon and tropical blue fish tanks enhance the wow-factor; there are four dining areas with the same vibe, while the street-level room (the others are subterranean) has a sushi bar, and, on the mezzanine above, a hip lounge bar all sleek in black. The kitchen turns out some accomplished modern Japanese food, conjured from quality ingredients and designed for sharing. Crispy chilli soft-shelled crab comes with garlic, chilli and spring onion, and there's the likes of pan-fried sea bream with mushrooms and soy sauce and lamb smoked with green tea and served with a moro miso (baby soya bean) sauce. There are cocktails, too.

Owner Madeira Group Assets Ltd **Times** 12-3/6-11 **Prices** Service added but optional 12.5% **Notes** 4 course Sakura menu £30 (based min 2 people)

Massimo Restaurant & Oyster Bar
PLAN 5 B6

@ Italian, Mediterranean

Grand Roman style in the West End

☎ 020 7998 0555
Northumberland Av WC2N 5AE
e-mail: information@massimo-restaurant.co.uk
dir: Nearest station: Embankment, Charing Cross. From Trafalgar Sq into Northumberland Av, restaurant within 2mins walk

The David Collins' designed interior certainly makes an impression with its soaring striped columns, magnificent light fittings, striking artworks and tables dressed up in white linen. It's a bold and exhilarating space to tuck into high quality seafood with an Italian flavour. There's a cool oyster bar where you can dive into Maldon, Loch Fyne, Irish Rock and Natives and accompany them with an oyster martini if it takes your fancy. There's loads of choice on the menu, so choosing may take a while: seared and peppered tuna with courgette fritters, or langoustines with rocket and Ligurian olive oil? Follow on with black tagliatelle with squid, carrot and courgette, and among 'carni' options you might find braised beef cheek with creamed potatoes. Top-quality seafood is the thing, though, such as a whole monkfish served with that Ligurian olive oil and Amalfi lemon, or lemon sole with tomato and anchovy sauce. To finish, Massimo's tiramisù is one way to go.

Times 12-3/6-11 Closed Sun

Mon Plaisir
PLAN 3 B2

Traditional French

A Francophile's delight in theatreland

☎ 020 7836 7243
19-21 Monmouth St WC2H 9DD
e-mail: monplaisirrestaurant@googlemail.com
web: www.monplaisir.co.uk
dir: Nearest station: Covent Garden, Leicester Square. Off Seven Dials

It is 'fashion police be dammed' at this cosily nostalgic veteran French restaurant. While the original front room has changed little since the '40s (with red and white checked cloths and wooden chairs), beyond a series of lighter, more modish areas (including a mezzanine-style loft and small bar) come decorated in French posters and paintings and quirky memorabilia. The place gets rammed with the pre- and post-theatre crowd, adding congenial buzz to French service and retro accordion music. The menu does safe and respectable French things and doesn't do impressions; take cuisine bourgeoise classics like foie gras parfait to snails in garlic and parsley butter or côte de boeuf, while scallops with pork belly and a pumpkin and ginger broth is as modish as it gets.

Chef Franck Raymond **Owner** Alain Lhermitte
Times noon-11.15 Closed Xmas, New Year, BHs, Sun
Prices Fixed L 2 course fr £12.95, Fixed D 3 course £15.95-£24.95, Starter £6.95-£11.95, Main £18.50-£25.95, Dessert £4.95-£8.95, Service added but optional 12.5% **Wines** 13 by glass **Notes** Fixed D pre-theatre 2/3 course incl coffee £13.95/£15.95, Vegetarian available, Dress restrictions, Smart casual **Seats** 100, Pr/dining room 25 **Children** Portions

The Opera Tavern
PLAN 3 C1

Spanish, Italian

Knock your socks off Spanish and Italian tapas

☎ 020 7836 3680
23 Catherine St, Covent Garden WC2B 5JS
e-mail: info@operatavern.co.uk
dir: Nearest station: Covent Garden

When busy, which it usually is, The Opera Tavern hits all the right notes like a soprano in full flow at the nearby Opera House. From the team behind Salt Yard and Dehesa (see entries), the winning idea of combining the best of the tastes of Italy and Spain in dishes to share brings in the crowds. The one-time pub in the heart of theatreland

has a vibrant ground-floor bar and grill (feel the heat at the far end of the room), with a little more refinement in the upstairs dining room; wherever you sit, the place positively throbs with energy. Friendly, clued-up staff will steer you through the entertaining fusion of Spanish and Italian ideas. The mini Ibérico pork and foie gras burger must surely be considered a classic by now, and the charcuterie and cheeses should not be ignored either. Smoked eel and pancetta brandade with free-range egg and horseradish velouté demonstrates the mettle of this kitchen. If tapas isn't your way, it's possible to stick to three-course convention.

Times 12-3/5-11.30 Closed 25-26 Dec, some BHs, D Sun

Orso
PLAN 3 C1

Modern Italian

Italian food in a lively basement

☎ 020 7240 5269
27 Wellington St WC2E 7DA
e-mail: info@orsorestaurant.co.uk
dir: Nearest station: Covent Garden. Between Exeter St & Tavistock St

While the street entrance could easily be missed, the clued-up crowds have been flocking downstairs to this relaxed, all-day Covent Garden Italian since the mid-'80s. The cavernous hide-away basement - once an orchid warehouse - buzzes with conversation and unstuffy, friendly quick-fire service, and is always busy pre-theatre. It's all endearingly rustic, charmingly authentic and classic Italian with a nod to the Milan of the '50s; from checked tablecloths to herringbone-patterned wood floors, white-tiled walls, pastel shades and black-and-white photos. In turn, crowd-pleasing menus are the drill, showcasing simple regional Italian cooking. All the usual pizza (roasted pepper, red onion, sun-dried tomato and mozzarella) and pasta (linguine with white crabmeat, garlic, parsley and cherry tomatoes) are here, otherwise expect roast halibut to arrive with tomatoes, black olives and new potatoes, and perhaps a pannacotta dessert with champagne rhubarb. A fixed-price pre-theatre option and all-Italian wines prove popular.

Times noon-mdnt Closed 24-25 Dec, L Sun (Jul-Aug)

Savoy Grill
PLAN 3 C1

British, French

A bedrock of classicism at a premier-league London address

☎ 020 7592 1600
1 Savoy Hill, Strand WC2R 0EU
e-mail: savoygrill@gordonramsay.com
dir: Nearest station: Charing Cross. Walk E through the riverside gardens to the hotel

From the Victorian literati to stars of the silent screen to the movers and shakers of today's business and politics, the Grill has always been a place to see and be seen. That seeing all goes on within the sacred confines of walnut panelling, art-deco mirrors and plush banquettes, beneath the glitter of chandeliers. The Savoy's recent

makeover refreshed the Grill as a Premier-League London restaurant space, and while the cuisine rests on a solid bedrock of Edwardian classicism, it doesn't feel in the least old-fashioned. What's that line about class never going out of style? The grills themselves, from the wood-fired oven, include 35-day, dry-aged beef in a plethora of cuts, lamb cutlets, pork chops, gammon steaks and sausages, but there are also roasts and braises that span the range from the elevated - thyme-roasted quail with Landes foie gras and horseradish mash in port jus - to the downright homeliness of a steak-and-ale pudding with onion sauce. It's all bookended by a good selection of hors d'oeuvres, including grilled kippers in lemon and parsley, and desserts that are unreconstructed because they haven't been deconstructed in the first place (rum baba with vanilla cream, for example). They've got some wines too, if you're up for pumping up the financial volume.

Times 12-3/5.30-11

Terroirs
PLAN 3 B1

Mediterranean, European NOTABLE WINE LIST

French provincial cooking with flavours to the fore

☎ 020 7036 0660
5 William IV St, Covent Garden WC2N 4DW
e-mail: enquiries@terroirswinebar.com
dir: Nearest station: Covent Garden, Charing Cross. Exit Charing Cross station turn right, along The Strand, first left onto William IV St

Head to the ground floor, which takes its inspiration from Parisian wine bars, and have a glass of something good with a plate of charcuterie (perhaps pork and pistachio terrine), or one of the plats du jour (rump of lamb with cime di rapa and anchovies) - or spread out at one of the tables downstairs. Either way, the inspiration is the cooking of a provincial grand-mère, with ideas pulled in from the Mediterranean and even further afield: lamb kofta, for instance, with the punch of harissa softened by mint and yoghurt, a careful balance of heat and fragrance. Dishes are carefully considered so the integrity of each ingredient is clear. A salad of beetroot, lentils and ricotta is a lovely blend of flavours, at the same time earthy and delicate. Equally impressive is the stronger taste of braised oxtail with gnocchi, while main courses may take in full-on cassoulet, or cod fillet with monk's beard and brown shrimps. Puddings are appreciated for their simplicity, among them perhaps rhubarb tarte fine with custard, or rich chocolate pot.

Chef Ed Wilson **Owner** Ed Wilson, Oli Barker, Eric Narioo **Times** 12-11 Closed Xmas, Etr, Sun **Prices** Fixed D 3 course £20-£30, Starter £6.50-£10, Main £16-£19, Dessert £5-£6.50, Service added but optional 12.5% **Wines** 200 bottles over £30, 30 bottles under £30, 18 by glass **Notes** Fixed 1 course L £10, Vegetarian available **Seats** 120 **Children** Portions

GREATER LONDON

BARNET
Map 6 TQ29

Savoro Restaurant with Rooms

◉ Modern European, British

Contemporary good looks and well-judged menu

☎ 020 8449 9888
206 High St EN5 5SZ
e-mail: savoro@savoro.co.uk
web: www.savoro.co.uk
dir: M25 junct 23 to A1081, continue to St Albans Rd, at lights turn left to A1000

Set back from Barnet's bustling high street, the traditional frontage of this snazzy neighbourhood restaurant with rooms belies its contemporary good looks. Done out in clean-cut fashionable manner, with neutral tones, etched glass screens, mirrors and cream tiled floors, it provides the perfect backdrop for the kitchen's modern approach. The cooking encompasses British classics with the flavours of the Med and Asia; begin with buffalo mozzarella salad or goats' cheese soufflé, for example, then follow up with chargrilled calves' liver teamed with smoked bacon, mash and onion gravy, or perhaps teriyaki roasted salmon or pan-seared halibut cooked with lemon and herbs. A range of steaks from the grill covers all the bases, while desserts continue the style with homespun Bakewell tart lining up alongside rhubarb and vanilla pannacotta.

Chef Jackson Lopes **Owner** Jack Antoni, Dino Paphiti **Times** 12-3/6-11 Closed 1 Jan, 1 wk New Year, D Sun **Prices** Prices not confirmed Service added but optional 12% **Wines** 12 by glass **Notes** Early eve menu Mon-Thu 2 course £11.95, Sunday L, Vegetarian available **Seats** 68 **Children** Portions **Parking** 9

BROMLEY

Chapter One
PLAN 1 H1

◉◉◉◉ – *see opposite*

ENFIELD
Map 6 TQ39

Royal Chace Hotel

◉ Modern British ◐

Imaginative cooking and rural views

☎ 020 8884 8181
162 The Ridgeway EN2 8AR
e-mail: reservations@royalchacehotel.co.uk
dir: 3m from M25 junct 24, 1.5m to Enfield

It might be on the outskirts of London, but the Royal Chace is set within its own peaceful grounds. The stylish restaurant, with well-spaced tables under a large skylight, shares the rural outlook and, even better, there's a courtyard for alfresco dining. An element of innovation runs through the cooking, so seared scallops are accompanied by sweetcorn and lemongrass pannacotta and pork belly lardons, seasonal asparagus is grilled with white truffle butter and plated with watercress purée, and a main course of baked pork fillet is wrapped in pancetta and served with apple croquettes rolled in crackling and a sauce of ginger and carrot. Dishes are well composed and timings are spot on, seen in seared salmon fillet, moist and full of flavour, with avocado and tomato consommé, new potatoes and crisp shallots. Desserts fulfil expectations too: perhaps rhubarb and vanilla cheesecake with apple salsa and orange syrup.

Chef Duncan Womack **Owner** B Nicholas **Times** 12-9.30 Closed D Sun **Prices** Fixed D 3 course fr £27.50, Starter £5.95-£6.95, Main £15.50-£26.95, Dessert £6.95, Service added but optional 10% **Wines** 14 bottles over £30, 58 bottles under £30, 10 by glass **Notes** Sunday L, Vegetarian available, Dress restrictions, Smart casual, Civ Wed 220 **Seats** 50, Pr/dining room 220 **Children** Portions, Menu **Parking** 220

HADLEY WOOD
Map 6 TQ29

West Lodge Park Hotel

◉ Modern British ◐

Polished cooking in a parkland setting

☎ 020 8216 3900
Cockfosters Rd EN4 0PY
e-mail: westlodgepark@bealeshotels.co.uk
web: www.bealeshotels.co.uk
dir: On A111, 1m S of M25 junct 24

A white Regency-style mansion - surrounded by 35 acres that include an arboretum of over 800 tree species - is the imposing setting for this hotel restaurant. Refurbishment has delivered a modern spin to the dining room's original features, its name dedicated to the 17th-century portrait artist Mary Beale (with family connection to the owners), whose original work adorns the walls. There's plenty to enjoy about the modish British cooking, with use of fresh quality local produce and provenance clearly a driving force behind the menus. Seared Denham Estate venison steak, for example, comes with roasted parsnip, beetroot purée, potato rösti and liquorice jus, whilst monkfish medallions might be wrapped in Parma ham and served with rocket, black noodles and tomato and olive oil sauce. To finish, a classic Belgian chocolate soufflé with Grand Marnier anglaise fits the bill.

Chef Wayne Turner **Owner** Beales Ltd **Times** 12.30-2.30/7-9.30 **Prices** Service optional, Groups min 12 service 12.5% **Wines** 7 by glass **Notes** Sunday L £31, Vegetarian available, Dress restrictions, Smart casual, jacket & tie recommended, Civ Wed 90 **Seats** 70, Pr/dining room 100 **Children** Portions **Parking** 75

HARROW ON THE HILL

Incanto Restaurant
PLAN 1 B5

◉◉ Modern Italian ▥ NOTABLE WINE LIST ◐

Regional Italian cooking with a light modern touch

☎ 020 8426 6767
The Old Post Office, 41 High St HA1 3HT
e-mail: info@incanto.co.uk
web: www.incanto.co.uk
dir: M4 junct 3 at Target rdbt, follow signs A312 Harrow. Continue through South Harrow, turn right at Roxeth Hill, turn left at top of hill

An old Victorian red-brick post office on the village green in Harrow on the Hill is the setting for this sleek modern Italian. Inside it is an expansive loft-like, split-level space with a soaring glass skylight, huge beams and bare darkwood tables on a pale wooden floor. The menu of southern Italian-inspired dishes eats as well as it reads, as it is all built on fresh produce combined creatively - ravioli filled with duck egg and matched with red onion purée, pancetta, wild mushrooms and black truffle, for example. Elsewhere, rump of Welsh Elwy Valley lamb could be served with a cannelloni of shoulder, beetroot Tatin and artichoke purée in a well-balanced idea, while monkfish arrives with a ragu of borlotti beans and shellfish, lime and roasted almond foam, and razor clam gremolata. Desserts keep the creative flow moving - perhaps banana parfait, cinnamon crumble, champagne jelly and mascarpone. Friendly, informed service and a deli-café for stocking up on authentic goodies to take home complete the picture.

Chef Quentin Dorangeville **Owner** David & Catherine Taylor **Times** 12-2.30/6.30-10.30 Closed 24-26 Dec, 1 Jan, Etr Sun, Mon, D Sun **Prices** Fixed L 2 course fr £17.95, Fixed D 3 course fr £23.95, Tasting menu fr £45, Starter £6.50-£9.50, Main £14.50-£19.50, Dessert £6-£7.50, Service added but optional 12.5% **Wines** 76 bottles over £30, 24 bottles under £30, 13 by glass **Notes** Sunday L, Vegetarian available **Seats** 64, Pr/dining room 30 **Children** Portions, Menu **Parking** On street

Chapter One

Modern European **V** NOTABLE WINE LIST

Strikingly refined cooking in out-of-town hotspot

☎ 01689 854848
Farnborough Common, Locksbottom BR6 8NF
e-mail: info@chaptersrestaurants.com
web: www.chaptersrestaurants.com
dir: On A21, 3m from Bromley. From M25 junct 4 onto A21 for 5m

The outskirts of a big city is not always the easiest place to do business when attention is so often focused up town, especially if that city is London, but Andrew McLeish and his team have well and truly put Farnborough Common on the map. If you want to wine and dine in fine style, make a beeline for BR6. The old Tudor house stands on a busy road junction, but no matter, for it makes finding the place straightforward and you'll be oblivious to the traffic once through the sharply contemporary entrance. The place is a little haven of civilisation, as swanky as any uptown joint, and a beacon for first-class, contemporary cooking. Attention to detail is evident from the precisely set tables - dressed in crisp white linen - to the upbeat and knowledgeable service team. It looks the part, too, with its coffee and cream colour scheme. Value for money can be a moot point, hard to pin down, but here it is black and white:

this is remarkably good value by any definition. The food is sharply focused, modern but grounded in classicism, and spectacular to look at. Start, perhaps, with a fabulous dish of jugged hare with pancetta, potato espuma and hare satay, the flavours perfectly judged, or the Asian-inspired, treacle-cured Loch Duart salmon partnered with charred spring onions, coriander, ginger and lemongrass purée, and a sesame dressing. The ingredients are sourced with diligence and the seasons followed to ensure everything is at its very best. Super-fresh gurnard, for example, is pan-fried and comes with a field mushroom purée, tiger prawns, gnocchi and chanterelles, while braised and crispy suckling pig is partnered with roast Jerusalem artichokes, potato purée and black truffle butter. There's a Josper grill, too, which does its very best with a piece of USDA prime rib-eye steak (served with twice-cooked chips and béarnaise sauce). Desserts are no less creative, beautiful to look at and even better to eat. Organic lemon tart, for example, with an apricot and yoghurt sorbet and crispy almond bracelet biscuit is a delightful combination, or go for all the comfort and joy of a hot Valrhona chocolate fondant with vanilla ice cream. The vegetarian menu is worthy of a mention for its ambition and originality. The attention to detail and high standards extend to the wine list, too, which is a fine piece of work with lots of well-chosen things to go for.

Chef Andrew McLeish **Owner** Selective Restaurants Group
Times 12-2.30/6.30-10.30 Closed 2-4 Jan **Prices** Fixed L 3 course fr £19.95, Starter fr £9.25, Main fr £20, Dessert fr £8.25, Service added but optional 12.5% **Wines** 13 by glass **Notes** Sunday L £22.95, Vegetarian menu, Dress restrictions, Smart casual **Seats** 120, Pr/dining room 55 **Children** Portions **Parking** 90

HARROW WEALD

Grim's Dyke Hotel
PLAN 1 B5

◉◉ British, European ✿

Modern British cooking and more in a country setting

☎ 020 8385 3100
Old Redding HA3 6SH
e-mail: reservations@grimsdyke.com
web: www.grimsdyke.com
dir: 3m from M1 between Harrow & Watford

An imposing part-timbered property in 40 acres of gardens and woodlands, Grim's Dyke was at one time the home of Sir William Gilbert, testament to his success as the librettist of Sir Arthur Sullivan. Gilbert's Restaurant, originally the billiard room, is a magnificent space, dominated by an inglenook and Gothic arches. Chef Daren Mason trained under Gary Rhodes and, like his mentor, his style is rooted in the great British traditions, so expect bubble-and-squeak with a poached duck egg and hollandaise, followed by confit pork belly with a faggot, apple croquettes and red wine glaze. He's also capable, though, of turning out the strong flavours of seared tuna with wasabi, pickled radishes and orange and soy dressing, then veal Holstein with fondant potato and anchovies. The Everyday Classics menu features time-honoured dishes like omelette Arnold Bennett and fish and chips with mushy peas and tartare sauce, while a skilled French pastry chef is responsible for desserts such as Bakewell tart with custard, and banana tarte Tatin.

Chef Daren Mason **Owner** Skerrits of Nottingham Holdings **Times** 12.30-2/7-9.30 Closed 24 Dec, 1 Jan, L Sat, D 25-26 Dec **Prices** Fixed L 2 course fr £12.95, Fixed D 3 course £16.95-£28.50, Starter £6-£8.25, Main £12-£25, Dessert £6.50-£9, Service optional **Wines** 25 bottles over £30, 20 bottles under £30, 10 by glass **Notes** Sunday L, Vegetarian available, Dress restrictions, No jeans or trainers (Fri-Sat), Civ Wed 60 **Seats** 60, Pr/dining room 88 **Children** Portions **Parking** 100

HEATHROW AIRPORT (LONDON)

The Continental Hotel
PLAN 1 B2

◉ Modern European NEW ✿

Modern European brasserie cooking near Heathrow

☎ 020 8572 3131 & 8538 5883
29-31 Lampton Rd TW3 1JA
e-mail: f&b@thecontinental-hotel.com
dir: A4, right onto A3006, left onto A3005 then left onto Lampton Rd

A spa hotel near Heathrow Airport will look like an essential resource if you've just spent nine hours in an economy seat, but is a useful addition all-round to the gastronomically impoverished Hounslow area. A stylish cocktail bar with gigantosaurus TV screen showing live sport is only the half of it. Youthful staff contribute to the vivacious ambience, and the menu in the Twentynine restaurant draws on modern European brasserie style to good effect in a rollcall of on-trend dishes. Start with venison ravioli topped with shaved parmesan, or seared

scallops with beignets and purée of cauliflower or butternut squash. Flavourful lamb shank comes with apposite garnishes of roast garlic mash, honeyed parsnip and a Madeira jus, while fish might be grilled salmon with creamed leeks in caviar beurre blanc. Finish with coconut and vanilla pannacotta and orange coulis, classic tiramisù, or an Anglo-European cheese selection with tomato relish.

Chef Palash Roy **Owner** Vistastar Leisure Plc **Times** 12.30-10.30 All-day dining **Prices** Fixed L 2 course fr £20, Fixed D 3 course fr £25, Starter £4.95-£7.95, Main £9.95-£16.95, Dessert £4.50-£5.95, Service added but optional 12.5%, Groups min 6 service 15% **Wines** 5 bottles over £30, 9 bottles under £30, 6 by glass **Notes** Pre-theatre 2/3 course £20/£25, Sunday L, Vegetarian available **Seats** 36 **Children** Portions, Menu **Parking** 19

London Heathrow Marriott Hotel
PLAN 1 A3

◉ Traditional Italian ✿

Tuscan-influenced cuisine at smart hotel

☎ 020 8990 1100
Bath Rd UB3 5AN
e-mail: mhrs.lhrhr.ays@marriotthotels.com
web: www.londonheathrowmarriott.co.uk
dir: M4 junct 4, follow signs for Heathrow Terminals 1 & 3. Left at rdbt onto A4 towards central London. Hotel 0.5m on left

Enlivened by the atmosphere and aromas of an open-to-view theatre kitchen, the intimate fine-dining option at this modern airport hotel offers simple Italian cooking and is justifiably popular, so booking is advisable. Modern and classical Italian food has its roots firmly set in Tuscany, with top-notch produce used to good effect to create hearty and rustic dishes where the main ingredient shines. From the seasonal menu, perhaps kick off with a light and subtly flavoured warm garlic and parmesan polenta cake with marinated peppers and rocket salad, then follow with pan-fried cod with sautéed spinach and an enjoyable prosecco and cream sauce. Leave room for a stunning vanilla pannacotta with a well-timed poached pear in a rich red wine sauce.

Chef Joe Beaver **Owner** Marriott International **Times** 6-10.30 Closed 23 Dec-4 Jan, L all week **Prices** Fixed D 3 course £39, Starter £7-£12, Main £14-£36, Dessert £7, Service added but optional 12.5%, Groups min 6 service 12.5% **Wines** 14 bottles over £30, 17 bottles under £30, 13 by glass **Notes** Vegetarian available, Dress restrictions, Smart casual, no jeans, trainers or shorts, Civ Wed 414 **Seats** 65 **Children** Portions, Menu **Parking** 280

Sofitel London Heathrow
PLAN 1 A2

◉◉ French NEW ✿

Fine-dining only a short walk from Terminal 5

☎ 020 8757 7777
Terminal 5, London Heathrow Airport TW6 2GD
e-mail: H6214-FB9@sofitel.com
dir: M25 junct 14, follow signs to Terminal 5

Connected to Heathrow's Terminal 5 by a covered walkway, the modern Sofitel is plugged into the international travel network like no other, but the fine-dining La Belle Epoque restaurant does bring a little touch of cultural refinement to proceedings. It occupies a vast space, but cleverly designed to bring it down to a human scale with a kind of inner gazebo and smart banquette seating at well-spaced tables. Bilingual menus reveal the French foundations on which the food is built, so you might start with a partridge, foie gras and pistachio terrine, served with a nicely-judged plum and galangal jam, or an inventive white onion and thyme brûlée partnered with a biscuit flavoured with caraway and chilli. There are a few Asian flavours along the way, such as a main-course lemon sole served with langoustine mousse and lemongrass broth. Apricot and almond tart with Amaretto cream looks beautiful on the plate and makes a fine finish to a meal.

Chef Daren Pavey **Owner** Surinder Arora **Times** 12-2.30/6-10 Closed Xmas, New Year, BH, Sun **Prices** Fixed L 3 course £27.95, Tasting menu £49.50, Starter £8.50-£11.50, Main £18-£29.50, Dessert £8.50-£11, Service added but optional 12.5% **Wines** 10 by glass **Notes** Vegetarian available **Seats** 88, Pr/dining room 20 **Children** Portions **Parking** 400

KESTON
Map 6 TQ46

Lujon

◉◉ Modern European ✿

Ambitious modern fare and a relaxing atmosphere

☎ 01689 855501
6 Comonside BR2 6BP
e-mail: info@lujon.co.uk
dir: M25 junct 4, follow A21 Bromley

A white property on Keston Common is the home of Lujon, an oak-floored space with oval-backed chairs at wooden-topped tables and a warm and relaxing atmosphere. A new chef is at the helm, continuing to cook in the modern European mode and to devise menus with headings such as 'stream and sea' and 'four legs (or two)'. Imaginative starters may run to prawns in white wine with gremolata, or pheasant ballottine with mushroom and beetroot dressing. Ingredients are well chosen and handled confidently so flavours are clear. Pork belly, served with apple sauce, red cabbage and pommes purée, is the sort of mainstream main course to expect, and fish is properly treated, seen in pan-fried mackerel partnered by pancetta, accompanied by cockle dressing, roast onions and new potatoes, and cod fillet given a kick from Madeira jus accompanied by ham hock mash. Finish with a comforting dessert like cinnamon-flavoured rice pudding with poached plums, or lemon curd tart with crème fraîche ice cream and passionfruit coulis.

Chef Andrew Demetriou **Owner** Angela Bell
Times 12-3/6.30-10 Closed Mon-Tue (excl BHs), D Sun
Prices Fixed L 2 course £14.50, Starter £5.90-£8.50, Main £12.50-£25.95, Dessert £6-£6.25, Service added but optional 12.5% **Wines** 10 by glass **Notes** Fixed L 2 course includes wine, D 3 course Wed-Fri, Sunday L £16.95-£19.95, Vegetarian available, Civ Wed 60 **Seats** 48, Pr/dining room 32 **Children** Portions, Menu **Parking** Free car park 1min walk away

KEW

The Glasshouse
PLAN 1 C3

▣▣▣ — *see page 378*

PINNER

Friends Restaurant
PLAN 1 B5

▣ French

Heartwarming French bistro fare in an old timbered house

☏ 020 8866 0286
11 High St HA5 5PJ
e-mail: info@friendsrestaurant.co.uk
web: www.friendsrestaurant.co.uk
dir: In centre of Pinner, 2 mins walk from underground station

In the 20 years or so since chef-patron Terry Farr established Friends in a picture-postcard black-and-white timbered 400-year-old cottage, it has become a fixture on the local foodie scene. The interior is similarly monochrome, but with a sharp, contemporary look - black leather seats at white linen tables, and modern Provençal artwork that hints at where the kitchen's heart lies. After two decades in business, local supply lines are strong, while top-grade meat and fish comes from Smithfield and Billingsgate markets. Tried-and-true French bistro cooking jazzed up with sound modern thinking is the deal here. To start, wild mushroom risotto is supercharged with porcini oil and parmesan tuile, followed by a classic trio of sautéed South Downs lamb fillet with creamy dauphinoise potatoes and flageolet beans. At the end, a compôte of rhubarb and balsamic and hazelnut biscotti prove the perfect foil to rhubarb pannacotta.

Friends Restaurant

Times 12-3/6.30-10.30 Closed 25 Dec, BHs, Mon in summer, D Sun

RICHMOND UPON THAMES

Bacco Restaurant Italiano
PLAN 1 C2

▣ Italian

Family hospitality and traditional Italian cooking

☏ 020 8332 0348
39-41 Kew Rd TW9 2NQ
e-mail: bookings@bacco-restaurant.co.uk
dir: A316 towards Richmond Station or town centre, 2 min walk from tube

There is a thoroughly charming air of family hospitality to this Italian eatery opposite Richmond Station and near to the Orange Tree Theatre. Linen-clothed tables look smart, and there is much to divert the eye in the shape of the colourful prints and paintings that crowd the pale yellow walls. Italian simplicity is the hallmark of the bilingual menus, although this isn't a kitchen to rest on its laurels. The pasta is freshly made in-house every day, perhaps for spaghetti served in a parmesan basket dressed in truffle oil. That might follow a bowl of traditional fish and shellfish soup with chick peas and garlic crostino, while mains run to calves' liver in sage butter with stewed cabbage, and well-seasoned sea bass with cherry tomatoes, black olives and capers in white wine sauce. Traditional tiramisù is a satisfying way to finish, or there may be vanilla pannacotta with mango coulis. A range of quality Italian wines completes the picture.

Chef Vincenzo Indelicato **Owner** Stefano Bergamin
Times 12-2.30/5.45-11 Closed Xmas, New Year, BHs, Sun **Prices** Prices not confirmed Service added 12.5% **Wines** 16 by glass **Notes** Vegetarian available, Dress restrictions, Smart casual **Seats** 50, Pr/dining room 27 **Children** Portions

Bingham
PLAN 1 C2

▣▣▣ — *see page 378*

La Buvette
PLAN 1 C2

▣ French, Mediterranean

Cheery bistro serving French classics and more

☏ 020 8940 6264
6 Church Walk TW9 1SN
e-mail: info@labuvette.co.uk
dir: 3 mins from train station, opposite St Mary Magdalene Church, off the main High St

Tucked away on a leafy walkway off the high street, this French neighbourhood bistro isn't easy to find, but once you know where it is you're bound to go back. Its alfresco courtyard is a sunny-day magnet, while inside the intimate space fits the bistro genre to a tee: all pastel shades, floorboards, close-set, brown-paper-covered tables and café-style chairs. The kitchen confidently turns out the requisite regional French fare, big on flavour and conjured from quality produce. So expect refined classics like a rustic fish soup with rouille, gruyère and croûtons, followed by chargrilled onglet. The roster also flirts with lighter, more current offerings: witness sparklingly fresh roasted monkfish with a balanced, clear-flavoured combo of Jerusalem artichokes, zesty gremolata, big-hit tapenade and a tempura of spring onion. Service is appropriately relaxed and informed, while clever prix-fixe deals are friendly on the wallet and appreciated by the pre-theatre crowds.

Chef Buck Carter **Owner** Bruce Duckett **Times** 12-3/6-10 Closed 25-26 Dec, 1 Jan, Good Fri, Etr Sun **Prices** Fixed L 2 course £15.50, Fixed D 3 course £22, Starter £5.25-£9.50, Main £12.50-£23.25, Dessert £5.25-£6.75, Service added but optional 12.5% **Wines** 20 bottles over £30, 17 bottles under £30, 12 by glass **Notes** Sunday L, Vegetarian available **Seats** 50 **Children** Portions, Menu **Parking** NCP - Paradise Road

The Dysart Arms
PLAN 1 C2

▣▣ British **NEW**

Fantastic ingredients used creatively

☏ 020 8940 8005
135 Petersham Rd, Petersham TW10 7AA

Looking over Richmond Park, The Dysart Arms occupies a lovely Arts and Crafts building dating from 1904 that was once a spit and sawdust boozer, but is now tastefully and sympathetically restored to its full glory with natural textures of wood and a neutral contemporary look. The food has also headed rather more upmarket under the direction of chef Kenneth Culhane, who is no stranger to stellar kitchens, and believes passionately in sourcing the best possible raw ingredients, including foraged seasonal materials, as the basis of his inventive, deeply-flavoured dishes. Home-made Irish soda bread with fennel pollen butter shows from the off that no corners are cut here in the quest to add interesting modern twists to the food, as does the kimchi (fermented cabbage) and lemon preserve that puts a novel spin on roasted quail. Next out, top-class Huntsham Court Farm pork belly is matched with apple polenta, curly kale, wild garlic and

continued

Bingham

RICHMOND UPON THAMES   PLAN 1 C2

Modern British V   NOTABLE WINE LIST

Instinctive, dynamic cooking by the river at Richmond

☎ 020 8940 0902
61-63 Petersham Rd TW10 6UT
e-mail: info@thebingham.co.uk
web: www.thebingham.co.uk
dir: On A307, near Richmond Bridge

If you like a substantial side order of chic to go with your food, the Bingham should hit the spot. The classy boutique hotel sits in an enviable riverside location just a short and rather pleasant stroll from the centre of Richmond - a setting that comes into its own in summer when you're dining out on the waterside terrace or balcony overlooking the Thames towpath. Originally a pair of knocked-together Georgian cottages, the interiors these days are straight from the pages of a glossy design magazine, all easy-on-the-eye neutral hues with statement teardrop chandeliers and cleverly-recessed lights softly illuminating the glamorous dining rooms - a sexy boudoir scene of velvety curvaceous banquettes, pale gold carpets, and silk curtains. Shay Cooper is a talented and ambitious chef whose complicated and intricate cooking produces dynamic results from components that will certainly have you wondering what they will actually taste like together. The results are never less than convincing thanks to top-level technical ability boosted by an instinctive feel for what works with what, and there's no recourse to fussy foams or jellies for showy effect, just great ingredients and spot-on flavours. Chicken soup sounds simple enough, but this one comes partnered inventively by confit egg yolk, glazed mushrooms, and a finger of fried ham and cheese sandwich. Next up, saddle of rabbit is wrapped in ham, stuffed with light truffled mousse and partnered by braised rabbit meat in wafer thin discs of celeriac, smoked celeriac purée, and truffle sauce, the whole edifice given a necessary fruity kick from chargrilled pear. Fish might appear as an inventive composition involving Cornish stone bass with braised endive, artichoke, glazed salsify, potato gnocchi, bergamot lemon and mushroom vinaigrette. To finish, tiramisù is the inspiration behind the exciting array of flavours and textures in a dessert of mascarpone mousse with candied pistachio, espresso ice cream and hot Valrhona chocolate sauce.

Chef Shay Cooper **Owner** Ruth & Samantha Trinder **Times** 12-2.30/7-10 Closed D Sun **Prices** Service added but optional 12.5% **Wines** 14 by glass **Notes** Tasting menu 8 course, Pre-theatre 2 course menu, Sunday L fr £38, Vegetarian menu, Civ Wed 90 **Seats** 40, Pr/dining room 90 **Children** Portions, Menu **Parking** 8, Town centre

The Glasshouse

KEW   PLAN 1 C3

Modern International   NOTABLE WINE LIST

French-based cooking of exemplary consistency

☎ 020 8940 6777
14 Station Pde TW9 3PZ
e-mail: info@glasshouserestaurant.co.uk
dir: Close to Kew Gardens underground station

No, this is not some fly-by-night pop-up affair that has set up shop in a Victorian greenhouse in Kew Gardens: this perennially popular neighbourhood restaurant's name comes from the floor-to-ceiling plate glass windows that make it stand out in the parade of shops leading away from Kew Gardens tube station, and make for a light-flooded and unbuttoned setting. With Bruce Poole and Nigel Platts-Martin (the team behind the equally in-vogue Chez Bruce in Wandsworth and La Trompette in Chiswick - see entries) at the helm, The Glasshouse seems to have found the Holy Grail that keeps the well-heeled denizens of Kew coming back again and again. Seasonally-driven modern European cooking that doesn't try any fancy smoke-and-mirrors trickery is what this place is all about: it trades in exactly the kind of food that modern gastronomes want to eat, built upon the solid foundations of classical French cuisine bourgeoise (rather than the stifling pretensions of the haute variety), and jazzed up with a switched-on lexicon of Mediterranean and Asian flavours. Typical of the style is a starter of rabbit tortellini with Serrano ham, rabbit consommé, carrots and baby artichokes, or there might be a globe-trotting array of guacamole, shiso and radish salad and yuzu dressing to partner deep-fried soft-shelled crab. Of course, it takes formidable technical skills to make compositions such as these seem effortless, and you can expect main courses to bring a similarly accomplished layering of flavours and textures: grilled sea bass, perhaps, supported by basil and shrimp ravioli, samphire, slow-cooked leeks, and shellfish espuma, while meatier ideas could bring the full-on pigginess of pork fillet and braised cheeks with boudin blanc, fennel choucroute, creamed potato, and mustard jus. Desserts such as Valrhona chocolate marquise with chicory mousse, nougatine and crème fraîche ice cream show a kitchen that has a firm grasp of how flavours work together. Conscientious and clued-up staff are the icing on the cake.

Chef Daniel Mertl **Owner** Nigel Platts-Martin, Bruce Poole **Times** 12-2.30/6.30-10.30 Closed Xmas, New Year **Prices** Fixed L 2 course £23.50-£27.50, Fixed D 3 course £42.50, Tasting menu £60-£95, Service added but optional 12.5% **Wines** 417 bottles over £30, 29 bottles under £30, 15 by glass **Notes** Tasting menu available D Sun-Fri, Sunday L, Vegetarian available **Seats** 60 **Children** Portions **Parking** On street (metered)

RICHMOND UPON THAMES *continued*

parsley purée, while dessert could be Valrhona Jivara chocolate and praline bar with miso salted caramel ice cream.

Chef Kenneth Culhane **Times** 11am-11.30pm **Prices** Prices not confirmed **Notes** Sunday L, Vegetarian available

The Petersham Hotel   PLAN 1 C2

◉◉ British, European **V** 🌱

Lovely Thames views and a varied modern menu

☎ 020 8939 1084 & 8940 7471
Nightingale Ln TW10 6UZ
e-mail: restaurant@petershamhotel.co.uk
web: www.petershamhotel.co.uk
dir: From Richmond Bridge rdbt A316 follow Ham & Petersham signs. Hotel in Nightingale Ln on left off Petersham Rd

An unmistakable mansion in floridly Italianate Gothic style, The Petersham was built as a hotel and opened its doors in 1865. Don't miss a glimpse of the magnificent Portland stone staircase winding its way up the building, with a painted ceiling and skylight at the top. Each table in the generously spaced restaurant, with its panelling and mirrors, has a wonderfully bucolic view over meadows to the Thames through full-length windows. High-quality ingredients form a solid base for the kitchen to work with on its seasonally-changing menus: lobster butter for potted shrimps with pickled cucumber, say, followed by Kiev-style chicken and foie gras, served with truffled haricot blanc purée and vin jaune. Classics like Dover sole meunière and grilled fillet steak with béarnaise put in an appearance alongside more modish ideas with no particular loyalty to any one cuisine: grilled ox tongue with pickled mushrooms and horseradish and parmesan toast, seared stone bass topped with olives, accompanied by a stew of octopus, chorizo, white beans and shallots, then apple galette with Calvados ice cream.

Chef Alex Bentley **Owner** The Petersham Hotel Ltd **Times** 12.15-2.15/7-9.45 Closed 25-26 Dec, 1 Jan, D 24 Dec **Prices** Fixed L 2 course £22.95, Fixed D 3 course £26.95, Starter £10.50-£14.50, Main £16.50-£34, Dessert £8, Service added but optional 12.5% **Wines** 93 bottles over £30, 34 bottles under £30, 8 by glass **Notes** Degustation menu 5 course £95, Sunday L, Vegetarian menu, Civ Wed 40 **Seats** 70, Pr/dining room 26 **Children** Portions, Menu **Parking** 60

Petersham Nurseries Café   PLAN 1 C2

◉ Modern 🌱

Fresh, vibrant cooking from garden to plate

☎ 020 8940 5230
Church Ln, Petersham Rd TW10 7AG
e-mail: info@petershamnurseries.com
dir: Adjacent to Richmond Park & Petersham Meadows. Best accessed on foot or bicycle along the river

Having gained a foodie following under Skye Gyngell ('til her departure in 2012), this charmingly ramshackle glasshouse restaurant still packs in the crowds. It's a romantically eccentric, shabby-chic place, best enjoyed on sunny days when it feels more Tuscany than Richmond, with its dirt floor, mismatched tables and chairs and riot of leafy fronds. It's a dress-down affair (old shoes rather than heels), but then that's all part of the fun. The kitchen's modern European approach is inspired by the seasons and the bounty of fresh produce that flows from the garden (including edible flowers and herbs straight from the walled potager). Witness simple, light dishes like a roast pepper and fennel salad (with basil aïoli) to accompany sea-fresh halibut, or a wild garlic, garden bean, and crème fraîche and almond partnership for a more gutsy flavoured lamb shoulder. Be warned though, prices are high and parking tricky. (The adjacent glasshouse is a more accessibly priced all-day teahouse.)

Chef Cat Ashton **Owner** Franceso & Gael Boglione **Times** 12-2.45 Closed Etr Sun, 25 Dec, Mon, D all week **Prices** Prices not confirmed Service added but optional 12.5% **Wines** 11 by glass **Notes** Vegetarian available **Parking** Town Centre, Paradise Road or The Quadrant

Richmond Hill Hotel   PLAN 1 C2

◉ Modern European

Riverside dining in Richmond

☎ 020 8939 0265
144-150 Richmond Hill TW10 6RW
e-mail: info.richmond@kewgreen.co.uk
dir: A316 for Richmond, hotel at top of Richmond Hill

The hotel, a Grade II listed building overlooking the Thames and Richmond Park, has a bar with comfortable leather sofas and chairs and a two-part restaurant, the first carpeted, the second with a wooden floor and a fireplace. A few influences from the East - Chinese ginger beef with coconut rice, or grilled salmon steak with teriyaki sauce, noodles and Asian greens - add some variety to the menu, which will otherwise be familiar enough, opening with carpaccio with a parmesan basket, and seared scallops with cauliflower purée and pancetta, and closing with crème brûlée, and sticky toffee pudding. In between might come pan-fried calves' liver and bacon with onion gravy and mash, or seared mackerel with grilled potatoes and salad.

Chef William Morvan **Owner** Kewgreen **Times** 10.30am-10.30pm **Prices** Starter £3.50-£10.50, Main £12.25-£29.50, Service added but optional 12% **Wines** 9 by glass **Notes** Sunday L, Vegetarian available,

Dress restrictions, Smart casual, Civ Wed 80 **Seats** 85, Pr/dining room 30 **Children** Portions, Menu **Parking** 150

RUISLIP

The Barn Hotel   PLAN 1 A5

◉◉ Modern French

Confident, creative cooking in Ruislip

☎ 01895 636057
West End Rd HA4 6JB
e-mail: info@thebarnhotel.co.uk
web: www.thebarnhotel.co.uk
dir: A40 onto A4180 (Polish War Memorial) exit to Ruislip. 2m to hotel entrance at mini-rdbt before Ruislip tube station

The Barn is a mix of period buildings and shiny new ones not very far from central London, reached via Ruislip tube station. It's handy for Heathrow and Wembley Stadium, Arena et al, too. But rather charmingly it is surrounded by three acres of pretty gardens and has that 'away from it all' feel. It's big on weddings and conferences, but due to the presence of its Hawtrey's Restaurant, it's a useful dining address as well. The dining room has been dressed up like a Jacobean baronial hall with acres of darkwood panelling, chandeliers and tables laid for fine dining. The cooking takes a bold contemporary French path, so you might start with pea velouté with a blue cheese beignet, or maybe seared yellowfin tuna with balsamic caviar and citrus vinaigrette. The food looks good on the plate and there is lots of creative thinking going on here. Main-course haunch of rabbit, for example, comes stuffed with mushrooms and pistachios, a sausage made with the leg meat, choucroute and braised radish.

Times 12-2.30/7-10.30 Closed L Sat, D Sun

SURBITON

The French Table
PLAN 1 C1

◎◎ French, Mediterranean **V** ☺

Contemporary French dining with panache in the suburbs

☎ 020 8399 2365
85 Maple Rd KT6 4AW
e-mail: enquiries@thefrenchtable.co.uk
dir: 5 min walk from Surbiton station, 1m from Kingston

It may be set in a modest parade of shops in Surbiton 'village', but Eric and Sarah Guignard's French Table has pedigree, and just keeps getting better. Eric's French/Mediterranean cooking is a fine-tuned affair: a progressive take on the classical theme, producing well-dressed, interesting dishes full of clean, clear flavours, fashioned from prime seasonal produce. Take an opening gambit of crushed peanut-coated mi-cuit salmon skilfully combined with light-and-airy cauliflower mousseline and soya and ginger dressing. Main course might bring on top-drawer slow-cooked lamb rump with a terrine of braised shoulder and piquant merguez sausage, with aubergine relish and ras el hanout jus giving a kick of spice, or perhaps braised ox cheek with home-made tagliatelle, wild mushrooms, roasted shallots and red wine sauce. The interior is a modern good-looker: all pastel shades, lime-green-backed banquettes and slate-tiled floor, and a relaxed, buzzy, high-decibel vibe. Sunny-natured service fits the brief too. (Its dinky sibling French Tart - a boulangère/patisserie/coffee house - is next-door.)

Chef Eric Guignard, Frederic Duval **Owner** Eric & Sarah Guignard **Times** 12-2.30/7-10.30 Closed 25-26 Dec, 1-3 Jan, Sun-Mon **Prices** Fixed L 2 course £19.50, Tasting menu £45-£75, Service added but optional 12.5% **Wines** 9 by glass **Notes** Tasting menu whole table only (with wine £75), Vegetarian menu, Dress restrictions, Smart casual **Seats** 48, Pr/dining room 32 **Children** Portions **Parking** On street

TEDDINGTON

Retro
PLAN 1 C1

◎◎ French **V** ☺

French bistro with bags of style and provincial cooking

☎ 020 8977 2239
114-116 High St TW11 8JB
e-mail: retrobistrot@aim.com
dir: A313 Teddington High St

This highly individual bistro certainly brings a taste of France to suburbia, standing out from the crowd not just for its bold-flavoured cooking and sassy avante-garde décor, but for the charming, flamboyant service of owner and front-of-house impresario Vincent Gerbeau. Bold-patterned wallpaper, glitzy chandeliers and vibrant-coloured banquettes and drapes deliver the retro-chic backdrop, along with Parisian café-style tables and chairs, bare floorboards, exposed brick and big mirrors. Appropriately, the kitchen turns out some retro French

classics like moules marinière, grilled snails, Chateaubriand and hot chocolate fondant, alongside more à la mode dishes like sea-fresh halibut fillet teamed with a striking risotto nero, piquant confit red peppers and naturally salty samphire, or perhaps melt-in-the-mouth braised pork belly with cavolo nero, root vegetables and a liquoricey anise jus. The flavours are simple and big-hearted and it's all fashioned from prime seasonal ingredients. Accompanying wines fittingly all speak with a patriotic French accent.

Chef Andrew West **Owner** Vincent Gerbeau **Times** 12-3.30/6.30-11 Closed Xmas, 1 Jan, BHs, Mon (open on request), D Sun **Prices** Fixed L 2 course fr £10.95, Service added but optional 12.5% **Wines** 25 by glass **Notes** Fixed D 2/3 course min price applies Tue-Thu, max Fri-Sat, Sunday L, Vegetarian menu **Seats** 110, Pr/dining room 50 **Children** Portions **Parking** On street

TWICKENHAM

A Cena
PLAN 1 C2

◎ Modern Italian

Reliable Italian cooking near Richmond Bridge

☎ 020 8288 0108
418 Richmond Rd TW1 2EB
e-mail: acenarichmond@gmail.com
dir: 100 yds from Richmond Bridge

An informal neighbourhood Italian smartly kitted out in bistro style, A Cena is certainly not your average pizza-pasta joint. True, pasta might make an appearance, but a thoughtful one: perhaps spaghetti con gamberoni (tiger prawns, chilli, rocket and lemon). The cooking reliably follows the seasons whilst speaking of sunnier climes. Take a fish main like pan-fried Sicilian-style marinated hake with its accompaniment of capers, white wine, lemon and green beans, or a veggie option like polenta fritters with Swiss chard, tomato and parmesan. For dessert there might be pannacotta (perhaps served old-school-style in a cocktail glass) with a brûlée-esque topping of salted peanut brittle and coffee caramel, while cheeses and wines all speak with an Italian accent. The dining room is a stylish mix of darkwood (floorboards, furniture and bar) and white walls hung with feature mirrors. Note that the restaurant is on the Twickenham side of Richmond Bridge.

Chef Nicola Parsons **Owner** Camilla & Tim Healy **Times** 12-2.30/7-10.30 Closed Xmas & BHs, L Mon, D Sun **Prices** Starter £7-£9, Main £12.95-£23.50, Dessert £6-£9.50, Service optional, Groups min 6 service 12.5% **Wines** 66 bottles over £30, 20 bottles under £30, 12 by glass **Notes** Fixed L 3 course available pre-rugby match £50, Sunday L £21-£25, Vegetarian available **Seats** 55 **Children** Portions **Parking** On street

MERSEYSIDE

BIRKENHEAD
MAP 15 SJ38

Fraiche

◎◎◎ – *see opposite*

FRANKBY
Map 15 SJ28

Stewart Warner at Hillbark

◎◎◎ – *see opposite*

LIVERPOOL
Map 15 SJ39

The London Carriage Works

◎◎ Modern European 🏅 NOTABLE WINE LIST ☺

Well-executed cooking in trendy hotel conversion

☎ 0151 705 2222
Hope Street Hotel, 40 Hope St L1 9DA
e-mail: eat@hopestreethotel.co.uk
dir: Follow cathedral & university signs on entering city, at the centre of Hope St between the two cathedrals

The Hope Street Hotel's restaurant gets its name from a sign uncovered during renovation: the property, built in the 1860s in the style of a Venetian palazzo, was once a coach and carriage works. The interior is now all stripped-down bare bricks and wooden floors, a trendy environment for some seriously ambitious cooking. The emphasis here is on fresh, regional produce, particularly fish and game, as demonstrated in a starter of Lakeland rabbit scented with sage and served with field mushrooms, baby leaf spinach and natural jus, which might be followed by Liverpool Bay sea bass with samphire, Puy lentils, Southport brown shrimp and Filey crab bisque. Dishes make an impact with their well considered combinations and good timings. Witness beautifully cooked scallops and braised pork cheek with morcilla, cauliflower purée and cider vinaigrette, and roast breast of Gressingham duck with a pink grapefruit and root ginger jus, spring cabbage, ratte potatoes, Southport smokehouse pancetta and new season peas.

Chef Paul Askew **Owner** David Brewitt **Times** 12-3/5-10 Closed D 25 Dec **Prices** Fixed L 2 course £15, Fixed D 3 course £20, Starter £4.95-£12.50, Main £13.95-£29.50, Dessert £5.95-£11.50, Service optional, Groups min 8 service 10% **Wines** 164 bottles over £30, 42 bottles under £30, 18 by glass **Notes** Pre-theatre & tasting menus available, Sunday L, Vegetarian available, Dress restrictions, Smart casual, Civ Wed 70 **Seats** 100, Pr/dining room 50 **Children** Portions, Menu **Parking** On street, car park opposite

Save on Hotels. Book at **theAA.com/hotel**

MERSEYSIDE 381 **ENGLAND**

Fraiche

BIRKENHEAD   **MAP 15 SJ38**

Modern French, European V

Restlessly creative cooking in a characterful venue

☎ 0151 652 2914
11 Rose Mount, Oxton CH43 5SG
e-mail: contact@restaurantfraiche.com
dir: M53 junct 3 towards Prenton. In 2m left towards Oxton. Fraiche on right

Fraiche may seem a remarkable venture to find in a conservation village on the Wirral peninsula, not far from Birkenhead, but the fact is it would be a remarkable restaurant to find anywhere. From start to finish, it offers a thoroughly idiosyncratic approach. The room itself may be done in familiar sandy and creamy hues (intended to reflect the local shoreline), but is given personality with bespoke artworks in glass and metal. An on-site shop

sells dining room accoutrements. The tone of the place is refreshingly informal, given that the cooking wears its culinary ambitions on its sleeve. Marc Wilkinson's cooking shows restlessly creative intelligence, welding contemporary technique on to a classical foundation. 'We propose to you our vision of modern cuisine using nature as our guide', announces the website, sounding faintly as though translated from the French, which isn't a bad indication of the centre of gravity. The Signature dinner menu offers a fixed six-course excursion through the style, with designations giving only a laconic hint of the combinations to be discovered: butternut squash, tangerine and yoghurt; cauliflower cheese, mint, Beaufort; wild brill fillet, parsley quinoa, grape and rose; loin of venison, pickled grelot, kohlrabi; lemongrass pannacotta; chocolate mousse, sea buckthorn and pear (the last assuming you don't decide instead to climb aboard the cheese chariot). The enigmatic Menu Black is not a festival of squid ink and truffle, but a menu surprise reserved to Fraiche members. Lunch offers a simpler

four-course format, but with no stinting on the impact, the main course perhaps offering Blackface Suffolk lamb with shallot purée and parsley root, coming after a marinated scallop with compressed avocado, and then textures of beetroot served with buttermilk. Roasted pineapple fragranced with coffee and lemon brings down the curtain. An imaginative slate of house wines has half-a-dozen by the glass.

Chef Marc Wilkinson **Owner** Marc Wilkinson
Times 12-1.30/7-9.30 Closed 25 Dec, 1 Jan, Mon-Tue, L Wed-Thu **Prices** Tasting menu £65, Service optional **Wines** 6 by glass **Notes** Sunday L £35, Vegetarian menu **Seats** 16, Pr/dining room 20 **Children** Portions **Parking** On street

Stewart Warner at Hillbark

FRANKBY   **MAP 15 SJ28**

Modern British V   🍷 NOTABLE WINE LIST

Outstanding cooking in luxury boutique hotel

☎ 0151 625 2400
Hillbark Hotel and Spa, Royden Park CH48 1NP
e-mail: enquiries@hillbarkhotel.co.uk
web: www.hillbarkhotel.co.uk
dir: M53 junct 3, A552 (Upton), right onto A551 (Arrowe Park Rd). 0.6m at lights left into Arrowe Brook Rd. 0.5m on left

Hillbark, completed in 1891, was built as a private residence, and it certainly reflects the great wealth and prestige of its then owners. It's said to be one of the finest examples of half-timbering in the country, and no expense was spared on the interior, with a profusion of panelling, stained-glass windows by William Morris and a fireplace dating from 1627. The Dining Room, where

Stewart Warner is in charge of the kitchen, is no exception, with portraits in oil on fabric-covered walls, chandeliers, an Adam fireplace, chairs upholstered in rich, colourful patterned fabrics, linen napery, crystal and fine china, and lovely views across the terrace towards the woodland beyond. In other words, it's an appropriate setting for Warner's finely wrought, imaginative modern cooking. Combinations of ingredients can at times sound implausible, but be assured this is a chef who really knows what works with what. A pickled herring fillet isn't perhaps the most obvious of starters, but here it's handled extremely well, combined with wafer-thin rounds of cucumber filled with crème fraîche - one with black toasted linseeds on top and the other with sweet maple syrup that contrasts nicely with the salty pickled fish - plus a cucumber granité, a chargrilled baby leek, borage flowers, nasturtium leaves and rye bread. A commitment to top-quality materials is abundantly evident, and ingredients need little embellishment, so pressed foie gras is accompanied simply by pear, almonds and

brioche, and crab with saffron-infused cauliflower purée and caviar. Middlewhite pork - a chop, crispy belly and a tender sausage - comes with dill-scented gnocchi and baby crayfish in an interesting but well-conceived and technically faultless main course, while perfectly timed fillet of turbot is given the Moroccan flavours of ras el hanout, along with swede, cumin and chicken. A pre-dessert - perhaps blood orange jelly topped with honey mousse, honeycomb adding a crunch - arrives before the real thing, which might be a multi-textured pud of nicely tart rhubarb combined with cream cheese and granola, or a theme on chocolate.

Chef Stewart Warner **Owner** Contessa Hotels
Times 12-2.30/7-10 Closed Sun-Mon **Prices** Fixed L 2 course £18, Fixed D 3 course £60, Tasting menu £80, Service added but optional 12.5% **Wines** 600 bottles over £30, 3 bottles under £30, 600 by glass **Notes** Sunday L, Vegetarian menu, Dress restrictions, Smart dress, Civ Wed 200 **Seats** 36, Pr/dining room 30 **Children** Portions, Menu **Parking** 160

LIVERPOOL *continued*

Malmaison Liverpool

◉ Modern British

Modern brasserie food on the Princes Dock

☎ 0151 229 5000
7 William Jessop Way, Princes Dock L3 1QZ
e-mail: liverpool@malmaison.com
dir: Located on Princes Dock near the Liver Building

The Liverpool 'Mal' was the first purpose-built hotel in this innovative chain. It sits on the rejuvenated Princes Dock, in the company of the famous Liver Birds, whose flight from their perch would, as the myth has it, cause the Mersey to engulf the city (perish the thought). Inside looks as contemporary as can be, with a stripped-down, industrial-chic feel from exposed brickwork and fat pipes, and there is a de rigueur chef's table next to the kitchen. Modern brasserie food is the name of the game; smoked salmon rösti with horseradish cream, two cuts of Gloucestershire Old Spot pork with beetroot, parsnip and chorizo, and chocolate fondant with espresso ice cream would be one satisfying route through the menu.

Times 12-2/6.30-10.30 Closed L Sat

60 Hope Street Restaurant

◉ Modern British **V**

Confident modern cooking near the cathedrals

☎ 0151 707 6060
60 Hope St L1 9BZ
e-mail: info@60hopestreet.com
web: www.60hopestreet.com
dir: From M62 follow city centre signs, then brown tourist signs for cathedral. Hope St near cathedral

The Georgian townhouse restaurant on Hope Street has been a presence on the Liverpool dining scene for over a dozen years now. It's in a good spot, close to the Philharmonic Hall and the two cathedrals, and it keeps pulling in the crowds. There's a relaxed bistro vibe on the ground floor, with a metal staircase leading to the restaurant and private dining room upstairs. It looks smart and contemporary but remains a reassuringly friendly place to eat and drink. Ham fritters with peach salad shows the style, as does goats' cheese and beetroot trifle - two modish starters full of flavour. Next

up, perhaps roast rump of Cumbrian lamb with confit potatoes, squash purée and sautéed wild mushrooms, or pan-seared fillet of turbot topped with a potato crust and served with Jerusalem artichoke and white wine velouté. Finish with cherry Bakewell with strawberry ice cream.

Chef Damien Flynn **Owner** Colin & Gary Manning
Times 12-2.30/5-10.30 Closed 26 Dec, 1 Jan, L Sat
Prices Fixed L 2 course fr £20, Fixed D 3 course fr £25, Starter £6.95-£16.95, Main £13.95-£35.95, Dessert £6.95-£12.95, Service optional, Groups min 8 service 10% **Wines** 60 bottles over £30, 9 bottles under £30, 6 by glass **Notes** Pre-theatre daily 5-7pm, Sunday L, Vegetarian menu, Dress restrictions, Smart casual, Civ Wed 50 **Seats** 90, Pr/dining room 40 **Children** Portions, Menu **Parking** On street

Spire

◉ Modern British, European ✪

Contemporary bistro comforts

☎ 0151 734 5040
Number One Church Rd L15 9EA
e-mail: spirerestaurant@btinternet.com

The name might lead you to think that this relaxed modern bistro lies in the shadow of one of Liverpool's two cathedrals, but it is actually a cab ride away in the Wavertree area, right by the one-and-only Penny Lane. The trip out of the centre is amply rewarded though: the friendly neighbourhood bistro venue has an unbuttoned vibe and looks the part too, with its well-trodden floorboards, bare brick and white-painted walls hung with colourful abstract art, and unclothed wooden tables. The kitchen deals in simple contemporary brasserie-style classics with a Mediterranean slant - chicken liver parfait with elderflower jelly and toasted brioche, say, while mains deliver the comforts of braised belly pork with swede purée, crispy black pudding, baby carrots and apple sauce, or roast mustard and herb-crumbed chump of salt marsh lamb partnered with ratatouille, lemongrass and oregano, and baby carrots. Chocolatey puddings - white chocolate pannacotta with chocolate ice cream, perhaps - will win friends, but there might also be apple tarte Tatin with caramel and vanilla sauce.

Chef Matt Locke **Owner** Matt & Adam Locke
Times 12-1.45/6-9.30 Closed BH Mon, 2wks from 2 Jan, Sun, L Sat, Mon **Prices** Fixed L 2 course £10.95-£14.95, Fixed D 3 course fr £17.95, Starter £6-£8.95, Main £13.95-£21.95, Dessert £5.95-£8.95, Service optional **Wines** 12 by glass **Notes** Vegetarian available, Dress restrictions, Smart casual **Seats** 70, Pr/dining room 40 **Children** Portions **Parking** On street, local pub car park

PORT SUNLIGHT Map 15 SJ38

Leverhulme Hotel

◉◉ Modern International **V** 🏆 ✪

Aspirational cooking in art deco gem

☎ 0151 644 6655 & 644 5555
Central Rd CH62 5EZ
e-mail: richardfox@leverhulmehotel.co.uk
web: www.leverhulmehotel.co.uk
dir: From Chester: M53 junct 5, A41 (Birkenhead) in approx 4m left into Bolton Rd, on at rdbt, 0.1m right into Church Drive. 0.2m hotel on right. From Liverpool: A41 (Chester), 2.7m, 3rd exit at 3rd rdbt into Bolton Rd (follow directions as above)

The centrepiece of Port Sunlight Garden Village on the Wirral is this splendid art deco boutique hotel. Built originally as a cottage hospital for the soap factory workers on Lord Leverhulme's pioneering philanthropic estate, the hotel has had a sprinkle of contemporary magic to bring its snow-white interiors up to meet 21st-century expectations, with cutting-edge modern dining in a striking designer setting. The space is airy and expansive with high ceilings, mirrored screens, leather chairs at glass tables and funky art-deco style carpets. Classics and grills feature on the menu, but it is the chef's approach to deconstructing dishes that has earned a reputation for cooking that is sharp, confident, and even edgy in places. Mackerel is served with gooseberry, crunchy onion rings and pointed up with a tartare sauce-style teaming of shallots, capers and gherkin, while main course Moroccan lamb arrives in the company of apricots, aubergines, couscous and a deeply-flavoured jus.

Chef Richard Fox **Owner** Contessa Hotels
Times 12-2.30/6-10 **Prices** Fixed L 2 course £14, Tasting menu £45, Service optional **Wines** 166 bottles over £30, 3 bottles under £30, 166 by glass **Notes** Sunday L, Vegetarian menu, Dress restrictions, Smart casual, Civ Wed 240 **Seats** 60, Pr/dining room 20 **Children** Portions, Menu **Parking** 70

SOUTHPORT Map 15 SD31

Bistrot Vérité

◉ French ✪

Traditional French cooking in Birkdale village

☎ 01704 564199
7 Liverpool Rd, Birkdale PR8 4AR

Marc Vérité's self-named bistro in Birkdale village flies the tricolor proudly for the old French culinary traditions, with the benefit that much of what he produces is based on prime Lancashire ingredients. Crammed-in tables, chalkboard menus and a friendly, breezy buzz characterise the operation, as does some accomplished cooking. A wooden board of hors d'oeuvres variés encompasses a generous range of hot and cold items, including a scallop with pickled veg, duck and game

Save on Hotels. Book at **theAA.com/hotel**

MERSEYSIDE 383 ENGLAND

terrine, battered frogs' legs, a snail simmered in Pernod, a goats' cheese croquette, and more. Main-course wood pigeon served with foie gras and wild mushrooms sautéed in garlic and parsley is a richly satisfying dish, and meals may end with a thickly caramelised classic crème brûlée.

Chef Marc Vérité **Owner** Marc & Michaela Vérité **Times** 12-1.30/5.30-late Closed 1 wk Feb & 1 wk Aug, Sun-Mon **Prices** Prices not confirmed Service optional **Notes** Vegetarian available **Seats** 45 **Children** Portions **Parking** Birkdale station

Gusto

◉ Italian **NEW**

A taste of Italy in Southport

☎ 01704 544255
58-62 Lord St PR8 1QB
e-mail: info@gustotrattoria.co.uk
dir: Located centre Southport

Gusto is a trattoria with a nice line in cheerful bonhomie and some good and proper Italian cooking. The two rooms are looked over by the charming service team and the open kitchen adds to the buzz of the place. The food does not attempt to reinvent the wheel, just to do things properly. The pizzas are very good - the 'boscaiola', for

example, with ham and mushrooms, or the 'Gusto', fired up with anchovies and chilli. Vegetali parmigiana is a first course filled with the flavours of the Med, or go for polpette piccanti (meatballs in a spicy Arrabiata sauce). Pasta is made in-house and should not be ignored: pappardelle al carciofo, maybe, which is cooked perfectly, or try the gnocchi al pesto. Desserts such as frutta caramellata and home-made tiramisù hit the spot, too, and it all comes at a very reasonable price.

Times 12-3/5-10 Closed Mon (excl BH) **Prices** Starter £3.95-£12.95, Main £6-£9.25, Dessert £1.25-£5.25 **Notes** Open all day Sat-Sun 12-10 **Children** Portions

Vincent Hotel

◉◉ British, European ⓒ

Skillful cooking in stylish hotel

☎ 01704 883800
98 Lord St PR8 1JR
e-mail: manager@thevincenthotel.com
dir: M58 junct 3, follow signs to Ormskirk & Southport

The V-Café and Sushi Bar at this stylish contemporary hotel is the place to be in the evening, when lights are dimmed and candles are lit. Tables are closely packed and floor-to-ceiling windows look onto bustling Lord Street, where there are tables for alfresco dining. The

menu roams around Britain and Europe before arriving in Japan with some platters of authentic sushi and sashimi, maki and temaki, with a section of 'gringo sushi for non-fish-lovers' - roasted crispy duck and mango maki for example, or barbecue pulled pork maki. Seafood dominates starters, among them an excellent smoked haddock and salmon fishcake with tartare sauce and endive salad. Dishes are noted for their freshness, accurate cooking times, and balanced combinations: moist fillet of salmon with a tarte fine of Mediterranean vegetables, say, or hearty braised lamb shank with rosemary sauce, honey-roast carrots and mash. Lovers of puddings will find much to entice, not least a trio of crème brûlées: Baileys, vanilla and mixed fruit.

Chef Andrew Carter **Owner** Paul Adams **Times** 7.30am-9.30pm All-day dining **Prices** Fixed D 3 course £14.95, Starter £3.95-£7.50, Main £12.95-£19.95, Dessert £5.95-£8.50, Service optional, Groups min 10 service 10% **Wines** 8 bottles over £30, 12 bottles under £30, 5 by glass **Notes** Fixed D 3 course available Sun-Thu, Sunday L, Vegetarian available, Dress restrictions, Smart casual **Seats** 85, Pr/dining room 12 **Children** Portions **Parking** 50, Valet parking

The Lawns Restaurant at Thornton Hall

Modern European **V**

Historic country-house hotel with contemporary cooking

☎ 0151 336 3938
Neston Rd CH63 1JF
e-mail: reservations@thorntonhallhotel.com
web: www.lawnsrestaurant.com
dir: M53 junct 4 onto B5151 & B5136, follow brown tourist signs (approx 2.5m) to Thornton Hall Hotel

Thornton Hall is an imposing Victorian manor house that has buffed up nicely, with a sheen of contemporary design adding lustre to its period grandeur. The place was built on a scale intended to impress: its public rooms all have the generous proportions that were so in-vogue in the 19th century, and its top-class facilities now

extend to a large spa and ample space to allow a thriving trade in conferences and weddings. The former billiards room must have played host to many a gentlemen's port and cigar session in its day, and certainly looks the part with its clubby sculpted mahogany panels, remarkable plasterwork friezes, and a vast crystal chandelier suspended from its carved and coffered mahogany ceiling. Nowadays, the big green baize table has been replaced by well-spaced, linen-swathed ones, and it trades as the fine-dining Lawns Restaurant. Led by executive chef David Gillmore, the kitchen continues to maintain a formidable pace, serving up seasonally-driven, robustly-flavoured modern food that draws on first-class local supplies. The menu is a tight-lipped affair that favours a laconic listing of components, so you may need to call on the friendly and well-briefed staff to spell out what is involved at each stage. An unmistakably modern approach sees stuffed saddle of rabbit matched with sweetcorn, popcorn, tarragon, and flower salad as a starter, followed by a two-way serving of Hebridean

mutton - rosemary-infused loin and treacle-glazed rib - partnered by aubergine fondant, goats' curd and charred kale. Voguish savoury jellies and slow cooking methods are extended even to fish-based dishes, such as John Dory, presented with chive gel, 55-minute egg yolk and fish pie crust. The cooking retains undeniable flair and remarkable depth of flavour, through to an outstanding dessert of floating island with poached rhubarb, custard and honeycomb, or there might be a deconstructed take on a 'Viennetta', involving blackberries, sorbet, violet, and white chocolate.

Chef David Gillmore **Owner** The Thompson family **Times** 12-2.30/7-9.30 Closed 1 Jan **Prices** Fixed L 2 course fr £17.50, Tasting menu fr £70, Starter £6-£14, Main £14-£28, Dessert £8-£10, Service optional **Wines** 100 bottles over £30, 34 bottles under £30, 11 by glass **Notes** Tasting menu available Mon-Sat, Sunday L fr £24, Vegetarian menu, Dress restrictions, Smart casual, no T-shirts or jeans, Civ Wed 70 **Seats** 45, Pr/dining room 24 **Children** Portions **Parking** 250

SOUTHPORT *continued*

Warehouse Kitchen & Bar

◎◎ International 🕒

Cool warehouse setting and smart modish cooking

☎ 01704 544662
30 West St PR8 1QN
e-mail: info@warehousekitchenandbar.com
dir: M58 junct 3, then A570 Southport

The stylish New York-esque Warehouse has white linen-clad tables against the bare-brick walls in a light and airy space and, up the stairs, a chic bar. Co-owned these days by Liverpool footballer Steven Gerrard, this town centre venue has been going strong for 15 years, its modern international cooking, cool design and relaxed vibe proving popular with the locals. Typical dishes include Ribble Valley pork croquettes with sweet honey mustard, crackling salad and baby pickles, followed perhaps by a trio of Cumbrian beef - steak and ale pie, fillet and oxtail sauce - and finishing with Wakefield rhubarb 'mayhem' - rhubarb Bakewell tart, tonka bean pannacotta and rhubarb sorbet.

Chef Mini Patel **Owner** Paul Adams, Steven Gerrard **Times** 12-2/5.30-10 Closed 26 Dec, 1 Jan, Sun **Prices** Fixed L 2 course fr £11.95, Fixed D 3 course fr £15.95, Starter £4.95-£10.95, Main £12.95-£26.95, Dessert £5.50-£6.50, Service optional, Groups min 8 service 10% **Wines** 10 bottles over £30, 14 bottles under £30, 9 by glass **Notes** Fixed D 2/3 course Mon-Thu all evening, Fri-Sat 5.30-6.30pm, Vegetarian available **Seats** 95, Pr/dining room 20 **Children** Portions, Menu **Parking** On street

THORNTON HOUGH   Map 15 SJ38

The Lawns Restaurant at Thornton Hall

◎◎◎ – *see page 383*

NORFOLK

ALBURGH   Map 13 TM28

The Dove Restaurant with Rooms

◎◎ Modern European

Classic cooking in charming restaurant with rooms

☎ 01986 788315
Holbrook IP20 0EP
e-mail: info@thedoverestaurant.co.uk
dir: On South Norfolk border between Harleston & Bungay, by A143, at junct of B1062

The owners have generated a French country auberge-style vibe in the pleasant Waveney Valley on the south Norfolk border. It's a traditional place sure enough, with refurbishment giving the dining room a cheerful countrified appearance; think blond-wood floors, pretty flowery wallpaper and clothed tables. The lounge or large raised terrace are the weather-dependent options for pre- or post-prandial drinks. This is a truly family-run

business having been in the hands of the Oberhoffers since 1980 (Robert is the fifth generation chef), with good local ingredients, unpretentiously prepared, the star of the show; thus you might start with soufflé Arnold Bennett (a perennial favourite), or go for cream of home-grown pumpkin soup, followed by roasted loin of Blythburgh pork with grain mustard, Savoy cabbage, celeriac and thyme gravy, with raspberry Pavlova bringing proceedings to a satisfying close.

Times 12-2/7-9 Closed Mon-Tue, L Wed-Sat, D Sun

BACTON   Map 13 TG33

The Keswick Hotel

◎ British 🕒

Unpretentious dining in small and friendly seaside hotel

☎ 01692 650468
Walcott Rd NR12 0LS
e-mail: margaret@keswickhotelbacton.co.uk
web: www.keswickhotelbacton.co.uk
dir: On B1159 coast road

Smack on the seafront in Bacton, this charming small hotel punches above its weight in culinary matters thanks to a kitchen that takes carefully-sourced seasonal and local materials - Cromer crab, Brancaster mussels, rare-breed meats - as the starting point for its vibrant modern cooking. No-one is trying to reinvent the wheel here: expect simple, classic combinations in unpretentious but skilfully-cooked dishes, starting out at its most emphatically seasonal with a summery idea such as crab cake with wasabi mayonnaise, pea shoots and a salad of micro leaves and herbs. Next, crisp-skinned, pan-fried sea bass arrives with rösti, wilted spinach, chorizo and brown shrimp butter, and for pudding there's condensed milk pannacotta with strawberry coulis and fresh strawberries.

Chef Russell Moore **Owner** Russell & Margaret Moore **Times** 12-3/6-9 Closed L Mon-Sat **Prices** Prices not confirmed Service optional **Wines** 6 by glass **Notes** Sunday L, Vegetarian available **Seats** 60 **Children** Menu **Parking** 75

BARNHAM BROOM   Map 13 TG00

Barnham Broom Hotel, Golf & Restaurant

◎◎ Modern British, European 🕒

Contemporary cooking with golfing views

☎ 01603 759393
Honingham Rd NR9 4DD
e-mail: enquiry@barnhambroomhotel.co.uk
web: www.barnham-broom.co.uk
dir: A11/A47 towards Swaffham, follow brown tourist signs

A sprawling, golf-centric hotel in 250 acres of bucolic Norfolk, Barnham Broom offers the full-dress country club and spa package, plus fine dining to views of the golf-course action in Flints Restaurant. A top-to-toe facelift in recent years has kept the place looking sharp, while the

kitchen continues to come up with the goods, sourcing top-grade produce as the foundations of its assured contemporary cooking. To start, you might fancy roast pigeon breast teamed with black pudding, confit potato and apple chutney, or a tried-and-true trio of pan-fried scallops, pork belly and butternut squash purée, while mains could stretch from an eastern-accented dish of Moroccan-marinated chicken suprême with tabouleh, aubergine caviar and preserved lemons, to a homely roast rump of English lamb served with a mini shepherd's pie, glazed carrots and wilted spinach. Finish with treacle tart with brown bread ice cream and salted caramel.

Chef John Batchelor **Owner** Barnham Broom Hotel **Times** 7-9.30 Closed L Mon-Sat **Prices** Fixed L 2 course £15.95-£18.95, Fixed D 3 course £28.95, Starter £5-£9, Main £15-£19, Dessert £6-£10, Service added but optional 10% **Wines** 15 bottles over £30, 45 bottles under £30, 14 by glass **Notes** Sunday L, Vegetarian available, Dress restrictions, Smart casual, no trainers, Civ Wed 150 **Seats** 90, Pr/dining room 50 **Children** Portions, Menu **Parking** 500

BLAKENEY   Map 13 TG04

The Blakeney Hotel

◎ Modern British **V** 🕒

Modern British cooking in a quayside hotel

☎ 01263 740797
The Quay NR25 7NE
e-mail: reception@blakeneyhotel.co.uk
web: www.blakeneyhotel.co.uk
dir: From A148 between Fakenham & Holt, take B1156 to Langham & Blakeney

The Blakeney's quayside terrace is one of North Norfolk's gems on a sunny day, with a big-sky panorama sweeping across the estuary and salt marshes to Blakeney Point, and the cries of wading birds providing a soulful soundtrack. When the weather forces you inside the lovely flint-faced hotel, the restaurant still has that view, and is a shipshape venue with an easygoing, friendly ambience. The kitchen is clearly on good terms with local suppliers, showing off their wares to great effect in uncomplicated modern ideas - local crab, perhaps, on Bloody Mary jelly with avocado, cucumber salad and basil oil, or you could take simplicity to its extreme and tuck into Brancaster oysters with raspberry shallot vinegar and lemon. Given the setting, fish is a good bet - try roasted fillet of halibut on horseradish mash with baby leeks, girolles and tarragon cream; meat is handled deftly too, though, in ideas such as a baby rack and slow-cooked shoulder of lamb with celeriac and potato gratin, fine beans, artichoke, and olive jus. Finally, the pudding trolley trundles in bearing comfort in the shape of warm spiced bread pudding with maple syrup.

Chef Martin Sewell **Owner** Stannard family **Times** 12-2/6.30-9 **Prices** Fixed D 3 course £29-£43.50, Service optional **Wines** 23 bottles over £30, 88 bottles under £30, 16 by glass **Notes** ALC 3 course £29-£43.50, No high chairs after 6.45pm, Sunday L, Vegetarian menu, Dress restrictions, Smart casual for D **Seats** 100, Pr/dining room 80 **Children** Portions **Parking** 60

Save on Hotels. Book at **theAA.com/hotel**

NORFOLK 385 **ENGLAND**

Morston Hall

BLAKENEY MAP 13 TG04

Modern British **V** NOTABLE WINE LIST

Assured country-house cooking on the covetable North Norfolk coast

☎ 01263 741041
Morston, Holt NR25 7AA
e-mail: reception@morstonhall.com
web: www.morstonhall.com
dir: On A149 (coast road) between Blakeney & Stiffkey

The North Norfolk coast has become one of England's most affectionately regarded slices of natural beauty, as resonant with greenness and pleasantness in the popular conception as the Lake District and the West Country. It's a more wild and wind-whipped area than either of those, but replete with country houses and landscaped gardens (Humphry Repton's Sheringham Park is near Morston), as well as the royal residence at Sandringham, of course. Galton and Tracy Blackiston cannily anticipated something of the region's present cachet when they opened here back in 1992, and time has proved them right. Sitting on the A149 coastal road, Morston Hall is an originally 17th-century house on the manageable scale (nothing like the imposing mansion you may be expecting), furnished in the country manner, but with a determined avoidance of twee, and offers the full package of conservatory dining, as well

as tables on the terrace. Blackiston's passion for cooking extends to running masterclasses and authoring recipe books, as well as hunting down the best of seasonal produce from local farms. The format for dinner is five courses, with choice only at the end (will it be a second dessert or cheeses?). Nothing about the cooking feels forced or out-of-joint, for all that a measured assimilation of contemporary technique is in evidence. A winter menu proceeds from a portion of rabbit with confit chestnuts and carrot and cumin purée, through skate dressed in egg-yolk with crackling, to a main course of Gressingham duck breast with pearl barley, curly kale and sage oil. After an interlude such as rice pudding with a little doughnut, the main dessert might be rhubarb tart with ginger ice cream. Wines of the month, available by the bottle or glass, are chosen with care, as is the whole list.

Chef Galton Blackiston **Owner** T & G Blackiston **Times** 12.30-7.30 Closed 2 wks Jan, L Mon-Sat (ex party booking) **Prices** Tasting menu £65, Service optional **Wines** 129 bottles over £30, 24 bottles under £30, 18 by glass **Notes** Sunday L £35-£37, Vegetarian menu, Dress restrictions, Smart casual **Seats** 50, Pr/dining room 26 **Children** Portions, Menu **Parking** 40

BLAKENEY *continued*

Morston Hall

◎◎◎ – *see page 385*

BRANCASTER STAITHE   Map 13 TF74

The White Horse

◎◎ Modern British ✪

Fine regional produce and marsh views

☎ 01485 210262
PE31 8BY
e-mail: reception@whitehorsebrancaster.co.uk
web: www.whitehorsebrancaster.co.uk
dir: On A149 (coast road) midway between Hunstanton & Wells-next-the-Sea

While this neat, traditional but much-extended inn comes with a big bolt-on conservatory restaurant and decked terrace, the real show-stopper here is its location on the North Norfolk coast, offering knock-your-socks-off-views over the tidal salt marshes. The brasserie-style dining room is a relaxed spot - all natural-wood tables and seascape tones - and takes in the vista, while the kitchen doesn't disappoint, bringing fashionable modernity to great regional produce. Given the location, marine life has its say; as well as Brancaster oysters (with shallot vinegar or tempura) or mussels (with white wine, garlic and cream), there's pan-fried sea bass fillet served with saffron potatoes, chargrilled leeks, ratatouille and tomato-butter sauce. But the menu makes the best of Norfolk's land larder, too: witness pan-roast Norfolk pheasant breast teamed with Brancaster braised vegetables, new potato fondant, sautéed kale and jus. There's a separate bar menu too.

Chef Avrum Frankel **Owner** Clifford Nye
Times 12-2/6.30-9 **Prices** Starter £5.25-£10.50, Main £12-£16.50, Dessert £6.95-£8, Service optional **Wines** 12 bottles over £30, 30 bottles under £30, 13 by glass **Notes** Sunday L £12.95, Vegetarian available **Seats** 100 **Children** Portions, Menu **Parking** 85

BRUNDALL   Map 13 TG30

The Lavender House

◎◎ Modern British V ✪

Engaging cooking in a modernised thatched cottage

☎ 01603 712215
39 The Street NR13 5AA
e-mail: lavenderhouse39@aol.com
dir: A47 E, 4m from Norwich city centre

The exterior may be an archetypally English thatched 16th-century cottage, but the interior of Lavender House has been reworked with a pared-back modern look involving exposed brickwork, modern art, high-backed leather chairs and crisp linen-clad tables beneath its head-skimming oak-beamed ceilings. Chef-proprietor Richard Hughes is the driving force in the kitchen, running a cookery school as well as the main business of

turning out what he defines as 'modern Norfolk' cuisine. This translates as plenty of local produce delivered in flavour-driven dishes - starting, perhaps, with Cley smokehouse salmon with cucumber, crème fraîche and treacle loaf, or a modish presentation of pig's head, involving terrine, cheeks, remoulade of tongue, crispy ear and capers. Main courses favour multi-cut presentations - lamb for example, might come in the shape of rack, breast and middle neck, accompanied by tomato, olive, basil and polenta. There are fine local cheeses to wrap things up on a savoury note, or desserts like prune and Armagnac ice cream with Earl Grey syrup and brandy snaps.

Chef Richard Hughes **Owner** Richard Hughes
Times 12-4/6.30-11 Closed Mon-Wed, L Thu-Sat, D Sun
Prices Tasting menu £55, Service optional **Wines** 8 by glass **Notes** Fixed D £45, Willi Opitz Table, Sunday L £28, Vegetarian menu **Seats** 50, Pr/dining room 36
Children Portions **Parking** 16

BURNHAM MARKET   Map 13 TF84

The Hoste

◎◎ Modern British, Pacific Rim ✪

Straightforward modern dishes in a historic Norfolk inn

☎ 01328 738777
The Green PE31 8HD
e-mail: reception@hostearms.co.uk
web: www.hostearms.co.uk
dir: 2m from A149 between Burnham & Wells

A couple of miles back from the heritage North Norfolk shoreline, Burnham Market has acquired the kind of gentrified reputation that has seen it nicknamed Little-Chelsea-on-Sea. The Hoste is a historic whitewashed inn, partially covered in climbing foliage in the shape of a trident. Recent extensive refurbishment has introduced a lodge dining area influenced by New Zealand restaurant style, and an open kitchen. Great emphasis is laid on sourcing as much produce from within a 30-mile Norfolk radius as possible, transforming it into an essentially simple modern idiom that avoids unnecessary frippery. Brancaster oysters thus come in straightforward options (red wine vinegar, garlic and parsley, tempura or Bloody Mary), as an appetising prelude to herb-crusted cannon of succulently pink lamb with curly kale and dauphinoise, or roast salmon with lemon tabbouleh, a tiger prawn in filo, and honey and mustard cream sauce. The on-the-money finisher is beautifully moist sticky toffee pudding with caramel sauce, a pecan tuile and nutmeg ice cream, and there are fine Norfolk cheeses with date and apple chutney.

Chef Aaron Smith **Times** 12-2/6-9 Closed D 25 Dec
Prices Starter £6-£22, Main £13-£22, Dessert £6-£17, Service optional **Wines** 21 by glass **Notes** Sunday L, Vegetarian available, Dress restrictions, Smart casual **Seats** 140, Pr/dining room 24 **Children** Menu **Parking** 45

COLTISHALL   Map 13 TG21

Norfolk Mead Hotel

◎ Modern British NEW ✪

Cooking with a local flavour in a charming small country-house hotel

☎ 01603 737531
Church Ln NR12 7DN
e-mail: info@norfolkmead.co.uk
web: www.norfolkmead.co.uk
dir: From Norwich take B1150 to Coltishall village, go right with petrol station on left, 200 yds church on right, go down driveway

The handsome old house in the heart of the beautiful Norfolk Broads has never looked so dapper. Refurbishment by new owners has given the Norfolk Mead a contemporary, country-chic look, none more so than in the restaurant, where period features combine with white walls broken up with abstract artwork, wooden floors and tables decorated with simple flower arrangements. Windows look out over the pretty gardens - a must for a pre- or post-prandial stroll down to the river - while the charming small bar offers a range of whiskies and real ales, with the bonus of a delightful sun-trap terrace. And so to the food: chef Anna Duttson sources the finest, freshest local ingredients for her attractively presented modern British cooking. Start, perhaps, with a well-made double-baked cheese soufflé, followed by something like black bream, perfectly cooked, served with a potato and crab cake. Apple tart Tatin with vanilla pod ice cream and caramel shard rounds things off nicely.

Chef Anna Duttson, Dave Potter **Owner** James Holliday, Anna Duttson **Times** 12-2.30/7-9 Closed L Mon-Sat
Prices Fixed D 3 course fr £30, Service optional **Wines** 22 bottles over £30, 31 bottles under £30, 8 by glass
Notes Afternoon tea £12.50 pp, Sunday L, Vegetarian available, Civ Wed 40 **Seats** 40, Pr/dining room 18
Children Portions **Parking** 45

CROMER   Map 13 TG24

See also **Sheringham**

Sea Marge Hotel

◎◎ Modern British ✪

Appealing modern menus on the North Norfolk coast

☎ 01263 579579
16 High St, Overstrand NR27 0AB
e-mail: seamarge@mackenziehotels.com
dir: A140 to Cromer, B1159 to Overstrand, 2nd left past Overstrand Church

Terraced lawns lead down to the coast path and beach from this 1908-built mansion. The property has been lovingly restored, with many original features retained, a notable one being a minstrels' gallery. It's a friendly and relaxing hotel, with professional, helpful staff serving in the restaurant. The menu, with around a handful of choices per course, is an appealing package of contemporary ideas, running from marinated wood pigeon with duck liver ravioli, parsnip purée and roast hazelnut dressing, to poached fillet of sea bass with a chowder of smoked haddock, brown shrimps and vegetables. Goats' cheese soufflé, served with apple and walnut salad, rises to the occasion, and may be followed by flavourful rump of local lamb with thyme jus and well-considered accompaniments of minted pea purée, smoked bacon mash and roast green beans. Puddings include a memorable chocolate torte with pineapple sorbet and peanut brittle.

Chef Rene Ilupar **Owner** Mr & Mrs Mackenzie **Times** 12-2/6.30-9.30 **Prices** Prices not confirmed Service optional **Wines** 6 by glass **Notes** Sunday L, Vegetarian available, Dress restrictions, Smart casual **Seats** 80, Pr/dining room 40 **Children** Portions, Menu **Parking** 50

The White Horse Overstrand
◎◎ Modern European

Great Norfolk produce cooked with flair

☎ 01263 579237
34 High St, Overstrand NR27 0AB
e-mail: enquiries@whitehorseoverstrand.co.uk
dir: From A140, before Cromer, turn right onto Mill Rd. At bottom turn right onto Station Rd. After 2m, bear left onto High St, White Horse Overstrand on left

The family-run Victorian inn in the village of Overstrand goes from strength to strength, with food occupying an ever-prominent place at the heart of the operation, whether it is glammed-up old favourites in the bar, themed grill, Spanish, or Italian nights, or vibrant modern dishes in the recently converted Barn restaurant. Large wrought-iron chandeliers hang from ceilings with original oak roof trusses above rustic Norfolk flint walls and solid oak tables in a clean-cut contemporary setting that suits the switched-on modern food. Top-class local and seasonal produce underpins the repertoire, whether it is a starter trio of Cromer crab remoulade, brown shrimp rillettes, and shallow-fried Cajun squid, or mains of pan-roast rump of Norfolk lamb with rösti potato, garden pea purée, sautéed baby leeks and lamb jus. Don't skip pudding, as bittersweet chocolate fondant with home-made coconut ice cream is a real treat.

Chef Nathan Boon **Owner** Darren Walsgrove **Times** 12-3/6-9.30 Closed D 25 Dec **Prices** Prices not confirmed Service optional **Notes** Sunday L, Vegetarian available **Seats** 80, Pr/dining room 40 **Children** Portions, Menu **Parking** 6, On street

---

GREAT BIRCHAM   Map 13 TF73

The Kings Head Hotel
◉ Modern British ☺

All-embracing menus near Sandringham

☎ 01485 578265
PE31 6RJ
e-mail: info@thekingsheadhotel.co.uk
web: www.the-kings-head-bircham.co.uk
dir: A148 to Hillington through village, 1st left Bircham

There's a new smartly appointed open-plan bar and lounge (think bright colours, patterned rugs on a wooden floor, tub chairs) at The Kings Head, where you can enjoy a drink (perhaps your choice from the 50-strong selection of gins) before moving through to the contemporary, spacious restaurant. The kitchen doesn't stray far from base to source its materials and uses them to good effect, with a versatile menu that embraces traditional fare and more modern concepts. Start with prawn cocktail or confit pork belly with roast spiced pear, a cider and sage reduction and crackling, and proceed to lemongrass-infused steamed salmon fillet wrapped in nori with stir-fried mooli, noodles and shellfish and soy soup, or a steak with béarnaise and the usual suspects. The specials might run to lobster, tarragon and tomato linguine with white wine butter, and desserts end strongly with the likes of warm chocolate pudding with pistachio ice cream.

Chef Nicholas Parker **Owner** Charlie & Holly Campbell **Times** 12-3/6.30-9 **Prices** Tasting menu £38-£70, Starter £6.25-£8.95, Main £7.95-£30, Dessert £5.50-£6, Service optional **Wines** 8 bottles over £30, 46 bottles under £30, 14 by glass **Notes** Sunday L £13.95-£15.95, Vegetarian available, Civ Wed 80 **Seats** 80, Pr/dining room 30 **Children** Portions, Menu **Parking** 25

GREAT YARMOUTH   Map 13 TG50

Andover House
◎◎ Modern British

Breezily contemporary cooking in townhouse

☎ 01493 843490
28-30 Camperdown NR30 3JB
e-mail: info@andoverhouse.co.uk
web: www.andoverhouse.co.uk
dir: Opposite Wellington Pier, turn onto Shadingfield Close, right onto Kimberley Terrace, follow onto Camperdown. Property on left

A touch of boutique styling has been sprinkled over the white-painted Victorian terrace that is Andover House, and these days it's a rather cool hotel, restaurant and bar, with a spruce look of fashionable muted pastel tones and a distinct lack of chintz. The restaurant is filled with blond wood with nary a tablecloth in sight and is a bright and breezy environment for the cooking, which fits the bill to a T. There's a daily specials board in support of the à la carte menu. The cooking treads a modish path and there are plenty of global flavours on show: first-course crispy beef and spring onion salad with a sweet chilli and

pimento dressing, for example, or a vegetarian main course tajine. It's back to Europe for a pasta starter - linguini with pan-fried squid, chorizo, ginger, chilli and lime - and main-courses such as tournedos Rossini or rack of English spring lamb with ratatouille, Parmentier potatoes, minted pears and rosemary jus. For dessert, the tasting plate removes any indecision.

Chef Sandra Meirovica, Simon Askew **Owner** Mr & Mrs Barry Armstrong **Times** 6-9.30 Closed Xmas, Sun-Mon, L all week **Prices** Prices not confirmed Service optional **Wines** 17 bottles under £30, 9 by glass **Notes** Vegetarian available **Seats** 37, Pr/dining room 18 **Parking** On street

---

Imperial Hotel
◉ Modern British ☺

Contemporary cooking by the sea

☎ 01493 842000
North Dr NR30 1EQ
e-mail: reception@imperialhotel.co.uk
web: www.cafecrurestaurant.co.uk
dir: Follow signs to seafront, turn left. Hotel opposite waterways

The grand old Imperial Hotel on Great Yarmouth's seafront has been providing generations of visitors with what they want, and in the 21st century that means the contemporary style of the made-over Café Cru Restaurant. It brings a younger vibe to the old girl's empire pomp with its city-slicker looks involving banquette seating, modish chrome lights resembling bunches of grapes, and palette of caramel, chocolate and cream. Daily-changing blackboard specials bolster a repertoire of unpretentious modern British dishes wrought from splendid local materials, while smart staff in black aprons lend a buzzy bistro vibe to proceedings. Local Morston mussels in white wine, garlic and parsley are a perennial favourite to start, then you might follow with roast cod matched with roasted artichokes, clams, and tomato, herb and flageolet bean casserole; those in the mood for meat could find braised ox cheek and mushroom suet pudding with swede and spring onion champ, crispy carrots and ox cheek jus, and to finish, a star anise crème brûlée with vanilla-poached pear.

continued

GREAT YARMOUTH *continued*

Chef Simon Wainwright **Owner** Mr N L & Mrs A Mobbs **Times** 12-2/6.30-10 Closed 24-28 & 31 Dec, L Sat & Mon, D Sun **Prices** Starter £5-£9, Main £12-£25, Dessert £6-£9, Service optional **Wines** 10 bottles over £30, 30 bottles under £30, 12 by glass **Notes** Sunday L £16-£20, Vegetarian available, Dress restrictions, Smart casual, no shorts or trainers, Civ Wed 140 **Seats** 60, Pr/dining room 140 **Children** Portions, Menu **Parking** 45

GRIMSTON — Map 12 TF72

Congham Hall Country House Hotel

@@ Modern British V 🍴

Creative cooking in charming Georgian house

☎ 01485 600250
Lynn Rd PE32 1AH
e-mail: info@conghamhallhotel.co.uk
dir: 6m NE of King's Lynn on A148, turn right towards Grimston. Hotel 2.5m on left (do not go to Congham)

With its pastoral location close to Her Majesty's Sandringham House, acres of peaceful grounds including a magnificent herb garden hosting a whopping 400 varieties, plus a swish spa, a visit to Congham is a genuine treat. The pretty Georgian house is done out handsomely, too, and has long been a destination dining address in the county. French windows lead onto a terrace from the newly refurbished dining room, and tables are dressed in their best whites. The kitchen makes excellent use of the garden and the wider locale to deliver some well-crafted, classically-minded cooking with an English flavour. Start with wild brown trout with sprouting broccoli, almonds and a fishcake, or a risotto of English asparagus. Main course might bring on breast of Aylesbury duck, its confit leg meat in an accompanying sausage, plus cabbage, swede and savoury granola, or fillet of turbot with curried lentils, cauliflower purée and bhaji. To finish, if you're lucky enough to arrive in season, perhaps garden rhubarb and custard with a rhubarb sorbet.

Chef Nick Claxton Webb **Owner** Nicholas Dickinson **Times** 12-2/7-9 **Prices** Fixed D 3 course £47.50, Tasting menu £67.50, Starter £6.50-£9.95, Main £12.50-£22.95, Dessert £6.50, Service optional **Wines** 10 by glass **Notes** Gourmand menu L £36, D £71.50 (with wines £101.50), Sunday L, Vegetarian menu, Dress restrictions, Smart casual, Civ Wed 100 **Seats** 50, Pr/dining room 18 **Children** Portions, Menu **Parking** 50

HEACHAM — Map 12 TF63

Heacham Manor Hotel

@ Modern European NEW

Fine local produce by the Norfolk coast

☎ 01485 536030 & 579800
Hunstanton Rd PE31 7JX
e-mail: info@heacham-manor.co.uk

The wide-open skies of Norfolk's fabulous coast make Heacham Manor an attractive prospect; the place even comes with its own coastal golf course if you're a player. Originally built as an Elizabethan manor, the hotel has been brought smartly up-to-date by complete renovation in recent years, and its airy conservatory-style Mulberry Restaurant is reason enough to pay a visit. The kitchen's output is simple, staunchly seasonal and driven by a sincere belief in local sourcing - salt marsh lamb comes from Wells-next-the-Sea, and the locally-landed fish and seafood racks up very few food miles on its way to the table. Goats' cheese cheesecake with red onion marmalade and mizuna leaf salad gets things off the blocks, followed by Gressingham duck breast teamed with grain mustard mash, Savoy cabbage, celeriac purée, and blackberry jus. At the end, rhubarb compôte provides a tangy foil to crème brûlée with fennel seed biscotti.

Chef Neil Rutland **Times** 12-2.30/6.30-9 **Prices** Prices not confirmed

---

HETHERSETT — Map 13 TG10

Park Farm Hotel

@ Modern British 🍴

Unfussy modern cooking in a spa hotel

☎ 01603 810264
NR9 3DL
e-mail: enq@parkfarm-hotel.co.uk
web: www.parkfarm-hotel.co.uk
dir: 6m S of Norwich on B1172

The family-run hotel has been modified over the past half-century from a rather grand Georgian farmhouse into a modern spa hotel, still surrounded by 200 acres of open countryside not far from Norwich. A smart orangery-style restaurant overlooking the gardens is where the main dining action goes on, in an atmosphere of bright informality, enhanced by boldly coloured paintings. The kitchen does simple things extremely well, turning out a decent Niçoise salad with new potatoes, fine beans, olives and a poached egg, all dressed in good olive oil, followed perhaps by five-spice pork belly, slow-roasted and served with chilli and soy egg noodles with stir-fried veg, or skate with wild mushrooms in red wine jus. The tiramisù is reassuringly doused in espresso and Tia Maria for a very moreish finish.

Chef David Bell **Owner** David Gowing **Times** 12-2/7-9.30 **Prices** Prices not confirmed Service optional **Wines** 12 by glass **Notes** Sunday L, Vegetarian available, Dress restrictions, Smart casual, Civ Wed 100 **Seats** 60, Pr/dining room 60 **Children** Portions, Menu **Parking** 150

HOLT — Map 13 TG03

Butlers Restaurant

@ Modern European

Crowd-pleasing bistro fare and a lovely courtyard garden

☎ 01263 710790
9 Appleyard NR25 6BN
e-mail: eat@butlersrestaurants.com
dir: Just off High Street, signed Appleyard

Just off the main street in charming Holt, Butlers is a light-filled, pleasant venue with double-doors opening on to a courtyard garden, where you can eat in the shade of a venerable copper beech tree. An upbeat, friendly tone prevails, thanks to proficient staff who know what they're about, and the seasonally based menus, supplemented by daily blackboard specials, deal in an extensive choice of readily comprehensible bistro fare. Niçoise salad looks a bit of a heap, to be honest, but has well-cooked tuna and properly marrying flavours, or there might be butternut squash gnocchi with walnuts, rocket and blue cheese. Parmesan-crusted chicken breast, sirloin steaks and burgers on focaccia please the crowds, as does accurately timed sea trout with crushed potato and spinach in a rollicking mustard sauce, topped with a poached egg. The reliable way to finish is with light-textured sticky toffee pudding, served with good vanilla ice cream.

Chef Manuel Ganzalez de Uzqueta **Owner** Charles Butler **Times** 12-3/6-9 Closed 25-26 Dec, D Sun **Prices** Fixed L 2 course £11.50, Starter £4.95-£6.95, Main £8.95-£16.50, Dessert £5.50-£6.95, Service optional **Wines** 20 bottles under £30, 8 by glass **Notes** Monthly events with special menu, Sunday L £10.95-£15.95, Vegetarian available **Seats** 50 **Children** Portions, Menu **Parking** On street (free after 6pm)

The Lawns Wine Bar

@ Modern European 🍴

Populist cooking in a Georgian townhouse

☎ 01263 713390
26 Station Rd NR25 6BS
e-mail: mail@lawnsatholt.co.uk
dir: A148 (Cromer road). 0.25m from Holt rdbt, turn left, 400yds along Station Rd

Fresh, seasonal local produce and a relaxed, please-all, modern brasserie-style are at the heart of the appeal of this smart Georgian townhouse restaurant, bar and hotel in the centre of town. The fashionably decked-out restaurant (darkwood tables and leather high-backed chairs), smart bar area, bright conservatory and terrace overlooking the garden, provides plenty of choice to suit the mood (and the weather), and, wherever you choose to sit, the vibe is unbuttoned and friendly. The cooking keeps things relatively uncomplicated: beer-battered haddock and rib-eye steak sit alongside slow-cooked belly of pork with sage mash and braised Savoy cabbage with bacon, and the more globetrotting green Thai curry.

Chef Leon Brookes, Adam Kobialka **Owner** Mr & Mrs Daniel Rees **Times** 12-2/6-9 **Prices** Starter £4.95-£7.95,

Save on Hotels. Book at **theAA.com/hotel**

NORFOLK 389 ENGLAND

Main £9.95-£17.95, Dessert £5-£6, Service optional
Wines 2 bottles over £30, 32 bottles under £30, 13 by
glass **Notes** Sunday L, Vegetarian available **Seats** 24
Children Portions, Menu **Parking** 18

Caley Hall Hotel

◎ Modern British V ♨

Well-judged menu on the North Norfolk coast

☎ 01485 533486
Old Hunstanton Rd PE36 6HH
e-mail: mail@caleyhallhotel.co.uk
web: www.caleyhallhotel.co.uk
dir: located on A149, Old Hunstanton

The core of Caley Hall, a 10-minute walk from wide
unspoiled beaches, is a 17th-century manor, with the

restaurant in an attractive, spacious former stable block,
with high-backed leather-look seats at wooden tables, a
tartan-patterned carpet and a vaulted ceiling. The
kitchen goes out of its way to find fresh local produce and
puts together a short, interesting menu with a handful of
dishes per course. One way to start is smooth cinnamon-
coated chicken liver parfait with apple chutney, an
alternative to crab tian with avocado mousse, grapefruit
and citrus dressing. Fish might get an airing as
marinated mackerel fillets with distinctively flavoured
accompaniments of fennel and potato salad, tomato
salsa and anchovy vinaigrette, and to finish, try treacle
tart with rum sorbet and toffee sauce.

Chef Amos Burrows **Owner** Caley Hall Hotel Ltd
Times 12-9 Closed 17-28 Dec, 3-16 Jan **Prices** Starter
£4.50-£9, Main £8.50-£19.50, Service optional **Wines** 7
by glass **Notes** Sunday L £10.95-£20.95, Vegetarian
menu **Seats** 80 **Children** Portions, Menu **Parking** 50

The Neptune Restaurant with Rooms

◎◎◎ — *see below*

Bank House Hotel

◎ Modern British ♨

Quality brasserie cooking in historic townhouse

☎ 01553 660492
King's Staithe Square PE30 1RD
e-mail: info@thebankhouse.co.uk
dir: Follow signs to Old Town and onto quayside, through
floodgate, hotel on right opposite Custom House

Stylishly revamped to inject a hit of eclectic modern
boutique style, this Georgian townhouse hotel with a slick
modern brasserie-style restaurant lies in the heart of
King's Lynn's historical quarter, right on the River Ouse
quayside. Bank House was once Gurney's bank in the
18th century (Gurney's was later absorbed by Barclays),
and its former counting house rooms are now the venue
for a bar serving a fine spread of local ales and excellent
wines, and the dark wood-furnished dining rooms. The
kitchen's precise, unpretentious modern brasserie dishes
kick off with a well-made chicken liver pâté with toasted
granary bread and red onion marmalade followed by roast
rump of lamb with rösti potato, parsnip purée and mint
salsa verde. Banoffee tartlet with Chantilly cream wraps
things up nicely.

Chef Stuart Deuchars **Owner** Jeannette & Anthony
Goodrich **Times** 12-2.30/6.30-9 **Prices** Starter £5-£7,

continued

The Neptune Restaurant with Rooms

Modern European V

Outstanding cooking on the North Norfolk coast

☎ 01485 532122
85 Old Hunstanton Rd PE36 6HZ
e-mail: reservations@theneptune.co.uk
web: www.theneptune.co.uk
dir: On A149

The North Norfolk coast has many attractions including
vast expanses of white sandy beaches, pretty flint-flecked
villages, and bird-watching aplenty. It is also home to
some fantastic ingredients - the bounty of the sea and
fertile land - and here at Kevin and Jacki Mangeolles'
place you are perfectly located to sample the best of
everything. Their restaurant with rooms resides within an
18th-century coaching inn close to the sea, with creepers

climbing the red-brick walls. Once you're over the
threshold, all is light and bright, with a touch of New
England beachcomber style in its white tongue-and-
groove panels, Lloyd Loom furniture, photographs of the
coast, and model boats. And what arrives on your plate
from the kitchen is perfectly balanced, creative food out
of the top drawer. Kevin seeks out first-class produce
from local boats and farms, giving his menus a genuine
sense of place. Start, perhaps, with skate wing with
pickled carrot and spiced crab salad, or ham hock and
Tornegus (an English cheese) terrine with quail's eggs,
cherry tomatoes and apple purée. Flavours and textures
are judged to a T and everything looks beautiful on the
plate. Main-course loin of local venison (from Houghton)
is partnered with a celeriac tart, baby onions and Savoy
cabbage, whilst local Brancaster mussels might feature
in a dish of monkfish with curly kale and apple. Desserts
are no less enticing: chestnut parfait, maybe, with
blueberries and a coconut sorbet, or sticky toffee pudding
with poached pear, tonka bean ice cream and

butterscotch. There's a multi-course tasting menu which
might take you from beetroot biscuit and spiced crab, via
sashimi scallop with passionfruit and chilli, to white
chocolate bavarois with raspberry and rose sorbet and
almond praline. Service, led by Jacki, is spot on, and a
well-chosen wine list rounds off an extremely appealing
package.

Chef Kevin Mangeolles **Owner** Kevin & Jacki Mangeolles
Times 12-1.30/7-9 Closed Jan, 2 wks Nov, 26 Dec, Mon, L
Tue-Sat (except by arrangement) **Prices** Fixed L 2 course
£26.50-£28.50, Fixed D 3 course £52, Tasting menu £70,
Service optional **Wines** 70 bottles over £30, 26 bottles
under £30, 14 by glass **Notes** Sunday L, Vegetarian menu,
Dress restrictions, Smart casual **Seats** 24
Children Portions **Parking** 6, On street

KING'S LYNN *continued*

Main £7-£15, Dessert £3-£6, Service optional, Groups min 8 service 10% **Wines** 6 by glass **Notes** Pre/post theatre menu available on request, Sunday L fr £11, Vegetarian available **Seats** 60, Pr/dining room 40 **Children** Portions, Menu **Parking** 5, On quayside or Baker Lane car park

NORTH WALSHAM Map 13 TG23

Beechwood Hotel

@@ Modern British **V** 🥄

Charming hotel with good local ingredients on the menu

☎ 01692 403231
20 Cromer Rd NR28 0HD
e-mail: info@beechwood-hotel.co.uk
web: www.beechwood-hotel.co.uk
dir: From Norwich on B1150, 13m to N Walsham. Left at lights, next right. Hotel 150mtrs on left

This handsome creeper-clad Georgian hotel should exert a strong pull for murder and mystery fans, since Agatha Christie came here frequently to visit when it was owned by family friends, and her framed letters are hung in the hallway. It is a lovely personal touch that sums up the exemplary attitude to service and attention to detail that is the hallmark of this charming small hotel. It all helps you to change down a gear into relaxation mode before settling into an elegantly traditional dining room, which is the setting for some well-crafted, contemporary cooking, delivered by a kitchen with a passion for sourcing top-grade Norfolk produce - much of it from within a 10-mile radius. A perfectly crisp and golden haddock and prawn fishcake with a poached egg, hollandaise sauce and pea shoot salad opens on fine form, ahead of loin of Aylsham lamb partnered simply by rosemary roast potatoes, parsnip purée, carrots and Savoy cabbage. Finally, a textbook crème brûlée is pointed up with vibrant raspberry compôte and coulis.

Chef Steven Norgate **Owner** Don Birch & Lindsay Spalding **Times** 12-1.45/7-9 Closed L Mon-Sat **Prices** Fixed D 3 course £39, Service optional **Wines** 11 by glass **Notes** Sunday L, Vegetarian menu, Dress restrictions, Smart casual **Seats** 60, Pr/dining room 20 **Children** Portions **Parking** 20

NORWICH Map 13 TG20

Best Western Annesley House Hotel

@@ Modern International 🥄

Georgian hotel with modish menu

☎ 01603 624553
6 Newmarket Rd NR2 2LA
e-mail: annesleyhouse@bestwestern.co.uk
dir: On A11, close to city centre

Georgian and Grade II listed, Annesley House is a pretty property a short walk from the centre of the city. It's got three acres of gardens to call its own, so really does feel like a little oasis. There are views over the garden from the conservatory restaurant, which has a decidedly contemporary finish with its wood-affect flooring, leather seats and darkwood tables. The kitchen matches the décor with its equally modish approach, which consists of sourcing good quality East Anglian ingredients and subjecting them to some fashionable Pan-European preparations. Thus hand-dived scallops, wrapped in smoky streaky bacon, are served with crisp pork belly, roast shallot purée and chicken jus. Next up, perhaps roast chump of lamb with fondant potato and chargrilled Mediterranean vegetables, or pan-fried salmon with fresh tagliatelle, braised baby gem, sautéed asparagus, broad beans and girolles. And to finish, Tunisian orange cake comes with a prune and orange compôte, stem ginger ice cream and crème anglaise.

Chef Steven Watkin **Owner** Mr & Mrs D Reynolds **Times** 12-2/6-9 Closed Xmas & New Year, L Sun **Prices** Fixed L 2 course £18.95-£21.95, Fixed D 3 course fr £34.75, Starter fr £6.95, Main fr £22.50, Dessert fr £6.95, Service optional **Wines** 10 bottles under £30, 7 by glass **Notes** Pre-theatre menu available from 6pm by arrangement, Vegetarian available **Seats** 30 **Children** Portions **Parking** 29

Best Western George Hotel

@ Modern British 🥄

Simple brasserie cooking at a family-run hotel

☎ 01603 617841
10 Arlington Ln, Newmarket Rd NR2 2DA
e-mail: reservations@georgehotel.co.uk
web: www.arlingtonhotelgroup.co.uk
dir: From A11 follow city centre signs, becomes Newmarket Rd. Hotel on left

A short stroll from the city centre, behind the frosted-glass frontage of the George, a family-run Victorian hotel, is a contemporary brasserie with leather banquette seating, dark wood panelling and mirrors setting the tone, and an open-to-view grill bringing a touch of restaurant theatre. Friendly, uniformed staff deliver formal service, and the kitchen makes good use of fresh seasonal produce, as well as of that grill. Fried corn-fed chicken breast comes with roast herbed new potatoes and red onion in a strong Madeira jus and among the desserts, an indulgent version of tiramisù is all present and correct.

Chef Paul Branford **Owner** David Easter, Kingsley Place Hotels Ltd **Times** 12-2/6-10 **Prices** Prices not confirmed Service optional **Wines** 10 by glass **Notes** Vegetarian available **Seats** 44, Pr/dining room 80 **Children** Portions, Menu **Parking** 40

Brasteds

@@ Modern European 🥄

Exciting cooking in a stylish barn conversion

☎ 01508 491112
Manor Farm Barns, Fox Rd, Framingham Pigot NR14 7PZ
e-mail: enquiries@brasteds.co.uk
web: www.brasteds.co.uk
dir: A11 onto A47 towards Great Yarmouth, then A146. After 0.5m turn right onto Fox Rd, 0.5m on left

Four miles from the city centre, in the privately owned village of Framingham Pigot, Brasteds is a combination of restaurant - a swish converted barn with beams in the vaulted ceiling, brick walls, an oak floor and cleverly angled spotlights - boutique B&B and wedding and event venue. A canny kitchen brigade assembles regularly-changing menus with the sort of über-modern ideas that would have left Mrs Beeton reaching for her smelling salts. How about cumin-roast scallops with Iberico ham, smoked eel and truffle vinaigrette, or a main course of roast venison tenderloin with pure cocoa, beetroot gel, peanut and vanilla crumble and blackcurrant espuma? Dishes are built on prime local produce and put together intelligently; expect potted salt beef with horseradish and apple, followed by steamed lemon sole fillets with cockle and caper fricassée, prawn mousse and watercress purée, and a finale of 'the rhubarb five' - clafoutis, poached fruit, syrup, granita and jelly.

Chef Chris Busby, Martin Recchi **Owner** Nick Mills, Chris Busby & Michael Zouvani **Times** 12-2.30/7-10 Closed Sun-Wed, L Sat, Thu **Prices** Prices not confirmed Service optional **Wines** 8 by glass **Notes** Vegetarian available, Dress restrictions, Smart dress advisable **Seats** 40, Pr/dining room 16 **Children** Portions **Parking** 50

Save on Hotels. Book at theAA.com/hotel

NORFOLK 391 ENGLAND

Brummells Seafood Restaurant

◉◉ International, Seafood

Venerable seafood restaurant in a 16th-century building

☎ 01603 625555
7 Magdalen St NR3 1LE
e-mail: brummell@brummells.co.uk
web: www.brummells.co.uk
dir: In city centre, 2 mins walk from Norwich Cathedral, 40yds from Colegate

In the oldest part of the city, Brummells shows its age with its beams, standing timbers and stone walls, candlelight adding a romantic glow to the rustic interior in the evening, and a log fire burning in winter. Seafood cooked to consistently high standards is the draw. Preparations vary from classics like skate wing pan-fried with black butter, lobster thermidor, or plainly grilled Dover sole, to the more adventurous: chargrilled yellowfin tuna, served pink, with curried fruit marmalade, or steamed sea bass fillets with prawn butter, ginger and leeks. Starters show the same broad sweep, from mussels with creamy white wine and garlic sauce, to blackened swordfish with citrus and mustard dressing. There are some meat dishes too, and to finish might be pear and nutmeg parfait with caramelised fruit.

Chef A Brummell, J O'Sullivan **Owner** A Brummell **Times** 12-flexible/6-flexible **Prices** Starter £7-£17, Main £18-£35, Dessert £6.50, Service optional, Groups min 7 service 10% **Wines** 38 bottles over £30, 44 bottles under £30, 6 by glass **Notes** Sunday L, Vegetarian available, Dress restrictions, Smart casual or jacket & tie **Seats** 25

Children Portions **Parking** On street after 6.30pm & Sun, Car park nearby

See advert on page 392

The Maids Head Hotel

◉ Modern British 🍽

Sound modern cooking in city-centre hotel

☎ 01603 209955
Tombland NR3 1LB
web: www.maidsheadhotel.co.uk
dir: A147 to north of the city. At rdbt for A1151, signed Wroxham, follow signs for Cathedral and Law Courts along Whitefriars. Hotel is approx 400 mtrs on right along Palace St

This part-timbered, part-brick building opposite the cathedral has its roots in the 13th century, although nowadays it provides conference facilities as well as all the other amenities expected of a modern hotel. Its restaurant is in a splendid room, once a courtyard, now glassed over with a pitched roof; it's airy and spacious, with a terracotta floor and well-appointed darkwood tables. Well-presented, modern British dishes are the kitchen's stock in trade. A trendy starter like properly cooked scallops with pancetta crisps and cauliflower purée may be followed by something old-fashioned and hearty like a game pie - its meat tender, its pastry perfectly crisp, with a rich gravy - served with roasted root vegetables. Finish with a lively, exotic pudding like smooth-textured coconut pannacotta with seared mango and caramel.

Chef Mark Lutkin **Owner** The Maids Head Hotel Ltd **Times** 12-3/6.30-9.30 **Prices** Prices not confirmed Service optional **Wines** 40 by glass **Notes** Fixed D 5 course with wine £45, Pre & post theatre menu, Sunday L, Vegetarian available **Seats** 70, Pr/dining room 8 **Children** Portions **Parking** 60

The Old Rectory

◉◉ Modern British V 🍽

Georgian rectory hotel with a local flavour

☎ 01603 700772
103 Yarmouth Rd, Thorpe St Andrew NR7 0HF
e-mail: enquiries@oldrectorynorwich.com
web: www.oldrectorynorwich.com
dir: From A47 southern bypass onto A1042 towards Norwich N & E. Left at mini rdbt onto A1242. After 0.3m through lights. Hotel 100mtrs on right

With its position by the River Yare and views over the Thorpe Marshes nature reserve, it's easy not to notice that the centre of Norwich is only two miles away. The Old Rectory is a handsome three-storey property with an adjoining Victorian coach house, offering a smart restaurant, an outdoor swimming pool and pretty gardens amongst its many assets. The dining room has great views over the garden, and with its panelled walls painted in neutral tones, fresh flowers and linen-clothed tables, it remains a cheerful spot day and night. The daily-changing menu is sensibly concise - three choices

per course - keeps things local where possible, and deals in gently modern ideas. You might start, perhaps, with local wild wood pigeon (marinated and roasted) in a salad with radicchio, roasted pecans, blood orange segments and gherkins. Seafood might be represented by fillet of black bream on lightly curried sweet potatoes, chick peas and parsnips, coriander spring onion salad and chilli tomato jam. To finish, you can't go far wrong with white chocolate tart with raspberry coulis.

Chef James Perry **Owner** Chris & Sally Entwistle **Times** 7-9 Closed Xmas, New Year, Sun, L all week **Prices** Fixed D 3 course £30-£35, Service optional **Wines** 5 bottles over £30, 16 bottles under £30, 5 by glass **Notes** Vegetarian menu **Seats** 18, Pr/dining room 16 **Children** Portions **Parking** 16

Roger Hickman's Restaurant

◉◉◉ – *see page 393*

St Benedicts Restaurant

◉ Modern British, French 🍽

Imaginative cooking in the heart of Norwich

☎ 01603 765377
9 St Benedicts St NR2 4PE
e-mail: stbenedicts@rafflesrestaurant.co.uk
dir: Just off inner ring road. Turn right by Toys-R-Us, 2nd right into St Benedicts St. Restaurant on left by pedestrian crossing

St Benedicts cuts a dash in the city centre with its smart French bistro looks, all duck-egg-blue-painted tongue and groove-panelled walls, jazzy fabrics, blond-wood floors and unclothed tables, and the place is no flash in the pan either, having been a stalwart of the Norwich dining scene for 20 years. Its evergreen success is down to straightforward cooking that stays in tune with the demand for feisty, clear-flavoured food built on seasonal, locally-sourced ingredients, and it delivers it all in an accessible, well-priced package. Get going with something like a double-baked cheese soufflé or pheasant sausage with Savoy cabbage and Puy lentils, then move on to sous-vide-cooked rabbit with pan-fried potato cake, curly kale and rosemary, and end with gooseberry and apple crumble with gooseberry ice cream.

Chef Nigel Raffles **Owner** Nigel & Jayne Raffles **Times** 12-2/6-10 Closed 25-31 Dec, Sun-Mon **Prices** Fixed L 2 course £10, Fixed D 3 course fr £14.95, Starter £4.95-£6.95, Main £13.95-£11.95, Dessert £5.95-£6.95, Groups min 10 service 10% **Wines** 8 by glass **Notes** Prix Fixe menu 6-7pm Tue-Sat 2 course £10, Vegetarian available **Seats** 42, Pr/dining room 24 **Children** Portions **Parking** On street, Car parks nearby

NORWICH *continued*

St Giles House Hotel

🏵🏵 🖐 Modern British 🍷

Classic and modern dishes in an architectural gem

☎ 01603 275180
41-45 St Giles St NR2 1JR
e-mail: reception@stgileshousehotel.com
web: www.stgileshousehotel.com
dir: A11 into central Norwich. Left at rdbt signed
Chapelfield Shopping Centre. 3rd exit at next rdbt. Left
onto St Giles St. Hotel on left

You could punctuate your perusal of Norwich city centre's
retail opportunities with a pitstop in St Giles House for
coffee, a massage, cocktails or something more
gastronomically satisfying in the SGH Bistro. The grand
Edwardian pile is worth a gander in its own right - beyond
its magnificent pillared façade is a palatial interior of
marble floors, oak panelling and elaborate plaster
ceilings, all sharpened with a slick contemporary
makeover. The art-deco bistro restaurant is a slick setting
for the kitchen's appealing repertoire of uncomplicated
modern dishes, as witnessed in a smooth and well-
flavoured chicken liver parfait served with celeriac
remoulade, tomato chutney and melba toast, ahead of
pan-fried chicken breast teamed with a leek and wild
mushroom pie, olive oil mash, sautéed baby carrots and
Marsala sauce. To finish, there's peanut butter and
chocolate parfait served with chocolate biscotti, peanut
brittle and salted caramel sauce. Smartly turned-out in
black, the front-of-house team are a polished act who
keep everything running smoothly.

Chef Stewart Jefferson **Owner** Rachel Roofe **Times** 11-10
All-day dining **Prices** Fixed D 3 course £32.50, Starter
£5.25-£7.50, Main £13.50-£24.50, Dessert £5-£7.50,
Service optional **Wines** 23 bottles over £30, 37 bottles
under £30, 19 by glass **Notes** Sunday L, Vegetarian
available **Seats** 50, Pr/dining room 48 **Children** Portions,
Menu **Parking** 30

Sprowston Manor, A Marriott Hotel & Country Club

🏵 Traditional, International

Grand manor house serving modernised classics

☎ 01603 410871
Sprowston Park, Wroxham Rd NR7 8RP
e-mail: mhrs.nwigs.frontdesk@marriotthotels.com
web: www.marriottsprowstonmanor.co.uk
dir: From A47 take Postwick exit onto Norwich outer ring
road, then take A1151. Hotel approx 3m and signed

With its splendid step-gabled façade, Sprowston Manor
presents an elegant and rather grand face to the world.
It's only a few miles from Norwich but feels a world away,
and serves up the full country-house package of golf (it
has its own championship course), spa and a couple of
dining options. The Zest Café is the informal choice, but
the main 1559 Restaurant keeps things relatively relaxed
and unpretentious, too, delivering a menu of modish
brasserie-style dishes. You might start with smoked duck
with pomegranate, toasted hazelnuts and parsnip crisps,
or king scallops with crispy pork belly and sweetcorn
purée. Next up, a steak cooked on the grill might appeal,
or a burger, or something like mackerel fillets with
mackerel cakes, beetroot and watercress sauce. Desserts
take the comfort route: hot chocolate fondant with vanilla
ice cream, for example.

Chef Martin Ng **Owner** Marriott International Inc
Times 12.30-3/6-10 Closed L Mon-Sat **Prices** Fixed L 2
course fr £16.50, Starter £6-£12, Main £12-£24, Dessert
£5.50-£7.50, Service optional **Wines** 3 bottles over £30,
22 bottles under £30, 10 by glass **Notes** Sunday L,
Vegetarian available, Dress restrictions, Smart casual, no
shorts, Civ Wed 300 **Seats** 70, Pr/dining room 150
Children Portions, Menu **Parking** 170

Stower Grange

🏵 Modern British 🍷

Eclectic dining in a Norfolk rectory

☎ 01603 860210
40 School Rd, Drayton NR8 6EF
e-mail: enquiries@stowergrange.co.uk
web: www.stowergrange.co.uk
dir: Norwich ring road N to ASDA supermarket. Take
A1067 (Fakenham road) at Drayton, right at lights into
School Rd. Hotel 150yds on right

The creeper-covered former rectory a few miles out of
Norwich makes a relaxing rural retreat, and is decorated
in classic country-house style, with a dining room done in
restful pastel shades looking out through full-drop
windows on to the well-tended gardens. Menus offer a
broad range of choice, from the oriental mash-up that is
Thai-spiced duck with mango and chilli chutney and duck
wonton, to mains such as slow-cooked belly of Blythburgh
pork with sweet potato fondant, spiced chick peas and
preserved lemon purée, or roast hake with braised lentils,
salsa verde and wilted spinach. It's good to see sharper
flavours being celebrated in desserts like lemon sponge
with lemon curd sauce and gooseberry ice cream.

Save on Hotels. Book at **theAA.com/hotel**

NORFOLK 393 **ENGLAND**

Chef Lee Parrette **Owner** Richard & Jane Fannon
Times 12-2.30/6.30-9.30 Closed 26-30 Dec, D Sun
Prices Starter £5.50-£6.95, Main £10.95-£19.50, Dessert
fr £6.50, Service optional **Wines** 8 by glass **Notes** Sunday
L fr £24, Vegetarian available, Civ Wed 120 **Seats** 25, Pr/
dining room 100 **Children** Portions **Parking** 40

The Sugar Hut

Thai

Vibrant Thai food near the castle

☎ 01603 766755
4 Opie St NR1 3DN
e-mail: lhongmo@hotmail.co.uk
dir: City centre next to Castle Meadow & Castle Mall car
park

Leelanooch Hongmo's expanding empire now incorporates
four restaurants - this venue not far from the castle, plus
two others in Norwich, and one in Coltishall. The ethos
throughout combines the famed courtesy of the Thai
service approach with some impeccably authentic
cookery. A yellow and blue colour scheme offsets the
black-clad staff to a tee, and the food is as bracing and
vibrant as can be. A house starter selection for two or
more is comprised of satay sticks, deep-fried minced pork
with chilli sauce, minced fish and prawn dumpling, won
tons and king prawn spring rolls, garnished with well-
dressed saladings. Lime-sharp tom yam gung soup is the
real thing, while a main dish of rump steak strips in hot
garlic sauce, with stir-fried veg, is robust and satisfying.

Good pad Thai, drunken noodles, or fried rice with
crabmeat provide a fragrant accompaniment.

Chef Chartchai Fodsungnoen, Saowanee Hongmo
Owner Leelanooch Hongmo **Times** 12-2.30/6-10.30
Closed Sun, L Mon **Prices** Fixed L 3 course £8.95-£9.95,
Fixed D 3 course £25-£27.50, Starter £4.95-£6.50, Main
£8.95-£16.95, Dessert £1.50-£5.95, Service optional,
Groups min 7 service 10% **Wines** 3 by glass
Notes Vegetarian available **Seats** 40 **Children** Portions
Parking Castle Mall

Tatlers

Modern British

Fashion-conscious brasserie cooking in Tombland

☎ 01603 766670
21 Tombland NR3 1RF
e-mail: info@tatlersrestaurant.co.uk
dir: In city centre in Tombland. Next to Erpingham Gate by
Norwich Cathedral

Hard by the cathedral in the Tombland district of the city,
the converted Victorian townhouse is the very image of a
modern restaurant, its three interlinked rooms done in
today's shabby chic, with unclothed tables and bare
floors offset by striking modern artworks in bold primary
colours. Expansive bay windows and high ceilings give
the place an airy feel, and in the evenings especially, it's
filled with the happy buzz of Norwich's gastro-
cognoscenti. Fashion-conscious combinations of seasonal

ingredients orientate the brasserie-style menus, where
truffled goats' cheese might appear with beetroot,
watercress purée and red onion jelly, as an overture to
pork mini-ribs with chips, garnished with rocket and
pomegranate salad, or salmon with cockles and courgette
'spaghetti', sauced in white wine. Desserts make
unashamed appeals to the sweet-toothed, with sticky
toffee pudding and pecan ice cream, as well as treacle
tart with an ice cream of honey. Spiced grape chutney is
the preferred accompaniment to cheeses.

Chef David Broada **Owner** Natasha & Christopher
Williams **Times** 12-2/6-9.15 Closed BHs, Sun
Prices Prices not confirmed Service optional, Groups min
6 service 10% **Wines** 7 by glass **Notes** Vegetarian
available **Seats** 75, Pr/dining room 35 **Children** Portions
Parking Law courts, Elm Hill, Colegate, St Andrews

Roger Hickman's Restaurant

NORWICH   **MAP 13 TG20**

Modern British

Well-crafted contemporary cooking

☎ 01603 633522
79 Upper St Giles St NR2 1AB
e-mail: info@rogerhickmansrestaurant.com
dir: In city centre, from A147 at rdbt into Cleveland Rd,
1st left into Upper St Giles St

Roger Hickman's name now hangs above the door of the
restaurant formerly known as Adlard's, a veteran of
Norwich's gastronomic scene where he once ran the
kitchen as head chef. 'If it ain't broke don't fix it' seems
to have been the approach since Hickman's return to his
old stomping ground: in terms of style and ambience, at
least, the place remains intimate, relaxed and with a
touch of class thanks to its linen-swathed tables on

stripped wooden floors, and clean-cut cream walls hung
with colourful prints. On the culinary front, however,
things have shifted gear into warp drive. After a spell as
sous-chef with Tom Aikens (see entry, London SW3),
Hickman has refined his already impressive technique
still further and is now turning out finger-on-the-pulse
cooking in a French-accented contemporary idiom. No
corners are cut here, after all the new boss is happiest
when he's at the stoves, so virtually everything is made
in-house, from breads to ice cream, and it's all built on
immaculate ingredients. An opening gambit of crab salad
with lemongrass mousse and avocado purée starts out on
the right foot with clean flavours and beautiful
presentation, then comes roast duck breast with fondant
potato and confit cabbage, a deceptively simple-sounding
description that fails to do justice to the fine ingredients,
accurate timing and spot-on textures of this well-
conceived dish. There's satisfaction too in the form of
spiced monkfish, its flavour complemented by aubergine
caviar, white beans and anchovy beignet. Dessert winds

up with an innovatively deconstructed carrot cake served
with carrot caramel and jelly and crème fraîche sorbet, or
there could be more emphatic flavours and textural
entertainment in a composition involving pear mousse
with apple tapioca, lemon granita and compressed apple.
The intelligently-assembled global wine list abounds with
quality producers and there's a fair choice of bottles that
won't send the bill into overdrive.

Chef Roger Hickman **Owner** Roger Hickman
Times 12-2.30/7-10 Closed 1 week Jan & Aug, Sun, Mon
Prices Fixed L 2 course fr £18, Fixed D 3 course fr £40,
Tasting menu £55, Service optional, Groups min 6 service
10% **Wines** 95 bottles over £30, 14 bottles under £30, 12
by glass **Notes** Pre-theatre menu £20/£24, Vegetarian
available **Seats** 40 **Children** Portions **Parking** On street &
St Giles multi-storey

NORWICH *continued*

Thailand Restaurant

◉ Thai

Vibrant traditional Thai cooking at popular out-of-town venue

☎ 01603 700444
9 Ring Rd, Thorpe St Andrew NR7 0XJ
e-mail: siamkidd@aol.com
dir: From Southern bypass, follow airport signs. Located at top of hill past Sainsbury's

The name tells you all you need to know about the cultural orientation of this abidingly popular restaurant on the outskirts of Norwich (booking seems essential), with traditionally dressed staff serving a repertoire of classic dishes from everybody's favourite southeast Asian cuisine. But the name alone doesn't sell the sheer quality of the cooking, which is as vibrantly and accurately seasoned and timed, and as carefully presented, as we hope to find. King prawns and mixed vegetables in tempura batter with plum sauce for dipping might start things off, or there are dinky little batter baskets of fried chicken, prawn and sweetcorn, before the main business of pork with ginger strips, peppers and mushrooms, chicken with baby corn and cashews, or mixed fish in coconut-milk curry. A versatile range of set menus for various headcounts is also offered. Iced fruity desserts such as orange sorbet or mango parfait refresh the palate.

Times 12-3/6-10 Closed 25 Dec, L Sat-Sun

The Gin Trap Inn

◉ British ◉

Charming 17th-century inn turned gastro-pub

☎ 01485 525264
6 High St PE36 5JU
e-mail: thegintrap@hotmail.co.uk
dir: A149 from King's Lynn towards Hunstanton. After 15m turn right at Heacham for Ringstead

Bikers and hikers on the Roman Peddars Way footpath - and anyone else passing through the tranquil village of Ringstead just inland from the North Norfolk coast - will find the 17th-century Gin Trap is an irresistible pitstop. It balances all the virtues of a well-run pub: genuine hospitality, local ales and good food, whether you go for the rustic bar with its bare bricks, gnarled beams and wood-burning stove in a walk-in fireplace, or the candlelit, linen-clad tables of the smart restaurant and conservatory. The kitchen is proud to buy its materials from local farmers and producers, and shows off its prowess with confidence. Beer-battered haddock with mushy peas and home-made tartare sauce keeps things pubby, but there's also smoked mackerel pâté with beetroot and onion compôte, pea shoots and reduced balsamic, ahead of seared venison loin with thyme creamed potatoes, carrots and braised red cabbage.

Chef Dale Edge **Owner** Steve Knowles & Cindy Cook
Times 12-2/6-9 **Prices** Starter £4-£6.50, Main £9-£17.50, Dessert £5.50-£7.50, Service optional **Wines** 2 bottles over £30, 25 bottles under £30, 9 by glass **Notes** Sun L all year, roasts during winter only, Sunday L, Vegetarian available **Seats** 60, Pr/dining room 18 **Children** Portions, Menu **Parking** 20, On street

Dales Country House Hotel

◉◉ British, European ◉

Smart modern cooking in rural Norfolk

☎ 01263 824555
Lodge Hill NR26 8TJ
e-mail: dales@mackenziehotels.com
dir: On B1157, 1m S of Sheringham. From A148 Cromer to Holt road, take turn at entrance to Sheringham Park. Hotel 0.5m on left

Handy for a stopover if you've been ogling the spectacular rhododendrons and azaleas in Humphry Repton's Sheringham Park gardens next door, you'll find that the grounds of the Dales Country House Hotel are no slouch either. Just a couple of miles from the big skies of the North Norfolk coast, the step-gabled Victorian house has heaps of period charm, although the cooking in Upchers restaurant takes a rather more contemporary European view of things. With the briny so near, fish and seafood is always going to be a good idea - perhaps gratin of local mussels with brown shrimps and Cromer crab velouté to start, then a delicate millefeuille of sea bass and lobster with fennel, chicory rösti potato, and girolles. Local meat plays its part too - maybe cannon of lamb partnered by confit lamb hash cake, butternut squash ratatouille, aubergine caviar and thyme sauce. To finish, try a sweetshop array of cinnamon doughnuts, strawberry jelly, chocolate sauce and caramel ice cream, or go savoury with a plate of Norfolk's finest cheeses.

Chef Rene Ilupar **Owner** Mr & Mrs Mackenzie
Times 12-2/7-9.30 **Prices** Fixed L 2 course fr £14.95, Fixed D 3 course fr £23, Starter £5.95-£7.25, Main £12.50-£23.50, Dessert £6-£8.75, Service optional **Wines** 4 bottles over £30, 28 bottles under £30, 7 by glass **Notes** Sunday L, Vegetarian available, Dress restrictions, No shorts or sportswear **Seats** 70, Pr/dining room 40 **Children** Portions **Parking** 50

The Rose & Crown

◉ British ◉

Bustling local with global dishes and British classics

☎ 01485 541382
Old Church Rd PE31 7LX
e-mail: info@roseandcrownsnettisham.co.uk
dir: From King's Lynn take A149 N towards Hunstanton. After 10m into Snettisham to village centre, then into Old Church Rd towards church. Hotel 100yds on left

Brim-full with period atmosphere, the 14th-century Rose & Crown is all rambling nooks and crannies, low beamed

ceilings, wobbly floors and log fires, but it has brought in summery colours and a hint of beachcomber-chic style to keep step with the times. The kitchen has also shifted up a gear, serving time-honoured pub classics done right - beer-battered haddock with hand-cut chips, mushy peas and tartare sauce, or local bangers and mash with onion gravy. If you want to trade up to unfussy contemporary ideas, expect to find hearty dishes that celebrate the Norfolk larder - perhaps Brancaster mussels marinière with crusty bread, or pork tenderloin with black pudding mousse, potato rösti, green beans, and apple purée. Finish with the comfort of sticky toffee pudding with butterscotch sauce and ginger ice cream.

Chef Jamie Clarke **Owner** Anthony & Jeanette Goodrich
Times 12-2/6.30-9 **Prices** Starter £5-£7, Main £8-£16, Dessert £3-£6, Service optional, Groups min 8 service 10% **Wines** 10 by glass **Notes** Sunday L, Vegetarian available **Seats** 160, Pr/dining room 30 **Children** Portions, Menu **Parking** 70

Elveden Café Restaurant

◉ Traditional British ◉

Farm produce and enterprising cooking on the Elveden Estate

☎ 01842 898068
London Rd, Elveden IP24 3TQ
e-mail: steve.pillinger@elveden.com
dir: On A11 between Newmarket & Thetford, 800 mtrs from junct with B1106

The 10,000-acre Elveden Estate is a busy operation producing vast amounts of vegetables, and acting as a local food hub selling local produce in a complex of shops in converted red-brick farm buildings. Its café-restaurant is a stylish place with a beamed vaulted ceiling, and expansive alfresco dining area with a barbecue in summer. Open from breakfast, through lunch to afternoon tea, the wide-ranging menu takes in unfussy, well-made classics. Bread is made in-house (to go with dipping oils and olives, for example), then to start there's home-made pork pie, or caramelised onion tart, followed by mains at their most simple - beef from the estate providing the prime protein in a burger with chunky chips and home-made relish; elsewhere there might be haunch of Elveden venison with fondant potato, braised carrot and onions. Dessert concludes on an equally comforting note with home-made treacle tart with golden syrup ice cream.

Chef Scott Taylor **Owner** The Earl of Iveagh
Times 9.30am-5pm Closed 25-26 Dec, D all week **Prices** Fixed L 2 course fr £16.50, Starter £2.95-£6.50, Main £8.95-£12.50, Dessert £5.50-£5.95, Service optional **Wines** 30 bottles over £30, 60 bottles under £30, 6 by glass **Notes** Sunday L £16.50-£19.50, Vegetarian available **Seats** 80 **Children** Portions, Menu **Parking** 200

Save on Hotels. Book at **theAA.com/hotel**

NORFOLK 395 ENGLAND

Titchwell Manor Hotel

TITCHWELL   MAP 13 TF74

Modern European

Art on a plate on the North Norfolk coast

☎ 01485 210221
PE31 8BB
e-mail: margaret@titchwellmanor.com
web: www.titchwellmanor.com
dir: On A149 (coast road) between Brancaster & Thornham

There are endless treasures in store for visitors to the North Norfolk coast, from its long, sandy beaches and wide, open skies, to its charming little towns and its multitude of great places to eat, drink and stay. Titchwell Manor has proven itself to be one of the greatest of those great places: a former Victorian farmhouse overlooking the coastal marshes, turned into an intimate and stylish boutique hotel. The neat little red-brick building has been owned by Margaret and Ian Snaith for close on 15 years and, this being a real family business, it's son Eric who looks after the food side of things. And what food. Eric's highly inventive seven-course tasting menus are served in the contemporary Conservatory Restaurant: an atmospheric setting for dinner with its twinkling lights wrapped around the ceiling beams, soft background music and views over the walled garden. If you need any clarification of the menu or have any questions about the 100-bin wine list, the highly attentive and passionate staff will be eager to assist, but alternatively you could just sit back and enjoy. The pick of North Norfolk's larder, including local fish and seafood, plus flowers and herbs grown in the hotel's own garden, is showcased in dishes that are by turns complex, innovative, exciting and as pretty as a picture. Pea custard tart with a fine, crisp pastry might get things off the ground, followed by a fresh-tasting dish of Brancaster crab with a sweetcorn purée, superbly textured brown crab ice cream, and marsh vegetables. Next up could be an accurately cooked, super-fresh fillet of brill with a mini pannacotta delicately flavoured with Applewood smoked cheese and textures of fennel (a purée, fennel leaves and poached), then best-end of Norfolk lamb, tender and moist, with black olive and yoghurt to cut through the natural sweetness of the meat. Lincolnshire Poacher cheddar with cherry and beetroot pickle and water biscuits might put in an appearance before attention turns to all things sweet: first up a delightfully moist gooseberry sponge with elderflower ice cream, then a richly satisfying chocolate délice with 'raspberry variations'. Less ambitious cooking is on offer in the hotel's more casual Eating Rooms.

Chef Eric Snaith **Owner** Margaret & Ian Snaith **Times** 12-5.30/6.30-9.30
Prices Tasting menu £45-£60, Starter £6-£13, Main £9-£27, Dessert £7-£9, Service optional, Groups min 8 service 10% **Wines** 9 by glass **Notes** Tasting menu D 5/8 course, Sunday L £23-£27, Vegetarian available, Civ Wed 70 **Seats** 80 **Children** Portions, Menu **Parking** 50

THURSFORD
Map 13 TF93

The Old Forge Seafood Restaurant

◉ Seafood ◔

Rustic seafood cooking in a historic former forge

☎ 01328 878345
Fakenham Rd NR21 0BD
e-mail: sarah.goldspink@btconnect.com
dir: On A148

The whitewashed former coaching station and forge used to be a resting place for pilgrims heading to Walsingham, and even merits a name-check in *The Pilgrim's Progress*. A sympathetic refurbishment means beams, York stone floor and walls, and even the original iron hooks where the horses were shod are in evidence in the cosy, buzzy restaurant. It's all about the seafood here and why not when you can get it in fresh every day from nearby Blakeney and Wells-next-the-Sea? Expect good, honest, rustic cooking, often with Spanish influences and using spices grown in the forge's garden. There might be sizzling tiger prawns in the Spanish way, served with chunks of bread, lobster grilled with garlic and parsley butter, or a zarzuela of fish - another Spanish dish with white fish and shellfish cooked in white wine, cream and tomatoes, served in a large paella-style pan.

Chef Colin Bowett **Owner** Colin & Sarah Bowett
Times 6.30-10 Closed Mon, BH, L all week, D Sun
Prices Fixed D 3 course £19.50, Starter £4.95-£12.50, Main £12.50-£36, Dessert £3.95-£5.75, Service optional **Wines** 1 bottle over £30, 12 bottles under £30, 5 by glass **Notes** Opening times vary (phone to check), no late bkgs Jan-Feb, Vegetarian available **Seats** 28 **Children** Portions **Parking** 12

TITCHWELL
Map 13 TF74

Titchwell Manor Hotel

◉◉◉ – see page 395

WIVETON
Map 13 TG04

Wiveton Bell

◉ British, European ◔

Distinctive cooking in village inn

☎ 01263 740101
The Green, Blakeney Rd NR25 7TL
e-mail: enquiries@wivetonbell.co.uk
dir: 1m S of Blakeney on the Holt road

There's a lively, cheerful atmosphere at the Bell, an 18th-century pub on the village green not far from North Norfolk's salt marshes, an Area of Outstanding Natural Beauty. Tables are bare wood, seating is from upholstered chairs and wooden pews, plain walls are hung with artwork, and young staff are upbeat and proactive. The

wide-ranging menus might feature chicken balti curry with mango chutney, an onion bhaji and basmati rice. Due deference is paid to seasonality: local asparagus, for instance, served with a soft-poached egg and hollandaise, and Brancaster mussels, steamed with white wine, shallots and cream. Local venison might appear in winter, casseroled in red wine and port, served with potato purée, sausage meat and thyme balls, and braised red cabbage, and fish is well handled, judging by well-timed fillet of sea bass with carrot and beetroot Lyonnaise and dill-flavoured crushed new potatoes. Tail off a meal with something like rich coffee pannacotta.

Chef Matt Gibbon **Owner** Berni Morritt & Sandy Butcher
Times 12-2.15/6-9.15 Closed 25 Dec **Prices** Starter £5.95-£7.95, Main £11.50-£19.95, Dessert £5.95, Service optional **Wines** 6 bottles over £30, 22 bottles under £30, 13 by glass **Notes** Sunday L fr £13.95, Vegetarian available **Seats** 60 **Children** Portions, Menu **Parking** 5, village green 50yds away

---

WYMONDHAM
Map 13 TG10

Number Twenty Four Restaurant

◉◉ Modern British ◔

Relaxed dining and market fresh produce

☎ 01953 607750
24 Middleton St NR18 0AD
web: www.number24.co.uk
dir: Town centre opposite war memorial

A row of Grade II listed 18th-century cottages in the historic heart of Wymondham is the setting for this smart, family-run restaurant. The dining room is a period gem done out with linen-clothed, widely-spaced tables set against warm, soothing colours, and the vibe is good humoured and unstuffy. There is dedication to good old-fashioned hard work in the kitchen, where everything is cooked from scratch and in tune with the seasons and local larder. The menu keeps things admirably to the point and works within the modern British idiom to deliver the likes of a local game hotpot with Cognac, red wine and onion gravy, caramelised onion and pancetta, as a prelude to grilled sea bass fillets, which could be partnered by roasted fennel and tomato, and smoked haddock and crayfish chowder. To finish, give in to temptation and go for steamed syrup sponge with vanilla custard.

Chef Jonathan Griffin **Owner** Jonathan Griffin
Times 12-2/7-9 Closed 26 Dec, 1 Jan, Mon, L Tue, D Sun **Prices** Fixed L 2 course fr £15.50, Fixed D 3 course fr £25.95 **Wines** 3 bottles over £30, 30 bottles under £30, 7 by glass **Notes** Sunday L, Vegetarian available, Dress restrictions, Smart casual, no shorts **Seats** 60, Pr/dining room 55 **Children** Portions **Parking** On street opposite, in town centre car park

---

NORTHAMPTONSHIRE

DAVENTRY
Map 11 SP56

Fawsley Hall

◉◉ Modern British ◔

Assertive modern British cooking

☎ 01327 892000
Fawsley NN11 3BA
e-mail: info@fawsleyhall.com
web: www.fawsleyhall.com
dir: A361 S of Daventry, between Badby & Charwelton, hotel signed (single track lane)

Plantagenets, Tudors and Georgians all had a go at Fawsley Hall over the centuries, resulting in the beguiling architectural mishmash we see before us. However mixed the stylistic messages, it all screams 'grand', and the interiors maintain the pace with oak panels, stone arches and the fabulous Equilibrium dining room, with its 25-foot-high beamed ceiling and huge inglenook, flagstone floor and flickering candlelight. That said, the number of covers is kept low, so that a proper feeling of intimacy pervades the place. An ingenious terrine of pigeon and foie gras is presented in Battenberg squares, while a bowl of deep-green parsley soup has its homogeneous silkiness offset with little chunks of smoked eel and a cloud of parmesan foam. A fish main course offers turbot with Evesham asparagus and Lyonnaise potatoes, together with a cucumber-wrapped herby mousse and a rather predominating note of grain mustard. Blythburgh pork belly is daringly paired with lobster and chive mash and red cabbage, and then dessert comes up with a slice of unmoulded burnt vanilla custard, alongside poached rhubarb and strawberry sorbet.

Chef Jon Rix **Owner** Bahram Holdings **Times** 7-9.30 Closed Xmas/New Year, Sun-Wed, L all week **Prices** Fixed D 3 course fr £59, Service added but optional 12.5% **Wines** 66 bottles over £30, 51 bottles under £30, 8 by glass **Notes** Sun L in Brasserie, Vegetarian available, Dress restrictions, Smart casual, Civ Wed 120 **Seats** 30, Pr/dining room 20 **Parking** 140

Save on Hotels. Book at **theAA.com/hotel**

NORTHAMPTONSHIRE 397 **ENGLAND**

EASTON-ON-THE-HILL   Map 11 TF00

The Exeter Arms

Modern British

Smartly revamped old inn with contemporary cooking

☎ 01780 756321
21 Stamford Rd PE9 3NS
e-mail: reservations@theexeterarms.net
dir: From A43 enter village, inn 300yds on left

If you're keen on the ideology of local sourcing, this spruced-up village inn should be up your street: the lion's share of the lamb, beef and pork is reared at the owners' family farm, while in the season you're never far from a bunch of asparagus from the same source. Inside, it is refurbished in an unpretentious blend of tradition - exposed beams and stonework - and contemporary style, while the smart Orangery dining area has doors that fold back, opening it out to the walled courtyard. The cooking has a suitably contemporary tone, serving seared scallops with parsnip purée and chicken wings, or in-house liquorice-cured salmon with potato salad and horseradish dressing, ahead of local wood pigeon Wellington with buttered mash, Savoy cabbage and jus. If you've room left for a sweet finish, go for something like white chocolate crème brûlée from the 'something naughty' section.

Chef Simon Pollendine **Owner** Michael Thurlby, Sue Olver **Times** 12-2.30/6-9.30 Closed D Sun **Prices** Starter £4-£5.95, Main £10.95-£18.95, Dessert £5.50, Service optional **Wines** 3 bottles over £30, 38 bottles under £30, 19 by glass **Notes** Sunday L, Vegetarian available **Seats** 80, Pr/dining room 24 **Children** Portions, Menu **Parking** 30

KETTERING   Map 11 SP87

Kettering Park Hotel & Spa

Modern British

Simple comfort food in a modern hotel restaurant

☎ 01536 416666
Kettering Parkway NN15 6XT
e-mail: kpark.reservations@shirehotels.com
web: www.ketteringparkhotel.com
dir: Off A14 junct 9 (M1 to A1 link road), hotel in Kettering Venture Park

It may well be located in a business park, yet there's a certain charm about this modern hotel. The restaurant overlooks the back garden and is an airy, open-plan, split-level space that welcomes with a large open fire. The extensive menu has something for everyone. There are global influences, but honest British food is to the fore here, and presentation is pleasingly simple. Smooth chicken liver parfait is partnered with Sauternes jelly and toasted brioche to start, or you might go for a classic tempura tiger prawns with chilli dipping sauce and grilled lime. For the main event, handmade Scottish salmon fishcakes are plump and come with fresh tomato and coriander salad, or you could choose a steak from the chargrill with fries and roasted vine tomato. Sticky toffee pudding with vanilla ice cream and hot treacle sauce ends proceedings firmly in the comfort zone.

Chef Jamie Mason **Owner** Shire Hotels **Times** 12-1.45/7-9.30 Closed Xmas, New Year (ex residents & pre-booked), L Mon-Sat **Prices** Fixed L 2 course £17.95-£19.95, Fixed D 3 course £20.95-£24.95, Starter £6.50-£15.50, Main £11.95-£57.50, Service optional **Wines** 40 bottles over £30, 60 bottles under £30, 15 by glass **Notes** Sunday L, Vegetarian available, Dress restrictions, Smart dress, Civ Wed 150 **Seats** 90, Pr/dining room 40 **Children** Portions, Menu **Parking** 200

Rushton Hall Hotel and Spa

@@@ – *see below*

Rushton Hall Hotel and Spa

@@@

KETTERING   MAP 11 SP87

Modern British

Innovative British cooking in a magnificent old hall

☎ 01536 713001
Rushton NN14 1RR
e-mail: enquiries@rushtonhall.com
web: www.rushtonhall.com
dir: A14 junct 7, A43 to Corby then A6003 to Rushton, turn after bridge

If you want grand, look no further. Rushton is a colossal slab of feudalist magnificence, which all started in the 15th century, when it was owned by various scions of the Tresham family. (Francis got caught up in the Gunpowder Plot. Frightful business). Extended further in the reign of Charles I, it was given its grandiosely French Empire interior makeover in the Victorian era, when Charles Dickens got himself repeat invitations from the then owners, returning the favour by immortalising the place as decomposing Havisham Hall in *Great Expectations*, cobwebbed wedding-cake and all. The figure representing Plenty above the massive entrance doors seems only apt, and prepares visitors for the panelled grandeur of the Tresham dining room, with its glazed fireplace and high windows gazing imperiously over an inner courtyard. Adrian Coulthard has girded his loins and delivered another Rosette to the Hall this year with cooking that energetically works the innovative vein of the modern British idiom. Beetroot-tinged cured salmon, as well as poached and smoked varieties, stars with fennel and lemon jelly as a prelude to a main that features a sausage, sticky drumstick and breast of corn-fed chicken, alongside puréed pickled carrot and leek in parsley jus. Or you might kick off with coriander-crusted scallops with matchsticks of celeriac and apple, zizzed up with capers, ahead of fillet, shredded leg and head terrine of profoundly succulent pork, which comes with sage gnocchi and pak choi. Rhubarb variations are comprised of poached, dried and sorbet, and offset with wobbling pistachio custard and a gently spicy ginger-beer jelly, while a startlingly straightforward prune and Armagnac soufflé comes with rich vanilla ice cream and roast apple. Artisan cheeses are the real thing, as is the full panoply of appetisers, petits fours and fantastic home-made breads.

Times 12-2/7-9 Closed L Mon-Fri

NASSINGTON Map 12 TL09

The Queens Head Inn

Modern British

Inviting riverside inn with treats from the grill

☎ 01780 784006
54 Station Rd PE8 6QB
e-mail: info@queensheadnassington.co.uk
dir: A1M N exit Wansford, follow signs to Yarwell & Nassington

The 200-year-old honey-hued stone inn on the banks of the River Nene looks like everyone's idea of a chocolate-box pretty village inn. There are all the requisite trappings - real ales on tap in a smart oak-floored and beamed bar - but these days it is a world apart from beer and dominos. The Queens Head has built a solid reputation for good food served in the rustic-chic restaurant. A charcoal-fired Josper Grill in the kitchen is a serious piece of kit that drives the cooking in the direction of unfussy meat and fish dishes sizzled to perfection on the flames. If you're up for some serious meat action, the steaks are impeccably sourced, and even extend to a rib-eye of Wagyu beef. Otherwise, you might take on slow-braised ox cheek ballottine with scorched Atlantic scallops, pickled ginger, wasabi pea purée and miso velouté, and finish with a novel take on trifle, made with plums, Jamaican ginger cake and grappa, vanilla custard and roasted almonds.

Chef Richard Crouch **Owner** Complete Hotels Ltd
Times 12-2/5.30-9.30 **Prices** Fixed D 2 course £14.25, Starter £4.50-£8.25, Main £10.50-£35, Dessert £5.95, Service optional **Wines** 11 bottles over £30, 21 bottles under £30, 8 by glass **Notes** Sunday L £16.95-£19.95, Vegetarian available **Seats** 40, Pr/dining room 70 **Children** Portions, Menu **Parking** 45

OUNDLE Map 11 TL08

Oundle Mill

Modern British NOTABLE WINE LIST

Confident cooking in comfortably converted mill

☎ 01832 272621
Barnwell Rd PE8 5PB
e-mail: info@oundlemill.co.uk
dir: Located just outside Oundle off A605

The River Nene that fueled the old mill for so many years wrought havoc in 2012, forcing the restaurant to close for four months until March 2013, but rest assured, the old mill is back. Oak beams, standing timbers and stone walls bring a rustic-chic character to the space, while the kitchen follows suit to some degree, with a successful rustic-chic style of its own. Country farmhouse terrine, for example, is a first course with accompanying spiced fruit chutney and toasted sourdough bread, or there might be squid ink risotto with fried squid and squid crackers. There's a good deal of technical ability in the kitchen and some good modish thinking. Thus North Atlantic cod appears in a main course with saffron polenta, chorizo tempura, Norfolk spinach and red sorrel cress, and wood

pigeon turns up in Wellington guise, with chicory and orange marmalade, thatched potatoes and sloe gin. Finish in style with a lemon sherbet jelly, lemon curd and lemon meringue ice cream.

Chef Gavin Austin **Owner** Mark & Sarah Harrod
Times 12-2.30/6.30-9.30 **Closed** 25-26 Dec, 1 Jan
Prices Fixed L 2 course fr £14.50, Fixed D 3 course fr £18.50, Starter £5.50-£9, Main £12.50-£20, Dessert £4.50-£7.50, Service optional **Wines** 151 bottles over £30, 49 bottles under £30, 18 by glass **Notes** Sunday L, Vegetarian available, Civ Wed 60 **Seats** 50, Pr/dining room 45 **Children** Portions, Menu **Parking** 60

The Talbot Hotel

British NEW

Brasserie favourites in an ancient hostelry

☎ 01832 273621
New St PE8 4EA
e-mail: talbot@bpcmail.co.uk
dir: A605 Northampton/Oundle at rdbt exit Oundle A427 - Station Road turn onto New Street

There has been a hostelry of some sort on this site since the seventh century, and the current manifestation of The Talbot certainly looks the ancient part. In the centre of charming Oundle, it now appears as a multi-faceted package, offering a hotel, eatery and coffee-house. The small dining room has been given a minimalistic modern makeover, with bare tables and fine cutlery, and is a comfortable space, although you are actually welcome to eat wherever you like, including the paved courtyard and garden. A long menu is comprised of today's brasserie favourites - smoked haddock and salmon fishcake, steak, ale and mushroom pie - as well as some more off-piste dishes. A generous bowl of crab linguine seasoned with chilli, dill and lemon in crème fraîche starts things off well, and may be succeeded by roast breast of Goosnargh duck with sweet potato in a distinctly retro raspberry dressing. Finish with a slice of bracingly tangy lemon tart sauced with blueberry coulis.

Chef David Simms **Owner** Bulldog Hotel Group
Times 12-2.30/6.30-9.30 **Prices** Starter £5-£13, Main £11-£19, Dessert £5-£6.50, Service optional **Wines** 12 bottles over £30, 30 bottles under £30, 15 by glass **Notes** Sunday L £18.50-£27.50, Vegetarian available, Civ Wed 80 **Seats** 48, Pr/dining room 64 **Children** Portions, Menu **Parking** 30

ROADE Map 11 SP75

Roade House Restaurant

Modern British

Much loved village restaurant with rooms

☎ 01604 863372
16 High St NN7 2NW
e-mail: info@roadehousehotel.co.uk
dir: M1 junct 15 (A508 Milton Keynes) to Roade, left at mini rdbt, 500yds on left

An enjoyable time is on the cards at this welcoming village restaurant with rooms near to the M1 and the high-octane thrills of Silverstone race track. Blackened beams and a neutral contemporary look involving cream walls and bentwood seats at white-linen tables add up to a soothing setting in the dining room, while Chris Kewley is the man directing the action at the stoves. His unfussy, flavour-driven modern cooking delivers intelligent combinations of taste and texture - perhaps rabbit terrine with brioche, walnuts and pickled mushrooms, while mains could see breast and confit leg of wild duck sharing a plate with a luxurious slab of seared foie gras, red cabbage, and apple and Calvados sauce. Hearty puddings could bring Santiago almond cake with spiced pears and red wine fruit.

Chef Chris Kewley **Owner** Mr & Mrs C M Kewley
Times 12-2/7-9.30 **Closed** 1 wk Xmas, BHs, L Sat, Mon, D Sun **Prices** Fixed L 2 course fr £20.50, Starter £5.75-£9, Main £16-£25, Dessert £6.50-£7.75, Service optional **Wines** 20 bottles over £30, 20 bottles under £30, 4 by glass **Notes** Sunday L £20.50-£23.50, Vegetarian available **Seats** 50, Pr/dining room 16 **Children** Portions **Parking** 20

TOWCESTER Map 11 SP64

Vine House Hotel & Restaurant

Modern British

Rural setting and a local flavour

☎ 01327 811267
100 High St, Paulerspury NN12 7NA
e-mail: info@vinehousehotel.com
dir: 2m S of Towcester, just off A5

A lovingly restored 300-year-old limestone cottage in a winsome village is the setting for this perfectly charming small restaurant and hotel. Inside, the vibe is homely and easygoing with Julie Springett taking care of front of house, while husband Marcus works with first-rate local and seasonal ingredients to deliver daily-changing three-course fixed-price menus. Choosing from three well-conceived ideas at each stage, plus a slate of artisan British cheeses at the end, you might get off the blocks with local black pudding with shallot cream and mustard pickle purée, and follow that with saddle of local lamb with salted butter crushed peas, potato terrine and salsa verde, or there might be line-caught cod with lemon, capers, shallots and croûtons. For afters, local Bramley apples go into a mousse, served enterprisingly with blue cheese and vanilla shortbread crumble. The romantic garden folly is a lovely spot for outdoor dining.

Chef Marcus Springett, K Kerley, J Bateman **Owner** Mr M & Mrs J Springett **Times** 12-1.30/6-9 Closed 1 wk winter, Sun, L Mon **Prices** Fixed L 2 course fr £27.50, Fixed D 3 course fr £30.95, Service added 12.5% **Wines** 5 by glass **Seats** 26, Pr/dining room 10 **Parking** 20

WHITTLEBURY   Map 11 SP64

Whittlebury Hall

◉◉ British, European

Contemporary fine dining and motor-racing

☎ 01327 857857
NN12 8QH
e-mail: reservations@whittleburyhall.co.uk
web: www.whittleburyhall.co.uk
dir: A43/A413 towards Buckingham, through Whittlebury, turn for hotel on right (signed)

The nearby goings-on at Silverstone inspire the catering thematics at this extensive spa hotel, where dining rooms called Astons, Bentleys and Murrays (after the voice of Formula One, Murray Walker) await the confirmed motorhead. The last is adorned with photos of the great man, alongside memorable quotes from his commentaries. There is some cooking going on too, as attested by the tableful of awards on display. It's contemporary stuff, as sleekly streamlined as a modern racing-car, and just as full of intricate engineering. A starter offers puffed wheat, pine nuts and truffle honey as textural foils to an artichoke custard, while mains furnish a serving of poached brill, wild mussels and sprouting broccoli with an underlay of sesame seed 'sand', or garnish 35-day dry-aged beef with the relatively classical accompaniments of ox tongue, onions and horseradish. Chocolate and banana mousse comes with banana jelly and hazelnuts.

Chef Craig Rose, Damyan Stefanov **Owner** Whittlebury Hall and Spa Ltd **Times** 7-9.30 Closed selected dates at Xmas, Sun-Mon, L all week **Prices** Prices not confirmed Service optional **Notes** Tasting menu available, Sunday L, Vegetarian available, Dress restrictions, Smart casual, No jeans, trainers or shorts **Seats** 32, Pr/dining room 10 **Children** Portions, Menu **Parking** 460

NORTHUMBERLAND

BAMBURGH   Map 21 NU13

Victoria Hotel

◉ Modern British

Glass-roofed brasserie with a modish menu

☎ 01668 214431
Front St NE69 7BP
e-mail: enquiries@thevictoriahotelbamburgh.co.uk
dir: Turn off A1, N of Alnwick onto B1342, follow signs to Bamburgh. Hotel opposite village green

With its position on the village green and views over to the historic castle, the Victoria Hotel is in a plum spot. The Baileys Bar & Restaurant consists of a number of dining areas, some under a glass atrium roof, with a decidedly modish sheen to the décor. There are trendy muted colour tones, some exposed stonework, nicely designed tables and chairs, and some smart fabric-covered banquettes, plus Milburn's bar which is decorated with black-and white pictures of the Magpies (that's Newcastle United football team) - it's named in honour of the legendary Jackie Milburn. The menu goes in for egalitarian modern Britishness, so you might go from Thai fishcakes with cucumber relish and chilli jam to Black Sheep ale-battered North Sea haddock with fat chips and mint-flavoured mushy peas, or locally-sourced 28-day aged Northumbrian beef (10oz rib-eye maybe) with a choice of traditional sauces.

Chef Harry Bailie **Times** 12-3/7-9 **Prices** Starter £2.95-£6.25, Main £10.25-£18.95, Dessert £5.25-£6.75

Waren House Hotel

◉ Modern British ✍

Local supplies for country-house cooking

☎ 01668 214581
Waren Mill NE70 7EE
e-mail: enquiries@warenhousehotel.co.uk
web: www.warenhousehotel.co.uk
dir: Exit A1 on B1342, follow signs to Bamburgh. Hotel in 2m in village Waren Mill

Handily placed for exploring the coast by Bamburgh Castle and Lindisfarne Island, Waren House is a Georgian mansion set in six acres of landscaped grounds with sea views. Everything cries out classic country-house style, from the grandfather clock and log fires to the oil paintings and soothing blue and gold hues of the restaurant, where burnished tables and gleaming glassware reflect the candlelight at dinner. Tradition is the watchword in the kitchen, too, starting with diligent sourcing of the region's finest ingredients which are brought together in a broadly modern British style. A well-made Doddington cheese soufflé is served simply with sweet beetroot chutney, followed by a more involved main course of pavé of halibut with wilted spinach, yellow pea purée, and mussels in leek, cream, and vermouth sauce with bacon crumbs. A dark chocolate fondant, its centre soft and oozing, is a good way to finish, especially when it

comes with white chocolate sorbet, crème fraîche, and chocolate streusel.

Chef Steven Owens **Owner** Mr & Mrs Laverack **Times** 6.30-8.30 **Prices** Fixed D 3 course £38.95, Service optional **Wines** 28 bottles under £30, 8 by glass **Notes** Vegetarian available, Dress restrictions, Smart casual **Seats** 28 **Parking** 20

CHATHILL   Map 21 NU12

Doxford Hall Hotel & Spa

◉◉ Modern British **V** ✍

Modish treatments of local supplies

☎ 01665 589700
NE67 5DN
e-mail: info@doxfordhall.com
dir: 8m N of Alnwick just off A1, signed Christon Bank & Seahouses. B6347 then follow signs for Doxford

A continuous programme of investment and generous dollops of TLC in recent years have brought food and rooms fully up to 21st-century spec at Doxford. Entered through a classic period portico, the late-Georgian pile is framed in ten acres of landscaped grounds (including a maze) just a short drive from Alnwick and the Northumbrian coast. For those intent on pampering and rejuvenation, there's a classy spa and leisure club, while gastronomes will find no fault with the elegant restaurant, where a huge stone fireplace, white linen, burnished wood panelling and full-length windows make for a luminous setting. Fresh, local and seasonal are clearly buzz words, and the kitchen takes a gently modern approach that sits comfortably alongside tried-and-tested classics. Seared rabbit and prawn with braised paella rice, chorizo, mussels and rabbit beignet is an intelligent reworking of the paella theme, while casserole of pheasant served with steamed suet and leek pudding, thyme and pancetta impresses with the quality of produce and power of its flavours. Warm pear and almond tart with pistachio ice cream is a good way to finish.

Chef Paul Blakey **Owner** Robert Parker **Times** 12-2/7-10 **Prices** Service optional **Wines** 32 bottles over £30, 27 bottles under £30, 15 by glass **Notes** Sunday L £17.50-£24.95, Vegetarian menu, Dress restrictions, Smart casual, Civ Wed 180 **Seats** 60, Pr/dining room 200 **Children** Portions, Menu **Parking** 100

CORNHILL-ON-TWEED · Map 21 NT83

Tillmouth Park Country House Hotel

◉ Modern British

Seasonal cooking in a splendid mansion

☎ 01890 882255
TD12 4UU
e-mail: reception@tillmouthpark.force9.co.uk
web: www.tillmouthpark.co.uk
dir: A698, 3m E from Cornhill-on-Tweed

Close to the Scottish border, this lovely old mansion, originally built in 1882 as a family home, is set in 15 acres of landscaped gardens. It's a peaceful and atmospheric place to stay, where real fires, comfy sofas and oil paintings abound. Dining here is leant a sense of occasion before you even sit down, as entry to the elevated Library Dining Room - with candlelit tables and views over the grounds - is via a beautiful wooden staircase around the edge of the tower. The kitchen turns out some classically based modern British food with menus informed by the best of local produce. Prawn cocktail or duck leg confit with orange chutney and chocolate and balsamic syrup might start you off, followed, perhaps, by pork fillet Wellington with an indulgent creamed mushroom sauce. Cinnamon and apple strudel with vanilla ice cream is another classic done well to bring things to a close.

Chef Piotr Dziedzic **Owner** Tillmouth Park Partnership **Times** 7-9 Closed 26-28 Dec, Jan-Mar, L all week **Prices** Fixed D 3 course £39.50, Starter £4.95-£7, Main £12.50-£18.95, Dessert £5.95-£6.95, Service optional **Wines** 18 bottles over £30, 28 bottles under £30, 7 by glass **Notes** Vegetarian available, Dress restrictions, Smart casual, No shorts, Civ Wed 50 **Seats** 40, Pr/dining room 20 **Children** Portions **Parking** 50

HEDDON-ON-THE-WALL · Map 21 NZ16

Close House

◉◉ Modern British

Vintage glamour and modern food

☎ 01661 852255
NE15 0HT
e-mail: reservations@closehouse.co.uk
web: www.closehouse.co.uk
dir: A1 N, A69 W. Follow B6528 at junct turn left, hotel signed

A boutique-style makeover has turned this 18th-century mansion into a sleekly modern venue that hits the spot for anyone with an interest in golf (there are two courses), getting hitched, or putting on the Ritz in the glamorous surroundings of the Argent d'Or restaurant. Wow factor is certainly not lacking in the palatial venue's soaring plasterwork ceilings, grandly neo-classical fireplace, crystal chandeliers and shimmering silk drapes - even the seats at the well-spaced tables are sheathed in gold fabric. It makes an unapologetically glamorous setting for cooking that works within a broadly modern British idiom, with a nod to the classics. Menus change to take advantage of the seasons, so spring brings fat and flavoursome seared scallops with black olive salsa and red pepper dressing, followed by a trio of Northumberland lamb served as confit shoulder, herb-crusted loin and slow-cooked rump with potato bake. To finish, there's an eye-catching chocolate dome with an orange brûlée centre.

Times 12-2.30/7-9.30

HEXHAM · Map 21 NY96

Barrasford Arms

◉ Traditional & Modern British NEW ◔

Well-rendered simple dishes in a genuine country pub

☎ 01434 681237
NE48 4AA
e-mail: contact@barrasfordarms.co.uk
dir: A69 at Acomb onto A6079 towards Chollerton. Turn left at church and follow signs to Barrasford

Sitting proudly at the heart of village life in this North Tyne valley hamlet, the Barrasford is a Victorian inn that hosts quoits tournaments and darts matches, like pubs did in the era before video games and Sky Sports. It enjoys a symbiotic relationship with the local community, its décor of fishing rods and shotguns reflecting the region's country pursuits, and Northumbrian produce naturally informs the bulk of Tony Binks's culinary output. Up-to-the-minute country pub dishes are big on flavour and accuracy of rendition, as witness the pease pudding portion served with pressed ham hock terrine with carrot and beetroot salad. Mains run to breadcrumbed veal escalope topped with tomato and Mull Cheddar, served with buttery Charlotte potatoes, as well as grilled mackerel jazzed up with lively dressings of tomato and chilli salsa and citrus crème fraîche. A well-rendered chocolate fondant is properly molten in the centre, made with rip-roaring chocolate, and sauced with espresso custard.

Chef Tony Binks **Owner** Tony Binks **Times** 12-2/6.30-close Closed 25-26 Dec, L Mon, D Sun **Prices** Fixed L 2 course £11.95, Starter £5-£6.95, Main £12.50-£17, Dessert £6, Service optional **Wines** 1 bottle over £30, 19 bottles under £30, 7 by glass **Notes** Sunday L £15-£17.50, Vegetarian available **Seats** 60, Pr/dining room 10 **Children** Portions

De Vere Slaley Hall

◉ Modern British ◔

Old and new in a grand Northumbrian manor

☎ 01434 673350
Slaley NE47 0BX
e-mail: slaley.hall@devere-hotels.com
web: www.devere.co.uk
dir: A1 from S to A68 link road follow signs for Slaley Hall. From N A69 to Corbridge then take A68 S and follow signs to Slaley Hall

One thousand acres of windswept Northumbrian moorland are the setting for the suitably grand Slaley Hall, a castellated edifice of colossal proportions, with flights of steps sweeping up majestically from the lawns. Inside is a bay-windowed dining room done in tasteful Edwardiana, with wing-backed chairs in claret upholstery, lit framed pictures and mirrors, and an air of unruffled calm. The cooking balances old and new: starters may be mussels in Chablis and cream, or ox cheek tortellini with beetroot purée, while mains offer a pair of you the chance to share a Chateaubriand, carved at table, and served with Pont-Neuf potatoes, béarnaise and Madeira jus. Sailfish isn't often seen - find it here with a tempura prawn, cauliflower purée and a pea dressing for company - while desserts mobilise vivid fruit flavours for lemon tart with mango sorbet and passionfruit and mango salsa, or chilled rhubarb crumble with a cherry doughnut and blackcurrant sorbet.

Chef Paul Patterson **Owner** De Vere Hotels **Times** 1-3/6.30-9.45 Closed Mon **Prices** Prices not confirmed Service added but optional 10% **Notes** Sunday L, Vegetarian available, Dress restrictions, Smart casual, Civ Wed 200 **Seats** 40, Pr/dining room 30 **Children** Portions **Parking** 200

Langley Castle Hotel

◎◎ Modern British 🍃

Ancient castle with contemporary food

☎ 01434 688888
Langley on Tyne NE47 5LU
e-mail: manager@langleycastle.com
web: www.langleycastle.com
dir: From A69 S on A686 for 2m. Hotel on right

This must be unique: a forbidding castle dating from 1350 complete with crenellations and seven-foot-thick walls, and an immaculately preserved interior. Josephine's Restaurant, recently extended and given a more contemporary look under its beamed ceiling, is where to head to for the fine-dining experience, which could be a five-course set-price affair including a sorbet or demitasse of soup and a pre-dessert, with plenty of choice at each of the other courses. Don't expect the roast beef of Old England; this is refined modern cooking with ideas culled from around Europe and beyond to add interest. Pan-fried pigeon breast, for instance, comes with almond and raisin polenta, squash purée and sage jus, and roast king prawns with avocado and chilli cream, mango salsa and lemongrass foam. The balance of flavours is clearly considered, seen in main courses of baked chicken roulade with pesto, courgette mousse spiked with lime, and red pepper purée, and cod fillet baked with cayenne served with spicy Puy lentils, spinach and cooling coriander yoghurt. End on a homely note with apple crumble and custard.

Chef Andy Smith **Owner** Dr S Madnick **Times** 12-2.30/7-9 **Prices** Fixed L 2 course fr £16.95, Starter £5.95-£10.50, Main £18.95-£26.50, Dessert £7.95, Service optional **Wines** 21 bottles over £30, 33 bottles under £30, 10 by glass **Notes** 4 course D £42.50, Sunday L £22.50-£24.50, Vegetarian available, Dress restrictions, Smart casual, Civ Wed 120 **Seats** 48, Pr/dining room 28 **Children** Portions, Menu **Parking** 57

LONGHORSLEY   **Map 21 NZ19**

Macdonald Linden Hall, Golf & Country Club

◎◎ Modern British 🍃

Appealing cooking in a grand Georgian manor

☎ 01670 500000
NE65 8XF
e-mail: lindenhall@macdonald-hotels.co.uk
web: www.macdonaldhotels.co.uk/lindenhall
dir: 7m NW of Morpeth on A697 off A1

Set in 450 acres of Northumbrian parkland, Linden Hall is a 19th-century manor house that exudes splendour from every brick. As one might expect from the upmarket Macdonald stable, the operation is run with consummate professionalism to ensure a relaxed stay. After a stroll through the vast grounds or a bit of me-time in the luxurious spa to sharpen the appetite, head to the claret-hued Dobson Restaurant: with its seductive views of the grounds through full-length windows, it makes a suitably refined setting for well-conceived dishes based on carefully-sourced raw materials. A posh surf and turf combo of king prawns, scallops and pork belly is a cracking way to set the ball rolling, and is all the better for a purée of curried parsnip. Following that, rabbit might arrive in a two-way treatment involving roast saddle and braised leg with tomato couscous, spinach, and rabbit jus. Finish with a classic apple tarte Tatin with hazelnut ice cream.

Chef David Kaleta **Owner** Macdonald Hotels **Times** 12.30-2/6.45-9.45 Closed Mon-Thu (winter), L Mon-Sat, D 31 Dec **Prices** Prices not confirmed Service optional **Wines** 16 by glass **Notes** Sunday L, Vegetarian available, Dress restrictions, Smart casual **Seats** 64, Pr/dining room 40 **Children** Portions, Menu **Parking** 300

MATFEN   **Map 21 NZ07**

Matfen Hall

◎◎ Modern British

Modern British dishes in the library of an ancestral seat

☎ 01661 886500 & 886400
NE20 0RH
e-mail: info@matfenhall.com
web: www.matfenhall.com
dir: A69 signed Hexham, leave at Heddon-on-the-Wall. Then B6318, through Rudchester & Harlow Hill. Follow signs on right for Matfen

Ancestral home of the Blackett family, Matfen was opened as a luxury spa hotel in 1999, so all may now enjoy its 300 acres of parkland, its grand public rooms, and the majestic, book-lined library with its ornate mouldings, panelling and magnificent views, which forms the dining room. The kitchen explores the modern British repertoire for inspiring stalwarts such as smoked haddock and pea risotto, king scallops with black pudding, and main courses such as seared salmon on lemon-crushed potatoes in dill beurre blanc, or roasted

beef fillet with thyme and garlic rösti and Jerusalem artichoke purée. Desserts bring on plenty of fruity creations, along the lines of lime cheesecake with mango sorbet and passionfruit jelly, or apple sponge with blueberry parfait and honeycomb.

Times 12-2.30/6.45-9.30 Closed L Mon-Sat

MORPETH   **Map 21 NZ18**

Eshott Hall

◎ British, European 🍃

Ambitious cooking of Northumbrian produce

☎ 01670 787454
Eshott NE65 9EN
e-mail: info@eshotthall.co.uk
dir: Eshott signed from A1. N of Morpeth

An elegantly proportioned Georgian property, its façade hung with wisteria, Eshott Hall is surrounded by gardens and woodlands. A magnificent stained-glass window looks over the entrance, and, in winter, expect open fires in the grandly appointed public rooms, including the dining room, with its soothing décor, pillars, moulded plasterwork and candelabra on crisply clothed tables. Seasonality is to the fore, with the hall's kitchen gardens responsible for much fresh produce, so expect seasonal game: perhaps roast guinea fowl with girolles, foie gras and pommes Anna. Fish might appear in the shape of halibut fillet with shellfish sauce, dill foam and fondant potato, while starters could take in perfectly cooked fillet of sea bass modishly accompanied by tomato and chorizo salsa and vierge dressing, or the full-bodied flavours of confit pork belly with black pudding beignets and carrot purée. Extras like canapés are appreciated, and to finish there may be Yorkshire rhubarb cheesecake.

Chef Chris Wood **Owner** Rev Robert Parker **Times** 1-2.30/6-9.30 Closed private functions **Prices** Starter £7-£10, Main £17-£26, Dessert £8-£10, Service optional **Wines** 12 bottles over £30, 20 bottles under £30, 14 by glass **Notes** Sunday L £14.50-£22, Vegetarian available, Dress restrictions, Smart casual, Civ Wed 100 **Seats** 30, Pr/dining room 30 **Children** Portions, Menu **Parking** 60

WARENFORD
Map 21 NU12

The White Swan
⊕ Modern British ☺

Rural pub serving fine local food

☎ 01668 213453 & 07500 080571
NE70 7HY
e-mail: dianecuthbert@yahoo.com
dir: 100yds E of A1, 10m N of Alnwick

Warenford is only a couple of miles off the A1, and yet it feels reassuringly remote, hiding away amid the rolling countryside. The White Swan is a locals' favourite, with a good reputation for its locally supplied meat, served in a raised dining area with unclothed chunky wood tables and a properly rustic feel. Staff are relaxed enough to chat, and what they bring you is hefty portions of carefully presented modern pub cooking. Salmon and dill fishcakes are generously constructed and offset with the nice surprise of a mango mayonnaise, while main might be well-crackled pork belly on a heap of parsnip, apple and black pudding, sauced powerfully with Calvados, or maybe a whole lemon sole with asparagus in vermouth and elderflower hollandaise. Cocoa potency is the selling point of a hunk of chocolate and Amaretto torte with vanilla ice cream.

Chef Mark Poole **Owner** Andrew & Diane Hay
Times 12-2.30/6-9 **Prices** Starter £4.75-£8.95, Main £8.50-£21.95, Dessert £4.95, Service optional **Wines** 3 bottles over £30, 31 bottles under £30, 10 by glass **Notes** Sunday L £8.50-£18.95, Vegetarian available **Seats** 65, Pr/dining room 30 **Children** Portions, Menu **Parking** 50

NOTTINGHAMSHIRE

FARNDON
Map 17 SK75

Farndon Boathouse
⊕ Modern European ☺

Up-to-date brasserie cooking in a riverside setting

☎ 01636 676578
Off Wyke Rd NG24 3SX
e-mail: info@farndonboathouse.co.uk
dir: From A46 rdbt (SW of Newark-on-Trent) take Fosse Way signed Farndon. Turn right into Main St signed Farndon. At T-junct turn right into Wyke Lane, follow Boathouse signs

The leafy banks of the meandering River Trent make an interesting contrast to the contemporary exposed ducting, industrial-style lighting, stone floors and glazed frontage of the stylish Boathouse. The kitchen is driven by the guiding principles of sourcing locally and seasonally, and using modern cooking techniques such as sous-vide to squeeze every molecule of flavour from the ingredients. Uncomplicated contemporary brasserie dishes run the gamut from starters such as in-house-smoked duck breast with marinated feta cheese, compressed melon and lamb's lettuce, and cashew crumb, to seared sea bass with home-made pesto and parmesan gnocchi,

squash purée and roast tomatoes; meaty ideas are along the lines of pan-fried pheasant breast with potato terrine, crispy ham, confit garlic and peas and roasting juices. Finish with the home comforts of sticky toffee pudding with milk ice cream and caramel sauce.

Chef Steve Munn, Dan Garner **Owner** Dan Garner, Nathan Barton **Times** 12-3/6-9.30 **Prices** Fixed L 2 course fr £14.95, Fixed D 3 course fr £17.95, Starter £5-£11, Main £8.95-£26, Dessert £6-£8.50, Service optional **Wines** 20 bottles over £30, 10 bottles under £30, 18 by glass **Notes** Early bird menu L & 6-7pm daily, Sunday L, Vegetarian available **Seats** 120 **Children** Portions, Menu **Parking** 18

GUNTHORPE
Map 11 SK64

Tom Browns Brasserie
⊕⊕ Modern International

Creative cooking in an old Victorian schoolhouse

☎ 0115 966 3642
The Old School House, Trentside NG14 7FB
e-mail: info@tombrowns.co.uk
web: www.tombrowns.co.uk
dir: A6097, Gunthorpe Bridge

The brasserie was once a Victorian schoolhouse, though you wouldn't know it. Any lingering echo of chanted multiplication tables is entirely muted in the cool, neutral-toned, wood-floored interior, and its outdoor mezzanine deck with views over the River Trent. The cooking, which is impeccably modern, is a few cuts above the brasserie norm, with dishes that sound satisfyingly multi-layered in the menu specifications, and look smart and alluring on the plate. Pears poached in red wine have shunted up the billing these days, from desserts to starters, and here's one with honey-glazed pork belly and celeriac remoulade, an inspired mix of flavours. The smoked salmon may appear with horseradish soufflé, puréed broad beans, pea shoots and salsa verde for another original composition, before mains such as fried stone bass in chilli, soy and ginger dressing with baby corn, red peppers, shiitake mushrooms and - just to ensure the final meeting of east and west - mushroom gnocchi. Meats include fine Scottish steaks from the chargrill and pudding might be Bakewell tart and custard. Theme nights are staged throughout the year.

Chef Peter Kirk **Owner** Adam & Robin Perkins
Times 12-2.30/6-9.30 Closed D 25-26 Dec **Prices** Fixed L 2 course fr £14.95, Fixed D 3 course £17.95-£30, Starter £5.50-£12.50, Main £12.95-£23.95, Dessert £6.50-£7.95, Service optional **Wines** 20 bottles over £30, 38 bottles

under £30, 17 by glass **Notes** Early bird L 12-3pm, Fixed D 6-7pm, Sunday L, Vegetarian available, Dress restrictions, Smart casual **Seats** 100, Pr/dining room 20 **Children** Portions, Menu **Parking** 28, On street

LANGAR
Map 11 SK73

Langar Hall
⊕⊕ Modern British ☺

A unique country house with a local flavour

☎ 01949 860559
Church Ln NG13 9HG
e-mail: info@langarhall.co.uk
web: www.langarhall.com
dir: Signed off A46 & A52 in Langar village centre (behind church)

It was never originally in the owner's game plan to run this handsome saffron-washed Victorian mansion as a hotel, but after dipping a toe into the water, she dived in with great enthusiasm and has infused the place with a one-off character. An avenue of lime trees runs past croquet lawns, a 12th-century church, and carp-filled medieval fishponds; inside, is an elegant scene of statues, crystal chandeliers, antiques and oil paintings, while dining takes place in a romantic marble-pillared dining room lit by silver candelabra, or in an airy conservatory. The kitchen's repertoire is built on ingredients from the garden, game from local estates and top-class stuff from local producers, and veers eclectically from simple classics - a twice-baked cheese soufflé, perhaps - to elaborate modern ideas, such as pan-fried brill with crème fraîche crushed new potatoes, braised fennel, brown shrimp and tarragon. Elsewhere, pig's cheek croquette might be partnered by smoked eel, salt-baked beetroot, pickled apple and mustard, while potato gnocchi, home-made ricotta, wild garlic and green olives could be the supporting cast for an assiette of Langar lamb.

Chef Gary Booth, Ross Jeffrey **Owner** Imogen Skirving **Times** 12-2/7-10 **Prices** Fixed L 2 course fr £20, Fixed D 3 course £30-£45, Service added but optional 10% **Wines** 8 by glass **Notes** Tasting menu 7 course, Sunday L, Vegetarian available, Civ Wed 50 **Seats** 30, Pr/dining room 20 **Children** Portions **Parking** 40

Save on Hotels. Book at theAA.com/hotel

NOTTINGHAMSHIRE 403 ENGLAND

NOTTINGHAM   Map 11 SK53

Cockliffe Country House

◉◉ Modern European

Intelligent flavour combinations in an elegant country setting

☎ 0115 968 0179
Burntstump Country Park, Burntstump Hill, Arnold NG5 8PQ
e-mail: enquiries@cockliffehouse.co.uk
dir: M1 junct 27, follow signs to Hucknall (A611), then B6011, right at T-junct, follow signs for Cockliffe House

It's hard to believe Cockliffe is a mere seven miles from the vibrant city centre of Nottingham, set as it is in three acres of garden with its own wood. Nevertheless, the grey-stone building has been here since the 17th century and is a lovely place to enjoy a peaceful break with some aesthetically pleasing cooking. The intimate dining room seats around 20 and is tastefully decorated with gilt mirrors, striking artwork and luxurious gold swag curtains framing the windows that look out over the gardens. Home-made individual brioche served with cep butter paves the way for a well-executed confit quail leg with seared breast, foie gras and white peaches, while another starter of Scottish scallops, pork pie purée, apples and trotter nuggets is typical of the kitchen's creative style. A sure hand at balancing contrasting flavours is evident in saddle of spring lamb, salsa verde, polenta cake and red pepper purée with a red wine jus. Lemon tart with crème anglaise and raspberry sorbet ends things on a high.

Times 6-9.30 Closed Sun, L all week

Hart's Hotel

◉◉ Modern British

Smart modish cooking from a skilled team

☎ 0115 988 1900
Standard Court, Park Row NG1 6GN
e-mail: ask@hartsnottingham.co.uk
web: www.hartsnottingham.co.uk
dir: At junct of Park Row & Ropewalk, close to city centre

Opposite the smart boutique hotel of the same name, in Nottingham's old General Hospital, Hart's has a contemporary finish (smart, neutral colour tones, some booth seating and tables laid with white linen) and a menu which deals in first-class produce, handled with intelligence and respect. The attention to detail shown all round is no surprise given the connections to Hambleton

Hall (see entry), including the wine list, which is compiled by Tim Hart. There are plenty of options here, from a great value set lunch, pre-theatre menu and a bespoke vegetarian menu which is a definite cut above the average. From the carte - with its sensible six or so choices per course - you might start with beetroot and walnut salad with goats' cheese beignets and compressed comice pear, which looks great on the plate and has well judged flavours and textures. Next up, perhaps rump of beef Diane with 'Koffmann' cabbage, rösti potato, crispy beef marrow, watercress and shallots, or a whole roast turbot with hollandaise sauce. To finish, kaffir lime baked Alaska, citrus and passionfruit is one way to go, or try apple crumble in soufflé form, served with crème anglaise.

Times 12-2/6-10.30 Closed 1 Jan, L 31 Dec, D 25-26 Dec

Park Plaza Nottingham

◉ Pan-Asian NEW

Vibrant, contemporary atmosphere and Pan-Asian flavours

☎ 0115 947 7200
41 Maid Marian Way NG1 8GD
web: www.chinolatino.eu
dir: A6200 (Derby Rd) into Wollaton St. 2nd exit into Maid Marian Way. Hotel on left

The Park Plaza is a modern hotel with all mod-cons and a cool and contemporary restaurant in the form of Chino Latino. The winning formula has been tried-and-tested in the group's London outpost, and it fits the bill in Nottingham, too. There's a moody club-like vibe to the space (set over two levels), views through to the kitchen, and the focus is on Latino cocktails and Pan-Asian food. Start with dim sum such as chicken sui mai dumplings with foie gras and shiitake mushrooms, or go Japanese with some sushi like spicy tuna roll with bonito flakes and chilli miso. Main-course duck breast toban-yaki arrives full of sizzle, or try the black cod with spicy miso. Desserts are no afterthought: banana spring roll, for example, with chocolate fudge sauce and vanilla ice cream.

Chef Paul Thacker **Times** 12-10.30 Closed Xmas, Sun All-day dining **Prices** Fixed L 3 course £9.95, Fixed D 2 course £25-£35, Starter £4-£12.50, Main £13-£30, Dessert £5-£6.50, Service optional, Groups min 6 service 10% **Wines** 28 bottles over £30, 7 bottles under £30, 11 by glass **Notes** 4 course dinner £45, Vegetarian available, Dress restrictions, Smart casual, Civ Wed 70 **Seats** Pr/dining room 70 **Children** Portions, Menu **Parking** On street, NCP

Restaurant Sat Bains with Rooms

◉◉◉◉◉ – see page 404

World Service

◉◉ Modern British ⬥NOTABLE WINE LIST ☺

Sharp cooking and idiosyncratic surroundings

☎ 0115 847 5587
Newdigate House, Castle Gate NG1 6AF
e-mail: info@worldservicerestaurant.com
web: www.worldservicerestaurant.com
dir: 200mtrs from city centre, 50mtrs from Nottingham Castle

Renaissance-styled Newdigate House was built in 1675, but what leaves its kitchen since it became home to World Service is distinctly contemporary work. The idiosyncratic interior mines a colonial vein, the warm orange and copper hues of the main dining room offset with Oriental artefacts: Buddha heads, Indian statuary and objets d'art in glass cases. It all combines to create a laid-back Zen ambience, but the staff are super-slick, smartly-suited and sharp on the uptake, while bassy background beats add a funky urban edge to proceedings. If the restaurant's name isn't enough of a hint, the cooking has a gentle East-meets-West theme, although western influences hold sway. This is a kitchen that thinks about textures, putting an imaginative spin onto classic ideas, as seen in a starter matching braised ox tongue with gremolata and Parmesan - a clever twist on classic carpaccio - followed by accurately-timed sea bass served with Korean sticky rice cakes, spring onion and bok choy. Carnivores might go for rump and shoulder of local lamb with potato terrine, butternut squash purée and shallot rings. At the end, banana parfait with banoffee caramel and palm sugar sorbet keeps the good ideas coming.

Chef Jacque Ferreira **Owner** Daniel Lindsay, Phillip Morgan, Ashley Walter **Times** 12-2.15/7-10 Closed 26 Dec, 1-7 Jan, D Sun (except Dec & BH Sun) **Prices** Fixed L 2 course £14.50, Fixed D 3 course £24.50, Starter £5-£15, Main £14.50-£25.95, Dessert £5.95-£8.50, Service added but optional 12% **Wines** 113 bottles over £30, 58 bottles under £30, 17 by glass **Notes** Sunday L, Vegetarian available, Civ Wed 50 **Seats** 80, Pr/dining room 34 **Children** Portions, Menu **Parking** NCP

Restaurant Sat Bains with Rooms

Modern British V **NOTABLE WINE LIST**

Analytical dining from a quicksilver creative intellect

☎ 0115 986 6566
Lenton Ln, Trentside NG7 2SA
e-mail: info@restaurantsatbains.net
web: www.restaurantsatbains.com
dir: M1 junct 24, A453 for approx 8m.
Through Clifton, road divides into 3 -
take middle lane signed 'Lenton Lane
Industrial Estate', then 1st left, left
again. Follow brown Restaurant Sat
Bains sign

It feels gloriously right that one of
Britain's A-list addresses for cutting-
edge concept dining isn't in the West
End of London, or on the Edinburgh
waterfront, or in Bray. With respect to all
those distinguished purlieus, a
renovated red-brick building on a lane
near a flyover on the edgelands of
Nottingham is so counter-intuitive as to
constitute a stroke of genius all in itself.
Especially when you consider you're not
necessarily here just to eat and go, but
are invited to stay in one of the eight
guest-rooms, currently under
refurbishment as we go to print. This is
a destination place if ever there was.
During its summer recess in 2012, the
kitchen was rejigged and redesigned,
which is important when you are
offering diners the chance of sitting in
it. A party of four can huddle on a

stylish new bench and watch Team
Bains in action. The book to accompany
the venture, *Too Many Chefs and Only
One Indian*, was published in November
2012. A truly excellent brigade of staff
has been assembled here, from sous to
sommelier level ('Laurent and Andreas
are available to discuss all your wine
requirements' - do they do house calls?
one wonders facetiously). It's another
world, and it all flows from the
quicksilver creative intellect of Satwant
Singh Bains himself. If you're at all
sceptical about the technological
movement in cookery, here is the place
to still those doubts. What Bains is good
at is not just the refinement of fabulous
dishes composed of thoroughbred
ingredients - we hope that comes with
the territory at five Rosettes - but all the
thinking that leads up to it too. The
template is an analytical approach to
the building-blocks of food, based on
the five western taste categories; the
seven- and ten-course menus are
flagged with colour-coded blobs in
varying permutations and strengths to
alert you to which dimensions of taste
you're about to be plunged into. A
concerto of all five is in play in the
opening black scallop, before bitter
recedes for a follow-up of roast roots
with béarnaise in dashi stock. Then all
five sound again in Cornish crab with
avocado and sea herbs. A principal dish
of braised ox cheek with pickled veg in a
smoked parsley emulsion is big on
umami, or there could be Wiltshire roe

deer with cauliflower, pear, blue cheese
and chocolate, while bitter plays off
sweet in the first dessert, a jelly and ice
cream job flavoured with pine and Earl
Grey. The ten-courser might end with
the famed treacle sponge with salted
apple and frozen cream, where nips of
sour and salt offset the sweetness of
parsnip (but of course) in the dough.
Call your own shots for the bespoke
menu package, 'Unique'.

Chef Sat Bains **Owner** Sat Bains,
Amanda Bains **Times** 12-1.30/7-8.30
Closed 2 wks Jan, 1 wk May, 2 wks Aug,
Sun-Mon, L all week **Prices** Tasting
menu £79-£89, Service added but
optional 12.5% **Wines** 30 by glass
Notes Tasting menu 7/10 course,
Vegetarian menu **Seats** 40, Pr/dining
room 14 **Parking** 22

Save on Hotels. Book at **theAA.com/hotel**

NOTTINGHAMSHIRE – OXFORDSHIRE 405   **ENGLAND**

OLLERTON
Map 16 SK66

Thoresby Hall Hotel

◉◉ Modern British ✿

Accomplished modern cooking in a grand Victorian pile

☎ 01623 821000 & 821025
Thoresby Park NG22 9WH
e-mail: thoresbyhall@bourne-leisure.co.uk

The first sight of Thoresby Hall is a jaw-dropping experience, its imposing creeper-hung façade a profusion of turrets, gables and bay windows. The interior is no less ornate, with wall tapestries, chandeliers, weapons and family portraits dotted about. The Blue Room is the foremost dining option, a room of soaring ceilings, mouldings, aqua-blue walls and views over the grounds. A new chef has taken over the stoves, but the style continues in the modern British mould. Fine produce is treated without too much fuss or elaboration, so seared scallops are partnered simply by broad bean purée spiked with chilli, and breast of wood pigeon is roasted and accompanied by nut 'crackling' and a balsamic-based sauce. Don't expect anything too flashy about main courses either, but what the kitchen does it does supremely well: shin of beef is braised in red wine and served with oxtail, and roast hake with crushed peas, confit potatoes and tartare sauce. To finish, go for something like a trio of lemon (tart, sorbet and a shot of limoncello).

Chef Mark Maris, Jason Wardill **Owner** Warner Leisure **Times** 12-2/6.30-9 Closed Mon **Prices** Fixed D 3 course fr £36, Service optional **Wines** 5 by glass **Notes** Sunday L, Vegetarian available, Dress restrictions, Smart casual **Seats** 50, Pr/dining room 50 **Parking** 140

OXFORDSHIRE

ASTON ROWANT
Map 5 SU79

Lambert Arms

◉ Modern British

Timbered coaching inn a stone's throw from the M40

☎ 01844 351496
London Rd OX49 5SB
e-mail: info.lambertarms@bespokehotels.com
web: www.bespokehotels.com
dir: M40 junct 6, at T-junct right towards Chinnor (B4009), back under motorway. 1st left to Postcombe/ Thame (A40)

The Lambert is a Georgian timbered coaching inn not far from Oxford, and a mere 500 yards from the M40. It works as a pub, if you're in the market for nothing more than a pint of real ale, but it's also a tastefully furnished modern hotel with a light and airy dining room. Pub food stalwarts like sausages and mash with onion gravy form the backbone of the menus, and there are some brasserie favourites such as chicken Caesar salad and steak burgers, but the kitchen also has a confident way with more contemporary classics. Goats' cheese and herb pannacotta with walnut dressing might be the prelude to Barbary duck breast with bok choi in five-spice jus, or sea bream with crab and parsley risotto in caper sauce. Round things off with pear and almond tart, served with Anglaise sauce and white chocolate ice cream, or a selection of West Country cheeses.

Chef Christopher Coaten **Owner** Bespoke Hotels **Times** 12-2.30/6.30-9 **Prices** Fixed L 2 course £10.95, Starter £4.95-£9.95, Main £11.95-£21.95, Dessert £4.95-£6.75, Service optional **Wines** 12 by glass **Notes** Sunday L £12.95-£21.75, Vegetarian available, Dress restrictions, Smart casual, Civ Wed 100 **Seats** 46, Pr/dining room 60 **Children** Portions, Menu **Parking** 80

BANBURY
Map 11 SP44

Best Western Plus Wroxton House Hotel

◉ Modern British

Charming inn with well-judged menu

☎ 01295 730777
Silver St, Wroxton OX15 6QB
e-mail: reservations@wroxtonhousehotel.com
dir: From M40 junct 11 follow A422 (signed Banbury, then Wroxton). After 3m, hotel on right

A row of delightful thatched cottages dating from the 17th century in a picturesque village between Banbury and Stratford-upon-Avon is the charming setting of Wroxton House Hotel. The contemporary-styled restaurant spreads through a trio of intimate rooms, where low oak-beamed ceilings, wall timbers and an inglenook impart a period country-house feel balanced with a distinctly 21st-century sheen. The kitchen follows suit, delivering a crowd-pleasing roster of dishes rooted in classic British ideas sexed up with a modern spin. Quality produce underpins it all, appearing first in a tried-and-true starter of chicken liver parfait with red onion marmalade and melba toast, then a generous main course showcasing baked Cornish cod fillet with Puy lentil cassoulet and sweet potato beignet. To finish, the deep comforts of warm sticky toffee pudding with butterscotch sauce and Devon clotted cream are faithfully rendered in a well-made example of this classic finale.

Chef Steve Mason-Tucker **Owner** John & Gill Smith **Times** 12-2/7-9 Closed L Mon-Sat **Prices** Fixed D 3 course fr £33, Service optional **Wines** 7 bottles over £30, 35 bottles under £30, 10 by glass **Notes** Sunday L, Vegetarian available, Dress restrictions, Smart casual, Civ Wed 80 **Seats** 60, Pr/dining room 80 **Children** Portions, Menu **Parking** 70

BURFORD
Map 5 SP21

The Angel at Burford

◉ Modern British **NEW** ✿

Creative cooking in a charming old pub

☎ 01993 822714
14 Witney St OX18 4SN
e-mail: enquiries@theangelatburford.co.uk

The Angel is a gem of a pub in historic Burford, a town with more than its fair share of chocolate-box charm. It's a proper pub, albeit an upmarket one, with a row of Hook Norton ales on the pumps and a roaring fire during the cool months of the year. It's the kind of place where your dog is made welcome. There's a serious approach to food, too, with due respect paid to local suppliers and the seasons. A first course such as beetroot tarte Tatin with frozen broad bean crème fraîche, micro herb salad and beetroot powder demonstrates that this is a kitchen of ambition, with lots of good ideas. Pickled red mullet and baby squid with red pepper bavarois and black olive tapenade is another creative starter, followed by pan-fried South Coast plaice with parsley pearl barley risotto, baby red chard and parsley foam. End with lemon tart with pistachio ice cream and raspberry coulis.

Chef Andrew Frost **Owner** Terence King, Gemma Finch **Times** 12-3/6-9.30 **Prices** Fixed L 2 course £17.50, Fixed D 3 course £23, Starter £6.50-£9.75, Main £12.95-£20.50, Dessert £6.55-£10.50, Service optional **Wines** 4 bottles over £30, 32 bottles under £30, 6 by glass **Notes** Sunday L, Vegetarian available **Seats** 28, Pr/dining room 14 **Children** Portions **Parking** On street, car park

BURFORD *continued*

The Bay Tree Hotel

⊛ Modern British

Modern British pub food in an elegant Cotswold inn

☎ 01993 822791
Sheep St OX18 4LW
e-mail: info@baytreehotel.info
web: www.cotswold-inns-hotels.co.uk/baytree
dir: A40 or A361 to Burford. From High St turn into Sheep St, next to old market square. Hotel on right

A Cotswold country inn smothered in wisteria with flagstone floors and leaded windows overlooking a garden is an appealing prospect, and The Bay Tree fills the bill. Candlelit in the evenings, and professionally run, the dining room is a cream-coloured space with high-backed chairs and cooking that takes a modern approach to its task. Accompanying cured salmon with excellent crab jelly and watercress cream works a treat, ahead of duck breast with the leg meat rolled in cannelloni, served with confit celeriac and braised, subtly spiced red cabbage. When rhubarb and custard got deconstructed, it got deconstructed for good, and here is a prime example, incorporating rhubarb jelly and custard mousse with almond crumble.

Chef Brian Andrews **Owner** Cotswold Inns & Hotels
Times 12-2/7-9.30 **Prices** Fixed L 2 course fr £12.95, Fixed D 3 course fr £33, Service added but optional 10% **Wines** 25 bottles over £30, 28 bottles under £30, 5 by glass **Notes** Sunday L, Vegetarian available, Dress restrictions, Smart casual, Civ Wed 80 **Seats** 70, Pr/dining room 24 **Parking** 55

The Bull at Burford

⊛⊛ Modern French ☺

Impressive cooking in a former coaching inn

☎ 01993 822220
105 High St OX18 4RG
e-mail: info@bullatburford.co.uk
dir: On A40 between Cheltenham & Oxford, in town centre

The Bull started life as a coaching inn in 1610 so it comes as no surprise to learn that it has seen some high-profile visitors over the centuries - Lord Nelson and Charles II to name but two. After a thorough facelift it is looking up to snuff, with a classy restaurant featuring bare Cotswold-stone walls, age-blackened beams, original artwork, and butterscotch-hued, high-backed seats at linen-swathed tables. The skilled kitchen team has quickly established The Bull on the local foodie map. A repertoire of modern French-influenced dishes shows serious ambition, starting with a multi-faceted plate of pan-seared scallops with confit pork belly, caramelised apple compôte, and a smoked haddock and potato purée. Next up, local beef gets a workout in an assiette of pan-seared fillet, oxtail ravioli and bone marrow boudin with horseradish pommes purée. Dessert could follow a caramel theme, in the forms of parfait, mousse, crème caramel and banana caramel ice cream.

Chef Peter Juszkiewicz **Owner** Mr & Mrs J-M Lauzier
Times 12-2.30/7-9.30 **Prices** Starter £5.95-£9.75, Main £14.25-£19.75, Dessert £6.75-£9.75, Service optional **Wines** 36 bottles over £30, 39 bottles under £30, 10 by glass **Notes** Sunday L, Vegetarian available **Seats** 40, Pr/dining room 12 **Children** Portions **Parking** 6, On street

The Lamb Inn

⊛⊛ Modern British V ☺

Imaginative modern cooking in classic village inn

☎ 01993 823155
Sheep St OX18 4LR
e-mail: info@lambinn-burford.co.uk
web: www.cotswold-inns-hotels.co.uk/lamb
dir: Exit A40 into Burford, down hill, take 1st left into Sheep St, hotel last on right

The setting is as chocolate-box English as you could ask - a wisteria-clad Cotswold stone 15th-century inn just off pretty Burford's high street - and the upmarket interior pursues the theme with beamed ceilings, flagstone floors, open fires, antiques, copper and brass, and squashy sofas. Outside in the buzzy, stone-walled courtyard is the place to be on a fine day, and the classy restaurant is none too shabby either, with its fuchsia and ivory walls, luminous skylights and mullioned windows. The kitchen delivers dishes that are more contemporary than the setting suggests, showing bags of ideas, careful preparation and flourishes of adventure - a starter of scallop and langoustine with cauliflower purée and seaweed salad, for example, followed by pan-fried Gressingham duck breast with braised cabbage, creamed potato, and confit duck and orange tortellini. Desserts such as cinnamon-poached apple with sun-dried cranberry gratin and apple sorbet are a treat.

Chef Sean Ducie **Owner** Cotswold Inns & Hotels
Times 12-2.30/7-9.30 **Prices** Fixed L 2 course £20, Fixed D 3 course £39, Tasting menu £55, Service added but optional 10% **Wines** 60 bottles over £30, 40 bottles under £30, 12 by glass **Notes** Tasting menu 8 course, with Dégustation wines, Sunday L, Vegetarian menu **Seats** 40 **Children** Portions **Parking** Care of The Bay Tree Hotel

CHECKENDON   Map 5 SU68

The Highwayman

⊛ Traditional British

Nice mix of menus in a welcoming country local

☎ 01491 682020
Exlade St RG8 0UA
dir: Exlade St signed off A4074 (Reading/Wallingford road), 0.4m

This Highwayman is a switched-on country dining pub that stands and delivers with its good honest cookery. A hike on the wooded Chiltern Hills nearby should bring on a keen appetite, and the setting is a rambling, 17th-century inn done out with exposed brickwork and beams and a wood-burner in a huge inglenook. Fine ales are on tap in the pubby bar, and all bases are covered in the food department by slabs of 28-day-aged Windsor Estate beef from the grill, home-made pies - venison, game, or wild boar, perhaps - and if you're in the market for something more contemporary, a carte with plenty of seasonal focus. Cod and crab cakes with garlic mayonnaise are a great way to start, followed by roast corn-fed chicken with chorizo risotto and seasonal vegetables. Round off with a trio of crème brûlée flavoured with coffee, vanilla and pistachio.

Chef Paul Burrows **Owner** Mr Ken O'Shea
Times 12-2.30/6-10 Closed 26 Dec, 1 Jan, Mon, D Sun
Prices Prices not confirmed Service optional, Groups min 8 service 10% **Wines** 5 by glass **Notes** Vegetarian available, Dress restrictions, No work clothes or vests **Seats** 55, Pr/dining room 40 **Children** Portions, Menu **Parking** 30

CHINNOR   Map 5 SP70

The Sir Charles Napier

⊛⊛⊛ *– see opposite*

CHIPPING NORTON   Map 10 SP32

The Chequers

⊛ British NEW

Pub classics done right in village gastro-pub

☎ 01608 659393
Church Rd, Churchill OX7 6NJ
e-mail: reservations@thechequerschurchill.com

Once you're inside, this unassuming stone pub in a pretty Cotswolds village has modern gastro-pub style in spades, but that's not to say you can't just have a pint in the cosy bar. The ambience is relaxed and unforced and there are plenty of interesting objets to catch the eye, as well as a small oyster bar that is also home to delicious arrays of charcuterie and cheese. The kitchen has an eye for top-notch local produce, which it turns into direct and purposeful dishes with clear, punchy flavours. The menu divides helpfully into starters, classics, steaks, and roasts, so begin with grilled squid with gremolata, rocket and lemon, then go for calves' liver and bacon with mashed potatoes and spinach from the classics section, which is a perfect example of what this place is all about: simple dishes done well. To finish, a well-made raspberry and almond tart comes with vanilla ice cream.

Times 12-3/6-9.30 Closed D Sun **Prices** Starter £5-£9, Main £12-£29

Save on Hotels. Book at **theAA.com/hotel**

OXFORDSHIRE 407 **ENGLAND**

The Kingham Plough

 Modern British

Revamped pub with creative cooking

☎ 01608 658327

The Green, Kingham OX7 6YD

e-mail: book@thekinghamplough.co.uk

dir: From Chipping Norton take B4450 to Churchill, left at T-junct signed Kingham. Plough on right

An idyllic inn on the green of a chocolate-box-pretty Cotswolds village, the Plough presents a quintessentially English face to the world. Inside, the place has been reinvented with a stylish rustic-chic décor to go with its venerable beams and exposed stone walls. In the bar there are large comfy armchairs and sofas, real ales and scrumpy, and proper bar food such as Scotched quail's eggs or home-made pheasant sausage and mash. But if you want to see what the kitchen brigade can really do, head for the stylishly informal restaurant where exec chef Emily Watkins, who used to work at Heston's Fat Duck, happily deploys traditional and up-to-the-minute cooking techniques to deliver intelligent interpretations of the modern British idiom. Spot-on pastry skills are evident in a starter of penny bun and girolle mushroom tart with tarragon butter sauce and pickled girolles, while rump and sweetbreads of Cotswold rose veal benefit from a well-matched accompaniment of runner beans and foraged mushrooms, exemplary mash and mustard sauce.

Puddings work a similar vein of clever comfort cooking with a bitter chocolate and salted caramel tart with popcorn ice cream.

Chef Emily Watkins, Ben Dulley **Owner** Emily & Miles Lampson **Times** 12-2/6.30-9 Closed 25 Dec, D Sun **Prices** Starter £7-£10, Main £12-£27, Dessert £5-£8, Service optional, Groups min 10 service 10% **Wines** 7 by glass **Notes** Sunday L, Vegetarian available **Seats** 54, Pr/dining room 20 **Children** Portions, Menu **Parking** 30

Wild Thyme Restaurant with Rooms

 Modern British

Contemporary style and modish cooking

☎ 01608 645060

10 New St OX7 5LJ

e-mail: enquiries@wildthymerestaurant.co.uk

dir: A44 Evesham, through Market Place. On left opposite Sainsbury's car park

The mood is relaxed and the food is bathed with Mediterranean warmth in this charming, chic restaurant in well-heeled Chipping Norton. Black beams are all that attest to the age of the building, otherwise the scene is one of rustic modernity - bare wooden floors, exposed stone or whitewashed walls hung with modern art, and chunky country-style tables. The kitchen goes about its business with quiet confidence, sending out robust flavours and plenty of seasonal ingredients in a spring dinner that starts with a delightful, well-conceived dish comprising Wye Valley asparagus, Cornish crab, poached quail's egg, pink grapefruit and hollandaise sauce. Next up, herb ravioli, peas and broad beans, trompette mushrooms, confit garlic, crispy pancetta and Madeira velouté are the accompaniments to a poached and roasted breast of guinea fowl, and it all ends happily with banana parfait, caramelised banana, and figgy pudding.

Chef Nicholas Pullen **Owner** Nicholas & Sally Pullen **Times** 12-2/7-9 Closed Jan 2 wks, Spring 1 wk, Sun-Mon **Prices** Fixed L 2 course fr £18, Starter £5.75-£11, Main £13-£22, Dessert £6.50-£8.50, Service optional **Wines** 11 by glass **Notes** Vegetarian available **Seats** 35, Pr/dining room 14 **Children** Portions **Parking** Public car park 3 min walk

The Sir Charles Napier

CHINNOR **MAP 5 SP70**

British, European **NOTABLE WINE LIST**

Compelling cooking in a unique pub restaurant

☎ 01494 483011

Sprigg's Alley OX39 4BX

e-mail: info@sircharlesnapier.co.uk

web: www.sircharlesnapier.co.uk

dir: M40 junct 6, B4009 to Chinnor. Right at rdbt to Sprigg's Alley

Ask a local if there's anywhere good to eat in the area and they're bound to direct you to this lovely old pub-restaurant, such is its reputation these days for the quality of its food. The old red-brick inn, perched high up in the Chiltern Hills overlooking beech woodlands, has had a stylish modern-country-pub makeover in recent years and the result is an interior that makes you feel right at home. Think open fires, beams, comfortable sofas, vases of fresh flowers and interesting original sculptures all around (a snail in the bar, a tiger and a polar bear in the large garden). Throw in some smooth jazz and friendly, casually dressed staff, and you've got the measure of the ambience of the place. When it comes to the food, head chef Chris Godfrey is firing on all cylinders, sourcing tip-top, seasonal ingredients and treating them with flair and imagination to produce clean, precise, beautifully presented dishes. Take a starter of ultra-fresh, hand-picked crab bound in a light mayonnaise and accompanied by a celeriac remoulade, finely sliced radish and a wonderfully gooey-centred salt-cod Scotch egg with a crispy breadcrumb coating. John Dory with cauliflower risotto, wasabi arancini and red kale is a truly awe-inspiring main course, the flavours acutely balanced, the quality of the fish superlative and the timing of its cooking – and that of the risotto – as accurate as can be. Proceedings end on a high with a first-class warm spiced apple financier with blackcurrant poached pear and frozen yoghurt – the kind of dessert you wish you could have second helpings of. All the peripherals are of an equally high standard, from the warm granary rolls and chunks of rosemary focaccia with unsalted butter, to the exemplary espresso with chocolate truffles.

Chef Chris Godfrey **Owner** Julie Griffiths **Times** 12-3.30/6.30-10 Closed 25-27 Dec, Mon, D Sun **Prices** Fixed L 2 course £17.50, Fixed D 3 course £25, Tasting menu £65, Starter £10.50-£15.50, Main £22.50-£32.50, Dessert £8.50, Service added but optional 12.5% **Wines** 9 by glass **Notes** Sunday L, Vegetarian available **Seats** 75, Pr/dining room 45 **Children** Portions, Menu **Parking** 60

DEDDINGTON
Map 11 SP43

Deddington Arms

◉ Modern British ◐

Good country-pub fare in a 16th-century inn

☎ 01869 338364
Horsefair OX15 0SH
e-mail: deddarms@oxfordshire-hotels.co.uk
web: www.deddington-arms-hotel.co.uk
dir: From S: M40 junct 10/A43. 1st rdbt left to Aynho
(B4100) & left to Deddington (B4031). From N: M40
junct 11 to hospital & Adderbury on A4260, then to
Deddington

Things continue to evolve at this 16th-century black-and-white coaching inn, with the addition of a range of old pasta and pizza favourites to its crowd-pleasing output of good, honest country-pub fodder. Kitted out with the requisite low beams, stone floors and cosy fireplaces, it remains a local watering hole with plenty of period allure in the bar, and a pared-back modernised sheen in the dining room. The kitchen sources its produce diligently from the local area, but it doesn't have to cast its net much wider than the front door when the farmers' market is in full swing on the village square. Home-made corned beef with Dijon mustard remoulade and rocket salad might start you off, before something like chicken breast with dauphinoise potato, woodland mushrooms and shallot and red wine sauce. Sticky date pudding with butterscotch sauce and vanilla ice cream ends things squarely in the comfort zone.

Chef Nick Porter **Owner** Oxfordshire Hotels Ltd
Times 12-2.30/6-9.30 Closed 25 Dec **Prices** Fixed L 2
course £11.95-£17.95, Fixed D 3 course £20.95, Starter
£5-£7, Main £9-£19, Dessert £1.25-£8, Service optional,
Groups min 6 service 10% **Wines** 9 bottles over £30, 37
bottles under £30, 10 by glass **Notes** Sunday L,
Vegetarian available **Seats** 60, Pr/dining room 30
Children Portions, Menu **Parking** 36

FARINGDON
Map 5 SU29

Best Western Sudbury House Hotel & Conference Centre

◉ Modern European

Good hotel dining between Oxford and Swindon

☎ 01367 241272
London St SN7 8AA
e-mail: events@sudburyhouse.co.uk
web: www.sudburyhouse.co.uk
dir: Off A420, signed Folly Hill

On the fringes of the Cotswolds and handy for the M4 and M40, this traditional hotel in nine acres of grounds has croquet and pitch and putt among its possible distractions, plus a large restaurant with pleasant views over the garden; order at the bar before heading on through to the dining room. There's plenty of clear-headed thinking going on in the kitchen, the good quality ingredients given room to shine. Tartlet of wild

mushrooms and Oxford Blue cheese might come with confit of tomato, while main-course seared lamb's liver is served up with colcannon, caramelised shallots and a redcurrant and rosemary scented sauce.

Times 11.30-2.30/6-9.15

The Eagle

◉◉ Modern European ◐

Accomplished cooking in revamped village inn

☎ 01367 241879
Little Coxwell SN7 7LW
e-mail: eaglelittlecoxwell@gmail.com
dir: A420, follow signs for 1m to Little Coxwell village

With chef Marcel Nerpas at the stoves, The Eagle is no ordinary local. A revamp has transformed the traditional country pub into a clean-lined contemporary operation furnished with chunky unclothed wooden tables lit by fat church candles, and art hung on soothing pastel-hued timbered walls. The ales are well kept in the casual bar, and the kitchen ensures the food toes a modern line, drawing on excellent local produce combined with hints of European influences (chef Nerpas hails from Slovakia). A lively streak of invention lifts the repertoire above the tried-and-tested category, scoring palpable hits with the likes of a deceptively simple sounding 'goats' cheese and beetroot' starter - a composition of goats' cheese spheres, roasted beets, brioche croûtons, and honey and truffle oil. Next up could be haunch of venison with Jerusalem artichoke purée, turned potatoes and wild mushroom sauce. A reinvented banoffee pie is presented with a touch of theatre: a globe of white chocolate on a biscuit base dissolves to reveal a filling of chopped banana and caramel sauce when a jug of hot milk chocolate sauce is poured onto it at the table.

Chef Marcel Nerpas **Owner** Marcel Nerpas
Times 12-2.30/5.30-11 Closed Mon, D Sun **Prices** Fixed L
2 course fr £8.50, Starter £3.95-£5.95, Main
£9.50-£15.95, Dessert £5.50-£5.95, Service optional
Wines 4 bottles over £30, 21 bottles under £30, 8 by
glass **Notes** Sunday L £9.95-£19.95, Vegetarian available
Seats 28 **Children** Portions, Menu **Parking** On street

The Trout at Tadpole Bridge

◉ Traditional British ◐

Classy pub grub in a traditional Thames-side inn

☎ 01367 870382
Buckland Marsh SN7 8RF
e-mail: info@troutinn.co.uk
web: www.troutinn.co.uk
dir: A415 from Abingdon signed Marcham, through
Frilford to Kingston Bagpuize. Left onto A420. 5m, right
signed Tadpole Bridge. Or M4 (E'bound) junct 15, A419
towards Cirencester. 4m, onto A420 towards Oxford. 10m,
left signed Tadpole Bridge

This historic inn on the River Thames is very much a traditional pub where diners mingle with locals and drinkers at the bar to reinforce that quintessential country-inn vibe. All the hoped for exposed beams, log

fires and plain wooden tables are present and correct, too, while if the weather is fine, the large garden proves a favoured spot to watch waterborne life float by. Otherwise settle into the laid-back atmosphere inside for some intelligently straightforward, flavour-driven cooking based around seasonal produce and an emphasis on fish dishes, with the daily-changing specials board showing the catch of the day. Go for roasted cod with Welsh rarebit and Lyonnaise potatoes, perhaps, while meat-lovers might tuck into pan-fried calves' liver served with fondant potato, cauliflower purée and wild mushrooms. To finish, how about green fig croissant bread pudding served with crème anglaise?

Chef Pascal Clavaud **Owner** Helen & Gareth Pugh
Times 12-2/7-9 Closed 25-26 Dec **Prices** Fixed L 2 course
£12.50, Starter £4.95-£9.95, Main £14.95-£19.95,
Dessert £5.95-£6.95, Service optional **Wines** 12 by glass
Notes Sunday L £4.95-£30, Vegetarian available, Civ Wed
100 **Seats** 50, Pr/dining room 40 **Children** Portions, Menu
Parking 40

FYFIELD
Map 5 SU49

The White Hart

◉◉ Modern British ◐

Confident cooking in a tranquil village inn

☎ 01865 390585
Main Rd OX13 5LW
e-mail: info@whitehart-fyfield.com
dir: A420 Oxford-Swindon, 7m S of Oxford A34

This historic Tudor coaching inn is a former chantry house, built during the reign of Henry VI, and sold to St John's college in Oxford after the Dissolution. Its many charms include a secret tunnel to Fyfield Manor (not so secret any more, then), and a minstrels' gallery - eat up here if you like, or stay down below with the cosy, pubby vibe of flagstoned floors, inglenooks, and enough timbers to build a galleon. Chef-proprietor Mark Chandler's appealing contemporary gastro-pub cooking draws in foodies from miles around with its impressive technical proficiency and ingredients that are local, fresh, seasonal, and may even be freshly plucked from the aromatic herb garden outside. A three-course approach gets going with goats' cheese and red onion tarte Tatin, followed by pan-fried duck breast and smoked duck spring roll pointed up with a tangy rhubarb and anise sauce, and a three-way treatment of sweet potato, served as purée, crisps and potato Anna. Finally, there's dark and white chocolate brownie with salted caramel ice cream and honeycomb.

Chef Mark Chandler **Owner** Kay & Mark Chandler
Times 12-2.30/7-9.30 Closed Mon (ex BHs), D Sun
Prices Fixed L 2 course fr £17, Starter £6.50-£9, Main
£12-£21, Dessert £6.50-£7.50, Service optional, Groups
min 8 service 10% **Wines** 29 bottles over £30, 29 bottles
under £30, 11 by glass **Notes** Chef's tasting menu
available on request, Sunday L £21-£24, Vegetarian
available **Seats** 65, Pr/dining room 32 **Children** Portions,
Menu **Parking** 60

Save on Hotels. Book at theAA.com/hotel

OXFORDSHIRE 409 ENGLAND

GORING
Map 5 SU68

The Leatherne Bottel

◉◉ British, French

Anglo-French cooking by the Thames

☎ 01491 872667
Bridle Way RG8 OHS
e-mail: leathernebottel@aol.com
web: www.leathernebottel.co.uk
dir: M4 junct 12 or M40 junct 6, signed from B4009 towards Wallingford

The Bottel floats serenely on the Thames with the Chilterns as backdrop. If you're arriving by your own launch, you can step straight on to the sun-dappled or windswept terrace, depending on the season. It's a lovely spot, and the place is a dining destination of long repute, weathering the vicissitudes of culinary fashion without getting stuck in any ruts. The accent is Anglo-French, perfectly seen in a meal that follows a petit crottin goats' cheese, roast fig and chestnut purée with beef Wellington, a beautifully moist recollection of the victory at Waterloo, complete with a porty reduction but rather uneven pastry. Lighter fish dishes might include seared turbot with shallot gratin in smoked haddock chowder, and meals come to a satisfying conclusion with something like a pear poached in pinot noir served with clotted cream and toasted almonds. The radio blaring out from the kitchen can make one wish all the more wistfully that someone would step up to the plate and give us something on the grand piano that stands in the centre of the dining room.

Chef Stuart Cockwell **Owner** Leatherne Bottle Ltd
Times 12-2/7-9 Closed D Sun **Prices** Fixed L 2 course fr £15, Fixed D 3 course fr £25, Tasting menu £70-£140, Service added 10% **Wines** 260 bottles over £30, 9 bottles under £30, 17 by glass **Notes** Tasting menus available, Sunday L, Vegetarian available **Seats** 45 **Children** Portions **Parking** 20

The Miller of Mansfield

◉◉ Modern British, European NEW

Elegant modern dishes at a refurbished coaching inn

☎ 01491 872829
High St RG8 9AW
e-mail: reservations@millerofmansfield.com
web: www.millerofmansfield.com
dir: M40 junct 7, S on A329 towards Benson, A4074 towards Reading, B4009 towards Goring. Or M4 junct 12, S on A4 towards Newbury. 3rd rdbt onto A340 to Pangbourne. A329 to Streatley, right at lights onto B4009 into Goring

In the middle of the Area of Outstanding Natural Beauty that is the Goring Gap, between Reading and Oxford, The Miller is a Georgian coaching inn luxuriantly covered in creepers. Extensive refurbishment has transformed it into a stylish venue that retains some its rustic allure, with solid oak tables and generously upholstered chairs in the rebooted dining room. Elegant modern dishes that avoid the tendency to overload, but show Lee Carter's acuity of judgment, are the name of the game. An oxtail croquette accompanies caramelised scallops, alongside powerful, fine-textured onion purée, to start things off with panache, while mains might offer shoulder, belly and noisette of local lamb in minty redcurrant jus, or a duo of roast red mullet and lobster, with crushed peas, cavolo nero and samphire in smoked butter dressing. There is impressive attention to detail in all these dishes, which doesn't flag at dessert stage, when peanut butter parfait appears with crunchy peanut brittle, raspberry sorbet and a tiny doughnut filled with custard.

Times 12-2.30/6-9.30

GREAT MILTON
Map 5 SP60

Le Manoir aux Quat' Saisons

◉◉◉◉◉ – see page 410

HENLEY-ON-THAMES
Map 5 SU78

The Cherry Tree Inn

◉ Modern British NEW ❧

Popular old inn serving good, honest food

☎ 01491 680430
Stoke Row RG9 5QA
e-mail: enquiries@thecherrytreeinn.co.uk
dir: On A4155 from Henley-on-Thames exit B481 to Sonning Common. Follow Stoke Row signs, turn right for inn

The Cherry Tree has been standing on this spot for 400 years and retains a palpable sense of history in its original flagstone floors, beamed ceilings and open fireplaces. New owners have freshened it all up lately though, and now that old-world look is nicely complemented by new wood furniture, rugs on stripped wooden floors, and tea lights and pot plants on the tables. Modern jazz plays in the background and super-friendly staff really keep the customers happy. There's

seating outside, too, if the weather's playing ball. The monthly changing menu is characterised by good honest food, well-prepared and presented and complemented by a few daily specials. Pan-fried scallops, pig's trotter and garlic mayonnaise makes a superb starter, with every component perfectly cooked. Berkshire pork cooked three ways with salt-baked celeriac and mash might follow, with hazelnut and gingerbread cookie with white chocolate ice cream Turkish Delight making an inventive ending.

Chef Nick Hope **Owner** Douglas Green
Times 12-3/6.30-9.30 **Prices** Service added but optional 10%, Groups min 6 service 10% **Notes** Sunday L £12.95-£19.50, Vegetarian available **Seats** 60, Pr/dining room 12 **Children** Portions, Menu **Parking** 30

Hotel du Vin Henley-on-Thames

◉◉ European

An old riverside brewery made over by HdV

☎ 01491 848400
New St RG9 2BP
e-mail: info.henley@hotelduvin.com
web: www.hotelduvin.com
dir: M4 junct 8/9 signed High Wycombe, take 2nd exit and onto A404 in 2m. A4130 into Henley, over bridge, through lights, up Hart St, right onto Bell St, right onto New St, hotel on right

Moving on from beer to wine usually results in a monumental headache, but the results here are a delight. The HdV brand has plenty of previous with its trademark chic contemporary makeovers, in this case converting the Georgian red-brick buildings encircling the yard of the former Brakspear's brewery with the customary Gallic inspiration. A central island of black leather banquettes is surrounded by copies of famous paintings on buttery-hued, panelled walls, and a plethora of paraphernalia references the wine-related theme, making an amenable setting for good bistro food. Home-grown and local are the buzzwords of the chain's sourcing ethos, although we will allow them a bit of leeway in an excellent crab and saffron tart starter, since the Thames hereabouts is not known for its crustaceans. Next up, chorizo and shellfish bring great flavours to a take on paella twinned with perfectly-timed, crisp-skinned hake and a chicken drumstick. A Black Forest gâteau done properly wraps things up on a fashionably retro note.

Times 12-2.30/6-10

Orwells

◉◉◉ – see page 411

Le Manoir aux Quat' Saisons

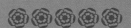

GREAT MILTON   MAP 5 SP60

Modern French V   NOTABLE WINE LIST

Incroyable cooking in magnifique setting

☎ 01844 278881
Church Rd OX44 7PD
e-mail: lemanoir@blanc.co.uk
web: www.manoir.com
dir: M40 junct 7 follow A329 towards Wallingford. After 1m turn right, signed Great Milton and Le Manoir aux Quat' Saisons

If there's one restaurant you should make sure you dine at at least once during your lifetime, this arguably has to be it. Raymond Blanc's delightful Oxfordshire manor house has been awarded five Rosettes in every single AA Restaurant Guide over the last 21 years, and that's not surprising when you consider that Le Manoir's raison d'être is to offer a standard of hospitality that's truly, consistently excellent. You'll experience that splendidly faultless hospitality as soon as you arrive, with immaculately attired staff almost falling over themselves to see to your every need from the off. Whether before or after your meal, make sure you fit in a stroll around the peaceful, beautiful grounds, complete with sculptures, well-stocked greenhouses, little bridges and even a Japanese tea garden. Blanc and his executive chef Gary Jones have never wavered from their belief that the quality of the raw produce is essential to the success or otherwise of every dish, thus the organic kitchen garden has long been at the heart of things here. These days it stretches for two acres and provides no fewer than 90 types of vegetable and 70 varieties of herbs for the kitchen, along with a good proportion of fruits and salad leaves. Dinner takes place in one of three rooms that make up the classically elegant restaurant, including an attractive conservatory with views over the manicured lawns. Tables are well spaced and dressed up to the nines, with candles at night enhancing the romance and intimacy of it all. The prices may be high, but this really is an experience to savour, to cherish. The food remains full of French soul, rooted in classic technique and never following fads or fashions, but at the same time it hasn't stood still. Flavour is always king, but presentations are modern and combinations of ingredients push the boundaries at times. Everything is stunningly good, from the canapés to the wonderful array of fresh, fresh breads. The seasonally changing menus - à la carte, découverte and a variety of fixed-price, multi-course options - are written in French but with clear English translations, and should you need any further explanation, the waiting staff clearly know the dishes inside out and back to front. Perhaps a simple, fresh-tasting salad of Devonshire crab with grapefruit and celery might appeal to start, or a technically impressive dish of quail's egg ravioli with spinach, parmesan and a poultry and rosemary jus. Cornish turbot, wonderfully fresh and cooked to perfection, with a delightful tortellini of crab and a zingy ginger consommé is a fine main course, or you might go for roasted fillet of Aberdeen Angus beef with pearl barley and red wine jus. Tough decisions are in store at dessert stage, with fruity desserts like a theme on citrus, and gariguette strawberries with Szechuan pepper and cream cheese crème glacée vying for your attention with 'flavours of tiramisu' with a Coeur de Guanaja chocolate cream. All the peripherals - amuse-bouche, pre-dessert and petits fours - demonstrate the same level of technical proficiency and well-judged flavour combinations, and if you bring your children, they'll be welcomed with open arms and given their own, rather special menu, such is the egalitarian approach of Monsieur Blanc.

Chef Raymond Blanc, Gary Jones
Owner Mr R Blanc & OE Hotels
Times 12-2.30/7-10 **Prices** Prices not confirmed Service optional **Wines** 1100 bottles over £30, 21 by glass
Notes Fixed L 5 course Mon-Fri, 7 course daily, D 6/9 course daily, Vegetarian menu, Dress restrictions, No trainers or shorts, Civ Wed 50 **Seats** 100, Pr/dining room 50 **Children** Portions, Menu **Parking** 60

KINGSTON BAGPUIZE   Map 5 SU49

Fallowfields Hotel and Restaurant

@@ Modern British V ☺

Contemporary British cooking in smart country hotel

☎ 01865 820416
Faringdon Rd OX13 5BH
e-mail: stay@fallowfields.com
web: www.fallowfields.com
dir: A34 (Oxford Ring Rd) take A420 towards Swindon. At junct with A415 left for 100yds then turn at mini rdbt. Hotel on left after 1m

This small country-house hotel has its roots in the 17th century, its restaurant nowadays smartly turned-out in shades of cream and gold, the room handsomely dressed, and benefitting from a wonderful outlook on lawns and paddocks. The kitchen has the enviable position of being able to monopolise meat and poultry from the owners' farm, and vegetables, herbs and fruit from the kitchen gardens and orchards. Rest assured other materials are equally well sourced: Cornish mackerel is smoked and served as a starter with cucumber spaghetti, confit lemon and herb salad, and locally-shot pheasant goes into a terrine, served with pineapple chutney and pineapple jelly - a fine contrast of flavours and textures. Chutneys accompany some main courses too, one of banana with a tasting of home-reared pork served with pork jus and confit potato, or go for roast rump of beef on red wine jus

with watercress and pommes Anna, and roast halibut with confit chicken wings, chicken jus, sauerkraut and braised shallots. Puddings keep up the high standards, from Amaretto crème brûlée to moist carrot cake with honey ice cream.

Chef Matt Weedon **Owner** Anthony & Peta Lloyd
Times 12-2.30/7-9.30 **Prices** Fixed L 2 course fr £22, Fixed D 3 course fr £25, Tasting menu fr £65, Starter £12.50-£14, Main £16.95-£25.99, Dessert £9-£9.50, Service added but optional 12.5% **Wines** 70 bottles over £30, 20 bottles under £30, 14 by glass **Notes** Tasting menu 7 course must be taken by the whole table, Sunday L, Vegetarian menu, Dress restrictions, Smart casual, Civ Wed 100 **Seats** 42, Pr/dining room 14 **Children** Portions, Menu **Parking** 50

MILTON COMMON   Map 5 SP60

The Oxfordshire

@ Modern British

Modern British cooking in golfing hotel

☎ 01844 278300
Rycote Ln OX9 2PU
e-mail: info@theoxfordshire.com
dir: From S M40 junct 7 onto A370 towards Thame. Hotel on right in 2m

The championship golf course is the main attraction at this new-built hotel in the Chilterns. Leisure facilities, a

spa and indoor pool add to the pleasure of a stay here, along with stylish bedrooms, while the first-floor restaurant has stunning views from its picture windows of the course and countryside, with friendly and efficient staff adding to the congenial atmosphere. The menu is built broadly around the modern British repertory with some European influences, so to start may be rich, smooth chicken liver parfait with nicely contrasting fruit chutney. Presentation is a strength, judging by blade of local beef braised in red wine, served with woodland mushrooms, carrots, spinach and mash - a commendably good marriage of flavours and textures. But you might find the kitchen saves the best till last, with vanilla pannacotta with sherbet-sprinkled mixed berries and raspberry coulis turning out to be the star of a meal.

Times 6-9.30 Closed Xmas, New Year, D Sun

Orwells

HENLEY-ON-THAMES   MAP 5 SU78

Modern British

Modern and trad cooking side by side in a popular country pub

☎ 0118 940 3673
Shiplake Row, Binfield Heath RG9 4DP
e-mail: eat@orwellsatshiplake.co.uk
dir: A4155 to Binfield Heath, take Plough Lane to Shiplake Row, restaurant on left

Ryan Simpson and Liam Trotman honed their approach at Orwells in 2012, moving away from the separate dining areas favoured by many country pubs, where serious eating goes on in a designated room and simpler dishes and bar food are served everywhere else. The faint air of sheep-and-goats that that arrangement can create is now banished, the appeal being that if one of you is in

the market for a plate of good old fish and chips, while the other has a hankering for some more technically intricate modern British cooking, you don't have to go your separate ways. Not entirely surprisingly, it's the latter that has people travelling from nearby Henley and from further afield. The proprietors' smallholding in Lower Shiplake supplies some of the kitchen's raw materials, with local farmers and foragers providing much of the rest. Combinations are inspired, as when crab and pink grapefruit are paired, together with a crab fritter and mixed pepper and apple, for a bracing opener, or there might be a version of beef tartare with shiitake mushrooms, onion 'ash' and a quail egg. At main, the aforesaid fish and chips is likely to be haddock coated in a light Brakspear beer batter, served with crushed peas, tartare sauce and triple-cooked chips, while the more intrepid aim for hay-smoked chicken with caramelised chicory, watercress and chanterelles, or seared black bream with clams, salt-roast Jerusalem artichokes and caviar. Finish off with a slice of goats' curd cheesecake

garnished with beetroot, walnut and pear, or perhaps orange and cardamom pannacotta with ginger biscuits and carrot, while your diehard traditionalist companion goes for sticky toffee pudding and vanilla ice cream. Sundays bring on roast Angus topside with all the trimmings. An enterprising wine list includes plenty of organic and biodynamic bottles, and an admirable choice by the glass.

Chef Ryan Simpson, Liam Trotman **Owner** Ryan Simpson, Liam Trotman **Times** 11.30-3/6.30-9.30 Closed 2 wks beg Jan, 1 wk Apr, 2 wks beg Sep, Mon, D Sun **Prices** Fixed L 2 course £10, Tasting menu £65-£105, Starter £5.50-£14.50, Main £13-£32.50, Dessert £6.50-£8.50, Service optional **Wines** 98 bottles over £30, 38 bottles under £30, 22 by glass **Notes** Tasting menu with/without wines, Sunday L £24.95-£29.95, Vegetarian available **Seats** 60, Pr/dining room 20 **Children** Portions **Parking** 40

The Nut Tree Inn

◎◎ Modern European V ▲ NOTABLE WINE LIST

Confident cooking in a pretty village inn

☎ 01865 331253
Main St OX5 2RE
e-mail: info@nuttreeinn.co.uk
dir: M40 junct 9. A34 towards Oxford, take 2nd exit for Islip. At Red Lion pub turn left, then 3rd right signed Murcott

The idyllic setting of this postcard-pretty thatched 14th-century inn deep in the Oxfordshire countryside, overlooking the village pond, is reason enough to visit The Nut Tree, and the prospect of propping up the bar with a pint of real ale is also a big plus. But the place is more about food these days, since chef-proprietor Mike North's confident cooking has turned the inn into a local foodie destination. Stone walls, gnarled beams and wood-burning stoves provide a cosy pubby backdrop for dishes that are unfussy, precise and assured, and designed to tease maximum flavour from ingredients of exemplary provenance - often wild, organic, or in the case of the rare breed pork, home-grown in the paddock outside. Wild mushrooms in pastry with a poached hen's egg is a typically straightforward starter; next out, a generous roast tranche of brill is served on the bone with braised leek and white wine sauce. To finish, there's sticky toffee pudding with a mini caramelised apple tart and praline ice cream.

Chef Michael & Mary North **Owner** Michael & Imogen North **Times** 12-2.30/7-9 Closed 27 Dec-3 Jan, Mon, D Sun **Prices** Fixed L 2 course £18, Fixed D 2 course £18, Tasting menu £55, Starter £7-£11, Main £16-£28, Dessert £7.50-£10, Service optional, Groups min 6 service 10% **Wines** 107 bottles over £30, 18 bottles under £30, 15 by glass **Notes** Sunday L £16-£22, Vegetarian available, Vegetarian menu **Seats** 70, Pr/dining room 36 **Children** Portions **Parking** 30

Gee's Restaurant

◎ Mediterranean

Well-judged menu in handsome Victorian conservatory

☎ 01865 553540
61 Banbury Rd OX2 6PE
e-mail: info@gees-restaurant.co.uk
dir: N off A4165, from city centre right onto Banbury Rd, located just past Bevington Rd

The setting within an impressive Victorian conservatory is a winning one indeed. Combine that with an unpretentious, clear-headed approach to culinary matters, including a dedication to well-sourced ingredients, and it is easy to see why Gee's is in its third decade satiating the good people of Oxford. Recent refurbishment has resulted in a smart bar with its vaulted roof and views to the kitchen, whilst the restaurant has thriving potted olive trees, garden-style

furniture, and a tiled floor within its luminous, handsome, Grade II listed frame. The menu suits the relaxed mood with a rustic and clearly-focused output, based on excellent produce, and served up in some style. Deep-fried soft-shelled crab is a great way to kick off a meal, served with a dollop of aïoli. Follow on, perhaps, with prime venison chops - pink and tender - with wilted spinach, roasted beetroot and green sauce, and finish with raspberry and chocolate torte or suchlike.

Chef Richard Allen **Times** 12-2.30/5.45-10.30 Closed 25-26 Dec

Macdonald Randolph Hotel

◎◎ Traditional British

Gently modernised British cooking in Oxford landmark

☎ 0844 879 9132 & 01865 256400
Beaumont St OX1 2LN
e-mail: foodservice.randolph@macdonald-hotels.co.uk
web: www.macdonaldhotels.co.uk
dir: M40 junct 8, A40 towards Oxford, follow city centre signs, leads to St Giles, hotel on right

The Randolph, opposite the Ashmolean, is an Oxford institution, with a plotting on the world tourist map through Colin Dexter's Inspector Morse novels. Built in Victorian Gothic style, it has a plethora of oak panelling and vaulted ceilings, while the restaurant is decorated with college shields on the walls and has an air of formality, with much use of trolleys. The cooking is a gently updated version of the great British tradition, with the kitchen skillfully treating top-notch ingredients, seen in starters of cured salmon with crab and apple salad and mixed cress, and game terrine with truffle dressing and pickled girolles. Game shows up among main courses in season - perhaps roast pheasant breast with rösti, Savoy cabbage, honey-roast parsnips and wild mushrooms; otherwise look for lamb chump roasted with garlic and rosemary, served with dauphinoise, spinach and root vegetables, or roast sea trout fillet with carrots, kale and roast potatoes. A good way to end is with almond frangipane tart with Amaretto parfait.

Owner Macdonald Hotels **Times** 12-2.30/6.30-10 **Prices** Fixed L 2 course fr £21, Fixed D 3 course fr £34.95, Starter £7.50-£11, Main £13.50-£27.50, Dessert £7.95-£11.50, Service optional **Wines** 15 by glass **Notes** Pre-theatre menu 2 course & glass of wine £19, Sunday L, Vegetarian available, Dress restrictions, Smart casual, Civ Wed 200 **Seats** 90, Pr/dining room 30 **Children** Portions, Menu **Parking** 50, Chargeable (pre-booking essential)

Malmaison Oxford

◎ Modern British, French V ☙

Egalitarian menu in former prison canteen

☎ 01865 268400
Oxford Castle, New Rd OX1 1AY
e-mail: oxford@malmaison.com
web: www.malmaison.com
dir: M40 junct 9 (signed Oxford/A34). Follow A34 S to Botley Interchange, then A420 to city centre

Who would have thought it? The city's former prison now has people turning up at its doors wanting to be let in. Reincarnated as a classy hotel by the boutique Malmaison chain, sybaritic bedrooms have been installed in the cells and there's a moodily-lit French-accented brasserie in the old basement canteen serving rather more than porridge. Cast-iron staircases and arched doorways are an atmospheric reminder of its past, but the mood is now pure 21st-century seduction dressed up in shades of chocolate brown and aubergine. The kitchen delivers French brasserie classics such as 28-day-aged slabs of prime bovine protein straight from the grill, as well as a please-all repertoire of simple modern dishes, and it is all built on good-quality materials. Cornish crab with avocado fritters and mint and shallot dressing gets things underway, ahead of a generous portion of baby back ribs with pickled coleslaw, barbecue sauce, fries and a rocket and Parmesan salad. Dessert reverts to France with Valrhona chocolate soufflé with milk ice cream.

Chef Daniel Bell **Owner** KSL **Times** 12-2.30/6-10.30 **Prices** Tasting menu £45, Starter £7.50-£11, Main £14.95-£49, Dessert £5.95-£7.95, Service added but optional 10%, Groups min 6 service 10% **Wines** 45 bottles over £30, 10 bottles under £30, 18 by glass **Notes** Tasting menu with wine 5 course, pre-theatre menu available, Sunday L £12.95-£19.95, Vegetarian menu, Civ Wed 110 **Seats** 100, Pr/dining room 35 **Children** Portions, Menu **Parking** Worcester St, Westgate

Mercure Oxford Eastgate Hotel

◎ Modern British

Vibrant brasserie in an historic building

☎ 01865 248695
73 High St OX1 4BE
e-mail: h6668-fb1@accor.com
web: www.thehightableoxford.co.uk
dir: A40 follow signs to Headington & city centre, over Magdalen Bridge, stay in left lane, through lights, left into Merton St, entrance to car park on left

The 17th-century building doesn't want for period charm with its mullioned windows and sandstone façade, but on the inside it's rather swanky in the contemporary manner - well-designed fixtures and fittings and a decidedly cool restaurant called the High Table Brasserie & Bar. Old regulars such as C.S. Lewis and J.R.R. Tolkien wouldn't recognise the place. It's a large open-plan space with whitewashed walls, white-tiled flooring, bare wooden tables and grey banquette seating; a perfect setting for

Save on Hotels. Book at theAA.com/hotel

OXFORDSHIRE 413 ENGLAND

its menu of British and Mediterranean-influenced food. Start with a single salmon fishcake served with a micro herb salad, follow on with a home-made burger with chips fried in duck fat, or roasted Cornish bass with braised Puy lentils, celeriac and pear remoulade. To finish, expect something like sticky toffee pudding with clotted cream ice cream and caramel sauce. And note it's close to all the city-centre action.

Chef Anthony Pitcher **Owner** MREF Trade Co **Times** 12-2.30/6-9.30 **Prices** Prices not confirmed Service added but optional 12.5%, Groups min 6 service 12.5% **Wines** 13 by glass **Notes** Tasting menu 12 course, Veg 10 course £25, 24 hrs notice req, Sunday L, Vegetarian available, Dress restrictions, Smart casual **Seats** 70, Pr/dining room 8 **Children** Portions, Menu **Parking** 40, Parking charges apply

The Oxford Hotel

◉ Modern British

Brasserie-style menu in modern hotel restaurant

☎ 01865 489988
Gidstow Rd, Wolvercote Roundabout OX2 8AL
e-mail: oxford@pumahotels.co.uk
web: www.pumahotels.co.uk
dir: A34 Peartree junct, follow signs to A40, take 4th exit at rdbt

Within easy striking distance of the city centre, this modern hotel has conference and leisure facilities aplenty, plus a number of options for unwinding before or after said activities. There's the Medio Bar for a cocktail and bar snack, the Cappuccino Lounge for a light meal or afternoon tea, and, up on the first floor, the smart and modish restaurant. The menu here has a lot to offer and satisfies contemporary expectations with its breadth and depth. You might start with ham hock terrine, for example, with a counter-pointing grape and apple chutney, or go for an Asian flavour with mussels steamed in a Thai sauce. The grill does its work on the steaks - 8oz rib-eye, maybe - served up in the traditional manner with a choice of sauces. And there are main courses like slow-cooked pork belly with bubble-and-squeak, or battered haddock fillet, or roasted artichoke and pea risotto. Finish with a pear and almond tart with clotted cream and caramel sauce.

Chef Gavin Chapman **Owner** Puma Hotels Collection **Times** 7-9.30 Closed L all week **Prices** Fixed D 3 course £29, Starter £4.95-£6.95, Main £13.95-£17.95, Dessert £4.95-£8.95, Service optional **Wines** 8 bottles over £30, 20 bottles under £30, 18 by glass **Notes** Sunday L, Vegetarian available, Dress restrictions, Smart casual, Civ Wed 200 **Seats** 180 **Children** Portions, Menu **Parking** 250

STADHAMPTON — Map 5 SU69

The Crazy Bear

◉◉ Modern British ◉

Charming 16th-century inn with some fine cooking

☎ 01865 890714
Bear Ln OX44 7UR
e-mail: enquiries@crazybear-stadhampton.co.uk
web: www.crazybeargroup.co.uk
dir: M40 junct 7, A329. In 4m left after petrol station, left into Bear Lane

With a name like that, The Crazy Bear is never going to be an identikit country inn. Accordingly, quirky character runs to the heart of this sprawling set-up in a 16th-century pub, remodelled to combine eclectic design with splendid gardens, an up-tempo vibe and great food, whether it comes from the English or Thai (see separate entry for the latter) side of the culinary fence. Candy-pink and crimson high-backed chairs, buttoned cream leather walls, crystal chandeliers, leopard-print floors, and a novel - if rather worrying - wine storage solution that racks bottles overhead certainly adds up to a setting of eclectic theatricality. A wide-ranging all-day menu of modern dishes covers most bases, and it's all commendably local (as local as meat and veg from the Crazy Bear farm) and seasonal. First out is charred squid pil-pil with home-cured pancetta, coriander and chilli, followed by rack and rump of the Bear's own lamb, served with pan-roasted potato, peas and beans. Pudding brings a bar of salted butter caramel with peanuts and pistachios, teamed with dark chocolate sorbet and a peanut and popcorn wafer.

Chef Martin Picken **Owner** Jason Hunt **Times** 12-10 All-day dining **Prices** Fixed L 2 course £14.50, Starter £7.95-£14.50, Main £11.95-£26.50, Dessert £8.95-£12.50, Service added but optional 12.5% **Wines** 20 by glass **Notes** Sunday L, Vegetarian available, Civ Wed 100 **Seats** 40, Pr/dining room 140 **Children** Portions **Parking** 100

Thai Thai at The Crazy Bear

◉◉ Modern Thai ◉

Thai cooking in an old coaching inn

☎ 01865 890714
The Crazy Bear, Bear Ln OX44 7UR
e-mail: enquiries@crazybear-stadhampton.co.uk
dir: M40 junct 7, A329. In 4m left after petrol station, left into Bear Lane

A 16th-century coaching inn in sleepy Oxfordshire countryside is not the sort of place one might expect to find a Thai restaurant, less still one that wears the costume of a velvet-sheathed Bedouin boudoir. But The Crazy Bear has never been one for toeing the line. The funky scene is set by etched brass and copper tables, a mirror-panelled ceiling, fretwork screens and bronze velvet banquettes, or on a fine day, move out to the oasis and dine to the music of birdsong and running water at a table in the garden. The cooking is an enticing blend of pukka Thai classics and fusion dishes that bring together

western and Pan-Asian ideas. Tom yam kung yai is a soup of king prawns, mushrooms, lemongrass, galangal, chillies and lime that falls into the former category, while mains sees crispy sea bream fillets paired with hot-and-sour sauce and Thai basil; a meaty option could be pot-roasted ox cheek with braised lettuce, shiitaki mushrooms, spring onions and roasted garlic. See entry above for the English dining option.

Chef Chalao Mansell **Owner** Jason Hunt **Times** 12-3/6-12 Closed L Sun **Prices** Fixed D 3 course £39.50-£49.50, Starter £6.95-£14.95, Main £9.95-£19.95, Dessert £8.95, Service added but optional 12.5% **Wines** 20 by glass **Notes** Sunday L, Vegetarian available, Civ Wed 100 **Seats** 30, Pr/dining room 140 **Children** Portions **Parking** 100

SWINBROOK — Map 10 SP21

The Swan Inn

◉◉ Modern British

Historic village inn with locally-sourced ingredients

☎ 01993 823339
OX18 4DY
e-mail: info@theswanswinbrook.co.uk
web: www.theswanswinbrook.co.uk
dir: A40 towards Cheltenham, turn left to Swinbrook

On the borders of Oxfordshire and Gloucestershire, this quintessential village pub, with an apple orchard to the rear and the Windrush River running by, takes the food-side of the operation seriously. It's owned by the Dowager Duchess of Devonshire and there is interesting memorabilia around the place relating to the Mitford sisters, including canvas prints of family portraits. Seasonal ingredients are sourced with care (traceability is a big deal here), and the fine produce turns up in dishes such as plum tomato and mozzarella tartlet with rocket and pesto, followed by confit belly of Cotswold lamb with spring vegetables, capers and mint, or locally-reared Aberdeen Angus steaks served with horseradish cream, green beans and skinny chips.

Times 12-2/7-9 Closed 25-26 Dec

TOOT BALDON
Map 5 SP50

The Mole Inn

◉◉ Modern European 🍷

Generously proportioned country-pub dishes in a splendidly named village

☎ 01865 340001
OX44 9NG
e-mail: info@themoleinn.com
dir: 5m S of Oxford, restaurant 15 mins from M40 junct 7

The Witchalls' sympathetically restored country inn in a village with a name straight out of Agatha Christie is only five miles from Oxford, and serves as a bucolic retreat from both town and gown. Garden tables under parasols, smart unclothed tables indoors, a brick bar and friendly, on-the-ball staff all contribute hugely to the appeal. Generously proportioned dishes in an adventurous vein are what's on the menu, which opens with the likes of Thai-spiced shredded duck and beansprouts in chilli, lime and coriander, or lightly curried risotto with undyed smoked haddock and a poached egg. Main dishes use premium local meats, as in lamb rump with a croquette of shoulder meat, cumin-spiked chickpeas, and minted radish and onion salad, while from the sea you might find a fish mixed grill with fries, rocket and cherry tomato salad and lime aïoli. Sticky date pudding is a fortifying finisher that needs some adjustment to its temperature, or there may be a tropical version of Eton mess made with mango, passionfruit and banana.

Chef Gary Witchalls **Owner** Gary Witchalls
Times 12-2.30/7-9.30 Closed 25 Dec **Prices** Fixed L 2 course £17.50, Fixed D 3 course £23, Starter £6.95-£7.95, Main £12.95-£17.95, Dessert £6.50, Service optional **Wines** 8 by glass **Notes** Sunday L, Vegetarian available **Seats** 70 **Children** Portions, Menu **Parking** 40

WALLINGFORD
Map 5 SU68

The Springs Hotel & Golf Club

◉ Modern British

Gentle country-house cooking and lakeside views

☎ 01491 836687
Wallingford Rd, North Stoke OX10 6BE
e-mail: info@thespringshotel.com
web: www.thespringshotel.com
dir: Edge of village of North Stoke

The Tudor-style timbered façade of this house in the glorious Oxfordshire countryside is actually a faithful Victorian copy. Set in landscaped gardens with a spring-fed lake (hence the name), The Springs Hotel now trades as a tranquil golf-oriented bolt-hole, and its Lakeside Restaurant is looking spruce after a makeover in 2012 brought in bare wooden floors and contemporary hues of beige and deep purple (in honour of a former rock band connection). Gently modernised country-house classics are the order of the day here - perhaps pan-fried pigeon breast with caramelised apple and black pudding, and redcurrant jus, followed by chargrilled rump steak with hand-cut chips, roasted tomato and garlic mayonnaise, or grilled whole Cornish plaice with roasted new potatoes, fine beans, sun-blushed tomatoes, and pesto dressing. End with sticky toffee pudding with treacle ice cream.

Times 12-2/6.30-9.45

WATLINGTON
Map 5 SU69

The Fat Fox Inn

◉ British NEW 🍷

Characterful inn with a local flavour

☎ 01491 613 040
13 Shurburn St OX49 5BU
e-mail: info@thefatfoxinn.co.uk

Right at the heart of this small market town, The Fat Fox is a proper inn with an unreconstructed bar, comfortable bedrooms and a serious approach to local food, cooked with flair and without fuss - hurrah! There's even a piano by the front door alongside some comfy sofas. It doesn't matter if you eat in the bar or the dining area, with its warm colour tones and laid-back service, and there's no background music, just the happy hubbub of the contented customers. Local farmers and producers get name-checked on the daily-changing menu, which keeps things fresh, seasonal and unpretentious. Britwell Farm

ox tongue, carrot and raisin salad, for example, is just the ticket, or try the excellent duck liver parfait with port jelly and red onion marmalade. Follow on with bavette steak with slow-roasted tomatoes, anchovy butter and chips, or its thanks again to Britwell Farm for its lamb belly, cooked with lentils and leeks.

Chef Stewart Lennox **Owner** John Riddell
Times 12-3/6.30-10 **Prices** Fixed L 2 course £10-£12, Starter fr £5, Main fr £12, Dessert fr £5 **Wines** 2 bottles over £30, 21 bottles under £30, 12 by glass **Notes** Sunday L £14-£16, Vegetarian available **Seats** 26 **Children** Portions **Parking** 20

WITNEY
Map 5 SP31

Old Swan & Minster Mill

◉ Traditional British NEW 🍷

Charming country pub by the River Windrush

☎ 01993 774441
Old Minster OX29 0RN
e-mail: reception@oldswanandminstermill.com
web: www.oldswanandminstermill.com

In a wonderful English setting, the Old Swan is a smart country pub (the more modishly done-out Minster Mill is next-door) with a good deal of rustic charm and a serious approach to food. It's very cosy on the inside, with lots of spaces to tuck yourself away, and there's real ale on tap if that's what you're after. There's a local flavour to the menu, a refreshing lack of pretension, and even ingredients grown in their own kitchen garden. At lunchtime there's a range of tip-top ploughman's, whilst there's always the option of going for broke and settling down for three courses: Wychwood Forest duck terrine, perhaps, with citrus salad and aged port dressing, followed by Oxfordshire farm steak and Hobgoblin ale pie with King Edward mash and Old Swan garden vegetables, with old fashioned treacle tart with vanilla seed custard for pudding. The garden is a gem.

Chef David Mwiti **Owner** DeSavary family
Times 12.30-3/6.30-9 **Prices** Fixed L 2 course £14.45, Starter £6.95-£9, Main £14-£22, Dessert £6.50-£9, Service optional **Wines** 33 bottles over £30, 19 bottles under £30 **Notes** Sunday L £16.95-£35, Vegetarian available, Civ Wed 50 **Seats** 110, Pr/dining room 55 **Children** Portions, Menu **Parking** 70

The Restaurant at Witney Lakes Resort

◉ Modern European 🍷

Modern brasserie cooking at a multi-purpose resort

☎ 01993 893012 & 893000
Downs Rd OX29 0SY
e-mail: restaurant@witney-lakes.co.uk
dir: 2m W of Witney town centre, off B4047 Witney to Burford road

An expansive resort venue in the prime minister's constituency has all eventualities nailed. It caters for business conferences and weddings, looks after golfers

Save on Hotels. Book at **theAA.com/hotel**

OXFORDSHIRE 415 ENGLAND

and fitness fanatics, and has a thoroughly modern restaurant, replete with bare oak tables, tea-lights, floral decorations and a large central bar. Thursday night is Foodie Night, when the culinary stops are pulled out, and there are wine evenings sponsored by champagne houses. The cooking is mostly modern brasserie fare, and highly reliable. A starter might pair smoked mackerel with white pudding and apple, or tempt you to try octopus dressed with preserved lemon and baby gem. Main-course meats are accurately cooked, as in rump of lamb with a kidney pudding, roast pumpkin and rosemary jus, or there may be haddock in a Brakspear beer batter with tartare sauce. To finish, a wodge of lime and ginger cheesecake might come haphazardly garnished with a stack of rhubarb.

Chef Sean Parker, Owen Little **Owner** Sean Parker **Times** 12-3/6.30-9 Closed 25 & 31 Dec, 1 Jan, L Sat, D Sun-Mon **Prices** Fixed L 2 course £13-£15, Fixed D 3 course £23, Service optional, Groups min 8 service 10% **Wines** 9 bottles over £30, 38 bottles under £30, 11 by glass **Notes** Themed evenings, Sunday L, Vegetarian available, Civ Wed 50 **Seats** 75 **Children** Portions, Menu **Parking** 400

WOODCOTE — Map 5 SU68

Woody Nook at Woodcote

◉ British, International

International flavours and top-notch Australian wines

☎ 01491 680775
Goring Rd RG8 0SD
e-mail: info@woodynookatwoodcote.co.uk
dir: Opposite village green

Given the quintessential English setting opposite the village green, with creepers and hanging baskets serving up a riot of foliage, you might be surprised to discover that there's a decidedly antipodean flavour at this pretty cottage restaurant. Named after the owners' award-winning boutique winery in the Margaret River region of Western Australia, you can sample the full range of wines here, plus tuck into a menu of dishes that draws inspiration from Australia, the UK, and a few places in between. So, king crab bound in ginger, chilli, lemon and coriander mayonnaise is one way to start a meal, or go for traditional Provençal fish soup with all the regulation accompaniments. There are fish specials such as cod with vine tomato sauce and parmesan fettuccine, and wild Pacific tiger prawns grilled with garlic and herb butter. Finish with vanilla and mango crème brûlée with ginger shortbread.

Times 12-2.30/7-9.30 Closed Xmas, Mon-Tue, D Sun

WOODSTOCK — Map 11 SP41

The Feathers Hotel

◉◉ Modern British ⚑ NOTABLE WINE LIST ✋

Bold design and imaginative cooking (and gin)

☎ 01993 812291
Market St OX20 1SX
e-mail: enquiries@feathers.co.uk
dir: From A44 (Oxford to Woodstock), 1st left after lights. Hotel on left

A feature in the historic Cotswold market town of Woodstock since the 17th century, The Feathers carries itself in a thoroughly modish manner these days, for this is boutique hotel territory, blending the indisputable traditional charms of the old building with a stylish

continued

WOODSTOCK *continued*

contemporary sheen. The dining room, split into two on quiet nights, has crisp white linen-clad tables with silver cutlery and sparkling glassware - a suitable setting for the refined modern British cooking courtesy of the team in the kitchen. Much is made of seasonality and locality in dishes such as confit foie gras (served on a square glass plate if you care for such details) with celeriac, pear, and quince jam, followed by a rustic, meltingly tender Longhorn beef (cooked sous-vide) with shallot pickle and red wine jus. Clementine cheesecake with oatmeal and orange jelly is typical of desserts. The gin bar is worth a visit, with over 100 varieties on offer, or, if you're up to it, there's the 'gin experience' tasting menu, where a different gin is paired with, or appears in, each of the seven courses.

The Feathers Hotel

Chef Kevin Barrett **Owner** Empire Ventures Ltd **Times** 12.30-2/7.10-9.30 **Prices** Fixed L 2 course £27-£38, Fixed D 3 course £35.50-£50.50, Tasting menu £55-£66, Starter £8-£12.25, Main £19-£25.75, Dessert £8.50, Service added but optional 10% **Wines** 8 bottles over £30, 10 bottles under £30, 16 by glass **Notes** Sunday L, Vegetarian available, Dress restrictions, No shorts or T-shirts **Seats** 40, Pr/dining room 24 **Children** Portions, Menu **Parking** On street

See advert on page 415

Kings Arms Hotel

◉ Modern British ⓒ

Stylishly revamped Georgian hotel

☎ 01993 813636
19 Market St OX20 1SU
e-mail: stay@kingshotelwoodstock.co.uk
web: www.kingshotelwoodstock.co.uk
dir: In town centre, on corner of Market St & A44

The white-painted Georgian Kings Arms fits in perfectly in well-to-do Woodstock with its air of distinction and handsome country décor within. It's only a short stroll from the splendour of Blenheim Palace after all. For all its period charm, there's a good deal of contemporary polish to the place, not least in the Atrium Restaurant with its sharp, modern good looks: think chunky wooden tables and black high-backed chairs on a black-and-white chequerboard floor, plus original artworks and huge antique mirrors with rococo frames. The menu is a happy mix of old and new, too, with lots of gently modish things to choose from. Game terrine with pear chutney and rustic toast to start, perhaps, followed by Kelmscott Farm ham with free-range egg and chips, or go for the more upmarket braised duck leg with rich plum sauce, celeriac dauphinoise and buttered chard. Finish with a treacle and roast walnut tart.

Chef Simon Cottrell **Owner** David & Sara Sykes **Times** 12-2.30/6.30-9.30 **Prices** Prices not confirmed Service optional, Groups min 10 service 10% **Wines** 13 by glass **Notes** Sunday L, Vegetarian available **Seats** 80 **Children** Portions **Parking** On street

Macdonald Bear Hotel

◉◉ Traditional British

Accomplished modern cooking in medieval hotel

☎ 01993 811124 & 08448 799143
Park St OX20 1SZ
e-mail: general.bear@macdonald-hotels.co.uk
web: www.thebearwoodstock.co.uk
dir: M40 junct 9 follow signs for Oxford & Blenheim Palace. A44 to town centre, hotel on left

Woodstock is not without its complement of attractive old buildings, and this creeper-covered hotel is one of them. Inside, evidence of the great age of the property is seen in the beams, stone walls and fireplaces in the traditional-looking dining rooms. The kitchen, though, keeps abreast of matters culinary, producing starters of ham hock roulade and crispy Stornoway black pudding with piccalilli vegetables and garlic ciabatta crisp, and Smoked John Ross Jr haddock fish cake with herb hollandaise. Beef is naturally reared in Scotland and aged for a minimum of 21 days, so perhaps you might go for a grilled rib-eye steak with Carroll's heritage hand-cut

chips and your choice of sauce (red wine, béarnaise or peppercorn), or if fish is more your thing, pan-fried fillet of skrie cod with saffron potatoes and mussel vinaigrette. Traditional lemon tart with crème fraîche provides a simple but effective finale, or there's all the comfort of rhubarb crumble with fresh egg custard.

Owner Macdonald Hotels **Times** 12.30-2.30/7-9.30 **Prices** Fixed L 2 course fr £19.95, Fixed D 3 course fr £35, Service optional **Wines** 30 bottles over £30, 20 bottles under £30, 16 by glass **Notes** Sunday L, Vegetarian available **Seats** 65, Pr/dining room 26 **Children** Portions, Menu **Parking** 50

RUTLAND

CLIPSHAM	Map 11 SK91

The Olive Branch

◉◉ British, European Ⓥ ⓒ

Refined modern pub dishes in a charming village inn

☎ 01780 410355
Main St LE15 7SH
e-mail: info@theolivebranchpub.com
dir: 2m from A1 at Stretton junct, 5m N of Stamford

Converted into a pub from a row of three cottages back in the Victorian era, today's Olive Branch satisfies on every level. They serve a fine pint of beer here for a start, plus offer a good range of wines, and even go as far as making their own lemonade and sloe gin. There is equal passion in the delivery of food, which can sort you out for a proper sandwich (minute steak with caramelised onions, perhaps), something traditional such as fish and chips with minted peas and tomato sauce, or a more restauranty dish like honey-roast pork belly with cider fondant. Whatever you eat, the produce is most likely local and, rather like the décor, the presentation has that appealing blend of slick rusticity. And in the true inn tradition, if you want to stay over, there are some charming rooms at your disposal.

Chef Sean Hope **Owner** Sean Hope, Ben Jones **Times** 12-2/7-9.30 Closed D 25 Dec **Prices** Fixed L 2 course £16.95, Fixed D 3 course £24.50, Starter £5.50-£10.50, Main £14.50-£23.95, Dessert £6.75-£7.50, Service optional, Groups min 12 service 10% **Wines** 53 bottles over £30, 27 bottles under £30, 16 by glass **Notes** Sat afternoon menu available 2.30-5.30pm, Sunday L, Vegetarian menu **Seats** 45, Pr/dining room 20 **Children** Portions, Menu **Parking** 15

Save on Hotels. Book at **theAA.com/hotel**

RUTLAND 417 ENGLAND

Hambleton Hall

British **V** NOTABLE WINE LIST

Superb fine-dining in majestic country-house hotel

☎ 01572 756991
Hambleton LE15 8TH
e-mail: hotel@hambletonhall.com
web: www.hambletonhall.com
dir: 8m W of A1 Stamford junct (A606),
3m E of Oakham

Fox hunting was a popular pursuit in these parts back in the day, and one lucky (and wealthy) Victorian brewer built Hambleton in 1881 as his home-from-home for the hunting season. The construction of Rutland Water reservoir (now a nature reserve) was not on the agenda back then, but its arrival on the hall's doorstep in 1970 has only succeeded in enhancing the splendour of the setting. Tim and Stefa Hart bought the place in 1979 and set about creating a country-house hotel of distinction. The formal gardens are truly delightful, surrounded by rolling Rutland countryside, with the shimmering waters a landmark feature whatever the weather. The house itself is handsome and rather grand, built on a manageable scale, which suits the friendly and professional approach of the team, while interiors, designed by Stefa, are breathtakingly elegant and charming. The two dining rooms are no less glamorous with splendid chandeliers, oil paintings, and tables dressed with reassuring formality. Aaron Patterson has headed up the kitchen since 1992 - people tend to stick around here, which is a very good sign indeed - and his food is refined, creative, and firmly rooted in sound culinary thinking. They have their own bakery, so it will come as no surprise to hear the bread is pretty good (served with excellent butter), and everything from the canapés to the petits fours is beautifully made. Roast breast of wood pigeon - a fabulous, tender bird - comes with beer-flavoured macadamia nuts, salt-baked turnips and burnt leek in an impressive first course, the flavours nicely judged, or try the assiette of beetroot with pear, walnut and a horseradish sorbet. Main-course variations of lamb is another winning combination of tastes and textures - superbly flavoured loin and delicious confit tongue among them - with a multitude of accompaniments from mint jelly to a rosemary-infused jus. The quality of the ingredients shines out here, everything sourced with due care and attention, and a good deal of it local to the area. Desserts are no less compelling and creative: 'The Pumpkin' for example, which is a spun-sugar ball filled with delights such as pumpkin and orange ices and a gingerbread pannacotta, or apple tarte fine with vanilla ice cream. The wine list is an equally impressive piece of work, and demonstrates the attention to detail and quality that runs right the way through Hambleton Hall.

Chef Aaron Patterson **Owner** Mr T Hart **Times** 12-2/7-9.30 **Prices** Fixed L 2 course fr £24, Fixed D 3 course £65, Tasting menu £72, Service added but optional 12.5% **Wines** 30 bottles under £30, 10 by glass **Notes** Sunday L, Vegetarian menu, Dress restrictions, Smart dress, no jeans, T-shirts or trainers, Civ Wed 64 **Seats** 60, Pr/dining room 20 **Children** Portions, Menu **Parking** 40

LYDDINGTON
Map 11 SP89

The Marquess of Exeter

🏵 Modern European NEW

Welcoming village inn with appealing menus

☎ 01572 822477

52 Main St LE15 9LT

e-mail: info@marquessexeter.co.uk

Chef-proprietor Brian Baker has done a lovely job of transforming this village pub into the sort of local we would all like on our patch. It is a relaxed and informal place with a fresh rustic look; in the cosy bar there are head-skimming gnarled beams, flagstoned floors and baskets of logs ready to go on the open fire - just the spot for a pre-dinner drink. The restaurant has a completely different feel: the open-plan layout is decluttered, and decorated with white walls and scrubbed pine tables; friendly, chatty staff jolly things along with an upbeat mood. Menus make the most of seasonal ingredients and local produce in good honest dishes: chicken liver parfait with fig chutney and grilled bread, for example, makes a triumphant start, ahead of rosemary and garlic roasted chicken with herb crushed potatoes, peas and mustard jus. For pudding, crème brûlée is made as per the textbook and served with buttery shortbread.

Chef Brian Baker **Owner** Brian Baker
Times 12-2.30/6.30-9.30 **Prices** Fixed L 2 course £13.50
Notes Sunday L £11.95-£14.25 **Children** Menu

OAKHAM
Map 11 SK80

Barnsdale Lodge Hotel

🏵 Modern British 🍷

Regionally-based cooking by Rutland Water

☎ 01572 724678

The Avenue, Rutland Water, North Shore LE15 8AH

e-mail: enquiries@barnsdalelodge.co.uk

web: www.barnsdalelodge.co.uk

dir: Turn off A1 at Stamford onto A606 to Oakham. Hotel 5m on right. (2m E of Oakham)

Thomas Noel's family have owned Barnsdale Lodge since 1760, and who can blame them for putting down roots in this splendid spot - it was once part of Exton Park, the seat of the Earls of Gainsborough - on the north shore of Rutland Water? Since 1989, the lodge has earned a crust as a small-scale, easygoing country hotel with a dinky spa and quietly stylish interior kitted out with old-school squidgy sofas blending with pastel-hued contemporary elegance. The cooking is on the money, too - produce is

hauled in from the kitchen garden and farms in the surrounding area to create simple, seasonal menus that wouldn't look out of place in a slick city brasserie. Expect the likes of smoked haddock risotto with a duck egg and rocket followed by roast Grasmere Farm pork chop with sautéed kale and a mixed bean and sausage casserole, or pan-fried hake with leek and prawn hash, mixed greens and pesto.

Chef Steve Conway **Owner** The Hon Thomas Noel
Times 12-2.15/7-9.30 **Prices** Fixed L 2 course £13.50, Starter £4.50-£9.95, Main £12.95-£21.95, Dessert £4.95-£7.95, Service added but optional 10% **Wines** 27 bottles over £30, 58 bottles under £30, 17 by glass **Notes** Sunday L £20.95, Vegetarian available, Civ Wed 200 **Seats** 120, Pr/dining room 200 **Children** Portions, Menu **Parking** 250

Hambleton Hall

🏵🏵🏵🏵 – *see page 417*

UPPINGHAM
Map 11 SP89

The Lake Isle

🏵🏵 British, French

Georgian townhouse hotel with confident cooking

☎ 01572 822951

16 High Street East LE15 9PZ

e-mail: info@lakeisle.co.uk

web: www.lakeisle.co.uk

dir: M1 junct 19 to A14 Kettering, at rdbt take A43 signed Corby and then A6003 to Rockingham/Uppingham. Continue to pedestrian lights Uppingham, right onto High St, Lake Isle on right after the square

Named for W. B. Yeats' *Lake Isle of Innisfree*, the hope is that visitors will experience a similar feeling of tranquillity in this Georgian townhouse with rooms in the lovely market town of Uppingham. On a pleasingly intimate scale, with a large window looking out onto the high street, inside there are panelled walls and original mahogany fittings, plus simply laid, heavy wooden tables attended by the friendly and efficient service team. French influences are in evidence on the broadly British menu, which changes every six weeks to keep flow with the seasons. There are some smart flavour combinations on show; take a starter of grilled medallion (well, fillet) of South Coast mackerel with crispy ham, bitter leaves, sautéed potatoes and a punchy piccalilli dressing. The quality of the lamb is indisputable in a duo including pan-roasted rack and medallion of braised shoulder,

served with creamed celeriac, Savoy cabbage and pancetta. Then, sit back and wait while the dark chocolate and baby pear fondant pudding (served with stem ginger ice cream) is cooked to order.

Times 12-2.30/7-9 Closed 26 Dec-1 Jan, L Mon, D Sun

WING
Map 11 SK80

Kings Arms Inn & Restaurant

🏵🏵 Modern British 🍷

Supplier-led hearty cooking in a traditional inn

☎ 01572 737634

13 Top St LE15 8SE

e-mail: info@thekingsarms-wing.co.uk

web: www.thekingsarms-wing.co.uk

dir: 1m off A6003, between Oakham & Uppingham

Not many village inns can say that they have their own smokehouse, produce their own charcuterie, bake the bread and generally make everything from jams to chutneys to sauces the hard way, from scratch. Amid the flagstone floors, low-beamed ceilings and open fires of the classic rustic interior you may also spot the map where local suppliers are proudly pinpointed. It all adds up to a deep commitment to real food at the Kings Arms, a 17th-century gem in a photogenic village near Rutland Water. Whether you stay in the bar with the ranks of splendid real ales and cider, or settle in the relaxed dining room, you can expect generous, big-hearted cooking with strong flavours from a kitchen that takes its work seriously. Home-smoked eel with horseradish potato salad, rocket and soft-boiled egg shows the no-nonsense style, while mains bring loin, liver and chipolata of local venison with juniper fondant, butternut purée and elderberry jus, or tournedos of hare loin wrapped in the in-house air-dried ham and teamed with red cabbage, sautéed potatoes and celeriac purée.

Chef James Goss **Owner** David, Gisa & James Goss
Times 12-2.30/6.30-9 Closed Mon, L Tue (Nov-Apr), D Sun **Prices** Tasting menu £32-£45, Starter £7-£12.50, Main £14-£32, Dessert £6-£20, Service optional, Groups min 7 service 10% **Wines** 30 bottles over £30, 20 bottles under £30, 33 by glass **Notes** Sunday L £10-£13, Vegetarian available **Seats** 32, Pr/dining room 20 **Children** Portions, Menu **Parking** 20

SHROPSHIRE

BRIDGNORTH   Map 10 SO79

The Old Vicarage Hotel

◉◉ British, European

Classic combinations in a conservatory-style hotel dining room

☎ 01746 716497
Hallow, Worfield WV15 5JZ
e-mail: admin@oldvicarageworfield.com
web: www.oldvicarageworfield.com
dir: Off A454, approx 3.5m NE of Bridgnorth, 5m S of Telford on A442, follow brown signs

Set in two acres of pleasant gardens in green-and-pleasant Shropshire countryside, and handily close to Bridgnorth and Telford, The Old Vicarage is an Edwardian house which earns its keep these days as a smart country house hotel. The airy conservatory-style dining room looking out over the gardens is one of its many charms. Flooded with sunlight on fine days and smartly done out with linen-clad tables, it is an agreeable spot for cooking that aims high and delivers a repertoire of classic and contemporary combinations based on top-class materials, much of it sourced from the local area. A well-presented starter matches ham hock ravioli with crushed peas, baby onions and pea mousse, ahead of free-range chicken breast teamed with spiced cauliflower purée, cardamom carrots and chicken cream. Local beef fillet might show up with parsley crust and jelly, crispy snails and red wine jus, while fish fans might find poached cod with River Exe mussels, marinière velouté and brandade bonbons. It all ends on a high note with bitter chocolate cream with lavender ice cream and candied flowers.

Times 12-2.30/7-9.30 Closed L Mon-Tue, Sat-Sun (by reservation only), D 24-26 Dec

CHURCH STRETTON   Map 15 SO49

The Studio

◉ British, French ☺

Homely village restaurant with a local flavour

☎ 01694 722672
59 High St SY6 6BY
e-mail: info@thestudiorestaurant.net
dir: Off A49 to town, left at T-junct onto High St, 300yds on left

A swinging palette sign greets customers at this erstwhile artist's studio on the high street. The arty theme continues indoors in a stylish room of summery yellow and exposed stone walls hung with artworks and ceramic pieces spread around; on mild summer evenings (this is a dinner-only operation) there's a delicious pocket-sized patio garden overlooking the Shropshire hills for alfresco dining. Run with considerable charm by chef-patrons Tony and Sheila Martland, the culinary focus is broadly modern British, unpretentious dishes with plenty of local input, although that doesn't preclude pan-fried scallops as a starter (since Shropshire is not known for

its shellfish), served with smoked salmon, and white wine, mustard and cheese velouté. Local Mortimer Forest venison could star in a main course, partnered by red cabbage, pickled pears, and a blackberry and port wine jus. Sheila's warm ginger parkin with poached rhubarb, vanilla ice cream and butterscotch sauce is a fortifying finale.

Chef Tony Martland **Owner** Tony & Sheila Martland **Times** 7-9 Closed 2 wks Jan, 1 wk Apr, 1 wk Nov, Sun-Wed, L all week **Prices** Fixed D 3 course £29.50-£36, Service optional **Wines** 6 bottles over £30, 33 bottles under £30, 6 by glass **Notes** Vegetarian available, Dress restrictions, Smart casual **Seats** 34 **Children** Portions **Parking** On street parking available

GRINSHILL   Map 15 SJ52

The Inn at Grinshill

◉◉ Modern British

Village coaching inn with inventive modern British cooking

☎ 01939 220410 & 07730 066451
High St SY4 3BL
e-mail: info@theinnatgrinshill.co.uk
web: www.theinnatgrinshill.co.uk
dir: 7m N of Shrewsbury towards Whitchurch on A49

Handily placed for stocking its larder with Shropshire's splendid bounty, this Georgian coaching inn now trades as a switched-on 21st-century restaurant with rooms. It's something of an inn for all seasons, welcoming all comers, whether you're piling into the pubby Elephant and Castle Bar with muddy boots off the local hills, or looking all sophisticated with a glass of pre-dinner fizz in the slick Bubbles Bar. The mood in the contemporary-styled restaurant is unbuttoned, and an open hatch lets you keep tabs on the talented young kitchen team as they turn out imaginative, up-to-date country-pub cooking. Staff are helpful and clued-up, which is a boon since the laconic menu merely lists the components of each dish, so a quail starter arrives as a pasty-like Wellington served with confit leg and wilted spinach, while crayfish risotto is enriched with creamy lobster bisque and pointed up with lemon and coriander. It all stays inventive through to a deconstructed Black Forest gâteau dessert involving chocolate mousse, cherries and cubes of cherry jelly.

Times 12-2.30/6.30-9.30 Closed Mon, D Sun

HADNALL   Map 15 SJ52

Saracens at Hadnall

◉◉ Modern British ☺

Modish cooking at village restaurant with rooms

☎ 01939 210877
Shrewsbury Rd SY4 4AG
e-mail: reception@saracensathadnall.co.uk
web: www.saracensathadnall.co.uk
dir: M54 onto A5, at junct of A5/A49 take A49 towards Whitchurch. Follow A49 to Hadnall, diagonally opposite church

This rather fine looking red-brick Georgian coaching inn is on good form these days. It's surely never looked better. There's a traditional bar with lots of burnished oak and leather sofas to sink into, but the pièce de résistance is the fine-dining restaurant, headed up by Jason Hodnett. There are two dining rooms, both modishly done out, one being a conservatory with a 40-foot-deep well. The food is ambitious, creative and confidently executed, and there's a good deal of regional produce on the menu, including meat from the owners' south Shropshire farm. The presence of two tasting menus shows the get-up-and-go of the kitchen, whilst the carte is sensibly short and focused. Start, perhaps, with Cornish mackerel tartar with yoghurt, lime, sesame and soy, or a luscious soup such as one of parsley velouté with thyme jelly and truffled cream cheese. Main-course belly of Welsh pork comes with Jerusalem artichokes, red-wine infused scallop, prune and Armagnac jus, and, for dessert, Irish stout might turn up in a pannacotta with accompanying blackcurrant sorbet.

Chef Jason Hodnett **Owner** Ben & Steve Christie **Times** 12-2.30/7-9.30 Closed 26 Dec-2 Jan, D Sun **Prices** Fixed L 2 course £19.95, Fixed D 3 course £22.95, Tasting menu £40-£55, Starter £6.50-£8.25, Main £14.95-£20.95, Dessert £5-£6.95, Service optional **Wines** 7 bottles over £30, 27 bottles under £30, 10 by glass **Notes** Sunday L, Vegetarian available, Dress restrictions, Smart casual **Seats** 45 **Children** Portions **Parking** 20

IRONBRIDGE — Map 10 SJ60

Restaurant Severn

◎◎ British, French 🍷

Country cooking beside the Ironbridge gorge

☎ 01952 432233
33 High St TF8 7AG
web: www.restaurantsevern.co.uk
dir: Travelling along High St pass Restaurant Severn on right, to mini rbdt, take 3rd exit onto Waterloo St, continue 50mtrs to car park on left

Eric and Beb Bruce's small neighbourhood restaurant blends in unobtrusively with the terrace of souvenir and tea shops facing Abraham Darby's World Heritage cast iron bridge. Inside, however, sunny yellow walls, bare wooden floors, unclothed tables and high-backed toffee leather chairs make for an intimate brasserie look. The supply lines to local producers are good in these parts, and full advantage is taken of the local larder, supplemented by home-grown organic seasonal materials from their own smallholding. Classical French influences are evident in starters such as a smooth chicken liver and malt whisky parfait served with red onion marmalade and melba toast, while mains plough a similarly simple and unfussy furrow, partnering medallions of Shropshire venison saddle with braised red cabbage, and Cognac and sun-dried cranberry sauce. Puddings are Beb Bruce's domain - perhaps dark Belgian chocolate délice with chocolate cannelloni - or you might be tempted by a platter of Shropshire cheeses served with home-made chutney and Beb's spiced bread.

Chef Eric & Beb Bruce **Owner** Eric & Beb Bruce **Times** 12-2/6.30-8.30 Closed BHs, Mon-Tue, L Wed-Sat, D Sun **Prices** Fixed L 2 course £16.95, Fixed D 3 course £25.95-£28.95, Service optional, Groups min 8 service 10% **Wines** 6 by glass **Notes** Monthly Gourmet evenings, Sunday L, Vegetarian available, Dress restrictions, Smart casual **Seats** 30 **Children** Portions **Parking** On street & car park opposite

LUDLOW — Map 10 SO57

La Bécasse

Rosettes not confirmed at time of going to print – see below

The Clive Bar & Restaurant with Rooms

◎◎ Modern British 🍷

Smart, modish cooking on Robert Clive's former estate

☎ 01584 856565 & 856665
Bromfield SY8 2JR
e-mail: info@theclive.co.uk
web: www.theclive.co.uk
dir: 2m N of Ludlow on A49, near Ludlow Golf Club, racecourse & adjacent to Ludlow food centre

Just off the A49 outside Ludlow, the converted farmhouse stands on an estate that once belonged to Clive of India. Uncovered wood is the modish decorative theme for both floors and tables, while the aubergine and sea-green walls are contrastingly smothered in pictures. Stephen Bennett has taken over the reins in the kitchen, and is clearly well capable of maintaining the technically polished, inventive British cooking for which the place has become noted. Seared Cornish scallops are partnered

---

La Bécasse

Rosettes not confirmed at time of going to print

LUDLOW — MAP 10 SO57

Modern French V

Thrilling modern cooking in charming 17th-century building

☎ 01584 872325
17 Corve St SY8 1DA
e-mail: info@labecasse.co.uk
dir: In town centre opposite Feathers Hotel, at bottom of hill

Please note: the Rosette award for this establishment has been suspended due to a change of chef. Reassessment will take place in due course under the new chef.

Number 17 Corve Street has long served as a culinary destination and, under the auspices of chef-patron Will Holland since 2007, the address goes from strength to strength. Part of Alan Murchison's powerhouse 10 in 8 Group, La Bécasse delivers exquisitely crafted food. The one-time coaching inn, dating from the 17th century, looks very smart with its oak panels, exposed brickwork and warren of interconnecting rooms. There's no hint of stuffiness here, though, helped by the extremely engaging service team. The smartly laid tables are well spaced, giving plenty of room to breathe, and there's now a private dining room called 'The Vault' with views into the kitchen and its own bespoke tasting menu. Will Holland takes supremely good quality produce, a good deal of which is very local indeed, and creates dishes of dynamism and bravura in the modern manner. You know you're in safe hands when a selection of rolls arrives straight from the oven - wild garlic and cheese, perhaps - along with some amuse-bouche such as chicken satay coated in coriander and lemongrass. It is the technical proficiency of the cooking and the intelligent combinations of flavours that distinguish the food here. First-course freshly picked Devon crab is as fresh and flavoursome as can be, served with four lightly spiced cod cakes, and perfectly partnered with a pickled papaya salsa. Main-course roast Herefordshire sirloin is impeccably tender, with a supporting cast that includes cauliflower as purée and beignet, and Shropshire blue cheese dauphinoise. The caramel soufflé is as light and well-risen as any you'll find, and the accompanying toasted marshmallows, popcorn and clotted cream ice cream are welcome additions - a stellar finale. It's not quite the finale, actually, for there are fab petits fours, too.

Owner Alan Murchison Restaurants Ltd **Times** 12-2/7-9.30 Closed Xmas-New Year, Mon, L Tue, D Sun **Prices** Fixed L 2 course £26, Fixed D 3 course £60, Tasting menu £65, Starter £15, Main £30, Dessert £15, Service added but optional 12.5% **Wines** 142 bottles over £30, 8 bottles under £30, 20 by glass **Notes** Tasting menu 7 course, Vegetarian menu, Dress restrictions, Smart casual **Seats** 40, Pr/dining room 14 **Children** Portions **Parking** 6

Save on Hotels. Book at **theAA.com/hotel**

SHROPSHIRE 421 **ENGLAND**

in classic fashion with a curry emulsion, along with warm potato, tomato and coriander to start, although you may be tempted instead by the confit duck leg terrine with smoked duck breast, mandarin, hibiscus and parsnip. A tranche of excellent sea bass arrives with crushed new potatoes with black olives, roasted salsify, sweet button onions and crab and saffron vinaigrette for main, and to finish it's a tough contest between the Bakewell tart with Seville orange marmalade and clotted cream ice cream, and the warm dark chocolate fondant with chocolate tuile and pistachio ice cream.

Chef Stephen Bennett **Owner** Paul & Barbara Brooks **Times** 12-3/6.30-10 Closed 25-26 Dec **Prices** Starter £5.50-£8.95, Main £10.95-£21.95, Dessert £5.50-£6.95, Service optional **Wines** 15 bottles over £30, 54 bottles under £30, 9 by glass **Notes** Sunday L £10.95-£12.95, Vegetarian available **Seats** 90 **Children** Portions **Parking** 80

Dinham Hall Hotel

◉◉ Modern British ◉

Opulent modern British cooking opposite the castle

☎ 01584 876464
By the Castle, Dinham SY8 1EJ
e-mail: info@dinhamhall.com
dir: Town centre, off Market Place, opposite Ludlow Castle

If you're contemplating a pilgrimage to Shropshire's foodie mecca of Ludlow, Dinham Hall is a dapper Georgian house cheek-by-jowl with the ruined medieval castle above the looping River Teme. All of the requisite oak floors, lofty plasterwork ceilings and bay windows are present and correct, but when you step into the glassed-over brasserie, it is fast forward to the contemporary world of clean-cut design and bare wooden tables. Wayne Smith's kitchen team also takes a clean, modern approach, drafting in prime seasonal produce from the local area to shine in a fine-tuned starter of ballottine of salmon, cucumber and crème fraîche. At main course, the unmistakable French accent continues in a loin of lamb with peas and bacon, boulangère potatoes and red wine sauce. Invention and flair continue through to dessert, as witnessed in a luscious trio of caramel parfait, banana bread and chocolate ice cream.

Chef Wayne Smith **Owner** Metzo Hotels Ltd **Times** 12.30-2.30/6.30-9.30 **Prices** Fixed D 3 course fr £39.95, Service added but optional 10% **Wines** 8 by glass **Notes** Sunday L **Seats** 36, Pr/dining room 60 **Parking** 16, On street

The Feathers Hotel

◉ British, European

Modern British cooking in 'the most handsome inn in the world' (official)

☎ 01584 875261
Bull Ring SY8 1AA
e-mail: enquiries@feathersatludlow.co.uk
web: www.feathersatludlow.co.uk
dir: from A49 follow town centre signs to centre. Hotel on left

The intricate timber-framed Jacobean façade of The Feathers is certainly a head-turning piece of woodwork: Pevsner bigs it up in *The Buildings of England*, and according to the *New York Times*, it is 'the most handsome inn in the world'. Luckily there is more to it than a handsome frontage, as the interior lives up to its promise with carved fireplaces, ornate 17th-century plaster ceilings and enough timbers to build a galleon. The restaurant's blackened beams, exposed stone walls and flagstones set the scene for sound contemporary cooking from a kitchen that delivers the goods. The quality of local raw materials is evident in starters such as pheasant and rabbit terrine with apple and celery chutney, while mains could team roast loin of venison with roast root vegetables, sweet potato mash, and a blackberry and red wine reduction. Finish with tarte Tatin with apple sorbet and cinnamon crème anglaise.

Chef Stuart Forman **Owner** Ceney Developments **Times** 7-9 Closed L all week **Prices** Fixed D 3 course £39.95-£41.45, Service optional, Groups min 12 service 10% **Wines** 7 bottles over £30, 30 bottles under £30, 10 by glass **Notes** Vegetarian available, Dress restrictions, Smart casual, Civ Wed 80 **Seats** 50, Pr/dining room 30 **Children** Portions, Menu **Parking** 36

Fishmore Hall

◉◉◉ – *see page 422*

Overton Grange Hotel and Restaurant

◉◉ Modern British ◉

Classic French cooking and attentive service in Ludlow

☎ 01584 873500
Old Hereford Rd SY8 4AD
e-mail: info@overtongrangehotel.com
dir: M5 junct 5. On B4361 approx 1.5m from Ludlow towards Leominster

This elegant Edwardian house in the Shropshire hills outside Ludlow has a recently built spa, pool and treatment room to further boost the feelgood factor. The dining room looks good too, with its lavender-shaded walls, and chocolate-coloured leather chairs at tables draped in floor-length linen, while the cooking is in the capable hands of head chef Thomas Jacks, who largely follows a classic French path which fits in nicely with the traditional country-house feel of the place. Feuillette of langoustine, buttered baby spinach and 'crustace coulis' to begin is typical of the style, or there might be chocolate raviolis of game in a fresh girolle mushroom velouté. Next up, perhaps a classic cassoulet of quail with Spanish white beans, or paupiette of wild sea bass with a red mullet farce. A rhubarb cup with lemon bavarois makes a refreshing, fruity finish in season, or you could go for a more indulgent croustillant of white chocolate with griottine cherry.

Chef Thomas Jacks **Owner** Metzo Hotels Ltd **Times** 12-2.30/7-9.30 **Prices** Fixed D 3 course fr £42.50, Tasting menu fr £59.50, Service added but optional 10%, Groups min 10 service 10% **Wines** 12 by glass **Notes** Sunday L, Vegetarian available, Dress restrictions, Smart casual, Civ Wed 100 **Seats** 40, Pr/dining room 24 **Parking** 50

Fishmore Hall

Modern European V

Compelling modern cooking in luxurious boutique hotel

☎ 01584 875148
Fishmore Rd SY8 3DP
e-mail: reception@fishmorehall.co.uk
web: www.fishmorehall.co.uk
dir: A49 from Shrewsbury, follow Ludlow & Bridgnorth signs. 1st left towards Bridgnorth, at next rdbt left onto Fishmore Rd. Hotel 0.5m on right after golf course

A Georgian country-house on a civilised scale, Fishmore Hall is a Shropshire gem. Its position in lush green countryside overlooking Ludlow helps set the tone, whilst the charming and stylish interior confirms its status as a first-class stopover, and a newly added NSpa treatment cabin in the grounds is another string to its boutique bow. The hotel's restaurant - in an orangery - has a new name too, Forelles, in honour of the pear trees in the garden. There are good views of said garden from Forelles, with its smartly laid tables and flickering candles, and better still from the terrace if you're lucky enough with the weather to sit outside. Head chef David Jaram draws inspiration from the surrounding landscape, sourcing a good deal of his ingredients from the farmers and artisan producers of the Shropshire Marches (seafood comes from Brixham

and Skye). There are six- and nine-course tasting menus to choose from, plus excellent vegetarian versions, and an à la carte, each packed with enticing and dynamic contemporary dishes. A first course crab, chilli and lime salad, for example, comes with warm potted shrimps and a chervil bavarois in a clever and compelling combination. Main-course monkfish is served with a cucumber and spring onion risotto, frogs' legs and ginger and lemongrass, or there might be saddle of rabbit with peanuts, tarragon and lime. These are bold, confident, modern dishes. Dessert might turn up a banana and custard slice with peanut ice cream, which, again, shows acute technical skills, or there is the hard to resist selection of artisan cheeses from the region, served with fig and almond cake, quince, warm fruit and nut bread and home-made biscuits.

Chef David Jaram **Owner** Laura Penman
Times 12-2.30/7-9.30 Closed D Sun, BH
Prices Fixed L 2 course fr £20, Fixed D 3 course fr £49, Tasting menu £59-£69, Service optional, Groups min 10 service 10% **Wines** 52 bottles over £30, 16 bottles under £30, 12 by glass
Notes Tasting menu 6/9 course, Vegetarian 2/3/6/9 course £30-£60, Sunday L, Vegetarian menu, Dress restrictions, Smart casual, Civ Wed 130
Seats 40, Pr/dining room 20
Children Portions, Menu **Parking** 36

Save on Hotels. Book at theAA.com/hotel

SHROPSHIRE 423 ENGLAND

Goldstone Hall

◎◎ Modern British 🍴

Modern British ideas in a manor-house hotel

☎ 01630 661202
Goldstone Rd, Goldstone TF9 2NA
e-mail: enquiries@goldstonehall.com
dir: 4m S of Market Drayton off A529 signed Goldstone
Hall Hotel. 4m N of Newport signed from A41

A Georgian manor house built around a medieval core, Goldstone is to be found a little off the A41, to the southeast of Market Drayton. It sits in beautifully tended gardens, which are well worth a wander. With a copiously productive kitchen garden and meat from neighbouring farms to call on, the culinary team keeps it eyes on the prize. The Orangery is the setting for informal eating, while the full-dress version happens in the handsome panelled dining room with its Arts and Crafts fireplace. A classically based menu works to the modern British template of rejigging familiar ideas in inventive ways, so that roast breast of pigeon comes with lentil and foie gras cromesqui and girolles in thyme jus to start, followed perhaps by halibut with lobster risotto in shellfish dressing, or roast breast of guinea fowl with a chicken and wild mushroom boudin and cep purée, sauced with Madeira. Baked desserts such as plum soufflé with bourbon ice cream are the alternative to a listing of pedigree British and Irish cheeses.

Chef Andrew McGeorge **Owner** John Cushing & Helen Ward **Times** 11-3/7-10 **Prices** Fixed L 2 course fr £22.50, Fixed D 3 course fr £26, Starter £7.50-£14.50, Main £16.50-£30, Dessert fr £8.95, Service optional **Wines** 30 bottles over £30, 70 bottles under £30, 15 by glass **Notes** Sunday L, Vegetarian available, Civ Wed 100 **Seats** 60, Pr/dining room 14 **Children** Portions **Parking** 70

Ternhill Farm House & The Cottage Restaurant

◎◎ Modern International 🍴

Ambitious cooking in homely Georgian farmhouse

☎ 01630 638984
Ternhill TF9 3PX
e-mail: info@ternhillfarm.co.uk
web: www.ternhillfarm.co.uk
dir: On junct A53 & A41, archway off A53 to back of
property

Mike and Jo Abraham have been hard at work for the last decade, unleashing a top-to-bottom facelift on their red-brick Georgian farmhouse and giving the place a new lease of life as a smart restaurant with rooms. The dining room occupies the old kitchen, complete with Aga, where they have pulled off a clean-cut modern look, blending original oak beams and pine flooring with leather seats and bare wooden tables, and custard yellow walls hung with mirrors and eclectic art. The cooking takes a hearty, crowd-pleasing approach, relying on the excellent quality

of the local and home-grown ingredients for its effect. A complex beetroot medley delivers chilli-spiced beetroot soup with chive cream, chilled beetroot and orange-cured salmon with mustard and lime dressing, and goats' cheese and beetroot bruschetta, while main course is another multi-faceted dish involving pan-fried partridge breast wrapped in honey-cured bacon, slow-braised leg, pheasant confit, rabbit, venison and pigeon with plum jus, spiced red cabbage, thyme dauphinoise potato and quince jelly.

Chef Michael Abraham **Owner** Michael & Joanne Abraham **Times** 6.30-mdnt Closed L all week, D Sun-Mon **Prices** Fixed D 2 course £14.95, Starter £4.50-£7.25, Main £11.95-£22.95, Dessert £4.95-£7.25, Service optional, Groups min 8 service 10% **Wines** 6 bottles over £30, 37 bottles under £30, 6 by glass **Notes** Fixed D 2 course available Tue-Fri, Credit cards 2% charge, Sunday L, Vegetarian available, Dress restrictions, Smart casual **Seats** 22, Pr/dining room 14 **Parking** 16

Raven Hotel

◎◎ British, Mediterranean

Ambitious cooking in the home of the Olympic Games (really)

☎ 01952 727251
30 Barrow St TF13 6EN
e-mail: enquiry@ravenhotel.com
web: www.ravenhotel.com
dir: 10m SW from Telford on A4169, 12m SE from
Shrewsbury. In town centre

Before the Olympic shenanigans in 2012 publicised the fact more widely, not a lot of people knew that the modern games started off in Much Wenlock, when local GP, William Penny Brookes, organised an Olympian event here in 1850. The 17th-century Raven no doubt played its part in refreshing the athletes back then, and continues the tradition nowadays in a smartly-updated setting. Venerable beams, log fires, and hand-pulled ales make for a cheerfully pubby vibe, while the kitchen hauls in splendid Shropshire produce as the backbone of its appealing repertoire. Sea bass and mullet escabèche might be served with a chilli and vegetable broth, then a sorbet offers breathing space before the main event - perhaps rack of Stottesdon lamb with fondant potato and pea and redcurrant fricassée, or pan-fried venison loin with boulangère potato, and creamed celeriac and bacon. Puddings such as double chocolate cheesecake with raspberry ripple ice cream aim straight at the comfort zone, if you're not tempted towards the splendid local artisan cheeses.

Chef Kirk Heywood, Steve Biggs **Owner** Kirk Heywood, Sheila Hartshorn **Times** 12-2.30/6.45-9.30 Closed 25 Dec **Prices** Fixed D 3 course £33, Starter £4.95-£8.95, Main £8.25-£13.95, Dessert £5.95-£6.25, Service optional **Wines** 14 by glass **Seats** 40, Pr/dining room 14 **Parking** 30

Crown Country Inn

◎◎ Modern British 🍴

Classy cooking in old village inn

☎ 01584 841205
SY7 9ET
e-mail: info@crowncountryinn.co.uk
dir: On B4368 between Craven Arms & Much Wenlock

A typical old English village coaching inn, the Crown has the usual exposed beams, inglenooks and flagstone floors. No surprises there, then. What elevates the place well above the gastro-pub norm is the quality of the food served in the upstairs restaurant. The kitchen works around a modern English style based on a well-mastered traditional repertoire, sourcing seasonal local produce in the process. Start with home-made bacon and herb black pudding with tomatoes topped with farm bacon, or a crisp fishcake of haddock, leeks and smoked cheese with chilli and tomato jam. Main courses are never over-elaborate, so flavours are clear: mushroom and barley risotto for smoked chicken breast with chorizo and chive sauce, say, and mushy peas and straw potatoes for crisply fried gurnard fillet with balsamic syrup. Summer may see a pudding like roast nectarine with vanilla pannacotta, the plate streaked with raspberry coulis and dotted with sugared almonds.

Chef Richard Arnold **Owner** Richard & Jane Arnold **Times** 12-2/6.45-8.45 Closed some days during Xmas, Mon, D Sun **Prices** Fixed L 2 course fr £13.50, Fixed D 3 course fr £20, Starter £5.95-£8.95, Main £14.95-£19.95, Dessert £6.50-£7.95, Service optional **Wines** 2 bottles over £30, 29 bottles under £30, 5 by glass **Notes** Sunday L, Vegetarian available **Seats** 65, Pr/dining room 42 **Children** Portions **Parking** 20

The Hundred House Hotel

◎◎ Traditional British, French

Hands-on family hotel where quirky charm meets skilled modern cuisine

☎ 01952 580240
Bridgnorth Rd TF11 9EE
e-mail: reservations@hundredhouse.co.uk
web: www.hundredhouse.co.uk
dir: Midway between Telford & Bridgnorth on A442. In
village of Norton

There are plenty of old Georgian coaching inns around the UK, but the hands-on family who have run Hundred House for a quarter of a century make this one stand out from the pack with a streak of mild eccentricity. There are stained glass Temperance Hall panels at the front door, and if you want to check in and take full advantage of the restaurant's delights, your bedroom will come with a swing hanging from the oak beams. Despite the quirky style, food is taken seriously; reminders of the local larder come in the shape of baskets of pumpkins and squashes,

continued

NORTON *continued*

and bunches of dried herbs are dotted around the warren of characterful rooms making up the bar, brasserie and main restaurant. Shropshire's superb produce, along with a hundred-odd herbs fresh from the kitchen garden, appears in flavour-driven, creative modern ideas; perhaps a platter of home-smoked trout, gravad lax and crab gâteau, grilled mussels and prawn filo, then duck breast with a duck confit and sage pasty and crab apple jelly sauce.

Times 12-2.30/6-9.30 Closed D 25 Dec

OSWESTRY   Map 15 SJ22

Pen-y-Dyffryn Country Hotel

◉◉ Modern British 🍴

Splendid views and superb Welsh produce

☎ 01691 653700
Rhydycroesau SY10 7JD
e-mail: stay@peny.co.uk
web: www.peny.co.uk
dir: 3m W of Oswestry on B4580

Sitting atop a hillside on the Welsh border (on the English side), Pen-y-Dyffryn is a fine Georgian rectory with a smart and intimate restaurant. Its position ensures that walkers will be in their element, but there are less strenuous ways to enjoy the glorious views, such as relaxing with a sundowner, or tea and cake, on the hotel's terrace looking across to the Welsh mountains to the west. The restaurant makes the most of what nature provides, too, with huge sash windows, plus elegant features like a marble mantle piece and ornate dresser. Each table is formally laid with a fresh flower, and what's on the menu is dictated by what local (often organic) produce is up to snuff. So you might start with terrine of Shropshire rose veal (welfare friendly), apricot and pistachio nuts with fig and date chutney and toasted soda bread. Next up, best end of Welsh lamb with gratin dauphinoise, ragoût of courgettes, red peppers and tomato, and a thyme jus, finishing with lemon crème brûlée with pressed Granny Smith apples, buttered shortbread and apple sorbet.

Chef David Morris **Owner** MJM & AA Hunter **Times** 6.45-11 Closed 20 Dec-21 Jan, L all week **Prices** Fixed D 3 course £30-£36, Service optional **Wines** 40 bottles over £30, 40 bottles under £30, 3 by glass **Notes** Vegetarian available **Seats** 25 **Children** Portions, Menu **Parking** 18

Sebastians

◉◉ International, French **NEW** 🍴

Skilled French cooking in boutique venue

☎ 01691 655444
45 Willow St SY11 1AQ
e-mail: sebastians.rest@virgin.net
dir: From town centre turn into Willow St signed Selatyn. Hotel on left in 400yds

Mark and Michelle Fisher have run their boutique restaurant with rooms for a couple of decades, and it

shows in the well-polished professionalism and amiability that pervades the place. The building is a 16th-century inn full of quaint beamed character, but not stuck in the past. For drinks and canapés, choose between a dinky bar or a comfy lounge with sofas and a roaring fire, before moving on to the oak-panelled, apricot-hued dining room with its tobacco leather chairs and crisp white linen. Orient Express-themed artwork hints at the French theme running through the menus: dinner takes you through four courses of well-crafted, Gallic-influenced ideas, or there's a great value market menu for tighter budgets. Pan-fried scallops with haricot cassoulet, red peppers, micro salad and raisin dressing is a cracking starter, followed by lamb (loin and ballottine of braised leg) matched to great effect with smoked aubergine purée, aubergine crisp, and rich jus spiked with goats' cheese. Of-the-moment techniques appear too, as in the sous-vide-cooked strawberries served with lemon pistachio cake and lemon verbena ice cream.

Chef Richard Jones, Mark Fisher **Owner** Mark & Michelle Fisher **Times** 6.30-9.30 Closed 25-26 Dec, 1 Jan, Etr Mon, Sun-Mon, L all week **Prices** Fixed D 3 course £19.95, Service optional **Wines** 40 bottles over £30, 5 bottles under £30, 2 by glass **Notes** 5 course D £39.50, Vegetarian available **Seats** 35 **Children** Portions **Parking** 6, On street

---

Wynnstay Hotel

◉◉ Modern European

Supplier-led cooking in an old coaching inn

☎ 01691 655261
Church St SY11 2SZ
e-mail: info@wynnstayhotel.com
web: www.wynnstayhotel.com
dir: In town centre, opposite church

Formerly a coaching inn for the London-to-Holyhead and Liverpool-to-Cardiff routes, this red-brick Georgian building is now home to over 30 bedrooms and a luxurious fitness club. The traditional Four Seasons restaurant has tables smartly dressed in cream linen with paintings of wine bottles and fruit adorning the walls. Unfussily presented dishes are based on well-sourced ingredients given a modern European spin; thus a generous portion of fresh crab and cucumber cannelloni with coriander, lime and chilli bursts with flavour, and tender roasted saddle of Welsh lamb is accompanied by confit aubergine and tomato, sweetbread beignet and rosemary jus. For those with a sweet tooth, the assiette gourmand's hot chocolate fondant, praline crème brûlée and rhubarb cheesecake will hit the spot.

Times 12-2/7-9.30 Closed 25 Dec

SHIFNAL   Map 10 SJ70

Park House Hotel

◉ Modern European 🍴

Modern cooking in singular market town hotel

☎ 01952 460128
Park St TF11 9BA
e-mail: reception02@parkhousehotel.net
dir: From M54 junct 4 take A464 through Shifnal; hotel 200yds after railway bridge

Two 17th-century country houses, one red-brick, one faced with white stucco have been pasted seamlessly together to make Park House, an upmarket venue in a pleasant Shropshire market town. Period oak panelling and ornate plasterwork combine with a dramatic contemporary colour scheme to provide a classy backdrop in the brasserie-style Butlers restaurant. The kitchen doesn't try to reinvent the wheel here, focusing instead on good quality local produce in a repertoire of straightforward modern European ideas. King scallops with pancetta and pea purée might lead the way, followed by rump of lamb served with Puy lentil and root vegetable cassoulet. At the end, local cheeses compete for your attention with crowd-pleasers such as hot chocolate fondant with pistachio ice cream.

Chef Paul Davies **Owner** Andrew Hughes **Times** noon-10 All-day dining **Prices** Fixed L 2 course £16.95, Fixed D 3 course £19.95, Starter £6.50-£7.95, Main £14.50-£22.95, Dessert £5.50-£7.50, Service optional **Wines** 7 bottles over £30, 24 bottles under £30, 10 by glass **Notes** Sunday L, Vegetarian available, Dress restrictions, Smart casual preferred, Civ Wed 180 **Seats** 50, Pr/dining room 180 **Children** Portions, Menu **Parking** 100

SHREWSBURY   Map 15 SJ41

Albright Hussey Manor Hotel & Restaurant

◉◉ Modern British 🍴

Medieval manor with refined contemporary cooking

☎ 01939 290571
Ellesmere Rd, Broad Oak SY4 3AF
e-mail: info@albrighthussey.co.uk
web: www.albrighthussey.co.uk
dir: 2.5m N of Shrewsbury on A528, follow signs for Ellesmere

The medieval manor, reached across a stone bridge, is actually a building of two halves: a timber-framed house next to a brick and stone wing. Inside are all the ancient features expected in a property of this age, the restaurant a chintzy, beamed room with a huge inglenook and period memorabilia like helmets and shields. There's nothing old-school about the menus, which list all the suppliers of top-quality materials. Leek and potato broth with three tortellini stuffed with smoked chicken is the sort of ambitious, successful starter to expect in winter, or there may be a blini with crabmeat and grapefruit salad. Loin of local venison, cooked pink, is imaginatively - even

Save on Hotels. Book at **theAA.com/hotel**

SHROPSHIRE 425 **ENGLAND**

daringly - crusted with praline and thyme and accompanied by hazelnut and celeriac purée to make a good balance of flavours and textures. A fish option might be roast fillet of sea bass with orzo pasta and ratatouille, and soufflés should not be overlooked, among them orange and Cointreau with lemon sorbet.

Chef Michel Nijsten **Owner** Franco, Vera & Paul Subbiani **Times** 12-2.15/7-10 **Prices** Fixed L 2 course £17.50-£24.50, Fixed D 3 course £24.50-£32.50, Tasting menu £45, Starter £5.95-£10.25, Main £15.50-£22.75, Service optional, Groups min 6 service 10% **Wines** 25 bottles over £30, 35 bottles under £30, 14 by glass **Notes** Tasting menu available, Sunday L, Vegetarian available, Dress restrictions, No jeans, trainers or T-shirts **Seats** 80, Pr/dining room 40 **Children** Portions **Parking** 100

Draper's Hall

◎◎ Modern, Traditional

Updated classic cooking in a medieval dining room

☎ 01743 344679
10 Saint Mary's Place SY1 1DZ
e-mail: goodfood@drapershallrestaurant.co.uk
dir: From A5191 (St Mary's St) on one-way system into St Mary's Place

Dating back to 1556, Draper's Hall restaurant with rooms is situated in the heart of Shrewsbury and offers the chance to dine in a lovingly restored period building. It's proud to be one of the oldest buildings in the market town, as evinced by its grand inglenook fireplaces, old wooden beams, medieval floors and wood-panelled walls. Striking candelabras dominate white-clothed tables with their tartan wool chairs. Ella Fitzgerald playing softly in the background adds to the civilised vibe. When it comes to the menu, tried and tested combinations benefit from some additional fashionable touches, so foams and jellies may crop up here and there. Roast quail, celeriac and vanilla purée and game jus is brimming with earthy flavours and might come before Cornish black bream with crab risotto and fish velouté, or a rib-sticking tartiflette with Reblochon cheese, potatoes and cream. Finish with a decadent dessert of baked dark chocolate, frangipane, cherries and amaretto ice cream.

Times 11-3.30/6-9.30 Closed D Sun

Lion & Pheasant Hotel

◎◎ British ◎

Vibrant brasserie cooking in a townhouse hotel

☎ 01743 770345
49-50 Wyle Cop SY1 1XJ
e-mail: info@lionandpheasant.co.uk
web: www.lionandpheasant.co.uk

The Lion & Pheasant, in Shrewsbury's historic town centre, is these days a hot-looking contemporary boutique townhouse hotel. The dove-grey façade offers a foretaste of the pared-back setting within: tongue-and-groove-panelled walls, chunky bleached wood tables and blond wood flooring all combine in a minimal look which you might call New England-style beachcomber chic, were it not for areas of bare brick and ancient gnarled beams as a reminder of the venerable age of this historic inn. The cooking works with the setting, delivering modern brasserie-style dishes that deploy British ingredients to telling effect. You might kick off with a skilfully-wrought idea such as pigeon breast partnered with clementine, medjool date and endive salad, and pistachio dressing, then follow with pan-fried fillet of brill with oxtail tortellini, winter greens and roast garlic sauce, or a tasting plate of Gloucestershire Old Spot pork with mustard mash, sage and sauce soubise, and roasting juices. Close the show with tarte Tatin and brown butter ice cream.

Chef Matthew Strefford **Owner** Jim Littler **Times** 12-2.30/6-9.30 Closed 25 Dec **Prices** Starter £6-£12, Main £14-£26, Dessert £6-£8, Service optional **Wines** 105 bottles over £30, 70 bottles under £30, 14 by glass **Notes** Early bird menu Mon-Thu 6-7pm 2/3 course £17/£22, Sunday L, Vegetarian available, Dress restrictions, Smart casual **Seats** 35, Pr/dining room 45 **Children** Portions, Menu **Parking** 14, NCP opposite

Mad Jack's Restaurant & Bar

◎ Modern British V

Modern brasserie food in the town centre

☎ 01743 358870
15 St Mary's St SY1 1EQ
e-mail: info@madjacks.uk.com
dir: In Shrewsbury town centre, on the one-way system, almost opposite St Mary's Church

Old Mad Jack himself would surely approve of what they've done with the place: he was a bit of a bon viveur by all accounts, back in the 18th century, but pushed it a little too far, hence the moniker. MJ's, as it is known, has a

cracking location right in the centre of town in a charming period building, but inside there's a thoroughly satisfying contemporary finish. Walls are hung with cartoon sketches of the man himself, and the courtyard garden is a hit in fair weather. The brasserie-style menu is packed with well-sourced ingredients - suppliers duly name-checked. Start with tempura of Perl Wen brie with pear chutney and Wenlock Edge pancetta, before moving on to 'A Taste of Shropshire' - ginger beer-infused pork belly and fillet with celeriac and mustard purée, apple fritter, ham hock hash and ginger beer jus, or a steak from the grill.

Chef Chris Geisler **Owner** Ann & Danny Ditella **Times** 12-10 Closed 25-26 Dec **Prices** Starter £5.50-£8, Main £10-£25, Dessert £6-£7 **Wines** 12 by glass **Notes** Sunday L, Vegetarian menu **Seats** 60, Pr/dining room 30 **Children** Portions **Parking** Town centre

Mytton & Mermaid Hotel

◎◎ Modern British V

Riverside setting and a true Shropshire flavour

☎ 01743 761220
Atcham SY5 6QG
e-mail: reception@myttonandmermaid.co.uk
web: www.myttonandmermaid.co.uk
dir: Just outside Shrewsbury on B4380 (old A5). Opposite NT Attingham Park

Named after a local reprobate who squandered his fortune, the Mytton & Mermaid is a creeper-clad Georgian coaching inn in a lovely spot near the Atcham Bridge on the banks of the River Severn close to Shrewsbury. The riverside tables are a magnet for a pre-dinner drink on a fine day, before moving into the elegant restaurant, which has the feel of a relaxed country house with its linen-clothed antique oak tables, gilt mirrors on terracotta walls and bare wooden floors. The kitchen shows ambition, putting together seasonal menus of modern British ideas built on a good showing of local materials. Start, perhaps, with pan-seared scallops with celeriac and truffle purée, warm apple jelly and bacon powder, before considering a venison 'mixed grill' comprising pan-fried loin, faggot, cottage pie, bonbon of fillet, roast beets, parsnip purée, rösti potato and game jus. Sloe gin crème brûlée with damson ice cream, shortbread crumble and blackberries is typical of the vibrantly flavoured desserts.

Chef Adrian Badland **Owner** Mr & Mrs Ditella **Times** 12-2.30/6.30-10 Closed 25 Dec, D 26 Dec, 1 Jan **Prices** Service optional **Wines** 12 by glass **Notes** Sunday L fr £18.95, Vegetarian menu, Civ Wed 90 **Seats** 100, Pr/dining room 12 **Children** Portions, Menu **Parking** 80

TELFORD | Map 10 SJ60

Chez Maw Restaurant

◉◉ Modern British V

Modern British food near the Ironbridge

☎ 01952 432247
Best Western Valley Hotel, Buildwas Rd TF8 7DW
e-mail: info@thevalleyhotel.co.uk
dir: M6/M54 from junct 6 take A5223 to Ironbridge for
4m. At mini island right, hotel 80yds on left

The polite chink of teacups has replaced the bedlam of heavy industry in Ironbridge these days, so go with the flow and explore the Coalbrookdale World Heritage area from this lovely Georgian mansion on the banks of the River Severn. The house was the Maws family's reward for their part in the industrial revolution when they kept the Victorian world supplied with lovely ceramic tiles. Updated in a soft-focus contemporary vein with warm tones of peach and caramel, bare wooden floors and tables, and modern art on the walls, the restaurant makes a fine end to a day around Ironbridge's museums. The wide-ranging menu of European-influenced dishes works throughout, thanks to a dedication to well-sourced local ingredients, which appear in a starter of pressed ham hock terrine teamed with black pudding beignets, piccalilli purée and quail's egg. Next up, roast butter-basted chicken with mushroom pâté, swede and potato dauphinoise, butternut squash purée and Madeira jus all comes together a treat, and chocolate brownie with peanut butter ice cream, caramelised peanuts and chocolate sauce ends on a high note.

Chef Barry Workman **Owner** Philip & Leslie Casson
Times 12-2/7-9.30 Closed 26 Dec-2 Jan, L Sat-Sun
Prices Fixed L 2 course fr £14.50, Starter £4.95-£7.25,
Main £12.95-£19.95, Dessert £4.95-£6.25, Service
optional **Wines** 2 bottles over £30, 37 bottles under £30,
7 by glass **Notes** Vegetarian menu, Dress restrictions,
Smart casual, Civ Wed 120 **Seats** 50, Pr/dining room 30
Children Portions, Menu **Parking** 100

Church Farm Guest House & Basil's Restaurant

◉ Modern British 🌱

Charming service and well-judged menu

☎ 01952 251927
Wrockwardine Village, Wellington TF6 5DG
e-mail: info@churchfarm-shropshire.co.uk
dir: M54 junct 7 towards Wellington, 1st left, 1st right,
right at end of road. 0.5m on left opposite St Peter's
Church

This family-run Georgian farmhouse has four bedrooms and a genuinely homely approach to hospitality. Basil's Restaurant, named after the family's obliging Staffordshire bull terrier, takes a flexible approach to proceedings. It's unlicensed - BYO - with a glowing fire in winter and lovely views out over the village and church. Martin Board does all of the cooking and dinner is served dinner-party style. On the regularly-changing menu you'll

find lots splendid Shropshire produce supplemented by Brixham fish; start with Jerusalem artichoke soup with confit duck ragoût, followed by fillet of venison with pickled red cabbage, butternut squash purée, toasted walnuts and red wine reduction, and finish in style with apple trifle with cider granita and doughnuts.

Chef Martin Board **Owner** Melanie & Martin Board
Times 7-close Closed Sat-Mon, L all week, D Sun
Prices Fixed D 3 course £30-£40, Service optional
Notes Sunday L, Vegetarian available **Seats** 12, Pr/dining
room 18 **Children** Portions **Parking** 10

SOMERSET

AXBRIDGE | Map 4 ST45

The Oak House

◉◉ Modern British NEW 🌱

A happy blend of rusticity and refinement in a chic restaurant with rooms

☎ 01934 732444
The Square BS26 2AP
e-mail: info@theoakhousesomerset.com
dir: M5 junct 22 onto A38 north, turn right to Axbridge,
signed

This stylish restaurant with rooms is a fine example of a characterful historic building given a classy contemporary spin for 21st century guests. High-beamed ceilings, exposed stone walls, flagstoned floors and rustic scrubbed wood tables tick all the right boxes for in-vogue aesthetics, while the kitchen turns out food that walks an intelligent line between earthy traditions and current culinary trends. The young, talented and enthusiastic team shows a clear passion for quality materials, supported by the technical wherewithal to coax the best out of it all. Bath chap and langoustine delivers a tender slice of pork cheek with a single fat crustacean, caramelised onion purée, quail's egg and quince, ahead of roast loin of venison with diced chorizo and potato haggerty well-matched with glazed onions and the sharp tang of blackberries. End with prune and Armagnac parfait with grape compôte and vanilla ice cream, or well-chosen West Country cheeses.

Chef Newstead Sayer **Owner** Hannah Brown
Times 12-2/6-9 Closed 2-3 Jan, L Mon-Wed, D Sun & Mon
Prices Fixed L 2 course £16, Starter £7-£9.50, Main
£14-£21, Dessert £7-£8.50, Service optional **Wines** 2
bottles over £30, 16 bottles under £30, 5 by glass
Notes Sunday L £9.95-£17.95, Vegetarian available
Seats 22 **Children** Portions, Menu **Parking** 100mtrs

BATH | Map 4 ST76

Abbey Hotel Bath

◉◉◉ – *see opposite*

The Bath Priory Hotel, Restaurant & Spa

◉◉◉ – *see opposite*

The Chequers

◉ Modern British NEW

Period pub with confident cooking

☎ 01225 360017
50 Rivers St BA1 2QA
e-mail: info@thechequersbath.com

This corner pub not far from the Royal Crescent and dating from 1776 has plenty of Georgian style and a focus on food. There's no lack of pub-like charm with its parquet floor, benches and wooden tables, and you can pop upstairs to the small dining room if you're in the mood for a little more refinement (soft lighting, flowers on the tables, and the like). Wherever you choose to sit, the menu is ambitious and full of good things. Start, perhaps, with confit sea trout with crispy egg, celeriac remoulade, beetroot, olives and fine beans, or rabbit with asparagus custard and bacon. These are well constructed dishes with bang-on flavours. Main-course haunch of venison comes with spring onion croquette, onion 'textures' and watercress, and fillet of Cornish hake with clams, pickled girolles, chicken wings and juices. Save room for a superb hot chocolate fondant with chocolate and orange rind mousse and honeycomb ice cream.

Times 12-2.30/6-9.30 **Prices** Fixed L 2 course £12
Notes Fixed L 2/3 course Mon-Fri, Sunday L

The Circus Café and Restaurant

◉ Modern British 🌱

Attention to detail all day long

☎ 01225 466020
34 Brock St BA1 2LN
e-mail: ali@allgolden.co.uk
dir: From West side of The Circus turn into Brock St,
second bldg on right heading towards the Royal Crescent

Bracketed by the great Georgian architectural landmarks of Bath - the eponymous Bath Circus and the iconic Royal Crescent - this trendy venue is rather more posh than its name suggests, with ladies who lunch piling into its classy olive-washed interior to refuel on an eclectic modern British menu of seasonally-driven ideas along the lines of spring nettle and lovage soup with a swirl of truffle cream, and celeriac crisps, or savoury cheddar éclairs filled with twice-baked Bath soft cheese soufflé, and served with roasted vine tomatoes and wild garlic pesto. Turn up for dinner, and a more intimate candlelit mood takes over, and the kitchen sends out starters such as monkfish cheeks with roasted peppers, butter beans, Bath Pig chorizo, and paprika and parsley sauce, followed by rack of lamb with rosemary and sweet garlic crust matched with crushed flageolet beans and red wine gravy. Puddings deliver more well-considered flavour combinations - perhaps rhubarb trifle with layers of vanilla sponge, rhubarb purée, jelly and fool served with honeycomb syllabub.

Chef Alison Golden **Owner** Alison & Geoffrey Golden
Times 10-mdnt Closed 3 wks from 24 Dec, Sun
Prices Fixed L 2 course £14-£19, Fixed D 3 course

continued

Save on Hotels. Book at **theAA.com/hotel**

SOMERSET 427 **ENGLAND**

Abbey Hotel Bath

BATH   MAP 4 ST76

Modern British **NEW**

Cooking out of the top drawer in the centre of the city

☎ 01225 809382
1 North Pde BA1 1LF
e-mail: reservations@abbeyhotelbath.co.uk
web: www.abbeyhotelbath.co.uk
dir: M4 junct 18/A46 for approx 8m. At rdbt right onto A4
for 2m. Once past Morrisons stay in left lane & turn left
at lights. Over bridge & right at lights. Over rdbt & right
at lights. Hotel at end of road

The city has its fair share of landmark buildings of
course, but the Abbey Hotel is no slouch in that
department: it's a fine construction of pristine Bath
stone, and just around the corner from the Pump Rooms
and all the city has to offer. It looks pretty good on the
inside, too, with a smart contemporary finish and
impressive modern artworks on the walls. So far, so good.
The ace in the hole, though, is the Allium Brasserie and
its chef, Chris Staines. Staines has worked at some pretty
plum addresses over the years and is an assured,
confident and creative practitioner of the culinary arts.
Large canvases of vivid contemporary artworks bring
splashes of colour to the well-proportioned restaurant,
with its large Georgian windows and pristine white walls,
and there's plenty of room between the darkwood tables.
The menu is jam-packed with good ideas and compelling
combinations, and everything is made using top quality
seasonal and often local ingredients. It's the kind of food
that doesn't just live up to its billing, it exceeds
expectations. Take a starter such as flame grilled
mackerel with salt and pepper prawns, Asian pickles and
satay sauce - sounds good, right? Well, it is very, very
good. The quality of the fish, the timing of the cooking,
the combination of flavours, everything comes together to
form a winning dish. Another starter to catch your eye
might be quail glazed in chilli and caramel with Chinese
cabbage, hearts of palm, lychee, peanuts and coriander.
Main-course chicken with Jerusalem artichokes sounds
like a happy marriage, and indeed it is, but so much
more: a complex construction of flavours and textures
that takes one's breath away. And for dessert, muscovado
sponge once again shows supreme technical ability and
sound judgement.

Chef Chris Staines **Owner** Ian & Christa Taylor
Times 12-3/5.30-9 **Prices** Fixed L 2 course £15.95, Fixed
D 3 course £21, Starter £7.25-£9.50, Main £14.50-£24
Wines 82 bottles over £30, 4 bottles under £30, 16 by
glass **Notes** Fixed L/D daily 12-7, Sun L 12-4, Afternoon
tea 3-5.30, Sunday L, Vegetarian available
Parking Manvers St, Southgate Centre (charge made)

The Bath Priory Hotel, Restaurant & Spa

BATH   MAP 4 ST76

Modern European 🍷 NOTABLE WINE LIST

**Impeccable modern cooking in a gorgeously decorated
house**

☎ 01225 331922
Weston Rd BA1 2XT
e-mail: mail@thebathpriory.co.uk
web: www.thebathpriory.co.uk
dir: Adjacent to Victoria Park

A major part of the appeal of this luxurious retreat is its
fantastic setting in four acres of magnificent gardens
just a short stroll from the city centre. The opulent
Regency mansion has all of the elements of a top-notch
country house - antiques, plush sofas, artworks on the
walls, and the obligatory glossy spa. More importantly for
gastronomes, the kitchen works under the direction of
Premier League chef Michael Caines, who also oversees
operations at the sibling hotel, Gidleigh Park (see entry).
With skilled head chef Sam Moody interpreting the Caines
style with aplomb, the cooking is everything you could ask
for: refined, inventive, with clean contemporary flavours
that are completely in tune with the seasons; sourcing of
raw materials is of the highest order - the Priory's kitchen
garden is the first port of call for supplies, while
everything else that finds its way into the larder ticks the
fresh, local and top-class boxes. A winter's dinner sets
out with melt-in-the-mouth pan-fried duck liver matched
with apricot and caraway chutney, crunchy walnut and
ginger topping and sherry jus, or there might be a modish
pairing of meat and fish - roast Brixham monkfish, say,
with caramelised chicken wing, cauliflower couscous and
truffles. Hearteningly simple main courses are not always
out to surprise - witness a plate of Middlewhite suckling
pig with butternut squash, apple compôte and paprika
jus; or there could be roast crown of partridge with a
ravioli of confit leg and mushrooms, and Gewürztraminer
sauce. Unwavering consistency and highly-skilled
execution are also the hallmarks of finely-crafted
desserts, delivering a well-balanced trio of pear fritter
with butterscotch sauce and vanilla ice cream, or
perhaps a delicate lemon verbena pannacotta with
poached blackcurrant, confit lemon and French sorrel.
Extras live up to the same promise, from the chicken
parfait on excellent home-made bread to the deeply
flavoured parsnip soup capped with foam.

Chef Sam Moody **Owner** Mr A Brownsword
Times 12.30-2.30/6.30-9.30 **Prices** Fixed D 3 course fr
£75, Tasting menu £80-£100, Service optional, Groups
min 10 service 12% **Wines** 14 by glass **Notes** Tasting
menu D 7 course, Sunday L, Vegetarian available, Dress
restrictions, No jeans, T-shirts or trainers, Civ Wed 64
Seats 64, Pr/dining room 64 **Children** Portions, Menu
Parking 40

BATH *continued*

£25-£28, Starter £6.10-£6.90, Main £14.90-£16.70, Dessert £4.50-£5.10, Service optional, Groups min 6 service 10% **Wines** 9 bottles over £30, 27 bottles under £30, 3 by glass **Notes** ALC D, Vegetarian available **Seats** 48, Pr/dining room 32 **Parking** On street, NCP Charlotte St

Combe Grove Manor Hotel

◉◉ British, European

Well-judged country-house cooking

☎ 01225 834644

Brassknocker Hill, Monkton Combe BA2 7HS
e-mail: combegrovemanor@pumahotels.co.uk
web: www.pumahotels.co.uk
dir: Exit A36 at Limpley Stoke onto Brassknocker Hill. Hotel 0.5m up hill on left

On the fabulously named Brassknocker Hill, just three miles from the centre of Bath, Combe Grove Manor has lots of Georgian charm. The surrounding 69 acres of gardens and woodland with views of the Limpley Stoke Valley only add to its appeal. The house is done out with respect for its heritage and neatly avoids appearing old hat. The Eden Brasserie in the vaulted cellar room is one dining option, the main event being The Georgian Room, with its pretty period decoration and smartly dressed, well-spaced tables. There's a tasting menu if you're up for it, but whichever route you choose, expect intelligently put together dishes built on high quality produce, a good deal of which comes from the region. Ham hock and foie gras terrine is one way to begin, served with a fruit chutney to cut the richness, followed by a rump and belly of lamb with couscous and a rosemary sauce. And for dessert, banana parfait with chocolate ganache and parfait.

Times 12-2/7-9.30

The Dower House Restaurant

◉◉◉ – *see opposite*

The Hare & Hounds

◉ Modern British NEW

Classy cooking in a roadside pub

☎ 01225 482682

Lansdown Rd BA1 1TJ
e-mail: info@hareandhoundsbath.com

Part of the same mini pub group as the Marlborough Tavern and The Chequers in the city centre (see entries), The Hare & Hounds is a mile and a bit away on the Lansdown Road. It's a sturdy stone building with spectacular views over the west side of the city and open countryside, best enjoyed from the terrace. The smart interior is done out with acres of darkwood - floors, panels, tables and chairs - and food is very much the

focus. You might start with pan-roasted scallops with chorizo and a lime and caper dressing, or a bright and breezy salad of heritage tomatoes, buffalo mozzarella, basil and melon. Pub classics, such as beer-battered cod served with fries, tartare sauce and herby garden peas, are done really well, or you might go for something more adventurous such as roast marinated rump of English lamb with spring greens, potato terrine and olive and thyme sauce. Sticky toffee pudding makes for a satisfying finale.

Times 12-3/5.30-9 **Prices** Fixed L 2 course £14 **Notes** Sunday L **Children** Menu

Jamie's Italian

◉ Modern Italian

Jamie's winning way with real Italian food

☎ 01225 432340

10 Milsom Place BA1 1BZ
e-mail: bath.office@jamiesitalian.com
dir: From A4 follow signs to city centre. Opposite Jolly's department store

They found a very nice Georgian building to house the Bath outpost of the brand, and inside it feels just as it should chez Jamie: rustic finishes and a wholesome lack of formality and fluff. It covers two floors and is relentlessly busy, so much so that a wait for a table is a probability (bookings are taken for large groups only). This popularity brings a surefire buzz to the place, matched by the energy and enthusiasm of the staff. On the menu is Jamie Oliver's style of rustic Italian food, based around the quality of the ingredients and little in the way of adulteration. Start with planks of excellent cured meats, Italian cheeses, pickles and vegetables, or dive straight into a pasta dish such as wild rabbit tagliolini. Main courses include braised shin of British beef and Jamie's Italian burger; note that side dishes are often necessary.

Chef Eric Bernard **Owner** Jamie's Italian **Times** 12-11 Closed 25-26 Dec, All-day dining **Prices** Prices not confirmed Service optional **Wines** 16 by glass **Notes** Vegetarian available **Seats** 180 **Children** Portions, Menu **Parking** Podium car park Walcot St (A3039)

Macdonald Bath Spa

◉◉ Modern British

Well-judged menu in grand Georgian hotel

☎ 0844 879 9106

Sydney Rd BA2 6JF
e-mail: sales.bathspa@macdonald-hotels.co.uk
web: www.macdonald-hotels.co.uk/bathspa
dir: From A4 follow city centre signs for 1m. At lights left signed A36. Turn right after pedestrian crossing, left into Sydney Place. Hotel 200yds on right

Overlooking landscaped gardens, and perfectly placed for exploring the city, the Bath Spa is a grand Georgian

mansion with a distinctly elegant finish. The classy (and formal) Vellore Restaurant is in the original ballroom - they partied in style back then - with its high-domed ceiling, pillars and all round stately air. There's also a canopied outdoor terrace. Engaging staff and a helpful sommelier keep things on track. On the menu, the crowd-pleasing and sensibly unfussy dishes have broad appeal, and are not beyond a few bright ideas too; beer battered scampi comes with dipping sauces (sweet chilli and Dijon mustard among them), followed by roast saddle of hare with braised haunch and chicory, or herb risotto with aubergine caviar and basil oil. Finish with dark chocolate pannacotta with a cocoa and almond crumble and toffee ice cream.

Times 12-2/6.15-10 Closed L Mon-Sat

Marlborough Tavern

◉◉ Modern British

Seasonal cooking and proper beer

☎ 01225 423731

35 Marlborough Buildings BA1 2LY
e-mail: info@marlborough-tavern.com
dir: 200mtrs from W end of Royal Crescent

The 18th-century Marlborough is built of mellow Bath stone and is only a short stroll from the iconic Royal Crescent. As for its credentials as a proper pub, there are local ales and ciders on tap, a pleasingly unstuffy atmosphere, and food that is decidedly 'gastro'. Seated at unadorned wooden tables you can tuck into some pretty impressive seasonal dishes which remain unpretentious and understated but with bags of good ideas on show. A first course among the daily specials might be a ballottine of pheasant and pistachio, served with the nicely pink breast in a salad with celeriac and apple, for example, or keep it simple with a half pint of prawns. The butcher who provides the steaks gets a name-check, and his locally-reared beef is available as sirloin, rump or rib-eye. Pistachio cake with lemon curd and sorbet, or West Country cheeses, are equally good ways to bring proceedings to a close. There's a good value set lunch available mid-week.

Times 12-2.30/6-10 Closed 25 Dec, D Sun

The Olive Tree at the Queensberry Hotel

◉◉◉ – *see opposite*

The Dower House Restaurant

BATH MAP 4 ST76

Modern British **NEW V** NOTABLE WINE LIST

Contemporary fine-dining in a splendid Georgian setting

☎ 01225 823333
The Royal Crescent Hotel, 16 Royal Crescent BA1 2LS
e-mail: info@royalcrescent.co.uk
dir: From A4, right at lights. 2nd left onto Bennett St. Continue into The Circus, 2nd exit onto Brock St

Probably the most photographed landmark in Bath, the sweeping terrace of townhouses that makes up The Royal Crescent is a true Georgian architectural gem. And The Royal Crescent Hotel, which sits bang in the middle of the terrace, is every bit a gem in its own right. A charming, elegant place to stay, it retains all of its Georgian splendour whilst offering every modern luxury, including a spa tucked away in the gardens behind. This is also where you'll find The Dower House Restaurant and Bar, a far more contemporary space than that of the main hotel, bathed in natural light that streams in through large windows swathed in mink-coloured silk trimmed in light olive-green. The dining area is spread across three rooms with well-spaced, linen clad tables with padded olive-green seats, and doors open out onto the gardens where you can dine on the terrace or on the manicured lawns in fine weather (having said all that, as we go to press we hear the place is undergoing a big refurbishment). Head chef David Campbell deals in bang up-to-date food, backed up by a passion for the finest, freshest ingredients, sourced as locally as possible, and sharp technical skills. A starter of foie gras rolled in black onion seeds with smoked eel, apple, radish, roast almond and nasturtium salad shows the style, the sharpness of the apple contrasting well with the richness of the foie gras and the whole dish appealingly colourful and finely balanced in flavour. Next up, accurately cooked, tender pigeon comes with local beetroot, smoked ratte potatoes, spinach, raisins, smoked carrot, glazed nectarine and star anise jus in a multi-dimensional main course that's, again, full of colour and interest. A soft, silky Valrhona chocolate pavé is teamed with roasted almond ice cream, raspberries and 'chocolate crunch' in a deeply indulgent dessert that leaves you wanting more. All the peripherals - canapés, amuse-bouche (perhaps a mushroom espuma with cracked hazelnuts and cress), bread and pre-dessert (peach schnapps, pannacotta and elderflower maybe) - are of equal finesse.

Chef David Campbell **Owner** Topland (Royal Crescent Hotel) Ltd **Times** 12.30-2/7-9.30 **Prices** Fixed L 2 course fr £23.50, Fixed D 3 course fr £55, Tasting menu £62.50-£78, Service optional **Wines** 200 bottles over £30, 18 bottles under £30, 10 by glass **Notes** Tasting & pre-theatre available, Sunday L, Vegetarian menu, Dress restrictions, Smart casual, no denim, Civ Wed 70 **Seats** 60, Pr/dining room 40 **Children** Portions, Menu **Parking** 17, Charlotte St (charge for on site parking)

The Olive Tree at the Queensberry Hotel

BATH MAP 4 ST76

Modern British NOTABLE WINE LIST

Creative modern cooking in a top-drawer hotel

☎ 01225 447928
4-7 Russel St BA1 2QF
e-mail: reservations@olivetreebath.co.uk
web: www.olivetreebath.co.uk
dir: 100mtrs from the Assembly Rooms

Named after the 8th Marquess of Queensbury, who built the row of terraced townhouses back in the Georgian era, this swish boutique hotel manages to tick all the chic style boxes without veering off into pretentious territory. Its Olive Tree restaurant has established itself firmly in recent years as a centre of serious gastronomy in Bath - quite an achievement in a city that is not exactly lacking for competition in the area of fine dining. The place occupies a series of low-lit, interconnecting basement rooms done out in cool neutral tones, with abstract modern art on the walls and chocolate-brown, high-backed leather chairs at white linen-clad tables; the service team here deserves particular plaudits for on-the-ball, well-considered and informed efforts in setting just the right tone. Chris Cleghorn took over the reins at the start of 2013 and hit the ground running at the head of a kitchen brigade that is turning out some impressive work. The trump card here is the clear dedication to superb local and seasonal ingredients of unimpeachable quality - the West Country is on the doorstep, after all - and it shows in the vivid flavours of slow-cooked salmon matched with charred leek, artichoke purée and horseradish cream. Next comes a pitch-perfect main course of Creedy Carver duck with sand carrot purée and orange-glazed chicory, the whole brought together with expert saucing. Fish can come in for robust treatment, as when halibut is partnered with parsley and garlic risotto, snails, fennel, and sherry foam. Visual appeal is also a strong point, as exemplified by a vibrant, beautifully-presented dessert of pineapple mousse with lime sponge and coconut sorbet. A superb wine list brings together an eclectic blend of traditional and new styles grouped by flavour types to help with food pairing.

Chef Chris Cleghorn **Owner** Mr & Mrs Beere **Times** 12-2/7-10 Closed L Mon-Thu **Prices** Fixed L 2 course £18.50, Fixed D 3 course £33, Starter £8.95-£14.50, Main £18-£26.50, Dessert £7.50-£10.50, Service added but optional 10% **Wines** 320 bottles over £30, 17 bottles under £30, 34 by glass **Notes** Sunday L, Vegetarian available **Seats** 60, Pr/dining room 30 **Children** Portions, Menu **Parking** On street pay & display

BATH *continued*

Woods Restaurant

Modern British, French

Contemporary bistro cooking in a Georgian setting

☎ 01225 314812 & 422493
9-13 Alfred St BA1 2QX
e-mail: woodsinbath@gmail.com

Opposite the Assembly Rooms, in a quiet cul-de-sac, Woods is furnished and decorated in the style of a French bistro, with pictures on the walls, curtains at the windows, a small bar area and tables outside. It's a relaxed and friendly place, and the menu, based mainly on a European foundation, accounts for its popularity, with Provençal fish soup, for instance, followed by pan-fried fillet of cod with salsa verde and parmesan dentelles. Cooking of a consistently high standard and variety aplenty keep regulars returning, perhaps for a starter of chilled king prawns with lime mayonnaise and spring onion and coriander salad, then slow-roast belly pork, two tender pieces with crisp crackling, in rich red Thai curry sauce served with bean sprouts sautéed with sesame seeds and seasonal vegetables. Thick slices of fresh bread are offered, and topping things off may be tangy lemon sorbet with lime Daiquiri.

Chef Stuart Ash **Owner** David & Claude Price
Times 12-2.30/5-10 Closed 25-26 Dec, D Sun
Prices Fixed L 2 course £16.95, Fixed D 2 course £16.95, Service optional **Notes** Pre-theatre D Mon-Sat 5-7pm, Sunday L, Vegetarian available **Seats** 100, Pr/dining room 40 **Children** Portions, Menu **Parking** On street, car park nearby

CASTLE CARY	Map 4 ST63

The Pilgrims

Modern British V

Impeccable West Country produce in a stone-built village inn

☎ 01963 240597
Lovington BA7 7PT
e-mail: jools@thepilgrimsatlovington.co.uk
web: www.thepilgrimsatlovington.co.uk
dir: On B3153, 1.5m E of lights on A37 at Lydford

The name distantly honours those brave souls who passed this way in centuries gone by on their quest to find King Arthur's tomb. The stone-built inn has been extended and repurposed in latter days into a welcoming restaurant-with-rooms, run by the Mitchisons with cheerful bonhomie. Jools runs the kitchen as a hive of activity, and a showcase for excellent local suppliers, so expect to see Jeff Cracknell's Langport duck, Brown and Forrest smoked eel, Lovington's ice cream and Hurdlebrook unpasteurised cream on the menu. That eel might be teamed with Denhay smoked bacon and horseradish potatoes for a successful opener, followed by pork in a blanket - full-flavoured tenderloin stuffed with Toulouse sausage, alongside black pudding and prunes macerated in cider brandy - for an impeccable West

Country array. Fish might be West Bay bouillabaisse, or sea bass in saffron-scented Noilly Prat, while the signature dessert is the simple but effective chocolate and ginger pot.

Chef Julian Mitchison **Owner** Julian & Sally Mitchison
Times 12-3/7-11 Closed 2 wks Oct, Sun-Mon, L Tue
Prices Fixed L 2 course £17, Fixed D 3 course £22, Starter £6-£9, Main £16-£24, Dessert £6-£8, Service optional **Wines** 7 bottles over £30, 21 bottles under £30, 15 by glass **Notes** Sunday L, Vegetarian menu **Seats** 25 **Children** Portions **Parking** 40

CHARD	Map 4 ST30

Cricket St Thomas Hotel

Italian

Tuscan specialities in Somerset cider country

☎ 01460 30111
TA20 4DD
e-mail: cricket.sales@bourne-leisure.co.uk
dir: A30 between Chard & Crewkerne, signed

In the buxom embrace of rolling Somerset hills, this porticoed Regency mansion sits in magnificent gardens that the 2nd Baron Bridport lavished a quarter of a million pounds on, including creating a chain of lakes. All of which historical trivia has nothing whatsoever to do with the cuisine of the Tuscan hills, which is the deal in Fenocchi's restaurant. The contemporary venue looks sharp with its darkwood tables, lime and chocolate-hued seats and grey-painted panelled walls, while the kitchen sends out simple classic pasta ideas along the lines of rigatoni alla bolognese, and mains such as prosciutto-wrapped chicken with sage butter, gnocchi, girolle and Italian bean casserole. End sweetly with panettone bread-and-butter pudding with orange zest mascarpone, or the Italian formaggi-board.

Chef Jason Eland **Owner** Bourne Leisure **Times** 6.30-9 Closed L all week **Prices** Prices not confirmed Service optional **Wines** 14 bottles under £30, 5 by glass **Notes** Vegetarian available, Civ Wed 50 **Seats** 80 **Parking** 200

CHEW MAGNA	Map 4 ST56

The Pony & Trap

Modern British

Big-hearted modern food in a country cottage inn

☎ 01275 332627
Knowle Hill BS40 8TQ
e-mail: info@theponyandtrap.co.uk
dir: Take A37 S from Bristol. After Pensford turn right at rdbt onto A368 towards Weston-Super-Mare. In 1.5m right signed Chew Magna & Winford. Pub 1m on right

The Pony & Trap looks like a traditional enough pub from the outside: a classic 200-year-old country cottage in lush Chew Valley countryside. Inside, there's a classic pubby bar with a relaxed and welcoming ambience, but a quick glance over the menu will tell you that chef Josh

Eggleton has transformed the place into an up-to-date inn driven by its switched-on, hearty cooking. Whether you go for the no-nonsense bare wooden tables in the bar, or trade up to the restaurant area with its slate floors, white linen and countryside views, the menu stays the same: punchy food with a big heart. High quality native ingredients are at the core of a culinary philosophy that delivers precise flavours and combinations that work, coming up with starters of devilled duck livers and hearts with mushrooms on toast, and main-course marinated pork fillet with Parma ham, rich braised shoulder, hodge podge, home-made black pudding, apple and celeriac. Apple and blackberry crumble with vanilla ice cream is a textbook example.

Chef Josh Eggleton **Owner** Josh Eggleton
Times 12-2.30/7-9.30 Closed Mon **Prices** Tasting menu £50-£45, Starter £5-£9.50, Main £11.50-£22, Dessert £4-£7.50, Service optional **Wines** 14 bottles over £30, 45 bottles under £30, 26 by glass **Notes** Tasting menu 7 course, Sunday L £12.50-£14.50, Vegetarian available **Seats** 60 **Children** Portions **Parking** 40

CORTON DENHAM	Map 4 ST62

The Queens Arms

Modern British

Compelling cooking in a village pub

☎ 01963 220317
DT9 4LR
e-mail: relax@thequeensarms.com
web: www.thequeensarms.com
dir: A303 exit Chapel Cross signed South Cadbury & Corton Denham. Follow signs to South Cadbury. Through village, after 0.25m turn left up hill signed Sherborne & Corton Denham. Left at top of hill, pub at end of village on right

In an ancient village on the Somerset-Dorset border, The Queens Arms is a late-18th-century pub overflowing with character. You can have a pork pie and a pint by the open fire in the bar (with its own menu) or a full meal in the adjoining restaurant. Food is a serious preoccupation here, the kitchen's inventive treatments seen in salmon and scallop céviche with pea vinaigrette and pea shoots, then slow-roast pork belly, rich, sticky and delicious, in a pepper and cider glaze served with poached rhubarb and an apple and potato cake. Lamb - loin and rump - is served straightforwardly with potato gratin, baby onions and spinach purée, or go for the seared tuna with seafood, tomato and chilli tagliatelle and a lime and ginger dressing. And who could resist a light, airy, well-risen pistachio soufflé with a pot of chocolate sauce?

Chef Boyd Macintosh, Tony Doyle, Chris Smith
Owner Jeanette & Gordon Reid **Times** 12-3/6-10 Closed D 1 Jan **Prices** Prices not confirmed Service optional **Wines** 25 bottles over £30, 33 bottles under £30, 20 by glass **Notes** Weekly menu L 2 course, Sunday L, Vegetarian available **Seats** 40, Pr/dining room 30 **Children** Portions, Menu **Parking** 20

Save on Hotels. Book at theAA.com/hotel

SOMERSET 431 ENGLAND

DULVERTON
Map 3 SS92

Tarr Farm Inn

◉ Modern British ⍟

Exmoor riverside inn with appealing brasserie menu

☎ 01643 851507
Tarr Steps, Liscombe TA22 9PY
e-mail: enquiries@tarrfarm.co.uk
web: www.tarrfarm.co.uk
dir: 6m NW of Dulverton. Off B3223 signed Tarr Steps, signs to Tarr Farm Inn

The Exmoor location deep in the Barle Valley, near the famous thousand-year-old Tarr Steps bridge over the river, feels as timeless and bucolic as just about anywhere in the UK. And the wild landscape turns provider when it comes to the menu at this 16th century inn. The bar has bags of rustic charm but there's a nicely contemporary edge to the place these days, not least in the dining room which has a brasserie vibe going on. The kitchen keeps things relatively simple, seasonal and local. River Fowey mussels with cider and cream is one way to begin, the high quality of the regional ingredients speaking for themselves. Next up, supreme of guinea fowl with wild mushroom rice, a pasta dish such as penne carbonara, or a Devon Ruby steak cooked on the grill (12oz T-bone, for example). Crème brûlée is a classic dessert done well.

Chef Paul Webber **Owner** Richard Benn & Judy Carless **Times** 12-3/6.30-12 Closed 1-10 Feb **Prices** Prices not confirmed Service optional **Wines** 12 by glass **Notes** Sunday L, Vegetarian available **Seats** 50, Pr/dining room 20 **Children** Portions **Parking** 40

Woods Bar & Dining Room

◉ Modern British, French

Well-judged menu and relaxed vibe

☎ 01398 324007
4 Banks Square TA22 9BU
e-mail: woodsdulverton@hotmail.com
dir: From Tiverton take A396 N. At Machine Cross take B3222 to Dulverton. Establishment adjacent to church

Looking something like a quaint little tea shop on the outside, the abidingly popular neighbourhood venue on the edge of Exmoor is consecrated to both eating and drinking, and doesn't much trouble to draw a strict dividing line between them. Indeed, the line between rusticity and refinement in the cooking itself is also appealingly blurred, and while there may be black plates and triangular plates, they get put down on chunky, unclothed tables in a place warmed by a log fire when needed. Good bistro accents are sounded in a twice-cooked Swiss cheese soufflé, served with fig chutney, walnut dressing and aged balsamic, followed by rump of Exmoor lamb - tender, accurately cooked and flavourful - with a miniature pie, wilted spinach and mash, in thyme-

scented juices. To finish, orange pannacotta is of the firm-textured school.

Times 12-2/7-9.30 Closed 25 Dec

EXFORD
Map 3 SS83

Crown Hotel

◉ Modern British ⍟

Good cooking in a handsome coaching inn

☎ 01643 831554
Park St TA24 7PP
e-mail: info@crownhotelexmoor.co.uk
web: www.crownhotelexmoor.co.uk
dir: From Taunton take A38 to A358. Turn left at B3224 & follow signs to Exford

Amid the gently rolling hills of Exmoor, in the charming village of Exford, the Crown has been doing business for 300 years or so. With three acres of grounds to explore, there's plenty to keep you close by, not least a menu of appealing dishes with a local flavour. Eat in the traditional bar (complete with stag's head) or the handsome dining room and expect well-crafted dishes such as Cornish mussels steamed in cider, followed by a steak from the grill with triple-cooked chips, or fillet of line-caught sea bass with Bombay crushed potatoes, braised fennel, aubergine caviar and curried velouté. Apple and raisin crumble with spiced poached pear and cinnamon ice cream brings it all to a comforting close. This is a dog- and horse-friendly establishment.

Chef Olivier Certain **Owner** Mr C Kirkbride, S & D Whittaker **Times** 6.45-9.15 Closed L all week **Prices** Fixed D 3 course £33-£38, Service optional **Wines** 20 bottles over £30, 12 bottles under £30, 19 by glass **Notes** Sunday L, Vegetarian available, Dress restrictions, Smart casual, no football shirts or shorts **Seats** 45, Pr/dining room 20 **Children** Portions **Parking** 30

HINTON CHARTERHOUSE
Map 4 ST75

Homewood Park Hotel & Spa

◉◉ British

Bright modern cooking in a grand Georgian house

☎ 01225 723731
Abbey Ln BA2 7TB
e-mail: info@homewoodpark.co.uk
web: www.homewoodpark.co.uk
dir: 6m SE of Bath on A36, turn left at 2nd sign for Freshford

Overlooking the Limpley Stoke valley not far from Bath, Homewood is a spiffing country house in the classic mould, with trimly manicured grounds and a dining room that looks out over them. The cooking is broadly contemporary and avoids undue showboating. Smoked ham tortellini with parmesan foam and rocket sounds an Italian note at the outset, as does the outstandingly

flavourful beetroot and blue cheese risotto with pea shoots. Rump of local lamb with thyme mash and parsnip purée and pork three ways (loin, belly and ears) are typical of the style. Fish could be a pavé of salmon in saffron-scented mussel and potato broth, and you might finish with the likes of an enthusiastically nutmegged egg custard tart, which boasts superb pastry and offsetting tang from a rhubarb sorbet.

Times 12-1.30/7-9.30

HOLCOMBE
Map 4 ST64

The Holcombe Inn

◉ British, International ⍟

Characterful inn with broad appeal

☎ 01761 232478
Stratton Rd BA3 5EB
e-mail: bookings@holcombeinn.co.uk
dir: From Bath or Shepton Mallet take A367 (Fosse Way) to Stratton. Follow inn signs

A genuine country inn with good food, real ales and comfortable bedrooms, The Holcombe is just what the doctor ordered. The whitewashed 17th-century property, near Downside Abbey, has plenty of character with oak beams, panelled walls and open fireplaces, and, if you visit when the weather is mild, outside tables with fabulous views. Indoors, eat in the bar or separate dining room and choose from a menu that follows a broad sweep of culinary thinking. Start with the likes of salt-and-pepper squid or devilled kidneys on toast, before moving on to the home-made pie of the day, a ploughman's, or pan-seared John Dory with baby vegetables and beurre blanc. There are steaks from a local farm - choose from rib-eye, fillet and rump - with accompanying sauces including chilli butter or Stilton. For dessert, crème caramel with toasted nuts and thyme is an appealing way to end a meal.

Chef David Beazer **Owner** Julie Berry **Times** 12-2.30/6.30-9 Closed D 25-26 Dec **Prices** Starter £5-£11.95, Main £9.95-£28.50, Dessert £5.95, Service optional **Wines** 9 bottles over £30, 30 bottles under £30, 16 by glass **Notes** Sunday L £9.95-£28.50, Vegetarian available **Seats** 65 **Children** Portions, Menu **Parking** 30

LOWER VOBSTER Map 4 ST74

The Vobster Inn

◉◉ British, European

Spanish-influenced menus in a country pub

☎ 01373 812920
BA3 5RJ
e-mail: info@vobsterinn.co.uk
dir: 4m W of Frome, between Wells & Leigh upon Mendip

The Vobster is a friendly and welcoming stone-built inn dating from the 17th century surrounded by four acres of rolling countryside. Food is an important part of the operation, with the lively bar serving baguettes, sausage and mash and cheese omelette with chips. A blackboard lists tapas (the chef-proprietor is Spanish) along the lines of chorizo, patatas bravas, and chick pea and beetroot houmus, while a full menu operates in the quieter dining room. Start with onion soup twirled with truffle oil, or seared pigeon breast with white pudding, and go on to tender rib-eye with garlic butter, crisp onion rings and a fried egg, roast sea bass with pesto, or roast chicken breast flavoured with thyme and saffron served with braised red cabbage and truffled potatoes. Finish with a straightforward dessert like crema catalana with orange sorbet, or chocolate mousse.

Chef Mr Rafael F Davila **Owner** Mr Rafael F Davila **Times** 12-3/6.30-11 **Closed** 25 Dec, Mon (check at BHs), D Sun **Prices** Prices not confirmed **Service** optional **Wines** 12 by glass **Notes** Sunday L, Vegetarian available **Seats** 40, Pr/dining room 40 **Children** Portions, Menu **Parking** 60

MILVERTON Map 3 ST12

The Globe

◉ Modern British

Modern culinary thinking in a country pub

☎ 01823 400534
Fore St TA4 1JX
e-mail: adele@theglobemilverton.co.uk
web: www.theglobemilverton.co.uk
dir: M5 junct 26 onto A38, then B3187 to Milverton

The Globe looks every inch the traditional red-brick coaching inn from the outside, but these days the village hostelry is more of a 'glasses of wine' rather than 'jars of ale' sort of place. Easy-on-the-eye good looks take in an airy and light modern décor - white paint and blond wood, local artwork on the walls - while the kitchen has its finger on the pulse of what people want to eat: unpretentious, up-to-the-minute ideas delivered via a constantly updated main menu and daily-changing specials. River Fowey mussels with cider and cream is a great example of letting the sheer quality of the ingredients shine, followed by guinea fowl suprême with wild mushroom sauce. Don't even think of passing on the home-made desserts when there's classic crème brûlée or sticky toffee pudding with toffee sauce and West Country clotted cream up for grabs.

Times 12-3/6-11.30 **Closed** L Mon, D Sun

OAKHILL Map 4 ST64

The Oakhill Inn

◉ Traditional British

Well-judged menu in a country inn

☎ 01749 840442
Fosse Rd BA3 5HU
e-mail: info@theoakhillinn.com
dir: On A367 between Stratton-on-the-Fosse & Shepton Mallet

A country inn on the A367, The Oakhill gazes out over the undulating Mendips, with the village church for company. Inside, the stone interiors present a mix of sofas and tables in the main bar, where locals knock back Orchard Pig cider and cask ales, and a quieter dining area with unclothed wooden tables and candles and a log fire. The kitchen uses quality regional produce in an uncomplicated way for pub cooking that's a cut above the norm. Tiger prawns dressed in sweet chilli sauce on a crisp salad with coriander fires up the taste buds, as a prelude to a venison steak with dauphinoise and seasonal greens in gin sauce, or roast salmon with Jersey Royals and kale in caper butter. Puddings include apple and pear crumble, bread-and-butter pudding with banana, and a fine, thin-shelled treacle tart served with excellent vanilla ice cream.

Chef Neil Creese **Times** 12-3/6-9 **Closed** 25-26 Dec **Prices** Starter £4.95-£7.50, Main £10.95-£14.95, Dessert £5.95, Service optional, Groups min 8 service 10% **Wines** 7 bottles over £30, 24 bottles under £30, 10 by glass **Notes** Sunday L £9.95-£14.95, Vegetarian available **Seats** 30 **Children** Portions **Parking** parking 20 yds

PORLOCK Map 3 SS84

The Oaks Hotel

◉ Traditional British ◉

Traditional cooking in the Exmoor National Park

☎ 01643 862265
TA24 8ES
e-mail: info@oakshotel.co.uk
dir: From E of A39, enter village (road narrows to single track) then follow hotel sign. From W: down Porlock Hill, through village, hotel sign on right

This Edwardian country house hotel is the kind of place where the genuine hospitality of the hands-on, husband-and-wife-team who run the place keeps the customers coming back. It helps that it's in a lovely spot, of course, on the outskirts of a village in the Exmoor National Park. The cheery yellow-walled restaurant has panoramic views and a short daily-changing dinner menu of unfussy, traditional dishes, cooked by Anne Riley. There's plenty of local produce and a genuine regional flavour; start with a delicious bacon, mushroom and cheese savoury, moving on to a tender breast of guinea fowl with morels, and finish with a flavoursome banana and ginger ice cream.

Chef Anne Riley **Owner** Tim & Anne Riley **Times** 7-8 **Closed** Nov-Mar, L all week **Prices** Prices not confirmed Service included **Notes** Weekly changing menu **Seats** 22 **Children** Portions **Parking** 12

SHEPTON MALLET Map 4 ST64

Charlton House Spa Hotel

◉◉ Modern British ◉

Contemporary cooking in a smart country house

☎ 01749 342008
Charlton Rd BA4 4PR
e-mail: enquiries.charltonhousehotel@bannatyne.co.uk
web: www.bannatyne.co.uk
dir: On A361 towards Frome, 1m from town centre

Charlton House aims squarely at the corporate market, with business facilities and spa pampering all part of the package. And its approach to dining is no mere afterthought. The décor in the restaurant keeps step with the classic country house theme, kitted out in best country-house chintz, with swagged curtains framing a view over the gardens. Owned by *Dragon's Den* star Duncan Bannatyne, you can expect the whole operation to be run on sharply professional lines, so service is from a keen, well-drilled young team, who maintain a relaxed atmosphere. The kitchen treats top-class, well-sourced produce with due respect to produce simple-but-effective contemporary dishes, starting out with tortelli of Brixham crab with bok choi, lotus root and lemongrass, while mains deliver well-timed Salisbury Plains venison in the company of red cabbage, apples, wild mushrooms and sage. If you're in the market for fish, there might be line-caught sea bass fillet with cannelloni of Cornish lobster, oven-fried tomatoes and salsa verde. Good technical skills keep everything on a high note to a fruity finale involving banana parfait, mango sorbet and pineapple salsa.

Chef Matt Lord **Owner** Bannatyne Hotels Ltd **Times** 12.30-2.15/7-9.15 **Prices** Fixed L 2 course £14.95, Fixed D 3 course £34.95, Service optional **Wines** 22 bottles over £30, 25 bottles under £30, 9 by glass **Notes** Sunday L, Vegetarian available, Dress restrictions, Smart casual, Civ Wed 120 **Seats** 60, Pr/dining room 80 **Children** Portions, Menu **Parking** 70

The Thatched Cottage Inn

◉ Modern British, European

Smart old inn with an industrious kitchen

☎ 01749 342058
Thatched Cottage, 63-67 Charlton Rd BA4 5QF
e-mail: david@thatchedcottage.info
dir: 0.6m E of Shepton Mallet, at lights on A361

The 17th-century Thatched Cottage Inn has the requisite chocolate-box appearance you would expect given its name, and a strong local fan base who come for its straightforward modern cooking based on good local produce, and the knowledge that its kitchen makes just about everything in-house. The interior looks the part too, made over with a gently contemporary polish without detracting from the intrinsic charm of its wooden beams and panelling, and vast stone fireplaces. You can do no wrong by starting with something as simple as mushrooms on toast, especially when the excellent fungi are served on garlic toast and pointed up with truffle oil.

Save on Hotels. Book at theAA.com/hotel

SOMERSET 433 ENGLAND

A well-thought-out main course brings pot-roast chicken breast with pearl barley and sage risotto, wilted spinach and lemon and thyme jus, while dessert winds proceedings up with a classic Bakewell tart served with marinated dried cherries and a dollop of clotted cream as an excellent foil to the tart.

Times 12-2.30/6.30-9.30

SOMERTON
Map 4 ST42

The Devonshire Arms
◉ Modern British 🌿

Good, honest cooking by the village green

☎ 01458 241271
Long Sutton TA10 9LP
e-mail: mail@thedevonshirearms.com
web: www.thedevonshirearms.com
dir: Off A303 onto A372 at Podimore rdbt. After 4m, left onto B3165, signed Martock and Long Sutton

Set on a picturesque village green, The Devonshire Arms is a Grade II listed former hunting lodge turned restaurant with rooms. A cheery atmosphere awaits whether you're after a pint or a full-blown meal in the restaurant with its modern, muted tones and unclothed tables, or outside in the courtyard or large walled garden. From the locally-sourced and daily-changing menu of well-judged dishes comes the like of roast fillet of bream with horseradish mousse and herb salad, and Quantock duck confit with pearl barley 'risotto'. Finish with a West Country cheeseboard or ginger sticky toffee pudding with Grand Marnier sauce and lime leaf ice cream.

Chef Max Pringle **Owner** Philip & Sheila Mepham **Times** 12-2.30/7-9.30 Closed 25-26 Dec, 1 Jan **Prices** Starter £5.95-£10.95, Main £11.75-£18.95, Dessert £5.85-£10.25, Service optional **Wines** 21 bottles over £30, 21 bottles under £30, 9 by glass **Notes** ALC menu served D, Sunday L £12.95-£16.50, Vegetarian available **Seats** 40 **Children** Portions, Menu **Parking** 6, On street

STON EASTON
Map 4 ST65

Ston Easton Park Hotel
◉◉ Modern British

Properly memorable cooking at a Palladian manor

☎ 01761 241631
BA3 4DF
e-mail: info@stoneaston.co.uk
web: www.stoneaston.co.uk
dir: A39 from Bath for approx 8m. Onto A37 (Shepton Mallet). Hotel in next village

A splendid snapshot of the early-Georgian Palladian style, Ston Easton is a treat. The 36 acres of grounds include gardens landscaped by Humphry Repton, as well as an 18th-century icehouse and a fountain in a ruined grotto, plus the babbling waters of the River Norr. There's also a Victorian walled kitchen garden that serves the Chefs well with organic fruit and veg, herbs and even edible flowers. You're positively invited to have a wander round, and get some green-fingered tips from the head gardener. It all ends up being transformed into the carefully worked-out menus of The Sorrel Restaurant, where intense flavours and pin-sharp presentations are the order of the day. A first-course plate bravely teams up poached salmon, Brixham crab, merguez sausage and heritage tomatoes from the garden for a stimulating composition, followed perhaps by a cleverly modulated take on classic French cuisine, as in the lapin aux pruneaux that features the fruit-stuffed saddle with braised lentils and a bubble-and-squeak croquette. Desserts bring on garden berries in the season, perhaps loaded on to a Pavlova and accompanied by a raspberry sorbet.

Times 12-2/7-9.30

TAUNTON
Map 4 ST22

The Mount Somerset Hotel
◉◉ British V 🌿

Luxurious cooking in a luxurious hotel

☎ 01823 442500
Lower Henlade TA3 5NB
e-mail: info@mountsomersethotel.co.uk
dir: M5 junct 25, A358 towards Chard/Ilminster, right in Henlade (Stoke St Mary), left at T-junct. Hotel 400yds on right

The surroundings of Mount Somerset have an undeniable serenity that is guaranteed to lift the spirits. The handsome Regency building sits in four acres of grounds in an elevated position between the Blackdown and Quantock Hills, and still tacks to a classic country-house style, its period features - high ceilings, ornate plasterwork, polished wooden floors, open fireplaces, and a sweeping spiral staircase for when you feel the need to make a grand entrance - all contributing to an air of luxury and refinement. Taking its name from the peacocks roaming the grounds, the dining room is a suitably formal setting for the kitchen's accomplished modern cooking. Golden raisin purée and apricot and chamomile jelly are a well-judged foil to duck liver parfait with smoked Creedy Carver breast, while an impressive main course sees boneless whole quail matched with sweet potato, ceps, baby onions and sherry vinegar jus. Seasonal fruits cascade forth from the dessert listings, offering the likes of a simple but effective pairing of poached pears with vanilla bean and apple mousse.

Chef Stephen Walker **Owner** Eden Hotels **Times** 12-2/7-9.30 **Prices** Fixed L 2 course £13.95, Fixed D 3 course £49, Tasting menu £69, Starter £5.95-£9.95, Main £10.95-£17.95, Dessert £6.95-£7.95, Service optional **Wines** 56 bottles over £30, 30 bottles under £30, 8 by glass **Notes** Sunday L, Vegetarian menu, Dress restrictions, Smart casual, Civ Wed 80 **Seats** 60, Pr/dining room 50 **Children** Portions, Menu **Parking** 100

The Willow Tree Restaurant
◉◉ Modern British 🌿

Pin-sharp cooking in a 17th-century townhouse

☎ 01823 352835
3 Tower Ln, Off Tower St TA1 4AR
e-mail: willowtreefood@hotmail.co.uk
dir: 200yds from Taunton bus station

Tucked away down a little lane beside a stream, The Willow Tree is a cosy and intimate sort of restaurant, beamed and tastefully furnished and decorated, with well-chosen artwork on the walls and high-backed chairs at clothed tables. Darren Sherlock applies his distinctively precise, thoughtful cooking style to tip-top produce to give it the maximum impact with the minimum of fuss. Cheddar soufflé is a light, well-risen classic of great flavour balanced by a creamy sauce of walnuts and celery, and another starter, of confit duck gizzard, served with Puy lentils, bacon, smoked celeriac purée and a pear and quince jelly, impresses for its well-thought-out marriage of flavours and textures. Main courses include pan-fried venison, tender and succulent, served simply with pan-fried root vegetables and contrasting sweet potato purée, and seared hake fillet topped with brandade sauced with chive beurre blanc. Baking skills are evident in breads, and thought and workmanship are behind even straightforward-sounding desserts like Muscovado crème brûlée with spicy fig compôte.

Chef Darren Sherlock **Owner** Darren Sherlock & Rita Rambellas **Times** 6.30-9 Closed Jan, Aug, Sun-Mon, Thu, L all week **Prices** Prices not confirmed Service added but optional 10% **Wines** 20 bottles over £30, 27 bottles under £30, 6 by glass **Notes** Vegetarian available, Dress restrictions, Smart casual **Seats** 25 **Parking** 20 yds, 300 spaces

TINTINHULL
Map 4 ST41

Crown & Victoria

◎ British

Good, honest cooking in a village pub

☎ 01935 823341
14 Farm St BA22 8PZ
e-mail: info@thecrownandvictoria.co.uk
web: www.thecrownandvictoria.co.uk
dir: W'bound off A303 follow signs for Tintinhull

Drinkers as well as diners are welcomed at this village pub in pretty, peaceful gardens, with a selection of real ales to choose from. It's a relaxing place, with friendly service and a jolly atmosphere. The kitchen prides itself on its use of free-range and organic produce, much sourced from local farms, and it makes good use of it, producing well-executed dishes of well-matched combinations - nothing too over-elaborate though. A thick slab of goats' cheese coated in almonds, orange and black pepper, served warm and melting with red onion marmalade, is an impressive opener, with perhaps a terrine of pigeon, ham and quail with gooseberry chutney an alternative. Familiar staples like beer-battered haddock with the usual accompaniments can be found among main courses, alongside pan-fried duck breast with Madeira sauce, rösti and spinach. Finish with impeccable vanilla pannacotta with wafer-thin slices of pineapple.

Chef Steven Yates **Owner** Isabel Thomas, Mark Hillyard **Times** 12-2.30/6.30-9.30 Closed D Sun **Prices** Prices not confirmed Service optional **Wines** 8 by glass **Notes** Sunday L, Vegetarian available **Seats** 100, Pr/dining room 45 **Children** Portions, Menu **Parking** 50

WELLS
Map 4 ST54

Ancient Gate House Hotel

◎ Modern Italian

A touch of Italy opposite the cathedral

☎ 01749 672029
20 Sadler St BA5 2SE
e-mail: info@ancientgatehouse.co.uk
web: www.ancientgatehouse.co.uk
dir: 1st hotel on left on cathedral green

Ancient the hotel certainly is; the building even incorporates the 15th-century Great West Gate, once part of the city's defensive walls. The Rugantino Restaurant looks the part too, with its large brick fireplace and ceiling beams. While it may look like something from England's yesteryear, its menu is resolutely Italian, with the kitchen focusing on quality ingredients and producing commendably unfussy dishes. Properly made risotto is a good way to start, perhaps with crab, smoked salmon and scallops, or wild mushrooms and parmesan, and there could also be classic carpaccio. Home-made pasta is a speciality - rigatoni with meatballs stuffed with dolcelatte, say - or follow with rump of lamb, served pink, successfully combined with lamb tortellini, minted pea purée and a rosemary and fennel jus. Puddings fly the flag with lightly textured vanilla pannacotta with fruit compôte, and plum and Amaretto semi-fredo with first-rate cantucci.

Chef Jamie Cundill **Owner** Nicholas & Jonathan Rossi **Times** 12-2.30/6-10 Closed 25-29 Dec **Prices** Fixed L 2 course £10.90-£13.90, Fixed D 3 course £25-£30, Starter £5.75-£8.25, Main £12.50-£21.50, Dessert £6-£8, Service added but optional 10% **Wines** 11 bottles over £30, 23 bottles under £30, 8 by glass **Notes** Tasting menu & pre/post cathedral concert menu available, Sunday L, Vegetarian available **Seats** 40, Pr/dining room 20 **Children** Portions **Parking** On street

Best Western Plus Swan Hotel

◎◎ Modern British

An ancient inn with creative contemporary cooking

☎ 01749 836300
Sadler St BA5 2RX
e-mail: info@swanhotelwells.co.uk
web: www.swanhotelwells.co.uk
dir: A39, A371, on entering Wells follow signs for Hotels & Deliveries. Hotel on right opposite cathedral

The Swan, in the shadow of the cathedral, has 600 years of history behind it, although restoration and extensions mean guests have all the amenities of a 21st-century hotel. The restaurant is a characterful room, with antiques, panelling, just-so table settings and comfortable upholstered seats. The menus offer much to interest, from teriyaki-grilled salmon fillet with lime-scented new potatoes and red pepper butter, to steak and chips with béarnaise. Top-notch produce is handled confidently, from partridge breast, cooked just right, served with chicory, wild mushrooms and apple jus, to fresh-tasting, well-timed fried halibut fillet with a rich saffron beurre blanc, three mussels, some kohlrabi and slices of chorizo. Puddings make an impact too: perhaps an assiette of chocolate desserts.

Chef Leigh Say **Owner** Kevin Newton **Times** 12-2/7-9.30 **Prices** Fixed L 2 course fr £12, Fixed D 3 course £27-£35, Starter £5.50-£8.95, Main £16.50-£21, Dessert £6-£7.50, Service optional **Wines** 14 bottles over £30, 21 bottles under £30, 7 by glass **Notes** Sunday L, Vegetarian available, Civ Wed 90 **Seats** 50, Pr/dining room 90 **Children** Portions, Menu **Parking** 25

Goodfellows

◎◎ Mediterranean, European

Creative fish restaurant with a café attached

☎ 01749 673866
5 Sadler St BA5 2RR
e-mail: goodfellows@btconnect.com
web: www.goodfellowswells.co.uk
dir: Town centre near Market Place

Virtually cheek by jowl with the Gothic cathedral, the Fellows' thriving business is recognisable by the distinctly regal purple of its frontal livery. The enterprise incorporates a café as well as more formal fish restaurant over two floors, so whether you're up for a hasty croissant on the way to work or a lingering three-course dinner, pretty well all bases are covered. An open kitchen on the ground floor allows spectacular views of the small, intensely focused brigade at work, and what they produce - creatively cooked fish, mostly from Brixham - is reliably good. A six-course tasting menu that reads like a shopping list (perhaps Crayfish, Salmon, Crab, Turbot, Scallops, Coconut) is a magical mystery tour for the open-minded, while the main menu offerings might take in brill in truffle dressing with parsnip purée, or a sunny southern-French composition of sea bass with grilled aubergine and courgette, saffron-braised fennel, black olives and capers. Start with tuna carpaccio, rocket and parmesan, and end on apple and blackcurrant crumble and custard, and happiness is complete.

Times 12-2/6.30-9.30 Closed 25-27 Dec, 1 & 7-20 Jan, Sun-Mon, D Tue

Save on Hotels. Book at theAA.com/hotel

SOMERSET 435 ENGLAND

The Old Spot

◎◎ Italian, French

Modern European cooking next to the cathedral

☎ 01749 689099
12 Sadler St BA5 2SE
e-mail: theoldspotwells@googlemail.com
dir: On entering Wells, follow signs for Hotels &
Deliveries. Sadler St leads into High St, Old Spot on left
opposite Swan Hotel

Hanging baskets prettify the frontage of the Bates' city
centre restaurant, while the proximity of Wells Cathedral,
whose west front can be seen from tables at the back,
does the rest. The décor within keeps things stylishly
plain, with bare wood tabletops, framed menus on the
walls, and a service approach that's refreshingly
unstuffy. Ian Bates trained with French master Michel
Guérard back in the day, and there is a streak of
Gallophilia still in his menus. A good way to start is with
excellent pork rillettes served terrine-style with onion
confit and toast, and you might then go on to calf's liver
with bacon, endive and duxelles, classically sauced with
Madeira. A more obviously Mediterranean leaning brings
on the likes of onion risotto with borlotti beans,
mozzarella and sage, and hake fillet with peperonata and
tapenade. The frangipane tart could do with a little more
almond, but a light and encouragingly quivery
pannacotta with praline and coffee syrup is a dessert
that inspires confidence.

Chef Ian Bates **Owner** Ian & Clare Bates
Times 12.30-2.30/7-10.30 Closed 1 wk Xmas, Mon, L Tue,
D Sun **Prices** Fixed L 2 course fr £15.50, Starter
£5.50-£10.50, Main £13-£21, Dessert £6-£6.50, Service
optional, Groups min 6 service 10% **Wines** 17 by glass
Notes Sunday L £18.50-£22.50, Vegetarian available
Seats 50 **Children** Portions **Parking** On street, Market
Square

WESTON-SUPER-MARE   Map 4 ST36

The Cove

◎ Modern British ✿

Cool seaside brasserie in rejuvenated Weston

☎ 01934 418217
Marine Lake, Birnbeck Rd BS23 2BX
e-mail: info@the-cove.co.uk
dir: From Grand Pier on Royal Parade N onto Knightstone
Rd. Left into Birnbeck Rd. Restaurant on left

Having lost its original pier to fire in 2008, Weston's
bounce back from trauma has been a heartening saga.
The new pier opened in 2010 and The Cove - which
launched in 2007 - fits in to the newly regenerated
seafront perfectly with its super-cool seaside brasserie
good looks. The views through the vast windows are
fantastic, and the menus, with their emphasis on fresh
fish and seafood, augmented by daily blackboard
specials, seal the deal. Deliveries from the Brixham and
Newlyn boats, fruit from Bristol market and local growers,
and properly matured meat from a Weston butcher all
add up to a picture of quality, manifested in the likes of
potted crab with sticks of brown crabmeat, served with
pickled fennel and orange salad, seared lamb rump with
sweet potato dauphinoise and spinach in rosemary jus,
and rich, soft pecan-dotted chocolate brownie with
honeycomb ice cream.

Chef Richard Tudor, Gemma Stacey **Owner** Heath Hardy &
Gemma Stacey **Times** 12-9.30 Closed 25 Dec, All-
day dining **Prices** Fixed L 3 course £16.50-£19.95, Starter
£4.25-£7.50, Main £9.95-£18.95, Dessert £4.50-£6,
Service optional **Wines** 4 bottles over £30, 20 bottles
under £30, 8 by glass **Notes** Early D 2 course £9.95
6-7pm, Sunday L £19.95, Vegetarian available **Seats** 65
Children Portions, Menu **Parking** On street/car park

Little Barwick House

YEOVIL   MAP 4 ST51

Modern European 🍷 NOTABLE
WINE LIST

**Classical Anglo-French cooking in a family-run
Georgian house**

☎ 01935 423902
Barwick Village BA22 9TD
e-mail: reservations@barwick7.fsnet.co.uk
dir: Turn off A371 Yeovil to Dorchester opposite Red
House rdbt, 0.25m on left

Perched on the Somerset-Dorset border, not far from
Yeovil, Little Barwick is a listed Georgian dower house
that's run these days very much as a family affair. Tim
and Emma Ford met while he was cooking at Sharrow Bay
in the Lake District (see entry), and their teenage sons do
their bit in helping run the dining room. Horses, cats and
a dog complete the harmonious menage. The place is
decorated in textbook country-house style, but without
choking you in chintz, the dining room itself being a
perfect example of how to create a sense of refinement
without over-egging any puddings. Good table linen and
glassware look the part, and the net curtains are parted
to reveal a view of some of the three acres of grounds.
Tim Ford's cooking is a considered approach to Anglo-
French fine dining with a strong seasonal air, with dishes
that are constructed of properly complementary elements
that pull together as they should. First up might be a
warm terrine of lemon sole and salmon, given depth with
an intense lobster sauce, or grilled red mullet dressed in
marinated carrot and orange. The palate thus primed,
main courses follow on with pinkly roasted roe deer,
classically served with braised red cabbage, beetroot
purée and rösti, or Cornish sea bass in white wine with
basil-scented crushed new potatoes. Nothing goes
against the grain of expectation, but is a sterling
representation of the tried and true, never more so than
when medallions of local beef fillet appear in the
company of dauphinoise, red onion confit and truffled
Madeira sauce. To finish, there may be a luxurious crème
brûlée laced with Grand Marnier, served with lemon curd
ice cream, two-tone chocolate terrine with griottine
cherries and white chocolate ice cream, or a selection of
West Country farmhouse cheeses with membrillo.

Chef Timothy Ford **Owner** Emma & Timothy Ford
Times 12-2/7-9 Closed New Year, 2 wks Jan, Sun-Mon, L
Tue **Prices** Fixed L 2 course £23.95, Fixed D 3 course
£43.95, Service optional **Wines** 6 by glass
Notes Vegetarian available **Seats** 40 **Children** Portions
Parking 25

WINCANTON   Map 4 ST72

Holbrook House

◎◎ Modern British ❧

Carefully considered cooking on an ancient West Country estate

☎ 01963 824466
Holbrook BA9 8BS
e-mail: enquiries@holbrookhouse.co.uk
web: www.holbrookhouse.co.uk
dir: From A303 at Wincanton, turn left on A371 towards Castle Cary & Shepton Mallet

A privately owned Georgian country-house hotel in 20 acres of West Country pasture and woodland, Holbrook has enough history to keep you absorbed over a long weekend. The estate can trace its lineage back to the 13th century, and the house itself was once owned by General Henry Shrapnel, whose claim to painful fame hardly needs guessing at. The elegant, peach-toned Cedar Restaurant enjoys restful views over the grounds, and is the setting for new chef James Forman's carefully considered, locally supplied British cooking. The vogue for Indian seasonings is celebrated in an opener that sees John Dory accompanied by curried lentils and a salad of beetroot, apple and sorrel, which might be followed by roast rib and braised belly of pork with anise-scented carrot purée in red wine jus, or accurately timed sea bass with langoustine tortellini in lemongrass and ginger broth. At the close of proceedings, a featherlight caramel soufflé is served with the contrasting temperatures of hot chocolate sauce and vanilla ice cream, or there are quality regional cheeses.

Chef James Forman **Owner** Mr & Mrs J McGinley
Times 12.30-2/7-9 Closed L Mon-Thu, D Sun
Prices Prices not confirmed **Wines** 10 by glass
Notes Sunday L, Vegetarian available, Dress restrictions, Smart casual, Civ Wed 250 **Seats** 70, Pr/dining room 140
Children Portions **Parking** 100

WOOKEY HOLE   Map 4 ST54

Wookey Hole Inn

◎ Modern European

Vibrant cooking in quirky Somerset inn

☎ 01749 676677
High St BA5 1BP
e-mail: mail@wookeyholeinn.com

The beamed exterior of this village inn opposite the eponymous tourist-magnet caves presents an orthodox face to the world, but inside there's a one-off maverick approach to interior décor, with a quirky collection of art and objets referencing the Mediterranean, North Africa and nearby Glastonbury. You may never make it out of the convivial bar unless you approach the arsenal of local ales, ciders and perries, and tongue-twisting, brain-scrambling Belgian brews with caution, which would be a shame as the eclectic menu sings in tune with the setting, referencing the Mediterranean and North Africa in an enticing repertoire. Ham and spinach potato cake with tomato and cardamom chutney, and smoked mayonnaise is a typical starter, while mains could bring on pan-roasted rump of lamb with dauphinoise potato, red onion tarte Tatin and carrot purée. Medjool date and custard tart with a shot glass of rhubarb and Campari jelly is an inventive way to finish.

Times 12-2.30/7-9.30 Closed 25-26 Dec, D Sun

YEOVIL   Map 4 ST51

Little Barwick House

◎◎◎ – **see page 435**

The Yeovil Court Hotel & Restaurant

◎◎ Modern European

Modern hotel with stimulating brasserie cooking

☎ 01935 863746
West Coker Rd BA20 2HE
e-mail: unwind@yeovilhotel.com
web: www.yeovilhotel.com
dir: 2.5m W of town centre on A30

On the outskirts of town, the sparkling white Yeovil Court has been kitted out with a modern makeover. It's all expansive, light-filled, airy spaces these days, and is run with a relaxed approach by a young team. The entire ground floor is given over to eating and drinking in one form or another, from the bar where lighter bites are served to the large restaurant with its black-and-white window blinds and elegant table settings. The cooking offers a stimulating version of modern brasserie food, influences drawn from far and wide for the likes of marinated tuna with Thai noodle salad dressed in chilli and sesame oil, followed by fillet of Dorset beef with satisfyingly textured pearl barley risotto and parsnip crisps, or grilled monkfish with red onion couscous and rocket. A classic combination of flavours and temperatures distinguishes a finisher of hot chocolate fondant with pistachio ice cream.

Chef Simon Walford **Owner** Brian Devonport
Times 12-1.45/7-9.30 Closed 26-30 Dec, L Sat
Prices Prices not confirmed Service optional **Wines** 8 by glass **Notes** Vegetarian available **Seats** 50, Pr/dining room 80 **Children** Portions **Parking** 65

Save on Hotels. Book at **theAA.com/hotel**

STAFFORDSHIRE 437 ENGLAND

STAFFORDSHIRE

BURTON UPON TRENT
Map 10 SK22

Three Queens Hotel

◉ Modern British

Central location, traditional home comforts

☎ 01283 523800
1 Bridge St DE14 1SY
e-mail: hotel@threequeenshotel.co.uk
dir: On A511, at junct of High St & Bridge St

The Three Queens Hotel dates from 1531 and sits at the centre of town close to the River Trent amid Burton's brewing heritage. Friendly staff make sure everyone gets a warm welcome, and the place exudes an easygoing, lived-in vibe. The relaxed Grill Room has a clubby intimacy with its wood panelling, screens and stained-glass windows that sits well with the kitchen's straightforward traditional cooking. Reliable hands in the kitchen conjure up comfortable mainstream ideas from well-sourced ingredients - seared scallops in garlic butter with salsify purée might appear among starters, while mains can be as simple as chargrilled steaks, braised lamb shank with roasted root vegetables and rosemary jus, or follow a more Mediterranean route by teaming chicken ballottine filled with sun-dried tomatoes with black olive mash and basil cream.

Times 6.15-10 **Closed** L all week

LEEK
Map 16 SJ95

Three Horseshoes Inn & Country Hotel

◉◉ Modern British V ✧

Grills and much more in a Peak District country inn

☎ 01538 300296
Buxton Rd, Blackshaw Moor ST13 8TW
e-mail: enquiries@threeshoesinn.co.uk
web: www.threeshoesinn.co.uk
dir: M6 junct 15 or 16 onto A500. Exit A53 towards Leek. Turn left onto A50 (Burslem)

The stone-built inn overlooked by lowering gritstone outcrops in the southern stretches of the Peak District does a good job of covering many bases. It's a country pub, a smart rural hotel and a chic brasserie and grill all in the one package. The original oak beams in the brasserie and grill are offset by contemporary styling, with an open-to-view kitchen augmenting the dynamic atmosphere. The odd Southeast Asian dish appears on the menu among the western stuff, so that chicken, rabbit and pigeon terrine must take its chances amid the excitements of three Thai ways with crab (spring roll with tamarind, in noodle salad, and crabcake) to start, followed by Penang red curry on pineapple fried rice, or a steak from the Inka charcoal grill served with beef dripping chips, roasted tomato, herb butter, roasted mushroom and your choice of sauces. Intensive labours pay off in a dessert that offers white chocolate and raspberry in the various manifestations of trifle, cheesecake, doughnut and Eton mess.

Chef Mark & Stephen Kirk **Owner** Bill, Jill, Mark & Stephen Kirk **Times** 6.30-9 **Closed** 26-30 Dec, 1-2 Jan, Sun, L all week **Prices** Starter £5.95-£7, Main £10.50-£19.95, Dessert £4.95-£6.50 **Wines** 47 bottles over £30, 67 bottles under £30, 10 by glass **Notes** £17-£19, Vegetarian menu, Dress restrictions, Smart casual, Civ Wed 178 **Seats** 50, Pr/dining room 150 **Children** Portions, Menu **Parking** 100

LICHFIELD
Map 10 SK10

Swinfen Hall Hotel

◉◉ Modern British V ✧

Classy modern cooking in a classic location

☎ 01543 481494
Swinfen WS14 9RE
e-mail: info@swinfenhallhotel.co.uk
web: www.swinfenhallhotel.co.uk
dir: 2m S of Lichfield on A38 between Weeford rdbt & Swinfen rdbt

Swinfen Hall is a neo-classical Georgian manor house that has the look of a costume drama film set, an impression which continues through to the Four Seasons Restaurant, where oak panelling, opulent swagged drapes at sash windows, and linen-clad tables set with shiny silver, Wedgwood china and crystal glasses create a suitably classical setting. The country-house cooking fits the bill, but it shows its mettle with some gently contemporary touches. An emphasis on local-sourcing sees head chef Adam Thomson curing his own meats and smoking his own fish, while the hotel's own walled garden supplies much of the seasonal fruit and vegetables. If you're not up to the full-dress tasting menu, the prix-fixe formula might set off with tortellini of lobster with confit tomatoes and basil purée, then proceed via a classy turf and surf combo of pan-fried John Dory and crisp pork belly matched with a leek tarte fine and pork jus, to conclude exotically with star anise pannacotta with pineapple and pink peppercorn salad and rum sorbet.

Chef Adam Thomson **Owner** Helen & Vic Wiser **Times** 12.30-2.30/7.30-9.30 **Closed** D Sun **Prices** Fixed L 2 course £18.90-£20.45, Tasting menu £60-£85, Service optional **Wines** 98 bottles over £30, 31 bottles under £30, 9 by glass **Notes** ALC D 3 course £48, Sunday L £26.50-£32.50, Vegetarian menu, Dress restrictions, No trainers or jeans, Civ Wed 120 **Seats** 50, Pr/dining room 20 **Parking** 80

STAFFORD
Map 10 SJ92

The Moat House

◉◉ Modern British ✧

Confident, creative cooking by a canal

☎ 01785 712217
Lower Penkridge Rd, Acton Trussell ST17 0RJ
e-mail: info@moathouse.co.uk
web: www.moathouse.co.uk
dir: M6 junct 13 towards Stafford, 1st right to Acton Trussell, hotel by church

This Grade II-listed moated manor house dating back to the 14th century has a lovely waterside location; diners in the Conservatory Restaurant get to watch the narrow boats wend their way along the canal from the comfort of their linen-clad tables, where candles flicker in the evening. The hotel competes in the wedding and business markets, while its restaurant is a hit for its ambitious contemporary cooking. The presence of a tasting menu nails their ambition to the mast (there's a veggie one too), with matching wines available if you wish to go the whole hog. From the à la carte, start with a decidedly modish Jerusalem artichoke velouté with caper and sultana purée, cauliflower beignet and micro coriander, before moving on to a flavoursome slow-cooked blade of beef with Savoy cabbage and bacon, creamed potatoes, chestnut mushrooms, glazed shallots and Guinness sauce. The creative thinking continues at dessert stage, too: banana and caramel parfait, perhaps, with toffee popcorn and bitter chocolate sorbet.

Chef Matthew Davies, James Cracknell **Owner** The Lewis Partnership **Times** 12-2/6.30-9.30 **Closed** 25 Dec **Prices** Fixed L 2 course £17-£20, Fixed D 3 course £22.95-£30, Tasting menu £60-£90, Starter £8-£12, Main £16-£28, Dessert £8-£10, Service optional **Wines** 61 bottles over £30, 87 bottles under £30, 16 by glass **Notes** Tasting & early doors menu available, Sunday L, Vegetarian available, Dress restrictions, Smart casual, Civ Wed 120 **Seats** 120, Pr/dining room 150 **Children** Portions, Menu **Parking** 200

UTTOXETER — Map 10 SK03

Restaurant Gilmore at Strine's Farm

◉◉ Modern British ✋

Locally-supplied kitchen in a Staffordshire farmhouse

☎ 01889 507100
Beamhurst ST14 5DZ
e-mail: paul@restaurantgilmore.com
dir: 1.5m N of Uttoxeter on A522 to Cheadle. Set 400yds back from road along fenced farm track

Sweep up the long drive to the Gilmores' converted farmhouse restaurant for hearty modern British cooking set in a pretty cottage garden. The house has the anticipated country charm and comforts, with the restaurant divided between a number of intimate ground-floor rooms decorated in warm neutral tones and tables laid with crisp white linen. The kitchen (with Paul Gilmore behind the stove) deals in quality produce, looking to the local Staffordshire larder wherever possible, including the property's own kitchen garden which supplies some of the fresh fruit, veg and herbs. Everything is home-made, while seasonality is a given and attention to detail reigns in dishes underpinned by a classical theme. Poached blade of Staffordshire beef 'bourguignonne' (with onions, mushrooms, bacon and mash), for example, or baked fillet of brill served with a spiced tomato and brown shrimp velouté, and to finish, maybe a signature bread-and-butter pudding with rich vanilla sauce anglaise.

Chef Paul Gilmore **Owner** Paul & Dee Gilmore
Times 12.30-2/7.30-9 Closed 1 wk Jan, 1 wk Etr, 1 wk Jul, 1 wk Oct, Mon-Tue, L Sat, Wed, D Sun **Prices** Fixed L 2 course £25, Fixed D 3 course £35, Service optional, Groups min 8 service 10% **Wines** 6 by glass **Notes** Fixed D 4/5 course £40/£45, Sunday L, Vegetarian available, Dress restrictions, Smart casual **Seats** 24
Children Portions **Parking** 12

SUFFOLK

ALDEBURGH — Map 13 TM45

Brudenell Hotel

◉◉ Modern British, European ✋

Sunny brasserie cooking in a beachfront hotel

☎ 01728 452071
The Parade IP15 5BU
e-mail: info@brudenellhotel.co.uk
web: www.brudenellhotel.co.uk
dir: A12/A1094, on reaching town, turn right at junct into High St. Hotel on seafront adjoining Fort Green car park

The elegant hotel stands proud on the Aldeburgh seafront, just a few steps from the shingle beach. As you might hope and expect, there are lovely panoramic marine views, especially from the terrace and the spacious, light-filled restaurant, attired in sunny yellow and sky-blue. A major refurbishment has enhanced the atmosphere of breezy freshness, and the casual approach of the service feels just right. James Barber steps up to the plate with bright modern brasserie dishes using good ingredients, many of them local. Start with potted venison and spiced apricot chutney, or a retro courgette flower stuffed with crab mousse, served in rich crab bisque. Mains range from classic British fare with a delicate twist, such as panko-crumbed plaice, mushy peas, chips and tartare sauce, to more cross-Channel offerings like duck leg with sauté potatoes in peppercorn sauce. The retro styling resurfaces in desserts such as textbook peach Melba, properly made with meringue, vibrant raspberry coulis, flaked almonds and a local vanilla ice cream.

Chef James Barber **Owner** TA Hotel Collection
Times 12-2.30/6-9 **Prices** Starter £6-£18, Main £10-£26, Dessert £6-£8.50, Service optional **Wines** 28 bottles over £30, 32 bottles under £30, 47 by glass **Notes** Sunday L £6-£18, Vegetarian available, Dress restrictions, Smart casual **Seats** 100, Pr/dining room 20 **Children** Portions, Menu **Parking** 15, Fort Green car park

152 Aldeburgh

◉ Modern British, European ✋

Modern European cooking near the beach

☎ 01728 454594
152 High St IP15 5AX
e-mail: andy.lister@virgin.net
dir: From A12, follow A1094 to Aldeburgh, located next to Tourist Information Centre

Step under the archway that links the High Street to the beach to find this bustling brasserie, which exactly fits the Aldeburgh bill. Light and clean-cut, with stripped wood floors, cream panelling, fresh flowers and cheerful service, it weaves a mood of relaxation that everyone, especially busy festival-goers, will appreciate. Seasonally oriented modern European dishes feature locally landed fish, quality meats and game at the appropriate times of year, and achieve a reliable degree of consistency. Start with coarse-textured smoked mackerel pâté and melba toast, or chicken and Parma ham Caesar, and then proceed to one of the fresh fish dishes, perhaps lightly grilled plaice with crayfish and lemon butter, or a hunk of rump steak with field mushroom, chips and garlic butter. British cheeses and chutney, or sweet treats such as honey and ginger sponge and custard, or milk chocolate and raspberry cheesecake with berry compote, bring things to a close.

Chef Andrew Lister **Owner** Andrew Lister **Times** 12-3/6-10 Closed 25 Dec **Prices** Fixed L 2 course £13.95, Starter £4.95-£9.95, Main £10.95-£19.95, Dessert £5.25-£7.50, Service optional **Wines** 10 bottles under £30, 9 by glass **Notes** Sunday L, Vegetarian available **Seats** 56
Children Portions, Menu **Parking** On street parking on High St & Kings St

Regatta Restaurant

◉ Modern British ✋

Buzzy bistro, local fish the star

☎ 01728 452011
171 High St IP15 5AN
e-mail: rob.mabey@btinternet.com
dir: Middle of High St, town centre

The sea is just a pebble's skim away, so it is only right that super-fresh fish landed on the beach in Aldeburgh is showcased in Robert and Johanna Mabey's cheery bistro. Regatta has been going for two decades, drawing in local foodies with its bright and breezy ambience, stylish seaside-themed décor, and of course, Robert's confident and accurate treatment of splendid locally-sourced raw materials. A blackboard of spanking fresh fish specials bolsters the carte, which might get going with home-smoked prawns with garlic mayonnaise, then continue with Thai-style crayfish with chick pea salad and prawn crackers. Meat eaters could set about confit crispy duck leg with carrot purée and sautéed foie gras, and for pudding, something like a classic vanilla crème brûlée.

Chef Robert Mabey **Owner** Mr & Mrs R Mabey
Times 12-2/6-10 Closed 24-26 & 31 Dec, 1 Jan, D Sun (Nov-Feb) **Prices** Fixed D 3 course £15.95-£18.95, Starter £4.50-£8.50, Main £10-£18.50, Dessert £4.50-£5.50

Save on Hotels. Book at **theAA.com/hotel**

SUFFOLK 439 ENGLAND

Wines 6 bottles over £30, 30 bottles under £30, 8 by glass
Notes Sunday L, Vegetarian available **Seats** 90, Pr/dining room 30 **Children** Portions, Menu **Parking** On street

Wentworth Hotel

@@ Modern British

Family-run hotel with impeccable traditional cooking

☎ 01728 452312
Wentworth Rd IP15 5BD
e-mail: stay@wentworth-aldeburgh.co.uk
web: www.wentworth-aldeburgh.com
dir: From A12 take A1094 to Aldeburgh. In Aldeburgh straight on at mini rdbt, turn left at x-roads into Wentworth Rd. Hotel on right

The Wentworth is in a peaceful spot on Aldeburgh's seafront. Its restaurant has claret-coloured walls hung with portraits, a thickly carpeted floor, crisp napery and sea views. The cooking has its roots in the traditional English repertory, with local produce the mainstay: meats from Suffolk farms, fish landed on the beach that morning. There may not be many modern culinary fireworks, but techniques are sound and tried-and-tested combinations mean that dishes hit the spot. Starters range from prawn and crayfish salad with Marie Rose sauce to baked mushrooms in a stilton crust with roast red pepper and rocket salad, while main courses take in perhaps guinea fowl casseroled with root vegetables and bacon, served with mash and kale, beef bourguignon, or beautifully fresh, perfectly grilled Dover sole. A separate seafood listing may

offer pan-fried skate wing with caper and lemon butter, and among puddings could be zesty lemon tart.

Wentworth Hotel

Times 12-2/7-9

See advert below

The White Lion Hotel

@ British, French

Modern brasserie dining on the Aldeburgh seafront

☎ 01728 452720
Market Cross Place IP15 5BJ
e-mail: info@whitelion.co.uk
web: www.whitelion.co.uk
dir: M25 junct 28 to A12 onto A1094, follow signs to Aldeburgh at junct on left. Hotel on right

The White Lion is the famous Suffolk festival town's oldest hotel, sitting in prime beachfront splendour by the shingle banks of Aldeburgh's strand. Bathed in a dramatic cobalt-blue light by night, the sparkling-white building revels in a fresh contemporary look inside, with its beautifully-carved inglenook in the bar and oak panels in the restaurant still holding pride of place. Unpretentious brasserie dining is the deal here, and it's all built on fine Suffolk ingredients. In fact, sourcing doesn't get more local than the fish landed but a few steps away on the beach, which turns up on the plate as exemplary haddock in Adnams beer batter with crisp golden chips and chunky tartare sauce. Topping and tailing this fine main course are cranberry and goats'

cheese beignets with candied onions and pickled beetroot salad to start, and a moresome finale of white and dark chocolate brownie with Baileys ice cream and bitter chocolate sauce.

Times 12-3/5.30-10

BILDESTON — Map 13 TL94

The Bildeston Crown

@@@ – see page 440

BRANDESTON — Map 13 TM26

The Queen's Head Inn

@ Modern, Traditional British

Superior pub cooking in relaxing village inn

☎ 01728 685307
The Street IP13 7AD
e-mail: thequeensheadinn@btconnect.com
dir: Signed from A1120 at Earl Soham, follow signs to village, on left

In the heart of a lovely historic village, the old red-brick Queen's Head is a cracking local, drawing a loyal crowd for its well-kept Adnams ales and straight-talking modern pub food. It's the sort of place that hosts the village fete, beer festivals and summer's day hog roasts. Inside, expect heaps of character, log fires crackling in winter, smart contemporary style, and a friendly service team. Whether you're in the market for something straightforward from the blackboard menus or more gastronomically ambitious ideas from the carte, you can be sure it has all been cooked from scratch using tip-top Suffolk ingredients. Keeping things simple, French onion soup is a fine example of its ilk, especially when it's served with crusty bread and melted cheese; next comes beer-battered haddock and chips with tartare sauce and salad, then apple crumble and home-made custard rounds it all off to perfection.

Times 12-2/6.30-9 Closed Mon, D Sun

The Bildeston Crown

BILDESTON   MAP 13 TL94

Modern British 🍷 NOTABLE WINE LIST

High-octane cooking in revamped old coaching inn

☎ 01449 740510
104 High St IP7 7EB
e-mail: hayley@thebildestoncrown.co.uk
web: www.thebildestoncrown.com
dir: A12 junct 31. B1070 to Hadleigh, B1115 to Bildeston

The 15th-century Crown is one of those Suffolk pubs that shows off its antiquity in its black beams and less than perfect symmetry. Yesterday's old coaching inn is today's updated 21st-century version of the genre - ambitious restaurant, classy pub and chic hotel rolled into one, with bags of character and a contemporary sheen. There's a space to suit your mood, so you might sit outside in the courtyard, relax into a deep leather armchair by the fireplace in the bar, or seek out one of the many areas where you can eat, which includes the spiffed up Ingrams with its fine-dining finish. The provenance of what appears on the menu is rightly a big deal here - the owner is a farmer - and chef-patron Chris Lee (who runs the place with wife Hayley) keeps it all as local as possible. This is a creative and ambitious kitchen. If you want to see what they're really capable of, book a table in Ingrams and go for the eight-course

tasting menu, but there's also the Crown Select and Crown Classics menus to choose from. And it doesn't matter if you sit in the calming, comfortable main dining room at a linen-clad table, or at a chunky wooden one in one of the other eating areas. The quality of the bread offered gets things off on the right foot - really top-notch stuff, including a choice of four rolls such as blue cheese and walnut. A starter off the Select menu might be cumin-roasted scallops, fresh as a daisy and perfectly timed, with some smoked eel, carrots and cardamom. Follow that with thoroughly local Semer lamb with its sweetbreads, peas, broad beans and asparagus, whilst on the tasting menu there might be grey mullet with braised lettuce and langoustine. Everything looks beautiful on the plate and flavours and textures are well judged, not least in a dessert such as chocolate and raspberry délice served with a raspberry sorbet.

Chef Chris Lee **Owner** Mrs G & Mr J K Buckle **Times** 12-3/7-10 Closed D 25-26 Dec, 1 Jan **Prices** Fixed L 3 course £20.13, Fixed D 3 course £45, Tasting menu £70-£100, Service optional, Groups min 10 service 12.5% **Wines** 11 by glass **Notes** Fixed L Mon-Sat, D 5 course £50, Tasting 8 course, Sunday L, Vegetarian available, Civ Wed 24 **Seats** 100, Pr/dining room 18 **Children** Portions **Parking** 36, Market Sq (overflow)

Save on Hotels. Book at **theAA.com/hotel**

SUFFOLK 441 **ENGLAND**

The Angel Hotel

◉◉ Modern British

Brasserie dining in creeper-covered hotel

☎ 01284 714000
Angel Hill IP33 1LT
e-mail: staying@theangel.co.uk
web: www.theangel.co.uk
dir: Town centre, right from lights at Northgate St

This former Georgian coaching inn on the historic town square includes Charles Dickens amongst its former visitors. Covered in deep-green creepers and purple-pink wisteria, it is a quintessential British inn, albeit at the grander end of the spectrum. Inside, alongside the period features, there's a more contemporary tone, nowhere more so than in its stylish, pine-floored Eaterie restaurant, with its stunning artworks and views across the square to the cathedral. Mediterranean-influenced modern brasserie food is what the kitchen's all about; Tuscan ribollita or bruschetta with wild mushrooms, poached egg, parmesan cream and tuile to start, perhaps. Follow on with roasted pork belly teamed with walnut and goats' cheese croquettes, cabbage and apple and celeriac purée. Unashamedly Anglo dishes have their say too, perhaps delivered in a rhubarb and apple crumble dessert with crème anglaise.

Chef Jason Scrimshaw **Owner** Robert Gough
Times 12-9.45 All-day dining **Prices** Fixed L 2 course £15.50, Starter £5.50-£10.50, Main £12.50-£18.50, Dessert £5-£9.50, Service added but optional 10% **Wines** 44 bottles over £30, 24 bottles under £30, 34 by glass **Notes** Sunday L £18.95-£22.95, Vegetarian available, Dress restrictions, Smart casual **Seats** 85, Pr/dining room 16 **Children** Portions, Menu **Parking** 20

Best Western Priory Hotel

◉ Modern British, International

Brasserie cooking in a tranquil priory

☎ 01284 766181
Mildenhall Rd IP32 6EH
e-mail: reservations@prioryhotel.co.uk
web: www.prioryhotel.co.uk
dir: From A14 take Bury St Edmunds W slip road. Follow signs to Brandon. At mini-rdbt turn right. Hotel 0.5m on left

The Priory is a Grade II-listed building a couple of miles from Bury St Edmunds town centre, making the most of its tranquil setting with landscaped gardens bounded by the old priory walls, as well as a thoroughly relaxing ambience inside. The dining room is divided into three areas, including a conservatory, where smartly clothed tables confer an air of gentility for inspired brasserie-style dishes from the modern cookbook. Pigeon and guinea fowl terrine with toasted brioche, or Manchego parfait with tomato and basil salsa, are sterling openers, setting the scene for something like roast monkfish with chorizo and sultanas in chardonnay vinegar, or Denham Estate venison loin with horseradish rösti and parsnip

purée, in a sauce enriched with bitter chocolate. The ever-dependable way to finish is with properly sticky toffee pudding, served with caramel sauce and good vanilla ice cream, but the local farmhouse cheeses, served with quince jelly, are tempting too.

Chef Peter Hobday **Owner** Peter Hobday **Times** 12-2/7-10 Closed L Sat (unless by arrangement) **Prices** Fixed L 3 course £25, Fixed D 3 course £32, Starter £2.50-£7, Main £7-£19, Dessert £2-£7 **Wines** 4 bottles over £30, 18 bottles under £30, 5 by glass **Notes** Sunday L, Vegetarian available, Civ Wed 75 **Seats** 72, Pr/dining room 28 **Children** Portions **Parking** 60, On street

Clarice House

◉ Modern European

Well-crafted, modish cooking at a spa retreat

☎ 01284 705550
Horringer Court, Horringer Rd IP29 5PH
e-mail: bury@claricehouse.co.uk
web: www.claricehouse .co.uk
dir: From Bury St Edmunds on A143 towards Horringer and Haverhill, hotel 1m from town centre on right

Sybaritic spa pampering is the first item on the agenda for many of the guests at Clarice House. After a restorative hit of massage and manipulation, followed by an appetite-stimulating stroll through the splendid grounds of the Jacobean-style country house, a table awaits in the smart oak-panelled restaurant, a suitably sumptuous backdrop for uncomplicated modern European cooking. Start with goats' cheese pannacotta served with hot and sour cherry tomatoes, confit pepper and parmesan tuile, followed by a more substantial minced venison ragù with horseradish mash, roasted carrots and parsnips. With that under your belt, you might as well throw caution to the wind and finish with an orange and Grand Marnier crème brûlée with clementine jam and pistachio Madeleine.

Chef Steve Winser **Owner** King family **Times** 12-2/7-9 Closed 25-26 Dec, 1 Jan **Prices** Starter £5-£8, Main £10-£16, Dessert £6, Service optional **Wines** 4 bottles over £30, 15 bottles under £30, 14 by glass **Notes** Sunday L, Vegetarian available, Dress restrictions, Smart casual D, Civ Wed 100 **Seats** 70, Pr/dining room 20 **Parking** 110

The Grange Hotel

◉ Modern British NEW

Charming country-house with ambitious kitchen

☎ 01359 231260
Barton Rd, Thurston IP31 3PQ
e-mail: info@grangecountryhousehotel.com
web: www.grangecountryhousehotel.com
dir: A14 junct 45 towards Gt Barton, right at T-junct. At x-rds left into Barton Rd to Thurston. At rdbt, left after 0.5m, hotel on right

Three miles outside of Bury St Edmunds, the faux-Tudor Grange is a Victorian hotel with lots of period charm inside and out. It has lovely gardens to explore and a reassuringly traditional décor within, and, to confirm its

country-house credentials, there's a spa here too. The dining room is suitably elegant and refined, with a good deal of period character, and tables smartly set for what is to come. And what is to come is some well-crafted, bright, contemporary cooking. Start, perhaps, with tea-smoked chicken and foie gras terrine with pickled walnuts and a tarragon yoghurt dressing, or a red onion tarte Tatin with glazed Crottin goats' cheese and a balsamic and basil ice cream. For main course, seared Barbary duck comes with dauphinoise potatoes, Savoy cabbage, bacon and red wine jus, and, for dessert, there's chocolate textures (tart, fondant and gin-flavoured bonbon), or sticky toffee pudding with gingerbread ice cream and caramel sauce.

Chef Darren Marchant **Owner** Sortpad Limited **Times** 12-2/7-9 Closed 1 Jan **Prices** Starter £5.95-£8.50, Main £13.25-£21.95, Dessert £5.50-£8.95, Service optional **Wines** 23 bottles over £30, 23 bottles under £30, 15 by glass **Notes** Afternoon tea, Sunday L £18.95, Vegetarian available **Seats** 32, Pr/dining room 40 **Children** Portions **Parking** 60

The Leaping Hare Restaurant & Country Store

◉◉ Modern British

Vineyard restaurant with contemporary menu

☎ 01359 250287
Wyken Vineyards, Stanton IP31 2DW
e-mail: info@wykenvineyards.co.uk
dir: 8m NE of Bury St Edmunds, 1m off A143. Follow brown signs at Ixworth to Wyken Vineyards

It is hard to think of a more appealing way to acquaint yourself with the foodie delights of Suffolk than to explore the local wine trail and turn up for lunch (lunch only, take note) at Wyken Vineyard's Leaping Hare Restaurant. The 1,200-acre estate keeps food miles to an absolute minimum, supplying game, and meat from its herd of Red Poll cattle and flock of Shetland sheep, fruit, herbs and veg from the kitchen garden, and wine from the seven-acre vineyard, while a farmers' market brings more to the doorstep every Saturday. The setting is a striking 400-year-old timbered barn with a soaring raftered ceiling, wood-burning stoves, exposed wall beams, wooden floors, leaping hare-themed paintings and tapestries, and large windows opening onto fields and ancient woodlands. A simple modern approach to cooking lets the flavours shine through in dishes such as Ellingham goats' cheese and spinach soufflé with red onion sauce, followed by Wyken wild rabbit pie with suet shortcrust pastry, roast potatoes and anise-glazed carrots.

Chef Jon Ellis **Owner** Kenneth & Carla Carlisle **Times** 12-2.30/7-9 Closed 2 wks Xmas, D Sun-Thu **Prices** Fixed L 2 course £16.95, Starter £5.95-£7.95, Main £10.95-£19.95, Dessert £5.95, Service optional, Groups min 6 service 10% **Wines** 5 bottles over £30, 19 bottles under £30, 22 by glass **Notes** Sunday L, Vegetarian available **Seats** 55 **Children** Portions **Parking** 50

BURY ST EDMUNDS *continued*

Maison Bleue

◉◉ Modern French 🍷

Classical French seafood specialities in historic Bury

☎ 01284 760623
30-31 Churchgate St IP33 1RG
e-mail: info@maisonbleue.co.uk
dir: A14 junct 43 (Sugar Beet, Central exit) to town
centre. Follow signs to the Abbey Gdns, Churchgate St is
opposite cathedral

The Blue House is secreted amid the backstreets of the
historic part of town, an outpost of French seafood
celebration in East Anglia. Any blueness is gently
sponged away by the colour-free interiors, where black
pillars, wood tones and cream upholstery take over, and
even the pictures of roiling seascapes are easy on the
eye. Subdued lighting helps to soften the scene still
further. Thus cocooned, you should be perfectly primed for
the classically based French dishes on offer, which might
begin with deboned frogs' legs in garlic velouté with
broad beans and asparagus, or textbook Provençal-style
fish soup with all its accoutrements, before main courses
like roast turbot with aubergine caviar in sage sauce, or
wild salmon seasoned with grain mustard in parsley
sauce. Meat dishes are available too, perhaps guinea-
fowl breast stuffed with almonds and sultanas, and
sauced with amaretto. Probably the best note to end on is
with seasonal fruits such as local strawberries in their
own soup, served with strawberry yoghurt ice cream.

Chef Pascal Canevet **Owner** Regis Crepy, Pascal & Karine
Canevet **Times** 12-2/7-9 Closed Jan, 2 wks summer, Sun-
Mon **Prices** Fixed L 2 course £18.50, Fixed D 3 course fr
£32.50, Starter £7.50-£11.95, Main £16.95-£29.95,
Dessert £7.50, Service optional **Wines** 12 by glass
Notes Vegetarian available, Dress restrictions, Smart
casual recommended **Seats** 65, Pr/dining room 35
Children Portions **Parking** On street

Pea Porridge

◉◉ Modern Bistro 🍷

**Technically accomplished cooking of upbeat modern
ideas**

☎ 01284 700200
28-29 Cannon St IP33 1JR
e-mail: enquiries@peaporridge.co.uk
dir: Off A14 towards town, in Northgate St turn left into
Cadney Lane. Restaurant opposite Old Cannon Brewery

Originally two cottages, then a bakery (the oven still in
situ), Pea Porridge is now a homely and unpretentious
three-roomed restaurant with wooden floors, pine tables,
exposed bricks and an open fire. A strong streak of
invention and innovation runs through the menu, taking
in as it does Lebanese-style lamb broth (with merguez,
apricots, chickpeas, coriander and harissa), and sea
bream fillet with chorizo, braised cocoa beans, spinach,
peppers and root vegetables. Dishes can be as forthright
of flavours as starters of lamb sweetbreads in curry
sauce, accompanied by roast sweet potato and spinach,

and black pudding and crispy pigs' ears with cavolo nero
and chanterelles. Raw materials are carefully chosen,
timings are impressively accurate and if dishes can seem
overladen with different elements they nonetheless work
well: witness a main course of hake fillet - an excellent
piece of fish, perfectly timed - with tempura cod cheek (a
triumph), olive oil mash, samphire, fennel, saffron and
chives. Desserts can seem quite ordinary in comparison,
among them perhaps silky-smooth vanilla yoghurt and
mango pannacotta.

Chef Justin Sharp **Owner** Justin Sharp
Times 12-2.30/6.30-10 Closed 2 wks Sep, 2 wks Xmas,
Sun-Mon, L Tue **Prices** Prices not confirmed Service
optional **Wines** 15 bottles over £30, 25 bottles under £30,
9 by glass **Notes** Vegetarian available **Seats** 46, Pr/dining
room 20 **Parking** On street

Ravenwood Hall Hotel

◉◉ Modern British 🍷

Reliably interesting food in a Tudor building

☎ 01359 270345
Rougham IP30 9JA
e-mail: enquiries@ravenwoodhall.co.uk
web: www.ravenwoodhall.co.uk
dir: 3m E off A14, junct 45. Hotel on left

If you like your country-house hotels to come with plenty
of history, Ravenwood Hall has 500 years under its belt.
Set in seven acres of bucolic Suffolk, the place has been
around since Henry VIII was in the top job, and it is
propped up by carved oak timbers and decorated with
rare 15th-century wall paintings, antiques and huge
inglenooks. With its warm terracotta-hued walls, oak
panelling, tapestry curtains, crisp white linen and soft
candlelight, the dining room is a delight, as is the
kitchen's approach to uniting harmonious flavours and
textures. Ingredients tick all the seasonal and local boxes
- meats and fish are smoked in-house, and fruit and
vegetables are preserved on the premises. A summer
dinner begins with a cocktail of Norfolk crab with
shredded lettuce, cucumber jelly and tomato dressing,
then proceeds to rack of Bildeston lamb with ratatouille,
glazed carrots, sprouting broccoli, rösti and a delicious
jus. Awaiting at the end, roasted peaches and hazelnut
with rum syrup, hazelnuts syrup, vanilla shortbread,
vanilla cream and peach purée.

Chef Shayne Wood **Owner** Craig Jarvis **Times** 12-2/7-9.30
Prices Fixed L 2 course £16.95, Fixed D 3 course £19.95,
Starter £7.95-£15.95, Main £15.95-£21.95, Dessert
£6.95, Service optional **Wines** 21 bottles over £30, 24
bottles under £30, 22 by glass **Notes** 7 Cheese platter
£14.50, Indulgent coffees £6.95, Sunday L, Vegetarian
available, Civ Wed 130 **Seats** 50, Pr/dining room 50
Children Portions, Menu **Parking** 150

The White Horse

◉ Modern British 🍷

Well-crafted, unfussy cooking in country gastro-pub

☎ 01284 735760 & 07778 996666
Rede Rd, Whepstead IP29 4SS
dir: 5m from Bury St Edmunds, 2m off A143 Bury/
Haverhill

Stylishly made over in recent years, this mustard-yellow
village inn now sits comfortably at the gastro-pub end of
the spectrum, but without losing any of the features one
hopes for - the interior is a series of smart and cosy
rooms with a copper-sheathed bar serving Suffolk ales,
and there are exposed beams, a huge inglenook, country-
style tables and chairs, artwork on the walls, and
soothing Farrow & Ball colour schemes. The kitchen here
appreciates the value of top-class local ingredients,
follows the seasons keenly, and cuts no corners, making
everything from scratch (including their own bangers -
how about pork, paprika and sun-dried tomato
sausages?). The blackboard menu lists joyously simple
ideas: country pâté with home-made chutney and French
bread, followed by a North African-influenced slow-
braised shoulder of Ickworth lamb with tomatoes and
black olives. Finish with baked apricot cheesecake, or
bow out on a savoury note with a plate of East Anglian
cheeses.

Chef Gareth Carter **Owner** Gary & Di Kingshott
Times 12-2/7-9.30 Closed 25-26 Dec, D Sun
Prices Starter £2.25-£6.95, Main £8.95-£16.95, Dessert
£5.95, Service optional **Wines** 8 by glass **Notes** Fixed L
Mon-Fri, Fixed D Mon-Thu, Sunday L, Vegetarian available
Seats 50, Pr/dining room 25 **Children** Portions
Parking 30

CAVENDISH Map 13 TL84

The George

◉ Modern British

Modish cooking in characterful inn

☎ 01787 280248
The Green CO10 8BA
e-mail: thegeorgecavendish@gmail.com
web: www.thecavendishgeorge.co.uk

The whitewashed inn is 16th-century and Grade II listed,
though better described as a restaurant with rooms in
today's parlance. Its interior is dominated by wood, from
the bare tables to the heavy beams that lend the place its

character, and the reassuring buzz of kitchen activity in the background reminds you what the main priority is. A Mediterranean-inflected repertoire of modern British dishes is on offer, from the olives and garlic focaccia nibbles to the smoked monkfish with risotto nero, or cod with borlotti beans and pancetta. In between come some less familiar but equally tempting ideas - starters of hickory-smoked venison saddle with truffled beurre noisette and hazelnuts, or breast and leg of partridge with garlic pommes purée and capers - and a meal might end with rice pudding, but a chilled lemon and ginger version with red berries and jelly.

Chef Lewis Bennet **Owner** Lewis Bennet, Bonnie Steel **Times** 12-2/6-9.30 Closed 25 Dec, 1 Jan, D Sun **Prices** Fixed L 2 course £12.50, Fixed D 3 course £15, Starter £4.50-£8, Main £9.50-£19.50, Dessert £4.50-£5, Service optional **Wines** 10 bottles over £30, 29 bottles under £30, 18 by glass **Notes** Sunday L, Vegetarian available **Seats** 50 **Children** Portions, Menu **Parking** On street directly outside

CHILLESFORD   Map 13 TM35

The Froize Freehouse Restaurant

◉ British, European ◉

Popular inn with cracking menu

☎ 01394 450282
The Street IP12 3PU
e-mail: dine@froize.co.uk
dir: On B1084 between Woodbridge & Orford

Converted from a brace of red-brick gamekeepers' cottages, The Froize is a welcoming Suffolk inn that is in fine shape after a contemporary makeover, and the mood is dressed-down and relaxed. Chef-proprietor David Grimwood is a local lad who likes to bang the drum for local materials, so his food taps into the current appetite for ingredients-led, honest-to-goodness dishes with clean-cut flavours - it's all so driven by what's in season locally that there are no menus at lunch, just blackboards with the day's specials. This is food straight from the heart - roast shoulder of locally-reared Gloucestershire Old Spot pork is served with proper pan juice gravy, fresh apple sauce, crisp crackling and stuffing, or there might be slow-cooked hare with chestnuts, ceps and blackberry brandy. Starters could see Orford crab cakes pointed up with sweet chilli sauce, whilst desserts are comfort classics along the lines of marmalade bread and butter pudding.

Chef David Grimwood **Owner** David Grimwood **Times** 12-2/7-close Closed Mon (ex BHs) **Prices** Prices not confirmed Service optional **Wines** 14 by glass **Notes** Vegetarian available **Seats** 48, Pr/dining room 20 **Children** Portions **Parking** 40

DUNWICH   Map 13 TM47

The Ship at Dunwich

◉ Modern British ◉

Enterprising gastro-pub in a coastal village

☎ 01728 648219
Saint James St IP17 3DT
e-mail: info@shipatdunwich.co.uk
dir: From N: A12, exit at Blythburgh onto B1125, then left to village. Inn at end of road. From S: A12, turn right to Westleton. Follow signs for Dunwich

An open fire in the traditional bar, with real ales on hand-pump, exposed brick walls, flagstone floors, rustic-style furniture, plus a conservatory, garden and further rooms for eating - what could be nicer in a charming coastal village? Add in an interesting, crowd-pleasing menu and an ambitious, professional kitchen and it's easy to see why The Ship is a popular dining destination. Locally landed fish - battered cod with chips and mushy peas, for instance, or whole plaice roasted and served with garlic and parsley butter, sautéed potatoes and salad - is a strength, but there's much more, from crispy duck leg glazed with home-made plum jam accompanied by spring onion and bacon croquettes and vegetables, to slow-cooked pork belly with date and apple purée, crackling, caraway carrots, spring greens and mash. Start with something like pork and apple rillettes with onion and orange marmalade, and end with a comforting pudding: perhaps treacle tart.

Chef Matthew Goodwin **Owner** Agellus Hotels Ltd **Times** 12-3/6-9 **Prices** Prices not confirmed Service optional **Wines** 3 bottles over £30, 17 bottles under £30, 7 by glass **Notes** Open all day for food Jul-Aug, Sunday L, Vegetarian available **Seats** 70, Pr/dining room 35 **Children** Portions, Menu **Parking** 20

EYE   Map 13 TM17

The Cornwallis Hotel

◉ Modern British

Simple brasserie dishes in a timbered manor house

☎ 01379 870326 & 0844 414 6524
Rectory Rd, Brome IP23 8AJ
e-mail: reservations.cornwallis@ohiml.com
web: www.oxfordhotelsandinns.com

The partly Tudor house with its timbered façade and 23 acres of gardens and woodland is to be found in a pleasantly tranquil corner of East Anglia, with the level expanses of the Broads not far off. Unspoiled rustic appeal pervades the bar, while the Lexington dining room has been done out in a challenging shade of bright raspberry, adorned with a mixture of black and red chairs

and black-clad, aproned staff. The kitchen doesn't try to overreach itself, but stays within a safe brasserie repertoire that may feature the likes of poached pear, caramelised walnut and blue cheese salad, dressed in honey and mustard, beef carpaccio with sun-dried tomatoes and pine nuts, and decently rich chocolate mousse served in a glass with a blob of mascarpone. Home-made breads are a commendable touch.

Times 12-3/6-9 Closed L Mon-Sat

FRESSINGFIELD   Map 13 TM27

Fox & Goose Inn

◉◉ Modern British ◉

Village restaurant and bar with modish cooking

☎ 01379 586247
Church Rd IP21 5PB
e-mail: foxandgoose@uk2.net
dir: A140 & B1116 (Stradbroke) left after 6m - in village centre by church

Abutting Fressingfield's medieval church, this one-time timber-framed Tudor guildhall turned local inn - set at the heart of a small chocolate-box village - ticks all the quintessential English boxes. But appearances can be deceiving; inside the place sports a thoroughly pared-back modern look, and, while there's a wealth of character in its old beams and open fires and the bar still serves real ales tapped straight from the barrel, it's much more a restro-pub these days. Accomplished and creative European ideas pepper the kitchen's modern cooking driven by Suffolk's abundant larder. Take lemon sole fillets served with crab and potato tempura, English asparagus, chervil mayo, micro greens and a hazelnut vinaigrette, or perhaps beef bourguignon with horseradish mash, glazed carrots and parsnip purée. Finish in classic style with vanilla crème brûlée accompanied by an oatmeal tuile and blackcurrant sorbet. The more formal evenings-only restaurant is upstairs, while downstairs there's a smaller dining room in the old lounge as well as the bar area.

Chef P Yaxley, M Wyatt **Owner** Paul Yaxley **Times** 12-2/7-8.30 Closed 25-30 Dec, 2nd wk Jan for 2 wks, Mon **Prices** Fixed L 2 course £14.95-£19.50, Fixed D 3 course £32, Tasting menu £45, Service optional **Wines** 9 bottles over £30, 43 bottles under £30, 8 by glass **Notes** Tasting menu 8 course, Sunday L, Vegetarian available **Seats** 70, Pr/dining room 35 **Children** Portions **Parking** 15

HINTLESHAM — Map 13 TM04

Hintlesham Hall Hotel

◉◉ Modern European V ✋

Polished cooking in top-ranking country-house hotel

☎ 01473 652334
IP8 3NS
e-mail: reservations@hintleshamhall.com
web: www.hintleshamhall.com
dir: 4m W of Ipswich on A1071

Just so you know what you're looking at, the original house was built in the 16th century, but the pink-painted façade is a creation of the 18th century (1720 to be precise). This beautiful and impressive building is these days a country-house hotel of considerable charm - traditional, luxurious and grand. There are three dining rooms and the pick of the bunch is The Salon, which really and truly would not look out of place in a stately home or royal palace with its soaring natural features and lavish period décor. The cooking of head chef Alan Ford is not so rooted in the past, but neither does it chase every modern fad and fashion. You might start with cider-braised pork belly, apple and leek terrine served with a golden sultana and apple relish, before moving on to breast of local Gressingham duck with a sweet potato and tarragon cake and wild mushroom sauce. Regional ingredients get a good showing on the menu. To finish, iced pistachio parfait comes with spiced roasted plums, and the cheeses hail from Britain and France.

Chef Alan Ford **Owner** Has Modi **Times** 12-2/7-9.30
Prices Fixed L 2 course fr £18, Fixed D 3 course fr £33, Starter fr £12, Main fr £24, Dessert fr £9, Service optional **Wines** 12 by glass **Notes** Sunday L, Vegetarian menu, Dress restrictions, Tailored jacket at D, smart casual at L, Civ Wed 100 **Seats** 80, Pr/dining room 80 **Children** Portions **Parking** 80

INGHAM — Map 13 TL87

The Cadogan Arms

◉ Traditional British ✋

Well-executed dishes in stylish gastro-pub

☎ 01284 728443
The Street IP31 1NG
e-mail: info@thecadogan.co.uk
dir: A134 4m from Bury St Edmunds

The interior of this former coaching inn has been reworked and spruced up with a stylish décor, subdued lighting, upholstered sofas and chairs and a curved bar dispensing real ales. Flexibility is the name of the game, with grazing boards for snackers and a lunch menu of sandwiches and dishes like local ham, eggs and chips. The kitchen moves up a couple of gears in the evening, its skills and nifty presentation evident in smoked chicken with home-made chorizo and a crisp poached egg, followed by confit shoulder of mutton with fondant potato and root vegetable purée. Seafood gets the modern treatment: battered shrimps cut by sweet chilli jam, and smoked coley fillet in Welsh rarebit with pea velouté and new potatoes.

Chef Ricky Calder **Owner** David Marjoram **Times** 12-2.30/6-9.30 Closed 25-31 Dec **Prices** Starter £4.50-£6.50, Main £8.50-£16, Dessert £5.50, Service optional **Wines** 8 bottles over £30, 37 bottles under £30, 12 by glass **Notes** Sunday L £8.50-£14.50, Vegetarian available **Seats** 72 **Children** Portions, Menu **Parking** 39

IPSWICH — Map 13 TM14

Best Western Claydon Country House Hotel

◉ Modern British V

Modern British cooking close to Ipswich

☎ 01473 830382
16-18 Ipswich Rd, Claydon IP6 0AR
e-mail: enquiries@hotelsipswich.com
dir: A14, junct 52 Claydon exit from rdbt, 300yds on left

Two old village houses were joined seamlessly together to form this friendly, small-scale hotel to the north west of Ipswich. The Victorian-style restaurant overlooks the gardens through a conservatory extension, although the classic look has been given a gentle update by ditching the cloths on its darkwood tables and adding high-backed leather chairs. Staff are smartly turned out to create a professional, welcoming vibe, and the kitchen draws on splendid locally-sourced produce as the bedrock of its unfussy European-accented modern British dishes. Expect starters along the lines of seafood risotto with rocket and parmesan, while mains could turn up roast rack of lamb with chive mash, wilted greens, and red wine and rosemary glaze. End with a warm Belgian chocolate muffin with chocolate sauce and vanilla ice cream.

Chef Frankie Manners **Owner** Mr Khurram Saeed **Times** 12-2/7-9.30 **Prices** Fixed D 3 course fr £24.95,

Service optional **Wines** 5 by glass **Notes** Sunday L, Vegetarian menu, Civ Wed 80 **Seats** 40, Pr/dining room 85 **Children** Portions, Menu **Parking** 80

Best Western Gatehouse Hotel

◉ Modern British V

Unfussy modern food in Regency-style country house

☎ 01473 741897
799 Old Norwich Rd IP1 6LH
dir: A14 junct 53 take A1156 Ipswich, left at lights onto Norwich Road, hotel on left

This small and friendly country house hotel on the outskirts of Ipswich offers a pleasant juxtaposition of town and country in a handsome Regency building. Three acres of immaculately-kept mature gardens provide seclusion as well as pleasant pre-dinner strolls to sharpen the appetite before settling into the easygoing ambience of the restaurant, where an elegant centrepiece fireplace and heaps of period character are set against a more contemporary look of smart high-backed leather seating and bare darkwood tables. The kitchen doesn't try to reinvent the wheel here, preferring to keep things simple and put its faith in the quality of local produce. You might set the ball rolling with something as straightforward as king prawns in crispy filo pastry with sweet chilli dipping sauce and baby leaf salad, followed by pan-seared rump steak with sautéed new potatoes, roasted red onions and wilted spinach. To finish, there's the comfort of steamed spotted dick with home-made custard.

Chef Frankie Manners **Owner** Khurram Saeed **Times** 12-2/7-9.30 **Prices** Fixed L 2 course fr £19.95, Fixed D 3 course fr £24.95, Service optional **Wines** 5 by glass **Notes** Sunday L, Vegetarian menu **Seats** 40 **Children** Portions, Menu **Parking** 30

Mariners

◉ French, Mediterranean

Honest Gallic fare afloat in Ipswich

☎ 01473 289748
Neptune Quay IP4 1AX
e-mail: info@marinersipswich.co.uk
dir: Accessed via Key St. Follow brown tourist signs to waterfront

Moored alongside Neptune Quay at Ipswich Marina, close to the town centre, this floating French brasserie on an old gunboat is a quirky destination to enjoy some good Gallic cuisine. The vessel might date back to 1899 when it was launched in Belgium, but inside it's all shipshape: original brass and woodwork are coupled with chandeliers and candles on the clothed tables, and you can even hear the calls of seagulls while you eat. Go up on deck for an alfresco lunch in the sun, but wherever you choose to eat, look forward to good, honest French food confidently presented. Maroille cheese tart and green leaves, perhaps, or moules marinière, followed by grilled halibut fillet with chive and shrimp sauce, or rabbit hotpot with prune and white wine sauce. To finish, an apple 'tart of Normandy' is served warm with vanilla ice cream.

Times 12-2.30/7-9.30 Closed Jan, Sun-Mon

Milsoms Kesgrave Hall

◉ Modern International ✪

Relaxed dining in a contemporary setting

☎ 01473 333741
Hall Rd, Kesgrave IP5 2PU
e-mail: reception@kesgravehall.com
web: www.kesgravehall.com
dir: A12 N of Ipswich/Woodbridge, rdbt onto B1214

A buzzy bistro is at the culinary heart of Kesgrave Hall, a Georgian mansion in thick woodland just north of Ipswich. Inside, however, a boutique makeover in recent years has reinvented the place as a stylish boutique hotel with a pared-back modern look involving oak floors, pine tables, leather chairs and muted shades of cream and sage; outdoors, there's a spacious terrace with a retractable awning that keeps the place on the boil whatever the weather. The crew in the open kitchen are nicely in tune with the surrounding landscape, serving modern brasserie dishes along the lines of smoked haddock fishcake with a soft boiled egg, pickled cucumber and lemon mustard mayonnaise, followed by braised Dedham Vale beef featherblade with carrot purée, cavolo nero and crispy bone marrow. Wrap it all up with pineapple tarte Tatin, with coconut sorbet, candied noodles and rum syrup.

Chef Stuart Oliver **Owner** Paul Milsom **Times** 12-9.30 All-day dining **Prices** Starter £5.75-£10.95, Main £10.95-£21.50, Dessert £5.95, Service optional **Wines** 38 bottles over £30, 43 bottles under £30, 18 by glass **Notes** Sunday L £14.25-£15.25, Vegetarian available **Seats** 80, Pr/dining room 24 **Children** Portions, Menu **Parking** 150

Salthouse Harbour Hotel

◉◉ Modern British ✪

Well-executed, modish dishes on the waterfront

☎ 01473 226789
1 Neptune Quay IP4 1AX
e-mail: reservations@salthouseharbour.co.uk
dir: A14 junct 53, A1156 to town centre & harbour, off Key St

Smack on the waterfront overlooking the marina, Salthouse Harbour is a converted warehouse reinvented

as a design-led contemporary boutique hotel. Ablaze with vivid colours and with its rich red-brick walls hung with an eclectic collection of striking modern art and installations and eye-catching kitsch curiosities, The Eaterie rather undersells itself with such a self-effacing name. It is an expansive, well-thought-out space kept ticking over by a switched-on young service team. The name of the game is clearly to combine good-quality, local and seasonal ingredients with lively contemporary treatments to produce a Mediterranean-accented menu with broad appeal. Plump scallops are teamed with a crisp sweet potato and chorizo croquette and roasted tomato salsa, while loin of venison wrapped in bacon stars in a main course with beetroot and blackberry purée, braised red cabbage, Parisienne potatoes and red wine venison jus. The flavours keep on coming right through to a dessert of affogato - vanilla ice cream with hot espresso poured over - with cinnamon doughnuts.

Chef Arron Jackson **Owner** Robert Gough **Times** 12-10 **Prices** Fixed L 2 course fr £13.95, Starter £6-£10, Main £12.95-£29, Dessert £5.95-£7.95, Service added but optional 10% **Wines** 44 bottles over £30, 24 bottles under £30, 34 by glass **Notes** Sunday L £17.95-£21.95, Vegetarian available **Seats** 70 **Children** Portions, Menu **Parking** 30

Theobalds Restaurant

◉◉ Modern British ✪

Seasonal country cooking in a Tudor inn

☎ 01359 231707
68 High St IP31 2HJ
dir: 7m from Bury St Edmunds on A143 (Bury to Diss road)

A Tudor inn in a village to the north of Bury St Edmunds, Theobalds could hardly be mistaken for anything else inside, with its abundance of uneven oak timbers, inglenook fireplace and plain whitewashed walls. Simon Theobald is an assiduous country chef, seeking out the best of seasonal produce, and letting it lead the transformation of his menus through the year. Autumn might bring a salad of shredded Serrano ham with gruyère, Cox's and croûtons in mustard seed vinaigrette, or poached mussels with shallots in cider cream, to start. Game crops up alluringly in the form of roast breast of partridge with golden sultanas in Calvados sauce, or there may be grilled plaice with brown shrimps in chive-strewn white wine butter sauce. Dishes boast well-defined flavours and confident timing, through to a serving of blackberry and apple clafoutis in a crisp pastry shell with apple ice cream.

Chef Simon Theobald **Owner** Simon & Geraldine Theobald **Times** 12.15-1.30/7-9 Closed 10 days in Spring/Summer, Mon, L Tue-Thu, Sat, D Sun **Prices** Fixed L 2 course £21.95-£22.95, Fixed D 3 course £31.95, Starter £7.50-£9.95, Main £15.95-£20.75, Dessert £7.50, Service optional **Wines** 16 bottles over £30, 34 bottles under £30, 7 by glass **Notes** Fixed L menu available Fri, Fixed D midweek & Fri, Sunday L, Vegetarian available **Seats** 42, Pr/dining room 16 **Children** Portions **Parking** On street

Lavenham Great House Restaurant with Rooms

◉◉ Modern French ✪

Modern French cooking in a medieval building

☎ 01787 247431
Market Place CO10 9QZ
e-mail: info@greathouse.co.uk
web: www.greathouse.co.uk
dir: In Market Place (turn onto Market Lane from High Street)

Opposite the 16th-century timber-framed Guildhall, owned by the National Trust, The Great House is itself pretty ancient behind its Georgian façade, though its dining room has been given a thoroughly modern look. It's a calm and soothing room, done out in soft tones, with a darkwood floor and comfortable upholstered chairs at white-clothed tables set with flowers and sparkling glasses. The cooking has its roots in the great French repertoire, so foie gras and tongue terrine with a veal jus, ratte potatoes and apple jelly may be followed by best end rack of lamb, served pink, accompanied by rosemary sauce, vegetable jardinière and a potato, onion and thyme pie. That's not to say there aren't some more global influences at play though: lobster gets the Thai treatment and comes with red curry sauce, while steamed fillet of sea bass is given a pancetta emulsion and accompanied by a marmalade of red cabbage and juniper berries. Finish off with rich chocolate terrine with raspberry jelly and crème anglaise. There's a new patio for warmer days.

Chef Regis Crepy **Owner** Mr & Mrs Crepy **Times** 12-2.30/7-9.30 Closed Jan & 2 wks summer, Mon, L Tue, D Sun **Prices** Fixed L 2 course £18.50, Fixed D 3 course £33.50, Starter £9-£18, Main £18-£28, Dessert £6.95, Service optional, Groups min 10 service 10% **Wines** 65 bottles over £30, 75 bottles under £30, 10 by glass **Notes** Sunday L, Vegetarian available **Seats** 40, Pr/dining room 15 **Children** Portions **Parking** Market Place

LAVENHAM *continued*

The Swan

◎◎ Modern British V

Modern dining in medieval splendour

☎ 01787 247477
High St CO10 9QA
e-mail: info@theswanatlavenham.co.uk
web: www.theswanatlavenham.co.uk
dir: From Bury St Edmunds take A134 (S) for 6m then take A1141 to Lavenham

The historic market town of Lavenham grew fat on the wool trade in Tudor times, and that is precisely how long The Swan has been feeding all-comers. The textbook 15th-century timber-framed inn is a tangle of sagging timbers both in and out - even its ancient brick floors are constructed of ballast from the wool ships that made the town's fortune - and there are oak panels, inglenook fireplaces, and cosy nooks and crannies which have hosted many a boozy session for Second World War pilots who came in from Lavenham airfield to let off steam. It's hard to imagine a more evocative setting for a repertoire of crowd-pleasing pub classics, or you could trade up to the atmospheric Gallery restaurant and tuck into modern British dishes beneath soaring barn-style rafters and the impressive minstrels' gallery. Seared sea bass with warm chickpea and onion cream and curried cauliflower purée shows the style, ahead of pan-fried cod with saffron and chorizo rice, mussels, smoked trout, and king prawn tempura. Finish with a deconstructed lemon meringue pie.

Chef Justin Kett **Owner** Thorpeness & Aldeburgh Hotels Ltd **Times** 12-2.30/7-9.30 **Prices** Fixed L 2 course £16.95, Starter £8, Main £21, Dessert £6.95, Service optional **Wines** 111 bottles over £30, 32 bottles under £30, 11 by glass **Notes** Sunday L £25.95, Vegetarian menu, Dress restrictions, No jeans or trainers, Civ Wed 100 **Seats** 90, Pr/dining room 32 **Children** Portions, Menu **Parking** 50

LONG MELFORD   **Map 13 TL84**

The Black Lion Hotel

◎◎ Modern British

Imaginative cooking in Georgian hotel

☎ 01787 312356
Church Walk, The Green CO10 9DN
e-mail: enquiries@blacklionhotel.net
web: www.blacklionhotel.net
dir: From Bury St Edmunds take A134 to Sudbury. Right onto B1064 to Long Melford. Right onto A1092 to Cavendish. Hotel on village green

Overlooking Long Melford's village green, and with the town's antiques and crafts shops, and the Tudor delights of Melford Hall to explore, the Georgian Black Lion is an inviting prospect. Expect full-flavoured modern British dishes with plenty of flair and imagination. You could keep things casual in the lovely bar, where there's a real fire, water bowl for Rover and views across the green, and tuck into the likes of smoked eel and ham hock Scotch egg with beetroot and apple chutney, followed by caramelised loin of cod with Shetland mussels, spinach, and curry and Sauternes velouté. Otherwise, the more formal Georgian room restaurant with its deep-green walls, antiques and oil paintings, opening into a Victorian walled garden, is the setting for similarly clever combinations: diver-caught scallops with pig's head, cumin and pickled apple, then perhaps saddle of rabbit with Alsace bacon, violet potatoes, parsnip, prune, and verjus.

Times 12-2/7-9.30

LOWESTOFT   **Map 13 TM59**

The Crooked Barn Restaurant

◎◎ Modern British

Locally-based cooking in a thatched barn

☎ 01502 501353
Ivy House Country Hotel, Ivy Ln, Oulton Broad NR33 8HY
e-mail: aa@ivyhousecountryhotel.co.uk
web: www.ivyhousecountryhotel.co.uk
dir: A146 into Ivy Lane

The thatched barn was built around 1800, and is a beautifully atmospheric edifice, complete with creaking floorboards and a welter of skew-whiff heavy beams. Views over pretty gardens and ornamental ponds are a draw, and on summer days you can sit in the courtyard and get close to nature. The culinary stock-in-trade is modern British and European dishes made with predominantly local prime ingredients, making a virtue of their simplicity and freshness. A densely textured terrine of pork and apricots with a wholegrain mustard dressing is a bold starter, and could be succeeded by crisp-skinned grilled sea bass with beetroot and samphire in hollandaise, or roast rack of lamb with red onions and peas in minted red wine sauce. A version of summer pudding stuffed with raspberries and strawberries is a

seasonal treat, and is served with fragrant lavender ice cream.

Chef Martin Whitelock **Owner** Paul & Caroline Coe **Times** 12-1.45/7-9.30 Closed 19 Dec-6 Jan **Prices** Starter £5.50-£9.95, Main £14.95-£25.50, Dessert £5.50-£8.95, Service optional **Wines** 6 bottles over £30, 31 bottles under £30, 6 by glass **Notes** Sunday L £5.50-£9.95, Vegetarian available, Dress restrictions, Smart casual, No shorts, Civ Wed 80 **Seats** 45, Pr/dining room 24 **Children** Portions **Parking** 50

MILDENHALL   **Map 12 TL77**

The Bull Inn

◎ Modern British 🕙

Local produce and appealing modern menus

☎ 01638 711001
The Street, Barton Mills IP28 6AA
e-mail: reception@bullinn-bartonmills.com
web: www.bullinn-bartonmills.com
dir: Off A11 between Newmarket & Mildenhall, signed Barton Mills. Hotel by Five Ways rdbt

The Bull has dropped the 'olde' from its name and gone back to its original moniker, which seems appropriate given the forward-thinking, boutique approach that's going down in Barton Mills. There are spiffing designer bedrooms, a bar where you can drink a pint and eat some smart bar food, and a brasserie-style restaurant with a nifty menu that's big on local ingredients. Kick off a meal with Suffolk ham hock with wholegrain mustard and tarragon and home-made chutney, or brie fritters with a winter berry purée, watercress and caramelised walnuts. Move on to roast rump of Norfolk lamb with sweet potato Parmentier, charred broccoli, rosemary and red wine jus, or a locally-farmed steak cooked on the chargrill and served with smoked garlic mash or hand-cut chips, plus a field mushroom, plum tomato and watercress salad. Dessert might be a spring berry Eton tidy (the clue is in the title).

Chef Cheryl Hickman, Shaun Jennings **Owner** Cheryl Hickman & Wayne Starling **Times** 12-9 Closed 25 Dec, All-day dining **Prices** Starter £5.75-£7, Main £13-£26, Dessert £6.50-£7.50, Service optional **Wines** 15 bottles over £30, 21 bottles under £30, 11 by glass **Notes** Sunday L £13-£21, Vegetarian available **Seats** 60, Pr/dining room 30 **Children** Portions, Menu **Parking** 60

| **MONKS ELEIGH** | **Map 13 TL94** |

The Swan Inn

◉◉ British, Mediterranean ☺

Thatched country pub with clearly-focused menu

☎ 01449 741391
The Street IP7 7AU
e-mail: carol@monkseleigh.com
dir: On B1115 between Sudbury & Hadleigh

The decidedly chocolate box village of Monks Eleigh is home to this attractive 16th-century thatched pub. It matters not if you're after a pint of local real ale, a bar snack or a full-on feed: flexibility is the name of the game. Old beamed ceilings and oak floors await, plus some intelligently unfussy bistro-style cooking which can be taken in any part of the building, including the smart bar. Sound judgement from the kitchen allows the main ingredient (often local) to shine through in the likes of coarse pork rillette with green tomato chutney, or chilled Suffolk asparagus with parmesan flakes and balsamic dressing. Next up, perhaps grilled fillet of turbot with lobster and crayfish sauce, crushed celeriac and new potatoes, and, for dessert, an individual apple pie with vanilla custard.

Chef Nigel Ramsbottom **Owner** Nigel Ramsbottom
Times 12-2/7-9 Closed 25-26 Dec, Mon (except BHs), D

Sun **Prices** Fixed L 2 course £14.75, Fixed D 3 course £17.75, Starter £4.95-£8.50, Main £9.75-£22.50, Dessert £8.95, Service optional **Wines** 20 bottles under £30, 10 by glass **Notes** Sunday L, Vegetarian available **Seats** 30, Pr/dining room 24 **Children** Portions **Parking** 12

| **NEWMARKET** | **Map 12 TL66** |

Bedford Lodge Hotel

◉◉ Modern International ☺

Brasserie dishes near the famous racecourse

☎ 01638 663175
Bury Rd CB8 7BX
e-mail: info@bedfordlodgehotel.co.uk
web: www.bedfordlodgehotel.co.uk
dir: From town centre take A1304 towards Bury St Edmunds, hotel 0.5m on left

A Georgian hunting lodge built for the Duke of Bedford in the 18th century, this place has been a hotel since the 1940s. Its position near the racing at Newmarket, England's centre of operations for the sport of kings since medieval times, means that no opportunity is lost in the decorative theming to celebrate the equestrian life, and if you've had a win at the races, there are plenty of ways of celebrating it, from spa treatments to a festive occasion in Squires restaurant. An extensive menu of brasserie

dishes spans the range from straightforward classics such as blue cheese soufflé and rosemary and garlic lamb cutlets, to more adventurous offerings like guinea fowl with pancetta, celeriac fondant and sprout leaves in game reduction, or spiced monkfish loin with curried risotto and mango. Desserts look like a proper indulge-athon, with doughnuts for dipping in chocolate and toffee, or cookies and ice cream served with Jack Daniel's honey liqueur and peanut butter, and there are local cheeses. The fixed-price menus are particularly good value.

Chef James Fairchild **Owner** Review Hotels Ltd
Times 12-2/7-9.30 Closed L Sat **Prices** Fixed L 2 course £21.50-£25, Fixed D 3 course £26.50-£32, Starter £6-£9, Main £11-£29, Dessert £6.50-£9, Service added but optional 10% **Wines** 89 bottles over £30, 51 bottles under £30, 23 by glass **Notes** Sunday L, Vegetarian available, Dress restrictions, No shorts, sandals, vests, Civ Wed 150 **Seats** 60, Pr/dining room 150 **Children** Portions, Menu **Parking** 120

Tuddenham Mill

| **NEWMARKET** | **MAP 12 TL66** |

Modern British

Imaginative cooking of unusual ingredients in a converted watermill

☎ 01638 713552
High St, Tuddenham St Mary IP28 6SQ
e-mail: info@tuddenhammill.co.uk
dir: M11 junct 9 towards Newmarket, then A14 exit junct 38 in direction of Norwich. Turn right at Herringswell road

One of the more striking hotel and dining venues in East Anglia is to be found at a converted watermill on the Suffolk-Cambridgeshire border, between Newmarket and Bury St Edmunds. Some conversions gently transmute the former function of a building, disguising it in the process, whereas at Tuddenham, it has become a central feature,

the gigantic waterwheel itself encased in glass in the first-floor restaurant, while inset window panels in the floor allow views of the water rushing by below. There are ducks and swans nesting on the River Kennett, and the view over open countryside from the terrace tables on a summer evening is of a well-nigh perfect English idyll. Old gnarled beams dominate the interiors, but are offset with plain modern restaurant design, in the form of unclad black tables with black napkins, black-clad staff and smart, simple tableware. Paul Foster and his team source and forage locally and therefore seasonally, but there is also a willingness to bring less familiar ingredients and techniques on to the menus. The celery-like alexanders gathered on one of those foraging trips might be the basis for a soup garnished with egg yolk, apple and seeds. One of the inaugural courses on the tasting menu might involve duck heart, accompanied by rhubarb, fennel and wild rice. The counterpointing of flavours and textures is ingenious, as when a starter of crisp-fried chicken wings turns up with puréed and

macerated sultanas, parmesan crisps and miniature chicory leaves. The penchant for slow and gentle cooking is marshalled for a main course of shoulder and rump of lamb, which appears with crunchy fennel-scented quinoa and the softening element of natural yoghurt. Fish could be Cornish hake robustly matched with oxtail potato hash, aubergine and hispi, while the final curtain is reached with an egg custard tart flavoured with apple, accompanied by set buttermilk.

Chef Paul Foster **Owner** Agellus Hotels
Times 12-2.15/6.30-9.15 **Prices** Fixed L 2 course £20, Tasting menu £65, Starter £7.25-£8.50, Main £20.50-£25.75, Dessert £7.25-£9.75, Service optional **Wines** 141 bottles over £30, 32 bottles under £30, 13 by glass **Notes** Tasting menu 8 course, Fixed L 5 course £35, Sunday L £25, Vegetarian available, Civ Wed 120 **Seats** 54, Pr/dining room 18 **Children** Portions, Menu **Parking** 40

NEWMARKET *continued*

The Rutland Arms Hotel

◉ British, European

Classic bistro cookery in a 17th-century coaching inn

☎ 01638 664251
33 High St CB8 8NB
e-mail: reservations.rutlandarms@bespokehotels.com
web: www.bespokehotels.com
dir: A14 junct 37 onto A142, or M11 junct 9 onto A11 then
A1304 - follow signs for town centre

A coaching inn with lots of period charm, The Rutland
Arms is at the heart of the action in the racing hotspot of
Newmarket. Runners and riders on the menu in the
informal, green-carpeted Carriages dining room take in
bistro classics, as well as one or two more modern
dishes. Start with deep-fried whitebait with lemon mayo,
or goats' cheese truffles with balsamic glaze and confit
tomatoes, before moving to sea bass on tagliatelle in
white wine and shellfish cream, or liver and bacon with
creamy mash and sage and onion gravy. Desserts come
in a range of sizes, depending on appetite, but feature
the comforting likes of poached pear in chocolate sauce,
or lemon tart with raspberry compôte.

Chef Raymond Revel **Owner** Bespoke Hotels
Times 12-2.30/7-9.30 **Prices** Service optional **Wines** 1
bottle over £30, 27 bottles under £30, 6 by glass
Notes Sunday L fr £9.95, Vegetarian available **Seats** 50,
Pr/dining room 30 **Children** Portions **Parking** 40

Tuddenham Mill

◉◉◉ – *see page 447*

see page 447

| ORFORD | Map 13 TM45 |

The Crown & Castle

◉◉ Italian, British V 🍷 NOTABLE WINE LIST 🕯

Very good eating in an old Suffolk inn

☎ 01394 450205
IP12 2LJ
e-mail: info@crownandcastle.co.uk
web: www.crownandcastle.co.uk
dir: Off A12, on B1084, 9m E of Woodbridge

In picturesque Orford on the Suffolk coast, this one-time
pub, now restaurant with rooms, was built eight centuries
ago and is separated from the castle by a little lane. It's
co-owned by the original Hotel Inspector off the telly,
Ruth Watson, so it's a safe bet for an overnight stay and/
or dinner in the Trinity Restaurant. Here, beams,
unclothed wooden tables and comfortable burgundy-
velvet cushioned chairs and benches create a
relaxed vibe which is aided by the friendly serving staff.
The place is still an inn popular with the locals as well as
being something of a foodie destination, with the daily-
changing, Italian-accented menu majoring on modern,
unpretentious and flavour-driven dishes that showcase
the best the area has to offer. There are a few British
favourites like proper steak and kidney pie with mash and

buttered cabbage, but more typical of the style is beef
fillet carpaccio with 'Harry's Bar dressing' and parmesan
shavings to start, before super-fresh Orford-landed sea
bass with samphire, brown shrimps and potato gnocchi.
A rustic-style warm nectarine and frangipane tart and
vanilla ice cream makes a fine finish.

Chef Ruth Watson, Charlene Gavazzi **Owner** David & Ruth
Watson, Tim Sunderland **Times** 12.15-2.15/7-9.30
Prices Starter £4.95-£12.50, Main £15.50-£25, Dessert
£6.95, Service added but optional 10% **Wines** 65 bottles
over £30, 62 bottles under £30, 16 by glass **Notes** Pre-
concert supper available (Prior booking essential),
Sunday L, Vegetarian menu **Seats** 60, Pr/dining room 10
Parking 17, Market Sq, on street

| SIBTON | Map 13 TM36 |

Sibton White Horse Inn

◉ Modern European 🕯

Classic country pub with impressive modern cooking

☎ 01728 660337
Halesworth Rd IP17 2JJ
e-mail: info@sibtonwhitehorseinn.co.uk

There's not a pool table or bleeping one-armed bandit in
sight at the White Horse, a textbook real pub in a
picturesque sleepy Suffolk village. The food may be great,
but the place hasn't gone all gastro, first and foremost it
is the village boozer where locals pop in for a pint and a
chat in a true-blue setting dating back to Tudor times, as
its raised gallery, blackened beams, huge inglenooks,
and ancient floors of recycled Roman tiles all attest. The
kitchen deals in unpretentious modern dishes created
with a passion that hauls in fish from the nearby Suffolk
coast, and meat and game from local farms and shoots,
offering among starters seared wood pigeon breast with
poached quail's egg and crispy bacon, then fillet of
Lowestoft cod with sweet potato fondant, stir-fried
vegetables and herb oil, or breast and leg of wild duck
teamed with dauphinoise potato, butternut squash purée,
braised red cabbage and cherry jus.

Chef Gill Mason, James Finch **Owner** Neil & Gill Mason
Times 12-2/6.45-9 Closed Xmas, Mon **Prices** Fixed L 2
course £13.25, Starter £5.25-£7, Main £14-£20, Dessert
£5.50-£7.50, Service optional **Wines** 3 bottles over £30,
26 bottles under £30, 7 by glass **Notes** Sunday L
£10.95-£12.95, Vegetarian available **Seats** 40, Pr/dining
room 18 **Children** Portions **Parking** 45

| SOUTHWOLD | Map 13 TM57 |

The Blyth Hotel

◉ Modern British

Family-run seaside hotel with accomplished cooking

☎ 01502 722632
Station Rd IP18 6AY
e-mail: reception@blythhotel.com
dir: Follow A1095 from the A12, signed Southwold. Hotel
on left after bridge

The Blyth ticks all of the contemporary style-led boxes
needed to figure among Southwold's on-trend addresses.
The beach is just a five-minute stroll away, and stripped
pine floors, chunky wooden tables and a switched-on
family- and dog-friendly attitude lend the place an
appropriately seasidey vibe. Adnams ales are almost de
rigueur in the brewery's home manor, so have a pint in
the relaxed bar, then move into the classier environs of
the contemporary restaurant, for appealing modern ideas
built on seasonal and local materials. Expect starters
along the lines of pan-fried pigeon breast with bacon,
black pudding, soft-boiled quail's egg and celeriac purée,
then intelligently composed main courses such as braised
Dingley Dell pork belly with apple mashed potato,
buttered Savoy cabbage, sage jus and crackling. Sweet
treats to finish might run to dark chocolate tart with
chocolate sauce, griottine cherries and chocolate brownie
ice cream.

Times 12-2/6.30-9

The Crown

◉◉ Modern British 🕯

Buzzy pub and restaurant in the heart of the action

☎ 01502 722275
90 High St IP18 6DP
e-mail: crown.reception@adnams.co.uk
web: www.adnams.co.uk
dir: A12 onto A1095 to Southwold. Hotel on left in High St

Right on the main street in the centre of town, this
Adnams' brewery-owned pub, restaurant and wine bar
within a hotel has something for everyone. It's informal
and lively throughout, whether you're in the pub-brasserie
or the restaurant with its scrubbed pine tables. The
Adnams wine list is as good as you'd expect with a great
selection by the glass. The young and enthusiastic
kitchen team turn out some appealing modern, rustic
British dishes, with plenty of Mediterranean sunshine
along the way, and good quality ingredients at the heart
of everything. There might be wild garlic risotto with
braised pig's cheek and parmesan, a fantastic
chargrilled pork rack with mustard mash, kale,
caramelised apple and roasted shallot jus, and smoked
haddock and prawn crumble with leeks, fennel and
dressed rocket. To bow out in style go for the limoncello
and lemon plate.

Chef Tyler Torrance **Owner** Adnams plc
Times 12-2/6.30-9 Closed D 25 Dec **Prices** Fixed L 2
course fr £15.95, Starter £6.50-£11.95, Main

Save on Hotels. Book at **theAA.com/hotel**

SUFFOLK 449 ENGLAND

£13.95-£19.95, Dessert £5.50-£7.50, Service optional **Wines** 35 bottles over £30, 70 bottles under £30, 18 by glass **Notes** Sunday L £16.95-£19.95, Vegetarian available **Seats** 65, Pr/dining room 40 **Children** Portions, Menu **Parking** 15, Free car parks within 5 mins walking distance

Sutherland House

◎◎ Modern British ✪

Neighbourhood fish restaurant with diligent sourcing

☎ 01502 724544
56 High St IP18 6DN
e-mail: enquiries@sutherlandhouse.co.uk
web: www.sutherlandhouse.co.uk
dir: A1095 into Southwold, on High St on left after Victoria St

Dating back to the 14th century, this Grade II listed place on Southwold High Street is packed full of fascinating period details - most of the wooden beams come from battle ships used in the battle of Sole Bay, plus there're ornate ceilings, coving and open fireplaces. In contrast the furniture cuts a contemporary dash - think plain wooden tables and high-backed chairs. Relaxed, casual service helps the buzzy feel, and fish, locally-landed daily, is a big part of the draw. The menu stalks a modern British path, ingredients are sourced with care and food miles get listed alongside each dish. Kick off with goats' cheese pannacotta with walnut pesto, carpaccio of beetroot and rocket, then move on to pan-roasted turbot (served on the bone) with rösti potato and brown shrimp and lemon butter. There are a couple of meat main courses, too, plus desserts such as lemon posset with candied lemon and Chantilly cream.

Chef Jed Tejada **Owner** Peter & Anna Banks
Times 12-2.30/7-9 Closed 25 Dec, 2 wks Jan, Mon (Oct-Mar) **Prices** Prices not confirmed Service optional **Wines** 10 bottles over £30, 20 bottles under £30, 10 by glass **Notes** Sunday L, Vegetarian available **Seats** 50, Pr/dining room 60 **Children** Portions, Menu **Parking** 1, On street

Swan Hotel

◎◎ Modern British

Smart British cooking at Adnams' flagship hotel

☎ 01502 722186
High St, Market Place IP18 6EG
e-mail: swan.hotel@adnams.co.uk
dir: A1095 to Southwold. Hotel in town centre. Parking via archway to left of building

The Adnams empire has things pretty tied up in Southwold, where it is the seaside town's brewer, main publican, wine merchant and hotelier. Just in front of the brewery, the Swan - a handsome bay-fronted Victorian façade occupying pole position among the boutiques - is the epicentre of operations. Inside, its 17th-century origins are revealed: there are wall panels, genuine 18th-century oil paintings and gilt chandeliers, but time has not stood still, so it is all leavened with smart contemporary styling. Afternoon tea in the drawing room is something of a local institution, but don't spoil your appetite for dinner in the smart dining room. As one would hope from a set-up with its roots deep into the local area, provenance of raw materials is emphatically regional, and the cooking is confident, full-flavoured stuff. That old stalwart of seared scallops and black pudding is matched here with celeriac, apple purée and pea shoots, and followed by a big-hearted dish of confit duck leg with bubble-and-squeak, roast parsnips, plum compôte and port jus.

Times 12-2.30/7-9.30

The Crown

◎◎ Modern British 🍷 NOTABLE WINE LIST

Boutique hotel and village inn in one

☎ 01206 262001
CO6 4SE
e-mail: info@crowninn.net
web: www.crowninn.net
dir: Stoke-by-Nayland signed from A12 & A134. Hotel in village off B1068 towards Higham

The 16th-century Crown has taken the fashionable boutique route, reinventing the one-time village inn with a stylish modern makeover and the addition of 11 classy bedrooms. There are still plenty of cosy corners to settle into though; whether it's in the beamed bar or the more contemporary dining areas, you'll find snug seats and log fires. Supplies are garnered from Suffolk's bountiful larder, and a daily-changing blackboard reflects the catch landed by local fishing boats working from the Blackwater Estuary: pan-fried mackerel fillets, for example, with pickled beetroot, soft-boiled egg, bacon, horseradish cream and potatoes. The kitchen's confident creative spirit also shows its hand in meat dishes: take roasted rump of lamb with rösti potato, smoked bacon, fresh peas and samphire and a port sauce. It's a perfect spot for Constable aficionados; The Crown lies in a sleepy village above the Stour and Box River valleys in deepest

Constable Country with the soaring tower of nearby St Mary's Church immortalised in the artist's works.

Times 12-2.30/6-9.30 Closed 25-26 Dec

The Shepherd and Dog

◎◎ Modern British, International

Revitalised village pub with creative cooking

☎ 01449 711361
Forward Green IP14 5HN
e-mail: marybruce@btinternet.com
web: www.theshepherdanddog.com
dir: On A1120 between A14 & A140

In the village of Forward Green, there's a lot of forward thinking going on. It's a village pub sure enough, but one with a good deal of contemporary swagger. The Wagyu burger on the menu gets a lot of attention, and deservedly so, for the only Wagyu herd in the UK is just down the road. An open-plan bar leads into the chic and contemporary restaurant, with pale wood tables, leather high-backed chairs, and a broad menu that would not look out of place in a big-city brasserie. Among starters tempura king prawns with tomato confit and chilli jam sits alongside grilled goats' cheese with beetroot carpaccio, walnut chutney and walnut praline. Next up, you could go for one of those Wagyu burgers served with hand-cut chips, or fish and chips in a tempura-style batter, and to finish, dark chocolate and honeycomb marquise or toffee apple sundae.

Chef Christopher & Daniela Bruce **Owner** Christopher & Mary Bruce **Times** 12-2/7-11 Closed mid Jan, Mon, D Sun **Prices** Service optional **Wines** 19 by glass **Notes** Sunday L £18.50-£21.50, Vegetarian available **Seats** 50, Pr/dining room 24 **Children** Portions, Menu **Parking** 35

SUDBURY — Map 13 TL84

The Case Restaurant with Rooms

Modern British

Characterful Suffolk inn with brasserie-style menu

☎ 01787 210483
Further St, Assington CO10 5LD
e-mail: restaurant@thecaserestaurantwithrooms.co.uk
dir: Located on A134 between Sudbury & Colchester.
0.5m past Newton Golf Club

Located in deepest Suffolk countryside, this great little property has bags of character. Dating back to about 1700, the whitewashed country inn used to be a private home and now there are beautiful bedrooms and a cosy little restaurant to attract paying customers. It's a little like eating in someone's front room (in a nice way), with a wood-burning stove, darkwood tables and low ceiling beams. Brasserie cooking is the name of the game and a highlight of the meal may well be the mini-beef Wellington that is a first-course option, but what follows on the daily-changing menu is sure to appeal too - a meaty Dingley Dell pork chop and sausage, perhaps, with apple tartlet, jacket potato, green vegetables and Suffolk Aspall cider sauce, or poached fillet of plaice filled with salmon mousse.

Times 12-2/6.30-9 Closed L Mon

THORPENESS — Map 13 TM45

Thorpeness Hotel

Modern British

Simple but sound cookery next to Britain's greenest golf course

☎ 01728 452176
Lakeside Av IP16 4NH
e-mail: manager@thorpeness.co.uk
web: www.thorpeness.co.uk
dir: A1094 towards Aldeburgh, take coast road N for 2m

A golfing hotel by the sea, Thorpeness boasts Britain's greenest course, laid out in 1922 and now replete with new bunkers and swales. If you're the understanding partner of a golfer, be it noted that there are fine walks hereabouts, the beach is only five minutes' stroll, and Aldeburgh beckons in the middle distance. Understated modern styling makes the hotel interiors look trim, and there are of course grand views of the fairways from the main restaurant, the covered patio bar and terrace. The food on a daily-changing menu doesn't aim for too much distraction from the main business, but achieves sound satisfaction by means of ham hock with melba toast, chutney and salad, followed perhaps by lamb shank with bubble-and-squeak and roasted winter veg in a richly assertive gravy, with solid comfort arriving at the final hole in the form of sticky toffee pudding, served with gooey toffee sauce and vanilla ice cream.

Chef Ronnie Hayes **Owner** Hotel Collection Ltd
Times 12.30-3/7-9.30 Closed L Mon-Sat **Prices** Starter £4.50-£7.25, Main £12.95-£17.95, Dessert £5.25-£5.95,

Service included **Wines** 3 bottles over £30, 28 bottles under £30, 15 by glass **Notes** Sunday L £9.95-£17.95, Vegetarian available, Dress restrictions, smart casual, Civ Wed 80 **Seats** 80, Pr/dining room 30
Children Portions, Menu **Parking** 80

WALBERSWICK — Map 13 TM47

The Anchor

Modern British

Globally influenced food in an eco-conscious village inn

☎ 01502 722112
Main St IP18 6UA
e-mail: info@anchoratwalberswick.com
dir: On entering village The Anchor on right, immediately after MG garage

The Dorbers took over The Anchor in 2004, and set about restoring it to its rightful place at the pulsing heart of pretty Walberswick by the sea. Solar panels, eco-timber and rainwater butts serve notice that The Anchor has been not only spruced up but conscientiously greened in the process, and it's a commendable approach that finds echoes in Sophie Dorber's culinary approach, which is anchored firmly to The Anchor's own allotment. Home-made breads are not just a dinner accoutrement, but are sold to locals in the bar. The net is cast far and wide for influences, which may be Asian (salt and chilli squid with dipping sauce), Italian (gnocchi with field mushrooms, leeks and Stilton), or more obviously home-grown in a main course of smoked haddock and salmon fishcake with chips, or a serving of beef short rib with mustard mash and hispi. A custard tart of creamed rice and apricot makes a very dashing end to proceedings, or there may be a baked cheesecake garnished with physalis and pine nuts.

Chef Sophie Dorber **Owner** Sophie & Mark Dorber
Times 11am-11pm All-day dining **Prices** Fixed L 2 course £14.50, Starter £5-£8.50, Main £9.50-£18.50, Dessert £4.50-£5.50, Service optional **Wines** 50 bottles over £30, 45 bottles under £30, 20 by glass **Notes** Breakfast from 8am £7.50-£10, 25 Dec drinks only, Sunday L, Vegetarian available **Seats** 55, Pr/dining room 26 **Children** Portions, Menu **Parking** 60

WESTLETON — Map 13 TM46

The Westleton Crown

Modern British V

Vibrant modern cooking in an ancient inn

☎ 01728 648777
The Street IP17 3AD
e-mail: info@westletoncrown.co.uk
web: www.westletoncrown.co.uk
dir: A12 N, turn right for Westleton just after Yoxford. Hotel opposite on entering village

This textbook red-brick Suffolk coaching inn may date from the 12th century, but there's nothing archaic about the gastronomic side of the operation. The Crown is still an endearingly cosy local with well-kept real ales, a log

fire and ancient beams in the bar, while the modern conservatory restaurant is done out in a clean-cut style with mismatched scrubbed wood tables and a wall of sliding glass doors that opens up to the lovely terraced gardens. The food also keeps its feet planted in the present with some cleverly-honed modern ideas wrought from first-rate local produce. Orford smoked haddock might provide the foundations for a puff pastry tart made with spinach and free-range eggs, ahead of main courses running from steamed halibut with cocotte potatoes, wilted red chard and a vegetable and herb nage, to a more gutsy four-way workout of local Suffolk chicken, in the form of poached breast, roasted thigh, confit leg, and breaded wing with pasta, parsley sauce and braised lettuce.

Chef Richard Bargewell **Owner** Agellus Hotels Ltd
Times 12-2.30/6.30-9.30 **Prices** Starter £5.50-£7, Main £13.25-£23.25, Dessert £4.75-£6, Service optional **Wines** 23 bottles over £30, 21 bottles under £30, 9 by glass **Notes** Afternoon tea, Sunday L £16-£26, Vegetarian menu, Civ Wed 90 **Seats** 85, Pr/dining room 50 **Children** Portions, Menu **Parking** 50

WOODBRIDGE — Map 13 TM24

The Crown at Woodbridge

Modern European

Distinguished brasserie cooking in a market town

☎ 01394 384242
2 Thoroughfare IP12 1AD
e-mail: info@thecrownatwoodbridge.co.uk
dir: A12 follow signs for Woodbridge onto B1438, after 1.25m from rdbt turn left into Quay Street & hotel on right, approx 100 yds from junct

A complete refurbishment saw The Crown triumphantly reopen for business in 2009, and become one of the prime draws of this attractive riverside market town. It still feels very much an inn, with food served throughout a range of different eating areas, all pervaded by a relaxed, easygoing ambience and a good mix of keen local clientele. The main business is brasserie cooking of genuine flair, based on local materials and mixing culinary ideas to good effect. Start with deep-fried crabcakes served with fennel escabèche dressed in soy, and follow up with roasted sea bass, samphire and lentils in anchovy vinaigrette, or succulently tender ox cheek braised in ale, with cavolo nero and horseradish mash. Desserts to indulge include chocolate brownie with banoffee ice cream, or pear sponge pudding and vanilla-pod custard.

Chef Stephen David, Luke Bailey **Owner** Thorpeness & Aldeburgh Hotels **Times** 12-2.15/6.15-9 Closed D 25 Dec (available for residents only) **Prices** Fixed L 2 course fr £18.50, Fixed D 3 course fr £23, Starter £5-£10, Main £12-£16, Dessert £6.50, Service optional **Wines** 14 by glass **Notes** Sunday L, Vegetarian available **Children** Portions, Menu

Save on Hotels. Book at **theAA.com/hotel**

SUFFOLK – SURREY 451 **ENGLAND**

Seckford Hall Hotel

◉◉ Modern European ✺

Castellated Tudor hall with modish menu

☎ 01394 385678
IP13 6NU
e-mail: reception@seckford.co.uk
web: www.seckford.co.uk
dir: Hotel signed on A12 (Woodbridge bypass). Do not follow signs for town centre

Approached by a sweeping drive, the imposing Tudor pile of Seckford - with its brick façade, soaring chimneys, carved-oak entrance door and well-preened grounds - is no less impressive than when Queen Elizabeth I held court here. Today, a country-house hotel for the 21st century it may be, but its interior successfully blends its regal past with modern-day comforts. The main dining room embodies that classical look, with oak panelling, rich tapestries, white linen and rich drapes, while the accomplished kitchen deals in country-house cooking with a modern spin, based on a good deal of local produce. Fillet of East Coast cod, for example, is accompanied by sautéed potatoes, chorizo and spinach, or there might be roast rump of salt marsh lamb teamed with sweet garlic and goats' cheese mash. Desserts continue the classic-with-a-twist trend in the form of glazed citrus tart served with a cinnamon doughnut and raspberry sorbet.

Chef Mark Archer **Times** 12.30-1.45/7-9.30 **Prices** Prices not confirmed Service available **Wines** 11 by glass **Notes** Sunday L, Vegetarian available, Dress restrictions, Smart casual, Civ Wed 120 **Seats** 70, Pr/dining room 100 **Children** Portions, Menu **Parking** 100

YAXLEY   Map 13 TM17

The Auberge

◉◉ Traditional, International ✺

Well-crafted dishes in a medieval Suffolk inn

☎ 01379 783604
Ipswich Rd IP23 8BZ
e-mail: aubmail@the-auberge.co.uk
web: www.the-auberge.co.uk
dir: 5m S of Diss on A140

Dating back to medieval times, The Auberge has been a public house for many centuries, and its reincarnation as a modern restaurant with rooms doesn't disguise the fact. The ancient beams and panelling and exposed brickwork make an atmospheric setting, whether you're after a cosy corner with a table for two, or a groaning board that will seat 20. As the name would suggest, French influence is in evidence in the cooking, but the kitchen relies solidly on local materials for its deft handling of modern pub food. Start perhaps with partridge and pork rillettes with green tomato and mango chutney, or a sustaining smoked haddock and fennel chowder, before moving to fried calves' liver with quince sauce and onion mash, or one of the speciality rump or rib steaks with garlic and herb butter or pink peppercorn sauce. Puddings go unashamedly for the populist vote,

with a concoction of dark chocolate, dried fruits and nuts in coffee and Marsala mascarpone, or ginger trifle with egg nog custard.

Chef John Stenhouse **Owner** John & Dee Stenhouse **Times** 12-2/7-9.30 Closed 1-7 Jan, Sun, L Sat-Mon **Prices** Fixed L 2 course £17.95-£19.95, Fixed D 3 course £22.95-£30, Starter £4.95-£10, Main £15-£30, Dessert £6.95-£10, Service optional **Wines** 22 bottles over £30, 28 bottles under £30, 13 by glass **Notes** Vegetarian available **Seats** 60, Pr/dining room 20 **Children** Portions **Parking** 25

YOXFORD   Map 5 TM36

Satis House Hotel

◉◉ Modern British

Piquant flavours in rural Suffolk

☎ 01728 668418
Main Rd IP17 3EX
e-mail: enquiries@satishouse.co.uk
web: www.satishouse.co.uk
dir: off A12 between Ipswich & Lowestoft. 9m E Aldeburgh & Snape

Satis House is a Grade II listed building dating from the 18th century with connections to Charles Dickens (it gets a name-check in *Great Expectations*). Today's incarnation has lost none of its period charm and it is decorated in such a way as to enhance the period features without seeming chintzy or dated. The restaurant has a decidedly contemporary sheen to it, with its polished wooden floor, bold red-flowered wallpaper and darkwood unclothed tables. Carefully-sourced local produce features prominently on the menu, which might take you from chicken liver parfait with onion marmalade to veal cutlet with olive and caper butter, or the more Eastern-inspired pan-fried scallops with crème fraîche and sweet chilli jam to Thai duck leg curry with pickled plums and duck spring roll. For dessert, chocolate mousse comes with a peanut parfait and brittle, while the seasonal celebration of rhubarb brings forth jelly, brulée and pudding (with ginger).

Times 12-3/6.30-11 Closed L Mon-Tue

SURREY

BAGSHOT   Map 6 SU96

The Brasserie at Pennyhill Park

◉◉ Modern British

Relaxed brasserie with contemporary cooking

☎ 01276 471774
Pennyhill Park Hotel & Spa, London Rd GU19 5EU
e-mail: enquiries@pennyhillpark.co.uk
dir: M3 junct 3, through Bagshot, left onto A30. 0.5m on right

The Brasserie is the more informal and relaxed alternative to Pennyhill Park's trailblazing Latymer (see entry), a large, bright room, with stone walls, lots of windows overlooking the pool, opposite the huge spa complex. The

kitchen puts a fresh spin on the brasserie repertoire, pairing roast fillet of sea bass with confit, squid ink gnocchi, a prawn and ginger 'cigar' and watercress purée, and beef Wellington with Parma ham, smoked potato purée and Madeira jus. Ideas are contemporary without being outlandish, as in successful starters of crab with tuna carpaccio, lime and tomato jelly, caper berries and pea shoots, and roast local quail with a cep and quail consommé. Grilled steaks are options too, and puddings might bring on chocolate fondant with a caramel centre, prettily arranged with raspberry compôte and sorbet.

Times 12-2.30/6-10 Closed L Sat

Michael Wignall at The Latymer

◉◉◉◉◉ – see page 453

CAMBERLEY   Map 6 SU86

Macdonald Frimley Hall Hotel & Spa

◉◉ Modern European

Smart modern cooking in peaceful setting

☎ 0844 879 9110
Lime Av GU15 2BG
e-mail: gm.frimleyhall@macdonald-hotels.co.uk
web: www.macdonaldhotels.co.uk
dir: M3 junct 3, A321 follow Bagshot signs. Through lights, left onto A30 signed Camberley & Basingstoke. To rdbt, 2nd exit onto A325, take 5th right

Readers of a certain age who remember Wright's Coal Tar Soap might be interested to know that this creeper-clad manor house ensconced in pretty gardens and unspoilt woodland was once the soap baron's family home. Nowadays, the country-house hotel has scrubbed up well: its grand looks - magnificent oak staircase and panelling, ornate plasterwork - are leavened with a pared-back modern style, plus the obligatory spa and health club are present and correct. The Linden Restaurant goes for a soothing, minimal look with a neutral colour scheme, deploying simple table settings as a backdrop to its modish cooking. The kitchen shows a solid focus on flavour whilst throwing some daredevil components into the mix, as in a starter of goats' cheese mousse teamed with poppy seed wafer, apple purée and olive tapenade. Next out, a porcine trio of pork fillet, pork belly and black pudding is served with vanilla-infused apple sauce, green beans and fondant potato, whilst the simplicity of a well-made classic crème brûlée is all that's needed for a satisfying finish.

Times 12.30-2/7-9.30 Closed L Sat, D 25 & 26 Dec

CHERTSEY · Map 6 TQ06

Hamilton's

◎ Modern European NEW

Skillful modern cooking in a charming restaurant-with-rooms

☎ 01932 560745
23 Windsor St KT16 8AY
e-mail: bookings@hamiltons23.com
dir: M25 junct 11 St Peters Way (A317). At rdbt 1st exit, Chertsey Rd (A317), next rdbt 2nd exit into Free Prae Rd, then Pound Rd. Left into London St, opposite church

Occupying a corner site in the town centre, Hamilton's is a small and intimate restaurant-with-rooms, with a warm and welcoming feel from its hands-on proprietors. Semi-frosted windows look out onto the street, allowing for a spot of people-watching as you take in the ambience in the stylishly done out space. Chef-patron Carter Williamson deals in thoughtfully presented modern European dishes using top-notch seasonal ingredients. Smoked venison carpaccio with mizuna cress salad, quail's egg, parsnip crisps and truffle oil is a simple starter done well, or you might go for seared king scallops (precisely timed) with wasabi potato purée, pickled cucumber and lotus root. Scallops turn up again in a main-course pairing with oriental belly pork, along with bok choy, sweet soy reduction and crispy lotus root – a winning combination of tastes and textures. Raspberry vodka jelly with raspberry and mint salad and vanilla bean ice cream ends things on a high.

Chef Carter Williamson Times 12-4/6-9.30 Closed Mon-Wed, L Mon-Sat, D Sun Prices Starter £6-£8, Main £15-£25, Dessert £6.50-£9, Groups min 8 service 10%

CHIDDINGFOLD · Map 6 SU93

The Swan Inn

◎ British, International ⊙

Wide-ranging menus in a former coaching inn

☎ 01428 684688
Petworth Rd GU8 4TY
e-mail: info@theswaninnchiddingfold.com
web: www.theswaninnchiddingfold.com
dir: On A283 Petworth road, towards Chichester

Expect to see lots of exposed brickwork, stripped floors, logs burning, and a comfortable and inviting dining room, with flowers on wooden tables, at this former coaching inn in a quintessential English village. The kitchen turns its hands to a principally British menu with some input from further afield, so roast chicken breast with merguez sausage and white bean cassoulet might appear next to rump of lamb with roast root vegetables, braised red cabbage and red wine jus. An innovative soup could kick things off – perhaps white onion, cider and sage – or go for soused mackerel with potato, cucumber and dill salad. End with a creditable trio of English cheeses or with passionfruit pannacotta with a kick of lime.

Chef Graham Digweed Owner Annemaria & Stuart Boomer Davies Times 12-3/6.30-10 Prices Starter £4.95-£12.25, Main £13-£19.95, Dessert £5-£8 Wines 18 bottles over £30, 33 bottles under £30, 16 by glass Notes Sunday L £11.75-£19.95, Vegetarian available Seats 40, Pr/dining room 40 Children Portions, Menu Parking 35

CHOBHAM · Map 6 SU96

Stovell's

◎◎ Contemporary European NEW

Accomplished modern European cooking in a Tudor farmhouse

☎ 01276 858000
125 Windsor Rd GU24 8QS
e-mail: enquiries@stovells.com

Husband and wife chef team Fernando and Kristy Stovell left the bright lights of the capital to turn this 16th century Tudor farmhouse in rural Surrey into their first restaurant in late 2012, and the residents of Chobham have welcomed them with open arms. The duo honed their skills cooking in London's celebrity hangout clubs before deciding to set up shop in this quaint old building which retains all of its original charm – lots of beams, low ceilings and open fireplaces – along with a welcome injection of contemporary style. The style of cooking is modern European, with bold flavours and creative presentation the kitchen's hallmarks. Dishes change with the seasons and are vibrantly colourful and built on top-quality produce, as in a starter of caramelised hand-caught Loch Leven scallops (perfectly timed) with chorizo, ratte potatoes and walnut dressing, and main-course roasted haddock, as fresh as can be, served with cockles, confit fennel, baby Charlotte potatoes, preserved lemons and saffron vinaigrette. Pud could be a simple, but textbook, dark chocolate fondant with Tudor Rose ice cream, or perhaps you might go for a refreshing orange and vanilla fool with raspberry ice cream and honeycomb.

Owner Fernando & Kristy Stovell Times 12-3.30/6-10.30 Closed Mon, L Sat, D Sun Prices Fixed L 2 course £15.50, Fixed D 3 course £38, Service added but optional 10% Notes Sunday L

CHURT · Map 5 SU83

Best Western Frensham Pond Hotel

◎ Modern British NEW ⊙

Modernised classic brasserie dishes overlooking a truly great pond

☎ 01252 795161
Bacon Ln GU10 2QB
e-mail: info@frenshampondhotel.co.uk
web: www.frenshampondhotel.co.uk
dir: A3 onto A287. 4m left at 'Beware Horses' sign. Hotel 0.25m

The house is originally 15th century, but only got into its stride in the hospitality game in the Georgian era. Sitting by the eponymous Great Pond, not far from Farnham, it's in a picturesque spot, and offers keep-fit facilities and all mod cons to the Home Counties traveller. The Watermark dining room enjoys a sweeping prospect of the pond, and is handsomely kitted out with crisp linen, fresh posies and well-upholstered seating. Modernised classic brasserie dishes are the order of the day, and soup fans are well served with a rotating list of changes being rung through the days of the week. Start, perhaps, with baked goats' cheese with salad leaves and croutons, then a well-timed pork loin steak with celeriac purée and caramelised onions in port and thyme reduction, before coming to rest with a good mixed berry cheesecake, or lemon tart with minty crème fraîche.

Chef Darren Grinstead Owner Aristel Hotels Times 12.30-2.30/7-10 Closed D Sun Prices Fixed L 2 course £14-£19, Fixed D 3 course £23.50-£28.50, Service added but optional 10% Wines 4 bottles over £30, 13 bottles under £30, 4 by glass Notes Vegetarian available Seats 60, Pr/dining room 50 Children Portions, Menu Parking 110

DORKING · Map 6 TQ14

Mercure Box Hill Burford Bridge Hotel

◎◎ British, European

Traditionally-based hotel cooking in rural Surrey

☎ 01306 884561
Burford Bridge, Box Hill RH5 6BX
e-mail: h6635@accor.com
web: www.mercure.com
dir: M25 junct 9, A245 towards Dorking. Hotel within 5m on A24

At the foot of Box Hill by the River Mole, the Burford Bridge is in a peaceful spot (though not far from the A24), as may be appreciated by those availing themselves of the outdoor pool or the croquet lawn. A beige-hued modern dining room, the Emlyn, is the setting for some gently tweaked, traditionally-based cooking, along the lines of oxtail soup with herb dumplings, grilled haddock with shrimp butter and parsley mash, or breast and cabbage-wrapped confit leg of duck in sloe gin sauce. Interesting ideas for pudding include chocolate and rosemary soufflé with orange biscotti, or praline parfait with wine- and cinnamon-poached pear.

Chef Andrew Barrass Owner MREF Ltd Times 12-2.30/7-9.30 Closed D Sun Prices Fixed L 2 course £20, Fixed D 3 course £25, Starter £6.95-£11.95, Main £15.95-£28.95, Dessert £7.50, Service included Wines 17 bottles over £30, 27 bottles under £30, 14 by glass Notes Sunday L, Vegetarian available, Civ Wed 200 Seats 70, Pr/dining room 200 Children Portions, Menu Parking 140

Save on Hotels. Book at **theAA.com/hotel**

SURREY 453 ENGLAND

Michael Wignall at The Latymer

BAGSHOT MAP 6 SU96

Modern European V NOTABLE WINE LIST

Stunningly-crafted contemporary cooking in a luxurious hotel

☎ 01276 471774
Pennyhill Park Hotel & Spa, London Rd GU19 5EU
e-mail: enquiries@pennyhillpark.co.uk
web: www.exclusivehotels.co.uk
dir: M3 junct 3, through Bagshot, left onto A30. 0.5m on right

It sounds lovely, doesn't it, Pennyhill Park? And as you approach the house along the tree-lined driveway, with rabbits dotted about on the grass enjoying their evening meal, you'll already be starting to think the place is living up to expectations. It would be fair to say that this luxurious hotel has it all: a bit of history and character in the main house (built in the 19th century for a high-flying businessman), a range of sumptuous bedrooms (those in the main house boasting period features, while others are more contemporary), 123 acres of lush wooded parkland, a golf course and other sporting facilities (including a rugby pitch which is a favoured training ground of the England squad), a world-class spa and two restaurants, with Michael Wignall at The Latymer the jewel in the crown (see also entry for The Brasserie). Situated in the main house, looking out over the beautiful grounds

(an aperitif on the terrace is a must if the weather is kind), The Latymer is an intimate room full of period character with its oak panelling and stained-glass windows, though with an injection of modernity thanks to a burnt orange, rust and pale green colour palette. There's plenty of modernity in Michael Wignall's cooking, which the man himself describes as, "complex, carefully crafted and very technical but not intimidating" - we couldn't have put it better ourselves. Ingredients are of the highest possible quality and treated with the utmost respect to produce dishes with clearly defined, fresh flavours that look like pieces of art on the plate. Choose from three, seven or, if your budget will stretch to it, ten courses, and sit back and enjoy a culinary journey that might begin (after a tantalisingly good amuse-bouche and some amazing breads fresh from the hotel's own bakery) with cod poached in single estate olive oil, with confit organic hen's yolk, rose harissa and potato, Monmouthshire ham and cabbage glass - a stunning dish demonstrating precision cooking, impressive technique and incredible flavours and textures. Next up, cannon, neck and belly of Cumbrian lamb - superb-quality meat, singing with flavour - comes with crisp tongue, carrot, hen of the wood and buttered kale in a plate of sheer Spring. Standout dishes from the ten-course tasting menu include 'eel and chicken' -

smoked eel and feuille de brick cigar, chicken poached in Asian stock, spiced aubergine, yoghurt and coriander - and cassoulet of cockles, razor and palourde clams, cuttlefish gnocchi, soya beans and poached quail egg. Sticking with the ten-course taster, desserts are also incredibly skillful, colourful, creative affairs, such as gariguette strawberry with peanut butter tuile and powder, warm doughnut, espuma, strawberry jelly and sorbet, or a thoroughly reworked tiramisù consisting of coffee parfait, jelly chocolate caramel, mocha butter, milk ice cream and almond espuma. The service team are a class act too, and if you prefer to get right to the heart of the culinary action, book yourself dinner at the chef's table (a handmade bubble-glass one with adjustable lighting, no less).

Chef Michael Wignall **Owner** Exclusive Hotels **Times** 12.30-2/7-9.30 Closed 1-14 Jan, Sun-Mon (Open Sun BHs but closed following Tue), L Tue, Sat **Prices** Fixed L 2 course fr £26, Fixed D 3 course £78-£92, Service added but optional 12.5% **Wines** 20 by glass **Notes** Tasting menu L 8 course, D 10 course, Vegetarian menu **Seats** 50, Pr/dining room 30 **Parking** 500

DORKING *continued*

Two To Four

◎◎ Modern European ✿

Modern cooking in a thriving neighbourhood venue

☎ 01306 889923
2-4 West St RH4 1BL
e-mail: two_to_four@hotmail.com
web: www.2to4.co.uk
dir: M25, exit at Leatherhead junct, follow signs to town centre

Occupying a period building in the town centre, this is the sort of friendly and welcoming neighbourhood restaurant we would all like on our manor. The décor goes in for a smart-casual look with unclothed tables, creaky floors and a blackboard specials menu that underlines the informal tone. First-class ingredients are the name of the game in a repertoire of uncomplicated modern European-style dishes; much of the meat is sourced from within a five-mile radius, and organic produce is used liberally. Seared scallops with artichoke purée, toasted hazelnuts and honey truffle vinaigrette is one way to start, while main courses take in roasted pork chop with parsnip mash, braised red cabbage and red wine jus, or perhaps pan-fried fillet of black bream with black olives, anchovy mayonnaise, Serrano ham and lemon gel, all realised with technical verve and presented with a modern flourish. For dessert, bread and butter pudding could be jazzed up with the addition of banana and peanut, and served with peanut butter ripple ice cream.

Chef Rob Gathercole **Owner** Restaurant 2to4 Ltd
Times 12-2.30/6.30-10 Closed Xmas, Mon (subject to change) **Prices** Fixed L 2 course £12, Fixed D 2 course £19, Starter £8-£9.95, Main £18.95-£26.95, Dessert £5-£8.50, Service added but optional 10% **Wines** 22 bottles over £30, 19 bottles under £30, 6 by glass **Notes** Sun L Oct-Mar, Sunday L £19.95-£24.95, Vegetarian available **Seats** 70, Pr/dining room 12 **Children** Portions **Parking** West St car park

---

The Estate Grill at Great Fosters

◎◎ Modern British NEW ⚑ NOTABLE WINE LIST ✿

Ingredient-led confident modern cooking

☎ 01784 433822
Great Fosters, Stroude Rd TW20 9UR
e-mail: reception@greatfosters.co.uk
dir: A30 (Bagshot to Staines) right at lights by Wheatsheaf pub into Christchurch Rd. Straight on at rdbt (pass 2 shop parades on right). Left at lights into Stroude Rd. Hotel 0.75m on right

The Estate Grill is the more informal eatery at Great Fosters (see also entry for The Tudor Room), a chapel-like room with a stone fireplace, beamed ceiling, plain cream walls hung with interesting modern artwork, and stone-mullioned windows. As its name suggests, the grill is much in evidence among main courses: flavourful and succulent rib-eye steak, for instance, dry-aged for 21 days and grilled over wood and charcoal embers in the Josper oven, sauced with tarragon mayonnaise and served with triple-cooked chips. Otherwise there may be sea bass baked with fennel and anise, or rack of lamb with Provençale vegetables. Herbs and vegetables come from the kitchen garden, honey from their own apiary, and there are even some home-reared pigs providing meat for the table. The Josper is also used to good effect among starters, seen in an attractive, simple dish of

---

The Tudor Room at Great Fosters

Rosettes not confirmed at time of going to print

Modern European NEW V ✿

All change at historic Surrey hotel

☎ 01784 433822
Stroude Rd TW20 9UR
e-mail: reception@greatfosters.co.uk
dir: A30 (Bagshot to Staines) right at lights by Wheatsheaf pub into Christchurch Rd. Straight on at rdbt (pass 2 shop parades on right). Left at lights into Stroude Rd. Hotel 0.75m on right

Great Fosters doesn't look like it's changed in a great many years: the Grade I listed manor house, dating back to the 16th century when it was built as a hunting lodge, is magnificently well preserved, with original features abounding both inside and out. But there has been a good deal of change lately in the dining department, with the former Oak Room restaurant transformed into a more casual, modern British eatery called The Estate Grill (see entry), and a new restaurant created in what was a private dining room. With just 24 covers, The Tudor Room is an intimate and elegant space decorated luxuriously with red silk on the walls, comfortable sofas pulled up at white linen-clad tables, and dominated by a giant 17th-century tapestry. With just a small number of guests to cater for, new chef Shane Hughes has the freedom to fully exercise his creativity and immense technical skills in two tasting menus - a four-course and an eight-course - while the dedicated front-of-house team deliver a pleasingly personal style of service (the very capable sommelier will sort you out with a perfectly matched flight of wines should you wish). Much of the produce used in the kitchen comes from the estate, including vegetables and herbs, along with Gloucestershire old spot pigs and longhorn cattle. An early course of pressed foie gras and artichoke with a light-as-air beetroot mousse, a purée of Cox's apple and pommes soufflé is a wonderful combination of flavours, textures and colours, while cod fillet marinated in sea salt, slowly cooked in clarified butter, with saffron and haddock brandade, lemon cream and brioche croutons is a beautiful dish both in the eating and the presentation. Excellent tortellini of spiced beef shin are paired up with Cardigan Bay lobster, garden vegetables and Madeira emulsion in an imaginative take on the surf and turf theme, and it could all end on a fun note with 'The Asian Forest' - lemongrass marshmallow, lime leaf pannacotta, green tea meringue, coconut cream and galangal ice cream.

Chef Shane Hughes **Owner** Great Fosters (1931) Ltd
Times 12-2/7-9.30 Closed Sun-Mon, L Sat **Prices** Prices not confirmed Service added but optional 12.5% **Wines** 270 bottles over £30, 15 by glass **Notes** Tasting menu 4/6 course L £28-£40, D £60-£75, Vegetarian menu, Civ Wed 180 **Seats** 24, Pr/dining room 20 **Children** Portions **Parking** 200

smoked mackerel with apple and truffled leeks, and mussels in cider and tarragon cream. Puddings make an impact too: perhaps cherry and tea pannacotta with bitter chocolate ice cream and griottines.

Chef Simon Bolsover **Owner** Great Fosters (1931) Ltd **Times** 12.30-9.30 All-day dining **Prices** Starter £8-£18, Main £12-£34, Dessert £9-£11, Service added but optional 10% **Wines** 67 bottles over £30, 15 bottles under £30, 17 by glass **Notes** Sunday L £32.50, Vegetarian available, Civ Wed 180 **Seats** 44, Pr/dining room 20 **Children** Portions, Menu **Parking** 200

The Tudor Room at Great Fosters

Rosettes not confirmed at time of going to print – see opposite

Rosettes not confirmed at time of going to print – see opposite

GODALMING   Map 6 SU94

La Luna

◉◉ Modern Italian 🍴NOTABLE WINE LIST 🌱

Stylish modern Italian venue

☎ 01483 414155
10-14 Wharf St GU7 1NN
e-mail: info@lalunarestaurant.co.uk
web: www.lalunarestaurant.co.uk
dir: In town centre, at junct of Wharf St & Flambard Way

Lucky Godalming locals have taken this smart contemporary Italian to their hearts - and who can blame them when it delivers on all counts: great-value lunch menus, charming, knowledgeable service, a modish interior in soothing hues of caramel, chocolate and black with oak tables, and a well-chosen Italian wine list to support an appealing modern repertoire of southern-leaning dishes. The menu follows the traditional route, starting out with antipasti such as smoked swordfish with shaved fennel, or well-sourced Italian charcuterie - wild boar and pork salami, or prosciutto from free-range Sicilian pigs - then Neapolitan scialatielli pasta with Sicilian fennel seed sausage ragù and smoked scamorza cheese. Main courses could bring rump of local South Downs lamb, meltingly tender (cooked sous-vide), teamed with Umbrian lentils and rosemary jus, while puddings run from a top-class tiramisù to chocolate and hazelnut torta Caprese with salted caramel truffles and crème brûlée ice cream.

Chef Valentino Gentile **Owner** Daniele Drago **Times** 12-2/7-10 Closed 2 wks Aug, BHs, Sun-Mon **Prices** Fixed L 2 course £13.50, Tasting menu £85, Starter £5.15-£10.95, Main £11.50-£19.50, Dessert

£4.50-£6.50, Service optional **Wines** 141 bottles over £30, 37 bottles under £30, 8 by glass **Notes** Tasting menu 7 course incl wine, Vegetarian available **Seats** 58, Pr/dining room 24 **Children** Portions **Parking** Public car park behind restaurant

---

HASLEMERE   Map 6 SU93

Lythe Hill Hotel & Spa

◉◉ Modern British, French

Innovative cooking in country-house hotel

☎ 01428 651251
Petworth Rd GU27 3BQ
e-mail: lythe@lythehill.co.uk
web: www.lythehill.co.uk
dir: 1m E of Haslemere on B2131

A splendid half-timbered Tudor property, this luxury country-house hotel is surrounded by 22 acres. Its restaurant is split into two distinct areas: towards the front is the original oak-panelled room, the other with a contemporary décor overlooking a lake and the grounds. The kitchen proactively works with local suppliers to source the best produce and changes the menu regularly to reflect availability. Flavour combinations can be beguiling, as in pan-fried cod cheeks with chorizo, popcorn, clam vinaigrette and creamy polenta. Braised shoulder of lamb with garlic mash, roast vegetables and mint and rosemary jus sounds familiar enough, while some innovative touches are given to other main courses: slowly cooked suckling pig with piquant pineapple jus, for instance, accompanied by bacon and Parma ham, potato terrine, Savoy cabbage and parsnips, or accurately roast cod fillet with crispy squid on a pungent caper and raisin vinaigrette served with potato confit and spinach. Puddings might bring on a successful combination of passionfruit mousse with lime meringue, pineapple confit and sorbet and coffee crumble.

Chef Malcom Campbell **Owner** Simon Drake (GM) **Times** 12-2.30/7-9.30 **Prices** Starter £6-£9, Main £11.50-£25, Dessert £6-£8.50, Service added but optional 10% **Wines** 23 bottles over £30, 25 bottles under £30, 9 by glass **Notes** Fixed L all week, Sunday L £15-£36.50, Vegetarian available, Dress restrictions, Smart casual, Civ Wed 120 **Seats** 70, Pr/dining room 34 **Children** Portions **Parking** 65

HORLEY

For restaurant details see Gatwick Airport (London), (Sussex, West)

For restaurant details see Gatwick Airport (London), (Sussex, West)

OCKLEY   Map 6 TQ14

Bryce's Seafood Restaurant & Country Pub

◉ Modern British, Seafood V 🌱

Enterprising seafood in a smart country inn

☎ 01306 627430
The Old School House, Stane St RH5 5TH
e-mail: fish@bryces.co.uk
dir: From M25 junct 9 take A24, then A29. 8m S of Dorking on A29

Serving up South Coast seafood in the Surrey countryside for over 20 years now, Bryce's is a restaurant and country pub with a lot going on. Once upon a time it was a boys' boarding school and the beamed restaurant served time as its gym, but these days you can expect to tuck into seafood landed at Shoreham Harbour or bought at Billingsgate. Trio of Devon crab comes as a pan-fried cake, quenelle of mousse and twice-baked soufflé, or try their home-cured gravad lax with dill and mustard sauce. Among main courses, red snapper gets an Eastern flavour with bok choy, soy, ginger and sesame dressing, while fillets of plaice are stuffed with smoked salmon and chive mousse and served with champagne sauce. There's a bar menu too with scampi, fish pie and the like, plus a vegetarian menu and steaks as an alternative to all the fishy things.

Chef B Bryce, Peter Howard **Owner** Mr W & Mrs E Bryce **Times** 12-2.30/7-9.30 Closed 25 Dec, 1 Jan, Mon in Jan, D Sun (Nov & Jan-Feb) **Prices** Fixed L 2 course £29-£34, Fixed D 2 course £29-£34, Service optional, Groups min 8 service 10% **Wines** 12 by glass **Notes** ALC 2/3 course £29/£34, Fixed 2/3 course £12.50/£16 Sun-Thu, Sunday L £29-£34, Vegetarian menu **Seats** 50 **Children** Portions **Parking** 35

OTTERSHAW   Map 6 TQ06

Foxhills Club and Resort

◉ Traditional & Modern British NEW 🌱

Contemporary and classic dining in a Victorian manor

☎ 01932 704480
Stonehill Rd KT16 0EL
e-mail: marketing@foxhills.co.uk
web: www.foxhills.co.uk
dir: From M25 junct 11 take A320 to Woking. At 2nd rdbt take last exit Cobham Rd, turn R into Foxhills Rd, follow until T-junct, turn L into Stonehill Rd

It's hard to believe that this 19th-century manor house is just a short hop from the frenzy of Heathrow, but you certainly don't need to think of leaving the country when there's a championship golf course, a spa and all manner of sporting pursuits spread around its 400-acre estate. That lot should help you work up an appetite for dining in the Manor Restaurant, an impressive setting with lofty vaulted ceilings within the oldest part of the building. Driven by locally-sourced ingredients - South Downs lamb

continued

OTTERSHAW *continued*

and Surrey-bred beef, for example - the food belongs mostly to the contemporary idiom. Seared parsley and garlic-crusted scallops with lemon purée and shaved parmesan opens the show, ahead of a trio of Blythburgh pork (braised cheek, slow-roasted belly, and poached fillet) teamed with sweet potato and apples. For dessert, there's hot chocolate soufflé with chocolate cream sauce.

Chef David Hanlon **Owner** Marc Hayton **Times** 12-2.30/6.30-9 **Prices** Fixed L 3 course £32, Fixed D 3 course £32, Starter £8.95-£9.95, Main £18.95-£29.50, Dessert £9.25-£9.95, Service added but optional 10% **Wines** 88 bottles over £30, 2 bottles under £30, 13 by glass **Notes** Sunday L, Vegetarian available, Dress restrictions, Smart casual **Seats** 100 **Children** Portions, Menu **Parking** 200

REDHILL
Map 6 TQ25

Nutfield Priory Hotel & Spa

☺☺ Modern British 🍷

Creative modern cooking in Gothic country pile

☎ 0845 072 7486 & 01737 824400
Nutfield Rd RH1 4EL
e-mail: nutfieldpriory@handpicked.co.uk
web: www.handpickedhotels.co.uk/nutfieldpriory
dir: On A25, 1m E of Redhill, off M25 junct 8 or M25 junct 6, follow A25 through Godstone

The priory's architect was inspired by Pugin's Palace of Westminster and he designed it in high Gothic style. Renovations have retained the original features of fine wood and stone carvings and panelling and added all the amenities of a modern country-house hotel, including a health club and spa. Cloisters Restaurant, aptly named, is smartly kitted out and gives breathtaking country views from its leaded mullioned windows. The kitchen shows sure-footed techniques, turning out ambitious starters like a terrine of foie gras, ham hock and poached chicken, its richness cut by piccalilli, and pan-fried scallops with parsnip purée, truffles and parsley 'air'. Main courses can be complex too, but ingredients are brought together with culinary good sense: amazingly fresh roast halibut fillet with brandade, mushrooms, cauliflower cream and chicken jus, say, or breast of duck with consommé, confit leg spring roll, parsnip rösti, a pistachio crumb and cherries. Chocoholics could end with a trio of brûlée, mousse and fondant.

Chef Roger Gadsden **Owner** Hand Picked Hotels **Times** 12.30-2/7-9.30 Closed L Sat **Prices** Fixed L 2 course fr £25, Fixed D 3 course £38-£52.90, Starter £9.50-£14.95, Main £19.95-£34.95, Dessert £10-£13.50, Service optional **Wines** 84 bottles over £30, 11 bottles under £30, 18 by glass **Notes** Sunday L, Vegetarian available, Dress restrictions, Smart casual, Civ Wed 80 **Seats** 60, Pr/dining room 60 **Children** Portions, Menu **Parking** 100

REIGATE
Map 6 TQ25

The Dining Room

☺☺ Modern British

Stimulating cooking on the High Street

☎ 01737 226650
59a High St RH2 9AE
dir: M25 junct 8/A217 follow one way system into High St. Restaurant on left

Tony Tobin may have TV chef status but he still heads up the brigade at his first-floor restaurant on the High Street. It's a smart-looking place, easy on the eye, with pictures on the walls and correctly set tables. A fixed-price deal pulls in the punters at lunchtime, drawn equally by a roster of bright contemporary ideas. Starters can vary from cauliflower soup enhanced by vanilla and curry oil, to a nicely presented dish of wild boar terrine with pear chutney, pistachios and truffle oil. There's no stinting on quality: fillet steak goes into meatballs (in tomato, pepper and chorizo sauce), and fillet of turbot comes roasted, moist and full of flavour, and served with Parmentier potatoes, girolles, broad beans and a complementary kick from smoked haddock foam. Breads are first rate, home-made chocolates come with coffee, and ingenuity extends to puddings such as lemon verbena Arctic roll with jelly-like balls of lemon syrup, or orange and lemon tart with blackcurrant sorbet.

Times 12-2/7-10 Closed Xmas, BHs, L Sat, D Sun

RIPLEY
Map 6 TQ05

Drake's Restaurant

☺☺☺ – *see opposite*

STOKE D'ABERNON
Map 6 TQ15

Woodlands Park Hotel

☺☺ Modern European

Formal dining in a grand Victorian country house

☎ 01372 843933
Woodlands Ln KT11 3QB
e-mail: woodlandspark@handpicked.co.uk
web: www.handpickedhotels.co.uk/woodlandspark
dir: A3 exit at Cobham. Through town centre & Stoke D'Abernon, left at garden centre into Woodlands Lane, hotel 0.5m on right

A fortune built on matches allowed Victorian industrialist William Bryant (of Bryant and May fame) to build this red-brick mansion, and simultaneously dispense with the need for his own products to light the gas lamps, by being one of the first houses in the UK to have electric lighting. He picked a lovely spot, set in landscaped gardens and grounds, and these days anyone with the cost of a meal to spend can enjoy it from the Oak Room restaurant, a period piece, all beautiful oak-panelled walls and splendid coffered oak ceilings, and well-padded leather seats at linen-swathed tables. It all adds up to an impressive scene for some vibrant modern

cooking, along the lines of crab ravioli teamed with seared scallops and shellfish bisque, followed by daube of Chanctonbury Estate venison with thyme fondant potato and horseradish cream. Desserts might be as creative as mint and chocolate millefeuille with a white chocolate sorbet shot and chocolate orange bonbon.

Times 12-2.30/7-9.30 Closed Mon, L Tue-Sat, D Sun

WEYBRIDGE
Map 6 TQ06

Brooklands Hotel

☺ British, European

Striking modern hotel where British motor-racing began

☎ 01932 335700
Brooklands Dr KT13 0SL
e-mail: brasserie@brooklandshotelsurrey.com

This hotel is very much about the future of Brooklands whilst acknowledging its historic past. It's a thrillingly modern hotel on a grand scale overlooking the race track - the first purpose-built circuit in the world, opening back in 1907. You get a great view of the track from the trendy bar, where you can sip on a cocktail such as a real dry martini, before heading into the 1907 Restaurant with its cool colour tones of charcoal and aubergine and darkwood surfaces giving a moody club-like vibe to the space. There's a modern brasserie feel to the food, with the grill offering up Casterbridge steaks from the West Country, and modish starters such as pressed ham hock, golden raisins, English mustard and sauce gribiche. Among main courses, butter-roasted monkfish comes with butternut squash purée, glazed lamb's sweetbreads and fennel 'textures', and, to finish, there might be banana tarte Tatin with fudge ice cream and banana crisps.

Times 12.30-2.30/6.30-10

Oatlands Park Hotel

☺ Modern British, French 🍷

Upmarket dining in Weybridge

☎ 01932 847242
146 Oatlands Dr KT13 9HB
e-mail: info@oatlandsparkhotel.com
web: www.oatlandsparkhotel.com
dir: From Weybridge town centre approach Monument Hill, follow road to mini rdbt. 1st left into Oatlands Drive. Hotel 500mtrs on left

The Broadwater Restaurant at Oatlands Park, part of which dates from Henry VIII's reign, is a large, traditional-looking room with ornate ceilings, well-spaced tables and views over the grounds. The cooking has a degree of ambition and elaboration and the kitchen team displays genuine confidence. Start with foie gras terrine lined with truffle butter and served with duck rillette and warm apple chutney, followed by tournedos sauced with wild mushrooms, served with oxtail ravioli, rösti and spinach. The food generally follows modern European

continued

Save on Hotels. Book at **theAA.com/hotel**

SURREY 457 ENGLAND

Drake's Restaurant

Modern British V

Outstanding cooking near the RHS gardens at Wisley

☎ 01483 224777
The Clock House, High St GU23 6AQ
e-mail: info@drakesrestaurant.co.uk
web: www.drakesrestaurant.co.uk
dir: M25 junct 10, A3 towards Guildford. Follow Ripley signs. Restaurant in village centre

If you're a first-timer, look for the clock reaching out from the Georgian red-brick façade. Of course, once you've sampled Steve Drake's majestically-crafted food, there's little doubt you will return. Steve and Serina have been here for nearly a decade now and their restaurant has evolved into a stylish, civilised spot which is very much a destination address. It looks the business - smart and nicely understated - with a bar area where you can sip on something before moving into the restaurant itself. The heritage of the building is reflected in the exposed beams and Georgian proportions, the chairs and tables bringing some contemporary chic to proceedings. Steve's food is modern and dynamic, but everything starts with the quality of the raw materials. He buys very well indeed, with 95% of what is used coming from the UK. His dishes demonstrate a good deal of technical

virtuosity in the making, and creative ideas abound. The attention to detail shown in the baking of the breads is a good sign indeed, and continues into first courses such as one of quail with rhubarb gel, foie gras and compressed lettuce. Everything looks beautiful on the plate, too. Another starter pairs scallops with sea broccoli, an oyster and capers, and main-course brill with burnt aubergine, parsley root and shrimp butter. The Flavour Discovery menu is a great way to go if you can persuade your guests to go with you, and the good-value lunch menu is a compelling deal offering two choices at each course. Desserts show no less skill and craft, so 'rhubarb' is a dish of rice pudding, gingerbread and burnt milk, and 'pear' includes a beurre noisette, goats' milk, hibiscus and crystalised vodka. A class act all round.

Chef Steve Drake **Owner** Steve & Serina Drake **Times** 12-2/7-9.30 Closed 1 wk Jan, 2 wks Aug, 1 wk Xmas, Sun-Mon, L Tue **Prices** Fixed L 2 course £22, Tasting menu £49.50-£80, Service added but optional 12.5% **Wines** 230 bottles over £30, 13 bottles under £30, 10 by glass **Notes** Discovery menu £80, Tasting menu 6/9 course, Vegetarian menu **Seats** 40 **Children** Portions **Parking** 2, 2 local car parks

WEYBRIDGE *continued*

conventions, but there are also eastern influences at work: a starter of seared scallops with coconut and coriander risotto, Thai cream and mango salsa, for example. Successful desserts include vanilla pannacotta with cinnamon doughnuts and raspberry syrup.

Chef Darren Kimber **Owner** Nawaz Jaual **Times** 1-3/7-10 Closed L Sat, D Sun **Prices** Fixed L 3 course £19.95, Fixed D 3 course fr £24.95, Starter £4.95-£14.95, Main £15.50-£25.95, Dessert £4.95-£9 **Wines** 5 bottles over £30, 7 bottles under £30, 12 by glass **Notes** BBQ on lawn summer, Sunday L, Vegetarian available, Civ Wed 220 **Seats** 100 **Children** Portions, Menu **Parking** 144

SUSSEX, EAST

ALFRISTON   Map 6 TQ50

Deans Place

◉◉ Modern British **V** ◔

Charming country hotel with confident cooking

☎ 01323 870248
Seaford Rd BN26 5TW
e-mail: mail@deansplacehotel.co.uk
web: www.deansplacehotel.co.uk
dir: off A27, signed Alfriston & Drusillas Zoo Park. Continue south through village

The setting on the edge of a pretty village in the South Downs National Park, with the River Cuckmere flowing past, is a winner. Once part of a vast farming estate, the house has lovely gardens and plenty of period charm, and, in the shape of Harcourts, a restaurant that puts it on the local map. It's a traditional room with well-spaced, well-dressed tables and garden views. Good use is made of regional ingredients on a menu that takes a decidedly modern British and Pan-European approach. Oxtail tart, for example, is a fabulous first course (with wholemeal and pine nut crust and Jerusalem artichoke purée), or go for the artichoke arancini with blue cheese and walnut dressing. Main-course cod is a good quality piece of fish, cooked with care, and served with brandade, crab bisque and caviar cream, whilst slow-roasted belly of pork comes with butter bean, chorizo and barley risotto. The confident cooking continues through to desserts such as spiced apple parfait with a cinnamon and blueberry syrup, and hazelnut crumble.

Chef Stuart Dunley **Owner** Steyne Hotels Ltd
Times 12.30-2.30/6.30-9.30 **Prices** Fixed D 3 course fr £35, Service optional **Wines** 20 bottles over £30, 45 bottles under £30, 10 by glass **Notes** Sunday L, Vegetarian menu, Dress restrictions, Smart casual, Civ Wed 140 **Seats** 60, Pr/dining room 50 **Children** Portions, Menu **Parking** 100

The Star Alfriston

◉ Modern British ◔

Ancient Sussex inn with unfussy modern food

☎ 01323 870495
High St BN26 5TA
e-mail: bookings@thestaralfriston.co.uk
dir: 2m off A27, at Drusillas rdbt follow Alfriston signs. Hotel on right in centre of High St

Whether you're a walker on the South Downs Way, or just pootling around Sussex in the car, The Star makes a tempting pitstop. On the pretty high street of a chocolate box-pretty Sussex village, the venerable timbered inn has been trading since the 13th century, and was run by the monks of Battle Abbey as a 'Holy House' - the wooden sanctuary post offering instant church protection is still in the bar. It hasn't saved the old place from a spot of updating through the centuries though: the Victorians added their bits, and there's a 1960s extension. The kitchen deals in straightforward ideas built on splendid Sussex ingredients, be it a quail's Scotch egg with tartare sauce, or pork tenderloin with château potatoes, braised red cabbage and celeriac purée. Dessert could be chocolate millefeuille with vanilla crème fraîche.

Chef Benoit Guay **Owner** Damian Martin & Martin Gobbee **Times** 7-9 Closed L Mon-Sat **Prices** Fixed D 3 course £29, Service added but optional 10% **Wines** 11 bottles over £30, 18 bottles under £30, 10 by glass **Notes** Vegetarian available, Civ Wed 120 **Seats** 50, Pr/dining room 32 **Children** Portions, Menu **Parking** 35

BATTLE   Map 7 TQ71

Powder Mills Hotel

◉ Modern British **V** ◔

Appealing modish cooking near the 1066 battlefield

☎ 01424 775511
Powdermill Ln TN33 0SP
e-mail: powdc@aol.com
web: www.powdermillshotel.com
dir: M25 junct 5, A21 towards Hastings. At St Johns Cross take A2100 to Battle. Pass abbey on right, 1st right into Powdermills Ln. 1m, hotel on right

Just outside Battle in the heart of 1066 country, Powder Mills is a lovely Georgian mansion set in 150 acres of splendid Sussex countryside made up of parkland, lakes and woods. Named after a gunpowder works whose materials helped fight off Napoleon, it now lives out a more tranquil existence, including leisurely dining in the bright and summery Orangery Restaurant. Wicker seats and linen-clothed tables on black and white marble floors, and Italian statuary reinforce the sunny feel, while the kitchen looks to the Sussex larder for the ingredients forming the bedrock of an appealing modern repertoire. You might start with that trusty combo of seared scallops and black pudding, pointed up by Calvados-marinated Cox's apples, then move on to loin of local venison with creamed potato, Savoy cabbage, butternut squash, and Cassis sauce. Finish with a luxurious Valrhona chocolate délice with griottine cherries.

Chef Callum O'Doherty **Owner** Mrs J Cowpland **Times** 12-2/7-9 **Prices** Fixed L 2 course £16.50-£21, Fixed D 3 course £29.50-£35, Service added but optional 10%, Groups min 10 service 10% **Wines** 4 by glass **Notes** Library menu £5-£21, Sunday L, Vegetarian menu, Dress restrictions, Smart casual, no jeans, shorts or T-shirts, Civ Wed 100 **Seats** 90, Pr/dining room 16 **Children** Portions, Menu **Parking** 100

BODIAM   Map 7 TQ72

The Curlew Restaurant

◉◉ Modern British **V** ◔

Sharply focused modern cooking

☎ 01580 861394 & 861202
Junction Rd TN32 5UY
e-mail: enquiries@thecurlewrestaurant.co.uk
dir: A21 south turn left at Hurst Green signed Bodiam. Restaurant on left at end of road

A mere few years is all it has taken to resurrect this simple white-painted clapboard coaching inn and transform it into one of East Sussex's foodie hotspots. The clean-cut décor would not look out of place in a chic urban venue, while cow motif wallpaper, antler coat hooks and stag's head mirrors serve as a playful reminder that you're out in the sticks. The vibe is suitably easygoing, helped along by a service team who are well-briefed on the innermost workings of the menu - they need to be, since it merely lists the components of each dish rather than giving any elucidation as to what has actually been done to them. Local produce drives the output, including foraged herbs and mushrooms, while line-caught fish travels a short way from the South Coast. The result is clever, of-the-moment, technically accomplished food: wood pigeon carpaccio with truffle custard, salt-baked artichoke and Madeira to get things going, followed by rump of Romney Marsh lamb teamed with grilled little gem lettuce, crispy lamb bacon and a dollop of sour cream. Finish with strawberry shortcake with buttermilk custard.

Chef Andrew Scott **Owner** Mark & Sara Colley **Times** 12-2.30/6.30-9.30 Closed 2 wks Jan, 1 wk Jun, 1 wk Nov, Mon-Tue **Prices** Fixed L 2 course £20, Fixed D 3 course £25, Starter £8.50-£10.50, Main £17-£23, Dessert £8-£9, Service optional **Wines** 19 by glass **Notes** Sunday L, Vegetarian menu **Seats** 64 **Children** Portions **Parking** 16

Save on Hotels. Book at theAA.com/hotel

SUSSEX, EAST 459 ENGLAND

BRIGHTON & HOVE
Map 6 TQ30

Chilli Pickle

◉◉ Regional Indian

Vibrant Indian flavours in buzzy venue

☎ 01273 900383
17 Jubilee St BN1 1GE
e-mail: info@thechillipickle.com
web: www.thechillipickle.com
dir: From the Steine (A23) right into Church Lane & right into Jubilee St. Next to myhotel Brighton, opposite Library

The Chilli Pickle has gone from strength to strength since it moved into capacious premises on a pedestrianised square in the regenerated North Laine quarter. Its full-length glass walls create the impression of dining alfresco whatever the weather, offering ringside seats for Brighton's ever-colourful street life. The interior works a contemporary rustic look with chunky wooden tables, blond-wood floors, and vivid splashes of blue and yellow to jazz up the almost Scandinavian minimalism of the place. The menu gives sub-continental clichés and curry house standards a swerve, dealing in smartly reworked thalis, dosai and Indian street-food-inspired dishes at lunchtime - fried coconut and coriander balls coated in potato and served with smoked red pepper, for example, ahead of Rajasthani mutton shoulder curry. At dinner, the kitchen cranks things up a gear, making good use of a brace of tandoors to produce the likes of a whole sea bream coated in green peppercorn chutney served with lemon rice and coconut chutney, or you could go all-out with a platter involving tandoor-roasted chicken, quail, clove-smoked venison, and spiced lamb chop.

Chef Alun Sperring **Owner** Alun & Dawn Sperring **Times** 12-3/6-10.30 Closed 25-26 Dec, 1 Jan **Prices** Fixed D 3 course £26.50, Starter £4.95-£7.95, Main £9.50-£18.50, Dessert £3-£5.95, Service optional, Groups min 8 service 10% **Wines** 6 bottles over £30, 26 bottles under £30, 7 by glass **Notes** King Thali menu daily £13, Sunday L, Vegetarian available, Civ Wed 130 **Seats** 115 **Children** Portions **Parking** NCP Church St

The De Vere Grand, Brighton

◉ Modern European

Fish specialities in the stylishly remodelled Grand

☎ 01273 224300 & 224309
King's Rd BN1 2FW
e-mail: reception@grandbrighton.co.uk
web: www.devere.co.uk
dir: On A259 (seafront road between piers) adjacent to Brighton Centre

It was all happening at The Grand in 2013, with an extensive makeover due to be completed by the late summer. Gone is the slightly frowsy air of formality that served the place well in Victorian and Edwardian times, and in has come a stylish champagne and oyster bar, while the main dining room is now remodelled as GB1, a fish and seafood venue. The views along the South Coast's most well-known seafront, with the spindly ruin of the West Pier standing ankle-deep in the sea, are continuing fixtures, but the menu now feels more in tune with Brighton's gastro-universe. Expect fried whitebait dusted in smoked paprika with garlic mayo, as well as crowd-pleasers like beer-battered pollock and triple-cooked chips, or classic fish pie. A strand of inventiveness also produces perfectly timed sea bass with confit celery, gnocchi and merguez, and there are fine local meats too. Dessert could be sensuously oozy Valrhôna chocolate fondant with spiced plum and star-anise ice cream.

Times 12.30-2/7-10 Closed L Sat

The Foragers

◉ Modern European 🍃

Foraged ingredients and more in a popular Hove pub

☎ 01273 733134
3 Stirling Place BN3 3YU
e-mail: info@theforagerspub.co.uk
web: www.theforagerspub.co.uk
dir: A2033 Sackville Rd, left Stirling Place, restaurant 200m on left

This buzzy backstreet pub tucked away behind Hove's main drag hums with a casual upbeat vibe. Refreshingly free of designer gastro pretensions, the dining area goes for a likeable shabby-chic look: simple pine-topped pub tables set against funky shades of turquoise and fuchsia pink, and a large mural in blocks of vivid paintbox colours inspired by a Brazilian favela scene that turns the brightness factor up to 11. This, however, has nothing whatsoever to do with the culinary theme, which

celebrates splendid seasonal Sussex produce. As its name suggests, the kitchen likes to use wild and foraged ingredients, so wood pigeon breast might start the show, together with sautéed Portobello mushrooms and parsnip purée, before a main course of tender duck breast with confit leg, potato fondant, red cabbage purée and orange jus. Dessert could be an intriguing and eclectic trio of ginger parkin with local Flower Marie cheese, and rosemary and hogweed seed honey.

The Foragers

Chef Josh Kitson **Owner** Paul Hutchison **Times** 12-3/6-10 Closed D Sun **Prices** Fixed L 2 course £12, Starter £5-£7, Main £10-£18, Dessert £5-£7.50, Service optional, Groups min 6 service 10% **Wines** 5 bottles over £30, 27 bottles under £30, 16 by glass **Notes** Sunday L £11-£14, Vegetarian available **Seats** 74 **Children** Portions, Menu **Parking** On street

The Gingerman Restaurant

◉◉ Modern British 🍃

Modern cooking without clichés near seafront

☎ 01273 326688
21A Norfolk Square BN1 2PD
e-mail: info@gingermanrestaurants.com
dir: A23 to Palace Pier rdbt. Turn right onto Kings Rd. At art-deco style Embassy building turn right into Norfolk Sq

The original venue of Ben McKellar's little Brighton & Hove empire, The Gingerman is tucked away in a former tea-room off the seafront. It's an intimate place, run with the unbuttoned familiarity that Brighton loves, decorated with pictures you may wish to purchase while you're buying the gutsy, well-wrought modern British food. A disinclination to rely on modern clichés produces starters such as lemon-marinated chargrilled cuttlefish with romesco sauce and rocket, and mains like roast guinea fowl with a gruyère croquette, crispy ham, spinach purée and Marsala jus. The fish special is usually worth a gander, supplementing menu offerings such as grilled sea bass with spiced crab gnocchi and puréed courgette in a reduction of Pernod. Dessert can be as inventive as orange and thyme pannacotta with orange and passionfruit sauce, or as satisfyingly old-fangled as tarte Tatin with cinnamon ice cream.

Chef Ben McKellar, Simon Neville Jones **Owner** Ben & Pamela McKellar **Times** 12.30-2/7-10 Closed 2 wks Xmas, Mon **Prices** Fixed L 2 course £15, Fixed D 3 course £35, Service optional, Groups min 6 service 12.5% **Wines** 16 bottles over £30, 24 bottles under £30, 10 by glass **Notes** Sunday L, Vegetarian available **Seats** 32 **Children** Portions **Parking** Regency Square NCP

BRIGHTON & HOVE *continued*

Graze Restaurant

◉◉ Modern British V ☺
- -

Ambitious contemporary cooking and charming Regency décor

☎ 01273 823707
42 Western Rd BN3 1JD
e-mail: info@graze-restaurant.co.uk
dir: Along A2010 Queens Rd, from clock tower head W on B2066 Western Rd. Restaurant on S/side of road just beyond Brunswick Sq

It's Hove, actually, but worth seeking out wherever you are in the city, for this is an ambitious restaurant that aims to impress with its bright, modish cooking. Just around the corner from the splendid Georgian Brunswick Square, and just a few minutes' stroll up from the seafront, the décor takes inspiration from the city's Regency heritage (think shades of rich reds and gold, lots of mirrors, artful objets and evocative lighting, plus well-spaced, well-dressed tables). The kitchen takes a contemporary approach in content and presentation of dishes, so expect foams, swipes of purées and gels, and some enticing combinations. A starter terrine of corn-fed chicken, for example, with leeks, tarragon and creamed livers is pointed up by its accompanying pickled shallots, or there might be seared hand-dived scallops with broccoli, bacon and almonds. Main-course halibut is topped with truffle and served with cauliflower cheese and hand-rolled macaroni, and for dessert, blood orange and vanilla pannacotta comes with a pistachio biscotti.

Chef Adrian Hawkins **Owner** Kate Alleston, Neil Mannifield **Times** 12-2/6.30-9.30 Closed 1-4 Jan, D Sun **Prices** Fixed L 3 course £18, Fixed D 3 course £34, Tasting menu £42-£47, Service added but optional 12% **Wines** 34 bottles over £30, 18 bottles under £30, 11 by glass **Notes** Vegetarian tasting menu £42, Tasting menu 7 course, Sunday L, Vegetarian menu, Dress restrictions, Smart casual **Seats** 50, Pr/dining room 24 **Children** Portions

Hotel du Vin Brighton

◉◉ Traditional British, French
- -

Upmarket bistro cooking off the seafront

☎ 01273 718588
2-6 Ship St BN1 1AD
e-mail: info@brighton.hotelduvin.com
web: www.hotelduvin.com
dir: A23 to seafront, at rdbt right, then right onto Middle St, bear right into Ship St, hotel at sea end on right

The Brighton branch of the chain, just off the seafront, has all the expected Francophile touches, its walls adorned with wine and spirit posters and risqué pictures, leather-look banquettes running back to back down the centre, and small wooden tables (easily pushed together by nifty staff for larger groups). A glance at the menu shows that this is more than your average bistro fare, with potted crab with caper berries and egg salad followed by ox cheek bourguignon, alongside chicken

terrine and bouillabaisse. Evidently the kitchen orders great-quality raw materials, often locally, and treats them with care and respect at the stoves. A simple starter of salmon ballottine with herbed fromage blanc might precede main-course chicken Dijonnaise, moist and full of flavour, with mousseline potatoes. Momentum doesn't falter at the final stretch, with light and tasty pistachio parfait with chocolate ice cream, the plate dotted with thick caramel sauce.

Times 12-2/7-10

Indian Summer

◉ Indian
- -

A cool venue for hot cuisine

☎ 01273 711001
69 East St BN1 1HQ
e-mail: manager@indian-summer.org.uk
dir: 500yds from Palace Pier

A Brighton treasure since it opened in 2001, this classy modern Indian continues to come up with the goods. Hidden away on the edge of the labyrinthine Lanes, what makes this place stand out from the sub-continental competition is its up-to-date pan-Indian cooking and commitment to using quality, fresh ingredients. The décor is contemporary and funky with bare blond-wood tables, darkwood floors, and huge pictures of Indian street food vendors on aubergine-hued walls. Classic street snacks such as bhel puri or masala dosa set things up for a range of zingy, fresh-tasting dishes, ranging from lamb kohlapuri - a robust dish of diced lamb with toasted peanuts, red chillies and coconut - to a Gujarati vegetarian thali platter, to hake marinated in fresh coriander, mint and cumin and served in a banana leaf. Often a weak element of the Indian repertoire, desserts here buck the trend with an excellent espresso cheesecake with amaretto crumb, or mango to put an exotic twist to a crème brûlée.

Chef Maharaj Jaswantsingh **Owner** Mikesh Aginlistri, Byron Swales **Times** 12-3/6-10.30 Closed 25-26 Dec, L Mon **Prices** Prices not confirmed Service added but optional 10%, Groups min 5 service 10% **Wines** 7 bottles over £30, 26 bottles under £30, 10 by glass **Notes** Vegetarian available **Seats** 60 **Children** Portions **Parking** On street, car park

Terre à Terre

◉ Modern Vegetarian V
- -

Ground-breaking vegetarian and vegan cooking

☎ 01273 729051
71 East St BN1 1HQ
e-mail: mail@terreaterre.co.uk
web: www.terreaterre.co.uk
dir: Town centre, close to Brighton Pier & The Lanes

Hitting its 20th year in 2013, Terre à Terre is a vegetarian restaurant of ambition which set the bar for creative, classy veggie-vegan food. It's just up from the seafront, not far from the pier, and generates a happy buzz within. The dining area is bigger than it looks from the outside, stretching back to a small terrace. The service team are a professional and cheerful bunch and happy to help with the menu. The food has made its mark with its highly creative combinations - and long, detailed dish descriptions - and everything is listed as to its status (gf = no gluten, v = vegan, etc.). Congee shiso yuzu and tempura shiitake is a satisfying hit of Japanese flavours, whilst main-course Terre à Tiffin includes cauliflower and ginger bhaji and confit brinjal pickle among its delights. The puds are a highlight: Moorish merlot molten mouthful (a take on a chocolate fondant, served with a merlot poached pear), for example.

Chef A Powley, P Taylor **Owner** A Powley & P Taylor **Times** 12-10.30 Closed 25-26 Dec, All-day dining **Prices** Fixed L 2 course fr £5, Fixed D 3 course £25-£30, Starter £4.50-£8.95, Main £13.95-£14.85, Dessert £5.55-£8.25, Service optional, Groups min 6 service 10% **Wines** 14 bottles over £30, 40 bottles under £30, 14 by glass **Notes** Promotional fixed price L & D menus available, Vegetarian menu **Seats** 110 **Children** Portions, Menu **Parking** NCP, on street

Save on Hotels. Book at **theAA.com/hotel**

SUSSEX, EAST 461 **ENGLAND**

CAMBER   Map 7 TV91

The Gallivant Hotel

Modern British **NEW**

Local flavours right on the Sussex coast

☎ 01797 225057
New Lydd Rd TN31 7RB
e-mail: beachbistro@thegallivanthotel.com
web: www.thebeachbistro.com
dir: M29 junct 10 to A2070, left Camber Road before Rye.
Hotel located on left in Camber Village

This shabby-chic hideaway hunkers down behind the
huge dunes and sweeping stretch of golden beach at
Camber Sands. With the fen-like landscapes of Romney
salt marshes all around, it's hard to believe you're in
Sussex, particularly when the Beach Bistro's style is
straight out of New England, flooded with light through
large glass doors opening onto the terrace, and done out
with distressed scrubbed pine tables and simple white
seats. After years of working in the kitchens of Marco and
Jean-Christophe (no surnames needed here), chef Trevor
Hambley believes in getting his hands on the best local
materials and treating them without fuss - fish landed by
day boats in Rye and Hastings is simply pan-fried and
served with Romney potatoes and sauces such as
hollandaise, crab and chilli, or salsa verde, while
fantastic Romney salt marsh lamb could appear with
braised little gem lettuce and gratin dauphinoise.

Chef Trevor Hambley **Owner** Harry Cragoe
Times 12-2.30/7-9 **Prices** Starter £6-£8.50, Main
£13.50-£24, Dessert £5.50-£7, Service added but
optional 10% **Wines** 17 bottles over £30, 28 bottles under
£30, 8 by glass **Notes** Sunday L £23-£27, Vegetarian
available, Dress restrictions, Smart casual, Civ Wed 150
Seats 55, Pr/dining room 100 **Children** Portions, Menu
Parking 20

EASTBOURNE   Map 6 TV69

The Grand Hotel

Modern, Classic NOTABLE WINE LIST

Grand seafront hotel with confident cooking

☎ 01323 412345
King Edward's Pde BN21 4EQ
e-mail: reservations@grandeastbourne.com
web: www.grandeastbourne.com
dir: Western end of seafront, 1m from Eastbourne station

If *Downton Abbey* and *Upstairs Downstairs* have
engendered a longing for a more elegant past, the
wedding cake pomp of Eastbourne's Grand Hotel - the
'White Palace' to its friends - should hit the spot. Built in
1875, the grande dame of the seafront still has a whiff of
the past about it that makes it easy to picture its
prestigious guests - Winston Churchill, Charlie Chaplin,
Elgar, and Debussy, who composed *La Mer* on his hols in
1905. Gastronomes might want to get in the mood with
afternoon tea, served in the marble-columned grandeur
of the Great Hall, then take a stroll on the prom to work
up an appetite for dinner in the fine dining Mirabelle
restaurant. Battalions of crisply uniformed staff pushing
trolleys certainly add to the old-school trappings, but
when the silver cloches are lifted, the plates beneath

reveal modern European flavour combinations and
textures to keep 21st-century guests sweet. You might be
treated to a warm salad of confit duck leg with Japanese-
spiced green pea ragoût, followed by slow-cooked navarin
of Kent Marsh lamb with potato purée and parsnip crisps.
A Thai basil pannacotta with blueberries, lime,
strawberries and mint makes a fine finale.

The Grand Hotel

Chef Keith Mitchell, Gerald Roser **Owner** Elite Hotels
Times 12.30-2/7-10 Closed 2-16 Jan, Sun-Mon
Prices Fixed L 3 course fr £21.50, Fixed D 3 course fr £38,
Service optional, Groups min 6 service 12.5% **Wines** 240
bottles over £30, 28 bottles under £30, 14 by glass
Notes Fixed L/D supplements added to price, Tasting
menu 5 course, Sunday L, Vegetarian available, Dress
restrictions, Jacket or tie for D **Seats** 50 **Parking** 70

See advert below

EASTBOURNE *continued*

Langham Hotel

Modern British

Enterprising cooking in seafront hotel

☎ 01323 731451
43-49 Royal Pde BN22 7AH
e-mail: neil@langhamhotel.co.uk
web: www.langhamhotel.co.uk
dir: A22 follow signs for seafront Sovereign Centre, take 3rd exit onto Royal Pde. Hotel on corner Royal Pde & Cambridge Rd

The Langham is in a great location bang on the seafront, and the décor of its Conservatory restaurant is intentionally low-key so as not to distract the eyes from the wonderful sea views. There's plenty of interest on the plate too, from Thai-style fish broth to roast rump of lamb in a rosemary and anchovy crust. The kitchen sources its raw materials from a narrow area - that lamb is from the South Downs, seafood from just a few yards away - and considers combinations carefully, producing perfectly seared mackerel fillets offset by a reduction of blackcurrants and cassis, served with girolles, and a main course of roast pancetta-wrapped breast of partridge with pear and juniper jus, accompanied by confit leg. Puddings can bring on some vibrant marriages of flavours and textures too: witness warm parkin pudding in sticky ginger sauce with damson chutney and oat ice cream.

Chef Michael Titherington **Owner** Neil & Wendy Kirby **Times** 12-2.30/6-9.30 **Prices** Prices not confirmed Service optional **Wines** 18 by glass **Notes** Sunday L, Vegetarian available **Seats** 24 **Children** Portions, Menu

Ashdown Park Hotel & Country Club

Modern British NOTABLE WINE LIST

Grand hotel dining in an upmarket country house

☎ 01342 824988
Wych Cross RH18 5JR
e-mail: reservations@ashdownpark.com
web: www.ashdownpark.com
dir: A264 to East Grinstead, then A22 to Eastbourne. 2m S of Forest Row at Wych Cross lights. Left to Hartfield, hotel on right 0.75m

Everything about the swanky Ashdown Park Hotel and Country Club is done in the high-flown style you would expect of an upscale Victorian country house: its 186 acres of landscaped gardens and parkland are secluded in the depths of Ashdown Forest, and there's an 18-hole golf course and a fitness and spa complex. Gents will need to pack a jacket and tie, and everyone can expect old-school formality in the Anderida Restaurant, where the front of house staff deliver all the precision of silver service. On the plate comes flamboyantly-presented classical cuisine, glossed up with modern takes on time-honoured ideas and fashionably-deconstructed dishes: a starter of smoked haddock fish 'pie', for example, presented in a Kilner jar with a scallop on top, pea purée, prawn toast and a tranche of fish terrine. Main course brings roasted rump of lamb with a pastilla of shoulder teamed with sweet tomato risotto and pesto, then a final flourish of brown sugar parfait with banana rice pudding, exotic foam and honeycomb brings down the curtain.

Ashdown Park Hotel & Country Club

Chef Andrew Wilson **Owner** Elite Hotels **Times** 12-2/7-10 **Prices** Fixed L 2 course fr £17.50, Fixed D 3 course £38.50, Tasting menu £82.50, Starter £8-£13.50, Main £19.50-£29.50, Dessert £9-£10, Service optional, Groups min 6 service 10% **Wines** 200 bottles over £30, 20 bottles under £30, 9 by glass **Notes** Tasting menu 8 course, Sunday L, Vegetarian available, Dress restrictions, Jacket or tie for gentlemen after 7pm, Civ Wed 150 **Seats** 120, Pr/dining room 160 **Children** Portions, Menu **Parking** 120

See advert below

Save on Hotels. Book at theAA.com/hotel

SUSSEX, EAST 463 ENGLAND

Jali Restaurant

◉ Traditional and Modern Indian

An Indian flavour by the seaside

☎ 01424 457300 & 720188
Chatsworth Hotel, 7-11 Carlisle Pde TN34 1JG
e-mail: info@chatsworthhotel.com
dir: On Hastings seafront, near railway station

The original in a small chain that now includes Crewe and Blackpool amongst its number, Jali is in the Chatsworth Hotel, with a prime seafront position close to the old town and the pier. It's all very civilised inside, with some Indian artefacts and artworks dotted around but resisting clichés, with tables smartly dressed in white linen cloths. The menu also avoids the typical curry house standards; start, perhaps, with gin-fried chicken, the meat marinated in the said booze and stir-fried with fresh herbs, and from the long kebab section there might be noorani seekh (minced lamb kebab) or salmon sula (grilled in the tandoor with a lime and herb crust). There's plenty for vegetarians, too, such as a main-course khumb kaju curry (mushrooms and cashew nuts in a spicy tomato, onion and yoghurt gravy) and meat course might be dal gosht (lamb cooked with lentils).

Chef Arun Ramachadran **Owner** Aristel Group of Hotels
Times 6-10.30 Closed Sun, L all week **Prices** Starter
£3.50-£8.50, Main £6.50-£13.50, Dessert £3.50-£6.50,
Service added but optional 10% **Wines** 5 by glass
Notes Vegetarian available, Dress restrictions, Smart
casual, no shorts **Seats** 52, Pr/dining room 35
Children Portions **Parking** 8

Jolly Sportsman

◉◉ Modern European, International V ☺

Rustic-chic inn serving up hearty food with a true Sussex flavour

☎ 01273 890400
Chapel Ln, East Chiltington BN7 3BA
e-mail: info@thejollysportsman.com
dir: From Lewes A275, East Grinstead road, left onto the B2116 Offham, 2nd right into Novington Lane. In approx 1m first left Chapel Lane

Tucked away among the meadows and rural lanes of the Sussex hinterland, chef-patron Bruce Wass's weatherboarded country inn is well worth hunting down. Inside, there's an inviting and cosy bar area with casks on trestles, but the place is clearly much more than a simple rustic boozer: sage-green walls hung with colourful works from local artists, mellow oak flooring and great rough-hewn oak slab tables add up to the tastefully uncluttered country-chic look of a switched-on modern dining inn. The kitchen delivers vibrant, contemporary cooking with a spot-on feel for sourcing the freshest, local and seasonal produce. Smoked ham hock terrine with celeriac remoulade and pickled shallot makes a robustly rustic opener, while superb, meltingly-tender

slow-cooked pork belly with home-made sausage roll, quince aïoli, cider gravy, colcannon and green beans is a superior version of an old favourite. Fans of local fish might find roast brill (landed in Newhaven) with chive sauce, white beans and salsa verde. Gingerbread pudding with rich sea salt butterscotch sauce and vanilla ice cream makes a richly comforting finish.

Chef Bruce Wass **Owner** Bruce Wass **Times** 12-3/6.30-10
Closed 25 Dec, D Sun **Prices** Fixed L 2 course fr £13.50,
Fixed D 2 course fr £19.50, Starter £5.45-£9.50, Main
£11.75-£19.85, Dessert £5.45-£11.75, Service optional,
Groups min 6 service 10% **Wines** 100 bottles over £30,
40 bottles under £30, 13 by glass **Notes** Sunday L
£19.50-£29.50, Vegetarian menu **Seats** 80, Pr/dining
room 20 **Children** Portions, Menu **Parking** 35

Newick Park Hotel & Country Estate

◉◉ Modern European ☺

Classy cooking on a sumptuous Sussex estate

☎ 01825 723633
BN8 4SB
e-mail: bookings@newickpark.co.uk
dir: Exit A272 at Newick Green, 1m, pass church & pub.
Turn left, hotel 0.25m on right

Aficionados of the blue-blooded country house idiom will go weak at the knees over Newick Park, a classy, intimate package of plush interiors laden with antiques and an unintimidating, easygoing mood set by personable staff. The handsome Georgian pile sits by the South Downs in 250 acres of parkland and gardens that are not just pretty to look at, but which also earn their keep, providing seasonal fruit, veg, herbs and game for Chris Moore's kitchen team who deliver a refined style of modernised country-house cooking perfectly in keeping with the surroundings. A spring lunch could open with crab salad with chorizo, potato, onion and lemon mayonnaise, then proceed to roast guinea fowl breast with thyme boudin, boulangère potatoes and garlic creamed cabbage. The intelligent Anglo-French polish continues through to desserts such as lime clafoutis with ginger ice cream and pomegranate dressing.

Newick Park Hotel & Country Estate

Chef Chris Moore **Owner** Michael & Virginia Childs
Times 12-1.45/7-9 Closed 31 Dec **Prices** Fixed L 2 course
£17.50-£29.50, Fixed D 3 course £42.50, Service optional
Wines 9 by glass **Notes** Sunday L, Vegetarian available,
Civ Wed 110 **Seats** 40, Pr/dining room 74
Children Portions, Menu **Parking** 100

The George in Rye

◉ Modern Mediterranean

Modern restaurant in historic town

☎ 01797 222114
98 High St TN31 7JT
e-mail: stay@thegeorgeinrye.com
dir: M20 junct 10, then A2070 to Brenzett then A259 to Rye

The 16th-century George has been transformed from a down-at-heel Tudor pub into a spiffy boutique hotel with a thoroughly modern roll-call of dishes coming out of the kitchen, and splendid wines from Sussex and Kent vineyards to bolster the sense of local terroir. The best bits are still there - beams from an Elizabethan ship, an 18th-century wig store, and the Georgian ballroom - but these are overlaid with a classy contemporary look, as typified in the George Grill, where olive-green walls, bare darkwood tables, buttoned banquettes and funky designer fabrics make a trendy setting for the kitchen's Mediterranean-accented ideas. Full advantage is taken of local supplies from the farms of Sussex and Kent, and the trawlers of Rye Bay, starting with the scallops that could come with cauliflower purée and raisin and caper vinaigrette. Next out, a Barnsley chop of Romney Marsh lamb might be paired with purple sprouting broccoli, and rosemary and anchovy dressing, while desserts supply the simple pleasures of sticky toffee pudding with stem ginger ice cream.

Times 12-3/6.30-9.30

RYE *continued*

Mermaid Inn

◎◎ British, Traditional French V 🖐

Atmospheric medieval inn with modish menu

☎ 01797 223065
Mermaid St TN31 7EY
e-mail: info@mermaidinn.com
web: www.mermaidinn.com
dir: A259, follow signs to town centre, then into Mermaid St

The cellars at the Mermaid Inn date from the 12th century, the inn itself from a mere 1420, so it is only 600 years old. In a town filled with spellbinding period buildings, this old inn has lots of historic charm and atmosphere. Check out the giant inglenook fireplace in the bar with its priest's hole, and the linenfold panels in the restaurant. The food takes an Anglo-French path and there are some appealingly contemporary dishes on the menu. You might start with the modish salt and pepper squid (from the south coast) with sweet chilli and coriander, or the more Francophile pressed duck leg terrine with toasted brioche, fruit chutney and watercress salad. Main course might serve up braised shoulder of Romney Marsh lamb (local ingredients get a good showing here) with chestnut mushrooms, baby onions, parsley creamed potatoes and pancetta. Finish with winter berry soufflé with orange crème anglaise and white chocolate ice cream.

Chef Kyle Tatner **Owner** J Blincow & G Kite
Times 12-2.30/7-9.30 **Prices** Fixed L 2 course £21-£22, Fixed D 3 course £37.50, Service added but optional 10% **Wines** 15 bottles over £30, 22 bottles under £30, 15 by glass **Notes** Sunday L, Vegetarian menu, Dress restrictions, Smart casual, no jeans or T-shirts **Seats** 64, Pr/dining room 14 **Children** Portions, Menu **Parking** 26

Webbes at The Fish Café

◎ Modern British

Local seafood in an informal converted warehouse

☎ 01797 222226
17 Tower St TN31 7AT
e-mail: info@thefishcafe.com
dir: 100mtrs before Landgate Arch

This three-storey converted warehouse in Rye's centre is home to a ground floor restaurant, above which is a private function room, with cookery demonstrations held on the top floor. There's a lively informal vibe in the restaurant making it popular with families and tourists alike. An open-plan kitchen provides some entertainment and red-brick walls showcase sea related artwork. Excellent quality fish and seafood, confidently prepared, comes mainly from Rye and Hastings ports, but meat eaters and veggies won't feel left out. Begin with a shellfish platter, or mackerel fritters with mirin and lime dressing, vegetable salad and chilli jam, or pork and wild mushroom rillette with red onion marmalade. Roast fillet of wild sea bass, brown shrimps, leek risotto and shellfish sauce hits the spot. Puddings might include vanilla pannacotta with strawberry ice cream and fresh strawberries. An affordable global wine list adds to the appeal.

Chef Paul Webbe, Matthew Drinkwater **Owner** Paul & Rebecca Webbe **Times** 11.30-2.30/6-9.30 **Closed** 24 Dec-10 Jan **Prices** Prices not confirmed Service optional **Wines** 10 by glass **Notes** Sunday L, Vegetarian available, Dress restrictions, Smart casual **Seats** 52, Pr/dining room 60 **Children** Portions, Menu **Parking** Cinque Port Street

TICEHURST	Map 6 TQ63

Dale Hill Hotel & Golf Club

◎ Modern European 🖐

Modern European menu in a golfing hotel

☎ 01580 200112
TN5 7DQ
e-mail: info@dalehill.co.uk
web: www.dalehill.co.uk
dir: M25 junct 5/A21. 5m after Lamberhurst turn right at lights onto B2087 to Flimwell. Hotel 1m on left

Golf is the signature dish at this hotel and country club in a fabulous location high on the Sussex Weald. A duo of 18-hole courses provide the main event, but for starters there are sweeping views over the hills of East Sussex, and side dishes taking in a heated indoor pool and gym. Of the two restaurants, the expansive fine-dining Wealden Restaurant is the star attraction, and it comes - perhaps inevitably - with vistas of the 18th green. Modern European cooking is par for this particular course, and it appears in some adventurous ideas: braised veal and mandarin ravioli teamed with marinated tuna carpaccio and caper berries, followed by fillet of monkfish in a cockle crust with braised pork belly, crab croquette, carrot purée and red pepper salsa. Finish with an apricot crème brûlée.

Chef Mark Carter **Owner** Mr & Mrs Paul Gibbons
Times 12-2.30/6.30-9 Closed 25 Dec, L Mon-Sat **Prices** Starter £5.50-£7, Main £8.50-£18.95, Dessert £1.50-£6.50, Service optional **Wines** 8 bottles over £30, 29 bottles under £30, 7 by glass **Notes** Sunday L, Vegetarian available, Dress restrictions, Smart casual, Civ Wed 120 **Seats** Pr/dining room 24 **Children** Portions, Menu **Parking** 220

UCKFIELD	Map 6 TQ42

Buxted Park Hotel

◎◎ Modern European V 🖐

Polished modern cooking in Palladian mansion

☎ 01825 733333
Buxted TN22 4AY
e-mail: buxtedpark@handpicked.co.uk
web: www.handpickedhotels.co.uk/buxtedpark
dir: From A26 (Uckfield bypass) take A272 signed Buxted. Through lights, hotel 1m on right

Buxted Park is a magnificent Palladian mansion in over 300 acres. Its architecture and the grand portico at the entrance are indicators of the sort of lavish interiors to expect, although the dining room has a more cutting-edge look, with rounded booth seating upholstered in purple under a skylight. On-the-ball, smartly dressed staff deliver Neil Davison's individualistic take on modern European cooking. A smoked cheese beignet adds interest to cream of cauliflower soup, an alternative perhaps to pheasant ballottine with glazed figs and tarragon mousse, or a tasting of duck. Seasonality is a prime concern, so samphire might accompany moist, meaty monkfish tail wrapped in Parma ham with well-judged, subtle chive cream sauce. More traditionally, rump of local lamb comes with rosemary jus, fondant potatoes and roast vegetables. Canapés start off proceedings, and a selection of petits fours comes with coffee. Puddings are along the lines of classic lemon tart with flavour-packed raspberry sorbet, or pistachio cake with roasted almond ganache.

Chef Neil Davison **Owner** Hand Picked Hotels
Times 12-2/7-9.30 **Prices** Fixed L 2 course £16, Fixed D 3 course £38, Tasting menu £64-£99, Starter £13.95-£15, Main £24.50-£30.95, Dessert £11.50-£13.50, Service optional **Wines** 95 bottles over £30, 5 bottles under £30, 18 by glass **Notes** Dégustation 7 course with/without wine, Sunday L, Vegetarian menu, Dress restrictions, Smart casual, Civ Wed 120 **Seats** 40, Pr/dining room 120 **Children** Portions, Menu **Parking** 100

Save on Hotels. Book at theAA.com/hotel

SUSSEX, EAST 465 ENGLAND

East Sussex National Golf Resort & Spa

◉ British, French ◐

Well-executed modern cooking and golf

☎ 01825 880088
Little Horsted TN22 5ES
e-mail: reception@eastsussexnational.co.uk
dir: M25 junct 6, A22 signed East Grinstead & Eastbourne. Straight on at rdbt junct of A22 & A26 (Little Horsted). At next rdbt right to hotel

The name nails this sprawling, purpose-built operation's colours to the mast. And if it would appear that you must be here for its two obvious core attractions - the fairways of its two championship golf courses and spa pampering treatments - there is a very good third reason to be here, and that is the fine dining on offer in the Pavilion restaurant. The setting is on the minimal end of the contemporary spectrum, and looks through a wall of full-length windows onto the greens and the rolling South Downs countryside. The kitchen has the bountiful produce of Sussex close to hand, which it deploys in appealing ideas along the lines of pan-seared rabbit loin with bacon and leek risotto balls and béarnaise sauce, followed by roast venison from the estate served with Lyonnaise potatoes, buttered curly kale, broad beans and wild mushroom jus.

Chef Mark Burton **Owner** East Sussex National Ltd **Times** 12-2.30/7-9 Closed L Sun **Prices** Fixed L 2 course £15.95, Fixed D 3 course £25, Starter £6-£8, Main £14-£23, Dessert £6.50-£8, Service optional **Wines** 14 by glass **Notes** Sunday L, Vegetarian available, Dress restrictions, Smart casual, Civ Wed 250 **Seats** 90 **Children** Portions, Menu **Parking** 500

Horsted Place

◉◉ Modern British ◐

Unpretentious country-house cooking in Victorian Gothic masterpiece

☎ 01825 750581
Little Horsted TN22 5TS
e-mail: hotel@horstedplace.co.uk
dir: From Uckfield 2m S on A26 towards Lewes

The house is one of the Home Counties' more head-turning examples of Victorian Gothic, built in 1850 by George Myers, with detailing by Pugin. The gardens were landscaped in the following century by Sir Geoffrey Jellicoe, so its starry credentials are hardly in question. Inside is as ornate as is to be expected, with a dining room done in pale green, where the tables are dressed in floor-length linen and the pictures are of landscapes and horses. The country-house cooking on offer does nothing to frighten those horses, but sticks to tried-and-true combinations, which it brings off with unpretentious style. Scallops appear with parsnip purée and plenty of fruity tang from pomegranate, lime and lemon, while mains might embrace venison loin with braised red cabbage and vanilla pear in game jus, or roast monkfish and spinach in ginger butter. Finish with baked vanilla cheesecake in orange and Grand Marnier sauce.

Chef Allan Garth **Owner** Perinon Ltd **Times** 12-2/7-9.30 Closed 1st wk Jan, L Sat **Prices** Fixed L 2 course £18.95, Starter £9.50, Main £20, Dessert £8.50, Service optional **Wines** 74 bottles over £30, 24 bottles under £30, 9 by glass **Notes** Afternoon tea £17.50, Sunday L £29.50, Vegetarian available, Dress restrictions, No jeans, Civ Wed 100 **Seats** 40, Pr/dining room 80 **Children** Portions **Parking** 50

WESTFIELD   Map 7 TQ81

The Wild Mushroom Restaurant

◉◉ Modern British

Modern British cooking in a charming converted farmhouse

☎ 01424 751137
Woodgate House, Westfield Ln TN35 4SB
e-mail: info@wildmushroom.co.uk
dir: From A21 towards Hastings, left onto A28 to Westfield. Restaurant 1.5m on left

A converted 19th century farmhouse surrounded by countryside just a short drive from Hastings, Paul and Rebecca Webbe's restaurant is part of a mini-empire that includes Webbe's at The Fish Café in Rye - see entry - and Rock-a-nore in Hastings Old Town. The restaurant takes up the whole of the ground floor, with a conservatory bar overlooking a small garden at the rear. There are original

features like flagged floors and low beams, and a smart country feel to the place, helped along by the friendly service. Sharp, contemporary cooking is the name of the game, with ingredients shipped in locally from trusted suppliers and due heed paid to the seasons. There are set lunch, à la carte and tasting menus to choose from, with canapés, an amuse-bouche and home-made breads all part of the package. Pork and wild mushroom rillette served with toasted granary bread and home-made piccalilli is a switched on starter, with slow-cooked ox cheek with garlic mash and Shiraz jus a hit among main courses.

Chef Paul Webbe, Christopher Weddle **Owner** Mr & Mrs P Webbe **Times** 12-2.30/7-10 Closed 25 Dec, 2 wks at New Year, Mon-Tue, D Sun **Prices** Prices not confirmed Tasting menu £35, Service optional **Wines** 6 by glass **Notes** Tasting menu 6 course, Sunday L, Vegetarian available, Dress restrictions, Smart casual **Seats** 40 **Children** Portions **Parking** 20

WILMINGTON   Map 6 TQ50

Crossways

◉◉ Modern British ◐

Country-house dining in relaxed restaurant with rooms

☎ 01323 482455
Lewes Rd BN26 5SG
e-mail: stay@crosswayshotel.co.uk
web: www.crosswayshotel.co.uk
dir: On A27, 2m W of Polegate

Crossways, a Georgian house below the South Downs Way, was at one time the home of Elizabeth David's parents, and foodies can pay their respects to the writer as her grave is a short distance away. A monthly-changing four-course dinner is served in the small and comfortable dining room, with its private party vibe created in part by relaxed service from the proprietors. The well-balanced menu could kick off with seafood pancake, or smoked duck and Asian pear salad, with a soup of the day to follow. Main courses reflect the kitchen's straightforward, uncluttered approach to its output - perhaps game pie in a rich gravy - and sauces and garnishes are well considered: wild mushroom sauce for sautéed loin of local venison, say, mango, ginger and cranberry for roast breast of Gressingham duck, and a maple glaze for pork tenderloin in a parmesan crumb coating.

Chef David Stott **Owner** David Stott, Clive James **Times** 7.30-8.30 Closed 24 Dec-24 Jan, Sun-Mon, L all week **Prices** Prices not confirmed Service optional **Wines** 11 bottles over £30, 28 bottles under £30, 10 by glass **Notes** 4 course D £39, Vegetarian available **Seats** 24 **Parking** 20

SUSSEX, WEST

ALBOURNE   Map 6 TQ21

The Ginger Fox

◉ Modern British ✿

Classy country gastro-pub

☎ 01273 857888
Muddleswood Rd BN6 9EA
e-mail: gingerfox@gingermanrestaurants.com
dir: On A281 at junct with B2117

Part of a small Brighton-based group (see entry for mothership Gingerman Restaurant), The Ginger Fox is a country pub with the South Downs as its backyard and food very much at its heart. Done out in modern gastro-pub fashion, it blends neutral tones, unclothed oak tables, black tiled floors and enough original features to remind you of the antiquity of the old thatched building. The kitchen deals in up-to-the-minute dishes conjured from locally-sourced ingredients and is not afraid to travel the globe for inspiration. Roasted harissa spring chicken with pea and mint tabouleh, baba ganoush and coriander yoghurt sits alongside pork and cider pie with mash, spring greens and gravy, and to finish, perhaps a tropically influenced passionfruit posset (with mango jelly and coconut tapioca) or crowd-pleasing dark chocolate brownie. There's a garden with views of the Downs too.

Chef Ben McKellar, Ben Limb **Owner** Ben & Pamela McKellar **Times** 12-2/6-10 Closed 25 Dec **Prices** Prices not confirmed Service optional, Groups min 6 service 12.5% **Notes** Fixed L 2 course Mon-Fri until 7pm, Sunday L, Vegetarian available **Seats** 50, Pr/dining room 24 **Children** Portions, Menu **Parking** 60

ARUNDEL   Map 6 TQ00

The Town House

◉◉ Modern V ✿

Accomplished cooking bang opposite the castle

☎ 01903 883847
65 High St BN18 9AJ
e-mail: enquiries@thetownhouse.co.uk
web: www.thetownhouse.co.uk
dir: Follow A27 to Arundel, onto High Street, establishment on left at top of hill

If you're looking for The Town House, just head for Arundel Castle and you're pretty much there. This elegant, three-storey, Grade II listed Regency townhouse perches on the hill right opposite the castle wall, so you can gaze out at the imposing residence of the Duke of Norfolk through the restaurant's large front window. But there's much to admire inside too: look up, and you'll see a marvellously ornate gilt ceiling, dating back to the 16th century and shipped over to West Sussex from Florence. The small, intimate dining room has been brought into the 21st century with high-backed black chairs, contemporary artworks and mirrors with funky striped frames. Chef-patron Lee Williams' food is pretty voguish too - using plenty of local and seasonal ingredients - and what's

more he offers a fashionably good value lunch menu. Start with Thai-spiced butternut squash soup or duck confit and foie gras terrine with fig and apple chutney, and, for a real treat in season, there might be among main courses a dish of expertly cooked fillet of local venison with confit haunch, spinach, dauphinoise and red wine jus. Dessert ends on a high with home-made apple tart with clotted cream.

Chef Lee Williams **Owner** Lee & Kate Williams **Times** 12-2.30/7-9.30 Closed 2 wks Etr, 2 wks Oct, Xmas, Sun-Mon **Prices** Fixed L 2 course fr £15.50, Fixed D 3 course fr £29, Service optional **Wines** 53 bottles over £30, 29 bottles under £30, 9 by glass **Notes** Vegetarian menu **Seats** 24 **Children** Portions **Parking** On street or nearby car park

BOSHAM   Map 5 SU80

The Millstream Hotel & Restaurant

◉◉ Modern British ✿

Stylish cooking in a quiet setting

☎ 01243 573234
Bosham Ln PO18 8HL
e-mail: info@millstreamhotel.com
web: www.millstreamhotel.com
dir: 4m W of Chichester on A259, left at Bosham rdbt. After 0.5m right at T-junct signed to church & quay. Hotel 0.5m on right

Originally three 17th-century workmen's cottages, The Millstream is these days a charming country-house hotel quietly located, as you may have guessed, beside a stream. The restaurant, overlooking the gardens, has undergone a recent makeover, though the cooking style continues in the same modern British vein as before. Neil Hiskey's menus are crowd-pleasing affairs, offering enough variety to keep even longer-term guests happy. Starters can be as classic as home-smoked salmon with celeriac remoulade, or chicken terrine with sauternes jelly and pickled vegetables, the boundaries extended by the likes of smoked haddock and leek tart with a crispy egg yolk and crème fraîche. Quality is clear in the raw materials, and combinations are intelligently thought through, so breast of duck is partnered by duck croquettes, Asian greens and Thai red curry sauce, and fillet of sea bass by shellfish bisque, a crab bonbon, crushed potatoes and spinach. Puddings are worth exploring: perhaps rhubarb trifle with ginger crumble. Also new to the hotel is the more informal Marwick's Brasserie.

Chef Neil Hiskey **Owner** The Wild family
Times 12.30-2/6.30-9 **Prices** Fixed L 2 course £21, Fixed D 3 course £34, Tasting menu £55, Service optional **Wines** 28 bottles over £30, 34 bottles under £30, 13 by glass **Notes** Tasting menu with wine 6 course, Pre-theatre menu, Sunday L, Vegetarian available, Dress restrictions, Smart casual, Civ Wed 75 **Seats** 60, Pr/dining room 40 **Children** Portions, Menu **Parking** 40

BURPHAM   Map 6 TQ00

George & Dragon

◉ British, French

Inspired gastro-pub cooking in 17th-century inn

☎ 01903 883131
BN18 9RR
e-mail: info@gdinn.co.uk
dir: Off A27 1m E of Arundel, signed Burpham, 2.5m pub on left

Dating from the 17th century, the George & Dragon is a traditional pub, a huge fireplace its focal point, with a bar dispensing real ales and a more formal-ish restaurant. It might be tucked away in a small village in the South Downs, but it's normally busy, with a great atmosphere, people drawn by the go-ahead menus and consistent standards, the term 'gastro-pub' fully justified. Everything is made on the premises, from the bread served with mussels and smoked bacon braised in cider, or pear chutney with rabbit and ham hock terrine, to inventive sea buckthorn ice cream with chocolate fondant. In between might be properly rested sirloin steak with béarnaise and the usual trimmings, or scrumpy-marinated belly pork with caramelised apple and cider cream and butternut squash, with a fish offering like fillet of sea bass with pea purée, braised cabbage and lime-infused new potatoes.

Times 12-2/7-9 Closed 25 Dec, D Sun

CHICHESTER   Map 5 SU80

Comme Ça

◉ French ✿

A taste of France close to the Festival Theatre

☎ 01243 788724 & 536307
67 Broyle Rd PO19 6BD
e-mail: comme.ca@commeca.co.uk
dir: On A286 near Festival Theatre

In case the name isn't enough of a clue, the blue-shuttered Georgian inn is the very image of rustic French charm, except it is located rather more conveniently on this side of the Channel, just a short walk from Chichester's Festival Theatre. Chef-patron Michel Navet was born in Normandy and despite spending a quarter of a century at the stoves in Sussex, his culinary heart has never left France. Boosting the already considerable Gallic factor are knowledgeable French staff, and a bilingual menu of old-school French country cooking that cherry picks its way through the country's varied regional cuisines. The good old French concept of terroir is alive and well in the use of local produce, so you can expect to see Selsey crab starring in a tartlet flavoured with saffron and sun-dried tomatoes, served simply with watercress; following this, perhaps slow-cooked leg of Sussex rabbit in a wholegrain mustard and Madeira sauce on a bed of crushed celeriac. Skipping dessert is out of the question when there is a véritable vanilla crème brûlée up for grabs.

Chef Michel Navet **Owner** Mr & Mrs Navet
Times 12-2/6-10.30 Closed Xmas & New Year wks, BHs, Mon, L Tue, D Sun **Prices** Prices not confirmed Service optional, Groups min 8 service 10% **Wines** 7 by glass **Notes** Sunday L, Dress restrictions, Smart casual **Seats** 100, Pr/dining room 14 **Children** Portions, Menu **Parking** 46

Crouchers Country Hotel & Restaurant

◎◎ Modern British

Imaginative cooking in stylish hotel

☎ 01243 784995 & 07887 744570
Birdham Rd PO20 7EH
e-mail: crouchers@btconnect.com
dir: From A27 Chichester bypass onto A286 towards West Wittering, 2m, hotel on left between Chichester Marina & Dell Quay

A fixture on the Chichester area's dining scene for many a year, Crouchers has morphed from a simple B&B to a smart modern hotel with an inviting wine bar and stylish oak-beamed restaurant looking over open green countryside near to Dell Quay and the marina. What keeps this well-run operation perennially popular is a pleasing lack of airs and graces, and a kitchen that takes a serious approach to its work - that means bringing out the best from splendid locally-sourced raw materials to produce well-composed, imaginative modern ideas, as in a starter of wild mushroom and white truffle risotto matched with deep-fried blue cheese beignets and garlic pesto. Main course brings an ambitious composition of rabbit loin stuffed with spinach and tarragon mousse, partnered by braised Puy lentils, butternut squash purée and tarragon reduction. Desserts are no mere afterthought either, as shown by the well-balanced flavours and textures of a salted caramel and white chocolate fondant served with a nibbed cocoa tuile and raspberry sorbet.

Times 12-2.30/7-9.30

Earl of March

◎ British

Classy cooking in revamped old pub

☎ 01243 533993 & 783991
Lavant Rd PO18 0BQ
e-mail: info@theearlofmarch.com
dir: On A286, 2m N of Chichester towards Midhurst, on the corner of Goodwood Estate

The view represents this part of Sussex through-and-through: the South Downs and Goodwood racecourse form the backdrop. This traditional 18th-century coaching inn

has been made-over for modern times, on the inside at least, and has an opened-up, smart finish which is very easy on the eye, with darkwood tables and swish leather chairs. During the summer months there's a seafood and champagne shack in the former bakehouse. The menu can sort you out for some classic pub dishes such as Sussex ham with free-range eggs and hand-cut chips, but equally you might go for 'double duck', which is honey-glazed breast with a faggot made from the leg meat, fondant potato and spiced plum sauce. And you might start with a fillet of red mullet with scallop mousseline, prawn tempura and Bloody Mary mayonnaise, and finish with white chocolate and rhubarb pannacotta with black pepper and chocolate crumb.

Chef Giles Thompson **Owner** Giles & Ruth Thompson **Times** 12-2.30/5.30-9.30 Closed D Sun **Prices** Prices not confirmed Service optional, Groups min 11 service 12.5% **Wines** 37 bottles over £30, 33 bottles under £30, 19 by glass **Notes** Pre-theatre/Early bird menu 2/3 course, Sunday L, Vegetarian available **Seats** 60, Pr/dining room 12 **Children** Portions, Menu **Parking** 30

Halliday's

◎◎ Modern British

Quality local produce cooked with flair

☎ 01243 575331
Watery Ln, Funtington PO18 9LF
e-mail: hallidaysdinners@aol.com
dir: 4m W of Chichester, on B2146

With its thatched roof and red-brick and flint exterior, Halliday's presents a decidedly traditional face to the world. Inside, everything remains respectful to its 13th-century origins, whilst setting the scene for some smart, well-crafted cooking. Andy Stephenson goes that extra mile when it comes to sourcing first-rate produce from the local area, including home-smoking and foraging in the woodland, and everything is made in-house with a good deal of finesse. Begin with a terrine packed with pigeon, veal and pistachios, with accompanying spiced oranges and sourdough toasts, or go for Selsey crabcakes with rocket leaves, lemon and caper dressing. Fish from the South Coast might include sea bass (served with steamed samphire and mussels) or turbot baked on the bone with seafood bouillabaisse. Among meaty options, pot roast rabbit with Serrano ham, aubergine and basil ragout is a bit of a treat, and, to finish, fine apple tart with cinnamon sugar and cinnamon ice cream shows off the sound technical abilities of the chef.

Chef Andrew Stephenson **Owner** Mr A & Mrs J Stephenson **Times** 12-2.15/7-10.15 Closed 1 wk Mar, 2 wks Aug, Mon-Tue, L Sat, D Sun **Prices** Fixed L 2 course £16, Fixed D 3 course fr £27.50, Starter £6-£9, Main £16-£21, Dessert £6-£6.75, Service optional **Wines** 26 bottles over £30, 36 bottles under £30, 8 by glass **Notes** Sunday L, Vegetarian available, Dress restrictions, No shorts **Seats** 26, Pr/dining room 12 **Children** Portions **Parking** 12

The Royal Oak Inn

◎ Modern British, European ⚘

Congenial pub restaurant with appealing menu

☎ 01243 527434
Pook Ln, East Lavant PO18 0AX
e-mail: info@royaloakeastlavant.co.uk
dir: From Chichester take A286 towards Midhurst, 2m to mini rdbt, turn right signed East Lavant. Inn on left

As well as functioning as the village pub, this 200-year-old inn is a welcoming restaurant, done out in rustic style, with exposed brick walls, beams, and leather-look chairs at wooden-topped tables. Contemporary ideas share the billing with well-established British favourites like cod and chips with pea purée. Starters can span game terrine with hedgerow jelly and a well-balanced dish of grilled plaice with chorizo and baby squid, and main courses can encompass moist and tasty pork belly with sage-flavoured rösti and roast apple, and sautéed fillet of sea bream with tapenade and potatoes crushed with lemon. Daily specials are listed on boards, and puddings can run to classics like vanilla crème brûlée or a crisp pastry tart of dark chocolate with raspberries.

Chef Daniel Ward **Owner** Charles Ullmann **Times** 10-3/6-10.30 **Prices** Fixed L 2 course £16.95-£17.95, Starter £7.95-£12.95, Main £14.90-£22.90, Dessert £3.50-£8.95, Service optional, Groups min 6 service 10% **Wines** 54 bottles over £30, 26 bottles under £30, 20 by glass **Notes** Pre-theatre menu from 5.30pm, Sunday L, Vegetarian available **Seats** 55 **Children** Portions **Parking** 25

See advert on page 468

Ockenden Manor Hotel & Spa

| **CUCKFIELD** | **MAP 6 TQ32** |

Modern British, French 🍴 NOTABLE WINE LIST

Gentle but effective country-house cooking overlooking the South Downs

☎ 01444 416111
Ockenden Ln RH17 5LD
e-mail: ockenden@hshotels.co.uk
web: www.hshotels.co.uk
dir: A23 towards Brighton. 4.5m left onto B2115 towards Haywards Heath. Cuckfield 3m. Ockenden Lane off High St. Hotel at end

The original Elizabethan manor house burned down in 1608, but rose again like a phoenix. It was bought in the mid-17th century by a local iron tycoon, one Burrell, and remained in the same family until the early years of the last century. It's to be found down a little lane off the centre of pretty Cuckfield, sitting in nine acres, and presents the twin facets we hope to see in a country-house hotel - a wood-panelled bar and plush country interiors in shimmering old-gold, together with state-of-the-art spa facilities, where the daylight pours in on a spring-water pool. Stephen Crane helms the kitchen, his productions these days more appealingly served in a room that looks out over the grounds towards the South Downs. Over the past decade and more he has honed a gentle but effective style of modern British cooking, sprinkled with bon-bons, croquettes and samosas as appropriate, but keeping its feet firmly on the Sussex ground. Local cheddar enriches a cauliflower soup, served in homely fashion with tomatoes on toast, or there might be salmon ballottine aromatic with fresh herbs, garnished with fromage blanc and caviar. Meats from just up the road in Balcombe star in main courses such as duck breast with braised chicory and a duck and mushroom tart, or pheasant breast, traditionally accompanied by smoked bacon, Brussels sprouts and chestnuts. An Indian approach to cod is on-trend, here forming a curry presentation with mussels, peppers and courgettes, all fragrant with coriander, or there may be a diverting vegetarian main course of butternut squash tarte fine, served with sweet-and-sour lentils, halloumi, chestnuts and sage. Cheeses come with home-made piccalilli and quince jelly, if you're not in the market for a dessert like white chocolate and pecan cheesecake with pear sorbet and maple syrup, or rhubarb clafoutis with almonds and ginger ice cream.

Chef Stephen Crane **Owner** The Goodman & Carminger family **Times** 12-2/7-9 **Prices** Fixed L 2 course £17.95, Fixed D 3 course £54, Tasting menu £75, Service optional, Groups min 10 service 10% **Wines** 214 bottles over £30, 35 bottles under £30, 11 by glass **Notes** ALC 3 course £54, Sunday L, Vegetarian available, Dress restrictions, No jeans or T-shirts, Civ Wed 150 **Seats** 70, Pr/dining room 96 **Children** Portions **Parking** 98

Save on Hotels. Book at theAA.com/hotel

SUSSEX, WEST 469 ENGLAND

CHICHESTER *continued*

The Ship Hotel

◎ Modern British NEW

Modern brasserie cooking in a boutique city-centre hotel

☎ 01243 778000
57 North St PO19 1NH
e-mail: enquiries@theshiphotel.net
dir: From A27 follow signs for town centre and Chichester Festival Theatre. Restaurant signed from Northgate rdbt

In the heart of historic Chichester, the brick-built Ship is a boutique hotel with style coming out of its ears. A dramatic stairwell ascends from the black-and-white checkerboard floor of the lobby, and a split-level dining room has a light and breezy feel, with white Venetian blinds, exposed floorboards and unclothed tables. Brasserie-style menus tick the right boxes, opening with generously loaded sharing 'planks' of seafood or vegetarian items, and going on with the likes of braised ham hock with crunchy-coated pea purée and a poached egg yolk, or crab tian with hazelnut slaw. Multiform presentations of lamb being quite the thing, expect a chop, a noisette and a portion of hot-pot for main, with puréed carrot and rosemary potatoes in damson jus, while fish might be sea bass with an oyster fritter and spaghetti-ed cucumber. Simple but effective finishers include well-rendered thin apple tart with cinnamon ice cream and berry coulis.

Chef Jon Lander **Owner** Chichester Hotel Company Ltd **Times** 10am-10pm All-day dining **Prices** Fixed L 2 course £15-£20, Fixed D 3 course £17.50-£25, Starter £4.95-£8.50, Main £10-£24.50, Dessert £4.95-£8, Service optional **Wines** 9 bottles over £30, 20 bottles under £30 **Notes** Pre-theatre prix fixe plus full ALC, Sunday L, Vegetarian available, Civ Wed 60 **Seats** 120, Pr/dining room 48 **Children** Portions **Parking** 25

CLIMPING   Map 6 SU90

Bailiffscourt Hotel & Spa

◎◎ Modern European  NOTABLE WINE LIST

Modern European cooking in a grand spa hotel

☎ 01903 723511
BN17 5RW
e-mail: bailiffscourt@hshotels.co.uk
web: www.hshotels.co.uk
dir: A259, follow Climping Beach signs. Hotel 0.5m on right

When your surname is Guinness, you may well find yourself with the wherewithal to indulge a folly or two - hence the creation of Bailiffscourt. When you arrive at this apparently medieval cluster of buildings in 30 acres of parkland just back from Climping Beach, the impression is of having stepped through a time portal to the Middle Ages, although this was actually an exercise in architectural salvage on a monumental scale, with the stone buildings, beamed ceilings and mullioned windows relocated from sites elsewhere. Naturally these days, the upscale bolt-hole is happy to pamper you in the glitzy spa before delivering the restored version of you to the Tapestry Restaurant. Here, the eponymous wall hangings are matched with opulent red and gold drapes, a coffered ceiling and candlelight for a scene of Gothic romance. The kitchen sends out an impeccably modern European repertoire built on top-notch materials, as in a starter of home-made pasta with sautéed baby squid, mussels and shrimps in dill butter, followed by roast rump of lamb with a braised lamb and onion faggot, and crisp-baked lemon-peppered goats' cheese with rosemary and pepper sauce.

Chef Russell Williams **Owner** Pontus & Miranda Carminger **Times** 12-2/7-9.30 **Prices** Fixed L 2 course £18.50, Fixed D 3 course £49.50, Starter £10, Main £29.50, Dessert £10, Service optional **Wines** 20 bottles under £30, 16 by glass **Notes** Sunset package incl 2

---

course meal & glass of champagne £89, Sunday L, Vegetarian available, Dress restrictions, Smart casual, no jeans or T-shirts, Civ Wed 75 **Seats** 70, Pr/dining room 70 **Children** Portions, Menu **Parking** 80

CUCKFIELD   Map 6 TQ32

Ockenden Manor Hotel & Spa

◎◎◎ – *see opposite*

EAST GRINSTEAD   Map 6 TQ33

The Felbridge Hotel & Spa

◎◎ Modern British 🍃

Inventive modern food in a spa hotel

☎ 01342 337700
London Rd RH19 2BH
e-mail: info@felbridgehotel.co.uk
dir: From W: M23 junct 10, follow signs to A22. From N: M25 junct 6. Hotel on A22 at Felbridge

When you're done with spoiling yourself in the treatment rooms of the classy Felbridge Hotel's spa and slipped a cocktail or two under the belt, it is time to move into the fine dining Anise Restaurant and let the kitchen team do their stuff. The venue is glossy, cosseting, and intimately-

continued

Gravetye Manor Hotel

EAST GRINSTEAD MAP 6 TQ33

Modern British V ⚑ NOTABLE WINE LIST

Superb dining in Elizabethan country-house hotel

☎ 01342 810567
Vowels Ln, West Hoathly RH19 4LJ
e-mail: info@gravetyemanor.co.uk
web: www.gravetyemanor.co.uk
dir: From M23 junct 10 take A264 towards East Grinstead. After 2m take B2028 to Haywards Heath. 1m after Turners Hill fork left towards Sharpthorne, immediate 1st left into Vowels Lane

A stunning mellow-stone Elizabethan manor, Gravetye is surrounded by acres of parkland and beautiful gardens: allow enough time for a stroll. Within are several comfortable lounges furnished in-keeping with the style of the property, and an oak-panelled dining room hung with oils, with plenty of well-trained and attentive staff on hand to add to the pleasure of a visit. Canapés - perhaps arancini with pea and herbs, and anchovy sticks with hummus - get things off to a flying start, and a glimpse at the menu shows a highly motivated kitchen with serious culinary ambition, clearly met by what appears on the plate. Some dishes get lavish country-house treatments, with luxuries appearing as butter-poached lobster with caviar beurre blanc and braised baby gem, followed by poached breast and braised leg of guinea fowl with Périgord black truffles, baby leeks and sautéed gnocchi. Dishes are intelligently composed, the results always impressive: for instance, a simple starter of beetroot, artichokes and textures of apple (julienne, purée and jelly), the plate dotted with horseradish, all beautifully presented and a good balance of flavours and textures, or a main course of tender, pink loin of lamb with spicy couscous, greens from the kitchen garden and a deeply flavoured jus. Fish is timed to the second, seen in fillet of red mullet, given the Provençal treatment with tapenade, ratatouille and bouillabaisse juices. 'All of our desserts are prepared to order' warns the menu, but that's okay because a first-class pre-dessert arrives to fill the gap - perhaps peach granita with marinated blackberries - and when the main event does arrive it's well worth the wait: perhaps blood orange soufflé, or vanilla pannacotta offset by poached plums (from the garden, of course) and jasmine rice sorbet. Excellent bread rolls with superb butter and all the extras contribute to a truly memorable dining experience.

Chef Rupert Gleadow **Owner** Jeremy & Elizabeth Hosking **Times** 12-2/6.30-9.30 **Prices** Fixed L 2 course £22.50, Tasting menu £75, Starter £16-£22, Main £27-£32, Dessert £10-£15, Service added but optional 12.5% **Wines** 5 bottles under £30, 10 by glass **Notes** 4 course D £40, All day menu 10am-10pm, Afternoon tea 3-5pm, Sunday L £35, Vegetarian menu, Dress restrictions, Smart casual, Civ Wed 60 **Seats** 40, Pr/dining room 20 **Children** Portions **Parking** 25

Save on Hotels. Book at **theAA.com/hotel**

SUSSEX, WEST 471 ENGLAND

EAST GRINSTEAD *continued*

lit - rather like sinking into a box of posh chocolates with its tones of cream, caramel and rich brown. The kitchen hauls in the best produce from the surrounding counties of Sussex, Surrey and Kent as the building blocks of a French-accented modern menu conceived with oodles of inventive flair and delivered with impressive technical skills. Roast loin of rabbit stars in a starter with piccalilli, cauliflower and watercress. Next comes fillet of halibut with crab and scallops, courgette and potato fondant, or confit duck with an anise jus. And to finish, carrot cake sits alongside ginger and brown sugar parfait, orange jelly and white chocolate mousse.

The Felbridge Hotel & Spa

Chef Leon Ash **Owner** New Century, East Grinstead Ltd **Times** 6-10 Closed L all week **Prices** Fixed D 3 course fr

£37.50, Service added but optional 10% **Wines** 50 bottles over £30, 35 bottles under £30, 16 by glass **Notes** Vegetarian available, Civ Wed 200 **Seats** 34, Pr/dining room 34 **Children** Portions, Menu **Parking** 200

See advert on page 469

Gravetye Manor Hotel

❀❀❀ – *see opposite*

GATWICK AIRPORT (LONDON)   Map 6 TQ24

Langshott Manor

❀❀❀ – *see below*

Sofitel London Gatwick

❀ British, French

Smart brasserie cooking by the North Terminal

☎ 01293 567070
North Terminal RH6 0PH
e-mail: h6204-re@accor.com
dir: M23 junct 9, follow to 2nd rdbt. Hotel straight ahead

It's fair to say not many people expect inspired dining in airport hotels, and yet the Sofitel close by Gatwick's North Terminal is making a determined effort to confound expectations. A range of dining options off the central atrium encompasses café snacking and Chinese, but it's La Brasserie where the principal action is. In a smart dining room decorated with striking artworks and furnished with quality table napery, a menu of appealing modern British dishes is offered. Quenelles of fresh crabmeat with avocado and chilli comes with retro Marie Rose dressing, while mains extend from sea bass cooked sous-vide with lemon and dill, pink fir potato, and bacon and citrus salad, to decent crisp-skinned corn-fed chicken with red onion jam and peppered cream cheese. Desserts show a slight tendency to lily-gilding: lemon tart is a zesty enough proposition not to need garnishes of avocado ice cream and frosted pine nuts.

Chef David Woods **Owner** S Arora **Times** 6.30-10.30 Closed L all week **Prices** Prices not confirmed Service added but optional 12.5% **Wines** 13 by glass **Notes** Vegetarian available, Dress restrictions, Smart casual **Seats** 70, Pr/dining room 40 **Children** Portions, Menu **Parking** 565

Langshott Manor

GATWICK AIRPORT (LONDON)   MAP 6 TQ24

Modern European V 🌱

Modern cooking in elegant manor house

☎ 01293 786680
Langshott Ln RH6 9LN
e-mail: admin@langshottmanor.com
dir: From A23 take Ladbroke Rd, off Chequers rdbt to Langshott, after 0.75m hotel on right

The herringbone-brickwork of this Elizabethan manor house and its three acres of landscaped gardens make a fine first impression, and satisfaction is further enhanced by the chic boutique styling of the interior. Gatwick Airport may be to hand if you need it, but it seems a million miles away, especially when you're seated in The Mulberry Restaurant, with its lovely views of the gardens and duck pond; it's a well-dressed space with lots of period charm (oak beams, leaded windows) and a veneer of contemporary sophistication thanks to the modern art on the walls, smart country-chic furnishings and formal, polished service. There are lots of regional ingredients on the menu and the hotel's garden delivers up its bounty, too. Start with canapés in the bar - perhaps a little serving of crème fraîche with mushroom and truffle and a cheese straw to dip into it, and a mini spiced butternut squash soup - before moving through to the restaurant where some excellent home-made breads (apricot and walnut perhaps) augur well for what is to come. And what is to come is some modern, well judged cooking that's full of good ideas. Take a first-course 64° hen's egg with 'preparations' of artichokes and hay, or Romney Marsh lamb, delightfully moist, tender and delicately flavoured, partnered by parsley and garlic. Next up, Sussex White pig's cheeks with butter beans, chorizo and sea scallops is a contemporary partnership with terrific balance of flavours and textural contrasts, or you might choose poached fillet of rainbow trout with brown butter quinoa, cauliflower and almond purée. A bitter chocolate cream with salted caramel and peanut ice cream is a virtuoso finale.

Chef Phil Dixon **Owner** Peter & Deborah Hinchcliffe **Times** 12-2.30/7-9.30 **Prices** Fixed L 2 course £15, Fixed D 3 course £45-£51, Tasting menu £50-£75, Service added but optional 12.5% **Wines** 76 bottles over £30, 8 bottles under £30, 16 by glass **Notes** Sunday L, Vegetarian menu, Dress restrictions, Smart casual, no jeans or shorts, Civ Wed 60 **Seats** 55, Pr/dining room 22 **Children** Portions, Menu **Parking** 25

GOODWOOD Map 6 SU80

The Goodwood Hotel

@@ Modern British 🌱

Contemporary cooking on the Goodwood Estate

☎ 01243 775537
PO18 0QB
e-mail: reservations@goodwood.com
web: www.goodwood.co.uk
dir: Off A285, 3m NE of Chichester

The luxury hotel, complete with health club and spa, is at the heart of the 12,000-acre Goodwood Estate, with the home farm, certified as organic, providing the kitchens of its various restaurants with pork, lamb and beef. The main dining option, the 17th century Richmond Arms, is elegantly kitted out, with an adjoining character bar serving a range of drinks from cask ales to cocktails. The menu follows a contemporary British path, offering dishes unlikely to startle with any newfangled and flashy innovation, but well-conceived and holding plenty of interest. Cheese soufflé, served with apple, chicory and caramelised walnuts, seems to be something of a signature starter, and may be offered alongside smoked salmon with horseradish slaw and pickled lemons, or a seasonal salad of winter vegetables with blood orange, yoghurt and seeds. Among main courses you might find pork belly with chive mash, pickled red cabbage and apple and rhubarb sauce, or confit duck and flageolet bean cassoulet. Vegetarians are not entirely overlooked, and a couple of fish options may include roast fillet of halibut with seafood and vegetable broth.

Chef Simon Wills **Owner** The Goodwood Estate Company Ltd **Times** 12.30-2.30/6.30-10.30 Closed L Mon-Sat **Prices** Starter £6.50-£9, Main £17-£27, Dessert £6.50-£8.50, Service optional **Wines** 50 bottles over £30, 29 bottles under £30, 12 by glass **Notes** Sunday L £22.50-£25.50, Vegetarian available, Civ Wed 100 **Seats** 85, Pr/dining room 120 **Children** Portions, Menu **Parking** 150

HAYWARDS HEATH Map 6 TQ32

Jeremy's at Borde Hill

@@ Modern European, Mediterranean 🌱

Confident cooking in idyllic garden setting

☎ 01444 441102
Balcombe Rd RH16 1XP
e-mail: reservations@jeremysrestaurant.com
web: www.jeremysrestaurant.com
dir: 1.5m N of Haywards Heath, 10mins from Gatwick Airport. From M23 junct 10a take A23 through Balcombe

The old estate agent's mantra of 'location, location, location' certainly holds true for chef-patron Jeremy Ashpool's relaxed country restaurant, set amid the classic English idyll of Borde Hill gardens. On fine days, you can bask in the Sussex sun on the south-facing terrace overlooking a Victorian walled garden; inside, the bright and airy converted stable block is done out with smart high-backed leather chairs, wooden floors and local artists' work on the walls. Big, bold flavours and colourful platefuls of thoroughly modern food are what to expect, delivered by a kitchen team that hauls in the best the bounteous Sussex larder has to offer, supported by super-fresh produce from the walled garden. On an early summer's day, the vivacious, Mediterranean-inflected repertoire might open with the clear, fresh flavours of sea trout ceviche with avocado, radish, yoghurt and mint. Black bream, fresh from the nearby South Coast, stars in a main course with vegetable risotto, and basil and rocket sauce. For dessert, pannacotta is flavoured thrillingly with garden herbs and matched with cucumber sorbet and a shot of Pimm's.

Chef Jimmy Gray, Jeremy Ashpool **Owner** Jeremy Ashpool **Times** 12-3/7-9.30 Closed after New Year for 7 days, Mon, D Sun **Prices** Fixed L 2 course fr £16, Fixed D 3 course fr £19, Tasting menu £40-£70, Starter £7.50-£10, Main £15-£22, Dessert fr £7, Service added but optional 10% **Wines** 10 by glass **Notes** Tasting menu 6 course (with wine £70), fixed D midweek, Sunday L, Vegetarian available **Seats** 55 **Children** Portions **Parking** 15, Overspill car park

HORSHAM Map 6 TQ13

Restaurant Tristan

@@ Modern British, French 🌱

Inventive cooking in a 500-year-old building

☎ 01403 255688
3 Stan's Way, East St RH12 1HU
e-mail: info@restauranttristan.co.uk

Set on the first floor of a 16th-century building in old Horsham, Tristan Mason's restaurant certainly looks the part as the base of operations for a rising star on the culinary scene with its striking beamed vaulted ceiling, wall timbers, bare floorboards, and contemporary black and cream floral wallpaper. Training with Marco Pierre White is certainly a good grounding before flying solo, and the cooking is firmly rooted in the 21st-century, displaying lively imagination backed by finely-honed technical ability. The menu confines itself to listing components, which are united in eclectic partnerships along the lines of scallops with cucumber, white chocolate risotto and dill, or rabbit with squid, wild mushrooms and pickled kohlrabi. Flavours are intense and clearly defined, as in a main course that delivers stunning fresh turbot with a crisp breadcrumbed ball of punchy wild mushroom and king prawn risotto, and roast garlic purée. Puddings offer thought-provoking reworkings of old favourites, such as a signature banana tarte Tatin with lemon sauce and caramelised walnut, and vibrant green parsley ice cream.

Chef Tristan Mason **Owner** Tristan Mason **Times** 12-2.30/6.30-9.30 Closed Sun-Mon **Prices** Prices not confirmed Service added but optional 12.5% **Wines** 12 by glass **Notes** Tasting menu 5 course (with wine £80), Vegetarian available, Dress restrictions, Smart casual **Seats** 40

Wabi

@@ Japanese V

Modern Japanese cuisine, prime British produce

☎ 01403 788140
38 East St RH12 1HL
e-mail: reservations@wabi.co.uk
dir: Corner Denne Rd & East St

In a change of career direction, this Horsham boozer began a new life as Wabi, a style-driven contemporary Japanese operation comprising a buzzy cocktail bar, an open ground-floor grill, where a long counter lets you get up close to the chefs at work, and up on the first floor, a more orthodox restaurant. Wherever takes your fancy, the décor goes for a pared-back minimal Japanese style with screens of timber and tatami, bare darkwood tables and luscious shades of chocolate and caramel brown. Japanese ideas are obviously the kitchen's primary inspiration, but that doesn't preclude input from a wider European idiom. Ingredients of unimpeachable pedigree arrive courtesy of the Japanese Nama Yasai organic farm in East Sussex, while fish for sushi and sashimi travels a short way from the South Coast. Roasted scallop and foie

Save on Hotels. Book at **theAA.com/hotel**

SUSSEX, WEST 473 **ENGLAND**

gras miso zuke is one way to get going (don't worry about the language barrier - friendly staff will talk you through the menu) or crispy soft-shelled crab tempura might tempt. From the robata grill, there could be tea-smoked lamb chops hoba-yaki with sweet-and-sour nasu and miso sauce, or among main courses, grilled Sussex unagi (freshwater eel) with foie gras, gobo and apple balsamic.

Owner Andre Cachia **Times** 12-2.30/6-10.30 Closed BHs, Sun-Mon **Prices** Prices not confirmed Service added but optional 12.5% **Wines** 7 bottles over £30, 8 bottles under £30, 8 by glass **Notes** Fixed L & D 6 course £33-£55, Vegetarian menu, Dress restrictions, Smart casual **Seats** 90, Pr/dining room 14 **Children** Portions, Menu **Parking** Car park

---

LODSWORTH Map 6 SU92

The Halfway Bridge Inn

◉ Modern British **NEW**

Updated pub classics in renovated old inn

☎ 01798 861281
Halfway Bridge GU28 9BP
e-mail: enquiries@halfwaybridge.co.uk
dir: From Petworth on A272 towards Midhurst, 3m on right

With the South Downs National Park all around, and the famous stately home and antique emporia of Petworth close by, you won't be short of ideas to fill the day when staying at this classy 18th-century roadside inn. Recently renovated from top to bottom, the interior works a cosy yet smartly-contemporary look, with muted tones set against its dark beams, exposed brickwork and herringbone parquet floors; wood burners and roaring fires boost the feel-good factor still further in winter. The ambience is friendly and unbuttoned, while the kitchen deals in traditional pub classics brought up-to-date, and built on materials that reflect the local area and what's in season. Kick off with the full-throttle flavours of duck liver faggots with wilted greens and bordelaise sauce, then follow with another rib-sticking idea - whole roast partridge with game jus, bread sauce, and pommes Anna. To finish, toffee apple crumble tart comes with excellent cinnamon ice cream.

The Halfway Bridge Inn

Chef Gavin Rees **Owner** Sam & Janet Bakose **Times** 12-2.30/6-10 **Prices** Fixed L 2 course £19.50, Starter £6-£10.50, Main £14.50-£28, Dessert £6.50-£8, Service optional **Wines** 24 bottles over £30, 23 bottles under £30, 22 by glass **Notes** Sunday L £14.50-£16.50, Vegetarian available **Seats** 55, Pr/dining room 16 **Children** Portions, Menu **Parking** 30

See advert below

LOWER BEEDING Map 6 TQ22

Camellia Restaurant at South Lodge Hotel

◉◉ British V ⌁NOTABLE WINE LIST 🍴

Contemporary cooking in comfortable hotel dining room

☎ 01403 891711
Brighton Rd RH13 6PS
e-mail: enquiries@southlodgehotel.co.uk
web: www.southlodgehotel.co.uk
dir: On A23 left onto B2110. Turn right through Handcross to A281 junct. Turn left, hotel on right

Camellia is the second dining option at South Lodge (see entry for The Pass), a neo-Jacobean pile dating from 1883. It's a smartly kitted-out room, with some panelling and camellia-patterned wallpaper, smartly set tables and views over the extensive grounds. The menus are built around contemporary renditions of traditional seasonal dishes, reflecting the culinary style of the day; vegetables, fruit and herbs come from the hotel's kitchen garden and supplies from local producers. Moist and flavoursome boned chicken leg is spiked with Cajun spices and served alongside a sweet and juicy seared scallop and sweetcorn purée, a nicely balanced starter that might be followed by loin of Rusper lamb with pearl barley, salsify and roast shallots. Seasonal game may appear as roast partridge breast with a chicory tart, pickled walnuts and quince, and seafood gets a decent showing: dressed crab with cauliflower, lime and peanuts, say, followed by skate wing with Jerusalem artichokes, capers and parsley. Desserts range from vanilla crème brûlée with orange sorbet, to warm chocolate fondant with coffee ice cream.

Chef Steven Edwards **Owner** Exclusive Hotels **Times** 12-2.30/7-10 **Prices** Fixed L 2 course £16.50, Fixed D 3 course £35, Starter £9-£14, Main £18-£30, Dessert £8, Service added but optional 10% **Wines** 196 bottles over £30, 8 bottles under £30, 200 by glass **Notes** Sunday L, Vegetarian menu, Civ Wed 130 **Seats** 75, Pr/dining room 140 **Children** Portions, Menu **Parking** 200

The Pass Restaurant at South Lodge Hotel

LOWER BEEDING MAP 6 TQ22

Modern British V 🍷 NOTABLE WINE LIST

Cutting-edge cooking before your very eyes

☎ 01403 891711
Brighton Rd RH13 6PS
e-mail: enquiries@southlodgehotel.co.uk
web: www.southlodgehotel.co.uk
dir: From A23 turn left onto B2110 & then right through Handcross to A281 junct. Turn left, hotel on right

With cooking having become a spectator sport in modern times, the chef's table concept is an enduring fascination for many. At South Lodge, a sophisticated country-house retreat not far from Horsham, the sophistication extends to an entire restaurant taking up residence in the kitchen. Elevated swivel chairs permit discreet oscillation between your dining companion and the culinary activity, and banks of live video screens give the feeling of sitting at the heart of the command centre. The fact is that it can be genuinely enlightening to see dishes being put together, the panoply of technique ranging from jaw-dropping to 'I could do that' (not very often for the latter, admittedly). Matt Gillan and his team work in preternatural quiet, which gives a more obvious impression of intense focus than if everybody was shouting over a blaring radio. Dishes mobilise all the tricks of the

contemporary gastronomic trade across a pair of fixed menus for lunch and dinner, with vegetarian alternatives and possible wine flights too. (The wines, incidentally, are stunning, worth the extra outlay if you're not counting.) Contrasting textures are a big theme, so an opening onion risotto is garnished with puffed rice and onion crisps, while the fish course sees pollock crusted in hazelnuts, its dressing of muscatel vinegar acknowledging another trending theme - the cutting edge of sourness. It works especially well with fish, as also seen in the accompaniment of pickled apple with charred cured trout and watermelon. The vogue for offering different cuts of meat brings on fillet and tongue of beef with relatively mainstream accoutrements of mushroom purée, shallots and parsley, but also a more unusual braised duck neck to go with the breast and leg, alongside chervil root and pomegranate. The selection of new-generation British cheeses may take in Somerset's Driftwood goats' cheese and the pungently distinguished Welsh blue, Perl Las, or a goats'-milk pannacotta with apple and sourdough bread may be the gentler alternative. Desserts then burst forth with further complexes of flavour, from pear parfait with smoked almonds and cinnamon, to rhubarb and liquorice tart with popcorn and fennel. The vegetarian menu may encompass, among other things, beetroot tartare and sorbet with blue cheese and orange;

salted charred leek with watermelon, pickled apple and olive; caramelised swede with butternut squash, clementine and grain mustard; and a main course of vegetable Wellington. It all constitutes one of the most singular dining experiences in the Home Counties.

Chef Matt Gillan **Owner** Exclusive Hotels **Times** 12-2/7-9 Closed 1st 2 wks Jan, Mon-Tue **Prices** Fixed L 3 course £25, Service added but optional 10% **Wines** 196 bottles over £30, 8 bottles under £30, 200 by glass **Notes** Fixed L 5/7 course £35/£55, Fixed D 6/8 course £60/£70, Sunday L £35-£55, Vegetarian menu **Seats** 26 **Children** Menu **Parking** 200

LOWER BEEDING *continued*

The Pass Restaurant at South Lodge Hotel

⊛⊛⊛⊛ — *see opposite*

PETWORTH   Map 6 SU92

The Leconfield

⊛ Modern British

Lots of creative energy in a lively and popular restaurant

☎ 01798 345111
New St GU28 0AS
e-mail: reservations@theleconfield.co.uk

The Leconfield's lively ground-floor restaurant, with its bar and white walls hung with artwork, opens on to a light and airy orangery leading to a cobbled courtyard; there's also a splendidly beamed room upstairs. All sorts of ideas find their way on to the menus, from foie gras parfait with cherry fluid gel and pickled walnuts, to crab salad with pickled daikon, pea shoots and crab mayonnaise. Crab and lobster bisque is a convincing rendition, and may be followed by accurately timed sesame-crusted tuna steak accompanied by ginger-flavoured glass noodles and a blob of wasabi, or herb-coated rack of lamb with white bean purée and tomato and garlic fondue. Good home-made breads come with dripping, and among interesting puddings may be rhubarb cheesecake with apple sorbet.

Times 12-3/6-9.30 Closed Mon, D Sun

ROWHOOK   Map 6 TQ13

The Chequers Inn

⊛ British 🍴

Ambitious modern cooking in village inn

☎ 01403 790480
RH12 3PY
e-mail: thechequersrowhook@googlemail.com
dir: From Horsham A281 towards Guildford. At rdbt take A29 signed London. In 200mtrs left, follow Rowhook signs

The Chequers may well have been around since the 15th century, but it has stayed in tune with modern tastes. It is a proper village local, and with flagstones, oak beams, chunky wooden tables, welcoming open fires and a battery of well-kept real ales on handpump, what's not to like? Chef-proprietor Tim Neal clearly loves to haul in the best Sussex ingredients he can find, some of them supplied as locally as from the pub's garden, as well as foraged goodies and game in season. There are no pretensions or gimmicks, just bang-on-the-money modern ideas, from pan-fried scallops with parsnip and vanilla purée, to crispy confit duck with Puy lentil and merguez ragoût, spinach and French beans. If you're up for fish, there may be crispy hake fillet with curried mussel and leek cream, new potatoes and buttered spinach, and you could end with sticky toffee pudding with caramel sauce and vanilla ice cream.

Chef Tim Neal **Owner** Mr & Mrs Neal **Times** 12-2/7-9 Closed 25 Dec, D Sun **Prices** Starter £5.50-£9.75, Main £14.50-£23, Dessert fr £5.95, Service optional, Groups min 8 service 10% **Wines** 8 by glass **Notes** Sunday L £15.50, Vegetarian available **Seats** 40 **Children** Portions **Parking** 40

RUSPER   Map 6 TQ23

Ghyll Manor

⊛ British

Traditionally-based cooking in a Tudor manor

☎ 0845 345 3426
High St RH12 4PX
e-mail: reception@ghyllmanor.co.uk
web: www.ghyllmanor.co.uk
dir: M23 junct 11, A264 signed Horsham. Continue 3rd rdbt, 3rd exit Faygate, follow signs for Rusper, 2m to village

The timbered Tudor manor sits in 40 acres of sumptuous grounds with the South Downs all around it. This sylvan setting can be enjoyed from a wide terrace that overlooks the lake and gardens, before you move indoors to the modern dining room with its woodblock floor, unclothed tables and white bucket chairs. Fixed-price menus (with supplements for appetisers and pre-desserts) offer engaging, traditionally inspired brasserie food, perhaps starting with fried scallops, seaweed and pancetta, or confit duck tian dressed in blood orange, before following on with rib-eye steak served with horseradish mash, balsamic shallots and carrot purée, or fish and chips. Puddings include banoffee tart with coffee ice cream.

Times 12-2/6.30-9

SIDLESHAM   Map 5 SZ89

The Crab & Lobster

◎◎ Modern British

Switched-on modern menu in a waterside restaurant
with rooms

☎ 01243 641233
Mill Ln PO20 7NB
e-mail: enquiries@crab-lobster.co.uk
dir: A27 S onto B2145 towards Selsey. At Sidlesham turn
left onto Rookery Ln, continue for 0.75m

The Crab & Lobster may sound (and even look) like a pub,
but gone are the days when this 350-year-old,
whitewashed inn on the fringes of the Pagham Harbour
nature reserve served pints and pork pies. The chic
restaurant with rooms ticks all the right boxes for a
switched-on contemporary operation - a sleek modern
dining area where ancient flagstoned floors and oak
beams are offset by chocolate leather, and cerise,
mushroom and sage-green fabrics, and there's a creative
modern British menu heaped with local produce. Given
the watery setting, expect plenty of piscine pleasures -
perhaps a parcel of Selsey crab, crayfish and smoked
salmon topped with Avruga caviar, then baked cod loin
wrapped in pancetta and matched with cavolo nero,
braised potato and tarragon cream. After such light
dishes there's always room for pudding, so go for
something like deep-fried coconut ice cream with exotic
fruit salad.

The Crab & Lobster

Chef Sam Bakose, Malcolm Goble, Simon Haynes
Owner Sam & Janet Bakose **Times** 12-2.30/6-10
Prices Fixed L 2 course £19.50, Starter £6.50-£13.50,
Main £15.50-£28, Dessert £6.75-£8.95, Service optional,
Groups min 7 service 10% **Wines** 25 bottles over £30, 25
bottles under £30, 23 by glass **Notes** Sunday L £16.95,
Vegetarian available **Seats** 54 **Children** Portions
Parking 12

See advert on page 475

TANGMERE   Map 6 SU90

Cassons Restaurant

◎ Modern British NEW 🖐

Good eating near Goodwood

☎ 01243 773294
Arundel Rd PO18 0DU
e-mail: cassonsresto@aol.com
dir: On Westbound carriageway of A27, 400mtrs from
Tangmere rdbt

Chef-patronne Viv Casson is a Kiwi who has run a
successful restaurant across the water in France, so you
can expect clear Gallic culinary influences to her work.
The setting is a couple of farm cottages beside the A27
handily close to Goodwood, reinvented with a rustic
simplicity that gains character from the huge inglenook
and low-beamed ceilings, while the modern menu takes
in straightforward, classically-influenced ideas as well as
some more daring forays into innovative territory. Opting
for the great-value fixed-price lunch menu offering five
choices at each stage, a crisp pastry parcel of smoked

AG's Restaurant at Alexander House Hotel

TURNERS HILL   MAP 6 TQ33

British, French

**Modern Anglo-French inventiveness in the Sussex
countryside**

☎ 01342 714914
Alexander House Hotel, East St RH10 4QD
e-mail: info@alexanderhouse.co.uk
web: www.alexanderhouse.co.uk
dir: 6m from M23 junct 10, on B2110 between Turners
Hill & East Grinstead

The red-brick mansion is one of those old piles whose
architect was clearly determined to make a statement. It
rises in square turrets and tall chimneys above 120 acres
of north Sussex countryside, not far from the Surrey
border (and therefore rather handy for Gatwick Airport,
did the architect but know it at the time of its
construction). The place is naturally equipped today to
cater for business types, and has the sort of spa facilities
in which a contemporary reworking of the *Satyricon* could
be staged. There are also more dining options than you
can shake a breadstick at, from the private rooms and
lounges for tea, to alfresco terraces, the informal
Reflections brasserie (see entry), and the main
restaurant, AG's, where executive chef Mark Budd and his
team offer a tour d'horizon of modern Anglo-French
cuisine, supplied by South Downs and South Coast
produce of obvious pedigree. Lightly butter-poached
native lobster is firm and tasty, dressed with a
mayonnaise of the coral, a brittle crab fritter and cubes
of quince jelly, or there could be superb rabbit loin and
'bacon' in consommé, along with halved kidney, for a
total bunny experience, served with truffled toast and
artichoke crisps. Mains might adopt a similar approach
to lamb, convoking as many bits and cuts as possible
(saddle, noisette and sweetbread) in a pleasingly varied
assembly, garnished with pommes Anna, morels and wild
garlic, or a fish option might be poached brill butched up
with oxtail and oysters, alongside a distinctly more fey
cauliflower mousse. Side dishes are more imaginative
than the usual bowl of enough greens to feed an army,
including as they do smoked mash with beef fat, or
truffled Gruyère dauphinoise. Desserts maintain the
creative standard with brilliantly textured peanut and
banana parfait, served with coffee sorbet, peanut butter
and dark rum.

Times 12-2.30/7-9.30 Closed Mon-Tue

haddock with spinach and curry foam gets things off the mark, ahead of belly of suckling pig teamed with wilted greens, shallot mash, caramelised apples, black pudding and cider jus. Things get quite avant-garde at dessert, when good technical skills bring together a composition involving blackcurrant gel, fresh blackberries, apple compôte, honeycomb, crème anglaise, and apple crisps.

Chef Viv Casson **Owner** Viv & Cass Casson **Times** 12-2/7-10 Closed between Xmas & New Year, Mon, L Tue, D Sun **Prices** Fixed L 2 course £15, Starter £8-£11, Main £23-£31, Dessert £8-£11, Service optional **Wines** 41 bottles over £30, 33 bottles under £30, 6 by glass **Notes** Gourmet & special events, Sunday L £22.50-£27, Vegetarian available, Dress restrictions, Smart casual no shorts **Seats** 36, Pr/dining room 14 **Children** Portions **Parking** 30

TILLINGTON   Map 6 SU92

The Horse Guards Inn

◉ Traditional British ◔

Skilful cooking near Petworth House

☎ 01798 342332
Upperton Rd GU28 9AF
e-mail: info@thehorseguardsinn.co.uk
dir: On A272, 1m west of Petworth, take road signed Tillington. Restaurant 500mtrs opposite church

The Horse Guards got its name in the 1840s, when part of the Household Cavalry frequented the place while their horses rested in nearby Petworth Park. It's full of rustic charm, with wooden furniture, the odd chesterfield, oak beams, bric-à-brac and log fires. The menu changes daily, depending on what the kitchen has bought from local farms or dug up from its vegetable garden, and ingredients are treated respectfully with no artifice. Bone marrow on toast with salsa verde is a simple, tasty starter, and may appear alongside salted fish fritters with aïoli. Game pitches up in season - perhaps partridge with root vegetable mash, kale and red wine sauce - with scope extended by something like prawns stir-fried with chilli, garlic and ginger accompanied by potato and aubergine salad. Finish with a British pud like Bakewell tart.

Chef Mark Robinson **Owner** Sam Beard & Michaela Hofirkova **Times** 12-2.30/6.30-9 **Prices** Starter £5.50-£10, Main £8-£22.50, Dessert £5.50-£12, Service optional, Groups min 12 service 12% **Wines** 14 by glass **Notes** Sunday L £14.50, Vegetarian available **Seats** 55, Pr/dining room 20 **Children** Portions, Menu **Parking** On street

TROTTON   Map 5 SU82

The Keepers Arms

◉ British, Mediterranean

Upmarket country pub with appealing menu

☎ 01730 813724 & 07506 693088
Love Hill, Terwick Ln GU31 5ER
e-mail: sharonmcgrath198@btinternet.com
dir: A272 towards Petersfield after 5m, restaurant on right just after narrow bridge. From Midhurst follow A272 for 3m, restaurant on left

The red tile-hung exterior of this 17th-century country inn is an inviting prospect on its perch above the A272, with a lovely garden and terrace that have plenty of alfresco appeal, and once inside, it is a gem of a pub. There's a proper friendly bar with a range of well-kept real ales, and the whole space has been opened out and given an easy-on-the-eye decluttered modern look, without sacrificing the inherent character in its plentiful beams and timbers. The stylish dining room looks out over the South Downs and aims for a contemporary hunting lodge look involving blond-wood tables, warm colours and funky tartans. Go for pubby classics from the chalkboards, or trade up to the carte of easy-eating contemporary ideas, and start with chicken liver and port parfait, followed by pan-fried sea bass fillet with truffle oil, crushed new potatoes, spinach and vanilla butter, and finish with chocolate fondant.

Times 11-3/6.30-9.30

TURNERS HILL   Map 6 TQ33

AG's Restaurant at Alexander House Hotel

◉◉◉ – see opposite

Reflections at Alexander House

◉ Modern International

Modern brasserie cooking in an elegant spa hotel

☎ 01342 714914
Alexander House Hotel, East St RH10 4QD
e-mail: admin@alexanderhouse.co.uk
web: www.alexanderhouse.co.uk
dir: 6m from M23 junct 10, on B2110 between Turners Hill & East Grinstead

The setting is impressive inside and out: 120 acres of gardens, woodland and parkland surround a handsome 17th-century mansion which has had a thoroughly modern makeover, moving it into boutique territory. Spa enthusiasts will be delighted by the restorative facilities at Alexander House, but there's also a buzzy brasserie - Reflections - to lift the spirits still further (the fine dining option is AG's Restaurant, see entry). Expect sleek chocolate-coloured leather banquettes, slate floors and subtle grey and peach tones on the walls, plus there's a champagne bar and tables in the courtyard for eating outdoors. Start with something like terrine of foie gras

and ham hock with sourdough toast, pork fritter and apricots, or gazpacho with avocado and cucumber, moving on to a classic beer battered fish and chips or a more adventurous Telmara duck breast with gooseberry compote and crisp radish salad. Banana parfait with toffee sauce and caramelised bananas makes for a richly indulgent pud, but then so does trad warm sticky toffee pudding with rum and raisin ice cream.

Times 12-3/6.30-10

TYNE & WEAR

GATESHEAD   Map 21 NZ26

Eslington Villa Hotel

◉ Modern British ◔

Simple modern cooking in a Victorian villa

☎ 0191 487 6017
8 Station Rd, Low Fell NE9 6DR
e-mail: home@eslingtonvilla.co.uk
dir: off A1(M) exit for Team Valley Trading Estate. Right at 2nd rdbt along Eastern Av. Left at car show room, hotel 100yds on left

A restyled Victorian villa with a pair of flights of steps sweeping up to the front has become a family-owned contemporary hotel of great character. It's run with a genuine sense of bonhomie by Nick and Melanie Tulip, and its popularity as a wedding venue isn't hard to fathom. Dining goes on mainly in a conservatory extension with tiled floor and commanding views over the lawns, as well as in the interior room behind it. Some ambitious ideas are tried out, as in a three-bird terrine with fine bean salad and sticky raisins, the last element rather dominating the whole, but the simpler things perhaps work best. Steamed salmon with mash in a dilled-up root vegetable nage is one way with fish, or there might be tender, flavourful braised venison with beetroot in a sweet jus. The vanilla pannacotta wobbles good and proper, and comes with luscious Italian amarena cherries.

Chef Jamie Walsh **Owner** Mr & Mrs N Tulip **Times** 12-2/5.30-9.45 Closed 25-26 Dec, 1 Jan, BHs **Prices** Fixed L 2 course £13.95, Fixed D 3 course £25.95, Service optional **Wines** 9 bottles over £30, 36 bottles under £30, 8 by glass **Notes** Early bird D 2/3 course £13.95/£16.95 from 5.30-6.45pm, Sunday L, Vegetarian available **Seats** 80, Pr/dining room 30 **Children** Portions **Parking** 30

NEWCASTLE UPON TYNE   Map 21 NZ26

Blackfriars Restaurant

◉ Traditional & Modern British ☺

Productive brasserie cooking in the old Dominican refectory

☎ 0191 261 5945
Friars St NE1 4XN
e-mail: info@blackfriarsrestaurant.co.uk
web: www.blackfriarsrestaurant.co.uk
dir: Take only small cobbled road off Stowell St (China Town). Blackfriars 100yds on left

The Dominican friary at the heart of medieval Newcastle is an integral part of the city's heritage, and a thriving modern restaurant has arisen on the site where they began serving food to the monks in 1239. Plenty of natural wood, exposed stonework and medieval artefacts establish the venerable tone, but the clientele is more mixed these days, with students and tourists mingling with football supporters fortifying themselves early, before setting off to St James's Park. The brasserie classics of today are given some productive twists, as in a dish of hand-rolled pasta with Northumberland oxtail in sage butter, or peppered mackerel with goats' cheese and chive soufflé and horseradish cream. Mains constructively pair well-timed cod with a haggis cake, alongside pea purée, spinach and a poached egg, and roasted gammon steak with pease pudding, while crowd-pleasers among desserts include dark chocolate torte with hazelnut brittle and Horlicks ice cream.

Blackfriars Restaurant

Chef Troy Terrington Owner Andy & Sam Hook
Times 12-2.30/5.30-12 Closed Good Fri & BHs, D Sun
Prices Fixed L 2 course fr £15, Fixed D 3 course fr £18, Starter £5-£11, Main £12-£21, Dessert £5-£6, Service added but optional 10% Wines 14 bottles over £30, 31 bottles under £30, 8 by glass Notes Fixed menu available 5.30-7pm, Sunday L, Vegetarian available, Civ Wed 50 Seats 80, Pr/dining room 50 Children Portions, Menu Parking Car park next to restaurant

Café 21 Newcastle

◉ Modern British V ☺

Brasserie buzz on the Newcastle quayside

☎ 0191 222 0755
Trinity Gardens, Quayside NE1 2HH
e-mail: enquiries@cafetwentyone.co.uk
dir: From Grey's Monument, S to Grey St & Dean St towards Quayside, left along the Quayside, 3rd left into Broad Chare. 1st right then 1st left into Trinity Gdns, restaurant on right

Still delivering on its promise of providing a great urban metropolis with great urban buzz, Terry Laybourne's spacious, bustling brasserie in the refurbished quayside area of the city sails majestically on. Multiple windows let the Geordie light shine in on the grey-walled, dark-floored space, and the kitchen is open to view from the bar area. A large brigade turns out a seasonally rotating menu, with daily specials keeping it fresh, and southern European culinary references abounding. A platter of Basque charcuterie and pickles encourages friendly commensality from the word go, or you might like to dunk sole goujons into a sweet-sour dipping sauce. Mains may encompass the familiar - smoked haddock and poached

---

Jesmond Dene House

NEWCASTLE UPON TYNE   MAP 21 NZ26

Modern British, European ▲ NOTABLE WINE LIST

Well-judged creativity in a splendid Georgian house

☎ 0191 212 3000
Jesmond Dene Rd NE2 2EY
e-mail: info@jesmonddenehouse.co.uk
web: www.jesmonddenehouse.co.uk
dir: From city centre follow A167 to junct with A184. Turn right towards Matthew Bank. Turn right into Jesmond Dene Rd

In a leafy residential area of the city (the centre of which seems a world away but is actually easily accessible), Jesmond Dene House is an Arts and Crafts townhouse in a woodland setting that makes a good impression. It's a boutique hotel with an appealing combination of designer chic and a pleasing lack of stuffiness. Original features and well-chosen furniture contribute to a refined and stylish interior, while the restaurant consists of two dining areas: the former music room and the light and bright garden room, with its lovely fair-weather terrace. Food-wise, what isn't grown in the grounds comes from carefully-chosen suppliers, a good deal of whom are from hereabouts. Head chef Michael Penaluna keeps a tight rein on the modern European idiom, keeping the focus on the ingredients, whilst producing dishes that show sound thinking, creativity and acute technical ability. Smoked eel stars in a first course with chorizo, pickled oysters and potato salad, and vegetarians et al will find happiness in the form of roasted figs with pickled celery and Colston Bassett salad. The outstanding quality of the produce is evident in main-course roast loin of venison (superb flavour) with pancetta, parsley roots, chanterelle mushrooms and bitter praline. Apple tarte fine with baked custard and Calvados ice cream shows the extent to which this kitchen understands how to balance flavours and textures, or you might go for the simplicity of one of their home-made sorbets and ice creams (pear sorbet or tonka bean ice cream, for example). There's a tasting menu if you fancy going the whole hog, and a wonderful vegetarian version which must surely be the best for miles around. The wine list, like everything here, is a class act.

Chef Michael Penaluna Owner Peter Candler, Tony Ganley
Times 12-2/7-9.30 Prices Fixed L 2 course fr £16.95, Fixed D 3 course £23.95-£36.95, Tasting menu fr £65, Starter £12.50-£15.50, Main £19.50-£35, Service added but optional 10% Wines 139 bottles over £30, 47 bottles under £30, 17 by glass Notes Tasting menu available, Sunday L, Vegetarian available, Dress restrictions, Smart casual, Civ Wed 100 Seats 80, Pr/dining room 24 Children Portions, Menu Parking 64

Save on Hotels. Book at **theAA.com/hotel**

TYNE & WEAR 479 ENGLAND

egg, or duck confit with Lyonnaise potatoes - but there is also room for delightfully tender roast Northumberland venison with sour cherries, grapes, bacon and walnuts in juniper sauce with spätzle. Dessert might offer counterpointing textures in the shape of apple parfait with cinder toffee.

Chef Chris Dobson **Owner** Terry Laybourne **Times** 12-2.30/5.30-10.30 Closed 25-26 Dec, 1 Jan, Etr Mon, D 24 Dec **Prices** Fixed L 2 course £16.50, Fixed D 3 course £20, Starter £5.50-£14.80, Main £15.50-£29.80, Dessert £6.20-£9.20, Service added but optional 10% **Wines** 42 bottles over £30, 41 bottles under £30, 17 by glass **Notes** Fixed L/D 2/3 course available Mon-Fri D 5.30-7pm, Sunday L, Vegetarian menu **Seats** 90, Pr/dining room 40 **Children** Portions **Parking** NCP/Council

David Kennedy's Food Social

◉ Modern British 🏵

Brasserie dining in a stylish commercial art gallery

☎ 0191 260 5411
The Biscuit Factory, 16 Stoddart St, Shieldfield NE2 1AN
e-mail: info@foodsocial.co.uk

There's a lot of creativity going on at the Biscuit Factory, a venue packed with contemporary art and workshops, plus, in the shape of Food Social, a restaurant that fits the bill. You get a sense of the industrial heritage of the building in the space, with its pictures, exposed brickwork and ducting, and the relaxed, cheerful mood of the place only adds to its appeal. On the menu are lots of local goodies, sourced with care and attention, and treated with respect. It's a little bit modern, a lit bit rustic, and the kind of stuff you want to eat. Rillette of slow-cooked pork with a black pudding fritter and red wine dressing to start, for example, followed by fillet of North Sea cod with creamed salsify and cod Kiev, or a chargrilled 10oz rib-eye steak. Finish with treacle tart with lemon curd.

Chef Andrew Wilkinson **Owner** Robin Price **Times** 12-2/5.30-9 Closed 25-26 Dec & 1 Jan, D Sun **Prices** Fixed L 2 course £10, Fixed D 3 course £15, Starter £4.50-£9.95, Main £11.50-£20.50, Dessert £4.95-£8.95, Service optional, Groups min 8 service 10% **Wines** 10 bottles over £30, 20 bottles under £30, 8 by glass **Notes** Sunday L, Vegetarian available **Seats** 70, Pr/dining room 24 **Children** Portions **Parking** 20, On street

Hotel du Vin Newcastle

◉◉ British, French ⬛NOTABLE WINE LIST 🏵

Stylish urban French bistro dining in designer hotel

☎ 0191 229 2200
Allan House, City Rd NE1 2BE
e-mail: reception.newcastle@hotelduvin.com
dir: A1 junct 65 slip road to A184 Gateshead/Newcastle, Quayside to City Rd

The Newcastle offshoot of the HdV chain conforms to the brand's values with its stylish reworking of a character-laden old building, in this case the red-brick Edwardian warehouse of the Tyne Tees Steamship Company. The riverside location puts it in pole position for shopping and taking in the city's arts and cultural attractions, with glorious urban landscapes along the Tyne to the iconic arching bridge as a backdrop. True to house style, the restaurant sports the trademark retro French bistro look, while the kitchen hauls in Northumberland's fine produce as the basis of its please-all modern brasserie repertoire - slow-cooked duck leg with wild mushrooms and Puy lentil jus, or roast cod with chorizo, butter beans, chilli and lemon are typical main course ideas. As is always the case in a Hotel du Vin, you can bank on a superb wine list of intelligently-chosen bottles that casts its net wide for quality drinking, with an expert sommelier on hand.

Chef Stuart Donaldson **Owner** KSL **Times** 12-2/6-10 **Prices** Prices not confirmed Service added but optional 10% **Wines** 350 bottles over £30, 15 bottles under £30, 14 by glass **Notes** Vegetarian available, Civ Wed 80 **Seats** 86, Pr/dining room 24 **Children** Portions **Parking** 15, On street (pay & display)

Jesmond Dene House

◉◉◉ – *see opposite*

Malmaison Newcastle

◉ French, British

Brasserie dining in a quayside setting

☎ 0844 6930658
104 Quayside NE1 3DX
e-mail: newcastle@malmaison.com
dir: A1 junct 65 to A184 signed Gateshead/Newcastle. Follow signs for city centre, then for Quayside/Law Courts. Hotel 100yds past Law Courts.

In a former warehouse on the lively quayside, Newcastle's 'Mal' enjoys a prime location on the River Tyne with views of the blinking Millennium Bridge. The trendy boutique hotel chain's set-up works a treat here, with the public areas decked out in the multi-textural tones of deep reds

and purples. Moody lighting in the bar sets the scene for a cocktail or something from the impressive wine list, taken seated at a purple velvet bar stool or tucked away in a velvet booth. The brasserie is typically relaxed and informal with the closely-packed tables leading to a happy hum, especially in the evening. Straightforward classics make the most of Northumberland's fine larder; Scotch quail's egg and bacon salad with piccalilli vinaigrette is one way to start, followed by Herdwick mutton masala with pilaf rice and naan bread, or, from the grill, lobster with garlic butter, herb aïoli and fries. Baked New York cheesecake and blueberries is a fitting finish.

Chef Gareth Marks **Owner** MWB **Times** 12-2.30/6-11 **Prices** Starter £4.95-£9.50, Main £12.50-£48, Service optional **Wines** 24 bottles over £30, 2 bottles under £30, 10 by glass **Notes** Sunday L £19.95, Vegetarian available **Seats** 84, Pr/dining room 20 **Children** Portions **Parking** 60, Sandgate (chargeable)

Pan Haggerty Restaurant

◉ Modern British 🏵

Classic British and more in relaxed quayside restaurant

☎ 0191 221 0904
21 Queen St NE1 3UG
e-mail: info@panhaggerty.com

A regional dish of potatoes and cheese, plus a few other ingredients, the constituents of which may well depend on whose granny you choose to believe, Pan Haggerty is also a thriving restaurant in an iconic Tyneside address. There is a local flavour to the menu, but this is bright, modish cooking that catches the eye. It's a great room with exposed brick and a lively buzz, and the service team keeps it all ticking along nicely. Spiced cauliflower soup with cauliflower bhaji and curry oil shows the modern British aspirations of the team in the kitchen, as does ox cheek tortellini with roast micro vegetables, mini squash fondant, truffle oil and thyme jus. There's a 'British Classics' section to the menu, too, which might deliver that pan haggerty with pan-fried black pudding, crispy quail's egg and smoked bacon, or from the carte, go for pan-fried plaice with parsnip and vanilla purée and an almond beurre noisette.

Chef Kelvin Linstead **Owner** Craig Potts, Mike Morely **Times** 12-2.30/5.30-9.30 Closed 25-26 & 31 Dec, 1 Jan, BHs, D Sun **Prices** Fixed L 2 course £14.95-£17.95, Fixed D 3 course £14.95-£17.95, Starter £5.95-£10.50, Main £11.95-£22.50, Dessert £6.50-£8.50, Service added but optional 10% **Wines** 19 bottles over £30, 26 bottles under £30, 7 by glass **Notes** Fixed D Mon-Fri, 5.30-7pm, Sat 5-6.30pm, Sunday L, Vegetarian available **Seats** 65 **Children** Portions **Parking** On street, NCP

NEWCASTLE UPON TYNE *continued*

Sangreela Indian Restaurant

◉ Indian, Bangladeshi V ⓔ

Indian and Bangladeshi cooking in smart venue

☎ 0191 266 2777 & 266 2444
North View House, Front St, Four Lane Ends NE7 7XF
e-mail: managementofsangreela@gmail.com

With its high vaulted ceiling, exposed brick walls, and smart linen-clothed tables, Sangreela certainly looks nothing like the average curry house, and a glance over the menu confirms that favourable impression. The traditional cuisines of India and Bangladesh are what this restaurant is all about, and it is all built on top-quality ingredients. If you're daunted by the mind-spinning choice on the menu, the affable front-of-house team will guide you knowledgeably through. Starting with excellent home-made chutneys, it's clear that this kitchen goes the extra mile in getting its accurate flavours and well-tuned spicing just right. Machli pakora is strips of haddock marinated in ginger, garlic and chillies and fried in gram-flour batter, then main course brings tandoor-roasted duck served with yoghurt and pistachio sauce and garnished with spicy honey, or chingri saag wala (prawns cooked with spinach, garlic, ginger, herbs and spices).

Chef Nazim Khan **Owner** Nazim Khan **Times** 4.30-11.30 Closed L all week **Prices** Fixed D 2 course £29.80-£45, Starter £5.90-£12.90, Main £11.90-£24.90, Dessert £3.90-£5.90 **Notes** Vegetarian menu, Dress restrictions, No T-shirts **Seats** 135 **Children** Portions, Menu **Parking** 16

Essence

◉ Modern British

Unfussy cooking in a friendly modern bistro

☎ 01789 762764
50 Birmingham Rd B49 5EP
e-mail: info@eatatessence.co.uk
dir: From town centre towards Birmingham & M42. Restaurant is opposite Alcester Grammar School

The columned frontage of this former cottage catches the eye along the main road leading into the small market town of Alcester, and once inside Essence presents a clean-cut contemporary look that blends 17th-century oak beams with modern art on cream walls, and leather chairs at darkwood tables. The vibe is the relaxed, friendly bustle of a well-loved neighbourhood eatery with easygoing, uncomplicated modern cooking to go with the surroundings. A terrine of pork and local game with spiced pear chutney has all the advertised flavours singing in tune, while main-course sea bass is accurately cooked and matched with a tomato and borlotti bean 'cassoulet'. Finish with warm pineapple tarte Tatin with coconut sorbet.

Chef Chris Short **Owner** Chris Short
Times 10-2.30/6.30-10 Closed Mon, D Sun **Prices** Fixed L 2 course £11.50, Fixed D 3 course £20, Starter £4.50-£8.50, Main £9.50-£22, Dessert £5.50-£8, Service optional **Wines** 8 bottles over £30, 27 bottles under £30, 7 by glass **Notes** Fixed price menu L & D Tue-Sat, Sunday L, Vegetarian available **Seats** 50 **Children** Portions, Menu **Parking** 19

Ettington Park Hotel

◉◉ Traditional & Modern British

Confident cooking in an impressive house

☎ 01789 450123
CV37 8BU
e-mail: ettingtonpark@handpicked.co.uk
web: www.handpickedhotels.co.uk/ettingtonpark
dir: M40 junct 15/A46 towards Stratford-upon-Avon, then A439 into town centre onto A3400 5m to Shipston. Hotel 0.5m on left

The grandly gothic Ettington Park makes a splendid first impression, what with its beautiful grounds (through which runs the River Stour) and majestic façade. It doesn't fail to impress on the inside either, with its array of antiques and fine period details. The Oak Room restaurant doesn't let the side down with its family heraldry, oak panelling, ornate plasterwork, smartly laid tables, and well-crafted contemporary cooking. The kitchen team serves up some bright, modish dishes rooted in classical thinking. Top-notch bread gets things off to a flying start before a deconstructed kedgeree with its tempura haddock and curried cream velouté, or potato

and gruyère scone with wilted baby spinach, poached duck's egg and hollandaise sauce. Next up, a duo of Lighthorne lamb (braised shoulder and crispy tongue) comes with textures of aubergine (caviar, crisps and purée), the dish finished with a lemon jus. The high level of skill and creativity continues at dessert stage, too, perhaps in the form of a pistachio meringue with autumnal fruits.

Times 12-2/7-9.30 Closed L Mon-Fri

Macdonald Ansty Hall

◉ British

Tried-and-tested modern dishes not far from Stratford

☎ 0844 879 9031
Main Rd CV7 9HZ
e-mail: ansty@macdonald-hotels.co.uk
web: www.macdonald-hotels.co.uk/anstyhall
dir: M6/M69 junct 2 through Ansty village approx 1.5m

Whether you're up in the area for the cultural enlightenment of the Shakespeare trail, or doing business in nearby Brum, Ansty Hall makes a rather tasty base. The handsome, three-storey, red-brick house sits in eight acres of landscaped grounds amid the rolling farmland and thatched cottages of Warwickshire. The elegantly furnished house is full of period character, not least in its classy Shilton dining room, where tall, lavishly-draped windows offer views of the surrounding landscape. Tables are clothed in their best white linen, clued-up staff preside over an ambience of assured informality, and the emphasis is firmly on British food wrought from good quality seasonal produce, cooked without pretension and served without undue fanfare and fuss. Pan-fried pigeon breast with black pudding and pea shoots gets things off the mark, ahead of a perfectly-timed suprême of salmon with wilted spinach, new potatoes, chive butter sauce and sun-dried tomatoes. Iced stem ginger parfait with sweet pickled roasted figs makes for a great finale.

Times 12.30-2.30/6.30-9.30 Closed D 25 Dec

Chapel House Restaurant With Rooms

◉ British, French ⓔ

Classic cooking in an elegant Georgian house

☎ 01827 718949
Friar's Gate CV9 1EY
e-mail: info@chapelhouse.eu
web: www.chapelhouse.eu
dir: Off Market Sq in Atherstone, behind High St

Built in 1728 as the dower house to the now-demolished Atherstone Hall, this Georgian restaurant with rooms on the market square is a charming place to stay and dine. If you do check in, you'll be following in the footsteps of one Florence Nightingale, who stayed here as a guest of the owners. The lounge-bar is a welcoming spot to enjoy a pre-dinner drink before moving through to the small and

Save on Hotels. Book at theAA.com/hotel

WARWICKSHIRE 481 ENGLAND

intimate restaurant - a classically decorated room with white linen and elegant silverware adorning the tables and views over the attractive walled gardens. Seasonal and local ingredients are simply prepared in well-executed dishes on the daily-changing menu. Excellent, smooth-textured duck pâté with malted brown bread gets things off to a fine start, followed by a summery dish of monkfish baxian with a sauce of spring onions, cucumber, tomato, ginger and prawns. Dessert might be a classic individual strawberry Pavlova. Chef-patron Richard Napper is passionate about wine, so be sure to give the list a decent look.

Chef Richard Henry Napper **Owner** Richard & Siobhan Napper **Times** 7-9.30 Closed 24 Dec-3 Jan, Etr wk, late Aug-early Sep, Sun, L unless booked in advance **Prices** Prices not confirmed Service optional **Wines** 9 by glass **Notes** Vegetarian available, Dress restrictions, Smart casual **Seats** 24, Pr/dining room 12 **Children** Portions **Parking** On street

BRANDON
Map 11 SP47

Mercure Coventry Brandon Hall Hotel & Spa

@ International NEW

Confident, unfussy cooking in a smart manor house hotel

☎ 024 7654 6000
Main St CV8 3FW
e-mail: h6625@accor.com
web: www.mercure.com
dir: A45 towards Coventry S. After Peugeot-Citroen garage on left, at island take 5th exit to M1 South/London (back onto A45). After 200yds, immediately after Texaco garage, left into Brandon Ln, hotel after 2.5m

Set in 17 acres of green-and-pleasant Warwickshire countryside, Brandon Hall is a smartly-revamped 19th-century manor that has something for everyone, whether you're in the area for business, or enjoying a spot of down time in the spa and fitness centre. Tones of chocolate and green predominate in the smart, contemporary-styled Clarendon restaurant, while service is as keen as mustard and the kitchen follows the seasons, drawing on conscientiously-sourced supplies for its straight-and-true menu of uncomplicated ideas. Well-made ham hock terrine is served with apple and celeriac salad and home-made piccalilli, or you could kick off with sautéed wild mushrooms in creamy white wine sauce on toasted brioche. Mains can be as straightforward as a 28-day-aged rib-eye steak with herb-roasted field mushrooms, plum tomatoes, chips and pesto hollandaise, or there might be cod fillet with Dorset crab risotto and lobster sauce. For pudding, a chocolate fondant releases the requisite hot sauce when cut open, and comes with raspberry ripple ice cream and marshmallows.

Times 7-9.30 Closed L Sat **Prices** Prices not confirmed **Notes** Sunday L

HENLEY-IN-ARDEN
Map 10 SP16

The Bluebell

@@ British 🍴

Highly polished cooking in a Tudor coaching inn

☎ 01564 793049
93 High St B95 5AT
e-mail: info@bluebellhenley.co.uk
dir: M4 junct 4, A3400 (Stratford Rd) to Henley-in-Arden

The timbered front of this Tudor coaching inn speaks of its venerability, and although the interiors have been freshened up, the design job hasn't overwhelmed the intrinsic character of the place: the original beams and fireplaces, and the flagstone floor, are all present and correct. The cooking works within the grain of modern British thinking, bringing some very polished classical technique to the broadly based repertoire. Dishes are cleverly thought out, so that even the relatively familiar can come as a revelation. A slab of duck and green peppercorn terrine offers the contrasts of rich meat, sweet cabbage and sharp peppercorns, offset by the juice of a poached pear accompaniment, the whole supported by a gently warming honey and mustard dressing. Fish is accurately timed and seasoned, as in the fillet of cod that comes with a razor sharp caper butter sauce. Two servings of local lamb with sweet-and-sour peppers in olive and rosemary jus is the kind of meat dish to expect. At dessert, the Valrhona chocolate brownie with salt caramel, candied pecans and banana ice cream is a surefire bet.

Chef Simon Malin **Owner** Leigh & Duncan Taylor **Times** 12-2.30/6-9.30 Closed Mon (ex BHs), D Sun **Prices** Fixed L 2 course £15, Fixed D 3 course £18, Starter £5.50-£9.45, Service optional **Wines** 15 bottles over £30, 18 bottles under £30, 12 by glass **Notes** Afternoon tea £18, Sunday L, Vegetarian available, Dress restrictions, Smart casual **Seats** 46, Pr/dining room 10 **Children** Portions **Parking** 20

LEA MARSTON
Map 10 SP29

Lea Marston Hotel & Spa

@@ Modern British 🍴

Modern cooking in a golf and spa hotel

☎ 01675 470468
Haunch Ln B76 0BY
e-mail: info@leamarstonhotel.co.uk
web: www.leamarstonhotel.co.uk
dir: From M42 junct 9/A4097 signed Kingsbury Hotel, 2nd turning right into Haunch Lane. Hotel 200yds on right

Handy for all that Brum has to offer, yet feeling away from it all in 54 acres of north Warwickshire countryside, the modern Lea Marston Hotel has a golf course and spa by way of pursuits and a good eating option in the shape of The Adderley Restaurant. Decked out in shades of aubergine and greys it's a swish, modish space for some breezy contemporary food. Black pudding and bacon terrine comes with a quail's egg and mesclun salad and makes a fine precursor to shin of beef served with an

oxtail faggot, parsley root and truffle mash, or go for duck three ways - confit leg, liver, breast - with braised cabbage and liquorice jus. Finish with a boozy chocolate and vodka parfait partnered with a blood orange sorbet.

Chef Richard Marshall **Owner** Blake family **Times** 1-3/7-9 Closed L Mon-Sat, D Sun **Prices** Fixed D 3 course fr £27.50, Starter £4.95-£9.50, Main £16.95-£21.50, Dessert £5.25-£7.95, Service optional **Wines** 6 bottles over £30, 23 bottles under £30 **Notes** Sunday L, Vegetarian available, Dress restrictions, Smart casual, Civ Wed 100 **Seats** Pr/dining room 120 **Children** Portions, Menu **Parking** 220

LEAMINGTON SPA (ROYAL)
Map 10 SP36

The Brasserie at Mallory Court

@@ Modern British V 🍴

Stylish brasserie in opulent country house

☎ 01926 453939 & 330214
Harbury Ln, Bishop's Tachbrook CV33 9QB
e-mail: thebrasserie@mallory.co.uk
dir: M40 junct 13 N'bound left, left again towards Bishop's Tachbrook, right onto Harbury Ln after 0.5m. M40 junct 14 S'bound A452 to Leamington, at 2nd rdbt left onto Harbury Ln

A second string to Mallory Court's bow (see separate entry for its three-Rosette fine-dining restaurant), The Brasserie is a short stroll from the main house and brings a little bit of art-deco glamour to proceedings. Mellow jazz music adds to the relaxed vibe of this gently glammed up venue, with the cocktail bar an appropriate starting point and the walled garden coming into its own in the summer. The menu fits its brasserie billing to a tee, so you might start with cream of white onion and caraway soup or the more esoteric kebab of mackerel with tempura squid and spiced ratatouille. It wouldn't be a brasserie menu without a steak - 8oz rib-eye, perhaps, with roasted tomatoes on the vine - but there're also the likes of pan-fried fillet of silver mullet with lemon and parsley risotto, braised chicory and sautéed baby squid, or fish and chips. For dessert go for lemon curd tartlet with Mallory Court blackcurrant sorbet and a pear poached in white wine.

Chef Simon Haigh, Jim Russell **Owner** Sir Peter Rigby **Times** 12-2.30/6.30-9.30 Closed D Sun **Prices** Starter £4.25-£6.75, Main £8.50-£18.50, Dessert £5.85, Service optional **Wines** 42 bottles over £30, 30 bottles under £30, 10 by glass **Notes** Sunday L fr £15.50, Vegetarian menu, Civ Wed 160 **Seats** 80, Pr/dining room 24 **Children** Portions, Menu **Parking** 100

LEAMINGTON SPA (ROYAL) continued

Mallory Court Hotel

⚛⚛⚛ – see opposite

Queans Restaurant

⚛ Modern European NEW

Charming restaurant with well-sourced menu

☎ 01926 315522
15 Dormer Place CV32 5AA
e-mail: laura@queans-restaurant.co.uk

You'd never guess from her cheerful and welcoming demeanor that chef-proprietor Laura Hamilton works alone in the kitchen - there are no outward signs that she feels any pressure! This is a delightful establishment with a good deal of genteel charm, where a smartly neutral décor meets an appealing menu of unpretentious dishes based on high quality regional produce. You might start with a vegetarian tart such as one filled with roasted beetroot and butternut squash, served with an accompanying walnut salad, or maybe a brie and hazelnut bake with a smoky bacon jam. Clearly a dab hand at vegetarian cookery, chef can also turn out some impressive meat and fish options, too, such as a main-course grilled whole black bream (marinated in coriander and lime mustard), or roast loin of lamb with caramelised onion and fig stuffing. Finish with strawberry and pink champagne cheesecake. Somehow Laura finds the time to produce her own ice cream which is sold locally (and here, of course).

Chef Laura Hamilton **Times** 12-2.30/6-10 Closed L Sat-Tue, D Sun-Mon **Prices** Fixed L 2 course £18.50, Fixed D 3 course £33, Groups min 6 service 10% **Notes** Available Sun-Mon for private hire 10+, contact in advance, Vegetarian available

Restaurant 23 & Morgan's Bar

⚛⚛⚛ – see opposite

The Red Lion

⚛ Traditional British

Tip-top Cotswold produce in a charming pub

☎ 01608 684221
Main St, Long Compton CV36 5JJ
e-mail: info@redlion-longcompton.co.uk
dir: 5m S on A3400

The nearby Roll Right Stones and some folklore regarding witches means there's plenty to ponder whilst sipping a pint of real ale at the bar of The Red Lion. Built as a coaching inn way back in 1748, the Grade II listed freehouse has a traditional interior of oak beams and inglenook fireplaces, plus some comfy leather armchairs to sink into. You can eat in the bar or the restaurant area that leads out onto a patio. Daily specials are chalked on the board to subsidise the frequently-changing menu; curried whitebait, mango and spring onion salad comes with minted yoghurt, followed by slow-cooked gammon with bubble-and-squeak, soft-poached egg and mustard hollandaise, with raspberry and toasted hazelnut Pavlova and raspberry sauce to finish. There's a good children's menu too.

Chef Sarah Keightley **Owner** Cropthorne Inns **Times** 12-2.30/6-9 Closed 25 Dec **Prices** Starter £5.50-£6.95, Main £12.95-£16.95, Dessert £5.95-£6.95, Service optional **Wines** 24 bottles under £30, 3 by glass **Notes** Pre fixed 2/3 course £12.50-£15.50 Mon-Thu L & 6-7pm, Sunday L fr £13.95, Vegetarian available **Seats** 50, Pr/dining room 20 **Children** Portions, Menu **Parking** 70

The Arden Hotel

⚛⚛ Modern British

Elegant modern brasserie dining in Shakespeare Central

☎ 01789 298682
Waterside CV37 6BA
e-mail: enquiries@theardenhotelstratford.com
web: www.theardenhotelstratford.com
dir: M40 junct 15 follow signs to town centre. At Barclays Bank rdbt left onto High St, 2nd left onto Chapel Lane (Nash's House on left). Hotel car park on right in 40yds

Just over the road from the concentrated Bardolatry going on at the RSC Theatre, The Arden has undergone a megabucks redecoration, its once rather dated air giving place to a seriously stylish grand hotel ambience. Portrait photographs of thesps in character line the walls, there's a champagne bar for after-show schmoozing and, best of all, the elegantly spacious Waterside Brasserie with its big windows, comfortable bucket chairs and buttoned banquettes in handsome claret. Here, the cooking draws a graceful arc through the brave new world of the modern British repertoire. A starter of pot-roast pigeon breast with oyster mushrooms, charred spring onions, quinoa and a Scotched quail egg has a lot going for it, and might be the prelude to lightly sautéed bream with red wine shallots, lemon and chilli potatoes and fennel, or twice-cooked pork belly with roasted carrots and mustard mash. A separate vegetarian menu is available. Desserts take a more straightforward approach for nutmeggy egg custard tart, copybook tiramisu, or milk chocolate crème brûlée with double choc shortbread.

Times 12-5 **Prices** Prices not confirmed **Notes** Pre-theatre menu **Children** Menu

Billesley Manor Hotel

⚛⚛ Modern European

Traditional Anglo-French cooking in Tudor manor house

☎ 01789 279955
Billesley, Alcester B49 6NF
e-mail: billesleymanor.reservations@pumahotels.co.uk
web: www.pumahotels.co.uk
dir: M40 junct 15, A46S towards Evesham. Over 3 rdbts, right for Billesley after 2m

Dating from the time of the Bard, Billesley Manor is a charming mellow-stone Elizabethan mansion in the heart of Shakespeare country. Eleven acres of primped and preened grounds with a century-old topiary garden and fountain are amongst its attractions, but for those with dining in mind, the classic oak-panelled Stuart Restaurant beckons. It is the quintessential English country-house setting - all plushly-upholstered comfort - and the kitchen has no intention of rocking this particular boat, sending out classically-inspired dishes with a nod to modern trends and presentation, and a keen eye on seasonal ingredients. King scallops with black pudding hash, glazed apples and celeriac purée gets things off the mark with all items accurately cooked and flavours in balance, ahead of pot-roasted lamb shank that falls from the bone alongside creamed potatoes, red wine-poached plums, glazed parsnips, buttered greens and Madeira jus. Standards remain high through to dessert - perhaps a blackberry and Bramley apple frozen parfait with apple crumble and proper vanilla custard.

Chef Ales Maurer **Owner** Puma Hotels Collection **Times** 12.30-2/7-9.30 **Prices** Fixed L 3 course £25, Fixed D 3 course £39.50, Starter £8.75-£12.25, Main £22-£29, Dessert £8.75-£12.50, Service optional **Wines** 16 bottles over £30, 46 bottles under £30, 26 by glass **Notes** Sunday L, Vegetarian available, Dress restrictions, Smart casual, Civ Wed 75 **Seats** 42, Pr/dining room 100 **Children** Portions, Menu **Parking** 100

Mallory Court Hotel

LEAMINGTON SPA (ROYAL)   **MAP 10 SP36**

Modern British V

Resourceful contemporary cooking in a fine manor house

☎ 01926 330214
Harbury Ln, Bishop's Tachbrook CV33 9QB
e-mail: reception@mallory.co.uk
web: www.mallory.co.uk
dir: M40 junct 13 N'bound. Left, left again towards Bishop's Tachbrook. 0.5m, right into Harbury Ln. M40 junct 14 S'bound, A452 for Leamington. At 2nd rdbt left into Harbury Ln

The court was built at the turn of the last century for an entrepreneur who had made his fortune in cotton, but it was cleverly designed to look at least 100 years older. Covered in neatly trimmed facial foliage, it stands in delightful grounds, all immaculate lawns and walled gardens, including plots that help provision the kitchen. The dining room is kitted out with oak panelling under a low ceiling, with fine fabrics and tableware rising to the occasion. Executive chef Simon Haigh oversees the menus, resourcefully mining East Asian and southern European seams to forge a contemporary amalgam of bright, upstanding dishes that always have plenty going on. Summer might see a scattering of nasturtiums and carrots from the garden splashing colour over a starter pairing of langoustines and pork belly, while winter brings warmer seasonings and preserves to bear when pickled pear, ginger and pistachio turn out in support of duck in two guises: smoked breast and a bonbon of confit. Incorporating chorizo into a dish is quite fashionable these days, but it so easily outshouts its partners, especially regrettable when they might be perfectly timed turbot and squid with cabbage and samphire. Better balance is seen in a main course of beef fillet crusted in truffle and bone marrow, served with brown beech mushrooms and sauced in red wine. Desserts are a strong suit, as when a lemon confection poised halfway between tart and meringue pie comes garnished with caramelised meringue shards, candied lemon, lemon jelly - wait, there's more - sugared pine nuts, pine nut butter and pine nut icecream. Your sweet tooth duly located, petits fours then arrive in exhilarating waves, transporting you back to childhood in a trail of space-dust and lollipops. There is also a Brasserie for more everyday food (see separate entry), and a magisterial wine list.

Chef Simon Haigh, John Footman **Owner** Sir Peter Rigby **Times** 12-1.45/6.30-8.45 Closed L Sat **Prices** Fixed L 2 course £27.50, Fixed D 3 course £45-£59.50, Tasting menu £79, Service optional **Wines** 200 bottles over £30, 25 bottles under £30, 12 by glass **Notes** Tasting menu 7 course, Sunday L, Vegetarian menu, Dress restrictions, No jeans or sportswear **Seats** 56, Pr/dining room 14 **Children** Portions, Menu **Parking** 100

Restaurant 23 & Morgan's Bar

LEAMINGTON SPA (ROYAL)   **MAP 10 SP36**

Modern European 🍃

Dynamic modern cooking and quality drinking in the town centre

☎ 01926 422422
34 Hamilton Ter CV32 4LY
e-mail: info@restaurant23.co.uk
dir: M40 junct 13 onto A452 towards Leamington Spa. Follow signs for town centre, just off Holly Walk, next to police station

A move around the corner in 2012 to a porticoed white Victorian building in Leamington town centre was an exciting development for Peter Knibb's impeccably stylish bar-restaurant. The first half of the enterprise is a comfortable, elegant bar with violet seating, serving glitzy cocktails and quality wines, while the latter is a formally toned room run with great professional aplomb, where tables are crisply covered, and lighting comes from a mixture of giant ceiling rings and candles. Knibb cooks a dynamic, and constantly developing, version of modern European cooking that has enough impact, freshness and originality to have gained a third Rosette this time. Dishes move with the seasons, using local suppliers, but are innovative and interesting too. Start with a kind of reworked ragout of smoked ham hock, globe artichoke, peas, cleverly crisped bone marrow and summer truffle, or brilliantly rich and comforting oxtail tortellini, its matching consommé poured on at table, the earthiness enhanced with puréed Jerusalem artichokes, a single chanterelle and pumpkin seeds. Fish main courses have been stunning, whether for aromatic roasted turbot with fennel, orange and razor-clams, or sea bass on buttery boulangère potato, alongside charred cauliflower and a shrimp and caper beurre noisette. Meat dishes offer different cuts and organs, as though following a butcher's illustrated manual, and might take in Lighthorne lamb three ways (loin, breast and sweetbread), with basil mash and an olive and tomato lamb jus, or belly and head of Blythburgh pork with raisin purée, candied fennel and langoustines. A fashionably disjointed approach to desserts sees a cherry Bakewell arrive as separate parfait, curd, sorbet, sponge and candied almonds, or there may be banana tarte Tatin with salt caramel ice cream, or poached apricots and raspberries with lemon curd, scented with elderflower. English and French cheeses with rhubarb chutney complete the bill.

Chef Peter Knibb **Owner** Peter & Antje Knibb, Richard Steeves **Times** 12-2/6.15-9.45 Closed 26 Dec, 1 Jan, D Sun **Prices** Fixed L 2 course fr £14.95, Fixed D 3 course fr £25, Tasting menu fr £60, Starter £10-£15, Main £18-£27, Dessert £7.95-£12, Service optional, Groups min 7 service 12.5% **Wines** 200 bottles over £30, 26 bottles under £30, 11 by glass **Notes** Afternoon tea all week 3-5pm, Sunday L, Vegetarian available **Seats** 65, Pr/dining room 25 **Parking** On street opposite

STRATFORD-UPON-AVON *continued*

The Legacy Falcon Hotel

⑩ British

Smart period hotel with confident cooking

☎ 0844 411 9005
Chapel St CV37 6HA
e-mail: res-falcon@legacy-hotels.co.uk
web: www.legacy-hotels.co.uk
dir: M40 junct 15, follow town centre signs towards
Barclays Bank on rdbt. Turn into High Street, between
Austin Reed & WH Smith. Turn 2nd right into Scholars
Lane & right again into hotel

If you have certain expectations when visiting Stratford,
rest assured The Falcon delivers: it's a stunning 16th-
century property with a black-and-white timber façade
and a good and proper lean. It looks pretty dapper inside
these days, with plenty of period detailing, smart fixtures
and fittings, and a contemporary finish. The updated old-
world charm has been carried through successfully into
the restaurant, a richly carpeted room with beams and
some exposed-stone walls. The kitchen keeps things
unfussy and focused, serving up the likes of a simple
Parma ham, asparagus, rocket and cherry tomato salad,
followed by braised shoulder of lamb with dauphinoise
potatoes, green beans, buttered cabbage and a carrot
and elderflower purée, with mango and passionfruit
pannacotta for dessert. The theatre is not very far away,
making the pre- and post-theatre menus a useful
addition.

Times 12.30-2/6-9

Macdonald Alveston Manor

⑩ Modern British

Deft modern cooking in an ancient manor-house hotel

☎ 01789 205478
Clopton Bridge CV37 7HP
e-mail: events.alvestonmanor@macdonald-hotels.co.uk
web: www.macdonald-hotels.co.uk/alvestonmanor
dir: 6m from M40 junct 15, (on edge of town) across
Clopton Bridge towards Banbury

Happily, historic Alveston Manor - set in primped grounds
with the scent of closely-mown lawns - hasn't lost all its
Tudor-house charm since its hotel makeover. The story
that its cedar tree was the backdrop for the debut
performance of *A Midsummer Night's Dream* will excite
those drawn to the area in pursuit of things
Shakespearean, while the Manor Restaurant does not let
the side down with its traditional charms (original oak
beams and timbers, mullioned windows and candlelight).
Granted it's an old-school conventional setting, but the
kitchen's smartly executed British cooking has a
decidedly modern spin. Pan-fried wild halibut fillet, for
example, comes with shrimp butter, roasted langoustine
and new potatoes, and pan-roasted free-range chicken
with fondant potato and a chorizo and broad bean
casserole.

Times 6-9.30 Closed L all week

Menzies Welcombe Hotel Spa & Golf Club

⑩⑩ Modern British, French 🕃

Modern Euro-cuisine in a refurbished Victorian hotel

☎ 01789 295252
Warwick Rd CV37 0NR
e-mail: welcombe@menzieshotels.co.uk
web: www.menzieshotels.co.uk
dir: M40 junct 15, A46 towards Stratford-upon-Avon, at
rdbt follow signs for A439. Hotel 3m on right

The mid-Victorian Welcombe Hotel is a gabled quasi-
Jacobean confection which the Menzies group has
recently treated to a comprehensive £2 million
refurbishment. Thankfully the integrity of features such
as the magnificent oak-panelled lounge with its open
fireplace remain undisturbed, while the dining room has
been done in corporate beige, with swagged brown drapes
to frame the view over a section of the 150 acres of
grounds. The kitchen pilots a course through the busy
waters of modern European cuisine, dressing spicy squid
with tomato, cucumber and red onion salsa, or savouring
up silky-smooth pea velouté with salty ham hock and
mustard grains. A bells-and-whistles main course sees
loin of local venison teamed with vanilla-poached pear,
puréed celeriac, baby leeks and chocolate oil, or there's a
more classical skate wing with brown shrimps dressed in
lemon and parsley. Pear and vanilla dispensed with at
main-course stage, dessert must mean time for parsnips,
turning up in the form of ice cream and crisps to
accompany chocolate tart.

Chef Dean Griffin **Owner** Menzies Hotels
Times 12.30-2/7-10 Closed L Sat **Prices** Fixed L 2 course
£20, Fixed D 3 course £25-£35, Starter £9-£11, Main
£20-£28, Dessert £7-£10, Service optional **Wines** 10
bottles over £30, 10 bottles under £30, 8 by glass
Notes Pre-theatre D menu available from 5.30pm, Sunday
L, Vegetarian available, Dress restrictions, Smart casual,
no sportswear or ripped jeans **Seats** 70, Pr/dining room
150 **Children** Portions, Menu **Parking** 150

Mercure Stratford-upon-Avon Shakespeare Hotel

⑩ British, European

Modish cooking in historic Tudor building

☎ 01789 294997
Chapel St CV37 6ER
e-mail: h6630@accor.com
dir: Follow signs to town centre. Round one-way system,
into Bridge St. At rdbt turn left. Hotel 200yds on left

From the outside, this link of the Mercure chain is all
you'd hope for given the location - the historic, black-
and-white timbered building is a real good looker. It's no
slouch on the inside either, with a well-judged
contemporary finish blending in nicely with the original
features. That goes for Othello's Bar Brasserie, too, with
its darkwood furniture, fireplace, smart table settings,
and splashes of colour from the upholstered chairs. On

the menu, modern British nicely sums up the aspiration,
with plenty of good British ingredients and some
preparations from farther afield. Thus chicken liver
parfait is perked up with an accompanying vodka jelly,
plus raspberry foam and toasted brioche, and among
main courses you might go for a 28-day aged
Casterbridge steak or wild mushroom tortellini with
spinach and parmesan. There is a good choice of wines
by the glass and the likes of lemon tart with passionfruit
soufflé to bring down the curtain.

Chef Marc Ward **Owner** Mercure Hotels **Times** 12-10
Prices Prices not confirmed Service added but optional
Wines 15 by glass **Notes** Vegetarian available **Seats** 80,
Pr/dining room 90 **Children** Portions, Menu **Parking** 31,
NCP nearby

WARWICK Map 10 SP26

Ardencote Manor Hotel & Spa

⑩⑩ Modern British V 🕃

Confident, creative cooking by a lake

☎ 01926 843111
The Cumsey, Lye Green Rd CV35 8LT
e-mail: hotel@ardencote.com
web: www.ardencote.com
dir: Off A4189. In Claverdon follow signs for Shrewley &
brown tourist signs for Ardencote Manor, approx 1.5m

Ardencote Manor occupies a prime piece of Warwickshire
countryside with a golf course, pretty gardens and
shimmering lakes to call its own. It's a popular wedding
venue for obvious reasons, but The Lodge Restaurant,
located in a separate building next to one of the lakes, is
a venue of ambition in its own right. A table outside is a
real fair-weather treat, but it looks great indoors, too,
with its high quality finish (leather seats, neutral tones,
linen tablecloths and glistening glassware). The cooking
is contemporary stuff and shows a good deal of craft and
creativity. A starter terrine of duck leg, for example, with
confit gizzards, quince jam, roast pistachios and
gingerbread shows classical sensibilities and a thorough
understanding of taste and texture. Follow on with roast
Atlantic turbot with vanilla-poached potatoes, cobnuts,
Salcombe cock crab, apple, sea kale and wild chervil, or
roast quail with pearl barley, artichokes, salted plums,
ransoms and bread sauce. The confident cooking
continues with desserts such as peanut butter
cheesecake with salted peanuts, caramel popcorn and
sweetcorn ice cream.

Chef Ian Buckle **Owner** Mr Huckerby **Times** 12.30-2/6-10
Prices Fixed L 2 course £15-£25, Tasting menu £45-£55,

Starter £7.95-£9.95, Main £15.95-£24.95, Dessert £7.50, Service included **Wines** 19 bottles over £30, 44 bottles under £30, 11 by glass **Notes** Sunday L £19.95-£21.95, Vegetarian menu, Civ Wed 60 **Seats** 65 **Children** Portions, Menu **Parking** 350

WELLESBOURNE   Map 10 SP25

Walton Hall

◎◎ British

- -

Creative modern flavour combinations in an old stately home

☎ 01789 842424
Walton CV35 9HU
dir: A429 through Bradford towards Wellesbourne, right after watermill, follow signs to hotel

Well-placed to explore Stratford-upon-Avon and Warwick, the luxurious Walton Hall dates back to the 16th century when it was built as an ancestral home for the Mordaunt family. Although the hall benefits from much modernisation, the Moncreiffe Restaurant is classically grand. Restored period details include large crystal chandeliers hanging from the ornate ceiling, antiques aplenty and an open fireplace. Uniformed staff provide formal yet friendly service, so dress for the occasion and leave your denim and sportswear at home. Simply presented, imaginative modern British food is what to expect. Start with the Walton Hall signature dish of confit

duck and foie gras, chilled roast breast, prune, port dressing and brioche loaf, or ham hock mayonnaise, soft boiled egg and bloody Mary jelly. Gilt head bream fillet, spinach and crayfish risotto is light and flavoursome, or you might go for rack of pork with butternut squash, capers and sultanas. Another signature dish - passionfruit soufflé in its own syrup with coconut ice cream - makes a refreshing end to a meal.

Times 7-9.30

WEST MIDLANDS

BALSALL COMMON   Map 10 SP27

Nailcote Hall

◎ Modern European

- -

Traditional and modern in a 17th-century house

☎ 024 7646 6174
Nailcote Ln, Berkswell CV7 7DE
e-mail: info@nailcotehall.co.uk
web: www.nailcotehall.co.uk
dir: On B4101 towards Tile Hill/Coventry, 10 mins from NEC/Birmingham Airport

A half-timbered 17th-century house sitting in 15 acres of Warwickshire, Nailcote Hall became a hotel in 1990. It's a country house on a human scale, not far from the Midlands business hubs, and there's a golf course on

hand. The low-ceilinged Oak Room restaurant with its inglenook fireplace and darkwood tables provides an atmospheric ambience in the evenings especially, when a resourceful repertoire of traditional British and more modern dishes is tried out. You might begin with well-seasoned asparagus velouté with a parmesan gougère and hazelnut oil, before tackling tender marinated loin of venison with spiced caramelised red cabbage and roast celeriac, finishing with prune and Armagnac soufflé with Earl Grey ice cream.

Times 12-2.30/7-9.30 Closed L Sat

BIRMINGHAM   Map 10 SP08

Adam's Restaurant

Rosettes not confirmed at time of going to print – see below

Adam's Restaurant

Rosettes not confirmed at time of going to print

BIRMINGHAM   Map 10 SP08

Modern British **NEW V**

- -

Dynamic contemporary cooking in the city centre

☎ 0121 643 3745
21A Bennetts Hill B2 5QP
e-mail: info@adamsrestaurant.co.uk
dir: Located Birmingham City Centre

As newcomers to Birmingham's dining scene, this is the way to make a good first impression. Adam's is a pop-up restaurant, you see, here for two years before they open a more permanent restaurant elsewhere in the city centre. By that time it is likely chef-patron Adam Stokes and his wife Natasha will have a legion of fans. Their restaurant is right at the heart of the city's action and looks rather good for a temporary address. There's a decidedly contemporary and city-slicker feel all round - inside and

out - with a deliberate lack of starchiness. Adam has experience in top-end kitchens and his cooking is creative and modern, but avoids look-at-me attention seeking - everything is on the plate for a reason. The format is based around tasting menus - five or nine courses - although there is a three-course lunch. Dish descriptions are pleasingly short and to the point: 'ham hock, foie gras, piccalilli', for example (looking beautiful on the plate), is a wonderfully well-balanced dish, the foie gras marinated with salt, frozen and grated, the piccalilli deconstructed. The technical ability of the cooking is undeniable, the produce first-class. Next up, 'chicken, celery, haggis' is another virtuoso plate of food, the concept of the dish a nod perhaps to chef's time in Scotland. On the nine-course tasting menu you might go from 'pig's trotter, smoked eel, bacon jam' to 'rhubarb, foie gras, anise', finishing with 'goats' curd, cherry and sorrel'. 'Lemon, sesame seeds, meringue' is another deconstruction dish - lemon meringue pie of course - and it's way, way better than any original version you will

have eaten. There is nothing temporary feeling about this place. It will be a central part of the Birmingham restaurant scene in its time here, and one can only look forward to their next venture. Get here while you can.

Chef Adam Stokes **Owner** Adam & Natasha Stokes **Times** 12-2/7-9.30 Closed Sun-Mon **Prices** Fixed L 2 course £21, Tasting menu £45-£75, Service added but optional 10% **Notes** Tasting menu 5 & 9 course, Vegetarian menu **Seats** 35 **Parking** On street

BIRMINGHAM *continued*

Hotel du Vin Birmingham

@ @ British, French ✍

Bistro dining in converted former eye hospital

☎ 0121 200 0600

25 Church St B3 2NR

e-mail: info@birmingham.hotelduvin.com

web: www.hotelduvin.com

dir: M6 junct 6/A38(M) to city centre, over flyover. Keep left & exit at St Chads Circus signed Jewellery Quarter. At lights & rdbt take 1st exit, follow signs for Colmore Row, opposite cathedral. Right into Church St, across Barwick St. Hotel on right

The former eye hospital is a grandiose Victorian red-brick edifice on a corner site in the regenerated Brummie hotspot of the Jewellery Quarter. A perfect location then, and thoroughly in keeping with the stylish brand's penchant for taking architecturally distinguished buildings to convert into its trademark boutique boltholes. The second city's branch of HdV retains oodles of period detail alongside cool modern styling. There's a classy champagne bar just off the central courtyard, and a clubby Pub du Vin serving up local ales in the former cellar bar. The bistro is an impressive space with lofty ceilings, bare floorboards, unclothed wooden tables, leather upholstered period chairs, and yellow ochre walls hung with framed, wine-themed pictures. Top-notch local produce drives the straightforward Anglo-French cooking

- expect simple crowd-pleasers such as French onion soup, steak tartare and moules-frites, or you might take a classic opener like creamy chicken liver parfait with toasted brioche and raisin chutney ahead of monkfish grand-mère, garnished with pearl onions, pancetta and wild mushrooms and served with potato rösti. Sticking with the Gallic theme, finish with apple tarte Tatin with crème Normande. The outstanding wine list is up to the usual HdV standards.

Chef Mark Nind **Owner** MWB **Times** 12-2/6-10 **Prices** Service added but optional 10% **Wines** 16 by glass **Notes** Sunday L £19.95, Vegetarian available **Seats** 85, Pr/dining room 120 **Children** Portions, Menu **Parking** NCP Livery St

Lasan Restaurant

@ Indian

Contemporary Indian cooking in the Jewellery Quarter

☎ 0121 212 3664 & 212 3665

3-4 Dakota Buildings, James St, St Paul's Square B3 1SD

e-mail: info@lasan.co.uk

dir: Near city centre, adjacent to Jewellery Quarter

Lasan is a Premier League contender in the new order of Brum's contemporary Indians. It has the de rigueur postcode in the trendy Jewellery Quarter, and minimal good looks in its expansive split-level layout - in fact, there's nothing obvious to suggest this is an Indian

restaurant except for a sitar on the wall and ethnic background music. The vibe is up-tempo and high-decibel, but the service team are on the case, while the kitchen brigade hails from all corners of the sub-continent to ensure pukka regional authenticity. What arrives on the plate is contemporary fusion thinking applied to top-class raw materials. Goan mackerel recheado is pan-fried fillets spiced with chilli and garlic, served with fresh cucumber and mooli salad, while Wiltshire Downs lamb is showcased in lamb lababdar, a trio of marinated cutlet, 10-hour confit shoulder, and braised shin pattie pointed up with spicy lentils and smoked bone marrow jus spiced with nutmeg and cinnamon.

Chef Aktar Islam, Gulsher Khan **Owner** Jabbar Khan **Times** 12-2.30/6-11 Closed 25 Dec, L Sat **Prices** Prices not confirmed Service included, Groups min 5 service 10% **Wines** 7 by glass **Notes** Sunday L, Vegetarian available, Dress restrictions, Smart casual **Seats** 64 **Parking** On street

Loves Restaurant

@ @ @ – *see below*

Loves Restaurant

Modern British V ◆ NOTABLE WINE LIST

Starry cooking on the Birmingham waterside

☎ 0121 454 5151

The Glasshouse, Canal Square, Browning St B16 8FL

e-mail: info@loves-restaurant.co.uk

dir: Turn off Broad St towards NEC & Sherbourne Wharf then left to Grosvenor St West & right into Sherbourne St, at end take right into Browning St

It is quite the happening metropolis these days - as it should be given it is England's second city - and the thriving restaurant scene reflects this confidence. At the epicentre of the culinary action is Steve and Claire Love's eponymous restaurant, overlooking one of the city's former industrial arteries (that would be a canal) through a huge wall of glass. The interior takes a relative

minimalist approach, free of flummery, with bold swirls of modern prints bringing splashes of colour and attitude, whilst tables are laid with evident attention to detail. Out front, Claire leads by example with professionalism and an easy charm. Steve's cooking shows contemporary dynamism and a rightly obsessive approach to the sourcing of ingredients - local stuff gets a very good showing indeed. There is precision in the cooking and the presentation of dishes, and every flavour on the plate plays its part. Start with Shropshire chicken wings, for example, with Berkswell cheese flavouring the accompanying gnocchi, plus braised lentils and a garlic cream, or how about seared baby squid with a brandade croquette, celery porridge and celery sauce? Among main courses, Warwickshire venison - seared loin and braised belly - comes with elderberry onions, buckwheat and parsnip, and Herefordshire beef (slow-cooked cheek and crispy tongue) with pickled carrots, kale and smoked potato mash. The good work continues with desserts such as a treatise on apples, which sees apple cheesecake,

caramelised apple, and apple and lemongrass sorbet accompanied by pecan nut granola, or a pineapple dish in which the fruit is marinated, served in a porridge and as a sorbet. It will come as no surprise that the wine list is given equal attention - put together by Claire - and has lots of interesting selections and a good choice by the glass.

Chef Steve Love **Owner** Steve & Claire Love **Times** 12-1.45/6-9.30 Closed 1 wk Etr, 2 wks Aug & Xmas, Sun-Mon **Prices** Tasting menu £68-£113, Service added 10% **Wines** 20 by glass **Notes** ALC 2/3 course £38/£45, Vegetarian menu **Seats** 32, Pr/dining room 8 **Children** Portions **Parking** Brindley Place car park

Purnell's

BIRMINGHAM MAP 10 SP08

Modern British 🍴 NOTABLE WINE LIST

Stellar cooking with bags of local pride

☎ 0121 212 9799
55 Cornwall St B3 2DH
e-mail: info@purnellsrestaurant.com
dir: Close to Birmingham Snow Hill railway station &
junct of Church St

Glynn Purnell is a celebrity chef these days by any
rationale. He's on the telly quite a bit, for a start, which is
no surprise given his naturally ebullient and
approachable personality, but if you want to get the
measure of the man, head on over to Cornwall Street and
sample his food for yourself. There's also Purnell's Bistro
and Ginger's Bar over at Newhall Street, if you want
something a little more laid-back (but still rather swish).

Here in the financial district, the slickly-converted red-
brick Victorian warehouse makes an ace dining venue,
what with its industrial-heritage chic and central
location. It's all very cool and classy, with a menu that
does not lack for contemporary dynamism and
excitement. Take 'The Purnell's Tour' if you want to give
chef free rein to take you on a journey (and why wouldn't
you?), with a wine flight to make it even more fun.
Otherwise, go for the seasonal fixed-price menu, or the
free-flowing lunch menu which allows a bit more
flexibility in the number of courses. Off the 'Winter Menu',
parsley risotto with crispy pork nuggets comes with
parsley, shallot and anchovy salad, which looks as pretty
as a picture and delivers bang-on flavours. Wild sea bass
with mushroom purée, orange, pumpkin and coriander is
another course where everything on the plate plays a part
in creating a greater whole. From the 'Tour' menu, 'A
Taste of British Seafood' consists of Devonshire crab, Isle
of Man scallops and King's Lynn shrimps, the quality of it
all second to none. These are well-crafted dishes of

panache and verve. For dessert, upside down pineapple
cake with mango parfait, pistachio and mango leather
will leave you happy as Larry. The wine list does justice to
the phenomenal food.

Chef Glynn Purnell **Owner** Glynn Purnell
Times 12-1.30/7-9 Closed 1 wk Etr, 2 wks end Jul-early
Aug, Xmas, New Year, Sun-Mon, L Sat **Prices** Prices not
confirmed Service added but optional 12.5% **Wines** 400
bottles over £30, 15 bottles under £30, 19 by glass
Notes Tasting menu 8 course, wine tasting fr £70, ALC 3
course £50, Vegetarian available, Dress restrictions,
Smart casual **Seats** 45, Pr/dining room 12 **Parking** On
street, Snow Hill car park nearby

Simpsons

BIRMINGHAM MAP 10 SP08

Modern British V 🍴 NOTABLE WINE LIST

Smart, confident cooking in classy Edgbaston favourite

☎ 0121 454 3434
20 Highfield Rd, Edgbaston B15 3DU
e-mail: info@simpsonsrestaurant.co.uk
dir: 1m from city centre, opposite St George's Church,
Edgbaston

Birmingham's gastronomic landscape has been
drastically reshaped over the last decade or so, and
Simpsons is unarguably in the top-flight of the new order.
The setting in the leafy, well-heeled 'burbs of Edgbaston
might make you expect something safe, a touch staid
perhaps, but while Simpsons doesn't pursue the path of
chemical experimentation or speculative eclecticism for
its own sake, executive chef Luke Tipping's inventive

modern cooking is not short of culinary fireworks. The
setting is a charming villa of fine proportions, with a
conservatory extension giving views over the pretty
garden, and four smart bedrooms that wouldn't look out
of place in a classy boutique hotel if you'd like to stop
over and enjoy the experience to the max (particularly if
you're keen to delve into the depths of the rather
impressive wine list). On sunny days, the garden is quite
the hotspot for alfresco dining, but there's no need to
despair when the weather doesn't play ball, as the
charming glassed-in dining rooms have a tasteful,
neutral charm, with tables dressed up in their best
whites, and tended by a switched-on service team. The
kitchen's output starts from where it should, with top-
notch ingredients sourced from named suppliers in the
surrounding area, backed by a passionately seasonal
approach, and a serious level of technical ability and
creative flair. A sprinkling of exotic flavours adds intrigue,
but solid classical foundations keep it all reined in so
that nothing strikes a discordant note. Start, perhaps,

with roast quail with carrots, date purée, cracked wheat,
feta, pomegranate and cumin, before loin of venison with
caramelised swede, haggis, blackberries and peppercorn
sauce. Cod is salted in-house and might come with globe
artichokes, lettuce, seaweed, prawns and caviar, and to
finish, rhubarb might come in for a multi-faceted
workout, accompanied by cheesecake ice cream and
pistachio.

Chef Luke Tipping **Owner** Andreas & Alison Antona
Times 12-2.30/7-9.30 Closed BHs, D Sun **Prices** Fixed L 3
course £40, Tasting menu £90, Starter £11.50-£15, Main
£25.50-£31, Dessert £9.50-£12.50, Service added but
optional 12.5% **Wines** 20 bottles over £30, 10 bottles
under £30, 11 by glass **Notes** Tasting menu 8 course,
Sunday L, Vegetarian menu, Dress restrictions, Smart
casual **Seats** 70, Pr/dining room 20 **Children** Portions,
Menu **Parking** 12, On street

BIRMINGHAM *continued*

Malmaison Birmingham

@ Traditional, Modern

Buzzy setting and smart brasserie-style cooking

☎ 0121 246 5000
1 Wharfside St, The Mailbox B1 1RD
e-mail: birmingham@malmaison.com
web: www.malmaison.com
dir: M6 junct 6, follow the A38 (city centre), via Queensway underpass. Left to Paradise Circus, 1st exit Brunel St, right T-junct, Malmaison directly opposite

Who knew a Royal Mail sorting office could look this good? Well, it doesn't sort post anymore, but The Mailbox development is home to designer shops galore along with the city's outpost of the Malmaison group, with all its flair for contemporary design. Pictures of Birmingham's canals in their industrial heyday adorn the walls of the first-floor brasserie, which has the group's trademark French brasserie vibe (banquette seating, darkwood tables topped with flickering candles). The menu plays the brasserie game, too, so you might start with wild mushrooms on a toasted bloomer with Madeira and garlic butter, or mussel and saffron soup served with cheese straws. There's steak cooked on the grill or salads such as a classic Caesar, and main courses along the lines of roast cod with chorizo and butterbean stew. Finish with a Valrhona chocolate fondant soufflé with milk ice cream.

Times 12-2.30/6-10.30

Opus Restaurant

@@ Modern British

Smart city favourite for modern British cooking

☎ 0121 200 2323
54 Cornwall St B3 2DE
e-mail: restaurant@opusrestaurant.co.uk
web: www.opusrestaurant.co.uk
dir: Close to Birmingham Snow Hill railway station in the city's business district

Opus has bags of big-city attitude and a vibrant buzz in a cavernous open-plan space. An eye-catching, full-length,

girder-framed glass frontage references the city's industrial heritage, while inside it's a stylish, cosmopolitan setting: darkwood floors, linen-clothed tables, olive green suede and black leather banquette seating, and earthy red ochre walls to relieve the muted palette. The menu has broad appeal, drawing in suited and booted execs from the financial and legal chambers nearby, as well as style-led shoppers doing lunch. Top-quality seasonal British produce anchors the whole operation, and it's all brought together in straightforward modern treatments - you'll find nothing fussy, over-complex or speculative in either composition or presentation of dishes. From the great-value market menu, a free-range ham hock and potato roulade might start you off, followed by cod with roasted artichokes, wild mushrooms, and wilted greens. Trade up to the carte, and pan-fried breast and herb-crusted leg of quail with leeks and bacon could get you going, followed by turbot fillet with spiced cauliflower purée, crushed potatoes and cod brandade.

Chef David Colcombe **Owner** Ann Tonks, Irene Allan, David Colcombe **Times** 12-2.45/6-10 Closed between Xmas & New Year, BHs, Sun, L Sat **Prices** Fixed L 2 course £15, Fixed D 3 course £17.50, Tasting menu £75, Service added but optional 12.5% **Wines** 20 bottles over £30, 12 bottles under £30, 8 by glass **Notes** Chef's tasting menu 6 course, Vegetarian available **Seats** 85, Pr/dining room 24 **Children** Portions, Menu **Parking** On street

Purnell's

@@@ — *see page 487*

Simpsons

@@@ — *see page 487*

Thai Edge Restaurant

@ Thai

Smart, modish Thai in Brindley Place

☎ 0121 643 3993
7 Oozells Square, Brindley Place B1 2HS
e-mail: birmingham@thaiedge.co.uk
dir: Brindley Place just off Broad St (approx 0.5m from B'ham New Street station)

The Birmingham outpost of this modern Thai restaurant chain (with siblings in Cardiff, Leeds and Bristol) looks smart with its glass partitions, tiled floor, plentiful Thai artefacts and orchids on the tables. Thai music plays in the background (unobtrusively so) and waitresses are dressed in traditional garb. The charming staff can advise about the heat of the dishes and can get them tweaked up or down according to your liking. The expansive menu runs the gamut of set banquets, soups and salads with familiar and not so familiar choices along the way; toro mun khoa pod is sweetcorn cakes with sweet plum sauce (light and packed with flavour) and phed nam makam is pan-fried duck with sweet-and-sour tamarind sauce (tender and sticky). Tago and Woon Ka Ti sees coconut cream with taro, sweetcorn and sago wrapped in pandanus leaf and served with coconut jelly cubes topped with water chestnut jelly.

Times 12-2.30/5.30-11 Closed 25-26 Dec, 1 Jan

Turners

@@ Modern French

Cooking up a gastronomic storm in a Birmingham suburb

☎ 0121 426 4440
69 High St, Harborne B17 9NS
e-mail: info@turnersrestaurantbirmingham.co.uk

You certainly won't forget where you are in this classy operation on des-res Harborne's high street, as chef-patron Richard Turner's name is etched all over the striking mirrors lining the walls of the bold, dark and moody charcoal-grey dining room. Equally unforgettable is the refined, confident and creative modern French cooking conjured from top-notch seasonal ingredients; well-judged professional service boosts the quality factor still further. Excellent home-made breads precede salt cod brandade with spiced fish soup and wild garlic leaf, a dish of punchy, clearly defined flavours all working together, while terrine of chicken, ham hock and duck liver is pointed up with beetroot (fresh, pickled, and smooth purée) and wafer-thin translucent discs of crunchy pickled mooli radish. Main course delivers perfectly timed garnet-red medallions of roast loin of hare with a delicate cannelloni of gamey, melt-in-the-mouth braised leg meat, velvety celeriac purée, purple sprouting and pickled prunes. Finally, a textbook blackcurrant soufflé is presented with a great bit of theatrical flourish: the waiter makes a hole in the top and pours in a rich blackcurrant coulis, followed by a quenelle of liquorice ice cream.

Chef Richard Turner **Owner** Richard Turner **Times** 12-2/7-9.30 Closed Sun-Mon, L Sat **Prices** Prices not confirmed Service added but optional 12.5% **Wines** 89 bottles over £30, 9 bottles under £30, 14 by glass **Notes** ALC 3 course £50, Menu du Jour D Wed-Thu £37.95, Vegetarian available **Seats** 30 **Parking** 50

DORRIDGE	Map 10 SP17

The Forest

@@ Modern European

Inspired modern cooking in a stylish hotel

☎ 01564 772120
Station Approach, 25 Station Rd B93 8JA
e-mail: info@forest-hotel.com
web: www.forest-hotel.com
dir: M42 junct 5, through Knowle right to Dorridge, left before bridge

Once a Victorian railway hotel, nowadays The Forest is a rather chic affair with modern-day boutique credentials and a bar and restaurant at its heart. A white-linen-free zone, the restaurant's fashionable banquette seating and chairs stand alongside wooden floors, feature wallpaper and a full-height wine cabinet. The brasserie-style menu is equally of-the-moment, delivering some appealing innovative ideas from quality produce with a broadly modern European accent. Think roasted turbot fillet with leek and mussel velouté and potato foam, and, for dessert, a plum tarte Tatin with cinnamon ice cream and

Save on Hotels. Book at **theAA.com/hotel**

WEST MIDLANDS 489 ENGLAND

hazelnuts. A range of classic dishes (steak-and-kidney pudding to fish and chips) keeps traditionalists happy.

Chef Dean Grubb **Owner** Gary & Tracy Perkins
Times 12-2.30/6.30-10 Closed 25 Dec, D Sun
Prices Fixed L 2 course fr £13.45, Fixed D 3 course fr £15.90, Starter £4.25-£7.50, Main £11.50-£22, Dessert £5.75-£6.50, Service added but optional 10% **Wines** 18 bottles over £30, 26 bottles under £30, 13 by glass
Notes Fixed L Mon-Sat, D Mon-Fri, Sunday L, Vegetarian available, Civ Wed 130 **Seats** 70, Pr/dining room 150
Children Portions, Menu **Parking** 40

HOCKLEY HEATH   Map 10 SP17

Nuthurst Grange Hotel

◉◉ Modern British

Inventive cooking in classy country-house hotel

☎ 01564 783972
Nuthurst Grange Ln B94 5NL
e-mail: info@nuthurst-grange.co.uk
web: www.nuthurst-grange.com
dir: Exit A3400, 0.5m S of Hockley Heath. Turn at sign into Nuthurst Grange Lane

It may come as no surprise, given the beautiful gardens and the handsomeness of the house inside and out, that Nuthurst Grange is a big hit for weddings. As for non-conjugal visitors, there's still plenty of reason to come,

not least for the food. There's a bistro in the orangery where you can order from the fine-dining carte if you wish, or you can choose to eat the same in the smart and elegant main dining room, with its country views, linen-clad tables and well-drilled service. The menu is a decidedly contemporary affair with lots of good ideas, carefully-executed and based on fine produce. A starter of quail three ways, for example, has the breast cooked at 64 degrees, the leg crisped up and the egg pickled, whilst venison carpaccio comes with red cabbage slaw, endive salad, and a Valrhona chocolate oil. Caraway-roasted pork tenderloin stars in a main course with crushed purple potato cake, curly kale and Dijon mustard cream, and there's a touch of sunshine in a dessert of tropical fruit soufflé with coconut ice cream and exotic fruit smoothie.

Nuthurst Grange Hotel

Times 12-2.30/7-9 Closed D Sun

See advert below

MERIDEN   Map 10 SP28

Best Western Plus Manor NEC Birmingham

◉◉ Modern British, French

Smart modish cooking in a Midlands manor

☎ 01676 522735
Main Rd CV7 7NH
e-mail: reservations@manorhotelmeriden.co.uk
web: www.manorhotelmeriden.co.uk
dir: M42 junct 6, A45 towards Coventry then A452 signed Leamington. At rdbt take B4102 signed Meriden, hotel on left

Handy if you're hitting the National Exhibition Centre, the restaurant at the family-run Manor Hotel in the small village of Meriden has also caught the eye of savvy locals, who come for the classy modish cooking. The large, traditionally-styled Regency Restaurant is hung with paintings depicting English country scenes, and combined with smartly dressed tables laid with sparkling glasses and fresh flowers, it's a charming spot for lunch or dinner. Young and upbeat staff ensure it all ticks along nicely. Modern British cooking is the order of the day; kick off with Loomswood Farm Gressingham duck and wild mushroom terrine with Provençale vegetable and celeriac velouté, before moving on to pan-roasted Cornish monkfish with cauliflower, pressed potato and garlic, mussel velouté, cumin-scented carrots and rocket pesto.

Chef Darion Smethurst **Owner** Bracebridge Holdings
Times 12-3/6-10 Closed L Mon-Sat **Prices** Fixed D 3 course £29, Starter £4.95-£7.95, Main £13.25-£18.50, Dessert £6.25-£6.75, Service optional **Wines** 1 bottle over £30, 34 bottles under £30, 16 by glass **Notes** Sunday L, Vegetarian available, Civ Wed 200 **Seats** 150, Pr/dining room 220 **Children** Portions, Menu **Parking** 190

MERIDEN *continued*

Forest of Arden Marriott Hotel & Country Club

◎ Modern British V

Good eating at a smart golfing hotel

☎ 01676 522335
Maxstoke Ln CV7 7HR
e-mail: nigel.parnaby@marriotthotels.com
web: www.marriottforestofarden.co.uk

A big hotel with lots going on - golf and spa for a start - the Forest of Arden Marriott is well-positioned for the East Midlands hub, and its Oaks Bar and Grill is a restaurant of note in its own right. There's a bold carpet, leather banquettes, straight-backed chairs and scatter cushions giving it a bright and breezy modish feel, and views over the grounds are an added bonus. On the menu, straightforward grills rub shoulders with more inventive things; a classic combination of warm figs and Parma ham is paired with bucks fizz jelly and sweet saffron syrup, followed perhaps by baked fillet of haddock with a poached egg, curried sauce and sautéed greens. To finish, strawberry Arctic roll, vanilla pannacotta and compôte is a good bet.

Chef Darcy Morgan **Times** 1-2.30/6.30-9.45 **Prices** Prices not confirmed Service optional **Wines** 16 by glass **Notes** Sunday L, Vegetarian menu, Dress restrictions, Smart casual **Seats** 192, Pr/dining room 18 **Children** Portions, Menu **Parking** 300

OLDBURY Map 10 SO98

Saffron Restaurant

◎ Modern Indian ✪

Smart modern setting for up-to-date Anglo-Indian fusion cooking

☎ 0121 552 1752
909 Wolverhampton Rd B69 4RR
e-mail: info@saffron-online.co.uk
dir: M5 junct 2. Follow A4123 (S) signs towards Harborne. Restaurant on right

This contemporary Indian in the heart of the Black Country goes for a bold colour scheme involving scarlet and black chairs arranged in a chequerboard pattern at darkwood tables, plushly padded booths and statement wallpaper, tempered by minimally white walls and dark wooden flooring. If you're not the adventurous type, tandoori staples and classics such as lamb rogan josh or chicken korma feature on a wide-reaching menu. But dig deeper, and you'll find more refined, delicately-spiced ideas built on quality, fresh ingredients. Among the seafood section, perhaps nilgiri machli, a traditional Parsee fish curry with garlic, green herbs and poppy paste. Catching the eye among starters is rabbit varuval, a South Indian speciality teaming tender rabbit with onion, curry leaves, mustard seeds and a palate-tingling hit of chilli. Choosing from the signature dishes reaps rewards too, in the shape of achari venison - meltingly tender pan-fried venison steak served with spiced potato

gâteau and sauced with the bittersweet citrus tang of achaar pickle.

Chef Sudha Shankar Saha **Owner** Abdul Rahman & A Momin **Times** 12-2.30/5.30-11 Closed D 25 Dec **Prices** Fixed L 2 course fr £6.95, Starter £3.50-£6.95, Main £7.95-£21.95, Dessert £3.75-£4.50, Groups min 8 service 10% **Wines** 38 bottles under £30, 8 by glass **Notes** Sunday L, Vegetarian available, Dress restrictions, Smart casual **Seats** 96 **Children** Portions **Parking** 25, On street

---

SUTTON COLDFIELD Map 10 SP19

New Hall Hotel & Spa

◎◎ Modern British ✪

Modern fine-dining in historic house

☎ 0121 378 2442 & 0845 072 7577
Walmley Rd, Walmley B76 1QX
e-mail: newhall@handpicked.co.uk
web: www.handpickedhotels.co.uk/newhall
dir: On B4148, E of Sutton Coldfield, close to M6 & M42 junct 9

It is hard to imagine, but before Birmingham's suburban sprawl engulfed the village of Sutton Coldfield, this 800-year-old moat house stood in empty countryside. The hall hasn't actually been 'new' since the 14th century, and does business nowadays as an upmarket operation that on one hand flaunts its age in medieval beams, flagstones, and heraldic crests, and on the other, supplies 21st-century spa pampering with all the bells and whistles, and it is all cushioned from the hurly-burly of modern Brum by 26 acres of fabulous grounds. The Bridge Restaurant is the top-end dining option, where mullioned stained-glass windows blend with a gently modern neutral décor as a setting for cooking whose roots are set in the classics but tweaked for today's tastes with modern techniques and presentation. Expect starters along the lines of smoked eel salad with new potato, red onion and apple, followed by slow-cooked Kentish lamb shoulder partnered with its sweetbreads, Jerusalem artichoke purée, and wholegrain mustard jus.

New Hall Hotel & Spa

Chef Paul Soczowka **Owner** Hand Picked Hotels **Times** 7-9.30 Closed L all week, D Mon-Wed **Prices** Prices not confirmed Service optional **Wines** 14 by glass **Notes** Vegetarian available, Dress restrictions, Smart casual, no jeans or T-shirts, Civ Wed 75 **Seats** 24, Pr/dining room 14 **Children** Portions, Menu **Parking** 60

WALSALL Map 10 SP09

Fairlawns Hotel & Spa

◎◎ Modern British V

Smart hotel with confident modern cooking

☎ 01922 455122
178 Little Aston Rd, Aldridge WS9 0NU
e-mail: reception@fairlawns.co.uk
web: www.fairlawns.co.uk
dir: Outskirts of Aldridge, 400yds from junction of A452 (Chester Rd) & A454

Well-insulated from the concrete sprawl of Greater Birmingham by nine acres of landscaped gardens, this family-run hotel north of Walsall is in a useful spot for plugging in to the big Midlands cities and the motorway network. The Victorian building at the heart of Fairlawns is smartly updated and extended, and comes with a spa and fitness centre. Completing the attractive package is the kitchen's deft line in modern British cooking, presented on a broad-ranging menu built on well-sourced materials. Things could kick off with Craster smoked haddock fishcakes with prawn and chive beurre blanc, followed by roast rack and confit shoulder of lamb served with fondant potato and roasted root vegetables. To wrap it all up, there may be a home-grown rhubarb soufflé.

Chef Neil Atkins **Owner** John Pette **Times** 12-2/7-10 Closed 25-26 Dec, 1 Jan, Good Fri, Etr Mon, May Day, BH Mon, L Sat **Prices** Fixed L 2 course fr £16.50, Fixed D 3 course fr £32.95, Service optional **Wines** 20 bottles over £30, 40 bottles under £30, 12 by glass **Notes** Sunday L, Vegetarian menu, Dress restrictions, No jeans, trainers or sports clothing **Seats** 80, Pr/dining room 100 **Children** Portions, Menu **Parking** 120

WOLVERHAMPTON   Map 10 SO99

Bilash

🌐 Indian 🍷

A happy mix of new and old ideas in longstanding Indian

☎ 01902 427762
2 Cheapside WV1 1TU
e-mail: m@thebilash.co.uk
dir: Opposite Civic Hall & St Peter's Church

In a quiet corner of the pedestrianised square overlooking St Peter's Church, Bilash has been pushing beyond the confines of mere curry for 30 years. The stylishly clean-cut interior works a colourful décor of caramel and burgundy high-backed leather seats at wooden tables set against pale lemon walls hung with modern Indian-themed pastel prints, a smart contemporary setting that reflects the kitchen's approach to its creative roll call of Bangladeshi and Indian regional dishes. Start with maachar shami kebab, a flat fishcake with lime, herbs and garam masala, served with tamarind sauce and excellent home-made chutneys, then follow with Goan tiger prawn masala - enormous tiger prawns marinated in spicy tomato paste and cooked with cumin, coriander, green chillies, roasted onions, curry leaves, mint and spring onions. Don't miss pukka Indian desserts such as rasmalai - an über-sweet dumpling made from Indian paneer (cottage cheese) flavoured with cardamom and saffron, poached in sweetened cardamom-flavoured milk and served with chopped almonds, pistachios and saffron.

Chef Sitab Khan **Owner** Sitab Khan
Times 12-2.30/5.30-10.30 Closed 25-26 Dec, 1 Jan, Sun **Prices** Prices not confirmed Service optional **Wines** 5 by glass **Notes** Pre-theatre D, tasting menu with wine, L specials, Vegetarian available, Dress restrictions, No tracksuits & trainers **Seats** 48, Pr/dining room 40 **Children** Portions, Menu **Parking** 15, Civic car park

WIGHT, ISLE OF

SEAVIEW   Map 5 SZ69

Priory Bay Hotel

🌐 Modern British 🍷

Attractive Regency dining room and creative menu

☎ 01983 613146
Priory Dr PO34 5BU
e-mail: enquiries@priorybay.co.uk
web: www.priorybay.co.uk
dir: B3330 towards Seaview, through Nettlestone. (Do not follow Seaview turn, but continue 0.5m to hotel sign)

Set within a 70-acre estate of gardens, woodlands and even with its own beach, this sumptuous former Tudor farmhouse is home to the elegant Island Room restaurant. The Regency-style dining room dazzles with murals of local scenery and gilded plasterwork, with floor-to-ceiling windows giving views across to the Solent. The fine-dining menu is based around local seafood, game and a good deal of fresh produce from the gardens and woodlands. Kick off with céviche of mackerel with horseradish pannacotta, pickled garden beetroot salad and beetroot jelly, followed by rump of island lamb with Medjool date purée, crushed pistachio, yeast extract-glazed potatoes and rosemary oil. The Oyster Bar & Grill does a fine line in unadulterated seafood.

Chef Ollie Stephens **Owner** Mr R & Mr J Palmer
Times 12.30-2.15/7-9.30 **Prices** Fixed L 2 course £15.50, Tasting menu £50-£70, Starter £5.50-£12, Main £10.50-£22, Dessert £6.50-£8.50, Service added but optional 12.5%, Groups min 8 service 12.5% **Wines** 59 bottles over £30, 30 bottles under £30, 14 by glass **Notes** Tasting menu available (blind tasting), Priory afternoon tea, Sunday L £12.95, Vegetarian available, Civ Wed 100 **Seats** 50, Pr/dining room 50 **Children** Portions, Menu **Parking** 50

The Seaview Hotel & Restaurant

🌐 Traditional British 🍷

Enterprising cooking in a sailing village

☎ 01983 612711
High St PO34 5EX
e-mail: reception@seaviewhotel.co.uk
web: www.seaviewhotel.co.uk
dir: Take B3330 from Ryde to Seaview, left into Puckpool Hill, follow signs for hotel

There's an appealing nautical charm to The Seaview Hotel. The water is very close, just down the road, but there's plenty of maritime charisma on the inside. There are two splendid bars, each with seafaring themes, including the Naval Bar modelled on a naval wardroom. When it comes to eating, there's a pleasingly egalitarian attitude - you can eat where you like, whether that's one of the bars or the two dining rooms. The Clock Room at the front is a breezy sea-blue room with wooden tables, or go for the Sunshine restaurant, which is a larger, more contemporary space with a conservatory vibe. On the

menu is some fine island produce. Start with a crab ramekin with ciabatta croûtons, or beef from the island served tartare with beef tea and dill pickle. Then follow on with fish pie, or slow-cooked ox cheek with tongue, fondant potato and creamed celeriac.

Chef Alan Staley **Owner** B E F Gardener
Times 12-2.30/6.30-9.30 Closed 23-27 Dec **Prices** Prices not confirmed Service optional **Wines** 10 bottles over £30, 16 bottles under £30, 5 by glass **Notes** Sunday L, Vegetarian available **Seats** 70, Pr/dining room 25 **Children** Portions, Menu **Parking** 8

VENTNOR   Map 5 SZ57

The Hambrough

Rosettes not confirmed at time of going to print – see page 492

The Leconfield

🌐 Traditional British **V** 🍷

Hotel with a local flavour and sea views

☎ 01983 852196
85 Leeson Rd, Upper Bonchurch PO38 1PU
e-mail: enquiries@leconfieldhotel.com
web: www.leconfieldhotel.com
dir: Situated Upper Bonchurch on A3055, 1m from Ventnor, 2m from Shanklin opposite turning, Bonchurch Shute

There are great views over the English Channel from inside and out of this ivy-clad hotel up on St Boniface Down above the village of Bonchurch. The Seascape Dining Room duly delivers the vista on a plate in the daylight hours, while the room's traditional charms should easily satisfy evening guests. There are plenty of local ingredients on the menu (beef and lobster, for example), which might take you from sautéed tiger prawns in garlic butter (served on toasted brioche) to orange Bakewell tart with Chantilly cream and chocolate sauce, via some of that local beef - fillet steak, perhaps, served Wellington style with a port sauce.

Chef Jason Lefley **Owner** Paul & Cheryl Judge
Times 6.30-8 Closed 24-26 Dec, 3 wks Jan, L all week (except by prior arrangement) **Prices** Fixed D 3 course £27-£41, Service optional **Wines** 5 bottles over £30, 25 bottles under £30, 8 by glass **Notes** Vegetarian menu, Dress restrictions, Smart casual **Seats** 26 **Parking** 14

The Pond Café

🌐 Modern European

Intimate little venue with an eclectic menu

☎ 01983 855666 & 856333
Bonchurch Village Rd, Bonchurch PO38 1RG
e-mail: reservations@robert-thompson.com
dir: A3055 to Leeson Rd follow Bonchurch signs until village turn off

In the tranquil environs of Bonchurch, The Pond is the sister restaurant to The Hambrough in Ventnor (see entry).

continued

VENTNOR continued

It's a simpler set-up as the café designation indicates, but not devoid of a certain romantic charm with its candles and intimate proportions. An outdoor terrace has been added for those balmier days. Under new ownership and with a new chef at the helm, the menu has gone all eclectic, taking in influences from all over. So interesting, inventive starters range from cured mackerel with salted peanut and cucumber kimchee, to crispy brawn, radish, shallot and XO sauce, and ramson ricotta angelotti with oyster emulsion. For main, lamb chump gets the Mediterranean treatment with fennel shoots, olive oil polenta and aubergine, while roast chicken comes with buckwheat waffle, sea kale, salted lemon and garlic crisps. Desserts are equally multi-dimensional and creative, such as sweet potato ice cream, Jamaican ginger cake, lime meringue and sour cream.

Chef Joe Gould **Times** 12-2.30/6-9.30 **Prices** Fixed L 2 course £15, Fixed D 3 course £20, Starter £7-£9, Main £14-£18.50, Dessert £5-£7, Service optional **Wines** 6 bottles over £30, 17 bottles under £30, 5 by glass **Notes** Early bird menu 2/3 course £15/£20 6-7pm, Sunday L, Vegetarian available **Seats** 26 **Children** Portions **Parking** On street

The Royal Hotel

◉◉ Modern British

Contemporary cooking in a reassuringly old-fashioned setting

☎ 01983 852186
Belgrave Rd PO38 1JJ
e-mail: enquiries@royalhoteliow.co.uk
dir: On A3055 (coast road) into Ventnor. Follow one-way system, left at lights into Church St. At top of hill left into Belgrave Rd, hotel on right

The Royal is a stone-built pile nestling amid sub-tropical gardens on the Isle of Wight's south-eastern coast, a spot that unblushingly styles itself 'the Madeira of England'. It's a formal seaside hotel in the classic manner, with beautifully turned-out interiors and a thoroughgoing professionalism in the service style, best seen in the Appuldurcombe Restaurant, where tied drapes, crisp table linen and little flower vases compose a picture of reassuring civility. The menus are distinctly in the contemporary vein, though, with seafood a particular forte. There is as much intuitive precision in balancing flavours and seasonings in a classical fish soup with rouille as there is in the succeeding dish of roast sea bass accompanied by a portion of moules marinière, saffron potatoes and samphire. Meats are given more traditional treatments, as when roast loin and braised neck of local lamb arrive with baby artichokes and some of the island's celebrated wild garlic, while desserts aim to cosset with the likes of baked almond ricotta

cheesecake with roasted peach and nectarine, and raspberry sorbet.

Times 12-1.45/6.45-9 Closed 2 wks Jan or 2 wks Dec, L Mon-Sat

The George Hotel

◉◉ British, Mediterranean ⬮

Refined seasonal cookery on The Solent

☎ 01983 760331
Quay St PO41 0PE
e-mail: res@thegeorge.co.uk
dir: Between castle & pier

Window seats are at a premium in The George's bright, conservatory-style brasserie - hardly surprising when you look at the location: smack on the water's edge

The Hambrough

Rosettes not confirmed at time of going to print

Modern European, French V ⬥ NOTABLE WINE LIST

Inspirational modern cooking overlooking the sea

☎ 01983 856333
Hambrough Rd PO38 1SQ
e-mail: reservations@robert-thompson.com
web: www.robert-thompson.com
dir: From A3055 follow signs to Ventnor & St Catherine's Church, turn right into Hambrough Rd, restaurant on left

Please note: the Rosette award for this establishment has been suspended due to a change of chef. Reassessment will take place in due course under the new chef.

Perched above the esplanade at Ventnor, The Hambrough is a smart Victorian villa turned sybaritic boutique hotel with uplifting views out to sea across the harbour. A

classy makeover has brought in a light and airy look of neutral refinement to the two front-facing rooms that comprise the restaurant, without detracting from their period character or those watery scenes stretching far beyond the bay windows. Robert Thompson made his name with immaculately-executed, labour-intensive modern French dishes inspired by the surrounding landscape, and here that means splendid produce hauled in from the local farms and fishing boats, as well as further afield. A signature pressing of lightly-smoked eel with foie gras, pork belly and Granny Smith apple served with celeriac remoulade and toasted brioche is typical of the full-throated flavours and rich textures on offer. Next out, roasted loin of New Forest venison might star in a perfectly-judged composition with snails, roast parsley root and field mushroom purée, and garlic and parsley butter. Puddings are equally intelligent combinations such as tarte Tatin of Pink Lady apples matched with cassia ice cream. On the wine front, there's more than

ample choice by the glass, and intelligent global coverage by the bottle.

Chef Darren Beevers **Times** 12-1.30/7-9.30 Closed 1.5 wks Apr, 2 wks Nov & Jan, Mon, D Sun **Prices** Fixed L 2 course £24, Fixed D 3 course £60, Tasting menu £85, Service optional **Wines** 10 by glass **Notes** ALC 3 course £60, Afternoon tea £30, Sunday L, Vegetarian menu, Dress restrictions, Smart casual, No sportswear, Civ Wed 45 **Seats** 45, Pr/dining room 22 **Children** Portions **Parking** On street

Save on Hotels. Book at theAA.com/hotel

WILTSHIRE 493 ENGLAND

overlooking the yachtie comings and goings on The Solent, the sweeping views extend over immaculate lawns to the castle, quay and pier beyond. Comfy banquettes, bare wooden tables, neutral colours and contemporary art set the scene for bright European-accented brasserie ideas punctuated with materials from the bountiful local larder. Isle of Wight rare-breed pork stars in a terrine served enterprisingly with crisp apple and watercress, raisin purée and cider jelly, or there might be local scallops with roast butternut squash and pancetta risotto. Fish fans will find plenty of interest too: roast organic salmon fillet with crushed new potatoes and smoked bacon and pea velouté scores a hit, or look for locally-landed cod, served with braised fennel, chilli and mint, and tempura oyster. A dessert of poached champagne rhubarb with shortbread biscuit, grenadine crème patissière, and champagne sorbet also passes with flying colours.

Chef Austin Gould **Owner** John Illsley, Jeremy Willcock **Times** 12-3/7-9.30 **Prices** Fixed L 2 course £17.95-£25, Starter £5.95-£9.50, Main £15.95-£24, Dessert £6.95-£7.95, Service optional **Wines** 31 bottles over £30, 12 bottles under £30, 11 by glass **Notes** Sunday L, Vegetarian available, Dress restrictions, Smart casual **Seats** 60 **Children** Portions, Menu **Parking** The Square

WILTSHIRE

AMESBURY   Map 5 SU14

Holiday Inn Salisbury - Stonehenge

◉ Modern International

Brisk brasserie food near Stonehenge

☎ 0845 241 3535 & 01980 677466
Midsummer Place, Solstice Park SP4 7SQ
e-mail: reservations@hisalisbury-stonehenge.co.uk
web: www.hisalisbury-stonehenge.co.uk
dir: Exit A303, follow signs into Solstice Park. Hotel adjacent to service area

The Salisbury Holiday Inn is a great glass ark of a building, grounded in the vicinity of England's ancient henges, with which it makes impressively little attempt to fit in. It's all airy spaciousness inside, with a giant open-plan dining room, windowed all round to afford views of rolling Wiltshire. A menu of brisk brasserie fare in the Solstice Bar and Grill does the business, whether you're flying through for a fishfinger roll on your way to join the Druids, or signing up for the Dinner Collection. The latter might offer warm herbed goats' cheese in roasted tomato, red pepper and rocket salad, followed by roast cod on pea purée with chilli prawns, oyster mushrooms and buttered kale, or decent calf's liver and smoked bacon with creamy mash, balsamic pearl onions and faintly pointless roasted courgette. Crème brûlée is pleasingly vanilla-ry and comes with a round of creditably home-made shortbread.

Chef Matthew Bills **Owner** Armani Hotels Ltd **Prices** Fixed L 2 course fr £9.95, Fixed D 3 course fr £19.95, Starter £5.25-£7.25, Main £13.25-£18.95, Dessert £5.25-£7.95, Service optional **Wines** 3 bottles over £30, 22 bottles under £30, 22 by glass **Notes** Sunday L, Vegetarian available **Seats** 80 **Children** Portions, Menu

BEANACRE   Map 4 ST96

Beechfield House Hotel, Restaurant & Gardens

◉ Modern British ❀

Contemporary country-house dining

☎ 01225 703700
SN12 7PU
e-mail: reception@beechfieldhouse.co.uk
web: www.beechfieldhouse.co.uk
dir: M4 junct 17, A350 S, bypass Chippenham, towards Melksham. Hotel on left after Beanacre

Externally, Beechfield House is a striking Venetian style late-Victorian country house built of Bath stone, but once inside it is clearly a switched-on operation that stays abreast of the times. An understated contemporary style has lightened up the look in the dining room: ornate period plasterwork sits well alongside a crystal chandelier above a de-cluttered setting of plush burgundy velvet seats, white linen-clad tables and an antique rug on stripped pine floors. Modern sensibilities are also assuaged by creative cooking founded on top-grade local produce - a simple, well-balanced starter involving duck breast 'bresaola', Medjool dates and blood orange might precede a chop and slow-cooked breast of Gloucestershire lamb, partnered by fondant potato, swede and leek. Finish with ginger parkin, marmalade ice cream, golden raisins and spiced syrup.

Chef Paul Horrell **Owner** Chris Whyte **Times** 12-2/7-9 Closed 23-26 Dec, D Sun **Prices** Fixed L 2 course £15, Starter £5.50-£6, Main £16.25-£20.50, Dessert £5.50-£8.50, Service optional **Wines** 15 bottles over £30, 27 bottles under £30, 5 by glass **Notes** Sunday L £17.50-£19.50, Vegetarian available, Dress restrictions, Smart casual, Civ Wed 70 **Seats** 22, Pr/dining room 20 **Children** Portions, Menu **Parking** 70

BRADFORD-ON-AVON   Map 4 ST86

The Three Gables

◉◉ Modern European V ⧓ NOTABLE WINE LIST ❀

Mediterranean-influenced menu in a venerable greystone inn

☎ 01225 781666
St Margaret St BA15 1DA
e-mail: info@thethreegables.com

The name reflects the trio of architectural eminences that surmount the façade of this venerable greystone inn opposite the town bridge. It's had an extensive restoration throughout, with a contemporary feel to the first-floor dining room, which extends across the three gable windows, where a mixture of exposed stonework and washed walls and a wood floor look the part. There's also a delightful raised terrace at the back for alfresco dining. Co-owner (and wine expert - hence the fantastic list) Vito Scaduto takes care of things out front with unfailing Italian charm, while chef Marc Salmon beavers away in the kitchen producing some highly refined Mediterranean-

influenced cuisine. A first-class terrine of Wiltshire pork with piccalilli and egg bhajee is an inventive take on a classic, or you might go for Cornish mackerel and horseradish pastry with cucumber oyster velouté. Cornish brill - a first-class piece of fish, perfectly cooked - comes with a crispy soft-shelled crab, rouille and samphire in an inspired main course, while dessert might actually be three puds in one: a rich dark chocolate mousse with moist pistachio polenta cake and moreish beetroot ice cream.

Chef Marc Salmon **Owner** Marc Salmon, Vito Scaduto **Times** 12-2/6.30-10 Closed 1-12 Jan, Sun-Mon **Prices** Prices not confirmed Service optional **Wines** 200 bottles over £30, 50 bottles under £30, 16 by glass **Notes** Vegetarian menu **Seats** 55 **Children** Portions **Parking** Public car park

CALNE   Map 14 ST97

The White Horse

◉ Modern British NEW ❀

A warm welcome and local produce

☎ 01249 813118
Compon Bassett SN11 8RG
e-mail: info@whitehorse-comptonbassett.co.uk
dir: M4 junct 16 onto A3102, after Hilmarton village turn left to Compton Bassett

Set in the Wiltshire countryside in the village of Compton Bassett, this freehouse guarantees a warm welcome from its hands-on owners. You can eat wherever you choose in the refurbished pub - be it in the modern and comfortable restaurant with its unclothed wooden tables, or in the bar which is well stocked with local ales and made cosy with a log burner. The kitchen supports local suppliers, both big and small, so if you've got good quality produce to spare, you're encouraged to bring it in and head chef Danny Adams will use it on the menu. Expect simple, honest cooking with some contemporary techniques on show, as in a superbly gamey seared breast of pigeon with celeriac purée, wild mushrooms and red wine jus. Roasted corn-fed chicken supreme supported by sweet potato mash, roasted root vegetables, chorizo and red wine jus makes a fine main course, while sticky toffee pudding with malted vanilla ice cream hits the spot for pud.

Chef Danny Adams **Owner** Danny & Tara Adams **Times** 12-9 Closed Mon, D Sun **Prices** Prices not confirmed Service optional **Wines** 7 bottles over £30, 34 bottles under £30, 8 by glass **Notes** Sunday L, Vegetarian available **Seats** 45, Pr/dining room 45 **Children** Portions, Menu **Parking** 45

CASTLE COMBE   Map 4 ST87

The Bybrook at The Manor House Hotel

◉◉◉ — see page 494

COLERNE
Map 4 ST87

The Brasserie

Modern British

Smart, modish brasserie in majestic country-house hotel

☎ 01225 742777

Lucknam Park Hotel & Spa SN14 8AZ
e-mail: brasserie@lucknampark.co.uk
dir: M4 junct 17, A350 towards Chippenham, then A420 towards Bristol for 3m. At Ford left to Colerne, 3m, right at x-rds, entrance on right

The second string to Lucknam Park's bow, The Brasserie offers a modernist, informal alternative to The Park Restaurant's fine-dinery (see separate entry). Located within the walled garden, with a wall of glass of its own, and right next-door to the spa, The Brasserie has a classy finish and serves up some pretty classy food, too. There's an open kitchen and a wood-burning oven to confirm those brasserie credentials. The kitchen knows what it's aiming for and keeps things simple and appealing. Start with creamed seasonal mushrooms, for example, with sweet sherry and brioche, or a Burford Brown Scotch egg with home-made tomato ketchup. Confit shoulder of pork might come in a main course spiced up with some ginger-braised pak choi, sweet potato and orange chutney, and there's a first-class burger and top-notch pizza, too. And to finish, who could resist churros with vanilla marshmallows and spiced chocolate dip?

Chef Hywel Jones **Owner** Lucknam Park Hotels Ltd **Times** 7.30am-10pm All-day dining **Prices** Fixed L 2 course £19, Starter £5.50-£8.50, Main £12.50-£28, Dessert £7, Service optional **Notes** Sunday L, Vegetarian available **Seats** 40 **Children** Portions, Menu **Parking** 80

The Park Restaurant

– *see page 496*

See advert opposite

CORSHAM
Map 4 ST87

Guyers House Hotel

Modern European

Creative ideas in a traditional country house

☎ 01249 713399

Pickwick SN13 0PS
e-mail: enquiries@guyershouse.com
dir: A4 between Pickwick & Corsham

Set in six acres of lovely English gardens with a tennis court and croquet lawn, Guyers House is a classic country-house hotel that is equally as happy to sort out your wedding or business needs as it is to put you up in serene comfort. When it comes to dining, the kitchen keeps fruitful connections with the local food network, as well as furnishing the larder with fresh, seasonal ingredients from its own vegetable and herb garden. Although the setting is resolutely traditional, the menu can come up with some surprising compositions that work well, as in a starter that sees creamy fennel velouté poured over a roll of smoked salmon with crème fraîche and mixed cress at the table, or an unusual dessert involving spiced chocolate and sweet potato dauphine matched with chestnut ice cream and a dark chocolate pavé. Sandwiched between these delicious ideas, there's a fashionable multi-cut tasting of top-quality local Biddestone pork, consisting of roast belly and fillet, braised shoulder and a full-flavoured faggot matched with caramelised onion purée and crispy shallots.

Chef Gareth John, Jamie Brandsbry, David Gale **Owner** Mr & Mrs Hungerford **Times** 12.30-2.30/7-9 **Closed** 30 Dec-3 Jan **Prices** Fixed D 3 course £25, Starter £7.50-£13.95, Main £17-£23.95, Dessert £7.25-£8.25, Service added but optional 10% **Wines** 9 bottles over £30, 24 bottles under £30, 5 by glass **Notes** Sunday L, Vegetarian available **Seats** 66, Pr/dining room 56 **Children** Portions, Menu **Parking** 60

The Bybrook at The Manor House Hotel

CASTLE COMBE
MAP 4 ST87

Modern British V

Complex contemporary cooking in a film-set medieval village

☎ 01249 782206

The Manor House Hotel SN14 7HR
e-mail: enquiries@manorhouse.co.uk
web: www.manorhouse.co.uk
dir: M4 junct 17, follow signs for Castle Combe via Chippenham

The village of Castle Combe finds itself at the heart of a particularly modern paradox. So beautifully preserved in aspic is it that it has earned itself a tidy living in recent years as a film-set, with Steven Spielberg's *War Horse* of 2011 among its more recent credits. When the sound technicians, makeup artists and Jeremy Irvine have left town, though, it settles back into unruffled pastoral tranquillity, a picture of serenity in which the originally 14th-century manor house is a key part, the thwock of golfballs notwithstanding. The interiors have not been spruced up by punk Parisian designers, but look as delightfully dated as its target constituency would wish. On the other hand, the cooking, under Richard Davies, aims to cut a contemporary dash, with tip-top ingredients and a gradually developing tendency to complexity in the armoury. That latter factor is seen in a main course of pork, a three-way assembly of richly gelatinous cheek, expressively flavoured rolled fillet and over-smoked belly, which are accompanied by boldly tart apple purée and shallot-studded mashed potato. Much of the produce is grown in the kitchen garden, and much else sourced from organic growers in the village, and helps to give liftoff to first courses such as seared scallops and chorizo with quince, cucumber and pickled mooli, or flame-grilled mackerel with puréed celeriac, compressed apple and shaved walnuts. The timing of truffled risotto is impressive, as too the oyster beignet and parsley purée accompanying it, and the confidence with assertive flavours brings on golden raisins and chocolate, not for afters but with main-course rump of Downland lamb. The technical wizardry ensures that interest is maintained at dessert stage, when a blackcurrant bavarois on a nutritious oat base comes with a portion of white chocolate ice cream and little lemon doughnuts.

Chef Richard Davies **Owner** Exclusive Hotels **Times** 12.30-2/7-9.30 **Closed** L Mon **Prices** Fixed L 2 course £25, Fixed D 3 course £60, Tasting menu £72, Service added but optional 12.5% **Wines** 270 bottles over £30, 29 bottles under £30, 12 by glass **Notes** Tasting menu 7 course, Sunday L, Vegetarian menu, Dress restrictions, Smart casual, Civ Wed 100 **Seats** 60, Pr/dining room 120 **Children** Portions, Menu **Parking** 100

The Park Restaurant

COLERNE MAP 4 ST87

Modern British V NOTABLE WINE LIST

Adventurous cooking in a stately home

☎ 01225 742777
Lucknam Park Hotel & Spa SN14 8AZ
e-mail: reservations@lucknampark.co.uk
web: www.lucknampark.co.uk
dir: M4 junct 17, A350 to Chippenham, then A420 towards Bristol for 3m. At Ford left towards Colerne. In 4m right into Doncombe Ln, then 300yds on right

The Lucknam Park experience is one to savour: beginning with an impressive approach along a tree-lined driveway, the anticipation builds until you reach the stunning Palladian mansion. Sitting serenely in 500 acres of lush parkland, it is a truly stately pile: built in the late 17th century by a wealthy cloth merchant with a sideline in tobacco importing, it has passed from one well-heeled family to another down the centuries, only becoming corporately owned in the 1980s. Once you're within the walls, the ambience is one of pure indulgence, with antiques, oil paintings and opulent fabrics sprinkled around with gay abandon. For the sybaritically inclined, there's the obligatory luxury spa and all manner of contemporary accoutrements. The house's erstwhile ballroom is an appropriate setting for the elegant restaurant, The Park, where swagged silk drapes and crystal

chandeliers frame garden views and the colour palette is tastefully unassertive. The formidably talented Hywel Jones continues to challenge preconceptions of staid country-house fine dining by delivering confident, brilliantly conceived modern British cooking. Liberally larded with luxury ingredients, the menu takes some serious digestion as dishes can be complex and there are plenty of them, but rest assured that you're in for a series of immaculately-presented plates of food realised with top-level technical virtuosity. The classicism of torchon of duck foie gras might be updated by bringing on board modish accompaniments such as pickled pear and chamomile jelly, while main course could bring an upmarket 'surf and turf' combination of roast line-caught sea bass and glazed chicken wings supported by Jerusalem artichokes, leek fondue, autumn truffles and hazelnut pesto. When game is in season, there might be pot-roast grey leg partridge with creamed Brussels sprouts, Morteau sausage, salt-baked potato and pan-fried foie gras. Desserts are equally entertaining confections - perhaps glazed passionfruit cream with lemongrass, lime leaf and mango.

Chef Hywel Jones **Owner** Lucknam Park Hotels Ltd **Times** 1-3/6.30-10 Closed Mon, L Tue-Sat, D Sun **Prices** Fixed D 3 course £70-£90, Tasting menu £90, Service optional **Wines** 15 by glass **Notes** Gourmand

menu available from £90, Sunday L, Vegetarian menu, Dress restrictions, Jacket & tie preferred, no jeans, Civ Wed 110 **Seats** 80, Pr/dining room 30 **Children** Portions, Menu **Parking** 80

Save on Hotels. Book at theAA.com/hotel

WILTSHIRE 497 ENGLAND

CORSHAM *continued*

The Methuen Arms

@@ British, European 🍴

Gimmick-free modern cookery

☎ 01249 717060
2 High St SN13 0HB
e-mail: info@themethuenarms.com
web: www.themethuenarms.com
dir: M4 junct 17 onto A350 towards Chippenham, at rdbt exit onto A4 towards Bath. 1m past lights, at next rdbt turn sharp left onto Pickwick Rd, 0.5m on left

The Methuen Arms is looking good after a classy refurb relaunched the place as a contemporary boutique inn and put the handsome porticoed Georgian house back in action at the hub of Corsham village life. Bare elm floorboards, log fires, ancient beams and exposed stone walls all add up to a rustic-chic look, there are hand-pulled real ales at the bar, and the extensive menu of confident up-to-date dishes is just what we like to eat these days. The kitchen has taken a stance against foams and swipes, and promises top-grade local ingredients treated without fuss. Expect the likes of duck, pigeon and pork terrine with Cumberland sauce, followed by slow-roasted Longhorn brisket with butter beans, sauté spinach, and sherry vinegar and caper sauce; fish fans might find roast monkfish in a Provençal partnership with aubergine ratatouille, olive oil mash and olive dressing. Desserts run to treacle tart with Wiltshire honey and yoghurt ice cream.

Chef Piero Boi **Owner** Still family **Times** 12-3/6-10 **Prices** Fixed L 2 course £15.50, Fixed D 3 course £24.95, Starter £5.95-£10.50, Main £14.50-£21.50, Dessert £5.50-£6.95, Service included **Wines** 29 bottles over £30, 37 bottles under £30, 14 by glass **Notes** Sunday L, Vegetarian available **Seats** 60, Pr/dining room 20 **Children** Portions, Menu **Parking** 40

Cricklade House

@@ Modern British NEW

Country-house dining in a Wiltshire conservatory

☎ 01793 750751
Common Hill SN6 6HA
e-mail: reception@crickladehotel.co.uk
web: www.crickladehotel.co.uk
dir: A419 onto B4040. Left at clock tower. Right at rdbt. Hotel 0.5m up hill on left

Built at the turn of the last century, Cricklade is a handsome country house on the edge of the Cotswolds. A flight of steps sweeps up from the lawns towards an original conservatory that runs across the full extent of the façade, its elevated position ensuring panoramic views over the acres of rolling golf course and Wiltshire downland. It's a delightful prospect for a light evening, and if the décor looks a touch retro, that's all in keeping with the period style. The menus are not about retro nostalgia at all but more the tried-and-true formula of gentle country-house cooking, which scores some notable successes. The in-vogue pairing of goats' cheese and beetroot produces fine contrast and visual appeal, garnished as it is with celeriac remoulade and dressed in aged balsamic. Main course might turn up simply cooked fish, such as a whole grilled lemon sole with prawn butter sauce, or pedigree meat like slow-cooked pork belly with a crisp-fried beignet, creamed potato and thyme-scented jus. Great citric zing brings a dessert of traditional key lime pie with lemon sherbet ice into pin-sharp focus.

Chef Aaron Conolly **Owner** Ambienza Ltd **Times** 12-2/7-9.30 **Prices** Fixed L 2 course fr £12.50, Fixed D 3 course fr £32.50, Service optional **Wines** 23 bottles over £30, 25 bottles under £30, 7 by glass **Notes** Sunday L, Vegetarian available **Children** Portions, Menu **Parking** 100

The Red Lion Inn

@ Modern British NEW 🍴

Hearty food in a beer-oriented inn

☎ 01793 750776
74 High St SN6 6JD
e-mail: info@theredlioncricklade.co.uk
dir: Just off A419 between Swindon & Cheltenham, 10m from M4 junct 15

Let's give a big cheer for beer, for The Red Lion is a temple to all things hoppy. This place really takes beer seriously: it has its own Hop Kettle micro brewery (where plans are afoot to install a chef's table), and offers dozens of hand-pulled and bottled artisan beers, which come with tasting notes and food matching suggestions. Choose between the traditionally pubby bar for pub

---

classics done right, or the contemporary country-chic look of the dining room, where the kitchen deals in the sort of switched-on, ingredients-led dishes that make you want to eat it all. Starters such as terrine of locally shot game, quince purée, and toasted home-made bread, or locally foraged pied bleu and grey oyster mushrooms with garlic butter on toast, show the style, and as the pub rears its own pigs, why not follow with a pork chop with grain mustard mash, broccoli, and honey-glazed carrots?

Chef Chris White **Owner** Tom Gee **Times** 12-2.30/6.30-9 **Prices** Starter £5-£6.50, Main £10-£22.95, Dessert £5-£6, Service added but optional 10% **Wines** 7 bottles over £30, 24 bottles under £30, 9 by glass **Notes** £12.95-£19.95, Vegetarian available **Seats** 40, Pr/dining room 15 **Children** Portions, Menu **Parking** On street

---

The Bear Hotel

@@ Modern British, European 🍴

Contemporary cooking in an elegant hotel

☎ 01380 722444
2-3 Market Place SN10 1HS
e-mail: info@thebearhotel.net
web: www.thebearhotel.net
dir: In town centre, follow Market Place signs

There has been a hostelry of one sort or another on this site since medieval times, but The Bear really came up in the world in the 18th century, when the Lawrence family acquired it. They were soon welcoming George III and Queen Charlotte, and the honour-roll of famous names has barely abated since. Its restaurant, Lambtons, is named after a painting by the Lawrences' most famous scion, the portraitist Sir Thomas. It's an elegant space, with smartly clothed tables, polished silver and chandeliers. Adam Harty's cooking plies a popular line, mixing modern European influences with classical technique. Flavour combinations are sharply defined, as in starters of cured salmon with crab mayonnaise and fennel coleslaw, or pressed pig's head, foie gras and apple with thin toast. Some enterprising things are done with fish, in main courses such as brill with lobster ravioli in a shellfish essence and basil syrup. A study in citrus juxtaposes lemon tart, lime posset and grapefruit sorbet, or there may be apple and toffee variations. A fine selection of unpasteurised English farmhouse cheeses looks tempting too.

Chef Adam Harty **Owner** Craneview (Roundway) Ltd **Times** 12-2.30/7-9.30 Closed Mon-Thu, L Fri-Sat, D Sun **Prices** Service optional **Wines** 14 bottles over £30, 41 bottles under £30, 16 by glass **Notes** £19-£22.50, Vegetarian available, Dress restrictions, Smart casual **Seats** 50, Pr/dining room 16 **Children** Portions, Menu **Parking** 14

The Harrow at Little Bedwyn

LITTLE BEDWYN — MAP 5 SU26

Modern British V NOTABLE WINE LIST

A shining beacon of quality food and wine in deepest Wiltshire

☎ 01672 870871
SN8 3JP
e-mail: reservations@harrowinn.co.uk
web: www.theharrowatlittlebedwyn.com
dir: Between Marlborough & Hungerford, well signed

The Harrow may sound like a village pub, and the location near the Kennet and Avon Canal in deepest Wiltshire would appear to support that proposition, but under the conscientious stewardship of chef-proprietor Roger Jones and his wife Sue, the place has been transformed into a shining beacon of culinary high achievement. A modest creeper-draped, red and grey brick exterior belies a tastefully made-over interior: a double-sided wood-burning stove adds cosiness to the interlinked dining rooms, a tawny palette is easy on the eye, original floorboards and tiles add period character, and high-backed leather chairs at smartly-dressed tables make a statement of serious intent. And if the Riedel wine glasses seem a touch OTT, you should be aware that the Joneses are serious wine experts. Now hitting its 15th anniversary, the place has plenty to celebrate: the food is a hymn to simplicity, driven by a sincere passion for the quality, freshness and

integrity of raw ingredients, and this admirable ethos means that what leaves the kitchen is gimmick- and fad-free, and crafted with a rare level of technical skill that allows each component to taste forthrightly of itself. Juxtapositions are fundamentally sound: a trinity of foie gras, scallop and black pudding might raise the curtain, ahead of a riff on four-week-hung Highland beef (fillet and 24-hour-braised cheek, tongue, shin and oxtail) matched with horseradish potato cake and king's cabbage. On the fish front, grilled line-caught turbot is married with the bold flavour of hen-of-the-woods mushrooms, while desserts could include bread-and-butter pudding with rum and prune parfait. As for the wine, the Joneses have put together one of England's premier-league wine lists, so why not put your faith in their knowledge and go with the suggestions that come with everything on the menu?

Chef Roger Jones, John Brown
Owner Roger & Sue Jones
Times 12-3/7-11 Closed Xmas & New Year, Sun-Tue **Prices** Tasting menu £70, Starter £15, Main £30, Dessert £9.50, Service optional **Wines** 750 bottles over £30, 250 bottles under £30, 20 by glass **Notes** Fixed L 5 course & wine £30, Gourmet menu 8 course £75, Vegetarian menu, Dress restrictions, Smart casual **Seats** 34
Children Portions, Menu **Parking** On street

Save on Hotels. Book at theAA.com/hotel

WILTSHIRE 499 ENGLAND

HINDON
Map 4 ST93

The Lamb at Hindon

Traditional British

Comforting cooking in an ancient inn

☎ 01747 820573
High St SP3 6DP
e-mail: info@lambathindon.co.uk
web: www.lambathindon.co.uk
dir: M3 junct 8 onto A303. Exit towards Hindon 4m after Salisbury exit & follow signs to Hindon

In case you are wondering why this 17th-century coaching inn in deepest Wiltshire has the feel of a Scottish hunting lodge, that could be because it is owned by the group that includes Boisdale of Belgravia (see entry) and brings the same signature Scottish-accented style, including north-of-the-border ingredients to rub shoulders with produce sourced from closer to home. Inside, it is all heavy beams, flagstoned floors, warm red walls, open fires in inglenooks, and an impressive listing of wines and malts to promote a convivial ambience. The kitchen deals in hearty contemporary comforts along the lines of Bury black pudding served with a poached hen's egg, chorizo, bacon and mushrooms to start, followed perhaps by pot-roasted loin of pork with cider and Calvados sauce, apple purée and crackling, or breast and confit leg of guinea fowl with sun-dried cranberry and Cognac sauce. A dark Belgian chocolate and cocoa liqueur torte with crème fraîche keeps the comfort factor topped up to the end.

Chef Andrzej Piechocki **Owner** Ranald Macdonald (Boisdale plc) **Times** 12-2.30/6-9.30 **Prices** Starter £4.50-£9, Main £7.75-£18.50, Dessert £5-£8.50, Service added but optional 10% **Wines** 9 by glass **Notes** Sunday L £11.95-£19.95, Vegetarian available **Seats** 52, Pr/dining room 32 **Children** Portions, Menu **Parking** 16

HORNINGSHAM
Map 4 ST84

The Bath Arms at Longleat

Modern, Traditional British

Charming boutique hotel with accomplished cooking

☎ 01985 844308
Longleat Estate BA12 7LY
e-mail: enquiries@batharms.co.uk
dir: A36 Warminster. At Cotley Hill rdbt 2nd exit (Longleat), Cleyhill rdbt 1st exit. Through Hitchcombe Bottom, right at x-rds. Hotel on the green

A solid-looking stone property covered in creepers, The Bath Arms is in a peaceful village within the Longleat Estate. The hotel's aim is to create an atmosphere of 'informality, fun, friendliness and efficiency' and it seems to succeed on all counts, from a welcoming bar with its own popular menu and local ales on handpump to a dining room with chandeliers and king-sized candles where young staff are friendly and eager. Local supplies are at the heart of the operation, the menu focusing on game in season: game sausage (actually more akin to partridge mousse) with deeply flavoured apple jelly, followed by roast pigeon with wild mushrooms and braised chicory, say. Dishes are marked by an absence of fuss and frills but the results hit the spot: duck pudding with pickled cherries and walnuts, followed by pan-fried sea bass with brown shrimps and white bean cassoulet, and, to finish, rhubarb and coconut crumble with coconut ice cream.

Times 12-2.30/7-9

LITTLE BEDWYN
Map 5 SU26

The Harrow at Little Bedwyn

— see opposite

LOWER CHICKSGROVE
Map 4 ST92

Compasses Inn

Modern British

Broadly appealing menu in an ancient inn

☎ 01722 714318
SP3 6NB
e-mail: thecompasses@aol.com
web: www.thecompassesinn.com
dir: Off A30 signed Lower Chicksgrove, 1st left onto Lagpond Ln, single-track lane to village

Approach down narrow lanes and catch sight of the thatched roof: it's a pub and no mistake. And it won't disappoint on the inside either: beams, standing timbers, open fires, nooks and crannies and high-backed wooden booths, and menus written up on blackboards. It's a friendly sort of place, very much used and appreciated by the local community, and food-wise it is most definitely a cut above. Whether you eat in the bar or the adjacent dining area, you can expect a mix of traditional favourites and more modish things, with local produce figuring prominently, including vegetables from nearby Rowswell's Farm. Start with pan-fried pigeon breast with a parsnip gratin, beetroot mousse and red wine glaze, and follow on with a traditional lamb hotpot or something like pan-fried fillets of sea bass with mussel and saffron cream sauce. Strawberry tart with Pimm's sorbet is a summertime treat among desserts.

Chef Dave Cousin, Geoff Mowlem **Owner** Alan & Susie Stoneham **Times** 12-3/6-11 Closed 25-26 Dec, L Mon

(Jan-Mar) **Prices** Starter £5.25-£8.50, Main £8.50-£17.95, Dessert £5.95-£6.95, Service optional **Wines** 2 bottles over £30, 28 bottles under £30, 8 by glass **Notes** Sunday L £11.50-£14.95, Vegetarian available **Seats** 50, Pr/dining room 14 **Children** Portions, Menu **Parking** 35

MALMESBURY
Map 4 ST98

Old Bell Hotel

Modern British, French

Nearly eight centuries of service to Malmesbury

☎ 01666 822344
Abbey Row SN16 0BW
e-mail: info@oldbellhotel.com
web: www.oldbellhotel.com
dir: M4 junct 17, follow A429 north. Left at 1st rdbt. Left at T-junct. Hotel next to Abbey

Laying claim to being the longest-serving hotel in England (we're talking 1220 here), the Old Bell's wisteria-clad, honey-hued Cotswold stone exterior certainly looks the part. It's an effortlessly charming place, with a rather grand dining room (high ceilings, mullioned windows, white linen) that adds a sense of occasion. But the accomplished kitchen is not stuck in the past, serving up modern British dishes underpinned by a classical theme. Interesting flavour combinations are fashioned from quality produce and delivered with cheffy presentation; sautéed monkfish, perhaps, served with cep consommé, oxtail and spinach to open proceedings, while to follow, rabbit loin might be wrapped in Parma ham accompanied by rabbit ragoût, fondant potato and carrots. Finish on a light note with Muscat mousse with almond foam and crème fraîche sorbet.

Chef Richard Synan **Owner** The Old Bell Hotel Ltd **Times** 12.15-2/7-9.30 Closed D Sun-Mon **Prices** Fixed D 3 course £42.50, Tasting menu £52.50, Service optional **Wines** 89 bottles over £30, 71 bottles under £30, 13 by glass **Notes** Sunday L, Vegetarian available, Dress restrictions, Smart dress preferred, Civ Wed 90 **Seats** 60, Pr/dining room 48 **Children** Portions, Menu **Parking** 35

Whatley Manor Hotel and Spa

— see page 500

Whatley Manor Hotel and Spa

Modern French 🍷 NOTABLE WINE LIST

Technically brilliant contemporary French cooking in a luxury spa hotel

☎ 01666 822888
Easton Grey SN16 0RB
e-mail: reservations@whatleymanor.com
web: www.whatleymanor.com
dir: M4 junct 17, follow signs to Malmesbury, continue over 2 rdbts. Follow B4040 & signs for Sherston, hotel 2m on left

It doesn't matter if you arrive under grey skies or in brilliant sunshine, whether it is snowing, drizzling, or if mist has descended over this part of Wiltshire: whatever the British weather can throw at you, Whatley Manor will look majestic, guaranteed. Once through the electric gates and into the cobbled courtyard, the honey-stone Cotswold manor awaits and there's every reason to feel content with the world. It's the kind of five-star country-house hotel that is comfortable in its own skin. Sure, it's posh and very luxurious, but Whatley Manor is the kind of place you could spend the rest of your life (if they'd let you, and if you could afford it). It stands in 12 acres of meadows, woodland and gardens, where you could take a different stroll every day of the year if you wished, and it has a luxurious spa, and even a cinema, to while away a few more hours in between

meals. And to the food. The kitchen is run by Martin Burge, a chef with a mightily impressive CV and the man who has made Whatley a culinary force to be reckoned with. He overseas Le Mazot brasserie, with its Swiss chalet vibe, where you can tuck into a wonderful blade of beef with buttered cabbage and a red wine jus infused with thyme, and The Dining Room, where the culinary activity is taken to another level (a very high level indeed in fact). The Dining Room is a quietly refined, understated space with an unusual pale bamboo floor, buttermilk walls, and subtle lighting. The cooking is French-focused, contemporary and beautifully judged, with every flavour and texture on the plate there for a reason, nothing out of place. A first course dish of foie gras - poached and roasted - is dressed with compressed pear and ginger and served with a sticky Sauternes sauce, or go for the braised snails set in a garlic cream and topped with a red wine sauce infused with veal kidney. Fabulous stuff. Main-course fillet of veal is roasted and poached and comes in the company of slow-braised cheek, textures of hazelnuts, caramelised sweetbreads and a Madeira sauce. The razor sharp technical skills and thorough good sense of the kitchen is further revealed at dessert stage: prune and orange soufflé, for example, with prune and Armagnac ice cream, or warm chocolate fondant with textures of caramel and

banana ice cream. A class act from top to bottom.

Chef Martin Burge **Owner** Christian & Alix Landolt **Times** 7-10 Closed Mon-Tue, L all week **Prices** Tasting menu £110, Service added but optional 10% **Wines** 350 bottles over £30, 5 bottles under £30, 16 by glass **Notes** ALC menu £85, Wine matching with tasting menu £65 extra, Vegetarian available, Civ Wed 120 **Seats** 40, Pr/dining room 30 **Children** Portions **Parking** 120

OAKSEY   Map 4 ST99

The Wheatsheaf at Oaksey

◉◉ Modern British ✪

Intelligent modish food in a lovely pub setting

☎ 01666 577348
Wheatsheaf Ln SN16 9TB
e-mail: info@thewheatsheafatoaksey.co.uk
dir: From Swindon A419 take Spine Rd E then continue onto Spine Rd W to Oaksey. From Kemble A429 at Airfield x-rds head to Oaksey on 'The Street'

This upmarket village inn on the fringes of the Cotswolds has oodles of character: there are logs piled by roaring fires, well-worn armchairs, and crosses carved into the ancient beams to ward off witches, should you be troubled by such cares. Jack Robson-Burrell has taken over the reins of the family business, and is certainly a safe pair of hands, having been trained at The Ritz. You could keep things as simple as burgers, although here the humble fast food staple is elevated to gourmet status with its own menu taking in versions made from local venison with sweet onion relish, Gloucestershire Old Spot pork with smoked apple sauce, or melt-in-the-mouth Wagyu beef. Otherwise, refined modern British pub food is the order of the day, with everything made in-house, from smoked salmon to ice cream and bread. Slow-braised pork with a fried bantam egg and red wine sauce could be one way to start, then pan-fried Cornish hake with spinach, new potatoes and sauce vierge. It all ends happily with Baileys cheesecake with chocolate cream.

Chef Jack Robson-Burrell **Owner** Tony & Holly Robson-Burrell **Times** 12-2/6.30-9.30 Closed Mon, D Sun **Prices** Starter £4.50-£7.50, Main £9-£19.50, Dessert £5-£6.50, Service optional **Wines** 16 bottles over £30, 18 bottles under £30, 10 by glass **Notes** £5 lunch menu available Tue-Sat, Sunday L £12.50-£15, Vegetarian available **Seats** 50, Pr/dining room 8 **Children** Portions, Menu **Parking** 15

PURTON   Map 5 SU08

The Pear Tree at Purton

◉◉ Modern British

Charming conservatory setting in a former vicarage

☎ 01793 772100
Church End SN5 4ED
e-mail: stay@peartreepurton.co.uk
dir: From M4 junct 16, follow signs to Purton. Turn right at Bestone shop, hotel 0.25m on right

It may sound like a humble pub, but this former Cotswold-stone vicarage on the edge of an old Saxon village is actually a country-house hotel with fabulous grounds which include a flower meadow, wetlands and a vineyard (three of their wines are on offer in the restaurant). Having reached a landmark 25 years here, owners Francis and Anne Young have made their mark and the hotel has lots to offer, from comfortable rooms to conference and wedding facilities, and the Conservatory Restaurant with its pleasing garden views and ambitious, gently modern menus. Smooth duck liver parfait is served as a first course with brioche and cauliflower pickle, followed perhaps by breast of wood pigeon in red wine flavoured with juniper and black treacle. A fish main course might be paupiettes of lemon sole served with a salmon and lemongrass mousseline and vegetable spaghetti, and among desserts, lemon and basil cheesecake with limoncello ice cream hits the spot.

Chef Alan Postill **Owner** Francis & Anne Young **Times** 12-2/7-9.15 Closed 26 Dec **Prices** Fixed L 2 course £15, Fixed D 3 course £35.50, Service optional **Wines** 36 bottles over £30, 44 bottles under £30, 11 by glass **Notes** Sunday L, Vegetarian available, Dress restrictions, Smart casual, no shorts **Seats** 50, Pr/dining room 50 **Children** Portions **Parking** 70

RAMSBURY   Map 5 SU27

The Bell at Ramsbury

◉ Modern British, European NEW

Ambitious cooking in made-over country inn

☎ 01672 520230
The Square SN8 2PE
e-mail: reservations@thebellramsbury.com
dir: M4 junct 14, A338 to Hungerford. B4192 towards Swindon. Left to Ramsbury

New owners have rung in a new era for the 300-year-old Bell. Dazzlingly whitewashed outside, and revamped in an almost Scandinavian-looking, pared-back modern style, the interior is what you'd expect from a smart contemporary food-oriented inn. Ramsbury Brewery ales, hand-pulled at the bar, go nicely with pub classics like daily pies, burgers, and fish and triple-cooked chips, or you could trade up to the more formal restaurant, where the deal is an ambitious output of dishes built on local materials, bolstered by home-grown produce from the kitchen garden and game from the Ramsbury Estate. Pan-fried foie gras with apricot and hazelnut crunch, mini brioche loaf and Sauternes gel is a typical starter that might be followed by bacon-wrapped tenderloin of free-range pork with celeriac and smoked bacon gratin, and pear and vanilla sauce. For dessert, there could be lemon meringue parfait with basil sorbet.

Chef Duncan Jones **Times** 12-3/6-9.30 Closed D Sun **Prices** Prices not confirmed Groups min 8 service 12.5%

ROWDE   Map 4 ST96

The George & Dragon

◉◉ Modern British V ✪

Old coaching inn with the focus on seafood

☎ 01380 723053
High St SN10 2PN
e-mail: thegandd@tiscali.co.uk
dir: On A342, 1m from Devizes towards Chippenham

This 16th-century coaching inn specialises in seafood brought up every day from St Mawes in Cornwall. It's a wonderfully atmospheric place with bags of period character, including a Tudor rose carved into one of the ancient beams. You can eat in the small bar or equally diminutive restaurant, which sports antique rugs on wooden floors and unclothed wooden tables. The food keeps things pleasingly straightforward and it's not entirely about seafood. You might kick off with fishy hors d'oeuvres or salt and pepper chilli squid salad, followed by whole grilled mackerel with anchovy butter, or salmon fillet teriyaki with soy, ginger and spinach. A meaty alternative might be roast rack of lamb with mint pea purée and red wine jus, with the reassuringly named ye olde lemon posset for afters.

Chef Christopher Day **Owner** Christopher Day, Philip & Michelle Hale **Times** 12-3/7-11 Closed D Sun **Prices** Fixed L 2 course fr £16.50, Fixed D 3 course fr £19.50, Starter £4.50-£7.50, Main £9.50-£21.50, Dessert £4.50-£7.50, Service added but optional 10% **Wines** 9 by glass **Notes** Sunday L, Vegetarian menu **Seats** 35 **Children** Portions, Menu **Parking** 14

SALISBURY
Map 5 SU12

Best Western Red Lion Hotel

⊛ Modern European

Contemporary cooking in an 800-year-old inn

☎ 01722 323334
Milford St SP1 2AN
e-mail: reception@the-redlion.co.uk
web: www.the-redlion.co.uk
dir: In city centre close to Guildhall Square

Whether or not the venerable Red Lion really is England's oldest surviving purpose-built hotel is something the historians can argue over, but you'll certainly find little to fault in the atmospheric vibes, ancient wattle-and-daub walls and gnarled beams of the Vine dining room, which is named in honour of the 300-year-old Virginia creeper in the courtyard. Hearty, uncomplicated flavours prevail on a menu of modern European ideas that could get under way with oak-smoked duck breast partnered with foie gras brûlée and apple and radish salad, followed by a main course of confit pork belly with pork and foie gras ballottine, pan-fried pork fillet, roasted pear, mash, choucroute, and mustard cream. At the end, perhaps rhubarb and custard iced parfait with popping candy, raspberry purée and raspberry crumble topping.

Times 12.30-2/6-9.30 Closed L Mon-Sat

Salisbury Seafood & Steakhouse

⊛ Modern, International 🖑

The clue is the name

☎ 01722 417411 & 424110
Milford Hall Hotel, 206 Castle St SP1 3TE
e-mail: info@salisburyseafoodandsteakhouse.co.uk
web: www.salisburyseafoodandsteakhouse.co.uk
dir: From A36 at rdbt on Salisbury ring road, right onto Churchill Way East. At St Marks rdbt left onto Churchill Way North to next rdbt, left in Castle St

Just a gentle stroll from Salisbury's historic market square, Milford Hall Hotel is a red-brick Georgian mansion on the outside, with a stylish blend of period elegance and clean-cut contemporary style within. In the aptly named Salisbury Seafood & Steakhouse, cream and brown leather high-backed chairs, wooden floors and walls lined with suede and stacked with wine bottles make a stylish setting for a hearty repertoire of surf and turf dishes. Old favourites strike a retro note - perhaps chicken liver and brandy terrine with Cumberland sauce to get things going, followed by a properly aged and chargrilled steak, or slow-braised beef sirloin with roast potatoes, shallots and a blue cheese, port and chive jus. On the surf side, you could go for a whole grilled plaice with crab, lime and ginger stuffing and lemongrass oil or chargrilled salmon steak with dill and lemon butter.

Chef Chris Gilbert **Owner** Simon Hughes **Times** 12-2/6-10 Closed 26 Dec, D 25 Dec **Prices** Fixed L 2 course £9.95, Fixed D 2 course £19.95, Starter £5.25-£8.25, Main £9.95-£22.50, Dessert £5.50-£7.25, Service optional, Groups min 6 service 10% **Wines** 4 bottles over £30, 25

bottles under £30, 12 by glass **Notes** Sunday L £8.95-£14.95, Vegetarian available, Dress restrictions, Smart casual **Seats** 55, Pr/dining room 20 **Children** Portions, Menu **Parking** 60

STANTON ST QUINTIN
Map 4 ST97

Stanton Manor Hotel

⊛ Modern British 🖑

Eclectic modern cooking in a rebuilt Elizabethan manor

☎ 01666 837552
SN14 6DQ
web: www.stantonmanor.co.uk
dir: M4 junct 17 onto A429 Malmesbury/Cirencester, in 200yds 1st left signed Stanton St Quintin. Hotel entrance on left just after church

Just off the M4 near Chippenham, Stanton Manor is a greystone Victorian rebuild of an Elizabethan manor house once owned by Elizabeth's financier, Lord Burghley. A dining room done in mint-green with Scandinavian-look light wood chairs and quality table linen opts for a cool contemporary feel, rather than heritage chintz, and the menus are situated firmly in the present day too, drawing European traditions into an eclectic mix. Start with smoked halibut served with horseradish mousse, pickled beetroot and capers, as a prelude to roast venison loin with celeriac and kale in red wine jus, or a pasta dish such as saffron cannelloni filled with chestnut mushrooms, goats' cheese and spinach, with truffle-oiled rocket salad. Comfort flavours stalk the dessert menu, in the likes of coffee pannacotta with caramelised banana and crushed walnuts. Home-made breads are a good sign, as are the thoroughbred West Country cheeses that come with cider chutney.

Chef Christopher Box **Owner** Robert David **Times** 12-2.30/7-9 Closed for wedding receptions **Prices** Fixed L 2 course £14.95-£16.95, Fixed D 3 course £29.95-£32.50, Starter £5.50-£6.50, Main £19.50-£22.50, Dessert £5.50-£6.50, Service optional **Wines** 4 by glass **Notes** Sunday L, Vegetarian available, Dress restrictions, Smart casual **Seats** 26, Pr/dining room 80 **Children** Portions, Menu **Parking** 60

SWINDON
Map 5 SU18

Chiseldon House Hotel

⊛ Modern European

Unfussy cooking in a Regency manor house

☎ 01793 741010
New Rd, Chiseldon SN4 0NE
e-mail: welcome@chiseldonhouse.com
web: www.chiseldonhouse.com
dir: M4 junct 15, A346 signed Marlborough. After 0.5m turn right onto B4500 for 0.25m, hotel on right

Chiseldon is an elegant Regency-era manor house in the Marlborough Downs, in the embrace of beautiful gardens where wedding parties are often to be found roaming. Inside, it is a relaxed and traditional place, with dining in the romantically candlelit Orangery restaurant. A young

front-of-house crew makes sure that everyone is at their ease, while the kitchen brigade has an eye for good-quality local produce, which it brings together in uncomplicated, tried-and-true combinations - duck liver parfait with apricot chutney and melba toast being a case in point. No horses will be scared either by a main course of roast chicken breast with fondant potato, crispy pancetta and thyme jus, but it is all nicely-balanced, flavoursome and comforting stuff. Rounding things off, there may be a bitter chocolate tart with vanilla pannacotta.

Chef Robert Harwood **Owner** Mark & David Pennells **Times** 12-2/7-9 **Prices** Fixed L 2 course fr £16.95, Fixed D 3 course fr £19.95, Starter £5.50-£7.50, Main £14.95-£22.95, Dessert £5.95-£9.95, Service optional **Wines** 7 by glass **Notes** Brunch served BHs, Sunday L, Vegetarian available, Civ Wed 85 **Seats** 65, Pr/dining room 32 **Children** Portions **Parking** 85

WARMINSTER
Map 4 ST84

The Bishopstrow Hotel & Spa

⊛ Modern British NEW V

Modish British cooking in a light-filled elegant Regency house

☎ 01985 212312
Boreham Rd BA12 9HH
e-mail: info@bishopstrow.co.uk
dir: From Warminster take B3414 (Salisbury). Hotel signed

Built towards the end of the Regency period, alongside the River Wylye, the creeper-covered Bishopstrow is a Cotswold-stone house that has been discreetly reconstituted as a modern spa hotel, only a few miles from the lions at Longleat. The tone throughout is airy and elegant, with pastel hues and light from full-drop windows pervading the dining rooms. Andy Britton has cooked in glam hotels all over, from the Caribbean to the Channel Islands, and offers a style of modish, but not confrontational, cooking. Expect poached trout with crabcakes and minted pea mousse, ahead of roast rack and stuffed leg of rabbit with aubergine purée and tarragon foam, or Longleat venison - loin and haunch - with pickled mushrooms in Stilton and juniper sauce. Asian spices lift lime-leaf crème brûlée into the exotic, helped along by cardamom ice cream, or there may be dark chocolate marquise with raspberry vodka sorbet. Local cheeses come with apple chutney and Bath Olivers.

Chef Andrew Britton **Owner** Longleat Enterprises Ltd **Times** 12-2/7-9.30 **Prices** Starter £6.50-£7.50, Main £11-£21.50, Dessert £6.50-£7.50, Service added but optional 10% **Wines** 50 bottles over £30, 5 bottles under £30, 8 by glass **Notes** Sunday L £19.95, Vegetarian menu, Dress restrictions, Smart casual, Civ Wed 70 **Seats** 65, Pr/dining room 28 **Children** Portions, Menu **Parking** 70

The Dove Inn

British, Mediterranean

Good simple pub cooking in the Wylye Valley

☎ 01985 850109
Corton BA12 0SZ
e-mail: info@thedove.co.uk
dir: A303 off A36, Salisbury to Bath road

A Victorian pub in the village of Corton, The Dove retains its bucolic appeal, with oak and flagstone floors inside, and an atmosphere of happy banter. A conservatory-style restaurant is as mod as the cons get, and outdoor tables make the most of fine days. Cask ales and decent wines lift the spirits of drinkers, and the approach to food is exactly what we expect - locally based, nice and simple, and cooked with care and attention. Blackboard fish specials supplement the printed menu, which also features beer-battered haddock with minty peas as a stalwart. A brace of giant field mushrooms stuffed with port-laced Stilton on toasted ciabatta might set the ball rolling, and be followed by fine, tender-as-anything lamb shank braised in spiced red wine, served with garlic mash and buttered greens. A lighter-than-usual strawberry cheesecake has a pleasing moussey texture and crumbly biscuit base, and comes with vibrant strawberry coulis.

Chef Bruno Fitas **Owner** William Harrison-Allan **Times** 12-3/6-11 **Prices** Prices not confirmed Service optional **Wines** 14 bottles under £30, 6 by glass **Notes** Sunday L, Vegetarian available **Seats** 60 **Children** Portions, Menu **Parking** 30

WORCESTERSHIRE

BEWDLEY   Map 10 SO77

The Mug House Inn

Modern British

Appealing modern cooking on the Severn

☎ 01299 402543
12 Severnside North DY12 2EE
e-mail: drew@mughousebewdley.co.uk
web: www.mughousebewdley.co.uk
dir: B4190 to Bewdley. On river, just over bridge on right

Its setting on the bank of the River Severn, in this picturesque town, could hardly be bettered. There's a traditional beamed bar dispensing real ales, and the smart Angry Chef restaurant with a lobster tank - the crustacean is the house speciality. The kitchen pulls off some ambitious ideas with impressive results, turning out starters like seared scallops on spinach purée in laverbread sauce, and quail Kiev with celeriac purée and parsley cream. 'Cod and chips' proclaims the menu, but here it comes as baked fillet coated in herb and garlic breadcrumbs served with remoulade sauce, sweet potato chips and minted pea purée. Elsewhere, the attention might be drawn to a well-considered mélange of pork (roast loin, slow-roast belly, as croquettes with apple and sage) served with black pudding, thyme-spiked onion purée, mustard mash and warm slaw. Pudding is a must when something like cinnamon pannacotta with pear compôte in mulled cider is on offer.

Chef Drew Clifford, Zac Birchley **Owner** Drew Clifford **Times** 12-2.30/6.30-9 Closed D Sun **Prices** Fixed L 2 course fr £12.95, Fixed D 3 course fr £15.95, Starter £3.95-£6.95, Main £11.75-£29.50, Dessert fr £5.95, Service optional **Wines** 10 by glass **Notes** Fixed D Mon-Thu only, Fixed L Mon-Sat only, Sunday L, Vegetarian available, Dress restrictions, Smart casual **Seats** 26, Pr/dining room 12 **Parking** Car park 100mtrs along river

---

Royal Forester Country Inn

Modern European

Contemporary dining in medieval inn

☎ 01299 266286
Callow Hill DY14 9XW
e-mail: royalforesterinn@btinternet.com

A sympathetic makeover has brought 21st-century comforts to this 15th-century inn while retaining the best of its venerable features. There's a bar with sofas and a baby grand, and a meandering restaurant full of nooks and crannies, with bare-brick walls and ancient timbers. The menus change daily on the basis of that morning's deliveries, with fish brought up from Cornwall (perhaps grilled tranche of turbot with clams and Parmentier potatoes) and game a speciality in season: perhaps a starter of guinea fowl and tarragon ballottine with pickled carrots and a verjus reduction. Consistently high standards can be seen throughout the wide-ranging menu, from mackerel three ways (pan-seared fillet, spicy tartare and pâté) to monkfish tails roasted with pancetta,

---

served with tomato and herb sauce, or roast duck breast with a damson gin jus, with chocolate bread-and-butter pudding to finish.

Chef Mark Hammond **Owner** Sean McGahern, Maxine Parker **Times** 12-3/6-9.30 **Prices** Fixed L 2 course £9.99-£11.99, Fixed D 3 course £14.99, Starter £4.95-£7.50, Main £14.95-£22, Dessert £4.50-£7.95, Service optional **Wines** 6 by glass **Notes** Gourmet menu with 4 glasses of wine £30 1st Tue of month, Sunday L, Vegetarian available **Seats** 60, Pr/dining room 18 **Children** Portions **Parking** 25

BROADWAY   Map 10 SP03

Dormy House Hotel

Modern British

Creative cooking in an impressive Cotswold house

☎ 01386 852711
Willersey Hill WR12 7LF
e-mail: reservations@dormyhouse.co.uk
web: www.dormyhouse.co.uk
dir: 2m E of Broadway off A44, at top of Fish Hill turn for Saintbury/Picnic area. In 0.5m turn left, hotel on left

In the green welly-wearing heart of the Cotswolds, Dormy House started its life in the 17th century as a lowly farmhouse. Nothing stands still for long in the modern world, so 2013 saw the honey-stone hotel above Broadway close for a megabucks refurbishment which has resulted in a luminous, romantic feel throughout, without sacrificing any of the charm that derives from its ancient oak beams and panelling. The understated contemporary dining room is an airy, open-plan space with views over the Cotswold Hills and a flannel-free menu of imaginative dishes in the modern country-house idiom. The kitchen keeps things refreshingly simple and follows the seasons keenly, coming up with well-judged ideas based on tried-and-true combinations, such as a mousse of crayfish and Cornish scallops with caviar and herb cream, followed by a triumphantly English roast rump of lamb with bubble and squeak, honey-glazed carrots, local sprouts and lamb jus. The skill level stays high all the way through to desserts such as dark chocolate marquise with mango sorbet.

Chef Paul Napper **Owner** Mrs I Philip-Sorensen **Times** 12-2/7-9 **Prices** Fixed D 3 course £40, Service optional **Wines** 71 bottles over £30, 29 bottles under £30, 20 by glass **Notes** Sunday L, Vegetarian available, Dress restrictions, Smart casual, Civ Wed 40 **Seats** 60, Pr/dining room 12 **Children** Portions, Menu **Parking** 70

BROADWAY *continued*

The Lygon Arms

◎◎ Modern British ⏱

Majestic Tudor hotel with 21st-century comforts

☎ 01386 852255
High St WR12 7DU
e-mail: thelygonarms@pumahotels.co.uk
web: www.pumahotels.co.uk
dir: From Evesham take A44 signed Oxford, 5m. Follow Broadway signs. Hotel on left

The old honey-stoned Lygon has borne witness to a great deal of history over its 500 or so years, not least hosting both Oliver Cromwell and his regal adversary, Charles I. These days a smart and rather luxurious country-house hotel, there is much to remind one of times gone by, not least the impressive great hall, with its barrel-vaulted ceiling and minstrels' gallery, which serves as the main restaurant. It is quite a space, with acres of oak panelling, two giant chandeliers (not trad ones though) and tables set with crisp white linen. And in keeping with the building, the cooking is built on classic foundations with an added touch of 21st-century vitality. An open ravioli first course is packed with wild mushrooms, Italian bacon, chestnuts and lentils, and finished with a deftly judged truffle and black vinegar dressing. Next up, perhaps a fillet of turbot with stir-fried kale and spring onions, and beetroots both roasted and puréed. For

dessert, lemon meringue pie with lemon jelly and citrus sorbet is dressed to kill.

Chef Peter Manner **Owner** Puma Hotels Collection **Times** 12-2/7-9.30 Closed L Sat **Prices** Fixed L 2 course £17.50-£20, Fixed D 3 course £39-£45, Starter £10-£15, Main £25-£32, Dessert £6.50-£9.50, Service optional **Wines** 45 bottles over £30, 9 bottles under £30, 16 by glass **Notes** Sunday L, Vegetarian available, Dress restrictions, Smart casual, no jeans, T-shirts or trainers, Civ Wed 100 **Seats** 80, Pr/dining room 110 **Children** Portions, Menu **Parking** 150

Russell's

◎◎ Modern British ⏱

Country-house cooking in a paradise of honey-coloured stone

☎ 01386 853555
20 High St WR12 7DT
e-mail: info@russellsofbroadway.co.uk
dir: A44 follow signs to Broadway, restaurant on High St opposite village green

Is it possible to have a surfeit of honeyed stone? The village of Broadway will certainly test lovers of the idiom to the max, but it looks undeniably lovely, with softly contoured countryside rolling around it to boot. This house was once an exhibition space for the work of furniture designer Sir Gordon Russell, and has settled into its modern role as a welcoming restaurant-with-rooms as though to the manner born. Blessedly free of muzak, the dining room is a relaxing venue furnished in simple contemporary style with bare-wood tables and a menu of appealing English country-house cooking based strongly on local produce. A starter of pressed local pig's head with smoked pineapple and crackling makes the point, though seafood dishes turn to Cornwall for something like scallops with parsnip variations and lemon balm. Main course might be roast breast and confit leg of properly hung pheasant, accompanied by olive oil mash, pancetta, chestnuts and curly kale. The witty dessert of cappuccino crème brûlée served in a coffee cup with a frothy top needs to be left to set a little longer, but good biscotti provide the more assured textural note.

Chef Neil Clarke **Owner** Andrew Riley **Times** 12-2.30/6-9.30 Closed BH Mon, D Sun **Prices** Fixed L 2 course £14.95-£21.95, Fixed D 3 course £17.95, Starter £6-£14, Main £15-£28, Dessert £6-£10.95, Service optional **Wines** 10 bottles under £30, 12 by glass **Notes** Sunday L, Vegetarian available **Seats** 60, Pr/dining room 14 **Children** Portions **Parking** 7

Brockencote Hall Country House Hotel

CHADDESLEY CORBETT   **MAP 10 S087**

Modern British

Up-to-date culinary wizardry in a Victorian manor house

☎ 01562 777876
DY10 4PY
e-mail: info@brockencotehall.com
web: www.brockencotehall.com
dir: M5 junct 4 to A38 Bromsgrove, then A448 just outside village, between Kidderminster & Bromsgrove

Great things are afoot at Brockencote these days. It's a classic Victorian manor-house hotel in the style of a Bordeaux château, sitting in 70 acres of landscaped parkland, complete with ornamental lake, with the gentle undulations of the Malvern Hills as backdrop. Interiors are framed in the Victorian style, but with freshness rather than faded splendour, so that the wood panelling, striped upholstery and Persian rugs look as new-minted as in the days when the place was young. In the Chaddesley dining room, a more modern decorative approach - splotches of claret and rich purple against a stone-grey foundation - is probably right. It creates a nice contrast, lifts the spirits and makes a sympathetic context for Adam Brown's unquestionably up-to-date culinary wizardry. Seafood makes a strong opening statement in the form of a partnering of baby squid and lightly caramelised scallop, dressed with the seeds and puréed flesh of pumpkin, and garnished with crunchy sea purslane. The modern obsession with textural contrasts is given free rein in another opener of roast rabbit fillet with more meat in a cannelloni tube, adorned with golden raisins and new carrots for a sweet taste of spring. Main courses draw on locally farmed meats: duck is exceptionally good, perhaps appearing as breast, leg and seared liver, with braised salsify, puréed chestnuts and chicory in autumn, or in spring as breast and gizzards,

accompanied by new season's morels, sprouting broccoli and a slash of acidity from blood-orange. An equally confident way with fish brings on sea bass with charred fennel, pickled pear and pine nuts, the array of cooking techniques working with the grain of the dish rather than complicating it unduly. Desserts are handled well, from carrot cake with mandarin sorbet and extra cream cheese, to a suite of rhubarb variations, including the hibiscus-scented poached article, sweetened with pistachio.

Times 12-3/6.45-9.45

Save on Hotels. Book at **theAA.com/hotel**

WORCESTERSHIRE 505 **ENGLAND**

BROMSGROVE | Map 10 SO97

The Vernon

◉ Modern European **NEW**

Enticing cooking in revamped 18th-century inn

☎ 01527 821236
Hanbury B60 4DB
e-mail: info@thevernonhanbury.com
web: www.thevernonhanbury.com
dir: A38 onto B4091 Hanbury Road, on junct with B4090

The Vernon reopened in mid-2012 after an extensive - and expensive - revamp, giving a stylishly contemporary sheen to the whole place. There's a good-looking bar with lightwood furniture, a classy restaurant with a wooden floor and chairs upholstered in different-coloured fabrics, and an extensive outdoor area. Food is a serious preoccupation, with the kitchen basing its modern style on fresh local produce. Asparagus in this area is not to be missed, served here with a deep-fried duck egg, parmesan shavings, watercress and truffle oil, an alternative to the full-on flavours of 'cheeky pig terrine' with blood orange, rum-soaked sultanas, carrots and toasted sourdough. Confident handling brings on, among well-judged main courses, succulent pan-fried chicken breast served with broad beans, baby gem, fondant potato and tarragon sauce, and seared sea bass fillets with clams, crushed potatoes, spring onion, mushrooms and lemon oil. Leave room for puddings like chocolate mousse with cherries and pistachio ice cream.

Chef Robert Powell **Owner** Vernon Leisure Ltd
Times 12-3/6-9.30 **Prices** Fixed L 2 course fr £11.95
Notes Sunday L £18.95-£24.95, Vegetarian available
Seats 73, Pr/dining room 8 **Children** Portions, Menu
Parking 20

CHADDESLEY CORBETT | Map 10 SO87

Brockencote Hall Country House Hotel

◉◉◉ *– see opposite*

KIDDERMINSTER | Map 10 SO87

The Granary Hotel & Restaurant

◉◉ Modern British 🍸

Smart, seasonal cooking in a boutique hotel

☎ 01562 777535
Heath Ln, Shenstone DY10 4BS
e-mail: info@granary-hotel.co.uk
web: www.granary-hotel.co.uk
dir: On A450 between Worcester & Stourbridge. 2m from Kidderminster

Close to the Midlands motorway arteries, yet nicely located in the countryside on the fringes of Kidderminster, the boutique-style Granary Hotel boasts its own market garden to supply the kitchen with the ultimate in low-mileage fruit and veg. The key players in the kitchen brigade have worked together for the best part of a decade and have developed a contemporary style of cooking that is all about working with the seasons and bringing great ingredients together in well-considered compositions. Given that the restaurant is about as far from the coast as it is possible to be in the UK, the team's dedication to sourcing fresh fish for the daily fish menu is impressive, and it is presented without fuss in simple dishes such as poached turbot with mussels, or pan-roast monkfish in Cajun spices. Elsewhere, there could be lambs' kidneys sautéed with mushrooms, bacon and cream as a curtain-raiser to marinated rump of lamb with dauphinoise potatoes, roasted root vegetables, spinach, and redcurrant jus.

The Granary Hotel & Restaurant

Chef Tom Court **Owner** Richard Fletcher
Times 12-2.30/7-11 Closed L Mon, Sat, D Sun
Prices Fixed L 2 course £10.95, Fixed D 3 course £17.95-£19.95, Starter £5.50-£9.95, Main £14.50-£23.95, Dessert £2.95, Service optional **Wines** 2 bottles over £30, 35 bottles under £30, 12 by glass
Notes Sunday L, Vegetarian available, Civ Wed 200
Seats 60, Pr/dining room 40 **Children** Portions
Parking 95

See advert below

KIDDERMINSTER *continued*

Stone Manor Hotel

◉ Modern British 🌱

Traditional comforts and good, modish eating

☎ 01562 777555
Stone DY10 4PJ
e-mail: enquiries@stonemanorhotel.co.uk
web: www.stonemanorhotel.co.uk
dir: 2.5m from Kidderminster on A448, hotel on right

The restaurant at this rambling property is notable for its standing timbers and ceiling beams; tables are well spaced, some in bays at banquettes, lighting is from ceiling spots and wall lights, and the room has a good vibe. The kitchen steers a course through a largely modern British repertoire, which means that seared scallops are served with black pudding, a purée of fennel, lemon and apple, and monkfish is wrapped in Parma ham and accompanied by lobster foam, saffron mash, roast chicory and pea purée. Dishes are well conceived - witness a crab tian, the plate dotted with horseradish cream and capers - and timings are accurate, as in a roast rump of lamb in herb and mustard crust served just pink along with thyme jus, scallion potatoes, and carrot purée. The kitchen's fond of flambéing, so finish with the theatre of crêpe Suzette.

Chef James McCarroll **Owner** Mr Dunn **Times** 12-2/7-10
Prices Prices not confirmed Service included **Wines** 10 by glass **Notes** Sunday L, Vegetarian available, Dress restrictions, No jeans, Civ Wed 150 **Seats** 90
Children Portions, Menu **Parking** 400

MALVERN
Map 10 SO74

L'Amuse Bouche Restaurant

◉◉ Traditional French, British 🌱

Updated classical cooking in an attractive country-house hotel

☎ 01684 572427
The Cotford Hotel, 51 Graham Rd WR14 2HU
e-mail: reservations@cotfordhotel.co.uk
web: www.cotfordhotel.co.uk
dir: From Worcester follow signs to Malvern on A449. Left into Graham Rd signed town centre, hotel on right

The Bishop of Worcester picked a fine spot for his summer residence back in 1851, right at the foot of the Malvern Hills, and nowadays it's a smart country-house hotel with grand (and Gothic) Victorian proportions and pretty gardens. The hotel's L'Amuse Bouche Restaurant is done out in warm pastel tones and looks very charming indeed, with the tables dressed up in white linen. The name of the restaurant is a clue to where the chef's inspiration lies, but it is first-class regional and organic produce that is at the heart of the French-focused menu. Start with pulled confit of corn-fed chicken with celeriac remoulade, pickled cucumber and date chutney, or go for the hand-dived scallops, served with green bean and cherry tomato confit, broad bean purée and pancetta dust. Next up, Welsh lamb shank with a confit onion

crust, buttered champ and sweet Burgundy and herb jus, and finish with a tarte au citron with passionfruit essence and blackcurrant sorbet.

Chef Christopher Morgan **Owner** Christopher & Barbara Morgan **Times** 12-1.30/6-8 Closed L Mon-Sat
Prices Service optional **Wines** 6 by glass **Notes** Pre-theatre menu available, Sunday L £19.95-£23.50, Vegetarian available, Dress restrictions, Smart casual **Seats** 40, Pr/dining room 12 **Parking** 15

Colwall Park Hotel

◉◉ Modern British 🌱

Excellent modern British cooking in the Malvern Hills

☎ 01684 540000
Walwyn Rd, Colwall WR13 6QG
e-mail: hotel@colwall.com
web: www.colwall.co.uk
dir: On B4218, off A449 from Malvern to Ledbury

Tucked beneath the glorious Malvern Hills, this substantial mock-Tudor timbered Edwardian country hotel has a fine pedigree, but is not stuck in an Elgar-themed past. The upmarket Seasons Restaurant provides an elegant backdrop, blending elements of old and new - pale oak panelling offset by vibrantly-coloured modern art, and wrought-iron chandeliers hanging from a vaulted ceiling. Contemporary British trends and an obvious penchant for top-grade local materials form the backbone of an accessible brasserie-style menu. Excellent home-made breads get things off on the right foot, then a crunchy fishcake of cod, haddock and salmon appears with a zesty shallot and tarragon dressing. Next comes herb-crumbed loin of Longdon Marsh lamb with thyme mash, peas, broad beans, in-house dried tomatoes, and a red wine and rosemary sauce, while pudding keeps up standards to the end with a refreshing lemon posset with blueberry sorbet and shortbread.

Chef James Garth **Owner** Mr & Mrs I Nesbitt
Times 12-2/7-9 Closed L all week (ex by arrangement)
Prices Fixed L 2 course £16.95, Starter £3.75-£9.25, Main £11.95-£21.95, Dessert £5.95-£9.50, Service optional **Wines** 22 bottles over £30, 66 bottles under £30, 9 by glass **Notes** Sunday L £16.95-£19.95, Vegetarian available **Seats** 40, Pr/dining room 100 **Children** Portions, Menu **Parking** 40

The Cottage in the Wood Hotel

◉◉ Modern British 🍷 NOTABLE WINE LIST 🌱

Ambitious cooking in charming hotel

☎ 01684 588860
Holywell Rd, Malvern Wells WR14 4LG
e-mail: reception@cottageinthewood.co.uk
web: www.cottageinthewood.co.uk
dir: 3m S of Great Malvern off A449, 500yds N of B4209, on opposite side of road

A visit during daylight hours has its own reward, for this is some view - a 30-mile sweep across the Severn Valley, in fact. Perched on a wooded hillside, the former Georgian dower house is a smart hotel and restaurant with appeal that goes beyond the undoubted beauty of its geographical situation. The Outlook Restaurant has the vista - as you might have guessed - and the space is suitably smart and comfortable. The family-run hotel's kitchen is headed up by one of the clan (Dominic Pattin), and his cooking is based on sound seasonal thinking. Start with confit shoulder of lamb with slow-roasted tomato, confit garlic, sweet tomato purée and thyme jus, or one of a choice of home-made soups. Next up, whole Cornish lemon sole is done in the classic manner, or go for pan-roasted guinea fowl with caramelised fennel gnocchi and shallot purée. Finish with a star-anise flavoured crème brûlée with a poached pear given a liquorice lift. The wine list is exceptional.

Chef Dominic Pattin **Owner** The Pattin family
Times 12.30-2/7-9.30 **Prices** Starter £5.45-£11.45, Main £12.55-£22.95, Dessert £2.75-£5.95, Service optional **Wines** 203 bottles over £30, 138 bottles under £30, 12 by glass **Notes** Pre-theatre D from 6pm, L menu Mon-Sat, Sunday L £18.95-£23.95, Vegetarian available **Seats** 70, Pr/dining room 20 **Children** Portions **Parking** 40

Save on Hotels. Book at theAA.com/hotel

WORCESTERSHIRE 507 ENGLAND

The Malvern

◉ Modern British 🕏

Contemporary brasserie dining in the Malvern Hills

☎ 01684 898290
Grovewood Rd WR14 1GD
e-mail: enquiries@themalvernspa.com
dir: A4440 to Malvern. Over 2 rdbts, at 3rd turn left. After 6m, left at rdbt, over 1st rdbt, hotel on right

The very first spa resort in the town, The Malvern opened its doors back in 1910 to satisfy the demands of the Edwardian public. It's changed a bit since then. In fact, the interior is spellbindingly modern and capacious. The spa has all the bells and whistles you might imagine, and there's also a brasserie restaurant if you're seeking fulfillment of a different kind. It's a fresh-looking contemporary space with muted neutral tones, wooden tables and local artworks on the walls. The menu follows a bright and breezy brasserie-style format, so you might start with something very of the moment such as slow-cooked pork belly with black pudding, cauliflower purée, spaghetti crackling and sage jus, or go for the Asian flavours of Thai green mussels. Main-course baked lemon sole is served on the bone, and for dessert, caramel, banana and rum pannacotta comes with raisin purée, banana sorbet and vanilla-poached prunes.

Chef Steve Rimmer **Owner** Huw Watson
Times 12-3/7-9.30 **Prices** Fixed L 2 course fr £15, Fixed D 3 course £25.20-£32.95, Starter £5.85-£8.95, Main £13-£16.50, Dessert £6.35-£7.50, Service optional **Wines** 8 bottles over £30, 12 bottles under £30, 9 by glass **Notes** Brunch every Sun, Themed menus every month, Vegetarian available, Dress restrictions, Smart casual **Seats** 34, Pr/dining room 24 **Parking** 82

The Venture In Restaurant

◉◉ British, French 🕏

Forthright flavours in a half-timbered medieval house

☎ 01905 620552
Main Rd WR9 0EW
dir: From Worcester N towards Kidderminster on A449 (approx 5m). Left at Ombersley turn. Restaurant 0.75m on right

Old meets new at this crooked 15th-century half-timbered building on sleepy Ombersley's high street. The name is an invitation, so step inside, and you'll find a bar with a huge inglenook, beams and stone walls, while the restaurant goes for a more contemporary look involving high-backed leather chairs, bare tables, and cream walls hung with tasteful prints. The place may exude antiquity (and a ghostly resident to go with it), but the kitchen is certainly not rooted in the past: it produces consistently interesting, thoughtful modern dishes based on judiciously-sourced produce. Seared Scottish scallops teamed with prawn, chicken and Parma ham boudin and red pepper beurre blanc is the preamble to a piggy main course of pan-roasted pork fillet with confit belly, sweet pickled red cabbage, and bubble and squeak, all of the elements complementing and contrasting in an entertaining way. Elsewhere, there may be pan-roasted breast of pheasant and game faggot with onion chutney, buttered spinach and game jus. Pudding might be a deeply smooth and creamy chocolate parfait with warm passionfruit, mango and banana compôte.

Chef Toby Fletcher **Owner** Toby Fletcher
Times 12-2/7-9.30 Closed 25 Dec-1 Jan, 2 wks summer & 2 wks winter, Mon, D Sun **Prices** Fixed L 2 course £25, Fixed D 3 course £39, Service optional **Wines** 38 bottles over £30, 35 bottles under £30, 6 by glass **Notes** Sunday L, Vegetarian available, Dress restrictions, Smart casual **Seats** 32, Pr/dining room 32 **Parking** 15, on street

---

Cadmore Lodge Hotel & Country Club

◉ British

Rural lakeside setting with trad cooking

☎ 01584 810044
Berrington Green, St Michaels WR15 8TQ
e-mail: reception.cadmore@cadmorelodge.com
web: www.cadmorelodge.com
dir: Off A4112 from Tenbury Wells to Leominster. 2m from Tenbury Wells, turn right opposite St Michael's Church

Cadmore is a small, modern family-run hotel set in peaceful countryside with the bonus of a nine-hole golf course and stunning lake within its 70-acre grounds. The country-style restaurant is old-school traditional, sporting neatly clothed tables, warm colours and an inglenook fireplace with log-burning stove, plus some great views over the grounds. The food makes use of some local ingredients and suits the mood of the place. Go retro with a classic prawn cocktail opener, and perhaps follow up with chicken Madeira and mash or lightly grilled fillet of plaice accompanied by spinach, new potatoes and hollandaise. To finish, there's nursery dessert heaven with apple crumble and custard or strawberry Bakewell tart.

Times 12-2/7-9.15 Closed 25 Dec

White Lion Hotel

◉ Modern British, European

Historic hotel with contemporary feel and flavour

☎ 01684 592551
21 High St WR8 0HJ
e-mail: info@whitelionhotel.biz
dir: From A422 take A38 towards Tewkesbury. After 8m take B4104 for 1m, after bridge turn left to hotel

The author Henry Fielding put up here while writing *Tom Jones*, and the White Lion also played a booze-fuelled part in the Civil War, but fascinating as the 16th-century inn's history may be, the place has stayed in tune with current trends without impacting on its immense character. Nowadays, the interior works a cheerfully-updated look in the Pepperpot Brasserie, blending black timbered walls filled with blocks of yellow ochre, apricot, and terracotta colour with bare chunky oak tables and high-backed chairs. Food-wise, the deal is straightforward combinations and big-hearted flavours on a menu that has something for all-comers. Seared scallops are skewered on a rosemary sprig and matched with roast butternut squash purée and chorizo, ahead of a hearty plate of mustard- and herb-crusted roast rump of lamb served with bubble and squeak, celeriac purée and rosemary jus. Baked apple crème brûlée with butterscotch sauce is a properly indulgent pudding.

Chef Jon Lear, Richard Thompson **Owner** Mr & Mrs Lear
Times 12-2/7-9.15 Closed 31 Dec-1 Jan, L few days between Xmas & New Year, D 24 Dec **Prices** Fixed L 2 course fr £13, Starter £5.50-£8.50, Main £9.95-£19, Dessert £6.45-£7.45, Service optional **Wines** 2 bottles over £30, 20 bottles under £30, 7 by glass **Notes** Sunday L, Vegetarian available **Seats** 45 **Children** Portions **Parking** 16

YORKSHIRE, EAST RIDING OF

BEVERLEY
Map 17 TA03

Beverley Tickton Grange Hotel

◉◉ Modern British

Period charm and fine local produce

☎ 01964 543666
Tickton HU17 9SH
e-mail: info@ticktongrange.co.uk
dir: From Beverley take A1035 towards Bridlington. After
3m hotel on left, just past Tickton

Tickton Grange is as English as warm beer and the sound
of leather on willow: a Grade II listed Georgian country
house in four acres of gardens with plenty of period
character. Just the sort of place, then, for celebrating a
special occasion in the fine-dining restaurant, which is
just the right side of elegant with its Georgian bits, linen-
clothed tables and rich, red leather chairs. There's a deft
team at work in the kitchen, turning great local
ingredients into stunning modern versions of classic
dishes. Hot-smoked sea trout with sea purslane and
liquorice gets things moving, and while there are drizzles,
swirls and jellies aplenty, it all packs plenty of punch,
whether it's local sea bass with saffron potatoes,
tempura squid rings and bouillabaisse sauce, or a pan-
fried steak of venison haunch with damson gin and
turnips. To finish, a slate of Yorkshire cheeses is a
savoury alternative to something like pistachio and
walnut baklava with rosewater ice cream and jelly.

Chef David Nowell **Owner** Mr & Mrs Whymant
Times 12-2/7-9.30 **Prices** Fixed L 2 course
£24.50-£29.50, Fixed D 3 course £25, Starter
£6.95-£8.95, Main £20.50-£28.95, Dessert £7.50-£12.50,
Service optional **Wines** 8 by glass **Notes** Sunday L,
Vegetarian available, Civ Wed 150 **Seats** 45, Pr/dining
room 20 **Children** Portions, Menu **Parking** 75

The Pipe and Glass Inn

◉◉ Modern British V 🏆NOTABLE WINE LIST 🍷

Superior modern cooking in stylish country inn

☎ 01430 810246
West End, South Dalton HU17 7PN
e-mail: email@pipeandglass.co.uk
dir: Just off B1248

The P and G's dedication to high quality food has not
been at the expense of its pub credentials: pop in and
have a pint to find out for yourself. It would be a shame
not to stay and eat, though, for there is some
exceptionally good stuff on offer. The 15th-century village
pub is looking good in the 21st with its rustic charms
enhanced by smart and rather classy decoration and
furniture; there's a new private dining room upstairs, too.
Chef-patron James Mackenzie runs an industrious
kitchen, cooks with a good deal of care and creativity,
and seeks out high quality ingredients. A little jar of
Gloucestershire Old Spot potted pork comes in a first
course with sticky apple, crackling salad and spelt toast,
or there might be fresh salmon pastrami with Jerusalem
artichokes, horseradish crème fraîche, crispy quail's egg
and coriander. Follow on with slow-cooked crispy shoulder
of lamb with spiced green lentils, cumin carrots, mint
yoghurt and cucumber pickle, and end happily with a
pear and almond tart with pear sorbet and Poire William
custard.

Chef James Mackenzie **Owner** James & Kate Mackenzie
Times 12-2/6.30-9.30 Closed 25 Dec, 2 wks Jan, Mon
(except BHs), D Sun **Prices** Starter £7.95-£11.95, Main
£9.95-£25.95, Dessert £5.45-£10.95, Service optional,
Groups min 8 service 10% **Wines** 13 by glass
Notes Sunday L, Vegetarian menu **Seats** 70, Pr/dining
room 36 **Children** Portions, Menu **Parking** 60

WILLERBY
Map 17 TA03

Best Western Willerby Manor Hotel

◉ Modern European 🍷

Extensive brasserie menu in countryside setting

☎ 01482 652616
Well Ln HU10 6ER
e-mail: willerbymanor@bestwestern.co.uk
web: www.willerbymanor.co.uk
dir: M62/A63, follow signs for Humber Bridge, then signs
for Beverley until Willerby Shopping Park. Hotel signed
from rdbt next to McDonald's

Four miles out of Hull, Willerby Manor is a modern spa
hotel in the East Yorkshire countryside. Its fine dining
goes on in Figs Brasserie, a relaxing room done in
avocado and coffee tones, which extends on to a paved
outdoor terrace on balmy evenings. An extensive menu of
brasserie dishes incorporates some neat ideas, such as a
starter of goats' cheese pannacotta with red wine-
poached pear and gingerbread, but also features many
classic ideas like Whitby scampi and chips, chicken
breast with black pudding, chestnuts, sprouts and mash
in red wine sauce, and apple and blueberry crumble with
vanilla cream.

Chef David Roberts, Ben Olley **Owner** Alexandra Townend
Times 10am-10pm Closed 25 Dec, All-day dining
Prices Starter £5.20-£5.50, Main £9.50-£19, Dessert
£4-£4.85, Service optional **Wines** 14 by glass
Notes Sunday L £10.95-£13.20, Vegetarian available, Civ
Wed 200 **Seats** 40, Pr/dining room 40 **Children** Portions,
Menu **Parking** 200

YORKSHIRE, NORTH

ALDWARK
Map 19 SE46

The Aldwark Arms

◉◉ Modern

Lively cooking in village gastro-pub

☎ 01347 838324
YO61 1UB
e-mail: enquiries@aldwarkarms.co.uk

The Aldwark is a well-maintained gastro-pub in a pretty
village, with a traditional bar complete with chesterfields,
a real fire, hand-pulled ales and pub food, and a light
and airy restaurant extending into a conservatory.
Seasonality is paramount on the monthly-changing menu,
backed up by daily specials, with the kitchen giving an
original spin to its output, serving curried tartare sauce
with good old fish and chips, for instance. Flavours can
be unapologetically forthright, as in black pudding on
tasty chunky apple and onion chutney, topped with a
poached egg and accompanied by chorizo. Enterprising
main courses might extend to monkfish 'fingers' coated in
parsley and breadcrumbs, served with potted shrimps
and classic pommes Anna, or hearty duck leg casseroled
in a rich gravy with garlic sausage, served with butternut
squash, green beans and dauphinoise. Bread is home-
made, and the momentum is carried through to pudding
stage: perhaps a glass of rich, smooth chocolate mousse
presented on a slate with a scoop of pistachio ice cream.

Times 12-2/5-9 Closed Mon, D Sun

ASENBY
Map 19 SE37

Crab Manor

◉◉ Modern British, European 🍷

Idiosyncratic restaurant with a strong line in seafood

☎ 01845 577286
Dishforth Rd YO7 3QL
e-mail: enquiries@crabandlobster.co.uk
dir: A1(M) junct 49, on outskirts of village

At first sight, this thatched and creeper-clad Georgian
inn could be the template for a classic Yorkshire country
pub, although an observant eye might spot the old
enamelled advertising signs that are a hint to the
Aladdin's cave of esoteric odds and ends that fills the
interior with endless visual entertainment. In case the
name isn't enough of a clue, fish and seafood is the
kitchen's main culinary focus, whether you choose to eat
in the sun-trap garden, the airy pavilion, the main
restaurant or the convivial bar. The choice is vast, taking
in starters such as seared hand-dived scallops with
confit belly pork, crisp black pudding, and roast butternut
squash cream, or fishcakes of local cod, pollock, and
cured fish served with creamed greens and a poached
egg. Next up, a chunk of local cod could come with spicy
sausage boulangère potatoes, buttered greens and gravy,
or you might take a meatier route with the likes of herb-
crusted roast rump of Faceby lamb with cumin-roasted
carrots, gratin potatoes, rosemary and redcurrant. To
finish, go for something like chilled Valrhona chocolate
fondant with honeycomb and caramelised banana
yoghurt ice cream.

Chef Steve Dean **Owner** Vimac Trading
Times 12-2.30/7-9 **Prices** Fixed L 2 course £16.50-£17,
Fixed D 3 course £35, Starter £8-£12, Main £17-£42,
Dessert £6-£16, Service optional **Wines** 12 bottles over
£30, 27 bottles under £30, 8 by glass **Notes** Sunday L,
Vegetarian available, Civ Wed 105 **Seats** 85, Pr/dining
room 16 **Children** Portions **Parking** 80

Save on Hotels. Book at theAA.com/hotel

YORKSHIRE, NORTH 509 ENGLAND

AUSTWICK
Map 18 SD76

The Traddock

◉◉ Modern British ©

Local and seasonal cooking at a Georgian house in the Dales

☎ 015242 51224
Settle LA2 8BY
e-mail: info@thetraddock.co.uk
dir: From Skipton take A65 towards Kendal, 3m after Settle turn right signed Austwick, cross hump back bridge, hotel 100yds on left

The stone-built house in the Yorkshire Dales is bountifully endowed with charm. It's a Georgian country hotel on the human scale with peaceful lawns for sitting and contemplating. A soothingly designed dining room with William Morris wallpaper and darkwood chairs (and muzak, sad to say) is the setting for cooking built on relationships with local artisan producers. Honey-roasted baby beetroot and goats' cheese with Burgundy jelly and black pepper toast is one way to start, or there may be crab from Whitby, properly dressed, served with Russian salad, capers and red caviar. The modish two-way serving of suckling pig - shoulder and belly - features fine Middlewhite meat alongside parmentier potatoes and spiced quince compote, sauced with cider. Main courses come with a plethora of those local vegetables, but look a little further afield for the chorizo and red pepper coulis that come with baked codling. Honey-roasting is a favoured technique, applied as enthusiastically to summer veg as to the plums in a tarte Tatin with a difference.

Chef John Pratt **Owner** The Reynolds family
Times 12-2.30/6.30-11 **Prices** Starter £4.95-£7.95, Main £12.95-£19.95, Dessert £6.25-£7.95, Service optional **Wines** 24 bottles over £30, 26 bottles under £30, 16 by glass **Notes** Sunday L £9.95-£17.95, Vegetarian available **Seats** 36, Pr/dining room 16 **Children** Portions, Menu **Parking** 20, On street

BAINBRIDGE
Map 18 SD99

Yorebridge House

◉◉ British, European

Bright, modish cooking in Wensleydale

☎ 01969 652060
DL8 3EE
e-mail: enquiries@yorebridgehouse.co.uk
dir: A648 to Bainbridge. Yorebridge House N of centre on right before river

In a peaceful setting on the edge of the village by the river in Wensleydale, Yorebridge House has been converted into a luxury boutique hotel, with a decently sized restaurant with a boarded floor, upholstered chairs at white-clothed tables, and plenty of light from skylights and a number of windows. The menu (there's a separate one in the bar) is a roll-call of fresh, vibrant ideas. Saddle of rabbit with langoustines, sweet potato purée, asparagus and morels is an unusual take on the surf and turf combination, followed perhaps by a more

conventional main course of loin and belly of pork with black pudding and apple sauce, an extra flavour dimension given by walnut jus. Sound materials, high technical skills and an imaginative approach are evident throughout. A starter of smoked duck and foie gras comes not just with rhubarb as a foil but with three ways with the fruit - purée, crisp and pickled - and desserts are as labour-intensive as the rest, judging by ginger pannacotta with poached quince, Poire William jelly and apple and blackberry sorbet.

Times 12-2.30/6.30-9.30

BOLTON ABBEY
Map 19 SE05

The Devonshire Arms Country House Hotel & Spa

Rosettes not confirmed at time of going to print – see page 510

The Devonshire Brasserie & Bar

◉ Modern British Ⓥ

Smart brasserie cooking in a top-class country hotel

☎ 01756 710710 & 710441
Bolton Abbey BD23 6AJ
e-mail: res@devonshirehotels.co.uk
dir: On B6160, 250yds N of junct with A59

This is the informal brasserie within The Devonshire Arms (see entry for The Burlington Restaurant), a room marked out by bright vibrant colours, contemporary artwork, comfortable seating, informal service, and a buzz in the air. The menu runs along modern British brasserie lines; ingredients cut the mustard, and the kitchen knows what it's about, producing starters of tender, crisply battered monkfish tails with a vegetable and noodle salad and sweet chilli, and chicken liver parfait with tangy red onion marmalade. Crowd-pleasing main courses vary from beer-battered haddock, through lamb shank hotpot to fillet of beef Wellington with Madeira sauce, and populist desserts might include sticky toffee pudding and profiteroles.

Chef Dan Field **Owner** The Duke & Duchess of Devonshire
Times 12-2.30/6-9.30 **Prices** Starter £4.95-£8.95, Main £7.25-£23.95, Dessert £4.50-£11.95, Service added but optional 12.5% **Notes** Sunday L £7.95-£12.95, Vegetarian menu, Civ Wed 90 **Seats** 60 **Children** Portions, Menu **Parking** 40

BOROUGHBRIDGE
Map 19 SE36

The Crown Inn

◉ Modern British Ⓥ ©

Old coaching inn with modish cooking

☎ 01423 322300
Roecliffe YO51 9LY
e-mail: info@crowninnroecliffe.com
web: www.crowninnroecliffe.com
dir: A1M junct 48, follow brown sign

The Crown is an old coaching inn which still radiates charm and hospitality within its 16th-century walls, with

the hoped for stone-flagged floors, chunky oak beams and roaring log fires all present and correct. It's been revamped with a keen eye by owners Karl and Amanda Mainey, blending traditional and contemporary touches into a pleasing whole. A good deal of local produce finds its way into the kitchen and is turned into brasserie-style dishes which have a regional flavour, and a bit more besides. Start with Whitby crab soup perked up with brandy, or a terrine of local rabbit studded with pickled walnuts and served with Wakefield rhubarb chutney and granary toast. Next up, there might be fish pie, or steak and kidney pie made with local ale, or the more outré spiced monkfish with chilli-spiked Puy lentils and a crab and coriander bhaji.

Chef Darryn Asher **Owner** Karl Mainey
Times 12-3.30/6-11 **Prices** Fixed L 2 course £16.95, Fixed D 3 course £16.95, Starter £4.50-£8.90, Main £13.95-£21.95, Dessert £6.95, Service optional **Wines** 20 bottles over £30, 20 bottles under £30, 19 by glass **Notes** Sunday L, Vegetarian menu, Civ Wed 120 **Seats** 60, Pr/dining room 20 **Children** Portions, Menu **Parking** 30

The Dining Room Restaurant

◉◉ British, French ©

Assured cooking in stylish neighbourhood restaurant

☎ 01423 326426
20 St James Square YO51 9AR
e-mail: chris@thediningroom.co.uk
dir: A1(M), Boroughbridge junct, follow signs to town. Opposite fountain in town square

This self-effacing restaurant in a bow-fronted Queen Anne building would be easy to pass by, but a horde of local fans would tell you the folly of your ways. Once inside there's a definite wow factor to its bright white contemporary looks, and there's a delightful walled terrace for alfresco aperitifs and open-air eating when the weather is up to scratch. Husband-and-wife-team Christopher and Lisa Astley run a tight ship, with Chris at the stoves and Lisa orchestrating front of house. Chris's cooking plays it straight, relying on mainstream flavour combinations that let the top-class local materials speak for themselves. Chicken liver parfait, melba toast, gherkins and chutney make reliable bedfellows in a well-flavoured starter, followed by free-range belly pork with black pudding mash, apple compôte and barbecue sauce. There's a classic crème brûlée with blackberries for a finale.

Chef Christopher Astley **Owner** Mr & Mrs C Astley
Times 12-2/7-9.30 Closed 26-28 Dec, 1 Jan, BHs, Mon, L Tue-Sat, D Sun **Prices** Fixed L 2 course £21.90, Fixed D 3 course £18.95, Starter £7.50-£10, Main £14.95-£22, Dessert £7-£8.50, Service optional **Wines** 24 bottles over £30, 34 bottles under £30, 12 by glass **Notes** Early bird set menu from 6pm, Sunday L, Vegetarian available, Dress restrictions, Smart casual, no T-shirts **Seats** 32 **Children** Portions **Parking** On street/Private on request

BURNSALL
Map 19 SE06

The Devonshire Fell

◉◉ Modern British V

Modern cooking in a made-over old building

☎ 01756 729000
BD23 6BT
e-mail: manager@devonshirefell.co.uk
web: www.devonshirefell.co.uk
dir: On B6160, 6m from Bolton Abbey rdbt A59 junct

The traditional stone exterior belies the contemporary makeover within at The Devonshire Fell, all vibrant colours, bold fabrics and attractive artwork. Part of the Devonshire Hotels & Restaurants group, which also includes The Devonshire Arms at Bolton Abbey (see entry), it's more of a boutique hotel than anything else these days, with attractive accommodation and a modern, funky-looking bistro, bar and conservatory all designed by the Duchess of Devonshire (who owns the group with her husband). The bright, airy and welcoming feel of the place is aided by informal, friendly service, while on the food front, the modern British cooking is based on top-notch local ingredients brought together in unfussy, appealing combinations by a small kitchen team. A starter of 'velouté - tomato, chilli and lime crème fraîche' is full of fresh, clean flavours, while main-course honey glazed duck breast comes perfectly cooked and accompanied by a smooth spring onion mash, buttered spinach, glazed baby carrots and blackberry jus. Homemade bread and butter pudding with clotted cream and apricot compote is as good as it gets.

Chef Oliver Adams **Owner** Duke & Duchess of Devonshire **Times** 12-2.30/6.30-9.30 **Prices** Starter £6.95-£7.95, Main £13.95-£18.50, Dessert £4.95-£6.95, Service added but optional 12.5% **Wines** 11 by glass **Notes** Fixed D 5 course £50, Sunday L, Vegetarian menu, Civ Wed 70 **Seats** 40, Pr/dining room 70 **Children** Portions, Menu **Parking** 40

CRATHORNE
Map 19 NZ40

Crathorne Hall Hotel

◉◉ Modern British ✤

Contemporary British style in stately Edwardian hotel

☎ 01642 700398
TS15 0AR
e-mail: crathornehall@handpicked.co.uk
web: www.handpickedhotels.co.uk/crathorne-hall
dir: Off A19, 2m E of Yarm. Access to A19 via A66 or A1, Thirsk

A grandiose Edwardian pile with four soaring columns above the front door, Crathorne Hall was the largest and last to be built in North Yorkshire in the twilight years of stately homes. While the décor and furnishings of the Leven Restaurant are a trip back to the early 20th century - oak half-panelled walls, heavy drapes at tall windows, oil paintings, and a gilt-edged coffered ceiling - it's fast forward to the 21st century in the kitchen, whose eye for the finest local ingredients and polished technical skills pays off with some accomplished modern cooking. Lobster risotto with avocado ice cream and coriander shoots shows the style, and this could be followed by a meat and fish partnership of stone bass fillet with oxtail, Chantenay carrots, baby leeks, and red wine reduction, or loin of venison, cooked sous-vide for maximum tenderness, and matched with textures of parsnip, and chocolate jus. Puddings bring on more carefully-considered combinations of flavour and texture, delivering passionfruit, for example, in the forms of brûlée, Alaska, sorbet, jelly and syrup.

Chef Alan Robinson **Owner** Hand Picked Hotels **Times** 12.30-2.30/7-9.30 **Prices** Fixed L 2 course fr £16.50, Fixed D 3 course fr £36, Starter £10.50-£11.95, Main £21.95-£25, Dessert £9.50-£10.95, Service included **Wines** 18 by glass **Notes** Sunday L, Vegetarian available, Civ Wed 90 **Seats** 45, Pr/dining room 26 **Children** Portions, Menu **Parking** 80

The Devonshire Arms Country House Hotel & Spa

Rosettes not confirmed at time of going to print

BOLTON ABBEY
Map 19 SE05

Modern French V

Stunning Yorkshire Dales setting for top-flight cooking

☎ 01756 710441 & 718111
BD23 6AJ
e-mail: res@devonshirehotels.co.uk
web: www.burlingtonrestaurant.co.uk
dir: On B6160 to Bolton Abbey, 250 yds N of junct with A59 rdbt

The Rosette award for this establishment has been suspended due to a change of chef. Reassessment will take place in due course under the new chef.

The Devonshire Arms has 30,000 acres of prime Yorkshire Dales to call its own, or at least the Duke of Devonshire does, for this magnificent one-time coaching inn dating back to the 17th century is part of his estate (technically it's in trust, but...). It's in an impressive position, surrounded by green rolling hills and close to the famously ruined priory, but The Devonshire has moved with the times - while remaining timeless to some degree - with sympathetic extensions over the centuries. These days it's a luxurious country-house hotel with a swish spa and a restaurant that has put it well and truly on the map. There are roaring log fires, elegant furniture, bags of antiques and grand pictures, plus plush sofas to sink into as you study the menu and bite into canapés. The Burlington Restaurant is the star of the show, where chef Steve Smith delivers food of craft and creativity, making good use of the estate's excellent produce (dining during the game season is a good idea) and the kitchen garden for herbs, vegetables and fruits. The setting is suitably elegant, with burnished darkwood tables dressed up for the business of fine dining, and the formal, traditionally decorated space watched over by the impeccable service team, including the wonderful sommelier (more of him later). It is jackets for the men, so come prepared. What follows is technically impressive, contemporary cooking, with lots of great ideas and compelling flavours. Things kick off with all the little freebies you might be expecting - perhaps an apple and pork cromesquis and a rather fun grapefruit and basil mojito - and the fabulous breads (baked in-house) come with two butters, including a fabulous seaweed and sea salt version. Hand-dived Orkney scallops are as delightfully fat as they come, cooked perfectly, served with smoked eel, celeriac and apple jelly, with truffle grated over the top at the table. Next up, main-course Hebridean lamb comes in various 'textures', including the slow-cooked shoulder and a superb, flavoursome piece of loin, partnered with goats' cheese bonbon, broccoli purée, tomato, and garlic and rosemary jus, or there's Brixham sea bass with fennel, figs, ceps and red wine. To finish, after the pre-requisite pre-dessert, comes coffee pannacotta and sponge with perfectly judged caramelised milk purée and liquorice ice cream. The wine list of some 2,500 bins is the domain of Nigel Fairclough and contains some of the best vintages to be found in the country. And note there's a brasserie on site, too (see entry).

Owner Duke & Duchess of Devonshire **Times** 12-2.30/7-9.30 Closed Xmas, 3-11 Jan, Mon, L Tue-Sat **Prices** Fixed L 3 course £35-£75, Fixed D 3 course £65-£75, Tasting menu £75, Service added but optional 12.5% **Wines** 12 by glass **Notes** Classic menu 5 course £65, Sunday L, Vegetarian menu, Dress restrictions, Smart dress, no jeans, shorts or T-shirts, Civ Wed 90 **Seats** 70, Pr/dining room 90 **Children** Portions **Parking** 100

The Parsonage Country House Hotel

⚫ Modern British V ☙

Victorian-era country house with creative cooking

☎ 01904 728111
York Rd YO19 6LF
e-mail: sales@parsonagehotel.co.uk
web: www.parsonagehotel.co.uk
dir: From A64 take A19 Selby. Follow to Escrick. Hotel on right of St Helen's Church

This 1940s former parsonage - now country-house hotel - is in six acres of formal gardens and woodlands and retains bags of period features. The smart Lascelles restaurant goes for a more modish vibe, which means pale-wood floors and vibrant colours, while white linen-clad tables make sure it doesn't get out of hand. The kitchen's modern approach fits the surroundings, with admirable emphasis on home-grown, local and seasonal produce and clear-cut flavours. Start with salmon and lobster ravioli served with lemongrass velouté and confit tomatoes, followed on with roast venison loin partnered with celeriac and potato dauphinoise, red wine and garlic purée and a redcurrant jus, and draw to a satisfying close with an assiette including pear terrine with stem ginger mousse, pear jelly and pear sorbet.

Chef Darren Davis **Owner** P Smith **Times** 12-2/6.30-9 Closed L Sat **Prices** Fixed L 2 course fr £12.95, Fixed D 3 course fr £19.95, Starter £5.90-£10.50, Main £15.90-£22.50, Dessert £5.95-£8.50, Service included **Wines** 4 bottles over £30, 22 bottles under £30, 11 by glass **Notes** Sunday L, Vegetarian menu, Dress restrictions, No shorts, Civ Wed 100 **Seats** 70, Pr/dining room 40 **Children** Portions, Menu **Parking** 100

Grassington House

⚫⚫ Modern European ☙

Inventive cooking in boutique surroundings

☎ 01756 752406
5 The Square BD23 5AQ
e-mail: bookings@grassingtonhousehotel.co.uk
web: www.grassingtonhousehotel.co.uk
dir: A59 into Grassington, in town square opposite post office

In the heart of Wharfedale in the Yorkshire Dales National Park, this charming three-storey Georgian restaurant with rooms has been stylishly modernised. Its location makes it ideal for walkers looking for a touch of luxury, or for couples on special breaks. A boutique feel dominates the small bar and cosy reception area and extends to the smart No. 5 Restaurant (part of which is in the conservatory), with its red tones and birdcage print wallpaper. Informal service comes courtesy of a young team. The modern European cooking puts the emphasis on local produce, including pigs home-reared by chef-patron John Rudden and his wife Sue. Expect inventive combinations such as local pheasant and prune

cannelloni with brown onion and wild mushroom dressing, or pigeon breast roasted in potato crisps with a textbook beetroot risotto, followed by pan-roasted Yorkshire venison haunch, Savoy cabbage faggot and juniper beetroot, or perhaps fillet of plaice with crab and lobster ravioli and sambuca shellfish sauce. To finish, you might treat yourself to date soufflé cooked to order and served with salt caramel ice cream.

Chef John Rudden **Owner** Susan & John Rudden **Times** 12-2.30/6-9.30 **Prices** Fixed L 2 course £13.50-£16.50, Fixed D 3 course £13.50-£16.50, Starter £4.50-£6.95, Main £11.95-£23.50, Dessert £5.50-£6.25, Service optional **Wines** 17 bottles over £30, 28 bottles under £30, 12 by glass **Notes** Fixed D 4 course Sun-Tue £39.50 per couple, Sunday L, Vegetarian available, Civ Wed 40 **Seats** 40 **Children** Portions, Menu

Gisborough Hall

⚫⚫ Modern British ☙

Well-crafted dishes in a Victorian country house

☎ 0844 879 9149 & 01287 593999
Whitby Ln TS14 6PT
e-mail: general.gisboroughhall@macdonald-hotels.co.uk
web: www.gisborough-hall.co.uk
dir: A171, follow signs for Whitby to Waterfall rdbt then 3rd exit into Whitby Lane, hotel 500yds on right

Only 20 minutes drive out of Middlesbrough, the Hall sits amid rolling grounds and woodland, with a backdrop of the Cleveland Hills. The Chaloner's dining room is named after the family who used to own Gisborough, and is spacious and gently formal, with white-upholstered chairs and unclothed tables, and glass partitions to divide the space. Simple but imaginative modern British menus are also divided - as between seasonal specials and signature dishes. A serving of duck liver pâté and toasted brioche is lifted out of the ordinary by its accompaniments of a cromesquis of the confit leg, shallot salad and orange purée, while that modern classic, monkfish wrapped in Parma ham, is generously partnered with a seared scallop and a well-timed risotto of tomatoes, fennel and basil. Finish with warm chocolate fondant with a properly gooey centre, served with blueberry and lavender compôte and vanilla ice cream.

Chef Dave Sotheran **Owner** Gisborough Estates Ltd **Times** 12.30-2.30/6.30-9.30 Closed L Mon-Sat **Prices** Fixed D 3 course £35-£48, Starter £6.75-£9.75, Main £18.50-£23.50, Dessert £6.75-£8.75, Service optional **Wines** 41 bottles over £30, 30 bottles under £30, 19 by glass **Notes** Sunday L, Vegetarian available, Dress restrictions, Smart casual, no trainers or sportswear, Civ Wed 300 **Seats** 90, Pr/dining room 33 **Children** Portions, Menu **Parking** 180

The Star Inn

⚫⚫ Traditional British V 🍷NOTABLE WINE LIST ☙

Exhilarating Yorkshire cooking in a thatched country inn

☎ 01439 770397
YO62 5JE
e-mail: reservations@thestaratharome.co.uk
dir: From Helmsley take A170 towards Kirkbymoorside, after 0.5m turn right towards Harome. After 1.5m, inn 1st building on right

The thatched country pub in a moorland village just outside Helmsley is a perfect crooked house: it's hard to get pictures to hang straight on 14th-century walls, as you'll see. Comprising a comfortable rustic bar with candles, an old dining room with chunky tables, a real fire and knick-knacks galore, and a newer one with a bright, opulent, contemporary feel, The Star has it all, not forgetting genuinely friendly staff and Andrew Pern's Yorkshire-rooted country cooking, which places a high premium on big, rugged flavours. It doesn't come much more rugged than Stinking Bishop, the prime ingredient in a twice-baked soufflé served with smoked bacon salad and red wine shallots. That could be followed by roast rump of Ryedale lamb, pink and tender, with pan haggerty and pearl barley, all hedged about with rosemary-scented pan juices, or breaded Scarborough woof with brown shrimps, buttered samphire and duck egg gribiche. The exhilarating sense of novelty extends into desserts such as spiced fig Bakewell with superb chestnut and honey ice cream and a little jug of almond anglaise.

Chef Andrew Pern **Owner** Andrew Pern **Times** 11.30-3/6.30-11 Closed 1 Jan, L Mon, D Sun **Prices** Fixed L 2 course £20, Fixed D 3 course £25, Tasting menu £75, Starter £5.95-£15, Main £17.95-£26.95, Dessert £6-£15, Service included **Wines** 77 bottles over £30, 32 bottles under £30, 24 by glass **Notes** Chef's table for 6-8 people, tasting menu 6-8 course, Sunday L, Vegetarian menu **Seats** 70, Pr/dining room 10 **Children** Portions, Menu **Parking** 30

HARROGATE
Map 19 SE35

Hotel du Vin Harrogate

@@ British, Mediterranean V ☺

Fine food and wine in chic Georgian townhouse setting

☎ 0844 7364257
Prospect Place HG1 1LB
e-mail: reception.harrogate@hotelduvin.com
web: www.hotelduvin.com
dir: A1(M) junct 47, A59 to Harrogate, follow town centre signs to Prince of Wales rdbt, 3rd exit, remain in right lane. Right at lights into Albert St, right into Prospect Place

This Victorian spa town's tea shops have a long tradition of spoiling its visitors, and the HdV's Harrogate outpost continues the tradition with dollops of 21st-century verve. The operation occupies a sybaritically-converted terrace of eight handsome Georgian townhouses opposite the 200-acre Stray common, and its interior will ring a bell with fans of the brand: style-savvy, unbuttoned luxury rubbing along seamlessly with the 18th-century grandeur of the rooms. The 'vin' part of the equation delivers fine wines at affordable prices to go with the French-influenced bistro-style menu. Terrine of belly pork with crisp black pudding and apple sauce is a typical starter, but it is the superb locally-sourced steaks that grab carnivores' attention at main course stage. On a fishy note, sea bass fillets are teamed with a deeply-flavoured cauliflower purée and crispy pancetta, and to finish, it just has to be a classic crème brûlée.

Chef Kevin Whiteford **Owner** Hotel du Vin Ltd
Times 12-2/5.30-10 **Prices** Starter £5.95-£11.50, Main £12.50-£55, Dessert £6.95, Service optional **Notes** Afternoon tea 2-5pm, Sunday L £19.95, Vegetarian menu, Civ Wed 75 **Seats** 86, Pr/dining room 60 **Children** Portions, Menu **Parking** 33

Nidd Hall Hotel

@@ Modern British

Culinary thrills in a Yorkshire country house

☎ 01423 771598
Nidd HG3 3BN
dir: A1M junct/A59 follow signs to Knaresborough. Continue through town centre & at Bond End lights turn left, then right onto B6165 signed Ripley & Pateley Bridge. Hotel on right in approx 4m

The hall was built during the reign of George IV for a Bradford wool merchant keen to display his success, and is a true English country house, down to its mature landscaped grounds, creeper-covered façade and elegant late-Georgian interiors. Of the dining options, the Terrace Restaurant is the prime site, a light room tinged with

verdant green décor, with antlered heads on the wall, and views over the gardens. A highly accomplished contemporary repertoire is in the practised hands of a large kitchen brigade, and the attention to detail in dishes such as butternut squash velouté with haricots and rabbit tortellini, laced with sherry, lifts them way above the humdrum. A main course of seared sea bass with more pasta parcels, this time of crab, is full of technical virtuosity, and benefits from accompaniments of fennel purée and a buttery shellfish and tomato sauce, while meats might offer venison saddle with textural contrasts of crispy celeriac, trompettes and sloe gin jelly. Fifteen minutes' wait seems a reasonable request for properly made cherry clafoutis, which comes with pistachio ice cream and Amaretto anglaise.

Times 6.30-9.30 Closed L Mon-Sat, D Tue-Wed

Rudding Park Hotel, Spa & Golf

@ Modern British V

Brasserie menu in an elegant Regency era hotel

☎ 01423 871350
Follifoot HG3 1JH
e-mail: reservations@ruddingpark.com
web: www.ruddingpark.co.uk
dir: A61 at rdbt with A658 follow signs 'Rudding Park'

Set in 300 acres of glorious parkland, the house is a Regency building with twin bowed façades and portico, now geared up for the expected range of modern amenities (spa pampering and golf, chiefly). Elegantly understated contemporary furnishings give a sense of space, especially in the airy Clocktower restaurant, where seating in charcoal and light green along with unclothed tables makes for a relaxed ambience. The menu is formatted brasserie-style, with daily specials such as tomato and basil soup with Parma ham and mozzarella, and grilled bream with red pepper coulis, heading up a lengthy classic repertoire. The grill delivers forth 28-day-aged beef cuts and burgers, and there are examples of well-thought modern dishes like pavé of salmon with a quail Scotch egg and samphire, or lamb three ways (cutlets, breast and shepherd's pie) in its own jus with heritage carrots. Finish with chocolate and cherry marquise and cherry ice cream.

Chef Eddie Gray **Owner** Simon Mackaness
Times 12-2.30/7-9.30 **Prices** Fixed L 2 course fr £14.95, Fixed D 3 course fr £37, Starter £8.50-£12.50, Main £17-£30, Dessert £8-£9, Service optional **Wines** 71 bottles over £30, 44 bottles under £30, 17 by glass **Notes** Sunday L, Vegetarian menu, Civ Wed 180 **Seats** 170, Pr/dining room 16 **Children** Portions, Menu **Parking** 250

Studley Hotel

@@ Pacific Rim

Smart hotel restaurant giving culinary tour of Asia

☎ 01423 560425
28 Swan Rd HG1 2SE
e-mail: info@studleyhotel.co.uk
web: www.orchidrestaurant.co.uk
dir: Adjacent to Valley Gardens, opposite Mercer Gallery

Mango and darkwood interiors divided by Japanese lattice-style screens are the setting for the Studley Hotel's Orchid restaurant, where the chefs give an eclectic pan-Asian array of cuisines from China, Indonesia, Japan, Korea, Malaysia, the Philippines, Thailand and Vietnam a thorough workout. A friendly team of attentive staff who know their way around the menu is a big plus, as is the large TV screen showing all the live cheffy action going on in the kitchen. Food miles are sacrificed in the name of authenticity as key ingredients are flown in regularly from Asia. A starter of aromatic Szechuan lamb brings slow-cooked lamb belly with cucumber, leek, red pepper, pancakes and yellow bean and honey dip, ahead of pan-fried chicken with Szechuan black pepper sauce and garlic cucumber. Desserts tend to be more successful when they stay within the Asian idiom - say Thai-style steamed banana cake cooked in a banana leaf and served with coconut ice cream.

Chef Kenneth Poon **Owner** Bokmun Chan
Times 12-2/6-10 Closed 25-26 Dec, L Sat **Prices** Fixed L 2 course £10.95, Fixed D 3 course £23.95-£31.95, Starter £4.60-£8.80, Main £8-£19.80, Dessert £4.90-£6.95, Service added but optional 10% **Wines** 13 bottles over £30, 26 bottles under £30, 10 by glass **Notes** Tue D sushi & sashimi, Vegetarian available **Seats** 72, Pr/dining room 20 **Parking** 18, On street

Save on Hotels. Book at theAA.com/hotel

YORKSHIRE, NORTH 513 ENGLAND

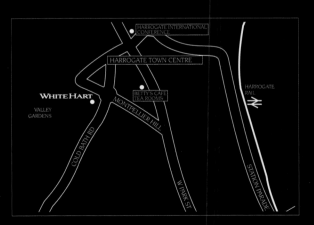

HARROGATE *continued*

van Zeller

⊛⊛ Modern British V ✋

Impressively creative cooking in Montpellier

☎ 01423 508762
8 Montpellier St HG1 2TQ
e-mail: info@vanzellerrestaurants.co.uk

On two levels, with tables on the lower looking out onto fashionable Montpellier, van Zeller is a smartly done-out restaurant, with brown leather-look chairs and banquettes at clothed tables, a dark wooden floor and subdued lighting providing a pleasant glow in the evening. Tom van Zeller has handed over the kitchen reins to his head chef, Neil Bentinck, and between them they've created a range of menus that are bursting with innovative ideas, from roasted onion 'tea' with peas, radish and spelt to a main course of roast Suffolk lamb with young nettles, celeriac dumplings, buttermilk and borage. Masterly technique is evident throughout, and a confident approach means that even unexpected compositions succeed, often using wild ingredients. Try pig's head with sorrel, dandelion, turnips and smoked eel, and go on to Goosnargh duck pie with lovage mash, roast onions, artichoke and lettuce. Seafood receives similar treatments, seen in halibut fillet with salt-baked beetroot, turnips, charred spring onions and brown shrimp and smoked butter, and for pudding there might be chocolate and peanut brownie with liquorice and raspberry.

Chef Tom van Zeller, Neil Bentinck **Owner** Tom van Zeller **Times** 12-2/6-10 Closed various dates throughout year, Mon, D Sun **Prices** Tasting menu fr £60, Service added but optional 12.5% **Wines** 9 by glass **Notes** 5 course £35, ALC £49.50, 10 course chef's menu from £85, Vegetarian menu, Dress restrictions, Smart casual **Seats** 34 **Children** Portions **Parking** Montpellier Hill

The White Hart Hotel

⊛⊛ British

Modern brasserie dishes in a Georgian landmark

☎ 01423 505681
2 Cold Bath Rd HG2 0NF
e-mail: reception@whitehart.net
web: www.whitehart.net
dir: A59 to Harrogate. A661 3rd exit on rdbt to Harrogate. Left at rdbt onto A6040 for 1m. Right onto A61. Bear left down Montpellier Hill

Not far from the Valley Gardens park, The White Hart is something of a Harrogate landmark, having been a comfortable resort of the discerning traveller since the Georgian era. The old dining room is now a trendy pub called the Fat Badger, while the main eating space is a light room done out in on-trend sandy neutral colours with a checkered pattern in curtains and seating. They call it a Brasserie, the logic of which is revealed at sight of a menu that deals in the likes of grilled scallops with leeks, bacon and cheddar, or oxtail risotto with a crisp-fried quail's egg and horseradish bubbles. An interesting fish offering is goujons of Scarborough woof (a catfish, despite its name) with baby clams in Cullen skink, and there's also a voguish three-way serving of pork - belly, fillet and cheek - seasoned with vanilla and purple sage. Puddings include the regional delicacy, Yorkshire curd tart, dolled up with cinnamon ice cream and blood orange, as well as peanut butter crumble with caramel.

Times 11.30-3.30/6-10 **Prices** Fixed L 2 course £12, Starter £4.95-£9.95, Main £8.95-£21.95 **Notes** L expresss menu Mon-Fri 11.30-3.30, Sunday L

See advert on page 513

The Inn at Hawnby

⊛ Modern British ✋

Hearty, honest cooking at a welcoming village inn

☎ 01439 798202
YO62 5QS
e-mail: info@innathawnby.co.uk
web: www.innathawnby.co.uk
dir: From the S, A1 to Thirsk & Teeside exit A19/A168 for Scarborough onto A170. 1st left through Felixkirk. Through Boltby into Hawnby

Hawnby is a lovely village with an unspoilt authenticity that attracts hikers and bikers who come to take on the North York Moors National Park, and this stone-built Victorian village inn makes an inviting prospect as a base, thanks to the sincere and friendly owners who make it stand out from the crowd. When it comes to feeding hungry souls in from the great outdoors, the kitchen takes a no-nonsense approach, drawing on quality local ingredients for its gutsy, crowd-pleasing contemporary dishes. You could nurse a pint and eat in the cosy bar, but then you would miss the splendid views and wildlife in the garden that is a backdrop to eating in the old-fashioned elegance of the dining room. Confit of Yorkshire duck leg served with roasted peppers, chorizo and courgettes and glazed with red onion marmalade is a satisfying starter, followed by a luxurious fish pie filled with halibut, haddock, smoked salmon, trout, crayfish and white wine and leek sauce. Finish with a trio of well-made desserts - strawberry Pavlova, dark chocolate mousse and fruit crumble.

Chef Jason Reeves **Owner** Kathryn & David Young **Times** 12-2/7-9 Closed 25 Dec, L Mon-Tue (limited opening Feb-Mar please phone) **Prices** Starter £5-£7.50, Main £10-£20, Dessert £5.50-£9.50, Service optional **Wines** 11 bottles under £30, 12 by glass **Notes** Sunday L £12.50-£17.50, Vegetarian available, Civ Wed 35 **Seats** 32, Pr/dining room 30 **Children** Portions, Menu **Parking** 22

Feversham Arms Hotel & Verbena Spa

Rosettes not confirmed at time of going to print

HELMSLEY MAP 19 SE68

Modern British V

Modern boutique hotel with equally modern culinary ideas

☎ 01439 770766
1-8 High St YO62 5AG
e-mail: info@fevershamarmshotel.com
web: www.fevershamarmshotel.com
dir: A1 junct 49 follow A168 to Thirsk, take A170 to Helmsley. Turn left at mini rdbt then right, hotel on right past church

The Rosette award for this establishment has been suspended due to a change of chef. Reassessment will take place in due course under the new chef.

The Feversham Arms gets its name from the earl who rebuilt an old coaching inn in 1855. He wouldn't recognise the distinctive hotel today, complete as it is with lovely gardens, spa and all-year heated outdoor swimming pool. The cosy lounge with its comfy sofas and open fire is an inviting place to enjoy a pre-dinner drink (and perhaps a post one too), before moving through to the very different look and feel of the restaurant - a fashionably smart conservatory-style room, with artwork hanging on red walls, banquettes and bucket seats at properly set tables, and a wonderfully intimate, romantic ambience at night. The cooking is based on Yorkshire's larder of pedigree goodies, and Simon Kelly displays a high degree of culinary skill and imagination. Dishes are intelligently composed to bring out distinct flavours without tipping over into pretension or gimmick. Foie gras mousse, for instance, is partnered by nothing more than lovage-infused blackberries, and Portland crab by watercress velouté and buttermilk. Among the handful or so of main courses may be corn-fed chicken, succulent and full of flavour, with Puy lentils, pancetta, oyster mushrooms and sauce Jacqueline, which sounds pretty standard but turns out to be a masterly multi-flavoured dish. Equally satisfying on the palate is a fish option: perhaps accurately timed fillet of wild halibut accompanied by truffle, fennel and shrimps in crumbed rye bread. Innovation is given free rein with puddings: witness ras el hanout bananas with coffee, Muscovado and treacle mayonnaise, or chocolate pannacotta with nougat and - wait for it - spiced mirin jelly.

Chef Simon Kelly **Owner** Feversham Arms Ltd
Times 12-2/6.30-9.30 Closed L Mon-Sat **Prices** Tasting menu fr £55, Starter £9-£13.50, Main £28-£29, Dessert £9.50-£10.50, Service optional **Wines** 11 by glass
Notes Tasting menu whole tables only, Sunday L £19.50-£25, Vegetarian menu, Dress restrictions, Smart casual, Civ Wed 70 **Seats** 65, Pr/dining room 24
Children Portions, Menu **Parking** 50

The Angel Inn

HETTON MAP 18 SD95

British NEW

Culinary delights in well-established Dales dining inn

☎ 01756 730263
BD23 6LT
e-mail: info@angelhetton.co.uk
web: www.angelhetton.co.uk
dir: 6m N Skipton, follow B6265 towards Grassington, left at duck pond & again at T-junct. The Angel up the hill on right

The creeper-covered Angel was in the vanguard of the foodie revolution that has transformed the dining scene in British inns and pubs over the last 20 years, and it remains as committed as ever to satisfying diners with top-class local produce and skillful, intelligent and polished cooking. Once discovered, hordes of loyal returnees head back to this oasis of good cheer and splendid flavour-driven food again and again, and it's easy to see why: set in a tiny village in the Yorkshire Dales National Park, and dating back around five centuries, the interior comes fully loaded with all the gnarled oak beams, nooks and crannies, and cockle-warming real fires you might hope for. A series of interconnecting rooms comprises a buzzy and informal beamed bar-brasserie with its own menu (order food at the bar) and the more sedate, full-dress experience in the restaurant, where high-backed upholstered chairs at smartly linen-swathed tables and waiter service set a more refined tone. The kitchen brigade is always firing on all cylinders, turning out the kind of cooking that allows the inherent quality of ingredients to shine. The freshest fish finds its way into blackboard specials such as pan-seared sea bass fillets with basil mash, courgettes, slow-roasted tomatoes, rocket and balsamic reduction, or pan-seared hake with prawn wonton, confit cherry tomatoes, buttered spinach, chive mash and lobster sauce. Elsewhere, well-thought-out ideas might include a parcel of slow-braised beef shin with marrowbone fritter, chervil root, and carrot crisps, followed by braised pork belly with pork popcorn, black pudding purée, mustard jelly, roasted carrots and creamed potatoes. Rich flavours and textures abound, and there's no let up when it comes to dessert, with memorable ideas such as iced apple Calvados parfait with apple and golden sultana compôte, or white chocolate and lemon tart with passionfruit syrup.

Chef Bruce Elsworth **Owner** Juliet Watkins
Times 12-2.30/6-10 Closed 25 Dec & 1 wk Jan, L Mon-Sat, D Sun **Prices** Prices not confirmed Service optional
Wines 26 by glass **Notes** Vegetarian available, Civ Wed 70 **Seats** 65, Pr/dining room 24 **Children** Portions, Menu
Parking 40

| HELMSLEY | Map 19 SE68 |

Black Swan Hotel

@ @ Modern British V 🕭

Yorkshire boutique inn with modish cooking

☎ 01439 770466
Market Place YO62 5BJ
e-mail: enquiries@blackswan-helmsley.co.uk
web: www.blackswan-helmsley.co.uk
dir: A170 towards Scarborough, on entering Helmsley
hotel at end of Market Place, just off mini-rdbt

Cantering through the centuries from Elizabethan to
Georgian to Victorian, the Black Swan mixes its historic
pedigree with a stylish 21st-century boutique look these
days. Smack on the square of this pretty North York Moors
village, the tea shop does a roaring trade in Yorkshire's
celebrated bakery indulgences, while the elegant Rutland
restaurant overlooking the walled garden is the scene for
vibrant, thoroughly modern cooking with an unerring eye
for splendid local produce. Pithivier of venison is served
with 'flavours and textures' of beetroot, horseradish
cream, and chocolate and balsamic dressing, and could
precede slow-braised featherblade of beef with pommes
purées, roasted shallot, baby onions and red wine jus.
Poached pear with cinnamon parfait and caramel sauce
is a typical finale.

Chef Paul Peters **Owner** John Jameson
Times 12.30-2.30/7-9.30 Closed L Mon-Sat **Prices** Fixed
D 3 course £36, Tasting menu £50, Service optional
Wines 134 bottles over £30, 59 bottles under £30, 15 by
glass **Notes** Tasting menu 6 course, Sunday L, Vegetarian
menu, Dress restrictions, Smart casual, Civ Wed 90
Seats 65, Pr/dining room 30 **Children** Portions, Menu
Parking 40

Feversham Arms Hotel & Verbena Spa

*Rosettes not confirmed at time of going to print –
see page 515*

| HETTON | Map 18 SD95 |

The Angel Inn

@ @ @ *– see page 515*

| KIRKBY FLEETHAM | Map 19 SE20 |

The Black Horse

@ @ Traditional & Modern 🕭

Modernised Yorkshire pub fare by the village green

☎ 01609 749010 & 749011
7 Lumley Ln DL7 0SH
e-mail: gm@blackhorsekirkbyfleetham.com
web: www.blackhorsekirkbyfleetham.com
dir: Exit A1 to Kirkby Fleetham, follow restaurant signs

The stone-built pub by a Yorkshire village green has been
given a confident but careful makeover, its guest rooms
full of modern comforts, and a range of regular events - a
wine club, fish-and-chip Fridays and weekly quiz nights -
to lure in an enthusiastic crowd of supporters. Sleek table
surfaces and a muted colour scheme distinguish the
stylish dining room, and there's garden seating for drinks
and nibbles and the chance to watch a game of quoits.
Up-to-date spins on traditional Yorkshire pub fare raise
the game, with openers such as salmon cured in malt
whisky with honey-mustard dressing, a breakfast salad
of black pudding, dry-cured bacon and a poached egg, or
a sharing board offering 'bits and bats' of all the
starters. Mains include an enterprising version of fish pie,
incorporating smoked haddock, mussels and
Wensleydale, while signature dishes embrace a textbook
take on braised lamb shank with roasted garlic mash,
confit roots, redcurrants and rosemary. You'd expect
Yorkshire rhubarb to feature strongly in the season, and it
does - in the form of a spicy crumble with vanilla ice
cream.

Chef Adrian Knowles **Owner** Inn Focus Group
Times 12-2.30/5-9 **Prices** Starter £3.95-£9.50, Main

£10.95-£18.95, Dessert £5-£7, Service optional **Wines** 10
by glass **Notes** Sunday L, Vegetarian available **Seats** 40
Children Portions, Menu **Parking** 40

| KNARESBOROUGH | Map 19 SE35 |

General Tarleton Inn

@ @ Modern British 🕭

Polished cooking in refined old coaching inn

☎ 01423 340284
Boroughbridge Rd, Ferrensby HG5 0PZ
e-mail: gti@generaltarleton.co.uk
dir: A1(M) junct 48 at Boroughbridge, take A6055 to
Knaresborough. 4m on right

This 18th-century coaching inn, in open countryside, is a
characterful place, with low beamed ceilings, rustic
walls, log fires and cosy corners. It has a private dining
room and separate cocktail bar - sure indicators of its
market - as well as a smart restaurant in what was the
stable. 'Food with Yorkshire Roots' is emblazoned on the
menu, and indeed a taste of Nidderdale salmon (smoked,
mousse, and seared with pickled fennel, accompanied by
horseradish ice cream) may precede chargrilled fillet of
Dales beef with foie gras tortellini and veal consommé.
Locally sourced or not, dishes are well rendered and
combinations intelligent: chilli-spiced crispy squid on a
julienne of peppers and coriander, say, then roast
pheasant breast rolled in sage and pancetta
accompanied by confit leg, Savoy cabbage, and
boulangère potatoes. The kitchen's momentum continues
into the final straight, with puddings like chocolate
fondant with orange ice cream and mandarin jelly, and
classic lemon tart with raspberry sorbet.

Chef John Topham **Owner** John & Claire Topham
Times 12-1.45/5.30-9.15 Closed L Mon-Sat, D 26 Dec, 1
Jan **Prices** Fixed L 2 course £15, Fixed D 3 course £18.50,
Starter £5.95-£9.95, Main £10.95-£22.50, Dessert
£4.95-£7.95, Service optional, Groups min 6 service 10%
Wines 74 bottles over £30, 48 bottles under £30, 13 by
glass **Notes** Sunday L, Vegetarian available, Dress
restrictions, Smart casual **Seats** 64, Pr/dining room 40
Children Portions, Menu **Parking** 40

Samuel's at Swinton Park

MASHAM   **MAP 19 SE28**

Modern British V

Exciting cooking in a castellated mansion

☎ 01765 680900
Swinton HG4 4JH
e-mail: enquiries@swintonpark.com
web: www.swintonpark.com
dir: Please telephone for detailed directions

Built on the 20,000-acre Swinton Estate and surrounded by 200 acres of gardens and parkland, the Cunliffe-Lister family's ancestral home is a hugely imposing castellated mansion complete with towers. The interior has the décor and fittings of a stately home, with antique furniture and walls hung with family portraits, while diners sit under the restaurant's gold-leaf ceiling and catch the views from the enormous windows of the lake and park. Discreet but unbuttoned staff add to the enjoyment of a visit, and Simon Crannage's imaginative cooking brings further pleasure.

The lunch and dinner menus follow a set-price pattern, with three or four choices per course, and there are separate vegetarian menus. Dinner might kick off with pheasant from the estate (chef Crannage is a lucky man, with four acres of kitchen garden to furnish him with fruit, vegetables and herbs as well) served as rillettes with date purée, mulled turnips and game chips. The fish that goes into a starter of smoked trout with house pickles, fennel toast and citrus crème fraîche also comes from the estate, so you can be assured of its freshness. Such well-judged compositions are typical of the kitchen's contemporary slant, adding exciting flavour elements to the main ingredient. Timings are pretty much flawless too, as in fillet of Scottish halibut with white beans and white cabbage, smoked chicken stock and confit wing adding depth and counterpoint. Braised blade of beef with seared foie gras, pommes purée, young vegetables and a Madeira sauce might be from the country-house school, but there could also be belly, fillet and pulled shoulder of pork, served with buckwheat, treacle-roasted carrots and onion purée infused with bay. Puddings end proceedings on a strong note: poached pears with a matching sorbet and set caramel praline, say, or a plate of local rhubarb with sorbet, yoghurt mousse and home-baked granola.

Chef Simon Crannage **Owner** Mr and Mrs Cunliffe-Lister **Times** 12.30-2/7-9.30 Closed L Mon (only Castle menu in bar) **Prices** Fixed L 2 course £22, Fixed D 3 course £52, Tasting menu £60, Service optional **Wines** 115 bottles over £30, 4 bottles under £30, 13 by glass **Notes** Sommelier pairing £28.50, Garden produce menu £52, Sunday L, Vegetarian menu, Civ Wed 120 **Seats** 60, Pr/dining room 20 **Children** Portions, Menu **Parking** 80

The Black Swan at Oldstead

OLDSTEAD   **MAP 19 SE57**

Modern British V

Top-notch cooking in charming country inn

☎ 01347 868387
YO61 4BL
e-mail: enquiries@blackswanoldstead.co.uk
dir: A1 junct 49, A168, A19 S (or from York A19 N), then Coxwold, Byland Abbey, Oldstead

There's a real sense of place to The Black Swan. Granted it has been on this spot for some 500 years (in the North York Moors National Park), and its old stone walls could tell a tale or two, but it's more the way the best features of its inherent character have been updated, upgraded and blended into a high end restaurant with rooms without the need to resort to every contemporary design concept. The bar, for example, is gloriously unreconstructed (flagged floor and all that) and serves a proper pint of real ale, and the dining room has Persian rugs, an open fire, and richly burnished darkwood tables topped with red roses. Into this soothing setting steps chef Adam Jackson with some rather exciting cooking. There's a tasting menu (with optional wine flight) if you feel like going where the chef wants to take you, and a carte that is packed with fabulous ingredients cooked in a modern manner. Japanese-style tuna tartare, for example, with wasabi, ginger, lime and coriander shows a light touch, or go for wood pigeon, served up with pickled vegetables, beetroot, watercress and walnuts. These are well considered combinations, cooked with skill and presented with flair. Next up, ox cheek comes with cauliflower cheese, macaroni, truffle and salsify, and halibut with squid, Jerusalem artichoke, Pink Fir potatoes and samphire. Rhubarb soufflé with stem ginger ice cream ends things on a high.

Chef Adam Jackson **Owner** The Banks family **Times** 12-2/6-9 Closed 1 wk Jan, L Mon-Wed **Prices** Fixed L 3 course fr £25, Fixed D 3 course fr £25, Tasting menu fr £70, Starter £11-£15, Main £21-£26, Dessert £9-£10, Service optional **Wines** 112 bottles over £30, 13 bottles under £30, 13 by glass **Notes** Tasting menu 7 course, Sunday L, Vegetarian menu **Seats** 40, Pr/dining room 12 **Children** Portions, Menu **Parking** 25

MALTON   Map 19 SE77

The Talbot Hotel

@@ British 🍷

Highly accomplished local cooking from a local chef

☎ 01653 639096
Yorkersgate YO17 7AJ
e-mail: reservations@talbotmalton.co.uk
dir: A46 Malton

The Talbot is a foursquare Yorkshire house that has been in the Naylor-Leyland family since 1739, and they've looked after it well over the centuries, from the landscaped gardens to the light-toned contemporary elegance with which today's hotel is furnished. If localism is a virtue in food sourcing, it's surely all the more so in the provenance of the chef himself, and James Martin was born in Malton, so has Yorkshire blood and Yorkshire pride flowing through him. The style of cooking he delivers (in an executive capacity) rises to the occasion of the smart, sophisticated dining room, where crisp white linen, silver cutlery and formal service play their parts. Modern British thinking is to the fore, with a mix of classical and up-to-date technique brought to bear on the fine ingredients the kitchen has at its disposal. A kind of croquette of lightly smoked kipper starts things off with a flourish, accompanied as it is by seasonal Sand Hutton asparagus and a capery Cambridge butter sauce. That's followed by superb lamb from Terrington, roasted in lavender and hay and partnered by braised shallots, peas and celery cress, with daringly savoury notes creeping into desserts too - dark chocolate fondant with caramel ice cream and black salt praline, for example.

Chef James Martin, Craig Atchinson **Owner** Fitzwilliam Estate **Times** 12.30-2.30/6.30-9.30 **Prices** Prices not confirmed Service optional **Wines** 14 by glass **Notes** Sunday L, Vegetarian available, Dress restrictions, No ripped jeans or football shirts, Civ Wed 40 **Seats** 40, Pr/dining room 40 **Children** Portions **Parking** 40

MASHAM   Map 19 SE28

Samuel's at Swinton Park

@@@ – see page 517

Vennell's

@@ Modern British 🍷

Lively modern cooking in stylish surroundings

☎ 01765 689000
7 Silver St HG4 4DX
e-mail: info@vennellsrestaurant.co.uk
dir: 8m from A1 Masham exit, 10m N of Ripon

Vennell's is a smartly appointed restaurant, with a small bar and split-level dining room done out in plum and taupe, with rich fabrics and crisp white napery. Jon Vennell's cooking is marked out by the high quality of the produce he uses, his eye for presentation and an unfussy approach that makes for well-defined flavours. Thus venison carpaccio (melt-in-the-mouth stuff) is

accompanied simply with pickled carrots and courgettes and parmesan strips in an attractive-looking, clear-flavoured starter, while main course might bring forth braised ox cheek, cooked to perfection, with creamy mash, wild mushrooms and shallots and a smattering of gremolata. The short menu normally encompasses a few seafood options: perhaps slowly poached salmon fillet enhanced by watercress sauce and crisp leeks, and well-timed, pan-fried sea bream inventively accompanied by mussels, broccoli, beetroot gnocchi and masala sauce. An impressive line-up of Yorkshire cheeses is a possibility for those who want to pass on a pudding like rich dark chocolate terrine with smooth white chocolate sauce.

Chef Jon Vennell **Owner** Jon & Laura Vennell **Times** 12-2/7.15-mdnt Closed 26-29 Dec, 1-14 Jan, 1 wk Sep, BHs, Mon, L Tue-Sat, D Sun **Prices** Fixed D 3 course £27.99-£32, Service optional **Wines** 27 bottles over £30, 28 bottles under £30, 11 by glass **Notes** Sunday L, Vegetarian available **Seats** 30, Pr/dining room 16 **Children** Portions **Parking** On street & Market Sq

MIDDLESBROUGH   Map 19 NZ41

Chadwicks Inn Maltby

@@ Modern British 🍷

Ambitious modern cooking in moorland country inn

☎ 01642 590300
High Ln, Maltby TS8 0BG
e-mail: enquiries@chadwicksinnmaltby.co.uk
dir: A19-A174(W)/A1045, follow signs to Yarm & Maltby, left at the Manor House, inn 500yds on left through village

Formerly known as The Pathfinders, in honour of Second World War flying aces, one of whom opened the place after hostilities were over, the country inn on the edge of the North York Moors still features a quantity of aviation memorabilia among its Victorian beams and stonework. A discreet boutique feel has crept in latterly, bringing hurricane lamps with church candles, banquette seating and swinging Sinatra coming from the speakers, and there is a partially open-to-view kitchen. The carte is all ambitious modern fare, offering scallops and clams with Avruga in fennel beurre blanc, and venison with a cherry Bakewell suet roll and bubble-and-squeak croquette. A menu of simpler bistro fare deals in velvety-rich chestnut mushroom soup with crispy shallots, and free-range chicken breast with béarnaise and chips. Wednesday night is grill night, when sirloins and rib-eyes, spatchcocked chicken and butterflied sea bream come into play. To finish, caramelised lemon syllabub with dots of meringue looks very pretty on its slab of black slate, and there are fine northern cheeses.

Chef John Appleby **Owner** Gary & Helen Gill, Lee Tolley & John Appleby **Times** 12-2.30/5-9.30 Closed 25 Dec, 1 Jan, Mon, D Sun **Prices** Fixed L 2 course £13.95, Starter £6.50-£9.50, Main £10.95-£26, Dessert £4.95-£6.95, Service optional, Groups min 8 service 10% **Wines** 23 bottles over £30, 21 bottles under £30, 8 by glass **Notes** Steak & grill night from £30, Bistro menu lunch & early eve, Sunday L £11.95-£17.95, Vegetarian available **Seats** 47 **Children** Portions, Menu **Parking** 50

OLDSTEAD   Map 19 SE57

The Black Swan at Oldstead

@@@ – see page 517

PICKERING   Map 19 SE78

Fox & Hounds Country Inn

@ Modern British 🍷

Quality fare in village gastro-pub

☎ 01751 431577
Main St, Sinnington YO62 6SQ
e-mail: fox.houndsinn@btconnect.com
dir: In Sinnington centre, 3m W of Pickering, off A170

The bar is a popular place at this 18th-century inn, originally three separate cottages (count the front doors), with its log burner, settles and beams. Just as popular with diners is the stylish restaurant, where upholstered chairs are pulled up at oak tables. Light lunches run from black pudding with sautéed potatoes, a poached egg and crispy bacon to fish pie, while the kitchen sets out its stall with a more ambitious evening menu. First-course sea bass fillet accompanied by chilli and ginger scallops, stir-fried shiitake mushrooms and Chinese greens might precede beef brisket slowly braised with red wine, bacon and shallots, served with croquette potatoes and roast root vegetables. Diehards could go for a steak with the usual trimmings, and desserts are a satisfying lot, among them perhaps apple and plum crumble with custard.

Chef Mark Caffrey **Owner** Mr & Mrs A Stephens **Times** 12-2/6.30-9 Closed 25-27 Dec **Prices** Starter £4.95-£7.95, Main £10.50-£18.95, Dessert £5.75-£10.95, Service optional **Wines** 9 bottles over £30, 32 bottles under £30, 9 by glass **Notes** Early eve menu Sun-Thu 5.30-6.30pm, Sunday L £21.20-£25.95, Vegetarian available, Dress restrictions, Smart casual, No shorts **Seats** 40, Pr/dining room 12 **Children** Portions, Menu **Parking** 35

The White Swan Inn

@@ Modern British

Smart market-town inn with well-judged menu

☎ 01751 472288
Market Place YO18 7AA
e-mail: welcome@white-swan.co.uk
web: www.white-swan.co.uk
dir: Just beyond junct of A169/A170 in Pickering, turn right off A170 into Market Place

Originally a refuelling post for the York to Whitby stagecoach, the centuries-old White Swan hasn't forgotten its pub roots, but neither has it stood still when it comes to embracing the country-chic interior design of today's top-ranking country inns. There's still a cosy bar with well-kept ales and a smart lounge with squashy sofas and log fire. The classy restaurant at the rear ups the ante with its modish country good looks: think ruby red walls, winter fire, stone floors and evening candlelight. Unfussy modern cooking fashioned from good quality seasonal Yorkshire produce (with an admirable eye on food miles) is the kitchen's mantra. Take an opener of Whitby fishcakes served with herbed shrimp salad and tartare, perhaps followed up with slow-cooked belly pork (Plum Pudding breed) matched with sweet red cabbage, brandy apple sauce, mustard mash and crackling.

Times 12-2/6.45-9

PICKHILL   Map 19 SE38

Nags Head Country Inn

◉◉ Modern British

Ambitious cooking in country inn

☎ 01845 567391
YO7 4JG
e-mail: reservations@nagsheadpickhill.co.uk
dir: Leave A1 junct 50 (travelling N) onto A6055; junct 51 (travelling S) onto A684, then A6055

In a quiet village just off the A1, The Nags Head is a civilised, welcoming inn, dating from the 17th century. The taproom dispenses real ales and has a separate menu, with the restaurant menu focused on seasonal ingredients, with game prominent in season: seared breast of wood pigeon with apple and blue cheese salad and mustard dressing, say, followed by game pie. New season's asparagus may appear in late spring, with a fried egg and ham shavings, alongside a more exotic starter of tempura king prawns with salt-and-pepper squid, wasabi and pickled ginger. Prime ingredients are sometimes given a surprising twist - foie gras terrine with pease pudding, for instance, in a starter with ham hock, tomato relish and crumbled crackling - and flavours can be piled up, although the results are normally successful, as when seared loin of lamb with confit breast and sautéed sweetbreads is joined by beetroot risotto, broad bean and lovage stew and nettle purée.

Times 12-2/6-9.30 Closed 25 Dec

RICHMOND   Map 19 NZ10

The Frenchgate Restaurant and Hotel

◉◉ Modern British ◐

Contemporary cooking in a swish Georgian townhouse

☎ 01748 822087 & 07921 136362
59-61 Frenchgate DL10 7AE
e-mail: info@thefrenchgate.co.uk
dir: From A1 (Scotch Corner) to Richmond on A6108. After lights, 1st left into Lile Close (leading to Flints Terrace) for hotel car park. Or for front entrance continue to 1st rdbt, left into Dundas St. At T-junct left into Frenchgate

Amid the cobbled streets of historic Richmond is this Georgian townhouse done-out with a good deal of panache. The blend of old and new is balanced to a tee in bedrooms and public rooms alike, with lots of local contemporary artworks on display (and for sale) providing an ever-changing backdrop. The diminutive and elegant

dining room (just seven tables) is the setting for some bright, creative contemporary cooking. Pressed foie gras terrine, for example, is served on slate, the accompanying sweet and sour cherry jam the perfect foil, or go for the Whitby white crab cocktail. Regional produce features in main courses, too, with roasted loin of Swaledale lamb served up with its braised leg meat in a mini pie, plus colcannon potatoes and a modish mint sauce gel. The slate is back at dessert stage, too, this time carrying a champagne jelly with raspberry sorbet and clotted cream. Service is led by the ebullient owner, David Todd.

Chef Lisa Miller **Owner** David & Luiza Todd **Times** 12-2/6-9.30 **Prices** Fixed L 2 course £12.95-£18.95, Fixed D 3 course £34, Starter £4.50-£6.95, Main £8.95-£16.95, Dessert £4.95-£5.95, Service optional, Groups min 6 service 10% **Wines** 32 bottles over £30, 35 bottles under £30, 9 by glass **Notes** Pre-theatre & tasting menu available, matching wine flights, Sunday L, Vegetarian available, Civ Wed 60 **Seats** 24, Pr/dining room 24 **Children** Portions **Parking** 12

RIPON   Map 19 SE37

The George at Wath

◉ Modern British

Revamped country inn with enterprising cooking

☎ 01765 641324
Main St, Wath HG4 5EN
e-mail: reception@georgeatwath.co.uk
web: www.georgeatwath.co.uk

The George's traditional bar, with its log-burner and mixture of oak and flagstone floors, leads to the smartly furnished restaurant, where helpful and genuinely friendly staff provide a good level of service. The menu has universal appeal, judging by openers of potted crab with a saffron brioche, and carpaccio with parmesan shavings, and main courses of steak and ale pie, and beer-battered haddock with the usual accompaniments. Presentation is carefully considered - seen in a colourful starter of ham knuckle terrine capped by a fried quail's egg, accompanied by a small jar of piccalilli topped with pea shoots - and quality meats are properly prepared: perfectly roast squab pigeon, tender and full of flavour, with confit leg, sauced with pan juices and served with red cabbage and carrot purées and hash browns.

Times 12-2.30/5.30-9 Closed D Sun

The Royal Oak

◉ Modern British ◐

Modernised traditional inn with food to suit

☎ 01765 602284
36 Kirkgate HG4 1PB
e-mail: info@royaloakripon.co.uk
dir: In town centre

The old coaching inn stands in the centre of this small cathedral city, with all the historic sights to hand and the famous racecourse only a short canter away. The old

place has been opened up within and has an uncluttered contemporary feel with wooden floors, real fires and leather sofas. It's still very much a pub, though, with real ales on tap, a separate dining area, and a small patio out back. The menu has broad appeal and plenty of old favourites among some perkier ideas. You might start, for example, with crabcake with potted shrimp butter and Bloody Mary ketchup, or chicken liver parfait with toasted spiced fruit loaf and Landlord ale chutney. Main courses include classic fish and chips, local steaks from Wateredge Farm, and Yorkshire Dales lamb with potatoes, red cabbage and garden peas, but you might also go for sticky Ripon beef with beetroot gnocchi, Paris mushrooms, horseradish cream and parmesan crackling.

Chef Jonathan Murray **Owner** Timothy Taylor & Co Ltd **Times** 12-2.30/5.30-9.30 **Prices** Starter fr £3.95, Main fr £7.95, Dessert fr £5.25, Service optional **Wines** 18 bottles under £30, 10 by glass **Notes** Quarterly seasonal tasting menu £9.95-£11.95, Vegetarian available **Seats** 50 **Children** Portions, Menu **Parking** 4, Market car park

SCARBOROUGH   Map 17 TA08

Beiderbecke's Hotel

◉ Modern British ◐

Modish hotel brasserie with good food

☎ 01723 365766 & 350349
1-3 The Crescent YO11 2PW
e-mail: info@beiderbeckes.com
dir: In town centre, 200mtrs from railway station

The name will need no introduction to trad jazz fans, but in case jazz is just not your bag, 'Bix' Beiderbecke was a famous American jazz horn player, pianist and composer. The hotel's upbeat Marmalade's Brasserie follows the jazz theme - the joint is jumping when live bands play at weekends, and the walls are hung with photos of famous musicians - but they don't flog it to death, ensuring that the result is an easygoing, stylish and contemporary venue with a good lively buzz. Local materials get a name check on a suitably modern brasserie repertoire that gets going with a workmanlike chicken and peppercorn terrine pointed up with a tangy cranberry chutney, followed by pan-fried sea bass with leek and pea risotto and herb oil. For the encore, a well-made traditional crème brûlée with shortbread biscuits hits the spot.

Chef Mark Huntley **Owner** Peter Bleach **Times** 12-10 All-day dining **Prices** Fixed L 2 course £17.95, Fixed D 3 course £21.95, Service optional **Wines** 3 bottles over £30, 29 bottles under £30, 6 by glass **Notes** Pre-theatre D 2 for 1 before 7.30pm selected nights, Vegetarian available, Dress restrictions, Smart casual, jacket & tie preferred **Seats** 60, Pr/dining room 20 **Children** Portions, Menu **Parking** 12, On street

SCARBOROUGH *continued*

Lanterna Ristorante

◉ Italian NEW ◐

Evergreen Italian on the Yorkshire coast

☎ 01723 363616
33 Queen St YO11 1HQ
e-mail: ralessio@lanterna-ristorante.co.uk
dir: Telephone restaurant for detailed directions

A central location, cheerful ambience and reliably good Italian cuisine have kept this Scarborough institution in business for four decades. And with a big anniversary refurb about to take place as we go to print, it's looking forward to the next 40 years with renewed energy. Chef-patron Giorgio Alessio stamps his affable personality over the operation, importing authentic ingredients from Italy to work alongside the finest fresh materials from Yorkshire. An ever-changing specials menu takes advantage of the splendid locally-landed fish, as in a simple but sublime starter of chunky pieces of monkfish served with a sauce of wild chanterelle and porcini mushrooms. Pasta is, of course, home-made: take agnolotti Montferrini - ravioli filled with beef, pork, parmesan cheese and spinach with a roasted beef sauce. If you've still room for secondi, fillet steak with a sauce of Taleggio cheese, cream and grappa is an option, and to finish, budino caramellato is crème caramel served Italian-style with rum poured on top.

Chef Giorgio Alessio **Owner** Giorgio & Rachel Alessio **Times** 7-9.30 Closed 2 wks Oct, 25-26 Dec, 1 Jan, Sun **Prices** Starter £7.50-£33, Main £14.25-£45, Dessert £7.50-£18, Service optional **Wines** 35 bottles over £30, 36 bottles under £30, 5 by glass **Notes** Vegetarian available, Dress restrictions, Smart casual **Seats** 35 **Children** Portions **Parking** on street, car park nearby

The Bull at Broughton

◉ Traditional British ◐

Confident, regional cooking in charming village inn

☎ 01756 792065
Broughton BD23 3AE
e-mail: enquiries@thebullatbroughton.com
dir: M65/A6068 (Vivary Way) for 1m, turn left onto A56 (Skipton Rd) for 7m, then right onto A59. Restaurant on right

The Bull is part of a mini empire of four gastro-pubs run by Nigel Haworth and Craig Bancroft of Northcote Manor (see entry), an enterprise whose praiseworthy aim is to showcase the best of Yorkshire and Lancashire produce in a switched-on, convivial, modern pub ambience. Accordingly, the stone-built Bull has received a smartly contemporary facelift, grafting a light and airy style and casually mis-matched furniture with traditional flagstoned floors and low beamed ceilings. Obliging staff play a key part in the Bull's welcoming vibe, backed up by good beer, and no-nonsense food. A glance at the menu shows a kitchen striving for local and seasonal output - a

filo pastry parcel of local seafood with Lancashire cheese fondue to start, followed by a pie of Goosnargh turkey, ham, leek and chestnuts with celeriac mash and Brussels sprouts. Puddings take no prisoners, offering deep comfort in the shape of sticky toffee pudding with vanilla ice cream or blackcurrant Bakewell tart with clotted cream.

Chef Michael Emminson **Owner** Craig Bancroft, Nigel Haworth, Richard Matthewman **Times** 12-2/5.30-8.30 Closed 25 Dec, Mon (ex BHs) **Prices** Starter £3.75-£6.50, Main £8.50-£19.50, Dessert £5, Service optional **Wines** 7 bottles over £30, 30 bottles under £30, 10 by glass **Notes** Fixed L & D Tue-Thu only 2/3 course £11.50/£15, Sunday L, Vegetarian available **Seats** 101 **Children** Portions, Menu **Parking** 41

The Coachman Inn

◉ Modern British ◐

Reinvented classics in a Georgian inn

☎ 01723 859231
Pickering Road West YO13 9PL
e-mail: info@coachmaninn.co.uk
web: www.coachmaninn.co.uk
dir: From A170 between Pickering & Scarborough onto B1258 (high St) in Snainton

In a rural setting halfway between Pickering and Scarborough, the Grade II listed Coachman dates back to 1776 when it was used as a staging post for mail coaches. Diners can eat in the characterful, quarry-tiled bar after warming up by the roaring fire, or in the more formal and elegant dining room with its sage green walls and crisp white linen. Modern takes on classics show the kitchen's skill and sense of fun, plus there are some more traditional pub options to choose from. Chicken liver parfait, textures of wild mushrooms and summer truffle is pretty as a picture and good to eat too, while local produce is used to great effect in a main of East Coast sea bream, garlic pommes purée, calamari, sweetcorn, chorizo and wild samphire. Who could resist 'The Fab' - tastes of the iconic ice cream lolly - for afters? Or, for comfort food nostalgics, 'School Days' - a brilliant confection of 'chocolate concrete', chilled rice pudding, bread and butter pudding and spotted Dick.

Chef Greg Wallace **Owner** Taylor family **Times** 12-9.30 **Prices** Starter £4.50-£6.95, Main £9.95-£15.95, Dessert £5.95-£8.95, Service optional **Wines** 5 bottles over £30, 22 bottles under £30, 16 by glass **Notes** Sunday L £10-£17, Vegetarian available **Seats** 42, Pr/dining room 12 **Children** Portions, Menu **Parking** 30

The Blackwell Ox Inn

◉ British ◐

Broadly appealing menu in a picturesque North York village

☎ 01347 810328
Huby Rd YO61 1DT
e-mail: enquiries@blackwelloxinn.co.uk
web: www.blackwelloxinn.co.uk
dir: Off A1237, onto B1363 to Sutton-on-the-Forest. Left at T-junct, 50yds on right

Named in honour of a legendary Shorthorn Teeswater ox that stood six feet at the crop before it met its fate, this Regency-era village inn is well placed for exploring the city of York and the wilds of the North York Moors. It's smartly done out with period colours and traditional furniture in both the bar and restaurant. The kitchen keeps a keen eye on what is in season locally and serves up a menu of classic and slightly more adventurous stuff. Thus you might start with a 'proper' prawn cocktail, Whitby crab salad, or the more trendy seared scallops with pulled pork and shallot purée. Among main courses a steak cooked on the grill seems fitting (rib-eye, maybe, served with chunky chips and onion rings), but there's also beef and ale pie, or chargrilled monkfish with confit duck, creamed cabbage and Puy lentils.

Chef Christopher Moscrop **Owner** Blackwell Ox Inns (York) Ltd **Times** 12-2/6-9.30 Closed 25 Dec, 1 Jan, D Sun **Prices** Starter £4.95-£7.95, Main £6.95-£19.95, Dessert £4.25-£5.95, Service optional **Wines** 20 by glass **Notes** Sunday L £9.45, Vegetarian available **Seats** 50, Pr/dining room 20 **Children** Portions, Menu **Parking** 19

THE ROSE & CROWN

The Rose & Crown, meet people, tell tales, make memories over glorious food and an intoxicating drink or two . . . !

Specialising in Steak & Seafood

Drop in for a drink in our bar where long evenings begin, or dine in our big room for fancy do's! We also have a large south facing country garden to relax in on a summers day.

Light Bites/Lunch/Supper Menu/Daily Changing Specials/Afternoon Teas/Bar Snacks & Snoopy Snacks for your Four Legged Friend.

We want to celebrate local produce in all it's glorious wonder, Knobbly Potatoes, Fresh Chicken Eggs, Twisty Carrots & Freshly Tugged Beetroot all come from down the road.

To Dine or if you fancy a chat over a local bitter, call 01347 811333 or drop in to The Rose & Crown/ Sutton-on-the-Forest/York/YO61 1DP

Please note we are 'apparently' the first to offer an order service, when you book you can request seafood or fish of your choice & we shall buy it in especially for you.

THE ROSE & CROWN, PUTTING THE TReat BACK IN TO eatING OUT

Main Street, Sutton on the Forest, York YO61 1DP
Tel: 01347 811333 • **Website:** www.theroseandcrownyork.co.uk

SUTTON-ON-THE-FOREST *continued*

The Rose & Crown

@ Modern British **V** ☺

Enterprising seafood - and more - in old village pub

☎ 01347 811333
Main St YO61 1DP
web: www.theroseandcrownyork.co.uk
dir: 8m N of York towards Helmsley on B1363

New owners have taken over this 200-year-old inn in an attractive village near York. Some things remain constant - wooden floors, low-beamed ceilings, a comfortable mix of traditional furniture and welcoming staff - while the menu has been updated. Seafood is now something of a speciality, with starters such as scallops with butternut squash purée and beetroot crisps, followed by super-fresh, accurately timed fish: perhaps swordfish steak chargrilled with chilli, lemon, garlic and spring onions, served with mixed-leaf salad, or roast monkfish wrapped in Parma ham, accompanied by spinach, roast potatoes, and tomato and basil coulis. Impressive results are seen in meat dishes too: say, pork and gammon terrine, then braised lamb shank with sweet potato mash, caramelised shallots and red wine sauce. Don't overlook puddings like chocolate mousse with matching ice cream and a mini cup of hot cocoa.

The Rose & Crown

Chef Richard Holden **Owner** Stuart & Sarah Temple
Times 12-2/6-9 Closed Jan, Mon, D Sun **Prices** Fixed L 2 course fr £15, Service optional **Wines** 10 bottles over £30, 23 bottles under £30, 8 by glass **Notes** Afternoon tea 2-5pm, Sunday L, Vegetarian menu, Civ Wed 70 **Seats** 70, Pr/dining room 30 **Children** Portions **Parking** 12

See advert on page 521

WEST WITTON Map 19 SE08

The Wensleydale Heifer

@ Modern British **V** ☺

Top-notch seafood and more in the heart of the Yorkshire Dales

☎ 01969 622322
Main St DL8 4LS
e-mail: info@wensleydaleheifer.co.uk
web: www.wensleydaleheifer.co.uk
dir: On A684 (3m W of Leyburn)

This whitewashed 17th-century coaching inn in the heart of the beautiful Yorkshire Dales National Park combines period atmosphere with a bit of boutique style in a winning combination; stay overnight and you can really get to know the place. There are two dining options: the more casual fish bar, with rattan chairs, wooden tables and pictures of seafaring cows as a nod to the heifer theme, and a smart restaurant done out with stylish chocolate leather chairs, linen-clothed tables and Doug Hyde artwork. There's a seafood focus here, but much more besides, and a desire to keep things local and relatively unfussy. So you will find good quality fish and chips, but you might also start with chilli-salt squid with Asian herb and noodle salad and sweet chilli dressing. Main-course roast Atlantic halibut competes for your attention with roast shoulder of lamb with goats' cheese and garlic gratin potatoes.

Chef David Moss **Owner** David & Lewis Moss
Times 12-2.30/6-9.30 **Prices** Fixed L 2 course £19.75, Fixed D 3 course £21.75, Tasting menu £50-£70, Starter £13.50, Main £17.50-£29.50, Dessert £4.50-£6, Service added but optional 10% **Wines** 25 bottles over £30, 29 bottles under £30, 14 by glass **Notes** Sunday L, Vegetarian menu **Seats** 70 **Children** Portions, Menu **Parking** 30

WHITBY Map 19 NZ81

The Cliffemount Hotel

@@ Modern British ☺

Pragmatic cooking in a Yorkshire clifftop hotel

☎ 01947 840103
Bank Top Ln, Runswick Bay TS13 5HU
e-mail: info@cliffemounthotel.co.uk
dir: Exit A174, 8m N of Whitby, 1m to end

Perched on the cliffs overlooking Runswick Bay, the hotel is blissfully insulated from almost any other sound but the distant plashing of waves below. That imperious view can be enjoyed from the Pasión dining room, where light boutique styling meets a country-pub approach to menu construction, with the day's specials chalked up on the board. Seafood is a particular lure, from crab spring rolls in sesame dressing, or roast mackerel with Yorkshire Blue rarebit and a salad of marinated apricot and red onion, to mains such as sea trout on brown shrimp and spring onion risotto. Homely dishes such as steak-and-ale pie and mash (made with Black Sheep ale) dispel any sense of pretentiousness, and that local beef might also appear roasted with a Yorkshire pudding and potatoes done in duck fat.

Chef David Spencer **Owner** Ian & Carol Rae
Times 12-2.30/6-9 **Prices** Starter £3.95-£9.95, Main £13.95-£25.95, Dessert £4.95-£9.75, Service optional **Wines** 8 by glass **Notes** Sunday L £12.95-£16.95, Vegetarian available **Seats** 50 **Children** Portions **Parking** 25

Dunsley Hall

@ Modern, Traditional

Accomplished cooking in a striking property

☎ 01947 893437
Dunsley YO21 3TL
e-mail: reception@dunsleyhall.com
web: www.dunsleyhall.com
dir: 3.5m from Whitby off A171(Teeside road)

Any self-respecting Victorian shipping magnate would want to impress the world at large, and this imposing mansion perched above the North Yorkshire coast sends out a clear message: this is the house of a gentleman of substance. Inside is all the oak panelling, mullioned and stained-glass windows and fine plasterwork that further reinforces a chap's taste and status. Naturally, this is no National Trust museum, so it's all tweaked to impress 21st-century sensibilities, while the kitchen tacks to a modern country-house course, using top-class Yorkshire ingredients to produce ☺ a well-thought-out repertoire. A

Save on Hotels. Book at **theAA.com/hotel**

YORKSHIRE, NORTH 523 **ENGLAND**

full-blooded salad of crispy lamb's sweetbreads, breast and confit shoulder with winter vegetables shows a keen eye for seasonality, and with Whitby's fishing fleet just up the road, it makes sense to go for a main course trio of roast pavé of sea bass, Whitby crab, and brown shrimp ravioli partnered with samphire and a nage of ginger, lemongrass and mussels.

Times 12-2/7.30-9.30

Estbek House

◉◉ Modern British

Fresh seafood by the sea near Whitby

☎ 01947 893424
East Row, Sandsend YO21 3SU
e-mail: info@estbekhouse.co.uk
dir: From Whitby follow A174 towards Sandsend. Estbek House just before bridge

Estbek House, a Grade II listed property built in the mid-18th century, stands on the beachfront a few miles out of Whitby. It's a small and comfortable restaurant with rooms, with a bright and modern dining room with a wooden floor, a neutral décor and comfortable high-backed leather-look chairs. Not surprisingly, fish is the speciality, whatever was landed that morning making its way on to the daily-changing menu. Fillet of cod, turbot,

halibut - whatever - is simply seared in the pan, offered with a choice of sauces - perhaps creamy lemon - and accompanied by fresh seasonal vegetables. Other options could extend to seafood pie or the extravagance of lobster thermidor. Seafood in a number of guises goes into starters - chowder, say, or smoked salmon and crayfish with seasonal samphire. For meat-eaters there may be moist and tender local lamb with rhubarb compôte and steamed vegetables, and you might end with white chocolate crème brûlée with raspberries.

Times 6-9

The Plough

◉◉ Modern British **NEW**

Exciting cooking in revamped country inn

☎ 01729 840243
BD23 4RJ
e-mail: info@theploughatwigglesworth.co.uk

Taken over by new owners in recent years, The Plough has raised its game impressively. The Georgian building has plenty of intrinsic character, and an eclectic eye has revamped the interiors - its venerable beams and wood panelling are painted white and cream to lighten the

ambience, and it comes kitted out with a cool, shabby-chic medley of reclaimed and salvaged materials, including a bar made from church pews, and unclothed rustic tables and chairs. There's an ambitious team at work in the kitchen with the clear technical ability and confidence to take top-quality local produce and cook it to deliver big flavours and vibrant, exciting combinations, as in a pressing of local pork and black pudding served with piccalilli vegetables and a quail Scotch egg. Next up, slow-braised shoulder of lamb stars in an intricate assemblage involving liver and onions, dauphinoise potatoes, asparagus, samphire, and rosemary jus, while a show-stopping dessert riffs on banana split by serving caramelised banana with moist pistachio cake, dark chocolate sauce and home-made ice cream.

Times 12-2/6.30-9 **Prices** Prices not confirmed **Seats** 60

Judges Country House Hotel

◉◉◉ **– see below**

Modern British V ⬥ NOTABLE WINE LIST

Confident modern cooking in an historic house

☎ 01642 789000
Kirklevington TS15 9LW
e-mail: enquiries@judgeshotel.co.uk
web: www.judgeshotel.co.uk
dir: 1.5m from junct W A19, take A67 towards Kirklevington, hotel 1.5m on left

This charming country house hotel close to the thriving market town of Yarm is set back from the road in 22 acres of mature gardens, a pleasing destination which was originally built for a Victorian engineering family. Towards the end of the Second World War the house, Kirklevington Hall, was taken over by the army, then in the 1970s it provided accommodation for circuit judges doing their rounds, and thus it got its current name. The well-preserved, grey-stone building certainly makes a fine country house

hotel, and if you're here for the business of eating, you're in for a bit of a treat. The main part of the dining room is in a conservatory facing south over the gardens, so you can gaze out the window and watch the resident wild animals going about their business as you tuck into dinner. Long-standing chef John Schwarz sources top quality ingredients and treats them with care and respect on varied menus that offer a pleasing mix of classic dishes and more out of the ordinary combinations. To start, caramelised foie gras, satay, radish and lime is a beautifully cooked piece of foie gras with broken peanuts, smooth peanut sauce, radish slivers and small wedges of sharp lime adding great flavour and textural contrast. Turbot, Morteau sausage and shellfish chowder brings all the elements together beautifully, while peaches, almonds, vanilla parfait and raspberry sorbet shows off the kitchen's technical skills. All the little extras - homemade bread rolls, petits fours such as bubble gum jelly and plum financier, and bar canapés - are all worth making a dent in your appetite, while the wine list is a bit of a corker and includes a decent choice by the glass.

Chef John Schwarz **Owner** Mr M Downs **Times** 12-2/7-9.30 **Prices** Fixed L 2 course £24.45-£27.45, Fixed D 3 course £37.50, Starter £10.95-£16.95, Main £33-£41, Dessert £10.95-£17.95, Service optional **Wines** 103 bottles over £30, 31 bottles under £30, 12 by glass **Notes** Early bird menu available, Sunday L, Vegetarian menu, Dress restrictions, Jacket & tie preferred, no jeans or trainers, Civ Wed 200 **Seats** 60, Pr/dining room 50 **Children** Portions, Menu **Parking** 110

YORK — Map 16 SE65

Best Western Plus Dean Court Hotel

@ Modern British 🍷

High quality ingredients and stunning Minster views

☎ 01904 625082
Duncombe Place YO1 7EF
e-mail: sales@deancourt-york.co.uk
web: www.deancourt-york.co.uk
dir: City centre, directly opposite York Minster

The boutique-style Dean Court Hotel - originally built to house the clergy of York Minster - makes the most of its pole position overlooking the Gothic masterpiece. The window tables at its elegant, contemporary-styled D.C.H restaurant offer the best views in town to a backing track of chiming Minster bells. The kitchen makes sterling use of local seasonal produce in unpretentious, eye-catching modish dishes. Breast of wild duck, perhaps, served with duck-leg faggots, smoked potatoes, roasted beetroot and orange-braised chicory salad, or baked cod accompanied by fennel bhaji and shellfish consommé. End in similar vein with an interesting fresh fig and griottine cherry tarte Tatin with cherry sorbet.

Chef Iain Weston **Owner** Mr B A Cleminson
Times 12.30-2/7-9.30 Closed 25 Dec eve, L Mon-Fri
Prices Fixed L 2 course £16-£19.50, Fixed D 2 course £25, Starter £6.25-£9.25, Main £16.50-£23, Dessert £6.50-£8.50 **Wines** 30 bottles over £30, 47 bottles under £30, 19 by glass **Notes** Pre-theatre menu available, Sunday L £19-£23.50, Vegetarian available, Dress restrictions, No T-Shirts, Civ Wed 50 **Seats** 60, Pr/dining room 40 **Children** Portions, Menu **Parking** Pay & display car park nearby

Burbridges Restaurant

@ Modern **NEW**

Skillful French-accented modern cooking

☎ 01904 619444
119 The Mount, The Mount Royale Hotel YO24 1GU
e-mail: info@burbridgesrestaurant.com
dir: W on A1036, 0.5m after racecourse. Hotel on right after lights

Part of the upmarket Mount Royale Hotel, this smart restaurant is a rather cool, contemporary affair with its wooden floors and well-spaced tables swathed in white linen. The vibe is relaxed, service is as keen as mustard, and the kitchen follows the seasons, drawing on the best local produce for its French-accented modern British repertoire. Starters set the tone for what is to follow: a wonderfully simple chicken liver terrine is paired with rhubarb, almonds, ginger crumble and home-made brioche. After that, loin of new season's lamb arrives with a rosemary and brioche crust, Lyonnaise potatoes, fine beans, roasted squash, and Puy lentil jus. Alternatively, if you're in the mood for local seafood, there could be sea bass with Whitby crab and pea risotto with spinach and parmesan shavings. Dessert puts a novel spin on a classic by flavouring crème brûlée with espresso and matching it with hazelnut biscotti.

Prices Fixed L 2 course £14.95, Starter £4.95-£9.95, Main £12.95-£24.95, Dessert £5.95-£8.95 **Notes** Fixed 2/3 course menu 12-6pm, Sunday L £10.95-£18.95, Vegetarian available

Cedar Court Grand Hotel & Spa

@@ Modern British 🍷

Elegant grill restaurant in a renovated Edwardian hotel

☎ 01904 380038
Station Rise YO1 6GD
e-mail: dining@cedarcourtgrand.co.uk
web: www.cedarcourtgrand.co.uk
dir: A1 junct 47, A59 signed York, Harrogate & Knaresborough. In city centre, near station

Overlooking the historic walls of one of northern England's best-loved cities, the imposing red-brick Edwardian edifice was given a major makeover, or 'reimagining' as design parlance now has it, in 2010. Huge windows let in plenty of light, and the principal restaurant, the Grill Room, is an expansive room done in today's favoured neutral colours, offset with lemon-yellow light-fittings, under which smartly dressed tables are set well apart. A formal service approach is quite in keeping with the overall tone, and the cooking plies a confident brasserie line, such as seared pigeon breast, wild mushroom risotto, or king scallops with black pudding (home-made) and creamed leeks, to start, followed ideally by something from the grill, be it a chicken breast, pork cutlet, or one of the first-rate and carefully timed steaks. Sauces are at an extra charge. Desserts can be of the deconstructed variety, as in a tiramisù which consists of a boozy sponge with whipped mascarpone, cubes of jelly and coffee sauce.

Chef Martin Henley **Owner** Cedar Court Hotels
Times 12.30-2.30/6.30-10 **Prices** Fixed L 2 course £19.95, Starter £9.50-£11.50, Main £23.50-£28.50, Dessert £9.50-£11.50, Service optional **Wines** 113 bottles over £30, 23 bottles under £30, 7 by glass **Notes** Sunday L £19.95-£24.95, Vegetarian available, Dress restrictions, Smart casual, no ripped jeans, Civ Wed 120 **Seats** 45, Pr/dining room 32 **Children** Portions **Parking** NCP Tanner Row

The Churchill Hotel

@@ Modern British

Imaginative food and piano music

☎ 01904 644456
65 Bootham YO30 7DQ
e-mail: info@churchillhotel.com
dir: On A19 (Bootham), W from York Minster, hotel 250yds on right

The set up is all rather civilised in this Georgian mansion in its own grounds just a short walk from York Minster. The Churchill blends the airy elegance of its period pedigree with the sharp looks of a contemporary boutique city hotel in a dining room that looks through those vast arching windows (that the Georgians did so well) into the garden, where the trees are spangled in fairy-lights. Laid-back live music floats from a softly-tinkling baby grand piano as the soundtrack to cooking that hits the target with its imaginative modern pairings of top-grade regional produce. Local wood pigeon, for example, is paired with black pudding bonbons, bitter chocolate and espresso jelly, while main-course saddle of venison might share a plate with Morteau sausage, choucroute, parsley root, and red wine salsify. To finish, duck eggs add extra oomph to a custard tart served with clementine, apricot, and vanilla ice cream.

Times 11-2.30/5-9.30

The Grange Hotel

🏵🏵 Modern

Classy brasserie in city-centre hotel

☎ 01904 644744
1 Clifton YO30 6AA
e-mail: info@grangehotel.co.uk
web: www.grangehotel.co.uk
dir: A19 (York/Thirsk road), approx 400yds from city centre

A short walk from the Minster, The Grange is an elegantly proportioned townhouse dating from the 1830s. The interior has all the style and comfort of a country-house hotel - open fires, deep sofas, antique paintings, swagged curtains - while the Ivy Brasserie has a more modish design, the most striking feature a mural of horseracing. The cooking is a cut above the brasserie norm, the kitchen clearly a creative and skilful powerhouse. Pressed ham hock and guinea fowl is vivified by zingy pineapple chutney, and curried crab goes into a salad with apple, almonds and cauliflower fritters to make another lively starter. Braised beef cheeks with parsnip purée and bourguignon sauce is a gutsy winter main course, and at other times there may be a lighter dish of pan-fried salmon fillet with shellfish chowder, creamed sweetcorn and baby leeks. Grilled steaks are possibilities, and proceedings can close with lemon and thyme pannacotta topped with lemon curd, meringue and blackberry jelly.

Times 12.30-2.30/6.30-9.30 Closed L Mon-Sat, D Sun

Guy Fawkes Inn

🏵 Traditional British

Historic city centre inn serving classic British food

☎ 01904 466674
25 High Petergate YO1 7HP
e-mail: reservations@gfyork.com
web: www.gfyork.com

The Gunpowder Plotter was born on this spot in 1570, in the shadow of York Minster, a fact which adds a frisson to the pub that has done business here for centuries. It is a darkly atmospheric, history-steeped den with an interior akin to stepping into an Old Master painting; recently restored and scrubbed up, there are roaring log fires, a timber staircase, wooden floors, gas lighting, cosy nooks and crannies, and cheerful service that suits the buzzy vibe. Monthly-changing menus and daily chalkboard specials follow a hearty modern pub grub course, treating great local produce with honest, down-to-earth simplicity - expect hearty main courses such as faggots in rich gravy with mushy peas and buttery mash, cider-braised rabbit with tarragon mash, or battered haddock with mushy peas and proper chips. And for pudding, it's Yorkshire parkin with butterscotch sauce.

Times 12-3/6-9 Closed D Sun

Hotel du Vin York

🏵 European, French

Winning bistro fare and outstanding wine list

☎ 01904 557350
89 The Mount YO24 1AX
e-mail: info.york@hotelduvin.com
dir: A1036 towards city centre, 6m. Hotel on right through lights

Not surprisingly for the Hotel du Vin chain, its York outpost is done out in the style of a French bistro, with wooden floors and tables softened by lighter-coloured walls hung with horsey images, reminders of the proximity of the city's racecourse. It's a smoothly run, easygoing sort of operation, with clued-up staff keeping wheels turning and offering advice about the wines on the outstanding list, and a menu of winning bistro fare, like escargots and cassoulet. Kick off a meal with rich and intense chicken liver parfait served with toasted brioche and raisin chutney, a fine starter if ever there was one, and go on to properly timed roast rack of lamb partnered by a seasonal fricassée of broad beans, peas and baby onions. Quality doesn't falter when it comes to desserts, among which could be chocolate pavé (layers of ganache and sponge) sprinkled with candied pistachios.

Times 12-2.30/6.30-10.30

The Lamb & Lion

🏵 Traditional & Modern British

Good honest cooking in a historic city centre pub

☎ 01904 654112
2-4 High Petergate YO1 7EH
e-mail: reservations@lambandlionyork.com
web: www.lambandlionyork.com

Built quite literally into the ancient city walls, and sitting in the shadow of York Minster, The Lamb & Lion offers everything you could reasonably ask of a historic pub: a labyrinth of cosy little rooms takes in a bar bristling with hand-pulled real ales and kitted out with church pews, bare wooden tables and a real fire, while skinny corridors lead to the back snugs and Parlour dining room. Straight-talking traditional food aims to please all comers, and you can rest assured that the quality of the ingredients is up to scratch. Pub classics such as home-made steak pie with mash and real gravy, or fish and chips with mushy peas and tartare sauce sit alongside unpretentious ideas - perhaps lamb shank with garlic and rosemary jus, or wild mushroom risotto with Parmesan crisp. Finish with

the comforting simplicity of chocolate brownie and ice cream or a retro knickerbocker glory.

The Lamb & Lion

Times 12-3/6-9

See advert on page 526

Melton's Restaurant

🏵 Modern British 🍷

Long-running favourite with well-judged menu

☎ 01904 634341
7 Scarcroft Rd YO23 1ND
e-mail: greatfood@meltonsrestaurant.co.uk
dir: South from centre across Skeldergate Bridge, restaurant opposite Bishopthorpe Road car park

Melton's remains as popular as ever, and it's been going for over 20 years. In a Victorian terrace, it's bright and modern, with mirrors and murals on the walls, a wooden floor, banquettes and unclothed tables - all very unpretentious, with friendly but efficient service. The kitchen conscientiously uses Yorkshire produce, dishes are well thought out and carefully cooked, and the menu of modern ideas offers plenty to enjoy. Typical starters include filo pissaladière with scallops, anchovies, capers and mint, and a dariole of warm chicken liver. Among main courses, a smoked haddock and crabcake is served on soft polenta with leeks, or there might be full-blooded pork trotter, belly and hock with cabbage, boulangère potatoes and Madeira jus. The regional approach extends to cheeses and iced rhubarb sticks with two custards.

Chef Michael Hjort, Calvin Goddard **Owner** Michael & Lucy Hjort **Times** 12-2/5.30-10 Closed 23 Dec-9 Jan, Sun-Mon **Prices** Fixed L 2 course fr £22, Service optional **Wines** 6 by glass **Notes** Pre-theatre D, early evening 2/3 course £22/£26, Vegetarian available **Seats** 30, Pr/dining room 16 **Children** Portions **Parking** Car park opposite

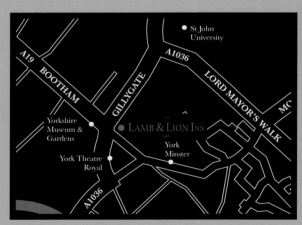

YORK *continued*

Middlethorpe Hall & Spa

◎◎ Modern British ▲ NOTABLE WINE LIST ⊙

Seasonal modern British cooking in a 17th-century mansion

☎ 01904 641241
Bishopthorpe Rd, Middlethorpe YO23 2GB
e-mail: info@middlethorpe.com
dir: A64 exit York West. Follow signs Middlethorpe & racecourse

Thomas Barlow, who made his fortune in Sheffield cutlery, had Middlethorpe built for himself at the end of the 17th century. It's a trim mansion house fashioned from red brick and limestone, furnished with antiques and fine paintings, and with a sublime panelled dining room at the heart of the operation. Formal service, layers of linen, a marble fireplace - it's all here - as is the up-to-the-minute seasonal British cooking of Nicholas Evans. A roast scallop teamed with confit pork belly is very much the mood of the moment, given further depth with pumpkin and sherry vinegar caramel. Meaty treatments for fish might see sea bream accompanied by ceps in a truffled chicken stock sauce, while meat itself is accurately timed and well-presented, as when breast of Cumbrian mallard makes an appearance with chestnuts and quince in a spiced-up version of bread sauce. Yorkshire's finest rhubarb is proudly featured in its season, perhaps in atavistic fashion as rhubarb and custard, but with the additions of crunchy granola and anise syrup.

Chef Nicholas Evans **Owner** The National Trust **Times** 12.30-2/7-9.45 **Prices** Fixed L 2 course fr £19.50, Starter £9.50-£14.50, Main £22.50-£28.50, Dessert £7.50-£13, Service included **Wines** 194 bottles over £30, 38 bottles under £30, 15 by glass **Notes** Gourmet 6 course menu £65 (with wine £95), Sunday L fr £26, Vegetarian available, Dress restrictions, Smart, no trainers, tracksuits or shorts, Civ Wed 56 **Seats** 60, Pr/dining room 56 **Children** Portions **Parking** 70

ROSSINGTON   **Map 16 SK69**

Best Western Premier Mount Pleasant Hotel

◎ Modern British

Sound country-house cooking in tip-top hotel

☎ 01302 868696 & 868219
Great North Rd DN11 0HW
e-mail: reception@mountpleasant.co.uk
web: www.mountpleasant.co.uk
dir: S of Doncaster, adjacent to Robin Hood Airport, on A638 between Bawtry & Doncaster

This smart 18th-century country-house hotel squirrelled away in 100 acres of beautiful woodland feels miles from anywhere, yet it is on the outskirts of Doncaster. While the grand old house is traditional in many aspects of its cosy décor and formal-yet-friendly service, Mount Pleasant comes fully geared for the 21st century with a full complement of glossy spa, leisure and conference facilities. The kitchen takes a broadly modern British line in its well-judged repertoire of comfort-oriented classics. You might get off the blocks with a black pudding Scotch egg with spiced apple marmalade and watercress ketchup, ahead of braised ox cheek with pommes purée, pancetta and braised shallots, and black truffle jus. For pudding it's back to school with 'jelly and ice cream', although this is a grown-up's take on the theme, comprising pear cider jelly, blackberry ripple ice cream, brioche and cinnamon.

Times 12-2/6.45-9.30 Closed 25 Dec

SHEFFIELD   **Map 16 SK38**

Copthorne Hotel Sheffield

◎ Modern European

Contemporary cooking at the home of the Blades

☎ 0114 252 5480
Sheffield United Football Club, Bramall Ln S2 4SU
e-mail: trevorvels@millenniumhotels.co.uk
dir: M1 junct 33, A57 Sheffield, A61 Chesterfield Rd, follow brown tourist signs for Bramall Lane

Although it is tucked away in a quiet corner of Sheffield United's football ground, the 18Fifty5 Restaurant is a clean-cut contemporary space with no obvious overtones related to the Beautiful Game. Understated and stylish, the setting goes for darkwood tables, neutral, earthy tones, and soft-focus lighting, while the kitchen has created a menu in the modern European mould, built on top-class, often local, ingredients. The menu keeps things accessible, focusing on intuitive combinations of flavour and texture, as seen in a starter that matches confit duck

---

leg with celeriac remoulade, ahead of main-course seared sea bream with moules marinière and crushed new potatoes. And it's straight in the back of the net for dark chocolate tart with honeycomb ice cream.

Chef Mark Jones **Owner** Millennium Copthorne Group **Times** 12.30-2.30/6.30-10 **Prices** Prices not confirmed Service optional **Wines** 12 by glass **Notes** Vegetarian available **Seats** 100, Pr/dining room 300 **Children** Portions, Menu **Parking** 250

The Milestone

◎ Modern British ⊙

Full-on flavours in industrial Sheffield

☎ 0114 272 8327
84 Green Lane at Ball St, Kelham Island S3 8SE
e-mail: bookings@the-milestone.co.uk

There's a genuine local flavour at The Milestone, which extends to local ales at the bar and the owners' rare-breed pigs on the menu. The spruced-up urban pub has a gastro vibe these days and it looks good with its bare wooden floors, mismatched chairs and tables, and hues of peppermint, coffee and cream. The industrious kitchen team has loads of good ideas and produces appealing dishes with flavour and no fuss. Start, perhaps, with a slow-cooked hen's egg with creamed leeks, Yorkshire mushrooms and parmesan, or a pressed leg of free-range chicken with smoked sweetcorn purée, confit garlic and a salad of peas and spiced black rice. There are light lunches, sandwiches - whatever you fancy really - and full-on main courses such as slow-cooked belly of pork with Milestone black pudding, carrot purée, buttered greens and mashed potatoes. For dessert, the quaking pudding (an English baked cream) comes with candied celery and a honey and walnut tart.

Chef Luke French **Owner** Matt Bigland, Marc Sheldon **Times** 12-4/5-10 Closed 25-26 Dec, 1 Jan **Prices** Fixed L 2 course £16, Tasting menu £35, Starter £4.95-£6.95, Main £10.95-£17.50, Dessert £4.95-£5.95, Service optional, Groups min 8 service 10% **Wines** 12 bottles over £30, 26 bottles under £30, 8 by glass **Notes** Early bird menu 2/3 course £14/£16.50, Sunday L £16-£18, Vegetarian available **Seats** 120 **Children** Portions **Parking** On street

SHEFFIELD *continued*

Nonnas

◉ Modern Italian V NOTABLE WINE LIST

Italian mini-chain with authentic cooking

☎ 0114 268 6166
535-541 Ecclesall Rd S11 8PR
e-mail: info@nonnas.co.uk
dir: From city centre onto Ecclesall Rd, large red building on left

Nonna's is the real deal, serving-up authentic Italian food and drink, from a shot of espresso or glass of prosecco taken at a high stool at the bar, to some full-flavoured home cooking at the table. Blending Yorkshire's best produce with specialist materials from Italy, Nonna's piles on the authenticity still further with its unabashedly Italian service. The place has a charming, relaxed, retro-Italian rusticity about it, with café-style marble-topped tables and olive green walls, while bread, biscotti, pizza, pasta and ice cream are all made daily in-house. The menu opens with the likes of vongole (steamed clams in white wine with garlic butter and chargrilled piadina bread), then pasta such as tagliatelle salsiccia (with eight-hour slow-cooked sausage sauce with tomato, bay leaf and red wine chilli), and secondi of roast rump of Yorkshire lamb with salsa di cipolle. Italian wines and artisan beers sing to the same song sheet.

Chef Jamie Taylor **Owner** Gian Bohian, Maurizio Mori **Times** 12-3.15/5-9.45 Closed 25 Dec, 1 Jan **Prices** Tasting menu £25, Service optional, Groups min 6 service 10% **Wines** 15 by glass **Notes** Brunch Sun 10am-1pm, Sunday L £12-£35, Vegetarian menu **Seats** 75, Pr/dining room 30 **Children** Portions, Menu **Parking** On street

Rafters Restaurant

◉◉ Modern British, European

Smart modern cooking in leafy neighbourhood

☎ 0114 230 4819
220 Oakbrook Rd, Nethergreen S11 7ED
e-mail: marcus.lane@tiscali.co.uk
web: www.raftersrestaurant.co.uk
dir: 5 mins from Ecclesall road, Hunters Bar rdbt

With 20 years under its belt serving the people of Sheffield, it's safe to call Rafters an institution. Run by chef-patron Marcus Lane since 2001, its setting atop a corner shop in a leafy part of the city speaks of a

neighbourhood restaurant, but the cooking is a cut above. There's a smart, rustic-chic vibe to the room and the well-informed service team contribute to the relaxed, happy atmosphere. People come here for the food - and they invariably come back. Lane takes first-class ingredients and cooks in a broadly European manner, and deciding what to eat is not easy: do you start with hickory-smoked duck breast with baby beets, toasted hazelnuts and raspberry vinaigrette, or dressed white crab meat with a baby smoked haddock fishcake and rouille? Next up, perhaps roast loin of Derbyshire lamb with Niçoise roast vegetables and rosemary jus, or grilled fillet of halibut with creamed potatoes, curly kale, lemon, caper and parsley sauce. To finish, how about a fabulous bitter chocolate and Seville orange terrine with marmalade Chantilly cream?

Chef Marcus Lane, Gareth Ducker **Owner** Marcus Lane **Times** 5-10 Closed 25-26 Dec, 1 wk Jan, 2 wks Aug, Sun, Tue, L all week **Prices** Fixed D 3 course fr £36.95, Service optional, Groups min 8 service 10% **Wines** 25 bottles over £30, 35 bottles under £30, 7 by glass **Notes** Fixed D 2 course with glass wine available Mon-Thu £25, Vegetarian available, Dress restrictions, Smart casual, no jeans **Seats** 38 **Children** Portions, Menu **Parking** 15

Staindrop Lodge Hotel

◉ Modern, Traditional

Far-reaching menus in art-deco-style brasserie

☎ 0114 284 3111
Lane End, Chapeltown S35 3UH
e-mail: info@staindroplodge.co.uk
dir: M1 junct 35, take A629 for 1m, straight over 1st rdbt, right at 2nd rdbt, hotel approx 0.5m on right

Seven miles from the city centre, within easy reach of both the M1 and the Peak District, Staindrop Lodge is a much-extended 19th-century hotel with conference facilities and an art-deco-style, split-level brasserie. The kitchen travels near and far for inspiration, with an eclectic menu running from starters of a simple plate of charcuterie, through seafood salad with garlic butter and crab mayonnaise, to sizzling chicken wings with chilli. Main courses are just as diverse: steak, ale and mushroom pie, say, Szechuan-style duck breast with plum sauce, wok-fried vegetables and deep-fried shrimps, and linguine with crab, tuna and prawns. Finish with a straightforward pudding like chocolate fudge cake, or crème brûlée.

Times 12-9.30

Whitley Hall Hotel

◉◉ Modern British

Imaginative British cooking in a stunning country hotel

☎ 0114 245 4444
Elliott Ln, Grenoside S35 8NR
e-mail: reservations@whitleyhall.com
web: www.whitleyhall.com
dir: A61 past football ground, then 2m, right just before Norfolk Arms, left at bottom of hill. Hotel on left

Whitley Hall is a textbook 16th-century ivy-clad country house set in 20 acres of immaculate grounds with lakes and superb gardens. It has stayed abreast of current trends in interior design and dining thanks to a modern facelift, and a restaurant that delivers a style of modernised country cooking perfectly in keeping with the surroundings. The oak panelling and white linen in the dining room may speak of old-school formality, and staff are suitably well-drilled and professionally correct in their ministrations, but what leaves the kitchen is switched-on contemporary cooking, presented in a way that is precise and well-considered, but not at all fussy. The newly-fashionable Scotch egg opens the show, made in this case from confit duck leg, and teamed with mature cheddar soufflé and plum chutney. Next out, a pan-fried fillet of wild sea bass arrives with mussels, steamed spinach dumplings, leeks, and saffron and tomato essence. Bringing down the curtain, an enterprising chocolate and beetroot cake is served with balsamic and raspberry sauce and goats' milk ice cream.

Times 12-2/7-9.30

The Wortley Arms

◉◉ Modern British V ☺

Up-to-the-minute brasserie food in a Georgian pub

☎ 0114 288 8749
Halifax Rd S35 7DB
e-mail: enquiries@wortley-arms.co.uk
dir: M1 junct 36. Follow Sheffield North signs, right at Tankersley garage, 1m on right

A two-pronged operation consists of The Wortley Arms, a traditional Georgian pub with panelled walls, a jumble of furniture and oak beams, and a more obviously modern urban-style restaurant upstairs that tends only to open at weekends now. The up-to-the-minute brasserie stylings of the menu are on offer throughout, though, so there's no need to miss out on tian of crab, squid and crayfish, or ham hock terrine with piccalilli and saladings, to start, followed by cod with garlic mash and walnut pesto, or a special such as breast of duck with a confit leg croquette, braised cabbage and puréed carrot. Treacle tart comes with cream to anoint it with, or there may be good sharp lemon posset with lavender shortbread.

Chef Andy Gabbitas **Owner** Andy Gabbitas **Times** 12-2.30/5-9 Closed D Sun **Prices** Starter £4.50-£8.50, Main £8.50-£27.50, Dessert £5.25-£6.25, Service optional **Wines** 5 bottles over £30, 24 bottles under £30, 8 by glass **Notes** Sunday L fr £12.50, Vegetarian menu **Seats** 80, Pr/dining room 12 **Children** Portions **Parking** 30

ADDINGHAM   Map 19 SE04

Craven Heifer

◎◎ Modern British **NEW**

Switched-on cooking in an ambitious gastro-pub

☎ 01943 830106
Main St LS29 0PL
e-mail: info@wellfedpubs.co.uk

This stylishly refurbished pub lies not far from Skipton and the wild moors, and offers seven luxurious rooms themed on Yorkshire characters should you want to stay over and take full advantage of the place's gastronomic possibilities - and a quick glance over the menu suggests this might be a good idea, as the output here aims way beyond pub staples. The kitchen team are certainly out to make an impact with an inventive roster of lively, flavour-driven modern ideas, hauling in top-drawer local ingredients, including daily fish specials, to supplement the weekly market menu and carte. Choosing from the latter, you might open with a tongue-in-cheek 'ham, egg and chips', which turns out to be a rather more involved assemblage of ham hock ballottine with home-made brown sauce, slow-cooked egg yolk, confit potatoes, and Pickering watercress. Main course could bring a similarly creative streak, matching butter-roasted John Dory with cauliflower (poached and purée) a mini fishcake, and chive velouté. End with baked stem ginger cheesecake with Yorkshire rhubarb (sorbet, poached and sherbet).

Chef Mark Owens **Times** 12-2/5.30-9 **Prices** Fixed L 2 course £20, Fixed D 3 course £23, Tasting menu fr £55, Service optional **Notes** Vegetarian available, Dress restrictions, Smart casual **Seats** 41 **Children** Portions **Parking** 20

BINGLEY   Map 19 SE13

Five Rise Locks Hotel & Restaurant

◎ Modern British **V** 🕯

Unfussy cooking in family-run hotel

☎ 01274 565296
Beck Ln BD16 4DD
e-mail: info@five-rise-locks.co.uk
dir: From A650 signed Bingley centre, turn right Park Rd. Beck Lane 300mtrs on left

Built by a successful Victorian businessman in 1875, this one-time mill owner's family home is now a family-run hotel on a pleasingly intimate scale (just nine bedrooms), with a restaurant that's worth knowing about. Done out in a smart manner with high-backed leather chairs, linen-clad tables and a splendid burgundy and cream paint job, it offers views in daylight hours over the garden and Aire Valley. On the menu you'll find some appealing combinations such as warm goats' cheese and red onion

confit served en croûte, or pigeon breast with rocket and beetroot salad to start. Next up, perhaps pan-fried calves' liver with crushed new potatoes, cabbage and onion confit, and, to finish, lemon posset or a selection of British cheeses.

Chef Steven Heaton, Richard Stoyle **Owner** Richard & Margaret Stoyle **Times** 12-2/6.30-9.15 Closed L Mon-Sat, D Sun (ex residents) **Prices** Starter £4-£8, Main £12.50-£21, Dessert £4.50-£5.50, Service optional **Wines** 4 bottles over £30, 26 bottles under £30, 10 by glass **Notes** Early bird ménu 2 course, Mon-Sat 6.30-7.30pm, Sunday L £14.50-£17, Vegetarian menu **Seats** 40, Pr/dining room 20 **Children** Portions **Parking** 15

BRADFORD   Map 19 SE13

Prashad

◎ Indian Vegetarian **V**

Indian vegetarian food of the highest order

☎ 0113 285 2037
137 Whitehall Rd, Drighlington BD11 1AT
e-mail: info@prashad.co.uk
dir: Follow A650 Wakefield Road then Whitehall Road

When it comes to pukka Indian cooking, the competition in Bradford is strong, but Mrs Kaushy Patel's take on the vegetarian repertoire ensures a zealous local following beats a path to her door in new premises after a relocation in late 2012. The new venue goes for a bright and cheerful look, with one wall taken up by a huge mural of a tumultuous Indian street scene. The all-in-one thali platter is a splendid way in to the vegetarian cuisine of the Gujarat, or you could head south for a spicy uttapam or masala dosa pancake served with spicy lentil soup and coconut chutney. Curries include chole - chick peas cooked with whole cumin seeds in a tomato and onion sauce, which goes great with light-as-air puri bread - and classic tarka dhal. Spicing is spot on throughout, and breads are cooked fresh to order.

Chef Kaushy & Minal Patel **Owner** Mohan Patel **Times** 12-5/6-11.30 Closed 25 Dec, Mon, L Tue-Thu **Prices** Prices not confirmed Service optional **Wines** 6 bottles over £30, 12 bottles under £30, 4 by glass **Notes** Vegetarian menu **Seats** 75, Pr/dining room 8 **Parking** 26

CLIFTON   Map 16 SE12

Black Horse Inn Restaurant with Rooms

◎ Modern British, Mediterranean 🕯

Bold British flavours in a Yorkshire inn

☎ 01484 713862
Westgate HD6 4HJ
e-mail: mail@blackhorseclifton.co.uk
web: www.blackhorseclifton.co.uk
dir: M62 junct 25, Brighouse, follow signs

This whitewashed 17th-century inn has the look of a traditional pub with its down-to-earth beamed bar with a real fire, and - more to the point - real ales. But give the menu a quick once-over, and it's clear that the Black Horse is more about food these days. A brace of stylish dining rooms offers different settings: one is more casual with high-backed leather chairs and bare darkwood tables, the other more formally dressed in white linen; on a fine day, the courtyard is an appealing spot too. Wherever you choose, the kitchen turns out contemporary ideas with a modish flourish here and there, all built on locally-sourced ingredients. Ox cheek croquette with onion purée, pickled chestnut mushrooms and blue cheese foam makes a punchy impact, followed by confit Gressingham duck leg with sticky red cabbage, bubble and squeak and plum jus. Dessert ends impressively with popcorn pannacotta with caramel popcorn and chocolate tuile.

Chef Richard Barrett **Owner** Andrew & Jane Russell **Times** 12-2.30/5.30-9.30 Closed D 25-26 Dec, 1 Jan **Prices** Prices not confirmed Service optional, Groups min 8 service 10% **Wines** 12 by glass **Notes** Sunday L, Vegetarian available, Dress restrictions, Smart casual, Civ Wed 60 **Seats** 70, Pr/dining room 60 **Children** Portions, Menu **Parking** 60

See advert on page 530

The Black Horse Inn

Clifton Village, Brighouse, West Yorkshire HD6 4HJ
Tel: 01484 713862   Fax: 01484 400582
E-mail: mail@blackhorseclifton.co.uk   Web: www.blackhorseclifton.co.uk

"The Black Horse Inn is a family owned village Inn, steeped in local history and bubbling with country charm. It is located in Clifton village, which is a real oasis and easily accessible only half a mile from Junction 25 off the M62.

With Passionate Chefs at the kitchen's helm - luscious food is at the heart of the Black Horse Inn, and the seasonal menu, sourced from Yorkshire's ambrosial larder, has won a loyal following, as well as an array of awards.

With two restaurant areas - private dining can be arranged if desired. The self contained function room is suitable for all events and there is a civil ceremony licence for wedding celebrations. There are 21 individually designed boutique bedrooms, perfect for the corporate traveller, or that special secret escape away from it all. The delightful flower filled courtyard is probably the property's best kept secret and yet in the summer months bathed in sunshine it is an idyllic place to relax with your favourite tipple.

With great food comes great drink – cask conditioned ales such as championship bitter from local brewer Timothy Taylor are served and also their own beer – Black Horse Brew, made exclusively for them by a small micro brewery. It has a well stocked bar including over 100 wine bins.

Why not take advantage of The Black Horse Inn Sleep Over Nights and events and enjoy a delicious combination of delectable food, excellent service and first class accommodation. Visit the website for more information www.blackhorseclifton.co.uk"

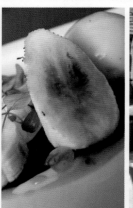

Save on Hotels. Book at theAA.com/hotel

YORKSHIRE, WEST 531 ENGLAND

HALIFAX
Map 19 SE02

Design House Restaurant

◎◎ Modern British NEW ☺

Local materials used with bags of creativity

☎ 01422 383242

Dean Clough, Arts & Business Centre HX3 5AX
dir: Telephone for detailed directions

The Design House occupies a converted mill and, despite its name, is not a case of style over substance. There's a central buzzy bar and an open-plan kitchen in the restaurant - an expansive, clean-cut space with white-topped tables, back-lit wall panels in caramel and cream, and colourful prints to punctuate the neutral palette. Chef-proprietor Lee Marshall is a Halifax lad who's keen to promote the best of the local larder in his imaginative contemporary cooking. Deconstructed classics are something of a theme, as in a seafood chowder whose individual components are presented on a dish before a waiter pours over the flavour-packed liquid at the table. Next up, an assiette of beef 'flavourings' with dauphinoise purée, ratatouille, and beef Marmite jus utilises humble cuts to great effect in a composition involving spicy meatball, perfectly-cooked shin, and a portion of tongue. It's all technically clever stuff, culminating in a chocolate soufflé tart that comes with a syringe of chocolate to squirt, Heston-style, into the soufflé.

Chef Lee Stevens Marshall, Christian Butterfield **Owner** Lee Stevens Marshall **Times** 12-2.30/5.30-9.30 Closed 26 Dec-9 Jan **Prices** Prices not confirmed Service optional, Groups min 10 service 12.5% **Wines** 12 by glass **Notes** Vegetarian available **Seats** 100 **Children** Portions **Parking** 100

Holdsworth House Hotel

◎◎ Modern British V ☺

Secluded manor house with well-crafted cooking

☎ 01422 240024

Holdsworth Rd, Holmfield HX2 9TG
e-mail: info@holdsworthhouse.co.uk
web: www.holdsworthhouse.co.uk
dir: From Halifax take A629 (Keighley road), in 2m right at garage to Holmfield, hotel 1.5m on right

It's little wonder that Holdsworth House is so popular with wedding parties - it really is a fairytale setting in secluded gardens. The oak-panelled rooms and roaring fires will certainly win you over, and the three inter-connecting rooms which make up the restaurant have oodles of period charm too (the building dates back to 1633), with low beams and mullioned windows, plus super views of the gardens. Yorkshire ingredients are much in evidence in traditional British cooking which is not adverse to some contemporary thinking. Start with sautéed black pearl scallops and marinated squid with pea purée and roasted red pepper sabayon, before Holme Farm venison Wellington with buttered spinach, gratin potatoes and juniper jus. Sarsaparilla and peanut butter cheesecake and honeycomb ice cream is a creative finish.

Chef Simon Allott **Owner** Gail Moss, Kim Wynn **Times** 12-2/7-9.30 Closed Xmas (open 25-26 Dec L only) **Prices** Tasting menu £45, Starter £5.95-£11.95, Main £15.50-£22.95, Dessert £7, Service optional, Groups min 10 service 10% **Wines** 47 bottles over £30, 37 bottles under £30, 13 by glass **Notes** Tasting menu 5 course, Sunday L, Vegetarian menu, Dress restrictions, Smart casual, No shorts, Civ Wed 120 **Seats** 45, Pr/dining room 120 **Children** Portions, Menu **Parking** 60

Shibden Mill Inn

◎◎ Modern British V ☺

Adventurous flavours in renovated corn mill

☎ 01422 365840

Shibden Mill Fold, Shibden HX3 7UL
e-mail: enquiries@shibdenmillinn.com
web: www.shibdenmillinn.com
dir: From A58 into Kell Lane, after 0.5m left into Blake Hill. Inn at bottom of hill on left

Converted from a 17th-century mill, the inn consists of a series of rooms connected by steps and stairs, with a rustic look generated by beams, exposed stone, and mismatched tables and chairs. Service is friendly but polished, and the whole place has a warm, good-humoured atmosphere. The kitchen's a hive of industry, judging by an assiette of pork: potted belly, a miniature pie, and crispy cheek, all accompanied by black pudding bread, beetroot and orange coleslaw, and beetroot chips - and that's just a starter. Another one combines pan-fried scallops with caramelised pistachio crumble and truffle and Jerusalem artichoke. The compositions of dishes may sound far-fetched, but the results are successful: Wellington-style baked salt cod, for instance, comes with spinach and mushrooms, smoked kippers and curried mussels. Cheeses are all made by Yorkshire artisan producers, or you could end with a plate of banana - crème brûlée, fritter and cake with salted toffee sauce.

Chef Darren Parkinson **Owner** Simon & Caitlin Heaton **Times** 12-2/6-9.30 Closed Xmas, D 24-26 Dec, 1 Jan

Prices Fixed L 2 course fr £12, Fixed D 3 course fr £15, Starter £8-£9, Main £17.50-£19, Dessert fr £6, Service optional **Wines** 32 bottles over £30, 54 bottles under £30, 22 by glass **Notes** Sunday L, Vegetarian menu **Seats** 50, Pr/dining room 8 **Children** Portions, Menu **Parking** 60

See advert on page 532

HAWORTH
Map 19 SE03

Ashmount Country House

◎ Modern British V ☺

Confident cooking in the Brontë village

☎ 01535 645726 & 07814 536044

Mytholmes Ln BD22 8EZ
e-mail: info@ashmounthaworth.co.uk
dir: M65 junct 13A Laneshaw Bridge, turn right over moors to Haworth. Turn left after car park on right, 100yds on right

A solid Victorian house with open fires and antique furniture, Ashmount is a short stroll from the Brontës' famous parsonage. Elegantly laid tables set the tone in the dining room, with its views over the hillside. The sensibly short menu, which changes every few days, is well planned to offer plenty of scope, the style set by a well-conceived main course of pan-fried sea bass fillet with tomato velouté, English asparagus, spinach and saffron-flavoured new potatoes. Equally, there may be honey-roast duck breast with blackberry jus, sweet potato dauphinoise and baked vegetables, with starters like a chunky galantine of duck and chicken with fruity marmalade, and puddings tend to the hearty: sticky toffee, say, or apple and raspberry crumble.

Chef Sarah Knighton **Owner** Ray & Gill Capeling **Times** 6.30-8.30 Closed L all week, D Mon-Tue **Prices** Starter £4.95-£7.95, Main £13.50-£19.95, Dessert £6.25-£8.50, Service optional **Wines** 10 bottles over £30, 17 bottles under £30, 11 by glass **Notes** Vegetarian menu, Civ Wed 40 **Seats** 26, Pr/dining room 20 **Parking** 12, On street

Shibden Mill Fold
Shibden, Halifax
West Yorkshire HX3 7UL
Tel: 01422 365840
Fax: 01422 362971
Email: enquiries@shibdenmillinn.com
Website: www.shibdenmillinn.com

For over 350 years *The Shibden Mill Inn* has been at the heart of life in West Yorkshire's Shibden Valley. It's a magical place where generation after generation of locals have enjoyed time well spent with friends and family, sharing in life's special moments and shaping memories to last a life time.

The Inn's reputation for warm hospitality, premier 2 Rosette gastro dining and 4 Star Inn accommodation draws people to the Shibden Valley from far and wide, and the Mill has naturally become a popular choice for those wishing to savour a sumptuous weekend break or mid-week stay.

Stunning countryside walks are in easy reach, as too the bright lights and city centre shopping on offer in Leeds. From its unique location, The Shibden Mill offers easy access to the very best to be found in this delightful part of West Yorkshire.

Opening times for breakfast, morning coffee & cake, afternoon teas, lunch and dinner can be found on the food page of the website www.shibdenmillinn.com

Save on Hotels. Book at **theAA.com/hotel**

YORKSHIRE, WEST 533 **ENGLAND**

HUDDERSFIELD Map 16 SE11

315 Bar and Restaurant

Modern V

Ambitious city-smart cooking in a reborn Yorkshire pub

☎ 01484 602613

315 Wakefield Rd HD8 0LX

e-mail: info@315barandrestaurant.co.uk

dir: M1 junct 38 to Huddersfield

Out in the sumptuous Yorkshire countryside not far from Huddersfield, 315 is a refurbished pub reborn as a city-smart restaurant and bar, with a fine conservatory room and a chef's table, which is pretty much all bases covered. Chairs upholstered in silver velvet and orchids on the tables make an aspirational statement, as does Jason Neilson's cooking, which is based on industrious in-house production of everything from breads to ice creams, and represents a successful alliance of English ingredients with modern French technique. A tall, thin, twice-cooked goats' cheese soufflé is an architectonic masterwork, and comes with a pecorino salad, the plate squiggled with sun-dried tomato sauce and pesto, while salmon and haddock are fashioned into a sausage that comes with warm potato salad and cauliflower cream. Local lamb gets a good outing, the best end crusted in garlic and rosemary, the liver sautéed, accompanied by fennel and red onion purée, or there might be sea bass with green-lip mussels and saffron potatoes. Desserts such as treacle apple tart with apple crumble ice cream on shortbread are a strength.

Chef Jason Neilson **Owner** Jason Neilson, Terry Dryden **Times** 12-9 Closed D Sun All-day dining **Prices** Fixed L 2 course £15, Starter £5-£7.50, Main £12.50-£23.50, Dessert fr £6.25, Service optional **Wines** 18 by glass **Notes** Sunday L £17.50-£19.95, Vegetarian menu, Civ Wed 150 **Seats** 90, Pr/dining room 115 **Children** Portions, Menu **Parking** 97

ILKLEY Map 19 SE14

Box Tree

— **see below**

LEEDS Map 19 SE23

De Vere Oulton Hall

British

Modernised British cooking in a splendid mansion

☎ 0871 222 4690

Rothwell Ln, Oulton LS26 8HN

e-mail: Oulton.hall@devere-hotels.com

web: www.devere-hotels.co.uk

dir: 2m from M62 junct 30, follow Rothwell signs, then 'Oulton 1m' sign. 1st exit at next 2 rdbts. Hotel on left. Or 1m from M1 junct 44, follow Castleford & Pontefract signs on A639

The De Vere group's Oulton Hall is a magnificent country mansion off the M62 to the south of Leeds. It's the kind of place that's grand enough to have staff swishing about the grounds on golf buggies, though ever mindful not to interrupt the outdoor Shakespeare that goes on in the summer. A stylish contemporary refurbishment has produced dashing interiors, and a strikingly elegant dining room done in black and crimson, with rich fabrics and lots of dark wood, and lighting low enough for an undercover rendezvous. The chosen culinary idiom is modernised classic British, with a fair bit of table side theatre if you don't mind the company, mixing up salads, slicing smoked salmon and carving the Chateaubriand before your very eyes. Baked cod with mushrooms, peas and pea shoots is an example of one of the attractively presented mains, or venison loin with poached pear and cocoa nibs in port. In the season, you could opt for a three-course rhubarb menu.

Chef Dean Rodgers **Owner** De Vere Hotels **Times** 7-9.45 Closed L all week **Prices** Prices not confirmed Service added but optional 10% **Wines** 13 by glass **Notes** Breakfast 7-10am, Sunday L, Vegetarian available, Dress restrictions, Smart casual, no T-shirts, shorts or trainers, Civ Wed 250 **Seats** 130, Pr/dining room 60 **Children** Portions, Menu **Parking** 200

Box Tree

ILKLEY MAP 19 SE14

Modern British, French V NOTABLE WINE LIST

Modern British meets classical French in a landmark Yorkshire venue

☎ 01943 608484

35-37 Church St LS29 9DR

e-mail: info@theboxtree.co.uk

dir: On A65 from Leeds through Ilkley, main lights approx 200yds on left

One of the foundational addresses of the culinary revival in England that emerged from postwar austerity, the Box Tree was conjured out of a stone-built former farmhouse on the main A65 road through town. From twee tearoom to beacon of gastronomy, the Tree has always punched above its weight, its reputation nurtured through successive changes of ownership and chef. There really was a moment in the 1980s when the career of the then unknown Marco Pierre White, his tempestuous London era still ahead of him, emerged in chrysalis - a moment nostalgically marked by White's returning now in part-ownership. Behind its neat box topiary, it still feels like an unusually elegant country house, the interiors smartly equipped in well-to-do Victorian style, with richly piled fabrics and diverting oil paintings abounding. There's always been an unabashed elegance about the food too, for all that it has consciously moved with the times. The haute cuisine de Yorkshire of a previous generation has now given place to a vigorous and imaginative rendition of modern British modes, while still underpinned by a principled commitment to pedigree regional produce. Simon Gueller still enjoys referencing classical French technique in dishes such as hazelnut-crusted foie gras with apple and pear, served with a glass of botrytised Coteaux du Layon, but then a starter like seared scallops with caramelised Jerusalem artichoke, with sea purslane and lemon jelly, makes an unmistakably contemporary statement. Move on to main, and dishes become deeper and fuller still, accompanying John Dory with truffled gnocchi, turnip and puréed salsify, or constructing an oxtail and snail croquette to go with beef fillet. Voguish textural explorations inform desserts like spiced ginger cake with poached plum, nut granola and star-anise ice cream. It's all served with effortless panache and a due sense of occasion, and there's a treasure-house of exciting wines.

Chef Mr S Gueller, Mr D Birk **Owner** Mrs R Gueller **Times** 12-2/7-9.30 Closed 27-31 Dec, 1-7 Jan, Mon, L Tue-Thu, D Sun **Prices** Fixed L 3 course £28-£35, Fixed D 3 course £6, Tasting menu £70, Groups min 8 service 10% **Wines** 11 bottles over £30, 12 bottles under £30, 7 by glass **Notes** Fixed L Fri & Sat only, Sunday L, Vegetarian menu, Dress restrictions, Smart dress preferred, Civ Wed 30 **Seats** 50, Pr/dining room 20 **Parking** NCP

LEEDS *continued*

Jamie's Italian, Leeds

◉ Italian V

Vibrant, branded Italian brasserie for all

☎ 0113 322 5400
35 Park Row LS1 5JL

The Jamie Oliver-branded chain now stretches the length and breadth of the UK, spreading its gospel of simple, colourful, rustic Italian lifestyle food. The Leeds city centre outpost works an open-plan warehouse look (it's actually an old bank building) with lots of exposed brick and girders, a splendid marquetry ceiling, and simple canteen-style table settings. Chirpy young staff are clearly chosen for their can-do attitude, which boosts further the upbeat vibe. The open-to-view kitchen sends out simple ideas that gain momentum from the quality of the raw ingredients (some of which are for sale). Planks of top-class Italian salumi, cheeses, or cured fish lead on to well-made creamy wild truffle risotto, or pappardelle with fennel sausage ragù in the pasta department, while mains run to straight-up steaks, burgers with smoked mozzarella and mortadella, or fish baked in a bag with clams, mussels, fennel, chilli, anchovies and Sicilian cracked wheat.

Times noon-11 **Prices** Starter £3.75-£8.20, Main £9.50-£19.50, Dessert £4.90-£4.95 **Notes** Vegetarian menu **Children** Menu

Malmaison Leeds

◉ Modern British ◐

Vibrant cooking in stylish city brasserie

☎ 0113 398 1000
1 Swinegate LS1 4AG
e-mail: leeds@malmaison.com
web: www.malmaison.com
dir: City centre. 5 mins walk from Leeds railway station. On junct 16 of loop road, Sovereign St & Swinegate

In pole position near the waterfront, and close by the intensive retail therapy provided by the city's chic boutiques and department stores, the Leeds outpost of the Mal stable delivers the expected house style of contemporary brasserie dining in a sultry, design-savvy venue. The building is converted from the offices of a bus and tram company and provides an atmospheric basis for a moodily-lit brasserie done out with intimate leather booths, dark wood galore, and a funky glass fireplace beneath a vaulted ceiling. Old friends from the British and European repertoire turn up on a please-all menu that works with the seasons and name-checks its Yorkshire food heroes. Expect the likes of smoked salmon rösti with horseradish cream, followed by venison haunch with roasted beetroot and grain mustard mash, or pan-fried cod with white bean and chorizo cassoulet.

Chef Andrew Lawson **Owner** Malmaison
Times 12-2.30/6.30-9.30 **Prices** Prices not confirmed Service added but optional 10% **Wines** 25 by glass **Notes** Sunday L, Vegetarian available, Civ Wed 80

Seats 85, Pr/dining room 12 **Children** Portions, Menu **Parking** Criterion Place car park, Q Park

The New Ellington

◉◉ Modern British ◐

Stylish boutique hotel with bold, modish cooking

☎ 0113 204 2150
23-25 York Place LS1 2EY
e-mail: info@thenewellington.com

The name references the late, great Duke who played the Leeds Music Festival in 1958, and there's a definite New Orleans, jazz-age vibe going on here. It's all very tasteful though and the hotel wears its 'boutique' billing very well indeed. If you're a fan of gin, head to The Gin Garden bar to take your pick from a head-spinning 84 varieties, before moving on down to the lower-ground floor to the plush Digby's Restaurant, where you'll find smart velour banquette seating and tables dressed up in crisp white linen. On the menu are some perky modish ideas and fun interpretations of classic dishes. Start, for example, with 'fish, chips & beans' or Digby's prawn cocktail, but you might also go for roast wood pigeon with oxtail pressing, chervil root and cabernet sauvignon. Main course delivers loin of Yorkshire lamb cooked sous-vide and served with crispy belly, smoked hotpot, asparagus, pancetta and barley, while for dessert, passionfruit tart with William Chase gin, palm sugar and pomegranate makes for a creative finale.

Chef Anton Scoones **Times** 12-2/5.30-10 **Closed** 25-26 Dec, D Sun **Prices** Fixed L 2 course £15.95-£19.95, Fixed D 3 course £19.95-£29.95, Tasting menu £44.95-£69.95, Starter £6.95-£8.95, Main £14.95-£21.95, Dessert £6.95-£8.95, Service optional **Wines** 10 bottles over £30, 10 bottles under £30, 8 by glass **Notes** Vegetarian available **Seats** 50, Pr/dining room 24 **Children** Portions, Menu **Parking** On street

Salvo's Restaurant & Salumeria

◉ Italian ◐

Popular Italian with salumeria (deli-café)

☎ 0113 275 5017 & 275 2752
115 Otley Rd, Headingley LS6 3PX
e-mail: dine@salvos.co.uk
dir: On A660 2m N of city centre

Since it first opened its doors back in 1976, Salvo's has served the local Headingley community and built a deserved reputation. It's lively, family-friendly and family-run (to this day) and can sort you out for a top-notch pizza or some regional Italian cooking of the rustic and hearty variety. Things have developed over the years with the arrival of the Salumeria a few doors down, which is a café-deli during the day and opens in the evening for musical soirees and the like. If you've come for a pizza because nothing else will do, you won't leave disappointed. But there is so much more: antipasti such as deep-fried squid and zucchini with caper mayonnaise, pasta - perhaps casareccie al anatra with confit duck, red onion and Sicilian sausage ragù - and main courses

run to the likes of pot-roasted beef with red wine and peppercorns.

Chef Giuseppe Schirripa, Geppino Dammone **Owner** John & Geppino Dammone **Times** 12-2/5.30-10.30 **Closed** 25-26 Dec, 1 Jan, L BHs **Prices** Fixed L 2 course £11.95, Fixed D 3 course £17.50, Starter £3.95-£8.50, Main £8.50-£19.50, Dessert £3.95-£10.50, Service optional **Wines** 9 bottles over £30, 33 bottles under £30, 6 by glass **Notes** Sunday L, Vegetarian available **Seats** 88, Pr/dining room 20 **Children** Portions, Menu **Parking** On street, Pay & display nearby

Thorpe Park Hotel & Spa

◉ Modern British ◐

Accomplished contemporary cooking in Thorpe Park

☎ 0113 264 1000
Century Way, Thorpe Park LS15 8ZB
e-mail: thorpepark@shirehotels.com
web: www.shirehotels.com
dir: M1 junct 46, follow signs off rdbt for Thorpe Park

On the edge of the city, convenient for the motorway, Thorpe Park is a smart hotel with popular leisure facilities and a spa. The restaurant is an open-plan, split-level room, with a pale wooden floor, artwork on the walls, and black leather-type chairs. The menu cleverly combines familiar with more contemporary ideas, so expect roast scallops with black pudding, potato purée and red wine sauce, alongside sirloin steak with béarnaise. Tempura tiger prawns with chilli dipping sauce is a popular starter, or go for something like Asian-style duck with watercress, cucumber and coriander salad. Fish is confidently handled, seen in grilled salmon, sea bass and scallops with salsa verde and thin fries, and a commitment to local product is evident: belly pork from Bacup, for instance, is slowly cooked and served with black pudding, champ, apple chutney and cider sauce, a satisfying combination of flavours and textures.

Chef Paul Woodward **Owner** Shire Hotels
Times 12-2/6.45-9.30 **Prices** Starter £5.95-£9.50, Main £11.50-£27, Dessert fr £6.50, Service optional **Wines** 35 bottles over £30, 47 bottles under £30, 10 by glass **Notes** Early bird Mon-Fri 5.45-6.45pm 2 course £12.95, Sunday L £15.95-£20.95, Civ Wed 90 **Seats** 120, Pr/dining room 50 **Children** Portions, Menu **Parking** 200

Town Hall Tavern

◉ Modern British ◐

Refined pub fare in the city centre

☎ 0113 244 0765
17 Westgate LS1 2RA
e-mail: info@townhalltavernleeds.co.uk
dir: Located in city centre, opposite the Law Courts

Located between the law courts and the Park Square Business Centre, this city-centre inn was at one time the haunt of policemen and solicitors. It dates from the 1920s, its more recent makeover creating a comfortable and homely atmosphere while retaining the building's original look. The menu sets out the pub's stall, emphasising that it buys from ethical local producers, and the kitchen's output is well up to the mark. Pub standards include gammon, egg and chips, and home-made burger, while a short 'perfect for lunch' section of the menu runs to omelettes and corned-beef hash. Those wanting the full works could go for salt-and-pepper squid with tempura prawns and honey and soy sauce, then slow-roast belly pork with passionfruit, braised fennel and mustard mash, and end with vanilla and ginger cheesecake with rhubarb.

Chef Stephen Carr **Owner** Timothy Taylor **Times** 11.30-9 Closed 25-26 Dec, BH Mon, D Sun All-day dining **Prices** Prices not confirmed Service optional **Wines** 2 bottles over £30, 19 bottles under £30, 8 by glass **Notes** Sunday L, Vegetarian available **Seats** 26 **Children** Portions, Menu **Parking** On street at rear

---

LIVERSEDGE   Map 16 SE12

Healds Hall Hotel & Restaurant

Modern British 🏵

Stimulating medley of styles in 18th-century hotel

☎ 01924 409112
Leeds Rd WF15 6JA
e-mail: enquire@healdshall.co.uk
web: www.healdshall.co.uk
dir: M1 junct 40, A638. From Dewsbury take A652 signed Bradford. Left at A62. Hotel 50yds on right

Healds Hall, an 18th-century mill owner's mansion, has two dining rooms: a contemporary, vibrantly decorated bistro, and more formal and demure Harringtons Restaurant. The long menu, served in both, has broad appeal, thus, tempura king prawns with tomato and chilli jam and coriander dressing may appear next to fennel and onion bhaji with raita, followed by duck leg confit with cassoulet-type casserole, or beef bourguignon with mash and root vegetables. Homelier dishes have included a simple plate of smoked salmon, and beer-battered haddock with mushy peas, while puddings can be as inspiring as rhubarb pancakes with ginger ice cream.

Chef Andrew Ward, David Winter **Owner** Mr N B & Mrs T Harrington **Times** 12-2/6-10 Closed 1 Jan, BHs, L Sat, D Sun (ex residents) **Prices** Service optional **Wines** 8 by glass **Notes** Sunday L £18.95-£23.95, Vegetarian available, Civ Wed 100 **Seats** 46, Pr/dining room 30 **Children** Portions **Parking** 90

OTLEY   Map 19 SE24

Chevin Country Park Hotel & Spa

Modern British

Modern cooking in a Scandinavian style log cabin

☎ 01943 467818
Yorkgate LS21 3NU
e-mail: gm.chevin@crerarhotels.com
dir: A658 towards Harrogate. Left at 1st turn towards Carlton, 2nd left towards Yorkgate

Tucked away in 40 acres of private Yorkshire woodland complete with three lakes, extensive gardens and abundant wildlife, it's seems hard to believe that Leeds/Bradford Airport is just a short drive away from this rather unusual, purpose-built hotel. The restaurant is housed in one of the UK's biggest log cabins (bedrooms are mostly scattered around the grounds in chalets) and it's all charmingly old fashioned with smartly dressed tables and lovely lakeside views through the picture windows. The modern menus - including a carte and steak and grill menu - are full of crowd-pleasers and local produce features strongly. Start, perhaps, with a well-made, smooth chicken liver parfait served with toasted brioche and red onion marmalade, before Scottish scallops sautéed with butter and pancetta lardons. Lemon tart with almond and ginger ice cream is a satisfying end to a meal.

Times 12-2.30/6-9

PONTEFRACT   Map 16 SE42

Wentbridge House Hotel

Modern British V 🍷 NOTABLE WINE LIST 🏵

Yorkshire flavour in a grand country house

☎ 01977 620444
The Great North Rd, Wentbridge WF8 3JJ
e-mail: info@wentbridgehouse.co.uk
web: www.wentbridgehouse.co.uk
dir: 4m S of M62/A1 junct, 0.5m off A1

With a heritage that includes ownership by the Leatham family of Barclays Bank fame, Wentbridge is these days a country-house hotel with a good deal of appeal. There are over 20 acres of grounds to explore in the lush Went Valley for a start and, inside the 300-year-old building, plenty of traditional charm. The Fleur de Lys is the main dining venue (The Wentbridge Brasserie the buzzy alternative), with its smartly dressed tables, chic upholstered chairs and banquettes, and a menu of updated classics, including beef Diane prepared at the table. Hand-dived scallops with Happy Trotters pork belly croquette, pea purée and crackling salad gets things off to a flying start, followed perhaps by saddle of Round Green Farm rose venison with venison faggot, spring cabbage, fennel purée and mushroom jus. The menu faithfully name-checks the many excellent regional ingredients, such as Flookburgh shrimp butter to accompany seared East Coast sea bass with steamed asparagus. To finish, perhaps something like Yorkshire treacle tart with raspberry ripple ice cream.

Chef Michael Ward **Owner** Mr G Page **Times** 7.15-9.30 Closed 25 Dec, L Mon-Sat, D Sun **Prices** Starter £7.95-£11.95, Main £18.50-£28.95, Dessert £6.50-£10.95, Service optional **Wines** 100 bottles over £30, 30 bottles under £30, 10 by glass **Notes** Sunday L £27, Vegetarian menu, Civ Wed 130 **Seats** 60, Pr/dining room 24 **Children** Portions **Parking** 100

WAKEFIELD   Map 16 SE32

Waterton Park Hotel

Traditional & Modern British V 🏵

Sound cooking by a huge lake

☎ 01924 257911
Walton Hall, The Balk, Walton WF2 6PW
e-mail: info@watertonparkhotel.co.uk
web: www.watertonparkhotel.co.uk
dir: 3m SE off B6378. Exit M1 junct 39 towards Wakefield. At 3rd rdbt right for Crofton. At 2nd lights right & follow signs

Locations don't come much more memorable than this Georgian mansion marooned on an island in the middle of a 26-acre lake, with an 18-hole golf course in the wooded parkland all around. An iron footbridge links the castaway to the shore, where you'll find the Bridgewalk restaurant in the hotel's modern, purpose-built annexe. Decorated in restful neutral shades and lined with books, the smart setting suits the contemporary country-house cooking. Ingredients are well-sourced and handled with care in a nice balance of simple and more labour-intensive dishes. Game terrine with beetroot relish and toasted brioche might be one way to get started, while mains could bring line-caught sea bass with pickled fennel and tarragon cream, or seared duck breast with black cherry confit. Wind things up with pear and almond frangipane with pear crumble and custard, or go for a savoury finish with a trio of Yorkshire cheeses.

Chef Armstrong Wgabi **Owner** The Kaye family **Times** 7-9.30 Closed D Sun **Prices** Service optional **Wines** 10 by glass **Notes** £21.50-£30, Vegetarian menu, Dress restrictions, Smart casual, Civ Wed 150 **Seats** 50, Pr/dining room 40 **Children** Portions, Menu **Parking** 200

| WETHERBY | Map 16 SE44 |

Wood Hall Hotel

Modern British V

Modish cooking in a grand Georgian hotel

☎ 01937 587271
Trip Ln, Linton LS22 4JA
e-mail: woodhall@handpicked.co.uk
web: www.handpickedhotels.co.uk/woodhall
dir: From Wetherby take A661 (Harrogate road) N for
0.5m. Left to Sicklinghall/Linton. Cross bridge, left to
Linton/Woodhall, right opposite Windmill Inn, 1.25m to
hotel (follow brown signs)

Built in 1750 as a country retreat for the Vavasour family,
Wood Hall retains a plethora of grand Georgian features
blended with more modern comforts. The long sweeping
driveway provides an excellent introduction to the 100-
plus acre estate, which, thanks to its position perched
atop a hill, enjoys wide-reaching views. The Georgian
Restaurant in the old dining hall has a formal air and
period details set against a fashionably muted biscuit-
coloured décor. Tables are stylishly laid with crisp white
linen and modern silver candlesticks, while service is as
professional as the stunning surroundings would lead you
to expect. Seasonal, local and homemade are true
buzzwords here - herbs come from the kitchen garden
and everything is made in-house. Skillfully updated
classics might include an attractively presented plate of
Wood Hall smoked salmon with 'cucumber and tomato
flavours' and crab parfait. Braised brisket of Yorkshire
beef, bourguignon jus and fondant potatoes is a
wonderfully hearty main course, while rhubarb
pannacotta, rosemary shortbread and almond praline ice
cream shows off the kitchen's competence in the pastry
department.

Chef Neal Birtwell **Owner** Hand Picked Hotels
Times 12-2.30/7-9.30 Closed L Mon-Sat **Prices** Fixed D 3
course £37, Starter £14-£18, Main £24-£29, Dessert
£8.50-£11, Service optional **Wines** 50 bottles over £30,
10 bottles under £30, 18 by glass **Notes** Sunday L,
Vegetarian menu, Dress restrictions, Smart casual, no
jeans or trainers, Civ Wed 100 **Seats** 40, Pr/dining room
100 **Children** Portions, Menu **Parking** 100

CHANNEL ISLANDS
ALDERNEY

| ALDERNEY | Map 24 |

Braye Beach Hotel

Modern British

Stylish cooking in beachside hotel

☎ 01481 824300
Braye St GY9 3XT
e-mail: reception@brayebeach.com
web: www.brayebeach.com
dir: Follow coast road from airport

Facing a magnificent sweep of white beach, the hotel is a
modern, gabled building with high levels of comfort.
Large windows in the stylish restaurant, with its subdued
décor, catch the sea views, and even better is the decked
terrace. Fresh, local produce is the kitchen's linchpin,
with seafood showing up strongly in season: perhaps a
mixed platter of shellfish. Grilled mackerel with slow-
cooked belly pork is the sort of contemporary idea found
among starters, dressed with soy, thin ribbons of
cucumber adding a refreshing dimension. Pan-fried
chicken breast, moist and full of flavour, may be among
main courses, partnered by a risotto of butternut squash
purée and thyme with parmesan crisps, and smooth,
intense dark chocolate mousse could round off a meal,
served with crème Chantilly and a white chocolate tuile.

Times 12-2.30/6.30-9.30 Closed Jan-Mar

GUERNSEY

| CASTEL | Map 24 |

Cobo Bay Hotel

Modern, Traditional

Superb views and admirable use of local produce

☎ 01481 257102 & 07781 156757
Cobo Coast Rd, Cobo GY5 7HB
e-mail: reservations@cobobayhotel.com
web: www.cobobayhotel.com
dir: From airport turn right, follow road to W coast at
L'Erée. Turn right onto coast road for 3m to Cobo Bay.
Hotel on right

The view across the eponymous bay is seen at its best if
you time it right for a sunset dinner at this west-facing
beachside hotel. If you're lucky you can dine alfresco on
the beach terrace, but if not it's no hardship to grab a
table indoors in the smart contemporary restaurant. As
you might hope in this wave-lapped setting, seafood is a
strong suit here, arriving slithery fresh from local boats,
and it is presented in straightforward contemporary
combinations, along with a cornucopia of other top-
quality locally-sourced produce. Courgette and red pepper
soup is a well-made opener, or you might prefer to head
straight for the fish - perhaps tempura monkfish or fritto
misto with lemon and caper mayonnaise - then move on
to pan-fried sea bass with pea and prawn risotto, garlic

king prawns, and crab and lobster bisque. Banana tarte
Tatin with caramel ice cream presses the comfort button
at the end.

Chef John Chapman **Owner** Mr D & Mrs J Nussbaumer
Times 12-2/6-9.30 **Prices** Fixed L 2 course £16.95, Fixed
D 3 course £25, Starter £6.95-£9.50, Main £8.95-£37.50,
Dessert £6.50-£7.50, Service optional **Wines** 14 bottles
over £30, 31 bottles under £30, 11 by glass **Notes** Sunday
L, Vegetarian available **Seats** 120, Pr/dining room 70
Children Portions, Menu **Parking** 100

| ST MARTIN | Map 24 |

The Auberge

Modern European

Seafood-led menu on a Guernsey clifftop

☎ 01481 238485
Jerbourg Rd GY4 6BH
e-mail: dine@theauberge.gg
dir: End of Jerbourg Rd at Jerbourg Point

Commandingly set on a Guernsey clifftop overlooking the
Channel and the neighbouring islands, The Auberge
enjoys a bracing maritime setting. Glass doors all round
open up to a decked terrace, and the light pine flooring
and rich purple and gold interior scheme make for a
pleasant contrast in the main room. A relaxed service
approach and piped Michael Bublé do their combined
best to put you at your ease, and the sense of amiability
is infectious. Daniel Green's cooking is big on fish and
seafood, with Herm oysters and scallop tempura amongst
the appealing starter options. Portions for main courses
are so Rabelaisian that you might wonder at the margins
the place must be running on, before shrugging off all
thought of them as you set about a loaded plateful of
king prawns and scallops fried in garlic butter, with
spring onion mash, crisp smoked lardons and pesto. A
hot chocolate fondant finale is a show-stopper.

Chef Daniel Green **Owner** Lapwing Trading Ltd
Times 12-2/7-9.30 Closed 25-26 Dec, D Sun **Prices** Fixed
L 2 course £14.50, Fixed D 3 course £17.95, Starter
£5.25-£12, Main £12.50-£30, Dessert £5.50-£7.50,
Service optional **Wines** 30 bottles over £30, 26 bottles
under £30, 12 by glass **Notes** Sunday L, Vegetarian
available **Seats** 70, Pr/dining room 20 **Children** Portions,
Menu **Parking** 25

La Barbarie Hotel

British, French

**Unpretentious country-house cooking in a charming
setting**

☎ 01481 235217
Saints Rd GY4 6ES
e-mail: reservations@labarbariehotel.com
web: www.labarbariehotel.com
dir: At lights in St Martin take road to Saints Bay. Hotel
on right at end of Saints Rd

Named after the Barbary Coast pirates who kidnapped
the owner of the building in the 17th century, this

Save on Hotels. Book at **theAA.com/hotel**

GUERNSEY 537 **ENGLAND**

country-house hotel benefits from a peaceful location close to Guernsey's stunning beaches and coves. It used to be a priory but became a hotel in the 1950s and is charmingly decorated throughout. Think traditional oak beams in the relaxing residents' lounge and white-clothed tables and whitewashed walls in the candlelit restaurant, where formal service manages to be friendly rather than stuffy. The kitchen, led by longstanding head chef Colin Pearson, does a good turn in unpretentious, seasonally-led cooking, influenced by the island's produce where possible. A flavoursome chicken liver parfait with tomato chutney and warm toast might precede a simple but effective main course of roast monkfish and tiger prawn with a light curry sauce, mange-tout and steamed basmati rice. Lemon verbena brûlée, lemon shortbread and lemon sorbet brings things to a zingy close.

Times 12-1.45/6-9.30 Closed mid Nov-mid Mar

Hotel Jerbourg

◉ French **NEW** 🍃

Ocean views and classic seafood dishes

☎ 01481 238826
Jerbourg Point GY4 6BJ
e-mail: stay@hoteljerbourg.com
dir: From airport turn left to St Martin, right at filter, straight on at lights, hotel at end of road on right

Magnificent views are a major pull at this modern hotel in lovely grounds out on the tip of the Jerbourg Peninsula. With the Atlantic lapping all around, thoughts are bound to turn to fish, so you will not be disappointed to see that the classic French repertoire is weighted in that direction. The kitchen resists the temptation to gild the lily, letting the sheer freshness and quality of prime piscine produce do the talking, serving Guernsey chancre crab with prawn and apple cocktail, ahead of turbot with crayfish and caviar butter sauce, or grilled brill fillet with sauté potatoes, spinach, and martini beurre blanc. Straight-up chargrilled steaks (entrecôte with dauphinoise potatoes and Roquefort sauce, say), or something requiring a touch more input from the kitchen - perhaps honey-glazed Barbary duck breast with potato rösti, asparagus and sherry vinegar jus - should keep the carnivores quiet. End with a classic crème brûlée.

Chef Kristian Gregg **Owner** Ess Ltd
Times 12-2.30/6.30-9.30 Closed 5 Jan-Mar **Prices** Fixed L 2 course £24.50, Fixed D 3 course £29, Starter £5.95-£8.50, Main £8.95-£24.95, Dessert £5, Service optional **Wines** 6 by glass **Notes** Sun L 3 course 12-2.30pm, Sunday L, Vegetarian available **Seats** 80 **Children** Portions, Menu **Parking** 30

ST PETER PORT   Map 24

The Absolute End

◉ Mediterranean, International

Italian-accented fish restaurant overlooking the harbour

☎ 01481 723822
St Georges Esplanade GY1 2BG
e-mail: the-absolute-end@cwgsy.net
dir: Less than 1m from town centre. N on seafront road towards St Sampson

Any faint note of exasperation in the name is entirely misleading. Peppe Rega's welcoming harbourside seafood place, formed from the knocking together of two former fishermen's cottages, is perfectly positioned to enjoy views over the sea, and draws in locals and holiday-makers for its softly Italian-accented menus of straightforward fish and shellfish. A light-filled ground-floor room in olive-green and white is supplemented by a terrace upstairs, and staff ensure a friendly tone to the proceedings. Reliable renditions of crisp-fried crab cakes with sweet chilli sauce, oysters alla fiorentina, and mains such as grilled sea bass with bitingly lemony meunière, all come up to snuff, but meat-eaters are not forgotten either. Fillet steaks, rack of lamb or veal saltimbocca should keep them happy. A slate of pasta and risotto variations provides carbs, and energetically garnished dessert plates feature the likes of milk chocolate fondant with Greek yoghurt and strawberry compôte.

Times 12-2.30/6.30-10 Closed Sun

The Duke of Richmond Hotel

◉ Modern International **NEW** 🍃

Leopard-spotted style in one of Guernsey's oldest hotels

☎ 01481 740866 & 726221
Cambridge Park GY1 1UY
web: www.dukeofrichmond.com
dir: Opposite Cambridge Park

A historically fascinating site once housed Guernsey's first hotel, Grover's, and subsequently the Richmond, the island's premier boarding-house. Following the rude interruption of occupation by the Nazis during wartime, the place once more became a hotel, but one that had come up in the world. An ennoblement of the name paved the way for the present incarnation, and what an incarnation it is. A rather fetching leopard-spotted theme has been introduced to the bar and dining room, and a screened-off kitchen provides the now de rigueur voyeur's

eye on the culinary action, rivalled for visual attention only by the views from the conservatory extension. Simple brasserie cooking is the chosen mode, with Caesar salad and excellent chicken liver pâté to start things off, followed by very mild lamb curry with basmati, classic fish and chips, or pasta primavera. Finish with a hefty wodge of baked American cheesecake. The concise list features the wines of Bouchard-Finlayson, one of South Africa's reference producers.

Chef Wesley Cadogan, Stamatis Loumousiotis **Owner** Red Carnation Hotels **Times** 12-2/6-10 **Prices** Fixed L 2 course fr £15.50, Starter £6-£9, Main £11-£18.50, Dessert £6.50-£8.50, Service added but optional 10% **Wines** 30 bottles over £30, 20 bottles under £30, 25 by glass **Notes** Sunday L £12.50-£18.50, Vegetarian available, Dress restrictions, Smart casual **Seats** 80, Pr/dining room 260 **Children** Portions, Menu **Parking** On street

Fermain Valley Hotel

◉◉ Modern European **V** 🍃

Brasserie-style dishes in a beautiful Guernsey valley

☎ 01481 235666
Fermain Ln GY1 1ZZ
e-mail: info@fermainvalley.com
dir: From town centre on Fort Rd follow St Martin signs. Fermain Ln on left. Hotel 0.5m on left

In a spectacularly sylvan setting, the white-painted Fermain Valley Hotel is close to the bay of the same name, the bright blue water glimpsed from the terrace over the treetops. It stands in beautiful gardens, too, so there's plenty of opportunity to unwind. The Valley Restaurant is the main dining option here - refurbished in 2013 - and makes a smart setting for some bright and gently contemporary cooking. Start with lemon sole and a fried oyster with cucumber and lemon, for example, or local Guernsey crab with tomato consommé jelly, avocado purée and brown crab toastie. There's a French and Italian flavour to the menu, thus a pork chop might come with Tuscan beans and a roast garlic and fennel crust, and the entrecôte steak with ceps pudding, oven-roasted tomatoes and parsley and garlic sauce. Finish with a rhubarb and champagne jelly with scorched meringue, or on a savoury note with potted cheddar with celery pickle and raisin toast.

Chef Christopher Archambault **Owner** Vista Hotels Ltd **Times** 12-2.30/6.30-9.30 **Prices** Fixed L 2 course £10, Fixed D 3 course £17, Starter £6-£9, Main £14-£21, Dessert £5-£8 **Wines** 8 by glass **Notes** Sunday L, Vegetarian menu, Dress restrictions, smart casual **Seats** 80 **Children** Portions, Menu **Parking** 50

ST PETER PORT *continued*

Mora Restaurant & Grill

◉ Traditional European ◐

Contemporary cooking in a stylish venue by the marina

☎ 01481 715053
The Quay GY1 2LE
e-mail: eat@mora.gg
dir: Facing Victoria Marina

Creative restyling has made Mora a more obviously engaging venue, without losing any of the firmly loyal local custom. The less formal ground floor has a brasserie menu alongside the carte, while upstairs it's just the latter. Reached via a sweeping metal staircase, it's a stylish, comfortable room with a vaulted ceiling and an open kitchen to add to the sense of theatre. The cooking essays some contemporary flourishes, but without leaving behind a solid foundation of tradition, so main-course hits might be generous calves' liver with bacon, bubble-and-squeak and creamy mustard onions, or brill with clams, spinach and puréed white beans. Preface either of those with potted smoked mackerel and anchovies, or crab cakes with lemon-and-chilli fennel, and the whole deal looks very attractive. Orange and Grand Marnier cheesecake with dark chocolate sauce is a good way to end, otherwise there are fine local cheeses.

Chef Trevor Baines **Owner** Nello Ciotti
Times 12-2.15/6-10 Closed 25 Dec **Prices** Fixed L 2 course £19.50, Fixed D 3 course £24.95, Starter £5-£9.50, Main £14-£19.50, Dessert £5.95-£6.95, Service optional **Wines** 30 bottles over £30, 40 bottles under £30, 11 by glass **Notes** Sunday L, Vegetarian available **Seats** 90 **Children** Portions, Menu **Parking** On pier

The Old Government House Hotel & Spa

◉◉ Indian ▨NOTABLE WINE LIST ◐

A taste of Asia at grand harbourside address

☎ 01481 724921
St Ann's Place GY1 2NU
e-mail: governors@theoghhotel.com
web: www.theoghhotel.com
dir: At junct of St Julian's Av & College St

Given it was once the official residence of the Governor, it is perhaps unsurprising that the OGH (as it is known) is in such a plum spot overlooking the old town and harbour. It dates from the mid-18th century and looks the part with its splendid white façade and classical proportions. It is doubtless no coincidence that with the appointment of a new executive chef who hails from India (Haridwar to be precise), there has been a change in direction of the culinary output too. Choose between the Curry Room or the Brasserie Restaurant. The latter is in a large conservatory dining room and serves up Guernsey crab Niçoise, grilled rib-eye steak and the like, whilst the hotel's fine-dining restaurant is now The Curry Room at the Governor's Restaurant. With a décor that recalls the days of the Raj, the menu delivers some smart modish-looking Indian dishes which steer clear of cliché. Start with pan-seared lamb with 'secret spices' and chick pea

masala, followed by Bengal king prawn curry with minted mushy peas and tempura spring onion.

Chef Arun Singh, Stamatis Loumousiotis **Owner** Red Carnation Hotels **Times** 12-2/7-11 Closed 25 & 31 Dec **Prices** Fixed L 3 course £28.50, Fixed D 3 course £28.50, Service added but optional 10% **Wines** 94 bottles over £30, 31 bottles under £30, 26 by glass **Notes** Vegetarian available, Dress restrictions, Smart casual **Seats** 20

ST SAVIOUR   Map 24

The Farmhouse Hotel

◉ Modern British ◐

Boutique hotel with resourceful cooking

☎ 01481 264181
Route des bas Courtils GY7 9YF
e-mail: enquiries@thefarmhouse.gg
web: www.thefarmhouse.gg
dir: From airport turn left. Approx 1m left at lights. 100mtrs, left, around airport runway perimeter. 1m, left at staggered junct. Hotel in 100mtrs on right

The same family has owned this 15th-century farmhouse, now a boutique hotel, for three generations. Beams, stone floors and granite are reminders of the property's antiquity, superimposed today with a modern décor and comfortable furnishings. Eating outside is an attractive proposition, while the restaurant is in the oldest part of the building. Seasonality is central to the kitchen's output, bringing on shellfish in summer: perhaps scallops with a simple white wine sauce. Game is abundant in the colder months: partridge tortellini, say, with confit leg, leeks and basil, followed by roast goose with leg meat stuffing cut by spot-on orange sauce. Otherwise, there might be boar's head with truffles, mushrooms and sauce gribiche, or fried fillet of cod with a smoked cod beignet, greens, fondant potatoes and parsley and caper beurre blanc, with a finale of chocolate and hazelnut tart, its pastry exemplary, with a hazelnut shard and vanilla crème fraîche.

Chef Robert Birch **Owner** David & Julie Nussbaumer **Times** 12-2.30/6.30-9.30 **Prices** Fixed L 2 course fr £15.95, Fixed D 3 course £19.95, Starter £6.50-£8.50, Main £17.50-£26, Dessert £5.95-£8.95, Service optional **Wines** 12 bottles over £30, 25 bottles under £30, 12 by glass **Notes** Sunday L, Vegetarian available, Dress restrictions, Smart casual **Seats** 60, Pr/dining room 162 **Children** Portions, Menu **Parking** 80

HERM

HERM   Map 24

White House Hotel

◉◉ European

Simple cooking and sea views in an island retreat

☎ 01481 722159
GY1 3HR
e-mail: admin@herm-island.com
web: www.herm-island.com
dir: Close to harbour. Access by regular 20 min boat trip from St Peter Port, Guernsey

If you hanker for a simpler, slower pace of life, how about the pocket-sized, car- and pollution-free island of Herm? The island's only hotel - the White House - even takes the concept of getting away from it all a step further by dispensing with TVs, phones and clocks, but that doesn't mean you can totally kick back and relax in the restaurant, since old-school values require gentlemen to wear jackets and/or ties. As its name suggests, the Conservatory Restaurant is light and airy, and every table has a sea view. The kitchen doesn't try to reinvent the wheel, sticking to unfussy dishes that rely on the sheer quality of the raw materials and simple, accurate cooking for their effect. The contemporary European menu opens with an easy-on-the-eye composition of seared Guernsey scallops with Puy lentil and pancetta casserole, and truffled celeriac purée, before reaching out into the realms of duck breast teamed with Waldorf croquettes, roasted figs, Chantenay carrots and whisky jus. To finish, there's classic apple tarte Tatin with vanilla crème anglaise.

Times 12.30-2/7-9 Closed Nov-Apr

JERSEY

GOREY   Map 24

The Moorings Hotel & Restaurant

◉◉ Traditional ◐

Local food on the quayside

☎ 01534 853633
Gorey Pier JE3 6EW
e-mail: reservations@themooringshotel.com
web: www.themooringshotel.com
dir: At foot of Mont Orgueil Castle

Right on the waterfront with the magnificent Mont Orgueil Castle looming large above it, The Moorings truly is at the centre of things. The wonderful beach is just a stroll away, there are outdoor tables for that continental vibe, and there's a passion for seafood within. It's not all about fish and shellfish, though, for both the bistro and Walkers Restaurant deliver the fruits of both land and sea. The restaurant is a pretty space with neatly laid tables and a warm, summery colour scheme. There's a Gallic imprint on the menu, with the kitchen making good use of the first-class ingredients in unfussy, clearly-focused dishes. Start, perhaps, with picked white chancre crab with a vegetable and miso soup, or pan-fried scallops with artichoke purée, wild rocket and truffle dressing. Next up, pan-fried fillet of sea bass with crushed potatoes, scallops and sauce vierge, or braised lamb fillets with parmesan risotto and stuffed Savoy cabbage. There's a great value fixed-price menu in support of the carte. Finish with a classic vanilla crème brûlée.

Chef Simon Walker **Owner** Simon & Joanne Walker **Times** 12-2/7-8.30 **Prices** Fixed L 2 course £12.50-£19, Fixed D 3 course £22.50-£27, Starter £8.95-£10.80, Main £18.25-£29, Dessert £6.50-£14, Service optional **Wines** 26 bottles over £30, 36 bottles under £30, 8 by glass **Notes** Sunday L, Vegetarian available, Dress restrictions, Smart casual **Seats** 65, Pr/dining room 35 **Children** Portions, Menu

Sumas

◎◎ Modern British

Inventive cooking and marina views

☎ 01534 853291
Gorey Hill JE3 6ET
e-mail: info@sumasrestaurant.com
web: www.sumasrestaurant.com
dir: From St Helier take A3 E for 5m to Gorey. Before castle take sharp left. Restaurant 100yds up hill on left (look for blue & white blind)

If beachside-chic is in your restaurant vocabulary, you'll have an idea what to expect here. Overlooking Gorey Bay, the vista changes with the ebb and flow of the tide, so you might be watching the boats bobbing in the harbour or locals digging for clams in the sands. The tables on the terrace have the best of those views. Inside is pretty peachy too, mind you, with whitewashed walls and plenty of splashes of blue giving a feeling of seaside bonhomie. There's a goodly amount of seafood on the menu, but not exclusively so, for this is a kitchen which also seeks out the best the local land has to offer. Expect well-crafted, modish dishes along the lines of local crab and pumpkin risotto with lemongrass and coriander, that's assuming you can resist the Royal Bay oysters. Main courses might deliver Angus rib-eye steak with hand-cut chips and Madeira sauce, or pan-fried local brill with crushed Charlotte potatoes mixed with crab, topped with a fish foam. For dessert, lemon tart with honey and Earl Grey ice cream will send you home content.

Chef Patrice Bouffaut **Owner** Mrs Bults & Paul Dufty **Times** 12-2.30/6-9.30 Closed late Dec-mid Jan (approx), D Sun **Prices** Fixed L 2 course fr £17.50, Fixed D 3 course fr £20, Starter £5.75-£12, Main £14.50-£25, Dessert

£5.75-£9.75, Service optional, Groups min 10 service 10% **Wines** 29 bottles over £30, 26 bottles under £30, 14 by glass **Notes** Sunday L, Vegetarian available **Seats** 40 **Children** Portions, Menu **Parking** On street

---

ROZEL	**Map 24**

Chateau La Chaire

◎◎ Traditional British, French Ⓥ ☺

Anglo-French panache in a sparkling-white hotel

☎ 01534 863354
Rozel Bay JE3 6AJ
e-mail: res@chateau-la-chaire.co.uk
web: www.chateau-la-chaire.co.uk
dir: From St Helier NE towards Five Oaks, Maufant, then St Martin's Church & Rozel. 1st left in village, hotel 100mtrs

The last word in formal elegance when it was built in the first half of the 19th century, La Chaire looks pristine and sparkling-white in the Jersey sun. Its gardens were laid out in 1841 by Samuel Curtis, erstwhile director of Kew Gardens, and there is an impressive air of the rococo to much of the interior. If the cherubs and intricate scrolled mouldings in the lounge positively scream 'France', that may be because they were once painstakingly removed from a château outside Paris. Dining activity spreads itself out over an oak-panelled room, a conservatory and a terrace, so nobody need feel stuck for choice, a point equally applicable to the resourceful Anglo-French cookery on offer. 'King prawns, chorizo, mango and coriander' is full of intelligent contrasts, while a main-course chargrill of local beef with bone marrow and Jersey Royals done in goose fat, sauced with a jus cautiously spiked with horseradish, is a well-wrought foray through classic British territory. Similarly, a superb buttery crumble of quince with vanilla sauce and cinnamon ice-cream rises above the sum of its parts to end things with a flourish.

Chef Marcin Ciehomski **Owner** The Hiscox family **Times** 12-2/7-9 **Prices** Fixed L 2 course £14.95, Fixed D 3 course £30, Starter £8.75-£10.25, Main £16.95-£21.50, Dessert £6.95-£7.95, Service added but optional 10% **Wines** 24 bottles over £30, 18 bottles under £30, 7 by glass **Notes** 'Taste of Jersey' Tasting menu with/out wines available, Sunday L, Vegetarian menu, Dress restrictions, Smart casual, Civ Wed 60 **Seats** 60, Pr/dining room 28 **Children** Portions, Menu **Parking** 30

ST AUBIN	**Map 24**

The Boat House

◎ Modern British

Modern cooking with harbourside views

☎ 01534 744226 & 747101
One North Quay JE3 8BS
e-mail: enquiries@theboathousegroup.com
dir: 3m W of St Helier

Walls of glass mean that every table in this buzzy modern venue gets fabulous views of the ranks of yachts moored in

St Aubin's busy harbour. In the daytime, the alfresco terrace exerts its own attraction, but you need to head upstairs to the aptly-named Sails Brasserie for a wide-ranging, globally-influenced menu of contemporary crowd pleasers. Fish and seafood are at the forefront of most people's minds in such a watery setting, so locally-dived scallops duly turn up in the company of hazelnuts and coriander butter to set the ball rolling, before a tip-top main course of turbot with creamy mash, crab mayonnaise, and mussel and scallop cream. Nor do carnivores get a raw deal - there could be Spanish-style slow-roasted shoulder of lamb with garlic, mash, and baked tomatoes and courgettes, while dessert brings a simple but effective pairing of vanilla pannacotta with poached plums.

Times 12-2/6-9.30 Closed 25 Dec & Jan, Mon-Tue (Winter), L Wed-Thu & Sat (Winter), D Sun (Winter)

The Salty Dog Bar & Bistro

◎ Modern International Ⓥ ☺

Vibrant seafood cooking (and more) by the harbour

☎ 01534 742760
Le Boulevard JE3 8AB
e-mail: info@saltydogbistro.com
web: www.saltydogbistro.com
dir: Walking from centre of St Aubin Village along harbour, approx halfway along, slightly set back

Nowhere is out of bounds for this salty dog, with a menu that happily globetrots around the Med, across the Indian Ocean, and back home to the English Channel. The harbourside location sets the tone, with the outside seating - plenty of it - coming into its own in the summer. Whenever you visit, though, this one-time smugglers' residence is a fun place to eat. Thai beef salad gets those Asian flavours spot on, there might be crab and crayfish risotto, or the Salty's tasting platter for two to share if you can't decide which way to go. Next up, from the 'spice kitchen', Malaysian Penang curry, or, from the grill, classic beef fillet cooked straight up or with an aged mustard and black pepper sauce. It's back to the Med for Spanish churros with a rich dark chocolate dipping sauce, or the crème brûlée of the day.

Chef Damon James Duffy **Owner** Damon & Natalie Duffy **Times** 12.30pm-1.30am Closed 25-26 Dec, 1 Jan, L Tue-Thu (Nov-Apr) **Prices** Fixed L 2 course fr £17.50, Fixed D 3 course £32, Starter £8.25-£9.95, Main £14-£30, Dessert £5.70-£6.50, Groups min 12 service 10% **Wines** 16 bottles over £30, 33 bottles under £30, 8 by glass **Notes** Sunday L, Vegetarian menu, Dress restrictions, Smart casual **Seats** 60 **Children** Portions, Menu **Parking** Car parks & on street parking nearby

ST BRELADE — Map 24

L'Horizon Hotel and Spa

◉◉ Modern, Traditional

Creative cooking and a touch of luxury on the beach

☎ 01534 743101
La Route de la Baie JE3 8EF
e-mail: lhorizon@handpicked.co.uk
web: www.handpickedhotels.co.uk/lhorizon
dir: From airport right at rdbt towards St Brelade & Red Houses. Through Red Houses, hotel 300mtrs on right in centre of bay

On a sunny day it may well feel like the Med, but this is Jersey, and the glorious sandy beach out front of this classy hotel is St Brelade, one of the island's finest. Needless to say a table on the terrace is the place to be. L'Horizon was built in 1850 by a colonel in the Bengal army and there's still plenty of Victorian elegance on show today alongside the luxe feel, swish spa, etc. The Grill is the big fish here when it comes to eating (there's a brasserie, too), and there's some bright, contemporary thinking going on. You can have a steak from the grill, of course - Aberdeen Angus rib-eye, for example - but equally you might start with pigeon and grouse set in a quail jelly with pumpkin sorbet and truffle mellow, followed by Jersey sea bass with crispy squid served with a razor clam and squid ink risotto. There's just as much creativity among desserts: quince tarte Tatin, for example, with brown bread ice cream and caramel sauce.

Times 6.45-10 Closed Sun-Mon, L all week

Hotel La Place

◉ Modern British

Modern bistro cooking near the harbour

☎ 01534 744261 & 748173
Route du Coin, La Haule JE3 8BT
e-mail: andy@hotellaplacejersey.com
dir: Off main St Helier/St Aubin coast road at La Haule Manor (B25). Up hill, 2nd left (to Red Houses), 1st right. Hotel 100mtrs on right

A short walk from St Aubin's harbour, the hotel is a collection of country cottages centred on an original 17th-century farmhouse in a particularly tranquil district of Jersey. Dining goes on in a pale beige and white room known as the Retreat, where modern bistro dishes in a light style are on the menu. Bresaola with fennel slaw, or crab fritters with beetroot and apple salsa, fire the starting gun, and may be followed by the likes of pollock on wilted spinach in parsley sauce, or braised ox cheeks on celeriac purée, served with braised leeks and rosemary roast potatoes. Finish up with lemon tart and blueberry compôte, or a canonical version of Eton Mess.

Times 6.30-9 Closed L Sat-Sun

Ocean Restaurant at the Atlantic Hotel

◉◉◉◉ — *see opposite*

Oyster Box

◉◉ Modern British ♨

A beachside setting for spankingly fresh seafood

☎ 01534 743311
St Brelade's Bay JE3 8EF
e-mail: eat@oysterbox.co.uk
dir: on the beach just east of Fishermen's chapel

With views during the day of kids building sandcastles, windsurfers, sand-yachters and the like, The Oyster Box's position right on lovely St Brelade beach really does take some beating, and a seat on the terrace is a prized position. At night, it's lit up and decidedly cool, with its open-to-view kitchen, slate floors and high-backed wicker chairs at wooden tables. The large menu is packed with fabulous seafood - Jersey Rock oysters, of course, served as you like them - plus plenty of non-fishy choices. You might start with confit duck spring rolls with celery, fennel and popcorn shoot salad, or squid a la plancha, before moving on to a risotto or pasta dish. There's sushi, too, plus whole lemon sole served on the bone with wilted spinach and garlic butter, Oyster Box fish and chips with pea purée and tartare sauce, or braised Irish ox cheek with smoked mashed potatoes and oxtail and bone marrow sauce. Attention to detail runs right the way through to desserts such as Frangelico pannacotta with fresh raspberries.

Chef Patrick Tweedie **Owner** Jersey Pottery
Times 12-2.30/6-9.30 Closed 25-26 Dec, Mon (Jan-Mar), L Mon, D Sun (winter only) **Prices** Prices not confirmed Service optional **Wines** 21 by glass **Notes** Sunday L, Vegetarian available **Seats** 100 **Children** Portions, Menu **Parking** Car park opposite

ST CLEMENT — Map 24

Green Island Restaurant

◉ Mediterranean

Great local seafood in bustling beach café

☎ 01534 857787
Green Island JE2 6LS
e-mail: info@greenisland.je

This laid-back beach café and restaurant stakes its claim to the title of most southerly eatery in the British Isles, so kick back and bask in its sun-kissed views over sandy Green Island bay. As you'd hope in this briny location, the emphasis is firmly on fish and shellfish, and the kitchen has the nouse to treat them with a light touch to let the freshness and quality do the talking, as in an ultra-simple dish of freshly-landed sole meunière with Jersey potatoes and salad. If it's meat you're after, tarragon-crusted roast rack and braised shank of lamb with boulangère potatoes, garlicky flageolet beans and baby carrots, roasted root vegetables and garlic might be up for grabs, and to finish, a classic crème brûlée with sablé biscuits should strike a suitably Gallic note.

Chef Dougal Anderson **Owner** Alan M Winch
Times 12-3/7-10 Closed Mon, D Sun **Prices** Fixed L 2 course £13.95, Starter £8.50-£9.75, Main £16.95-£26.95,

Dessert £6.50-£8.95, Service optional, Groups min 8 service 10% **Wines** 3 by glass **Notes** Fixed D £21.50 Tue-Thu, Sunday L £19.50 **Seats** 40 **Children** Portions **Parking** Public car park adjacent

ST HELIER — Map 24

Best Western Royal Hotel

◉ Modern European ♨

Trendily presented food in a smart hotel

☎ 01534 726521
26 David Place JE2 4TD
e-mail: manager@royalhoteljersey.com
web: www.morvanhotels.com
dir: Follow signs for Ring Rd, pass Queen Victoria rdbt keep left, left at lights, left into Piersons Rd. Follow one-way system to Cheapside, Rouge Bouillon, at A14 turn to Midvale Rd, hotel on left

The Royal has been accommodating guests since the early Victorian era, when it was more humbly known as Bree's Boarding House. A wide stone-coloured frontage makes a bright and fresh impression, as does the light-filled white dining room known as Seasons, where smartly clothed tables and comfortable leather upholstery make for a relaxing ambience. Trendy presentations on black slate distinguish beginners such as tea-smoked duck with a salad of celeriac, apple, raisins and hazelnuts, while scallops get paired modishly with chorizo in red pepper coulis. Main courses up the ante for classic luxuries such as tournedos Rossini in wild mushrooms and Madeira with potato and bacon gratin, or sea bass with shellfish risotto in chive beurre blanc. Tarte Tatin with Jersey butter ice cream is a beautifully rendered dessert, only thrown off balance by the addition of no fewer than three sauces where one would do perfectly well, or there may be black cherry clafoutis.

Chef Alun Williams **Owner** Morvan Hotels **Times** 6.30-9 Closed L all week **Prices** Fixed D 3 course £23.95-£25.95, Service optional **Wines** 3 bottles over £30, 38 bottles under £30, 7 by glass **Notes** Vegetarian available, Civ Wed 50 **Seats** 90, Pr/dining room 12 **Children** Portions, Menu **Parking** 14

Bohemia Restaurant

◉◉◉ — *see page 542*

Grand Jersey

◉◉◉ — *see page 542*

Save on Hotels. Book at **theAA.com/hotel**

JERSEY 541 **ENGLAND**

Ocean Restaurant at the Atlantic Hotel

ST BRELADE   MAP 24

Modern British **V** NOTABLE WINE LIST

Top-class Jersey produce treated with skill in a breathtakingly beautiful location

☎ 01534 744101
Le Mont de la Pulente JE3 8HE
e-mail: info@theatlantichotel.com
web: www.theatlantichotel.com
dir: A13 to Petit Port, turn right into Rue de la Sergente & right again, hotel signed

More than 40 years after it first opened its doors, The Atlantic Hotel has aged extremely well. Still family owned to this day, the hotel on Jersey's stunning west coast has been lovingly maintained and updated over the years, and it's a luxurious, glamorous place to stay with a welcoming, relaxed feel and a first-class restaurant amongst its many attractions (the others include six acres of sub-tropical gardens and a championship golf course next-door). The Ocean Restaurant has views out over the gardens towards the sea beyond, and a design that reflects its coastal setting, with a colour palette of blues, whites and beiges, comfortable hand-crafted furniture and modern artwork on the walls. It's a wonderfully light and airy setting, classic in style but at the same time contemporary, in which to appreciate the undeniable talents of executive chef Mark Jordan and his team. There's a seasonal à la carte and a series of daily-changing set menus, including a seven-course tasting and, at the other end of the spectrum, a spectacular value lunch menu. Whichever you choose, each is chock-full of splendid Jersey produce, while dishes demonstrate some finely tuned technical skills, and a sharp eye for presentation. Superb goats' cheese and olive bread, and an amuse-bouche of a parsnip espuma with real depth of flavour, accompanied by a perfectly timed roasted scallop, might begin proceedings. Next, a starter entitled 'sea shore' comprises a mixture of local fish (extremely high quality and precisely cooked) presented on a plate alongside some foraged seaweed and anchovy 'sand', with a tomato essence poured over at the table. Main course might be loin of roe deer - accurately cooked and full of rich natural flavour - with a smooth celeriac purée, subtly spiced pear and a vanilla scented jus, or you might choose pan-roasted fillet of Jersey brill (exemplary quality again) with melt-in-the-mouth braised oxtail, salsify and wild mushrooms and parmesan shavings. Vegetarians are admirably well catered for here, with a dedicated vegetarian menu alongside the regular carte, offering the likes of potato and garden herb gnocchi with parmesan cream to start, followed by baked tian of aubergine, garlic and thyme roasted vegetables, black olive and salsa verde. Decisions get really tough at dessert stage, with a 70 per cent cocoa Guanaja chocolate jelly with chocolate streusel and coffee ice cream vying for your attention with a colourful and creative pud of raspberry and banana granité with a pistachio biscuit and salted milk chocolate and caramel mousse. The wine list has plenty to entice, and head sommelier Sergio dos Santos is a safe pair of hands should you need any assistance.

Chef Mark Jordan **Owner** Patrick Burke
Times 12.30-2.30/7-10 Closed Jan
Prices Fixed L 2 course £20, Fixed D 3 course £55, Tasting menu £80, Service included **Wines** 509 bottles over £30, 41 bottles under £30, 35 by glass
Notes Fixed ALC 2/3 course £55/£65, Tasting menu 7 course, Sunday L, Vegetarian menu, Dress restrictions, Smart dress, Civ Wed 80 **Seats** 60, Pr/dining room 60 **Children** Portions, Menu **Parking** 60

Bohemia Restaurant

Modern European V

Pace-setting contemporary cooking in a smart spa hotel

☎ 01534 880588 & 876500
The Club Hotel & Spa, Green St JE2 4UH
e-mail: bohemia@huggler.com
web: www.bohemiajersey.com
dir: In town centre. 5 mins walk from main shopping centre

If you've heard that old chestnut about Jersey being a trip back to the 1950s, think again: the Club Hotel & Spa is a sophisticated boutique hotel as sharp and contemporary as any slick big-city operation, and its Bohemia Restaurant offers destination dining that should have you hot-footing it to the Channel Islands. Jersey's smart set hangs out in the heaving, hyper-trendy Bohemia Bar, so if you're not here to see and be seen with a cocktail or a glass of bubbly in hand, push on through the scrum to take a seat in the design-conscious restaurant, where darkwood, chrome, chocolate-hued leather chairs, and tables laid with crisp white linen come together in a suave exercise in pared-back contemporary chic. Chef Steve Smith took over the reins at the start of 2013, and has quickly made Jersey his home, cooking up a storm with the produce from the land and waters around the island. His prodigious talent and creativity produces dishes of refinement, craft and contemporary dynamism, delivered via multi-course tasting menus - although you could come in at the bargain basement end by turning up for the good-value two- or three-course lunch menu. Descriptions are minimal, so it's comforting that proceedings are watched over by a professional service team who are entirely up to speed with the menu. Expect a relentlessly entertaining interplay of tastes and textures, starting with an up-to-the-minute 'smoked haddock - hen's yolk - mustard', the yolk added at table to smoked haddock velouté and mustard ice cream. Elsewhere, truffle is grated onto a plump scallop, perfuming a composition involving smoked eel, apple purée and jelly, while salty shrimps, cauliflower purée, pickled grape, and oxalis support a perfect piece of brill. The high point sees an intricately contrived riff on lamb (loin, sweetbread and rolled, breaded confit) with punchy morels, pungent Jerusalem artichoke purée, and leaves and buds of wild garlic.

Chef Steve Smith **Owner** Lawrence Huggler
Times 12-2.30/6.30-10 Closed 24-30 Dec **Prices** Fixed L 2 course £25, Fixed D 3 course £59, Tasting menu £75-£85, Starter £25, Main £35, Dessert £10, Service added but optional 10% **Wines** 24 by glass **Notes** ALC 3 course £59, Market D menu Mon-Thu, Vegetarian menu, Dress restrictions, Smart casual, Civ Wed 80 **Seats** 60, Pr/dining room 24 **Children** Portions **Parking** 20, Opposite

Grand Jersey

Modern British 🍷 NOTABLE WINE LIST

Top-end contemporary cooking in landmark hotel

☎ 01534 722301
The Esplanade JE2 3QA
e-mail: reservations@grandjersey.com
web: www.grandjersey.com
dir: Located on St Helier seafront

Situated in pole position on the esplanade, and bracketed by heavenly views across St Aubin's Bay to the front, and the buzz of St Helier's streets inland, the Grand is a much-loved local landmark. The crunch might be hurting, but inside, it's five-star luxury all the way as an antidote to the downturn. With over 100 bottles of fizz to mull over, the glam champagne lounge offers an unavoidable prelude to dinner. In the Tassili restaurant, the sleek looks of the hotel are matched in a space that goes for a palette of unassuming, neutral shades punctuated by abstract modern art to ring the changes, although it is nature's beauty in the dreamy vista across the bay which will inevitably grab diners' attention. Executive chef Richard Allen has allowed Jersey's larder to shape his style, drawing on local day boats and island producers, as well as a spot of foraging, for his excellent raw materials. He brings razor sharp technical skills to bear and aims to surprise and delight with curveball combinations of flavour and texture. A well-crafted starter puts confit pork belly centre stage, with a supporting cast of squash purée, chorizo, popcorn and roasted seeds. Next up, scallops are seared and matched with haddock risotto, lemongrass, and eel beignets, while meatier fare could see fillet of Black Angus beef teamed with the luxury of roast foie gras, celeriac and truffle. Dessert calls on the arsenal of modern techniques to pull off an exciting, mouth-filling dish of caramelised banana with satay ice cream, green tea foam, lime jelly and sesame brittle. Turophiles will swoon over the array of cheese which runs to over a dozen perfectly-ripened examples from British artisan producers, all served with superb breads and individually matched with home-made accompaniments such as truffled honey, 'mustard bubble', or prune foam.

Chef Richard Allen **Owner** BDL Hotels
Times 12-2.30/7-9.30 Closed Sun-Mon, L Sun-Thu **Prices** Prices not confirmed Service optional **Wines** 14 by glass **Notes** Tasting menu 6 course, Chef's surprise menu 9 course, Sunday L, Vegetarian available, Dress restrictions, Smart casual, Civ Wed 150 **Seats** 25 **Parking** 32, NCP

Restaurant Sirocco @ The Royal Yacht

The Royal Yacht, Weighbridge, St Helier, Jersey, Channel Islands JE2 3NF
Tel: 01534 720511 • **Fax:** 01534 767729
Website: www.theroyalyacht.com • **Email:** reception@theroyalyacht.com

Chic and sophisticated *Restaurant Sirocco* at the *Royal Yacht Hotel* in Jersey is an experience for all your senses. With menus created from the freshest of the season's produce, classic Jersey dishes are served with a modern twist using delicate flavours cooked to perfection. A contemporary approach to menu design is coupled with innovative presentation of dishes, such as flambé at your table, providing an experience for all the senses. The superb Sunday Lunch is available throughout the year offering a carvery with a range of choices to satisfy any appetite, while the comprehensive wine list caters for all tastes. The Sirocco Terrace is available during the summer months, offering dinner with a view and fresh sea air.

ST HELIER *continued*

Hotel Savoy

◉ Modern British ✿

Smart hotel dining room specialising in local seafood

☎ 01534 727521
37 Rouge Bouillon JE2 3ZA
e-mail: info@thesavoy.biz
web: www.thesavoy.biz
dir: From airport 1st exit at rdbt. At next rdbt take 2nd exit right, down Beaumont Hill. At bottom turn left, along coast onto dual carriageway. At 3rd lights turn 1st left. Right at end. Remain in right lane, into left lane before hospital. Hotel on left opposite police station

Jersey's version of the iconic name occupies a Victorian manor house on the outskirts of St Helier which has been given a more boutique-style spin by a recent revamp. As you might hope in this island setting, seafood and fish landed on the Jersey coast figure prominently on the menu in the Montana restaurant - a compact but stylish space with service on the correctly formal end of the spectrum. The kitchen plays out well-rehearsed flavour combinations - sautéed seafood in garlic butter, or smoked salmon pâté with horseradish cream and blinis, perhaps, ahead of grilled Jersey plaice with Jersey Royals (what else?), and buttered vegetables. On the meat front there may be roast rack of lamb with dauphinoise potatoes, broccoli purée and thyme jus, and with the French coast so close, it seems right to end with a classic crème brûlée. Note that the Savoy is home to Roberto's Jazz Bar if you like a side order of cool jazz.

Chef Samuel Sherwood **Owner** Mr J Lora **Times** 7-9.30 Closed L ex by prior arrangement **Prices** Fixed L 3 course £18.95-£26, Fixed D 3 course £25-£35, Starter £8.95-£12.50, Main £16.50-£25, Dessert £6.95-£9.95, Service included **Wines** 21 bottles over £30, 36 bottles under £30, 14 by glass **Notes** Sunday L, Vegetarian available, Dress restrictions, Smart dress, Civ Wed 80 **Seats** 36, Pr/dining room 120 **Children** Portions, Menu **Parking** 35

Restaurant Sirocco@ The Royal Yacht

◉◉ Modern British NEW

Cool, contemporary hotel with confident team in the kitchen

☎ 01534 720511
The Weighbridge JE2 3NF
e-mail: reception@theroyalyacht.com
web: www.theroyalyacht.com
dir: Adjacent to Weighbridge Park overlooking Jersey Harbour

The Royal Yacht, a spick and span modern hotel with bags of style, occupies a plum spot right on the harbour. There's no shortage of things to do, whether that is chill out in the fab spa, or chill out with a glass of something in one of the hotel's numerous bars (no less than four). There's a choice of dining options, too, the pick of the bunch being Restaurant Sirocco, with its classy décor and focus on first-class Jersey produce. The cooking takes a smart, modish approach, with some pretty hot technical skills on show. Start, maybe, with a tarte fine of wild mushrooms with gruyère and tarragon espuma and a Scotch quail's egg, or poached lobster minestrone with tempura claw and coconut foam. Flavours are to the fore in main courses such as slow-cooked Anjou pigeon with curried parsnips, potato and garlic gratin, and in desserts like black berry soufflé served with an apple fool.

Chef Steve Walker **Owner** Lodestar Group, The Royal Yacht **Times** 12-4/7-10 Closed L Mon-Sat **Prices** Fixed D

3 course £55, Tasting menu £64-£94, Starter £8-£8.50, Main £15.10-£30.50, Dessert £7-£9, Service added but optional 10% **Wines** 19 by glass **Notes** Tasting menu available, weekly rotating Table d'hote menu, Sunday L, Vegetarian available, Dress restrictions, Smart casual **Seats** 65, Pr/dining room 20 **Children** Portions **Parking** Car park

See advert on page 543

ST PETER   Map 24

Greenhills Country Hotel

◉ Mediterranean ✿

Contemporary cooking of Jersey's fine produce

☎ 01534 481042
Mont de L'Ecole JE3 7EL
e-mail: reserve@greenhillshotel.com
dir: A1 signed St Peters Valley (A11). 4m, turn right onto E112

A riot of colour, the hotel's garden is a treat, but then again, there is a lot to like about Greenhills. Dating from the 17th century, the building has traditional charm inside and out, and a restaurant where the tables are dressed in white linen ready and waiting for the Anglo-European output from the team in the kitchen. The ambitious repertoire might see Jersey Bay scallops served with a pancetta crisp, caper berries, sweetcorn purée and a garnish of fresh raspberries, before main-course lamb Wellington or pan-fried sea bass with asparagus salad, warm potatoes, baby vegetables, tomato concasse, tarragon vinegar and champagne sauce. There's no less endeavour in the desserts, with yoghurt and mango tart served on a raspberry coulis with blackcurrant sorbet and fresh fruit garnish.

Chef Marcin Dudek **Owner** Seymour Hotels **Times** 12.30-2/7-9.30 Closed 23 Dec-14 Feb **Prices** Fixed L 2 course fr £13, Fixed D 3 course fr £28.50, Service added but optional 10% **Wines** 19 bottles over £30, 62 bottles under £30, 8 by glass **Notes** A la carte specialities, Sunday L, Vegetarian available, Dress restrictions, Smart casual, Civ Wed 60 **Seats** 90, Pr/dining room 40 **Children** Portions, Menu **Parking** 45

Mark Jordan at the Beach

◉◉ Modern British ✿

Simple but stunning food by the St Peter plage

☎ 01534 780180
La Plage, La Route de la Haule JE3 7YD
e-mail: bookings@markjordanthebeach.com
dir: A1 W from St Helier, left mini-rdbt towards St Aubin, follow sign 50mtrs on left

The website shows a picture of a solitary table with two chairs actually dug into the sand on the plage at St Peter, but Mark Jordan - he of the Ocean Restaurant at the

Save on Hotels. Book at **theAA.com/hotel**

JERSEY 545 ENGLAND

Atlantic Hotel (see entry) - isn't quite as much 'at the beach' as that. Nonetheless, the restaurant is right next to the golden sands, with views of the castle and St Aubin harbour. A breezy seaside feel pervades the place, its chunky wood tables and broad-beam flooring offset with pictures of local scenes, and a smart, voguish air distinguishes the cookery. It all sounds beautifully simple, and is in fact, but impresses with depth and quality in all the right places. Crab and sweetcorn risotto dressed in vivid herb oil is a masterpiece of timing and intensity, and continuing the seafood route into mains might turn up an improbably spectacular grilled fillet of plaice with prawn, cockle and caper butter, served with indigenous Jersey Royals. While seafood is thus a strong point, there are pedigree meats too: steak burger with foie gras, rump of lamb with lentils, or the pairing of curried pork loin with mussel marinière. Note the richly yellow pastry (made with incomparable local butter) of a salted chocolate tart before you set about it, its melting filling echoed by good pistachio ice cream.

Chef Mark Jordan, Karl Tarjani **Owner** Mark Jordan, Patrick Burke **Times** 12-2.30/6-9.30 Closed Jan, Mon (winter), D Sun (winter) **Prices** Fixed L 2 course £19.50, Fixed D 3 course £27.50, Starter £7-£12.50, Main

£14.50-£35, Dessert £4.50-£9.50, Service optional **Wines** 28 bottles over £30, 28 bottles under £30, 7 by glass **Notes** Sunday L, Vegetarian available **Seats** 50 **Children** Portions **Parking** 16

ST SAVIOUR Map 24

Longueville Manor Hotel

◉ ◉ ◉ – *see below*

TRINITY Map 24

Water's Edge Hotel

◉ Modern British NEW

Sea views and cooking that aims high

☎ 01534 862777
Bouley Bay JE3 5AS
e-mail: info@watersedgejersey.com
dir: 10-15 mins from St Helier, A9 N onto A8 then onto B31, follow signs to Bouley Bay

Tucked into the cliffs of Bouley Bay a wave's lap from the briny, the Water's Edge is aptly named. The view from the

restaurant is hard to beat, looking across an unbroken expanse of sea to the distant coast of France, and the food also merits serious attention. A new kitchen team took the reins in April 2013 and is keen to stamp its mark on the local foodie scene, hauling in the finest local produce and delivering it in well-executed, easy-on-the-eye dishes. Fish and seafood are naturally a strong suit - perhaps salmon tartare to start, ahead of braised shin of Jersey Angus beef which arrives with slices of fillet and foie gras, roasted baby beets, glazed carrots, sautéed leeks and horseradish duchesse potatoes. The ambition continues to a well-crafted finale involving pear tarte Tatin and an unusual yet effective ice cream of Jersey Blue cheese and walnuts.

Chef John Gilbert **Times** 12-2.30/6.30-9 **Prices** Fixed D 3 course £19.95, Starter £6.50-£12.50, Main £13.95-£19.95, Dessert £6-£7.95, Service included **Wines** 5 bottles over £30, 20 bottles under £30, 4 by glass **Notes** Reservations essential, Sun L all day carvery 12.30-8pm, Sunday L, Vegetarian available, Dress restrictions, Smart casual, No trainers, jeans or T-shirts **Seats** 100, Pr/dining room 40 **Children** Menu **Parking** 20, On street

---

Longueville Manor Hotel

ST SAVIOUR MAP 24

Modern British V 📖 NOTABLE WINE LIST

Finely wrought cooking in luxury hotel

☎ 01534 725501
JE2 7WF
e-mail: info@longuevillemanor.com
web: www.longuevillemanor.com
dir: From St Helier take A3 to Gorey, hotel 0.75m on left

The manor has its roots in the Middle Ages, with upgrading and modernisation over the years making it into what it is today: the epitome of a luxury country-house hotel, with sumptuous soft furnishings and a classy décor amid the oak panelling and exposed stone. It's not at all stuffy or pretentious, with professional and obliging staff personally greeting guests as they arrive. Dinner is served in the 15th-century Oak Room, with its

dark panelling and original beams, and in the more contemporary Garden Room. Andrew Baird capitalises fully on the fruit, vegetables and salads grown in the hotel's own gardens and on supplies from the island's farmers and fishermen. Cooking skills are impeccable, and dishes are intelligently composed. Wafer-thin tortellini is crafted to hold a whole langoustine, topped with soft, pink langoustine mousse, with dashes of sweet pea purée and a Malibu foam adding an exotic coconut flavour. Other seafood dishes might be a starter of scallops and prawns sauced simply with coral butter, or an extravagant main-course seafood platter. Meat is equally well handled: venison tartare with potato and horseradish salad perhaps, followed by a labour-intensive dish of a chunky roll of roast saddle of rabbit bound in Parma ham, a perfectly sautéed kidney sitting on top, a couple of slices of punchily flavoured liver alongside, served with deeply flavoured gravy, some cannelloni and cumin-enhanced carrot purée. Puddings are a class act too, among them a light orange and Grand Marnier

soufflé with cookies ice cream, and an indulgent 'pandora' of Valrhona chocolate mousse with banana and warm vanilla cream.

Chef Andrew Baird **Owner** Malcolm Lewis **Times** 12.30-2/7-10 **Prices** Fixed L 2 course fr £22.50, Fixed D 3 course £57.50-£72, Service included **Wines** 300 bottles over £30, 69 bottles under £30, 25 by glass **Notes** Discovery menu with/without wine £75-£102, Sunday L, Vegetarian menu, Dress restrictions, Smart casual, Civ Wed 40 **Seats** 65, Pr/dining room 22 **Children** Portions, Menu **Parking** 45

SARK

SARK
Map 24

La Sablonnerie

🔘 Modern, Traditional International 🍸

Imaginative ways with home-grown produce on a special island

☎ 01481 832061
Little Sark GY10 1SD
e-mail: reservations@sablonneriesark.com
web: www.sablonneriesark.com
dir: On southern part of island. Horse & carriage transport to hotel

Blankets of wild flowers, wonderful scenery, sparkling, clear sea, lack of crowds or traffic (a horse-drawn carriage collects guests from the ferry from Guernsey) mean that a visit to Sark is a truly idyllic experience, and La Sablonnerie makes the perfect base. Have a drink in the stone-walled bar before dining in the beamed, candlelit restaurant (or outside in summer). Lobster is a speciality, and other seafood is turned to good effect, perhaps as scallop and halibut ravioli with hollandaise. Most produce comes from the hotel's own farm and gardens, guaranteeing freshness and seasonality. Look for duck liver parfait with onion confit and orange and watercress salad, followed by best-end of lamb, cooked pink, stuffed with veal and tarragon purée, served on a spinach gâteau with a light garlic sauce. To finish there might be lemon tart with Sark cream, or pineapple ravioli with lemongrass syrup and strawberry cream.

La Sablonnerie

Chef Colin Day **Owner** Elizabeth Perrée
Times 12-2.30/7-9.30 Closed mid Oct-Etr **Prices** Fixed L 2 course £24.50, Fixed D 3 course £32.50, Tasting menu £37.50, Starter £9.80, Main £16.50, Dessert £8.80, Service added but optional 10% **Wines** 16 bottles over £30, 50 bottles under £30, 6 by glass **Notes** Sunday L, Vegetarian available **Seats** 39 **Children** Portions, Menu

ISLE OF MAN

DOUGLAS
Map 24 SC37

JAR Restaurant

◉◉ Modern 🍸

Sharp cooking using prime Manx produce in grand Victorian hotel

☎ 01624 663553 & 629551
Admiral House Hotel, 12 Loch Promenade IM1 2LX
e-mail: jar@admiralhouse.com
dir: Located 2 mins from Douglas Ferry Terminal. 20 mins from airport

Given the prime position on the promenade and its new-found contemporary swagger, it is perhaps no surprise that Admiral House is the talk of the town. Longstanding chef Malcolm Bartolo has developed good links to local supply chains over the years, so you can be assured that all the produce used in his kitchen will be of the highest standard. Shellfish risotto with mussels, prawns, crab, queen scallops, courgette ribbons, cherry vine tomatoes and young herbs sounds like a good way to start in these parts, moving on, perhaps, to fillet of Manx pork with confit belly, champ, seasonal greens and balsamic jus, or fillet of wild sea bass with crevettes, new potatoes, ratatouille, asparagus, pesto and sun-dried tomato oil. Finish with Malc's lemon curd or spiced pannacotta.

JAR Restaurant

Chef Malcolm Bartolo **Owner** Branwell Ltd
Times 12-2/6-10 Closed 26-30 Dec, Sun, L Sat
Prices Prices not confirmed Service optional
Notes Tasting menu available, Vegetarian available, Dress restrictions, Smart casual **Seats** 48
Children Portions **Parking** Free parking opposite

See advert opposite

Scotland

Dunvegan Village and Loch Dunvegan, Skye

CITY OF ABERDEEN

ABERDEEN
Map 23 NJ90

Holiday Inn Aberdeen West

⊛ Contemporary Italian

Sound Italian cooking in Westhill

☎ 01224 270300
Westhill Dr, Westhill AB32 6TT
e-mail: marc.jones@hiaberdeenwest.co.uk
dir: On A944 in Westhill

Located in a dormitory town to the west of the city, the Holiday Inn offers an unexpectedly authentic Italian restaurant called Luigi's. The chef isn't called Luigi, but does know how to mix well-researched Italian dishes with local Scottish ingredients to create a style of straightforward, neatly presented food that has some undoubted high points. Tuscan-style soft-baked egg with cheese and pancetta, or mussels marinara, might start you off, and be followed by sea bream with gnocchi primavera in garlic cream, accurately timed king prawn tagliatelle with courgette strips, garlic and chilli, or hearty Tuscan meat stew with pork belly, Italian sausage and beans in herb-scented tomato sauce. Finish with tiramisù or sharply flavoured lemon tart.

Times 6.30-9.30 Closed Sun, L all week

Malmaison Aberdeen

⊛ Modern British

Cool brasserie with theatre kitchen

☎ 01224 327370
49-53 Queens Rd AB15 4YP
e-mail: info.aberdeen@malmaison.com
dir: A90, 3rd exit onto Queens Rd at 3rd rdbt, hotel on right

The Granite City's outpost of the boutique Malmaison chain has all the buzz, bold colours and sensual textures that you expect from the brand; the industrial-chic interior certainly making a good first impression. Dark wood tables and funky modern tartans make for a sassy, cool setting in the cavernous, moodily-lit Brasserie restaurant; high stools overlook the centrepiece Josper grill, where a busy chorus of chefs turn out fuss-free modern dishes using top-notch Scottish produce. Slow-cooked leg of mutton, perhaps, simply served with pommes purée and black olive sauce, or from the Josper, 28-day aged rib-eye steak, and to finish, tiramisù or jam roly-poly. Great wines are a trademark and you get to walk through a glassed-in wine tunnel with the cellar visible through a glass floor.

Times 12-2.30/5.30-10.30 Closed D 25 Dec

Maryculter House Hotel

⊛ Modern British

Lively cooking beside the River Dee

☎ 01224 732124
South Deeside Rd, Maryculter AB12 5GB
e-mail: info@maryculterhousehotel.com
web: www.maryculterhousehotel.com
dir: Off A90 to S of Aberdeen and onto B9077. Hotel is located 8m on right, 0.5m beyond Lower Deeside Caravan Park

Maryculter House dates from the 13th century, when it was a stronghold of the Knights Templar, with evidence of the order within the old building and in a chapel in the grounds. The Priory restaurant, with its stone walls and flickering candles after dark, looks out on the River Dee, a rather formal setting contrasting with some exuberant contemporary cooking. Cullen skink sounds familiar enough, but here it's made into a tart and served with pea and parmesan ice cream and tomato and tarragon coulis, and traditional game terrine is given an oomph from beetroot emulsion, plum chutney, a quail's egg and citrus brioche. Globetrotting main courses might take in Thai red seafood curry with fragrant rice and lychees, Caesar salad, or braised duck leg with a ragout of tomatoes, chick peas and chorizo, served with sautéed potatoes. Puddings deliver the likes of iced honeycomb parfait with macerated strawberries.

Chef Adam McKenzie **Owner** James Gilbert **Times** 7-9 Closed L all week **Prices** Service optional **Wines** 19 bottles over £30, 13 bottles under £30, 3 by glass **Notes** 8 course gourmet menu available Fri-Sun, Sunday L £13.50-£20, Vegetarian available, Dress restrictions, Smart casual, no jeans or T-shirts, Civ Wed 225 **Seats** 40, Pr/dining room 18 **Children** Portions **Parking** 150

Mercure Aberdeen Ardoe House Hotel & Spa

⊛ Modern Scottish, French ☺

19th-century hotel with 21st-century cooking

☎ 01224 860600
South Deeside Rd AB12 5YP
e-mail: h6626-dm@accor.com
web: www.mercure.com
dir: 4m W of city off B9077

This fine old greystone house does a fine impression of a castle - think soaring towers and grand gables - but it was built as a family home back in the 1870s. Three miles from the city centre and surrounded by 30 acres of grounds, these days it's a smart hotel with a spa and all mod-cons. The overall impression is one of traditional comfort, elegance and even a bit of old-world grandeur. Blair's Restaurant fits the bill with its hand-carved ceilings, tapestry-clad walls, and smartly laid tables. The menu treads a more modish path, going from Cullen skink in salad form or chicken, leek and Arran mustard terrine, to main-course slow-braised pork belly with sour apple purée, braised red cabbage and Vichy carrots.

Chef Richard Yearnshire **Owner** Accor
Times 12.30-3.30/6.30-9.30 **Prices** Fixed D 3 course £32.50-£36, Starter £4.50-£8.50, Main £12.50-£28.50, Dessert £7.50-£9.50, Service optional **Wines** 15 bottles over £30, 15 bottles under £30, 17 by glass **Notes** Afternoon tea from £6, Vegetarian available, Civ Wed 400 **Seats** 100, Pr/dining room 25 **Children** Portions, Menu **Parking** 90

Norwood Hall Hotel

⊛ Modern British ☺

Victorian mansion showcasing fine Scottish produce

☎ 01224 868951
Garthdee Rd, Cults AB15 9FX
e-mail: info@norwood-hall.co.uk
web: www.norwood-hall.co.uk
dir: Off A90, at 1st rdbt cross Bridge of Dee, left at rdbt onto Garthdee Rd (B&Q & Sainsburys on left) continue to hotel sign

Built in 1881 on the site of 15th-century Pitfodels Castle, Norwood is a magnificent Victorian mansion with all of its period grandeur still present and correct. A sweeping oak staircase, stained-glass windows and ornate fireplaces are all as impressive as you might expect, while the restaurant is a suitably grand oak-panelled room hung with tapestries. Friendly and efficient service sets the right tone to banish any trace of starchiness, and the menu takes an accessible modern approach based on top-class seasonal produce. You might open proceedings with venison, black pudding and pork terrine with honey pickled beetroot and date purée, then move on to something like pan-fried fillet of wild sea bass with curried lentils and spicy carrot salad. Meat eaters could tackle navarin of lamb with root vegetables, potato purée and red wine jus, and for pudding, a please-all approach takes in sticky toffee pudding with vanilla ice cream or cranachan cheesecake with raspberry coulis.

Chef Cyril Strub **Owner** Monument Leisure
Times 12-2.30/6-9.45 **Prices** Starter £6-£9, Main £13-£28, Dessert £5-£8, Service optional **Wines** 46 bottles over £30, 24 bottles under £30, 12 by glass **Notes** Sunday L £6-£28, Vegetarian available, Dress restrictions, Smart casual, no T-shirts or sportswear, Civ Wed 200 **Seats** 48, Pr/dining room 180 **Children** Portions, Menu **Parking** 140

The Silver Darling

⊛⊛ French, Seafood

Interesting ways with superbly fresh seafood

☎ 01224 576229
Pocra Quay, North Pier AB11 5DQ
e-mail: silverdarling@hotmail.co.uk
dir: At Aberdeen Harbour entrance

Reached by a spiral metal staircase, Silver Darling is on the first floor of a crenallated quayside building with floor-to-ceiling windows looking over the harbour out to sea. It gets its name from the local colloquialism for herring, and sure enough this is predominantly a seafood restaurant. The kitchen takes its inspiration from France but exhibits a flexible, contemporary approach to its output. 'Seafood Darling', for instance, is a mixture of fish and shellfish, served with samphire, saffron potatoes, rouille and croûtons, and steamed fillet of lemon sole is wrapped in lettuce and served with shellfish fricassée, seaweed risotto and saffron broth. Dishes can be multi-layered - a starter of pan-fried tiger prawns and bacon comes with curried courgette and fennel salpicon and piperade dressing, a main course of steamed turbot with cockle and seaweed risotto, spring onions, a poached oyster and watercress sauce - but supremely confident handling means results are nothing less than satisfying.

Chef Didier Dejean **Owner** Didier Dejean & Karen Murray **Times** 12-1.45/6.30-10 Closed Xmas-New Year, Sun, L Sat **Prices** Fixed L 2 course fr £19.50, Starter £9.50-£14.50, Main £16.50-£26.50, Dessert £8.50-£10.50, Service added but optional 10% **Wines** 25 bottles over £30, 15 bottles under £30, 8 by glass **Notes** Vegetarian available **Seats** 50, Pr/dining room 8 **Children** Portions **Parking** On quayside

La Stella

◉ Modern British ◔

Starry little restaurant in the Adelphi district

☎ 01224 211414 & 07912 666256
28 Adelphi AB11 5BL
e-mail: info@lastella.co.uk
dir: Off Union St

Chris and Lynsey Tonner opened in the Adelphi district of the city in the late 1990s, and have painstakingly established an elevated reputation for their appropriately starry-named restaurant. It's a small, smart place, decorated with framed pictures of the local area, the modishly monochrome look offset with shell-pink napkins. Chris works within defined parameters of simplicity and balance to create some dynamic, carefully crafted and popular dishes. A pairing of pressed ham and apple terrine with Waldorf salad in chive oil is an appealing opener followed by a main course that matches king scallops with chorizo, pea purée and crisp-fried kale, dressed in white truffle oil. A bells-and-whistles presentation of rabbit offers no fewer than four treatments on one plate, including the rolled saddle and a pastry-clad Wellington. Fish specials and desserts are written up on the board, the latter perhaps including a flawlessly caramelised coffee crème brûlée with cappuccino foam and shortbread.

Chef Chris Tonner **Owner** Beetroot Restaurants Ltd **Times** 12-2.30/5-9.45 Closed 1st 2 wks Jan, Sun **Prices** Fixed L 2 course £12.95-£15, Fixed D 2 course £35-£40, Starter £8-£12, Main £16-£28, Dessert £8-£10, Service included, Groups min 6 service 10% **Wines** 4 by glass **Notes** Vegetarian available **Seats** 37 **Children** Portions **Parking** On street

---

ABERDEENSHIRE

BALLATER   Map 23 NO39

Darroch Learg Hotel

◉◉ Modern Scottish ▮ NOTABLE WINE LIST

Traditional country house with modern Scottish cooking and wonderful views

☎ 01339 755443
56 Braemar Rd AB35 5UX
e-mail: enquiries@darrochlearg.co.uk
web: www.darrochlearg.co.uk
dir: On A93 at the W end of village

Darroch Learg means 'the oak wood on the sunny hillside' in old Gaelic, and this small country-house hotel, which has been in the Franks family for over 40 years, is every bit as appealing as its name suggests. There are lovely walks from the hotel grounds to the top of the hill, where you're rewarded with a fantastic view over Ballater. Originally built as a country residence in 1888, the hotel is no less special inside: oak panelling and antiques abound, and diners can soak up the views across the valley in the restaurant, which extends into a conservatory. The kitchen team proudly uses the best of the local larder in its modern Scottish cooking, presented on daily-changing menus. Pan-fried Loch Fyne scallops are perfectly cooked and come with curried cauliflower purée, apple shallot vinaigrette and pakora, while breast of Gressingham duck is pan-seared and served with celeriac purée, pak choi and Puy lentil jus in a beautifully presented main course. Finish with classic lemon tart and berry sauce.

Chef John Jeremiah **Owner** The Franks family **Times** 12.30-2/7-9 Closed Xmas, last 3 wks Jan, L Mon-Sat **Prices** Fixed D 3 course £45-£51, Service included **Wines** 71 bottles over £30, 35 bottles under £30, 4 by glass **Notes** Sunday L, Vegetarian available, Dress restrictions, Smart casual **Seats** 48 **Children** Portions, Menu **Parking** 15

Loch Kinord Hotel

◉ Modern British

Imaginative Scottish-focused cooking in Royal Deeside

☎ 01339 885229
Ballater Rd, Dinnet AB34 5JY
e-mail: stay@lochkinord.com
web: www.lochkinord.com
dir: Between Aboyne & Ballater, on A93, in Dinnet

Whether you're drawn to Royal Deeside for rod-and-fly-related activities on the salmon fishing beats of the River Dee, or a malt-tasting tour of the Speyside distilleries, this sturdy family-run Victorian hotel is an ideal spot to finish the day with local bounty on the table. The restaurant is a snug, smartly-updated space of colourful fabrics and rugs on the pale wooden floor, which chimes in tune with the kitchen's French-inflected modern cooking. Great store is set by the provenance of raw materials, much of them local and, where possible, organic. Pan-fried hand-dived scallops with cauliflower purée and caper and apple dressing shows the style, while mains could be roast saddle and confit leg of local rabbit matched with spring cabbage, dauphinoise potato and prune essence. To conclude, there might be glazed lemon tart with clotted cream ice cream and raspberry coulis.

Times 6.30-9 Closed L all week

BALMEDIE
Map 23 NJ91

Cock & Bull

Modern Scottish, British 🍷

Big flavours at a distinctive country inn

☎ 01358 743249
Ellon Rd, Blairton AB23 8XY
e-mail: info@thecockandbull.co.uk
web: www.thecockandbull.co.uk
dir: 6m N of Aberdeen on A90

This low-slung 19th-century coaching inn is a foodie destination these days, happily describing itself as a restaurant and bar and offering up a menu with broad appeal and a local flavour. It has all the wooden beams and log fires you might expect, plus a good deal of style with contemporary artworks covering the walls (for sale if something catches your eye), and smart fixtures and fittings. You can eat in the atmospheric restaurant or the modish conservatory extension, but wherever you sit, expect some well-crafted food based on carefully-sourced ingredients. Start with Cullen skink, perhaps, or chicken liver parfait with a tangy plum chutney and toasted brioche. Follow on with supreme of free-range chicken stuffed with award-winning Huntly haggis, clapshot, smoked bacon wafers and whisky sauce, and finish with a pear and frangipane tart with vanilla anglaise.

Chef Michael Middleton **Owner** Rodger Morrison
Times 10.30-late Closed 26 Dec, 2 Jan, All-day dining
Prices Service optional **Wines** 11 bottles over £30, 24 bottles under £30, 7 by glass **Notes** Sunday L £15.50-£24.95, Vegetarian available **Seats** 80, Pr/dining room 30 **Children** Portions, Menu

BANCHORY
Map 23 NO69

Cow Shed

Modern Scottish NEW 🍷

Regional Scottish cuisine in a converted dairy

☎ 01330 820813
Beamoir Rd AB31 5QB
e-mail: info@cowshedrestaurant.co.uk
dir: A93 from Aberdeen, right at Tesco on Hill of Banchory East, at T-junct right onto A980, second left

You won't actually be eating in the old cowshed here - that's still standing in the neighbouring field - but Graham Buchan's enterprising contemporary brasserie stands on the site of the old dairy. It's as pastoral a Highland setting as you could wish, in other words, with views over ploughed fields towards the Hill of Fayre. Any hint of twee rusticity has been banished though, thanks to an interior design featuring a viewable kitchen behind a sliding glass panel, an extensive wine store, and natural wood tones throughout. The infectious buzz that animates the place drifts up to the high ceiling, and the modern Scottish dishes do the rest. Deeside partridge is an impeccable example of the local bounty, the caramelised breast served with confit leg in an alternating stack along with sliced potato, puréed parsnip, crispy kale and a 'scorched' poached pear. That may follow a bowl of celeriac and mushroom velouté containing a fat raviolo stuffed complicatedly with ham hock, ricotta and black garlic purée. The technically skilful desserts include an unmoulded pumpkin brûlée topped with nougatine, garnished with cocoa nibs in syrup and coffee ice cream.

Chef Graham Buchan **Owner** Graham & Joy Buchan
Times 12.30-3/6.30-9.30 Closed 1st wk Jan, Mon-Tue (Jan-Feb & Nov-Dec), L Mon-Sat, D Sun **Prices** Fixed D 3 course £37, Service optional **Wines** 46 bottles over £30, 17 bottles under £30, 6 by glass **Notes** Sunday L, Vegetarian available **Seats** 62 **Children** Portions **Parking** 36

Raemoir House Hotel

Modern and Traditional British 🏅NOTABLE WINE LIST 🍷

Modern country-house cooking in Royal Deeside

☎ 01330 824884
Raemoir AB31 4ED
e-mail: hotel@raemoir.com
dir: A93 to Banchory then A980, hotel at x-rds after 2.5m

Raemoir House is set in 11 acres surrounded by the hills and forests of Royal Deeside. It was built in the Georgian period, its restaurant in what was the Oval Ballroom - all dark flocked velvet, 19th-century portraits and mirrors, a chandelier hanging from the corniced ceiling, and fires blazing in winter. Dinner is a set-price deal of four courses, plus coffee, with around four choices per course. A soup - perhaps spiced parsnip, with moreish breads - normally follows the starter, which might be something like a plate of smoked salmon with lemon curd, compressed cucumber and Keta caviar. Main courses are updated classical ideas: four slices of pink venison in

rich gravy on a fricassee of wild mushrooms and shallots with green beans, parsnip purée and golden-topped dauphinoise, or perhaps smoked pollock fillet with sauce vierge, polenta and wilted greens. Dishes are artfully presented, as seen in puddings like white chocolate mousse sandwiched by sponge with a scoop of vivid passionfruit sorbet studded with cocoa nibs, the plate drizzled with rhubarb syrup and butterscotch sauce.

Chef David Littlewood **Owner** Neil & Julie Rae
Times 12-2.30/5.30-9.30 **Prices** Prices not confirmed Service optional **Wines** 12 by glass **Notes** Tasting menu available, Sunday L, Vegetarian available, Dress restrictions, smart casual, Civ Wed 70 **Seats** 40, Pr/dining room 16 **Children** Portions **Parking** 40

CRATHES
Map 23 NO79

The Milton Restaurant

Traditional British

Accomplished cooking at the gateway to Royal Deeside

☎ 01330 844566 & 844474
AB31 5QH
e-mail: jay@themilton.co.uk
dir: On the A93, 15m W of Aberdeen, opposite Crathes Castle

Part of a complex of shops, studios and a steam rail museum, The Milton occupies one of a cluster of farm buildings, with a beamed vaulted ceiling, white walls dotted with pictures and tall-backed dining chairs covered in red or blue fabric. The menu kicks off with a list of 'classics' - dishes customers clearly can't live without - running from Cullen skink, through minute steak with chips, to vanilla crème brûlée. Otherwise there are more modern, peppier ideas such as duck rillette with orange compôte, then tender, crisp-skinned chicken breast on a potato pancake with a tasty sauce of mustard and café au lait. End with a trio of rhubarb: crumble, jelly and ice cream.

Times 9.30am-9.30pm Closed 25 Dec, 1 Jan, D Sun-Tue

Save on Hotels. Book at **theAA.com/hotel**

ABERDEENSHIRE 553 | SCOTLAND

ELLON	Map 23 NJ93

Eat on the Green

◉◉ Traditional British and Scottish ☙

Eclectic cooking in a starry village inn

☎ 01651 842337
Udny Green AB41 7RS
e-mail: enquiries@eatonthegreen.co.uk
web: www.eatonthegreen.co.uk
dir: A920 towards Udny Green/Ellon

The stone-built inn on the village green is quite a magnet for the titled great and good of the Scottish arts, politics and football scenes, but is nonetheless a hospitably unstuffy venue for the thoughtfully composed eclectic cooking of its kilted chef-patron, Craig Wilson. As we were going to print, a chef's table and a champagne lounge were in the offing, so there is clearly no resting on laurels. A taster assemblage of starters works on analogy with a dessert assiette, a good idea that incorporates a brie and red onion tart, a spiced haggis meatball, ham and apricot terrine, roasted veg in pesto, and a sip of soup. Mains run to steamed sea bass in a bhuna sauce of chick peas, ginger and chilli, as well as quality local meats such as lamb loin in brandy cream with cabbage, peas and pancetta, or fillet and belly of pork in mushroom and thyme jus. Finish with salted chocolate torte and passionfruit cream, or a cheese slate garnished with quince, grapes and frosted nuts.

Chef Craig Wilson **Owner** Craig & Lindsay Wilson
Times 12-2/6-9.30 Closed 1st wk Jan, Mon-Tue, L Sat
Prices Prices not confirmed Service optional **Wines** 9 by glass **Notes** Tasting menu 8 course 48hr notice required,

Sunday L, Vegetarian available, Civ Wed 70 **Seats** 82, Pr/ dining room 28 **Children** Portions **Parking** 7, On street

See advert on page 554

INVERURIE	Map 23 NJ72

Macdonald Pittodrie House

◉ Traditional, Modern Scottish ☙

Consummate cooking in historical property

☎ 0870 194 2111 & 01467 622437
Chapel of Garioch, Pitcaple AB51 5HS
e-mail: pittodrie@macdonald-hotels.co.uk
web: www.macdonald-hotels.com/pittodrie

In an estate of over 2,000 acres, this solidly built property has its roots in the 15th century. It's a comfortable place, with an open fire in the lounge and a candlelit restaurant hung with oil paintings. Materials are sourced with due diligence, with meat from Scottish farms, smoked fish from a traditional red-brick kiln, and fruit and vegetables organic whenever possible. Dishes are thoughtfully composed, with impressive results: seared fillet of cod, for instance, is accompanied by mussel and spring onion broth and wilted spinach, and an industrious kitchen is clearly behind roast rump and braised shoulder of lamb with red wine jus, onion marmalade, squash purée, salsify and mash. Starters are equally impressive - perhaps ham hock terrine with grape chutney and oatcakes, or a simple assiette of smoked salmon with avruga caviar, crème fraîche and herb dressing. Vanilla pannacotta with poached rhubarb and ginger granita is one way to finish.

Chef Neil Ireland **Owner** Monument Leisure
Times 12-3/7-9.30 **Prices** Fixed L 2 course fr £19.50, Fixed D 3 course fr £35, Starter £6-£12.50, Main £13.75-£32, Dessert £7.50-£9.50, Service included **Wines** 103 bottles over £30, 29 bottles under £30 **Notes** Sunday L, Vegetarian available, Dress restrictions, Smart casual, Civ Wed 150 **Seats** 28 **Children** Portions, Menu **Parking** 300

OLDMELDRUM	Map 23 NJ82

Meldrum House Country Hotel & Golf Course

◉◉ Modern British ☙

Smart country-house hotel with a local flavour

☎ 01651 872294
AB51 0AE
e-mail: enquiries@meldrumhouse.com
web: www.meldrumhouse.com
dir: 11m from Aberdeen on A947 (Aberdeen to Banff road)

There's a lot more to Meldrum House than golf, but golf there is should you wish to indulge. The grand old house, dating from the 12th century and now much extended, looks handsome in the baronial style, and the inside matches expectations with a chic and luxurious décor that blends original features with well-chosen, high quality furniture and objets d'art. The dining room strikes a traditional pose with its splendid proportions, portraits, real fire and burnished darkwood tables, and makes a grand setting for some gently contemporary cooking rooted in the terroir of these parts. Thus you might start with a duo of Deeside game (wood pigeon and venison as it happens) with pearl barley, or an Arbroath smoked haddock risotto with a Kintore quail's egg and chive cream. Next up, roast grouse with malt barley, parsnip purée and game chips is hard to resist in season, and, to finish, sticky toffee pudding soufflé is one alternative to Scottish cheeses with oatcakes and chutney.

Chef Walter Walker **Owner** Peter Walker
Times 12-2/6.30-9 **Prices** Starter £5.90-£13, Main £14-£30, Dessert £5-£9.50, Service optional **Wines** 8 by glass **Notes** Sunday L £29.50, Vegetarian available, Dress restrictions, Smart casual, Civ Wed 150 **Seats** 40, Pr/ dining room 16 **Children** Portions, Menu **Parking** 70

Eat on the Green

Udny Green, near Ellon AB41 7RS • Tel: 01651 842337

Savour the best of Scotland's larder in a rural idyll

Situated in the tranquil village of Udny Green, just 20 minutes' drive from Aberdeen city, good food and service is at the heart of everything we do here at *Eat on the Green*. From birthday celebrations to anniversaries, our aim is to make these moments '*Something Rather Special*'. Guests can celebrate their special occasions in one of our beautifully-designed private dining rooms or main restaurant. And, in our recently launched stunning *Chef's Table*, guests can dine intimately with family and friends, whilst watching the chefs hard at work safely behind glass!

As well as the lunch and dinner offering, *Eat on the Green* now offer *Afternoon Tea* daily from Wednesday to Sunday. With the promise of delicious sandwiches, bespoke homemade cakes and sweet treats, Afternoon Teas have proved extremely popular and attract customers from near and far.

Enjoy the ulimate gourmet experience by taking a culinary journey through our specially created seven-course Tasting Menu. This elaborate menu (which can be enjoyed with or without matched wines) highlights Craig's passion for food and showcases the best of what Scotland's larder has to offer.

Located only 10 minutes by car from Trump International, *Eat on the Green* offers a luxurious and welcoming ambience to help you unwind after a challenging round of golf. And, before your meal, perhaps you'd like to enjoy a glass of Laurent Perrier Champagne with canapés in our stunning new Garden Room. Booking essential.

It is easy to see that *Eat on the Green* is more than just a Restaurant, but don't just take our word for it, come and see for yourself.

Website: www.eatonthegreen.co.uk • **Email:** enquiries@eatonthegreen.co.uk
Facebook: https://www.facebook.com/EatOnTheGreen
Twitter: https://twitter.com/EatOnTheGreen1

Buchan Braes Hotel

◉ Modern Scottish, European ✪

Local produce getting top billing

☎ 01779 871471
Boddam AB42 3AR
e-mail: info@buchanbraes.co.uk
dir: From Aberdeen take A90, follow Peterhead signs. 1st right in Stirling signed Boddam. 50mtrs, 1st right

When it opened in 2008, Buchan Braes quickly acquired a reputation for good food. You could say it has cooking in its roots, as it was once the officers' mess at RAF Buchan, although the building was totally remodelled before its relaunch as a smart and contemporary hotel and restaurant. The open-plan Grill Room has a buzzy vibe and a thoroughly modern look, with its eye-catching chandeliers and open-to-view kitchen. Local produce is the driving force here - meats come from the surrounding area, smoked fish courtesy of the ancient Ugie smokehouse; the individual boats supplying the fish even get a name-check. A seasonal focus means they seek out and deliver it on weekly-changing menus of unaffected modern Scottish ideas. Scallops baked with herbs in Silver Birch Moniack wine is a typically appealing starter, while mains could be poached fillet of lemon sole with Boddam crab risotto and Jerusalem artichoke velouté.

Chef Gary Christie, Paul McLean **Owner** Kenneth Watt, Tony Jackson **Times** 11.45-2.30/6-9.30 **Prices** Fixed L 2 course £12.95, Fixed D 3 course £27.85, Starter £3.50-£11.50, Main £15-£26, Dessert £6, Service optional **Wines** 10 bottles over £30, 24 bottles under £30, 7 by glass **Notes** Sunday L, Vegetarian available, Civ Wed 150 **Seats** 70, Pr/dining room 80 **Children** Portions, Menu **Parking** 100

Carron Art Deco Restaurant

◉ Modern British ✪

Seasonal brasserie food in an art deco masterpiece

☎ 01569 760460
20 Cameron St AB39 2HS
e-mail: jacki@cleaverhotels.eclipse.co.uk
dir: From Aberdeen, right at town centre lights, 2nd left onto Ann St, right at road end, 3rd building on right

The Carron is an impressive piece of Highlands art deco, with its sleek white bow-fronted rear façade. This was once solely the restaurant entrance (there were shops on the other side), and is preserved today pretty much as it looked in the 1930s, with steps like overlapping ripples ascending amid a floral rockery. Inside it feels expansive and properly stylish, with 500 lightbulbs (hang the electricity bill) and a tall mirror gorgeously etched with a naked female form in the Picasso idiom. A carte of seasonally-evolving brasserie food is supplemented by blackboard specials, and there is a distinctive Scottish note to proceedings. Start, perhaps, with the abidingly popular beetroot and red onion bhaji with matching jelly and coulis and chunky mango salsa, moving on to a thoroughly hearty game casserole: venison, pheasant and rabbit enriched with Marsala, smoked bacon and button mushrooms, with a herby suet dumpling floating in it. Crumbly-textured pastry appears in a very grown-up bitter chocolate tart with orange compôte and a creamy white chocolate sorbet.

Chef Robert Cleaver **Owner** Robert Cleaver **Times** 12-2/6-9.30 Closed 24 Dec-10 Jan, Sun-Mon **Prices** Starter £4.35-£7.25, Main £11.95-£18.95, Dessert £5.95-£6.95, Service optional **Wines** 5 by glass **Notes** Vegetarian available **Seats** 80, Pr/dining room 30 **Children** Portions, Menu **Parking** Town Square

The Tolbooth Restaurant

◉ Modern British

Speciality seafood restaurant overlooking the harbour

☎ 01569 762287
Old Pier, Stonehaven Harbour AB39 2JU
e-mail: enquiries@tolbooth-restaurant.co.uk
dir: 15m S of Aberdeen on A90, located in Stonehaven harbour

Right on the harbour wall - where it has stood for over 400 years - this stone building houses the local museum on the ground floor and this gem of a seafood restaurant above. (Note the old stone steps make access tricky for anyone who might need assistance). With its relaxed bistro atmosphere, open-plan layout, maritime décor and views out over the quay, it's an ideal spot to tuck into some of the area's fine seafood. What's on the menu depends on what's been pulled out of the water, but Stonehaven crab soup is a perennial favourite, or there might be something a little more outré such as tempura of soft-shelled crab with daikon and carrot salad, micro coriander, mango and vanilla dressing (all the flavours working in harmony). Among main courses, pan-seared hand-dived scallops come with samphire and broad bean risotto, Parma ham crisp and chorizo foam, and there are always a few meat and veggie alternatives on offer.

Chef Craig Somers **Owner** J Edward Abbott **Times** 12-4/6-12 Closed 1st 3 wks Jan, Sun (Oct-Apr) & Mon **Prices** Fixed L 2 course £15.95-£19.95, Starter £6.50-£12.50, Main £15.95-£25, Dessert £6.25-£7.95, Service optional, Groups min 10 service 10% **Wines** 21 bottles over £30, 13 bottles under £30, 6 by glass **Notes** Sun L & D (May-Sep), Sunday L £20-£25, Vegetarian available **Seats** 46 **Children** Portions **Parking** Public car park, 100 spaces

Carnoustie Golf Hotel & Spa

◉ British

Fine dining and premium golf course views

☎ 0843 178 7109
The Links DD7 7JE
e-mail: reservations.carnoustie@bespokehotels.com
web: www.bespokehotels.com/carnoustiegolfhotel
dir: From A92 exit at Upper Victoria junct, follow signs for town centre, then signs for golf course

The golf course needs no introduction. The fact the Dalhousie Restaurant overlooks the legendary links (scene of the 136th British Open) is worth shouting about. It's a large hotel with its eyes on the prize of the corporate market, with leisure and spa facilities aplenty to further broaden its appeal. The restaurant is a traditional-looking space with those iconic golfing views and some bright contemporary cooking. Start, perhaps, with a modern classic such as Stornoway black pudding with a soft poached egg, pancetta crisp and hollandaise sauce. There's a good deal of regional produce on the menu bringing a local flavour to proceedings. For main course, braised daube and cheeks of beef come in a 'duo' with leek roulade and curly kale, and for dessert, there's excellent pastry skills on show in a caramelised apple frangipane tart with vanilla ice cream.

Chef Graeme Ball **Owner** Bespoke Hotels Ltd **Times** 7-9.30 Closed L all week **Prices** Prices not confirmed Service optional **Wines** 8 by glass **Notes** Dress restrictions, Smart casual **Children** Portions, Menu

FORFAR — Map 23 NO45

Drovers

Modern British **NEW**

Country inn serving rustic modern Scottish cooking

☎ 01307 860322
Memus By Forfar DD8 3TY
e-mail: info@the-drovers.com
dir: Forth Road bridge onto A823 then M90. Dundee through to Forfar onto A90, then B9128 Memus, Cortachy, The Glens

Tucked away off the beaten track, the Drovers Inn is the sort of place that really hits the spot after a day's walking in the glens. The rustic interior is an intriguing space with arching beams and whitewashed walls made cosy by open fires, and furnished with darkwood tables and chairs. Huge bullock horns and antlers on the walls and a sprinkling of droving objets are a nod to its livestock-related past, but if you're expecting the cattle theme to extend to the kitchen's output, the deal here is rather more contemporary and inventive than simple animal protein. From a menu that faithfully name-checks suppliers, grilled red mullet Niçoise rubs shoulders with a true-blue Scottish opener such as haggis croquettes with Dalmore whisky sauce, while mains bring pan-fried monkfish served on a bed of Puy lentils with chorizo and oven-dried cherry tomatoes. To end, crème brûlée might get a boozy twist of local terroir with the addition of Drambuie and home-made shortbread.

Chef Eden Sinclair **Owner** John Dodd
Times 12-2.30/5.30-9 **Prices** Fixed L 2 course £12-£25, Fixed D 3 course £16-£30, Tasting menu £45-£65, Starter £5.50-£9, Main £12.50-£21, Dessert £5-£7, Service optional **Wines** 11 bottles over £30, 18 bottles under £30, 7 by glass **Notes** Sunday L, Vegetarian available
Seats 60, Pr/dining room 16 **Children** Portions, Menu **Parking** 35

INVERKEILOR — Map 23 NO64

Gordon's

– *see below*

ARGYLL & BUTE

ARDUAINE — Map 20 NM71

Loch Melfort Hotel

Modern British

Ambitious contemporary cooking and stellar views

☎ 01852 200233
PA34 4XG
e-mail: reception@lochmelfort.co.uk
web: www.lochmelfort.co.uk
dir: On A816, midway between Oban & Lochgilphead

There is something very special about the West Coast of Scotland and the Loch Melfort Hotel presents it to you on a plate - the landscape (metaphorically speaking) and the wonderful ingredients (quite literally). The position of the hotel is nothing short of magnificent, on the shore of Asknish Bay, with views over the loch to copious islands, and the famous Arduaine Gardens right next door. The Asknish Bay Restaurant is positioned to make the best of the view, and note it is first-come-first-served at the best positioned tables. The team in the kitchen serve up ambitious contemporary dishes based on first-class regional produce, thus pan-fried rabbit loin is served with a plump langoustine, girolles and chicory, and roast Barbreck marrow bone with caper and shallot relish and toasted soda bread among first courses. Follow on with steamed pavé of halibut with Puy lentils, artichoke purée,

Gordon's

INVERKEILOR — MAP 23 NO64

Modern British

Outstanding cooking in a friendly, family-run restaurant

☎ 01241 830364
Main St DD11 5RN
e-mail: gordonsrest@aol.com
dir: From A92 exit at signs for Inverkeilor (between Arbroath & Montrose)

This splendid family-run restaurant plies its trade in a Victorian house in a tiny village close by lovely Lunan Bay. The colourful red and blue frontage makes it an unmissable local landmark, and the enterprise represents an equally unmissable presence on the local foodie scene, thanks to the sterling efforts of father and son chef duo Gordon and Garry Watson. Completing the family team is mother Maria, who runs front-of-house with genuine friendliness and good cheer. A recent makeover has given the intimate beamed interior a lighter, more contemporary look, but the place has lost none of the charm and atmosphere that keeps its loyal fan base on side. And so to the food, which is a very impressive blend of classic combinations taken to another level by some adventurous modern thinking, all built on seasonal local produce of exceptional quality. Garry Watson's inventive spirit pushes the repertoire ever onward into creative territory without losing sight of the importance of pitch-perfect natural flavours. Two cuts of the same meat is clearly a format they like to explore here - perhaps feather blade of locally-farmed beef cooked at low temperature for 24 hours, paired with braised ox cheek, shallot and hazelnut purée, parsley root, and Sarladaise potato. This might be preceded by a starter that showcases the quality of Isle of Mull Tobermory cheddar in a simple double-baked soufflé, or a more complex, well-thought-out combination involving a mosaic of foie gras and ham hock alongside pea pannacotta and pickled girolles. It is all punctuated by equally accomplished and intriguing incidentals - a mid-course velouté of cauliflower and Jersey Royal with brunoise scallop, or an excellent pre-dessert of passionfruit posset with banana sorbet and star anise meringues - before ending with memorable desserts such as hot Valrhona chocolate pudding with a centre of liquid Drambuie served with honeycomb ice cream and cherry and basil compôte.

Chef Gordon Watson, Garry Watson **Owner** Gordon & Maria Watson **Times** 12-1.45/7-9 Closed 2 wks Jan, Mon, L Sat, D Sun (in Winter) **Prices** Fixed L 3 course £28, Fixed D 3 course £50, Service optional **Wines** 11 bottles over £30, 33 bottles under £30, 5 by glass
Notes Bookings essential, Vegetarian available, Dress restrictions, Smart casual **Seats** 24, Pr/dining room 8 **Parking** 6

foie gras, kale and port sauce, finishing with glazed lemon curd tart with raspberry sorbet. The Chartroom II Bistro is another dining option.

Chef Peter Carr **Owner** Calum & Rachel Ross **Times** 6.30-9 Closed mid 2 weeks Jan, midweek Nov-Mar, L all week, D Tue-Wed (Nov-Mar) **Prices** Starter £8-£12.75, Main £12.50-£28, Dessert £6.50-£8.95, Service optional **Wines** 21 bottles over £30, 54 bottles under £30, 8 by glass **Notes** 4 course D £39.50, Vegetarian available, Dress restrictions, Smart casual, no jeans, Civ Wed 100 **Seats** 60, Pr/dining room 14 **Children** Portions, Menu **Parking** 65

KILCHRENAN　　　　　　　　　**Map 20 NN02**

The Ardanaiseig Hotel

Rosettes not confirmed at time of going to print – see page 558

Taychreggan Hotel

◉◉ Modern British **V** ⬮

Inventive cooking with sublime loch views

☎ 01866 833211 & 833366
PA35 1HQ
e-mail: info@taychreggan.co.uk
web: www.taychreggan.co.uk
dir: W from Crianlarich on A85 to Taynuilt, S for 7m on B845 (single track) to Kilchrenan

This plush 17th-century country-house hotel is a million miles from the primitive drovers' inn that once put up herders who swam their cattle across Loch Awe. Although not far from Oban, it also feels a very long way from anywhere, standing in glorious isolation in 40 acres of well-kept grounds freckled with colourful rhododendrons on a peninsula jutting into Loch Awe, and with wrap-around views of timeless Highland scenery - views that can be soaked up at leisure from the floor-to-ceiling arched windows of the low-slung restaurant. On the food front, the kitchen delivers a well-judged and inventive fusion of contemporary Scottish and French influences. The chefs forage for wild herbs and flowers, as well as putting great care into sourcing the prime ingredients for five-course set dinner menus. It all begins with an espresso cup of onion and star anise soup with bacon and chives, then progresses via pressed pork belly with apples, horseradish cream, celeriac remoulade, herbs and flowers, to a main course of slow-cooked Argyll beef with almonds, sorrel, and potato fondant in chicken stock. Dessert brings pistachio and dried apricot tart with yoghurt sorbet, spiced mascarpone and caramelised walnuts.

Chef Ondrej Kasan **Owner** North American Country Inns **Times** 7-8.45 Closed 3-21 Jan **Prices** Prices not confirmed Service optional **Wines** 11 by glass **Notes** Fixed 5 course menu £45, Vegetarian menu, Dress restrictions, Smart casual, Civ Wed 70 **Seats** 45, Pr/dining room 18 **Children** Portions, Menu **Parking** 40

LOCHGILPHEAD　　　　　　　　**Map 20 NR88**

Cairnbaan Hotel

◉ British, European ⬮

Canal views and local ingredients

☎ 01546 603668
Crinan Canal, Cairnbaan PA31 8SJ
e-mail: info@cairnbaan.com
web: www.cairnbaan.com
dir: From Lochgilphead 2m N to Cairnbaan on A83, hotel 1st on left

At the halfway point of the beautiful nine-mile stretch of the Crinan Canal connecting Loch Fyne to the Sound Of Jura, the Cairnbaan has been serving fishermen, walkers and waterborne traffic since 1801. The restaurant makes the most of the waterside views of 'Britain's most beautiful short cut' with its split-level layout, while the décor has a jaunty nautical edge with its polished brass handrails, high-backed leather chairs and colourful artworks, and the whole operation is run with easygoing charm. As you might hope, the straightforward modern European menu has a strong line in local fish and seafood - perhaps grilled sea bass with a Provençal-style stew of fennel, tomato and black olives, or monkfish wrapped in Parma ham and stuffed with rosemary pesto; for fans of local meat, there could be a pie of local game with chestnuts, mash and vegetables.

Chef Vicki Ure **Owner** Darren & Christine Dobson **Times** 12-2.30/6-9.30 **Prices** Starter £4.25-£8.20, Main £9.50-£18.50, Dessert fr £5.50, Service optional **Wines** 6 by glass **Notes** Civ Wed 120 **Seats** 40, Pr/dining room 30 **Children** Portions, Menu **Parking** 30

LUSS　　　　　　　　　　　　**Map 20 NS39**

The Lodge on Loch Lomond

◉◉◉ Modern British, International ⬮

Wide-ranging menus and unequalled loch views

☎ 01436 860201
G83 8PA
e-mail: res@loch-lomond.co.uk
web: www.loch-lomond.co.uk
dir: N of Glasgow on A82

What a location! This low-slung hotel is slap-bang on the water's edge within pine woods. Pine is used on the walls and pillars in Colquhoun's restaurant, where floor-to-ceiling windows give magnificent loch views and, even better, there's a decked terrace for alfresco dining when it stops drizzling. The introduction of a Josper oven means that the kitchen focuses on grills among main courses: steaks, spatchcock chicken and pork chops, for instance, with a choice of sauces, including truffle butter and veal jus. The kitchen's not stuck in a culinary rut, though, with plenty of other dishes to choose, ranging from grilled cod with chilli and ginger greens and soya noodles, to twice-cooked lamb rump with tapenade mash, tomato fondue and pepper dressing. Starters cover a broad sweep, from bradan rost confit with fennel jam, or smoked kipper parfait with salsa verde, to smoked ham hock with pickled vegetables and mustard aïoli, and to crown a meal might be chocolate mousse with pistachio ice cream, or rhubarb and lemongrass tart.

Chef Donn Eadie **Owner** Niall Colquhoun **Times** 12-5/6-9.45 **Prices** Fixed L 2 course £11.95-£13.95, Starter £4.95-£6.95, Main £13.95-£28.95, Dessert £5.95-£11.95, Service optional **Wines** 7 by glass **Notes** Sunday L, Vegetarian available, Civ Wed 100 **Seats** 100, Pr/dining room 40 **Children** Portions, Menu **Parking** 70

The Ardanaiseig Hotel

Rosettes not confirmed at time of going to print

KILCHRENAN   **MAP 20 NN02**

Modern British **V** NOTABLE WINE LIST

Wild foods and high comfort in a stunning lochside hotel

☎ 01866 833333
PA35 1HE
e-mail: marcel@ardanaiseig.com
dir: From A85 at Taynuilt onto B845 to Kilchrenan. Left in front of pub (road very narrow) signed 'Ardanaiseig Hotel' & 'No Through Road'. Continue for 3m

The Rosette award for this establishment has been suspended due to a change of chef. Reassessment will take place in due course under the new chef.

William Burn is a big name in Scottish architecture and he did some very good work here back in 1834, knocking up a magnificent baronial manor for a colonel of Clan Campbell. And at what a spot: it overlooks the aptly named Loch Awe and the soaring peak of Ben Cruachan. Fast-forward to the 21st century and you'll find a country-house hotel that delivers satisfaction whether you want to lose yourself in the wild landscape or simply read a book in the splendid lounge. The period details within show respect for the fine work of Mr Burn and are decorated handsomely and grandly, making for a luxurious stay. The wonderful views glimpsed through the generously-proportioned windows beat any artwork, and that

goes for the dining room, too, which is the setting for some rather splendid modern Scottish cooking courtesy of chef Gary Goldie and his team. It's the kind of menu that seems entirely in keeping with the location, yet manages to meet contemporary expectations. The diligent sourcing of regional ingredients extends to foraging in the surrounding landscape, with no stone left unturned in the search for a local flavour. A meal includes all the little intermediaries you might expect at this level, plus some pretty fine bread such as a winning rosemary and olive version. To begin, golden beetroot might come in a deliciously velvety soup topped with bonnet goats' cheese, followed by two plump Tiree langoustines served with parsley root purée and wild herbs (including pennywort and dandelion). Next up, perhaps a best-end of Argyll lamb with the slow-cooked shoulder served stovie style, plus Cevenne onion purée, artichokes, wild mushrooms and wild garlic. For dessert, how about russet apples with a cobnut cake and cobnut ice cream? The on-song staff make sure everything goes swimmingly.

Owner Bennie Gray **Times** 12-2.30/7-11
Prices Prices not confirmed Service optional **Wines** 12 by glass
Notes Tasting menu 6 course, Sunday L, Vegetarian menu, Dress restrictions, Smart casual, Civ Wed 40 **Seats** 38
Children Portions, Menu **Parking** 20

OBAN   Map 20 NM82

Best Western The Queens Hotel

◉ French, Scottish **NEW** ✪

Creative modern dishes in revamped seafront hotel

☎ 01631 562505 & 570230
Corran Esplanade PA34 5AG
e-mail: thequeenshoteloban@hotmail.co.uk
dir: Entering Oban on A85 take 2nd exit rdbt to seaside, next rdbt Ganavan Sands, hotel 0.4m on right

The Queens Hotel is an unmissable presence along the esplanade with its high-gabled frontage looking rather like a trio of bishops in a meeting. After recent refurbishment it's all looking spick and span inside, with the grandly-proportioned Glen Campa Restaurant perfectly positioned to make the most of the seafront vistas. Bare darkwood tables on a colourful tartan carpet make a smart setting for well-conceived contemporary dishes. Diligent sourcing of fine Scottish ingredients is clearly on the agenda of a kitchen that deals in starters such as gruth dhu mousse - translation courtesy of the knowledgeable and friendly staff reveals this to be black crowdie cheese which is served with marinated beetroot, fennel pollen oatcakes, and salted caramel walnuts. Main course stars Argyll pork, delivered as a trio of cured fillet, cannelloni of braised collar, and roasted belly with wilted spinach; with the briny just a few steps away, you might be tempted by Oban-landed wild sea bass with sea spinach, plantain purée, chick pea and chorizo, and fried baby squid.

Chef Romi Denesle **Owner** Raymond & Susan Ayavis **Times** 12-2/5.30-9 Closed Xmas & Jan **Prices** Fixed D 3 course £28-£30.50, Service optional **Wines** 2 bottles over £30, 24 bottles under £30, 5 by glass **Notes** Sunday L, Vegetarian available, Civ Wed 100 **Children** Portions, Menu **Parking** 16

Coast

◉ Modern British ✪

Seafood-led bistro food at a popular high-street eatery

☎ 01631 569900
104 George St PA34 5NT
e-mail: coastoban@yahoo.co.uk
dir: On main street in town centre

Next to the art gallery on Oban's main drag, Coast occupies a corner site and a place in the hearts of locals. Its rather stern black-and-white frontage belies a closely packed but comfortable bustle of business within, where polished wood tables and dark green walls set the tone, and staff are knowledgeable and professional. Its stock-in-trade is reliable, well-conceived modern bistro dishes, with seafood the undoubted star. A trio of scallops arrives lined up as though for parade inspection with a mirepoix of vegetables, lentils and smoked bacon as well as a

heap of saladings big on parsley, before herb-crusted sole fillets on broccoli and parmesan risotto with fennel dressing follows up. If fish isn't your catch, there's also haunch of venison with juniper cabbage and puréed celeriac in red wine jus, or Angus steaks and mash, before the perennially popular duo of salted caramel and chocolate turn up as components of a thin-shelled tart, served with a scoop of berry sorbet.

Chef Richard Fowler **Owner** Richard & Nicola Fowler **Times** 12-2/5.30-9.30 Closed 25 Dec, 2 wks Jan, Sun (Nov-Mar), L Sun **Prices** Fixed L 2 course fr £12.95, Starter £4.50-£8.95, Main £13.50-£22.95, Dessert £5.95, Service optional, Groups min 8 service 10% **Wines** 5 by glass **Notes** Fixed D available early evening, Vegetarian available **Seats** 46 **Parking** On street

---

Manor House Hotel

◉ Scottish, European

Modern Scottish food overlooking Oban harbour

☎ 01631 562087
Gallanach Rd PA34 4LS
e-mail: info@manorhouseoban.com
web: www.manorhouseoban.com
dir: follow MacBrayne Ferries signs, pass ferry entrance for hotel on right

The house is a Georgian villa built for the Duke of Argyll during the reign of George III. With panoramic views over Oban harbour, the ground-floor dining room is an elegant space with dark green walls and original paintings on maritime themes. Knowledgeable staff contribute to the professionalism that imbues the place, and a restrained style of modern Scottish cooking is the order of the day. A warm roulade of corn-fed chicken and Stornoway black pudding with sun-dried tomato stuffing and tarragon cream is a gentle opener, and could be succeeded (after intervening soup and sorbet offerings) by well-timed grilled halibut on courgette risotto with tomato confit. Marmalade from the Isle of Kerrera, which you can see across the water, might be used to glaze a peppered duck breast, served with creamed leeks and fennel potatoes, and meals end happily with loose-textured orange crème brûlée, garnished with a pair of pistachio tuiles.

Times 12-2.30/6.45-8.45 Closed 25-26 Dec

PORT APPIN   Map 20 NM94

Airds Hotel and Restaurant

◉◉◉ – **see page 560**

The Pierhouse Hotel

◉ Modern, International ✪

Top-notch fish and seafood with stunning views

☎ 01631 730302 & 730622
PA38 4DE
e-mail: reservations@pierhousehotel.co.uk
web: www.pierhousehotel.co.uk
dir: M8, A82 to Crianlarich & Fort William. At Ballachulish take A828 towards Oban. Turn right in Appin for Port Appin & Lismore Ferry

The one-time residence of the pier master is these days a hotel and restaurant with Loch Linnhe right outside the door. The loch supplies a good deal of what appears on the menu - fish and shellfish are the star of the show here - as well as providing a breathtaking backdrop. Crabs and lobsters await in creels off the jetty outside, day boats drop off fish at the door, oysters come from Loch Creran, and mussels and langoustines from Loch Linnhe's waters. Pierhouse Cullen skink is a traditional way to start, or keep things very simple with those langoustines served in their shells either warm with garlic butter or cold with garlic mayonnaise. The glorious simplicity and freshness of the seafood platters is hard to ignore, but there are the likes of baked fillet of sea bass with rosemary potato cake and vermouth cream, too. Sticky toffee pudding for afters, then go home replete.

Chef Tim Morris **Owner** Nicholas & Nicolette Horne **Times** 12.30-2.30/6.30-9.30 Closed 25-26 Dec **Prices** Starter £5-£12, Main £15-£35, Dessert £5-£10, Groups min 10 service 15% **Wines** 8 bottles over £30, 27 bottles under £30, 6 by glass **Notes** Vegetarian available, Civ Wed 100 **Seats** 45, Pr/dining room 25 **Children** Portions, Menu **Parking** 25

RHU
Map 20 NS28

Rosslea Hall Hotel

Modern British **NEW**

Spectacular views and seasonal cooking from Scotland's abundant larder

☎ 01436 439955
Ferry Rd G84 8NF
e-mail: enquiries@rossleahallhotel.co.uk
web: www.rossleahallhotel.co.uk
dir: From Erskine Bridge A82 to Dumbarton to junct with A814, follow to Helensburgh. Along waterfront 2m on left

Enjoying views out over the Firth of Clyde, this stunning Victorian mansion, originally built for a wealthy merchant, is looking dapper after a hefty £1 million refurbishment. The new light and airy conservatory dining room makes the most of the views through large, knee-to-ceiling windows with luxuriant drapes. Dark-blue patterned carpets, gold wallpaper and linen-clothed tables decorated with small vases of vibrantly colourful flowers complete the look. Smartly dressed and attentive staff ensure everything ticks along nicely, and the modern British menu is founded in top-notch Scottish produce. Pan-fried scallop with seafood tortellini, summer pea sauce and tarragon oil might start you off, followed by a

trio of pork - roast fillet, crispy belly and Stornoway black pudding - with pommes purée and roast shallot jus. A standout vanilla pannacotta with a strawberry consommé and summer berries makes a delightful finish.

Chef Ian Dunn **Owner** BDL Select Hotel
Times 12-3/6.30-9.30 **Prices** Fixed L 2 course £9.95-£12.95, Fixed D 3 course £19.95-£29.95, Starter £3.95-£7.95, Main £11.95-£22.95, Dessert £3.95-£6.95, Service optional **Wines** 8 bottles over £30, 28 bottles under £30, 6 by glass **Notes** Traditional afternoon tea for 2 £14.95, Sunday L, Vegetarian available, Civ Wed 100 **Seats** 48, Pr/dining room 40 **Children** Portions, Menu **Parking** 60

STRACHUR
Map 20 NN00

The Creggans Inn

Modern British, French

Locally-sourced cooking on the shore of Loch Fyne

☎ 01369 860279
PA27 8BX
e-mail: info@creggans-inn.co.uk
web: www.creggans-inn.co.uk
dir: A82 from Glasgow, at Tarbet take A83 towards Cairndow, left onto A815 to Strachur Or by ferry from Gourock to Dunoon onto A815

Rather more handsome than the word 'inn' might suggest, Creggans is a smart yet homely whitewashed hotel and restaurant on the banks of Loch Fyne. This to-die-for location not only adds an extra level of well-being to proceedings for diners, but also comes in pretty handy for the kitchen's sourcing of spanking fresh fish and seafood, and game from the hills all around. Staff in black and white uniforms, and softly burbling classical music add a refined note to dinner, kicking off with hand-dived Loch Fyne scallops twinned with Stornoway black pudding and served with a sharp citrus butter sauce to cut through the richness. Main-course keeps the big flavours coming - roast loin of venison appears with

Airds Hotel and Restaurant

PORT APPIN
MAP 20 NM94

Modern British

Splendid Argyll views and first-class cooking

☎ 01631 730236
PA38 4DF
e-mail: airds@airds-hotel.com
dir: From A828 (Oban to Fort William road), turn at Appin signed Port Appin. Hotel 2.5m on left

Hidden away along a winding road skirting the serene shores of Loch Linnhe, Airds is an intimate and sophisticated country-house hotel that consistently gets all of the details right. The whitewashed 18th-century ferry inn once put up farmers and livestock on their way to market, but is run these days with a high degree of polish, consummate professionalism, and furnished in opulent style. The views from the dining room are reason

enough to come, sweeping across the Sound of Lismore to Loch Linnhe and the Morven Mountains beyond, but top-class food has always been a vital part of the Airds experience, and chef David Barnett's impressive culinary talents, honed to a fine edge after eight years working with Martin Wishart (see entry), would bring diners out here even if the views were of the local power station. Superlative local produce is the starting point, with fish and seafood coming fresh from the Oban fleet, and all ingredients chosen for seasonality. There's plenty going on in a starter of seared scallops matched with aubergine purée, cauliflower (served pickled and as crispy pakora), charred shallot, yoghurt and mango, and it all adds up to a cleverly balanced plate of contrasting texture and flavours. A main course of Argyll pork chop is perfectly timed and paired effectively with smoked ham haugh bonbon, garlic and shallot purée, rhubarb, and creamed kale, while dessert culminates with an impressive assemblage of well-risen banana soufflé, zingy passionfruit sorbet, rich milk chocolate crémeux, and

banana foam. All of the peripheral items, from bacon brioche to haggis bonbon canapés and delicious petits fours are equally impressive and wrought with a keen eye for detail. For such a small operation, the wide-reaching wine list punches well above its weight, and refreshingly unstuffy service is the icing on the cake.

Chef David Barnett, Alan Hunter **Owner** Mr & Mrs S McKivragan **Times** 12-1.45/7.30-9.30 **Prices** Fixed L 3 course £23.95, Fixed D 3 course £53, Tasting menu £72, Starter £4.50-£8.95, Main £8.90-£22.50, Dessert £5.50-£6.50, Service optional **Wines** 12 by glass **Notes** Tasting menu 7 course, wine dinners, Sunday L, Vegetarian menu, Dress restrictions, Smart casual at D, no jeans, T-shirts **Seats** 32 **Children** Portions, Menu **Parking** 20

gratin potatoes, pickled red cabbage, celeriac purée, earthy wild mushrooms and a sticky raspberry vinegar reduction. To conclude, it's showtime with a beautifully presented bitter chocolate tear drop with milk chocolate mousse and boozy griottine cherries.

Chef Robbie Hutchinson **Owner** The MacLellan family **Times** 7-9 Closed 25-26 Dec, L all week **Prices** Prices not confirmed Service optional **Wines** 6 by glass **Notes** Vegetarian available, Dress restrictions, Smart casual, Civ Wed 80 **Seats** 35 **Children** Portions, Menu **Parking** 25

TARBERT LOCH FYNE	Map 20 NR86

Stonefield Castle Hotel

◉ Modern British

Modern British cooking in a Victorian castle

☎ 01880 820836
PA29 6YJ
e-mail: reservations.stonefieldcastle@ohiml.com
web: www.oxfordhotelsandinns.com
dir: From Arrochar follow signs for A83 through Inveraray & Lochgilphead, hotel on left 2m before Tarbert

Finely detailed down to the last crenallation, Stonefield is a hubristic piece of Victorian pastiche, a medieval-effect castle sitting high on the Kintyre peninsula. The décor inside matches the exterior grandiosity, and the views over the water from the wide-screen picture windows in the dining room are a rare old treat. The cooking keeps things relatively simple, opening with a serving of langoustines with shallot and caper hollandaise, and following up with beef in three guises - medallion, burger and mini-pie - served with cauliflower purée strongly spiked with Lanark Blue, all sauced with port, or lobster glazed in Arran mustard and Mull cheddar. Finish with apple, toffee and almond tart with apple syrup and cinnamon ice cream.

Times 12-9

Braidwoods

◉◉ Modern Scottish

Creative cooking from a gifted husband-and-wife-team

☎ 01294 833544
Drumastle Mill Cottage KA24 4LN
e-mail: keithbraidwood@btconnect.com
dir: 1m from Dalry on Saltcoats road

In a cottage in the middle of a field near Dalry, Braidwoods is a small, unpretentious restaurant, its two rooms split by a central fireplace, with beams in the low ceilings, close-set tables, an informal, relaxed atmosphere, and young and helpful staff. Dinner, of three or four courses, could open with a well-balanced dish of seared scallops on pea purée along with crispy chicken wings, or perhaps even more modish beetroot-cured gravad lax on beetroot and clementine salad with a potato cake. Main courses impress with their timing and presentation: melt-in-the-mouth roast best end of local lamb on wilted spinach, with a mound of cauliflower purée topped with confit neck fillet and a square of dauphinoise, all complemented by rosemary jus, or grilled turbot fillet crowned with tapenade served on herb risotto and a rich shellfish jus. Canapés make a great introduction to a meal, and puddings impress too, among them Valrhona truffle cake with prune and Armagnac ice cream.

Chef Keith & Nicola Braidwood **Owner** Mr & Mrs Braidwood **Times** 12-1.45/7-9 Closed 25-26 Dec, 1st 3 wks Jan, 1st 2 wks Sep, Mon, L Tue (Sun Etr-Sep), D Sun **Prices** Fixed L 3 course £43, Fixed D 3 course £26, Service optional, Service included **Wines** 4 by glass **Notes** Sun L mid Sep-Apr, Dress restrictions, Smart casual **Seats** 24 **Parking** 10

Enterkine Country House

◉◉ Modern British V ✿

Well-crafted contemporary cooking in an elegant 1930s country house

☎ 01292 520580
Annbank KA6 5AL
e-mail: mail@enterkine.com
dir: 5m E of Ayr on B743

An avenue of mature trees leads to the door of Enterkine, a pristine art-deco mansion that is run with the relaxed intimacy of a small-scale family residence rather than the tweedy grandeur of a full-dress country house. The restaurant was renamed Browne's in recent years to go with its new contemporary look, and comes with the extra bonus of uplifting views over the Ayr Valley through vast picture windows. The kitchen takes a suitably contemporary line with its output, sending out well-sourced Scottish produce in dishes bursting with full-on flavours - an Arbroath smokie soufflé backed up by goats' cheese, chorizo and lobster bisque to start, then rump of Borders lamb with mashed potatoes and Toulouse sausage, Provençal vegetables, smoked anchovy and cubes of redcurrant jelly. A line-up of superb Scottish cheeses is one way to finish, or you might opt for something more complex such as Bramley apple crumble parfait with spiced apple pithivier, toffee sauce and shortbread.

Chef Paul Moffat **Owner** Mr Browne **Times** 12-2/7-9 **Prices** Fixed L 2 course £10-£16.95, Fixed D 3 course £22-£35, Tasting menu £70, Starter £5-£8, Main £10-£25, Dessert £5-£7, Service optional **Wines** 37 bottles over £30, 19 bottles under £30, 4 by glass **Notes** Sunday L, Vegetarian menu, Dress restrictions, Smart casual, Civ Wed 200 **Seats** 40, Pr/dining room 14 **Children** Portions, Menu **Parking** 20

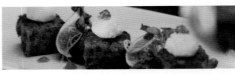

AYR *continued*

Fairfield House Hotel

◉◉ Modern International

Great views and cooking with broad appeal

☎ 01292 267461
12 Fairfield Rd KA7 2AS
e-mail: reservations@fairfieldhotel.co.uk
dir: From A77 to Ayr South. Follow signs for town centre. Left into Miller Rd. At lights turn left, then right into Fairfield Rd

Built as the seaside home of a Glasgow tea merchant who clearly had an eye for a rapturous view, this Victorian mansion looks across to the Firth of Clyde and the Isle of Arran. The owners have brought the old girl gently up to date with a tasteful, neutral modern look without losing any of the period charm inherent in its lofty plasterwork ceilings. In Martin's Bar and Grill - the culinary heart of the enterprise - you could keep things simple with something from the grill - a steak, say - or go for Arran ale-battered haddock and chunky chips, or trade up to the Rosette menu which has its heart in fine Scottish produce, as in a simply-cooked trio of scallops, squid and Tarbet crab. Local game is always a good idea, particularly when it happens to be Athol Estate venison Wellington served with spiced red cabbage, parsnip mash and Madeira sauce. It is all prepared in a positive, confident style that delivers clear, well-judged flavours, culminating in a zesty passionfruit baked Alaska with passionfruit syrup and the textural contrast of praline crisp.

Fairfield House Hotel

Times 11am-9.30pm

See advert on page 561

The Western House Hotel

◉◉ Modern British ✪

Modern cooking at Ayr racecourse

☎ 0870 055 5510
2 Craigie Rd KA8 0HA
e-mail: msimpson@ayr-racecourse.co.uk
web: www.westernhousehotel.co.uk
dir: From Glasgow M77 then A77 towards Ayr. At Whitletts rdbt take A719 towards town centre

The Ayr racecourse hotel extends over two buildings, a main house and a courtyard section, which is where most of the guest rooms are. Well-tended gardens and a patio area make it a pleasant place on a summer's day in the Lowlands, and the equestrian theme is given the thorough airing you would expect in pictures of the thoroughbred champions of yesteryear on the walls of the Jockey Club restaurant. Here, the net is cast widely for culinary influences from hither and yon, hauling in smoked haddock and tiger prawn gratin with creamed leeks and gruyère, a version of cassoulet with confit duck leg, merguez, pancetta and white beans, and steamed lemon sponge with cardamom anglaise and ginger ice cream. Look to the grill for steaks of 28-day, dry-aged prime Scottish beef from the Carrick Hills.

Chef Donald McInnes **Owner** Alan MacDonald, Richard Johnstone **Times** 12-2/7-9.30 **Prices** Starter £3.50-£8.95, Main £8.95-£19.95, Dessert £4.50, Service optional **Wines** 9 by glass **Notes** Sunday L, Vegetarian available, Dress restrictions, Smart casual **Seats** 40, Pr/dining room 60 **Children** Portions **Parking** 200

Glenapp Castle

BALLANTRAE	**MAP 20 NX08**

Modern British V ✪

Inventive contemporary cooking in a Victorian castle

☎ 01465 831212
KA26 0NZ
e-mail: info@glenappcastle.com
web: www.glenappcastle.com
dir: S through Ballantrae, cross bridge over River Stinchar, 1st right, castle gates in 1m, use entry system

The castle was built in 1870 for a Lord Lieutenant of Ayrshire, and is a fittingly hubristic example of the Scots baronial manner, all stolid turrets and towers rising above the sandstone battlements. Not that you were likely to be besieged by anything more minatory than the odd flock of pigeons by 1870, but still, it looked the part. Lengthily reworked to its former magnificence by present owners the Cowans, it emerges as a masterpiece of the restorer's art, the interiors replete with rich fabrics, gilt-framed mirrors and oil paintings. The dining room is split across either side of the lounge, the main room done in regal red, with views towards Ailsa Craig, the coastline and the Mull of Kintyre. Matt Worswick arrived at the stoves at the beginning of 2013, having previously been sous-chef at Cheltenham's reference address, Le Champignon Sauvage (see entry). He's certainly made a good early impression, although the format remains unchanged, a six-course fixed dinner menu (four for lunch) with a pair of alternatives at main and dessert. Intense sea-fresh flavours distinguish an opener of seared red mullet with crispy squid and ink-black quinoa, ahead of a beautifully composed course of foie gras ballottine accompanied by fragrant, soft jasmine jelly and sweet apricot chutney. The principal fish dish may be crisply fried halibut on cauliflower purée with powdered smoked almonds, which acts as an outrider to the main meat, perhaps roast venison loin of exquisite tenderness, served with heritage carrots, braised leek hearts and roasted orange. Pause for breath before selecting from the compendious array of quality Scottish cheeses, anointed with a spoonful of white truffle honey, and then choose a dessert such as evenly risen raspberry soufflé with deeply intense elderflower sorbet, or perhaps burdock root crème brûlée with burdock meringue and coffee ice cream.

Chef Matt Worswick **Owner** Graham & Fay Cowan **Times** 12.30-2/7-10 Closed 3 Jan-25 Mar, Xmas **Prices** Fixed L 3 course £39.50, Service optional **Wines** 9 by glass **Notes** Fixed Gourmet D 6 course £65, Sun L 3 course, bookings req, Sunday L £29.50, Vegetarian menu, Civ Wed 40 **Seats** 34, Pr/dining room 20 **Children** Portions, Menu **Parking** 20

Save on Hotels. Book at **theAA.com/hotel**

AYRSHIRE, SOUTH 563 SCOTLAND

Lochgreen House Hotel

TROON   MAP 20 NS33

Modern French

Modern French cooking in a stunningly restored manor house

☎ 01292 313343
Monktonhill Rd, Southwood KA10 7EN
e-mail: lochgreen@costley-hotels.co.uk
web: www.costley-hotels.co.uk
dir: From A77 follow Prestwick Airport signs, take B749 to Troon, hotel on left, 1m from junct

Lochgreen House Hotel approaches its 25th anniversary in fine fettle. Built in 1905 for a wealthy lace mill owner and bought by the Costley family back in 1989, the handsome white-painted mansion is a stellar country-house hotel of considerable charm and class. It has an esteemed neighbour in the shape of the Royal Troon golf course and it isn't all that far from Glasgow's Prestwick Airport if you fancy flying in. The 30 acres of woodlands and immaculately-tended gardens overlook the Ayrshire coastline, and there are good views of the grounds from the Tapestry Restaurant. Located in a sympathetic and expansive extension, pull up a tapestry-upholstered seat at one of the well-spaced, well-dressed tables beneath a lofty beamed ceiling hung with vast crystal chandeliers. The spruce and proficient service team play their part in making dining here a memorable experience. Andrew Costley, son of the owners, leads the team in the kitchen with head chef Jordan Annabi, and they deliver dishes based on superb seasonal Scottish produce, sound French classical thinking, and no shortage of good ideas. Imaginative canapés get the ball rolling - chorizo doughnut, perhaps - before a first course such as crisp belly of Ayrshire pork with curried langoustines, fennel remoulade and a light lemongrass dressing. Next up, poached fillet of halibut is the star of the show - a fabulous piece of fish - with cauliflower couscous, wilted sea greens and lemon butter sauce, or try the Gressingham duck breast with Scottish beetroot, skin crisp and an orange and beetroot reduction. There's sharp technique at dessert stage, too: rhubarb and custard, for example, with spiced gingerbread and popcorn, or praline noisette semi-fredo with cherry sorbet and sour cherry compôte.

Chef Andrew Costley, Jordan Annabi **Owner** Mr W Costley **Times** 12-2/7-10 **Prices** Fixed L 2 course £17.95, Fixed D 3 course £39.95, Service optional **Wines** 10 by glass **Notes** Sunday L, Vegetarian available, Dress restrictions, Smart casual, Civ Wed 140 **Seats** 80, Pr/dining room 40 **Children** Portions, Menu **Parking** 70

The James Miller Room

TURNBERRY   MAP 20 NS20

Modern V NOTABLE WINE LIST

Imaginative cooking in famous golfing hotel

☎ 01655 331000
Turnberry Resort, Scotland, Maidens Rd KA26 9LT
e-mail: turnberry@luxurycollection.com
dir: From Glasgow take A77/M77 S towards Stranraer, 2m past Kirkoswald, follow signs for A719/Turnberry. Hotel 500mtrs on right

It is not compulsory to turn up at this luxurious hotel on the fabulous Ayrshire coast with golf in mind, since the world-famous Turnberry Resort also stakes its claim as a dining destination worth going out of the way for. It has a brace of top-notch food operations, the more exclusive of which goes by the name of The James Miller Room. Tucked away just off the main 1906 dining room (see entry), the setting brings together a more romantic and exclusive mood amid the contemporary verve of curvaceous crimson chairs and darkwood blended seamlessly with the Edwardian pomp of high ceilings, ornate plaster cornicing and a grand centrepiece fireplace. Better still, with a maximum capacity of just 14 diners to cater for, staff can deliver a more attentive service, and head chef Justin Galea can cook at a more refined level than can be achieved in the busy main dining room. For the select few who have bagged a table in the JMR, the kitchen has a commendable open door policy, inviting diners in for a close-up look at the action at the stoves. The kitchen's commitment to superb locally-sourced ingredients is mightily impressive, right down to the sustainably-sourced fish and seafood deployed in dishes such as Sound of Kilbrannan scallops matched with the textural interest of tabouleh, cauliflower and a Gran Reserva wine sauce. Naturally in such a high-end setting, luxurious produce is never far off, whether it's foie gras with grapes, caramel and brioche, or a main course of peppered roe deer alongside cabbage, beetroot and liquorice. Desserts are perfectly conceived and impeccably balanced constructions - perhaps banana soufflé with bee pollen ice cream and spiced butter cake, or an irresistibly named 'ten layers of Valrhona chocolate' with pistachio ice cream. Presenting the impressive wine list on an iPad is a switched-on quirky detail that adds to the enjoyment.

Chef Justin Galea **Owner** Leisurecorp **Times** 7-9.30 Closed 8 Dec-17 Jan, Sun-Mon **Prices** Prices not confirmed Service optional **Wines** 26 by glass **Notes** Vegetarian menu, Dress restrictions, Smart casual **Seats** 14, Pr/dining room 10 **Parking** 200

BALLANTRAE   Map 20 NX08

Glenapp Castle

⊛⊛⊛ – *see page 562*

TROON   Map 20 NS33

Lochgreen House Hotel

⊛⊛⊛ – *see page 563*

MacCallums of Troon

⊛ Seafood ☺

Simple, fresh seafood on the harbourside

☎ 01292 319339
The Harbour KA10 6DH

Watching the waves crash against Troon's harbour wall as the fishing fleet lands its catch, thoughts turn inescapably to the prospect of dining on fish and seafood. And this harbourside restaurant in an attractively converted pump house is guaranteed to come up with the goods. Inside it is a businesslike space of high rafters, exposed brick walls liberally layered with maritime memorabilia, and bare, rustic wooden tables set in a simple manner that echoes the unfussy treatments meted out to the spanking-fresh seafood (whose journey from boat to table can be measured in feet). What has just come in on the quayside gets star billing on the chalkboard. The Cullen skink delivers a creamy, smoky opener filled with chunks of haddock, potatoes and leek, while a splendid fillet of halibut is showcased in a main course beside a supporting cast of baked ratatouille, saffron potatoes and fish fumet. Dessert is no mere sideshow either, as seen in a light bitter chocolate mousse with orange and white chocolate ice cream.

Chef Philip Burgess **Owner** John & James MacCallums
Times 12-2.30/6.30-9.30 Closed Xmas, New Year, Mon, D Sun **Prices** Starter £4.85-£8.95, Main £9.95-£27.50, Dessert £5.85-£7.95, Service optional, Groups min 12 service 10% **Wines** 1 bottle over £30, 20 bottles under £30, 4 by glass **Notes** Sunday L **Seats** 43
Children Portions **Parking** 12

The Marine Hotel

⊛⊛ Modern British ☺

Colourful cooking and fantastic coastal views

☎ 01292 314444
Crosbie Rd KA10 6HE
e-mail: marine@pumahotels.co.uk
web: www.pumahotels.co.uk
dir: A77, A78, A79 onto B749. Hotel on left after golf course

The tripartite, split-level Fairways dining room at the Troon Marine enjoys fantastic views over the Firth of Clyde towards the Isle of Arran; the sunsets are amazing. Formally dressed tables and formally drilled service establish a civilised tone, with colourful artworks on the warm orange walls and a wine store that seems to invite

exploration. Equally as colourful as the surroundings is a starter of beetroot-stained mackerel with red onion confit in orange and tomato dressing, seasoned with sesame oil and soy. A brace of pork servings - roast fillet and cider-braised belly - with a smear of garlic and chive mash makes for an elegant main course, its creamy cider sauce adding to the dish, or there could be salmon with aubergine purée, king scallop and sesame-fried pak choi. The filling of a slice of dark chocolate tart is thickly luxurious, and is partnered with vanilla ice cream and a garnish of orange.

Owner Puma Hotels Collection **Times** 7-9.30 Closed L all week **Prices** Fixed L 2 course fr £29.50, Service optional **Notes** Vegetarian available, Dress restrictions, Smart casual, Civ Wed 50 **Seats** 120, Pr/dining room 50 **Children** Portions, Menu **Parking** 220

TURNBERRY   Map 20 NS20

The James Miller Room

⊛⊛⊛ – *see page 563*

Turnberry Resort, Scotland

⊛⊛ Traditional French ☺

Classical dining at renowned coastal golf resort

☎ 01655 331000
Maidens Rd KA26 9LT
e-mail: turnberry@luxurycollection.com
dir: From Glasgow take A77, M77 S towards Stranraer, 2m past Kirkoswald, follow signs for A719/Turnberry. Hotel 500mtrs on right

The 1906 Restaurant of this upscale golfing resort is named after the year it opened, so the place has had plenty of time to polish its act to a high gloss. With the wild Ayrshire coast to explore, plus golf (of course) and a state of the art spa, there's plenty to keep you busy before slotting in the genteel custom of afternoon tea. There's no denying the splendour of the 1906 Restaurant, which is somewhat akin to dining inside a vast white wedding cake, and thus an entirely appropriate setting for the output of a kitchen that takes its spiritual inspiration from Escoffier's classics, with luxury ingredients aplenty. You might as well stick with the theme and start with a torchon of foie gras marinated in white port and Sauternes and served with poached pear and toasted brioche, then follow that with something from Escoffier's recipe book - perhaps halibut Trouvillaise, the fish pot-roasted with shrimp and mussel salpicon, or beef Diane flambéed with brandy and finished with cream. For more table-side theatre, finish with the indulgence of a Grand Marnier-flambéed crêpe Suzette. See separate entry for The James Miller Room which is also in the hotel.

Chef Justin Galea **Owner** Leisurecorp **Times** 6.30-10 Closed 8-22 Dec, L all week **Prices** Service optional **Wines** 16 by glass **Notes** Brunch 1st & 3rd Sun of month 12.30-3pm, Sunday L £25, Vegetarian available, Dress restrictions, Smart casual **Seats** 120, Pr/dining room 10 **Children** Portions, Menu **Parking** 200

DUMFRIES & GALLOWAY

ANNAN   Map 21 NY16

Del Amitri Restaurant

⊛ Modern European

Creative cooking in the Borders

☎ 01461 201999
95a High St DG12 6DJ
e-mail: enquiries@del-amitri.co.uk
web: www.del-amitri.co.uk
dir: Located above the Café Royal

The name might have an Italian ring about it, but this stylish first-floor restaurant on Annan High Street is definitely not in the business of Italophile cuisine. The venue is a long, narrow room in tones of chocolate and plum, with wooden floors, brown leather seats at clothed tables, and splashes of colour courtesy of artworks from a local gallery. The vibe is relaxed - the table is yours for the evening, so no need to watch the clock - while the kitchen turns out well-executed modern dishes with a French accent. The fine produce of Scotland is well to the fore, as in a starter of smoked haddock kedgeree with soft-boiled quail's eggs and curried mayonnaise. Next out, North Sea halibut is baked under a layer of herb crumb and served with crushed new potatoes, butternut squash cream and buttered kale. Chocoholics are well catered for by an assiette comprising dark chocolate brownie, white chocolate ice cream and milk chocolate mousse.

Times 12-2/6-10 Closed Mon, L Tue-Sat, D Sun (Nov-May)

AUCHENCAIRN   Map 21 NX75

Balcary Bay Hotel

⊛⊛ Modern French, European

Modern country-house cooking on the Solway coast

☎ 01556 640217 & 640311
Shore Rd DG7 1QZ
e-mail: reservations@balcary-bay-hotel.co.uk
web: www.balcary-bay-hotel.co.uk
dir: on A711 between Dalbeattie & Kirkcudbright. In Auchencairn follow signs to Balcary along shore road for 2m

Named for the beautiful bay whose waters lap on its doorstep, this snow-white hotel on the Solway coast sits in splendid isolation at the end of a single-track lane with uninterrupted views sweeping as far as the distant

Cumbrian peaks. The arty enclave of Kirkcudbright is nearby, and there is magnificent hiking to be had along the coastline, and when the day is done, the restaurant is ready with an accomplished repertoire of inviting modern European ideas built on the peerless produce of the Dumfries & Galloway region. The area's marine bounty is always at hand, perhaps in a starter of breaded langoustine tails with saffron linguine and sauce antiboise, followed by pan-fried hake fillet with vegetable cannelloni, roast salsify and herb foam. This is prime farming country too, so meatier ideas could be Galloway beef fillet layered between puff pastry with oxtail tongue and veal jus, or loin, braised cheek and belly of pork with pea purée and cider jus. End with dark chocolate marquise with cherry ice cream, or a spread of artisan Scottish cheeses with home-made chutney.

Chef Craig McWilliam **Owner** Graeme A Lamb & family **Times** 12-2/7-8.30 Closed Dec-Jan, L Mon-Sat **Prices** Fixed D 3 course £39.75, Service optional **Wines** 52 bottles over £30, 55 bottles under £30, 12 by glass **Notes** Sunday L, Vegetarian available, Dress restrictions, Smart casual **Seats** 55 **Children** Portions **Parking** 50

GATEHOUSE OF FLEET   Map 20 NX55

Cally Palace Hotel

◎ Traditional V

Formal dining on the Solway coast

☎ 01557 814341
Cally Dr DG7 2DL
e-mail: info@callypalace.co.uk
web: www.callypalace.co.uk
dir: From A74(M) take A75, at Gatehouse take B727. Hotel on left

Although golf rules the roost in this Georgian country manor in 150 acres of parkland on the Solway coast, you don't need to have any interest at all in the game to have a great time here. There are hiking and biking trails criss-crossing the area, and every imaginable leisure activity for pampering or punishing yourself in readiness for dinner in the formal restaurant, where that starchy institution of jacket and tie for gentlemen still holds sway. A pianist tinkling away in the background adds a softer note to proceedings as a repertoire of gently-modernised country-house classics built on soundly-sourced Scottish produce gets under way with the likes of chicken, mozzarella and roast pepper terrine with pesto dressing. This might be followed by pan-fried pork fillet with Stornoway black pudding, Bramley apple purée, fondant potato, celeriac purée, and Calvados jus; awaiting at the end, there may be caramelised banana parfait with passionfruit and lime syrup and coconut tuile.

Chef Jamie Muirhead **Owner** McMillan Hotels **Times** 12-1/6.45-9 Closed 3 Jan-early Feb **Prices** Fixed L 2 course £18.95, Fixed D 3 course £29.50, Starter £3.75-£5.75, Main £10.95-£14.95, Dessert £4.75, Service optional **Wines** 35 bottles over £30, 55 bottles under £30, 11 by glass **Notes** Sunday L, Vegetarian menu, Dress

restrictions, Jacket and tie **Seats** 110 **Children** Portions, Menu **Parking** 70

GRETNA   Map 21 NY36

Smiths at Gretna Green

◎◎ Modern British ✿

Inventive cooking in a striking modern hotel

☎ 01461 337007
Gretna Green DG16 5EA
e-mail: info@smithsgretnagreen.com
web: www.smithsgretnagreen.com
dir: From M74 junct 22 follow signs to Old Blacksmith's Shop. Hotel opposite

Gretna's sterling service to the wedding industry continues unabated, an island of romance in a cynical world, and Smiths hotel doesn't stint when it comes to hosting some of the brisk nuptial business. Not surprisingly, the place is always turned out in its special-occasion best, not least in the fascinating chainmailed area of the restaurant, where a floor-to-ceiling cordon marks off a striking mirrored space. Concept starters set the tone, perhaps an artist's impression of ham, egg and chips incorporating 'liquid peas', or a 'winter picnic' comprised of a chunk of hot-smoked salmon, a smoked salmon sandwich, a quail Scotch egg, champagne jelly and caviar. Fish and meat combinations, often a risk, are handled persuasively, mixing pork belly, turbot, scallops and black pudding in one majestic main-course dish that manages not to lose any of its component flavours, and dessert could be well-executed orange and lemon tart with razor-sharp gin-and-tonic sorbet. And with that, you'll be ready to depart on your honeymoon.

Chef Stephen Myers **Owner** Alasdair Houston **Times** 12-9.30 Closed 25 Dec **Prices** Fixed L 2 course £12.95, Starter £6.50-£29.50, Service optional **Wines** 31 bottles over £30, 37 bottles under £30, 12 by glass **Notes** Tea time menu 3 course £10.95 4.30-6pm, Sunday L £15.95, Vegetarian available, Civ Wed 150 **Seats** 60, Pr/dining room 18 **Children** Portions, Menu **Parking** 115

MOFFAT   Map 21 NT00

Annandale Arms Hotel

◎ Modern Scottish

250-year-old inn serving well-cooked local produce

☎ 01683 220013
High St DG10 9HF
e-mail: reception@annandalearmshotel.co.uk
web: www.annandalearmshotel.co.uk
dir: M74 junct 15/A701. Hotel on west side of central square that forms High St

Still very much a pub and the hub of Moffat life for 250 years, this fine old inn draws loyal locals into the oak-panelled bar for tip-top real ales, decent malt whiskies, and the relaxing atmosphere. Food is also worth more than a passing glance, served at bare darkwood tables with imperial purple velvet seats in a good-looking contemporary venue. Regularly-changing menus make

sound use of meat, game and fish sourced from north of the border and dishes are given a modern spin to keep things interesting. Typically, kick off with pan-fried pigeon breast on black pudding with blueberry sauce, then move on to roast monkfish wrapped in Parma ham with a tarragon and dill cream sauce, or venison loin with red wine jus. Finish with raspberry cranachan.

Times 12-2/6-8.45 Closed 25-26 Dec

Brodies

◎ Modern British ✿

Smart modish cooking in contemporary setting

☎ 01683 222870
Holm St DG10 9EB
e-mail: whatscooking@brodiesofmoffat.co.uk
web: www.brodiesofmoffat.co.uk
dir: M74 junct 15 towards Selkirk, take 2nd right turn

Natural light floods in during the day through its glass frontage, but this restaurant, just off the high street, serves up bright modern food day and night. There's a decidedly modish sheen to the room with its trendy neutral colour scheme, darkwood tables with little goldfish bowl flower arrangements and decorative stencils on the walls. A large bar is just the ticket for pre- or post-prandial drinks. Local ingredients from Dumfries & Galloway pop up in the likes of double-baked cheese soufflé made with mature Lockerbie cheddar, followed by trout and clam chowder with Parmentier potatoes and smoked Ayrshire bacon. There's a decent veggie selection too, including sweetcorn fritters with warm cannellini beans, spinach and tomato, and, for dessert, perhaps apple and custard galette with cinnamon ice cream.

Chef Russell Pearce **Owner** Russell & Danyella Pearce **Times** 10am-11pm Closed 25-26 Dec, D Wed (Oct-Mar) All-day dining **Prices** Service optional **Wines** 15 bottles under £30, 7 by glass **Notes** Early door menu available 5.30-7pm, Sunday L £13.95-£16.95, Vegetarian available **Seats** 40 **Children** Portions **Parking** On street

MOFFAT ***continued***

Hartfell House & The Limetree Restaurant

Modern British

Confident global cooking in a Victorian house

01683 220153
Hartfell Crescent DG10 9AL
e-mail: enquiries@hartfellhouse.co.uk
web: www.hartfellhouse.co.uk
dir: Off High St at war memorial onto Well St & Old Well Rd. Hartfell Crescent on right

In a peaceful setting in an area of Outstanding Natural Beauty, Hartfell House is built of local stone and dates back to around 1850. Its period features are all perfectly intact, both outside and in. The residents' lounge is the place to linger over drinks either before or after dinner in the intimate Limetree Restaurant, which dazzles with gold cornices and ceiling roses. Non-residents would do well to book as this is a popular place to eat thanks to its eclectic menus informed by top-quality local produce. Malaysian spiced coconut milk soup with prawns, rice noodles, lime and coriander could precede loin of roe deer and Barony venison sausage with mushroom gratin dauphinoise, roast celeriac and carrots with thyme, and braised shallot sauce. For dessert you might well return to home territory with something like sticky gingerbread pudding with vanilla ice cream and treacle toffee sauce.

Chef Matt Seddon **Owner** Robert & Mhairi Ash
Times 12.30-2.30/6.30-9 Closed Xmas, Mon, L Tue-Sat, D Sun **Prices** Fixed L 2 course £19.50, Fixed D 3 course £27.50, Service optional **Wines** 6 bottles over £30, 21 bottles under £30, 4 by glass **Notes** Sun L by arrangement, Vegetarian available **Seats** 26
Children Portions **Parking** 6

NEWTON STEWART — Map 20 NX46

Kirroughtree House

Modern British

Historic mansion serving up fine Scottish produce

01671 402141
Minnigaff DG8 6AN
e-mail: info@kirroughtreehouse.co.uk
web: www.kirroughtreehouse.co.uk
dir: From A75 take A712, entrance to hotel 300yds on left

The splendid white-painted baronial country mansion dating from the early 1700s has connections to Rabbie Burns, who was a friend of the owner, but even without that association, the house oozes with historic charm. The setting within the Galloway Forest Park, just outside Newton Stewart, is hard to beat, too. Inside, none of the character of the original house has been lost, the lofty corniced ceilings and expanses of wood panelling joined by antiques and plush carpets. The restaurant is suitably traditional - and grand - with swagged curtains, darkwood chairs and linen-clad tables. Dinner is a formal four-course affair starting, perhaps, with smoked chicken and tarragon risotto with parmesan shavings, or pan-fried salmon with parsley mashed potatoes and lemon sauce. After that, an intermediary course is a bonus, such as sweet potato and lime soup, before the main event: loin of Scottish lamb, maybe, with creamed potatoes, pea purée, broad beans and mint jus. To finish, there's an excellent choice of Scottish cheeses, or something like lemon posset with shortbread.

Chef Matthew McWhir **Owner** Mr D McMillan
Times 12-1.30/7-9 Closed 2 Jan-1 Feb **Prices** Fixed L 3 course £18, Fixed D 3 course £35, Service optional
Wines 6 by glass **Notes** ALC L only, Sunday L, Vegetarian available, Dress restrictions, Smart casual **Seats** 45
Parking 50

PORTPATRICK — Map 20 NW95

Knockinaam Lodge

– see opposite

SANQUHAR — Map 20 NS70

Blackaddie House Hotel

Modern British

Traditional country-house hotel with engaging modern cooking

01659 50270
Blackaddie Rd DG4 6JJ
e-mail: ian@blackaddiehotel.co.uk
dir: 300 mtrs off A76 on north side of Sanquhar

A veteran of many a stellar kitchen, chef-patron Ian McAndrew has been busily establishing the restaurant at Blackaddie as a dining destination for fans of locally-sourced, vibrant modern cooking - some of it as local as the seasonal veg, herbs and fruit that come but a few steps from the kitchen garden. The honey-hued stone hotel was once a rectory and sits in heavenly tranquil grounds alongside the River Nith, a renowned salmon fishing spot, and while its smart restaurant may be small, it certainly punches above its weight with such an experienced hand directing the action in the kitchen. The daily-changing menus fizz with good ideas and dishes impress with their depth of flavour and elegant presentation, such as a starter of seared diver-caught scallops with Parma ham, spiced apples, smoked Cairnsmore cheese, macadamia nuts and red wine dressing. Main course could bring roast monkfish with red wine rice, parsnip purée and bacon dust, then more well-conceived intricacy in a finale of white chocolate cheesecake with caramel-poached pineapple and Amaretto sorbet.

Chef Ian McAndrew **Owner** Ian McAndrew
Times 12-2/6.30-9 **Prices** Fixed D 2 course £22.50, Tasting menu £60, Service optional **Wines** 10 by glass
Notes Gourmet tasting menu available, 4 course D £48, Sunday L £17.50-£28.50, Vegetarian available, Civ Wed 25 **Seats** 20, Pr/dining room 20 **Children** Portions, Menu
Parking 20

STRANRAER — Map 20 NX06

Corsewall Lighthouse Hotel

Modern Scottish V

A unique location with a true local flavour

01776 853220
Corsewall Point, Kirkcolm DG9 0QG
e-mail: info@lighthousehotel.co.uk
web: www.lighthousehotel.co.uk
dir: Take A718 from Stranraer to Kirkcolm, then follow B718 signed Lighthouse

Corsewall still earns its keep as a beacon for passing mariners heading into Loch Ryan, but it's also a hotel and restaurant. Needless to say the setting is something special, reached via a winding single-track road, with fabulous sea views towards Arran and Ailsa Craig waiting at the end. The accommodation and restaurant are in what used to be the keeper's living quarters and stores. There's a maritime theme in the restaurant, a traditionally-decorated room with bare wooden tables and a friendly, relaxed vibe. The menu keeps things relatively simple, so you might start with goats' cheese and red onion tartlet with a pesto dressing, before moving on to smoked haddock with a creamy Tobermory cheddar cheese sauce, or roast rack of Galloway lamb with a rich sherry, redcurrant and thyme reduction. Dessert extends to Amaretto and vanilla cheesecake with raspberry coulis.

Chef Andrew Downie **Owner** Gordon, Kay & Pamela Ward **Times** 12-2.15/7-9.15 **Prices** Fixed L 2 course £15.95, Starter £3.85-£7.75, Main £8.75-£21.70, Dessert £6.75, Service optional **Wines** 12 bottles over £30, 25 bottles under £30, 4 by glass **Notes** Fixed D 5 course £35-£39.75, Sunday L £15.95-£19.50, Vegetarian menu, Dress restrictions, Smart casual, Civ Wed 28 **Seats** 28 **Children** Portions, Menu **Parking** 20

DUNBARTONSHIRE, WEST

BALLOCH   Map 20 NS38

The Cameron Grill

@@ Modern British 🍃

Classy grill in grand lochside hotel

☎ 01389 722582 & 755565
Cameron House on Loch Lomond G83 8QZ
e-mail: reservations@cameronhouse.co.uk
web: www.devere.co.uk
dir: M8 (W) junct 30 for Erskine Bridge. A82 for Crianlarich. 14m, at rdbt signed Luss, hotel on right

Cameron House sits in a great location on the banks of Loch Lomond, pulling off a classy act with its stylish blend of tartans and sybaritic contemporary looks. The décor in The Cameron Grill typifies the style with its dark and clubby masculinity - tobacco-brown leather chairs and banquettes, burnished darkwood, and a huge mural showing how clansmen caroused back in the day. It's not all about steak, but they are truly exceptional slabs of protein, cooked on a Josper grill, and the locally-reared stuff is joined by American grain-fed USDA Creekstone and Casterbridge from Devon. If you're a touch peckish and up for some red meat action, take a man-sized 500g rib-eye (we're in metric land here), from Angus-Limousin cattle bred at Cairnhill Farm in Ayrshire. Otherwise, start with ham hock and foie gras terrine with pineapple, parsley purée and dried tomato, then move onto

Gressingham duck with leg meat pastilla, creamed Savoy cabbage, blackberries, and vanilla foam. The hotel is also home to the fine-dining Martin Wishart at Loch Lomond (see entry).

Chef Pavan Panday **Owner** De Vere Hotels **Times** 6.30-10 Closed L all week, D 26 Dec **Prices** Fixed D 3 course £35, Starter £7.25-£14.50, Main £15.95-£55, Dessert £6.25-£13.95, Service added but optional 10% **Wines** 82 bottles over £30, 18 bottles under £30, 13 by glass **Notes** Vegetarian available, Dress restrictions, Smart casual, Civ Wed 220 **Seats** 120, Pr/dining room 16 **Children** Portions, Menu **Parking** 30

Martin Wishart at Loch Lomond

@@@ – *see page 568*

Knockinaam Lodge

PORTPATRICK   MAP 20 NW95

Modern Scottish V

Well-judged, classically-based cooking in splendid Galloway isolation

☎ 01776 810471
DG9 9AD
e-mail: reservations@knockinaamlodge.com
web: www.knockinaamlodge.com
dir: From A77, follow signs to Portpatrick, follow tourist signs to Knockinaam Lodge

The long drive down winding single-track lanes is amply rewarded when you crest the brow of a hill, and there is Knockinaam Lodge ahead of you with the sea crashing against the rocks of the rugged Galloway coastline at the foot of its 30 acres of gardens. Built in laird-of-the-manor style, the Victorian hunting lodge is gloriously cut

off in its own inlet, so isolated in fact, that Eisenhower and Churchill met here safe from spying eyes in wartime. Within, the scene is easy to conjure: a clubby setting of an oak-panelled gentlemen's club, well-stocked with malts, although wreaths of cigar smoke are a thing of the past. Scottish romance continues in spades in the classic country-house restaurant, where soothing pastels are matched with antique chairs at linen tables and swagged toile de jouy drapes - a decorative style that suits to perfection the classically-influenced cuisine. Dinner is a five-course, set-menu affair that changes every day, so you can take it as read that it is all driven by whatever the season has to offer. The kitchen team hauls in the finest materials sourced, shot and caught locally, boosted by ingredients plucked from the gardens or foraged in the woods. Chef Tony Pierce cooks with the confidence to know that less really is more, deploying classic French influences to support well-thought-through flavour combinations. A winter dinner begins with grilled fillet of salted cod with red pepper emulsion and green olive

tapenade, then proceeds to a bowl of celeriac and white onion soup pointed up with a hint of Stilton. After that, slow-roasted fillet of Speyside Angus beef is served with shallot purée, thyme pomme fondant, root vegetables and a port and tarragon reduction. At the end it's a tough call between dessert and cheese, the former being a superbly crafted hot apple crumble soufflé with caramelised milk ice cream. Stocked by a knowledgeable owner, the cellar at Knockinaam is a thing of great joy, running to over 450 bins of globe-trotting, hand-picked bottles.

Chef Anthony Pierce **Owner** David & Sian Ibbotson **Times** 12.30-2/7-9 **Prices** Prices not confirmed **Wines** 7 by glass **Notes** Fixed L 4 course £40, D 5 course £58, Sunday L, Vegetarian menu, Dress restrictions, No jeans, Civ Wed 36 **Seats** 32, Pr/dining room 18 **Children** Menu **Parking** 20

CLYDEBANK   Map 20 NS47

Beardmore Hotel

◉ Modern British ✪

Gently modish cooking on the banks of the Clyde

☎ 0141 951 6000
Beardmore St G81 4SA
e-mail: info@beardmore.scot.nhs.uk
web: www.thebeardmore.com
dir: M8 junct 19, follow signs for Clydeside Expressway to Glasgow road, then A814 (Dumbarton road), then follow Clydebank Business Park signs. Hotel on left

Handy for the M8 and overlooking the River Clyde, the Beardmore is a hive of activity. The large, modern hotel does a roaring business trade and has a health club (yin and yang, perhaps), a bar with its own menu, and a fine-dining restaurant. The latter is an intimate space lacking in natural light but not in charm, with abstract artworks, darkwood tables and a well-drilled service team. Respect is shown to the producers (some of whom are name-checked on the menu), there's a general appreciation of healthy living, and gluten-free dishes are clearly marked as such. Start, perhaps, with mosaic of Scottish game with spiced pear chutney and sourdough croûton served prettily on a black slate. Next up, braised cheek and roast tail of monkfish with rösti potato, creamed cabbage and tomato and chive beurre blanc, and, to finish, vanilla crème brûlée with flapjack biscuits.

Chef Iain Ramsay **Owner** NHS **Times** 6.30-10 Closed Sun, L all week **Prices** Prices not confirmed Service optional **Wines** 12 by glass **Notes** Vegetarian available, Civ Wed 120 **Seats** 36, Pr/dining room 200 **Children** Menu **Parking** 300

CITY OF DUNDEE

DUNDEE   Map 21 NO43

The Landmark Hotel

◉ Modern British

Contemporary setting for modish and trad food

☎ 01382 641122
Kingsway West DD2 5JT
e-mail: meetings@thelandmarkdundee.co.uk
web: www.thelandmarkdundee.co.uk
dir: A90 at Landmark rdbt, west Dundee city centre

The original stone-built baronial mansion bristling with turrets makes an impressive sight, but The Landmark has spread its wings into modern extensions and been brought up to speed with a smart leisure club, spanking new bedrooms and a classy conservatory restaurant. The Garden Room looks into the hotel's lovely grounds and mature gardens from an upmarket setting with linen-swathed tables and moody lighting at dinner. The kitchen steers a crowd-pleasing course with its appealing menus of tried-and-trusted modern ideas. You could encounter turnip soup with haggis croquette, ahead of chargrilled

venison loin teamed with braised red cabbage, carrot and parsnip purée, and thyme jus; fish could put in an appearance as a combo of roast monkfish wrapped in Parma ham, served with dauphinoise potato and rosemary jus. Ending it all, there might be iced hazelnut parfait with rhubarb coulis.

Times 12-2.30/6.30-9.30 Closed L Mon-Sat

CITY OF EDINBURGH

EDINBURGH   Map 21 NT27

Apex City Hotel

◉ Scottish, International ✪

Modern brasserie cooking in a contemporary hotel

☎ 0845 365 0002
61 Grassmarket EH1 2HJ
e-mail: agua@apexhotels.co.uk
web: www.apexhotels.co.uk
dir: Into Lothian Rd at west end of Princes St, 1st left into King Stables Rd. Leads into Grassmarket

With its position on the Grassmarket and contemporary good looks, there's plenty to like about Edinburgh's branch of the Apex group. The Agua restaurant cuts quite a dash too, with its modernist clean lines, banquette seating and mellow contemporary colour tones. No starchy linen tablecloths here. The menu keeps in step with its brasserie-style offerings which match broad

---

Martin Wishart at Loch Lomond

BALLOCH   MAP 20 NS38

Modern French V 🍷NOTABLE WINE LIST

Refined, intelligent cooking on the shores of Loch Lomond

☎ 01389 722504
Cameron House on Loch Lomond G83 8QZ
e-mail: info@mwlochlomond.co.uk
dir: From A82, follow signs for Loch Lomond. Restaurant 1m after Stoneymullan rdbt on right

Standing majestically by the banks of Scotland's largest loch, Cameron House is a multi-turreted baronial manor house of some grandeur. It seems only fitting that it should possess a restaurant to live up to the setting, and in the form of Martin Wishart at Loch Lomond, it does. Mr Wishart is a big fish in the UK dining scene, his Edinburgh restaurant winning awards from far and wide,

and here by the loch it is Graeme Cheevers who delivers the Wishart style to good effect. The heather and tan colour scheme is a reminder of the provenance of much of what is served on the menu, and the room has an air of easy refinement about it, plus a charming service team to match. Attention to detail runs right through. Scottish produce - and the very best Scottish produce at that - figures large on menus that follow a modern French path, built on a bedrock of sound classical thinking, with plenty of contemporary thrills along the way. There's a tasting menu, of course, and a vegetarian version that might even convert a hardened carnivore. From the carte, roasted Orkney scallop is partnered with poached bone marrow, artichoke purée and smoked herring caviar in a compelling first course, but, then again, every dish catches the eye. North Sea cod cheek and brown shrimp gratin comes as a main course with smoked eel, Arran mustard and parsley purée, or you might go for breast of Goosnargh duck with spiced orange purée and roasted chervil root. Nothing is out of place on the plate, and all

the flavours work in harmony. Finish with Valrhona dark chocolate creméux with banana ice cream and peanuts, and be sure not to leave without appreciating the magnificent wine list.

Chef Graeme Cheevers **Owner** Martin Wishart **Times** 12-2.30/6.30-10 Closed 25-26 Dec, 1 Jan, Mon-Tue, L Wed-Fri **Prices** Fixed D 3 course £70, Tasting menu £75, Service added but optional 10% **Wines** 240 bottles over £30, 12 bottles under £30, 12 by glass **Notes** Tasting menu 6 course, Sunday L, Vegetarian menu, Dress restrictions, Smart casual **Seats** 40 **Children** Portions **Parking** 150

appeal with an inventive streak. Crab and lime bonbon with mango and basil is one way to kick off, or there may be rabbit terrine with cabbage and ceps, pea purée and pickled carrot. Main-course duo of lamb (seared rump and slow-cooked shoulder) is cooked with skill, and comes with aubergine, goats' cheese and potato bake. There's a market fish dish of the day and steak, too, plus desserts such as home-made Jaffa cake, which consists of syrup-spiked sponge, marmalade jelly filling, chocolate ganache and orange anglaise.

Chef James McCann **Owner** Norman Springford **Times** 12-2/4-9.45 Closed Xmas **Prices** Fixed L 2 course £14.95-£19.95, Fixed D 3 course £14.95-£19.95, Starter £5.50-£6.95, Main £14.50-£19.95, Dessert £5.95-£9.95 **Wines** 15 bottles under £30, 11 by glass **Notes** Pre-theatre menu available until 6.30pm daily, Sunday L, Vegetarian available, Civ Wed 80 **Seats** 60, Pr/dining room 60 **Children** Portions, Menu **Parking** On street & NCP

Apex International Hotel

◎◎ Modern Scottish

Modern hotel with views of the Castle

☎ 0845 365 0002
31-35 Grassmarket EH1 2HS
e-mail: heights@apexhotels.co.uk
web: www.apexhotels.co.uk
dir: Into Lothian Rd at west end of Princes St, then 1st left into King Stables Rd, leads into Grassmarket

The full-drop windows that constitute one side of the fifth-floor Heights dining room at the Apex International frame stunning views of the Castle, theatrically illuminated on its mound after dark. Here, a fixed-price menu deals in modern cooking using good Scottish ingredients in stimulating ways. Start perhaps with a two-tone mousse of red and yellow peppers, served with a polenta muffin and a pesto-ish basil and pine nut purée. That might lead on to sea bass and fennel with puréed artichoke and sweet cicely in a sauce of liquorice and red wine, or to braised Scottish beef cheeks with caramelised shallots, salsify crisps and barley. Finish fragrantly with lavender pannacotta, summer berries and sabayon gratin. Cheeses come with beetroot and apple chutney and home-made walnut and fruit bread.

Chef John Newton **Owner** Norman Springford **Times** 5.30-10 Closed Sun-Mon, L all week **Prices** Starter £5.50-£8.25, Main £14.95-£22.50, Dessert fr £7.50, Service optional **Wines** 13 bottles over £30, 16 bottles under £30, 9 by glass **Notes** Pre-theatre Tue-Sat 2 course £30 for 2 people, Vegetarian available, Civ Wed 100 **Seats** 120 **Children** Menu **Parking** 65

Café Royal

◎ Modern Scottish

Brasserie food in a heritage Scots-Parisian landmark

☎ 0131 556 1884
19 West Register St EH2 2AA
e-mail: info@caferoyal.org.uk
dir: Just off Princes St, close to Waverley Station

A Victorian plumber, one Robert Hume, put up this exquisite slice of Parisian rococo in the 1860s, with the intention of taking Edinburgh's breath away with the latest designs in bathroom furniture. Alas (though it's only a small alas), the washbasins and bathtubs never saw the light of day, as the place was commandeered to become the latest venue for the recently demolished Café Royal, which had once stood across the road. The stained glass, plaster mouldings and ceramic murals are as gasp-inducing now as they must have been when horse-drawn carriages clattered along outside, and the place was saved from the indignity of being sold to Woolworths (who remembers them now?) in 1969. This remarkable venue is thus preserved as a setting for modern brasserie cuisine, of the likes of accurately cooked mussels in a Thai broth of coconut, ginger, coriander and chilli, generous crab linguine with tiger prawns and chorizo, prosciutto-wrapped lamb with garlic mash in red wine, and warm chocolate and raspberry torte with vanilla ice-cream.

Times 12-2.30/5-9.30

Castle Terrace Restaurant

◎◎◎ – see page 570

Chop Chop

◎ Chinese 🌶

Reliable Manchurian café dining

☎ 0131 221 1155
248 Morrison St, Haymarket EH3 8DT
e-mail: info@chop-chop.co.uk
dir: From Haymarket Station, restaurant 150 yds up Morrison St

Specialising in the culinary ways of China's Manchurian northeast (Dongbei) region, this enjoyable venue is effectively a Chinese café. The menu makes a courteous point of explaining the format to newbies, but basically anyone familiar with dim sum ordering will understand the drill. Choose from a slate of jiaozi or guo tie dumplings (boiled and fried, respectively), and get stuck in as the dishes arrive. The main menu deals in many well-rendered northern Chinese standards, among them crispy beef in ginger and vinegar, Changchun hotpot, and pork with ginger and coriander. Boiled and stir-fried noodle dishes are also highly reliable. The DIY dessert of sugar-string apple or pancake, which you crisp up for yourself by dunking them in iced water, is an entertaining way to finish, or there are yet more dumplings to ponder, of mixed fruits or peanuts. There's a sister branch in Leith (see entry).

Chef Yu Xu Wei **Owner** Jian Wang **Times** 12-2/5.30-10 **Prices** Prices not confirmed Service added but optional 10%, Groups min 5 service 10% **Wines** 7 by glass **Notes** Unlimited banquet £19.50 (min 2 people), Sunday L, Vegetarian available **Seats** 60

Chop Chop Leith

◎ Chinese

Chop Chop's cooking brought to Leith

☎ 0131 553 1818
76 Commercial St, Commercial Quay, Leith EH6 6LX
e-mail: info@chop-chop.co.uk
dir: From Ocean Terminal follow Commercial St for 400 yds

Opposite the Scottish Office in the heart of Leith, this is the younger sister of the original Chop Chop (see entry), with a more upmarket vibe: glass-topped metal tables, red-upholstered chairs, and Chinese fans and prints on the walls. The menus at both are identical, concentrating on the cuisine of Dongbei, and staff are as charming and helpful as they are at Morrison Street. Go for a banquet or order a selection of dishes and create your own beanfeast: prawn, vegetable and chicken boiled and fried dumplings zinging with flavour, tender strips of stir-fried chilli beef, noodles in a sweet-and-sour sauce with crisp battered shreds of tender chicken breast and mushrooms, and aubergine flash-fried with garlic and spring onions. Don't leave without trying the fruit dumplings with vanilla ice cream.

Times 12-2/6-10 Closed L Mon-Fri

Dalmahoy, A Marriott Hotel & Country Club

◎ Modern, Traditional

Georgian manor serving up a genuine Scottish flavour

☎ 0131 333 1845
Kirknewton EH27 8EB
e-mail: mhrs.edigs.frontdesk@marriotthotels.com
web: www.marriottdalmahoy.co.uk
dir: Edinburgh City bypass (A720) turn onto A71 towards Livingston, hotel on left in 2m

The impressive baronial manor has a long and illustrious history and is these days part of the Marriott group. It's handy for Edinburgh, but there's plenty to keep you on site, not least the two golf courses woven into 1,000 acres of wooded parkland. In the hotel's Pentland Restaurant, a split-level layout means everyone gets a view of the rolling hills (the Pentland Hills no less) whilst tucking into the unfussy, regionally-minded menu. Start with Campbell's haggis spring roll - a new take on an old favourite - with red cabbage and pea shoot salad and plum sauce dressing, or air-dried ham with pickled melon and rocket. Next up, pappardelle pasta is served with slow-cooked rabbit, ceps and rosemary sauce, or go for hot-smoked bream with lemon and parsley risotto. There are steaks and a daily roast, too, and for dessert,

continued

EDINBURGH *continued*

something like passionfruit cheesecake with raspberries from a nearby farm and ginger nut crumbs.

Chef James Thomson **Owner** Marriott Hotels Ltd **Times** 7-10 Closed L all week **Prices** Prices not confirmed Service optional **Wines** 15 by glass **Notes** Sunday L, Vegetarian available, Dress restrictions, Smart casual, Civ Wed 300 **Seats** 150, Pr/dining room 18 **Children** Portions, Menu **Parking** 350

Divino Enoteca

Modern Italian **NEW** NOTABLE WINE LIST

Exemplary Italian cooking and wines

☎ 0131 225 1770
5 Merchant St EH1 2QD
e-mail: info@divinoedinburgh.com
dir: Near National Museum of Scotland and The Grassmarket

Leave the cobbled street and descend the stairs leading into Divino Enoteca's stygian gloom punctured by candles and spotlights picking out the artwork on the bare-brick walls, a number of wine displays underlining that this is 'not just a wine bar but a wine library', to quote the restaurant. Clued-up staff are as knowledgeable about the wines as they are about the all-Italian menu, with the cooking based on the very best Italian produce. Pan-fried scallops on a bed of salad drizzled with sweet chilli sauce

is a simple but effective starter, an alternative to one of the hand-made pastas: perhaps gnocchi with crisp Italian bacon, peppers and courgettes topped with parmesan and balsamic. Main courses can be as straightforward as pan-fried fillet of sea bream on orange-flavoured risotto with a julienne of vegetables, or as complex as baked quail wrapped in pancetta, stuffed with sausage meat and chestnuts, on a bed of spinach and honey-glazed butternut squash. The tiramisù here is in a league of its own.

Chef Lorenzo Magnani **Owner** Tony Crolla **Times** 4-mdnt Closed Sun **Prices** Fixed D 3 course £15-£30, Starter £5-£10, Main £8-£16, Dessert £4-£7, Groups min 6 service 10% **Notes** Vegetarian available **Seats** 85, Pr/dining room 14 **Children** Portions **Parking** On street

The Dungeon Restaurant at Dalhousie Castle

Traditional European

Creative cuisine in a truly unique setting

☎ 01875 820153
Dalhousie Castle & Aqueous Spa, Bonnyrigg EH19 3JB
e-mail: info@dalhousiecastle.co.uk
web: www.dalhousiecastle.co.uk
dir: From A720 (Edinburgh bypass) take A7 south, turn right onto B704. Castle 0.5m on right

Dalhousie Castle is a pukka 13th-century fortress in acreages of wooded parkland on the banks of the River

Esk, so you know you're in for something a bit special when you're heading for the Dungeon Restaurant. And the reality does not disappoint: the barrel-vaulted chamber comes with a full complement of romantic medieval candlelit vibes and enough weaponry - suits of armour, battleaxes and broadswords - to sort out the French all over again. Mentioning our cross-Channel cousins, the cooking here has its roots in French classicism, and is built on top-class ingredients with plenty of luxury factor. But the kitchen doesn't rely on the one-off setting and posh ingredients for its effect: a spirit of eclectic creativity reworks it all with a clever contemporary spin that might see wild garlic and cream cheese terrine matched with roast plum tomato jelly and Bloody Mary foam, ahead of lavender and honey-glazed pork fillet served with artichoke barigoule and onion textures. To finish, consider date and walnut soufflé with coffee mocha sauce and honey madeleines.

Chef Francois Giraud **Owner** Robert & Gina Parker **Times** 7-10 Closed L all week **Prices** Service optional **Wines** 15 by glass **Notes** ALC 5 course £49.50, Sunday L £18.95-£23.95, Vegetarian available, Civ Wed 100 **Seats** 45, Pr/dining room 100 **Children** Portions **Parking** 150

Castle Terrace Restaurant

EDINBURGH **MAP 21 NT27**

Scottish, French V NOTABLE WINE LIST

Refined, intelligent cooking near the castle

☎ 0131 229 1222
33-35 Castle Ter EH1 2EL
e-mail: info@castleterracerestaurant.com
dir: Close Edinburgh Castle, at the bottom of Lady Lawson St on Castle Terrace

Since Castle Terrace opened in 2010 it has shot straight into the top flight of Edinburgh's Premier League dining destinations, benefitting from a strong synergy with its sibling restaurant The Kitchin (see entry). Chef-patron Dominic Jack made his bones in big-name Parisian kitchens, fine-tuning his technical skills before coming home to Edinburgh to set up Castle Terrace in conjunction with his old mate Tom Kitchin. The two restaurants bear a

resemblance in their interior design aesthetic: the Georgian townhouse is overlaid with a glossy fine-dining sheen comprising opulent purple fabrics matched with darkwood tables, dove-grey walls, designer wallpapers and a shimmering golden ceiling. The two operations also share a common culinary direction, although Jack is his own man. His modern Scottish food follows the 'from nature to plate' ethos printed on the carte, and is driven by a passion verging on obsession for seasonal Scottish ingredients from the best regional supply lines. This is elegant and precise cooking with a noticeable French accent in the willingness to use the kinds of earthy raw ingredients that others shy away from - perhaps a starter of crispy pan-fried ox tongue served with a quail's egg and celeriac soup, while game season might produce roasted mallard, partridge or hare à la royale. An autumn menu kicks off with grouse pâté en croûte served with pear sauce, prune jelly and port, followed by saddle of Winton Estate roe deer with quince Tatin, seared pumpkin, and chestnut and pepper sauce, all looking as

pretty as a picture and realised with high-level technical skills that ensure flavours are all full-on and as clear as a bell. The humble blackberry stars at dessert, in a layered blackberry and black cardamom pannacotta pointed up by lemon ice cream and black cardamom sorbet. The cooking is solidly supported by efficient staff who display excellent menu knowledge, and an intelligently composed wine list. For those on an austerity-era budget, the set lunch menu offers good value.

Chef Dominic Jack **Owner** Dominic Jack **Times** 12-2/6.30-10 Closed Xmas, New Year (subject to change), Sun-Mon **Prices** Fixed L 3 course £26.50, Tasting menu £70, Starter £13-£17, Main £25-£34, Dessert £9-£11, Service optional, Groups min 8 service 10% **Wines** 286 bottles over £30, 6 bottles under £30, 18 by glass **Notes** Tasting menu 6 course, Vegetarian menu, Dress restrictions, Smart casual **Seats** 65, Pr/dining room 16 **Children** Portions **Parking** NCP, on street

La Favorita

◉ Modern Italian

Log-fired pizzas and contemporary Italian cooking

☎ 0131 554 2430 & 555 5564
325-331 Leith Walk EH6 8SA
e-mail: info@la-favorita.com
dir: On A900 from Edinburgh to South Leith

La Favorita has had a bit of a makeover, with a more contemporary colour scheme and new seating booths. It's a large space, busy and buzzy, people drawn by the authentic Italian cooking, with produce imported from the mother country. Wonderful crisp-based pizzas are made in the log-fired ovens and take in simple margherita and the luxurious mare blue (topped with prawns and king scallops), with the rest of the long menu a slate of crowd-pleasers. Pasta never fails to impress - perhaps ravioli alla norcina (stuffed with porcini, ricotta and parmesan, topped with Italian sausage, rocket and tomatoes), and elsewhere there may be baked pork ribs with a spicy dipping sauce, followed by pesto-crusted swordfish steak, served on sautéed spinach with capers and peanuts, or vitello milanese. Desserts cross frontiers, so crème brûlée may appear alongside Italian stars like tiramisù.

Chef Japeck Splawski **Owner** Tony Crolla **Times** 12-11 Closed 25 Dec-1 Jan, All-day dining **Prices** Fixed L 2 course fr £11.95, Fixed D 3 course fr £27, Tasting menu fr £33, Starter £3.95-£7.70, Main £7.95-£25.95, Dessert £2.50-£7.95, Service added but optional 10%, Groups min 10 service 10% **Wines** 4 bottles over £30, 26 bottles under £30, 7 by glass **Notes** Sunday L, Vegetarian available **Seats** 120, Pr/dining room 30 **Children** Portions, Menu **Parking** On street

Galvin Brasserie de Luxe

◉ French NEW

Timeless French brasserie dishes à la Galvin

☎ 0131 2228888
The Caledonian, A Waldorf Astoria Hotel, Princes St EH1 2AB
e-mail: guest_caledonian@waldorfastoria.com

The well-composed menu at the more accessible of the Galvin brothers' Edinburgh operations (see also entry for The Pompadour) pleases diners hankering for a hit of cross-Channel classicism built on top-class Scottish produce. Housed in the luxurious Caledonian Waldorf Astoria, the setting also aims straight at the heart of Francophiles with its Parisian brasserie-styled looks: there are navy-blue banquettes, darkwood flooring and tables around a circular island seafood bar, and waiting staff in time-honoured black-and-white uniforms. As for the food, it's a trip to France without needing to fly: steak tartare, Burgundian snails, terrine of chicken, ham hock and foie gras with sauce gribiche are all present and correct, while mains take in the rich flavours and textures of duck confit with boudin noir and red wine sauce, or pork cutlet with pommes mousseline and Agen prunes. Classic desserts take in tarte Tatin with crème fraîche and rum baba with Chantilly.

Owner Chris & Jeff Galvin **Times** 12-3/6-10.30 **Prices** Fixed L 2 course £15.50, Fixed D 3 course £18.50, Starter £5.50-£19, Main £12.50-£26.50, Dessert £5.50-£10.50

La Garrigue

◉◉ Traditional French, Mediterranean 🍷NOTABLE WINE LIST

Charming French bistro in the heart of Edinburgh

☎ 0131 557 3032
31 Jeffrey St EH1 1DH
e-mail: reservations@lagarrigue.co.uk
web: www.lagarrigue.co.uk
dir: Halfway along Royal Mile towards Holyrood Palace, turn left at lights into Jeffrey St

To paraphrase Rupert Brooke, this bustling bistro is a corner of Edinburgh's Old Town that will be forever France. Chef Jean-Michel Gauffre has brought the honest rustic cooking of his native Languedoc into a suitably contemporary rustic interior kitted out with delicious plain wooden tables and chairs hand-made by artist and woodcarver Tim Stead. There are no foams or jellies here, just straight down-the-line authentique French country dishes done properly. The menu is a joy to read - rabbit rillettes with herb and lentil salad, or fish soup with croûtons and rouille to start, and as Gauffre hails from the heartlands of cassoulet, dig into his version of the rich stew of pork, duck, Toulouse sausage and white beans, or go for a slow-cooked stew of beef cheeks in a Provençal sauce of red wine, tomatoes and olives, and finish with a lavender crème brûlée. La Garrigue has clearly given Edinburgh's foodies a formula they like as the original Jeffrey Street operation has spread its wings into branches in Leith and the New Town.

Chef Jean-Michel Gauffre **Owner** Jean-Michel Gauffre **Times** 12-3/6.30-10.30 Closed 26-27 Dec, 1-2 Jan **Prices** Fixed L 2 course £12.50, Fixed D 3 course £30, Starter £4.50-£8, Main £9.50-£18, Dessert £4.50-£6, Service added but optional 10% **Wines** 20 bottles over £30, 30 bottles under £30, 11 by glass **Notes** Sunday L, Vegetarian available **Seats** 48, Pr/dining room 11 **Children** Portions **Parking** On street, NCP

Hadrian's

◉ Modern Scottish

Classy brasserie in landmark hotel

☎ 0131 557 5000 & 557 2414
The Balmoral Hotel, 1 Princes St EH2 2EQ
e-mail: hadrians.balmoral@roccofortecollection.com
dir: Follow city centre signs. Hotel at E end of Princes St, adjacent to Waverley Station

Not to be outfaced by its fine-dining sibling at the landmark Balmoral Hotel (see entry for Number One), Hadrian's, the more casual venue, is a useful address in its own right. The handsome art-deco styling of the chic brasserie is quite a head turner with its walnut floors, darkwood tables and subtle shades of violet and lime, while nattily turned-out staff in long white aprons and black waistcoats set the right tone for its repertoire of European-accented, yet unmistakably Scottish, dishes. Tuna carpaccio with oriental salad, sesame and coriander dressing is a starter that could pop up anywhere in the world, but move on to loin of Perthshire venison, served tender and pink, with red cabbage and gnocchi, or Isle of Gigha halibut with crab brandade and dill sauce, and you're clearly knee-deep in Scottish terroir. Awaiting at the finale are classic ideas - tiramisù with Baileys ice cream, or classic vanilla crème brûlée.

Times 12-2.30/6.30-10.30

Harvey Nichols Forth Floor Restaurant

◉ British, Modern, International 🍷NOTABLE WINE LIST 🍽

City views and modern Scottish cooking

☎ 0131 524 8350
30-34 St Andrew Square EH2 2AD
e-mail: forthfloor.reservations@harveynichols.com
web: www.harveynichols.com
dir: Located on St Andrew Square at the east end of George Street, 2 min walk from Princes Street

Harvey Nic's has a habit of naming its classy restaurants after the floor on which they are found. In the case of the Edinburgh outpost, the name is not further evidence of a

continued

EDINBURGH *continued*

decline in national standards of literacy: from its open-plan perch on the store's top floor you get 360-degree views of the Edinburgh cityscape and, of course, the Forth. The kitchen sends out dishes as modish as the glossy clientele who like to take the weight off their Louboutin's after a hard day's shopping. The foodie paradise here comprises the adjacent food hall, brasserie and seafood bar as well as the restaurant, where an excellent chicken liver parfait with apple and pear chutney and toasted sourdough bread leads on to Toulouse sausage with warm potato salad, grain mustard and the contrasting crunch of onion rings. Rounding things off, there may be damson parfait with olive oil and thyme sablé.

Chef Stuart Muir **Owner** Harvey Nichols **Times** 12-3/6-10 Closed 25 Dec, 1 Jan, D Sun-Mon, 24 & 26 Dec, 2 Jan **Prices** Tasting menu £60-£85, Starter £6-£11, Main £15-£23, Dessert £7-£9, Service added but optional 10% **Wines** 266 bottles over £30, 46 bottles under £30, 16 by glass **Notes** Tasting menu 6 course, Afternoon tea £20 Sun-Fri 3-4pm, Sunday L £30, Vegetarian available **Seats** 47, Pr/dining room 14 **Children** Portions **Parking** 20

The Honours

◉◉ Modern French ♻

Classic French brasserie food Wishart style

☎ 0131 220 2513
58a North Castle St EH2 3LU
e-mail: info@thehonours.co.uk
dir: In city centre

Opened in 2011, here is the latest side project of Edinburgh's hot-shot chef Martin Wishart. In the heart of the New Town, it aims at the style of a classic French brasserie, a restaurant mode that has long enjoyed great purchase in the Scottish capital. It's split into a large bar area with comfortable seating for informal eating, with restaurant tables on the next level up. Service is impeccably practised and professional, and the kitchen's orientation is modern French food interpreted through quality Scots produce, with accurate, well-honed flavours and eye-catching presentation. Pork and duck rillettes are wonderfully earthy and savoury, accompanied by spiced prune chutney, cornichons and toasted hazelnuts for texture in a bravura starter. Alternatives take in crab Marie Rose, sea bream tartare, and portions of jamón Bellota. Main courses offer grilled steaks, ox cheeks bordelaise or lamb tagine, as well as beautifully expressive fish dishes like sautéed fillets of John Dory with leeks and mussels topped with an evanescent curry foam and sauced with Sauternes. A crème brûlée to finish is boosted with Kirsch and textured with marinated cherries.

Chef Paul Tamburrini **Owner** Martin Wishart
Times 12-2.30/6-10 Closed Xmas, 1-3 Jan, Sun-Mon **Prices** Fixed L 3 course £17.50, Fixed D 3 course £19.50, Starter £6.75-£10.50, Main £14-£32.50, Dessert £4.75-£7.95, Service optional, Groups min 6 service 10% **Wines** 34 bottles over £30, 22 bottles under £30, 20 by glass **Notes** Fixed D Tue-Fri 6-7pm, Vegetarian available **Seats** 65 **Children** Portions, Menu **Parking** On street

Hotel du Vin Edinburgh

◉ Modern British, French ♻

Bags of HdV style and sound brasserie cooking

☎ 0131 247 4900 & 0844 736 9255
11 Bristo Place EH1 1EZ
e-mail: reception.edinburgh@hotelduvin.com
dir: M8 junct 1, A720 (signed Kilmarnock/W Calder/Edinburgh W). Right at fork, follow A720 signs, merge onto A720. Take exit signed A703. At rdbt take A702/Biggar Rd. 3.5m. Right into Lauriston Pl which becomes Forrest Rd. Right at Bedlam Theatre. Hotel on right

The former city asylum is the setting for HdV's Edinburgh outpost. These days the setting is considerably more cheerful thanks to the group's trademark clubby look of well-worn leather seats and woody textures. There's a splendid tartan-clad whisky snug, plus a buzzy mezzanine bar overlooking the bistro, which offers the usual nods to France with its wine-related paraphernalia and hearty, rustic contemporary brasserie cooking that the group specialises in everywhere from Royal Tunbridge Wells to the Scottish capital. An Isle of Mull cheese soufflé is the signature starter, which you might follow with a classic plate of haggis, neeps and tatties, or hake paella.

Chef Gavin Lindsay **Owner** Hotel du Vin & Malmaison
Times 12-2.30/5.30-10.30 Closed D 25 Dec **Prices** Fixed L 2 course £15.50, Fixed D 3 course £19.50, Starter £5.95-£11.50, Main £14.75-£29.50, Dessert £6.95, Service added but optional 10% **Wines** 150 bottles over £30, 75 bottles under £30, 18 by glass **Notes** Pre-theatre 2 course with wine £14.50, Sun brunch £19.95, Sunday L, Vegetarian available **Seats** 88, Pr/dining room 26 **Children** Portions **Parking** NCP

Hotel Missoni Edinburgh

◉◉ Italian

Modern Italian cucina in a glamorous Royal Mile hotel

☎ 0131 220 6666 & 240 1666
1 George IV Bridge EH1 1AD
e-mail: cucina.edinburgh@hotelmissoni.com

This luxurious style-slave hotel delivers a colourful hit of in-your-face Italian glamour amid the Royal Mile's dour grandeur. The boutique bolt-hole oozes contemporary chic, with loud and proud design touches throughout - check out those gigantic vases sitting in the lobby windows - and its rooms come fully loaded with all the latest gizmos. The food, obviously enough, is Italian too, served in the bustling, light-flooded Cucina, where la dolce vita is enthusiastically celebrated amid a lively décor of bold slabs of paintbox colours and psychedelic abstract art. Chef Mattia Camorani comes from the Locatelli stable and offers a gently-modernised take on Italian cooking. Pasta and risotto dishes hit the spot - linguine with octopus, chilli and tomato is simple but oh-so good. Elsewhere, risotto with nettles and

Gorgonzola might catch the eye, followed, perhaps, by saddle of rabbit with polenta and grilled radicchio, or steamed halibut with lentil stew. For pudding, how about a boozy baba soaked in Grand Marnier and served with orange sauce and yoghurt ice cream?

Times 12.30-3/6-10 Closed D 25 Dec

The Howard

◉ Modern Scottish ♻

Modern Scottish cooking in a swanky hotel

☎ 0131 557 3500
34 Great King St EH3 6QH
e-mail: reception@thehoward.com
web: www.thehoward.com
dir: E on Queen St, 2nd left, Dundas St. Through 3 lights, right, hotel on left

Just a short stroll off the bustling main drag of Princes Street in Edinburgh's New Town, a trio of elegant Georgian townhouses have been stylishly converted into the small-scale luxury of The Howard. If it's personal service you want, there are butlers on call, while the décor hits the heights of opulence, matching Georgian period authenticity with rich fabrics, oil paintings and period furniture. Take it all in over pre-dinner drinks in the drawing room before settling into The Atholl restaurant; with space for just 14 diners, the setting amid hand-painted murals dating from the 1820s is something rather special. The kitchen deals in modern Scottish ideas, beginning perhaps with pan-fried Mallaig scallops with celeriac purée, crispy pancetta and lemon oil, followed by guinea fowl suprême with wilted spinach, château potatoes and bourguignon garnish. Finish with excellent cheeses from Mellis, or warm plum pudding with crème anglaise and vanilla ice cream.

Chef William Poncelet **Owner** Ricky Kapoor
Times 12-2/6-9.30 **Prices** Fixed L 2 course £28-£36, Fixed D 3 course £34-£40, Tasting menu £55-£80, Starter £7-£9, Main £21-£36, Dessert £5.50-£9.50, Service optional **Wines** 50 bottles over £30, 10 bottles under £30, 10 by glass **Notes** Pre-theatre menu available, Sunday L, Vegetarian available, Civ Wed 40 **Seats** 14, Pr/dining room 40 **Children** Portions **Parking** 10

Iggs

◉ Modern 🔺 NOTABLE WINE LIST 🕲

Enterprising modern Spanish cooking in the city centre

☎ 0131 557 8184
15-19 Jeffrey St EH1 1DR
e-mail: info@iggs.co.uk
web: www.iggs.co.uk
dir: In heart of Old Town, 0.5m from castle, just off Royal Mile

Consisting of a restaurant and adjacent barioja (tapas bar), Iggs is the lifetime work of Ignacio Campos (Iggy to one and all) and 2014 sees it celebrate its 25th year. The restaurant has contemporary good looks and a fun, positive approach to life: there are no starchy tablecloths, black and white photos hang on the walls, and the music has a Latin vibe. The menu is full of Spanish heart and soul. Start with sopa de judias blanca (white bean soup - the menu is bilingual), which is full of flavour, or go for grilled sardines with black olive tapenade and cauliflower couscous. The famous acorn-fed Ibérian pigs might feature in a main course with spinach and olive oil purée and Rioja jus - the meat as tender and delightfully sticky as can be - or go for deep-fried hake served on the bone. Desserts can be as traditional as churros with a warm chocolate sauce.

Chef Mark Spence-Ishaq **Owner** Mr I Campos
Times 12-2.30/6-10.30 Closed Sun **Prices** Prices not confirmed Service added but optional 10% **Wines** 50 bottles over £30, 73 bottles under £30, 18 by glass **Notes** Vegetarian available **Seats** 80, Pr/dining room 40 **Children** Portions **Parking** On street, NCP

The Indian Cavalry Club

◉ Indian

The West End's Indian star

☎ 0131 220 0138
22 Coates Crescent EH3 7AF
e-mail: info@indiancavalryclub.co.uk
dir: Few mins walk from Haymarket Railway Station & the west end of Princes St

Edinburgh's slickest Indian restaurant offers a classy quartet of dining spaces all kitted out in an upmarket modern vein with wooden floors, coffee and cream hues, and tended by well-drilled staff happy to talk you through the menu. As with any restaurant that stands out from the herd, dedication to top-class materials is key to the Pan-Indian repertoire on offer here. An impressive regiment of pakora and tandoori classics leads the charge into dishes that span the sub-continent, running the gamut of Kashmiri, Punjabi, Jaipuri, Afghan and Keralan specialities, all with clearly-defined, fresh flavours. Red Fort lamb delivers tender tandoori-cooked meat in a mild sauce of yoghurt and ground almonds - perfect with a side dish of sag makkai (spinach with sweetcorn) - or you might go for a blowout seafood banquet comprising tandoori salmon tikka, sea bass chargrilled with mustard seeds, tomato and coriander, and jumbo king prawns curried with spring onions sweetcorn and potatoes.

Chef M D Qayum, Biplob **Owner** Shahid Chowdhury
Times 12-5/5.30-11.30 **Prices** Fixed L 3 course fr £8.95, Fixed D 3 course £26.90-£38.90, Starter £4.85-£9.95, Main £11.25-£24.50, Dessert £3.85-£6.50, Service added but optional 10% **Wines** 9 bottles over £30, 23 bottles under £30, 2 by glass **Notes** Sunday L, Vegetarian available **Seats** 120, Pr/dining room 50 **Parking** On street

Jamie's Italian Restaurant

◉ Italian NEW V

The Oliver empire lands in Edinburgh

☎ 0131 202 5452
The Assembly Rooms, 54 George St EH2 2LR

The second of Jamie Oliver's mushrooming chain to open north of the border, the Edinburgh branch has set up shop in the magnificent Georgian pomp of the Assembly Rooms. Beneath huge crystal chandeliers hanging from ornate plasterwork ceilings it's all very matey, with elbow-to-elbow bench seating and marble topped tables overseen by eager young staff. Hams and sausages hang above the bar to get you in the mood for sharing 'planks' of artisan cured meats or Italian cheeses, while the menu offers an affordable, unfussy roll-call of the lively Latin food that the man himself has championed on the telly for so many years. Crispy fried squid with garlic mayo, lemon and chilli is a typical offering from the antipasti department, while pasta dishes run to wild rabbit tagliolini with garlic, herbs, mascarpone and lemon. Hearty mains take in the likes of chargrilled prime rib with wild mushrooms and endives.

Times 12-11 **Prices** Prices not confirmed
Notes Vegetarian menu **Children** Menu

Kanpai Sushi

◉ Japanese 🕲

On-trend Japanese fast food in the cultural district

☎ 0131 228 1602
8-10 Grindlay St EH3 9AS
dir: Parallel to Lothian Road behind Usher Hall

Kanpai is the Japanese for 'cheers!', and neatly sums up the hospitable informality of this sushi bar near the Usher Hall and Lyceum Theatre. Split between two rooms, the interiors utilise the light wood tones favoured by such places, with chefs on view chopping and sculpting amid an air of minimalist purity. The expected things are done well, with diamond-bright seasonings, ultra-fresh fish and bags of umami underpinning the menus. Miso soup and squid tempura with dipping sauce kick things off well, there are well-made sticky maki rolls of tuna or crispy chicken and avocado, topped with fish roe, and of course an array of fine sushi and sashimi. Regularly replenished side-plates of hot wasabi dumplings and pickled ginger keep you going, while you wait perhaps for salmon teriyaki or a piece of expertly grilled sirloin. Sake, plum wine and Japanese beers flesh out the drinks list.

Chef Jack Zhang **Owner** Monica Wang
Times 12-2.30/5-10.30 Closed Mon **Prices** Starter £2.50-£9.90, Main £7.90-£14.90, Dessert £4.20, Service optional **Wines** 3 bottles over £30, 5 bottles under £30, 3 by glass **Notes** Vegetarian available **Seats** 45, Pr/dining room 8 **Children** Portions **Parking** On street

The Kitchin

◉◉◉◉ – *see page 574*

The Kitchin

Scottish, French V

Benchmark modern Scottish cooking of great impact

☎ 0131 555 1755
78 Commercial Quay, Leith EH6 6LX
e-mail: info@thekitchin.com
dir: In Leith opposite Scottish Executive building

Tom and Michaela Kitchin opened in a converted bonded whisky warehouse in the Leith redevelopment in 2006. It's been a wild ride since then, involving TV appearances for Tom (never the most obviously self-publicising of chefs) and a reputation that has rippled out from the waterfront of the Scottish capital to far-distant shores. That reputation has been built on a thoroughgoing approach to freshness and seasonality, of course (who doesn't claim that?), but here, the seriousness of intent is reflected in the buying of meat and fish in as close to its natural state as possible, so that all the butchering and filleting is done on the premises. The dedication and skill that involves reflects Kitchin's classical training under Ducasse and Koffmann, two of the French maîtres still casting long shadows over the global restaurant world, but the focus is naturally on Scotland's own produce (from spoots to Highland Wagyu), in a philosophy where the tagline 'From nature to plate' actually means something. What really distinguishes Kitchin's cooking, though, is that it is conceived first and foremost with attention to impact on the palate, rather than ideas in the head. The spoots (razor clams) from Arisaig are cooked à point, having nothing of the leathery blandness so often encountered, adorned with diced vegetables, crumbled chorizo and preserved lemon for a mouthful of fabulous sea-savoury richness. Marine flora is brought widely into play, with sea purslane a salty, textural garnish to potato and seaweed terrine with braised squid, and to seared scallops with puréed fennel. It's hard to tear yourself away from the bounty of the seas, when mains might include poached Scrabster monkfish cooked on its iron rod of a bone with squid and winkles and saffron, accompanied dramatically by black squid pasta. Meats are unmissable too, however, perhaps duck breast and leg pastilla with a caramelised endive tart and a dazzling take on classic orange sauce, or Orkney beef shin, braised osso buco-style and served with potatoes cooked with the bone marrow. There are nods to much older traditions in these modern compositions, which give the diner welcome relief from the relentless avante-garderie found elsewhere, and also a real understanding of how flavours develop to the point of utmost concentration through the ancient arts of cooking and seasoning, rather than goofball technological intervention.

Dessert might be simple rhubarb cheesecake with jelly and sorbet, or a more daring coffee soufflé with an ice cream made from Alloa's Midnight Sun stout.

Chef Tom Kitchin **Owner** Tom & Michaela Kitchin **Times** 12.15-3/6.45-10 Closed Xmas, New Year, 1st 2 wks Jan, Sun-Mon **Prices** Fixed L 3 course £26.50, Tasting menu £75, Starter £16.50-£25, Main £28-£40, Dessert £10.50-£14, Service optional, Groups min 8 service 10% **Wines** 250 bottles over £30, 20 by glass **Notes** Tasting menu 6 course, Vegetarian menu **Seats** 50 **Children** Portions **Parking** 30, On site parking evening only, all day Sat

EDINBURGH *continued*

Locanda De Gusti

◉◉ Italian ○

Neapolitan-accented cooking in the heart of the city

☎ 0131 558 9581
7-11 East London St EH7 4BN
e-mail: info@locandadegusti.com
dir: Corner of Broughton & East London St, 5 min walk from the Playhouse

Neapolitan-inspired food, authentically executed, gives this city centre restaurant an edge when it comes to eating Italian in Edinburgh. It looks nicely contemporary in a clean-lined minimalist sort of way; think terracotta floors, whitewashed walls hung with bright artworks, bare tables and an open-plan kitchen. A new wine and beer cellar is spot on for pre- and post-prandial drinking. There's a good amount of great Scottish seafood on the menu, plus a generous sprinkling of imported Italian ingredients. Start with foccacia topped with cream of salted cod, smoked pancetta and Sardinian pecorino cheese, before a pasta dish such as linguine with plenty of top-notch seafood (langoustines, prawns, squid, mussels and clams). Among secondi might be braised Scottish Borders lamb shank or breaded escalope of swordfish with a sweet Sicilian-style ratatouille, and, to finish, how about tortino ricotta e pere?

Chef Rosario Sartore **Owner** Rosario Sartore
Times 12-2.30/5-11 Closed Sun **Prices** Fixed L 2 course fr £10.95, Tasting menu £30-£50, Starter £4.95-£8.95, Main £9.95-£25, Dessert £4.95-£6.95, Service optional **Wines** 7 by glass **Notes** Fixed L 2 course available until 6.30pm (Tue-Sat until 4pm), Vegetarian available **Seats** 60, Pr/dining room 30 **Children** Portions **Parking** On street

Malmaison Edinburgh

◉ British, French ○

Dockside brasserie Mal style

☎ 0844 693652
One Tower Place, Leith EH6 7DB
e-mail: edinburgh@malmaison.com
web: www.malmaison.com
dir: A900 from city centre towards Leith, at end of Leith Walk through 3 lights, left into Tower St. Hotel on right at end of road

Edinburgh's branch of the Mal is stylishly set in the capital's dynamic Leith development, with views over the water. Dining goes on amid an ambience of retro wood panelling, brown leather upholstery and unclothed tables, a surprisingly clubby feel for what is impeccably contemporary, defiantly simple brasserie food. Moules marinière is a benchmark, its liquor excellent, the mussels fresh and plump, while a main course of braised ox cheek with shallot purée and polenta croûtons brings on well-seasoned, resonantly flavoured meat and good textural contrasts. Blowtorched crème brûlée is singing with vanilla, and arrives with a spiced madeleine.

Chef Martin Kelly **Owner** Malmaison Hotels Ltd
Times 12-2.30/6-10.30 **Prices** Fixed D 3 course £19.95, Starter £6.95-£8.50, Main £11.95-£39, Service added but optional 10% **Wines** 49 bottles over £30, 23 bottles under £30, 18 by glass **Notes** Sunday L, Vegetarian available, Civ Wed 100 **Seats** 60, Pr/dining room 60 **Children** Portions, Menu **Parking** 45

Mithas

◉◉ Modern Indian NEW V ○

Modern Indian cooking at the docks

☎ 0131 554 0008
7 Dock Place EH6 6LU
e-mail: dine@mithas.co.uk
dir: Commercial St, Commercial quay, near to Scottish executive building

The Leith dock area does not want for good places to eat, but Mithias is a great addition to the community - a modern Indian restaurant with real va-va-voom. It avoids clichés in the décor and on the menu, whilst respecting tradition. The kitchen is open to view so the tantalising sight and smells of the searing grill and tandoori ovens gets you in the mood. The quality of the ingredients deserves a mention, as does the fact that they have a BYO policy with no corkage charge for table wine or fizz. The à la carte menu is supported by tasting versions that are worth checking out. Start with partridge, marinated in honey and mustard and cooked in the tandoor, served with three sauces (plum chutney, sweet chilli and a dried spice), followed by samudri khazana, which is scallops, monkfish, mussels, clams, sea bass and langoustines served in a spring onion and coconut gravy - superb seafood and a great flavour. The carrot taster dessert makes a fabulous finale.

Chef Pramod Nawani **Owner** Islam Mohammed
Times 12-2.30/5.30-10 Closed Xmas D, 26 Dec & 1 Jan, Mon **Prices** Fixed L 2 course £9.95-£11.95, Tasting menu £29.95-£49.95, Starter £4.95-£11.95, Main £9.95-£29.95, Dessert £5.95-£7.95 **Notes** Sunday L, Vegetarian menu, Dress restrictions, Smart dress **Seats** 72, Pr/dining room 14 **Parking** On street

North Bridge Brasserie

◉ Modern Scottish ○

Compelling cooking in a stylishly converted newspaper office

☎ 0131 622 2900 & 556 5565
The Scotsman Hotel, 20 North Bridge EH1 1TR
e-mail: scotsman-northbridge@thescotsmanhotel.co.uk
web: www.northbridgebrasserie.com
dir: Town centre, next to railway station, 1 min from Royal Mile & 2 mins to Princes St

North Bridge Brasserie is a triumphant conversion of the old Scotsman newspaper offices, housed in what was the reception hall and retaining all the impressive original features of marble pillars, intricate cornicing, panelling and a balcony with tables and chairs. The kitchen's pride in Scotland's produce is evident from the menu, which may open with maple-cured Pitlochry pigeon with a piquant salad of pickled mushrooms and carrot, or citrus-cured Scottish salmon fashionably partnered by beetroot textures, horseradish and rocket arancini. High levels of skill and innovation continue into main courses, accompanying roast squid with crisp smoked mussel fritters, chorizo, black tagliatelle and lemon yoghurt, for instance, and serving slow-cooked Borders lamb shank with basil mousse, goats' cheese, bean cassoulet and curly kale. A fine selection of Scottish artisan cheeses with chutney and oatcakes is an alternative to something sweeter like dark chocolate pithivier with crème fraîche.

Chef Paul Hart **Owner** The Scotsman Hotel Ltd
Times 12-2/6-10 **Prices** Starter £6.75-£12, Main £11.75-£32, Dessert £5.50-£10, Service added but optional 10% **Wines** 12 bottles over £30, 20 bottles under £30, 12 by glass **Notes** Afternoon tea £16.95, Vegetarian available, Dress restrictions, Smart casual, Civ Wed 80 **Seats** 80, Pr/dining room 80 **Children** Portions, Menu **Parking** Station car park

Norton House Hotel & Spa

EDINBURGH   **MAP 21 NT27**

Modern British, French

Smart contemporary cooking in a peaceful spot

☎ 0131 333 1275
Ingliston EH28 8LX
e-mail: nortonhouse@handpicked.co.uk
web: www.handpickedhotels.co.uk/nortonhouse
dir: M8 junct 2, off A8, 0.5m past Edinburgh Airport

Standing in 55 acres of grounds, Norton House offers a taste of the country close to Edinburgh (20 minutes from the city centre, ten from the airport), and has the full complement of leisure and conference facilities, plus, in the shape of Ushers, a restaurant that is a destination in its own right. There's a brasserie, too, to service the need for a more informal dining experience. Open only in the evening, Ushers is done out in a classical manner; a windowless room, smart and formal, it's the domain of the talented Graeme Shaw and his team. The cooking on show is refined, creative, and everything looks beautiful on the plate - and it certainly doesn't disappoint in the eating either. This is a place where you can expect amuse-bouche and pre-dessert (crab salad with fennel, smoked tomatoes and smoked goats' milk foam, and lemon pannacotta with lemon granité respectively) and attention to detail throughout. Millefeuille of foie gras with plums and almonds shows wonderful balance of taste and texture, or go for Loch Duart salmon partnered with oyster mayonnaise and an apple and sorrel dressing. There's plenty of local and regional produce on show, not least in the signature wild grouse with Jerusalem artichoke purée and soured cabbage. Monkfish might turn up in a main course with chorizo and razor clams, and among desserts the happy marriage of apple and caramel comes with a toffee sponge pudding and Granny Smith ice cream. There's a tasting menu, too.

Chef Graeme Shaw, Glen Bilins **Owner** Hand Picked Hotels **Times** 7-9.30 Closed Jan-Feb, Sun-Tue, L all week **Prices** Tasting menu fr £65, Starter £7.50-£10.50, Main £16.95-£32.50, Dessert £6.50-£8.95, Service optional **Wines** 80 bottles over £30, 15 bottles under £30, 12 by glass **Notes** Tasting menu 8 course, Vegetarian available, Civ Wed 140 **Seats** 22, Pr/dining room 40 **Children** Portions **Parking** 100

Number One, The Balmoral

EDINBURGH   **MAP 21 NT27**

Modern Scottish V NOTABLE WINE LIST

Dynamic cooking at an opulent address

☎ 0131 557 6727 & 556 2414
1 Princes St EH2 2EQ
e-mail: numberone@roccofortecollection.com
web: www.roccofortecollection.com
dir: follow city centre signs. Hotel at E end of Princes St, adjacent to Waverley Station

A classic of the great Railway Age, The Balmoral even has its own clock tower, and, with its Princes Street address, location next to Waverley Station, and views over the castle, it really is at the heart of the city. It's built to grand Victorian proportions and inside the scale and five-star luxury of it all will leave an impression. There are dining options aplenty - see also entry for Hadrian's - but it is the Number One restaurant that holds the number one position. It's a smartly done-out space courtesy of Olga Polizzi with copious artworks on richly lacquered walls, deep carpets, lavishly upholstered chairs and plenty of room between the crisply laid tables. The cooking is based on classical French thinking, but it looks and feels contemporary, with a good deal of creativity and technical flair on show. A meal consists of all the bells and whistles - canapé, amuse and petits fours - and there's even a trolley bringing round the array of breads on offer (spelt bread, perhaps, cut from a loaf at the table, or a smoked cheese version). Whether you go for the tasting menu with its tantalisingly brief dish descriptions, or delve into the fixed-price carte, you'll find first-class ingredients from top to bottom. Start with a perfectly balanced first course of sautéed foie gras with peach, gingerbread and truffle, or Corra Linn cheese and beetroot with hazelnuts and frozen apple. Main-course sirloin of beef is cooked sous-vide and comes with tongue and sweetbreads, asparagus spelt risotto and truffle sauce, or there might be turbot with squid linguine, parsnips and shellfish sauce. To finish, poached rhubarb with white chocolate pannacotta and custard doughnut is a stellar combination. The wine list does justice to the wonderful food, and so do the highly professional service team.

Chef Jeff Bland, Billy Boyter **Owner** Rocco Forte Collection **Times** 6.30-10 Closed 1st 2 wks Jan, L all week **Prices** Fixed D 3 course fr £64, Tasting menu fr £70, Service optional, Groups min 6 service 10% **Wines** 10 bottles over £30, 8 by glass **Notes** Tasting menu 8 course, Vegetarian menu, Dress restrictions, Smart casual preferred, Civ Wed 60 **Seats** 50, Pr/dining room 50 **Children** Portions **Parking** NCP Greenside/St James Centre

Save on Hotels. Book at **theAA.com/hotel**

CITY OF EDINBURGH 577 | SCOTLAND

EDINBURGH *continued*

Norton House Hotel & Spa

◉◉◉ – *see opposite*

Number One, The Balmoral

◉◉◉ – *see opposite*

Ondine Restaurant

◉◉ Seafood

Contemporary seafood restaurant with ethical outlook

☎ 0131 226 1888
2 George IV Bridge EH1 1AD
e-mail: enquiries@ondinerestaurant.co.uk
dir: Located Edinburgh City Centre, just off the Royal Mile

There's always a lively buzz at Ondine – in fact it's got such a loyal following, it's hard to believe the place hasn't been here for years. The central horseshoe-shaped crustacea bar is both a feature in the room and a declaration of intent – this place is about seafood, and top-notch sustainable Scottish seafood at that. Just off the Royal Mile, on George IV Bridge, it's a modish space with great views out over the old town. Start with rock oysters (Loch Fyne, Cumbrae, Carlingford), either as they come or cooked (tempura or thermidor, perhaps), or something like a textbook fish and shellfish soup with the trad accompaniments of rouille, gruyère and croutons. Chef Roy Brett shows a sensibly steady hand when it comes to treating the first-class piscine produce at his disposal, so nothing is overworked and everything tastes just so. Thus main course might be a simple roast shellfish platter, risotto nero with grilled chilli squid, Shetland mussel marinière, fish curry, or good old-fashioned deep-fried haddock and chips with minted pea purée.

Chef Roy Brett **Owner** Roy Brett **Times** 12-3/5.30-10 Closed 1st wk Jan, Sun **Prices** Fixed L 2 course £17.95, Starter £8.50-£14.50, Main £14.95-£32, Dessert £7.95, Service optional **Wines** 60 bottles over £30, 6 bottles under £30, 25 by glass **Notes** Pre-theatre menu 2/3 course 5.30-6.30pm, Vegetarian available **Seats** 70, Pr/dining room 8 **Children** Portions, Menu **Parking** On street or Castle Terrace car park

One Square

◉ Modern British

Smart modern cooking in a setting to match

☎ 0131 221 6422
The Sheraton Grand Hotel & Spa, 1 Festival Square EH3 9SR
e-mail: info@onesquareedinburgh.co.uk
dir: Off Lothian Road. Entrance to hotel behind Standard Life building

The location by Edinburgh Castle is a boon, but The Sheraton Grand hotel - home to the contemporary One Square restaurant - has plenty to keep you occupied before and after exploring the city, or doing business if that's why you're in town. It's a big, bright and very smart contemporary space, with lots of neat designer touches and top-notch facilities, including a fab spa. In the sleekly designed One Square, the kitchen deals in a broad range of appealing, classically-inspired dishes using top-notch Scottish produce. Pan-fried Tarbert crabcake with a spinach and walnut salad and mustard cream sauce stands alongside Macsween haggis with a fried duck's egg among starters, and from there you can go on to trad fish and chips with tartare sauce and mushy peas, or venison Wellington with wild mushrooms, peas and blackcurrant sauce. There's a decidedly trendy bar, too, and an outdoor terrace to soak up those occasional Scottish rays.

Chef Malcolm Webster **Owner** Sheraton Grand **Times** 7-11 All-day dining **Prices** Starter £4.50-£13, Main £7-£37, Dessert £2-£8.50, Service added but optional 10% **Wines** 35 bottles over £30, 36 bottles under £30, 14 by glass **Notes** Sunday L £29, Vegetarian available, Civ Wed 40 **Seats** 90, Pr/dining room 40 **Children** Portions, Menu **Parking** 125

Plumed Horse

◉◉◉ – *see page 578*

Pompadour by Galvin

◉◉◉ – *see page 578*

Restaurant Martin Wishart

◉◉◉◉ – *see page 579*

Rhubarb at Prestonfield House

◉◉ Traditional British ⚑ NOTABLE WINE LIST

Opulent surroundings for high-impact cooking

☎ 0131 225 1333
Priestfield Rd EH16 5UT
e-mail: reservations@prestonfield.com
web: www.rhubarb-restaurant.com
dir: Exit city centre on Nicholson St, onto Dalkeith Rd. At lights turn left into Priestfield Rd. Prestonfield on left

Amateur food historians might like to take note that this restaurant has more right than most to name itself after the eponymous Asian vegetable, since it was the former owner of Prestonfield, Sir Alexander Dick, who brought the exotic rarity to Scotland in 1746. The blue-blooded 17th-century mansion wears a rather different set of clothes these days: the designers have done their stuff, kitting out the old girl with a decadent, theatrical and rather glam boudoir look that delivers all the wow-factor you'd expect from Regency rooms done out with chandeliers and oil paintings set against darkly opulent shades of blood red and burgundy. The food is no wallflower either, thanks to a kitchen that makes its own luxurious contribution, blending old-school classicism with an eclectic contemporary spirit. Hand-dived scallops appear with a supporting cast of cauliflower purée, lovage, chorizo, apple and truffle dressing and confit lemon, all staged to make maximum visual impact. Next up, roast loin of Strathspey venison with black pudding crumble, red cabbage purée, and Arran mustard and potato mousse. An intricate dessert brings together top-notch chocolate flavoured with extra-virgin olive oil with financiers, coconut ice cream, and a sphere of Earl Grey tea-flavoured gel.

Rhubarb at Prestonfield House

Times 12-2/6.30-10

Plumed Horse

EDINBURGH   MAP 21 NT27

Modern European V

Consistently impressive contemporary cuisine near the Leith dockland

☎ 0131 554 5556 & 05601 123266
50-54 Henderson St, Leith EH6 6DE
e-mail: plumedhorse@aol.com
web: www.plumedhorse.co.uk
dir: From city centre N on Leith Walk, left into Great Junction St & 1st right into Henderson St. Restaurant 200mtrs on right

Not in the prettiest part of Leith, chances are you won't stumble across the Plumed Horse, but once you've found it and crossed the threshold, you'll want to come back. Tony Borthwick is his own man and his restaurant, like his food, is classy, distinctive and refined. With high-backed cream leather seats, smartly laid tables and vivid contemporary artworks, the look says fine-dining and no mistake, and there's a definite appreciation for classical culinary traditions on show. If you really want to push the boat out, go for the tasting menu (with optional wine flight), or if your means are a little more modest the lunch menu is spectacular value by any standards. Top-notch ingredients lie at the heart of every good-looking dish, and this is a kitchen that takes the time to get the small things right. A lunchtime starter might be a venison terrine wrapped in bacon and served with a Cumberland sauce - a classic done perfectly - whilst the kitchen is not adverse to the idea of dressing a dish with a foam (a curried brown crab version, perhaps, atop a crab and oyster quiche). Next up, sautéed halibut comes in the happy company of a lobster ravioli and lemon risotto, and roast loin of French rabbit with its leg meat stuffed into cabbage leaves, kidney, garlic and potato gratin, mustard sauce and a Madeira-spiked rabbit stock. There's sound judgement and spot-on balancing of flavours at dessert stage, too: a lemon tart with mandarin and Grand Marnier sorbet, for example, or forced rhubarb and orange chiboust with orange and ginger sauce. The excellent wine list has a good choice by the glass and half bottle.

Chef Tony Borthwick **Owner** The Company of The Plumed Horse Ltd **Times** 12-1.30/7-9 Closed Xmas, New Year, 2 wks summer, 1 wk Etr, Sun-Mon **Prices** Fixed L 3 course £24, Fixed D 3 course £55, Tasting menu £69-£117, Service optional, Groups min 6 service 10% **Wines** 16 by glass **Notes** Vegetarian menu **Seats** 40 **Parking** On street

Pompadour by Galvin

EDINBURGH   MAP 21 NT27

Modern French NEW V

Haute cuisine Galvin-style comes to Edinburgh

☎ 0131 222 8975 & 222 8777
The Caledonian, A Waldorf Astoria Hotel, Princes St EH1 2AB
e-mail: pompadour.reservations@waldorfastoria.com
dir: Situated on east end of Princes St, on Rutland St & Lothian Rd

The empire-building Galvin brothers have taken Edinburgh with a show of force, setting up their high-end gastronomic HQ in the palatial environs of The Caledonian Waldorf Astoria, a grand Victorian railway-era hotel restored to its full glory after a megabucks refurbishment. 'The Pomp' - as locals affectionately know this grande dame of a restaurant - has been a byword for opulence since it opened its doors in 1925, and was always considered to be the hottest ticket in town before the culinary opposition upped the ante in recent years. The belle époque extravaganza still manages to provoke sharp intakes of breath from awe-struck diners as they take in its wedding cake plasterwork, delicate hand-painted panelling, peerless views of Edinburgh Castle perched upon its lofty crag, and perhaps wonder whether Madame de Pompadour herself will be turning up. They've certainly nailed the luxurious service vibe with a full-works, classical French hierarchy - as professional, charming and efficient a team as you're ever likely to encounter, including a seriously knowledgeable sommelier to guide you through the oh-so French listings. Naturally, The Pompadour shows the same Francophile culinary direction as the Galvins' much-lauded London establishments, delivering rich seasonal ingredients that sit together happily, prepared with razor-sharp technical ability and realised with haute cuisine flair. A procession of intricately-presented dishes might begin with ravioli of rabbit and ricotta, partnered with sarriette and the contrasting acidic tang of artichokes barigoule, or a show-stopping roulade of foie gras and ham hock with pineapple purée and fennel croûtons. Next up, loin and meltingly-tender braised cheek of Tamworth pork, and boudin noir, deliver phenomenal depth of flavour when pointed up with caramelised apple, white beans and parsley. Finally, an impeccable banana soufflé is matched with rum and raisin parfait. For a taste of the Galvin magic at more accessible prices, try the ground-floor Brasserie de Luxe (see entry).

Chef Craig Sandle **Owner** Chris & Jeff Galvin **Times** 6.30-10 Closed 2 wks Jan, Sun-Mon, L all week **Prices** Fixed D 3 course £58, Tasting menu fr £65, Service added but optional 10% **Wines** 28 by glass **Notes** 7 course tasting menu, Vegetarian menu **Children** Portions, Menu **Parking** 42

Restaurant Martin Wishart

EDINBURGH   MAP 21 NT27

Modern French **V** ⚑ NOTABLE WINE LIST

Contemporary French cooking from Scotland's darling of the restaurant scene

☎ 0131 553 3557
54 The Shore, Leith EH6 6RA
e-mail: info@martin-wishart.co.uk
dir: off the A199

Dedicated foodies from the world over hotfoot it to dine at Martin Wishart's eponymous restaurant, such is the reputation of the Scottish chef who trained with some of the greats of French cuisine before setting up shop here in 1999. In the heart of Leith, the restaurant was a leading light in the transformation of this part of the city from disused docklands to a trendy foodie quarter, and it's going as strong as ever. The elegant, sumptuously furnished dining room overlooks the water, and is an undeniably pleasant environment in which to dine, with tables dressed in their finest linen and set with sparkling glassware, comfortable chairs, and a mellow colour palette of creams and natural wood shades. Guests' every needs are looked after by a large team of immaculately presented and consummately professional staff, whose knowledge of the menu is impeccable (a good job, as the menu descriptions give little away). And if the views out the window and the people watching aren't enough to entertain you while you eat, there are little touches of theatre, such as a special leg of lamb (roast leg of native Shetland lamb from Vementry, no less) carved at the table, while the cheese trolley that regularly traverses the room is an impressive sight in itself. Scottish produce of the highest order is the starting point of every dish, and while the kitchen employs no shortage of impressive technique, it has the sense not to resort to any off-the-wall ideas simply for effect. There's a six-course tasting menu (and a vegetarian version) but if you go down the à la carte route you might start with sauté of duck foie gras pointed up with soft-poached Mouneyrac pear and caramelised endive, a wonderfully sticky bitter orange sauce, and a savoury Szechuan meringue which melts in the mouth to release a soft pepper flavour - a stunning dish, beautifully presented, which leaves you wanting more. Next up, tranche of roast turbot is super-fresh, flaky and moist and comes with a Vivaldi potato and artichoke galette, bone marrow, preserved truffle jus and a salad of lamb's lettuce dressed in a sharp vinaigrette which ably cuts through the richness. A meatier main course might be roast loin and civet of hare with caramelised onion and grey chanterelle on brioche, braised red cabbage and grand veneur sauce - a smile-inducing combination of flavours and textures, and all cooked to perfection, too. Valrhona Manjari chocolate cremeux with exotic fruit sorbet and chocolate sablé shows no lack of skill in the pastry department: two small cylinders of wafer-thin chocolate come filled with the chocolate cremeux, which is matched perfectly with the exotic fruit flavours in the sorbet and a gel-like coulis. It's certainly worth ordering coffee if only to indulge a little further in the excellent home-made chocolates (flavoured with raspberry, fresh mint, salted caramel, praline or passionfruit). The superb breads, canapés and amuse-bouche complete a truly class act.

Chef Martin Wishart, Joe Taggart **Owner** Martin Wishart **Times** 12-2/6.30-10 Closed 25-26 Dec, 1 Jan, 2 wks Jan, Sun-Mon **Prices** Fixed L 3 course fr £28.50, Fixed D 3 course fr £70, Tasting menu fr £75, Service optional, Groups min 6 service 10% **Wines** 250 bottles over £30, 9 bottles under £30, 17 by glass **Notes** Tasting menu 6 course, Vegetarian menu, Dress restrictions, Smart casual **Seats** 50, Pr/dining room 10 **Children** Portions, Menu **Parking** On street

EDINBURGH *continued*

The Sheep Heid

◉ British

Hearty dining in the city's oldest pub

☎ 0131 661 7974
43-45 The Causeway EH15 3QA
e-mail: enquire@thesheepheidedinburgh.co.uk
dir: From A1 from city centre towards Musselburgh, right
at lights into Duddingston Road West, take 4th or 5th
right into The Causeway

Said to be Edinburgh's oldest pub, The Sheep Heid has
fed and watered the residents of Duddingston village
since 1360. After an appetite sharpening ramble in
nearby Holyrood Park, it makes for a convivial pitstop
with its relaxed, shabby-chic décor of olive-green painted
panelling, traditional pews and mismatched chairs at
bare wooden tables. If you prefer the pubby setting,
complete with antique skittle alley, stay downstairs;
alternatively, go up to the eclectically-furnished first-floor
restaurant. Wherever you settle, expect straight-talking
food with generous portions, big flavours and splendid
ingredients. Sautéed Portobello and oyster mushrooms in
Marsala cream sauce on toasted ciabatta is a good way
to start, followed by smoked loin of cod served with
spiced Puy lentils, wilted greens and a salt-cod fritter.
For pudding, rich Columbian chocolate provides the
oomph in a glazed brownie with vanilla ice cream.

Times 12-10

Stac Polly

◉ Scottish

City centre cellar with Franco-Scottish flavour

☎ 0131 556 2231
29-33 Dublin St EH3 6NL
e-mail: bookings@stacpolly.com
dir: On corner of Albany St & Dublin St

In the New Town area of Edinburgh, Stac Polly occupies a
labyrinthine cellar and serves up Scottish dishes with the
twang of a French accent. Housed in a 200-year-old
building, the place has loads of character thanks to stone
floors, bare-brick walls, linen-clad tables, and there's
even a small outside courtyard if you fancy a bit of
alfresco eating. The well-judged cooking sees some
interesting flavour combinations and a few firm
favourites such as haggis filo pastry parcels stay on the
menu by popular demand. Start perhaps with queen
scallops grilled in the shell and topped with a smoked
salmon and citrus butter, followed by a multi-component
main course such as suprême of halibut with a parsley
crust, citrus and dill mash, broccoli and creamy curry
sauce with fresh mussels. There's another branch in St
Mary's Street.

Times 12-2/6-10 Closed L Sat-Sun

The Stockbridge Restaurant

◉◉ Modern European ✿

Spirited flavours in distinctive surroundings

☎ 0131 226 6766
54 Saint Stephen St EH3 5AL
e-mail: jane@thestockbridgerestaurant.com
web: www.thestockbridgerestaurant.com
dir: From A90 towards city centre, left Craigleith Rd
B900, 2nd exit at rdbt B900, straight on to Kerr St, turn
left onto Saint Stephen St

The Stockbridge occupies the basement of a large
Georgian property in the area it takes its name from. It's
at the same time dramatic and cosy, with large still lifes
and mirrors hanging on the dark walls and clever lighting
adding a cosseting glow to the white-clothed tables and
gold-upholstered seats. The menu delivers a broadly
European range of full-bodied flavours showcasing
seasonal Scottish produce. Start with seared scallops
with crisp pork belly, black pudding, parsnip purée and
cider vinegar syrup, or a fun mini version of cod, chips
and tartare sauce. Pork belly may crop up again in a
gutsy main course with cheeks and crispy ear, served
with creamed potato, Puy lentils and apple purée, the
kitchen pulling off another winner with the unlikely but
successful blend of seared sea bass and crispy squid
with roast beetroot, chorizo, and sautéed Pink Fir Apple
potatoes.

The Stockbridge Restaurant

Chef Jason Gallagher **Owner** Jason Gallagher & Jane
Walker **Times** 7-9.30 Closed 1st 2 wks Jan after New
Year, Mon, L all week (open on request only) **Prices** Fixed
L 2 course £13.95-£14.95, Fixed D 3 course
£24.95-£28.95, Starter £6.95-£11.95, Main
£18.95-£24.95, Dessert £6.95-£8.95, Service optional,
Groups min 6 service 10% **Wines** 5 by glass **Notes** Pre-
theatre Aug only, open L only on request min 6 people,
Vegetarian available **Seats** 40 **Children** Portions
Parking On street

21212

◉◉◉◉ – *see opposite*

Save on Hotels. Book at **theAA.com/hotel**

CITY OF EDINBURGH 581 SCOTLAND

21212

EDINBURGH   **MAP 21 NT27**

Modern French 🍷 NOTABLE WINE LIST

Intense flavours and fun, creative cooking from a true culinary genius

☎ 0131 523 1030 & 0845 222 1212
3 Royal Ter EH7 5AB
e-mail: reservation@21212restaurant.co.uk
dir: Calton Hill, city centre

The name may at first appear rather odd: is it the restaurant's phone number by any chance? Or could it just be that 1 and 2 are the chef's lucky numbers? Thankfully, 21212 makes slightly more sense than that: it depicts the format of a meal here, in that you'll get five courses with a choice of two starters, two mains and two desserts, with one soup course and a cheese course in between (that is, unless you dine at lunchtime when you can choose from three, four or five courses). In an elegant Georgian townhouse right in the heart of Edinburgh's Royal Terrace, 21212 is the culmination of a lifelong dream for Paul Kitching, a prodigiously talented chef who champions a style of cooking that many aspire to but few achieve thanks to his classical French training complemented by his exhaustive knowledge of food and, in particular, combinations of ingredients. Together with his partner Katie O'Brien (who looks after things out front with endless charm and professionalism), Kitching

has created a sumptuously stylish restaurant with rooms (four rather luxurious ones at that). The high-ceilinged dining room retains its original ornate plasterwork and is enhanced with curvaceous banquettes, muslin-draped walls and a chocolate-brown carpet decorated with giant moths. At one end of the room there are windows looking out over the Royal Terrace and the gardens beyond, while at the other a patterned glass partition separates diners from the kitchen, where Kitching and his seven-strong team can be seen hard at work day in, day out. And so, back to that menu: dishes are described, unusually, in great detail, with every ingredient listed, as in a starter of 'all things mushroom and cauliflower' which is 'creamy Italian style risotto, an assiette of exotic mushrooms, truffles and morels, romanesque and button cauliflowers, breakfast radish and crosnes, mozzarella cheese and greens, piccalilli mayonnaise'. It may well sound confused but when the dish arrives it all makes sense - all those ingredients mentioned are there, presented immaculately in a small, high-sided bowl, and the balance of flavours is mind-blowingly good. Next up could be 'French corn-fed chicken, potatoes and spicy popcorn' - an exercise in textural contrasts with a multitude of cooking techniques in evidence and a combination of flavours that works incredibly well ('sweetcorn, garlic and

swede fries, capers and pistachio nuts, hot spicy popcorn, leeks, white beans, streaky bacon, crispy pancake and sweet pickle, curried yellow pea purée, smoked ham'). And there are more treats in store at dessert stage when the likes of 'apricot and ginger, white chocolate and almonds, banana and mango' arrive to tantalise your taste buds and take you on a journey like no other. With such fun, imaginative, exciting, creative and yet technically brilliant cooking on offer, it's no wonder 21212 has joined the ranks of the UK's destination restaurants.

Chef Paul Kitching **Owner** P Kitching, K O'Brien, J Revle
Times 12-1.45/6.45-9.30 Closed 2 wks Jan, 2 wks summer, Sun-Mon
Prices Fixed L 3 course fr £28, Service optional **Wines** 222 bottles over £30, 14 bottles under £30, 6 by glass
Notes Fixed L 4/5 course £38/£52, D 5 course £68, Vegetarian available
Seats 36, Pr/dining room 10 **Parking** On street

EDINBURGH *continued*

The Witchery by the Castle

Traditional Scottish NOTABLE WINE LIST

Confident Scottish cooking in magnificent surroundings

☎ 0131 225 5613
Castlehill, The Royal Mile EH1 2NF
e-mail: mail@thewitchery.com
web: www.thewitchery.com
dir: Top of Royal Mile at gates of Edinburgh Castle

This place is the real deal. Where so many strive for individuality by adding 'boutique' character, The Witchery is as strikingly unique, intriguing and lavish as they come. The higgledy piggledy collection of 16th-century buildings in the old town right by the castle has a slate of glamorous rooms and a restaurant that really takes the biscuit. The two dining rooms (Witchery and Secret Garden) leave a lasting impression: the former with its fabulous oak panelling and tapestries, the latter with its ornately painted ceiling and French windows onto a secluded terrace with great views. On the menu is some smart Scottish cooking, rooted in tradition but with a contemporary sheen. Haggis, neeps and tatties is blended into a chicken mousse to begin, followed by a seafood platter, slow-cooked monkfish with an Asian broth, or steamed saddle of rabbit served with a suet pudding filled with braised shoulder and kidney.

Times 12-4/5.30-11.30 Closed 25 Dec

BANKNOCK   Map 21 NS77

Glenskirlie House & Castle

Modern British, European

Pan-European cooking next to a photogenic modern castle

☎ 01324 840201
Kilsyth Rd FK4 1UF
e-mail: macaloneys@glenskirliehouse.com
web: www.glenskirliehouse.com
dir: Follow A803 signed Kilsyth/Bonnybridge, at T-junct turn right. Hotel 1m on right

As castles go, Glenskirlie's is a little more Disney World than medieval, but it makes a fine backdrop for wedding photos and a good setting for a private bash. The dining room - in the house next-door - has a small conservatory for aperitifs, while the low-ceilinged room itself is done in faintly retro glam, with elaborate wallpaper in cream and black, large mirrors and low lighting. The cooking incorporates elements of the modern technical repertoire for a Pan-European style that embraces confit chicken and wild mushroom ravioli with sharply pungent balsamic foam, and mains such as baked sea trout with Cullen skink risotto and pancetta, or brilliantly executed roast saddle and panko-crumbed shoulder of venison with parsnip purée, Chantenay carrots and spinach in a glossy juniper jus. The chocolate creations can be a little under-powered - better look to the zestier likes of lemon meringue torte with lime and cucumber sorbet, or blackberry and vanilla parfait with violet sorbet and a poppy seed tuile.

Times 12-2/6-9.30 Closed 26-27 Dec, 1-4 Jan, D Mon

CUPAR   Map 21 NO31

Ostlers Close Restaurant

Modern British V 🕒

Fabulous seasonal produce and skilled hand in the kitchen

☎ 01334 655574
Bonnygate KY15 4BU
dir: In small lane off main street, A91

Down a narrow alley just off the main street, this one-time scullery of a 17th-century Temperance hotel has

---

been a favoured foodie bolt-hole since 1981. That's when James (Jimmy) and Amanda Graham bought the place, and their passion and dedication has put it well and truly on the map. With red-painted walls and linen-clad tables, it's an intimate space (just 26 covers), which is watched over by Amanda with a good deal of charm and enthusiasm. Jimmy's pleasingly concise, hand-written menus make the most of fruit, veg and herbs from the restaurant's garden (and polytunnel), and at the right time of year he can be found gathering wild mushrooms from the local woods. Seasonal Scottish produce takes centre stage, and you might spot an occasional Spanish influence amid the well-crafted modern repertoire. Dishes are packed with flavour, never over worked, with the ingredients given room to shine. Start, perhaps, with roast breast of Perthshire partridge with Stornoway black pudding mash and pork belly confit, before moving on to fillet of wild Scottish halibut (perfectly cooked) served with Pittenweem prawns, winter greens and saffron sauce. Vanilla pannacotta with a compôte of fruits, damson gin coulis and damson sorbet makes a fine and refreshing finale.

Chef James Graham **Owner** James & Amanda Graham **Times** 12.15-1.30/7-9.30 Closed 25-26 Dec, 1-2 Jan, 2 wks Apr, 2 wks Oct, Sun-Mon, L Tue-Fri **Prices** Prices not confirmed Service optional **Wines** 6 by glass **Notes** Fixed D 3 course only available Tue-Fri, Nov-May £28.50, Vegetarian menu **Seats** 26 **Children** Portions **Parking** On street, public car park

---

ELIE   Map 21 NO40

Sangsters

Modern British

Modern cooking on the village high street

☎ 01333 331001
51 High St KY9 1BZ
dir: From St Andrews on A917 take B9131 to Anstruther, right at rdbt onto A917 to Elie. (11m from St Andrews)

Bruce and Jackie Sangster set up shop plum in the middle of the main street of this unassuming Fife village, and set about wowing the locals with finely-crafted modern Scottish cooking that showcases plenty of local produce, including apples and herbs from the back garden. It all takes place in a smart dining room hung with landscape pictures, and furnished with crisply dressed tables and high-backed chairs. Dinner follows a four-course, fixed-price format, kicking off perhaps with seared Ross-shire scallops in a Thai-fragrant dressing of chilli, ginger, galangal and lemongrass, before an intermediate fish course, which could be steamed stuffed Loch Duart salmon, teamed with Arbroath smokie and Finnan haddock, in Sauternes and ginger sauce. Main course might be pork two ways, braised cheek and fillet stuffed with black pudding and apricot, with fennel, cabbage and braising juices, while mango and white chocolate parfait with tropical fruits and a sesame and poppy seed biscuit brings things to a close in style.

Times 12.30-1.30/7-8.30 Closed 25-26 Dec, Jan, 1st wk Nov, Mon (also Tue winter), L Tue-Sat, D Sun

PEAT INN   Map 21 NO40

The Peat Inn

⊛⊛⊛ – *see below*

ST ANDREWS   Map 21 NO51

Esperante at Fairmont St Andrews

⊛⊛ Modern Mediterranean ☺

Mediterranean flavour at a coastal golf resort

☎ 01334 837000 & 837021
KY16 8PN
e-mail: standrews.scotland@fairmont.com
dir: 1.5m outside St Andrews on A917 towards Crail

The sprawling Fairmont resort stands in 520 acres in a grand coastal setting. There are all the facilities you could wish for, including golf, massages, and a butler to run your bath for you, as well as the Esperante dining room, named after a classic racing car. Done in autumnal hues of terracotta, brown and olive, it's a relaxing venue for cooking that makes a virtue of healthy eating. A terrine of smoked salmon and caper butter is fruitily garnished with poached apple and peach jelly, and there's mango purée with the duck rillettes. Mediterranean influences waft over mains such as cod with chorizo fricassée, sun-blush tomatoes and beans, while a winning pasta combination offers goats' cheese

cannelloni with sweet potato tortellini in sauce vierge. Finish with a dark chocolate and Frangelico mousse with praline ice cream, perhaps with a glass of Muscat de Beaumes-de-Venise.

Chef Alan Matthew **Owner** Apollo European Real Estate **Times** 6.30-9.30 Closed L all week, D Mon-Tue **Prices** Tasting menu £42-£69, Starter £6.95-£11.95, Main £17.95-£29.95, Dessert £6.95-£8.95, Service optional **Wines** 49 bottles over £30, 2 bottles under £30, 11 by glass **Notes** Tasting menu 6 course, Vegetarian available, Civ Wed 300 **Seats** 60, Pr/dining room 60 **Children** Portions **Parking** 250

The Inn at Lathones

⊛⊛ Modern European ☺

Well-judged, locally-focused menu in a characterful coaching inn

☎ 01334 840494
Largoward KY9 1JE
e-mail: innatlathones.com
web: www.innatlathones.com
dir: 5m SW of St Andrews on A915. In 0.5m before Largoward on left, just after hidden dip

With a history that stretches back some 400 years, The Inn at Lathones is smartly done out these days, with modish accommodation in the refurbished outbuildings (an old forge and the like) and a restaurant that brings in

the punters to sample the locally-minded menu. The inn is close to St Andrews (golfers duly note) and the coast, and it is also the setting for live music (see the website for a list of gigs). The décor blends whitewashed walls, stone fireplaces and contemporary artworks with new oak tables. On the menu is a good amount of regional produce and a decidedly local flavour. Start, perhaps, with a classic Cullen skink, or pan-fried scallops with micro-herb salad and chorizo and onion marmalade. Next up, pan-fried sea trout with caper butter, or rack of Black Isle lamb with baby turnips, boulangère potatoes, braised cabbage and mint reduction, and for dessert, something like iced vanilla yoghurt parfait with blueberry compôte and sorbet.

Chef Chris Wright **Owner** Mr N White
Times 12-2.30/6-9.30 Closed 26 Dec, 1st 2 wks Jan **Prices** Prices not confirmed Service optional, Groups min 8 service 10% **Wines** 5 by glass **Notes** Sunday L, Vegetarian available, Dress restrictions, Smart casual, Civ Wed 40 **Seats** 40, Pr/dining room 40 **Children** Portions, Menu **Parking** 35

The Peat Inn

PEAT INN   MAP 21 NO40

Modern British 🍷NOTABLE
WINE LIST

Virtuoso skills in village institution

☎ 01334 840206
KY15 5LH
e-mail: stay@thepeatinn.co.uk
dir: At junct of B940/B941, 6m SW of St Andrews

Geoffrey and Katherine Smeddle have run this one-time coaching inn with professionalism and charm since 2006, and it remains one of the stand-out destinations in Scotland's culinary firmament. It may look humble from the outside, but that belies the unfettered comforts within, where luxurious bedroom suites mean you don't have to worry about getting home afterwards. It's the kind of place where you study the menu in the comfort of a plush lounge, aperitif in hand, with a roaring log fire adding to the cossetting feel. Then it's into one of the smart, beamed

dining rooms (three small rooms make up the space), which reflect the cottagey feel of the original building whilst maintaining the fine-dining factor. Geoffrey Smeddle's cooking is first and foremost based on superb produce, these prime ingredients drawn substantially from Scotland's fabulous larder, and prepared with craft, care and creativity. Things kick off with canapés and an amuse-bouche such as cauliflower pannacotta with parmesan crisps and foam, before a first course such as wood pigeon, served as smoked breast and cannelloni, alongside a crisp tongue bonbon, ceps purée, figs and cob nuts. Next up, perhaps lemon sole fillets with poached lobster, Jerusalem artichoke fricassée, young fennel and lobster sauce, or roast breast and confit leg of wild Mallard, served in earthy partnership with black pudding, girolles, damson compôte, rösti potato, pearl barley and autumn roots and fruits. Fads and fashions are tempered by a cool head, but these are complex, ambitious dishes with a good deal going on. To finish, hot strawberry soufflé with balsamic sorbet rises to the occasion. There is a tasting menu, with optional wine

flight, and whilst we're on the subject, the wonderful wine list is clearly a labour of love.

Chef Geoffrey Smeddle **Owner** Geoffrey & Katherine Smeddle **Times** 12.30-1.30/7-9 Closed 25-26 Dec, 1-14 Jan, Sun-Mon **Prices** Fixed L 3 course £20, Fixed D 3 course £45, Tasting menu £65, Starter £13-£16, Main £22-£27, Dessert £9.50-£10.50, Service optional **Wines** 350 bottles over £30, 10 bottles under £30, 16 by glass **Notes** Tasting menu 6 course D, Chef's menu 4 course L, Vegetarian available **Seats** 40, Pr/dining room 14 **Parking** 24

FIFE *continued*

Nahm-Jim & the L'Orient Lounge

◉ Japanese, Thai

The flavours of Thailand in the town centre

☎ 01334 470000 & 474000
60-62 Market St KY16 9NT
e-mail: manager@nahm-jim.co.uk

Nahm-Jim is a popular family-run Thai restaurant over two floors, often full, in the town centre, with red and white walls, a wooden floor and some South-East Asian decorations. Produce is flown in weekly from Bangkok, the cooking is consistently of a high standard, and presentation is ever attractive. After a starter like spicy fishcakes, move on to a curry (lamb massaman, perhaps, slowly braised with shallots and potatoes in a gentle sauce), Thai-style local scallops, pan-fried in a garlic, oyster and miso sauce served with a spicy dip, and end with a deep-fried banana in coconut and honey with coconut ice cream. The long menu of authentic dishes gives plenty of scope and includes a selection from Japan as well as around half a dozen banquets.

Times 12-10 Closed 25-26 Dec, 1 Jan

Road Hole Restaurant

◉◉◉ *– see opposite*

Rocca Grill

◉◉◉ *– see below*

Rufflets Country House

◉◉ British, European ⚑ NOTABLE WINE LIST ✋

Appealing menus in tasteful country-house hotel

☎ 01334 472594
Strathkinness Low Rd KY16 9TX
e-mail: reservations@rufflets.co.uk
web: www.rufflets.co.uk
dir: 1.5m W of St Andrews on B939

Built in the 1920s for the widow of a Dundee jute baron, Rufflets is an imposing turreted and creeper-clad mansion standing in 10 acres of delicious flowery gardens. The smart contemporary-styled restaurant looks over those lovely grounds; it is an airy space, done out with colourful artwork on rich terracotta walls, and upholstered seats at linen-swathed tables. The kitchen has a commitment to quality produce prepared with respect and creativity, delivering menus of carefully composed, eye-catching modern dishes with a clear Mediterranean accent. Keeping things strictly local, you might start with Highland game terrine with braised pork cheek, home-made chutney and Arran oatcakes, before heading south for the sunnier flavours of roast monkfish partnered by fregola, smoked ham, sweetcorn, sun-blushed tomato, baby baked potatoes, and chilli and lime syrup. Meat eaters could find roast rump of Fife lamb in the company of fondant potato, pea purée, chorizo, chanterelle mushrooms, and rosemary and garlic jus. Desserts work interesting combinations of flavour and texture - say blackcurrant and semolina cake with blackcurrant curd, gooseberry sorbet and blackberry milkshake.

Chef David Kinnes **Owner** Ann Murray-Smith
Times 12.30-2.30/7-9.30 Closed L Mon-Sat **Prices** Fixed L 2 course £12.50-£16.50, Fixed D 3 course £35-£39.50, Service optional, Groups min 20 service 10% **Wines** 9 by glass **Notes** Sunday L, Vegetarian available, Dress restrictions, Smart casual, Civ Wed 150 **Seats** 60, Pr/dining room 130 **Children** Portions, Menu **Parking** 50

Rocca Grill

ST ANDREWS	**MAP 21 NO51**

Italian, Scottish V

Smart, modish food with top-class golfing views

☎ 01334 472549
Macdonald Rusacks Hotel, The Links KY16 9JQ
e-mail: info@roccagrill.com
web: www.roccagrill.com
dir: M90 junct 8, A91 to St Andrews. Turn left onto Golf Place, then right onto the links

For many people, particularly the hordes of international pilgrims who jet in from the States and Asia, St Andrews is only about one thing, and that is golf. Sure, the town is, and always will be, the cradle of the game, and the Macdonald Rusacks Hotel sits within a short putt of the hallowed greensward of the 18th hole of the Old Course, but hard though it may be to ignore, golf isn't the only reason to come here: you could simply turn up for the contemporary Italian-accented cooking in the Rocca Grill. Naturally, huge windows offer ringside seats over the golfing action and West Sands beach (where some scenes of *Chariots of Fire* were shot). It's an expansive, well-lit space with high ceilings, big feature lights, drapes and a chic décor, but friendly and relaxed staff dispel any suspicion of stuffiness, and under the guidance of executive chef Davey Aspin, the kitchen is firing on all cylinders. 'Classical Scottish cooking with a creative Italian twist' is the restaurant's mantra, so things may well begin with local salmon and lobster packed into a single ravioli served with wilted spinach and a vibrant, intense and creamy bisque that would make a stand-out dish in its own right. Otherwise, you could start with saffron risotto served with braised veal and gremolata. The kitchen's technical skills don't miss a beat, as witnessed in the immaculate timing of a main course comprising venison served with a supporting cast of chicory, quince, beetroot, velvet-smooth potato purée, and red wine-poached pear. Fish is handled just as confidently - perhaps sea trout with cima di rape greens, Ayrshire potato and wild fennel. Rounding things off in style, rhubarb is served poached, dried and as a delicate yet intensely flavoured mousse matched with creamy vanilla custard, wafer-thin meringue and palate-refreshing blood orange sorbet.

Chef Davey Aspin **Owner** APSP Restaurants Ltd
Times 6.30-9.30 Closed L all week, D Sun (Oct-Mar)
Prices Prices not confirmed Service optional, Groups min 8 service 10% **Wines** 10 by glass **Notes** Tasting menu available, Vegetarian menu, Dress restrictions, Smart casual, Civ Wed 40 **Seats** 80, Pr/dining room 34 **Children** Portions, Menu **Parking** 23

Save on Hotels. Book at **theAA.com/hotel**

FIFE 585 SCOTLAND

Road Hole Restaurant

British NOTABLE WINE LIST

Stylish modern Scots cooking overlooking the 17th hole

☎ 01334 474371
The Old Course Hotel, Golf Resort & Spa KY16 9SP
e-mail: reservations@oldcoursehotel.co.uk
dir: M90 junct 8 then A91 to St Andrews

There is no dearth of five-star hotels on the Scottish golfing circuit, but The Old Course, as its name announces without a blush for false modesty, enjoys the shortest handicap. Overlooking the world-famous links at St Andrews, specifically the famous Road Hole of the 17th green, it's certainly in a prime location. The views also stretch to the West Sands beach and the majestic sweep of coastline below this old university town, so there's something for everyone. And that's truest of all in the fine-dining restaurant, where an elegant design job of dark walls, framed prints and quality table settings is the backdrop for the stylishly presented modern Scots cooking on offer. Dishes are turned out in that clinically clean-looking fashion, their components arranged in neat rows on oblong or square glass plates, and while there is plenty of inventive mixing and matching of ingredients going on, the basic foundations are refreshingly

straightforward, with prime materials proudly accorded their origins. East Neuk lobster gratin seasoned with Arran mustard and parsley purée might be one way of starting, prior to a tripartite presentation of Black Isle lamb, in the guises of braised neck, a cutlet and sweetbreads, served with kale and turnips, the last simmered in red wine. Alternatively, a pasta starter might see Falkland venison tortellini with celeriac and Ayrshire bacon pave the way for Gigha halibut with curried leeks in warm tomato vinaigrette. Fish treatments are pretty robust all round, as is also seen when Scrabster monkfish comes bandaged in ham, accompanied by artichokes, salsify and trompettes. Finish with plum crumble soufflé and anise ice cream, or a pairing of honeycomb parfait and poached pear, with a macadamia biscuit and pear sorbet. Alternatively, opt for a plate of Scottish cheeses. The seriously upmarket wine list opens with eight by the glass.

Chef Ross Marshall **Owner** Kohler Company **Times** 12-2/7-9.30 Closed Jan **Prices** Fixed L 3 course fr £16.50, Fixed D 3 course fr £35, Tasting menu £50-£95, Starter £6-£12, Main £12-£22, Dessert £6-£8, Service optional **Wines** 11 by glass **Notes** Sunday L, Vegetarian available, Dress restrictions, Smart, collared shirt required, Civ Wed 260 **Seats** 70, Pr/dining room 16 **Parking** 100

FIFE *continued*

Russell Hotel

◉ Scottish, International

Scottish-influenced menus in small townhouse hotel

☎ 01334 473447
26 The Scores KY16 9AS
e-mail: enquiries@russellhotelstandrews.co.uk
web: www.russellhotelstandrews.co.uk
dir: From A91 left at 2nd rdbt into Golf Place, right in
200yds into The Scores, hotel in 300yds on left

A two-minute stroll from the breakfast table to the first
tee of the Old Course, the world-famous cradle of golf,
coupled with spectacular views over St Andrews Bay,
make this family-run Victorian townhouse an attractive
prospect. And when you have finished with the mashies
and niblicks, or had a bit of fun recreating the slow-mo
running scene from *Chariots of Fire* along the endless
sands, there's imaginative Scottish cooking to round off
the day in the cosy candlelit restaurant. Ham hock and
confit duck terrine with home-made piccalilli is a
dependable starter, then local materials come into play in
a main course such as roast saddle of Highland venison
with glazed pear, apricot and honey stuffing and red wine
jus. The addition of egg nog makes for an interesting take
on pannacotta, served with, what else, shortbread
biscuit.

Chef Michael Smith **Owner** Gordon De Vries
Times 12-2/6.30-9.30 Closed Xmas **Prices** Fixed D 3
course £27.50, Service optional **Wines** 12 by glass
Notes Civ Wed 40 **Seats** 40, Pr/dining room 10
Children Portions, Menu **Parking** 80, On street

Sands Grill

◉ Steak, Seafood

Locally-inspired brasserie-style cooking

☎ 01334 474371 & 468228
The Old Course Hotel, Golf Resort & Spa KY16 9SP
e-mail: reservations@oldcoursehotel.co.uk
dir: M90 junct 8 then A91 to St Andrews

The Old Course has a range of dining options in its
favour, plus quite possibly the most famous golf course
in the world on its doorstep. It's a luxurious five-star
affair and Sands Grill, as the name suggests, is the
informal (relatively speaking) dining venue, done out with
lots of black leather and darkwood, and looked over by a
slick and unstuffy service team. From the Josper grill
come excellent locally-sourced meats (10oz Scotch Black
Isle rib-eye, 8oz flat iron, and whole baby chicken,
perhaps), whilst among fish main courses might be roast
wild Shetland pollock with chorizo, mussels and borlotti
bean chowder. Finish with a warm hazelnut brownie with
praline ice cream.

Times 6-10 Closed L all week

The Seafood Restaurant

◉◉ Modern Seafood

Racy contemporary fish cookery on the coast

☎ 01334 479475
Bruce Embankment KY16 9AB
e-mail: standrews@theseafoodrestaurant.com
dir: On A917 turn left along Golf Place

From unassuming beginnings in a former fishermen's
pub in St Monans in the 1990s, The Seafood Restaurant
spread its wings and arrived at this perch on the St
Andrews coast nearly a decade ago. Glass-walled on all
sides, cantilevered out at one end over the embankment,
so that you can watch the four seasons that often go by
in a day on the east coast, it's a suitably dramatic
environment for the racy, contemporary fish cookery that's
on offer. Smoked haddock rarebit is a popular starter,
chunks of fine fish in rich rarebit on sliced baguette,
possibly coming with creamed leeks and pancetta, while
crab from East Neuk is not merely dressed, but tricked
out too with avocado espuma, confit tomato and
sweetcorn sorbet. An in-betweenie at dinner - smoked
salmon terrine, or half-a-dozen oysters with shallot
vinegar and Bloody Mary - precedes a main such as
crisp-skinned sea trout with sun-dried tomato linguini,
tapenade and basil. Desserts have got it going on, in the
form of complicated assemblages like apple and
cinnamon pannacotta, cinnamon and almond crumble,
caramel custard and apple sorbet.

Times 12-2.30/6.30-10 Closed 25-26 Dec, 1 Jan

Craig Millar @ 16 West End

◉◉ Modern Scottish   🍷 NOTABLE WINE LIST

Eclectic cooking with sweeping harbour views

☎ 01333 730327
16 West End KY10 2BX
e-mail: craigmillar@16westend.com
dir: Take A959 from St Andrews to Anstruther, then W on
A917 through Pittenweem. In St Monans to harbour then
right

Sweeping views of the Firth of Forth and St Monans
harbour can get dramatic when winter waves surge over
the sea wall, but all of the briny turmoil just serves to
remind you of the business in hand here: serving fabulous
fish and seafood with an exciting, modern spin. Large
windows flood the uncluttered space with natural light,
while unbuttoned service enhances the chilled out vibe.
Chef-patron Craig Millar succeeds in blending fabulous
Scottish produce with well-honed technique to deliver
precise, Asian and European-influenced dishes in the
modern idiom. Hand-dived scallops with Jerusalem
artichoke purée, smoked bacon, nuts and seeds opens the
show with a burst of intense flavour, while simplicity is
the key in a main course of top-quality stone bass
matched with couscous and satay sauce. Of course, it's
not all about fish - braised ox cheek with Puy lentils and
root vegetables should satisfy the carnivores at main
course. On-the-money flavour combinations see chocolate
tart matched with banana ice cream and salt caramel to
finish.

Chef Craig Millar **Owner** Craig Millar
Times 12.30-2/6.30-9 Closed 25-26 Dec, 1-2 Jan, 2 wks
Jan, Mon-Tue **Prices** Fixed L 2 course fr £22, Fixed D 3
course fr £42, Tasting menu fr £60, Service optional
Wines 77 bottles over £30, 11 bottles under £30, 7 by
glass **Notes** Tasting menu available, Sunday L,
Vegetarian available **Seats** 35, Pr/dining room 25
Children Portions **Parking** 10

Save on Hotels. Book at theAA.com/hotel

CITY OF GLASGOW 587 SCOTLAND

Blythswood Square

◎◎ Modern British ♥

Contemporary and classic cooking in former automobile headquarters

☎ 0141 248 8888
11 Blythswood Square G2 4AD
e-mail: reserve@blythswoodsquare.com

Glasgow's Blythswood Square, with its leafy aspect and upscale atmosphere, is home to a boutique hotel of real verve. The grand old HQ of the Royal Scottish Automobile Club (built in 1821) has never looked so...snazzy. It's on a big scale and those generous proportions have been put to good use. A drink in the palatial Salon Lounge surrounded by fluted columns topped with gilt capitals makes a fine first impression, before heading into the restaurant in the erstwhile ballroom, where a stylish décor works a blend of period splendour and ultra-modern. You wouldn't expect the menu to be stuck in the past, and it ain't. They've got a Josper grill - the signature of a 'serious' kitchen these days - so go for one of the excellent Scottish steaks (Buccleuch Estate fillet, maybe), or otherwise something like a poached Gigha halibut with oyster ravioli, heritage potatoes, salsify and vanilla jus. Top and tail a meal with chicken liver parfait with a bramble gel and melba toast, and a classic lemon tart.

Chef Derek Donaldson **Owner** Peter Taylor
Times 12-2.30/6-10 **Prices** Fixed L 2 course £18.50, Fixed D 3 course £22, Starter £4.95-£11.95, Main £12.95-£36, Dessert £2-£6.95, Service added but optional 10% **Wines** 40 bottles over £30, 10 bottles under £30, 14 by glass **Notes** Sunday L, Vegetarian available, Civ Wed 80 **Seats** 120, Pr/dining room 80 **Children** Portions, Menu **Parking** On street

La Bonne Auberge

◎ French, Mediterranean

The flavours of the Mediterranean and beyond in theatreland

☎ 0141 352 8310
Holiday Inn Theatreland, 161 West Nile St G1 2RL
e-mail: info@higlasgow.com
web: www.labonneauberge.co.uk
dir: M8 junct 16, follow signs for Royal Concert Hall, hotel opposite

Refurbishment and redecoration have given a high degree of comfort and elegance to La Bonne Auberge, with its plush seating, smart décor, drapes over the windows, and soft lighting from chandeliers and sconces. The kitchen still follows a broadly French and Mediterranean path without being too rigid, producing, for instance, Cajun-spiced salmon fillet with lemon butter, or tender and flavourful grilled rump of lamb rubbed with herbs, accompanied by spicy couscous, wilted spinach and orange and cardamom jus. More central to the style are

such well-conceived starters as ham hock and leek terrine wrapped in Parma ham served with apple purée, and pan-fried scallops with smoked bacon and cauliflower purée. Purées seem to be a hallmark of the kitchen, serving one of sweetcorn with chicken breast in red wine jus, accompanied by creamed oyster mushrooms and spinach. Finish with a classic rendition of lemon bavarois, dense and creamy, with strawberry ice cream.

Chef Gerry Sharkey **Owner** Chardon Leisure Ltd
Times 12-2.15/5-10 **Prices** Fixed L 2 course £16.95, Fixed D 3 course £22.95, Starter £7-£9.50, Main £12.50-£22.50, Dessert £6.95-£7.50, Service added but optional 12.5% **Wines** 10 by glass **Notes** Pre-theatre menu £16.95 from 5pm, Sunday L, Vegetarian available **Seats** 90, Pr/dining room 100 **Children** Portions, Menu **Parking** NCP opposite

Cail Bruich

◎◎ Modern European ♥

Artful modern cookery using the best of regional produce

☎ 0141 334 6265
752 Great Western Rd G12 8QX
e-mail: info@cailbruich.co.uk

The Charalambous brothers' Glasgow bistro is in the West End, adjacent to a stretch of the Botanical Gardens and not far from the university. The interior scheme emphasises bare wood, softened by leather upholstery and colourful artwork, as well as a floor-to-ceiling wine store. There is imagination at work throughout the menu, which utilises artful modern technique in ways that underline the unquestioned quality of the produce. Arran crab with a salad of fennel, tomato and cucumber keeps things simple enough, but there is also smoked Perthshire pigeon tricked out with pickled veg and dressed in raisins and capers. A more classical foie gras ballotine comes with dots of sublime almond milk, compressed plum and a napkin-swaddled slice of warm gingerbread. The seafood dishes are cause for celebration: a rolled fillet of Scrabster lemon sole on shredded leek set about with smoked haddock and potato, together with garlicky potato purée and an emulsion of smoked butter is a hauntingly aromatic dish. The finale might be an exotic chiboust of mango and sea-buckthorn with mango curd, candied carrots and carrot sorbet for a ravishing study in gold.

Chef Chris Charalambous **Owner** Paul & Chris Charalambous **Times** 12-2.30/5.30-9.30 Closed Xmas, New Year, 1 wk summer, 1 wk winter, Mon **Prices** Fixed L 2 course £14.95, Fixed D 3 course £17.95, Tasting menu £45-£54.50, Starter £6.50-£10.50, Main £14.50-£34, Dessert £6.95-£9.50, Service optional, Groups min 6 service 10% **Wines** 18 bottles over £30, 24 bottles under £30, 16 by glass **Notes** Pre-theatre offer Tue-Sun, Sunday L, Vegetarian available **Seats** 48 **Children** Portions, Menu **Parking** On street

Gamba

◎◎ Scottish, Seafood

Vibrant fish and seafood in the West End

☎ 0141 572 0899
225a West George St G2 2ND
e-mail: info@gamba.co.uk
dir: On the corner of West Campbell St & West George St, close to Blythswood Sq

Down in the basement - but none the worse for that - of a Georgian townhouse in the fashionable West End, Gamba is a perennial favourite with a stellar reputation for top-notch seafood. Its popularity is also a testament to its friendly approach to service. The clean-cut contemporary interior takes in terracotta tiled or boarded floors, pale wooden tables, fashionable seating and plenty of piscine references in its fish-themed artwork. The kitchen draws on Mediterranean and Asian influences and is passionate about sourcing the best seasonal produce from the Scottish larder, with fish from sustainable stocks cooked with simplicity and flair. The menu takes in a classic combo of grilled or pan-fried lemon sole with browned lemon and parsley butter, to the Med-inspired red mullet with chorizo peperonata and chick peas, and the Asian flavours of whole line-caught sea bass teriyaki with wasabi and fragrant rice.

Chef Derek Marshall **Owner** Mr D Marshall
Times 12-2.30/5-10.30 Closed 25-26 Dec, 1st wk Jan, L Sun **Prices** Fixed L 2 course £16.95, Fixed D 3 course £19.95-£25, Starter £7.50-£14.50, Main £16.50-£26, Dessert £5.50-£8.95, Service optional, Groups min 6 service 10% **Wines** 21 bottles over £30, 14 bottles under £30, 6 by glass **Notes** Pre-theatre menu, 3 course winter menu incl wine £25, Vegetarian available **Seats** 66 **Parking** On street

GLASGOW *continued*

The Hanoi Bike Shop

Vietnamese **NEW**

Exciting Vietnamese street food

☎ 0141 334 7165
8 Ruthven Ln G12 9BG
e-mail: pho@thehanoibikeshop.co.uk
web: www.thehanoibikeshop.co.uk

Run by the Glasgow group behind the ever-popular Ubiquitous Chip and Stravaigin (see entries), this venture takes aim at an entirely different culinary concept, with its menus based loosely around Vietnamese street food. The canteen-style setting is fun and funky, an explosion of riotous colours lit by silken lanterns and decorated with (what else?) dismembered bits of bikes from Uncle Ho's Communist era. And the food is similarly explosive, bursting with the authentic pungent, perfumed, palate-thrilling tastes of Vietnam. If you're not familiar with the style, friendly staff will guide you through the menu. Start with classic bun cha - pork meatballs and chargrilled pork belly with vermicelli noodles and fresh herbs - or pho ('fuh'), the noodle broth spiked with chilli and herbs that is eaten round the clock in Vietnam, then follow with slow-cooked beef and anise stew with lemongrass, ginger, chilli and spring onion, or caramel hake flavoured with sweet galangal, coconut, chilli and garlic.

The Hanoi Bike Shop

Chef Tad McLean **Owner** Colin Clydesdale & Carol Wright **Times** 12-11 Closed 25-26 Dec, 1 Jan **Prices** Prices not confirmed Service optional **Wines** 4 by glass **Notes** Sun brunch 11am-5pm, Vegetarian available **Seats** 75 **Children** Portions **Parking** On street

Hotel du Vin at One Devonshire Gardens

— *see below*

Hotel du Vin at One Devonshire Gardens

GLASGOW   **MAP 20 NS56**

French, European **NOTABLE WINE LIST**

Smart, creative cooking in an elegant townhouse hotel

☎ 0844 736 4256
1 Devonshire Gardens G12 0UX
e-mail: bistro.odg@hotelduvin.com
web: www.hotelduvin.com
dir: M8 junct 17, follow signs for A82 after 1.5m turn left into Hyndland Rd

One Devonshire Gardens is a swanky address in Glasgow's West End and is these days home to what must surely be considered the Hotel du Vin group's shining star. The row of porticoed townhouses in a tree-lined terrace makes a fine first impression and the interior is done out with a good deal of boutique chic - a luxe blend of old and new, with rich fabrics, well-chosen furniture and a good deal of style. For those seeking out a bit of old-school entertainment, there's even a cigar shack and whisky room. The trademark HdV Bistro is a shade grander than many others in the group, with burnished oak panelling aplenty and crisp white linen on the tables, which matches the kitchen's ambitious and refined output. Darin Campbell and his team cook up a storm delivering creative contemporary food underpinned with French classicism and top-notch Scottish ingredients. Thus Cullen skink as a first course is a modish interpretation, with velouté of potato and onion, poached haddock and hen's egg from Corrie Mains farm in Ayrshire, and a dish of Loch Fyne langoustines comes with a salted lemon fluid gel and smoked gnocchi. Among main courses, Newtonmore venison might come with Savoy cabbage, pommes dauphine and a beetroot and juniper sauce, line-caught sea bass (from Cornwall) with samphire, clams, calamari and a saffron velouté, and Chateaubriand is a classic treat for two. There's a menu dégustation if you really want to push the boat out.

Among desserts, blood orange and chocolate soufflé with caramel and fresh ginger ice cream, or red velvet cake with pecan brittle and cheesecake ice cream will end things in style. The wine list is full of good things and worth a moment of anybody's time.

Chef Darin Campbell **Owner** MWB/Hotel Du Vin **Times** 12-2/6-10 Closed L Sat **Prices** Fixed L 2 course £15.95, Fixed D 3 course £19.95, Tasting menu £69, Starter £8.25-£14.25, Main £17.95-£25.25, Dessert £6.95-£14.50, Service added but optional 10% **Wines** 12 by glass **Notes** Tasting menu 6 course, Sunday L, Vegetarian available, Dress restrictions, Smart casual, Civ Wed 70 **Seats** 78, Pr/dining room 70 **Children** Portions **Parking** On street

Ian Brown Food & Drink

◉ Modern Scottish ⏱

Impressive modern Scottish cooking in Giffnock

☎ 0141 638 8422
55 Eastwood Mains Rd G46 6PW
e-mail: ian@ianbrownrestaurant.co.uk
dir: Group of shops on Eastwoodmains Rd next to railway bridge

Ian Brown was head chef at Ubiquitous Chip (see entry) for many years before finally opening his own restaurant in Giffnock. It's a friendly, family-run place, with much light wood in evidence, splashes of colour brought to the neutral décor by red lampshades and works by local artists on the walls. Dishes can sound deceptively simple, but they are big on flavour, as seen in a starter of melt-in-the-mouth pig's cheek with smooth Madeira sauce and herbed polenta, and main-course collops of venison, their richness cut by sweet-and-sour bramble sauce, nicely accompanied by celeriac purée, kale and sesame potatoes. Produce is of the first order, and the menus of contemporary ideas give plenty to consider, including a couple of fish options (baked sea bass fillet with clapshot and lemon hollandaise, perhaps). Don't miss out on a pudding like chocolate and ginger fondant with satsuma sauce.

Chef Ian Brown **Owner** Ian & Sheila Brown
Times 12-2/5.30-9.30 Closed 1 Jan, Mon **Prices** Fixed L 2 course £12.50, Fixed D 3 course £15.50, Starter £3.60-£7.10, Main £9.20-£27.50, Dessert £5.50-£7, Service optional **Wines** 5 bottles over £30, 29 bottles under £30, 7 by glass **Notes** Fixed L/D 2/3 course £11/£14.40 (except Fri-Sat), Sunday L, Vegetarian available **Seats** 40 **Children** Portions **Parking** 6

Malmaison Glasgow

◉ Modern French, Scottish ⏱

Reliable brasserie food in a former church

☎ 0844 693 0653
278 West George St G2 4LL
e-mail: reception.glasgow@malmaison.com
web: www.malmaison.com
dir: From George Square take St Vincent St to Pitt St. Hotel on corner with West George St

You can rely on the Malmaison chain to come up with out-of-the-ordinary settings for their design-led boutique hotels: the Glasgow Mal occupies the old Greek Orthodox church and its brasserie lies at the bottom of a spiral staircase in the original crypt. With its vaulted ceilings, comfy banquettes, darkly atmospheric colour scheme, and low lighting to lend the place an intimate vibe, it's a memorable setting for modern brasserie food. The eclectic menu takes in comfort classics from the grill - the burger stack, say, which comes with foie gras, celeriac slaw and onion rings - otherwise, start with beef consommé with braised oxtail, celeriac, field mushrooms and orzo pasta, followed by coriander-crusted rack of lamb with spiced potatoes and mint yoghurt. Also look for blackboard specials driven by what's available locally and in season.

For pudding, treacle tart with clotted cream provides a typically comfort-oriented finale.

Chef Colin Manson **Owner** Malmaison Hotels Ltd
Times 12-2.30/5.30-10.30 **Prices** Prices not confirmed Service added but optional 10%, Groups min 10 service 10% **Wines** 39 bottles over £30, 21 bottles under £30, 11 by glass **Notes** Pre-theatre menu available, Brunch £19.95, Sunday L, Vegetarian available, Civ Wed 40 **Seats** 85, Pr/dining room 12 **Children** Portions, Menu **Parking** Q Park Waterloo St

Number Sixteen

◉ Modern International ⏱

Buzzy neighbourhood venue

☎ 0141 339 2544 & 07957 423615
16 Byres Rd G11 5JY
dir: 2 mins walk from Kelvinhall tube station, at bottom of Byres Rd

This tiny neighbourhood restaurant on Glasgow's vibrant Byres Road has a strong local following who appreciate its unbuttoned approach and the kitchen's creative mission. It is an elbow-to-elbow sort of space with a pocket-sized downstairs area, and a mini-mezzanine above, all decorated with colourful artwork, and kept ticking over by casually dressed, on-the-ball staff. The chefs beavering away in the open-to-view kitchen aren't scared to experiment with novel flavour combinations, so a starter might bring together a galette of Jerusalem artichoke purée with roast beetroot, figs, crumbled feta, sumac and roast onion vinaigrette. Next up, braised pork belly is served with crackling, piccalilli, pumpkin and sage gratin, apple purée and red wine sauce. Pudding delivers an exotic combo of passionfruit and coconut tart with passionfruit ice cream.

Chef Gerard Mulholland **Owner** Gerard Mulholland, Joel Pomfret **Times** 12-2.30/5.30-9.30 Closed 25-26 Dec, 1-2 Jan **Prices** Fixed L 2 course fr £11.95, Fixed D 3 course fr £16.95, Starter £4.95-£7.50, Main £13.50-£18.95, Dessert £6.50-£7.50, Service optional **Wines** 2 bottles over £30, 31 bottles under £30, 6 by glass **Notes** Sunday L, Vegetarian available **Seats** 36, Pr/dining room 17 **Children** Portions **Parking** On street

Opium

◉ Chinese, Oriental fusion NEW ⏱

Asian fusion from a Hong Kong masterchef

☎ 0141 332 6668
191 Hope St G2 2UL
e-mail: eat@opiumrestaurant.co.uk

The name might evoke images of hallucinogenic drug stupors, but what we have here is a pin-sharp, contemporary-styled East-Asian fusion restaurant in the pulsing heart of Glasgow. Big picture-windows let the light stream in on a brown study, where communal tables with high chairs share the space with conventional restaurant seating. Kwan Yu Lee learned his skills from virtual boyhood in Hong Kong, but has honed an on-trend mélange of classical and modern Asian dishes to suit

current British taste. An array of dim sum shows basic skills are not forgotten, with shu mai and har gau dumplings full of crisp, clean flavours. A huge plate of Malay seafood noodles incorporates octopus, king prawns and more with racy levels of fresh chilli, while the likes of slow-cooked claypot Hong Kong beef and Thai green curry extend the range. Coconut-coated, deep-fried ice cream with dark chocolate and honey sauce is the grandest of finales.

Chef Kwan Yu Lee **Owner** Trevor Lee **Times** 12-2.30/5-10 **Prices** Prices not confirmed Service optional, Groups min 6 service 10% **Wines** 2 bottles over £30, 19 bottles under £30, 8 by glass **Notes** Pre-theatre 2/3 course menu, Sunday L, Vegetarian available **Seats** 54

La Parmigiana

◉◉ Italian, Mediterranean ⏱

West End Italian institution

☎ 0141 334 0686
447 Great Western Rd, Kelvinbridge G12 8HH
e-mail: sgiovanazzi@btclick.com
web: www.laparmigiana.co.uk
dir: Next to Kelvinbridge underground

Reaching its 35th birthday in 2013, La Parmigiana has earned its place as a Glasgow institution. Family-run, the small restaurant with its warm red walls, smartly dressed tables, and equally well turned-out staff, garners a loyal following for its traditional Italian cooking. The place is not preserved in aspic, though, and there is a nicely restrained modish influence to the menu, with the fine Scottish ingredients allowed to shine. Excellent home-made pasta is a good place to start, perhaps flavoursome lobster ravioli with a cream and basil sauce. Roast fillet of venison comes with a rich Brunello, porcini and Italian sausage ragù, plus a polenta croûton - a wonderful, hearty plate of food - while an elegantly put-together Calvados crème brûlée with apple confit and apple crumble ice cream makes a memorable finish.

Chef Peppino Camilli **Owner** Sandro & Stefano Giovanazzi
Times 12-2.30/5.30-10.30 Closed 25-26 Dec, 1 Jan **Prices** Fixed L 3 course fr £16.20, Fixed D 3 course fr £18.95, Starter £5.60-£11.90, Main £19.30-£27.95, Dessert £5.90-£6.15, Service optional **Wines** 35 bottles over £30, 15 bottles under £30, 8 by glass **Notes** Pre-theatre 2/3 course 5.30-7pm £16.10/£18.25, Sunday L, Vegetarian available **Seats** 50 **Children** Portions **Parking** On street

GLASGOW *continued*

Rogano

◉◉ Scottish, Seafood V 🐾

Modern cooking with a sense of occasion in an art deco masterpiece

☎ 0141 248 4055
11 Exchange Place G1 3AN
e-mail: info@roganoglasgow.com

Fast approaching its 80th birthday, it's fair to call Rogano a Glasgow institution. The art-deco look of the place never fails to leave an impression, particularly the oyster bar, and there's a sense of bygone sophistication running right through. The charming service team plays a big part in maintaining a sense of occasion. Some classic seafood dishes have been on the menu since 1935 - platefuls of Scottish fruits de mer, for example, and lobster thermidor - but you might also start with haggis, neeps and tatties with an Arran mustard cream, and follow up with rabbit wrapped in Parma ham. But seafood is king here. Langoustines en croûte with aïoli is a starter featuring wonderfully fresh shellfish, or go for Scottish oysters from Cumbrae. Among main courses, grilled fillets of red mullet with couscous, chargrilled vegetables and harissa dressing competes for your attention with lemon sole, either grilled or meunière, and served on or off the bone. And for dessert there might be vanilla and honeycomb parfait with butterscotch sauce.

Chef Andy Cumming **Owner** Lynnet Leisure **Times** 12-2.30/6-10.30 Closed 1 Jan **Prices** Prices not confirmed Service added but optional 12.5% **Wines** 14 by glass **Notes** Tasting menu 4 course, Sunday L, Vegetarian menu, Dress restrictions, Smart casual **Seats** 70, Pr/dining room 16 **Children** Portions **Parking** NCP car parks

Shish Mahal

◉ Indian

Long-standing Indian in a quiet part of the city

☎ 0141 339 8256
60-68 Park Rd G4 9JF
e-mail: reservations@shishmahal.co.uk
dir: From M8/A8 take exit towards Dumbarton. On Great Western Rd 1st left into Park Rd

A Glaswegian institution since the '60s, the Shish Mahal has seen generations of curry fans pass through its doors to sample Mr Ali's reliable classic Indian cooking. The house motto may be 'unspoilt by progress', but the décor has moved with the times - there's a smart modern feel to its warm Asian colour scheme, while leather seating and linen-clad tables do their bit to bolster the feel-good factor, and service is friendly and knowledgeable. The extensive menu explores familiar regional variations, taking in old favourites from the Madras, vindaloo and bhuna stables, but there are plenty of intriguing ideas to broaden your horizons too. Murgh tikka achari is chicken breasts in a tikka-spiced marinade, pan-fried with onion seeds and cracked coriander, while mains head north to the Punjab for an aromatic nashedar banjara - succulent

lamb in a rich sauce of ginger, garlic, coriander, tomato and green pepper.

Chef Mr I Humayun **Owner** Ali A Aslam, Nasim Ahmed **Times** 12-2/5-11 Closed 25 Dec, L Sun **Prices** Fixed L 2 course £13-£22, Starter £3.25-£7.95, Main £8.95-£17.95, Dessert £2.95-£4.95, Service optional, Groups min 5 service 10% **Wines** 2 bottles over £30, 18 bottles under £30, 1 by glass **Notes** Fixed L 4 course, Vegetarian available **Seats** 95, Pr/dining room 14 **Children** Portions **Parking** Side street, Underground station car park

Stravaigin

◉◉ Modern International

Popular eatery with creative, multi-national flavour

☎ 0141 334 2665
28-30 Gibson St, Kelvinbridge G12 8NX
e-mail: stravaigin@btinternet.com
web: www.stravaigin.com
dir: Next to Glasgow University. 200yds from Kelvinbridge underground

The tagline of this switched-on stalwart of the Glasgow foodie scene - 'Think global, eat local' - neatly sums up its culinary ideology. Spread over two floors of café-bar and a basement restaurant, the operation goes for a quirky contemporary look - reclaimed and reinvented pieces of modern art and interesting objets set against rough stone walls, wallpaper with a cleaver motif, and beamed ceilings - that is a perfect foil to its consistently imaginative, flavour-driven cooking. The kitchen plunders Scotland's magnificent larder for its raw materials, which are allied with an eclectic approach to the world's cuisines: a starter of Mull cheddar and polenta cakes with sweetcorn and chilli velouté, plum tomato and jalapeño salsa is a typical case in point. Caramelised pork belly and cheek with butternut squash gratin, salsify and thyme purée and soused red cabbage makes a similarly full-frontal attack on the taste buds, while desserts keep exploring interesting combos of flavour and texture with stem ginger parfait teamed with prune Metaxa ice cream, mulled wine reduction and cinnamon crumb.

Stravaigin

Chef Kenny Mackay **Owner** Colin Clydesdale, Carol Wright **Times** 5-11 Closed 25 Dec, 1 Jan, L Mon-Fri **Prices** Prices not confirmed Service optional **Wines** 23 by glass **Notes** Pre-theatre menu 2/3 £13.95/£15.95, Sunday L, Vegetarian available **Seats** 50, Pr/dining room 50 **Children** Portions, Menu **Parking** On street, car park 100yds

Ubiquitous Chip

◉◉ Scottish ⚱ NOTABLE WINE LIST

Iconic address for modern Scottish cooking

☎ 0141 334 5007
12 Ashton Ln G12 8SJ
e-mail: mail@ubiquitouschip.co.uk
web: www.ubiquitouschip.co.uk
dir: In West End, off Byres Rd. Adjacent to Hillhead underground station

Part of the West End scene since 1971, the Chip is many things to many people. First and foremost it represents the best of Scotland, flying the flag for Scottish ingredients (and culture even), and it matters not if you just want to pop in to drink in one of the three bars or dine heartily under the glassed-over roof of the courtyard restaurant. Inside it's a warren of four dining areas, including a brasserie, the courtyard and a mezzanine,

Save on Hotels. Book at theAA.com/hotel

CITY OF GLASGOW – HIGHLAND 591 SCOTLAND

and all around are sprawling colourful murals and the buzz of contented customers. The cooking is more sophisticated than you might imagine, but it is always clear-headed and based on superb Scottish ingredients. You might start with the long-running favourite, venison haggis, but equally you could go for torchon of foie gras with pain d'épice, Gewürztraminer jelly and apple. Main course might deliver fillet of sole with squid ink spätzle, grilled leek and langoustine sauce, or a fabulous Aberdeen Angus steak, and for dessert, there's always the Caledonian oatmeal ice cream to tempt you.

Ubiquitous Chip

Chef Andrew Mitchell **Owner** Colin Clydesdale **Times** 12-2.30/5-11 Closed 25 Dec, 1 Jan **Prices** Fixed L 2 course fr £15.95, Starter £6-£16, Main £16-£35, Dessert £6-£15, Service optional **Wines** 215 bottles over £30, 58 bottles under £30, 37 by glass **Notes** Pre-theatre 2/3 course fr £15.95/£19.95, 5-6.30pm, Sunday L, Vegetarian available, Civ Wed 60 **Seats** 100, Pr/dining room 45 **Children** Portions, Menu **Parking** Lilybank Gardens (50mtrs)

Urban Bar and Brasserie

◉ Modern British, French ◉

Updated brasserie fare in a former bank

☎ 0141 248 5636
23-25 St Vincent Place G1 2DT
e-mail: info@urbanbrasserie.co.uk
dir: In city centre between George Sq & Buchanan St

Climb the small set of stairs, pass the champagne bar and enter the spacious dining room, where the décor, leather-look banquettes and booths, black-clad staff wearing long white aprons, and the bustle are all reminiscent of a Parisian brasserie. The menu runs to Serrano ham with borlotti beans, marinated artichokes and parmesan and steamed fillets of plaice with chorizo, fennel and sticky rice. The kitchen knows its stuff, producing smooth, rich foie gras and chicken liver parfait cut by Oxford sauce, then accurately cooked crisp-fried salmon fillet on a velvety, buttery lemon and vanilla sauce accompanied by crabmeat and truffled new potatoes. Francophiles will be pleased to see boeuf bourguignon, served with parsnip champ, and who could

resist a jam jar filled with popcorn-flavoured pannacotta topped with salted caramel?

Chef David Clunas **Owner** Alan Tomkins **Times** noon-10 Closed 25 Dec, 1 Jan, All-day dining **Prices** Fixed L 2 course £15-£17, Fixed D 3 course £25-£45, Starter £6-£13, Main £12-£24, Dessert £6-£9, Service optional, Groups min 6 service 10% **Wines** 20 bottles over £30, 20 bottles under £30, 13 by glass **Notes** Pre-theatre, Fixed D menu available, Sunday L, Vegetarian available **Seats** 110, Pr/dining room 20 **Children** Portions **Parking** NCP West Nile St

La Vallée Blanche

◉ French ◉

French bistro cooking in a Glasgow ski lodge

☎ 0141 334 3333
360 Byres Rd G12 8AW
e-mail: enquiries@lavalleeblanche.com

If you're pining for the French slopes, this thriving venue in the West End named after one of the ski districts in the Haute-Savoie may offer some comfort. But, hey, the real reason to visit is to tuck into some great unfussy modern bistro cooking. The log cabin décor, flickering candlelight in the evening, and good-natured atmosphere is all part of the appeal. Kick off with smoked haddock with soft-boiled egg, crisp potato and a light curry foam for a simple and satisfying first course, or maybe go for the roast poussin and courgette tarte fine with caramelised onion and walnut salad. Main-course confit pork belly, caramelised apple purée, black pudding and poached dates is a good and hearty dish, or try the fillet of halibut with olive-crushed potatoes, roast fennel, baby leeks and saffron velouté. Hot apricot soufflé with salted almond ice cream is a modish finale.

Chef David Maxwell **Times** 12-2.15/5.30-9.45 Closed 25 Dec, 1 Jan, Mon **Prices** Fixed L 2 course fr £12.95, Fixed D 3 course fr £14.95, Starter £5.95-£7.95, Main £12.95-£24.95, Dessert £5.50-£6.50, Service optional, Groups min 8 service 10% **Wines** 14 bottles over £30, 21 bottles under £30, 8 by glass **Notes** Brunch available, Sunday L, Vegetarian available **Seats** 78 **Children** Portions

Wee Lochan

◉ Modern Scottish

Polished contemporary cooking in the West End

☎ 0141 338 6606
340 Crow Rd, Broomhill G11 7HT
e-mail: eat@an-lochan.com

You could keep things as simple as coffee and a scone at this welcoming family-run operation, but you would be missing out if you didn't stay for the lively, modern Scottish cooking. Bag a seat at one of the pavement tables outside if the weather is being kind, but no matter if it's not, for it's lovely inside too: simple and inviting, with white walls hung with bright artwork and white leather-look chairs at wooden tables. The local-is-best philosophy reigns in the kitchen, finding its expression in

seared scallops with Jerusalem artichoke purée, chorizo and vinaigrette, followed by crispy panko-crumbed fillet of hake given an Asian spin by coconut rice, pak choi, and soy and ginger dressing, or there may be roast crown of partridge wrapped in Parma ham with pan-fried foie gras, bubble-and-squeak and red wine sauce. Finish with vanilla pannacotta with poached rhubarb and ginger crumble.

Chef Rupert Staniforth **Owner** Aisla & Rupert Staniforth **Times** 12-3/5-10 Closed 25 Dec, 1-2 Jan **Prices** Fixed L 2 course £11.95-£14.95, Fixed D 3 course £15.95-£17.95, Service optional, Groups min 8 service 10% **Wines** 6 bottles over £30, 30 bottles under £30, 18 by glass **Notes** Sun breakfast, Pre-theatre set menu available, Sunday L, Vegetarian available **Seats** 50 **Children** Portions **Parking** On street (no charge)

HIGHLAND

BOAT OF GARTEN	Map 23 NH91

Boat Hotel

◉◉ Modern British ◉

Modern bistro classics in a majestic Cairngorm setting

☎ 01479 831258
Deshar Rd PH24 3BH
e-mail: info@boathotel.co.uk
dir: Turn off A9 N of Aviemore onto A95. Follow signs to Boat of Garten

In such a traditional-looking Scottish country hotel in the heart of the Cairngorms, you might be forgiven for expecting the full-monty formal approach to dining. But its panelled Boat Bistro has moved with the times and gone all refreshingly unbuttoned and chilled, with unclothed wooden tables, tealights and relaxed service. Quality local and seasonal produce underpins the kitchen's well-presented modernised bistro repertoire; think hand-dived scallops teamed with butternut squash purée and crispy pancetta, or loin of Speyside venison with skirlie potato cake, Chantenay carrots and juniper jus. To finish, go for saffron and orange frangipane tart with vanilla ice cream or fresh raspberry cranachan pepped-up with toasted oatmeal and whisky cream. (Lighter options - classic Caesar salad to fish and chips - are available in the adjoining bar.)

Chef Tomi Burns **Owner** Mr J Erasmus & Mr R Drummond **Times** 12-3/5-9 **Prices** Fixed L 2 course fr £11.95, Fixed D 3 course fr £24, Starter £4.95-£9.95, Main £9.95-£24.95, Dessert £4.95-£8.95 **Wines** 15 bottles over £30, 15 bottles under £30, 8 by glass **Notes** Early bird menu available daily, Sunday L, Vegetarian available, Civ Wed 65 **Seats** 70, Pr/dining room 40 **Children** Portions, Menu **Parking** 36

BRORA — Map 23 NC90

Royal Marine Hotel, Restaurant & Spa

◉ Modern Scottish

Traditional Highland hotel with reliable cooking

☎ 01408 621252
Golf Rd KW9 6QS
e-mail: info@royalmarinebrora.com
web: www.royalmarinebrora.com
dir: off A9 in village towards beach & golf course

It's no surprise that this smartly refurbished Edwardian country-house hotel does good service as a 19th hole, with Brora's renowned golf links on the doorstep. Lorimer's Restaurant - the hotel's fine-dining option - is the nattily traditional setting for dinner, formally attired in blue-themed Scottish baronial style, carpeted for comfort, with heavy tartan drapes and white linen-dressed tables. The kitchen keeps things intelligently simple, allowing quality produce from the local Scottish larder to shine in hearty portions. West Coast haddock, perhaps, lightly grilled with lemon and simply served with sautéed garden vegetables and new potatoes, or saddle of Highland venison accompanied by crunchy champ (studded with toasted seeds), roasted root vegetables and a rich port and red wine jus.

Times 12-2/6.30-8.45 Closed L (pre booking only)

DORNOCH — Map 23 NH78

Dornoch Castle Hotel

◉ Modern Scottish

Medieval castle hotel with a true Scottish flavour

☎ 01862 810216
Castle St IV25 3SD
e-mail: enquiries@dornochcastlehotel.com
web: www.dornochcastlehotel.com
dir: 2m N of Dornoch Bridge on A9, turn right to Dornoch. Hotel in village centre opp Cathedral

Situated on Dornoch's quaint Market Square, opposite the 12th-century cathedral, this dramatic 15th-century castle turned hotel and restaurant flies the flag for Scottish good looks and a happy mix of modern and traditional cooking. There's a small, internal courtyard and cosy bar complete with a fire and exposed brick castle walls, while the conservatory style dining room embraces its Scottish heritage: think tartan table runners over burgundy tablecloths, burgundy napkins and some interesting Tain Pottery (plates, cruets and vases). Tea lights and soft music create a relaxing atmosphere, and black-clad staff display good knowledge of a menu that sees some Scottish tradition amongst the mainly modern British, well-presented dishes. Start with pressed ham hock terrine, prune purée and chargrilled focaccia before a fantastic pan-fried fillet of John Dory, vegetables, new potatoes, caper and herb butter sauce. Deconstructed cranachan - raspberry jelly, whisky parfait and oatmeal cream - works well as a modern take on an old favourite.

Times 12-3/6-9.30 Closed 25-26 Dec, 2nd wk Jan

FORT AUGUSTUS — Map 23 NH30

Inchnacardoch Lodge Hotel

◉ Modern Scottish ☺

Unfussy, produce-led cooking beside Loch Ness

☎ 01456 450900
Inchnacardoch Bay PH32 4BL
e-mail: info@inchhotel.com
dir: On A82. Turn right before entering Fort Augustus from Inverness

On the banks of Loch Ness, this 150-year-old former hunting lodge is now a traditionally done out country-house hotel with a lot going for it. Affectionately known as the Inch, it has smart bedrooms and, in the form of the Yard, a restaurant with fabulous views. Original polished floors, high ceilings and local artwork (for sale) set the scene, whilst well-laid tables and leather chairs crank up the comfort factor. Good quality local ingredients figure large in the slate of unfussy dishes; start, perhaps, with haggis, neaps and tatties, before moving on to oven-baked fillet of haddock with baby potatoes, red onion, courgettes and a creamy fish sauce, finishing with a four-layer chocolate cake served with caramel ice cream. It's worth noting that the bar lounge is home to 60 malt whiskies.

Chef Paul Draper **Times** 7.30-10 Closed L all week **Prices** Prices not confirmed **Wines** 3 by glass **Notes** Vegetarian available, Civ Wed 35 **Seats** 24, Pr/dining room 6 **Children** Portions **Parking** 15

The Lovat, Loch Ness

◉◉ Modern British V ☺

Ingenious cookery in a lochside eco-hotel

☎ 01456 459250 & 0845 450 1100
Loch Ness PH32 4DU
e-mail: info@thelovat.com
web: www.thelovat.com
dir: On A82 between Fort William & Inverness

Sitting at the southern tip of Loch Ness, The Lovat is run on sound eco-principles, ensuring it does nothing to disturb the monster's environment. Its elevated position enjoys commanding views of both water and town, and a programme of improvements within the Victorian building has produced a set of elegant public spaces, none more so than the dining room, which looks out imperiously over the grounds. Elaborate light fittings, linen-clad tables and smart staff who explain each dish as it appears, all add to the allure. Sean Kelly is skilled at thinking outside the box, producing a cylinder of foie gras filled with mulled wine jelly, alongside rolled smoked duck and crackling, to start, followed by a picture of the sea-bed constructed of shellfish, seaweed, samphire and oyster foam, tingling with seafood freshness. Main might be garlic-crumbed lamb loin, a cone of shoulder, sweetbreads and shepherd's pie, with a smear of vivid pea purée, while dessert includes a witty take on breakfast, with baked yoghurt cream, whisky marmalade, muesli and dried raspberries, topped with a piece of sweet melba toast.

Chef Sean Kelly **Owner** Caroline Gregory **Times** 7-9 Closed Nov-Mar, Sun-Mon, L all week **Prices** Prices not confirmed Service optional **Wines** 25 bottles over £30, 35 bottles under £30, 13 by glass **Notes** Vegetarian menu, Civ Wed 120 **Seats** 24, Pr/dining room 50 **Parking** 30

See advert opposite

FORT WILLIAM — Map 22 NN17

Inverlochy Castle Hotel

◉◉◉ – *see opposite*

Inverlochy Castle Hotel

FORT WILLIAM MAP 22 NN17

Modern British V NOTABLE WINE LIST

Grand formal dining in the foothills of Ben Nevis

☎ 01397 702177
Torlundy PH33 6SN
e-mail: info@inverlochy.co.uk
web: www.inverlochycastlehotel.com
dir: 3m N of Fort William on A82, just past Golf Club, N towards Inverness

A Victorian castle hotel overlooked by Ben Nevis, Inverlochy stands proud in 500 acres, a goodly portion of which can be surveyed from the deep dining room windows. Its namesake, the ruined 13th-century castle itself, resides nearby, adding an air of longue durée to the setting. The house was a private residence until the 1960s, but has found its calling as a country-house hotel in the full-dress idiom. Abundant staff and a highly polished, formal approach confer distinction on the whole package. What better than to spend a day fishing in tranquillity, before dressing for dinner, where harpist or pianist await in the splendidly opulent restaurant to provide melodious accompaniment to your tales of the one that got away? Philip Carnegie oversees an ambitious, high-achieving kitchen that has stuck tenaciously and productively to the presentational style and techniques of haute cuisine, as witness the signature opener of baked quail with foie gras. Lustrous sauces give depth to gently rich compositions of immaculate prime materials, and contrasting textures abound. Start with a trio of fat Loch Linnhe prawns, lined up smartly on a parmesan potato cake, with wild mushrooms and tarragon cream, or a palate-awakening serving of curry-dusted veal sweetbreads with pickled nectarine and rosemary. Main-course chef's specials see the stops pulled out for the likes of roast mallard with confit leg, cabbage and chestnuts in orange and cinnamon jus, but it's hard to tear yourself away from sleekly refined fish dishes such as grilled turbot with razor clams, all beautifully timed and served with girolles, broad beans and a tangle of linguine. A clever spin on cranachan becomes a hot honey and whisky soufflé topped with oatmeal, alongside raspberry sorbet, or there could be lightly whipped cinnamon brûlée with caramelised banana and yoghurt. An extensive fine wine list does the food justice.

Chef Philip Carnegie **Owner** Inverlochy Hotel Ltd **Times** 12.30-1.45/6.30-10 **Prices** Fixed L 2 course fr £28, Fixed D 3 course fr £67, Tasting menu fr £85, Service added but optional 10% **Wines** 240 bottles over £30, 4 bottles under £30, 11 by glass **Notes** Vegetarian menu, Dress restrictions, Jacket & tie for D, Civ Wed 80 **Seats** 40, Pr/dining room 20 **Children** Portions, Menu **Parking** 20

FORT WILLIAM *continued*

Lime Tree Hotel & Restaurant

◉◉ Modern Scottish ✦

A place of culinary and artistic creativity

☎ 01397 701806
The Old Manse, Achintore Rd PH33 6RQ
e-mail: info@limetreefortwilliam.co.uk
dir: On the A82 on entering Fort William

The Lime Tree has a lot going for it. For a start, it has a fully working beamed art gallery, staging national exhibitions, as well as being a modern hotel and destination restaurant with Loch Linnhe and the mountains as backdrop. The name given to the gallery is An Ealdhain, Gaelic for 'the place of creativity', and it's a title that applies just as much to what's going on in the restaurant under new chef William MacDonald. In a relaxed ambience of candlelight and warm hospitality, the food served is a considered tour through the modern Scottish repertoire, using much local produce. Start with smoked haddock and leek terrine in Cullen skink sauce, or with a warm salad of crowdie cream cheese, figs, celeriac and pine nuts, before the main show brings on beetroot-cured, hot-smoked salmon on citrus mash in a balsamic reduction, or saddle of Glenfinnan venison with puréed quince, a violet potato scone and braised red cabbage in juniper jus. The regionally apposite dessert is Laphroaig whisky bavarois with tempered chocolate and cranachan ice cream.

Chef William MacDonald **Owner** David Wilson & Charlotte Wright **Times** 6-9 Closed 24-25 Dec & 3-31 Jan, L all week **Prices** Fixed D 3 course £29.95, Service optional **Wines** 26 bottles over £30, 25 bottles under £30, 10 by glass **Notes** Vegetarian available, Civ Wed 50 **Seats** 32, Pr/dining room 50 **Children** Portions **Parking** 10

Moorings Hotel

◉ Modern European ✦

Popular Highland hotel with accomplished cooking

☎ 01397 772797
Banavie PH33 7LY
e-mail: reservations@moorings-fortwilliam.co.uk
web: www.moorings-fortwilliam.co.uk
dir: From A82 take A830 W for 1m. 1st right over Caledonian Canal on B8004, signed Banavie

The location may be tranquillity itself, but there's plenty going on around this Highland hotel on the Caledonian

Canal. Feeling energetic? Then go for a hike in the steps of World War II commandos who trained in the Great Glen; if you want more sedate pursuits, you could watch boats stepping up the flight of locks known as Neptune's Staircase on the canal as it leaves Loch Linnhe, or wave at the Jacobite train as it chuffs by on its way to the fishing port of Mallaig. When the day's activities are done, The Moorings' beamed Neptune's Restaurant serves unfussy modern European dishes made with a good showing of local seafood and game - perhaps peat-smoked salmon with cucumber salad, caviar dressing and quail's egg, ahead of Scotch beef fillet teamed with oxtail croquette, celeriac purée, woodland mushrooms, and shallot and red wine sauce. Finish with Belgian dark chocolate custard with cinnamon beignets.

Chef Paul Smith **Owner** Mr S Leitch **Times** 7-9.30 Closed 24-26 Dec, Sun in winter, L all week **Prices** Fixed D 3 course £30, Service optional **Wines** 7 by glass **Notes** Vegetarian available, Dress restrictions, Smart casual, Civ Wed 120 **Seats** 40, Pr/dining room 120 **Children** Portions **Parking** 50

Craigdarroch House

◉ British ✦

Skilled Scottish cooking in Loch Ness country house

☎ 01456 486400
IV2 6XU
e-mail: info@hotel-loch-ness.co.uk
dir: Take B862 from either end of the Loch, then B852 signed Foyers

Traditional dark oak panelling, high corniced ceilings and crackling log fires are all part of the Highland appeal at Craigdarroch. The house is tucked away in a forest near the Falls of Foyers, and basks in splendid views down to the wild east bank of Loch Ness, which form the backdrop to dining in the romantic candlelit restaurant. Chef-proprietor Martin Donnelly mans the stoves single-handed, cooking everything from scratch in daily-changing set dinner menus that work within the modern British idiom. Elegantly-presented dishes start out with black pudding with sautéed mushrooms and brioche topped with a poached egg and pointed up with a subtly spicy sherry and Tabasco sauce. Next up, fillet of Highland beef is served simply with creamed cabbage and pepperoni, intricately-carved carrots and swede, and roast potatoes. Skilled execution is also the hallmark of a well-crafted apple tart and a punchy apple sorbet.

Chef Martin Donnelly **Owner** Martin & Elinor Donnelly **Times** 8 **Prices** Prices not confirmed Service optional **Wines** 4 by glass **Notes** Vegetarian available, Civ Wed 30 **Seats** 20 **Children** Portions **Parking** 30

The Prince's House

◉◉ Modern British ✦

Warm hospitality and confident cooking

☎ 01397 722246
PH37 4LT
e-mail: princeshouse@glenfinnan.co.uk
web: www.glenfinnan.co.uk
dir: From Fort William N on A82 for 2m. Turn left on to A830 Mallaig Rd for 15m to hotel

Not far from the breathtakingly beautiful spot where, in 1745, Bonnie Prince Charlie raised the last rebel army ever to be mustered on British soil (don't miss the enclosed stone monument), the white-fronted hotel certainly has location going for it. It also has warmth and hospitality too, all the more welcome when you're miles from anywhere, and the white-painted dining room, complete with log-fire and framed pictures of an assortment of ladies, is the setting for confident cooking that capitalises on the respective bounties of the hill country and the coastal waters. A seared fillet of sea bass is accompanied by Provençal sunshine in the forms of roast peppers, aubergine fondant, salted lemon and herbs, while mains may offer the signature loin of hill lamb with a baked mushroom in green peppercorn jus, or a classy trio of Moidart venison medallion, loin of rabbit and breast of wood pigeon with their separate garnishes. Consistent finishers include chocolate and banana parfait with rum syrup.

Chef Kieron Kelly **Owner** Kieron & Ina Kelly **Times** 7-9 Closed Xmas, Jan-Feb, Low season (booking only), L all week **Prices** Fixed D 3 course £30-£32, Starter £7-£11, Main £17-£27, Dessert £7-£8, Service included **Wines** 42 bottles over £30, 19 bottles under £30, 8 by glass **Notes** Vegetarian available **Seats** 30 **Children** Portions **Parking** 18

Glengarry Castle Hotel

◉ Scottish, International

Country-house comfort food by Loch Oich

☎ 01809 501254
PH35 4HW
e-mail: castle@glengarry.net
web: www.glengarry.net
dir: 1m S of Invergarry on A82

Peering through dense woodland cloaking the hillsides above Loch Oich, and with the ruins of Invergarry Castle in its grounds, this grand Victorian mansion was built for the Ellice family, who got rich in the Canada fur and logging trades. Glengarry is a classic small-scale country house, replete with the traditional comfort of tartans,

Save on Hotels. Book at **theAA.com/hotel**

HIGHLAND 595 SCOTLAND

chintz and antlers on the walls, and Victorian period charm in the classy dining room. Daily-changing dinner menus keep things traditional and uncomplicated - locally-smoked venison with cherry tomato and quail's egg salad to start, followed by roast loin of lamb with garlic-roasted vegetables and port wine jus. Given the setting, the finale just has to be a luxurious cranachan, with the requisite raspberries, Drambuie, honey-flavoured cream and toasted oatmeal all present and correct.

Chef John McDonald **Owner** Mrs MacCallum & Sons **Times** 12-1.45/7-8.30 Closed mid Nov-mid Mar **Prices** Prices not confirmed Service included **Wines** 9 by glass **Notes** Vegetarian available **Seats** 40 **Children** Portions, Menu **Parking** 30

INVERGORDON
Map 23 NH76

Kincraig Castle Hotel

◉ Modern British V ✪

Fine dining in a splendid castle setting

☎ 01349 852587
IV18 0LF
e-mail: info@kincraig-castle-hotel.co.uk
web: www.kincraig-castle-hotel.co.uk
dir: Off A9, past Alness towards Tain. Hotel is 0.25m on left past church

When you're a laird, you want an impressive base of operations, thus the former seat of the Mackenzie clan is a suitably Baronial castle complete with mini turrets and gables and heavenly views over the Cromarty Firth and Black Isle. Inside, it looks the part too - this is a house of some magnificence, but it is run with a hands-on style that makes guests feel relaxed. The vibe continues in the romantically candlelit restaurant, where the scene is set by a centrepiece stone hearth, cherry-red walls and tables draped in pristine white linen. Excellent local produce takes a starring role in a modern repertoire that might get going with smoked ham hock terrine with confit cherry tomatoes and melba toasts, then proceed to fillets of sea bass served with mussel and saffron broth, baby potatoes and braised fennel.

Chef Mark Fairgrieve **Owner** Kevin Wickman **Times** 12-2/6.30-9 **Prices** Fixed L 2 course fr £14.95, Service optional **Wines** 27 bottles over £30, 27 bottles under £30, 6 by glass **Notes** Fixed D 7 course £40, Sunday L £12.95-£14.95, Vegetarian menu, Dress restrictions, Smart casual, Civ Wed 50 **Seats** 30, Pr/dining room 50 **Children** Portions, Menu **Parking** 40

INVERNESS
Map 23 NH64

Abstract Restaurant & Bar

◉ Modern French

Top Scottish produce in intimate restaurant by the river

☎ 01463 223777
Glenmoriston Town House Hotel, 20 Ness Bank IV2 4SF
e-mail: reception@glenmoristontownhouse.com
web: www.glenmoristontownhouse.com
dir: 2 mins from city centre, on river opposite theatre

The contemporary Glenmoriston Town House Hotel sits on the banks of the River Ness, close to Inverness city centre. The piano bar, with live music on Fridays and Saturdays, is the place to head to for a pre- or post-dinner drink (perhaps your choice from the impressive list of 200-plus malt whiskies), while the Abstract Restaurant is an atmospheric place to dine, with tea lights on the tables and modern artwork on the walls. There's a tasting menu should you wish to splash out on a seat at the chef's table, otherwise the carte offers prettily presented, French-influenced dishes based on top Scottish produce. Start with seared hand-dived scallops from the West Coast with celeriac and white truffle purée, before a duo of Ross-shire lamb - roasted rack and braised shoulder - with aubergine purée, fondant potatoes and balsamic jus.

Times 6-10 Closed Sun-Mon, L all week

Bunchrew House Hotel

◉◉ Scottish ✪

A touch of Scottish baronial splendour

☎ 01463 234917
Bunchrew IV3 8TA
e-mail: welcome@bunchrewhousehotel.com
web: www.bunchrewhousehotel.com
dir: 3m W of Inverness on A862 towards Beauly

With 400 years of history to its name, Bunchrew is a baronial-style country-house hotel in a glorious position on the banks of Beauly Firth. Spires rise into the Highland sky, 20 acres of gardens and woodlands await to be explored, and the sunsets over the distant hills may well leave a lasting impression. The dining room, resplendent with its wood-panelled walls, old portraits and smartly laid tables, serves up some excellent Scottish produce, including the harvest of the hotel's own gardens. Slices of salt-roasted duck might come in a first course with caramelised red onion tartlet and a sloe gin sauce, followed by local salmon with a Savoy cabbage parcel and shellfish sauce, or go for breast and thigh of guinea fowl with Stornoway black pudding. To finish, pannacotta gets perked up with blueberry and orange.

Chef Mark Dickson **Owner** Terry & Irina Mackay **Times** 12-1.45/7-9 Closed 23-26 Dec **Prices** Fixed D 3 course £39.50, Service optional **Wines** 15 bottles over £30, 25 bottles under £30, 4 by glass **Notes** Sunday L, Vegetarian available, Civ Wed 92 **Seats** 32, Pr/dining room 14 **Children** Portions, Menu **Parking** 40

Loch Ness Country House Hotel

◉◉ Modern British ✪

Exciting contemporary cooking near Loch Ness

☎ 01463 230512
Loch Ness Rd IV3 8JN
e-mail: info@lochnesscountryhousehotel.co.uk
web: www.lochnesscountryhousehotel.co.uk
dir: On A82 (S), 1m from Inverness town boundary

The hotel is far enough away from the loch so as to reassure any believers that they're safe (that's from the mythical Nessie, by the way), and the appeal of this splendid Georgian mansion is undoubtedly in its lovely secluded setting and the little dose of luxury it provides. It's done out from top-to-bottom in a smart and traditional manner, including the elegant restaurant with its three inter-linked period rooms. The kitchen seeks out the excellent regional produce and serves it up like a picture on the plate. There are some rather exciting things on the menu, such as a starter of octopus carpaccio with queen scallops, radish, orange, cardamom and chorizo oil, or a jazzed up soup such as garden pea and pancetta with braised ham knuckle, wild garlic and soft quail's egg. Main courses and desserts are no less creative and appealing: breast of corn-fed chicken and braised Gloucestershire Old Spot pork belly with celeriac and black truffle millefeuille, mustard and parmesan froth, for example, and Blairgowrie strawberry shortcake with strawberry and Bacardi soup and lime and basil sorbet.

Chef Chris Crombie **Owner** Loch Ness Hospitality Ltd **Times** 12-2.30/6-9 Closed D 31 Dec **Prices** Fixed L 2 course fr £14.95, Fixed D 3 course fr £36.50, Starter £5-£12, Main £14-£23, Dessert £5-£9, Service optional **Wines** 9 by glass **Notes** Sunday L, Vegetarian available, Civ Wed 150 **Seats** 42, Pr/dining room 14 **Children** Portions, Menu **Parking** 50

INVERNESS *continued*

The New Drumossie Hotel

◎◎ Modern Scottish

Confident, seasonal cooking at an art deco hotel

☎ 01463 236451
Old Perth Rd IV2 5BE
e-mail: stay@drumossiehotel.co.uk
dir: From A9 follow signs for Culloden Battlefield, hotel on left after 1m

Just a short drive from Inverness, the Drumossie is a delightful place, an immaculately-white art-deco beauty in acres of well-tended grounds framed all around by the Scottish Highlands. Its charm is due in no small part to the staff who treat guests with engaging politeness and feed them with high-class Scottish cuisine in the Grill Room. The quality of the raw materials shines out in a starter of hand-dived scallops teamed with Stornoway black pudding, cauliflower purée and a crispy shard of Parma ham, while mains bring on perfectly-timed honey-roast Gressingham duck with fondant potato, red cabbage and star anise jus. If something sizzling from the grill appeals, the meat delivered is impeccable Scottish rib-eye and sirloin steaks, with a choice of sauces that includes Arran mustard or whisky cream. Form stays true to the end with superb regional cheeses, or an intense dark chocolate ganache balanced by the counterpoint of orange sorbet, and kumquat and ginger compôte.

Chef Kenny McMillan **Owner** Ness Valley Leisure **Times** 12.30-2/7-9.30 **Prices** Prices not confirmed Service included **Wines** 13 by glass **Notes** Vegetarian available, Civ Wed 400 **Seats** 90, Pr/dining room 30 **Children** Portions, Menu **Parking** 200

Rocpool

◎◎ Modern European

Riverside setting and smart modern cooking

☎ 01463 717274
1 Ness Walk IV3 5NE
e-mail: info@rocpoolrestaurant.com
web: www.rocpoolrestaurant.com
dir: On W bank of River Ness close to the Eden Court Theatre

This buzzy contemporary brasserie operation capitalises on its corner site on the banks of the River Ness, with sweeping windows on two sides to open up floodlit views of the river and castle at night. The interior is a cool exercise in contemporary design flair featuring lots of wood and a décor of natural tones. On the menu is an appealing cast of crowd-pleasing modern European dishes built on top-class Scottish produce. Start with roast pork belly with Granny Smith apple purée, black pudding and zingy grain mustard, or you might go for West Coast mussels with Thai red curry, fresh coriander and coconut cream. Next could be the full-on flavours of rump of lamb roasted with garlic and thyme with cassoulet of butter beans, chorizo, pancetta and parsley, and crisp golden polenta to soak it all up. Elsewhere, there might be roast fillet of halibut with brown shrimp, parsley and lemon butter, pecorino mash and wilted spinach with a soft poached egg. Dessert delivers an indulgent finish via an intricately presented white chocolate and coconut cheesecake with caramelised bananas and toffee sauce.

Chef Steven Devlin **Owner** Steven Devlin **Times** 12-2.30/5.45-10 Closed 25-26 Dec, 1-3 Jan, Sun, L Sun **Prices** Fixed L 2 course £14.95, Fixed D 2 course £16.95, Starter £3.95-£10.95, Main £12.95-£23.95, Dessert £6.95, Service optional **Wines** 15 bottles over £30, 28 bottles under £30, 11 by glass **Notes** Early D 5.45-6.45pm 2 course £16.95, Vegetarian available **Seats** 55 **Children** Portions **Parking** On street

The Cross

◎◎ Modern Scottish V ⚑NOTABLE WINE LIST 🐲

Modern Scottish cooking in an old water mill

☎ 01540 661166
Tweed Mill Brae, Ardbroilach Rd PH21 1LB
e-mail: relax@thecross.co.uk
dir: From lights in Kingussie centre along Ardbroilach Rd, 300yds left onto Tweed Mill Brae

Originally a water-powered tweed mill built in the late 1800s, The Cross sits in a secluded enclave of the town of Kingussie, in the heart of the Cairngorm National Park. The old building is surrounded by four acres of woodland and garden beside the Gynack Burn, and if the weather is kind there's a terrace beside the river where you can take in the tranquillity of the setting - and, if you're lucky, spot a red squirrel or two. Inside, the small restaurant seats around 20 and is full of period features including exposed beams, white-painted stone walls and an open fireplace. The set menu of modern Scottish dishes changes daily depending on what produce is at its peak. An imaginative starter of local grouse chipolatas, parsley root purée, cobnuts, and caper and sherry vinegar jus is typical of the style, and might be followed by Scottish beef fillet, pan-fried duck foie gras, pommes Anna, chef's foraged mushrooms and Madeira jus. End on a high with Alvie Estate raspberry soufflé, tarragon crème anglaise and honey ice cream, or a selection of artisan cheeses with hand-made Ullapool oatcakes and apple, pear and fig chutney.

Chef Ross Sutherland **Owner** Derek & Celia Kitchingman **Times** 12-2.30/7-8.30 Closed Xmas & Jan (ex New Year), Sun-Mon **Prices** Fixed L 3 course £17, Starter £5, Main £10, Dessert £5, Service optional **Wines** 98 bottles over £30, 27 bottles under £30, 4 by glass **Notes** 5 course D £50, Afternoon tea, Vegetarian menu **Seats** 30 **Children** Portions, Menu **Parking** 12

Map 22 NG72

The Waterside Seafood Restaurant

Modern, Traditional Seafood

Popular fish restaurant in the old railway waiting room

☎ 01599 534813
Railway Station Buildings, Station Rd IV40 8AE
e-mail: seafoodrestaurant@btinternet.com
dir: Off A87

Located in the old railway station waiting room, with original carved British Rail chairs (you weren't expecting Rennie Mackintosh, were you?), the nautical-hued blue and yellow restaurant is simple and informal. Fish and seafood specials are the name of the game, the menu updated as items sell out, the staff doing their efficient best to cope with the press of business. Among the popular dishes are lightly spiced crabcakes with red pepper and coriander salsa, smoked mackerel with sour cream and dill, and mains such as fat scallops complete with their roe, fried in herb butter and served in the shell with rice, red Thai seafood curry replete with hot spice and coconut milk, and the all-important seafood platters with salads and dips. Finish straightforwardly with a chunky and nutty chocolate brownie, served with vanilla ice cream.

Chef Jann MacRae **Owner** Jann & Neil MacRae **Times** 5-9.30 Closed end Oct-early Mar, Sun (please phone to confirm opening hrs), L Sat **Prices** Prices not confirmed Service optional **Wines** 2 by glass **Notes** Vegetarian available **Seats** 35 **Children** Portions, Menu **Parking** 5

Map 20 NM64

The Whitehouse Restaurant

Modern British NEW V

Vibrant, ingredient-led modern cooking

☎ 01967 421777 & 07866 586698
PA80 5XT
e-mail: info@thewhitehouserestaurant.co.uk

In a remote spot near the ferry crossing to Mull, this restaurant does indeed occupy an unassuming white house overlooking Lochaline bay. Inside, it looks every inch the unpretentious modern eatery, from its pale wooden tables and flooring to the whitewashed walls hung with maritime and food-themed art. Blessed with a remarkable natural larder close to hand, the kitchen is passionate in its local sourcing ethos, and skilled when it comes to wringing every molecule of flavour from the peerless produce. Daily-changing chalkboards reference the provenance of the main element of each dish, starting with Lochaber chicken liver parfait served with spiced apple chutney and toasted raisin and walnut bread. Next out, a vibrantly colourful dish sees Gigha halibut poached in sea water and matched with Creran oysters, sweet cicely, and caper butter. Dessert brings a clever take on pear Belle Hélène: rich chocolate marquise layered with spiced poached pears and quenelles of chocolate sorbet.

Chef Michael Burgoyne, Lee Myers **Owner** Jane Stuart Smith, Sarah Jones **Times** 12-3/6-9.30 Closed Nov-Mar, Sun-Mon **Prices** Fixed L 2 course £15.95-£17.95, Fixed D 3 course £19.95-£22.95, Tasting menu £45-£55, Starter £6-£12.95, Main £15.95-£22, Dessert £5.95-£10, Service optional, Groups min 6 service 12% **Wines** 9 bottles over £30, 17 bottles under £30, 5 by glass **Notes** Vegetarian menu **Seats** 26 **Children** Portions **Parking** 10

Map 23 NH55

Ord House Hotel

British, French

Comforting bistro cooking in a 17th-century house

☎ 01463 870492
Ord Dr IV6 7UH
e-mail: admin@ord-house.co.uk
dir: Off A9 at Tore rdbt onto A832. 5m, through Muir of Ord. Left towards Ullapool (A832). Hotel 0.5m on left

A Stuart country house in its own expansive and manicured gardens not far from Inverness, Ord House is popular among local anglers and country sports people. Log fires and a snug bar make a comforting scene in winter, and the first-floor dining room is small enough to feel intimate, with views over the grounds. Residents may make the acquaintance of the lady ghost who stalks the place after dark. A vegetable garden supplies much of the kitchen's fresh produce, and local suppliers the bulk of the rest. The culinary style is modern bistro, starting with the likes of tempura king prawns and sweet chilli dip, or foie gras with baked egg, and then going on to well-judged baked halibut in dill hollandaise, or Highland pheasant with crumble-topped leeks and mushrooms. Finish with defiantly textbook crème brûlée.

Chef Eliza Allen **Owner** Eliza & John Allen **Times** 12-2/7-9 Closed Nov-end Feb **Prices** Starter £7.25-£9.50, Main £15.75-£22.50, Dessert £4.75-£6.95, Service included **Wines** 9 bottles over £30, 37 bottles under £30, 4 by glass **Notes** Vegetarian available **Seats** 26 **Children** Portions **Parking** 24

Map 23 NH85

Boath House

— *see page 598*

The Golf View Hotel and Spa

Traditional Scottish V

Fine Scottish produce and sea views

☎ 01667 452301
Seabank Rd IV12 4HD
e-mail: golfview@crerarhotels.com
dir: Off A96 into Seabank Rd & continue to end

The hotel could just as well be named 'Sea View', as it has wonderful views over the Moray Firth, with access to long sandy beaches, the picture windows in the restaurant giving the same magical vista. There's a lot to recommend on a menu that's built on Scotland's bounty, from goats' cheese vol-au-vent to smoked haddock and langoustine chowder. The kitchen tends to favour a traditional approach, seen in a quenelle of salmon, and a main course of pavé of lamb with roast garlic and rosemary. There's no better way to finish than with cranachan with shortbread.

Chef Darren Munro **Owner** Crerar Hotels **Times** 6.45-9 Closed L Mon-Sat **Prices** Prices not confirmed Service optional **Wines** 11 bottles over £30, 35 bottles under £30, 8 by glass **Notes** Steak night Thu, Sunday L, Vegetarian menu, Dress restrictions, Smart casual, Civ Wed 120 **Seats** 50 **Children** Portions, Menu **Parking** 30, Next to hotel on street

Newton Hotel

Modern British

Well-considered dishes in baronial-style hotel

☎ 01667 453144
Inverness Rd IV12 4RX
e-mail: salesnewton@ohiml.com
web: www.oxfordhotelsandinns.com
dir: A96 from Inverness to Nairn. In Nairn hotel signed on left

Within 21 acres of wooded grounds, the Newton Hotel was built in the late 19th century in the baronial style, with a complement of crenellations and turrets. The restaurant is in a conservatory-like room with a relaxing décor of pale grey-blue. Dishes generally show a good balance of flavours, the kitchen applying sound technical skills to quality local produce and taking great care with presentation. A starter of duck confit studded with asparagus and leeks is accompanied by a refreshing pea and mint salad, a smear of parsnip and apple purée, and grain mustard dressing. Purées seem to be a favoured garnish, one of rich-tasting pumpkin surrounding a disc of spicy Puy lentils under fanned slices of medium-rare (as requested) duck breast in a port reduction, served with dauphinoise potatoes. A selection of breads is offered, and puddings might run to baked apple crème (like brûlée without the topping) with home-made shortbread.

Times 12-2/6-9 Closed D 25 Dec

Boath House

NAIRN   **MAP 23 NH85**

Modern British V 🍷 NOTABLE WINE LIST

Astonishing culinary intricacy in a restored Georgian manor house

☎ 01667 454896
Auldearn IV12 5TE
e-mail: wendy@boath-house.com
web: www.boath-house.com
dir: 2m E of Nairn on A96 (Inverness to Aberdeen road)

Built in the 1820s, Boath House has justly been called one of Scotland's finest Georgian houses, and yet not long ago, it had very definitely seen better days. When Don and Wendy Matheson happened on it in the 1990s, it was in a sorry state of disrepair. Scotland has cause to be proud of their achievement in restoring it to its full dignity, not just as an architectural museum piece, but as a fully operational hotel and restaurant, its impeccably laid-out gardens incorporating kitchen plots, just as they would have done in its first heyday. On the exposed northeast coast, not too distant from Inverness, it stands in 20 acres that incorporate a trout lake and orchard, as well as the walled kitchen garden. Behind a pillared portico that suggests a Greek temple, the interiors bear all the evidence of lavish attention to detail, not least in the circular dining room, where the walls are done in an appetising shade of raspberry, and French windows look out on the lawns. Fine artworks in painting and sculpture are on sale, if you feel like taking home a souvenir of your visit. Charlie Lockley's long tenure with Boath House has been immensely productive, not only in forging and developing links with regional suppliers, but in establishing a culinary continuity that is founded on constant innovation. The six-course fixed price dinner menus change nightly, and embrace a formidable range of technical skill. First up might be a demi-tasse of sweet onion squash soup sprinkled with seeds and oil, a gentle overture to a small loin portion of rabbit dusted in powdered ceps, alongside home-made black pudding and a spurt of cashew-flavoured foam. Then a single scallop arrives next to a heap of squid-black quinoa, grated celery and oatmeal skirlie. For the main course, stems and leaves of pennywort from the garden garnish a liquorice-dusted slab of roe deer loin, which comes with delicately textured onion rings and wine-poached salsify. A single cheese (perhaps Snowdonia Black Bomber with oat biscuits and fig chutney) precedes something like a study in chocolate, comprised of fondant, cake crumbs, cocoa nibs and a tuile, offset with a scoop of nutmeg ice cream. Breads are extremely fine, notably the soda bread served with fish, while canapés and petits fours (the latter including a passion fruit marshmallow dotted with crystalised rose petal) maintain the same astonishing intricacy that typifies the whole production.

Chef Charles Lockley **Owner** Mr & Mrs D Matheson **Times** 12.30-1.15/7-7.30 **Prices** Fixed L 2 course fr £24, Tasting menu fr £70, Service included **Wines** 9 by glass **Notes** Tasting menu 6 course, Sunday L £24-£30, Vegetarian menu, Dress restrictions, Smart casual, no shorts, T-shirts or jeans, Civ Wed 32 **Seats** 28, Pr/dining room 8 **Children** Portions **Parking** 25

SHIEL BRIDGE

Map 22 NG91

Grants at Craigellachie

Modern Scottish

Well-crafted cooking in charming setting

☎ 01599 511331
Craigellachie, Ratagan IV40 8HP
e-mail: info@housebytheloch.co.uk
dir: A87 to Glenelg, 1st right to Ratagan opposite the Youth Hostel sign

A great little restaurant with rooms in a splendid location just off the main road to Skye, Grants is run by a hands-on husband-and-wife-team. There are (perhaps unsurprisingly in this neck of the woods) superb views from the white-painted house (over Loch Duich as it happens, across to the Five Sisters of Kintail mountains). The conservatory restaurant has just four tables so booking is advisable to say the least. It's a charming and elegant place to eat, with tables laid with crisp white linen and fresh flowers. Co-owner Liz Taylor runs front of house with relaxed charm while hubby Tony works his magic in the kitchen, championing local producers as he goes. Warm mousse of Loch Hourn queen scallops with Corran Red Velvet crab and squat lobster bisque is a beautifully flavoured first course, followed perhaps by braised tongue of Highland beef with glazed baby onions and an Amontillado sherry and rosemary reduction. To finish, a pear poached in mulled wine comes with banana crème caramel and mascarpone, almond and Amaretto ice cream.

Times 7-11 Closed Dec-mid Feb, L all week, D Sun, Mon

SHIELDAIG

Map 22 NG85

Tigh an Eilean

Modern Scottish

Imaginative cooking with loch views

☎ 01520 755251
IV54 8XN
e-mail: tighaneilean@keme.co.uk
dir: From A896 follow signs for Shieldaig. Hotel in village centre on water's edge

In a charming village on the shore of Loch Torridon, Tigh an Eilean Hotel has a small and intimate restaurant, its green walls hung with colourful posters, with fabulous sea views (so window seats are at a premium). Locally-landed seafood runs like a rich seam through the daily-changing menu, perhaps as a straightforward starter of potted shrimps, and a main course of well-timed fillet of salmon on fettuccine with saffron sauce. Imaginative ideas are culled globally, so a taster of sopa de guisantes (spicy pea soup) may precede tricolore salad, to be followed by tender duck breast roasted with plums on a ginger, honey and soy sauce accompanied by pak choi and spicy sautéed potatoes. Local game pops up in season - perhaps as quail with grapes - and dinner ends strongly with a pudding like classic cherry clafoutis.

Times 7-9 Closed end Oct-mid Mar (except private booking), L all week

SPEAN BRIDGE

Map 22 NN28

Russell's at Smiddy House

Modern Scottish

Seasonal cooking amid elegant pastoral surroundings

☎ 01397 712335
Roy Bridge Rd PH34 4EU
e-mail: enquiry@smiddyhouse.com
web: www.smiddyhouse.com
dir: In village centre, 9m N of Fort William, on A82 towards Inverness

The low-roofed white building stands on a corner on the main road through the village, in front of a cottage that was once the village blacksmith's (hence 'Smiddy'). It's a gentle, pastoral setting with elegant country décor, and serves as a fine backdrop for Glen Russell's modish seasonal Scottish cooking. A salad of warm figs with caramelised pecans and avocado ice cream offers nice contrasts of texture and temperature, and ushers in main courses built around pedigree raw materials. Grilled hake in smoked haddock chowder is a robustly satisfying fish dish, while saddle of Highland venison comes with pancetta, Puy lentils and mushrooms in red wine jus. Piquant flavours at dessert stage are mobilised for rhubarb cheesecake or lemon and fennel tart.

Times 6-9 Closed 2 days a week (Nov-Apr), L Mon-Sat

STRONTIAN

Map 22 NM86

Kilcamb Lodge Hotel & Restaurant

Modern European, Scottish V

Idyllically situated lodge with skilful cooking

☎ 01967 402257
PH36 4HY
e-mail: enquiries@kilcamblodge.co.uk
web: www.kilcamblodge.co.uk
dir: Take Corran ferry off A82. Follow A861 to Strontian. 1st left over bridge after village

It takes effort to get to Kilcamb Lodge out on the remote Ardnamurchan Peninsula, but when you arrive the rewards are more than ample. The setting in 22 acres of lochside meadows and woodland on the wild shores of Loch Sunart, with the mountains all around, is one that stays with you forever, while the elegant house is run with easygoing, unpretentious charm. As an escape from the daily grind, it can't be beaten, and with views like this you need to try to bag a window table in the restaurant, where intelligent contemporary country-house cooking showcases top-class local produce. Game and shellfish, often sourced from local estates and fishing boats, is a particular focus - perhaps Oban Bay scallops and Orkney crabcake with oriental dressing as an opener, while main course partners twice-cooked belly of Tamworth pork with spinach, salsify, mushroom tortellini and crackling. At the end, a fine plum crumble and pear frangipane tart is served with home-made vanilla ice cream.

Chef Gary Phillips **Owner** Sally & David Fox
Times 12-2/5.30-9.30 Closed 1 Jan-1 Feb **Prices** Starter £5.50-£10, Main £9.95-£24, Dessert fr £7, Service optional, Groups min 10 service 10% **Wines** 53 bottles over £30, 16 bottles under £30, 10 by glass **Notes** 5 course D £49.50, Sunday L fr £16.50, Vegetarian menu, Dress restrictions, Smart casual, no jeans, T-shirts or trainers, Civ Wed 120 **Seats** 26 **Parking** 28

TAIN

Map 23 NH78

The Glenmorangie Highland Home at Cadboll

British, French

Dinner party dining in a magnificent Highland location

☎ 01862 871671
Cadboll, Fearn IV20 1XP
e-mail: relax@glenmorangie.co.uk
web: www.theglenmorangiehouse.com
dir: N on A9, at Nigg Rdbt turn right onto B9175 (before Tain) & follow signs for hotel

Set in fantastic grounds with a large walled garden and a tree-lined walk down to its own private beach, The Glenmorangie has appeal in spades. It's owned by Moët Hennessy, who in turn own the nearby Glenmorangie Distillery, making it something of a whisky lover's paradise (whisky tasting weekends prove a big pull), and as if that weren't enough, the French-influenced cuisine is out of the top drawer. Guests dine dinner-party-style here, meeting first in the lounge for drinks and canapés before moving through to the green-hued dining room and taking a seat at the long oak table. Seasonal produce might come straight from the walled garden to take a star turn in technically impressive creations on four-course, no-choice menus. Squab pigeon, truffle and goats' cheese gnocchi might precede 'textures of Caithness carrot, fondant potato, Hispi cabbage, Cullisse girolle mushrooms, root vegetables and grand veneur sauce' - a dish with real 'wow factor'. The pastry chef's skills are undeniable at dessert stage when Valrhona chocolate mousse cannelloni with poached cherries, curd and an intensely flavoured cherry sorbet is brought to the table.

Chef David Graham, John Wilson **Owner** Glenmorangie Ltd **Times** 8-close Closed Xmas, New Year & Jan, L except by prior arrangement **Prices** Prices not confirmed Service optional **Wines** 15 by glass **Notes** D single sitting, guests seated 7.30 for 8, Vegetarian available, Dress restrictions, Smart casual, no jeans or T-shirts, Civ Wed 26 **Seats** 30, Pr/dining room 12 **Parking** 60

Forss House Hotel

◉◉ Modern Scottish 🍷

Confident cooking in Georgian country-house hotel

☎ 01847 861201
Forss KW14 7XY
e-mail: anne@forsshousehotel.co.uk
web: www.forsshousehotel.co.uk
dir: On A836, 5m outside Thurso

Built as a private home in 1810, Forss House is surrounded by 20 acres of woodland and overlooks the river from which it takes its name; small wonder, then, that it's a popular base for anglers and game sportsmen. The restaurant is a high-ceilinged room with large portraits and an elegant fireplace; seats are comfortable, with shoulder-height backs, and staff add to a sense of well-being. Modern Scottish cooking is the name of the game, and dishes demonstrate that a confident, experienced team is at the stoves. A starter of scallop and lobster raviolo comes with the pasta on a bed of spinach, the shellfish on top in a rich bisque, all the flavours working in harmony. There could also be a soup - perhaps sweetcorn - followed by roast medallions of venison, cooked pink, sitting on roast salsify with a mini pie of minced meat and a dollop of beetroot fondant, with monkfish with crushed potatoes and olives a fishy alternative. To finish, a perfectly made, intensely

flavoured banana soufflé is served with rum and raisin ice cream.

Chef Gary Stevenson **Owner** Ian & Sabine Richards **Times** 7-9 Closed 23 Dec-4 Jan, L all week **Prices** Starter £5.95-£7.50, Main £15-£24.50, Dessert £6.50-£7.50, Service optional **Wines** 14 bottles over £30, 18 bottles under £30, 4 by glass **Notes** Vegetarian available **Seats** 26, Pr/dining room 14 **Children** Portions **Parking** 14

The Torridon Restaurant

◉◉◉ – *see below*

The Westerwood House & Golf Resort

◉ Modern Scottish 🍷

Confident modern cooking and top-drawer service

☎ 01236 457171
1 St Andrews Dr, Westerwood G68 0EW
e-mail: stewartgoldie@qhotels.co.uk
web: www.qhotels.co.uk
dir: A80 junct signed Dullatur, from junct follow signs for hotel

Westerwood House is a stylish contemporary golf and spa-oriented hotel in extensive grounds overlooking the Campsie Hills, yet only a 15-minute drive from the bright lights of Glasgow city centre. On the food front, Fleming's Restaurant fits the bill with its clean-cut modern look, all darkwood tables and seats upholstered in warm hues of tangerine and sage-green, while a switched-on professional team make sure it all goes with a swing. The kitchen follows a broadly modern Scottish path, enlivened with a splash of well-considered creativity here and there. Pan-fried scallops with chorizo and sweetcorn salsa and sweetcorn purée is a typical starter, while mains might run to roast rump of Perthshire lamb with Provençal vegetables, pan juices and pesto. To round

The Torridon Restaurant

British, French V 📖NOTABLE WINE LIST

A piece of loch-side Highland luxury

☎ 01445 791242
IV22 2EY
e-mail: info@thetorridon.com
web: www.thetorridon.com
dir: From Inverness take A9 N, follow signs to Ullapool (A835). At Garve take A832 to Kinlochewe, take A896 to Torridon. Do not turn off to Torridon Village. Hotel on right after Annat

There is every imaginable opportunity to work up an appetite at this magnificent turreted Victorian shooting lodge at the head of a sea loch in remote Wester Ross, starting with 58 acres of wooded grounds to lose yourself in, as well as bracing walks on the shores of Loch

Torridon. And when you simply want to put your feet up and indulge in a little well-deserved R&R, the interiors provide a rather chic blend of traditional features and contemporary style. There's also a mind-boggling array of over 350 malts awaiting at the whisky bar when you feel in need of a touch of spirit-based relaxation. The restaurant, in two interconnecting dining rooms, is a suitably grand setting for the top-class cooking of chef 'Bruno' Birkbeck: acres of cosseting clubby oak panelling, ornate plasterwork ceilings, crisp white linen on the tables, and that splendid wilderness view makes for an inspirational backdrop; charming staff do credit to the operation with their clued-up approach to food and wine, whilst keeping things moving along at a well-orchestrated pace. The skilled modern cooking puts spectacular regional produce to the fore, kicking off with up-to-date canapés in the form of trendy bar snacks - perhaps crispy pig's ear served with a shandy shot - before the five-course table d'hôte dinner performance begins in earnest with a silky smooth wild mushroom

velouté teamed with hand-rolled macaroni and locally-foraged mushrooms with tarragon oil. Next out, Wester Ross cured salmon and Shieldaig crab with caviar and vegetables à la Grecque, all pointed up with the acidity of saffron pickle jelly, is a preamble to the main event, a three-way serving of lamb - oven-roast chump, confit shoulder and shepherd's pie - with swede purée, pickled red cabbage and lamb jus. After an outstanding pre-dessert of deconstructed banoffee pie, the curtain comes down with a white chocolate parfait with foraged blackberries served as sorbet, compôte and in a cannelloni.

Chef Jason 'Bruno' Birkbeck **Owner** Daniel & Rohaise Rose-Bristow **Times** 12-2/7-9 Closed 2 Jan for 5 wks, L all week **Prices** Tasting menu £55-£67.50, Service optional **Wines** 8 by glass **Notes** Fixed D 5 course £55, Vegetarian menu, Dress restrictions, No jeans or trainers, Civ Wed 42 **Seats** 38, Pr/dining room 16 **Children** Portions, Menu **Parking** 20

things off, an irresistibly Scottish Irn Bru baked Alaska should hit the spot.

Chef Stewart Goldie **Owner** Q Hotels **Times** 6.30-9.30 Closed Sun-Mon, L all week **Prices** Prices not confirmed Service optional **Notes** Vegetarian available **Seats** 180, Pr/dining room 60 **Children** Portions, Menu **Parking** 250

LANARKSHIRE, SOUTH

EAST KILBRIDE   Map 20 NS65

Macdonald Crutherland House

◎◎ British

Elegant hotel dining room with accomplished cooking

☎ 01355 577000
Strathaven Rd G75 0QZ
e-mail: general.crutherland@macdonald-hotels.co.uk
web: www.macdonald-hotels.co.uk
dir: Follow A726 signed Strathaven, straight over Torrance rdbt, hotel on left after 250yds

With the original parts of the building dating from the early 1700s, Crutherland House stands in nearly 40 acres of peaceful grounds. There are conference facilities aplenty these days, plus a spa in which to unwind and detox. The hotel is done out in a traditional manner, not least in the restaurant, with its panelled walls, paintings and well-spaced, burnished darkwood tables. The menu takes a comforting classical approach to culinary matters, with plenty of Scottish ingredients on show. Start with traditional smoked salmon from John Ross Jnr of Aberdeen, for example, or smoked haddock and leek fishcakes with lemon and parsley mayonnaise. Among main courses there are steaks cooked on the grill (21-day hung Scottish sirloin, maybe), or the likes of pan-roasted venison with dauphinoise potatoes, honey-glazed parsnips and blackberry jus. Among desserts, citrus tart competes with dark chocolate truffle cake with coffee anglaise and chocolate ice cream. There are Scottish cheeses, too.

Times 7-9 Closed L all week

STRATHAVEN   Map 20 NS74

Rissons at Springvale

◎ Modern Scottish ◔

Modern Scottish bistro cooking in a comfortable restaurant-with-rooms

☎ 01357 520234 & 521131
18 Lethame Rd ML10 6AD
e-mail: info@rissons.co.uk
dir: M74 junct 8, A71, through Stonehouse to Strathaven

A bright, airy restaurant-with-rooms in the small town of Strathaven near East Kilbride, Rissons caters to an enthusiastic local crowd. The main dining room is a fairly intimate space overlooking the gardens, with linen-clad tables and subdued lighting in the evenings, and wooden blinds to mitigate the glare through conservatory-style windows on sunny days. The modern Scottish bistro cooking makes a good fist of local supplies, with

respectable portion sizes and unfussy presentations. Scott Baxter can turn out a well-executed twice-baked goats' cheese soufflé with interesting fruity 'winter coleslaw', or produce a hearty fish casserole of sea bream and scallops in the robust company of chorizo, beans and tomato. Properly crackled pork belly of tip-top flavour comes with assertive haggis croquettes and creamed cabbage in port sauce, and satisfaction is guaranteed for fans of both chocolate and salty caramel in the form of a softly bitter terrine accompanied by crunchy honeycomb ice cream.

Chef Scott Baxter **Owner** Scott & Anne Baxter **Times** 12-2.30/6-9.30 Closed New Year, 1 wk Jan, 1st wk Jul, Mon-Tue, L Wed-Fri, D Sun **Prices** Fixed L 2 course £15.95, Starter £4.50-£10, Main £11.95-£20, Dessert £5.25-£6.50, Service optional **Wines** 6 by glass **Notes** Early evening menu Wed-Fri, Sunday L £15.95-£17.95, Vegetarian available **Seats** 40 **Children** Portions, Menu **Parking** 10

LOTHIAN, EAST

ABERLADY   Map 21 NT47

Ducks at Kilspindie

◎◎ Modern British ⭑ NOTABLE WINE LIST ◔

Inventive modern cooking in smart restaurant with rooms

☎ 01875 870682
EH32 0RE
e-mail: kilspindie@ducks.co.uk
web: www.ducks.co.uk
dir: A1 (Bankton junct) take 1st exit to North Berwick. At next rdbt 3rd exit onto A198 signed Longniddry, left towards Aberlady. At T-junct, facing river, right to Aberlady

In the heart of golfing country with no less than 21 courses within striking distance, Ducks has a lot to offer. Here on the high street of an East Lothian village, Malcolm Duck offers relaxation and fortification in the form of restaurant, bistro and bedrooms. The main culinary attraction is the diminutive main restaurant - just ten tables - with its charming mix of objets and artworks, and a menu based around good quality local ingredients. There's lots of craft and imagination on display throughout. Start, perhaps, with a winter soup flavoured with pumpkin and ginger, or steak tartare with a lime cure, pear, and mustard seasoning. Next up, cannelloni of sea fish with chick pea and rosemary sauce and seaweed competes for your attention with a duo of quail with a cider-cooked apple, a filo pastry nest and tempura vegetables. White chocolate cheesecake with raspberry jelly brings things to a close. Donald's Bar Bistro serves up real ale and whisky (over 50) alongside the likes of sandwiches and 40-day aged steaks.

Chef Alessandro Grillo **Owner** Malcolm Duck **Times** 12-3/6-10 Closed 25 Dec **Prices** Starter £7-£10.95, Main £12-£27, Dessert £6.50-£7, Service optional **Wines** 121 bottles over £30, 48 bottles under £30, 9 by glass **Notes** Sunday L, Vegetarian available,

Dress restrictions, Smart casual **Seats** 22, Pr/dining room 22 **Children** Portions **Parking** 15

GULLANE   Map 21 NT48

La Potinière

◎◎ Modern British ◔

Long-running gastronomic landmark

☎ 01620 843214
Main St EH31 2AA
dir: 5m from North Berwick on A198

A modest-looking, intimate high-street restaurant that put Gullane on the gastronomic map a generation ago, La Potinière is done out in a fetching shade of raspberry, both outside and in. Essentially a two-handed operation, in which both partners cook and occasionally serve, it's the very model of a small fine-dining restaurant, as its band of regulars attests. Clearly not all the out-of-towners are here for the Muirfield golf nearby. An array of local suppliers is credited on menus that offer a pair of choices at each stage. Proceedings might open with a cheddar soufflé teamed with a tomato tart, alongside rocket and pesto, to be followed at dinner by an intervening soup, perhaps Thai-style coconut with poached scallops. The fish or meat choice at main could be between halibut, braised and served with sole and smoked salmon mousse and chive mash in saffron sauce, or fine Scotch beef, the fillet poached and then seared, alongside dauphinoise, in red wine and shallot sauce. A world of sweet satisfaction arrives in the shape of gooey-centred chocolate moelleux with a poached pear, caramel sauce and vanilla ice cream, and there are thoroughbred Scottish cheeses too.

Chef Mary Runciman, Keith Marley **Owner** Mary Runciman **Times** 12.30-1.30/7-8.30 Closed Xmas, Jan, BHs, Mon-Tue, D Sun (Oct-May) **Prices** Fixed L 2 course fr £20.50, Fixed D 3 course fr £38, Tasting menu fr £43, Service optional **Wines** 22 bottles over £30, 26 bottles under £30, 7 by glass **Notes** Sunday L, Vegetarian available, Dress restrictions, Smart casual **Seats** 24 **Children** Portions **Parking** 10

NORTH BERWICK — Map 21 NT58

Macdonald Marine Hotel & Spa

@@ European

Impressive Victorian pile with confident cooking

☎ 01620 897300
Cromwell Rd EH39 4LZ
e-mail: sales.marine@macdonald-hotels.co.uk
web: www.macdonaldhotels.co.uk/marine
dir: from A198 turn into Hamilton Rd at lights then 2nd right

The views over the Firth of Forth and the East Lothian golf course give the Marine Hotel a sense of place - this is the east coast of Scotland and no mistake. The house is of 19th-century provenance, with all the expected Grade II listed grandeur, and its restaurant, named after the man at the stoves (John Paul McLachlan), serves up plenty of fine Scottish produce. The dining room is done out in rich, warming colours, with panelling and traditional portraits on the walls, but the darkwood tables remain clothless and the service keeps things suitably friendly and relaxed. John Paul is up to speed with contemporary culinary goings on, while his food shows respect for classical thinking. Ravioli filled with salmon and lobster and finished with lobster bisque is one way to start, or try the chef's modish take on the Arbroath smokie. Next up, perhaps slowly-braised Scottish beef cheeks with creamed potatoes and rosemary jus, and, to finish, hot chocolate fondant might come with griottine cherries and milk sorbet.

Times 12.30-2.30/6.30-9.30

LOTHIAN, WEST

LINLITHGOW — Map 21 NS97

Champany Inn

@@ Traditional British

Upmarket steakhouse in a characterful old mill

☎ 01506 834532 & 834388
Champany Corner EH49 7LU
e-mail: reception@champany.com
dir: 2m NE of Linlithgow. From M9 (N) junct 3, at top of slip road turn right. Champany 500yds on right

The Champany Inn deals in the polar opposite of fussy, faddy food and sticks to what it knows best: this is the destination of choice for fans of properly-hung, expertly-butchered and chargrilled slabs of Class-A meat. The rambling cluster of buildings dates from the 16th century, and focuses on the main circular restaurant, which was once a horse-powered flour mill. The place has a baronial charm, with candle-lit burnished wooden tables, and oil paintings on bare-stone walls beneath a vaulted roof. Loch Gruinart oysters or hot-smoked salmon or cod from the Champany smokepot are a good way to get going, or you might opt for Brechin black pudding fried in a skillet with potato and apple rösti and red onion marmalade. But this is a mecca for beef, so the main event offers up your favourite cut - T-bone, porterhouse, rib-eye, Chateaubriand and all points in between - whacks it on a charcoal grill, and delivers the result timed to perfection. Quality of the raw materials is second to none, and consequently it's expensive. If you're on a budget, go for the more wallet-friendly Chop and Ale House.

Times 12.30-2/7-10 Closed 25-26 Dec, 1-2 Jan, Sun, L Sat

Livingston's Restaurant

@@ Modern European V ♥

Modern European cookery at a family-run place

☎ 01506 846565
52 High St EH49 7AE
e-mail: contact@livingstons-restaurant.co.uk
web: www.livingstons-restaurant.co.uk
dir: On high street opposite old post office

Accessed via a sweet little alley off the main high street, which opens up into a pretty garden with a summer house, Livingston's is a family-run restaurant with a good deal of traditional charm. There's plenty of period character on the inside with stone floors in two of the dining areas (the third being a conservatory extension with views over the garden). The menu treads a modish path with a good showing of Scottish ingredients and some bright, Pan-European ideas. Start, for example, with braised Tamworth pork cheek with pickled apple, apple jelly and maple bacon, or a pea velouté with coconut foam. Among main courses, Shetland monkfish tail is roasted with Bayonne ham and served with fennel and leek purée and spiced lentils, or go for the poached loin of Highland venison with beetroot rösti, celeriac milk gel, syboes (spring onions) and port-glazed baby beetroot. There's no less creativity at dessert stage: strawberry and elderflower cannelloni, for example, with honeycomb, strawberry bonbon and balsamic ice cream.

Chef Max Hogg **Owner** The Livingston Family
Times 12-2.30/6-9.30 Closed 1 wk Jun, 1 wk Oct, 2 wks Jan, Sun-Mon (ex Mothering & Etr Sun) **Prices** Fixed L 2 course fr £17.25, Fixed D 3 course fr £40.25, Service optional, Groups min 8 service 10% **Wines** 32 bottles over £30, 29 bottles under £30, 6 by glass
Notes Vegetarian menu, Dress restrictions, Smart casual **Seats** 60, Pr/dining room 15 **Children** Portions
Parking NCP Linlithgow Cross, on street

UPHALL — Map 21 NT07

Macdonald Houstoun House

@@ Traditional British, Scottish ♥

Scottish cooking in an atmospheric tower restaurant

☎ 0844 879 9043
EH52 6JS
e-mail: houstoun@macdonald-hotels.co.uk
web: www.macdonaldhotels.co.uk/houstoun.house
dir: M8 junct 3 follow Broxburn signs, straight over rdbt then at mini-rdbt turn right towards Uphall, hotel 1m on right

The white-painted house sits in a secluded spot surrounded by 22 acres of peaceful woodlands to the west of Edinburgh. It dates from the 16th century and Mary Queen of Scots is said to be a past visitor. Recently redecorated, up in the tower the four rooms that make up the restaurant - now renamed Jeremy Wares at Houstoun House - sport deep burgundy walls, grand chandeliers and elegant unclothed tables lit by a single tall candle. The kitchen relies heavily on quality Scottish ingredients and presents them in a modern, unfussy style. You might start with thin onion and thyme tart and beetroot relish, or seared Skye scallops with red wine risotto and tomato pesto, before moving on to a traditional ashet (a pie) of ox cheek with creamy mash and root vegetables. The patriotic mood continues with a rich Caledonia burnt cream with rhubarb, or seasonal cranachan mess, amongst the desserts.

Chef Jeremy Wares, David Murray **Owner** Macdonald Hotels **Times** 6.30-9.30 Closed L all week **Prices** Starter £6.50-£9, Main £14-£22.50, Dessert £6.95-£9, Service optional **Wines** 13 by glass **Notes** Sunday L fr £17, Vegetarian available, Dress restrictions, Smart casual, no jeans or trainers **Seats** 65, Pr/dining room 30 **Children** Portions, Menu **Parking** 200

MIDLOTHIAN

DALKEITH — Map 21 NT36

The Sun Inn

@ Traditional ♥

Winning menus in a popular gastro-pub

☎ 0131 663 2456 & 663 1534
Lothian Bridge EH22 4TR
e-mail: thesuninn@live.co.uk
dir: Opposite Newbattle Viaduct on the A7 near Eskbank

This is a real gem of a pub. In fact, it's more than a pub, but still a pub. And that's a good thing. A winner of the AA Pub of the Year for Scotland a few years ago, the old inn was revitalised in 2009 and these days it has fabulous boutique bedrooms, a good deal of smart-yet-rustic charm, and a menu that champions local producers. There are beams aplenty, real fires and an all-round bonhomie to the place. The menu is supported by blackboards and follows the seasons to deliver some inventive but not over-blown contemporary dishes: a pork tapas plate, for example, which includes Scotch egg, belly pork, barbecued slider and winter slaw. Pheasant and ham pie with sherried bay leaf cream is a fine pie indeed, and the beef Wellington with Hornig's haggis is a surefire hit. There's beer from the independent Stewart's of Edinburgh and a well-chosen wine list to complete the picture.

Chef Ian Minto, Barry Drummond **Owner** Bernadette McCarron **Times** 12-2/6-9 Closed 26 Dec, 1 Jan **Prices** Prices not confirmed Service optional **Wines** 33 by glass **Notes** Set menu 2/3 course £15/£18, Vegetarian available, Dress restrictions, Smart casual **Seats** 90 **Children** Portions, Menu **Parking** 125

LASSWADE   Map 21 NT36

The Paper Mill

⊛ British, Scottish **NEW**

Uncomplicated brasserie cooking overlooking the Esk

☎ 0131 663 1412
2-4 Westmill Rd EH18 1LR
e-mail: info@thepapermill-lasswade.co.uk
dir: In centre of Lasswade village

There are no prizes for guessing what this place used to be. They stopped making esparto-grass paper at Lasswade as recently as 2004, but if that seems a shame, this diverting modern eatery goes a long way to making up for it. Overlooking the banks of the River Esk, it's been creatively decorated with reclaimed materials and objets trouvés, as well as striking artworks, and there is an infectiously relaxing tone to the service approach. There's also the benefit of outdoor tables to enjoy when the valley is bathed in sunshine. An uncomplicated brasserie menu draws on regional produce, but with an international culinary philosophy, so expect Ullapool scallops to come with chorizo and spinach as one possible opener. Sharing platters of charcuterie and pickles are always a good thing, while mains extend from well-worked duck en croûte with fairly pugnacious cracked pepper sauce to sea bass with gnocchi, tomato and parmesan. High-octane chocolate mousse served warm is offset by white chocolate ice cream and crumbled pistachios.

Chef David Millar **Owner** Karen Calvert & David Johnston **Times** 12-10 Closed 25 Dec, All-day dining **Prices** Starter £4.25-£8.95, Main £6.95-£21.95, Dessert £3.95-£5.95 **Wines** 13 bottles over £30, 35 bottles under £30, 16 by glass **Notes** Sunday L £11.95, Vegetarian available **Seats** Pr/dining room 12 **Children** Portions, Menu **Parking** 25

MORAY

CRAIGELLACHIE   Map 23 NJ24

Craigellachie Hotel

⊛ Scottish ✿

Neatly presented Scottish cooking in a Highland valley

☎ 01340 881204
Victoria St AB38 9SR
e-mail: reservations.craigellachie@ohiml.com
web: www.oxfordhotelsandinns.com
dir: 12m S of Elgin, in village centre

Sitting aloof on a valley slope in Speyside, the white-fronted Victorian hotel with its pitched roofs surveys the rivers and mountains of a particularly ravishing section of the Highlands, and represents a wonderful setting to enjoy one (or more) of the hundreds of single-malt whiskies available in the Quaich Bar. The Ben Aigan dining room recalls the Highland retreats of old, with its high ceiling and appealingly weathered look. Neatly presented modern Scottish cooking mobilises plenty of regional ingredients for such dishes as a Strathdon Blue cheese and leek soufflé, twice-cooked and turned out in the company of braised celery, confit apple and chestnut purée, before roast saddle of lamb with root veg in bordelaise sauce, or seared cod with spinach in sauce vierge. Fantastic tang is achieved in the orange marmalade ice cream that accompanies a shortbread-based caramelised lemon tart. Otherwise, there are thoroughbred Scottish cheeses, served with oatcakes and fruity chutney.

Chef John Geddes **Owner** Oxford Hotels & Inns **Times** 12-2/6-9 **Prices** Prices not confirmed Service optional **Wines** 7 by glass **Notes** Booking essential for Sun L, Sunday L, Vegetarian available, Dress restrictions, Smart casual, Civ Wed 60 **Seats** 30, Pr/dining room 60 **Children** Portions, Menu **Parking** 25

PERTH & KINROSS

AUCHTERARDER   Map 21 NN91

Andrew Fairlie @ Gleneagles

⊛⊛⊛⊛ – *see page 604*

The Strathearn

⊛⊛ British, French

Classical cooking in a grand but intimate dining room

☎ 01764 694270
The Gleneagles Hotel PH3 1NF
e-mail: gleneagles.restaurant.reservations@gleneagles.com
web: www.gleneagles.com
dir: Off A9 at exit for A823 follow signs for Gleneagles Hotel

In the sprawling Gleneagles Hotel (see also Andrew Fairlie), The Strathearn dining room has been given a refurbishment in the interests of a slightly more intimate

atmosphere. That said, the art deco grandeur of the surroundings, from the moulded ceilings to the table lights, are still something to see, and the tableside labours of carving smoked salmon and setting fire to various items retain their allure. Sixes of oysters and dollops of caviar are the high-rolling ways to start, and the Franco-Scottish remit of the kitchen is ably fulfilled in the pairing of a clootie dumpling with foie gras in ginger wine. Mains bring on lobster thermidor, whole Dover soles, and a range of grilled meats, and also rack of lamb with boulangère potatoes in olive and thyme jus. At dessert stage, chocoholics can get stuck into the Valrhona menu, while the rest gravitate towards something like classic tarte Tatin, served with Calvados anglaise and clotted cream ice cream.

Chef Paul Devonshire **Owner** Diageo plc **Times** 12.30-2.30/7-10 Closed L Mon-Sat **Prices** Tasting menu fr £59, Service optional **Wines** 15 by glass **Notes** Sunday L fr £42, Vegetarian available, Dress restrictions, Smart casual, no jeans or trainers, Civ Wed 250 **Seats** 322 **Children** Portions, Menu **Parking** 300

COMRIE   Map 21 NN72

Royal Hotel

⊛ Traditional British

Luxury small hotel with confident cooking

☎ 01764 679200
Melville Square PH6 2DN
e-mail: reception@royalhotel.co.uk
web: www.royalhotel.co.uk
dir: In main square, 7m from Crieff, on A85

The Royal, at one time a coaching inn, is a small luxury hotel, its two dining rooms linked by double doors, the more traditional restaurant decorated with patterned wallpaper hung with numerous pictures. The menus may not hold too many surprises, but the kitchen is conscientious about sourcing fresh local produce, timing and seasoning are spot on, and presentation is a strength. Devilled lamb's kidneys could precede sea bass fillet atop curly kale in prawn butter sauce with new potatoes, or moist, crisp-skinned pan-fried chicken breast with a good Madeira and mushroom sauce and truffle-scented mash. Meals end happily enough with desserts like bread-and-butter pudding or hot chocolate fondant, both served with vanilla ice cream.

Times 12-2/6.30-9 Closed 25-26 Dec

Andrew Fairlie @ Gleneagles

AUCHTERARDER   **MAP 21 NN91**

Modern French V 🍷 NOTABLE WINE LIST

Franco-Scottish cooking at the hermetic heart of a golfing hotel

☎ 01764 694267
The Gleneagles Hotel PH3 1NF
e-mail: reservations@andrewfairlie.
co.uk
dir: From A9 take Gleneagles exit, hotel in 1m

The Gleneagles was built in 1924 during the period of hedonism that followed the depredations of the Great War. There may not seem an obvious connection these days, but a golfing habit was quite the sophisticated thing as part of the lifestyle of the smart set, and Gleneagles did its best to look and feel like somewhere on the French Riviera, for all that it sits in hundreds of acres of Perthshire highland, near what was once its own railway station. If you're something less than passionate about golf, this may not be the most obvious resort. The broad windows of the lounge-bar look out over the greens after all. At the pulsing heart of its culinary enterprise, however, Andrew Fairlie has single-handedly turned the place into a magnet for serious eating, worth the journey out from Edinburgh (at least), and it presumably isn't a coincidence that his self-named restaurant is so entirely careless of the business of golf that it doesn't survey

the fairways, or anything at all. It sits like a giant anechoic chamber at the centre of the ground floor, lit like an exhibition of fragile antiquities inside, with framed prints and striking paintings, including a portrait of Fairlie himself, enlivening the crepuscular repose. The service approach is all soft-spoken, hyper-efficient courtesy, and it all makes a pointedly subdued backdrop for the gastronomic activity to come. Fairlie's kitchen is a celebration of the Auld (and indeed Modern) Alliance of French and Scottish pedigree, with prime ingredients flown in from Paris's Rungis market each morning, to take their place alongside the scallops and lobster, the roe deer, free-range chicken and duck from closer to home. What turns up is a highly worked, intelligently conceived contemporary cooking that is fluent in the modern discourse, but with a keen eye for sound gustatory principle. Start with a seafood medley combining roast scallops and sea bass with oyster parfait (a brave idea) and grilled squid, as a prelude to roast breast of duck, its density of texture and expressive flavour offset with the earthy vegetal accompaniments of cauliflower cream and wild garlic, rather than the usual fruit. Another route might be to open with creamy roasted veal sweetbreads and grilled lettuce in tomato fondue, before progressing to John Dory with artichokes and langoustines in red wine jus. Desserts mobilise an array of fruits for grapefruit and pistachio rapeseed oil

cake, pineapple soufflé with coconut sauce, or poached rhubarb with crowdie ice cream.

Chef Andrew Fairlie **Owner** Andrew Fairlie **Times** 6.30-10 Closed 24-25 Dec, 3 wks Jan, Sun, L all week **Prices** Fixed D 3 course £95-£105, Tasting menu £95-£125, Starter £31-£41, Main £46, Dessert £18 **Wines** 12 by glass **Notes** ALC 3 course £85, 6 course Degustation £125/Du Marché £95, Vegetarian menu, Dress restrictions, Smart casual **Seats** 54 **Parking** 300

Save on Hotels. Book at **theAA.com/hotel**

PERTH & KINROSS 605 SCOTLAND

Fortingall Hotel

◎◎ Modern Scottish

Well-balanced menu in Arts and Crafts village

☎ 01887 830367 & 829012
PH15 2NQ
e-mail: enquiries@fortingall.com
dir: B846 from Aberfeldy for 6m, left signed Fortingall for 3m. Hotel in village centre

Fortingall Hotel, near Loch Tay with views down Glen Lyon, is a solidly built property, and within is a lounge bar that serves pub-style food and a choice of two dining rooms, one in Arts and Craft style, the other slightly less formal; staff are knowledgeable and approachable throughout. Set dinners offer a trio of choices at each course, the kitchen utilising as much local produce as it can; Perthshire lamb, for example, as a main course of pink-roast loin with thyme jus, creamed cabbage, artichoke purée and pommes en cocotte. Meals might kick off with a platter of smoked salmon, quail's eggs and Avruga caviar adding touches of luxury, or foie gras and game terrine complemented by Sauternes jelly, Cumberland sauce and poached figs. Fish is well handled, judging by pan-fried fillet of halibut served on two balls of saffron-flavoured noodles with caviar butter and pak choi. Go for cranachan if offered - the real thing, served with whisky jelly.

Chef Alasdair Calwell, David Gray **Owner** Robbie & Mags Cairns **Times** 12-2/6.30-9 **Prices** Prices not confirmed Service optional **Wines** 15 bottles over £30, 20 bottles under £30, 12 by glass **Notes** Sunday L, Vegetarian available, Civ Wed 50 **Seats** 30, Pr/dining room 30 **Children** Portions, Menu **Parking** 20

The Famous Bein Inn

◎ Modern British

Traditional inn serving up good Scottish food

☎ 01577 830216
PH2 9PY
e-mail: enquiries@beininn.com
web: www.beininn.com
dir: 2m N of Glenfarg, on the intersection of A912 & B996

Once a grand Georgian manor house and old drovers' inn in a wooded glen just off the M90 south of Perth, the Bein has joined the ranks of the gastro brigade, offering

admirably fuss-free cooking with a side order of hearty Scottish welcome. It's a cheery, traditional place with a Saltire flapping from the flagpole and tartan on the floor of the lounge bar, and whether you choose to eat in the bistro or the Balvaird restaurant, the kitchen deploys top-class local and seasonal produce as the basis of an unpretentious menu. Work your way through the likes of pan-roasted loin of pork with apple purée, black pudding tempura and real ale sauce, or lamb rump steak with pommes Anna, baby veg, pea purée and pan juices. To finish, consider sticky toffee pudding with rich toffee sauce, or keep things savoury with Scottish cheeses served with oatcakes and chutney.

Times 12-9 Closed 25 Dec

Killiecrankie Hotel

◎◎ Modern British V ◑

Satisfying country-house cooking in tranquil Perthshire

☎ 01796 473220
PH16 5LG
e-mail: enquiries@killiecrankiehotel.co.uk
dir: off A9 at Pitlochry, hotel 3m along B8079 on right

There's a sense of splendid isolation at Killicrankie, and you'd never guess the A9 was so handy if you hadn't come that way yourself. The charming early Victorian house was built for a church minister, but these days administers a different type of absolution - a chance to escape from the real world and get a little taste of comfort and joy. It's in a plum spot, surrounded by soaring trees, with four acres of grounds to call its own and the River Garry flowing past. There's a soothing and smart traditionalism to the interior, including the dining room, with its linen-clad tables, one of which is yours for the night. The menu features plenty of regional ingredients and does not attempt to rock the boat. You might start with sautéed wild mushroom and chorizo tartlet with a leek cream sauce, followed by monkfish wrapped in Parma ham with seared king scallops, potato and sunblushed tomato rösti, and a roasted garlic and parsley butter sauce. Warm frangipane and pear flan with crème fraîche hits the spot at dessert.

Chef Mark Easton **Owner** Henrietta Fergusson **Times** 6.30-8.30 Closed Jan-Feb, L all week **Prices** Service optional, Groups min 8 service 10% **Wines** 32 bottles over £30, 47 bottles under £30, 9 by glass **Notes** Pre-theatre menu from 6.15pm Mon-Sat, 4 course D £42, Sunday L £4.50-£27.50, Vegetarian menu, Dress restrictions, No shorts **Seats** 30, Pr/dining room 12 **Children** Portions, Menu **Parking** 20

Ballathie House Hotel

◎◎ Classic

Modern country-house cooking by the Tay

☎ 01250 883268
PH1 4QN
e-mail: info@ballathiehousehotel.com
web: www.ballathiehousehotel.com
dir: From A9, 2m N of Perth, take B9099 through Stanley & follow signs, or from A93 at Beech Hedge follow signs for Ballathie, 2.5m

The Glasgow to Aberdeen train used to deliver anglers to this turreted Scottish mansion by the River Tay, and although Ballathie is still a prime spot for the rod and line brigade, you don't need to dangle your fly into frigid waters to enjoy a stay here. The gastronomically inclined will appreciate the elegant buttercup-hued restaurant, and a kitchen team that takes native produce - much of it from the surrounding estate - as its starting point. Cooking is unapologetically in the tried-and-tested modern country-house idiom, and succeeds thanks to its superb ingredients and refusal to veer off course into faddish trends. Judicious balance and luxury touches combine in a starter of confit duck croustillant with seared foie gras, macerated apricots and carrot and orange purée, ahead of loin and truffled haunch of Sutherland venison with thyme rösti, red wine salsify, celeriac purée and praline sauce. Dessert wraps things up with a melting chocolate fondant with cherry compôte and pistachio ice cream.

Times 12.30-2/7-9

Barley Bree Restaurant with Rooms

◎◎ British, French

Well-crafted contemporary cooking

☎ 01764 681451
6 Willoughby St PH5 2AB
e-mail: info@barleybree.com
dir: A9 onto A822 in centre of Muthill

Barley Bree is a smart restaurant with rooms in a quiet conservation village, just a mile from the magnificent Drummond Castle Gardens. A one-time coaching inn dating from the 18th-century, it oozes spruced up rustic charm these days, with candles and flowers on scrubbed wooden tables, stone walls adorned with original artwork, old beams and boarded floors, and a double-sided wood burning stove that pumps out heat in the main dining room. Expect a cosy, informal atmosphere and good modish cooking with a distinct Gallic twist from Fabrice Bouteloup, the French chef-patron. Top-notch local ingredients are well sourced and traditional and contemporary techniques combine to good effect. A starter of succulent red mullet with a crisp fennel salad and rich, anchovy-infused caper dressing might precede

continued

MUTHILL *continued*

melt-in-the-mouth slow-cooked blade of Aberdeen Angus with wild mushroom gratin, Jerusalem artichoke purée, roseval potatoes and back pepper jus. Round off with a simple, beautifully caramelised apple tarte Tatin.

Chef Fabrice Bouteloup **Owner** Fabrice & Alison Bouteloup **Times** 12-2/6.45-9 Closed Xmas, Mon-Tue **Prices** Starter £7.50-£11, Main £16.50-£22.50, Dessert £6.50-£8.50, Service included **Wines** 23 bottles over £30, 50 bottles under £30, 15 by glass **Notes** Sunday L £6-£14.50, Vegetarian available **Seats** 35 **Children** Portions, Menu **Parking** 12

PERTH
Map 21 NO12

Deans@ Let's Eat
◉◉ Modern Scottish ◐

Dazzling cooking in stylish restaurant

☎ 01738 643377
77-79 Kinnoull St PH1 5EZ
e-mail: deans@letseatperth.co.uk
web: www.letseatperth.co.uk
dir: On corner of Kinnoull St & Atholl St, close to North Inch & cinema

On the corner of a busy street in the centre of town, Deans is a smart, relaxed and inviting place, with a large display of wines, colourful prints on a vinous theme, and comfortable seats at bare-topped tables. Chef Willie Deans deals in innovative dishes prepared from splendid Scottish produce. Take shortcrust tart of smoked haddock, for example, an ultra-thin pastry case filled generously, topped with small chunks of spinach, a poached egg covered in melted cheddar flecked with bacon, with a smear of cauliflower purée and a rich seafood and tomato sauce on the side. Haggis cake with turnip purée, confit onions, mash and whisky cream might be an alternative, while for the main event there might be beef medallion topped with duxelle served with roast vegetables, or spankingly fresh trout fillets with green beans, grapes stewed with Sauternes and vanilla, saffron potatoes and a rich lobster and red wine bisque. Puddings make an impact too: perhaps dense chocolate tart with candied fruit, caramelised banana, banana ice cream and sauce anglaise.

Chef Willie Deans **Owner** Mr & Mrs W Deans **Times** 12-3/6-10 Closed 1st 2 wks Jan, Sun-Mon **Prices** Fixed L 2 course £12.50, Fixed D 3 course £20.50, Starter £4.95-£9.95, Main £13.25-£22.95, Dessert £2-£8.95, Service optional **Wines** 23 bottles over £30, 36

bottles under £30, 14 by glass **Notes** Pre-theatre 2/3 course £15.50/£20.50 Tue-Fri 6-9pm, Vegetarian available, Dress restrictions, Smart casual **Seats** 70 **Children** Portions **Parking** Multi-storey car park (100 yds)

Murrayshall House Hotel & Golf Course
◉◉ Modern British ◐

Polished cooking amid the rolling Lowland acres

☎ 01738 551171
New Scone PH2 7PH
e-mail: info@murrayshall.co.uk
web: www.murrayshall.co.uk
dir: From Perth A94 (Coupar Angus) turn right signed Murrayshall before New Scone

With a brace of 18-hole courses woven into its densely-wooded 350-acre estate, it's fair to say that most of Murrayshall's guests have golf in mind, but there are other attractions too, not least the fine dining to be had in its Old Masters restaurant. Bag a window table to soak up the views which stretch all the way to the city of Perth, and take in the leaded windows, original artworks and faultlessly elegant tone of the room. Menus bang the drum for Scottish produce and offer much to please traditionalists, plus a few creative flourishes to assuage modern tastes. The fatty richness of a duck liver pâté is offset with the acid twang of tart gooseberries and smoked bacon salad, while main course brings layers of pork belly and black pudding atop crushed apple purée spiked with Calvados and served with Savoy cabbage, mushrooms and rich jus. Puddings take refuge in classily-tweaked old favourites - cherry Bakewell tart with cherry ice cream and a shot glass of cranberry punch, for example.

Chef Craig Jackson **Owner** Old Scone Ltd **Times** 12-2.30/7-9.45 Closed 26 Dec, L Sat-Mon **Prices** Fixed D 3 course £25, Service optional **Wines** 8 by glass **Notes** Sunday L, Vegetarian available, Civ Wed 130 **Seats** 55, Pr/dining room 40 **Children** Portions, Menu **Parking** 120

The New County Hotel
◉◉ Modern British V ◐

Modish cooking in city-centre boutique hotel

☎ 01738 623355
22-30 County Place PH2 8EE
e-mail: enquiries@newcountyhotel.com
web: www.opusone-restaurant.co.uk
dir: A9 junct 11, Perth. Follow signs for town centre. Hotel on right after library

Part of the boutique New County Hotel in Perth centre, the Opus One restaurant is a hotspot for business lunches, while culture vultures turn up to refuel on forays to the city's theatre, concert hall and galleries. The hotel goes for a cosmopolitan city-slicker look in Opus One that brings together bare darkwood tables and floors with chocolate-brown high-backed leather seats, soft lighting, and cool jazz burbling in the background. On the food front, the kitchen clearly reads from a French-influenced

script and has the necessary technique and creativity to make the most of the top-drawer ingredients from Perthshire's larder. A switched-on menu kicks off with goats' cheese soufflé with cauliflower, served both pickled and as a curried purée, and Grana Padano crisp; next up, slow-cooked beef blade comes with a bone filled with marrow and garlic snails, pearl barley and parsley, or there might be braised pork neck with Jerusalem artichoke, hazelnut, apple and red wine reduction. The good ideas keep coming to the end with a mincemeat pithivier matched with a nutmeg tuile and vanilla bean ice cream.

Chef Rory Lovie **Owner** Mr Owen & Mrs Sarah Boyle **Times** 12-2/5.30-9 Closed Sun-Mon, L Sun-Thu **Prices** Prices not confirmed Service optional **Wines** 20 bottles over £30, 19 bottles under £30, 7 by glass **Notes** Early bird menu available, Vegetarian menu **Seats** 48 **Children** Portions **Parking** 10, plus opposite on street

---

63@Parklands
◉◉ Modern European V

Smart contemporary cooking in a chic hotel

☎ 01738 622451
Parklands Hotel, St Leonards Bank PH2 8EB
e-mail: info@63atparklandshotel.com
web: www.63atparklands.com
dir: Adjacent to Perth station, overlooking South Inch Park

Sister restaurant to 63 Tay Street (see entry), 63@ Parklands is located in a smart hotel near the river, and comes complete with a lovely patio area for alfresco dining. It offers the same style of technically adept, well-focused and creative cooking from chef Graeme Pallister as its ever-popular sibling. Fixed-price menus with choices of two at the principal stages are the business, opening perhaps with Loch Nevis langoustine fricassée with shimeji mushrooms and penne. A soup is interposed before the main-course alternatives of Kirriemuir lamb rump crusted in olives and pine nuts, with tomato, basil and garlic, or salmon roasted in Hebridean salt and herbs with smoked salmon noodles in salmon roe butter sauce. Cheeses are followed by creative desserts such as rhubarb burnt cream with a salty ginger ice cream doughnut.

Chef Graeme Pallister **Owner** Scott & Penny Edwards **Times** 7-9 Closed 25 Dec-6 Jan, Tue-Wed, L all week **Prices** Prices not confirmed Service optional, Groups min 8 service 10% **Wines** 8 by glass **Notes** Vegetarian menu, Civ Wed 30 **Seats** 32, Pr/dining room 22 **Children** Portions **Parking** 25

63 Tay Street

◎◎ Modern Scottish V 🅝NOTABLE WINE LIST 🅒

Enterprising neighbourhood restaurant by the River Tay

☎ 01738 441451
63 Tay St PH2 8NN
e-mail: info@63taystreet.com
dir: In town centre, on river

This Tayside restaurant is decorated in neutral shades, with a wooden floor, small porthole-size mirrors and artwork lining the walls. The menus reflect the pick of Scottish produce, and the kitchen treats it with enthusiasm and originality, making a velouté of smoked haddock and partnering it with scallops, bacon and curried apple for example, and serving chicken with langoustines, risotto and leek fondue. Another juxtaposition of surf 'n' turf impresses - this time Parma ham-wrapped rabbit terrine surrounded by a scattering of broad beans and peas, two small caramelised scallops, two deep-fried balls of smoked scallop roe, scallop purée and foam. Dishes can be elaborate but are none the worse for it: slices of barbecued Gressingham duck breast, for instance, succulent and full of flavour, are served atop buttery pommes purée and garnished with pickled cherries, foie gras, watercress and caramelised lemongrass sauce. Puddings make an impact too - perhaps dense chocolate ganache topped with raspberry sorbet, with scoops of white chocolate mousse and coffee ice cream, all surrounded by sugar syrup and caramelised pistachios.

Chef Graeme Pallister **Owner** Scott & Penny Edwards, Graeme Pallister **Times** 12-2/6.30-9 Closed Xmas, New Year, 1st wk Jul, Sun-Mon, L Wed **Prices** Fixed L 2 course £18-£24, Fixed D 3 course £25, Starter £8, Main £21-£25, Dessert £8-£10, Service optional, Groups min 8 service 10% **Wines** 124 bottles over £30, 66 bottles under £30, 7 by glass **Notes** Fixed D 4 course £25, 5 course £35-£39 Tue-Fri, Vegetarian menu **Seats** 38 **Children** Portions **Parking** On street

Tabla

◎ Indian NEW V

Exemplary and authentic Indian dishes

☎ 01738 444630
173 South St PH2 8NY
e-mail: thirmalreddy@yahoo.com

The palate-tickling flavours on offer in Tabla are built on spices grown in chef Praveen Kumar's family fields in India - proof, perhaps, that it is sometimes worth sacrificing the fashionable dogma of local sourcing in the name of authenticity. The menu offers a roster of familiar old ideas that take their inspiration from all over the sub-continent; there's no attempt to deliver trendy hybrid nouveau Indian cuisine, since the staff are staunchly proud of their culinary heritage and eager to explain what's going on in the dishes they offer. Crispy deep-fried pakora - take your pick from salmon, squid, chicken or vegetable - are a good way to get going, then you might follow with a rich and spicy South Indian garlic chicken,

bursting with the flavours of fresh chilli, coriander and tamarind (make sure to order an excellent naan bread to mop up all of the sauce). Finish with sweet and sticky gulab jamun.

Owner Praveen Kumar & Saroo **Times** 12-2.30/5-10.30 Closed L Sun **Prices** Starter £3.95-£5.95, Main £8.95-£13.95 **Notes** Pre-theatre 2 course fr £11.95, Wine & Dine 2 people £34.95, Vegetarian menu

---

PITLOCHRY   **Map 23 NN95**

Green Park Hotel

◎ British 🅒

Country-house cooking with magnificent views

☎ 01796 473248
Clunie Bridge Rd PH16 5JY
e-mail: bookings@thegreenpark.co.uk
web: www.thegreenpark.co.uk
dir: Turn off A9 at Pitlochry, follow signs for 0.25m through town, turn left at Clunie Bridge Rd

The Green Park has one of those dining rooms where the injunction to 'bag a table by the window' is worth heeding, the reward being prime views over Loch Faskally, with the forests and mountains as backdrop. It's a long room with a chintzy feel, where tables are clad in floor-length coverings, respectably spaced and individually adorned with blooms. A gentle version of country-house cooking is in the offing, so avocado mousse is garnished with Serrano ham, shaved parmesan and dried tomato, while main courses run to braised rose veal osso buco with basil mash, in a dressing of tomatoes, olive oil and herbs, or a seafood assemblage of poached salmon, prawns, mackerel and anchovies with saffron mayonnaise and salad. Finish up with moreish gingerbread pudding served with a moat of caramel sauce and a garnish of banana ice cream.

Chef Chris Tamblin **Owner** Green Park Ltd
Times 12-2/6.30-8.30 **Prices** Prices not confirmed Service optional **Wines** 6 bottles over £30, 70 bottles under £30, 8 by glass **Notes** Pre-theatre menu available from 5.45pm, Sunday L, Vegetarian available, Dress restrictions, Smart casual **Seats** 100 **Children** Portions, Menu **Parking** 52

Knockendarroch House Hotel

◎ Traditional British

Resourceful cooking at elegantly appointed hotel

☎ 01796 473473 & 07802 878231
Higher Oakfield PH16 5HT
e-mail: bookings@knockendarroch.co.uk
dir: On entering town from Perth, 1st right (East Moulin Road) after railway bridge, then 2nd left, last hotel on left

An imposing property with great views over the town and surrounding hills, Knockendarroch has been elegantly furnished and makes a stylish place to stay as well as dine. The restaurant is a grand room, with ornate ceiling cornicing and delicate rose-work around the chandeliers making an appropriate setting for fine dining. Quality

Scottish produce is the kitchen's stock-in-trade, which it uses inventively with memorable results. Successes have included hake fillet with mussel sauce, served with chive mash, mange-tout and cucumber spaghetti, and sautéed medallion of Angus fillet with shin croquette, red wine sauce, pommes Anna, spinach and root vegetables. The kitchen's care with timing and presentation is clear throughout, seen in starters like a warm salad of wood pigeon with black pudding and mushrooms, or terrine of smoked ham hock with butter beans and home-made apple chutney, and puddings such as warm almond and cherry tart with custard and vanilla ice cream.

Chef Angus McNab **Owner** Liz Martin & Elaine Muldoon **Times** 5.30-8.30 Closed mid Nov-mid Jan, L all week **Prices** Starter £4.45-£7.30, Main £13.50-£22.60, Dessert £6.25-£7.75, Service optional **Wines** 8 bottles over £30, 25 bottles under £30, 5 by glass **Notes** Pre-theatre D Jun-Oct, Vegetarian available, Dress restrictions, Smart casual **Seats** 24 **Parking** 12

ST FILLANS   **Map 20 NN62**

The Four Seasons Hotel

◎◎ Modern British V 🅒

Breathtaking loch views and appealing modern cooking

☎ 01764 685333
Lochside PH6 2NF
e-mail: info@thefourseasonshotel.co.uk
web: www.thefourseasonshotel.co.uk
dir: From Perth take A85 W, through Crieff & Comrie. Hotel at west end of village

Perched on the edge of Loch Earn, The Four Seasons has breathtaking south-westerly views over the water and wooded hills. The hotel dates from the 19th century, with additions and modifications made over the years to meet modern sensibilities. The Meall Reamhar restaurant is a spacious room, with colourful fabric chairs at rectangular and circular tables and a display of artwork (for sale) on neutral-coloured walls - and that spectacle of the loch. The kitchen takes full advantage of Scotland's natural larder, and its cooking makes an impact with its sharply modern combinations. A pavé of salmon wrapped in ham, on a sorrel and lemon balm potato cake, surrounded by braised fennel and a Bloody Mary nage is typical of main courses. Starters can range from smoked duck with apple chutney and red wine jelly to crab and mussel risotto, and winning desserts have included pear and honey frangipane tart with whisky-soaked prunes and custard lightly flavoured with tarragon.

Chef Mathew Martin **Owner** Andrew Low
Times 12-2.30/6-9.30 Closed Jan-Feb & some wkdays Mar, Nov & Dec **Prices** Fixed D 2 course £28-£39.90, Service optional **Wines** 8 by glass **Notes** 4 course D £38-£49.90, Sunday L £15.95, Vegetarian menu, Dress restrictions, No jeans or trainers, Civ Wed 80 **Seats** 40, Pr/dining room 20 **Children** Portions, Menu **Parking** 30

RENFREWSHIRE, EAST

UPLAWMOOR   Map 10 NS45

Uplawmoor Hotel

◉ Modern Scottish

Good cooking in a Georgian coaching inn

☎ 01505 850565
66 Neilston Rd G78 4AF
e-mail: info@uplawmoor.co.uk
web: www.uplawmoor.co.uk
dir: M77 junct 2, A736 signed Barrhead & Irvine. Hotel 4m beyond Barrhead

Many of Britain's coaching inns saw unofficial service in the past as staging-posts for smugglers, and this Georgian hostelry was smack on the route from the Ayrshire coast to Glasgow. What was its stable-block, complete with copper-canopied fireplace surmounted with quotations from Robert Burns, is now a weekend dining room with darkwood tables, a small wood-fired stove and many good pictures. A homely style of Scots bistro cooking, built around fine local meats and fresh fish, provides plenty to satisfy. Cullen skink is a properly pungent, smoky, creamy version with good bite from leek, potato and celery, while mains run the gamut from pink-cooked haunch of Highland venison with dauphinoise in redcurrant jus, to poached sole, cheddar-glazed leeks and chive mash. The toffee pudding has all the stickiness one could wish from butterscotch sauce, as well as a scoop of smooth vanilla ice cream.

Times 12-3/6-9.30 Closed 26 Dec, 1 Jan, L Mon-Sat

SCOTTISH BORDERS

EDDLESTON   Map 21 NT24

The Horseshoe Inn

◉◉ Modern Scottish 🏆NOTABLE WINE LIST 🥂

Inventive Scottish cooking in an old smithy

☎ 01721 730225
Edinburgh Rd EH45 8QP
e-mail: reservations@horseshoeinn.co.uk
web: www.horseshoeinn.co.uk
dir: On A703, 5m N of Peebles

The one-time smithy (hence the name) hasn't looked back since its transformation into a restaurant with rooms and these days offers hospitality and even a little bit of luxury to travellers on the road from Peebles to Edinburgh. It's a destination in its own right these days, of course. There's a good deal of character on the inside with the restaurant done out handsomely in a stylish traditional manner with richly upholstered chairs and tables dressed up in white linen for what is to come. And what is to come is some smart, inspired and rather modish food. A starter of pan-fried scallops comes with wild leek, spiced parsnip purée and black pudding in a neat interpretation of a modern classic, followed perhaps by braised ox cheek and brisket with celeriac purée, confit tomatoes, lentils and red wine sauce. There are daily specials supplementing the carte

(split-pea soup with pork croquette and parsley dressing, maybe), and desserts such as black cherry soufflé with jellies and vanilla ice cream.

Chef Alistair Craig **Owner** Border Steelwork Structures Ltd **Times** 12-2.30/7-9 Closed 2 wks Jan, Mon-Tue **Prices** Fixed L 2 course £15, Fixed D 3 course £50, Starter £6.50-£9.50, Main £12-£25, Dessert £6.50-£9.50, Service optional, Groups min 8 service 10% **Wines** 89 bottles over £30, 35 bottles under £30, 12 by glass **Notes** Tasting menu available, Sunday L, Vegetarian available, Dress restrictions, Smart casual **Seats** 40, Pr/dining room 14 **Children** Menu **Parking** 20

KELSO   Map 21 NT73

The Cobbles Freehouse & Dining

◉ British, Pacific Rim 🥂

Appealing menu in lively pub setting

☎ 01573 223548
7 Bowmont St TD5 7JH
e-mail: info@thecobbleskelso.co.uk
dir: A6089 from Edinburgh, turn right at rdbt into Bowmont Rd. Restaurant in 0.3m

Festooned with hanging baskets in the summer, this 19th-century inn is just off the town's main square. It's the brewery tap for the Tempest Brewing Co just up the road, so a pint or two should hit the spot, but there are plenty of other good reasons to visit. The beamed bar has bags of atmosphere with a roaring log fire in winter, there's live music on Friday nights, plus no shortage of nice things to eat. You might opt for a home-made burger off the bar menu, or settle down in the cosy restaurant and choose something like seared breast of wood pigeon with crumbled Stornoway black pudding, red cabbage and port jus, followed by crispy-skin sea bass with pea purée, crushed lemon new potatoes, confit cherry tomatoes and tomato Choron sauce. There's a good showing of regional ingredients, and the beer might even sneak into dessert in the form of Tempest mocha porter ice cream served with a chocolate fondant and poached blueberries.

Chef Gavin Meiklejohn, John Addy **Owner** Annika & Gavin Meiklejohn **Times** 12-2/6-9 Closed 25-26 Dec, Mon in winter **Prices** Fixed D 3 course £24.95-£28.95, Starter £4-£5.95, Main £8.95-£20.95, Dessert £5.15-£6.50, Service optional **Wines** 4 bottles over £30, 26 bottles under £30, 7 by glass **Notes** Sunday L, Vegetarian available **Seats** 35, Pr/dining room 30 **Children** Portions, Menu **Parking** Behind restaurant

The Roxburghe Hotel & Golf Course

◉◉ Modern British

Fine country setting for modern British cooking

☎ 01573 450331
TD5 8JZ
e-mail: hotel@roxburghe.net
web: www.roxburghe-hotel.com
dir: From A68, 1m N of Jedburgh, take A698 for 5m to Heiton

Owned by the eponymous Duke, this turreted country-house hotel is a treat for those in search of outdoor country pursuits, and there's a bit of pampering on the cards, too, in the health and beauty salon, but there is no better reason to visit than to eat in the restaurant. The dining room delivers all the ducal finery you might expect, with its grand proportions, views over the manicured lawns, plush fabrics, horse-racing prints, crisp linen tablecloths, and a tartan carpet to put you in your place. Needless to say the estate provides a good deal of what turns up on the menu and there's a tendency towards modernism in the culinary thinking. A terrine of Scottish hare is partnered with Assam consommé and candied hazelnuts amongst first courses, for example, or there might be Scottish beef served tartare with quail's egg and horseradish crème fraîche. Pan-fried halibut forms a meaty partnership with Oxtail broth and girolles among main courses, or go for slow-cooked Peelham Farm pork belly with braised cheek ragout, langoustines and wild garlic.

Times 12.30-2/7-9.30

MELROSE   Map 21 NT53

Burt's Hotel

◉◉ Modern Scottish 🏆NOTABLE WINE LIST 🥂

Contemporary cooking at an old favourite

☎ 01896 822285
Market Square TD6 9PL
e-mail: enquiries@burtshotel.co.uk
web: www.burtshotel.co.uk
dir: A6091, 2m from A68, 3m S of Earlston. Hotel in market square

Burt's, on the attractive 18th-century Market Square, manages successfully to combine the roles of hotel, bar and restaurant, as it has done for years. The restaurant itself is a stylish room, with high-backed chairs, crisp napery and a paean to sports in its hunting, fishing and

Save on Hotels. Book at **theAA.com/hotel**

SCOTTISH BORDERS 609 SCOTLAND

shooting theme; it also has strong rugby links with the town's club. The kitchen moves with the times, laying its own inventive take on Scottish materials. Crisp belly pork comes with squid marinated in red wine, balsamic onions and apples, and well-timed fried halibut is served with gooey pancetta sauce, shallot purée, salsify in red wine, and wilted kale. A tian of beetroot and goats' cheese mousse, accompanied by apple compôte, beetroot jelly and pickled shallots, sounds thoroughly cosmopolitan, and, as this is Scotland, expect accurately roast venison with a game boudin, shallots, Savoy cabbage and parsnip purée. Finish with rum crème brûlée with caramelised bananas, chocolate fondant and banana sorbet.

Chef Trevor Williams **Owner** The Henderson family **Times** 12-2/7-9 Closed 26 Dec, 3-8 Jan, L Mon-Fri **Prices** Starter £4.50-£9, Main £12.95-£23.50, Dessert £6.95, Service optional **Wines** 33 bottles over £30, 27 bottles under £30, 8 by glass **Notes** Sunday L £22-£30, Vegetarian available, Dress restrictions, Jacket & tie preferred **Seats** 50, Pr/dining room 25 **Children** Portions **Parking** 40

PEEBLES   **Map 21 NT24**

Cringletie House

◉◉◉ *— see below*

Macdonald Cardrona Hotel, Golf & Spa

◉ Modern British

Modish cooking and ravishing country views

☎ 0844 879 9024 & 01896 833600
Cardrona EH45 8NE
e-mail: general.cardrona@macdonald-hotels.co.uk
web: www.macdonald-hotels.co.uk
dir: From Edinburgh on A701 signed Penicuik/Peebles. Then A703, at 1st rdbt beside garage turn left onto A72, hotel 3m on right

Part of the Macdonald group, the Cardrona is a classy modern hotel that has most bases covered: it is on the banks of the Tweed, so fishing is sorted, and golf is taken care of by the 18-hole course. All around are the rolling Borders hills, perfect for biking and hiking, or if that is all too outdoorsy to contemplate, you can get pampered in the glossy spa. Nor is dining neglected: from its vantage point on the second-floor, Renwicks restaurant provides outstanding views to go with a well-thought-out repertoire of uncomplicated modern dishes, running from seared peppered tuna loin with couscous, and coriander and lime butter sauce, to mains along the lines of braised

shoulder of Highland lamb with roast root vegetables and garlic mash, or grilled fillet of cod with spring onion and pancetta crust, braised leeks and herb mash. To finish, perhaps rhubarb and ginger crumble tart with crème anglaise.

Chef Ivor Clark **Owner** Macdonald Hotels **Times** 12.30-2/6.30-9.45 **Prices** Fixed D 3 course fr £27.95, Service optional **Wines** 18 by glass **Notes** Sunday L, Vegetarian available, Dress restrictions, Smart casual, no jeans or T-shirts, Civ Wed 200 **Seats** 70, Pr/dining room 200 **Children** Portions, Menu **Parking** 200

Cringletie House

Modern French V

Intelligent and refined cooking in baronial-style country house

☎ 01721 725750
Edinburgh Rd EH45 8PL
e-mail: enquiries@cringletie.com
web: www.cringletie.com
dir: 2.5m N of Peebles on A703

Amid beautiful rolling hills just 30 minutes' drive from Edinburgh, Cringletie is a handsome baronial house indeed. Built to impress in 1861 and standing in 28 acres of magnificent grounds, today's country-house hotel is truly delightful. It's on a manageable scale for a start - just 12 bedrooms - which enhances the get-away-from-it-all feel and means you're unlikely to encounter too

many people when exploring the walled gardens and woodland. There's a good deal of period charm on the inside, with elegant furnishings filling the well-proportioned rooms. The restaurant is up on the first floor - so lovely views in the daylight hours - and has an ornately painted ceiling, lots of period detailing, and tables dressed up for fine dining. Chef Patrick Bardoulet's cooking is rooted in French classicism, but is also creative and contemporary, and pays due homage to the superb Scottish produce to hand. A meal kicks off with canapés and amuse-bouche before a first course such as celeriac velouté with truffle oil and gingerbread croûtons, the flavours judged to a T. Two beautiful fillets of plaice star in a main course, sitting atop shellfish risotto and served with baby leeks and a Sauternes sauce, whilst on the 'Indulgence Menu' (the à la carte), 'loin of venison PH20' (from up in the Highlands) comes with a game sausage, mulled pear and red wine sauce. Dexterity and craft is on display once again at dessert stage in the form of coco caramel tartlet with salted caramel ice

cream. The 'Grand Experience' menu is the tasting version. Everything from the bread to the petits fours shows this to be a dedicated, industrious and skilled kitchen team. All this and engaging and effective service, too.

Chef Patrick Bardoulet **Owner** Jacob & Johanna van Houdt **Times** 12.30-2.30/6.30-9 Closed 2-23 Jan **Prices** Fixed D 3 course £35, Tasting menu £55, Service optional **Wines** 8 by glass **Notes** ALC 3 course £45, Sunday L, Vegetarian menu, Dress restrictions, Smart casual, no jeans or trainers, Civ Wed 60 **Seats** 60, Pr/dining room 14 **Children** Portions, Menu **Parking** 30

STIRLING

ST BOSWELLS   Map 21 NT53

Dryburgh Abbey Hotel

◉◉ Modern British ⟡

Exciting modern cooking and superb river views

☎ 01835 822261
TD6 0RQ
e-mail: enquiries@dryburgh.co.uk
web: www.dryburgh.co.uk
dir: From A68 to St Boswells. Take B6404 for 2m. Take
B6356 for about 2m to hotel

The evocative ruins of Dryburgh Abbey, Sir Walter Scott's
final resting place, make a romantic backdrop to this
Victorian baronial mansion turned country-house hotel. A
ten-acre estate makes the modern world seem a long way
off, whilst also paying its way by providing a useful chunk
of the kitchen's seasonal vegetables and herbs from an
expansive walled garden. After a day's hiking or biking in
the Borders hills, or fishing on the eponymous river, the
hotel's Tweed Restaurant makes a grand setting with its
high ceilings, fancy plasterwork and ornate chandeliers,
while the kitchen deals in modern Scottish food that
takes its cue from the surrounding landscape. The
humble carrot gets star billing in a starter of carrot
velouté matched with carrot pakora, crisps, and curried
oil, while haggis stuffing adds a neat touch of Scottish
terroir to roast corn-fed chicken served with fondant
potatoes, silverskin onions, Savoy cabbage, and sage
crisps and jus. Finally, Tasmanian beans supply the
backbone for bitter chocolate tart with hazelnut, Kirsch
cherries, and smoked praline ice cream.

Chef Peter Snelgar **Owner** Dryburgh Abbey Hotel Limited
Times 7-9 Closed L all week **Prices** Fixed D 3 course £35,
Service optional **Wines** 36 bottles over £30, 20 bottles
under £30, 11 by glass **Notes** Vegetarian available, Dress
restrictions, No sportswear, Civ Wed 120 **Seats** 78, Pr/
dining room 40 **Children** Portions, Menu **Parking** 50

STIRLING

ABERFOYLE   Map 20 NN50

Macdonald Forest Hills Hotel & Resort

◉ Modern Scottish

Modern cooking in a happening resort hotel

☎ 01877 389500
Kinlochard FK8 3TL
e-mail: general.forest-hills@macdonald-hotels.co.uk
dir: 4m from Aberfoyle on B829

Whether you're here to roam the Trossachs, soak up the
fabulous views of Loch Ard, de-stress in the spa, get
pumped up with the plentiful indoor and outdoor sports
facilities, or do a bit of everything, the friendly team at
Forest Hills will make sure that it all goes with a swing.
When you're done with the day's activities, the classy
restaurant provides a relaxed and informal setting for
unchallenging modern cooking built on solid French-
accented foundations. The kitchen's commitment to well-
sourced ingredients is impressive, starting, say, with a

fillet of seared sea trout with potato and horseradish
compôte and aïoli, and continuing through to main-
course ideas such as poached organic salmon and wild
halibut matched with saffron and shellfish broth. To
finish, expect orange crème brûlée with white wine-
poached pear or Scottish cheeses with home-made
chutney and oatcakes.

Times 6.30-9.30

CALLANDER   Map 20 NN60

Callander Meadows

◉ Traditional British ⟡

**Flavour-focused cooking in charming restaurant with
rooms**

☎ 01877 330181
24 Main St FK17 8BB
e-mail: mail@callandermeadows.co.uk
web: www.callandermeadows.co.uk
dir: M9 junct 10, A84 for 15m, restaurant 1m in village
on left past lights

The Parkes' restaurant with rooms - within a charming
Georgian townhouse at the centre of town - has the bonus
of a sun-trap garden for a spot of dining alfresco. Inside,
the intimate dining room is a light-filled, unpretentious
kind of place, with bare-wood floors and undressed
tables, crimson walls and fresh flowers. Both proprietors
are chefs and have cooked at top restaurants, including
the Gleneagles Hotel, but the cooking here takes a much
simpler approach than any grand hotel dining, with fresh,
quality local seasonal produce, simplicity and flavour
doing the talking. Roast rump of lamb, for example, is
teamed with couscous, ratatouille and a rosemary jus, or
go for pan-fried salmon with roasted garlic mash,
spinach and citrus segments. Steak lovers will be drawn
to the likes of grilled Scottish sirloin with horseradish
mash, red onion marmalade and thyme sauce.

Chef Nick & Susannah Parkes **Owner** Nick & Susannah
Parkes **Times** 12-2.30/6-9 Closed 25-26 Dec, Tue-Wed
Prices Fixed L 2 course £8.95-£15.95, Starter
£3.95-£6.95, Main £11.95-£27.95, Dessert £4.95-£7.95
Wines 10 bottles over £30, 30 bottles under £30, 10 by
glass **Notes** Sunday L £8.95-£15.95, Vegetarian available
Seats 40, Pr/dining room 16 **Children** Portions **Parking** 4,
80 yds council car park

Roman Camp Country House Hotel

◉◉◉ – *see opposite*

KILLIN

The Ardeonaig Hotel & Restaurant

◉◉◉ – *see opposite*

STIRLING   Map 21 NS79

The Stirling Highland Hotel

◉ British, European **NEW**

**Commanding valley views and confident cooking in an
old school**

☎ 01786 272727
Spittal St FK8 1DU
e-mail: stirling@pumahotels.co.uk
web: www.pumahotels.co.uk
dir: In road leading to Stirling Castle - follow Castle signs

Perched high up on the hillside next to Stirling Castle,
this former 1850s high school boasts panoramic views
across the Forth Valley. Don't feel nervous about being
asked to the Headmaster's Study, it's actually a rather
relaxing place to enjoy a drink before your meal in the
Scholar's Restaurant. Consisting of three grand rooms
with vaulted ceilings, it's a bit like eating in Hogwarts.
The confident modern cooking makes the most of fine
Scottish produce, so you might start with an earthy dish
of caramelised pan-fried pigeon breast with black
pudding, watercress salad and beetroot dressing, moving
on to a technically impressive fillet of steamed sea bass
with pancetta mousse, bean purée, confit tomato and
asparagus. Dessert might be something a little more
classic, such as a crème brûlée with some wonderfully
buttery home-made shortbread just to remind you where
you are.

Chef Clark Gillespie **Owner** Puma Hotels Collection
Times 7-9.45 Closed L all week **Prices** Prices not
confirmed Service included **Wines** 20 by glass **Notes** Civ
Wed 100 **Seats** 96, Pr/dining room 100 **Children** Portions,
Menu **Parking** 106

Save on Hotels. Book at **theAA.com/hotel**

STIRLING 611 SCOTLAND

Roman Camp Country House Hotel

CALLANDER	MAP 20 NN60

Modern French **V**

Ritzy luxury and immaculate modern cooking

☎ 01877 330003
FK17 8BG
e-mail: mail@romancamphotel.co.uk
web: www.romancamphotel.co.uk
dir: N on A84 through Callander, Main St turn left at East End into drive

The Roman earthworks you can see in the meadows beyond the gardens are what give this upmarket country house its name. Built in the 17th century as a shooting lodge for the Earls of Moray, the prestigious house has put up prime ministers, generals, painters and famous thespians during the social whirl of the Victorian and Edwardian periods. Even in the 21st century it is still a place where tradition holds sway - there have been no incongruous makeovers here: it remains a peaceful and opulent bolt-hole for getting away from it all amid a plush setting of oak linenfold panelling, ornate plasterwork ceilings, luxurious fabrics and open fires in its snug lounges. The grand oval dining room is a pastel-shaded, soft-focus space where tables are set formally with crisp linen, fine silverware and crystal, and romantically lit by candles at dinner. Immaculate service, courtesy of professionally polite and well-briefed staff, completes the picture. The larder is clearly stocked with top-class Scottish produce, skilfully cooked by a chef who evidently has a sound grip of what works with what. The results are French-influenced, modern Scottish ideas presented in a four-course format that opens with the likes of perfectly-timed sea bass matched to great visual effect with a golden goats' cheese bonbon, red pepper purée and squid ink taramasalata. A full-throttle Jerusalem artichoke velouté keeps things moving along before the main event - perhaps Goosnargh duck breast, with great depth of flavour, elegantly paired with a pressing of leg meat, pineapple purée, foie gras, red cabbage and ginger-infused jus. Dessert brings a bitter dark chocolate crémeux offset by sweet coconut sorbet and pistachio syrup. All of the accompanying canapés, amuses and pre-dessert nibbles are well up to the mark, and supporting it all is an unshowy, judiciously chosen traditional wine list with some special bins at the top end for big spenders.

Chef Ian McNaught **Owner** Eric Brown **Times** 12-2/7-9 **Prices** Fixed L 2 course £25, Tasting menu £50-£54, Starter £19-£27, Main £24-£34, Dessert £12-£16, Service optional **Wines** 16 by glass **Notes** Tasting menu 4 course dishes change daily, Sunday L £30-£34, Vegetarian menu, Dress restrictions, Smart casual, Civ Wed 150 **Seats** 120, Pr/dining room 36 **Children** Portions **Parking** 80

The Ardeonaig Hotel & Restaurant

KILLIN	MAP 20 NN63

French **NEW V**

Creative food in an enchanting setting

☎ 01567 820400
South Loch Tay Side FK21 8SU
e-mail: info@ardeonaighotel.co.uk
dir: From E via Kenmore take South Loch Tay Rd for 7m. From W via Killin take South Loch Tay Rd for 7m

It takes determination to get to Ardeonaig, winding along miles of deserted single-track roads until the pretty flower-decked and whitewashed inn hoves into view in its gloriously isolated spot on the south bank of Loch Tay. From its lowly beginnings as a 16th-century drover's inn that put up herdsmen taking their flocks to market, it has morphed into a more contemporary hideaway with sybaritic guest rooms, unforgettable loch views, and the guarantee of exciting top-flight cuisine at the end of the day. The kitchen pursues its commitment to local produce with heartfelt conviction, sourcing organically-farmed meat, wild game, fresh fish and seasonally-foraged ingredients - girolle mushrooms and wild garlic, to name but two - from practically on the doorstep. The cooking is continually developing and fires on all cylinders with an unusual level of technical skills and creative flair. A starter of tortellini filled with truffled chicken mousse and partnered with cauliflower velouté, truffle oil and pancetta shows an intuitive understanding of flavours and textures that make happy bedfellows. Main course sees the full-bore flavours of loin and cheek of Perthshire pork working wonders with buttery pommes purée, a swipe of boudin noir purée, and thyme jus, or if the hotel's owner has had a good morning with rod and reel, Loch Tay salmon is matched with beetroot purée, cucumber pearls, lemon, and beurre blanc sauce. Desserts, too, are fashioned with technical mastery and an unerring feel for contrast and texture, as witnessed in an über-rich ganache of Valrhona's Tainori chocolate served with raspberry sorbet and crunchy crushed pistachios. Backing this up is a well-thought-out wine list, usefully arranged by grape variety, packed with quality growers, and knowledgeably served. If you're up for a bottle of bubbly, the sommelier is a keen exponent of sabrage, popping the cork theatrically with a flourish of a sabre blade.

Chef Grant Walker **Owner** Riverlane Ltd **Times** 12-2/6.30-9 Closed Mon-Tue (may open non-residents in main season) **Prices** Fixed L 3 course £28.50 **Notes** D 7 course + veg menu £55, L & D must be pre-booked, Sunday L, Vegetarian menu, Dress restrictions, Smart casual **Seats** 40 **Children** Portions **Parking** 30

STRATHYRE

Map 20 NN51

Creagan House

◎◎ French, Scottish ♨

17th-century Trossachs farmhouse with good food

☎ 01877 384638
FK18 8ND
e-mail: eatandstay@creaganhouse.co.uk
web: www.creaganhouse.co.uk
dir: 0.25m N of village, off A84

Gordon and Cherry Gunn's long-established restaurant with rooms stands at the head of Loch Lubnaig, surrounded by mountains, rivers and forests, with free access to peaceful walks and wonderful views. The converted 17th-century farmhouse is well worth seeking out for Gordon's bold, classically-inspired French dishes, served at large wooden tables in the impressive dining room with its stripped floors, grand open fireplace and fabulous views. Cooking is well executed and sourcing of top-notch local produce is a priority and reflected on the sensibly short yet well balanced dinner menu. Herbs and vegetables come from the garden and local small-holdings, while meat is all reared on Perthshire farms. Typically, begin with breast of grouse with boudin of leg and compôte liver, served with apple and smoked bacon, then follow with John Dory with puréed plum chutney and a scallop and mussel sauce. To finish, try the steamed butterscotch and pecan pudding with Macallan whisky sauce.

Chef Gordon Gunn **Owner** Gordon & Cherry Gunn
Times 7.30-8.30 Closed 5-20 Nov, Xmas, 15 Jan-13 Mar, Wed-Thu, L all week (ex parties) **Prices** Fixed D 3 course fr £35, Service optional **Wines** 34 bottles over £30, 33 bottles under £30, 7 by glass **Notes** Vegetarian available, Dress restrictions, Smart casual **Seats** 15, Pr/dining room 6 **Children** Portions **Parking** 15

SCOTTISH ISLANDS

ARRAN, ISLE OF

BRODICK

Map 20 NS03

Kilmichael Country House Hotel

◎◎ Modern British ♨

Classical cooking in a refined country-house hotel

☎ 01770 302219
Glen Cloy KA27 8BY
e-mail: enquiries@kilmichael.com
web: www.kilmichael.com
dir: Turn right on leaving ferry terminal, through Brodick & left at golf club. Follow brown sign. Continue past church & onto private drive

This small country-house hotel is run by hands-on proprietors, and sits in its own secluded gardens - home to 14 friendly peacocks running free, rolling lawns, water features and attractive flowerbeds. It's by no means all for show, for they grow all their own fruit, vegetables, salad leaves, herbs and edible flowers here, as well as keeping chickens and ducks. Inside is no less beguiling, as antiques and artwork abound in the tastefully decorated rooms (no wonder guests return again and again). Co-owner Geoffrey Botterill looks after guests - only around 16 at a time - in the small and intimate, red-hued dining room, while chef-patron Antony Butterworth takes care single-handedly of the classic country-house cooking. The daily-changing, no-choice menu might feature salmon tartare with avocado and coriander sorbet followed by a full-flavoured prime fillet of lamb spiked with garlic and fresh lavender and baked with Scottish heather honey. A trio of autumnal desserts - damson and soured cream brûlée, wild bramble cobbler, and a 'wee' toffee apple with home-made toffee and walnut ice cream - makes a smile-inducing finale.

Chef Antony Butterworth **Owner** G Botterill & A Butterworth **Times** 7-8.30 Closed Nov-Mar, Tue, L all week **Prices** Prices not confirmed Service optional **Wines** 3 by glass **Notes** 4 course D £45, Vegetarian available, Dress restrictions, Smart casual, no T-shirts **Seats** 18 **Parking** 12

HARRIS, ISLE OF

SCARISTA (SGARASTA BHEAG)

Map 22 NG09

Scarista House

◎◎ Modern Scottish

Modern Scottish cooking and stunning sea views

☎ 01859 550238
HS3 3HX
e-mail: timandpatricia@scaristahouse.com
dir: On A859 15m S of Tarbert

When you head for the Isle of Harris, the idea is usually to get away from it all, and the remoteness and beauty boxes are certainly ticked at this Georgian manse. Jaw-dropping views are of a three-mile-long white beach and

---

the Atlantic, and within is a civilised, soothing, TV-free space with antiques, open fires in the library and drawing room, and a great CD collection to set the mood. The island's bounty is the star of the show in the two elegant dining rooms - seafood tends to feature prominently, and there is lamb, beef and game, all full of freshness and flavour, and backed by accurate timings and attention to detail. Dinner menus are no-choice affairs that could kick off with porcini risotto with grilled breast of quail, followed by Stornoway-landed monkfish tail wrapped in smoked Argyll ham roasted with lemon, saffron and basil, and served with broccoli, pea and mint purée. Dessert - perhaps chocolate truffle with coffee ice cream and raspberry coulis - precedes a finale of Scottish farmhouse cheeses.

Times 7.30-8 Closed 25 Dec, Jan-Feb, L all week

TARBERT (TAIRBEART)

Map 22 NB10

Hotel Hebrides

◎ Scottish

A thoroughly Scottish menu with views to match

☎ 01859 502364
Pier Rd HS3 3DG
e-mail: stay@hotel-hebrides.com
dir: To Tarbert via ferry from Uig (Isle of Skye); or ferry from Ullapool to Stornaway, A859 to Tarbert; or by plane to Stornaway from Glasgow, Edinburgh or Inverness

Right beside the Tarbert ferry terminal, this modern boutique hotel is a great base for exploring the Hebridean islands. As you might imagine, the views from here across the pier and out to sea - with the hills of Harris in the opposite direction - are stunning, hence proprietors Angus and Chirsty Macleod have gone for an understated, simple look inside The Pierhouse Restaurant so as not to compete with that fantastic vista. Food is served pretty much all day, with coffees and home-made cakes available in the morning and a lounge bar menu served throughout the afternoon. In the evening, the carte brims with local and seasonal produce, offering the likes of hand-dived Harris scallops with mango salsa and caramelised pineapple to start with, followed by local smoked haddock with chive mash, a poached egg and cheese sauce. The Harris cranachan with vanilla shortbread makes a suitably Scottish finale.

Times 12-4/5-9 **Prices** Prices not confirmed **Children** Menu

MULL, ISLE OF

TOBERMORY   Map 22 NM55

Highland Cottage

◉◉ Modern Scottish, International

Hospitable island hotel with locally-sourced menu

☎ 01688 302030
24 Breadalbane St PA75 6PD
e-mail: davidandjo@highlandcottage.co.uk
web: www.highlandcottage.co.uk
dir: Opposite fire station. Main St up Back Brae, turn at
top by White House. Follow road to right, left at next
junct into Breadalbane St

David and Jo Currie's small-scale hotel and restaurant
couldn't be better placed for hauling in the freshest fish
and seafood imaginable, as it lies just a few minutes'
stroll from the colourful Tobermory waterfront. There's a
bit more to the operation than the word 'cottage' might
suggest but it is nonetheless a cosy, welcoming place
crammed with interesting art and objets. The dedication
to local sourcing is admirable, and the materials are
brought together in well-conceived and well-balanced
dishes that run the gamut from crabcakes with mixed
leaves and chilli caper sauce, to mains such as roast
halibut fillet with boulangère potatoes, and leek and
smoked mussel cream sauce. Carnivores are not sent
away unhappy - roast loin and braised shoulder of lamb
with dauphinoise potato and redcurrant and rosemary
gravy might be on the cards, and to finish there may be
chocolate and orange truffle torte.

Times 7-9 Closed Nov-Mar, L all week

ORKNEY ISLANDS

ST MARGARET'S HOPE   Map 24 ND49

The Creel Restaurant with Rooms

◉◉ British ◔

First-class cooking of outstanding produce

☎ 01856 831311
The Creel, Front Rd KW17 2SL
e-mail: creelorkney@btinternet.com
web: www.thecreel.co.uk
dir: A961 into village, on seafront

The cream-painted house in the quiet village overlooking
the bay looks modest enough, while inside is an
unassuming stone-floored dining room with bare wooden
tables, a stove and local artwork on the walls - and on
the cards is the highly accomplished cooking from Alan
Craigie. What marks out his cooking is his professional,
imaginative handling of top-rate Orcadian produce, from
the island's new potatoes via seafood to seaweed-feeding
North Ronaldsay mutton, which might appear in a
pithivier with parsnip purée and barley gravy alongside
another successful starter of crab salad, with apple
mayonnaise, avocado salsa and pickled cucumber. Main
courses are never too elaborate, so flavours are clearly
defined: pan-fried scallops with steamed halibut and
braised lentils, say, or slowly braised beef brisket with
onion marmalade and glazed carrots. Less familiar but
sustainable varieties of fish also find their way on to the
menu - seared wolf fish, for example, with spinach and
roast courgettes.

Chef Alan Craigie **Owner** Alan & Joyce Craigie **Times** 7-8
Closed mid Oct-Apr, Sun-Mon, L all week **Prices** Fixed D 3
course £40, Service optional **Wines** 2 by glass
Notes Vegetarian available **Seats** 20, Pr/dining room 12
Children Portions **Parking** 10

SHETLAND

SCALLOWAY   Map 24 HU43

Scalloway Hotel

◉ Modern Scottish **NEW V** ◔

A rising star in the far north

☎ 01595 880444
Main St ZE1 0TR
e-mail: info@scallowayhotel.com
dir: 7m from Lerwick on west mainland on A970

Overlooking the Scalloway Voe, just a short drive from
Lerwick, this simple whitewashed hotel is steadily
building itself an enviable reputation for great food. The
location is defined by the waters around it, so the kitchen
makes full use of the massive catches of fish and seafood
that are landed on Shetland, as well as excellent lamb
bred on the rugged local hills. At the core of the menu are
classic ideas, often enlivened with flavours from further
afield. Typical of the style is an open ravioli of Shetland
crab, queen scallop and parsley with rocket pesto, and
main-course halibut poached in pomace oil teamed with
a smoked haddock croquette, black pudding with Isle of
Mull cheddar, and pancetta and chive sauce. That superb
local lamb might turn up as a leg steak served on minced
lamb with Puy lentils, Savoy cabbage and rosemary jus.
Pudding could be an ambitious assemblage of
lemongrass and lime leaf pannacotta with chilli syrup
and mango and passionfruit sorbet.

Chef Colin McLean **Owner** P McKenzie **Times** 12-3/5-9
Prices Starter £5.25-£7.95, Main £13.95-£30, Dessert
£5.95-£6.95, Service optional **Wines** 10 bottles over £30,
16 bottles under £30, 10 by glass **Notes** Sunday L £20-
£40, Vegetarian menu **Seats** 36 **Children** Portions
Parking 10

SKYE, ISLE OF

COLBOST   Map 22 NG24

The Three Chimneys

◉◉◉ — *see page 614*

ISLEORNSAY   Map 22 NG71

Duisdale House Hotel

◉◉ Modern Scottish ◔

Modern Scottish cooking in remotest southern Skye

☎ 01471 833202
Sleat IV43 8QW
e-mail: info@duisdale.com
web: www.duisdale.com
dir: 7m N of Armadale ferry & 12m S of Skye Bridge on
A851

Overlooking the mournful beauty of the Sound of Sleat at
the southern tip of Skye, the conservatory dining room
has the best seats in the house for sunset-washed
mountain views. And when the weather draws a veil over
nature's splendour, the darkly intimate interior room is a
stylish setting with its red arched walls, cream high-
backed chairs and views over the garden. The cooking
reflects the surrounding landscapes with its
unchallenging modern compositions - scallops are hand
dived from the wine-dark waters that lay before your eyes,
then sautéed with precision to capture their sweetness,
and served with pimento relish, smoked vine tomato and
butter sauce. Moving on, roast loin of venison is matched
with mash, carrots, spinach and juniper jus, and to close
the show, there's banana tarte Tatin with vanilla ice
cream and orange syrup.

Chef David Allan **Owner** K Gunn & A Gracie
Times 12-2.30/6.30-9 **Prices** Fixed L 2 course fr £16,
Fixed D 3 course £45, Starter £4.50-£9, Main £10.50-£22,
Dessert £4.50-£6.50, Service optional **Wines** 30 bottles
over £30, 30 bottles under £30, 6 by glass **Notes** Sunday
L, Vegetarian available, Dress restrictions, Smart casual,
Civ Wed 60 **Seats** 50 **Children** Portions **Parking** 30

Hotel Eilean Iarmain

◉◉ Traditional Scottish ◔

Spectacular sea views and consummate cooking

☎ 01471 833332
Sleat IV43 8QR
e-mail: hotel@eileaniarmain.co.uk
web: www.eileaniarmain.co.uk
dir: Mallaig & cross by ferry to Armadale, 8m to hotel or
via Kyle of Lochalsh

The whitewashed old building in well-maintained grounds
looks across the waters of the Sound of Sleat to the
mainland's Knoydart Hills, and the restaurant - a
continued

ISLEORNSAY *continued*

panelled room hung with works by a local artist, with a log fire in winter and a conservatory extension - takes full advantage of the spectacular views. The lack of fuss and artifice in the décor extends to the kitchen's output, with its reliance on the island's glorious resources: venison from the estate, for instance, and langoustines landed at the pier outside. The cooking is not without a high level of refinement and ambition, though: chicken ballotine is stuffed with mushrooms and spinach, wrapped in Parma ham and served on a dollop of walnut mayonnaise, with blobs of red onion marmalade around the square glass plate. Main courses are as well composed, seen in accurately grilled salmon fillet with crayfish risotto, grilled fennel and saffron velouté, or fanned slices of roast breast of guinea fowl, cooked just so, straightforwardly accompanied by silky parsnip purée, fondant potato, Savoy cabbage and red wine jus.

Chef Marius Wilczynski **Owner** Lady Lucilla Noble **Times** 12-2.30/6.30-8.45 **Prices** Fixed D 3 course fr £39.95, Service optional **Wines** 14 bottles over £30, 21 bottles under £30, 7 by glass **Notes** Sunday L, Vegetarian available, Dress restrictions, Smart casual, Civ Wed 80 **Seats** 40, Pr/dining room 22 **Children** Portions, Menu

Kinloch Lodge

◎◎◎ – *see opposite*

Toravaig House Hotel

◎◎ Modern Scottish ☝

Plush island retreat with modern Scottish cooking

☎ 01471 820200
Knock Bay, Sleat IV44 8RE
e-mail: info@skyehotel.co.uk
web: www.skyehotel.co.uk
dir: From Skye Bridge, left at Broadford onto A851, hotel 11m on left. Or from ferry at Armadale take A851, hotel 6m on right

What is now the Toravaig House Hotel was in something of a sorry state when the present owners took it under their wing in 2003, and set about laying on the TLC. Its location, overlooking the Sound of Sleat in southern Skye, demanded nothing less. Amid the gentle Hebridean wildness, it's now a welcoming retreat, with plush, smartly finished interiors and a candlelit dining room, the Islay, that looks out over the gardens and the distant hills. Dinner comes in the form of a short menu of three choices each for first course and main, with a sorbet in between. A highly polished version of modern Scottish cooking draws on local seafood for a starter of lobster and crab tortellini with fennel and apple in a light bisque, served with radish and confit tomato, and a main course of cod fillet in mussel broth with cauliflower beignets, beetroot and samphire. Meatier appetites may be lured by rack of Highland lamb with a fricassée of Savoy cabbage and carrot, butternut squash and onion jam. The concluding choice of savoury or sweet is between Scottish and European artisan cheeses with oatcakes, or something like warm walnut and banana bread with a cinnamon and caramel doughnut and marmalade ice cream.

Chef Richard Massey **Owner** Anne Gracie & Ken Gunn **Times** 12.30-2.30/6.30-9.30 **Prices** Fixed L 2 course £15, Fixed D 3 course £48, Service optional **Wines** 40 bottles over £30, 25 bottles under £30, 6 by glass **Notes** Sunday L, Vegetarian available, Dress restrictions, Smart casual **Seats** 25 **Children** Portions **Parking** 20

The Three Chimneys

◎◎◎

COLBOST   **MAP 22 NG24**

Modern British 🍷 NOTABLE WINE LIST

Exceptional cooking in a wild, romantic setting

☎ 01470 511258
IV55 8ZT
e-mail: eatandstay@threechimneys.co.uk
web: www.threechimneys.co.uk
dir: 5m W of Dunvegan take B884 signed Glendale. On left beside loch

It's well worth taking the single-track road to reach this warm and welcoming restaurant with rooms, which has been run by Eddie and Shirley Spear for well-nigh 30 years. It's in what were two crofter's cottages, with a restaurant of stone walls, beams in the ceiling, high-backed dining chairs and polished wooden tables. While Skye's landscape and the views over the loch towards the

Western Isles are attractions in themselves, the overriding draw is Michael Smith's trailblazing cooking, its bedrock top-notch produce from land and sea, seen in a summer main course of steamed lobster served simply with a shellfish and tarragon butter, crushed new potatoes and locally-grown vegetables, a straightforward but brilliant amalgam of flavours. Equally impressive are more labour-intensive dishes, intelligently assembled and of peerless timing: for instance, roast loin, pressed shoulder and haggis of Blackface lamb, sauced with a peaty gravy and accompanied by rosemary-scented maize, greens and neeps, or roast crown and skirlie-stuffed leg of chicken with tattie scones, bacon, chanterelles, young leeks and nettles. The same unswerving consideration for combinations of flavours and textures shows up in starters too, perhaps ranging from just-landed mackerel fillet, grilled and served with a robustly flavoured fennel and mussel risotto with sorrel and spiced oil, to a beguiling pairing of smoked haddie and hough in a terrine with a quail's egg, orange and

nasturtium and a dill and mustard dressing. Not-to-be-missed puddings might include iced toddy syllabub and strawberries offset by aniseed brittle, and traditional cranachan. A 'Seven Courses of Skye' tasting menu is also available, and a table seating up to eight covers has been installed in the kitchen for guests who want to be at the centre of the action.

Chef Michael Smith **Owner** Eddie & Shirley Spear **Times** 12.15-1.45/6.15-9.45 Closed 1 Dec-23 Jan, L Sun & Nov-Mar **Prices** Fixed L 2 course £28.50-£32, Fixed D 3 course £60-£65, Service optional **Wines** 105 bottles over £30, 4 bottles under £30, 13 by glass **Notes** Tasting menu 7 course, Sun lunch Jun-Aug, Vegetarian available, Dress restrictions, Smart casual preferred **Seats** 40, Pr/dining room 12 **Parking** 12

Save on Hotels. Book at **theAA.com/hotel**

SKYE, ISLE OF 615 SCOTLAND

Kinloch Lodge

ISLEORNSAY
MAP 22 NG71

French, Scottish **V** NOTABLE WINE LIST

A stunning setting for highland hospitality that's second to none

☎ 01471 833214 & 833333
Sleat IV43 8QY
e-mail: reservations@kinloch-lodge.co.uk
web: www.kinloch-lodge.co.uk
dir: 1m off main road, 6m S of Broadford on A851, 10m N of Armadale

Set in extensive grounds with a wonderfully secluded location, Kinloch Lodge on the Isle of Skye has a reputation that extends far beyond the Scottish border. It occupies a setting so magical it might have come out of a fairytale, nestled as it is at the foot of Kinloch Hill on the sea loch Na-Dal in Sleat. It's renowned not just for its majestic location and its heritage as ancestral home to the 34th High Chief of Clan Donald, but for Lady Claire Macdonald's role as an award-winning cookery writer and tutor, and general champion of all things to do with traditional highland hospitality. The dining room at Kinloch seats around 30 and is every bit as romantic as the location, with views over the hills to the sea beyond. Green painted walls play host to portraits of Macdonald ancestors who gaze down upon diners as they enjoy the daily set or tasting menu. As you'd expect from such a rarefied place,

and given Lady Macdonald's ambassadorial role, the hospitality is excellent here. She and her husband Godfrey Macdonald regularly put in appearances to speak to guests, while staff are smartly dressed and service is formal but in no way stuffy. Chef Marcello Tully deploys modern French techniques to highlight the best Scotland has to offer in deceptively simple dishes whose flavours pack a tremendous punch. Excellently cooked roast Mallaig monkfish, Moray pork cheeks and caramelised passionfruit jus matches seemingly disparate tastes together perfectly, then you might choose a delicately presented fillet of Black Isle lamb, caramelised apples and pears, pancetta lardons, shallots and potato dauphinoise. The kitchen is strong on the sweet stuff - a vanilla crème fraîche pannacotta is a textbook example of the Italian favourite, and comes with a deeply fruity raspberry sauce and Caipirinha sorbet. Petits fours, particularly Drambuie truffles and pecan brittle, are also exemplary. The excellent wine list is broken down into comprehensive sections with extensive tasting notes and surprisingly reasonable prices. Diners can take a wine flight with their meal or, if you'd like to be a bit alternative, there are whisky and beer flights on offer.

Chef Marcello Tully **Owner** Lord & Lady Macdonald **Times** 12-2.30/6.30-9 **Prices** Fixed L 2 course £29.99, Fixed D

3 course £65, Service optional **Wines** 16 by glass **Notes** Tasting menu available, Sunday L, Vegetarian menu **Seats** 40, Pr/dining room 20 **Children** Portions **Parking** 20

PORTREE
Map 22 NG44

Cuillin Hills Hotel

@@@ Modern Scottish ☺

Creative dining and breathtaking views

☎ 01478 612003
IV51 9QU
e-mail: info@cuillinhills-hotel-skye.co.uk
web: www.cuillinhills-hotel-skye.co.uk
dir: 0.25m N of Portree on A855

Built originally as a hunting lodge, this splendid country-house hotel perches above Portree Bay in 15 acres of mature grounds - a jaw-dropping location where views unfurl endlessly across the bay to the Sound of Raasay and the dragon's back crags of the Cuillin Mountain range. And it is with just cause that the restaurant is named 'The View' since it is visible from all tables. The split-level room is none too shabby either, decked out in classic ivory and white tones, with cream leather chairs at linen-swathed tables and regularly-changing works by local artists. Ingredients from the sea and hills all around get pride of place on the European-accented modern menu, perhaps braised shoulder of Skye lamb with shallot purée, Savoy cabbage, potato almondine and caper jus, followed by pan-fried John Dory with spoots (that's razor clams in the local lingo), apple and fennel salad, chorizo and red pepper salsa, and watercress sauce. If you need any further reminder that you're in Scotland, a

'deconstructed cranachan' pulls off an exciting array of flavours and textures for dessert.

Chef Andrew Baillie **Owner** Wickman Hotels **Times** 6.30-9 Closed L all week **Prices** Prices not confirmed **Service** optional **Wines** 8 by glass **Notes** Sunday L, Vegetarian available, Civ Wed 60 **Seats** 40 **Children** Portions, Menu **Parking** 56

SKEABOST BRIDGE
Map 22 NG44

Skeabost Country House

@ British V ☺

Country-house cooking in a lochside hunting lodge

☎ 01470 532202 & 0843 178 7139
IV51 9NP
e-mail: generalmanager.skeabost@bespokehotels.com
web: www.bespokehotels.com/skeabostcountryhouse
dir: Follow A87 over Skye Bridge to Portree then Uig. Left onto A850, Skeabost on right

Originally built in the 19th century by the Macdonald clan as a rather grand hunting lodge, Skeabost's pristine whitewashed façade stands out against the verdant hills fringing Loch Snizort (bless you!). Nowadays, it is a luxurious small hotel with a picturesque lochside golf course, and even if the game holds no interest for you, the elemental landscapes of Skye all around are to die for. When it comes to dining, an attractive wood-panelled room overlooks it all, and you can expect well-executed traditional Scottish country-house cooking, with locally-landed seafood a strong point - perhaps clams cooked in garlic and dill butter, or scallops with black pudding and dressed rocket salad. Otherwise, you might start with quenelles of haggis with neeps and tatties and whisky sauce, continue with pan-seared venison haunch with dauphinoise potatoes, braised red cabbage, carrot purée and red wine jus, and end with Normandy apple tart with home-made vanilla ice cream.

Chef James Cosgrove **Owner** Bespoke Hotels **Times** 12-3/5-9 **Prices** Fixed L 2 course £9-£17, Fixed D 3 course £25-£45, Starter £4-£10, Main £12-£25, Dessert £4-£9, Service optional **Wines** 10 bottles over £30, 33 bottles under £30, 6 by glass **Notes** Tasting menus available, buffet for events, Sunday L, Vegetarian menu, Dress restrictions, Smart casual, Civ Wed 120 **Seats** 40, Pr/dining room 80 **Children** Portions, Menu **Parking** 40

STAFFIN
Map 22 NG46

The Glenview

@@@ British, French

Skilled cooking with local ingredients

☎ 01470 562248
Culnacnoc IV51 9JH
e-mail: enquiries@glenviewskye.co.uk
dir: 12m N of Portree on A855, 4m S of Staffin

On the wild Trotternish Peninsula in the north of the Isle of Skye, where snow-dusted peaks march across the

Ullinish Country Lodge

Rosettes not confirmed at time of going to print

STRUAN
Map 22 NG33

Modern French V ☺

Electrifying cooking in a Skye hideaway

☎ 01470 572214
IV56 8FD
e-mail: ullinish@theisleofskye.co.uk
dir: 9m S of Dunvegan on A863

The Rosette award for this establishment has been suspended due to a change of chef. Reassessment will take place in due course under the new chef.

The breathtaking views alone make the journey to this white-painted hotel worthwhile, with lochs on three sides and the rugged beauty of the Black Cuillins and MacLeod's Tables. The interior is comfortingly traditional, with tartan used in moderation in the panelled restaurant, where service is relaxed, friendly and polished. A daily 'link van' collects meat, seafood and garden produce from a network of the island's small suppliers and delivers them to the kitchen, where Craig Halliday works his wizardry. Dishes sound convoluted, but Halliday shows considerable talent when it comes to the art of balancing flavours. Take a starter of poached quail breast which arrives perfectly cooked, with a crisp samosa of rich-tasting confit leg, together with a port and plum reduction, crisp nuggets of bread sauce, lightly pickled shimeji mushrooms and orange butter, all beautifully presented and working in harmony. Langoustine grilled with garlic butter and parsley, served with leaves, herbs and flowers, is as straight and true as they come. Among main courses, three slices of melt-in-the-mouth venison comes with beetroot and apple risotto, with sprinkles of pomegranate vinaigrette, and four firm blocks of balsamic jelly arranged around the plate - another resounding success. The fish alternative (just two main courses are offered) might be fillet of turbot with crepinette of oxtail, red wine vinaigrette and pommes purée. Extras like canapés are not only plentiful but exemplary, as are puddings, among which is a stunning blueberry soufflé with ripple ice cream.

Chef Chris Leisk **Owner** Brian & Pam Howard **Times** 7.30-8.30 Closed mid Dec-Jan, L all week **Prices** Prices not confirmed Service optional **Wines** 36 bottles over £30, 40 bottles under £30, 16 by glass **Notes** 4 course D £48-£52.50, Vegetarian menu, Dress restrictions, Smart casual, No T-shirts **Seats** 22 **Parking** 10

Save on Hotels. Book at **theAA.com/hotel**

SKYE, ISLE OF 617 SCOTLAND

skyline, this delightful whitewashed restaurant with rooms certainly lives up to its name. Housed in a Victorian croft that was once the Culnacnoc village shop, it now deals in unpretentious modern cooking built on splendid materials, many of which have travelled but a short distance from producers and fishermen on the island. These prime ingredients are then handled with due confidence and care, as in a simple but perfectly-executed starter of braised and glazed Staffin pork belly with pickled carrot salad and sweet chilli dressing. Next out, the venison from MacLeod's Table - a hill range near the hotel - couldn't be more local, and it appears with roast garlic and rosemary sauce, gratin potatoes and spring greens. A chocolate fudge tart with crème fraîche sorbet and sugared macadamia nuts ends on a note of splendid indulgence.

Times 7-8.30 Closed Jan, 8 Feb, Sun-Mon, L all week

STEIN	Map 22 NG25

Loch Bay Seafood Restaurant

◉ British Seafood 🍷

Pleasingly straightforward seafood cookery by the bay

☎ 01470 592235
MacLeod Ter IV55 8GA
e-mail: lochbay@gmail.com
dir: 4m off A850 by B886

A show-stopping location - secreted away in unruffled silence in one of a straddle of former 18th-century fishermen's cottages on the loch shore - this homely little nautical-themed restaurant is a fish-and-seafood lovers' nirvana. In summer there's the whiff of sea air through the open door, or you can perch on a table outside, while the vibe is friendly and informal. Expect intelligently simple cooking where freshness and local provenance are king (check-out the blackboard for the day's catch);

grilled Isle of Gigha halibut, perhaps, seasoned with an emulsion of olive oil and fresh citrus juice, or maybe collops of monkfish with herb and garlic butter, or whole young turbot. Apple and plum crumble might be among desserts.

Chef David Wilkinson **Owner** David & Alison Wilkinson **Times** 12-2/6-9 Closed mid Oct-Etr, Sun-Mon, L Mon-Tue & Fri-Sun **Prices** Starter £5.95-£10.80, Main £14-£23, Dessert £5.40-£5.70, Service optional, Groups min 7 service 10% **Wines** 6 by glass **Notes** Blackboard choices, child portions L, veg menu on request, Vegetarian available **Seats** 23 **Parking** 6

STRUAN	Map 22 NG33

Ullinish Country Lodge

Rosettes not confirmed at time of going to print – see opposite

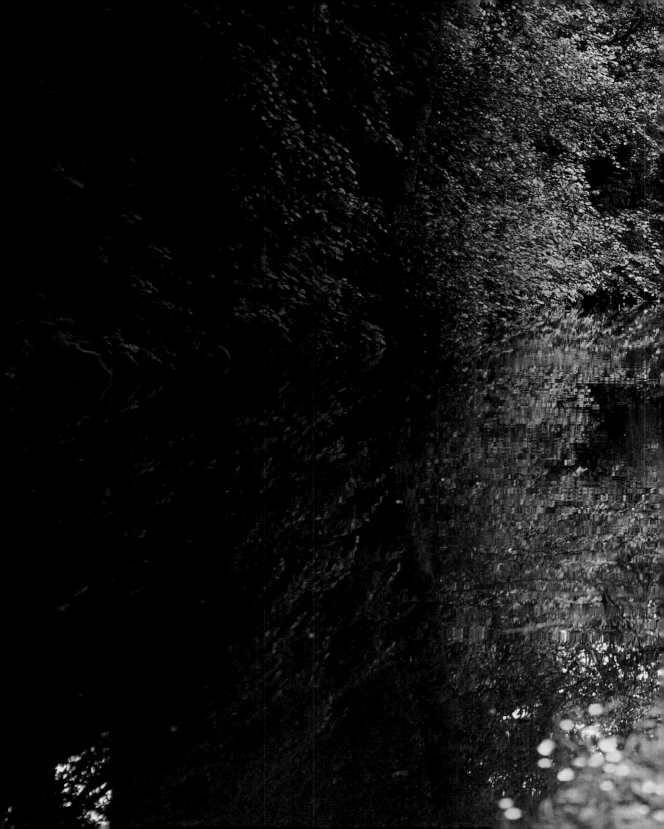

Wales

Brecon Canal at Talybont-On-Usk, Brecon Beacons National Park

ANGLESEY, ISLE OF

BEAUMARIS — Map 14 SH67

Bishopsgate House Hotel

@ Traditional Welsh V 🖑

Bistro cookery on the Beaumaris waterfront

☎ 01248 810302
54 Castle St LL58 8BB
e-mail: hazel@bishopsgatehotel.co.uk
dir: from Menai Bridge onto A545 to Beaumaris. Hotel on left in main street

The Georgian townhouse done in minty green, outside and in, looks out from the Beaumaris waterfront over the Menai Strait. It's a cheering place all round, through to the dining room at the back, where stained-glass windows give the impression of looking out over the mainland. Simple bistro dishes are capably rendered, starting with a duo of black and white puddings and Carmarthen ham for a meaty starter, or a parcel of smoked salmon and white crabmeat for something from the sea. Well-sauced fish main courses may include halibut, richly served with mushrooms in tarragon and Pernod, or there might also be loin of lamb on crushed new potatoes in port and redcurrant jus. Finish with pecan tart and vanilla ice cream.

Chef I Sankey **Owner** Hazel Johnson Ollier
Times 12.30-2.30/6.30-9.30 Closed L Mon-Sat
Prices Fixed D 3 course £22.75, Starter £4.95-£6.50, Main £11.95-£22.50, Service optional **Wines** 5 bottles over £30, 26 bottles under £30, 4 by glass **Notes** Early bird menu 6.30-7.30pm 2 course £14, Sunday L, Vegetarian menu, Dress restrictions, Smart dress **Seats** 40 **Children** Portions **Parking** 10

AA RESTAURANT OF THE YEAR FOR WALES

Ye Olde Bulls Head Inn

@@@ – *see opposite*

BRIDGEND

BRIDGEND — Map 9 SS97

Bokhara Brasserie

@ Indian V 🖑

A salute to Indian cuisine in a country-house hotel

☎ 01656 720212
Court Colman Manor, Pen-y-Fai CF31 4NG
e-mail: experience@court-colman-manor.com
dir: M4 junct 36/A4063 in direction of Maesteg, after lights take 1st exit at rdbt to Bridgend continue under motorway, take next right & follow hotel signs

Set within the Court Colman Manor country-house hotel, the Bokhara is decked out in warm colours, with an open-to-view kitchen, and a wall of slate a relatively new feature. New too is the revamped menu, which now concentrates on the cuisine of the sub-continent, with a number of dishes taken from the old North-West Frontier. The kitchen prides itself on not using colourings or ghee and on buying only locally grown and reared produce and meat. Thus Welsh lamb could appear as barrah kebab (chunks of marinated chargrilled meat), as a whole leg (for six people) cooked in aromatic spices, or in a mutton saag curry. The tandoor is used to good effect, from fish tikka to murgh makhani (chicken in a creamy tomato sauce with cashew nuts, ginger and garlic), and prawns masala. The hotel carte, meanwhile, offers 'a taste of Wales', among which are Glamorgan sausages, cawl, and laverbread.

Chef Sarvesh Jadon **Owner** Sanjeev Bhagotra **Times** 7-10 Closed 25 Dec, L all week **Prices** Starter £3.95-£9.95, Main £8.95-£16.95, Dessert £3.95, Service optional **Wines** 11 bottles under £30, 3 by glass **Notes** All you can eat buffet Sun, Vegetarian menu, Civ Wed 120 **Seats** 80, Pr/dining room 120 **Children** Portions, Menu **Parking** 100

CARDIFF

CARDIFF — Map 9 ST17

Bully's

@ French, European 🖑

Lively modern dishes in relaxed restaurant

☎ 029 2022 1905
5 Romilly Crescent CF11 9NP
e-mail: info@bullysrestaurant.co.uk
dir: 5 mins from city centre

'Shabby chic, eclectic' is the self-styled description of Bully's: walls crammed with pictures, gilt mirrors and framed restaurant menus and bills, wooden tables, Persian rugs on the floor and books everywhere. The kitchen takes its inspiration from France, adding some modern European and Asian touches, and depends on local produce with some imports - foie gras, for instance, fried and served with rhubarb compôte and sake dressing as a starter. Or there may be pickled herring with fennel and apple salad and beetroot dressing, followed by chargrilled beef fillet, accurately cooked, with port jus, kale and dauphinoise, or seared loin of yellowfin tuna with green pepper sauce, braised fennel and confit potatoes. Finish with pear tarte Tatin with pear drop ice cream.

Chef Gareth Farr **Owner** Russell Bullimore
Times 12-2/6.30-9 Closed Mon-Tue, D Sun **Prices** Fixed L 2 course £14, Tasting menu £21-£35, Starter £5-£9.50, Main £14-£25, Dessert £6-£9.50, Service added but optional 10% **Wines** 42 bottles over £30, 8 bottles under £30, 9 by glass **Notes** Gourmet menu 7 course, Sunday L £16-£19.50, Vegetarian available **Seats** 40 **Children** Portions **Parking** On street

Cardiff Marriott Hotel

@ British, French

Cuisine Française near the home of Welsh rugby

☎ 029 2078 5872 & 2039 9944
Mill Ln CF10 1EZ
web: www.cardiffmarriott.co.uk
dir: M4 junct 29, A48M E follow signs city centre & Cardiff Bay. 3m, right into Mill Lane

Centrally placed in the capital, handy for a cultural excursion to the castle or the rugby at the Millennium Stadium, the Cardiff Marriott is a corporate hotel that's very much in with the in-crowd. An elegant bar that opens on to a terrace looks a good recourse when the sun's shining, while the smartly toned restaurant offers occasional live music from the baby grand, and a brasserie menu of indubitably French orientation, as is indicated by the carefully researched bilingual descriptions. The house special mussel dish offers a clutch of steamed bivalves with merguez sausage in white wine and garlic, which could be followed by peppered lamb rump with fries, or megrim sole with capers and cornichons in shallot butter. Finish with chocolate tart and crème anglaise, an evenly caramelised crème brûlée, or a selection of French cheeses with Muscat grapes and honeycomb.

Chef Anthony Barnes **Owner** Marriott International
Times 12.30-2.30/6-10 Closed D Sun **Prices** Service optional **Wines** 12 by glass **Notes** Pre-concert D 2/3 course £15.75/£19.50, Sunday L fr £14.95, Vegetarian available, Civ Wed 150 **Seats** 120 **Children** Portions, Menu **Parking** 140

Save on Hotels. Book at **theAA.com/hotel**

CARDIFF 621 WALES

Ye Olde Bulls Head Inn

BEAUMARIS MAP 14 SH67

Modern British 🍃

Creative modern British dishes in a medieval inn

☎ 01248 810329
Castle St LL58 8AP
e-mail: info@bullsheadinn.co.uk
dir: Town centre, main street

This particular Bull has impeccable pedigree. Dating from the 15th century, the inn stands just a stone's throw from the walls of Beaumaris Castle and comes with a serious weight of history, having provided lodgings for parliamentary forces when Cromwell's General Mytton requisitioned the place during the Civil War, as well as less belligerent illustrious patrons, including diarist Dr Samuel Johnson and Charles Dickens. Having undergone numerous transformations over the years, it now offers swish boutique accommodation for the style-conscious 21st-century traveller, as well as bang up-to-date dining possibilities. Head chef Hefin Roberts pulls out all the stops to deliver an ambitious and exciting style of cooking in the flagship Loft Restaurant up under the eaves of the oldest part of the inn. Formerly the hayloft serving the stables, its ancient beams extend over a classy and intimate contemporary space done in shades of oatmeal and cream,

with swirly-patterned designer wallpaper and smartly-clothed tables. Imaginative and stylishly-presented modern British dishes built from premium Welsh ingredients are the deal here, starting with the punchy flavours of poached gurnard fillet with spiced crab meat, garlic gnocchi, toasted seed quinoa, and sweet-and-sour vegetables. Next up, roast loin and marinated rump of Anglesey lamb comes with the Mediterranean notes of courgettes, spiced aubergine purée, red onions, spinach, cumin-spiced potatoes, and an intense jus. The creative juxtapositions are applied equally to fish, with the likes of garlic butter, razor clams, charred potatoes, leeks, fennel, confit lemon, and parsley purée supporting roast loin of monkfish. Full-on flavours keep coming all the way to a dessert of pistachio and chocolate cake with spiced chocolate and orange mousse, and chocolate oil. Served by a separate kitchen, the buzzy ground-floor conservatory brasserie delivers a more casual, crowd-pleasing roster of bright contemporary ideas in a setting of Welsh slate floors and chunky oak tables.

Chef Hefin Roberts **Owner** D Robertson, K Rothwell **Times** 7-9.30 Closed 25-26 Dec, 1 Jan, Sun-Mon, L all week **Prices** Fixed D 3 course £42.50, Service optional **Wines** 60 bottles over £30, 40 bottles under £30, 4 by glass **Notes** Vegetarian available **Seats** 45 **Parking** 10

CARDIFF *continued*

The Parc Hotel, Cardiff

⊛ Modern European

Appealing cooking in remodelled Victorian hotel

☎ 0871 376 9011 & 029 2078 5593
Park Place CF10 3UD
e-mail: restaurant-cardiff@thistle.co.uk
web: www.thistle.com/theparchotel
dir: M4 junct 29, A48, 4th exit signed City Centre/A470.
At rdbt 2nd exit signed City Centre/A470

Cool big-city vibes and a lively crowd are big selling
points at the Parc's thoroughly contemporary Social
restaurant and bar. It is a slick but relaxed city-centre
hangout where you might just drop in to people-watch
over a drink, but it would be a shame to miss out on the
rather good food in the dining area. Clever lighting
creates the right mood in the modish space, divided up
by see-through floor-to-ceiling shelves, and there's plenty
of banquette seating at tables left fashionably bare. The
sensibly restricted menu plays a straight bat, relying on
fine Welsh produce and an uncomplicated approach to
deliver clearly defined, often robust flavours. A well-made
game terrine with macerated raisin purée makes for a
satisfyingly rich and tasty opening gambit, followed by
roast monkfish tail with mussels and squid, with quinoa
and chorizo to add further interest. Puddings also play to
the crowd with simple ideas such as apple tarte Tatin
with apple sorbet.

Chef Iain Inman **Owner** Curzon Hotel Ltd
Times 12-2/6-9.30 **Prices** Fixed L 2 course £16.95, Fixed
D 3 course £19.50, Tasting menu £45, Starter
£4.95-£5.95, Main £11.50-£15.50, Dessert £3.95-£6.95,
Service optional **Wines** 52 bottles over £30, 25 bottles
under £30, 10 by glass **Notes** Afternoon tea, Champagne
jazz brunch, Pre-theatre meal, Sunday L, Vegetarian
available, Dress restrictions, Smart casual **Seats** 80, Pr/
dining room 14 **Children** Portions, Menu **Parking** 50

WINNER OF THE AA WINE AWARD FOR WALES

Park House

⊛⊛ British, International **NEW** V ⚑ NOTABLE WINE LIST

**Contemporary cooking in a gothic revival architectural
masterpiece**

☎ 029 2022 4343
20 Park Place CF10 3DQ
e-mail: bookings@parkhouseclub.com
dir: Opposite Cardiff Museum

Once a private club, Park House is one of the Welsh
capital's finest pieces of architectural extravagance.
Designed by William Burges, one of the premier
practitioners of the gothic revival, it overlooks the
gardens of the National Museum of Wales. The architect
is celebrated in the name of the restaurant, which is done
out in gently clashing tones of pinks and peaches against
a background of solid oak panelling, and offers the added

bonus of a pianist and singer at the weekends. Chef
Jonathan Edwards offers an ambitiously lengthy menu
that features much prime produce. A mastery of
contemporary technique is exhibited in a classic pairing
of scallop and black pudding which gains depth from
seared foie gras and a sparse swipe of treacle-rich PX
caramel. Meanwhile, peas and butter beans form the
base for a composition of oriental mushrooms, apple and
crispy konbu with beetroot jelly and dashi consommé, and
top-quality Shorthorn beef fillet appears with St Brides
Bay lobster alongside a mound of vigorously spiced tarka
dhal and mushroom and sherry sabayon. Desserts like
buttermilk ice cream and honeycomb with sherry caramel
and puréed apple round off a polished act.

Chef Jonathan Edwards **Owner** Adam & Claire Pledger
Times 11-4/6-11 Closed 25-26 Dec & some BHs, Sun-
Mon, D Tue **Prices** Fixed L 2 course £15, Fixed D 3 course
£42, Tasting menu £59, Starter £10-£12, Main £26,
Dessert £7-£10, Service added but optional 8%, Groups
min 6 service 8% **Wines** 450 bottles over £30, 60 bottles
under £30, 10 by glass **Notes** Pre-theatre a la carte D
menu 25% discount, Vegetarian menu, Dress restrictions,
Smart casual, Civ Wed 100 **Seats** 80, Pr/dining room 40
Parking NCP 50mtrs away

Park Plaza Cardiff

⊛ British, European **NEW** V

Efficient classic cooking in a chic city-centre hotel

☎ 029 2011 1111 & 2011 1103
Greyfriars Rd CF10 3AL
e-mail: jlewis@parkplazahotels.co.uk
web: www.lagunakitchenandbar.com
dir: Located on Greyfriars Rd inside Park Plaza Hotel

In the centre of the city, and therefore handy for just
about everything that's going on in the Welsh capital, the
Park Plaza offers contemporary comfort with plenty of
imaginative design features. Ring-form chandeliers and
bright upholstery in the bar give way to a more neutral
look in the restaurant, where darkwood boards, cream
banquettes, a wine store, and big windows giving on to a
decked area are the order of the day. The kitchen offers
efficient classic cooking with some modern touches.
Expect to start with a fishcake of smoked Grimsby
haddock and spring onion with Indian accoutrements, or
strongly flavoured duck liver and foie gras parfait with
spiced plum and ginger chutney, before the main part of
the show brings on rump and shoulder of lamb with
caponata, celeriac purée and Kalamata olive jus, or well-
handled sea bass with gnocchi, wild mushrooms, peas
and tarragon. Dessert could be a rich dark chocolate and
Penderyn whisky torte with apple and pear sauce and
vanilla mascarpone.

Chef Justin Llewellyn **Owner** Martin Morris
Times 12-2.30/5.30-9.30 Closed 25 Dec **Prices** Fixed L 2
course £12.95, Starter £4.95-£8.25, Main £11.95-£24.95,
Dessert £4.50-£7.95, Service added but optional 10%
Wines 44 bottles over £30, 38 bottles under £30, 9 by
glass **Notes** Pre-theatre fr £12.95, Afternoon tea fr £15,
Sunday L £15.95-£18.95, Vegetarian menu
Children Portions, Menu **Parking** NCP

The Thai House Restaurant

⊛ Thai V

Top Thai cooking in the centre of the city

☎ 029 2038 7404
3-5 Guildford Crescent, Churchill Way CF10 2HJ
e-mail: info@thaihouse.biz
web: www.thaihouse.biz
dir: At junct of Newport Rd & Queen St turn left past
Queen St station, before lights turn left into Guildford
Crescent

When Thai House set up shop in the heart of Cardiff back
in 1985 it was the only place outside of London serving
those fragrant and fiery flavours of south-east Asia. It is
still a hugely popular venue that has stood the test of
time with a sound policy of sourcing its raw materials
from the local area, and flying in authentic exotica from
Bangkok; pleasant and helpful staff in national costume
add to the relaxed ambience, while the kitchen turns out
confidently cooked traditional Thai dishes with full-
throttle flavours. Get going with gung sarong - king
prawns deep-fried in filo pastry with sweet chilli dipping
sauce and fresh herbs - before the house speciality hor
moak (salmon and broccoli marinated in red curry paste
and steamed in banana leaves), or gaeng pat kee mow
(venison marinated in Welsh whisky with sweet basil,
galingale, and Thai aubergines). End with rich, creamy
pumpkin pudding, known as sankaya fak tong.

Chef Sujan Klingson **Owner** Noi & Arlene Ramasut
Times 12-2.30/5.30-10.30 Closed Xmas, 1 Jan, Sun
Prices Fixed L 2 course fr £10.95, Fixed D 3 course
£27.95-£42.95, Starter £5.50-£13.50, Main
£9.95-£19.95, Dessert £5.50-£8.95, Service optional,

Groups min 8 service 10% **Wines** 18 bottles over £30, 19 bottles under £30, 16 by glass **Notes** Vegetarian menu, Dress restrictions, Smart casual **Seats** 130, Pr/dining room 20 **Parking** On street, NCP opposite

See advert below

Woods Brasserie

Modern European

Modern brasserie fare in trendy Cardiff Bay

☎ 029 2049 2400
Pilotage Building, Stuart St CF10 5BW
e-mail: woods@knifeandforkfood.co.uk
dir: In heart of Cardiff Bay. From M4 junct 33 towards Cardiff Bay, large stone building on right

A vast expanse of full-length windows capitalises on the views over Cardiff Bay from the Victorian grey-stone Pilotage Building. Inside, a grey-tiled floor, lime-green banquettes, and bare pale wood tables give the place a thoroughly contemporary look, while the kitchen has strong supply lines to local farms, butchers and fishermen, so you can take top-quality ingredients and a healthy approach to seasonality as read. Modern brasserie ideas form the backbone of a crowd-pleasing, great-value table d'hôte menu and an imaginative carte. You might start with steamed Gower coast mussels with chorizo and olive oil, or caramelised ox cheek and foie gras ballotine with star anise pickle and crispy bread, then follow with pan-fried fillet of hake with wilted spinach, saffron potato mousse, and bouillabaisse sauce. Carnivores can head straight to the grill for slabs of prime Welsh protein with thick-cut chips and flavoured butters. Desserts such as bitter chocolate tart with salted caramel and cappuccino ice cream bow out on a high note.

Owner Knife & Fork Food Ltd **Times** 12-2/5.30-10 Closed 25-26 Dec & 1 Jan, D Sun (Sep-May) **Prices** Prices not confirmed Service optional, Groups min 6 service 10%

Wines 20 by glass **Notes** Fixed L & D Mon-Sat, Sunday L, Vegetarian available **Seats** 90, Pr/dining room 40 **Children** Portions, Menu **Parking** Multi-storey car park opposite

CARMARTHENSHIRE

LAUGHARNE   Map 8 SN31

The Cors Restaurant

Modern

Charming restaurant in Dylan Thomas country

☎ 01994 427219
Newbridge Rd SA33 4SH
e-mail: nick@thecors.co.uk
dir: A40 from Carmarthen, left at St Clears & 4m to Laugharne

Chef-proprietor Nick Priestland has taken a lovely Victorian rectory and transformed it into a one-off, idiosyncratic restaurant with rooms. Just off Laugharne's main street in Dylan Thomas country, the trees, shrubs, ponds, and modern sculptures in the magical bog garden ('cors' is Welsh for bog) are unmissable when lit up at night, while the moody interior has a gothic edge with its deep claret-hued walls, wrought-iron seats and stained-glass windows; an atmospheric setting for unaffected, precise cooking that trumpets the virtues of excellent local ingredients. Full-on flavours are more important here than fancy presentation, thus smoked haddock brûlée certainly grabs the attention at the start of a summer's dinner, before roast rack of Welsh lamb arrives with the punchy flavours of a rosemary and garlic crust, dauphinoise potatoes and caramelised onion gravy, and it all ends happily with a summer fruit Pavlova.

Chef Nick Priestland **Owner** Nick Priestland **Times** 7-9.30 Closed 25 Dec, Sun-Wed, L all week **Prices** Prices not confirmed Service optional **Wines** 6 by glass **Seats** 24 **Parking** 8

LLANDEILO   Map 8 SN62

The Plough Inn

Modern International

Broad menu in friendly roadside hotel

☎ 01558 823431
Rhosmaen SA19 6NP
e-mail: info@ploughrhosmaen.com
web: www.ploughrhosmaen.com
dir: On A40 1m N of Llandeilo towards Llandovery. From M4 onto A483 at Pont Abraham

The Plough may sound like a pub, but it has morphed into a smartly-updated small hotel and restaurant overlooking the Towy Valley on the edge of the Brecon Beacons National Park. Whether you go for the convivial bar or stylish dining room, there's a please-all menu built on tip-top ingredients sourced from Welsh suppliers, taking in everything from old favourites - steaks from the grill, or crisp belly pork with black pudding, caramelised apple, buttered mash and cider jus, say - to more ambitious, modern ideas along the lines of crayfish and prawn ravioli with seafood bouillabaisse and chervil foam, followed by braised shoulder of Welsh lamb with goats' cheese tarte Tatin and Madeira sauce.

Chef Andrew Roberts **Owner** Andrew Roberts **Times** 11.30-3.30/5.30-9.30 Closed 26 Dec **Prices** Fixed L 2 course £13.75, Fixed D 3 course £21.95, Starter £4.95-£7.95, Main £9.95-£19.95, Dessert £5-£6, Service optional **Wines** 5 bottles over £30, 37 bottles under £30, 7 by glass **Notes** Sunday L, Vegetarian available, Civ Wed 140 **Seats** 190, Pr/dining room 10 **Children** Portions, Menu **Parking** 70

Sosban Restaurant

◉◉ British, French 🍷

Dockside brasserie dining in a local landmark

☎ 01554 270020
The Pumphouse, North Dock SA15 2LF
e-mail: ian@sosbanrestaurant.com
web: www.sosbanrestaurant.com

The Victorian building that once provided hydraulic power for Llanelli's docks has been revitalised as an industrial-chic powerhouse on the local gastronomic scene. The 90-foot-high castellated stone tower is a local landmark, which makes it easy enough to find; once inside, the setting is certainly impressive with walls of arched glass windows looking out to sea, Welsh slate floors, and classy bare wooden tables beneath the exposed industrial skeleton of the heritage building. At work inside an open-to-view kitchen, the team at the stoves turns out a French-accented brasserie-style repertoire with a broad appeal and maximum input from local suppliers and producers all over Wales. A signature starter of crab lasagne shows the unfussy style, followed by hearty crowd-pleasers along the lines of breast and confit leg of Barbary duck with Puy lentils and red wine sauce, or braised Brecon venison with red cabbage and celeriac purée. To finish, the Welsh cheeseboard is hard to overlook, otherwise prune and Armagnac parfait makes a grown-up pudding.

Chef Sian Rees **Owner** Robert Williams & Partners
Times 12-2.45/6-9.45 Closed D Sun **Prices** Fixed L 2 course £15, Fixed D 3 course £17, Starter £2-£9.50, Main £14-£23, Dessert £4.50-£8, Service included **Wines** 49 bottles over £30, 34 bottles under £30, 14 by glass **Notes** Fixed D available until 6.45pm, Sunday L, Vegetarian available **Seats** Pr/dining room 20 **Children** Portions **Parking** 100

Y Polyn

◉◉ Modern British 🍷

Locally-inspired cooking in a country pub

☎ 01267 290000
SA32 7LH
e-mail: ypolyn@hotmail.com
dir: Follow brown tourist signs to National Botanic Gardens, Y Polyn signed from rdbt in front of gardens

The Mansons' welcoming country pub makes no bones about its unpretentiousness. The service approach is friendly, chatty and informal, the place is furnished in true rustic style with bare wood tables, and the happy buzz of customers is testimony to the success of the cooking. There is no desire to innovate for its own sake, just reliable local ingredients cooked with bravura. Start with fried mackerel, served with vegetable slaw in blood orange and ginger dressing, and follow up with a shepherd's pie made with duck, served with celeriac, parsnip and parmesan mash, or a restorative vegetable tagine with a dressing of coriander yoghurt. Favourite puddings such as knickerbocker glory with flavours of chocolate and orange, or plum frangipane tart served warm, will send everyone home happy. Home-baked bread and mineral water are included in the menu price.

Chef Susan Manson **Owner** Mark & Susan Manson
Times 12-2/7-9 Closed Mon, D Sun **Prices** Fixed L 2

Plas Ynyshir Hall Hotel

Modern British 🏆 NOTABLE WINE LIST

Daring contemporary cooking amid birdsong and ancient trees

☎ 01654 781209
SY20 8TA
e-mail: ynyshir@relaischateaux.com
web: www.ynyshir-hall.co.uk
dir: On A487, 6m S of Machynlleth

We are used to places that Queen Victoria once passed through on her travels through her realm, but Ynyshir bears rather more of the regal imprint than most. It was owned by the Queen, who had many of the still-surviving trees planted, and who saw its value as an ornithological paradise. Indeed, a thousand acres of the original estate were eventually acquired by the RSPB for the bird sanctuary that may still be enjoyed today. It's no exaggeration to say that Rob and Joan Reen have contributed in their own way to the illustrious history of the hall over the past generation, making it one of the gastronomic magnets of west Wales, and running the whole show with solicitous care and attention. A lavender-hued dining room is gentle on the visual senses, with quality table appointments as befits the tone, the better to let Paul Croasdale's culinary magic weave its spell. Fish from Cardigan Bay and the local rivers, produce from the hall's own gardens and foraged wild ingredients, as well as pedigree meats from the valleys, form the basis of an abundant and thoughtful kitchen production, seen in menus that subtly incorporate some of the surreal elements of modern British cooking into an essentially classical methodology. A daring excursion into sweetness at the outset produces a lobe of foie gras roasted in sherry, alongside hazelnut caramel, a foie gras ice cream and gingerbread crisps. That might be counterpointed by the thoroughgoing savoury impact of a main course of thyme-scented turbot with fragrant herb risotto and truffled pig's cheek salad, while meat might be rump of lamb subjected to the sun-lamp cooking temperature of a mere 52 degrees C, and served with Jerusalem artichokes and clams. If meals begin sweet, they may as easily end in a beguiling acid key, with a balsamic note wafting through wild strawberry cheesecake and basil ice cream.

Chef Paul Croasdale **Owner** Rob & Joan Reen and John & Jen Talbot **Times** 12.30-2/7-9 Closed Jan **Prices** Fixed L 3 course fr £20, Tasting menu £45-£90, Starter £12-£17, Main £20-£28, Dessert £8-£12, Service optional **Wines** 191 bottles over £30, 27 bottles under £30, 17 by glass **Notes** Tasting menu 10 course, Fixed D 5 course £72.50, Sunday L £25-£29.50, Vegetarian available, Dress restrictions, No jeans, beachwear shorts or trainers, Civ Wed 28 **Seats** 30, Pr/dining room 16 **Children** Portions **Parking** 15

course £12, Fixed D 3 course £32.50-£35.50, Starter £5-£9, Main £11.50-£16.50, Dessert £6.50, Service optional **Wines** 25 bottles over £30, 51 bottles under £30, 9 by glass **Notes** ALC prices for L only, Sunday L, Vegetarian available **Seats** 40 **Children** Portions **Parking** 25

CEREDIGION

ABERAERON   Map 8 SN46

Ty Mawr Mansion

◉◉ Modern British, Welsh ◔

Food from within ten miles of a handsome Georgian mansion

☎ 01570 470033
Cilcennin, Lampeter SA48 8DB
e-mail: info@tymawrmansion.co.uk
web: www.tymawrmansion.co.uk
dir: 4m from Aberaeron on A482 to Lampeter road

In a lofty position above the Aeron Valley, this stone-built Georgian mansion is tucked away in 12 acres of gorgeous grounds. Inside, it is an authentically-restored gem right down to its heritage colour schemes - sunny yellows lighten the feel, while lavender walls combine with darkwood floors and blue and white Regency-striped chairs at bare wooden tables in the rather splendid restaurant. Lots of hotels go on about their organic and local ingredients, but in this case it is not empty bluster: most of the materials come from within a ten-mile radius, including organic produce from Cilcennin village's farms on the doorstep, while the coast (four miles distant) supplies the fishy stuff. Start, perhaps, with seared Cardigan Bay scallops with cauliflower risotto, chorizo and tempura caper berries, then move on via a sorbet, to pan-seared fillet and confit belly of local pork served with crackling, parsnip purée and pan juices. For pudding there may be duck egg tart with garden rhubarb in the form of compôte and sorbet.

Chef Geraint Morgan **Owner** Martin & Catherine McAlpine **Times** 7-9 Closed 26 Dec-7 Jan, Sun, L all week **Prices** Fixed D 3 course £29.95, Starter £6.95-£9.95, Main £18.95-£24.95, Dessert £6.95-£8.95, Service optional **Wines** 5 bottles over £30, 23 bottles under £30, 6 by glass **Notes** ALC 5 course available, Vegetarian available, Dress restrictions, Smart casual, Civ Wed 35 **Seats** 35, Pr/dining room 12 **Parking** 20

EGLWYS FACH   Map 14 SN69

Plas Ynyshir Hall Hotel

◉◉◉ – see opposite

LAMPETER   Map 8 SN54

The Falcondale Hotel & Restaurant

◉◉ Modern British V ◔

Fine Welsh produce cooked in a lovely rural setting

☎ 01570 422910
Falcondale Dr SA48 7RX
e-mail: info@thefalcondale.co.uk
web: www.thefalcondale.co.uk
dir: 1m from Lampeter take A482 to Cardigan, turn right at petrol station, follow for 0.75m

Built on a Victorian banking fortune, this handsome Italianate mansion stands in 14 acres of grounds ensconced in lovely mid-Wales countryside. The Falcondale earns its living as an easygoing country-house hotel these days, with a classy dining room gently updated to assuage contemporary sensibilities - rugs on wooden floors, unclothed darkwood tables set against period features, and a relaxed and friendly ambience. Local hills and valleys and the nearby coastline supply the lion's share of the kitchen's raw materials for menus of broadly modern British ideas - Cardigan Bay lobster and crab, perhaps, served simply with tagliatelle and saffron sauce, followed by a winter season main course of roast loin of Pembrokeshire venison with braised red cabbage, caramelised walnuts and quince purée. For those who fancy fish, there could be a duo of salmon and sea bass served with wilted spinach, dauphinoise potatoes, artichoke 'textures' and shellfish bisque. At the end, Welsh cheeses are delivered with home-made chutney and oatcakes, and finely-crafted desserts could extend to a peppermint custard tart with bitter chocolate mousse, candyfloss and coconut sorbet.

Chef Michael Green **Owner** Chris & Lisa Hutton **Times** 12-2/6.30-9 **Prices** Fixed L 2 course £15.95-£22, Fixed D 3 course fr £40, Service optional, Groups min 8 service 10% **Wines** 50 bottles over £30, 52 bottles under £30, 18 by glass **Notes** Tasting menu 7 course (pre-booked), Sunday L, Vegetarian menu, Dress restrictions, Smart casual, no shorts, Civ Wed 100 **Seats** 36, Pr/dining room 20 **Children** Portions **Parking** 60

CONWY

ABERGELE   Map 14 SH97

The Kinmel Arms

◉◉ Modern Welsh ◔

Sophisticated cooking in the Elwy Valley

☎ 01745 832207
The Village, St George LL22 9BP
e-mail: info@thekinmelarms.co.uk
dir: From A55 junct 24a to St George. E on A55, junct 25. 1st left to Rhuddlan, then 1st right into St George. Take 2nd right

In a village near the coast, this 18th-century stone coaching inn is a combination of bar, with a wood-burning stove and real ales, and restaurant with rooms. The restaurant itself has a conservatory feel, with light

wooden furniture and exposed brickwork and a lively bustle. The kitchen focuses on the best quality ingredients it can find in Wales and the Marches and turns out accomplished, imaginative dishes. A pressing of belly pork, for instance, is served with braised turnips, pickled carrots and rhubarb compôte, and another starter may be scallops sautéed with smoked paprika accompanied by lemon purée and chorizo foam. Influences are culled from here and there to create some adventurous, palate-pleasing compositions - accurately grilled sea bass fillet, for instance, on a bed of sautéed pak choi and steamed mooli with saffron tempura mussels, chilli and spring onion dressing and galangal chips - although pink-roast sirloin gets a more mainstream treatment, served with red wine purée and Madeira jus. Pudding fanciers can end with rum baba or apple tarte Tatin.

Chef Wes Oakley **Owner** Tim & Lynn Watson **Times** 12-3/6-9.30 Closed 25 Dec, 1-2 Jan, Sun-Mon **Prices** Fixed L 2 course £22.95-£29.95, Starter £4.60-£9.95, Main £14.95-£22.95, Dessert £5.45-£6.95, Service optional **Wines** 49 bottles over £30, 49 bottles under £30, 20 by glass **Notes** Vegetarian available **Seats** 88 **Children** Portions, Menu **Parking** 60

BETWS-Y-COED   Map 14 SH75

Craig-y-Dderwen Riverside Hotel

◉ Traditional, International ◔

Idyllic riverside setting for fine Welsh ingredients

☎ 01690 710293
LL24 0AS
e-mail: info@snowdoniahotel.com
web: www.snowdoniahotel.com
dir: A5 to Betws-y-Coed, cross Waterloo Bridge, take 1st left

Elgar was a great fan of the peace and seclusion he found at this half-timbered Victorian country-house hotel tucked away at the end of a tree-lined drive in well-maintained gardens on the River Conwy - a view that is opened up to the max by a wall of glass in the dining room. The kitchen is clearly passionate about the produce from this landscape, growing vegetables, herbs and fruit in the extensive kitchen garden, and sourcing the rest from local and Welsh suppliers. Gently contemporary ideas take their cue from Europe and further afield, starting with Conwy crabcake with chive, rocket and warm potato salad, and proceeding to slow-braised neck of Conwy Valley lamb with roast vegetables and fondant potatoes. An apple tarte fine is as good as it should be to finish.

Chef Paul Goosey **Owner** Martin Carpenter **Times** 12-2.30/6.30-9 Closed 2 Jan-1 Feb **Prices** Prices not confirmed Service optional **Wines** 50 bottles over £30, 60 bottles under £30, 7 by glass **Notes** Sunday L, Vegetarian available, Dress restrictions, Smart casual, Civ Wed 125 **Seats** 82, Pr/dining room 40 **Children** Portions, Menu **Parking** 50

BETWS-Y-COED *continued*

Llugwy River Restaurant @ Royal Oak Hotel

Modern British, Welsh

Former coaching inn with quality Welsh cuisine

☎ 01690 710219
Holyhead Rd LL24 0AY
e-mail: royaloakmail@btopenworld.com
web: www.royaloakhotel.net
dir: on A5 in town centre, next to St Mary's church

The Royal Oak Hotel will never lack for custom in the tourist honeypot of Betws-y-Coed, where ambling day-trippers and hardy hikers fresh off the peaks of Snowdonia are all in need of refuelling. After a thorough facelift, the Victorian coaching inn sports a smart contemporary interior that has also given the Llugwy River Restaurant a swish new look involving cappuccino walls, crystal chandeliers, LED wall panels and bare blond-wood tables. The kitchen takes a suitably modern Welsh line with top-grade local materials - perhaps ballottine of local pheasant with spinach and walnut mousse and red onion marmalade to start, followed by Welsh lamb starring as a half rump, rillettes of slow-cooked shoulder, and a lamb and mint shortcrust pie teamed with leek dauphinoise potatoes. Welsh cheeses with bara brith fruitcake make a savoury alternative to puddings such as rich dark chocolate terrine with amaretti biscuits and pistachio.

Chef Dylan Edwards **Owner** Royal Oak Hotel Ltd
Times 12-3/6.30-9 Closed 25-26 Dec, Mon-Tue, L Wed-Sat, D Sun **Prices** Fixed L 2 course £12.50-£13.95, Fixed D 3 course £25-£35, Starter £5.95-£12.95, Main £13.75-£25, Dessert £5.75-£7.95, Service optional **Wines** 11 by glass **Notes** Sunday L, Vegetarian available, Dress restrictions, Smart casual, no jeans, shorts or T-shirts, Civ Wed 60 **Seats** 60, Pr/dining room 20 **Children** Portions, Menu **Parking** 100

Tan-y-Foel Country Guest House

— *see below*

CONWY   Map 14 SH77

Castle Hotel Conwy

British, International

Fine Welsh produce in local landmark

☎ 01492 582800
High St LL32 8DB
e-mail: mail@castlewales.co.uk
web: www.castlewales.co.uk
dir: A55 junct 18, follow town centre signs, cross estuary (castle on left). Right then left at mini-rdbts onto one-way system. Right at Town Wall Gate, right onto Berry St then High St

It's a PhD project in the waiting to track the evolution of this hotel through history: suffice to say, built on the site of a Cistercian abbey, with a Victorian bell-gabled façade of local green granite and red Ruabon bricks, and first open for a jug of ale in the 15th century, there's no shortage of character. But this is no museum, with today's hotel positioning itself somewhere on the 'boutique' side of the spectrum and a restaurant, Dawsons, that has a satisfyingly contemporary finish. There's plenty of local flavour on the long menu in the shape of some excellent regional produce - Conwy mussels, for example - and there's attention to detail in the execution. The modish repertoire extends from Thai-style crab and salmon fishcakes with crispy 'seaweed', radish and bean sprout salad and sweet chilli sauce, to

Tan-y-Foel Country Guest House

BETWS-Y-COED   MAP 14 SH75

Modern British

Compelling, accomplished cooking in small country hotel

☎ 01690 710507
Capel Garmon LL26 0RE
e-mail: enquiries@tyfhotel.co.uk
web: www.tyfhotel.co.uk
dir: A5 onto A470, 2m N towards Llanrwst, then turning for Capel Garmon. House on left 1m before village

On a hill just outside the pretty village, Tan-y-Foel, parts dating from the 16th century, is set in landscaped grounds with views of the Conwy Valley and the Snowdonia National Park. The interior is a happy marriage of period features and modern style, while the dining room has a clean, uncluttered look. The deal is a fixed-price dinner, the menu changing daily, with two choices per course, with Welsh farmhouse cheeses an alternative to pudding. Janet Pitman shows guests her menus in advance so they can decide what they'd like, and works alone in the kitchen. To say that hers is a labour of love is no exaggeration, and she gives her own highly distinctive style to her cooking, creating a dressing of caramelised vinegar and basil to go with perfectly grilled mackerel fillet with aubergine relish and crisp-fried aubergine wafers, and one of apple, prune and pecan for an alternative starter of duck pithivier with Madeira sauce. Dishes are complex enough to be interesting without becoming implausible or overwrought, seen in an assiette of local lamb - breadcrumbed loin, braised shoulder and sautéed liver - accompanied by tomato fondue, wilted spinach and potato and onion purée hinting of garlic. A fillet of trawler-fresh fish - maybe baked sea bass - could be the other choice, served with leek and smoked salmon risotto and creamy mustard sauce. Janet Pitman's care, precision and integrity are evident throughout, from canapés to desserts like dark chocolate soufflé with cappuccino-style frothy topping, or sabayon of apricots and white Stilton.

Chef Janet Pitman **Owner** Mr & Mrs P Pitman **Times** 7.30-close Closed Dec-Jan, L all week, D Sun-Mon **Prices** Fixed D 3 course £50, Service optional **Wines** 6 by glass **Notes** D single sitting, Dress restrictions, No jeans, trainers or walking boots **Seats** 10 **Parking** 6

main-course fillet of sea bass with a risotto of those excellent mussels, or Welsh lamb hotpot. To finish, warm cherry tart with Amarena cherry ice cream and fresh berry compôte competes with the slate of excellent Welsh cheeses.

Chef Andrew Nelson **Owner** Lavin Family **Times** 12-10 Closed D 25 Dec All-day dining **Prices** Starter £5.75-£8.95, Main £14.95-£22.95, Dessert £6.95-£9.95, Service added but optional 10% **Wines** 20 bottles over £30, 21 bottles under £30, 16 by glass **Notes** Small plates menu spring & summer, Sunday L £11.95-£13.95, Vegetarian available **Seats** 70 **Children** Portions, Menu **Parking** 36

The Groes Inn

⬡ Traditional British

Historic inn serving simple pub grub

☎ 01492 650545
Tyn-y-Groes LL32 8TN
e-mail: reception@groesinn.com
web: www.groesinn.com
dir: On B5106, 3m from Conwy

Once a stopping point for weary stagecoach passengers, the 16th-century Groes is said to be Wales's first licensed house. The white-fronted inn has all the expected beamed ceilings and roaring fires, plus some interesting paraphernalia you probably wouldn't expect such as Victorian portraits, a collection of military hats and some historic cooking utensils. Try a pint or bottle of the inn's own Groes ale - a light ale with citrus tones. Food can be taken in the welcoming bar, cosy restaurant, airy conservatory or the garden, which has wonderful views. Fresh pub cooking using classic combinations defines the kitchen's output. Start with a smooth chicken liver pâté with toast and chutney before oven-baked whole rainbow trout, which slides off the bone, served with fennel and king prawns, carrots and roasted new potatoes with lemon and dill butter. Poached pears with cider ice cream provides a satisfying finish.

Times 12-2.15/6.30-9

DEGANWY   Map 14 SH77

Quay Hotel & Spa

⬡⬡ Modern European 🍃

Steaks and seafood on the Conwy estuary

☎ 01492 564100 & 564165
Deganwy Quay LL31 9DJ
e-mail: reservations@quayhotel.com
web: www.quayhotel.com
dir: M56, A494, A55 junct 18, straight across 2 rdbts. At lights bear left into The Quay. Hotel/Restaurant on right

A stylish boutique hotel on the Conwy estuary, the Quay is a north Welsh destination for getting away from it all. Within striking distance of Snowdonia, it offers golf and spa treatments in the modern way, and boasts a smart eatery, the Grill Room, upholstered in muted greens and lilacs. Locally-landed fish and seafood are a strong draw,

naturally, with oysters in shallots and red wine vinegar, crab croquettes with capers and 'tartare hollandaise', or mussels either Thai-style or marinière to get things going. A charcoal-fired oven ensures more sizzle for the steaks, which come in various cuts, all aged for 28 days, or stay fishy with monkfish medallions with butter-poached langoustines in shellfish bisque. The slapstick kitchen antics depicted on the dessert menu shouldn't be deemed to indicate that any less care has been taken over your hot apple crumble soufflé, served with apple and toffee ripple ice cream. High rollers may opt for the five-course tasting menu with wine flight.

Chef Sue Leacy **Owner** Exclusive Hotels **Times** 12-3/6.30-9.30 **Prices** Fixed L 2 course £14.95, Fixed D 2 course £29.95, Tasting menu £60, Starter £6.95-£12, Main £18.95-£65, Dessert £7.95, Service optional **Wines** 18 bottles over £30, 40 bottles under £30, 19 by glass **Notes** Sunday L, Vegetarian available, Civ Wed 180 **Seats** 120, Pr/dining room 40 **Children** Portions, Menu **Parking** 110

LLANDUDNO   Map 14 SH78

Bodysgallen Hall and Spa

⬡⬡⬡ – *see page 628*

Empire Hotel & Spa

⬡ Modern British 🍃

Handsome Victorian spa hotel with brasserie-style menu

☎ 01492 860555
Church Walks LL30 2HE
e-mail: reservations@empirehotel.co.uk
web: www.empirehotel.co.uk
dir: From Chester, A55 junct 19 for Llandudno. Follow signs to Promenade, turn right at war memorial & left at rdbt. Hotel 100yds on right

Built as part of the mercantile boom of the early Victorian era (1856 to be precise), opening as a hotel in 1904, and run by the same family since 1946, the Empire is part of the town's history. The Watkins & Co restaurant is named after the wine merchants business that once inhabited the premises, and serves a menu of brasserie-style dishes in a bright and modish setting. Kick off with chicken satay with peanut sauce before moving on to grilled sea bass with crushed peas and garlic, or roast duck breast (served pink) with onion stuffing, red cabbage and orange sauce. There are steaks, too - rib-eye, perhaps - with accompanying sauces, and desserts such as dark chocolate cheesecake with raspberry coulis. The hotel also has a spa and swimming pool, so plenty of opportunity to work off any over indulgence.

Chef Michael Waddy, Larry Mustisya **Owner** Len & Elizabeth Maddocks **Times** 12.30-2/6.30-9.30 Closed 22-30 Dec, L Mon-Sat **Prices** Fixed L 3 course £15.95, Fixed D 3 course £22.95, Service optional **Wines** 9 bottles over £30, 37 bottles under £30, 11 by glass **Notes** Fixed L Sun only, Sunday L, Vegetarian available, Dress restrictions, Smart casual **Seats** 110 **Children** Portions, Menu **Parking** 54, On street

Imperial Hotel

⬡ Modern, Traditional British

Grand hotel cooking with views of the sea

☎ 01492 877466
The Promenade LL30 1AP
e-mail: reception@theimperial.co.uk
web: www.theimperial.co.uk
dir: A470 to Llandudno

Where Snowdonia drops away to the sea, Llandudno's promenade basks in the sun, a vision of Victorian leisure in the grand manner, with the flesh-coloured Imperial ruling the roost. Chantrey's Restaurant surveys the maritime scene from panoramic windows, and there are outdoor tables too, for those who want to hear the murmuring surf. The kitchen works within the parameters of what's expected in such a context, but productively and with a few modern touches: smoked haddock mousse is wrapped in smoked salmon and garnished with radishes, capers and lemon, before a little fillet of Welsh beef appears, all tricked out with leek and horseradish rösti, smoked bacon, wild mushrooms, and a sauce lusty with Great Orme ale. Fish might be sea bass with roasted chicory and samphire in sauce vierge, while dessert brings on classic crème brûlée with apple and blueberry compôte, or pecan treacle tart with ginger cake and clotted cream ice cream.

Times 12.30-3/6.30-9.30

LLANDUDNO *continued*

The Lilly Restaurant with Rooms

Modern Welsh

Modern Welsh cooking overlooking the sea

☎ 01492 876513
West Pde LL30 2BD
e-mail: thelilly@live.co.uk
dir: Just off A546 at Llandudno, follow signs for the Pier, beach front on right

Parked right on the seafront at the West Shore, the Ashes' family-run restaurant with rooms is quite a looker inside. The dining room is done in ecclesiastical purples, with black-and-white table settings, the many-windowed space capitalising on views of the Llandudno headland and the sea. The bill of fare is modern Welsh cooking, presented cleanly and mobilising plenty of good local materials, such as rump of excellent Elwy lamb on creamed cabbage, served with a little chop and a portion of meaty suet pudding in minty juices. Other dishes are more obviously from the European mainstream, perhaps chicken and chorizo risotto, or truffled wild mushroom tagliatelle with shaved parmesan. The pork taster dish enterprisingly incorporates a Scotch egg along with the expected belly and tenderloin. Finish with passionfruit tart and honeycomb ice cream. Fine home-made breads, appetisers and pre-desserts show this to be a kitchen of serious intent.

Chef Phillip Ashe, Jonathon Goodman **Owner** Roxanne & Phillip Ashe **Times** 12-3/6-9 Closed Mon-Tue, L Tue-Sat, D Sun-Tue **Prices** Fixed L 2 course £14.95-£16.95, Starter £6.95-£9.95, Main £15.95-£24.95, Dessert £5.95-£6.95, Service included **Wines** 22 bottles over £30, 98 bottles under £30, 43 by glass **Notes** Sunday L £16.95-£19.95, Vegetarian available, Dress restrictions, Smart **Seats** 35 **Children** Portions, Menu

Osborne House

Modern British

All-day brasserie menu on the promenade

☎ 01492 860330
17 North Pde LL30 2LP
e-mail: sales@osbornehouse.co.uk
web: www.osbornehouse.co.uk
dir: A55 at junct 19, follow signs for Llandudno then Promenade, at War Memorial turn right, Osborne House on left opposite entrance to pier

Smack on the seafront promenade, this grand townhouse hotel is luxuriously and romantically decorated. The dining room is a real show-stopper, where beautifully restored period features abound; think Roman pillars, large paintings, opulent drapes, gilt mirrors and dazzling statement chandeliers. So, in these opulent surroundings - formally decked out in white-linen dressed tables and with uniformed staff - you might not ordinarily expect a more relaxed café/brasserie-style operation. But here it

is. The long, all-day, please-all menu offers bags of choice whatever the time of day; from a sandwich and bakery menu to more substantial things like grilled sea bass on bacon creamed cabbage, or braised lamb shank with crushed root vegetables and rosemary jus. To finish, retro desserts like treacle tart or sherry trifle hit the spot.

Chef Michael Waddy, Tim McAll **Owner** Len & Elizabeth Maddocks **Times** 10.30am-10pm Closed 22-30 Dec, All-day dining **Prices** Fixed L 2 course £11.50-£12.50, Fixed D 3 course £21.95-£22.95, Starter £4.50-£7.50, Main £10.50-£19.95, Dessert £5.25-£5.95, Service optional, Groups min 12 service 10% **Wines** 9 bottles over £30, 44 bottles under £30, 8 by glass **Notes** Pre-theatre menu 5pm, Sunday L, Vegetarian available, Dress restrictions, Smart casual **Seats** 70, Pr/dining room 24 **Children** Portions **Parking** 6, On street

St George's Hotel

Modern, Traditional

Patriotic Welsh cooking in a grand seafront hotel

☎ 01492 877544 & 862184
The Promenade LL30 2LG
e-mail: info@stgeorgeswales.co.uk
web: www.stgeorgeswales.co.uk
dir: A55, exit at Glan Conwy for Llandudno. A470 follow signs for seafront (distinctive tower identifies hotel)

Llandudno's prom is the place to be for splendid sunsets and sweeping views across the bay, and St George's Hotel

Bodysgallen Hall and Spa

LLANDUDNO   MAP 14 SH78

Modern British V NOTABLE WINE LIST

Classy country-house cooking in a splendid mansion

☎ 01492 584466
LL30 1RS
e-mail: info@bodysgallen.com
web: www.bodysgallen.com
dir: A55 junct 19, A470 towards Llandudno. Hotel 2m on right

There is inevitably a sense of occasion as you approach Bodysgallen: set in 200 acres of parkland, rose gardens and parterres, the 17th-century hall is the sort of country-house for which the word stately was coined. Little wonder, then, that the National Trust has taken over custodianship of the old girl since 2008. Take in the view, which sweeps across the skyline to Snowdonia, Conwy

Castle and the Isle of Anglesey, before pushing on indoors into a bygone era of antiques, oil paintings, dark oak panelling and stone mullioned windows. In such a setting, the vibe could end up a tad moribund, but the obliging, courteous and always on-the-ball staff banish any hint of starchy formality. And so to the food, which is a productive blend of traditional and gently-modernised country house ideas. Head chef Michael Cheetham has worked in Bodysgallen's kitchen for over a decade, and continues to deliver the light, fresh, seasonal cuisine that is the house's trademark. Virtuoso classic French technique is brought to bear on top-class Welsh materials, which could produce the likes of seared hand-dived scallops with curried cauliflower, raita and coriander, or poached breast and crisp leg of partridge with chicory, smoked bacon, and roasted chestnut granola. A sorbet - perhaps lemon and thyme - intervenes before main course, when roasted fillet of turbot might be matched simply with clams and saffron broth, or there could be a more robust idea involving poached fillet and

sticky cheek of Welsh beef supported by creamed celeriac, glazed onions, onion ash, and red wine shallot sauce. Dessert winds things up in the same elegant vein, perhaps presenting blood orange and ginger in the form of pannacotta, purée, crumb, sorbet and brittle. For something less formal, try the Bistro 1620 in the old coach house.

Chef Michael Cheetham **Owner** The National Trust **Times** 12.30-1.45/7-9.30 Closed Mon-Tue (winter), L Mon, D Mon (Tue in winter) **Prices** Prices not confirmed Service included **Wines** 6 bottles under £30, 8 by glass **Notes** Pre-theatre D available, Tasting menu on request, Sunday L, Vegetarian menu, Dress restrictions, Smart casual, no trainers or T-shirts **Seats** 60, Pr/dining room 40 **Children** Portions **Parking** 40

Save on Hotels. Book at theAA.com/hotel

CONWY – GWYNEDD 629 WALES

sits centre stage among a grand line-up of seafront buildings. The place is a timeless slice of Victorian wedding cake pomp, whose terrace is the place to be on balmy days, although the floor-to-ceiling windows of the eponymous restaurant allow you to enjoy the same views when the weather isn't playing ball. Balancing trends with tradition, the kitchen brings together excellent local ingredients with confident simplicity: crab, saffron and chilli risotto cake with aïoli is a typical starter, while main courses could see thyme-roasted rump of lamb served with creamed root vegetables and roasted garlic, or monkfish starring in a casserole with shallots, white beans, saffron and tomato. Desserts conclude in a similar vein, perhaps warm bara brith-and-butter pudding with almond sabayon and Penderyn ice cream.

Owner Anderbury Ltd **Times** 12-2.30/6.30-9.30 **Prices** Fixed L 2 course £15-£20, Fixed D 3 course £25-£35, Starter £5-£10, Main £18-£25, Dessert £5-£8, Service optional **Wines** 10 bottles over £30, 10 bottles under £30, 10 by glass **Notes** Pre-theatre menu available, Sunday L, Vegetarian available, Dress restrictions, Smart casual, Civ Wed 150 **Seats** 110, Pr/dining room 12 **Children** Portions, Menu **Parking** 36

St Tudno Hotel and Restaurant

@@ Modern British 🍸

Modern Welsh cooking overlooking the bay

☎ 01492 874411
The Promenade LL30 2LP
e-mail: sttudnohotel@btinternet.com
web: www.st-tudno.co.uk
dir: On Promenade towards pier, hotel opposite pier entrance

Sitting snugly in a prime location overlooking the sandy beaches and the bay, the hotel was fashioned from a former convalescent home in the 1970s. It retains something of the style of the seaside hotels of yesteryear, its Terrace Restaurant decorated with a mural depicting the tranquillity of Lake Como, for the enjoyment of those not positioned facing the tranquillity of Llandudno. The cooking is much more in the modern vein, and scores many hits with an unfussy, confident approach to quality Welsh ingredients. Start with seared Anglesey scallops and bacon, garnished with peas, broad beans and shallots, or butternut squash risotto with red onion and Pont Gâr cheese, as a prelude to roast tenderloin and braised cheek of pork with Lyonnaise potatoes, Cos lettuce, roasted apple purée and Madeira jus. A seafood array is generously comprised of plaice, crab, brandade and mussel chowder, with peas, tomato and samphire.

The whole show might close with a lemony version of baked Alaska decorated with raspberries, or with Welsh farmhouse cheeses and grape chutney.

Chef Andrew Foster **Owner** Mr Bland
Times 12.30-2/5.30-9.30 **Prices** Fixed L 2 course £22.50, Fixed D 3 course £27.50, Starter £7.95-£9.95, Main £19.95-£25.95, Dessert £5.95-£7.95, Service optional **Wines** 91 bottles over £30, 60 bottles under £30, 12 by glass **Notes** Pre-theatre menu available, Sunday L, Vegetarian available, Dress restrictions, Smart casual, no shorts, tracksuits or jeans, Civ Wed 70 **Seats** 60 **Children** Portions, Menu **Parking** 9, On street

---

LLANRWST   Map 14 SH86

Plas Meanan Country House

@@ Traditional British 🍸

Wonderful views and country-house cooking

☎ 01492 660232
Meanan LL26 0YR
e-mail: caroline.burt@btconnect.com
dir: On A470 between Glan Conwy & Llanrwst

At 300 feet above the Conwy Valley, this Edwardian manor gives stunning views over the river and Snowdonia National Park. The whole property has been traditionally decorated, and the restaurant, candlelit at night, is no exception with its country-house good looks. The kitchen knows its market and generally follows a traditional route, from herb-crusted scallops with smoked salmon and tartare sauce, or venison carpaccio with morels, parmesan and truffle cream, to pannacotta, or chocolate and orange mousse. Ingredients are chosen and cooked with care: pheasant casseroled with girolles, bacon, potatoes, and prunes, say, or roast fillet of sea bass well matched by its accompaniments of broad beans, peas, wild mushrooms, baby potatoes and vermouth sauce.

Chef Karmel Bougchiche **Owner** James & Caroline Burt **Times** 12-2.30/6-9 Closed Mon, D Sun **Prices** Fixed L 2 course fr £12.95, Starter £5.25-£6.75, Main £15.95-£22.95, Dessert £5.75, Service optional **Wines** 7 bottles over £30, 21 bottles under £30, 6 by glass **Notes** Afternoon tea £9.95, Sunday L fr £10.95, Vegetarian available, Dress restrictions, No shorts or vests, Civ Wed 100 **Seats** 30, Pr/dining room 40 **Children** Portions **Parking** 60

ABERSOCH   Map 14 SH32

Porth Tocyn Hotel

@@ Modern British 🍷 NOTABLE WINE LIST 🍸

Well-established country house with first-class cooking

☎ 01758 713303
Bwlch Tocyn LL53 7BU
e-mail: bookings@porthtocyn.fsnet.co.uk
web: www.porthtocynhotel.co.uk
dir: 2m S of Abersoch, through Sarn Bach & Bwlch Tocyn. Follow brown signs

Three generations of the Fletcher-Brewer family have run Porth Tocyn since 1948, converting a lowly terrace of lead miners' cottages and building the place up into the comfy, relaxed and unstuffy small-scale country house we see today. You can see why they put down such deep roots: who would want to move on from that spectacular view of Cardigan Bay with the peaks of Snowdonia rising in the distance? Inside, all is homely, relaxed and unstuffy, with a lived-in patina in its interconnecting antique-filled lounges. Vast picture windows in the smart restaurant capitalise on that remarkable panorama across the bay, while Louise Fletcher-Brewer oversees the kitchen team as it cooks up an assured repertoire that combines traditional values with more modern sensibilities. Carefully-sourced local, seasonal produce underpins it all, starting with the likes of pan-fried tournedos of hare with black pudding bonbons, sweet potato purée and port jus, followed by pan-fried, herb-crusted cannon of Welsh lamb teamed with carrot and cumin purée, green beans, toasted almonds, crushed potatoes and redcurrant and port jus. Finish with a comfort food classic - warm treacle tart with Chantilly cream.

Chef L Fletcher-Brewer, C Wild **Owner** The Fletcher-Brewer family **Times** 12.15-2.30/7.30-9 Closed mid Nov, 2 wks before Etr, occasional low season **Prices** Fixed D 3 course £44, Service included **Wines** 26 bottles over £30, 71 bottles under £30, 6 by glass **Notes** Light lunches Mon-Sat, Sunday L, Vegetarian available, Dress restrictions, Smart casual preferred **Seats** 50 **Children** Portions, Menu **Parking** 50

CAERNARFON   Map 14 SH46

Seiont Manor Hotel

◎◎◎ Modern British V ✪

Compelling cooking in farmhouse hotel

☎ 01286 673366
Llanrug LL55 2AQ
e-mail: seiontmanor@handpicked.co.uk
web: www.handpickedhotels.co.uk/seiontmanor
dir: From Bangor follow signs for Caernarfon. Leave
Caernarfon on A4086. Hotel 3m on left

This charming grey-silver stone building started life in
the 18th century as a working farmstead and is now a
prestigious country-house hotel. With Snowdonia National
Park nearby and Anglesey over the water, there's no
shortage of country pursuits; guests can even catch their
own fish in the hotel's lake (the River Seiont flows through
the 150-acre grounds) and get the chef to cook it. An
identifiably Welsh trait runs through the cooking, which is
chock-full of appealing ideas. Start with rabbit terrine
with watercress purée and pickled carrots, and proceed to
roast duck breast with sweet-and-sour walnut compôte,
glazed turnips and wilted kale. Good local materials are
handled deftly, with seafood given due consideration:
Jerusalem artichoke and clam chowder with laverbread,
for instance, then fillet of sea trout with a fricassee of
mussels, broccoli, potatoes and smoked bacon. Cheeses
are as local as can be, and interesting puddings might
include pineapple tarte Tatin with pink peppercorn ice
cream.

Owner Hand Picked Hotels **Times** 12-2/7-9.30
Prices Fixed L 2 course fr £10, Fixed D 3 course £37,
Service optional **Wines** 104 bottles over £30, 2 bottles
under £30, 18 by glass **Notes** Sun brunch 11am-4pm,
Vegetarian menu, Dress restrictions, Smart casual, Civ
Wed 100 **Seats** 55, Pr/dining room 30 **Children** Portions,
Menu **Parking** 60

CRICCIETH   Map 14 SH53

Bron Eifion Country House Hotel

◎ Modern British ✪

Elegant country-house hotel in stunning setting

☎ 01766 522385
LL52 0SA
e-mail: enquiries@broneifion.co.uk
dir: A497, between Porthmadog & Pwllheli

Set in lovely landscaped gardens with uplifting views
over Snowdonia and the coastline of the Lleyn Peninsula,
Bron Eifion is a small-scale Victorian country-house in
the classic vein. Inside, its period features have survived
unscathed, and include the impressive Great Hall with a
minstrels' gallery as a perfect spot for aperitifs. The
Orangery Restaurant offers panoramic views as a
backdrop to a repertoire of modern ideas. Driven by well-
sourced ingredients - top-class fish and shellfish from
nearby Pwllheli, and locally-reared beef and lamb - and
unfussy execution, the kitchen sends out a wide-ranging
menu that might start with Tyddyn Mawr pork belly

teamed with pan-seared scallops, caramelised apple
purée and rosemary jus, then proceed to fillet of Welsh
Black beef with blue cheese rösti, wilted spinach with
nutmeg, root vegetables and wild mushroom jus.

Chef Matthew Philips **Owner** John & Mary Heenan
Times 12-2/6.30-9 **Prices** Fixed L 2 course £11.95, Fixed
D 3 course fr £30, Starter £6.75-£9.95, Main
£16.95-£24.95, Dessert £6.95-£7.95, Service optional
Wines 6 by glass **Notes** Gourmand menu 8 course £65,
Sunday L, Vegetarian available, Civ Wed 150 **Seats** 150,
Pr/dining room 24 **Children** Portions, Menu **Parking** 50

DOLGELLAU   Map 14 SH71

Bwyty Mawddach Restaurant

◎ Modern British ✪

Confident modern British cooking in barn conversion

☎ 01341 424020
Pen Y Garnedd, Llanelltyd LL40 2TA
e-mail: enquiries@mawddach.com
dir: A470 Llanelltyd to A496 Barmouth, restaurant 0.2m
on left after primary school

Ifan Dunn has transformed an old granite barn on his
family farm into a restaurant. Now you might be picturing
a chintzy farmhouse bistro with flowery tablecloths and
walls adorned with farming implements, but nothing
could be further from the truth. The conversion is modern,
simple and clean lined, whilst respecting the nature of
the building, and the only cheese here is a fine selection
of Welsh favourites served with oat biscuits and home-
made pear and Bramley apple fruit cheese. Spread over
two floors, there are exposed beams in the vaulted ceiling
upstairs, slate floors on the ground floor, and a glass
frontage that gives views over the Mawddach Estuary and
Cader Idris (the second highest mountain in Wales). It
will come as no surprise in such a pastoral setting that
local and home-grown produce figures large on a menu
packed with well considered dishes. Pressed Bala pork to
start, perhaps, with grilled sourdough bread (home-
made), lemon and quick pickled onions, followed by pan-
fried salted hake with butter beans, slow-cooked tomato
and balsamic sauce and salsa verde, with hot vanilla rice
pudding or those cheeses to finish.

Chef Ifan Dunn **Owner** Roger, Will & Ifan Dunn
Times 12-2.30/6-9.30 Closed 26 Dec, 1 wk Jan, 1 wk Apr,
2 wks Nov, Mon-Tue, D Sun **Prices** Starter £5.50-£7, Main
£12-£19.50, Dessert £6-£6.50, Service optional **Wines** 8
bottles over £30, 19 bottles under £30, 7 by glass
Notes Fixed L only Sun £17.95-£19.95, Vegetarian
available, Civ Wed 100 **Seats** 75 **Children** Menu
Parking 20

Penmaenuchaf Hall Hotel

◎◎ Modern British ♦ NOTABLE WINE LIST

Modern British cooking in a Snowdonia garden room

☎ 01341 422129
Penmaenpool LL40 1YB
e-mail: relax@penhall.co.uk
web: www.penhall.co.uk
dir: From A470 take A493 (Tywyn/Fairbourne), entrance
1.5m on left by sign for Penmaenpool

The setting of this 1860s grey-stone mansion is a treat to
savour, embraced by the flanks of lofty Cader Idris, and
with the glorious Mawddach Estuary spread before its 21
wooded and landscaped acres. Inside are grand stone
fireplaces and all of the oak panelling you would expect of
a handsome Victorian pile; dining goes on in the
luminous conservatory-style Llygad yr Haul restaurant - a
tasteful setting floored with Welsh slate and romantically
candlelit at dinner. The kitchen has its heart in French
classicism, which it applies to pedigree Welsh produce to
deliver essentially modern British cooking driven by
flavour and seasonality, and presented with panache. A
duo of duck - boudin and smoked - is served with celeriac
remoulade and toasted brioche to get things off the
blocks, then an unmistakably modern approach at main
course stage sees a splendid slab of seared turbot paired
robustly with oxtail, braised baby gem lettuce and herb
oil. At the end, coffee pannacotta shares a plate with
chocolate brownies and Kahlua syrup.

Chef J Pilkington, T Reeve **Owner** Mark Watson, Lorraine
Fielding **Times** 12-2/7-9.30 **Prices** Fixed L 2 course fr
£16.95, Fixed D 3 course fr £25, Starter fr £8.50, Main fr
£25.50, Dessert fr £8.50, Service optional **Wines** 53
bottles over £30, 66 bottles under £30, 6 by glass
Notes Sunday L, Vegetarian available, Dress restrictions,
Smart casual, no jeans or T-shirts, Civ Wed 50 **Seats** 36,
Pr/dining room 20 **Children** Portions, Menu **Parking** 36

PORTHMADOG   Map 14 SH53

Royal Sportsman Hotel

◎◎ Modern British ✪

Innovative cooking in friendly old coaching inn

☎ 01766 512015
131 High St LL49 9HB
e-mail: enquiries@royalsportsman.co.uk
dir: At rdbt junct of A497 & A487

It might have been built as a coaching inn in 1862, but
this unpretentious family-run hotel has been thoroughly
updated. The stone and slate fireplaces are still in place
in the lounge and bar (great places for a pre-prandial
snifter) and renovation uncovered the original darkwood
floor in the restaurant, now done out in pastel shades.
The kitchen is committed to fresh Welsh produce and
displays a sense of adventure without straying too far off
the beaten track. Perfectly roast scallops are joined in a
starter by cauliflower three ways (couscous, purée and
tempura), and carpaccio comes with 'corned beef' and a
purée of celeriac and horseradish. Main courses can
seem a tad more traditional: fillet of beef with potato

terrine, kale and mushroom purée, roast partridge with a game faggot, swede and carrots. Desserts show a high level of skill and imagination: limoncello tart, say, or chocolate fondant, its richness cut by ginger and tangerine ice cream.

Chef Dan & Ian Owen **Owner** L Naudi **Times** 12-2.30/6-9 **Prices** Prices not confirmed Service optional **Wines** 11 by glass **Notes** Sunday L, Vegetarian available, Dress restrictions, Smart casual **Seats** 50 **Children** Portions, Menu **Parking** 17, On street

PORTMEIRION   Map 14 SH53

Castell Deudraeth

◉ Modern Welsh ◔

Clean and simple brasserie dishes in a Victorian Gothic pile

☎ 01766 772400
LL48 6ER
e-mail: castell@portmeirion-village.com
web: www.portmeirion-village.com
dir: Off A487 at Minffordd. Between Porthmadog & Penryndeudraeth

Sir Clough Williams-Ellis, designer of the eye-popping Welsh Disneyland that is Portmeirion, reckoned the Castell "the most imposing single building on the estate", and you can see what he meant. It's a textbook essay in Victorian pastiche, a battlemented Gothic castle suited to the era of wing-collars and bustles. Wood, slate and plain white walls hung with paintings by Sir Clough's granddaughter make a refreshing contemporary statement today, and the clean and simple brasserie dishes back it up. Neatly presented smoked duck breast accompanied by glazed cherries and hazelnuts is an assertive opener, to be followed by gently-cooked salmon with crushed potatoes flavoured with prawns and chives, as well as artichokes, in a simultaneously rich and sharp lemon sauce, or braised lamb shank in redcurrant jus. Pudding could be a soft-topped apple crumble with salted caramel ice cream. The menus are bilingual and the staff are fluent too.

Chef Mark Muscroft **Owner** Portmeirion Ltd
Times 12-2.30/6.30-9.30 Closed 7 Jan-7 Feb
Prices Prices not confirmed Service optional **Wines** 8 by glass **Notes** Vegetarian available **Seats** 80, Pr/dining room 40 **Children** Portions, Menu **Parking** 40

The Hotel Portmeirion

◉◉ Modern Welsh

Modern Welsh cooking and sea views

☎ 01766 770000 & 772324
Minffordd LL48 6ET
e-mail: hotel@portmeirion-village.com
web: www.portmeirion-village.com
dir: Off A487 at Minffordd

The hotel is at the foot of the unique Italianate village, close to the shore, looking over the estuary to Snowdonia beyond. It's a striking place, filled with antiques and artwork, the curvilinear restaurant, sharing that sea view, decorated in shades of blue and green. Dishes are well executed and nicely presented without being too flashy. Pan-fried lamb's kidneys appear as a starter with bacon, garlic mash and rich Madeira sauce, and main courses could see pan-fried turbot served up with a cannelloni of crab and an orange and cardamom sauce, or protein-rich lamb cutlets, shoulder and liver with braised potatoes. Finish with an excellent citrus financier with accompanying caramelised blood oranges and crème fraîche sorbet.

Times 12-2.30/6.30-9.30 Closed 2 wks Nov

PWLLHELI   Map 14 SH33

Plas Bodegroes

◉◉ Modern British ◔

First-rate cooking in a small-scale country house

☎ 01758 612363
Nefyn Rd LL53 5TH
e-mail: gunna@bodegroes.co.uk
dir: On A497, 1m W of Pwllheli

Husband and wife Chris and Gunna Chown have been running Plas Bodegroes as a restaurant with rooms since 1986. It's easy to see why the business has been going strong for so long: the white-painted Georgian manor is full of charm and surrounded by stunning gardens brimming with beautiful flowers. Add to that some luxuriously furnished accommodation, a friendly vibe, and top-notch cooking from Chris in the modern but elegant restaurant decorated with colourful artworks, and all the bases are covered. Chris diligently sources ingredients for his modern British menus from local suppliers, with some herbs, fruits and vegetables picked fresh from the garden, and everything (including the excellent breads) is made in-house. Flavour combinations are well-considered, as in a starter of crispy smoked pork cheek with black pudding, Scotch egg and spiced lentil dressing. Fabulous Welsh mountain lamb turns up in a main-course roast rump with slow-cooked shoulder cake, pea sausage and mint jus, and you can bet that the grilled fillet of hake (on a bed of spinach with tomato and garlic casserole) will be sustainably sourced. For dessert it could be a toss up between lemon curd parfait with Eton Mess, or plum tart with plum ripple ice cream.

Chef Chris Chown, Hugh Bracegirdle **Owner** Mr C & Mrs G Chown **Times** 12.30-2.30/7-9.30 Closed Dec-Feb, Mon, L Tue-Sat, D Sun **Prices** Prices not confirmed Service optional **Wines** 8 by glass **Notes** Sunday L, Vegetarian available **Seats** 40, Pr/dining room 24 **Parking** 20

MONMOUTHSHIRE

ABERGAVENNY   Map 9 SO21

Angel Hotel

◉ Modern, Traditional ◔

Old coaching inn with broadly appealing menu

☎ 01873 857121
15 Cross St NP7 5EN
e-mail: mail@angelabergavenny.com
web: www.angelabergavenny.com
dir: From A40 & A465 junct follow town centre signs, S of Abergavenny, past rail & bus stations

In its heyday a staging post on the Fishguard to London route, this Georgian hotel is still a refuge for travellers, although nowadays a good proportion of its patrons will have come here to dine. Eating in the popular bar is an option, while the menu in the restaurant, with its well-spaced neat tables under the chandeliers, follows a modern brasserie format - even down to moules et frites. Thai fishcake with spicy mayonnaise, followed by seared scallops with chorizo, gnocchi and red pepper sauce, and steak sandwich with chips show the diversity on offer, while desserts can stretch to pannacotta with grilled pineapple, or crème brûlée.

Chef Wesley Hammond **Owner** Caradog Hotels Ltd
Times 12-2.30/7-10 Closed 25 Dec, D 24-30 Dec
Prices Fixed L 2 course fr £25, Fixed D 3 course fr £25, Starter £5.90-£12.80, Main £11.90-£25, Dessert £4.90-£6.80, Service optional **Wines** 47 bottles over £30, 47 bottles under £30, 10 by glass **Notes** Pre-theatre menu 2 course & coffee £15, Sunday L, Vegetarian available, Civ Wed 120 **Seats** 80, Pr/dining room 120 **Children** Portions, Menu **Parking** 30

ABERGAVENNY *continued*

The Foxhunter

◉◉ Modern British ⬇ NOTABLE WINE LIST ✋

Carefully-sourced ingredients cooked with flair

☎ 01873 881101
Nantyderry NP7 9DN
e-mail: info@thefoxhunter.com
dir: Just off A4042 between Usk & Abergavenny

Matt Tebbutt - he off the telly - practices what he preaches at his pub in a quiet hamlet on the fringes of the Brecon Beacons. It's a one-time stationmaster's house named in honour of an Olympic gold-medal winning horse, and it's been done out with a good deal of charm with wooden and Welsh stone floors, food-related paintings on cream walls, gleaming glassware on smart clothed tables, and a log fire for the chillier months. Tebbutt's food is modern inasmuch as it pays attention to seasonality, provenance (he's an advocate of foraging, too) and flavour, and his menus are a joy to behold. Sautéed scallops come with crisp pork belly, shallot purée and sherry caramel, for example, or there might be a game terrine with toasted brioche and onion jam. This is hearty and unpretentious stuff and it looks good on the plate. Main-course marinated leg of lamb is beautifully tender and served nicely pink, with Jansson's temptation (a Scandinavian potato dish) and purple sprouting broccoli. Red-wine-poached pear and almond Bakewell tart with crème fraîche brings up the rear.

Chef Matt Tebbutt **Owner** Lisa & Matt Tebbutt
Times 12-2.30/7-9.30 Closed Xmas, 1 Jan, BHs, Mon, D Sun **Prices** Fixed L 2 course fr £22.95, Starter £7.25-£10.95, Main £16.50-£22.50, Dessert £5.95-£7.25, Service optional, Groups min 8 service 10% **Wines** 19 bottles over £30, 38 bottles under £30, 5 by glass **Notes** Foraging trip and wild food lunch, Sunday L £23.95-£28.95, Vegetarian available **Seats** 40, Pr/dining room 30 **Children** Portions **Parking** 25

The Hardwick

◉◉ Modern British ⬇ NOTABLE WINE LIST

Compelling modern cooking in revamped country pub

☎ 01873 854220
Old Raglan Rd NP7 9AA
e-mail: info@thehardwick.co.uk

Stephen Terry has set out his stall in a former pub, now extended and with an unpretentious, rustic-chic look. His starting point is his suppliers, all duly name-checked on the menu, and his commitment to using fresh ingredients, along with his love for his craft, shows in every dish. Moist, loosely structured duck liver hash is a great match for confit leg, served with a fried duck egg and leaves in mustardy dressing to start. An alternative might be roast scallops with black pudding, potato purée, and an effective foil of brown butter with shallots, capers and lemon. The same imaginative and confident touch is given to main courses: three ways with rabbit, for instance (poached loin, faggots and burger, with deep-fried polenta and rocket), and pan-fried hake fillet with

chorizo, saffron risotto cake, peas and broad beans. Puddings have a high wow factor: perhaps a Kilner jar of lemon crunch - layers of curd, custard, biscuit and caramel topped with meringue.

Times 12-3/6.30-10 Closed 25 Dec, D Sun Jan-Etr

Llansantffraed Court Hotel

◉◉ Modern British ⬇ NOTABLE WINE LIST ✋

Good views and accomplished cooking

☎ 01873 840678
Old Raglan Rd, Llanvihangel Gobion, Clytha NP7 9BA
e-mail: reception@llch.co.uk
web: www.llch.co.uk
dir: M4 junct 24/A449 to Raglan. At rdbt take last exit to Clytha. Hotel on right in 4.5m

The wild beauty of the Brecon Beacons makes a memorable backdrop to this elegant Georgian mansion in 20 acres of landscaped grounds on the edge of the Usk Valley. Plushly-decorated lounges and blazing log fires in winter provide the requisite country-house comforts within, and friendly, unobtrusive staff add to the sense of luxury. The restaurant, in the oldest part of the house, goes for a surprisingly contemporary contrast, with its high-backed chairs, and church candles on smartly-laid tables beneath a black-beamed ceiling. The kitchen is ideally placed to access prime materials from Monmouthshire's army of small artisan producers, which are put to effective use in unfussy dishes prepared with good technical skill. Expect well-considered combinations delivered in good-looking modern presentations - perhaps air-dried Welsh Longhorn beef teamed with shaved Caerphilly cheese, rocket and lemon, followed by roast loin and rib of local lamb with spring greens, creamed potato and cawl jus, or if you're in the mood for fish, maybe fillet of sea bream partnered with squid, lime and chilli tagliatelle, roast carrots and fennel and crushed potatoes. Round it off with milk chocolate and almond brownie with Baileys ice cream.

Chef Mike Hendry **Owner** Mike Morgan **Times** 12-2/7-9 **Prices** Fixed L 2 course £15, Fixed D 3 course £27.50-£38, Tasting menu £45-£70, Starter £6.50-£12, Main £15-£24, Dessert £6-£9, Service optional **Wines** 94 by glass **Notes** Tasting menu 7 course with matched wines, Sunday L, Vegetarian available **Seats** 50, Pr/dining room 35 **Children** Portions, Menu **Parking** 300

Restaurant 1861

◉◉ Modern British **V** ✋

Charming country setting and confident cooking

☎ 0845 388 1861 & 01873 821297
Cross Ash NP7 8PB
web: www.18-61.co.uk
dir: On B4521, 9m from Abergavenny, 15m from Ross-on-Wye, on outskirts of Cross Ash

Under the stewardship of Simon and Kate King, this restaurant in the hamlet of Cross Ash near Abergavenny has become a force to be reckoned with on the Monmouthshire foodie scene. The Victorian building (no prizes for guessing in what year it was built) was once a pub, and has been thoroughly made over with a clean-lined, gently contemporary look involving black beams, stone walls, and Welsh slate place mats on bare wooden tables. Simon's cooking certainly makes an impact as he brings his sound classical technique to bear on pedigree local ingredients. Tortellini of braised lamb could arrive with black olives and capers, or there might be a duo of smoked and confit goose with sweet-and-sour cherries to start. Main courses again give those quality meats and fish star billing, whether in fricassée of pheasant with grain mustard, or fillet of brill poached in red wine, while honey and lavender pannacotta with mulled pear makes a splendid finale.

Chef Simon King **Owner** Simon & Kate King
Times 12-2/7-9 Closed 1st 2 wks Jan, Mon, D Sun
Prices Fixed L 2 course £19, Fixed D 3 course £34, Tasting menu £49.50, Starter £8-£13.50, Main £18-£24, Dessert £7-£8.50, Service optional **Wines** 30 bottles over £30, 32 bottles under £30, 7 by glass **Notes** Tasting menu 7 course, Sunday L, Vegetarian menu **Seats** 40 **Children** Portions **Parking** 20

Walnut Tree Inn

◉◉◉ *– see opposite*

Save on Hotels. Book at **theAA.com/hotel**

MONMOUTHSHIRE 633 WALES

Walnut Tree Inn

ABERGAVENNY MAP 9 SO21

Modern British ◗NOTABLE WINE LIST

Blissfully unfussy and focused cooking by a culinary mastermind

☎ 01873 852797
Llandewi Skirrid NP7 8AW
e-mail: mail@thewalnuttreeinn.com
web: www.thewalnuttreeinn.com
dir: 3m NE of Abergavenny on B4521

The simple white-painted inn in a hamlet not far from Abergavenny has been known for excellent food for over 50 years, and looks set to be a firm fixture on the UK's foodie map as long as Shaun Hill, one of the heroes of the modern British cooking scene, is running the show. The place had a period in the doldrums after renowned chef Franco Taruschio's 30-year reign came to an end, but Hill stepped into the breach and pulled the inn up by its bootstraps after moving on from The Merchant House in Ludlow in 2005, and he's still here most days, hands-on at the stoves with a crack brigade of hand-picked chefs. Hill has always gone his own way, resisting ephemeral culinary fads and fashions; a quick glance at the restaurant's straight-talking website shows that this is a man who has no truck with pretentions or cheffy grandstanding. The ambience is similarly unaffected: around 20 simply-laid tables are set against plain walls and serviced by a friendly team without

any intrusive hovering or faffing around to top up glasses. The cooking echoes Hill's unpretentious style at The Merchant House, pulling together the finest seasonal ingredients and turning it all into deceptively straightforward dishes that belie the immense technical skills needed to coax every molecule of flavour from the raw materials. From veal sweetbreads with pig's head cromesquis to spätzle with venison stew, there is ample choice from the robust end of the spectrum, but for a lighter touch, look for something like a silky bourride of sea bass and John Dory, or super-fresh turbot with blood orange and hollandaise sauce. Desserts range from muscat crème caramel with Agen prunes to a first-class baked chocolate mousse with honey ice cream. There is no attempt to soft talk you into trading up your wine choice, although the compact list is full of quality and interest.

Chef Shaun Hill **Owner** Shaun Hill, William Griffiths **Times** 12-2.30/7-10 Closed 1 wk Xmas, Sun-Mon **Prices** Fixed D 3 course £27.50, Starter £8-£14, Main £15-£25, Dessert £8, Service optional **Wines** 50 bottles over £30, 40 bottles under £30, 8 by glass **Notes** Vegetarian available **Seats** 70, Pr/dining room 26 **Children** Portions, Menu **Parking** 30

CHEPSTOW
Map 4 ST59

St Pierre, A Marriott Hotel & Country Club

◉ Modern British

Classic cooking in upscale 14th-century manor

☎ 01291 625261
St Pierre Park NP16 6YA
e-mail: mhrs.cwigs.frontdesk@marriotthotels.com
web: www.marriottstpierre.co.uk
dir: M48 junct 2, A466 for Chepstow. At next rdbt 1st exit signed Caerwent A48. Hotel approx 2m on left

The upmarket Marriott St Pierre Hotel does country-house splendour with knobs on, but then it does have a head start: it is an authentic 14th-century manor with turrets and battlements set in 400 acres of rolling South Wales hill country near Chepstow. That means enough space for its own golf course, so the game is naturally high on the agenda for many guests, but there's also the full complement of leisure and fitness facilities you'd expect in a hotel of this standing. In keeping with the hotel's blend of ancient and modern, Morgan's Restaurant works a clean-lined contemporary look that sits well with its simple, please-all modern repertoire. Mussels in a white wine and garlic sauce with laverbread might start you off, followed by a taster plate of Welsh lamb, or fillet of salmon with hollandaise sauce. Desserts are well-made versions of straightforward classics like bread-and-butter pudding, chocolate tart with vanilla ice cream, or cheesecake.

Chef Darren Pryer **Owner** Marriott Hotels **Times** 1-3/7-10 **Prices** Prices not confirmed Service optional **Wines** 11 by glass **Notes** Sunday L, Vegetarian available, Dress restrictions, smart casual **Seats** 120, Pr/dining room 40 **Children** Portions, Menu **Parking** 440

LLANGYBI
Map 9 ST39

The White Hart Village Inn

◉◉ Modern British ☺

Impressive gastro-pub cooking in a smart village inn

☎ 01633 450258 & 07748 114838
Old Usk Rd NP15 1NP
e-mail: enquiries@thewhitehartvillageinn.com
dir: M4 junct 25 onto B4596 Caerleon road, through town centre on High St, straight over rdbt onto Usk Rd continue to Llangybi

Rich in history and atmosphere, the handsomely revamped 16th-century White Hart is the hub of Llangybi and stands close to the Roman settlement of Caerleon in the beautiful Usk Valley. The traditional bar has low-slung windows, black-painted beams and a blazing fire in the grand inglenook fireplace, while the more contemporary dining areas are the setting for some top-notch gastro-pub food. Regional produce is supplemented by fish deliveries from Brixham, and it all finds its way on to the enticing modern British menus and daily-changing blackboards. Cooking is accurate with good, well-

balanced flavours and presentation is simple with no flowery garnishes. Well-seasoned leek and potato soup may get the ball rolling, followed by a moist, well-cooked bream served on an oblong piece of slate with crushed parsnip, sweet-tasting beetroot and orange chicory. A light apple trifle served with refreshing cider granité rounds off the meal nicely. The individual mini-loaves of bread are spot-on - great texture and flavour.

Chef Adam & Liam Whittle **Owner** Michael Bates **Times** 12-3/6-10 Closed Mon (ex BHs), D Sun **Prices** Fixed L 2 course £14.95-£18.50, Fixed D 3 course £18.95, Tasting menu £45, Starter £5.95-£9.50, Main £12.85-£22, Dessert £5.50-£8.50, Service optional **Wines** 4 bottles over £30, 25 bottles under £30, 13 by glass **Notes** Fixed D Tue-Thu, Tasting menu 6 course Tue-Sat, Sunday L, Vegetarian available **Seats** 46, Pr/dining room 36 **Children** Portions, Menu **Parking** 30

MONMOUTH
Map 10 SO51

Bistro Prego

◉ Modern Italian **NEW** ☺

Buzzy bistro with an Italian edge

☎ 01600 712600
7 Church St NP25 3BX
e-mail: enquiries@pregomonmouth.co.uk
dir: Travelling N A40 at lights left turn, T-junct left turn, 2nd right, hotel at rear of car park

This welcoming little café and bistro in the heart of Monmouth's old town is simple in style but big on charm. Prego hums with a constant bustle of local fans won over by its all-day approach, serving everything from light snacks to lunch - perhaps local hare braised in red wine served simply with mashed potato and roasted balsamic onions - through to a more involved evening bistro offering. The food here is all about sourcing top-class local ingredients which are brought together without undue fuss or complicated flim-flam. As you may have spotted in the name, a strongly Italophile vein courses through it all: the menu skips with flair and imagination from a starter of home-made tagliatelle with a rich ragù of wild boar and mushrooms, to rump of Welsh lamb with buttered Savoy cabbage and smoked bacon. For pudding, you can't go wrong with the home-made ice creams, or there might be chocolate and walnut torta Caprese with crème fraîche.

Chef Stephen Robbins **Owner** Stephen Robbins, Tom David, Sue Howell **Times** 12-2.30/6.30-9.30 Closed 24-26 & 31 Dec, 1 Jan **Prices** Starter £4-£8, Main £8-£22.50, Dessert £4-£6, Service optional **Wines** 14 bottles over £30, 31 bottles under £30, 15 by glass **Notes** Pre-theatre from 6pm, Sunday L £10.50-£12.50, Vegetarian available **Seats** 40 **Children** Portions **Parking** Pay & display at rear of restaurant

The Inn at Penallt

◉ Modern British ☺

Straightforward, honest cooking in the Wye Valley

☎ 01600 772765
Penallt NP25 4SE
e-mail: enquiries@theinnatpenallt.co.uk
web: www.theinnatpenallt.co.uk

Slate floors, ceiling beams, lots of wooden furniture, a fireplace in the bar and a jolly atmosphere throughout - all nicely traditional and reassuring in a 17th-century inn in a tiny village in the Wye Valley. The food is the draw here, its appeal due to good-quality materials treated straightforwardly, so belly pork is breadcrumbed, fried and served with herby leaf salad and mustard dressing, and ham is roasted in honey and served with chips, a duck egg and caper mayonnaise. Fish gets a fair showing - perhaps accurately grilled sea bass fillet, from Anglesey, with simple beurre blanc, buttery new potatoes and a warm salad of asparagus and curly endive - and well-presented desserts might extend to chocolate pannacotta spiked with rosemary accompanied by stewed plums.

Chef Peter Hulsmann **Owner** Andrew & Jackie Murphy **Times** 12-2.30/6-9 Closed Mon, L Tue **Prices** Fixed L 2 course £15.95, Starter £5.95-£11.95, Main £14.95-£20.95, Dessert £6.45, Service optional **Wines** 9 by glass **Notes** Wed evening meal & drink £9.95, Sunday L £14.95-£22.95, Vegetarian available **Seats** 28, Pr/dining room 28 **Children** Portions, Menu **Parking** 26

RAGLAN
Map 9 SO40

The Beaufort Raglan Coaching Inn & Brasserie

◉ Modern British ☺

Historic Welsh Marches inn with modern food

☎ 01291 690412
High St NP15 2DY
e-mail: enquiries@beaufortraglan.co.uk
web: www.beaufortraglan.co.uk
dir: M4 junct 24 (Newport/Abergavenny), north on A449 to junct with A40, 1 min from turning to Abergavenny

With over 400 years of history behind it, The Beaufort Raglan stands proud in the village, famed for its rather splendid 15th-century castle. The old coaching inn presents a traditional façade to the world, but there's been a bit of a contemporary makeover within, not least in the self-styled Brasserie with its tones of cappuccino, cream and cerise, and designer Lloyd loom chairs at unclothed darkwood tables. There is still plenty of period character on show, though, and a good deal of local ingredients on the menu, which is backed up by daily specials and shows clear-headed, unpretentious thinking. There are steaks cooked on the chargrill, or the likes of sea bass with fennel, asparagus, sauté potatoes and lemon butter sauce among main courses. Start with a goats' cheese and beetroot salad, and finish with a baked egg custard with nutmeg ice cream.

Save on Hotels. Book at **theAA.com/hotel**

MONMOUTHSHIRE 635 **WALES**

Chef Will Harmer, Eliot Lewis **Owner** Eliot & Jana Lewis **Times** 12-3/6-10 Closed 25 Dec **Prices** Fixed L 2 course £12.95, Service optional **Wines** 26 bottles over £30, 45 bottles under £30, 12 by glass **Notes** Sunday L £16.50-£19.50, Vegetarian available **Seats** 60, Pr/dining room 26 **Children** Menu **Parking** 30

ROCKFIELD   Map 9 S041

The Stonemill & Steppes Farm Cottages

⊛⊛ Modern British, International ☺

Clearly-focused cooking in a 16th-century cider mill

☎ 01600 716273

NP25 5SW

e-mail: enquiries@thestonemill.co.uk

dir: A48 to Monmouth, B4233 to Rockfield. 2.6m from Monmouth town centre

The 16th-century mill's grinding stone remains in the centre of the room as a reminder of the old building's former working life. There's plenty of toil going on in the kitchen today, mind you, to deliver some well-crafted Modern British food to the hungry 21st-century customer. Oak-timbered ceilings and simple wooden tables keep things rustic and relaxed, and there's a good showing of local ingredients to remind you where you are. Start, perhaps, with roasted butternut squash soup perked up with white truffle oil and parmesan and sage crostini, before moving on to slow-cooked shoulder of Raglan lamb with a carrot and swede scone, buttered curly kale and confit garlic. Whole baked sea bass with wild mushrooms is one way to go with seafood, and, for dessert, apple and pear tart with cinnamon ice cream competes with the excellent slate of cheeses from Wales and the Borders, including the likes of Black Bomber and Perl Las (you could have both, of course).

Chef Carl Hammett, Jordan Simons **Owner** Mrs M L Decloedt **Times** 12-2/6-9 Closed 25-26 Dec, 2 wks Jan, Mon, D Sun **Prices** Fixed L 2 course £13.95, Fixed D 3 course £19.95, Starter £6.50-£8.75, Main £15.95-£24.50, Dessert fr £5.95, Service optional **Wines** 10 bottles over £30, 36 bottles under £30, 7 by glass **Notes** Sunday L, Vegetarian available, Civ Wed 120 **Seats** 56, Pr/dining room 12 **Children** Portions **Parking** 40

SKENFRITH   Map 9 S042

The Bell at Skenfrith

⊛⊛ Modern British ▲NOTABLE WINE LIST ☺

Creative cookery in an old coaching inn

☎ 01600 750235

NP7 8UH

e-mail: enquiries@skenfrith.co.uk

web: www.skenfrith.co.uk

dir: N of Monmouth on A466 for 4m. Left on B4521 towards Abergavenny, 3m on left

The Bell is a white-fronted 17th-century coaching inn in the middle of nowhere, 'nowhere' in this case being the

lustrous Monnow Valley. Sensitive refurbishment has eased it into the present day, lending the place the feel of a modern restaurant with rooms. Pastel yellow walls hung with many pictures, slender beams and chunky rustic furniture set the tone, and the kitchen naturally draws on the local produce of the abundant surrounding countryside (and The Bell garden) for some colourful, artfully presented creations. Main ingredients done in variations are very 'now', and might extend to three ways with garden beetroot, served with orange dressing and a goats' cheese bonbon. Dishes are painstakingly worked throughout, wrapping up a fillet of turbot in courgette ribbons alongside tarragon-crusted mussels, for example, or producing fillet and belly of pork with fantastic crackling and a breadcrumbed ball of champ. Neat spins on homely desserts include spiced apple trifle with cider granita and fennel-seed doughnuts.

Chef Kieran Gough **Owner** Mr & Mrs W Hutchings **Times** 12-2.30/7-9.30 Closed Tue (Nov-Mar) **Prices** Fixed L 2 course £18, Starter £6-£11, Main £15-£21.50, Dessert £7-£8.50, Service optional **Wines** 47 bottles over £30, 44 bottles under £30, 12 by glass **Notes** Sunday L £22-£26, Vegetarian available, Dress restrictions, Smart casual **Seats** 60, Pr/dining room 40 **Children** Portions, Menu **Parking** 35

USK   Map 9 S030

Newbridge on Usk

⊛⊛ Traditional British

Idyllic riverside setting for contemporary country inn fare

☎ 01633 451000 & 410262

Tredunnock NP15 1LY

e-mail: newbridgeonusk@celtic-manor.com

web: www.newbridgeonusk.co.uk

dir: A449 to Usk exit through town & turn left after bridge through Llangibby. After approx 1m Cwrt Bleddyn Hotel on right, turn left opposite hotel up lane. Drive through village of Tredunnock, down hill, inn on banks of River Usk

In an exceptionally tranquil spot at a bend in the River Usk, this charming inn is owned by the nearby Celtic Manor hotel. The idyllic location makes it a popular haunt for those who want to explore the stunning countryside or enjoy a spot of fishing. The two-tiered beamed dining room makes the most of its location with window tables overlooking the river and bridge, while the menu of updated country inn fare offers plenty to appeal. Rare seared tuna 'Niçoise-style' with crispy gem lettuce, soft

boiled hen's egg, heritage tomatoes, split green beans, black anchovies and shaved red radish is crisp, fresh and delightfully presented, while Welsh Black ox cheek and Penclawdd mussels, Savoy cabbage, Welsh farmed mushrooms and creamed potatoes utilises the best of the local larder. Save room for an indulgent parkin, butterscotch sauce, rum and raisin ice cream, and gingersnap tuile. And if you like your Sunday lunch accompanied by the sounds of live jazz and swing, Newbridge will delight.

Times 12-2.30/7-10

Raglan Arms

⊛ Modern British ☺

Unpretentious atmosphere and good, honest food

☎ 01291 690800

Llandenny NP15 1DL

e-mail: theraglanarms@gmail.com

dir: M4 junct 24. Turn off A449 towards Usk, then immediately right towards Llandenny

This flint-built pub traded up from a local boozer to lure in diners with a winning combo of great locally-sourced food and a relaxed, informal ambience. It is in a peaceful Monmouthshire village, and if you're into the pubby side of things, there's a cosy feel to the flagstoned bar serving well-kept real ales, but it's clear that culinary matters are what drives the place these days, the action focused in the conservatory extension. Taking its spiritual inspiration from France and Italy, and its ingredients from the surrounding area, the kitchen delivers snappy crowd-pleasers such as traditional Welsh lamb broth 'cawl', or local goose rillettes with home-made chutney to start, then mains such as locally-farmed pork and smoked paprika meatballs in tomato sauce with bucatini and Manchego cheese. Finish with Valrhona chocolate and orange fool.

Chef Giles A Cunliffe **Owner** Giles A Cunliffe **Times** 12-2.30/7-9.30 Closed 25-26 Dec, Mon, D Sun **Prices** Starter £5.50-£8, Main £10.50-£20, Dessert £4.50-£7, Service optional **Wines** 15 bottles over £30, 45 bottles under £30, 12 by glass **Notes** Sunday L £12-£24, Vegetarian available **Seats** 65 **Children** Portions **Parking** 20

USK *continued*

The Three Salmons Hotel

◉◉ Modern Welsh

Smart cooking in a revamped old coaching inn

☎ 01291 672133
Bridge St NP15 1RY
e-mail: general@threesalmons.co.uk
dir: M4 junct 24/A449, 1st exit signed Usk. On entering town hotel on main road

This old coaching inn has served the community and weary travellers for over 300 years, yet while the Grade II listed building presents a traditional face to the world, inside it has moved with the times (albeit without scaring the horses). The restaurant combines the character of the old building with gently contemporary fixtures and fittings, or you could choose to eat in the less formal bar. It's a flexible kind of place. The menu shows evident passion for the produce of this area, some of which is grown in the hotel's own garden, and there is a welcome egalitarian approach and lack of pretension, too. A starter of smoked eel ravioli with pickled carrot, velouté and fennel seed wafer shows this to be a kitchen of ambition and confidence, but you might opt to follow that with a burger with smoked cheese and chips. Breast of duck with vanilla mash, braised red cabbage and parsnip purée is another way to go, and for dessert, treacle tart with gingerbread ice cream hits the spot.

Times 12-2.30/6.30-9.30

NEWPORT

NEWPORT   Map 9 ST38

Le Patio at the Manor House

◉ Modern French ✿

French country cooking in a Welsh golf resort

☎ 01633 413000
The Celtic Manor Resort, The Manor House, Coldra Woods NP18 1HQ
e-mail: bookings@celtic-manor.com
web: www.celtic-manor.com
dir: M4 junct 24, B4237 towards Newport. Hotel 1st on right

If you're splashing out on a golfing week at the sprawling Celtic Manor Resort, you can ring the changes by eating in a different venue every day you're there. Tucked away in the historic part of the old manor house, Le Patio is the

place to head for when you need a hit of hearty French country cooking, served in an informal glass-roofed extension done out with bare blond-wood tables and wicker seats. Starters are as simple as onion soup with croûtons and gruyère, or confit pork terrine with almonds, herbs and sweet garlic served with plum and ginger chutney and onion bread, while mains take in regional classics such as beef bourguignon with mash, bouillabaisse with rouille and toasted garlic bread, and Alsatian chicken slow-cooked in Riesling with cream, lardons, mushrooms and served with sweet potato purée. End with cinnamon and apple bavarois with apple sorbet.

Chef Mikael le Cuziat **Owner** Celtic Manor Resort **Times** 6.30-10 Closed L all week **Prices** Prices not confirmed Service optional **Wines** 15 bottles over £30, 34 bottles under £30, 8 by glass **Notes** Sunday L, Vegetarian available, Civ Wed 100 **Seats** 65, Pr/dining room 20 **Children** Portions, Menu **Parking** 400

Rafters

◉ Modern British ✿

Grill classics at the 19th hole

☎ 01633 413000
The Celtic Manor Resort, Coldra Woods NP18 1HQ
e-mail: bookings@celtic-manor.com
web: www.celtic-manor.com
dir: M4 junct 24, B4237 towards Newport. Hotel 1st on right

The upmarket golf-centric Celtic Manor Resort offers a huge spread of eating venues, but golfers who fancy eating without having to miss the action can get the best of both worlds in Rafters grill, where the Ryder Cup course fills the view outside the window. The restaurant is striking in its own right, with soaring cedar wood beams climbing high to the ceiling, and a smart contemporary look. The kitchen's main culinary building blocks come from Welsh suppliers, but also cast the net a bit wider for starters such as Severn and Wye smoked salmon with Sakura cress and honey, mustard and dill sauce. At the heart of things is prime Welsh beef - not the national rugby team, but rib-eye, sirloin, fillet, or - pushing the boat out - a Chateaubriand for two, served with triple-cooked chips, watercress and classic sauces. End with crème brûlée with cardamom-spiced oranges, or an updated take on sherry trifle.

Chef Simon Searle **Owner** Celtic Manor Resort **Times** 12-2.30/6-10 Closed D Mon-Wed (Oct-Mar) **Prices** Fixed L 2 course fr £10.95, Starter £5.50-£11.50, Main £14.50-£36.50, Dessert £5.25-£9.25, Service

optional **Wines** 6 by glass **Notes** Sunday L £18.50-£22.50, Vegetarian available, Dress restrictions, Smart casual, no trainers or flip-flops, Civ Wed 100 **Seats** 80, Pr/dining room 96 **Children** Portions **Parking** 115

Terry M at The Celtic Manor Resort

◉◉◉ – *see opposite*

PEMBROKESHIRE

HAVERFORDWEST   Map 8 SM91

Wolfscastle Country Hotel

◉ Modern British ✿

Appealing menu in peaceful country hotel

☎ 01437 741225
Wolf's Castle SA62 5LZ
e-mail: info@wolfscastle.com
web: www.wolfscastle.com
dir: From Haverfordwest take A40 towards Fishguard. Hotel in centre of Wolf's Castle

The restaurant of this ancient stone-built hotel now sports a spiffy new brasserie look, with more space for diners and a bright and airy ambience. The place sits on a promontory above the confluence of two rivers in lush Pembrokeshire countryside, and is a hit locally for weddings and meetings, as well as its straightforward food based on good Welsh produce. The kitchen plays a straight bat, delivering an unfussy repertoire spiced up with a few global influences here and there. The Wales-meets-Asia style might start with the likes of pan-fried local sea bass with a laverbread, chilli, ginger and basil sauce, while mains could bring pan-fried venison fillet with parsnip rösti, foie gras, smoked bacon and porcini mushrooms sauce. Finish with iced coffee and Tia Maria parfait with coffee syrup, or revert to local mode with a bara brith pain perdu served with roasted plums and maple syrup ice cream.

Chef Tom Simmons **Owner** Mr A Stirling **Times** 12-2/6.30-9 Closed 24-26 Dec **Prices** Fixed L 2 course £11-£14, Starter £5.95-£8.50, Main £10.95-£23.95, Dessert £5.50-£6.95, Service optional **Wines** 6 bottles over £30, 39 bottles under £30, 14 by glass **Notes** Sunday L £10.50-£17.50, Vegetarian available **Seats** 55, Pr/dining room 32 **Children** Portions, Menu **Parking** 75

NARBERTH　　　　　Map 8 SN11

The Grove

 Modern British 🍷NOTABLE WINE LIST 🐾

Elegant restaurant with rooms making the most of its kitchen garden

☎ 01834 860915
Molleston SA67 8BX
e-mail: info@thegrove-narberth.co.uk
web: www.thegrove-narberth.co.uk
dir: From A40, take A478 to Narberth. Continue past castle & Herons Brook, turn right bottom of hill

There's quite a history to the house, with the final architectural tinkering taking place in the 1870s, but all you really need to know is that it is really beautiful. And the fact it is surrounded by 24 acres of lush green gently rolling countryside and flower gardens only adds to its impact. It makes an impression on the inside, too, with a touch of individuality and character to the glorious period features of the house. The restaurant has plenty of traditional charm, local artworks on the walls and tables dressed up for what lies ahead. And what lies ahead is some smart, clearly-focused contemporary cooking. The kitchen garden delivers its bounty, but what can't be grown in situ is sourced locally and with care. Start with goats' curd with burnt onion, shallot and toasted brioche, before moving onto a superb loin of Brecon red deer, served with turnip, glazed shallot and a nifty venison

pudding. Jerusalem artichoke cheesecake is a creative finale, aided by its mandarin sorbet and blackberry coulis accompaniments.

Chef Duncan Barham **Owner** Neil Kedward & Zoe Agar **Times** 12-2.30/6-9.30 **Prices** Fixed L 2 course £18, Fixed D 3 course £49, Tasting menu £64-£79, Service optional **Wines** 216 bottles over £30, 46 bottles under £30, 18 by glass **Notes** Tasting menu 5/7 course, Sunday L, Vegetarian available **Seats** 55, Pr/dining room 25 **Children** Portions, Menu **Parking** 42

NEWPORT　　　　　Map 8 SN03

Llys Meddyg

◉◉ British 🐾

Accomplished cooking in a former coaching inn

☎ 01239 820008 & 821050
East St SA42 0SY
e-mail: contact@llysmeddyg.com
dir: A487 to Newport, located on the Main Street, through the centre of town

Llys Meddyg is easy to spot in the centre of Newport, a village a few miles from Fishguard within the Pembrokeshire Coast National Park. It used to be a coaching inn and is now a comfortable, smartly done out restaurant with rooms. There's a stone-walled cellar bar with a wood-burner, a compact and elegant restaurant and a lovely garden for pre-dinner drinks. The kitchen

takes great pains to buy local produce, from sustainable sources whenever possible, or goes foraging; thus a salad of pennywort, wild sorrel and beetroot to partner home-smoked salmon. Main courses are praiseworthy for their lack of gimmick and for their precision: roast rump of Preseli lamb, served pink, with boulangère potatoes and parsnip purée flavoured with cumin, or fillet of hake poached in olive oil accompanied by mushroom macaroni. Seasonality applies to puddings too, with blackcurrant soufflé and Eton Mess coming on the menu in summer.

Chef Patrick Szenasi **Owner** Ed & Louise Sykes **Times** 6-9 Closed L all week (excl summer L kitchen garden) **Prices** Starter £7.50-£8, Main £14-£24, Dessert £5-£9, Service optional **Wines** 4 by glass **Notes** Vegetarian available, Civ Wed 40 **Seats** 30, Pr/dining room 14 **Children** Portions **Parking** 8, On street

Terry M at The Celtic Manor Resort

🌹🌹🌹

NEWPORT　　　　　MAP 9 ST38

Modern British 🍷NOTABLE WINE LIST

Outstanding cooking at world-class golfing hotel

☎ 01633 413000
Coldra Woods NP18 1HQ
e-mail: terrym@celtic-manor.com
web: www.celtic-manor.com
dir: From M4 junct 24 take B4237 towards Newport, turn right after 300yds

The Celtic Manor is a vast hotel complex with spacious public rooms off a soaring atrium, tournament-level golfing, a spa, fitness centre, and even a kiddies' club. It has its fair share of eating options too, with the jewel in the crown, the crème de la crème, being Terry M, named after its chef-patron Tim (you thought it would be Terry, didn't you?) McDougall. The restaurant celebrated five years with three AA Rosettes in 2013, an achievement that's testament to McDougall's unwavering passion for top-notch ingredients, combined with

considerable technical skill and creative flair. The elegant restaurant has a tasteful décor of plain walls hung with mirrors, polished floorboards, and distinctive dangling crystal chandeliers, while the highly professional and slightly formal style of service adds to the sense of occasion. Carefully sourced, seasonal materials - meat from selected Welsh farms, fish delivered daily from Cornwall - are given upfront modern treatments, resulting in dishes with fresh, powerful flavours: crab ravioli with crab broth and spiced tomato, for instance, is accompanied by gésier salad, and may be followed by accurately-timed fillet of red mullet with rocket and passionfruit sauce and roast vegetables. The menu, with around half a dozen choices per course (there's a tasting option too), holds plenty of interest and variety, and dishes are notable for their judicious combinations, so chicken boudin is a striking contrast to a starter of seared scallops with white beans, and truffle butter jus complements rib of beef with potato galette. Vegetarian options are approached with the same level of imagination and skill, as in a main course of truffled polenta with parsley root fondant, herb coulis and wild mushrooms. A pre-dessert - caramelised apricot with liquorice ice cream, say - heralds the goodies to

come, which may run to blueberry soufflé triumphantly partnered by sweet chilli jelly and banana ice cream.

Chef Tim McDougall **Owner** Celtic Manor Resort **Times** 12-2.30/7-9.30 Closed 1-14 Jan, Mon-Tue **Prices** Prices not confirmed Service optional, Groups min 8 service 10% **Wines** 195 bottles over £30, 40 bottles under £30, 12 by glass **Notes** Tasting menu 6 course, Sunday L, Vegetarian available, Dress restrictions, Smart casual **Seats** 50, Pr/dining room 12 **Children** Portions **Parking** 100

PEMBROKE   Map 8 SM90

Best Western Lamphey Court Hotel & Spa

◉ Modern British

Local approach at a grandiose Georgian villa

☎ 01646 672273
Lamphey SA71 5NT
e-mail: info@lampheycourt.co.uk
web: www.lampheycourt.co.uk
dir: A477 to Pembroke. Left at Milton for Lamphey, hotel on right

Lamphey Court is a grandiose Georgian villa, complete with massive portico entrance, standing in extensive grounds amid the Pembrokeshire Coast National park. Relaunched on the world as a contemporary spa hotel, it loses nothing of its august dignity, although the main dining now goes on in a conservatory extension with marble-topped tables and views of the gardens from three sides. Localism is the watchword, with Black beef, salt marsh lamb and pork from local farms, Cardigan Bay fish and seafood from the dayboats at Milford, and a plethora of Welsh cheeses all on hand. The menus don't try anything too daring, but keep the focus on quality and simplicity, producing a rarebit starter into which smoked haddock has been productively inveigled. Main courses run to maple-glazed salmon dressed in curry oil, and pan-roasted venison with Lyonnaise potatoes and puréed butternut squash in port jus. Hazelnut praline brings texture to crème brûlée.

Times 6.15-10 **Prices** Starter fr £5, Main fr £9.95
Notes Sunday L

PORTHGAIN   Map 8 SM83

The Shed

◉ Traditional British, Mediterranean ✿

Spanking-fresh seafood on the harbour

☎ 01348 831518
SA62 5BN
e-mail: caroline@theshedporthgain.co.uk
web: www.theshedporthgain.co.uk
dir: 7m from St Davids. Off A487

The Shed is right on the harbour of this tiny village within the Pembrokeshire Coast National Park. It's a friendly, relaxed and informal place, simply decorated and furnished, with fish and shellfish delivered daily the main

business. Timings are spot on, whatever the cooking medium, and sauces and seasonings are a well-considered match for the main component, with nothing too elaborate. Start with prawns simply fried in butter with lots of garlic and parsley, or cockle chowder, and progress to seafood stew with rouille, or whole sea bream baked en papillote with lemon, garlic and thyme. Beer-battered fillets are options too, chips or colcannon are the accompaniments, and you can end with a simple dessert like rhubarb crumble with custard.

Chef Viv Folan, Rob Jones **Owner** Rob & Caroline Jones
Times 12-3/5.30-9 Closed Nov-Apr (open only wknds except half term & Xmas hols), D Tue (off peak)
Prices Prices not confirmed Service optional **Wines** 7 by glass **Notes** Sunday L, Vegetarian available **Seats** 60
Children Portions, Menu **Parking** On village street

ST DAVIDS   Map 8 SM72

Cwtch

◉ Modern British ✿

The taste of Wales in the smallest city

☎ 01437 720491
22 High St SA62 6SD
e-mail: info@cwtchrestaurant.co.uk
dir: A487 St Davids, restaurant on left before Cross Square

If your Welsh isn't up to scratch, the name is pronounced 'cutsh' and it has all the cosseting connotations of hug, snug, and cosy. The restaurant lives up to its name as far as the ambience goes, with three small dining rooms spread over two floors, and done out with the pared-back simplicity of whitewashed stone walls, sturdy cross-beams and a mini-library of foodie books for diners to leaf through. The cooking takes a similarly restrained approach, leaving peerless Pembrokeshire produce to do the talking without unwelcome interference from trendy ideas or foams and froths. It's clearly a formula that works, as the local following is loyal and keen for more: the place now opens for lunch, when soul-soothing Welsh lamb cawl, full of the goodness of cabbage, onion, carrot and swede, is served with Caerfai cheddar and granary bread. Turn up in the evening, and you might trade up to pan-fried sea bass with sauce vierge, cockles and samphire, and round things off with puddings that fly the Welsh dragon - sticky toffee bara brith pudding with vanilla ice cream, or dark chocolate Merlyn liqueur torte with berry compôte and raspberry sorbet.

Chef Andy Holcroft **Owner** Rachael Copley **Times** 6-10 Closed 25-26 Dec, Sun-Wed (Nov-Mar), D Sun-Mon
Prices Fixed D 3 course fr £30, Service optional **Wines** 3 bottles over £30, 16 bottles under £30, 8 by glass
Notes Early evening offer 6-6.45pm 2/3 course £17/£20, Vegetarian available **Seats** 50 **Children** Portions, Menu
Parking On street

SAUNDERSFOOT   Map 8 SN10

St Brides Spa Hotel

◉ Modern British

Pleasingly unfussy food and fabulous sea views

☎ 01834 812304
St Brides Hill SA69 9NH
e-mail: reservations@stbridesspahotel.com
web: www.stbridesspahotel.com
dir: A478 onto B4310 to Saundersfoot. Hotel above harbour

Built to make the very best of the views out across Saundersfoot harbour and Carmarthen Bay, this spa hotel is a good option in fair weather or foul. There is the spa for a start, to sooth the mind and body, and in the form of the Cliff Restaurant, a dining option that delivers some classic dishes based on high quality regional produce. There's also a bar (the Gallery) with its own menu, and a terrace that is the hot ticket in warmer months. The genuinely charming and friendly staff are also a big part of the hotel's appeal. In the Cliff Restaurant, you might start with Welsh beef in carpaccio form, marinated in lime, coriander and chilli, before main-course breast of Gressingham duck with wild garlic mash, finishing with orange and cinnamon crème brûlée served with a lemon tuile, or go for the Welsh cheeses.

Chef Toby Goodwin **Owner** Andrew & Lindsey Evans
Times 11-6.30 **Prices** Starter £6.50-£8, Main £16-£25, Dessert £6.25-£7.25, Service optional **Wines** 104 bottles over £30, 79 bottles under £30, 14 by glass **Notes** All day Gallery menu, L all day from 11am, Sunday L £25, Vegetarian available, Dress restrictions, Smart dress, Civ Wed 60 **Seats** 100, Pr/dining room 50 **Children** Portions, Menu **Parking** 60

POWYS

BRECON   Map 9 SO02

Peterstone Court

◉◉ Modern British, European ✿

Excellent local food on the edge of the Brecon Beacons

☎ 01874 665387
Brecon Rd, Llanhamlach LD3 7YB
e-mail: info@peterstone-court.com
web: www.peterstone-court.com
dir: 1m from Brecon on A40 to Abergavenny

Peterstone Court is impressive on several levels. The handsome Georgian house overlooks the River Usk beneath the brooding peak of Pen-y-Fan in the Brecon Beacons National Park, a perfect location for hiking with our four-legged friends, who are made equally welcome as their owners. Inside, the place is a class act, blending eclectic contemporary style with period elegance; there's a lovely pocket-sized spa to de-stress in, and a classy pared-back contemporary restaurant with unclothed antique tables, oak floors and white walls. The team behind this polished modern country-house operation are passionate about food, starting with a thoroughly local

Save on Hotels. Book at **theAA.com/hotel**

POWYS 639 WALES

approach that keeps food miles to a minimum - meat and poultry are bred just seven miles up the road at the family's Glaisfer farm, and handled with skill to produce intelligently-considered juxtapositions of flavour and texture. Chicken terrine might appear with pickled wild mushrooms and carrots, carrot purée and pea cress salad, then rump and braised shoulder of lamb from the farm is teamed with garlic mash, parsnip and rosemary purée, roasted parsnip, and mint jus.

Chef Sean Gerrard, Kelvin Parry **Owner** Jessica & Glyn Bridgeman, Sean Gerrard **Times** 12-2.30/7-9.30 **Prices** Fixed L 2 course fr £12, Starter £5-£9, Main £17-£19, Dessert £6-£9, Service optional **Wines** 12 by glass **Notes** Mid week 3 course L £15, D £19.50, Sunday L £19-£22.50, Vegetarian available, Civ Wed 120 **Seats** 45, Pr/dining room 120 **Children** Portions, Menu **Parking** 40

CRICKHOWELL · Map 9 SO21

The Bear Hotel

◉ Modern British, International 🕲

Convivial dining in a thriving 15th-century village inn

☎ 01873 810408
High St NP8 1BW
e-mail: bearhotel@aol.com
dir: Town centre, off A40 (Brecon road). 6m from Abergavenny

If you're tired of village inns that have inflicted identikit contemporary makeovers on their venerable heritage, head for The Bear which has been the heart and soul of its village community between Abergavenny and the Brecon Beacons since 1432. Its enduring appeal is due to its custodians, the Hindmarsh family, who have run the place for over 30 years without being blown around in the ephemeral winds of fashion. Just look inside: what's not to like about flagstoned floors, cosy log fires, venerable oak beams and stone walls? And the kitchen only has to look to the hills, valleys and rivers all around for the supplies that are the backbone of its unpretentious modern comfort food repertoire. Evergreen ideas such as platters of smoked salmon and trout from the Black Mountains served with lemon and tarragon dressing, or chicken liver and Cognac parfait with red onion marmalade lead on to mains starring slow-braised Welsh lamb shank with spring onion mash and braising juices, or slow-roasted belly pork with colcannon, black pudding, and cider cream reduction.

Chef Iain Sampson **Owner** Mrs J & Mr S Hindmarsh **Times** 12-2/7-9.30 Closed 25 Dec, L Mon-Sat, D Sun **Prices** Service optional **Wines** 6 bottles over £30, 45 bottles under £30, 10 by glass **Notes** Vegetarian available, Dress restrictions, Smart casual **Seats** 60, Pr/dining room 30 **Children** Portions, Menu **Parking** 40

Manor Hotel

◉ Modern British 🕲

Local produce and stunning mountain views

☎ 01873 810212
Brecon Rd NP8 1SE
e-mail: info@manorhotel.co.uk
web: www.manorhotel.co.uk
dir: On A40, 0.5m from Crickhowell

The whitewashed frontage with its elegant Georgian portico is framed by the elemental Black Mountains and the verdant valley of the River Usk. Fantastic walking country, then, and these hills and valleys also produce the peerless local produce you will be tucking into at the end of the day. A recent refurb has laid bare the original oak flooring in the Manor's relaxed bistro, a smart contemporary setting with food to match. If you're bothered by such things, food miles are minimal since much of the meat comes from the family farm seven miles down the road. The unfussy and gently modish repertoire takes in the likes of confit duck leg with braised Puy lentils, bacon and red wine jus to start, followed by pan-fried Gower sea bass with potato rösti, purple broccoli, green sauce and roasted beets, or braised belly pork with bubble-and-squeak, honey-roasted parsnips, and cider and tarragon sauce.

Chef Glyn Bridgeman **Owner** Glyn & Jessica Bridgeman, Sean Gerrard **Times** 12-2.30/6-9.30 **Prices** Starter £4.95-£8.95, Main £10.95-£18.95, Dessert £4.50-£6, Service optional **Wines** 17 by glass **Notes** Simple and Seasonal menu 2/3 course £15/£17.50, Sunday L £14.95-£18.95, Vegetarian available, Civ Wed 150 **Seats** 54, Pr/dining room 26 **Children** Portions, Menu **Parking** 200

HAY-ON-WYE · Map 9 SO24

Old Black Lion Inn

◉ Modern International 🕲

Traditional and modern cookery in an historic inn

☎ 01497 820841
26 Lion St HR3 5AD
e-mail: info@oldblacklion.co.uk
web: www.oldblacklion.co.uk
dir: 1m off A438. From TIC car park turn right along Oxford Rd, pass NatWest Bank, next left (Lion St), hotel 20yds on right

The 17th-century Black Lion is tucked away on a quiet side street just a short stroll from the bookworm paradise at the centre of Hay-on-Wye. The place is just what a historic old inn should be: laden with heaps of creaky charm and period character, it has an unpretentious, unspoilt vibe and wonky beamed ceilings that once sheltered Oliver Cromwell while the Roundheads besieged Hay Castle. The old regicide probably wouldn't have dined as well as present-day visitors, who can choose between the restaurant and bar areas, both cosily informal spaces, to tuck into a medley of staunchly traditional and hearty modern British dishes. In the former camp are the likes of Herefordshire rib-eye steak with peppercorn or

mushroom sauce, or beer-battered cod with proper chips, peas and tartare sauce, while modernists might go for red mullet fillets rubbed with garlic and chilli and served with Mediterranean vegetable couscous, spinach, and chilli and red pepper sauce.

Chef Rod Lewis, Maximillion Evilio **Owner** Dolan Leighton **Times** 12-2/6.30-9 Closed 24-26 Dec **Prices** Starter £4.95-£7.95, Main £8.95-£18.95, Dessert £4.95-£5.50, Service optional **Wines** 7 by glass **Notes** Sunday L, Vegetarian available **Seats** 40, Pr/dining room 20 **Children** Portions, Menu **Parking** 10

KNIGHTON · Map 9 SO27

Milebrook House Hotel

◉◉ Modern, Traditional Ⓥ 🕲

Quality British food on the Welsh-English border

☎ 01547 528632
Milebrook LD7 1LT
e-mail: hotel@milebrookhouse.co.uk
web: www.milebrookhouse.co.uk
dir: 2m E of Knighton on A4113 (Ludlow)

When the legendary explorer and travel writer Sir Wilfred Thesiger took time out from crossing Arabia's Empty Quarter on a camel, he returned home to this handsome 18th-century Marches mansion in the Teme Valley. The riotously colourful gardens must have been balm to his soul, and are not merely decorative, since they supply the kitchen with heaps of fresh, seasonal fruit, veg and herbs. The kitchen delivers deceptively-simple and well-balanced modern British country-house dishes that impress with their light touch and flavour combos. Rhubarb and mustard seed sauce might be used as a sharpening foil for a pan-fried fillet of Cornish mackerel, while main courses could see rump of local Welsh lamb in a time-honoured partnership with dauphinoise potatoes, spring cabbage, creamed leeks and rosemary juice. Desserts such as garden rhubarb and ginger crème brûlée hit the spot, or there are artisan cheeses from both sides of the border.

Chef Chris Lovell **Owner** Mr & Mrs R T Marsden **Times** 12-2/6.30-9 Closed L Mon **Prices** Fixed L 2 course fr £13.75, Fixed D 3 course £25-£32, Starter £6.50-£8.75, Main £16.75-£19.75, Dessert £6.75-£7.25, Service optional **Wines** 6 bottles over £30, 36 bottles under £30, 8 by glass **Notes** Sunday L, Vegetarian menu **Seats** 40, Pr/dining room 16 **Children** Portions **Parking** 24

LLANDRINDOD WELLS
Map 9 SO06

The Metropole

Modern British V

Stylish spa hotel with sound modern cooking

☎ 01597 823700
Temple St LD1 5DY
e-mail: info@metropole.co.uk
web: www.metropole.co.uk
dir: In centre of town off A483, car park at rear

The emerald green hexagonal turrets of The Metropole have been a landmark since the height of the Victorian vogue for taking the waters in spa towns, and incredibly, the hotel has been in the hands of the same family since Queen Victoria was on the throne. In the Radnor restaurant, however, there's a rather more contemporary approach, both in the décor of tobacco-hued leather high-backed chairs at white linen-clad tables, and in what leaves the kitchen. The chefs haul in the best locally-farmed Welsh lamb, Black beef, game, cheeses, and are to be seen foraging the local woods when ceps and chanterelles are in season. A sensibly concise menu offers the likes of ham hock and chestnut terrine with caramelised onion marmalade, and pursues the unpretentious theme on through main courses like confit Welsh White belly pork with bashed apple and butter beans, pak choi and Asian broth, to conclude with the comforts of sticky date pudding with toffee sauce and vanilla ice cream.

Chef Nick Edwards **Owner** Justin Baird-Murray
Times 12-2.15/6-9.30 **Prices** Starter £4.95-£6.25, Main £11.75-£22, Dessert £4.75-£5.25, Service included **Wines** 4 bottles over £30, 29 bottles under £30, 9 by glass **Notes** Sunday L £12.95-£14.95, Vegetarian menu, Civ Wed 150 **Seats** 46, Pr/dining room 250 **Children** Portions, Menu **Parking** 150

LLANFYLLIN
Map 15 SJ11

Seeds

Modern British

Accurate cooking in an intimate, relaxed setting

☎ 01691 648604
5-6 Penybryn Cottages, High St SY22 5AP
dir: In village centre. Take A490 N from Welshpool, follow signs to Llanfyllin

Run by an amiable husband and wife and their cheery and personable front-of-house team, Seeds is a totally chilled little bistro in a 500-year-old terrace. Artworks and eclectic travel souvenirs decorate the low-beamed, slate-floored dining room, and cool jazz is the soundtrack to chef-proprietor Mark Seager's full-flavoured and unpretentious classic bistro dishes. Starters can be as simple as grilled goats' cheese salad with sweet chilli sauce, while mains could take in rack of Welsh lamb with a Dijon mustard and herb crust, or grilled sea bass fillet with tagliolini and rich tomato sauce. Puddings aim for the classic comforts of treacle tart or sticky toffee pudding with cream, ice cream or custard.

Chef Mark Seager **Owner** Felicity & Mark Seager **Times** 11-2.30/7-9 Closed 25 Dec, 1 wk Aug, 1 wk Oct, Sun-Mon (Sun-Wed winter) **Prices** Fixed L 2 course £12.50-£16.25, Fixed D 3 course £27.50-£30.50, Starter £4.50-£6.95, Main £8.95-£17.25, Dessert £4.95-£6.95, Service optional **Wines** 19 bottles over £30, 93 bottles under £30, 3 by glass **Notes** Pre-music festival menu Jun-Jul, Vegetarian available **Seats** 20 **Children** Portions **Parking** Free town car park, on street

LLANGAMMARCH WELLS
Map 9 SN94

The Lake Country House & Spa

Modern British

Classy modern cooking in a relaxing country house

☎ 01591 620202 & 620474
LD4 4BS
e-mail: info@lakecountryhouse.co.uk
web: www.lakecountryhouse.co.uk
dir: W from Builth Wells on A483 to Garth (approx 6m). Left for Llangammarch Wells, follow hotel signs

If you're looking to escape for a few days, The Lake Country House has everything to keep you happy whatever floats your boat. Whether you come for the golf or fishing, to pamper yourself in the spa or simply lose yourself in the gardens for a little while, it's all here. The house has a good deal of period charm - it dates from the 1840s - and the fixtures and fittings give the place an air of understated classical grandeur, not least in the dining room with its smartly dressed tables. The kitchen is not adverse to a touch of modernism, albeit discreetly so, and on a bedrock of sound classical thinking. After canapés in the lounge, you might start with ham hock rillettes with a spiced apple purée, or a terrine filled with Swansea seafood and leeks served with saffron and tomato dressing and caviar. Amongst main courses, fillet of sea bass comes with roasted tomatoes, salsa verde, confit leeks and tempura scallop, and to finish, sticky toffee pudding has accompanying honeycomb, rosemary ice cream and roasted fig.

Chef Russell Stach **Owner** Jean Pierre & Jan Mifsud **Times** 12.30-2.30/7-9 **Prices** Fixed D 3 course £38.50, Tasting menu £60, Service optional **Wines** 120 bottles over £30, 15 bottles under £30, 11 by glass **Notes** Sunday L, Vegetarian available, Dress restrictions, Smart casual, Civ Wed 100 **Seats** 80, Pr/dining room 70 **Children** Portions **Parking** 40

LLANWDDYN
Map 15 SJ01

Lake Vyrnwy Hotel & Spa

Modern British

Interesting menus, breathtaking views

☎ 01691 870692
Lake Vyrnwy SY10 0LY
e-mail: info@lakevyrnwyhotel.co.uk
web: www.lakevyrnwy.com
dir: on A4393, 200yds past dam turn sharp right into drive

This stylishly converted Victorian sporting lodge is in a superb spot above the eponymous lake. For the breathtaking view, try to bag a window seat in the conservatory-style restaurant, a long room divided by a sliding door. The frequently-changing menus showcase Welsh produce, which the kitchen treats with skill and accuracy. Starters hit the mark, from lightly pickled mackerel on a bed of leaves with saffron aïoli to chicken and wild mushroom terrine with pineapple chutney. Main courses can vary from traditional roast loin of lamb, served unusually with herby confit, accompanied by mash and Savoy cabbage, to medallions of monkfish marinated in yoghurt, chilli and lime, served with leek dauphinoise and fennel purée. Puddings like runny-centred baked chocolate fondant with vanilla ice cream maintain standards to the end.

Times 12-2/6.45-9.15

LLANWRTYD WELLS
Map 9 SN84

Carlton Riverside

Modern British

Creative cooking in family-run riverside restaurant

☎ 01591 610248
Irfon Crescent LD5 4SP
e-mail: info@carltonriverside.com
dir: In town centre beside bridge

Its name is a bit of a giveaway: this small restaurant is beside the River Irfon running through the village. The restaurant's large windows let in plenty of light, while at night, when the beige-patterned curtains are closed, the lighting level is pitched to create an intimate feel in the elegantly decorated room. An amuse-bouche of leek and potato soup can get things off to a resounding start before chicken and pork terrine with plum chutney, or a plate of charcuterie with a textbook version of celeriac remoulade. The kitchen's clearly well versed in the classical repertory, and technical skills are evident too in a main course of Dover sole with salmon mousse, chive beurre blanc and crushed potatoes. While some dishes can appear busy, a steady nerve keeps them balanced and flavours pull together, not apart, as in partridge breast on cabbage and bacon, served with a venison noisette, and game pie in a ramekin under a pastry lid, all accompanied by port and game jus and dauphinoise. Finish with a trio of rhubarb: jelly, fool and crumble.

Chef Mary Ann Gilchrist **Owner** Dr & Mrs Gilchrist **Times** 7-9 Closed Sun, L all week **Prices** Fixed D 3 course £27.50-£43.50, Starter £4.95-£11, Main £11.95-£24, Dessert £5.95-£9, Service optional **Wines** 13 bottles over £30, 35 bottles under £30, 4 by glass **Notes** Vegetarian available **Seats** 20 **Children** Portions, Menu **Parking** Car park opposite

Lasswade Country House

◉◉ Modern British ◉

Organic focus in an Edwardian country house

☎ 01591 610515
Station Rd LD5 4RW
e-mail: info@lasswadehotel.co.uk
web: www.lasswadehotel.co.uk
dir: Exit A483 into Irfon Terrace, right into Station Rd, 350yds on right

Run with great charm by owners Roger and Emma Stevens, this grand Edwardian house sits at the edge of the Victorian spa town with 360-degree views of the Cambrian Mountains and Brecon Beacons. It's a soothing spot, and when you add the chef-proprietor's skilled modern British cooking into the deal, the whole package is an inviting prospect. After pre-dinner drinks in the homely lounge, it all takes place in a traditional-style dining room kitted out with burnished mahogany furniture. Driven by a passion for sourcing organic and sustainable produce from Wales and the Marches area, Roger keeps combinations straightforward, timings accurate, and interweaves flavours intelligently. Expect daily-changing dinner menus to get going with home-smoked trout fillets matched with potato and radish salad, and lemon and thyme oil, followed, perhaps, by a plate of that splendid Cambrian mountain lamb, comprising roast rump, braised breast and sautéed kidneys in grain mustard and tomato sauce with leek soufflé and Madeira wine reduction.

Chef Roger Stevens **Owner** Roger & Emma Stevens **Times** 7.30-9.30 Closed 25 Dec, L all week **Prices** Fixed D 3 course fr £35, Service optional **Wines** 3 bottles over £30, 17 bottles under £30, 4 by glass **Notes** Vegetarian available, Dress restrictions, Smart casual **Seats** 20, Pr/dining room 20 **Parking** 6

LLYSWEN   **Map 9 SO13**

Llangoed Hall

◉◉ Modern British ◉

Confident cooking in an impressive house

☎ 01874 754525
LD3 0YP
e-mail: enquiries@llangoedhall.co.uk
dir: On A470, 2m from Llyswen towards Builth Wells

Surrounded by the lush green Wye Valley, Llangoed has enjoyed its prime position since 1632 but hasn't stood still in that time (metaphorically speaking). It is a grand house indeed, with some parts going back to the early Stuart era, and a sweeping pillared gallery added by none other than Clough Williams-Ellis (of Portmeirion fame) just before the Great War. The traditional and elegant dining room is done out in Wedgwood blue and tables are dressed in crisp white linen. New chef Nick Brodie cooks up some smart, well-crafted dishes with a light touch and the good sense to let the flavours shine. Start with wafer-thin cannelloni packed with excellent crab meat, the flavours of lemongrass and ginger kept reined in, or go for ham hock, foie gras and black pudding terrine with toasted brioche and home-made piccalilli. Follow on with an excellent piece of venison served with potato rösti and honeyed-parsnip purée, and end on a high with pineapple cheesecake with cardamom and passionfruit.

Chef Nick Brodie **Owner** Llangoed Ltd **Times** 12.30-2/6.30-9.30 **Prices** Fixed L 3 course £25-£28.50, Fixed D 3 course £55-£60, Tasting menu £90-£95, Service optional **Wines** 7 by glass **Notes** Sunday L, Vegetarian available, Dress restrictions, Smart dress, Civ Wed 90 **Seats** 40, Pr/dining room 80 **Children** Portions **Parking** 50

MONTGOMERY   **Map 15 SO29**

The Dragon

◉ British

Appealing bistro cooking in a timbered inn

☎ 01686 668359
Market Square SY15 6PA
e-mail: reception@dragonhotel.com
dir: Behind town hall

With its striking black-and-white timbered frontage and an interior dating back to the mid-1600s, there is plenty to catch the eye at this old coaching inn set on the town square. The homely, split-level dining room boasts ancient black timbers and a slate fireplace, and service is friendly and efficient from welcoming staff. The cooking style is traditional British, with accurately cooked and simply presented dishes making good use of locally-sourced ingredients. Choose from the short table d'hôte of reliable bistro favourites, or look to the carte for home-made Stilton soup, followed by slow-cooked Welsh lamb shank with roasted garlic mash and Cumberland sauce, with traditional sticky toffee pudding to finish.

Chef Matthew Smith **Owner** M & S Michaels **Times** 12-2/7-9 **Prices** Fixed L 3 course £17-£19.50, Fixed D 3 course £17-£19.50, Starter £4.50-£5.25, Main £9.50-£16.95, Dessert £4.50-£5.60, Service optional **Wines** 3 bottles over £30, 36 bottles under £30, 12 by glass **Notes** Sunday L, Vegetarian available, Civ Wed 40 **Seats** 42, Pr/dining room 50 **Children** Portions **Parking** 20

RHONDDA CYNON TAFF

MISKIN   **Map 9 ST08**

Miskin Manor Country Hotel

◉◉ Modern, Traditional British V ◉

Inventive modern British cooking in tranquil setting

☎ 01443 224204
Pendoylan Rd CF72 8ND
e-mail: info@miskin-manor.co.uk
web: www.miskin-manor.co.uk
dir: M4 junct 34, exit onto A4119, signed Llantrisant, hotel 300yds on left

Buffered from the frenetic M4 and Cardiff's outskirts by 22 acres of grounds with fabulously colourful gardens, Miskin Manor supplies history and contemporary style in equal measure. The romantic Meisgyn Restaurant has an atmospheric Gothic edge, thanks to its curvaceous wrought-iron seats, oak panelling and swagged-back gauzy curtains, but the kitchen team is on-message with modern culinary trends. The brigade takes a serious approach, growing vegetables and herbs in the gardens, and turning out top-notch bread, cakes and desserts from its in-house pastry section. To start, grouse comes in a modish three-way format - confit leg, breast, and mini Scotch egg - while main course might see another trio, lamb this time, served as mini rack, loin, and rolled shoulder, with bubble-and-squeak mash, pumpkin purée, wilted chard, and garden mint sauce. Dessert plays a riff on the rhubarb and custard theme, delivering creamy custard tart with nutmeg and a custard-filled doughnut with a contrasting hit of slightly sharp poached rhubarb.

Chef Mark Beck **Owner** Mr & Mrs Rosenberg **Times** 12-2.30/6-10 Closed D 25-26 Dec **Prices** Fixed L 2 course £17.95, Fixed D 3 course £23.95, Starter £6.50-£8.25, Main £19.95-£25.95, Dessert £6.75, Service optional **Wines** 16 bottles over £30, 27 bottles under £30, 12 by glass **Notes** Sunday L, Vegetarian menu, Dress restrictions, Smart casual, Civ Wed 130 **Seats** 50, Pr/dining room 30 **Children** Portions, Menu **Parking** 200

La Luna

◉ Modern International

Relaxed bistro dining near the shops

☎ 01443 239600
79-81 Talbot Rd, Talbot Green CF72 8AE
e-mail: info@la-lunarestaurant.com
dir: M4 junct 34, follow signs for Llantrisant, turn left at 2nd lights

Describing itself as a brasserie and lounge bar, La Luna is opposite the village's retail park and is not surprisingly a big hit for lunchtime shoppers seeking out the bargain fixed-price offer. There's an excellent value early evening menu, too. The place has an unpretentious, modish vibe on the inside, and a few tables outside for when the sun shines on South Wales. The menu suits the relaxed mood with its unfussy brasserie repertoire; start with chorizo and roasted vegetable risotto, for example, and move on to slow-cooked pork belly with crushed potatoes and rich jus. There are steaks cooked on the grill - sourced from the Usk Valley and matured for 21 days - while a fish main course might be pan-fried sea bass with warm crab Niçoise and a Spanish-style coriander sauce. When it comes to dessert, how about a chocolate fondant?

Chef Craig Brookes **Owner** Craig & Kevin Brookes **Times** 12-3/6-10 Closed 24 Dec, 1 Jan & BHs, Mon, D Sun **Prices** Fixed L 2 course £10.99, Fixed D 3 course £16.95, Starter £4.50-£7.95, Main £9.95-£21.95, Dessert £4.95-£7.95, Service optional **Wines** 2 by glass **Notes** Fixed L Tue-Sat 12-3, D Tue-Fri 6-7 (last orders) **Seats** 91, Pr/dining room 50 **Children** Menu **Parking** On street

Llechwen Hall Hotel

◉ Modern Welsh

Scenic, historical setting for unfussy cooking

☎ 01443 742050
Llanfabon CF37 4HP
e-mail: reservations@llechwenhall.co.uk
dir: A470 N towards Merthyr Tydfil. 3rd exit at large rdbt then 3rd exit at mini rdbt, hotel signed 0.5m on left

Overlooking four valleys from its hilltop perch, and set in six acres of gorgeous grounds, it's easy to see why Llechwen Hall does such a roaring trade with the wedding parties - there's even a permanent marquee in the grounds. But you don't need to be tying the knot to come here, since the Oak Beam Restaurant is an attractive proposition for a romantic dinner, housed in the traditional 17th-century beamed longhouse, where well-appointed tables are laid with crisp white linen. Taking its cue from carefully-sourced local ingredients, the kitchen deals in a straightforward, modern repertoire that might start with mature Welsh cheese brûlée with asparagus and poppy seed biscuits, before moving on to sautéed cod with crab beignets, celeriac, and dill and lemon remoulade. Whether you go for a savoury or sweet

ending, do it on a Welsh note with either a slate of Welsh cheeses, or pice ar y maen baked cheesecake with strawberry compôte.

Chef Paul Trask **Owner** Ramish Gor **Times** 12-2/7-9 **Prices** Starter £4.95-£6.95, Main £12.50-£20.95, Dessert £3.95-£6.95, Service optional **Wines** 4 by glass **Notes** Sunday L £9.95-£12.95, Vegetarian available, Dress restrictions, Smart casual, Civ Wed 80 **Seats** 35, Pr/dining room 300 **Children** Portions, Menu **Parking** 100

Fairyhill

◉◉ Modern British V ▮ NOTABLE WINE LIST ◉

Elegant country-house hotel with real local flavour

☎ 01792 390139
SA3 1BS
e-mail: postbox@fairyhill.net
web: www.fairyhill.net
dir: M4 junct 47, take A483 then A484 to Llanelli, Gower, Gowerton. At Gowerton follow B4295 for approx 10m

For a restorative retreat, this lovely 18th-century country house is hard to beat. In the heart of Gower, Fairyhill has bags of style in an interior kitted out in the hybrid of old and new that defines a modern country house. And with just eight bedrooms, 24 acres of delightful grounds with mature woodland, a lake and trout stream, you won't have difficulty shaking off the other guests. Better still, you don't need to head off into the wilds to look for dinner, as the best table for miles around is right here. The kitchen stocks its larder with Welsh Black beef, salt marsh lamb, Penclawdd cockles and fresh fish, most of which comes from a ten-mile radius around Gower. Simple, fresh and local are the watchwords of the modern Welsh menu; for the least food miles, open with Gower crab with chilli and apple, toast, rocket and endives, and follow with loin, rib and sweetbread of Cefn Stylle salt marsh lamb matched with spring greens, mash and cawl jus. Round it off with chocolate brownie, coffee pannacotta and milk ice cream.

Chef Paul Davies, Neil Hollis **Owner** Mr Hetherington, Mr Davies **Times** 12-2/7-9 Closed 26 Dec, 1-25 Jan **Prices** Fixed L 2 course fr £20, Fixed D 3 course fr £45, Service optional **Wines** 10 by glass **Notes** Sunday L, Vegetarian menu, Civ Wed 40 **Seats** 60, Pr/dining room 40 **Children** Portions **Parking** 45

The Dragon Hotel

◉ Modern European ◉

A touch of modern style in the heart of Swansea

☎ 01792 657100 & 657159
Kingsway Circle SA1 5LS
e-mail: enquiries@dragon-hotel.co.uk
web: www.dragon-hotel.co.uk
dir: M4 junct 42, A483 follow signs for city centre A4067. After lights at Sainsbury's right onto The Strand then left into Kings Ln. Hotel straight ahead

The Dragon is breathing fire after a megabucks renovation has brought everything up to full contemporary spec, making the most of its location in the thick of Swansea's town centre action. The buzzy Dragon Brasserie is in pole position for watching the world go by: ringside seats look through floor-to-ceiling windows onto the high street in a thoroughly modern venue with exposed industrial ducting and spotlights above bare darkwood tables and pale wooden floors. The cooking is well-focused and in tune with the setting, offering straightforward modern European dishes built from local produce; keenly-priced two or three-course dinner menus could get going with smooth chicken liver parfait with pear and ginger chutney, then move on to confit belly pork with pork and apple sausage and spring onion mash. Dessert might be saffron and vanilla crème brûlée with chocolate shortbread.

Chef Steve Williams **Owner** Dragon Hotel Ltd **Times** 12-2.30/6-9.30 **Prices** Fixed L 2 course fr £10.50, Fixed D 3 course fr £19.95, Service optional **Wines** 5 bottles over £30, 33 bottles under £30, 12 by glass **Notes** Tasting menu & pre-theatre menu by reservation only, Sunday L, Vegetarian available, Civ Wed 200 **Seats** 65, Pr/dining room 80 **Children** Menu **Parking** 50

Hanson at the Chelsea Restaurant

◉◉ Modern Welsh, French

Modern bistro-style fare in relaxed restaurant

☎ 01792 464068
17 St Mary St SA1 3LH
e-mail: andrew_hanson@live.co.uk
dir: In small lane between St Mary Church & Wine St

Lemon-coloured walls give a fresh feel to this small restaurant in a terrace on a narrow city-centre side street. Banquettes and high-backed wooden chairs with padded seats, clothed tables, a board listing seafood specials, and friendly uniformed staff all add to the appeal. The weekly-changing menu is a roll-call of contemporary British and French bistro-style dishes, from fishcake with pommes allumette and tartare sauce to duck rillette with cornichons. Seafood is a forte and receives inventive treatment, partnering pan-fried scallops with a cockle and laverbread crumble and parmesan and rocket. Elsewhere, shoulder of local lamb is slowly cooked French-style with navarin of vegetables, served with mash, and veal rump is simmered in Madeira with mushrooms and accompanied by potato gratin.

Desserts are a familiar enough bunch, among them chocolate tart with clotted cream.

Chef Andrew Hanson, Gareth Sillman, Sam Beddoe **Owner** Andrew & Michelle Hanson **Times** 12-2/7-10 Closed 25-26 Dec, BHs, Sun **Prices** Fixed L 2 course £12.95-£16.95, Fixed D 3 course £19.95, Starter £2.50-£8.95, Main £11.95-£23.50, Dessert £5.50 **Wines** 8 by glass **Notes** Vegetarian available, Dress restrictions, Smart casual **Seats** 50, Pr/dining room 20 **Children** Portions, Menu

VALE OF GLAMORGAN

HENSOL   Map 9 ST07

Vale Resort

🌐 Modern British

Welsh resort hotel with local flavour

☎ 01443 667800
Hensol Park CF72 8JY
e-mail: sales@vale-hotel.com
web: www.vale-hotel.com
dir: M4 junct 34, exit signed Pendoylan, turn 1st right twice, then 1st left before white house on bend. Hotel on right

This large and luxurious contemporary resort hotel has it all, in spades: a great location near Cardiff and the Glamorgan coast, 650 acres of grounds with a brace of golf courses, and the largest spa complex in Wales. Appetite, therefore, should not be lacking for the kitchen's straightforward modern repertoire, served in the smart bistro-style Vale Grill, a clean-cut space with bare darkwood tables and views of the cheffy action in the open kitchen. Locally-sourced ingredients get a good showing, particularly prime Welsh beef - no, not the Welsh rugby team, who you might meet here after a training session - but a slab of sirloin steak served sizzling from the open grill with béarnaise and triple-cooked chips. On a more delicate note, there could be

grey mullet fillet with rocket and pesto risotto, broad beans, salsify, and tapenade dressing, and to finish, apricot bavarois and jelly paired with Earl Grey tea ice cream.

Times 7-11 Closed L all week

WREXHAM

LLANARMON DYFFRYN CEIRIOG   Map 15 SJ13

The Hand at Llanarmon

🌐 Modern British

Well-executed country-pub food in the Ceiriog Valley

☎ 01691 600666
Ceiriog Valley LL20 7LD
e-mail: reception@thehandhotel.co.uk
dir: Leave A5 at Chirk onto B4500 signed Ceiriog Valley, continue for 11m

If you're looking for a traditional country inn with a voluble, friendly ambience and classy cooking in the Ceiriog Valley, talk to the Hand. The surrounding landscape of moor and mountain makes a haunting backdrop to the simple but well-executed pub dishes on offer. A plate of crab from the Llyn peninsula combines fresh white and brown meat, a crab and ginger bhaji and a filo parcel of crab and tiger prawn. Then it's grilled mackerel with smoked salmon and pea shoot salad, topped with a poached egg, or slow-braised lamb shoulder in redcurrant and lamb jus. Banana fritters with berry compôte and honey makes a fitting finale.

Times 12-2.20/6.30-8.45 Closed 25 Dec

West Arms

🌐 Modern British, French 🍷

Traditional and modern cooking in an ancient inn

☎ 01691 600665 & 600612
LL20 7LD
e-mail: info@thewestarms.co.uk
dir: Exit A483 (A5) at Chirk (mid-way between Oswestry & Llangollen). Follow signs for Ceiriog Valley (B4500), 11m

The West Arms has been standing in the foothills of the Berwyn Mountains since 1570, and with its slate-flagged floors, exposed beams and inglenook fireplaces, it's easy to imagine the drovers dropping in for some good food and good cheer on their way back from the market in the inn's early days. Produce from trusted local suppliers informs the largely traditional menu, thus an evening meal might kick off with the chef's watercress, leek and home-grown Jerusalem artichoke soup finished with cream and herb croûtons. Medallions of Welsh beef fillet with wild mushrooms, dauphinoise potato and a Burgundy sauce could be on the cards for the main event, while an iced lemon and ginger semi-fredo layered with biscuit shows that the chef has no lack of ambition when it comes to dessert stage.

Chef Grant Williams **Owner** Geoff & Gill Leigh-Ford **Times** 12-2/7-9 Closed L Mon-Sat **Prices** Fixed D 3 course fr £32.95, Starter £5.95-£8.95, Main £11.95-£19.95, Dessert £5.95, Service optional **Wines** 5+ bottles over £30, 10+ bottles under £30, 9 by glass **Notes** Sunday L, Vegetarian available, Civ Wed 70 **Seats** 34, Pr/dining room 10 **Children** Portions, Menu **Parking** 20

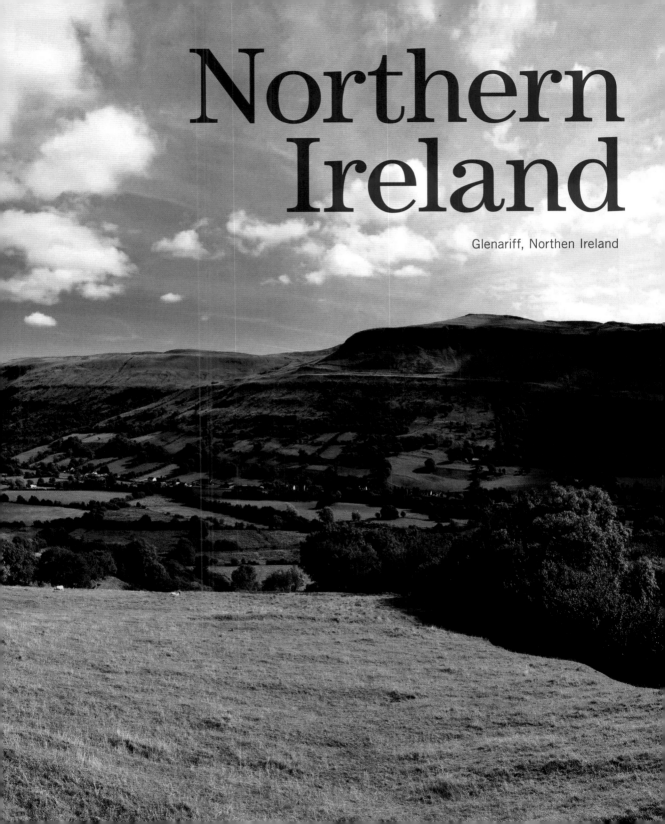

Northern Ireland

Glenariff, Northen Ireland

NORTHERN IRELAND
CO ANTRIM

BALLYMENA   Map 1 D5

Galgorm Resort & Spa

Modern Brtitish V

Modish cooking by the river

☎ 028 2588 1001
136 Fenaghy Rd, Galgorm BT42 1EA
e-mail: sales@galgorm.com
dir: 1m from Ballymena on A42, between Galgorm & Cullybackey

The River Room Restaurant at the Galgorm Resort delivers on its billing with the fast-flowing River Maine serving up a charming vista. And the floor-to-ceiling windows ensure everyone gets a gander, with the river floodlit at night to create an alluring atmosphere. It all takes place in a swanky resort with three dining options, luxurious rooms, swish spa and posh conference facilities, on a 163-acre estate. The kitchen is the forward-looking, dynamic engine of the place, with a good deal of ambition on show. Things start in style with an amuse-bouche such as pan-fried scallop with wild garlic cream before a first-course ravioli of local rabbit with black pudding purée, apples (caramelised and au naturel), English mustard and watercress sauce. Next up, pan roasted halibut with a crab rösti, cauliflower, samphire, wild garlic, lobster and fennel shows considered balancing of flavours and textures, and for dessert, liquorice parfait comes with poached rhubarb, rhubarb jelly and sorbet, honeycomb and strawberry.

Galgorm Resort & Spa

Chef Chris Bell **Owner** Nicholas & Paul Hill **Times** 12-3/6.30-9.30 Closed Mon-Tue, L Wed-Sat **Prices** Fixed L 3 course £24-£28, Tasting menu fr £60, Starter £8-£9, Main £23-£26, Service added but optional 10% **Wines** 211 bottles over £30, 60 bottles under £30, 12 by glass **Notes** Sunday L £24-£28, Vegetarian menu, Civ Wed 100 **Seats** 42 **Children** Portions **Parking** 200

BUSHMILLS   Map 1 C6

Bushmills Inn Hotel

Traditional

Locally-based cooking near the Giant's Causeway

☎ 028 2073 3000 & 2073 2339
9 Dunluce Rd BT57 8QG
e-mail: mail@bushmillsinn.com
web: www.bushmillsinn.com
dir: 2m from Giant's Causeway on A2 in Bushmills after crossing river

Whiskey, golf and historic landmarks, Bushmills has proximity to the traveller's holy trinity around these parts: the Old Bushmills Distillery, Royal Portrush Golf Club and the Giant's Causeway. The old 17th-century coaching inn is these days a refuge with bags of boutique style and charm. There's a bar done out with lavishly burnished wood, a 30-seater cinema even, and a restaurant that keeps pace with the times. There's a good deal of local produce on show, from land and sea, so you might start with Ulster beef carpaccio, or smoked haddock and leek risotto, before moving on to Barbary duck served with spiced red cabbage, celeriac purée and red wine jus, or sea bass fillets with razor clams, buttered spinach and seafood 'essence'. And to finish, chocolate and caramel tart is made with hazelnut and almond pastry, and comes with a Morello cherry sorbet.

Times 12-9.30

BELFAST

BELFAST   Map 1 D5

Beatrice Kennedy

Modern, Traditional V

Modern bistro food in the university district

☎ 028 9020 2290
44 University Rd BT7 1NJ
e-mail: reservations@beatricekennedy.co.uk
dir: Adjacent to Queens University

The continent never feels far away in this quirky restaurant in the university district, whether you're taken across the Channel by the rich pink and green walls with shelves of books, wooden floors, and leather chairs that give off the ambience of a wartime bistro, or the plentiful European references on the eclectic menu. It is a buzzy little venue where all of the front-of-house team pitch in with an unfussy hands-on attitude. Chef-patron Jim McCarthy shows sound talent and avoids complication by concentrating attention on the main ingredients, serving up seared foie gras with gingerbread, apple and cinnamon compôte and a port reduction, followed by rump of wild Irish venison with a croquette of braised shin, squash gnocchi, and parsnip purée. On the fish front, baked Atlantic cod could appear alongside artichoke and salsify risotto, white onion and truffle. For dessert, how about sticky toffee pudding with butterscotch sauce and vanilla ice cream?

Chef Jim McCarthy, Dave O'Callaghan **Owner** Jim McCarthy **Times** 12.30-3/5-10.30 Closed 24-26 Dec, 1 Jan, Etr, Mon, L Mon-Sat, D Mon **Prices** Fixed L 3 course fr £18.50, Tasting menu £40, Starter £4-£9, Main £14-£20, Dessert £5-£6, Service optional, Groups min 6 service 10% **Wines** 6 bottles over £30, 25 bottles under £30, 4 by glass **Notes** Pre-theatre menu 5-7pm £14.95, 6 course £40, Sunday L £18.50, Vegetarian menu **Seats** 75, Pr/dining room 25 **Children** Portions, Menu **Parking** On street

Café Vaudeville

French NEW

Big-flavoured brasserie dishes in a historic city-centre building

☎ 028 9043 9160
25-39 Arthur St BT1 4GQ
e-mail: info@cafevaudeville.com

In the early 19th century, the premises belonged to an entrepreneur named Dunville, dealer in tea and fine whiskies. After a long incarnation as a bank, the grand city-centre edifice is now a stylish contemporary eatery, its high-ceilinged spaces ringing with swing jazz (with live music on selected evenings). The aptly named Luxebar is one part of the operation, but the modern brasserie menus are a strong attraction too. Dishes are not too precious in their execution, but big on flavour, as in a starter of goats' cheese fritters rolled in crushed walnuts, with beetroot and apple balls in a robust cabernet sauvignon dressing. That could be followed by

Save on Hotels. Book at theAA.com/hotel

BELFAST 647 IRELAND

smoked salmon and cod fishcakes with lemon aïoli, or moistly tender pork belly cooked for 18 hours, and served with Pommery mustard mash and garlic sausage in a sauce of the braising juices. Finish with professionally executed chocolate fondant and peanut butter ice cream.

Times 12-3/5-9 Closed Sun **Prices** Fixed D 2 course £13.95, Starter £3-£11, Main £10.95-£19.95, Dessert £3-£5.95 **Notes** Fixed D 2 course Wed-Fri 5-6.45, includes glass wine

Deanes at Queens

◉ Modern European 🍃

Buzzy brasserie dining near the university

☎ 028 9038 2111
1 College Gardens BT9 6BQ
e-mail: deanesatqueens@michaeldeane.co.uk

The name Michael Deane needs no introduction in these parts (see entry for Deanes Restaurant), and his buzzy bar and grill restaurant in the University Quarter is a hot-ticket in the city. The smart space has large windows to take in the view over the Botanic Gardens and a menu that favours a modish European approach. Start, perhaps, with duck rillettes with celeriac, red onion jam and country bread, or smoked haddock and leek fishcake served with an apple, cabbage and raisin coleslaw. Among main courses, Glenarm salmon is cooked perfectly (deliciously crisp skin) and comes with chorizo orzo pasta, crisp tempura vegetables and gremolata, or go for the 12-hour braised beef in a risotto with leek and parmesan, Serrano ham and Chianti. Finish with all the comfort and joy of a chocolate steamed pudding, with accompanying mint chocolate chip ice cream.

Chef Chris Fearon **Owner** Michael Deane
Times 12-3/5.30-10 Closed 25-26 Dec, D Sun
Prices Fixed L 2 course £12.50, Fixed D 3 course £19.50, Starter £5-£9, Main £11-£18.50, Dessert £5-£6.50, Service added but optional 10% **Wines** 17 bottles over £30, 24 bottles under £30, 12 by glass **Notes** Prix-fixe menu 3 course £19.50 Mon-Thu 5.30-7, Sunday L, Vegetarian available **Seats** 120, Pr/dining room 44 **Children** Portions, Menu **Parking** On street

Deanes Restaurant

◉◉◉ — *see page 648*

James Street South Restaurant & Bar

◉◉ Modern European 🍃

Confident modern cooking in the city centre

☎ 028 9043 4310
21 James Street South BT2 7GA
e-mail: info@jamesstreetsouth.co.uk
dir: Located between Brunswick St & Bedford St

Tucked away behind city hall, this slick central restaurant has a strong local fan base for all the right reasons. Light floods the bright and spacious dining room through high-arched windows, revealing a pared-back contemporary look involving abstract art on white walls and dark brown leather seats on a blond-wood floor. The man directing the action at the stoves is Niall McKenna, who has built his reputation on solid foundations. Strong bonds with local suppliers are key to sourcing the best local materials, which he subjects to well-honed French techniques in a blend of classical, and bright, up-to-date ideas. Red gurnard comes with a concasse of tomato, chorizo and capers, and seaweed beurre blanc, ahead of a melt-in-the-mouth veal osso buco with raisin, roasted parsnips, and truffle and ricotta gnocchi, or there might be fillet of Antrim beef teamed with girolles, cauliflower and ox tongue. Dessert hits the spot with an imaginative confection of lemon vacherin with crispy pistachios, curd and fromage frais sorbet.

Chef Niall McKenna **Owner** Niall & Joanne McKenna
Times 12-2.45/5.45-10.45 Closed 25-26 Dec, 1 Jan, Etr Sun & Mon, 12-15 Jul, Sun **Prices** Fixed L 2 course fr £15.50, Fixed D 3 course fr £26.50, Tasting menu fr £55, Starter £4.50-£10.50, Main £15.50-£22, Dessert £5.50-£9, Service optional, Groups min 5 service 10% **Wines** 35 bottles over £30, 40 bottles under £30, 8 by glass **Notes** Pre-theatre menu Mon-Sat 2/3 course, Vegetarian available **Seats** 60, Pr/dining room 40 **Children** Portions **Parking** On street

Malmaison Belfast

◉ French

Confident Anglo-French brasserie cooking

☎ 028 9022 0200 & 9022 0201
34-38 Victoria St BT1 3GH
e-mail: belfast@malmaison.com
web: www.malmaison.com
dir: M1 along Westlink to Grosvenor Rd. Follow city centre signs. Pass City Hall on right, turn left onto Victoria St. Hotel on right

The Malmaison hotel group has been extremely resourceful when it comes to finding places to pitch camp, and in Belfast a former seed warehouse is the chosen setting. Boutique design gives the venue as much idiosyncratic class as the rest of the chain has, offering a mixture of wall-mounted objets and boldly striped upholstery in the Brasserie. Head chef Ip Wai oversees a confident version of the Anglo-French brasserie idiom, from a high-impact smoked ham hock and foie gras terrine with spiced apple chutney, through tender and unctuous duck confit with garlic potatoes and pickled girolles, to a warming wintry dessert of creamy rice pudding with mulled cherries.

Times 12-2.30/6-12.30

Malone Lodge Hotel

◉ Modern European

Refurbished hotel with modish menu

☎ 028 9038 8000
60 Eglantine Av, Malone Rd BT9 6DY
e-mail: info@malonelodgehotel.com
web: www.malonelodgehotelbelfast.com
dir: At hospital rdbt exit towards Bouchar Rd, left at 1st rdbt, right at lights at top, then 1st left

Close to the famous Queens University, this townhouse hotel is well placed for exploring the city. A refurbishment in 2013 has given the restaurant its own entrance from the street and, thus, a little more individual identity, while the banqueting and conference facilities have been spruced up as well. So raise a glass to celebrate this investment in the city in the new bar, or head through to the modish Green Door restaurant and tuck into some good contemporary food. Butternut squash and pea risotto is a first course with broad appeal, followed by pan-seared fillet of salmon with samphire and seaweed beurre blanc, or rib-eye steak with black pepper cream. Chocolate and toffee brownie with clotted cream and caramel ice cream delivers the comfort factor among desserts.

Times 12.30-3/5-10 Closed L Mon-Sat, D Sun

Deanes Restaurant

Modern French, Irish **V** 🍷 NOTABLE WINE LIST

Classy and confident cooking chez Michael Deane

☎ 028 9033 1134
36-40 Howard St BT1 6PF
e-mail: info@michaeldeane.co.uk
web: www.michaeldeane.co.uk
dir: At rear of City Hall. Howard St on left opposite Spires building

Michael Deane is a talented chef who has made his mark in the Northern Irish dining scene over many years. These days he has a number of addresses in the city (see entry for Deanes at Queens, for example), providing the kind of food people want to eat. This Howard Street location has changed a little in recent years, moving away from the sharp end of fine dining to a more relaxed approach. Don't go thinking corners are being cut, though, for this remains a serious restaurant of serious intent, and you can still delve into a tasting menu if you wish. It's smart and a little posh, but won't scare the horses; neatly laid, linen-dressed tables stand on a blond-wood floor and warm vermillion tones cover the walls. The cooking takes a Franco-Irish route through contemporary culinary thinking, with first-rate ingredients allowed to shine. There's plenty of shellfish to choose from - note there's also a seafood bar at this address - so seared scallop might come with samphire and pancetta, or Carlingford rock oyster with shallot vinaigrette. Pressed duck confit comes as a first course in the company of a pastila and pickled mushrooms, or go for the earthy comfort of mushroom risotto with truffle oil. Regional Fermanagh chicken might feature in a main course with onion tarte fine, morels and thyme, or roast halibut with spinach, mussels and chive velouté. There's plenty of interesting stuff among desserts, too: chocolate and espresso mousse, for example, with Kahlúa jelly, mascarpone and amaretti, or warm hazelnut cake with pistachio ice cream, candied orange and Frangelico syrup.

Chef Michael Deane, Simon Toye
Owner Michael Deane
Times 12-3/5.30-10 Closed 25 Dec, BHs, Sun **Prices** Tasting menu £55-£85, Starter £4.50-£11, Main £14-£28, Dessert £6.50-£8.50, Service added but optional 10% **Wines** 97 bottles over £30, 39 bottles under £30, 11 by glass **Notes** 6 course tasting menu, Vegetarian menu **Seats** 80, Pr/dining room 50 **Children** Portions, Menu **Parking** On street (after 6pm), car park Clarence St

Save on Hotels. Book at **theAA.com/hotel**

BELFAST – CO DOWN 649 IRELAND

BELFAST *continued*

The Merchant Hotel

◉◉ Modern European ☺

Magnificent setting for contemporary cooking

☎ 028 9023 4888
16 Skipper St, Cathedral Quarter BT1 2DZ
e-mail: thegreatroom@merchanthotel.com
dir: In city centre, 2nd left at Albert clock onto Waring St.
Hotel on left

The architects of this grand Italianate building certainly succeeded in their aim to create a bank headquarters that would overawe, and no less successful has been its redevelopment into a 21st-century hotel. The Great Room is the apposite name of the restaurant, a jaw-droppingly magnificent room, all cherubs, marble columns and plasterwork under a glass-domed ceiling, with banquettes and chairs upholstered in vivid red. The cooking is based on the classical repertoire, updated to meet today's expectations, and the kitchen concentrates on top-drawer produce: duck from Fermanagh, for instance, cod landed at Portavogie. Start, perhaps, with caramelised scallops with glazed pork and smoked Alsace foam, moving on to something labour-intensive such as three ways with rabbit - saddle ballottine, crispy leg, braised shoulder - cooked just so and of excellent flavour, with rosemary gnocchi and sweet potato purée. Fish holds up equally well: parsley-crusted salmon fillet with seafood tagliatelle and lemon and herb velouté, for example. End with a textbook bitter chocolate tart with orange honeycomb and coffee foam.

Chef John Paul Leake **Owner** The Merchant Hotel
Times 12-2.30/6-10 Closed L Sat **Prices** Fixed L 2 course
£19.50-£24.50, Fixed D 3 course £26.50-£31.50, Tasting
menu £65-£85, Starter £6.50-£10.50, Main
£19.50-£28.50, Dessert £8.50-£15.50, Service added but
optional 10% **Wines** 91 bottles over £30, 48 bottles under
£30, 13 by glass **Notes** Pre-theatre 2/3 course
£18.50/£22.50, Sunday L, Vegetarian available, Dress
restrictions, Smart casual, Civ Wed 120 **Seats** 85, Pr/
dining room 18 **Children** Portions, Menu **Parking** On
street

Shu

◉◉ Modern European ☺

Contemporary Irish cooking with a buzz

☎ 028 9038 1655
253-255 Lisburn Rd BT9 7EN
e-mail: eat@shu-restaurant.com
dir: From city centre take Lisburn Rd (lower end).
Restaurant in 1m, on corner of Lower Windsor Avenue

A terrace of whitewashed Victorian houses in the fashionable Lisburn shopping district of Belfast is the setting for this sleek modern restaurant. The name might hint at something Oriental, but this Shu is named after the Egyptian God of atmosphere, who seems pleased by what is going on and has obligingly breathed a real buzz into the air of the breezy, open-plan venue. An open-to-view kitchen throws its culinary theatre and enticing smells into the mix as the chefs turn out some real treats in a repertoire of Irish-accented modern European dishes. Expect well-conceived ideas such as crispy pork cromesquis with Jerusalem artichoke purée and hazelnuts, followed by Clandeboye wood pigeon scented with lapsang souchong tea, beetroot, celeriac purée, kale and purple carrots. To close the show, only the finest Amedei chocolate will do for a finale of chocolate mousse with hazelnuts and banana cream.

Chef Brian McCann **Owner** Alan Reid **Times** 12-2.30/6-10
Closed 25-26 Dec, 1 Jan, 12-13 Jul, Sun **Prices** Fixed L 2
course £13.25, Fixed D 3 course £28-£30.50, Starter
£4.50-£9, Main £12-£21, Dessert £5.75, Service optional,
Groups min 6 service 10% **Wines** 18 bottles over £30, 48
bottles under £30, 19 by glass **Notes** Vegetarian
available **Seats** 100, Pr/dining room 24 **Children** Portions,
Menu **Parking** 4, On street

CRAWFORDSBURN Map 1 D5

The Old Inn

◉◉ Modern European ☺

Revamped restaurant in historic old inn

☎ 028 9185 3255
15 Main St BT19 1JH
e-mail: info@theoldinn.com
web: www.theoldinn.com
dir: From Belfast along A2, past Belfast City Airport.
Contine past Holywood & Belfast Folk & Transport
museum. 2m after museum left at lights onto B20 for
1.2m

As the oldest thatched part of the building dates from the early 17th century, it's fair to say that this sprawling low-slung hotel deserves its title. Over the centuries, an entertaining cast of famous writers and poets as well as the usual motley crew of smugglers has been fed and watered here. Nowadays, guests head for the smartly-refurbished Lewis restaurant, named after author C. S. Lewis who hung out here with his literary pals in the 1950s. The style is that of a contemporary bistro with a modish open-to-view kitchen turning out assured modern European-inflected ideas based on well-sourced Irish meat and game, and spanking-fresh seafood landed in the local ports of Strangford and Portavogie. The result is clear, bold flavours, as seen in a starter of chilled white crab with guacamole. At main course stage, take your pick from rosemary-skewered monkfish and salmon served with chargrilled fennel, smoked paprika, sautéed potatoes and lobster velouté, or a duo of duck breast and confit leg with chicken livers, pommes Anna, and passionfruit and redcurrant jus.

Chef Gavin Murphy **Owner** Danny, Paul & Garvan Rice
Times 12-9.30 Closed 25 Dec, All-day dining **Prices** Fixed
L 2 course £8.95, Fixed D 2 course £52.50, Starter
£4.95-£8.95, Main £12-£26, Dessert £4.95, Service
added but optional 10%, Groups min 6 service 10%
Wines 8 bottles over £30, 38 bottles under £30, 11 by
glass **Notes** Sunday L £13.50-£22.50, Vegetarian
available **Seats** 134, Pr/dining room 25 **Children** Portions,
Menu **Parking** 80

DUNDRUM Map 1 D5

Mourne Seafood Bar

◉ Seafood ☺

Vibrant fish restaurant 30 minutes from Belfast

☎ 028 4375 1377
10 Main St BT33 0LU
e-mail: bob@mourneseafood.com
dir: On main road from Belfast to The Mournes, on village
main street

The name of this famous seafood joint says it all really -
set in a handsome Georgian building in a pretty fishing
village, it comes with the Mourne Mountains as a
backdrop and seafood centre stage. Inside there's none of
that big-city cool, just an easygoing, relaxed kind of place
with wooden floors and chunky wooden tables buoyed up
by vibrant artwork, smiley staff and a warm, buzzy
atmosphere. Straightforward fish and shellfish dishes
that allow sea-fresh produce (and local organic veg) to
shine is the key to success here, with the kitchen even
garnering oysters and mussels from its own beds. Expect
Mourne seafood chowder perhaps, modish hake fillet with
chick pea and chorizo, or monkfish with avocado salsa,
while for the traditionalists, fish 'n' chips with mushy
peas.

Chef Wayne Carville **Owner** Bob & Joanne McCoubrey
Times 12.30-9.30 Closed 25 Dec, Mon-Thu (winter)
Prices Prices not confirmed Service optional, Groups min
6 service 10% **Wines** 5 by glass **Notes** Fixed D menu Sat
only, Sunday L, Vegetarian available **Seats** 75, Pr/dining
room 20 **Children** Portions, Menu **Parking** On street

NEWTOWNARDS Map 1 D5

Balloo House

◉ Traditional European NEW ☺

Lively bistro and serene dining room in a venerable old house

☎ 028 9754 1210
1 Comber Rd, Killinchy BT23 6PA
e-mail: info@balloohouse.com
web: www.balloohouse.com
dir: A22 from Belfast, through Dundonald. 6m from Comber

A coaching inn in the Georgian era and a farmhouse in the Victorian, the venerable whitewashed house near Strangford Lough has pretty much seen it all. Stone walls and flagged floors bear witness to its age, and the dining offers two moods - a ground-floor bistro with plenty of happy hubbub, and a more serene evening-only restaurant upstairs, where exposed walls are offset by champagne upholstery and an aura of relaxing civility. A cheery lunch down below might bring on salt and chilli squid with Asian slaw, chilli jam and garlic mayo, Gloucestershire Old Spot pork belly with roast apples, boxty (potato pancakes) and baconed cabbage, with dark chocolate torte and salt caramel ice cream to conclude, all served to a background of REM's greatest hits. Up above, creativity takes wing for Lough Neagh eel teriyaki with smoked eel fritter, apple and radish, duck breast with orange and fennel polenta and sweet-sour cherries, and buttermilk pannacotta with roast peach and raspberries. Certainly one to watch.

Chef Grainne Donnelly **Owner** Danny Millar
Times Noon-9pm Closed 25 Dec **Prices** Fixed L 2 course £12.95-£17.95, Fixed D 3 course £17.95-£26.95, Starter £3.25-£6.95, Main £9.95-£18.95, Dessert £3.95-£4.50, Service optional, Groups min 8 service 10% **Wines** 19 bottles over £30, 44 bottles under £30, 7 by glass
Notes Sunday L, Vegetarian available **Seats** 80, Pr/dining room 30 **Children** Portions, Menu

CO FERMANAGH

ENNISKILLEN Map 1 C5

Lough Erne Resort

◉◉ Modern, Traditional V

Great Irish produce in golfer's paradise

☎ 028 6632 3230
Belleek Rd BT93 7ED
e-mail: info@lougherneresort.com
web: www.lougherneresort.com
dir: A46 from Enniskillen towards Donegal, hotel in 3m

This vast and luxurious, purpose-built golfing hotel guarantees panoramic views, located on its own 60-acre peninsula jutting into the lough. It's a golfer's haven, with one of its two championship courses designed by Nick Faldo. The Catalina is the fine-dining option here, named after the famous seaplanes that were based on the lough during the Second World War and commemorated in framed photos on the walls. It's an expansive space sporting a classic look and formal vibe, with vaulted ceilings and views of the course and water through its arched windows. Home-grown chef Noel McMeel's menus showcase quality seasonal produce from the local larder in creative dishes underpinned by classical foundations. Think pan-fried breast of Lissara duck with mixed bean cassoulet, marinated cherries, beetroot, parsnip purée and red wine jus, or perhaps roast fillet of Irish hake with citrus-infused lentils, confit carrot and Madeira Jus. Otherwise, try the signature 'Lough Erne mixed grill' and perhaps an apple duo finish - bavarois and tarte Tatin with vanilla ice cream.

Chef Noel McMeel **Owner** Jim & Eileen Treacy
Times 1-2.30/6.30-10 Closed L Mon-Sat **Prices** Fixed D 3 course £34-£39.50, Service added but optional 10% **Wines** 3 by glass **Notes** Sunday L, Vegetarian menu, Civ Wed 315 **Seats** 75, Pr/dining room 30 **Children** Menu **Parking** 200

Manor House Country Hotel

◉◉ Irish ☺

Laudable cooking and loch views

☎ 028 6862 2200
Killadeas BT94 1NY
e-mail: info@manorhousecountryhotel.com
dir: On B82, 7m N of Enniskillen

The original manor is a striking building, much modified in the Victorian period when the Italianate tower was added. The Balleek Restaurant is in two parts, one in the old building, the other in a conservatory-style extension with views over Lower Lough Erne. The kitchen deploys the freshest produce from local suppliers and uses it to good effect on a compact menu that manages to encompass modern ideas as well as the more familiar. Roast chicken breast, for instance, served simply in its own juices with Savoy cabbage and mash, preceded by a starter of lobster ravioli, stuffed with a generous amount of the crustacean, its flavour enhanced by a sauce of rocket, basil and lemongrass. A degree of complexity can be seen in some main courses - take roast olive-encrusted cannon of lamb, of excellent quality, with braised neck, fennel jam, rosemary jus, swede and broad beans - and a meal can end with a classic version of crème brûlée with cherry compôte.

Chef Ryan Murphy **Owner** Manor House Country Hotel Ltd
Times 12.30-3/6-10 Closed L Mon-Fri **Prices** Fixed D 3 course £35-£40, Service optional **Notes** Sunday L, Vegetarian available, Dress restrictions, Smart casual, Civ Wed 350 **Seats** 90, Pr/dining room 350 **Children** Portions, Menu **Parking** 300

Save on Hotels. Book at theAA.com/hotel

CO LONDONDERRY 651 IRELAND

CO LONDONDERRY

CASTLEDAWSON — Map 1 C5

The Inn Castledawson

◉◉ Modern Irish

Creative cooking in Seamus Heaney's birth place

☎ 028 7946 9777
47 Main St BT45 8AA
e-mail: info@theinncastledawson.com
web: www.theinncastledawson.com
dir: Castledawson rdbt, from Belfast take 3rd exit, from Londonderry take 1st exit

The custard-yellow inn at the heart of Castledawson village was brought into the world of contemporary design with a classy makeover in 2009, transforming its restaurant with a glossy new look. Beneath its high, blond-wood beamed ceilings are chocolate and cream leather high-backed chairs at linen-clad tables, a centrepiece fireplace resplendent in gold designer wallpaper, cream walls hung with photos of Castledawson in the old days, and a large rear window looking across the decking terrace to the River Moyola. The kitchen makes the most of fine regionally-sourced produce in creative modern ideas - perhaps breast of local estate wood pigeon teamed with a croquette of confit leg, onion purée and Clonakilty black pudding, while mains extend to a boozy dish of perry-poached pheasant with mulled wine cabbage and walnuts; fishy ideas might offer pan-fried skate wing with caper and orange butter and parsley gnocchi.

Times 12-8.30 Closed 25-26 Dec, 1 wk Jan

LIMAVADY — Map 1 C6

The Lime Tree

◉ Traditional Mediterranean ✎

Long-running neighbourhood restaurant showcasing the pick of the province

☎ 028 7776 4300
60 Catherine St BT49 9DB
e-mail: info@limetreerest.com
dir: Enter Limavady from Derry side. Restaurant on right on small slip road

Stanley and Maria Matthews have run their appealing neighbourhood restaurant since 1996 and it's a firmly entrenched presence on the local gastronomic scene. Named after the lime trees planted in Limavady in honour of local lad William Massey landing the top job as PM in New Zealand, the operation is intimate, cosy and impeccably run by Maria out front. Stanley mans the stoves, delivering the best of what Northern Ireland has to offer via Mediterranean-accented menus that continually evolve to take advantage of the splendid, slithering-fresh, locally-landed fish and seafood. The home-made crabcakes are quite rightly a fixture, and could be accompanied by apple salad and a cider and rapeseed oil dressing, while all that fresh fish might find its way into a Spanish-influenced stew laden with tomato and garlic; carnivores can expect chicken tajine with lemon, chilli and coriander. Finish with the deep comfort of steamed Seville orange marmalade sponge with vanilla custard.

Chef Stanley Matthews **Owner** Mr & Mrs S Matthews **Times** 12-2/5.30-9 Closed 25-26 Dec, 12 Jul, Sun-Mon, L Sun-Wed **Prices** Fixed L 2 course £11.50-£14.50, Starter £4.95-£8.95, Main £14.75-£23.50, Dessert £4.95-£7, Service optional **Wines** 5 bottles over £30, 26 bottles under £30, 5 by glass **Notes** Early bird menu 2/3 course Tue-Fri 6-7pm, Vegetarian available **Seats** 30 **Children** Portions, Menu **Parking** On street

Roe Park Resort

◉ Modern, Traditional ✎

Traditional dining in a relaxed resort hotel

☎ 028 7772 2222
BT49 9LB
e-mail: reservations@roeparkresort.com
web: www.roeparkresort.com
dir: On A6 (Londonderry-Limavady road), 0.5m from Limavady. 8m from Derry airport

Built as a country mansion in the 18th century, surrounded by 150 acres of grounds beside the River Roe, Roe Park has been extended in recent years into a vast modern golfing and leisure resort. Just one of several dining options here, Greens Restaurant is a stylish, split-level space offering mostly traditional cooking with the odd modern twist. Start, perhaps, with confit duck rillette with toasted sourdough, beetroot and orange relish, moving on to fillet of Irish beef with potato croquette, confit garlic, button mushrooms and jus, or grilled salmon supreme with oriental noodles and a ginger and soy dressing. If cheesecake is your thing, there's a daily-changing selection of flavours, or you may want to go down the comfort route with the steamed banana and ginger pudding with fresh cream and sauce anglaise.

Chef Emma Gormley **Owner** Mr Conn, Mr McKeever, Mr Wilton **Times** 12-3/6.30-9 **Prices** Prices not confirmed Service optional **Wines** 8 by glass **Notes** Sunday L, Vegetarian available, Dress restrictions, Smart casual, Civ Wed 250 **Seats** 160, Pr/dining room 50 **Children** Portions, Menu **Parking** 250

LONDONDERRY — Map 1 C5

Browns Restaurant and Champagne Lounge

◉ Modern Irish **NEW V**

On-the-money modern Irish cooking

☎ 028 7134 5180
1 Bonds Hill, Waterside BT47 6DW
e-mail: eat@brownsrestaurant.com

Situated on the edge of the city centre by Lough Foyle, Browns has quickly garnered a loyal local following since it opened its doors in 2009. Get in the mood with a glass of bubbly on a squidgy sofa in the champagne lounge, then head for one of the white linen-swathed tables in the dining room, where toffee-hued walls and leather seating, stripy banquettes, and pale wooden floors add up to a sharp contemporary look. Driven by well-sourced local ingredients and unfussy execution, the kitchen turns out an appealing roll-call of modern Irish ideas, with fish and seafood a strong suit. Pan-seared scallops are matched with braised pork cheek, honey and soy sauce, and apple and star anise purée, ahead of roast fillet of monkfish with cauliflower served crispy and in a curried cream sauce. To finish, Turkish Delight, chocolate cookies and ginger cream put a novel spin on crème brûlée.

Chef Ian Orr **Prices** Fixed L 2 course £14, Tasting menu £40-£60, Starter £7-£9.95, Main £17-£22.95, Dessert £5.50 **Notes** Tasting menu 6 course, Early Bird £19.95 Tue-Sat, Vegetarian menu **Children** Menu

Republic of Ireland

Blarney Castle, County Cork

REPUBLIC OF IRELAND

CO CARLOW

TULLOW
Map 1 C3

Mount Wolseley Hotel, Spa & Country Club

◉ Modern European V 🖑

Intriguing modern dining at a luxury golfing hotel

☎ 059 9180100 & 9151674
e-mail: info@mountwolseley.ie
dir: N7 from Dublin. In Naas, take N9 towards Carlow. In Castledermot left for Tullow

The 200-acre country estate once owned by Frederick Wolseley, of car making renown, is now a splendiferous golf resort with all of the spa and leisure bells and whistles you can imagine. The championship course attracts golfers from all over the world, so the hotel's main restaurant duly serves up a wide-ranging repertoire of modern European ideas on a menu spiked with dishes with supplementary charges. Fine local materials are to the fore - seared Kilmore scallops, say, teamed with hot cacao, potato popcorn and hollandaise sauce, while mains could see Cajun-spiced Slaney Valley lamb served with rosemary fondant potatoes, asparagus, celeriac purée and minted yoghurt. Finish with pineapple beignet, crispy sweet tagliatelle, and pineapple and coconut cappuccino.

Chef David Cuddihy, Fabien Riquet **Owner** The Morrissey Family **Times** 12.30-2.30/6-9.30 Closed 24-26 Dec, L Mon-Sat **Prices** Service optional **Wines** 15 bottles over €30, 35 bottles under €30, 6 by glass **Notes** Sunday L €25-€40, Vegetarian menu, Civ Wed 450 **Seats** 150, Pr/dining room 40 **Children** Portions, Menu **Parking** 500

CO CAVAN

CAVAN
Map 1 C4

Radisson Blu Farnham Estate Hotel

◉ French, European NEW

Irish produce, French-influenced cooking

☎ 049 4377700
Farnham Estate
e-mail: info.farnham@radissonblu.com
dir: From Dublin take N3 to Cavan. From Cavan take Killeshandra road for 4km

With lakes, rivers and ancient oak forests all around on this massive 1300-acre, 16th-century estate, you're never short of outdoor pursuits to work up a keen appetite at Farnham, a historic stately home that has morphed into an upmarket country hotel offering the full corporate package of spa, golf, wedding and meeting facilities. Clever use of plush drapes and screens helps to soften the capacious space that is the Botanica Restaurant, and a friendly service team is well-versed in the ins and outs of each dish. The kitchen places its faith in local ingredients, bringing it all together with French-inspired

flair. Spicy tiger prawns, orange and dill-infused salmon, and smoked mackerel rillettes make up a seafood platter, then roast rack and slow-cooked rump of local lamb is delivered with aubergine caviar and buttery potato mash. Dessert could be a riff on lemon, in the shape of a zesty tart, Madeleines, and jelly.

Chef Philippe Farineau **Times** 1-3/7-9.15 Closed L Mon-Sat **Prices** Fixed D 3 course €32 **Wines** 23 bottles over €30, 22 bottles under €30, 9 by glass **Notes** D 4 course €40.00, Sun L buffet style, pre-booking essential **Seats** Pr/dining room 35 **Parking** 600

KINGSCOURT
Map 1 C4

Cabra Castle Hotel

◉ European NEW 🖑

Grand house with a traditional menu

☎ 042 9667030
Cabra Castle
e-mail: sales@cabracastle.com
dir: R165 between Kingscourt & Carrickmacross

With a long history going back to the 17th century, the structure of Cabra Castle is in fact rather newer than that, but it is still old and looks mightily impressive, carrying the castle moniker very well indeed. The hotel's Courtroom Restaurant occupies a series of first-floor rooms which provide fabulous views over the 100-acre estate. The elegant, traditional décor and well-spaced, smartly laid tables set the scene for the classical cooking that follows. Start with prawn and smoked salmon tart with sakura salad and pesto oil, followed by a mid-course - iced cranberry granita or such like. Next up, main course might be roast rack of lamb on a bed of champ, finished with a rosemary gravy. Among desserts, mascarpone and passionfruit curd comes with excellent home-made meringues (nicely soft and chewy on the inside).

Chef Clare Gloukhova **Owner** Corscadden Family **Times** 7-9 Closed 24-27 Dec, L Mon-Sat **Prices** Prices not confirmed Service optional **Wines** 8 by glass **Notes** Sunday L, Dress restrictions, Smart casual **Seats** 65, Pr/dining room 60 **Children** Portions **Parking** 120

CO CLARE

BALLYVAUGHAN
Map 1 B3

Gregans Castle

◉◉◉ – see opposite

DOOLIN
Map 1 B3

Cullinan's Seafood Restaurant & Guest House

◉◉ Modern French 🖑

Artistically presented seafood and meat by the river Aille

☎ 065 7074183
e-mail: cullinans@eircom.net
dir: Located in Doolin town centre R479

The Cullinans' guesthouse in rural Clare overlooks the Aille River meadow, the sumptuous views captured by broad windows on two sides of the dining room. A large seascape mural provides alternative optical diversion. Tables are shoehorned in close enough to encourage happy converse between guests, and James Cullinan's confident, supremely professional knack with seafood is another essential part of the picture. Dishes are presented with a certain artistry, and deliver on freshness, flavour and accuracy, as in a starter assembly of salmon, cod, monkfish and langoustine with two sauces, a bisque and a white wine cream. If you're moving on to meat for main, you might encounter superlative Barbary duck breast rubbed with cinnamon and lime zest, served with a ragoût of wild mushrooms and shallots, in an apple and cider sauce, or there could be Black Angus fillet with chorizo and Savoy cabbage in a rich reduction of burgundy. Finish self-indulgently with the likes of milk chocolate tart and raspberry sorbet, or Tia Maria cheesecake with an ice cream made of Ferrero Rocher.

Chef James Cullinan **Owner** James & Carol Cullinan **Times** 6-9 Closed Nov-Etr, Wed, Sun, L all week **Prices** Fixed D 3 course €27.50, Starter €6-€9.95, Main €20-€27, Dessert €6.75-€8.75, Service optional, Groups min 8 service 10% **Wines** 2 bottles over €30, 24 bottles under €30, 6 by glass **Notes** Vegetarian available **Seats** 24 **Children** Portions **Parking** 20

Save on Hotels. Book at **theAA.com/hotel**

CO CLARE 655 **IRELAND**

ENNIS   Map 1 B3

Temple Gate Hotel

◉ Modern International V ✍

Modern bistro cooking in a former convent

☎ 065 6823300
The Square
e-mail: info@templegatehotel.com
dir: Exit N18 onto Tulla Rd for 0.25m, hotel on left

The Sisters of Mercy having relocated to a new home nearby in 1995, their Victorian convent not far from the cobbled town centre became a modern hotel, with a pub called Preachers and a dining room named Legends. That latter is a three-part room with big windows and plenty of natural daylight, where modern bistro cooking is the order of the day. Fried garlic mushrooms or a smoked chicken salad start things off, with follow-ups of salmon darne and pea purée in smoked salmon and dill cream sauce, or nutty pork (an escalope coated in nutty breadcrumbs with colcannon in apple and cider sauce). Finish with an ice cream meringue nest and dark chocolate mousse, or lemon cheesecake.

Chef Paul Shortt **Owner** John Madden
Times 12.30-2.30/5.30-9.30 Closed 25-26 Dec
Prices Fixed L 2 course €16.95, Fixed D 3 course €22.95, Service optional **Wines** 7 bottles over €30, 10 bottles under €30, 6 by glass **Notes** Early bird menu, Sunday L,

Vegetarian menu, Civ Wed 70 **Seats** 100, Pr/dining room 60 **Children** Portions, Menu

---

LAHINCH   Map 1 B3

Moy House

◉◉ Modern French V ✍

Modern cooking and fabulous sea views

☎ 065 7082800
e-mail: moyhouse@eircom.net
web: www.moyhouse.com
dir: Located 1km from Lahinch on the Miltown Malbay road

Moy House looks spruce with its whitewashed 18th-century Italianate tower lording it over picturesque Lahinch Bay. The small-scale country house stands in 15 acres of grounds with mature woodlands and a river to stroll along, while a classy contemporary makeover has added a dollop of up-to-date style to the period elegance of its interior. The conservatory restaurant is easy on the eye with its burnished wooden floors and cream-jacketed high-backed chairs at romantically candlelit linen-clothed tables, while a floor-to-ceiling wall of windows makes the most of the fabulous sea views. The wealth of excellent ingredients available locally means that the kitchen is never lost for inspiration when composing its menus of modern French ideas, so you might see smoked salmon from the Burren area adding interest to potato-

filled agnolotti pasta with sauce soubise and spring onions. Next up, local beef could be partnered with potato millefeuille, mushroom duxelles, confit garlic, wilted spinach and sauce Bordelaise, before almond cake with lemon curd and meringue closes the show.

Chef Gerard O'Connor **Owner** Antoin O'Looney
Times 7-8.30 Closed Jan-Mar, Nov-Dec, Sun-Mon (off peak) **Prices** Tasting menu €55, Service optional **Wines** 4 bottles under €30, 4 by glass **Notes** Fixed D 5 course €55 (reservation req), Vegetarian menu, Dress restrictions, Smart casual **Seats** 35, Pr/dining room 22
Children Portions, Menu **Parking** 50

Gregans Castle

BALLYVAUGHAN   MAP 1 B3

Modern European

Outstanding contemporary food at a little house in the Burren

☎ 065 7077005
e-mail: stay@gregans.ie
dir: On N67, 3.5m S of Ballyvaughan

The Burren is a wild and beautiful landscape - Ireland's smallest National Park, as it happens - and it is the setting for this 18th-century manor turned country-house hotel. It isn't actually a castle, but if that's a deal breaker, you're really losing out. (There is a castle opposite, which was the seat of the Princes of the Burren.) Gregans is a luxurious hideaway filled with antiques and period Georgian elegance. The restaurant is a romantic and refined room where picture windows open onto a view across the gardens to Galway Bay; candlelight flickers in the evening, and as the summer sun sets, diners are treated to an eerie light show as the dying rays ignite the grey limestone rocks. And if it's a light show you're after, there are some fireworks on the plate too, for this is sharp modern cooking out of the top drawer. The local landscape provides a good deal of the ingredients and the cooking techniques of the team in the kitchen favour modernist culinary thinking. Confit sea trout is a first course with well-judged flavours and bags of invention, with beetroot, avocado, horseradish and smoked eel combining to form a hugely satisfying whole. Next up, perhaps lightly salted cod with lobster, cauliflower and chorizo, or wild Tipperary rabbit served up with celeriac, lovage and sherry-poached raisins. Among desserts, forced rhubarb soufflé with white chocolate sorbet and crispy brown bread is a creative and compelling combination, but no more so than yoghurt bavarois with lemon, celery, thyme and olive oil. All the peripheral appetisers, pre-desserts and petits fours that you take as read with this style of dining are equally labour intensive, intelligently conceived and on the money.

Chef David Hurley **Owner** Simon Haden **Times** 6-9.30 Closed mid Nov-mid Feb, Wed, Sun (ex BH Sun), L all week **Prices** Fixed D 3 course €55, Service included **Wines** 14 by glass **Notes** Vegetarian available, Dress restrictions, Smart casual, no shorts, Civ Wed 65 **Seats** 50, Pr/dining room 36 **Children** Portions, Menu **Parking** 20

LISDOONVARNA   Map 1 B3

Sheedy's Country House Hotel

◉◉ Modern Irish

Flavour-led cooking in small rural hotel

☎ 065 7074026
e-mail: info@sheedys.com
dir: 20m from Ennis on N87

Chef-patron John Sheedy is the latest in a long line of Sheedys who have run the family business since the 18th century. The small-scale country house hotel is the oldest house in the village, which lies on the fringes of the Burren close by the coast, and exudes the sort of family-run, unpretentious tradition that keeps a loyal fan base returning again and again. It goes without saying, then, that John Sheedy has long-established local supply lines to support his passion for authentic ingredients: the kitchen garden provides fresh herbs and vegetables to supplement local organic meat and fish landed at nearby Doolin. Full-on, clearly defined flavours are what to expect in a repertoire of uncomplicated modern dishes, such as rillettes of rabbit with dried plum and brandied chutney, followed by roast rack of Burren lamb with a crisp crust of parsley and mustard, served with confit shoulder, spinach, and a ragoût of broad beans and tomato concasse. A classic lemon posset with raspberry coulis and sorbet and langue de chat biscuits makes a creamy, crunchy and refreshing finish.

Chef John Sheedy **Owner** John & Martina Sheedy
Times 6.30-8.30 Closed mid Oct-mid Mar, 1 day a week Mar-Apr **Prices** Starter €6.50-€12.50, Main €19.50-€28, Dessert €7.80, Service optional **Wines** 2 by glass **Notes** Vegetarian available **Seats** 28 **Children** Portions **Parking** 25

Wild Honey Inn

◉◉ Modern Irish **NEW**

Simple cooking done right

☎ 065 7074300
Kincora
e-mail: info@wildhoneyinn.com
dir: N18 from Ennis to Ennistymon. Continue through Ennistymon towards Lisdoonvarna, located on the right at edge of town

The culinary emphasis is on wild, free-range and seasonal produce at this characterful family-run inn. Wild Honey has been around since 1860, and although a makeover in recent years has grafted on a smart contemporary sheen, the place still oozes heaps of cosy character. The bar is utterly unpretentious with its pubby tables and 'first come first served' no bookings policy, so you'd best arrive early to dig into Aidan McGrath's no-nonsense modern bistro cooking. Driven by the splendid produce of the rugged West Coast, his hearty repertoire is simplicity itself, delivered with confidence and well-defined flavours, whether it's a starter of poached Liscannor crab claws with garlic and chilli butter sauce,

or a posh take on fish and chips, the fish pan-fried in olive oil and butter and served with sauce gribiche and twice-cooked chips. Meatier fare might run to marinated lamb neck fillet with buttered greens, black olives, capers, parsley and garlic, while comforting desserts, such as apple and blueberry crumble or classic vanilla crème brûlée, complete the picture.

Chef Aidan McGrath **Owner** Aidan McGrath
Times 1-3.30/5-9 Closed Jan-mid Feb, Tue, L Mon & Wed **Prices** Starter €7.50-€9.90, Main €14.50-€26.90, Dessert €6-€9.50 **Notes** Restricted opening winter, Sunday L

NEWMARKET-ON-FERGUS   Map 1 B3

Dromoland Castle

◉◉ Traditional Irish, European

Classical haute cuisine in a spectacular castle

☎ 061 368144
e-mail: sales@dromoland.ie
dir: From Ennis take N18, follow signs for Shannon/Limerick. 7m follow Quin. Newmarket-on-Fergus sign. Hotel 0.5m. From Shannon take N18 towards Ennis

It's a castle and no mistake. Turrets and ramparts are present and correct at this top-end country-house hotel, with a golf course on the magnificent estate, a spa lurking within its 15th-century walls, and plenty of good eating to be had. The Fig Tree restaurant is the more informal dining option and there's a plush cocktail bar too, but the main deal here is the Earl of Thomond restaurant, located in a spectacular room filled with antiques and oak-panelled period character. The cooking fits the bill with its classical good taste and high quality produce drawn from the local area, including the estate itself. Fricassée of wild mussels and monkfish is a starter that gives a thrilling taste of the sea, followed perhaps by milk-fed mignon of veal - beautifully tender - with leeks, scallions, courgettes, carrot and ginger purée and raisin sauce. Service is formal (expect a cloche or two) and everything looks wonderful on the plate. For dessert, a bitter-sweet chocolate 'dome' ends proceedings in style.

Times 7-10 Closed 24-27 Dec, L all week

CO CORK

BALLYCOTTON   Map 1 C2

Bayview Hotel

◉◉ Modern Irish, French

Imaginative contemporary cooking and sea views

☎ 021 4646746
e-mail: res@thebayviewhotel.com
dir: At Castlemartyr on N25 (Cork-Waterford road) turn onto R632 to Garryvoe, then follow signs for Shanagarry & Ballycotton

Bayview Hotel has a prime position above the bay and the harbour, and expansive windows through which you can admire the whole, lovely panorama as you eat. It's a gently contemporary space with muted colour tones,

looked over by a charming service team who are pretty much all local. There's a lot of local influence here, in fact, with a passion for the fruits of the countryside and sea around these parts. The seafood is landed down the road, farmers deliver their wares to the door, and the chef and his team know how to make the very best of them in creative, clearly-focused dishes. Start with the humble mackerel, perhaps, which comes three ways on a slate plate - pickled, smoked and pan-fried - with cucumber jelly, wasabi cream, mango mayonnaise and sesame crisps. Next up, roast rack and braised shank of lamb - nice and pink, perfectly rested - comes with spaghetti squash purée, glazed carrots and ras el hanout, and to finish, a well-made lemon tart hits the spot.

Times 1-3/7-9 Closed Nov-Apr, L Mon-Sat

BALLYLICKEY   Map 1 B2

Sea View House

◉◉ Traditional **V** ☙

Polished cooking in smart country-house hotel

☎ 027 50073
e-mail: info@seaviewhousehotel.com
web: www.seaviewhousehotel.com
dir: 3m N of Bantry towards Glengarriff, 70yds off main road, N71

The grand white-painted Seaview has the promised vista over Bantry Bay, glimpsed through the trees in the pretty gardens, but all the better from the first- and second-floor bedrooms. The restaurant is done out in a traditional manner, traversing three well-proportioned rooms, one of which is a conservatory with lush garden views. There's a good deal of local produce on the menu - crabs out of the bay, perhaps, or lamb from west Cork - and everything is handled with care and attention to detail. Start, perhaps, with a light and flavourful scallop mousse, served with a vermouth sauce and topped with the scallop roe. Next up, a superb piece of sole, grilled on the bone which is removed before service, and partnered with a caper butter served in a pot, plus mashed potatoes, wilted spinach, broccoli and cauliflower. Chocolate mousse with white chocolate sauce is a typical dessert.

Save on Hotels. Book at **theAA.com/hotel**

CO CORK 657 **IRELAND**

Sea View House

Chef Eleanor O'Donavon **Owner** Kathleen O'Sullivan **Times** 12.30-1.45/7-9.30 Closed Nov-Mar, L Mon-Sat **Prices** Prices not confirmed Service included, Groups min 10 service 10% **Wines** 10 by glass **Notes** Sunday L, Vegetarian menu, Dress restrictions, Smart casual, Civ Wed 75 **Seats** 50 **Children** Portions, Menu **Parking** 32

BALTIMORE Map 1 B1

Rolfs Country House

◎ French, European V ♨

Continental classics in a heavenly spot

☎ 028 20289
e-mail: info@rolfscountryhouse.com
dir: Into Baltimore, sharp left, follow restaurant signs, up hill

The Haffner family have been in business here since 1979, and who could blame them for staying put when you see the location. Set in beautiful sub-tropical gardens, the stone-built restaurant has world-class views overlooking Baltimore Harbour to Roaringwater Bay and Carbery's 100 islands. Johannes Haffner is the current incumbent at the stoves, and he runs the restaurant with his sister Frederica, bringing a dedication to the job that ensures produce is locally grown, reared and caught, organic whenever possible, and pastries and breads are all home-baked. The beamed restaurant provides a cosy and informal setting for a classic European repertoire: king scallops flambéed in Cognac come simply with salad leaves from the garden, while monkfish gets an equally fuss-free treatment: medallions poached in white wine and butter and served with chive and white wine sauce. End with a properly buttery caramelised apple tarte Tatin.

Rolfs Country House

Chef Johannes Haffner **Owner** Johannes Haffner **Times** 6-9.30 Closed Xmas, Mon-Tue (winter) **Prices** Service included **Wines** 12 by glass **Notes** Sunday L €25, Vegetarian menu **Seats** 50 **Children** Portions, Menu **Parking** 45

CASTLEMARTYR Map 1 C2

Castlemartyr Resort

◎◎ Modern Irish

Fine-dining in elegant surroundings

☎ 021 4219000
e-mail: reception@castlemartyrresort.ie
dir: N25 from Cork City, located between Midleton and Youghal

History lies thick on the ground at this 18th-century manor house, which stands in 320 acres of mature parkland with streams, a lake, classic parterre gardens, and the ruins of an 800-year-old castle built by the Knights Templar. Once the home of Sir Walter Raleigh, Castlemartyr now earns its crust as an upmarket R & R bolthole, sporting the inevitable package of health club, spa and golf course. For the full formal fine-dining experience complete with crisp, floor-length linen on the tables, head to the elegant Bell Tower Restaurant. Expect uncomplicated modern Irish cooking based around the best seasonal ingredients hauled in from the surrounding countryside. Summer brings pan-fried scallops from nearby Ballycotton teamed with cauliflower beignets and purée and white raisin butter to start, followed by a delicate dish of poached wild salmon served in a light and clear seafood and vegetable broth with seasonal vegetables, herb hollandaise and whipped potatoes. A colourful composition of Wexford strawberries with honeycomb, white chocolate mousse and strawberry sorbet brings things to a close.

Times 6.30-10 Closed Sun (Nov-Mar), L all week

CLONAKILTY Map 1 B2

Inchydoney Island Lodge & Spa

◎◎ Modern Mediterranean ♨

Fine West Cork ingredients in a glorious coastal setting

☎ 023 8833143
Inchydoney
e-mail: reservations@inchydoneyisland.com
dir: From Cork take N71 following West Cork signs. Through Innishannon, Bandon & Clonakilty, then follow signs for Inchydoney Island

The Atlantic Ocean makes for an impressive vista come rain or shine, and as you cross the short causeway from the mainland to reach Inchydoney Island, well, you know you're in for a treat. The expansive white-painted hotel and spa has all the sybaritic distractions one needs, and inside all is smart, elegant and rather luxurious. And in its Gulfstream Restaurant, there's some good eating to be had, too. Up on the first floor to maximise the view, it is a chic, contemporary space with a good deal of style. West Cork's best produce is quite rightly the focus of attention here, and turns up in prettily presented dishes with compelling flavour combinations. Roasted breast and confit leg of squab pigeon, for example, comes with parsnip purée, plum tomato compôte, pickled pear and leek dressing - a good start indeed. Follow on with baked fillet of Castletownbere hake with root vegetable gâteau, Savoy cabbage, baby carrots with chorizo, and tarragon cream, and finish with milk chocolate, caramel and hazelnut cream.

Chef Adam Medcalf **Owner** Des O'Dowd **Times** 6.30-9.30 Closed 24-25 Dec **Prices** Tasting menu €75, Starter €12, Main €32, Dessert €12, Service optional **Wines** 24 bottles over €30, 29 bottles under €30, 9 by glass **Notes** Fixed D 5 course €59, Vegetarian available, Dress restrictions, Smart casual, Civ Wed 180 **Seats** 80, Pr/dining room 250 **Children** Portions, Menu **Parking** 200

CORK | Map 1 B2

Maryborough Hotel & Spa

◉ Modern International V ◔

Traditional and modern in a 300-year-old country house

☎ 021 4365555
Maryborough Hill, Douglas
e-mail: info@maryborough.ie
dir: From Jack Lynch Tunnel take 2nd exit signed Douglas. Right at 1st rdbt, follow Rochestown road to fingerpost rdbt. Left, hotel on left 0.5m up hill

The 300-year-old country house near Cork stands in 14 acres of luxurious grounds and woodland, full of rare plant species and with a magnificent display of rhododendrons. It has been brought thoroughly up-to-date inside, with the promisingly named Zings restaurant featuring a walk-in wine cellar on the lower of its two levels. A congenial mix of traditional and modern thinking is in evidence from the kitchen, which delivers some well-rendered, satisfying dishes. Panko-crumbed fishcakes of salmon and cod, blended with tarragon and wholegrain mustard, served with wilted spinach and sorrel cream, get things off to a good savoury start. Main courses might see lamb in two presentations - roast rack and braised shank - with canny accompaniments of roast red and yellow peppers, citrus-spiked onion compôte and a rosemary jus. Finish with passionfruit crème brûlée and macadamia cookies.

Chef Gerry Allen **Owner** Dan O'Sullivan **Times** 12.30-10 Closed 24-26 Dec, All-day dining **Prices** Fixed L 2 course fr €25, Fixed D 3 course fr €35, Starter €5.50-€10.50, Main €15.50-€24.50, Dessert €4.95-€7.50, Service optional, Groups min 10 service 10% **Wines** 15 bottles over €30, 13 bottles under €30, 8 by glass **Notes** Sunday L, Vegetarian menu, Dress restrictions, Smart casual, Civ Wed 300 **Seats** 170, Pr/dining room 60 **Children** Portions, Menu **Parking** 300

DURRUS | Map 1 B2

Blairscove House & Restaurant

◉◉ Modern British ◔

Local produce in magnificent converted stables

☎ 027 61127
e-mail: mail@blairscove.ie
dir: R591 from Durrus to Crookhaven, in 1.5m restaurant on right through blue gate

This Georgian manor house with uplifting views over Dunmanus Bay hides a real treat in the stylishly converted stables and outbuildings. Bare stone walls hung with vivid contemporary art soar upwards to a crystal chandelier suspended from a church-like beamed ceiling, making for a memorable setting in which to explore the local larder. Fresh, local and seasonal are buzz words, and the kitchen doesn't need to worry about food miles as the materials all come from nearby ports or

the surrounding hills. It's a case of helping yourself to starters from the buffet - perhaps duck rillettes or spiced calves' tongue - before perfectly caramelised lambs' kidneys with Dijon mustard-spiked garlicky spinach, or a well-hung rib-eye cooked before your eyes on the beech wood grill. Dessert reverts to the help-yourself format, so go for something like a classic crème brûlée or pannacotta with strawberry compôte.

Chef Ronald Klötzer **Owner** P & S De Mey **Times** 6.30-9.30 Closed Nov-17 Mar, Sun-Mon, L all week **Prices** Prices not confirmed Service optional, Groups min 8 service 10% **Notes** Vegetarian available, Dress restrictions, Smart casual, Civ Wed 30 **Seats** 75, Pr/dining room 48 **Children** Portions **Parking** 30

GARRYVOE | Map 1 C2

Garryvoe Hotel

◉ Modern Irish

Modern Irish cooking in a grand seafront hotel

☎ 021 4646718
Ballycotton Bay, Castlemartyr
e-mail: res@garryvoehotel.com
web: www.garryvoehotel.com
dir: From N25 at Castlemartyr (Cork-Rosslare road) take R632 to Garryvoe

Right on the seafront overlooking Ballycotton Bay, the Garryvoe is something of a local institution, but one that has moved with the times, modernising and aggrandising in the process. The high-ceilinged dining room naturally makes the most of those Cork coastal views, with well-spaced tables set with high-class accoutrements. The cooking might be described as modern Irish, but with no inhibitions about featuring retro dishes too. Start with crab croquette with chilli jam, citrus crab millefeuille and celeriac in wild mushroom bisque, moving onto a classic main course such as roast rump of local lamb with creamed cabbage and root veg in red wine reduction. The finale could be chocolate fondant with pistachio ice cream and raspberry coulis.

Times 1-2.30/6.30-8.45 Closed 24-25 Dec, L Mon-Sat

GOLEEN | Map 1 A1

The Heron's Cove

◉ Traditional Irish ◔

Unbroken sea views, super-fresh seafood and more

☎ 028 35225
The Harbour
e-mail: suehill@eircom.net
web: www.heronscove.com
dir: In Goleen village, turn left to harbour

Head for the most south-westerly tip of the country where the beam of the Fastnet Rock lighthouse scans the Atlantic at Mizen Head, and pull in at this charming rustic restaurant with rooms in Goleen Harbour. In summer, it is a magical spot when you can eat out to

sublime sea views on the balcony overlooking the tiny inlet, and the menu offers a roll call of fabulous local seafood and meats prepared with forthright simplicity. Starters might include crabcakes with wasabi mayonnaise, while variety is ensured at main course stage by seared Dunmanus Bay scallops with creamy smoked bacon sauce or pan-fried John Dory with balsamic butter alongside local lamb chops with rosemary jus. Sticky toffee pudding with vanilla ice cream wraps things up on a comforting note.

Chef Irene Coughlan **Owner** Sue Hill **Times** 7-9.30 Closed Xmas, Oct-Apr (only open for pre-bookings), L all week (ex private functions) **Prices** Fixed D 3 course €25-€27.50, Starter €5.50-€11.95, Main €19.50-€29.95, Dessert €6.95-€8.50, Service optional **Wines** 25 bottles over €30, 35 bottles under €30, 2 by glass **Notes** Vegetarian available **Seats** 30 **Children** Portions, Menu **Parking** 10

GOUGANE BARRA | Map 1 B2

Gougane Barra Hotel

◉ Irish, French

Tried-and-true country cooking in hauntingly beautiful setting

☎ 026 47069
e-mail: info@gouganebarrahotel.com
dir: Off R584 between N22 at Macroom & N71 at Bantry. Take Keimaneigh junct for hotel

The Cronin family has owned property in hauntingly beautiful Gougane Barra since Victorian times, when its potential as an idyllic retreat was first fully realised, though the present hotel dates back only to the 1930s. Those views over the lake towards the mountains of Cork look especially magnificent from the ample windows of the dining room, where fine seasonal artisan produce takes centre-stage. There are no airs and graces to the cooking, just careful presentation in tried-and-true formulas that never lack for support. Dingle Bay smoked salmon, or a double-act of Clonakilty black and De Róiste white pudding, with bacon and apple sauce, might fire the starting-gun, before grilled cutlets of exemplary West Cork lamb with colcannon and port gravy make their appearance. Fish could be herb-crusted hake with creamed leeks and peas in prawn sauce, with flourless pear frangipane and butterscotch ice cream to round things off in style.

Times 12.30-2.30/6-8.30 Closed 20 Oct-10 Apr, L Mon-Sat (ex group bookings)

Save on Hotels. Book at **theAA.com/hotel**

CO CORK – CO DONEGAL 659 **IRELAND**

Carlton Hotel Kinsale

◉ Modern European V ✋

A local flavour in a classy contemporary hotel

☎ 021 4706000
Rathmore Rd
e-mail: reservations.kinsale@carlton.ie
dir: Before Kinsale turn left signed Charles Fort. 3kms, hotel on left

With wonderful views over Oysterhaven Bay and the headland, the Carlton Hotel is a modernist vision built of stone, wood and glass. There's a leisure club and spa, conference facilities and the like, but another good reason to visit is to sample the cooking from the new team in the kitchen. The first-floor Rockpool Restaurant gets the great views; a wall of glass keeps out the worst of the weather, the terrace comes into its own when the climate allows. It's all very bright and contemporary, and, the cooking has a new focus on regional ingredients, much of it from artisan producers. On the lunch menu, Kinsale seafood stars in a creamy chowder, served with home-made seed bread, and spinach and ricotta is stuffed into tortellini and served with a rocket and pesto crème. The evening menu cranks things up a bit to deliver the likes of polenta-crusted Castletownbere sole with local smoked salmon and shrimp sauce.

Chef Dean Diplock **Owner** Bank of Scotland
Times 12-2.30/6-9.30 Closed Xmas **Prices** Fixed D 3 course €35, Starter €4.95-€9.95, Main €16.95-€24.95, Dessert €7.95-€9.95, Service optional **Wines** 15 bottles over €30, 15 bottles under €30, 9 by glass **Notes** Sunday L, Vegetarian menu, Civ Wed 209 **Seats** 90, Pr/dining room 15 **Children** Portions, Menu **Parking** 100

The White House

◉ Traditional, International ✋

Broadly appealing menu in a gastronomic hub

☎ 021 4772125
Pearse St, The Glen
e-mail: whitehse@indigo.ie
dir: Located in town centre

The White House has been in the hospitality game since the mid-19th century, and occupies a prime site in the centre of a town that holds a renowned Gourmet Festival every autumn. That means there's plenty to live up to in the gastronomic stakes, and the kitchen here rises to the occasion with a resourceful repertoire of modern Irish dishes that draws inspiration from far and wide, but is also a dab hand at Irish stews, fish pies and the like. Baked cod fillet is coated in Cajun spices for a satisfying main course, accompanied by ratatouille topped with melted cheese. Local mussels make a fine starter, with a creamy dressing of white wine, garlic and lemongrass, and favourite puddings take in apple and cinnamon crumble with well-churned vanilla ice cream, or passionfruit and mango cheesecake.

Chef Martin El Sahen **Owner** Michael Frawley
Times 12-10 Closed 25 Dec **Prices** Prices not confirmed
Service optional **Wines** 9 by glass **Notes** Vegetarian available **Seats** 45 **Children** Portions, Menu **Parking** Car park at rear of building

Springfort Hall Country House Hotel

◉ Modern Irish

Modern dining in a Georgian country house

☎ 022 21278 & 30620
e-mail: stay@springfort-hall.com
web: www.springfort-hall.com
dir: N20 onto R581 at Two Pot House, hotel 500mtrs on right

The kitchen team in this immaculately-preserved Georgian country house certainly aren't scared of a bit of domestic hard graft: no corners are cut here - meat and fish is smoked in-house and everything is made from scratch from fresh, judiciously-sourced local produce. The setting for all of this laudable culinary endeavour is the palatial Lime Tree Restaurant, where all the detail of the original ornate plasterwork is picked out in gold paint, and a crystal chandelier hangs above pristine white linen-clothed tables on polished timber flooring. The kitchen deals in a broadly modern Irish style of cookery, sending out ideas such as black pudding and glazed pork belly with pickled leeks, apple purée and cider jelly, followed by seared wild venison with butternut squash purée, Savoy cabbage, pickled mushrooms and candied pumpkin seeds.

Times 12-9.30 Closed 25-26 Dec

Ballymaloe House

◉◉ Traditional ✋

Fabulous food in a classic country-house setting

☎ 021 4652531
e-mail: res@ballymaloe.ie
dir: From R630 at Whitegate rdbt, left onto R631, left onto Cloyne. Continue for 2m on Ballycotton Rd

The concept of sourcing local, seasonal produce is taken to extremes at Ballymaloe, where most of what turns up on your plate comes from the 400 acres of their East Cork estate, which includes 100 acres of organic farm, and pretty walled gardens that supply herbs, fruit and vegetables. The Allen family have followed the ethos of taking the best regional ingredients and treating them simply and with respect for 40 years - long before it became fashionable to trumpet such credentials - and it is all served up in four traditional dining rooms. The daily menus are driven by what the chefs bring in from the garden and what has been landed by the boats at Ballycotton, so you might find roast hake with chilli, parsley and garlic oil alongside locally-smoked salmon rillettes with pickled cucumber, then raise the comfort rating further still with slow-roast free-range pork with

Bramley apple sauce and roast Jerusalem artichokes, or an equally unfussy pairing of grilled cod and lobster with wild watercress relish and leek Julienne.

Chef Jason Fahey **Owner** The Allen Family
Times 1-1.30/7-9.30 Closed Xmas, 2 wks Jan, Mon & Tue in Feb, D Sun in Feb **Prices** Fixed D 2 course €50, Starter €10-€15, Main €40-€45, Dessert €15, Service optional **Wines** 300 bottles over €30, 20 bottles under €30, 18 by glass **Notes** Fixed D 5 course €70, Pre-theatre menu from €45, Sunday L €36-€40, Vegetarian available, Dress restrictions, Smart casual, no jeans or T-shirts, Civ Wed 120 **Seats** 110, Pr/dining room 50 **Children** Portions, Menu **Parking** 100

Harvey's Point Hotel

◉◉ Modern Irish ✋

Modern Irish food in a family-run hotel overlooking Lough Eske

☎ 074 9722208
Lough Eske
e-mail: stay@harveyspoint.com
web: www.harveyspoint.com
dir: From Donegal 2m towards Lifford, left at Harvey's Point sign, follow signs, take 3 right turns to hotel gates

Adrift in the hills of the wild northwest, the family-owned Harvey's Point is a well-developed country retreat overlooking Lough Eske. The Gyslings have had the place since 1989, and have turned it into the full package, with new features coming on stream all the time (a seafood bar and grill was due to open as we went to print). New chef Gavin O'Rourke maintains the style and standard set by his predecessor for a menu of modern Irish cooking that draws on European techniques in a broad range of choice. A duo of coriander-crusted halibut and soy-glazed chicken thigh, with pak choi and spiced carrot purée, might be the bravura opener for loin and confit breast of lamb with polenta, roast onion and garlic, or perhaps a mi-cuit of sea trout, served with a crab croquette and poached spring veg in a smooth emulsified sauce made with pearl barley. At the conclusion comes chocolate marquise, garnished with spears of caramelised hazelnut and blackberry sorbet. Fine Irish cheeses rumble round temptingly on a trolley.

Chef Gavin O'Rourke **Owner** Marc & Deirdre Gysling
Times 6.30-9.30 Closed Sun-Thu (Nov-Apr), Sun, Wed (Jun-Oct), L all week **Prices** Fixed L 2 course €25, Fixed D 3 course €50, Starter €12, Main €32, Dessert €8, Service optional **Wines** 70 bottles over €30, 17 bottles under €30, 17 by glass **Notes** Sunday L, Vegetarian available, Dress restrictions, Smart casual, Civ Wed 220 **Seats** 108 **Children** Portions **Parking** 200

DUNFANAGHY
Map 1 C6

Arnolds Hotel

◉ Traditional ✋

Good Irish cooking on the coast

☎ 074 9136208
Main St
e-mail: enquiries@arnoldshotel.com
dir: On N56 from Letterkenny, hotel on left on entering the village

In a village overlooking Sheephaven Bay, with Killahoey Beach a stroll away, Arnolds Hotel has been welcoming guests since 1922. It's a friendly, comfortable and comforting place, with open fires in the winter, and a restaurant capitalising on those coastal views. The kitchen takes a fuss-free approach, relying on quality raw materials and sound technique to make the most of flavours. To start there may be steamed mussels in garlic and dill cream, or balls of mushroom risotto coated in oatmeal, fried and dressed with white truffle and parmesan. Fish is well handled, seen in baked fillet of turbot served simply on pea purée with red pesto, or there might be honey-glazed roast duckling on rösti with a rich orange sauce, or fillet steak with grilled mushrooms, mustard mash and a bourbon and pepper cream. Desserts are of the home-baked, comfort food variety, such as Arnolds Hotel Pavlova, apple pie and rhubarb crumble.

Chef John Corcoran **Owner** Arnold Family **Times** 6-9.30 Closed Nov-Apr **Prices** Fixed L 3 course €19.50-€25, Fixed D 3 course €35-€40, Starter €5.75-€7.95, Main €17.95-€27.50, Dessert €5.95-€7.95, Service optional **Notes** Sunday L, Vegetarian available, Civ Wed 90 **Seats** 60 **Children** Portions, Menu **Parking** 40

LETTERKENNY
Map 1 C5

Radisson Blu Hotel Letterkenny

◉ Modern Irish

Unpretentious cooking in a modern hotel

☎ 074 9194444
Paddy Harte Rd
e-mail: info.letterkenny@radissonblu.com
dir: N14 into Letterkenny. At Polestar Rdbt take 1st exit, to hotel

Donegal's timeless attractions are on the doorstep of this contemporary-styled hotel. The building is bright and airy thanks to the liberal use of glass, wood and steel in its construction, a style which is used to good effect in the clean-cut TriBeCa Brasserie. Done out with plenty of light wood, warm tones, unclothed tables and a large screen showing the action in the kitchen, the place certainly looks the part, and if the buzz of contented diners is anything to go by, the formula works a treat. The kitchen builds its crowd-pleasing repertoire of modern brasserie dishes on well-sourced ingredients. A starter of pan-seared sea trout with roasted asparagus and prosciutto and red pepper dressing sets the tone, ahead of roast glazed rump of Slaney Valley lamb with fondant potato,

carrots and wild mushroom sauce. At the end, rice krispies make a quirky base for a lime and chocolate pie with lime sorbet.

Chef Collette Langan **Owner** Paul Byrne **Times** 12.30-3.30/6-9.30 Closed L Mon-Sat **Prices** Fixed D 3 course €82.50, Starter €4.95-€9.95, Main €14.95-€23.95, Dessert €5.95-€10.95, Service optional **Wines** 22 bottles under €30, 5 by glass **Notes** Early bird menu 6-7pm €19.95, Fixed L 2/3 course Sun only, Sunday L, Vegetarian available, Civ Wed 600 **Seats** 120, Pr/dining room 320 **Children** Portions, Menu **Parking** 150

MOVILLE
Map 1 C6

Redcastle Hotel, Golf & Spa Resort

◉ Modern, International **NEW** ✋

Lough views and Irish ingredients

☎ 074 9385555
Inishowen Peninsula
e-mail: info@redcastlehotel.com
dir: On R238 between Derby & Greencastle

Location is everything and tranquillity reigns at this golf and spa resort in a glorious waterfront setting on the Inishowen Peninsula. It's an uplifting prospect that forms the backdrop to dining in the contemporary-styled The Edge Restaurant (no connection with U2's guitarist, by the way), with its fabulous view across Lough Foyle through vast picture windows. Those trawlers you can see chugging across the lough are bound for Greencastle port, carrying the fish that finds its way onto your plate. Uniformed staff keep their eye on the ball and know their way around the menu and wine list, with carefully-sourced Irish produce at the heart of things, whether it's Donegal smoked salmon that appears in a terrine with horseradish, globe artichoke, salsa verde and toasted soda bread, or a duo of pan-fried Greencastle cod teamed with caramelised pork belly, red pepper piperade and chorizo.

Chef Gordon Smyth **Owner** Pisona Developments **Times** 12-4/6-9.30 Closed 25 Dec **Prices** Fixed L 2 course €15-€25, Fixed D 3 course €25-€36, Tasting menu €45-€65, Starter €6.50-€11.25, Main €16.25-€26, Dessert €6.95-€7.25, Service optional **Wines** 16 bottles over €30, 11 bottles under €30, 6 by glass **Notes** Early bird offer off peak, Sunday L, Vegetarian available, Civ Wed 200 **Seats** 120 **Children** Portions, Menu **Parking** 360

RATHMULLAN
Map 1 C6

Rathmullan House

◉◉ Modern Irish

Charming country hotel with contemporary cooking

☎ 074 9158188
e-mail: info@rathmullanhouse.com
dir: R245 Letterkenny to Ramelton, over bridge right onto R247 to Rathmullan. On entering village turn at Mace shop through village gates. Hotel on right

Rathmullan is an elegant Regency-era mansion in wooded grounds overlooking Lough Swilly, and just a short stroll from a two-mile golden sand beach. Run by the second generation of the Wheeler family, who celebrated 50 years in business as a country-house hotel in 2012, the whole operation has a well-established feel and ticks along with discreet charm. The Weeping Elm restaurant is housed in a modern extension with a tented ceiling, wooden floors and views through the trees to the Lough. Chef Kelan McMichael runs an industrious kitchen supporting local artisan suppliers, and raiding the hotel's Victorian walled garden for seasonal organic fruit, salad and herbs. Mackerel caught a few hours previously from the lough appears seared and teamed with wild garlic tapenade, a punchy horseradish and rhubarb compôte, and pickled beetroot, while main course stars Rathmullan lamb from a neighbouring farm - roast loin, rolled breast and a breadcrumbed croquette of braised neck, to be precise - served with a ragoût of morels and sweet garlic, olive oil mash and rosemary jus. To finish, there's a delicate rhubarb treacle tart with praline ice cream.

Chef Kelan McMichael **Owner** Wheeler Family **Times** 7-8.45 Closed Jan-mid Feb **Prices** Fixed D 3 course €45-€55, Starter €10-€15, Main €20-€30, Dessert €10-€15, Service added but optional 10% **Wines** 10 by glass **Notes** Vegetarian available, Dress restrictions, Smart casual, Civ Wed 100 **Seats** 70, Pr/dining room 30 **Children** Portions, Menu **Parking** 40

DUBLIN

DUBLIN
Map 1 D4

Castleknock Hotel & Country Club

◉ European, International

Contemporary dining in country club setting

☎ 01 6406300
Porterstown Rd, Castleknock
e-mail: info@chcc.ie
web: www.castleknockhotel.com
dir: M50 from airport. Exit at junct 6 (signed Navan, Cavan & M3) onto N3, becomes M3. Exit at junct 3. At top of slip road 1st left signed Consilla (R121). At T-junct left. 1km to hotel

When the All Blacks rugby team are on tour in this hemisphere they hole up at this glossy contemporary country club hotel to wash off the mud and relax with a spot of pampering and beauty therapy between tussles on the pitch. Although it is just 15 minutes from Dublin city centre, it feels surprisingly rural - perhaps because it sits surrounded by its own 18-hole golf course. A slew of bars, a brasserie and the Park Restaurant cover all of the eating and drinking bases, the latter being a modern bistro and steak house with views of the club-swinging action as a backdrop. Using plenty of Irish produce, the kitchen keeps things modern, upbeat and uncomplicated - perhaps warm grilled smoked duck breast with saffron and pea risotto, and parmesan mousse, ahead of chargrilled slabs of 21-day-aged Irish beef; for something less primordial, yet equally full-flavoured, there may be slow-roasted pork belly with Clonakilty black pudding, pan-fried scallops, creamy celeriac, and Calvados jus. Fine Irish cheeses are the alternative to desserts like chocolate fondant with vanilla and bourbon ice cream.

Chef Robert Reid **Owner** FBD Group
Times 12.30-3/5.30-10 Closed 24-26 Dec **Prices** Starter €5.50-€11.50, Main €15.50-€54.50, Dessert €6.25-€9.50 **Wines** 12 by glass **Notes** Fixed 4 course D 2 people & includes wine, Sunday L, Vegetarian available, Civ Wed 120 **Seats** 65, Pr/dining room 400 **Children** Portions, Menu **Parking** 200

The Cellar Restaurant

◎◎ Modern Irish 🖐

Smart cooking of fine local produce

☎ 01 6030600 & 6030630
Merrion Hotel, Upper Merrion St
e-mail: info@merrionhotel.com
dir: Top Upper Merrion Street, opp Government buildings

The Merrion Hotel's Cellar Restaurant (see also Restaurant Patrick Guilbaud) may have no natural light, but it's a bright room under its vaulted ceiling, with lots of nooks and crannies and top-end fittings and furnishings. The kitchen bases its cooking on indigenous ingredients and promotes local and artisan producers whenever possible, seen in imaginative starters like confit of Galway salmon with horseradish and potato salad, pickled cucumber and cucumber gel, and saddleback pork and pistachio terrine with fig chutney, a cherry and balsamic treacle adding another flavour dimension. Main courses pull some punches too, without being overwrought or fussy: meltingly tender veal liver with rich onion gravy laced with red wine, accompanied by bacon and buttery mash, say, or roast skate wing with lemon and brown shrimp beurre noisette and garlicky spinach. Cheeses are Irish, with ingredients in some puddings coming from wilder shores: a smooth light soufflé of exotic fruits, for instance, with mango ice cream and coconut liqueur-infused custard.

Chef Ed Cooney **Times** 12.30-2/6-10 Closed L Sat **Prices** Fixed L 2 course fr €20, Fixed D 3 course fr €29.95, Starter €8-€14, Main €23-€40, Dessert €8-€14, Service included **Notes** Sun brunch 12.30-2.30pm, Vegetarian available, Dress restrictions, Smart casual, Civ Wed 55 **Children** Portions, Menu **Parking** Merrion Square

Crowne Plaza Dublin Northwood

◉ Asian Fusion, International 🖐

Fusion food and more in modern hotel

☎ 01 8628888
Northwood Park, Santry Demesne, Santry
e-mail: info@crowneplazadublin.ie
web: www.cpdublin.crowneplaza.com
dir: M50 junct 4, left into Northwood Park, 1km, hotel on left

In a quiet location on the edge of Northwood Park, 10 minutes from the airport, the Crowne Plaza is a modern hotel, its restaurant a bright and airy space, overlooking the courtyard gardens. The kitchen takes its inspiration from the techniques and flavours of Asia and the Pacific Rim, with crisp duck spring roll with an Asian-style salad and yoghurt and chilli dressing to start, followed by chicken stir-fried with noodles and vegetables sauced with coconut green curry. But this is no style slave, so asparagus and Parma ham with a poached egg and hollandaise may appear before roast halibut fillet with tapenade and a casserole of haricot beans, chorizo and red peppers, with lemon tart for pudding.

Chef Logan Inwin **Owner** Tifco Ltd **Times** 5.30-10 Closed 25 Dec, L all week **Prices** Fixed D 3 course €24.95, Starter €5-€10.95, Main €9.95-€26.95, Dessert €5-€7.50, Service included **Wines** 34 bottles over €30, 17 bottles under €30, 15 by glass **Notes** Vegetarian available, Dress restrictions, Smart dress, Civ Wed 100 **Seats** 156, Pr/dining room 15 **Children** Portions, Menu **Parking** 360

Crowne Plaza Hotel Dublin - Blanchardstown

◉ Italian 🖐

Italian dining in funky modern venue

☎ 01 8977777
The Blanchardstown Centre
e-mail: info@cpireland.crowneplaza.com
dir: M50 junct 6 (Blanchardstown)

The Blanchardstown branch of the Crowne Plaza empire fits the bill, whether you're suited and booted for business, or dropping by to refuel after a hit of retail therapy in the shops and boutiques of the nearby Blanchardstown Centre. The Forchetta restaurant works a loud and proud contemporary look with bold floral wallpaper and bare dark wood tables - it's a buzzy, breezy setting that suits the crowd-pleasing modern Italian menu. The usual suspects from the world of pizza and pasta are all present and correct, or you might ignore convention and start with a fish soup involving mussels, clams, prawns, salmon and cod in a tomato and white wine broth, and follow with a chargrilled Irish steak, or lamb shank roasted in red wine, garlic and rosemary. Puddings are Italian classics - pannacotta or tiramisù, for example.

Chef Jason Hayde **Owner** Tifco Hotels
Times 12-2.30/6-9.30 Closed 24-25 Dec **Prices** Fixed L 2 course €19.95-€25, Fixed D 3 course €25-€40, Starter €7-

€15, Main €9.95-€25.95, Dessert €6.95-€8.95, Service optional **Wines** 20 bottles over €30, 27 bottles under €30, 6 by glass **Notes** Carvery L served Sanctuary Bar, Bar food daily noon-10, Vegetarian available, Civ Wed 400 **Seats** 100, Pr/dining room 45 **Children** Portions, Menu **Parking** 200

Restaurant Patrick Guilbaud

◎◎◎◎ – *see page 662*

The Shelbourne Dublin, a Renaissance Hotel

◎◎ Irish, European 🖐

Grand hotel with top-notch steak and seafood

☎ 01 6634500
27 St Stephen's Green
e-mail: eamonn.casey@marriott.com
web: www.theshelbourne.ie
dir: M1 to city centre, along Parnell St to O'Connell St towards Trinity College, 3rd right into Kildare St, hotel on left

The Victorian builders of the Shelbourne set out to impress with this neo-classical Grand Hotel on St Stephen's Green in the heart of Dublin. Lavishly restored to its former glory, it is a splendid sight as soon as you're through the doors with its domed stained-glass ceiling and sweeping staircase. It is fast forward to a more contemporary clubby look in the Saddle Room restaurant, however, where leather banquettes, dark oak walls and curtained booths with buttoned bronze leather dividing screens set an opulent and intimate stage for tucking into oysters, steaks and seafood dishes. Classic brasserie staples are all built on materials of peerless provenance, whether it is a starter of pan-seared Dublin Bay prawns with artichoke, and shellfish sabayon, or prime Irish beef from the grill. Otherwise, go for Wicklow venison loin with braised red cabbage and Chinese leaves, or if you're up for fish, there could be seared halibut fillet with a buttered broth of root vegetables and kale. To finish, it has to be a classic crème brûlée with a palmier biscuit.

Chef Garry Hughes **Owner** Renaissance Hotels
Times 12.30-2.30/6-10.30 **Prices** Fixed L 2 course €21.95-€26.95, Fixed D 3 course €39.50, Tasting menu €59.95-€79.50, Starter €12-€18, Main €28-€69.95, Dessert €8.95, Service optional **Wines** 100 bottles over €30, 10 bottles under €30, 12 by glass **Notes** Daily pre-theatre menu 2/3 course available 6-7pm, Sunday L, Vegetarian available, Dress restrictions, No sports wear, Civ Wed 300 **Seats** 120, Pr/dining room 20 **Children** Portions, Menu **Parking** Valet parking

Restaurant Patrick Guilbaud

DUBLIN   MAP 1 D4

Modern French **V**

Outstanding French cooking at the pre-eminent Dublin address

☎ 01 6764192
Merrion Hotel, 21 Upper Merrion St
e-mail: info@
restaurantpatrickguilbaud.ie
dir: Opposite government buildings, next to Merrion Hotel

From its striking collection of modern Irish artworks to its unyielding pursuit of culinary nirvana, Restaurant Patrick Guilbaud is a class act. The eponymous Frenchman opened in Dublin in 1981 and for over 30 years has not wavered in his ambition to deliver striking food to the people of the city, and with Guillaume Lebrun heading up the kitchen, the consistency and creative drive of this winning team is nothing short of remarkable. They've got a lovely spot to work in: the five-star Merrion Hotel is a handsome pile indeed with its generous Georgian proportions, not least in the restaurant itself, where the arched ceiling and pure-white paint job give it an almost spiritual demeanour. The well-spaced tables are dressed with precision and the service team is out of the top drawer. It is perhaps not surprising that France provides a good deal of the inspiration for the kitchen's output, but at the heart of everything is the very best Irish produce, sourced when it is at its very best. The technical abilities on show are mightily impressive, with plenty of contemporary ideas and pin-sharp presentation. You know you're in for a treat when the amuse-bouche arrives: perhaps a confit of baby bell pepper filled with goats' cheese, topped with a savoury crumble, herb oil and a parmesan tuile. There is refinement and exceptional balance of flavour in every dish - a first-course duck and foie gras terrine for example, with sea buckthorn and pickled radish, or caramelised veal sweetbreads with steamed spinach, crispy tubers and roast juices. The creativity extends to some intriguing flavour combinations, so roast breast of duck, for example, might come with Amaretto milk, spicy popcorn, poached figs and cardamom jus in a main course that delivers a compelling whole. Fish is no less beautifully handled: a superb piece of John Dory, perhaps, with octopus served as a punchy citrus escabèche. Among desserts, a classic opera gâteau gets elevated to fine-dining status with seven delicious layers and an accompanying hazelnut ice cream. The cheese selection, perhaps symbolic of the whole establishment, brings together the very best of France and Ireland in perfect harmony. The wine list, though, cannot oblige the same equanimity for obvious reasons, and is instead a powerhouse of French classics and lots more besides.

Chef Guillaume Lebrun **Owner** Patrick Guilbaud **Times** 12.30-2.15/7.30-10.15 Closed 25 Dec, 1st wk Jan, Sun-Mon **Prices** Fixed L 2 course €40, Tasting menu fr €90, Service optional **Wines** 12 by glass **Notes** A la carte menu 2/3/4 course €85/ €105/ €130, Vegetarian menu, Dress restrictions, Smart casual **Seats** 80, Pr/dining room 25 **Children** Portions **Parking** Parking in square

DUBLIN *continued*

Stillorgan Park Hotel

◉ Traditional Mediterranean, International 🍽

Striking-looking restaurant with ambitious cooking

☎ 01 2001800
Stillorgan Rd
e-mail: info@stillorganpark.com
web: www.stillorganpark.com
dir: On N11 follow signs for Wexford, pass RTE studios on left, through next 5 sets of lights. Hotel on left

Moody lighting and intimate alcoves combine with funky floral fabrics, vibrant colours and modern art in the upmarket Stillorgan Park Hotel's Purple Sage restaurant. As you might expect in such a contemporary setting, the cooking takes a distinctly modern tack, serving up an eclectic output of dishes that can be as simple as smoked haddock, leek and potato chowder, or as labour intensive as a main course of grilled corn-fed chicken stuffed with sun-dried tomato pesto, wrapped in Parma ham, and served with potato gnocchi and herb sauce. Fish dishes might see pan-fried sea bass fillet teamed with pak choi, parmesan polenta, citrus fruit segments, and chilli and lime butter, while artisan Irish cheeses offer a savoury alternative to comfort-oriented desserts such as apple and blackberry crumble with vanilla ice cream.

Chef Enda Dunne **Owner** Des Pettitt
Times 12-3/5.45-10.15 Closed 25 Dec, L Sat, D Sun
Prices Fixed L 2 course fr €19.25, Fixed D 3 course fr €29.95, Service optional **Wines** 5 bottles over €30, 20 bottles under €30, 14 by glass **Notes** Early bird menu 2,3 course €21, €25, Sunday L, Vegetarian available, Civ Wed 120 **Seats** 140, Pr/dining room 60 **Children** Portions, Menu **Parking** 300

The Westbury Hotel

◉◉ Modern Irish 🍽

Refined modern cooking in city-centre hotel

☎ 01 6791122
Grafton St
e-mail: westbury@doylecollection.com
dir: Adjacent to Grafton St, half way between Trinity College & St Stephen's Green

The restaurant at this city centre hotel is a swishly decorated and furnished room dedicated to Oscar Wilde. The kitchen picks the cream of Ireland's produce and showcases it to good effect on a menu that's a beguiling mix of modern ideas. Prawn and crab cocktail with Marie Rose sauce sounds familiar enough, but here it's an exemplary example of the beast, and jostles for attention with foie gras crusted in pain d'épice, served with pear salad and caramelised walnuts. Among main courses, spicy duck has been given the Eastern treatment, served with honey and soy sauce, a spring roll and squash purée spiked with chilli. Alternatively you might go for a daily fish dish - say, properly timed fillet of halibut with smoked bacon essence, Jerusalem artichokes and roast

salsify. Puddings are a strong suit too, among them perhaps red berry vacherin with blackberry sorbet.

Chef Thomas Haughton **Owner** The Doyle Collection
Times 6.30-10.30 Closed Sun-Mon, L all week
Prices Fixed D 3 course fr €35, Starter €9-€18, Main €21-€38, Service optional **Wines** 56 bottles over €30, 14 bottles under €30, 10 by glass **Notes** Pre-theatre available, Vegetarian available, Civ Wed 80 **Seats** 95 **Children** Portions, Menu

CO DUBLIN

KILLINEY   Map 1 D4

Fitzpatrick Castle Hotel

◉ Traditional, International 🍽

Fine dining overlooking Dublin Bay

☎ 01 2305400
e-mail: info@fitzpatricks.com
web: www. fitzpatrickcastle.com
dir: From Dun Laoghaire port turn left, on coast road right at lights, left at next lights. Follow to Dalkey, right at Ivory pub, immediate left, up hill, hotel at top

The sweeping views across Dublin Bay from this grand 18th-century pile atop Killiney Hill are worth driving the nine miles out of Dublin for in their own right, but it's worth factoring in a pitstop at the hotel's classy fine-dining restaurant PJ's while you're there. Crystal chandeliers and well-spaced tables dressed in crisp linen create a sense of occasion for tackling the wide-ranging menu of skilfully-cooked seasonal dishes built on excellent local ingredients. You might start with plum tomato and roasted pepper soup with fresh ricotta and basil croûton, and follow with rack of lamb with a mustard and pistachio crust, mint mash, and red wine jus. Finish with luscious black cherry crêpes with Cognac ice cream.

Chef Sean Dempsey **Owner** Eithne Fitzpatrick **Times** 6-10 Closed 25 Dec, L Mon-Sat **Prices** Fixed L 2 course €22-€30, Fixed D 3 course €28-€36, Starter €5.50-€12.95, Main €15.50-€26, Dessert €6.50-€10.50, Service optional **Wines** 7 bottles over €30, 16 bottles under €30, 13 by glass **Notes** Sunday L, Vegetarian available **Seats** 65, Pr/dining room 50 **Children** Portions, Menu **Parking** 200

LUCAN   Map 1 D4

Finnstown Country House Hotel

◉ Traditional European 🍽

Accomplished cooking in 18th-century manor hotel

☎ 01 6010700
Newcastle Rd
e-mail: edwina@finnstown-hotel.ie
dir: N4 S/bound exit 4, left on slip road straight across rdbt & lights. Hotel on left

This creeper-hung 18th-century hotel, a portico over the front door, is on a 45-acre estate but is only a half-hour from the city centre. Its Peacock restaurant is a handsome room for dining, offering honest-to-goodness

cooking of fine ingredients from a menu that doesn't try to change the world. Mango and chilli salsa, for grilled duck and spring roll sausage, is about as exotic as things get with tian of crab and prawns Marie Rose more typical. Crabmeat may turn up again in a main course as a partner for baked fillet of sea trout in a herb crust with shellfish and brandy bisque, an alternative to seared peppered duck breast with mushroom and basil cream and sautéed spinach. End with a straightforward dessert, such as lemon tart or chocolate mousse.

Chef Steve McPhillips **Owner** Finnstown Country House Hotel **Times** 12.30-2.30/7-9 Closed 24-26 Dec, D Sun **Prices** Fixed L 2 course €25-€30, Fixed D 3 course €30-€45 **Wines** 5 by glass **Notes** Fri D, Dine out €58 for 2 people incl bottle of wine, Sunday L, Vegetarian available, Dress restrictions, Smart casual, Civ Wed 180 **Seats** 150 **Children** Portions, Menu **Parking** 300

CO GALWAY

BARNA   Map 1 B3

The Pins at The Twelve

◉ International, Italian NEW

Eclectic dining in design-led venue

☎ 091 597000
Barna Village
e-mail: enquire@thetwelvehotel.ie
dir: Coast road Barna village, 10 mins from Galway

Part of the boutique-style Twelve Hotel, gastronomes will be pleased to learn that The Pins is actually an unusual amalgam of bar, bakery, bistro and pizzeria: the on-site Pins Bakery means that bread and pastries are as fresh as it gets, and if you want to keep things simple, the Dozzina pizzeria turns out traditional artisan pizzas made in an oven hewn from Vesuvian stone. But if you want to put the kitchen through its paces, there's also a menu of 'casual, local' food that champions regional suppliers in uncomplicated ideas along the lines of seared venison steak with venison sausage roll, braised red cabbage, root vegetables, and truffle mash and jus. If you're in the mood for fish, organic Connemara sea trout might be served with white beans, chorizo and chard in a mussel and wine broth. For more ambitious modern fare, head up to the first-floor West Restaurant (see separate entry under The Twelve).

Times breakfast-10 All-day dining **Notes** BBQ menu private functions, Sun L 12-5.30, Sunday L **Children** Menu

BARNA *continued*

Upstairs@ West, The Twelve

◉◉ Modern Irish ◐

Well-conceived modern dishes in seaside hotel

☎ 091 597000
Barna Village
e-mail: west@thetwelvehotel.ie
dir: Coast road Barna village, 10 mins from Galway

In a coastal village but only 10 minutes from the centre of Galway, The Twelve is a boutique hotel stylishly furnished and decorated. The Upstairs at West Restaurant, with its displays of wine and a menu built on the finest local produce, is the place to head for some lively modern cooking (the Pins Gastro Bar is the more casual eating option - see entry). Expect seafood to be star attractions, from a theme on sea trout (cured, confit and tartare) with pea shoots and garlic dressing, to a main course of seared scallops paired with quail quiche and pan-fried breast, served with sautéed artichokes and parsley velouté. Imaginatively thought-out meat options might include turf-smoked rabbit loin with warm potato salad, parsnip hash and port reduction, and seared fillet steak with glazed onions, purple garlic and salsify, and horseradish suet pudding. A memorable way to finish is with the hand-crafted cheeses, especially with the sommelier's wine flight selection.

Chef Martin O'Donnell **Owner** Fergus O'Halloran **Times** 1-4/6-10 Closed Mon-Tue, L Wed-Fri **Prices** Prices not confirmed Service optional **Wines** 300 bottles over €30, 60 bottles under €30, 35 by glass **Notes** Gourmet menu 5 course with wine, Wine tutorials, Sunday L, Vegetarian available, Dress restrictions, Smart casual, Civ Wed 100 **Seats** 94, Pr/dining room 100 **Children** Portions, Menu **Parking** 120

CASHEL   Map 1 A4

Cashel House

◉◉ Traditional **V** ◐

A heavenly location and top-notch regional produce

☎ 095 31001
e-mail: res@cashel-house-hotel.com
web: www.cashel-house-hotel.com
dir: S of N59. 1m W of Recess

Run by the McEvilly family since 1968, the house was actually built by a great, great grandfather of the current owners back in 1840. It's a gem of a location, surrounded by beautiful gardens filled with rare plants, woodland and even mountain streams. You can stroll along the beach and through woodland up to Cashel Hill - it's quite something. But the house is rather lovely, too, and it is the setting for some first-class food to boot. The restaurant spans three rooms, decorated in a smart and traditional manner, one of which is a handsome conservatory. The garden provides some of the fruits and vegetables for the table, and everything that isn't home-grown is sourced with care. Start with hot kipper pâté with shallots and red wine sauce, or warm Cleggan

mussels with tomato, chilli and garlic. Next up, a sorbet (lemon perhaps), before baked fillet of hake gratin comes topped with tomato and white onion concasse and a sprinkling of crumbled cheddar. Warm rhubarb tart with ginger ice cream makes a fine finale.

Chef Arturo Tillo, John O'Toole **Owner** Kay McEvilly & family **Times** 12.30-2.30/6.30-9 Closed 2 Jan-2 Feb **Prices** Fixed L 2 course €25-€32, Fixed D 2 course €32.50-€55, Starter €6-€12.75, Main €16.50-€32, Dessert €9.50, Service added 12.5% **Wines** 5 by glass **Notes** Sunday L €30-€40, Vegetarian menu, Dress restrictions, Smart casual, Civ Wed 80 **Seats** 70, Pr/dining room 20 **Children** Portions, Menu **Parking** 30

CLIFDEN   Map 1 A4

Abbeyglen Castle Hotel

◉ French, International

Fresh local produce in a charming old property

☎ 095 21201
Sky Rd
e-mail: info@abbeyglen.ie
web: www.abbeyglen.ie
dir: N59 from Galway towards Clifden. Hotel 1km from Clifden on Sky Rd

The crenallated Victorian fantasy of Abbeyglen Castle basks in views sweeping from Connemara's Twelve Bens mountains to the shores of Clifden Bay. Ensconced in 12 acres of lovely grounds, it is just a five-minute walk from the bustle and cosy pubs of Clifden village, but you might find it hard to drag yourself away from its classic country-house comforts. In the restaurant at dinner, the décor is bold and bright with artworks on cherry-red walls, crystal chandeliers, and a pianist tinkles away on a grand piano. Expect classic cooking built on excellent local materials. As you'd hope, given the closeness to the briny, fish and seafood makes a good showing - fresh oysters, seafood chowder, or poached salmon with hollandaise - while meat could turn up as slow-roasted suckling pig teamed with braised belly pork, apple chutney, celeriac crisps and a grain mustard reduction. Puddings finish slap in the comfort zone with the likes of chocolate bread-and-butter pudding or rhubarb crumble with crème anglaise.

Times 7-9 Closed 6 -31 Jan, L all week

GALWAY   Map 1 B3/4

Ardilaun Hotel & Leisure Club

◉ Modern International ◐

Contemporary cooking in a quietly set hotel

☎ 091 521433
Taylor's Hill
e-mail: info@theardilaunhotel.ie
web: www.theardilaunhotel.ie
dir: 1m from city centre, towards Salthill on west side of city, near Galway Bay

In a quiet spot on the outskirts of the city towards Galway Bay, the Ardilaun Hotel has been built up around a 19th-

century property, with the restaurant looking out on its five acres of grounds. The kitchen takes a European-wide stance, with starters along the lines of smoked haddock and potato cake on spinach with sauce vierge and pickled cucumber, and a salad of crisp pancetta, radish, peas and mozzarella with coriander and green pepper dressing. Well-chosen ingredients go into main courses too: a medley of Galway Bay seafood with a ragoût of sweetcorn, fennel and spring onions and truffle and chive cream, and roast bacon-wrapped chicken breast stuffed with sage and onions on cauliflower purée with mushroom sauce. Lemon meringue pie with berry compôte is a good way to end.

Chef David O'Donnell **Owner** John Ryan & family **Times** 1-2.30/6.30-9.15 Closed 23-26 Dec, L Mon-Sat **Prices** Fixed L 2 course €12.50, Fixed D 3 course €31.50, Tasting menu €39, Starter €8.75-€10.50, Main €17.25-€52, Dessert €6.95-€7.95, Service included **Wines** 62 bottles over €30, 9 bottles under €30, 9 by glass **Notes** Meal deal in Bistro 2,3 course €24, €27.50, Sunday L, Vegetarian available, Dress restrictions, Smart casual, Civ Wed 650 **Seats** 180, Pr/dining room 380 **Children** Portions, Menu **Parking** 300

The G Hotel

◉◉ Modern French

Ultra-modern cooking in a hotel setting to match

☎ 091 865200
Wellpark, Dublin Rd
e-mail: info@theg.ie

Gigi's restaurant on the ground floor of the ultra-modern town centre hotel looks every inch a 21st-century dining experience. Designed in the main by society milliner Philip Treacy (note the hat-related prints on the walls), it's a riot of dayglo-coloured seats in a sepulchrally lit space with subdued spotlights and candles. Modern Euro-cuisine is the order of the day, with artistically presented dishes appearing on a range of eccentrically shaped plates. A beautifully rendered pearl barley risotto topped with local black pudding and a couple of seared Clew Bay scallops, surrounded by a ribbon of beurre blanc, is a confident opener, followed perhaps by seared breast of crisp-skinned duck, accompanied by a cauliflower fritter and a combined purée of celeriac and sweet potato eased into a hollowed-out fondant potato, with two dressings - one of hazelnut oil, the other a deeply glossy port-based jus. A dish from the Sea section of the menu might be grilled turbot in a spicy mussel and clam broth, garnished with a crisp-textured abalone and beetroot 'tagliatelle'. The architectural complexity of dishes continues through to spectacular desserts such as the banana bavarois.

Times 1-3/6-9 Closed 23-26 Dec, L Mon-Sat

Save on Hotels. Book at theAA.com/hotel

CO GALWAY – CO KERRY 665 IRELAND

Park House Hotel & Restaurant

Modern Irish, International

Appealing menu in bustling city-centre hotel

☎ 091 564924
Forster St, Eyre Square
e-mail: parkhousehotel@eircom.net
web: www.parkhousehotel.ie

Standing just off the city's Eyre Square and built of striking pink granite, Park House has been offering high standards of food and accommodation for well over 35 years. Its celebrated Park Restaurant - where paintings of old Galway help keep the past alive - fairly bustles at lunchtime and mellows in the evening. Endearing classical design - in reds and golds with banquette seating and chairs and closely-set tables - suits the surroundings, likewise the traditional-inspired cooking is classically underpinned, while making good use of traceable local ingredients on a menu with broad appeal. Orange- and honey-glazed breast of duckling with a peppercorn sauce, for instance, or prime fillet steak au poivre to Dublin Bay prawns thermidor. Finish with profiteroles, apple pie or Pavlova.

Chef Robert O'Keefe, Martin Keane **Owner** Eamon Doyle, Kitty Carr **Times** 12-3/6-10 Closed 24-26 Dec **Prices** Prices not confirmed Service optional **Wines** 4 by glass **Notes** Early evening menu €33.95, Sunday L, Vegetarian available **Seats** 145, Pr/dining room 45 **Children** Portions, Menu **Parking** 40, Adjacent to hotel

RECESS (SRAITH SALACH)　　Map 1 A4

Lough Inagh Lodge

Irish, French

Spectacular scenery and Irish country-house cooking

☎ 095 34706 & 34694
Inagh Valley
e-mail: inagh@iol.ie
dir: From Galway take N344. After 3.5m hotel on right

Right on the shores of Lough Inagh, with Connemara's wild mountains all around, this 19th-century fishing lodge will melt the heart of anyone with an eye for beautiful landscapes. You can fill the daylight hours with fishing the lake and hiking around the Inagh Valley, before returning to the comfy country house for a pre-dinner snifter by an open fire in the lounge or the oak-panelled bar. Top-drawer native ingredients form the cornerstones of the kitchen's efforts, which aim for all-round satisfaction with the likes of smoked salmon with walnuts and raspberry vinaigrette preceding equally straightforward main courses - perhaps roast duck with French beans and cherry sauce, lobster from the lough, or Irish fillet steak with braised red cabbage and onion jus. Finish with Irish artisan cheeses or classic profiteroles with vanilla cream and chocolate sauce.

Chef J O'Flaherty, M Linne **Owner** Marie O'Connor **Times** 7-8.45 Closed mid Dec-mid Mar **Prices** Prices not confirmed Service added 10% **Notes** Civ Wed 36 **Seats** 30

CO KERRY

DINGLE (AN DAINGEAN)　　Map 1 A2

Gormans Clifftop House & Restaurant

Modern, Traditional

Clifftop cracker with splendid local produce

☎ 066 9155162 & 083 0033133
Glaise Bheag, Ballydavid (Baile na nGall)
e-mail: info@gormans-clifftophouse.com
dir: R559 to An Mhuirioch, turn right at T-junct, N for 3km

Simplicity is the key to this delightful restaurant with rooms out on the north-western tip of the Dingle Peninsula. The stone-built house perches on the clifftops above Smerwick harbour; this is about as far west as you can expect to eat in Europe, so there's nothing to get in the way of the dining room's sweeping views across the Atlantic. The Gorman family have owned the house since the 18th century, which might explain why chef-proprietor Vincent Gorman has an innate passion for sourcing as much as possible of his materials from the local farms and ports. Produce as spanking fresh as this doesn't need to be messed with, so the menu is appropriately to the point, offering five choices at each stage. You might start with Annascaul black pudding served with traditional potato cakes, glazed apples and grain mustard sauce, and follow with Dingle Bay prawns stir-fried with vegetables, herbs, garlic and white wine, or a Moroccan-style tajine of West Kerry lamb. To finish, there could be stewed rhubarb from the garden topped with a buttery walnut crumble and served with vanilla ice cream.

Times 7-8 Closed Oct-Mar, Sun, L all week

KENMARE　　Map 1 B2

Sheen Falls Lodge

Modern European V

Memorable cooking and waterfall views

☎ 064 6641600
Sheen Falls Lodge
e-mail: info@sheenfallslodge.ie
dir: From Kenmare take N71 to Glengarriff. Take 1st left after suspension bridge. 1m from Kenmare

High on a promontory in woodland and gardens, this modern building has views of Kenmare Bay to one side and of Sheen Falls on the other. La Cascade restaurant has views of the falls too - floodlit after dark - although the attention is likely to be diverted to the enticements on the menu. The cooking is based on a contemporary European repertory, with the kitchen applying its own creative spin on things, adding confit pork belly ravioli to green pea soup, for instance, and making another starter of veal carpaccio and pan-fried sweetbreads and serving them with a 'dust' of aged balsamic, and watermelon and samphire marinated in salted olive oil. Main courses are intelligently composed, offering much to interest, with fillet of local hake paired with a crab beignet and served with thyme risotto, bell pepper jus and seasonal

vegetables, and pan-fried smoked duck breast accompanied by confit drumstick, dandelion leaves, sage butter and gnocchi. A touch of novelty is seen in puddings like mojito sponge with pineapple sorbet and pineapple and chilli kebab.

Chef Heiko Riebandt **Owner** Palladium Hotels & Resorts **Times** 7-9.30 Closed 2 Jan-1 Feb, L all week **Prices** Fixed D 3 course €65, Tasting menu €95, Service optional **Wines** 16 by glass **Notes** Vegetarian menu, Dress restrictions, Smart casual (jacket), no jeans or T-shirts, Civ Wed 150 **Seats** 120, Pr/dining room 40 **Children** Portions, Menu **Parking** 75

KILLARNEY　　Map 1 B2

Cahernane House Hotel

Modern European, International V

Modern country-house cooking in a tranquil setting

☎ 064 6631895
Muckross Rd
e-mail: info@cahernane.com
web: www.cahernane.com
dir: From Killarney follow signs for Kenmare, then from Muckross Rd over bridge. Hotel signed on right. Hotel 1m from town centre

Reached via an impressive driveway lined with mature trees, and only a short stroll from the shores of Lough Leane, Cahernane House is on a private estate on the edge of Killarney National Park. It was once the seat of the Earls of Pembroke, so it will come as no surprise that the 17th-century house is rather grand and packed with original features such as fireplaces, ornate ceilings and ancestral oil portraits. The Herbert Room restaurant is suitably well dressed and traditional - crisp white linen, sparkling glassware and the like - and the service is from a professional and confident team. The daily-changing menu is based on first-class regional ingredients and displays the creativity and craft in the kitchen. Cahernane chicken liver might turn up in a first-course parfait in the company of red onion marmalade, redcurrant syrup and warm toasted brioche, whilst among main courses, duck breast is roasted on the bone and served with braised Savoy cabbage with raisins, caramelised pineapple and chutney juices, plus an array of accompanying vegetables.

Chef David Norris **Owner** Mr & Mrs J Browne **Times** 12-2.30/7-9.30 Closed Jan-Feb, L all week ex by arrangement, D Sun **Prices** Fixed D 3 course €48, Starter €9, Main €30, Dessert €9, Service optional **Wines** 20 by glass **Notes** Tasting menu available, Sunday L, Vegetarian menu, Dress restrictions, Smart casual, no shorts, Civ Wed 80 **Seats** 50, Pr/dining room 18 **Children** Portions, Menu **Parking** 50

KILLARNEY *continued*

The Lake Hotel

🏵 Traditional European **V** 🕙

Lough views and successful modern cooking

☎ 064 6631035
On the Shore, Muckross Rd
e-mail: info@lakehotel.com
dir: 2 km from town centre on N71 Muckross Rd

The Lake Hotel earns its name, as it's bang on the shore of Lough Lein, with glorious views over water and mountains. The hotel has been much extended over the years, and The Castlelough Restaurant, built as part of the original 1820 house, has itself seen total refurbishment while retaining its high ceilings, cornicing and vast windows catching those views. The kitchen works around a slate of modern ideas based on classical traditions, using the area's tip-top ingredients. An assiette of duck, for instance, comes as terrine, smoked, with hazelnuts and orange, and warm pithivier, and a plate of smoked fish as salmon blini, sea trout with lemon and caviar dressing, and haddock fishcake with caper aïoli. Main courses can seem more mainstream, as in chicken breast with fondant potato, pea purée, and leek and mushroom ragout, although roast saddle of rabbit partnered by monkfish and served with black pudding, carrots and a savoury jus brings an interesting interpretation of surf 'n' turf.

Chef Paul O'Connor **Owner** The Huggard family
Times 12-4.30/6.30-9 Closed Dec-Jan, L all week
Prices Fixed L 2 course €18-€22, Fixed D 3 course €35, Starter €5.50-€12, Main €17-€29, Dessert €6-€8.50, Service optional **Wines** 25 bottles over €30, 14 bottles under €30, 7 by glass **Notes** Signature tasting menu available, Sunday L, Vegetarian menu, Civ Wed 150 **Seats** 90, Pr/dining room 120 **Children** Portions, Menu **Parking** 150

Muckross Park Hotel & Cloisters Spa

🏵 Modern Irish **NEW V** 🕙

Modern food in a characterful country house

☎ 064 6623400
Lakes of Killarney
e-mail: info@muckrosspark.com
dir: From Killarney take N71 towards Kenmare

This upmarket hotel and spa occupies a venerable old house that first opened its doors as the Herbert Arms in 1795. The location overlooking the Killarney National Park, with the Blue Pool River running through the grounds, is a dream, and there's history too: Queen Victoria stayed here, and George Bernard Shaw holed up in the summer of 1923 to write *Pygmalion*; his sojourn is referenced in the fine-dining GB Shaw's Restaurant. The venue sports a smart contemporary sheen, and local produce is the name of the game, appearing in appealing modern European-accented dishes. Duck foie gras with apple membrillo and truffled brioche might be one way to start, while main course could see venison partnered by celeriac purée, pear, and chocolate jus; fish turns up in

the shape of monkfish with aubergine purée, pancetta and tomato. To end, blood orange jelly and sorbet add an up-to-date edge to vanilla rice pudding.

Chef Mike Hayes **Owner** Jackie Lavin **Times** 6.30-9.30 Closed midweek Nov-Feb, Mon, L all week, D Mon
Prices Fixed L 2 course €20-€25, Fixed D 3 course €35-€55, Tasting menu €45-€65, Starter €7-€13, Main €18-€35, Dessert €7-€8.50, Service optional **Wines** 38 bottles over €30, 31 bottles under €30, 10 by glass **Notes** Vegetarian menu, Dress restrictions, Smart casual, Civ Wed 250 **Seats** 70, Pr/dining room 60 **Children** Portions, Menu **Parking** 150

KILLORGLIN | Map 1 A2

Carrig House Country House & Restaurant

🏵 Modern Irish, European

Fine dining with expansive lough views

☎ 066 9769100
Caragh Lake
e-mail: info@carrighouse.com
dir: N70 to Killorglin

Carrig is a lovingly restored Victorian country manor in acres of colourful woodland gardens with views across Caragh Lake to the Kerry Mountains. Inside, the genteel house is done out in period style, with turf fires sizzling in cosy, chintzy lounges, while the dining room is the very image of 19th-century chic; all William Morris wallpapers, swagged curtains, polished floorboards, and formally laid tables. The cooking, on the other hand, takes a more up-to-date approach, lining up superb local ingredients and sending them to finishing school: crab could get a modish three-way treatment as ravioli, soup and pasty, and might be followed by Skeganore duck breast with vanilla and lime potato purée, and sweet port and brandy jus. For dessert, maybe prune and Armagnac crème brûlée.

Times 7-9 **Notes** D 4 course fr €45, Menus alternate & ALC menu

---

TRALEE | Map 1 A2

Ballygarry House Hotel and Spa

🏵 Modern Irish **NEW**

Excellent Irish ingredients in well-established family-run hotel

☎ 066 7123322
Killarney Rd
e-mail: info@ballygarryhouse.com
web: www.ballygarryhouse.com
dir: 1.5km from Tralee, on N21

After 50 years in the hands of the same family, you might expect service at this upmarket country house hotel with a delicious pampering spa to run like a well-oiled clock, and you'd be right. The location, too, is a big plus: set in six acres of gorgeous gardens at the foot of the Kerry Mountains. Landscapes hereabouts run the gamut from mountains to lakes, woodland, and ocean - a perfect

environment, then, for the kitchen to get its hands on the finest local materials from land and sea, so on the food front you can expect well-executed Irish cooking served in the bright and cheerful surroundings of the Brooks Restaurant. Start with heartwarming seafood chowder served with home-made brown soda bread, and go on with roast rack of lamb with wild mushrooms and sherry jus, or baked sea bass with potato rösti, crab meat, and fresh pea cream.

Chef John O'Sullivan **Owner** Padraig McGillicudy
Times 12.30-2.30/6.30-9.30 Closed 22-26 Dec
Prices Fixed L 3 course fr €25, Fixed D 3 course fr €35, Starter €5.95-€10.95, Main €19.95-€28.95, Dessert €5.75-€6.95, Service optional **Wines** 14 bottles over €30, 20 bottles under €30, 6 by glass **Notes** Sunday L, Vegetarian available, Civ Wed 200 **Seats** 90 **Children** Portions, Menu **Parking** 200

Ballyseede Castle

🏵 Traditional European

Appealing food in a historic castle

☎ 066 7125799
e-mail: info@ballyseedecastle.com
dir: On N21 just after N21/N22 junct

Crenallated and turreted, and with a pedigree dating back to the 1590s, Ballyseede certainly delivers the full-dress stately home experience. With its deep green walls, heavy swagged-back drapes, crystal chandelier and gilt-framed oil paintings, the fine-dining O'Connell Restaurant makes a suitably plush setting for food that calls on top-class Irish materials for its crowd-pleasing menus, which essay a broad sweep from pan-fried tiger prawns with garlic butter as a simple opener, to a main course that sees roast suprême of chicken partnered with Irish cider velouté, foie gras risotto and white truffle oil. For fish fans, there could be roast loin of cod with mussel, chorizo, black olive and roast tomato cream sauce, and comfort-oriented desserts such as sticky toffee pudding with butterscotch sauce and vanilla ice cream will help to fill any holes.

Owner Marnie & Rory O'Sullivan **Times** 12.30-2.30/7-9 Closed Jan-3 Mar, L Mon-Sat **Prices** Prices not confirmed **Wines** 4 by glass **Notes** Sunday L, Vegetarian available, Civ Wed 130 **Seats** 40, Pr/dining room 70 **Children** Portions, Menu **Parking** 180

Save on Hotels. Book at **theAA.com/hotel**

CO KILDARE – CO KILKENNY 667   IRELAND

CO KILDARE

STRAFFAN   Map 1 C/D4

Barberstown Castle

◉◉ Irish, French

Classic cooking in a 13th-century castle

☎ 01 6288157
e-mail: info@barberstowncastle.ie
web: www.barberstowncastle.ie
dir: R406, follow signs for Barberstown

Close to Dublin city centre and the airport, Barberstown Castle presents a fascinating timeline running through eight centuries of history from its 13th-century crenallated tower to wings added by Elizabethan and Victorian inhabitants, which now house the elegant dining rooms. You can take oodles of period character as read: amid walls hung with tapestries, wooden and flagstoned floors, and throne-like wooden chairs at candlelit, linen-clad tables, dinner is always a bit special, and staff make sure it all ticks along in a smooth and professional manner. Classical country-house influences are to the fore - the man directing the culinary action is French, after all - in a repertoire built on prime local materials and a pitch-perfect grasp of how flavours and textures work together. Expect main courses such as chargrilled Irish beef fillet with fondant potato, baby spinach, celeriac purée and foie gras sauce, or wild sea bass matched with scallops, fennel compôte, vine tomatoes, and star anise cream. Bringing up the rear are desserts that might include buttermilk pannacotta with Irish rhubarb compôte and jelly.

Times 7.30-10 Closed 24-26 Dec, Jan, Sun-Thu, L all week

CO KILKENNY

KILKENNY   Map 1 C3

Kilkenny River Court Hotel

◉ Modern, Traditional

Historic castle setting for ambitious cooking

☎ 056 7723388
The Bridge, John St
e-mail: info@rivercourthotel.com
dir: In town centre, opposite castle

This contemporary hotel has a clear line of sight across to the battlements of 12th-century Kilkenny Castle and the free-flowing River Nore. It's a treat day or night as the castle is lit up in the evening and floor-to-ceiling windows mean you get the best view in town. The restaurant is done out in a smart modish manner with well-dressed tables, high-backed leather seats and moody lighting to set the upmarket tone. The menu matches the contemporary disposition with some well-crafted, well-presented food. Start with teriyaki-flavoured flaked salmon with buffalo mozzarella, curly endive and plum tomato salad, before moving on to fillet of hake with a fricassee of fennel, garden peas, capers and a herby beurre blanc, or cider-braised pork belly with creamed leeks, Savoy cabbage and champ. There's good cooking at dessert stage, too: a trio of Cox's Orange Pippin (strudel, parfait and jelly), for example.

Chef Gerrard Dunne **Owner** Rubyside Ltd
Times 12.30-3/6-9.30 Closed Xmas, L Mon-Sat, D Sun
Prices Fixed D 3 course fr €29.50, Service optional
Wines 21 bottles over €30, 15 bottles under €30, 4 by glass **Notes** Early bird from €21.95, Sunday L, Vegetarian available, Civ Wed 260 **Seats** 80 **Children** Portions, Menu
Parking 120

The Lady Helen Restaurant

THOMASTOWN   MAP 1 C3

Modern Irish V

Modern Irish cooking on an extensive country estate

☎ 056 7773000
Mount Juliet Hotel
e-mail: info@mountjuliet.ie
dir: M7 from Dublin, N9 towards Waterford, exit at junct 9/Danesfort for hotel

The Mount Juliet Hotel is part of a premier country estate in the southeast of Ireland. There is golf, of course, as well as equestrian facilities, salmon and trout fishing and archery, and a club for the juniors called the Little Rascals, which surely seals the deal. The jewel in the crown of the catering activities is The Lady Helen Restaurant, which enjoys sweeping views over the estate and the River Nore, an elegant elliptical space with ornate plasterwork ceiling, top-notch table appointments and staff who are the last word in solicitous professionalism. Local (and therefore seasonal) produce is bought in, and seasoned aromatically with herbs picked fresh each day from the hotel's own garden. Multi-course taster menus, including an aperitif, prove popular, and come with the option of a pre-selected wine flight in the modern manner, while the carte offers a broad variety of appealing choice. First off might be a pressed terrine of veal and foie gras adorned with sea buckthorn and pickled vegetables, or seared scallops with sea-lettuce and cauliflower in apple-sweetened chicken consommé. Mains might offer a modish pairing of rabbit loin and langoustine, furnished with contemporary stylings in the shapes of fennel purée, pickled watermelon, marsh samphire and fennel pollen gnocchi, or perhaps a faintly North African presentation of squab pigeon cooked in almond milk, with medjool date purée and cabbage in a reduction of the roasting juices. Desserts maintain the pace-setting standard with baked lemon cream, accompanied by goats' curd parfait, raspberry sorbet and yuzu jelly, or caramelised apple bavarois with walnut sponge and vanilla ice cream. Fabulous Irish cheeses are served with poached figs, pickled pear and linseed crackers, while coffee comes with batches of beautifully made petits fours to round things off in style. The hotel sells its own range of stemware, and naturally lists some extremely fine gear to pour into it.

Chef Cormac Rowe **Owner** Kileen Investments
Times 6.30-9.45 Closed L all week, D Sun, Tue
Prices Fixed D 3 course fr €65, Tasting menu €55-€75, Service optional **Wines** 10 by glass **Notes** Fixed D 4 course, Tasting menu 8 course, Vegetarian menu, Dress restrictions, No jeans or T-shirts, Civ Wed 100 **Seats** 60, Pr/dining room 80 **Children** Portions, Menu **Parking** 200

THOMASTOWN — Map 1 C3

Kendals Brasserie

French, European

A taste of France beside the golf course

☎ 056 7773000
Mount Juliet Hotel
e-mail: info@mountjuliet.ie
dir: Just outside Thomastown S on N9

The name might not have a cross-Channel ring to it, but French brasserie classics are the name of the game at Kendals, which is the more casual venue at the swanky 18th-century Mount Juliet Hotel. Housed in the estate's converted stables - now the golf clubhouse - the setting is light and airy in the day, looking over the fairways through large windows, and more romantic when it is candlelit for dinner. Top-class local ingredients underpin the repertoire of French brasserie classics, which could kick off with salade Lyonnaise, beef carpaccio, or salt-cod brandade with marinated cherry tomatoes and curly endive, ahead of local Slaney lamb, slow-cooked for 15 hours and served with pommes Anna, Chantenay carrots and peas, and thyme jus. Finish with banana tarte Tatin with home-made rum and raisin ice cream. If you want to trade up on another visit, the posh option is The Lady Helen Restaurant (see entry below).

Chef Cormac Rowe **Owner** Mount Juliet **Times** 6-9.30 Closed Mon & Wed (seasonal) **Prices** Starter €6.50-€12.50, Main €16.50-€31, Dessert €6.50-€8.50 **Wines** 38 bottles over €30, 25 bottles under €30, 10 by glass **Notes** Early bird menu 6-7pm, 3 course €25, Vegetarian available, Civ Wed 160 **Seats** 70 **Children** Portions, Menu **Parking** 200

The Lady Helen Restaurant

– see page 667

CO LEITRIM

MOHILL — Map 1 C4

Lough Rynn Castle

Modern, Traditional Irish V

Contemporary flavours in a peaceful location

☎ 071 9632700
e-mail: enquiries@loughrynn.ie
dir: N4 (Dublin to Sligo), hotel 8km off N4 & 2km from Mohill

The Earl of Leitrim's old place makes a rather splendid country-house hotel, its handsome gothic architecture and position by the lough making a fine first impression. There's a golf course on the estate these days, too. Within, the well-proportioned rooms are decorated traditionally and comfortably and are packed with period character. The Sandstone Restaurant is in the former stable block, the aforementioned stone a design feature of the smart-looking room, where tables are dressed to impress. The menu meets the fine-dining expectations of

the setting, with an ambitious repertoire of confident, contemporary dishes. Start, perhaps, with monkfish wrapped in Parma ham and spinach and served with red onion marmalade, sautéed samphire and a saffron froth, following on with seared duck breast partnered with confit leg, vanilla-flavoured sweet potato mash and an anise reduction, and end with an impressive warm pineapple financier.

Chef Clare O'Leary **Owner** Hanly Group/Alan Hanly **Times** 12-2.30/7-9 Closed L Mon-Sat **Prices** Fixed L 2 course €13.95-€27.50, Fixed D 2 course €38-€45, Starter €8.50-€13.50, Main €28-€42.50, Dessert €8.20-€16.95, Service optional **Wines** 12 by glass **Notes** Sunday L, Vegetarian menu, Civ Wed 350 **Seats** 90, Pr/dining room 10 **Children** Portions, Menu

CO LIMERICK

LIMERICK — Map 1 B3

Limerick Strand Hotel

Modern, International V

River views and comforting food

☎ 061 421800
Ennis St
e-mail: info@strandlimerick.ie
dir: On the Shannon side of Sorsfield Bridge, on River Shannon

The aptly-named River Restaurant of the spanking-new contemporary Limerick Strand Hotel is the place to head for dining with the best views in town. Floor-to-ceiling glass walls mean everyone gets a view of the Shannon flowing by to go with a well-prepared and presented repertoire of straightforward modern European food. There's an abundance of splendid raw materials in these parts, and they find their way into dishes such as beef carpaccio with rocket, parmesan, horseradish crisp and citrus vinaigrette, while mains run to mixed grills, steaks or herb-crusted rack of new season Kerry lamb with fondant potato, carrot gratin, and red wine jus. For pudding, perhaps a refreshing lemon vacherin with raspberry sauce.

Chef Tom Flavin **Times** 6-10 Closed D Sun **Prices** Prices not confirmed Service optional **Notes** Sunday L, Vegetarian menu **Seats** 120, Pr/dining room 400 **Children** Portions, Menu **Parking** 100

CO LOUTH

CARLINGFORD — Map 1 D4

Ghan House

Modern Irish

Wide-ranging menus on the lough

☎ 042 9373682
e-mail: info@ghanhouse.com
dir: M1 junct 18 signed Carlingford, 5mtrs on left after 50kph speed sign

On the shore of Carlingford Lough in a walled garden, Ghan House is a family-run hotel and restaurant with views over the water. The kitchen's a busy place, making everything in-house, from bread to ice cream; herbs, fruit and vegetables come from the hotel's garden and shellfish from the lough. The eclectic menu picks up ideas from international cuisines, so to start might come seafood chowder, confit duck leg with cassoulet and thyme jus, and mackerel escabèche with black onion seed crackers, potato salad and smoked haddock cream. The menu name-checks sources - Cooley lamb and beef, fish landed at Kilkeel harbour - so quality and freshness are guaranteed. Fillet of cod is marinated in Indian spices, accurately fried and served with fennel compôte, curried yoghurt and pineapple salsa, and pink-seared duck breast is accompanied by beetroot ketchup, candied parsnips and parsnip purée. Puddings seem to be rooted in a more familiar repertoire, among them vanilla crème brûlée, and dark chocolate fondant with vanilla ice cream.

Chef Stephane Le Sourne **Owner** Joyce & Paul Carroll **Times** 1-3/6-11 Closed 24-26 & 31 Dec, 1-2 Jan, 1 day a week (varies), L Mon-Sat (open most Sun or by arrangement), D 1 day a week (varies) **Prices** Fixed L 2 course fr €21.50, Fixed D 3 course €40-€46.50, Tasting menu €29.50-€33.50, Service optional **Wines** 19 bottles over €30, 33 bottles under €30, 13 by glass **Notes** Tasting menu 6 course Mon-Thu 5.30-8, Sunday L, Vegetarian available, Civ Wed 45 **Seats** 50, Pr/dining room 34 **Children** Portions **Parking** 24

CO MAYO

BALLINA   Map 1 B4

Belleek Castle

◉◉ Modern Irish V ✆

Special occasion dining in historic castle

☎ 096 22400 & 21878
Belleek
e-mail: info@belleekcastle.com

Belleek may call itself a castle and even look like one, but this pocket-sized stately home in a thousand-acre forested estate on the banks of the River Moy is actually a Victorian folly whose dainty 19th-century Gothic gables and skinny turrets wouldn't put up much of a fight if shots were fired in anger. In fact, the only popping noises to be heard are caused by the opening of champagne bottles at one of the many weddings taking place. Inside, oak panelling, coffered ceilings, chandeliers, and crimson walls hung with tapestries make for a suitably faux-medieval baronial setting in the dining room, which was originally the library of the manor house. The kitchen takes well-sourced local ingredients - some foraged seasonally in the surrounding grounds and woodlands - as the eminently solid building blocks of a straightforward country-house menu. Fresh hot-smoked salmon makes for a deliciously simple starter, ahead of a duo of duck (pan-roasted breast, and braised leg in pastry) served with potato and swede gratin and light veal jus.

Chef Stephen Lenahan **Owner** Paul Marshal Doran **Times** 1-5.30/6-9.30 Closed Xmas & Jan **Prices** Tasting menu €49.50-€65.50, Starter €8.90-€12.90, Main €17.90-€32.50, Dessert €8.90-€12.50, Service optional **Wines** 57 bottles over €30, 7 bottles under €30, 5 by glass **Notes** Early bird menu 3 course €28.50, Gourmet menu €65.50, Vegetarian menu, Civ Wed 200 **Seats** 55, Pr/dining room 30 **Children** Portions, Menu **Parking** 90

Mount Falcon Estate

◉◉ Traditional French, International

Polished cooking using exemplary local materials

☎ 096 74472
Mount Falcon Country House, Foxford Rd
e-mail: info@mountfalcon.com
web: www.mountfalcon.com
dir: On N26, 6m from Foxford & 3m from Ballina. Hotel on left

On the banks of the River Moy, the Mount Falcon is a splendidly baronial-looking pile sitting in its own 100-acre estate, and in its Kitchen Restaurant, it has a dining address that elevates it above the country-house norm. It will come as no surprise that the restaurant is in the old kitchen and pantry of this grand old house, and it is done out with a good degree of style, with linen-clad tables and food-related prints on the walls. Head chef Philippe Farineau hails from France and has a passion for cooking - in a mostly French classical style - with local and regional ingredients. The wares of small-scale and

artisan producers and suppliers are bolstered by home-grown stuff (from the kitchen's own poly-tunnel). Start, perhaps, with an assiette of local seafood which includes salmon rillette, glazed oyster, gravad lax and a crab beignet, and move on to loin of venison served with a venison sausage, leek and cep tart, celeriac and cauliflower purée, finished with a game jus. End in fine style with a stunningly presented plate dedicated to the pear: poached in saffron syrup, in a tart with almond, and a light pear mousse.

Times 6.30-9 Closed Xmas, L Mon-Sat

CONG   Map 1 B4

The George V Dining Room

◉◉ Traditional European, International V ✆

Classy cooking in magnificent castle

☎ 094 9546003
Ashford Castle
e-mail: ashford@ashford.ie
web: www.ashford.ie
dir: In Cross, turn left at church onto R345 signed Cong. Turn left at hotel sign & continue through castle gates

There need be no quibbling about castle credentials here, for it's a castle and no mistake. Once the Guinness family summer retreat, it's a magnificent building with parts that date back to the 13th century. With its position by a lough, surrounded by the beautiful estate, Ashford Castle is a luxurious escape from the real world. The magnificence outside is matched within, not least in the George V Dining Room with its opulent fixtures and fittings and grand proportions - chandeliers, panelled walls, rich fabrics and well-dressed tables generously spaced around the room. There's a good deal of fine Irish produce on the classically-minded menu, and a roast of the day is carved at the table. Start, perhaps, with butter-seared Irish scallops served with crisp risotto cakes, pesto foam and raspberry coulis, followed by roast loin of local venison accompanied by a crisp samosa filled with venison and girolle mousse, plus a cheddar potato, carrot purée and blackberry jus. Finish with a well-crafted dessert of white chocolate and blackberries that shows sharp technical skills.

Chef Stefan Matz **Owner** Edward Holdings **Times** 7-9.30 Closed L all week **Prices** Fixed D 3 course €59, Tasting menu €75, Starter €9-€22, Main €25-€32, Dessert €10-€15, Service added 15% **Wines** 500 bottles over €30, 12 bottles under €30, 12 by glass **Notes** Fixed D 4 course €67, Sunday L, Vegetarian menu, Dress restrictions, Jacket & tie, Civ Wed 166 **Seats** 166, Pr/dining room 44 **Children** Portions, Menu **Parking** 115

MULRANY   Map 1 A4

Mulranny Park Hotel

◉◉ Modern ✆

Local produce and dramatic Atlantic views

☎ 098 36000
e-mail: info@mulrannyparkhotel.ie
web: www.mulrannyparkhotel.ie
dir: R311 from Castlebar to Newport onto N59. Hotel on right

This smart modern restaurant in a refurbished Victorian railway hotel benefits from breathtaking views across Clew Bay and out to sea. Unsurprisingly window tables are worth their weight in gold while professional service is underpinned by a genuine friendliness. Classically-based cooking lets its hair down in the presentation stakes but make no mistake, this is sound cooking using well-sourced, local ingredients. You might be offered chilled Irish Cashel Blue cheese and Guinness parfait, tomato and mint chutney and pickled pear, followed by a perfectly cooked baked suprême of organic Clare Island salmon, crab and chive orzo, aubergine caviar and cep jus. Honey and yoghurt pannacotta is a delicate finale.

Chef Ollie O'Regan **Owner** Tom Bohan & Tom Duggan **Times** 6.30-9 Closed Jan **Prices** Fixed D 3 course €40, Service optional **Wines** 6 bottles over €30, 14 bottles under €30, 3 by glass **Notes** Vegetarian available, Civ Wed 100 **Seats** 100, Pr/dining room 50 **Children** Portions, Menu **Parking** 200

WESTPORT   Map 1 B4

Hotel Westport Leisure, Spa & Conference

◉ Irish, European ✆

Exemplary local produce at riverside hotel

☎ 098 25122
Newport Rd
e-mail: reservations@hotelwestport.ie
web: www.hotelwestport.ie
dir: N5 to Westport. Right at end of Castlebar St, 1st right before bridge, right at lights, left before church. Follow to end of street

Heavenly scenery frames this expansive family-run hotel and spa set in seven acres of mature woodland. And with miles of walking and cycling on the Great Western Greenway close to hand, there's no excuse for failing to bring a keen appetite to table. After a recent top-to-tail refurbishment, the place is looking pretty nifty, with plush carpets and seating beneath an ornate ceiling, while views overlooking the Carrowbeg River are timeless. Expect a bedrock of straightforward modern ideas built on the finest local, seasonal materials - perhaps home-cured organic Clare Island salmon with cucumber jelly, shaved fennel and lemon oil, followed by the simplicity of roast rib of beef with horseradish jus and pan juices, or grilled fillet of wild Atlantic hake matched with roast

continued

WESTPORT *continued*

vegetables and salsa verde. Finish with rich chocolate fondant with pistachio ice cream, or bow out on a savoury note with Irish artisan cheeses.

Chef Stephen Fitzmaurice **Owner** Cathal Hughes **Times** 1-2.30/6-9.30 **Prices** Fixed L 2 course €19.50-€21.50, Fixed D 3 course €35-€36, Tasting menu €35-€36, Service optional **Wines** 20 bottles over €30, 31 bottles under €30, 10 by glass **Notes** Sunday L, Vegetarian available, Civ Wed 200 **Seats** 120, Pr/dining room 45 **Children** Portions, Menu **Parking** 220

Knockranny House Hotel

◎◎ Modern International ✍

Fresh culinary ideas in a luxurious hotel setting

☎ 098 28600
e-mail: info@khh.ie
web: www.knockrannyhousehotel.ie
dir: On N5 (Dublin to Castlebar road), hotel on left before entering Westport

Opening in the 1990s in a splendidly tranquil setting on the west coast, Knockranny enjoys commanding views of the mountain pilgrimage site of Croagh Patrick and the many-islanded Clew Bay. Its split-level dining room, La Fougère, takes full advantage of this seductive setting, with elegant furnishings and appointments and confident, formally-attired staff. The kitchen works seasonally to produce appealingly presented modern dishes. Langoustines from the Bay outside the windows turn up with a fine tortellini of earthy mushrooms in an accurately seasoned seafood bisque with chervil jelly. Next up could be roast pork tenderloin wrapped in caul, served with a thin cigar of black pudding encased in filo, sharply pickled sauerkraut, parsnip purée and an apple paste. Similar contrasts of sweet and sour are mobilised for a dessert of parfait and purée of rhubarb, served with buttery shortbread, rich vanilla anglaise and a rapidly vanishing yoghurt foam.

Chef Seamus Commons **Owner** Adrian & Geraldine Noonan **Times** 6.30-9.30 Closed Xmas, L Mon-Sat (open selected Sun) **Prices** Tasting menu €74, Starter €16-€17, Main €29-€32, Dessert €14.50, Service optional **Wines** 6 by glass **Notes** Table d'hôte menu €52, Sunday L, Vegetarian available, Dress restrictions, Smart casual, Civ Wed 350 **Seats** 90, Pr/dining room 120 **Children** Portions, Menu **Parking** 200

CO MEATH

KILMESSAN — Map 1 D5

The Station House Hotel

◎ European, Mediterranean V ✍

Extensive menu in converted railway station

☎ 046 9025239 & 9025565
e-mail: info@stationhousehotel.ie
web: www.stationhousehotel.ie
dir: From Dublin N3 junct 6 to Dunshaughlin, R125 to Kilmessan

Is there anything more poignant than a disused railway station? The last passenger trains clattered through Kilmessan in the 1940s, freight stopped passing through in the sixties, but the station house has survived the rustication of the rail network to become a charming country hotel, complete with a suite occupying the old signal box. The restaurant is in the former waiting-room, now an uplifting bright space with smartly dressed tables and unfailingly friendly staff. There's a cornucopia of choice at various fixed price-points, with the kitchen confident enough in its abilities to stretch from lamb samosa with apple and mint jelly, to duck confit with braised red cabbage in mango and orange coulis. Mains might take in sea bass with caponata and pesto, or a venison medallions with sweet potato purée in a fruity game jus incorporating blackberries and Cassis. Finish with a boozy trifle made with mascarpone and rum.

Chef David Mulvihill **Owner** Chris & Thelma Slattery **Times** 12.30-4.30/5-10.30 **Prices** Fixed D 3 course fr €23.95, Starter €4.95-€8.95, Main €16.95-€26.95, Dessert €5.95-€9.50, Service optional **Wines** 20 bottles over €30, 20 bottles under €30, 6 by glass **Notes** Fixed D 4 course €29.95, Sunday L, Vegetarian menu, Civ Wed 180 **Seats** 90, Pr/dining room 180 **Children** Portions, Menu **Parking** 200

SLANE — Map 1 D4

Tankardstown

◎◎ Modern Irish ✍

Modern Irish cooking in a classy rustic setting

☎ 041 9824621
e-mail: info@tankardstown.ie
dir: N51 (Navan-Slane road), take turn directly opposite main entrance to Slane Castle, signed Kells. Continue for 5km

There's a fine Georgian manor house at the heart of the Tankardstown estate, but much more besides. It's a big hit on the wedding scene, not surprisingly given the charm of the place and its superb setting, whilst its Brabazon restaurant puts the place on the culinary map. Housed in a one-time cow house, the restaurant has plenty of charm of its own and a lavender-scented garden terrace which is a real boon in the warmer months. The kitchen - headed up by Richard Luckey - gets a good amount of its ingredients from the walled organic gardens and the estate's flock of hens, as well as top-

---

class local and seasonal materials from a trusty network of suppliers, and the cooking is modern and precise. Pressed ham hock with apple and elderflower purée, pain d'épice crumbs, quail's egg and pea soup is a first-course with well-judged flavours. Next up, perhaps fillet of turbot poached in red wine and served with palourde clams, oxtail, ratte potatoes and a chicken and tomato consommé, and to finish, raspberry soufflé with raspberry sauce.

Chef Richard Luckey **Owner** Patricia & Brian Conroy **Times** 12-4/6-9 Closed 3 days Xmas, Mon-Thu (seasonal), L Mon-Thu (seasonal), D Mon-Wed (seasonal) **Prices** Fixed L 2 course €25-€35, Fixed D 3 course €40-€48, Tasting menu €45, Service optional **Wines** 9 by glass **Notes** Fixed 3 course menu available for groups over 10 €35, Sunday L, Vegetarian available, Civ Wed 50 **Seats** 70, Pr/dining room 50 **Children** Portions, Menu

---

CO MONAGHAN

GLASLOUGH — Map 1 C5

The Lodge at Castle Leslie Estate

◎◎ Traditional Irish, International ✍

Modern country-house cooking in splendid isolation

☎ 047 88100
The Lodge, Castle Leslie Estate
e-mail: info@castleleslie.com
dir: M1 junct 14 N Belfast signed Ardee/Derry. Follow N2 Derry Monaghan bypass, then N12 to Armagh for 2m, left N185 to Glaslough

The Castle Leslie Estate extends over 1,000 acres, and both the castle and The Lodge are separate country-house hotels within the estate. Snaffles, in the latter, is a large, stylish restaurant where a glass wall gives country views, and a baby grand piano adds to the atmosphere. The kitchen keeps its finger on the pulse of culinary trends, turning its hands to crab salad with citrus fruit and herb salad, and duck confit with pickled girolles and pear chutney. Among main courses, Fermanagh Saddleback pork comes as glazed rib, rolled roasted fillet and black pudding with Parmentier potatoes and sauerkraut, with an Armagh cider sauce and sultanas, and pan-fried halibut is fashionably partnered by bean and chorizo cassoulet. Finish with a lemon tartlet with Italian meringue and blackberry purée - beautifully presented and bursting with vibrant flavours.

Chef Andrew Bradley **Owner** Samantha Leslie **Times** 6-9.30 Closed Xmas, L all week **Prices** Prices not confirmed Service optional **Wines** 27 bottles over €30, 37 bottles under €30, 14 by glass **Notes** Tasting menu available, Vegetarian available **Seats** 110, Pr/dining room 50 **Children** Portions, Menu **Parking** 200

CO ROSCOMMON

ROSCOMMON Map 1 B4

Kilronan Castle Estate & Spa

◉ French NEW

Country house classics amid Victorian Gothic grandeur

☎ 071 9618000
Ballyfarnon
e-mail: enquiries@kilronancastle.ie
dir: M4 to N4, exit R299 towards R207 Droim ar Snámh/
Drumsna/Droim. Exit R207 for R280, turn left Keadue
Road R284

Kilronan certainly looks like a real castle complete with a
foursquare crenellated turret, but it is actually a mere
stripling, dating from the early 19th century, and after a
thorough restoration as recently as 2006, it now trades as
an upmarket hotel with luxurious spa and leisure
facilities. The interior sports the full-dress Victorian
Gothic look, a style which works to particularly impressive
effect in the Douglas Hyde restaurant, where oak
panelling galore and a magnificent carved fireplace
combine with crystal chandeliers and heavy swagged
drapes. Perhaps unsurprisingly, given the grand setting,
the kitchen looks to French classicism for its inspiration,
spiked here and there with oriental notes. Seasonal wild
garlic is used together with ginger and chilli to lift a tian
of crabmeat, while main course sees loin of venison
glazed with honey, crushed pepper and herbs and served
with roast squash and red wine sauce.

Times 1-3.30/6-10 Closed L Mon-Sat **Prices** Prices not
confirmed **Notes** ALC menu available, Sunday L

CO SLIGO

SLIGO Map 1 B5

Radisson Blu Hotel & Spa Sligo

◉ Modern Irish 🍷

Classy hotel serving top-grade local produce

☎ 071 9140008 & 9192400
Rosses Point Rd, Ballincar
e-mail: info.sligo@radissonblu.com
dir: From N4 into Sligo to main bridge. Take R291 on left.
Hotel 1.5m on right

Named after a castle once owned by Lord Mountbatten,
the Classiebawn Restaurant is the culinary focus of this
clean-cut modern hotel. Although the décor is faultlessly
upmarket, it is the breathtaking views of Sligo Bay and
Knockhaven Mountain that immediately grab your
attention. The kitchen stays abreast of modern trends
and serves up contemporary, internationally-inspired food
made with fresh, seasonal, locally-sourced ingredients.
Fussy embellishments are kicked into touch here in tried-
and-tested stalwarts such as seared scallops with
Clonakilty black pudding, creamed potatoes and chive
butter sauce, or rump of Connemara lamb with braised
Puy lentils teamed with confit garlic and thyme jus.
Flavours are on the money to the end - a Classiebawn
lemon tart made with an unstinting hand on the lemon
zest, served with lime curd.

Chef Joe Shannon **Owner** Radisson Blu **Times** 6-10
Prices Fixed L 2 course fr €15.50, Fixed D 3 course €24-
€34, Starter €6.50-€9.50, Main €15.50-€28.50, Dessert
€6-€8.50 **Wines** 6 bottles over €30, 6 bottles under €30,
7 by glass **Notes** Seasonal early bird menu, Vegetarian
available, Civ Wed 450 **Seats** 120, Pr/dining room 60
Children Portions, Menu **Parking** 600

CO TIPPERARY

THURLES Map 1 C3

Inch House Country House & Restaurant

◉ Irish

Splendid ingredients cooked simply in Georgian manor

☎ 050 451348
e-mail: mairin@inchhouse.ie
dir: 6.5km NE of Thurles on R498

Inch House is a lovingly restored Georgian manor house
at the heart of a working farm run with hands-on charm
by the Egan family. Provenance of food is key here: if it's
not local, seasonal, organic or sourced from an artisan
producer, it doesn't make it onto the table, and the Inch
House own-label black pudding and range of preserves
and chutneys are renowned in these parts. The setting for
dinner is a classically elegant claret and gold-hued
dining room with polished wood floors and white linen on
the tables. When the raw materials are as good as we
have here, you don't need to gild the lily, so the kitchen
treats them with simple, accurately-cooked care in
classic dishes that could see the celebrated black
pudding appearing in a tartlet with red onion marmalade
and Knockdrinna goats' cheese, followed by roast belly of
locally-farmed pork served with creamed cabbage, apple
sauce and red wine jus.

Times 6-9.15 Closed Xmas, Sun-Mon, L all week

CO WATERFORD

ARDMORE Map 1 C2

Cliff House Hotel

◉◉◉◉ – **see page 672**

BALLYMACARBRY Map 1 C2

Hanoras Cottage

◉ Modern Traditional NEW 🍷

Charming country hotel with good honest cooking

☎ 052 6136104 & 6136442
Nire Valley
e-mail: hanorascottage@eircom.net
dir: From Clonmel or Dungarvan to Ballymacarbry. Exit by
pub, 3m, establishment by Nire Church

With its glorious setting in the lush Nire Valley, forays
into nature's beauty are very much on the agenda for
walkers, twitchers and nature lovers of all shades at this
small-scale country house hotel beside the church and

river. The smart restaurant is as classic and
unpretentious as the cooking, which is built on solid
foundations of carefully-sourced local materials treated
with the respect they deserve. Husband and wife team
Eoin Wall and Judith Hovenden run a kitchen that cuts no
corners, making everything in-house and delivering
honest, full-flavoured and accurately cooked dishes. Pan-
fried lamb's kidneys with blue cheese and cream are
served with a Cashel Blue cheese muffin to soak up the
sauce, while a simple grilled fillet of spanking fresh hake
is matched with tomato confit, buttery mash, braised red
cabbage and sauced with Bay Lough cheese, which is
made just five kilometres away, for those interested in
food mileage. For pudding, there's pear and meringue
roulade with crunchy toasted walnuts and decadent
fudge sauce.

Chef Eoin & Judith Wall **Owner** Mary & Eoin Wall
Times 6.30-9 Closed 25-28 Dec, Sun **Prices** Prices not
confirmed **Notes** Vegetarian available, Dress restrictions,
Smart, Civ Wed 40 **Seats** 40 **Children** Menu **Parking** 20

WATERFORD Map 1 C2

Faithlegg House Hotel & Golf Resort

◉ Modern Irish, French

Country-house cooking in a historic Waterford hotel

☎ 051 382000
Faithlegg
e-mail: liammoran@fhh.ie
web: www.faithlegg.com
dir: From Waterford follow Dunmore East Rd then
Cheekpoint Rd

The present house arose in the 1780s, after Cromwell's
ravages in Ireland had gifted the original property to the
Bolton family. For a large part of the 20th century, it was
a monastic novitiate, with the modern hotel opening in
1998. Overlooking the gardens, the Roseville dining room,
with its high ceilings, is fashioned from a pair of original
drawing rooms, with a conservatory extension to boot.
Modern country-house cooking in a fixed-price format is
what to expect, with smoked salmon and guacamole tian
and tomato and apple salsa to start, leading to lamb
shank Cajun-style with chick peas, bulgar and spiced
tomato sauce, or poached haddock with honey-roast
parsnips in grain mustard sauce, topped with a poached
egg. Finish with crème brûlée, enriched with Tia Maria
and served with poppy seed biscuits.

Times 1-2.30/6-9.30 Closed 25 Dec, L pre-book only

Cliff House Hotel

ARDMORE   **MAP 1 C2**

Modern Irish V

Thrilling cooking at the sea's edge

☎ 024 87800 & 87803
e-mail: info@thecliffhousehotel.com
dir: N25 to Ardmore. Hotel at the end of village via The Middle Road

Ocean views don't come much more dramatic than at Cliff House. Originally built in the 1930s, the striking modernist structure is grafted onto the cliffs of Ardmore Bay, with waves breaking on the rocks just a few feet beneath. There's no beach, but it is the kind of place that has a speedboat laid on to whisk guests away to picnics on secluded coves. The place was completely reinvented in the noughties and makes quite an architectural statement in slate, glass, granite and wood, the hard edges softened by opulent, comfortable and colourful fixtures and fittings. It is a glamorous and inspirational look that is typified in the bar and restaurant, which stare out to sea over a terrace, anticipating yet another glorious sunset. Quite where chef Martijn Kajuiter gets inspiration is difficult to judge, but he certainly has an eye for exceptional ingredients of local provenance, and he's completely at home in the realms of of-the-moment, technically-adept cooking, producing extraordinarily creative, complex dishes - even reading the menu takes some concentration. Take a starter of Irish rose veal, which comes grilled, confit, and as a punchy tartare, served with cooked and carpaccio langoustines, girolles, white asparagus, and the edible nasturtium flowers that are a trademark, giving his beautifully-presented dishes that extra wow factor like a riotous, flowery meadow on the plate. Another tour de force, and just as prettily arranged, is a main course of oh-so-perfect grilled halibut fillet, accompanied by delicious grilled shrimp, beech mushrooms, fennel (from the abundant kitchen garden), black quinoa, chicken jus, and watercress oil. There's no let up in technical wizardry and inventiveness at dessert stage either: a riff on local rhubarb delivers the vegetable compressed, as sorbet and meringue, together with white chocolate caramel and mousse encased in a ribbon of rhubarb jelly, hibiscus, cucumber syrup, and gin and tonic gel.

Chef Martijn Kajuiter **Owner** Valshan Ltd **Times** 6.30-10 Closed Xmas, Sun-Mon (occasional Tue), L all week **Prices** Fixed D 3 course €68, Tasting menu €95-€145, Service included **Wines** 12 by glass **Notes** 3 course ALC €68, Sunday L, Vegetarian menu **Seats** 64, Pr/dining room 20 **Children** Portions **Parking** 30

WATERFORD *continued*

Waterford Castle Hotel and Golf Resort

◉◉ French, European 🍴

Traditional setting for confident, modish cooking

☎ 051 878203
The Island
e-mail: info@waterfordcastle.com
dir: From city centre turn onto Dunmore East Rd, 1.5m, past hospital, 0.5m left after lights, ferry at bottom of road

As a reminder that you're heading for somewhere a bit special, it's hard to beat the ferry that takes you across Waterford Harbour to the titular 15th-century castle ensconced on its own private 300-acre island. The estate is expansive enough to have its own 18-hole golf course, while the hotel itself comes fully loaded with Elizabethan oak panelling, elaborate plasterwork ceilings, and stone mullioned windows. Gentlemen probably won't be taken aback by being asked to don a jacket in the Munster Dining Room, where a pianist tinkles away in a grand oak-panelled space hung with ancestral artworks. Food-wise, however, it's fast forward to a repertoire of modern ideas with a distinct French accent, wrought from top-notch Irish materials. A starter of seared scallops with Puy lentils, ceps, scallop cream and vanilla salt shows the style, followed by an assiette of pork comprising confit belly, braised cheek and roast loin matched with shiitaki mushrooms and fennel jus. To finish, there might be apple and blueberry crumble with ginger ice cream.

Chef Michael Quinn **Owner** Munster Dining Room **Times** 6.30-9 Closed Xmas, early Jan, L all week **Prices** Fixed L 3 course €38, Tasting menu €70, Starter €8.50-€14, Main €28-€36, Dessert €12-€14.50, Service optional **Wines** 40 bottles over €30, 21 bottles under €30, 8 by glass **Notes** 4 course D €40, Early bird menu 6-7.30, Vegetarian available, Dress restrictions, Jacket or tie required for D, Civ Wed 120 **Seats** 60, Pr/dining room 30 **Children** Portions, Menu **Parking** 80

CO WEXFORD

GOREY   Map 1 D3

Amber Springs Hotel

◉ Modern European NEW

Modern hotel with food to match

☎ 053 9484000
Wexford Rd
e-mail: info@ambersprings.ie
dir: N11 junct 23, 500mtrs from Gorey by-pass at junct 23

This spanking-new contemporary hotel in historic Gorey opened in 2006 and has something for everyone, whether you're tying the knot, planning a spot of down time in the spa, setting up a corporate team building session, or just looking to de-stress by the coast and eat well. The latter is taken care of by Kelby's Bistro, a clean-cut, neutral modern space up on the first floor, where sweeping

picture windows open up views across the gardens to fields beyond. Straightforward, easygoing comfort food is the deal here, with much of the seasonal produce - particularly beef - provided by the owners' farm, as in a main course of dry-aged Angus sirloin steak served with onion and truffle purée, smoked butter hollandaise, and cherry tomatoes. This might come book-ended by crispy deep-fried lemon and pepper-coated calamari with a spicy kick from mango and chilli purée, and glazed chocolate mousse with pistachio ice cream to finish.

Chef Michael Thomas **Times** 6-9 Closed 25-26 Dec, L all week **Prices** Prices not confirmed **Parking** 178

Ashdown Park Hotel

◉ Mediterranean, European 🍴

Crowd-pleasing menu in an elegant setting

☎ 053 9480500
Station Rd
e-mail: info@ashdownparkhotel.com
web: www.ashdownparkhotel.com
dir: On approach to Gorey town take N11 from Dublin. Take left signed for Courtown. Hotel on left

With sandy beaches and golf courses nearby, this modern hotel on a grand scale, within walking distance of the centre of Gorey, has plenty of attractions of its own. There's a spa and conference facilities, for a start, plus some 22 acres of grounds to explore. It is also home to the Rowan Tree Restaurant, where tables are dressed up in crisp white linen, and the kitchen turns out some pleasingly straightforward dishes based on good local ingredients, including some things from the grounds. Start with a Caesar salad with croûtons, smoked bacon and parmesan, or prawn and pineapple skewers with an Asian dressing. Next up, rump of Wexford lamb is roasted and served with buttered cabbage and thyme jus, or there might be a duo of cod and rainbow trout with braised leeks and almond and dill butter, and for dessert, something like mango cheesecake with blackcurrant coulis.

Chef Jason Wall **Owner** Thomas & Patrick Redmond **Times** 12.30-3/5.30-9 Closed 24-26 Dec, L Mon-Fri **Prices** Prices not confirmed Service optional **Wines** 4 by glass **Notes** Sunday L, Vegetarian available, Dress restrictions, Smart casual, Civ Wed 400 **Seats** 104, Pr/dining room 100 **Children** Portions, Menu **Parking** 150

Marlfield House

◉◉ Classical

Grand hotel dining in the heart of Wexford

☎ 053 9421124
Courtown Rd
e-mail: info@marlfieldhouse.ie
web: www.marlfieldhouse.com
dir: N11 junct 23, follow signs to Courtown. Turn left for Gorey at Courtown Road Rdbt, hotel 1m on the left

If you hanker after a touch of country-house luxury and you're in the south east of Ireland, head on over to Marlfield House. It's been a while since the Earls of

Courtown held grand house parties in this opulent Regency era home, but you can get a taste of it in today's smart and luxurious hotel. The dining room consists of more than one handsomely decorated space, leading into an impressive conservatory, whilst murals and mirrors are interspersed with huge windows which open onto the immaculate garden. The kitchen garden plays its part in delivering first-rate seasonal produce, and the chefs do the rest. The contemporary Mediterranean-inflected menu might see you starting with crab and lemon crumble with roast beetroot salad, or pan-roasted quail with ragoût of fennel peppers and thyme jus. Next up, seared North Atlantic monkish with a cassoulet of saffron potatoes, or pan-fried rib-eye of Wexford beef, and for dessert, buttermilk pannacotta with Wexford berries, sesame seed tuile and toasted almond flakes.

Times 12.30-2.30/7-9 Closed Xmas, Jan-Feb, Mon-Tue (Mar-Apr, Nov-Dec), L Mon-Sat

Seafield Golf & Spa Hotel

◉ Modern European

Contemporary cooking in a modern spa hotel

☎ 053 942 4000
Ballymoney
e-mail: reservations@seafieldhotel.com

A contemporary, Italian-designed hotel on the shore at Ballymoney, less than an hour's drive out of Dublin, caters for modern tastes, in the familiar spectrum from fairways to massage-tables, with some fine dining in the intervals between. A nine-foot-high bronze female centaur stands guard over the dining room, where lighting and music levels are kept soft, and the décor is in fashionable black, from the marble walls to the chandeliers. The modern European cooking makes all the right noises, starting with a rectangular plate of salmon variations - poached, confit, lime-cured with dill, and a smoked salmon crème brûlée - followed by more variations on a theme, this time of aubergine, with seared best end of Wicklow lamb, served with a single roasted polenta chip and air-dried cherry tomatoes, finished at the table with a reduced lamb jus.

Times 12.30-3/6.30-9.30

ROSSLARE — Map 1 D2

Beaches Restaurant at Kelly's Resort Hotel

◉ European

Beachside resort hotel with modern cooking

☎ 053 9132114
e-mail: info@kellys.ie
dir: From N25 take Rosslare/Wexford road signed Rosslare Strand

The Beaches restaurant is aptly named, as it sits on five miles of golden sands in Rosslare. The Kelly family have run their resort hotel since 1895 - why move when you can work in a setting like this? - and the venue is set up to capitalise on the views, bathed in light through good-sized windows, and with restful pastel hues, white linen on the tables, and a mini gallery of original artworks on the walls. Local produce is as good as it gets, and the kitchen has the experience and confidence to treat it all simply and let the sheer quality do the talking in simple contemporary dishes. Confit duck arrives in an unfussy combo with spiced pears and baked plums with five spice, while local goose from a local artisan producer is roasted and pointed up with chestnut stuffing, braised ham, caramelised pear and glazed pearl onions. Yoghurt and lime pannacotta with raspberry sorbet provides a refreshing finale.

Times 1-2/7.30-9 Closed mid Dec-mid Feb

La Marine Bistro

◉ Modern

Bistro-style cooking at a smart seaside resort hotel

☎ 053 9132114
Kelly's Resort Hotel & Spa
e-mail: info@kellys.ie
dir: From N25 take Rosslare/Wexford road signed Rosslare Strand

The more casual stand-alone restaurant of Kelly's Resort Hotel is an easygoing venue with views of the chefs at work in the open kitchen. The shipshape French bistro theme suits the beachside setting to a T, as does its menu of classic Gallic bistro fare, which is all built on the eminently solid foundations of spanking fresh local produce. Top-class fish and seafood comes but a short way from Kilmore Quay to be treated simply and sent out in ideas such as monkfish medallions with warm saffron and garlic mayonnaise, or scallops with creamy spiced Puy lentils and coconut crème fraîche. Meat eaters are not sent home hungry either - there may be roast rack of lamb with gratin dauphinoise and redcurrant sauce, and to finish, pear, chocolate and almond pithivier or well-chosen local cheeses.

Times 12.30-2/6.30-9 Closed mid Dec-Feb

WEXFORD — Map 1 D3

Whitford House Hotel Health & Leisure Club

◉ Traditional European NEW ✿

Traditionally based cooking in a family-run hotel

☎ 053 9143444
New Line Rd
e-mail: info@whitford.ie
web: www.whitford.ie
dir: From Rosslare ferry port take N25. At Duncannon Rd rdbt right onto R733, hotel immediately on left. 1.5m from Wexford

A family-run boutique hotel since the 1960s, not far from the town centre and within reach of the Rosslare ferry, Whitford House is a haven of contemporary creature comforts. State-of-the-art spa facilities and a little cocktail bar are among the various ways to indulge yourself, but best of all is the Seasons dining room. Primrose-coloured walls and gaily striped upholstery make an uplifting impression, and the cooking tacks to a traditionally based route, but with plenty of style. Start in Mediterranean fashion with a puff pastry tart piled with roasted tomatoes, mozzarella and basil, served with a balsamic-dressed salad of rocket, pine nuts and parmesan, before going on to slow-roast lamb rump in its own juices, or steamed salmon on spinach, sauced with white wine. Comforting pudding options include strawberry pavlova, sherry trifle or sticky toffee pudding and butterscotch sauce, and there are great Irish cheeses, served with Gubbeen cheese crackers.

Chef Siobhan Devereux **Owner** The Whitty Family **Times** 12.30-3/7-9 Closed 24-27 Dec, Sun-Tue (out of season), L Mon-Sat **Prices** Fixed L 2 course €17.95-€18.95, Fixed D 3 course €29.95, Service optional **Wines** 8 bottles over €30, 28 bottles under €30, 4 by glass **Notes** Sunday L, Vegetarian available, Civ Wed 100 **Seats** 100 **Children** Portions, Menu **Parking** 150

CO WICKLOW

ENNISKERRY — Map 1 D3

Gordon Ramsay at The Ritz Carlton Powerscourt

◉◉ Modern European ⒱

Ramsay-style fine dining in a Palladian hotel

☎ 01 2748888
Powerscourt Estate
e-mail: powerscourtgordonramsay@ritzcarlton.com
dir: N11 to R117 Enniskerry, follow signs for Powerscourt Gardens

An imposing Palladian mansion just a short drive out of Dublin, The Ritz Carlton Powerscourt is a vast resort where you can play golf, fish, walk or chill out in a spa to your heart's content. It also houses an outpost of the Gordon Ramsay empire. On the third floor (which is the garden level, it's that big), the restaurant occupies a grand space with masses of room between the pristine, linen-clad tables. There are views over Sugar Loaf mountain through the full-drop windows, and a terrace to make the best of the view when the Wicklow weather allows. On the menu are some sharp, precise and creative dishes, cooked with a good deal of flair, and with local ingredients getting a decent showing. Start with Kilmore Quay crab brandade with two tempura claws and a fennel and samphire dressing, before loin of venison Wellington with pumpkin purée, red cabbage and a boldly successful chocolate and balsamic sauce. For dessert, a tiramisù cylinder with white chocolate and coffee ice cream is a creative take on an old favourite.

Chef Peter Byrne **Owner** Sugar Loaf Ventures **Times** 1-2.30/6-10 Closed Mon, L Tue-Fri **Prices** Fixed L 2 course €33, Starter €9-€16, Main €29-€32, Dessert €9-€11, Service optional **Wines** 15 by glass **Notes** Table for 2 menu 3 course €33 Sat-Sun L/Tue-Thu D fr €33, Vegetarian menu **Seats** 120, Pr/dining room 24 **Children** Portions, Menu **Parking** 214

MACREDDIN — Map 1 D3

BrookLodge & Wells Spa

◉◉ Modern Irish

Dramatic dining venue, organic and wild food

☎ 0402 36444
e-mail: info@brooklodge.com
web: www.brooklodge.com
dir: N11 to Rathnew, R752 to Rathdrum, R753 to Aughrim, follow signs to Macreddin Village

Looking every inch the luxurious country-house retreat, the BrookLodge hotel is the heart of the purpose-built Macreddin Village. The upmarket operation comprises an 18-hole golf course and spa, a pub and brewery, café, bakery, smokehouse, and Italian restaurant. The Strawberry Tree (dinner-only) is the top foodie option of the whole set-up, a strikingly opulent setting spreading through three grand, moodily Gothic rooms with mirrored ceilings reflecting twinkling modern chandeliers, bare burnished mahogany tables, and gilt-framed mirrors on midnight-blue walls. Given its status as Ireland's first certified organic restaurant, provenance of seasonal ingredients is king, so if it's not wild or foraged, it's sourced from certified organic producers, with herbs and soft fruit grown in the estate's own walled garden. The kitchen brings all of this peerless produce together creatively, showing its skill in simple dishes such as wild wood pigeon terrine with strawberry and green pepper jam, followed by guinea fowl with dried fruit compôte, or organic Irish Angus beef roasted in a crust of Irish turf for that true touch of terroir.

Times 7-9.30 Closed varies, check web, L all week

Save on Hotels. Book at **theAA.com/hotel**

CO WICKLOW 675 IRELAND

RATHNEW	Map 1 D3

Hunter's Hotel

◉ Traditional French

Classical cooking in an ancestral family hotel

☎ 0404 40106
Newrath Bridge
e-mail: reception@hunters.ie
dir: N11 exit at Wicklow/Rathnew junct. 1st left onto R761. Restaurant 0.25m before village

Great venerability resides not just in the stones of Hunter's, Ireland's oldest coaching inn, but in the ownership, which has passed through generations of the Gelletlie family since 1825. Barely half-an-hour from the Dun Laoghaire ferry, it sits in riotously colourful gardens, its dining room a vision of crisp linen, mahogany and fine living. A small team of dedicated, volubly friendly staff runs the show. Expect daily-changing menus of classically informed cooking, starting with spanking-fresh crab tian in dill mayonnaise, and progressing via an intermediate course (perhaps leek and potato soup or lime and ginger sorbet) to the likes of crisply roasted breast and leg of duckling with blueberry sauce and pomme purée, or a loaded seafood brochette in curry dressing. Strawberry pannacotta to finish comes in a cocktail glass, lifted with a portion of balsamic-marinated strawberries, or you might be tempted by a selection of Ireland's new generation of artisan cheeses.

Chef Mark Barry **Owner** M Gelletlie **Times** 12.45-3/7.30-9 Closed 3 days Xmas **Prices** Fixed L 2 course fr €18.75, Fixed D 3 course fr €36.50, Service optional **Notes** Afternoon tea €12, Sunday L **Seats** 54, Pr/dining room 30 **Children** Portions **Parking** 30

Tinakilly Country House & Restaurant

◉◉ Modern Irish NEW

Updated classics in an elegant small country-house hotel

☎ 0404 69274
e-mail: reservations@tinakilly.ie
dir: From Dublin Airport follow N11/M11 to Rathnew. Continue on R750 towards Wicklow. Hotel entrance approx 500mtrs from village on left

An oak-lined drive leads your way up to the handsome grey-stone Tinakilly Country House, sitting in seven acres of landscaped gardens overlooking the Irish Sea. Built by the British government in 1883 for Captain Robert Halpin, mariner supreme who laid 2,600 miles of telegraphic cable joining Europe to America in 1866, it's nice to know that - in the shape of this neat, elegantly proportioned house - he was well looked after having completed such a feat. The split-level Brunel Restaurant, with tables dressed in their finest linen and lovely views over the gardens, is the setting for some well crafted French-influenced cooking based on top-class seasonal and local ingredients. Accurately seared scallops with chargrilled white and green asparagus and an emulsion of pink grapefruit, pork belly and muscovado sugar might start you off, followed by a superb tasting of Wicklow lamb (cutlet, fillet, kidney, braised shoulder) with wild garlic polenta, spring vegetable bouquet and lamb jus. Chocolate and jasmine crème brûlée with buttermilk mousse and wilted redcurrant is an unusual but highly successful take on a classic.

Chef Guillane Lerays **Owner** Raymond & Josephine Power **Times** 12.30-4/6.30-8.30 Closed 24-26 & 31 Dec, 1-2 Jan, L Mon-Sat **Prices** Starter €12-€15, Main €22.50-€30, Dessert €7.50-€8.50 **Notes** Early bird menu 3 course €33.50, Sunday L **Seats** 80 **Children** Menu

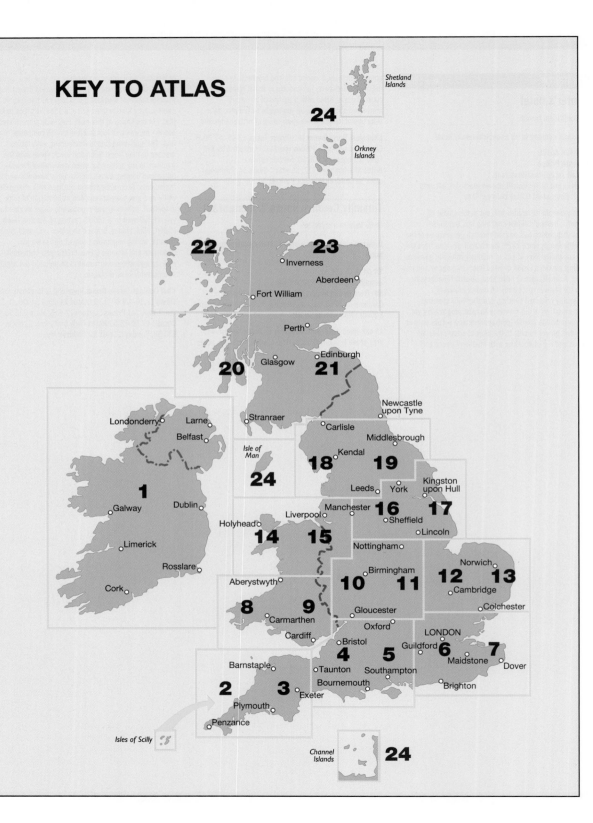

KEY TO ATLAS

Shetland Islands
24

Orkney Islands

22 **23**
Inverness
Aberdeen
Fort William

20 **21**
Perth
Glasgow Edinburgh
Stranraer

Londonderry Larne
Belfast

Isle of Man
24

Newcastle upon Tyne
Carlisle
Middlesbrough
18 Kendal **19**
Leeds York Kingston upon Hull
16 **17**
Manchester
Liverpool Sheffield
Lincoln

1
Galway Dublin
Limerick
Rosslare
Cork

Holyhead
14 **15**
Nottingham
Aberystwyth
10 Birmingham **11**
8 **9**
Carmarthen Gloucester **12** Norwich **13**
Cardiff Oxford Cambridge
Bristol LONDON Colchester
4 **5** Guildford **6** **7**
Barnstaple Taunton Southampton Maidstone Dover
2 **3** Bournemouth Brighton
Plymouth Exeter
Penzance

Isles of Scilly

Channel Islands **24**

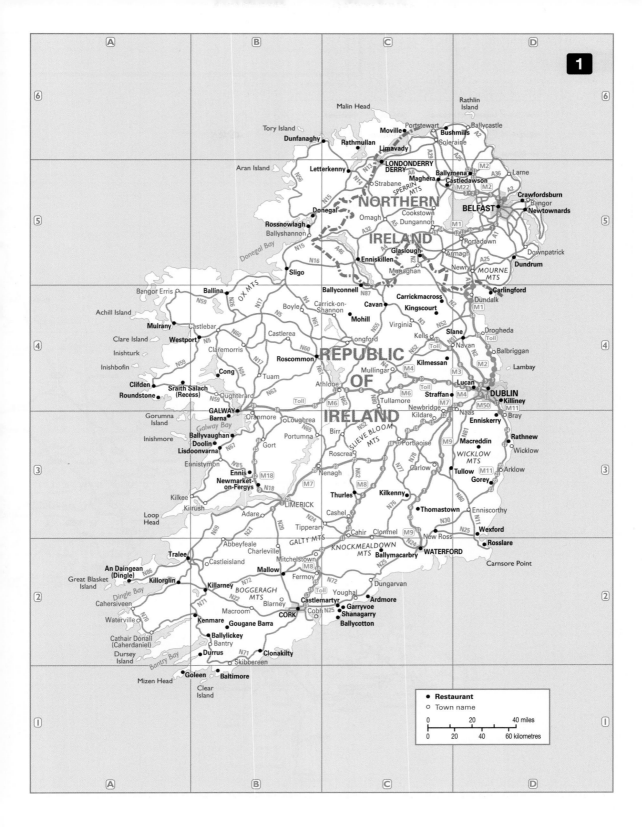

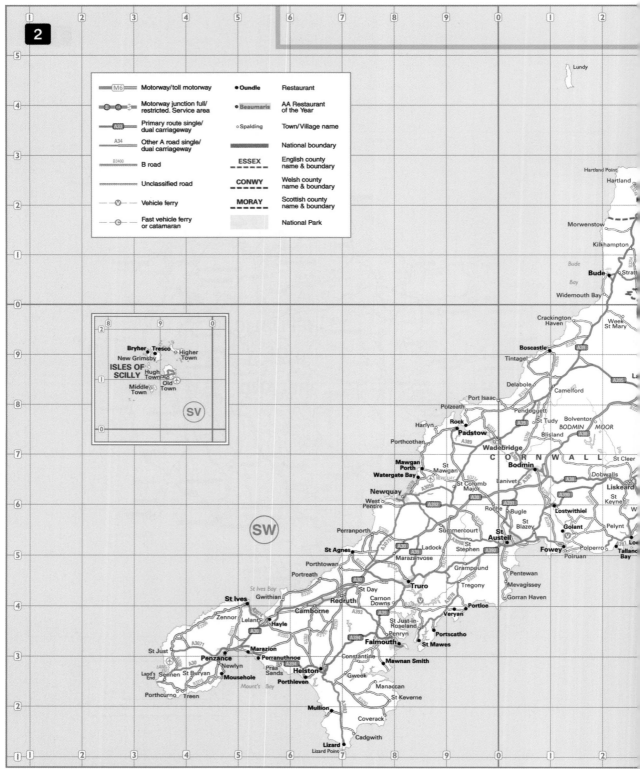

Legend

M6	Motorway/toll motorway
	Motorway junction full/restricted. Service area
A31	Primary route single/dual carriageway
A34	Other A road single/dual carriageway
B3400	B road
	Unclassified road
V	Vehicle ferry
C	Fast vehicle ferry or catamaran
● Oundle	Restaurant
● Beaumaris	AA Restaurant of the Year
○ Spalding	Town/Village name
	National boundary
ESSEX	English county name & boundary
CONWY	Welsh county name & boundary
MORAY	Scottish county name & boundary
	National Park

ISLES OF SCILLY

Bryher New Grimsby — Tresco — Higher Town — Hugh Town — Old Town — Middle Town

SV

SW

Lundy

Hartland Point
Hartland

Morwenstow
Kilkhampton
Bude Bay
Bude Strat
Widemouth Bay

Crackington Haven
Week St Mary
Boscastle
Tintagel
L
Delabole
Camelford
Port Isaac
Polzeath
Pendoggett
St Tudy Bolventor
BODMIN MOOR
Harlyn Rock Blisland
Porthcothan Padstow
A389 Wadebridge
Mawgan Porth St Mawgan
Watergate Bay CORNWALL St Cleer
St Columb Major Bodmin
Newquay Lanivet A38 Dobwalls
West Pentire A392 Roche Liskeard
Bugle St St Keyne
Summercourt St Blazey W
Perranporth Ladock St Lostwithiel
St Agnes Marazanvose Stephen A390 Golant Pelynt
Porthtowan St Austell Fowey Polperro Loo
Portreath St Day Grampound Polruan Tallan Bay
St Ives Bay Gwithian Truro Pentewan
St Ives Carnon Downs Tregony Mevagissey
Zennor Lelant Redruth Gorran Haven
Hayle Camborne Portloe
Lelant A393 Veryan
St Just-in-Roseland
St Just Penryn Portscatho
Penzance Marazion Falmouth St Mawes
Newlyn Perranuthnoe Constantine Mawnan Smith
Land's End Sennen St Buryan Praa Helston Gweek
Mousehole Sands Porthleven Manaccan
Porthcurno Treen Mount's Bay St Keverne
Mullion Coverack
Cadgwith
Lizard
Lizard Point

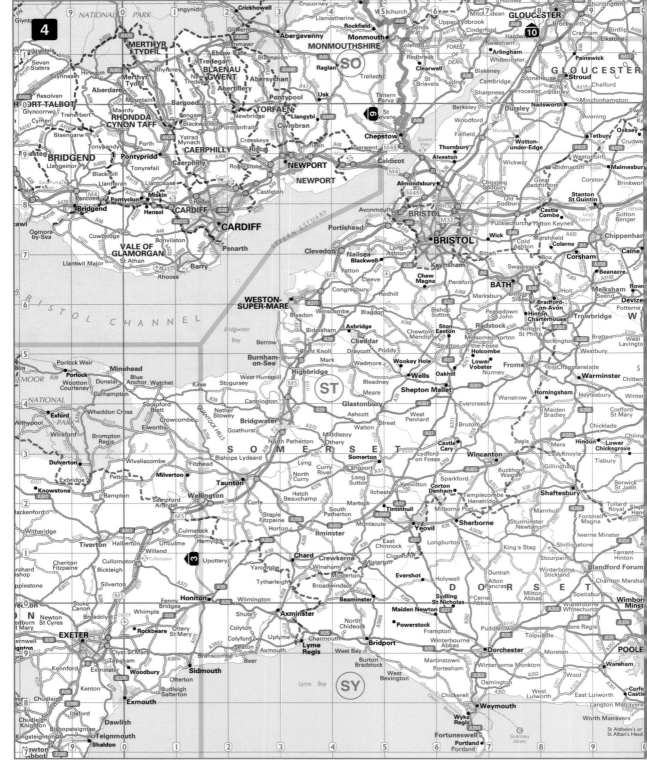

For continuation pages refer to numbered arrows

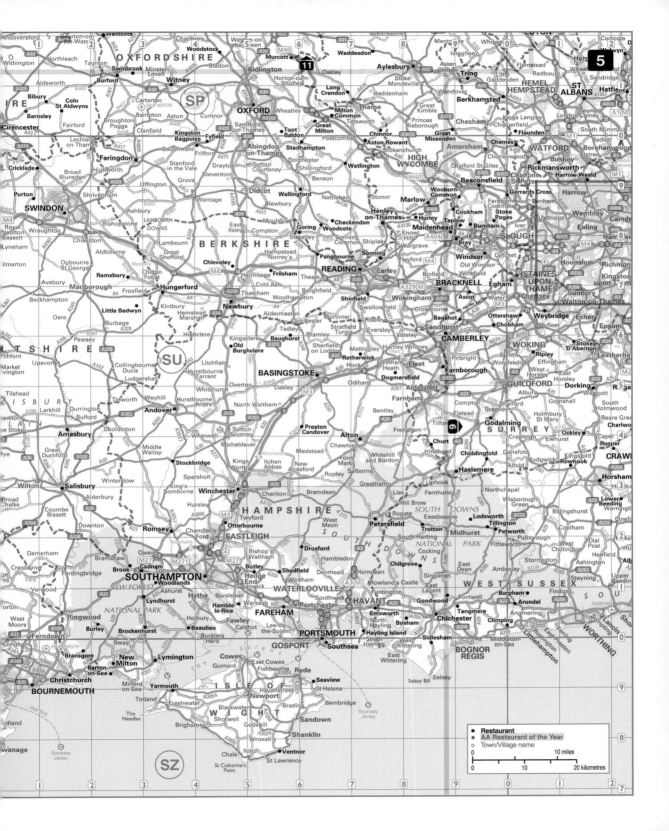

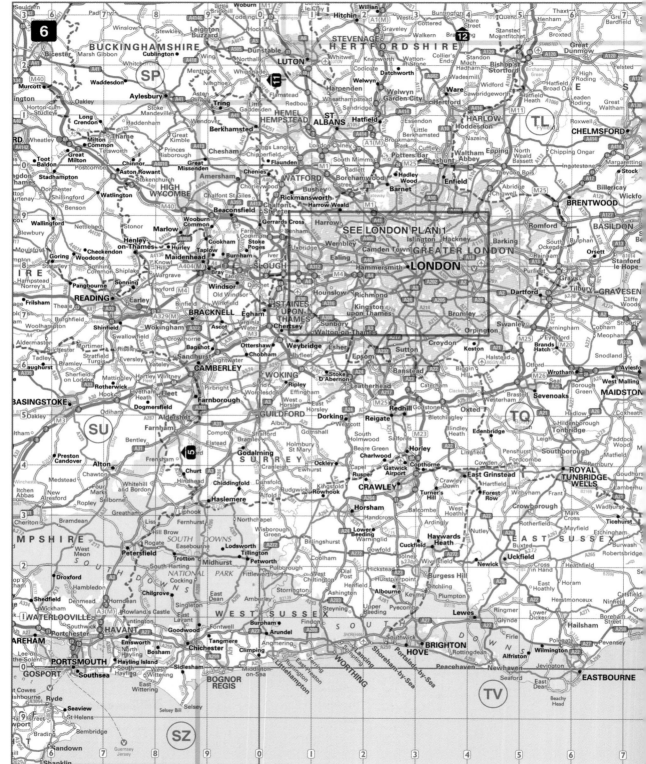

TM

TR

Restaurant
AA Restaurant of the Year
Town/Village name

0   10 miles

0   10   20 kilometres

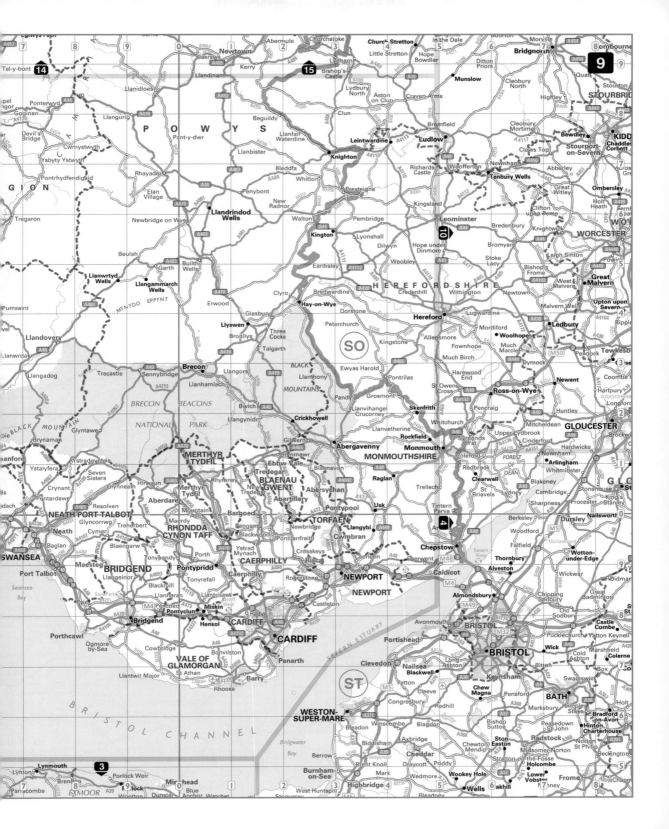

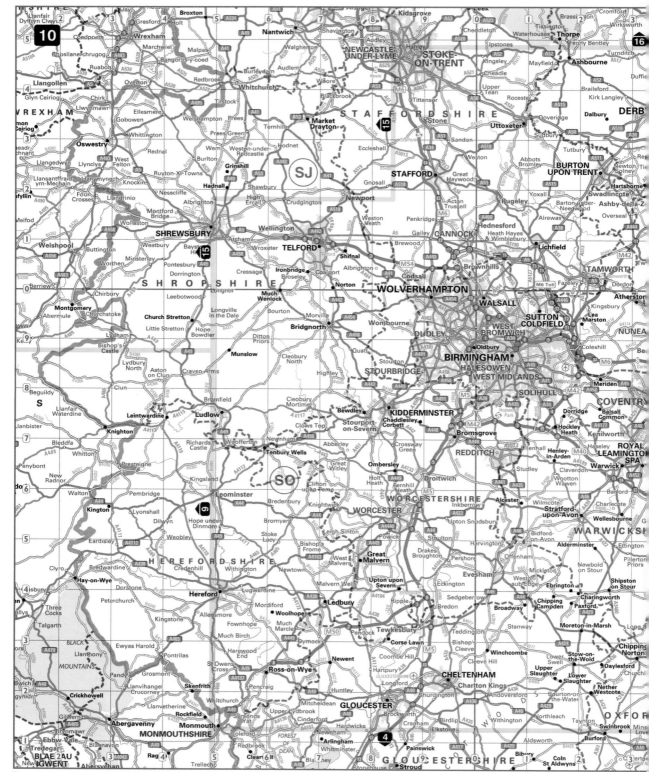

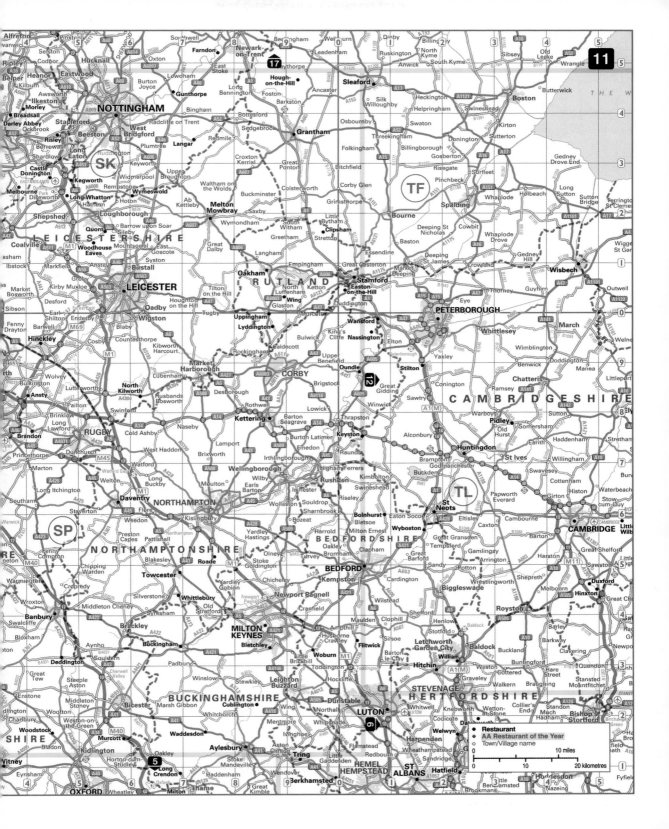

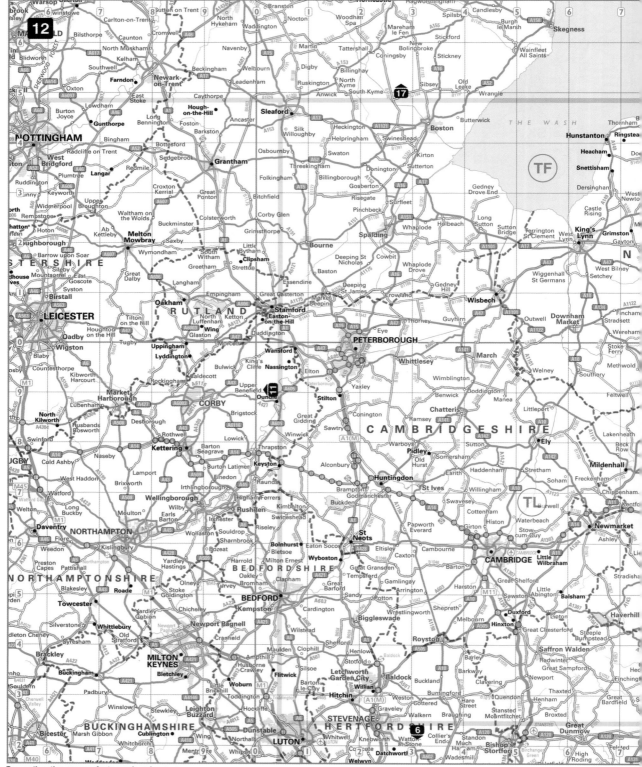

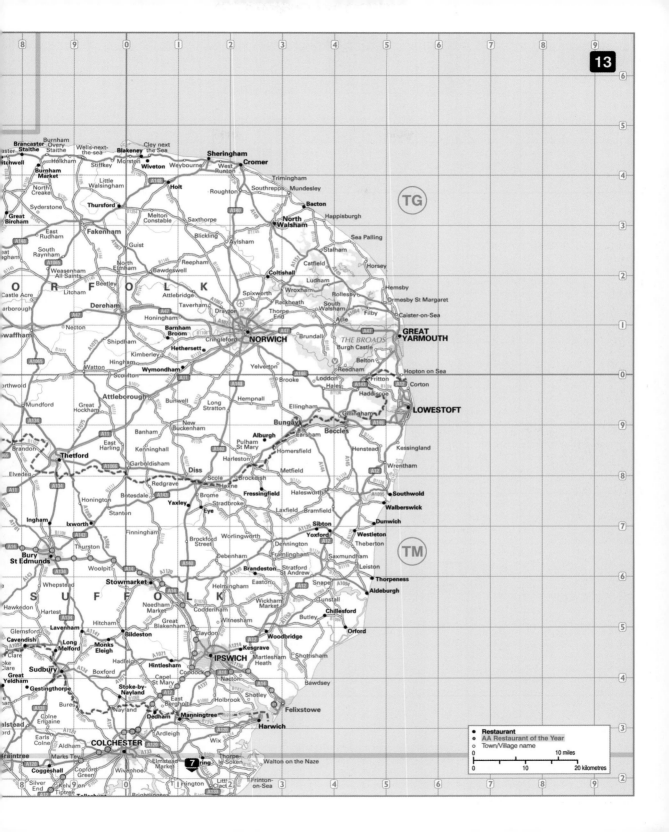

NORFOLK

SUFFOLK

THE BROADS

NORWICH

GREAT YARMOUTH

LOWESTOFT

IPSWICH

COLCHESTER

Bury St Edmunds

Thetford

Diss

Sudbury

Harwich

Felixstowe

TG

TM

●	**Restaurant**	
●	**AA Restaurant of the Year**	
○	Town/Village name	

0   10 miles

0   10   20 kilometres

ISLE OF
ANGLESEY

Cemaes
Amlwch
Llanerchymedd
Holyhead
Llanfachraeth
Benllech
Red
Wharf Bay
Trearddur Bay
Llangoed
Holy
Island
Pentraeth
Rhosneigr
Llangefni
Beaumaris
Menai
Bridge
Bangor
Aberffraw
Llanfair
P.G.
Y Felinheli
Newborough
Penmaenmawr
Conwy
Llanfairfechan
Llandudno
Deganwy
Colwyn Bay
Rhôs-
on-Sea
Rh
Abergel
Llanddulas
Llansanffraid
Glan Conwy
Betws-yn-Rhos
Tal-y-Cafn
Llan
Caernarfon
Bentnewydd
Llanrug
Llanllechid
Bethesda
Tal-y-Bont
Trefriw
Llanrwst
Llanfair
Talhaiarn
Llangernyw
Llansannan
Bylchau
CONWY
Llandwrog
Llanwnda
Llanberis
Capel Curig
Betws-y-Coed
Penmachno
Pentrefoelas
Cerrigydrudion
Y Maer
Caernarfon
Bay
Clynnog-fawr
Penygroes
Rhyd-Ddu
Beddgelert
Dolwyddelan
SH
Blaenau Ffestiniog
Llanaelhaearn
Prenteg
Ffestiniog
Morfa Nefyn
Nefyn
PENINSULA
Tremadog
Maentwrog
Bodfuan
Llanystumdwy
Porthmadog
Penrhyndeudraeth
Handder
Criccieth
Portmeirion
Bala
Borth-y-Gest
Talsarnau
LLEYN
Sarn
Trawsfynydd
SNOWDONIA
Pwllheli
Harlech
GWYNEDD
NATIONAL
Llanbedrog
Llanuwchllyn
PARK
Aberdaron
Y Rhiw
Abersoch
Llanbedr
Bardsey
Island
Dyffryn Ardudwy
Ganllwyd
Tal-y-bont
Barmouth
Dolgellau
Dinas-Mawddwy
Fairbourne
Mallwyd
Llangadfa
Llwyngwril
Corris
Cemmaes
Road
Llanbrynmair
Bryncrug
Pennal
Tywyn
Machynlleth
SN
Aberdyfi
Eglwys Fach
Carno
Borth
Tal-y-bont
9
Llandre
Llanidloes
Aberystwyth
Capel
Bangor
Ponterwyd

Restaurant
AA Restaurant of the Year
Town/Village name
0   10 miles
0   10   20 kilometres

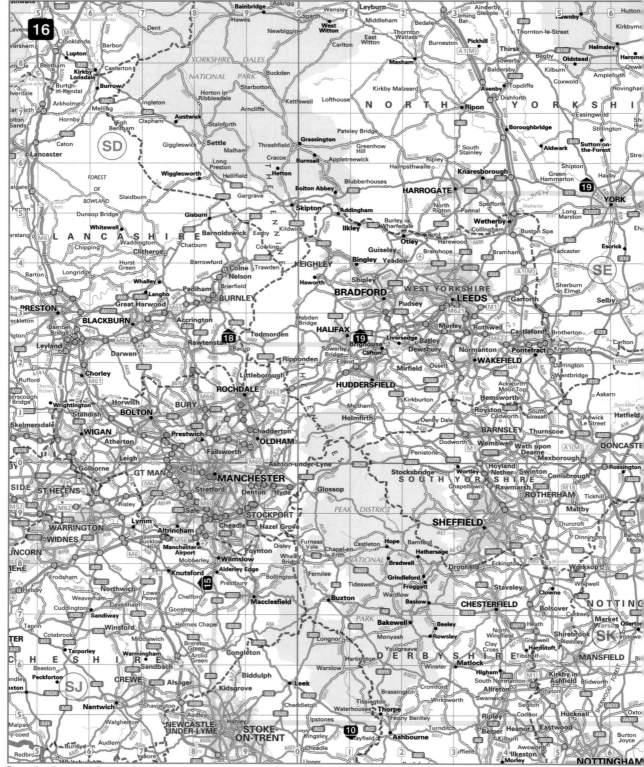

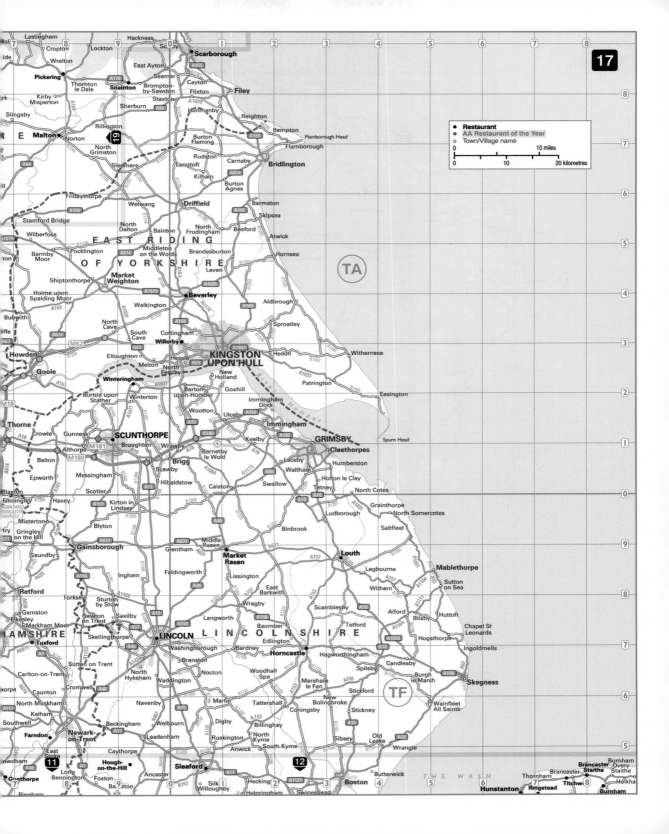

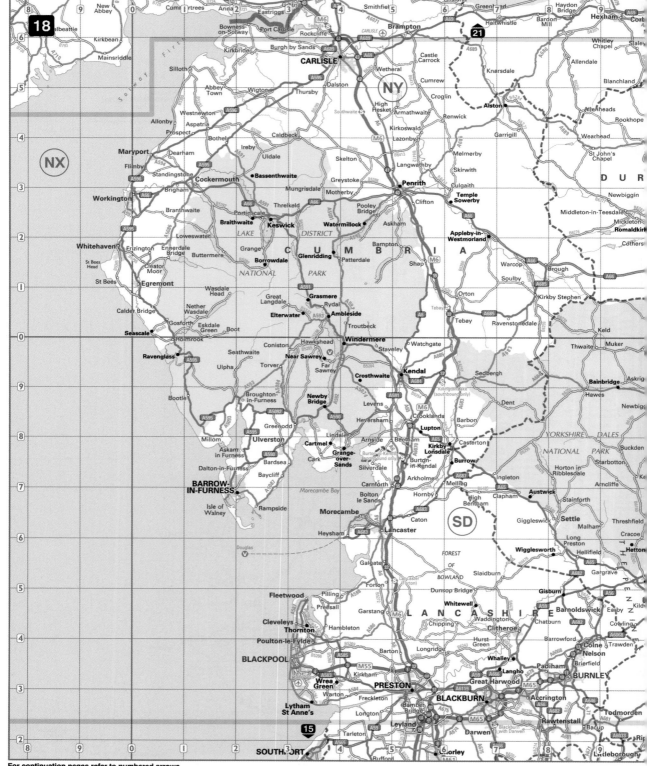

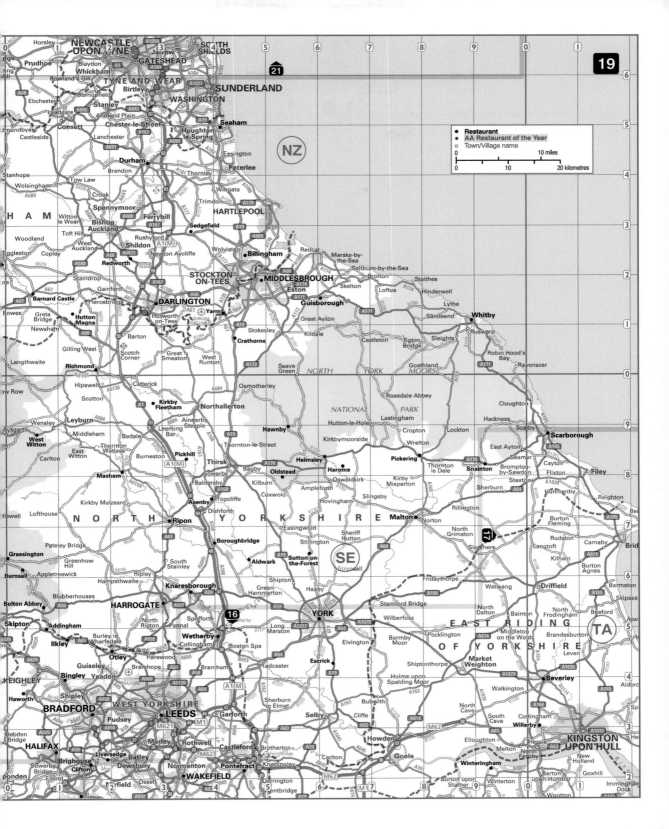

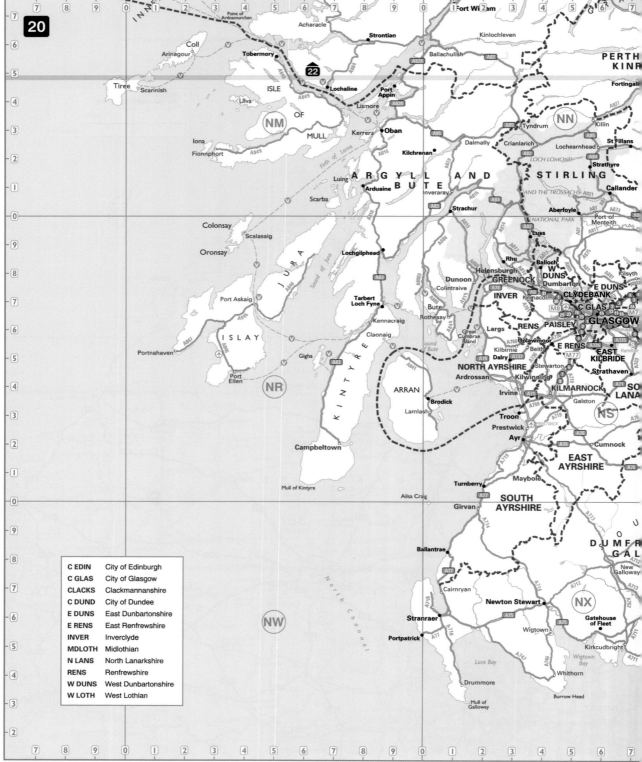

C EDIN	City of Edinburgh
C GLAS	City of Glasgow
CLACKS	Clackmannanshire
C DUND	City of Dundee
E DUNS	East Dunbartonshire
E RENS	East Renfrewshire
INVER	Inverclyde
MDLOTH	Midlothian
N LANS	North Lanarkshire
RENS	Renfrewshire
W DUNS	West Dunbartonshire
W LOTH	West Lothian

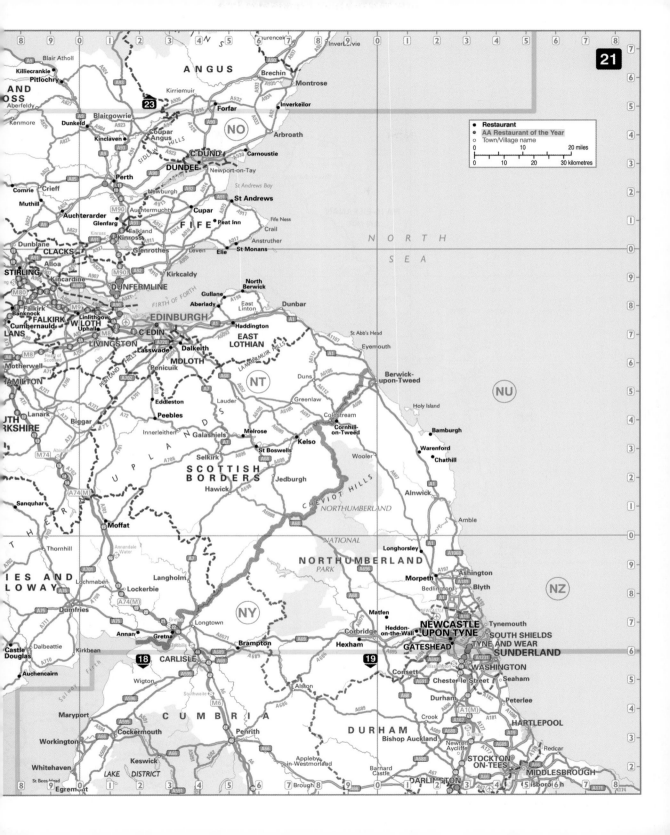

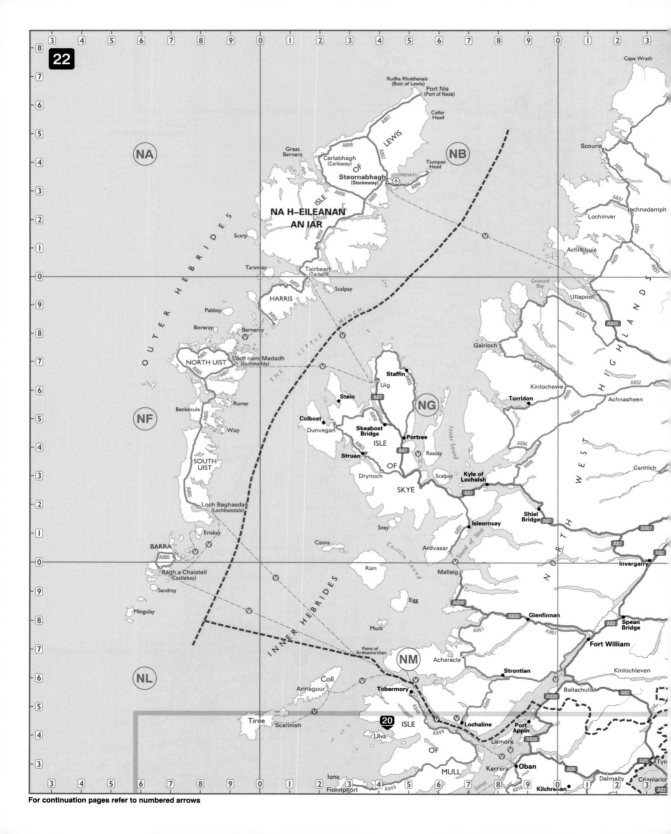

For continuation pages refer to numbered arrows

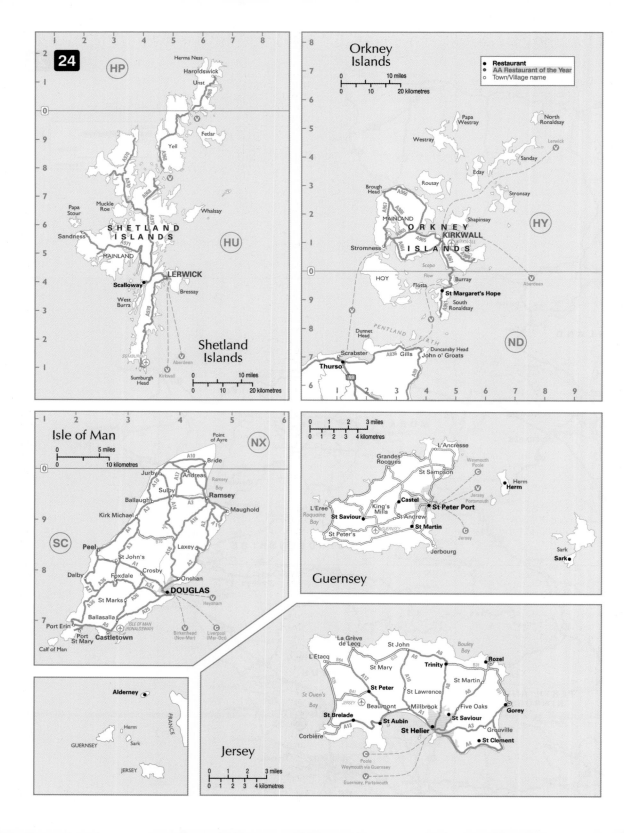

24

HP

Herma Ness
Haroldswick
Unst

Fetlar

Yell

Muckle Roe
Papa Stour

Whalsay

SHETLAND
ISLANDS

Sandness

HU

MAINLAND

LERWICK

Scalloway

Bressay

West Burra

Sumburgh Head
Kirkwall
Aberdeen

Shetland Islands

0   10 miles
0   10   20 kilometres

Orkney Islands

Restaurant
AA Restaurant of the Year
Town/Village name

0   10 miles
0   10   20 kilometres

Papa Westray
North Ronaldsay

Westray
Lerwick

Sanday

Brough Head
Rousay
Eday
Stronsay

HY

MAINLAND
ORKNEY
KIRKWALL
Shapinsay

Stromness
ISLANDS

Scapa Flow

HOY
Burray
Aberdeen

Flotta
St Margaret's Hope

South Ronaldsay

ND

Dunnet Head
PENTLAND FIRTH
Duncansby Head
John o' Groats

Scrabster
Gills

Thurso
A836
A9

Isle of Man

0   5 miles
0   10 kilometres

Point of Ayre
NX

A10
Bride
Jurby
Andreas
Ramsey Bay
Sulby
Ballaugh
Ramsey
Kirk Michael
Maughold

SC

Peel
St John's
Laxey
Crosby
Onchan
Dalby
Foxdale

St Marks
DOUGLAS
Ballasalla
Heysham

Port Erin
Port St Mary
Castletown
ISLE OF MAN (RONALDSWAY)
Birkenhead (Nov-Mar)
Liverpool (Mar-Oct)
Calf of Man

0   1   2   3 miles
0   1   2   3   4 kilometres

L'Ancresse
Grandes Rocques
St Sampson
Weymouth Poole
Herm
Jersey Portsmouth
King's Mills
Castel
St Saviour
L'Eree Rocquaine Bay
St Andrew
St Peter Port
St Peter's
St Martin
Jersey

Sark
Jerbourg
Sark

Guernsey

Alderney

FRANCE

Herm

GUERNSEY
Sark

JERSEY

Jersey

La Grève de Lecq
St John
Bouley Bay
L'Etacq
St Mary
A9
Trinity
Rozel
St Peter
St Lawrence
St Martin
St Ouen's Bay
Beaumont
Millbrook
Five Oaks
St Brelade
St Aubin
St Saviour
Gorey
Corbière
St Helier
Grouville
St Clement
Poole
Weymouth via Guernsey
Guernsey, Portsmouth

0   1   2   3 miles
0   1   2   3   4 kilometres

Index of Restaurants

0/9

10 Greek St, LONDON W1	353
11 The Quay, ILFRACOMBE	138
22 Mill Street Restaurant & Rooms, CHAGFORD	134
36 on the Quay, EMSWORTH	192
60 Hope Street Restaurant, LIVERPOOL	382
63 Tay Street, PERTH	607
63@Parklands, PERTH	606
140 Park Lane Restaurant & Bar, LONDON W1	340
152 Aldeburgh, ALDEBURGH	438
315 Bar and Restaurant, HUDDERSFIELD	533
1851 Restaurant at Peckforton Castle, PECKFORTON	92
1901 Restaurant, LONDON EC2	268
2850 Wine Workshop & Kitchen, LONDON EC4	271
21212, EDINBURGH	580

A

A Cena, TWICKENHAM	380
Abbeville Kitchen, The, LONDON SW5	306
Abbey Hotel Bath, BATH	426
Abbeyglen Castle Hotel, CLIFDEN	664
Absolute End, The, ST PETER PORT	537
Abstract Restaurant & Bar, INVERNESS	595
Acorn Inn, The, EVERSHOT	154
Adam Simmonds at Danesfield House, MARLOW	73
Adam's Brasserie at Luton Hoo, LUTON	48
Adam's Restaurant, BIRMINGHAM	485
Advocate Arms, The, MARKET RASEN	237
AG's Restaurant at Alexander House Hotel, TURNERS HILL	477
Agaric, ASHBURTON	133
Airds Hotel and Restaurant, PORT APPIN	559
Al Duca, LONDON SW1	283
Alain Ducasse at The Dorchester, LONDON W1	314
Albright Hussey Manor Hotel & Restaurant, SHREWSBURY	424
Alderley Restaurant, The, ALDERLEY EDGE	87
Aldwark Arms, The, ALDWARK	508
Alloro, LONDON W1	314
Almeida Restaurant, LONDON N1	272
Alveston House Hotel, ALVESTON	167
Alyn Williams at The Westbury, LONDON W1	314
Amaya, LONDON SW1	284
Amber Springs Hotel, GOREY	673
Ambrette, The, MARGATE	221
Ametsa with Arzak Instruction, LONDON SW1	284
Anchor & Hope, The, LONDON SE1	276
Anchor Inn, The, ALTON	186
Anchor Inn, The, ELY	84
Anchor, The, WALBERSWICK	450
Ancient Gate House Hotel, WELLS	434
Andover House, GREAT YARMOUTH	387
Andrew Edmunds, LONDON W1	314
Andrew Fairlie @ Gleneagles, AUCHTERARDER	603
Angel at Burford, The, BURFORD	405
Angel Hotel, ABERGAVENNY	631
Angel Hotel, The, BURY ST EDMUNDS	441
Angel Inn, The, HETTON	516
Angel Restaurant, The, LONG CRENDON	73
Angelus Restaurant, LONDON W2	357
Anglesea Arms, LONDON W6	360
Annandale Arms Hotel, MOFFAT	565
Annie Jones Restaurant, PETERSFIELD	199
Apex City Hotel, EDINBURGH	568
Apex City of London Hotel, LONDON EC3	268

Apex International Hotel, EDINBURGH	569
Apicius, CRANBROOK	218
Apollo Hotel, BASINGSTOKE	187
Appleby Manor Country House Hotel, APPLEBY-IN-WESTMORLAND	109
Apsleys at The Lanesborough, LONDON SW1	284
Aqua Kyoto, LONDON W1	316
Aqua Nueva, LONDON W1	316
Arbutus Restaurant, LONDON W1	317
Ardanaiseig Hotel, The, KILCHRENAN	557
Arden Hotel, The, STRATFORD-UPON-AVON	482
Ardencote Manor Hotel & Spa, WARWICK	484
Ardeonaig Hotel & Restaurant, The, KILLIN	610
Ardilaun Hotel & Leisure Club, GALWAY	664
Armathwaite Hall Country House & Spa, BASSENTHWAITE	109
Arnolds Hotel, DUNFANAGHY	660
Artichoke, The, AMERSHAM	69
Artillery Tower Restaurant, PLYMOUTH	141
Arundell Arms, LIFTON	139
Ashdown Park Hotel & Country Club, FOREST ROW	462
Ashdown Park Hotel, GOREY	673
Ashmount Country House, HAWORTH	531
Asquiths Restaurant, LOSTWITHIEL	97
Assaggi, LONDON W2	357
Athenaeum Hotel & Apartments, LONDON W1	317
Auberge du Lac, WELWYN	213
Auberge, The, ST MARTIN	536
Auberge, The, YAXLEY	451
Aubergine at the Compleat Angler, MARLOW	73
Audleys Wood, BASINGSTOKE	187
Aumbry, PRESTWICH	185
Aurelia, LONDON W1	317
Austell's, ST AUSTELL	102
Avenue Restaurant at Lainston House Hotel, WINCHESTER	204
Avenue, LONDON SW1	284
Aviator, FARNBOROUGH	193
Avista, LONDON W1	318
Avon Gorge Hotel, The, BRISTOL	65
Aynsome Manor Hotel, CARTMEL	112
Aztec Hotel & Spa, ALMONDSBURY	167

B

Babur, LONDON SE23	282
Babylon, LONDON W8	361
Bacco Restaurant Italiano, RICHMOND UPON THAMES	377
Baglioni Hotel, LONDON SW7	308
Bailiffscourt Hotel & Spa, CLIMPING	469
Bakers Arms, DROXFORD	192
Balcary Bay Hotel, AUCHENCAIRN	564
Ballathie House Hotel, KINCLAVEN	605
Balloo House, NEWTOWNARDS	650
Ballygarry House Hotel and Spa, TRALEE	666
Ballymaloe House, SHANAGARRY	659
Ballyseede Castle, TRALEE	666
Balmer Lawn Hotel, The, BROCKENHURST	190
Balthazar, LONDON WC2	368
Bank House Hotel, KING'S LYNN	389
Bar Boulud, LONDON SW1	284
Bar Trattoria Semplice, LONDON W1	318
Barbecoa, LONDON EC4	270
Barberstown Castle, STRAFFAN	667
Barbican Kitchen, PLYMOUTH	141
Barclay House, LOOE	96
Barley Bree Restaurant with Rooms, MUTHILL	605
Barn at Coworth, The, ASCOT	51
Barn Hotel, The, RUISLIP	379
Barnham Broom Hotel, Golf & Restaurant, BARNHAM BROOM	384
Barnsdale Lodge Hotel, OAKHAM	418

Barnsley House, BARNSLEY	168
Barrafina, LONDON W1	318
Barrasford Arms, HEXHAM	400
Bartley Lodge Hotel, CADNAM	191
Barton Cross Hotel & Restaurant, EXETER	137
Basingstoke Country Hotel, BASINGSTOKE	188
Bath Arms at Longleat, The, HORNINGSHAM	499
Bath Priory Hotel, Restaurant & Spa, The, BATH	426
Baumann's Brasserie, COGGESHALL	163
Bay @ Hotel Penzance, The, PENZANCE	99
Bay Tree Hotel, The, BURFORD	406
Bay Tree, The, MELBOURNE	129
Bayview Hotel, BALLYCOTTON	656
Beaches Restaurant at Kelly's Resort Hotel, ROSSLARE	674
Beales Hotel, HATFIELD	210
Bear Hotel, The, CRICKHOWELL	639
Bear Hotel, The, DEVIZES	497
Bear Hotel, The, HUNGERFORD	57
Bear's Paw, The, WARMINGHAM	93
Beardmore Hotel, CLYDEBANK	568
Beatrice Kennedy, BELFAST	646
Beaufort Raglan Coaching Inn & Brasserie, The, RAGLAN	634
Beaulieu Hotel, BEAULIEU	188
Bedford Arms Hotel, The, CHENIES	72
Bedford Hotel, LYTHAM ST ANNES	225
Bedford Hotel, TAVISTOCK	145
Bedford Lodge Hotel, NEWMARKET	447
Bedford Swan Hotel, The, BEDFORD	48
Beech Hill Hotel, WINDERMERE	119
Beechfield House Hotel, Restaurant & Gardens, BEANACRE	493
Beechwood Hotel, NORTH WALSHAM	390
Beiderbecke's Hotel, SCARBOROUGH	519
Bell at Ramsbury, The, RAMSBURY	501
Bell at Skenfrith, The, SKENFRITH	635
Bell Inn Hotel, STILTON	86
Bell Inn, The, BROOK	191
Bella Vista Cucina Italiana, LONDON SE3	281
Bellamy's, LONDON W1	319
Belleek Castle, BALLINA	669
Belvedere, LONDON W8	362
Ben's Cornish Kitchen, PENZANCE	99
Benares Restaurant, LONDON W1	319
Bentley's Oyster Bar & Grill, LONDON W1	319
Best Western Annesley House Hotel, NORWICH	390
Best Western Castle Green Hotel in Kendal, KENDAL	115
Best Western Claydon Country House Hotel, IPSWICH	444
Best Western Frensham Pond Hotel, CHURT	452
Best Western Gatehouse Hotel, IPSWICH	444
Best Western George Hotel, NORWICH	390
Best Western Hardwick Hall Hotel, SEDGEFIELD	162
Best Western Henbury Lodge Hotel, BRISTOL	65
Best Western Lamphey Court Hotel & Spa, PEMBROKE	638
Best Western Lee Wood Hotel, BUXTON	126
Best Western Plus Cambridge Quy Mill Hotel, CAMBRIDGE	79
Best Western Plus Dean Court Hotel, YORK	524
Best Western Plus Manor NEC Birmingham, MERIDEN	489
Best Western Plus Orton Hall Hotel & Spa, PETERBOROUGH	85
Best Western Plus Swan Hotel, WELLS	434
Best Western Plus Wroxton House Hotel, BANBURY	405
Best Western Premier Mount Pleasant Hotel, ROSSINGTON	527
Best Western Premier Yew Lodge Hotel & Spa, EAST MIDLANDS AIRPORT	232
Best Western Priory Hotel, BURY ST EDMUNDS	441
Best Western Red Lion Hotel, SALISBURY	502
Best Western Royal Chase Hotel, SHAFTESBURY	156
Best Western Royal Hotel, ST HELIER	540
Best Western Sudbury House Hotel & Conference Centre, FARINGDON	408
Best Western The Connaught Hotel, BOURNEMOUTH	148
Best Western The Grange at Oborne, SHERBORNE	156
Best Western The Queens Hotel, OBAN	559
Best Western Willerby Manor Hotel, WILLERBY	508
Beverley Tickton Grange Hotel, BEVERLEY	508
Bibendum Restaurant, LONDON SW3	300
Bibury Court Hotel, BIBURY	168
Bilash, WOLVERHAMPTON	491
Bildeston Crown, The, BILDESTON	439
Billesley Manor Hotel, STRATFORD-UPON-AVON	482
Bingham, RICHMOND UPON THAMES	377
Bishopsgate House Hotel, BEAUMARIS	620
Bishopstrow Hotel & Spa, The, WARMINSTER	502
Bistro 21, DURHAM	161
Bistro Prego, MONMOUTH	634
Bistro Union, LONDON SW4	305
Bistrot Bruno Loubet, LONDON EC1	263
Bistrot Vérité, SOUTHPORT	382
Black Boys Inn, HURLEY	57
Black Bull Inn, The, BALSHAM	79
Black Cow, The, DALBURY	126
Black Horse Inn Restaurant with Rooms, CLIFTON	529
Black Horse, The, KIRKBY FLEETHAM	516
Black Lion Hotel, The, LONG MELFORD	446
Black Rat, The, WINCHESTER	204
Black Swan at Oldstead, The, OLDSTEAD	518
Black Swan Hotel, HELMSLEY	516
Blackaddie House Hotel, SANQUHAR	566
Blackfriars Restaurant, NEWCASTLE UPON TYNE	478
Blackwell Ox Inn, The, SUTTON-ON-THE-FOREST	520
Blairscove House & Restaurant, DURRUS	658
Blakeney Hotel, The, BLAKENEY	384
Bleeding Heart, The, LONDON EC1	263
Blue Elephant, LONDON SW6	307
Bluebell, The, HENLEY-IN-ARDEN	481
Bluebells Restaurant & Garden Bar, ASCOT	51
Bluefish Restaurant, The, PORTLAND	156
Blyth Hotel, The, SOUTHWOLD	448
Blythswood Square, GLASGOW	587
Boat Hotel, BOAT OF GARTEN	591
Boat House, The, ST AUBIN	539
Boath House, NAIRN	597
Bocca di Lupo, LONDON W1	319
Bodysgallen Hall and Spa, LLANDUDNO	627
Bohemia Restaurant, ST HELIER	540
Boisdale of Belgravia, LONDON SW1	284
Boisdale of Bishopsgate, LONDON EC2	266
Bokhara Brasserie, BRIDGEND	620
Bombay Brasserie, LONDON SW7	308
Bonds, LONDON EC2	266
Bordeaux Quay, BRISTOL	65
Botleigh Grange Hotel, SOUTHAMPTON	202
Boulters Riverside Brasserie, MAIDENHEAD	58
Bournemouth Highcliff Marriott Hotel, BOURNEMOUTH	149
Bowaters, MARLOW	73
Box Tree, ILKLEY	533
Brackenborough Hotel, LOUTH	237
Braidwoods, DALRY	561
Brandshatch Place Hotel & Spa, BRANDS HATCH	217
Branston Hall Hotel, LINCOLN	235
Brasserie at Mallory Court, The, LEAMINGTON SPA (ROYAL)	481
Brasserie at Pennyhill Park, The, BAGSHOT	451
Brasserie at The Cumberland, LONDON W1	320
Brasserie Chavot, LONDON W1	320
Brasserie Zedel, LONDON W1	320
Brasserie, The, COLERNE	494
Brasteds, NORWICH	390
Brawn, LONDON E2	261

Braye Beach Hotel, ALDERNEY 536
Bread Street Kitchen, LONDON EC4 270
Breadsall Priory, A Marriott Hotel & Country Club, BREADSALL 124
Bricklayers Arms, FLAUNDEN 209
BridgeHouse, BEAMINSTER 148
Brigade, LONDON SE1 276
Bristol Marriott Royal Hotel, BRISTOL 65
Brockencote Hall Country House Hotel, CHADDESLEY CORBETT 505
Brodies, MOFFAT 565
Bron Eifion Country House Hotel, CRICCIETH 630
Brooklands Hotel, WEYBRIDGE 456
BrookLodge & Wells Spa, MACREDDIN 674
Brownlow Arms, The, HOUGH-ON-THE-HILL 235
Browns Restaurant and Champagne Lounge, LONDONDERRY 651
Brudenell Hotel, ALDEBURGH 438
Brummells Seafood Restaurant, NORWICH 391
Bryce's Seafood Restaurant & Country Pub, OCKLEY 455
Buchan Braes Hotel, PETERHEAD 555
Buckland-Tout-Saints, KINGSBRIDGE 139
Budock Vean - The Hotel on the River, MAWNAN SMITH 98
Bugle, The, HAMBLE-LE-RICE 193
Bulgari Hotel & Residences, LONDON SW7 308
Bull & Swan at Burghley, The, STAMFORD 238
Bull & Willow Room at Great Totham, The, GREAT TOTHAM 165
Bull at Broughton, The, SKIPTON 520
Bull at Burford, The, BURFORD 406
Bull Hotel, PETERBOROUGH 85
Bull Hotel, The, GERRARDS CROSS 72
Bull Inn, The, MILDENHALL 446
Bull, The, WROTHAM 224
Bully's, CARDIFF 620
Bunchrew House Hotel, INVERNESS 595
Burbridges Restaurant, YORK 524
Burleigh Court Hotel, STROUD 178
Burnham Beeches Hotel, BURNHAM 71
Burt's Hotel, MELROSE 608
Bushmills Inn Hotel, BUSHMILLS 646
Bustard Inn & Restaurant, The, SLEAFORD 238
Bustophers Bar Bistro, TRURO 106
Butcher & Grill, The, LONDON SW11 311
Butchers Arms, WOOLHOPE 208
Butlers Restaurant, HOLT 388
Buxted Park Hotel, UCKFIELD 464
Bwyty Mawddach Restaurant, DOLGELLAU 630
Bybrook at the Manor House Hotel, The, CASTLE COMBE 493

C
C London, LONDON W1 323
Cabra Castle Hotel, KINGSCOURT 654
Cadmore Lodge Hotel & Country Club, TENBURY WELLS 507
Cadogan Arms, The, INGHAM 444
Café 21 Newcastle, NEWCASTLE UPON TYNE 478
Café Royal, EDINBURGH 569
Café Spice Namasté, LONDON E1 258
Café Vaudeville, BELFAST 646
Cahernane House Hotel, KILLARNEY 665
Cail Bruich, GLASGOW 587
Cairnbaan Hotel, LOCHGILPHEAD 557
Calcot Manor, TETBURY 179
Caldesi in Campagna, BRAY 52
Caley Hall Hotel, HUNSTANTON 389
Callander Meadows, CALLANDER 610
Callow Hall Hotel, ASHBOURNE 123
Cally Palace Hotel, GATEHOUSE OF FLEET 565
Cambio de Tercio, LONDON SW5 306
Camellia Restaurant at South Lodge Hotel, LOWER BEEDING 473
Cameron Grill, The, BALLOCH 567

Cannizaro House, LONDON SW19 312
Cantina del Ponte, LONDON SE1 276
Cantina Vinopolis, LONDON SE1 277
Capote y Toros, LONDON SW5 307
Captain's Club Hotel and Spa, CHRISTCHURCH 151
Caravaggio, LONDON EC3 269
Carbis Bay Hotel, ST IVES 104
Cardiff Marriott Hotel, CARDIFF 620
Careys Manor Hotel & Senspa, BROCKENHURST 190
Carlton Hotel Kinsale, KINSALE 659
Carlton Riverside, LLANWRTYD WELLS 640
Carlyon Bay Hotel, ST AUSTELL 102
Carnoustie Golf Hotel & Spa, CARNOUSTIE 555
Carrig House Country House & Restaurant, KILLORGLIN 666
Carron Art Deco Restaurant, STONEHAVEN 555
Casa Hotel, CHESTERFIELD 126
Casamia Restaurant, BRISTOL 65
Case Restaurant with Rooms, The, SUDBURY 450
Cashel House, CASHEL 664
Cassis Bistro, LONDON SW3 300
Cassons Restaurant, TANGMERE 476
Castell Deudraeth, PORTMEIRION 631
Castle Hotel Conwy, CONWY 626
Castle House, HEREFORD 206
Castle Restaurant, The, BUDE 94
Castle Terrace Restaurant, EDINBURGH 569
Castleknock Hotel & Country Club, DUBLIN 660
Castlemartyr Resort, CASTLEMARTYR 657
Catch 22 Restaurant, TOLLESHUNT KNIGHTS 167
Cavendish Hotel, BASLOW 124
Cavendish London, LONDON SW1 286
Cecconi's, LONDON W1 321
Cedar Court Grand Hotel & Spa, YORK 524
Cedar Manor Hotel & Restaurant, WINDERMERE 119
Cellar Restaurant, The, DUBLIN 661
Cerise Restaurant at The Forbury Hotel, READING 61
Chabrot, LONDON SW1 286
Chadwicks Inn Maltby, MIDDLESBROUGH 518
Chakra, LONDON W11 366
Chamberlains Restaurant, LONDON EC3 269
Champany Inn, LINLITHGOW 602
Chancery, The, LONDON EC4 270
Chapel House Restaurant With Rooms, ATHERSTONE 480
Chapter One, BROMLEY 374
Chapters All Day Dining, LONDON SE3 282
Charingworth Manor Hotel, CHARINGWORTH 169
Charlotte's Place, LONDON W5 359
Charlton House Spa Hotel, SHEPTON MALLET 432
Chase Hotel, The, ROSS-ON-WYE 207
Chateau La Chaire, ROZEL 539
Chef Collin Brown, LONDON E14 262
Chelsea Riverside Brasserie, LONDON SW10 309
Cheltenham Park Hotel, CHELTENHAM 169
Chequers Inn, The, FROGGATT 127
Chequers Inn, The, ROWHOOK 475
Chequers Inn, WOOBURN COMMON 79
Chequers, The, BATH 426
Chequers, The, CHIPPING NORTON 406
Cherry Tree Inn, The, HENLEY-ON-THAMES 409
Chesil Rectory, The, WINCHESTER 204
Chesterfield Mayfair, The, LONDON W1 321
Chevin Country Park Hotel & Spa, OTLEY 535
Chewton Glen Hotel & Spa, NEW MILTON 195
Chez Bruce, LONDON SW17 312
Chez Maw Restaurant, TELFORD 426
Chez Mumtaj, ST ALBANS 211
Chilli Pickle, BRIGHTON & HOVE 459

Chilston Park Hotel, LENHAM	220
China Tang at The Dorchester, LONDON W1	323
Chinese Cricket Club, LONDON EC4	270
Chino Latino London, LONDON SE1	277
Chiseldon House Hotel, SWINDON	502
Chop Chop Leith, EDINBURGH	569
Chop Chop, EDINBURGH	569
Christchurch Harbour Hotel, CHRISTCHURCH	151
Christopher's, LONDON WC2	369
Church Farm Guest House & Basil's Restaurant, TELFORD	426
Church Green British Grill, The, LYMM	91
Churchill Arms, PAXFORD	178
Churchill Hotel, The, YORK	524
Chutney Mary Restaurant, LONDON SW10	310
Cibo, LONDON W14	368
Cicada, LONDON EC1	264
Cielo, LONDON W1	323
Cigalon, LONDON WC2	369
Cinnamon Club, The, LONDON SW1	286
Cinnamon Kitchen, LONDON EC2	266
Circus Café and Restaurant, The, BATH	426
Clare House, GRANGE-OVER-SANDS	114
Clarence House Country Hotel & Restaurant, BARROW-IN-FURNESS	109
Clarice House, BURY ST EDMUNDS	441
Clarke's, LONDON W8	362
Cliff House Hotel, ARDMORE	671
Cliffemount Hotel, The, WHITBY	522
Clifton Arms Hotel, LYTHAM ST ANNES	225
Clive Bar & Restaurant with Rooms, The, LUDLOW	420
Clog & Billycock, The, BLACKBURN	224
Clos Maggiore, LONDON WC2	369
Close House, HEDDON-ON-THE-WALL	400
Club Gascon, LONDON EC1	264
Coachman Inn, The, SNAINTON	520
Coast, OBAN	559
Cobbles Freehouse & Dining, The, KELSO	608
Cobo Bay Hotel, CASTEL	536
Cock & Bull, BALMEDIE	552
Cockliffe Country House, NOTTINGHAM	403
Cocochan, LONDON W1	323
Colbert, LONDON SW1	287
Colchis, LONDON W2	357
Coldstreamer Inn, The, PENZANCE	99
Colette's at The Grove, RICKMANSWORTH	210
Colwall Park Hotel, MALVERN	506
Combe Grove Manor Hotel, BATH	428
Comme Ça, CHICHESTER	466
Compasses Inn, LOWER CHICKSGROVE	499
Congham Hall Country House Hotel, GRIMSTON	388
Continental Hotel, The, HEATHROW AIRPORT (LONDON)	376
Coppid Beech, BRACKNELL	52
Copthorne Hotel Sheffield, SHEFFIELD	527
Coq d'Argent, LONDON EC2	267
Corinthia Hotel London, LONDON SW1	287
Cormorant Hotel & Restaurant, GOLANT	96
Corner House, WRIGHTINGTON	231
Cornish Range Restaurant with Rooms, The, MOUSEHOLE	98
Cornwall Hotel, Spa & Estate, The, ST AUSTELL	102
Cornwallis Hotel, The, EYE	443
Corrigan's Mayfair, LONDON W1	323
Cors Restaurant, The, LAUGHARNE	623
Corse Lawn House Hotel, CORSE LAWN	174
Corsewall Lighthouse Hotel, STRANRAER	566
Cotswolds88Hotel, PAINSWICK	176
Cottage in the Wood Hotel, The, MALVERN	506
Cottage in the Wood, The, BRAITHWAITE	110
Cottons Hotel & Spa, KNUTSFORD	89
County Hotel, CHELMSFORD	163
Cove, The, WESTON-SUPER-MARE	435
Cow Shed, BANCHORY	552
Crab & Lobster, The, SIDLESHAM	476
Crab at Bournemouth, The, BOURNEMOUTH	149
Crab at Chieveley, The, CHIEVELEY	56
Crab House Café, WYKE REGIS	158
Crab Manor, ASENBY	508
Craig Millar @ 16 West End, ST MONANS	586
Craig-y-Dderwen Riverside Hotel, BETWS-Y-COED	625
Craigdarroch House, FOYERS	594
Craigellachie Hotel, CRAIGELLACHIE	603
Crathorne Hall Hotel, CRATHORNE	510
Craven Heifer, ADDINGHAM	529
Crazy Bear Beaconsfield, BEACONSFIELD	69
Crazy Bear, The, STADHAMPTON	413
Creagan House, STRATHYRE	612
Creel Restaurant with Rooms, The, ST MARGARET'S HOPE	613
Creggans Inn, The, STRACHUR	560
Crewe Hall, CREWE	89
Cricket Inn, The, BEESANDS	133
Cricket St Thomas Hotel, CHARD	430
Cricklade House, CRICKLADE	497
Cringletie House, PEEBLES	609
Criterion, LONDON W1	323
Crooked Barn Restaurant, The, LOWESTOFT	446
Crooked Beam Restaurant, CHRISTCHURCH	151
Crooked Billet, The, BLETCHLEY	71
Cross, The, KINGUSSIE	596
Crossways, WILMINGTON	465
Crouchers Country Hotel & Restaurant, CHICHESTER	467
Crown & Castle, The, ORFORD	448
Crown & Victoria, TINTINHULL	434
Crown at Woodbridge, The, WOODBRIDGE	450
Crown Country Inn, MUNSLOW	423
Crown Hotel, CARLISLE	112
Crown Hotel, EXFORD	431
Crown Inn, The, BOROUGHBRIDGE	509
Crown Lodge Hotel, WISBECH	86
Crown, The, AMERSHAM	69
Crown, The, BRAY	53
Crown, The, SOUTHWOLD	448
Crown, The, STOKE-BY-NAYLAND	449
Crowne Plaza Dublin Northwood, DUBLIN	661
Crowne Plaza Hotel Dublin - Blanchardstown, DUBLIN	661
Crowne Plaza London - Ealing, LONDON W5	360
Crowne Plaza Marlow, MARLOW	73
Crowne Plaza Resort Colchester - Five Lakes, TOLLESHUNT KNIGHTS	167
Cuillin Hills Hotel, PORTREE	616
Cullinan's Seafood Restaurant & Guest House, DOOLIN	654
Cumberland Hotel, BOURNEMOUTH	149
Curlew Restaurant, The, BODIAM	458
Curry Corner, The, CHELTENHAM	169
CUT at 45 Park Lane, LONDON W1	324
Cwtch, ST DAVIDS	638

D

Dabbous, LONDON W1	324
Daffodil, The, CHELTENHAM	171
Dairy, The, LONDON SW4	305
Dale Hill Hotel & Golf Club, TICEHURST	464
Dales Country House Hotel, SHERINGHAM	394
Dalmahoy, A Marriott Hotel & Country Club, EDINBURGH	569
Darleys Restaurant, DARLEY ABBEY	126
Darroch Learg Hotel, BALLATER	551
Dart Marina Hotel, The, DARTMOUTH	134
Dartmoor Inn, LYDFORD	140

David Kennedy's Food Social, NEWCASTLE UPON TYNE   479
Daylesford Farm Café, DAYLESFORD   174
De Vere Carden Park, BROXTON   87
De Vere Grand, Brighton, The, BRIGHTON & HOVE   459
De Vere Oulton Hall, LEEDS   533
De Vere Slaley Hall, HEXHAM   400
Deanes at Queens, BELFAST   647
Deanes Restaurant, BELFAST   647
Deans Place, ALFRISTON   458
Deans@ Let's Eat, PERTH   606
Deddington Arms, DEDDINGTON   408
Degò, LONDON W1   324
Dehesa, LONDON W1   324
Del Amitri Restaurant, ANNAN   564
Delaunay, The, LONDON WC2   371
Depot, The, LONDON SW14   312
Design House Restaurant, HALIFAX   531
Devonshire Arms at Beeley, The, BEELEY   124
Devonshire Arms Country House Hotel & Spa, The, BOLTON ABBEY   509
Devonshire Arms, The, SOMERTON   433
Devonshire Brasserie & Bar, The, BOLTON ABBEY   509
Devonshire Fell, The, BURNSALL   510
Dew Pond Restaurant, The, OLD BURGHCLERE   195
Diciannove, LONDON EC4   270
Dinham Hall Hotel, LUDLOW   421
Dining Room Restaurant, The, BOROUGHBRIDGE   509
Dining Room, The, REIGATE   456
Dining Rooms @ Worsley Park, The, MANCHESTER   182
Dinings, LONDON W1   325
Dinner by Heston Blumenthal, LONDON SW1   287
Divino Enoteca, EDINBURGH   570
Dock Kitchen, The, LONDON W10   366
Donnington Valley Hotel & Spa, NEWBURY   58
Dormy House Hotel, BROADWAY   503
Dornoch Castle Hotel, DORNOCH   592
Dove Inn, The, CANTERBURY   217
Dove Inn, The, WARMINSTER   503
Dove Restaurant with Rooms, The, ALBURGH   384
Dower House Restaurant, The, BATH   428
Downtown Mayfair, LONDON W1   325
Doxford Hall Hotel & Spa, CHATHILL   399
Dragon Hotel, The, SWANSEA   642
Dragon, The, MONTGOMERY   641
Drake's Restaurant, RIPLEY   456
Draper's Hall, SHREWSBURY   425
Drapers Arms, The, LONDON N1   272
Driftwood, PORTSCATHO   102
Dromoland Castle, NEWMARKET-ON-FERGUS   656
Drovers, FORFAR   556
Drunken Duck Inn, AMBLESIDE   108
Dryburgh Abbey Hotel, ST BOSWELLS   610
DSTRKT, LONDON W1   326
Duck & Waffle, LONDON EC2   267
Ducks at Kilspindie, ABERLADY   601
Duisdale House Hotel, ISLEORNSAY   613
Duke of Cornwall Hotel, PLYMOUTH   142
Duke of Richmond Hotel, The, ST PETER PORT   537
Dungeon Restaurant at Dalhousie Castle, The, EDINBURGH   570
Dunkerleys Hotel & Restaurant, DEAL   218
Dunsley Hall, WHITBY   522
Duxford Lodge Hotel, DUXFORD   80
Dysart Arms, The, RICHMOND UPON THAMES   377

E

E&O, LONDON W11   367
Eagle, The, FARINGDON   408
Earl of March, CHICHESTER   467

Earle by Simon Rimmer, ALTRINCHAM   182
East Lodge Country House Hotel, ROWSLEY   132
East Sussex National Golf Resort & Spa, UCKFIELD   465
Eastbury Hotel, SHERBORNE   156
Eastwell Manor, ASHFORD   215
Eat on the Green, ELLON   553
Ebrington Arms, The, EBRINGTON   174
Edera, LONDON W11   367
Ees Wyke Country House, NEAR SAWREY   117
Egerton House Hotel, BOLTON   182
Eight Over Eight, LONDON SW3   301
El Pirata Detapas, LONDON W2   357
Elephant at Pangbourne, The, PANGBOURNE   61
Elephant Restaurant and Brasserie, The, TORQUAY   146
Ellenborough Park, CHELTENHAM   171
Elveden Café Restaurant, THETFORD   394
Empire Hotel & Spa, LLANDUDNO   627
Empress, The, LONDON E9   261
Enoteca Turi, LONDON SW15   312
Enterkine Country House, AYR   561
Entrée Restaurant and Bar, LONDON SW11   311
Eshott Hall, MORPETH   401
Eslington Villa Hotel, GATESHEAD   477
Esperante at Fairmont St Andrews, ST ANDREWS   583
Esseborne Manor, ANDOVER   187
Essence, ALCESTER   480
Estate Grill at Great Fosters, The, EGHAM   454
Estbek House, WHITBY   523
Etrop Grange Hotel, MANCHESTER AIRPORT   185
Ettington Park Hotel, ALDERMINSTER   480
Exeter Arms, The, EASTON-ON-THE-HILL   397
Eyre Brothers, LONDON EC2   268

F

Fairfield House Hotel, AYR   562
Fairlawns Hotel & Spa, WALSALL   490
Fairwater Head Hotel, AXMINSTER   133
Fairyhill, REYNOLDSTON   642
Faithlegg House Hotel & Golf Resort, WATERFORD   671
Falcondale Hotel & Restaurant, The, LAMPETER   625
Fallowfields Hotel and Restaurant, KINGSTON BAGPUIZE   411
Falmouth Hotel, FALMOUTH   94
Famous Bein Inn, The, GLENFARG   605
Farlam Hall Hotel, BRAMPTON   110
Farmhouse Hotel, The, ST SAVIOUR   538
Farndon Boathouse, FARNDON   402
Fat Duck, The, BRAY   53
Fat Fox Inn, The, WATLINGTON   414
Fat Goose, The, TENDRING   167
Fat Olives, EMSWORTH   192
Fawsley Hall, DAVENTRY   396
Feathered Nest Country Inn, The, NETHER WESTCOTE   176
Feathers Hotel, LEDBURY   206
Feathers Hotel, The, LUDLOW   421
Feathers Hotel, The, WOODSTOCK   415
Felbridge Hotel & Spa, The, EAST GRINSTEAD   469
Fermain Valley Hotel, ST PETER PORT   537
Feversham Arms Hotel & Verbena Spa, HELMSLEY   516
Fifteen Cornwall, WATERGATE BAY   107
Fifteen London - The Restaurant, LONDON N1   272
Fifteen Thirty Nine Bar & Restaurant, CHESTER   87
Finnstown Country House Hotel, LUCAN   663
Fino, LONDON W1   327
Fischer's Baslow Hall, BASLOW   124
Fish on the Green, MAIDSTONE   220
Fishmore Hall, LUDLOW   421
Fitzpatrick Castle Hotel, KILLINEY   663

Five Arrows, The, WADDESDON	79
Five Rise Locks Hotel & Restaurant, BINGLEY	529
Flemings Mayfair, LONDON W1	327
Foragers, The, BRIGHTON & HOVE	459
Forbury's Restaurant, READING	61
Forest of Arden Marriott Hotel & Country Club, MERIDEN	490
Forest Pines Hotel & Golf Resort, SCUNTHORPE	237
Forest, The, DORRIDGE	488
Forss House Hotel, THURSO	600
Fortingall Hotel, FORTINGALL	605
Fosse Manor, STOW-ON-THE-WOLD	178
Four Seasons Hotel Hampshire, DOGMERSFIELD	191
Four Seasons Hotel London at Canary Wharf, LONDON E14	262
Four Seasons Hotel London at Park Lane, LONDON W1	327
Four Seasons Hotel, The, ST FILLANS	607
Fowey Hotel, The, FOWEY	95
Fox & Goose Inn, FRESSINGFIELD	443
Fox & Grapes, The, LONDON SW19	313
Fox & Hounds Country Hotel, EGGESFORD	137
Fox & Hounds Country Inn, PICKERING	518
Fox, The, WILLIAN	215
Foxhills Club and Resort, OTTERSHAW	455
Foxhunter, The, ABERGAVENNY	632
Fraiche, BIRKENHEAD	380
Franklins, LONDON SE22	282
Frederick's Restaurant, LONDON N1	272
Fredrick's Hotel Restaurant Spa, MAIDENHEAD	58
Freemasons at Wiswell, The, WHALLEY	231
French by Simon Rogan, The, MANCHESTER	182
French Horn, The, READING	61
French Table, The, SURBITON	380
Frenchgate Restaurant and Hotel, The, RICHMOND	519
Friends Restaurant, PINNER	377
Froize Freehouse Restaurant, The, CHILLESFORD	443

G

G Hotel, The, GALWAY	664
Galgorm Resort & Spa, BALLYMENA	646
Gallivant Hotel, The, CAMBER	461
Galvin at Windows Restaurant & Bar, LONDON W1	327
Galvin Bistrot de Luxe, LONDON W1	327
Galvin Brasserie de Luxe, EDINBURGH	571
Galvin Café a Vin, LONDON E1	258
Galvin La Chapelle, LONDON E1	258
Gamba, GLASGOW	587
Garrack Hotel & Restaurant, ST IVES	104
Garryvoe, GARRYVOE	658
Gate, The, LONDON W6	360
Gatsby, The, BERKHAMSTED	209
Gauthier Soho, LONDON W1	328
Gavin Gregg Restaurant, SEVENOAKS	221
Gee's Restaurant, OXFORD	412
General Tarleton Inn, KNARESBOROUGH	516
George & Dragon, BURPHAM	466
George & Dragon, The, ROWDE	501
George Albert Hotel, EVERSHOT	154
George at Wath, RIPON	519
George Hotel & Brasserie, The, ST NEOTS	86
George Hotel, HATHERSAGE	128
George Hotel, The, YARMOUTH	492
George in Rye, The, RYE	463
George of Stamford, The, STAMFORD	239
George V Dining Room, The, CONG	669
George, The, CAVENDISH	442
Ghan House, CARLINGFORD	668
Ghyll Manor, RUSPER	475
Gidleigh Park, CHAGFORD	134

Gilbert Scott, The, LONDON NW1	273
Gilbey's Restaurant, AMERSHAM	69
Gilgamesh Restaurant Lounge, LONDON NW1	273
Gillray's Steakhouse & Bar, LONDON SE1	278
Gilpin Hotel & Lake House, WINDERMERE	119
Gin Trap Inn, The, RINGSTEAD	394
Ginger Fox, The, ALBOURNE	466
Gingerman Restaurant, The, BRIGHTON & HOVE	459
Gisborough Hall, GUISBOROUGH	511
Glass Boat Restaurant, BRISTOL	65
Glasshouse, The, KEW	377
Glasshouse, The, LYNDHURST	195
Glazebrook House, SOUTH BRENT	144
Glenapp Castle, BALLANTRAE	564
Glengarry Castle Hotel, INVERGARRY	594
Glenmorangie Highland Home at Cadboll, The, TAIN	599
Glenskirlie House & Castle, BANKNOCK	582
Glenview, The, STAFFIN	616
Glewstone Court Country House Hotel & Restaurant, ROSS-ON-WYE	208
Globe, The, MILVERTON	432
Goldbrick House, BRISTOL	67
Goldstone Hall, MARKET DRAYTON	423
Golf View Hotel and Spa, The, NAIRN	597
Goodfellows, WELLS	434
Goodman, LONDON W1	328
Goods Shed Restaurant, The, CANTERBURY	218
Goodwood Hotel, The, GOODWOOD	472
Gordon Ramsay at The Ritz Carlton Powerscourt, ENNISKERRY	674
Gordon's, INVERKEILOR	556
Goring, The, LONDON SW1	288
Gormans Clifftop House & Restaurant, DINGLE (AN DAINGEAN)	665
Gougane Barra Hotel, GOUGANE BARRA	658
Granary Hotel & Restaurant, The, KIDDERMINSTER	505
Grand Hotel, The, EASTBOURNE	461
Grand Hotel, TORQUAY	146
Grand Jersey, ST HELIER	540
Grange Hotel, The, BURY ST EDMUNDS	441
Grange Hotel, The, YORK	525
Grants at Craigellachie, SHIEL BRIDGE	599
Grassington House, GRASSINGTON	511
Gravetye Manor Hotel, EAST GRINSTEAD	471
Graze Restaurant, BRIGHTON & HOVE	460
Great British Restaurant, LONDON W1	328
Great Queen Street, LONDON WC2	371
Green House, The, BOURNEMOUTH	149
Green Island Restaurant, ST CLEMENT	540
Green Man and French Horn, LONDON WC2	371
Green Park Hotel, PITLOCHRY	607
Green, The, SHERBORNE	157
Greenbank Hotel, The, FALMOUTH	95
Greene Oak, The, WINDSOR	64
Greenhills Country Hotel, ST PETER	544
Greenhouse, The, LONDON W1	328
Greens Bistro, LYTHAM ST ANNES	228
Greens, MANCHESTER	184
Greenway Hotel & Spa, The, CHELTENHAM	171
Gregans Castle, BALLYVAUGHAN	654
Gregg's Bar and Grill, LONDON SE1	278
Greyhound Inn, The, SYDLING ST NICHOLAS	157
Greyhound on the Test, STOCKBRIDGE	203
Grill at The Dorchester, The, LONDON W1	328
Grim's Dyke Hotel, HARROW WEALD	376
Groes Inn, The, CONWY	627
Grosvenor Pulford Hotel & Spa, CHESTER	87
Grove, The, NARBERTH	637
Grovefield House Hotel, The, BURNHAM	71
Gun, The, LONDON E14	262

Gusto, SOUTHPORT — 383
Guy Fawkes Inn, YORK — 525
Guyers House Hotel, CORSHAM — 494

H

H10 London Waterloo Hotel, LONDON SE1 — 278
Hadrian's, EDINBURGH — 571
Hakkasan Mayfair, LONDON W1 — 328
Hakkasan, LONDON W1 — 328
Halfway Bridge Inn, The, LODSWORTH — 473
Halliday's, CHICHESTER — 467
Hambleton Hall, OAKHAM — 418
Hambrough, The, VENTNOR — 491
Hamilton's, CHERTSEY — 452
Hammer & Pincers, WYMESWOLD — 234
Hanbury Manor, A Marriott Hotel & Country Club, WARE — 212
Hand & Flowers, The, MARLOW — 75
Hand at Llanarmon, The, LLANARMON DYFFRYN CEIRIOG — 643
Hanoi Bike Shop, The, GLASGOW — 588
Hanoras Cottage, BALLYMACARBRY — 671
Hanson at the Chelsea Restaurant, SWANSEA — 642
Haozhan, LONDON W1 — 331
Harbour Heights, POOLE — 155
Hardwick, The, ABERGAVENNY — 632
Hare & Hounds Hotel, TETBURY — 179
Hare & Hounds, The, BATH — 428
Harris's Restaurant, PENZANCE — 101
Harrison's, LONDON SW12 — 311
Harrow at Little Bedwyn, The, LITTLE BEDWYN — 499
Harry's Place, GRANTHAM — 234
Hart's Hotel, NOTTINGHAM — 403
Hartfell House & The Limetree Restaurant, MOFFAT — 566
Hartnett Holder & Co, LYNDHURST — 195
Hartwell House Hotel, Restaurant & Spa, AYLESBURY — 69
Harvey Nichols Forth Floor Restaurant, EDINBURGH — 571
Harvey Nichols Second Floor Restaurant, MANCHESTER — 184
Harvey's Point Hotel, DONEGAL — 659
Harwood Arms, The, LONDON SW6 — 307
Haven, The, POOLE — 155
Haxted Mill Restaurant, EDENBRIDGE — 218
Haycock Hotel, The, WANSFORD — 86
Heacham Manor Hotel, HEACHAM — 388
Headlam Hall, DARLINGTON — 158
Healds Hall Hotel & Restaurant, LIVERSEDGE — 535
Hedone, LONDON W4 — 358
Hélène Darroze at The Connaught, LONDON W1 — 331
Hell Bay, BRYHER — 107
Hempstead House Country Hotel, SITTINGBOURNE — 222
Hendon Hall Hotel, LONDON NW4 — 276
Hengist Restaurant, AYLESFORD — 216
Hermitage Hotel, BOURNEMOUTH — 149
Heron's Cove, The, GOLEEN — 658
Hibiscus, LONDON W1 — 331
High Road Brasserie, LONDON W4 — 358
Highland Cottage, TOBERMORY — 613
Highwayman, The, BURROW — 224
Highwayman, The, CHECKENDON — 406
Hinds Head, BRAY — 53
Hintlesham Hall Hotel, HINTLESHAM — 444
Hipping Hall, KIRKBY LONSDALE — 116
HIX Mayfair, LONDON W1 — 334
Hix Oyster & Chop House, LONDON EC1 — 264
HIX, LONDON W1 — 331
Holbeck Ghyll Country House Hotel, WINDERMERE — 119
Holbrook House, WINCANTON — 436
Holcombe Inn, The, HOLCOMBE — 431
Holdsworth House Hotel, HALIFAX — 531

Hole in the Wall, LITTLE WILBRAHAM — 85
Holiday Inn Aberdeen West, ABERDEEN — 550
Holiday Inn Reading M4 Jct 10, READING — 62
Holiday Inn Salisbury - Stonehenge, AMESBURY — 493
Holiday Inn Winchester, WINCHESTER — 204
Holme Lacy House Hotel, HEREFORD — 206
Holt Bar & Restaurant, The, HONITON — 138
Homewood Park Hotel & Spa, HINTON CHARTERHOUSE — 431
Honest Lawyer Hotel, DURHAM — 161
Honours, The, EDINBURGH — 572
Hoop, The, STOCK — 166
Horn of Plenty, The, TAVISTOCK — 145
Horse Guards Inn, The, TILLINGTON — 477
Horseshoe Inn, The, EDDLESTON — 608
Horsted Place, UCKFIELD — 465
Hoste, The, BURNHAM MARKET — 386
Hotel du Vin at One Devonshire Gardens, GLASGOW — 588
Hotel du Vin Birmingham, BIRMINGHAM — 486
Hotel du Vin Brighton, BRIGHTON & HOVE — 460
Hotel du Vin Bristol, BRISTOL — 67
Hotel du Vin Cambridge, CAMBRIDGE — 80
Hotel du Vin Cheltenham, CHELTENHAM — 172
Hotel du Vin Edinburgh, EDINBURGH — 572
Hotel du Vin Harrogate, HARROGATE — 512
Hotel du Vin Henley-on-Thames, HENLEY-ON-THAMES — 409
Hotel du Vin Newcastle, NEWCASTLE UPON TYNE — 479
Hotel du Vin Poole, POOLE — 155
Hotel du Vin Tunbridge Wells, TUNBRIDGE WELLS (ROYAL) — 222
Hotel du Vin Winchester, WINCHESTER — 204
Hotel du Vin York, YORK — 525
Hotel Eilean Iarmain, ISLEORNSAY — 613
Hotel Felix, CAMBRIDGE — 80
Hotel Hebrides, TARBERT (TAIRBEART) — 612
Hotel Jerbourg, ST MARTIN — 537
Hotel La Place, ST BRELADE — 540
Hotel Maiyango, LEICESTER — 232
Hotel Missoni Edinburgh, EDINBURGH — 572
Hotel Portmeirion, The, PORTMEIRION — 631
Hotel Savoy, ST HELIER — 544
Hotel Tresanton, ST MAWES — 105
Hotel Van Dyk, CLOWNE — 126
Hotel Westport Leisure, Spa & Conference, WESTPORT — 669
Housel Bay Hotel, LIZARD — 96
Howard, The, EDINBURGH — 572
Humphry's at Stoke Park, STOKE POGES — 75
Hundred House Hotel, The, NORTON — 423
Hunter's Hotel, RATHNEW — 675

I

Ian Brown Food & Drink, GLASGOW — 589
Iberica Marylebone, LONDON W1 — 334
Iggs, EDINBURGH — 573
Il Convivio, LONDON SW1 — 288
Ilsington Country House Hotel, ILSINGTON — 139
Imperial Hotel, GREAT YARMOUTH — 387
Imperial Hotel, LLANDUDNO — 627
Imperial Hotel, The, TORQUAY — 146
Incanto Restaurant, HARROW ON THE HILL — 374
Inch House Country House & Restaurant, THURLES — 671
Inchnacardoch Lodge Hotel, FORT AUGUSTUS — 592
Inchydoney Island Lodge & Spa, CLONAKILTY — 657
Indaba Fish, TRURO — 106
Indian Cavalry Club, The, EDINBURGH — 573
Indian Summer, BRIGHTON & HOVE — 460
Inn at Grinshill, The, GRINSHILL — 419
Inn at Hawnby, The, HAWNBY — 514
Inn at Lathones, The, ST ANDREWS — 583

Inn at Penallt, The, MONMOUTH 634
Inn at Whitewell, The, WHITEWELL 231
Inn at Woburn, The, WOBURN 51
Inn Castledawson, The, CASTLEDAWSON 651
Inn on the Lake, The, GLENRIDDING 113
Inn the Park, LONDON SW1 288
Inverlochy Castle Hotel, FORT WILLIAM 592
Island Restaurant & Bar, LONDON W2 358
Ivy, The, LONDON WC2 371

J
J. Sheekey & J. Sheekey Oyster Bar, LONDON WC2 372
Jack In The Green Inn, The, ROCKBEARE 143
Jali Restaurant, HASTINGS & ST LEONARDS 463
James Miller Room, The, TURNBERRY 564
James Street South Restaurant & Bar, BELFAST 647
Jamie's Italian Restaurant, EDINBURGH 573
Jamie's Italian, BATH 428
Jamie's Italian, Leeds, LEEDS 534
Jamie's Italian, LONDON WC2 371
JAR Restaurant, DOUGLAS 546
Jeremy's at Borde Hill, HAYWARDS HEATH 472
Jerichos, WINDERMERE 119
Jesmond Dene House, NEWCASTLE UPON TYNE 479
Jesse's Bistro, CIRENCESTER 173
Jetty, The, CHRISTCHURCH 152
Jim's Yard, STAMFORD 239
Jolly Cricketers, The, BEACONSFIELD 71
Jolly Sportsman, LEWES 463
JSW, PETERSFIELD 199
Judges Country House Hotel, YARM 523
Juniper, BRISTOL 67
JW Steakhouse, LONDON W1 334

K
Kai Mayfair, LONDON W1 334
Kanpai Sushi, EDINBURGH 573
Karpo, LONDON NW1 273
Kaspar's Seafood Bar & Grill, LONDON WC2 372
Keepers Arms, The, TROTTON 477
Kemps Country House, WAREHAM 157
Ken Lo's Memories of China, LONDON SW1 288
Kendals Brasserie, THOMASTOWN 668
Kensington Place, LONDON W8 363
Keswick Hotel, The, BACTON 384
Kettering Park Hotel & Spa, KETTERING 397
Kilcamb Lodge Hotel & Restaurant, STRONTIAN 599
Kilkenny River Court Hotel, KILKENNY 667
Killiecrankie Hotel, KILLIECRANKIE 605
Kilmichael Country House Hotel, BRODICK 612
Kilronan Castle Estate & Spa, ROSCOMMON 671
Kilworth House Hotel & Theatre, NORTH KILWORTH 233
Kincraig Castle Hotel, INVERGORDON 595
Kingham Plough, The, CHIPPING NORTON 407
Kings Arms Hotel, WOODSTOCK 416
Kings Arms Inn & Restaurant, WING 418
Kings Head Hotel, The, GREAT BIRCHAM 387
Kings Head Inn, The, STOW-ON-THE-WOLD 178
Kings, The, CHIPPING CAMPDEN 172
Kinloch Lodge, ISLEORNSAY 614
Kinmel Arms, The, ABERGELE 625
Kirroughtree House, NEWTON STEWART 566
Kitchen Joël Antunès at Embassy Mayfair, LONDON W1 335
Kitchen W8, LONDON W8 363
Kitchin, The, EDINBURGH 573
Knockendarroch House Hotel, PITLOCHRY 607
Knockinaam Lodge, PORTPATRICK 566

Knockranny House Hotel, WESTPORT 670
Koffmann's, LONDON SW1 289
Kopapa, LONDON WC2 372
Kota Restaurant with Rooms, PORTHLEVEN 101
Kyashii, LONDON WC2 372

L
L' Anima, LONDON EC2 266
L'Amuse Bouche Restaurant, MALVERN 506
L'Atelier de Joël Robuchon, LONDON WC2 368
L'Autre Pied, LONDON W1 317
L'Enclume, CARTMEL 112
L'Escargot - The Ground Floor Restaurant, LONDON W1 326
L'Etranger, LONDON SW7 308
L'Horizon Hotel and Spa, ST BRELADE 540
L'ortolan, SHINFIELD 62
La Barbarie Hotel, ST MARTIN 536
La Bécasse, LUDLOW 420
La Bonne Auberge, GLASGOW 587
La Brasserie at The Chester Grosvenor & Spa, CHESTER 87
La Buvette, RICHMOND UPON THAMES 377
La Collina, LONDON NW1 273
La Favorita, EDINBURGH 571
La Fleur de Lys Restaurant with Rooms, SHAFTESBURY 156
La Garrigue, EDINBURGH 571
La Luna, GODALMING 455
La Luna, PONTYCLUN 642
La Marine Bistro, ROSSLARE 674
La Parmigiana, GLASGOW 589
La Petite Maison, LONDON W1 341
La Potinière, GULLANE 601
La Sablonnerie, SARK 546
La Stella, ABERDEEN 551
La Trompette, LONDON W4 359
La Vallée Blanche, GLASGOW 591
Lady Helen Restaurant, The, THOMASTOWN 668
Lake Country House & Spa, The, LLANGAMMARCH WELLS 640
Lake Hotel, The, KILLARNEY 666
Lake Isle, The, UPPINGHAM 418
Lake Vyrnwy Hotel & Spa, LLANWDDYN 640
Lakeside Hotel Lake Windermere, NEWBY BRIDGE 117
Lamb & Lion, The, YORK 525
Lamb at Hindon, The, HINDON 499
Lamb Inn, The, BURFORD 406
Lambert Arms, ASTON ROWANT 405
Lamberts, LONDON SW12 311
Lambourne, The, LONDON SW19 313
Landmark Hotel, The, DUNDEE 568
Langar Hall, LANGAR 402
Langdale Hotel & Spa, ELTERWATER 113
Langdon Court Hotel & Restaurant, DOWN THOMAS 136
Langham Hotel, EASTBOURNE 462
Langley Castle Hotel, HEXHAM 401
Langmans Restaurant, CALLINGTON 94
Langrish House, PETERSFIELD 199
Langshott Manor, GATWICK AIRPORT (LONDON) 471
Langstone Hotel, HAYLING ISLAND 193
Lanterna Ristorante, SCARBOROUGH 520
Lasan Restaurant, BIRMINGHAM 486
Lasswade Country House, LLANWRTYD WELLS 641
Latium, LONDON W1 335
Laughing Monk, The, STRETE 145
Launceston Place Restaurant, LONDON W8 363
Lavender House, The, BRUNDALL 386
Lavenham Great House Restaurant with Rooms, LAVENHAM 445
Lawn Bistro, The, LONDON SW19 314
Lawns Restaurant at Thornton Hall, The, THORNTON HOUGH 384

Lawns Wine Bar, The, HOLT	388
Le Café Anglais, LONDON W2	357
Le Café du Marché, LONDON EC1	264
Le Caprice, LONDON SW1	286
Le Cercle, LONDON SW1	286
Le Champignon Sauvage, CHELTENHAM	169
Le Colombier, LONDON SW3	300
Le Comptoir Gascon, LONDON EC1	264
Le Gavroche Restaurant, LONDON W1	328
Le Manoir aux Quat' Saisons, GREAT MILTON	409
Le Meridien Piccadilly, LONDON W1	337
Le Patio at the Manor House, NEWPORT	636
Le Petit Canard, MAIDEN NEWTON	154
Le Pont de la Tour, LONDON SE1	280
Le Talbooth, DEDHAM	164
Le Vacherin, LONDON W4	359
Lea Marston Hotel & Spa, LEA MARSTON	481
Leaping Hare Restaurant & Country Store, The, BURY ST EDMUNDS	441
Leatherne Bottel, The, GORING	409
Leathes Head Hotel, BORROWDALE	110
Leconfield, The, PETWORTH	475
Leconfield, The, VENTNOR	491
Ledbury, The, LONDON W11	367
Legacy Falcon Hotel, The, STRATFORD-UPON-AVON	484
Les Bouviers Restaurant with Rooms, WIMBORNE MINSTER	157
Les Deux Salons, LONDON WC2	371
Les Saveurs, EXMOUTH	137
Les Trois Garçons, LONDON E1	260
Levant, LONDON W1	335
Leverhulme Hotel, PORT SUNLIGHT	382
Lewtrenchard Manor, LEWDOWN	139
Library @ Browns, The, TAVISTOCK	145
Light House Restaurant, The, LONDON SW19	314
Lilly Restaurant with Rooms, The, LLANDUDNO	628
Lima, LONDON W1	335
Lime Tree Hotel & Restaurant, FORT WILLIAM	594
Lime Tree, The, LIMAVADY	651
Limerick Strand Hotel, LIMERICK	668
Lincoln Hotel, The, LINCOLN	236
Lindeth Howe Country House Hotel & Restaurant, WINDERMERE	122
Linthwaite House Hotel & Restaurant, WINDERMERE	122
Lion & Pheasant Hotel, SHREWSBURY	425
Lion, The, LEINTWARDINE	207
Little Barwick House, YEOVIL	436
Little Social, LONDON W1	335
Littlecote House Hotel, HUNGERFORD	57
Livingston's Restaurant, LINLITHGOW	602
Llangoed Hall, LLYSWEN	641
Llansantffraed Court Hotel, ABERGAVENNY	632
Llechwen Hall Hotel, PONTYPRIDD	642
Llugwy River Restaurant @ Royal Oak Hotel, BETWS-Y-COED	626
Llys Meddyg, NEWPORT	637
Locanda De Gusti, EDINBURGH	575
Locanda Locatelli, LONDON W1	335
Loch Bay Seafood Restaurant, STEIN	617
Loch Kinord Hotel, BALLATER	551
Loch Melfort Hotel, ARDUAINE	556
Loch Ness Country House Hotel, INVERNESS	595
Lochgreen House Hotel, TROON	564
Lodge at Castle Leslie Estate, The, GLASLOUGH	670
Lodge at Prince's, The, SANDWICH	221
Lodge on Loch Lomond, The, LUSS	557
London Carriage Works, The, LIVERPOOL	380
London Heathrow Marriott Hotel, HEATHROW AIRPORT (LONDON)	376
Longueville Manor Hotel, ST SAVIOUR	545
Lonsdale, LONDON W11	368
Lord Bute & Restaurant, The, CHRISTCHURCH	152
Lords of the Manor, UPPER SLAUGHTER	180
Losehill House Hotel & Spa, HOPE	129
Lough Erne Resort, ENNISKILLEN	650
Lough Inagh Lodge, RECESS (SRAITH SALACH)	665
Lough Rynn Castle, MOHILL	668
Lovat, Loch Ness, The, FORT AUGUSTUS	592
Lovelady Shield Country House Hotel, ALSTON	108
Loves Restaurant, BIRMINGHAM	486
Lower Slaughter Manor, LOWER SLAUGHTER	175
Lowry Hotel, The, MANCHESTER	184
Lugger Hotel, The, PORTLOE	101
Lujon, KESTON	376
Lumière, CHELTENHAM	172
Lutyens Restaurant, LONDON EC4	271
Luxe, First-Floor Brasserie, The, LONDON E1	258
Lygon Arms, The, BROADWAY	504
Lythe Hill Hotel & Spa, HASLEMERE	455

M

MacCallums of Troon, TROON	564
Macdonald Alveston Manor, STRATFORD-UPON-AVON	484
Macdonald Ansty Hall, ANSTY	480
Macdonald Bath Spa, BATH	428
Macdonald Bear Hotel, WOODSTOCK	416
Macdonald Berystede Hotel & Spa, ASCOT	52
Macdonald Botley Park, Golf & Spa, BOTLEY	189
Macdonald Cardrona Hotel, Golf & Spa, PEEBLES	609
Macdonald Craxton Wood Hotel, PUDDINGTON	92
Macdonald Crutherland House, EAST KILBRIDE	601
Macdonald Forest Hills Hotel & Resort, ABERFOYLE	610
Macdonald Frimley Hall Hotel & Spa, CAMBERLEY	451
Macdonald Houstoun House, UPHALL	602
Macdonald Kilhey Court Hotel, WIGAN	186
Macdonald Leeming House, WATERMILLOCK	118
Macdonald Linden Hall, Golf & Country Club, LONGHORSLEY	401
Macdonald Manchester Hotel, MANCHESTER	184
Macdonald Marine Hotel & Spa, NORTH BERWICK	602
Macdonald Old England Hotel & Spa, WINDERMERE	122
Macdonald Pittodrie House, INVERURIE	553
Macdonald Portal Hotel Golf & Spa, TARPORLEY	93
Macdonald Randolph Hotel, OXFORD	412
Macdonald Swan Hotel, GRASMERE	114
Macdonald Windsor Hotel, WINDSOR	64
Mad Jack's Restaurant & Bar, SHREWSBURY	425
Magdalen, LONDON SE1	278
Magpies Restaurant with Rooms, HORNCASTLE	234
Maids Head Hotel, The, NORWICH	391
Maison Bleue, BURY ST EDMUNDS	442
Mall Tavern, The, LONDON W8	363
Mallory Court Hotel, LEAMINGTON SPA (ROYAL)	482
Malmaison Aberdeen, ABERDEEN	550
Malmaison Belfast, BELFAST	647
Malmaison Birmingham, BIRMINGHAM	488
Malmaison Charterhouse Square, LONDON EC1	264
Malmaison Edinburgh, EDINBURGH	575
Malmaison Glasgow, GLASGOW	589
Malmaison Leeds, LEEDS	534
Malmaison Liverpool, LIVERPOOL	382
Malmaison Manchester, MANCHESTER	184
Malmaison Newcastle, NEWCASTLE UPON TYNE	479
Malmaison Oxford, OXFORD	412
Malmaison Reading, READING	62
Malone Lodge Hotel, BELFAST	647
Malvern, The, MALVERN	507
Mandeville Hotel, The, LONDON W1	337
Manicomio - City, LONDON EC2	268
Manicomio, LONDON SW3	301

Manna, LONDON NW3 — 275
Manor Hotel, CRICKHOWELL — 639
Manor House Country Hotel, ENNISKILLEN — 650
Manor House Hotel, MORETON-IN-MARSH — 175
Manor House Hotel, OBAN — 559
Marcello@ the barn, PIDLEY — 86
Marco Pierre White Steak & Alehouse, LONDON E1 — 258
Marco, LONDON SW6 — 308
Marcus Wareing at the Berkeley, LONDON SW1 — 289
Margot's, PADSTOW — 98
Marine Hotel, The, TROON — 564
Mariners, IPSWICH — 444
Mariners, The, LYME REGIS — 154
Mark Jordan at the Beach, ST PETER — 544
Marlborough Tavern, BATH — 428
Marlfield House, GOREY — 673
Marquess of Exeter, The, LYDDINGTON — 418
Marquis at Alkham, The, DOVER — 218
Martin Wishart at Loch Lomond, BALLOCH — 567
Marwell Hotel, WINCHESTER — 205
Maryborough Hotel & Spa, CORK — 658
Maryculter House Hotel, ABERDEEN — 550
Marygreen Manor Hotel, BRENTWOOD — 162
Masa Restaurant, DERBY — 127
Masons Arms, The, KNOWSTONE — 139
Masons at Tracy Park, WICK — 180
Massimo Restaurant & Oyster Bar, LONDON WC2 — 372
Matfen Hall, MATFEN — 401
Maynard, The, GRINDLEFORD — 127
Maze Grill, LONDON W1 — 337
Maze, LONDON W1 — 337
Medlar Restaurant, LONDON SW10 — 310
Meldrum House Country Hotel & Golf Course, OLDMELDRUM — 553
Mele e Pere, LONDON W1 — 337
Meliá White House, LONDON NW1 — 273
Melton's Restaurant, YORK — 525
Mennula, LONDON W1 — 337
Menzies Cambridge Hotel & Golf Club, CAMBRIDGE — 80
Menzies Hotels Bournemouth - Carlton, BOURNEMOUTH — 149
Menzies Hotels London Luton - Strathmore, LUTON — 49
Menzies Hotels Woburn Flitwick Manor, FLITWICK — 48
Menzies Welcombe Hotel Spa & Golf Club, STRATFORD-UPON-AVON — 484
Meon Valley, A Marriott Hotel & Country Club, SHEDFIELD — 202
Merchant Hotel, The, BELFAST — 649
Mercure Aberdeen Ardoe House Hotel & Spa, ABERDEEN — 550
Mercure Box Hill Burford Bridge Hotel, DORKING — 452
Mercure Coventry Brandon Hall Hotel & Spa, BRANDON — 481
Mercure Milton Keynes Parkside Hotel, MILTON KEYNES — 75
Mercure Oxford Eastgate Hotel, OXFORD — 412
Mercure Southampton Centre Dolphin Hotel, SOUTHAMPTON — 202
Mercure Stratford-upon-Avon Shakespeare Hotel, STRATFORD-UPON-AVON — 484
Mercure Windsor Castle Hotel, WINDSOR — 64
Mere Court Hotel & Conference Centre, KNUTSFORD — 89
Mere Golf Resort & Spa, The, KNUTSFORD — 91
Mermaid Inn, RYE — 464
Methuen Arms, The, CORSHAM — 497
Metropole, The, LLANDRINDOD WELLS — 640
Metropole, The, PADSTOW — 98
Mews of Mayfair, LONDON W1 — 338
Michael Nadra Primrose Hill, LONDON NW1 — 274
Michael Wignall at The Latymer, BAGSHOT — 451
Middlethorpe Hall & Spa, YORK — 527
Midsummer House, CAMBRIDGE — 80
Milebrook House Hotel, KNIGHTON — 639
Milestone Hotel, The, LONDON W8 — 365
Milestone, The, SHEFFIELD — 527
Mill Wheel, The, HARTSHORNE — 128

Millennium Bailey's Hotel London Kensington, LONDON SW7 — 309
Millennium Madejski Hotel Reading, READING — 62
Miller Howe Hotel, WINDERMERE — 123
Miller of Mansfield, The, GORING — 409
Millstone at Mellor, The, BLACKBURN — 224
Millstream Hotel & Restaurant, The, BOSHAM — 466
Milsoms Kesgrave Hall, IPSWICH — 445
milsoms, DEDHAM — 164
Milton Restaurant, The, CRATHES — 552
Min Jiang, LONDON W8 — 365
Mint Leaf, LONDON SW1 — 289
Miskin Manor Country Hotel, MISKIN — 641
Mistley Thorn, The, MANNINGTREE — 166
Mithas, EDINBURGH — 575
Mitsukoshi, LONDON SW1 — 289
Miyako, LONDON EC2 — 268
Moat House, The, STAFFORD — 437
Modern Pantry, The, LONDON EC1 — 264
Mole Inn, The, TOOT BALDON — 414
Mon Plaisir, LONDON WC2 — 373
Monkton Court, HONITON — 138
Montagu Arms Hotel, The, BEAULIEU — 188
Montagu, The, LONDON W1 — 338
Montague on the Gardens, The, LONDON WC1 — 368
Montcalm London City at The Brewery, The, LONDON EC1 — 265
Montrose Restaurant, TUNBRIDGE WELLS (ROYAL) — 222
Monty's Brasserie, CHELTENHAM — 172
Moorhill House Hotel, BURLEY — 191
Moorings Hotel & Restaurant, The, GOREY — 538
Moorings Hotel, FORT WILLIAM — 594
Mora Restaurant & Grill, ST PETER PORT — 538
Morgan M, LONDON EC1 — 265
Morley Hayes Hotel, The, MORLEY — 132
Moro, LONDON EC1 — 265
Morrels, KESWICK — 115
Morritt, The, BARNARD CASTLE — 158
Morston Hall, BLAKENEY — 386
Mortons House Hotel, CORFE CASTLE — 152
Mount Falcon Estate, BALLINA — 669
Mount Haven Hotel & Restaurant, MARAZION — 97
Mount Somerset Hotel, The, TAUNTON — 433
Mount Wolseley Hotel, Spa & Country Club, TULLOW — 654
Mourne Seafood Bar, DUNDRUM — 649
Moy House, LAHINCH — 655
MU at Millennium Knightsbridge, LONDON SW1 — 291
Muckross Park Hotel & Cloisters Spa, KILLARNEY — 666
Mug House Inn, The, BEWDLEY — 503
Mulberry Tree, The, BOUGHTON MONCHELSEA — 216
Mullion Cove Hotel, MULLION — 98
Mulranny Park Hotel, MULRANY — 669
Murano, LONDON W1 — 338
Murrayshall House Hotel & Golf Course, PERTH — 606
Muset Restaurant, The, BRISTOL — 67
Mya Lacarte, READING — 62
Mytton & Mermaid Hotel, SHREWSBURY — 425

N

Nags Head Country Inn, PICKHILL — 519
Nags Head Inn & Restaurant, GREAT MISSENDEN — 73
Nahm-Jim & the L'Orient Lounge, ST ANDREWS — 584
Nailcote Hall, BALSALL COMMON — 485
Nare, The, VERYAN — 106
Navy Inn, The, PENZANCE — 101
Neptune Restaurant with Rooms, The, HUNSTANTON — 389
New County Hotel, The, PERTH — 606
New Drumossie Hotel, The, INVERNESS — 596
New Ellington, The, LEEDS — 534

New Hall Hotel & Spa, SUTTON COLDFIELD 490
New Inn at Coln, The, COLN ST ALDWYNS 174
New Inn, TRESCO 108
New Lotus Garden, LONDON SW5 307
New Yard Restaurant, HELSTON 96
Newbridge on Usk, USK 635
Newbury Manor Hotel, NEWBURY 60
Newick Park Hotel & Country Estate, NEWICK 463
Newman Street Tavern, LONDON W1 338
Newton Hotel, NAIRN 597
Nidd Hall Hotel, HARROGATE 512
Nipa, LONDON W2 358
No.4 Clifton Village, BRISTOL 67
Nobu Berkeley ST, LONDON W1 338
Nobu, LONDON W1 338
Nonnas, SHEFFIELD 528
NOPI, LONDON W1 340
Norfolk Mead Hotel, COLTISHALL 386
Normandy Arms, The, BLACKAWTON 133
North Bridge Brasserie, EDINBURGH 575
North Hill Hotel, The, COLCHESTER 163
North Lakes Hotel & Spa, PENRITH 117
Northcote Manor, BURRINGTON 134
Northcote, LANGHO 225
Norton House Hotel & Spa, EDINBURGH 577
Norwood Hall Hotel, ABERDEEN 550
Novikov Asian Restaurant, LONDON W1 340
Novikov Italian Restaurant, LONDON W1 340
Novotel London West, LONDON W6 361
Nozomi, LONDON SW3 301
Number 9, WIMBORNE MINSTER 157
Number Four at Stow Hotel & Restaurant, STOW-ON-THE-WOLD 178
Number One, The Balmoral, EDINBURGH 577
Number Sixteen, GLASGOW 589
Number Twenty Four Restaurant, WYMONDHAM 396
Nunsmere Hall Hotel, SANDIWAY 92
Nut Tree Inn, The, MURCOTT 412
Nutfield Priory Hotel & Spa, REDHILL 456
Nuthurst Grange Hotel, HOCKLEY HEATH 489
Nutters, ROCHDALE 185

O

Oak Bank Hotel, GRASMERE 114
Oak House, The, AXBRIDGE 426
Oak Tree Inn, The, HUTTON MAGNA 161
Oakhill Inn, The, OAKHILL 432
Oakley Court Hotel, WINDSOR 64
Oakley Hall Hotel, BASINGSTOKE 188
Oaks Hotel, The, PORLOCK 432
Oatlands Park Hotel, WEYBRIDGE 456
Ocean Restaurant at the Atlantic Hotel, ST BRELADE 540
Ockenden Manor Hotel & Spa, CUCKFIELD 469
Oddfellows, CHESTER 89
ODE dining, SHALDON 144
Odette's Restaurant & Bar, LONDON NW1 274
Old Bakery, The, LINCOLN 236
Old Bell Hotel, MALMESBURY 499
Old Black Lion Inn, HAY-ON-WYE 639
Old Bridge Hotel, The, HUNTINGDON 84
Old Drum, The, PETERSFIELD 200
Old Forge Seafood Restaurant, The, THURSFORD 396
Old Government House Hotel & Spa, The, ST PETER PORT 538
Old Inn, The, CRAWFORDSBURN 649
Old Inn, The, DREWSTEIGNTON 136
Old Passage Inn, The, ARLINGHAM 168
Old Rectory, The, NORWICH 391
Old Spot, The, WELLS 435

Old Swan & Minster Mill, WITNEY 414
Old Vicarage Hotel, The, BRIDGNORTH 419
Olde Bell Inn, The, HURLEY 57
Olive Branch, The, CLIPSHAM 416
Olive Tree at the Queensberry Hotel, The, BATH 428
Olive Tree Restaurant at the Queens Court Hotel, The, EXETER 137
Ondine Restaurant, EDINBURGH 577
One Square, EDINBURGH 577
One-O-One, LONDON SW1 291
Only Running Footman, The, LONDON W1 340
Opera Tavern, The, LONDON WC2 373
Opium, GLASGOW 589
Opus Restaurant, BIRMINGHAM 488
Ord House Hotel, MUIR OF ORD 597
Orestone Manor, TORQUAY 147
Orrery, LONDON W1 340
Orsett Hall Banqueting & Conference Centre, ORSETT 166
Orso, LONDON WC2 373
Orwells, HENLEY-ON-THAMES 409
Osborne House, LLANDUDNO 628
Osteria Dell'Angolo, LONDON SW1 291
Ostlers Close Restaurant, CUPAR 582
Oundle Mill, OUNDLE 398
Outlaw's at The Capital, LONDON SW3 301
Overton Grange Hotel and Restaurant, LUDLOW 421
Overwater Hall, IREBY 115
Oxford Hotel, The, OXFORD 413
Oxfordshire, The, MILTON COMMON 411
Oxo Tower Restaurant, The, LONDON SE1 279
Oyster Box, ST BRELADE 540
Ozer Restaurant, LONDON W1 341
Ozone Restaurant, The, SEAHAM 162

P

Painted Heron, The, LONDON SW10 310
Palmerston, The, LONDON SE22 282
Pan Haggerty Restaurant, NEWCASTLE UPON TYNE 479
Paper Mill, The, LASSWADE 603
Paramount, LONDON WC1 368
Parc Hotel, Cardiff, The, CARDIFF 622
Paris House Restaurant, WOBURN 51
Park Farm Hotel, HETHERSETT 388
Park House Hotel & Restaurant, GALWAY 665
Park House Hotel, SHIFNAL 424
Park House, CARDIFF 622
Park Plaza Cardiff, CARDIFF 622
Park Plaza County Hall, LONDON SE1 279
Park Plaza Nottingham, NOTTINGHAM 403
Park Plaza Sherlock Holmes, LONDON W1 341
Park Plaza Victoria London, LONDON SW1 292
Park Plaza Westminster Bridge, LONDON SE1 279
Park Restaurant, The, COLERNE 494
Park Terrace Restaurant, LONDON W8 366
Parsonage Country House Hotel, The, ESCRICK 511
Pass Restaurant at South Lodge Hotel, The, LOWER BEEDING 475
Paul Ainsworth at No. 6, PADSTOW 99
Pea Porridge, BURY ST EDMUNDS 442
Peacock at Rowsley, The, ROWSLEY 132
Peacock Room, The, ROCHDALE 186
Pear Tree at Purton, The, PURTON 501
Peat Inn, The, PEAT INN 583
Peat Spade Inn, The, STOCKBRIDGE 204
Pebble Beach, BARTON-ON-SEA 187
Pen-y-Dyffryn Country Hotel, OSWESTRY 424
Pendley Manor Hotel, TRING 212
Penmaenuchaf Hall Hotel, DOLGELLAU 630
Pennington Hotel, The, RAVENGLASS 118

Perkin Reveller, The, LONDON EC3 — 269
Petersham Hotel, The, RICHMOND UPON THAMES — 379
Petersham Nurseries Café, RICHMOND UPON THAMES — 379
Peterstone Court, BRECON — 638
Pétrus, LONDON SW1 — 292
Pheasant Inn, KEYSTON — 84
Pheasant, The, BASSENTHWAITE — 110
Pheasant, The, GESTINGTHORPE — 165
Pied à Terre, LONDON W1 — 341
Piedaniel's, BAKEWELL — 123
Pier at Harwich, The, HARWICH — 165
Pierhouse Hotel, The, PORT APPIN — 559
Pig, The, BROCKENHURST — 190
Pilgrims, The, CASTLE CARY — 430
Pines Hotel, The, PRESTON — 228
Pins at The Twelve, The, BARNA — 663
Pipe and Glass Inn, The, BEVERLEY — 508
Pizarro, LONDON SE1 — 279
Plantation House, ERMINGTON — 137
Plas Bodegroes, PWLLHELI — 631
Plas Meanan Country House, LLANRWST — 629
Plas Ynyshir Hall Hotel, EGLWYS FACH — 625
Plateau, LONDON E14 — 262
Plough at Bolnhurst, The, BOLNHURST — 48
Plough Inn Lupton, The, LUPTON — 116
Plough Inn, The, ANDOVER — 187
Plough Inn, The, HATHERSAGE — 128
Plough Inn, The, LLANDEILO — 623
Plough, The, WIGGLESWORTH — 523
Plum Valley, LONDON W1 — 341
Plumed Horse, EDINBURGH — 577
Pollen Street Social, LONDON W1 — 341
Polpo, LONDON W1 — 341
Pompadour by Galvin, EDINBURGH — 577
Pond Café, The, VENTNOR — 491
Pony & Trap, The, CHEW MAGNA — 430
Porth Tocyn Hotel, ABERSOCH — 629
Porthminster Beach Restaurant, ST IVES — 104
Portsmouth Marriott Hotel, PORTSMOUTH & SOUTHSEA — 200
Pot Kiln, The, FRILSHAM — 57
Powder Mills Hotel, BATTLE — 458
Prashad, BRADFORD — 529
Priest House Hotel, The, EAST MIDLANDS AIRPORT — 232
Prince's House, The, GLENFINNAN — 594
Print Room & Ink Bar & Brasserie, The, BOURNEMOUTH — 150
Priory Bay Hotel, SEAVIEW — 491
Prism Brasserie and Bar, LONDON EC3 — 269
Probus Lamplighter Restaurant, TRURO — 106
Providores and Tapa Room, The, LONDON W1 — 344
Pullman London St Pancras, LONDON NW1 — 274
Pump House, The, BRISTOL — 68
Punchbowl Inn at Crosthwaite, The, CROSTHWAITE — 112
Purefoy Arms, PRESTON CANDOVER — 200
Purnell's, BIRMINGHAM — 488

Q

Quaglino's, LONDON SW1 — 292
Quarterdeck at the Nare, The, VERYAN — 107
Quay Hotel & Spa, DEGANWY — 627
Quayside Hotel, BRIXHAM — 134
Queens Restaurant, LEAMINGTON SPA (ROYAL) — 482
Queen's Head Inn, The, BRANDESTON — 439
Queens Arms, The, CORTON DENHAM — 430
Queens Head Inn, The, NASSINGTON — 398
Queens, The, ST IVES — 104
Quilon, LONDON SW1 — 292

Quo Vadis, LONDON W1 — 344
Quorn Country Hotel, QUORN — 233

R

Racine, LONDON SW3 — 301
Radisson Blu Farnham Estate Hotel, CAVAN — 654
Radisson Blu Hotel & Spa Sligo, SLIGO — 671
Radisson Blu Hotel Letterkenny, LETTERKENNY — 660
Raemoir House Hotel, BANCHORY — 552
Rafters Restaurant, SHEFFIELD — 528
Rafters, NEWPORT — 636
Raglan Arms, USK — 635
Rampsbeck Country House Hotel, WATERMILLOCK — 118
Ramside Hall Hotel, DURHAM — 161
Ransome's Dock, LONDON SW11 — 311
Rasoi Restaurant, LONDON SW3 — 301
Rathmullan House, RATHMULLAN — 660
Raven Hotel, MUCH WENLOCK — 423
Ravenwood Hall Hotel, BURY ST EDMUNDS — 442
Read's Restaurant, FAVERSHAM — 220
Red Cat, The, CHORLEY — 225
Red Fort, The, LONDON W1 — 344
Red Lion Inn, The, CRICKLADE — 497
Red Lion Inn, The, HINXTON — 84
Red Lion, The, SHIPSTON ON STOUR — 482
Red Lyon, HURLEY — 58
Redcastle Hotel, Golf & Spa Resort, MOVILLE — 660
Redcoats Farmhouse Hotel, HITCHIN — 210
Redesdale Arms, MORETON-IN-MARSH — 175
Redworth Hall Hotel, REDWORTH — 161
Reflections at Alexander House, TURNERS HILL — 477
Regatta Restaurant, ALDEBURGH — 438
Regency Park Hotel, NEWBURY — 60
Restaurant 22, CAMBRIDGE — 80
Restaurant 23 & Morgan's Bar, LEAMINGTON SPA (ROYAL) — 482
Restaurant 27, PORTSMOUTH & SOUTHSEA — 200
Restaurant 1861, ABERGAVENNY — 632
Restaurant Alimentum, CAMBRIDGE — 80
Restaurant at Witney Lakes Resort, The, WITNEY — 414
Restaurant Coworth Park, ASCOT — 52
Restaurant Gilmore at Strine's Farm, UTTOXETER — 438
Restaurant Gordon Ramsey, LONDON SW3 — 301
Restaurant Martin Wishart, EDINBURGH — 577
Restaurant Michael Nadra, LONDON W4 — 358
Restaurant Nathan Outlaw, ROCK — 102
Restaurant Patrick Guilbaud, DUBLIN — 661
Restaurant Sat Bains with Rooms, NOTTINGHAM — 403
Restaurant Sauterelle, LONDON EC3 — 270
Restaurant Severn, IRONBRIDGE — 420
Restaurant Sirocco@ The Royal Yacht, ST HELIER — 544
Restaurant Story, LONDON SE1 — 280
Restaurant Tristan, HORSHAM — 472
Retro, TEDDINGTON — 380
Rhinefield House, BROCKENHURST — 190
Rhodes@ The Dome, PLYMOUTH — 142
Rhubarb at Prestonfield House, EDINBURGH — 577
Rib Room, The, LONDON SW1 — 294
Richmond Hill Hotel, RICHMOND UPON THAMES — 379
Riding House Café, The, LONDON W1 — 344
Rising Sun Hotel, LYNMOUTH — 141
Risley Hall Hotel & Spa, RISLEY — 132
Rissons at Springvale, STRATHAVEN — 601
Ristorante Semplice, LONDON W1 — 345
Ritz Restaurant, The, LONDON W1 — 345
River Café, The, LONDON W6 — 361
Riverford Field Kitchen, The, TOTNES — 147

Riverside Brasserie, The, BRAY 56
Riverside Restaurant, BRIDPORT 151
riverstation, BRISTOL 68
Riviera Hotel, SIDMOUTH 144
Road Hole Restaurant, ST ANDREWS 584
Roade House Restaurant, ROADE 398
Roast, LONDON SE1 280
Rocca Grill, ST ANDREWS 584
Rock Inn, HAYTOR VALE 138
Rock Restaurant, BOURNEMOUTH 150
Rockfish Grill & Seafood Market, The, BRISTOL 68
Rockliffe Hall, DARLINGTON 158
Rocksalt Rooms, FOLKESTONE 220
Rocpool, INVERNESS 596
Roe Park Resort, LIMAVADY 651
Rogan & Company Restaurant, CARTMEL 112
Rogano, GLASGOW 590
Roger Hickman's Restaurant, NORWICH 391
Roka, LONDON E14 262
Roka, LONDON W1 345
Rolfs Country House, BALTIMORE 657
Roman Camp Country House Hotel, CALLANDER 610
Ronnie's of Thornbury, THORNBURY 179
Rookery Hall Hotel & Spa, NANTWICH 91
Room Manchester, MANCHESTER 184
Rose & Crown Hotel, ROMALDKIRK 162
Rose & Crown, The, SNETTISHAM 394
Rose & Crown, The, SUTTON-ON-THE-FOREST 522
Rose-in-Vale Country House Hotel, ST AGNES 102
Rosewarne Manor, HAYLE 96
Roslin Beach Hotel, The, SOUTHEND-ON-SEA 166
Rosslea Hall Hotel, RHU 560
Rothay Garden Hotel, GRASMERE 114
Rothay Manor, AMBLESIDE 108
Roti Chai, LONDON W1 345
Roux at Parliament Square, LONDON SW1 294
Roux at The Landau, LONDON W1 346
Rowhill Grange Hotel & Utopia Spa, DARTFORD 218
Rowton Hall Country House Hotel & Spa, CHESTER 89
Roxburghe Hotel & Golf Course, The, KELSO 608
Royal Chace Hotel, ENFIELD 374
Royal Duchy Hotel, The, FALMOUTH 95
Royal Forester Country Inn, BEWDLEY 503
Royal Horseguards, The, LONDON SW1 294
Royal Hotel, COMRIE 603
Royal Hotel, The, VENTNOR 492
Royal Marine Hotel, Restaurant & Spa, BRORA 592
Royal Oak Inn, The, CHICHESTER 467
Royal Oak Paley Street, The, MAIDENHEAD 58
Royal Oak, The, LONG WHATTON 233
Royal Oak, The, RIPON 519
Royal Sportsman Hotel, PORTHMADOG 630
RSJ, The Restaurant on the South Bank, LONDON SE1 281
Rubens at the Palace, The, LONDON SW1 294
Rudding Park Hotel, Spa & Golf, HARROGATE 512
Rufflets Country House, ST ANDREWS 584
Running Horse Inn, WINCHESTER 205
Rushton Hall Hotel and Spa, KETTERING 397
Russell Hotel, ST ANDREWS 586
Russell's at Smiddy House, SPEAN BRIDGE 599
Russell's, BROADWAY 504
Rutland Arms Hotel, The, NEWMARKET 448

S

Saffron Restaurant, OLDBURY 490
Sagar, LONDON W6 361

St Benedicts Restaurant, NORWICH 391
St Brides Spa Hotel, SAUNDERSFOOT 638
St Ermin's Hotel, LONDON SW1 294
St George's Hotel, LLANDUDNO 628
St Giles House Hotel, NORWICH 392
St John Bread & Wine, LONDON E1 260
St John, LONDON EC1 265
St Mellion International Resort, ST MELLION 105
St Michael's Hotel and Spa, FALMOUTH 95
St Michael's Manor, ST ALBANS 212
St Pancras Grand Brasserie, LONDON NW1 275
St Petroc's Hotel and Bistro, PADSTOW 99
St Pierre, A Marriott Hotel & Country Club, CHEPSTOW 634
St Tudno Hotel and Restaurant, LLANDUDNO 629
Sake No Hana, LONDON SW1 294
Salisbury Seafood & Steakhouse, SALISBURY 502
Salloos Restaurant, LONDON SW1 297
Salt Yard, LONDON W1 346
Salthouse Harbour Hotel, IPSWICH 445
Salty Dog Bar & Bistro, The, ST AUBIN 539
Salty Monk, The, SIDMOUTH 144
Salvo's Restaurant & Salumeria, LEEDS 534
Sam's Brasserie & Bar, LONDON W4 359
Samling, The, WINDERMERE 123
Samuel Fox Country Inn, The, BRADWELL 124
Samuel's at Swinton Park, MASHAM 518
Sandbanks, The, POOLE 155
Sands Grill, ST ANDREWS 586
Sandy Cove Hotel, ILFRACOMBE 139
Sangreela Indian Restaurant, NEWCASTLE UPON TYNE 480
Sangsters, ELIE 582
Santini Restaurant, LONDON SW1 297
Santo's Higham Farm Hotel, HIGHAM 129
Saracens at Hadnall, HADNALL 419
Sartoria, LONDON W1 347
Satis House Hotel, YOXFORD 451
Saunton Sands Hotel, SAUNTON 143
Savoro Restaurant with Rooms, BARNET 374
Savoy Grill, LONDON WC2 373
Scalloway Hotel, SCALLOWAY 613
Scarista House, SCARISTA (SGARASTA BHEAG) 612
Scarlet Hotel, The, MAWGAN PORTH 97
Scott's Restaurant, LONDON W1 347
Sea Marge Hotel, CROMER 386
Sea View House, BALLYLICKEY 656
Seafield Golf & Spa Hotel, GOREY 673
Seafood Restaurant, The, PADSTOW 99
Seafood Restaurant, The, ST ANDREWS 586
Seagrass Restaurant, ST IVES 104
Seagrave Arms, CHIPPING CAMPDEN 172
Seahorse, The, DARTMOUTH 136
Season at The Fifth Floor Restaurant, LONDON SW1 297
Seaview Hotel & Restaurant, The, SEAVIEW 491
Sebastians, OSWESTRY 424
Seckford Hall Hotel, WOODBRIDGE 451
Second Floor Restaurant, BRISTOL 68
Seeds, LLANFYLLIN 640
Seiont Manor Hotel, CAERNARFON 630
Sella Park House Hotel, SEASCALE 118
Seven Park Place by William Drabble, LONDON SW1 297
Sharrow Bay Country House Hotel, HOWTOWN 115
Shed, The, PORTHGAIN 638
Sheedy's Country House Hotel, LISDOONVARNA 656
Sheen Falls Lodge, KENMARE 665
Sheep Heid, The, EDINBURGH 580
Shelbourne Dublin, a Renaissance Hotel, The, DUBLIN 661

Shepherd and Dog, The, STOWMARKET 449
Shibden Mill Inn, HALIFAX 531
Ship at Dunwich, The, DUNWICH 443
Ship Hotel, The, CHICHESTER 469
Shish Mahal, GLASGOW 590
Shogun, Millennium Hotel Mayfair, LONDON W1 347
Shoulder at Hardstoft, The, HARDSTOFT 127
Shrigley Hall Hotel, Golf & Country Club, MACCLESFIELD 91
Shu, BELFAST 649
Sibton White Horse Inn, SIBTON 448
Sienna, DORCHESTER 152
Silver Darling, The, ABERDEEN 550
Simon Radley at The Chester Grosvenor, CHESTER 89
Simpsons, BIRMINGHAM 488
Sir Charles Napier, The, CHINNOR 406
Sir Christopher Wren Hotel and Spa, WINDSOR 64
Skeabost Country House, SKEABOST BRIDGE 616
Sketch (Lecture Room & Library), LONDON W1 347
Sketch (The Gallery), LONDON W1 347
Sketch (The Parlour), LONDON W1 347
Sketchley Grange Hotel, HINCKLEY 232
Skylon, LONDON SE1 281
Smiths at Gretna Green, GRETNA 565
Smiths of Smithfield, Top Floor, LONDON EC1 266
So Restaurant, LONDON W1 350
Soar Mill Cove Hotel, SALCOMBE 143
Social Eating House, LONDON W1 350
Sofitel London Gatwick, GATWICK AIRPORT (LONDON) 471
Sofitel London Heathrow, HEATHROW AIRPORT (LONDON) 376
Sofitel London St James, LONDON SW1 297
Solent Hotel & Spa, FAREHAM 193
Sonny's Kitchen, LONDON SW13 312
Sopwell House, ST ALBANS 212
Sosban Restaurant, LLANELLI 624
Soufflé Restaurant, BEARSTED 216
Spa Hotel at Ribby Hall Village, The, WREA GREEN 231
Spa Hotel, The, TUNBRIDGE WELLS (ROYAL) 222
Spire, LIVERPOOL 382
Splinters Restaurant, CHRISTCHURCH 152
Sportsman, The, WHITSTABLE 223
Springfort Hall Country House Hotel, MALLOW 659
Springs Hotel & Golf Club, The, WALLINGFORD 414
Sprowston Manor, A Marriott Hotel & Country Club, NORWICH 392
Square, The, LONDON W1 350
Stables Restaurant at The Grove, The, RICKMANSWORTH 211
Stac Polly, EDINBURGH 580
Stafford London by Kempinski, The, LONDON SW1 299
Stagg Inn and Restaurant, The, KINGTON 206
Staindrop Lodge Hotel, SHEFFIELD 528
Stanneylands Hotel, WILMSLOW 93
Stanton Manor Hotel, STANTON ST QUINTIN 502
Stanwell House Hotel, LYMINGTON 195
Stapleford Park, MELTON MOWBRAY 233
Star Alfriston, The, ALFRISTON 458
Star Inn, The, HAROME 511
Station House Hotel, The, KILMESSAN 670
Stewart Warner at Hillbark, FRANKBY 380
Stillorgan Park Hotel, DUBLIN 663
Stirk House Hotel, GISBURN 225
Stirling Highland Hotel, The, STIRLING 610
Stockbridge Restaurant, The, EDINBURGH 580
Stoke by Nayland Hotel, Golf & Spa, COLCHESTER 163
Stoke Place, STOKE POGES 78
Ston Easton Park Hotel, STON EASTON 433
Stone Manor Hotel, KIDDERMINSTER 506
Stonefield Castle Hotel, TARBERT LOCH FYNE 561
Stonemill & Steppes Farm Cottages, The, ROCKFIELD 635

Stones Restaurant, MATLOCK 129
Storrs Hall Hotel, WINDERMERE 123
Stovell's, CHOBHAM 452
Stower Grange, NORWICH 392
Strathearn, The, AUCHTERARDER 603
Stravaigin, GLASGOW 590
Studio, The, CHURCH STRETTON 419
Studley Hotel, HARROGATE 512
Sugar Hut, The, NORWICH 393
Sumas, GOREY 539
Summer Lodge Country House Hotel, Restaurant & Spa, EVERSHOT 154
Sumosan Restaurant, LONDON W1 350
Sun Inn, The, DALKEITH 602
Sun Inn, The, DEDHAM 164
Sun Inn, The, KIRKBY LONSDALE 116
Super Tuscan, LONDON E1 260
Sushinho, LONDON SW3 305
Sushisamba London, LONDON EC2 268
Sutherland House, SOUTHWOLD 449
Swan English Restaurant, TENTERDEN 222
Swan Hotel, BIBURY 169
Swan Hotel, SOUTHWOLD 449
Swan Inn, The, CHIDDINGFOLD 452
Swan Inn, The, MONKS ELEIGH 447
Swan Inn, The, SWINBROOK 413
Swan, The, LAVENHAM 446
Swan, The, WEST MALLING 223
Sweet Mandarin, MANCHESTER 185
Swinfen Hall Hotel, LICHFIELD 437
Swinside Lodge Country House Hotel, KESWICK 116

T

Tabb's, TRURO 106
Tabla, PERTH 607
Talbot Hotel, The, MALTON 518
Talbot Hotel, The, OUNDLE 398
Talland Bay Hotel, TALLAND BAY 105
Tamarind, LONDON W1 353
Tan-y-Foel Country Guest House, BETWS-Y-COED 626
Tankardstown, SLANE 670
Tanners Restaurant, PLYMOUTH 142
Taplow House Hotel, TAPLOW 78
Tarr Farm Inn, DULVERTON 431
Tatlers, NORWICH 393
Taychreggan Hotel, KILCHRENAN 557
Temple Gate Hotel, ENNIS 655
Temple Sowerby House Hotel & Restaurant, TEMPLE SOWERBY 118
Ternhill Farm House & The Cottage Restaurant, MARKET DRAYTON 423
Terrace Dining Room, Cliveden, The, TAPLOW 78
Terre à Terre, BRIGHTON & HOVE 460
Terroirs, LONDON WC2 373
Terry M at The Celtic Manor Resort, NEWPORT 636
Tewin Bury Farm Hotel, WELWYN 213
Texture Restaurant, LONDON W1 353
Thackeray's, TUNBRIDGE WELLS (ROYAL) 223
Thai Edge Restaurant, BIRMINGHAM 488
Thai House Restaurant, The, CARDIFF 622
Thai Thai at The Crazy Bear, STADHAMPTON 413
Thailand Restaurant, NORWICH 394
Thatched Cottage Inn, The, SHEPTON MALLET 432
Theo Randall, LONDON W1 353
Theobalds Restaurant, IXWORTH 445
Thirty Six by Nigel Mendham at Dukes London, LONDON SW1 299
Thomas Lord, The, PETERSFIELD 200
Thoresby Hall Hotel, OLLERTON 405
Thornbury Castle, THORNBURY 179
Thorpe Park Hotel & Spa, LEEDS 534

Thorpeness Hotel, THORPENESS	450
Three Chimneys, The, COLBOST	613
Three Choirs Vineyards, NETHER WESTCOTE	176
Three Fishes, The, WHALLEY	231
Three Gables, The, BRADFORD-ON-AVON	493
Three Horseshoes Inn & Country Hotel, LEEK	437
Three Horseshoes Inn, POWERSTOCK	156
Three Queens Hotel, BURTON UPON TRENT	437
Three Salmons Hotel, The, USK	636
Three Tuns, The, BRANSGORE	189
Three Tuns, The, ROMSEY	201
Three Ways House, CHIPPING CAMPDEN	173
Thurlestone Hotel, THURLESTONE	145
Tides Reach Hotel, SALCOMBE	143
Tigh an Eilean, SHIELDAIG	599
Tilbury, The, DATCHWORTH	209
Tillmouth Park Country House Hotel, CORNHILL-ON-TWEED	400
Time & Space, LONDON W1	353
Tinakilly Country House & Restaurant, RATHNEW	675
Tinello, LONDON SW1	299
Tinhay Mill Guest House and Restaurant, LIFTON	140
Titchwell Manor Hotel, TITCHWELL	396
Tolbooth Restaurant, The, STONEHAVEN	555
Tom Aikens, LONDON SW3	305
Tom Browns Brasserie, GUNTHORPE	402
Tom Ilic, LONDON SW8	309
Tom's Kitchen, LONDON SW3	305
Topes Restaurant, ROCHESTER	221
Toravaig House Hotel, ISLEORNSAY	614
Torridon Restaurant, The, TORRIDON	600
Tors Hotel, LYNMOUTH	141
Tortworth Court Four Pillars Hotel, WOTTON-UNDER-EDGE	181
Tower Hotel, LINCOLN	236
Town Hall Tavern, LEEDS	534
Town House, The, ARUNDEL	466
Traddock, The, AUSTWICK	509
Treby Arms, PLYMPTON	142
Trehellas House Hotel & Restaurant, BODMIN	94
Trelaske Hotel & Restaurant, LOOE	97
Trinity Restaurant, LONDON SW4	305
Trishna, LONDON W1	353
Trout at Tadpole Bridge, The, FARINGDON	408
Trullo, LONDON N1	272
Tsunami, LONDON SW4	306
Tuddenham Mill, NEWMARKET	448
Tudor Farmhouse Hotel & Restaurant, CLEARWELL	173
Tudor Room at Great Fosters, The, EGHAM	455
Turnberry Resort, Scotland, TURNBERRY	564
Turners, BIRMINGHAM	488
Twelve Restaurant and Lounge Bar, THORNTON	228
Two Bridges Hotel, TWO BRIDGES	147
Two To Four, DORKING	454
Ty Mawr Mansion, ABERAERON	625
Tylney Hall Hotel, ROTHERWICK	202

U

Ubiquitous Chip, GLASGOW	590
Ullinish Country Lodge, STRUAN	617
Umu, LONDON W1	353
Unicorn, The, CUBLINGTON	72
Uplawmoor Hotel, UPLAWMOOR	608
Upstairs@ West, The Twelve, BARNA	664
Urban Bar and Brasserie, GLASGOW	591

V

Vale Resort, HENSOL	643
van Zeller, HARROGATE	514

Vanilla Black, LONDON EC4	271
Vanilla Pod, The, MARLOW	75
Vasco & Piero's Pavilion Restaurant, LONDON W1	355
Veeraswamy Restaurant, LONDON W1	355
Vennell's, MASHAM	518
Venture In Restaurant, The, OMBERSLEY	507
Vernon, The, BROMSGROVE	505
Verru Restaurant, LONDON W1	355
Viajante, LONDON E2	261
Victoria Hotel, BAMBURGH	399
Victoria Hotel, The, SIDMOUTH	144
Victoria Inn, The, PERRANUTHNOE	101
Village Pub, The, BARNSLEY	168
Villandry, LONDON W1	355
Villiers Hotel, BUCKINGHAM	71
Vincent Hotel, SOUTHPORT	383
Vine House Hotel & Restaurant, TOWCESTER	398
Vineyard, The, NEWBURY	61
Vobster Inn, The, LOWER VOBSTER	432

W

Wabi, HORSHAM	472
Waggoners, The, WELWYN	213
Wallett's Court Country House Hotel & Spa, DOVER	218
Walnut Tree Inn, ABERGAVENNY	632
Walton Hall, WELLESBOURNE	485
Wapping Food, LONDON E1	260
Warehouse Kitchen & Bar, SOUTHPORT	384
Waren House Hotel, BAMBURGH	399
Washingborough Hall Hotel, LINCOLN	236
Water's Edge Hotel, TRINITY	545
Waterford Castle Hotel and Golf Resort, WATERFORD	673
Waterhead Hotel, AMBLESIDE	109
Waterside Inn, BRAY	56
Waterside Seafood Restaurant, The, KYLE OF LOCHALSH	597
Watersmeet Hotel, WOOLACOMBE	148
Waterton Park Hotel, WAKEFIELD	535
Webbes at The Fish Café, RYE	464
Wee Lochan, GLASGOW	591
Wellington Arms, The, BAUGHURST	188
Wellington Hotel, The, BOSCASTLE	94
Wellington, The, WELWYN	215
Wensleydale Heifer, The, WEST WITTON	522
Wentbridge House Hotel, PONTEFRACT	535
Wentworth Hotel, ALDEBURGH	439
Wernher Restaurant at Luton Hoo, LUTON	49
Wesley House Wine Bar & Grill, WINCHCOMBE	181
Wesley House, WINCHCOMBE	180
West Arms, LLANARMON DYFFRYN CEIRIOG	643
West Beach, BOURNEMOUTH	150
West House, The, BIDDENDEN	216
West Lodge Park Hotel, HADLEY WOOD	374
Westbury Hotel, The, DUBLIN	663
Western House Hotel, The, AYR	562
Westerwood House & Golf Resort, The, CUMBERNAULD	600
Westleton Crown, The, WESTLETON	450
Wharf House Restaurant with Rooms, The, GLOUCESTER	174
Whatley Manor Hotel and Spa, MALMESBURY	499
Wheatsheaf at Oaksey, The, OAKSEY	501
Wheeler's, LONDON SW1	300
White Hart Hotel, The, HARROGATE	514
White Hart Hotel, The, WELWYN	215
White Hart Inn, The, OLDHAM	185
White Hart Royal Hotel, MORETON-IN-MARSH	175
White Hart Village Inn, The, LLANGYBI	634
White Hart, The, FYFIELD	408
White Hart, The, GREAT YELDHAM	165

White Horse Hotel & Brasserie, The, ROMSEY	201
White Horse Overstrand, The, CROMER	387
White Horse, The, BRANCASTER STAITHE	386
White Horse, The, BURY ST EDMUNDS	442
White Horse, The, CALNE	493
White Horse, The, OTTERBOURNE	195
White House Hotel, HERM	538
White House, The, KINSALE	659
White Lion Hotel, The, ALDEBURGH	439
White Lion Hotel, UPTON UPON SEVERN	507
White Oak, The, COOKHAM	56
White Star Tavern, Dining and Rooms, SOUTHAMPTON	203
White Swan Inn, The, PICKERING	518
White Swan Pub & Dining Room, The, LONDON EC4	271
White Swan, The, WARENFORD	402
Whitechapel Gallery Dining Room, LONDON E1	260
Whitehouse Restaurant, The, LOCHALINE	597
Whitewater Hotel, NEWBY BRIDGE	117
Whitford House Hotel Health & Leisure Club, WEXFORD	674
Whitley Hall Hotel, SHEFFIELD	528
Whittlebury Hall, WHITTLEBURY	399
Who'd A Thought It, GRAFTY GREEN	220
Wife of Bath, The, ASHFORD	216
Wild Garlic Restaurant and Rooms, NAILSWORTH	176
Wild Garlic, The, BEAMINSTER	148
Wild Honey Inn, LISDOONVARNA	656
Wild Honey, LONDON W1	355
Wild Mushroom Restaurant, The, WESTFIELD	465
Wild Thyme Restaurant with Rooms, CHIPPING NORTON	407
William Cecil, The, STAMFORD	239
Willow Tree Restaurant, The, TAUNTON	433
Wilton Court Restaurant with Rooms, ROSS-ON-WYE	208
Winchester Hotel and Spa, The, WINCHESTER	205
Winter Garden, The, LONDON NW1	275
Winteringham Fields, WINTERINGHAM	239
Witchery by the Castle, The, EDINBURGH	582
Wivenhoe House Hotel, COLCHESTER	163
Wiveton Bell, WIVETON	396
Wolfscastle Country Hotel, HAVERFORDWEST	636
Wolseley, The, LONDON W1	355
Wood Hall Hotel, WETHERBY	536
Woodbury Park Hotel and Golf Club, WOODBURY	147
Woodhouse, The, WOODHOUSE EAVES	234
Woodlands Lodge Hotel, WOODLANDS	205
Woodlands Park Hotel, STOKE D'ABERNON	456
Woods Bar & Dining Room, DULVERTON	431
Woods Brasserie, CARDIFF	623
Woods Restaurant, BATH	430
Woody Nook at Woodcote, WOODCOTE	415
Wookey Hole Inn, WOOKEY HOLE	436
Wordsworth Hotel & Spa, GRASMERE	114
World Service, NOTTINGHAM	403
Wortley Arms, The, WORTLEY	528
Wrightington Hotel & Country Club, WIGAN	186
Wyboston Lakes Hotel, WYBOSTON	51
Wyck Hill House Hotel & Spa, STOW-ON-THE-WOLD	178
Wykeham Arms, The, WINCHESTER	205
Wyndham Arms Hotel, The, CLEARWELL	173
Wynnstay Hotel, OSWESTRY	424
Wynyard Hall Hotel, BILLINGHAM	158

X

XO, LONDON NW3	276

Y

Y Polyn, NANTGAREDIG	624
Yauatcha, LONDON W1	356
Ye Olde Bulls Head Inn, BEAUMARIS	620
Yeoldon House Hotel, BIDEFORD	133
Yeovil Court Hotel & Restaurant, The, YEOVIL	436
YMing Restaurant, LONDON W1	356
Yorebridge House, BAINBRIDGE	509

Z

Zafferano, LONDON SW1	300
Zaika of Kensington, LONDON W8	366
Zen Garden Restaurant, The, BROCKENHURST	190
Zucca, LONDON SE1	281
Zuma, LONDON SW7	309

Acknowledgments

The Automobile Association wishes to thank the following photographers and organisations for their assistance in the preparation of this book.

Abbreviations for the picture credits are as follows – (t) top; (b) bottom; (l) left; (r) right; (c) centre; (AA) AA World Travel Library

1 Ashley Palmer Watts; 2 AA/Mockford/Bonetti; 3 AA/James Tims; 4 AA/Karl Blackwell; 5 AA/James Tims; 7 The Vineyard; 8 Ashley Palmer Watts; 9 Mark Poynton; 10 Hand & Flowers Restaurant; 11 Hand & Flowers Restaurant; 12l Lucknam Park Hotel & Spa; 12r Lucknam Park Hotel & Spa; 13t Waterside Restaurant, Bray; 13b Waterside Restaurant, Bray; 14l The Artichoke, Amersham; 14r Medlar, London; 15l Ondine, Edinburgh; 15r Ye Olde Bulls Head Inn, Beamaris; 16bl AA/James Tims; 17l Northcote, Blackburn; 17c The Witchery By the Castle, Edinburgh; 17r Park House, Cardiff; 18 Aiden Byrne; 19 Aiden Byrne; 20 Aiden Byrne; 21 Aiden Byrne; 23 Mark Poynton; 24 Ashley Palmer Watts; 25 Aiden Byrne; 26 Mat Follas; 28 Mat Follas; 29 Mat Follas; 30/1 The Vineyard, Stockcross; 32 The Vineyard, Stockcross; 33 The Vineyard, Stockcross; 34 The Vineyard, Stockcross; 35 The Vineyard, Stockcross; 36 The Vineyard, Stockcross; 37 The Vineyard, Stockcross; 46/7 AA/John Wood; 225 AA/David Clapp; 240/1 AA/James Tims; 257 AA/James Tims; 365 AA/James Tims; 548/9 AA/Stephen Whitehorne; 618/9 AA/Nick Jenkins; 644/5 AA/Chris Hill.

Every effort has been made to trace the copyright holders, and we apologise in advance for any unintentional omissions or errors. We would be pleased to apply any corrections in a following edition of this publication.

Readers' Report Form

Please send this form to:–
Editor, The Restaurant Guide,
Lifestyle Guides,
AA Media,
Fanum House,
Basingstoke RG21 4EA

e-mail: lifestyleguides@theAA.com

Please use this form to recommend any restaurant you have visited, whether it is in the guide or not currently listed. Feedback from readers helps us to keep our guide accurate and up to date. Please note, however, that if you have a complaint to make during your visit, we strongly recommend that you discuss the matter with the restaurant management there and then, so that they have a chance to put things right before your visit is spoilt.

Please note that the AA does not undertake to arbitrate between you and the restaurant management, or to obtain compensation or engage in protracted correspondence.

Date

Your name (BLOCK CAPITALS)

Your address (BLOCK CAPITALS)

Post code

E-mail address

Restaurant name and address: (if you are recommending a new restaurant please enclose a menu or note the dishes that you ate.)

Comments

(please attach a separate sheet if necessary)

Please tick here ☐ if you DO NOT wish to receive details of AA offers or products

PTO

Readers' Report Form *continued*

Have you bought this guide before? ☐ YES ☐ NO

Please list any other similar guides that you use regularly

What do you find most useful about The AA Restaurant Guide?

Please answer these questions to help us make improvements to the guide:

What are your main reasons for visiting restaurants? (tick all that apply)

Business entertaining ☐   Business travel ☐   Trying famous restaurants ☐   Family celebrations ☐
Leisure travel ☐   Trying new food ☐   Enjoying not having to cook yourself ☐
To eat food you couldn't cook yourself ☐   Because I enjoy eating out regularly ☐
Other (please state)

How often do you visit a restaurant for lunch or dinner? (tick one choice)

Once a week ☐   Once a fortnight ☐   Once a month ☐   Less than once a month ☐
Other (please state)

Do you use the location atlas? ☐ YES ☐ NO

Do you generally agree with the Rosette ratings at the restaurants you visit in the guide?
(If not please give examples)

Who is your favourite chef?

Which is your favourite restaurant?

Which type of cuisine is your first choice e.g. French?

Which of these factors is the most important when choosing a restaurant? (tick one choice)

Price ☐   Service ☐   Location ☐   Type of food ☐
Awards/ratings ☐   Decor/surroundings ☐
Other (please state)

What elements of the guide do you find most useful when choosing a restaurant? (tick all that apply)

Description ☐   Photo ☐   Rosette rating ☐   Price ☐
Other (please state)

Readers' Report Form

Please send this form to:–
Editor, The Restaurant Guide,
Lifestyle Guides,
AA Media,
Fanum House,
Basingstoke RG21 4EA

e-mail: lifestyleguides@theAA.com

Please use this form to recommend any restaurant you have visited, whether it is in the guide or not currently listed. Feedback from readers helps us to keep our guide accurate and up to date. Please note, however, that if you have a complaint to make during your visit, we strongly recommend that you discuss the matter with the restaurant management there and then, so that they have a chance to put things right before your visit is spoilt.

Please note that the AA does not undertake to arbitrate between you and the restaurant management, or to obtain compensation or engage in protracted correspondence.

Date
_____

Your name (BLOCK CAPITALS)
_____

Your address (BLOCK CAPITALS)
_____

_____

_____
                                            Post code
_____

E-mail address
_____

Restaurant name and address: (if you are recommending a new restaurant please enclose a menu or note the dishes that you ate.)
_____

_____

Comments
_____

_____

_____

_____

_____

(please attach a separate sheet if necessary)

Please tick here ☐ if you DO NOT wish to receive details of AA offers or products   PTO

Readers' Report Form *continued*

Have you bought this guide before? ☐ YES ☐ NO

Please list any other similar guides that you use regularly

What do you find most useful about The AA Restaurant Guide?

Please answer these questions to help us make improvements to the guide:

What are your main reasons for visiting restaurants? (tick all that apply)

Business entertaining ☐   Business travel ☐   Trying famous restaurants ☐   Family celebrations ☐

Leisure travel ☐   Trying new food ☐   Enjoying not having to cook yourself ☐

To eat food you couldn't cook yourself ☐   Because I enjoy eating out regularly ☐

Other (please state)

How often do you visit a restaurant for lunch or dinner? (tick one choice)

Once a week ☐   Once a fortnight ☐   Once a month ☐   Less than once a month ☐

Other (please state)

Do you use the location atlas? ☐ YES ☐ NO

Do you generally agree with the Rosette ratings at the restaurants you visit in the guide?
(If not please give examples)

Who is your favourite chef?

Which is your favourite restaurant?

Which type of cuisine is your first choice e.g. French?

Which of these factors is the most important when choosing a restaurant? (tick one choice)

Price ☐   Service ☐   Location ☐   Type of food ☐

Awards/ratings ☐   Decor/surroundings ☐

Other (please state)

What elements of the guide do you find most useful when choosing a restaurant? (tick all that apply)

Description ☐   Photo ☐   Rosette rating ☐   Price ☐

Other (please state)